Great Britain & Ireland

2006

Contents

Sommaire
Sommario
Inhaltsverzeichnis

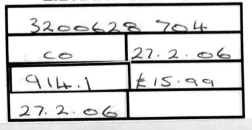

INTRODUCTION

→ INTRODUCTION

→ INTRODUZIONE

→ EINLEITUNG

Commitments

"This volume was created at the turn of the century and will last at least as long".

This foreword to the very first edition of the MICHELIN Guide, written in 1900, has become famous over the years and the Guide has lived up to the prediction. It is read across the world and the key to its popularity is the consistency of its commitment to its readers, which is based on the following promises.

The MICHELIN Guide's commitments :

Anonymous inspections: our inspectors make regular and anonymous visits to hotels and restaurants to gauge the quality of products and services offered to an ordinary customer. They settle their own bill and may then introduce themselves and ask for more information about the establishment. Our readers' comments are also a valuable source of information, which we can then follow up with another visit of our own.

Independence: Our choice of establishments is a completely independent one, made for the benefit of our readers alone. The decisions to be taken are discussed around the table by the inspectors and the editor. The most important awards are decided at a European level. Inclusion in the Guide is completely free of charge.

Selection and choice: The Guide offers a selection of the best hotels and restaurants in every category of comfort and price. This is only possible because all the inspectors rigorously apply the same methods.

Annual updates: All the practical information, the classifications and awards are revised and updated every single year to give the most reliable information possible.

Consistency: The criteria for the classifications are the same in every country covered by the Michelin Guide.

... and our aim: to do everything possible to make travel, holidays and eating out a pleasure, as part of Michelin's ongoing commitment to improving travel and mobility.

Dear reader

Dear reader,

We are delighted to introduce the 33rd edition of The Michelin Guide Great Britain & Ireland.

This selection of the best hotels and restaurants in every price category is chosen by a team of full-time inspectors with a professional background in the industry. They cover every corner of the country, visiting new establishments and testing the quality and consistency of the hotels and restaurants already listed in the Guide.

Every year we pick out the best restaurants by awarding them from ✿ to ✿✿✿. Stars are awarded for cuisine of the highest standards and reflect the quality of the ingredients, the skill in their preparation, the combination of flavours, the levels of creativity and value for money, and the ability to combine all these qualities not just once, but time and time again.
This year sees two important additions.One highlights those restaurants which, over the last year, have raised the quality of their cooking to a new level. Whether they have gained a first star, risen from one to two stars, or moved from two to three, these newly promoted restaurants are marked with an '**N**' next to their entry to signal their new status in 2006.

We have also picked out a selection of « *Rising Stars* ». These establishments, listed in red, are the best in their present category. They have the potential to rise further, and already have an element of superior quality; as soon as they produce this quality consistently, and in all aspects of their cuisine, they will be hot tips for a higher award. We've highlighted these promising restaurants so you can try them for yourselves; we think they offer a foretaste of the gastronomy of the future.
We're very interested to hear what you think of our selection, particularly the " *Rising Stars* ", so please continue to send us your comments. Your opinions and suggestions help to shape your Guide, and help us to keep improving it, year after year. Thank you for your support. We hope you enjoy travelling with the Michelin Guide 2006.

Consult the Michelin Guide at **www.ViaMichelin.com**
and write to us at:
themichelinguide-gbirl@uk.michelin.com

Classification & awards

CATEGORIES OF COMFORT

The Michelin Guide selection lists the best hotels and restaurants in each category of comfort and price. The establishments we choose are classified according to their levels of comfort and, within each category, are listed in order of preference.

- Luxury in the traditional style
- Top class comfort
- Very comfortable
- Comfortable
- Quite comfortable
- Traditional pubs serving good food
- Other recommended accommodation (Guesthouses, farmhouses and private homes)
- without rest. — This hotel has no restaurant
- with rm — This restaurant also offers accommodation

THE AWARDS

To help you make the best choice, some exceptional establishments have been given an award in this year's Guide. They are marked or and **Rest**.

THE BEST CUISINE

Michelin stars are awarded to establishments serving cuisine, of whatever style, which is of the highest quality. The cuisine is judged on the quality of ingredients, the skill in their preparation, the combination of flavours, the levels of creativity, the value for money and the consistency of culinary standards.

Exceptional cuisine, worth a special journey
One always eats extremely well here, sometimes superbly.

Excellent cooking, worth a detour

A very good restaurant in its category

GOOD FOOD AND ACCOMMODATION AT MODERATE PRICES

Bib Gourmand
Establishment offering good quality cuisine for under £27 or €38 in the Republic of Ireland (price of a 3 course meal not including drinks).

Bib Hotel
Establishment offering good levels of comfort and service, with most rooms priced at under £75 or under €105 in the Republic of Ireland (price of a room for 2 people, including breakfast).

PLEASANT HOTELS AND RESTAURANTS

Symbols shown in red indicate particularly pleasant or restful establishments: the character of the building, its décor, the setting, the welcome and services offered may all contribute to this special appeal.

⌂, ⌂ to ⌂⌂⌂⌂⌂ **Pleasant hotels**

🍺, ✗ to ✗✗✗✗✗ **Pleasant restaurants**

OTHER SPECIAL FEATURES

As well as the categories and awards given to the establishment, Michelin inspectors also make special note of other criteria which can be important when choosing an establishment.

LOCATION

If you are looking for a particularly restful establishment, or one with a special view, look out for the following symbols:

- **Quiet hotel**
- **Very quiet hotel**
- < **Interesting view**
- < **Exceptional view**

WINE LIST

If you are looking for an establishment with a particularly interesting wine list, look out for the following symbol:

Particularly interesting wine list

This symbol might cover the list presented by a sommelier in a luxury restaurant or that of a simple pub or restaurant where the owner has a passion for wine. The two lists will offer something exceptional but very different, so beware of comparing them by each other's standards.

Facilities & services

30 rm	Number of rooms
	Lift (elevator)
	Air conditioning (in all or part of the establishment)
	Establishment with areas reserved for non-smokers. In the Republic of Ireland the law prohibits smoking in all pubs, restaurants and hotel public areas
	Fast Internet access in bedrooms
	Establishment at least partly accessible to those of restricted mobility
	Special facilities for children
	Meals served in garden or on terrace
	Wellness centre: an extensive facility for relaxation and well-being
	Sauna – Exercise room
	Swimming pool: outdoor or indoor
	Garden – Park
18	Tennis court – Golf course and number of holes
	Landing stage
	Fishing available to hotel guests. A charge may be made
150	Equipped conference room: maximum capacity
12	Private dining rooms: maximum capacity
	Hotel garage (additional charge in most cases)
P	Car park for customers only
	No dogs allowed (in all or part of the establishment)
	Nearest Underground station (in London)
May-October	Dates when open, as indicated by the hotelier

Prices

Prices quoted in this Guide are for autumn 2005 and apply to high season. They are subject to alteration if goods and service costs are revised. By supplying the information, hotels and restaurants have undertaken to maintain these rates for our readers.
In some towns, when commercial, cultural or sporting events are taking place the hotel rates are likely to be considerably higher.
Prices are given in £ sterling, except for the Republic of Ireland where € euro are quoted.

All accommodation prices include both service and V.A.T. All restaurant prices include V.A.T. Service is also included when an **s.** appears after the prices. Where no **s.** is shown, prices may be subject to the addition of a variable service charge which is usually between 10 % - 15 %.
(V.A.T. does not apply in the Channel Islands).
Out of season, certain establishments offer special rates. Ask when booking.

RESERVATION AND DEPOSITS

Some hotels will require a deposit which confirms the commitment of both the customer and the hotelier.
Ask the hotelier to provide you with all the terms and conditions applicable to your reservation in their written confirmation.

CREDIT CARDS

AE ① MC VISA	Credit cards accepted by the establishment: American Express – Diners Club – MasterCard – Visa

ROOMS

rm 🚹 50.00/90.00	Lowest price 50.00 and highest price 90.00 for a comfortable single room
rm 🚹🚹 70.00/120.00	Lowest price 70.00 and highest price 120.00 for a double or twin room for 2 people
rm ☕ 55.00/85.00	Full cooked breakfast (whether taken or not) is included in the price of the room
☕ 6.00	Price of breakfast

SHORT BREAKS

Many hotels offer a special rate for a stay of two or more nights which comprises dinner, room and breakfast usually for a minimum of two people. Please enquire at hotel for rates.

RESTAURANT

Set meals: lowest price £13.00, highest price £28.00, usually for a 3 course meal. The lowest priced set menu is often only available at lunchtimes.
A la carte meals:
The prices represent the range of charges from a simple to an elaborate 3 course meal.

s.	Service included
🎭	Restaurants offering lower priced pre and/or post theatre menus
🍷	Wine served by the glass

⌂: Dinner in this category of establishment will generally be offered from a fixed price menu of limited choice, served at a set time to residents only. Lunch is rarely offered. Many will not be licensed to sell alcohol.

Towns

GENERAL INFORMATION

✉ *York*	Postal address
501 M27, ⑩	Michelin map and co-ordinates or fold
Great Britain G.	See the Michelin Green Guide Great Britain
pop. 1057	Population Source: 2001 Census (Key Statistics for Urban Areas) Crown copyright 2004
BX A	Letters giving the location of a place on a town plan
18	Golf course and number of holes (handicap sometimes required, telephone reservation strongly advised)
	Panoramic view, viewpoint
	Airport
	Shipping line (passengers & cars)
	Passenger transport only
	Tourist Information Centre

STANDARD TIME

In winter, standard time throughout the British Isles is Greenwich Mean Time (GMT). In summer, British clocks are advanced by one hour to give British Summer Time (BST). The actual dates are announced annually but always occur over weekends in March and October.

TOURIST INFORMATION

STAR-RATING

★★★	Highly recommended
★★	Recommended
★	Interesting
AC	Admission charge

LOCATION

See	Sights in town
Envir.	On the outskirts
Exc.	In the surrounding area
N, S, E, W	The sight lies north, south, east or west of the town
A 22	Take road A 22, indicated by the same symbol on the Guide map
2m.	Distance in miles (In the Republic of Ireland kilometres are quoted).

Town plans

a ● a Hotels – restaurants

SIGHTS

Place of interest
Interesting place of worship

ROADS

M 1 Motorway
4 4 Numbered junctions: complete, limited
Dual carriageway with motorway characteristics
Main traffic artery
A 2 Primary route (GB) and National route (IRL)
One-way street – Unsuitable for traffic or street subject to restrictions
Pedestrian street – Tramway
Piccadilly P R Shopping street – Car park – Park and Ride
Gateway – Street passing under arch – Tunnel
15'5 Low headroom (16'6" max.) on major through routes
Station and railway
Funicular – Cable-car
B Lever bridge – Car ferry

VARIOUS SIGNS

Tourist Information Centre
Church/Place of worship - Mosque – Synagogue
Communications tower or mast – Ruins
Garden, park, wood – Cemetery
9 Stadium - Racecourse - Golf course
Golf course (with restrictions for visitors) – Skating rink
Outdoor or indoor swimming pool
View – Panorama
Monument – Fountain – Hospital – Covered market
Pleasure boat harbour – Lighthouse
Airport – Underground station – Coach station
Ferry services: passengers and cars
Main post office
Public buildings located by letter:
C H J - County Council Offices – Town Hall – Law Courts
M T U - Museum – Theatre – University, College
POL. - Police (in large towns police headquarters)

LONDON

BRENT WEMBLEY Borough – Area
Borough boundary
Congestion Zone – Charge applies Monday-Friday 07.00-18.30
Nearest Underground station to the hotel or restaurant

Local maps

MAY WE SUGGEST THAT YOU CONSULT THEM

Sould you be looking for a hotel or restaurant not too far from Leeds, for example, you can now consult the map along with the town plan.

The local map (opposite) draws your attention to all places around the town or city selected, provided they are mentioned in the Guide.

Places located within a range of 16 miles/25 km are clearly identified by the use of a different coloured background.

The various facilities recommended near the different regional capitals can be located quickly and easily.

NOTE:

Entries in the Guide provide information on distances to nearby towns.

Whenever a place appears on one of the local maps, the name of the town or city to which it is attached is printed in BLUE.

EXAMPLE:

ILKLEY W. Yorks **502** O 22
– *pop. 13 472.*
18 Myddleton (01943) 607277
Station Rd (01943) 602319
London 210 – Bradford 13 – Harrogate 17 – Leeds 16 – Preston 46

ILKLEY is to be found on the local map LEEDS.

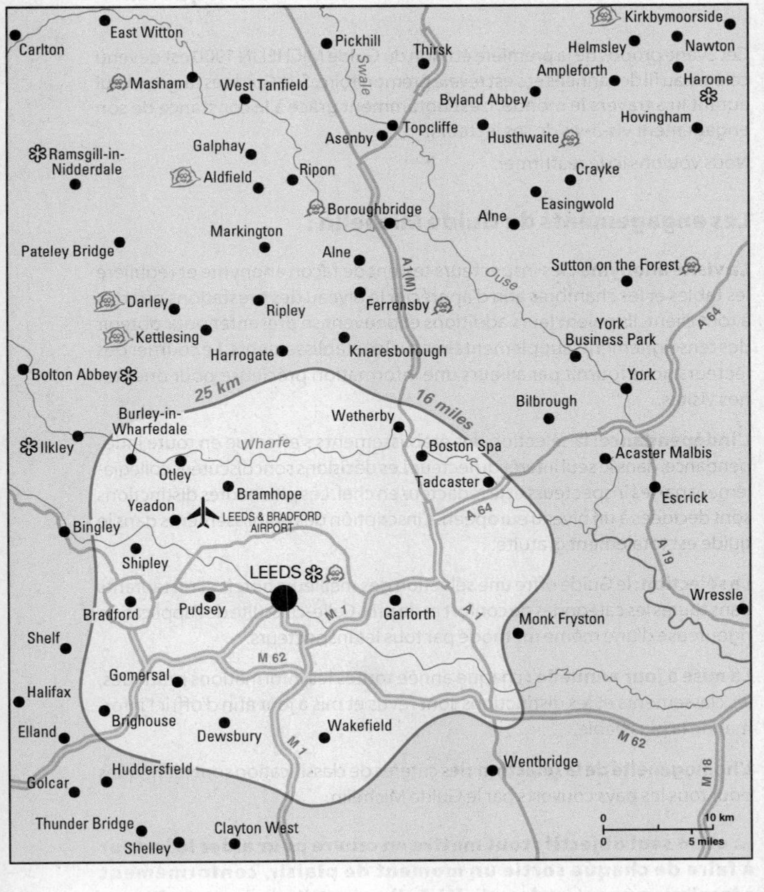

Kirkbymoorside
Carlton
East Witton
Pickhill
Thirsk
Helmsley
Nawton
Swale
Ampleforth
Harome
Masham
West Tanfield
Byland Abbey
Hovingham
Topcliffe
Asenby
Husthwaite
Galphay
Ramsgill-in-
Nidderdale
Aldfield
Ripon
Crayke
Easingwold
Boroughbridge
Alne
Markington
Pateley Bridge
Alne
A1(M)
Sutton on the Forest
Ouse
Darley
Ripley
Ferrensby
York
Business Park
A 64
Kettlesing
Harrogate
Knaresborough
Bolton Abbey
York
25 km
16 miles
Bilbrough
Burley-in-
Wharfedale
Wetherby
Ilkley
Wharfe
Boston Spa
Acaster Malbis
Otley
Tadcaster
Escrick
Bramhope
Yeadon
LEEDS & BRADFORD
AIRPORT
A 64
Bingley
A 19
Shipley
LEEDS
Wressle
Bradford
Pudsey
M 1
Garforth
A 1
Monk Fryston
Shelf
M 62
Gomersal
Halifax
Brighouse
Dewsbury
Wakefield
Elland
M 62
M 1
Wentbridge
Huddersfield
Golcar
M 18
0
10 km
0
5 miles
Thunder Bridge
Clayton West
Shelley

Engagements

« Ce guide est né avec le siècle et il durera autant que lui. »

Cet avant-propos de la première édition du Guide MICHELIN 1900 est devenu célèbre au fil des années et s'est révélé prémonitoire. Si le Guide est aujourd'hui autant lu à travers le monde, c'est notamment grâce à la constance de son engagement vis-à-vis de ses lecteurs.

Nous voulons ici le réaffirmer.

Les engagements du Guide Michelin :

La visite anonyme : les inspecteurs testent de façon anonyme et régulière les tables et les chambres afin d'apprécier le niveau des prestations offertes à tout client. Ils paient leurs additions et peuvent se présenter pour obtenir des renseignements supplémentaires sur les établissements. Le courrier des lecteurs nous fournit par ailleurs une information précieuse pour orienter nos visites.

L'indépendance: la sélection des établissements s'effectue en toute indépendance, dans le seul intérêt du lecteur. Les décisions sont discutées collégialement par les inspecteurs et le rédacteur en chef. Les plus hautes distinctions sont décidées à un niveau européen. L'inscription des établissements dans le guide est totalement gratuite.

La sélection: le Guide offre une sélection des meilleurs hôtels et restaurants dans toutes les catégories de confort et de prix. Celle-ci résulte de l'application rigoureuse d'une même méthode par tous les inspecteurs.

La mise à jour annuelle : chaque année toutes les informations pratiques, les classements et les distinctions sont revus et mis à jour afin d'offrir l'information la plus fiable.

L'homogénéité de la sélection : les critères de classification sont identiques pour tous les pays couverts par le Guide Michelin.

... et un seul objectif : tout mettre en œuvre pour aider le lecteur à faire de chaque sortie un moment de plaisir, conformément à la mission que s'est donnée Michelin : contribuer à une meilleure mobilité.

Édito

Cher lecteur,

Nous avons le plaisir de vous proposer notre 33e édition du Guide Michelin Great Britain & Ireland. Cette sélection des meilleurs hôtels et restaurants dans chaque catégorie de prix est effectuée par une équipe d'inspecteurs professionnels, de formation hôtelière. Tous les ans, ils sillonnent le pays pour visiter de nouveaux établissements et vérifier le niveau des prestations de ceux déjà cités dans le Guide.

Au sein de la sélection, nous reconnaissons également chaque année les meilleures tables en leur décernant de ✿ a ✿✿✿. Les étoiles distinguent les établissements qui proposent la meilleure qualité de cuisine, dans tous les styles, en tenant compte des choix de produits, de la créativité, de la maîtrise des cuissons et des saveurs, du rapport qualité/prix ainsi que de la régularité.

Cette année encore, de nombreuses tables ont été remarquées pour l'évolution de leur cuisine. Un « **N** » accompagne les nouveaux promus de ce millésime 2006, annonçant leur arrivée parmi les établissements ayant une, deux ou trois étoiles.

De plus, nous souhaitons indiquer les établissements « *espoirs* » pour la catégorie supérieure. Ces établissements, mentionnés en rouge dans notre liste, sont les meilleurs de leur catégorie. Ils pourront accéder à la distinction supérieure dès lors que la régularité de leurs prestations, dans le temps et sur l'ensemble de la carte, aura progressé. Par cette mention spéciale, nous entendons vous faire connaître les tables qui constituent à nos yeux, les espoirs de la gastronomie de demain.

Votre avis nous intéresse, en particulier sur ces « espoirs » ; n'hésitez pas à nous écrire. Votre participation est importante pour orienter nos visites et améliorer sans cesse votre Guide. Merci encore de votre fidélité. Nous vous souhaitons de bons voyages avec le Guide Michelin 2006.

Consultez le Guide Michelin sur **www.ViaMichelin.com**
Et écrivez-nous à : **themichelinguide-gbirl@uk.michelin.com**

Classement & distinctions

LES CATÉGORIES DE CONFORT

Le Guide Michelin retient dans sa sélection les meilleures adresses dans chaque catégorie de confort et de prix. Les établissements sélectionnés sont classés selon leur confort et cités par ordre de préférence dans chaque catégorie.

🏨	XXXXX	Grand luxe et tradition
🏨	XXXX	Grand confort
🏨	XXX	Très confortable
🏨	XX	De bon confort
🏨	X	Assez confortable
	🍺	Pub traditionnel servant des repas
⌂		Autres formes d'hébergement conseillées (b&b, logis à la ferme et cottages)
without rest.		L'hôtel n'a pas de restaurant
with rm		Le restaurant possède des chambres

LES DISTINCTIONS

Pour vous aider à faire le meilleur choix, certaines adresses particulièrement remarquables ont reçu une distinction : étoiles ou Bib Gourmand. Elles sont repérables dans la marge par ✿ ou ☺ et dans le texte par **Rest.**

LES ÉTOILES : LES MEILLEURES TABLES

Les étoiles distinguent les établissements, tous les styles de cuisine confondus, qui proposent la meilleure qualité de cuisine. Les critères retenus sont : le choix des produits, la créativité, la maîtrise des cuissons et des saveurs, le rapport qualité/prix ainsi que la régularité.

✿✿✿ **Cuisine remarquable, cette table vaut le voyage**
On y mange toujours très bien, parfois merveilleusement.

✿✿ **Cuisine excellente, cette table mérite un détour**

✿ **Une très bonne cuisine dans sa catégorie**

LES BIB : LES MEILLEURES ADRESSES À PETIT PRIX

☺ **Bib Gourmand**
Établissement proposant une cuisine de qualité à moins de £27 ou €38 en République d'Irlande (repas composé de 3 plats, hors boisson).

☺ **Bib Hôtel**
Établissement offrant une prestation de qualité avec une majorité des chambres à moins de £75 ou moins de €105 en République d'Irlande (prix d'une chambre double, petit-déjeuner compris).

LES ADRESSES LES PLUS AGRÉABLES

Le rouge signale les établissements particulièrement agréables. Cela peut tenir au caractère de l'édifice, à l'originalité du décor, au site, à l'accueil ou aux services proposés.

⌂, ⌂ to ⌂⌂⌂⌂⌂ **Hôtels agréables**

⌂, X to XXXXX **Restaurants agréables**

LES MENTIONS PARTICULIÈRES

En dehors des distinctions décernées aux établissements, les inspecteurs Michelin apprécient d'autres critères souvent importants dans le choix d'un établissement.

SITUATION

Vous cherchez un établissement tranquille ou offrant une vue attractive ? Suivez les symboles suivants :

Hôtel tranquille

Hôtel très tranquille

Vue intéressante

Vue exceptionnelle

CARTE DES VINS

Vous cherchez un restaurant dont la carte des vins offre un choix particulièrement intéressant ? Suivez le symbole suivant :

Carte des vins particulièrement attractive

Toutefois, ne comparez pas la carte présentée par le sommelier d'un grand restaurant avec celle d'un pub ou d'un restaurant beaucoup plus simple. Les deux cartes vous offriront de l'exceptionnel, mais de niveau très différent.

Équipements & services

30 rm	Nombre de chambres
	Ascenseur
	Air conditionné (dans tout ou partie de l'établissement)
	Établissement possédant des zones réservées aux non-fumeurs. En République d'Irlande, il est formellement interdit de fumer dans les pubs, restaurants et hôtels.
	Connexion Internet à Haut débit dans la chambre
	Établissement en partie accessible aux personnes à mobilité réduite.
	Équipements d'acceuil pour les enfants
	Repas servi au jardin ou en terrasse
	Wellness centre : bel espace de bien-être et de relaxation
	Sauna - Salle de remise en forme
	Piscine : de plein air ou couverte
	Jardin – Parc
18	Court de tennis, golf et nombre de trous
	Ponton d'amarrage
	Pêche ouverte aux clients de l'hôtel (éventuellement payant)
150	Salles de conférences : capacité maximum
12	Salon privé : capacité maximum
	Garage dans l'hôtel (généralement payant)
P	Parking réservé à la clientèle
	Accès interdit au chiens (dans tout ou partie de l'établissement)
	Station de métro à proximité (Londres)
May-October	Période d'ouverture (ou fermeture), communiquée par l'hôtelier

Prix

Les prix indiqués dans ce guide ont été établis à l'automne 2005 et s'appliquent à la haute saison. Ils sont susceptibles de modifications, notamment en cas de variation des prix des biens et des services.
Les hôteliers et restaurateurs se sont engagés, sous leur propre responsabilité, à appliquer ces prix aux clients.
Dans certaines villes, à l'occasion de manifestations commerciales ou touristiques, les prix demandés par les hôteliers risquent d'être considérablement majorés.
Les prix sont indiqués en livres sterling sauf en République d'Irlande où ils sont donnés en euros.

Les tarifs de l'hébergement comprennent le service et la T.V.A. La T.V.A. est également incluse dans les prix des repas. Toutefois, le service est uniquement compris dans les repas si la mention « **s.** » apparaît après le prix.
Dans le cas contraire, une charge supplémentaire variant de 10 à 15% du montant de l'addition est demandée.
(La T.V.A. n'est pas appliquée dans les Channel Islands).
Hors saison, certains établissements proposent des conditions avantageuses, renseignez-vous dès votre réservation.

LES ARRHES

Certains hôteliers demandent le versement d'arrhes. Il s'agit d'un dépôt-garantie qui engage l'hôtelier comme le client. Bien demander à l'hôtelier de vous fournir dans sa lettre d'accord toutes les précisions utiles sur la réservation et les conditions de séjour.

CARTES DE PAIEMENT

AE Ⓓ MC VISA	Carte de paiement acceptées : American Express – Diners Club – Mastercard – Visa.

CHAMBRES

rm 50.00/90.00	Prix minimum/maximum pour une chambre confortable d'une personne
rm 70.00/120.00	Prix minimum/maximum pour une chambre de deux personnes
rm 55.00/85.00	Prix de la chambre petit-déjeuner compris
6.00	Prix du petit-déjeuner si non inclus

SHORT BREAKS

Certains hôtels proposent des conditions avantageuses pour un séjour de deux ou trois nuits. Ce forfait, calculé par personne pour 2 personnes au minimum, comprend le dîner, la chambre et le petit-déjeuner. Se renseigner auprès de l'hôtelier.

RESTAURANT

Menu à prix fixe : minimum £13, maximum £28 comprenant généralement 3 plats. Le prix minimum correspond souvent à celui d'un déjeuner.

Repas à la carte

Le 1er prix correspond à un repas simple comprenant une entrée, un plat du jour et un dessert. Le 2e prix concerne un repas plus complet (avec spécialité) comprenant un hors d'œuvre, un plat principal, fromage ou dessert

s.	Service compris
	Restaurants proposant des menus à prix attractifs servis avant ou après le théâtre
	Vin servi au verre

: Dans les établissements de cette catégorie, le dîner est servi à heure fixe exclusivement aux personnes résidentes. Le menu à prix unique offre un choix limité de plats. Le déjeuner est rarement proposé. Beaucoup de ces établissements ne sont pas autorisés à vendre des boissons alcoolisées.

Villes

GÉNÉRALITÉS

✉ *York*	Numéro de code postal et nom du bureau distributeur du courrier
501 M27, ⑩	Numéro des cartes Michelin et carroyage ou numéro du pli
Great Britain G.	Voir le Guide Vert Michelin Grande-Bretagne
pop. 1057	Population (d'après le recensement de 2001)
BX A	Lettre repérant un emplacement sur le plan
18	Golf et nombre de trous (handicap parfois demandé, réservation par téléphone vivement recommandée)
	Panorama, point de vue
	Aéroport
	Transports maritimes
	Transports maritimes (pour passagers seulement)
	Information touristique

HEURE LÉGALE

Les visiteurs devront tenir compte de l'heure officielle en Grande-Bretagne : une heure de retard sur l'heure française.

INFORMATIONS TOURISTIQUES

INTÉRÊT TOURISTIQUE

★★★	Vaut le voyage
★★	Mérite un détour
★	Intéressant
AC	Entrée payante

SITUATION

See	Dans la ville
Envir.	Aux environs de la ville
Exc.	Excursions dans la région
N, S, E, W	La curiosité est située : au Nord, au Sud, à l'Est, à l'Ouest
A 22	On s'y rend par la route A 22, repérée par le même signe que sur le plan du Guide
2 m.	Distance en miles (calculée en kilomètre pour la République d'Irlande)

Plans

a ● a Hôtels – Restaurants

CURIOSITÉS

Bâtiment intéressant
Édifice religieux intéressant

VOIRIE

M 1 Autoroute
Numéro d'échangeur : complet, partiel
Route à chaussée séparées de type autoroutier
Grande voie de circulation
A 2 Itinéraire principal (GB) - Route nationale (IRL)
Sens unique – Rue impraticable, réglementée
Rue piétonne – Tramway
Piccadilly Rue commerçante – Parking – Parking Relais
Porte – Passage sous voûte – Tunnel
15'5 Passage bas (inférieur à 16'6'') sur les grandes voies de circulation
Gare et voie ferrée
Funiculaire – Téléphérique, télécabine
B Pont mobile – Bac pour autos

SIGNES DIVERS

Information touristique
Église/édifice religieux – Mosquée – Synagogue
Tour ou pylône de télécommunication – Ruines
Jardin, parc, bois – Cimetière
Stade – Hippodrome – Golf
Golf (réservé) – Patinoire
Piscine de plein air, couverte
Vue – Panorama
Monument – Fontaine – Hôpital – Marché couvert
Port de plaisance – Phare
Aéroport – Station de métro – Gare routière
Transport par bateau :
– passagers et voitures
Bureau principal
Bâtiment public repéré par une lettre :
C H J - Bureau de l'Administration du comté – Hôtel de ville – Palais de justice
M T U - Musée - Théâtre - Université, grande école
POL. - Police (Commissariat central)

LONDRES

BRENT WEMBLEY Nom d'arrondissement (borough) - de quartier (area)
Limite de « borough »
Zone à péage du centre-ville lundi-vendredi 7h-18h30
Station de métro à proximité de l'hôtel ou du restaurant

Cartes de voisinage

AVEZ-VOUS PENSÉ À LES CONSULTER ?

Vous souhaitez trouver une bonne adresse, par exemple, aux environs de Leeds ?
Consultez la carte qui accompagne le plan de la ville.

La "carte de voisinage" (ci-contre) attire votre attention sur toutes les localités citées au Guide autour de la ville choisie, et particulièrement celles situées dans un rayon de 16 miles/25 km (limite de couleur).

Les "cartes de voisinage" vous permettent ainsi le repérage rapide de toutes les ressources proposées par le Guide autour des métropoles régionales.

NOTA :

Lorsqu'une localité est présente sur une "carte de voisinage", sa métropole de rattachement est imprimée en BLEU sur la ligne des distances de ville à ville.

EXEMPLE :

ILKLEY is to be found on the local map LEEDS.

ILKLEY W. Yorks 502 O 22
– *pop. 13 472.*
18 *Myddleton* ☏ *(01943) 607277*
ℹ *Station Rd* ☏ *(01943) 602319*
London 210 – Bradford 13 – Harrogate 17 – Leeds 16 – Preston 46

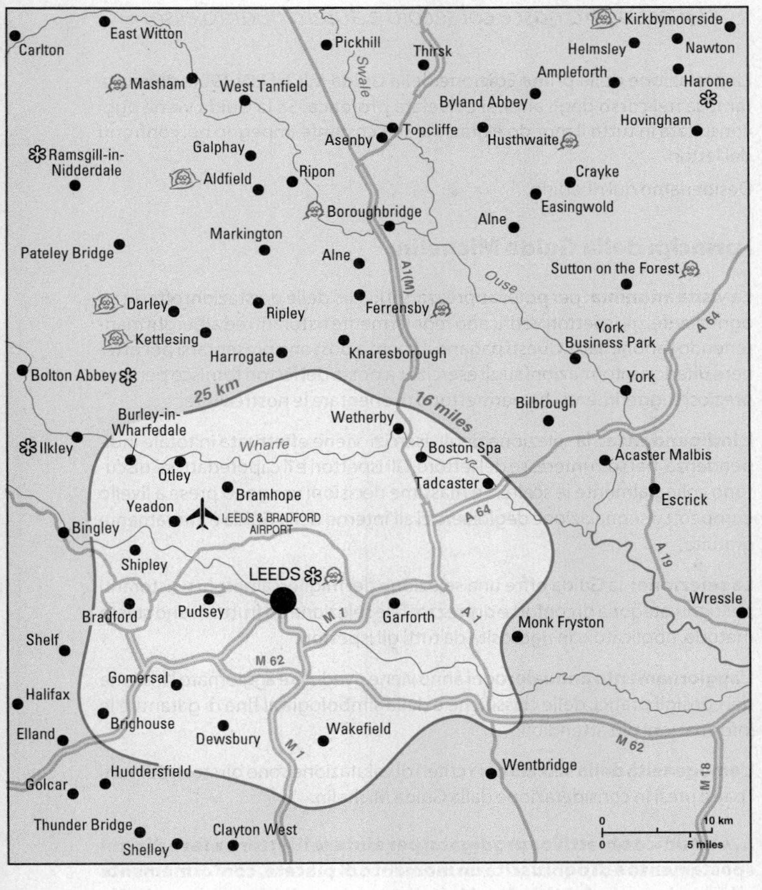
Carlton
East Witton
Masham
West Tanfield
Pickhill
Swale
Thirsk
Kirkbymoorside
Helmsley
Nawton
Ampleforth
Harome
Byland Abbey
Hovingham
Topcliffe
Asenby
Husthwaite
Ramsgill-in-Nidderdale
Galphay
Aldfield
Ripon
Crayke
Easingwold
Boroughbridge
Alne
Markington
Pateley Bridge
Alne
A1(M)
Ouse
Sutton on the Forest
Darley
Ripley
Ferrensby
Kettlesing
York Business Park
A 64
Harrogate
Knaresborough
Bolton Abbey
York
25 km
16 miles
Bilbrough
Burley-in-Wharfedale
Wetherby
Ilkley
Wharfe
Boston Spa
Acaster Malbis
Otley
Tadcaster
Bramhope
Escrick
Yeadon
LEEDS & BRADFORD AIRPORT
A 64
Bingley
A 19
Shipley
LEEDS
Wressle
Bradford
Pudsey
M 1
Garforth
A 1
Monk Fryston
Shelf
M 62
Gomersal
Halifax
Brighouse
Dewsbury
Wakefield
Elland
M 1
M 62
Huddersfield
Wentbridge
M 18
Golcar
Thunder Bridge
Clayton West
Shelley
10 km
5 miles

Principi

« Quest'opera nasce col secolo e durerà quanto esso. »

La prefazione della prima Edizione della Guida MICHELIN 1900, divenuta famosa nel corso degli anni, si è rivelata profetica. Se la Guida viene oggi consultata in tutto il mondo è grazie al suo costante impegno nei confronti dei lettori.

Desideriamo qui ribadirlo.

I principi della Guida Michelin:

La visita anonima: per poter apprezzare il livello delle prestazioni offerte ad ogni cliente, gli ispettori verificano regolarmente ristoranti ed alberghi mantenendo l'anonimato. Questi pagano il conto e possono presentarsi per ottenere ulteriori informazioni sugli esercizi. La posta dei lettori fornisce peraltro preziosi suggerimenti che permettono di orientare le nostre visite.

L'indipendenza: la selezione degli esercizi viene effettuata in totale indipendenza, nel solo interesse del lettore. Gli ispettori e il caporedattore discutono collegialmente le scelte. Le massime decisioni vengono prese a livello europeo. La segnalazione degli esercizi all'interno della Guida è interamente gratuita.

La selezione: la Guida offre una selezione dei migliori alberghi e ristoranti per ogni categoria di confort e di prezzo. Tale selezione è il frutto di uno stesso metodo, applicato con rigorosità da tutti gli ispettori.

L'aggiornamento annuale: ogni anno viene riveduto e aggiornato l'insieme dei consigli pratici, delle classifiche e della simbologia al fine di garantire le informazioni più attendibili.

L'omogeneità della selezione: i criteri di valutazione sono gli stessi per tutti i paesi presi in considerazione dalla Guida Michelin.

... e un unico obiettivo: prodigarsi per aiutare il lettore a fare di ogni spostamento e di ogni uscita un momento di piacere, conformemente alla missione che la Michelin si è prefissata: contribuire ad una miglior mobilità.

Editoriale

Caro lettore,

Abbiamo il piacere di presentarle la nostra 33a edizione della Guida Michelin Gran Bretagna & Irlanda.
Questa selezione, che comprende i migliori alberghi e ristoranti per ogni categoria di prezzo, viene effettuata da un'équipe di ispettori professionisti di formazione alberghiera. Ogni anno, percorrono l'intero paese per visitare nuovi esercizi e verificare il livello delle prestazioni di quelli già inseriti nella Guida.

All'interno della selezione, vengono inoltre assegnate ogni anno da ✿ a ✿✿✿ alle migliori tavole. Le stelle contraddistinguono gli esercizi che propongono la miglior cucina, in tutti gli stili, tenendo conto della scelta dei prodotti, della creatività, dell'abilità nel raggiungimento della giusta cottura e nell'abbinamento dei sapori, del rapporto qualità/prezzo, nonché della costanza.

Anche quest'anno, numerose tavole sono state notate per l'evoluzione della loro cucina. Una « **N** » accanto ad ogni esercizio prescelto dell'annata 2006, ne indica l'inserimento fra gli esercizi con una, due o tre stelle.

Desideriamo inoltre segnalare le « *promesse* » per la categoria superiore. Questi esercizi, evidenziati in rosso nella nostra lista, sono i migliori della loro categoria e potranno accedere alla categoria superiore non appena le loro prestazioni avranno raggiunto un livello costante nel tempo, e nelle proposte della carta. Con questa segnalazione speciale, è nostra intenzione farvi conoscere le tavole che costituiscono, dal nostro punto di vista, le principali promesse della gastronomia di domani.

Il vostro parere ci interessa, specialmente riguardo a queste « *promesse* ». Non esitate quindi a scriverci, la vostra partecipazione è importante per orientare le nostre visite e migliorare costantemente la vostra Guida. Grazie ancora per la vostra fedeltà e vi auguriamo buon viaggio con la Guida Michelin 2006.

Consultate la Guida Michelin su
www.ViaMichelin.com
e scriveteci a:
themichelinguide-gbirl@uk.michelin.com

Categorie & simboli distintivi

LE CATEGORIE DI CONFORT

Nella selezione della Guida Michelin vengono segnalati i migliori indirizzi per ogni categoria di confort e di prezzo.Gli esercizi selezionati sono classificati in base al confort che offrono e vengono citati in ordine di preferenza per ogni categoria.

🏨🏨🏨🏨🏨	XXXXX	Gran lusso e tradizione
🏨🏨🏨🏨	XXXX	Gran confort
🏨🏨🏨	XXX	Molto confortevole
🏨🏨	XX	Di buon confort
🏨	X	Abbastanza confortevole
	🍺	Pub tradizionali con cucina
⌂		Pensione, fattorie, case private (forme alternative di ospitalità)
without rest.		L'albergo non ha ristorante
with rm		Il ristorante dispone di camere

I SIMBOLI DISTINTIVI

Per aiutarvi ad effettuare la scelta migliore, segnaliamo gli esercizi che si distinguono in modo particolare. Questi ristoranti sono evidenziati nel testo con ✿ o 😋 e **Rest.**

LE MIGLIORI TAVOLE

Le stelle distinguono gli esercizi che propongono la miglior qualità in campo gastronomico, indipendentemente dagli stili di cucina. I criteri presi in considerazione sono: la scelta dei prodotti, l'abilità nel raggiungimento della giusta cottura e nell'abbinamento dei sapori, il rapporto qualità/prezzo nonché la costanza.

✿✿✿ **Una delle migliori cucine, questa tavola vale il viaggio**
Vi si mangia sempre molto bene, a volte meravigliosamente.

✿✿ **Cucina eccellente, questa tavola merita una deviazione**

✿ **Un'ottima cucina nella sua categoria**

I MIGLIORI ESERCIZI A PREZZI CONTENUTI

😋 **Bib Gourmand**
Esercizio che offre una cucina di qualità a meno di £27 (€38 per l'Irlanda). Prezzo di un pasto, bevanda esclusa.

🛏 **Bib Hotel**
Esercizio che offre un soggiorno di qualità a meno di £75 (€105 per l'Irlanda) per la maggior parte delle camere. Prezzi per 2 persone, prima colazione esclusa.

GLI ESERCIZI AMENI

Il rosso indica gli esercizi particolarmente ameni. Questo per le caratteristiche dell'edificio, le decorazioni non comuni, la sua posizione ed il servizio offerto.

⌂, ⌂ to ⌂⌂⌂⌂⌂ **Alberghi ameni**

🍴, X to XXXXX **Ristoranti ameni**

LE SEGNALAZIONI PARTICOLARI

Oltre alle distinzioni conferite agli esercizi, gli ispettori Michelin apprezzano altri criteri spesso importanti nella scelta di un esercizio.

POSIZIONE

Cercate un esercizio tranquillo o che offre una vista piacevole ? Seguite i simboli seguenti:

Albergo tranquillo

Albergo molto tranquillo

Vista interessante

Vista eccezionale

CARTA DEI VINI

Cercate un ristorante la cui carta dei vini offre una scelta particolarmente interessante ? Seguite il simbolo seguente:

Carta dei vini particolarmente interessante

Attenzione a non confrontare la carta presentata da un sommelier in un grande ristorante con quella di un pub o di un ristorante più semplice. Le due carte vi offriranno degli ottimi vini di diverso livello.

Installazioni & servizi

30 rm	Numero di camere
	Ascensore
	Aria condizionata (in tutto o in parte dell'esercizio)
	Esercizio riservato in parte ai non fumatori. In Irlanda la legge vieta il fumo in tutti i pub, ristoranti e le zone comuni degli alberghi.
	Connessione Internet ad alta velocità in camera
	Esercizio accessibile in parte alle persone con difficoltà motorie
	Attrezzatura per accoglienza e ricreazione dei bambini
	Pasti serviti in giardino o in terrazza
	Wellness centre: centro attrezzato per il benessere ed il relax
	Sauna - Palestra
	Piscina: all'aperto, coperta
	Giardino – Parco
18	Campo di tennis – Golf e numero di buche
	Pontile d'ormeggio
	Pesca aperta ai clienti dell'albergo (eventualmente a pagamento)
150	Sale per conferenze: capienza massima
120	Saloni particolari: capienza massima
	Garage nell'albergo (generalmente a pagamento)
P	Parcheggio riservato alla clientela
	Accesso vietato ai cani (in tutto o in parte dell'esercizio)
	Stazione della metropolitana più vicina (a Londra)
May-October	Periodo di apertura, comunicato dall'albergatore

Prezzi

I prezzi che indichiamo in questa guida sono stati stabiliti nell'autunno 2005; potranno subire delle variazioni in relazione ai cambiamenti dei prezzi di beni e servizi. Gli albergatori e i ristoratori si sono impegnati, sotto la propria responsabilità, a praticare questi prezzi ai clienti.
In occasione di alcune manifestazioni commerciali o turistiche i prezzi richiesti dagli albergatori potrebbero subire un sensibile aumento nelle località interessate e nei loro dintorni.
I prezzi sono indicati in lire sterline (1 £ = 100 pence) ad eccezione per la Repubblica d'Irlanda dove sono indicati in euro.

Prezzi

Tutte le tariffe per il soggiorno includono sia servizio che I.V.A. Tutti i prezzi dei ristoranti includono l'I.V.A., il servizio è incluso quando dopo il prezzo appare « **s.** ». Quando non compare « **s.** », il prezzo può essere soggetto ad un aumento per il servizio solitamente compreso tra il 10 % e il 15 %.
In bassa stagione, alcuni esercizi applicano condizioni più vantaggiose, informatevi al momento della prenotazione.
Entrate nell'albergo o nel ristorante con la guida in mano, dismostrando in tal modo la fiducia in chi vi ha indirizzato.

LA CAPARRA

Alcuni albergatori chiedono il versamento di una caparra. Si tratta di un deposito-garanzia che impegna sia l'albergatore che il cliente. Vi consigliamo di farvi precisare le norme riguardanti la reciproca garanzia di tale caparra.

CARTE DI CREDITO

AE ⦶ MC VISA — Carte di credito accettate: American Express – Diners Club – MasterCard – Visa

CAMERE

rm 🚹 50.00/90.00	Prezzo minimo e massimo per una camera singola di buon confort
rm 🚹🚹 70.00/120.00	Prezzo minimo e massimo per una camera doppia per due persone
rm ☕ 55.00/85.00	Prezzo della camera compresa la prima colazione
☕ 6.00	Prezzo della prima colazione

SHORT BREAKS

Alcuni alberghi propongono delle condizioni particolarmente vantaggiose o short break per un soggiorno minimo di due notti. Questo prezzo, calcolato per persona e per un minimo di due persone, comprende: camera, cena e prima colazione. Informarsi presso l'albergatore.

RISTORANTE

Menu a prezzo fisso: prezzo minimo £13 e massimo £28 comprendente generalmente 3 piatti. Il menu a prezzo minimo è spesso disponibile solo a pranzo.

Pasto alla carta

Il primo prezzo corrisponde ad un pasto semplice comprendente: primo, piatto del giorno e dessert. Il secondo prezzo corrisponde ad un pasto più completo (con specialità) comprendente: due piatti e dessert.

s.	Servizio compresso
🎭	Ristoranti che offrono menu a prezzi ridotti prima e/o dopo gli spettacoli teatrali
🍷	Vino servito al bicchiere

⌂ : Negli alberghi di questa categoria, la cena viene servita, ad un'ora stabilita, esclusivamente a chi vi allogia. Il menu, a prezzo fisso, offre una scelta limitata di piatti. Raramente viene servito anche il pranzo. Molti di questi esercizi non hanno l'autorizzazione a vendere alcolici.

Città

GENERALITÀ

✉ *York*	Codice di avviamento postale
501 M27, ⑩	Numero della carta Michelin e del riquadro
Great Britain G.	Vedere la Guida Verde Michelin Gran Bretagna
pop. 1057	Popolazione residente
BX A	Lettere indicanti l'ubicazione sulla pianta
18	Golf e numero di buche (handicap generalmente richiesto, prenotazione telefonica vivamente consigliata)
	Panorama, vista
	Aeroporto
	Trasporti marittimi
	Trasporti marittimi (solo passeggeri)
	Ufficio informazioni turistiche

ORA LEGALE

I visitatori dovranno tenere in considerazione l'ora ufficiale nelle Isole Britanniche: un'ora di ritardo sull'ora italiana.

INFORMAZIONI TURISTICHE

INTERESSE TURISTICO

★★★	Vale il viaggio
★★	Merita una deviazione
★	Interessante
AC	Entrata a pagamento

UBICAZIONE

See	Nella città
Envir.	Nei dintorni della città
Exc.	Nella regione
N, S, E, W	Il luogo si trova a Nord, a Sud, a Est, a Ovest della località
A 22	Ci si va per la strada A 22 indicata con lo stesso segno sulla pianta
2 m.	Distanza in miglia (solo per la Gran Bretagna)

Piante

ⓐ ● a	Alberghi – Ristoranti

CURIOSITÀ

Edificio interessante
Costruzione religiosa interessante

VIABILITÀ

M 1	Autostrada
4 4	numero dello svincolo: completo, parziale
	Strada a carreggiate separate
	Grande via di circolazione
A 2	Itinerario principale: Primary route (GB) o National route (IRL)
	Senso unico – Via impraticabile, a circolazione regolamentata
	Via pedonale – Tranvia
Piccadilly P	Via commerciale – Parcheggio – Parcheggio Ristoro
	Porta – Sottopassaggio – Galleria
15'5	Sottopassaggio (altezza inferiore a 15'5) sulle grandi vie di circolazione
	Stazione e ferrovia
	Funicolare – Funivia, cabinovia
B	Ponte mobile – Traghetto per auto

SIMBOLI VARI

	Ufficio informazioni turistiche
	Chiesa – Moschea – Sinagoga
	Torre o pilone per telecomunicazioni – Ruderi
	Giardino, parco, bosco – Cimitero
9	Stadio – Ippodromo – Golf
	Golf riservato – Pattinaggio
	Piscina: all'aperto, coperta
	Vista – Panorama
	Monumento – Fontana – Ospedale – Mercato coperto
	Porto turistico – Faro
	Aeroporto – Stazione della metropolitana – Autostazione
	Trasporto con traghetto: passeggeri ed autovetture
	Ufficio postale centrale
	Edificio pubblico indicato con lettera:
C H J	Sede dell'Amministrazione di Contea – Municipio – Palazzo di Giustizia
M T U	Museo – Teatro – Università, Scuola superiore
POL.	Polizia (Questura, nelle grandi città)

LONDRA

BRENT WEMBLEY	Distretto amministrativo (Borough) – Quartiere (Area)
	Limite del Borough
	Area con circolazione a pagamento Lunedì-Venerdì 07.00-18.30
	Stazione della metropolitana più vicina all'albergo o al ristorante

Carte dei dintorni

SAPETE COME USARLE?

Se desiderate, per esempio, trovare un buon indirizzo nei dintorni di Leeds, la "carta dei dintorni" (qui accanto) richiama la vostra attenzione su tutte le località citate nella Guida che si trovino nei dintorni della città prescelta, e in particolare su quelle raggiungibili nel raggio di 16 miles/25 km (limite di colore).

Le "carte dei dintorni" coprono l'intero territorio e permettono la localizzazione rapida di tutte le risorse proposte dalla Guida nei dintorni delle metropoli regionali.

NOTA:

Quando una località è presente su una "carta dei dintorni", la città a cui ci si riferisce è scritta in BLU nella linea delle distanze da città a città.

ESEMPIO:

ILKLEY is to be found on the local map LEEDS.

ILKLEY W. Yorks 502 O 22
– pop. 13 472.
Myddleton ✆ (01943) 607277
Station Rd ✆ (01943) 602319
London 210 – Bradford 13 – Harrogate 17 – Leeds 16 – Preston 46

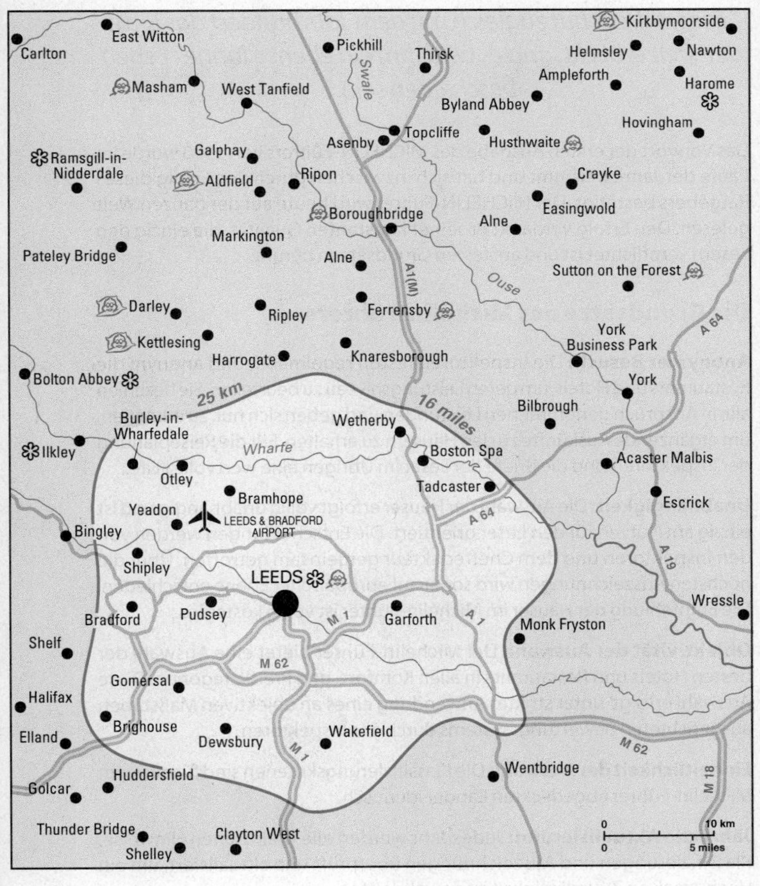

Kirkbymoorside
Carlton
East Witton
Pickhill
Thirsk
Helmsley
Nawton
Swale
Masham
West Tanfield
Ampleforth
Harome
Byland Abbey
Hovingham
Topcliffe
Asenby
Husthwaite
Galphay
Ramsgill-in-
Nidderdale
Aldfield
Ripon
Crayke
Easingwold
Boroughbridge
Alne
Markington
Pateley Bridge
Alne
A1(M)
Sutton on the Forest
Ouse
Darley
Ripley
Ferrensby
A 64
Kettlesing
York
Business Park
Harrogate
Knaresborough
Bolton Abbey
York
25 km
16 miles
Bilbrough
Burley-in-
Wharfedale
Wetherby
Ilkley
Wharfe
Boston Spa
Acaster Malbis
Otley
Tadcaster
Bramhope
Escrick
Yeadon
A 64
LEEDS & BRADFORD
AIRPORT
Bingley
A 19
Shipley
LEEDS
Wressle
Bradford
Pudsey
M 1
Garforth
A 1
Monk Fryston
Shelf
M 62
Gomersal
Halifax
Brighouse
Dewsbury
Wakefield
Elland
M 1
M 62
Huddersfield
Wentbridge
M 18
Golcar
Thunder Bridge
Clayton West
Shelley
0
10 km
0
5 miles

Grundsätze

„Dieses Werk hat zugleich mit dem Jahrhundert das Licht der Welt erblickt, und es wird ihm ein ebenso langes Leben beschieden sein."

Das Vorwort der ersten Ausgabe des MICHELIN-Führers von 1900 wurde im Laufe der Jahre berühmt und hat sich inzwischen durch den Erfolg dieses Ratgebers bestätigt. Der MICHELIN-Führer wird heute auf der ganzen Welt gelesen. Den Erfolg verdankt er seiner konstanten Qualität, die einzig den Lesern verpflichtet ist und auf festen Grundsätzen beruht.

Die Grundsätze des Michelin-Führers:

Anonymer Besuch: Die Inspektoren testen regelmäßig und anonym die Restaurants und Hotels, um deren Leistungsniveau zu beurteilen. Sie bezahlen alle in Anspruch genommenen Leistungen und geben sich nur zu erkennen, um ergänzende Auskünfte zu den Häusern zu erhalten. Für die Reiseplanung der Inspektoren sind die Briefe der Leser im Übrigen eine wertvolle Hilfe.

Unabhängigkeit: Die Auswahl der Häuser erfolgt völlig unabhängig und ist einzig am Nutzen für den Leser orientiert. Die Entscheidungen werden von den Inspektoren und dem Chefredakteur gemeinsam getroffen. Über die höchsten Auszeichnungen wird sogar auf europäischer Ebene entschieden. Die Empfehlung der Häuser im Michelin-Führer ist völlig kostenlos.

Objektivität der Auswahl: Der Michelin-Führer bietet eine Auswahl der besten Hotels und Restaurants in allen Komfort- und Preiskategorien. Diese Auswahl erfolgt unter strikter Anwendung eines an objektiven Maßstäben ausgerichteten Bewertungssystems durch alle Inspektoren.

Einheitlichkeit der Auswahl: Die Klassifizierungskriterien sind für alle vom Michelin-Führer abgedeckten Länder identisch.

Jährliche Aktualisierung: Jedes Jahr werden alle praktischen Hinweise, Klassifizierungen und Auszeichnungen überprüft und aktualisiert, um ein Höchstmaß an Zuverlässigkeit zu gewährleisten.

... und sein einziges Ziel – dem Leser bestmöglich behilflich zu sein, damit jede Reise und jeder Restaurantbesuch zu einem Vergnügen werden, entsprechend der Aufgabe, die sich Michelin gesetzt hat: die Mobilität in den Vordergrund zu stellen.

Lieber Leser

Lieber Leser,

Wir freuen uns, Ihnen die 33. Ausgabe des Michelin-Führers Great Britain & Ireland vorstellen zu dürfen. Diese Auswahl der besten Hotels und Restaurants in allen Preiskategorien wird von einem Team von Inspektoren mit Ausbildung in der Hotellerie erstellt. Sie bereisen das ganze Jahr hindurch das Land. Ihre Aufgabe ist es, die Qualität und Leistung der bereits empfohlenen und der neu hinzu kommenden Hotels und Restaurants kritisch zu prüfen. In unserer Auswahl weisen wir jedes Jahr auf die besten Restaurants hin, die wir mit ✿ bis ✿✿✿ kennzeichnen. Die Sterne zeichnen die Häuser mit der besten Küche aus, wobei unterschiedliche Küchenstilrichtungen vertreten sind. Als Kriterien dienen die Wahl der Produkte, die fachgerechte Zubereitung, der Geschmack der Gerichte, die Kreativität und das Preis-Leistungs-Verhältnis, sowie die Beständigkeit der Küchenleistung. Dieses Jahr werden ferner zahlreiche Restaurants für die Weiterentwicklung ihrer Küche hervorgehoben. Um die neu hinzugekommenen Häuser des Jahrgangs 2006 mit einem, zwei oder drei Sternen zu präsentieren, haben wir diese mit einem "**N**" gekennzeichnet.

Außerdem möchten wir die *"Hoffnungsträger"* für die nächsthöheren Kategorien hervorheben. Diese Häuser, die in der Liste in Rot aufgeführt sind, sind die besten ihrer Kategorie und könnten in Zukunft aufsteigen, wenn sich die Qualität ihrer Leistungen dauerhaft und auf die gesamte Karte bezogen bestätigt hat. Mit dieser besonderen Kennzeichnung möchten wir Ihnen die Restaurants aufzeigen, die in unseren Augen die Hoffnung für die Gastronomie von morgen sind. Ihre Meinung interessiert uns! Bitte teilen Sie uns diese mit, insbesondere hinsichtlich dieser *"Hoffnungsträger"*. Ihre Mitarbeit ist für die Planung unserer Besuche und für die ständige Verbesserung des Michelin-Führers von großer Bedeutung.

Wir danken Ihnen für Ihre Treue und wünschen Ihnen angenehme Reisen mit dem Michelin-Führer 2006.

Den Michelin-Führer finden Sie auch im Internet unter
www.ViaMichelin.com
oder schreiben Sie uns eine E-Mail:
themichelinguide-gbirl@uk.michelin.com

Kategorien & Auszeichnungen

KOMFORTKATEGORIEN

Der Michelin-Führer bietet in seiner Auswahl die besten Adressen jeder Komfort- und Preiskategorie. Die ausgewählten Häuser sind nach dem gebotenen Komfort geordnet; die Reihenfolge innerhalb jeder Kategorie drückt eine weitere Rangordnung aus.

- Großer Luxus und Tradition
- Großer Komfort
- Sehr komfortabel
- Mit gutem Komfort
- Mit Standard-Komfort
- Traditionelle Pubs, die Speisen anbieten
- Andere empfohlene Übernachtungsmöglichkeiten (Gästehäuser, Bauernhäuser und private Übernachtungs möglichkeiten)

without rest. Hotel ohne Restaurant

with rm Restaurant vermietet auch Zimmer

AUSZEICHNUNGEN

Um ihnen behilflich zu sein, die bestmögliche Wahl zu treffen, haben einige besonders bemerkenswerte Adressen dieses Jahr eine Auszeichnung erhalten. Die Sterne bzw. „Bib Gourmand" sind durch das entsprechende Symbol bzw. und **Rest** gekennzeichnet.

DIE BESTEN RESTAURANTS

Die Häuser, die eine überdurchschnittlich gute Küche bieten, wobei alle Stilrichtungen vertreten sind, wurden mit einem Stern ausgezeichnet. Die Kriterien sind: die Wahl der Produkte, die Kreativität, die fachgerechte Zubereitung und der Geschmack, sowie das Preis-Leistungs-Verhältnis und die immer gleich bleibende Qualität.

Eine der besten Küchen: eine Reise wert
Man isst hier immer sehr gut, öfters auch exzellent.

Eine hervorragende Küche: verdient einen Umweg

Ein sehr gutes Restaurant in seiner Kategorie

DIE BESTEN PREISWERTEN HÄUSER

Bib Gourmand
Häuser, die eine gute Küche für weniger als £27 (GB) bzw. €38 (IRE) bieten (Preis für eine dreigängige Mahlzeit ohne Getränke).

Bib Hotel
Häuser, die eine Mehrzahl ihrer komfortablen Zimmer für weniger als £75 (GB) bzw. €105 (IRE) anbieten (Preis für 2 Personen inkl. Frühstück).

DIE ANGENEHMSTEN ADRESSEN

Die rote Kennzeichnung weist auf besonders angenehme Häuser hin. Dies kann sich auf den besonderen Charakter des Gebäudes, die nicht alltägliche Einrichtung, die Lage, den Empfang oder den gebotenen Service beziehen.

⌂, 🏠 to 🏠🏠🏠🏠🏠 **Angenehme Hotels**

🍺, ✗ to ✗✗✗✗✗ **Angenehme Restaurants**

BESONDERE ANGABEN

Neben den Auszeichnungen, die den Häusern verliehen werden, legen die Michelin-Inspektoren auch Wert auf andere Kriterien, die bei der Wahl einer Adresse oft von Bedeutung sind.

LAGE

Wenn Sie eine ruhige Adresse oder ein Haus mit einer schönen Aussicht suchen, achten Sie auf diese Symbole:

- Ruhiges Hotel
- Sehr ruhiges Hotel
- ← Interessante Sicht
- ← Besonders schöne Aussicht

WEINKARTE

Wenn Sie ein Restaurant mit einer besonders interessanten Weinauswahl suchen, achten Sie auf dieses Symbol:

Weinkarte mit besonders attraktivem Angebot

Aber vergleichen Sie bitte nicht die Weinkarte, die Ihnen vom Sommelier eines großen Hauses präsentiert wird, mit der Auswahl eines Gasthauses, dessen Besitzer die Weine der Region mit Sorgfalt zusammenstellt.

Einrichtung & Service

30 rm	Anzahl der Zimmer
	Fahrstuhl
	Klimaanlage (im ganzen Haus bzw. in den Zimmern oder im Restaurant)
	Nichtraucherzimmer vorhanden. In der Republik Irland ist Rauchen per Gesetz verboten: in allen Pubs, Restaurants und in den öffentlichen Bereichen der Hotels.
	High-Speed Internetzugang in den Zimmern möglich
	Für Körperbehinderte leicht zugängliches Haus
	Spezielle Angebote für Kinder
	Terrasse mit Speisenservice
	Wellnessbereich
	Sauna - Fitnessraum
	Freibad oder Hallenbad
	Liegewiese, Garten – Park
18	Tennisplatz – Golfplatz und Lochzahl
	Bootssteg
	Angelmöglichkeit für Hotelgäste, evtl. gegen Gebühr
150	Konferenzraum mit Kapazität
120	Veranstaltungsraum mit Kapazität
	Hotelgarage (wird gewöhnlich berechnet)
P	Parkplatz reserviert für Gäste
	Hunde sind unerwünscht (im ganzen Haus bzw. in den Zimmern oder im Restaurant)
	Nächstgelegene U-Bahnstation (in London)
May-October	Öffnungszeit, vom Hotelier mitgeteilt

Preise

Die in diesem Führer genannten Preise wurden uns im Herbst 2005 angegeben und beziehen sich auf die Hauptsaison. Sie können sich mit den Preisen von Waren und Dienstleistungen ändern.
Die Häuser haben sich verpflichtet, die von den Hoteliers selbst angegebenen Preise den Kunden zu berechnen.
Anlässlich größerer Veranstaltungen, Messen und Ausstellungen werden von den Hotels in manchen Städten und deren Umgebung erhöhte Preise verlangt.
Die Preise sind in Pfund Sterling angegeben (1 £ = 100 pence) mit Ausnahme der Republik Irland, wo sie in Euro angegeben sind.

Alle Übernachtungspreise enthalten Bedienung und MWSt. Die Restaurantpreise enthalten die MWSt., Bedienung ist enthalten, wenn ein **s.** nach dem Preis steht.
Wo kein **s.** angegeben ist, können unterschiedliche Zuschläge erhoben werden, normalerweise zwischen 10%-15% (keine MWSt. auf den Kanalinseln). Erkundigen Sie sich bei den Hoteliers nach eventuellen Sonderbedingungen.

RESERVIERUNG UND ANZAHLUNG

Einige Hoteliers verlangen zur Bestätigung der Reservierung eine Anzahlung. Dies ist als Garantie sowohl für den Hotelier als auch für den Gast anzusehen. Bitten Sie den Hotelier, dass er Ihnen in seinem Bestätigungsschreiben alle seine Bedingungen mitteilt.

KREDITKARTEN

AE ⓓ MC VISA	Akzeptierte Kreditkarten: American Express – Diners Club – Mastercard – Visa

ZIMMER

rm 🚹 50.00/90.00	Mindestpreis 50.00 und Höchstpreis 90.00 für ein Einzelzimmer
rm 🚹🚹 70.00/120.00	Mindestpreis 70.00 und Höchstpreis 120.00 für ein Doppelzimmer
rm ☕ 55.00/85.00	Zimmerpreis inkl. Frühstück (selbst wenn dieses nicht eingenommen wird)
☕ 6.00	Preis des Frühstücks

SHORT BREAKS

Einige Hotels bieten Vorzugskonditionen für einen Mindestaufenthalt von zwei Nächten oder mehr (Short break). Der Preis ist pro Person kalkuliert, bei einer Mindestbeteiligung von zwei Personen und schließt das Zimmer, Abendessen und Frühstück ein. Bitte fragen Sie im Hotel nach dieser Rate.

RESTAURANT

Menupreise: mindestens £13.00, höchstens £28.00 für eine dreigängige Mahlzeit. Das Menu mit dem niedrigen Preis ist oft nur mittags erhältlich.
Mahlzeiten „à la carte": Die Preise entsprechen einer dreigängigen Mahlzeit.

s.	Bedienung inkl.
🎭	Restaurants mit preiswerten Menus vor oder nach dem Theaterbesuch
🍷	Wein wird glasweise ausgeschenkt

⌂ : In dieser Hotelkategorie wird ein Abendessen normalerweise nur zu bestimmten Zeiten für Hotelgäste angeboten. Es besteht aus einem Menu mit begrenzter Auswahl zu festgesetztem Preis. Mittagessen wird selten angeboten. Viele dieser Hotels sind nicht berechtigt, alkoholische Getränke auszuschenken.

Städte

ALLGEMEINES

✉ *York*	Postadresse
501 M27, ⑩	Nummer der Michelin-Karte mit Koordinaten
Great Britain G.	Siehe Grünen Michelin-Reiseführer Großbritannien
pop. 1057	Einwohnerzahl
BX A	Markierung auf dem Stadtplan
18	Golfplatz mit Lochzahl (Handicap manchmal erforderlich, telefonische Reservierung empfehlenswert)
	Rundblick, Aussichtspunkt
	Flughafen
	Autofähre
	Personenfähre
	Informationsstelle

UHRZEIT

In Großbritannien ist eine Zeitverschiebung zu beachten und die Uhr gegenüber der deutschen Zeit um 1 Stunde zurückzustellen.

SEHENSWÜRDIGKEITEN

BEWERTUNG

★★★	Eine Reise wert
★★	Verdient einen Umweg
★	Sehenswert
AC	Eintrittspreis

LAGE

See	In der Stadt
Envir.	In der Umgebung der Stadt
Exc.	Ausflugsziele
N, S, E, W	Im Norden, Süden, Osten, Westen der Stadt
A 22	Zu erreichen über die Straße A 22
2m.	Entfernung in Meilen (in der Republik Irland in Kilometern)

Stadtpläne

ⓐ● a Hotels – Restaurants

SEHENSWÜRDIGKEITEN

Sehenswertes Gebäude
Sehenswerte Kirche

STRASSEN

M 1 Autobahn
4 4 Nummern der Anschlussstellen: Autobahnein- und/oder -ausfahrt
Schnellstraße
Hauptverkehrsstraße
A 2 Fernverkehrsstraße (Primary route: GB – National route: IRL))
Einbahnstraße – Gesperrte Straße, mit Verkehrsbeschränkungen
Fußgängerzone – Straßenbahn
Piccadilly P R Einkaufsstraße – Parkplatz, Parkhaus – Park -and-Ride-Plätze
Tor – Passage – Tunnel
15'5 Unterführung (Höhe bis 16'6'') auf Hauptverkehrsstraßen
Bahnhof und Bahnlinie
Standseilbahn – Cable Car
B Bewegliche Brücke – Autofähre

SONSTIGE ZEICHEN

Informationsstelle
Kirche/Gebetshaus – Moschee – Synagoge
Funk-, Fernsehturm – Ruine
Garten, Park, Wäldchen – Friedhof
9 Stadion – Pferderennbahn – Golfplatz
Golfplatz (Zutritt bedingt erlaubt) – Eisbahn
Freibad – Hallenbad
Aussicht – Rundblick
Denkmal – Brunnen – Krankenhaus – Markthalle
Jachthafen – Leuchtturm
Flughafen – U-Bahnstation – Autobusbahnhof
Schiffsverbindungen: Autofähre – Personenfähre
Hauptpostamt
Öffentliches Gebäude, durch einen Buchstaben gekennzeichnet:
C H J – Sitz der Grafschaftsverwaltung – Rathaus-Gerichtsgebäude
M T U – Museum – Theater – Universität, Hochschule
POL. – Polizei (in größeren Städten Polizeipräsidium)

LONDON

BRENT WEMBLEY – Name des Stadtteils (borough) – Name des Viertels (area)
– Grenze des «borough»
– Gebührenpflichtiger Innenstadtbereich (Mo-Fr 7-18.30 Uhr)
⊖ – Dem Hotel oder Restaurant nächstgelegene U-Bahnstation

Umgebungskarten

DENKEN SIE DARAN, SIE ZU BENUTZEN

Die Umgebungskarten sollen Ihnen die Suche eines Hotels oder Restaurants in der Nähe der größeren Städte erleichtern.

Wenn Sie beispielsweise eine gute Adresse in der Nähe von Leeds brauchen, gibt Ihnen die Karte schnell einen Überblick über alle Orte, die in diesem Michelin-Führer erwähnt sind.

Innerhalb der in Kontrastfarbe gedruckten Grenze liegen Gemeinden, die im Umkreis von 16 miles/ 25 km zu erreichen sind.

ANMERKUNG:

Auf der Linie der Entfernungen zu anderen Orten erscheint im Ortstext die jeweils nächste Stadt mit Umgebungskarte in „BLAU".

BEISPIEL:

ILKLEY W. Yorks 502 O 22
– pop. 13 472.

ILKLEY	*18 Myddleton ℘ (01943) 607277*
is to be found	*Station Rd ℘ (01943) 602319*
on the local map	*London 210 – Bradford 13 – Harrogate 17 –*
LEEDS.	*Leeds 16 – Preston 46*

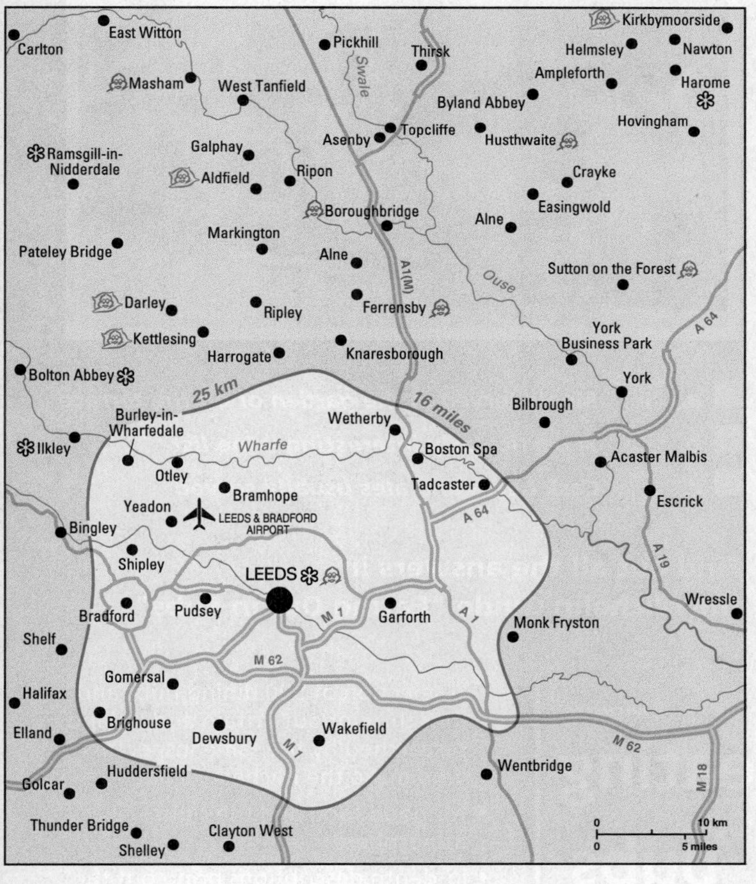
Kirkbymoorside
Carlton
East Witton
Pickhill
Thirsk
Helmsley
Nawton
Swale
Masham
West Tanfield
Ampleforth
Harome
Byland Abbey
Hovingham
Topcliffe
Asenby
Husthwaite
Galphay
Ramsgill-in-Nidderdale
Ripon
Crayke
Aldfield
Easingwold
Boroughbridge
Alne
Markington
Pateley Bridge
Alne
A1(M)
Ouse
Sutton on the Forest
Darley
Ripley
Ferrensby
A 64
Kettlesing
York Business Park
Harrogate
Knaresborough
Bolton Abbey
York
25 km
16 miles
Bilbrough
Burley-in-Wharfedale
Wetherby
Wharfe
Ilkley
Boston Spa
Acaster Malbis
Otley
Tadcaster
Bramhope
Escrick
Yeadon
LEEDS & BRADFORD AIRPORT
A 64
Bingley
A 19
Shipley
LEEDS
Wressle
Bradford
Pudsey
M 1
Garforth
A 1
Monk Fryston
Shelf
M 62
Gomersal
Halifax
Brighouse
Elland
Dewsbury
Wakefield
M 1
M 62
Huddersfield
Wentbridge
M 18
Golcar
Thunder Bridge
Clayton West
Shelley
0
10 km
0
5 miles

Awards 2006

Distinctions 2006
Le distinzioni 2006
Auszeichnungen 2006

Starred establishments

Les tables étoilées
Esercizi con stelle
Sterne-Restaurants

✿✿✿

ENGLAND

Bray-on-Thames	*Fat Duck*
–	*The Waterside Inn*
London	*Gordon Ramsay*

✿✿

ENGLAND

Cambridge	*Midsummer House*
Chagford	*Gidleigh Park*
Cheltenham	*Le Champignon Sauvage*
London	*Capital*
–	*Le Gavroche*
–	*Pied à Terre*
–	*The Square*
Ludlow	*Hibiscus*
Oxford	*Le Manoir aux Quat' Saisons*

SCOTLAND

Auchterarder	*Andrew Fairlie at Gleneagles*	**N**

IRELAND

Republic of Ireland

Dublin	*Patrick Guilbaud*

✿

In red, *the 2006 Rising Stars for* ✿✿
→ **En rouge,** *les espoirs 2006 pour* ✿✿
→ **In rosso,** *le promesse 2006 per* ✿✿
→ **In roter Schrift,** *die Hoffnungsträger 2006 für* ✿✿

ENGLAND

Abinger Hammer	*Drakes on the Pond*	
Altrincham	*Juniper*	
Baslow	*Fischer's at Baslow Hall*	
Bath	*Bath Priory*	
–	*Lucknam Park*	**N**
Biddenden	*The West House*	
Birmingham	*Jessica's*	
–	*Simpsons*	
Blackburn	*Northcote Manor*	
Blakeney	*Morston Hall*	
Bolton Abbey	*The Devonshire Arms Country House*	
Britwell Salome	*The Goose*	
Brockenhurst	*Le Poussin at Whitley Ridge*	**N**

N *New* ✿, ✿✿
→ *Nouveau* ✿, ✿✿ → *Nuovo* ✿, ✿✿ → *Neu* ✿, ✿✿

Chester	*Arkle*	
Cuckfield	*Ockenden Manor*	
Dartmouth	*The New Angel*	
East Grinstead	*Gravetye Manor*	
Emsworth	*36 on the Quay*	
Faversham	*Read's*	
Grange-over-Sands	*L'Enclume*	
Grantham	*Harry's Place*	
Helmsley	*The Star Inn*	
Henley-in-Arden	*Edmunds*	
Hungerford	*The Hare*	**N**
Ilkley	*Box Tree*	
Jersey	*Bohemia*	
Kington	*Stagg Inn*	
Leeds	*Pool Court at 42*	
London	*Amaya*	**N**
–	*Angela Hartnett at The Connaught*	
–	*Assaggi*	
–	*Aubergine*	
–	*Chapter One*	
–	*Chez Bruce*	
–	*Club Gascon*	
–	*L'Escargot*	
–	*Foliage*	
–	*The Glasshouse*	
–	*Gordon Ramsay at Claridge's*	
–	*The Greenhouse*	
–	*Hakkasan*	
–	*The Ledbury*	**N**
–	*Locanda Locatelli*	
–	*Maze*	**N**
–	*Mirabelle*	
–	*Nahm*	
–	*Nobu*	
–	*Nobu Berkeley*	
–	*1 Lombard Street (Restaurant)*	
–	*Orrery*	
–	*Pétrus*	
–	*Rasoi Vineet Bhatia*	**N**
–	*Rhodes Twenty Four*	
–	*Richard Corrigan at Lindsay House*	
–	*River Café*	
–	*Roussillon*	
–	*The Savoy Grill*	
–	*Sketch (The Lecture Room)*	
–	*Tamarind*	
–	*Tom Aikens*	
–	*Umu*	
–	*Yauatcha*	
–	*Zafferano*	
Longridge	*The Longridge Restaurant*	
Ludlow	*Mr Underhill's at Dinham Weir*	
Malmesbury	*Whatley Manor*	
Marlow	*The Hand & Flowers*	**N**
Midsomer Norton	*The Moody Goose At The Old Priory*	**N**
Newbury	*Vineyard*	
Nottingham	*Restaurant Sat Bains*	
Oakham	*Hambleton Hall*	
Padstow	*Ripleys*	
–	*St Ervan Manor*	**N**
Pateley Bridge	*Yorke Arms*	
Petersfield	*JSW*	
Reading	*L'Ortolan*	
Ripley	*Drake's*	
Royal Leamington Spa	*Mallory Court*	
Sheffield	*Old Vicarage*	
South Molton	*The Masons Arms*	**N**
Stamford	*The Olive Branch*	
Stockbridge	*The Greyhound*	
Taplow	*Waldo's (at Cliveden H.)*	**N**
Taunton	*The Castle*	
Tavistock	*Horn of Plenty*	
Tetbury	*The Trouble House*	
Torquay	*The Elephant*	**N**
–	*Orestone Manor*	**N**
Ullswater	*Sharrow Bay Country House*	
Winchcombe	*5 North St.*	
Windermere	*Gilpin Lodge*	**N**
–	*Holbeck Ghyll*	
Winteringham	*Winteringham Fields*	
Yarmouth	*The George*	

SCOTLAND

Achiltibuie	*Summer Isles*	
Ballachulish	*Ballachulish House*	
Castle Douglas	*Plumed Horse*	
Dalry	*Braidwoods*	
Edinburgh	*Martin Wishart*	
–	*Number One (at Balmoral H.)*	
Fort William	*Inverlochy Castle*	
Portpatrick	*Knockinaam Lodge*	

WALES

Machynlleth	*Ynyshir Hall*	**N**
Pwllheli	*Plas Bodegroes*	

IRELAND

Northern Ireland

Belfast	*Restaurant Michael Deane*

Republic of Ireland

Dublin	*L'Ecrivain*
–	*Thornton's (at The Fitzwilliam H.)*

In red, the 2006 Rising Stars for ✿
→ **En rouge,** les espoirs 2006 pour ✿
→ **In rosso,** le promesse 2006 per ✿
→ **In roter Schrift,** die Hoffnungsträger 2006 für ✿

Birkenhead	*Fraiche*
Jersey	*Atlantic*
Hungerford	*The Harrow*

Bib Gourmand

Good food at moderate prices
Repas soignés à prix modérés
Pasti accurati a prezzi contenuti
Sorgfältig zubereitete, preiswerte Mahlzeiten

ENGLAND

Aldeburgh	*The Lighthouse*	
Alderley Edge	*The Wizard*	
Birmingham	*La Toque d'Or*	
Blackpool	*Twelve*	
Boroughbridge	*thediningroom*	
Bray-on-Thames	*Hinds Head*	
Brighton and Hove	*The Real Eating Company*	**N**
–	*Terre à Terre*	
Bromsgrove	*Epic*	
Burnham Market	*The Restaurant (at The Hoste Arms)*	
Cambridge	*22 Chesterton Road*	
Canterbury	*The Granville*	**N**
Castle Cary	*The Camelot*	**N**
Chipping Campden	*Churchill Arms*	
Cranbrook	*Apicius*	**N**
Danehill	*Coach & Horses*	
Dorking	*The Stephan Langton Inn*	
Durham	*Bistro 21*	
Exeter	*Jack in the Green Inn*	
Faversham	*The Dove*	
Guernsey	*The Pavilion*	
Haddenham	*Green Dragon*	
Hurley	*Black Boys Inn*	**N**
Husthwaite	*The Roasted Pepper*	
Itteringham	*Walpole Arms*	
Jersey	*Green Island*	
–	*Village Bistro*	
Kenilworth	*Simply Simpsons*	
Knaresborough	*The General*	
–	*Tarleton Inn*	
Leeds	*Brasserie Forty Four*	
–	*The Calls Grill*	
Liverpool	*Simply Heathcotes*	
London	*L'Accento*	
–	*Agni*	**N**
–	*Al Duca*	
–	*Anchor & Hope*	
–	*Brasserie La Trouvaille*	
–	*Brasserie Roux*	
–	*Brula Bistrot*	
–	*Café Spice Namaste*	
–	*Chapter Two*	
–	*Comptoir Gascon*	**N**
–	*Cotto*	
–	*Galvin*	**N**
–	*Ma Cuisine (Kew)*	
–	*Ma Cuisine (Twickenham)*	
–	*Malabar*	
–	*Mello*	**N**
–	*Metrogusto*	
–	*The Parsee*	
–	*Le Petit Max*	
–	*Racine*	
–	*Salt Yard*	**N**
–	*Sarkhel's*	
Loughborough	*Lang's*	
Lowick	*Snooty Fox*	
Manchester	*Café Jem&I*	

N *New*
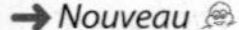
→ *Nouveau* → *Nuovo* → *Neu*

Masham	*Vennell's*	**N**
Melton Mowbray	*Red Lion Inn*	
Mistley	*The Mistley Thorn*	
Newcastle upon Tyne	*Café 21*	
Norwich	*1 Up at The Mad Moose Arms*	
–	*Wildebeest Arms*	
Oldham	*Brasserie (at White Hart Inn)*	
Ombersley	*Epic*	**N**
Orford	*The Trinity (at Crown and Castle H.)*	
Oxford	*Mole Inn*	
Padstow	*Rick Stein's Café*	**N**
Preston	*Inside Out*	
–	*Winckley Square Chop House*	
Ramsbottom	*Ramsons*	
Ross-on-Wye	*The Lough Pool Inn*	
Royal Tunbridge Wells	*George and Dragon*	**N**
Rushlake Green	*Stone House*	
St Albans	*Sukiyaki*	
Saxmundham	*The Bell*	
Sheffield	*Thyme*	
Skipton	*Angel Inn*	
Southport	*Warehouse Brasserie*	
Sowerby Bridge	*The Millbank*	
Stamford	*The Jackson Stops Inn*	
Standish	*The Mulberry Tree*	
Stow-on-the-Wold	*The Old Butchers*	**N**
Summercourt	*Viners*	
Sutton-on-the-Forest	*Rose & Crown*	
Tynemouth	*Sidney's*	
Ullingswick	*Three Crowns Inn*	
Westfield	*The Wild Mushroom*	**N**
West Malling	*The Swan*	
Whitstable	*The Sportsman*	
Windsor	*Al Fassia*	
Witney	*The Navy Oak*	
Woodbridge	*The Captain's Table*	

SCOTLAND

Crieff	*The Bank*	**N**
Edinburgh	*Atrium*	
Kintyre (Peninsula)		
Kilberry	*Kilberry Inn*	**N**
Sorn	*Sorn Inn*	
Strathyre	*Creagan House*	

WALES

Llandudno	*Nikki Ip's*
Newport	*The Chandlery*

IRELAND

Northern Ireland

Belfast	*Aldens*
–	*Cayenne*
–	*Deanes Brasserie*
Holywood	*Fontana*

Republic of Ireland

Baltimore	*Customs House*
Cashel	*Cafe Hans*
Dingle	*The Chart House*
Dublin	*Bang Café*
–	*Jacobs Ladder*
–	*La Maison des Gourmets*
Durrus	*Good Things Cafe*
Kenmare	*An Leath Phingin*
–	*The Lime Tree*
Kilbrittain	*Casino House*
Kinsale	*Fishy Fishy Cafe*

Bib Hotel

Good accommodation at moderate prices
Bonnes nuits à petits prix
Buona sistemazione a prezzo contenuto
Hier übernachten Sie gut und preiswert

ENGLAND

Alderney	*Maison Bourgage*	**N**
Appletreewick	*Knowles Lodge*	**N**
Armscote	*Willow Corner*	
Askrigg	*The Apothecary's House*	**N**
Barnard Castle	*Greta House*	
Battle	*Fox Hole Farm*	**N**
Biddenden	*Barclay Farmhouse*	**N**
Bishop's Stortford	*Chimneys*	
Bodmin	*Bokiddick Farm*	**N**
Broad Oak	*Fairacres*	**N**
Bury St Edmunds	*Manorhouse*	
Cambridge	*Red House Farm*	
Carlisle	*Aldingham House*	
Cheddleton	*Choir Cottage*	**N**
Chipping Campden	*Myrtle House*	
Darley	*Cold Cotes*	**N**
Devizes	*Blounts Court Farm*	**N**
Dunster	*Exmoor House*	**N**
Eastbourne	*Brayscroft*	**N**
East Dereham	*Peacock House*	
East Mersea	*Mersea Vineyard*	
Ely	*Springfields*	
Exeter	*Silversprings*	
Great Malvern	*Brook House*	**N**
Halland	*Shortgate Manor Farm*	
Harrogate	*Knabbs House*	**N**
Hastings	*Tower House*	**N**
Helston	*Cobblers Cottage*	
Henfield	*Frylands*	**N**
Hexham	*West Close House*	
Ipswich	*Highfield*	
Ironbridge	*Bridge House*	
–	*The Library House*	
Kedington	*The White House*	
Kirkby Lonsdale	*Pickle Farm*	
Kirkbymoorside	*Brickfields Farm*	**N**
Littlehampton	*Amberley Court*	**N**
Longtown	*Bessiestown Farm*	
Ludlow	*Lower House Farm*	**N**
Nantwich	*The Limes*	
North Bovey	*The Gate House*	
Norwich	*Beaufort Lodge*	**N**
Oxhill	*Oxbourne House*	
Penrith	*The Old School*	
Pickering	*Bramwood*	
–	*Burr Bank*	**N**
Ripon	*Bay Tree Farm*	**N**
–	*Sharrow Cross House*	**N**
Rochdale	*Hindle Pastures*	
Ross-on-Wye	*Lumleys*	**N**
Saffron Walden	*Chaff House*	
St Just	*Boscean Country*	**N**
Stratford-upon-Avon	*Pear Tree Cottage*	
Symonds Yat West	*Norton House*	
Taunton	*Tilbury Farm*	
Telford	*Dovecote Grange*	**N**
Upton-on-Severn	*Yew Tree House*	**N**
Wareham	*Gold Court House*	
Wells	*Beaconsfield Farm*	
Whitby	*The Lawns*	
Winchelsea	*Strand House*	
Woodstock	*The Laurels*	

N *New* 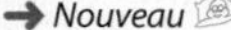
→ *Nouveau* → *Nuovo* → *Neu*

SCOTLAND

Aboyne	*Arbor Lodge*	
Anstruther	*The Spindrift*	
Aviemore	*The Old Minster's Guest House*	
Ayr	*No. 26 The Crescent*	
Banchory	*The Old West Manse*	
Blairgowrie	*Gilmore House*	**N**
Brora	*Glenaveron*	
Carnoustie	*The Old Manor*	**N**
Crieff	*Merlindale*	**N**
Dalry	*Langside Farm*	
Dumfries	*Redbank House*	
Dunkeld	*Letter Farm*	
Edinburgh	*The Beverley*	
Killin	*Breadalbane House*	
Linlithgow	*Arden House*	
Lochearnhead	*Mansewood Country House*	
Melrose	*Twelve of Melrose*	
Moffat	*Burnside*	
North Berwick	*Beach Lodge*	
Oban	*The Barriemore*	
Perth	*Taythorpe*	**N**
St. Boswells	*Clint Lodge*	
Stirling	*Ashgrove House*	
Strathpeffer	*Craigvar*	
Thornhill	*Gillbank House*	
Ullapool	*Point Cottage*	

WALES

Colwyn Bay	*Rathlin Country House*	**N**
Dolgellau	*Tyddyn Mawr*	
Llandrindod Wells	*Guidfa House*	
Llangollen	*Oakmere*	
Ruthin	*Firgrove*	

NORTHERN IRELAND

Bangor	*Cairn Bay Lodge*
Belfast	*Ravenhill House*
Crumlin	*Caldhame Lodge*
Downpatrick	*Pheasants' Hill Farm*

REPUBLIC OF IRELAND

Ballyvaughan	*Drumcreehy House*
Carlingford	*Beaufort House*
Carlow	*Barrowville Town House*
Cashel	*Aulber House*
Castlegregory	*Strand View House*
–	*The Shores Country House*
Drogheda	*Boyne Haven House*
Dungarvan	*An Bohreen*
Ennis	*Fountain Court*
Glengarriff	*Cois Coille*
Killarney	*Kingfisher Lodge*
Listowel	*Allo's*
New Ross	*Riversdale House*
Oughterard	*Waterfall Lodge*
Schull	*Corthna Lodge*
Toormore	*Fortview House*
Tramore	*Glenorney*

Particularly pleasant hotels

Hôtels agréables
Alberghi ameni
Angenehme Hotels

ENGLAND

London *The Berkeley*
– *Claridge's*
– *Dorchester*
– *Mandarin Oriental Hyde Park*
– *Ritz*
– *Savoy*
New Milton *Chewton Glen*
Taplow *Cliveden*

IRELAND *Republic of Ireland*

Straffan *The K Club*

ENGLAND

Aylesbury *Hartwell House*
Bath *Lucknam Park*
– *The Royal Crescent*
Daventry *Fawsley Hall*
Ipswich *Hintlesham Hall*
London *The Bentley Kempinski*
– *Connaught*
– *The Goring*
– *The Soho*
Malmesbury *Whatley Manor*
Newbury *Vineyard*
Oxford *Le Manoir aux Quat' Saisons*
St Saviour (Jersey) *Longueville Manor*

SCOTLAND

Ballantrae *Glenapp Castle*
Bishopton *Mar Hall*
Dunkeld *Kinnaird*
Eriska *(Isle of)* *Isle of Eriska*
Fort William *Inverlochy Castle*

WALES

Llyswen *Llangoed Hall*

IRELAND
Republic of Ireland

Dublin *The Merrion*
Kenmare *Park*
– *Sheen Falls Lodge*
Killarney *Killarney Park*

ENGLAND

Amberley *Amberley Castle*
Bath *Bath Priory*
Bolton Abbey *The Devonshire Arms Country House*
Bourton-on-the-Water *Lower Slaughter Manor*
Broadway *Buckland Manor*
Castle Combe *Manor House*
Chagford *Gidleigh Park*
Chipping Campden *Cotswold House*
Dedham *Maison Talbooth*
East Grinstead *Gravetye Manor*

Evershot	*Summer Lodge*
Gillingham	*Stock Hill Country House*
La Pulente (Jersey)	*Atlantic*
Littlehampton	*Bailiffscourt*
London	*Blakes*
–	*Capital*
–	*Charlotte Street*
–	*Covent Garden*
–	*The Draycott*
–	*The Halkin*
–	*The Milestone*
–	*One Aldwych*
–	*The Pelham*
Oakham	*Hambleton Hall*
Royal Leamington Spa	*Mallory Court*
Sandiway	*Nunsmere Hall*
Scilly (Isles of)	
St Martin's	*St Martin's on the Isle*
Tresco	*The Island*
Seaham	*Seaham Hall*
Taunton	*The Castle*
Tetbury	*Calcot Manor*
Ullswater	*Sharrow Bay Country House*
Windermere	*Gilpin Lodge*
York	*Middlethorpe Hall*

SCOTLAND

Blairgowrie	*Kinloch House*
Edinburgh	*The Howard*
–	*Prestonfield*
Inverness	*Culloden House*
Newton Stewart	*Kirroughtree House*
Torridon	*Loch Torridon*

WALES

Llandudno	*Bodysgallen Hall*
–	*Osborne House*
Llangammarch Wells	*Lake Country House*

IRELAND

Republic of Ireland

Dublin	*The Clarence*
Gorey	*Marlfield House*
Mallow	*Longueville House*

ENGLAND

Ambleside	*The Samling*
Bath	*Queensberry*
Brampton	*Farlam Hall*
Burnham Market	*The Hoste Arms*
Cheltenham	*On the Park*
Cirencester	*Barnsley House*
Cuckfield	*Ockenden Manor*
Frome	*Babington House*
Helmsley	*Feversham Arms*
Hereford	*Castle House*
Horley	*Langshott Manor*
Kingsbridge	*Buckland-Tout-Saints*
King's Lynn	*Congham Hall*
Lewdown	*Lewtrenchard Manor*
London	*Knightsbridge*
–	*Number Sixteen*
Milford-on-Sea	*Westover Hall*
Oxford	*Old Parsonage*
Purton	*Pear Tree at Purton*
Rushlake Green	*Stone House*
St Helier (Jersey)	*Eulah Country House*
St Mawes	*Tresanton*
Tavistock	*Hotel Endsleigh*
Torquay	*Orestone Manor*
Wareham	*Priory*
Wellington	*Bindon Country House*
Wight *(Isle of)*	
Yarmouth	*The George*
Windermere	*Holbeck Ghyll*
Woodstock	*Feathers*

SCOTLAND

Achiltibuie	*Summer Isles*
Arran *(Isle of)*	*Kilmichael Country House*
Gullane	*Greywalls*
Port Appin	*Airds*
Portpatrick	*Knockinaam Lodge*

WALES

Machynlleth	*Ynyshir Hall*
Swansea	*Fairyhill*
Talsarnau	*Maes-y-Neuadd*

IRELAND

Republic of Ireland

Arthurstown	*Dunbrody Country House*
Athlone	*Wineport Lodge*
Ballingarry	*Mustard Seed at Echo Lodge*
Castlebaldwin	*Cromleach Lodge*
Craughwell	*St Clerans*
Glin	*Glin Castle*
Kinsale	*Perryville House*
Shanagarry	*Ballymaloe House*

ENGLAND

Ashwater	*Blagdon Manor*
Blakeney	*Morston Hall*
Bourton-on-the-Water	*The Dial House*
Chipping Campden	*Malt House*
Coln St Aldwyns	*New Inn at Coln*
Dartmouth	*Nonsuch House*
Dorchester	*Birkin House*
Dulverton	*Ashwick House*
Helmsley	*Cross House Lodge At The Star Inn*
Keswick	*Swinside Lodge*
Leominster	*Ford abbey*
Lynton	*Hewitt's*
North Walsham	*Beechwood*
Porlock	*Oaks*
Portscatho	*Driftwood*
St Ives	*Blues Hayes*
Salisbury	*Howard's House*
Staverton	*Kingston House*
Teignmouth	*Thomas Luny House*
Ullswater	*Old Church*
Wight (Isle of)	
Seaview	*Seaview*

SCOTLAND

Annbank	*Enterkine*
Ballater	*Balgonie Country House*
Kelso	*Edenwater House*
Killin	*Ardeonaig*
Maybole	*Ladyburn*
Muir of Ord	*Dower House*
Nairn	*Boath House*
Tain	*Glenmorangie House*

WALES

Betws-y-Coed	*Tan-y-Foel Country House*
Llansanffraid Glan Conwy	*Old Rectory Country House*

IRELAND

Republic of Ireland

Bagenalstown	*Kilgraney Country House*
Clifden	*Dolphin Beach Country House*
Dingle	*Emlagh House*
Lahinch	*Moy House*
Riverstown	*Coopershill*

ENGLAND

Ash	*Great Weddington*
Askrigg	*Helm*
Bath	*Haydon House*
Billingshurst	*Old Wharf*
Blackpool	*Number One*
Bury St Edmunds	*Northgate House*
Calne	*Chilvester Hill House*
Clun	*Birches Mill*
Crackington Haven	*Manor Farm*
Cranbrook	*Cloth Hall Oast*
East Hoathly	*Old Whyly*
Faversham	*Frith Farm House*
Hawkshead	*West Vale*
Helmsley	*Oldstead Grange*
Honiton	*Cokesputt House*
Ilminster	*Old Rectory*
Iron Bridge	*Severn Lodge*
Ivychurch	*Olde Moat House*
Kendal	*Beech House*
Lavenham	*Lavenham Priory*
Ledbury	*Hall End*
Lizard	*Landewednack House*
Ludlow	*Bromley Court*
Malpas	*Tilston Lodge*
Man *(Isle of)*	*Aaron House*
Marazion	*Ednovean Farm*
North Bovey	*The Gate House*
Norton St. Philip	*Monmouth Lodge*
Petworth	*Old Railway Station*

Pickering	*The Moorlands Country House*
Ripon	*Sharrow Cross House*
St Austell	*Anchorage House*
St Blazey	*Nanscawen Manor House*
Shrewsbury	*Pinewood House*
Stow-on-the-Wold	*Rectory Farmhouse*
Tavistock	*Quither Mill*
–	*Tor Cottage*
Thursford Green	*Holly Lodge*
Veryan	*Crugsillick Manor*
Wareham	*Gold Court House*
York	*Alexander House*

SCOTLAND

Ballantrae	*Cosses Country House*
Bute *(Isle of)*	*Balmory Hall*
Edinburgh	*Kingsburgh House*
Fort William	*Crolinnhe*
–	*The Grange*
Glenborrodale	*Feorag House*
Inverness	*Millwood House*
Islay *(Isle of)*	*Kilmeny Country Guest House*
Linlithgow	*Arden House*
Mull *(Isle of)*	*Gruline Home Farm*
Perth	*Over Kinfauns*
Skirling	*Skirling House*
Skye *(Isle of)*	*Kinlochfollart*
Stathpeffer	*Craigvar*

WALES

Pwllheli	*The Old Rectory*

IRELAND

Northern Ireland

Dungannon	*Grange Lodge*
Holywood	*Beech Hill*

Republic of Ireland

Castlegregory	*The Shores Country House*
Castlelyons	*Ballyvolane House*
Cong	*Ballywarren House*
Enniscorthy	*Monfin House*
Fethard	*Mobarnane House*
Galway	*Killeen House*
Kanturk	*Glenlohane*
Kenmare	*Sallyport House*
Kilkenny	*Blanchville House*
Portlaoise	*Ivyleigh House*

Particularly pleasant restaurants

Restaurants agréables

Ristoranti ameni

Angenehme Restaurants

XXXXX

ENGLAND

London *The Restaurant (at Ritz H.)*

XXXX

ENGLAND

Bray-on-Thames *Waterside Inn (with rm)*
London *Angela Hartnett at The Connaught*
– *Grill Room (at Dorchester H.)*
– *1880 (at The Bentley Kempinski)*
– *Pétrus (at The Berkeley H.)*
– *The Savoy Grill*
Taplow *Waldo's (at Cliveden H.)*

IRELAND

Republic of Ireland
Dublin *Patrick Guilbaud*

XXX

ENGLAND

Baslow *Fischer's at Baslow Hall (with rm)*
Birmingham *Simpsons (with rm)*
Cambridge *Midsummer House*
Dedham *Le Talbooth*
Emsworth *36 on the Quay (with rm)*
Grange-over-Sands *L'Enclume (with rm)*
London *Bibendum*
– *The Capital Restaurant (at Capital H.)*
– *Orrery*
– *Oxo Tower*
– *Le Pont de la Tour*
– *The Wolseley*
Newcastle upon Tyne *Fisherman's Lodge*
Skipton *Angel Inn & Barn Lodgings (with rm)*
Tavistock *Horn of Plenty (with rm)*
Welwyn Garden City *Auberge du Lac*

WALES

Llandrillo *Tyddyn Llan (with rm)*

XX

ENGLAND

Channel Islands
Jersey *Jersey Pottery (Garden Rest)*
– *Suma's*
Derby *Darleys*
Goring *Leatherne Bottel*
Grantham *Harry's Place*
London *Le Caprice*
– *J. Sheekey*
– *Mon Plaisir*
– *Rules*
Ludlow *Mr Underhill's at Dinham Weir (with rm)*
Malmesbury *Le Mazot (at Whatley Manor)*

Medbourne	*Horse & Trumpet (with rm)*
Nayland	*White Hart Inn (with rm)*
Padstow	*The Seafood (with rm)*
Pateley Bridge	*Yorke Arms (with rm)*
Winchcombe	*Wesley House (with rm)*
Windermere	*Miller Howe (with rm)*
Yeovil	*Little Barwick House (with rm)*

SCOTLAND

Aberdeen	*Silver Darling*
Kingussie	*The Cross (with rm)*
Lochinver	*The Albannach (with rm)*
Skye *(Isle of)*	*Three Chimneys & The House Over-By (with rm)*

WALES

Builth Wells	*The Drawing Room (with rm)*
Pwllheli	*Plas Bodegroes (with rm)*

IRELAND

Republic of Ireland

Kenmare	*The Lime Tree*
Kilbrittain	*Casino House*
Tramore	*Coast (with rm)*

ENGLAND

Burford	*Jonathans at the Angel brasserie (with rm)*
Burnham Market	*The Restaurant (at The Hoste Arms)*
High Ongar	*The Wheatsheaf*
London	*Al Duca*
–	*Blueprint Café*
–	*Oxo Tower Brasserie*
Mousehole	*Cornish Range (with rm)*
Stanton	*Leaping Hare*
Studland	*Shell Bay*

WALES

Aberaeron	*Harbourmaster (with rm)*

IRELAND

Republic of Ireland

Dingle	*The Chart House*

ENGLAND

Ambleside	*Drunken Duck Inn (with rm)*
Barnard Castle	*Rose & Crown (with rm)*
Biggleswade	*The Hare & Hounds*
Broadhembury	*Drewe Arms*
Chichester	*The Royal Oak Inn (with rm)*
Cirencester	*The Bell*
Corscombe	*The Fox Inn (with rm)*
Evershot	*Acorn Inn (with rm)*
Helmsley	*The Star Inn*
Henley-in-Arden	*Crabmill*
Ilmington	*The Howard Arms (with rm)*
Kendal	*The Punch Bowl (with rm)*
Keyston	*Pheasant*
Lydford	*Dartmoor Inn*
Melksham	*Pear Tree Inn (with rm)*
Milton Keynes	*Crooked Billet*
Oundle	*The Falcon Inn*
Royston	*The Cabinet at Reed*
Shefford	*The Black Horse (with rm)*
Skipton	*Angel Inn*
Stadhampton	*Crazy Bear (with rm)*
Stow-on-the-Wold	*Fox Inn (with rm)*
Sutton-on-the-Forest	*Rose & Crown*
Tarr Steps	*Tarr Farm Inn (with rm)*
Taunton	*Blue Ball Inn (with rm)*
Winchester	*Wykeham Arms (with rm)*
Woburn	*The Birch*

WALES

Brecon	*Felin Fach Griffin (with rm)*
Caersws	*Talkhouse (with rm)*
Newport	*The Newbridge (with rm)*
Skenfrith	*The Bell (with rm)*

IRELAND

Northern Ireland

Donaghadee	*Grace Neills*

Further information

Pour en savoir plus

Per saperne di piú

Gut zu wissen

Beer

Beer is one of the oldest and most popular alcoholic drinks in the world. Traditional draught beer is made by grinding malted barley, heating it with water and adding hops which add the familiar aroma and bitterness. Beers in Britain can be divided into 2 principal types: Ales and Lagers which differ principally in their respective warm and cool fermentations. In terms of sales the split between the two is approximately equal. Beer can also be divided into keg or cask.

Keg beer – is filtered, pasteurised and chilled and then packed into pressurised containers from which it gets its name.

Cask beer – or `Real Ale' as it is often referred to, is not filtered, pasteurised or chilled and is served from casks using simple pumps. It is considered by some to be a more characterful, flavoursome and natural beer.

There are several different beer styles in Britain and Ireland:

Bitter – whilst it is the most popular traditional beer in England and Wales it is now outsold by lager. Although no precise definition exists it is usually paler and dryer than Mild with a high hop content and slightly bitter taste.

Mild – is largely found in Wales, the West Midlands and the North West of England. The name refers to the hop character as it is gentle, sweetish and full flavoured beer. It is generally lower in alcohol and sometimes darker in colour, caused by the addition of caramel or by using dark malt.

Stout – the great dry stouts are brewed in Ireland and are instantly recognisable by their black colour and creamy head. They have a pronounced roast flavour with plenty of hop bitterness.

In Scotland the beers produced are full bodied and malty and are often known simply as Light, Heavy, or Export which refers to the body and strength of the beer.

Although Ireland is most famous for its stouts, it also makes a range of beers which have variously been described as malty, buttery, rounded and fruity with a reddish tinge.

Whisky

The term whisky is derived from the Scottish Gaelic *uisage beatha* and the Irish Gaelic *uisce beathadh*, both meaning "water of life". When spelt without an e it usually refers to Scotch Whisky which can only be produced in Scotland by the distillation of malted and unmalted barley, maize, rye, and mixtures of two or more of these. Often simply referred to as Scotch it can be divided into 2 basic types: malt whisky and grain whisky.

Malt whisky – is made only from malted barley which is traditionally dried over peat fires. The malt is then milled and mixed with hot water before mashing turns the starches into sugars and the resulting liquid, called wort, is filtered out. Yeast is added and fermentation takes place followed by two distilling processes using a pot still. The whisky is matured in oak, ideally sherry casks, for at least three years which affects both its colour and flavour. All malts have a more distinctive smell and intense flavour than grain whiskies and each distillery will produce a completely individual whisky of great complexity. A single malt is the product of an individual distillery. There are approximately 100 malt whisky distilleries in Scotland.

Grain whisky – is made from a mixture of any malted or unmalted cereal such as maize or wheat and is distilled in the Coffey, or patent still, by a continuous process. Very little grain whisky is ever drunk unblended.

Blended whisky – is a mix of more than one malt whisky or a mix of malt and grain whiskies to produce a soft, smooth and consistent drink. There are over 2,000 such blends which form the vast majority of Scottish whisky production.

Irish Whiskey – differs from Scotch whisky both in its spelling and method of production.
It is traditionally made from cereals, distilled three times and matured for at least 7 years. The different brands are as individual as straight malt and considered by some to be gentler in character.

La bière

La bière est l'une des plus anciennes et populaires boissons alcoolisées dans le monde. Pour produire la bière pression traditionnelle, on écrase l'orge maltée que l'on chauffe ensuite avec de l'eau à laquelle on ajoute le houblon. C'est ce qui lui donne son arôme et son goût amer bien connus. Deux types de bières sont principalement vendues en Grande-Bretagne : les Ales fermentées à chaud et les Lagers fermentées à froid. Elles se divisent en « keg beer » et en « cask beer ».

Bière en keg : elle est filtrée, pasteurisée et refroidie, puis versée dans des tonnelets pressurisés appelés kegs.

Bière en cask ou « Real Ale » : elle n'est ni filtrée, ni pasteurisée, ni refroidie mais tirée directement du tonneau à l'aide d'une simple pompe. Selon certains, cette bière, de qualité bien distincte, a plus de saveur et est plus naturelle.

Types de bières vendues au Royaume-Uni et en Irlande :

Bitter – C'est la bière traditionnelle la plus populaire en Angleterre et au pays de Galles mais ses ventes diminuent au profit des lagers. La Bitter est généralement plus pâle et son goût plus sec que la Mild. Son contenu en houblon est élevé et elle a un goût légèrement amer.

La Mild se consomme surtout au pays de Galles, dans le Midlands de l'Ouest et dans le Nord-Ouest de l'Angleterre. On l'appelle ainsi en raison de son goût moelleux légèrement douceâtre conféré par le houblon. Cette bière, généralement moins alcoolisée, est plus foncée par le caramel qui lui est ajouté ou par l'utilisation de malt plus brun.

Stout – les grandes marques de bières brunes sont brassées en Irlande et sont reconnaissables par leur couleur noire rehaussée de mousse crémeuse. Elles ont un goût prononcé de houblon grillé et une saveur amère.

Celles produites en Écosse sont maltées ; elles ont du corps et se dénomment le plus souvent Light, Heavy ou Export en référence au corps et à leur teneur en alcool. buttery, rounded and fruity with a reddish tinge.

Whisky

Le mot whisky est un dérivé du gaélique écossais *uisage beatha* et du gaélique irlandais *uisce beathadh* signifiant tous deux « eau de vie ». Quand il est écrit sans e, il se réfère au whisky écossais qui ne peut être produit qu'en Écosse par la distillation de céréales maltées ou non comme l'orge, le maïs, le seigle ou d'un mélange de deux ou plus de ces céréales. Souvent appelé tout simplement Scotch il se réfère à deux types de whiskies : whisky pur malt ou whisky de grain.

Le whisky pur malt est fait seulement à partir d'orge maltée qui est traditionnellement séchée au-dessus de feux de tourbe. Le malt est moulu et mélangé avec de l'eau chaude, puis le brassage transforme l'amidon en sucre ; le moût est ensuite filtré. On y ajoute de la levure et après la fermentation on fait distiller deux fois dans un alambic. Le whisky est alors vieilli pendant au moins trois ans dans des fûts de chêne, ayant contenu de préférence du sherry, ce qui transforme son goût et sa couleur. Tous les whiskies pur malt ont un arôme particulier et une saveur plus intense que les whiskies de grain et chaque distillerie produit son propre whisky avec des qualités bien distinctes. Il y a environ une centaine de distilleries de whiskies pur malt en Écosse.

Le whisky de grain est fait d'un mélange de céréales, maltées ou non, comme le maïs ou le froment et est distillé dans un alambic de type Coffey suivant un procédé continu. Très peu de whiskies de grain sont consommés à l'état pur. On procède à des mélanges pour la consommation.

Blended whisky est le mélange d'un ou de plusieurs whiskies pur malt et de whiskies de grain afin de produire un alcool léger, moelleux et de qualité. Il existe plus de 2 000 marques de blended whiskies qui forment la majeure partie de la production écossaise.

Le whisky irlandais, différent du whisky écossais par sa fabrication, est traditionnellement produit à partir de céréales ; il est ensuite distillé trois fois et vieilli pendant au moins sept ans. Certains le trouvent plus moelleux.

La Birra

La birra è una delle bevande alcoliche più antiche e popolari. La tradizionale birra alla spina si ottiene macinando l'orzo, riscaldandolo con l'acqua e aggiungendo il luppolo, che le conferiscono l'aroma e il tipico sapore amaro.

Le birre britanniche si dividono in due tipi principali: Ales e Lagers, che differiscono essenzialmente per la fermentazione, rispettivamente calda e fredda. In termini di vendita, i due tipi approssimativamente si equivalgono. La birra può anche dividersi in keg (lett, barilotto), e cask (lett botte).

La keg beer è filtrata, pastorizzata e raffreddata, e poi messa in contenitori pressurizzati, da cui deriva il nome.

La cask beer, o Real Ale, come viene comunemente indicata, non è filtrata, pastorizzata o raffeddata, ed è servita dalle botti, usando semplici pompe. Alcuni la considerano una birra più ricca di carattere e di gusto e più naturale.

In Gran Bretagna e Irlanda, le birre si caratterizzano anche in base a « stili » diversi.

Le bitter costituisce la birra tradizionalmente più popolare in Inghilterra e nel Galles, ma è ora « superata » dalla lager. Non esiste definizione specifica per la birra bitter, ma si può dire che si tratta in genere di una birra più pallida e secca della mild, dall'alto contenuto di luppolo e dal gusto leggermente amaro.

La mild è diffusa in Galles, West Midlands e Inghilterra nord-occidentale. Il nome richiama il carattere del luppolo, essendo delicata, dolce e dal gusto pieno. Contiene solitamente una limitata quantità di alcol ed è talvolta scura per l'aggiunta di caramello e per l'impiego di malto scuro.

La secche stouts vengono prodotte in Irlanda e sono immediatamente riconoscibili dal colore nero e dalla schiuma cremosa. Hanno una decisa fragranza di tostatura e un gusto amaro di luppolo.

Whisky

Il termine whisky deriva dal gealico scozzese *uisage beatha* e dal gaelico irlandese *uisce beathadh*, che significano « acqua di vita ». Se scritto senza la e, indica di solito lo Scotch Whisky, che può essere unicamente prodotto in Scozia dalla distillazione di malto e orzo, granturco e segale, e dall'unione di due o più di questi ingredienti. Spesso chiamato semplicemente Scoveri, si divide in due tipi: malt whisky e grain whisky.

Il malt whisky viene prodotto unicamente con malto, tradizionalmente seccato su fuochi alimentati con torba. Il malto viene poi macinato e gli viene aggiunta acqua bollente prima che l'impasto muti gli amidi in zuccheri e il liquido che ne deriva, chiamato wort (mosto di malto), venga filtrato. Si amalgama poi il lievito e avviene la fermentazione, seguita da due processi di distillazione nell'alambicco. Il whisky è lasciato invecchiare in legno di quercia, idealmente in botti di sherry, per almeno tre anni, perchè acquisti colore e sapore. Ogni tipo di malt whisky ha un profumo più distintivo e un gusto più intenso del grain whisky. Ogni distilleria produce un whisky dal carattere individuale, che richiede un processo di grande complessità. Un solo malt whisky è il prodotto di una specifica distilleria. In Scozia, esistono circa 100 distillerie di malt whisky.

Il grain whisky è il risultato della fusione di qualsiasi cereale con o senza malto, come il granturco o il frumento, es viene distillato nel Coffey, o alambicco brevettato, grazie ad un processo continuo. È molto scarsa la quantità di grain whisky che si beve puro.

Il blended whisky nasce dalla fusione di più di un malt whisky, o da quella di *malt* e grain whiskies. Il risultato è una bevanda dal gusto delicato, dolce e pieno. Esistono più di 2000 whisky di questo tipo, che costituiscono la parte più consistente della produzione scozzese.

Bier

Bier ist eines der ältesten und beliebtesten alkoholischen Getränke der Welt. Das traditionelle Fassbier wird aus gemahlener und gemalzter Gerste hergestellt, die in Wasser erhitzt wird. Durch Beigabe von Hopfen werden das bekannte Aroma und der typische bittere Geschmack erzeugt.

Die Biersorten in Großbritannien unterteilen sich in zwei Hauptgruppen: Ales und Lagers, wobei die Art der Gärung – im einen Fall warm, im anderen kalt – ausschlaggebend für das Endresultat ist. Beide Sorten haben hierzulande einen ungefähr gleichen Marktanteil. Da sich die meisten Brauvorgänge anfangs gleichen, entscheiden erst die Endphasen des Brauens, welche der verschiedenen Biersorten entsteht.

Darüber hinaus kann das englische Bier auch nach der Art seiner Abfüllung in Keg- bzw. Cask-Bier unterschieden werden:

Keg beer wird gefiltert, pasteurisiert, abgekühlt und anschließend in luftdichte, unter Druck gesetzte Metallbehälter gefüllt, von denen das Bier auch seinen Namen erhält.

Cask beer, gewöhnlich Real Ale genannt, wird weder gefiltert, noch pasteurisiert oder gekühlt, sondern mit einfachen (zumeist Hand-) Pumpen vom Faß gezapft.

Es gibt folgende Biersorten in Großbritannien und Irland: Bitter ist das meistbekannte traditionelle Bier in England und Wales. Eine genaue Definition, was ein Bitter ausmacht, sucht man vergeblich; es ist gewöhnlich heller und trockener als das Mild, hat einen hohen Hopfenanteil und einen leicht bitteren Geschmack. In den letzten Jahren hat das – meist importierte oder in Lizenz gebraute – Lager ihm jedoch den Rang abgelaufen.

Mild ist übergwiegend in Wales, in den westlichen Midlands und Nordwestengland zu finden. Der Name bezieht sich auf den Hopfenanteil, der es zu einem milden, etwas süßlichen und vollmundigen Bier macht. Es hat einen geringeren Alkoholgehalt und besitzt wegen der Zugabe von Karamel oder dunklem Malz bisweilen eine dunklere Farbe.

Stouts von hervorragendem trockenem Geschmack werden in Irland gebraut und sind unmittelbar an ihrer schwarzen Farbe und der cremigen Blume erkennbar. Sie haben einen ausgesprochen starken Geschmack nach bitterem Hopfen.

In Schottland hergestellte Biere sind alkoholstark und malzig; sie sind oft einfach bekannt als: Light, Heavy oder Export – Bezeichnungen, die auf Körper und Stärke des Bieres hinweisen.

Whisky

Die Bezeichnung Whisky entstammt dem Gälischen, wo im Schottischen der Ausdruck *uisage beatha*, im Irischen des Ausdruck *uisce beathadh* jeweils « Wasser des Lebens » bedeuten. Wird Whisky ohne ein e am Ende geschrieben, ist Scotch Whisky gemeint, der nur in Schottland aus gemalzter und ungemalzter Gerste, Mais, Roggen oder aus Mischungen zweier oder mehrerer dieser Zutaten gebrannt werden darf. Oft auch nur als Scotch bezeichnet, kann dieser in zwei Grundarten unterschieden werden: malt whisky und grain whisky.

Malt (Malz) whisky wird nur aus gemalzter Gerste hergestellt, die traditionell über Torffeuern getrocknet wird. Danach wird das Malz gemahlen und mit heißem Wasser vermischt, wonach in der Maische die Stärke in Zucker umgewandelt wird. Die dadurch entstandene Flüssigkeit, « wort » genannt, wird gefiltert und mit Hefe versetzt, was den Gärungsprozess einleitet. Anschließend folgen zwei Destillierungen im herkömmlichen Topf über offenem Feuer. Der Whisky reift danach mindestens drei Jahre lang in Eichenholz, idealerweise in Sherry-Fässern, was sich sowohl auf Farbe wie auf Geschmack des Whiskys auswirkt. Alle malts haben einen ausgeprägteren Geruch und intensiveren Geschmack als die grain-Whiskies; und jede Destillerie erzeugt einen völlig eigenen Whisky mit individueller Geschmacksnote und großer Komplexität. Ein sogenannter single malt enstammt aus einer einzigen Destillerie. Es gibt ungefähr 100 Malt Whisky-Destillerien in Schottland.

Grain (Korn) whisky wird aus Mischungen von gemalzten und ungemalzten Getreidesorten, wie Mais oder Weizen, hergestellt und wird in einem kontinuierlichen Prozeß in dem sogenannten « Coffey » destilliert. Nur sehr wenige Kornwhisky-Sorten sind nicht das Ergebnis von blending, dem Abstimmen des Geschmacks durch Mischung.

Blended whisky wird aus mehr als einer Sorte Malt Whisky oder aus Malt und Grain Whiskies gemischt, um ein weiches, geschmacklich harmonisches Getränk von beständiger Güte zu garantieren. Die über 2000 im Handel zu findenden blends stellen den Großteil der schottischen Whiskyerzeugung dar.

Irish Whiskey unterscheidet sich vom Scotch Whisky sowohl in der Schreibweise wie auch dem Herstellungsverfahren. Er wird traditionell aus Getreide hergestellt, wird dreifach destilliert und reift mindestens sieben Jahre lang. Die verschiedenen Sorten sind so individuell ausgeprägt wie reine Malt Whiskies und werden oft als weicher und gefälliger empfunden.

B. Pérousse/MICHELIN

Tower Bridge

Towns
from A to Z

Villes
de A à Z

Città
de A a Z

Städte
von A bis Z

England
Channel Islands
Isle of Man

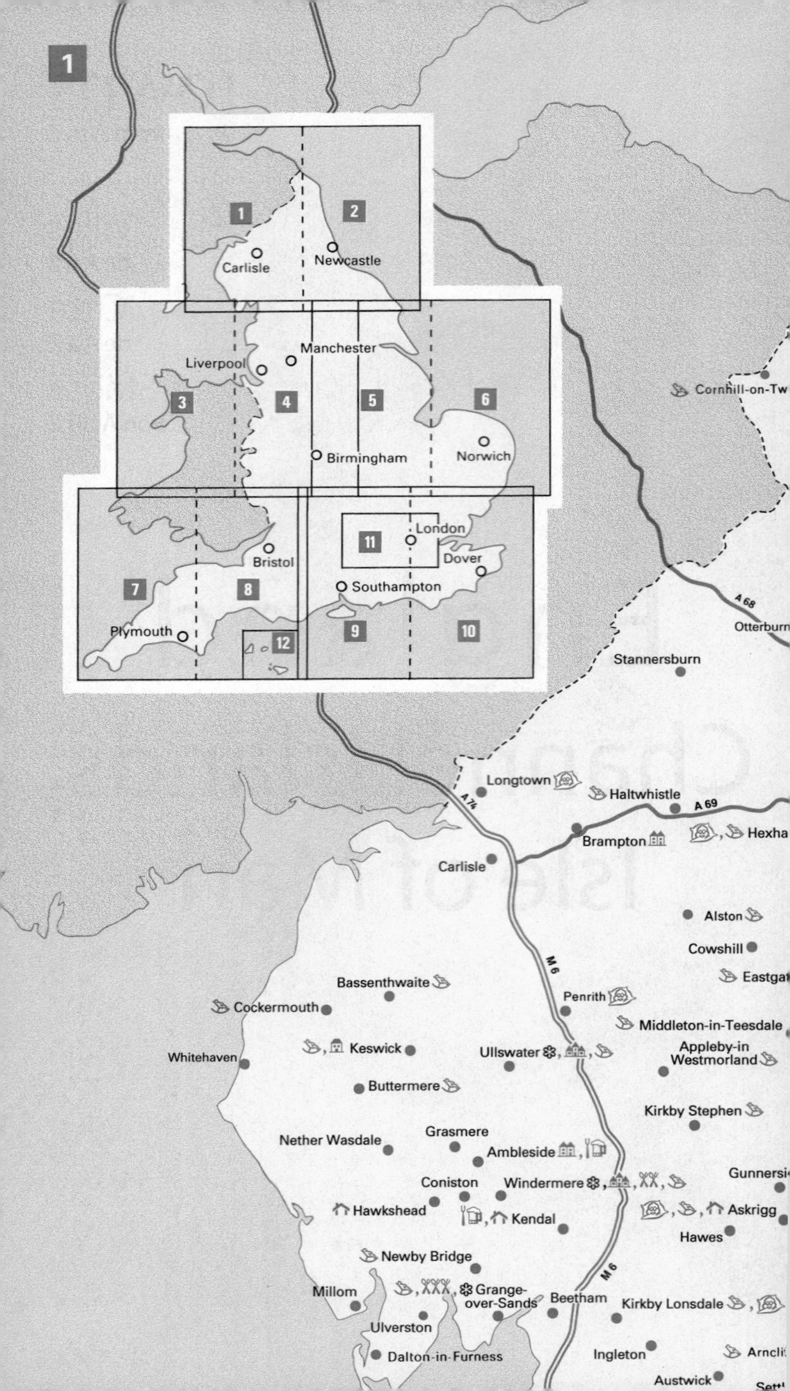
1
1
2
Carlisle
Newcastle
Manchester
Liverpool
3
4
5
6
Birmingham
Norwich
London
11
Dover
Bristol
7
8
Southampton
Plymouth
12
9
10
Cornhill-on-Tw
A 68
Otterburn
Stannersburn
Longtown
Haltwhistle
A 74
A 69
Brampton
Hexha
Carlisle
Alston
Cowshill
Eastgat
M 6
Bassenthwaite
Penrith
Cockermouth
Middleton-in-Teesdale
Keswick
Ullswater
Appleby-in Westmorland
Whitehaven
Buttermere
Kirkby Stephen
Grasmere
Nether Wasdale
Ambleside
Gunnersi
Coniston
Windermere
Hawkshead
Kendal
Askrigg
Hawes
Newby Bridge
M 6
Millom
Grange-over-Sands
Beetham
Kirkby Lonsdale
Ulverston
Dalton-in-Furness
Ingleton
Arnclif
Austwick
Settl

2
Place with at least
a hotel or restaurant
Ripon
a pleasant hotel or restaurant
Good accommodation at moderate prices
a quiet, secluded hotel
a restaurant with
Rest
Town with a local map
Localité offrant au moins
une ressource hôtelière
Ripon
un hôtel ou restaurant agréable
Bonnes nuits à petits prix
un hôtel très tranquille, isolé
une bonne table à
Rest
Carte de voisinage : voir à la ville choisie
La località possiede come minimo
una risorsa alberghiera
Ripon
Albergo o ristorante ameno
Buona sistemazione a prezzi contenuti
un albergo molto tranquillo, isolato
un'ottima tavola con
Rest
Città con carta dei dintorni
Ort mit mindestens
einem Hotel oder Restaurant
Ripon
einem angenehmen Hotel oder Restaurant
Hier übernachten Sie gut und preiswert
einem sehr ruhigen und abgelegenen Hotel
einem Restaurant mit
Rest
Stadt mit Umgebungskarte
Berwick-upon-Tweed
Belford
Bamburgh
Seahouses
Beadnell
Alnwick
Rothbury
Kirkwhelpington
Morpeth
A 696
Whitley Bay
Matfen
Tynemouth
Newcastle-Upon-Tyne
Heddon-on-the-Wall
Gateshead
Sunderland
Washington
Carterway Heads
Seaham
Chester-le-Street
Durham
A1
Spennymoor
Hartlepool
Stockton-on-Tees
Staithes
Runswick Bay
Middlesbrough
Yarm
Guisborough
Darlington
Whitby
Stokesley
Moulton
Great Broughton
Goathland
Richmond
Osmotherley
Rosedale Abbey
Leyburn
Patrick Brompton
Northallerton
Hutton-le-Hole
Lastingham
Scarborough
Middleham
Kirkbymoorside
Hawnby
E. Witton
Pickhill
Pickering
Snainton
Masham
Thirsk
Helmsley
W. Tanfield
Husthwaite
Hovingham
Ripon
Wold Newton
Easingwold
Whitwell-on-the-Hill
Pateley Bridge
Westow
Boroughbridge

3

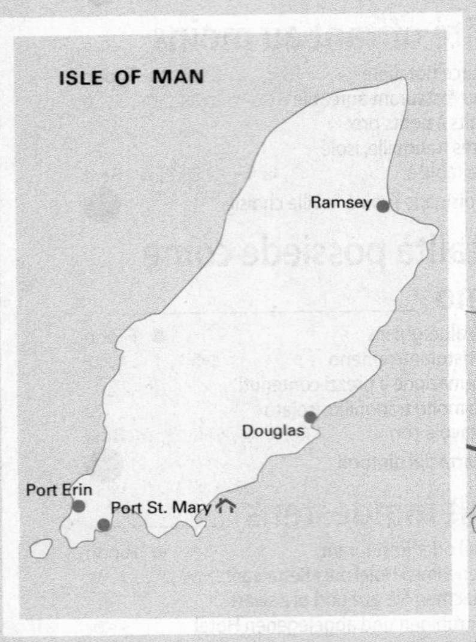

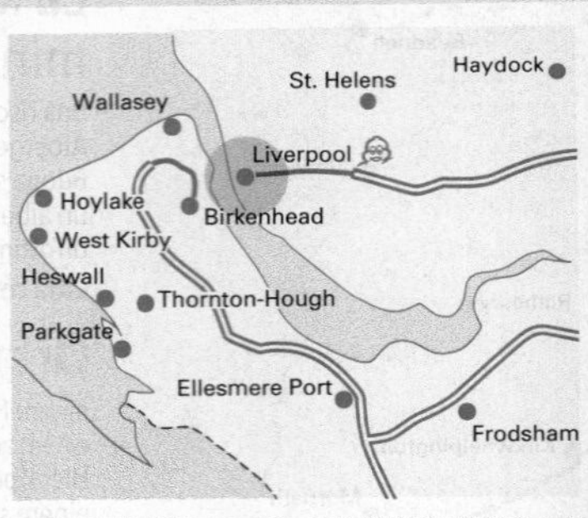

ST GEORGE'S CHANNEL

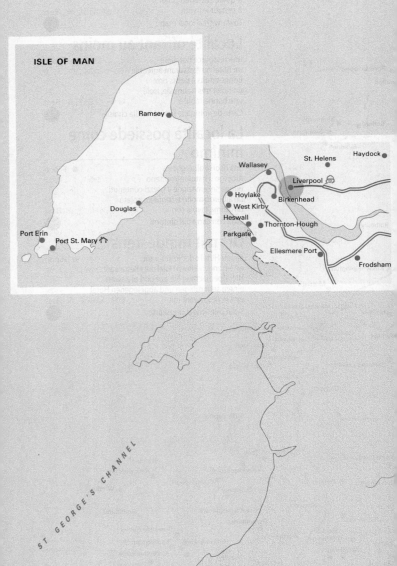

4
Dalton-in-Furness
Ingleton
Arncliffe
Kilnsey
Ripon
Pateley Bridge
Austwick
Settle
Grassington
Borough
Lancaster
Burnsall
Darley
Appletreewick
Ripley
Bolton-by-Bowland
Bolton Abbey
Skipton
Harrogate
Forton
Whitewell
Burley-in-Wharfedale
Fleetwood
Pilling
Sawley
Addingham
Garstang
Ilkley
Boston Spa
Chipping
Clitheroe
Otley
St-Michaels-on-Wyre
Longridge
Hurst Green
Haworth
Bingley
Blackpool
Whalley
Padiham
Shipley
Goosnargh
Burnley
Bradford
Kirkham
Blackburn
Leeds
Preston
Clayton-le-Moors
Brighouse
Lytham St. Anne's
Halifax
Clayton le Woods
Darwen
Todmorden
Dewsbury
Ramsbottom
Sowerby Bridge
Elland
Southport
Chorley
Wakefield
Eccleston
Rochdale
Huddersfield
Horwich
M 62
Clayton West
Bury
Marsden
Standish
Denby Dale
Oldham
Barnsley
Wigan
M 1
Manchester
Denton
Hyde
Glossop
Liverpool
M 62
Sale
Marple
Altrincham
Sheffield
Hope
Warrington
Cheadle
Bradwell
Hathersage
Knutsford
Wilmslow
Froggatt Edge
M 56
Lower Whitley
Prestbury
Grindleford
Alderley Edge
Buxton
Baslow
Macclesfield
Sandiway
M 6
Chester
Holmes Chapel
Bakewell
Rowsley
Tarporley
Middlewich
Hartington
Congleton
Matlock
Aldford
Tattenhall
Sandbach
Broxton
Crewe
Cheddleton
Nantwich
Thorpe
Stoke-on-Trent
Malpas
Belper
Newcastle-under-Lyme
Ashbourne
Whitchurch
Derby
Market Drayton
Oswestry
Uttoxeter
Burlton
Stafford
Burton-upon-Trent
East Midlands Airport
Newport
Shrewsbury
Alrewas
Telford
A 5
M 54
Lichfield
Market Bosworth
Tamworth
Marton
Ironbridge
Aldridge
R. Severn
Much Wenlock
Wolverhampton
Sutton Coldfield
Walsall
Church Stretton
Bridgnorth
Dudley
Munslow
Nuneaton
Birmingham
Clun
Hampton in Arden
Clent
Dorridge
Barston
Ludlow
Kidderminster
Solihull
Coventry
Leintwardine
Chadwick End
Barnt Green
Kenilworth
Stourport-on-Severn
Hockley Heath
Abberley
Bromsgrove
Royal Leamington
Tenbury Wells
Henley-in-Arden
Shobdon
Droitwich Spa
Redditch
Studley
Warwick
Kington
Leominster
Ombersley
Aston Cantlow
Alcester
Pembridge
Worcester
Stratford-upon-Avon
M 5
Pillerton Hersey
Weobley
Ullingswick
M 40
Great Malvern
Pershore
Upper Quinton
Ilmington
Winforton
Evesham
Armscote
Upton upon Severn
Hereford
Chipping Campden
Ledbury
Broadway
Great Wolford

5
Easingwold
Whitwell-on-the-Hill
Westow
Boroughbridge
Sutton-on-the-Forest
Ripley
Knaresborough
Bolton Abbey
Harrogate
York
Burley-in-Wharfedale
Wetherby
Bilborough
Brandesburton
Boston Spa
Otley
Tadcaster
Bingley
Beverley
Shipley
Leeds
Wressle
M 62
Kingston-upon-Hull
Monk Fryston
A 63
Dewsbury
Elland
M 62
Winteringham
Wakefield
Wentbridge
Clayton West
Grimsby
Denby Dale
Scunthorpe
Barnsley
Cleethorpes
Doncaster
A 1
M 1
Rotherham
Market Rasen
Hope
Sheffield
M 18
Blyth
Bradwell
Hathersage
Retford
Marton
Froggatt Edge
Grindleford
Baslow
Lincoln
Chesterfield
R. Trent
Horncastle
Bakewell
Rowsley
Mansfield
Woodhall Spa
Matlock
South Normanton
Halam
Thorpe
Southwell
Newark-on-Trent
M 1
Boston
A 17
Sleaford
Belper
Ashbourne
Nottingham
Bingham
Grantham
Derby
Langar
Uttoxeter
Kegworth
Colston Bassett
Knipton
Holbeach
Castle Donington
Buckminster
East Midlands Airport
Loughborough
Melton Mowbray
Alrewas
Oakham
Market Bosworth
A 1
Tamworth
Leicester
Stamford
Hallaton
Uppingham
Peterborough
Sutton Coldfield
Kibworth Beauchamp
Medbourne
Hinckley
Stilton
Nuneaton
Bruntingthorpe
M 69
Thorpe Langton
Hampton in Arden
Oundle
North Kilworth
Dorridge
Barston
M 6
Kettering
Market Harborough
Lowick
Coventry
Chadwick End
Rugby
A 14
Huntingdon
Hockley Heath
Kenilworth
Keyston
St. Ives
Royal Leamington Spa
Wellingborough
Henley-in-Arden
Great Staughton
Buckden
Daventry
Warwick
M 1
Aston Cantlow
Northampton
Bolnhurst
Stratford-upon-Avon
Pillerton Hersey
Roade
Bedford
Sandy
M 40
Towcester
Stoke Bruerne
Ilmington
Oxhill
Newport Pagnell
Biggleswade
Armscote
Farnborough
Shefford
Milton Keynes
Steppingley
Royston
Banbury
Great Wolford
Aspley Guise

NORTH SEA

Holkham
Wells-next-the-Sea
Blakeney
Sheringham
West Runton
Cromer
Hunstanton
Burnham Market
Hindringham
Holt
Heacham
Thursford Green
Erpingham
Thorpe Market
Walcott
Great Bircham
Itteringham
North Walsham
King's Lynn
Wellingham
Coltishall
Wroxham
East Dereham
A 47
Brundall
Watton
Norwich
Great Yarmouth
Wymondham
Bungay
Lowestoft
A 11
Pulham Market
Ely
Stanton
Diss
Fressingfield
Bramfield
Southwold
Thornham Magna
Westleton
Bury St. Edmunds
Framlingham
Kelsale
Newmarket
Saxmundham
mbridge
Snape
Aldeburgh
hittlesford
A 14
Cavendish
Lavenham
Woodbridge
Duxford
Long Melford
Orford
Monks Eleigh
Kedington
Ipswich
Clare
Hadleigh
Levington
Stoke-by-Nayland
Saffron Walden
Dedham
Mistley

BRISTOL CHANNEL
ISLE OF LUNDY
Ilfracombe
Woolacombe
Croyde
Saunton
Barnsta
Appledore
Bideford
Clovelly
Parkham
Bude
Crackington Haven
Boscastle
Virginstow
Ashwater
Lewdown
Lifton
Lydf
Tavistock
Rock
Padstow
Bodmin
Liskeard
Callington
Yelver
St. Mawgan
Newquay
Fraddon
A 30
Plymouth
St. Blazey
Summercourt
St. Austell
Fowey
St. Agnes
Ladock
Looe
Polperro
Grampound
Illogan
Truro
Veryan
Mevagissey
Noss May
St. Ives
Philleigh
Portloe
Hayle
Portscatho
Penzance
Falmouth
St. Mawes
Marazion
St. Just
Constantine
Mousehole
Helston
Porthleven
St. Keverne
Mullion
Coverack
Lizard
ISLES OF SCILLY
Bryher
St. Martin's
Tresco
St.Mary's

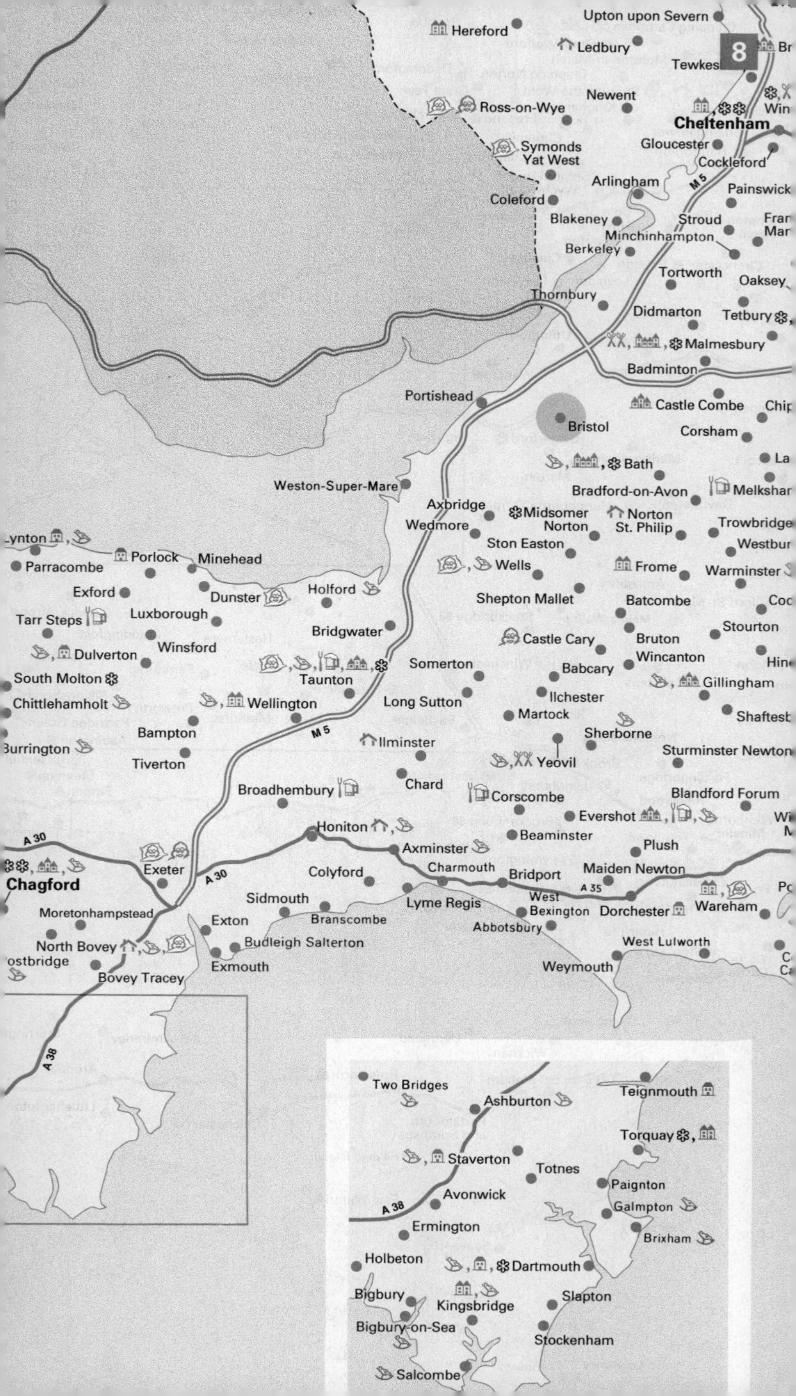
8
Upton upon Severn
Hereford
Ledbury
Tewkes
Newent
Ross-on-Wye
Cheltenham
Gloucester
Symonds Yat West
Cockleford
Arlingham
M 5
Painswick
Coleford
Blakeney
Stroud
Minchinhampton
Berkeley
Tortworth
Oaksey
Thornbury
Didmarton
Tetbury
Malmesbury
Badminton
Portishead
Castle Combe
Bristol
Corsham
Bath
Bradford-on-Avon
Melkshar
Weston-Super-Mare
Axbridge
Midsomer Norton
Norton St. Philip
Wedmore
Trowbridge
Ston Easton
Westbur
Lynton
Porlock
Minehead
Parracombe
Wells
Frome
Warminster
Exford
Holford
Dunster
Shepton Mallet
Batcombe
Luxborough
Tarr Steps
Bridgwater
Stourton
Castle Cary
Bruton
Winsford
Dulverton
Wincanton
Somerton
Babcary
Taunton
South Molton
Gillingham
Ilchester
Chittlehamholt
Wellington
Long Sutton
Martock
Bampton
Sherborne
M 5
Ilminster
Burrington
Sturminster Newton
Tiverton
Yeovil
Chard
Broadhembury
Corscombe
Blandford Forum
Evershot
Honiton
Beaminster
A 30
Axminster
Plush
Charmouth
Maiden Newton
Exeter
Colyford
Bridport
Chagford
A 30
A 35
Sidmouth
Lyme Regis
West Bexington
Dorchester
Wareham
Moretonhampstead
Branscombe
Abbotsbury
Exton
North Bovey
Budleigh Salterton
West Lulworth
Postbridge
Exmouth
Weymouth
Bovey Tracey
A 38
Two Bridges
Teignmouth
Ashburton
Torquay
Staverton
Totnes
Paignton
Avonwick
A 38
Galmpton
Ermington
Brixham
Holbeton
Dartmouth
Bigbury
Kingsbridge
Slapton
Bigbury-on-Sea
Stockenham
Salcombe

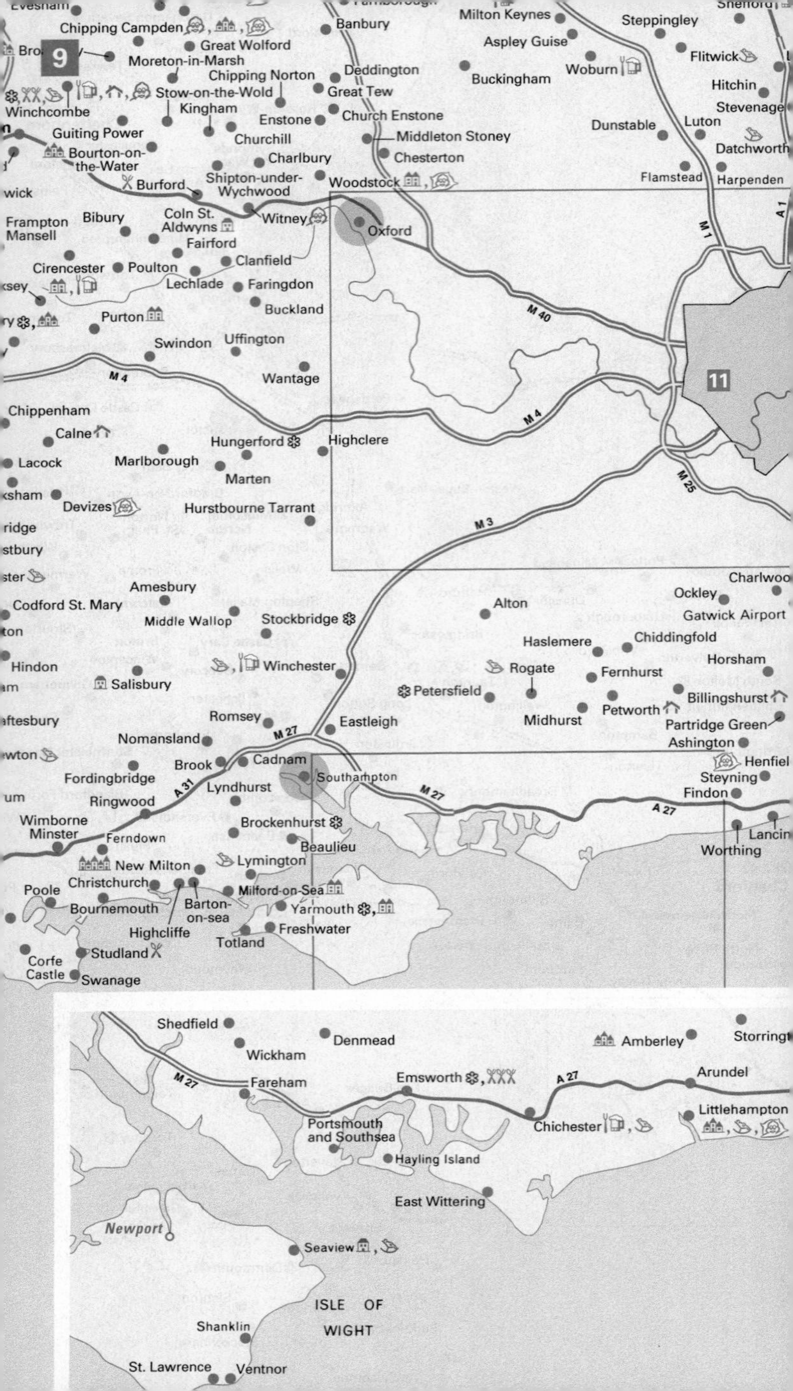

9
Chipping Campden
Great Wolford
Moreton-in-Marsh
Chipping Norton
Stow-on-the-Wold
Kingham
Winchcombe
Guiting Power
Bourton-on-the-Water
Burford
Churchill
Charlbury
Shipton-under-Wychwood
Banbury
Deddington
Great Tew
Enstone
Church Enstone
Middleton Stoney
Chesterton
Woodstock
Milton Keynes
Aspley Guise
Buckingham
Woburn
Steppingley
Flitwick
Hitchin
Stevenage
Luton
Dunstable
Datchworth
Flamstead
Harpenden
Frampton Mansell
Bibury
Coln St. Aldwyns
Witney
Oxford
Fairford
Clanfield
Cirencester
Poulton
Lechlade
Faringdon
Buckland
Purton
Swindon
Uffington
Wantage
M 4
M 40
M 1
A 1
11
Chippenham
Calne
Hungerford
Highclere
Lacock
Marlborough
Marten
Devizes
Hurstbourne Tarrant
M 25
M 3
Amesbury
Codford St. Mary
Middle Wallop
Stockbridge
Alton
Ockley
Gatwick Airport
Haslemere
Chiddingfold
Hindon
Winchester
Rogate
Fernhurst
Horsham
Salisbury
Petersfield
Billingshurst
Petworth
Midhurst
Romsey
Eastleigh
Partridge Green
Ashington
Nomansland
M 27
Cadnam
Brook
Southampton
Henfield
Steyning
Findon
Fordingbridge
Lyndhurst
A 31
Ringwood
A 27
Wimborne Minster
Ferndown
Brockenhurst
Beaulieu
Lancing
Worthing
New Milton
Lymington
Poole
Christchurch
Milford-on-Sea
Bournemouth
Barton-on-sea
Yarmouth
Freshwater
Highcliffe
Totland
Studland
Corfe Castle
Swanage
Shedfield
Denmead
Wickham
Amberley
Fareham
Emsworth
Arundel
Littlehampton
Portsmouth and Southsea
Chichester
Hayling Island
East Wittering
Newport
Seaview
ISLE OF WIGHT
Shanklin
St. Lawrence
Ventnor

Clare
Hadleigh
Levington
Stoke-by-Nayland
Dedham
Mistley
Saffron Walden
Nayland
Clavering
Thaxted
Manningtree
Wix
Harwich and Dovercourt
M 11
Stansted Airport
Earls Colne
Bishop's Stortford
Great Dunmow
Braintree
Coggeshall
Colchester
Ware
Fuller Street
Clacton-on-Sea
Hatfield Peverel
East Mersea
Chelmsford
Maldon
M 25
Stock
Burnham-on-Crouch
Basildon
Leigh-on-Sea
Rayleigh
LONDON
Horndon-on-the-Hill
Southend-on-Sea
Canvey Island
North Stifford
Gravesend
Whitstable
Margate
Rochester
Cobham
Sittingbourne
Broadstairs
M 20
Faversham
Aylesford
West Malling
Canterbury
Ash
Sandwich
Lenham
Hunton
Barham
Maidstone
Deal
M 23
Wye
Pluckley
Horley
Edenbridge
Bodsham
Ashford
Turners Hill
Royal Tunbridge Wells
Dover
Biddenden
East Grinstead
Cranbrook
Folkestone
Crawley
Forest Row
A 259
Goudhurst
Hythe
Danehill
Tenterden
Ticehurst
Bodiam
Ivychurch
Uckfield
Fletching
Sedlescombe
New Romney
Uckfield
Broad Oak
Brookland
Channel Tunnel
Haywards Heath
Halland
Rushlake Green
Battle
Rye
Newick
Herstmonceux
Winchelsea
Lewes
East Hoathly
Westfield
Icklesham
Hailsham
Hastings and St. Leonards
Brighton and Hove
Alfriston
Newhaven
Eastbourne
ENGLISH CHANNEL

11
Easington
Cuddington
Waddesdon
Aylesbury
Aston Clinton
Tring
Ford
Long Crendon
Stoke Mandeville
Haddenham
Thame
M 40
ford
Berkhamsted
St.Albans
Hemel Hempstead
Kings Langley
M 1
Welwyn
A 1
Welwyn Garden City
Hertford
Hatfield
Harlow
High Ongar
Blackmore
Fryerning
Brentwood
Waltham Abbey
Buckhurst Hill
M 11
Great Missenden
Chipperfield
Bricket Wood
Stadhampton
Chinnor
M 40
Chenies
Watford
Bushey
Amersham
Speen
High Wycombe
ngdon
Dorchester
Britwell Salome
Christmas Common
Didcot
Turville
Beaconsfield
Harwell
Wallingford
Denham
Nettlebed
Marlow
Stoke Row
Moulsford
Cookham
Stoke Poges
Hurley
Cookham Dean
Taplow
Henley-on-Thames
Burchett's Green
Farnham Royal
Streatley
Goring
Wargrave
Knowl Hill
Maidenhead
Slough
Iver
M 25
BRAY-ON-THAMES
A 41
A 11
LONDON
A 40
A 4
M 4
Thames
Thurrock
Rainham
Dartford
M 25
hieveley
Yattendon
Sonning-on-Thames
Windsor
Thames
Reading
M 4
Staines
A 316
A 20
Bracknell
Ascot
Egham
Thatcham
Woolhampton
ewbury
Padworth
Crowthorne
Windlesham
Weybridge
Esher
A 23
Farningham
Brands Hatch
d Burghclere
Silchester
Bagshot
Stratfield Turgis
Yateley
Camberley
West End
Chobham
Cobham
Epsom
M 20
Woking
Ripley
M 26
Sevenoaks
Hook
M 3
Farnborough
Basingstoke
Aldershot
Mickleham
Redhill
M 25
M 23
Abinger Hammer
Guildford
Odiham
Dogmersfield

Channels Islands

12

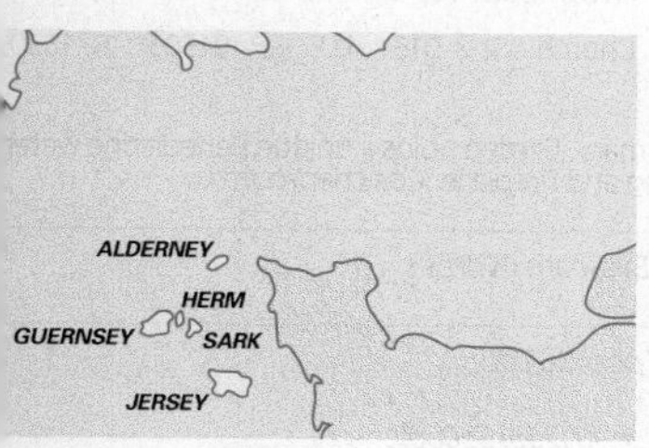

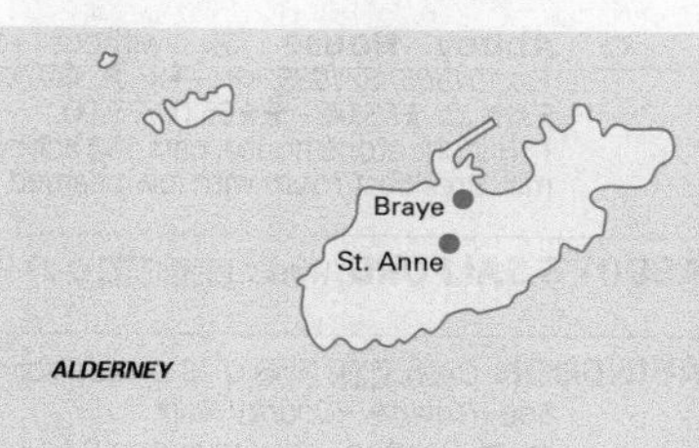

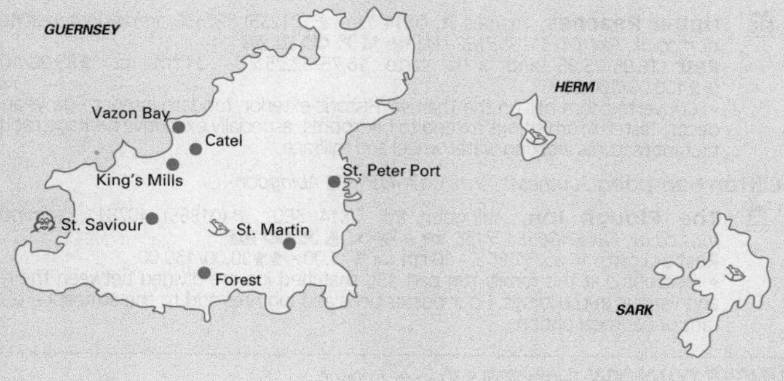

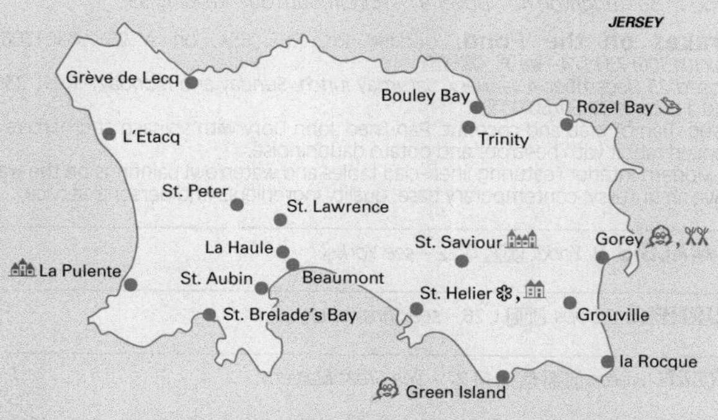

ABBERLEY *Worcs.* 503 504 M 27 – *pop. 654* – ✉ *Worcester.*
London 137 – Birmingham 27 – Worcester 13.

The Elms, WR6 6AT, West : 2 m. on A 443 ✆ (01299) 896666, *info@theelmshotel.co.uk Fax (01299) 896804,* ≤, 🐶, ♨, 🎾 – ⇥ rest, P – 🏛 50. MO AE ① VISA. ✂
Rest 18.50/55.00 and a la carte 35.00/45.00 **s.** ♀ – **21 rm** ☕ ★70.00/80.00 – ★★130.00.
◆ Queen Anne mansion with sweeping gardens and croquet lawn. Period details include carved wooden fireplace and ornate plasterwork. Antique furnishings and spacious bedrooms. Restaurant makes good use of fresh herbs from kitchen garden.

ABBOTSBURY *Dorset* 503 504 M 32 *The West Country G.* – *pop. 422.*
See : *Town★★ - Chesil Beach★★ - Swannery★ AC – Sub-Tropical Gardens★ AC.*
Env. : *St Catherine's Chapel★, ½ m. uphill (30 mn rtn on foot).*
Exc. : *Maiden Castle★★ (≤★) NE : 7½ m.*
London 146 – Bournemouth 44 – Exeter 50 – Weymouth 10.

Abbey House ⛰ without rest., Church St, DT3 4JJ, ✆ (01305) 871330 *Fax (01305) 871088,* 🐶 – ⇥ P. MO. ✂
5 rm ☕ ★65.00 – ★★65.00/75.00.
◆ Historic stone house, part 15C abbey infirmary. Garden holds a unique Benedictine water mill. Breakfast room with low beamed ceiling and fireplace. Cosy bedrooms.

ABBOT'S SALFORD *Warks.* 503 504 O 27 – *see Evesham (Worcs.).*

ABINGDON *Oxon.* 503 504 Q 28 *Great Britain G.* – *pop. 36 010.*
See : *Town★ – County Hall★.*
18, 9 *Drayton Park, Steventon Rd, Drayton ✆ (01235) 550607.*
⛴ *from Abingdon Bridge to Oxford (Salter Bros. Ltd) 2 daily (summer only).*
ℹ *25 Bridge St ✆ (01235) 522711, abingdontic@btconnect.com.*
London 64 – Oxford 6 – Reading 25.

Upper Reaches, Thames St, OX14 3JA, ✆ (01235) 522536, *info@upperreaches-abingdon.co.uk, Fax (01235) 555182* – ⚓ ⇥ ✆ P. MO AE VISA
Rest 16.95/25.95 and a la carte 16.75/32.25 ♀ – **31 rm** ☕ ★85.00/100.00 – ★★100.00/160.00.
◆ Converted corn mill on the Thames. Historic exterior, modern interior - greys and beige décor. Tasteful furnishings extend to bedrooms, especially executive heritage rooms. Restaurant features working water wheel and millrace.

at Clifton Hampden *Southeast : 3 m. on A 415* – ✉ *Abingdon.*

The Plough Inn, Abingdon Rd, OX14 3EG, ✆ (01865) 407811, *admin@ploughinns.co.uk, Fax (01865) 407136,* 🐶 – ⇥ ✆ ♿ P. MO VISA
Rest a la carte 16.85/31.85 ♀ – **10 rm** ☕ ★75.00 – ★★90.00/130.00.
◆ Bedrooms at this family-run part 16C thatched inn are divided between the main inn and various outbuildings. Four poster beds and log fires add to the atmosphere. Restaurant or bar meal options.

ABINGER COMMON *Surrey* 504 S 30 – *see Dorking.*

ABINGER HAMMER *Surrey* 504 S 30.
London 35 – Brighton 40 – Dover 91 – Portsmouth 50 – Reading 33.

Drakes on the Pond, Dorking Rd, RH5 6SA, on A 25 ✆ (01306) 731174 *Fax (01306) 731174* – ▤ P. MO VISA
closed 25 December-4 January, Saturday lunch, Sunday and Monday – **Rest** 23.50 (lunch) and a la carte 37.50/50.00 ♀.
Spec. Tian of crab and coconut. Pan-fried John Dory with spinach and herb ravioli. Slow-cooked rabbit with beetroot and potato dauphinoise.
◆ Modern interior featuring linen-clad tables and waterfowl paintings on the walls. Menus have an unfussy, contemporary base; quality ingredients and personal service.

ACASTER MALBIS *N. Yorks.* 502 Q 22 – *see York.*

ACTON BURNELL *Shrops.* 503 L 26 – *see Shrewsbury.*

ACTON GREEN *Worcs.* 503 504 M 27 – *see Great Malvern.*

ADDINGHAM *W. Yorks.* 502 O 22 *Great Britain G. – pop. 3 215.*
Env. : *Bolton Abbey★ AC, N : 3.5 m. on B 6160.*
London 225 – Bradford 16 – Ilkley 4.

Fleece, 154 Main St, LS29 0LY, ☎ (01943) 830491 – P. MO VISA
Rest a la carte 15.00/25.00 ♀.
◆ Personally run pub on village main street. Open fires, solid stone floor, rustic walls filled with country prints. Wide ranging menu with good use of seasonal ingredients.

AINTREE *Mersey.* 502 503 L 23 – *see Liverpool.*

ALBRIGHTON *Shrops.* 502 503 L 25 – *see Shrewsbury.*

ALCESTER *Warks.* 503 504 O 27 – *pop. 7 068.*
London 104 – Birmingham 20 – Cheltenham 27 – Stratford-upon-Avon 8.

Kings Court, Kings Coughton, B49 5QQ, North : 1 ½ m. on A 435 ☎ (01789) 763111, *info@kingscourthotel.co.uk, Fax (01789) 400242,* – ♿ P – 130. MO AE VISA
closed 25-30 December – **Rest** 12.85 (lunch) and dinner a la carte 17.15/26.15 ♀ – **41 rm** ⊐ ★68.00/73.00 – ★★90.00.
◆ Refurbished hotel popular for weddings and conferences. Some bedrooms in original Tudor part of building retain oak beams lending them a certain rustic charm. Welcoming dining room with courtyard garden; log fire in bar.

ALDEBURGH *Suffolk* 504 Y 27 – *pop. 2 654.*
Thorpeness Golf Hotel, Thorpeness ☎ (01728) 452176.
152 High St ☎ (01728) 453637, atic@suffolkcoastal.gov.uk.
London 97 – Ipswich 24 – Norwich 41.

Wentworth, Wentworth Rd, IP15 5BD, ☎ (01728) 452312, *stay@wentworth-aldeburgh.co.uk, Fax (01728) 454343,* ←, , – P. MO AE VISA
Rest (bar lunch)/dinner 18.00 ♀ – **35 rm** ⊐ ★73.00/105.00 – ★★155.00/195.00.
◆ Carefully furnished, traditional seaside hotel; coast view bedrooms are equipped with binoculars and all have a copy of "Orlando the Marmalade Cat", a story set in the area. Enjoy Aldeburgh sprats on the dining room terrace.

Brudenell, The Parade, IP15 5BU, ☎ (01728) 452071, *info@brudenellhotel.co.uk, Fax (01728) 454082,* ←, – ♿ P. MO AE VISA
Rest 25.00 (dinner) and a la carte 18.85/46.70 ♀ – **41 rm** ⊐ ★67.00/102.00 – ★★124.00/163.00, 1 suite.
◆ Seaside hotel facing pebble beach and sea. Contemporary décor in pastel shades. Good rooms with modern amenities; most with view. Bright and modern dining room with terrace. Light informal menus offering modern dishes and British classics, using local produce.

Flint House, Aldeburgh Rd, IP17 1PD, Northwest : 2 ¾ m. on A 1094 ☎ (01728) 689123, *flinthouse@eidosnet.co.uk, Fax (01728) 687406,* – P.
Rest 15.00 – **4 rm** ⊐ ★35.00/45.00 – ★★70.00.
◆ Two rebuilt 19C terraced flint cottages with modern extensions and rural outlook. Good value accommodation with homely, colourfully decorated bedrooms. Organic breakfasts.

The Lighthouse, 77 High St, IP15 5AU, ☎ (01728) 453377, *sarafox@diron.co.uk, Fax (01728) 4543831,* – . MO AE VISA
closed 2 weeks January – **Rest** (booking essential) a la carte 16.25/30.20 ♀.
◆ Busy, unpretentious bistro boasts a wealth of Suffolk produce from local meats to Aldeburgh cod and potted shrimps. Good choice of wines; amiable service.

152, 152 High St, IP15 5AX, ☎ (01728) 454594, *info@152aldeburgh.co.uk, Fax (01728) 454618,* – MO AE VISA
Rest 17.50 and a la carte 20.50/30.00 ♀.
◆ Choose between the bright, informal restaurant or the courtyard terrace on summer days to enjoy the keenly priced menu that features a wide variety of local produce.

Regatta, 171-173 High St, IP15 5AN, ☎ (01728) 452011, *Fax (01728) 453324* – . MO AE VISA
closed Sunday dinner-Tuesday, November-March – **Rest** - Seafood specialities - a la carte 16.00/28.50 s.
◆ Maritime murals on the walls and the modest priced menus make this fish-inspired eatery a good catch. Local seafood is a speciality as are the inventive puddings.

at Friston *Northwest : 4 m. by A 1094 on B 1121 – ✉ Aldeburgh.*

The Old School without rest., IP17 1NP, ✆ (01728) 688173, – **P**.
3 rm ☕ ★50.00 – ★★58.00.
◆ Redbrick former school house in pleasant garden. Good breakfast served family style in spacious room. Comfortable modern rooms with good amenities in the house or annexe.

ALDERLEY EDGE *Ches.* 502 503 504 N 24 – *pop. 5 280.*
Wilmslow, Great Warford, Mobberley ✆ (01565) 872148.
London 187 – Chester 34 – Manchester 14 – Stoke-on-Trent 25.

Alderley Edge, Macclesfield Rd, SK9 7BJ, ✆ (01625) 583033, *sales@alderleyedgehotel.com, Fax (01625) 586343,* – **P** – 90. AE VISA.
Rest – (see ***The Alderley*** below) – ☕ 12.50 – **51 rm** ★120.00/135.00 – ★★170.00, 1 suite.
◆ A substantial late Victorian house with an easy-going style. Relaxing lounges furnished with cushion-clad easy chairs. Well-furnished, comfortable bedrooms, some with views.

The Alderley (at Alderley Edge H.), Macclesfield Rd, SK9 7BJ, ✆ (01625) 583033, *sales@alderleyedgehotel.com, Fax (01625) 586343,* – **P**. AE VISA
Rest 17.95/30.00 and a la carte 34.50/50.00 ♀.
◆ Conservatory dining room; comfortably spaced tables. The cuisine, served by dinner-suited staff, is modern British. Particularly proud of 500 wine list and 100 Champagnes.

The Alderley Bar & Grill, 50 London Rd, SK9 7DZ, ✆ (01625) 599999, *Fax (01625) 599913,* – . AE VISA
Rest a la carte 16.90/28.00 ♀.
◆ High street restaurant with wood-decked pavement terrace. Stylish interior on two floors with old slapstick movies projected onto walls. Modern menus, world-wide influences.

The Wizard, Macclesfield Rd, SK10 4UB, Southeast : 1¼ m. on B 5087 ✆ (01625) 584000, *Fax (01625) 585105,* , – **P**. AE VISA
closed Christmas-New Year – **Rest** a la carte 20.00/45.00 ♀.
◆ Located in a National Trust area, this 200-year old pub restaurant serves up-to-date dishes at reasonable prices. Sticky puddings of chocolate, toffee or caramel feature.

Undecided between two equivalent establishments?
Within each category, establishments are classified
in our order of preference.

ALDERNEY *C.I.* 503 Q 33 and 517 ⑨ – *see Channel Islands.*

ALDERSHOT *Hants.* 504 R 30.
35-39 The High St ✆ (01252) 320968.
London 45 – Portsmouth 38 – Reading 22 – Southampton 45 – Winchester 32.

Premier Travel Inn, 7 Wellington Ave, GU11 1SQ, East : on A 323 ✆ (01252) 344063, *Fax (01252) 344073* – rm, rest, **P**. AE VISA.
Rest (grill rest.) – **60 rm** ★49.95/49.95 – ★★52.95/52.95.
◆ Suitable for families and the business traveller. 24 hour self-service eateries and range of hot and cold food available. Comfortable, modern bedrooms.

ALDFIELD *N. Yorks. – see Ripon.*

ALDFORD *Ches.* 502 L 24.
London 189 – Chester 6 – Liverpool 25.

The Grosvenor Arms, Chester Rd, CH3 6HJ, ✆ (01244) 620228, *grosvenor-arms@brunningandprice.co.uk, Fax (01244) 620247,* , – **P**. AE VISA
closed dinner 25-26 December and 1 January – **Rest** a la carte 15.65/29.20 ♀.
◆ Large, red-brick 19C pub in rural village with sprawling summer terrace and conservatory. Equally spacious, bustling interior. Daily changing menus offer modern/rustic dishes.

ALDRIDGE *W. Mids.* 502 503 504 O 26 – *pop. 15 659* – ✉ *Walsall.*
London 130 – *Birmingham 12* – *Derby 32* – *Leicester 40* – *Stoke-on-Trent 38.*

Plan : see Birmingham p. 5

Fairlawns, 178 Little Aston Rd, WS9 0NU, East : 1 m. on A 454 ✆ (01922) 455122, *welcome@fairlawns.co.uk, Fax (01922) 743210,* , , , , , – , rest, – 60. MC AE VISA CT n
closed 24 December-1 January – **Rest** *(closed Bank Holidays)* 18.95/30.00 **s.** – **54 rm** 79.50/92.50 – 95.00/129.00, 6 suites.
◆ Privately owned hotel with well-equipped leisure facility. A choice range of rooms from budget to superior, all comfy and spacious, some with good views over open countryside. Restaurant gains from its rural ambience.

ALFRISTON *E. Sussex* 504 U 31 – *pop. 1 721* – ✉ *Polegate.*
London 66 – *Eastbourne 9* – *Lewes 10* – *Newhaven 8.*

Star Inn, High St, BN26 5TA, ✆ (01323) 870495, *bookings@star-inn-alfriston.com, Fax (01323) 870922* – – 30. MC AE VISA
Rest (bar lunch Monday-Saturday)/dinner 24.50 – **37 rm** 44.00/64.00 – 88.00/128.00.
◆ 14C coaching inn with original half-timbered façade where smugglers once met. Décor includes flagstone floor and beamed ceilings; bar serves real ale. Well-kept bedrooms. Atmospheric Tudor style restaurant.

George Inn with rm, High St, BN26 5SY, ✆ (01323) 870319, *Fax (01323) 871384,* , – rm, rm. MC VISA
Closed 25-26 December – **Rest** a la carte 12.00/25.00 – **6 rm** 50.00 – 120.00.
◆ Revered 15C timbered pub with dried hops, open fire, original floor boards. Popular with walkers. Local suppliers provide backbone to eclectic menus. Carefully restored rooms.

ALNE *N. Yorks.* 502 Q 21 – *see Easingwold.*

ALNWICK *Northd.* 501 502 O 17 *Great Britain G.* – *pop. 7 767.*
See : *Town* ★ – *Castle*★★ *AC.*
Exc. : *Dunstanburgh Castle*★ *AC, NE : 8 m. by B 1340 and Dunstan rd (last 2½ m. on foot).*
18 *Swansfield Park* ✆ *(01665) 602632.*
2 The Shambles ✆ *(01665) 510665, alnwicktic@alnwick.gov.uk.*
London 320 – *Edinburgh 86* – *Newcastle upon Tyne 34.*

Charlton House without rest., 2 Aydon Gdns, South Rd, NE66 2NT, Southeast : ½ m. on B 6346 ✆ (01665) 605185 – .
closed 5 November - 16 February – **5 rm** 27.00/30.00 – 60.00.
◆ 19C semi-detached townhouse, the first to be lit by hydro-electricity. Breakfast in colourful front room with garden: Craster kippers served. Bedrooms with bright personality.

at North Charlton *North : 6¾ m. by A 1* – ✉ *Alnwick.*

North Charlton Farm without rest., NE67 5HP, ✆ (01665) 579443, *stay@northcharltonfarm.co.uk, Fax (01665) 579407,* , , – .
Easter-October – **3 rm** 40.00 – 70.00.
◆ Attractive house on working farm with agricultural museum. Offers cosy, traditional accommodation. Each bedroom is individually decorated and has countryside views.

at Newton on the Moor *South : 5½ m. by A 1* – ✉ *Alnwick.*

Cook and Barker Inn with rm, NE65 9JY, ✆ (01665) 575234, *Fax (01665) 575234,* , – . MC AE VISA.
closed dinner 25 December – **Rest** 19.50 (dinner) and a la carte 25.00/35.00 – **19 rm** 47.00 – 70.00.
◆ Attractive stone-faced inn with traditional décor. Extensive blackboard menu - traditional pub food and more adventurous dishes. Spacious modern en suite bedrooms in annexe.

at Swarland *South : 7¾ m. by A 1* – ✉ *Alnwick.*

Swarland Old Hall without rest., NE65 9HU, Southwest : 1 m. on B 6345 ✆ (01670) 787642, *proctor@swarlandoldhall.fsnet.co.uk,* , , – .
3 rm 30.00 – 60.00.
◆ Grade II listed building, on working farm, with unusual castellated wall. Well-run accommodation. Comfortable bedrooms with views of the coast on clear days.

ALREWAS *Staffs.* 502 503 504 O 25.
London 128.5 – Burton-upon-Trent 10 – Derby 20.

The Old Boat, Kings Bromley Rd, DE13 7DB, ☎ (01283) 791468, *Fax (01283) 792886,* – P. VISA
closed Sunday dinner – **Rest** 10.95 (lunch) and a la carte 18.00/29.00 ♀.
◆ Tucked away in corner of village, with regular canal boat clientele. An informal pub/restaurant, it boasts a strong range of dishes from bangers and mash to modern creations.

ALSTON *Cumbria* 501 502 M 19 – *pop. 2 218.*
Alston Moor, The Hermitage ☎ (01434) 381675.
The Alstonmorry Information Centre, Town Hall ☎ (01434) 382244.
London 309 – Carlisle 28 – Newcastle upon Tyne 45.

Lovelady Shield Country House, Nenthead Rd, CA9 3LF, East : 2½ m. on A 689 ☎ (01434) 381203, *enquiries@lovelady.co.uk, Fax (01434) 381515,* ←, – P. AE VISA
weekends only in January – **Rest** (booking essential to non-residents) (dinner only) 36.50 ♀ – **12 rm** (dinner included) 100.00 – 200.00.
◆ Stately, personally run 18C Georgian house in very quiet position by River Nent. Open fires and restful atmosphere throughout. Bedrooms boast a quality, up-to-date feel. Peaceful dining room with modern English cooking.

ALTON *Hants.* 504 R 30 – *pop. 16 005.*
Old Odiham Rd ☎ (01420) 82042.
7 Cross and Pillory Lane ☎ (01420) 88448, altoninfo@btconnect.com.
London 53 – Reading 24 – Southampton 29 – Winchester 18.

Alton Grange, London Rd, GU34 4EG, Northeast : 1 m. on A 3004 ☎ (01420) 86565, *info@altongrange.co.uk, Fax (01420) 541346,* – P – 100. AE VISA.
closed 24-30 December – ***Truffles :*** Rest a la carte 29.95/36.50 ♀ – **30 rm** 90.00/110.00 – 120.00/160.00.
◆ Hotel set in well-kept, oriental inspired gardens. The bar serves bistro-style snacks. Bedrooms are individually decorated, particularly junior suites and Saxon room. Dining room boasts myriad of Tiffany lamps and fusion cuisine.

ALTRINCHAM *Gtr Manchester* 502 503 504 N 23 – *pop. 40 695.*
Altrincham Municipal, Stockport Rd, Timperley ☎ (0161) 928 0761 – Dunham Forest, Oldfield Lane ☎ (0161) 928 2605 – Ringway, Hale Mount, Hale Barns ☎ (0161) 904 9609.
20 Stamford New Rd ☎ (0161) 912 5931, tourist.information@trafford.gov.uk.
London 191 – Chester 30 – Liverpool 30 – Manchester 8.

Juniper (Kitching), 21 The Downs, WA14 2QD, ☎ (0161) 929 4008, *reservations@juniper-restaurant.co.uk, Fax (0161) 929 4009* – . AE VISA
restricted opening Christmas and closed 1 week February, 2 weeks summer, Sunday, Monday and lunch Tuesday-Thursday. – **Rest** 20.00 (lunch) and a la carte 32.00/48.00.
Spec. Baked trout with caviar, lentils and chocolate. Fillet of beef, white asparagus, pinenuts and sultanas. Blueberry muffin soufflé, cream cheese ice cream.
◆ Smooth service and highly original, creative cooking are the notable hallmarks here. Try the 20-course gastronomic menu to sample the memorable style.

Dilli, 60 Stamford New Rd, WA14 1EE, ☎ (0161) 929 7484, *info@dilli.co.uk, Fax (0161) 929 1213* – 40. AE VISA
Rest - Indian - 14.95 (lunch) a la carte 20.35/28.85.
◆ Intriguing interior: the décor is a mix of Indian wooden fretwork and minimalism. Totally authentic Indian dishes use quality ingredients. Lunches are particularly good value.

Snockers, 9 Goose Green, WA14 1DW, ☎ (0161) 929 8929, *chris@snockers.com, Fax (0161) 474 1312,* – AE VISA
closed Sunday – **Rest** 14.95/19.95 and a la carte 21.50/31.50.
◆ Eccentrically named restaurant in courtyard; the food, as well as the monicker, ensnares curious diners. Original dishes can be enjoyed on the pleasant summer terrace.

at Hale Barns *Southeast : 3 m. on A 538 – ✉ Altrincham.*

Marriott Manchester Airport, Manchester Airport, Hale Rd, WA15 8XW, ☎ (0870) 4007271, *reservations.manchesterairport@marriotthotels.co.uk, Fax (0161) 980 1787,* , , – , rm, P – 180. AE VISA.
Four Seasons : Rest a la carte 21.15/36.90 **s.** ♀ – 14.95 – **142 rm** 129.00 – 129.00.
◆ A group owned hotel convenient for both the airport and the motorway. Guests can unwind in the well-equipped leisure facilities or the spacious bar. Comfortable bedrooms. Fine dining restaurant with interesting modern dishes.

at Little Bollington *Southwest : 3¼ m. on A 56 – ✉ Altrincham.*

Ash Farm without rest., Park Lane, WA14 4TJ, ✆ (0161) 929 9290, *jan@ashfarm97.fsnet.co.uk, Fax (0161) 928 5002,* – P.
closed 5-17 January – **4 rm** ☕ ♦49.00/54.00 – ♦♦63.00/75.00.
◆ Attractive, creeper-clad 18C former farmhouse in quiet location, a short walk from Dunham Deer Park. Pretty stone-flagged breakfast room; cosy, individually styled bedrooms.

ALVELEY *Shrops. – see Bridgnorth.*

ALVESTON *Warks. – see Stratford-upon-Avon.*

ALWALTON *Cambs.* 502 504 T 26 *– see Peterborough.*

ALWESTON *Dorset* 503 504 M 31 *– see Sherborne.*

AMBERLEY *W. Sussex* 504 S 31 *Great Britain G. – pop. 525 – ✉ Arundel.*
Env. : *Bignor Roman Villa (mosaics★) AC, NW : 3½ m. by B 2139 via Bury.*
London 56 – Brighton 24 – Portsmouth 31.

Amberley Castle , BN18 9LT, Southwest : ½ m. on B 2139 ✆ (01798) 831992, *info@amberleycastle.co.uk, Fax (01798) 831998,* , , – P – 40. MC AE VISA.
Queen's Room : **Rest** (booking essential) 20.00/50.00 – ☕ 16.50 – **13 rm** ♦155.00/375.00 – ♦♦155.00/375.00, 6 suites.
◆ Historic yet intimate, a 14C castle in the South Downs - majestic battlements and luxurious rooms with jacuzzis. White peacocks and black swans inhabit the serene gardens. Barrel-vaulted dining room with graceful lancet windows and mural.

AMBLESIDE *Cumbria* 502 L 20 *Great Britain G. – pop. 3 064.*
Env. : *Lake Windermere★★ – Dove Cottage, Grasmere★ AC* AY A *– Brockhole National Park Centre★ AC, SE : 3 m. by A 591* AZ.
Exc. : *Wrynose Pass★★, W : 7½ m. by A 593* AY *– Hard Knott Pass★★, W : 10 m. by A 593* AY.
Central Buildings, Market Cross ✆ (015394) 32582 AZ, *amblesidetic@southlakeland.gov.uk – Main Car Park, Waterhead ✆ (015394) 32729 (summer only)* BY.
London 278 – Carlisle 47 – Kendal 14.

Plan on next page

The Samling , Ambleside Rd, LA23 1LR, South : 1½ m. on A 591 ✆ (015394) 31922, *info@thesamling.com, Fax (015394) 30400,* < Lake Windermere and mountains, , – P. MC AE VISA.
Rest (booking essential for non-residents) 48.00 **s.** – **9 rm** ☕ ♦195.00 – ♦♦415.00, 2 suites.
◆ Late 18C Lakeland house with superb views of Lake Windermere and surrounding mountains. Stylishly relaxing and informal environment. Elegant, individually decorated rooms. Imaginative, modern cuisine in smart dining room.

The Waterhead, Lake Rd, LA22 0ER, ✆ (015394) 32566, *waterhead@elhmail.co.uk, Fax (015394) 31255,* <, , – P – 40. MC AE VISA BY x
The Bay : **Rest** (light lunch Monday-Saturday)/dinner 30.00 **s.** – **41 rm** ☕ ♦80.00/115.00 – ♦♦160.00/220.00.
◆ Set close to Lake Windermere; modernised in 2004, resulting in a stylish, airy, open plan feel. Bedrooms, in modish creams and browns, have flat screen TVs and DVDs. Restaurant boasts original cooking, sleek décor and lovely terrace views to lake.

Rothay Manor, Rothay Bridge, LA22 0EH, South : ½ m. on A 593 ✆ (015394) 33605, *hotel@rothaymanor.co.uk, Fax (015394) 33607,* – P. MC AE VISA. BY r
closed 3 January - 26 February – **Rest** 19.50/37.00 and lunch a la carte 17.50/18.50 – **16 rm** ☕ ♦70.00/120.00 – ♦♦125.00/165.00, 3 suites.
◆ Elegant Regency country house in landscaped gardens. Family run with long traditions: many regulars. Bedrooms furnished in modern tones. Free use of nearby leisure club. Gardens can be admired from dining room windows.

Brathay Lodge without rest., Rothay Rd, LA22 0EE, ✆ (01539) 432000, *brathay@globalnet.co.uk* – P. MC VISA AZ e
21 rm ♦40.00/60.00 – ♦♦70.00/95.00.
◆ Stylish accommodation in the heart of Ambleside. Unfussy, bright and warm décor. Continental breakfast only. All bedrooms have spa baths and some boast four posters.

AMBLESIDE

Borrans Rd . . . . . BY 2
Cheapside . . . . . AZ 4
Church St . . . . . AZ 6
Compston St . . . . . AZ 8
Kelsick Rd . . . . . AZ 12
King St . . . . . AZ 13
Lake Rd . . . . . AZ
Market Pl. . . . . . AZ 14
North Rd . . . . . AZ 17
Old Lake Rd . . . . . AZ 20
St Mary's Lane . . . . . AZ 22
Smithy Brow . . . . . AZ 23

GRASMERE

Broadgate . . . . . BZ 3
Easedale Rd . . . . . BZ 10
Swan Hill . . . . . AY 24

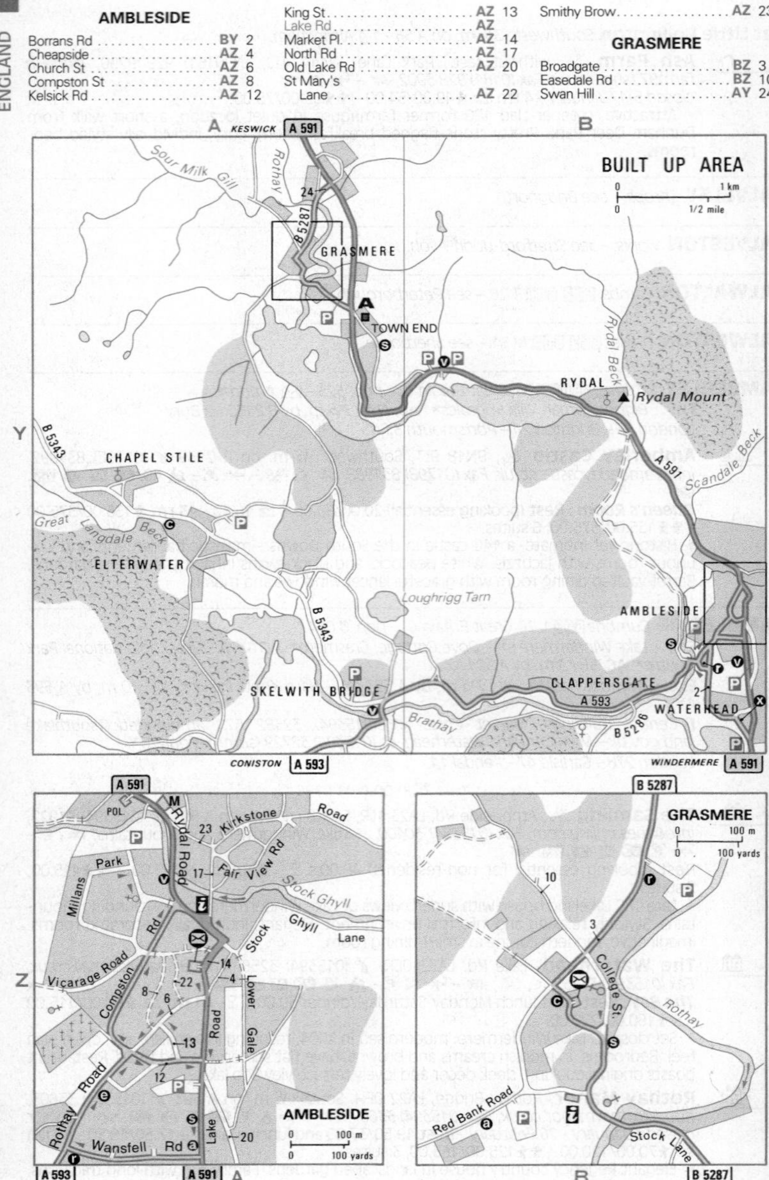

Lakes Lodge without rest., Lake Rd, LA22 0DB, ☎ (015394) 33240, *u@lakeslodge.co.uk, Fax (015394) 33240* – P. MO AE VISA AZ s
12 rm ★49.00/79.00 – ★★79.00/99.00.
◆ Characterful house with traditional exterior but modern facilities and relaxed atmosphere. Good size bedrooms with contemporary style. Buffet style Continental breakfast.

Elder Grove without rest., Lake Rd, LA22 0DB, ☎ (015394) 32504, *info@eldergrove.co.uk, Fax (015394) 32251* – P. MO VISA AZ a
restricted opening December and January – **10 rm** ★27.00/40.00 – ★★54.00/80.00.
◆ Homely establishment with warm, family run appeal. Distinctive cosy bar has firemen's memorabilia. Traditionally furnished throughout, including bedrooms. Cumbrian breakfasts.

Red Bank without rest., Wansfell Rd, LA22 0EG, ☎ (015394) 34637, *info@redbank.co.uk, Fax (015394) 34637*, – P. MO VISA. AZ r
closed 1-15 November and 23 December - 2 January – **3 rm** ★60.00/70.00 – ★★76.00.
◆ Edwardian house, well sited a minute's walk from town. Cosy central lounge and pleasant breakfast room overlooking garden. Attractively furnished rooms with wrought iron beds.

Riverside without rest., Under Loughrigg, LA22 9LJ, ☎ (015394) 32395, *info@riverside-ambleside.co.uk, Fax (015394) 32240*, – P. MO VISA. BY s
closed Christmas-New Year – **6 rm** ★45.00/60.00 – ★★76.00/96.00.
◆ 19C country house with river Rothay on the doorstep and access to Loughrigg Fell. Lovely rear fellside garden. Nicely decorated bedrooms commanding admirable views.

The Log House with rm, Lake Rd, LA22 0DN, ☎ (015394) 31077, *steve@loghouse.co.uk* – MO VISA BY v
Rest 21.95 and a la carte 23.85/34.45 ♀ – **3 rm** ★45.00/55.00 – ★★60.00/80.00.
◆ Artist Alfred Heaton Cooper imported this house from Norway for use as a studio. It's now a polished restaurant serving tasty cooking with imaginative touches. Comfy bedrooms.

Glass House, Rydal Rd, LA22 9AN, ☎ (015394) 32137, *info@theglasshouserestaurant.co.uk, Fax (015394) 33384*, – MO VISA AZ v
closed 25 December and Tuesday – **Rest** (booking essential) a la carte 21.30/31.00 ♀.
◆ Chic, split-level, converted 15C mill with water wheel next to glass making studio; maker of dining room light fittings. Sophisticated, well-executed dishes; classy snacks.

Drunken Duck Inn with rm, Barngates, LA22 0NG, Southwest : 3 m. by A 593 and B 5286 on Tarn Hows rd ☎ (015394) 36347, *info@drunkenduckinn.co.uk, Fax (015394) 36781*, ←, – P. MO AE VISA.
closed 25 December – **Rest** a la carte 25.95/39.95 ♀ – **16 rm** ★71.25 – ★★210.00.
◆ Named after a 19C landlady who found her ducks drunk, this part 16C inn boasts an on-site brewery, cosy bar with oak settles and restaurant serving modern fare. Smart rooms.

at Skelwith Bridge *West : 2½ m. on A 593 – ✉ Ambleside.*

Skelwith Bridge, LA22 9NJ, ☎ (015394) 32115, *skelwithbr@aol.com, Fax (015394) 34254* – P. MO VISA AY v
The Bridge : Rest (dinner only and Sunday lunch)/dinner 27.45 **s.** ♀ – **28 rm** ★40.00/95.00 – ★★70.00/110.00.
◆ 17C Lakeland inn at entrance to the stunningly picturesque Langdale Valley. Traditional, simple bedrooms; panelled, clubby bar; busy Badgers Bar for walkers. Popular restaurant has large windows overlooking fells.

at Elterwater *West : 4½ m. by A 593 off B 5343 – ✉ Ambleside.*

Langdale H. & Country Club, Great Langdale, LA22 9JD, Northwest : ½ m. on B 5343 ☎ (015394) 37302, Reservations (Freephone) 0500 051197, *info@langdale.co.uk, Fax (015394) 37130*, squash – rest, P – 60. MO AE VISA. AY c
Purdeys : Rest 25.00 (dinner) and a la carte 19.95/30.40 ♀ – ***The Terrace :*** Rest a la carte 12.40/19.95 – **57 rm** ★75.00/90.00 – ★★210.00.
◆ Family friendly, part-timeshare estate hidden in a forest, on site of former gunpowder works. Lots of ponds and streams; smart leisure centre. Hotel and lodge rooms available. Purdeys with local stone and water features. Informal Terrace boasts wi-fi access.

at Little Langdale *West : 5 m. by A 593 – ✉ Langdale.*

Three Shires Inn, LA22 9NZ, ☎ (015394) 37215, *enquiry@threeshiresinn.co.uk, Fax (015394) 37127*, ←, – P. MO AE VISA. AY c
restricted opening December-January – **Rest** (bar lunch)/dinner a la carte 15.45/24.40 – **10 rm** ★40.00/70.00 – ★★74.00/100.00.
◆ Traditional slate inn, built 1872; named after meeting point of old counties of Cumberland, Westmorland, Lancashire. Neatly turned rooms in quiet colours; some have views. Dining room boasts hearty, rustic atmosphere.

AMERSHAM (Old Town) *Bucks.* 504 S 29 – *pop. 21 470.*

Little Chalfont, Lodge Lane ℘ (01494) 764877.

Tesco's Car Park, London Road West ℘ (01494) 729492 (April-September).

London 29 – Aylesbury 16 – Oxford 33.

Artichoke, 9 Market Sq., HP7 0DF, ℘ (01494) 726611, *info@theartichokerestaurant.co.uk* – . MC VISA

closed 2 weeks August, 1 week Spring, 1 week Christmas, Sunday and Monday – **Rest** 22.50/32.50 and lunch a la carte 31.50/37.50.

• Charmingly converted from its 16C origins but still retaining much period detail: thick walls, exposed beams. Distinctive modern cooking using interesting combinations.

Gilbey's, 1 Market Sq, HP7 0DF, ℘ (01494) 727242, *gilbeysamersham@aol.com, Fax (01494) 431243,* – MC AE VISA

closed 24-28 December and 1 January – **Rest** (booking essential) a la carte 22.40/28.40.

• Atmospheric exposed brick dining room. The bold menu includes inventive accompaniments such as bacon and cabbage hash, black bean salsa and grain mustard creamed potatoes.

AMESBURY *Wilts.* 503 504 O 30 *The West Country G.* – *pop. 8 312.*

Env. : *Stonehenge**** *AC, W : 2 m. by A 303.*

Exc. : *Wilton Village** *(Wilton House*** *AC, Wilton Carpet Factory** *AC), SW : 13 m. by A 303, B 3083 and A 36.*

Amesbury Library, Smithfield St ℘ (01980) 622833, amesburytic@salisbury.gov.uk.

London 87 – Bristol 52 – Southampton 32 – Taunton 66.

Mandalay without rest., 15 Stonehenge Rd, SP4 7BA, via Church St ℘ (01980) 623733, *Fax (01980) 626642,* – P. MC AE VISA.

5 rm 38.00/50.00 – 65.00.

• Only two minutes' drive from Stonehenge, this brick-built house boasts a bygone style and pleasant garden. Varied breakfasts. Individual rooms, named after famous authors.

Good food without spending a fortune? Look out for the Bib Gourmand

AMPLEFORTH *N. Yorks.* 502 Q 21 – *see Helmsley.*

ANSTY *W. Mids.* – *see Coventry.*

APPLEBY-IN-WESTMORLAND *Cumbria* 502 M 20 – *pop. 2 570 (inc. Bongate).*

Appleby, Brackenber Moor ℘ (017683) 51432.

Moot Hall, Boroughgate ℘ (017683) 51177, tic@applebytown.org.uk.

London 285 – Carlisle 33 – Kendal 24 – Middlesbrough 58.

Appleby Manor Country House, Roman Rd, CA16 6JB, East : 1 m. by B 6542 and Station Rd ℘ (017683) 51571, *reception@applebymanor.co.uk, Fax (017683) 52888,* , – P – 40. MC AE VISA.

closed 24-26 December – **Rest** a la carte 22.00/34.00 **s.** – **30 rm** 80.00/85.00 – 120.00/140.00.

• Wooded grounds and good views of Appleby Castle at this elevated 19C pink sandstone country manor. Main house bedrooms have most character; coach house annex welcomes dogs. Dining options: oak ceilinged restaurant or lighter, chandelier equipped room.

Tufton Arms, Market Sq, CA16 6XA, ℘ (017683) 51593, *info@tuftonarmshotel.co.uk, Fax (017683) 52761,* – P – 100. MC AE VISA

closed 25-26 December – **Rest** 27.50 (dinner) and a la carte 18.40/27.50 – **22 rm** 63.50/73.50 – 100.00/155.00.

• 19C coaching inn; quaint, atmospheric interiors. Homely, country rooms and bar adorned with sepia photographs. Inn runs a sporting agency; fly fishing can be arranged. Charming conservatory restaurant overlooking cobbled mews courtyard.

at Maulds Meaburn *Southwest : 5¾ m. by B 6260 – Appleby-in-Westmorland.*

Crake Trees Manor, CA10 3JG, South : ½ m. on Crosby Ravensworth rd ℘ (01931) 715205, *ruth@craketreesmanor.co.uk,* The Pennine Hills, – P. MC AE VISA – **Rest** (by arrangement) (communal dining) 20.00 – **5 rm** 40.00/50.00 – 80.00/84.00.

• Superbly located modern barn conversion built of stone, slate, ash and oak. Splendid Pennine views; guests encouraged to walk the paths. Comfy public areas and tasteful rooms. Dining room where good home cooking is a mainstay.

APPLEDORE *Devon* 503 H 30 *The West Country G. – pop. 2 114.*
See : Town★.
London 228 – Barnstaple 12 – Exeter 46 – Plymouth 61 – Taunton 63.

West Farm without rest., Irsha St, EX39 1RY, West : ¼ m. ✆ (01237) 425269, *west farm@appledore-devon.co.uk*, – .
3 rm ★54.00/60.00 – ★★88.00/94.00.
◆ A 17C house with a particularly charming garden at the back. Delightfully appointed sitting room. Bedrooms feel comfortable and homely.

APPLETREEWICK *N. Yorks.* 502 O 21.
London 236 – Harrogate 25 – Skipton 11.

Knowles Lodge without rest., BD23 6DQ, South : 1 m. on Bolton Abbey rd ✆ (01756) 720228, *pam@knowleslodge.com, Fax (01756) 720381*, , – P. VISA
closed January-February – **Rest** 20.00 – **3 rm** ★45.00 – ★★70.00.
◆ Unusual Canadian ranch-house style guesthouse, clad in timber and sited in quiet dales location. Large sitting room with fine outlook. Cosy bedrooms have garden views.

ARDENS GRAFTON *Warks. – see Stratford-upon-Avon.*

ARLINGHAM *Glos.* 503 504 M 28 – *pop. 377 – ✉ Gloucester.*
London 120 – Birmingham 69 – Bristol 34 – Gloucester 16.

Old Passage Inn with rm, Passage Rd, GL2 7JR, West : ¾ m ✆ (01452) 740547, *oldpassageinn@ukonline.co.uk, Fax (01452) 741871*, ≤, – P. AE VISA.
closed 24 December-3 January – **Rest** - Seafood - *(closed Sunday dinner and Monday)* a la carte 23.50/33.50 – **3 rm** ★55.00/65.00 – ★★85.00/95.00.
◆ Former inn with simple style and bright ambience afforded by large windows. Friendly, relaxed dining. Seafood based menu. Modern, funky bedrooms in a vivid palette.

ARMSCOTE *Warks.* 504 P 27.
London 91 – Birmingham 36 – Oxford 38.

Willow Corner without rest., CV37 8DE, ✆ (01608) 682391, *trishandalan@willow corner.co.uk*, – P.
closed Christmas-New Year – **3 rm** ★48.00 – ★★68.00.
◆ Cosy 18C cottage at village periphery, personally run by dedicated owner. Thatched roof; snug interiors plus a vast inglenook. Well-kept rooms with host of thoughtful extras.

Fox and Goose Inn with rm, CV37 8DD, ✆ (01608) 682293, *email@foxandgoose.co.uk, Fax (01608) 682293*, – P. VISA.
closed 1 January and 25-26 December – **Rest** a la carte 20.00/30.00 – **4 rm** ★55.00/70.00 – ★★85.00/120.00.
◆ Rustic inn with stone floor, wattle walls and warming log fires. Traditional country cooking in "olde worlde" setting with cask ales from bar. Eccentrically styled bedrooms.

ARNCLIFFE *N. Yorks.* 502 N 21 – *pop. 79 – ✉ Skipton.*
London 232 – Kendal 41 – Leeds 41 – Preston 50 – York 52.

Amerdale House , BD23 5QE, ✆ (01756) 770250, *amerdalehouse@btopen world.com, Fax (01756) 770250*, ≤, – rest, P. VISA.
mid March-October – **Rest** (booking essential to non-residents) (dinner only) 34.50 – **11 rm** (dinner included) ★99.00/101.00 – ★★168.00/176.00.
◆ Nestling in the secluded Dales, this country house offers tranquillity and a superb rural panorama. Comfy bedrooms and library stocked with books on local topography. Dining room employs fresh ingredients from the garden.

ARUNDEL *W. Sussex* 504 S 31 *Great Britain G. – pop. 3 297.*
See : Castle★★ AC.
61 High St ✆ (01903) 882268, tourism@arun.gov.uk.
London 58 – Brighton 21 – Southampton 41 – Worthing 9.

Swan, 27-29 High St, BN18 9AG, ✆ (01903) 882314, *info@swan-hotel.co.uk, Fax (01903) 883759* – , rest. AE VISA.
Rest a la carte 13.70/21.25 – **15 rm** ★65.00/85.00 – ★★79.00/95.00.
◆ Elegant Victorian hotel provides traditional comforts with modern facilities. The Brewery Tap bar of English oak serves real ale. Compact bedrooms boast quality furnishings. Restaurant proud of 200-year old wine cellar.

at Burpham *Northeast : 3 m. by A 27 – ✉ Arundel.*

Old Parsonage without rest., BN18 9RJ, ☎ (01903) 882160, *info@oldparsonage.co.uk, Fax (01903) 884627,* ←, – P. MO AE VISA.
10 rm ★45.00 – ★★120.00.
• Reputedly a hunting lodge for the Duke of Norfolk, this quiet hotel constitutes the ideal "stress remedy break". Calm, pastel coloured bedrooms overlook exquisite gardens.

George and Dragon, BN18 9RR, ☎ (01903) 883131 – P. MO VISA
closed 25 December and Sunday dinner – **Rest** a la carte 22.00/35.00.
• Pleasant, characterful pub in pretty village. Bar and more formal restaurant both serve robust British menus, prepared with care and attention, employing seasonal produce.

at Walberton *West : 3 m. by A 27 off B 2132 – ✉ Arundel.*

Hilton Avisford Park, Yapton Lane, BN18 0LS, on B 2132 ☎ (01243) 551215, *general.manager@hilton.com, Fax (01243) 552485,* ←, , heated, , 18, , , , squash – P. – 500. MO AE VISA
Rest (bar lunch Monday-Saturday)/dinner 25.95 **s.** – 15.95 – **134 rm** ★75.00/140.00 – ★★95.00/170.00, 5 suites.
• Former school and one-time home of Baronet Montagu, Nelson's admiral; retains a stately air with grand façade and 62-acre grounds. Generous drapes and furnishings in rooms. Dining room features honours board listing prefects of yesteryear.

ASCOT *Windsor & Maidenhead* 504 R 29 – *pop. 17 509 (inc. Sunningdale).*
18 *Mill Ride, Ascot* ☎ *(01344) 886777.*
London 36 – Reading 15.

Royal Berkshire Ramada Plaza, London Rd, Sunninghill, SL5 OPP, East : 2 m. on A 329 ☎ (01344) 623322, *sales.royalberkshire@ramadajarvis.co.uk, Fax (01344) 874240,* , , , , – P. – 100. MO AE VISA
Rest *(closed Saturday lunch)* (booking essential) 29.50 and a la carte 22.85/33.40 **s.** – **60 rm** ★225.00 – ★★245.00, 3 suites.
• Former home to the Churchill family, this Queen Anne mansion welcomes with tasteful, elegant furnishings and lounge bar with private library. Light, spacious bedrooms. Sedate, imposing restaurant.

Berystede, Bagshot Rd, Sunninghill, SL5 9JH, South : 1½ m. on A 330 ☎ (0870) 4008111, *general.berystede@macdonald-hotels.co.uk, Fax (01344) 872061,* heated, – , rest, P. – 120. MO AE VISA.
Rest *(closed Saturday lunch)* 18.95/27.50 and a la carte approx 18.95 **s.** – **118 rm** ★135.00/194.00 – ★★145.00/204.00, 7 suites.
• Popular with the sporting fraternity, this turreted, ivy clad hotel includes a bar styled on a gentleman's smoking room, a panelled library lounge and immaculate bedrooms. Restaurant overlooks the open air swimming pool.

at Sunninghill *South : 1½ m. by A 329 on B 3020 – ✉ Ascot.*

Highclere, Kings Rd, SL5 9AD, ☎ (01344) 625220, *info@highclerehotel.com, Fax (01344) 872528* – P. MO AE VISA.
Rest (residents only) (dinner only) 15.00 and a la carte 15.50/21.50 – **11 rm** ★75.00 – ★★110.00.
• "A home from home", exuding the personal touch, typified by comfy conservatory chairs for after-dinner coffee. Cosseted bedrooms: the Executive style a little more spacious.

XX **Jade Fountain,** 38 High St, SL5 9NE, ☎ (01344) 627070, *jadefountain328@aol.com, Fax (01344) 627070* – . MO AE VISA
closed 24-28 December – **Rest** - Chinese (Canton, Peking) - 20.00/25.00 (dinner) and a la carte 16.00/30.00.
• Smart Chinese restaurant specialising in sizzling dishes from Szechuan and Beijing -Peking duck, spring rolls and noodles amongst them. Also some Thai specialities.

ASENBY *N. Yorks. – see Thirsk.*

The ✿ award is the crème de la crème. This is awarded to restaurants which are really worth travelling miles for!

ASH *Kent* 504 X 30.
London 70 – Canterbury 9.5 – Dover 15.5.

Great Weddington, CT3 2AR, Northeast : ½ m. by A 257 on Weddington rd (01304) 813407, *traveltale@aol.com, Fax (01304) 812531,* AE VISA.
closed Christmas and New Year – **Rest** (by arrangement) (communal dining) 29.50 – **3 rm** 65.00 – 96.00.
◆ Charming Regency country house, ideally located for Canterbury and Dover. Well appointed drawing room and terrace. Thoughtfully furnished, carefully co-ordinated rooms. Communal dining room; owner an avid cook.

ASHBOURNE *Derbs.* 502 503 504 O 24 *Great Britain G. – pop. 5 020.*
Env. : *Dovedale★★ (Ilam Rock★) NW : 6 m. by A 515.*
13 Market Pl (01335) 343666, ashbourneinfo@derbyshiredales.gov.uk.
London 146 – Birmingham 47 – Manchester 48 – Nottingham 33 – Sheffield 44.

Callow Hall, Mappleton Rd, DE6 2AA, West : ¾ m. by Union St (off Market Pl) (01335) 300900, *reservations@callowhall.co.uk, Fax (01335) 300512,* AE VISA
closed 25-26 December and 1 January – **Rest** – (see ***The Restaurant*** below) – **15 rm** 95.00/120.00 – 135.00/185.00, 1 suite.
◆ Owned originally by a corset manufacturer earning it the nickname of "Corset Castle", this Victorian country house overlooks the River Dove valley. Some rooms with views.

The Restaurant (at Callow Hall), Mappleton Rd, DE6 2AA, West : ¾ m. by Union St (off Market Pl) (01335) 300900, *Fax (01335) 300512* – AE VISA
closed Sunday dinner to non-residents, 25-26 December and 1 January – **Rest** (dinner only and Sunday lunch)/dinner 39.50 and a la carte 29.75/37.65.
◆ Proud of its culinary traditions which include homebaking, smoking and curing, crafts that have been passed down through the generations. Local game and range of fine wines.

the dining room, 33 St Johns St, DE6 1GP, (01335) 300666 – VISA
closed 26 December-9 January, 1 week March, 1 week September, Sunday and Monday – **Rest** 22.00 (lunch) and a la carte 26.85/36.00.
◆ 17C building in central location. Huge display of orchids as part of contemporary décor. Wooden tables and wine display case. Wide ranging menu of modern dishes.

Bramhall's with rm, 6 Buxton Rd, DE6 1EX, (01335) 346158, *info@bramhalls.co.uk,* VISA.
closed 25-26 December and 1 January – **Rest** 12.95 (lunch) and a la carte 20.00/30.00 – **10 rm** 27.50 – 65.00.
◆ An unassuming inn just off the Market Square with dining terrace and stepped garden. Modern style cooking with daily blackboard specials. Contemporary bedrooms.

at Marston Montgomery *Southeast : 7½ m. by A 515 – ✉ Ashbourne.*

Bramhall's at The Crown Inn with rm, Rigg Lane, DE6 2FF, (01889) 590541, *info@bramhalls.co.uk,* VISA.
closed 25 December and 1 January – **Rest** *(closed Sunday dinner)* 12.95 (lunch) and a la carte 20.00/30.00 – **7 rm** 50.00 – 70.00.
◆ Relaxed and welcoming pub with exposed beams and open fire. Daily blackboard menu of good simple dishes. Cosy but modern bedrooms.

ASHBURTON *Devon* 503 I 32 *The West Country G. – pop. 3 309.*
Env. : *Dartmoor National Park★★.*
London 220 – Exeter 20 – Plymouth 25.

Holne Chase, TQ13 7NS, West : 3 m. on Two Bridges rd (01364) 631471, *info@holne-chase.co.uk, Fax (01364) 631453,* rest, VISA
Rest *(closed Monday lunch)* 20.00/34.50 – **9 rm** 115.00/125.00 – 170.00, **8 suites** 200.00/210.00.
◆ Former hunting lodge to Buckfast Abbey, set in 70 acres of woodland in Dartmoor National Park. This is walking country; dogs are welcome. Rooms are in main house and stables. Country style dining room utilising local produce.

Gages Mill without rest., Buckfastleigh Rd, TQ13 7JW, Southwest : 1 m. on Buckfastleigh/Totnes rd (01364) 652391, *richards@gagesmill.co.uk, Fax (01364) 652641,*
March-24 October – **7 rm** 26.00/45.00 – 52.00/68.00.
◆ 14C former wool mill in farmland on the edge of Dartmoor National Park. All bedrooms overlook countryside and benefit from a crisp freshness. Cottage-style breakfast room.

ENGLAND

Agaric, 30 North St, TQ13 7QD, ☏ (01364) 654478, *eat@agaricrestaurant.co.uk* – ⇆. MC VISA
closed last 2 weeks August, 2 weeks Christmas, Sunday-Tuesday and Saturday lunch – **Rest** a la carte 27.85/34.85.
◆ 200 year-old house in the centre of town. Windows full of home-made jams, fudge and olives, all for sale. Relaxed neighbourhood restaurant using a blend of cooking styles.

Rising Sun with rm, Woodland, TQ13 7JT, Southeast : 2 ½ m. by A 38 and Woodland rd ☏ (01364) 652544, *mail@risingsunwoodland.co.uk, Fax (01364) 653628*, ≈, ⇆ rm, P. MC AE VISA
closed 25 December and Monday except Bank Holidays – **Rest** a la carte 15.00/22.00 ♀ – **6 rm** ☕ ★40.00 – ★★68.00.
◆ Once a drovers' inn, set down a rural track, in fine country setting. Cosy interior with beams and log fires. Traditional fare with a strong Devon base. Simple bedrooms.

ASHFORD *Kent* 504 W 30.

Channel Tunnel : Eurostar information and reservations ☏ (08705) 186186.
i 18 The Churchyard ☏ (01233) 629165, tourism@ashford.gov.uk.
London 56 – Canterbury 14 – Dover 24 – Hastings 30 – Maidstone 19.

Eastwell Manor ⋟, Eastwell Park, Boughton Lees, TN25 4HR, North : 3 m. by A 28 on A 251 ☏ (01233) 213000, *enquiries@eastwellmanor.co.uk, Fax (01233) 635530*, ≤, ⑩, Ls, ≘s, ☒ heated, ☒, ≈, ♤, ✂ – |≑|, ⇆ rest, ☏ P – 🏛 250. MC AE ① VISA
Manor : **Rest** 15.00/60.00 and a la carte 33.40/85.95 ♀ – ***Brasserie :*** **Rest** 15.00/45.00 and a la carte 23.85/32.75 – **20 rm** ☕ ★190.00 – ★★285.00, 3 suites.
◆ Mansion house in formal gardens, replete with interesting detail including carved panelled rooms and stone fireplaces. Smart individual bedrooms. Manor offers seasonal menus. Swish brasserie in luxury spa with marbled entrance hall.

Ashford International, Simone Weil Ave, TN24 8UX, North : 1½ m. by A 20 ☏ (01233) 219988, *sales@ashfordinthotel.com, Fax (01233) 647743*, Ls, ≘s, ☒ – |≑| ⇆ ♿ P – 🏛 400. MC AE ① VISA
closed 24-27 December – ***Alhambra :*** **Rest** *(closed Sunday dinner and Bank Holidays)* 14.95/25.00 ♀ – ***Mistral Brasserie :*** **Rest** *(closed Sunday)* (carvery) (dinner only and Sunday lunch) 20.00 ♀ – ☕ 10.95 – **201 rm** ★135.00 – ★★135.00/150.00.
◆ Enormous corporate oriented hotel with large central atrium containing shops and coffee bars to relax in. Modern, comfortable bedrooms. Alhambra noted for range of modern dishes. Informal, relaxed Mistral.

Premier Travel Inn, Hall Ave, Orbital Park, Sevington, TN24 0GA, Southeast : 3 m. by A 292 off A 2070 ☏ (08701) 977305, *Fax (01233) 500742* – |≑|, ⇆ rm, ▤ rest, ♿ P. MC AE ① VISA. ⋟
Rest (grill rest.) – **60 rm** ★49.95 – ★★49.95.
◆ Group-owned lodge with comfortable modern bedrooms, ideal for family or business stopovers. A handy address for those travelling to the continent on Eurostar.

ASHFORD-IN-THE-WATER *Derbs.* 502 503 504 O 24 – *see Bakewell.*

ASHINGTON *W. Sussex* 504 S 31 – *pop. 2 351* – ✉ *Pulborough.*

London 50 – Brighton 20 – Worthing 9.

Mill House, Mill Lane, RH20 3BZ, ☏ (01903) 892426, *ashingtonmill@aol.com, Fax (01903) 892855*, ≈ – P – 🏛 30. MC AE VISA
closed 23 December - 5 January **Rest** (dinner only) 23.95 ♀ – **10 rm** ☕ ★52.00/60.00 – ★★92.00.
◆ Once the home of the owners of Ashington Water and Wind Mills, this 17C cottage with conservatory, inglenook fireplace and pastel painted rooms makes a quiet retreat. Restaurant with tranquil blue décor and watercolours on the walls.

ASHURST *W. Sussex* 504 T 31 – *see Steyning.*

We try to be as accurate as possible when giving room rates.
But prices are susceptible to change,
so please check rates when booking.

ASHWATER *Devon.*
London 218 – Bude 16.5 – Virginstow 3.

Blagdon Manor, Beaworthy, EX21 5DF, Northwest : 2 m. by Holsworthy rd on Blagdon rd (01409) 211224, *stay@blagdon.com, Fax (01409) 211634*, – P. VISA
closed 2 weeks January and 2 weeks autumn – **Rest** *(closed lunch Monday and Tuesday)* (booking essential) (residents only Monday and Sunday dinner) 18.00/32.00 – **7 rm** 80.00 – 110.00.
◆ Idyllic rural setting, with splendid views to match. Charming breakfast conservatory; characterful bar has original flagstone floors. Carefully styled rooms designed by owner. Country house dining: local produce to fore on classic dishes with modern touch.

ASKRIGG *N. Yorks.* 502 N 21 – *pop. 1 002* – *Leyburn.*
London 251 – Kendal 32 – Leeds 70 – Newcastle upon Tyne 70 – York 63.

Helm without rest., Helm, DL8 3JF, West : 1½ m., turning right at Helm rd after 1 m. (01969) 650443, *holiday@helmyorkshire.com, Fax (01969) 650443*, Wensleydale – P. VISA.
closed Christmas-New Year – **3 rm** 60.00 – 85.00.
◆ A steep lane winds up to this 17C stone farmhouse still in possession of an underground dairy with cheese press used in making Wensleydale cheese. Compact, homely bedrooms.

The Apothecary's House without rest., Market Pl, DL8 3HT, (01969) 650626, *bookings@apothecaryhouse.co.uk* – P.
closed 25 and 31 December and 1 January – **3 rm** 35.00 – 60.00/65.00.
◆ Built in 1756 by the local apothecary in centre of village; overlooks church. Combined lounge and breakfast room has fresh, modern feel. Rear bedroom boasts exposed timbers.

Hotels and restaurants change every year, so change your Michelin guide every year!

ASPLEY GUISE *Beds.* 504 S 27 – *pop. 2 236.*
Woburn Sands, West Hill (01908) 583596 – Lyshott Heath, Ampthill (01525) 840252.
London 52 – Bedford 13 – Luton 16 – Northampton 22 – Oxford 46.

Moore Place, The Square, MK17 8DW, (01908) 282000, *manager@mooreplace.com, Fax (01908) 281888*, – P – 40. AE VISA
closed 27 December - 2 January – **Rest** *(closed Saturday lunch and Bank Holidays* 18.50 (lunch) and dinner a la carte 24.45/38.00 – **62 rm** 125.00/135.00 – 145.00, 1 suite.
◆ Elegant Georgian mansion house with waterfall in garden, lobby lounge and bar. Bedrooms each have bowls of fruit and two small "welcome" drinks decanters. Restaurant with tried-and-tested menu and lighter options.

ASTON CANTLOW *Warks.* 503 504 O 27 *Great Britain G.*
Env. : *Mary Arden's House★ AC, SE : 2 m. by Wilmcote Lane and Aston Cantlow Rd.*
London 106 – Birmingham 20 – Stratford-upon-Avon 5.

King's Head, Bearley Rd, B95 6HY, (01789) 488242, *Fax (01789) 488137*, , – P. AE VISA
closed 25-26 December – **Rest** a la carte 18.00/27.00.
◆ Charming, cottagey 15C pub with timbers. Pleasant terrace and garden; real fire and polished flag flooring. Hearty, eclectic range of dishes with a real gastro feel.

ASTON CLINTON *Bucks.* 504 R 28 – *pop. 3 467* – *Aylesbury.*
London 42 – Aylesbury 4 – Oxford 26.

West Lodge without rest., 45 London Rd, HP22 5HL, (01296) 630362, *jibwl@westlodge.co.uk, Fax (01296) 630151*, , – P. AE VISA.
10 rm 58.00/65.00 – 85.00.
◆ 19C former lodge house and part of the Rothschild estate, boasting a beautiful garden with tranquil fish pond. Elegant public areas and cosy, well-kept bedrooms. Montgolfier Room enlivened by hot-air balloon décor.

ATCHAM *Shrops.* 503 504 L 25 – *see Shrewsbury.*

AUSTWICK *N. Yorks.* 502 M 21 – *pop. 467* – ✉ *Lancaster (Lancs.).*

London 259 – Kendal 28 – Lancaster 20 – Leeds 46.

Austwick Traddock, LA2 8BY, ℘ (015242) 51224, *info@austwicktraddock.co.uk, Fax (015242) 51796*, – P. MC AE VISA
Rest (booking essential to non-residents) (dinner only and Sunday lunch)/dinner 29.00 and a la carte 23.00/28.00 – **10 rm** ☕ ★60.00/90.00 – ★★150.00/160.00.
◆ A Georgian country house decorated with both English and Asian antiques. Bedrooms are individually styled to a high standard and overlook the secluded gardens. Dining room split into two rooms and lit by candlelight.

Wood View without rest., The Green, LA2 8BB, ℘ (015242) 51190, *stay@woodviewbandb.com, Fax (015242) 51190*, – P. MC VISA
6 rm ☕ ★40.00 – ★★70.00.
◆ In a charming spot on the village green, the cottage dates back to 17C with many of the original features still in place including exposed rafters in several bedrooms.

AVONWICK *Devon.*

London 202 – Plymouth 17.5 – Totnes 8.

The Avon Inn, TQ10 9NB, ℘ (01364) 73475, – rest, P. MC AE VISA
closed Monday lunch – **Rest** a la carte 12.95/24.95.
◆ Homely, village centre pub with an interior of beams and hop bines. French owner/chef serves accomplished dishes with classic Gallic base and plenty of local seafood and fish.

AXBRIDGE *Somerset* 503 L 30 – *pop. 2 025.*

London 142 – Bristol 17 – Taunton 27 – Weston-Super-Mare 11.

The Parsonage without rest., Parsonage Lane, Cheddar Rd, BS26 2DN, East : ¾ m. on A 371 ℘ (01934) 733078, *Fax (01934) 733078*, ←, – P.
3 rm ☕ ★44.00 – ★★52.00.
◆ Former Victorian parsonage nestling in the southern slopes of the Mendip Hills overlooking the Somerset Levels. The comfortable bedrooms are tastefully furnished.

AXMINSTER *Devon* 503 L 31 *The West Country G.* – *pop. 4 952.*

Env. : *Lyme Regis★ - The Cobb★, SE : 5½ m. by A 35 and A 3070.*
The Old Courthouse, Church St ℘ (01297) 34386, axminster@btopenworld.com.
London 156 – Exeter 27 – Lyme Regis 5.5 – Taunton 22 – Yeovil 24.

Fairwater Head Country House, Hawkchurch, EX13 5TX, Northeast : 5 ¼ m. by B 3261 and A 35 off B 3165 ℘ (01297) 678349, *reception@fairwaterhead.demon.co.uk, Fax (01297) 678459*, ← Axe Vale, , – P. MC AE VISA
closed 27 December-12 January – **Rest** (bar lunch Monday-Saturday)/dinner 32.50 – **20 rm** ☕ ★80.00/115.00 – ★★180.00/210.00.
◆ Edwardian house in flower-filled gardens. Tea and fresh cakes served in the afternoon. Many bedrooms have views across the Axe Valley. Hotel arranges themed tours of area. Piano accompanies romantic candlelit meals on Wednesdays and Saturdays.

Kerrington House, Musbury Rd, EX13 5JR, Southwest : ½ m. ℘ (01297) 35333, *ja.reaney@kerringtonhouse.com, Fax (01297) 35345*, – P. MC VISA.
Rest (by arrangement) 28.00 – **6 rm** ☕ ★75.00 – ★★110.00.
◆ Pleasantly converted Victorian house with original tiles and homely character; close to town centre. Warm, welcoming owners. Spacious sitting room. Large, comfy bedrooms. Attractive dining room with formal air.

at Membury *North : 4½ m. by A 35 and Stockland rd* – ✉ *Axminster.*

Lea Hill without rest., EX13 7AQ, South : ½ m. ℘ (01404) 881881, *reception@leahill.co.uk*, ←, – P
3 rm ☕ ★45.00 – ★★70.00/90.00.
◆ Down a country lane, this 14C thatched longhouse is the essence of tranquillity. Bedrooms are in the converted barns and main house: surrounded by pleasant gardens.

at Dalwood *Northwest : 3½ m. off A 35* – ✉ *Axminster.*

The Tuckers Arms with rm, EX13 7EG, ℘ (01404) 881342, *davidbeck@tuckersarms.freeserve.co.uk, Fax (01404) 881138*, – P. MC VISA.
closed 25-26 December – **Rest** a la carte 10.95/23.00 – **4 rm** ☕ ★65.00 – ★★65.00.
◆ 13C thatched longhouse with low beams, stone floors and inglenooks guaranteeing a cosy atmosphere. Tasty menus with local seafood the highlight. Well-kept, comfy rooms.

AYCLIFFE *Darlington – see Darlington.*

AYLESBURY *Bucks.* 504 R 28 *Great Britain G. – pop. 69 021.*

Env. : *Waddesdon Manor★★, NW : 5½ m. by A 41 – Chiltern Hills★.*

Weston Turville, New Rd (01296) 424084 – Hulcott Lane, Bierton (01296) 393644.

8 Bourbon St (01296) 330559, info@aylesbury-tourist.org.uk.

London 46 – Birmingham 72 – Northampton 37 – Oxford 22.

Hartwell House, Oxford Rd, HP17 8NL, Southwest : 2 m. on A 418 (01296) 747444, *info@hartwell-house.com, Fax (01296) 747450,* – 80.

Rest 22.00/46.00 – 4.00 – **33 rm** ★165.00/210.00 – ★★270.00, 13 suites 370.00/700.00.

◆ Magnificent stately home rich in history; Louis XVIII was exiled here in 1809. Gothic hall and carved stairway lead to superb heritage bedrooms. Many have four-poster beds. Fine dining in peacefully located restaurant with garden aspect.

AYLESFORD *Kent* 504 V 30.

London 37 – Maidstone 3.5 – Rochester 8.

Hengist, 7-9 High St, ME20 7AX, (01622) 719273, *the.hengist@btconnect.com, Fax (01622) 715077* – 12.

closed 26-27 December and 1 January – **Rest** 18.50 (lunch) and a la carte 21.45/35.00.

◆ Converted 16C town house, elegantly appointed throughout, with bonus of exposed rafters and smart private dining room upstairs. Accomplished modern cooking with seasonal base.

BABCARY *Somerset* 403 M 30.

London 128.5 – Glastonbury 12 – Yeovil 12.

Red Lion Inn, TA11 7ED, (01458) 223230, *Fax (01458) 224510,* – .

closed 25 December and Sunday dinner – **Rest** a la carte 18.50/25.00.

◆ Attractive thatched pub in cosy village. Tasteful interior that's full of squashy sofas and dining pub style. Accomplished menus, modern in substance, suit the surroundings.

BADMINTON *South Glos.* 503 504 N 29.

London 114 – Bristol 19 – Gloucester 26 – Swindon 33.

Bodkin House, Petty France, GL9 1AF, Northwest : 3 m. on A 46 (01454) 238310, *info@bodkin-house-hotel.co.uk, Fax (01454) 238422,* – , rest, .

Rest 27.95 – **11 rm** ★70.00 – ★★105.00.

◆ White-painted former coaching inn, now extended, refurbished and family run. Neat rooms, named after authors, in pine and classic patterns; cosy bar with log fire. Candlelit tables in unpretentious dining room.

BAGSHOT *Surrey* 504 R 29 – *pop. 5 247.*

Windlesham, Grove End (01276) 452220.

London 37 – Reading 17 – Southampton 49.

Pennyhill Park, London Rd, GU19 5EU, Southwest : 1 m. on A 30 (01276) 471774, *enquiries@pennyhillpark.co.uk, Fax (01276) 473217,* heated, – rest, – 150.

Brasserie and Oyster bar: **Rest** (buffet lunch) 18.95/30.00 and dinner a la carte 31.90/51.50 – (see also ***The Latymer*** below) – 17.50 – **113 rm** ★211.50 – ★★229.00, 10 suites.

◆ Sympathetically extended ivy-clad 19C manor house in wooded parkland. Intimate lounges. Outstanding spa. Rooms with fine antique furniture share a relaxing period elegance. Marble and stained glass enhanced restaurant overlooks garden.

Premier Travel Inn, 1 London Rd, GU19 5HR, North : ½ m. on A 30 (01276) 473196, *Fax (01276) 451357,* – rm, rest, .

Rest (grill rest.) – **40 rm** ★49.95/49.95 – ★★54.95/54.95.

◆ Group-owned hotel offering bright, modern budget rooms, many suitable for families. Sports enthusiasts will appreciate the excellent road connections to Ascot and Wentworth.

XXX **The Latymer** (at Pennyhill Park H.), London Rd, GU19 5EU, Southwest : 1 m. on A 30
✆ (01276) 471774, *pennyhillpark@msn.com, Fax (01276) 473217,* – P. VISA
closed 26-30 December, Sunday, Monday and Saturday lunch – **Rest** (booking essential) 25.00/50.00 ♀.
• Robust flavours in an ambitious, elaborately presented modern British menu. Oak panels, oil lamps and attentive service uphold Victorian country house tradition.

BAKEWELL *Derbs.* 502 503 504 O 24 *Great Britain G. – pop. 3 676.*
Env. : *Chatsworth★★★ (Park and Garden★★★) AC, NE : 2½ m. by A 619 – Haddon Hall★★ AC, SE : 2 m. by A 6.*
Old Market Hall, Bridge St ✆ *(01629) 813227, bakewell@peakdistrict-mpa.gov.uk.*
London 160 – Derby 26 – Manchester 37 – Nottingham 33 – Sheffield 17.

Haddon House Farm without rest., Haddon Rd, DE45 1BN, South : ½ m. on A 6
✆ (01629) 814024, *m@great-place.co.uk* – P.
4 rm ☕ ★45.00/50.00 – ★★75.00/90.00.
• Friendly guesthouse, just out of town. Cottagey breakfast room with Aga. Individual rooms: ask for the Monet, painted to make you feel you're in the middle of a waterfall.

at Ashford-in-the-Water *Northwest : 1¾ m. by A 6 and A 6020 – ✉ Bakewell.*

Riverside House, Fennel St, DE45 1QF, ✆ (01629) 814275, *riversidehouse@enta.net, Fax (01629) 812873,* – P. VISA.
Rest – (see ***The Riverside Room*** below) – **14 rm** (dinner included) ☕ ★100.00/140.00 – ★★190.00/230.00.
• Extended 18C country house on the banks of the Wye; immaculate, tastefully appointed and individually furnished bedrooms, comfortable drawing room and modern conservatory.

XX **The Riverside Room** (at Riverside House), Fennel St, DE45 1QE, ✆ (01629) 814275, *Fax (01629) 812875* – P. VISA
Rest 26.95/60.00.
• Panelled bar adjoins two intimate dining rooms, one centred around a gleaming Victorian range. Seasonal modern cuisine, flavourful and well-prepared. Welcoming service.

BALSALL COMMON *W. Mids. – see Coventry.*

BAMBURGH *Northd.* 501 502 O 17 *Great Britain G.*
See : *Castle★ AC.*
London 337 – Edinburgh 77 – Newcastle upon Tyne 51.

Lord Crewe Arms, Front St, NE69 7BL, ✆ (01668) 214243, *Fax (01668) 214273* – rest, P. VISA
closed December-January – **Rest** a la carte 22.00/33.00 – **18 rm** ☕ ★47.00/74.00 – ★★88.00/126.00.
• In the shadow of the Norman castle, a neat and traditional market town hotel, still in private hands. Smartly fitted bedrooms; spacious, comfy lounge. Characterful beamed bar. Alluring timber and stone retaurant.

at Waren Mill *West : 2¾ m. on B 1342 – ✉ Belford.*

Waren House, NE70 7EE, ✆ (01668) 214581, *enquiries@warenhousehotel.co.uk, Fax (01668) 214484,* – P – 30. VISA
Rest (dinner only) 26.00 ♀ – **11 rm** ☕ ★79.00/95.00 – ★★112.50/150.00, 2 suites.
• A Georgian country house in attractive grounds and formal gardens, with views to Lindisfarne. Individually decorated bedrooms with themes ranging from Oriental to Edwardian. Classical dining room overlooking gardens.

BAMPTON *Devon* 503 J 31 – *pop. 1 617.*
London 189 – Exeter 18 – Minehead 21 – Taunton 15.

Bark House, Oakfordbridge, EX16 9HZ, West : 3 m. by B 3227 on A 396 ✆ (01398) 351236, – P
Rest (booking essential) (residents only) (dinner only) (set menu only) 28.50 **s.** – **5 rm** ☕ ★47.50/54.00 – ★★93.00/119.50.
• Neat, personally run stone cottages which once stored wood from Exmoor forest. Bright bedrooms of different sizes are decorated in pretty floral fabrics. Terraced rear garden. Home-cooking proudly served in neat dining room.

Newhouse Farm, Oakford, EX16 9JE, West : 5 m. on B 3227 (01398) 351347, *anne.boldry@btconnect.com, Fax (01398) 351347*, – P. MC VISA.
closed Christmas and New Year – **Rest** (by arrangement) 17.50 – **3 rm** 30.00 – 60.00.
• Sweet 17C cottage reached down a long lane through fields of sheep; peaceful garden to stream. Original beams throughout. Surprisingly spacious rooms. Lots of local maps. Pretty little dining room.

BANBURY *Oxon.* 503 504 P 27 *Great Britain G. – pop. 43 867.*
Exc. : *Upton House* AC, NW : 7 m. by A 422.*
Cherwell Edge, Chacombe (01295) 711591.
Spiceball Park Rd (01295) 259855.
London 76 – Birmingham 40 – Coventry 25 – Oxford 23.

Whately Hall, Horsefair, by Banbury Cross, OX16 0AN, (0870) 4008104, *sales.whatelyhall@macdonald-hotels.co.uk, Fax (01295) 271736*, – P – 80. MC AE VISA
Rest (bar lunch Monday-Friday)/dinner 21.95 and a la carte 25.35/30.60 – **63 rm** 60.00/120.00 – 90.00/135.00, 6 suites.

• Renowned for hidden staircases, priest holes and a resident ghost, this part 17C inn has an eccentric floor plan of well-appointed rooms and panelled, black-beamed corridors. Dining room of local stone and leaded windows overlooks croquet lawn.

Banbury House, Oxford Rd, OX16 9AH, (01295) 259361, *sales@banburyhouse.co.uk, Fax (01295) 270954* – rm, P – 70. MC AE VISA.
closed 24 December-2 January – **Rest** (bar lunch)/dinner 20.00/22.50 – 15.00 – **63 rm** 115.00/140.00 – 140.00.
• Handsome, extensive Georgian house, smartly and enthusiastically managed. Rear facing rooms are quieter, but all are spacious and well kept, modernised with taste and care. Subdued dining room with potted palms and botanical prints.

at North Newington *West : 2¼ m. by B 4035 – Banbury.*

The Mill House without rest., OX15 6AA, (01295) 730212, *lamadonett@aol.com, Fax (01295) 730363*, – P. MC AE VISA.
closed 2 weeks Christmas – **7 rm** 55.00 – 99.00/120.00.
• Friendly, personally run guesthouse in 17C paper mill, set in peaceful gardens beside a stream. Comfortable bedrooms, prettily decorated with individual touches.

at Sibford Gower *West : 8 m. by B 4035 – Banbury.*

The Wykham Arms, Temple Mill Rd, OX15 5RX, (01295) 788808, *ianwallace@wykhamarms.co.uk, Fax (01295) 788806*, , – P. MC AE VISA
closed 25 December, Sunday dinner and Monday – **Rest** a la carte 16.00/28.00.
• Former 17C farmhouse, now a pretty thatched pub, refurbished in spring 2004. Bright interior with original inglenook and low beams. Local ingredients to fore on modern menus.

at Hanwell *Northwest : 3½ m. by A 422 and B 4100 – Oxon.*

Moon & Sixpence, OX17 1HW, (01295) 730549, *info@moonandsixpencehanwell.com*, – MC P VISA
Rest a la carte 23.90/27.15.
• Personally run by two brothers who've re-established the community pub. Spacious interior exudes warm traditionality. Appealing menus offer an eclectic range of styles.

at Shenington *Northwest : 6 m. by B 4100 off A 422 – Banbury.*

Sugarswell Farm, OX15 6HW, Northwest : 2 ¼ m. on Edge Hill rd (01295) 680512, *Fax (01295) 688149*, , – P.
Rest (by arrangement) (communal dining) 30.00 – **3 rm** 65.00/75.00 – 75.00/85.00.
• In quiet rolling fields on the Warwickshire border, this sandstone house is the centre of a working farm; spacious, well-kept rooms retain their individual rustic character. Home-cooked dishes served at a communal table.

BARFORD *Warks.* 503 504 P 27 – *see Warwick.*

"Rest" appears in red for establishments with a (star) or (Bib Gourmand).

BARHAM *Kent* 504 X 30.
London 66 – Canterbury 7 – Dover 11.

Elmstone Court, Out Elmstead Lane, CT4 6PH, North : ¾ m. ✆ (01227) 832091, *info@elmstonecourt.com, Fax (01227) 832403,* – P.
Rest (by arrangement) (communal dining) 25.00 – **4 rm** ☕ ✝50.00/60.00 – ✝✝90.00/100.00.
◆ Georgian house with earlier origins on cusp of village; striking gardens. Modern artwork in all areas; period style drawing room with open fire. All rooms individually themed. Communal dining room; local organic produce to the fore.

BAR HILL *Cambs.* 504 U 27 – *see Cambridge.*

BARNARD CASTLE *Durham* 502 O 20 *Great Britain G. – pop. 6 714.*
See : *Bowes Museum★ AC.*
Exc. : *Raby Castle★ AC, NE : 6½ m. by A 688.*
18 *Harmire Rd ✆ (01833) 638355.*
Woodleigh, Flatts Rd ✆ (01833) 690909.
London 258 – Carlisle 63 – Leeds 68 – Middlesbrough 31 – Newcastle upon Tyne 39.

Demesnes Mill without rest., DL12 8PE, Southeast : ½ m. by The Bank and Gray Lane, through the playing field ✆ (01833) 637929, *themillbarnardcastle@btopenworld.com, Fax (01833) 637974,* <, – .
May-October – **3 rm** ☕ ✝40.00 – ✝✝55.00/75.00.
◆ Set in peaceful gardens, a sensitively restored 15C mill abounding in period character. Large bedrooms, including one with an open fire. Conservatory with views of the Tees.

Homelands without rest., 85 Galgate, DL12 8ES, ✆ (01833) 638757, *enquiries@homelandsguesthouse.co.uk,* – . MC VISA.
closed 23 December-2 January – **5 rm** ☕ ✝28.00/36.00 – ✝✝56.00/65.00.
◆ Immaculately maintained 19C terraced house on main road. Cosy lounge and compact but pleasantly furnished, well-priced rooms, some overlooking the long mature rear garden.

Greta House without rest., 89 Galgate, DL12 8ES, ✆ (01833) 631193, *gretahousebc@btclick.com, Fax (01833) 631193,* – .
3 rm ☕ ✝45.00 – ✝✝58.00.
◆ Part of a Victorian terrace with leafy garden. Bedrooms are spacious and individually decorated. Evening snacks may be taken in your room; plenty of books to browse through.

at Greta Bridge *Southeast : 4½ m. by B 6277 off A 66 – ✉ Barnard Castle.*

Morritt Arms, DL12 9SE, ✆ (01833) 627232, *relax@themorritt.co.uk, Fax (01833) 627392,* – P – 270. MC AE VISA
Gilroy's : Rest a la carte 14.95/40.00 ♀ – ***Pallatts :*** Rest 35.00/45.00 ♀ – **27 rm** ☕ ✝70.00/120.00 – ✝✝100.00/160.00.
◆ 19C coaching inn where Charles Dickens stayed in 1839. The Dickens bar has murals by John Gilroy, historian of the Guinness firm. All rooms individually designed. Gilroy's is oak panelled restaurant. Bistro ambience at Pallatts.

The Coach House, DL12 9SD, ✆ (01833) 627201, *info@coachhousegreta.co.uk,* – P. MC VISA
Rest (by arrangement) 22.50 – **3 rm** ☕ ✝45.00 – ✝✝75.00.
◆ Relax by the log fire in the smart sitting room full of books or enjoy home-cooked breakfasts in the dining room. The 18C bedrooms are attractively decorated and comfortable.

at Romaldkirk *Northwest : 6 m. by A 67 on B 6277 – ✉ Barnard Castle.*

Rose and Crown with rm, DL12 9EB, ✆ (01833) 650213, *hotel@rose-and-crown.co.uk, Fax (01833) 650828,* – P. MC VISA
closed 24-26 December – ***The Restaurant :*** Rest (bar lunch Monday-Saturday)/dinner 26.00 ♀ – **12 rm** ☕ ✝75.00 – ✝✝126.00.
◆ Fine 1733 coaching inn set back from the green. Characterful, well thought-out rooms. Firelit lounge and bar; beams and rough stone walls hung with brasses and etchings. Dining room decorated with curios and antique china.

BARNARD GATE *Oxon.* 503 504 P 28 – *see Witney.*

BARNSLEY *Glos.* 503 504 O 28 – *see Cirencester.*

BARNSLEY *S. Yorks.* 502 504 P 23 – *pop. 71 599.*

Wakefield Rd, Staincross (01226) 382856 – Silkstone, Field Head, Elmhirst Lane (01226) 790328 – Wombwell Hillies, Wentworth View, Wombwell (01226) 754433.

46 Eldon St (01226) 206757.

London 177 – Leeds 21 – Manchester 36 – Sheffield 15.

Tankersley Manor, Church Lane, S75 3DQ, South : 6 ¼ m. on A 61 (01226) 744700, *tankersley@marstonhotels.com, Fax (01226) 745405,* – rest, – 400. VISA.
Rest *(closed Saturday lunch)* a la carte 18.95/28.00 – 14.50 – **97 rm** 118.00 – 142.00, 2 suites.
◆ Part 17C house, sympathetically enlarged to cater for corporate functions and weddings. Low-beamed lounge and bar with Regency-style furniture. Rooms have useful mod cons. Formal or informal option: characterful pub or stone-walled dining room.

Premier Travel Inn, Maple Rd, Tankersley, S75 3DL, South : 6 ½ m. by A 61 at junction with A 616 (01226) 350035, *Fax (01226) 741524* – rm, rest, VISA.
Rest (grill rest.) – **42 rm** 46.95/46.95 – 48.95/48.95.
◆ Moderately priced lodge provides reliable standard of compact, modern accommodation for leisure breaks or business travel. Informal dining in adjacent restaurant.

Look out for red symbols, indicating particularly pleasant establishments.

BARNSTAPLE *Devon* 503 H 30 *The West Country G. – pop. 30 765.*

See : *Town★ - Long Bridge★.*

Env. : *Arlington Court★★ (Carriage Collection★) AC, NE : 6 m. by A 39.*

Chulmleigh, Leigh Rd (01769) 580519.

Museum of North Devon, The Square (01271) 375000.

London 222 – Exeter 40 – Taunton 51.

Imperial, Taw Vale Parade, EX32 8NB, (01271) 345861, *info@brend-imperial.co.uk, Fax (01271) 324448* – rest, rest, – 60. VISA.
Rest 15.00/25.00 s. – 12.50 – **63 rm** 85.00/90.00 – 160.00.
◆ Group hotel dating from the turn of 20C. Convivial bar on a regimental theme and smart accommodation: deluxe front bedrooms have balconies overlooking the river Taw. Grand, bay-windowed dining room.

Barnstaple, Braunton Rd, EX31 1LE, West : 1 ½ m. on A 361 (01271) 376221, *info@barnstaplehotel.co.uk, Fax (01271) 324101,* heated, – rest, rest, – 350. VISA.
Rest 23.00 s. – 10.00 – **60 rm** 65.00/85.00 – 75.00/95.00.
◆ Built in the 1970s to meet the needs of the growing commercial market. Impressive leisure facilities and well-equipped bedrooms; deluxe rooms have balconies. Classically inspired dining room.

Premier Travel Inn, Eastern Ave, Whiddon Valley, EX32 8RY, on A 361 (01271) 377830, *Fax (01271) 377710* – rm, rest, VISA.
Rest (grill rest.) – **40 rm** 49.95 – 49.95.
◆ Adjacent to the North Devon link road, conveniently located for North Devon Museum and Queen Anne Heritage Centre. Suitable for business and family stopovers. Neat rooms.

at Bishop's Tawton *South : 2 ¾ m. by A 39 on A 377 – Barnstaple.*

Halmpstone Manor without rest., EX32 0EA, Southeast : 3 m. by Chittlehampton rd (01271) 830321, *charles@halmpstonemanor.co.uk, Fax (01271) 830826,* – VISA
closed Christmas and New Year – **4 rm** 70.00 – 140.00.
◆ A 400 year old manor set in charming Devon countryside. Log fires, deep sofas, sherry decanters, four poster and brass coronet beds; peace and relaxation assured.

BARNT GREEN *Birmingham.*

London 114.5 – Birmingham 11 – Bromsgrove 9.5.

The Barnt Green Inn, 22 Kendal End Rd, B45 8PZ, on B 4120 (0121) 445 4949, *Fax (0121) 447 9912,* – VISA
closed Sunday dinner – **Rest** a la carte 14.65/32.85.
◆ Huge mock Tudor establishment in the Birmingham hinterland. Smoochy lounge area and bar; separate restaurant with an informal air: modern international menus predominate.

BARSTON *W. Mids.* 504 O 26.

London 110 – Birmingham 17 – Coventry 11.

Malt Shovel, Barston Lane, B92 0JP, West : ¾ m *(01675) 443223, Fax (01675) 443223,* – P. MO AE VISA

closed 25 December and Sunday dinner – **Rest** (lunch bookings not accepted) 25.00 (dinner) and a la carte 21.00/29.95 ♀.

◆ Modern dining pub, an oasis in a rustic hideaway, with large garden and patio. Good sized menus: noteworthy seafood specials. Busy at lunchtimes - you can't book so go early!

BARTON-ON-SEA *Hants.* 503 504 P 31.

London 108 – Bournemouth 11 – Southampton 24 – Winchester 35.

Tower House without rest., Christchurch Rd, BH25 6QQ, West : 1 m. on A 337 *(01425) 629508, bandb@towerhouse-newforest.co.uk, Fax (01425) 629508,* – P.

closed Christmas, January and February – **3 rm** ★60.00 – ★★60.00.

◆ Proudly run Edwardian guesthouse close to main road. Particularly good breakfasts, with ingredients sourced from local farm shop. Bright, cheery and very comfortable bedrooms.

Pebble Beach with rm, Marine Drive, BH25 7DZ, (01425) 627777, *email@pebblebeach-uk.com, Fax (01425) 610689,* – P. MO AE VISA

Rest - Seafood specialities - *(closed dinner 25 December and 1 January)* a la carte 20.90/47.00 ♀ – 4.95 – **3 rm** ★49.95/69.95 – ★★69.95/89.95.

◆ Cliff-top position: striking terrace views over Solent and The Needles. Bright, modish interior with large windows. Wide range of choice on modern menus. Well-equipped rooms.

The sun's out – let's eat al fresco! Look for a terrace:

BARWICK *Somerset* 503 504 M 31 – *see Yeovil.*

BASILDON *Essex* 504 V 29 – *pop. 102 913 (inc. North Benfleet).*

18 Clayhill Lane, Sparrow's Hearne (01268) 533297 – 9 Langdon Hills, Lower Dunton Rd, Bulphan (01268) 548444.

London 30 – Chelmsford 17 – Southend-on-Sea 13.

at Wickford *North : 5¼ m. by A 132 – Basildon.*

Chichester, Old London Rd, Rawreth, SS11 8UE, East : 2 ¾ m. by A 129 (01268) 560555, *Fax (01268) 560580,* – rest, rest, P. MO AE VISA.

Rest (dinner only and Sunday lunch)/dinner a la carte 17.30/24.85 – 8.95 – **35 rm** ★57.75/58.75 – ★★67.75.

◆ Surrounded by open farmland, a traditional hotel with a relaxing open-plan bar and lounge and well-proportioned rooms around a central courtyard. Restaurant has tried-and-tested dishes.

BASINGSTOKE *Hants.* 503 504 Q 30 – *pop. 90 171.*

18 Test Valley, Micheldever Rd, Overton (08707) 459020 – 18 Weybrook Park, Rooksdown Lane, Basingstoke (01256) 320347.

Willis Museum, Old Town Hall, Market Pl (01256) 817618.

London 55 – Reading 17 – Southampton 31 – Winchester 18.

Plan opposite

Apollo, Aldermaston Roundabout, RG24 9NU, North : 1 m. on A 340 (01256) 796700, *Fax (01256) 796794,* – rm, rest, P – 250. MO AE VISA. Z A

***Vespers :* Rest** (dinner only) 26.50 ♀ – ***Brasserie :* Rest** (buffet) 14.50/19.95 and a la carte 23.00/27.50 ♀ – 15.00 – **122 rm** ★150.00 – ★★170.00, 3 suites.

◆ Recently refurbished hotel aimed at business clients; well situated on Basingstoke ring road. Extensive conference and leisure facilities. Modern, well equipped rooms. Vespers is an intimate fine dining room. Large, modern Brasserie with centre servery.

Premier Travel Inn, Basingstoke Leisure Park, Worting Rd, RG22 6PG, (01256) 811477, *Fax (01256) 819329* – rm, P. MO AE VISA. Z C

Rest (grill rest.) – **71 rm** ★49.95/49.95 – ★★52.95/52.95.

◆ Trim, practical, reasonably priced rooms in a modern two-storey lodge hotel. A multiplex cinema, ice rink, bowling alley - and the Anvil Theatre - are a short walk away.

BASINGSTOKE

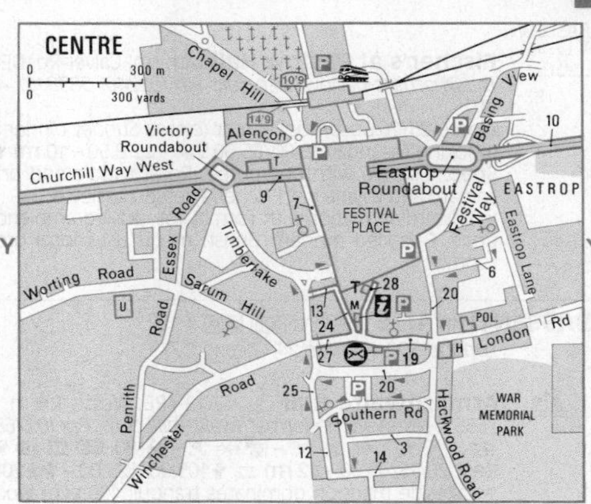

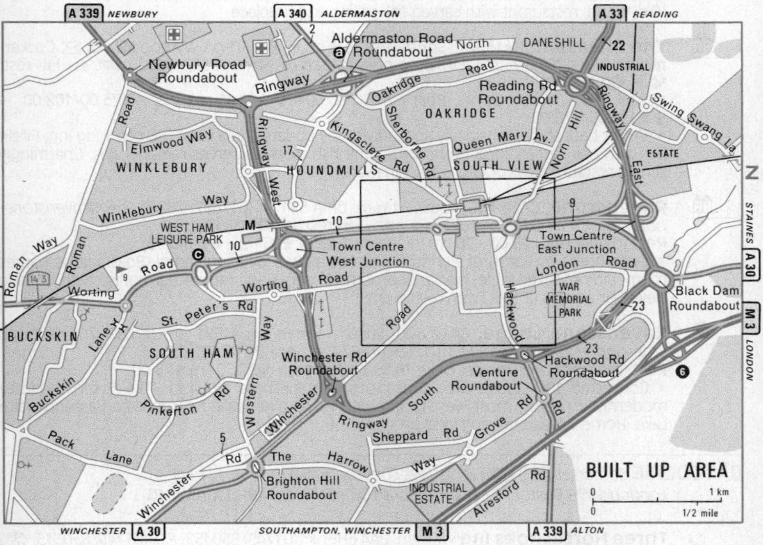

Good food without spending a fortune? Look out for the Bib Gourmand

BASLOW *Derbs.* 502 503 504 P 24 *Great Britain G.* – ✉ *Bakewell.*

See : *Chatsworth*★★★ *(Park and Garden*★★★*) AC.*

London 161 – Derby 27 – Manchester 35 – Sheffield 13.

Cavendish, Church Lane, DE45 1SP, on A 619 ☎ (01246) 582311, *info@cavendish-hotel.net, Fax (01246) 582312,* ≤ Chatsworth Park, 🐟, – ⇆ rest, 📞 P – 🏛 25. MC AE ⓞ *VISA*. ✂

The Gallery : **Rest** a la carte 27.95/37.20 – ***Garden Room :*** **Rest** a la carte 20.65/32.20 **s.** – ☕ 14.95 – **23 rm** ★108.00/115.00 – ★★162.75/168.00, 1 suite.

◆ Antiques and fine art complement an elegant, welcoming, country house interior. Well-proportioned rooms, handsomely decorated in the 18C wing, overlook Chatsworth Park. The Gallery includes one table in the kitchen. Conservatory Garden Room has rural views.

XXX **Fischer's at Baslow Hall** with rm, Calver Rd, DE45 1RR, on A 623 ✆ (01246) 583259, *m.s@fischers-baslowhall.co.uk, Fax (01246) 583818,* – rest, .
closed 25-26 December – **Rest** *(closed Sunday dinner to non-residents and Monday lunch)* (booking essential) 35.00/65.00 – 8.50 – **10 rm** 100.00/130.00 – 180.00, 1 suite.
Spec. Fish pie with pea purée. Roast saddle and braised shoulder of Derbyshire lamb, tomato and thyme jus. Fischer's dessert assiette.
◆ Edwardian manor with formal yet relaxed ambience: smooth service and elegant settings. Balanced modern British menu uses local produce to imaginative effect. Smart rooms.

BASSENTHWAITE *Cumbria* 501 502 K 19.

London 300 – Carlisle 24 – Keswick 7.

Armathwaite Hall, CA12 4RE, West : 1 ½ m. on B 5291, ✉ Keswick ✆ (017687) 76551, *reservations@armathwaite-hall.com, Fax (017687) 76220,* ← Bassenthwaite Lake, – – 80.
Rest 20.95/42.00 – **42 rm** 105.00/125.00 – 200.00/310.00.
◆ Lakeside mansion dominates tranquil 400-acre woods and deer park. Rooms, some in rebuilt stables, vary in size and, like the panelled hall, marry modern and period fittings. 'Old-World' restaurant with carved oak ceiling and fireplace.

The Pheasant, CA13 9YE, Southwest : 3 ¼ m. by B 5291 on Wythop Mill rd, ✉ Cockermouth ✆ (017687) 76234, *info@the-pheasant.co.uk, Fax (017687) 76002,* – rest, .
closed 25 December – **Rest** 24.50/35.00 s. – **15 rm** 73.00/102.00 – 132.00/178.00.
◆ Bright bedrooms, sensitively and individually updated, in a rural 16C coaching inn. Firelit bar with oak settles, local prints and game fish trophies serves regional ales. Charmingly simple restaurant decorated with chinaware.

Ravenstone, CA12 4QG, South : 1 ½ m. on A 591 ✆ (017687) 76240, *info@ravenstone-hotel.co.uk, Fax (017687) 76733,* ←, – rest, .
Rest (dinner only) 25.00 – **20 rm** (dinner included) 65.00 – 140.00.
◆ Once home to Baron of Penrith's mother, now a well-kept hotel. Boasts large games room with snooker table, piano. Bedrooms in soft floral fabrics harmonise with outside views. Fine vistas of lake from restaurant.

Ravenstone Lodge, CA12 4QG, South : 1 ½ m. on A 591 ✆ (017687) 76629, *ravenstone.lodge@talk21.com, Fax (017687) 76629,* ←, –
Rest (residents only) (dinner only) 18.50 – **10 rm** 37.50 – 75.00.
◆ Converted 19C stables with conservatory at the base of Ullock Pike. Sympathetically modernised rooms, most west-facing with views over walled gardens to Bassenthwaite Lake. Homely meals utilising local produce.

BATCOMBE *Somerset* 503 504 M 30 – ✉ *Shepton Mallet.*

London 130 – Bristol 24 – Bournemouth 50 – Salisbury 40 – Taunton 40.

Three Horseshoes Inn with rm, BA4 6HE, ✆ (01749) 850359, *Fax (01749) 850615,* –
Rest a la carte 15.00/30.00 – **3 rm** 45.00 – 60.00.
◆ By the parish church, a rustic bar in exposed stone and timber with a stove and inglenook fireplace. Varied blackboard menu: imaginative and well-prepared. Well-kept bedrooms.

- *Discover the best restaurant ?*
- *Find the nearest hotel ?*
- *Find your bearings using our maps and guides ?*
- *Understand the symbols used in the guide...*

Follow the red Bibs !

Advice on restaurants from Chef Bib.

Advice on hotels from Bellboy Bib.

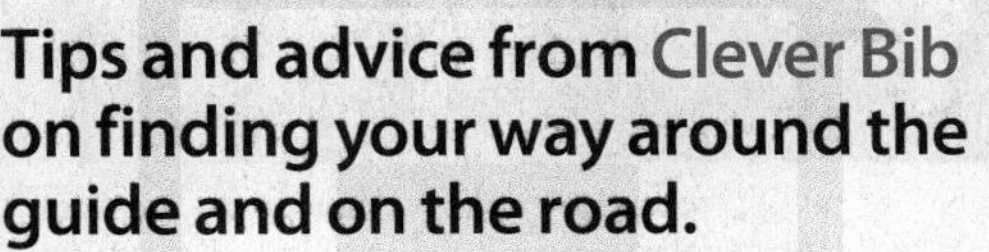

Tips and advice from Clever Bib on finding your way around the guide and on the road.

Bath, Royal Crescent

BATH

Bath & North East Somerset 503 504 M 29 *Great Britain G. – pop. 90 144.*

London 119 – Bristol 13 – Southampton 63 – Taunton 49.

TOURIST INFORMATION

Abbey Chambers, Abbey Church Yard (0870) 4201278; tourism@bathnes.gov.uk.

PRACTICAL INFORMATION

9, 9, 9, *Tracy Park, Bath Rd, Wick (0117) 937 2251.*
18 *Lansdown (01225) 422138.*
9 *Entry Hill (01225) 834248.*

SIGHTS

See: *City★★★ – Royal Crescent★★★* **AV** *(No. 1 Royal Crescent★★ AC* **AV A**) *– The Circus★★★* **AV** *– Museum of Costume★★★ AC* **AV M7** *– Roman Baths★★ AC* **BX D** *– Holburne Museum and Crafts Study Centre★★ AC* **Y M5** *– Pump Room★* **BX B** *- Assembly Rooms★* **AV** *– Bath Abbey★* **BX** *– Pulteney Bridge★* **BV** *– Bath Industrial Heritage Centre★ AC* **AV M1** *– Lansdown Crescent★★ (Somerset Place★)* **Y** *– Camden Crescent★* **Y** *– Beckford Tower and Museum AC (prospect★)* **Y M6** *– Museum of East Asian Art★* **AV M9** *– Orange Grove★* **BX**.

Env.: *Claverton (American Museum★★ AC, Claverton Pumping Station★ AC) E: 3 m. by A 36* **Y**.

Exc.: *Corsham Court★★ AC, NE: 8½ m. by A 4 – Dyrham Park★ AC, N: 6½ m. by A 4 and A 46.*

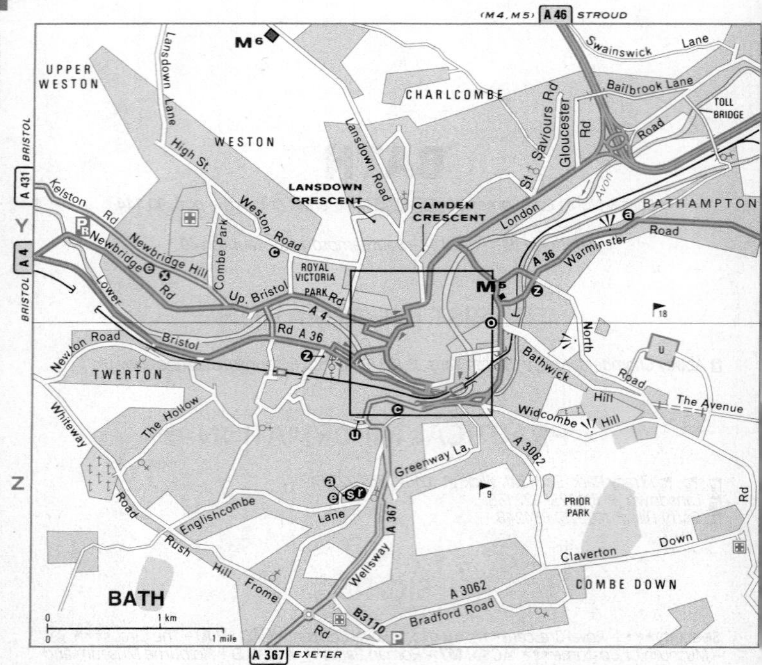

The Royal Crescent, 16 Royal Crescent, BA1 2LS, ☎ (01225) 823333, *info@royalcrescent.co.uk, Fax (01225) 339401,* – 40. VISA
AV a

Pimpernels : **Rest** 25.00/55.00 – 18.50 – **35 rm** 210.00/280.00 – 220.00/290.00, 10 suites 520.00/840.00.

◆ Meticulously restored historic town house in sweeping Georgian crescent. Service, like the superbly appointed rooms and lounges, is flawless in every charming detail. Dower house restaurant with French windows opening onto beautiful lawned garden.

Bath Spa, Sydney Rd, BA2 6JF, ☎ (0870) 4008222, *sales.bathspa@macdonald-hotels.co.uk, Fax (01225) 444006,* – 120. VISA
Y z

Vellore : **Rest** (dinner only and Sunday lunch) 37.50 and a la carte 43.95/48.45 –
Alfresco : **Rest** - Mediterranean - *(closed Sunday lunch)* 17.95 (lunch) and a la carte 22.40/49.45 – 17.95 – **102 rm** 250.00 – 290.00, 2 suites.

◆ Part 19C mansion in formal gardens: from the classical lobby to luxuriously appointed, high ceilinged rooms, all is space, elegance and English refinement. Alfresco features murals and exotic palms. Vellore for formal dining beneath a grand domed ceiling.

Bath Priory, Weston Rd, BA1 2XT, ☎ (01225) 331922, *mail@thebathpriory.co.uk, Fax (01225) 448276,* heated, – 18 – 30. VISA
Y c

Rest 25.00/49.50 – **23 rm** 200.00 – 245.00/360.00, 4 suites.

Spec. Salad of quail with garden flowers and beetroot syrup. Loin of pork, braised belly tortellini, sage emulsion. Mango with passion fruit foam and poached apricot.

◆ Set in beautiful gardens, a stunning 19C series of houses in Bath stone. Charmingly appointed rooms, varying in style, and comfy firelit lounges with vivid artwork on walls. Showpiece cuisine in two rooms: one modern and panelled, one warm and traditional.

Homewood Park, Hinton Charterhouse, BA2 7TB, Southeast : 6 ½ m. on A 36 ☎ (01225) 723731, *info@homewoodpark.co.uk, Fax (01225) 723820,* heated, – rest, VISA

Rest 21.00/52.00 – **19 rm** 120.00/150.00 – 155.00/175.00.

◆ Well-proportioned bedrooms, with views of the idyllic wooded gardens and croquet lawn, and cosy country house drawing rooms retain strong elements of the Georgian interior. Ask for dining room window table when garden is in full bloom.

BATH

Street	Grid	No.
Ambury	BX	2
Argyle St	BV	3
Bennett St	AV	4
Bridge St	BVX	6
Broad Quay	BX	7
Chapel Row	AVX	9
Charles St	AX	10
Charlotte St	AV	12
Cheap St	BX	13
Churchill Bridge	BX	14
Circus Pl.	AV	16
Gay St	AV	
Grand Parade	BX	17
Great Stanhope St	AV	18
Green St	BV	21
Guinea Lane	BV	23
Henry St	BX	24
Lower Borough Walls	BX	26
Milsom St	ABV	
Monmouth Pl.	AVX	28
Monmouth St	AX	30
New Bond St	BV	31
New Orchard St	BX	32
Nile St	AV	34
Northgate St	BVX	35
Old Bond St	BX	36
Orange Grove	BX	38
Pierrepont St	BX	39
Quiet St	BV	40
Railway St	BX	41
Russell St	AV	42
Southgate St	BX	43
Terrace Walk	BX	46
Upper Borough Walls	BX	48
Westgate Buildings	AX	49
Westgate St	ABX	50
Wood St	AV	52
York St	BX	53

Queensberry, Russell St, BA1 2QF, ☎ (01225) 447928, *reservations@thequeensberry.co.uk, Fax (01225) 446065,* – [lift] [P]. [MC] [AE] [VISA]. — AV x
Rest – (see ***Olive Tree*** below) – 14.00 – **29 rm** 105.00/145.00 – 105.00/145.00.
◆ Classy boutique merger of Georgian town house décor with contemporary furnishing, understated style and well-chosen detail. Ample, unfussy rooms; pretty courtyard garden.

Dukes, Great Pulteney St, BA2 4DN, ☎ (01225) 787960, *info@dukesbath.co.uk, Fax (01225) 787961,* – . [MC] [AE] [VISA] — BV n
***Cavendish :* Rest** 12.95 (lunch) and dinner a la carte 23.85/33.40 – **13 rm** 85.00/95.00 – 105.00/145.00, 4 suites.
◆ Attractive townhouse in fine Georgian street. Paved terrace with parasols. Spacious, autumnally coloured bar with leather sofas. Classically styled rooms with rich décor. Lower ground floor restaurant for modern British cuisine.

Menzies Waterside, Rossiter Rd, Widcombe Basin, BA2 4JP, (01225) 338855, *waterside@menzies-hotels.co.uk, Fax (01225) 428941* – , rest, – 140. BX r

The Brasserie : Rest 11.95/22.50 and a la carte 26.70/30.45 – 15.95 – **112 rm** 79.00/149.00 – 109.00/179.00.

◆ On the canal bank below Beechen Cliff, a well-maintained hotel, purpose-built with business travellers in mind. Comfortable, modern rooms, four with balconies over the Basin. Smart brasserie with conservatory.

The Windsor, 69 Great Pulteney St, BA2 4DL, (01225) 422100, *sales@bathwindsorhotel.com, Fax (01225) 422550* – . BV c

closed 1 week Christmas – ***Sakura :*** Rest - Japanese - *(closed Sunday-Monday)* (booking essential) (dinner only) 25.00/28.00 s. – **14 rm** 85.00/135.00 – 135.00/195.00.

◆ Grade I listed building in Georgian boulevard. Fine furniture and tastefully co-ordinated floral fabrics in individually styled rooms, some overlooking a Japanese garden. Small Japanese restaurant specialising in teppan-yaki and shabu-shabu.

The County without rest., 18-19 Pulteney Rd, BA2 4EZ, (01225) 425003, *reservations@county-hotel.co.uk, Fax (01225) 466493* – . Z o

closed 22 December-10 January – **22 rm** 75.00/100.00 – 112.00/190.00.

◆ Well-maintained Edwardian house in sight of the Abbey and rugby ground. Comprehensively but sensitively updated rooms, larger on first floor, and comfortable Reading Room.

The Ayrlington without rest., 24-25 Pulteney Rd, BA2 4EZ, (01225) 425495, *mail@ayrlington.com, Fax (01225) 469029*, – . Z v

closed 23 December-6 January – **14 rm** 75.00/100.00 – 100.00/175.00.

◆ An interesting blend of Georgian styling and Asian artefacts develops through twelve spacious, subtly themed rooms. Charming cherry tree garden overlooks croquet club.

Paradise House without rest., 86-88 Holloway, BA2 4PX, (01225) 317723, *info@paradise-house.co.uk, Fax (01225) 482005*, <, – . Z c

closed 3 days Christmas – **11 rm** 65.00/110.00 – 65.00/165.00.

◆ Elegant yet homely hotel on Beechen Cliff. Most rear-facing rooms have exceptional city views; all reflect 18C origins in their décor and boast Jacuzzis. Beautiful gardens.

Oldfields without rest., 102 Wells Rd, BA2 3AL, (01225) 317984, *info@oldfields.co.uk, Fax (01225) 444471*, – . Z u

closed 24-25 December – **16 rm** 49.00/99.00 – 150.00.

◆ Spaciously elegant Victorian house with comfy, well-furnished drawing room, breakfast room boasting 'Bath rooftops' view and bedrooms that exude a high standard of comfort.

Apsley House without rest., 141 Newbridge Hill, BA1 3PT, (01225) 336966, *info@apsley-house.co.uk, Fax (01225) 425462*, – . Y x

closed 22-27 December – **10 rm** 60.00/120.00 – 145.00/160.00.

◆ Built for the Duke of Wellington and staffed with the unobtrusive calm of an English private house. Spacious individual rooms; two open on to a peaceful, mature rear garden.

Kennard without rest., 11 Henrietta St, BA2 6LL, (01225) 310472, *reception@kennard.co.uk, Fax (01225) 460054* – . BV u

closed 24 December-1 January – **12 rm** 54.00/70.00 – 110.00/118.00.

◆ Beautifully furnished townhouse from Bath's golden age; each bedroom individually appointed in classic or contemporary style to very high standard. Charming breakfast room.

Cheriton House without rest., 9 Upper Oldfield Park, BA2 3JX, (01225) 429862, *info@cheritonhouse.co.uk, Fax (01225) 428403*, – . Z u

13 rm 50.00/70.00 – 70.00/100.00.

◆ Comfortable, sizeable rooms and lounge, refurbished in keeping with the house's 19C origins, with some fine tiled fireplaces. Conservatory breakfast room. Charming hosts.

Dorian House without rest., 1 Upper Oldfield Park, BA2 3JX, (01225) 426336, *info@dorianhouse.co.uk, Fax (01225) 444699*, <, – . Z u

11 rm 47.00/78.00 – 95.00/150.00.

◆ Charming 19C house preserves original tiling and stained glass; attic rooms are refreshingly modern, others Victorian. Breakfast to recordings of owner's cello performances.

Bloomfield House without rest., 146 Bloomfield Rd, BA2 2AS, (01225) 420105, *info@ecobloomfield.com*, <, – . Z r

6 rm 65.00 – 140.00.

◆ Bath's first eco-hotel is in this Grade II listed Georgian building. Breakfast produce is organic, fair trade or, whenever possible, locally sourced. Tastefully elegant rooms.

Tasburgh House without rest., Warminster Rd, BA2 6SH, East : 1 m. on A 36 ☎ (01225) 425096, *hotel@bathtasburgh.co.uk, Fax (01225) 463842*, ←, – P. MC AE VISA. Y a
closed Christmas – **12 rm** ☕ ★65.00/75.00 – ★★130.00.
◆ Personally run by charming owner. Rear bedrooms, decorated with original artwork and named after British authors, overlook Avon Valley. Walk along the canal into Bath.

Villa Magdala without rest., Henrietta Rd, BA2 6LX, ☎ (01225) 466329, *office@villamagdala.co.uk, Fax (01225) 483207*, – P. MC VISA. BV r
18 rm ★75.00/85.00 – ★★90.00/150.00.
◆ Named after Napier's 1868 victory. Well-equipped rooms, floral furnishings; carefully preserved ornate balustrade and showpiece bedroom with four-poster and chaise longue.

Harington's, 8-10 Queen St, BA1 1HE, ☎ (01225) 461728, *post@haringtonshotel.co.uk, Fax (01225) 444804* – P. MC AE VISA. AV s
Rest a la carte 19.00/25.00 s. – **13 rm** ☕ ★65.00/114.00 – ★★88.00/134.00.
◆ 18C houses on a cobbled street in the heart of the city and perfectly located for the shops. Simply styled but diligently maintained accommodation on offer. Bar in hot ochre and yellow adjoins restaurant.

Express by Holiday Inn without rest., Lower Bristol Rd, Brougham Hayes, BA2 3QU, ☎ (0870) 4442792, *bath@expressholidayinn.co.uk, Fax (0870) 4442793* – P – 30. MC AE VISA Z z
126 rm ★69.00/99.00 – ★★69.00/99.00.
◆ Lodge style accommodation close to main railway station: the city centre is just five minutes' walk away. Modern bedrooms with power showers. Breakfast area near foyer.

Haydon House without rest., 9 Bloomfield Park, off Bloomfield Rd, BA2 2BY, ☎ (01225) 444919, *stay@haydonhouse.co.uk, Fax (01225) 427351*, – . MC AE VISA. Z a
5 rm ☕ ★50.00/80.00 – ★★80.00/135.00.
◆ Pristine bedrooms and lounge in calm pastels, full of the charming, thoughtful details of a family home. Leafy bowers and trellises. Friendly hosts serve delicious breakfasts.

The Town House without rest., 7 Bennett St, BA1 2QJ, ☎ (01225) 422505, *stay@thetownhousebath.co.uk, Fax (01225) 422505* – . MC AE VISA AV c
closed 5 January-12 February – **3 rm** ☕ ★70.00 – ★★85.00.
◆ Welcoming 18C house in excellent location, designed by John Wood and rebuilt after war damage. Spacious bedrooms with South African wildlife décor. Communal breakfast.

Lavender House without rest., 17 Bloomfield Park, off Bloomfield Rd, BA2 2BY, ☎ (01225) 314500, *lavenderhouse@btinternet.com, Fax (01225) 448564*, – . MC VISA. Z s
5 rm ☕ ★52.00/75.00 – ★★80.00/95.00.
◆ Edwardian house run with confidence and brio. Comfortable, smartly refurbished rooms in rose, blue, gold, terracotta and lavender. Guesthouse cats patrol a pleasant garden. Smart dining room overlooks garden.

Meadowland without rest., 36 Bloomfield Park, off Bloomfield Rd, BA2 2BX, ☎ (01225) 311079, *stay@meadowlandbath.co.uk, Fax (01225) 311079*, – P. MC VISA. Z e
closed 25-26 December – **3 rm** ☕ ★50.00/60.00 – ★★85.00/95.00.
◆ Small suburban guesthouse with a welcoming ambience; comfortably furnished and immaculately maintained accommodation. A neat breakfast room gives onto a lawned garden.

Brocks without rest., 32 Brock St, BA1 2LN, ☎ (01225) 338374, *marion@brocksguesthouse.co.uk, Fax (01225) 334245* – . MC VISA. AV e
closed Christmas and New Year – **6 rm** ☕ ★52.00/60.00 – ★★72.00/88.00.
◆ Between the Circus and the Royal Crescent, a 1765 terraced house, welcoming and well run, offering homely, comfortable en suite rooms. Well-priced for its excellent location.

Athole without rest., 33 Upper Oldfield Park, BA2 3JX, ☎ (01225) 334307, *info@atholehouse.co.uk, Fax (01225) 320009*, – P. MC AE VISA. Z i
3 rm ☕ ★48.00 – ★★78.00.
◆ Spacious, bay windowed Victorian guesthouse with large garden, away from city centre. Bright breakfast room; conservatory lounge. Light, airy, contemporary bedrooms.

Cranleigh without rest., 159 Newbridge Hill, BA1 3PX, ☎ (01225) 310197, *cranleigh@btinternet.com, Fax (01225) 423143*, – P. Y e
closed 25-26 December – **9 rm** ☕ ★45.00/65.00 – ★★60.00/95.00.
◆ Airy, high-ceilinged bedrooms, the largest ideal for families, with brightly patterned fabrics. Pleasant south-facing garden. Smoked salmon and eggs a breakfast speciality.

Olive Tree (at Queensberry H.), Russell St, BA1 2QF, ☎ (01225) 447928, *reservations@thequeensberry.co.uk, Fax (01225) 446065* – . MC AE VISA AV x
closed Monday lunch – **Rest** 16.50 (lunch) and a la carte 29.45/38.95 .
◆ Restaurant refurbishment has resulted in a classy, stylish and contemporary ambience. Modern artworks adorn the split-level basement. Modern British cooking. Helpful staff.

ENGLAND

Hole in the Wall, 16 George St, BA1 2EH, ☎ (01225) 425242, *info@theholeinthewall.co.uk, Fax (01225) 425242* – 8. AV n
closed 25-26 December and Sunday lunch – **Rest** 13.95 and a la carte 18.20/29.50 ♀.
◆ Once a starting point of British culinary renaissance; former coal hole mixes white-washed walls, antique chairs and a relaxed mood. Slightly eclectic cuisine.

No.5, 5 Argyle St, BA2 4BA, ☎ (01225) 444499, *Fax (01225) 444499* – AE VISA BV s
closed 25-26 December and 1-3 January – **Rest** a la carte 22.00/30.00 ♀.
◆ Unfussy bistro with a distinctly buzzy feel. Personally run by cheery French owner. Fish night on Wednesday a speciality. Menus offer ample variety; some are good value, too.

Fishworks, 6 Green St, BA1 2JY, ☎ (01225) 448707, *bath@fishworks.co.uk,* – AE VISA BV a
closed Christmas, Sunday, Monday and Bank Holidays – **Rest** - Seafood - (booking essential) a la carte 20.00/40.00 ♀.
◆ Behind a quality fish shop, whose produce appears on menus. Bustling ambience. Extensive, daily changing blackboard specials; the cooking is straightforward and unfussy.

at Box *Northeast : 4¾ m. on A 4 – Y – ✉ Bath.*

The Northey, Bath Rd, SN13 8AE, ☎ (01225) 742333, *Fax (01225) 742333,* – P. AE.
closed 25-26 December – **Rest** a la carte 20.40/29.95 ♀.
◆ Spacious roadside pub with pleasant rear terrace. Modern interior dominated by chunky wooden tables and rattan chairs. Serious modern cooking lays claim to restaurant style.

at Colerne *(Wilts.) Northeast : 6½ m. by A 4 – Y – , Batheaston rd and Bannerdown Rd – ✉ Chippenham.*

Lucknam Park , SN14 8AZ, North : ½ m. on Marshfield rd ☎ (01225) 742777, *reservations@lucknampark.co.uk, Fax (01225) 743536,* – rest, P – 40. AE VISA.
Rest (light lunch Monday-Saturday)/dinner 55.00 **s.** ♀ – 18.50 – **37 rm** 235.00 – 510.00, 4 suites.
Spec. Devon duck four ways with endive Tatin. Roast fillets of John Dory, braised pork belly and white onion purée. Coconut parfait with bitter chocolate sorbet, passion fruit coulis.
◆ Luxurious Palladian mansion set in 500 acres of listed parkland and superb gardens. Drawing rooms, panelled library and spacious bedrooms, all in delightful period style. Chandeliered restaurant where accomplished cuisine matches the style of the surroundings.

at Monkton Combe *Southeast : 4½ m. by A 36 – Y – ✉ Bath.*

Monkshill without rest., Shaft Rd, BA2 7HL, ☎ (01225) 833028, *monks.hill@virgin.net, Fax (01225) 833028,* ≤ Limpley Stoke Valley, – P. AE VISA
closed Christmas and New Year – **3 rm** 60.00/75.00 – 80.00/90.00.
◆ Victorian house in pretty gardens enjoying superb views of Limpley Stoke Valley. Comfortable, sensitively refurbished bedrooms and an intriguing collection of antiques.

Do not confuse X with ✿! X defines comfort, while stars are awarded for the best cuisine, across all categories of comfort.

BATTLE *E. Sussex* 504 V 31 *Great Britain G. – pop. 5 190.*
See : *Town★ – Abbey and Site of the Battle of Hastings★ AC.*
Battle Abbey Gatehouse ☎ (01424) 773721, battletic@rother.gov.uk.
London 55 – Brighton 34 – Folkestone 43 – Maidstone 30.

PowderMills , Powdermill Lane, TN33 0SP, South : 1½ m. by A 2100 on Catsfield rd ☎ (01424) 775511, *powdc@aol.com, Fax (01424) 774540,* ≤, – rest, P – 250. AE VISA
Orangery : **Rest** 18.50/30.00 and dinner a la carte 35.00/40.00 – **40 rm** 105.00 – 155.00/190.00.
◆ Part Georgian gunpowder mill in 150 acres of woods and lakes. Individually decorated rooms - more sizable in annex and with better views - combine antiques and modern pieces. Dining room terrace overlooks pool.

Fox Hole Farm without rest., Kane Hythe Rd, TN33 9QU, Northwest : 2 ½ m. by A 2100 and A 271 on B 2096 (Netherfield rd) (01424) 772053, *foxholefarm@amserve.com, Fax (01424) 772053*, – **P**. VISA
closed Christmas and January – **3 rm** ★40.00 – ★★59.00/63.00.
◆ Peaceful 18C woodcutters cottage by 1000 acres of protected forest. Simple pine furnished bedrooms with sea-grass matting. Timbered lounge centred around a log stove.

BAWBURGH *Norfolk* 504 X 26 – *see Norwich.*

BEACONSFIELD *Bucks.* 504 S 29 – *pop. 12 292.*
Beaconsfield Seer Green (01494) 676545.
London 26 – Aylesbury 19 – Oxford 32.

Bellhouse, Oxford Rd, HP9 2XE, East : 1 ¾ m. on A 40 (01753) 887211, *info@bellhousehotel.co.uk, Fax (01753) 888231*, , , , – – **P** – 400. AE VISA
Archways : **Rest** *(closed lunch Saturday and Bank Holidays)* (buffet lunch)/dinner 28.00 –
Aquarium : **Rest** *(closed lunch Saturday and Bank Holidays)* (a la carte) 16.15/22.15 **s.** –
135 rm ★160.00/180.00 – ★★200.00, 1 suites.
◆ A splendid level of modern facilities, particularly in the more boldly decorated executive rooms. Smartly run and commercially driven, with extensive conference suites. Archways is centred round a gleaming grand piano. Café Bar tables overlook pool.

at Wooburn Common *Southwest : 3½ m. by A 40 – ✉ Beaconsfield.*

Chequers Inn , Kiln Lane, HP10 0JQ, Southwest : 1 m. on Bourne End rd (01628) 529575, *info@chequers-inn.com, Fax (01628) 850124*, , – **P** – 45. AE VISA.
Rest a la carte 25.00/30.00 – **17 rm** ★72.50/99.50 – ★★107.50.
◆ Coaching inn dating from 18C. Good-sized bedrooms with leaded lattice windows and something of a country cottage feel. Popular with business travellers. Restaurant boasts exposed beams and brickwork.

Undecided between two equivalent establishments?
Within each category, establishments are classified
in our order of preference.

BEADNELL *Northd.* 501 502 P 17.
London 341 – Edinburgh 81 – Newcastle upon Tyne 47.

Beach Court without rest., Harbour Rd, NE67 5BJ, (01665) 720225, *info@beachcourt.com, Fax (01665) 721499*, ≤ Beadnell Bay – **P**. AE VISA
closed 1 week Christmas – 3.95 – **3 rm** ★54.50 – ★★99.00/119.00.
◆ Turreted house enjoys fine views of Beadnell Bay. Simple, traditional en suite rooms; leafy little conservatory. Hospitable owners with a real enthusiasm for entertaining.

BEAMHURST *Staffs. – see Uttoxeter.*

BEAMINSTER *Dorset* 503 L 31 – *pop. 2 791.*
Chedington Court, South Perrott (01935) 891413.
London 154 – Exeter 45 – Taunton 30 – Weymouth 29.

Bridge House, 3 Prout Bridge, DT8 3AY, (01308) 862200, *enquiries@bridgehouse.co.uk, Fax (01308) 863700*, – **P**. AE VISA
closed 29-31 December – **Rest** (residents only Sunday and Monday dinner) 33.50 (dinner) and a la carte 32.50/41.75 – **14 rm** ★62.00/102.00 – ★★166.00/174.00.
◆ Priest's house reputed to date back to the 1200s. Large bedrooms, in the new block, with cheerful floral fabrics. Firelit lounge, charming walled garden, informal, rural feel. Oak beamed restaurant with conservatory.

BEARSTED *Kent* 504 V 30 – *see Maidstone.*

BEAULIEU *Hants.* 503 504 P 31 *Great Britain G.* – ✉ *Brockenhurst.*
See : *Town*★★ - *National Motor Museum*★★ *AC.*
Env. : *Buckler's Hard*★ *(Maritime Museum*★ *AC) SE : 2 m.*
London 102 – Bournemouth 24 – Southampton 13 – Winchester 23.

Montagu Arms, Palace Lane, SO42 7ZL, ☎ (01590) 612324, *reservations@montaguarmshotel.co.uk, Fax (01590) 612188,* – P – 40. AE VISA.
Terrace : Rest 39.00 **s.** – ***Monty's Brasserie :*** Rest a la carte 20.95/26.50 **s.** – **21 rm** ★125.00/135.00 – ★★180.00, 2 suites.
• Ivy-covered 18C inn. Bedrooms, in various shapes and sizes, can't quite match the warmth of the inviting panelled lounge with log fires, but are tidy with useful mod cons. A pretty garden adjoins panelled Terrace. Monty's is bright, warm brasserie.

at Bucklers Hard *South : 2½ m.* – ✉ *Brockenhurst.*

Master Builder's House, SO42 7XB, ☎ (01590) 616253, *res@themasterbuilders.co.uk, Fax (01590) 616297,* – rm, P – 40. VISA.
Riverview : Rest 22.50/34.50 and a la carte approx 31.50 – **23 rm** ★135.00/155.00 – ★★190.00/205.00, 2 suites.
• In 18C village, once home to the master shipwright. Lounge boasts inglenook, restored with easy country house style. Rooms in the old house have naval prints and sea chests. Riverview is smartly set by Beaulieu River.

BEAUMONT *Channel Islands – see Jersey.*

BEDFORD *Beds.* 504 S 27 – *pop. 82 488.*
Bedfordshire, Bromham Rd, Biddenham ☎ (01234) 261669 Y – Mowsbury, Kimbolton Rd ☎ (01234) 771041.
The Old Town Hall, St Paul's Sq ☎ (01234) 215226, tourisminfo@bedford.gov.uk.
London 59 – Cambridge 31 – Colchester 70 – Leicester 51 – Lincoln 95 – Luton 20 – Oxford 52 – Southend-on-Sea 85.

Plan opposite

Corus H. Bedford, Cardington Rd, MK44 3SA, East : 2 m. on A 603 ☎ (0870) 609 6108, *reservations.barns@corushotels.com, Fax (01234) 273102,* – P – 120. AE VISA. Y n
Rest *(closed Saturday lunch)* a la carte 21.50/32.50 – 10.50 – **48 rm** ★92.00 – ★★92.00/135.00.
• In 3 acres of gardens on the banks of the Great Ouse. Spacious, well equipped rooms. Fine 13C tithe barn, now a function room: lofty timbered ceiling, agricultural curios. Adjoining cocktail bar and riverside brasserie.

Bedford Swan, The Embankment, MK40 1RW, ☎ (01234) 346565, *info@bedfordswanhotel.co.uk, Fax (01234) 212009,* – rest, P – 250. AE VISA. X a
Rest 14.95/21.50 and a la carte 22.00/28.90 **s.** – 11.95 – **113 rm** ★130.00 – ★★135.00.
• Impressive Georgian house, built in 1794 for the Duke of Bedford. The more modern bedrooms have ample work space, and a grandiose indoor pool has ancient Roman style. Restaurant on the banks of the Great Ouse.

Premier Travel Inn, Priory Country Park, Barkers Lane, MK41 9DJ, ☎ (0870) 1977030, *Fax (01234) 325697* – rm, P. AE VISA. Y s
Rest (grill rest.) – **32 rm** ★47.95/47.95 – ★★50.95/50.95.
• Well-proportioned modern bedrooms, some overlooking a country park and lake, suitable for family stopovers or business travel. Informal dining in adjoining Beefeater.

at Elstow *South : 2 m. by A 6* – ✉ *Bedford.*

St Helena, High St, MK42 9XP, ☎ (01234) 344848, – P. AE VISA Y r
closed Saturday lunch, Sunday and Monday – **Rest** 21.00/35.00.
• Part light, modern conservatory, part antique-furnished dining room of 16C origin. Personally run. Creative, seasonal menus and appetising daily specials. Attentive service.

at Houghton Conquest *South : 6½ m. by A 6 – Y –* ✉ *Bedford.*

Knife and Cleaver, The Grove, MK45 3LA, ☎ (01234) 740387, *info@knifeandcleaver.com, Fax (01234) 740900,* – rest, P. AE VISA
closed 27-30 December – **Rest** *(closed dinner Sunday and Bank Holidays)* 15.95/22.00 and a la carte 22.25/35.40 – **9 rm** ★53.00 – ★★78.00.
• An intimate bar, panelled in Jacobean oak and serving real ales and ciders, plus traditionally styled bedrooms in a redbrick village pub opposite All Saints church. Leafy conservatory restaurant spread with rugs.

BEDFORD

Street	Grid	No.
Alexandra Rd	X	3
Ampthill Rd	X	4
Ashburnham Rd	Y	6
Castle Rd	XY	7
Church Lane	Y	9
Church Square	X	10
Clapham Rd	Y	12
Commercial Rd	X	13
Eastcotts Rd	Y	15
Embankment (The)	X	16
Ford End Rd	Y	18
Goldington Rd	X	19
Harpur Shopping Centre	X	
Harpur St	X	21
Hassett St	X	22
Haylands Way	Y	24
High St	Y	25
Hillgrounds Rd	Y	26
Horne Lane	X	27
Interchange Retail Park	Y	
Longholme Way	Y	28
Manton Lane	Y	31
Newnham Ave	Y	33
Newnham Rd	X	34
Queen's Drive	Y	36
River St	X	37
Rope Walk	Y	39
St Pauls Square	X	40
St Loyes St	X	30
Shakespeare Rd	Y	42
Silver St	X	43
Thurlow St	X	45
West End Lane	Y	46

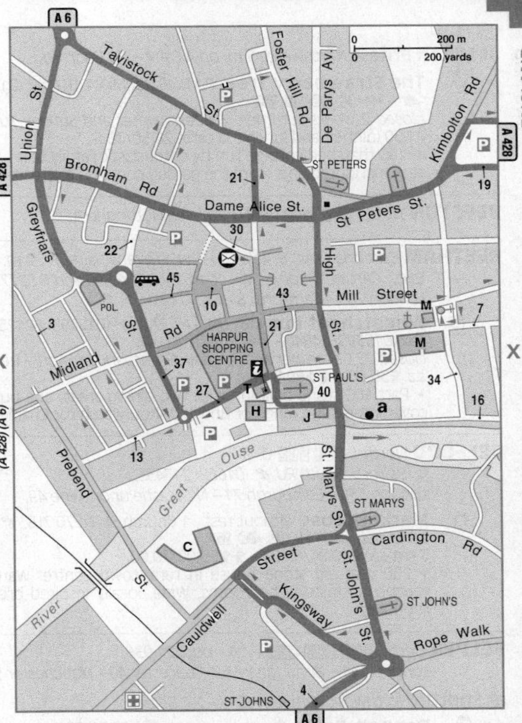

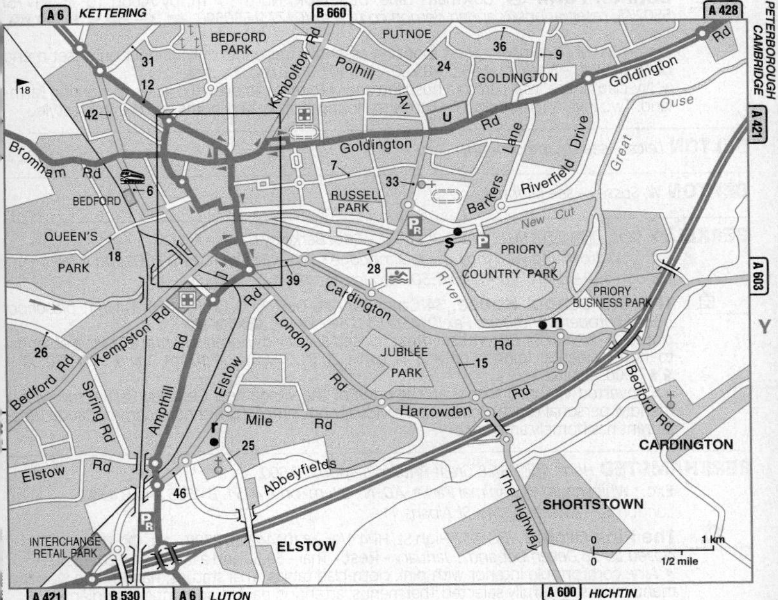

A 6 KETTERING — B 660 — A 428 — PETERBOROUGH CAMBRIDGE — A 421 — A 603 — Y

BEDFORD PARK, PUTNOE, GOLDINGTON, Polhill Av., Kimbolton Rd, Goldington Rd, Bromham Rd, BEDFORD, RUSSELL PARK, Barkers Lane, Riverfield Drive, Great Ouse, New Cut, QUEEN'S PARK, PRIORY COUNTRY PARK, PRIORY BUSINESS PARK, Cardington Rd, River, Kempston Rd, London Rd, Bedford Rd, Spring Rd, Ampthill Rd, Elstow Rd, JUBILEE PARK, Harrowden Rd, Mile Rd, Bedford Rd, CARDINGTON, Elstow Rd, Abbeyfields, The Highway, SHORTSTOWN, INTERCHANGE RETAIL PARK, ELSTOW

0 1 km
0 1/2 mile

A 421 — B 530 — A 6 LUTON — A 600 HICHTIN

at Milton Ernest *Northwest : 5 m. on A 6 – Y – ✉ Bedford.*

XX **The Strawberry Tree,** Radwell Rd, MK44 1RY, ✆ (01234) 823633, *Fax (01234) 823633* – ⇔ – ✈ P. MC ⦿ VISA
closed 2 weeks summer, 2 weeks winter and Sunday-Tuesday – **Rest** (booking essential) 41.50 (dinner) and lunch a la carte 26.50/36.50.
◆ 18C thatched cottage run by enthusiastic family team. Market-fresh produce and some seasonal ingredients from the garden combine to create a confident, well-balanced menu.

BEESTON *Notts.* 502 503 504 Q 25 – *see Nottingham.*

BEETHAM *Cumbria Great Britain G.* – **Env.** : *Levens Hall*★, *N : 2 m. by A 6.*
Exc. : *Cartmel Priory*★, *W : 10 m. by A 6, A 590 and B 5277.*
London 263 – Carnforth 8 – Milnthorpe 1.

Wheatsheaf Inn with rm, LA7 7AL, ✆ (015395) 62123, *wheatsheafbeetham@aol.com, Fax (015395) 64840* – ✈ P. MC VISA. ✗
closed 25 December and Sunday dinner January-April – **Rest** a la carte 16.90/28.00 ♀ – **6 rm** ☐ ★55.00 – ★★69.50.
◆ Part 16C stone built inn with two dining areas, one bustling, the other relaxed. Menus cover interesting range of British dishes: watch for Charlie the parrot! Homely rooms.

BELFORD *Northd.* 501 502 O 17.
⛳9 *Belford, South Rd* ✆ *(01668) 213433.*
London 335 – Edinburgh 71 – Newcastle upon Tyne 49.

Market Cross without rest., 1 Church St, NE70 7LS, ✆ (01668) 213013, *details@marketcross.net,* ⇔ – ✈ P. MC VISA
3 rm ☐ ★40.00/65.00 – ★★55.00/70.00.
◆ 200 year-old stone house in rural town centre. Warmly decorated lounge, homely touches in tasteful bedrooms. Wide, locally inspired breakfast choice in cosy pine surroundings.

BELPER *Derbs.* 502 503 504 P 24 – *pop. 21 938.*
London 141 – Birmingham 59 – Leicester 40 – Manchester 55 – Nottingham 17.

at Shottle *Northwest : 4 m. by A 517 – ✉ Belper.*

Dannah Farm ⛰, Bowmans Lane, DE56 2DR, North : ¼ m. by Alport rd ✆ (01773) 550273, *reservations@dannah.demon.co.uk, Fax (01773) 550590,* ⇔, ⛰ – ✈ ✆ P. MC VISA. ✗
closed 24-26 December – **Rest** (booking essential) (residents only) (dinner only) (set menu only) 24.50 **s.** – **8 rm** ☐ ★65.00/85.00 – ★★90.00/160.00, 2 suites.
◆ Ivy-clad house, well run by a husband and wife team, in over 100 acres of working farmland. Two inviting, thoughtfully furnished lounges; cosy bedrooms in old-English style.

BELTON *Leics.* – *see Loughborough.*

BEPTON *W. Sussex* – *see Midhurst.*

BERKELEY *Glos.* 503 504 M 28 *Great Britain G.* – **See**: *Berkeley Castle*★★ *AC.*
Exc. : *Wildfowl and Wetlands Trust, Slimbridge*★ *AC, NE : 6½ m. by B 4066 and A 38.*
London 129 – Bristol 20 – Cardiff 50 – Gloucester 18.

The Old School House, 34 Canonbury St, GL13 9BG, ✆ (01453) 811711, *oldschoolhouse@btopenworld.com, Fax (01453) 511761* – ✈ P. MC ⦿ VISA
closed 25-26 and 31 December – **Rest** *(closed Sunday to non-residents)* (booking essential to non-residents) (dinner only) a la carte 20.85/27.85 **s.** – **10 rm** ☐ ★55.00/60.00 – ★★79.00, 1 suite.
◆ Converted Victorian school on the edge of the village near Berkeley Castle, run with a friendly, personal touch. Spacious, individually but simply furnished accommodation. Restaurant has homely ambience.

BERKHAMSTED *Herts.* 504 S 28 *Great Britain G.* – *pop. 18 800.*
Exc. : *Whipsnade Wild Animal Park*★ *AC, N : 9½ m. on A 4251, B 4506 and B 4540.*
London 34 – Aylesbury 14 – St Albans 11.

XX **The Pink Orchid,** 333-337 High St, HP4 1AL, ✆ (01442) 878799 – ▤. MC VISA
closed 25-26 December and 1 January – **Rest** - Thai - 39.50 and a la carte 24.20/32.40.
◆ Airy, comfortable interior with pink cloth-clad tables, Thai statues; hand-made wooden menu covers. Carefully selected Thai menus: attention paid to authentic ingredients.

BERWICK-UPON-TWEED *Northd.* 501 502 O 16 *Great Britain and Scotland G. – pop. 12 870.*
See : *Town*★ - *Walls*★.
Env. : *Foulden*★, *NW : 5 m. – Paxton House (Chippendale furniture*★*) AC, W : 5 m. by A 6105, A 1 and B 6461.*
Exc. : *St Abb's Head*★★ *(≤*★*), NW : 12 m. by A 1, A 1107 and B 6438 – SW : Tweed Valley*★★ *– Eyemouth Museum*★ *AC, N : 7½ m. by A 1 and A 1107 – Holy Island*★ *(Priory ruins*★ *AC, Lindisfarne Castle*★ *AC), SE : 9 m. by A 1167 and A 1 – Manderston*★ *(stables*★*), W : 13 m. by A 6105 – Ladykirk (Kirk o'Steil*★*), SW : 8½ m. by A 698 and B 6470.*
Goswick ☎ (01289) 387256 – Magdalene Fields ☎ (01289) 306384.
106 Marygate ☎ (01289) 330733, tourism@berwick-upon-tweed.gov.uk.
London 349 – Edinburgh 57 – Newcastle upon Tyne 63.

Marshall Meadows Country House, TD15 1UT, North : 2 ¾ m. by A 1 ☎ (01289) 331133, *stay@marshallmeadows.co.uk, Fax (01289) 331438,* – P – 180. MC AE VISA
closed 16-29 December – **Rest** (lunch booking essential) 14.95/34.00 – **18 rm** ★85.00/95.00 – ★★115.00/150.00, 1 suite.
◆ Privately owned Georgian country house with sympathetic extension, neat lawned gardens, woodland walks. Co-ordinated country house style rooms; larger in original building. Two traditional, formal dining rooms.

Sallyport, 1 Sallyport, TD15 1EZ, off Bridge St ☎ (01289) 308827, *info@sallyport.co.uk* – P. MC VISA
Rest (communal dining) 35.00 – **5 rm** ★120.00 – ★★155.00.
◆ 17C Grade II listed house on cobbled alley. The bedrooms are a strong point: they boast a boutique style, with a high standard of facilities, and lots of homely extra touches. Characterful farmhouse kitchen style dining room.

BEVERLEY *East Riding* 502 S 22 *Great Britain G. – pop. 29 110 – ✉ Kingston-upon-Hull.*
See : *Town*★ - *Minster*★★ – *St Mary's Church*★.
The Westwood ☎ (01482) 867190.
34 Butcher Row ☎ (01482) 867430, beverley.tic@eastriding.gov.uk.
London 188 – Kingston-upon-Hull 8 – Leeds 52 – York 29.

Tickton Grange, Tickton, HU17 9SH, Northeast : 3 ¾ m. on A 1035 ☎ (01964) 543666, *info@ticktongrange.co.uk, Fax (01964) 542556,* – P – 200. MC AE VISA.
Squires Dining Room : **Rest** 20.00/35.00 and dinner a la carte 29.20/34.95 – 10.00 – **17 rm** ★80.00 – ★★100.00/120.00.
◆ Carefully renovated bedrooms blend Georgian and contemporary architecture, antique and period-inspired furniture. Richly swagged fabrics and open fires in an inviting lounge. Dine in the Georgian style; large bay windows look out onto the lawn.

BEYTON *Suffolk* 504 W 27 – *see Bury St Edmunds.*

BIBURY *Glos.* 503 504 O 28 *Great Britain G. – ✉ Cirencester.*
See : *Village*★.
London 86 – Gloucester 26 – Oxford 30.

Swan, GL7 5NW, ☎ (01285) 740695, *info@swanhotel.co.uk, Fax (01285) 740473,* – P – 50. MC AE VISA.
Gallery : **Rest** (dinner only) 29.95 – ***Café Swan :*** **Rest** a la carte 20.50/26.40 – **18 rm** ★140.00/180.00 – ★★220.00/260.00.
◆ Ivy-clad 17C coaching inn with private gardens; idyllic location by a trout stream. Comfortable rooms in pretty country style, some with canopied beds. Gallery is formally stylish and spacious. Café Swan is a brasserie with stone-flagged courtyard.

Cotteswold House without rest., Arlington, GL7 5ND, on B 4425 ☎ (01285) 740609, *enquiries@cotteswoldhouse.org.uk, Fax (01285) 740609* – P. MC VISA.
3 rm ★40.00 – ★★58.00.
◆ Set in a manicured garden outside the picturesque village. Simple, spotless and modestly priced bedrooms, comprehensively remodelled behind a Victorian façade. Non smoking.

The red symbol? This denotes the very essence of peace – only the sound of birdsong first thing in the morning ...

BIDDENDEN *Kent* 504 V 30 *Great Britain G. – pop. 2 205.*

Exc. : *Bodiam Castle★★, S : 10 m. by A 262, A 229 and B 2244 – Sissinghurst Garden★, W : 3 m. by A 262 – Battle Abbey★, S : 20 m. by A 262, A 229, A 21 and A 2100.*

London 52 – Ashford 13 – Maidstone 16.

Barclay Farmhouse without rest., Woolpack Corner, TN27 8BQ, South : ½ m. by A 262 on Benenden rd ☎ (01580) 292626, *info@barclayfarmhouse.co.uk, Fax (01580) 292288,* – P.

3 rm ☕ ★50.00/80.00 – ★★55.00/85.00.

◆ Set in an acre of pleasant garden: well-priced, very comfortable accommodation with fine French oak flooring and furniture. Inventive breakfasts in granary or barn conversion.

Bishopsdale Oast, TN27 8DR, South : 3 m. by A 262 and Benenden rd on Tenterden rd ☎ (01580) 291027, *drysdale@bishopsdaleoast.co.uk,* – P. MC VISA

closed Christmas – **Rest** (by arrangement) (communal dining) 28.20 – **5 rm** ☕ ★56.40 – ★★70.50.

◆ Extended oast house in four acres of mature grounds with wild flower garden. Comfy lounge with log fire; plenty of trinkets and books in bright, clean, good sized rooms. Family size dining table; interesting meals employ home-grown, organic produce.

The West House (Garrett), 28 High St, TN27 8AH, ☎ (01580) 291341, *thewesthouse@btconnect.com, Fax (01580) 291341* – P. MC VISA

closed Christmas-New Year, 2 weeks August, Saturday lunch, Sunday dinner and Monday – **Rest** 24.00/29.50 ♀.

Spec. Foie gras "crème caramel", sherry vinegar and raisins. Marsh samphire and lobster hollandaise. Elderflower fritters, vanilla ice cream.

◆ Characterful timbered cottages - with wood-burner and golden beams - on pretty street. Dine on refined, original dishes making good use of carefully sourced ingredients.

Three Chimneys, TN27 8LW, West : 1 ½ m. off A 262 ☎ (01580) 291472, – P. MC VISA

closed 25 and 31 December – **Rest** (booking essential) a la carte 26.00/32.00.

◆ 15C pub with coir mat, yellow walls, dried hops, characterful original beams. Smart rear restaurant facing garden. Tasty, regularly changing menus: home-made puds of renown.

**We try to be as accurate as possible when giving room rates.
But prices are susceptible to change,
so please check rates when booking.**

BIDEFORD *Devon* 503 H 30 *The West Country G. – pop. 16 262.*

See : *Bridge★★ – Burton Art Gallery★ AC.*

Env. : *Appledore★, N : 2 m.*

Exc. : *Clovelly★★, W : 11 m. by A 39 and B 3237 – Lundy Island★★, NW : by ferry – Rosemoor★ – Great Torrington (Dartington Crystal★ AC) SE : 7½ m. by A 386.*

18 Royal North Devon, Golf Links Rd, Westward Ho ☎ (01237) 473824 – 9 Torrington, Weare Trees ☎ (01805) 622229.

to Lundy Island (Lundy Co. Ltd) (1 h 45 mn).

Victoria Park, The Quay ☎ (01237) 477676, bidefordtic@torridge.gov.uk.

London 231 – Exeter 43 – Plymouth 58 – Taunton 60.

Yeoldon House, Durrant Lane, EX39 2RL, North : 1 ½ m. by B 3235 off A 386 ☎ (01237) 474400, *yeoldonhouse@aol.com, Fax (01237) 476618,* – P. MC AE VISA

closed 24-28 December – **Rest** *(closed Sunday)* (dinner only) 27.50 **s.** – **10 rm** ☕ ★70.00 – ★★115.00.

◆ Privately run 19C house, its lawns leading down to the river Torridge. Comfortable lounge bar with books, dried flowers and curios. Period-style rooms, some with balconies. Smart restaurant overlooking river.

Memories, 8 Fore St, Northam, EX39 1AW, North : 2 m. by B 3235 off A 386 ✆ (01237) 473419, *Fax (01237) 473419* – .
closed 25-26 December, Sunday-Tuesday and Bank Holidays – **Rest** (dinner only) 16.50 (mid week) and a la carte at weekends 25.40.
◆ Simple, blue and white painted restaurant with vibrant local ambience. Enthusiastic owners serve well-prepared, traditional menus at a reasonable price.

at Instow *North : 3 m. by A 386 on B 3233 – ✉ Bideford.*

Commodore, Marine Parade, EX39 4JN, ✆ (01271) 860347, *admin@commodore-instow.co.uk, Fax (01271) 861233,* < Taw and Torridge estuaries, – rest, – 250.
Rest (dinner only and Sunday lunch)/dinner 24.00/28.00 and dinner a la carte 13.50/55.00 – **25 rm** (dinner included) 49.00/90.00 – 150.00/200.00.
◆ Extended former gentleman's residence, family run in a friendly spirit for over 30 years. Trim, comfy accommodation: front-facing balcony rooms overlook the estuary. Immaculate, classically styled dining room.

BIGBURY *Devon* 503 I 33 *The West Country G.*
Exc. : *Kingsbridge*★ *, E : 13 m. by B 3392 and A 379.*
London 195 – Exeter 41 – Plymouth 22.

The Oyster Shack, Milburn Orchard Farm, Stakes Hill, TQ7 4BE, ✆ (01548) 810876, *info@oystershack.co.uk,* – .
closed lunch Monday-Thursday – **Rest** - Seafood Bistro - (booking essential) (unlicensed) a la carte 19.95/28.00.
◆ Eccentric seaside venue, decorated with fishing nets. Seafood, particularly various oyster dishes; classic and modern dishes using the freshest produce.

BIGBURY-ON-SEA *Devon* 503 I 33 – ✉ *Kingsbridge.*
London 196 – Exeter 42 – Plymouth 23.

Burgh Island , TQ7 4BG, South : ½ m. by sea tractor ✆ (01548) 810514, *reception@burghisland.com, Fax (01548) 810243,* < Bigbury Bay, , , , , – .
closed 3 weeks January – **Rest** (booking essential to non-residents) (dancing Wednesday and Saturday evening) 35.00/50.00 – **13 rm** (dinner included) 230.00 – 320.00 11 suites 300.00/480.00.
◆ Unique Grade II listed 1930s country house in private island setting: stylishly romantic Art Deco interior. Charmingly individual rooms with views: some have fantastic style. Ballroom dining: owners pride themselves on local, seasonal, daily changing menus.

Henley , Folly Hill, TQ7 4AR, ✆ (01548) 810240, *enquiries@thehenleyhotel.co.uk, Fax (01548) 810240,* < Bigbury Bay and Bolt Tail, – .
March-October – **Rest** (booking essential to non-residents) (dinner only) 28.00 – **6 rm** 55.00/70.00 – 110.00/120.00.
◆ Personally run cottage of 16C origin. Stunning views of the bay and Bolt Tail from the modern conservatory with deep wicker chairs and simple, compact rooms in pastel tones. Homely dining room with magnificent sea views.

BIGGLESWADE *Beds.* 504 T 27 – *pop. 15 383.*
London 46 – Bedford 12 – Luton 24.

at Old Warden *West : 3½ m. by A 6001 off B 658 – ✉ Biggleswade.*

The Hare & Hounds, SG18 9HQ, ✆ (01767) 627225, *Fax (01767) 627588,* , –
closed 26 December, 1 January, Sunday dinner and Monday except Bank Holidays – **Rest** 20.00/30.00 ♀.
◆ Stylish dining pub with lawn and terrace. Very pleasant restaurant section boasts autumnal shades and tweeds. Winning mix of modern or classic dishes; locally sourced produce.

Good food without spending a fortune? Look out for the Bib Gourmand

BILBROUGH *N. Yorks* 502 Q 22.

The Three Hares, Main St, YO23 3PH, ☎ (01937) 832128, *info@thethreehares.co.uk, Fax (01937) 834626,* – P. MC VISA
Rest *(closed Sunday dinner)* a la carte 20.00/30.00.
◆ Immaculately extended inn with 18C origins. There are four different rooms in which to dine: menus, featuring much that is local, mix Yorkshire staples and modish invention.

BILLESLEY *Warks. – see Stratford-upon-Avon.*

BILLINGSHURST *W. Sussex* 504 S 30 – *pop. 5 465.*
London 44 – Brighton 24 – Guildford 25 – Portsmouth 40.

Old Wharf without rest., Wharf Farm, Newbridge, RH14 0JG, West : 1¾ m. on A 272 ☎ (01403) 784096, *david.mitchell@farming.co.uk, Fax (01403) 784096,* – P.
closed 2 weeks Christmas, New Year and restricted opening in winter – **3 rm** 55.00 – 80.00/100.00.
◆ Charming touches to former 19C canalside warehouse: antiques, dried flowers and brimming bookshelves. Breakfast in farmhouse kitchen; cosy country house rooms overlook water.

The ✿ award is the crème de la crème. This is awarded to restaurants which are really worth travelling miles for!

BILSBORROW *Lancs. – see Garstang.*

BINFIELD HEATH *Oxon. – see Henley-on-Thames.*

BINGHAM *Notts.* 502 504 R 25 – *pop. 8 658.*
London 125 – Leicester 26 – Lincoln 28 – Nottingham 11 – Sheffield 35.

Yeung Sing with rm, Market St, NG13 8AB, ☎ (01949) 831222, *manager@yeung-sing.co.uk, Fax (01949) 838833* – P. MC AE VISA
closed 25-26 December – **Rest** - Chinese (Canton) - (closed lunch Monday-Wednesday) 12.50/30.00 and a la carte 20.50/35.00 – **16 rm** 46.00/64.00 – 64.00.
◆ Carefully prepared, authentic Cantonese and regional Chinese cuisine served amid Oriental prints and wall-hangings. Smartly attired staff in discreet, friendly attendance.

BINGLEY *W. Yorks.* 502 O 22 – *pop. 19 884* – ✉ *Bradford.*
18 *St Ives Est.* ☎ *(01274) 562436.*
London 204 – Bradford 6 – Leeds 15 – Skipton 13.

Five Rise Locks, Beck Lane, BD16 4DD, via Park Rd ☎ (01274) 565296, *info@five-rise-locks.co.uk, Fax (01274) 568828,* – P. MC VISA
Rest *(closed Sunday dinner)* (dinner only and lunch Friday and Sunday) 9.95 (lunch) and dinner a la carte 16.75/24.00 – **9 rm** 50.00/60.00 – 72.00.
◆ Neat mid-Victorian house named after the locks on the nearby Leeds-Liverpool canal. Cheerful, modern, individually styled rooms, some with views of the distant dales. Well-kept dining room employs local produce on menus.

Premier Travel Inn, 502 Bradford Rd, Sandbeds, BD20 5NH, Northwest : 1½ m. by A 650 ☎ (01274) 566662, *Fax (01274) 566114* – rm, rest, P. MC AE VISA.
Rest (grill rest.) – **40 rm** 46.95/46.95 – 48.95/48.95.
◆ Competitively priced hotel offers bright, simple rooms, useful for leisure or business travel. A short drive from Titus Salt's 19C mill and model village at Saltaire.

BINLEY *W. Mids. – see Coventry.*

BIRCHOVER *Derbs. – see Matlock.*

BIRKENHEAD *Mersey.* 502 503 K 23 – *pop. 83 729.*

Arrowe Park, Woodchurch ℘ (0151) 677 1527 – Prenton, Golf Links Rd, Prenton ℘ (0151) 608 1461.

Mersey Tunnels (toll).

to Liverpool and Wallasey (Mersey Ferries) frequent services daily.

Woodside Ferry Booking Hall ℘ (0151) 647 6780, touristinfo@wirral.gov.uk.

London 222 – Liverpool 2.

Plan : see Liverpool p. 3

River Hill, Talbot Rd, Oxton, CH43 2HJ, Southwest : 2 ¼ m. by A 552 on B 5151 ℘ (0151) 653 3773, *reception@theriverhill.co.uk, Fax (0151) 653 7162,* – P. MC AE VISA
Rest (dinner only and Sunday lunch)/dinner 17.95 and a la carte 20.70/28.95 – 7.95 – **15 rm** 69.75 – 79.75.
◆ Imposing redbrick Victorian house with purpose-built extension. Sizeable lounge and bar. Spacious, characterful rooms with chintz décor and fabrics. Carefully tended garden adjoins restaurant.

XXX **Fraiche,** 11 Rosemount, Oxton, CH43 5SG, Southwest : 2 ¼ m. by A 552 and B 5151 ℘ (0151) 652 2914 – . MC VISA
closed Sunday and Monday – **Rest** (booking essential) (dinner only and lunch Friday and Saturday) 32.00/40.00.
◆ Immaculately appointed neighbourhood restaurant, enhanced by vivid pieces of modern glassware. Gourmet and tasting menus a highlight of the inspired, original cooking.

X **Sleep Station** with rm, 24-28 Hamilton St, CH41 1AL, ℘ (0151) 647 1047, *info@sleepstation.co.uk, Fax (0151) 650 1155* – – 40. MC AE VISA AX a
closed 23 December-2 January – **Rest** *(closed Sunday)* 15.00 (dinner) and a la carte 19.95/28.05 – 5.25 – **4 rm** 55.00/70.00 – 75.00/90.00, 1 suite.
◆ Modern restaurant with an appealingly relaxed ambience. Brasserie style menus; try getting a bench seat along the window. Stylish, contemporary bedrooms.

K. Blackwell/MICHELIN

Birmingham, the Bullring

BIRMINGHAM

W. Mids. 503 504 O 26 *Great Britain G. – pop. 970 892.*

London 122 – Bristol 91 – Liverpool 103 – Manchester 86 – Nottingham 50.

TOURIST INFORMATION

The Rotunda, 150 New St ☎ (0121) 202 5099, Fax (0121) 616 1038.
Tourism Centre, National Exhibition Centre ☎ (0121) 202 5099.

PRACTICAL INFORMATION

18 *Edgbaston, Church Road ☎ (0121) 454 1736,* **FX.**
18 *Hilltop, Park Lane, Handsworth ☎ (0121) 554 4463,* **CU.**
18 *Hatchford Brook, Coventry Road, Sheldon ☎ (0121) 743 9821.*
18 *Brandhall, Heron Road, Oldbury, Warley ☎ (0121) 552 7475,* **BU.**
9 *Harborne Church Farm, Vicarage Road, Harborne ☎ (0121) 427 1204,* **EX**
✈ *Birmingham International Airport : ☎ (08707) 335511, E : 6½ m. by A 45* **DU.**

SIGHTS

See : *City★ – Museum and Art Gallery★★* **LY M2** *– Barber Institute of Fine Arts★★ (at Birmingham University)* **EX U** *– Cathedral of St Philip (stained glass portrayals★)* **LMY** *– Thinktank★, Millennium Point* **FV.**

Env. : *Aston Hall★★* **FV M.**

Exc. : *Black Country Museum★, Dudley, NW : 10 m. by A 456 and A 4123* **AU** *– Bournville★, SW : 4 m. on A 38 and A 441.*

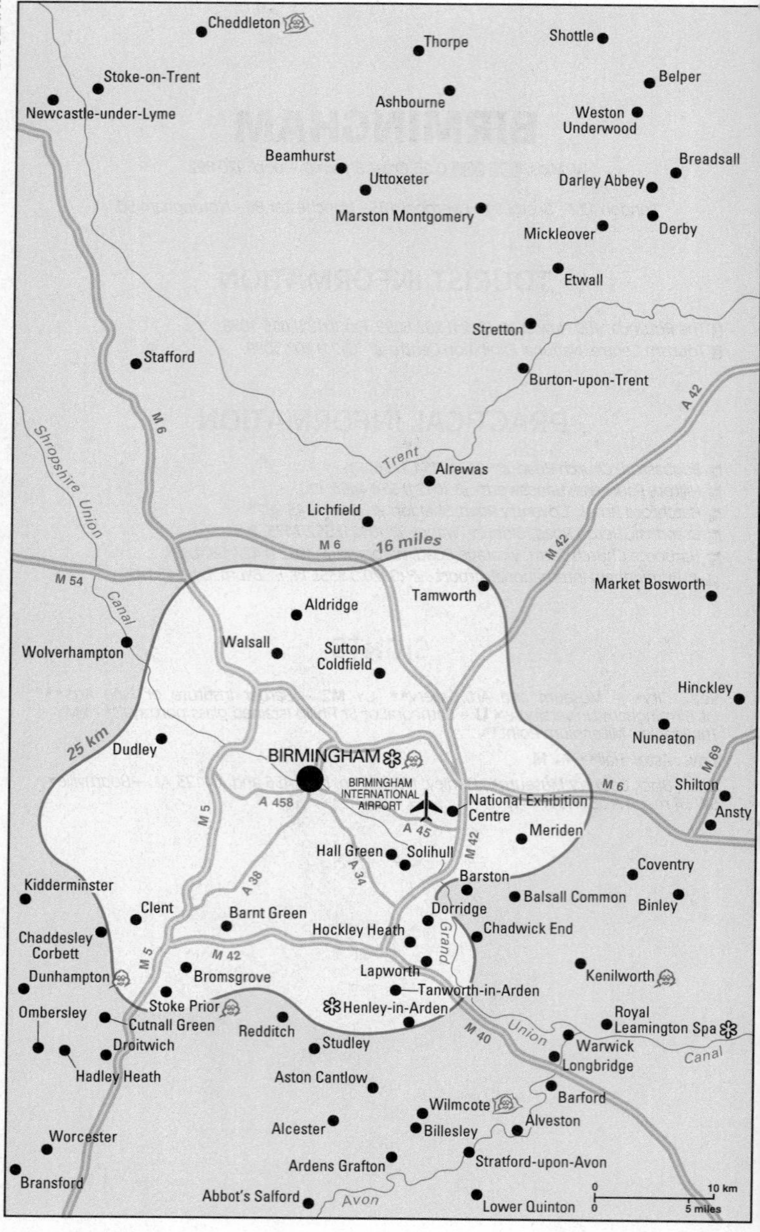
Cheddleton
Thorpe
Shottle
Stoke-on-Trent
Belper
Newcastle-under-Lyme
Ashbourne
Weston Underwood
Beamhurst
Breadsall
Uttoxeter
Darley Abbey
Marston Montgomery
Mickleover
Derby
Etwall
Stretton
Stafford
Burton-upon-Trent
A 42
M 6
Shropshire Union
Trent
Alrewas
Lichfield
M 6
16 miles
M 42
M 54
Canal
Market Bosworth
Tamworth
Aldridge
Wolverhampton
Walsall
Sutton Coldfield
Hinckley
Nuneaton
25 km
Dudley
BIRMINGHAM
M 69
Shilton
M 6
BIRMINGHAM INTERNATIONAL AIRPORT
A 458
National Exhibition Centre
Ansty
M 5
A 45
Meriden
M 42
Hall Green
Solihull
Coventry
A 34
A 38
Barston
Kidderminster
Balsall Common
Binley
Clent
Dorridge
Barnt Green
Chaddesley Corbett
Hockley Heath
Chadwick End
Grand
M 5
M 42
Dunhampton
Lapworth
Kenilworth
Bromsgrove
Tanworth-in-Arden
Stoke Prior
Henley-in-Arden
Ombersley
Royal Leamington Spa
Cutnall Green
Union
Redditch
M 40
Warwick
Droitwich
Studley
Longbridge
Canal
Hadley Heath
Aston Cantlow
Barford
Wilmcote
Alveston
Alcester
Billesley
Worcester
Stratford-upon-Avon
Ardens Grafton
Bransford
0
10 km
Abbot's Salford
Avon
Lower Quinton
0
5 miles

INDEX OF STREET NAMES IN BIRMINGHAM

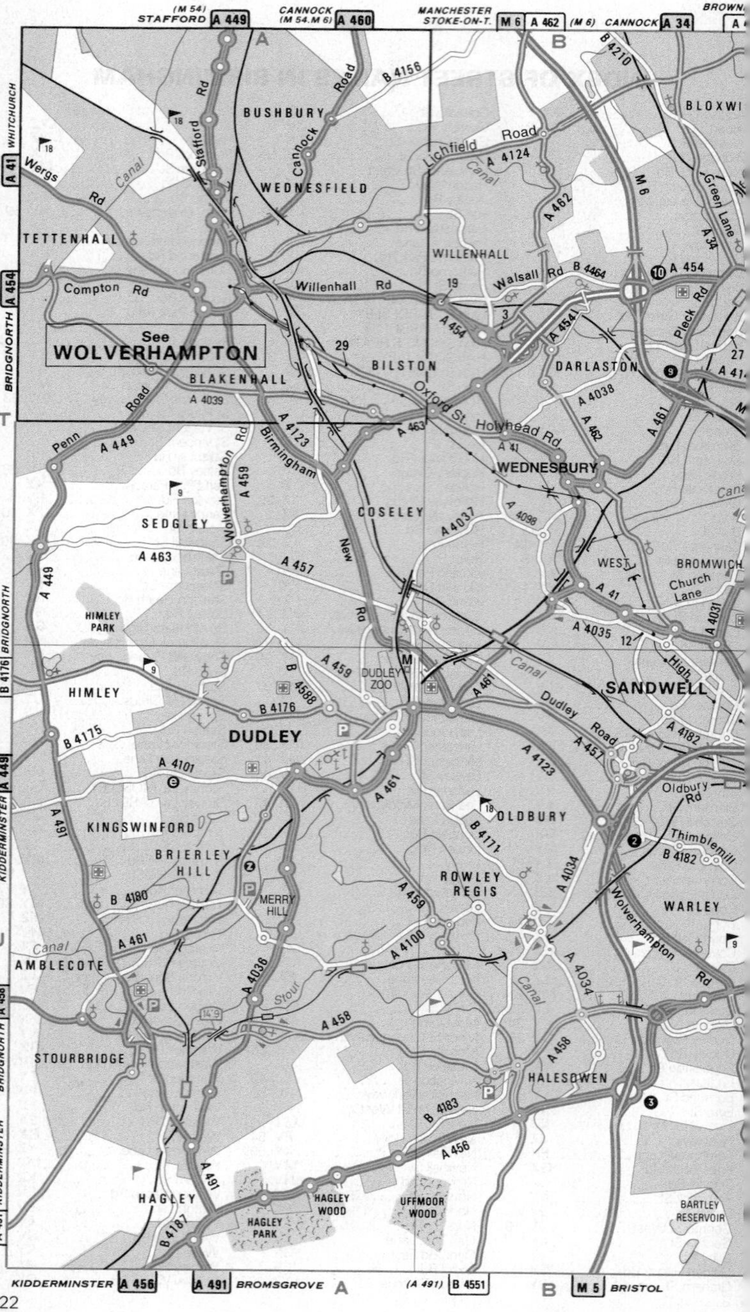
(M 54)
STAFFORD A 449
CANNOCK
(M 54.M 6) A 460
MANCHESTER
STOKE-ON-T. M 6 A 462 (M 6) CANNOCK A 34
A
B
B 4210
B 4156
BLOXWI
BUSHBURY
Stafford Rd
Cannock Road
WEDNESFIELD
Lichfield Road
A 4124
Canal
M 6
Green Lane
A 34
A 462
WHITCHURCH
A 41
Wergs Rd
Canal
TETTENHALL
WILLENHALL
A 454
Compton Rd
Willenhall Rd
19
Walsall Rd B 4464
A 454
BRIDGNORTH
See
WOLVERHAMPTON
29
BILSTON
3
A 454
Pleck Rd
DARLASTON
27
A 41
BLAKENHALL
A 4039
Oxford St.
A 4038
Holyhead Rd
A 462
A 461
T
Road
A 463
A 41
Penn
A 449
Birmingham
A 4123
Wolverhampton Rd
A 459
WEDNESBURY
Canal
SEDGLEY
COSELEY
A 4037
A 4098
A 463
A 457
New Rd
WEST
BROMWICH
Church Lane
A 449
A 41
A 4031
BRIDGNORTH
HIMLEY PARK
A 4035
12
B 4176
HIMLEY
A 459
DUDLEY ZOO
B 4588
Canal
High
SANDWELL
A 461
Dudley Road
B 4176
DUDLEY
A 4182
B 4175
A 457
A 449
A 4101
A 461
A 4123
Oldbury Rd
KIDDERMINSTER
A 491
KINGSWINFORD
OLDBURY
B 4171
Thimblemill
B 4182
BRIERLEY HILL
ROWLEY REGIS
A 4034
MERRY HILL
B 4180
A 459
WARLEY
U
Canal
A 461
A 4100
Wolverhampton Rd
AMBLECOTE
A 4036
Stour
Canal
A 4034
A 458
A 458
BRIDGNORTH
STOURBRIDGE
A 458
HALESOWEN
B 4183
KIDDERMINSTER
A 456
A 491
A 451
HAGLEY
HAGLEY WOOD
UFFMOOR WOOD
BARTLEY RESERVOIR
B 4187
HAGLEY PARK
KIDDERMINSTER A 456 A 491 BROMSGROVE A (A 491) B 4551 B M 5 BRISTOL

BIRMINGHAM AND WOLVERHAMPTON

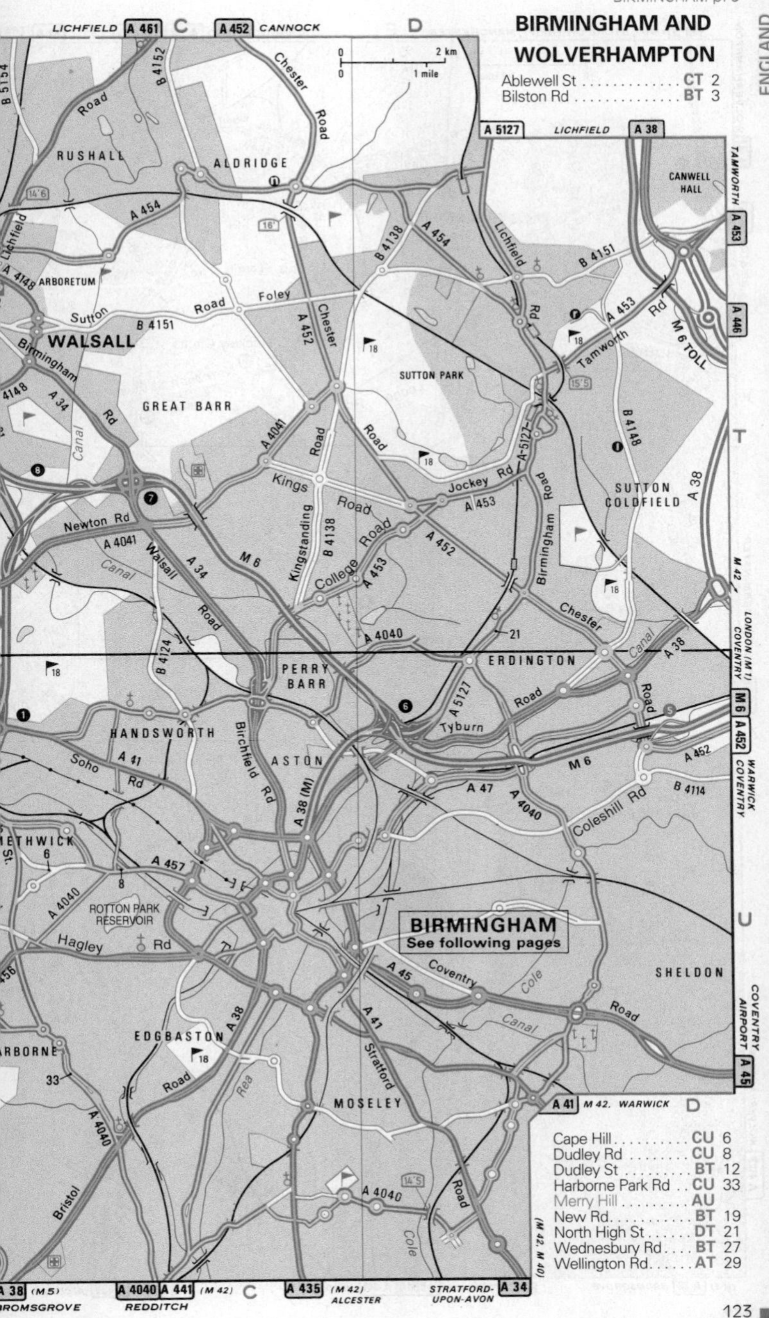

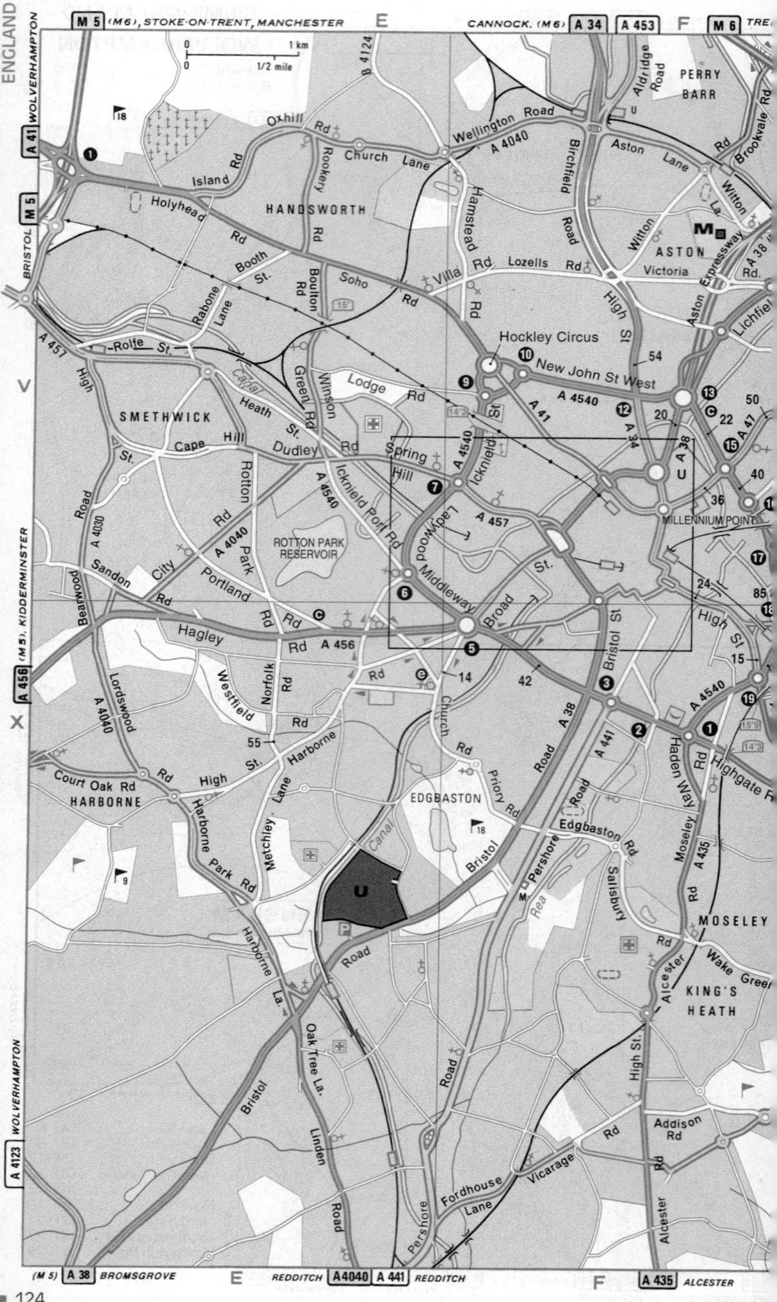

ENGLAND
M 5 (M6), STOKE-ON-TRENT, MANCHESTER
CANNOCK, (M6) A 34 A 453
M 6
WOLVERHAMPTON A 41
BRISTOL M 5
(M5), KIDDERMINSTER A 456
WOLVERHAMPTON A 4123
(M 5) A 38 BROMSGROVE
REDDITCH A4040 A 441 REDDITCH
A 435 ALCESTER
E
F
V
X
PERRY BARR
HANDSWORTH
ASTON
SMETHWICK
HARBORNE
EDGBASTON
MOSELEY
KING'S HEATH
Hockley Circus
MILLENNIUM POINT
ROTTON PARK RESERVOIR
Wellington Road
Aldridge Road
Aston Lane
Brookvale Rd
Witton La
Witton Rd
Oxhill Rd
Rookery Rd
Church Lane
Island Rd
Holyhead Rd
Hamstead Rd
Birchfield Road
Booth St.
Boulton Rd
Soho Rd
Villa Rd
Lozells Rd
Victoria Rd.
Aston Expressway
High St
Lichfield
Rabone Lane
Rolfe St.
New John St West
A 4540
A 41
A 34
A 38
A 47
Heath St.
Winson Green Rd
Lodge Rd
Dudley Rd
Cape Hill
Spring Hill
Icknield St
Icknield Port Rd
Ladywood Middleway
A 457
Broad St.
Bristol St
Rotton Park
City Rd
A 4040
Sandon Rd
Portland Rd
Bearwood Road
A 4030
High St
Hagley Rd
A 456
Norfolk Rd
Westfield Rd
Lordswood Rd
Church Rd
Harborne Rd
High St.
Court Oak Rd
Harborne Park Rd
Metchley Lane
Canal
Priory Rd
Bristol Road
Pershore Road
Edgbaston Rd
Salisbury Rd
Haden Way
Highgate Rd
Moseley Rd
A 435
A 441
A 4540
Wake Green Rd
Alcester Rd
High St.
Addison Rd
Vicarage Rd
Fordhouse Lane
Pershore Road
Harborne La.
Oak Tree La.
Linden Road
Bristol Road
Alcester Road
Road
Rea
B 4124
0 1 km
0 1/2 mile

BIRMINGHAM

Calthorpe Rd . . . . . FX 14
Camp Hill . . . . FX 15
Corporation St . . . . FV 20
Darmouth Middleway . . . . . FV 22
Digbeth . . . . FV 24
Dudley Park Rd . . . GX 25
High St SALTLEY . GV 31
Jennen's Rd . . . . . . FV 36
Lawley St. . . . . FV 40
Lee Bank Middleway . . . . . FX 42
Nechell's Parkway . FV 50
New Town Row . . . . FV 54
Nursery Rd . . . . EX 55
Saltley Rd . . . . GV 66
Sandy Lane . . . . . . FX 10
Solihull Lane . . . . . GX 74
Watery Lane . . . . . FV 85
Westley Rd . . . . . . GX 87

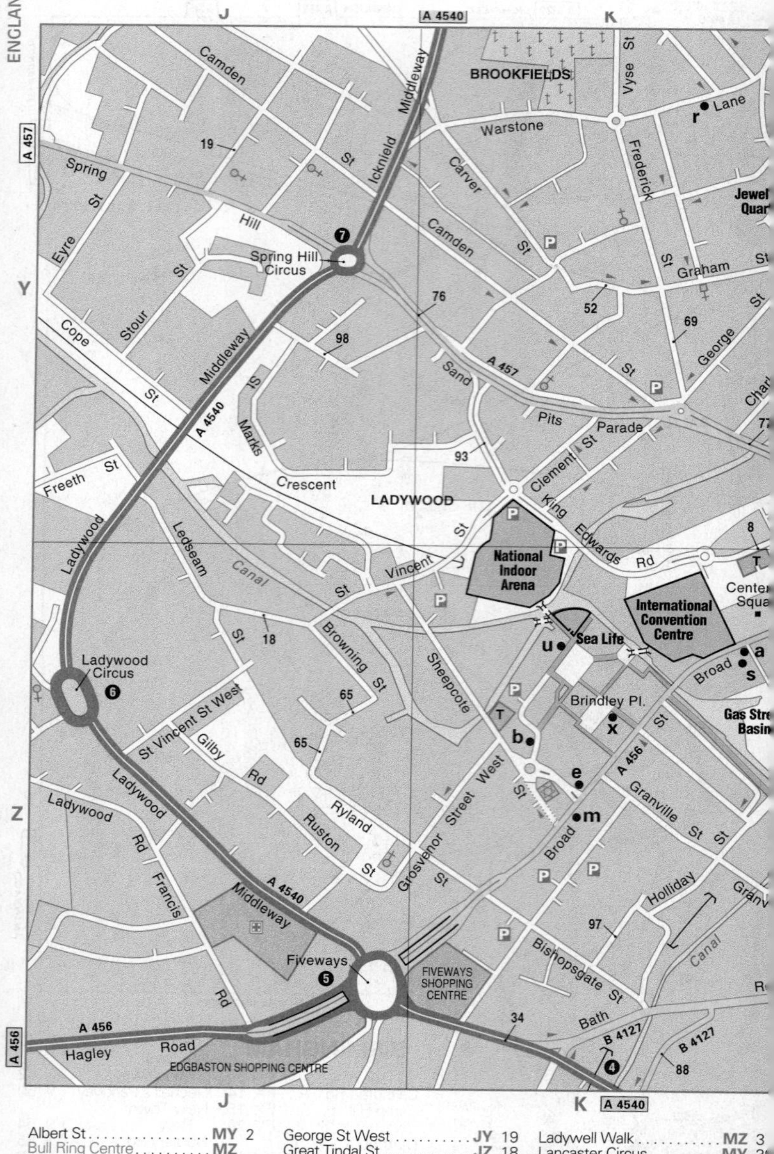
J
A 4540
K
A 457
BROOKFIELDS
Vyse St
Lane
Camden
Middleway
Icknield
Warstone
Frederick
19
Spring
St
Hill
Carver
Camden
St
Jewel
Quar
Eyre
St
Spring Hill
Circus
Graham
St
Y
Stour
76
52
69
George
Cope
98
Sand
A 457
St
Middleway
St
Pits
Parade
Char
77
A 4540
Marks
93
Clement
St
Freeth
St
Crescent
LADYWOOD
King
Edwards
Rd
8
T
Ladywood
Ledsam
Canal
St
National
Indoor
Arena
Center
Squa
Vincent
St
International
Convention
Centre
St
18
Browning
Sea Life
Ladywood
Circus
Sheepcote
St
Broad
65
Brindley Pl.
Gas Stre
Basin
St Vincent St West
Gilby
65
St
A 456
Rd
West
Ladywood
St
Granville
Z
Ladywood
Ryland
Street
St
St
Rd
Ruston
Broad
Francis
Grosvenor
St
Holliday
Granv
A 4540
Middleway
St
97
Fiveways
FIVEWAYS
SHOPPING
CENTRE
Bishopsgate St
Canal
Rd
34
Bath
A 456
B 4127
B 4127
A 456
Hagley
Road
EDGBASTON SHOPPING CENTRE
88
J
K
A 4540

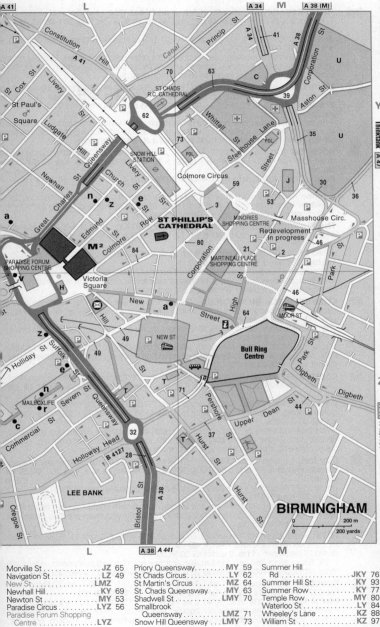

BIRMINGHAM

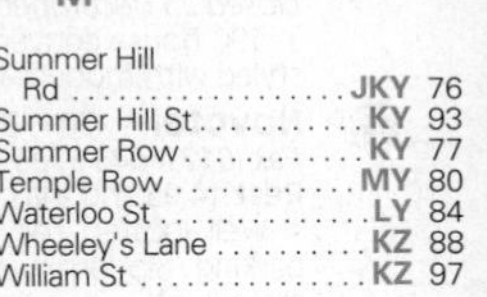

ENGLAND

Town plans: Birmingham pp. 3-9

Hyatt Regency, 2 Bridge St, B1 2JZ, ☎ (0121) 643 1234, *birmingham@hyattintl.com, Fax (0121) 616 2323,* ≤, Ⓢ, Ⓛ, ≘s, ▣ - |♦|, ✗ rm, ▤ ✆ ♿ ⇔ - 🔔 200. MC AE ◐ VISA. ✗ KZ a

Aria : Rest 16.75 and a la carte 28.50/33.50 ♀ - ☐ 15.25 - **315 rm** ♦99.00/169.00 - ♦♦99.00/169.00, 4 suites.

• Striking mirrored exterior. Glass enclosed lifts offer panoramic views. Sizeable rooms with floor to ceiling windows. Covered link with International Convention Centre. Contemporary style restaurant in central atrium; modish cooking.

Malmaison, Mailbox, 1 Wharfside St, B1 1RD, ☎ (0121) 246 5000, *birmingham@malmaison.com, Fax (0121) 246 5002,* Ⓛ, ≘s - |♦| ✗ ▤ ✆ ♿ - 🔔 45. MC AE ◐ VISA. ✗ LZ e

Brasserie : Rest a la carte 21.90/36.75 ♀ - ☐ 13.50 - **184 rm** ♦140.00 - ♦♦140.00, 5 suites.

• Stylish, modern boutique hotel, forms centrepiece of Mailbox development. Stylish bar. Spacious contemporary bedrooms with every modern facility; superb petit spa. Brasserie serving contemporary French influenced cooking at reasonable prices.

Hotel Du Vin, 25 Church St, B3 2NR, ☎ (0121) 200 0600, *info@birmingham.hotelduvin.com, Fax (0121) 236 0889,* ☂, Ⓛ, ≘s - |♦|, ✗ rest, ▤ rm, ✆ ♿ - 🔔 85. MC AE ◐ VISA. ✗ LY e

Bistro : Rest 14.50 (lunch) and a la carte 30.50/33.70 ❀ - ☐ 14.50 - **66 rm** ♦130.00 - ♦♦130.00.

• Former 19C eye hospital in heart of shopping centre; has relaxed, individual, boutique style. Low lighting in rooms of muted tones: Egyptian cotton and superb bathrooms. Champagne in "bubble lounge"; Parisian style brasserie.

The Burlington, Burlington Arcade, 126 New St, B2 4JQ, ☎ (0121) 643 9191, *mail@burlingtonhotel.com, Fax (0121) 643 5075,* Ⓛ, ≘s - |♦| ✗ ▤ ✆ ♿ - 🔔 400. MC AE ◐ VISA LZ a

closed 25-26 December - ***Berlioz :*** Rest 22.95 and a la carte 25.00/35.00 - ☐ 14.95 - **110 rm** ♦155.00 - ♦♦155.00, 2 suites.

• Approached by a period arcade. Restored Victorian former railway hotel retains much of its original charm. Period décor to bedrooms yet with fax, modem and voice mail. Elegant dining room: ornate ceiling, chandeliers and vast mirrors.

Crowne Plaza Birmingham, Central Sq, B1 1HH, ☎ (0870) 4009150, *reservations.bhamcity@ichotelsgroup.com, Fax (0121) 643 9018,* Ⓛ, ≘s, ▣ - |♦|, ✗ rm, ▤ ✆ ♿ ⇔ - 🔔 150. MC AE ◐ VISA LZ z

The Conservatory : Rest 15.95/18.95 and a la carte 21.95/29.95 **s.** ♀ - **281 rm** ☐ ♦159.00/179.00 - ♦♦179.00/189.00, 3 suites.

• Ideal for both corporate and leisure guests. Extensive leisure facilities include children's pool. Well-equipped bedrooms with air-conditioning and triple glazing. Conservatory restaurant with views across city.

Copthorne, Paradise Circus, B3 3HJ, ☎ (0121) 200 2727, *reservations.birmingham@millcop.com, Fax (0121) 200 1197,* Ⓛ, ≘s - |♦| ✗, ▤ rest, ♿ Ⓟ - 🔔 250. MC AE ◐ VISA. ✗ LZ v

Goldsmiths : Rest *(closed Sunday)* (dinner only) 25.00/35.00 and a la carte 26.00/36.00 ♀ - ***Goldies :*** Rest 10.95/18.95 and a la carte 20.95/33.95 ♀ - ☐ 15.75 - **209 rm** ♦165.00 - ♦♦185.00, 3 suites.

• Overlooking Centenary Square. Corporate hotel with extensive leisure club and cardiovascular gym. Cricket themed bar. Connoisseur rooms offer additional comforts. Flambé dishes offered in intimate Goldsmiths. Goldies is all-day relaxed brasserie.

City Inn, 1 Brunswick Sq, Brindley Pl, B1 2HW, ☎ (0121) 643 1003, *birmingham.reservations@cityinn.com, Fax (0121) 643 1005,* ☂, Ⓛ - |♦|, ✗ rm, ▤ ✆ ♿ - 🔔 100. MC AE ◐ VISA. ✗ KZ b

closed 26-28 December - ***City Café :*** Rest 12.50/16.50 and a la carte 18.95/31.45 **s.** ♀ - ☐ 10.50 - **238 rm** ♦149.00 - ♦♦149.00.

• In heart of vibrant Brindley Place; the spacious atrium with bright rugs and blond wood sets the tone for equally stylish rooms. Corporate friendly with many meeting rooms. Eat in restaurant, terrace or bar.

TOTEL without rest., 19 Portland Rd, Edgbaston, B16 9HN, ☎ (0121) 454 5282, *info@toteluk.com, Fax (0121) 456 4668* - ✗ Ⓟ. MC ◐ VISA EX c

closed 25 December - **1 rm, 9 suites** 65.00/95.00.

• 19C house converted into comfortable, spacious fully-serviced apartments, individually styled with modern facilities. Friendly service. Continental breakfast served in room.

Novotel, 70 Broad St, B1 2HT, ☎ (0121) 643 2000, *h1077@accor.com, Fax (0121) 643 9796,* Ⓛ, ≘s - |♦| ✗ ✆ ♿ ⇔ - 🔔 300. MC AE ◐ VISA KZ e

Rest 14.95 and a la carte 16.60/24.40 **s.** ♀ - **148 rm** ☐ ♦158.00/165.00 - ♦♦165.00.

• Well located for the increasingly popular Brindleyplace development. Underground parking. Modern, well-kept, branded bedrooms suitable for families. Modern, open-plan restaurant.

Express by Holiday Inn without rest., 65 Lionel St, B3 1JE, (0121) 200 1900, *ebhi-bhamcity@btconnect.com, Fax (0121) 200 1910* – 30. VISA. LY a
120 rm 55.00/95.00 – 55.00/95.00.
◆ Well-kept, well-managed hotel situated in a handy location for visitors to the city centre. Tidy, comfortable accommodation to suit tourists or business travellers alike.

Premier Travel Inn, Richard St, Aston, B7 4AA, (0870) 2383312, *Fax (0121) 333 6490* – rm, rest, VISA. FV c
Rest (grill rest.) (dinner only) – **60 rm** 49.95/49.95 – 52.95/52.95.
◆ Between M6 motorway and city centre; this modern and well kept lodge offers family rooms at no extra charge. Close to both Aston Villa and Birmingham City football grounds.

Simpsons (Antona) with rm, 20 Highfield Rd, Edgbaston, B15 3DU, (0121) 454 3434, *info@simpsonsrestaurant.co.uk, Fax (0121) 454 3399*, , – , rest, 18. VISA EX e
closed 27-28 August and 25-26 December – **Rest** 20.00/30.00 and a la carte 38.20/53.70 – **4 rm** 140.00 – 190.00.
Spec. Torte of smoked salmon, crab and creamed guacamole. Fillet of Aberdeenshire beef cooked on the bone, red wine shallot sauce. Black forest cake, cherry sorbet.
◆ Restored Georgian residence; its interior a careful blend of Victorian features and contemporary style. Refined, classically based cooking. Elegant bedrooms.

Jessica's (Purnell), 1 Montague Rd, B15 9HN, (0121) 455 0999, *Fax (0121) 455 8222* – . VISA EX c
closed last 2 weeks July, 1 week Easter, 24 December-2 January, Saturday lunch, Sunday and Monday – **Rest** 23.50/32.95.
Spec. Salted Cornish cod with smoked black olives and frozen passion fruit. Gressingham duck in two ways. Chocolate soufflé with compote of strawberry.
◆ Georgian 'outbuilding' and conservatory offering excellently presented, highly original French influenced modern British cooking sourced from quality Midland suppliers.

Paris, 109-111 Wharfside St, The Mailbox, B1 1RF, (0121) 632 1488, *paris.restaurant@virgin.net, Fax (0121) 632 1489* – 12. VISA LZ n
closed Sunday and Monday – **Rest** 21.50 (lunch) and a la carte 40.00/52.50.
◆ Located in fashionable Mailbox area and painted in a deep chocolate brown palette with stylish tan leather chairs. Fine dining, with chef's gourmand menu also available.

Opus, 54 Cornwall St, B3 2DE, (0121) 200 2323, *restaurant@opusrestaurant.co.uk, Fax (0121) 200 2090* – 64. VISA LY z
closed last week July, first week August, 1 week Christmas, Sunday, Saturday lunch and Bank Holidays – **Rest** 15.00/17.50 (lunch) and a la carte 24.50/34.75.
◆ Restaurant of floor-to-ceiling glass in evolving area of city. Seafood and shellfish bar for diners on the move. Assured cooking underpins modern menus with traditional base.

Lasan, 3-4 Dakota Buildings, James St, B3 1SD, (0121) 212 3664, *info@lasan.co.uk, Fax (0121) 212 3665* – . VISA KY a
closed 25-26 December and Sunday – **Rest** - Indian - (dinner only) a la carte 14.20/19.45 s..
◆ Jewellery quarter restaurant of sophistication and style; good quality ingredients allow the clarity of the spices to shine through in this well-run Indian establishment.

Bank, 4 Brindleyplace, B1 2JB, (0121) 633 4466, *birmres@bankrestaurants.com, Fax (0121) 633 4465*, – 100. VISA KZ u
closed 1-2 January, August Bank Holiday and dinner Bank Holiday Mondays – **Rest** 15.00 (lunch) and a la carte 29.70/48.00.
◆ Capacious, modern and busy bar-restaurant where chefs can be watched through a glass wall preparing the tasty modern dishes. Pleasant terrace area.

La Toque D'Or, 27 Warstone Lane, Hockley, B18 6JQ, (0121) 233 3655, *didier@latoquedor.co.uk, Fax (0121) 233 3655* – VISA KY r
closed Easter, 2 weeks August, 1 week Christmas, Sunday, Monday and Saturday lunch – **Rest** - French - (booking essential) 19.50/24.50 **s.**
◆ A different type of gem in the Jewellery Quarter. Personally run former rolling mill: bare brick and stained glass. Well-judged seasonal menu bears classic French hallmarks.

Metro Bar and Grill, 73 Cornwall St, B3 2DF, (0121) 200 1911, *Fax (0121) 200 1611* – . VISA LY n
closed 25 December-1 January, Sunday and Bank Holidays – **Rest** (booking essential) a la carte 21.15/28.85.
◆ Gleaming chrome and mirrors in a bright, contemporary basement restaurant. Modern cooking with rotisserie specialities. Spacious, ever-lively bar serves lighter meals.

Shimla Pinks, 214 Broad St, B15 1AY, (0121) 633 0366, *info@shimlapinks.com, Fax (0121) 643 3325* – . VISA KZ m
closed lunch Saturday and Sunday – **Rest** - Indian - a la carte 17.40/28.40.
◆ A vast establishment in a street full of restaurants. Buzzy ambience prevails: open-plan kitchen adds to atmosphere. Authentic, modern Indian cuisine; impressive set menus.

ENGLAND

XX **Zinc Bar and Grill,** Regency Wharf, Broad St, B1 2DS, ✆ (0121) 200 0620, *zinc-birmingham@conran-restaurants.co.uk, Fax (0121) 200 0630,* – ⊞ ⇔ 40. MO AE ① VISA KZ
closed 25-26 December and Sunday dinner – **Rest** a la carte 17.00/31.50 ♀.
◆ Purpose-built restaurant in lively pub and club area of city. Spiral staircase leads to dining area, including terrace overlooking canal. Modern, classically toned, dishes.

X **Le Petit Blanc,** 9 Brindley Place, B1 2HS, ✆ (0121) 633 7333, *birmingham@lepetitblanc.co.uk, Fax (0121) 633 7444,* – ⊞. MO AE VISA KZ
Rest 14.50 (lunch) and a la carte 21.25/29.40 ♀.
◆ Outside, a central square and offices. Within, an atmospheric brasserie in relaxed, contemporary environment serving predominantly French classics. Special menu for children.

X **Fino,** 120-122 Wharfside St, The Mailbox, B1 1RQ, ✆ (0121) 632 1232, *finobar@fsmail.net, Fax (0121) 632 1231,* – ⊞. MO AE VISA LZ
Rest - Italian - a la carte 18.50/28.50 ♀.
◆ Located in trendy Mailbox area, this informal bar eatery is perched by the side of the renovated canal. A distinct Italian influence provides the base for the large menus.

X **Cafe Lazeez,** 116 Wharfside St, The Mailbox, B1 1RF, ✆ (0121) 643 7979, *birmingham@cafelazeez.com, Fax (0121) 643 4546,* – ⊞. MO AE ① VISA LZ
closed 25 December – **Rest** - Indian - a la carte 17.85/23.40 ♀.
◆ Located in fashionable Mailbox. Large, open plan establishment, kitchen included. Polite friendly service. Authentic accurate Indian cooking with quality ingredients.

at Hall Green *Southeast : 5¾ m. by A 41 on A 34 – ✉ Birmingham.*

XX **Liaison,** 1558 Stratford Rd, B28 9HA, ✆ (0121) 733 7336, *Fax (0121) 733 1677* – . MO ① VISA GX
closed 2 weeks Christmas-New Year, 1 week September, Sunday and Monday – **Rest** 16.95/28.95 ♀.
◆ Pleasant restaurant with understated décor in residential location. Linen table cloths and friendly service. Classically based modern eclectic cooking.

at Birmingham Airport *Southeast : 9 m. by A 45 – DU – ✉ Birmingham.*

Novotel Birmingham Airport, Passenger Terminal, B26 3QL, ✆ (0121) 782 7000 *h1158@accor.com, Fax (0121) 782 0445* – |≡| – 35. MO AE ① VISA
Rest (bar lunch Saturday, Sunday and Bank Holidays) 16.95/22.95 and a la carte 17.00/29.15 **s.** ♀ – ☕ 12.95 – **195 rm** ★125.00 – ★★125.00.
◆ Opposite main terminal building: modern hotel benefits from sound proofed doors and double glazing. Mini bars and power showers provided in spacious rooms with sofa beds. Open-plan garden brasserie.

at National Exhibition Centre *Southeast : 9½ m. on A 45 – DU – ✉ Birmingham.*

Crowne Plaza, Pendigo Way, B40 1PS, ✆ (0870) 400 9160, *necroomsales@ichotelsgroup.com, Fax (0121) 781 4321,* – |≡| ⊞ [P] – 200. MO AE ① VISA.
Rest *(closed Saturday lunch)* a la carte 20.50/35.95 – ☕ 15.95 – **242 rm** ★89.00 – ★★89.00.
◆ Modern hotel adjacent to NEC. Small terrace area overlooks lake. Extensive conference facilities. State-of-the-art bedrooms with a host of extras. Basement dining room: food with a Yorkshire twist.

Express by Holiday Inn without rest., Bickenhill Parkway, Bickenhill, B40 1QA, ✆ (0121) 782 3222, *exhi-nec@foremosthotels.co.uk, Fax (0121) 780 4224* – |≡| [P] – 100. MO AE ① VISA
179 rm ★115.00 – ★★115.00.
◆ Handy for the NEC and airport. Modern budget hotel ideal for the corporate traveller. Extensive cold buffet breakfast included.

BIRMINGHAM AIRPORT *W. Mids.* 503 504 O 26 – *see Birmingham.*

BISHOP'S STORTFORD *Herts.* 504 U 28 *Great Britain G. – pop. 35 325.*

Env. : *Audley End★★ AC, N : 11 m. by B 1383.*

✈ *Stansted Airport : ✆ (0870) 0000303, NE : 3½ m.*

🅸 *The Old Monastery, Windhill ✆ (01279) 655831, tic@bishopsstortford.org.*

London 34 – Cambridge 27 – Chelmsford 19 – Colchester 33.

The Cottage without rest., 71 Birchanger Lane, CM23 5QA, Northeast : 2 ¼ m. by B 1383 on Birchanger rd ✆ (01279) 812349, *bookings@thecottagebirchanger.co.uk, Fax (01279) 815045,* – [P]. MO AE ① VISA.
closed Christmas and New Year – **14 rm** ☕ ★50.00/60.00 – ★★80.00.
◆ Part 17C and 18C cottages in 2-acre garden. Conservatory breakfast room and comfortable panelled lounge. Bedrooms are simple but pristine and spacious. Convenient for airport.

The Lemon Tree, 14-16 Water Lane, CM23 2LB, (01279) 757788, *mail@lemontree.co.uk, Fax (01279) 757766* – . VISA
closed 25-26 December, 1 January, Sunday dinner and Monday – **Rest** 18.00 and dinner a la carte 23.75/32.75.
◆ Indebted to the London scene in concept and cooking. A bright, informal, smartly run restaurant; its Mediterranean accented dishes are satisfying and modestly priced.

Host, 4 The Corn Exchange, Market Sq, CM23 3UU, (01279) 657000, *Fax (01279) 655566,* – . AE VISA
closed Sunday dinner – **Rest** 15.00 and a la carte 16.50/28.50.
◆ Grade I listed building, situated in former Corn Exchange. Airy, modern restaurant with unique rooftop terrace and relaxed atmosphere. Eclectic, well priced brasserie menus.

at Stansted Mountfitchet *Northeast : 3½ m. by B 1383 on B 1051 – Bishop's Stortford.*

Chimneys without rest., 44 Lower St, CM24 8LR, on B 1351 (01279) 813388, *info@chimneysguesthouse.co.uk* – P. VISA
4 rm ★47.00/55.00 – ★★72.00.
◆ 17C Grade II listed house boasts immaculate interior: lounge with log fire, cloth-clad breakfast room with fresh flowers. Personally decorated, thoughtfully designed bedrooms.

at Hatfield Heath *(Essex) Southeast : 6 m. on A 1060 – Bishop's Stortford.*

Down Hall Country House, CM22 7AS, South : 1 ½ m. by Matching Lane (01279) 731441, *reservations@downhall.co.uk, Fax (01279) 730416,* – , rest, P – 200. AE VISA
Ibbetsons : **Rest** *(closed Sunday, Monday and Saturday lunch)* a la carte 33.00/42.00 –
Downham : **Rest** (booking essential to non-residents) 24.50 – **100 rm** ★120.00/140.00 – ★★160.00.
◆ In expansively landscaped grounds, a 19C Italianate mansion touching on the palatial. Period-style bedrooms in mahogany, brass and swagged fabrics, half in the new wing. Ibbetsons exudes contemporary elegance. Downham has light, formal feel.

BISHOP'S TAWTON *Devon* 503 H 30 – *see Barnstaple.*

BLABY *Leics.* 502 503 504 Q 26 – *see Leicester.*

BLACKBURN *Blackburn* 502 M 22 – *pop. 105 085.*

18 Pleasington (01254) 202177 – 18 Wilpshire, 72 Whalley Rd (01254) 248260 – 9 Great Harwood, Harwood Bar (01254) 884391.
ASKUS, 15-17 Railway Rd, Blackburn, BB1 5AX (01254) 53277, askus@blackburn.gov.uk.
London 228 – Leeds 47 – Liverpool 39 – Manchester 24 – Preston 11.

at Langho *North : 4½ m. on A 666 – Whalley.*

The Avenue, Brockhall Village, Old Lango, BB6 8AY, North : 1 ¼ m. by A 666 and A 59 on Northcote rd (01254) 244811, *bookingenquiries@theavenuehotel.co.uk, Fax (01254) 244812* – rm, rest, P – 40. AE VISA.
closed 25-26 December – **Rest** *(closed Sunday)* (bar lunch)/dinner a la carte 15.00/22.50 – 10.95 – **19 rm** ★40.00 – ★★55.00, 2 suites.
◆ Modern hotel located within a new village near old Langho, and ideal for football fans as it overlooks Blackburn Rovers' training ground. Stylish, contemporary bedrooms. Modern, informal café/bar style restaurant.

Northcote Manor (Haworth) with rm, Northcote Rd, BB6 8BE, North : ½ m. on A 59 at junction with A 666 (01254) 240555, *sales@northcotemanor.com, Fax (01254) 246568,* – rest, P 26 – 40. AE VISA.
closed 25 December and 1 January – **Rest** *(closed Bank Holiday Mondays)* 20.00 (lunch) and a la carte 36.90/49.90 – **14 rm** ★110.00/145.00 – ★★140.00/175.00.
Spec. Black pudding and trout with mustard and nettle sauce. Roe deer with shiitake mushrooms, pastry leaves, spinach and redcurrants. Queen of puddings soufflé, lemon and crème fraîche ice cream.
◆ Elegant dining room within substantial 19C house. Renowned and accomplished cuisine with Lancastrian dishes a proven speciality. Individually furnished bedrooms.

at Mellor *Northwest : 3¼ m. by A 677 – Blackburn.*

Stanley House, BB2 7NP, Southwest : ¾ m. by A 677 and Further Lane (01254) 769200, *info@stanleyhouse.co.uk, Fax (01254) 769206,* – P – 250. AE VISA.
Rest – (see ***Cassis*** below) – **12 rm** ★145.00 – ★★195.00.
◆ 17C manor with superb rural views. Relaxing, tastefully toned bar. Strong emphasis on conference facilities. Elegantly proportioned rooms defined by wonderfully rich colours.

ENGLAND

Millstone, Church Lane, BB2 7JR, ✆ (01254) 813333, *info@millstonehotel.co.u* *Fax (01254) 812628* – ⇎ ✆ P – 25. MC AE D VISA. ✗
***Millers*: Rest** 25.95 and a la carte 25.00/31.40 s. ♀ – **22 rm** ☕ ★105.00 – ★★140.00.
◆ Attractive little sandstone former coaching inn in quiet village. Lounge bar with log fir and comfy sofas. Cosy bedrooms: matching floral patterns, botanical prints. Elegant woo panelled dining room warmed by fire.

XXX **Cassis** (at Stanley House), BB2 7NP, Southwest : ¾ m. by A 677 and Further Lan ✆ (01254) 769220, *Fax (01254) 769206* – ⇎ ▤ P. MC AE D VISA
closed lunch Monday, Tuesday and Saturday – **Rest** 22.00 (lunch) and a la cart 32.75/42.95 ♀.
◆ Independent from main hotel. Name derives from rich blackcurrant theme throughout Vast raised mezzanine for apéritifs. Weekly evolving menus with vibrant Lancashire accent

BLACKMORE *Essex.*

London 26 – Brentwood 7 – Chelmsford 8.

Leather Bottle, The Green, CM4 0RL, ✆ (01277) 823538, *leatherbottle@tiscali.co.uk* – P. MC VISA
closed 26 December, 1 January and Sunday dinner – **Rest** a la carte 17.50/30.00.
◆ Characterful black-and-white pub on the green. Real fire in a wood burner; conservatory room and paved terrace. Satisfying modern menus with an evolving, eclectic influence.

BLACKPOOL *Blackpool 502 K 22 Great Britain G.* – *pop. 142 283.*

See : *Tower*★ *AC* AY **A.**

18 Blackpool Park, North Park Drive ✆ *(01253) 397910* **BY** – *9 Poulton-le-Fylde, Myrtle Farm, Breck Rd* ✆ *(01253) 892444.*

Blackpool Airport : ✆ *(08700) 273777, S : 3 m. by A 584.*

1 Clifton St ✆ *(01253) 478222 – Pleasure Beach, Unit 25, Ocean Boulevard, South Promenade* ✆ *(01253) 403223.*

London 246 – Leeds 88 – Liverpool 56 – Manchester 51 – Middlesbrough 123.

Plan opposite

Imperial, North Promenade, FY1 2HB, ✆ (01253) 623971, *imperialblackpool@paramount-hotels.co.uk, Fax (01253) 751784,* ←, Ls, ≘s, ☐ – ⧉ ⇎ ✆ P – 500. MC AE D VISA AY c
***Palm Court*: Rest** (carvery lunch)/dinner a la carte 27.15/43.15 ♀ – ☕ 12.95 – **173 rm** ☕ ★70.00/180.00 – ★★90.00/190.00, 7 suites.
◆ Imposing, classic 19C promenade hotel. Grand columned lobby, well-appointed rooms, many with views. Photos in the convivial No.10 bar recall PMs and past party conferences. Elegant restaurant with smartly liveried staff.

Hilton Blackpool, North Promenade, FY1 2JQ, ✆ (01253) 623434, *reservations.blackpool@hilton.com, Fax (01253) 294371,* ←, Ls, ≘s, ☐ – ⧉ ⇎, ▤ rest, ♿ P – 700. MC AE D VISA. ✗ AY x
***The Promenade*: Rest** (bar lunch Monday-Saturday)/dinner 21.95/30.95 and a la carte 17.70/29.45 s. ♀ – ☕ 14.50 – **268 rm** ★90.00/252.00 – ★★115.00/262.00, 6 suites.
◆ Open-plan, marble-floored lobby and smartly equipped rooms in contemporary style, almost all with views over the sea-front. Cabaret shows on most Fridays and Saturdays. Informal dining after cocktail lounge aperitifs.

De Vere Herons' Reach, East Park Drive, FY3 8LL, ✆ (01253) 838866, *Fax (01253) 798800,* Ls, ≘s, ☐, 18, squash – ⧉ ⇎, ▤ rest, ♿ P – 600. MC AE VISA. ✗ BZ a
***Brasserie*: Rest** (bar lunch Monday-Saturday)/dinner 24.50 and a la carte approx 29.00/35.00 s. ♀ – **170 rm** ☕ ★80.00/110.00 – ★★120.00/140.00, 2 suites.
◆ Purpose-built hotel: state-of-the-art leisure club and floodlit driving range. Comfortable, well-equipped bedrooms; some, like the clubby bar, overlook the golf course. Extensive modern restaurant.

Premier Travel Inn, Whitehills Park, Preston New Rd, FY4 5NZ, Southeast : 4 m. on A 583 ✆ (0870) 7001514, *Fax (0870) 7001515* – ⧉, ⇎ rm, ▤ rest, ♿ P. MC AE D VISA. ✗
Rest (grill rest.) – **81 rm** ★49.95/49.95 – ★★52.95/52.95.
◆ Situated just off junction 4 of the M55, not far from the pleasure beach and the city centre. Well-equipped bedrooms decorated in a contemporary style. Restaurant has a 10ft waterfall, water wheel and cobbled floor.

Premier Travel Inn, Yeadon Way, South Shore, FY1 6BF, ✆ (01253) 341415, *Fax (01253) 343805* – ⇎ rm, ▤ rest, ♿ P – 40. MC AE D VISA. ✗ AZ e
Rest (grill rest.) – **79 rm** ★52.95 – ★★52.95.
◆ Simply furnished and brightly decorated bedrooms in a purpose-built lodge, ideal for short breaks and within walking distance of the Pleasure Beach and South Shore.

BLACKPOOL

Street	Grid	No.
Abingdon St	AY	2
Adelaide St	AY	3
Ansdell Rd	BZ	4
Blackpool Old Rd	BY	5
Burlington Rd West	AZ	6
Caunce St	AY	7
Central Drive	BZ	8
Cherry Tree Rd	BZ	9
Church St	AY	
Clifton St	AY	12
Condor Grove	BZ	13
Cookson St	AY	14
Deansgate	AY	15
Garstang Rd West	BY	16
George St	AY	17
Grange Rd	BY	19
Grasmere Rd	BZ	20
Grosvenor St	AY	21
High St	AY	22
Hornby Rd	BY	
Hounds Hill Centre	AY	
King St	AY	23
Lark Hill St	AY	24
New Bonny St	AY	25
North Park Drive	BY	26
Pleasant St	AY	27
Plymouth Rd	BY	28
Poulton Rd	BY	29
Queen's Promenade	BY	
Reads Ave	BZ	32
Rigby Rd	BZ	33
Seaside Way	BZ	34
South King St	AY	35
South Park Drive	BZ	36
Talbot Square	AY	39
Topping St	AY	40
Westcliffe Drive	BY	41

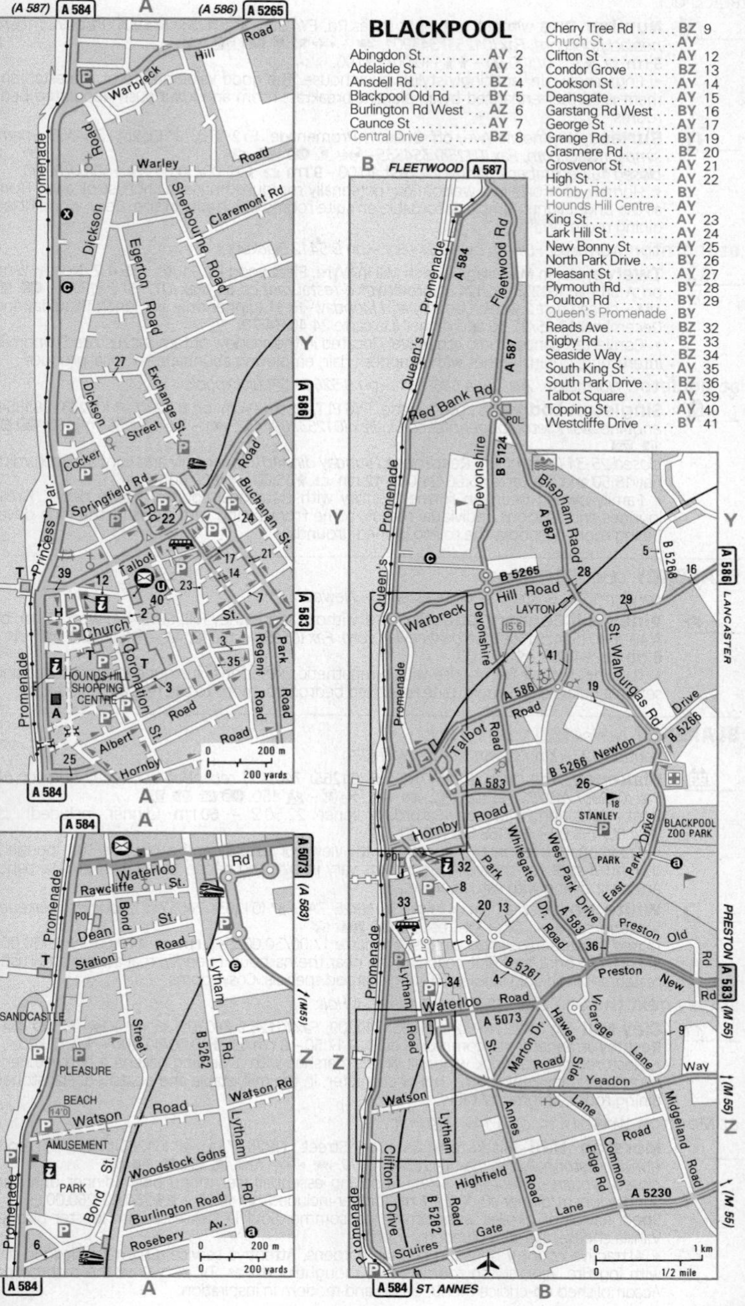

ENGLAND

Number One without rest., 1 St Lukes Rd, FY4 2EL, ☎ (01253) 343901, *info@numberonelackpool.com, Fax (01253) 343901*, – – P. MC VISA. AZ
3 rm ☐ ★70.00/100.00 – ★★110.00/130.00.
◆ Engagingly run, enticingly stylish guesthouse. The good value nature of the establishment is further enhanced by an elegant breakfast room and luxuriously appointed bedrooms.

Burlees, 40 Knowle Ave, off Queen's Promenade, FY2 9TQ, ☎ (01253) 354535, *marrsimpson@aol.com, Fax (01253) 354535* – P. MC VISA. BY
closed 16 December-6 January – **Rest** 10.00 – **9 rm** ☐ ★25.00/50.00 – ★★50.00/60.00.
◆ Homely comforts in a welcoming, personally run guesthouse, a short stroll away from all the bright lights. Simple, affordable en suite rooms which vary in size. Cosy, wood fitted dining room.

at Thornton *Northeast : 5½ m. by A 584 –* **BY** *– on B 5412 Blackpool.*

Twelve, Marsh Mill Village, Marsh Mill in Wyre, Fleetwood Rd South, FY5 4JZ, North : ½ m. on A 585 ☎ (01253) 821212, *info@twelve-restaurant.co.uk, Fax (01253) 821212* – MC AE VISA *– closed first 2 weeks January and Monday* – **Rest** (dinner only and lunch Thursday and December) 13.95/22.50 and dinner a la carte 24.40/34.70.
◆ Converted dance studio attractively located in the shadow of famous restored windmill. Interesting, original dishes with a modern flair, employing abundance of local produce.

at Singleton *Northeast : 7 m. by A 586 –* **BY** *– on B 5260 – ✉ Blackpool.*

Singleton Lodge , Lodge Lane, FY6 8LT, North : ¼ m. on B 5260 ☎ (01253) 883854, *enquiries@singletonlodgehotel.co.uk, Fax (01253) 894432*, – rest, P – 60. MC AE VISA
closed 25-31 December – **Rest** *(closed Sunday dinner)* (dinner only and Sunday lunch)/dinner 15.50 and a la carte 15.00/21.00 – **12 rm** ☐ ★55.00 – ★★80.00.
◆ Family owned Georgian former rectory with traditional country house décor. Firelit lounges and spacious, individual rooms, some front-facing with views of the long drive. Dining room overlooks the rolling lawned grounds.

BLAKENEY *Glos.* 503 504 M 28.
London 134 – Bristol 31 – Gloucester 16 – Newport 31.

Viney Hill Country Guesthouse without rest., Viney Hill, GL15 4LT, West : ¾ m. by A 48 ☎ (01594) 516000, *info@vineyhill.com, Fax (01594) 516018*, – P. MC VISA.
6 rm ☐ ★40.00 – ★★70.00.
◆ Part 18C former farmhouse with sympathetic extensions, surrounded by gardens and set on a quiet road. Simple, pine furnished bedrooms, those to the rear are quieter.

BLAKENEY *Norfolk* 504 X 25 – ✉ *Holt.*
London 127 – King's Lynn 37 – Norwich 28.

Blakeney, The Quay, NR25 7NE, ☎ (01263) 740797, *reception@blakeney-hotel.co.uk, Fax (01263) 740795*, <, , , – – P – 150. MC AE VISA
Rest (light lunch Monday-Saturday)/dinner 22.50 ♀ – **60 rm** (dinner included) ☐ ★84.00/155.00 – ★★168.00/190.00.
◆ Traditional hotel on the quayside with views of estuary and a big sky! Sun lounge a delightful spot for the vista. Bedrooms vary in size and décor, some with private patio. Armchair dining with estuary views.

White Horse with rm, 4 High St, NR25 7AL, ☎ (01263) 740574, *enquiries@blakeneywhitehorse.co.uk*, – rest, P. MC VISA.
closed 2 weeks mid January – **Rest** a la carte 17.00/30.00 ♀ – **9 rm** ☐ ★70.00 – ★★130.00.
◆ Part 17C brick-and-flint coaching inn near the harbour. Friendly, real ale bar and rustic restaurant in the old stables offering seafood specials. Cosy rooms.

at Cley next the Sea *East : 1½ m. on A 149 – ✉ Holt.*

Cley Mill , NR25 7RP, ☎ (01263) 740209, *Fax (01263) 740209*, <, – P. MC VISA
Rest (by arrangement) (communal dining) 17.50 – **8 rm** ☐ ★40.00/124.00 – ★★126.00.
◆ Restored 18C redbrick windmill in salt marshes with a viewing gallery: a birdwatcher's paradise. Neatly kept rooms, full of character, in the mill, stable and boatshed. Flagstoned dining room; communal table.

at Morston *West : 1½ m. on A 149 – ✉ Holt.*

Morston Hall (Blackiston) , The Street, NR25 7AA, ☎ (01263) 741041, *reception@morstonhall.com, Fax (01263) 740419*, – rest, P. MC AE VISA
closed January-3 February – **Rest** (booking essential) (set menu only) (dinner only and Sunday lunch)/dinner 42.00 ♀ – **7 rm** (dinner included) ★140.00 – ★★250.00/260.00.
Spec. Ravioli of girolles with tomato consommé. Soufflé Suissesse with lobster bisque. Vanilla cheesecake with blueberry soufflé.
◆ Attractive country house in pristine gardens. Attentive service. Charming flagged hall with log fire. Airy, stylish rooms boast thoughtful extras. TV in two of the bathrooms! Accomplished no-choice menu, classic and modern in inspiration.

BLANDFORD FORUM *Dorset* 503 504 N 31 *The West Country G. – pop. 9 854.*
See : *Town*★.
Env. : *Kingston Lacy*★★ *AC, SE : 5½ m. by B 3082 – Royal Signals Museum*★*, NE : 2 m. by B 3082.*
Exc. : *Milton Abbas*★*, SW : 8 m. by A 354 – Sturminster Newton*★*, NW : 8 m. by A 357.*
Ashley Wood, Wimbourne Rd ✆ *(01258) 452253.*
1 Greyhound Yard ✆ *(01258) 454770.*
London 124 – Bournemouth 17 – Dorchester 17 – Salisbury 24.

at Chettle *Northeast : 7¼ m. by A 354 – ✉ Blandford Forum.*

XX **Castleman** with rm, DT11 8DB, ✆ (01258) 830096, *chettle@globalnet.co.uk, Fax (01258) 830051,* ≤, – rest, P. MC VISA.
closed February and 25-26 December – **Rest** (dinner only and Sunday lunch)/dinner a la carte 16.00/26.50 – **8 rm** ★50.00 – ★★90.00.
◆ Attractive part 16C dower house with Victorian extensions. Ingredients sourced from small local producers: game from their own estate. Classic cooking with a French base.

at Farnham *Northeast : 7½ m. by A 354 – ✉ Blandford Forum.*

The Museum Inn with rm, DT11 8DE, ✆ (01725) 516261, *enquiries@museuminn.co.uk, Fax (01725) 516988,* – P. MC VISA
closed 25, 26 and 31 December – **Rest** (bookings not accepted) a la carte 25.00/32.00 ♀ – **8 rm** ★85.00 – ★★140.00.
◆ Part thatched 17C inn offering locally produced and carefully prepared modern British cooking. Dine in the bar or more formal Shed restaurant. Comfortable bedrooms.

BLEDINGTON *Glos.* 503 504 P 28 – *see Stow-on-the-Wold.*

BLUNDELLSANDS *Mersey.* 502 503 L 23 – *see Liverpool.*

BLUNSDON *Wilts.* 503 504 O 29 – *see Swindon.*

BLYTH *Notts.* 502 503 504 Q 23 – ✉ *Worksop.*
London 166 – Doncaster 13 – Lincoln 30 – Nottingham 32 – Sheffield 20.

Charnwood, Sheffield Rd, S81 8HF, West : ¾ m. on A 634 ✆ (01909) 591610, *charnwood@bestwestern.co.uk, Fax (01909) 591429,* – rest, P – 120. MC AE VISA
closed 26 December – ***The Lantern :*** **Rest** 14.95/23.95 and a la carte 23.85/49.90 ♀ – **30 rm** ★77.50 – ★★92.50/140.00.
◆ Privately owned hotel designed largely with the business traveller in mind. Practically appointed bedrooms are consistently well kept; some overlook the landscaped gardens. Restaurant with hanging lanterns and exposed beams.

BODIAM *E. Sussex* 504 V 30 *Great Britain G.*
See : *Castle*★★.
Exc. : *Battle Abbey*★*, S : 10 m. by B 2244, B 2089, A 21 and minor rd – Rye*★★*, SW : 13 m. by A 268.*
London 58 – Cranbrook 7 – Hastings 13.

The Curlew, Junction Rd, TN32 5UY, Northwest : 1 ½ m. at junction with B 2244 ✆ (01580) 861394, *enquiries@thecurlewatbodiam.co.uk,* – P. MC VISA
closed dinner Sunday and Monday – **Rest** 19.95 and a la carte approx 32.00 ♀.
◆ Smart, serious dining pub in deep burgundy with beams, dried hops and elegant tableware. Simple or elaborate traditional menus with French base; notable fine wine list.

BODMIN *Cornwall* 503 F 32 *The West Country G. – pop. 12 778.*
See : *St Petroc Church*★.
Env. : *Bodmin Moor*★★ *– Lanhydrock*★★*, S : 3 m. by B 3269 – Blisland*★ *(Church*★*), N : 5½ m. by A 30 and minor roads – Pencarrow*★*, NW : 4 m. by A 389 and minor roads – Cardinham (Church*★*), NE : 4 m. by A 30 and minor rd – St Mabyn (Church*★*), N : 5½ m. by A 389, B 3266 and minor rd.*
Exc. : *St Tudy*★*, N : 7 m. by A 389, B 3266 and minor rd.*
Shire Hall, Mount Folly Sq ✆ *(01208) 76616.*
London 270 – Newquay 18 – Plymouth 32 – Truro 23.

ENGLAND

Trehellas House, Washaway, PL30 3AD, Northwest: 3 m. on A 389 ☎ (01208) 72700 *trehellashouse@btconnect.com, Fax (01208) 73336,* heated, – P. VISA
closed Christmas and New Year – **Rest** *(closed Sunday)* (dinner only) a la carte approx 28.00 – **11 rm** ☕ ★65.00/80.00 – ★★100.00/115.00.
◆ Relaxed, personally run country house with a cottage facade. Owners' original Cornish art on show in listed room. Cosy lounges with flag floors. Airy, pastel painted bedrooms. Characterful restaurant; owners take pride in local, fresh, seasonal produce.

Bokiddick Farm without rest., Lanivet, PL30 5HP, South : 5 m. by A 30 following signs for Lanhydrock and Bokiddick ☎ (01208) 831481, *gillhugo@bokiddickfarm.co.uk Fax (01208) 831481,* – P. VISA.
closed Christmas and New Year – **5** rm ☕ ★45.00/50.00 – ★★60.00/75.00.
◆ Sizeable house on dairy farm: do take a quick tour. Warm welcome assured. Neat, well priced rooms with added amenities in old house; smart stable conversion for more rooms.

at Helland *Northeast : 4½ m. by A 389 off B 3266 – ✉ Bodmin.*

Tredethy Country House without rest., Helland Bridge, PL30 4QS, ☎ (01208) 841262, *tredethyhouse@aol.com, Fax (01208) 841707,* <, heated, – P. AE VISA
closed Christmas-second week January – – **11 rm** ☕ ★75.00/85.00 – ★★130.00/145.00.
◆ Victorian house overlooking the Camel Valley. Books and family photos of former resident, Prince Chula of Thailand, in the reading room. Spacious well appointed bedrooms. Ornate dining room with view of Camel Valley; traditional menu set each evening.

BODSHAM *Kent.*

London 65 – Ashford 10 – Canterbury 10.

Froggies at the Timber Batts, School Lane, TN25 5JQ, ☎ (01233) 750237 *Fax (01233) 750176,* – P. VISA
closed 1 week January, 1 week September, Sunday dinner, Monday except Bank Holidays when closed on Tuesday – **Rest** - French - a la carte 23.00/30.00.
◆ Creeper-clad, 15C pub with welcoming Gallic owner. Large dining area has menus in French: staff readily translate. Fine local produce in unfussy, French country style dishes.

BOLNHURST *Beds..*

London 64.5 – Bedford 8 – St Neots 7.

The Plough at Bolnhurst, Kimbolton Rd, MK44 2EX, South : ½ m. on B 660 ☎ (01234) 376274, *theplough@bolnhurst.com,* – P. VISA
closed 25 December, Sunday dinner and Monday – **Rest** a la carte 20.00/28.00 ♀.
◆ Sympathetically refurbished15C pub with terraces boasting charmingly rustic interior inducing pronounced feel of relaxation. Local produce a speciality in seasonal dishes.

BOLTON ABBEY *N. Yorks.* 502 O 22 *Great Britain G.* – ✉ *Skipton.*

See : *Bolton Priory★ AC.*
London 216 – Harrogate 18 – Leeds 23 – Skipton 6.

The Devonshire Arms Country House , BD23 6AJ, ☎ (01756) 710441 *sales@thedevonshirearms.co.uk, Fax (01756) 710564,* <, , , , , , , , – P – 90. AE VISA
The Burlington *:* **Rest** *(closed Monday)* (dinner only and Sunday lunch) 58.00 ♀ – **38 rm** ☕ ★165.00 – ★★195.00/350.00, 2 suites.
Spec. Poached loin of rabbit, mousseline of sweetcorn and langoustine beignets. Duckling with osso bucco cannelloni and butternut squash purée. Lime mousse with bitter chocolate, coconut ice cream.
◆ Extended part 17C coaching inn owned by Duke and Duchess of Devonshire: elegant country house rooms with art and antiques. Close to spectacular ruins of 12C Bolton Priory. Candlelit refined dining with views of Italian Garden.

BOLTON-BY-BOWLAND *Lancs.* 502 M/N 22 *Great Britain G.*

Exc. : *Skipton - Castle★, E : 12 m. by A 59 – Bolton Priory★, E : 17 m. by A 59.*
London 246 – Blackburn 17 – Skipton 15.

Middle Flass Lodge , Settle Rd, BB7 4NY, North : 2½ m. by Clitheroe rd on Settle rd ☎ (01200) 447259, *info@middleflasslodge.fsnet.co.uk, Fax (01200) 447300,* <, – P. VISA.
Rest (by arrangement) 27.00 – **7 rm** ☕ ★36.00/45.00 – ★★56.00/65.00.
◆ Friendly, welcoming owners in a delightfully located barn conversion. Plenty of beams add to rustic effect. Pleasantly decorated, comfy rooms with countryside outlook. Dining room features blackboard menu with good range of dishes.

BOROUGHBRIDGE *N.Yorks.* 502 P 21 – *pop. 3 311.*
Fishergate (01423) 323373 (summer only).
London 215 – Leeds 19 – Middlesbrough 36 – York 16.

thediningroom, 20 St James's Sq, YO51 9AR, (01423) 326426, *lisa.astley@virgin.net.(pop.net), Fax (01423) 326426* – . VISA
closed 2 weeks June, 25-26 December, Sunday dinner and Monday – **Rest** (booking essential) (dinner only and Sunday lunch) 25.00.
◆ Characterful cottage with beamed dining room. Vivid fireside sofas and Impressionist oils, as modern as the well-prepared dishes: duck on rocket and pesto features.

BORROWDALE *Cumbria* 502 K 20 – *see Keswick.*

BOSCASTLE *Cornwall* 503 F 31 *The West Country G.*
See : *Village*★.
Env. : *Church*★ – *Old Post Office*★.
London 260 – Bude 14 – Exeter 59 – Plymouth 43.

The Bottreaux, PL35 0BG, South : ¾ m. by B 3263 on B 3266 (01840) 250231, *info@boscastlecornwall.co.uk, Fax (01840) 250170* – . VISA.
closed 1 month in winter – **Rest** *(closed Sunday-Monday)* (booking essential in winter) (dinner only) 25.00 – **9 rm** 55.00/65.00 – 75.00/90.00.
◆ On a hill outside the village, a privately owned, well-run hotel. The rooms, some with king-size beds, and the public areas have a sleek, stylish ambience. Dining room offers well-sourced, local, modern dishes.

Trerosewill Farm without rest., Paradise, PL35 0BL, South : 1 m. off B 3263 (01840) 250545, *cheryl@trerosewill.co.uk, Fax (01840) 250545*, , , – . VISA.
mid February - mid November – **6 rm** 40.00/60.00 – 59.00/79.00.
◆ Modern house on 50-acre working farm: fine views of the coast and good clifftop walks. Lovely conservatory breakfast room. Bedrooms in matching patterns, some with Jacuzzis.

BOSHAM *W. Sussex* 504 R 31 – *see Chichester.*

BOSTON *Lincs.* 502 504 T 25 *Great Britain G.* – *pop. 35 124.*
See : *St Botolph's Church*★.
Exc. : *Tattershal Castle*★*, NW : 15 m. by A 1121, B 1192 and A 153 – Battle of Britain Memorial Flight, RAF Coningsby*★*, NW : 14 m. on A 1121, B 1192 and A 153.*
18 *Cowbridge, Horncastle Rd (01205) 362306.*
Market Pl (01205) 356656.
London 122 – Lincoln 35 – Nottingham 55.

Premier Travel Inn, Wainfleet Rd, PE21 9RW, North : 1 ½ m. on A 52 (01205) 362307, *Fax (01205) 366494* – rm, – 35. AE VISA.
Rest (grill rest.) – **34 rm** 48.95 – 48.95.
◆ A spacious lodge usefully located to the north of Boston and within easy reach of St Botolph's church and the Pilgrim Father's memorial. Modern, well-proportioned rooms.

BOSTON SPA *W. Yorks.* 502 P 22 – *pop. 5 952.*
London 127 – Harrogate 12 – Leeds 12 – York 16.

Four Gables without rest., Oaks Lane, LS23 6DS, West : ¼ m. by A 659 (01937) 845592, *info@fourgables.co.uk, Fax (01937) 849031*, – .
closed Christmas and New Year – **4 rm** 46.00/48.00 – 70.00.
◆ Down a quiet private road, a 1900 house, after Lutyens: period fireplaces, stripped oak and terracotta tile floors. Traditional, individually decorated rooms. Croquet lawn.

Spice Box, 152 High St, LS23 6BW, (01937) 842558, *info@thespicebox.com, Fax (01937) 849955* – . VISA
closed Sunday dinner and Monday – **Rest** 14.95 (lunch) and a la carte approx 24.00.
◆ Former chemist shop, evidenced by display of original artefacts. Smart, modern, two-roomed restaurant with warm burgundy décor. Carefully prepared modern British cooking.

BOULEY BAY *Jersey (Channel Islands)* 503 L 33 – *see Channel Islands.*

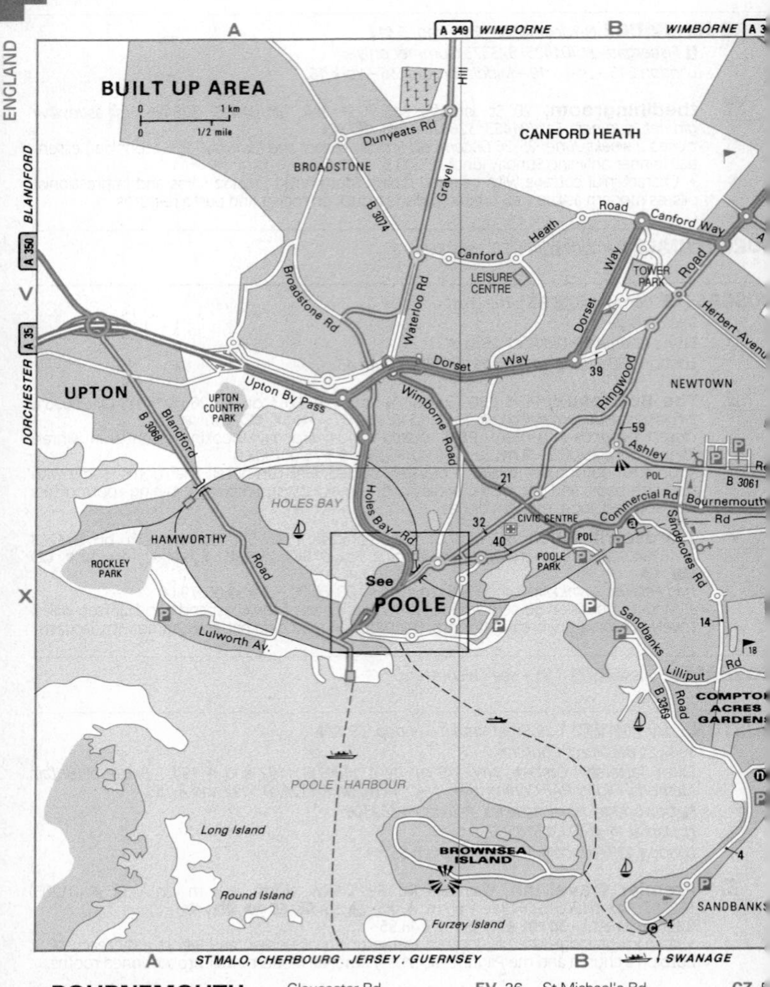

BOURNEMOUTH AND POOLE

Street	Grid	No.
Archway Rd	BX	2
Banks Rd	BX	4
Boscombe Overcliff Rd	EX	6
Boscombe Spa Rd	DX	7
Branksome Wood Rd	CY	9
Chessel Ave	EX	10
Clarendon Rd	CX	12
Commercial Rd	CY	13
Compton Ave	BX	14
Cranleigh Rd	EV	16
Durley Rd	CZ	17
Ensbury Park Rd	CV	19
Exeter Rd	CDZ	20
Fernside Rd	ABX	21
Fir Vale Rd	DY	23
Gervis Pl.	DY	24
Gloucester Rd	EV	26
Hampshire Centre	DV	
Hinton Rd	DZ	27
Lansdowne (The)	DY	28
Lansdowne Rd	DY	30
Leven Ave	CX	31
Longfleet Rd	BX	32
Madeira Rd	DY	34
Manor Rd	EY	35
Meyrick Rd	EYZ	36
Old Christchurch Rd	DY	
Old Wareham Rd	BV	39
Parkstone Rd	BX	40
Pinecliff Rd	CX	42
Post Office Rd	CY	43
Priory Rd	CZ	45
Queen's Rd	CX	46
Richmond Hill	CY	47
Richmond Park Rd	DV	48
Russell Cotes Rd	DZ	49
St Michael's Rd	CZ	5
St Paul's Rd	EY	5
St Peter's Rd	DY	5
St Stephen's Rd	CY	5
St Swithuns Rd South	EY	5
Sea View Rd	BV	5
Seabourne Rd	EV	5
Seamoor Rd	CX	5
Southbourne Grove	EX	6
Southbourne Overcliff Drive	EX	6
Sovereign Shopping Centre	EX	
Square (The)	CY	6
Suffolk Rd	CY	6
Surrey Rd	CX	6
Triangle (The)	CY	6
Upper Hinton Rd	DZ	6
Wessex Way	CX	7
West Cliff Promenade	CZ	7
Western Rd	CX	7
Westover Rd	DZ	7

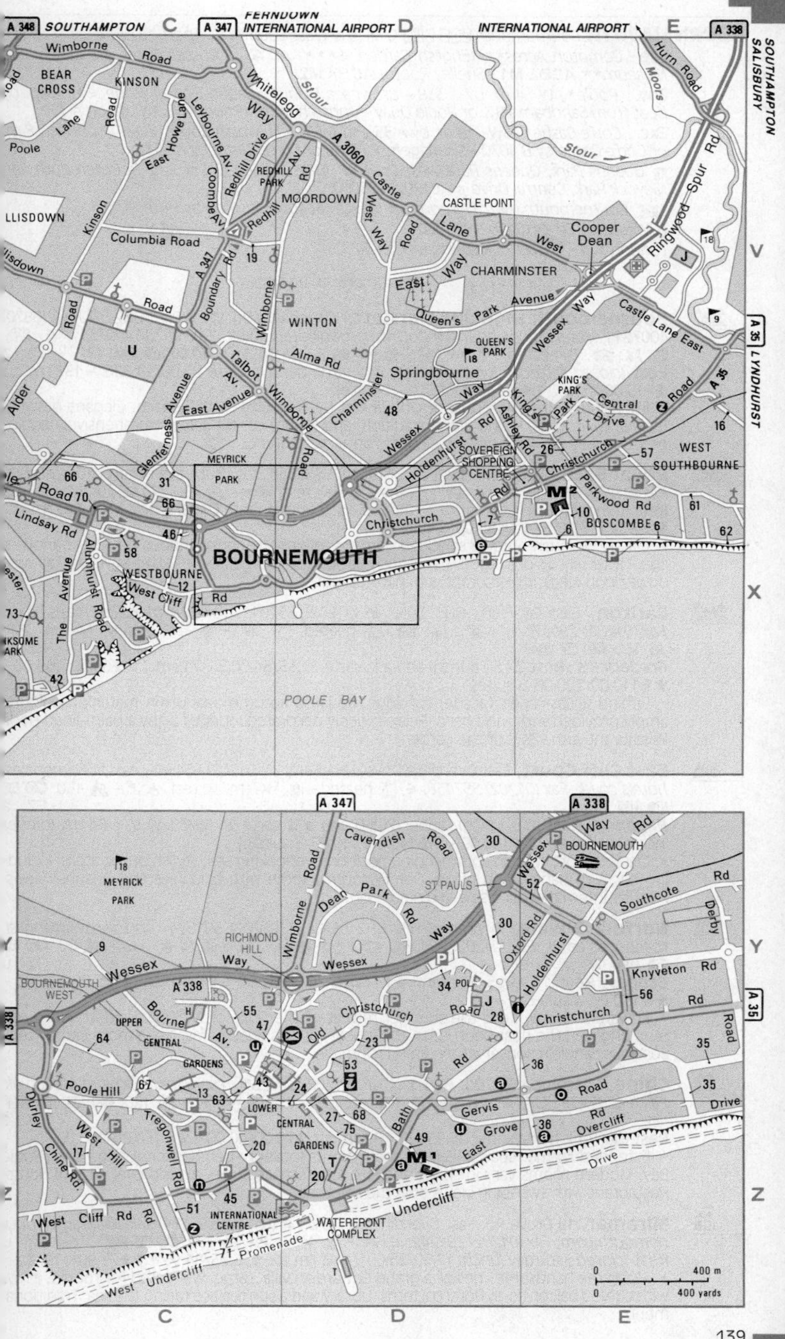

A 348 SOUTHAMPTON
A 347 FERNDOWN INTERNATIONAL AIRPORT
INTERNATIONAL AIRPORT
A 338 SOUTHAMPTON SALISBURY
A 35 LYNDHURST
C
D
E
V
X
Y
Z
Wimborne Road
BEAR CROSS
KINSON
Poole Lane
Kinson Road
East Howe Lane
Leybourne Av.
Coombe Av.
Redhill Drive
Whitelegg Way
Stour
REDHILL PARK
Redhill Av.
Rd
MOORDOWN
A 3060
Castle Lane West
West Way
Castle Road
CASTLE POINT
Cooper Dean
Moors
Hurn Road
Spur Rd
Ringwood
LLISDOWN
Columbia Road
Boundary Rd
A 347
19
Wimborne Road
WINTON
East Way
CHARMINSTER
Queen's Park Avenue
Wessex Way
Castle Lane East
U
Talbot Av.
Alma Rd
QUEEN'S PARK
Springbourne
KING'S PARK
Central Drive
Road
A 35
Alder
Glenferness Avenue
East Avenue
Wimborne Road
Charminster
48
Wessex Way
Holdenhurst Rd
Ashley Rd
King's Park
SOVEREIGN SHOPPING CENTRE
26
Christchurch
57
WEST SOUTHBOURNE
16
MEYRICK PARK
66
31
66
Road 70
Lindsay Rd
Alumhurst Road
The Avenue
58
46
Christchurch
Rd
7
Parkwood Rd
BOSCOMBE
10
6
6
61
62
M2
BOURNEMOUTH
WESTBOURNE
West Cliff
12
Rd
73
KSOME PARK
42
POOLE BAY
A 347
A 338
Cavendish Road
30
Wessex Way
Rd
BOURNEMOUTH
MEYRICK PARK
Wimborne Road
Dean Park Rd
ST PAULS
52
Southcote
Rd
Derby
30
Oxford Rd
Holdenhurst
RICHMOND HILL
Way
Wessex
9
Wessex
BOURNEMOUTH WEST
A 338
Way
Knyveton Rd
34 POL
Christchurch Road
J
28
Rd
56
Christchurch
A 35
Road
UPPER CENTRAL GARDENS
Bourne Av.
55
47
Old
23
64
53
36
35
Poole Hill
67
13
63
43
24
Rd
Road
35
Drive
Durley Chine Rd
West Hill
Tregonwell Rd
LOWER CENTRAL GARDENS
27
68
75
Gervis
Bath
Grove
36
Overcliff Rd
17
20
49
M1
East
Drive
20
51
45
Undercliff
West Cliff Rd
Rd
INTERNATIONAL CENTRE
WATERFRONT COMPLEX
71
Promenade
West Undercliff
0 400 m
0 400 yards

BOURNEMOUTH *Bournemouth* 503 504 O 31 *The West Country G. – pop. 167 527.*
See : *Compton Acres★★ (English Garden ≤★★★) AC* AX – *Russell-Cotes Art Gallery and Museum★★ AC* DZ **M1** - *Shelley Rooms AC* EX **M2**.
Env. : *Poole★, W : 4 m. by A 338 – Brownsea Island★ (Baden-Powell Stone ≤★★) AC, by boat from Sandbanks* BX *or Poole Quay – Christchurch★ (Priory★) E : 4½ m. on A 35.*
Exc. : *Corfe Castle★, SW : 18 m. by A 35 and A 351 – Lulworth Cove★ (Blue Pool★) W : 8 m. of Corfe Castle by B 3070 – Swanage★, E : 5 m. of Corfe Castle by A 351.*
Queens Park, Queens Park West Drive ✆ (01202) 396198, DV – *Bournemouth and Meyrick Park, Central Drive ✆ (01202) 786000,* CY.
Bournemouth (Hurn) Airport : ✆ (01202) 364000, N : 5 m. by Hurn - DV.
Westover Rd ✆ (01202) 451700.
London 114 – Bristol 76 – Southampton 34.

Plans on preceding pages

Bournemouth Highcliff Marriott, St Michael's Rd, West Cliff, BH2 5DU, ✆ (0870) 4007211, *reservations.bournemouth@marriotthotels.co.uk, Fax (0870) 4007311,* ≤, heated, – 350. VISA. CZ z
Rest *(closed Saturday lunch)* (carvery lunch)/dinner a la carte 22.00/29.00 – **158 rm** 115.00/135.00 – 130.00/150.00, 2 suites.
◆ Imposing white clifftop landmark, linked by funicular to the beach. Elegant drawing rooms; bedrooms, in the grand tradition, and leisure centre are comprehensively equipped. Secure a bay view table in elegant formal restaurant.

Royal Bath, Bath Rd, BH1 2EW, ✆ (01202) 555555, *royalbathhotel@devere-hotel.com, Fax (01202) 554158,* ≤, – rest, – 400. DZ a
Rest (dinner only) a la carte 25.00/35.50 **s.** – (see also ***Oscars*** below) – **133 rm** 120.00/175.00 – 185.00, 7 suites.
◆ Classic Victorian hotel in secluded gardens retains the conscientious service of another age. Tastefully co-ordinated, generously appointed rooms, some with sea views. Tall windows flood elegant restaurant with natural light.

Carlton, East Overcliff, BH1 3DN, ✆ (01202) 552011, *carlton@menzies-hotels.co.uk, Fax (01202) 299573,* ≤, heated, – rest, – 160. VISA EZ a
***Frederick's* : Rest** 22.50 (lunch) and a la carte 25.35/54.00 – **71 rm** 65.00/149.00 – 110.00/220.00, 5 suites.
◆ Behind a 30s-styled façade, spacious, updated accommodation in matching colours, amply provided with mod cons. Relax in richly decorated lounges or by a palm-lined pool. Restaurant with views of the garden.

East Cliff Court, East Overcliffe Drive, BH1 3AN, ✆ (01202) 554545, *eastcliff@menzies-hotels.co.uk, Fax (01202) 557456,* ≤, heated – rm, rest, – 150. VISA EZ a
***Regency* : Rest** (bar lunch)/dinner 26.50 and a la carte 26.85/39.40 **s.** – **64 rm** (dinner included) 70.00/160.00 – 140.00/260.00, 3 suites.
◆ Classic resort hotel in commanding position overlooking sea. Stylish public areas, including bar with baby grand piano. Comfy rooms, some with balconies and Channel views. Popular international cuisine in dining room.

Norfolk Royale, Richmond Hill, BH2 6EN, ✆ (01202) 551521, *norfolkroyal@englishrosehotels.co.uk, Fax (01202) 294031,* – rest, – 90. VISA. CY u
***Echoes* : Rest** 15.90/25.00 **s.** and a la carte 26.00/37.50 – **91 rm** 115.00/125.00 – 150.00, 4 suites.
◆ Edwardian hotel, once the summer retreat of the Duke of Norfolk. Bold, modern colours brighten the neat bedrooms; the lobby, with its deep sofas, has a more clubby feel. Spacious candlelit conservatory dining room.

Chine, Boscombe Spa Rd, BH5 1AX, ✆ (01202) 396234, *reservations@chinehotel.co.uk, Fax (01202) 391737,* ≤, heated, – – 120. VISA DX e
Rest (buffet lunch)/dinner 26.95 **s.** – **89 rm** 70.00/90.00 – 120.00/180.00.
◆ Extended former spa takes its name from its location, perched on a ridge over Poole Bay. Modern rooms vary in shape and size; conference suites extend over several floors. Restaurant with sweeping views over the treetops.

Miramar, 19 Grove Rd, East Overcliff, BH1 3AL, ✆ (01202) 556581, *sales@miramar-bournemouth.com, Fax (01202) 291242,* ≤, – – 200. VISA DZ u
Rest *(closed Saturday lunch)* 17.50/25.00 – **43 rm** 36.95/84.95 – 73.90/119.90.
◆ Along the handsome lines of a grand Edwardian villa. Large, well cared for rooms, a few with curved balconies, in floral patterns. Library and a sun terrace facing the sea. Traditional menu.

Collingwood, 11 Priory Rd, BH2 5DF, (01202) 557575, *info@hotel-collingwood.co.uk, Fax (01202) 293219,* , – , rest, . CZ n
Rest (bar lunch Monday-Saturday)/dinner 16.95 – **53 rm** (dinner included) 64.00/120.00 – 128.00/138.00.
◆ A smoothly run, family owned hotel of long standing, its modern accommodation comfortably decorated in warm pastel shades. Bar terrace and reverently hushed snooker room. Effusively decorative dining room.

The Orchid without rest., 34 Gervis Rd, BH1 3DH, (01202) 551600, *enquiries@orchid-hotel.co.uk, Fax (01202) 553731* – – 100. DY a
closed 24-30 December – **33 rm** 30.00/75.00 – 60.00/120.00.
◆ As you might expect, images of the orchid abound in this personally run hotel with lovely rear courtyard. Modern, minimalist style prevails. Comfy rooms with designer touches.

Tudor Grange without rest., 31 Gervis Rd, East Cliff, BH1 3EE, (01202) 291472, *Fax (01202) 311503,* – . EY o
closed 24 December-1 January – **11 rm** 30.00/52.00 – 60.00/70.00.
◆ Well-priced rooms in dark wood, in keeping with the rest of the half-timbered mock Tudor house. Greenery and oak panels surround the deep wing armchairs in a restful lounge.

Oscars (at Royal Bath H.), Bath Rd, BH1 2EW, (01202) 555555, *Fax (01202) 554158* – . DZ a
closed Sunday dinner and Monday – **Rest** 16.50/19.50 (lunch) and dinner a la carte 36.50/52.75.
◆ Pristine settings and discreet, impeccable service distinguish this elegant restaurant, serving modern British dishes, many infused with flavours of French country cooking.

Noble House, 3-5 Lansdowne Rd, BH1 1RZ, (01202) 291277, *Fax (01202) 291312* – . DEY i
Rest - Chinese - 6.00/28.00 and a la carte 11.90/23.40.
◆ A hospitable family team are behind a comprehensive menu of authentic Chinese cuisine, carefully prepared from fresh ingredients. Smoothly run; handy town centre location.

Salathai, 1066 Christchurch Rd, Boscombe East, BH7 6DS, (01202) 420772 – . EV z
Rest - Thai - 8.95/18.95 and a la carte 12.85/19.80.
◆ Extensive, traditional menu from well-sourced produce. Charming, welcoming service keeps the regulars coming back to this neighbourhood Thai restaurant.

"Rest" appears in red for establishments with a (star) or (Bib Gourmand).

OURTON-ON-THE-WATER *Glos.* 503 504 O 28 *Great Britain G.* – *pop. 3 093.*

See : *Town*★.
Env. : *Northleach (Church of SS. Peter and Paul*★, *Wool Merchants' Brasses*★ *), SW : 5 m. by A 429.*
London 91 – Birmingham 47 – Gloucester 24 – Oxford 36.

The Dial House, The Chestnuts, High St, GL54 2AN, (01451) 822244, *info@dialhouse hotel.com, Fax (01451) 810126,* , – .
Rest (booking essential to non-residents) a la carte 17.00/33.00 – **13 rm** 55.00/89.00 – 80.00/180.00.
◆ Charming and personally run, this is the oldest Cotswold stone property in the village. Delightful, individually styled rooms: four in 18C former dairy are most characterful. Two intimate dining rooms with original fireplaces.

Coombe House without rest., Rissington Rd, GL54 2DT, (01451) 821966, *info@coombehouse.net, Fax (01451) 810477,* – .
restricted opening in winter – **6 rm** 45.00/50.00 – 70.00/80.00.
◆ Creeper-clad 1920s house on the quiet outskirts of the village, near the local bird sanctuary. Homely lounge and spotless, comfortable, cottage style bedrooms in soft chintz.

Broadlands without rest., Clapton Row, GL54 2DN, by Coronation Bridge (01451) 822002, *marco@broadlands-guest-house.co.uk, Fax (01451) 821776* – .
closed January – **11 rm** 48.00 – 60.00/75.00.
◆ Abundant baskets of summer flowers brighten this enthusiastically run sandstone farmhouse and converted stable. Homely, leather furnished lounge and well-appointed bedrooms.

ENGLAND

Manor Close without rest., High St, GL54 2AP, ✆ (01451) 820339, – P. closed 25 December – **3 rm** ★45.00/50.00 – ★★55.00/65.00.
◆ Superb central but quiet location. Lounge and breakfast room in Cotswold stone house comfortable floral rooms in purpose-built garden annexe, one on ground floor.

Alderley without rest., Rissington Rd, GL54 2DX, ✆ (01451) 822788, *alderleygues house@hotmail.com, Fax (01451) 822788* – P.
closed 24-25 December – **3 rm** ★55.00 – ★★65.00.
◆ Short walk from town centre on main road. Combined lounge and eating room; terrac for summer breakfasts; good quality local produce used. Bright, homely, floral bedrooms

at Lower Slaughter *Northwest : 1¾ m. by A 429 – ✉ Cheltenham.*

Lower Slaughter Manor, GL54 2HP, ✆ (01451) 820456, *info@lowerslaug ter.co.uk, Fax (01451) 822150*, ←, – rest, P – 25. MC AE VISA
Rest 19.95/45.00 – **13 rm** ★185.00/215.00 – ★★275.00/295.00, 3 suites.
◆ Listed part 17C manor in warm Cotswold stone. A wealth of objets d'art, fine oils and sense of enveloping period comfort extends from spacious bedrooms to the firelit hal Ornate dining room with lithographs and Wedgewood.

Washbourne Court, GL54 2HS, ✆ (01451) 822143, *info@washbournecourt.co.u Fax (01451) 821045*, – rest, P. MC AE VISA
Rest (bar lunch Monday-Saturday)/dinner 30.00/50.00 and a la carte 28.75/43.50 **s.**
24 rm ★90.00/110.00 – ★★140.00/170.00, 5 suites.
◆ Privately owned part 1800s manor house by the Eyre. Spacious rooms in floral fabrics a their traditional best in the old building. Flag-floored, timbered bar with terrace. Restau rant offers views of tree-lined lawns.

BOVEY TRACEY *Devon* 503 I 32 *The West Country G.* – ✉ *Newton Abbot.*
See : *St Peter, St Paul and St Thomas of Canterbury Church*★.
Env. : *Dartmoor National Park*★★.
18 *Newton Abbot* ✆ *(01626) 52460.*
London 214 – Exeter 14 – Plymouth 32.

Edgemoor, Haytor Rd, TQ13 9LE, West : 1 m. on B 3387 ✆ (01626) 832466, *reser tions@edgemoor.co.uk, Fax (01626) 834760*, – rest, P – 50. MC VISA
closed 27 December-9 January – **Rest** (dinner only) 32.50 **s.** – **16 rm** ★90.00/115.00 ★★135.00.
◆ Creeper-clad country house run by a friendly couple. Firelit lounge - lofty beame ceiling and deep chintz armchairs. Smartly kept, pine furnished bedrooms in floral print Elegantly proportioned dining room.

Brookfield House without restaurant, Challabrook Lane, TQ13 9DF, Southwest ¾ m. off Brimley rd ✆ (01626) 836181, *brookfieldH@tinyworld.co.uk, Fax (01626) 83618* – P. MC VISA.
closed December and January – – **3 rm** ★45.00/52.00 – ★★60.00/74.00.
◆ Well-kept early Edwardian house in two acres of attractive gardens surrounded by Dart moor. The three large bedrooms have expansive windows and are immaculately appoi ted.

at Haytor Vale *West : 3½ m. by B 3387 – ✉ Newton Abbot.*

Rock Inn with rm, TQ13 9XP, ✆ (01364) 661305, *inn@rock-inn.co.uk, Fax (01364) 66124* – rm, P. MC AE VISA.
closed 25 December – **Rest** 26.95 (dinner) and a la carte 20.00/35.00 – **9 rm** ★66.95 ★★106.95.
◆ Steadfastly traditional 18C inn; relaxed, firelit bar in polished oak and brass. En suit rooms, named after Grand National winners, are true to the old-world style.

BOWNESS-ON-WINDERMERE *Cumbria* 502 L 20 – *see Windermere.*

Good food and accommodation at moderate prices? Look for the Bib symbols: red Bib Gourmand for food, blue Bib Hotel for hotels

BOX *Bath & North East Somerset* 503 504 N 29 – *see Bath.*

BRACKNELL *Bracknell Forest* 504 R 29 – *pop. 70 795.*

18 *Downshire, Easthampstead Park, Wokingham ℘ (01344) 302030.*
The Look Out, Discovery Park, Nine Mile Ride ℘ (01344) 354409.
London 35 – Reading 11 – Southampton 51.

Coppid Beech, John Nike Way, RG12 8TF, Northwest : 3 m. on B 3408 ℘ (01344) 303333, *sales@coppid-beech-hotel.co.uk, Fax (01344) 302045,* – rm, rest, – 350. MO AE VISA
Rowans : Rest 17.95/25.95 and a la carte 31.00/41.75 – ***Brasserie in the Keller :*** Rest *(closed Sunday)* (dinner only) a la carte 13.90/25.30 **s.** – **203 rm** 65.00/165.00 – 75.00/185.00, 2 suites.
◆ Striking, alpine style hotel offering modern rooms; meticulously kept throughout, with a full range of mod cons. Large open-plan lounge bar and a discreetly located nightclub. Rowans is formal with a sage-green palette. German themed Brasserie in the Keller.

Premier Travel Inn, Wokingham Rd, RG42 1NA, West : ½ m. on B 3048 at "3.M." roundabout ℘ (0870) 1977036, *Fax (01344) 319526* – rm, rest, MO AE VISA
Rest (grill rest.) – **60 rm** 57.95/57.95 – 59.95/59.95.
◆ Well-proportioned modern bedrooms, suitable for business and family stopovers, designed with practicality and price in mind. Informal dining at the nearby Brewers Fayre.

Red = Pleasant. Look for the red and symbols.

BRADFORD *W. Yorks.* 502 O 22 *Great Britain G. – pop. 293 717.*

See : *City★ – National Museum of Photography, Film and Television★* AZ **M.**
18 *West Bowling, Newall Hall, Rooley Lane ℘ (01274) 724449* BY – 18 *Woodhall Hills, Woodhall Rd, Calverley, Pudsey ℘ (0113) 256 4771,* – 9 *Bradford Moor, Scarr Hill, Pollard Lane ℘ (01274) 771716* BX – 9 *East Brierley, South View Rd ℘ (01274) 681023* BX – 9 *Queensbury, Brighouse Rd, Queensbury ℘ (01274) 882155* AY.
Leeds and Bradford Airport : ℘ (0113) 250 9696, NE : 6 m. by A 658 BX.
City Hall ℘ (01274) 433678.
London 212 – Leeds 9 – Manchester 39 – Middlesbrough 75 – Sheffield 45.

Plan of Enlarged Area : see Leeds

Hilton Bradford, Hall Ings, BD1 5SH, ℘ (01274) 734734, *Fax (01274) 306146* – , rest, – 600. MO AE VISA BZ e
closed Christmas – ***Britisserie :*** Rest a la carte 15.00/25.00 **s.** – 15.95 – **116 rm** 51.00/105.00 – 61.00/115.00, 4 suites.
◆ City centre hotel, convenient for rail travellers. Don't be put off by dated 60s exterior. Neatly equipped modern accommodation; smart and comfortable cocktail lounge. Easy informality is the by-word in restaurant.

Cedar Court, Mayo Ave, off Rooley Lane, BD5 8HZ, ℘ (01274) 406606, *sales@cedarcourtbradford.co.uk, Fax (01274) 406600,* – , rest, – 800. MO AE VISA. BY a
Four Seasons : Rest 15.95/21.95 and a la carte 18.50/21.95 **s.** – 12.95 – **130 rm** 48.00/125.00 – 65.00/125.00, 1 suite.
◆ Subtly co-ordinated décor and mod cons make this a popular business option. Comfortable modern lounge by a long mahogany bar. Near the home of rugby league's Bradford Bulls. Restaurant exudes relaxing informality.

Express By Holiday Inn without rest., The Leisure Exchange, Vicar Lane, BD1 5LD, ℘ (0870) 7872064, *bradford@exbhi.fsnet.co.uk, Fax (0870) 7872066* – – 40. MO AE VISA. BZ a
120 rm 70.00 – 70.00.
◆ Located above a large entertainment centre in the heart of the city. Aimed at business travellers with ample desk space and meeting rooms. Good value accommodation.

t Gomersal *Southeast : 7 m. by A 650 on A 651 – Bradford.*

Gomersal Park, Moor Lane, BD19 4LJ, Northeast : 1½ m. by A 651 off A 652 ℘ (01274) 869386, *enquiries@gomersalparkhotel.com, Fax (01274) 861042,* – , rest, – 200. MO AE VISA BU u
Brasserie 101 : Rest *(closed Saturday lunch)* a la carte 21.50/29.50 **s.** – **100 rm** 99.00 – 99.00/240.00.
◆ Well-equipped corporate hotel on greenfield site; comprehensive conference facilities. Modern bedrooms: the executive style provides more comfort. Well-stocked, comfortable bar is ideal stopping point before dining.

BRADFORD

KEIGHLEY A 650
HARROGATE A 658
0 1 km
0 1/2 mile
HEATON
LISTER PARK
BOLTON
UNDERCLIFFE
PEEL PARK
MANNINGHAM
BRADFORD CITY F.C.
FORSTER SQUARE RETAIL PARK
MOOR PARK
GREAT HORTON
HORTON PARK
LITTLE HORTON
WEST BOWLING
BOWLING PARK
BIERLEY
WIBSEY
SPORTS CENTRE
HALIFAX A 647
HALIFAX A 6036 A 641 HUDDERSFIELD
M 606 MANCHESTER (M 62)

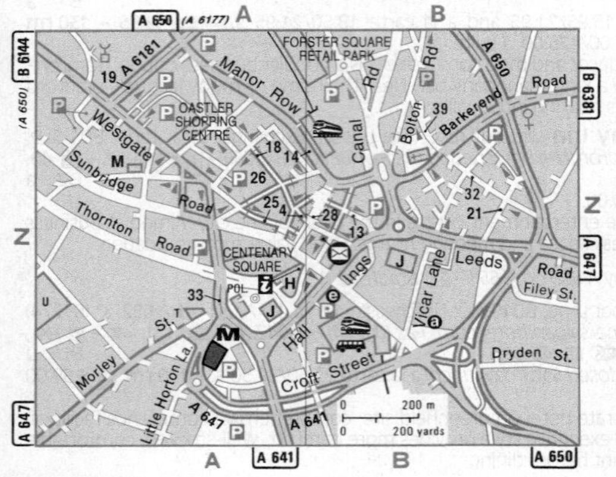
A 650 (A 6177)
B 6144
B 6381
A 647
FORSTER SQUARE RETAIL PARK
OASTLER SHOPPING CENTRE
CENTENARY SQUARE
Manor Row
Westgate
Sunbridge Road
Thornton Road
Canal Rd
Bolton Rd
Barkerend Road
Leeds Road
Vicar Lane
Filey St.
Dryden St.
Croft Street
Hall Ings
Morley St.
Little Horton La.
0 200 m
0 200 yards
A 641
A 650

BRADFORD-ON-AVON *Wilts.* 503 504 N 29 *The West Country G. – pop. 9 072.*
See : *Town★★ - Saxon Church of St Lawrence★★ - Tithe Barn★ – Bridge★.*
Env. : *Great Chalfield Manor★ (All Saints★) AC, NE : 3 m. by B 3109 – Westwood Manor★ AC, S : 1½ m. by B 3109 – Top Rank Tory (<★).*
Exc. : *Bath★★★, NW : 7½ m. by A 363 and A 4 – Corsham Court★★ AC, NE : 6½ m. by B 3109 and A 4.*
The Greenhouse, 50 Margaret's Street ☎ (01225) 865797.
London 118 – Bristol 24 – Salisbury 35 – Swindon 33.

Woolley Grange, Woolley Green, BA15 1TX, Northeast : ¾ m. by B 3107 on Woolley St ☎ (01225) 864705, *info@woolleygrange.com, Fax (01225) 864059,* heated, – P – 30. MC AE VISA
Rest 35.50 (dinner) and a la carte 21.00/35.50 – **19 rm** (dinner included) ★95.00/200.00 – ★★165.00/220.00, 7 suites.
◆ Modern art, period furniture: innumerable charming details spread through the rooms of a beautiful Jacobean manor. This is an hotel very much geared to families. Classic British cooking in restaurant, conservatory or terrace.

Widbrook Grange, Trowbridge Rd, Widbrook, BA15 1UH, Southeast : 1 m. on A 363 ☎ (01225) 864750, *stay@widbrookgrange.com, Fax (01225) 862890,* – P – 25. MC AE VISA
closed 24 December- 1 January – ***The Medlar Tree :*** **Rest** *(closed Sunday)* (dinner only) a la carte 26.50/31.00 – **20 rm** ★95.00/110.00 – ★★120.00/130.00.
◆ Georgian house and outbuildings, once the centre of an 11-acre model farm; cosy bedrooms, subtly reflecting the past, overlook peaceful fields and a pleasant mature garden. Pre-prandial relaxation in comfy drawing rooms.

Bradford Old Windmill, 4 Masons Lane, BA15 1QN, on A 363 ☎ (01225) 866842, *Fax (01225) 866648,* < , – P. MC VISA.
3 March-October – **Rest** - Vegetarian - (by arrangement) (communal dining) 21.00 – **3 rm** ★59.00/99.00 – ★★79.00/109.00.
◆ 1807 windmill in redressed local stone; Gothic windows and restored bridge. Rooms and circular lounge, stacked with books and curios, share a homely, unaffected quirkiness. Flavourful vegetarian menus.

The Beeches Farmhouse without rest., Holt Rd, BA15 1TS, East : 1 ¼ m. on B 3107 ☎ (01225) 865170, *beeches-farmhouse@netgates.co.uk, Fax (01225) 865170,* – P. MC VISA.
4 rm ★40.00/45.00 – ★★80.00/85.00.
◆ 18C farmhouse where sheep and ducks roam. Charming main bedroom boasts Victorian bath; log stove heats a cosy lounge. Pine furnished bedrooms in converted outbuildings.

at Holt *East : 2 m. on B 3107 – ✉ Bradford-on-Avon.*

Tollgate Inn with rm, Ham Green, BA14 6PX, ☎ (01225) 782326, *alison@tollgateholt.co.uk, Fax (01225) 782805,* – P. MC VISA
closed 25-26 December, first week January, Sunday dinner and Monday – **Rest** (booking essential) 11.95 (lunch) and a la carte 20.00/29.00 – **4 rm** ★50.00 – ★★95.00.
◆ Friendly, log-fired pub built of Bath stone. Twin dining areas with simple wooden tables and chairs. Interesting à la carte menu serves food with international elements.

at Winsley *West : 2½ m. by A 363 off B 3108 – ✉ Bradford-on-Avon.*

Burghope Manor without rest., BA15 2LA, ☎ (01225) 723557, *info@burghope.co.uk, Fax (01225) 723113,* – P. MC AE VISA.
closed Christmas and New Year – **5 rm** ★85.00/95.00 – ★★100.00.
◆ Historic gabled 13C manor in secluded gardens: pleasing combination of sensitively modernised, classically English rooms with Tudor fireplaces and portraits of past owners.

at Monkton Farleigh *Northwest : 4 m. by A 363 – ✉ Bradford-on-Avon.*

Fern Cottage without rest., BA15 2QJ, ☎ (01225) 859412, *enquiries@fern-cottage.co.uk,* – P.
3 rm ★40.00 – ★★60.00.
◆ Creeper-clad, listed cottage, dating back to the 1680s, run with pride and affable bonhomie by a husband and wife team. Trim bedrooms. Communal breakfast.

Do not confuse ✗ with ✿! ✗ defines comfort, while stars are awarded for the best cuisine, across all categories of comfort.

BRADWELL *Derbs.* 502 503 504 O 24 – *pop. 1 728* – ✉ *Sheffield.*
London 181 – Derby 51 – Manchester 32 – Sheffield 16 – Stoke-on-Trent 41.

Stoney Ridge without rest., Granby Rd, S33 9HU, West : ¾ m. via Town Lan
(01433) 620538, *toneyridge@aol.com, Fax (01433) 623154*, ≤, – P. VISA
4 rm 40.00 – 62.00.
◆ Extensive, modern hilltop bungalow with views of the village and distant moors. Cos lounge with open fire and family ornaments. Homely bedrooms in individual floral fabrics

BRAINTREE *Essex* 504 V 28 – *pop. 42 393.*
Kings Lane, Stisted (01376) 346079 – Towerlands, Panfield Rd (01376) 326802.
Town Hall Centre, Market Pl (01376) 550066.
London 45 – Cambridge 38 – Chelmsford 12 – Colchester 15.

Express by Holiday Inn without rest., Galley's Corner, Cressing Rd, CM77 8DJ, South east : 2 ¼ m. on B 1018 (01376) 551141, *Fax (01376) 551142* – P – 30. VISA.
47 rm 65.00 – 65.00.
◆ Purpose-built hotel offering smart, contemporary rooms, well lit with ample wor space, on the outskirts of the town. Take-away breakfast option for travellers in a hurry.

BRAITHWAITE *Cumbria* 502 K 20 – *see Keswick.*

BRAMFIELD *Suffolk* 504 Y 27 – *pop. 1 778 (inc. Cratfield)* – ✉ *Ipswich.*
London 215 – Ipswich 27 – Norwich 28.

Queen's Head, The Street, IP19 9HT, (01986) 784214, *qhbfield@aol.com Fax (01986) 784797*, – rest, P. VISA
closed 26 December – **Rest** a la carte 16.95/27.00.
◆ Village pub with real rustic character draws on local, organic farm produce, including rare-breed meats, for an eclectic menu. Roaring log fires in winter.

BRAMHOPE *W. Yorks.* 502 P 22 – *see Leeds.*

BRAMPTON *Cambs.* 504 T 27 – *pop. 5 030* – *see Huntingdon.*

BRAMPTON *Cumbria* 501 502 L 19 *Great Britain G.* – *pop. 3 965.*
Env. : *Hadrian's Wall*★★, *NW : by A 6077.*
Talkin Tarn (016977) 2255 – Brampton Park, Huntingdon (01480) 434700.
Moot Hall, Market Pl (016977) 3433.
London 317 – Carlisle 9 – Newcastle upon Tyne 49.

Farlam Hall , CA8 2NG, Southeast : 2 ¾ m. on A 689 (016977) 46234 *Fax (016977) 46683*, ≤, – P. VISA
closed 26-30 December – **Rest** (booking essential to non-residents) (dinner only) 36.00 -
12 rm (dinner included) 140.00/160.00 – 270.00/310.00.
◆ Family run 19C coal baron's country seat in fine established gardens with an ornamenta lake. Luxuriously furnished drawing rooms, comfortable bedrooms in bold floral décor Period styled dining room with staff in eveningwear.

at Kirkcambeck *North : 7¾ m. by A 6071 and Walton rd* – ✉ *Brampton.*

Cracrop Farm without rest., CA8 2BW, West : 1 m. by B 6318 on Stapleton rc
(016977) 48245, *cracrop@aol.com, Fax (016977) 48333*, ≤, , , – P. VISA.
closed 1 week Christmas – **4 rm** 30.00/45.00 – 65.00/70.00.
◆ Run with real friendliness, a spotlessly kept house on a working farm. Comfy rooms furnished in solid pine overlook rolling fields. Breakfasts at antique dining table.

at Castle Carrock *South : 4 m. on B 6413* – ✉ *Brampton.*

The Weary with rm, CA8 9LU, (01228) 670230, *relax@theweary.com Fax (01228) 670089*, – P. VISA.
closed 25-26 December, 1 January and Mondays to non-residents – **Rest** a la carte 22.75/35.00 – **5 rm** 55.00 – 85.00.
◆ Based in a small village near the Talkin Tarn beauty spot. Bold, stylish interior. Dine or sofas, in the conservatory or on the terrace. Tasty modern dishes. Modish bedrooms.

BRANDESBURTON *East Riding* 502 T 22 – *pop. 1 835* – ✉ *Great Driffield.*
London 197 – Kingston-upon-Hull 16 – York 37.

Burton Lodge, YO25 8RU, Southwest : ½ m. on Leven rd ☎ (01964) 542847, *email@burtonlodge.fsnet.co.uk, Fax (01964) 544771,* 18, – P. MC AE VISA
closed 25-26, 31 December and 1 January – **Rest** (residents only) (dinner only) 17.50 **s.** ♀ – **9 rm** ☕ ★42.00/50.00 – ★★62.00.
◆ Personally run, extended 1930s house. Neat, modern bedrooms in soft pastels, some overlooking the golf course - perfect for an early round. A short drive to Beverley Minster.

BRANDS HATCH *Kent* 504 U 29 – ✉ *Dartford.*
9 *Corinthian, Gay Dawn Farm, Fawkham, Dartford ☎ (01474) 707559.*
London 22 – Maidstone 18.

at Fawkham Green *East : 1½ m. by A 20 –* ✉ *Ash Green.*

Brands Hatch Place, DA3 8NQ, ☎ (01474) 875000, *brandshatchplace@handpicked.co.uk, Fax (01474) 879652,* , , , , , , , squash – , rest, , P – 120. MC AE VISA
Rest *(closed Saturday lunch)* 28.50 **s.** – ☕ 12.95 – **38 rm** ★155.00 – ★★155.00.
◆ Sensitively extended Georgian house in 12 acres offering smart bedrooms, some in the annexe, with hi-tech facilities. Also, a range of conference and entertainment packages. Smart, contemporary restaurant.

BRANSCOMBE *Devon* 503 K 31 *The West Country G.* – ✉ *Seaton.*
See : *Village*★.
Env. : *Seaton (≤★★), NW : 3 m – Colyton*★.
London 167 – Exeter 20 – Lyme Regis 11.

Masons Arms, EX12 3DJ, ☎ (01297) 680300, *reception@masonsarms.co.uk, Fax (01297) 680500,* – rest, rest, P. MC VISA
Rest (bar lunch)/dinner 25.00 and a la carte 15.20/27.00 ♀ – **21 rm** ☕ ★30.00 – ★★150.00.
◆ Family run 14C inn; cosy, unspoilt bar with slate floors and ships' timbers, popular with locals. Bedrooms in the inn have more character; those in the annex are much larger. Restaurant with dressed stone interior and huge open fire.

BRANSFORD *Worcs.* – *see Worcester.*

BRATTON *Wrekin – see Telford.*

BRAYE *Alderney (Channel Islands)* 503 Q 33 and 517 A 34 – *see Channel Islands.*

BRAY MARINA *Windsor & Maidenhead – see Bray-on-Thames.*

BRAY-ON-THAMES *Windsor & Maidenhead* 504 R 29 – ✉ *Maidenhead.*
London 34 – Reading 13.

Plan : see Maidenhead

Monkey Island, SL6 2EE, Southeast : ¾ m. by Upper Bray Rd and Old Mill Lane ☎ (01628) 623400, *eveco@monkeyisland.co.uk, Fax (01628) 675432,* ≤, , , , – , rest, rest, P – 120. MC AE VISA.
Rest 24.50/35.00 and a la carte 32.95/45.00 ♀ – **25 rm** ☕ ★110.00/170.00 – ★★160.00/190.00, 1 suite.
◆ Two elegant 18C Thames island pavilions with neat garden and fine setting. Ornate lounge ceilings and Wedgwood conference room. Modern bedrooms, some with riverside balconies. Restaurant, with terrace, faces upriver.

✿✿✿

The Waterside Inn (Roux) with rm, Ferry Rd, SL6 2AT, ☎ (01628) 620691, *reservations@waterside-inn.co.uk, Fax (01628) 784710,* ≤ Thames-side setting – P 16. MC AE VISA.
X s
closed 26 December-2 February and 19-20 April – **Rest** - French - *(closed Tuesday except dinner June-August and Monday)* (booking essential) 40.00/89.50 and a la carte 77.00/117.70 – **8 rm** ☕ ★165.00/215.00 – ★★165.00/215.00, 3 suites.
Spec. Tronçonnettes de homard poêlées minute au Porto blanc. Filets de lapereau grillés aux marrons glacés. Péché Gourmand.
◆ Thames-side idyll still delights: opulent dining room, drinks in the summer houses, exquisite French cuisine and matchless service. Bedrooms are restful and classically chic.

ENGLAND

XX ✿✿✿ **Fat Duck** (Blumenthal), High St, SL6 2AQ, ✆ (01628) 580333, *Fax (01628) 776188* – ⇔ MC AE VISA X

closed 2 weeks Christmas, Sunday dinner and Monday – **Rest** 67.75/97.75 ♀.
Spec. Roast foie gras, almond fluid gel, cherry and chamomile. "Nitro" scrambled egg and bacon ice cream, parsnip cereal.
◆ History and science combine in an innovative alchemy of contrasting flavours and textures. Modern art, stylish, relaxing milieu, confident service.

Hinds Head, High St, SL6 2AB, ✆ (01628) 626151, *Fax (01628) 623394* – ⇔ P ⇔ 24. MC VISA X

closed 25 December, 1 January and dinner Sundays and Bank Holiday Mondays – **Rest** a la carte 25.00/35.00 ♀.
◆ Characterful 17C village pub; inside a wealth of panelling and charm. Enjoy a sip of mead or a glass of perry with tasty and heart-warming classic British cooking.

Royal Oak, Paley St, SL6 3JN, Southwest : 3½ m. by A 308, A 330 on B 3024 ✆ (01628) 620541 – P. MC AE VISA
closed 27 December-2 January and Sunday dinner – **Rest** 19.50 (lunch) and a la carte 23.00/30.00.
◆ A very welcoming, traditional pub; plenty of charm and character with exposed beams and wattle walls. Fine selection of real ales; snug bar area. Seasonally based, tasty food.

at Bray Marina *Southeast : 2 m. by B 3208, A 308 – X – on Monkey Island Lane – ✉ Bray-on-Thames.*

X **Riverside Brasserie,** SL6 2EB, (follow road through the marina) ✆ (01628) 780553, *Fax (01628) 674312,* – ⇔ P. MC AE VISA
closed Christmas, New Year, Sunday dinner and Monday – **Rest** a la carte 25.95/30.45 ♀.
◆ Marina boathouse, idylically set on the banks of the Thames. Very simply appointed interior and decked terrace. Inventive cooking in informal, busy and buzzy surroundings.

BREADSALL *Derby* – *see Derby.*

BREEDON ON THE HILL *Leics.* – *see Castle Donington.*

BRENTWOOD *Essex* 504 V 29 – *pop. 47 593.*

Bentley G. & C.C., Ongar Rd ✆ (01277) 373179 – 18, 9 Warley Park, Magpie Lane, Little Warley ✆ (01277) 224891.

Pepperell House, 44 High St ✆ (01277) 200300.

London 22 – Chelmsford 11 – Southend-on-Sea 21.

Marygreen Manor, London Rd, CM14 4NR, Southwest : 1¼ m. on A 1023 ✆ (01277) 225252, *info@marygreenmanor.co.uk, Fax (01277) 262809,* – ⇔ ▤ ♿ P – 50. MC AE VISA.
Rest *(closed Sunday dinner)* 25.50/35.00 and a la carte 33.45/46.95 **s.** ♀ – ☕ 14.50 – **55 rm** ♦135.00 – ♦♦150.00, 1 suite.
◆ Half timbered 16C house. Some rooms, named after Henry VIII's wives, with carved oak beds, others off a courtyard garden: all well-equipped. Cosy lounge with ornate ceiling. Dining hall with spiral oak pillars, criss-crossing beams.

BRICKET WOOD *Herts.*

London 23 – St Albans 4 – Watford 4.

Premier Travel Inn, Smug Oak Lane, AL2 3TY, ✆ (01727) 875557, *Fax (01727) 873289* – ⇔ rm, ♿ P. MC AE VISA.
Rest (grill rest.) – **56 rm** ♦55.95/55.95 – ♦♦57.95/57.95.
◆ Situated in a busy motorway area. Offers simply furnished, brightly decorated rooms with ample work space. Family rooms have sofa beds. Grill restaurant for meals.

Your opinions are important to us:
please write and let us know about your discoveries and experiences – good and bad!

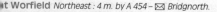

BRIDGNORTH *Shrops.* 502 503 504 M 26 *Great Britain G. – pop. 11 891.*

Exc. : *Ironbridge Gorge Museum★★ AC (The Iron Bridge★★ - Coalport China Museum★★ - Blists Hill Open Air Museum★★ - Museum of the River and Visitor Centre★) NW : 8 m. by B 4373.*

Stanley Lane ☎ (01746) 763315.

The Library, Listley St ☎ (01746) 763257.

London 146 – Birmingham 26 – Shrewsbury 20 – Worcester 29.

at Worfield *Northeast : 4 m. by A 454 – ✉ Bridgnorth.*

The Old Vicarage, WV15 5JZ, ☎ (01746) 716497, *admin@the-old-vicarage.demon.co.uk, Fax (01746) 716552,* – VISA

Rest *(closed Saturday lunch)* (booking essential) 21.50 (lunch) and dinner a la carte 31.85/45.45 – **13 rm** ★85.00 – ★★135.00, 1 suite.

◆ Antiques, rare prints and rustic pottery: a personally run Edwardian parsonage in a rural setting with thoughtfully appointed bedrooms, some in the coach house. Delightful orangery dining room overlooking garden; modern British cooking.

at Alveley *Southeast : 7 m. by A 442 – ✉ Bridgnorth.*

Mill, Birdsgreen, WV15 6HL, Northeast : ¾ m. ☎ (01746) 780437, *info@themill-hotel.co.uk, Fax (01746) 780850,* – 250. VISA.

Waterside : **Rest** 15.00/30.00 and a la carte 21.60/41.10 – 8.50 – **41 rm** ★80.00/90.00 – ★★110.00/190.00.

◆ Hugely extended water mill. Below traditionally styled rooms in flowery patterns, ducks paddle around the pond and fountain. Popular wedding venue. Capacious restaurant, busy at weekends, overlooks garden and duck pond.

We try to be as accurate as possible when giving room rates. But prices are susceptible to change, so please check rates when booking.

BRIDGWATER *Somerset* 503 L 30 *The West Country G. – pop. 35 563.*

See : *Town★ – Castle Street★ – St Mary's★ – Admiral Blake Museum★ AC.*

Env. : *Westonzoyland (St Mary's Church★★) SE : 4 m. by A 372 – North Petherton (Church Tower★★) S : 3½ m. by A 38.*

Exc. : *Stogursey Priory Church★★, NW : 14 m. by A 39.*

Enmore Park, Enmore ☎ (01278) 671244.

50 High St ☎ (01278) 472652.

London 160 – Bristol 39 – Taunton 11.

at Woolavington *Northeast : 5 m. by A 39 on B 3141 – ✉ Bridgwater.*

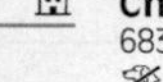

Chestnut House Village H., Hectors Stones Lower Road, TA7 8EF, ☎ (01278) 683658, *brandons@chestnuthousehotel.com, Fax (01278) 684333,* – VISA.

Rest (residents only) (dinner only) 22.50 – **7 rm** ★65.00 – ★★85.00.

◆ Converted farmhouse, spotless and personally run, the exposed stone and beams in the homely lounge testify to its 16C origins. Rooms are neat, comfortable; and all en suite. Dining room with comfy wicker chairs and garden views.

at Cannington *Northwest : 3½ m. by A 39 – ✉ Bridgwater.*

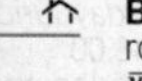

Blackmore Farm without rest., TA5 2NE, Southwest : 1½ m. by A 39 on Bradley Green rd ☎ (01278) 653442, *dyerfarm@aol.com, Fax (01278) 653427,* – VISA.

6 rm ★38.00/45.00 – ★★60.00/80.00.

◆ Part 15C manor, now a working dairy farm, with great hall and chapel, set against a backdrop of the Quantocks. Huge, well-priced bedrooms brimming with character.

BRIDPORT *Dorset* 503 L 31 *The West Country G. – pop. 12 977.*

Env. : *Parnham House★★ AC, N : 6 m. by A 3066 – Mapperton Gardens★, N : 4 m. by A 3066 and minor rd.*

Exc. : *Lyme Regis★ – The Cobb★, W : 11 m. by A 35 and A 3052.*

Bridport and West Dorset, East Cliff, West Bay ☎ (01308) 422597.

47 South St ☎ (01308) 424901.

London 150 – Exeter 38 – Taunton 33 – Weymouth 19.

ENGLAND

Roundham House without rest., Roundham Gdns, West Bay Rd, DT6 4BD, South : 1 m by B 3157 ☏ (01308) 422753, *cyprencom@compuserve.com, Fax (01308) 421500*, ≤, – P. VISA
March-October – **8 rm** ☕ ♦41.00/80.00 – ♦♦72.00/94.00.
◆ Elegant 1903 house with trim, spacious bedrooms, their broad windows overlooking woods, fields and a lawned garden. Coffee in the smart lounge with its marble fireplace Breakfast room has pleasant views of the countryside.

Britmead House without rest., West Bay Rd, DT6 4EG, South : 1 m. on B 3157 ☏ (01308) 422941, *britmead@talk21.com, Fax (01308) 422516*, – P. VISA
8 rm ☕ ♦42.00/50.00 – ♦♦68.00.
◆ On the road to West Bay and the Dorset Coast Path, a neat, redbrick Edwardian house with well-proportioned rooms and a comfortable lounge leading out to the garden.

Riverside, West Bay, DT6 4EZ, South : 1 ¾ m. by B 3157 ☏ (01308) 422011, *Fax (01308) 458808*, ≤, – VISA
11 February-3 December – **Rest** - Seafood - *(closed Sunday dinner and Monday except Bank Holidays)* (booking essential) (restricted opening February-April and October-November) a la carte 21.00/35.00 ♀.
◆ Follow the footbridge across the river to this popular seafood café overlooking the harbour, renowned for its extensive choice of specials and its friendly service.

Chez Cuddy, 47 East St, DT6 3JX, ☏ (01308) 458770 – . VISA
closed 24-30 December, Sunday, Monday and Tuesday dinner – **Rest** (light lunch) a la carte 19.00/27.45.
◆ Inviting, personably run, centrally located, café style eatery. Simple décor enhanced by vivid artwork. Interesting seasonal menus: accomplished execution of modern dishes.

at Shipton Gorge *Southeast : 3 m. by A 35 – ✉ Bridport.*

Innsacre Farmhouse , Shipton Lane, DT6 4LJ, North : 1 m. ☏ (01308) 456137, *innsacre.farmhouse@btinternet.com, Fax (01308) 421187*, , – P. VISA
closed October and 24 December-2 January – **Rest** (by arrangement) 19.50 – **4 rm** ☕ ♦90.00 – ♦♦90.00.
◆ 17C farmhouse in acres of lawns and orchards. Simple comfortable lounge centred on old fireplace. Sizeable rooms in bold colours. Intimate dining room using carefully sourced ingredients.

BRIGGSWATH *N. Yorks.* 502 S 20 – *see Whitby.*

BRIGHOUSE *W. Yorks.* 502 O 22 – *pop. 32 360.*
Crow Nest Park, Coach Rd, Hove Edge ☏ (01484) 401121.
London 213 – Bradford 12 – Burnley 28 – Leeds 15 – Manchester 35 – Sheffield 39.

Waterfront Lodge, Huddersfield Rd, HD6 1JZ, ☏ (01484) 715566, *info@waterfrontlodge.co.uk, Fax (01484) 715588* – , rm, rest, – 100. VISA.
closed 25-26 December and 1 January – ***Prego* : Rest** - Italian - *(closed Saturday lunch)* 13.50 (dinner) and a la carte 13.70/31.90 – ☕ 6.95 – **42 rm** ♦39.00/46.00 – ♦♦46.00.
◆ A privately owned converted flour mill on the canal in the centre of town. Lodge-style accommodation with uniform décor of colourful fabrics and good bedroom facilities. Ask for a window table to enjoy restaurant's canal views.

Brook's, 6 Bradford Rd, HD6 1RW, ☏ (01484) 715284, *info@brooks-restaurant.co.uk, Fax (01484) 712641* – 20. VISA
closed 2 weeks January, 1 week July and Sunday – **Rest** (dinner only and lunch in December)/dinner 26.00.
◆ Eclectic art collection fills the walls of this informal restaurant and wine bar with its vaguely Edwardian upstairs lounge. Robust, tasty cooking with 'Spam' on the menu!

BRIGHSTONE *Isle of Wight* 504 P 32 – *see Wight (Isle of).*

BRIGHTON AND HOVE Brighton and Hove 504 T 31 *Great Britain G. – pop. 206 628.*

See : *Town*★★ - *Royal Pavilion*★★★ AC CZ – *Seafront*★★ – *The Lanes*★ BCZ – *St Bartholomew's*★ AC CX B – *Art Gallery and Museum (20C decorative arts*★ *)* CY M.

Env. : *Devil's Dyke (<★) NW : 5 m. by Dyke Rd (B 2121)* BY.

East Brighton, Roedean Rd ☎ (01273) 604838 CV – *The Dyke, Devil's Dyke, Dyke Rd ☎ (01273) 857296,* BV – *Hollingbury Park, Ditchling Rd ☎ (01273) 552010,* CV – *Waterhall, Waterhall Rd ☎ (01273) 508658,* AV.

Shoreham Airport : ☎ (01273) 296900, W : 8 m. by A 27 AV.

10 Bartholomew Sq ☎ (0906) 711 2255.

London 53 – Portsmouth 48 – Southampton 61.

Plans on following pages

Grand, Kings Rd, BN1 2FW, ☎ (01273) 224300, *general@grandbrighton.co.uk, Fax (01273) 224321,* <, , , – , & , – 800. MC AE VISA BZ v
Kings : **Rest** a la carte 27.85/47.00 **s.** – **196 rm** ★120.00/275.00 – ★★120.00/275.00, 4 suites.
◆ Imposing, white Victorian edifice with a prime place in the sun. Ornate marble, striking staircase, elegant rooms, indulgent cream teas in a quintessentially English lounge. Discreet, traditional grandeur distinguishes restaurant.

Hilton Brighton Metropole, Kings Rd, BN1 2FU, ☎ (01273) 775432, *reservations.brightonmet@hilton.com, Fax (01273) 207764,* <, , , , – , , rest, & – 1300. MC AE VISA. BZ s
Rest *(closed Saturday lunch)* (buffet lunch) 19.50 – 15.50 – **327 rm** ★66.00/165.00 – ★★66.00/165.00, 7 suites.
◆ Impressive late 19C hotel, thoroughly updated: vast conference centres; leisure and beauty suites in the west wing. Spacious, well-kept, modern rooms, some with sea views. Strong traditionality underpins restaurant.

Hotel du Vin, Ship St, BN1 1AD, ☎ (01273) 718588, *info@brighton.hotelduvin.com, Fax (01273) 718599* – – 30. MC AE VISA. CZ a
Bistro : **Rest** (booking essential) a la carte approx 28.40 – 13.50 – **37 rm** ★135.00 – ★★135.00.
◆ 19C part Gothic building. Style is the keyword here: lounge bar full of wine books; mezzanine cigar gallery has billiard table. Striking, minimalist rooms, some with terraces. Bistro with bohemian slant: cellar stocks predictably huge wine selection.

drakes, 43-44 Marine Parade, BN2 1PE, ☎ (01273) 696934, *info@drakesofbrighton.com, Fax (01273) 684805,* < – . MC AE VISA. CZ u
Rest – (see ***The Gingerman*** below) – 12.50 – **20 rm** ★95.00/115.00 – ★★245.00.
◆ Refurbished seaside hotel, now with Asian ambience, including Thai artwork. Informal lounge/reception. Stylish rooms with plasma TVs: choose between sea or city views.

Seattle, Brighton Marina, BN2 5WA, ☎ (01273) 679799, *seattle@aliashotels.com, Fax (01273) 679899,* <, – , rest, rest, & – 120. MC AE VISA CV c
Café Paradiso : **Rest** a la carte 22.50/28.00 **s.** – 13.50 – **71 rm** ★105.00 – ★★155.00.
◆ Striking marina setting: exploits its position with delightful "Saloon" lounge and decked terrace. Cocktail bar with Beatles portraits. Light, airy rooms in modish palette. Informal restaurant with totally relaxed feel; absorbing marina views.

Blanch House, 17 Atlingworth St, BN2 1PL, ☎ (01273) 603504, *info@blanchhouse.co.uk, Fax (01273) 689813* – rest, . MC AE VISA CZ o
closed 25-26 December, minimum stay 2 nights at weekends – **Rest** *(closed Sunday dinner and Monday)* 16.00/30.00 – **12 rm** ★80.00 – ★★220.00.
◆ For something different, this is the place to be. Individually themed bedrooms, all with CDs and videos. Red roses are pinned up in one room; another is full of snow shakers. Stark, minimalist restaurant beyond famed cocktail bar.

Nineteen without rest., 19 Broad St, BN2 1TJ, ☎ (01273) 675529, *info@hotelnineteen.co.uk, Fax (01273) 675531* – . MC AE VISA CZ z
minimum stay 2 nights at weekends – **8 rm** ★90.00 – ★★250.00.
◆ Sleek white bedrooms, some have beds with glass base of panels illuminated by blue lighting. Other attractive features include complimentary Champagne with Sunday breakfast.

Adelaide without rest., 51 Regency Sq, BN1 2FF, ☎ (01273) 205286, *info@adelaidehotel.co.uk, Fax (01273) 220904* – MC VISA. BZ z
closed 1 week Christmas and first 2 weeks January – **12 rm** ★39.00/55.00 – ★★70.00/95.00.
◆ Listed Regency town house run by friendly owners. Pretty, period-inspired rooms in floral patterns, some with coronet draped bed heads, and a spacious bow fronted lounge.

BRIGHTON AND HOVE

A 293 (A 27) WORTHING LEWES — A 2038 LONDON — LONDON A 23 — LEWES (A 27) A 270 Stanmer Park — A 259 WORTHING (A27) — NEWHAVEN

See following page

BUILT UP AREA

0 — 1 km

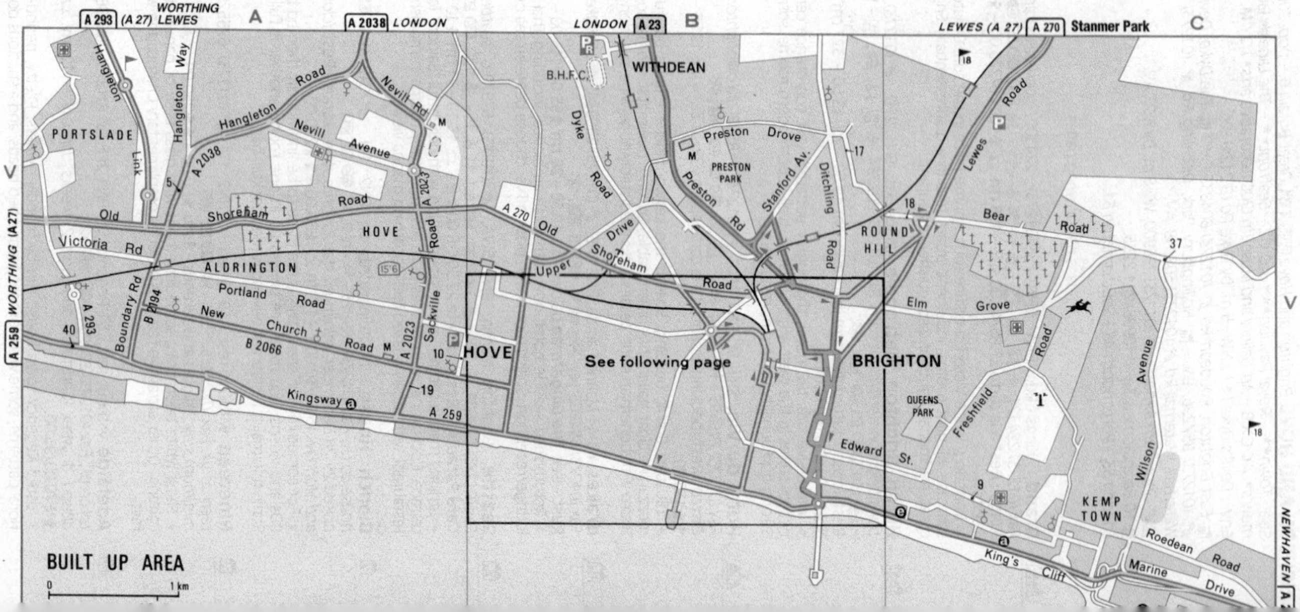

A 2073
A 259
B 2066
A 259
X
Y
Z
A
B
C
CENTRE
0
300 m
0
300 yards
BRIGHTON
HOVE
ROYAL PAVILION
THE LANES
CHURCHILL SQ. SHOPPING CENTRE
THE BRIGHTON CENTRE
ST. ANN'S WELL GARDENS
Redevelopment in progress
Viaduct Road
Ditchling Rd
Southover St.
Albion Hill
Sussex Street
Carlton Hill
John St.
Grand Parade
Edward Street
St. James's St.
Marine Parade
Madeira Drive
London Road
New England Street
New England Rd
Trafalgar Street
North Road
Church St.
North St.
Queen's Road
West St.
King's Road
Buckingham Road
Buckingham Pl.
Dyke Road
Dyke Rd
Clifton Hill
Upper North St.
Western Road
Montpelier Road
Preston St.
Vernon Ter.
Old Shoreham Road
New Road
Davigdor Road
Lansdowne Road
Holland Road
Palmeira Avenue
Selborne Rd
First Avenue
Wilbury Road
Second Av.
Cromwell Road
Eaton Road
The Drive
Tisbury Road
Grand Avenue
Norton Rd
Third Av.
Church Road
Fourth Av.
Kingsway
A 23
A 2010
B 2119
B 2121
B 2122
B 2120
A 259
POL.

ENGLAND

Brighton Pavilions without rest., 7 Charlotte St, BN2 1AG, (01273) 621750, *brigh onpavilions@tiscali.co.uk, Fax (01273) 622477* – . CV
10 rm ☐ ★45.00/65.00 – ★★100.00.
◆ Terraced house yards from seafront with something a little different - bedrooms all hav individual themes: for example, Titanic Room has clock set at time it hit iceberg!

Brighton House without rest., 52 Regency Sq, BN1 2FF, (01273) 323282 – BZ
14 rm ☐ ★35.00/75.00 – ★★50.00/130.00.
◆ Beautiful Regency house on four floors in charming square. Clean, classic déco throughout. Rooms benefit from period detail such as high ceilings and plenty o space.

Esteban without rest., 35 Upper Rock Gdns, BN2 1QF, (01273) 681161, *reserv tions@estebanhotel.co.uk, Fax (01273) 676945* – . CZ
closed November-December – **12 rm** ☐ ★35.00/65.00 – ★★75.00/90.00.
◆ To the east of the centre, a smartly kept, personally run, 19C hotel. Compact, affordable co-ordinated rooms with modern bathrooms.

One Paston Place, 1 Paston Pl, Kemp Town, BN2 1HA, (01273) 606933, *info@on pastonplace.co.uk, Fax (01273) 675686* – . CV
closed 2 weeks January, 1 week August, Sunday and Monday – **Rest** 16.50/39.00.
◆ Elegant framed mirrors run the length of this stylish, personally run restaurant, a bus local favourite. Appealing menu; assured, balanced and carefully sourced.

The Gingerman at drakes, 44 Marine Parade, BN2 1PE, (01273) 696934 *info@gingermanrestaurants.com, Fax (01273) 684805* – 10. CZ
Rest a la carte 15.00/25.00 ♀.
◆ Set in hotel basement, this cool, contemporary eatery conveys a soft, moody atmos phere. The menus present a good balanced choice of modern British dishes with Gallic twists.

Sevendials, 1 Buckingham Pl, BN1 3TD, (01273) 885555, *sam@sevendialsrestau ant.co.uk, Fax (01273) 888911*, – 20. BX
closed 24 December-3 January and Monday – **Rest** 15.00/26.50 and a la carte 18.00/27.00 ♀.
◆ Former bank on street corner: the vault now acts as function room. Light, airy fee with high ceiling. Modern menus with local ingredients admirably to fore. Good value lunch.

Terre à Terre, 71 East St, BN1 1HQ, (01273) 729051, *mail@terreaterre.co.uk Fax (01273) 327561*, – . CZ
closed 25-26 December, 1 January, Monday and lunch Tuesday – **Rest** - Vegetarian - a la carte 19.95/30.00 ♀.
◆ Hearty helpings of bold, original vegetarian cuisine lyrically evoked on an eclectic menu Despite fast-growing popularity, still friendly, hip and suitably down-to-earth.

Havana, 32 Duke St, BN1 1AG, (01273) 773388, *Fax (01273) 748923* – CZ
Rest 18.95/32.95 and a la carte 25.70/48.95.
◆ 1790s theatre, now a busy, spacious, two-tiered restaurant, its pediments and balustrades combined with mock-colonial styling. International dishes and exotic combinations.

The Gingerman, 21A Norfolk Sq, BN1 2PD, (01273) 326688, *info@gingermanre taurants.com, Fax (01273) 326688* – . BZ
closed 1 week Christmas and Monday – **Rest** (booking essential) 14.95/25.00.
◆ Tucked away off the promenade; French and Mediterranean flavours to the fore in a confident, affordable, modern repertoire: genuine neighbourhood feel.

The Real Eating Company, 86-87 Western Rd, BN3 1JB, (01273) 221444 – AY
closed Christmas and dinner Sunday (except at Bank Holidays)-Tuesday – **Rest** (booking essential at dinner) a la carte 15.00/24.00 ♀.
◆ Unique food store, bursting with speciality foods and 'food to go'. Ground floor dining area exudes buzzy ambience: superb in-house cooking using produce sold in the shop.

Due South, 139 King's Rd Arches, BN1 2FN, (01273) 821218, *info@duesouth.co.uk Fax (0871) 7334359*, – . BZ
Rest a la carte 24.50/39.20 ♀.
◆ Beside the beach, with lovely arch interior: best tables upstairs facing half-moon window overlooking sea. Organic prominence in modern menus using distinctly local produce.

t Hove.

Claremont House without rest., Second Ave, BN3 2LL, ✆ (01273) 735161, *info@claremonthouse.co.uk, Fax (01273) 735161,* – . AY c
12 rm ★55.00/70.00 – ★★135.00/145.00.
◆ Personally run Victorian town house with a neat garden; its tall windows and high ceilings lend a sense of space to the spotlessly kept, traditionally decorated bedrooms. Straightforward home cooking.

Quentin's, 42 Western Rd, BN3 1JD, ✆ (01273) 822734 – . AY a
closed 1 week Christmas, Sunday dinner and Monday – **Rest** 10.00 (lunch) and a la carte 27.00/35.00 ♀.
◆ Announces itself in vivid scarlet; inside is the comfortable, neighbourhood style dining room in cream with artwork on the walls. Modish menus; good value lunches.

BRIMFIELD *Herefordshire* 503 504 L 27 – *see Ludlow.*

BRIMSCOMBE *Glos.* 503 504 N 28 – *see Stroud.*

C. Bowman/SCOPE

Bristol, the Clifton Suspension Bridge

BRISTOL

503 504 M 29 *Great Britain G. – pop. 420 556.*

London 121 – Birmingham 91.

TOURIST INFORMATION

The Annexe, Wildscreen Walk, Harbourside ☎ (0845) 4080474; bristol@tourism.bristol.gov.uk

PRACTICAL INFORMATION

Mangotsfield, Carsons Rd ☎ (0117) 956 5501, **BV**.
Beggar Bush Lane, Failand, Clifton ☎ (01275) 393117, **AX**.
Knowle, Fairway, West Town Lane, Brislington ☎ (0117) 977 6341, **BX**.
Long Ashton, Clarken Coombe ☎ (01275) 392229, **AX**.
Stockwood Vale, Stockwood Lane, Keynsham ☎ (0117) 986 6505, **BX**.
Severn Bridge (toll).
Bristol Airport : ☎ (0870) 1212747, SW : 7 m. by A 38 **AX**.

SIGHTS

See : *City★★ – St Mary Redcliffe★★* **DZ** *– At-Bristol★★* **CZ** *– Brandon Hill★★* **AX** *– Georgian House★★* **AX K** *– Harbourside Industrial Museum★★* **CZ M3** *– SS Great Britain★★ AC* **AX S2** *– The Old City★* **CYZ** *: Theatre Royal★★* **CZ T** *– Merchant Seamen's Almshouses★* **CZ Q** *– St Stephen's City★* **CY S1** *– St John the Baptist★* **CY** *– College Green★* **CYZ** *(Bristol Cathedral★, Lord Mayor's Chapel★) – City Museum and Art Gallery★* **AX M1**.

Env. : *Clifton★★* **AX** *(Suspension Bridge★★ (toll), RC Cathedral of St Peter and St Paul★★* **F1**, *Bristol Zoological Gardens★★ AC, Village★) – Blaise Hamlet★★ – Blaise Castle House Museum★, NW : 5 m. by A 4018 and B 4057* **AV**.

Exc. : *Bath★★★, SE : 13 m. by A 4* **BX** *– Chew Magna★ (Stanton Drew Stone Circles★ AC) S : 8 m. by A 37 –* **BX** *– and B 3130 – Clevedon★ (Clevedon Court★ AC, ≤★) W : 11½ m. by A 370, B 3128 –* **AX** *– and B 3130.*

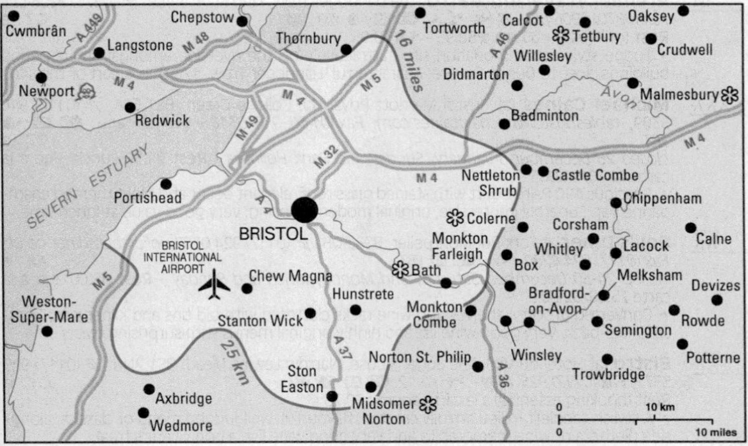

Bristol Marriott Royal, College Green, BS1 5TA, (0870) 4007220, *reservations.bristolroyal@marriotthotels.co.uk, Fax (0870) 4007320*, – – 250. MC AE VISA. CZ a
Terrace : **Rest** (dinner only and Sunday lunch) 27.00 and a la carte approx 28.00 **s.** – (see also ***Michael Caines*** below) – 15.95 – **230 rm** 149.00 – 149.00, 12 suites.
◆ Striking Victorian building next to the cathedral and facing College Green. Bedrooms, classic and individual, combine period styling and an array of modern facilities. Classic style at Terrace: wide variety of dishes to suit all tastes.

Bristol Marriott City Centre, 2 Lower Castle St, Old Market, BS1 3AD, (0870) 4007210, *events.bristolcity@marriotthotels.co.uk, Fax (0117) 930 4341*, – – 600. MC AE VISA. DY s
Mediterrano : **Rest** (bar lunch) a la carte 18.45/32.15 – 14.95 – **301 rm** 135.00 – 135.00/185.00.
◆ Stalwart, purpose-built block with smart, well-proportioned rooms, aimed at the business market, and providing many mod cons. Spacious modern lounges and coffee shop. Light, modern Mediterranean cooking.

Hotel du Vin, The Sugar House, Narrow Lewins Mead, BS1 2NU, (0117) 925 5577, *info@bristol.hotelduvin.com, Fax (0117) 925 1199* – rm, – 65. MC AE VISA CY e
Rest – (see ***Bistro*** below) – 13.50 – **40 rm** 130.00 – 350.00.
◆ A massive chimney towers over the 18C sugar refinery; stylish loft rooms in minimalist tones: dark leather and wood, low-slung beds, Egyptian linen and subtle wine curios.

The Brigstow, 5-7 Welsh Back, BS1 4SP, (0117) 929 1030, *brigstow@fullers.co.uk, Fax (0117) 929 2030*, – rm, – 60. MC AE VISA. CY n
Ellipse : **Rest** a la carte 20.00/25.50 – 12.00 – **115 rm** 145.00/169.00 – 145.00/169.00, 1 suite.
◆ Smart city centre hotel with charming riverside position. Stylish public areas typified by lounges and mezzanine. 21C rooms, full of curves, bright colours and plasma TVs. Modern brasserie and bar overlooking river.

City Inn, Temple Way, BS1 6BF, (0117) 925 1001, *bristol.reservations@cityinn.com, Fax (0117) 910 2727*, – – 45. MC AE VISA. DZ e
closed 26-28 December – ***City Café :*** **Rest** 14.95/16.50 (lunch) and a la carte 19.70/33.45 – 12.50 – **167 rm** 139.00 – 139.00.
◆ An affordable, central hotel. Airy, well-insulated rooms in intelligent contemporary designs and usefully supplied with mod cons. Sharp brasserie; terrace overlooks Temple Gardens.

Novotel, Victoria St, BS1 6HY, (0117) 976 9988, *h5622@accor.com, Fax (0117) 925 5040*, – – 150. MC AE VISA DZ n
Rest a la carte approx 20.00 – **130 rm** 130.00 – 130.00, 1 suite.
◆ Purpose-built hotel in heart of business district, close to Temple Meads station. Ample conference facilities. Bedrooms are spacious and up-to-date. Open-plan lounge bar and restaurant catering for many tastes.

Premier Travel Inn Metro, The Llandoger Trow, King St, BS1 4ER, (0870) 9906424, *Fax (0870) 9906425* – . MC AE VISA. CZ e
Rest (grill rest.) – **60 rm** 58.95 – 58.95.
◆ Lodge-style accommodation sited attractively on the riverside amongst smart period buildings close to Queen Square. Characterful 'Llandoger Trow' 17C pub is part of the site.

Michael Caines (at Bristol Marriott Royal H.), College Green, BS1 5TA, (0117) 910 5309, *tablesbristol@michaelcaines.com, Fax (0117) 910 5310* – . MC AE VISA CZ a
closed 26 December-5 January, Sunday and Bank Holidays – **Rest** 21.50 (lunch) and a la carte 41.75/51.00 .
◆ Spacious 19C Palm Court with stained glass roof, elegant décor and Moet themed champagne bar. Superbly impressive, original modern cooking; very good value at lunch time.

Bell's Diner, 1 York Rd, Montpelier, BS6 5QB, (0117) 924 0357, *info@bellsdiner.co.uk, Fax (0117) 924 4280* – . MC AE VISA AX s
closed 24-30 December, Saturday and Monday lunch and Sunday – **Rest** 45.00 and a la carte 25.50/32.50 .
◆ Converted grocery; shelves and wine racks cluttered with old tins and Kilner jars. Pleasantly laid-back. Very good wine list and highly original menus with surprising twists.

Bistro (at Hotel du Vin), The Sugar House, Narrow Lewins Mead, BS1 2NU, (0117) 925 5577, *Fax (0117) 925 1199* – 12. MC AE VISA CY e
Rest (booking essential) a la carte approx 30.75 .
◆ A stylish candlelit milieu artfully created; flavourful, well-judged menu of classics, alongside plethora of wine memorabilia and very good wine list: a bon viveur's treat.

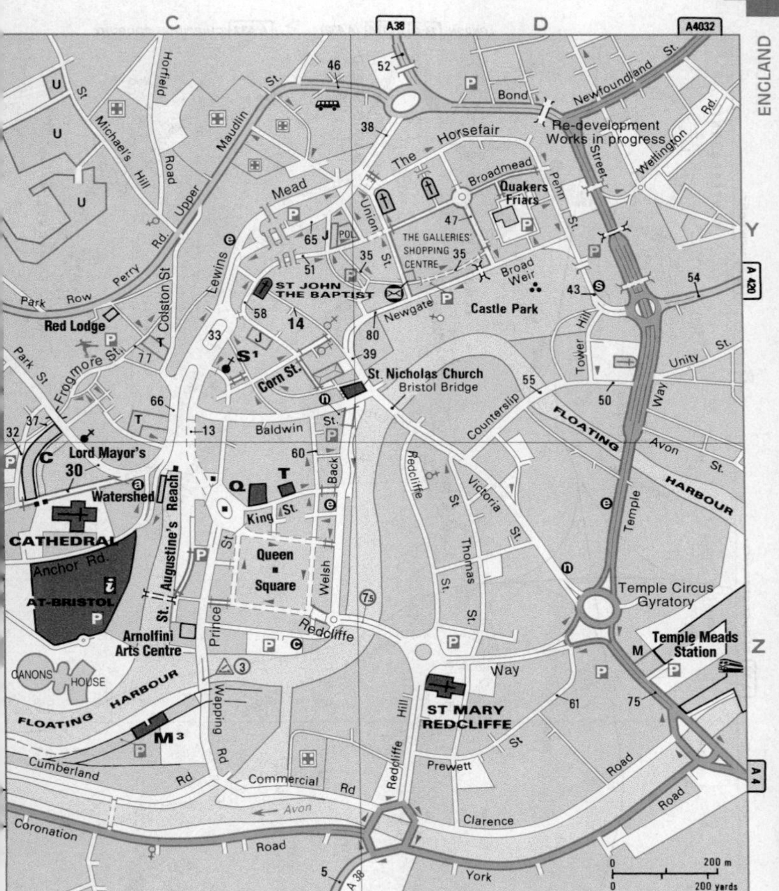

INDEX OF STREET NAMES IN BRISTOL

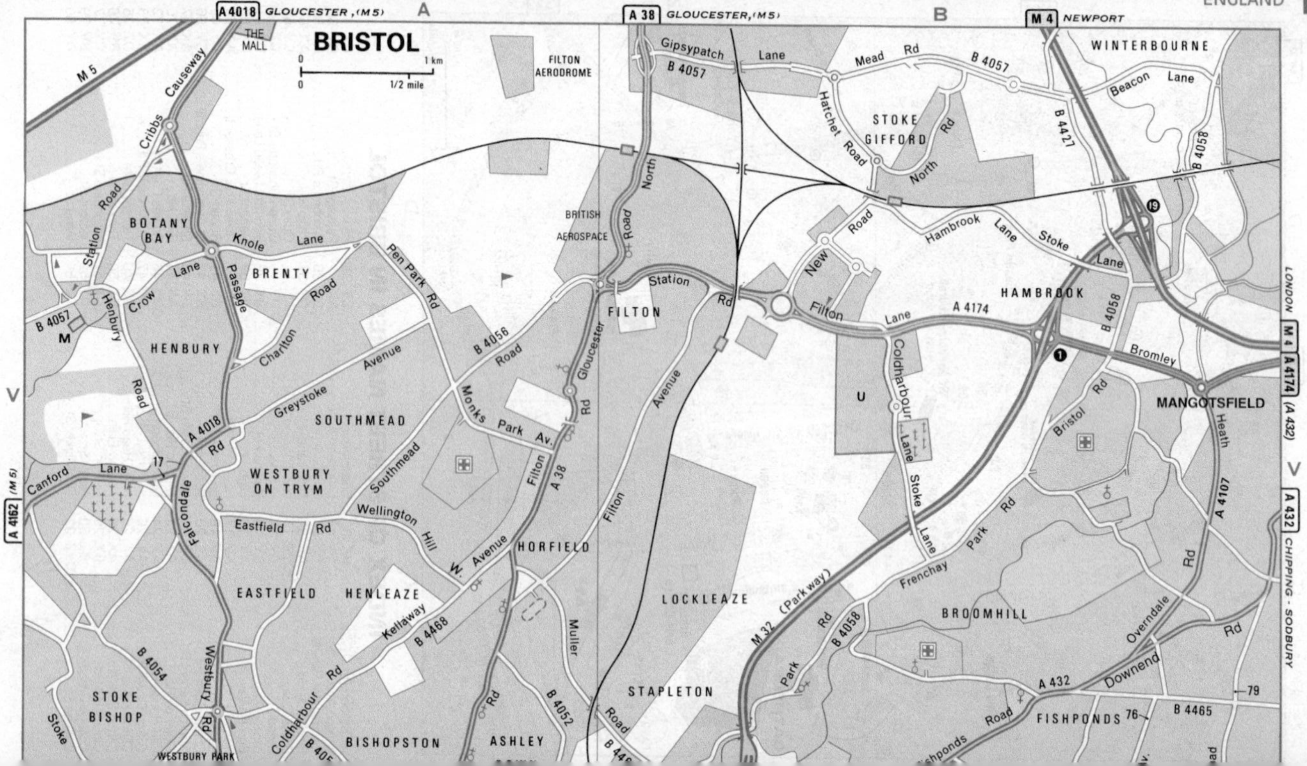

BRISTOL

0 — 1 km
0 — 1/2 mile

A 4018 GLOUCESTER, (M5)
A 38 GLOUCESTER, (M5)
M 4 NEWPORT
M 4 A 4174 (A 432) LONDON
A 432 CHIPPING - SODBURY
A 4162 (M 5)

A
B

THE MALL
M 5
Cribbs Causeway
FILTON AERODROME
BRITISH AEROSPACE
WINTERBOURNE
STOKE GIFFORD
HAMBROOK
MANGOTSFIELD
BOTANY BAY
BRENTY
FILTON
HENBURY
SOUTHMEAD
WESTBURY ON TRYM
HORFIELD
LOCKLEAZE
BROOMHILL
EASTFIELD
HENLEAZE
STAPLETON
FISHPONDS
STOKE BISHOP
BISHOPSTON
ASHLEY
WESTBURY PARK

Gipsypatch Lane
B 4057
Mead Rd
Beacon Lane
B 4427
B 4058
Hatchet Road
North Rd
North Road
Hambrook Lane
Stoke Lane
New Road
Station Rd
Filton Lane
A 4174
Bromley Heath
A 4107
Coldharbour Lane
Stoke Lane
Bristol Rd
Park Rd
Frenchay Park Rd
M 32 (Parkway)
Overndale Rd
Downend Road
A 432
B 4465
Fishponds Road
Station Road
Knole Lane
Passage
Crow Lane
Henbury Road
Charlton Road
Pen Park Rd
B 4056 Road
Gloucester Rd
Monks Park Av.
Filton Avenue
Greystoke Avenue
A 4018 Rd
Southmead
Filton A 38
Canford Lane
Falcondale
Eastfield Rd
Wellington Hill
W. Avenue
Kellaway
B 4468
Muller Rd
B 4052
B 4054
Westbury Rd
Coldharbour Rd
Stoke
Road
B 440
B 444
U
M
17
19
1
76
79

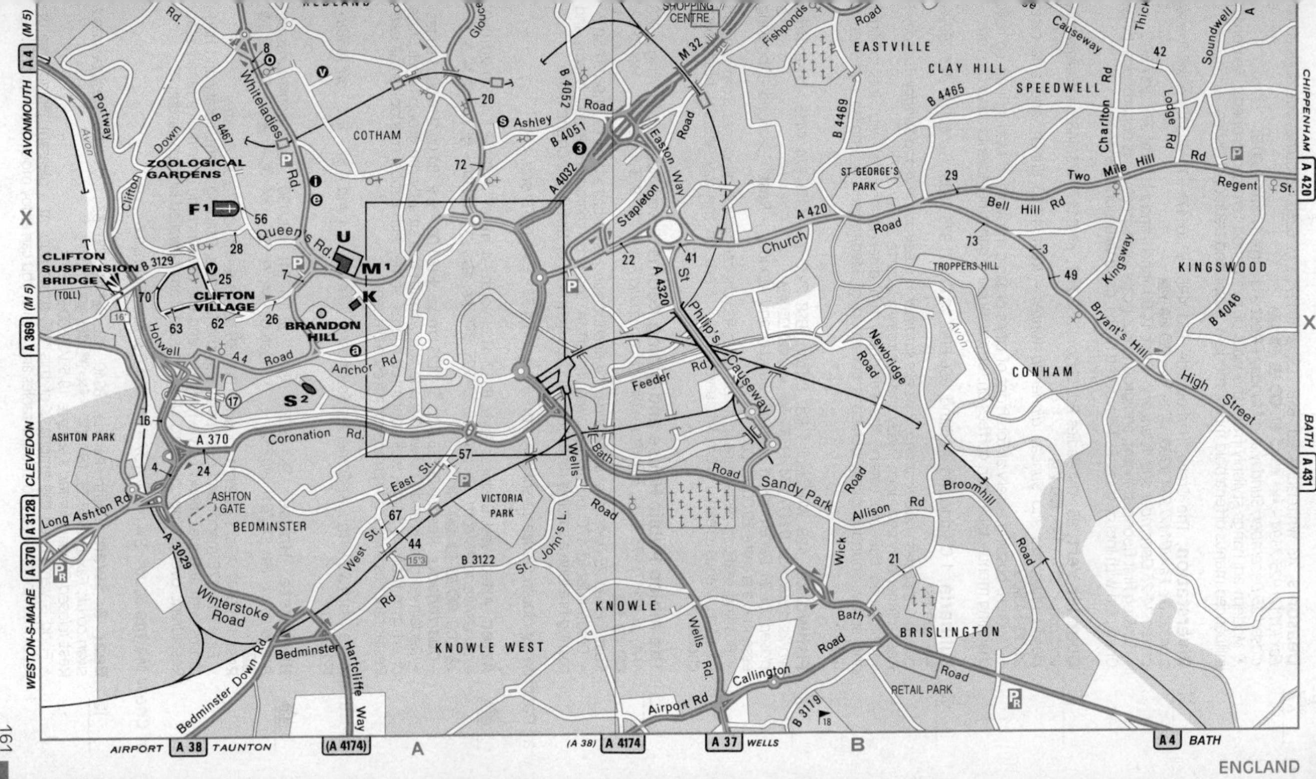
AVONMOUTH A 4 (M 5)
A 369 (M 5)
CLEVEDON A 3128
WESTON-S-MARE A 370
CHIPPENHAM A 420
BATH A 431
AIRPORT A 38 TAUNTON
(A 4174)
(A 38) A 4174
A 37 WELLS
A 4 BATH
A
B
EASTVILLE
CLAY HILL
SPEEDWELL
KINGSWOOD
CONHAM
TROPPERS HILL
BRISLINGTON
RETAIL PARK
KNOWLE
KNOWLE WEST
BEDMINSTER
ASHTON GATE
ASHTON PARK
VICTORIA PARK
ST GEORGE'S PARK
COTHAM
ZOOLOGICAL GARDENS
CLIFTON SUSPENSION BRIDGE
(TOLL)
CLIFTON VILLAGE
BRANDON HILL
SHOPPING CENTRE
Portway
Avon
Clifton Down
B 4467
Whiteladies Rd.
Queen's Rd.
B 3129
Hotwell
A 4 Road
Anchor Rd
A 370
Coronation Rd.
Long Ashton Rd
A 3029
Winterstoke Road
Bedminster Down Rd
Bedminster
Hartcliffe Way
East St.
West St.
B 3122
St. John's L.
Wells Road
Wells Rd.
Airport Rd
Callington
B 3119
Bath Road
Road
Sandy Park
Wick Road
Allison Rd
Broomhill Road
Newbridge Road
Feeder Rd
Philip's Causeway
A 4320
St
Stapleton
Easton Way
Road
M 32
Fishponds
Road
B 4052
Ashley
B 4051
A 4032
Gloucester
B 4469
B 4465
Causeway
Charlton Rd
Lodge Rd
Soundwell
Two Mile Hill
Rd
Regent St.
Bell Hill Rd
Church Road
A 420
Kingsway
Bryant's Hill
B 4046
High Street

ENGLAND

XX **Deason's,** 43 Whiteladies Rd, BS8 2LS, ✆ (0117) 973 6230, *enquiries@deasons.co.uk, Fax (0117) 923 7394* – ⇔ ▤ ⇔ 12. MC AE ⓓ VISA AX e
closed 25 December, Sunday and Monday – **Rest** a la carte 17.50/29.00 ♀.
◆ Modern art hangs stylishly from the walls of this period terraced property. Seasonally influenced menus offer a bold mix of modern, classic and traditional dishes.

X **Riverstation,** The Grove, Harbourside, BS1 4RB, ✆ (0117) 914 4434, *relax@riverstation.co.uk, Fax (0117) 934 9990,* ⛱ – ⇔. MC ⓓ VISA CZ c
closed 24-26 December and 1 January – **Rest** 14.50 (lunch) and a la carte 27.50/37.50 ♀.
◆ Striking first floor restaurant, and ground floor café, with great views of harbour activity. Open plan with lots of glass. Full-flavoured mains; good value lunches, too.

X **Quartier Vert,** 85 Whiteladies Rd, Clifton, BS8 2NT, ✆ (0117) 973 4482, *info@quartiervert.co.uk,* ⛱ – ⇔. MC VISA AX i
closed Christmas and Sunday dinner in winter – **Rest** 19.50 (lunch) and a la carte 21.00/34.50 ♀.
◆ Modern, bustling eatery at forefront of city's organic movement. Med influenced daily changing menus, tapas bar, coffees on terrace. Good organic ingredients always to fore.

X **Culinaria,** 1 Chandos Rd, Redland, BS6 6PG, ✆ (0117) 973 7999, *Fax (0117) 973 7999* – ⇔. MC VISA AX v
closed Christmas, 1 week spring, 2 weeks summer, 1 week autumn and Sunday-Tuesday – **Rest** (dinner only and lunch Friday and Saturday) a la carte 22.70/26.75.
◆ Combined deli and eatery; the personally run diner is informal with lots of light and space. Sound cooking behind a collection of Mediterranean, English and French dishes.

X **Fishworks,** 128 Whiteladies Rd, Clifton, BS8 2RS, ✆ (0117) 974 4433, *bristol@fishworks.co.uk, Fax (0117) 974 4933* – ⇔ ▤. MC AE VISA AX o
closed 25-26 December, 1 January, Sunday and Monday – **Rest** - Seafood - (booking essential) a la carte 20.00/40.00 ♀.
◆ Bustling seafood restaurant in a fishmongers: choose your ingredients from the fish counter. Menus created from whatever arrives fresh on the day. Vibrant blackboard choice.

The Albion Public House and Dining Rooms, Boyces Ave, Clifton Village, BS8 4AA, ✆ (0117) 973 3522, *info@thealbionclifton.co.uk, Fax (0117) 973 9768,* ⛱ – ⇔ ⇔ 12. MC ⓓ VISA AX v
Rest *(closed 25 December and Sunday dinner)* (booking essential) a la carte 21.00/37.50 ♀.
◆ Grade II listed 17C inn hidden away in Clifton. Loads of character: settles, beams and roaring fire lend a suitably rustic feel for the enjoyment of tasty West Country fare.

at Patchway *(South Gloucestershire) North : 6½ m. on A 38* – **BV** – ✉ *Bristol.*

Aztec, Aztec West Business Park, BS32 4TS, North : 1 m. by A 38 ✆ (01454) 201090, *aztec@shirehotels.com, Fax (01454) 201593,* ⛱, Ⅰ₅, ≘s, ⊠, squash – |‡| ⇔ ▤ ✆ ♿ P – 🏛 200. MC AE ⓓ VISA. ✂
– ***Quarterjacks :*** **Rest** 30.00/35.00 **s.** ♀ – **125 rm** ☐ ✝164.00 – ✝✝184.00/214.00, 3 suites.
◆ Reclaimed beams and Cotswold stone add warmth to a smartly run group hotel. State of art gym facilities. Large, well-appointed rooms; some, with patios, overlook small lake. Restaurant has sheltered terrace for alfresco dinners.

at Hunstrete *(Bath & North East Somerset) Southeast : 10 m. by A 4 and A 37* – **BX** – *off A 368* – ✉ *Bristol.*

Hunstrete House ⛭, BS39 4NS, ✆ (01761) 490490, *reception@hunstretehouse.co.uk, Fax (01761) 490732,* ≤, ⛆ heated, ⛲, ⛳, ✂ – ⇔ P – 🏛 40. MC AE ⓓ VISA
Rest 19.95/47.75 **s.** ♀ – **22 rm** ☐ ✝105.00/135.00 – ✝✝150.00/170.00, 3 suites.
◆ Fine late 17C manor and deer park near the Mendips. Drawing room, library and bedrooms with antiques, period style furniture and the idiosyncratic charm of a family seat. Restaurant, overlooking courtyard, uses produce from its walled kitchen garden.

at Chew Magna *South : 8¼ m. by A 37* – **BX** – *on B 3130* – ✉ *Bristol.*

Bear & Swan, South Parade, BS40 8SL, ✆ (01275) 331100, *enquiries@bearandswan.co.uk, Fax (01275) 332187,* ⛱ – ⇔ P. MC VISA
Rest *(closed Sunday dinner)* a la carte 19.50/29.00 ♀.
◆ Food is very much the emphasis of this 19C stone pub. At a pleasant dining area of reclaimed floorboards and antique tables and chairs, you can enjoy modern eclectic dishes.

at Stanton Wick *(Bath & North East Somerset) South : 9 m. by A 37 –* **BX** *– and A 368 on Stanton Wick rd – ✉ Bristol.*

Carpenters Arms with rm, BS39 4BX, ✆ (01761) 490202, *carpenters@buccaneer.co.uk, Fax (01761) 490763,* – P. VISA.
closed dinner 25-26 December – **Rest** a la carte 21.00/25.00 – **12 rm** 64.50 – 89.50.
◆ A row of converted miners' cottages in a rural village: cosy, firelit real ale bar with exposed stone walls and good-sized, pine furnished rooms in subtle floral patterns. Popular beamed "parlour" for meals.

BRITWELL SALOME *Oxon.*
London 75 – Oxford 21 – Reading 19.

The Goose, OX49 5LG, ✆ (01491) 612304, *thegooseatbritwellsalome@fsmail.net, Fax (01491) 613945,* – P. VISA
closed Sunday dinner – **Rest** 18.00 (lunch) and a la carte 22.50/34.50.
Spec. Fillet of sea bream, scallop and tiger prawn with soused vegetables. Ballottine of chicken with morels and sweetbreads, truffle jus. Passion fruit soufflé and sorbet.
◆ Well-established, simply styled pub, offering local game, fish and organic food: concise, assured, modern and classic menu.

BRIXHAM *Devon* 503 *J 32 The West Country G. – pop. 17 457.*
Env. : Berry Head★ (≤★★★) NE : 1½ m.
The Old Market House, The Quay ✆ (01803) 852861.
London 230 – Exeter 30 – Plymouth 32 – Torquay 8.

Berry Head , Berry Head Rd, TQ5 9AJ, ✆ (01803) 853225, *stay@berryheadhotel.com, Fax (01803) 882084,* ≤ Torbay, , , – rest, P – 300. VISA
Rest 12.50/22.00 and a la carte 16.50/29.50 s. – **32 rm** 48.00/88.00 – 120.00/172.00.
◆ Clifftop 18C hotel, once a military hospital, with lovely coastal views. Panelled lounge, a lively, locally popular bar and terrace and trim, bright rooms in modern prints. Restaurant affords fine panorama of the Channel.

Quayside, 41 King St, TQ5 9TJ, ✆ (01803) 855751, *reservations@quaysidehotel.co.uk, Fax (01803) 882733,* ≤ – P. VISA
Rest (bar lunch)/dinner a la carte 11.50/29.00 – **29 rm** 57.00/73.00 – 115.00/135.00.
◆ Six converted fishermen's cottages with colourfully decorated rooms, at their best on the harbour side: some have pleasant window seats. Friendly bar; a popular local choice. Soft-toned restaurant showcases freshly landed seafood.

BROAD CAMPDEN *Glos. –* *see Chipping Campden.*

BROAD CHALKE *Wilts.* 503 504 *O 30 –* *see Salisbury.*

BROADHEMBURY *Devon* 503 *K 31 – ✉ Honiton.*
London 191 – Exeter 17 – Honiton 5 – Taunton 23.

Drewe Arms, EX14 3NF, ✆ (01404) 841267, *nigelburge@btconnect.com, Fax (01404) 841118,* – P. VISA
closed Sunday dinner, 25 and 31 December – **Rest** - Seafood - (booking essential) a la carte 10.00/30.00.
◆ Intimate and instantly likeable medieval thatched pub with flagged floor and log fire. Robust chalkboard menu, featuring prime local seafood; simple and flavourful. Local ale.

BROAD OAK *E. Sussex.*
London 62.5 – Hastings 8 – Rye 7.

Fairacres without rest., Udimore Rd, TN31 6DG, on B 2089 ✆ (01424) 883236, *johnshelagh@fairacres.fsworld.co.uk, Fax (01424) 883236,* – P
closed Christmas and New Year – **3 rm** 59.00 – 75.00.
◆ Listed 17C cottage in picture-postcard pink. Big breakfasts under low beams. Individual rooms: one overlooks superb magnolia tree in garden. All have many thoughtful extras.

BROADSTAIRS *Kent* 504 Y 29.

London 77.5 – Canterbury 18.5 – Ramsgate 2.

The Victoria without rest., 23 Victoria Parade, CT10 1QL, ☎ (01843) 871010, *mu lin@thevictoriabroadstairs.co.uk, Fax (01843) 860888,* ←, – ✻ ☎ P. MC VISA.
6 rm ☐ ★41.00/88.00 – ★★129.00.
◆ Large 19C house with views to Viking Bay, harbour and gardens. Proud use of Kentish produce at breakfast. Spotless rooms: The Balcony, in prime position, overlooks the front

Marchesi, 16-18 Albion St, CT10 1AN, ☎ (01843) 862481, *enquiries@marchesi.co.uk Fax (01843) 861509,* ←, – ✻. MC AE VISA
closed Sunday dinner and Monday except in summer – **Rest** 16.95 (lunch) and a la carte 21.85/32.90 ♀.
◆ Family owned since 1886; traditionality the key to dining room, conservatory and delightful terrace. Balanced, modern menus with local fish, and classics brought up-to-date.

BROADWAY *Worcs.* 503 504 O 27 *Great Britain G. – pop. 2 496.*

See : *Town*★.
Env. : *Country Park (Broadway Tower* ✻★★*), SE : 2 m. by A 44 – Snowshill Manor*★ *(Terrace Garden*★*) AC, S : 2½ m.*
ℹ *1 Cotswold Court* ☎ *(01386) 852937.*
London 93 – Birmingham 36 – Cheltenham 15 – Oxford 38 – Worcester 22.

The Lygon Arms, High St, WR12 7DU, ☎ (01386) 852255, *info@thelygonarms.co.uk Fax (01386) 854470,* ⓦ, Ꮀ, ≘, , , – ✻, ▤ rest, P – 80. MC AE ① VISA
The Great Hall : **Rest** 28.00/44.50 and dinner a la carte 47.75/66.45 ♀ – (see also ***Goblets*** below) – **66 rm** ☐ ★139.00/260.00 – ★★260.00/305.00, 3 suites.
◆ Superbly enticing, quintessentially English coaching inn with many 16C architectural details in its panelled, beamed interiors and rooms Charles I and Cromwell once stayed in. Refined dining and baronial splendours: heraldic friezes and minstrels' gallery.

Dormy House, Willersey Hill, WR12 7LF, East : 3¼ m. by A 44 and Broadway Golf Club rd ☎ (01386) 852711, *reservations@dormyhouse.co.uk, Fax (01386) 858636,* , Ꮀ, ≘, – ✻ ♿ P – 170. MC AE ① VISA
closed 24-27 December – ***The Dining Room :*** **Rest** (dinner only and Sunday lunch)/dinner 34.00 and a la carte 28.50/38.50 ♀ – ***Barn Owl :*** **Rest** a la carte approx 20.00 ♀ – **42 rm** ☐ ★120.00 – ★★175.00, 5 suites.
◆ Creeper-clad 17C farmhouse and outbuildings. Sizeable rooms and comfortable lounge open fires, wing armchairs and a warm country house palette. Dine in cosy, rustic rooms or conservatory. Barn Owl is an A-framed hall with flagged floors.

The Broadway, The Green, WR12 7AA, ☎ (01386) 852401, *info@broadwayhotel.info, Fax (01386) 853879,* , – ✻ P. MC AE VISA
The Courtyard : **Rest** 12.50/23.95 ♀ – **20 rm** ☐ ★80.00/90.00 – ★★150.00.
◆ A 16C inn on the green, built as an abbot's retreat; sympathetically updated rooms in a pretty mix of rural patterns with an atmospheric, horse racing themed, timbered bar. Half-timbered restaurant with leaded windows.

The Olive Branch without rest., 78 High St, WR12 7AJ, ☎ (01386) 853440, *david pam@theolivebranch-broadway.fsnet.co.uk, Fax (01386) 859070* – ✻ P. MC VISA
8 rm ☐ ★40.00/65.00 – ★★65.00/88.00.
◆ A 1590s former staging post on the high street run by a friendly husband and wife team. Flagged floors, sandstone walls and compact bedrooms with a few charming touches.

Barn House without rest., 152 High St, WR12 7AJ, ☎ (01386) 858633, *barn house@btinternet.com,* , , – ✻ P
4 rm ☐ ★45.00/60.00 – ★★60.00/80.00.
◆ Traditional 17C house in 16 acres of garden, paddock and croquet lawn, its vast, open galleried hall dominated by a Tudor fireplace. Well-stocked library, spacious rooms.

Windrush House, Station Rd, WR12 7DE, ☎ (01386) 853577, *richard@broadway-wind rush.co.uk, Fax (01386) 853790,* – ✻ P. MC ① VISA
Rest (by arrangement) 18.00 **5 rm** ☐ ★30.00/50.00 – ★★50.00/65.00.
◆ Personally run guesthouse, built at the turn of 20C, with a charming, subtle period style, and a pleasant rear garden. Well-proportioned, affordable rooms.

Whiteacres without rest., Station Rd, WR12 7DE, ☎ (01386) 852320, *whiteacres@btin ternet.com, Fax (01386) 852674,* – ✻ P. MC ① VISA
5 rm ☐ ★35.00/45.00 – ★★50.00/65.00.
◆ Spacious accommodation - homely, pleasantly updated and modestly priced - in a personally owned Victorian house, a short walk from the village centre.

XX **Russell's** with rm, 20 High St, WR12 7DT, ☎ (01386) 853555, *info@russellsofbroadway.com*, – ⊬ 🅿. MC VISA
Rest *(closed Sunday dinner)* 19.95/21.95 and a la carte 25.00/35.00 ♀ – **4 rm** ☕ ♦75.00 – ♦♦75.00/180.00.
◆ Behind the splendid Cotswold stone façade lies a stylish modern restaurant with terrace front and rear. Seasonally influenced, regularly changing menus. Smart, comfy bedrooms.

X **Goblets,** High St, WR12 7DU, ☎ (01386) 854418, *Fax (01386) 858611* – ⊬ 🅿. MC AE ⦿ VISA
Rest (booking essential) a la carte 23.90/31.70 ♀.
◆ Characterfully firelit in rustic dark oak. Modern dining room at front more atmospheric than one to rear. Menus of light,, tasty, seasonal dishes offered.

at Buckland *(Glos.) Southwest : 2¼ m. by B 4632 – ✉ Broadway.*

Buckland Manor ⛰, WR12 7LY, ☎ (01386) 852626, *info@bucklandmanor.co.uk*, *Fax (01386) 853557*, ←, ⛱, ⛹, ✂ – ⊬ rest, 🅿. MC AE VISA. ✂
Rest (booking essential to non-residents) 25.50 (lunch) and dinner a la carte 39.20/53.00 ♀ – **14 rm** ☕ ♦240.00 – ♦♦420.00.
◆ Secluded part 13C country house with beautiful gardens. Individually furnished bedrooms boast high degree of luxury. Fine service throughout as old-world serenity prevails. Restaurant boasts elegant crystal, fine china and smooth service.

For a pleasant stay in a charming hotel,
look for the red 🏠 ... 🏰 symbols.

BROCKDISH *Norfolk* 504 X 26 – *see Diss.*

BROCKENHURST *Hants.* 503 504 P 31 *Great Britain G. – pop. 2 865.*
Env. : *New Forest★★ (Rhinefield Ornamental Drive★★, Bolderwood Ornamental Drive★★).*
⛳18 *Brockenhurst Manor, Sway Rd ☎ (01590) 623332.*
London 99 – Bournemouth 17 – Southampton 14 – Winchester 27.

Rhinefield House ⛰, Rhinefield Rd, SO42 7QB, Northwest : 3 m. ☎ (01590) 622922, *rhinefieldhouse@handpicked.co.uk*, *Fax (01590) 622800*, ⊛, ⛱, ⛹, ⛳, ✂ – ⊬ 🅿 – 🎪 120. MC AE ⦿ VISA. ✂
Armada : Rest 19.95/34.95 ♀ – **34 rm** ☕ ♦210.00 – ♦♦270.00/310.00.
◆ A long ornamental pond reflects this imposing 19C New Forest mansion, surveying parterres and a yew maze. Panelled drawing room. Handsomely appointed bedrooms in new wing. Dining room in gleaming oak with forest views.

Careys Manor, Lyndhurst Rd, SO42 7RH, on A 337 ☎ (08707) 512305, *stay@careysmanor.com*, *Fax (08707) 512306*, ⊛, Ꮀ, ≘s, ⛱, ⛹ – ⊬ 🅿 – 🎪 150. MC AE ⦿ VISA. ✂
Rest (dinner only) 29.50 and a la carte 42.45/45.95 – ***Blaireau's*** *(☎ (01590) 623032)* ***: Rest*** - French - a la carte 16.70/29.25 – ***The Zen Garden :*** Rest - Thai - *(closed dinner Sunday and Monday)* a la carte 21.85/29.85 – **79 rm** ☕ ♦79.00/139.00 – ♦♦158.00/190.00, 1 suite.
◆ Smartly run, substantial 19C house with modern additions, near the main road. Some bedrooms have balcony overlooking gardens; the manor house rooms are the best. Fine dining in smart restaurant. Blaireau's is informal bistro with hints of French styling.

New Park Manor ⛰, Lyndhurst Rd, SO42 7QH, North : 1½ m. on A 337 ☎ (01590) 623467, *info@newparkmanorhotel.co.uk*, *Fax (01590) 622268*, ←, ⊛, Ꮀ, ≘s, ⛱ heated, ⛱, ⛹, ⛳, ✂ – ⊬ 🅿 – 🎪 120. MC AE ⦿ VISA
Stag : Rest 19.50/38.00 s. – **24 rm** ☕ ♦110.00/135.00 – ♦♦275.00.
◆ Extended, elegantly proportioned hunting lodge with equestrian centre for guided forest treks. Rooms, some in former servants' quarters, have four posters and parkland views. Candlelit fine dining.

Cloud, Meerut Rd, SO42 7TD, ☎ (01590) 622165, *enquiries@cloudhotel.co.uk*, *Fax (01590) 622818*, – ⊬ 🅿. MC VISA
closed 27 December-13 January – **Rest** 13.50/29.00 – **18 rm** ☕ ♦67.00/196.00 – ♦♦176.00/196.00.
◆ Well-kept, comfortable and personally owned, with something of a country cottage character. Simple, pine furnished accommodation; views over the wooded countryside. Intimate little restaurant with pleasant covered terrace.

The Cottage without rest., Sway Rd, SO42 7SH, ☎ (01590) 622296, *chris@cottagehotel.org*, *Fax (01590) 623014*, ⛹ – ⊬ 🅿. MC ⦿ VISA. ✂
closed Christmas – **6 rm** ☕ ♦50.00/85.00 – ♦♦75.00/100.00.
◆ 300-year old former forester's cottage in the heart of the village: family run and faultlessly kept. Low oak beamed ceiling, cosy snug bar and large, neatly appointed rooms.

ENGLAND

XXX **Le Poussin at Whitley Ridge** (Aitken) with rm, Beaulieu Rd, SO42 7QL, East 1 m. on B 3055 ✆ (01590) 622354, *sales@lepoussin.co.uk, Fax (01590) 622856*, ≤, – ⇔ P. MO AE VISA
closed 2 weeks January – **Le Poussin : Rest** 15.00/40.00 and a la carte 34.00/53.50 – ☐ 10.00 – **22 rm** ✝70.00/100.00 – ✝✝180.00/200.00, 1 suite.
Spec. Pork and prawns with lime and ginger. Quail and foie gras "pie". New Forest venison with "haggis".
◆ Secluded Georgian house, surrounded by acres of parkland. Two period style dining rooms serving accomplished, classically based menus. Individual rooms, some with steam cabin.

XX **Simply Poussin,** The Courtyard, rear of 49-51 Brookley Rd, SO42 7FZ, ✆ (01590) 623063, *simply@lepoussin.co.uk, Fax (01590) 623144* – ⇔. MO AE VISA
closed Sunday-Monday – **Rest** (booking essential) 15.00 (lunch) and a la carte 23.00/28.00 ♀.
◆ Intimate little mews restaurant, tucked away off the village centre, with well-spaced subtly spotlit tables. Capable, flavourful modern British menu; unobtrusive service.

XX **Thatched Cottage** with rm, 16 Brookley Rd, SO42 7RR, ✆ (01590) 623090, *sales@thatchedcottage.co.uk, Fax (01590) 623479* – ⇔ rest, P. MO AE VISA
closed 1 January-10 February – **Rest** *(closed Sunday dinner, Tuesday lunch and Monday)* (booking essential) (light lunch)/dinner a la carte 34.00/45.00 – **5 rm** ☐ ✝70.00/90.00 – ✝✝90.00/150.00.
◆ 17C farmhouse and one-off rooms with a touch of eccentricity to their blend of curios, pictures and bright flowers. Open kitchen; elaborate, locally sourced menu.

at Sway *Southwest : 3 m. by B 3055 – ✉ Lymington.*

XX **The Nurse's Cottage** with rm, Station Rd, SO41 6BA, ✆ (01590) 683402, *nurses.cottage@lineone.net, Fax (01590) 683402*, – ⇔ P. MO AE VISA
closed 3 weeks March and 3 weeks November – **Rest** (booking essential) (dinner only) 22.50 ♀ – **4 rm** (dinner included) ☐ ✝80.00/90.00 – ✝✝160.00.
◆ Personally run, welcoming conservatory restaurant with an intimate charm. Traditional menus make good use of Hampshire's larder. Pristine, comfy rooms with pretty details.

BROCKTON *Shrops. – see Much Wenlock.*

BROCKWORTH *Glos.* 504 N 28 – *see Cheltenham.*

BROME *Suffolk* 504 X 26 – *see Diss (Norfolk).*

BROMFIELD *Shrops.* 503 L 26 – *see Ludlow.*

BROMSGROVE *Worcs.* 503 504 N 26 – *pop. 29 237.*
Bromsgrove Museum, 26 Birmingham Rd ✆ (01527) 831809.
London 117 – Birmingham 14 – Bristol 71 – Worcester 13.

Premier Travel Inn, Birmingham Rd, B61 0BA, North : ½ m. by A 38 ✆ (0870) 1977044, *Fax (01527) 834719* – ⇔, ▤ rest, ♿ P. MO AE VISA. ⚮
Rest (grill rest.) – **78 rm** ✝46.95/46.95 – ✝✝49.95/49.95.
◆ Useful and spacious hotel, opened in 2004. The airy rooms offer affordable, stylish accommodation, handy for visitors to the nearby Cadbury World experience.

Bromsgrove Country House without rest., 249 Worcester Rd, Stoke Heath, B61 7JA, Southwest : 2 m. on B 4091 ✆ (01527) 835522, *Fax (01527) 871257*, – ⇔ P. MO VISA. ⚮
closed 2 weeks Christmas-New Year – ☐ 4.50 – **7 rm** ✝49.00/59.00 – ✝✝64.00.
◆ Personally run, redbrick Victorian house, on a main road, converted but with original tiling and other period features intact. Sizeable rooms are homely and well kept.

at Stoke Prior *Southwest : 2¼ m. by A 38 on B 4091 – ✉ Bromsgrove.*

XX **Epic,** 68 Hanbury rd, B60 4DN, ✆ (01527) 871929, *epic.bromsgrove@virgin.net, Fax (01527) 575647*, – ⇔ P. ⇔ 12. MO AE VISA
closed Sunday dinner – **Rest** 12.95 (lunch) and a la carte 25.00/32.00 ♀.
◆ Heavily extended former roadside pub: tiled floor and some beams remain. Vast bar; brick and wood cleverly worked into open-plan dining area. Large menus of modern classics.

BROOK *Hants.* 503 504 P 31 – ✉ *Lyndhurst.*
London 92 – Bournemouth 24 – Southampton 14.

Bell Inn, SO43 7HE, ☎ (023) 8081 2214, *bell@bramshaw.co.uk, Fax (023) 8081 3958,* 18, – P – 40. MO AE VISA.
Rest (bar lunch Monday-Saturday)/dinner 31.00 and a la carte 18.70/23.00 – **25 rm** 65.00/110.00 – 90.00/110.00.
◆ Family owned for over 200 years, an extended inn with golf course and clubhouse. Cosy, clubby bar with an open fire and tasty light menu; neat, modern, pine fitted rooms.

BROOKLAND *Kent.*
London 69 – Ashford 12.5 – Rye 7.

Yew and Ewe, High St, TN29 9QR, ☎ (01797) 344215, *info@yewandewe.co.uk, Fax (01797) 344373,* – P. MO VISA
closed Sunday except July-September – **Rest** a la carte 16.00/25.00.
◆ Listed, 15C pub given a facelift. Original beams, real log fire, chunky oak tables, worn effect leather chairs. Local artwork for sale. Modern menus change with the seasons.

BROUGHTON *Cambs. – see Huntingdon.*

BROUGHTON *Lancs.* 502 L 22 *– see Preston.*

BROXTON *Ches.* 502 503 L 24.
London 197 – Birmingham 68 – Chester 12 – Manchester 44 – Stoke-on-Trent 29.

De Vere Carden Park, CH3 9DQ, West : 1 ½ m. on A 534 ☎ (01829) 731000, *reservations.carden@devere-hotels.co.uk, Fax (01829) 731599,* 18, – , rest, P – 400. MO AE VISA.
Garden Restaurant : Rest (dinner only and Sunday lunch)/dinner 27.50 and a la carte 26.45/41.45 **s.** 17.45/29.95 **189 rm** 80.00/170.00 – 180.00, 7 suites.
◆ Very well equipped and up-to-date leisure hotel with extensive grounds in a rural location. Golf breaks a speciality. Main house or courtyard rooms are equally comfortable. Formal Garden Restaurant with Carden estate wines.

BRUNDALL *Norfolk* 504 Y 26.
London 118.5 – Great Yarmouth 15 – Norwich 8.

The Lavender House, 39 The Street, NR13 5AA, ☎ (01603) 712215 – P. MO VISA
closed 23-31 December, Sunday and Monday – **Rest** (booking essential) (dinner only and Friday lunch)/dinner 32.50 **s.**
◆ Locally renowned restaurant with pleasant lounge for pre-prandials. Intimate, beamed dining room. Proudly local menus with the suppliers listed; ingredients are in season.

BRUNTINGTHORPE *Leics. Great Britain G.*
Exc. : *Leicester - Museum and Art Gallery★, Guildhall★ and St Mary de Castro Church★, N : 11 m. by minor rd and A 5199.*
London 96 – Leicester 10 – Market Harborough 15.

Joiners Arms, Church Walk, LE17 5QH, ☎ (0116) 247 8258, *stephen@joinersarmsbruntingthorpe.co.uk, Fax (0116) 247 8258* – P. MO VISA
closed 25 December, Sunday dinner, Monday and Bank Holidays – **Rest** (booking essential) a la carte 19.50/30.00.
◆ 18C pub with beams in small rural village; cosy drinking area. The compact menus and blackboard specials provide well executed, good value dishes with a country flavour.

BRUSHFORD *Somerset* 503 J 30 *– see Dulverton.*

BRUTON *Somerset* 503 504 M 30 *The West Country G. – pop. 2 982.*
Exc. : *Stourhead★★★ AC, W : 8 m. by B 3081.*
London 118 – Bristol 27 – Bournemouth 44 – Salisbury 35 – Taunton 36.

Bruton House, 2-4 High St, BA10 0AA, ☎ (01749) 813395, *info@brutonhouse.co.uk* – . MO AE VISA
closed Sunday dinner and Monday – **Rest** 35.00 (dinner) and lunch a la carte 20.95/26.40 **s.**.
◆ 15C/18C townhouse; beams and fireplace of yore meet interesting contrast in modern art work on walls. Quality locally sourced produce in imaginative, well-executed dishes.

Truffles, 95 High St, BA10 0AR, ✆ (01749) 812255, *deborah@trufflesbruton.co.uk* – ⇔ ▤. MC VISA
closed Monday-Wednesday lunch – **Rest** 15.00/26.95 ♀.
◆ Cottagey façade; intimate and cosy two-level interior. Personally run, the husband and wife team take pride in a small, well prepared menu rich in market fresh local produce.

BRYHER *Cornwall* 503 ㉚ – *see Scilly (Isles of).*

BUCKDEN *Cambs.* 504 T 27 – *pop. 2 385* – ✉ *Huntingdon.*
London 65 – Bedford 15 – Cambridge 20 – Northampton 31.

The George, High St, PE19 5XA, ✆ (01480) 812300, *manager@thegeorgebuckden.com, Fax (01480) 813920,* – ⇔ P. MC AE VISA.
Rest – (see ***Brasserie*** below) – **12 rm** ☆70.00 – ☆☆130.00.
◆ 19C former coaching inn in village centre, now refurbished with individuality and high quality soft furnishings. Smart, stylish rooms, all named after famous 'Georges'.

Lion, High St, PE19 5XA, ✆ (01480) 810313, *reception.lionhotel@virgin.net, Fax (01480) 811070* – ⇔ rest, P. MC AE VISA.
closed 26 December and 1 January – **Rest** 17.50 and a la carte 20.35/28.15 – **15 rm** ☆65.00/73.50 – ☆☆90.00.
◆ 15C Grade II listed with attendant period details: original fireplace with carved Tudor Rose, five spoke ceiling with Lamb and Papal pennant. Has resident ghost. Cosy rooms. Silver service in large panelled restaurant.

Brasserie (at The George H.), High St, PE19 5XA, ✆ (01480) 812300, *manager@thegeorgebuckden.com, Fax (01480) 813920,* – ⇔ P. MC AE VISA.
Rest a la carte 30.00/50.00 ♀.
◆ Modish bar leads into brasserie where modern cooking holds plenty of appeal. Outside is a lovely courtyard terrace with olive trees, whitewashed walls and waxed wood tables.

BUCKHURST HILL *Essex* – *pop. 11 243.*
London 12 – Brighton 82 – Cambridge 48 – Ipswich 73 – Oxford 68.
Plan : see Greater London (North-East) 4

Express by Holiday Inn, High Rd, IG9 5HT, on A 121 ✆ (020) 8504 4450, *Fax (020) 8498 0011* – ⇔ rm, ♿ P – 🔬 30. MC AE ⊕ VISA HT e
Rest (grill rest.) – **49 rm** ☆69.00 – ☆☆69.00.
◆ With Epping Forest on the doorstep, and golfing facilities 3km away, this conveniently positioned lodge offers modern, comfortable accommodation. Toby carvery for meals.

BUCKINGHAM *Bucks.* 503 504 Q 27 *Great Britain G.*
Env. : *Stowe Gardens*★★, *NW : 3 m. by minor rd.*
Exc. : *Claydon House*★ *AC, S : 8 m. by A 413.*
18 *Silverstone, Silverstone Rd, Stowe* ✆ *(01280) 850005* – 18 *Tingewick Rd* ✆ *(01280) 813282.*
London 64 – Birmingham 61 – Northampton 20 – Oxford 25.

Villiers, 3 Castle St, MK18 1BS, ✆ (01280) 822444, *buckingham@villiershotels.com, Fax (01280) 822113* – ♿ P – 🔬 200. MC AE ⊕ VISA.
Henrys **:** **Rest** *(closed Sunday dinner)* (dinner only and Sunday lunch)/dinner 32.00/40.00 ♀ – **42 rm** ☆105.00/135.00 – ☆☆120.00/150.00, 4 suites.
◆ Former coaching inn built around a cobbled courtyard; a town centre landmark ever since its Cromwellian heyday, with a characterful beamed bar and modern lounge and bedrooms. Intimate restaurant to rear of hotel.

BUCKLAND *Glos.* 503 504 O 27 – *see Broadway (Worcs.).*

BUCKLAND *Oxon.* 503 504 P 28 – ✉ *Faringdon.*
London 78 – Oxford 16 – Swindon 15.

Lamb Inn, Lamb Lane, SN7 8QN, ✆ (01367) 870484, *enquiries@thelambatbuckland.co.uk, Fax (01367) 870675,* – ⇔ P. MC ⊕ VISA.
closed 2 weeks Christmas-New Year, Sunday dinner and Monday – **Rest** a la carte 20.00/35.00 ♀.
◆ Sheep motifs appear in paintings, curios and carpet of this 18C real ale pub, well established and family owned. Tasty traditional menu: seafood fricassee, summer pudding.

BUCKLERS HARD *Hants.* 503 504 P 31 – *see Beaulieu.*

BUCKMINSTER *Leics.* 502 504 R 25.
London 114 – Grantham 11 – Melton Mowbray 10.

Tollemache Arms with rm, 48 Main St, NG33 5SA, ✆ (01476) 860007, *enquiries@thetollemachearms.com*, – rm, P 16. MC AE VISA
closed Sunday dinner and Monday – **Rest** 15.00 (lunch) and a la carte 21.00/36.00 – **5 rm** ☕ ✝45.00 – ✝✝60.00.
◆ Late 19C former coaching inn with 21C interior: wood floor, stainless steel bar, huge leather sofas. Modern British à la carte served in evenings. Simple, good value rooms.

BUDE *Cornwall* 503 G 31 *The West Country G. – pop. 8 071 (inc. Stratton).*
See : *The Breakwater★★ – Compass Point (≤★).*
Env. : *Poughill★ (church★★), N : 2½ m. – E : Tamar River★★ – Kilkhampton (Church★), NE : 5½ m. by A 39 – Stratton (Church★), E : 1½ m. – Launcells (Church★), E : 3 m. by A 3072 – Marhamchurch (St Morwenne's Church★), SE : 2 ½ m. by A 39 – Poundstock★ (≤★★, church★, guildhouse★), S : 4½ m. by A 39.*
Exc. : *Morwenstow (cliffs★★, church★), N : 8½ m. by A 39 and minor roads – Jacobstow (Church★), S : 7 m. by A 39.*
Burn View ✆ (01288) 352006.
Bude Visitor Centre, The Crescent ✆ (01288) 354240.
London 252 – Exeter 51 – Plymouth 50 – Truro 53.

Falcon, Breakwater Rd, EX23 8SD, ✆ (01288) 352005, *reception@falconhotel.com, Fax (01288) 356359*, ≤, – P – 180. MC AE VISA.
closed 25 December – **Rest** (bar lunch Monday-Saturday)/dinner a la carte 15.50/22.95 **s.** – **27 rm** ☕ ✝52.50/67.50 – ✝✝105.00/125.00.
◆ An imposing, personally run hotel with the proudly traditional character of a bygone age. Contemporary and classic blend in bedrooms. Separate private garden. Formal dining.

Hartland, Hartland Terrace, EX23 8JY, ✆ (01288) 355661, *hartlandhotel@aol.com, Fax (01288) 355664*, ≤, heated – P
closed December-February except Christmas and New Year – **Rest** (bar lunch)/dinner 23.00/25.00 – **28 rm** ☕ ✝51.00/67.00 – ✝✝94.00/100.00.
◆ Sizeable seaside hotel, family owned and run for over 30 years. Individually appointed rooms mix modern or period furniture with African, Egyptian and nautical themes. Dine by the dance floor on red leather banquettes.

Bude Haven, Flexbury Ave, EX23 8NS, ✆ (01288) 352305, *enquiries@budehavenhotel.com, Fax (01288) 352662* – P. MC AE VISA
Rest *(closed Sunday and Wednesday)* (booking essential to non-residents) (dinner only) a la carte 15.00/22.50 – **10 rm** ☕ ✝40.00 – ✝✝100.00.
◆ Large, privately owned Edwardian house on the quiet outskirts of the town. Comfortable lounge, traditionally styled rooms with hot-tubs; affordable and well kept. Dining room with jazz piano on a Saturday night.

BUDLEIGH SALTERTON *Devon* 503 K 32 *The West Country G. – pop. 4 801.*
Env. : *East Budleigh (Church★), N : 2½ m. by A 376 – Bicton★ (Gardens★) AC, N : 3 m. by A 376.*
East Devon, North View Rd ✆ (01395) 442018.
Fore St ✆ (01395) 445275.
London 182 – Exeter 16 – Plymouth 55.

The Long Range, 5 Vales Rd, EX9 6HS, by Raleigh Rd ✆ (01395) 443321, *info@thelongrangehotel.co.uk, Fax (01395) 442132*, – P. MC VISA.
Rest *(closed Monday dinner)* (dinner only and Sunday lunch)/dinner 22.95 – **7 rm** ☕ ✝39.00/60.00 – ✝✝79.00/88.00.
◆ Homely and unassuming little hotel, personally run in quiet residential street. Sun lounge with bright aspect, overlooking broad lawn and neat borders. Simple, unfussy rooms. Tasty, locally sourced dishes in a comfy dining room.

at Yettington *North : 3 m. by B 3178 – ✉ Budleigh Salterton.*

Lufflands without rest., EX9 7BP, ✆ (01395) 568422, *stay@lufflands.co.uk, Fax (01395) 568810*, – P. MC VISA.
3 rm ☕ ✝29.00/34.00 – ✝✝58.00.
◆ 400 year-old farmhouse with Victorian additions in pleasant rural setting. Simple breakfast room doubles as cosy lounge area: inglenook fireplace. Well-kept bedrooms.

BUDOCK WATER *Cornwall* – *see Falmouth.*

BUNBURY *Ches.* 502 503 504 M 24 – *see Tarporley.*

BUNGAY *Suffolk* 504 Y 26 *Great Britain G.* – *pop. 4 895.*
Exc. : *Norwich★★ - Cathedral★★, Castle Museum★, Market Place★, NW : 15 m. by B 1332 and A 146.*
London 108 – Beccles 6 – Ipswich 38.

at Earsham *Southwest : 3 m. by A 144 and A 143 – ✉ Bungay.*

Earsham Park Farm without rest., Harleston Rd, NR35 2AQ, on A 143 ✆ (01986) 892180, *bobbie@earsham-parkfarm.co.uk, Fax (01986) 892180,* – P. MO VISA
3 rm ★42.00/62.00 – ★★84.00/86.00.
• Isolated red-brick Victorian farmhouse, surrounded by working farm. Admire the view while enjoying local produce for breakfast. Well appointed rooms with rural names.

BURCHETT'S GREEN *Windsor & Maidenhead.*
London 35 – Maidenhead 6 – Oxford 33 – Reading 12 – Southampton 61.

Burchett's Place Country House without rest., Burchett's Green Rd, SL6 6QZ, ✆ (01628) 825023, *Fax (01628) 826672,* – P.
4 rm ★45.00 – ★★75.00.
• Tudor style country house set in fields. Breakfast cooked on Aga, served in conservatory dining room. Rooms decorated by interior designer owner; those to rear are quieter.

BURCOMBE *Wilts. – see Salisbury.*

BURFORD *Oxon.* 503 504 P 28.
18 ✆ *(01993) 822583.*
The Brewery, Sheep St ✆ (01993) 823558.
London 76 – Birmingham 55 – Gloucester 32 – Oxford 20.

Bay Tree, 12-14 Sheep St, OX18 4LW, ✆ (01993) 822791, *info@baytreehotel.info, Fax (01993) 823008,* – rest, P. – 30. MO AE VISA
Rest 18.95/27.95 and a la carte 21.85/44.85 ♀ – **21 rm** ★119.00/165.00 – ★★215.00, 3 suites.
• Handsome, ivy-clad 16C hotel. Warm, antique furnished library lounge. Hunting trophies over a broad stone fireplace. Thoughtfully appointed rooms in rich chintz and tartans. Flagged country dining room overlooks walled rose and herb garden.

Lamb Inn, Sheep St, OX18 4LR, ✆ (01993) 823155, *info@lambinn-burford.co.uk, Fax (01993) 822228,* – MO AE VISA
– **Rest** (bar lunch Monday-Saturday)/dinner 32.50 and a la carte 21.90/32.95 ♀ – **15 rm** ★115.00 – ★★235.00.
• Relaxing, part 14C inn in weathered local stone. Window seats, broad rugs and age-old wooden armchairs in a charming lounge. Trim cottage rooms: floral fabrics and antiques. Classically formal restaurant reflects inn's age.

Burford House without rest., 99 High St, OX18 4QA, ✆ (01993) 823151, *stay@burfordhouse.co.uk, Fax (01993) 823240,* – MO AE VISA.
closed 2 weeks January – **8 rm** ★85.00/110.00 – ★★110.00/155.00.
• 17C town house. Paintings, antiques and rich fabrics in welcoming lounges and elegantly composed rooms, some with Victorian baths. Lavish afternoon teas with home-made cakes.

Inn For All Seasons, The Barringtons, OX18 4TN, West : 3 ¼ m. on A 40 ✆ (01451) 844324, *sharp@innforallseasons.com, Fax (01451) 844375,* – P. – 35. MO AE VISA
Rest 15.00/20.00 and a la carte 18.75/32.50 **s.** ♀ – **10 rm** ★56.50/59.50 – ★★97.00/147.00.
• Sizeable, well cared-for rooms in a family owned roadside inn; flagstone floor and traditional booths in a pleasant bar, hung with burnished brass. Cask ales. Convivial dining room with seafood specialities.

Jonathan's at the Angel brasserie with rm, 14 Witney St, OX18 4SN, ✆ (01993) 822714, *jo@theangel-uk.com, Fax (01993) 822069,* – MO VISA.
closed 18 January-9 February, Sunday dinner except at Bank Holidays and Monday, minimum stay 2 nights at weekends – **Rest** (booking essential) a la carte 22.95/34.50 ♀ – **3 rm** ★75.00 – ★★85.00.
• Splendid mellow 16C former coaching inn. Modern yet rustic restaurant with natural wood tables. Brasserie dishes from Thai to Mediterranean. Approachable staff. Restful rooms.

BURLEY IN WHARFEDALE *W. Yorks.* 502 O 22 – *pop. 5 865.*
London 218 – Bradford 14 – Harrogate 15 – Leeds 14 – Preston 52.

XX **Mantra,** 78 Main St, LS29 7BT, ✆ (01943) 864602, *david@mantra.uk.net, Fax (01943) 865239* – ⇔. MC VISA
closed Sunday dinner – **Rest** (dinner only and Sunday lunch)/dinner a la carte 18.00/29.25 ♀.
• Busy, personally run neighbourhood restaurant: high backed chairs, closely set tables and colourful modern décor. Extensive British menu with some unusual combinations.

BURLEYDAM *Ches. – see Whitchurch (Shrops.).*

BURLTON *Shrops. – ✉ Shrewsbury.*
London 235 – Shrewsbury 10 – Wrexham 20.

Burlton Inn with rm, SY4 5TB, ✆ (01939) 270284, *bean@burltoninn.co.uk, Fax (01939) 270214,* – P. MC VISA
closed 25-26 December, 1 January and lunch Bank Holiday Monday – **Rest** (restricted lunch Monday) a la carte 17.00/29.65 ♀ – **6 rm** ☕ ★50.00 – ★★80.00.
• Bustling, family run pub with a characterful, wood furnished interior. Extensive menus of traditional fare. Bedrooms in contemporary style. Four Poster bed available.

BURNHAM MARKET *Norfolk* 504 W 25 *Great Britain G.*
Env. : *Holkham Hall★★ AC, E : 3 m. by B 1155.*
18 *Lambourne, Dropmore Rd ✆ (01628) 666755.*
London 128 – Cambridge 71 – Norwich 36.

The Hoste Arms, The Green, PE31 8HD, ✆ (01328) 738777, *reception@hostearms.co.uk, Fax (01328) 730103,* – ⇔ P ⇔ 26 – 25. MC VISA
Rest – (see ***The Restaurant*** below) – **35 rm** ☕ ★82.00 – ★★248.00, 1 suite.
• Renowned and restored 17C inn in this pretty village. Intriguing wing in Zulu style. Individually designed rooms provide a high level of comfort. Informal ambience.

X **The Restaurant** (at The Hoste Arms), The Green, PE31 8HD, ✆ (01328) 738777, *Fax (01328) 730103,* – ⇔ P ⇔ 26. MC VISA
Rest (booking essential) a la carte 19.25/33.95 ♀.
• North Sea fish features in an Anglo-European and oriental fusion menu. Delightful terrace with Moroccan theme for summer dining. Invariably friendly staff.

X **Fishes,** Market Pl, PE31 8HE, ✆ (01328) 738588, *ob1@sizzel.net, Fax (01328) 730534* – ⇔. MC VISA
closed 3 weeks January, 1 week Christmas, Sunday dinner and Monday except last week July, August and Bank Holidays – **Rest** - Seafood - 19.50/35.00 ♀.
• Attractive restaurant in centre of popular North Norfolk town. Locally caught seafood dishes are well prepared and tasty; lunches are good value.

at Burnham Thorpe *Southeast : 1¼ m. by B 1355 – ✉ Burnham Market.*

The Lord Nelson, Walsingham Rd, PE31 8HL, ✆ (01328) 738241, *enquiries@nelsonslocal.co.uk, Fax (01328) 738241,* – ⇔ P. MC VISA
closed dinner 25-26 December, Sunday dinner and Monday except summer and Bank Holidays – **Rest** 23.95 (dinner) and a la carte 20.95/30.40 ♀.
• Cosy, characterful pub in small village - Nelson was indeed born here: much memorabilia to remind you. Flagged floors, beams and a tiny bar. Good value, tasty dishes.

BURNHAM-ON-CROUCH *Essex* 504 W 29 – *pop. 7 636.*
18 *Burnham-on-Crouch, Ferry Rd, Creeksea ✆ (01621) 782282.*
London 52 – Chelmsford 19 – Colchester 32 – Southend-on-Sea 25.

XX **The Contented Sole,** 80 High St, CM0 8AA, ✆ (01621) 782139, *thesole@aol.com* – ⇔. MC VISA
closed January, Saturday lunch, Sunday dinner, and Monday and Tuesday – **Rest** a la carte 21.85/34.90.
• Personally run, comfortable and softly lit, mixing pastel shades and modern art. Tasty menu on a traditional base with a more ambitious à la carte alongside.

BURNHAM THORPE *Norfolk* 504 W 25 – *see Burnham Market.*

BURNLEY *Lancs.* 502 N 22 – *pop. 73 021.*

Towneley, Towneley Park, Todmorden Rd (01282) 451636 – Glen View (01282) 451281.

Bus Station, Croft St (01282) 664421.

London 236 – Bradford 32 – Leeds 37 – Liverpool 55 – Manchester 25 – Middlesbrough 104 – Preston 22 – Sheffield 68.

Oaks, Colne Rd, Reedley, BB10 2LF, Northeast : 2 ½ m. on A 56 (01282) 414141, *oaks@shirehotels.co.uk, Fax (01282) 433401,* – 120. VISA.
Quills : Rest (dinner only) a la carte 24.25/29.65 – ***Archives Brasserie :*** Rest *(closed Saturday-Sunday)* (lunch only) (buffet) a la carte 11.50 – **51 rm** 104.00 – 129.00.
◆ Extended 19C house with accent on business traveller. Clubby lounge with leather sofas and mahogany staircase dappled in colour from superb stained glass window. Comfy rooms. Quills boasts views over neat lawns. Archives Brasserie in brick vaulted cellars.

Rosehill House, Rosehill Ave, Manchester Rd, BB11 2PW, South : 1 ¼ m. by A 56 (01282) 453931, *rhhotel@provider.co.uk, Fax (01282) 455628,* – rest, VISA.
Dugdales : Rest a la carte 19.00/28.00 **s.** – ***El Nino's :*** Rest - Tapas - a la carte 10.00/18.00 **s.** – **32 rm** 50.00/60.00 – 75.00/85.00, 2 suites.
◆ Turreted 19C house in wooded grounds; residentially set. Spacious lounge with long leather Chesterfields. Ornate ceilings are a particular feature of various rooms. Imposing, panelled Dugdales. El Nino's, in rear conservatory, has tapas style.

Premier Travel Inn, Queen Victoria Rd, BB10 3EF, Northeast : ¾ m. on A 6114 (08701) 977045, *Fax (01282) 448431* – rm, rest, – 40. VISA.
Rest (grill rest.) – **40 rm** 46.95/46.95 – 48.95/48.95.
◆ Sandstone lodge, set in a wooded valley next to Queen Victoria's Park. Bright modern bedrooms, designed with practicality and price in mind, ideal for short breaks.

BURNSALL *N. Yorks.* 502 O 21 – *Skipton.*

London 223 – Bradford 26 – Leeds 29.

Red Lion, BD23 6BU, (01756) 720204, *info@redlion.co.uk, Fax (01756) 720292,* – – 90. VISA
Rest – (see ***The Restaurant*** below) – **15 rm** 69.00 – 145.00, 3 suites.
◆ Part 16C inn on the River Wharfe, ideal for walks, fishing and shooting. Cosy bedrooms, some in adjacent cottage: all have 19C brass beds or overlook the village green.

Devonshire Fell, BD23 6BT, (01756) 729000, *reservations@thedevonshirearms.co.uk, Fax (01756) 729009,* – – 70. VISA
Rest a la carte 17.25/24.75 – **10 rm** 75.00/130.00 – 120.00/170.00, 2 suites.
◆ Once a club for 19C mill owners; strikingly updated by Lady Hartington with vivid colours and Hockney prints. Wide-ranging modern menu. Stylish rooms with Dales views.

The Restaurant (at Red Lion H.), BD23 6BU, (01756) 720204, *Fax (01756) 720292,* – VISA
Rest (bar lunch Monday-Saturday)/dinner 21.95/31.95 and a la carte 20.00/30.00.
◆ Dales meat, game and local cheeses in robust, seasonal menu. Eat in the firelit, oak-panelled bar or the dining room with mullioned windows facing the green. Keen local staff.

BURPHAM *W. Sussex* 504 S 30 – *see Arundel.*

BURRINGTON *Devon* 503 I 31.

London 260 – Barnstaple 14 – Exeter 28 – Taunton 50.

Northcote Manor , EX37 9LZ, Northwest : 2 m. on A 377 (01769) 560501, *rest@northcotemanor.co.uk, Fax (01769) 560770,* – VISA
Rest (booking essential) (lunch by arrangement)/dinner 25.00/38.00 – **10 rm** 90.00/100.00 – 210.00, 1 suite.
◆ Creeper-clad hall above River Tew dating from 1716. Fine fabrics and antiques in elegant, individually styled rooms; attention to well-judged detail lends air of idyllic calm. Country house restaurant features eye-catching murals.

BURTON-ON-THE-WOLDS *Leics.* 502 503 504 Q 25 – *see Loughborough.*

Good food and accommodation at moderate prices? Look for the Bib symbols: red Bib Gourmand for food, blue Bib Hotel for hotels

BURTON-UPON-TRENT *Staffs.* 502 503 504 O 25 – *pop. 43 784.*

Branston G. & C.C., Burton Rd (01283) 543207 – Craythorne, Craythorne Rd, Stretton (01283) 564329.

Coors Visitor Centre, Horninglow St (01283) 508111.

London 128 – Birmingham 29 – Leicester 27 – Nottingham 27 – Stafford 27.

Express by Holiday Inn without rest., 2nd Ave, Centrum 100, DE14 2WF, Southwest : 2 m. by A 5121 (01283) 504300, *info@exhiburton.co.uk, Fax (01283) 504301* – P – 60. VISA
82 rm 72.00 – 72.00.
◆ On the outskirts of the town near a business park, a short drive from the Bass Brewery Museum. Comfortable, carefully designed bedrooms in a modern hotel.

at Stretton *North : 3¼ m. by A 5121 (A 38 Derby) – Burton-upon-Trent.*

Dovecliff Hall, Dovecliff Rd, DE13 0DJ, (01283) 531818, *enquiries@dovecliffhall hotel.com, Fax (01283) 516546,* rest, P. VISA.
Rest *(closed Sunday dinner and Monday lunch)* 16.50/28.50 and a la carte 28.00/41.00 –
16 rm 80.00/90.00 – 110.00/170.00.
◆ Imposing, listed 1790s house with lovely gardens and spacious rooms, nestling in an elevated position above the Trent. Airy bedrooms, most boasting garden vistas. Formal dining rooms in restaurant and delightful orangery.

BURY *Gtr Manchester* 502 N 23 503 ③ 504 N 23 – *pop. 60 718.*

Greenmount (01204) 883712.

The Met Art Centre, Market St (0161) 253 5111.

London 211 – Leeds 45 – Liverpool 35 – Manchester 9.

The Waggon, 131 Bury and Rochdale Old Rd, Birtle, BL9 6UE, East : 2 m. on B 6222 (01706) 622955, *Fax (01706) 620094* – P. VISA
closed 2 weeks July-August, 25-26 December, 1 week January, Saturday lunch, Monday and Tuesday – **Rest** a la carte 17.70/26.40.
◆ Despite the unprepossessing exterior, this little former pub is now a pleasantly decorated eatery with good value, no-nonsense cooking featuring the famous Bury Black Pudding.

BURY ST EDMUNDS *Suffolk* 504 W 27 *Great Britain G. – pop. 36 218.*

See : *Town*★ – *Abbey and Cathedral*★.

Env. : *Ickworth House*★ *AC, SW : 3 m. by A 143.*

Suffolk G. & C.C., St John's Hill Plantation, The Street, Fornham All Saints (01284) 706777.

6 Angel Hill (01284) 764667.

London 79 – Cambridge 27 – Ipswich 26 – Norwich 41.

Angel, 3 Angel Hill, IP33 1LT, (01284) 714000, *reservations@theangel.co.uk, Fax (01284) 714001* – rm, P – 90. VISA
The Vaults : **Rest** *(closed Sunday)* a la carte 25.85/34.00 s. – **74 rm** 75.00/125.00 – 135.00, 2 suites.
◆ 15C inn near the Abbey Gardens with a fine Georgian façade. Rooms offer a bright, modern take on classic style: a few, named after famous visitors, have four poster beds. The Vaults are in atmospheric 12C cellars.

Priory, Tollgate, IP32 6EH, North : 1¾ m. on A 1101 (01284) 766181, *reservations@prioryhotel.co.uk, Fax (01284) 767604,* P – 40. VISA
closed 26-30 December – ***The Garden :*** **Rest** *(closed Saturday lunch)* 22.00/31.00 – **39 rm** 93.00/99.00 – 140.00.
◆ 13C former Franciscan Priory with a listed Georgian façade. Traditionally styled in the main house with some usefully appointed modern rooms in the later Garden wings. Conservatory restaurant overlooks neatly manicured garden.

Ounce House without rest., Northgate St, IP33 1HP, (01284) 761779, *pott@globalnet.co.uk, Fax (01284) 768315,* P. VISA.
3 rm 65.00/85.00 – 90.00/120.00.
◆ 1870s redbrick town house; very well furnished with Victorian elegance. Spacious, individually styled bedrooms; well-chosen antiques contribute to a characterful interior.

Northgate House without rest., Northgate St, IP33 1HQ, (01284) 760469, *northgate-hse@hotmail.com, Fax (01284) 724008,* P. VISA.
closed Christmas and New Year – **3 rm** 65.00/70.00 – 110.00.
◆ Restored Georgian townhouse of Tudor origins in walled garden with stunning Queen Anne façade to west. Peerless interiors: airy, panelled rooms; antiques, claw foot baths.

ENGLAND

Maison Bleue, 30-31 Churchgate St, IP33 1RG, ✆ (01284) 760623, *info@maisonbleue.co.uk, Fax (01284) 761611* – ⅀. MC AE VISA
closed January, 1 week Summer, Sunday and Monday – **Rest** - Seafood - 15.95 and a la carte 18.85/30.40.
◆ 17C house with attractive façade and window boxes. Timbered interior with maritime memorabilia. A number of different rooms to eat in; predominantly seafood menu.

at Ixworth *Northeast : 7 m. by A 143 – ✉ Bury St Edmunds.*

Theobalds, 68 High St, IP31 2HJ, ✆ (01359) 231707, *Fax (01359) 231707* – ⅀. MC VISA
closed 1 week Spring, 26 December, 1 January, dinner Sunday and Monday – **Rest** (dinner only and lunch Sunday, Wednesday and Friday)/dinner 25.00 (midweek) and a la carte at weekends 29.15/34.25.
◆ Beamed part 16C cottage with a cosy firelit lounge. Friendly service and well-judged seasonal menus combine heartwarming favourites and contemporary dishes.

at Rougham Green *East : 4 m. by A 14 – ✉ Bury St Edmunds.*

Ravenwood Hall, IP30 9JA, ✆ (01359) 270345, *enquiries@ravenwood.co.uk, Fax (01359) 270788,* , heated, , – [P] – 150. MC AE VISA
Rest 25.75 and a la carte approx 34.00 ♀ – **14 rm** ☕ ✝87.50/118.50 – ✝✝113.50/170.00.
◆ Tudor dower house set in seven acres of calm lawns and woods. Welcoming lounge and individually designed bedrooms, more compact in the mews, are furnished with antiques. Restaurant with old wooden beams and inglenook fireplace.

at Beyton *East : 6 m. by A 14 – ✉ Bury St Edmunds.*

Manorhouse, The Green, IP30 9AF, ✆ (01359) 270960, *manorhouse@beyton.com,* – [P].
closed Christmas and New Year – **Rest** (by arrangement) 17.00 – **4 rm** ☕ ✝45.00/55.00 – ✝✝56.00/65.00.
◆ Part 15C Suffolk longhouse in idyllic spot overlooking village green. Two rooms are in converted barn; all have a rustic feel to them. Breakfast of eggs from owner's hens.

at Horringer *Southwest : 3 m. on A 143 – ✉ Bury St Edmunds.*

The Ickworth , IP29 5QE, ✆ (01284) 735350, *info@ickworthhotel.com, Fax (01284) 736300,* , heated, , – [P] – 30. MC AE VISA
Fredericks : **Rest** (dinner only) 37.50 – ***Cafe Inferno :*** **Rest** *(closed lunch June-September)* a la carte 19.70/30.75 ♀ – **28 rm** (dinner included) ☕ ✝150.00/180.00 – ✝✝480.00/585.00, 10 suites.
◆ Ickworth House's east wing mixes modern and country house styles. Three airy drawing rooms; conservatory breakfasts. Comfy rooms with views. A favourite with young families. Fredericks overlooks gardens. Bustling, basement-based Café Inferno.

The Beehive, IP29 5SN, ✆ (01284) 735260, – [P]. MC VISA
closed 25-26 December – **Rest** a la carte 19.50/26.40 ♀.
◆ Rustic, low-ceilinged, brick-and-flint pub near Ickworth House. Tasty daily specials like scallops in garlic butter affably served at pine tables or on a sheltered terrace.

BUSHEY *Herts.* 504 S 29.

Bushey Hall, Bushey Hall Drive ✆ (01923) 222253, **BT** – *Bushey G. & C.C., High St ✆ (020) 8950 2283,* **BT**.
London 18 – Luton 21 – Watford 3.

Plan : see Greater London (North-West) 1

st James, 30 High St, WD23 3HL, ✆ (020) 8950 2480, *Fax (020) 8950 4107* – ▤. MC VISA
closed 25-26 December and Sunday – **Rest** a la carte 21.15/28.40 ♀. BT c
◆ Likeable neighbourhood venue - choose the airy, wood floored front room by the wine bar. Flavourful chalkboard specials from the modern British repertory, helpful service.

BUTTERMERE *Cumbria* 502 K 20 – ✉ *Cockermouth.*

London 306 – Carlisle 35 – Kendal 43.

Bridge, CA13 9UZ, ✆ (017687) 70252, *enquiries@bridge-hotel.com, Fax (017687) 70215,* [P]. MC VISA
closed 2 weeks January **Rest** (booking essential) (bar lunch Monday-Saturday)/dinner 25.00 – **21 rm** ☕ ✝45.00/90.00 – ✝✝90.00/150.00.
◆ A family-run Lakeland hotel, first licensed as a coaching inn in 1735. After a day's walking in the Fells relax in front of the log fire. Some bedrooms have four-posters. Warm yellow dining room is oldest part of house.

Wood House, CA13 9XA, Northwest : ½ m. on B 5289 ☎ (017687) 70208, *woodhouse.guest@virgin.net, Fax (017687) 70241*, ≤ Crummock Water and Melbreak, –
March-November – **Rest** (by arrangement) (communal dining) 29.00 – **3 rm** ☐ ★55.00 – ★★90.00.
◆ This period house boasts a stunning lakeside setting, providing views of Crummock Water and the mountains. Tranquility is assured. Charming sitting room, simple bedrooms. Dinner is served around a single antique table.

BUXTON *Derbs.* 502 503 504 O 24 – *pop. 20 836.*
Buxton and High Peak, Townend ☎ (01298) 26263.
The Crescent ☎ (01298) 25106.
London 172 – Derby 38 – Manchester 25 – Stoke-on-Trent 24.

Lee Wood, The Park, SK17 6TQ, on A 5004 ☎ (01298) 23002, *leewoodhotel@btinternet.com, Fax (01298) 23228*, – rm, – 100. VISA
Garden : Rest 15.95/25.00 and a la carte 23.95/33.50 – ☐ 12.00 – **40 rm** ★50.00/100.00 – ★★80.00/146.00.
◆ An extended country house dating back to Buxton's heyday. Front-facing rooms overlook the gardens; others, in the annex, are quieter - all are sizeable and neatly kept. Spacious conservatory dining room.

Buxton's Victorian without rest., 3A Broad Walk, SK17 6JE, ☎ (01298) 78759, *buxtonvictoria@btconnect.com, Fax (01298) 74732* – VISA.
closed Christmas – **8 rm** ☐ ★45.00/74.00 – ★★80.00/88.00.
◆ Spacious, charming Victorian house overlooking delightful gardens. Oriental themed breakfast room with wall-mounted kimono. Comfy sitting room. Immaculately kept bedrooms.

Grendon without rest., Bishops Lane, SK17 6UN, ☎ (01298) 78831, *grendonguesthouse@hotmail.com, Fax (01298) 79257*, – VISA
closed 5-25 January and 15-22 May – **4 rm** ☐ ★30.00/50.00 – ★★70.00/79.00.
◆ A serene Edwardian house down a country lane which leads to a hill, ideal for ramblers. Comfortable rooms in pastel colours with guide books and armchairs to read them in.

BYFORD *Herefordshire* 503 L 27 – *see Hereford.*

BYLAND ABBEY *N. Yorks.* 502 Q 21 – *see Helmsley.*

CADNAM *Hants.* 503 504 P 31 – *pop. 1 875.*
London 91 – Salisbury 16 – Southampton 8 – Winchester 19.

Walnut Cottage without rest., Old Romsey Rd, SO40 2NP, off A 3090 ☎ (023) 8081 2275, *Fax (023) 8081 2275*, –
closed 25-26 December – **3 rm** ☐ ★40.00 – ★★55.00.
◆ A pretty white Victorian forester's cottage with views over the garden and good for forays into the New Forest. Charming, simply furnished bedrooms.

CALCOT *Glos. – see Tetbury.*

CALLINGTON *Cornwall* 503 H 32.
London 237 – Exeter 53 – Plymouth 15 – Truro 46.

Langmans, 3 Church St, PL17 7RE, ☎ (01579) 384933, *dine@langmansrestaurant.co.uk, Fax (01579) 384933* – . VISA
closed Sunday-Wednesday – **Rest** (booking essential) (dinner only) (set menu only) 31.95.
◆ Truly individual establishment: seven course tasting menus change monthly, employing skilful cooking with finesse; ingredients from small local suppliers. Booking essential.

at Rilla Mill *Northwest : 6½ m. by A 388 off B 3257 – ✉ Callington.*

The Manor House Inn, PL17 7NT, ☎ (01579) 362354, *Fax (01579) 364056*, –
VISA
closed 25 December and Tuesday – **Rest** a la carte 20.00/25.40.
◆ 17C inn that's had a total refurbishment: very pleasant bar, perfectly shelved books, homely touches. Thoughtfully appointed dining areas with local, seasonal menus.

CALNE *Wilts.* 503 504 O 29 *The West Country G.* – *pop. 13 789.*
Env. : *Bowood House★ AC, (Library ≤★) SW : 2 m. by A 4 – Avebury★★ (The Stones★, Church★) E : 6 m. by A 4.*
London 91 – Bristol 33 – Southampton 63 – Swindon 17.

Chilvester Hill House, SN11 0LP, West : ¾ m. by A 4 on Bremhill rd ✆ (01249) 813981, *gill.dilley@talk21.com, Fax (01249) 814217,* – rest, P. MC AE VISA.
Rest (by arrangement) (communal dining) 20.00/25.00 – **3 rm** ☐ 55.00/65.00 – 85.00/95.00.
◆ 19C Bath stone house with lots of William Morris wallpapering, Persian carpeted drawing room, and spacious bedrooms. Charming mature owners are its very heart and soul.

CAMBER *E. Sussex* 504 W 31 – *see Rye.*

CAMBERLEY *Surrey* 504 R 29 – *pop. 47 123 (inc. Frimley).*

Camberley Heath, Golf Drive ✆ (01276) 23258.
London 40 – Reading 13 – Southampton 48.

Frimley Hall, Lime Ave via Conifer Drive, GU15 2BG, East : ¾ m. off Portsmouth Rd (A 325) ✆ (0870) 400 8224, *sales.frimleyhall@macdonald-hotels.co.uk, Fax (01276) 691253,* P – 250. MC AE VISA
Linden : Rest 18.95/27.50 s. – ☐ 14.95 – **98 rm** 211.00 – 211.00.
◆ Ivy-clad Victorian manor. A carved wooden staircase leads to the bedrooms; some are traditional with inlaid mahogany furniture, others are bright and modern. 19C restaurant with contemporary furnishings.

CAMBOURNE *Cambs. – see Cambridge.*

CAMBRIDGE *Cambs.* 504 U 27 *Great Britain G. – pop. 117 717.*

See : *Town*★★★ – *St John's College*★★★ AC Y – *King's College*★★ *(King's College Chapel*★★★ *)* Z *The Backs*★★ YZ – *Fitzwilliam Museum*★★ Z **M1** – *Trinity College*★★ Y – *Clare College*★ Z **B** – *Kettle's Yard*★ Y **M2** – *Queen's College*★ AC Z.
Exc. : *Audley End*★★, *S : 13 m. on Trumpington Rd, A 1309, A 1301 and B 1383* – *Imperial War Museum*★, *Duxford, S : 9 m. on M 11.*
Cambridgeshire Moat House Hotel, Bar Hill ✆ (01954) 249988 **X**.
Cambridge Airport : ✆ (01223) 373737, E : 2 m. on A 1303 **X**.
The Old Library, Wheeler St ✆ (01223) 457581, tourism@cambridge.gov.uk.
London 55 – Coventry 88 – Ipswich 54 – Kingston-upon-Hull 137 – Leicester 74 – Norwich 61 – Nottingham 88 – Oxford 100.

Plan opposite

Hotel Felix, Whitehouse Lane, Huntingdon Rd, CB3 0LX, Northwest : 1 ½ m. by A 1307 ✆ (01223) 277977, *help@hotelfelix.co.uk, Fax (01223) 277973,* P – 50. MC AE VISA
Graffiti : Rest 16.50 (lunch) and a la carte 25.20/35.50 – ☐ 7.50 – **52 rm** 136.00 – 168.00/255.00.
◆ Built as a private house in 1852, now with modern extensions. Public areas are smart, modern and stylish. The contemporary rooms include state-of-the art facilities. Sleek restaurant overlooks garden and terrace.

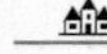

Crowne Plaza, Downing St, CB2 3DT, ✆ (0870) 4009180, *reservations-cambridgecp@ichotelsgroup.com, Fax (01223) 464440,* – rm, P – 250. MC AE VISA Z a
Rest a la carte approx 25.50 – **198 rm** ☐ 160.00 – 160.00/350.00.
◆ Concierge parking to greet you, then unwind in the Bloomsbury bar on the mezzanine level. Modern bedrooms: King Superior and Junior suites offer highest levels of comfort. A la carte restaurant or Irish themed bar.

University Arms, Regent St, CB2 1AD, ✆ (01223) 351241, *dua.sales@devere-hotels.com, Fax (01223) 315256* – P – 300. MC AE VISA Z e
Rest *(closed Sunday lunch)* (bar lunch)/dinner a la carte 22.75/32.00 **s.** – **119 rm** ☐ 85.00/189.00 – 99.00/189.00, 1 suite.
◆ Extended Victorian hotel overlooking Parker's Piece with grand lounge and bar. Spacious bedrooms, some with balconies and views over the green. Contemporary restaurant with street entrance.

Gonville, Gonville Pl, CB1 1LY, ✆ (01223) 366611, *info@gonvillehotel.co.uk, Fax (01223) 315470* – rest, P – 200. MC AE VISA. Z r
Rest (bar lunch)/dinner a la carte 13.95/20.40 s – ☐ 11.50 – **73 rm** 89.00/150.00 – 99.00/160.00.
◆ Overlooks the green where cricketer Jack Hobbs honed his talents. Caters for corporate visitors and tourists. Bedrooms in newer extension benefit from air conditioning. International menu served in the relaxed atrium.

CAMBRIDGE

ıdge St	Y	2
ıldham's Lane	X	5
ırn Exchange St	Z	6
ıwning St	Z	7
ee School Lane	Z	12
afton Centre	Y	
ıbson St	Y	14
ng's Parade	Z	15
ın Yard Centre	Z	
adingley Rd	X	16
agdalene St	Y	17
arket Hill	YZ	18
arket St	Y	19
Milton Rd	Y	20
Newmarket Rd	Y	21
Northampton St	Y	22
Parker St	Z	23
Peas Hill	Z	25
Pembroke St	Z	26
Petty Cury	Z	27
Rose Crescent	Y	28
St Andrew's St	Z	30
St John's St	Y	31
Short St	Y	32
Sidney St	Y	34
Trinity St	Y	36
Trumpington Rd	Z	37
Wheeler St	Z	39

COLLEGES

Christ's	Y	A
Churchill	X	B
Clare Hall	X	N
Clare	Z	B
Corpus Christi	Z	G[1]
Darwin	Z	D
Downing	Z	E[1]
Emmanuel	Z	F
Fitzwilliam	X	G
Gonville and Caius	Y	G[2]
Hugues Hall	Z	K
Jesus	Y	K
King's	Z	
Lucy Cavendish	Y	O[1]
Magdalene	Y	N
New Hall	X	D
Newnham	X	E[2]
Pembroke	Z	N
Peterhouse	Z	O[2]
Queen's	Z	
Robinson	X	K
St Catharine's	Z	R
St Edmund's House	Y	U
St John's	Y	
Selwyn	X	F
Sidney Sussex	Y	P
Trinity Hall	Y	V
Trinity	Y	
Wolfson	X	U

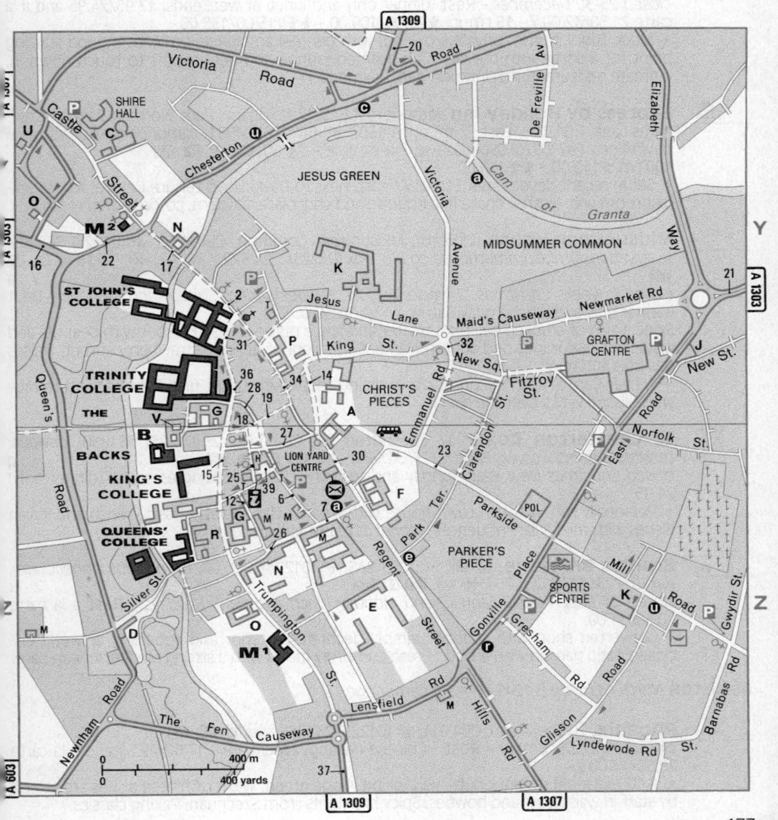

ENGLAND

Arundel House, Chesterton Rd, CB4 3AN, ✆ (01223) 367701, *info@arundelhousehotels.co.uk, Fax (01223) 367721,* – , rest, P – 50. VISA. Y u
closed 25-26 December – ***Restaurant :*** **Rest** 20.75 and a la carte 21.65/34.15 – ***Conservatory :*** **Rest** a la carte 14.40/20.75 – 6.95 – **105 rm** 75.00/95.00 – 95.00/120.00.
◆ Privately owned, traditional hotel, formerly a terrace of 19C houses. Coach House rooms, overlooking tranquil gardens, were once part of the city's horse-drawn coach system. Colourful, eclectic Restaurant. Magnificent Conservatory boasts rattan armchairs.

Meadowcroft without rest., 16 Trumpington Rd, CB2 2EX, South : 1 ¼ m. on A 1134 ✆ (01223) 346120, *meadowcroft@meadowcrofthotel.co.uk, Fax (01223) 346138,* – P. VISA X e
closed 23 December-2 January – **18 rm** 85.00/180.00 – 110.00/200.
◆ Victorian house with striking original features such as hall tiling and staircase. Decorated throughout in period style. Individually furnished, light, airy bedrooms.

Centennial, 63-71 Hills Rd, CB2 1PG, ✆ (01223) 314652, *reception@centennialhotel.co.uk, Fax (01223) 315443* – P. VISA. X x
closed 23 December-2 January – **Rest** (dinner only) 15.50 and a la carte approx 30.00 **s.** – **39 rm** 70.00/80.00 – 96.00.
◆ Converted terraced Victorian houses with chesterfield sofas, chairs and dresser in a smart lounge. Friendly bar. Traditional bedrooms, some with canopied beds. Table flowers prettify the dining room.

Cambridge Lodge, 139 Huntingdon Rd, CB3 0DQ, ✆ (01223) 352833, *cambridge.lodge@bt.connect.com, Fax (01223) 355166,* – P. VISA. X i
closed 25-30 December – **Rest** (dinner only and lunch at weekends) 17.95/24.95 and a la carte 21.50/32.00 – **15 rm** 75.00/100.00 – 115.00/135.00.
◆ Mock Tudor house, privately owned, with genteel ambience, provides a good starting point for a sortie into the city. Oak beamed lounge and neat rooms to touch down in. Intimate restaurant: rich interior, dark beamed.

Express by Holiday Inn without rest., 15-17 Coldhams Park, Norman Way off Coldhams Lane, CB1 3LH, East : 2 m. off A 1303 ✆ (0870) 9904081, *cambridge@expressbyholidayinn.net, Fax (0870) 9904082* – P – 50. VISA
100 rm 110.00 – 110.00.
◆ Set in recent development to city's east, next to David Lloyd Leisure Centre. Airy breakfast room with leather chairs in turquoise and chocolate. Modern, co-ordinated rooms.

Midsummer House (Clifford), Midsummer Common, CB4 1HA, ✆ (01223) 369299, *reservations@midsummerhouse.co.uk, Fax (01223) 302672,* – 16. VISA Y a
closed 2 weeks Christmas, 2 weeks August, 1 week spring, Sunday and Monday – **Rest** (dinner only and lunch Friday-Saturday) 30.00/50.00 .
Spec. Salad of smoked eel, pig's trotter and apple purée. Braised turbot with peanuts and pistachios, asparagus and squash pureé. Cannelloni of apricot, strawberry sorbet, fraises des bois and mint.
◆ A river Cam idyll. Chic conservatory dining room with smart first floor bar and terrace with blissful views over the river.

22 Chesterton Road, 22 Chesterton Rd, CB4 3AX, ✆ (01223) 351880, *davidcarter@restaurant22.co.uk, Fax (01223) 323814* – . VISA Y c
closed Christmas-New Year, Sunday and Monday – **Rest** (booking essential) (dinner only) 24.95.
◆ Personally run Victorian town house with smartly clad tables. Classic French and Italian dishes with mild Asian influences, served at reasonable prices.

Bruno's Brasserie, 52 Mill Rd, CB1 2AS, ✆ (01223) 312702, *brunos@btconnect.com, Fax (01223) 312702,* – . VISA Z u
closed 24 December-8 January and Monday lunch and Bank Holidays – **Rest** a la carte 20.50/31.00.
◆ Converted shop with spacious simply decorated interior and appealing artwork. Enclosed patio garden with arbour. Fresh and zingy menu with a strong Mediterranean base.

at Histon *North : 3 m. on B 1049* – X – ✉ *Cambridge.*

Phoenix, 20 The Green, CB4 9JA, ✆ (01223) 233766 – P. VISA
closed 25-27 December – **Rest** - Chinese (Peking, Szechuan) - 17.50/29.50 and a la carte 29.50/43.00 **s.**
◆ A 100-year old redbrick pub overlooking village green. Within, Chinese dishes are served by staff in waistcoats and bowties. Spicy highlights from Szechuan; Peking classics.

at Horningsea *Northeast : 4 m. by A 1303 – X – and B 1047 on Horningsea rd – ✉ Cambridge.*

Crown & Punchbowl with rm, High St, CB5 9JG, ✆ (01223) 860643, *rd@cambscuisine.com, Fax (01223) 441814,* – P. MC AE VISA
closed dinner Sunday – **Rest** and a la carte 16.00/30.00 – **5 rm** ☐ ★59.95 – ★★79.95.
◆ Former 17C village inn with characterful beams. Farmhouse tables and chairs sit cosily by real fire. Blend of tasty dishes amiably served. Clean, modern rooms.

at Little Shelford *South : 5½ m. by A 1309 – X – off A 10 – ✉ Cambridge.*

Sycamore House, 1 Church St, CB2 5HG, ✆ (01223) 843396 – P. MC VISA
closed Christmas-New Year and Sunday-Tuesday – **Rest** (booking essential) (dinner only) 25.00.
◆ Restaurant divided by central brick chimney with cast-iron, coal burning stove in centre. Fresh produce, fish and game available on set menu. Simple, honest cooking.

at Great Eversden *Southwest : 7½ m. by A 603 – Z – ✉ Cambridge.*

Red House Farm without rest., 44 High St, CB3 7HW, ✆ (01223) 262154, *info@redhousefarmuk.com, Fax (01223) 264875,* – P.
closed 2 weeks Christmas-New Year – **3 rm** ☐ ★38.00 – ★★60.00.
◆ Red-brick 18C listed farmhouse on a working farm; house overlooks meadow. Sunny garden room for breakfast, including home-made bread and preserves. Immaculate rooms.

at Madingley *West : 4½ m. by A 1303 – X – ✉ Cambridge.*

Three Horseshoes, High St, CB3 8AB, ✆ (01954) 210221, *threehorseshoes@huntsbridge.co.uk, Fax (01954) 212043,* – P. AE VISA
Rest a la carte 26.00/36.00.
◆ Thatched yet modern pub. Eat in the bar and sample the bar-grill menu or the conservatory restaurant for innovative cuisine. Excellent range of wine by the glass.

at Hardwick *West : 5 m. by A 1303 – X – ✉ Cambridge.*

Wallis Farmhouse without rest., 98 Main St, CB3 7QU, ✆ (01954) 210347, *enquiries@wallisfarmhouse.co.uk, Fax (01954) 210988,* – P. MC VISA.
4 rm ☐ ★42.00/48.00 – ★★60.00/65.00.
◆ Spacious, timbered bedrooms, all en suite, in converted stables of a redbrick Georgian farmhouse: Wimpole Way bridle path to the rear. Friendly owner serves hearty breakfasts.

at Cambourne *West : 7 m. by A 428 – X – ✉ Cambridge.*

The Cambridge Belfry, Back Lane, CB3 6BN, ✆ (01954) 714995, *cambridge@marstonhotels.com, Fax (01954) 714998,* – rest, P – 220. MC AE VISA.
***Bridge* : Rest** *(closed Saturday lunch and Sunday dinner)* a la carte 29.00/34.50 – ***Brookes Brasserie* : Rest** a la carte 25.00 – **110 rm** ☐ ★149.50 – ★★208.00, 10 suites.
◆ Brick-built hotel, constructed around central courtyard and opened in 2004, in modern village. Well-equipped leisure centre. Bedrooms boast a pleasant, contemporary style. Formal, linen-clad Bridge. All-day, informal dining at Brookes Brasserie.

at Bar Hill *Northwest : 5½ m. by A 1307 – X – off A 14 – ✉ Cambridge.*

Cambridgeshire Moat House, CB3 8EU, ✆ (01954) 249988, *reservations.cambridgeshire@moathousehotels.com, Fax (01954) 249970,* – rest, P – 200. MC AE VISA
Rest *(closed lunch Saturday and Sunday)* (buffet lunch)/dinner 17.95 and a la carte – **134 rm** ★109.00 – ★★129.00.
◆ Distinguished by its golf course. Caters for business visitors as well as sightseers which is reflected in the range of rooms. Executive suites have chestnut veneer décor. Well-run, family-friendly dining room.

Undecided between two equivalent establishments? Within each category, establishments are classified in our order of preference.

CANNINGTON *Somerset* 503 K 30 – *see Bridgwater.*

CANTERBURY *Kent* 504 X 30 *Great Britain G. – pop. 43 552.*

See : City★★★ - Cathedral★★★ **Y** *- St Augustine's Abbey★★ AC* **YZ K** *– King's School★* **Y** *– Mercery Lane★* **Y 12** *- Christ Church Gate★* **Y D** *– Weavers★* **Y B** *– Hospital of St Thomas the Martyr, Eastbridge★* **Y E** *– Museum of Canterbury★ AC* **Y M1** *– St Martin's Church★* **Y N** *– West Gate★ AC* **Y R**.

12-13 Sun St, Buttermarket ✆ (01227) 378100, canterburyinformation@canterbury.gov.uk.

London 59 – Brighton 76 – Dover 15 – Maidstone 28 – Margate 17.

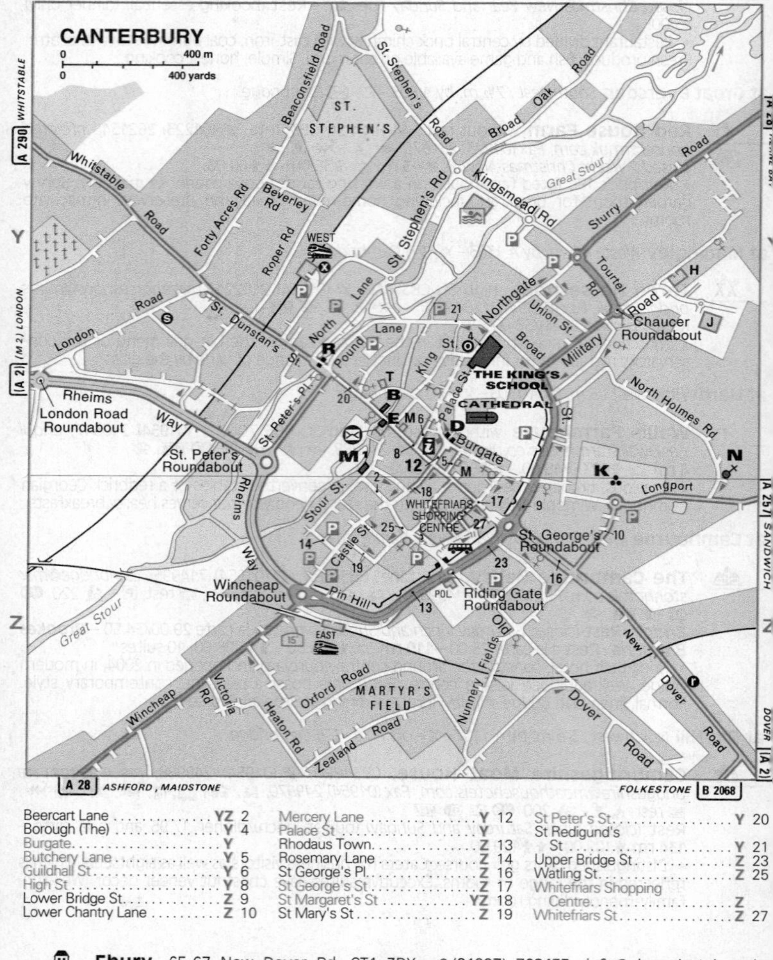

Ebury, 65-67 New Dover Rd, CT1 3DX, ✆ (01227) 768433, *info@ebury-hotel.co.uk, Fax (01227) 459187,* – MO AE VISA **Z r**
closed 20 December-7 January – **Rest** *(closed Sunday)* (dinner only) 21.00/27.00 – **15 rm** ☕ ★65.00/85.00 – ★★85.00/105.00.
◆ 1850s redbrick hotel where drinks are served in a lounge holding a collection of Bulls Eye clocks. Bedrooms are all spacious and comfortable. Restaurant ambience reflects age of hotel.

Magnolia House without rest., 36 St Dunstan's Terr, CT2 8AX, ☎ (01227) 765121, *info@magnoliahousecanterbury.co.uk*, *Fax (01227) 765121*, – P. MO AE VISA.
Y s
closed 25 December – **7 rm** ★55.00/65.00 – ★★85.00/125.00.
◆ Gracious Georgian house with calm, sunny interior and plush bedrooms including four-poster suite. Breakfast room offers good choice, and boasts charming garden outlook.

Tuo e Mio, 16 The Borough, CT1 2DR, ☎ (01227) 761471, *Fax (01227) 784924* – MO AE VISA
Y o
– **Rest** - Italian - 14.00 (lunch) and a la carte 19.90/29.15.
◆ Personally run Italian restaurant with variations on popular dishes. Well-sourced, rustic ingredients; attentive service is guaranteed. Look out for the blackboard specials.

The Goods Shed, Station Rd West, St Dunstans, CT2 8AN, ☎ (01227) 459153 – P. MO AE VISA
Y x
closed Sunday dinner and Monday – **Rest** a la carte 20.00/29.00.
◆ Once derelict railway shed, now a farmers' market that's open all day. Its eating area offers superbly fresh produce with no frills and real flavours very much to the fore.

at Lower Hardres *South : 3 m. on B 2068* – **Z** – ✉ *Canterbury.*

The Granville, Street end, CT4 7AL, ☎ (01227) 700402, *Fax (01227) 700925*, , – P. MO VISA
closed 25 December, Monday and Sunday dinner – **Rest** a la carte 17.50/31.40 ♀.
◆ A close relative to The Sportsman in Whitstable. Relax in leather sofas, then enjoy quality ingredients on a well-priced, very interesting modern menu featuring superb fish.

at Chartham Hatch *West : 3¼ m. by A 28* – **Z** – ✉ *Canterbury.*

Howfield Manor, Howfield Lane, CT4 7HQ, Southeast : 1 m. ☎ (01227) 738294, *howfieldmanor@londoninns.com*, *Fax (01227) 731535*, – P – 100. MO AE VISA.
closed 25-30 December – ***Old Well* :** **Rest** 22.95/24.95 – **15 rm** ★85.00/100.00 – ★★112.00/115.00.
◆ Once part of the estate of Priory of St Gregory, this 19C manor is set amongst deciduous trees and lawned garden. Sunny rooms; "Manor Suite" has dance floor, cocktail bar. Restaurant takes name from well hole where monks once drew water.

at Upper Harbledown Service Area *West : 4 m. on A 2* – **Y** – ✉ *Canterbury.*

Express by Holiday Inn without rest., CT2 9HX, (eastbound carriageway) ☎ (01227) 865000, *canterbury@oriel-leisure.co.uk*, *Fax (01227) 865100* – P – 35. MO AE VISA
89 rm ★72.00 – ★★72.00.
◆ A standard lodge; simply furnished rooms. Well placed for Canterbury Cathedral and Canterbury Heritage museum.

CANVEY ISLAND *Essex* 504 V 29 – *pop. 37 479.*

Castle Point, Waterside Farm, Somnes Ave ☎ (01268) 510830.
London 35 – Chelmsford 19 – Maidstone 44 – Southend-on-Sea 13.

Oysterfleet, Knightswick Rd, SS8 7UX, ☎ (01268) 510111, *Fax (01268) 511420*, – , rest, P – 200. MO VISA.
Rest *(closed Sunday dinner)* (grill rest.) (carvery lunch Sunday) a la carte 13.80/24.55 – 5.00 – **41 rm** ★42.50 – ★★50.00.
◆ Modern hotel stands on site of the eponymous pub. Functional bedrooms, some with floral furnishings and views of the lake. Family restaurant adjoins bar; conservatory also available for dining.

CARBIS BAY *Cornwall* 503 D 33 – *see St Ives.*

CARLISLE *Cumbria* 501 502 L 19 *Great Britain G.* – *pop. 71 773.*

See : *Town★ - Cathedral★ (Painted Ceiling★)* **AY E** – *Tithe Barn★* **BY A**.
Env. : *Hadrian's Wall★★, N : by A 7* **AY**.
Aglionby ☎ (01228) 513029 **BY** – *Stony Holme, St Aidan's Rd ☎ (01228) 625511* **BY** – *Dalston Hall, Dalston ☎ (01228) 710165,* **AZ**.
Carlisle Airport ☎ (01228) 573641, NW : 5½ m. by A 7 – **BY** – *and B 6264* – **Terminal :** *Bus Station, Lowther St.*
Carlisle Visitor Centre, Old Town Hall, Green Market ☎ (01228) 625600.
London 317 – Blackpool 95 – Edinburgh 101 – Glasgow 100 – Leeds 124 – Liverpool 127 – Manchester 122 – Newcastle upon Tyne 59.

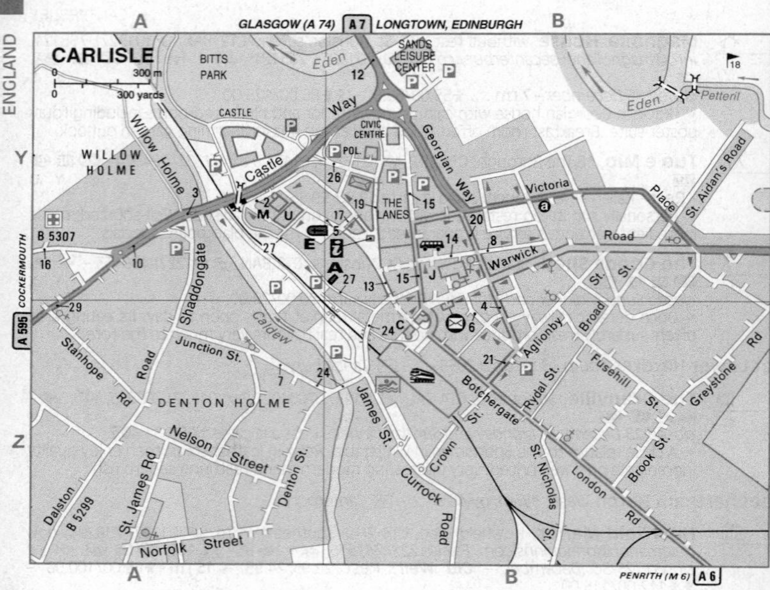

Annetwell St	AY 2	Church St	AY 10	Spencer St	BY 20
Botchergate	BZ	Eden Bridge	BY 12	Tait St	BZ 21
Bridge St	AY 3	English St	BY 13	The Lanes Shopping Centre	BY
Brunswick St	BZ 4	Lonsdale St	BY 14	Victoria Viaduct	ABZ 24
Castle St	BY 5	Lowther St	BY 15	West Tower St	BY 26
Cecil St	BZ 6	Port Rd	AY 16	West Walls	ABY 27
Charlotte St	AZ 7	St Marys Gate	BY 17	Wigton Rd	AZ 29
Chiswick St	BY 8	Scotch St	BY 19		

Cumbria Park, 32 Scotland Rd, CA3 9DG, North : 1 m. on A 7 ℘ (01228) 522887, *enquiries@cumbriaparkhotel.co.uk, Fax (01228) 514796,* – rest, – 120. *VISA*.
closed 25-26 December – **Rest** 12.95/16.95 and a la carte 21.85/27.40 – **47 rm** 76.00 – 98.50/125.00.
◆ Personally run hotel, tiny piece of Hadrian's Wall visible in car park.Smart gym and sauna. Family curios decorate interiors. Sizeable rooms; some have whirlpool baths. Eat in bar among the fishtanks, or more formal 'Roman' themed restaurant.

Premier Travel Inn, Walkmill Crescent, CA1 2WF, East : 1 ½ m. on A 69 ℘ (0870) 1977053, *Fax (01228) 534096* – rest, *VISA*.
Rest (grill rest.) – **44 rm** 52.95 – 52.95.
◆ Lodge accommodation next to Lakeland Gate Brewers Fayre and handy for Carlisle Castle, the Cathedral and city centre. Informal eatery and well-kept bedrooms.

Number Thirty One, 31 Howard Pl, CA1 1HR, ℘ (01228) 597080, *pruirving@aol.com, Fax (01228) 597080* – *VISA*. BY a
Rest (by arrangement) 20.00 – **3 rm** 60.00/69.00 – 100.00.
◆ Classic 19C town house in residential area. Luxuriously and stylishly furnished throughout with many thoughtful extras. Three rooms decorated in either yellow, green or blue.

Aldingham House without rest., 1 Eden Mount, Stanwix, CA3 9LZ, North : ¾ m. on A 7 ℘ (01228) 522554, *stay@aldinghamhouse.co.uk, Fax (0871) 2771644* – *VISA*.
closed 18 December-2 January – **3 rm** 50.00 – 75.00.
◆ Classic 19C townhouse in terrace of matching properties; original features firmly in situ. Delightful drawing room with grand piano. Rooms decorated with considerable style.

No.10, 10 Eden Mount, Stanwix, CA3 9LY, North : ¾ m. on A 7. ℘ (01228) 524183, *Fax (01228) 524183* – *VISA*
closed February, last week October, Sunday and Monday – **Rest** (booking essential) (dinner only) a la carte 21.10/28.50.
◆ Popular little neighbourhood restaurant with friendly air away from city bustle. The appealing menus contain much local produce: cheese, sausages, lamb and beef.

XX **Gallo Rosso,** Parkhouse Rd, Kingstown, CA6 4BY, Northwest : 2 ¾ m. by A 7 on Rockcliffe rd ✆ (01228) 526037, *Fax (01228) 550074* – ⇔ ▤ P. MC VISA
closed Tuesday – **Rest** - Italian - a la carte 16.00/27.50.
◆ City outskirts setting: watch chef at work in central open plan kitchen. Bright, airy surroundings. Soundly prepared Italian dishes, from pasta to meat and fish classics.

at Crosby-on-Eden *Northeast : 5 m. by A 7 – BY – and B 6264 off A 689 – ✉ Carlisle.*

Crosby Lodge Country House ⛵, High Crosby, CA6 4QZ, ✆ (01228) 573618, *enquiries@crosbylodge.co.uk, Fax (01228) 573428*, <, ⚘ – ⇔ rest, P. MC AE VISA
closed Christmas-mid January – **Rest** (Sunday dinner residents only) 35.00 (dinner) and a la carte 25.00/40.50 ♀ – **11 rm** ☕ ✝85.00/95.00 – ✝✝180.00.
◆ Secluded castellated 19C country mansion with walled gardens in rural setting. Plenty of period character including antiques and curios.Pets allowed in converted stable rooms. Elegant restaurant boasts silver cutlery and crystal glassware.

at Wetheral *East : 6¼ m. by A 69 – BY – ✉ Carlisle.*

Crown, CA4 8ES, ✆ (01228) 561888, *info@crownhotelwetheral.co.uk, Fax (01228) 561637*, ⚘, ⚲, ≘s, ▣, ⚘, squash – ⇔ ♿ P. – 🔺 175. MC AE ⊙ VISA
Rest *(closed lunch Saturday and Sunday)* 21.95 (dinner) and a la carte 21.95/33.00 ♀ – **49 rm** ☕ ✝110.00 – ✝✝136.00, 2 suites.
◆ Former 18C farmhouse: period character visible in lounges and rustic bar. Clean-cut, unfussy rooms. Executive rooms have balconies and garden views. Good leisure facilities. Main conservatory or bar dining options.

CARLTON-IN-COVERDALE *N. Yorks.* 502 O 21 – *see Middleham.*

CARLYON BAY *Cornwall* 503 F 33 – *see St Austell.*

CARNFORTH *Lancs.* 502 L 21 – *see Lancaster.*

CARNON DOWNS *Cornwall* 503 E 33 – *see Truro.*

CARTERWAY HEADS *Northd.* 501 502 O 19 – ✉ *Shotley Bridge.*
London 272 – Carlisle 59 – Newcastle upon Tyne 21.

Manor House Inn with rm, DH8 9LX, on A 68 ✆ (01207) 255268, *manor@carterwayheads.com, Fax (01207) 255268* – ⇔ P. MC AE VISA
closed dinner 25 December – **Rest** a la carte 18.00/27.00 ♀ – **4 rm** ☕ ✝38.00/49.00 – ✝✝67.00/70.00.
◆ 18C inn with views over the moors; whet your whistle in the bar or dine in the jug-festooned restaurant. Tasty dishes and home-made desserts. Smart rooms with views.

CARTMEL *Cumbria* 502 L 21 – *see Grange-over-Sands.*

CARTMEL FELL *Cumbria* 502 L 21 – *see Newby Bridge.*

CASTERTON *Cumbria* 502 M 21 – *see Kirkby Lonsdale.*

CASTLE CARROCK *Cumbria* 502 L 19 – *see Brampton.*

CASTLE CARY *Somerset* 503 M 30 – *pop. 3 056.*
London 127 – Bristol 28 – Wells 13.

Clanville Manor without rest., BA7 7PJ, West : 2 m. by B 3152 and A 371 on B 3153 ✆ (01963) 350124, *info@clanvillemanor.co.uk, Fax (01963) 350719*, ⛆ heated, ⚘, ⚘ – ⇔ P. MC VISA. ⚘
closed Christmas and New Year – – **4 rm** ☕ ✝30.00/50.00 – ✝✝60.00/70.00.
◆ Comely 18C house full of period style and charm. Heirlooms and antiques abound. Breakfasts served from the Aga. Walled garden boasts heated pool. Individualistic rooms.

at South Cadbury *South : 4½ m. by B 3152 off A 359 – ✉ Castle Cary.*

Lower Camelot without rest., Church Rd, BA22 7HA, ✆ (01963) 440581, *info@southcadbury.co.uk*, ⚘ – ⇔ ✆ P. MC AE VISA. ⚘
closed 25-31 December and mid January-March – **3 rm** ☕ ✝42.50 – ✝✝65.00.
◆ Owners go out of their way to make your stay pleasurable in guesthouse named after King Arthur's castle. Lovely garden; good breakfasts in the conservatory. Smart rooms.

ENGLAND

The Camelot, Chapel Rd, BA22 7EX, ☎ (01963) 440448, *Fax (01963) 441462*, – P. VISA.
Rest a la carte 16.50/27.10.
• Owned by award-winning cheese makers who've modernised this old pub, alongside the restored skittle alley. Upstairs restaurant-style dining room serves good value dishes.

at Lovington *West : 4 m. by B 3152 and A 371 on B 3153 – ✉ Castle Cary.*

The Pilgrims, BA7 7PT, ☎ (01963) 240597, *thejades@btinternet.com*, – P. AE VISA
closed 3 weeks October, Sunday dinner, Tuesday lunch and Monday – **Rest** a la carte 20.00/34.00.
• Unprepossessing façade disguises lovely olive green rustic interior with watercolours and beams. Interesting, hearty menus include meat, ice cream and beer from the village!

CASTLE COMBE *Wilts.* 503 504 N 29 *The West Country G. – ✉ Chippenham.*
See : *Village*★★.
London 110 – Bristol 23 – Chippenham 6.

Manor House H. and Golf Club, SN14 7HR, ☎ (01249) 782206, *enquiries@manor-housecc.co.uk, Fax (01249) 783100*, 18, – P – 100. AE VISA
The Bybrook : **Rest** *(closed Saturday lunch)* 25.00/45.00 – 16.00 – **44 rm** 185.00 – 185.00, 4 suites.
• Particularly peaceful manor in a sweeping green with trout in the river. Fine fabrics and oak panelling exude history. Luxurious bedrooms in mews cottages or main house. Smart restaurant: English country style menus.

Castle Inn, SN14 7HN, ☎ (01249) 783030, *enquiries@castle-inn.info, Fax (01249) 782315* – . AE VISA
closed 25 December – **Rest** a la carte 17.75/27.75 – **11 rm** 60.00/75.00 – 100.00/140.00.
• A hostelry dating back to the 12C in the middle of a delightful and historic village. Much character, from the wooden beams in the bedrooms to the rustic bar. Large glass ceiling creates light-flooded dining room.

at Nettleton Shrub *West : 2 m. by B 4039 on Nettleton rd (Fosse Way) – ✉ Chippenham.*

Fosse Farmhouse , SN14 7NJ, ☎ (01249) 782286, *caroncooper@compuserve.com, Fax (01249) 783066*, – P. VISA.
Rest (by arrangement) 30.00 – **3 rm** 55.00/65.00 – 85.00/130.00.
• 18C Cotswold Stone farmhouse personally run by enthusiastic owner. Cream teas served in the garden in summer. Welcoming bedrooms with French artefacts and Gallic style.

CASTLE DONINGTON *Leics.* 502 503 504 P 25 – *pop. 5 977 – ✉ Derby.*
Nottingham East Midlands Airport : ☎ (01332) 852852, S : by B 6540 and A 453.
London 123 – Birmingham 38 – Leicester 23 – Nottingham 13.

Priest House on the River, Kings Mills, DE74 2RR, West : 1 ¾ m. by Park Lane ☎ (01332) 810649, *Fax (01332) 811141*, – rest, P – 130. AE VISA.
Rest *(closed Sunday dinner)* (dinner only and Sunday lunch)/dinner 32.50 **s.** – 14.95 – **42 rm** 155.00 – 225.00, 3 suites.
• Extended mill where modernity holds sway: plasma TVs in the bedrooms, which are divided between the main house with Trent views, and charming former mill workers' cottages. Elegantly formal main dining room, or relaxing informal brasserie.

at Breedon on the Hill *Southwest : 4 m. by Breedon rd off A 453 – ✉ Castle Donington.*

The Three Horseshoes Inn, DE73 8AN, ☎ (01332) 695129, *Fax (01332) 695128*, – P. VISA
closed 26 December and 1 January – **Rest** *(closed Sunday)* a la carte 20.00/35.00.
• 18C pub where locals gather round the bar's open fire. Eat here or in two dining areas: large blackboard menus offer dishes using carefully sourced and combined ingredients.

CATEL *Guernsey (Channel Islands)* 503 P 33 and 517 ⑨ – *see Channel Islands.*

CAUNTON *Notts.* 502 504 R 24 – *see Newark-on-Trent.*

CAVENDISH *Suffolk* 504 V 27.

London 70 – Cambridge 30 – Colchester 20.

Embleton House without rest., Melford Rd, CO10 8AA, ✆ (01787) 280447, *silverned@aol.com, Fax (01787) 282396,* heated, – **P**
5 rm ☕ ✝35.00/50.00 – ✝✝70.00.
◆ Spacious, comfy Edwardian house in attractive, mature gardens. Breakfast with extensive menu served at large communal table. Well-kept rooms. Holistic therapies available.

CHADDESLEY CORBETT *Worcs.* 503 504 N 26 – *see Kidderminster.*

CHADWICK END *W. Mids.* 503 504 O 26.

London 106 – Birmingham 13 – Leicester 40 – Stratford-upon-Avon 16.

The Orange Tree, Warwick Rd, B93 0BN, on A 4141 ✆ (01564) 785364, *Fax (01564) 782988,* – **P**. MO AE VISA
closed 25 December and Sunday dinner – **Rest** (booking essential) a la carte 25.00/35.00 ♀.
◆ Modern roadside dining pub with attractive exterior and stylish interior. The menu of modish classics is good value and has an appealing, flexible range.

CHAGFORD *Devon* 503 I 31 *The West Country G.*

Env. : *Dartmoor National Park★★.*

London 218 – Exeter 17 – Plymouth 27.

Gidleigh Park , TQ13 8HH, Northwest : 2 m. by Gidleigh Rd ✆ (01647) 432367, *gidleighpark@gidleigh.co.uk, Fax (01647) 432574,* ≤ Teign Valley, woodland and Meldon Hill, – rest, **P**. MO AE VISA
June-December – **Rest** (booking essential) 35.00/80.00 ♀ – **12 rm** (dinner included) ☕ – ✝✝440.00/600.00, 3 suites.
Spec. Roast scallops with aubergine, tomato, peppers and tapenade. Lobster fricassée with summer vegetables and herbs. Best end and saddle of lamb with fondant potato, roast garlic and tapenade jus.
◆ Spectacular hotel of sensual delights. Outstanding rooms decorated in a flourish of style. Oak panelled lounge with watercolours. Water garden and herb beds. Excellent cuisine showcases local produce. Hotel closed until June 2006 for extensive refurbishment.

Cherryford House , Gidleigh, TQ13 8HS, Northwest : 2 m. by Gidleigh Rd on Scovhill rd ✆ (01647) 433260, *stay@cherryford.freeserve.co.uk, Fax (01647) 433637,* ≤, – **P**.
Rest (by arrangement) (communal dining) 26.50 – **3 rm** ☕ ✝70.00 – ✝✝70.00.
◆ Modern house with spacious grounds in country location. Comfortable sitting room overlooking gardens. Coordinated modern bedrooms, one on ground floor. Communal dining by arrangement; fresh, local produce.

22 Mill Street with rm, 22 Mill St, TQ13 8AW, ✆ (01647) 432244, *Fax (01647) 433101* – rest. MO VISA
closed January and 1 week June – **Rest** *(closed Sunday-Monday)* 22.60/39.50 **s.** – ☕ 5.50 – **2 rm** ✝45.00 – ✝✝75.00.
◆ Unusual dishes served in friendly two-roomed restaurant with well-spaced tables. Roast calves sweetbreads on braised cabbage sets the standard. Comfortable bedrooms.

at Easton *Northeast : 1½ m. on A 382 – ✉ Chagford.*

Easton Court without rest., Easton Cross, TQ13 8JL, ✆ (01647) 433469, *stay@easton.co.uk, Fax (01647) 433654,* – **P**. MO VISA
5 rm ☕ ✝45.00/49.00 – ✝✝60.00/72.00.
◆ Well appointed accommodation and a high ceilinged lounge overlooking the immaculate gardens. Home made marmalade a speciality. Friendly atmosphere.

at Sandypark *Northeast : 2¼ m. on A 382 – ✉ Chagford.*

Mill End, TQ13 8JN, on A 382 ✆ (01647) 432282, *info@millendhotel.com, Fax (01647) 433106,* – rest, **P**. MO AE VISA
Rest (light lunch)/dinner 35.00 ♀ – **15 rm** ☕ ✝75.00/110.00 – ✝✝115.00/150.00.
◆ Country house with mill wheel; river Teign runs through garden. Framed pictures, curios grace interiors. Upstairs bedrooms have views; those downstairs have private patios. Pretty restaurant, bright and comfortable.

Parford Well without rest., TQ13 8JW, on Drewsteignton rd ✆ (01647) 433353, *tim@parfordwell.co.uk,* – .
closed 25 December and January – **3 rm** ☕ ✝45.00/65.00 – ✝✝75.00.
◆ Tastefully maintained with superbly tended gardens. Elegant sitting room has plenty of books and French windows to garden. Two breakfast rooms. Homely, immaculate rooms.

A. Zezmer/SCOPE

Gorey: the impressive Mont Orgueil Castle

CHANNEL ISLANDS 503 OPQ 33 and 517 ⑨ ⑩ ⑪ *The West Country G.*

ALDERNEY

C.I. 503 Q 33 and 517 ⑨ *The West Country G. – pop. 2 294*

See: *Braye Bay★ – Mannez Garenne (≤★ from Quesnard Lighthouse) – Telegraph Bay★ – Vallee des Trois Vaux★ – Clonque Bay★.*

(01481) 822624 - Booking Office : Aurigny Air Services (01481) 822888.

States Office, Queen Elizabeth II St (01481) 823737.

Braye *C.I.*

First and Last, GY9 3TH, (01481) 823162, ≤ harbour – VISA
Easter-September – **Rest** - Seafood specialities - *(closed Monday except Bank Holidays)* (dinner only) a la carte 21.50/30.50.
◆ Positioned by the harbour with scenic views. Simple pine furniture, blue gingham tablecloths. Nautical theme prevails. Keen use of island produce with seafood base.

St Anne *C.I.*

Farm Court without rest., Le Petit Val, GY9 3UX, (01481) 822075, *relax@farmcourt-alderney.co.uk, Fax (01481) 822075,* – . VISA.
closed 1 week Christmas – **9 rm** ★35.00/60.00 – ★★70.00/90.00.
◆ Converted stone farm buildings around cobbled courtyard and garden. Sitting room and breakfast room. Spacious well-appointed bedrooms with contemporary and antique furniture.

Maison Bourgage without rest., 2 Le Bourgage, GY9 3TL, (01481) 824097, – . VISA.
closed 4 January-28 February – **3 rm** ★40.00/60.00 – ★★52.00/72.00.
◆ Part Georgian house on quiet, cobbled, town centre street. Neat, enclosed decked patio and garden face south. Leather furnished lounge and breakfast room. Bright, airy rooms.

GUERNSEY

C.I. 503 OP 33 and 517 ⑨ ⑩ *The West Country G. – pop. 58 867*

See: *Island★ – Pezeries Point★★ – Icart Point★★ – Côbo Bay★★ – St Martin's Point★★ – St Apolline's Chapel★ – Vale Castle★ – Fort Doyle★ – La Gran'mere du Chimquiere★ – Rocquaine Bay★ – Jerbourg Point★.*

Service Air (01481) 237766, Aurigny Air (01481) 822888.

from St Peter Port to France (St Malo) and Jersey (St Helier) (Emeraude Lines) – from St Peter Port to Jersey (St Helier) and Weymouth (Condor Ferries Ltd).

– from St Peter Port to France (St Malo) and Jersey (St Helier) (Condor Ferries Ltd) 2 weekly – from St Peter Port to France (Dielette) (Emeraude Lines) (summer only) (1 h 15 mn) – from St Peter Port to Herm (Herm Seaway) (25 mn) – from St Peter Port to Sark (Isle of Sark Shipping Co. Ltd) (45 mn) – from St Peter Port to Jersey (St Helier) (Emeraude Lines) (50 mn) – from St Peter Port to Jersey (St Helier) (Condor Ferries Ltd) daily except Sunday.

P.O. Box 23, North Plantation (01481) 723552 – Passenger Terminal, New Jetty (01481) 715885 – The Airport, La Villiaze, Forest (01481) 237267.

Catel/Castel *C.I.*

Hougue du Pommier, Hougue du Pommier Rd, GY5 7FQ, (01481) 256531, *hotel@houguedupommier.guernsey.net, Fax (01481) 256260,* , , heated, , – VISA
Tudor Bar : **Rest** a la carte 12.20/17.85 – ***The Restaurant :*** **Rest** (dinner only and Sunday lunch)/dinner a la carte 18.95/33.25 – **43 rm** ★40.00/74.00 – ★★80.00/183.00.
◆ A personally run 18C farmhouse with later extensions. Lovely outdoor pool and decking area. Occasional medieval banquets. Comfortable bedrooms, warmly decorated. Restaurant with beams and oak panelling. Tudor Bar for unique Feu du Bois cooking over open flame.

Cobo Bay, Cobo Coast Rd, GY5 7HB, (01481) 257102, *reservations@cobobayhotel.com, Fax (01481) 254542,* ≤, – , rest, rest, VISA.
closed January-February – **Rest** (dinner only and Sunday lunch)/dinner 15.50/25.00 – **36 rm** ★49.00 – ★★118.00.
◆ Modern hotel on peaceful, sandy Cobo Bay; an ideal location for families. The rooms are pleasant with bright décor and some have the delightful addition of seaview balconies. Romantic dining with views of sunsets.

Harton Lodge, Rue de Galaad, GY5 7FJ, (01481) 256341, *Fax (01481) 255716,* , , – VISA
Rest (bar lunch)/dinner 10.00/20.00 and a la carte 10.50/20.00 **s.** – **20 rm** ★40.00/60.00 – ★★80.00/120.00.
◆ Sunny yellow painted house with a neat and tidy appeal; close to beach. Two bars, one with a pool table. Decking to rear with small pool and sauna. Bright bedrooms. Linen-laid dining room: conservatory extension boasts comfy leather sofas.

Forest *C.I. – pop. 1 386.*

Maison Bel Air without rest., Le Chene, GY8 0AL, (01481) 238503, *juliette@maisonbelair.com, Fax (01481) 239403*, – P. VISA.
March-October – **6 rm** 32.00/39.00 – 44.00/60.00.
◆ Welcoming peach and white guesthouse, near airport; overlooking Petit Bot Valley with shady, peaceful, south facing garden. Smart breakfast room. Comfortable bedrooms.

Kings Mills *C.I.*

Fleur du Jardin with rm, GY5 7JT, (01481) 257996, *info@fleurdujardin.com, Fax (01481) 256834*, heated, – rest, P. VISA.
Rest (bar lunch)/dinner a la carte 15.00/25.00 – **17 rm** 47.00/86.00 – 116.00.
◆ Daily menus of local seafood give this granite 15C inn a standing of quiet renown. Cosy interior: rough hewn walls, alcoves, stone fireplace. Cottagey, traditional rooms.

St Martin *C.I. – pop. 6 082.*
St Peter Port 2.

Bon Port, Moulin Huet Bay, GY4 6EW, (01481) 239249, *mail@bonport.com, Fax (01481) 239596*, ≤ Moulin Huet Bay and Jerbourg Point, – P. VISA
closed January-February – **Rest** (bar lunch Monday-Saturday)/dinner 23.95 and a la carte 26.00/38.00 – **17 rm** 50.00/105.00 – 65.00/160.00, 1 suite.
◆ Perched on the top of the cliff, with a commanding view of the bay, this hotel is very keenly and personally run. Rooms vary in size and style and some have balconies. Large two tier dining room with bay views.

Jerbourg, Jerbourg Point, GY4 6BJ, (01481) 238826, *stay@hoteljerbourg.com, Fax (01481) 238238*, ≤ sea and neighbouring Channel Islands, – , rest, P. VISA.
mid March-mid October – **Rest** (bar lunch Monday-Saturday)/dinner 19.50 and a la carte 13.00/22.50 **s.** – **30 rm** 50.00/80.00 – 95.00/150.00.
◆ In a prime position for walks to sandy bays. Popular terrace for afternoon teas. Equipped with solar heated outdoor pool and garden patio. Most rooms have pleasant sea views. Finely presented, fish based cuisine.

La Barbarie, Saints Bay, GY4 6ES, (01481) 235217, *reservations@labarbariehotel.com, Fax (01481) 235208*, heated, – P. VISA.
10 March-October – **Rest** (carvery lunch Sunday) 18.95 (dinner) and a la carte 17.40/27.95 – **22 rm** 50.00/68.00 – 60.00/96.00, 10 suites 90.00/126.00.
◆ Stone-built former farmhouse with a welcoming, cottagey style. Characterful bar; well-kept pool and terrace. Eclectic range of rooms, including 10 larger annexed apartments. Mediterranean buzz from the restaurant.

Saints Bay, Icart, GY4 6JG, (01481) 238888, *info@saintsbayhotel.com, Fax (01481) 235558*, heated, – rm, P. VISA.
Rest (bar lunch Monday-Saturday)/dinner 18.50/30.00 and a la carte – **35 rm** 34.50/74.50 – 69.00/128.00.
◆ Located on Icart Point, overlooking Fisherman's Harbour, the southern tip of the island, perfect for cliff top walks. Multilingual staff; neat bedrooms with all amenities. Broad choice of menus.

La Michele, Les Hubits, GY4 6NB, (01481) 238065, *info@lamichelehotel.com, Fax (01481) 239492*, heated, – P. VISA.
mid March-mid October – **Rest** (residents only) (dinner only) – **16 rm** (dinner included) 39.00/55.00 – 78.00/110.00.
◆ Painted and canopied façade with conservatory lounge and secluded garden. Lovely seating area around the pool. Fermain bay is nearby; pleasant, unfussy bedrooms.

Sunnydene without rest., Rue des Marettes, GY4 6JH, (01481) 236870, *info@sunnydenecountryhotel.com, Fax (01481) 237468*, heated, – P. VISA.
Easter-early October – **20 rm** 40.00/55.00 – 70.00/80.00.
◆ Neat and tidy guesthouse with pitch and putt to rear of garden! Comfortable, homely lounge; linen-laid breakfast room. Pretty pool and terrace area. Rooms in house or garden.

The Auberge, Jerbourg Rd, GY4 6BH, (01481) 238485, *theauberge@cwgsy.net, Fax (01481) 710936*, ≤ Sea and neighbouring Channel Islands, – P. VISA
Rest (booking essential) a la carte 21.95/28.70.
◆ A splendid spot to sample contemporary brasserie-style dishes. Modern informal style, attractive terrace and excellent views of sea and islands.

St Peter Port *C.I. The West Country G. – pop. 16 648.*

See : *Town*★★ – *St Peter's Church*★ **Z** – *Hauteville House*★ **AC Z** – *Castle Cornet*★ (< ★) **AC Z**.

Env. : *Saumarez Park*★ *(Guernsey Folk Museum*★*), W : 2 m. by road to Catel* **Z** *– Little Chapel*★*, SW : 2¼ m. by Mount Durand road* **Z**.

18 *Rohais, St Pierre Park* ✆ *(01481) 727039,* **Z**.

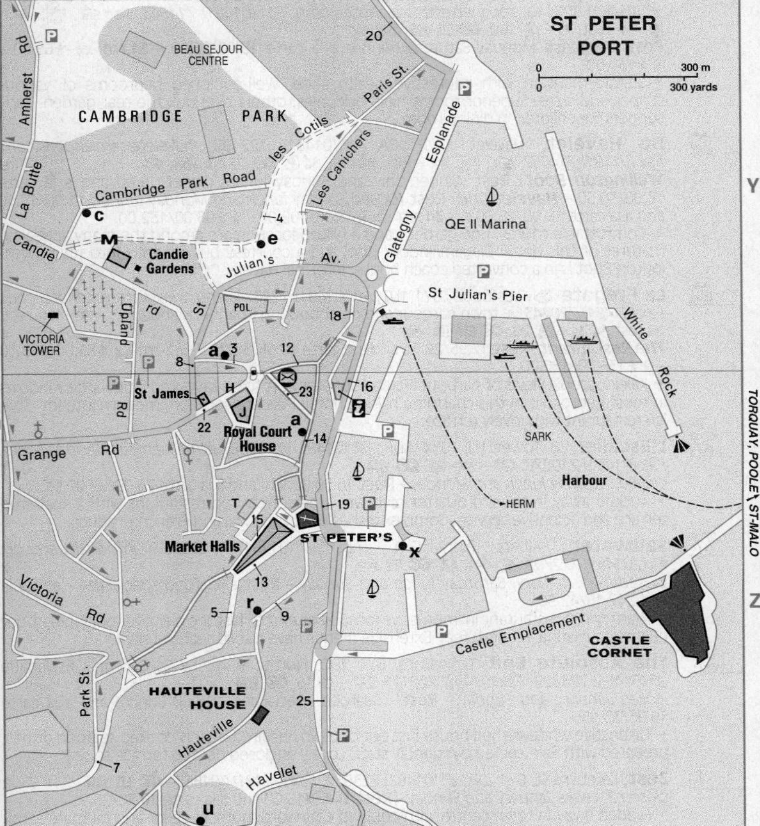

Y

Z

Street	Square	No.
Ann's Place	Y	3
Beauregard Lane	Y	4
Bordage	Z	5
Charroterie	Z	7
College Street	YZ	8
Cornet Street	Z	9
Forest Lane	Y	12
Fountain Street	Z	13
High Street	Z	14
Market Street	Z	15
North Esplanade	YZ	16
Pollet	Y	18
Quay (The)	Z	19
St-George's Esplanade	Y	20
St-James Street	Z	22
Smith Street	Z	23
South Esplanade	Z	25

Old Government House, St Ann's Pl, GY1 2NU, ✆ (01481) 724921, *ogh@theoghhotel.com, Fax (01481) 724429,* <, ♨, Fō, ≘s, ⛱ heated, 🛏 – 🛗 ⚭ 📞 ♿ 🅿 – 🏛 300. MC AE ⓓ VISA. ✈ **Y a**

***Governors* :** Rest (booking essential) a la carte 23.50/28.15 s. 🍷 – ***The Brasserie* :** Rest a la carte 24.75/31.75 s. – **63 rm** ☕ ★115.00/145.00 – ★★165.00/245.00.

◆ Refurbished hotel in 18C house, built for island governors. State-of-art leisure facilities. Conservatory is popular for tea. Comfortable rooms, some boasting harbour views. Impressively spacious Governors. Informal Mediterranean favourites at the Brasserie.

Duke of Richmond, Cambridge Park, GY1 1UY, (01481) 726221, *duke@guernsey.net, Fax (01481) 728945,* ←, heated – – 100. Y c
Rest closed lunch Monday-Friday 12.95/19.95 and a la carte 19.95/25.00 **s.** – **73 rm** 60.00/77.50 – 100.00/125.00, 1 suite.
◆ Boasts views over Candie Gardens. Equipped with rooms of pine and co-ordinated furnishings. Rear rooms overlook pool and gardens. Resident band plays in the ballroom. Basement dining room.

Les Rocquettes, Les Gravees, GY1 1RN, West : 1 m. by St Julian's Ave and Grange Rd (01481) 722146, *rocquettes@sarniahotels.com, Fax (01481) 714543,* , , , – , rest, – 100. .
Rest (bar lunch Monday-Saturday)/dinner a la carte 15.00/25.00 – **51 rm** 65.00 – 130.00.
◆ Stately mansion with impressive health suite. Well-equipped bedrooms of various shapes and sizes. Superior rooms have balconies; others overlook the rear garden. Early suppers for children in dining room.

De Havelet, Havelet, GY1 1BA, (01481) 722199, *havelet@sarniahotels.com, Fax (01481) 714057,* , , – , rest, . . Z u
Wellington Boot : **Rest** (dinner only and Sunday lunch)/dinner 19.00 and a la carte 16.00/30.50 – ***Havelet Grill :*** **Rest** *(closed Sunday lunch and Monday dinner)* 11.00/18.50 and a la carte 18.00/28.00 **s.** – **34 rm** 48.00/102.00 – 96.00/132.00.
◆ Comfortable rooms, fine gardens and a hilltop location are among the many appealing features of this hotel. Elegant indoor pool and a courtesy bus for trips into town. Wellington Boot is in a converted coach house. Informal Havelet Grill.

La Frégate , Les Cotils, GY1 1UT, (01481) 724624, *enquiries@lafregatehotel.com, Fax (01481) 720443,* ← town harbour and neighbouring Channel Islands, , – rest, rest, – 25. Y e
The Restaurant : **Rest** 17.95/26.50 and a la carte 19.95/35.75 – **12 rm** 85.00/165.00 – 135.00/180.00.
◆ Kaleidoscopic views of harbour life and St Peter Port to be savoured from large windows in most bedrooms in this charming hillside hotel. Peaceful location; modern interior. Stylish restaurant with lovely terrace.

L'Escalier, 6 Tower Hill, GY1 1DF, (01481) 710088, *armelleetdean@hotmail.com, Fax (01481) 710878,* – . Z r
closed Saturday lunch and Monday – **Rest** 16.50 (lunch) and a la carte 25.00/39.00 **s** .
◆ Tucked away in the old quarter of town, a personally run restaurant with a sheltered terrace and attentive service. Complex dishes use both local and French produce.

Saltwater, Albert Pier, GY1 1AD, (01481) 720823, *info@saltwater.gg, Fax (01481) 772702,* ← – . Z x
closed 1-21 January, Saturday lunch and Sunday – **Rest** - Seafood specialities - and a la carte 17.15/42.90.
◆ Warmly run restaurant in impressive location at end of historic pier overlooking harbour near large marina. Modern feel. Extensive menus have a solid seafood slant.

The Absolute End, Longstore, GY1 2BG, North : ¾ m. by St George's Esplanade (01481) 723822, *Fax (01481) 729129,* – 16.
closed January and Sunday – **Rest** - Seafood specialities - 15.00 (lunch) and a la carte 19.95/35.95.
◆ Distinctive whitewashed house just out of town. Inspired freshly cooked seafood dishes, prepared with flair, served by friendly staff. Lovely enclosed decked terrace to rear.

Zest, Lefebvre St, GY1 2JP, (01481) 723052, *Fax (01481) 701662* – Z a
closed 2 weeks January and Sunday – **Rest** 14.50/15.00 and a la carte 16.70/25.95.
◆ Hidden away in town centre with cobbled courtyard, homely décor and intimate semi-boothed seating. Wide-ranging, good quality dishes with a traditional base.

St Saviour *C.I. – pop. 2 419.*

St Peter Port 4.

Atlantique, Perelle Bay, GY7 9NA, (01481) 264056, *enquiries@perellebay.com, Fax (01481) 263800,* ←, heated, – , rest, . .
Easter-November – ***Atlantique :*** **Rest** (dinner only) a la carte 17.00/35.95 – **22 rm** 40.00/80.00 – 60.00/120.00, 1 suite.
◆ Traditionally styled hotel in a delightful spot on Perelle Bay, only a few metres from the sea: fine views from front-facing rooms. Charmingly formal Atlantique.

The Pavilion, Le Gron, GY7 9RN, (01481) 264165, *lecknleck@cwgsy.net, Fax (01481) 267396,* , – .
closed Monday in winter, Christmas and January – **Rest** (lunch only) a la carte 17.95/23.65 .
◆ Located in grounds of jewellers Bruce Russell and Son. Pleasant interior of exposed stone and beams. Excellent value, well executed dishes using good quality local produce.

Vazon Bay *C.I. – ✉ Catel.*

La Grande Mare, Vazon Coast Rd, GY5 7LL, ✆ (01481) 256576, *hotellagrandemare@cwgsy.net, Fax (01481) 256532,* ←, heated, – 30. VISA.

Rest a la carte 21.50/33.50 ♀ – **10 rm** ★89.00/99.00 – ★★158.00/178.00, **27 suites** 208.00/260.00.

◆ Resort complex with large bedrooms of magnolia and pine furnishings; some have balconies, some well-equipped small kitchens. Family friendly, with indoor/outdoor activities. Formal dining room overlooks golf course.

HERM

C.I. 503 P 33 *and* 517 ⑩ *The West Country G. – pop. 97*

See: *Le Grand Monceau★.*

to Guernsey (St Peter Port) (Herm Seaway) (20 mn).

White House , GY1 3HR, ✆ (01481) 722159, *hotel@herm-island.com, Fax (01481) 710066,* ← Belle Greve Bay and Guernsey, heated, – rest. VISA.

April-September – ***Conservatory :*** **Rest** (booking essential) 23.00 (dinner) and lunch a la carte 19.85/24.85 – ***Ship Inn :*** **Rest** (bar lunch)/dinner 17.00 and lunch a la carte approx 13.20/18.85 – **40 rm** (dinner included) ★73.00/103.00 – ★★146.00/188.00.

◆ Hotel with real country house feel: offset by verdant hills, the beach extends to the door. Guernsey and Jethou can be viewed from the hushed lounge. Attractive rooms. Formal Conservatory with seafood emphasis. Relaxed Ship Inn.

Good food and accommodation at moderate prices? Look for the Bib symbols: red Bib Gourmand for food, blue Bib Hotel for hotels

JERSEY

C.I. 503 OP 33 *and* 517 ⑪ *The West Country G. – pop. 87 500*

See: *Island★★ – Jersey Zoo★★ AC – Jersey Museum★ – Eric Young Orchid Foundation★ – St Catherine's Bay★ (←★★) – Grosnez Point★ – Devil's Hole★ – St Matthews Church, Millbrook (glasswork★) – La Hougue Bie★ (Neolithic tomb★ AC) – Waterworks Valley - Hamptonne Country Life Museum★ – St Catherine's Bay★ (←★★) – Noirmont Point★.*

✈ *States of Jersey Airport : ✆ (01534) 492000.*

from St Helier to France (St Malo) and Guernsey (St Peter Port) (Emeraude Lines) – from St Helier to France (Granville) (Emeraude Lines) (summer only) (1 h) – from St Helier to France (Dielette) (Emeraude Lines) (summer only) (1 h 10 mn) – from St Helier to France (Carteret) (Emeraude Lines) (summer only) (55 mn) – from St Helier to Sark (Emeraude Lines) (50 mn) – from St Helier to Guernsey (St Peter Port) and Weymouth (Condor Ferries Ltd).

from St Helier to France (Granville and St Malo) (Emeraude Lines and Condor Ferries Ltd) (summer only) – from St Helier to France (St Malo) (Condor Ferries Ltd) 3 weekly – from Gorey to France (Carteret) (Emeraude Lines) (summer only) (30-40 mn) – from St Helier to Guernsey (St Peter Port) (Condor Ferries Ltd) (50 mn) – from St Helier to Guernsey (St Peter Port) (Condor Ferries Ltd) daily except Sunday.

ℹ *Liberation Sq, St Helier ✆ (01534) 500777.*

Beaumont *C.I.*

Bistro Soleil, La Route de la Haule, JE3 7BA, ✆ (01534) 720249, *Fax (01534) 625621,* ← St Aubins Bay, – VISA

closed Sunday dinner, Monday and Bank Holidays – **Rest** 15.85/25.85 and a la carte 21.60/29.70 ♀.

◆ Series of connected rooms with superb views over St Aubins Bay. Minimalist style: just a couple of modern pictures. Freshly prepared, bold menus with Mediterranean accent.

Bouley Bay *C.I.*

St Helier 6.

The Water's Edge, JE3 5AS, ✆ (01534) 862777, *mail@watersedgehotel.co.je,* ← Bouley Bay, heated, – rest, – 40. VISA.

mid April-mid October – ***Waterside :*** **Rest** (dinner only) 22.00 and a la carte 29.20/48.00 – ***Black Dog Bar :*** **Rest** a la carte 13.75/19.40 s. – **47 rm** ★65.00/90.00 – ★★100.00/150.00, 3 suites.

◆ Refurbished, revitalised hotel of long standing that boasts breathtaking bay views. Secluded garden with well-manicured lawns. Comfortable, well-appointed accommodation. Formal Waterside for tables-with-a-view. Black Dog Bar with quarterdeck al fresco area.

Gorey *C.I. The West Country G. – ✉ St Martin.*

See : Mont Orgueil Castle★ (≤★★) AC.
St Helier 4.

Old Court House, Gorey Village, JE3 9FS, ☎ (01534) 854444, *ochhotel@itl.net, Fax (01534) 853587,* , heated, – P. VISA
mid April-early October – **Rest** (bar lunch)/dinner 18.00 – **58 rm** (dinner included) ★58.00/104.50 – ★★116.00/149.00.
◆ A popular, spacious hotel opposite three miles of sandy beach of the Royal Bay of Grouville. Large balconies in the second and third floor bedrooms. Pleasant gardens. Part 15C dining room: low beamed ceilings, exposed granite walls.

Moorings, Gorey Pier, JE3 6EW, ☎ (01534) 853633, *reservations@themooringshotel.com, Fax (01534) 857618* – rest. AE VISA
Rest 20.50/27.50 and a la carte 26.50/43.75 – **16 rm** ★46.00/114.00 – ★★92.00/114.00.
◆ Located at the base of Gorey Castle, overlooking the waterfront, once the heart of the oyster fishing industry. Well-priced; the first floor bedrooms have terraces. Pleasant decked area at front of restaurant.

Jersey Pottery (Garden Restaurant), Gorey Village, JE3 9EP, ☎ (01534) 851119, *admin@jerseypottery.com, Fax (01534) 856403,* , – P. VISA
closed October-March, Sunday and Monday – **Rest** - Seafood specialities - (lunch only) 21.00 and a la carte 21.20/31.00 **s.**
◆ Unusual restaurant in a working pottery: polished service and an impressive choice of seafood specialities. Dine among rich foliage in the orangery-style covered terrace.

Suma's, Gorey Hill, JE3 6ET, ☎ (01534) 853291, *Fax (01534) 851913,* ≤ Gorey harbour and castle, – . AE VISA
closed Christmas-New Year – **Rest** (booking essential) 15.00 (lunch) and a la carte 25.00/31.75 **s.**
◆ Cheerful and contemporary; fine terrace views of Gorey Castle and harbour. Dishes are carefully prepared and innovatively presented; pleasant service enhances the enjoyment.

Village Bistro, Gorey Village, JE3 9EP, ☎ (01534) 853429, *thevillagebistro@yahoo.co.uk, Fax (01534) 858730,* – . VISA
closed 3 weeks November, Sunday dinner and Monday – **Rest** 14.50 (lunch) and a la carte 22.20/25.70.
◆ Local produce sourced daily from small suppliers. Unpretentious feel; interesting choices to be made, particularly of seafood dishes.

Green Island *C.I.*

Green Island, St Clement, JE2 6LS, ☎ (01534) 857787, *greenislandrestaurant@jerseymail.co.uk,* – VISA
closed 30 October-16 November, 24-31 December, Sunday dinner and Monday – **Rest** - Seafood specialities - (booking essential) 15.00 (lunch) and a la carte 25.15/30.90.
◆ Lovely location on the beach; coir carpeted, nautically fitted restaurant with wide ranging, daily changing menu at affordable prices. Welcoming, casual atmosphere.

Grève De Lecq *C.I. – ✉ St Ouen.*

Des Pierres, JE3 2DT, on B 65 ☎ (01534) 481858, *despierres@localdial.com, Fax (01534) 485273* – P. VISA.
closed mid November-mid February – **Rest** (residents only) (dinner only) 14.50 **s.** – **16 rm** ★33.50/52.00 – ★★58.00/64.00.
◆ A personally run hotel, well situated for exploring the north of the island; close to the old smuggling harbour of Grève de Lecq. Simply furnished rooms; some have views.

Grouville *C.I.*

St Helier 3.

Cafe Poste, La Grande Route des Sablons, JE3 9FY, ☎ (01534) 859696, – P. VISA
closed 2 weeks early March, 2 weeks early November Monday and Tuesday – **Rest** (booking essential) a la carte 22.20/31.00.
◆ Former post office and general store with hidden decked area for outdoor dining. Very much a neighbourhood favourite. Strong use of island produce on eclectic, modish menus.

La Haule *C.I. – ✉ St Brelade.*

La Place, Route du Coin, JE3 8BT, by B 25 on B 43 ☎ (01534) 744261, *reservations@hotellaplacejersey.com, Fax (01534) 745164*, heated, – 100. VISA
*closed January – **The Retreat :*** **Rest** (dinner only and Sunday lunch) 27.00 and a la carte – **42 rm** 70.00/99.00 – 140.00/198.00.
◆ Built round the remains of a 17C farmhouse; peaceful gardens and pool. Suited to both holiday makers and business clientele; spacious rooms, includes executive study rooms. Medieval inspired restaurant and adjoining conservatory.

La Haule Manor without rest., St Aubin's Bay, JE3 8BS, ☎ (01534) 746013, *mariefore ster@msn.com, Fax (01534) 745501*, ≤ St Aubin's Fort and Bay, – VISA.
10 rm 57.75/82.00 – 70.00/100.00.
◆ Attractive, extended Georgian house with fine coastal outlook. Period style sitting room; stylish breakfast room; large basement bar. Airy, well-kept bedrooms with good view.

Au Caprice, Route de la Haule, JE3 8BA, on A 1 ☎ (01534) 722083, *aucaprice@jersey mail.co.uk, Fax (01534) 280058* – VISA.
April-October – **Rest** (by arrangement) 9.00 – **12 rm** 42.00/62.00 – 42.00/72.00.
◆ Clean-lined white guesthouse with French windows; light and airy, providing homely good value rooms: two of them share large balcony at the front. Close to large sandy beach. Each morning, guests told dining room menu.

La Pulente *C.I. – ✉ St Brelade.*

Les Mielles G. & C.C., St Ouens Bay ☎ (01534) 482787.
St Helier 7.

Atlantic, Le Mont de la Pulente, JE3 8HE, on B 35 ☎ (01534) 744101, *info@theatlanti chotel.com, Fax (01534) 744102*, ≤, heated, – rest, – 60. VISA.
closed January-10 February – ***Ocean :*** **Rest** 19.50/35.00 – **49 rm** 145.00/185.00 – 190.00/550.00, 1 suite.
◆ Luxury hotel fringed by gardens and golf course. Stylish twist enhances modern rooms in pale, cool colours. Garden suites have own terrace; fine views from upper floors. Cool, clean, relaxing restaurant; enjoy modern dishes utilising Jersey's fine larder.

La Rocque *C.I.*

St Helier 8.

Borsalino Rocque, JE3 9FF, ☎ (01534) 852111, *Fax (01534) 856404*, – VISA
closed 25-26 December and Tuesday – **Rest** - Seafood - 23.50 and a la carte 19.95/30.25.
◆ Well-spaced tables in large conservatory and dining room filled with curios. A long-established family business, popular with island residents. Wide choice in menus.

Rozel Bay *C.I. – ✉ St Martin.*

St Helier 6.

Chateau La Chaire, Rozel Valley, JE3 6AJ, ☎ (01534) 863354, *res@chateau-la-chaire.co.uk, Fax (01534) 865137*, – rest, VISA.
Rest 24.95 (dinner) and a la carte 28.85/39.85 – **12 rm** 121.00/149.00 – 256.00/274.00, 2 suites.
◆ Imposing chateau dated 1843, rich in paintings and antiques: individually decorated bedrooms overlook the quiet wooded grounds. Ornate sitting room. Conservatory dining room; terrace popular in summer.

Beau Couperon, JE3 6AN, ☎ (01534) 865522, *beaucouperon@southernhotels.com, Fax (01534) 865332*, ≤, heated – rest, VISA
25 March-October – **Rest** 12.90/22.55 and a la carte 15.00/30.00 s. – **34 rm** 42.40/88.65 – 164.20.
◆ A converted Napoleonic fortress with splendid views of the bay and harbour. The famous zoo and wildlife trust are very close by. Most of the well-sized rooms have balconies. Cool blue dining room with sea views.

Le Frère, Le Mont de Rozel, JE3 6AN, East : ½ m. on B 38 ☎ (01534) 861000, *lefrere@jer seymail.co.uk, Fax (01534) 864007*, ≤ Sea and French coastline, – 32. VISA.
closed January, Sunday dinner and Monday – **Rest** - Seafood specialities - 16.50 (lunch) and a la carte 23.00/51.00.
◆ Dine alfresco with the sea breeze on your face or inside with views from panoramic windows. Menus with strong fish base. Classic style and service.

ENGLAND

St Aubin *C.I. – St Brelade.*

St Helier 4.

Somerville, Mont du Boulevard, JE3 8AD, South : ¾ m. via harbour (01534) 741226, *somerville@dolanhotels.com, Fax (01534) 746621,* ≤ St Aubin's Bay, heated, – rest, rest, P. VISA.
Tides : **Rest** a la carte 10.95/19.50 **s.** – **59 rm** 61.00 – 150.00.
◆ Delightful views of the harbour, bay and village. Courtesy bus runs from hotel into town. Evening entertainment laid on. Cheerful rooms, some in superior style. Cloth clad, classic dining room.

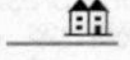

Mont de La Roque, Mont de La Roque, JE3 8BQ, (01534) 742942, *Fax (01534) 747841,* ≤ St Aubin's Fort and Bay, – rest, P. VISA.
March-October – ***Le Mirage :*** **Rest** *(closed Monday)* (dinner only and Sunday lunch)/dinner a la carte 21.50/37.00 – **29 rm** 45.00/70.00 – 75.00/110.00, 2 suites.
◆ This brightly furnished hotel in a stunning position has some of the best views on the island. Matching floral fabrics in rooms, some of which have balconies. Restaurant with views and the gentle sounds of Spanish guitar.

Panorama without rest., La Rue du Crocquet, JE3 8BZ, (01534) 742429, *info@panoramajersey.com, Fax (01534) 745940,* ≤ St Aubin's Fort and Bay, – VISA.
mid April-mid October – **14 rm** 35.00/87.00 – 88.00/116.00.
◆ Personally run hotel with conservatory, garden and bay views. Also boasts a teapot collection. The superior style bedrooms are very pleasant. All rooms boast good amenities.

Sabots d'or, High St, JE3 8BZ, (01534) 43732, *sandralecorre@yahoo.co.uk, Fax (01534) 490142 –* rest. VISA
Rest (by arrangement) 9.00 – **11 rm** 21.00/35.00 – 46.00/60.00.
◆ Traditional floral furnishings in homely and cosy bedrooms. Well located for shops, watersports; its cobbled high street position not far from picturesque harbour. Home-made desserts a dining room highlight.

Porthole Cottage without rest., La Route au Moestre (Market Hill), JE3 8AE, (01534) 745007, *portcott@itl.net, Fax (01534) 490336,* ≤, – P. VISA.
8 March-13 October – **11 rm** 38.00 – 76.00.
◆ Brick and stone guesthouse overlooking St Aubins harbour; shrub-filled, elevated rear garden. Nautically inspired breakfast room with beams and galley window. Cottagey rooms.

Old Court House Inn with rm, St Aubin's Harbour, JE3 8AB, (01534) 746433, *Fax (01534) 745103,* ≤, – VISA.
closed 25 December – **Rest** 10.00/21.00 and a la carte 20.00/60.00 – **9 rm** 40.00/60.00 – 80.00/120.00.
◆ Atmospheric quayside inn, once a courthouse and merchant's house, dating from 15C. Bar featured in Bergerac TV series. Cosmopolitan menu with seafood emphasis. Neat bedrooms.

St Brelade's Bay *C.I. The West Country G. – pop. 9 560 – St Brelade.*

See : *Fishermen's Chapel (frescoes★).*

St Helier 6.

L'Horizon, JE3 8EF, (01534) 743101, *lhorizon@handpicked.co.uk, Fax (01534) 746269,* ≤ St Brelade's Bay, – rm, rest, P – 300. VISA.
Brasserie : **Rest** a la carte approx 24.50 – (see also ***The Grill*** below) – **99 rm** 100.00/150.00 – 260.00/330.00, 7 suites.
◆ Period hotel right on the beach and consequently popular for its stunning views from the terrace and some of its tastefully decorated front bedrooms. Serene indoor pool. Informal brasserie adjacent to the sea.

St Brelade's Bay, Rue de la Baie, JE3 8EF, (01534) 746141, *info@stbreladesbayhotel.com, Fax (01534) 747278,* ≤ St Brelade's Bay, heated, – rest, P. VISA.
15 April-9 October – **Rest** 25.00/35.00 (dinner) and a la carte 28.00/38.00 – **78 rm** 75.00/154.00 – 170.00/248.00, 3 suites.
◆ Traditional seafront hotel with mouth-watering views of bay and resplendent gardens with pool. Rattan furnished sitting room and spacious bedrooms. Friendly and family run. Front, sea-facing restaurant.

ENGLAND

Golden Sands, La Route de la Baie, JE3 8EF, ☎ (01534) 741241, *goldensands@dolanhotels.com, Fax (01534) 499366*, ≤ - |‡|, ⇸ rest. MC AE VISA. ✗
April-mid October – **Rest** (bar lunch)/dinner a la carte 15.40/25.70 – **62 rm** ☐ ✝60.00/105.00 – ✝✝120.00/160.00.
◆ With adjacent sweep of a sandy bay and many of the bedrooms south-facing with balconies, this hotel is a popular spot. Within easy reach of the airport and St Helier. Seasonal menus.

The Grill (at L'Horizon H.), JE3 8EF, ☎ (01534) 490082, *Fax (01534) 746269*, ≤ St Brelade's Bay, ♨ – ⇸ ▤ P. MC AE ⓓ VISA
closed Sunday and Monday – **Rest** (dinner only) 37.00 and a la carte approx 33.50 ♀.
◆ Intimately styled grill room with tasteful cream and brown banquettes and framed photos of film stars. Seafood stars but faces competition from a strong suit of meat dishes.

St Helier *C.I. The West Country G. – pop. 27 523.*

See : *Jersey Museum★ AC* Z – *Elizabeth Castle (≤★) AC* Z – *Fort Regent (≤★ AC)* Z.
Env. : *St Peter's Valley - German Underground Hospital★ AC, NW : 4 m. by A 1, A 11 St Peter's Valley rd and C 112.*

Plan on next page

The Club Hotel & Spa, Green St, JE2 4UH, ☎ (01534) 876500, *reservations@theclubjersey.com, Fax (01534) 720371*, ⊛, ≘s, ⊡ – |‡| ⇸ ▤ ✆ ♿ P – 🏛 30. MC AE ⓓ VISA. ✗
Rest a la carte 20.45/31.90 – (see also ***Bohemia*** below) – ☐ 7.50 – **42 rm** ✝195.00 – ✝✝195.00, 4 suites.
◆ Above the Bohemia restaurant, a town house hotel of contemporary luxury with particularly pleasant roof terrace; the cosy bedrooms are fitted with many stylish mod cons. Small New York café style restaurant.

Hotel de France, St Saviours Rd, JE1 7XP, ☎ (01534) 614000, *general@defrance.co.uk, Fax (01534) 614999*, ♨, ⊛, Fб, ≘s, ⛱ heated, ⊡, ⛶ – |‡| ▤ P – 🏛 800. MC AE ⓓ VISA. ✗ Y b
closed 19 December-9 January – ***Gallery :*** **Rest** *(closed Sunday)* (dinner only) a la carte approx 35.10 **s.** ♀ – ***Orangery :*** **Rest** a la carte 24.95/33.95 ♀ – **276 rm** ☐ ✝99.00/125.00 – ✝✝150.00, 13 suites.
◆ A well-located grand hotel with sweeping balustraded staircase leading to neatly furnished rooms. Cinema on complex and extensive range of business facilities. Gallery restaurant boasts intimate, fine dining experience. Informal Atrium Brasserie.

De Vere Grand, Esplanade, JE4 8WD, ☎ (01534) 722301, *grand.jersey@devere-hotels.com, Fax (01534) 737815*, ≤, Fб, ≘s, ⊡ – |‡| ⇸, ▤ rest, ♿ – 🏛 180. MC AE ⓓ VISA. ✗ Y u
The Regency : **Rest** (dinner only and Sunday lunch)/dinner 19.95 and a la carte 13.45/23.95 – **113 rm** ☐ ✝70.00/145.00 – ✝✝100.00/150.00, 5 suites.
◆ Impressive Victorian hotel with pitched white façade overlooking St Aubins Bay. Elegant wing armchairs in smart lounge. Strong leisure facilities and comfortable bedrooms. Smart dining room.

Eulah Country House without rest., Mont Cochon, JE2 3JA, Northwest : 2 m. by A 1 on B 27 ☎ (01534) 626626, *eulah@jerseymail.co.uk, Fax (01534) 626600*, ≤ St Aubin's Bay, ≘s, ⛱ heated, ⛶ – ⇸ P. MC AE VISA. ✗
9 rm ☐ ✝105.00/145.00 – ✝✝190.00/230.00.
◆ Informally run Edwardian country house proves pleasantly unconventional. Stylish combined lounge and breakfast room, luxurious bedrooms and superb views of St Aubin's Bay.

La Bonne Vie without rest., Roseville St, JE2 4PL, ☎ (01534) 735955, *labonneviequesthouse@yahoo.com, Fax (01534) 733357* – ⇸ ✆. MC VISA. ✗ Z a
10 rm ☐ ✝25.00/62.00 – ✝✝50.00/65.00.
◆ Floral fabrics and pastel colours enliven interiors in this "home from home" guesthouse. Comfy lounge and breakfast room. All bedrooms have showers; some have four posters.

Bohemia (at The Club Hotel & Spa), Green St, JE2 4UH, ☎ (01534) 880588, *bohemia@huggler.com, Fax (01534) 875054* – ⇸ ▤. MC AE ⓓ VISA Z e
closed Sunday – **Rest** 19.50/45.00 ♀.
Spec. Velouté of Jersey crab, scallop ravioli, buttered lobster and sweetcorn. Confit of belly pork with glazed pig cheek and roast foie gras. Lemon soufflé, milk chocolate semifreddo.
◆ Smart modern restaurant with a touch of West-End style: its bar is very popular at weekends. Original, contemporary cooking and very good service set the tone.

ST HELIER

Street	Grid	No.	Street	Grid	No.	Street	Grid	No.
Beresford Street	Z	2	Gloucester Street	Y	10	Royal Square	Z	20
Broad Street	Z	3	Halkett Place	Z	13	St-Saviours Hill	Y	23
Burrard Street	Z	4	King Street	Z		Simon Place	Y	24
Cannon Street	Y	5	La Colomberie	Z	16	Union Street	Y	26
Charing Cross	Z	6	La Motte Street	Z	17	Victoria Street	Y	27
Cheapside	Y	7	Minden Place	Z	18	Windsor Road	Y	28
Conway Street	Z	8	Queen's Road	Y	19	York Street	Y	30
Elizabeth Place	Y	9	Queen Street	Z				

XX **La Capannina,** 65-67 Halkett Pl, JE2 4WG, ☎ (01534) 734602, *Fax (01534) 877628* – ▤ ⇔ 16. MO AE D VISA Z n

closed 10 days Christmas, Sunday and Bank Holidays – **Rest** - Italian - 14.00/22.00 and a la carte 17.00/36.00.

◆ A buffet display of seafood and Parma ham preside over airy dining room with prints of Venice and Pisa. Choose between Jersey fish and Italian pasta. Dessert from the trolley.

St Lawrence C.I.

Cristina, Mont Felard, JE3 1JA, ✆ (01534) 758024, *cristina@dolanhotels.com, Fax (01534) 758028*, ←, heated, – rest, P. MC AE VISA.
April-October – ***Indigo :*** **Rest** (bar lunch)/dinner 21.00 and a la carte 14.40/26.60 ♀ – **63 rm** ★69.30/106.20 – ★★77.00/156.00.
◆ Traditional, white painted hotel in elevated position. Well-kept pool and garden terrace area. Spacious bar and wicker furnished lounge. Modern, pristine bedrooms. Tiled floors, suede fabrics add character to restaurant.

St Peter *C.I. The West Country G. – pop. 4 228.*

See : *Living Legend*★.
St Helier 5.

Greenhill's Country H., Mont de l'Ecole, Coin Varin, JE3 7EL, on C 112 ✆ (01534) 481042, *greenhills@messages.co.uk, Fax (01534) 485322*, heated, – rest, rest, P. MC AE VISA.
9 February-17 December – **Rest** 13.50/26.50 and a la carte 22.70/37.65 ♀ – **30 rm** ★50.00/101.00 – ★★110.00/152.00, 1 suite.
◆ Very popular with regular guests, this part 17C stone farmhouse is a fine place to settle down in, with flower-filled gardens, country style rooms and wood panelled lounge. Restaurant with plush pink predominating.

St Saviour *C.I. – pop. 12 680.*

St Helier 1.

Longueville Manor, Longueville Rd, JE2 7WF, on A 3 ✆ (01534) 725501, *longuevillemanor@relaischateaux.com, Fax (01534) 731613*, heated, , , – , rest, P. MC AE VISA
Rest 15.00 (lunch) and a la carte 42.00/55.50 **s.** ♀ – **28 rm** ★190.00/205.00 – ★★230.00/260.00, 2 suites.
◆ Exemplary part 14C manor for a special stay; every detail from furnishings to service is considered. Sumptuous rooms, delightful garden, poolside terrace. Panelled restaurant and terrace room overlooking garden; locally-inspired classics with modern twists.

Trinity *C.I. – pop. 2 639.*

The Highfield Country H., Route d'Ebenezer, JE3 5DT, Northwest : ½ m. on A 8 ✆ (01534) 862194, *reservations@highfieldjersey.com, Fax (01534) 865342*, , , , – , P. MC AE VISA.
April-October – **Rest** (bar lunch)/dinner 18.50 and a la carte 19.00/23.00 ♀ – **28 rm** ★65.00/90.00 – ★★100.00/130.00, 10 suites 115.00/145.00.
◆ Family oriented hotel, well placed for zoo and coast. Bedrooms are particularly large, some with equally spacious sitting rooms. Equipped with games room and conservatory. Children's options appear on the seafood based menu.

SARK

C.I. **503** P 33 and **517** ⑩ *The West Country G. – pop. 550*

See: *Island*★★ – *La Coupée*★★★ – *Port du Moulin*★★ – *Creux Harbour*★ – *La Seigneurie*★ *AC* – *Pilcher Monument*★ – *Hog's Back*★.
to Jersey (St Helier) (Emeraude Lines) (50 mn).
– to Guernsey (St Peter Port) (Isle of Sark Shipping Co. Ltd) (summer only) (45 mn).
Harbour Hill ✆ *(01481) 832345.*

Aval du Creux, Harbour Hill, GY9 0SB, ✆ (01481) 832036, *avalducreux@freeuk.com, Fax (01481) 832368*, , heated, – rest. MC AE VISA
May-September – ***The Lobster :*** **Rest** 23.00 (dinner) and a la carte 20.00/30.50 – **20 rm** ★70.00/82.00 – ★★100.00/124.00.
◆ Secluded stone built hotel - the closest to the harbour - with 21C extensions. South facing mature gardens. Comfortable modern bedrooms. Dining room and terrace overlook garden and pool.

Stocks Island, GY9 0SD, ✆ (01481) 832001, *stocks@sark.net, Fax (01481) 832130*, , , – . MC AE VISA
Rest (bar lunch)/dinner 20.00/34.00 and a la carte 17.00/25.00 **s.** ♀ – **18 rm** (dinner included) ★50.00/90.00 – ★★140.00/180.00.
◆ A mellow granite former farmhouse built in 1741, family owned and very personally run. Quiet location facing wooded valley. Well-kept bedrooms and period beamed bar. Organic produce to fore in charming restaurant.

ENGLAND

Petit Champ, GY9 0SF, (01481) 832046, *info@hotelpetitchamp.co.uk*, *Fax (01481) 832469*, ≤ coast, Herm, Jetou and Guernsey, heated, – rest.
Easter - October – **Rest** 20.25 (dinner) and a la carte 13.45/24.50 – **10 rm** (dinner included) 59.50/69.00 – 115.00/134.00.
◆ Ideal for views of neighbouring islands, with three sun lounges to enjoy them from; neat, trim rooms. Quarry, from which hotel's stone comes, is site of solar heated pool. Dining room features Sark specialities.

La Sablonnerie with rm, Little Sark, GY9 0SD, (01481) 832061, *Fax (01481) 832408*, –
Easter-mid October – **Rest** 25.80/28.80 and a la carte 21.60/28.80 – **21 rm** (dinner included) 59.50/89.25 – 135.00/169.00, 1 suite.
◆ Immaculately whitewashed 16C former farmhouse: a long low building. Diners greeted from jetty by Victorian horse and carriage. Home-produced ingredients to fore. Smart rooms.

CHANNEL TUNNEL *Kent* 504 X 30 – *see Folkestone.*

CHAPELTOWN *N. Yorks.* 502 503 504 P 23 – *see Sheffield.*

CHARD *Somerset* 503 L 31 – *pop. 12 008.*
15 High St (01460) 67463.
London 157 – Exeter 32 – Lyme Regis 12 – Taunton 18 – Yeovil 17.

Bellplot House, High St, TA20 1QB, (01460) 62600, *info@bellplothouse.co.uk*, *Fax (01460) 62600*, – rest,
Rest *(closed Sunday)* (dinner only) a la carte 19.40/32.00 – 9.00 – **7 rm** 68.00/78.00 – 78.00.
◆ Impressive mid-Georgian house named after shape of original plot of land. Lounge with plush sofas and fitted bar. Bedrooms stylishly modern with bright yellow décor. Restaurant with antique tables; well-sourced local ingredients feature.

CHARLBURY *Oxon.* 503 504 P 28 – *pop. 2 984.*
London 72 – Birmingham 50 – Oxford 15.

Bull Inn with rm, Sheep St, OX7 3RR, (01608) 810689, *info@bullinn-charlbury.com* –
closed 25 December and 1 January **Rest** *(closed Monday in winter and Sunday dinner)* a la carte 16.95/25.00 – **3 rm** 60.00 – 85.00.
◆ Charming part 17C inn with friendly ambience. Simple bar menu; restaurant dishes are more elaborate without sacrificing personal touch. Neat, well-kept bedrooms.

CHARLESTOWN *Cornwall* 503 F 32 – *see St Austell.*

CHARLTON *W. Sussex* 504 R 31 – *see Chichester.*

CHARLWOOD *Surrey* 504 T 30 – ✉ *Horley.*
London 30 – Brighton 29 – Royal Tunbridge Wells 28.

Stanhill Court, Stan Hill, RH6 0EP, Northwest : 1 m. by Norwood Hill Rd (01293) 862166, *enquiries@stanhillcourthotel.co.uk*, *Fax (01293) 862773*, ≤, – 250.
Rest (booking essential to non-residents) 15.95/45.00 and a la carte 32.00/46.90 – **15 rm** 75.00/105.00 – 125.00/180.00.
◆ Attractive Victorian country house in 30 acres of parkland. Striking panelled baronial hall with stained glass. Huge conservatory. Bedrooms retain some original features. Pleasant dining room in classic style.

**We try to be as accurate as possible when giving room rates.
But prices are susceptible to change,
so please check rates when booking.**

CHARMOUTH *Dorset* 503 L 31 – ✉ *Bridport.*

London 157 – Dorchester 22 – Exeter 31 – Taunton 27.

White House, 2 Hillside, The Street, DT6 6PJ, ☎ (01297) 560411, *Fax (01297) 560702* – ⇎ P. MC VISA. ✗

closed January and restricted opening in winter and Monday – **Rest** *(closed Sunday)* (dinner only) 30.00 – **7 rm** ☕ ♦40.00/106.00 – ♦♦106.00/130.00.

◆ Gleaming white Regency hotel a stone's throw from magnificent coastal scenery; popular with fossil hunters. Tasteful rooms, with pretty furnishings and a bold palette. Garden herbs and fruit used in home-cooked meals.

CHARTHAM HATCH *Kent* 504 X 30 – *see Canterbury.*

CHEADLE *Ches.* 502 503 N 23.

London 200 – Manchester 7 – Stoke-on-Trent 33.

Village H. & Leisure Club, Cheadle Rd, SK8 1HW, South : ¾ m. by A 5149 ☎ (0161) 428 0404, *village.cheadle@village-hotels.com, Fax (0161) 428 1191,* ⓘ, ₣₆, ≘s, ▢, squash – |‡| ⇎, ▤ rest, ♿ P – 🏛 200. MC AE ⓓ VISA

Rest 9.95/17.50 and a la carte 17.00/25.00 ♀ – **78 rm** ☕ ♦85.00/135.00 – ♦♦85.00/150.00.

◆ Corporate hotel in leafy suburb, convenient for Manchester airport and offering range of rooms; the executive rooms are larger with extra touches. Excellent leisure club. Bustling restaurant with cosmopolitan offerings.

"Rest" appears in red for establishments with a ✿ (star) or ☺ (Bib Gourmand).

CHEDDLETON *Staffs.* 502 503 504 N 24 – *pop. 2 719* – ✉ *Leek.*

London 125 – Birmingham 48 – Derby 33 – Manchester 42 – Stoke-on-Trent 11.

Choir Cottage without rest., Ostlers Lane, via Hollow Lane (opposite Red Lion on A 520), ST13 7HS, ☎ (01538) 360561, *enquiries@choircottage.co.uk,* ⚘ – ⇎ P. ✗

3 rm ☕ ♦45.00/50.00 – ♦♦60.00/80.00.

◆ Personally run 17C stone cottage, formerly church owned, and let to the poor, rent used to buy choir gowns. Individually furnished bedrooms with four-posters.

CHELMSFORD *Essex* 504 V 28 – *pop. 99 962.*

ℹ *County Hall, Market Rd* ☎ *(01245) 283400, tic@cheltenham.gov.uk.*

London 33 – Cambridge 46 – Ipswich 40 – Southend-on-Sea 19.

Premier Travel Inn, Main Rd, Boreham, CM3 3HJ, Northeast : 3 m. on B 1137 ☎ (0870) 9906394, *Fax (0870) 9906395* – |‡|, ⇎ rm, ▤ rest, ♿ P – 🏛 35. MC AE ⓓ VISA. ✗

Rest (grill rest.) – **78 rm** ♦49.95/49.95 – ♦♦52.95/52.95.

◆ Handily placed lodge-style accommodation with good road connections. Well-equipped modern rooms: ask for one overlooking car park as these have the benefit of being quieter. Busy grill restaurant has an international menu.

✗ **Barda,** 30-32 Broomfield Rd, CM1 1SW, ☎ (01245) 357799, *martin@barda-restaurnat.com, Fax (01245) 350333,* ⛱ – ▤. MC AE ⓓ VISA

closed 24-28 December, Saturday lunch, Sunday and Monday – **Rest** 18.00 (lunch) and a la carte 26.00/36.00 ☺ ♀.

◆ Former bank, near main railway station. Intimate and minimal, with bare, candle-lit tables and plain walls. Eclectic European dishes, with a flavoursome modern style.

at Great Baddow *Southeast : 3 m. by A 1114* – ✉ *Chelmsford.*

Pontlands Park ⛰, West Hanningfield Rd, CM2 8HR, ☎ (01245) 476444, *sales@pontlandsparkhotel.co.uk, Fax (01245) 478393,* ≤, ₣₆, ≘s, ⛱ heated, ▢, ⚘ – P – 🏛 100. MC AE ⓓ VISA. ✗

closed 23 December-3 January – **Rest** *(closed Saturday lunch)* 15.00/17.00 and a la carte 26.00/34.00 – ☕ 12.00 – **32 rm** ♦75.00/105.00 – ♦♦130.00/150.00, 4 suites.

◆ Family run converted and extended Victorian house with commanding views of countryside. Many rooms share vistas; all are individually furnished, some with brass bedsteads. Formal linen-clad dining in the main house.

CHELTENHAM *Glos.* 503 504 N 28 *Great Britain G. – pop. 98 875.*
See : Town★.
Exc. : *Sudeley Castle★ (Paintings★) AC, NE : 7 m. by B 4632 A.*
Cleeve Hill ✆ (01242) 672025 A – Cotswold Hills, Ullenwood ✆ (01242) 515264 A.
77 Promenade ✆ (01242) 522878.
London 99 – Birmingham 48 – Bristol 40 – Gloucester 9 – Oxford 43.

Plan opposite

The Queen's, Promenade, GL50 1NN, ✆ (0870) 4008107, *general.queens@macdonald-hotels.co.uk, Fax (01242) 224145,* – – – 120. BZ n
Napier **:** Rest 19.95/24.95 and a la carte 26.50/35.95 ♀ – 14.95 – **79 rm** ★75.00/170.00 – ★★105.00/220.00.
◆ A white columned neo-classical building with views over Imperial Square and the Ladies College. Grand reception and wood panelled bar. Individually styled bedrooms. Restaurant named after the famous British general.

On the Park, 38 Evesham Rd, GL52 2AH, ✆ (01242) 518898, *stay@hotelonthepark.com, Fax (01242) 511526,* – . CY r
Rest – (see ***Parkers*** below) – 9.50 – **12 rm** ★99.00/169.00 – ★★184.00.
◆ Regency town house of distinction. Bedrooms are named after dukes and dignitaries; individually decorated with paintings, antiques, mirrors and lamps. Stately library.

Kandinsky, Bayshill Rd, GL50 3AS, ✆ (01242) 527788, *info@aliaskandinsky.com, Fax (01242) 226412,* – , rest, BZ x
Café Paradiso **:** Rest 16.50 (lunch) amd a la carte 18.50/28.40 ♀ – 10.95 – **47 rm** ★75.00/99.00 – ★★99.00/125.00, 1 suite.
◆ Bohemian set-up with distressed furniture in minimalist bedrooms; each contains a different Kandinsky print. Sparkle in 1950s style basement club; live jazz some nights. Restaurant boasts long, open-plan kitchen with wood fired pizza oven.

The George, St George's Rd, GL50 3DZ, ✆ (01242) 235751, *hotel@stayatthegeorge.co.uk, Fax (01242) 224359* – – 26. . BY a
closed 24-26 December – **Rest** (bar lunch Monday-Saturday)/dinner 30.00/35.00 and a la carte 19.50/34.50 **s.** ♀ – **38 rm** ★85.00/95.00 – ★★120.00.
◆ White Regency hotel in quiet central location. Bright, modern, well-equipped bedrooms; larger rooms have extra facilities. Spacious period style restaurant with formal decor. Seasonal menu of traditional dishes with a touch of international influence.

Milton House without rest., 12 Bayshill Rd, GL50 3AY, ✆ (01242) 582601, *info@miltonhousehotel.co.uk, Fax (01242) 222326,* – . . BZ e
closed 18 December-31 January – **7 rm** ★70.00/78.00 – ★★95.00/115.00.
◆ A warm, Cotswold stone hotel in Regency style. Bedrooms with quality traditional wallpaper and discreet charm. Relax in the conservatory with honesty bar and garden views.

Lypiatt House without rest., Lypiatt Rd, GL50 2QW, ✆ (01242) 224994, *stay@lypiatt.co.uk, Fax (01242) 224996,* – . . BZ c
– **10 rm** ★70.00 – ★★90.00.
◆ A privately owned, serene Victorian house with friendly service. Rooms on top floor with dormer roof tend to be smaller than those on the ground floor. Soft, pale colours.

Beaumont House without rest., 56 Shurdington Rd, GL53 0JE, ✆ (01242) 245986, *reservations@bhhotel.co.uk, Fax (01242) 520044,* – . . AX u
15 rm ★59.00/69.00 – ★★139.00.
◆ Escape the rat race in sleek, bay windowed 19C comfort. Colour co-ordinated rooms named after racehorses; some with views of Leckhampton Hill. Neat garden by breakfast room.

Charlton Kings, London Rd, Charlton Kings, GL52 6UU, ✆ (01242) 231061, *enquiries@charltonkingshotel.co.uk, Fax (01242) 241900,* – . AX c
Rest (bar lunch Monday-Saturday)/dinner a la carte 18.50/27.50 – **13 rm** ★65.00/85.00 – ★★120.00.
◆ A clean-lined, white purpose-built hotel with unfussy pastel interiors. Pristine, plainly painted bedrooms with light wood furniture. The rural setting bestows tranquillity. Subdued lighting endows atmosphere to dining room.

Butlers without rest., Western Rd, GL50 3RN, ✆ (01242) 570771, *info@butlers-hotel.co.uk, Fax (01242) 528724,* – . BY v
9 rm ★50.00/70.00 – ★★80.00/120.00.
◆ Personally managed hotel where bedrooms constitute a peaceful haven with stylish drapes and canopies. Rooms named after famous butlers; some overlook wooded garden to rear.

Premier Travel Inn, 374 Gloucester Rd, GL51 7AY, ✆ (01242) 260103, *Fax (01242) 260042* – , rm, rest, . . AX v
Rest (grill rest.) – **42 rm** ★49.95 – ★★49.95.
◆ White painted lodge next to TGI Fridays, close to supermarket. Large, popular, pubby grill restaurant offering range of dishes. Comfortable bedrooms with mod cons.

CHELTENHAM

Berkeley St . . . . CYZ 4
Clarence St . . . . CY 6
Crescent Terrace . . . . . BY 7
Deep St . . . . AX 9
Dunalley St . . . . CY 10
Henrietta St . . . . CY 13
High St PRESTBURY . AX 14
High St . . . . BCY
Knapp Rd . . . . BY 16
Montpellier Ave . . . . . . BZ 17
Montpellier Walk . . . . . BZ 18
North St . . . . CY 20
Norwood Rd . . . . BZ 21
Oriel Rd . . . . CZ 22
Pittville St . . . . CY 26
Portland St . . . . CY 27
Promenade (The) . . . . BZCY 28
Centre . . . . CY
Regent St . . . . CY 29
Rodney Rd . . . . CY 30
Royal Well Rd . . . . . . BCY 32
St James St . . . . CY 33
St Johns Ave . . . . CY 34
St Margaret's Rd . . . . . CY 35
Sandford Mill Rd . . . . . CZ 36
Sandford Terrace . . . . . CZ 37
Winchcombe St . . . . . . CY 38

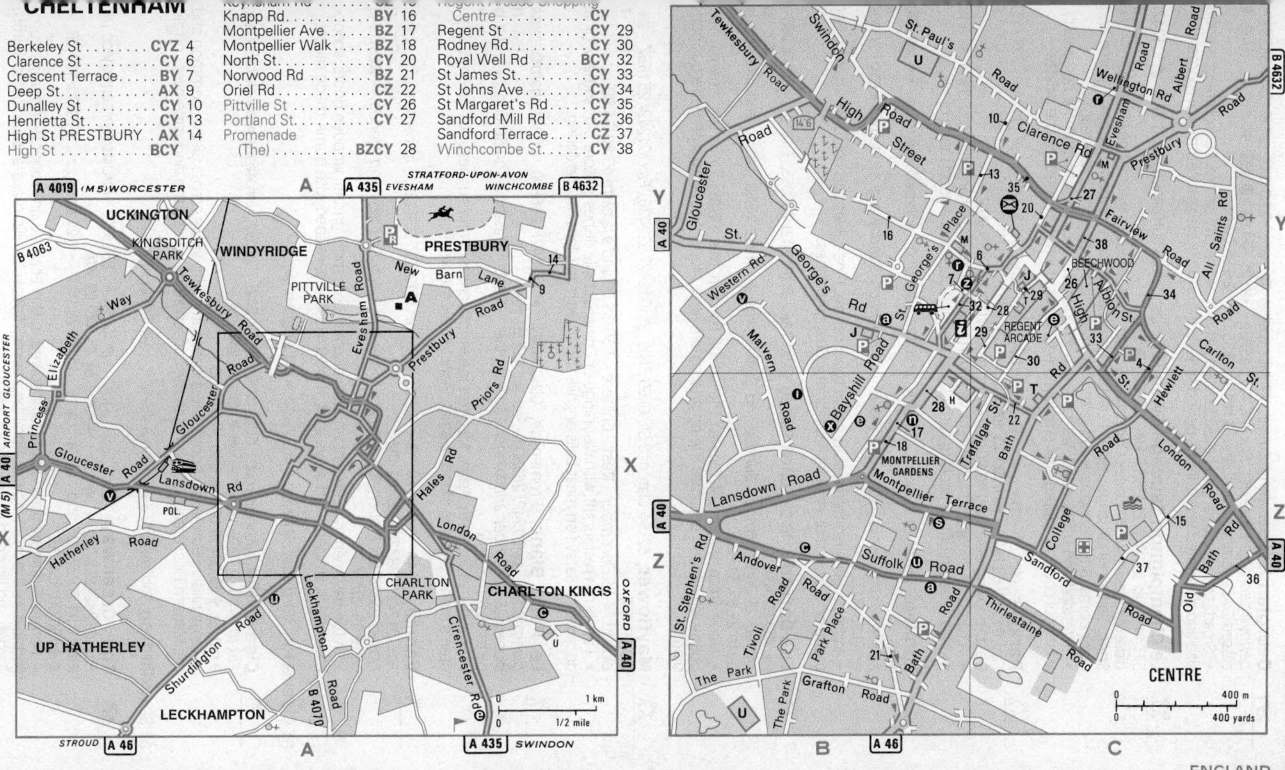

Georgian House without rest., 77 Montpellier Terrace, GL50 1XA, ☎ (01242) 515577, *penny@georgianhouse.net, Fax (01242) 545929* – P. MC AE VISA. BZ s
closed 24 December-2 January – **3 rm** ☕ ★55.00 – ★★85.00.
◆ Smart, terraced Georgian house located just out of the city centre. Bedrooms of a good size and decorated in authentic period style. Comfortable, elegant communal rooms.

Le Champignon Sauvage (Everitt-Matthias), 24-26 Suffolk Rd, GL50 2AQ, ☎ (01242) 573449, *Fax (01242) 254365* – . MC AE VISA BZ a
closed 3 weeks June, 1 week Christmas, Sunday and Monday – **Rest** 27.00/47.60 ♀.
Spec. Tortelloni of langoustine. Poached and roasted belly of pork, pumpkin purée and razor clams. Bitter chocolate and salted caramel délice, malted milk ice cream.
◆ Extended and refurbished, yet retaining its colourful artwork and intimate personality. Masterful cooking: ingredients employed with great invention to seduce the palette.

Parkers (at On the Park H.), 38 Evesham Rd, GL52 2AH, ☎ (01242) 227713, *Fax (01242) 511526* – . MC AE VISA CY r
Rest (booking essential) 19.00/35.00 and a la carte 19.55/35.00 ♀.
◆ A carefully decorated restaurant with mirrors, high ceilings, hand painted cornices and murals. Modern British cooking with classical undertones and a good range of wine.

Lumière, Clarence Parade, GL50 3PA, ☎ (01242) 222200, *dinner@lumiere.cc* – . MC VISA BC z
closed first 2 weeks January, 2 weeks late summer, Sunday and Monday – **Rest** (dinner only) 38.00.
◆ Intimate glass fronted restaurant in town centre. Pine tables and colourful artwork. Set menu offers original, eclectic Pacific rim influenced dishes.

The Daffodil, 18-20 Suffolk Parade, GL50 2AE, ☎ (01242) 700055, *Fax (01242) 700088* – . MC AE VISA BZ u
closed 25-26 December, Sunday and Bank Holidays – **Rest** 14.50 (lunch) and dinner a la carte 22.65/31.95 ♀.
◆ Move from the art of film to the art of food in this 1920s converted cinema. The open-plan kitchen occupies the original screen area. Modern cooking with generous puddings.

Mayflower, 32-34 Clarence St, GL50 3NX, ☎ (01242) 522426, *Fax (01242) 251667* – . MC AE VISA BY r
closed 24-26 December – **Rest** - Chinese - 7.50/35.00 and a la carte 15.80/34.80.
◆ Family run restaurant with vast range of Chinese staple dishes in store plus some original departures. Satay fish meat balls or chilli and garlic frog's legs for the daring.

Le Petit Blanc, Promenade, GL50 1NN, ☎ (01242) 266800, *cheltenham@lepetitblanc.co.uk, Fax (01242) 266801* – . MC AE VISA BZ n
closed 25 December and dinner 26 December – **Rest** - Brasserie - 14.50 (lunch) and a la carte 18.50/33.20 ♀.
◆ French cuisine with Asian, Mediterranean influences. Wine suggestions offered. Children's menu. Floating Island "Maman Blanc" steals the limelight.

Vanilla, 9-10 Cambray Pl, GL50 1JS, ☎ (01242) 228228, *info@vanillainc.co.uk, Fax (01242) 228228* – MC AE VISA CY e
closed 25-26 December, 1 January, Sunday and lunch Saturday and Monday – **Rest** a la carte 18.95/27.75.
◆ In the basement of a Regency house; discreet, soft spot lighting, wooden floors, scoop-back chairs. Efficient staff serve light, modern dishes garnished with home-made sauces.

at Cleeve Hill *Northeast : 4 m. on B 4632 – AX – ✉ Cheltenham.*

Cleeve Hill without rest., GL52 3PR, ☎ (01242) 672052, *info@cleevehill-hotel.co.uk, Fax (01242) 679969,* ←, – P. MC AE VISA.
9 rm ☕ ★45.00/55.00 – ★★85.00/100.00.
◆ Large hillside Edwardian house; most bedrooms with views across Cleeve Common and the Malvern Hills. Breakfast room is in the conservatory; admire the landscape over coffee.

at Shurdington *Southwest : 3¾ m. on A 46 – AX – ✉ Cheltenham.*

The Greenway, GL51 4UG, ☎ (01242) 862352, *info@thegreenway.co.uk, Fax (01242) 862780,* ←, – P – 45. MC AE VISA
Rest 21.00/32.00 and a la carte 45.00/75.00 ♀ – **21 rm** ☕ ★79.00/109.00 – ★★130.00/150.00.
◆ Former Prime minister John Major stayed in this Elizabethan manor. Particularly comfortable in the main house; floral bedrooms; Cotswold hills make a pleasant backdrop. Garden and lily pond on view from restaurant.

at Brockworth *Southwest : 5½ m. on A 46 – AX – Cheltenham.*

Cheltenham and Gloucester Moat House, Shurdington Rd, GL3 4PB, on A 46 (01452) 519988, *reservations.cheltenham@moathousehotels.com, Fax (01452) 519977,* rest, – 340.
Rest *(closed Saturday lunch)* (carvery Sunday lunch) 18.00/19.50 and dinner a la carte 21.40/30.50 **s** – **118 rm** 56.00/112.00 – 70.00/120.00, 2 suites.
◆ A modern corporate hotel located in landscaped grounds on the edge of the Cotswolds. Good leisure facilities. The "Crown Executive" rooms are particularly well equipped. Restaurant furnished in polished wood, daily changing menu and a la carte..

at Great Witcombe *Southwest : 6 m. by A 46 – AX – Cheltenham.*

Crickley Court without rest., Dog Lane, GL3 4UF, North : 1 m. by Bentham rd (01452) 863634, *geoff-pm@fsmail.net, Fax (01452) 863634,*
4 rm 30.00 – 60.00.
◆ Old inn dating from 16C. Lounge provided with an array of books. Family style breakfast. Outdoor pool. Spacious, bright and clean rooms with modern amenities.

CHENIES *Bucks.* 504 S 28 – *Rickmansworth (Herts.).*
London 30 – Aylesbury 18 – Watford 7.

Bedford Arms, WD3 6EQ, (01923) 283301, *contact@bedfordarms.co.uk, Fax (01923) 284825,* rm,
Rest *(closed Saturday lunch and Sunday dinner)* a la carte 19.50/31.20 – **18 rm** 90.00/110.00 – 130.00.
◆ A homely hotel, pub-like in character. Well proportioned rooms, some with views of a pretty garden. Country house style bars and a meeting room for business guests. Oak panelled dining room; adjacent cocktail bar.

CHESTER *Ches.* 502 503 L 24 *Great Britain G. – pop. 80 121.*
See : *City*★★ - *The Rows*★★ B – *Cathedral*★ B – *City Walls*★ B.
Env. : *Chester Zoo*★ AC, N : 3 m. by A 5116.
18 *Upton-by-Chester, Upton Lane (01244) 381183* A – 18 *Curzon Park (01244) 675130* A.
Town Hall, Northgate St (01244) 402111 – Chester Visitor and Craft Centre, Vicars Lane (01244) 402111.
London 207 – Birkenhead 7 – Birmingham 91 – Liverpool 21 – Manchester 40 – Preston 52 – Sheffield 76 – Stoke-on-Trent 38.

Plans on following pages

The Chester Grosvenor and Spa, Eastgate, CH1 1LT, (01244) 324024, *hotel@chestergrosvenor.com, Fax (01244) 313246,* – 250. B a
closed 24 December - 19 January – **Rest** – (see ***Arkle*** and ***La Brasserie*** below) – 17.50 – **77 rm** 217.40/264.40 – 311.40, 3 suites.
◆ 19C coaching inn in heart of city. Lavishly furnished with antiques and oil paintings. Superb spa facilities. Luxuriously appointed, individually styled bedrooms.

Crabwall Manor, Parkgate Rd, Mollington, CH1 6NE, Northwest : 2 ¼ m. on A 540 (01244) 851666, *crabwallmanor@marstonhotels.com, Fax (01244) 851400,* rest, – 100. A d
***Conservatory* :** **Rest** *(dinner only and Sunday lunch)* a la carte 26.95/36.40 **s.** – **43 rm** 110.00/160.00 – 150.00/189.00, 5 suites.
◆ 17C manor with castellated façade and mature grounds heavily extended into an individually furnished and comfortable business and leisure hotel. Amply proportioned bedrooms. Fine dining at classic conservatory restaurant.

Green Bough, 60 Hoole Rd, CH2 3NL, on A 56 (01244) 326241, *luxury@greenbough.co.uk, Fax (01244) 326265* – – 30. A t
closed 25-26 December and 1 January – ***Olive Tree* :** **Rest** (dinner only) 20.00/40.00 **s.** – **13 rm** 95.00 – 180.00, 2 suites.
◆ Personally run and very comfortable, boasting high quality decor; owner pays notable attention to detail. Individually styled, generously sized rooms with wrought iron beds. Dine formally in attractive surroundings.

Alton Lodge, 78 Hoole Rd, CH2 3NT, (01244) 310213, *reception@altonlodge.co.uk, Fax (01244) 319206* – A t
closed Christmas and New Year – **Rest** *(closed Friday-Sunday)* (residents only) (dinner only) a la carte 18.50/26.50 **s.** – **17 rm** 60.00/78.00 – 80.00/98.00.
◆ A family run, good value hotel. Pine furnished breakfast room, bar and lounge. Compact, annexed rooms provide a comfy night's accommodation after enjoying the city's sights.

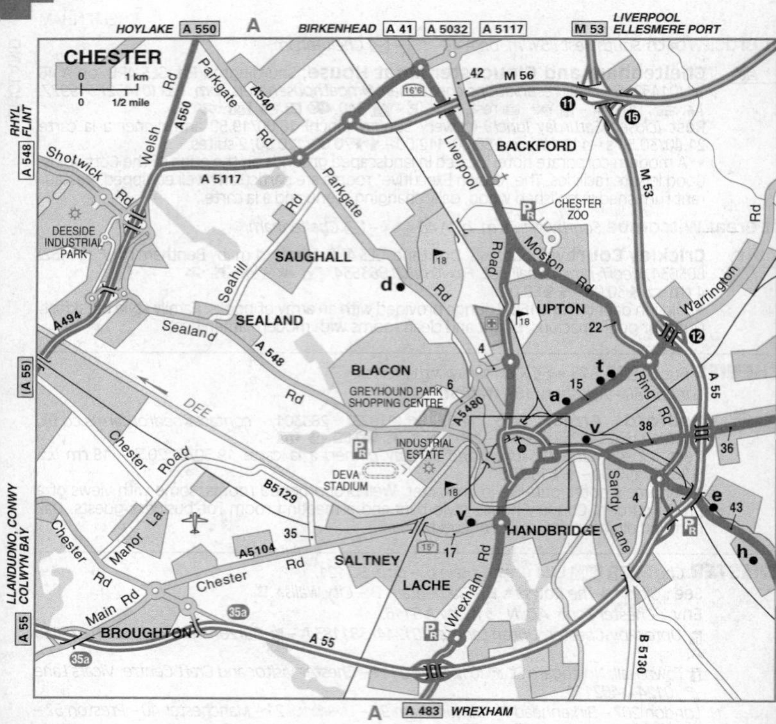

Caldy Valley Rd . . . . A 4
Countess Way . . . . A 5
Deva Link. . . . . A 6
Greyhound Park Shopping Centre . . . . A
Hoole Rd . . . . A 15
Hough Green. . . . . A 17
Long Lane . . . . A 22
Saltney Ferry Rd. . . . . A 35
Tarvin Rd . . . . A 36
Vicar's Cross Rd. . . . . A 38
Whitby Lane . . . . A 42
Whitchurch Rd . . . . A 43

Express by Holiday Inn without rest., The Racecourse, New Crane St, CH11 2LY, ℘ (0870) 9904065, *Fax (0870) 9904066*, ⇐ – |‡| ⇔ ♿ P – 🏃 30. MC AE ◑ VISA — B c
97 rm ★80.00 – ★★85.00.
◆ Ultimate race-goers accommodation: by the main stand of Chester race course. Very comfortable, good value, well-equipped rooms: some have great views of final furlong.

Mitchell's of Chester without rest., 28 Hough Green, CH4 8JQ, Southwest : 1 m. by A 483 on A 5104 ℘ (01244) 679004, *mitoches@dialstart.net, Fax (01244) 659567*, 🚗 – ⇔ P. MC VISA. ⊘ — A v
closed 20-29 December – **7 rm** ☕ ★38.00/50.00 – ★★64.00.
◆ Large Victorian house, attractively restored and privately run. Homely breakfast room with large central table; lounge with views to garden. Individually decorated bedrooms.

The Limes without rest., 12 Hoole Rd, CH2 3NJ, ℘ (01244) 328239, *malcolm@thelimes.co.uk, Fax (01244) 322874* – ⇔ P. MC VISA — A a
9 rm ☕ ★35.00/65.00 – ★★60.00/80.00.
◆ Personally run guesthouse in a redbrick Victorian property. Good value accommodation in well-maintained and furnished bedrooms, with convenient access to city centre.

Chester Town House without rest., 23 King St, CH1 2AH, ℘ (01244) 350021, *davidbellis@chestertownhouse.co.uk* – ⇔ ☎ P. MC VISA. ⊘ — B z
5 rm ☕ ★40.00/55.00 – ★★60.00/65.00.
◆ 17C redbrick house on a quiet, cobbled, lamplit street in a conservation area. Bedrooms have matching furnishings. Sunny breakfast room and period lounge.

CHESTER

XXXX **Arkle** (at The Chester Grosvenor and Spa), Eastgate, CH1 1LT, ✆ (01244) 324024, *Fax (01244) 313246* – ⊬ ▤ P. MC AE ⓪ VISA — B a

✿ *closed 24 December-19 January, Sunday and Monday* – **Rest** (dinner only) a la carte 55.00/65.00 **s.** ♀ ❀.

Spec. Cod flakes, caramelised pork cheeks and nettle coulis. Whole roast duck with truffle honey rub and foie gras cannelloni. Chocolate soufflé with lime jelly and granité.

◆ Named after the racehorse; distinguishes itself by its excellent, modern dishes using top quality ingredients and its renowned wine cellar of over 600 bins.

XX **La Brasserie** (at The Chester Grosvenor and Spa), Eastgate, CH1 1LT, ✆ (01244) 324024, *Fax (01244) 313246* – ▤ P. MC AE ⓪ VISA — B a

– **Rest** a la carte 25.95/44.20 ♀.

◆ Burnished interior, Parisian-style eatery with mirrors and glass frontage. Eclectic menu with classic French and Italian staples of pasta and meat dishes. Weekend live music.

XX **Locus,** 111 Boughton, CH3 5BH, ✆ (01244) 311112, *Fax (01244) 344860* – ⊬ P. MC AE ⓪ VISA — A v

closed 25-26 December and Monday – **Rest** (dinner only) a la carte 22.25/29.40 ♀.

◆ Unprepossessing exterior, but this small restaurant has a stylish, modern interior with atmospheric low lighting. Varied, interesting menus using well-sourced ingredients.

ENGLAND

XX **Brasserie 10/16,** Brookdale Pl, CH1 3DY, (01244) 322288, *Fax (01244) 322325* – MC AE VISA B s
Rest a la carte 15.70/28.20 **s.**
• Contemporary brasserie on two levels. Open plan kitchen on ground floor. Large modern British menu with Mediterranean touches, including plenty for the more adventurous.

X **Blue Bell,** 65 Northgate St, CH1 2HQ, (01244) 317758, *info@bluebellrestaurant.co.uk, Fax (01244) 317759,* – . MC AE VISA B n
closed 25-26 December, 1 January and Sunday – **Rest** 10.75 (lunch) and a la carte 21.95/32.50
• Reputedly the oldest domestic structure in the city, dating from 11C; purportedly named after Chester's very own curfew bell. Traditional cooking with atmosphere!

Old Harkers Arms, 1 Russell St, CH3 5AL, (01244) 344525, *harkers.arms@brunningandprice.co.uk, Fax (01244) 344812* – MC AE VISA B v
closed 25-26 December – **Rest** a la carte 14.00/25.00 **s.**
• Pub set in converted warehouse by canal. Homespun personality in interior décor of prints, bookshelves and wooden flooring. Offers traditional English meals and sandwiches.

at Little Barrow *Northeast : 6½ m. by A 56 (Warrington Rd) – A – on B 5132 – Chester.*

X **The Foxcote,** Station Lane, CH3 7JN, (01244) 301343, *Fax (01244) 303287* – P. MC VISA
closed Sunday dinner – **Rest** - Seafood - 9.95 (lunch) and a la carte 17.00/26.00
• Off the beaten track; traditional inn now given over to dining tables. Vast number of blackboard specials, mostly seafood dishes utilising broad range of fresh ingredients.

at Rowton *Southeast : 3 m. on A 41 – Chester.*

Rowton Hall, Whitchurch Rd, CH3 6AD, (01244) 335262, *rowtonhall@rowtonhall.co.uk, Fax (01244) 335464,* , , , , , – , rest, P – 170. MC AE VISA. A h
Langdale : **Rest** 14.50/19.50 and a la carte 27.75/38.00 – 12.50 – **36 rm** 90.00/125.00 – 135.00, 2 suites.
• Gracious 18C sandstone hotel with many original features: hand-carved staircase, Robert Adam fireplace, range of bedrooms. Business facilities offered. Country house style. Colonial style restaurant with wooden blinds and rattan furniture.

CHESTERFIELD *Derbs.* 502 503 504 P 24 *Great Britain G. – pop. 70 260.*

Env. : *Bolsover Castle* ★ *AC, E : 5 m. by A 632.*
18, 9 *Chesterfield Municipal, Murray House, Crow Lane (01246) 273887* – 18 *Grassmoor, North Wingfield Rd (01246) 856044.*
Rykneld Square (01246) 345777.
London 152 – Derby 24 – Nottingham 25 – Sheffield 12.

Ibis without rest., Lordsmill St, S41 7RW, at junction of A 619 and A 632 (01246) 221333, *h3160@accorhotels.com, Fax (01246) 221444* – P – 30. MC AE VISA
4.95 – **86 rm** 50.95 – 50.95.
• Lodge within walking distance of the town, yet on the main ring road. All mod cons which include in-house movies in up-to-date bedrooms. A Continental buffet for breakfast.

CHESTER-LE-STREET *Durham* 501 502 P 19.

18 *Lumley Park (0191) 388 3218* – 18 *Roseberry Grange, Grange Villa (0191) 370 0670.*
London 275 – Durham 7 – Newcastle upon Tyne 8.

Lumley Castle , DH3 4NX, East : 1 m. on B 1284 (0191) 389 1111, *reservations@lumleycastle.com, Fax (0191) 389 1881,* – P – 150. MC AE VISA.
closed 25-26 December and 1 January – ***Black Knight :*** **Rest** *(closed Saturday lunch)* 18.50/29.75 and dinner a la carte 25.75/45.25 **s.** – 13.95 – **58 rm** 65.00/120.00 – 195.00, 1 suite.
• Norman castle, without additions, underscoring its uniqueness. Rich, gothic interiors of carved wood, chandeliers, statues, tapestries, rugs. Rooms imbued with atmosphere.

Inn on the Green, Waldridge, DH2 3RY, West : 1 ¾ m. on Waldridge rd (0191) 389 0439, , – P. MC AE VISA
closed Monday and dinner Sunday – **Rest** a la carte 17.95/24.25
• Don't be put off by drab exterior: inside is a revelation, with smart, modish décor in browns, creams and chocolates. Modern British cooking with Northumbrian produce to fore.

CHESTERTON *Oxon.* 504 Q 28 – ✉ *Bicester.*
Bicester ✆ *(01869) 241204.*
London 69 – Birmingham 65 – Northampton 36 – Oxford 15.

Bignell Park, OX26 1UE, on A 4095 ✆ (01869) 326550, *enq@bignellparkhotel.co.uk, Fax (01869) 322729,* – ♿ P – 25. MC AE VISA.
Rest a la carte 22.00 – **23 rm** ☕ ★80.00/85.00 – ★★90.00/145.00.
◆ A traditional Cotswold house built in 1740, sits in lovely gardens. A homely lounge and bar set the tone of a warm, friendly atmosphere. Sizeable, comfy bedrooms. Oak beamed cocktail bar; restaurant with minstrels gallery.

CHETTLE *Dorset – see Blandford Forum.*

CHEW MAGNA *Somerset* 503 504 M 29 – *see Bristol.*

CHICHESTER *W. Sussex* 504 R 31 *Great Britain G. – pop. 27 477.*
See : *City★ – Cathedral★* **BZ A** – *St Mary's Hospital★* **BY D** – *Pallant House★* *AC* **BZ M.**
Env. : *Fishbourne Roman Palace (mosaics★) AC* **AZ R.**
Exc. : *Weald and Downland Open Air Museum★ AC, N : 6 m. by A 286* **AY**
Goodwood, Kennel Hill ✆ *(01243) 774968,* **AY** – *Chichester Golf Centre, Hunston Village* ✆ *(01243) 533833,* **AZ.**
29a South St ✆ *(01243) 775888.*
London 69 – Brighton 31 – Portsmouth 18 – Southampton 30.

CHICHESTER

Street	Grid	No.
Birdham Rd	AZ	2
Bognor Rd	AZ	3
Chapel St	BY	6
Chartres (Av. de)	BZ	7
Chichester Arundel Rd	AY	8
East Pallant	BZ	9
East St	BZ	
Florence Rd	AZ	10
Hornet (The)	BZ	12
Kingsham Rd	BZ	13
Lavant Rd	AY	14
Little London	BY	15
Market Rd	BZ	16
North Pallant	BZ	19
North St	BYZ	
Northgate	BY	17
St Jame's	AZ	21
St John's St	BZ	23
St Martin's Square	BY	24
St Pancras	BY	25
St Paul's Rd	BY	27
Sherborne Rd	AZ	28
South Pallant	BZ	31
South St	BZ	
Southgate	BZ	29
Spitalfield Lane	BY	32
Stockbridge Rd	AZ	33
Tower St	BY	35
Via Ravenna	AZ	37
West Pallant	BZ	39
Westhampnett Rd	AYZ	38

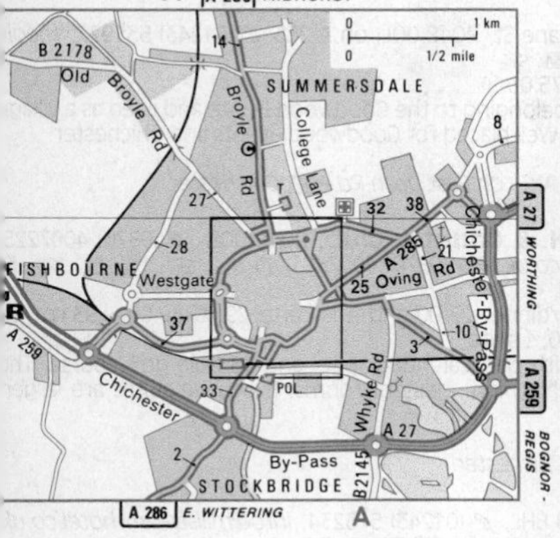

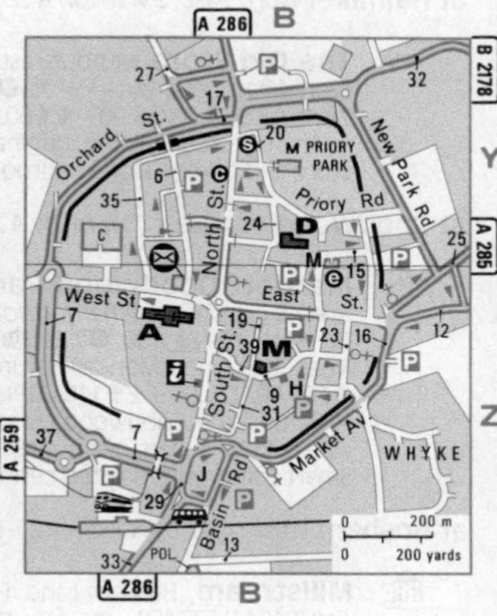

Crouchers Country H., Birdham Rd, Apuldram, PO20 7EH, Southwest : 2 ½ m. on A 286 ✆ (01243) 784995, *info@crouchersbottom.com, Fax (01243) 539797,* – ♿ P. MC AE VISA
Rest 17.50/19.50 and a la carte 23.40/33.40 – **18 rm** ☕ ★65.00/85.00 – ★★105.00/125.00.
◆ 1900s farmhouse surrounded by fields. Bedrooms are in a separate coach house, some on ground floor; furnished with matching floral fabrics. Admire waterfowl in nearby pond. Bright, modern dining room.

ENGLAND

Comme ça, 67 Broyle Rd, PO19 6BD, on A 286 ℘ (01243) 788724, *comme.ca@commeca.co.uk, Fax (01243) 530052,* , – P 12. AE VISA AY c
closed 2 weeks Christmas, New Year, Monday, Tuesday lunch and Sunday dinner – **Rest** - French - 21.95 (lunch) and a la carte 28.45/29.45 ♀.
◆ Strong French cooking ministered by Normand chef; generous à la carte, set menus and French family lunch on Sundays. Festoons of hops on exposed beams complete the décor.

The Dining Room at Purchases, 31 North St, PO19 1LY, ℘ (01243) 537352, *info@thediningroom.biz, Fax (01243) 533397,* – . AE VISA BY c
closed 25 December, Sunday and Bank Holidays – **Rest** a la carte 21.45/35.00 ♀.
◆ Charming Georgian house with garden terrace. Interior of wood floors, vividly painted walls, leading to conservatory/orangery. Appealingly varied dishes, prepared with care.

at East Lavant *North : 2½ m. off A 286 – AY – ✉ Chichester.*

The Royal Oak Inn with rm, Pook Lane, PO18 0AX, ℘ (01243) 527434, *roethesussexpub.co.uk, Fax (01243) 775062,* – P. AE VISA
Rest *(closed 25 December)* a la carte 20.00/30.00 ♀ – **6 rm** ☐ ☆60.00 – ☆☆110.00.
◆ Utterly charming village pub with summer terraces. Modern rustic feel enhanced by leather sofas. All-encompassing restaurant: very well executed cooking. Comfy, modern rooms.

at Charlton *North : 6¼ m. by A 286 – AY – ✉ Chichester.*

Woodstock House without rest., PO18 0HU, ℘ (01243) 811666, *info@woodstockhousehotel.co.uk, Fax (01243) 811666,* – P. AE VISA
13 rm ☐ ☆52.00/75.00 – ☆☆88.00/106.00.
◆ A row of flint and whitewashed cottages close to Goodwood Racecourse. Indoors, relax in the mulberry coloured, cottage style lounge or the floral furnished bedrooms. Enjoy the home cooking, undertaken with pride, in mellow restaurant.

The Fox Goes Free with rm, PO18 0HU, ℘ (01243) 811461, *thefoxgoesfree.always@virgin.net, Fax (01243) 811946,* – P. VISA
closed 25 December – **Rest** a la carte 18.50/27.50 – **5 rm** ☐ ☆50.00 – ☆☆70.00.
◆ Flint and brick pub, oozing 14C charm, balanced by appealing, modern tones. Antique church furniture, huge fire, cosy snug; hearty, fresh cooking. Welcoming beamed bedrooms.

at Halnaker *Northeast : 3¼ m. on A 285 – BY – ✉ Chichester.*

The Old Store without rest., Stane St, PO18 0QL, on A 285 ℘ (01243) 531977, *theoldstore4@aol.com,* – P. VISA.
7 rm ☐ ☆35.00/75.00 – ☆☆60.00/75.00.
◆ An 18C listed building, originally belonging to the Goodwood Estate and used as a village store and bakery. Floral bedrooms. Well placed for Goodwood events and Chichester.

at Goodwood *Northeast : 3½ m. by A 27 – AY – on East Dean Rd – ✉ Chichester.*

Marriott Goodwood Park H. & Country Club, PO18 0QB, ℘ (0870) 4007225 *events.goodwood@marriotthotels.co.uk, Fax (0870) 4007325,* , , , , 18, , – P – 150. AE VISA
Rest (bar lunch Monday-Saturday)/dinner 25.00 and a la carte 29.00/39.00 – **93 rm** ☐ ☆109.00/125.00 – ☆☆119.00/135.00, 1 suite.
◆ Part of the Goodwood estate with classical indoor pool and 18 hole golf course. The cocktail bar is part of an 18C coaching inn. Pleasant rooms: Executive suites are larger Smart eatery with painted ceiling.

at Bosham *West : 4 m. by A 259 – AZ – ✉ Chichester.*

Millstream, Bosham Lane, PO18 8HL, ℘ (01243) 573234, *info@millstream-hotel.co.uk Fax (01243) 573459,* – , rest, , P. AE VISA.
Rest 21.50/30.00 ♀ – **32 rm** ☐ ☆85.00/119.00 – ☆☆139.00/159.00, 3 suites.
◆ Pretty hotel with garden that backs onto stream bobbing with ducks. Cosy bedrooms individually co-ordinated fabric furnishings, sandwash fitted furniture and large windows.

Hatpins without rest., Bosham Lane, PO18 8HG, ℘ (01243) 572644, *mary@hatpins.co.uk Fax (01243) 572644,* – P.
5 rm ☐ ☆50.00 – ☆☆120.00.
◆ Owner is a former designer of hats and wedding dresses, and her decorative skills are on display in the interiors. Plenty of prints and flowers and lacy cushions in bedrooms.

at West Stoke *Northwest : 2¾ m. by B 2178 – AY – off B 2146 – ✉ Chichester.*

XX **West Stoke** with rm, Downs Rd, PO18 9BN, ✆ (01243) 575226, *info@weststoke house.co.uk, Fax (01243) 574655*, <, , – , P. MC AE VISA
closed 25-26 December – **Rest** *(closed Monday-Tuesday)* 25.00/35.00 – **6 rm** ☕ ★75.00/85.00 – ★★130.00/150.00.
◆ Charmingly peaceful part 17C manor, set in very pleasant gardens. Reception with log burner seamlessly blends subtle elegance to modern art; strikingly understated rooms. Modish menus at full linen tables.

at Funtington *Northwest : 4¾ m. by B 2178 – AY – on B 2146 – ✉ Chichester.*

XX **Hallidays,** Watery Lane, PO18 9LF, ✆ (01243) 575331 – P. MC VISA
closed 2 weeks March, 1 week late August, Monday, Tuesday, Saturday lunch and Sunday dinner – **Rest** 18.50/30.50 and lunch a la carte 23.00/32.50.
◆ A row of part 13C thatched cottages; confident and keen chef delivers a lively medley of frequently changing set menus and à la carte. Modern meals sit alongside classics.

CHIDDINGFOLD *Surrey* 504 S 30.

London 47 – Guildford 10 – Haslemere 5.

The Swan Inn with rm, Petworth Rd, GU8 4TY, ✆ (01428) 682073, *Fax (01428) 683259*, – P. MC AE VISA
Rest a la carte 18.00/27.00 – ☕ 5.00 – **11 rm** ★65.00 – ★★120.00.
◆ Located on the main road of a leafy, red-brick village; refurbishment has created a pub with a neo-rustic atmosphere. Elaborate menus. Smart, contemporary bedrooms.

CHIEVELEY *Berks.* 503 504 Q 29.

London 60 – Newbury 5 – Swindon 25.

Crab at Chieveley with rm, Wantage Rd, RG20 8UE, West : 2 ½ m. by School Rd on B 4494 ✆ (01635) 247550, *info@crabatchieveley.com, Fax (01635) 247440*, – P. MC AE VISA
Rest - Seafood - 19.50 (lunch) and a la carte 19.50/45.00 – **10 rm** ☕ ★120.00 – ★★170.00.
◆ Thatched inn on a country road surrounded by wheat fields. Choice of two dining areas: both serve extensive seafood menus. Highly original bedrooms themed as famous hotels.

CHILLATON *Devon* 503 H 32 – *see Tavistock.*

CHINNOR *Oxon.* 504 R 28 *Great Britain G.* – *pop. 5 407.*

Exc. : *Ridgeway Path★★.*
London 45 – Oxford 19.

Cross Lanes Cottage without rest., West Lane, Bledlow, HP27 9PF, Northeast : 1½ m. on B 4009 ✆ (01844) 345339, *ronaldcou@aol.com, Fax (01844) 274165*, – P. MC VISA.
3 rm ☕ ★45.00/50.00 – ★★55.00/60.00.
◆ Friendly part 16C guesthouse with homely lounge of rafters, lamps and ornaments. Rooms are in cream and white with co-ordinated fabrics, baskets of toiletries.

at Sprigg's Alley *Southeast : 2½ m. by Bledlow Ridge rd – ✉ Chinnor.*

XX **Sir Charles Napier,** OX39 4BX, ✆ (01494) 483011, *Fax (01494) 485311*, , – P. MC AE VISA
closed 3 days Christmas, Sunday dinner and Monday – **Rest** a la carte 27.50/35.00 .
◆ Off the beaten track for exciting menus where fish features alongside game (mallard, roast partridge) and funghi and berries brought in by locals. Sculptural ornamentation.

at Kingston Blount *Southwest : 1¾ m. on B 4009 – ✉ Chinnor.*

Lakeside Town Farm without rest., Brook St, OX3 4RZ, (off Sydenham rd) ✆ (01844) 352152, *townfarmcottage@oxfree.com, Fax (01844) 352152*, – P. MC VISA.
3 rm ☕ ★45.00 – ★★75.00.
◆ Modern building, on a working farm, in a sympathetic style that engenders a traditional, old-fashioned ambience. Charming, Victorian-style bedrooms. Attractive gardens.

Your opinions are important to us:
please write and let us know about your discoveries and experiences – good and bad!

CHIPPENHAM *Wilts.* 503 504 N 29 *The West Country G.* – *pop. 33 189.*
See : *Yelde Hall*★.
Env. : *Corsham Court*★★ *AC, SW : 4 m. by A 4* – *Sheldon Manor*★ *AC, W : 1½ m. by A 420* – *Biddestone*★, *W : 3½ m.* – *Bowood House*★ *AC (Library* ★) *SE : 5 m. by A 4 and A 342.*
Exc. : *Castle Combe*★★, *NW : 6 m. by A 420 and B 4039.*
Monkton Park (Par Three) ☎ *(01249) 653928.*
Yelde Hall, Market Place ☎ *(01249) 706333.*
London 106 – *Bristol 27* – *Southampton 64* – *Swindon 21.*

Premier Travel Inn, Cepen Park, West Cepen Way, SN14 6UZ, North : 1 ¾ m. on A 350 ☎ (0870) 1977061, *Fax (01249) 461359* – rest, rest, P. MC AE VISA.
Rest (grill rest.) – **79 rm** ★49.95/49.95 – ★★52.95/52.95.
◆ Situated at busy road junction just out of town centre. Modern, well-proportioned rooms. Adjacent pub restaurant has extensive popular menus.

at Stanton Saint Quintin *North : 5 m. by A 429* – ✉ *Chippenham.*

Stanton Manor, SN14 6DQ, ☎ (0870) 8902880, *reception@stantonmanor.co.uk, Fax (0870) 8902881*, – P – 50. MC AE VISA
Rest 15.00/27.00 ♀ – **23 rm** ★110.00/120.00 – ★★135.00/210.00.
◆ Extended 19C manor in formal gardens; popular commercial/wedding venue. There's some noise from adjacent M4, but this is more than made up for by appealing range of bedrooms. Elegant restaurant uses produce from the garden.

CHIPPERFIELD *Herts.* 504 S 28 – ✉ *Kings Langley.*
London 27 – *Hemel Hempstead 5* – *Watford 6.*

Two Brewers Inn, The Common, WD4 9BS, ☎ (01923) 265266, *two.brewers.4086@thespiritgroup.com, Fax (01923) 261884* – rm, P. MC AE VISA.
Rest a la carte 12.00/23.35 ♀ – **20 rm** ★99.50 – ★★99.50.
◆ A row of pretty white terraced cottages overlooking the common and run by friendly staff. Rooms are all of a similar standard, comfortable and practically furnished. Open-plan restaurant with extensive blackboard menus.

CHIPPING *Lancs.* 502 M 22 – ✉ *Preston.*
London 233 – *Lancaster 30* – *Leeds 54* – *Manchester 40* – *Preston 12.*

Gibbon Bridge, PR3 2TQ, East : 1 m. on Clitheroe rd ☎ (01995) 61456, *reception@gibbon-bridge.co.uk, Fax (01995) 61277*, – rest, P – 120. MC AE VISA.
Rest 16.00 (lunch) and dinner a la carte approx. 25.00/29.00 ♀ – **11 rm** ★80.00 – ★★120.00, **18 suites** 150.00/230.00.
◆ Converted stone farm buildings set in the heart of the Trough of Bowland. Bedrooms, all of which are very comfy and individual, include split-level suites with four-posters. Own bakery produce in restaurant, which overlooks delightful gardens.

CHIPPING CAMPDEN *Glos.* 503 504 O 27 *Great Britain G.* – *pop. 1 943.*
See : *Town*★.
Env. : *Hidcote Manor Garden*★★ *AC, NE : 2½ m.*
Old Police Station ☎ *(01386) 841206.*
London 93 – *Cheltenham 21* – *Oxford 37* – *Stratford-upon-Avon 12.*

Cotswold House, The Square, GL55 6AN, ☎ (01386) 840330, *reception@cotswoldhouse.com, Fax (01386) 840310*, – P – 50. MC AE VISA
Juliana's : **Rest** (dinner only and Sunday lunch)/dinner 45.00 ♀ – (see also ***Hicks'*** below) – **27 rm** ★130.00/285.00 – ★★215.00/295.00, 2 suites.
◆ Regency town house with graceful spiral staircase winding upwards to stylish bedrooms. Particularly superior cottage rooms. Delightful formal walled gardens. Genteel Juliana's with French windows.

Noel Arms, High St, GL55 6AT, ☎ (01386) 840317, *reception@noelarmshotel.com, Fax (01386) 841136* – rest, P – 50. MC AE VISA
Rest - Asian - (bar lunch)/dinner 22.50 and a la carte 18.50/24.00 ♀ – **26 rm** ★85.00/110.00 – ★★120.00/195.00.
◆ A 14C former coaching inn; lounge and reception decked in civil war armoury and antique furniture. This extends to some heritage style rooms, one has 14C ornate four poster. Colourful, intimate dining room with menu of Asian dishes.

Hicks' (at Cotswold House), The Square, GL55 6AN, ☎ (01386) 840330 *Fax (01386) 840310*, – P. MC AE VISA
Rest (booking essential) a la carte 22.00/30.00 **s.** ♀.
◆ Named after local benefactor. Booking advised; open all day serving locals and residents with modern varied menu. Morning coffees, afternoon teas, home-made cake available.

King's with rm, The Square, GL55 6AW, ✆ (01386) 840256, *info@kingscampden.co.uk, Fax (01386) 841598*, – MO AE VISA
closed 25 December – **Rest** a la carte 20.00/30.00 – **12 rm** ☐ ✝85.00/115.00 – ✝✝165.00.
◆ Pub with 17C Cotswold stone walls on the main street. Characterful interiorwith rustic charm. Splendid rear courtyard. Skilfully created, quality dishes. Smart bedrooms.

Eight Bells Inn with rm, Church St, GL55 6JG, ✆ (01386) 840371, *neilhargreaves@bellinn.fsnet.co.uk, Fax (01386) 841669*, – . MO VISA
closed 25 December – **Rest** a la carte 19.50/28.50 ♀ – **7 rm** ☐ ✝50.00 – ✝✝95.00/115.00.
◆ A 14C stone inn, once used by stonemasons working on church; still exudes history in wood and stone interior. Traditional robust menu: blackboard specials.

at Mickleton *North : 3¼ m. by B 4035 and B 4081 on B 4632 – ✉ Chipping Campden.*

Three Ways House, GL55 6SB, ✆ (01386) 438429, *reception@puddingclub.com, Fax (01386) 438118*, – , rest, P – 80. MO AE VISA
Rest (bar lunch Monday-Saturday)/dinner 32.00 **s.** ♀ – **48 rm** ☐ ✝75.00/92.00 – ✝✝120.00/180.00.
◆ Built in 1870; renowned as home of the "Pudding Club". Two types of room, in the original house and in modern block - some named after puddings. Bar with antique tiled floor. Arcaded dining room; Pudding Club meets here to vote after tastings.

Myrtle House without rest., GL55 6SA, ✆ (01386) 430032, *kate@myrtlehouse.co.uk*, – P. MO VISA
5 rm ☐ ✝45.00 – ✝✝75.00.
◆ Part Georgian house with large lawned garden. Bedrooms named and styled after flowers and plants, those on top floor most characterful.

Nineveh Farm without rest., GL55 6PS, on B 4081 ✆ (01386) 438923, *ninevehfarm@hotmail.com*, – P. MO VISA.
5 rm ☐ ✝55.00/60.00 – ✝✝65.00/70.00.
◆ Georgian farmhouse in pleasant garden. Warm welcome; local information in resident's lounge. Comfortable rooms with view in house or with French windows in garden house.

at Paxford *Southeast : 3 m. by B 4035 – ✉ Chipping Campden.*

Churchill Arms with rm, GL55 6XH, ✆ (01386) 594000, *info@thechurchillarms.com, Fax (01386) 594005*, – rm. MO VISA.
Rest (bookings not accepted) a la carte 18.00/28.00 ♀ – **4 rm** ☐ ✝40.00 – ✝✝70.00.
◆ Popular Cotswold stone and brick pub; mellow interior. Good value menus chalked on blackboard. Organic local produce used. Comfortable bedrooms.

at Broad Campden *South : 1¼ m. by B 4081 – ✉ Chipping Campden.*

Malt House without rest., GL55 6UU, ✆ (01386) 840295, *info@malt-house.co.uk, Fax (01386) 841334*, – P. MO AE VISA
closed 1 week Christmas – **6 rm** ☐ ✝87.50 – ✝✝134.00, 1 suite.
◆ For a rare experience of the countryside idyll, this 16C malting house is a must. Cut flowers from the gardens on view in bedrooms decked out in fabrics to delight the eye.

Marnic House without rest., GL55 6UR, ✆ (01386) 840014, *marnic@zoom.co.uk, Fax (01386) 840441*, – P.
March-November – **3 rm** ☐ ✝50.00/60.00 – ✝✝65.00/75.00.
◆ A stone built cottage with pleasing, well tended back gardens and views over countryside. Rear rooms share vistas and are quieter. Full breakfasts served on large oak table.

CHIPPING NORTON *Oxon.* 503 504 P 28 – *pop. 5 688.*
London 77 – Oxford 22 – Stow-on-the-Wold 9.

Masons Arms, Banbury Rd, Swerford, OX7 4AP, Northeast : 5 m. by A 361 ✆ (01608) 683212, *themasonschef@hotmail.com, Fax (01608) 683105*, – P. MO VISA
closed 25-26 December – **Rest** a la carte 18.00/25.00 ♀.
◆ Cotswold stone roadside inn with pleasant terrace, garden and fine views. Bright, contemporary interior. Appealing menus make use of local, well-chosen ingredients.

Do not confuse X with ✿! X defines comfort, while stars are awarded for the best cuisine, across all categories of comfort.

CHISELDON *Wilts.* 503 504 O 29 – *see Swindon.*

CHITTLEHAMHOLT *Devon* 503 I 31 – ✉ *Umberleigh.*
London 216 – Barnstaple 14 – Exeter 28 – Taunton 45.

Highbullen, EX37 9HD, ☎ (01769) 540561, *info@highbullen.co.uk*
Fax (01769) 540492, ←, Fб, ≘s, heated, , 18, , , indoor/outdoor, squash
– rest, P. MO VISA.
Rest (lunch by arrangement)/dinner 25.00 – ☕ 8.00 – **40 rm** (dinner included)
★78.00/90.00 – ★★210.00.
◆ 19C Gothic mansion enjoys tranquil elevated position and impressive leisure facilities. Bedrooms are divided between the main house (with fine views) and converted barns. Magnificent outlook from large dining room window.

CHOBHAM *Surrey* 504 S 29 – *pop. 2 773* – ✉ *Woking.*
London 35 – Reading 21 – Southampton 53.

Zinfandel, 1 Bagshot Rd, GU24 8BP, ☎ (01276) 858491, *mail@zinfandel.org.uk*
Fax (01276) 858491 – . MO AE VISA
closed 25-26 December, 1 January, Sunday, Monday and Saturday lunch – **Rest** a la carte
19.95/27.20 ♀.
◆ Informal, welcoming restaurant with stylish modern décor. Napa Valley cuisine - American-style dishes with global twists - prepared with flair; char-grilled specialities.

Undecided between two equivalent establishments?
Within each category, establishments are classified
in our order of preference.

CHOLLERTON *Northd.* 501 502 N 18 – *see Hexham.*

CHORLEY *Lancs.* 502 504 M 23 – *pop. 33 536.*
18 *Duxbury Park, Duxbury Hall Rd* ☎ *(01257) 265380* – 18 *Shaw Hill Hotel G. & C.C., Preston Rd, Whittle-le-Woods* ☎ *(01257) 269221.*
London 222 – Blackpool 30 – Liverpool 33 – Manchester 26.

Premier Travel Inn, Malthouse Farm, Moss Lane, Whittle-le-Woods, PR6 8AB, North-east : 1½ m. by A 6 and A 674 on B 6229 ☎ (0870) 7001354, *Fax (01257) 232912*, –
rm, rest, ♿ P. MO AE VISA.
Rest (grill rest.) – **81 rm** ★46.95/46.95 – ★★48.95/48.95.
◆ Purpose-built lodge adjacent to a canal with some rooms in separate, converted stable. Modern bedrooms. Well located for Reebok Stadium and city shopping centres. Restaurant in picturesque canal bank setting.

at Whittle-le-Woods *North : 2 m. on A 6* – ✉ *Chorley.*

Shaw Hill H. Golf & Country Club, Preston Rd, PR6 7PP, ☎ (01257) 26922
info@shaw-hill.co.uk, Fax (01257) 261223, Fб, ≘s, , 18 – rest, P – 200. MO AE VISA
closed 26-27 December – ***Vardon*** : **Rest** *(closed Saturday lunch)* 14.95/21.95 and a la carte
22.50/37.00 s. – **30 rm** ☕ ★78.00/82.00 – ★★92.00/130.00.
◆ Dignified Georgian hotel presides over 18 hole golf course. Golfing memorabilia adorn smart interiors. Variety of rooms, tastefully wallpapered; some overlook course. Classic dining room with golfing views.

Parkville Country House, 174 Preston Rd, PR6 7HE, ☎ (01257) 26188
Fax (01257) 273171, – P. MO AE VISA.
Rest (dinner only and Sunday lunch)/dinner 16.95 and a la carte 19.40/31.40 s. – ☕ 5.00
6 rm ★50.00/60.00 – ★★60.00/70.00.
◆ A large converted house with conservatory extension not far from Shaw Hill Golf Club. Tidy bedrooms, all similarly furnished, some with jacuzzis. Well tended lawned garden. Conservatory restaurant with gourmet club.

CHORLTON-CUM-HARDY *Gtr. Manchester 502 503 504 N 23 – see Manchester.*

CHRISTCHURCH *Dorset 503 504 O 31 The West Country G. – pop. 40 208.*
See : *Town★ – Priory★.*
Env. : *Hengistbury Head★ (≤★★) SW : 4½ m. by A 35 and B 3059.*
18 Highcliffe Castle, 107 Lymington Rd, Highcliffe-on-Sea ☎ (01425) 272953 – 9 Riverside Ave ☎ (01202) 436436.
49 High St ☎ (01202) 471780.
London 111 – Bournemouth 6 – Salisbury 26 – Southampton 24 – Winchester 39.

Premier Travel Inn, Barrack Rd, BH23 2BN, West : ¾ m. on A 35 ☎ (01202) 485215 – rm, P. MO AE VISA.
Rest (grill rest.) – **40 rm** ★49.95 – ★★49.95.
◆ Comfortable, modern bedrooms suitable for families and the business traveller. 24 hour self-service eateries. Well placed for Christchurch Priory, Red House Museum.

Druid House without rest., 26 Sopers Lane, BH23 1JE, ☎ (01202) 485615, *reservations@druid-house.co.uk, Fax (01202) 473484,* – rm, P. MO AE VISA.
8 rm ★30.00/60.00 – ★★60.00/80.00.
◆ 1930s house that appeals with bright, fresh ambience: cottagey breakfast room, light and airy conservatory sitting room, smart bar. Spacious bedrooms, two with balconies.

Splinters, 12 Church St, BH23 1BW, ☎ (01202) 483454, *eating@splinters.uk.com, Fax (01202) 480180* – 21. MO VISA
closed 1-9 January, 26 December, Sunday and Monday – **Rest** 25.95/36.95 ♀.
◆ Brasserie-like exterior; two dining areas inside: one has intimate pine booths; upstairs more formal with high-backed chairs. French-influenced cuisine.

Fishworks, 10 Church St, BH23 1BW, ☎ (01202) 487000, *christchurch@fishworks.co.uk, Fax (01202) 487001* – . MO AE VISA
closed 25-26 December, Sunday and Monday – **Rest** - Seafood - (booking essential) a la carte 20.00/40.00 ♀.
◆ An informal eatery which has its own well-stocked fish counter: choose your selection with the aid of helpful chefs. Tasty, prime quality produce.

at Mudeford *Southeast : 2 m. – ✉ Christchurch.*

Avonmouth, 95 Mudeford, BH23 3NT, ☎ (01202) 483434, *info@avonmouth-hotel.co.uk, Fax (01202) 479004,* ≤, heated, – P – 60. MO AE VISA
Rest a la carte 18.00/29.00 ♀ – **38 rm** ★80.00/90.00 – ★★120.00/140.00, 3 suites.
◆ Built in the 1820s, affording splendid views of estuary and Mudeford Quay; sailing craft on hire for the beachcomber. Feature bedrooms particularly good; all are well-kept. Harbour view restaurant.

Waterford Lodge, 87 Bure Lane, Friars Cliff, BH23 4DN, ☎ (01425) 272948, *waterford@bestwestern.co.uk, Fax (01425) 279130,* – rest, P – 80. MO AE VISA
Rest 16.50/30.50 – **18 rm** ★73.00/85.00 – ★★96.00/115.00.
◆ Family run hotel. Take a sea stroll with the dog, as they are welcome, or enjoy free swimming at local leisure centre. Rooms overlook rooftops and countryside on top floor. Hand-made truffles round off tasty meals.

CHRISTMAS COMMON *Oxon.*
London 41 – Oxford 18 – Reading 13.

The Fox & Hounds, OX49 5HL, ☎ (01491) 612599, – P. MO VISA
closed Sunday dinner – **Rest** a la carte 18.00/29.00 ♀.
◆ Red brick and flint pub with beamed bar, fire and distinctive red and black tiled floor. Eat in barn conversion: carefully chosen local suppliers. Blend of cooking styles.

The ✿ award is the crème de la crème. This is awarded to restaurants which are really worth travelling miles for!

CHURCH ENSTONE *Oxon. – ✉ Chipping Norton.*

London 72 – Banbury 13 – Oxford 38.

Crown Inn, Mill Lane, OX7 4NN, ✆ (01608) 677262, *Fax (01608) 677394*, – P. MC VISA

closed 26 December, 1 January, Sunday dinner and Monday lunch – **Rest** a la carte 20.00/25.00 ♀.

◆ 17C Cotswold stone pub in charming village. Bar with seagrass carpet; bright dining room boasts red-hued walls and conservatory extension. Expansive menus, honest cooking.

CHURCHILL *Oxon.* 503 504 P 28 – ✉ *Chipping Norton.*

London 79 – Birmingham 46 – Cheltenham 29 – Oxford 23 – Swindon 31.

The Forge without rest., OX7 6NJ, ✆ (01608) 658173, *theforge@rushbrooke.co.uk* – P. MC VISA.

5 rm ☕ ★50.00/65.00 – ★★75.00.

◆ Converted smithy run by friendly owners. Limitless hot drinks at breakfast. Thoughtful extras in bedrooms; some have four-posters, two with jacuzzi. Non smoking.

The Chequers, Church Rd, OX7 6NJ, ✆ (01608) 659393, – P. MC VISA

closed 25 December – **Rest** a la carte approx 20.00.

◆ Recently renovated honeystone Cotswold pub. Spacious contemporary interior with high ceiling and beams; upstairs lounge. Appealing mix of British menus with local ingredients.

CHURCH HANBOROUGH *Oxon. – see Woodstock.*

CHURCH STRETTON *Shrops.* 502 503 L 26 *Great Britain G. – pop. 3 941.*

Env. : *Wenlock Edge★, E : by B 4371.*

18 Trevor Hill ✆ (01694) 722281.

London 166 – Birmingham 46 – Hereford 39 – Shrewsbury 14.

Jinlye without rest., Castle Hill, All Stretton, SY6 6JP, North : 2¼ m. by B 4370 turning left beside telephone box in All Stretton ✆ (01694) 723243, *info@jinlye.co.uk, Fax (01694) 723243*, ≤, , – P. MC VISA.

7 rm ☕ ★45.00/55.00 – ★★60.00/80.00.

◆ Enjoy wonderful views of Long Mynd from this characterful crofter's cottage high in the hills, run by charming owner and daughter. Grandiose breakfast room. 19C conservatory.

The Studio, 59 High St, SY6 6BY, ✆ (01694) 722672, , – . MC VISA

closed Sunday and Monday – **Rest** (dinner only and Sunday lunch)/dinner a la carte 23.70/29.45 ♀.

◆ Personally run former art studio; walls enhanced by local artwork. Pleasant rear terrace for sunny lunches. Tried-and-tested dishes: much care taken over local produce.

CIRENCESTER *Glos.* 503 504 O 28 *Great Britain G. – pop. 15 861.*

See : *Town★ – Church of St John the Baptist★ – Corinium Museum★ (Mosaic pavements★) AC.*

Env. : *Fairford : Church of St Mary★ (stained glass windows★★) E : 7 m. by A 417.*

18 Cheltenham Rd, Bagendon ✆ (01285) 652465.

Corn Hall, Market Pl ✆ (01285) 654180.

London 97 – Bristol 37 – Gloucester 19 – Oxford 37.

Corinium, 12 Gloucester St, GL7 2DG, by Spitalgate Lane off A 417 ✆ (01285) 659711, *info@coriniumhotel.co.uk, Fax (01285) 885807*, – P. MC AE VISA

Rest a la carte 15.15/24.45 ♀ – **15 rm** ☕ ★65.00/75.00 – ★★79.00.

◆ Classic market town hotel, built as an Elizabethan wool merchant's house. All rooms decorated in co-ordinated traditional style, those on top floor with exposed beams. Restaurant in former stables and coach house.

Hotel Le Spa, Stratton Pl, Gloucester Rd, GL7 2LA, Northwest : 1 ½ m. on A 417 ✆ (01285) 648768, *bookings@lespa.com, Fax (01285) 659293*, , , , , , – P – 25. MC VISA.

closed 25-26 December and 1 January – **Rest** a la carte 18.25/33.15 – ☕ 5.95 – **9 rm** ★69.00 – ★★99.00.

◆ Mellow stone 19C manor set in manicured terraced gardens with pool and gym complex: constantly busy with predominance of spa guests. Chic rooms, richly decorated in silks. Informal, contemporary bistro overlooks the gardens.

The Ivy House without rest., 2 Victoria Rd, GL7 1EN, ✆ (01285) 656626, *info@ivyhousecotswolds.com* – ⇔ P. MO VISA. ✂
closed Christmas and New Year – **4 rm** ☐ ✝45.00/50.00 – ✝✝55.00.
◆ Ivy shrouded, stone Victorian house with pleasant, well-sized bedrooms and sunny breakfast room. A noteworthy full English breakfast is served. Non-smoking establishment.

at Barnsley *Northeast : 4 m. by A 429 on B 4425 – ✉ Cirencester.*

Barnsley House ⛵, GL7 5EE, ✆ (01285) 740000, *info@barnsleyhouse.com, Fax (01285) 740925,* ≤, ⛱, ☗, ⚓, ✂ – ✆ P. MO VISA. ✂
Rest - Italian - 25.50/39.50 – (see also ***Village Pub*** below) – ☐ 15.00 – **5 rm** ✝270.00 – ✝✝270.00/385.00, **5 suites** 325.00/475.00.
◆ 17C manor house in Cotswold stone with magnificent gardens. Original features retained in contemporary décor. Stunning bedrooms with every modern comfort. Dining room opening on to terrace and gardens. Interesting modern Italian menu using home-grown produce.

Village Pub with rm, GL7 5EF, ✆ (01285) 740421, *reservations@thevillagepub.co.uk, Fax (01285) 740900,* ⛱ – ⇔ rm, P. MO VISA
Rest a la carte 23.75/32.50 ♀ – **6 rm** ☐ ✝75.00 – ✝✝125.00.
◆ 17C pub: flagstone and oak floors, exposed timbers, open fireplaces. Home-made bread, local drinks, organic ingredients allied to modern English cooking. Rustic bedrooms.

at Ewen *Southwest : 3¼ m. by A 429 – ✉ Cirencester.*

Wild Duck Inn with rm, Drake's Island, GL7 6BY, ✆ (01285) 770310, *wduckinn@aol.com, Fax (01285) 770924,* ⛱, ☗ – P. MO AE VISA
closed 25 December – **Rest** a la carte 25.00/40.00 ♀ – **12 rm** ☐ ✝70.00 – ✝✝95.00/150.00.
◆ Cotswold stone Elizabethan inn; rich interiors, beams garlanded with hops. Country style cooking: game and fresh fish feature; blackboard selection. Relaxed, friendly staff.

at Sapperton *West : 5 m. by A 419 – ✉ Cirencester.*

The Bell, GL7 6LE, ✆ (01285) 760298, *thebell@sapperton66.freeserve.co.uk, Fax (01285) 760761,* ⛱, ☗ – P. MO VISA
closed 25 December – **Rest** a la carte 21.00/35.00 ♀.
◆ Charming pub made up of three cottages. Log fires and beams inside and a terrace outside. Mix of English and European cooking: cassoulet alongside fish and chips.

CLACTON-ON-SEA *Essex 504 X 28 – pop. 51 284.*

West Rd ✆ (01255) 421919.
Town Hall, Station Rd ✆ (01255) 423400.
London 76 – Chelmsford 37 – Colchester 14 – Ipswich 28.

Chudleigh without rest., 13 Agate Rd, Marine Parade West, CO15 1RA, ✆ (01255) 425407, *reception@chudleighhotel.com, Fax (01255) 470280* – ⇔ P. MO VISA
restricted opening October-January – **10 rm** ☐ ✝39.00/48.50 – ✝✝58.00/60.00.
◆ Victorian terraced house within easy reach of pier, seafront and the shops. Decorated in a traditional style with simple, comfortable lounge and floral bedrooms.

CLANFIELD *Oxon. 503 504 P 28 – pop. 1 709 (inc. Shilton).*

London 75 – Oxford 24 – Swindon 16.

Plough at Clanfield, Bourton Rd, OX18 2RB, on A 4095 ✆ (01367) 810222, *ploughatclanfield@hotmail.com, Fax (01367) 810596,* ☗ – ⇔ ♿ P. MO ◑ VISA
closed 3-10 January – **Rest** a la carte 19.50/28.50 ♀ – **12 rm** ☐ ✝79.00 – ✝✝118.00/128.00.
◆ Restored Elizabethan manor (1560), sitting in pretty gardens. Serene lounge with original fireplace; choice of rooms with character in main house and larger, newer rooms. Intimate restaurant.

**We try to be as accurate as possible when giving room rates.
But prices are susceptible to change,
so please check rates when booking.**

CLARE *Suffolk* 504 V 27 – *pop. 1 975* – ✉ *Sudbury.*
London 67 – Bury St Edmunds 16 – Cambridge 27 – Colchester 24 – Ipswich 32.

Ship Stores without rest., 22 Callis St, CO10 8PX, ✆ (01787) 277834, *shipclare@aol.com*
Fax (01787) 277183 – ⇹ ✆. MC VISA. ✂
7 rm ☐ ☆35.00/55.00 – ☆☆58.00/60.00.
• Three converted cottages which once sheltered sheep farmers and now double as the village shop. Simple, pine furnished rooms, four in the adjacent annex. Breakfast room with low ceiling, nooks and crannies.

CLAVERING *Essex* 504 U 28 – *pop. 1 663* – ✉ *Saffron Walden.*
London 44 – Cambridge 25 – Colchester 44 – Luton 29.

Cricketers with rm, CB11 4QT, ✆ (01799) 550442, *cricketers@lineone.net*
Fax (01799) 550882, ☂, ☂ – ⇹ ♿ P. MC AE VISA. ✂
closed 25-26 December – **Rest** a la carte 15.00/26.00 ♀ – **14 rm** ☐ ☆70.00 – ☆☆100.00.
• Jamie Oliver grew up in this 16C inn and cooked here; it's still owned by the family. Exciting dishes with influences old and new. Rooms, too, have modern or traditional feel.

CLAYTON-LE-MOORS *Lancs.* 502 M 22 – *pop. 8 289* – ✉ *Accrington.*
London 232 – Blackburn 3.5 – Lancaster 37 – Leeds 44 – Preston 14.

Sparth House, Whalley Rd, BB5 5RP, ✆ (01254) 872263, *mail.sparth@btinternet.com*
Fax (01254) 872263, ☂ – ⇹ rest, ✆ P – 🎤 100. MC AE ⦿ VISA. ✂
Rest a la carte 19.85/26.40 ♀ – **16 rm** ☐ ☆68.00/78.00 – ☆☆90.00/110.00.
• A Georgian house in wooded grounds with wood panelled interiors. Some rooms are modern, others traditional; one has antiques from the Titanic's sister liner. Traditional dining in wood-panelled room with open fire.

CLAYTON-LE-WOODS *Lancs.* 502 M 24 – *pop. 14 173* – ✉ *Chorley.*
London 220 – Liverpool 34 – Manchester 26 – Preston 5.5.

The Pines, 570 Preston Rd, PR6 7ED, on A 6 at junction with B 5256 ✆ (01772) 33855
mail@thepineshotel.co.uk, Fax (01772) 629002, ☂, ☂ – ⇹ rm, ✆ P – 🎤 300. MC AE ⦿ VISA. ✂
closed 24-26 December – ***Haworths Bistro :*** **Rest** 12.50 and a la carte 23.00/33.00 s. ♀
34 rm ☐ ☆65.00 – ☆☆100.00/120.00, 2 suites.
• Prospering on a heady round of weddings and cabarets, this redbrick Victorian hotel boasts two fashionable lounges and a smart set of bedrooms, all individually decorated. Light, airy restaurant with a unique stained glass roof.

CLAYTON WEST *W. Yorks.* 502 504 P 23 – *pop. 7 932 (inc. Skelmanthorpe)* – ✉ *Huddersfield.*
London 190 – Leeds 19 – Manchester 35 – Sheffield 24.

Bagden Hall, Wakefield Rd, Scissett, HD8 9LE, Southwest : 1 m. on A 636 ✆ (01484) 865330, *info@bagdenhallhotel.co.uk, Fax (01484) 861001*, ☂, ⛳, ☂, ✿ – ⇹ rest, ▤ rest, ♿ P – 🎤 220. MC AE ⦿ VISA. ✂
closed 25-26 December and 1 January – ***Glendale :*** **Rest** 19.95/28.95 and dinner a la carte 19.40/35.85 ♀ – ***Pippins :*** **Rest** a la carte 14.95/21.95 – **36 rm** ☐ ☆70.00/90.00 ☆☆90.00/130.00.
• 19C house in Georgian style with extensive, mature gardens, lake, 16C boathouse and golf course. Suites and bedrooms in country house style. Bar with conservatory extension. Formal dining in Glendale. Pippins brasserie named after racehorse buried in grounds!

CLEARWELL *Glos.* – *see Coleford.*

Do not confuse ✗ with ✿! ✗ defines comfort, while stars are awarded for the best cuisine, across all categories of comfort.

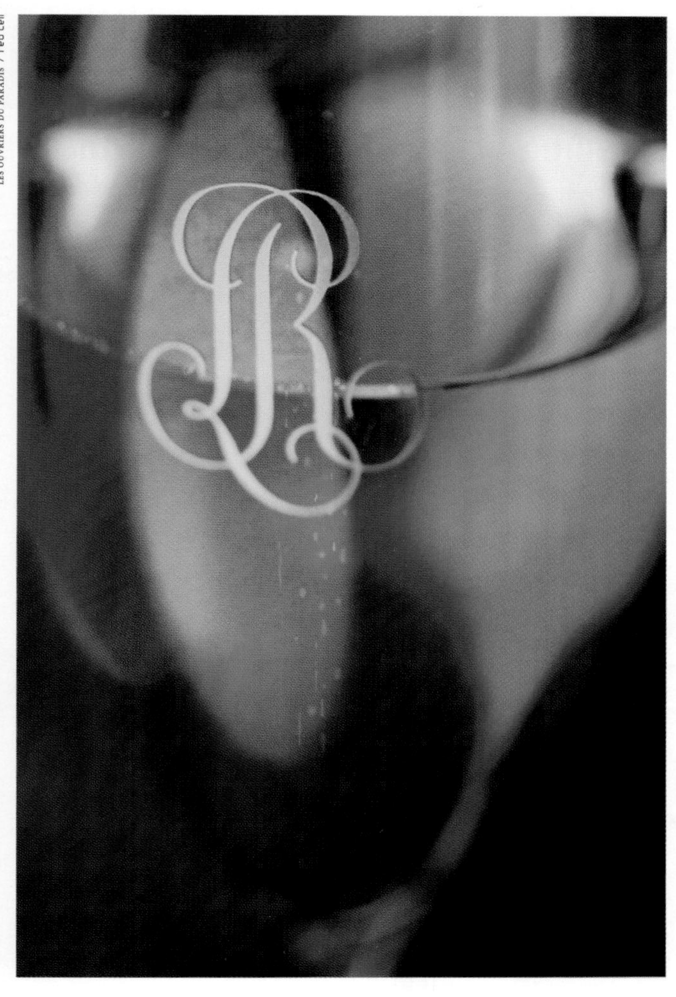

CLEEDOWNTON *Shrops.* 503 L 26 – *see Ludlow.*

CLEETHORPES *N.E. Lincs.* 502 504 U 23 – *pop. 31 853.*
Humberside Airport : ☎ (01652) 688456, W : 16 m. by A 46 and A 18 Y.
42-43 Alexandra Rd ☎ (01472) 323111.
London 171 – Lincoln 38 – Sheffield 77.

XX **Riverside Bar and Restaurant,** 2 Alexandra Rd, DN35 0SP, ☎ (01472) 600515, *chris@theriversidebarandrestaurant.com, Fax (01472) 290270* – ⇔ 20. MC VISA
closed 25-26 December, Sunday dinner and Monday – **Rest** a la carte 24.40/33.15 ♀.
◆ Actually looking out to sea, this 19C terraced property has a modern interior with a ground floor bar and smart restaurant upstairs where modern classics take centre stage.

CLEEVE HILL *Glos.* 503 504 N 28 – *see Cheltenham.*

CLENT *Worcs.* 504 N 26 *Great Britain G.*
Exc. : *Black Country Museum★, N : 7 m. by A 491 and A 4036 – Birmingham★ - Museum and Art Gallery★★, Aston Hall★★, NE : 10 m. by A 491 and A 456.*
London 127 – Birmingham 12 – Hagley 2.

Bell & Cross, Holy Cross, DY9 9QL, West : ½ m. off A 491 (northbound carriageway) (Bromsgrove rd) ☎ (01562) 730319, *Fax (01562) 731733,* – P. MC VISA
closed 25 December – **Rest** a la carte 18.50/24.50.
◆ Early 19C village pub with gardens and dining terrace. Traditional public bar and five intimate dining rooms. Friendly service; blackboard specials and seasonal produce.

Your opinions are important to us:
please write and let us know about your discoveries and experiences – good and bad!

CLEY NEXT THE SEA *Norfolk* 504 X 25 – *see Blakeney.*

CLIFFORD'S MESNE *Glos.* – *see Newent.*

CLIFTON HAMPDEN *Devon* 503 504 Q 29 – *see Abingdon.*

CLIMPING *W. Sussex* 504 S 31 – *see Littlehampton.*

CLIPSHAM *Rutland* – *see Stamford.*

CLITHEROE *Lancs.* 502 M 22 – *pop. 14 697.*
Whalley Rd ☎ (01200) 422618.
12-14 Market Pl ☎ (01200) 425566.
London 64 – Blackpool 35 – Manchester 31.

Brooklyn without rest., 32 Pimlico Rd, BB7 2AH, ☎ (01200) 428268 – ⇔. MC VISA.
4 rm ★29.00/30.00 – ★★50.00.
◆ Stone 19C house, two minutes' walk from town, with floral furnished rooms, quieter at the rear. Homely lounge to relax in after a day's exploration of the Trough of Bowland.

CLOVELLY *Devon* 503 G 31 *The West Country G.* – *pop. 439* – ✉ *Bideford.*
See : *Village★★.*
Env. : *SW : Tamar River★★.*
Exc. : *Hartland : Hartland Church★ – Hartland Quay★ (viewpoint★★) – Hartland Point ≤★★★, W : 6½ m. by B 3237 and B 3248 – Morwenstow (Church★, cliffs★★), SW : 11½ m. by A 39.*
London 241 – Barnstaple 18 – Exeter 52 – Penzance 92.

ENGLAND

Red Lion , The Quay, EX39 5TF, ☎ (01237) 431237, *redlion@clovelly.co.uk Fax (01237) 431044*, ← – ⇔ rest, P. MC VISA. ⅍
Rest (bar lunch)/dinner 25.00 **s.** – **11 rm** ☐ ♀51.50/66.50 – ♀♀103.00/111.00.
◆ Once a beer house for fishermen; stands on quayside. All rooms enjoy sea and harbour views and are decorated in soft, understated colours, providing a quiet resting place. Simple dining room looks out to harbour.

CLUN *Shrops.* 503 K 26.
London 173 – Church Stretton 16 – Ludlow 16.

Birches Mill , SY7 8NL, Northwest : 3 m. by A 488, Bicton rd, Mainstone rd and Burlow rd ☎ (01588) 640409, *gill@birchesmill.fsnet.co.uk, Fax (01588) 640409*, – ⇔ P. MC AE VISA. ⅍
mid March-October – **Rest** (by arrangement) (communal dining) – **3 rm** ☐ ♀52.00 – ♀♀80.00.
◆ High quality comforts in remote former corn mill: interior has characterful 17C/18C structures. Flagged lounge with lovely inglenook. Simple but tastefully decorated rooms. Quality organic Shropshire produce served in candle-lit dining room with fellow guests.

COATHAM MUNDEVILLE *Durham* 502 P 20 – *see Darlington.*

COBALT BUSINESS PARK *Tyne and Wear – see Newcastle upon Tyne.*

COBHAM *Surrey* 504 S 30 – *pop. 16 360 (inc. Oxshott).*
London 24 – Guildford 10.

Plan : see Greater London (South-West) 5

Hilton Cobham, Seven Hills Road South, KT11 1EW, West : 1½ m. by A 245 ☎ (01932) 864471, *gm-cobham@hilton.com, Fax (01932) 868017*, , , , , , – , ⇔ rm, ▤ rest, , P – 300. MC AE VISA
Rest (bar lunch Saturday) (dancing Saturday evening) a la carte 19.70/25.70 ♀ – ☐ 17.95 – **155 rm** ♀189.00 – ♀♀199.00, 3 suites.
◆ Designed with the corporate traveller in mind, this large hotel set in woodland offers comfortable, well-kept rooms fitted with pine furniture. Mediterranean influenced menus.

at Stoke D'Abernon *Southeast : 1½ m. on A 245 – ✉ Cobham.*

Woodlands Park, Woodlands Lane, KT11 3QB, on A 245 ☎ (01372) 843933, *woodlandspark@handpicked.co.uk, Fax (01372) 842704*, , , – , ⇔ rm, ♿ P – 150. MC AE VISA. ⅍
Oak Room : **Rest** *(closed Sunday dinner and Monday)* (dinner only and Sunday lunch)/dinner a la carte approx 39.00 – ***Brasserie :*** **Rest** a la carte approx 19.00 – ☐ 12.50 – **57 rm** ♀185.00 – ♀♀215.00.
◆ Designed in 1885 for son of founder of Bryant and May match company; one of first houses with electricity. Frequented by Prince of Wales and Lillie Langtry. Modish rooms. Appealingly welcoming Oak Room restaurant; also brasserie.

COCKERMOUTH *Cumbria* 501 502 J 20 – *pop. 7 446.*
Embleton ☎ (017687) 76223.
Town Hall, Market St ☎ (01900) 822634.
London 306 – Carlisle 25 – Keswick 13.

Trout, Crown St, CA13 0EJ, ☎ (01900) 823591, *enquiries@trouthotel.co.uk, Fax (01900) 827514*, , , – ⇔ P – 50. MC AE VISA
The Restaurant : **Rest** (dinner only and Sunday lunch)/dinner 25.95 and a la carte 25.95/40.40 ♀ – ***The Terrace :*** **Rest** a la carte approx 18.95 – **43 rm** ☐ ♀89.95/129.00 – ♀♀109.00/149.00.
◆ Extended 17C house on the banks of the River Derwent, now a hotel catering for trout and salmon fishing. Rooms in modern wing or stick with rustic style in original house. Two dining options.

at Lorton *Southeast : 4¼ m. by B 5292 – ✉ Cockermouth.*

Winder Hall Country House , CA13 9UP, on B 5289 ☎ (01900) 85107, *nick@winderhall.co.uk, Fax (01900) 85479*, ←, – ⇔ P. MC VISA. ⅍
closed January – **Rest** (booking essential to non-residents) (dinner only) 25.00/32.50 **s.** – **7 rm** (dinner included) ☐ ♀110.00/120.00 – ♀♀160.00/180.00.
◆ A mellow manor house by the river Cocker dating from 14C. Stone mullions and leaded windows. Slip into peaceful rooms with flowers and chocolates and views of the fells. Classic white and black dining room with oak panelling.

New House Farm, CA13 9UU, South : 1 ¼ m. on B 5289 ☎ (01900) 85404, *hazel@newhouse-farm.co.uk, Fax (01900) 85478,* ←, ⛆, 🐴 – ⇔ P. MC VISA
Rest 25.00 s. – **6 rm** ☕ 🚹56.00/66.00 – 🚹🚹112.00/132.00.
◆ A converted 17C-19C farmhouse in spectacular countryside of hills and lakes. Fine rambling territory but if wet, sit back and admire the scenery from the bedroom window. Home cooking with local ingredients.

COCKLEFORD *Glos.* – ✉ *Cheltenham.*

London 95 – Bristol 48 – Cheltenham 7.

The Green Dragon with rm, GL53 9NW, ☎ (01242) 870271, ⛱ – ⇔ P. MC AE VISA
closed 25-26 December and dinner 1 January – **Rest** a la carte 20.00/28.00 – **9 rm** ☕ 🚹57.00 – 🚹🚹70.00.
◆ 17C country inn of old Cotswold stone, "in the middle of nowhere", with beams, log fire and large outside terrace. Tasty meals employing good use of local ingredients.

CODFORD ST MARY *Wilts.* 504 N 30 *Great Britain G.*

Exc. : *Stonehenge★★★ AC, E : 10½ m. by A 36 and A 303.*
London 101 – Bristol 38 – Warminster 8.

George with rm, High St, BA12 0NG, ☎ (01985) 850270 – ⇔ rm, P. MC VISA. ✂
Rest *(closed Tuesday and Sunday dinner to non-residents)* a la carte 18.00/35.00 – **3 rm** ☕ 🚹45.00 – 🚹🚹65.00.
◆ Whitewashed 18C pub/hotel in pretty village. Large bar with real ales, mix and match furniture. Concise menu, accomplished dishes using fresh produce. Simply appointed rooms.

Do not confuse X with ✿! X defines comfort, while stars are awarded for the best cuisine, across all categories of comfort.

COGGESHALL *Essex* 504 W 28 – *pop. 3 919* – ✉ *Colchester.*

London 49 – Braintree 6 – Chelmsford 16 – Colchester 9.

White Hart, Market End, CO6 1NH, ☎ (01376) 561654, *whitehart.coggeshall@greenek ing.co.uk, Fax (01376) 561789* – P. MC AE ◑ VISA
Rest (in bar Sunday dinner) 18.50 (lunch) and a la carte 28.85/37.85 ♀ – **18 rm** ☕ 🚹75.00 – 🚹🚹99.00.
◆ Part 15C guildhall, a meeting place for merchants (the south road used to pass between entrance hall and reception). Individually furnished rooms have contemporary style. Timbered 'olde worlde' restaurant.

Baumann's Brasserie, 4-6 Stoneham St, CO6 1TT, ☎ (01376) 561453, *food@baumanns.brasserie.co.uk, Fax (01376) 563762* – MC AE VISA
closed first 2 weeks January, Monday and Tuesday – **Rest** 13.50/21.00 and a la carte 27.95/31.50 ♀.
◆ A local institution. The colourful pictures on the walls help create an agreeably relaxed ambience in which to sample exciting, traditional cuisine in a wide variety of menus.

COLCHESTER *Essex* 504 W 28 *Great Britain G.* – *pop. 104 390.*

See : *Castle and Museum★ AC BZ.*
⛳ *Birch Grove, Layer Rd ☎ (01206) 734276.*
ℹ *Visitor Information Centre, 1 Queen St ☎ (01206) 282920.*
London 52 – Cambridge 48 – Ipswich 18 – Luton 76 – Southend-on-Sea 41.

Plan on next page

George, 116 High St, CO1 1TD, ☎ (01206) 578494, *colcgeorge@aol.com, Fax (01206) 761732,* ⛱ – ⇔ rm, ▤ rest, P – 🏛 70. MC AE VISA BZ b
Rest 11.95 and a la carte 18.55/27.65 ♀ – ☕ 9.95 – **47 rm** 🚹88.95 – 🚹🚹98.95/114.95.
◆ The atmosphere of a 500-year old coaching inn pervades the hotel with its arched and timbered interior, beamed ceilings and wooden floors. Bedrooms have charm of bygone age. Relaxed brasserie and sumptuous lounge.

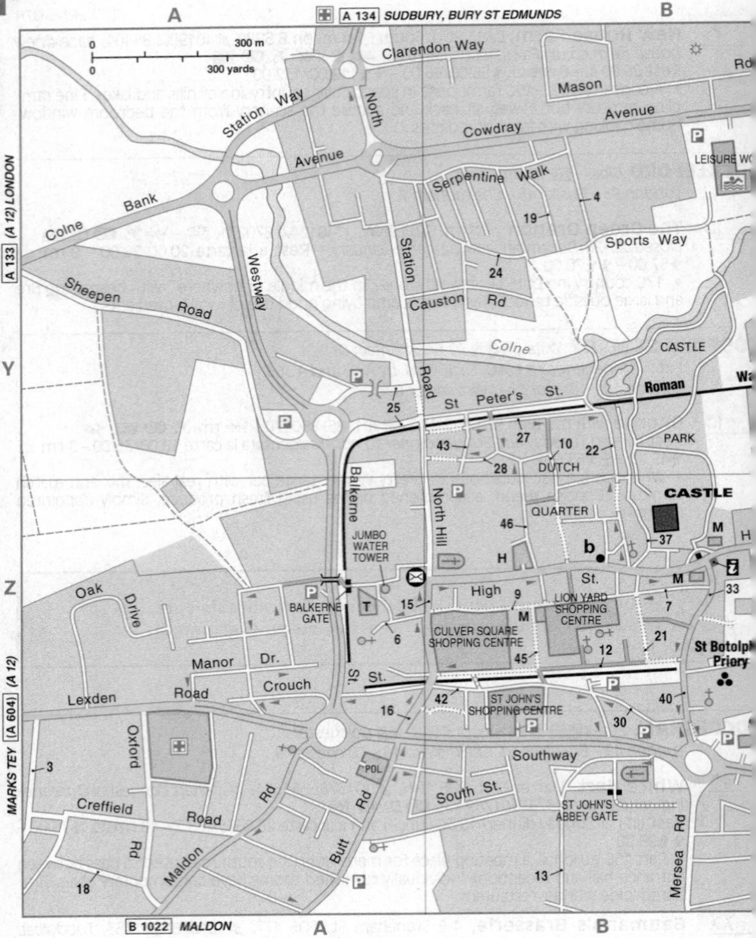

Rose and Crown, East St, Eastgates, CO1 2TZ, ✆ (01206) 866677, *info@rose-and crown.com, Fax (01206) 866616* – ⊭ ♿ P – 🏛 100. MC AE ① VISA. ✗ CZ
Rest *(closed Sunday dinner)* 19.95 (lunch) and dinner a la carte 21.75/33.45 **s.** – ☕ 9.95
38 rm ☨70.00/85.00 – ☨☨80.00/95.00.
◆ The Tudor bar sits snug in the oldest part of this 14C extended timbered inn wher locally brewed beer is served. Beamed bedrooms rub shoulders with those in moder style. Warm, atmospheric dining room; menu of Indian and French fusion cuisine.

Red House without rest., 29 Wimpole Rd, CO1 2DL, ✆ (01206) 509005, *theredhousec chester@hotmail.com, Fax (01206) 500311,* 🌳 – ⊭. ✗ CZ
3 rm ☕ ☨40.00 – ☨☨60.00.
◆ Red-brick Victorian house within walking distance of the centre. Pleasant period styl lounge; ample breakfast choice. Well-appointed rooms with good level of amenities.

Luxury pad or humble abode? ✗ and 🏠 denote categories of comfort.

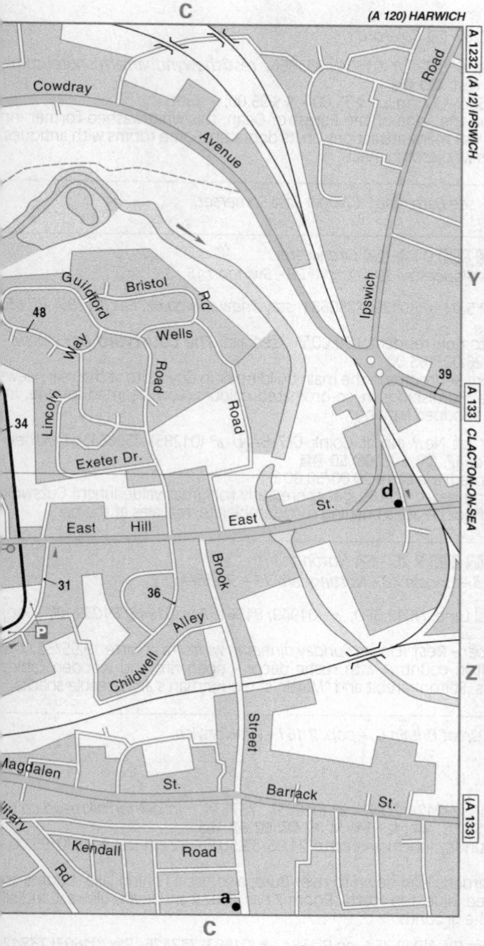

COLCHESTER

Street	Grid	No.
Beverley Rd	AZ	3
Catchpool Rd	BY	4
Church St	AZ	6
Culver Square Shopping Centre	BZ	
Culver St East	BZ	7
Culver St West	BZ	9
East Stockwell St	BYZ	10
Eld Lane	BZ	12
Flagstaff Rd	BZ	13
Head St	BZ	15
Headgate	ABZ	16
High St	BZ	
Inglis Rd	AZ	18
Kings Meadow Rd	BY	19
Lion Yard Shopping Centre	BZ	
Long Wyre St	BZ	21
Maidenburgh St	BYZ	22
Margaret Rd	BY	24
Middleborough	AY	25
Northgate St	BY	27
Nunn's Rd	BY	28
Osborne St	BZ	30
Priory St	BCZ	31
Queen St	BZ	33
Roman Rd	CY	34
Rosebery Ave	CY	36
Ryegate Rd	BYZ	37
St Andrews Ave	CY	39
St Botolph's St	BZ	40
St John's Shopping Centre	BZ	
St John's St	BZ	42
Short Cut Rd	BY	43
Trinity St	BZ	45
West Stockwell St	BYZ	46
Worcester Rd	CY	48

Good food without spending a fortune? Look out for the Bib Gourmand

COLEFORD *Glos.* 503 504 M 28 *Great Britain G. – pop. 10 145.*

Env. : *W : Wye Valley★.*

Forest of Dean, Lords Hills ☎ (01594) 832583 – Forest Hills, Mile End Rd ☎ (01594) 810620.

High St ☎ (01594) 812388.

London 143 – Bristol 28 – Gloucester 19 – Newport 29.

Speech House, Forest of Dean, GL16 7EL, Northeast : 3 m. by B 4028 on B 4226 ☎ (01594) 822607, *relax@thespeechhouse.co.uk, Fax (01594) 823658,* – – 50. VISA

Rest (bar lunch Monday-Saturday)/dinner 27.00 **s.** – **32 rm** 60.00/70.00 – 90.00.

◆ Charles II's hunting lodge in Forest of Dean; poachers executed in courtroom - gibbet now removed. Fine four-posters; disabled facilities in ground floor room. Dogs welcome. Dining room wooden dais and bench hint at royal history.

ENGLAND

at Clearwell *South : 2 m. by B 4228 – ✉ Coleford.*

Wyndham Arms, GL16 8JT, ✆ (01594) 833666, *res@thewyndhamarmshotel.co.uk*
Fax (01594) 836450 – rest. VISA
Rest a la carte 17.50/27.50 – **17 rm** 55.00 – 95.00, 1 suite.
◆ Set in a quiet village on the edge of the Forest of Dean, this whitewashed former inn dates back 600 years and has many attractions on its doorstep. Some rooms with antiques. Homely restaurant serves wholesome meals.

COLERNE *Wilts.* 503 504 M 29 – *see Bath (Bath & North East Somerset).*

COLN ST ALDWYNS *Glos.* 503 504 O 28 – ✉ *Cirencester.*
London 101 – Bristol 53 – Gloucester 20 – Oxford 28 – Swindon 15.

New Inn At Coln, GL7 5AN, ✆ (01285) 750651, *stay@new-inn.co.uk, Fax (01285) 75065*
– P. AE VISA
Rest (booking essential to non-residents) 39.00 – (see also ***The Courtyard Bar*** below) –
14 rm 95.00 – 126.00/163.00.
◆ Pretty 16C coaching inn. Bedrooms in the main building or in dovecote at the rear; views over fields or the village. Furnishings in co-ordinated colours. Low beamed lounge. Intimate dining room with subdued lighting.

The Courtyard Bar (at New Inn at Coln), GL7 5AN, ✆ (01285) 750651, *stay@new-inn.co.uk, Fax (01285) 750657,* – P. AE VISA
Rest (bookings not accepted) a la carte 20.00/38.00.
◆ Popular hostelry serving hearty meals: get there early for great value lunch! Cotswold stone walls, quarry-tiled floor create a bustling rustic ambience; real ales at the bar.

COLSTON BASSETT *Notts.* 502 504 R 25 – ✉ *Nottingham.*
London 129 – Leicester 23 – Lincoln 40 – Nottingham 15 – Sheffield 51.

Martins Arms, School Lane, NG12 3FD, ✆ (01949) 81361, *Fax (01949) 81039,*
P. AE VISA
closed dinner 25 December – **Rest** *(closed Sunday dinner in winter)* a la carte 19.95/33.00
◆ Charming pub in "Stilton country" with rustic décor - open fire and wooden tables. Makes good use of assets: Stilton rarebit and "Martin's" ploughman's are sizeable snacks.

COLTISHALL *Norfolk* 504 Y 25 *Great Britain G. – pop. 2 161 –* ✉ *Norwich.*
Env. : *The Broads*★.
London 133 – Norwich 8.

Norfolk Mead , NR12 7DN, ✆ (01603) 737531, *info@norfolkmead.co.uk*
Fax (01603) 737521, ←, – P. AE VISA
Rest (dinner only and Sunday lunch) a la carte 21.95/33.50 – **12 rm** 70.00/95.00
140.00/160.00.
◆ Restful 18C manor; gardens lead down to river Bure; also has a fishing lake. Rooms are individually colour themed: blue, terracotta. Room 7 has jacuzzi and lovely views. Candlelit restaurant overlooking the grounds.

King's Head, Wroxham Rd, NR12 7EA, on B 1354 ✆ (01603) 737426, *Fax (01603) 73742*
– P 15. AE VISA.
closed 26 December – **Rest** 9.95 (lunch) and a la carte 21.50/29.50.
◆ Fishing curios hang from the roof of this unassuming pub by the Bure. Modern menu served in the firelit bar or more formal dining room. Good choice blackboard menus.

COLWALL *Herefordshire – see Great Malvern.*

COLYFORD *Devon* 503 K 31 *Great Britain G.* – ✉ *Colyton.*
Env. : *Colyton*★ *(Church*★*), N : 1 m. on B 3161 – Axmouth (*←★*), S : 1 m. by A 3052 and B 3172.*
London 168 – Exeter 21 – Taunton 30 – Torquay 46 – Yeovil 32.

Swallows Eaves, EX24 6QJ, ✆ (01297) 553184, *Fax (01297) 553574,* – P.
VISA.
Rest (dinner only) 26.00 **s.** – **8 rm** 49.00/55.00 – 86.00/106.00.
◆ Pristine 1920s house with brightly coloured, sprightly furnished bedrooms, some with views over the Axe Valley. An ornithologist's dream: marshes crammed with birdsong nearby. Adventurous home cooking by the owner.

COMPTON ABBAS *Dorset – see Shaftesbury.*

CONGLETON *Ches.* 502 503 504 N 24 *Great Britain G. – pop. 25 400.*
Env. : *Little Moreton Hall★★ AC, SW : 3 m. by A 34.*
Biddulph Rd ℘ (01260) 273540.
Town Hall, High St ℘ (01260) 271095.
London 183 – Liverpool 50 – Manchester 25 – Sheffield 46 – Stoke-on-Trent 13.

Sandhole Farm without rest., Hulme Walfield, CW12 2JH, North : 2 ¼ m. on A 34 ℘ (01260) 224419, *veronica@sandholefarm.co.uk, Fax (01260) 224766,* – P. MC AE VISA.
15 rm ★52.00 – ★★62.00.
◆ Former farm with its stable block converted into comfy, well-equipped bedrooms with a rustic feel. Breakfast taken in the farmhouse's conservatory overlooking the countryside.

Pecks, Newcastle Rd, Moreton, CW12 4SB, South : 2 ¾ m. on A 34 ℘ (01260) 275161, *Fax (01260) 299640* – P. MC AE VISA
closed 24-30 December, Sunday dinner and Monday – **Rest** 14.50/35.00 and lunch a la carte 13.70/26.65 **s.** ♀.
◆ Light, airy restaurant with jaunty yellow décor: well regarded locally. 5 or 7 course dinners served sharp at 8pm. The cuisine is an interesting mix of modern and traditional.

L'Endroit, 70-72 Lawton St, CW12 1RS, ℘ (01260) 299548, *Fax (01260) 299548* – . MC VISA
closed 2 weeks February, 1 week late June, 1 week late September, Saturday lunch, Sunday dinner and Monday – **Rest** - French - a la carte 18.40/29.65.
◆ Relaxing eatery, away from town centre, boasting the tangible feel of a bistro: vivid walls with foodie prints, chunky wood tables. Tasty French dishes with seasonal specials.

CONISTON *Cumbria* 502 K 20 *Great Britain G. – pop. 1 304.*
Env. : *Coniston Water★ – Brantwood★ AC, SE : 2 m. on east side of Coniston Water.*
Exc. : *Hard Knott Pass★★, Wrynose Pass★★, NW : 10 m. by A 593 and minor road.*
Ruskin Ave ℘ (015394) 41533, conistontic@lake-district.gov.uk.
London 285 – Carlisle 55 – Kendal 22 – Lancaster 42.

Coniston Lodge, Station Rd, LA21 8HH, ℘ (015394) 41201, *info@coniston-lodge.com, Fax (015394) 41201* – P. MC VISA.
restricted opening in winter – **Rest** (by arrangement) – **6 rm** ★59.50 – ★★98.00.
◆ Personally run hotel; Donald Campbell's Bluebird memorabilia adorns lounge. Home-made jams for sale - and for breakfast. Rooms named after tarns; some overlook garden.

at Torver *Southwest : 2¼ m. on A 593 – ✉ Coniston.*

Old Rectory, LA21 8AX, Northeast : ¼ m. by A 593 ℘ (015394) 41353, *enquire@theoldrectoryhotel.com, Fax (015394) 41156,* – P. MC VISA
Rest (residents only) (dinner only) 24.00 **s.** – **9 rm** (dinner included) ★62.50/67.00 – ★★112.00/118.00.
◆ Beneath the Coniston Old Man, close to Coniston Water stands this country house built in 1868 for the Rev Thomas Ellwood. Snug bedrooms afford panoramic views of landscape. Fine meadow vistas from conservatory style dining room.

Wheelgate Country Guest House without rest., Little Arrow, LA21 8AU, Northeast : ¾ m. on A 593 ℘ (015394) 41418, *enquiry@wheelgate.co.uk, Fax (015394) 41114,* – P. MC VISA.
5 rm ★39.00/70.00 – ★★78.00.
◆ Pretty, wisteria-clad, converted 17C farmhouse in mature gardens. Quaint interiors: oak beams, low ceilings, antique furniture. Cottage-style bedrooms and snug rustic bar.

CONSTABLE BURTON *N. Yorks.* 502 O 21 *– see Leyburn.*

CONSTANTINE *Cornwall* 503 E 33 *The West Country G. – ✉ Falmouth.*
Env. : *Mawgan-in-Meneage (Church★), S : 3 m. by minor roads.*
London 303 – Falmouth 15 – Penzance 25 – Truro 24.

Trengilly Wartha Inn with rm, Nancenoy, TR11 5RP, South : 1½ m. by Fore St off Port Navas rd ℘ (01326) 340332, *reception@trengilly.co.uk, Fax (01326) 341121,* – P. MC AE VISA
Rest *(closed 25 and 31 December)* 29.00 (dinner) and a la carte 14.00/26.00 ♀ – **8 rm** ★50.00 – ★★80.00.
◆ Well-established landmark. Name means "settlement above the trees": stands in area of natural beauty. Dishes of local meat, game and fish with rich desserts. Cosy rooms.

CONSTANTINE BAY *Cornwall* 503 E 32 – *see Padstow.*

COOKHAM *Windsor & Maidenhead* 504 R 29 *Great Britain G.* – *pop.* 5 304 – ✉ *Maidenhead.*
See : *Stanley Spencer Gallery★ AC.*
to Marlow, Maidenhead and Windsor (Salter Bros. Ltd) (summer only).
London 32 – High Wycombe 7 – Oxford 31 – Reading 16.

XX **Manzano's,** 19-21 Station Hill Parade, SL6 9BR, ☎ (01628) 525775 – MC VISA
closed 2 weeks August, Saturday lunch, Sunday and Bank Holidays – **Rest** 19.00/21.00 and a la carte 28.50/38.50.
◆ Popular, personally run neighbourhood restaurant situated on busy parade. Warm homely feel pervades. Frequently changing seasonal Spanish menus with a classical base.

The Ferry, Sutton Rd, SL6 9SN, ☎ (01628) 525123, – P. MC AE VISA
Rest a la carte 21.00/34.00.
◆ Part 14C riverside inn with its own landing stage. Delightful 'woody' dining terrace inside, characterful beams and sofas mix the modern and the rustic. Eclectic pub dishes.

COOKHAM DEAN *Windsor and Maidenhead Great Britain G.*
Env. : *Windsor Castle★★★, Eton★★ and Windsor★, S : 5 m. by B 4447, A 4 (westbound) and A 308.*
London 32 – High Wycombe 7 – Oxford 31 – Reading 16.

XX **The Inn on the Green** with rm, The Old Cricket Common, SL6 9NZ, ☎ (01628) 482638 *reception@theinnonthegreen.com, Fax (01628) 487474,* – rm, P. MC AE VISA
Rest *(closed Monday and Sunday dinner)* (booking essential) (dinner only and Sunday lunch) a la carte 26.70/47.00 – **9 rm** ★80.00/120.00 – ★★100.00/160.00.
◆ Part timbered inn with delightful patio terrace. Stylish bar; two dining rooms and conservatory: menus are original with French base. Sumptuous rooms with individual appeal.

COPTHORNE *W. Sussex* 504 T 30 – *see Crawley.*

CORBRIDGE *Northd.* 501 502 N 19 *Great Britain G.* – *pop.* 2 800.
Env. : *Hadrian's Wall★★, N : 3 m. by A 68 – Corstopitum★ AC, NW : ½ m.*
Hill St ☎ (01434) 632815 (Easter-October).
London 300 – Hexham 3 – Newcastle upon Tyne 18.

Town Barns without rest., NE45 5HP, by Middle St and Hexham rd ☎ (01434) 633345 – P.
March-September – **3 rm** ★60.00 – ★★60.00.
◆ Modern cottage-style house on edge of town enjoys views of the Tyne Valley. Spacious comfortable guests' sitting room and well-furnished bedrooms.

XX **Valley,** The Old Station House, Station Rd, NE45 5AY, South : ½ m. by Riding Mill rd ☎ (01434) 633434, *Fax (01434) 633923* – . MC AE VISA
closed 25 December and Sunday – **Rest** - Indian - (dinner only) a la carte 19.25/31.00.
◆ As the former station house for the railway, one can still see the platform from the rear of this welcoming Indian restaurant. Smoothly run, with a bar for pre-dinner drinks.

at Great Whittington *North : 5½ m. by A 68 off B 6318* – ✉ *Corbridge.*

Queens Head Inn, NE19 2HP, ☎ (01434) 672267 – P. MC VISA.
closed 1 week Spring, Sunday dinner and Monday – **Rest** a la carte 19.00/30.00.
◆ Personally run 17C pub in sleepy village. Real ales in pleasant timbered bar. Traditional menus employ locally sourced produce - game, cheese and meat all from Northumberland.

CORFE CASTLE *Dorset* 503 504 N 32 *The West Country G.* – ✉ *Wareham.*
See : *Castle★ (≤★★) AC.*
London 129 – Bournemouth 18 – Weymouth 23.

Mortons House, 45 East St, BH20 5EE, ☎ (01929) 480988, *stay@mortonshouse.co.uk Fax (01929) 480820,* ≤, – & P. MC VISA.
Rest a la carte 33.00/50.00 – **16 rm** ★75.00/150.00 – ★★150.00, 3 suites.
◆ Elizabethan manor built in the shape of an "E" in Queen's honour. Wood panelled drawing room; range of bedrooms, some themed: the Victoria room has original Victorian bath. Colourful dining room with views over courtyard.

CORNHILL-ON-TWEED *Northd.* 501 502 N 17 *Scotland G.*
Env. : *Ladykirk (Kirk o'Steil★), NE : 6 m. by A 698 and B 6470.*
London 345 – Edinburgh 49 – Newcastle upon Tyne 59.

Tillmouth Park, TD12 4UU, Northeast : 2 ½ m. on A 698 (01890) 882255, *reception@tillmouthpark.f9.co.uk, Fax (01890) 882540*, – P. MO VISA
Rest (dinner only and Sunday lunch)/dinner 35.00 – ***The Library :*** **Rest** (bar lunch Monday-Saturday)/dinner 22.50/32.50 and a la carte 22.50/32.50 – **14 rm** 60.00/90.00 – 180.00.
• In an area renowned for its fishing, a 19C country house in mature grounds and woodland. Inside one finds stained glass windows, grand staircases and antique furniture. Light meals in bistro. Large, panelled Library restaurant has good views of grounds.

Coach House, Crookham, TD12 4TD, East : 4 m. on A 697 (01890) 820293, *stay@coachhousecrookham.com, Fax (01890) 820284*, – rest, P. MO VISA
*closed 24-26 December***Rest** (residents only) (dinner only) 19.50 – **10 rm** 35.00 – 60.00.
• Converted from a collection of farm buildings, including a 1680s dower house, and set around a courtyard. Afternoon tea by the fire, with home-made cakes, is a speciality.

CORSCOMBE *Dorset* 503 L 31 – *Dorchester.*
London 153 – Exeter 47 – Taunton 30 – Weymouth 24.

The Fox Inn with rm, DT2 0NS, Northeast : ¾ m. on Halstock rd (01935) 891330, *Fax (01935) 891330* – rm, P. MO VISA.
closed 25 December – **Rest** a la carte 19.00/28.00 – **4 rm** 55.00 – 100.00.
• Popular thatched inn with quaint interior: gingham tablecloths, beamed ceiling and conservatory. Light, modern cooking with fine fish dishes. Country style bedrooms.

CORSE LAWN *Worcs. – see Tewkesbury (Glos.).*

CORSHAM *Wilts.* 504 N 29 – *pop. 11 318.*
London 107 – Bristol 22 – Chippenham 5.

Heatherly Cottage without rest., Ladbrook Lane, Gastard, SN13 9PE, Southeast : 1 ¼ m. by B 3353 (01249) 701402, *ladbrookl@aol.com, Fax (01249) 701412*, – P.
March-November – **3 rm** 45.00 – 64.00/66.00.
• Part 17C stone cottage set down a quiet country road close to small village. Three very good value rooms: spacious, individually furnished and with good facilities.

CORSLEY *Wilts. – see Warminster.*

CORTON DENHAM *Somerset – see Sherborne.*

COSHAM *Portsmouth* 503 504 Q 31 – *see Portsmouth and Southsea.*

COTEBROOK *Ches. – see Tarporley.*

COTTINGHAM *Kingston-upon-Hull* 502 S 22 – *see Kingston-upon-Hull.*

COVENTRY *W. Mids.* 503 504 P 26 *Great Britain G. – pop. 303 475.*
See : *City★ - Cathedral★★★* **AC** AV – *Old Cathedral★* AV **B** – *Museum of British Road Transport★* *AC* AV **M2.**
18 *Windmill Village, Birmingham Rd, Allesley (024) 7640 4041* – 9 *Sphinx, Sphinx Drive (024) 7645 1361.*
4 Priory Row (024) 7622 7264.
London 100 – Birmingham 18 – Bristol 96 – Leicester 24 – Nottingham 52.

Plans on following pages

Brooklands Grange, Holyhead Rd, CV5 8HX, Northwest : 2 ½ m. on A 4114 (024) 7660 1601, *info@brooklands-grange.co.uk, Fax (024) 7660 1277*, – P. MO AE VISA
AY e
closed 25 December - 2 January – **Rest** *(closed Saturday lunch)* 25.95 and a la carte 19.85/30.85 – **31 rm** 105.00/135.00 – 120.00/155.00.
• Part 16C yeoman's farmhouse with comfy, snug bar and neatly kept rooms furnished in dainty prints. Attentive service. On main route into city with good motorway connections. Victorian restaurant and conservatory.

COVENTRY

Street	Grid	Ref
Bayley Lane	AV	3
Bishop St.	AV	5
Broadgate	AV	6
Burges Cross	AV	7
Central Six Retail Park Shopping	AV	
Corporation St.	AV	
Earl St	AV	10
Fairfax St.	AV	12
Far Gosford St.	AV	13
Gallagher Retail Park	BX	
Gosford St.	AV	15
Greyfriars Lane	AV	16
Hales St.	AV	17
Hearsall Lane	AY	21
High St	AV	22
Ironmonger Rd	AV	23
Jordan Well	AV	26
Leicester Row	AV	29
Light Lane	AV	30
Little Park St	AV	31
Precincts Shopping	AV	
Primrose Hill St	AV	34
Queen Victoria Rd	AV	35
St Johns (Ringway)	AV	38
St Nicholas (Ringway)	AV	39
Swanswell (Ringway)	AV	40
Trinity St	AV	41
Upper Well St	AV	43
Vecqueray St	AV	45
Victoria St	AV	46
Warwick Rd	AV	49
White Friars (Ringway)	AV	54
White St	AV	51
Windsor St	AV	52

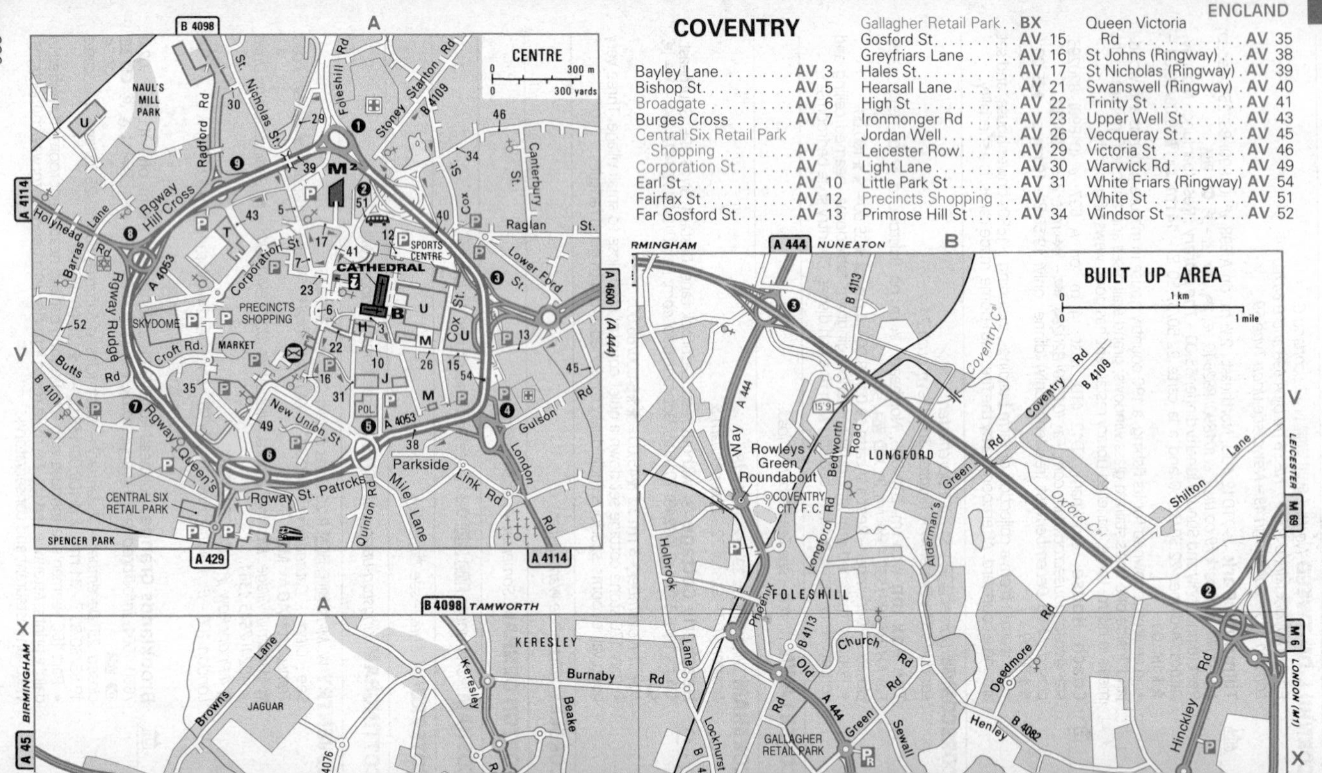

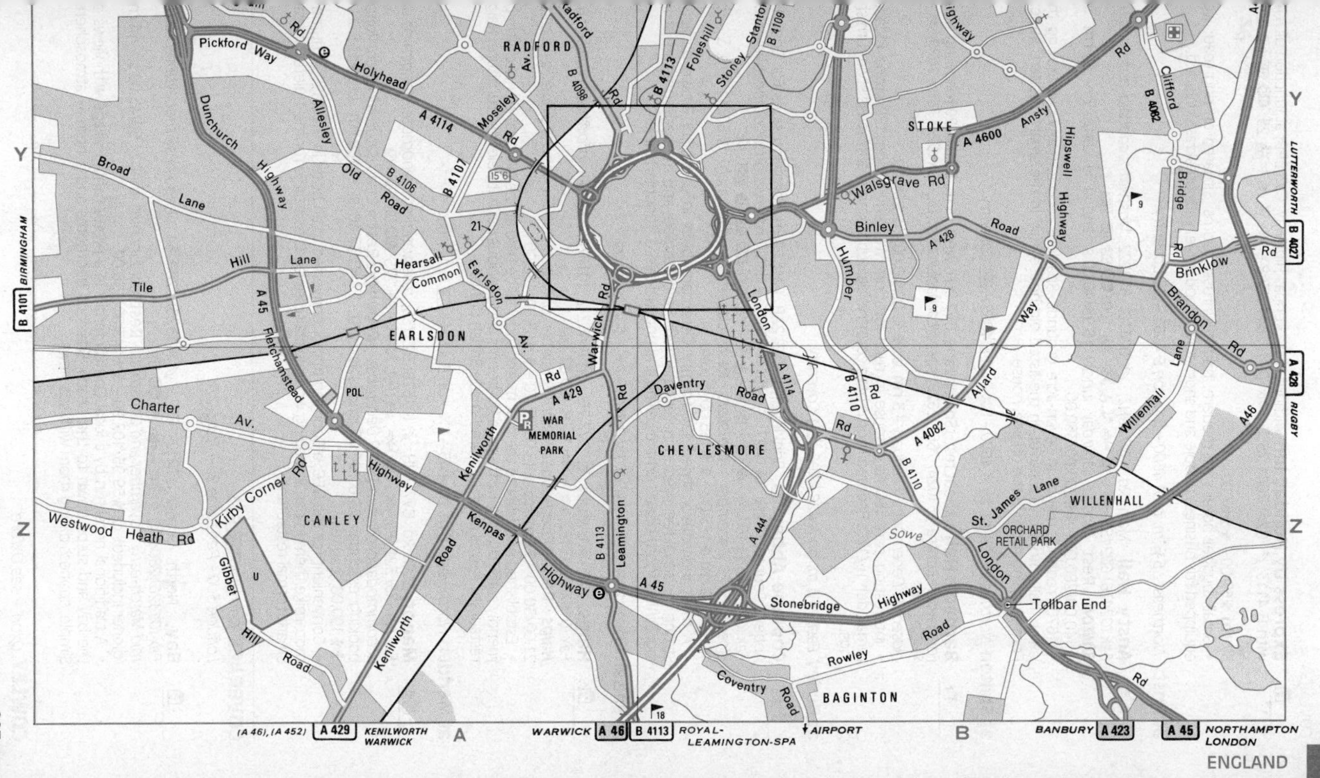

RADFORD
Pickford Way
Holyhead
A 4114
Moseley
Rd
Av.
B 4098
Radford
B 4113
Foleshill
Stoney
Stanton
B 4109
Dunchurch
Highway
Allesley
Old
Road
B 4106
B 4107
Broad
Lane
Hill
Lane
Tile
Hearsall
Common
Earlsdon
A 45
Fletchamstead
EARLSDON
Av.
Rd
Warwick
Rd
A 429
POL.
Charter
Av.
Kirby Corner Rd
Westwood Heath Rd
Gibbet
Hill
Road
CANLEY
Highway
Kenilworth
WAR MEMORIAL PARK
Kenpas
Road
Kenilworth
Highway
B 4113
Leamington
Rd
Daventry
Road
CHEYLESMORE
A 45
A 444
London
A 4114
Stonebridge
Highway
Coventry
Road
Rowley
Road
BAGINTON
STOKE
A 4600
Ansty
Walsgrave Rd
Binley
A 428
Road
Humber
Hipswell
Highway
Clifford
B 4082
Bridge
Rd
Brinklow
Rd
Brandon
Rd
Way
Allard
A 4082
B 4110
Rd
Rd
B 4110
Lane
Willenhall
A46
WILLENHALL
St. James Lane
ORCHARD RETAIL PARK
Sowe
London
Tollbar End
Rd
Y
Z
B 4101 BIRMINGHAM
LUTTERWORTH B 4027
A 428 RUGBY
(A 46), (A 452) A 429 KENILWORTH WARWICK
A
WARWICK A 46
B 4113 ROYAL-LEAMINGTON-SPA
AIRPORT
B
BANBURY A 423
A 45 NORTHAMPTON LONDON

Express by Holiday Inn without rest., Kenpas Highway, CV3 6PB, at junction of A 4 with B 4113 ✆ (024) 7641 7555, *Fax (024) 7641 3388* – ⇔ ♿ P – 🚣 25. MO AE ① VIS ⚡ AZ
37 rm ✝67.00 – ✝✝67.00.
◆ Small, budget hotel with modern, bright, unfussy rooms. Situated on ring road: we equipped for business people and short stays. Good value, with breakfast included.

at Ansty *Northeast : 5¾ m. by A 4600 – BX – on B 4065 – ✉ Coventry.*

Ansty Hall, Main Rd, CV7 9HZ, ✆ (02476) 612222, *ansty@macdonald-hotels.co.u* *Fax (02476) 602155,* – ⇔ ♿ P – 🚣 120. MO AE ① VISA
Shilton : **Rest** *(closed Saturday lunch)* 16.95/40.00 **s.** and a la carte ♀ – **62 rm** ✝140.00/280.00 – ✝✝200.00/360.00.
◆ 1670s redbrick manor in seven-acre grounds. Spacious rooms, many overlooking th lawns: half, more characterful, in the listed old house, half in the smart, modern anne Formal dining room in the original house.

at Shilton *Northeast : 6¾ m. by A 4600 – BX – on B 4065 – ✉ Coventry.*

Barnacle Hall without rest., Shilton Lane, CV7 9LH, West : 1 m. by B 4029 following sign for garden centre ✆ (024) 7661 2629, *rose@barnaclehall.co.uk, Fax (024) 7661 2629,* ⇔ P. ⚡
closed 24 December - 2 January – **3 rm** ✝30.00/40.00 – ✝✝60.00.
◆ Interesting part 16C farmhouse in rural location. Westerly facing 18C stone façad remainder 16/17C. Beamed rooms have countryside outlook and farmhouse style furnish ings.

at Binley *East : 3½ m. on A 428 – BY – ✉ Coventry.*

Coombe Abbey , Brinklow Rd, CV3 2AB, East : 2 m. following signs for Coomb Abbey Country Park (A 427) ✆ (024) 7645 0450, *reservations@combeabbey.com* *Fax (024) 7663 5101,* ←, – ⇔ ♿ P – 🚣 120. MO AE ① VISA. ⚡
closed 25-26 December – ***Cloisters :*** **Rest** *(closed Saturday lunch)* 18.50/32.50 **s.** ♀ – 13.50 – **82 rm** ✝135.00 – ✝✝155.00, 1 suite.
◆ A most individually styled 12C former Cistercian abbey in Capability Brown garden Strong medieval feel predominates: the staff are costumed, and the bedrooms are strik ing. Dining room boasts ornate ceiling and unusual raised, canopied tables.

at Balsall Common *West : 6¾ m. by B 4101 – AY – ✉ Coventry.*

Haigs, 273 Kenilworth Rd, CV7 7EL, on A 452 ✆ (01676) 533004, *info@haigsemail.co.u* *Fax (01676) 535132,* – ⇔ P. MO AE VISA
Haigs : **Rest** *(closed Sunday dinner)* (dinner only and Sunday lunch)/dinner a la cart 21.00/30.00 – **23 rm** ✝45.00/87.50 – ✝✝65.00/120.00.
◆ Established hotel where the first motor show to be held at the NEC was planned; run b friendly staff. Light floral themed bedrooms and spacious bar with elegant furniture. Haig restaurant serves carefully home-made British dishes.

at Meriden *Northwest : 6 m. by A 45 – AX – on B 4104 – ✉ Coventry.*

Manor, Main Rd, CV7 7NH, ✆ (01676) 522735, *reservations@manorhotelmeriden.co.u* *Fax (01676) 522186,* – ⇔, rest, P – 🚣 275. MO AE ① VISA
accommodation closed 24-30 December – ***Regency :*** **Rest** *(closed Saturday lunch)* (lunc booking essential) 25.00/26.00 and a la carte 27.40/37.40 **s.** – **108 rm** ✝135.00 ✝✝190.00, 2 suites.
◆ Convenient for the NEC, a Georgian manor converted to an hotel in the 1950s. Triump motorbike themed bar. Sweeping wooden staircase leads to sizable rooms, quieter at rea Smart, formal restaurant.

COVERACK *Cornwall* 503 E 33.
London 300 – Penzance 25 – Truro 27.

Bay, North Corner, TR12 6TF, ✆ (01326) 280464, *enquiries@thebayhotel.co.u* *Fax (01326) 280464,* ←, – ⇔ P. MO VISA
mid March-early November and Christmas – **Rest** (bar lunch)/dinner 21.50/45.00 **s.** – **14 rr** (dinner included) ✝59.95/107.90 – ✝✝143.00/156.00.
◆ A traditional hotel run by a local Cornish family in a pretty fishing village with views c the bay and steps down to the beach. Spacious bedrooms and a homely atmospher Simple, spotless dining room with sea views.

COWLEY *Oxon.* – *see Oxford.*

COWSHILL *Durham* 502 N 19.
London 295 – Newcastle upon Tyne 42 – Stanhope 10 – Wolsingham 16.

Low Comriggs Farm ⛰, Weardale, DL13 1AQ, Northwest : ¾ m. on A 689 ☎ (01388) 537600, *enquiries@lowcomriggsfarm.fsnet.co.uk, Fax (01388) 537777*, ≤, 🌳, 🐴 – ⇔ P.
closed Christmas – **Rest** (by arrangement) 15.00 – **3 rm** ☕ ✝30.00/32.00 – ✝✝48.00/50.00.
◆ Stone-built 300 year-old farmhouse boasting some superb views over Teesdale. Forms part of adjacent riding centre. Conservatory breakfast room; cosy, pine-furnished bedrooms. Beamed dining room offers hearty, home-cooked, organic dishes.

CRACKINGTON HAVEN *Cornwall* 503 G 31 *The West Country G.* – ✉ *Bude.*
Env. : *Poundstock★ (≤★★, church★, guildhouse★), NE : 5 ½ m. by A 39 – Jacobstow (Church★), E : 3½ m.*
London 262 – Bude 11 – Plymouth 44 – Truro 42.

Manor Farm ⛰, EX23 0JW, Southeast : 1 ¼ m. by Boscastle rd taking left turn onto Church Park Rd after 1.1 m. then taking first right onto unmarked lane ☎ (01840) 230304, ≤, 🌳, 🐴 – ⇔ P.
closed 25 December – **Rest** (by arrangement) (communal dining) 23.00 – **3 rm** ☕ ✝40.00/45.00 – ✝✝80.00.
◆ Appears in the Domesday Book and belonged to William the Conqueror's half brother. A lovely manor in beautifully manicured grounds. Affable owner and comfortable rooms. Dinner party ambience: diners sit at one table.

Trevigue ⛰, EX23 0LQ, Southeast : 1 ¼ m. on High Cliff rd ☎ (01840) 230492, *trevigue@talk21.com, Fax (01840) 230418*, 🌳 – ⇔ P. MC VISA.
March-October – **Rest** (by arrangement) 22.00 – **3 rm** ☕ ✝40.00/50.00 – ✝✝60.00/70.00.
◆ 16C working farm in a peaceful, secluded area. Walking and wildlife expeditions organised. Friendly owners oversee comfortable, rustic accommodation. Well-furnished rooms. Communal dining; hearty Cornish fare.

CRANBROOK *Kent* 504 V 30 *Great Britain G.* – *pop. 4 225.*
Env. : *Sissinghurst Castle★ AC, NE : 2½ m. by A 229 and A 262.*
Vestry Hall, Stone St ☎ (01580) 712538 (summer only).
London 53 – Hastings 19 – Maidstone 15.

Cloth Hall Oast ⛰, Coursehorn Lane, TN17 3NR, East : 1 m. by Tenterden rd ☎ (01580) 712220, *clothhalloast@aol.com, Fax (01580) 712220*, ≋ heated, 🌳 – ⇔ rm, P.
closed Christmas – **Rest** (by arrangement) (communal dining) 24.00 – **3 rm** ☕ ✝60.00/75.00 – ✝✝120.00.
◆ Run by former owner of Old Cloth Hall, with well-tended garden, rhododendrons lining the drive. Peaceful spot. Charming sitting room. Immaculate bedrooms exude personal style.

Apicius, 23 Stone St, TN17 3HE, ☎ (01580) 714666 – ⇔. MC VISA
closed Sunday dinner, Monday and Tuesday lunch – **Rest** 24.00 ♀.
◆ Stylish restaurant in Grade II listed building; named after Greek author of world's first cookbook. Smartly priced, modern French menus proffer a well-executed originality.

at Sissinghurst *Northeast : 1¾ m. by B 2189 on A 262 –* ✉ *Cranbrook.*

Rankins, The Street, TN17 2JH, on A 262 ☎ (01580) 713964, *rankins@btconnect.com* – ⇔. MC VISA
closed Sunday dinner, Monday, Tuesday and Bank Holidays – **Rest** (booking essential) (dinner only and Sunday lunch)/dinner 30.50.
◆ A friendly, well-established, family run bistro-style restaurant, not far from Sissinghurst Castle. The set menu has an international focus.

CRANTOCK *Cornwall* 503 E 32 – *see Newquay.*

CRAWLEY *W. Sussex* 504 T 30 – *pop. 100 547.*
18, 18 Cottesmore, Buchan Hill, Pease Pottage ☎ (01293) 528256 – 18, 9 Tilgate Forest, Titmus Drive, Tilgate ☎ (01293) 530103 – 9 Gatwick Manor, London Rd, Lowfield Heath ☎ (01293) 538587 – 9 Pease Pottage, Horsham Rd ☎ (01293) 521706.
County Mall Shopping Centre ☎ (01293) 846968, vip@countymall.co.uk.
London 33 – Brighton 21 – Lewes 23 – Royal Tunbridge Wells 23.
Plan of enlarged Area : see Gatwick

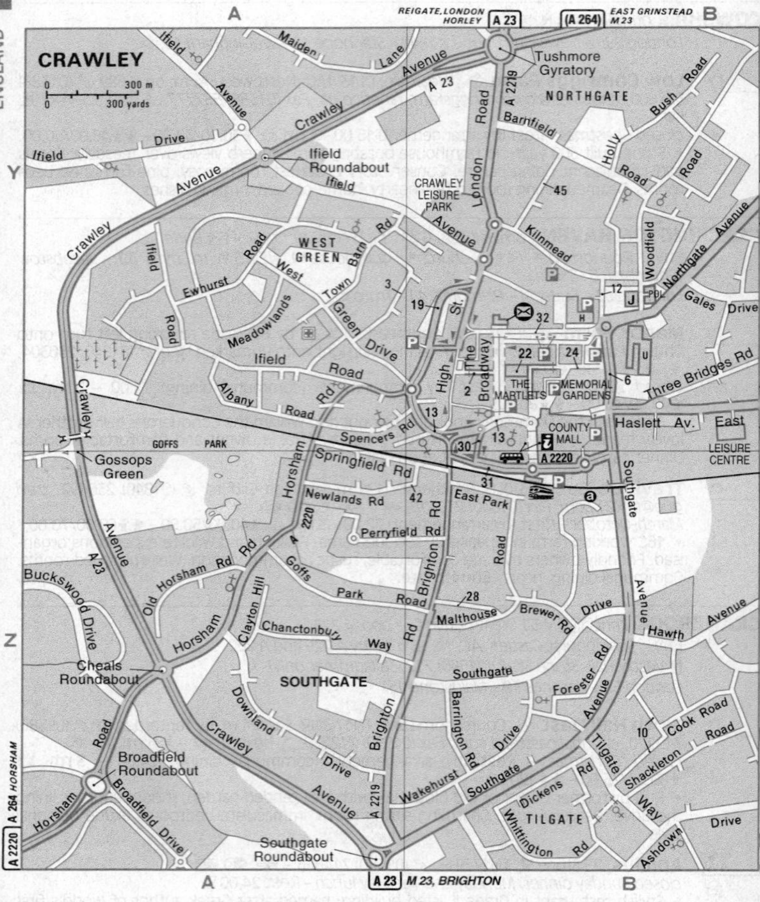

Broad Walk	BY 2		Haslett Ave West	BY 13		Station Way	BZ 31
Bruckmans Rd	AY 3		High St	BY		The Boulevard	BY 32
College Rd	BY 6		Orchard St	BY 19		The Broadway	BY
County Mall Shopping Centre	BZ		Queens Square	BY 22		The Martlets	BY
Drake Rd	BZ 10		Queensway	BY 24		Titmus Drive	BZ 34
Exchange Rd	BY 12		Southgate Rd	BZ 28		West St	ABZ 42
			Station Rd	BY 30		Woolborough Rd	BY 45

Arora International, Southgate Ave, Southgate, RH10 6LW, ✆ (01293) 530000, *gatwickreservations@arorainternational.com, Fax (01293) 515515,* – ⌂, ⌧ rm, ▤ ✆ ♿ P – 🏛 270. MC AE ① VISA. ✂ BZ a

***mono brasserie*:** Rest a la carte 17.50/28.50 s. ⚲ – ☕ 11.95 – **431 rm** ✝155.00 – ✝✝155.00, 1 suite.

◆ Futuristically designed, business oriented hotel with airport rail access. Calming water features and striking open-plan atrium. Impressive leisure facilities and bedrooms. Easy-going brasserie offers tried-and-tested menus.

Express by Holiday Inn without rest., The Squareabout, Haslett Ave East, RH10 1UA, ✆ (01293) 525523, *Fax (01293) 525529* – ⌂ ⌧ ♿ P – 🏛 35. MC AE ① VISA. ✂
74 rm ✝69.95 – ✝✝69.95. on Gatwick town plan Z a

◆ A bright, modern lodge with tiled and tasteful reception area and fresh, crisp bedrooms. Within easy reach of Crawley town centre and leisure complex. Grill and pub nearby.

at Copthorne *Northeast : 4½ m. on A 264 – BY – ✉ Crawley.*

Copthorne London Gatwick, Copthorne Way, RH10 3PG, ☎ (01342) 348800, *Fax (01342) 348833,* squash – rm, rest, – 100. MC AE VISA

Lion D'Or : **Rest** a la carte 30.00/40.50 **s.** – ***Brasserie :*** **Rest** 15.00/27.50 and a la carte 24.00/32.00 **s.** – 15.75 – **227 rm** 175.00 – 175.00.

◆ Hotel incorporates 16C farmhouse in woodlands, a retreat from hectic bustle of airport. Fine range of rooms: "Connoisseur" with spa bath, bedrooms with disabled facilities. Lion D'Or has rustic interiors of red and gold. Brasserie adjoins a smart garden room.

Copthorne Effingham Park, West Park Rd, RH10 3EU, on B 2028 ☎ (0870) 8900214, *sales.effingham@mill-cop.com, Fax (0870) 8900215,* – – 600. MC AE VISA.

Rest (bar lunch)/dinner 25.00 and a la carte 24.00/33.00 – 15.75 – **122 rm** 175.00 – 175.00.

◆ Modern hotel in 40 acres of grounds with 9 hole golf course, floodlit tennis courts and jogging track. 6 miles to airport. Superior rooms have private balconies with views. Restaurant or bar meal alternatives.

CRAYKE *N. Yorks. – see Easingwold.*

CRAY'S POND *Oxon. – see Goring.*

CREWE *Ches. 502 503 504 M 24 – pop. 67 683.*

Queen's Park, Queen's Park Drive ☎ (01270) 666724 – Fields Rd, Haslington ☎ (01270) 584227.

London 174 – Chester 24 – Liverpool 49 – Manchester 36 – Stoke-on-Trent 15.

Crewe Hall, Western Rd, CW1 6UZ, Southeast : 1 ¾ m. on A 5020 ☎ (01270) 253333, *crewehall@marstonhotels.com, Fax (01270) 253322,* – – 230. MC AE VISA.

Ranulph Room : **Rest** *(closed Sunday dinner and Monday)* 35.00 **s.** – ***Brasserie :*** **Rest** a la carte 24.70/41.95 **s.** – **60 rm** 154.50 – 224.00, 5 suites.

◆ Impressive 17C mansion with formal gardens. Victorian décor featuring alabaster, marble and stained glass. Rooms offer luxurious comfort. Formal dining in Ranulph Room with its wood panelling and ornate plaster work. Popular modern menu in the chic Brasserie.

Premier Travel Inn, Coppenhall Lane, Woolstanwood, CW2 8SD, West : 2 m. on A 532 at junction with A 530 ☎ (01270) 251126, *Fax (01270) 256316* – rm, rest, . MC AE VISA.

Rest (grill rest.) – **41 rm** 46.95/46.95 – 49.95/49.95.

◆ Located next to a Beefeater. Popular branded menus served in grill restaurant. Simple and spacious rooms with modern facilities. Not far from Nantwich Museum.

CRICK *Northants. 503 504 Q 26 – see Rugby.*

CRICKET MALHERBIE *Somerset 503 L 31 – see Ilminster.*

CROFT-ON-TEES *Durham 502 P 20 – see Darlington.*

CROMER *Norfolk 504 X 25 – pop. 8 836.*

Royal Cromer, Overstrand Rd ☎ (01263) 512884.

Prince of Wales Rd ☎ (01263) 512497.

London 132 – Norwich 23.

at Overstrand *Southeast : 2½ m. by B 1159 – ✉ Cromer.*

Sea Marge, 16 High St, NR27 0AB, ☎ (01263) 579579, *info@mackenziehotels.com, Fax (01263) 579524,* – . MC VISA

Rest (bar lunch)/dinner a la carte 20.20/25.95 – **23 rm** 78.00/116.00 – 116.00/138.00.

◆ Mock Elizabethan house built in 1908; gardens lead down to beach. Interiors feature Delft tiles alongside panelled bar, minstrel gallery. Most bedrooms have sea views. Restaurant offers views from a large leaded window.

ENGLAND

at Northrepps *Southeast : 3 m. by A 149 and Northrepps rd – ✉ Cromer.*

Shrublands Farm without rest., NR27 0AA, ☎ (01263) 579297, *youngman@farming.co.uk, Fax (01263) 579297,* – ⇔ P. MC VISA. ✂
3 rm ☕ ★37.00 – ★★58.00.
◆ Whitewashed part 18C arable farm in wooded gardens. Conservatory, lounge, neat rooms with cut flowers and garden views. Guests are encouraged to explore the farm.

CROPTON *N. Yorks.* 502 R 21 – *see Pickering.*

CROSBY-ON-EDEN *Cumbria* 501 502 L 19 – *see Carlisle.*

CROSTHWAITE *Cumbria* 502 L 21 – *see Kendal.*

CROWTHORNE *Bracknell Forest* 504 R 29 – *pop. 24 082.*
London 42 – Reading 15 – Southampton 46.

XX **Beijing,** 103 Old Wokingham Rd, RG45 6LH, Northeast : ¾ m. by A 3095 ☎ (01344) 778802 – ▤ P. MC AE ① VISA
Rest - Chinese - a la carte 10.50/16.00 s..
◆ Friendly Chinese restaurant serves authentic dishes; includes vegetarian and "sizzlers". Stuffed crab claw, prawns on toast, oyster omelette are among the unusual offerings.

CROYDE *Devon* 503 H 30 – ✉ *Braunton.*
London 232 – Barnstaple 10 – Exeter 50 – Taunton 61.

Whiteleaf, Hobbs Hill, EX33 1PN, ☎ (01271) 890266, – ⇔ P. MC VISA
closed 25-26 December – **Rest** (by arrangement) a la carte 20.50/29.15 – **5 rm** ☕ ★42.00/49.00 – ★★66.00/76.00.
◆ Homely guesthouse close to North Devon and Somerset coastal path; views of Baggy Point, Lundy Island. Rooms have mini-bars, books and are furnished in co-ordinated fabrics. Restaurant looks out onto garden.

CRUDWELL *Wilts.* 503 504 N 29 – *see Malmesbury.*

CRUMPSALL *Gtr Manchester – see Manchester.*

CUCKFIELD *W. Sussex* 504 T 30 – *pop. 2 879.*
London 40 – Brighton 15.

Ockenden Manor ⛭, Ockenden Lane, RH17 5LD, ☎ (01444) 416111, *reservations@ockenden-manor.com, Fax (01444) 415549,* , – ⇔ rest, ☎ P – 🏛 50. MC AE ① VISA. ✂
✿
Rest (lunch booking essential) 24.00/46.00 ♀ – **19 rm** ☕ ★108.00 – ★★290.00, 3 suites.
Spec. Lobster salad with Marie Rose sauce. Breast of chicken with white asparagus and risotto primavera. Apricot and almond tart with crème fraîche sorbet.
◆ Secluded part 16C manor; heritage is on display in antique furnished bedrooms, many named after previous owners. Ideal for golfers, historians and the romantic. Wood panelled dining room offers some of Sussex's finest cooking.

CUDDINGTON *Bucks.* 503 504 M 24 *Great Britain G.*
Env. : *Waddesdon Manor★★ AC, NE : 6 m. via Cuddington Hill, Cannon's Hill, Waddesdon Hill and A 41.*
London 48 – Aylesbury 6 – Oxford 17.

Crown, Aylesbury Rd, HP18 0BB, ☎ (01844) 292222 – P. MC AE VISA. ✂
closed 25 December – **Rest** a la carte 19.50/27.00.
◆ Thatched, Grade II listed inn in pretty village: small windows, flag floors and period fireplaces. Tasty food mixing modern British with pub staples and heartwarming puddings.

CUTNALL GREEN *Worcs.* 503 504 N 27 – *see Droitwich Spa.*

DALTON *N. Yorks.* 502 O 20 – *see Richmond.*

DALTON-IN-FURNESS *Cumbria* 502 K 21 – *pop. 8 057.*

The Dunnerholme, Duddon Rd, Askham-in-Furness ℘ (01229) 462675.

London 283 – Barrow-in-Furness 3.5 – Kendal 30 – Lancaster 41.

Clarence House Country, Skelgate, LA15 8BQ, North : ½ m. on Askam rd ℘ (01229) 462508, *clarencehsehotel@aol.com, Fax (01229) 467177,* – – 100. VISA

closed 25-26 December – ***The Orangery :*** Rest 26.00 – **18 rm** 79.00 – 105.00.

◆ Welcoming hotel with spacious, comfortable bedrooms in a distinctive 19C building. Features a conservatory sitting room and fine period tiling in the entrance hall. Dine in a most attractive conservatory overlooking gardens.

Park Cottage without rest., Park, LA15 8JZ, North : 1½ m. by Askam rd off Romney Park Rd ℘ (01229) 462850, *joan@parkcottagedalton.co.uk,* –

closed January – – **3 rm** 35.00/40.00 – 50.00/56.00.

◆ Quaint little 18C house hidden away in four wooded acres. Two cosy lounges: from one you can observe garden's many feathered visitors. Pleasant rooms overlook garden and lake.

DALWOOD *Devon* – *see Axminster.*

DANEHILL *E. Sussex Great Britain G.*

Env. : *Sheffield Park Garden*★, *S : 3 m. on A 275.*

London 53 – Brighton 21 – East Grinstead 7.

Coach & Horses, School Lane, RH17 7JF, Northeast : ¾ m. on Chelwood Common rd ℘ (01825) 740369, – VISA

closed 25-26 December, 1 January and Sunday dinner – **Rest** a la carte 20.00/23.50.

◆ An atmospheric 'locals' bar leads to two separate dining areas: one is a converted beamed stable. Modern menus have a distinctly French base and fine dining style.

DARESBURY *Warrington* 502 M 23 – *see Warrington.*

DARGATE *Kent* – *see Faversham.*

DARLEY *N. Yorks..*

London 217.5 – Harrogate 8.5 – Ripon 16.5.

Cold Cotes without rest., Cold Cotes Rd, Felliscliffe, HG3 2LW, South : 2 m. by Kettlesing rd, going straight over crossroads and on Harrogate rd ℘ (01423) 770937, *cold cotes@btopenworld.com, Fax (01423) 779284,* – VISA.

closed 22 December-1 February – **3 rm** 45.00/65.00 – 65.00.

◆ Victorian farmhouse in five acres of lovely gardens. Cosy lounge with open fire. Communal breakfasts overlooking grounds. Extra touches adorn the pleasant, well-priced rooms.

DARLEY ABBEY *Derbs.* 502 503 504 P 25 – *see Derby.*

DARLINGTON *Darlington* 502 P 20 – *pop. 86 082.*

Blackwell Grange, Briar Close ℘ (01325) 464458 – *Stressholme, Snipe Lane ℘ (01325) 461002.*

Teesside Airport : ℘ (01325) 332811, E : 6 m. by A 67.

13 Horsemarket ℘ (01325) 388666.

London 251 – Leeds 61 – Middlesbrough 14 – Newcastle upon Tyne 35.

Bannatyne, Southend Ave, DL3 7HZ, Southwest : ¾ m. by A 167 ℘ (01325) 365859, *en quiries@thenewgrangehotel.com, Fax (01325) 487111,* – rest, – 100. VISA

Maxine's : **Rest** (light lunch)/dinner a la carte 19.20/26.20 s. – **60 rm** 65.00/80.00 – 80.00/105.00.

◆ In a converted late Georgian villa with recent sympathetic extensions, the hotel has generally modern décor with spacious, stylish rooms. Book a rear one for enhanced peace. Uncluttered dining room with bar.

Premier Travel Inn, Morton Park Way, Morton Park, DL1 4PJ, East : 2¼ m. on B 6280 ℘ (01325) 373340, *Fax (01325) 373341* – rm, rest, VISA.

Rest (grill rest.) – **58 rm** 46.95/46.95 – 49.95/49.95.

◆ Modern, recently opened lodge accommodation situated just out of town centre. Well-equipped, comfortable rooms. Convenient for Teeside Airport. Large grill restaurant.

ENGLAND

at Coatham Mundeville *North : 4 m. on A 167 – ✉ Darlington.*

Hall Garth Golf & Country Club, DL1 3LU, East : ¼ m. on Brafferton rd ☎ (01325) 300400, *Fax (01325) 310083,* – 250.
Hugo's : **Rest** (dinner only and Sunday lunch)/dinner a la carte 18.15/37.20 **s.** – 11.75 – **48 rm** 98.00/118.00 – 118.00, 3 suites.
◆ 16C building which retains much of its country house character. Spacious and traditional rooms, especially in the older wing. Country pub and extensive leisure facilities. Candlelit dining at Hugo's.

at Aycliffe *North : 5½ m. on A 167 – ✉ Darlington.*

The County, 13 The Green, DL5 6LX, ☎ (01325) 312273, *Fax (01325) 308780* – VISA.
closed 25-26 December, 1 January and Sunday – **Rest** (booking essential) a la carte 19.90/32.40.
◆ A village pub, overlooking the green, with minimalist décor and a busy atmosphere. Friendly staff serve tasty, balanced modern dishes. Seasonally inspired blackboard specials.

at Croft-on-Tees *South : 3½ m. on A 167 – ✉ Darlington.*

Clow Beck House, Monk End Farm, DL2 2SW, West : ¾ m. by A 167 off Barton rd ☎ (01325) 721075, *heather@clowbeckhouse.co.uk, Fax (01325) 720419,* – VISA.
closed 24 December-2 January – **Rest** (residents only) (dinner only) a la carte 21.00/35.00 **s.** – **13 rm** 75.00 – 110.00.
◆ Collection of stone houses on a working farm. The residence has a friendly, homely atmosphere and plenty of amenities for children. Spacious rooms with individual character.

at Headlam *Northwest : 6 m. by A 67 – ✉ Gainford.*

Headlam Hall, DL2 3HA, ☎ (01325) 730238, *admin@headlamhall.co.uk, Fax (01325) 730790,* – 150. VISA
closed 24-26 December – ***The Panelled Restaurant :*** **Rest** 17.50 (lunch) and a la carte 27.00/31.00 **s.** – 5.00 – **33 rm** 85.00 – 100.00, 1 suite.
◆ Part Georgian, part Jacobean manor house in delightful, secluded countryside with charming walled gardens. Period interior furnishings and antiques. Good leisure facilities. Country house restaurant in four distinctively decorated rooms.

at Redworth *Northwest : 7 m. by A 68 on A 6072 – ✉ Bishop Auckland.*

Redworth Hall, DL5 6NL, ☎ (01388) 770600, *redworthhall@paramount-hotels.co.uk, Fax (01388) 770654,* – 250. VISA
Conservatory : **Rest** 18.50 (dinner) and a la carte 22.40/31.45 **s.** – (see also ***1744*** below) – **100 rm** 69.00/125.00 – 89.00/150.00.
◆ 18C and 19C manor house of Elizabethan origins with a tranquil ambience. Original features include a period banqueting hall. Comfortable, traditional bedrooms. Good leisure. Conservatory restaurant has light, open atmosphere.

XXX **1744** (at Redworth Hall), DL5 6NL, ☎ (01388) 770600, *Fax (01388) 770654,* – VISA
closed Sunday-Monday – **Rest** (dinner only) 31.00 **s.**
◆ Part painted, wood-panelled room, named after year original house was built. Well-spaced tables with immaculate settings; detailed, attentive service. Creative, modern menus.

DARTFORD *Kent* 504 U 29 – *pop. 56 818.*
Dartford Tunnel and Bridge (toll).
London 20 – Hastings 51 – Maidstone 22.

Express by Holiday Inn Dartford Bridge without rest., University Way, DA1 5PA, Northeast : 3 m. by A 226 and Cotton Lane on A 206 (westbound carriageway) ☎ (01322) 290333, *dartford-reservations@khl.uk.com, Fax (01322) 290444* – 40. VISA.
126 rm 72.50 – 72.50.
◆ A modern, budget hotel with spacious and bright public areas. Rooms are well equipped and uniformly decorated. A limited light supper is available.

at Wilmington *Southwest : 1½ m. A 225 on B 258 – ✉ Dartford.*

Rowhill Grange, DA2 7QH, Southwest : 2 m. on Hextable rd (B 258) ☎ (01322) 615136, *admin@rowhillgrange.com, Fax (01322) 615137*, – 160.
Truffles :* Rest** *(closed Saturday lunch)* 25.00/35.00 a la carte 35.00/42.50 **s.** – ***Brasserie : **Rest** a la carte approx 24.00 – **37 rm** 125.00/185.00 – 180.00/230.00, 1 suite.
♦ Extended 19C thatched house set in pretty, nine-acre gardens. Bold-coloured rooms with teak beds, eight in the converted clockhouse. Smart, up-to-date leisure club. Kentish ingredients to fore in modern Restaurant. Flag-floored Brasserie next to Leisure.

DARTMOUTH *Devon* 503 J 32 *The West Country G. – pop. 5 512.*
See : *Town★★ (≤★) – Old Town - Butterwalk★ - Dartmouth Castle (≤★★★) AC.*
Exc. : *Start Point (≤★) S : 13 m. (including 1 m. on foot).*
The Engine House, Mayor's Ave ☎ (01803) 834224, enquire@dartmouth-tourism.org.uk.
London 236 – Exeter 36 – Plymouth 35.

Dart Marina, Sandquay, TQ6 9PH, ☎ (01803) 832580, *info@dartmarinahotel.com, Fax (01803) 835040*, ≤ Dart Marina, rest, VISA
Rest 27.95 (dinner) and a la carte 18.00/36.00 – **49 rm** 79.50/126.50 – 129.00/213.00.
♦ Lovely location with excellent views over the Dart Marina. The hotel has smart, comfortable bedrooms, many with balconies. Welcoming, bright, modern public areas. Stylish restaurant; terrace overlooks river.

Royal Castle, 11 The Quay, TQ6 9PS, ☎ (01803) 833033, *enquiry@royalcastle.co.uk, Fax (01803) 835445*, ≤ – VISA
Rest 19.50/25.00 and a la carte 19.50/40.00 – **25 rm** 75.00/85.00 – 165.00/195.00.
♦ Harbour views and 18C origins enhance this smart hotel with its cosy bar and open log fires. Each of the comfortable rooms is individually styled, some boast four-poster beds. Harbour-facing restaurant particularly proud of sourcing fresh fish.

Brown's Hotel, 27-29 Victoria Rd, TQ6 9RT, ☎ (01803) 832572, *info@little-admiral.co.uk, Fax (01803) 835815* – rm. VISA
closed Christmas-mid February – **Rest** *(closed Sunday and Monday)* (dinner only) a la carte approx 20.00 – **10 rm** 60.00/80.00 – 155.00.
♦ Georgian townhouse close to the harbour. Stylish "Racing Green" window frames. Modern lounge with local artists' work. Bright, cream coloured bedrooms. Informal tapas-style dining.

Wadstray House without rest., Blackawton, TQ9 7DE, West : 4 ½ m. on A 3122 ☎ (01803) 712539, *wadstraym@aol.com, Fax (01803) 712539*,
closed 25-26 December – **3 rm** 60.00 – 80.00.
♦ An attractive house with beautifully kept gardens, delightful courtyard and verandah. Highly individual rooms decorated in pretty hues. Library sitting room.

Woodside Cottage without rest., Blackawton, TQ9 7BL, West : 5½ m. by A 3122 on Blackawton rd ☎ (01803) 712375, *stay@woodsidedartmouth.co.uk*, ≤,
closed 24-26 December – **3 rm** 45.00/55.00 – 65.00/80.00.
♦ Pretty countryside location for this quiet guesthouse. Well-furnished sitting room with conservatory. Bright, airy rooms with simple cream and white décor.

Broome Court without rest., Broomhill, TQ6 0LD, West : 2 m. by A 3122 and Venn Lane ☎ (01803) 834275, *Fax (01803) 833260*, ≤,
3 rm 45.00/50.00 – 90.00/100.00.
♦ Pretty house in a stunning, secluded location. Two sitting rooms: one for winter, one for summer. Breakfast "en famille" in huge kitchen, complete with Aga. Cottagey bedrooms.

The New Angel (Burton-Race), 2 South Embankment, TQ6 9BH, ☎ (01803) 839425, *reservations@thenewangel.co.uk, Fax (01803) 839567*, ≤ Dart Estuary VISA
closed January, first week September, dinner 25-26 December, Sunday dinner and Monday except Bank Holidays – **Rest** (booking essential) a la carte 28.50/50.50.
Spec. Roast quail with molasses butter and spiced basmati rice. Fillet of Brixham turbot with clams, cockles, mussels and pasta. Plum tart with almond ice cream.
♦ The famous "Carved Angel" reborn under TV personality chef John Burton-Race. Modern décor; open-plan kitchen. Refined cooking concentrates on local ingredients.

at Kingswear *East : via lower ferry taking first right onto Church Hill before Steam Packet Inn – ✉ Dartmouth.*

Nonsuch House, Church Hill, TQ6 0BX, ✆ (01803) 752829, *enquiries@nonsuch-house.co.uk, Fax (01803) 752357,* ≤ Dartmouth Castle and Warfleet, – . VISA.
Rest *(closed Tuesday, Wednesday and Saturday)* (residents only) (dinner only) (set menu only) (unlicensed) 25.00 – **3 rm** ☕ ✝65.00/75.00 – ✝✝90.00/100.00.
◆ Charming Edwardian house with great views to Dartmouth Castle and Warfleet from the conservatory terrace and large, well appointed bedrooms. Good, homely breakfasts.

at Strete *Southwest : 4 m. on A 379 – ✉ Dartmouth.*

The Kings Arms, TQ6 0RW, on A 379 ✆ (01803) 770377, *Fax (01803) 771008,* , – P. AE VISA
Rest - Seafood - a la carte 23.50/30.00 ♀.
◆ Mid-18C pub with rear terrace that looks to sea. Smart restaurant is where serious, accomplished cooking takes place: local, seasonal produce well utilised on modern menus.

DARWEN *Blackburn* 502 504 M 22.

18 Winter Hill ✆ (01254) 701287.
London 222 – Blackburn 5 – Blackpool 34 – Leeds 59 – Liverpool 43 – Manchester 24.

Astley Bank, Bolton Rd, BB3 2QB, South : ¾ m. on A 666 ✆ (01254) 777700, *sales@astleybank.co.uk, Fax (01254) 777707,* – P – 70. AE VISA.
Rest a la carte 19.75/32.25 – **37 rm** ☕ ✝82.00/102.00 – ✝✝92.00/132.00.
◆ Part Georgian, part Victorian privately owned hotel in elevated position above town. Varied rooms overlook the pleasant gardens. Well-equipped conference rooms. Conservatory dining room.

The red symbol? This denotes the very essence of peace – only the sound of birdsong first thing in the morning …

DATCHWORTH *Herts.* 504 T 28.

London 31 – Luton 15 – Stevenage 6.

Coltsfoot Country Retreat , Coltsfoot Lane, Bulls Green, SG3 6SB, South : ¾ m. by Bramfield Rd ✆ (01438) 212800, *info@coltsfoot.com, Fax (01438) 212840,* , – P. AE VISA.
closed 1 week Christmas – **Rest** *(closed Sunday)* (booking essential) (dinner only) a la carte 27.40/32.50 – **15 rm** ☕ ✝125.00 – ✝✝145.00.
◆ Stylish hotel, once a working farm, in 40 rural acres. Lounge bar with log-burning stove. Highly individual rooms around courtyard have vaulted ceilings and rich furnishings. Main barn houses restaurant: concise modern menus employ good seasonal produce.

DAVENTRY *Northants.* 504 Q 27 – *pop. 21 731.*

9 Norton Rd ✆ (01327) 702829 – 18, 9 Hellidon Lakes H. & C.C., Hellidon ✆ (01327) 62550 – 18 Staverton Park, Staverton ✆ (01327) 302000.
Moot Hall, Market Sq ✆ (01327) 300277.
London 79 – Coventry 23 – Leicester 31 – Northampton 13 – Oxford 46.

Fawsley Hall , Fawsley, NN11 3BA, South : 6 ½ m. by A 45 off A 361 ✆ (01327) 892000, *reservations@fawsleyhall.com, Fax (01327) 892001,* ≤, , , , , , – P – 100. AE VISA
The Knightley : **Rest** 35.00/49.50 and a la carte 30.70/39.00 ♀ – ☕ 8.00 – **41 rm** ✝145.00/155.00 – ✝✝295.00/358.00, 2 suites.
◆ Magnificent Tudor manor house with Georgian and Victorian additions in a secluded rural location. Open fires, a great hall and impressive period interiors throughout. Interesting, Italian influenced dishes, in three-roomed restaurant.

The Daventry, Sedgemoor Way, off Ashby Rd, NN11 5SG, North : 2 m. on A 361 ✆ (01327) 307000, *daventry@paramount-hotels.co.uk, Fax (01327) 706313,* , , – , rest, P – 600. AE VISA.
Rest *(closed Saturday lunch)* (carvery lunch)/dinner a la carte 25.40/38.45 **s.** ♀ – ☕ 11.95 – **136 rm** ✝125.00 – ✝✝125.00, 2 suites.
◆ A large and spacious modern hotel with comprehensive conference facilities and a well equipped leisure centre. Contemporary, comfy rooms, some with "study areas". Restaurant has pleasant views over Drayton Water.

at Staverton *Southwest : 2¾ m. by A 45 off A 425 – ✉ Daventry.*

Colledges House, Oakham Lane, NN11 6JQ, off Glebe Lane ✆ (01327) 702737, *lizjarrett@colledgeshouse.co.uk, Fax (01327) 300851,* – rm, P. VISA.
Rest (by arrangement) (communal dining) 28.50 – **4 rm** ☕ 59.50/62.50 – 95.00.
◆ Part 17C house in a quiet village. Full of charm with antiques, curios, portraits and an inglenook fireplace. Homely rooms are in the main house and an adjacent cottage. Evening meals served at elegant oak table.

DEAL *Kent* 504 Y 30 – *pop. 29 248.*
Walmer & Kingsdown, The Leas, Kingsdown ✆ (01304) 373256.
Deal Library, Broad St ✆ (01304) 369576.
London 78 – Canterbury 19 – Dover 8.5 – Margate 16.

Dunkerley's, 19 Beach St, CT14 7AH, ✆ (01304) 375016, *dunkerleysofdeal@btinternet.com, Fax (01304) 380187,* ← – . AE VISA.
Rest – (see ***Restaurant*** below) – **16 rm** ☕ 70.00 – 170.00.
◆ The hotel faces the beach and the Channel. Bedrooms are comfortably furnished and the principal rooms have jacuzzis. Comfortable bar offers a lighter menu than the restaurant.

Sutherland House, 186 London Rd, CT14 9PT, ✆ (01304) 362853, *info@sutherlandhouse.fsnet.co.uk, Fax (01304) 381146,* – P. AE VISA
Rest (by arrangement) 21.00 – **4 rm** ☕ 45.00/50.00 – 55.00/60.00.
◆ An Edwardian house with garden in a quiet residential area. Stylish, welcoming bedrooms are individually decorated. Friendly, relaxed atmosphere. Refined dining room with homely ambience.

Restaurant (at Dunkerley's H.), 19 Beach St, CT14 7AH, ✆ (01304) 375016, *Fax (01304) 380187* – . AE VISA
closed Monday lunch – **Rest** 13.95/25.00 and a la carte 24.95/42.85 ♀.
◆ With views of the Channel, the restaurant is best known for preparing locally caught seafood, although non-seafood options are also available. Wide ranging wine list.

Undecided between two equivalent establishments?
Within each category, establishments are classified
in our order of preference.

DEDDINGTON *Oxon.* 503 504 Q 28 – *pop. 1 595.*
London 72 – Birmingham 46 – Coventry 33 – Oxford 18.

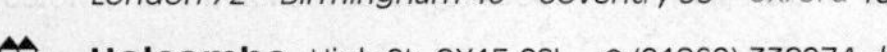

Holcombe, High St, OX15 0SL, ✆ (01869) 338274, *holcombe@oxfordshire-hotels.co.uk, Fax (01869) 337010,* – , rest, P. AE VISA.
Rest a la carte 13.85/28.70 ♀ – **15 rm** ☕ 85.00 – 95.00.
◆ A traditional 17C stone house on village main road. Exposed oak beams and tidy public areas contribute to the relaxed ambience. Each bedroom is individually decorated. Bright, informal, Mediterranean style dining.

Deddington Arms, Horsefair, OX15 0SH, ✆ (01869) 338364, *deddarms@oxfordshire-hotels.co.uk, Fax (01869) 337010* – rm, rest, P – 30. AE VISA.
Rest 11.50 (lunch) and a la carte 22.70/30.15 ♀ – **27 rm** ☕ 85.00 – 95.00/120.00.
◆ Traditional coaching inn with a smart, modish ambience, on the market place. Spacious modern bedrooms in rear extension. Stylish rooms, two four-postered, in the main house. The restaurant is decorated in a warm and contemporary style.

DEDHAM *Essex* 504 W 28 *Great Britain G.* – ✉ *Colchester.*
Env. : *Stour Valley★ – Flatford Mill★, E : 6 m. by B 1029, A 12 and B 1070.*
London 63 – Chelmsford 30 – Colchester 8 – Ipswich 12.

Maison Talbooth , Stratford Rd, CO7 6HN, West : ½ m. ✆ (01206) 322367, *maison@milsomhotels.com, Fax (01206) 322752,* ←, – P. AE VISA.
Rest – (see ***Le Talbooth*** below) – **9 rm** ☕ 120.00 – 325.00, 1 suite.
◆ Quiet, Victorian country house with intimate atmosphere, lawned gardens and views over river valley. Some rooms are smart and contemporary, others more traditional in style.

ENGLAND

Milsoms, Stratford Rd, CO7 6HW, West : ¾ m. ✆ (01206) 322795, *milsoms@milsomhotels.co.uk, Fax (01206) 323689,* ≡ rest, P. MC AE VISA
Rest (bookings not accepted) a la carte 17.20/31.35 ♀ – ☕ 15.00 – **15 rm** ☕ ✝75.00 – ✝✝135.00.
◆ Modern hotel overlooking Constable's Dedham Vale with attractive garden and stylish lounge. Bright, airy and welcoming rooms feature unfussy décor and modern colours. Likeably modish, wood-floored bistro.

XXX **Le Talbooth,** Gun Hill, CO7 6HP, West : 1 m. ✆ (01206) 323150, *talbooth@milsomhotels.com, Fax (01206) 322309,* – P. MC AE VISA
closed Sunday dinner, October-April – **Rest** 25.00 (lunch) and a la carte 30.75/51.00 ♀.
◆ Part Tudor house in attractive riverside setting. Exposed beams and real fires contribute to the traditional atmosphere matched by a traditional menu. Well chosen wine list.

XX **Fountain House & Dedham Hall** with rm, Brook St, CO7 6AD, ✆ (01206) 323027, *sarton@dedhamhall.demon.co.uk, Fax (01206) 323293,* – rest, P. MC VISA.
closed 4 days Christmas-New Year – **Rest** *(closed Sunday-Monday)* (booking essential) (dinner only) 27.50 ♀ – **5 rm** ☕ ✝55.00 – ✝✝95.00.
◆ In a quiet, country house dating back to 15C with traditional, uncluttered ambience. Weekly changing traditionally based set menu. Comfortable rooms also available.

The Sun Inn with rm, High St, CO7 6DF, ✆ (01206) 323351, *thesuninndedham@btconnect.com, Fax (01206) 323964,* – rm, P. MC VISA.
closed 25-27 and 31 December – **Rest** *(closed Sunday dinner)* a la carte 20.00/25.00 ♀ – **4 rm** ☕ ✝55.00/105.00 – ✝✝70.00/130.00.
◆ Modernised 15C coaching inn in heart of village. Welcoming sunny yellow façade; spacious interior. Interesting, original Mediterranean style menus. Boutique bedrooms.

The ✿ award is the crème de la crème. This is awarded to restaurants which are really worth travelling miles for!

DENBY DALE *W. Yorks.* 502 504 P 23.
London 192 – Leeds 22 – Manchester 37.

XX **Aagrah,** 250 Wakefield Rd, HD8 8SU, Northeast : ¾ m. on A 636 ✆ (01484) 866266 – P. MC AE VISA
closed 25 December – **Rest** - Indian (Kashmiri) - (booking essential) (dinner only) 15.00 and a la carte approx 18.00 s.
◆ The Eastern influenced interior décor reflects the authentic feel of the good quality Indian-Kashmiri dishes on offer. A busy, bustling atmosphere prevails.

DENHAM *Bucks.* 504 S 29 *Great Britain G. – pop. 2 269.*
Env. : *Windsor Castle★★★, Eton★★ and Windsor★, S : 10 m. by A 412.*
London 20 – Buckingham 42 – Oxford 41.

The Swan Inn, Village Rd, UB9 5BH, ✆ (01895) 832085, *info@swaninndenham.co.uk, Fax (01895) 835516,* – P. MC AE VISA
closed 25-26 December – **Rest** (booking essential) a la carte 17.75/25.00 ♀.
◆ Ivy-covered inn; part bar, part restaurant leading through to pleasant terrace and spacious garden. Good modern dishes with blackboard specials changing daily.

DENMEAD *Hants.* 503 Q 31 – *pop. 5 788.*
London 70 – Portsmouth 11 – Southampton 27.

XX **Barnard's,** Hambledon Rd, PO7 6NU, ✆ (023) 9225 7788, *Fax (023) 9225 7788,* MC AE VISA
closed 1 week Christmas, 1 week May, 1 week August, Saturday lunch, Sunday and Monday – **Rest** (light lunch)/dinner a la carte 22.65/32.45 ♀.
◆ Friendly village centre shop conversion; bright and airy with a small bar area. Classic and modern dishes: ricotta and basil gnocchi, chorizo salad or pork in mustard sauce.

DENTON *Gtr Manchester* 502 504 N 23 – *pop. 26 866.*

Denton, Manchester Rd ☎ (0161) 336 3218.

London 196 – Chesterfield 41 – Manchester 6.

Premier Travel Inn, Alphagate Drive, Manchester Road South, M34 3SH, West : 1 m. by A 57 at junction of M 60 and M 67 ☎ (0161) 320 1116, *Fax (0161) 337 9652* – rm, rest, P. VISA
Rest (grill rest.) – **40 rm** 47.95/47.95 – 50.95/50.95.
◆ Easy links to Stockport and close to golf facilities and Old Trafford stadium. A good value budget hotel with family rooms. Brewers Fayre next door.

DERBY *Derby* 502 503 504 P 25 *Great Britain G.* – *pop. 229 407.*

See : *City★ – Museum and Art Gallery★ (Collection of Derby Porcelain★) YZ* **M1** – *Royal Crown Derby Museum★ AC Z* **M2.**

Env. : *Kedleston Hall★★ AC, NW : 4½ m. by Kedleston Rd X.*

Wilmore Rd, Sinfin ☎ (01332) 766323 – Mickleover, Uttoxeter Rd ☎ (01332) 513339 – Kedleston Park, Kedlston, Quardon ☎ (01332) 840035 – , Marriott Breadsall Priory H. & C.C., Moor Rd, Morley ☎ (01332) 832235 – Allestree Park, Allestree Hall, Allestree ☎ (01332) 550616.

Nottingham East Midlands Airport, Castle Donington : ☎ (0871) 919 9000, SE : 12 m. by A 6 X.

Assembly Rooms, Market Pl ☎ (01332) 255802.

London 132 – Birmingham 40 – Coventry 49 – Leicester 29 – Manchester 62 – Nottingham 16 – Sheffield 47 – Stoke-on-Trent 35.

Plan on next page

Midland, Midland Rd, DE1 2SQ, ☎ (01332) 345894, *sales@midland-derby.co.uk, Fax (01332) 293522,* – |‡|, rm, P – 150. VISA. Z i
closed 24 December - 2 January – **Rest** *(closed Saturday lunch)* a la carte 18.45/35.00 **s.** – 13.50 – **99 rm** 99.00/137.00 – 117.00/137.00, 1 suite.
◆ A pleasant, early-Victorian railway hotel with good sized modern rooms and traditionally decorated public areas. Wide array of conference rooms. Pretty dining room in the Victorian style of the hotel.

Premier Travel Inn, Foresters Leisure Park, Osmaston Park Rd, DE23 8AG, ☎ (01332) 270027, *Fax (01332) 270528* – rm, P – 40. VISA. X e
Rest (grill rest.) – **26 rm** 49.95/49.95 – 52.95/52.95.
◆ Spacious commercial hotel with conference facilities. Adjacent to cinema and entertainment complex. Convenient for Derby's attractions and transport links. Efficient, airy restaurant.

at Darley Abbey *North : 2½ m. off A 6 – X – ✉ Derby.*

Darleys, Darley Abbey Mill, DE22 1DZ, ☎ (01332) 364987, *info@darleys.com, Fax (01332) 364987* – P. VISA
closed Sunday dinner and Bank Holidays – **Rest** 15.95 (lunch) and dinner a la carte 28.50/32.50 ♀.
◆ A converted cotton mill in an attractive riverside setting. The interior is modern, stylish and comfortable. High quality British cuisine of satisfying, classical character.

at Breadsall *Northeast : 4 m. by A 52 – X – off A 61 – ✉ Derby.*

Marriott Breadsall Priory H. & Country Club , Moor Rd, Morley, DE7 6DL, Northeast : 1 ¼ m. by Rectory Lane ☎ (01332) 832235, *Fax (01332) 833509,* <, , , , , , , , – |‡| , rest, P – 110. VISA
***Priory* : Rest** (dinner only and Sunday lunch) 30.00 ♀ – ***Long Weekend* : Rest** a la carte approx 20.00 ♀ – **107 rm** 145.00 – 145.00, 5 suites.
◆ Quiet, characterful hotel with main house of 13C origins retaining original elements. Mixture of modern and period rooms. Good leisure facilities and parkland. Priory restaurant housed within arches of building's old wine cellars. Long Weekend is all day bistro.

at Etwall *Southwest : 5 m. by A 38 – X – and A 516 – ✉ Derby.*

Blenheim House with rm, Main St, DE65 6LP, ☎ (01283) 732254, *info@theblenheimhouse.com, Fax (01283) 733860* – P. VISA
Rest *(closed dinner 25 December and Sunday)* 15.95 (lunch) and a la carte 21.85/31.85 ♀ – **10 rm** 65.00 – 85.00/130.00.
◆ Extended red-brick farmhouse. Dining areas enhanced by good-sized, linen-clad tables. Polite service. Well executed, extensive menus. Some bedrooms in the annexe.

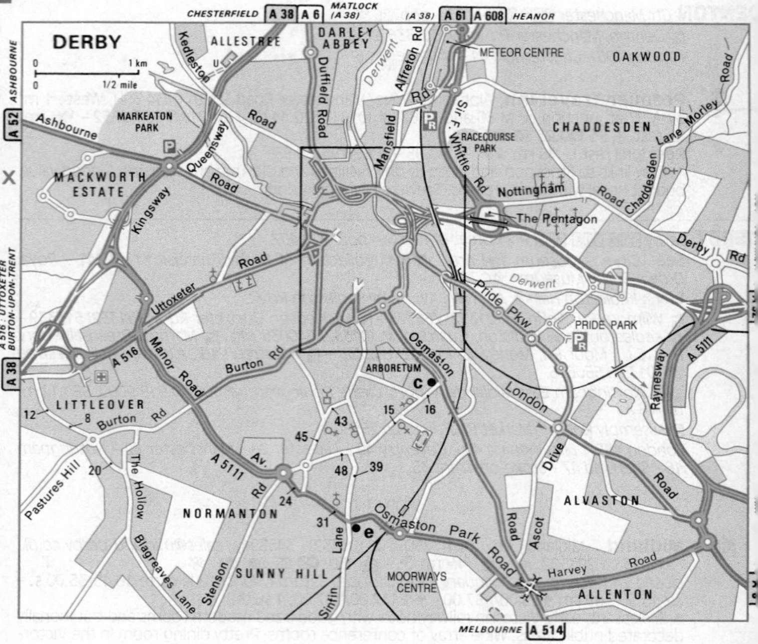

DERBY
CHESTERFIELD
A 38
A 6
MATLOCK (A 38)
(A 38)
A 61
A 608
HEANOR
ASHBOURNE
A 52
A 516 : UTTOXETER BURTON-UPON-TRENT
A 38
MELBOURNE
A 514
X
0 1 km
0 1/2 mile
ALLESTREE
DARLEY ABBEY
METEOR CENTRE
OAKWOOD
MARKEATON PARK
CHADDESDEN
RACECOURSE PARK
MACKWORTH ESTATE
The Pentagon
PRIDE PARK
ARBORETUM
LITTLEOVER
NORMANTON
SUNNY HILL
MOORWAYS CENTRE
ALVASTON
ALLENTON
Kedleston
Road
Duffield Road
Derwent
Alfreton Rd
Mansfield Rd.
Sir F. Whittle Rd
Ashbourne
Queensway
Road
Kingsway
Uttoxeter Road
Nottingham Road
Chaddesden Lane
Morley Road
Derby Rd
Pride Pkw
Raynesway
A 5111
A 516
Manor Road
Burton Rd
Osmaston
London Road
Drive
Ascot
Road
Burton Rd
Pastures Hill
The Hollow
A 5111
Av.
Rd
Blagreaves Lane
Stenson
Lane
Sinfin
Osmaston Park Road
Harvey Road
c
e
12
8
20
24
31
43
45
48
39
15
16
CENTRE
0 200 m
0 200 yards
A 6
A 61
A 52
A 516
A 5250 (A 38)
A 514
Y
Z
Garden St.
Lodge La.
Alkmund's
Way
Mansfield Road
Fox Street
Nottingham Road
Stores Road
Sir F. Whittle Road
Eastgate
POL.
LEISURE CENTRE
Ford St.
Friar Gate
Derwent St.
Curzon St.
Macklin St.
Wilson St.
Green La.
The Cock Pitt
MARKET
EAGLE CENTRE
Pride Parkway
Siddals Rd
Traffic St.
Osmaston
London Road
Canal St.
Railway Ter.
MIDLAND
Street
Gerard St.
Abbey
Burton
Rd
Leopold St.
Mill Hill Lane
Litchurch St.
Road
Derwent
M
M1
M2
17
25
7
34
19
23
4
36
22
27
14
50
13
29
2
42
46
37
18
3
26
40
5
9
30
33
28

Albert St . . . . Z 2
Babington Lane . . . . Z 3
Bold Lane . . . . Y 4
Bradshaw Way . . . . Z 5
Cathedral Rd . . . . Y 7
Chain Lane . . . . X 8
Charnwood St . . . . Z 9
Corden Ave . . . . X 12
Corn Market . . . . Z 13
Corporation St . . . . YZ 14
Dairy House Rd . . . . X 15
Douglas St . . . . X 16
Duffield Rd . . . . Y 17
Eagle Shopping Centre . . . Z
East St . . . . Z 18
Full St . . . . Y 19
Hillsway . . . . X 20
Iron Gate . . . . Y 22
Jury St . . . . Y 23
Kenilworth Ave . . . . X 24
King St . . . . Y 25
Liversage St . . . . Z 26
Market Pl. . . . . YZ 27
Midland Rd . . . . Z 28
Morledge . . . . Z 29
Mount St . . . . Z 30
Newdigate St. . . . . X 31
Normanton Rd . . . . Z 33
Queen St . . . . Y 34
Sacheveral St . . . . Z 40
St Mary's Gate . . . . Y 36
St Peter's St . . . . Z 37
St Thomas Rd . . . . X 39
Stafford St . . . . Z 42
Stanhope St . . . . X 43
Upper Dale Rd . . . . X 45
Victoria St . . . . Z 46
Walbrook Rd . . . . X 48
Wardwick . . . . Z 50

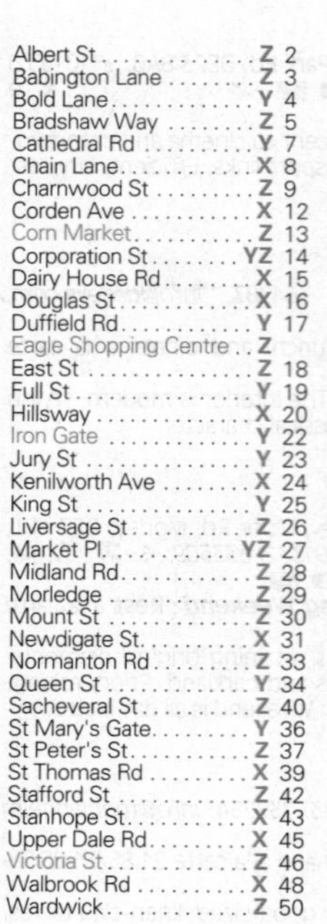

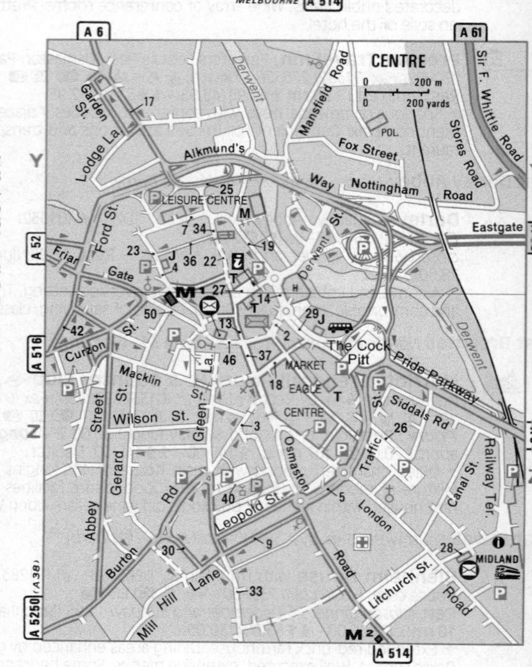

at Mickleover *Southwest : 3 m. by A 38 – X – and A 516 – ✉ Derby.*

Mickleover Court, Etwall Rd, DE3 0XX, ✆ (01332) 521234, *mickleover@menzies-hotels.co.uk, Fax (01332) 521238,* ⚇, ≘s, ☐ – ⊞, ⅍ rm, ▤ ♿ P – 🏛 200. MC AE ① VISA
The Brasserie : Rest 16.50/26.00 and a la carte 22.40/34.40 – ***Stelline Trattoria :*** Rest - Italian - *(closed Sunday-Tuesday)* (dinner only) 22.50 and a la carte 16.85/24.45 – ☕ 14.95 – **91 rm** ✝150.00 – ✝✝150.00, 8 suites.
◆ A large central atrium with 2 café-bar areas. Rooms are spacious and well equipped, with good use of natural light. Comprehensive leisure and conference facilities. Vibrant, spacious Brasserie. Stelline Trattoria is authentic Italian restaurant.

at Weston Underwood *Northwest : 5½ m. by A 52 – X – and Kedleston Rd – ✉ Derby.*

Park View Farm without rest., DE6 4PA, ✆ (01335) 360352, *enquiries@parkviewfarm.co.uk, Fax (01335) 360352,* ⋞, ⚐ – ⅍ P. ⚐
closed Christmas-New Year – **3 rm** ☕ ✝50.00/60.00 – ✝✝80.00/90.00.
◆ Friendly couple run this elegant house on a working farm, in sight of Kedleston Hall. Antique-filled lounge with oils and a Victorian fireplace. Simple rooms in stripped pine.

DEVIZES *Wilts.* 503 504 O 29 *The West Country G. – pop. 14 379.*
See : *St John's Church★★ – Market Place★ – Devizes Museum★ AC.*
Env. : *Potterne (Porch House★★) S : 2½ m. by A 360 – E : Vale of Pewsey★.*
Exc. : *Stonehenge★★★ AC, SE : 16 m. by A 360 and A 344 – Avebury★★ (The Stones★, Church★) NE : 7 m. by A 361.*
18 *Erlestoke Sands, Erlestoke ✆ (01380) 831069.*
ℹ *Cromwell House, Market Sq ✆ (01380) 729408.*
London 98 – Bristol 38 – Salisbury 25 – Southampton 50 – Swindon 19.

at Marden *Southeast : 6½ m. by A 342 – ✉ Devizes.*

The Millstream, SN10 3RH, ✆ (01380) 848308, *mail@the-millstream.co.uk, Fax (01380) 848337,* ⛱, ⚐ – ⅍ P. MC ① VISA
closed 25 December and Monday lunch – **Rest** a la carte 20.00/37.50 ♀.
◆ Refurbished in 2004: smart outside terrace; modern rusticity invoked in stylish interior. Carefully prepared, tasty, modish menus. Champagne always available!

at Potterne *South : 2¼ m. on A 360 – ✉ Devizes.*

Blounts Court Farm ⛐ without rest., Coxhill Lane, SN10 5PH, ✆ (01380) 727180, *caroline@blountscourtfarm.co.uk,* ⚐, ⚐ – ⅍ P. MC VISA. ⚐
3 rm ☕ ✝38.00 – ✝✝60.00.
◆ Working farm personally run by charming owner: good value accommodation in blissful spot. Cosy rooms in converted barn are handsomely furnished with interesting artefacts.

at Rowde *Northwest : 2 m. by A 361 on A 342 – ✉ Devizes.*

The George & Dragon, High St, SN10 2PN, ✆ (01380) 723053, *thegandd@tiscali.co.uk,* ⛱, ⚐ – ⅍ P. MC VISA
closed 1-8 January, Sunday dinner and Monday – **Rest** - Seafood specialities - (booking essential) 14.50 (lunch) and a la carte 25.00/40.00 ♀.
◆ Characterful little pub with rustic fittings and open fire. Robust modern classics and fish specials hold sway in a cosy, personally run atmosphere. Real ale.

DEWSBURY *W. Yorks.* 502 P 22 – *pop. 54 341.*
London 205 – Leeds 9 – Manchester 40 – Middlesbrough 76 – Sheffield 31.

Heath Cottage, Wakefield Rd, WF12 8ET, East : ¾ m. on A 638 ✆ (01924) 465399, *bookings@heathcottage.co.uk, Fax (01924) 459405* – ⅍, ▤ rest, P – 🏛 70. MC VISA. ⚐
Rest 14.95/25.00 **s.** – **29 rm** ☕ ✝39.00/63.00 – ✝✝68.00/74.00.
◆ Extended Victorian house; former doctors' surgery. Bright décor and furnishings throughout with rooms of varying shapes and sizes. Cocktail bar in comfortable lounge area. Tried-and-tested cuisine.

DICKLEBURGH *Norfolk* 504 X 26 – *see Diss.*

The sun's out – let's eat al fresco! Look for a terrace: ⛱

DIDCOT *Oxon.* 503 504 Q 29 – ✉ *Abingdon.*
118 Broadway ℘ (01235) 813243.
London 58 – Oxford 15 – Reading 20 – Swindon 31.

Premier Travel Inn, Marcham Rd, OX14 1AD, Northwest : 3 ¼ m. by B 4493 on A 4130 ℘ (01235) 835168, *Fax (01235) 820465* – ✕ rm, ▤ rest, ♿ P. MC AE VISA.
Rest (grill rest.) – **60 rm** ☆50.95 – ☆☆50.95.
◆ Branded modern lodge accommodation conveniently located for Oxford city and its historic attractions and major transport links. Benefits from a popular grill restaurant.

DIDMARTON *Glos.* 503 504 N 29 – ✉ *Tetbury.*
London 120 – Bristol 20 – Gloucester 27 – Swindon 33.

Kings Arms with rm, The Street, GL9 1DT, on A 433 ℘ (01454) 238245, *bookings@kingsarmsdidmarton.co.uk, Fax (01454) 238249,* – ✕ P 24. MC VISA
Rest a la carte 15.00/25.00 ♀ – **4 rm** ☕ ☆45.00 – ☆☆70.00.
◆ Busy, bustling pub with 17C façade, open fires and low beams. Large, traditional pub menu served in bar or dining area. Comfortable rooms available. Lawned garden.

Good food without spending a fortune? Look out for the Bib Gourmand

DIDSBURY *Gtr Manchester* 502 503 504 N 23 – *see Manchester.*

DISS *Norfolk* 504 X 26 – *pop. 7 444.*
Meres Mouth, Mere St ℘ (01379) 650523.
London 98 – Ipswich 25 – Norwich 21 – Thetford 17.

at Dickleburgh *Northeast : 4½ m. by A 1066 off A 140 – ✉ Diss.*

Dickleburgh Hall Country House without rest., Semere Green Lane, IP21 4NT, North : 1 m. ℘ (01379) 741259, *johnandberyl@dickhall.freeserve.co.uk,* 18, – ✕ P.
closed Christmas-New Year – **3 rm** ☕ ☆40.00 – ☆☆70.00/80.00.
◆ 16C house still in private hands. Trim rooms in traditional patterns, beamed lounge with an inglenook fireplace; snooker room and golf course.

at Brockdish *East : 7 m. by A 1066, A 140 and A 143 – ✉ Diss.*

Grove Thorpe without rest., Grove Rd, IP21 4JR, North : ¾ m. ℘ (01379) 668305, *b-b@grovethorpe.co.uk,* – ✕ ♿ P.
closed Christmas and New Year – **3 rm** ☕ ☆50.00/55.00 – ☆☆78.00.
◆ Pretty 17C bailiff's house in peaceful pastureland with fishing; very welcoming owners. Cosy ambience. Characterful interior with oak beams, inglenook and antique furniture.

at Brome *(Suffolk) Southeast : 2¾ m. by A 1066 on B 1077 – ✉ Eye.*

The Cornwallis, IP23 8AJ, ℘ (01379) 870326, *info@thecornwallis.com, Fax (01379) 870051,* – ✕ P – 30. MC VISA.
Rest (booking essential) 27.00 and a la carte 20.00/30.50 ♀ – **16 rm** ☕ ☆99.00 – ☆☆120.00/175.00.
◆ Part 16C dower house with quiet topiary gardens. Spacious, individually decorated timbered rooms with antique furniture. 60ft well in very characterful bar dating from 1561. Dining room with delightful conservatory lounge overlooking gardens.

DODDISCOMBSLEIGH *Devon* 503 J 31 – *see Exeter.*

DOGMERSFIELD *Hants.*
London 44.5 – Farnham 6 – Fleet 2.

Four Seasons, Dogmersfield Park, Chalky Lane, RG27 8TD, ℘ (01252) 853000, *Fax (01252) 853010,* – ✕ ▤ ♿ P – 240. MC AE VISA
***Seasons* :** **Rest** 27.00/34.00 and a la carte 36.00/49.00 s. – ☕ 25.00 – **111 rm** ☆280.00 – ☆☆280.00, 22 suites.
◆ Part Georgian splendour in extensive woodlands; many original features in situ. Superb spa facilities: vast selection of leisure pursuits. Luxurious, highly equipped bedrooms. Restaurant has thoroughly modish, relaxing feel.

DONCASTER *S. Yorks.* 502 503 504 Q 23 – *pop. 67 977.*

18 Doncaster Town Moor, Bawtry Rd, Belle Vue ℘ (01302) 533778, B – 18 Crookhill Park, Conisborough ℘ (01709) 862979 – 18 Wheatley, Amthorpe Rd ℘ (01302) 831655, B – 9 Owston Park, Owston Hall, Owston ℘ (01302) 330821.

Central Library, Waterdale ℘ (01302) 734309.

London 173 – Kingston-upon-Hull 46 – Leeds 30 – Nottingham 46 – Sheffield 19.

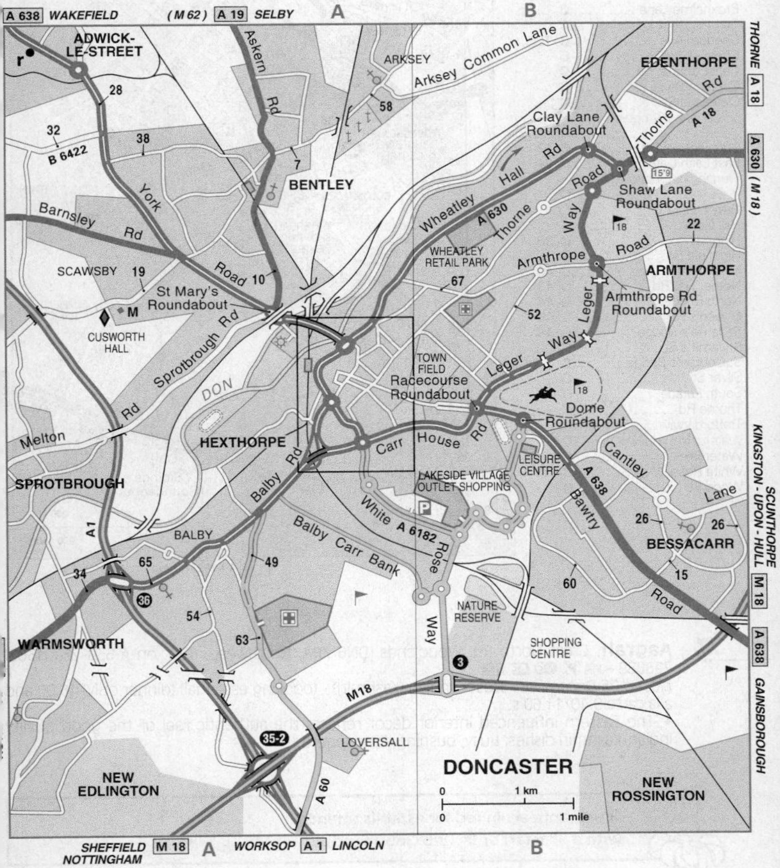

Mount Pleasant, Great North Rd, DN11 0HW, Southeast : 6 m. on A 638 ℘ (01302) 868219, *mountpleasant@fax.co.uk, Fax (01302) 865130,* – , rest, – 200. MC AE VISA.
closed 25-26 December ***Garden :*** **Rest** 16.95/32.95 and dinner a la carte 21.70/34.65 **s.** – **43 rm** 79.00/125.00 – 99.00/150.00, 2 suites.
◆ Stone-built farmhouse with sympathetic extension. Traditionally styled throughout: wood panelled lounges and a small bar. Well-kept bedrooms, including one with a five-poster! Restaurant with garden views.

DONCASTER

Albion Pl. . . . . C 3
Apley Rd . . . . C 5
Balby Rd . . . . C 8
Broxholme Lane C
Carr House Rd. C
Chequer Ave . . . . C 12
Chequer Rd C
Christ Church Rd. C
Church Way. C
Cleveland St C
Colonnades Shopping Centre C
Cunningham Rd . . . . C 17
East Laith Gate . . . . C 24
Frenchgate Shopping Centre C
Grey Friars Rd C
Hall Gate C
High St. . . . . C 36
Highfield Rd. C
Milton Walk. . . . . C 40
Nether Hall Rd. . . . . C 43
North Bridge Rd . . . . C 44
Queen's Rd. . . . . C 46
St Jame's Bridge. . . . . C 48
St Jame's St C
St George's Bridge C
Silver St C
South Parade. C
Thorne Rd C
Trafford Way C
Waterdale Shopping Centre C
Waterdale C
White Rose Way. . . . . C 70
Wood St. C

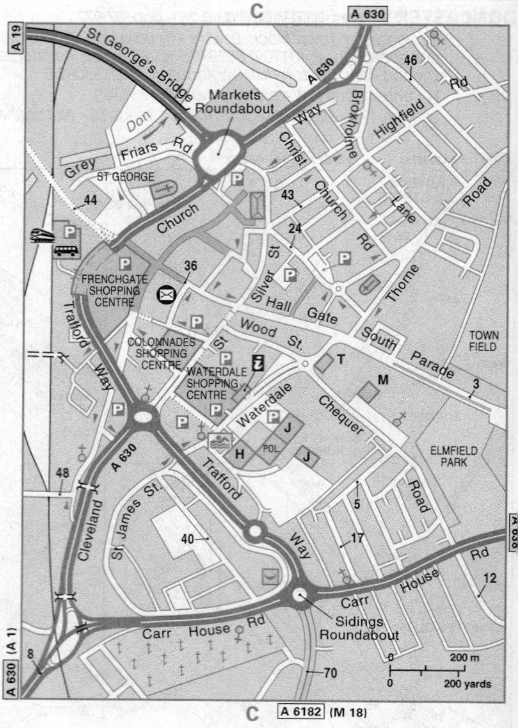

XX **Aagrah,** Great North Rd, Woodlands, DN6 7RA, Northwest : 4 m. on A 638 ✆ (01302) 728888 – ▤ P. MC AE VISA A r
closed 25 December – **Rest** - Indian (Kashmiri) - (booking essential) (dinner only) 16.00 and a la carte 9.40/11.60 s.
• The Eastern influenced interior décor reflects the authentic feel of the good quality Indian-Kashmiri dishes. Busy, bustling atmosphere.

"Rest" appears in red for establishments with a ✿ (star) or ☺ (Bib Gourmand).

DONHEAD ST ANDREW *Wilts.* 503 504 N 30 – *see Shaftesbury (Dorset).*

DORCHESTER *Dorset* 503 504 M 31 *The West Country G. – pop. 16 171.*
See : *Town★ - Dorset County Museum★ AC.*
Env. : *Maiden Castle★★ (≤★) SW : 2½ m. – Puddletown Church★, NE : 5½ m. by A 35.*
Exc. : *Moreton Church★★, E : 7½ m. – Bere Regis★ (St John the Baptist Church★ - Roof★★) NE : 11 m. by A 35 – Athelhampton House★ AC, NE : 6½ m. by A 35 - Cerne Abbas★, N : 7 m. by A 352 – Milton Abbas★, NE : 12 m. on A 354 and by-road.*
⛳18 *Came Down ✆ (01305) 813494.*
ℹ *11 Antelope Walk ✆ (01305) 267992.*
London 135 – Bournemouth 27 – Exeter 53 – Southampton 53.

Birkin House without rest., Stinsford, DT2 8QD, East : 1 ¼ m. by B 3150 ☎ (01305) 260262, *info@birkinhouse.com, Fax (01305) 259510*, P. VISA.
closed Christmas-New Year – **12 rm** ★55.00 – ★★180.00.
◆ Greystone Victorian mansion in formal gardens. Brims with antiques and style. Imposing hallway; elegant lounge; opulent drawing room; cosy bar/library. Well furnished rooms.

Casterbridge without rest., 49 High East St, DT1 1HU, ☎ (01305) 264043, *reception@casterbridgehotel.co.uk, Fax (01305) 260884* – AE VISA.
closed 25-26 December – **15 rm** ★58.00/85.00 – ★★95.00/125.00.
◆ A Georgian town house with courtyard and conservatory at the bottom of the high street. Well decorated throughout in a comfortable, traditional style. Bar and quiet lounge.

Yalbury Cottage, Lower Bockhampton, DT2 8PZ, East : 2 ¼ m. by B 3150 and Bockhampton rd ☎ (01305) 262382, *yalburyemails@aol.com, Fax (01305) 266412*, – P. VISA
closed 2 weeks January – **Rest** (dinner only) 32.00 – **8 rm** ★60.00 – ★★96.00.
◆ Characterful converted 17C cottages with pretty garden and quiet country location. Uncluttered lounge with original fireplace. Rooms are simply furnished and spacious. Dining room boasts beamed ceiling and stone walls.

Westwood House without rest., 29 High West St, DT1 1UP, ☎ (01305) 268018, *reservations@westwoodhouse.co.uk, Fax (01305) 250282* – VISA.
closed 1 week christmas – **7 rm** ★40.00/55.00 – ★★60.00/85.00.
◆ Georgian town house on the high street with a welcoming atmosphere. Breakfast served in the conservatory. Rooms are decorated in bold colours and are well kept and spacious.

Sienna, 36 High West St, DT1 1UP, ☎ (01305) 250022, *browns@siennarestaurant.co.uk* – VISA
closed 2 weeks Spring, 2 weeks Autumn, Sunday and Monday – **Rest** (booking essential) 17.50/31.00 ♀.
◆ Charming, intimate restaurant at top of high street. Cheerful yellow walls with modern artwork and banquette seating on one side. Modern British dishes using local produce.

at Winterbourne Steepleton *West : 4¾ m. by B 3150 and A 35 on B 3159 – ✉ Dorchester.*

Old Rectory without rest., DT2 9LG, ☎ (01305) 889468, *trees@eurobell.co.uk, Fax (01305) 889737*, – P.
closed Christmas and New Year – **4 rm** ★55.00 – ★★58.00/68.00.
◆ Built in 1850 and having a characterful exterior. Situated in the middle of a charming village. Well kept, good sized rooms overlook the pleasant garden.

Red = Pleasant. Look for the red and symbols.

DORCHESTER-ON-THAMES *Oxon.* 503 504 Q 29 *Great Britain G. – pop. 2 256.*

See : *Town*★.
Exc. : *Ridgeway Path*★★.
London 51 – Abingdon 6 – Oxford 8 – Reading 17.

White Hart, 26 High St, OX10 7HN, ☎ (01865) 340074, *whitehart@oxfordshire-hotels.co.uk, Fax (01865) 341082* – P – 40. AE VISA.
Rest 15.00 (lunch) and a la carte 21.50/39.45 ♀ – **26 rm** ★65.00/95.00 – ★★95.00/105.00, 2 suites.
◆ 17C coaching inn with charm and character. The comfortable bar has large leather armchairs. Well-kept pretty bedrooms with smart bathrooms. Striking beamed dining room.

DORKING *Surrey* 504 T 30 – *pop. 16 071.*

18 *Betchworth Park, Reigate Rd ☎ (01306) 882052.*
London 26 – Brighton 39 – Guildford 12 – Worthing 33.

Burford Bridge, Box Hill, RH5 6BX, North : 1 ½ m. on A 24 ☎ (0870) 4008283, *generalburfordbridge@macdonald-hotels.co.uk, Fax (01306) 880386*, heated, – P – 300. AE VISA
Rest 17.95/28.50 and a la carte ♀ – **57 rm** ★120.00/150.00 – ★★130.00/160.00.
◆ Wordsworth and Sheridan frequented this part 16C hotel. Well run, high quality feel throughout. Antique paintings in public areas, embossed wallpaper in bedrooms. The dining room has a smart, well kept air.

at Abinger Common *Southwest : 4½ m. by A 25 – ✉ Dorking.*

The Stephan Langton Inn, Friday Street, RH5 6JR, East : 1 ¼ m. by Friday Street Rd taking first turn on the right before duck pond ☎ (01306) 730775, – 🚭 P. MC VISA
closed 25 December, 1 week January, Sunday dinner and Monday – **Rest** a la carte 19.00/24.00 ♀.
◆ Hidden away in the Surrey countryside, a busy, friendly local favourite named after 13C Archbishop of Canterbury. Satisfying, locally sourced country cooking and real ales.

DORRIDGE *W. Mids.* 503 504 O 26 – ✉ *Birmingham.*
London 109 – Birmingham 11 – Warwick 11.

The Forest with rm, 25 Station Approach, B93 8JA, ☎ (01564) 772120, *info@forest-hotel.com, Fax (01564) 732680,* – 🚭, rest, P. – 100. MC AE VISA
closed 25 December – **Rest** *(closed Sunday dinner)* a la carte 19.20/31.40 ♀ – 7.50 – **12 rm** ★87.50/92.50 – ★★97.50.
◆ Attractive red-brick and timber former pub with a busy ambience. Food is its backbone: modern classics served in stylish bar and restaurant. Cool, modern bedrooms.

Look out for red symbols, indicating particularly pleasant establishments.

DORRINGTON *Shrops.* 502 503 L 26 – *see Shrewsbury.*

DOUGLAS *Isle of Man* 502 G 21 – *see Man (Isle of).*

DOVER *Kent* 504 Y 30 *Great Britain G. – pop. 34 087.*
See : *Castle★★ AC* Y.
Env. : *White Cliffs★★, Langdon Cliffs, NE : 1 m. on A 2* Z *and A 258.*
to France (Calais) (P & O Stena Line) frequent services daily (1 h 15 mn) – to France (Calais) (SeaFrance S.A.) frequent services daily (1 h 30 mn) – to France (Calais) (Hoverspeed Ltd) frequent services daily (55 mn) – to France (Boulogne) (SpeedFerries) 3-5 daily (50 mn).
The Old Town Gaol, Biggin ☎ (01304) 205108, tic@doveruk.com.
London 76 – Brighton 84.

Plan opposite

Premier Travel Inn, Marine Court, Marine Parade, CT16 1LW, ☎ (0870) 9906516, *Fax (0870) 9906517,* – |‡|, 🚭 rm, rest, ♿ P. MC AE VISA. Y a
Rest (grill rest.) – **100 rm** ★52.95 – ★★52.95.
◆ Recently built lodge on the seafront, with half the rooms having sea views. Well-equipped modern bedrooms, all with work stations. Dining room specialises in grills.

East Lee without rest., 108 Maison Dieu Rd, CT16 1RT, ☎ (01304) 210176, *elgh@eclipse.co.uk, Fax (01304) 206705* – 🚭 P. MC VISA. Y o
closed 24-26 December – **4 rm** ★35.00/40.00 – ★★50.00/58.00.
◆ Tile hung, mid-terraced Victorian residence. Thoughtfully restored with attractive breakfast room and antique pine furnished bedrooms. A totally non-smoking establishment.

Number One without rest., 1 Castle St, CT16 1QH, ☎ (01304) 202007, *res@number1guesthouse.co.uk, Fax (01304) 214078,* – . MC VISA. Y c
4 rm ★30.00/35.00 – ★★50.00/56.00.
◆ Peach painted Georgian townhouse with traditional guesthouse appeal. Breakfast offered in bedrooms: these are compact, and cosy with a cottagey feel.

at St Margaret's at Cliffe *Northeast : 4 m. by A 258* – Z – ✉ *Dover.*

Wallett's Court, West Cliffe, CT15 6EW, Northwest : ¾ m. on Dover rd ☎ (01304) 852424, *wc@wallettscourt.com, Fax (01304) 853430,* , , , , , – 🚭 P. MC AE VISA.
closed 24-27 December – **Rest** – (see ***The Restaurant*** below) – **17 rm** ★99.00 – ★★119.00/159.00.
◆ With origins dating back to the Doomsday Book, a wealth of Jacobean features remain in this relaxed country house. Most characterful rooms in main house; luxurious spa rooms.

The Restaurant (at Wallett's Court H.), West Cliffe, CT15 6EW, Northwest : ¾ m. on Dover rd ☎ (01304) 852424, *Fax (01304) 853430,* – 🚭 P. MC AE VISA
closed 24-27 December and lunch Monday and Saturday – **Rest** 19.50/35.00 ♀.
◆ Local produce dominates the imaginative, monthly changing, seasonal menu. Dine by candlelight in the beamed restaurant after drinks are taken by the open fire.

DOVER

Bench St	Y	3
Biggin St	Y	4
Cannon St	Y	5
Castle St	Y	6
Charlton Green	Y	7
Crabble Hill	Z	9
Eaton Rd	Z	10
High St	Y	
King St	Y	13
Ladywell Park St	Y	15
London Rd	Y	17
Pencester Rd	Y	
Priory Rd	Y	18
Priory St	Y	19
Queen St	Y	20
Sandwich Rd	Z	21
Tower St	Z	24
Worthington St	Y	25

The sun's out – let's eat al fresco! Look for a terrace:

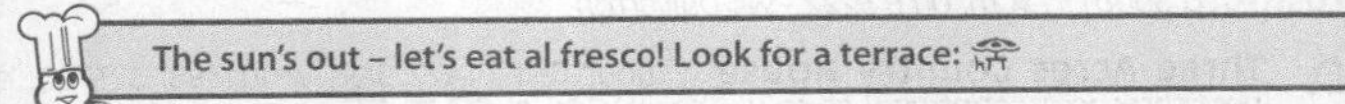

DOWNHOLME *N. Yorks.* 502 O 20 – *see Richmond.*

DOWNTON *Hants.* 503 504 P 31 – *see Lymington.*

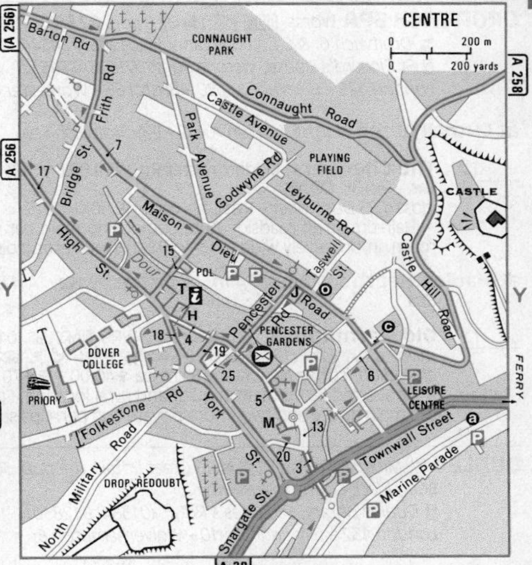

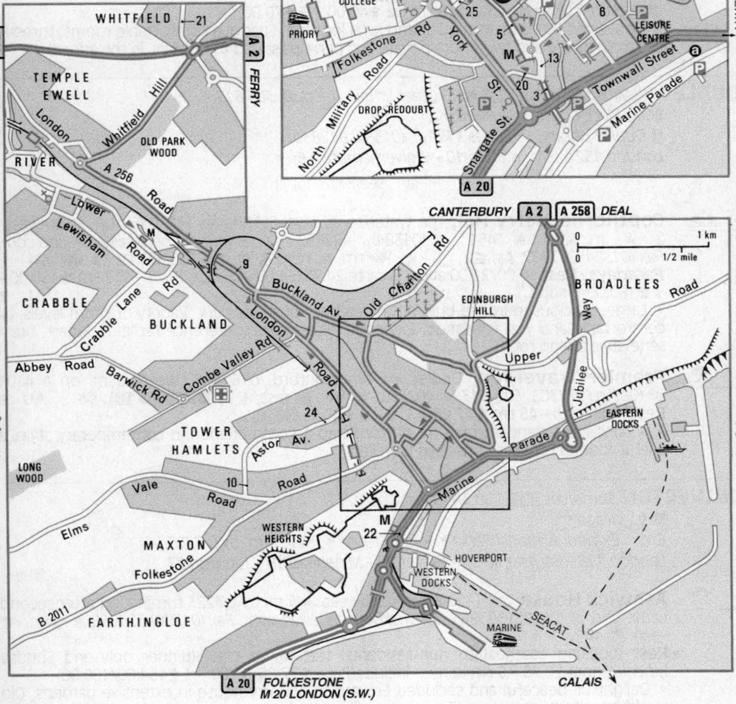

DRIFT *Cornwall – see Penzance.*

DROITWICH SPA *Worcs.* 503 504 *N 27 – pop. 22 585.*
Droitwich G. & C.C., Ford Lane ℘ (01905) 774344.
St Richard's House, Victoria Sq ℘ (01905) 774312.
London 129 – Birmingham 20 – Bristol 66 – Worcester 6.

at Cutnall Green *North : 3 m. on A 442 – ✉ Droitwich Spa.*

The Chequers, Kidderminster Rd, WR9 0PJ, ℘ (01299) 851292, *Fax (01299) 851744*, – P. VISA
closed 25 December – **Rest** a la carte 18.50/24.50 ♀.
• Half-timbered roadside pub, comprising main bar with beams and fire or cosy garden room. Impressively wide range of highly interesting dishes, firmly traditional or modern.

at Hadley Heath *Southwest : 4 m. by Ombersley Way, A 4133 and Ladywood rd – ✉ Droitwich Spa.*

Old Farmhouse without rest., WR9 0AR, ℘ (01905) 620837, *lambe@ombersley.demon.co.uk, Fax (01905) 621722*, – P.
closed Christmas-New Year – **5 rm** ☕ ★40.00 – ★★70.00.
• Converted farmhouse in quiet and rural location. Spacious comfortable rooms, three in the main house and two, more private and perhaps suited to families, in the annex.

DUDLEY *W. Mids.* 502 503 504 N 26 *Great Britain G. – pop. 304 615.*
See : *Black Country Museum*★.
Dudley Library, St James's Rd ℘ (01384) 812830.
London 132 – Birmingham 10 – Wolverhampton 6.

Plan : see Birmingham p. 4

Copthorne Merry Hill, The Waterfront, Level St, Brierley Hill, DY5 1UR, Southwest : 2 ¼ m. by A 461 ℘ (01384) 482882, *reservations.merryhill@mill-cop.com, Fax (01384) 263282*, , – , rm, rest, P – 500. AE VISA.
Faradays : **Rest** 16.00/21.00 and a la carte 24.75/34.00 **s.** ♀ – ☕ 15.75 – **137 rm** ★150.00 – ★★160.00, 1 suite. AU z
• Large, spacious, purpose-built hotel in a busy business park. Variety of room levels, all comfortable and well furnished. Extensive leisure and conference facilities. Smart, brasserie-style dining room.

Premier Travel Inn, Dudley Rd, Kingswinford, DY6 8WT, West : 3 m. on A 4101 ℘ (08701) 977303, *Fax (01384) 402736* – , rest, P. AE VISA. AU e
Rest (grill rest.) – **45 rm** ★47.95/47.95 – ★★50.95/50.95.
• A consistent standard of trim, simply fitted accommodation in contemporary style; a useful address for cost-conscious travellers.

DULVERTON *Somerset* 503 J 30 *The West Country G.*
See : *Village*★.
Env. : *Exmoor National Park*★★ *– Tarr Steps*★★, *NW : 6 m. by B 3223.*
London 198 – Barnstaple 27 – Exeter 26 – Minehead 18 – Taunton 27.

Ashwick House , TA22 9QD, Northwest : 4 ¼ m. by B 3223 turning left after second cattle grid ℘ (01398) 323868, *ashwickhouse@talk21.com, Fax (01398) 323868*, ←, , – P.
Rest (booking essential to non-residents) (set menu only) (dinner only and Sunday lunch)/dinner 22.75 – **6 rm** (dinner included) ☕ ★77.00/95.00 – ★★134.00/160.00.
• Delightful, peaceful and secluded Edwardian country house in extensive gardens. Old world hospitality writ large. Traditionally furnished, airy rooms with thoughtful touches. Home-cooked meals; personalised menus presented as scrolls.

at Brushford *South : 1¾ m. on B 3222 – ✉ Dulverton.*

Three Acres Country House without rest., TA22 9AR, ℘ (01398) 323730, *enquiries@threeacrescountryhouse.co.uk*, – P. AE VISA
6 rm ☕ ★50.00/55.00 – ★★100.00.
• Keenly run 20C guesthouse that's more impressive in than out: super-comfy bedrooms are the strong point. There's an airy lounge, cosy bar and breakfasts are locally sourced.

DUNHAMPTON *Worcs. – see Ombersley.*

DUNSLEY *N. Yorks. – see Whitby.*

DUNSTABLE *Beds.* 504 S 28 *Great Britain G. – pop. 50 775.*

Env. : *Whipsnade Wild Animal Park★.*

Tilsworth, Dunstable Rd ☎ (01525) 210721.

The Library, Vernon Pl ☎ (01582) 471012.

London 40 – Bedford 24 – Luton 4.5 – Northampton 35.

Premier Travel Inn, 350 Luton Rd, LU5 4LL, Northeast : 1 ¾ m. on A 505 ☎ (0870) 1977083, *Fax (01582) 664114* – rest, P. MC AE VISA
Rest (grill rest.) – **42 rm** ★47.95/47.95 – ★★50.95/50.95.
◆ Economical hotel with well proportioned modern bedrooms, suitable for business and family stopovers. Convenient for Woburn Safari Park, Whipsnade Zoo and Luton airport.

DUNSTER *Somerset* 503 J 30.

London 185 – Minehead 3 – Taunton 23.

Exmoor House without rest., 12 West St, TA24 6SN, ☎ (01643) 821268, *stay@exmoorhousehotel.co.uk, Fax (01643) 821268,* – . MC VISA.
early February-early November – **6 rm** ★35.00/40.00 – ★★65.00.
◆ Georgian terraced house with pink exterior, enhanced by colourful window boxes. Spacious, comfy lounge and welcoming breakfast room. Chintz rooms with pleasing extra touches.

Dollons House without rest., Church St, TA24 6SH, ☎ (01643) 821880, *jmott@onetel.com* – P. MC VISA.
closed 24-26 December – **3 rm** ★37.50 – ★★55.00.
◆ Grade II listed guesthouse in centre of attractive village. Entrance via busy gift shop to homely lounge cum breakfast room. Cottagey rooms: two have views of Dunster Castle.

DURHAM *Durham* 501 502 P 19 *Great Britain G. – pop. 42 939.*

See : *City★★★ - Cathedral★★★ (Nave★★★, Chapel of the Nine Altars★★★, Sanctuary Knocker★)* B *– Oriental Museum★★ AC (at Durham University by A 167)* B *– City and Riverside (Prebends' Bridge ≤★★★* A *, Framwellgate Bridge ≤★★* B*) – Monastic Buildings (Cathedral Treasury★, Central Tower≤★)* B *– Castle★ (Norman chapel★) AC* B.

Exc. : *Hartlepool Historic Quay★, SE : 14 m. by A 181, A 19 and A 179.*

Mount Oswald, South Rd ☎ (0191) 386 7527.

2 Millennium Pl ☎ (0191) 384 3720.

London 267 – Leeds 77 – Middlesbrough 23 – Newcastle upon Tyne 20 – Sunderland 12.

Plan on next page

Durham Marriott H. Royal County, Old Elvet, DH1 3JN, ☎ (0191) 386 6821, *durham.royal@marriotthotels.co.uk, Fax (0191) 386 0704,* – P – 120. MC AE VISA B a
County : Rest (dinner only) a la carte 30.00/46.50 ♀ – ***Cruz :*** Rest a la carte 22.00/30.00 s. ♀ – **146 rm** ★135.00/145.00 – ★★155.00/175.00, 4 suites.
◆ Scene of miners' rallies in the 50s and 60s. The quality of accommodation at this town centre hotel is of a comfortable, refined, modern standard. Good leisure facilities. County has elegant décor and linen settings. Bright, relaxed Cruz brasserie.

Ramside Hall, Carrville, DH1 1TD, Northeast : 3 m. on A 690 ☎ (0191) 386 5282, *mail@ramsidehallhotel.co.uk, Fax (0191) 386 0399,* 18, 9, – P – 400. MC AE VISA
The Restaurant : Rest a la carte 15.80/32.00 ♀ – **78 rm** ★125.00 – ★★165.00, 2 suites.
◆ Large, stately home with castellated appearance. Various lounge and bar areas are spacious, as are the bedrooms. Well geared to large conferences and banqueting. Restaurant has attractive garden outlook.

Farnley Tower without rest., The Avenue, DH1 4DX, ☎ (0191) 375 0011, *enquiries@farnleytower.freeservenet.co.uk, Fax (0191) 383 9694,* – P. MC VISA A c
13 rm ★55.00/65.00 – ★★80.00/90.00.
◆ Spacious Victorian house in quiet residential area close to city centre. Neat and tidy breakfast room. Modern, airy, well-equipped bedrooms with a good degree of comfort.

Premier Travel Inn, Broomside Park, Belmont Industrial Estate, DH1 1GG, Northeast : 1 ¾ m. by A 690 on Dragonville rd ☎ (0191) 370 6500, *Fax (0191) 370 6501* – rm, rest, P. MC AE VISA.
Rest (grill rest.) – **40 rm** ★52.95 – ★★52.95.
◆ A consistent standard of trim, simply fitted accommodation in contemporary style; a useful address for cost-conscious travellers. Adjacent grill restaurant. Handy for A1.

Cathedral View Town House without rest., 212 Lower Gilesgate, DH1 1QN, ☎ (0191) 386 9566, *cathedralview@hotmail.com,* – . MC VISA. B n
6 rm ★60.00/80.00 – ★★70.00/80.00.
◆ Alluring Georgian townhouse with terraced garden in older part of the city near the centre. Attractive breakfast room with good views. Spacious, individually named rooms.

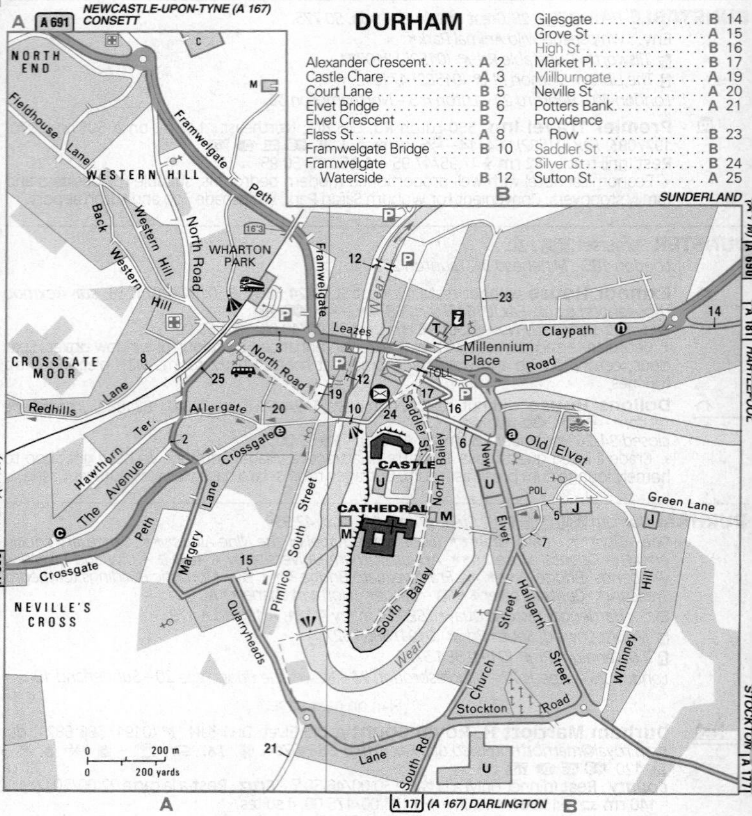

DURHAM

NEWCASTLE-UPON-TYNE (A 167) CONSETT – A 691

Street	Square	No.
Alexander Crescent	A	2
Castle Chare	A	3
Court Lane	B	5
Elvet Bridge	B	6
Elvet Crescent	B	7
Flass St	A	8
Framwelgate Bridge	B	10
Framwelgate Waterside	B	12
Gilesgate	B	14
Grove St	A	15
High St	B	16
Market Pl.	B	17
Millburngate	A	19
Neville St	A	20
Potters Bank	A	21
Providence Row	B	23
Saddler St.	B	
Silver St.	B	24
Sutton St.	A	25

SUNDERLAND A 690 – HARTLEPOOL A 181 – STOCKTON A 177 – CROOK, (A 167) A 690 – A 177 (A 167) DARLINGTON

Castle View without rest., 4 Crossgate, DH1 4PS, ✆ (0191) 386 8852, *castle-view@hotmail.com* – ⇎. MC Ⓓ VISA. ⚮ A e
closed Christmas and New Year – **6 rm** ☕ ✝45.00/75.00 – ✝✝75.00.
◆ Attractive Georgian townhouse off steep cobbled hill, reputedly once the vicarage to adjacent church. Breakfast on terrace in summer. Individually furnished bedrooms.

Bistro 21, Aykley Heads House, Aykley Heads, DH1 5TS, Northwest : 1½ m. by A 691 and B 6532 ✆ (0191) 384 4354, *Fax (0191) 384 1149,* 斋 – ⇎ P. MC AE Ⓓ VISA
closed Sunday and Bank Holidays – **Rest** 15.50 (lunch) and a la carte 23.50/34.50 ♀.
◆ Part 17C villa with an interior modelled on a simple, Mediterranean style. Good modern British food, with some rustic tone, served in a beamed room or an enclosed courtyard.

at Shincliffe *Southeast : 2 m. on A 177 – B – ✉ Durham.*

Bracken, Shincliffe, DH1 2PD, on A 177 ✆ (0191) 386 2966, *r.whitley.brackenhol@amserve.com, Fax (0191) 384 5423* – ⇎ ♿ P. MC VISA. ⚮
Rest *(closed Sunday)* (residents only) (dinner only) a la carte 11.50/24.00 **s.** ♀ – **13 rm** ☕ ✝50.00/65.00 – ✝✝120.00.
◆ Just outside the city and with good access, lying just off busy main road. The family owned hotel is in a much extended building. Compact bedrooms with modern furnishings.

If breakfast is included the ☕ symbol appears after the number of rooms.

DUXFORD *Cambs.* 504 U 27 – *pop. 1 836* – ✉ *Cambridge.*
London 50 – Cambridge 11 – Colchester 45 – Peterborough 45.

Duxford Lodge, Ickleton Rd, CB2 4RT, ☎ (01223) 836444, *admin@duxfordlodgehotel.co.uk, Fax (01223) 832271,* – P – 30. VISA
closed 25 December-January – ***Le Paradis :*** **Rest** *(closed Saturday lunch)* 18.00/30.00 and a la carte 35.00/45.00 – **15 rm** 85.00/100.00 – 120.00/140.00.
◆ Large, smart, redbrick building set in an acre of garden in a quiet village. Public areas and bedrooms, which are tidy and well proportioned, have co-ordinated chintz décor. Themed dining room overlooks garden.

EAGLESCLIFFE *Stockton-on-Tees* 502 P 20 – *see Stockton-on-Tees.*

EARLS COLNE *Essex* 504 W 28 *Great Britain G.* – *pop. 3 504* – ✉ *Colchester.*
Exc. : *Colchester - Castle and Museum★, E : 11 m. by A 1124 and A 12.*
London 53 – Cambridge 37 – Colchester 11.

de Vere Arms, 53 High St, CO6 2PB, ☎ (01787) 223353, *info@deverearms.com, Fax (01787) 223365* – P. VISA.
Rest *(closed Saturday lunch)* 19.50/23.00 and a la carte 19.50/35.00 **s.** – 7.50 – **9 rm** 80.00/125.00 – 95.00/175.00.
◆ High Street hotel. Comfortable lounge bar with deep sofas and modern artwork. Well-appointed individually-styled bedrooms, three in annexe. Dining room with slate floor, red walls, beams and elegant tableware. Assured modern British cooking.

Carved Angel, Upper Holt St, CO6 2PG, ☎ (01787) 222330, *info@carvedangel.com, Fax (01787) 220013,* – P. VISA.
closed 26 December – **Rest** 12.95 lunch and a la carte 17.95/25.00.
◆ Traditional 15C inn with pleasant conservatory and terrace. Very stylish interior typified by sage green painted walls. Pleasing mixture of traditional and modern dishes.

Do not confuse X with ✿! X defines comfort, while stars are awarded for the best cuisine, across all categories of comfort.

EARSHAM *Suffolk* 504 Y 26 – *see Bungay.*

EASINGTON *Bucks.*
London 54 – Aylesbury 13 – Oxford 18.

Mole & Chicken with rm, The Terrace, HP18 9EY, ☎ (01844) 208387, *Fax (01844) 208250* – rm, P. VISA.
closed Christmas – **Rest** (booking essential) a la carte 20.00/25.00 – **5 rm** 50.00 – 65.00.
◆ Friendly pub with country style character and décor. Regularly changing menu of international modern dishes. Bedrooms in adjoining cottages have rural feel and good views.

EASINGWOLD *N. Yorks.* 502 Q 21 – *pop. 3 975* – ✉ *York.*
Stillington Rd ☎ (01347) 821486.
Chapel Lane ☎ (01347) 821530.
London 217 – Leeds 38 – Middlesbrough 37 – York 14.

Old Vicarage without rest., Market Pl, YO61 3AL, ☎ (01347) 821015, *kirman@oldvic-easingwold.freeserve.co.uk, Fax (01347) 823465,* – P.
closed December-January – **4 rm** 55.00 – 80.00.
◆ Spacious, part Georgian country house with walled rose garden and adjacent croquet lawn. Immaculately kept throughout with fine period antiques in the elegant sitting room.

at Crayke *East : 2 m. on Helmsley Rd* – ✉ *York.*

The Durham Ox with rm, Westway, YO61 4TE, ☎ (01347) 821506, *enquiries@thedurhamox.com, Fax (01347) 823326,* – rest, P 16. VISA
closed 25 December – **Rest** (booking essential) a la carte 15.00/32.50 – **8 rm** 60.00/80.00 – 120.00.
◆ Open fires, finest English oak bar panelling and exposed beams create a great country pub atmosphere. Hearty dishes from local ingredients. Well-kept rooms.

ENGLAND

at Alne *Southwest : 4½ m. by A 19 – ✉ Easingwold.*

Aldwark Manor, YO61 1UF, Southwest : 3 ½ m. by Aldwark Bridge rd on Aldwark rd ℘ (01347) 838146, *aldwark@marstonhotels.com, Fax (01347) 838867,* – 240. VISA.
Rest (dinner only and Sunday lunch)/dinner a la carte 25.50/33.50 ♀ – **54 rm** ☐ ✶129.00 – ✶✶166.00, 1 suite.
◆ Part Victorian manor house surrounded by parkland and golf course. Contemporary styling in some rooms and a country house feel in those in the original house. Classic formal dining.

EASTBOURNE *E. Sussex* 504 U 31 *Great Britain G. – pop. 106 562.*
See : *Seafront*★.
Env. : *Beachy Head*★★★, *SW : 3 m. by B 2103 Z.*
Royal Eastbourne, Paradise Drive ℘ (01323) 729738 Z – Eastbourne Downs, East Dean Rd ℘ (01323) 720827 – Eastbourne Golfing Park, Lottbridge Drove ℘ (01323) 520400.
Cornfield Rd ℘ (01323) 411400, tic@eastbourne.gov.uk.
London 68 – Brighton 25 – Dover 61 – Maidstone 49.

Plan opposite

Grand, King Edward's Parade, BN21 4EQ, ℘ (01323) 412345, *reservations@grandeastbourne.co.uk, Fax (01323) 412233,* heated, – rest, rest, – 300. VISA Z x
Garden Restaurant **:** **Rest** a la carte 31.50/44.50 **s.** ♀ – (see also ***Mirabelle*** below) – **128 rm** ☐ ✶135.00 – ✶✶165.00, 24 suites.
◆ Huge, pillared lobby with ornate plasterwork sets the tone of this opulently refurbished, Victorian hotel in prime seafront location. High levels of comfort throughout. Garden Restaurant exudes a light, comfy atmosphere.

Lansdowne, King Edward's Parade, BN21 4EE, ℘ (01323) 725174, *reception@lansdowne-hotel.co.uk, Fax (01323) 739721,* – – 80. VISA Z z
closed 2-12 January – **Rest** (bar lunch Monday-Saturday)/dinner 21.95 and a la carte 26.45/28.00 **s.** ♀ – **101 rm** ☐ ✶45.00/140.00 – ✶✶120.00/165.00.
◆ Traditional seaside hotel in the same family since 1912. Bedrooms are a mix of décor, either traditional or modern, some with sea views. Dining room has classic feel.

Cherry Tree without rest., 15 Silverdale Rd, BN20 7AJ, ℘ (01323) 722406, *lynda@cherrytree-eastbourne.co.uk, Fax (01323) 648838* – . VISA. Z u
9 rm ☐ ✶30.00/60.00 – ✶✶60.00/90.00.
◆ Comfy guesthouse in semi-detached redbrick building, in quiet residential area near the seafront. Interior of traditional standard and spotlessly kept. A non smoking house.

Brayscroft, 13 South Cliff Ave, BN20 7AH, ℘ (01323) 647005, *brayscroft@hotmail.com* – . VISA. Z n
Rest (by arrangement) 14.00 – **6** rm ☐ ✶33.00/45.00 – ✶✶66.00/70.00.
◆ Immaculately kept with individual style, antiques, original local art and comfy furnishings throughout. Well run by charming owners. Dining room overlooks a smart terrace.

XXXX **Mirabelle** (at Grand H.), King Edward's Parade, BN21 4EQ, ℘ (01323) 435066, *reservations@grandeastbourne.co.uk, Fax (01323) 412233* – . VISA Z x
closed 1-14 January, Sunday and Monday – **Rest** (booking essential) 19.00/55.00 and dinner a la carte 29.50/46.50 **s.** ♀.
◆ Elegant, comfortable restaurant with a seasonally changing menu of original dishes. A bar lounge in the basement and wine list of impressive names.

at Jevington *Northwest : 6 m. by A 259 – Z – on Jevington Rd – ✉ Polegate.*

XX **Hungry Monk,** The Street, BN26 5QF, ℘ (01323) 482178, *Fax (01323) 483989* – 16. VISA
closed 24-25 December – **Rest** (booking essential) (dinner only and Sunday lunch)/dinner 29.95 ♀.
◆ Part 17C Elizabethan cottages with garden. Welcoming, relaxed atmosphere; antique chairs and log fires add to the charm. Menu offers good and hearty, traditional fare.

at Wilmington *Northwest : 6½ m. by A 22 on A 27 – Y – ✉ Eastbourne.*

Crossways, Lewes Rd, BN26 5SG, ℘ (01323) 482455, *stay@crosswayshotel.co.uk, Fax (01323) 487811,* – . VISA.
closed 24 December-24 January – **Rest** *(closed Sunday-Monday)* (dinner only) 34.95 – **7 rm** ☐ ✶62.00/95.00 – ✶✶110.00.
◆ Pretty, detached country house with well tended garden. Linen covered tables in cosy dining room. Cuisine acknowledges the classics with locally sourced, seasonal dishes.

EASTBOURNE

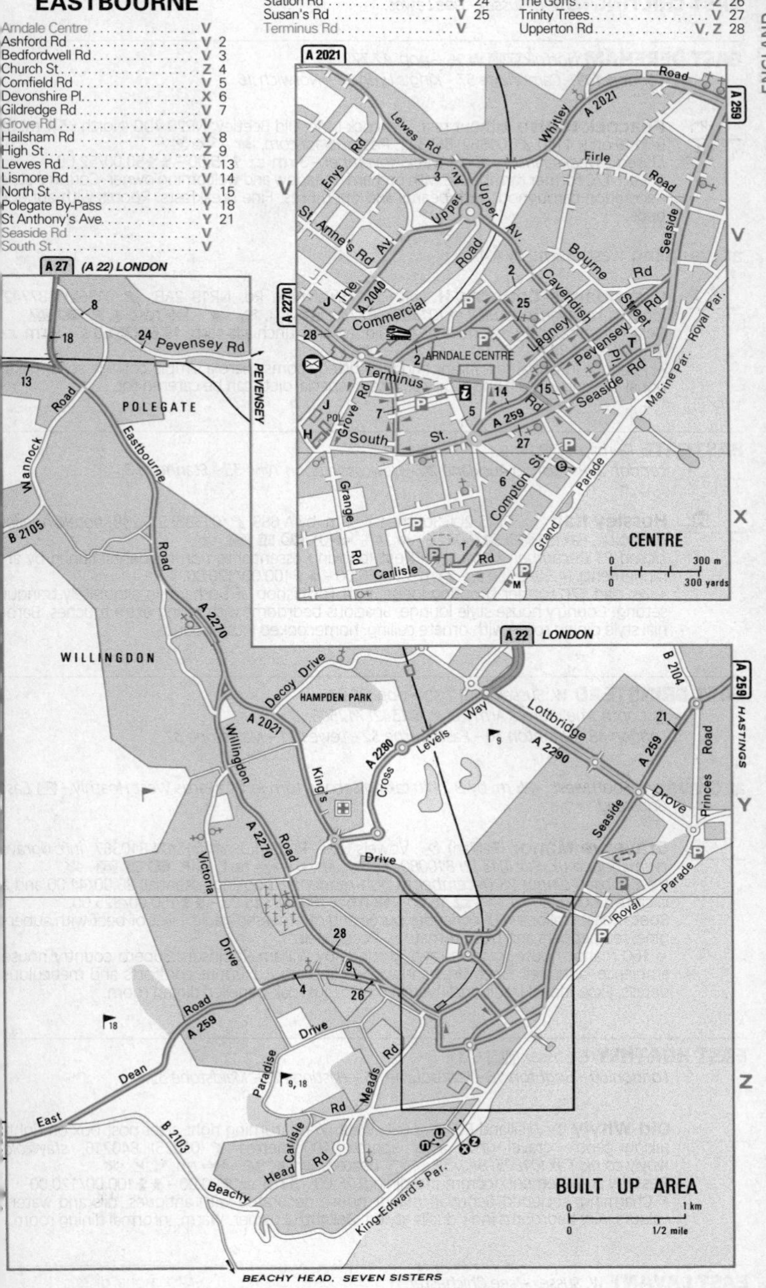

A 2021
A 27
(A 22) LONDON
A 2270
A 259
Lewes Rd
Whitley Road
Firle Road
Enys Rd
Upper Av.
St. Anne's Rd
The Av.
A 2040
Commercial Road
Bourne Rd
Cavendish Pl.
Seaside
Lagney Street
Pevensey Rd
Seaside Rd
Royal Par.
Marine Par.
ARNDALE CENTRE
Terminus
Grove Rd
POL
South St.
Grange Rd
Carlisle Rd
Compton St.
Grand Parade
CENTRE
300 m
300 yards
V
X
Pevensey Rd
PEVENSEY
POLEGATE
Wannock Road
Eastbourne Road
B 2105
WILLINGDON
A 22 LONDON
Decoy Drive
HAMPDEN PARK
A 2021
Willingdon Road
A 2280
Levels Way
Lottbridge Drove
A 2290
B 2104
HASTINGS
Princes Road
Cross Drive
King's Road
Victoria Drive
A 2270
Seaside
Royal Parade
Y
Road
Drive
Paradise Drive
Meads Rd
Dean
East
B 2103
Carlisle Rd
Head
Beachy
King-Edward's Par.
BUILT UP AREA
1 km
1/2 mile
Z
BEACHY HEAD. SEVEN SISTERS

EAST CHILTINGTON *E. Sussex – see Lewes.*

EAST DEREHAM *Norfolk* 504 *W 25 – pop. 17 779.*
London 109 – Cambridge 57 – King's Lynn 27 – Norwich 16.

Peacock House without rest., Peacock Lane, Old Beetley, NR20 4DG, North : 3½ m. by B 1146 on B 1110 ☎ (01362) 860371, *PeackH@aol.com,* – P
closed 2 weeks January and 1 week November – **3 rm** ☐ ★35.00 – ★★50.00/52.00.
◆ Part 17C former farmhouse with orchard, meadow and welcoming owner. Country-style decoration throughout with beams and open fires. Fine breakfasts. Rooms with antique beds.

at Wendling *West : 5½ m. by A 47.*

Greenbanks Country H. with rm, Swaffham Rd, NR19 2AB, ☎ (01362) 687742, *jenny@greenbanks.co.uk, Fax (01362) 687760,* , , , – rest, P. MC VISA
Rest (lunch booking essential) 23.00 (dinner) and lunch a la carte 19.60/25.60 **s.** – **9 rm** ☐ ★65.00 – ★★88.00/108.00.
◆ Friendly, informal restaurant and pine fitted rooms share a simple cottage style. Traditional cooking is fresh and locally sourced - special diets can be catered for.

EASTGATE *Durham* 502 *N 19.*
London 288 – Bishop Auckland 20 – Newcastle upon Tyne 35 – Stanhope 3.

Horsley Hall , DL13 2LJ, Southeast : 1 m. by A 689 ☎ (01388) 517239, *hotel@horsleyhall.co.uk, Fax (01388) 517608,* ←, , – P. MC AE VISA.
closed 23 December-2 January – **Rest** (booking essential to non-residents) (lunch by arrangement) 14.50/23.50 **s.** – **7 rm** ☐ ★65.00 – ★★100.00/120.00.
◆ Ivy-clad 17C former shooting lodge, built for Bishop of Durham, in exquisitely tranquil setting. Country house style lounge. Spacious bedrooms with telling extra touches. Baronial style dining room with ornate ceiling: homecooked local produce.

EAST GRINSTEAD *W. Sussex* 504 *T 30 – pop. 26 222.*
18 *Copthorne, Borers Arm Rd ☎ (01342) 712508.*
London 48 – Brighton 30 – Eastbourne 32 – Lewes 21 – Maidstone 37.

at Gravetye *Southwest : 4½ m. by B 2110 taking second turn left towards West Hoathly – ✉ East Grinstead.*

Gravetye Manor (Raffan) , Vowels Lane, RH19 4LJ, ☎ (01342) 810567, *info@gravetyemanor.co.uk, Fax (01342) 810080,* ←, , , – rest, P. MC AE VISA.
Rest *(closed dinner 25 December to non-residents)* (booking essential) 28.00/41.00 and a la carte 37.00/52.00 **s.** – ☐ 16.00 – **18 rm** ★100.00/325.00 – ★★150.00/325.00.
Spec. Roast scallops with coriander purée and caramelised garlic. Fillet of beef with aubergine, red peppers and plum tomatoes. Peach Melba.
◆ 16C manor house; gardens and grounds by William Robinson. Superb country house ambience: antiques, open fires and wood panelling. Luxurious comforts and meticulous details. Exceptional traditional food in marvellous, oak-panelled dining room.

EAST HOATHLY *E. Sussex* 504 *U 31.*
London 60 – Brighton 16 – Eastbourne 13 – Hastings 25 – Maidstone 32.

Old Whyly , Halland Rd, BN8 6EL, West : ½ m., turning right after post box on right, taking centre gravel drive after approx. 400 metres ☎ (01825) 840216, *stay@oldwhyly.co.uk, Fax (01825) 840738,* ←, heated, , , – rm, P.
Rest (by arrangement) (communal dining) 25.00 – **3 rm** ☐ ★80.00 – ★★100.00/120.00.
◆ Charming, secluded Georgian manor house decorated with antiques, oils and watercolours. Airy bedrooms individually styled. Delightful owner. Warm, informal dining room.

EAST LAVANT *W. Sussex – see Chichester.*

EASTLEIGH *Hants.* 503 P 31 – *pop. 52 894.*
Fleming Park, Magpie Lane ☎ (023) 8061 2797.
Southampton (Eastleigh) Airport : ☎ (0870) 0400009.
London 74 – Southampton 4 – Winchester 8.

Premier Travel Inn, Leigh Rd, SO50 9YX, West : ½ m. on A 335 ☎ (023) 8065 0541, *Fax (023) 8065 0531* – rm, P. VISA
Rest (grill rest.) – **60 rm** 50.95 – 50.95.
◆ Sizeable, modern bedrooms, good for business and family stopovers, designed for practicality and price. Convenient for Southampton airport and family attractions.

EASTLING *Kent* 504 W 30 – *see Faversham.*

EAST MERSEA *Essex.*
London 72 – Colchester 13 – Ipswich 29.

Mersea Vineyard without rest., Rewsalls Lane, CO5 8SX, ☎ (01206) 385900, *accommodation@merseawine.com, Fax (01206) 383600,* P
closed 25-26 December – **3** rm 40.00 – 60.00.
◆ Serious working vineyard producing about 15,000 bottles a year. Sunny courtyard; family style breakfast room. Well priced. Carefully co-ordinated rooms have vineyard views.

EASTON *Devon* 503 I 31 – *see Chagford.*

EASTON *Hants. – see Winchester.*

EASTON *Somerset – see Wells.*

EAST WITTERING *W. Sussex* 504 R 31 – *pop. 5 172* – ✉ *Chichester.*
London 74 – Brighton 37 – Portsmouth 25 – Southampton 36.

Clifford's Cottage, Bracklesham Lane, Bracklesham Bay, PO20 8JA, East : 1 m. by B 2179 on B 2198 ☎ (01243) 670250 – P. VISA
closed 2 weeks autumn, 1 week spring, Wednesday in winter, Monday, Tuesday and Sunday dinner – **Rest** (dinner only and Sunday lunch)/dinner 21.00 and a la carte 24.40/31.15.
◆ A well established, bustling restaurant with friendly service in a characterful part 17C cottage. Traditional menu using seasonal produce. Classic, rich puddings are popular.

EAST WITTON *N. Yorks.* 502 O 21 – ✉ *Leyburn.*
London 238 – Leeds 45 – Middlesbrough 30 – York 39.

Blue Lion with rm, DL8 4SN, ☎ (01969) 624273, *bluelion@breathemail.net, Fax (10969) 624189,* – P. VISA
Rest *(closed lunch 25 December)* (booking essential) a la carte 24.45/32.65 – **12 rm** 59.00 – 99.00.
◆ Characterful, rustic feel throughout: flagstone floors, log fires, antiques and curios. Good value, traditional bar food. Extensive wine list and hand-pumped ales.

ECCLESTON *Lancs.* 502 L 23 – *pop. 4 708 (inc. Heskin).*
London 219 – Birmingham 103 – Liverpool 29 – Preston 11.

Parr Hall Farm without rest., Parr Lane, PR7 5SL, ☎ (01257) 451917, *parrhall@talk21.com, Fax (01257) 453749,* – P. VISA.
12 rm 30.00 – 50.00.
◆ Part 18C former farmhouse with neat lawned gardens in small, pleasant town. Warmly decorated breakfast room with pine dressers. Cosy bedrooms with flowery fabrics.

Undecided between two equivalent establishments?
Within each category, establishments are classified in our order of preference.

EDENBRIDGE *Kent* 504 U 30 *Great Britain G. – pop. 7 196.*
Env. : *Hever Castle★ AC, E : 2½ m. – Chartwell★ AC, N : 3 m. by B 2026.*
18, 18, 9 *Edenbridge G & C.C., Crouch House Rd ☎ (01732) 867381.*
London 35 – Brighton 36 – Maidstone 29.

Haxted Mill, Haxted Rd, TN8 6PU, West : 2 ¼ m. on Haxted Rd ☎ (01732) 862914, *david@haxtedmill.co.uk,* – P. MC VISA
closed 22 December-13 January, Sunday dinner and Monday (except bank holidays) – **Rest** 22.95/27.95 and a la carte 28.90/41.90 ♀.
◆ Converted 17C clapboard stables located next to the watermill with large terrace overlooking the river Eden. Seasonally changing menu with emphasis on seafood in the summer.

at Four Elms *Northeast : 2½ m. on B 2027 – ✉ Edenbridge.*

Oak House Barn without rest., Mapleton Rd, TN8 6PL, Northwest : 1 m. off B 269 ☎ (01732) 700725, *christinaking01@aol.com,* – P.
closed December - 30 January – **3 rm** ★45.00 – ★★60.00.
◆ Converted part 16C barn located close to Chartwell in a quiet setting. Rooms are simply decorated and guest areas include a conservatory lounge next to courtyard garden.

EGHAM *Surrey* 504 S 29 – *pop. 27 666.*
London 29 – Reading 21.

Runnymede, Windsor Rd, TW20 0AG, on A 308 ☎ (01784) 436171, *info@runnymedehotel.com, Fax (01784) 436340,* – rm, P – 350. MC AE VISA.
Left Bank : Rest 22.95 (lunch) and dinner a la carte 25.50/33.25 ♀ – 13.95 – **177 rm** ★205.00/246.00 – ★★305.00, 3 suites.
◆ Riverside setting; indeed some of the comfortable, co-ordinated rooms have river views. Well maintained with smart, modern décor throughout. Good leisure and fitness. Bustling, Mediterranean influenced brasserie-style restaurant.

Great Fosters, Stroude Rd, TW20 9UR, South : 1 ¼ m. by B 388 ☎ (01784) 433822, *enquiries@greatfosters.co.uk, Fax (01784) 472455,* heated, – rest, P – 130. MC AE VISA.
Rest *(closed Saturday lunch)* 25.00/32.50 and a la carte 41.00/46.00 ♀ – 15.50 – **40 rm** ★120.00/210.00 – ★★325.00, 3 suites.
◆ Elizabethan mansion with magnificent gardens. Delightfully original interior has tapestries, oak panelling and antiques. Bedooms in the main house especially notable. Two historic dining rooms: one an ancient tithe barn, the other in 16C French style.

Monsoon, 20 High St, TW20 9DT, ☎ (01784) 432141, *Fax (01784) 432194* – . MC AE VISA
closed 25-26 December – **Rest** - Indian - a la carte 11.75/20.20.
◆ Smart, stylish restaurant that prides itself on immaculate upkeep and personable service. Contemporary artwork enlivens the walls. Freshly cooked, authentic Indian dishes.

ELLAND *W. Yorks.* 502 O 22 – *pop. 14 554 – ✉ Halifax.*
9 *Hammerstones Leach Lane, Hullen Edge ☎ (01422) 372505.*
London 204 – Bradford 12 – Burnley 29 – Leeds 17 – Manchester 30.

La Cachette, 31 Huddersfield Rd, HX5 9AW, ☎ (01422) 378833, *Fax (01422) 327567* – . MC VISA
closed last 2 weeks August, 26 December-4 January, Sunday and Bank Holidays – **Rest** a la carte 16.95/29.40 **s.** ♀.
◆ A busy, bustling brasserie-style restaurant with sprinkling of French panache. Menu of eclectically blended interpretations served in the dining room or well-stocked wine bar.

ELLESMERE PORT *Mersey.* 502 503 L 24 – *pop. 66 265.*
London 211 – Birkenhead 9 – Chester 9 – Liverpool 12 – Manchester 44.

Holiday Inn Ellesmere Port Cheshire Oaks, Centre Island, Waterways, Lower Mersey St, CH65 2AL, Northeast : 1 ½ m. by A 5032 (M 53 junction 9) ☎ (0151) 356 8111, *sales@hiellesmereport.com, Fax (0151) 356 8444,* – rm, P – 250. MC AE VISA
closed 24-26 December – ***The Locks :*** Rest *(closed Sunday lunch)* 16.95 (dinner) and a la carte 21.00/35.00 – 11.95 – **83 rm** ★112.00 – ★★122.00/150.00.
◆ Purpose-built hotel on marina beside boat museum. Uniform styling in carefully designed, modern rooms, all with waterway views. Convenient for land and air transport links. Bustling, split-level restaurant.

ELSTED *W. Sussex* 504 R 31 – *see Midhurst.*

ELSTOW *Beds.* 504 S 27 – *see Bedford.*

ELTERWATER *Cumbria – see Ambleside.*

ELY *Cambs.* 504 U 26 *Great Britain G. – pop. 13 954.*
See : Cathedral★★ AC.
Exc. : *Wicken Fen★, SE : 9 m. by A 10 and A 1123.*
18 107 Cambridge Rd ☎ (01353) 662751.
Oliver Cromwell's House, 29 St Mary's St ☎ (01353) 662062.
London 74 – Cambridge 16 – Norwich 60.

at Little Thetford *South : 2¾ m. off A 10 – ✉ Ely.*

Springfields without rest., CB6 3HJ, North : ½ m. on A 10 ☎ (01353) 663637, *springfields@talk21.com, Fax (01353) 663130,* – P.
closed Christmas and New Year – **3 rm** ★50.00 – ★★65.00.
◆ Spotlessly kept guesthouse and gardens. Breakfast served at communal table. Chintz bedrooms with bric-a-brac and extras such as perfume, fresh flowers and sweets.

at Sutton Gault *West : 8 m. by A 142 off B 1381 – ✉ Ely.*

Anchor Inn with rm, CB6 2BD, ☎ (01353) 778537, *anchorinn@popmail.bta.com, Fax (01353) 776180,* – P. MC AE VISA.
closed 26 December – **Rest** 14.50 (lunch) and a la carte 27.00/33.00 ♀ – **2 rm** ★55.00 – ★★115.00.
◆ Part 17C inn on the western edge of the Isle of Ely. Gas light and open fires. Balanced à la carte menu of traditional British food from the blackboard. Comfortable bedrooms.

The ✿ award is the crème de la crème. This is awarded to restaurants which are really worth travelling miles for!

EMSWORTH *Hants.* 504 R 31 – *pop. 18 139 (inc. Southbourne).*
London 75 – Brighton 37 – Portsmouth 10 – Southampton 22.

36 on the Quay (Farthing) with rm, 47 South St, The Quay, PO10 7EG, ☎ (01243) 375592, *Fax (01243) 375593,* ← – . MC AE VISA
closed 1-24 January, 1 week late October and Christmas – **Rest** *(closed Sunday-Monday)* (booking essential) 22.95/42.95 – **4 rm** ★65.00 – ★★90.00/115.00, 1 suite.
Spec. Seared scallops on pork belly with creamed parsnip. Veal fillet with calf's liver and spinach lasagne, Madeira and truffle sauce. Banana and caramel desserts.
◆ A delightful quayside restaurant with very comfortable, warm pastel interior and chic, sleek bedrooms. Outstanding, innovative modern British food with global influences.

Spencers, 36 North St, PO10 7DG, ☎ (01243) 372744, *Fax (01243) 372744* – . MC AE VISA
closed 25-26 December and Sunday – **Rest** a la carte 19.70/27.70 ♀.
◆ Ground floor brasserie-style with central bar and wood flooring, first floor more formal with brightly coloured dining-booths. Good variety of modern English dishes.

Fat Olives, 30 South St, PO10 7EH, ☎ (01243) 377914, *info@fatolives.co.uk,* – . MC VISA
closed 1 week October, 3 weeks Christmas and New Year, Sunday and Monday – **Rest** (booking essential) 17.50 (lunch) and a la carte 22.70/31.70.
◆ Small terraced house with a welcoming ambience. Simply decorated with wood floor and rough plaster walls. Tasty modern British menu and, yes, fat olives are available!

ENSTONE *Oxon.* 503 504 P 28 – ✉ *Chipping Norton.*
London 73 – Birmingham 48 – Gloucester 32 – Oxford 18.

Swan Lodge without rest., OX7 4NE, on A 44 ☎ (01608) 678736, *Fax (01608) 677963,* – P.
3 rm ★45.00/55.00 – ★★65.00/70.00.
◆ 18C former coaching inn ideally situated for the Cotswolds. Well kept and furnished with antiques and log fires. Sizeable, comfy, mahogany furnished bedrooms.

EPSOM *Surrey* 504 T 30 – *pop. 64 493 (inc. Ewell).*
Longdown Lane South, Epsom Downs (01372) 721666 – , Horton Park C.C., Hook Rd (020) 8393 8400.
London 17 – *Guildford* 16.

Chalk Lane, Chalk Lane, KT18 7BB, Southwest : ½ m. by A 24 and Woodcote Rd (01372) 721179, *smcgregor@chalklanehotel.com, Fax (01372) 727878,* – rm, – 140. MC AE VISA
Rest *(closed Saturday lunch)* 15.00 (lunch) and dinner a la carte 25.00/42.00 – **22 rm** 95.00/150.00 – 180.00.
◆ At the foot of the Epsom Downs and near to the racecourse. Quality furnishings throughout; the neatly kept bedrooms are most comfortable. Smart, modern dining room.

Premier Travel Inn, 2-4 St Margarets Drive, off Dorking Rd, KT18 7LB, Southwest : ½ m. on A 24 (01372) 739786, *Fax (01372) 739761* – rm, rest, – 40. MC AE VISA
Rest (grill rest.) – **58 rm** 59.95/59.95 – 62.95/62.95.
◆ A consistent standard of trim, simply fitted accommodation in contemporary style; a useful address for cost-conscious travellers. Brewers Fayre restaurant adjacent.

Le Raj, 211 Fir Tree Rd, Epsom Downs, KT17 3LB, Southeast : 2 ¼ m. by B 289 and B 284 on B 291 (01737) 371371, *bookings@lerajrestaurant.co.uk, Fax (01737) 211903* – . MC AE VISA
closed 25-26 December – **Rest** - Bangladeshi - a la carte 16.85/30.85.
◆ Original, interesting menu makes good use of fresh ingredients and brings a modern style to traditional Bangladeshi cuisine. Smart, vibrant, contemporary interior décor.

ERMINGTON *Devon.*
London 216 – *Plymouth* 11 – *Salcombe* 15.

Plantation House, PL21 9NS, Southwest : ½ m. on A 3121 (01548) 831100, *enquiries@plantationhousehotel.com,* , – MC AE VISA
Matisse : **Rest** *(closed Monday lunch and Sunday)* (residents only dinner) 16.00/29.00 – **10 rm** 50.00/79.00 – 119.00.
◆ Appealing, converted Georgian rectory with pleasant gardens and terraced seating area. Personally run. Individually styled bedrooms are all named after cocktails. Modish dining room makes good use of local produce.

ERPINGHAM *Norfolk* 504 X 25.
London 123 – *Cromer* 8 – *King's Lynn* 46 – *Norwich* 16.

Saracen's Head with rm, Wolterton, NR11 7LX, West : 1 ½ m. on Itteringham rd (01263) 768909, *saracenshead@wolterton.freeserve.co.uk, Fax (01263) 768993,* , – rm, MC AE VISA
closed 25 December and dinner 26 December (minimum 2 night stay at weekends) – **Rest** (booking essential) a la carte 20.50/27.95 – **6 rm** 45.00 – 80.00/85.00.
◆ Personally run 19C coaching inn with courtyard and walled garden. Log fires, stone floors and bright en suite rooms. Blackboard menu of unpretentious, country dishes.

ESCRICK *N. Yorks.* 502 Q 22 – *see York.*

ESHER *Surrey* 504 S 29 – *pop. 50 344 (inc. Molesey).*
Thames Ditton & Esher, Portsmouth Rd (020) 8398 1551 **BZ** – *Moore Place, Portsmouth Rd (01372) 463533* **BZ** – , *Sandown Park, More Lane (01372) 461234* **BZ**.
London 20 – *Portsmouth* 58.

Plan : see Greater London (South-West) 5

Good Earth, 14-18 High St, KT10 9RT, (01372) 462489, *Fax (01372) 460668* – . MC AE VISA **BZ** e
closed 22-30 December – **Rest** - Chinese - 10.00/35.00 and a la carte 14.60/56.60.
◆ A large Chinese restaurant with a smart, smooth style in décor and service. Well presented menu with much choice including vegetarian sections.

ETWALL *Derby* 502 503 504 P 25 – *see Derby.*

EVERSHOT *Dorset* 503 504 M 31 – ✉ *Dorchester.*

London 149 – Bournemouth 39 – Dorchester 12 – Salisbury 53 – Taunton 30 – Yeovil 10.

Summer Lodge, 9 Fore St, DT2 0JR, ☎ (01935) 482000, *reservations@summerlodgehotel.com, Fax (01935) 482040,* – VISA

Rest 25.00/37.50 and a la carte 25.00/45.00 – **20 rm** (dinner included) 245.00 – 550.00, 4 suites.

◆ Part Georgian dower house in quiet village, in the best tradition of stylish, English country hotels. Extensive refurbishment in 2004: sleek, smart, up-to-date bedrooms. Elegant dining room overlooking walled garden and terrace.

Acorn Inn with rm, 28 Fore St, DT2 0JW, ☎ (01935) 83228, *stay@acorn-inn.co.uk, Fax (01935) 83707* – rm, VISA

Rest a la carte 20.00/30.00 – **9 rm** 75.00 – 140.00.

◆ 16C inn in idyllically archetypal English setting. Characterful main bar with open fire and beamed ceiling. Hearty British cooking with modern touches. Smart, cottagey rooms.

EVESHAM *Worcs.* 503 504 O 27 – *pop. 22 179.*

The Almonry, Abbey Gate ☎ (01386) 446944.

London 99 – Birmingham 30 – Cheltenham 16 – Coventry 32.

Wood Norton Hall, WR11 4WN, Northwest : 2 ¼ m. on A 4538 ☎ (01386) 425780, *info@wnhall.co.uk, Fax (01386) 425781,* – 70. VISA.

Le Duc's : Rest (booking essential) 25.95/30.00 – **44 rm** 100.00/120.00 – 150.00/160.00, 1 suite.

◆ Superbly wood-panelled 19C Vale of Evesham country house. Built by a French duke, and once a BBC training centre. Antiques, original fittings and a library. Large, airy rooms. Formal elements define restaurant.

Evesham, Coopers Lane, WR11 1DA, off Waterside ☎ (01386) 765566, Reservations (Freephone) 0800 716969, *reception@eveshamhotel.com, Fax (01386) 765443,* – VISA

closed 25-26 December – ***Cedar :*** Rest a la carte 24.25/28.50 **s.** – **40 rm** 76.00/90.00 – 122.00/140.00.

◆ Idiosyncratic family run hotel in a quiet location. Guest families well catered for, with jolly japes at every turn. Individual rooms with cottage décor and eclectic themes. Unconventional menus in keeping with hotel style.

at Abbot's Salford *(Warks.) Northeast : 5 m. by A 4184 and B 4088 on Bidford rd* – ✉ *Evesham.*

Salford Hall, WR11 8UT, ☎ (01386) 871300, *reception@salfordhall.co.uk, Fax (01386) 871301,* – 50. VISA.

closed 24-30 December – ***Standford Room :*** Rest *(closed Saturday lunch)* 16.25/29.75 – **33 rm** 60.00/95.00 – 100.00/150.00.

◆ Tudor mansion with early 17C extension and gatehouse. Some very characterful public areas with exposed brickwork conducive to a more formal ambience. Eclectic bedrooms. Oak-panelled, candlelit dining room.

EWEN *Glos.* 503 504 O 28 – *see Cirencester.*

EXETER *Devon* 503 J 31 *The West Country G.* – *pop. 106 772.*

See : *City*★★ – *Cathedral*★★ **Z** – *Royal Albert Memorial Museum*★ **Y**.

Exc. : *Killerton*★★ *AC, NE : 7 m. by B 3181* **V** – *Ottery St Mary*★ *(St Mary's*★*) E : 12 m. by B 3183* – **Y** – *A 30 and B 3174* – *Crediton (Holy Cross Church*★*), NW : 9 m. by A 377.*

Downes Crediton, Hookway ☎ (01363) 773025.

Exeter Airport : ☎ (01392) 367433, E : 5 m. by A 30 **V** – **Terminal :** *St. David's and Central Stations.*

Civic Centre, Paris St ☎ (01392) 265700.

London 201 – Bournemouth 83 – Bristol 83 – Plymouth 46 – Southampton 110.

Plans on following pages

Barcelona, Magdalen St, EX2 4HY, ☎ (01392) 281000, *barcelona@aliashotels.com, Fax (01392) 281001,* rest, – 35. VISA **Z s**

Café Paradiso : Rest a la carte 17.35/31.90 – 11.50 – **46 rm** 85.00/99.00 – 125.00.

◆ Trendy hotel located in Victorian former infirmary. Informal atmosphere. Two fashionable lounges with contemporary furniture. Autumnal coloured rooms with modern facilities. Bright restaurant with very relaxed ambience.

EXETER

Street	Grid	No.	Street	Grid	No.	Street	Grid	No.
Blackboy Rd.	V	8	North St HEAVITREE	X	32	Sweetbriar Lane	VX	52
Buddle Lane	X	9	Old Tiverton Rd	V	35	Trusham Rd	X	53
Butts Rd	X	12	Polsloe Rd	V	39	Union Rd	V	54
East Wonford Hill	X	17	Prince Charles Rd	V	41	Whipton Lane	X	55
Heavitree Rd	VX	20	Prince of Wales Rd	V	42	Wonford Rd	X	57
Hill Lane	V	21	St Andrew's Rd	V	48	Wonford St	X	58
Marsh Barton Rd	X	25	Summer Lane	V	51	Woodwater Lane	X	60
Mount Pleasant Rd	V	29						

Royal Clarence, Cathedral Yard, EX1 1HD, ✆ (01392) 319955, *Fax (01392) 439423* – ⊞ ✂ ✆ – 🏛 120. MC AE ⓓ VISA. ✈ Y z
Rest – (see ***Michael Caines*** below) – ☕ 14.50 – **52 rm** ☆125.00/165.00 – ☆☆125.00/165.00, 1 suite.
◆ Boasts Georgian-style frontage; located on the doorstep of the cathedral. The interior is co-ordinated and comfortably modern, with a classic and uncluttered tone.

The Queens Court, Bystock Terrace, EX4 4HY, ✆ (01392) 272709, *enquiries@queenscourt-hotel.co.uk, Fax (01392) 491390,* – ⊞ ✂ P – 🏛 50. MC AE VISA. ✈ Y n
closed 25-31 December – ***Olive Tree :*** **Rest** - Mediterranean - (closed lunch Sunday and Bank Holidays) 12.95 (lunch) and a la carte 21.00/27.00 ♀ – **18 rm** ☕ ☆77.00/87.00 – ☆☆101.00/111.00.
◆ A town house hotel located close to Central train station. Bright public areas decorated in a clean, modern style. Well-equipped, tidily furnished and co-ordinated bedrooms. Brightly painted, clean-lined restaurant.

St Olaves, Mary Arches St, EX4 3AZ, ✆ (01392) 217736, *info@olaves.co.uk, Fax (01392) 413054,* – ✂ ✆ P. MC VISA. ✈ Z e
Rest 14.95/31.95 ♀ – **13 rm** ☕ ☆85.00/105.00 – ☆☆105.00/115.00, 2 suites.
◆ A Grade II listed and centrally located Georgian town house with walled garden. Décor has a fresh modern feel; some original elements retained. Comfortable bedrooms. Warmly decorated dining room.

St Andrews, 28 Alphington Rd, EX2 8HN, ✆ (01392) 276784, *standrewsexeter@aol.com, Fax (01392) 250249* – ✂ ♿ P. MC AE VISA. ✈ X c
closed 23 December-4 January – **Rest** *(closed Friday-Sunday)* (dinner only) a la carte 16.00/19.50 **s.** – **17 rm** ☕ ☆53.00/60.00 – ☆☆76.00/80.00.
◆ Well established hotel in a converted Victorian family house. Overall ambience is traditionally English with unfussy décor and a well-kept air. Large bay-windowed dining room.

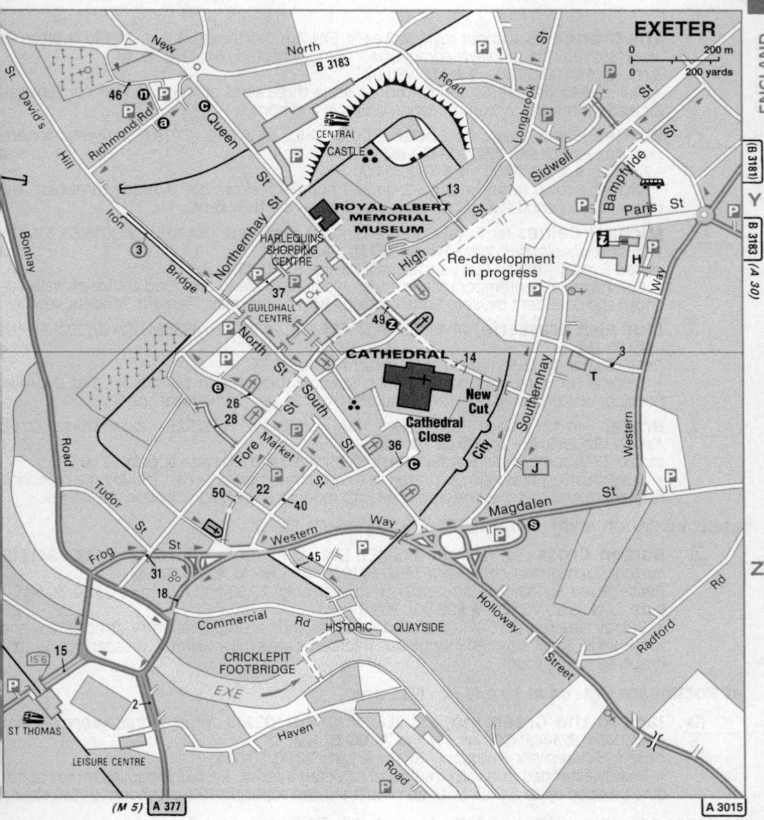

The Edwardian without rest., 30-32 Heavitree Rd, EX1 2LQ, (01392) 276102, *michael@edwardianexeter.co.uk, Fax (01392) 253393* – ✕. MC AE VISA V a
closed 25-26 December – **12 rm** ☕ ★48.00/58.00 – ★★60.00/70.00.
◆ The emphasis is on homely atmosphere and this is reflected in the traditional décor throughout. Private hotel with a welcoming ambience. Some rooms with four-poster beds.

Express by Holiday Inn without rest., Exeter Business Park, EX1 3PE, East : 2 ¾ m. on Honiton Rd (A 30) (junction 29 M 5) (01392) 261000, *Fax (01392) 261061* – ✕ & P – 30. MC AE VISA
122 rm ★79.00 – ★★79.00.
◆ A consistent standard of trim, simply fitted accommodation in contemporary style; a useful address for the business person. Convenient road links.

Silversprings without rest., 12 Richmond Rd, EX4 4JA, (01392) 494040, *reservations@silversprings.co.uk, Fax (01392) 494040*, – ✕. MC VISA Y a
10 rm ☕ ★42.00/65.00 – ★★70.00/90.00.
◆ Cream coloured Georgian terraced house in Roman part of town. Warm and friendly, with immaculately kept public areas. Varied palettes and cathedral views distinguish rooms.

ENGLAND

The Grange without rest., Stoke Hill, EX4 7JH, Northeast : 1¾ m. by Old Tiverton Rd
(01392) 259723, *dudleythegrange@aol.com*, heated, – P.
3 rm ★50.00/55.00 – ★★50.00/55.00.
• Quiet, detached, 1930s country house set in three acres of woodland yet conveniently located for the city. Accommodation is simple and homely.

Raffles without rest., 11 Blackall Rd, EX4 4HD, (01392) 270200, *raffleshtl@btinternet.com, Fax (01392) 270200* – VISA V e
– 7 rm ★40.00/50.00 – ★★62.00/64.00.
• Victorian town house in a quiet area; a homely feel prevails. Antique furnished, and decorated in period style. Comfortable bedrooms are tidily kept.

Michael Caines (at Royal Clarence H.), Cathedral Yard, EX1 1HD, (01392) 310031, *tables@michaelcaines.com* – . AE VISA Y z
closed Sunday – **Rest** 17.00 (lunch) and a la carte 33.40/48.45 ♀.
• Comfortable, contemporary and stylish restaurant. Menu has good choice of well- balanced and confident modern British cooking with a French air. Pleasant, efficient service.

Blue Fish Brasserie, 44-45 Queen St, EX4 3SR, (01392) 493581, *Fax (01392) 219019* – AE VISA Y c
Rest - Seafood - 15.95 (lunch) and a la carte 25.90/33.85.
• Tropical fish tank links bar to bright, spacious brasserie in a Grade II listed Georgian building. Well prepared fish dishes sourced from St. Ives. Some meat specials, too.

Brazz, 10-12 Palace Gate, EX1 1JA, (01392) 252525, *exeter@brazz.co.uk, Fax (01392) 253045* – . AE VISA Z c
closed 25 December and Sunday – **Rest** 12.95/14.95 and a la carte approx 22.00 ♀.
• Busy, bustling brasserie decorated in smart, contemporary style, including a cylindrical fish tank. Menu matches the ambience with modern English and Continental staples.

at Stoke Canon *North : 5 m. by A 377 off A 396 – V – ✉ Exeter.*

Barton Cross , Huxham, EX5 4EJ, East : ½ m. on Huxham rd (01392) 841245, *bartonxhuxham@aol.com, Fax (01392) 841942*, – P. AE VISA
Rest *(closed Sunday to non-residents)* (dinner only) 27.50 and a la carte 23.00/30.50 ♀ – 9 rm ★69.50/72.50 – ★★98.00/120.00.
• Quietly situated part 17C thatched cottages with a simple, country atmosphere and furnishings. Small, beamed lounge bar. Bedrooms are similarly simple yet spacious. Pretty, timbered dining room.

at Rockbeare *East : 6¼ m. by A 30 – V – ✉ Exeter.*

Jack in the Green Inn, EX5 2EE, (01404) 822240, *info@jackinthegreen.uk.com, Fax (01404) 823445*, , – P. AE VISA.
closed 25 December-5 January – **Rest** a la carte 20.00/30.00 ♀.
• Heavily extended pub with traditional carpeted interior. Restaurant spans three rooms: dine on good value dishes, both accomplished and sophisticated, in modern British style.

at Kenton *Southeast : 7 m. by A 3015 – X – on A 379 – ✉ Exeter.*

Rodean, The Triangle, EX6 8LS, (01626) 890195, *excellence@rodeanrestaurant.co.uk, Fax (01626) 891781* – . VISA
closed 1-7 January, 1-14 August, Sunday dinner and Monday – **Rest** (dinner only and Sunday lunch)/dinner a la carte 19.75/34.20 ♀.
• Former 1900s butchers shop in pretty location. Bar area for pre-prandials. Restaurant in two rooms with beams and local photos. Menus employ good use of local ingredients.

at Kennford *South : 5 m. on A 30 off A 38 – X – ✉ Exeter.*

Fairwinds, EX6 7UD, (01392) 832911, *fairwindshotbun@aol.com* – P. VISA.
closed 16 November-31 December – **Rest** (residents only) (dinner only) a la carte 17.40/19.25 **s.** – **6 rm** ★48.00/49.00 – ★★64.00/66.00.
• Simple post-war building providing unfussy, spacious accommodation. A friendly ambience prevails. Compact bar area; wholly non-smoking. Useful road links.

at Doddiscombsleigh *Southwest : 10 m. by B 3212 off B 3193 – X – ✉ Exeter.*

Nobody Inn, EX6 7PS, (01647) 252394, *info@nobodyinn.co.uk, Fax (01647) 252978*, – P. AE VISA
closed 25-26 December and 1 January – **Rest** a la carte 19.40/29.90 ♀.
• Well established, characterful, part 16C pub. Low-beamed ceiling and antique furniture. Traditionally based food; excellent cellar, choice of whiskies and cheeseboard.

Red = Pleasant. Look for the red and symbols.

EXFORD *Somerset* 503 J 30 *The West Country G.*

See : *Church*★.

Env. : *Exmoor National Park*★★.

London 193 – Exeter 41 – Minehead 14 – Taunton 33.

The Crown, TA24 7PP, ✆ (01643) 831554, *info@crownhotelexmoor.co.uk, Fax (01643) 831665,* , – P. MC AE VISA

Rest (bar lunch)/dinner a la carte approx 32.50 – **16 rm** ★65.00 – ★★130.00.

◆ Pretty 17C coaching inn with a delightful rear water garden. Open fires and country prints. Comfy, individualistic rooms, some retaining period features.

EXMOUTH *Devon* 503 J 32 *The West Country G. – pop. 32 972.*

Env. : *A la Ronde*★ *AC, N : 2 m. by B 3180.*

Alexandra Terr ✆ (01395) 222299.

London 210 – Exeter 11.

Barn , Foxholes Hill, EX8 2DF, East : 1 m. via Esplanade and Queens Drive ✆ (01395) 224411, *info@barnhotel.co.uk, Fax (01395) 225445,* ⩽, heated, – P – 100. MC VISA.

closed 21 December-8 January – **Rest** (dinner only and Sunday lunch)/dinner 20.00 **s.** – **11 rm** ★39.00/94.00 – ★★78.00/94.00.

◆ Grade II listed Arts and Crafts house in a peacefully elevated position offering sea views from many bedrooms. Personal and friendly service. Simple dining room looks out to gardens.

The Seafood, 9 Tower St, EX8 1NT, ✆ (01395) 269459, *seafoodexmouth@aol.com* – MC VISA

closed Sunday dinner, Monday and lunch Tuesday and Wednesday – **Rest** - Seafood - (dinner only) a la carte 24.45/28.45.

◆ Cosy, traditional and unpretentious restaurant in the centre of town, run by a husband and wife team. Interestingly varied, flavoursome seafood menu.

EXTON *Devon.*

London 176.5 – Exmouth 4.5 – Topsham 3.

The Puffing Billy, Station Rd, EX3 0PR, ✆ (01392) 877888, *food@thepuffingbilly.com, Fax (01392) 876232,* – P. MC AE VISA.

Rest *(closed Sunday dinner)* a la carte 16.00/36.00 ♀.

◆ Rough textured 16C pub with late 20C extension. Relaxed ambience: comfy leather seating in lounge bar. Menus designed to please all, from informal favourites to fine dining.

FADMOOR *N. Yorks. – see Kirkbymoorside.*

FAIRFORD *Glos.* 503 504 O 28 *Great Britain G. – pop. 2 960.*

See : *Church of St Mary*★ *(Stained glass windows*★★*).*

Exc. : *Cirencester*★ *- Church of St John the Baptist*★ *- Corinium Museum*★ *(Mosaic Pavements*★*), W : 9 m. on A 429, A 435, Spitalgate Lane and Dollar St – Swindon - Great Railway Museum*★ *AC - Railway Village Museum*★ *AC, S : 17 m. on A 419, A 4312, A 4259 and B 4289.*

London 88 – Cirencester 9 – Oxford 29.

XXX **Allium,** 1 London St, Market Pl, GL7 4AH, ✆ (01285) 712200, *restaurant@allium.uk.net, Fax (01285) 712658* – . MC VISA

closed 2 weeks January, 25-26 December, Sunday and Monday – **Rest** 19.50/34.50 ♀.

◆ Mellow Cotswold stone property with large bay window, lounge and bar boasting modern sofas, and elegant dining room, where modern dishes are prepared with skill and care.

FALMOUTH *Cornwall* 503 E 33 *The West Country G. – pop. 21 635.*

See : *Town*★ *– Pendennis Castle*★ *(⩽★★) AC* B.

Env. : *Glendurgan Garden*★★ *AC – Trebah Garden*★*, SW : 4½ m. by Swanpool Rd* A *– Mawnan Parish Church*★ *(⩽★★) S : 4 m. by Swanpool Rd* A *– Cruise along Helford River*★.

Exc. : *Trelissick*★★ *(⩽★★) NW : 13 m. by A 39 and B 3289* A *– Carn Brea (⩽★★) NW : 10 m. by A 393* A *– Gweek (Setting*★*, Seal Sanctuary*★*) SW : 8 m. by A 39 and Treverva rd – Wendron (Poldark Mine*★*) AC, SW : 12½ m. by A 39 –* A *– and A 394.*

18 *Swanpool Rd ✆ (01326) 311262* A – 9 *Budock Vean Hotel, Mawnan Smith ✆ (01326) 252102.*

11 Market Strand, Prince of Wales Pier ✆ (01326) 312300.

London 308 – Penzance 26 – Plymouth 65 – Truro 11.

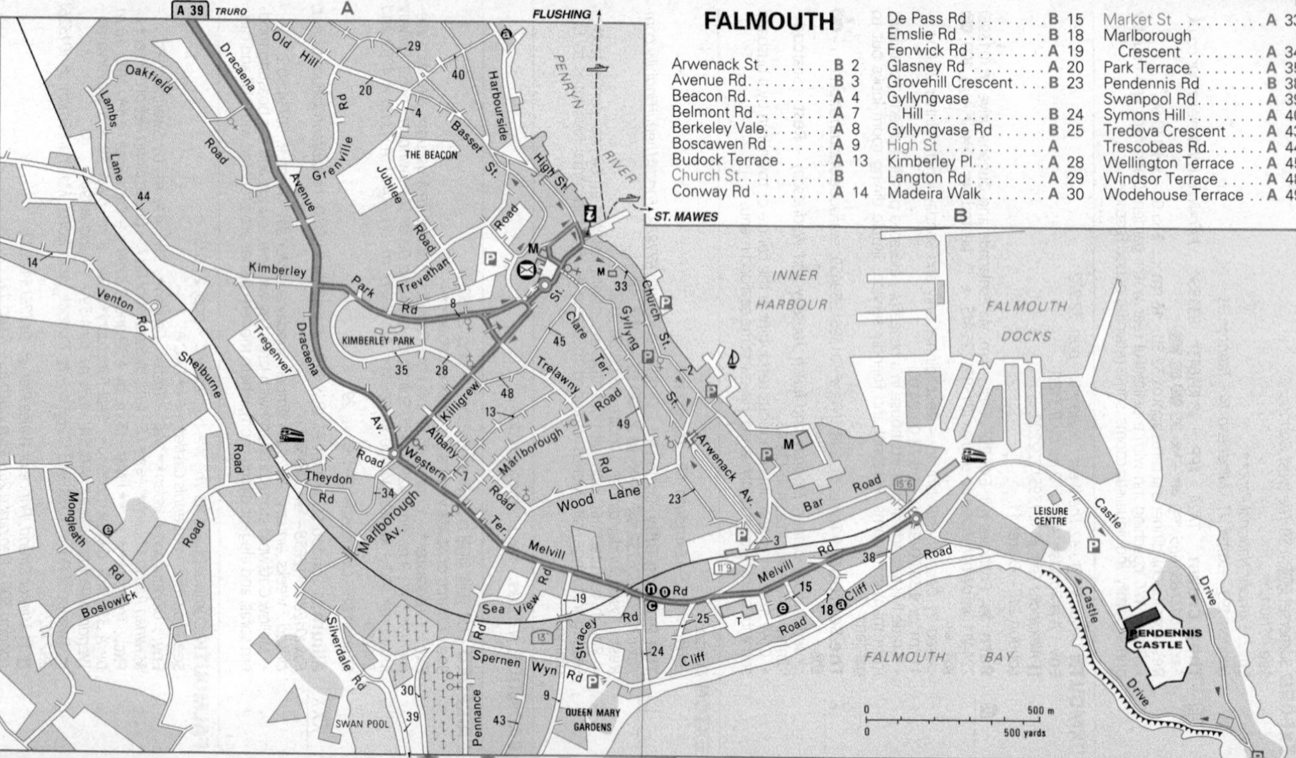
FALMOUTH
Arwenack St . . . . B 2
Avenue Rd . . . . B 3
Beacon Rd . . . . A 4
Belmont Rd . . . . A 7
Berkeley Vale . . . . A 8
Boscawen Rd . . . . A 9
Budock Terrace . . . . . . A 13
Church St . . . . B
Conway Rd . . . . A 14
De Pass Rd . . . . B 15
Emslie Rd . . . . B 18
Fenwick Rd . . . . A 19
Glasney Rd . . . . A 20
Grovehill Crescent . . . . B 23
Gyllyngvase Hill . . . . . . B 24
Gyllyngvase Rd . . . . . . B 25
High St . . . . A
Kimberley Pl . . . . A 28
Langton Rd . . . . A 29
Madeira Walk . . . . A 30
Market St . . . . A 33
Marlborough Crescent . . . A 34
Park Terrace . . . . A 35
Pendennis Rd . . . . B 38
Swanpool Rd . . . . A 39
Symons Hill . . . . A 40
Tredova Crescent . . . . . A 43
Trescobeas Rd . . . . A 44
Wellington Terrace . . . . A 45
Windsor Terrace . . . . . A 48
Wodehouse Terrace . . . . A 49
A 39 TRURO
A
B
FLUSHING
ST. MAWES
PENRYN RIVER
INNER HARBOUR
FALMOUTH DOCKS
FALMOUTH BAY
PENDENNIS CASTLE
LEISURE CENTRE
THE BEACON
KIMBERLEY PARK
QUEEN MARY GARDENS
SWAN POOL
Dracaena Avenue
Old Hill
Oakfield Road
Lambs Lane
Grenville Rd
Jubilee Road
Basset St.
Harbourside
High St.
Trevethan Road
Kimberley Park Rd
Venton Rd
Tregenver Road
Shelburne Road
Killigrew St.
Clare Ter.
Trelawny Road
Gyllyng St.
Church St.
Arwenack Av.
Bar Road
Marlborough Rd
Albany Road
Western Ter.
Wood Lane
Melvill Rd
Theydon Rd
Marlborough Av.
Mongleath Rd
Boslowick Road
Silverdale Rd
Sea View Rd
Stracey Rd
Sperrnen Wyn Rd
Pennance Rd
Cliff Road
Castle Drive
0 500 m
0 500 yards

Greenbank, Harbourside, TR11 2SR, ✆ (01326) 312440, *sales@greenbank-hotel.com, Fax (01326) 211362,* ≤ harbour – |‡| ⚓ ✈ 🚗 P. MC AE ◑ VISA A a
Harbourside **:** **Rest** *(closed Saturday lunch)* 12.95/29.50 **s.** ♀ – **57 rm** ☐ ★65.00/100.00 – ★★105.00/180.00, 1 suite.
◆ Flagstones and sweeping staircase greet your arrival in this ex-17C coaching inn, just as they once did for Florence Nightingale and Kenneth Grahame. Rooms with harbour views. Fine vista of bay from modern restaurant.

Royal Duchy, Cliff Rd, TR11 4NX, ✆ (01326) 313042, *info@royalduchy.com, Fax (01326) 319420,* ≤, ☂, ≘s, ☐, ☐ – |‡| ✈ P. MC AE ◑ VISA. ✈ B a
Restaurant **:** **Rest** 13.95/28.00 **s.** ♀ – **42 rm** ☐ ★70.00/100.00 – ★★105.00/115.00, 1 suite.
◆ Located on clifftop next to beach with stunning views of Pendennis Castle on headland beyond. Indoor swimming pool and leisure area. Comfortable bedrooms, many with sea views. Restaurant has good choice menus promoting local, seasonal dishes.

Penmere Manor ☐, Mongleath Rd, TR11 4PN, ✆ (01326) 211411, *reservations@penmere.co.uk, Fax (01326) 317588,* ☐, ≘s, ☐ heated, ☐, ☐ – ✈ P. – ☐ 60. MC AE ◑ VISA A e
closed 24 December – ***Bolitho's*** **:** **Rest** (bar lunch)/dinner 23.75 and a la carte 23.75/29.15 **s.** ♀ – **37 rm** ☐ ★51.00/83.00 – ★★102.00/130.00.
◆ Victorian whitewashed hotel in five acres of sub-tropical gardens and woodland. Well-kept lounge. Extensive leisure facilities. Immaculate rooms in varying styles. Formal dining in rural setting.

Dolvean without rest., 50 Melvill Rd, TR11 4DQ, ✆ (01326) 313658, *reservations@dolvean.co.uk, Fax (01326) 313995* – ✈ P. MC AE VISA. ✈ B n
closed 24-26 December – **11 rm** ☐ ★40.00/45.00 – ★★80.00/95.00.
◆ Smart cream property with local books and guides in parlour: exceptionally good detail wherever you look. Elegant, neatly laid breakfast room. Bright, well-kept bedrooms.

Prospect House without rest., 1 Church Rd, Penryn, TR10 8DA, Northwest : 2 m. by A 39 on B 3292 ✆ (01326) 373198, *stay@prospecthouse.co.uk,* ☐ – ✈ P. MC VISA
3 rm ☐ ★35.00 – ★★65.00.
◆ Large Georgian guesthouse on Penryn river, set within walled garden, run by welcoming owner. Super breakfasts with local produce in abundance. Individually styled rooms.

Rosemullion without rest., Gyllyngvase Hill, TR11 4DF, ✆ (01326) 314690, *gail@rosemullionhotel.demon.co.uk, Fax (01326) 210098* – ✈ P. ✈ B c
closed Christmas – **3 rm** ☐ ★30.00/40.00 – ★★60.00/64.00.
◆ Spacious, whitewashed Tudor guesthouse. Wood panelled breakfast room and well-kept chintz lounge. Comfortable rooms. Personally run by pleasant owner.

Melvill House without rest., 52 Melvill Rd, TR11 4DQ, ✆ (01326) 316645, *enquiries@melvill-eurobell.co.uk, Fax (01326) 211608* – ✈ P. MC VISA. ✈ B o
7 rm ☐ ★22.00/45.00 – ★★44.00/54.00.
◆ Elegant Victorian house in pink, 200 yards from sandy beach. Guest lounge at the front; newspapers provided at breakfast. Well-kept, simple rooms.

Chelsea House without rest., 2 Emslie Rd, TR11 4BG, ✆ (01326) 212230, *info@chelseahousehotel.com,* ≤, ☐ – ✈. MC VISA. ✈ B e
restricted opening in winter – **8 rm** ☐ ★35.00/45.00 – ★★60.00/75.00.
◆ Large Victorian house in quiet residential area with partial sea-view at front. Neat breakfast room; well-appointed bedrooms, two with their own balconies.

The Three Mackerel, Swanpool Beach, TR11 5BG, South : ¾ m. off Pennance Rd ✆ (01326) 311886, *Fax (01326) 316014,* ≤, ☂ – ✈. MC AE VISA A n
closed 25 December and 1 January – **Rest** a la carte 15.85/27.85 ♀.
◆ Casually informal beachside restaurant with white clapperboard façade. Super terrace or light interior. Seasonal, local ingredients provide the core of modern menus.

at Mylor Bridge *North : 4½ m. by A 39 – A – and B 3292 on Mylor rd –* ✉ *Falmouth.*

Pandora Inn, Restronguet Creek, TR11 5ST, Northeast : 1 m. by Passage Hill off Restronguet Hill ✆ (01326) 372678, *Fax (01326) 378958,* ≤, ☂ – ⚓ P ⇔ 8. MC VISA
Rest a la carte 19.00/25.00 ♀.
◆ A very characterful thatched inn of 13C origins in stunning location next to harbour. Flagstone flooring, low ceilings, exposed beams. Dining room has more formal style.

at Mawnan Smith *Southwest : 5 m. by Trescobeas Rd – A –* ✉ *Falmouth.*

Meudon ☐, TR11 5HT, East : ½ m. by Carwinion Rd ✆ (01326) 250541, *wecare@meudon.co.uk, Fax (01326) 250543,* ☐, ☐ – ✈ rest, P. MC AE ◑ VISA
closed 31 December-31 January – **Rest** 29.50 (dinner) and a la carte 22.50/43.00 – **27 rm** (dinner included) ☐ ★86.00/115.00 – ★★172.00/230.00, 2 suites.
◆ Landscaped sub-tropical gardens are the abiding allure of this elegant hotel. Antiques, oil paintings, log fires and fresh flowers abound. Comfy rooms, many with views. Conservatory restaurant highlighted by fruiting vine.

ENGLAND

Trelawne ⛺, Maenporth, TR11 5HS, East : ¾ m. by Carwinion Rd ☎ (01326) 250226, *info@trelawnehotel.co.uk, Fax (01326) 250909*, ≤, ☐, 🐕 – ⇍ P. MC AE ⊕ VISA
closed 20 December-10 February – ***The Hutches*** **:** Rest (bar lunch)/dinner 23.50/28.50 – **14 rm** (dinner included) ☐ ★58.00/91.00 – ★★106.00/178.00.
• Purpose-built hotel with neat gardens in two acres of grounds. Good views across bay. Traditionally charming open lounge and very well-kept, individually furnished rooms. Smartly dressed dining room with fine bay views.

at Budock Water *West : 2¼ m. by Trescobeas Rd – A – ✉ Falmouth.*

Crill Manor ⛺, TR11 5BL, South : ¾ m. ☎ (01326) 211880, *info@crillmanor.com, Fax (01326) 211229*, 🐕 – ⇍ P. MC VISA. ✂
Rest (dinner only and Sunday lunch)/dinner 24.50 – **14 rm** (dinner included) ☐ ★57.00/94.00 – ★★114.00/138.00.
• Small country house hotel in secluded location near Helford river. Spacious, well-furnished lounge. Individually styled, smartly appointed bedrooms. Smart dining room for meals featuring Cornish produce.

FAREHAM *Hants.* 503 504 Q 31 *Great Britain G. – pop. 56 160 (inc. Portchester).*
Env. : *Portchester castle★ AC, SE : 2½ m. by A 27.*
🅘 *Westbury Manor, West St ☎ (01329) 221342.*
London 77 – Portsmouth 9 – Southampton 13 – Winchester 19.

Solent, Rookery Ave, Whiteley, PO15 7AJ, Northwest : 5 m. by A 27 ☎ (01489) 880000, *solent@shirehotels.co.uk, Fax (01489) 880007*, ⛺, Ⅎ6, ≘s, ☐, ✂ – |‡| ⇍ ▤ ✆ ♿ P – 🏛 250. MC AE ⊕ VISA. ✂
Rest (bar lunch)/dinner a la carte 29.50/34.00 ♀ – **107 rm** ☐ ★91.00/120.00 – ★★132.00/185.00, 4 suites.
• Nestling in acres of woodland. Beamed lounge and gallery; leisure facilities include sauna, solarium and hi-tech gym. Sizeable rooms boast sofa and ample work area. Timbered ceilings add to restaurant's warm and rustic feel.

Lysses House, 51 High St, PO16 7BQ, ☎ (01329) 822622, *lysses@lysses.co.uk, Fax (01329) 822762*, 🐕 – |‡|, ⇍ rest, ✆ P – 🏛 100. MC AE ⊕ VISA. ✂
closed 24 December-2 January – ***The Richmond*** **:** Rest *(closed Saturday lunch, Sunday and Bank Holidays)* 16.00/21.50 and a la carte 24.70/28.70 ♀ – **21 rm** ☐ ★80.00/95.00 – ★★100.00.
• Former private residence built in the Georgian era. Elegant and stylish, in the heart of town. Quiet rear garden. Bright, smart bedrooms, practically appointed. Busy dining room caters for breakfasts to four course dinners.

Premier Travel Inn, Southampton Rd, Park Gate, SO31 6AF, West : 4 m. by A 27 ☎ (01489) 579857, *Fax (01489) 577238* – ⇍ rm, ♿ P. MC AE ⊕ VISA. ✂
Rest (grill rest.) – **40 rm** ★50.95 – ★★50.95.
• Trim, simply fitted accommodation in contemporary style. Family rooms with sofa beds. Popular grill restaurant located on other side of large car park.

Springfield without rest., 67 The Avenue, PO14 1PE, West : 1 m. on A 27 ☎ (01329) 828325, 🐕 – ⇍ P. MC VISA. ✂
6 rm ☐ ★45.00 – ★★55.00.
• Sizeable redbrick guesthouse, both comfortable and well-equipped - quieter rear bedrooms face a pleasant garden. The friendly owner cooks a hearty full breakfast at weekends.

Lauro's brasserie, 8 High St, PO16 7AN, ☎ (01329) 234179, *lauros@ntlworld.com, Fax (01329) 822776* – ⇍ ▤. MC ⊕ VISA
closed 25-26 December, 1 January, Sunday dinner and Monday – **Rest** 11.50/19.50 and a la carte 23.80/30.80 ♀.
• Picture-window façade; long narrow interior with red hued walls and open-plan kitchen. The unpretentious cooking has influences ranging from the Mediterranean to Japan.

FARINGDON *Oxon.* 503 504 P 29.
🅘 *7A Market Pl ☎ (01367) 242191.*
London 81 – Newbury 29 – Oxford 19 – Swindon 12.

The Trout at Tadpole Bridge with rm, Buckland Marsh, SN7 8RF, Northeast : 4½ m. by A 417 off A 420 on Bampton rd ☎ (01367) 870382, *info@troutinn.co.uk*, ⛺, 🐕 – ⇍ rm, ♿ P. MC VISA
closed 25-26 and 31 December, 1 January and last week January – **Rest** *(closed Sunday dinner)* a la carte 18.40/31.40 ♀ – **6 rm** ☐ ★55.00 – ★★80.00.
• Thames-side pub next to pretty bridge. Meat supplied by local farmer; marinated medallions of venison a speciality. Trout caught by local fisherman. Welcoming rooms..

at Littleworth *Northeast : 3 m. by A 417 off A 420 – ✉ Faringdon.*

The Snooty Fox Inn, SN7 8PW, on A 420 ✆ (01367) 240549, – P. MC VISA
Rest a la carte 15.00/25.00.
◆ Modern, cream painted pub on main road with minimalistic style and real fire. Friendly service. Interesting signature dishes range from char-grills to fish and fresh pasta.

FARNBOROUGH *Hants.* 504 R 30 – *pop. 57 147.*
Southwood, Ively Rd ✆ (01252) 548700.
London 41 – Reading 17 – Southampton 44 – Winchester 33.

Falcon, 68 Farnborough Rd, GU14 6TH, South : ¾ m. on A 325 ✆ (01252) 545378, *hotel@falconfarnborough.com, Fax (01252) 522539* – rest, P. MC AE VISA.
Rest *(closed lunch Saturday, Sunday and Bank Holidays)* 19.50 (dinner) and a la carte 19.50/29.00 – **30 rm** ☕ ✝98.00/108.00 – ✝✝112.00.
◆ Purpose-built whitewashed hotel offering traditional comfort. Ideal for business travellers. Rich oak panelling dominates Lobby bar. Neat bedrooms in bright colours. Well-kept, efficiently run dining room.

Premier Travel Inn, Ively Rd, Southwood, GU14 0JP, Southwest : 2 m. by A 325 on A 327 ✆ (01252) 546654, *Fax (01252) 546427* – rm, P. MC AE VISA.
Rest (grill rest.) – **40 rm** ✝49.95/49.95 – ✝✝52.95/52.95.
◆ Simply furnished and brightly decorated bedrooms. Useful address for cost-conscious travellers. Popular with visitors to the world-famous local Air Show.

FARNBOROUGH *Warks.* 503 504 P 27 *Great Britain G.*
Env. : *Upton House*★, *SW : 6 m. on B 4086 and A 422.*
London 83 – Banbury 6 – Birmingham 41.

Inn at Farnborough, OX17 1DZ, ✆ (01295) 690615, *enquiries@innatfarnborough.co.uk, Fax (01295) 690032,* – P. MC AE VISA
Rest 12.95 (lunch) and a la carte 20.00/35.00 ♀.
◆ Solid 17C village centre pub. Inviting rustic interior typified by open fire and stone floor. Tasty dishes: much time and effort is involved in sourcing local ingredients.

FARNHAM *Dorset* 503 N 31 – *see Blandford Forum.*

FARNHAM *Surrey* 504 R 30 – *pop. 36 298.*
Farnham Park (Par Three) ✆ (01252) 715216.
Council Offices, South St ✆ (01252) 715109.
London 45 – Reading 22 – Southampton 39 – Winchester 28.

Bishop's Table, 27 West St, GU9 7DR, ✆ (01252) 710222, *welcome@bishopstable.com, Fax (01252) 733494,* – rest. MC AE VISA.
closed 24 December-4 January – **Rest** *(closed Monday lunch)* 15.00 (lunch) and a la carte 29.45/39.70 – ☕ 12.50 – **15 rm** ✝97.00 – ✝✝107.00/120.00.
◆ Stylish Georgian hotel once owned by the Marquis of Lothian and a former training school for clergy. Take a drink in secluded walled garden. Individually decorated rooms. Original dishes in pastel pink restaurant.

FARNHAM ROYAL *Bucks.* 503 504 S 29.
London 27.5 – Burnham 2 – Windsor 5.5.

The King of Prussia, Blackpond Lane, SL2 3EG, off A 355, by Cherry Tree Rd ✆ (01753) 643006, *info@tkop.co.uk, Fax (01753) 648645,* – P. MC AE VISA
closed Sunday dinner – **Rest** a la carte 28.95/37.40.
◆ TV chef Phil Vickery part owns this charming village pub. Three dining areas - best of all is the barn conversion - for constantly evolving menus full of fresh, local produce.

FARNINGHAM *Kent* 504 U 29.
London 22 – Dartford 7 – Maidstone 20.

Beesfield Farm without rest., Beesfield Lane, DA4 0LA, off A 225 ✆ (01322) 863900, *kim.vingoe@btinternet.com, Fax (01322) 863900,* – P.
closed 14 December-1 February – **3 rm** ☕ ✝65.00/70.00 – ✝✝80.00/90.00.
◆ Peaceful valley setting, with attractive garden. Exudes character: oldest part is 400 year-old Kentish longhouse. Comfy sitting room; bedrooms boast beams and garden outlook.

FAR SAWREY *Cumbria 502 L 20 – see Hawkshead.*

FAVERSHAM *Kent 504 W 30 – pop. 18 222.*

Fleur de Lis Heritage Centre, 13 Preston St (01795) 534542.
London 52 – Dover 26 – Maidstone 21 – Margate 25.

XXX **Read's** (Pitchford) with rm, Macknade Manor, Canterbury Rd, ME13 8XE, East : 1 m. on A 2 (01795) 535344, *enquiries@reads.com, Fax (01795) 591200,* , – rm, P 20. MC AE VISA.
closed 25-26 December, first week January, Sunday and Monday – **Rest** 21.00/45.00 –
6 rm 120.00 – 175.00.
Spec. Terrine of ham hock, prune and apples with walnuts and pickled raisins. Fillet of sea bass with celeriac purée and herb gnocchi. Honey and nougatine parfait.
◆ Georgian house with immaculate grounds and kitchen garden. Relax in bar before indulging in classic dishes making best use of delicious local produce. Very comfortable rooms.

at Dargate *East : 6 m. by A 2 off A 299 – Faversham.*

The Dove, Plum Pudding Lane, ME13 9HB, (01227) 751360, – P. MC VISA
closed Monday and dinner Sunday and Tuesday – **Rest** (booking essential) a la carte 23.50/32.00 s.
◆ Relaxed, well-run village pub: cosy interior of wooden tables, church-pew chairs and black and white photos of old Dargate. Good, locally sourced food, affordably priced.

at Eastling *Southwest : 5 m. by A 2 – Faversham.*

Frith Farm House without rest., Otterden, ME13 0DD, Southwest : 2 m. by Otterden rd on Newnham rd (01795) 890701, *enquiries@frithfarmhouse.co.uk, Fax (01795) 890009,* , – P. MC VISA.
3 rm 45.00 – 75.00.
◆ Lovingly restored Georgian farmhouse in six acres of orchards which enhance the wonderfully relaxed atmosphere. Plush sitting room with fireplace; exquisitely varied rooms.

FAWKHAM GREEN *Kent 504 U 29 – see Brands Hatch.*

FENCE *Blackburn – see Padiham.*

FERNDOWN *Dorset 503 504 O 31 – pop. 25 246.*

Ferndown Forest, Forest Links Rd (01202) 876096.
London 108 – Bournemouth 6 – Dorchester 27 – Salisbury 23.

Premier Travel Inn, Ringwood Rd, Tricketts Cross, BH22 9BB, Northeast : 1 m. on A 347 (01202) 874210, *Fax (01202) 897794* – rm, P. MC AE VISA.
Rest (grill rest.) – **32 rm** 55.95 – 55.95.
◆ Half-timbered lodge featuring well-proportioned modern bedrooms, suitable for business and family stopovers. Thatched Beefeater pub in front.

FERNHURST *W. Sussex 504 R 30.*

London 50 – Brighton 40 – Southampton 46.

King's Arms, Midhurst Rd, GU27 3HA, South : 1 m. on A 286 (01428) 652005, – P. MC VISA
closed 25 December and Sunday dinner – **Rest** a la carte 19.50/24.95 .
◆ Cosy, warm, friendly pub with exposed beams, roaring fire and real ales. Well-priced selection of modern and traditional dishes, with local produce and fresh fish to fore.

FERRENSBY *N. Yorks. – see Knaresborough.*

FINDON *W. Sussex 504 S 31 – pop. 1 720 – Worthing.*

London 49 – Brighton 13 – Southampton 50 – Worthing 4.

Findon Manor, High St, BN14 0TA, off A 24 (01903) 872733, *hotel@findonmanor.com, Fax (01903) 877473,* – rest, P – 40. MC AE VISA.
closed 25-26 December – **Rest** (bar lunch Monday-Saturday)/dinner 27.50 and a la carte 18.00/27.50 s. – **11 rm** 64.00/74.00 – 140.00.
◆ Flint-built former rectory dating from the 16C. Characterful lounge with heavy drapes, real fire and flagstones. Spacious, country house bedrooms. Elegant restaurant opening onto secluded gardens.

LAMSTEAD *Herts.* 504 S 28 – ✉ *St Albans.*
London 32 – Luton 5.

Express by Holiday Inn without rest., London Rd, AL3 8HT, Northeast : 1 m. on A 5 at junction 9 of M 1 ✆ (01582) 841332, *ebhi-flamstead@btconnect.com, Fax (01582) 842486* – ⇔ ♿ P – 🏛 30. MC AE ⓓ VISA. ✻
75 rm ☐ ✝55.00/69.95 – ✝✝55.00/69.95.
◆ Modern, purpose-built lodge on busy M1 junction, sited just along from a Harvester grill restaurant. Informal breakfast area. Clean, well-kept bedrooms.

LEETWOOD *Lancs.* 502 K 22 – *pop. 26 841.*
Fleetwood, Golf House, Princes Way ✆ (01253) 873114.
to Northern Ireland (Larne) (Stena Line).
Old Ferry Office, The Esplanade ✆ (01253) 773953.
London 245 – Blackpool 10 – Lancaster 28 – Manchester 53.

North Euston, The Esplanade, FY7 6BN, ✆ (01253) 876525, *elizabeth.fleetwood@elizabethhotels.co.uk, Fax (01253) 777842,* ≤ Wyre estuary and Lake District hills – |≑| ⇔ ✆ P – 🏛 200. MC AE VISA. ✻
The Restaurant : **Rest** *(closed Saturday lunch)* 12.50/21.95 and dinner a la carte – **53 rm** ☐ ✝59.80/67.00 – ✝✝72.00/92.00.
◆ Impressive crescent-shaped Victorian hotel on fishing port esplanade with views to Lake District. Softly furnished bedrooms, most with sea views. Family run individuality. Restaurant with potted ferns overlooks Irish Sea.

LETCHING *E. Sussex* 504 U 30/31.
London 45 – Brighton 20 – Eastbourne 24 – Maidstone 20.

The Griffin Inn with rm, TN22 3SS, ✆ (01825) 722890, *thegriffininn@hotmail.com, Fax (01825) 722810,* , – ⇔ rm, P. MC AE ⓓ VISA. ✻
closed 25 December and 1 January – **Rest** (meals in bar Sunday dinner) a la carte 20.00/32.00 ♀ – **8 rm** ☐ ✝60.00/80.00 – ✝✝95.00/130.00.
◆ 16C coaching inn; rustic ambience with real fire, stone floor. Generous, traditional cooking. Beamed rooms with four-poster beds, rushmat flooring, hand-painted wall murals.

LITWICK *Beds.* 504 S 27 – *pop. 12 700.*
London 45 – Bedford 13 – Luton 12 – Northampton 28.

Flitwick Manor , Church Rd, MK45 1AE, off Dunstable Rd ✆ (01525) 712242, *flitwick@menzies-hotels.co.uk, Fax (01525) 718753,* ≤, , , – ⇔ P. MC AE ⓓ VISA
Rest 25.00/45.00 – ☐ 19.00 – **17 rm** ✝99.00/195.00 – ✝✝159.00/210.00.
◆ Georgian manor house set in 27 acres. Elegant lounge. Individually decorated rooms: those on ground floor have garden seating areas, others overlook 300-year old cedar tree. Formal restaurant in Georgian house style.

FOLKESTONE *Kent* 504 X 30 *Great Britain G.* – *pop. 45 273.*
See : *The Leas★ (≤★) Z.*
Channel Tunnel : Eurotunnel information and reservations ✆ (08705) 353535.
Harbour St ✆ (01303) 258594, tourism@folkestone.org.uk.
London 76 – Brighton 76 – Dover 8 – Maidstone 33.

Plan on next page

Clifton, The Leas, CT20 2EB, ✆ (01303) 851231, *enquiries@thecliftonhotel.com, Fax (01303) 223949,* ≤, – |≑|, ⇔ rm, ✆ – 🏛 80. MC AE ⓓ VISA. ✻ Z r
Rest 14.50/20.00 and dinner a la carte 20.70/30.40 **s.** – ☐ 9.50 – **80 rm** ✝58.00/72.00 – ✝✝92.00.
◆ Seafront hotel with gardens and views over Channel. Traditional style; bar has sun terrace and flower-boxes. Comfortable bedrooms. Traditionally appointed restaurant.

Relish without rest., 4 Augusta Gardens, CT20 2RR, ✆ (01303) 850952, *Fax (01303) 850958* – ⇔ ✆. MC ⓓ VISA Z n
(2 night stay at weekends) – **10 rm** ☐ ✝55.00/68.00 – ✝✝89.00/130.00.
◆ Large Regency townhouse overlooking private parkland. Stylish black canopy to entrance; modish furnishings. Handy food and drink area at foot of stairs. Light, airy rooms.

Harbourside without rest., 12-14 Wear Bay Rd, CT19 6AT, ✆ (01303) 256528, *joy@harboursidehotel.com, Fax (01303) 241299,* ≤, , – ⇔ ♿. MC AE ⓓ VISA. ✻ X e
16 rm ☐ ✝40.00/60.00 – ✝✝80.00/120.00.
◆ Well-kept hotel with clifftop views over harbour. Relax in garden or luxuriate in hot tub. Several comfortable lounges include music and games rooms. Very individual rooms.

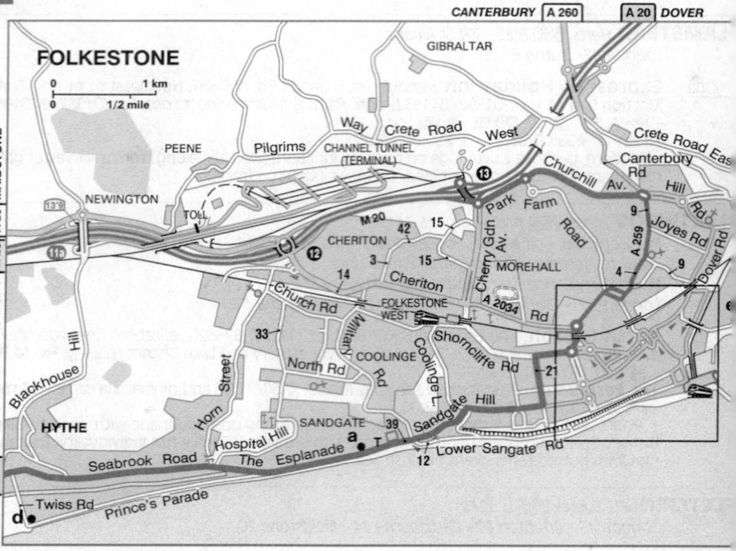

FOLKESTONE

Street	Grid	No.
Ashley Ave	X	3
Black Bull Rd	X, Y	4
Bouverie Pl.	Z	6
Bradstone Rd	Y	8
Canterbury Rd	X	9
Castle Rd	X	12
Cheriton High St.	X	14
Cheriton Pl.	Z	13
Cherry Garden Lane	X	15
Clifton Crescent	Z	16
Clifton Rd.	Z	17
Durlocks (The)	Y	20
Earl's Ave	X	21
Grace Hill	Y	22
Guildhall St	YZ	23
Harbour App. Rd.	Z	25
Harbour St.	Z	24
Langhorne Gardens	Z	27
Manor Rd	Z	28
Marine Terrace	Z	29
Middelburg Sq.	Z	30
North St.	Y	32
Old High St.	YZ	
Pond Hill Rd	X	33
Radnor Bridge Rd.	Y	34
Remembrance (Rd of)	Z	35
Rendezvous St.	Y	37
Ryland Pl.	Y	38
Sandgate High St.	X	39
Sandgate Rd	Z	
Shorncliffe Rd	Y	41
Tilekiln Lane	X	42
Tontine St	Y	
Trinity Gardens	Z	43
Victoria Grove	Y	45
West Terrace	Z	47

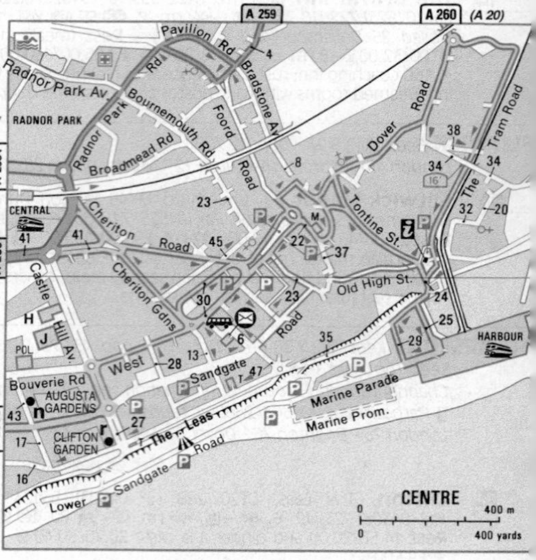

at Sandgate *West : 1¾ m. on A 259 – ✉ Folkestone.*

Sandgate, 8-9 Wellington Terrace, CT20 3DY, ✆ (01303) 220444, *info@sandgatehotel.com, Fax (01303) 220496,* ←, – ⊞ ⋡. MC AE VISA X a
closed 25-26 December – ***Restaurant :*** Rest a la carte 19.50/31.50 – **15 rm** ☕
†50.00/80.00 – ††80.00/85.00.

◆ 19C seafront hotel with smart beige and brown façade. Relaxed, modern boutique style public areas. Bedrooms have a crisp, simple freshness; some boast seaviews and balconies. Distinctively modern restaurant; very pleasant terrace.

FORD *Bucks. Great Britain G.*

Exc. : *Waddesdon Manor★★ AC, NW : 7 m. on A 418, Cuddington Rd, Aylesbury Rd and Cannon's Hill.*
London 43 – Aylesbury 5 – Oxford 20.

Dinton Hermit with rm, Water Lane, HP17 8XH, ☎ (01296) 747473, *dintonhermit@btconnect.com, Fax (01296) 748819,* – ⅔ & P. MO AE VISA
closed 25-26 December – **Rest** *(closed Sunday dinner)* a la carte 20.00/35.00 ♀ – **13 rm** ☐ ★80.00 – ★★125.00.
◆ Charming 17C inn in pretty village; landscaped gardens, roaring fires and beams. Freshly prepared menus using local produce. Mix of rooms in main house, extension and barn.

FORDINGBRIDGE *Hants.* 503 504 O 31 – *pop. 5 755.*

Kings Yard, Salisbury St ☎ (01425) 654560 (summer only).
London 101 – Bournemouth 17 – Salisbury 11 – Southampton 22 – Winchester 30.

XX **The Hour Glass** with rm, Salisbury Rd, SP6 1LX, North : 1 m. on A 338 ☎ (01425) 652348, *hglassrestaurant@aol.com, Fax (01425) 656002* – P. MO AE VISA
closed first 2 weeks January, 25-26 December, Sunday dinner and Monday – **Rest** a la carte 21.65/30.90 ♀ – ☐ 5.00 – **3 rm** ★55.00/65.00 – ★★60.00/75.00.
◆ Thatched cottage restaurant on main Salisbury road. Exposed black beams create a cosy ambience. Eclectic modern menu with a traditional base; carefully sourced local produce.

at Stuckton *Southeast : 1 m. by B 3078 – ✉ Fordingbridge.*

X **Three Lions** with rm, Stuckton Rd, SP6 2HF, ☎ (01425) 652489, *Fax (01425) 656144,* – rm, P. MO VISA
closed last 2 weeks January and first week February – **Rest** *(closed Sunday dinner and Monday)* a la carte 30.75/33.75 ♀ – ☐ 7.50 – **7 rm** ★65.00/95.00 – ★★75.00/115.00.
◆ Personally run former farmhouse. Impressive blackboard menu includes local produce like wild New Forest mushrooms or venison. Bright, cosy rooms with thoughtful extras.

FOREST *Guernsey (Channel Islands)* 503 P 33 and 517 ⑨ ⑩ – *see Channel Islands.*

FOREST ROW *E. Sussex* 504 U 30 – *pop. 3 623.*

18, 18 *Royal Ashdown Forest, Chapel Lane, Forest Row ☎ (01342) 822018.*
London 35 – Brighton 26 – Eastbourne 30 – Maidstone 32.

at Wych Cross *South : 2½ m. on A 22 – ✉ Forest Row.*

Ashdown Park, RH18 5JR, East : ¾ m. on Hartfield rd ☎ (01342) 824988, *reservations@ashdownpark.com, Fax (01342) 826206,* ←, 18, – & P – 150. MO AE VISA
Anderida : **Rest** 23.00/46.00 s. ♀ – **100 rm** ☐ ★135.00/165.00 – ★★230.00, 6 suites.
◆ Part 19C manor in landscaped woodland with antiques, real fires. Former convent. Extensive leisure facilities. Immaculate rooms in two wings boast writing desks, armchairs. Ornate ceiling dominates formal restaurant.

FORTON *Lancs.* 502 M 25 *Great Britain G.* – ✉ *Lancaster.*

Env. : *Lancaster - Castle★, N : 5½ m. by A 6.*
London 236 – Blackpool 18 – Manchester 45.

Bay Horse Inn, LA2 0HR, North : 1¼ m. by A 6 on Quernmore rd ☎ (01524) 791204, *wilkicraig@aol.com* – P. MO AE VISA
closed 25 December, 1 January, Sunday dinner and Monday (except Bank Holidays when closed Tuesday instead) – **Rest** a la carte 20.00/35.00 ♀.
◆ Rurally set inn dating from 18C with open fires, exposed beams and enthusiastic owners. Good selection of real ales. Tasty, well-prepared, home-made dishes.

Good food and accommodation at moderate prices? Look for the Bib symbols: red Bib Gourmand for food, blue Bib Hotel for hotels

FOUR ELMS *Kent* 504 U 30 – *see Edenbridge.*

FOWEY *Cornwall* 503 G 32 *The West Country G.* – *pop. 2 064.*
See : *Town*★★.
Env. : *Gribbin Head*★★ (≤★★) *6 m. rtn on foot* – *Bodinnick* (≤★★) - *Lanteglos Church*★, *E 5 m. by ferry* – *Polruan* (≤★★) *SE : 6 m. by ferry* – *Polkerris*★, *W : 2 m. by A 3082.*
5 South St ✆ *(01726) 833616, info@fowey.co.uk.*
London 277 – *Newquay 24* – *Plymouth 34* – *Truro 22.*

Fowey Hall, Hanson Drive, PL23 1ET, West : ½ m. off A 3082 ✆ (01726) 833866, *fowey@luxuryfamilyhotels.com, Fax (01726) 834100*, ≤, – – P – 40
VISA
Rest (light lunch Monday-Saturday)/dinner 32.50 – **23 rm** (dinner included) ★170.00/210.00 – ★★170.00/210.00, 13 suites.
◆ Imposing 19C country house within walled garden. Two spacious lounges with real fires wicker furnished garden room. Smart, plush rooms. Special facilities for children. Impressive oak-panelled restaurant.

Marina Villa Hotel, 17 The Esplanade, PL23 1HY, ✆ (01726) 833315, *enquiries@themarinahotel.co.uk, Fax (01726) 832779*, ≤ Fowey river and harbour, – . VISA
Rest – (see ***Waterside*** below) – **17 rm** ★100.00/150.00 – ★★144.00/200.00, 1 suite.
◆ Small house in tiny street with splendid views of river and quay. Attractive interior with well-kept lounge, and rooms of varying size with a contemporary, individual feel.

Old Quay House, 28 Fore St, PL23 1AQ, ✆ (01726) 833302, *info@theoldquayhouse.com, Fax (01726) 833668*, ≤, – . VISA.
Rest *(closed lunch in low season)* a la carte 27.00/37.50 – **12 rm** ★120.00 – ★★200.00.
◆ Former Victorian seamen's mission idyllically set on the waterfront. Stylish, contemporary lounge. Rear terrace overlooks the river. Smart, individually decorated bedrooms. Spacious restaurant with wicker and wood furniture, serving modern British dishes.

Waterside (at Marina Villa H.), 17 The Esplanade, PL23 1HY, ✆ (01726) 833315, *Fax (01726) 832779*, ≤ Fowey River and harbour, – . VISA
Rest - Seafood specialities - 25.00/45.00 s.
◆ Smart, comfortable restaurant adding a stylish feel to well-established Georgian hotel. Enjoy lovely river views to the accompaniment of very competent cooking.

FRADDON *Cornwall* 503 F 32 – ✉ *St Columbus Major.*
London 264 – *Exeter 77* – *Newquay 7* – *Penzance 35* – *Plymouth 44* – *Truro 12.*

Premier Travel Inn, Penhale, TR9 6NA, on A 30 (eastbound carriageway) ✆ (01726) 861148, *Fax (01726) 861336* – rm, rest, P. VISA.
Rest (grill rest.) – **40 rm** ★49.95 – ★★49.95.
◆ A consistent standard of trim, simply fitted accommodation. Family rooms with sofa beds. Useful address for cost-conscious travellers, especially surfers for Newquay.

FRAMLINGHAM *Suffolk* 504 Y 27 – *pop. 2 839* – ✉ *Woodbridge.*
London 92 – *Ipswich 19* – *Norwich 42.*

Colston Hall without rest., Badingham, IP13 8LB, ✆ (01728) 638375, *lizjohn@colstonhall.com, Fax (01728) 638084*, , – P. VISA.
6 rm ★40.00 – ★★90.00.
◆ Part Elizabethan farmhouse in rural location with lakes and garden. Simple breakfast room. Comfortable bedrooms with character: plenty of timbers and small sitting areas.

Undecided between two equivalent establishments?
Within each category, establishments are classified in our order of preference.

FRAMPTON MANSELL *Glos. Great Britain G.*
Env. : *Cirencester★ - Corinium Museum★, E : 7 m. by A 419.*
London 106 – Bristol 34 – Gloucester 17.

White Horse, Cirencester Rd, GL6 8HZ, on A 419 ☎ (01285) 760960, – P. VISA
closed 24-26 December, 1 January and Sunday dinner – **Rest** a la carte 21.00/40.00 ♀.
◆ Stone-built public house on main road. Cosy small bar and attractive dining room. Friendly service. Daily menu of classic and modern British dishes with original touches.

FRESHWATER BAY *I.O.W.* 503 504 P 31 – *see Wight (Isle of).*

FRESSINGFIELD *Suffolk* 504 X 26.
London 104 – Ipswich 34 – Lowestoft 27.

XX **The Fox & Goose Inn,** Church Rd, IP21 5PB, ☎ (01379) 586247, *foxandgoose@uk2.net, Fax (01379) 586106* – P. VISA
closed 27-30 December, 10 days mid January and Monday – **Rest** (booking essential) 13.95 (lunch) and a la carte 25.00/32.00 ♀.
◆ Spacious black and white inn with leaded panes. Beams and wooden floor in dining room. Extensive menu of traditional dishes with modern influence; some use of local produce.

Your opinions are important to us:
please write and let us know about your discoveries and experiences – good and bad!

FRISTON *Suffolk – see Aldeburgh.*

FRITHSDEN *Herts. – see Hemel Hempstead.*

FRODSHAM *Ches.* 502 503 L 24.
London 198 – Liverpool 20 – Runcorn 5.5.

Netherton Hall, Chester Rd, WA6 6UL, Southwest : ¾ m. on A 56 ☎ (01928) 732342, *Fax (01928) 739140,* – P. AE VISA.
closed 25-26 December – **Rest** a la carte 25.00/35.00.
◆ Converted Georgian farmhouse with spacious gardens. Homely interior: walls lined with books and curios. Four separate dining areas serving freshly prepared, eclectic menus.

FROGGATT EDGE *Derbs.* 502 503 504 P 24.
London 167 – Bakewell 6 – Sheffield 11.

Chequers Inn with rm, Hope Valley, S32 3ZJ, ☎ (01433) 630231, *info@chequers-froggatt.com, Fax (01433) 631072,* – P. AE VISA.
closed 25 December – **Rest** a la carte 18.50/26.40 ♀ – **5 rm** ★65.00/90.00 – ★★65.00/90.00.
◆ Refurbished 16C Grade II listed building, retaining many period features. Wide-ranging, modern menus enhanced by accomplished cooking. Pleasant, cosy bedrooms.

FROME *Somerset* 503 504 M/N 30.
London 118 – Bristol 24 – Southampton 52 – Swindon 44.

Babington House, Babington, BA11 3RW, Northwest : 6½ m. by A 362 on Vobster rd ☎ (01373) 812266, *enquiries@babingtonhouse.co.uk, Fax (01373) 812112,* , , , , heated, , , , – – P – 45. AE VISA
The Log Room : **Rest** (residents and members only) a la carte 24.00/30.00 ♀ – 12.50 – **23 rm** ★215.00/315.00 – ★★360.00/390.00, 5 suites.
◆ Country house with vivid difference: Georgian exterior; cool, trendy interior. Laidback dining, health club, even a cinema: modern minimalism prevails. Trendy 21C rooms.

XX **The Settle,** 16 Cheap St, off Market Pl, BA11 1BN, ☎ (01373) 465975, *Fax (01373) 465975* – . AE VISA
closed 2 weeks Christmas-New Year and 2 weeks in summer – **Rest** (dinner only Thursday-Saturday) 24.50.
◆ First-floor restaurant above tea shop in town centre. Vivid red and blue linen colour scheme adds panache to compact dining area. Well-prepared dishes using local produce.

FRYERNING *Essex.*
London 33 – Brentwood 6 – Chelmsford 7.

XX **The Woolpack,** Mill Green Rd, CM4 0MS, ✆ (01277) 352189, *info@thewoolpack-fryerring.co.uk, Fax (01277) 356802,* – P. MC AE VISA
closed 2 weeks mid August, 26 December-7 January, Monday, Sunday dinner and lunch Tuesday and Saturday – **Rest** 19.95 and a la carte 31.85/41.85.
◆ 19C inn located in a delightful rural village. Neighbourhood feel prevails with distinctive modish interior full of stylish charm. Accomplished cooking in the modern vein.

FULLER STREET *Essex* – ✉ *Chelmsford.*
London 45 – Cambridge 46 – Colchester 24 – Southend-on-Sea 30.

Square & Compasses, CM3 2BB, ✆ (01245) 361477, – P. MC VISA
closed Sunday dinner and Monday – **Rest** a la carte 17.00/28.00 ♀.
◆ Dining pub converted from timbered cottages. Rustic interior with log fire, wood-burning stove and countryside artefacts. Well-cooked fare utilising local seasonal produce.

FUNTINGTON *W. Sussex* 504 R 31 – *see Chichester.*

Do not confuse X with ✿! X defines comfort, while stars are awarded for the best cuisine, across all categories of comfort.

GALMPTON *Devon* 503 J 32 – ✉ *Brixham.*
London 229 – Plymouth 32 – Torquay 6.

Maypool Park, Maypool, TQ5 0ET, Southwest : 1 m. by Greenway Rd ✆ (01803) 842442, *peacock@maypoolpark.co.uk,* ≤, – P.
Rest (residents only) (dinner only) 25.00 **s.** – **3 rm** ☐ ✝60.00 – ✝✝100.00.
◆ Hotel of converted 19C cottages in heart of estate bought by Agatha Christie in 1938. Secluded, 300 feet above river Dart. Terrace with good views. Country style bedrooms. Restaurant with rural views specialises in local produce.

GALPHAY *N. Yorks. – see Ripon.*

GARFORTH *W. Yorks.* 502 P 22 – *see Leeds.*

GARSTANG *Lancs.* 502 L 22 – *pop. 6 293.*
Discovery Centre, Council Offices, High St ✆ (01995) 602125.
London 233 – Blackpool 13 – Manchester 41.

Garstang Country H. and Golf Club, Bowgreave, PR3 1YE, South : 1 ¼ m. on B 6430 ✆ (01995) 600100, *reception@garstanghotelandgolf.co.uk, Fax (01995) 600950,* 18, – P – 250. MC AE VISA
Rest (bar lunch Monday-Saturday)/dinner 16.50 **s.** ♀ – **32 rm** ☐ ✝60.00 – ✝✝113.00.
◆ Stone-built hotel, privately owned. Rooms overlook golf course and driving range. Golfing breaks throughout year. Uniformly sized rooms with colourful fabrics and drapes. Restaurant with course outlook.

at Bilsborrow *South : 3¾ m. by B 6430 on A 6 – ✉ Preston.*

Guy's Thatched Hamlet, Canalside, St Michaels Rd, PR3 0RS, off A 6 ✆ (01995) 640010, *info@guysthatchedhamlet.com, Fax (01995) 640141,* – rm, P – 70. MC AE VISA
closed 25 December – **Rest** a la carte 13.50/28.00 **s.** ♀ – ☐ 6.00 – **65 rm** ✝48.00 – ✝✝62.50/69.50.
◆ Nestles in small, thatched, whitewashed, themed village by canal. Has its own bowling green and cricket pitch with pavilion. Cosy rooms with pine furniture, floral curtains. Two-floored, wood-beamed restaurant.

Premier Travel Inn, Garstang Rd, PR3 0RN, ✆ (0870) 7001516, *Fax (0870) 7001517* – P. MC AE VISA.
Rest (grill rest.) – **40 rm** ✝46.95/46.95 – ✝✝48.95/48.95.
◆ Neat, modern rooms, spacious and carefully designed, in a modern group-owned lodge. Suitable for business and family stopovers, designed with practicality and price in mind. Family friendly restaurant.

Olde Duncombe House without rest., Garstang Rd, PR3 0RE, ☎ (01995) 640336, *oldedunc@aol.com, Fax (01995) 640336,* – P. MC AE VISA
9 rm ☐ ★39.50 – ★★55.00.
◆ Whitewashed, stonebuilt guesthouse, formerly three cottages dating back 400 years. Simple rooms with free-standing pine furniture. Rear rooms overlook the canal.

GATESHEAD *Tyne and Wear* 501 502 P 19 *Great Britain G. – pop. 78 403.*

Exc. : *Beamish : North of England Open Air Museum★★ AC, SW : 6 m. by A 692 and A 6076* BX.

Ravensworth, Moss Heaps, Wrekenton ☎ (0191) 487 6014 – Heworth, Gingling Gate ☎ (0191) 469 4424 BX.

Tyne Tunnel (toll).

Central Library, Prince Consort Rd ☎ (0191) 477 3478 BX *– Metrocentre, Portcullis, 7 The Arcade ☎ (0191) 460 6345* AX.

London 282 – Durham 16 – Middlesbrough 38 – Newcastle upon Tyne *1 – Sunderland 11.*

Plan : see Newcastle upon Tyne

Hilton Newcastle Gateshead, Bottle Bank, NE8 2AR, ☎ (0191) 490 9700, *Fax (0191) 490 9800,* – – P – 700. MC AE VISA CZ e
Windows on the Tyne : **Rest** *(closed Saturday lunch)* a la carte 22.65/40.90 **s.** – ☐ 15.95 – **251 rm** ★125.00/175.00 – ★★125.00/175.00, 3 suites.
◆ Modern hotel on steep riverbank, with fine views across the Tyne. Well-equipped leisure centre. Extensive conference facilities. Stylish, modern rooms, many with river vistas. Informal, split-level restaurant.

Express by Holiday Inn without rest., Riverside Way, Derwenthaugh, NE16 3BE, ☎ (01207) 541100, *gateshead@premierhotels.co.uk, Fax (0191) 414 6967* – P – 25. MC AE VISA AX a
100 rm ★90.00 – ★★90.00.
◆ Conveniently positioned lodge hotel with economical, modern bedrooms. Competitively priced, purpose-built accommodation that is compact and comfortable.

Premier Travel Inn, Derwent Haugh Rd, Swalwell, NE16 3BL, ☎ (0191) 414 6308, *Fax (0191) 414 5032* – , rest, P. MC AE VISA AX c
Rest (grill rest.) – **40 rm** ★50.95 – ★★50.95.
◆ Well-proportioned modern bedrooms, suitable for business and family stopovers, designed with practicality and price in mind. A useful address for cost-conscious travellers.

McCoys at the Rooftop, 6th Floor, Baltic Centre, South Shore Rd, NE8 3BA, ☎ (0191) 440 4949, *mccoys@balticmill.com, Fax (0191) 440 4950,* ≤ City skyline – . MC AE VISA BX c
closed 25-26 December and 1 January – **Rest** (booking essential) 19.95 (lunch) and a la carte 35.00/40.00 ♀.
◆ Restaurant atop the Baltic Arts Centre; glass walls give fine city views. Stylish modern décor; original cooking to match the inventive art on show elsewhere in the building.

at Low Fell *South : 2 m. on A 167* – BX – ✉ *Gateshead.*

Eslington Villa, 8 Station Rd, NE9 6DR, West : ¾ m. by Belle Vue Bank, turning left at T junction, right at roundabout then taking first turn right ☎ (0191) 487 6017, *eslington villa@freeuk.com, Fax (0191) 420 0667,* – P – 35. MC AE VISA.
closed 25 December – **Rest** – (see ***The Restaurant*** below) – **18 rm** ☐ ★74.50 – ★★84.50.
◆ Well-run, stylish, privately owned hotel 10 minutes' drive from city centre. Nicely furnished lounge bar leads from smart reception. Attractively styled, modern bedrooms.

The Restaurant (at Eslington Villa), 8 Station Rd, NE9 6DR, West : ¾ by Belle Vue Bank, turning left at T junction, right at roundabout then taking first turn right ☎ (0191) 487 6017, *eslingtonvilla@freeuk.com, Fax (0191) 420 0667,* – P. MC AE VISA
closed 25 December, Saturday lunch, Sunday dinner and Bank Holidays – **Rest** 15.50/19.50 and a la carte 21.50/30.00 ♀.
◆ Two separate dining areas, one of which is a conservatory. Both are classically decorated and serve good range of traditionally based dishes with modern twists.

at Whickham *West : 4 m. by A 184, A 1, A 692 on B 6317* – ✉ *Gateshead.*

Gibside, Front St, NE16 4JG, ☎ (0191) 488 9292, *reception@gibside-hotel.co.uk, Fax (0191) 488 8000* – rm, rest, – 150. MC AE VISA AX s
Rest (bar lunch Monday-Saturday)/dinner a la carte 15.95/26.70 **s.** ♀ – ☐ 8.95 – **45 rm** ★62.50/75.00 – ★★72.50/85.00.
◆ Purpose-built hotel in small town near Gateshead with views over Tyne Valley. Set on hill, so its up to date facilities are on different levels. Comfortable, spacious rooms. Pleasant dining room.

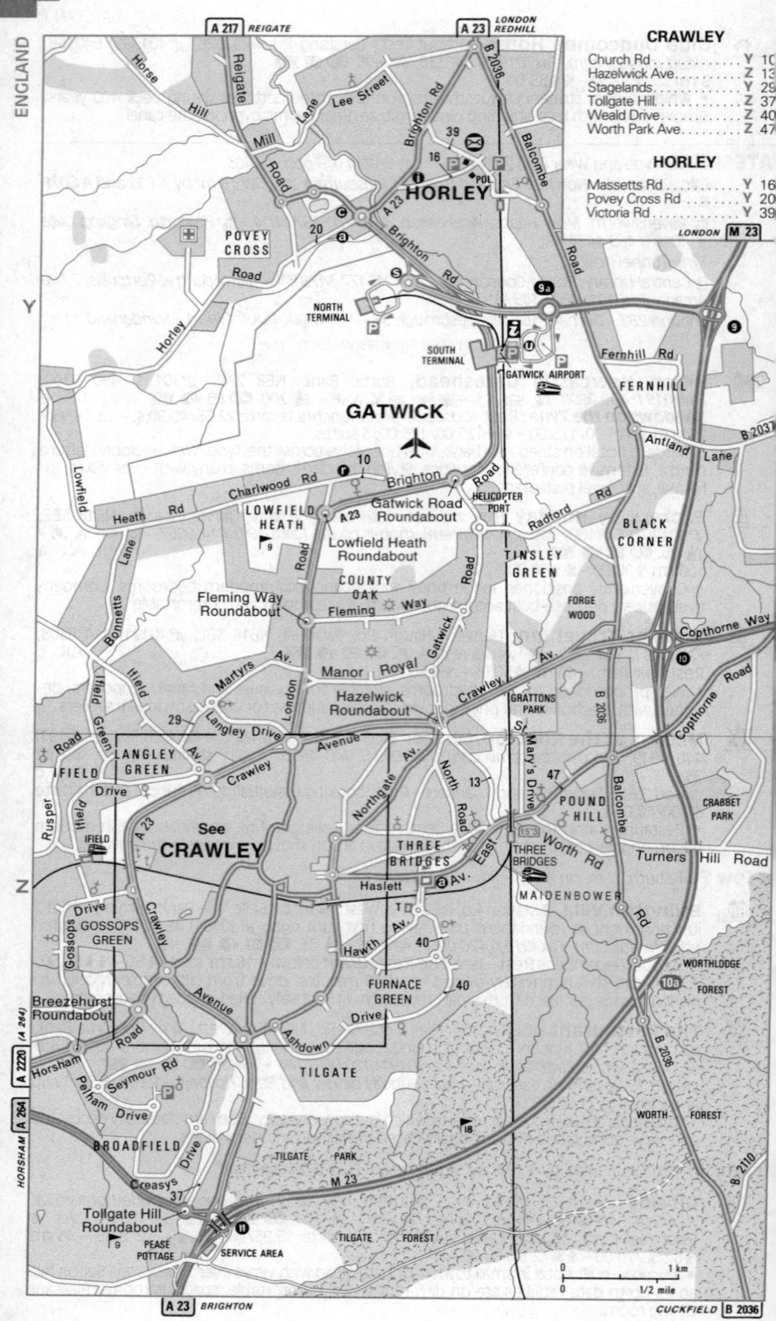
CRAWLEY
Church Rd .... Y 10
Hazelwick Ave .... Z 13
Stagelands .... Y 29
Tollgate Hill .... Z 37
Weald Drive .... Z 40
Worth Park Ave .... Z 47
HORLEY
Massetts Rd .... Y 16
Povey Cross Rd .... Y 20
Victoria Rd .... Y 39
A 217 REIGATE
A 23 LONDON REDHILL
LONDON M 23
A 23 BRIGHTON
CUCKFIELD B 2036
HORSHAM A 264
A 2220 (A 264)
HORLEY
GATWICK
See CRAWLEY
POVEY CROSS
NORTH TERMINAL
SOUTH TERMINAL
GATWICK AIRPORT
HELICOPTER PORT
FERNHILL
LOWFIELD HEATH
Lowfield Heath Roundabout
Gatwick Road Roundabout
BLACK CORNER
TINSLEY GREEN
COUNTY OAK
Fleming Way Roundabout
FORGE WOOD
GRATTONS PARK
Hazelwick Roundabout
LANGLEY GREEN
IFIELD
POUND HILL
CRABBET PARK
THREE BRIDGES
MAIDENBOWER
GOSSOPS GREEN
Breezehurst Roundabout
FURNACE GREEN
WORTHLODGE FOREST
TILGATE
BROADFIELD
TILGATE PARK
WORTH FOREST
Tollgate Hill Roundabout
PEASE POTTAGE
SERVICE AREA
TILGATE FOREST
Horse Hill
Reigate Road
Mill Lane
Lee Street
Brighton Rd
Balcombe Road
B 2036
Povey Cross Road
Horley Road
Fernhill Rd
Antland Lane
B 2037
Charlwood Rd
Heath Rd
Lowfield
Radford Rd
London Road
Gatwick Road
Fleming Way
Manor Royal
Martyrs Av.
Copthorne Way
Copthorne Road
Crawley Av.
Langley Drive
Crawley Avenue
Ifield Green
Ifield Road
Ifield Drive
Bonnetts Lane
Rusper Road
Northgate Av.
North Road
St. Mary's Drive
Worth Rd
Turners Hill Road
Haslett Av. East
Hawth Av.
Gossops Drive
Horsham Road
Seymour Rd
Pelham Drive
Ashdown Drive
Creasys Drive
M 23
B 2110
0 1 km
0 1/2 mile

GATWICK AIRPORT *W. Sussex* 504 T 30 – ✉ *Crawley.*
Gatwick Airport : (0870) 0002468.
London 29 – Brighton 28.

Plan opposite

Hilton London Gatwick Airport, South Terminal, RH6 0LL, (01293) 518080, *londongatwick@hilton.com, Fax (01293) 528980,* – |, rm, – 500. MC AE VISA. Y u
Rest 25.95 (dinner) and a la carte 22.50/31.50 – 17.95 – **791 rm** 117.50/274.75 – 117.50/274.75.
• Large, well-established hotel, popular with business travellers. Two ground floor bars, lounge and leisure facilities. Older rooms co-ordinated, newer in minimalist style. Restaurant enlivened by floral profusions.

Renaissance London Gatwick, Povey Cross Rd, RH6 0BE, (01293) 820169, *Fax (01293) 820259,* , , , squash – |, rm, – 220. MC AE VISA Y a
Rest (bar lunch)/dinner 19.50 and a la carte 38.00/53.95 **s.** – 15.50 – **252 rm** 119.00/176.00 – 119.00/176.00, 2 suites.
• Large red-brick hotel. Good recreational facilities including indoor pool, solarium. Bedrooms are spacious and decorated in smart, chintzy style. Small brasserie area open all day serving popular meals.

Premier Travel Inn, North Terminal, Longbridge Way, Gatwick Airport, RH6 0NX, (0870) 2383305, *Fax (01293) 568278* – |, rm, rest, . MC AE VISA. Y s
Rest (grill rest.) – **220 rm** 54.95/54.95 – 59.95/59.95.
• Consistent standard of trim, simply fitted accommodation in contemporary style. Family rooms with sofa beds. Ideal for corporate or leisure travel.

Undecided between two equivalent establishments? Within each category, establishments are classified in our order of preference.

GILLINGHAM *Dorset* 503 504 N 30 *The West Country G. – pop. 8 630.*
Exc. : *Stourhead★★★ AC, N : 9 m. by B 3092, B 3095 and B 3092.*
London 116 – Bournemouth 34 – Bristol 46 – Southampton 52.

Stock Hill Country House , Stock Hill, SP8 5NR, West : 1½ m. on B 3081 (01747) 823626, *reception@stockhillhouse.co.uk, Fax (01747) 825628,* , , – rest, . MC VISA.
Rest *(closed lunch Monday and Saturday)* (booking essential) 25.00/36.00 – **8 rm** (dinner included) 125.00/165.00 – 260.00/300.00.
• Idyllically peaceful Victorian country house set in eleven acres of mature woodland. Classically furnished. Individually decorated bedrooms, including antique beds. Very comfortable restaurant with rich drapes, attentive service.

GITTISHAM *Devon* 503 K 31 – *see Honiton.*

GLENRIDDING *Cumbria* 502 L 20 – *see Ullswater.*

GLEWSTONE *Herefordshire – see Ross-on-Wye.*

GLOSSOP *Derbs.* 502 503 504 O 23 – *pop. 32 219 (inc. Hollingworth).*
Sheffield Rd (01457) 865247.
The Gatehouse, Victoria St (01457) 855920.
London 194 – Manchester 18 – Sheffield 25.

The Wind in the Willows , Derbyshire Level, SK13 7PT, East : 1 m. by A 57 (01457) 868001, *info@windinthewillows.co.uk, Fax (01457) 853354,* – . MC AE VISA.
Rest (dinner only) 29.00 – **12 rm** 88.00 – 145.00.
• Victorian country house in Peak District, named after trees in garden. Adjacent golf course. Snug, fully-panelled sitting room. Bedrooms individually styled with antiques. Eat on carved chairs at gleaming wooden tables.

GLOUCESTER

Y

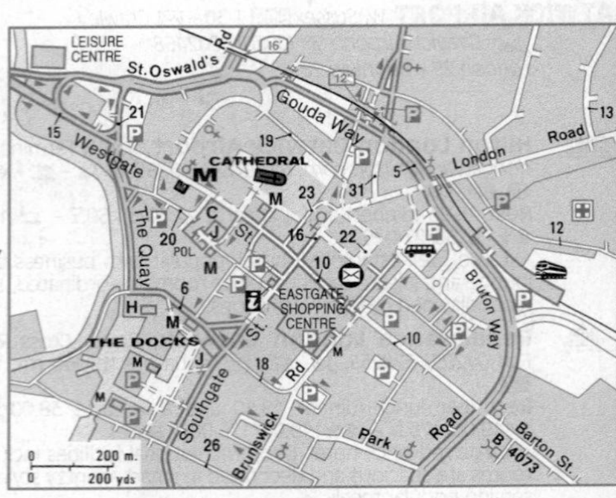

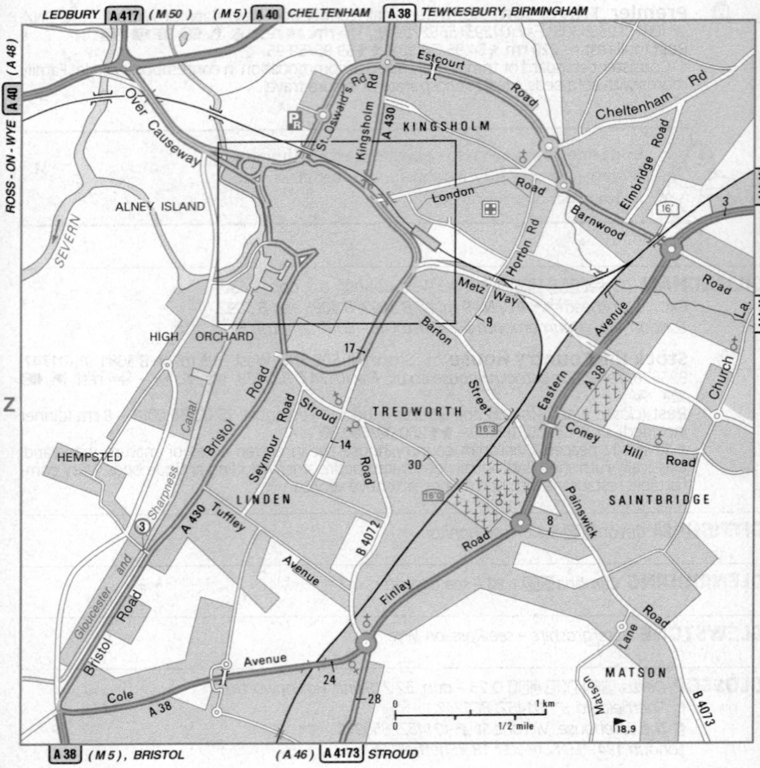

LEDBURY A 417 (M 50) (M 5) A 40 CHELTENHAM A 38 TEWKESBURY, BIRMINGHAM

ROSS-ON-WYE A 40 (A 48)

Over Causeway
St. Oswald's Rd
Kingsholm Rd
A 430
Estcourt Road
KINGSHOLM
Cheltenham Rd
Elmbridge Road
ALNEY ISLAND
SEVERN
London Road
Horton Rd
Barnwood Road
Metz Way
Barton Street
Avenue
Road
La.
Church
HIGH ORCHARD
Eastern
A 38
Z
Canal
Bristol Road
Seymour Road
Stroud Road
TREDWORTH
Coney Hill Road
HEMPSTED
Sharpness
LINDEN
A 430
Tuffley Avenue
B 4072
Painswick Road
SAINTBRIDGE
Gloucester and
Bristol Road
Finlay Road
Avenue
Cole
A 38
Lane
Road
MATSON
Matson
B 4073
1 km
1/2 mile

A 38 (M 5), BRISTOL (A 46) A 4173 STROUD

GLOUCESTER *Glos.* 503 504 N 28 *Great Britain G. – pop. 123 205.*

See : *City★ - Cathedral★★* Y – *The Docks★* Y – *Bishop Hooper's Lodging★* AC Y **M**.

18, 9 *Gloucester Hotel, Matson Lane ☎ (01452) 525653.*

28 Southgate St ☎ (01452) 396572, *tourism@gloucester.gov.uk.*

London 106 – Birmingham 52 – Bristol 38 – Cardiff 66 – Coventry 57 – Northampton 83 – Oxford 48 – Southampton 98 – Swansea 92 – Swindon 35.

Plan opposite

Express by Holiday Inn without rest., Waterwells Business Park, Telford Way, Nr Quedgeley, GL2 2AB, Southwest : 3 m. on A 38 ☎ (0870) 7200953, *gloucester@morethanhotels.com, Fax (0870) 7200954* – P – 35. MC AE VISA
106 rm 67.00 – 67.00.
◆ Purpose-built lodge hotel conveniently located close to M5, three miles from cathedral. Designed for cost-conscious business or leisure travellers. Light, modern bedrooms.

GOATHLAND *N. Yorks.* 502 R 20 – ✉ *Whitby.*

London 248 – Middlesbrough 36 – York 38.

Heatherdene, The Old Vicarage, The Common, YO22 5AN, ☎ (01947) 896334, *info@heatherdenehotel.co.uk, Fax (01947) 896074,* ←, – P. MC VISA.
closed 25 December and restricted opening in winter – **Rest** *(closed Sunday dinner)* (booking essential to non-residents) (dinner only and Sunday lunch) 17.95 – **7 rm**
37.50/55.00 – 80.00/90.00.
◆ Country house hotel in converted vicarage with good village views. Sitting room has contemporary styling, which is reflected to slightly lesser degree in the bedrooms. Hearty, home-cooked meals in modern dining room.

GOLCAR *W. Yorks. – see Huddersfield.*

GOMERSAL *W. Yorks.* 502 O 22 – *see Bradford.*

GOODWOOD *W. Sussex* 504 R 31 – *see Chichester.*

GOOSNARGH *Lancs.* 502 L 22 – ✉ *Preston.*

London 238 – Blackpool 18 – Preston 6.

Solo, Goosnargh Lane, PR3 2BN, ☎ (01772) 865206, *Fax (01772) 865206* – P. MC VISA
closed Sunday dinner and Monday – **Rest** (dinner only and Sunday lunch)/dinner a la carte 23.50/29.50.
◆ Long-standing and very personally run on the edge of the village; renowned locally. Comfortable, tried-and-tested ambience. Traditional cuisine with Mediterranean influences.

GOREY *Jersey (Channel Islands)* 503 P 33 and 517 ⑪ – *see Channel Islands.*

GORING *Oxon.* 503 504 Q 29 *Great Britain G. – pop. 3 934 (inc. Streatley).*

Exc. : *Ridgeway Path★★.*

London 56 – Oxford 16 – Reading 12.

Leatherne Bottel, The Bridleway, RG8 0HS, North : 1 ½ m. by B 4009 ☎ (01491) 872667, *leathernebottel@aol.com, Fax (01491) 875308,* ←, – P. MC AE VISA
closed 31 December and Sunday dinner – **Rest** (booking essential) 24.50 (Monday-Thursday dinner) and a la carte 31.20/37.70.
◆ Charming Thames-side restaurant; idyllic views of Berkshire Downs. Neat, linen-clad round tables, sparkling windows, travel photos on walls. Imaginative international menu.

at Cray's Pond *East : 2 m. on B 4526 – ✉ Goring.*

The White Lion, Goring Rd, Goring Heath, RG8 7SH, ☎ (01491) 680471, *reservations@innastew.com, Fax (01491) 681654,* , – P. MC
closed 25-26 December, 1 January, Sunday dinner and Monday – **Rest** (booking essential) 16.95 and a la carte 25.00/30.00.
◆ Part 18C pub sporting 21C appearance. Front terrace for summer dining. Stylish interior: mix of old beams, low ceilings and soft lights. Eclectic dishes and British staples.

GOSFORTH *Tyne and Wear* 501 502 P 18 – *see Newcastle upon Tyne.*

GOUDHURST *Kent* 504 V 30.
London 50 – Hastings 25 – Maidstone 17.

West Winchet without rest., Winchet Hill, TN17 1JX, North : 2 ½ m. on B 2079 (01580) 212024, *annieparker@jpa-ltd.co.uk*, *Fax (01580) 212250*, – P
closed Christmas and New Year – **3 rm** ☐ 45.00 – 65.00.
◆ Victorian house with large, attractive rear garden. Breakfast taken in vast and attractively decorated drawing room. Traditional bedrooms offer country style décor.

GRAMPOUND *Cornwall* 503 F 33 *The West Country G.* – ✉ *Truro.*
Env. : *Trewithen★★★ AC, W : 2 m. by A 390 – Probus★ (tower★, Country Demonstration Garden★ AC) W : 2½ m. by A 390.*
London 287 – Newquay 16 – Plymouth 44 – Truro 8.

Creed House without rest., Creed, TR2 4SL, South : 1 m. by Creed rd turning left just past the church (01872) 530372, ←, – P.
closed Christmas-New Year – **3 rm** ☐ 60.00 – 90.00.
◆ Smart Georgian rectory with restful gardens featured in several Cornish gardening books. Well-appointed sitting room. Fine art in breakfast room. Country house bedrooms.

Eastern Promise, 1 Moor View, TR2 4RT, (01726) 883033, *Fax (01726) 882311* – P. VISA
closed Wednesday – **Rest** - Chinese - (booking essential) (dinner only) 22.00 and a la carte.
◆ Cosy Chinese restaurant on busy main road close to Truro. Wall paintings in comfortable lounge. Lengthy menu with good, fresh cooking; clear flavours throughout.

The ✿ award is the crème de la crème. This is awarded to restaurants which are really worth travelling miles for!

GRANGE-IN-BORROWDALE *Cumbria* 502 K 20 – *see Keswick.*

GRANGE-OVER-SANDS *Cumbria* 502 L 21 *Great Britain G. – pop. 4 835.*
Env. : *Cartmel Priory★, NW : 3 m.*
Meathop Rd (015395) 33180.
Victoria Hall, Main St (015395) 34026.
London 268 – Kendal 13 – Lancaster 24.

Netherwood, Lindale Rd, LA11 6ET, (015395) 32552, *enquiries@netherwood-hotel.co.uk*, *Fax (015395) 34121*, ← Morecambe Bay, rest, P – 150. VISA
Rest 16.00/32.00 – **32 rm** ☐ 80.00/100.00 – 140.00/180.00.
◆ Unusual, castellated late 18C hotel offering fine view of Morecambe Bay. Atmospheric wood-panelled lounges, each boasting open log fire. Comfy rooms with good mod cons. Dine formally and enjoy superb bay vistas.

Graythwaite Manor, Fernhill Rd, LA11 7JE, (015395) 32001, *enquiries@graythwaitemanor.co.uk*, *Fax (015395) 35549*, ←, P. VISA.
Rest 14.50/22.50 and lunch a la carte 14.00/22.50 – **20 rm** (dinner included) ☐ 60.75/84.00 – 107.00/136.00.
◆ Victorian manor house. Extensive garden with distinctive floral base. Open fires enhance semi-panelled bar. Atmospheric billiard room. Very traditionally furnished bedrooms. Pervasive etched glass windows add gravitas to dining room.

Clare House, Park Rd, LA11 7HQ, (015395) 33026, *info@clarehousehotel.co.uk*, *Fax (015395) 34310*, ←, – rest, P. VISA.
late March-early November – **Rest** (booking essential for non-residents) (dinner only) 30.00 – **19 rm** (dinner included) ☐ 68.00/119.00 – 136.00.
◆ Longstanding family run hotel, its lovely lawned garden looking over Morecambe Bay. Two smartly furnished lounges. Traditionally styled rooms, most with bay views. Two pleasant dining rooms; daily changing five-course menus show care and interest.

at Lindale *Northeast : 2 m. on B 5277* – ✉ *Grange-over-Sands.*

Greenacres without rest., LA11 6LP, (015395) 34578, *greenacres-lindale@hotmail.com* – P. VISA.
closed Christmas – **4 rm** ☐ 32.00/35.00 – 60.00/64.00.
◆ Pleasant guesthouse with distinctive Cumbrian feel: small slate-lined sitting room with open log fire and adjacent, homely breakfast room. Good-sized, very well-kept rooms. Cosy lounge and conservatory.

at Cartmel *Northwest : 3 m – ✉ Grange-over-Sands.*

Aynsome Manor ⛳, LA11 6HH, North : ¾ m. by Cartmel Priory rd on Wood Broughton rd ✆ (015395) 36653, *info@aynsomemanorhotel.co.uk, Fax (015395) 36016*, – rest, P. MC AE VISA
closed 25-26 December and 2-28 January – **Rest** *(closed Sunday dinner to non-residents)* (dinner only and Sunday lunch)/dinner 22.00 ♀ – **12 rm** (dinner included) ☕ ✝79.00/89.00 – ✝✝118.00/160.00.
◆ Country house, personally run by two generations of the same family. Open fired snug bar and lounge with fine clocks. Sitting room has Priory view. Airy, traditional rooms. Dine on candle-lit, polished wood tables with silver.

Uplands ⛳, Haggs Lane, LA11 6HD, East : 1 m. ✆ (015395) 36248, *enquiries@uplandshotel.co.uk, Fax (015395) 36848*, ←, – rest, P. MC AE VISA
closed January-February – **Rest** *(closed Monday)* (booking essential) (dinner only and lunch Friday and Sunday) 33.50 ♀ – **5 rm** (dinner included) ☕ ✝89.00/99.00 – ✝✝172.00/192.00.
◆ Personally run, attractive hotel affording enviable views to the Leven Estuary. Situated in two acres of lovely gardens. Light, spacious bedrooms. Pleasantly bright décor in dining room; well-sourced ingredients enhance the accomplished cooking.

Hill Farm ⛳ without rest., LA11 7SS, Northwest : 1½ m. bearing to right of village shop in Market Square then left onto Cul-de-Sac rd after the racecourse ✆ (015395) 36477, ←, , – P.
February-October – **3 rm** ☕ ✝35.00/40.00 – ✝✝80.00/90.00.
◆ Superb hospitality a feature of this 16C farmhouse with cottagey interior and lovely gardens: a peaceful setting. Individual colour schemes enhance the pretty bedrooms.

L'Enclume (Rogan) with rm, Cavendish St, LA11 6PZ, ✆ (015395) 36362, *info@lenclume.co.uk, Fax (015395) 38907*, – P. MC AE VISA
✿ *closed 1 week January and 1 week November* – **Rest** *(closed Monday-Tuesday)* 25.00 (lunch) and a la carte 45.00/52.00 ♀ – **7 rm** ☕ ✝80.00/170.00 – ✝✝170.00/200.00.
Spec. "Cubism" in foie gras. John Dory with pistachio basmati and bitter caramel. Roquefort soufflé.
◆ Stylish and modern conversion of a former blacksmith's. Highly original modern cooking with some very unusual ingredients. Individual, well-furnished rooms.

GRANTHAM *Lincs.* 502 504 S 25 *Great Britain G. – pop. 34 592.*
See : *St Wulfram's Church★.*
Env. : *Belton House★ AC, N : 2½ m. by A 607.*
Exc. : *Belvoir Castle★★ AC, W : 6 m. by A 607.*
⛳9, ⛳9, ⛳9 *Belton Park, Belton Lane, Londonthorpe Rd ✆ (01476) 567399* – ⛳18, ⛳18, ⛳9 *Belton Woods H. ✆ (01476) 593200.*
ℹ *The Guildhall Centre, St Peter's Hill ✆ (01476) 406166.*
London 113 – Leicester 31 – Lincoln 29 – Nottingham 24.

Belton Woods, Belton, NG32 2LN, North : 2 m. on A 607 ✆ (01476) 593200, *belton.woods@devere-hotels.com, Fax (01476) 574547*, , , Ⅎ6, , , ⛳18, ⛳9, , , , squash – ǀ, , – P – 🏛 245. MC AE VISA
Manor Brasserie **:** Rest *(closed Monday-Tuesday)* (dinner only) a la carte 31.00/42.00 ♀ –
Plus Fours **:** Rest 16.00/23.95 ♀ – **132 rm** ☕ ✝69.00/135.00 – ✝✝79.00/155.00, 4 suites.
◆ Set in acres of countryside, this modern hotel offers impressive leisure facilities, including three golf courses. Range of conference suites. Spacious bedrooms. Brasserie style Manor has vast cocktail bar. Light, modern décor in traditional Plus Fours.

Grantham Marriott, Swingbridge Rd, NG31 7XT, South : 1¼ m. at junction of A 607 with A 1 southbound sliproad ✆ (01476) 593000, *grantham.reservations@whitbread.com, Fax (01476) 592592*, , Ⅎ6, , – , rest, , P – 🏛 200. MC AE VISA
Rest 21.00 and dinner a la carte approx 40.00 – **90 rm** ☕ ✝95.00/105.00 – ✝✝95.00/105.00.
◆ Purpose-built hotel on A1 motorway, convenient for East Midlands airport. Impressive leisure facilities in light, airy surroundings. Smart, comfortable, modern bedrooms. Stylish restaurant with classic menus.

at Great Gonerby *Northwest : 2 m. on B 1174 – ✉ Grantham.*

Harry's Place (Hallam), 17 High St, NG31 8JS, ✆ (01476) 561780 – P. MC VISA
✿ *closed Christmas-New Year, Sunday, Monday and Bank Holidays* – **Rest** (booking essential) a la carte 47.00/59.50.
Spec. Breast of guinea fowl with foie gras and Serrano ham. Fillet of beef with herb, onion and horseradish farce. Apricot soufflé.
◆ Discreet terraced house with old pine interior. Just three tables, bedecked with lilies and candles.Charming and attentive service. Robust, exquisite modern cooking.

at Woolsthorpe-by-Belvoir *West : 7½ m. by A 607 – ✉ Grantham.*

The Chequers with rm, NG32 1LU, ☎ (01476) 870701, *justinnabar@chequers-inn.net* – P. MO VISA.
Rest *(closed Sunday dinner in winter)* 12.50 (lunch) and a la carte 18.00/28.00 ♀ – 5.00 – **4 rm** ☆49.00 – ☆☆59.00.
◆ Attractive pub, orginally built as 17C farmhouse. Various nooks, crannies, exposed bricks and beams. Traditional English cuisine with emphasis on game. Simple, clean rooms.

GRASMERE *Cumbria* 502 K 20 *Great Britain G.* – ✉ *Ambleside.*
See : *Dove Cottage*★ **AC AY A.**
Env. : *Lake Windermere*★★, *SE : by A 591* **AZ.**
ℹ *Redbank Rd ☎ (015394) 35245 (summer only)* **BZ.**
London 282 – Carlisle 43 – Kendal 18.
Plans : see Ambleside

The Wordsworth, Stock Lane, LA22 9SW, ☎ (015394) 35592, *enquiry@wordsworth grasmere.co.uk, Fax (015394) 35765,* – rest, rest, P – 100. MO AE VISA. **BZ**
Prelude : **Rest** 21.95/65.00 **s.** – **35 rm** ☆55.00/100.00 – ☆☆150.00/180.00, 2 suites.
◆ This imposing Victorian hotel next to Wordsworth's burial ground has lovely rear gardens. Lily adorned sitting room and conservatory bar. Attractive, comfortable bedrooms Immaculately traditional dining room.

Gold Rill, Red Bank Rd, LA22 9PU, ☎ (015394) 35486, *reception@gold-rill.com Fax (015394) 85486,* – rest, P. MO VISA. **BZ**
closed mid December-mid January – **Rest** (bar lunch)/dinner 24.00 ♀ – **31 rm** (dinner included) ☆51.00/79.00 – ☆☆102.00/148.00, 1 suite.
◆ Liberally proportioned, privately owned hotel in quiet part of town. Good views, open fires, slate based walls, traditional décor. Large bar with fine ales. Homely bedrooms. Quiet rear dining room overlooking lake.

Red Lion, Red Lion Sq, LA22 9SS, ☎ (015394) 35456, *enquiries@hotelgrasmere.uk.com Fax (015394) 35579,* – rest, P – 60. MO AE VISA **BZ**
Rest (bar lunch)/dinner 20.00 **s.** ♀ – **48 rm** ☆48.00/87.00 – ☆☆96.00/124.00, 1 suite.
◆ Centrally located hotel with good fell views. Squashy sofas in reception. Light, airy conservatory. Real ales in adjoining Lamb Inn. Most bedrooms boast jacuzzis. Central raised atrium enhances restaurant.

White Moss House, Rydal Water, LA22 9SE, South : 1½ m. on A 591 ☎ (015394) 35295 *sue@whitemoss.com, Fax (015394) 35516,* – rest, P. MO VISA. **BY**
closed December and January – **Rest** *(closed Sunday)* (booking essential) (dinner only) (set menu only) 36.50 ♀ – **6 rm** (dinner included) ☆85.00/95.00 – ☆☆170.00/190.00, 1 suite.
◆ This solid Lakeland house close to Rydal Water was once home to Wordsworth and his family. Elegant lounge with antiques, oils, curios and slate tables. Well-kept bedrooms. Dine at polished wooden tables with fine glassware.

Grasmere, Broadgate, LA22 9TA, ☎ (015394) 35277, *enquiries@grasmerehotel.co.uk Fax (015394) 35277,* P. MO VISA **BZ**
closed 4 January-5 February – **Rest** (dinner only) 27.50 – **13 rm** (dinner included) ☆55.00/105.00 – ☆☆110.00/140.00.
◆ Small Victorian country house with pleasant acre of garden through which River Rothay flows. Snug, open-fired bar with good malt whisky selection. Individually styled rooms. Pleasant pine roofed rear dining room.

Woodland Crag without rest., How Head Lane, LA22 9SG, Southeast : ¾ m. by B 5287 ☎ (015394) 35351, *info@woodlandcrag.co.uk, Fax (015394) 33971,* P MO VISA. **AY**
closed mid November-mid February – **5 rm** ☆30.00/60.00 – ☆☆70.00/80.00.
◆ Dove Cottage stands tantalisingly close to this solid stone guesthouse with its very pleasant gardens and homely lounge. Cottage-style breakfast room. Comfortable rooms.

GRASSENDALE *Mersey.* 502 503 L 23 – *see Liverpool.*

We try to be as accurate as possible when giving room rates.
But prices are susceptible to change,
so please check rates when booking.

GRASSINGTON *N. Yorks.* 502 O 21 – ✉ *Skipton.*

National Park Centre, Colvend, Hebden Rd ☎ (01756) 752774.
London 240 – Bradford 30 – Burnley 28 – Leeds 37.

Ashfield House, Summers Fold, BD23 5AE, off Main St ☎ (01756) 752584, *sales@ashfieldhouse.co.uk, Fax (01756) 752584,* – P. MC AE VISA.
closed 20-27 December – **Rest** (booking essential to non-residents) (dinner only) 25.00 – **7 rm** ☕ ★61.00/79.50 – ★★80.00/85.00.
◆ Sturdy 17C small stone hotel with beams and flagged floors: oozes period charm. Individually decorated, cottagey bedrooms with occasional exposed timber. Delightful garden.

Grassington Lodge without rest., 8 Wood Lane, BD23 5LU, ☎ (01756) 752518, *relax@grassingtonlodge.co.uk, Fax (01756) 752518* – P.
closed 24-25 December – **8 rm** ☕ ★50.00 – ★★80.00/90.00.
◆ Modern guesthouse at gateway to Yorkshire Dales. Built over 100 years ago as home of village doctor. Gallery of local photos on display around the house. Stylish, smart rooms.

GRAVESEND *Kent* 504 V 29 – *pop. 53 045.*

18a St George's Sq ☎ (01474) 337600.
London 25 – Dover 54 – Maidstone 16 – Margate 53.

Manor, Hever Court Rd, Singlewell, DA12 5UQ, Southeast : 2½ m. by A 227 off A 2 (eastbound carriageway) ☎ (01474) 353100, *manor@bestwestern.co.uk, Fax (01474) 354978,* – rest, P – 200. MC AE VISA.
closed 24 December-2 January – **Rest** *(closed Sunday)* (dinner only) a la carte 21.20/29.28 s. – **58 rm** ☕ ★70.00/89.00 – ★★75.00/150.00.
◆ Privately owned hotel close to A2 motorway. Useful for visitors to Bluewater shopping complex. Bar, small health club. Comfortable bedrooms with limed oak style furniture. Cosy, wood floored restaurant.

Premier Travel Inn, Wrotham Rd, DA11 7LF, South : 1 m. on A 227 ☎ (08701) 977118, *Fax (01474) 323776* – rm, P. MC AE VISA
Rest (grill rest.) – **36 rm** ★49.95/49.95 – ★★52.95/52.95.
◆ Well-proportioned modern bedrooms, suitable for business travellers and visitors to nearby shopping complex. Family rooms with sofa beds. Adjacent to grill restaurant.

"Rest" appears in red for establishments with a ✿ (star) or ☺ (Bib Gourmand).

GRAVETYE *W. Sussex – see East Grinstead.*

GRAZELEY GREEN *Wokingham – see Reading.*

GREAT BADDOW *Essex* 504 V 28 – *see Chelmsford.*

GREAT BIRCHAM *Norfolk* 502 504 V 25.

London 115.5 – Hunstanton 10.5 – King's Lynn 15.

King's Head, PE31 6RJ, ☎ (01485) 578265, *welcome@the-kings-head.bircham.co.uk, Fax (01485) 578635,* – rest, P. MC VISA
Rest a la carte 24.25/32.15 ♀ – **9 rm** ☕ ★69.50/99.50 – ★★125.00/175.00.
◆ Sign saying '1860' denotes age of property. Smart interior: relaxed bar and stylish residents lounge with big leather chairs. Well-equipped rooms in striking, earthy tones. Modern menus in a contemporary restaurant boasting sheltered courtyard terrace.

GREAT BROUGHTON *N. Yorks.* 502 Q 20 – ✉ *Middlesbrough.*

London 241 – Leeds 61 – Middlesbrough 10 – Newcastle upon Tyne 51 – York 54.

Wainstones, 31 High St, TS9 7EW, ☎ (01642) 712268, *reception@wainstoneshotel.co.uk, Fax (01642) 711560* – rest, P – 120. MC AE VISA.
Rest *(closed Sunday dinner)* 27.00 – **24 rm** ☕ ★77.50/82.50 – ★★109.00.
◆ Converted 17C farmhouse named after local outcrop of rocks. A good base for exploring North Yorkshire Moors. Large, atmospheric bar and sitting room. Good-sized bedrooms. Unfussy dining room.

GREAT DUNMOW *Essex* 504 V 28 – *pop. 5 943.*
London 42 – Cambridge 27 – Chelmsford 13 – Colchester 24.

XXX **The Starr** with rm, Market Pl, CM6 1AX, ✆ (01371) 874321, *starrestaurant@btinternet.com, Fax (01371) 876337* – ⇆ ✆ P – 🔑 35. MC AE ① VISA
closed 27-30 December and 2-8 January – **Rest** *(closed Sunday dinner)* 35.00/42.50 ♀ – **8 rm** ☕ ★80.00 – ★★120.00/145.00.
◆ Former 15C pub with rustic bar and fire. Characterful restaurant has exposed beams and conservatory. Strong, interesting cooking, traditionally inspired. Smart bedrooms.

X **Dish,** 15 High St, CM6 1AB, ✆ (01371) 859922, *Fax (01371) 859888* – MC AE VISA
closed 25-26 December, 1 January and Sunday dinner – **Rest** 13.50/15.00 dinner a la carte 22.95/28.75 ♀.
◆ Modern family-run restaurant in 14C monastic reading room. Stylish interior with vibrant artwork and open plan kitchen. Contemporary menu with subtle Mediterranean feel.

GREAT EVERSDEN *Cambs.* – *see Cambridge.*

GREAT GONERBY *Lincs.* 502 504 S 25 – *see Grantham.*

GREAT MALVERN *Worcs.* 503 504 N 27 – *pop. 35 588.*
21 Church St ✆ (01684) 892289 B.
London 127 – Birmingham 34 – Cardiff 66 – Gloucester 24.

Plan opposite

Bredon House without rest., 34 Worcester Rd, WR14 4AA, ✆ (01684) 566990, *rayella@brendonhouse.co.uk, Fax (01684) 577530,* ← Severn Valley, – P. MC VISA B a
closed Christmas – **10 rm** ☕ ★55.00/65.00 – ★★80.00/90.00.
◆ Elegant, Grade II listed Regency house with spectacular views. Personable owners make breakfast a special event. Most of the individually styled rooms enjoy the fine vista.

Cowleigh Park Farm without rest., Cowleigh Rd, WR13 5HJ, Northwest : 1 ½ m. by B 4232 on B 4219 ✆ (01684) 566750, *cowleighpark@ukonline.co.uk,* – ⇆ P A
closed Christmas - New Year – **3 rm** ☕ ★40.00/60.00 – ★★62.00/65.00.
◆ Part 17C farmhouse nestling in rustic position by gurgling stream. Vast inglenook fireplace complements comfy, adjacent sitting room. Cosy, snug bedrooms with exposed beams.

at Malvern Wells *South : 2 m. on A 449 – ✉ Malvern.*

Cottage in the Wood ⛰, Holywell Rd, WR14 4LG, ✆ (01684) 575859, *reception@cottageinthewood.co.uk, Fax (01684) 560662,* ← Severn and Evesham Vales, , – ⇆ rest, P. MC AE VISA A
Rest 14.75 (lunch) and dinner a la carte 32.85/37.85 ♀ – **31 rm** ☕ ★79.00/105.00 – ★★99.00/175.00.
◆ Early Victorian house, family owned and run, with superb view over surrounding vales. Very comfortable sitting room and bar. Individually furnished rooms in traditional style. Lovely restaurant with Oriental silk prints and Vale views.

at Colwall *Southwest : 3 m. on B 4218 – ✉ Great Malvern.*

Colwall Park, WR13 6QG, ✆ (01684) 540000, *hotel@colwall.com, Fax (01684) 540847,* – ⇆ ✆ P – 🔑 120. MC AE VISA A
Rest – (see ***Seasons*** below) ♀ – **20 rm** ☕ ★79.00/89.00 – ★★120.00, 2 suites.
◆ Built in 1903, this personally run hotel has a distinct Edwardian feel. Play croquet in the garden or wander into the nearby Malvern Hills. Individually decorated bedrooms.

Brook House ⛰ without rest., Walwyn Rd, WR13 6QX, ✆ (01684) 540604, *maggie@brookhouse-colwall.fsnet.co.uk, Fax (01684) 540604,* – ⇆ P.
4 rm ☕ ★42.50 – ★★71.00.
◆ Characterful Jacobean manor house with delightful gardens, stream and arboretum. Local prints in breakfast room. Beamed ceilings and antique furniture. All rooms individual.

XX **Seasons** (at Colwall Park H.), WR13 6QG, ✆ (01684) 540000, *hotel@colwall.com, Fax (01684) 540847,* – ⇆ P. MC AE VISA A
Rest (lunch booking essential)/dinner 28.45/35.15 **s.** ♀.
◆ Predominant oak panelling merges seamlessly with modern styling in a spacious location for formal dining. Accomplished and interesting modern British cooking.

at Acton Green *Northwest : 7 m. by A 449 – B –, B 4219, A 4103 on B 4220 – ✉ Bromyard.*

Hidelow House ⛰ without rest., Acton Beauchamp, WR6 5AH, South : ¾ m. on B 4220 ✆ (01886) 884547, *mg@hidelow.co.uk, Fax (01886) 884658,* – ⇆ P. MC VISA.
3 rm ☕ ★39.95 – ★★73.90.
◆ Secluded, privately run guesthouse with pleasant views down the Leadon Valley. Sizeable bedrooms with a homely feel. Boudoir grand piano in the firelit lounge.

GREAT MALVERN

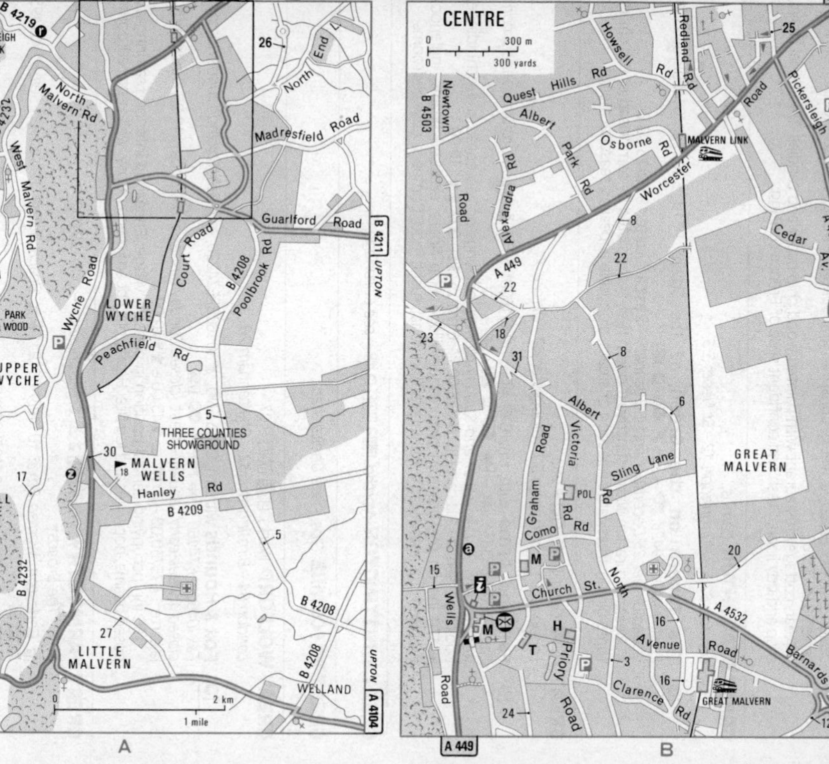

GREAT MILTON *Oxon.* 503 504 Q 28 – *see Oxford.*

GREAT MISSENDEN *Bucks.* 504 R 28 – *pop. 7 070 (inc. Prestwood).*
London 34 – Aylesbury 10 – Maidenhead 19 – Oxford 35.

XX **La Petite Auberge,** 107 High St, HP16 0BB, ☎ (01494) 865370 – MO VISA
closed 2 weeks Easter, 2 weeks Christmas and Sunday – **Rest** - French - (dinner only) a la carte 28.80/35.60.
◆ Neat, cottagey restaurant with painted wood chip paper and candles. Traditional chairs, crisp and tidy linen. Fresh and confident style of French cooking.

GREAT STAUGHTON *Cambs..*
London 62.5 – Huntingdon 12 – St Neots 5.5.

The Tavern on the Green, 12 The Green, PE19 5DG, ☎ (01480) 860336 *Fax (01480) 869426,* – P. MO VISA
closed dinner 25 December and 1-2 January – **Rest** a la carte 18.00/25.00 ♀.
◆ Pleasant rural inn with distinctive modern feel, accentuated by comfy leather tub chairs. Three dining areas: large selection of steaks, alongside appealing seasonal menus.

GREAT TEW *Oxon.* 503 504 P 28.
London 75 – Birmingham 50 – Gloucester 42 – Oxford 21.

Falkland Arms with rm, OX7 4DB, ☎ (01608) 683653, *sjcourage@btconnect.com* *Fax (01608) 683656,* – . MO AE VISA.
Rest *(closed 25 December and Sunday dinner)* (bookings not accepted at lunch) (dinner booking essential) a la carte 15.00/25.00 ♀ – **6 rm** ☐ ✝50.00 – ✝✝110.00.
◆ 17C inn on the green in picturesque village. Flag floors, exposed beams, inglenook fireplace guarantee warm ambience. Traditional, rustic food. Compact, cosy bedrooms.

GREAT WHITTINGTON *Northd.* 501 502 O 18 – *see Corbridge.*

GREAT WITCOMBE *Glos. – see Cheltenham.*

GREAT WOLFORD *Warks.* 503 504 P 27.
London 84 – Birmingham 37 – Cheltenham 26.

Fox & Hounds with rm, CV36 5NQ, ☎ (01608) 674220, *info@thefoxandhoundsinn.com* *Fax (01608) 674160* – rm, P. MO VISA
closed 1 week early January – **Rest** *(closed Sunday dinner and Monday)* 12.95 (lunch) and a la carte 17.75/30.00 – **3 rm** ☐ ✝45.00 – ✝✝70.00.
◆ 16C inn occupying central position in pleasant village. Endearing interior, featuring exposed beams, hop vines and log fire. Hearty blackboard menus. Cosy, well-kept bedrooms.

GREAT YARMOUTH *Norfolk* 504 Z 26 *Great Britain G. – pop. 58 032.*
Env. : *The Broads*★.
18 *Gorleston, Warren Rd* ☎ *(01493) 661911* – 18 *Beach House, Caister-on-Sea* ☎ *(01493) 728699.*
25 Marine Parade ☎ *(01493) 842195.*
London 126 – Cambridge 81 – Ipswich 53 – Norwich 20.

Imperial, North Drive, NR30 1EQ, ☎ (01493) 842000, *reception@imperialhotel.co.uk* *Fax (01493) 852229,* ← – rest, P – 140. MO AE VISA
***Rambouillet* : Rest** *(dinner only and Sunday lunch)* 15.00 and a la carte 21.00/38.00 **s.** ♀ – **39 rm** ☐ ✝76.00 – ✝✝94.00.
◆ Turn of 20C classic promenade hotel, still privately owned. Imposing exterior with large public areas. Pleasant bedrooms in light fabrics include four wine-themed rooms. French feel pervades basement restaurant.

XX **Seafood,** 85 North Quay, NR30 1JF, ☎ (01493) 856009, *Fax (01493) 332256* – . MO AE VISA
closed Saturday lunch, Sunday and Bank Holidays – **Rest** - Seafood - a la carte 21.40/40.95.
◆ Run by a husband and wife team, a long-standing neighbourhood restaurant. Lobster tank, fish display, fresh, generous seafood, attentive service oh, and home-made chocolates.

GREEN ISLAND *Jersey (Channel Islands) – see Channel Islands.*

GRETA BRIDGE *Durham* 502 O 20 – *see Barnard Castle.*

GREVE DE LECQ *Jersey (Channel Islands)* 503 P 33 and 517 ⑪ – *see Channel Islands.*

GRIMSBY *N.E. Lincs.* 502 504 T 23.
London 173 – Boston 51 – Kingston-upon-Hull 33 – Lincoln 37 – Sheffield 73.

Premier Travel Inn, Europa Park, Appian Way, off Gilbey Rd, DN31 2UT, ✆ (01472) 242630, *Fax (01472) 250281* – ⇔ rm, ▤ rest, ♿ P. MO AE ① VISA. ✗
Rest (grill rest.) – **40 rm** ★46.95/46.95 – ★★49.95/49.95.
◆ Simply furnished and brightly decorated bedrooms with ample work space. Family rooms have sofa beds. Designed with practicality and price in mind.

GRIMSTON *Norfolk* 504 V 25 – *see King's Lynn.*

GRINDLEFORD *Derbs.* 502 503 504 P 24 – ✉ *Sheffield (S. Yorks.).*
London 165 – Derby 31 – Manchester 34 – Sheffield 10.

Maynard Arms, Main Rd, S32 2HE, on B 6521 ✆ (01433) 630321, *info@maynardarms.co.uk, Fax (01433) 630445,* ←, ⚘ – ⇔ rest, P – 🏛 130. MO VISA
Padley **: Rest** *(closed Saturday lunch and dinner Sunday-Monday)* a la carte 15.00/27.95 ♀ – **8 rm** ☕ ★55.00/75.00 – ★★65.00/95.00, 2 suites.
◆ Nestling in the Peak District, this late Victorian hotel has oak-panelled reception area and superb stained glass. Sepia photographs on walls. Open fires, immaculate bedrooms. Restaurant has imposing hill views.

GRINSHILL *Shrops.* 503 L 25 – *see Shrewsbury.*

GROUVILLE *Jersey (Channel Islands)* 503 M 33 – *see Channel Islands.*

GUERNSEY *C.I.* 503 OP 33 and 517 ⑨ ⑩ – *see Channel Islands.*

GUILDFORD *Surrey* 504 S 30 – *pop. 69 400.*
Env. : *Clandon Park*★★, *E : 3 m. by A 246 Z – Hatchlands Park*★, *E : 6 m. by A 246 Z.*
Exc. : *Painshill*★★, *Cobham, NE : 10 m – Polesden Lacey*★, *E : 13 m. by A 246 Z and minor rd.*
ℹ *14 Tunsgate* ✆ *(01483) 444333* Y.
London 33 – Brighton 43 – Reading 27 – Southampton 49.

Plan on next page

Angel Posting House and Livery without rest., High St, GU1 3DP, ✆ (01483) 564555, *reservations@angelpostinghouse.com, Fax (01483) 533770* – 🛗 ✆ ♿ – 🏛 70. MO AE VISA. ✗ Y e
☕ 13.50 – **14 rm** ★150.00 – ★★150.00, 7 suites.
◆ Prominent 16C exterior. Front lounge timbered with plush sofas and dried flowers; rear lounge has brick Jacobean fireplace, 17C parliamentary clock. Warm, welcoming bedrooms.

Premier Travel Inn, Parkway, GU1 1UP, North : 1 ½ m. by A 320 on A 25 ✆ (01483) 304932, *Fax (01483) 304935* – 🛗, ⇔ rm, ▤ rest, ♿ P – 🏛 45. MO AE ① VISA. ✗ Z a
Rest (grill rest.) – **87 rm** ★57.95/57.95 – ★★59.95/59.95.
◆ Consistent standard of trim, simply fitted accommodation in contemporary style. Well-proportioned modern bedrooms, suitable for business and family guests.

Café de Paris, 35 Castle St, GU1 3UQ, ✆ (01483) 534896, *Fax (01483) 300411,* ☂ – MO AE VISA Y u
closed Sunday dinner – **Rest** - French - (booking essential) a la carte 18.95/37.95 ☺.
◆ French-style backstreet eatery. Take your pick of brasserie in front or restaurant at back. Prix fixe or à la carte dishes with traditional twist and seasonal changes.

Zinfandel, 4-5 Chapel St, GU1 3UH, ✆ (01483) 455155, *mail@zinfandel.org.uk* – ▤. MO AE VISA Y v
closed 25-26 December, 1 January and Sunday dinner – **Rest** a la carte 17.95/27.20 ☺ ♀.
◆ Welcoming, modern and irresistibly laid back; Napa Valley cuisine mixes grills, Pacific Rim salads, full-flavoured, wood-fired pizzas and picket-fence classics like pecan pie.

GUILDFORD

Bedford Rd	Y	2
Bridge St	Y	3
Castle St.	Y	5
Chertsey St	Y	6
Commercial Rd	Y	8
Eastgate Gardens	Y	9
Friary Bridge	Y	12
Friary Centre	Y	
High St	Y	
Ladymead	Z	13
Leapale Lane	Y	15
Leapale Rd	Y	16
Leas Rd	Y	17
Market St	Y	18
Mary Rd	Y	19
Midleton Rd	Z	20
Millbrook	Y	21
New Inn Lane	Z	22
North St	Y	
One Tree Hill Rd	Z	24
Onslow St	Y	25
Park St	Y	27
Quarry St	Y	28
Stoughton Rd	Z	30
Trood's Lane	Z	31
Tunsgate Shopping Centre	Y	
Tunsgate	Y	33
Warwick's Bench	Y	34
Woodbridge Rd	Z	37

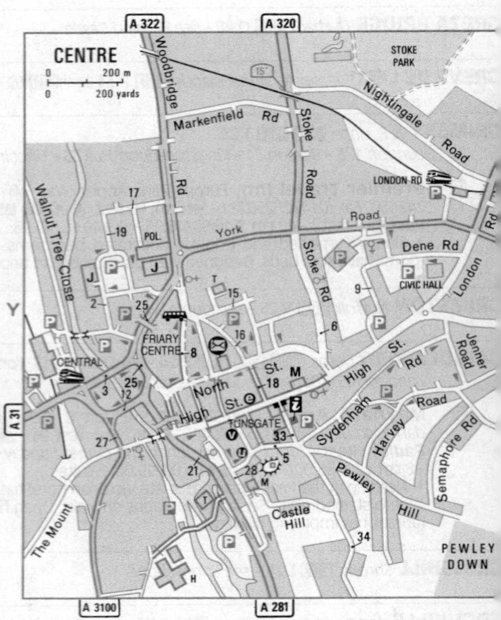

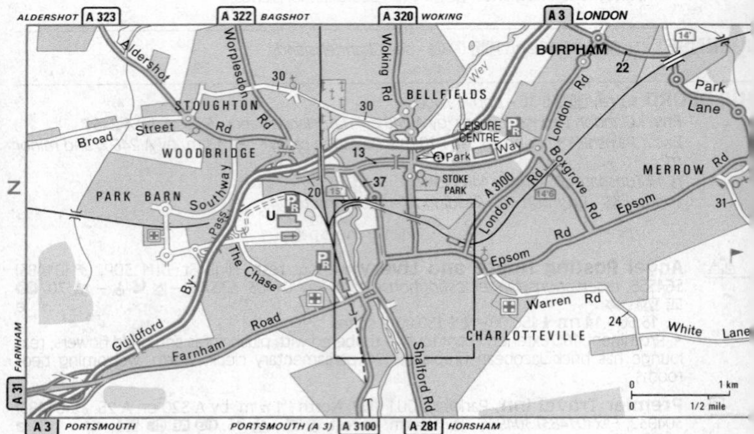

at Shere *East : 6¾ m. by A 246 off A 25 – Z – ✉ Guildford.*

XX **Kinghams,** Gomshall Lane, GU5 9HE, ✆ (01483) 202168, *paul@kinghams-resta rant.co.uk* – P. MC AE ⓓ VISA
closed 25 December-8 January, Sunday dinner and Monday – **Rest** (booking essentia 21.70 and a la carte 21.65/34.85.
◆ Popular restaurant in 17C cottage in appealing village. Daily blackboard and fis specials are particularly good value. Adventurous modern menus with bold comb nations.

Domaines
Ott★

GUISBOROUGH *Redcar and Cleveland 502 Q 20.*
London 265 – Middlesbrough 9 – Newcastle upon Tyne 50 – Whitby 22.

Gisborough Hall, Whitby Lane, TS14 6PT, East : 1 m. on Whitby rd ☎ (01287) 4008191, *Fax (01287) 610844*, – 350.
Tocketts **:** Rest 15.90/27.90 – 12.95 – **70 rm** 160.00 – 160.00, 1 suite.
◆ Imposing, ivy-clad 19C country house with modern wing. Very comfy drawing room; main hall has minstrel gallery; cosy library bar. Rooms more individually styled in main house. Restaurant, set in billiard room, infused with classical style.

GUITING POWER *Glos. 503 504 O 28 – ✉ Cheltenham.*
London 95 – Birmingham 47 – Gloucester 30 – Oxford 39.

Guiting Guest House, Post Office Lane, GL54 5TZ, ☎ (01451) 850470, *info@guitingguesthouse.com, Fax (01451) 850034* –
Rest (by arrangement) 26.95 – **6 rm** 38.50/45.00 – 77.00.
◆ 16C stone-built former Cotswold farmhouse in centre of small village. Cosy lounge, wood floors and original open fire. Two particularly comfortable converted cottage rooms. Intimate, low-beamed dining-room.

GULWORTHY *Devon 503 H 32 – see Tavistock.*

GUNNERSIDE *N. Yorks. 502 N 20 – ✉ Darlington.*
London 268 – Newcastle upon Tyne 60 – Richmond 17.

Oxnop Hall without rest., Low Oxnop, DL11 6JJ, West : 1½ m. on B 6270 ☎ (01748) 886253, *Fax (01748) 886253*,
March-October – **5 rm** 31.00/39.00 – 60.00/70.00.
◆ Pleasant stone-built 17C farmhouse and working sheep farm in agreeable hillside position. Cosy little lounge. Bedrooms feature beams, mullion windows and rural views.

GUNWALLOE *Cornwall 503 E 33 – see Helston.*

HACKNESS *N. Yorks. 502 S 21 – see Scarborough.*

HADDENHAM *Bucks. 504 R 28 – pop. 4 720.*
London 54 – Aylesbury 8 – Oxford 21.

Green Dragon, Churchway, HP17 8AA, ☎ (01844) 291403, *Fax (01844) 299532*, –
closed 25 December, 1 January and Sunday dinner – **Rest** (booking essential) a la carte 18.00/28.00.
◆ Warmly decorated, modern-style pub-restaurant with a friendly atmosphere and pleasant service. Very good value, from simple pub food to more elaborate restaurant-style dishes.

HADLEIGH *Suffolk 504 W 27 – pop. 7 124.*
Hadleigh Library, 29 High St ☎ (01473) 823778.
London 72 – Cambridge 49 – Colchester 17 – Ipswich 10.

Edge Hall without rest., 2 High St, IP7 5AP, ☎ (01473) 822458, *r.rolfe@edgehall-hotel.co.uk, Fax (01473) 827751*,
6 rm 45.00/75.00 – 75.00/135.00.
◆ One of the oldest houses in the town (1590), with a Georgian façade. Spacious, comfy bedrooms are traditionally furnished, as are the communal areas. Very well-kept gardens.

HADLEY HEATH *Worcs. – see Droitwich Spa.*

Your opinions are important to us:
please write and let us know about your discoveries and experiences – good and bad!

HAILSHAM *E. Sussex* 504 U 31 – *pop. 19 177.*

Wellshurst G. & C.C., North St, Hellingly ☎ (01435) 813636.
London 57 – Brighton 23 – Eastbourne 7 – Hastings 20.

at Magham Down *Northeast : 2 m. by A 295 on A 271 – ✉ Hailsham.*

Olde Forge, BN27 1PN, ☎ (01323) 842893, *theoldeforgehotel@tesco.ne*
Fax (01323) 842893 – P. MC VISA
Rest (dinner only) 23.50 – **7 rm** ★48.00 – ★★70.00.
◆ Privately owned timbered house with cottage feel, charmingly run by helpful, friendl owners. Rooms are individually furnished in elegant pine; one boasts a four-poster bec Beamed restaurant with carefully compiled menu.

HALAM *Notts. Great Britain G..*

Env. : *Southwell Minster★★ AC, E : 2 m. on Mansfield Rd, Halam Hill, Market Pl and A 612.*
London 134 – Derby 8 – Nottingham 8.

Waggon and Horses, Mansfield Rd, NG22 8AE, ☎ (01636) 813109, *w-h@btco nect.com, Fax (01636) 816228* – P. MC VISA
closed 25-26 December and Sunday dinner – **Rest** 14.50 and a la carte 20.00/28.00.
◆ Cosy, low-beamed pub with well-stocked bar and cricket themed curios. Owners ar members of 'Campaign For Real Food' and menus have emphasis on fresh, local, seasona produce.

HALE BARNS *Gtr Manchester* 502 503 504 N 23 – *see Altrincham.*

HALFWAY BRIDGE *W. Sussex* 504 R 31 – *see Petworth.*

HALIFAX *W. Yorks.* 502 O 22 – *pop. 83 570.*

Halifax Bradley Hall, Holywell Green ☎ (01422) 374108 – Halifax West End, Paddoc Lane, Highroad Well ☎ (01422) 341878, Union Lane, Ogden ☎ (01422) 244171 – Ryburn, Norland, Sowerby Bridge ☎ (01422) 831355 – Lightcliffe, Knowle Top R ☎ (01422) 202459.
Piece Hall ☎ (01422) 368725.
London 205 – Bradford 8 – Burnley 21 – Leeds 15 – Manchester 28.

Holdsworth House , Holmfield, HX2 9TG, North : 3 m. by A 629 and Shay Lan ☎ (01422) 240024, *info@holdsworthhouse.co.uk, Fax (01422) 245174*, – P – 150. MC AE VISA
(closed 27-30 December) **Rest** *(closed lunch Saturday and Sunday)* 15.95 (lunch) and a l carte 25.95/36.00 – 8.95 – **36 rm** ★105.00/120.00 – ★★170.00, 4 suites.
◆ Characterful and extended part 17C manor house in a quiet location. Comfortable, tradi tionally decorated rooms with wood furniture. Country house-style throughout. Three roomed, wood-panelled restaurant overlooks garden.

Design House, Dean Clough (Gate 5), HX3 5AX, ☎ (01422) 383242, *enquiries@desig houserestaurant.co.uk, Fax (01422) 322732* – P 12. MC AE VISA
closed 1 week mid August, 26 December-January, Saturday lunch, Sunday and Bank Hol days – **Rest** 13.95 (dinner and a la carte 21.85/33.00.
◆ Located within converted mill on outskirts of town, an impressively stylish and moderr restaurant with Philippe Starck furniture. Varied menu of contemporary British cooking.

Shibden Mill Inn with rm, Shibden Mill Fold, HX3 7UL, Northeast : 2 ¼ m. by A 58 anc Kell Lane (turning left at Stump Cross public house) on Blake Hill Rd ☎ (01422) 365840 *Fax (01422) 362971*, – P 8. MC AE VISA
(closed 25-26 December and 1 January) **Rest** 11.95 (lunch) and a la carte 19.00/29.65 – **12 rm** ★68.00 – ★★130.00.
◆ Part 17C inn hidden away in wooded Shibden Valley. Beamed areas and open fires; firs floor restaurant. Classic or modern English dishes. Comfy rooms in converted barn.

at Shelf *Northeast : 3 m. on A 6036 – ✉ Halifax.*

Bentley's, 12 Wadehouse Rd, HX3 7PB, ☎ (01274) 690992, *bentleys@btinternet.com Fax (01274) 690011* – . MC VISA
closed 25-26 December, January, Saturday lunch, Sunday and Monday – **Rest** 10.95 (lunch and a la carte 19.45/30.50.
◆ Converted terraced house with characterful interior, highlighted by rustic brickwork Appealing, wide-ranging blackboard menu serving hearty food with a Yorkshire base.

ALLAND *E. Sussex* 504 U 31 – ✉ *Lewes.*
London 59 – Brighton 17 – Eastbourne 15 – Maidstone 35.

Shortgate Manor Farm without rest., BN8 6PJ, Southwest : 1 m. on B 2192 ℘ (01825) 840320, *ewalt@shortgate.co.uk, Fax (01825) 840320,* – P.
3 rm ☕ ★40.00/45.00 – ★★65.00/80.00.
• Extended 18C shepherd's cottage with extensive, pretty gardens. Neat and spacious bedrooms. Communal rooms decorated with home-grown dried flowers.

ALLATON *Leics.* 504 R 26.
London 95 – Leicester 17 – Market Harborough 9.

Bewicke Arms with rm, 1 Eastgate, LE16 8UB, ℘ (01858) 555217, *Fax (01858) 555598,* – rm, P. MC VISA.
Rest *(closed Sunday dinner in winter)* (booking essential) a la carte 15.95/19.50 ♀ **3 rm** ☕ ★40.00 – ★★55.00.
• Located in picturesque village, this part thatched 17C inn boasts hop vines, beams and a crackling fire. Seasonal, regionally inspired dishes served by friendly staff.

ALL GREEN *W. Mids.* 502 503 504 O 26 – *see Birmingham.*

ALNAKER *W. Sussex – see Chichester.*

ALTWHISTLE *Northd.* 501 502 M 19 *Great Britain G. – pop. 3 811.*
Env. : *Hadrian's Wall★★, N : 4½ m. by A 6079 – Housesteads★★ AC, NE : 6 m. by B 6318 – Roman Army Museum★ AC, NW : 5 m. by A 69 and B 6318 – Vindolanda (Museum★) AC, NE : 5 m. by A 69 – Steel Rig (≤★) NE : 5½ m. by B 6318.*
18 *Wallend Farm, Greenhead ℘ (01697) 747367.*
Railway Station, Station Rd ℘ (01434) 322002.
London 335 – Carlisle 22 – Newcastle upon Tyne 37.

Centre of Britain, Main St, NE49 0BH, ℘ (01434) 322422, *enquiries@centre-of-britain.org.uk, Fax (01434) 322655* – P. – 25. MC AE VISA
(closed 24-27 December) **Rest** (dinner only) 19.95 – **12 rm** ☕ ★55.00 – ★★100.00.
• Attractive hotel on busy main street. Oldest part, a pele tower, dates from 15C. Comfortable modern décor, including bedrooms, incorporates original architectural features. Glass-roofed restaurant with light, airy feel.

Ashcroft without rest., Lantys Lonnen, NE49 0DA, ℘ (01434) 320213, *ashcroft.1@btconnect.com, Fax (01434) 321641,* – P. MC AE VISA.
closed 25 December – **7 rm** ☕ ★30.00 – ★★60.00/68.00.
• Large Victorian house, formerly a vicarage, with beautifully kept gardens. Family run and attractively furnished throughout creating a welcoming atmosphere. Large bedrooms.

Broomshaw Hill Farm without rest., Willia Rd, NE49 9NP, North : 1 m. by Aesica Rd on Willia Rd ℘ (01434) 320866, *stay@broomshaw.co.uk, Fax (01434) 320866,* – P.
March-October, minimum stay 2 nights – **3 rm** ☕ ★45.00 – ★★60.00.
• In the heart of Hadrian's Wall country; 18C farmhouse: one bedroom points to origins with impressive stone walls, timberwork. Remaining rooms are spacious and comfortable.

AMBLETON *Rutland – see Oakham.*

AMPTON-IN-ARDEN *W. Mids.* 502 O 26.
London 114 – Birmingham 16 – Coventry 11.

The White Lion with rm, High St, B92 0AA, ℘ (01675) 442833, *Fax (01675) 443168* – P. MC VISA.
Rest *(closed Monday dinner and Sunday)* (booking essential) a la carte 19.50/29.95 ♀ – ☕ 7.50 – **8 rm** ★49.00 – ★★59.00.
• Pleasantly updated pub. Atmospheric front bar with lots of real ales. The rear dining room is stylish and spacious, serving tasty, modern dishes. Retire to simple bedrooms.

ANLEY SWAN *Worcs.* 503 504 N 27 – *see Upton-upon-Severn.*

ANWELL *Oxon. – see Banbury.*

ARDWICK *Cambs. – see Cambridge.*

HARLOW Essex  U 28 – pop. 88 296.

Nazeing, Middle St ✆ (01992) 893798.
London 22 – Cambridge 37 – Ipswich 60.

Swallow Churchgate, Churchgate St, Old Harlow, CM17 0JT, East : 3 ¼ m. by A 41 and B 183 ✆ (01279) 420246, *reservations.oldharlow@swallowhotels.cor* *Fax (01279) 437720,* – 170.
Rest *(closed Saturday lunch)* a la carte 21.00/28.00 s. – **83 rm** 85.00/111.00 – 85.00/116.00, 2 suites.
◆ Modern hotel built around a Jacobean building. The bedrooms, many of which overloo the gardens, are modern and co-ordinated, and the executive rooms have oak furnitur Country house restaurant with inglenook.

Harlow/Stansted Moat House, Southern Way, CM18 7BA, Southeast : 2 ¼ m. b A 1025 on A 414 ✆ (01279) 829988, *reservations.harlow@moathousehotels.cor* *Fax (01279) 635094,* – rest, – 200.
Rest (bar lunch Monday-Saturday and Sunday) a la carte approx 27.50 – 11.50 – **119 r** 61.00/81.00 – 122.00/162.00.
◆ Geared to the business traveller, a purpose-built hotel close to Stansted airport. Bed rooms are compact with modern fitted furniture. Coffee bar and business centre. Bistro style dining.

Corus H. Harlow, Mulberry Green, Old Harlow, CM17 0ET, East : 2 ¼ m. by A 414 ar B 183 ✆ (0870) 609 6146, *reservations@corushotels.com, Fax (01279) 626113,* – – 60.
Rest *(closed Sunday dinner)* (bar lunch)/dinner a la carte 16.85/34.85 **s.** – 10.95 **55 rm** 94.00 – 94.00.
◆ Part timbered 14C coaching inn with bright, contemporary fabrics, furnishings an décor throughout, except in the bar which has a traditional, timbered pub style. Bright coloured restaurant with timbered ceiling and joists.

Premier Travel Inn, Cambridge Rd, Old Harlow, CM20 2EP, Northeast : 3 ¼ m. by A 41 on A 1184 ✆ (0870) 1977125, *Fax (01279) 452169* – rm, .
Rest (grill rest.) – **61 rm** 52.95 – 52.95.
◆ Well-proportioned modern bedrooms, suitable for business and family stopovers, de signed with practicality and price in mind. Convenient for Stansted airport.

HAROME N. Yorks. – see Helmsley.

HARPENDEN Herts. 504 S 28 – pop. 28 452.

Harpenden Common, East Commmon ✆ (01582) 711320 – Hammonds End ✆ (01582) 712580.
London 32 – Luton 6.

The Bean Tree, 20A Leyton Rd, AL5 2HU, ✆ (01582) 460901, *enquiries@thebea tree.com, Fax (01582) 460826,* – .
closed 1 January, Saturday lunch, Sunday dinner and Monday – **Rest** a la cart 22.50/46.00 .
◆ Converted red-brick cottage with bean tree and smart terrace. Intimate, softly lit restau rant with sage green palette. Carefully sought ingredients; precise modern cooking.

HARROGATE N. Yorks. 502 P 22 Great Britain G. – pop. 85 128.

See : *Town*★.
Exc. : *Fountains Abbey*★★★ *AC :- Studley Royal*★★ *AC (≤★ from Anne Boleyn's Seat) Fountains Hall (Façade*★*), N : 13 m. by A 61 and B 6265 AY – Harewood House*★★ *(Th Gallery*★*) AC, S : 7½ m. by A 61 BZ.*
Forest Lane Head ✆ (01423) 863158 – Follifoot Rd, Pannal ✆ (01423) 871641 – Oakdale ✆ (01423) 567162 – Crimple Valley, Hookstone Wood Rd ✆ (01423) 883485.
Royal Baths, Crescent Rd ✆ (01423) 537300, tic@harrogate.gov.uk.
London 211 – Bradford 18 – Leeds 15 – Newcastle upon Tyne 76 – York 22.

Plan opposite

Rudding Park, Rudding Park, Follifoot, HG3 1JH, Southeast : 3 ¾ m. by A 661 ✆ (01423 871350, *sales@ruddingpark.com, Fax (01423) 872286,* – , rm, res – 300.
The Clocktower : **Rest** a la carte 25.75/31.25 – **49 rm** 140.00 – 170.00, 2 suites
◆ Grade I listed Georgian house in rural location with modern extension. Comfortable elegant style throughout. Rooms are simple and classical with modern, colourful fabrics Smart, contemporary brasserie with oak floors.

HARROGATE

Albert St	BZ	2
Cambridge St	BZ	3
Cheltenham Cres.	BYZ	4
Cheltenham Parade	BYZ	7
Commercial St	BY	8
Crescent Rd	AZ	10
Hampsthwaite Rd	AY	13
James St	BZ	15
Knapping Hill	AY	16
Montpellier Parade	AZ	18
North Park Rd	BCZ	19
Oxford St	BZ	20
Parliament St	AZ	22
Springfield Ave	ABY	23
Swan Rd	AYZ	24
Westmorland St	BY	26
Wheatlands Rd East	CZ	27

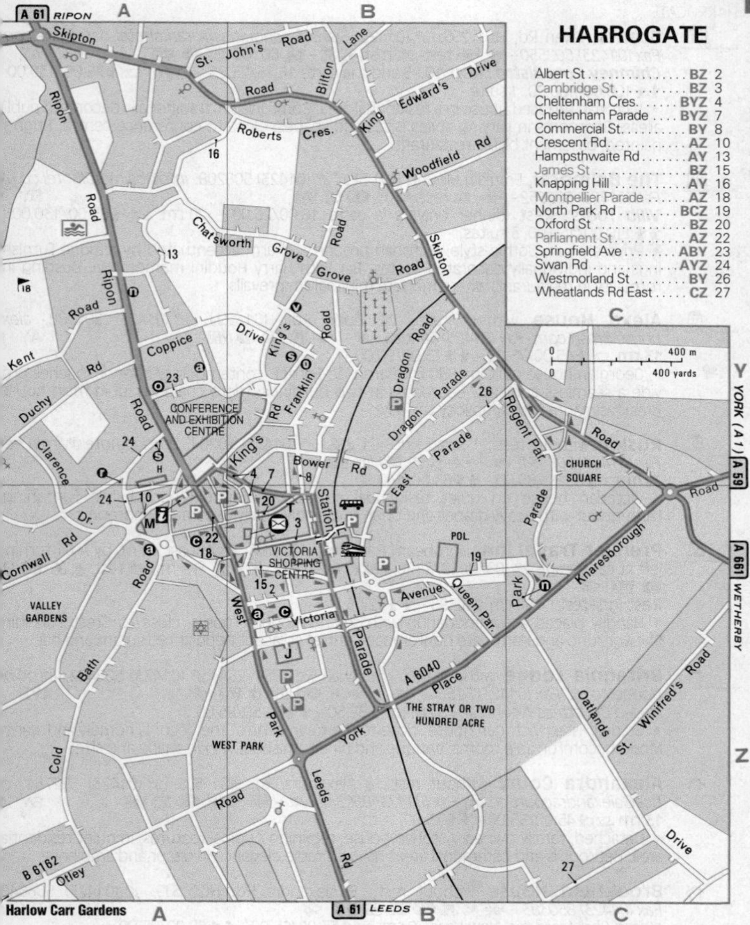

Hotel du Vin, Prospect Pl, HG1 1LB, ✆ (01423) 856800, *info@harrogate.hotelduvin.com, Fax (01423) 856801*, – – 60. BZ a
Bistro : Rest a la carte 28.00/32.00 – 13.50 – **43 rm** 95.00 – 125.00.
◆ Terrace of Georgian houses overlooking pleasant green. Individually appointed bedrooms with wine-theme decor and modern facilities. Buzzy, modern, stylish French bistro and private dining rooms. Good menu of Gallic influenced dishes.

Cedar Court, Queen Building, Park Parade, HG1 5AH, ✆ (01423) 858585, *sales@cedarcourt.karoo.co.uk, Fax (01423) 504950*, – , rest, – 325. VISA. CZ n
Brasserie Tour d'Argent : Rest a la carte 18.20/27.00 s. – **97 rm** 110.00/140.00 – 120.00/160.00, 3 suites.
◆ Large, thoroughly modernised hotel with 17C origins, on edge of town but convenient for the centre. Modern rooms have largely chintz fabrics and furnishings. Compact, modern restaurant.

ENGLAND

Grants, Swan Rd, HG1 2SS, ☎ (01423) 560666, *enquiries@grantshotel-harrogate.com* *Fax (01423) 502550* – |♿|, ⇍ rest, ▤ rest, ✆ P – 🏔 60. MC AE ◑ VISA AY
Chimney Pots Bistro : **Rest** 10.95 and a la carte 16.75/25.25 – **41 rm** ☕ ✝75.00/130.00 – ✝✝100.00/160.00, 1 suite.
◆ Victorian terraced house in a residential area. Comfortable, traditionally decorated public areas. Bedrooms in varying styles, sizes and shapes. Close to conference centre. Brightly painted, basement bistro restaurant.

The Balmoral, Franklin Mount, HG1 5EJ, ☎ (01423) 508208, *info@balmoralhotel.co.uk* *Fax (01423) 530652* – ⇍, ▤ rest, ✆ P. MC AE VISA BY
Villu Toots : **Rest** (dinner only) a la carte 16.00/26.00 – **20 rm** ☕ ✝85.00/130.00 – ✝✝110.00/150.00, 3 suites.
◆ Privately run, Gothic-style, Victorian property; charm accentuated by antique furnishings and individually decorated rooms. Bar with Harry Houdini memorabilia. Bustling informality in restaurant, where modern minimalism prevails.

Alexa House without rest., 26 Ripon Rd, HG1 2JJ, ☎ (01423) 501988, *alexa house@msn.com, Fax (01423) 504086*, 🚗 – ⇍ P. MC ◑ VISA AY
13 rm ☕ ✝45.00/75.00 – ✝✝75.00/90.00.
◆ Georgian house built in 1830 for Baron-de-Ferrier: contemporary interior touches provide a seamless contrast. Bedrooms in two buildings: more characterful in main house. Breakfast room with simplicity the key.

Ruskin without rest., 1 Swan Rd, HG1 2SS, ☎ (01423) 502045, *ruskin.hotel@virgin.net* *Fax (01423) 506131*, 🚗 – ⇍ ✆ P. MC AE VISA AY
7 rm ☕ ✝65.00/85.00 – ✝✝85.00/140.00.
◆ Victorian house on quiet residential street. Comfortable period-style furnishings throughout with heavy drapes and open fires; individually decorated bedrooms.

Premier Travel Inn, Hornbeam Park Ave, HG2 8RA, Southeast : 2 m. by A 61 turning left at car garage ☎ (0870) 1977126, *Fax (01423) 878581* – |♿|, ⇍ rm, ▤ rest, ♿ P. MC AE ◑ VISA. ✗
Rest (grill rest.) – **50 rm** ✝52.95 – ✝✝52.95.
◆ Handily placed accommodation with smart, modern rooms, close to Great Yorkshire Showground and Harrogate Conference Centre. Adjacent popular restaurant and bar.

Britannia Lodge without rest., 16 Swan Rd, HG1 2SA, ☎ (01423) 508482, *info@britlodge.co.uk, Fax (01423) 526840*, 🚗 – ⇍ P. MC AE ◑ VISA. ✗ AYZ
closed Christmas-New Year – **3 rm** ☕ ✝82.50 – ✝✝82.50/95.00.
◆ Grade II listed Victorian house, close to the town centre. The décor is homely and warm. Modern, comfortable rooms, antique and pine furnished, vary in shape and size.

Alexandra Court without rest., 8 Alexandra Rd, HG1 5JS, ☎ (01423) 502764, *office@alexandracourt.co.uk, Fax (01423) 850383*, 🚗 – ⇍ ✆ P. MC AE VISA BY
13 rm ☕ ✝45.00/55.00 – ✝✝75.00.
◆ Detached, family owned Victorian house, retaining original features, in quiet residential area. Bedrooms and communal areas have a simple elegance in décor and ambience.

Brookfield House without rest., 5 Alexandra Rd, HG1 5JS, ☎ (01423) 506646 *Fax (01423) 850383* – ⇍ ✆ P. MC AE ◑ VISA. ✗ BY
closed Christmas and New Year – **6 rm** ☕ ✝55.00/65.00 – ✝✝68.00/85.00.
◆ Family owned Victorian property in a quiet, residential location close to the town centre. Homely feel in communal areas and comfortable bedrooms with a mix of styles.

Acacia without rest., 3 Springfield Ave, HG1 2HR, ☎ (01423) 560752 – ⇍ P. ✗ AY
restricted opening November-March, minimum stay 2 nights – **4 rm** ☕ ✝55.00/75.00 – ✝✝75.00/85.00.
◆ Centrally located Victorian solid stone guesthouse, within a few minutes' walk of the shops; very personably run. Immaculately kept throughout. Attractive, pine-clad bedrooms.

Ashwood House without rest., 7 Spring Grove, HG1 2HS, ☎ (01423) 560081, *ashwoodhouse@aol.com, Fax (01423) 527928* – ⇍ P. MC VISA. ✗ AY
closed 20 December-2 January – **5 rm** ☕ ✝35.00/55.00 – ✝✝60.00/70.00.
◆ An Edwardian house minutes from the International Conference Centre. Simply decorated, pine furnished rooms and communal areas have a homely ambience.

Quantro, 3 Royal Par, HG1 2SZ, ☎ (01423) 503034, *info@quantro.co.uk* *Fax (01423) 503034* – ⇍ ▤. MC AE VISA AZ
closed 25-26 December, 1 January and Sunday – **Rest** 12.95 and a la carte 22.40/29.00
◆ Modern art murals and mirrors adorn this smart restaurant. Comfy banquettes and black tables. Good value mix of interesting dishes with Mediterranean underpinnings.

ENGLAND

XX **Orchid,** 28 Swan Rd, HG1 2SE, ☎ (01423) 560425, *info@orchidrestaurant.co.uk* – ⇜ ▤ P ⇔ 16. MC AE D VISA
closed 10 days early February and Saturday lunch – **Rest** - South East Asian - a la carte 20.00/37.00 ♀.
◆ Unfussy, uncluttered restaurant with Asian styling. Polite, friendly service adds to the enjoyment of richly authentic dishes from a wide range of south-east Asian countries.

X **Courtyard,** 1 Montpellier Mews, HG1 2TQ, ☎ (01423) 530708, *Fax (01423) 530708*, ⛱ – ⇜. MC AE VISA
AZ c
closed Sunday – **Rest** 14.95 (lunch) and a la carte 25.00/35.00 ♀.
◆ Former stables with Jacob's ladder, set in Victorian mews area; cosy, contemporary interior. Charming cobbled terrace. Traditional menus with modern Mediterranean twist.

X **Sasso,** 8-10 Princes Sq, HG1 1LX, ☎ (01423) 508838, *Fax (01423) 508838* – ⇜. MC VISA
BZ c
closed 1 week Spring, 1 week September, 25-26 December, 1 January, Sunday, Monday lunch and Bank Holidays – **Rest** - Italian - a la carte 20.70/31.50 ♀.
◆ In the basement of a 19C property. Antiques, ceramics and modern art embellish the interior. The menu offers a good choice of authentic Italian dishes with modern influences.

t Kettlesing *West : 6½ m. by A 59 – AY – ✉ Harrogate.*

⌂ **Knabbs Ash** without rest., Skipton Rd, HG3 2LT, on A 59 ☎ (01423) 771040, *sheila@knabbsash.freeserve.co.uk*, ≤, ⛱, ⚘ – ⇜ P. ✗
closed Christmas – 3 rm ☐ ★40.00/45.00 – ★★60.00/65.00.
◆ Stone built cottage with spacious gardens and grounds. Cosy lounge; pine furnished breakfast room. Homely and simple, largely floral interior; rooms individually decorated.

Do not confuse X with ✿! X defines comfort, while stars are awarded for the best cuisine, across all categories of comfort.

ARTINGTON *Derbs.* 502 503 504 O 24 – ✉ *Buxton.*
London 168 – Derby 36 – Manchester 40 – Sheffield 34 – Stoke-on-Trent 22.

🏠 **Biggin Hall** ⛱, Biggin, SK17 0DH, Southeast : 2 m. by B 5054 ☎ (01298) 84451, *enquiries@bigginhall.co.uk, Fax (01298) 84681*, ≤, ⛱ – ⇜ rest, P. MC AE VISA
Rest (booking essential to non-residents) (dinner only) 17.50 s. – ☐ 4.50 – **20 rm** ★60.00/80.00 – ★★110.00/124.00.
◆ Charming house with much rustic personality and individuality. Stone floored lounges and open fires. Antique furnished bedrooms vary in size and shape. Elegant dining room with low beams.

ARTLEPOOL *Hartlepool* 502 Q 19 – *pop. 86 075.*
18, 18 Seaton Carew, Tees Rd ☎ (01429) 266249 – 18 Castle Eden & Peterlee ☎ (01429) 836220 – 18 Hart Warren ☎ (01429) 274398.
✈ Teesside Airport : ☎ (01325) 332811, SW : 20 m. by A 689, A 1027, A 135 and A 67.
ℹ Hartlepool Art Gallery Information Centre, Church Sq ☎ (01429) 869706.
London 263 – Durham 19 – Middlesbrough 9 – Newcastle upon Tyne 33 – Sunderland 21.

🏠 **Premier Travel Inn,** Maritime Ave, Hartlepool Marina, TS24 0YG, ☎ (01429) 890115, *Fax (01429) 233105*, ≤ – ⇜, ▤ rest, ♿ P. MC AE D VISA. ✗
Rest (grill rest.) – **40 rm** ★46.95/46.95 – ★★49.95/49.95.
◆ Well-proportioned modern rooms, suitable for business or family guests; overlooks the marina. Practical, economical accommodation. Convenient for Hartlepool football ground.

X **Krimo's,** Neptune House, The Marina, TS24 0BY, by Maritime Ave and Fleet Ave ☎ (01429) 266120, *krimo@krimos.co.uk, Fax (01429) 222111* – ⇜ ▤ P. MC VISA
closed 25-26 December, 1 January, Sunday dinner and Monday – **Rest** a la carte 17.10/29.85 s.
◆ Well situated in the marina area overlooking the lock and boats. An informal, almost Mediterranean style reflected in the menu alongside Algerian dishes.

ENGLAND

HARWELL *Oxon.* 503 504 Q 29 – *pop. 2 015.*

London 64 – Oxford 16 – Reading 18 – Swindon 22.

Kingswell, Reading Rd, OX11 0LZ, South : ¾ m. on A 417 ☎ (01235) 833043, *kir swell@breathemail.net, Fax (01235) 833193* – rm, P – 30. AE VISA.
closed 24-30 December – **Rest** 15.95/18.95 and a la carte 19.50/33.00 **s.** ♀ – **19 rm**
✝85.00/99.00 – ✝✝99.00/115.00.
• Large redbrick hotel located on the south Oxfordshire Downs. Convenient for Didc rail and Oxford. Spacious, uniform, traditional bedrooms and pubby public areas. Class menus served in traditional dining room.

HARWICH and DOVERCOURT *Essex* 504 X 28 – *pop. 20 130 (Harwich).*

Station Rd, Parkeston ☎ (01255) 503616.
to Germany (Cuxhaven) (DFDS Seaways A/S) 4 per week (19 h) – to Denmark (Esbjer (DFDS Seaways A/S) 1-3 daily (20 h) – to The Netherlands (Hook of Holland) (Stena Line) daily (3 h 30 mn).
Iconfield Park, Parkeston ☎ (01255) 506139.
London 78 – Chelmsford 41 – Colchester 20 – Ipswich 23.

Pier at Harwich, The Quay, CO12 3HH, ☎ (01255) 241212, *pier@milsomhotels.cor Fax (01255) 551922,* ← – P. AE VISA.
Harbourside : **Rest** - Seafood - 20.00 (lunch) and a la carte 20.85/47.45 ♀ – **14 rm**
✝75.00 – ✝✝180.00.
• Bright Victorian building located on the quayside giving many bedrooms views of th area's busy sea lanes. Décor is comfortably stylish and contemporary with a nautic theme. Seafood restaurant with North Sea outlook.

Undecided between two equivalent establishments? Within each category, establishments are classified in our order of preference.

HASLEMERE *Surrey* 504 R 30 – *pop. 11 663.*

London 47 – Brighton 46 – Southampton 44.

Lythe Hill and Spa, Petworth Rd, GU27 3BQ, East : 1½ m. on B 2131 ☎ (01428) 65125 *lythe@lythehill.co.uk, Fax (01428) 644131,* ←, – rest,
– 100. AE VISA
Auberge de France : **Rest** - French - 15.00 (lunch) and a la carte 29.00/47.00 – 12.00
30 rm ✝160.00 – ✝✝160.00, 11 suites.
• Accommodation focused around a delightful Tudor building which houses breakfa room and suites. Good leisure facilities. Spotlessly kept, traditional and period room Robust cuisine under ancient beams in Auberge de France.

HASTINGS and ST LEONARDS *E. Sussex* 504 V 31 – *pop. 85 828 (Hastings).*

Beauport Park, Battle Rd, St Leonards-on-Sea ☎ (01424) 854243.
Town Hall, Queen's Sq, Priory Meadow ☎ (01424) 781111, hic-info@hastings.gov.uk
The Stade, Old Town Hall ☎ (01424) 781111.
London 65 – Brighton 37 – Folkestone 37 – Maidstone 34.

Plan opposite

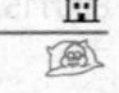

Tower House, 26-28 Tower Road West, TN38 0RG, ☎ (01424) 427217, *reser tions@towerhousehotel.com, Fax (01424) 430165,* – . VISA. AY
closed Christmas – **Rest** (residents only) (dinner only) (set menu only) 18.50 ♀ – **10** rm
✝49.50/55.00 – ✝✝75.00.
• Friendly and well run, a redbrick Victorian house in a residential area. Comfortably fu nished with individually decorated bedrooms and a conservatory bar lounge area.

Parkside House without rest., 59 Lower Park Rd, TN34 2LD, ☎ (01424) 43309 *bkent.parksidehouse@talk21.com, Fax (01424) 421431* – . AE VISA. BY
5 rm ✝35.00/45.00 – ✝✝65.00.
• Detached Victorian house in quiet area of town overlooking a park. Traditionally decora ted; the spacious bedrooms all boast television and video.

HASTINGS ST. LEONARDS

bert Rd . . . . BZ 3
ourne (The). . . . . BY 4
ambridge Gardens . . . . . BZ 5
astle Hill Rd . . . . BZ 8
astle St. . . . . BZ 7
ornwallis Gardens. . . . . . BZ 9
ornwallis Terrace . . . . . . BZ 10
Denmark Pl. . . . . BZ 13
Dorset Pl. . . . . BZ 15
Gensing Rd. . . . . AZ 16
George St. . . . . BY 18
Grosvenor Crescent . . . . . AY 19
Harold Pl. . . . . BZ 20
Havelock Rd . . . . BZ 21
King's Rd . . . . AZ 22
London Rd . . . . AZ
Marine Court . . . . AZ 23
Middle St . . . . BZ 24
Norman Rd. . . . . AZ
Priory Meadow Shopping Centre . . . . BZ
Queen's Rd. . . . . BZ
Robertson St . . . . BZ 27
Rock-a-Nore Rd . . . . BY 30
St Helen's Park Rd . . . . . . BY 31
Sedlescombe Rd South . . AY 32
Silchester Rd . . . . AZ 33
Warrior Square . . . . AZ 34
Wellington Pl. . . . . BZ 35
Wellington Square . . . . . . BZ 36
White Rock Road . . . . BZ 38

A 21 LONDON
B 2093 (A 21), BATTLE
A
B
Y
A 259
RYE, FOLKESTONE FAIRLIGHT COUNTRY PARK
HOLLINGTON
ST-HELEN'S WOOD
ST-HELEN'S
SILVERHILL
ALEXANDRA PARK
HASTINGS
OLD TOWN
ST. CLEMENT'S CAVES
ST.LEONARDS
Sedlescombe Rd
North
A 21
St. Helen's
A 2101
Battle
B 2159
Blackman Av.
Ironlatch Av.
Gillsmans Hill
Amherst Rd
Bohemia Road
London
The Green
Dane Rd
Road
Filsham
Marina
Harley Shute Rd
B 2092
Downs Rd
Elphinstone Road
Mt Pleasant Rd
Priory
The Ridge
Frederick Rd
Rock Lane
Rye Rd
London Road
Old London
Harold Rd
Saxon Road
0
1 km
1 mile

A 2102 (A 21)
A 21
A 259 (A 21) A 2101
CRICKET GROUND
SUMMER FIELDS
POL.
SUMMERFIELDS LEISURE CENTRE
HASTINGS
PRIORY MEADOW
1066 STORY AT HASTINGS CASTLE
WARRIOR SQ.
GENSING GARDENS
ST.LEONARDS
WHITE ROCKS GARDENS
Woodland Vale Rd
A 2102
Southwater Road
Chapel Park Rd
Church Rd
Bohemia Road
Magdalen Rd
Falaise Rd
Linton Rd
Braybrooke
Priory Av.
Road
South Ter.
Queen's Road
Milward Road
Cambridge Rd
White Rock
Carlisle Parade
St. John's Rd
Pevensey Rd
London Road
Western Rd
St.Margaret's Rd
Eversfield Place
Norman Road
Grand Parade
CENTRE
0
400 m
400 yards
A
B
N

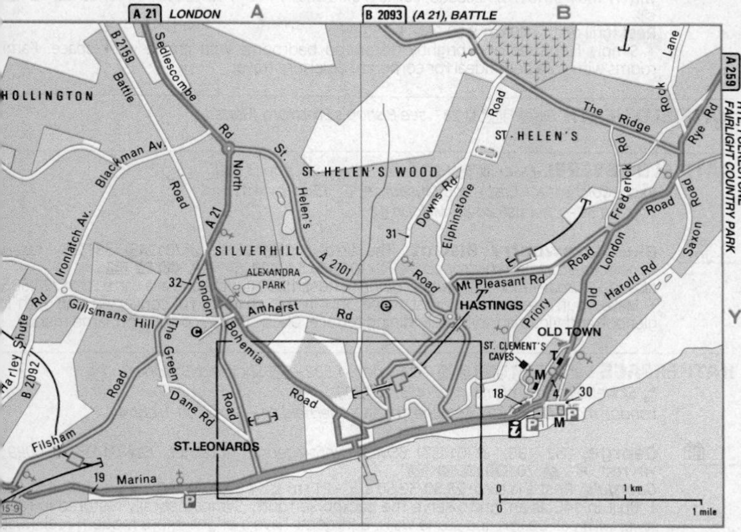

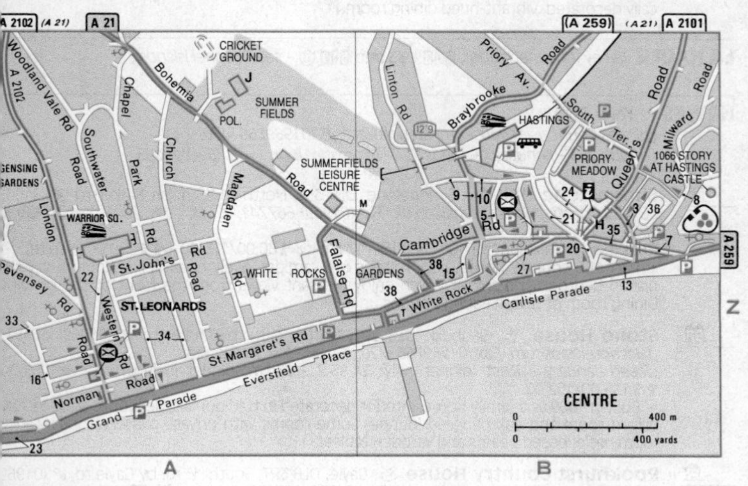

Good food without spending a fortune? Look out for the Bib Gourmand

HATCH BEAUCHAMP *Somerset* 503 K 30 – *see Taunton.*

HATFIELD *Herts.* 504 T 28 *Great Britain G. – pop. 32 281.*
See : *Hatfield House★★ AC.*
Hatfield London C.C., Bedwell Park, Essendon ☎ (01707) 260360.
London 27 – Bedford 38 – Cambridge 39.

Premier Travel Inn, Lemsford Rd, AL10 0DA, Northwest : 1 m. by B 197 at junctio with A 1001 ☎ (01707) 268990, *Fax (01707) 256054* – rm, rest, P. MC AE VISA
Rest (grill rest.) – **40 rm** 52.95 – 52.95.
◆ Simply furnished and brightly decorated bedrooms with ample work space. Fami rooms with sofa beds. Ideal for corporate or leisure travel.

HATFIELD HEATH *Essex* 504 U 28 – *see Bishop's Stortford (Herts.).*

HATFIELD PEVEREL *Essex* 504 V 28 *Great Britain G. – pop. 3 258.*
Exc. : *Colchester - Castle and Museum★, E : 13 m. by A 12.*
London 39 – Chelmsford 8 – Maldon 12.

Blue Strawberry Bistrot, The Street, CM3 2DW, ☎ (01245) 381333, *reserv tions@bluestrawberrybistrot.co.uk, Fax (01245) 340498,* – P. MC AE VISA
closed Saturday lunch and Sunday dinner – **Rest** 15.00 (lunch) and a la carte 20.15/28.50
◆ Make your reservation by first name only in this characterful converted pub with ir glenook and Victorian style. Rear dining terrace. Classic British cooking off large menus.

HATHERSAGE *Derbs.* 502 503 504 P 24 – *pop. 1 582* – ✉ *Sheffield (S. Yorks.).*
Sickleholme, Bamford ☎ (01433) 651306.
London 177 – Derby 39 – Manchester 34 – Sheffield 11 – Stoke-on-Trent 44.

George, S32 1BB, ☎ (01433) 650436, *info@george-hotel.net, Fax (01433) 650099* rest, P – 70. MC AE VISA
George's : **Rest** a la carte 23.50/32.50 **s.** – **21 rm** 82.00/92.00 – 111.00/114.00.
◆ Built in 14C as an inn to serve the packhorse route. Sympathetically restored in rusti style, with oak beams and stone walls. Bedrooms have a bright, more modern feel. Rust cally decorated, vibrant-hued dining room.

LA HAULE *Jersey (Channel Islands)* 503 L 33 and 517 ⑪ – *see Channel Islands.*

HAWES *N. Yorks.* 502 N 21.
Dales Countryside Museum, Station Yard ☎ (01969) 667450.
London 253 – Kendal 27 – Leeds 72 – Newcastle upon Tyne 76 – York 65.

Simonstone Hall , Simonstone, DL8 3LY, North : 1 ½ m. on Muker rd ☎ (0196 667255, *info@simonstonehall.co.uk, Fax (01969) 667741,* ←, , , – P. MC A VISA
Rest (bar lunch)/dinner 27.00/35.00 – **17 rm** 60.00/120.00 – 120.00, 1 suite.
◆ Part 18C country house, with historic feel, amidst lovely countryside. Individually fur nished bedrooms, many of which enjoy pleasant views from the front of the building Dining room or tavern eating options.

Stone House , Sedbusk, DL8 3PT, North : 1 m. by Muker rd ☎ (01969) 66757 *daleshotel@aol.com, Fax (01969) 667720,* ←, – P. MC VISA
closed January – **Rest** (dinner only) 24.95 – **23 rm** (dinner included) 125.00 135.00/152.00.
◆ Built in 1908 as a family home. Interior decorated in traditional style; public areas includ billiard room and oak panelled lounge. Some rooms with private conservatories. Dinin room has exposed beams and wooden tables.

Rookhurst Country House , Gayle, DL8 3RT, South : ½ m. by Gayle rd ☎ (0196 667454, *enquiries@rookhurst.co.uk, Fax (01969) 667128,* – P. MC VISA.
closed Christmas and New Year – **Rest** (booking essential) (residents only) (dinner onl 25.00 **s.** – **5 rm** 55.00 – 120.00/130.00.
◆ Spacious yet cosy country house with a very comfortable, smart, traditional atmospher that's friendly and informal. Convenient for the Pennine Way. Uncluttered bedrooms.

Cockett's, Market Pl, DL8 3RD, ✆ (01969) 667312, *enquiries@cocketts.co.uk, Fax (01969) 667162,* – . MC AE VISA.
closed 25-26 December and 10-26 January – **Rest** *(closed Tuesday)* (dinner only) 16.95 and a la carte 16.15/24.85 – **8 rm** ☐ ✝45.00/50.00 – ✝✝69.00/74.00.
◆ Grade II listed building with a historic inscribed door lintel - reputedly the most photographed doorway in the country. Cosy, traditional atmosphere throughout. Dining room with enticing, age-old ambience.

Bulls Head without rest., Market Pl, DL8 3RD, ✆ (01969) 667437, *ann@bullsheadhotel.com, Fax (01969) 667048* – . MC VISA
6 rm ☐ ✝45.00/65.00 – ✝✝55.00/65.00.
◆ Substantial, listed 19C house, in former incarnations a bank and a pub. Lounge with original range and crackling fire. Pleasant rooms; two are vaulted and in the cellars.

East House without rest., Gayle, DL8 3RZ, South : ½ m. by Gayle rd on Bainbridge rd ✆ (01969) 667405, *lornaward@lineone.net,* ≤, – P.
closed Christmas and January – **3 rm** ☐ ✝25.00 – ✝✝50.00.
◆ Attractive, very tidily run stone house dating from early 1800s in peaceful hamlet: lovely views over Wensleydale. Combined breakfast and lounge area. Pleasant bedrooms.

HAWKSHEAD *Cumbria* 502 L 20 *Great Britain G.* – *pop. 570* – ✉ *Ambleside.*
See : *Village*★.
Env. : *Lake Windermere*★★ – *Coniston Water*★ *(Brantwood*★, *on east side), SW : by B 5285.*
ℹ *Main Car Park* ✆ *(015394) 36525 (summer only).*
London 283 – *Carlisle 52* – *Kendal 19.*

Ivy House, Main St, LA22 ONS, ✆ (015394) 36204, *ivyhousehotel@btinternet.com, Fax (015394) 36204,* – P. MC VISA
Rest (by arrangement) 20.00/45.00 – **6 rm** (dinner included) ☐ ✝53.00 – ✝✝106.00.
◆ Georgian house, in centre of village, retains architectural features such as a period spiral staircase. Traditional style public areas; bedrooms feature four-poster beds. Simple dining room with fine Georgian furnishings.

at Near Sawrey *Southeast : 2 m. on B 5285* – ✉ *Ambleside.*

Sawrey House Country H., LA22 OLF, ✆ (015394) 36387, *enquiries@sawreyhouse.com, Fax (015394) 36010,* ≤ Esthwaite Water and Grizedale Forest, – P. MC VISA
closed November-January – **Rest** (booking essential) (dinner only) 25.00/35.00 a la carte 29.50/36.50 – **12 rm** ☐ ✝40.00/75.00 – ✝✝150.00/170.00.
◆ Victorian house with idyllic views of Esthwaite Water and Grizedale Forest and adjacent to Beatrix Potter's house. Traditional interior with individually styled bedrooms. Restaurant with great views by day, candlelight by night.

Ees Wyke Country House, LA22 OJZ, ✆ (015394) 36393, *mail@eeswyke.co.uk, Fax (015394) 36740,* ≤ Esthwaite Water and Grizedale Forest, – rest, P. MC VISA
*restricted opening in winter***Rest** (booking essential) (dinner only) 30.00 – **8 rm** (dinner included) ☐ ✝72.00/105.00 – ✝✝144.00/176.00.
◆ Panoramic views of Esthwaite Water and Grizedale Forest from this large, impressive Georgian house. Good sized bedrooms with distinctive, homely charm. Dining room's large windows afford lovely views.

at Far Sawrey *Southeast : 2½ m. on B 5285* – ✉ *Ambleside.*

West Vale, LA22 OLQ, ✆ (015394) 42817, *enquiries@westvalecountryhouse.co.uk, Fax (015394) 45302,* ≤ – P. MC AE VISA.
closed 25-26 December – **Rest** (by arrangement) 34.00 – **7 rm** ☐ ✝52.00/77.00 – ✝✝128.00/146.00.
◆ Victorian house on edge of hamlet with attractive country views. A warm welcome to an interior with open-fired, stone-floored sitting room and snug bedrooms. Meals locally sourced, proudly home cooked.

HAWNBY *N. Yorks.* 502 Q 21 – ✉ *Helmsley.*
London 245 – *Middlesbrough 27* – *Newcastle upon Tyne 69* – *York 30.*

Hawnby, YO62 5QS, ✆ (01439) 798202, *info@hawnbyhotel.co.uk, Fax (01439) 798344,* ≤, – P. MC VISA.
Rest a la carte 11.85/22.50 ♀ – **9 rm** ☐ ✝59.00 – ✝✝79.00.
◆ Personally run small hotel in a very rural location with commanding views of nearby countryside - ideal for walking in the Dales. Snug bedrooms with a cottage feel. Tried-and-tested menus.

ENGLAND

at Laskill *Northeast : 2¼ m. by Osmotherley rd – ✉ Hawnby.*

Laskill Grange without rest., Easterside, YO62 5NB, ✆ (01439) 798268, *suesmith@killfarm.fsnet.co.uk, Fax (01439) 798498,* – ✉ P. VISA
4 rm ★35.00/50.00 – ★★70.00.
◆ A working farm with four cottagey bedrooms set in two converted Victorian stab blocks, surrounded by 1000 acres of rolling farmland. Breakfast served in sunny co servatory.

HAWORTH *W. Yorks.* 502 O 22 *Great Britain G. – pop. 6 078 – ✉ Keighley.*
See : *Town*★.
ℹ *2-4 West Lane ✆ (01535) 642329, haworth@ytbtic.co.uk.*
London 213 – Burnley 22 – Leeds 22 – Manchester 34.

Hill Top Farmhouse, Haworth Moor, BD22 0EL, West : 1 m. by Colne rd a Penistone Hill rd on Brontë Waterfall rd ✆ (01535) 643524, ≤ Haworth Moor,
Rest (by arrangement) 16.00 – **3 rm** ★48.00 – ★★60.00.
◆ Attractive 17C farmhouse wonderfully set on the moors, close to Brontë Parsona Museum. Welcoming fires, wood carved furniture. Cosy rooms with fresh flowers and fi views. Good home cooking is assured.

Rosebud Cottage, 1 Belle Isle Rd, BD22 8QQ, ✆ (01535) 640321, *info@rosebudc tage.co.uk,* – P. VISA.
closed 25-26 December – **Rest** (by arrangement) 14.00 – **5 rm** ★27.50/40.00 ★★60.00/65.00.
◆ Compact, cosy sandstone end-of-terrace cottage built in 1752, next to station on pr served railway line. The homely bedrooms are all very different with individual theme Pine-furnished dining room overlooks conservatory; home-cooked dishes.

Aitches, 11 West Lane, BD22 8DU, ✆ (01535) 642501, *aitches@talk21.com* – . VI
Rest (by arrangement) 17.50 ♀ – **4 rm** ★40.00 – ★★55.00.
◆ Imposing Victorian house in centre of historic town: two minutes' walk from Bron parsonage, and adjacent to famous cobbled streets. Distinctive homely feel; comfy room

Weaver's with rm, 15 West Lane, BD22 8DU, ✆ (01535) 643822, *weavers@aol.co Fax (01535) 644832* – rest, rest, ✆. VISA.
closed 26 December-4 January – **Rest** *(closed Tuesday lunch, Sunday dinner and Monda* 17.50 (lunch) and a la carte 19.85/29.50 ♀ – **3 rm** ★55.00/65.00 – ★★85.00.
◆ Former weavers cottages with an informal atmosphere and some charm. Characterf cluttered lounge with ornaments and artefacts. Homely cooking, surroundings and be rooms.

HAYDOCK *Mersey.* 502 503 504 M 23 – ✉ *St. Helens.*
London 198 – Liverpool 19 – Manchester 18.

Premier Travel Inn, Yew Tree Way, Golbourne, WA3 3JD, East : 2 ½ m. by A 5 ✆ (01942) 273422, *Fax (01942) 296100* – rm, rest, P. VISA.
Rest (grill rest.) – **60 rm** ★46.95/46.95 – ★★48.95/48.95.
◆ Conveniently located for the racecourse with modern, comfortable rooms - those aw from road are quieter. A wood fitted restaurant with conservatory extension for meals.

HAYDON BRIDGE *Northd* 501 502 N 19 – *see Hexham.*

HAYLE *Cornwall* 503 D 33.
London 288 – Penzance 9 – Truro 20.

Premier Travel Inn, Carwin Rise, Loggans, TR27 4PN, North : 1 m. by B 3301 junction with A 30 ✆ (08701) 977133, *Fax (01736) 759514* – rm, rest, P. VISA.
Rest (grill rest.) – **56 rm** ★49.95 – ★★49.95.
◆ Well-proportioned modern bedrooms, suitable for business and family stopovers, d signed with practicality and price in mind. Wood fitted pub-style restaurant.

HAYLING ISLAND *Hants.* 504 R 31 – *pop. 14 842.*
18 *Links Lane ✆ (023) 9246 3712.*
ℹ *Beachlands, Seafront ✆ (023) 9246 7111 (summer only).*
London 77 – Brighton 45 – Southampton 28.

Cockle Warren Cottage without rest., 36 Seafront, PO11 9HL, ☎ (023) 9246 4961, *Fax (023) 9246 4838*, heated, – P. VISA
6 rm ☐ ★40.00/50.00 – ★★65.00/75.00.
◆ A pleasant cottage just across the road from the beach. Conservatory breakfast room overlooks pool. Comfortable, well-kept bedrooms. Families particularly welcome.

HAYTOR VALE *Devon – see Bovey Tracey.*

HAYWARDS HEATH *W. Sussex* 504 T 31 *Great Britain G. – pop. 29 110.*
Env. : *Sheffield Park Garden★, E : 5 m. on A 272 and A 275.*
Paxhill Park, East Mascalls Lane, Lindfield ☎ (01444) 484467.
London 41 – Brighton 16.

Jeremy's at Borde Hill, Borde Hill Gdns, RH16 1XP, North : 1 ¾ m. by B 2028 on Balcombe Rd ☎ (01444) 441102, *reservations@jeremysrestaurant.com, Fax (01494) 441355,* – P. AE VISA
closed 1 week January, Sunday dinner and Monday except Bank Holidays – **Rest** 22.00 (lunch) and a la carte 37.50.
◆ Converted 19C stables with delightful views to Victorian walled garden. Contemporary interior with modern art. Confident, vibrant cooking in a light Mediterranean style.

HEACHAM *Norfolk* 504 V 25.
London 116 – Hunstanton 2.5 – King's Lynn 15.5.

The Grove without rest., 17 Collins Lane, PE31 7DZ, ☎ (01485) 570513, *tm.shannon@virgin.net,* – P.
3 rm ☐ ★35.00/60.00 – ★★60.00.
◆ Victorian house set on high street continuation. Cosy, book-strewn guest lounge. Full cooked breakfasts with fruit plates. Two rooms homely and spotless; secluded stable room.

HEADLAM *Durham* 502 O 20 – *see Darlington.*

HEATHROW AIRPORT *Middx.* 504 S 29 – *see Hillingdon (Greater London).*

HEDDON ON THE WALL *Northd..*
London 288.5 – Blaydon 7.5 – Newcastle upon Tyne 8.5.

Close House, NE15 0HT, Southwest : 2 ¼ m. by B 6528 ☎ (01661) 852255, *events@closehouse.co.uk, Fax (01661) 853322,* – P – 80. AE VISA.
closed 25-26 December – **Rest** *(closed Saturday lunch and Sunday dinner)* 18.95 (lunch) and dinner a la carte 32.95/41.45 **s.** – ☐ 5.00 – **7 rm** ★100.00/112.50 – ★★150.00/175.00.
◆ Conference oriented Georgian manor house in 300 acres of grounds in Hadrian's Wall country. Marble-floored reception leads to sofa-strewn lounge. Stylish Regency style rooms. Dining room in warm burgundy serves modern menus.

HELLAND *Cornwall – see Bodmin.*

HELMSLEY *N. Yorks.* 502 Q 21 *Great Britain G. – pop. 1 559.*
Env. : *Rievaulx Abbey★★ AC, NW : 2½ m. by B 1257.*
Ampleforth College, Court Cottage, Cawton, York ☎ (01653) 628555.
Helmsley Castle, Castlegate ☎ (01439) 770173.
London 239 – Leeds 51 – Middlesbrough 28 – York 24.

The Black Swan, Market Pl, YO62 5BJ, ☎ (01439) 770466, *blackswan@macdonald-hotels.co.uk, Fax (01439) 770174,* – P. AE VISA
The Rutland Room : **Rest** 25.00 (dinner) and a la carte 22.50/32.00 – **45 rm** (dinner included) ☐ ★100.00/125.00 – ★★140.00/160.00.
◆ Part 16C coaching inn in a historic market town; indeed it overlooks the market. Charming rustic interior with exposed beams. Many bedrooms with period fittings and features. Formal dining in classically furnished restaurant.

Feversham Arms, YO62 5AG, on B 1257 ✆ (01439) 770766, *info@fevershamarmshotel.com, Fax (01439) 770346*, , heated, , – – . 35.
Conservatory : Rest 16.95 and a la carte 30.00/38.50 – **19 rm** 130.00 – 160.00/210.00.
◆ A former coaching inn; its stone façade conceals surprisingly modern rooms of a quiet restful nature: walls, floors in muted colours, spot lighting, quality fabrics. Range of dining locations, including around the pool.

No.54, 54 Bondgate, YO62 5EZ, ✆ (01439) 771533, *Fax (01439) 771533*, –
Rest (by arrangement) (communal dining) – **4 rm** 30.00/45.00 – 78.00.
◆ Victorian terraced cottage, formerly the village vet's. Charming owner. Bedrooms are strong point: set around flagged courtyard, they're airy, bright and very well-equipped. Dine round antique communal table in homely lounge.

Carlton Lodge without rest., Bondgate, YO62 5EY, ✆ (01439) 770557, *b+b@carlton-lodge.com, Fax (01439) 770623* – .
8 rm 35.00/45.00 – 75.00.
◆ Late 19C house set just out of town. Homely and traditional air to the décor in the communal areas and the bedrooms, some of which have period features. Cosy breakfast room.

at Nawton *East : 3¼ m. on A 170 – ✉ York.*

Plumpton Court without rest., High St, YO62 7TT, ✆ (01439) 771223, *mail@plumptoncourt.com*, – . .
closed December and January – **9 rm** 40.00 – 62.00.
◆ The emphasis here is on homeliness; this is well provided by cottage-style traditional décor, open fires and a friendly welcome. Top floor bedrooms have modern style.

at Harome *Southeast : 2¾ m. by A 170 – ✉ York.*

The Pheasant, YO62 5JG, ✆ (01439) 771241, *Fax (01439) 771744*, , – rest, .
mid March-mid December – **Rest** (bar lunch)/dinner 25.00 – **12 rm** (dinner included) 75.50/89.50 – 151.00/160.00, 2 suites.
◆ Family run and hidden away in picturesque hamlet with a duck pond and mill stream close by. Open fires and beams in traditionally styled building with modern furniture. Conservatory dining room.

Cross House Lodge at The Star Inn, YO62 5JE, ✆ (01439) 770397, *Fax (01439) 771833*, – rm, .
The Piggery : **Rest** *(closed Sunday dinner and Monday)* (booking essential) (residents only) (set menu only) 45.00 - (see also ***The Star Inn*** below) – **11 rm** 120.00 – 210.00.
◆ Converted farm building set opposite pub in pretty village. Open-plan, split-level lounge. Ultra-stylish, super-smart rooms in either main building, annex or local cottages.

The Star Inn (Pern), High St, YO62 5JE, ✆ (01439) 770397, *Fax (01439) 771833*, , – . .
closed 2 weeks January, Sunday dinner, Monday and Bank Holidays – **Rest** (booking essential) a la carte 25.00/40.00 .
Spec. Grilled black pudding with foie gras and watercress. Fillet of John Dory, cauliflower purée and braised oxtail. Elderflower rice pudding with strawberry jam.
◆ Delightful thatched inn with appealing rustic character. Eat in the beamed bar or elegant dining room. Modern original cooking heavy with Yorkshire influences.

at Ampleforth *Southwest : 4½ m. by A 170 off B 1257 – ✉ Helmsley.*

Shallowdale House , YO62 4DY, West : ½ m. ✆ (01439) 788325, *stay@shallowdalehouse.co.uk, Fax (01439) 788885*, Gilling Gap, – . .
closed Christmas - New Year – **Rest** (by arrangement) 30.00 – **3 rm** 65.00/75.00 – 82.00/99.00.
◆ Modern guesthouse with spectacular views of the Howardian Hills; an area of outstanding beauty. Spacious rooms with large picture windows for the scenery. Warm and relaxed. Owners proud of their home-cooked menus.

at Byland Abbey *Southwest : 6½ m. by A 170 – ✉ Helmsley.*

Oldstead Grange without rest., Oldstead, YO61 4BJ, Northwest : 1 ¼ m. on Oldstead rd ✆ (01347) 868634, *oldsteadgrange@yorkshireuk.com*, , – . .
closed Christmas and New Year – **3 rm** – 64.00/84.00.
◆ Comfort is paramount in this part 17C farmhouse on working farm. Cosy, warm lounge with real fire. Hand-made oak furniture adorns bedrooms which benefit from rural outlook.

Abbey Inn with rm, YO61 4BD, ☎ (01347) 868204, *Fax (01347) 868678*, – rest, P. MC VISA.
closed 25 December – **Rest** *(closed Sunday dinner and Monday lunch)* (booking essential) a la carte 18.50/27.95 – **3 rm** ☐ ★70.00 – ★★155.00.
◆ Characterful part 17C ivy-clad inn uniquely positioned overlooking Byland Abbey ruins. Tasty mix of modern and traditional food and very smart, stylish bedrooms.

HELSTON *Cornwall* 503 E 33 *The West Country G.* – *pop. 10 578.*
See : *The Flora Day Furry Dance*★★.
Env. : *Lizard Peninsula*★ – *Gunwalloe Fishing Cove*★, *S : 4 m. by A 3083 and minor rd* – *Culdrose (Flambards Village Theme Park*★*), SE : 1 m. – Wendron (Poldark Mine*★*), NE : 2½ m. by B 3297 – Gweek (Seal Sanctuary*★ *– setting*★*), E : 4 m. by A 394 and minor rd.*
London 306 – Falmouth 13 – Penzance 14 – Truro 17.

at Trelowarren *Southeast : 4 m. by A 394 and A 3083 on B 3293 – ✉ Helston.*

New Yard (at Trelowarren Estate), TR12 6AF, ☎ (01326) 221595, *newyardrestaurant@trelowarren.com, Fax (01326) 221595*, – P. MC VISA
closed January, Monday October-May and Sunday dinner – **Rest** a la carte 21.50/34.00 ♀.
◆ Converted country house stable yard adjoining craft gallery. Terrace view from modern tables and chairs. Dinner offers full menus of locally inspired dishes; lunch is simpler.

at Nantithet *Southeast : 4 m. by A 3083 on Cury Rd – ✉ Helston.*

Cobblers Cottage, TR12 7RB, ☎ (01326) 241342, *Fax (01326) 241342* – P.
April-October – **Rest** (by arrangement) – **3 rm** ☐ ★56.00 – ★★56.00.
◆ Rurally set, converted 17C cobbler's shop, boasting an acre of mature, immaculately kept gardens. Homely style throughout; exposed beams enrich character. Superior bedrooms.

at Gunwalloe *South : 5 m. by A 394 off A 3083 – ✉ Helston.*

The Halzephron Inn with rm, TR12 7QB, ☎ (01326) 240406, *halzephroninn@gunwalloe1.fsnet.co.uk, Fax (01326) 241442*, – rest, P. MC AE VISA.
closed 25 December and dinner Sunday and Monday in winter – **Rest** a la carte 16.90/30.00 ♀ – **2 rm** ☐ ★45.00 – ★★80.00.
◆ Country pub in pretty coastal setting. Gleaming copper, original paintings. Adventurous or traditional dishes using local produce. Selection of Cornish cheeses. Neat rooms.

HEMEL HEMPSTEAD *Herts.* 504 S 28 – *pop. 83 118.*
Env. : *Whipsnade Wild Animal Park*★.
18 *Little Hay Golf Complex, Box Lane, Bovingdon ☎ (01442) 833798* – 9 *Boxmoor, 18 Box Lane ☎ (01442) 242434.*
Dacorum Information Centre, Marlowes ☎ (01442) 234222.
London 30 – Aylesbury 16 – Luton 10 – Northampton 46.

Premier Travel Inn, Stoney Lane, Bourne End, HP1 2SB, West : 3½ m. by A 4251 off A 41 ☎ (0870) 2383309, *Fax (01442) 879147* – rm, rest, P – 60. MC AE VISA.
Rest (grill rest.) – **61 rm** ★49.95/49.95 – ★★55.95/55.95.
◆ A consistent standard of trim, simply fitted accommodation in contemporary style; a useful address for cost-conscious travellers. Close to Whipsnade Zoo.

at Frithsden *Northwest : 4½ m. by A 4146 – ✉ Hemel Hempstead.*

The Alford Arms, HP1 3DD, ☎ (01442) 864480, *info@alfordarms.co.uk, Fax (01442) 876893*, – P. MC AE VISA
closed 25-26 December – **Rest** a la carte 17.50/25.00 ♀.
◆ Tucked away in a small hamlet, popular with cyclists and walkers. A pleasant, modern interior of terracotta and cream hues; stylish dishes with interesting combinations.

HEMINGFORD GREY *Cambs.* 504 T 27 – *see Huntingdon.*

Look out for red symbols, indicating particularly pleasant establishments.

HENFIELD *W. Sussex* 504 T 31 – *pop. 4 527.*

London 47 – Brighton 10 – Worthing 11.

at Wineham *Northeast : 3½ m. by A 281, B 2116 and Wineham Lane – ✉ Henfield.*

Frylands without rest., BN5 9BP, West : ¼ m. taking left turn at telephone bo (01403) 710214, *b+b@frylands.co.uk, Fax (01403) 711449,* ←, heated, – P.
closed 21 December-1 January – **3** rm ★35.00 – ★★55.00.
• Part Elizabethan farmhouse in 250 acres with woodlands and fishing. Fresh home cooked breakfasts. Bedrooms exude charm and character with homely furnishings, original features.

HENLADE *Somerset – see Taunton.*

HENLEY-IN-ARDEN *Warks.* 503 504 O 27 – *pop. 2 797.*

London 104 – Birmingham 15 – Stratford-upon-Avon 8 – Warwick 8.5.

Ardencote Manor H. & Country Club and Spa, Lye Green Rd, Claverdon CV35 8LS, East : 3¾ m. by A 4189 on Shrewley rd (01926) 843111, *hotel@ardencote.com Fax (01926) 842646,* , squash – rm, P – 200 . VISA.
The Lodge : **Rest** a la carte 24.50/30.25 s. – **75 rm** ★90.00/160.00 – ★★120.00/160.00.
• Secluded manor house with modern extension and spacious leisure facilities, in formal gardens and grounds. Bedrooms are generally large and traditionally furnished. Informal dining room.

Edmunds (Waters), 64 High St, B95 5BX, (planned relocation in 2006), (01564) 795666 *edmunds@bmwaters.freeserve.co.uk, Fax (01564) 795666* – . VISA
closed Sunday, Monday and Saturday lunch – **Rest** (booking essential) 15.00/28.50.
Spec. Langoustine spring roll with ginger and watercress. Saddle of lamb with pistachio fondant, vanilla and parsnip purée. Assiette of desserts.
• Characterful beamed cottage in centre of market town. Rustic, homely interior. Modern style of refined cooking with a classical base, competitively priced.

Crabmill, Preston Bagot, Claverdon, B95 5EE, East : 1 m. on A 4189 (01926) 843342 *thecrabmill@aol.com, Fax (01926) 843989,* – P. VISA
closed 25 December and Sunday dinner – **Rest** (booking essential) a la carte 22.00/32.00 ♀.
• Stylish pub with a contemporary feel. Dining room has an intimate air, rustic décor and modern prints. Contemporary food with Mediterranean touches on a classic foundation.

at Tanworth-in-Arden *Northwest : 4½ m. by A 3400 and Tanworth Rd – ✉ Henley-in-Arden.*

The Bell with rm, The Green, B94 5AL, (01564) 742212, *info@thebellattanworthinarden.co.uk* – rm, P. VISA.
closed Sunday dinner – **Rest** a la carte 16.00/22.00 – **4 rm** ★55.00 – ★★75.00.
• Very pleasant modern pub with rustic tones in pretty village; spacious bar. Intimate dining room serving good food with modish twists. Stylish rooms with designer touches.

HENLEY-ON-THAMES *Oxon.* 504 R 29 – *pop. 10 513.*

Huntercombe, Nuffield (01491) 641207.
to Reading (Salter Bros. Ltd) (summer only) daily (2 h 15 mn) – to Marlow (Salter Bros. Ltd) (summer only) daily (2 h 15 mn).
Kings Arms Barn, Kings Rd (01491) 578034.
London 40 – Oxford 23 – Reading 9.

Hotel du Vin, New St, RG9 2BP, (01491) 848400, *info@henley.hotelduvin.com, Fax (01491) 848401,* – , rm, P – 35. VISA
Bistro : **Rest** a la carte 26.00/28.00 ♀ – 14.50 – **43 rm** ★115.00/175.00 – ★★115.00/175.00.
• Former brewery premises; now an easy-going, designer styled boutique hotel. Stunning rooms: studios with outdoor terrace and bath tub or airy doubles with great amenities. Bistro with resolutely Gallic style, French influenced menus and excellent wine list.

Red Lion, Hart St, RG9 2AR, (01491) 572161, *reservations@redlionhenley.co.uk, Fax (01491) 410039,* ← – P – 30. VISA.
Rest a la carte 24.95/40.90 – 12.50 – **26 rm** ★95.00/130.00 – ★★115.00/145.00.
• Hostelry since 15C; has accommodated three kings and overlooks the regatta course. Rooms are well furnished with antiques; an elegant, traditional style pervades throughout. Dining room exudes crisp, light feel.

Thamesmead House without rest., Remenham Lane, RG9 2LR, ☎ (01491) 574745, *thamesmead@supanet.com, Fax (01491) 579944* – ⇔ ☎ P. MC AE VISA. ✗
closed Christmas and New Year – **6 rm** ☐ ★110.00/125.00 – ★★130.00/135.00.
◆ Victorian hotel with smart contemporary interiors. Comfy, informal breakfast lounge with stripey banquette seating. Bright, airy Scandinavian style rooms in pastel shades.

Alushta without rest., 23 Queen St, RG9 1AR, ☎ (01491) 636041, *sdr@alushta.co.uk, Fax (01491) 636042* – ⇔ P. ✗
5 rm ☐ ★30.00/50.00 – ★★50.00/75.00.
◆ Centrally located guesthouse, built in late 18C. Very pleasant breakfast room: display shelves boast Russian china. Well-appointed bedrooms with thoughtful extras.

Alftrudis without rest., 8 Norman Ave, RG9 1SG, ☎ (01491) 573099, *sue@alftrudis.co.uk, Fax (01491) 411747* – ⇔. ✗
closed Christmas – **3 rm** ☐ ★45.00/55.00 – ★★60.00/70.00.
◆ Grade II listed Victorian guesthouse in private cul-de-sac. Two well-furnished, comfortable lounges. Inviting breakfast room. Well-appointed, extremely spacious rooms.

Lenwade without rest., 3 Western Rd (off St Andrews Rd), RG9 1JL, ☎ (01491) 573468, *lenwadeuk@aol.com, Fax (01491) 411664,* ⛬ – ⇔ ☎ P. ✗
closed 25-26 December – **3 rm** ☐ ★45.00/50.00 – ★★70.00.
◆ Late 19C home in a quiet residential area. Neatly kept throughout with modern appointments. Bedrooms are of a good size and pine furnished.

The Three Tuns Foodhouse, 5 The Market Pl, RG9 2AA, ☎ (01491) 573260, *thefoodhouse@btconnect.com,* ⛱ – ⇔. MC VISA
closed Sunday dinner – **Rest** a la carte 20.00/35.00 **s.** ♀.
◆ Sandwiched between shops in attractive market place, this early 16C pub has a quirky front bar and cosy rear dining area. Market fresh produce employed on original menus.

at Lower Shiplake *South : 2 m. by A 4155 – ✉ Henley-on-Thames.*

The Knoll ⛯ without rest., Crowsley Rd, RG9 3JT, ☎ (0118) 940 2705, *enquiries@theknollhenley.co.uk, Fax (0118) 940 2705,* ⛬ – ⇔ P
closed April, September and October – **3 rm** ☐ ★50.00/55.00 – ★★70.00.
◆ Pleasant riverside village location. 19C house in charming garden with summer house. Breakfast served in dining room. Comfortable and spacious bedrooms on ground floor.

at Binfield Heath *Southwest : 4 m. by A 4155 – ✉ Henley-on-Thames.*

Holmwood ⛯ without rest., Shiplake Row, RG9 4DP, ☎ (0118) 947 8747, *wendy.cook@freenet.co.uk, Fax (0118) 947 8637,* ⛬, ⛹, ✗ – P. MC VISA. ✗
closed 22-28 December – **5 rm** ☐ ★50.00/60.00 – ★★70.00.
◆ Part Georgian country house set in peaceful gardens. Charming drawing room facing south with extensive views of the Thames valley. Spacious bedrooms and good home comforts.

HEREFORD *Herefordshire* 503 L 27 *Great Britain G. – pop. 56 373.*
See : *City*★ - *Cathedral*★★ *(Mappa Mundi*★*)* A A – *Old House*★ A B.
Exc. : *Kilpeck (Church of SS. Mary and David*★★*) SW : 8 m. by A 465* B.
⛳18 *Raven's Causeway, Wormsley* ☎ *(01432) 830219* – ⛳18 *Belmont Lodge, Belmont* ☎ *(01432) 352666* – ⛳18 *Burghill Valley, Tillington Rd, Burghill* ☎ *(01432) 760456* – ⛳9 *Hereford Municipal, Holmer Rd* ☎ *(01432) 344376* B.
ℹ *1 King St* ☎ *(01432) 268430.*
London 133 – Birmingham 51 – Cardiff 56.

Plan on next page

Castle House, Castle St, HR1 2NW, ☎ (01432) 356321, *info@castlehse.co.uk, Fax (01432) 365909,* ⛱, ⛬ – ⛶, ⇔ rest, ▤ rest, ♿ P. MC AE VISA — A e
La Rive : **Rest** a la carte 27.65/42.35 ♀ – **15 rm** ☐ ★113.50/180.00 – ★★200.00/245.00.
◆ Stylish and exclusive air to this contemporarily furnished, classically proportioned Georgian house, near the cathedral. Excellent quality and attention to detail throughout. Smart restaurant overlooks gardens and Wye.

Aylestone Court, 2 Aylestone Hill, HR1 1HS, ☎ (01432) 341891, *enquiries@aylestonecourt.com, Fax (01432) 267691,* ⛬ – ⇔ P – 🎓 40. MC AE ⓓ VISA. ✗ — B a
Rest *(closed Sunday dinner)* a la carte 19.50/25.00 – **10 rm** ☐ ★55.00/75.00 – ★★85.00/110.00.
◆ Characterful Georgian house, retaining many original features, a close walk from the city centre. Cosy bar. Bedrooms are decorated in a striking Louis XV style. Intimate dining room.

HEREFORD

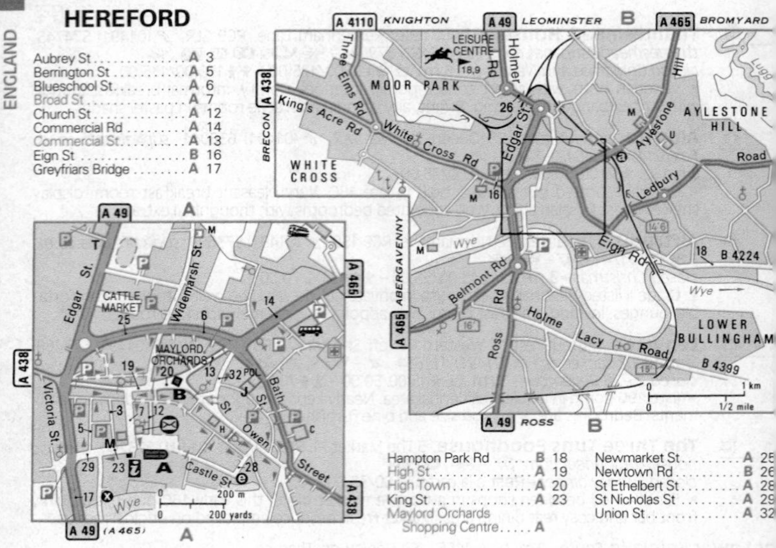

Brandon Lodge without rest., Ross Rd, HR2 8BH, South : 1 ¾ m. on A 49 ☎ (01432) 355621, *info@brandonlodge.co.uk, Fax (01432) 355621*, – P. VISA.
10 rm ☕ ★40.00/45.00 – ★★55.00/58.00.
◆ A good value hotel with 18C origins, charmingly overseen by owner. Bedrooms in main building or adjacent annex: all are spacious, boasting a cheery warmth and good facilities.

Grafton Villa Farm without rest., Grafton, HR2 8ED, South : 2 ¼ m. on A 49 ☎ (01432) 268689, *jennielayton@ereal.net, Fax (01432) 268689*, – P.
closed December and January – **3 rm** ☕ ★40.00/50.00 – ★★60.00/70.00.
◆ Early 18C farmhouse, on a working farm with extensive grounds. Antique furnished homely bedrooms and fresh, substantial country breakfasts.

Floodgates Brasserie, Left Bank Village, Bridge St, HR4 9DG, ☎ (01432) 349009, *info@leftbank.co.uk, Fax (01432) 349012*, – P. AE VISA — A x
Rest a la carte 13.05/23.35 s.
◆ Excellently located, with dining on the river terrace, in the Left Bank Village. A relaxed and informal, though smart, ambience matched by an internationally influenced menu.

at Kingstone *Southwest : 6¾ m. by A 465 – B – and B 4349 – ✉ Hereford.*

Mill Orchard without rest., HR2 9ES, ☎ (01981) 250326, *relax@millorchard.co.uk*, – P.
March-November – **3 rm** ☕ ★36.00 – ★★64.00.
◆ An acre of lawned gardens accentuates the peaceful position of this personally run guesthouse. Cosy lounge and warmly welcoming breakfast room. Well-equipped bedrooms.

at Ruckhall *West : 5 m. by A 49 off A 465 – B – ✉ Eaton Bishop.*

Ancient Camp Inn with rm, HR2 9QX, ☎ (01981) 250449, *Fax (01981) 251581*, ← River Wye and countryside, – P. VISA.
closed 2 weeks February, Sunday dinner, Monday and Tuesday – **Rest** a la carte 21.00/30.00 – **5 rm** ☕ ★70.00 – ★★90.00.
◆ Dating back to the 18C, a friendly, privately owned inn in peaceful countryside. Homely accommodation; ask for one of the front rooms with superb views down to the river Wye.

at Byford *West : 7½ m. by A 438 – B – ✉ Hereford.*

Old Rectory without rest., HR4 7LD, ☎ (01981) 590218, *Fax (01981) 590499*, – P.
March-October – **3 rm** ☕ ★40.00/55.00 – ★★60.00/65.00.
◆ Rurally set Georgian-style 19C rectory with pleasant gardens. Spacious yet homely atmosphere and décor; the bedrooms are furnished in a simple, traditional style.

HERM 503 P 33 and 517 ⑩ – see Channel Islands.

HERMITAGE *Dorset* – *see Sherborne.*

HERSTMONCEUX *E. Sussex* 504 U 31.
London 63 – Eastbourne 12 – Hastings 14 – Lewes 16.

Sundial, Gardner St, BN27 4LA, ✆ (01323) 832217, *sundialrestaurant@hotmail.com, Fax (01323) 832909,* – P. VISA
closed Sunday dinner and Monday – **Rest** - French - 21.00 and a la carte 44.75.
◆ Converted 16C cottage retaining leaded windows and a beamed ceiling. Comfortable chairs in a well spaced dining room. Menu is French with a classic, familiar style.

at Wartling *Southeast : 3¾ m. by A 271 and Wartling rd* – ✉ *Herstmonceux.*

Wartling Place without rest., BN27 1RY, ✆ (01323) 832590, *accom@wartlingplace.prestel.co.uk, Fax (01323) 831558,* – P. AE VISA.
3 rm ☐ ✝68.00/95.00 – ✝✝135.00/175.00.
◆ Part Georgian house with three acres of gardens, sited in the village. Pleasantly furnished, with some antiques; two of the rooms have four-poster beds.

HERTFORD *Herts.* 504 T 28.
London 25 – Bishop's Stortford 16 – Stevenage 11.

The Hillside, 45 Port Hill, Bengeo, SG14 3EP, North : ¼ m. on B 158 ✆ (01992) 554556, *Fax (01992) 583709* – P. AE VISA.
closed Sunday dinner – **Rest** a la carte 25.00/40.00 ♀.
◆ Refurbished 17C pub next to deli and farm shop. Intimate and cosy, with sofas by the fire. Dine in an airy, sunny environment. Fashionable brasserie dishes with global range.

HESWALL *Mersey.* 502 503 K 24 – *pop. 29 977.*
London 212 – Birkenhead 12 – Chester 14 – Liverpool 11.

Gem, 1 Milner Rd, CH60 5RT, ✆ (0151) 342 4811, *enquiries@gemrestaurant.co.uk, Fax (0151) 342 4811* – VISA
closed 2 weeks September, Sunday and Monday – **Rest** (booking essential) (dinner only) 17.95 (mid week) and a la carte 24.40/31.70.
◆ Personally run, friendly neighbourhood restaurant; unassuming exterior and simple, modern interior with intimate ambience. Country cooking with distinctive departures.

HETHERSETT *Norfolk* 504 X 26 – *see Norwich.*

HETTON *N. Yorks.* 502 N 21 – *see Skipton.*

HEXHAM *Northd.* 501 502 N 19 *Great Britain G.* – *pop. 10 682.*
See : *Abbey★ (Saxon Crypt★★, Leschman chantry★).*
Env. : *Hadrian's Wall★★, N : 4½ m. by A 6079.*
Exc. : *Housesteads★★, NW : 12½ m. by A 6079 and B 6318.*
18 *Spital Park ✆ (01434) 603072* – 18 *De Vere Slaley Hall G. & C.C., Slaley ✆ (01434) 673350* – 9 *Tynedale, Tyne Green ✆ (01434) 608154.*
Wentworth Car Park ✆ (01434) 652220.
London 304 – Carlisle 37 – Newcastle upon Tyne 21.

Beaumont, Beaumont St, NE46 3LT, ✆ (01434) 602331, *reservations@beaumonthotel.eclipse.co.uk, Fax (01434) 606184* – P – 100. AE VISA.
The Park : **Rest** 12.50/20.50 ♀ – **25 rm** ☐ ✝75.00/90.00 – ✝✝105.00/110.00.
◆ Victorian building of local stone overlooking park and the town's ancient abbey - which is visible from some of the comfortable rooms. Personally run with a warm atmosphere. Park restaurant on the first floor with views of the abbey.

Hallbank, Hallgate, NE46 1XA, ✆ (01434) 606656, *Fax (01434) 605567* – P. VISA.
Rest (by arrangement) 23.00 – **8 rm** ☐ ✝60.00/60.00 – ✝✝60.00/80.00.
◆ Red-brick Georgian house close to market square, set in the shadow of the old gaol. Fully refurbished rooms exhibit a warm, classic style with good modern facilities. Dine in adjacent, informal café/bistro.

ENGLAND

West Close House without rest., Hextol Terrace, NE46 2AD, Southwest : ½ m. o
B 6305 ☎ (01434) 603307, – P.
closed Christmas and New Year – **4** rm ★22.00/47.00 – ★★48.00/64.00.
◆ Detached house in a residential area providing a high standard of simple, good valu
accommodation. Polished wood floors and immaculately kept.

Dene House without rest., Juniper, NE46 1SJ, South : 3 ¾ m. by B 6306 followin
signs for Dye House ☎ (01434) 673413, *margaret@denehouse-hexham.co.uk*, –
VISA.
closed Christmas – **3 rm** ★27.50/40.00 – ★★55.00.
◆ Attractive stone cottage in a quiet spot with pleasant views, numerous country walks i
the environs. Cosy feel throughout. Simple, homely rooms.

Roué, Gilesgate House, 4-6 Gilesgate, NE46 3NJ, ☎ (01434) 602110, *info@roue.bi*
Fax (01434) 608259 – . AE VISA
closed 25 December, Sunday-Monday – **Rest** 23.95 (dinner) and a la carte 25.90/36.95.
◆ Set over three floors, this bohemian styled restaurant offers accomplished, complex an
interesting dishes, plus a comfy, velvet strewn lounge for post-prandial relaxation.

Valley Connection 301, Market Pl, NE46 3NX, ☎ (01434) 601234, *Fax (01434) 60662*
– . AE VISA
closed 25 December and Monday except at Bank Holidays – **Rest** - Indian - (dinner only) a l
carte 19.25/31.00.
◆ Near Hexham Abbey; views of the market place from the second floor. Old favourite
interspersed with modern dishes in a tasty Indian menu.

The Green Room, Hexham Railway Station, Station Rd, NE46 1EZ, ☎ (01434) 60880(
Fax (01434) 608800, – . AE VISA
closed 2 weeks August, 1 week Christmas, Sunday dinner, Monday and Bank Holidays
Rest a la carte 15.15/30.85 s.
◆ Located in former luggage room and named after 19C architect who designed Hexhar
station. Pleasant rustic feel; accomplished, wide ranging menus exude eclectic appeal.

at Chollerton *North : 6 m. on A 6079 – ✉ Hexham.*

The Hermitage without rest., NE48 4DG, North : 1 m. on A 6079 (entrance throug
Gate House) ☎ (01434) 681248, *katie.stewart@themeet.co.uk, Fax (01434) 681110*,
– P.
March-September – **3 rm** ★50.00 – ★★80.00.
◆ A hospitable country house in tranquil setting with a garden terrace to sit out on i
summer and a log fire to snuggle up to in winter. Peaceful bedrooms with rural views.

at Slaley *Southeast : 5½ m. by B 6306 – ✉ Hexham.*

Slaley Hall , NE47 0BX, Southeast : 2 ¼ m. ☎ (01434) 673350, *slaley.hall@devere*
hotels.com, Fax (01434) 673962, , , , , , – – P – 400
AE VISA.
The Restaurant : **Rest** (dinner only and Sunday lunch)/dinner 26.95 and a la cart
27.50/43.50 s. – **129 rm** ★175.00/195.00 – ★★210.00/230.00, 10 suites.
◆ Extended Edwardian manor house, now a leisure oriented hotel, grounds with wood
land and two golf courses. Spacious bedrooms with up-to-date facilities and country views
Formal restaurant offering menus based on a modern English style.

at Haydon Bridge *West : 7½ m. on A 69 – ✉ Hexham.*

Langley Castle , Langley-on-Tyne, NE47 5LU, South : 2 m. by A 69 on A 68
☎ (01434) 688888, *manager@langleycastle.com, Fax (01434) 684019*, , – rest,
P – 100. AE VISA
Rest 32.95 (dinner) and lunch a la carte 14.50/32.95 – **18 rm** ★119.50/185.00 -
★★229.00/239.00.
◆ Turreted stone castle in 12 acres. Impressive staircase, tapestry style fabrics, heraldi
themed ornaments, open fire. Spacious rooms in house or converted stables. Forma
restaurant with beams and stone floor; classic dishes using local produce.

HEYTESBURY *Wilts.* 503 504 N 30 – *see Warminster.*

HIGHCLERE *Hants.* 503 P 29 – *pop. 2 409* – ✉ *Newbury.*
London 69 – Newbury 5 – Reading 25.

The Yew Tree with rm, Hollington Cross, Andover Rd, RG20 9SE, South : 1 m. off A 343
☎ (01635) 253360, *www.theyewtree.net, Fax (01635) 255035*, – rest, P. AE
VISA
closed Sunday dinner – **Rest** 15.50 (lunch) and a la carte 20.00/57.00 – **6 rm** ★60.00 -
★★60.00.
◆ 17C pub with smart front terrace, old rafters and no less than four elegant, candle-lit
rear dining rooms with a classical style of modern cooking finding favour with locals.

HIGHCLIFFE *Dorset* 503 504 O 31.
London 112 – Bournemouth 10 – Salisbury 21 – Southampton 26 – Winchester 37.

Lord Bute, Lymington Rd, BH23 4JS, ℘ (01425) 278884, *mail@lordbute.co.uk, Fax (01425) 279258* – ⇔ rest, ▤ P – 🏛 25. MC AE VISA
Rest *(closed Sunday dinner and Monday)* 15.95/28.95 and dinner a la carte 18.85/35.85 **s.** – ☕ 5.95 – **12 rm** ✝75.00 – ✝✝95.00/140.00.
◆ Modern property with a traditional style. Well designed, light, airy lounge. Bedrooms are well appointed and include safes and spa baths.. Formal dining room adjacent to Orangery lounge.

HIGHER BURWARDSLEY *Ches. – see Tattenhall.*

HIGH ONGAR *Essex.*
London 24 – Brentwood 11 – Chelmsford 10.

The Wheatsheaf Brasserie, King St, CM5 9NS, East : 2 m. by A 414 on Blackmore rd ℘ (01277) 822220, *Fax (01277) 822441*, 🌳, 🌲 – P. MC AE ⊙ VISA
closed 2 weeks late December-early January, 1 week June, 1 week October, Saturday lunch, Sunday dinner, Monday and Bank Holidays – **Rest** (booking essential) a la carte 23.00/35.00 ♀.
◆ Pretty, converted pub with large garden and terrace. Dine in four different rooms with open fires and homely ornamentation. Good value, accomplished British cuisine.

HIGH WYCOMBE *Bucks.* 504 R 29 *Great Britain G. – pop. 77 178.*
Env. : *Chiltern Hills*★.
⛳18 *Hazlemere G & C.C., Penn Rd, Hazlemere* ℘ *(01494) 719300* – ⛳18, ⛳18 *Wycombe Heights, Rayners Ave, Loudwater* ℘ *(01494) 816686.*
ℹ *Paul's Row* ℘ *(01494) 421892.*
London 34 – Aylesbury 17 – Oxford 26 – Reading 18.

Premier Travel Inn, Thanstead Farm, London Rd, Loudwater, HP10 9YL, Southeast : 3 m. on A 40 ℘ (01494) 537080, *Fax (01494) 446855* – ⇔ rm, ▤ rest, ♿ P. MC AE ⊙ VISA.
Rest (grill rest.) – **108 rm** ✝49.95/49.95 – ✝✝55.95/55.95.
◆ Simply furnished and brightly decorated bedrooms with ample work space. Family rooms with sofa beds. Ideal for corporate or leisure travel. Convenient A40-M40 location.

Eat-Thai, 14-15 Easton St, HP11 1NJ, ℘ (01494) 532888, *Fax (01494) 532889* – ⇔. MC AE VISA
closed 25-28 December – **Rest** - Thai - 12.00/40.00 and a la carte 15.40/26.85 **s.**
◆ Modern restaurant with wood floors and well-spaced tables. Three distinct areas serving fresh, tasty dishes with ingredients flown regularly from Thailand. Attentive service.

HINCKLEY *Leics.* 502 503 504 P 26 *– pop. 43 246.*
ℹ *Hinckley Library, Lancaster Rd* ℘ *(01455) 635106.*
London 103 – Birmingham 31 – Coventry 12 – Leicester 14.

Sketchley Grange, Sketchley Lane, LE10 3HU, South : 1 ½ m. by B 4109 (Rugby Rd) ℘ (01455) 251133, *reservations@sketchleygrange.co.uk, Fax (01455) 631384*, 🏊, 🏋, ≘s, ▣, 🌲 – |♣| ⇔, ▤ rest, 🐕 P – 🏛 280. MC AE VISA
The Willow : **Rest** *(closed Sunday-Monday)* (dinner only and Sunday lunch)/dinner a la carte 26.30/37.75 – ***The Terrace Bistro*** : **Rest** a la carte 18.85/32.65 – ☕ 10.95 – **51 rm** ✝121.00 – ✝✝142.00, 1 suite.
◆ Privately owned, spacious hotel with good leisure and an array of conference facilities. Bedrooms are well proportioned, and furniture is comfortable and well chosen. The Willow exudes elegance and garden views. The Terrace Bistro is bright and spacious.

HINDON *Wilts.* 503 N 30.
London 103.5 – Shaftesbury 7.5 – Warminster 10.

The Lamb Inn with rm, High St, SP3 6DP, ℘ (01747) 820573, *info@lambathindon.co.uk, Fax (01747) 820605*, 🌳, 🌲 – ⇔ rest, P. MC AE VISA
Rest *(closed Sunday)* a la carte 18.00/30.00 ♀ – **14 rm** ☕ ✝65.00 – ✝✝90.00.
◆ 15C former coaching inn. Attractively creeper clad with picture-strewn deep burgundy interior. Large blackboards offer heartily traditional English menus. Characterful rooms.

HINDRINGHAM *Norfolk.*

London 118.5 – Fakenham 8.5 – Holt 8.

Field House, Moorgate Rd, NR21 0PT, ✆ (01328) 878726, *stay@fieldhousehindringham.co.uk,* – ⊁ ♿ 🅿. ⊁
closed Christmas – **Rest** (by arrangement) 29.50 – **3 rm** ☐ ★60.00/70.00 – ★★80.00/100.00.
◆ Well-kept flint stone house with pretty garden and summer house. Pristine lounge with books and magazines. Extensive breakfast menus. Carefully co-ordinated rooms with extras. Conservatory dining: full dinner with canapés can be arranged.

HINTLESHAM *Suffolk* 504 X 27 – *see Ipswich.*

HISTON *Cambs.* 504 U 27 – *see Cambridge.*

HITCHIN *Herts.* 504 T 28 – *pop. 33 352.*

London 40 – Bedford 14 – Cambridge 26 – Luton 9.

Just 32, 32 Sun St, SG5 1AH, ✆ (01462) 455666 – MC AE ⓓ VISA
closed 26 December, Sunday and Monday – **Rest** a la carte 24.20/36.25 ♀.
◆ Friendly bistro, located just off the town square, with hatch to kitchen from which an interestingly eclectic range of dishes arrive at table. Keen service.

HOCKLEY HEATH *W. Mids.* 503 504 O 26 – *pop. 13 616* – ✉ *Solihull.*

London 117 – Birmingham 11 – Coventry 17.

Nuthurst Grange Country House, Nuthurst Grange Lane, B94 5NL, South : ¾ m by A 3400 ✆ (01564) 783972, *info@nuthurst-grange.co.uk, Fax (01564) 783919,* – 🅿 – 80. MC AE VISA. ⊁
closed 26-30 December – **Rest** – (see ***The Restaurant*** below) – **15 rm** ☐ ★139.00 – ★★165.00/195.00.
◆ Part Edwardian manor house, overlooking M40 and convenient for Birmingham airport. Classic English country décor throughout. Spacious rooms with high level of comfort.

Premier Travel Inn Metro, Stratford Rd, B94 6NX, on A 3400 ✆ (01564) 782144, *Fax (01564) 783197* – ⊁, ▤ rest, ♿ 🅿 – 30. MC AE ⓓ VISA. ⊁
Rest (grill rest.) – **55 rm** ★49.95/49.95 – ★★52.95/52.95.
◆ Consistent standard of trim, simply fitted accommodation in contemporary style; useful address for cost-conscious travellers. Close to Birmingham International and the NEC.

The Restaurant (at Nuthurst Grange Country House), Nuthurst Grange Lane, B94 5NL, South : ¾ m. by A 3400 ✆ (01564) 783972, *Fax (01564) 783919,* – ⊁ 🅿 ⇔ 30. MC AE VISA
closed 26-30 December and Saturday lunch – **Rest** 22.95/29.50 and a la carte 29.50/59.50 **s.** ♀.
◆ Thoroughly traditional tone in the dining room's décor which contributes to a formal ambience. Seasonal menu draws on British and French traditions.

at Lapworth *Southeast : 2 m. on B 4439* – ✉ *Warwick.*

Boot Inn, Old Warwick Rd, B94 6JU, on B 4439 ✆ (01564) 782464, *bootinn@hotmail.com, Fax (01564) 784989,* , – ⊁ 🅿. MC AE VISA
closed 25 December and 1 January – **Rest** (booking essential) 21.95/25.00 and a la carte 18.50/25.00 ♀.
◆ Bustling modern dining pub, with traditional bucolic character at the front and spacious dining room to rear. Appealing rustic dishes supplemented by daily changing specials.

HOLBEACH *Lincs.* 502 504 U 25 – *pop. 7 247.*

London 117 – Kingston-upon-Hull 81 – Norwich 62 – Nottingham 60 – Peterborough 25.

Pipwell Manor without rest., Washway Rd, Saracen's Head, PE12 8AL, Northeast : 1 ½ m. by A 17 ✆ (01406) 423119, *honnor@pipwellmanor.freeserve.co.uk, Fax (01406) 423119,* – ⊁ 🅿. ⊁
closed 20 December-1 January – **4 rm** ☐ ★36.00 – ★★50.00.
◆ Georgian manor built on site of Cisterian Grange, close to solitude of the Wash. Garden railway for train spotters. Complimentary tea, cake on arrival. Country style rooms.

A good night's sleep without spending a fortune? Look for a Bib Hotel

OLBETON *Devon.*
London 211.5 – Ivybridge 6 – Plymouth 10.5.

The Dartmoor Union, Fore St, PL8 1NE, ✆ (01752) 830288, *info@dartmoorunion.co.uk, Fax (01752) 830296,* – P. MC VISA
Rest 13.95 (lunch) and a la carte 19.15/25.45 ♀.
◆ Subtle brass plaque signage; inside, though, a conspicuous 19C log fire crackles in the bar and rose pink walls light up the restaurant. Seasonal dishes offer local flavours.

OLBROOK *Suffolk* 504 X 28 – *see Ipswich.*

OLFORD *Somerset* 503 K 30 *Great Britain G.* – ✉ *Bridgwater.*
Env. : *Stogursey Priory Church★★, W : 4½ m.*
London 171 – Bristol 48 – Minehead 15 – Taunton 22.

Combe House, TA5 1RZ, Southwest : ¾ m. by Youth Hostel rd ✆ (01278) 741382, *enquiries@combehouse.co.uk, Fax (01278) 741322,* – P. MC VISA
Rest a la carte 24.85/28.85 – **13 rm** ☐ 55.00/77.50 – 110.00/115.00.
◆ Interesting Edwardian country house with a water wheel in pleasant Quantock Hills location. Informal relaxed ambience with plenty of books and beams. Rooms overlook garden. Restaurant with spaced beams; locally sourced produce to the fore.

Luxury pad or humble abode? and denote categories of comfort.

OLKHAM *Norfolk* 504 W 25.
London 124 – King's Lynn 32 – Norwich 39.

The Victoria, Park Rd, NR23 1RG, ✆ (01328) 711008, *victoria@holkham.co.uk, Fax (01328) 711009,* – P. MC VISA.
Rest – (see *The Restaurant* below) – **10 rm** ☐ 90.00/110.00 – 110.00/140.00.
◆ Trendy, stylish hotel, built in 1838, overlooking Holkham nature reserve. Bedrooms are individually styled with much of the furniture sourced from Rajasthan.

The Restaurant (at Victoria H.), Park Rd, NR23 1RG, ✆ (01328) 711008, *victoria@holkham.co.uk, Fax (01328) 711009,* – P. MC VISA
Rest a la carte 21.00/31.00 ♀.
◆ Extensive dining areas, now including conservatory option, specialise in modish menus as well as fine fish and seafood dishes. The bar offers a buzzy alternative.

OLMES CHAPEL *Ches.* 502 503 504 M 24 – *pop. 5 669.*
London 181 – Chester 25 – Liverpool 41 – Manchester 24 – Stoke-on-Trent 20.

Cottage Rest. and Lodge, London Rd, Allostock, WA16 9LU, North : 3 m. on A 50 ✆ (01565) 722470, *cottage-restaurant@btopenworld.com, Fax (01565) 722749* – P – 60. MC AE VISA.
closed 1 January – **Rest** *(closed Sunday dinner and Bank Holidays)* 12.95 (lunch) and dinner a la carte 21.40/34.85 s. – **12 rm** ☐ 79.00 – 95.00.
◆ Brick-built cottage notable for an abundant degree of rustic allure and charm. Up-to-date, spacious bedrooms are the feature of its annex extension. Characterfully beamed restaurant is part of original cottage.

OLT *Norfolk* 504 X 25 – *pop. 3 550.*
London 124 – King's Lynn 34 – Norwich 22.

Byfords, Shirehall Plain, NR25 6BG, ✆ (01263) 711400, *Fax (01263) 713520,* – P. MC VISA.
Rest a la carte 17.00/25.00 – **7 rm** ☐ 90.00 – 150.00.
◆ Flint-fronted Grade II listed house that boasts something different: a well-stocked deli; rustic cellar café; and stunning rooms, with Egyptian cotton and under-floor heating.

Yetman's, 37 Norwich Rd, NR25 6SA, ✆ (01263) 713320 – . MC AE VISA
restricted opening in winter and closed Monday, Tuesday and Sunday dinner (except at Bank Holidays) – **Rest** (dinner only and Sunday lunch)/dinner 34.00 ♀.
◆ A relaxed and cosy atmosphere in prettily painted Georgian cottages. Interesting and well balanced dishes, with a British feel, using local produce.

OLT *Wilts.* 503 504 N 29 – *see Bradford-on-Avon.*

HONITON *Devon* 503 K 31 *The West Country G. – pop. 11 213.*

See : *All Hallows Museum★ AC.*
Env. : *Ottery St Mary★ (St Mary's★) SW : 5 m. by A 30 and B 3177.*
Exc. : *Faraway Countryside Park (≤★) AC, SE : 6½ m. by A 375 and B 3174.*
Lace Walk Car Park ✆ (01404) 43716.
London 186 – Exeter 17 – Southampton 93 – Taunton 18.

Deer Park , Buckerell Village, Weston, EX14 3PG, West : 2 ½ m. by A 30 ✆ (01404) 41266, *admin@deerparkcountryhotel.com, Fax (01404) 46598*, ≤, heated, , , – P – 70.
Rest 16.00/25.00 – **25 rm** ★65.00/85.00 – ★★125.00.
◆ Characterful house pleasantly located down narrow country lane. Extensive rural sporting facilities and a country house feel throughout. Spacious, individually styled rooms. Dining room decorated in keeping with country house surroundings.

at Yarcombe *Northeast : 8 m. on A 30 – ✉ Honiton.*

Belfry Country H., EX14 9BD, on A 30 ✆ (01404) 861234, *stay@thebelfrycountryhotel.com, Fax (01404) 861579*, ≤ P. .
closed Christmas-New Year – **Rest** *(closed Monday-Tuesday)* (dinner only) 24.00 **s.** – **6 rm** ★45.00 – ★★80.00.
◆ Pretty cottage, formerly the village school, opposite 14C church. Immaculately kept property with light and cosy bedrooms, named after poets, featuring stained glass windows. Comfy restaurant decorated with light, stripped wood.

at Wilmington *East : 3 m. on A 35 – ✉ Honiton.*

Home Farm, EX14 9JR, on A 35 ✆ (01404) 831278, *homefarmhotel@breathemail.net, Fax (01404) 831411*, – P.
Rest and a la carte 18.25/28.75 – **13 rm** ★45.00 – ★★60.00/100.00.
◆ Part 16C thatched farmhouse offering a simple and comfortable standard of accommodation. Characterful lounges and bedrooms with individual country personality. Snug, cosy dining room with inglenook.

at Gittisham *Southwest : 3 m. by A 30 – ✉ Honiton.*

Combe House , EX14 3AD, ✆ (01404) 540400, *stay@thishotel.com, Fax (01404) 46004*, ≤, , , – P – 60.
closed 17-29 January – **Rest** (booking essential to non-residents) 26.00/39.00 – **14 rm** ★133.00/148.00 – ★★153.00/168.00, 1 suite.
◆ Elizabethan mansion set in glorious Devon countryside. See the original Victorian kitchen. Oak-panelling and 18C paintings. Individually designed rooms with fine antiques. Elegant restaurant with murals.

at Payhembury *Northwest : 7 m. by A 373 – ✉ Honiton.*

Cokesputt House , EX14 3HD, West : ¼ m. on Tale rd ✆ (01404) 841289, *aeac.forbes@virgin.net*, ≤, – P. .
closed Christmas and January – **Rest** (booking essential) (communal dining) 27.00 – **3 rm** ★38.50/48.50 – ★★77.00.
◆ Part 17C and 18C house with gardens. Elegant antique furnished interior, in the best traditions of English country style. Charming bedrooms. Home-grown meals at welcoming communal table.

HOO GREEN *Ches. – see Knutsford.*

HOOK *Hants.* 504 R 30 *– pop. 6 869 – ✉ Basingstoke.*
London 47 – Oxford 39 – Reading 13 – Southampton 31.

at Rotherwick *North : 2 m. by A 30 and B 3349 on Rotherwick rd – ✉ Basingstoke.*

Tylney Hall , RG27 9AZ, South : 1 ½ m. by Newnham rd on Ridge Lane ✆ (01256) 764881, *sales@tylneyhall.com, Fax (01256) 768141*, , , , heated, , , , rm, P – 120. .
Rest 18.00/46.00 **s.** and a la carte – **103 rm** ★140.00 – ★★430.00, 9 suites.
◆ Grand and beautifully restored 19C mansion in delightful, extensive Gertrude Jekyll gardens. Country house rooms, some with private conservatories or suites over two floors. Classically English dining room with oak panelling and garden views.

HOPE *Derbs.* 502 503 504 O 23 – ✉ *Sheffield.*
London 180 – Derby 50 – Manchester 31 – Sheffield 15 – Stoke-on-Trent 40.

Underleigh House without rest., Hope Valley, S33 6RF, North : 1 m. by Edale rd ✆ (01433) 621372, *underleigh.house@btconnect.com, Fax (01433) 621324*, ≤, – P. MC VISA.
closed 25, 26, 31 December and 1 January – **6 rm** ☕ ✝50.00 – ✝✝72.00/85.00.
◆ Converted Victorian property, rurally located and personally run, well located for the Peak District. Countryside views and a welcoming country ambience.

HOPE COVE *Devon* 503 I 33 – *see Salcombe.*

HORLEY *Surrey* 504 T 30 – *pop. 22 582.*
London 27 – Brighton 26 – Royal Tunbridge Wells 22.

Plan : see Gatwick

Langshott Manor, Langshott, RH6 9LN, North : by A 23 turning right at Thistle Gatwick H. onto Ladbroke Rd ✆ (01293) 786680, *admin@langshottmanor.com, Fax (01293) 783905*, , – P. MC AE VISA.
Mulberry : **Rest** (booking essential) 25.00/39.00 and dinner a la carte 19.50/52.50 – **21 rm** ☕ ✝125.00/170.00 – ✝✝190.00, 1 suite.
◆ Part Elizabethan manor house set amidst gardens of roses, vines and ponds. For centuries the home of aristocrats, now a refined and harmonious country house hotel. Country house-style dining room with intimate ambience.

Lawn without rest., 30 Massetts Rd, RH6 7DF, ✆ (01293) 775751, *info@lawnguest house.co.uk, Fax (01293) 821803*, – P. MC AE VISA Y r
12 rm ☕ ✝40.00/45.00 – ✝✝58.00/60.00.
◆ Privately owned and personally run with home comforts and ambience. Close to the station and convenient for Gatwick airport. Chintz decorated bedrooms are pine furnished.

The Turret without rest., 48 Massetts Rd, RH6 7DS, ✆ (01293) 782490, *info@thetur ret.com, Fax (01293) 431492* – P. MC VISA. Y i
10 rm ☕ ✝39.00 – ✝✝54.00.
◆ Victorian home, with turrets, offering a warm welcome and simple comforts with homely style. Magnolia rooms with co-ordinated soft furnishings. Courtesy airport transport.

HORNCASTLE *Lincs.* 502 504 T 24 – *pop. 6 090.*
ℹ *The Trinity Centre, 52 East St* ✆ *(01507) 526636.*
London 143 – Lincoln 22 – Nottingham 62.

XX **Magpies,** 71-75 East St, LN9 6AA, ✆ (01507) 527004, *Fax (01507) 525068* – . MC VISA
closed last week December-first week January, Monday and Tuesday – **Rest** (dinner only and Sunday lunch) 32.00.
◆ Renowned, family run restaurant in a converted 18C house. Snug, comfortable, beamed interior. Local ingredients used in accomplished, refined dishes in a modern style.

HORNDON-ON-THE-HILL *Essex* 504 V 29.
London 25 – Chelmsford 22 – Maidstone 34 – Southend-on-Sea 16.

The Bell with rm, High Rd, SS17 8LD, ✆ (01375) 642463, *info@bell-inn.co.uk, Fax (01375) 361611*, – P. MC AE VISA
closed 25-26 December – **Rest** *(closed Bank Holiday Mondays)* a la carte 22.95/26.95 ♀ – ☕ 9.50 – **5 rm** ✝40.00/85.00 – ✝✝85.00.
◆ 16C part timbered coaching inn. Log fire in bar and beamed ceiling in restaurant. Eclectically influenced range of menus. Comfortable, individually furnished bedrooms.

We try to be as accurate as possible when giving room rates. But prices are susceptible to change, so please check rates when booking.

HORNINGSEA *Cambs. – see Cambridge.*

HORN'S CROSS *Devon* 503 H 31 *Great Britain G.* – ✉ *Bideford.*

Exc. : *Clovelly★★, W : 6½ m. on A 39 and B 3237 – Bideford : Bridge★★ - Burton Art Gallery AC - Lundy Island★★ (by ferry), NE : 7 m. on a 39 and B 3235 – Hartland : Hartland Church - Hartland Quay★ (★★) - Hartland Point ★★★, W : 9 m. on A 39 and B 3248 – Gre Torrington (Dartington Crystal★ AC), SE 15 m. on A 39 and A 386 – Rosemoor★, SE : 16 r on A 39, A 386 and B 3220.*

London 222 – Barnstaple 15 – Exeter 46.

The Hoops Inn with rm, EX39 5DL, ✆ (01237) 451222, *info@hoopsinn.co.u Fax (01237) 451247,* – P. VISA

closed 25 December – **Rest** a la carte 11.00/35.00 – **13 rm** ★65.00 – ★★140.00.

◆ Nestling in the hills and dating from 13C, this archetypal Devonshire inn has timber thick cob walls and oak panels. Menus feature quality local produce. Comfy rooms.

HORRINGER *Suffolk* 504 W 27 *– see Bury St Edmunds.*

HORSHAM *W. Sussex* 504 T 30 – *pop. 47 804.*

18, 18 Fullers, Hammerpond Rd, Mannings Heath ✆ (01403) 210228.

9 Causeway ✆ (01403) 211661, tourist.information@horsham.gov.uk.

London 39 – Brighton 23 – Guildford 20 – Lewes 25 – Worthing 20.

South Lodge, Brighton Rd, Lower Beeding, RH13 6PS, Southeast : 5 m. on A 28 ✆ (01403) 891711, *enquiries@southlodgehotel.co.uk, Fax (01403) 891766,* 18, – rest, P – 160. VISA

Rest (booking essential to non-residents) 17.50/46.00 – 15.00 – **42 rm** – ★★229.0 3 suites.

◆ Victorian mansion in 93 acres of immaculate gardens and parkland, overlooking Sout Downs. Opulent yet relaxed antique furnished public areas. Charming individual bedroom Rich, refined dining room includes tapestry hung walls.

Premier Travel Inn, The Station, 57 North St, RH12 1RB, ✆ (01403) 25014 *Fax (01403) 270797* – rm, rest, P. VISA.

Rest (grill rest.) – **40 rm** ★47.95/47.95 – ★★52.95/52.95.

◆ Well-proportioned modern bedrooms, suitable for business and family stopovers, de signed with practicality and price in mind. Directly opposite the train station.

Les Deux Garçons, Piries Pl, RH12 1DF, ✆ (01403) 271125, *info@lesdeuxgarcons.com Fax (01403) 271022* – . VISA

closed 1 week Christmas, Sunday and Monday – **Rest** 11.90 (lunch) and a la cart 23.80/40.85.

◆ A low sloped ceiling and candles enhance the appeal of this casually informal restaurant Menus range widely within a strong Gallic base: from menu rapide to gourmet.

Stan's Way House, 3 Stans Way, East St, RH12 1HU, ✆ (01403) 255688, *sl@stanswa house.co.uk, Fax (01403) 266144* – . VISA

closed 22 August-5 September, 25-26 December, 1 January and Sunday – **Rest** a la cart 18.45/27.45.

◆ Attractive part 15C building: upstairs restaurant is in striking, vaulted room with beame ceiling: rustic, yet modern. Relaxed service. Well-priced, modish European menus.

at Slinfold *West : 4 m. by A 281 off A 264 – ✉ Horsham.*

Random Hall, Stane St, RH13 0QX, West : ½ m. on A 29 ✆ (01403) 790558, *nigelrandor hall@btconnect.com, Fax (01403) 791046* – P. VISA.

closed 2 weeks Christmas-New Year – **Rest** *(closed Friday-Sunday)* (residents only) (dinne only) 21.95 – **13 rm** ★69.00/76.00 – ★★95.00.

◆ Restored part 16C farmhouse characterised by books, paintings, nooks and crannies The Tudor bar boasts oak beams and flagstone flooring; beams continue through t bedrooms.

HORWICH *Lancs.* 502 504 M 23 – ✉ *Bolton.*

London 217 – Liverpool 35 – Manchester 21 – Preston 16.

Whites, The Reebok Stadium, (Car Park A), De Havilland Way, BL6 6SF, Southeast : 2½ m by A 673 on A 6027 ✆ (01204) 667788, *whites@devere-hotel.com, Fax (01204) 673721,* , – , rest, P – 1700. VISA.

Brasserie at Whites : **Rest** a la carte approx 20.00 **s.** – (see also ***Reflections*** below) **119 rm** ★55.00/135.00 – ★★140.00/145.00, 6 suites.

◆ Modern business hotel, uniquely part of Bolton Wanderers' football stadium. Well equip ped all round with good, modern bedrooms. Corporate clients can use stadium facilities Brasserie at Whites is a "must" for Wanderers fans.

Express by Holiday Inn without rest., 3 Arena Approach, BL6 6LB, Southeast : 2½ m. by A 673 on A 6027 ☎ (01204) 469111, *ebhi-bolton@btconnect.com, Fax (01204) 469222* – ♿ P – 🏨 25. MC AE VISA.
74 rm 59.95 – 59.95.
◆ Simple good quality furnishings in brightly decorated rooms with ample work space. Contemporary styling throughout and two popular grill restaurants adjacent.

Premier Travel Inn, 991 Chorley New Rd, BL6 4BA, Southeast : 1 ¾ m. on A 673 ☎ (08701) 977282, *Fax (01204) 692585* – rm, ♿ P. MC AE VISA.
Rest (grill rest.) – **60 rm** 46.95/46.95 – 49.95/49.95.
◆ Located on the main road, close to the Reebok Stadium, and its adjoining retail park. Comfortable accommodation for business travellers or families. Adjacent pub-style eatery.

XXX **Reflections** (at Whites H.), The Reebok Stadium (car park A), De Havilland Way, BL6 6SF, ☎ (01204) 667788, *Fax (01204) 673721* – P. MC AE VISA
closed Sunday-Tuesday – **Rest** (dinner only) a la carte 30.00/45.00 ♀.
◆ Notable for its elevated position overlooking the pitch at the Reebok Stadium. Formal dining experience, though dishes have a distinctly modern, original style.

HOUGHTON *Cambs. – see Huntingdon.*

HOUGHTON CONQUEST *Beds.* 504 S 27 *– see Bedford.*

HOVE *Brighton and Hove* 504 T 31 *– see Brighton and Hove.*

HOVINGHAM *N. Yorks.* 502 R 21 – ✉ *York.*
London 235 – Leeds 47 – Middlesbrough 36 – York 25.

Worsley Arms, YO62 4LA, ☎ (01653) 628234, *worsleyarms@aol.com, Fax (01653) 628130,* – P – 🏨 50. MC AE VISA
Cricketer's Bistro : **Rest** a la carte 15.00/30.00 s. ♀ – ***The Restaurant :*** **Rest** (dinner only and Sunday lunch) a la carte 15.50/31.00 s. ♀ – **20 rm** 85.00/110.00 – 115.00/135.00.
◆ Part 19C coaching inn set in delightful Yorkshire stone village. Charm and character throughout the classically traditional public rooms. Comfortable individual bedrooms. Informal Cricketer's Bistro. Calm, refined Restaurant.

HOYLAKE *Wirral* 502 504 K 23 *Great Britain G. – pop. 25 524.*
Exc. : *Liverpool★ - Cathedrals★★, Walker Art Gallery★★, Merseyside Maritime Museum★ and Albert Dock★, E : 13½ m. by A 553.*
London 220 – Chester 20 – Liverpool 11.

XX **Ruby,** 22-24 Market St, CH47 2AE, ☎ (0151) 632 3344 – . MC AE VISA
closed 26 December, 1 January, Sunday and Monday – **Rest** (dinner only) 15.95 and a la carte 18.45/26.25 ♀.
◆ Stylish restaurant with modern lighting and a bold palette. The eclectic menus take their inspiration from Cajun, French, Jamaican and Oriental styles, to name but a few.

HUDDERSFIELD *W. Yorks.* 502 504 O 23 *– pop. 146 234.*
18, 9 *Bradley Park, Bradley Rd ☎ (01484) 223772* – 18 *Woodsome Hall, Fenay Bridge ☎ (01484) 602971* – 18 *Outlane, Slack Lane ☎ (01422) 374762* **A** – 18 *Meltham, Thick Hollins Hall ☎ (01484) 850227* – 18 *Fixby Hall, Lightridge Rd ☎ (01484) 426203* **B** – 18 *Crosland Heath, Felks Stile Rd ☎ (01484) 653216* **A**.
3 Albion St ☎ (01484) 223200.
London 191 – Bradford 11 – Leeds 15 – Manchester 25 – Sheffield 26.

Plans on following pages

at Thunder Bridge *Southeast : 5¾ m. by A 629 –* **C** *– ✉ Huddersfield.*

Woodman Inn with rm, HD8 0PX, ☎ (01484) 605778, *thewoodman@connectfree.co.uk, Fax (01484) 604110* – rest, P. MC VISA.
Rest a la carte 14.00/20.00 ♀ – **12 rm** 45.00 – 65.00.
◆ A collection of 19C cottage style buildings, set in Last of the Summer Wine country. Freshly prepared dishes from bar or restaurant. Compact rooms in former weavers' cottages.

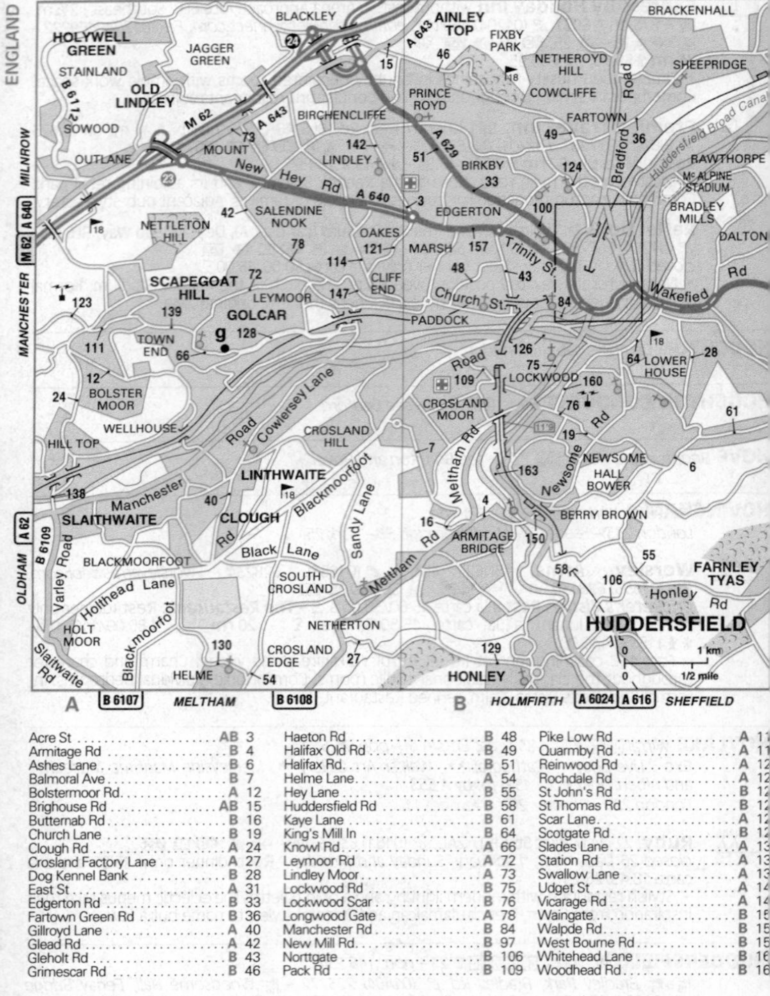

- Acre St . . . . AB 3
- Armitage Rd . . . . B 4
- Ashes Lane . . . . B 6
- Balmoral Ave . . . . B 7
- Bolstermoor Rd . . . . A 12
- Brighouse Rd . . . . AB 15
- Butternab Rd . . . . B 16
- Church Lane . . . . B 19
- Clough Rd . . . . A 24
- Crosland Factory Lane . . . . A 27
- Dog Kennel Bank . . . . B 28
- East St . . . . A 31
- Edgerton Rd . . . . B 33
- Fartown Green Rd . . . . B 36
- Gillroyd Lane . . . . A 40
- Glead Rd . . . . A 42
- Gleholt Rd . . . . B 43
- Grimescar Rd . . . . B 46
- Haeton Rd . . . . B 48
- Halifax Old Rd . . . . B 49
- Halifax Rd . . . . B 51
- Helme Lane . . . . A 54
- Hey Lane . . . . B 55
- Huddersfield Rd . . . . B 58
- Kaye Lane . . . . B 61
- King's Mill In . . . . B 64
- Knowl Rd . . . . B 66
- Leymoor Rd . . . . A 72
- Lindley Moor . . . . A 73
- Lockwood Rd . . . . B 75
- Lockwood Scar . . . . B 76
- Longwood Gate . . . . A 78
- Manchester Rd . . . . B 84
- New Mill Rd . . . . B 97
- Norttgate . . . . B 106
- Pack Rd . . . . B 109
- Pike Low Rd . . . . A 11
- Quarmby Rd . . . . A 11
- Reinwood Rd . . . . A 12
- Rochdale Rd . . . . A 12
- St John's Rd . . . . B 12
- St Thomas Rd . . . . B 12
- Scar Lane . . . . A 12
- Scotgate Rd . . . . B 12
- Slades Lane . . . . A 13
- Station Rd . . . . A 13
- Swallow Lane . . . . A 13
- Udget St . . . . A 14
- Vicarage Rd . . . . A 14
- Waingate . . . . B 15
- Walpde Rd . . . . B 15
- West Bourne Rd . . . . B 15
- Whitehead Lane . . . . B 16
- Woodhead Rd . . . . B 16

at Shelley *Southeast : 6¼ m. by A 629 – B – on B 6116 – ✉ Huddersfield.*

The Three Acres, Roydhouse, HD8 8LR, Northeast : 1 ½ m. on Flockton rd ℘ (01484) 602606, *3acres@globalnet.co.uk, Fax (01484) 608411,* ≤, – ⇔ rest, ▤ rest, **P.** MO AE VISA. ✗
closed 25 December-3 January
Rest *(closed Saturday lunch)* (booking essential) a la carte 24.40/44.45
20 rm ☕ ☆60.00/80.00 – ☆☆80.00/120.00.
◆ Well-established stone inn in rural location. Annex rooms more spacious and quiet; those in main house closer to the bar and dining room; all warm, modern and comfortable. Agreeably busy restaurant with open fires: fish dishes prepared at open seafood bar.

HUDDERSFIELD

Chapel Hill . . . . C 18
Claremont St . . . . C 21
Fitzwilliam St . . . . C 37
Gaswoors St . . . . C 39
Great Northern St . . . . C 45
Imperial Arcade . . . . C 60
King St . . . . C 63
Kingsgate Shopping Centre C
Lower Fitzwilliam St . . . . . . C 79
Manchester Rd . . . . C 84
Market Pl. . . . . C 85
Market St . . . . C 87
Merton St. . . . . C 91
New North Rd . . . . C 100
Northumberland St . . . . C 105
Outcote Bank . . . . C 108
Piazza Shopping Centre C
Portland St . . . . C 112
Queen St South. . . . . C 117
Queen St . . . . C 115
Railway St . . . . C 120
St Peter's St. . . . . C 125
Spring St . . . . C 133
Springwood Ave . . . . C 136
Trinity St . . . . C 141
Venn St. . . . . C 145
Victoria Lane . . . . C 148
Wakefield Rd . . . . C 151
Water St. . . . . C 156

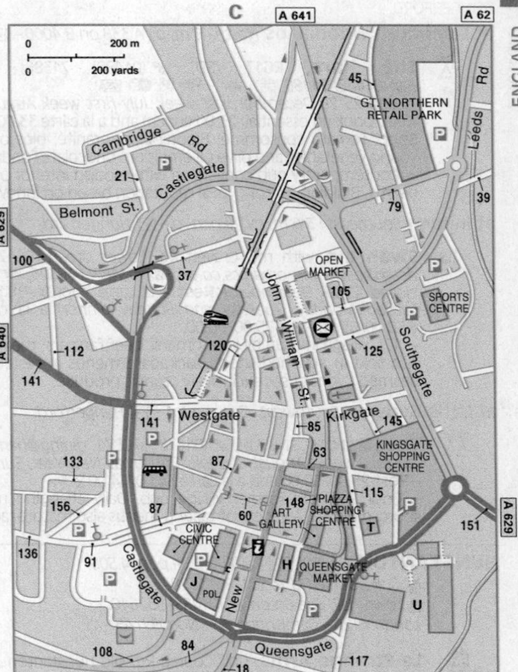

at Golcar *West : 3½ m. by A 62 on B 6111 – ✉ Huddersfield.*

XXX **The Weavers Shed** with rm, Knowl Rd, via Scar Lane, HD7 4AN, ☎ (01484) 654284, *info@weaversshed.co.uk, Fax (01484) 650980,* – rest, P. MC AE VISA
closed Christmas-New Year – **Rest** *(closed Saturday lunch, Sunday and Monday)* 15.95 (lunch) and a la carte 29.85/46.50 ♀ – **5 rm** ☕ ★70.00 – ★★90.00.
◆ Converted 18C cloth finishing mill. Stone floored dining area with low beamed ceiling. Select, modern British menu supplied by an extensive kitchen garden. Smart bedrooms.

HULL *Kingston-upon-Hull* 502 S 22 – *see Kingston-upon-Hull.*

HUNGERFORD *Newbury* 503 504 P 29 *The West Country G. – pop. 4 938.*
Exc. : *Savernake Forest★★ (Grand Avenue★★★), W : 7 m. by A 4 – Crofton Beam Engines★, SW : 8 m. by A 338 and minor roads.*
London 74 – Bristol 57 – Oxford 28 – Reading 26 – Southampton 46.

Marshgate Cottage without rest., Marsh Lane, RG17 0QN, West : ¾ m. by Church St ☎ (01488) 682307, *reservations@marshgate.co.uk, Fax (01488) 685475,* ⋖, – P. MC VISA
10 rm ☕ ★50.00 – ★★68.00.
◆ A quiet location, just a towpath walk away from the town centre. Pine-furnished and well-equipped bedrooms have pastoral views and some overlook the Kennet and Avon canal.

Fishers Farm without rest., Shefford Woodlands, RG17 7AB, Northeast : 4 m. by A 4 and A 338 on B 4000 ☎ (01488) 648466, *mail@fishersfarm.co.uk, Fax (01488) 648706,* , – P.
3 rm ☕ ★45.00 – ★★62.00.
◆ Attractive redbrick farmhouse in a quiet location on a working farm. Well-appointed sitting room. Breakfast served family style. Individually styled rooms with country views.

ENGLAND

at Lambourn Woodlands *North : 6 m. by A 338 on B 4000 – ✉ Hungerford.*

The Hare, RG17 7SD, ☎ (01488) 71386, *cuisine@theharerestaurant.co.u* *Fax (01488) 71186,* – **P**. VISA
closed 25-26 December, last week July-first week August, Sunday and Monday dinner
Rest (booking essential) 23.00 (lunch) and a la carte 33.00/41.00 ♀.
Spec. Tomato consommé, Bloody Mary granité, blossom fritter. Breast of chicken wit young vegetables and olive oil emulsion. Chocolate fondant with mascarpone ice cream.
◆ Contemporary pub conversion with modish interior of three dining rooms and origin beams. Building a strong local reputation based on innovative cooking of a high standard

at Inkpen *Southeast : 3½ m. by Inkpen rd – ✉ Hungerford.*

Swan Inn with rm, Craven Rd, Lower Green, RG17 9DX, ☎ (01488) 668326, *enqu ries@theswaninn-organics.co.uk, Fax (01488) 668306,* – **P**. VISA.
closed 25-26 December – **Rest** a la carte approx. 18.50 – ***Cygnet Restaurant*** **:** **Res** *(closed Monday, Tuesday and Sunday dinner)* a la carte approx 30.50 – **10 rm** ★50.00/65.00 – ★★75.00/90.00.
◆ 17C village inn run by local organic beef farmers; their produce is used in the meals an also sold in attached shop. Blackboard menus in restaurant and bar. Cosy rooms. Oak beamed Cygnet uses exclusively organic produce.

at Little Bedwyn *Southwest : 3 m. by A 4 – ✉ Hungerford.*

The Harrow, SN8 3JP, ☎ (01672) 870871, *dining@harrowinn.co.uk,* – . VISA
closed 2 weeks August, 2 weeks Christmas-New Year, Sunday dinner, Monday and Tuesda – **Rest** 25.00/30.00 and a la carte 34.00/44.00 ♀.
◆ Cosy, intimate former village pub. Daily changing menus offer well crafted, locall sourced dishes. A variety of tasting menus also feature, accompanied by impressive wines

HUNSTANTON *Norfolk 502 504 V 25 – pop. 4 505.*

18 Golf Course Rd ☎ (01485) 532811.
Town Hall, The Green ☎ (01485) 532610.
London 120 – Cambridge 60 – Norwich 45.

Le Strange Arms, Golf Course Rd, Old Hunstanton, PE36 6JJ, North : 1 m. by A 14 ☎ (01485) 534411, *reception@lestrangearms.co.uk, Fax (01485) 534724,* ←, – **P** – 150. AE VISA
Rest (bar lunch Monday-Saturday)/dinner 25.00 and a la carte 22.40/26.40 – **38 rm** ★72.00 – ★★140.00.
◆ Imposing Georgian building with fine views across the Wash, immediate access to the beach and opposite an arts and crafts centre. Good sized, traditionally styled bedrooms Sea view from restaurant.

The Gables, 28 Austin St, PE36 6AW, ☎ (01485) 532514, *bbatthegables@aol.com* – AE VISA
Rest (by arrangement) 15.00 – **6 rm** ★33.00/46.00 – ★★46.00/66.00.
◆ Large Edwardian house built of traditional Norfolk stone: well located for beach and town centre. Neat guest lounge; family photos decorate hallway. Personally styled rooms Cloth-clad dining room: extensive breakfasts and home-cooked meals.

Narara House without rest., 9 Lincoln Sq, PE36 6DW, ☎ (01485) 534290, ←, –
closed Christmas and New Year – **5 rm** ★32.00/45.00 – ★★56.00.
◆ Substantial 100 year-old house in quiet position; beach only a short walk away. Traditionally decorated, airy bedrooms, most with sea outlook. Full English breakfast served.

Claremont without rest., 35 Greevegate, PE36 6AF, ☎ (01485) 533171, *claremont@am serve.com* –
mid February-mid November – **7 rm** ★25.00/35.00 – ★★50.00/56.00.
◆ Classic seaside guesthouse in a Victorian building close to beach, shops and gardens. Well-kept, traditional interior and a toaster on each table at breakfast.

at Ringstead *East : 3¾ m. by A 149 – ✉ Hunstanton.*

The Gin Trap Inn with rm, 6 High St, PE36 5JU, ☎ (01485) 525264, *gintrap@aol.com, Fax (01485) 525321,* – **P**. VISA
Rest a la carte 17.75/34.80 ♀ – **3 rm** ★70.00 – ★★160.00.
◆ Charming 17C inn with tasteful, uncluttered style, but with rural mainstays like beams and open fire. Lunchtime bar favourites; well executed gourmet evenings. Stylish rooms.

HUNSTRETE *Bath & North East Somerset 503 504 M 29 – see Bristol.*

HUNTINGDON *Cambs.* 504 T 26 – *pop. 20 600* – *Hemingford Abbots, New Farm Lodge, Cambridge Rd (01480) 495000.*
The Library, Princes St (01480) 388588.
London 69 – Bedford 21 – Cambridge 16.

Huntingdon Marriott, Kingfisher Way, Hinchingbrooke Business Park, PE29 6FL, West : 1 ½ m. by A 141 at junction with A 14 (0870) 4007257, *reservations.huntingdon@marriotthotels.co.uk, Fax (0870) 4007357,* – – 260. AE VISA
Rest *(closed Saturday lunch)* (buffet lunch)/dinner 21.00 and a la carte 26.95/36.50 **s.** – 14.95 – **146 rm** 62.00/140.00 – 90.00/155.00, 4 suites.
◆ Purpose-built 1990s hotel, well geared to the modern business traveller. Good standard of brand furniture in public areas and well-equipped rooms which include data ports. Smart, airy dining room.

Old Bridge, 1 High St, PE29 3TQ, (01480) 424300, *oldbridge@huntsbridge.co.uk, Fax (01480) 411017,* – , rm, – 50. AE VISA
Rest – (see ***Terrace*** below) – **24 rm** 95.00/105.00 – 175.00.
◆ 18C former private bank overlooking the river. All bedrooms, some very contemporary, are decorated to a good standard and bathrooms often have deep Victorian-style baths.

Terrace (at Old Bridge H.), 1 High St, PE29 3TQ, (01480) 424300, *Fax (01480) 411017,* , – . AE VISA
Rest 16.50 (lunch) and a la carte 23.40/32.40 **s.** .
◆ Two dining areas: a formal wood panelled room and a more casual conservatory with terrace. Hearty rustic Italian dishes provide the basis for menus.

at Broughton *Northeast : 6 m. by B 1514 off A 141 – Huntingdon.*

The Crown, Bridge Rd, PE28 3AY, (01487) 824428, *simon@thecrownbroughton.co.uk, Fax (01487) 824912,* , – . VISA
closed 1-11 January and Monday (except lunch Bank Holidays) -Tuesday – **Rest** 13.50 (lunch) and a la carte 18.00/27.00 .
◆ Bay-windowed pub next to church in sleepy village. Uncluttered feel punctuated by bare tables and farmhouse chairs. Well-priced, modern meals with classic French base.

at Houghton *East : 3½ m. by B 1514 off A 1123 – Huntingdon.*

Cheriton House without rest., PE28 2AZ, (01480) 464004, *sales@cheritonhousecambs.co.uk, Fax (01480) 496960,* – . VISA.
5 rm 55.00/65.00 – 60.00/80.00.
◆ Cream painted 19C house with lovely garden. Place your order overnight for memorable breakfast. Relaxing conservatory-lounge. Co-ordinated rooms with thoughtful touches.

at Hemingford Grey *Southeast : 5 m. by A 1198 off A 14 – Huntingdon.*

The Willow without rest., 45 High St, PE28 9BJ, (01480) 494748, *info@thewillowguesthouse.co.uk, Fax (01480) 464456* – . VISA.
11 rm 45.00 – 55.00.
◆ Very personally run guesthouse in picturesque village location: its vivid yellow exterior makes it easy to spot. Good value, and close to The Cock. Immaculately kept bedrooms.

The Cock, 47 High St, PE28 9BJ, (01480) 463609, *info@cambscuisine.com, Fax (01480) 461747,* – . VISA
closed 25-26 December – **Rest** 11.95 (lunch) and a la carte 18.85/29.85 .
◆ Real ale pub with spacious dining area that features a wood-burning stove and oil paintings for sale. Good choice of dishes: fresh fish or sausage selections are a speciality.

at Brampton *West : 2 m. by A 141 off A 14 on B 1514 – Huntingdon.*

The Grange with rm, 115 High St, PE28 4RA, (01480) 459516, *info@grangehotelbrampton.com, Fax (01480) 459391,* – . AE VISA
closed 26-27 December and 1-2 January – **Rest** *(closed Sunday)* a la carte 18.50/32.00 – **7 rm** 70.00/80.00 – 100.00.
◆ Red-brick Georgian house, once a girls' school. Light, airy dining room with trendy pale grey walls. Well executed classic and modern menus. Colourful, contemporary rooms.

at Spaldwick *West : 7½ m. by A 141 off A 14 – Huntingdon.*

The George, 5 High St, PE28 0TD, (01480) 890293, *Fax (01480) 896847,* – . VISA
closed dinner 25 December and 1 January – **Rest** a la carte 17.95/31.95 .
◆ Built in the early 1500s, now sporting lilac and aubergine walls and an imposing fireplace. Characterful beamed restaurant: menus mix modern European with home-grown classics.

HUNTON *Kent* 504 V 30 – ✉ *Maidstone.*
London 37 – Canterbury 28 – Folkestone 34 – Hastings 35 – Maidstone 5.

Goldings without rest., Elphicks Farm, ME15 0SG, Pass the school and sharp bend, left after Durrants Cottage down unmarked drive ✆ (01622) 820758, *goldingsoast@btinternet.com, Fax (01622) 850754,* , – P
closed 20 December-24 January – **3 rm** ☕ 60.00/75.00 – 70.00/80.00.
◆ Built in 1840 for drying hops; set in 100 riverside acres on arable working farm. Striking façade; simpler interior: relaxed guest lounge, and airy, modern, well-fitted rooms.

HURLEY *Berks..*
London 35.5 – Maidenhead 5.5 – Reading 18.

Black Boys Inn with rm, Henley Rd, SL6 5NQ, Southwest : 1½ m. on A 4130 ✆ (01628) 824212, *info@blackboysinn.co.uk,* – P. MC VISA
closed 2 weeks Christmas – **Rest** *(closed Sunday dinner)* a la carte 21.00/27.00 ♀ – **8 rm** ☕ 65.00 – 75.00.
◆ Restored 16C inn: delightful interior, with sage walls and central fire. Appealing, well-priced menus: Newlyn fish, game from Hambledon Estate. Comfy, characterful rooms.

HURST *Berks.* 503 504 Q 29 – *see Reading.*

HURSTBOURNE TARRANT *Hants.* 503 504 P 30 – ✉ *Andover.*
London 77 – Bristol 77 – Oxford 38 – Southampton 33.

Esseborne Manor , SP11 0ER, Northeast : 1½ m. on A 343 ✆ (01264) 736444, *info@esseborne-manor.co.uk, Fax (01264) 736725,* , – rest, P – 60. MC AE VISA
Rest 18.00/22.00 and a la carte 25.00/42.00 s. ♀ – **20 rm** ☕ 95.00 – 180.00.
◆ 100 year old country house in attractive grounds with herb garden. Smart, well-appointed bedrooms, three in garden cottages. Ferndown room boasts a spa bath and private patio. Long, narrow dining room with large windows.

HURST GREEN *Lancs.* 502 M 22 – ✉ *Clitheroe.*
London 236 – Blackburn 12 – Burnley 13 – Preston 12.

Shireburn Arms, Whalley Rd, BB7 9QJ, on B 6243 ✆ (01254) 826518, *sales@shireburnarmshotel.com, Fax (01254) 826208,* , – rest, P. MC AE VISA
Rest 9.50/9.95 and a la carte 13.50/23.50 ♀ – **19 rm** ☕ 50.00 – 80.00/100.00.
◆ Ivy clad 17C former farmhouse located in a charming village. Traditional cottage décor and views of the Ribble valley. Reputedly haunted by a long deceased nun. Valley outlook from spacious dining room.

HUSTHWAITE *N. Yorks. Great Britain G.*
Exc. : *Castle Howard★★, E : 15 m. by minor roads.*
London 230 – Easingwold 4 – Leeds 41 – Thirsk 8.

The Roasted Pepper, Low St, YO61 4QA, ✆ (01347) 868007, *info@roastedpepper.co.uk, Fax (01347) 868776,* – P. MC VISA
closed Sunday dinner and Monday – **Rest** a la carte 15.70/24.20 ♀.
◆ Immaculately whitewashed and refurbished village pub. Chunky wood tables give it the ambience of rustic restaurant. Good value, Mediterranean themed dishes. Friendly service.

HUTTON-LE-HOLE *N. Yorks.* 502 R 21.
London 244 – Scarborough 27 – York 33.

Burnley House without rest., YO62 6UA, ✆ (01751) 417548, *info@burnleyhouse.co.uk,* – P
6 rm ☕ 45.00 – 75.00.
◆ Attractive part 16C, part Georgian house, Grade II listed in a picturesque Moors village. Brown trout in beck winding through garden. Simple, individually styled bedrooms.

HUTTON MAGNA *Durham Great Britain G. – pop. 86.*
Env. : *Raby Castle★, N : 5 m. by B 6274.*
Exc. : *Richmond★, S : 8 m. by B 6274 – Bowes Museum★, W : 8 m. by A 66.*
London 258 – Darlington 17 – Newcastle upon Tyne 53 – Scarborough 75.

Oak Tree Inn, DL11 7HH, ✆ (01833) 627371 – MC VISA
closed 25-26 December, 1 January and Monday – **Rest** (dinner only and Sunday lunch)/dinner a la carte approx 28.00.
◆ Part 18C inn in rural location. Interior beams and stone walls with homely décor. Blackboard menus offering modern pub food.

HUTTON ROOF *Cumbria – see Kirkby Lonsdale.*

HYDE *Gtr Manchester* 502 503 504 N 23 – *pop. 31 253.*
London 202 – Manchester 10.

Premier Travel Inn, Stockport Rd, Mottram, SK14 3AU, East : 2 m. by A 57 ✆ (0870) 7001478, *Fax (0870) 7001479* – rest, MC AE VISA.
Rest (grill rest.) – **83 rm** 47.95/47.95 – 50.95/50.95.
◆ Purpose-built hotel offering a dependable standard of accommodation - compact and functional, yet comfortable. Inner facing rooms quieter. Tried-and-tested menus in airy restaurant.

HYTHE *Kent* 504 X 30 – *pop. 14 766.*
Sene Valley, Sene, Folkestone ✆ (01303) 268513.
En Route Building, Red Lion Sq ✆ (01303) 267799.
London 68 – Folkestone 6 – Hastings 33 – Maidstone 31.

Plan : see Folkestone

Hythe Imperial, Prince's Parade, CT21 6AE, ✆ (01303) 267441, *hytheimperial@marstonhotels.com, Fax (01303) 264610,* squash – 250. MC AE VISA. X d
The Princes Room : **Rest** *(closed Saturday lunch)* 17.50/32.50 – **100 rm** 108.00/129.00 – 166.00/216.00.
◆ Set in a 50 acre estate, this classic Victorian hotel retains the elegance of a former age. Wide range of bedrooms cater for everyone from families to business travellers. Spacious restaurant with classic style and menus to match.

Hythe Bay, Marine Parade, CT21 6AW, ✆ (01303) 267024, *enquiries@thehythebay.co.uk, Fax (01303) 230651,* MC AE VISA
Rest - Seafood - (buffet lunch Sunday) a la carte 16.50/53.90.
◆ Originally built as tea rooms and in a great position just feet from the beach. Bright, airy room with views out to Channel. Seafood menus - ideal for lunch on a summer's day.

ICKLESHAM *E. Sussex* 504 V/W 31.
London 66 – Brighton 42 – Hastings 7.

Manor Farm Oast , Workhouse Lane, TN36 4AJ, South : ½ m. ✆ (01424) 813787, *manor.farm.oast@lineone.net, Fax (01424) 813787,* MC VISA.
closed Christmas-New Year and January – **Rest** (by arrangement) 25.00 – **3 rm** 54.00/74.00 – 74.00/84.00.
◆ 19C former oast house retaining original features and surrounded by orchards. Welcoming beamed lounge with open fire. One of the comfy bedrooms is completely in the round! Home-cooked menus in circular dining room.

IFFLEY *Oxon. – see Oxford.*

IGHTHAM COMMON *Kent – see Sevenoaks.*

ILCHESTER *Somerset* 503 L 30 – *pop. 2 123.*
London 138 – Bridgwater 21 – Exeter 48 – Taunton 24 – Yeovil 5.

Ilchester Arms with rm, The Square, BA22 8LN, ✆ (01935) 840220, *Fax (01935) 841353,* MC AE VISA.
closed 26 December – **Rest** *(closed Sunday dinner)* a la carte 15.00/26.00 – **7 rm** 60.00 – 75.00.
◆ Attractive-looking, ivy-covered 18C coaching inn. Relaxing, intimate public areas enhanced by flagstone flooring in bar. Hearty bistro menus. Clean and comfy bedrooms.

ILFRACOMBE *Devon* 503 H 30 *Great Britain G.*

Env. : *Mortehoe★★ : St Mary's Church - Morte Point★, SW : 5 ½ m. on B 3343 – Lundy Island★★ (by ferry).*
Exc. : *Braunton : St Brannock's Church★, Braunton Burrows★, S : 8 m. on A 361 – Barnstaple★ : Bridge★, S : 12 m. on A 3123, B 3230, A 39, A 361 and B 3233.*
London 218 – Barnstaple 13 – Exeter 53.

The Quay, 11 The Quay, EX34 9EQ, ✆ (01271) 868090, *info@thequay.co.uk, Fax (01271) 865599,* ← – MC AE VISA
closed 2 weeks January – ***Atlantic Dining Room and Harbourside :*** Rest *(closed Sunday dinner, Monday and Tuesday)* 18.50 (lunch) and a la carte 17.50/45.00 ♀ – ***Bar :*** Rest - World tapas - 15.50 and a la carte 10.00/25.00.
◆ Tall brick harbourside building, part owned by Damien Hirst. Cool, modish interior. Two restaurants; ground floor tapas bar. Modern international cooking in Atlantic.

ILKLEY *W. Yorks.* 502 O 22 – *pop. 13 472.*

Myddleton ✆ (01943) 607277.
Station Rd ✆ (01943) 602319.
London 210 – Bradford 13 – Harrogate 17 – Leeds 16 – Preston 46.

Rombalds, 11 West View, Wells Rd, LS29 9JG, ✆ (01943) 603201, *reception@rombalds.demon.co.uk, Fax (01943) 816586* – P – 70. MC AE VISA
closed 27 December-5 January – **Rest** 16.95 (lunch) and a la carte 14.85/28.85 **s.** – **11 rm** ★65.00/89.00 – ★★90.00/105.00, 4 suites.
◆ Privately owned Georgian town house on edge of Moor. Elegant fixtures and fittings adorn its sitting room. Individually styled bedrooms have matching fabrics and drapes. Yorkshire produce to fore in cool blue restaurant.

Box Tree (Gueller), 37 Church St, LS29 9DR, on A 65 ✆ (01943) 608484, *info@theboxtree.co.uk, Fax (01943) 607186* – 14. MC VISA
closed 27-30 December, 1-7 January, Sunday dinner and Monday – **Rest** (dinner only and lunch Friday-Sunday)/dinner 28.00 a la carte ♀.
Spec. Seared scallops with celeriac purée and truffles. Herb risotto with ceps and truffle oil. Châteaubriand with pomme purée, Choron sauce.
◆ Stone farmhouse built in 1720. Antiques, ornaments and oils adorn lounges and restaurant. Light, delicate cuisine with classic French and English combinations.

ILLOGAN *Cornwall* 503 E 33 *The West Country G.* – ✉ *Redruth.*

Env. : *Portreath★, NW : 2 m. by B 3300 – Hell's Mouth★, SW : 5 m. by B 3301.*
London 305 – Falmouth 14 – Penzance 17 – Truro 11.

Aviary Court, Mary's Well, TR16 4QZ, Northwest : ¾ m. by Alexandra Rd ✆ (01209) 842256, *info@aviarycourthotel.co.uk, Fax (01209) 843744,* – P. MC VISA.
Rest *(closed Sunday dinner to non-residents)* (dinner only and Sunday lunch) 17.50 – **6 rm** ★50.00 – ★★75.00.
◆ Tranquillity reigns at this cosy Cornish hotel with its neat, well-kept gardens. Traditional ambience prevails throughout with colourful furnishings and traditional rooms. Cornish ingredients dominate cuisine.

ILMINGTON *Warks.* 504 O 27 *Great Britain G.*

Env. : *Hidcote Manor Garden★★, SW : 2 m. by minor rd – Chipping Campden★★, SW : 4 m. by minor rd.*
London 91 – Birmingham 31 – Oxford 34 – Stratford-upon-Avon 9.

Folly Farm Cottage without rest., Back St, CV36 4LJ, ✆ (01608) 682425, *Fax (01608) 682425,* – P.
closed 25-26 December – **3 rm** ★45.00 – ★★80.00.
◆ Welcoming, cosy guesthouse with snug interior. Notable, sunny seating area in rear garden. Spacious breakfast room. Immaculate bedrooms, where breakfast may also be taken.

The Howard Arms with rm, Lower Green, CV36 4LT, ✆ (01608) 682226, *info@howardarms.com, Fax (01608) 682226,* rest, P. MC VISA.
closed 25 December – **Rest** a la carte 25.00/30.00 ♀ – **3 rm** ★77.50 – ★★115.00.
◆ Cotswold stone inn facing village green. Spacious pub with various rooms and snugs. Good British pub cooking; varied blackboard menu. Bright rooms with modern facilities.

Hotels and restaurants change every year, so change your Michelin guide every year!

ILMINSTER *Somerset* 503 L 31 *The West Country G. – pop. 4 451.*
See : *Town★ – Minster★★.*
Env. : *Barrington Court Gardens★* AC, *NE : 3½ m. by B 3168 – Chard (Museum★), S : 6 m. by B 3168 and A 358.*
London 145 – Taunton 12 – Yeovil 17.

at Cricket Malherbie *South : 2½ m. by Chard rd – ✉ Ilminster.*

The Old Rectory, TA19 0PW, ✆ (01460) 54364, *info@malherbie.co.uk, Fax (01460) 57374*, – ⇔ P. MC VISA. ✻
closed Christmas – **Rest** (by arrangement) (communal dining) 30.00 – **5 rm** ★55.00 – ★★105.00.
◆ Warmly run 16C thatched house in enticingly tranquil spot off beaten track. Delightful gardens. Carved oak beams draw you into sitting rooms's deep sofas. Inviting bedrooms.

INGLETON *N. Yorks.* 502 M 21 *– pop. 1 641 – ✉ Carnforth (Lancs.).*
The Community Centre ✆ (015242) 41049.
London 266 – Kendal 21 – Lancaster 18 – Leeds 53.

Pines Country House, Kendal Rd, LA6 3HN, Northwest : ¼ m. on A 65 ✆ (015242) 41252, *pineshotel@aol.com, Fax (015242) 41252*, – ⇔ P. MC VISA
February-October – **Rest** (booking essential) (residents only) (dinner only) 16.00 – **8 rm** ★35.00/45.00 – ★★56.00/62.00.
◆ Spacious early Victorian house, set on busy main road, near White Scar caves. Homely lounge. Good-sized, immaculately kept rooms. Conservatory dining room with fell views.

Riverside Lodge, 24 Main St, LA6 3HJ, ✆ (015242) 41359, *info@riversideingleton.co.uk*, <, – ⇔ P. MC VISA. ✻
closed 24-25 December – **Rest** (by arrangement) 15.00 – **7 rm** ★36.00 – ★★52.00.
◆ Pleasant 19C house close to famous pot-holing caves. Conservatory dining room with great views across Yorkshire Dales. Informal gardens. Cosy sitting room and homely bedrooms.

INKPEN *Newbury* 503 504 P 29 – *see Hungerford.*

INSTOW *Devon* 503 H 30 – *see Bideford.*

IPSWICH *Suffolk* 504 X 27 *Great Britain G. – pop. 138 718.*
See : *Christchurch Mansion (collection of paintings★)* X **B.**
Exc. : *Sutton Hoo★, NE : 12 m. by A 12* Y *and B 1083 from Woodbridge.*
18 *Rushmere, Rushmere Heath ✆ (01473) 725648 –* 18, 9 *Purdis Heath, Bucklesham Rd ✆ (01473) 727474 –* 18, 9 *Fynn Valley, Witnesham ✆ (01473) 785267.*
St Stephens Church, St Stephens Lane ✆ (01473) 258070, ipswich@eetb.info.
London 76 – Norwich 43.

Plan on next page

Salthouse Harbour, 1 Neptune Quay, IP4 1AS, ✆ (01473) 226789, *staying@salthouseharbour.co.uk, Fax (01473) 226927*, <, – |‡|, ⇔ rest, & P. MC AE VISA X a
Brasserie : **Rest** a la carte 15.45/30.45 – **41 rm** ★100.00/125.00 – ★★130.00/140.00, 2 suites.
◆ Converted 7-storey warehouse overlooking the marina. Lounge with seagrass seats. Designer style bedrooms with modern facilities; some with good views; two penthouse suites. Modern brasserie with a Mediterranean touch.

The Gatehouse, 799 Old Norwich Rd, IP1 6LH, ✆ (01473) 741897, *info@gatehousehotel.co.uk, Fax (01473) 744236*, – ⇔ rest, P. MC VISA. ✻ Y c
closed Christmas – **Rest** (booking essential to non-residents) (dinner only) 24.00 – **9 rm** ★70.00/90.00 – ★★90.00/100.00.
◆ Regency style house in large garden on edge of town. Wood-panelled drawing room. Spacious rooms, including 4 singles, with individual colour schemes and attractive furniture. Smart dining room with cloth-clad tables at dinner.

Express by Holiday Inn without rest., Old Hadleigh Rd, Sproughton, IP8 3AR, West : 2½ m. by A 1214 and A 1071 on B 1113 ✆ (01473) 222279, *Fax (01473) 222297*, – ⇔ & P – 30. MC AE VISA. ✻
49 rm ★49.95 – ★★62.00.
◆ A modern hotel within easy reach of the A12 and A14 junction, not far from the town centre. The Beagle Inn next door serves popular grill dishes. Well-equipped bedrooms.

IPSWICH

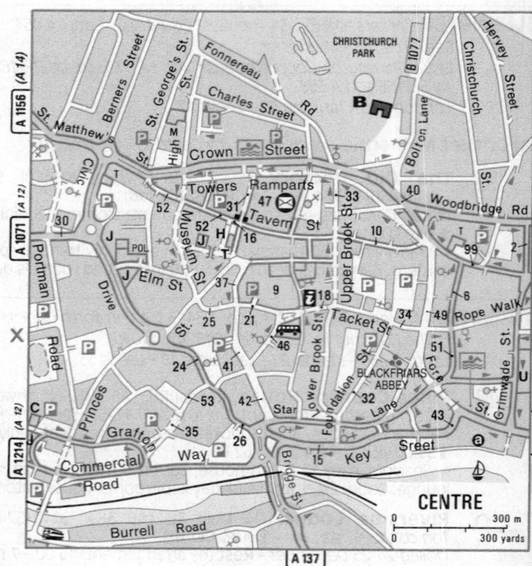

(A 140) A 14 BURY

WHITTON
CASTLE HILL
WHITE HOUSE
INDUSTRIAL ESTATE
BROOMHILL
ST. MARGARET'S
RUSHMERE
CHRISTCHURCH PARK
ST. JOHN'S
ALEXANDRA PARK
ST. CLEMENT'S
CHANTRY
CHANTRY PARK
SPRITES
STOKE PARK
BRIDGE
BOURNE PARK
HOLYWELLS PARK
LANDSEER PARK
GAINSBOROUGH
PRIORY HEATH

Bury Rd, Lovetofts Dr., Bramford Rd, Norwich Rd, Dales Rd., Henley Road, Valley Rd, Park Rd, Westerfield Road, Tuddenham Rd, Humber Doucy Lane, Colchester Rd, Woodbridge Road, Rushmere Road, Spring Road, Cauldwell Hall Rd, Heath Road, Foxhall Road, Sproughton Rd, London Road, Hadleigh Road, Ranelagh Rd, Hawthorn Drive, Belstead Rd., Stoke Park Drive, Wherstead Road, Hawes St, Landseer Road, Cliff Lane, Clapgate Lane, Nacton Road, Felixstowe Road, Bixley Road, Orwell

A 14 HADLEIGH (A 12)
A 1071
A 1214 COLCHESTER (A 12)
(A 12) (A 14) A 137 MANNINGTREE
(A 14)
A 1156 FELIXSTOWE
A 1214 (A 12) GREAT YARMOUTH
0 1 km
0 1/2 mile

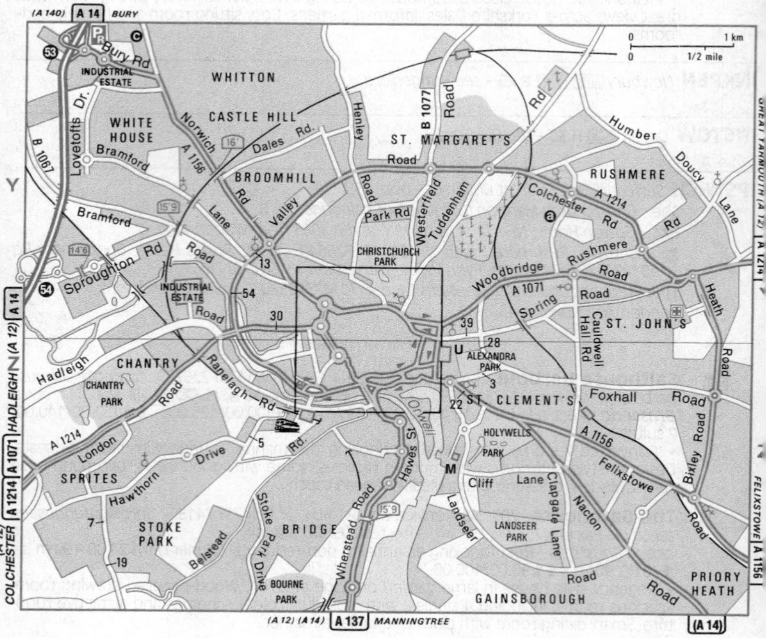

Look out for red symbols, indicating particularly pleasant establishments.

Premier Travel Inn, Bourne Hill, Wherstead, IP2 8ND, South : 1 3/4 m. by A 137 (Wherstead Rd) (01473) 692372, *Fax (01473) 692283* – rm, P. VISA
Rest (grill rest.) – **40 rm** 46.95/46.95 – 49.95/49.95.
◆ Well-proportioned modern bedrooms, suitable for business and family stopovers; simply fitted accommodation. Sited behind Beefeater restaurant.

Sidegate Guest House without rest., 121 Sidegate Lane, IP4 4JB, (01473) 728714, *sidegate.guesthouse@btinternet.com, Fax (01473) 728714,* – P Y a
6 rm 37.00/57.00 – 70.00.
◆ Compact, friendly guesthouse in residential area. Comfy lounge with terraced doors onto garden. Neatly laid breakfast room. Well-kept, cosy rooms.

at Holbrook *South : 5 3/4 m. by A 137 – Z – and B 1456 on B 1080 – Ipswich.*

Highfield without rest., Harkstead Rd, IP9 2RA, East : 1/2 m. by Fishponds Lane (01473) 328250, *Fax (01473) 328250,* – P.
closed December-January – **3 rm** 41.00 – 56.00.
◆ Rurally located guesthouse set in gardens with good views of River Stour. Peaceful ambience pervades lounge and communal breakfast room. Large, individually furnished rooms.

at Hintlesham *West : 5 m. by A 1214 on A 1071 – Y – Ipswich.*

Hintlesham Hall , IP8 3NS, (01473) 652334, *reservations@hintleshamhall.com, Fax (01473) 652463,* , heated, – rest, P – 80. VISA
Rest 27.50/30.00 (mid week) and a la carte 40.00/56.50 **s.** – 9.50 – **31 rm** 195.00 – 295.00, 2 suites.
◆ Grand and impressive Georgian manor house of 16C origins set in parkland with golf course. Stuart carved oak staircase. Ornate wedding room. Individually decorated rooms. Opulent room for fine dining.

IRONBRIDGE *Wrekin* 503 504 M 26 *Great Britain G. – pop. 1 560.*

See : *Ironbridge Gorge Museum★★ AC (The Iron Bridge★★, Coalport China Museum★★, Blists Hill Open Air Museum★★, Museum of the River and visitors centre★).*
The Toll House, The Iron Bridge, info@ironbridge.org.uk.
London 135 – Birmingham 36 – Shrewsbury 18.

Severn Lodge without rest., New Rd, TF8 7AU, (01952) 432147, *julia@severnlodge.com, Fax (01952) 432812,* – P.
closed 15 December-5 January – **3 rm** 59.00/64.00 – 72.00/79.00.
◆ Redbrick Georgian detached house with garden overlooking Iron Bridge, a World Heritage site. Quiet position. Cosy breakfast room. Antiques and pine furnishings in bedrooms.

The Library House without rest., 11 Severn Bank, TF8 7AN, (01952) 432299, *info@libraryhouse.com, Fax (01952) 433967,* – .
4 rm 60.00 – 70.00.
◆ Nicely hidden, albeit tricky to find, guesthouse with rear terrace. Homely sitting room. Cottage style breakfast room. Compact, comfy rooms, with a touch of style about them.

Bridge House without rest., Buildwas Rd, TF8 7BN, West : 2 m. on B 4380 (01952) 432105, *Fax (01952) 432105,* – P. VISA.
closed Christmas and New Year – **4** rm 48.00/50.00 – 65.00/70.00.
◆ Characterful 17C cottage with interesting turn of 20C machines in garden. Comfy reception room, fine collection of local objects and photos. Individually decorated rooms.

da Vinci's, 26 High St, TF8 7AD, (01952) 432250 – . VISA
closed 2 weeks Christmas, 1 week spring, 1 week autumn, Sunday and Monday – **Rest** - Italian - (booking essential) (dinner only) a la carte 15.65/32.85.
◆ Buzzy, personally run town centre restaurant with its rustic interior, painted boards, exposed brickwork and framed Leonardo prints. Tasty, authentic Italian cooking.

ISLE OF MAN *I.O.M.* 502 FG 21 – *see Man (Isle of).*

ITTERINGHAM *Norfolk – Aylsham.*

London 126 – Cromer 11 – Norwich 17.

Walpole Arms, The Common, NR11 7AR, (01263) 587258, *goodfood@thewalpolearms.co.uk, Fax (01263) 587074,* , – P. VISA
closed dinner 25 December and Sunday – **Rest** a la carte 19.00/25.00 .
◆ Charming, friendly, part 18C inn. Seasonal British menu draws intelligently on global ideas: dine at linen-clad parlour tables or in inviting, oak-beamed bar. Regional ale.

IVER *Bucks.* 504 S 29.
London 23 – Langley 2 – Slough 6.

The Swan at Iver, 2 High St, SL0 9NG, ☎ (01753) 655776, *Fax (01753) 655090* – ⇎ P. MC AE ⓓ VISA
closed Sunday dinner and Monday – **Rest** 25.00.
◆ A warm, traditional pub, complemented by 21C updates. Etched glass enhances rear dining room, as does the food, which is well executed in a distinctly modern British style.

IVYCHURCH *Kent* 504 W 30 *Great Britain G.*
Exc. : *Rye Old Town★★ : Mermaid St★ - St Mary's Church (<★), SW : 9 m. on A 2070 and A 259.*
London 67 – Ashford 11 – Rye 10.

Olde Moat House ⛵, TN29 0AZ, Northwest : ¾ m. on B 2070 ☎ (01797) 344700, *oldemoathouse@hotmail.com,* – ⇎ P. MC VISA. ✗
– **3 rm** ☕ ★40.00/60.00 – ★★60.00/95.00.
◆ Blissfully characterful guesthouse with 15C origins, set in over three acres, encircled by small moat. Beamed sitting room with inglenook. Individual, homely styled rooms.

IXWORTH *Suffolk* 504 W 27 – *see Bury St Edmunds.*

JERSEY *C.I.* 503 OP 33 and 517 ⑩ ⑪ – *see Channel Islands.*

JEVINGTON *E. Sussex* 504 U 31 – *see Eastbourne.*

KEDINGTON *Suffolk* 504 V 27 – *pop. 1 815* – ✉ *Haverhill.*
London 63 – Cambridge 23 – Haverhill 3.

The White House without rest., Silver St, CB9 7QG, ☎ (01440) 707731, *tobybarclay@netsparks.co.uk, Fax (01440) 705753,* – ⇎ P. ✗
3 rm ☕ ★40.00/65.00 – ★★65.00.
◆ Attractive former mill and bacon smokery with 16C origins. Beamed sitting room with wood burning stove and honesty bar. Rooms individually decorated with considerable taste.

KEGWORTH *Derbs.* 502 503 405 Q 25 *Great Britain G.*
Exc. : *Calke Abbey★, SW : 7 m. by A 6 (northbound) and A 453 (southbound) – Derby★ - Museum and Art Gallery★, Royal Crown Derby Museum★, NW : 9 m. by A 50 – Nottingham Castle Museum★, N : 11 m. by A 453 and A 52.*
London 123 – Leicester 18 – Loughborough 6 – Nottingham 13.

Kegworth House, 42 High St, DE74 2DA, ☎ (01509) 672575, *tony@kegworthhouse.co.uk, Fax (01509) 670645,* – ⇎ P. MC AE ⓓ VISA
closed Christmas-New Year – **Rest** (by arrangement) 25.00 – **11 rm** ☕ ★75.00 – ★★125.00/195.00.
◆ Georgian manor house in village, secluded in walled garden. Fine interior with original decorative features. Individually-decorated bedrooms of charm and character. Home cooking by arrangement.

KELSALE *Suffolk* 504 Y 27 – ✉ *Saxmundham.*
London 103 – Cambridge 68 – Ipswich 23 – Norwich 37.

Mile Hill Barn, North Green, IP17 2RG, North : 1½ m. on (main) A 12 ☎ (01728) 668519, *mail@mile-hill-barn.co.uk,* – ⇎ P. ✗
Rest (by arrangement) 23.00 – **3 rm** ☕ ★60.00/65.00 – ★★80.00/90.00.
◆ Converted 16C barn in heart of glorious Suffolk countryside. Timbered ceiling invokes rustic feel in pleasant lounge. Comfortable bedrooms with pine and chintz furnishings. Fresh English dishes cooked in owner's Aga.

KENDAL *Cumbria* 502 L 21 *Great Britain G.* – *pop. 28 030.*
Env. : *Levens Hall and Garden★ AC, S : 4½ m. by A 591, A 590 and A 6.*
Exc. : *Lake Windermere★★, NW : 8 m. by A 5284 and A 591.*
18 *The Heights ☎ (01539) 723499.*
B *Town Hall, Highgate ☎ (01539) 725758.*
London 270 – Bradford 64 – Burnley 63 – Carlisle 49 – Lancaster 22 – Leeds 72 – Middlesbrough 77 – Newcastle upon Tyne 104 – Preston 44 – Sunderland 88.

Beech House without rest., 40 Greenside, LA9 4LD, by All Hallows Lane ✆ (01539) 720385, *hilary.claxton@virgin.net, Fax (01539) 724082*, – . VISA.
closed 24-26 December – **6 rm** ★45.00/70.00 – ★★70.00/90.00.
◆ Tasteful and stylish semi-detached Georgian villa. Open-plan lounge; communal breakfasts. Individually decorated rooms are particularly tasteful and comfortable.

Bridge House, Bridge St, LA9 7DD, ✆ (01539) 738855, *info@bridgehousekendal.co.uk, Fax (01539) 738855* – . VISA
closed 25-26 December, 1 January, Sunday and Monday – **Rest** (lunch booking essential) 18.00 (lunch) and a la carte 19.50/33.65.
◆ Sited within a Georgian building by the River Kent. Modern ground-floor lounge; dining upstairs in two rooms. Assured cooking that stays within tried-and-tested boundaries.

at Crosthwaite *West : 5¼ m. by All Hallows Lane – ✉ Kendal.*

Crosthwaite House, LA8 8BP, ✆ (015395) 68264, *bookings@crosthwaitehouse.co.uk, Fax (015395) 68264*, ≤, – . AE
March-mid November – **Rest** (by arrangement) 15.00 – **6 rm** ★23.00/27.50 – ★★46.00/55.00.
◆ Comfortable Georgian style guesthouse in rural location with good views of nearby valley and a large, rear damson orchard. Rustic décor. Spacious bedrooms have a cottage feel. Cool dining room with shelves of curios; food from orchard.

The Punch Bowl with rm, LA8 8HR, ✆ (015395) 68237, *info@the-punchbowl.co.uk, Fax (015395) 68875*, – . AE VISA.
Rest a la carte 20.00/37.50 ♀ – **9 rm** ★71.25/93.75 – ★★95.00/150.00.
◆ Superbly refurbished 17C inn with heart-warming rustic ambience. Dine at bar or in formal room: accomplished seasonal dishes strike the right note. Luxuriously stylish rooms.

KENILWORTH *Warks.* 503 504 P 26 *Great Britain G.* – *pop. 22 218.*

See : *Castle★ AC.*
The Library, 11 Smalley Pl ✆ (01926) 748900.
London 102 – Birmingham 19 – Coventry 5 – Leicester 32 – Warwick 5.

Chesford Grange, Chesford Bridge, CV8 2LD, Southeast : 1 ¾ m. by A 452 on B 4115 ✆ (01926) 859331, *Fax (01926) 855272*, , , , – – 700. AE VISA
Rest 14.50/23.50 and a la carte 21.40/31.40 s. – **209 rm** ★170.00 – ★★170.00/220.00.
◆ Sizeable hotel in 17 acres of private gardens near Warwick Castle. Characterful foyer and staircase of oak. Extensive meeting facilities and leisure club. Spacious bedrooms. Smart dining room exudes comfy air.

Castle Laurels without rest., 22 Castle Rd, CV8 1NG, North : ½ m. on Stonebridge rd ✆ (01926) 856179, *mat.belson@btinternet.com, Fax (01926) 854954* – . AE VISA.
closed Christmas – **11 rm** ★45.00/60.00 – ★★75.00.
◆ Characterful Victorian house adjacent to Kenilworth Castle. Semi-panelled entrance, stained glass windows, original tiled floor. Homely sitting room and ample sized rooms.

Victoria Lodge without rest., 180 Warwick Rd, CV8 1HU, ✆ (01926) 512020, *info@victorialodgehotel.co.uk, Fax (01926) 858703*, – . AE VISA.
closed 1 week Christmas – **10 rm** ★47.00/60.00 – ★★70.00/75.00.
◆ Personally run hotel situated close to town centre. Small sitting room with adjacent bar. Simple and homely breakfast room. Immaculately kept, ample sized rooms.

Simply Simpsons, 101-103 Warwick Rd, CV8 1HL, ✆ (01926) 864567, *info@simplysimpsons.co.uk, Fax (01926) 864510* – . AE VISA
closed 1 week Christmas, last 2 weeks August, Sunday and Monday – **Rest** 22.50 (lunch) and a la carte 22.40/29.40.
◆ Boasts contemporary feel, typified by striking mirrors and artwork. Good value, hearty, robust classically based dishes supplemented by tried-and-tested daily specials.

Bosquet, 97a Warwick Rd, CV8 1HP, ✆ (01926) 852463, *rest.bosquet@aol.com, Fax (01926) 852463* – AE VISA
closed 2 weeks July-August, 1 week Christmas, Sunday and Monday – **Rest** - French - (lunch by arrangement) 29.50 and a la carte approx 34.50.
◆ Well-established French restaurant near centre of town. Contemporary interior with wooden floor and well-spaced tables accommodating stylish leather chairs.

KENNFORD *Devon* 503 J 32 – *see Exeter.*

KENTON *Exeter* 503 J 31 – *see Exeter.*

KERNE BRIDGE *Herefordshire* 503 504 M 28 – *see Ross-on-Wye.*

KESWICK *Cumbria* 502 K 20 *Great Britain G.* – *pop. 4 984.*

Env. : *Derwentwater*★ X – *Thirlmere (Castlerigg Stone Circle*★ *), E : 1½ m.* X A.

Threlkeld Hall ☎ *(017687) 79324.*

Moot Hall, Market Sq. ☎ *(017687) 72645, seatollertic@lake-district.gov.uk – at Seatoller, Seatoller Barn, Borrowdale* ☎ *(017687) 77294.*

London 294 – Carlisle 31 – Kendal 30.

Plan opposite

Underscar Manor ⑤, Applethwaite, CA12 4PH, North : 1 ¾ m. by A 591 on Underscar rd ☎ (017687) 75000, *Fax (017687) 74904,* ← Derwent Water and Fells, – P. MC AE VISA.

closed 2-4 January – **Rest** – (see ***The Restaurant*** below) – **11 rm** (dinner included) ★125.00 – ★★275.00.

◆ Blissfully located Victorian Italianate manor with commanding views of Derwent Water and Fells. Two comfortable sitting rooms. Modern leisure centre. Large, well kept rooms.

Dale Head Hall Lakeside ⑤, Thirlmere, CA12 4TN, Southeast : 5 ¾ m. on A 591 ☎ (017687) 72478, *onthelakeside@daleheadhall.co.uk, Fax (017687) 71070,* ← Lake Thirlmere, – P. MC AE VISA.

closed January – **Rest** (booking essential to non-residents) (dinner only) 40.00 **s.** – **12 rm** ★75.00/85.00 – ★★100.00/120.00.

◆ Wonderfully set 18C house on Lake Thirlmere. The family run friendliness lends a rich country house ambience. Log fired lounges, smart rooms. Daily changing dinner menu shows a careful touch; choose lake views or a rustic 16C dining room.

Highfield, The Heads, CA12 5ER, ☎ (017687) 72508, *info@highfield.co.uk,* ← Derwent Water and Borrowdale Valley, – P. MC AE VISA. Z n

closed December and January – **Rest** (dinner only) 32.50 – **19 rm** (dinner included) ★70.00/90.00 – ★★170.00.

◆ Substantial, keenly run 19C house with fine views across Derwent Water to Borrowdale Valley. Most bedrooms offer the vista; all are spacious and individually decorated. Traditional restaurant has big windows and imaginatively created dishes.

Lyzzick Hall ⑤, Underskiddaw, CA12 4PY, Northwest : 2 ½ m. on A 591 ☎ (017687) 72277, *lyzzickhall@btconnect.com, Fax (017687) 72278,* ←, – rest, P. MC VISA.

closed 24-26 December and January – **Rest** 30.00 (dinner) and lunch a la carte – **31 rm** ★53.00/56.00 – ★★106.00/112.00.

◆ Pleasant country house and gardens situated on slopes of Skiddaw. Welcoming lounge with plenty of plush chairs. Swimming pool and pretty terrace. Comfy, traditional bedrooms. L-shaped dining room filled with Lakeland pictures.

Lairbeck ⑤, Vicarage Hill, CA12 5QB, ☎ (017687) 73373, *mg@lairbeckhotel-keswick.co.uk, Fax (017687) 73144,* – P. MC VISA. X a

closed January and February – **Rest** (residents only) (dinner only) 19.50 – **14 rm** ★41.00/70.00 – ★★82.00/94.00.

◆ Victorian country house with original fittings still in place: beautiful panelling and wooden staircase. Good views of Skiddaw. Homely bar and sitting room. Spacious bedrooms. Golden hued dining room with thick russet drapes.

Abacourt House without rest., 26 Stanger St, CA12 5JU, ☎ (017687) 72967, *abacourt@btinternet.com* – P. Z e

5 rm ★45.00 – ★★56.00.

◆ Converted Victorian town house close to town centre. Boasts original features such as pitch pine doors and staircase. Simple, cosy breakfast room. Immaculately kept bedrooms.

Claremont House without rest., Chestnut Hill, CA12 4LT, ☎ (017687) 72089, *claremonthouse@btinternet.com,* ←, – P. X e

closed 24-26 December – **6 rm** ★30.00/60.00 – ★★46.00/70.00.

◆ Built 150 years ago, this former lodge house has good views over Keswick. Lounge filled with lovely prints and lithographs. Extensive breakfast menu. Spotless, homely rooms.

Acorn House without rest., Ambleside Rd, CA12 4DL, ☎ (017687) 72553, *info@acornhousehotel.co.uk* – P. MC VISA. Z s

closed 1-28 December – **10 rm** ★45.00 – ★★76.00.

◆ Characterful Georgian house in residential part of town. Well cared for gardens are a step away from elegant, comfortable lounge. Very bright, traditional, spacious bedrooms.

XXX **The Restaurant** (at Underscar Manor H.), Applethwaite, CA12 4PH, North : 1 ¾ m. by A 591 on Underscar rd ☎ (017687) 75000, *Fax (017687) 74904,* ← Derwent Water and Fells, – P. MC AE VISA

closed 2-4 January – **Rest** 28.00/45.00 and a la carte 38.00/43.50.

◆ Conservatory dining room of impressive height. Formal ambience with lace clothed tables and elegant glassware. Traditional menus: à la carte with classic base.

KESWICK

A 66 WORKINGTON COCKERMOUTH
A 591 CARLISLE
PENRITH, M 6
By-Pass
Greta
Derwent
PORTINSCALE
B 5292
BRAITHWAITE
A 66
A 591 WINDERMERE
Brockle Beck
GREAT WOOD
Borrowdale Road
STAIR
DERWENTWATER
Newlands Beck
BRANDELHOW PARK
HOGS EARTH
Watendlath Beck
BORROWDALE
DERWENT FELLS
Derwent
GRANGE
ROSTHWAITE
B 5289
BUTTERMERE
1 km
1/2 mile
X
Y

(A 66)
LEISURE CENTRE
LOWER FITZ PARK
UPPER FITZ PARK
A 5271
Main Street
Stanger St.
Victoria St.
Station Road
Greta
Penrith Road
Windebrowe Av.
Heads Road
The Headlands
The Heads
Lake Road
Lake Rd
St. John's St.
Southey St.
Blencathra St.
Helvellyn St.
Greta St.
Wordsworth St.
Skiddaw St.
Eskin Street
Manor Park
Ambleside Rd.
POL
CENTRE
200 m
200 yards
B 5289
Z

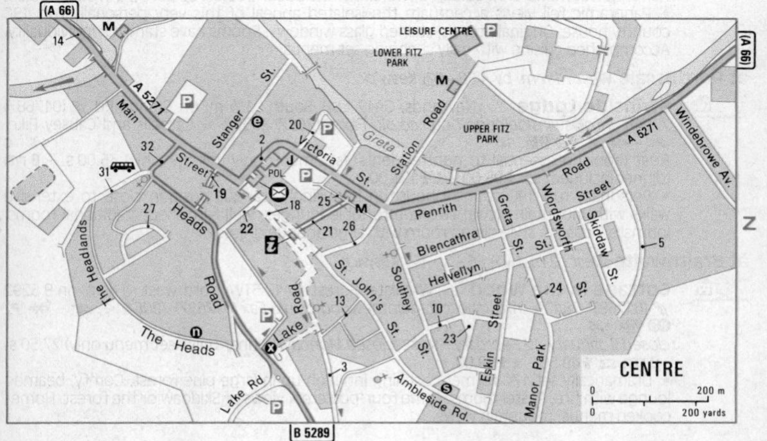

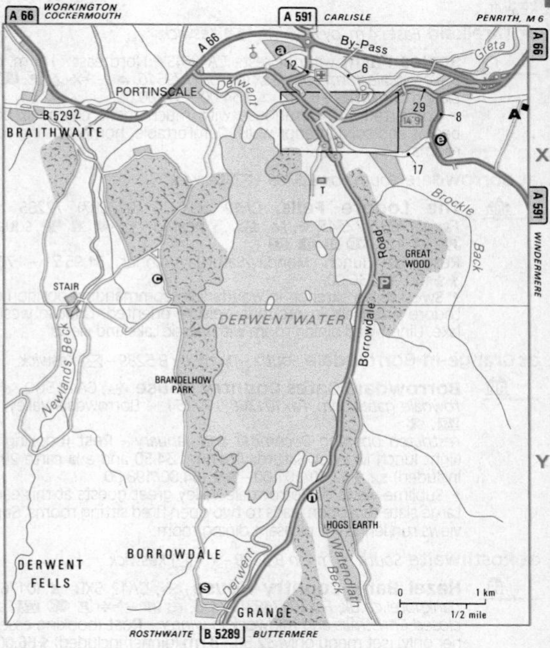

Morrel's, 34 Lake Rd, CA12 5AQ, ✆ (017687) 72666, *info@morrels.co.uk* – ⇔. MC VISA Z x

closed 25-26 December, 1 week January and Monday – **Rest** (dinner only) a la carte 16.75/30.00.

◆ Pleasingly refurbished and personally run. Etched glass and vivid artwork dominate interior. Menus designed to appeal to all: an agreeable blend of traditional and modern.

at Threlkeld *East : 4 m. by A 66 – X – ✉ Keswick.*

Scales Farm without rest., CA12 4SY, Northeast : 1 ½ m. off A 66 ☎ (017687) 79660, *scales@scalesfarm.com, Fax (017687) 79510,* – ⊬ ♿ P. MC VISA
closed Christmas – **6 rm** ☐ ✝34.00 – ✝✝60.00.
◆ Converted 17C farmhouse with much rustic charm. It boasts open stove, exposed beams and solid interior walls. Comfortable, homely sitting room. Spacious cottage style rooms.

at Borrowdale *South : on B 5289 – ✉ Keswick.*

The Lodore Falls, CA12 5UX, ☎ (017687) 77285, *info@lodorefallshotel.co.uk, Fax (017687) 77343,* ≤, heated, squash – |‡|, ⊬ rest, P – 120. MC AE ⓓ VISA Y n
Rest (bar lunch Monday-Saturday)/dinner 31.95 ♀ – **70 rm** ☐ ✝75.00/95.00 – ✝✝150.00/236.00.
◆ Swiss-styled exterior, in wonderfully commanding position overlooking Derwent Water; Lodore waterfalls in grounds. Leisure oriented. Choose west facing rooms overlooking lake. Llinen-clad dining room with classic Lakeland views.

at Grange-in-Borrowdale *South : 4¾ m. by B 5289 – ✉ Keswick.*

Borrowdale Gates Country House , CA12 5UQ, ☎ (017687) 77204, *hotel@borrowdale-gates.com, Fax (017687) 77254,* ≤ Borrowdale Valley, – ⊬ rest, P. MC AE ⓓ VISA. Y s
restricted opening December and January – **Rest** (booking essential to non-residents) (light lunch Monday-Saturday)/dinner 34.50 and a la carte 29.75/38.50 ♀ – **29 rm** (dinner included) ☐ ✝67.00/101.00 – ✝✝164.00/198.00.
◆ Sublime views of Borrowdale Valley greet guests at this early Victorian country house. Large slate reception leads to two open fired sitting rooms. Superior styled bedrooms. Fell views run length of pleasant dining room.

at Rosthwaite *South : 6 m. on B 5289 – Y – ✉ Keswick.*

Hazel Bank Country House , CA12 5XB, ☎ (017687) 77248, *enquiries@hazelbankhotel.co.uk, Fax (017687) 77373,* ≤, – ⊬ P. MC VISA.
closed Christmas and midweek in winter – **Rest** (booking essential to non-residents) (dinner only) (set menu only) 32.50 – **8 rm** (dinner included) ✝66.00/82.00 – ✝✝170.00/190.00.
◆ Panoramic fell views accentuate the isolated appeal of this very personally run 19C country house. Original fittings; stained glass windows. Rooms have stamp of individuality. Accomplished cuisine with daily changing set menus.

at Portinscale *West : 1½ m. by A 66 – ✉ Keswick.*

Swinside Lodge , Newlands, CA12 5UE, South : 1 ½ m. on Grange Rd ☎ (017687) 72948, *info@swinsidelodge-hotel.co.uk, Fax (017687) 73312,* ≤ Catbells and Causey Pike, – ⊬ P. MC VISA. X c
Rest (booking essential to non-residents) (set menu only) (dinner only) 35.00 **s.** – **8 rm** (dinner included) ☐ ✝98.00 – ✝✝196.00.
◆ Personally run 19C country house in beguilingly tranquil position close to extensive walks with mountain views. Two comfortable lounges; well furnished, traditional rooms. Intimate Victorian style dining room with large antique dresser.

at Braithwaite *West : 2 m. by A 66 – X – ✉ Keswick.*

Cottage in the Wood , Whinlater Forest, CA12 5TW, Northwest : 1 ¾ m. on B 5292 ☎ (017687) 78409, *info@thecottageinthewood.co.uk, Fax (017687) 78064,* ≤, – ⊬ P. MC VISA.
closed 2 January-12 February – **Rest** *(closed Monday)* (dinner only) (set menu only) 27.50 **s.** – **9 rm** ☐ ✝49.50 – ✝✝99.00.
◆ Dramatically set 17C former coaching inn high up in large pine forest. Comfy, beamed lounge with fire. Pastel rooms, some four-postered; views of Skiddaw or the forest. Home-cooked menus; mountain views.

KETTERING *Northants.* 504 R 26 – *pop. 51 063.*
The Coach House, Sheep St ☎ (01536) 410266.
London 88 – Birmingham 54 – Leicester 16 – Northampton 24.

Premier Travel Inn, Rothwell Rd, NN16 8XF, West : 1 ¼ m. at junction of A 14 with A 43 ☎ (01536) 310082, *Fax (01536) 310104* – ⊬ rm, rest, ♿ P. MC AE ⓓ VISA.
Rest (grill rest.) – **39 rm** ✝46.95 – ✝✝48.95.
◆ Simply furnished and brightly decorated bedrooms with ample work space, suitable for business and family stopovers. Grill restaurant serves popular menu.

KETTLESING *N. Yorks.* 502 P 21 – *see Harrogate.*

KETTLEWELL *N. Yorks.* 502 N 21.
London 246 – Darlington 42 – Harrogate 30 – Lancaster 42.

Littlebeck without rest., The Green, BD23 5RD, take turning at the Old Smithy shop by the bridge (01756) 760378, *stay@little-beck.co.uk* –
closed Christmas – **3 rm** 45.00 – 70.00.
◆ Characterful stone house from 13C with Georgian façade overlooking village maypole. Cosy lounge; extensive dales breakfast served. Attractively decorated bedrooms.

KEYSTON *Cambs.* 504 S 26 – *Huntingdon.*
London 75 – Cambridge 29 – Northampton 24.

Pheasant Inn, Village Loop Rd, PE28 0RE, (01832) 710241, *pheasant@huntsbridge.co.uk, Fax (01832) 710340,* – VISA
Rest (booking essential) a la carte 24.00/29.50.
◆ Attractive thatched country inn with beams and open fires serving good monthly menu of eclectic dishes. Wood floors and country bric-a-brac complete the rustic feel.

KIBWORTH BEAUCHAMP *Leics. – pop. 4 788 – Leicester.*
London 85 – Birmingham 49 – Leicester 6 – Northampton 17.

Firenze, 9 Station St, LE8 0LN, (0116) 279 6260, *info@firenze.co.uk, Fax (0116) 279 3646* – VISA
closed 10 days Christmas-New Year, Easter, Saturday lunch, Sunday and Monday – **Rest** - Italian - a la carte 18.00/43.75.
◆ Modern Italian restaurant in village centre. Beamed interior; contemporary décor. High-back wood-framed chairs. Expect king prawns with pancetta or quail with sage and garlic.

KIDDERMINSTER *Worcestershire* 503 504 N 26 – *pop. 55 348.*
Severn Valley Railway Station, Comberton Hill (01562) 829400 (summer only).
London 139 – Birmingham 17 – Shrewsbury 34 – Worcester 15.

at Chaddesley Corbett *Southeast : 4½ m. by A 448 – Kidderminster.*

Brockencote Hall, DY10 4PY, on A 448 (01562) 777876, *info@brockencotehall.com, Fax (01562) 777872,* – 25. VISA.
closed 1-17 January – **Rest** – (see ***The Restaurant*** below) – **17 rm** 96.00/120.00 – 116.00/180.00.
◆ Reminiscent of a French château, a 19C mansion in extensive parkland. Pine and maple library, chintz furnished conservatory. Good-sized rooms, all unique in style and décor.

The Restaurant (at Brockencote Hall), DY10 4PY, on A 448 (01562) 777876, *Fax (01562) 777872,* – VISA
closed 1-17 January and Saturday lunch – **Rest** - French 17.00/52.30 and a la carte 37.50/44.50 s.
◆ Two adjacent dining rooms: impressive high ceilings, fine oak panelled walls, a formal but discreet and relaxed atmosphere and fine modern dishes from local produce.

KILNSEY *N. Yorks.* 502 O 21 *Great Britain G.*
Exc. : *Skipton Castle★, S : 12 m. by B 6160 and B 6265 – Bolton Priory★, SE : 13 m. by B 6160.*
London 245 – Harrogate 31 – Skipton 14.

Kilnsey Old Hall without rest., BD23 5PS, (01756) 753887, *oldhall.kilnsey@virgin.net,* Wharfdale valley, –
closed 1 week Christmas – **3 rm** 50.00 – 75.00.
◆ Stone-built 17C hall set below huge limestone crag. Inglenooks a highlight. "Pigeon Loft" crammed with maps, painting materials and books. Thoughtful touches in each bedroom.

KIMBOLTON *Herefordshire* 503 L 27 – *see Leominster.*

"Rest" appears in red for establishments with a (star) or (Bib Gourmand).

KINGHAM *Oxon.* 503 504 P 28.
London 81 – Gloucester 32 – Oxford 25.

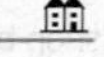

Mill House , OX7 6UH, ℘ (01608) 658188, *stay@millhousehotel.co.uk, Fax (01608) 658492*, , – rest, P – 70. VISA
Rest 16.50/28.00 and a la carte 28.00/37.50 – **23 rm** (dinner included) 90.00 – 170.00/187.50.
◆ Privately run house in 10 acres of lawned gardens with brook flowing through grounds. Spacious lounge with comfortable armchairs and books. Country house style bedrooms. Modern décor suffuses restaurant.

KINGSBRIDGE *Devon* 503 I 33 *The West Country G. – pop. 5 521.*
See : *Town★ – Boat Trip to Salcombe★★ AC.*
Exc. : *Prawle Point (≤★★★) SE : 10 m. around coast by A 379.*
18 *Thurlestone ℘ (01548) 560405.*
The Quay ℘ (01548) 853195.
London 236 – Exeter 36 – Plymouth 24 – Torquay 21.

Buckland-Tout-Saints , Goveton, TQ7 2DS, Northeast : 2½ m. by A 381 ℘ (01548) 853055, *buckland@tout-saints.co.uk, Fax (01548) 856261*, ≤, – rest, P – 100. VISA
closed 3 weeks January – **Rest** 19.00/37.50 and a la carte 19.00/35.50 – **10 rm** 65.00/85.00 – 130.00/150.00, 2 suites.
◆ Immaculate, impressive Queen Anne mansion with neat lawned gardens in rural location. Wood panelled lounge; all other areas full of antiques. Well-furnished bedrooms. Classic twin-roomed country house restaurant.

Your opinions are important to us:
please write and let us know about your discoveries and experiences – good and bad!

KINGSDON *Somerset* 503 L 30 – *see Somerton.*

KINGS LANGLEY *Herts.* 504 S 28 – *pop. 7 072.*
London 26 – Luton 14.

Premier Travel Inn, Hempstead Rd, WD4 8BR, ℘ (0870) 7001568, *Fax (0870) 7001569* – rm, rest, P. VISA.
Rest (grill rest.) – **60 rm** 45.95/45.95 – 59.95/59.95.
◆ Handily placed one mile from M25 motorway, this modern hotel provides ample facilities for business guests and families alike. Comfortable bedrooms. Bright, modern restaurant.

KING'S LYNN *Norfolk* 502 504 V 25 *Great Britain G. – pop. 41 281.*
Exc. : *Houghton Hall★★ AC, NE : 14½ m. by A 148 – Four Fenland Churches★ (Terrington St Clement, Walpole St Peter, West Walton, Walsoken) SW : by A 47.*
9 *Eagles, School Rd, Tilney All Saints ℘ (01553) 827147.*
The Custom House, Purfleet Quay ℘ (01553) 763044, kings-lynn.tic@west-norfolk.gov.uk.
London 103 – Cambridge 45 – Leicester 75 – Norwich 44.

Premier Travel Inn, Clenchwarten Rd, West Lynn, PE34 3LJ, Southwest : 3 ¼ m. by Hardwick Rd at junction of A 47 with A 17 ℘ (08701) 977149, *Fax (01553) 775827* – rm, rest, P. VISA.
Rest (grill rest.) – **40 rm** 49.95 – 49.95.
◆ Simply furnished and brightly decorated bedrooms with ample work space; a useful address for cost-conscious travellers. Handy for north Norfolk coast.

Old Rectory without rest., 33 Goodwins Rd, PE30 5QX, ℘ (01553) 768544, *clive@theoldrectory-kingslynn.com, Fax (01553) 691553*, – P
4 rm 38.00 – 48.00.
◆ Personally run Georgian styled Victorian residence with garden. Bright breakfast room is matched by colourful bedrooms that are sizable and furnished in modern style..

XX **Rococo,** 11 Saturday Market Pl, PE30 5DQ, ℘ (01553) 771483, *nickandersonchef@hotmail.com, Fax (01553) 771483* – . VISA
closed Sunday-Monday – **Rest** a la carte 26.60/38.00.
◆ Centrally located, in 17C house with vivid sitting room ceiling, exposed beams and bold artwork. Internationally influenced modern cooking with a distinctive seasonal base.

at Grimston *East : 6¼ m. by A 148 – ✉ King's Lynn.*

Congham Hall 🐎, Lynn Rd, PE32 1AH, ✆ (01485) 600250, *info@conghamhallhotel.co.uk, Fax (01485) 601191*, ≤, 🏊, 🏞, 🎾 – ⇔ P – 🎤 30. MC AE D VISA. ✂
Orangery : **Rest** 19.50/42.00 ♀ – **12 rm** ☕ ♠99.00/130.00 – ♠♠215.00, 2 suites.
◆ Immaculately peaceful cream-washed part Georgian house with herb and salad garden. Classic country house style lounges with many antiques. Elegant bedrooms of varying sizes. Pleasant, classic restaurant using herb garden produce.

KINGS MILLS *Guernsey (Channel Islands) – see Channel Islands.*

KINGSTON BAGPUIZE *Oxon.* 503 504 P 28 *– see Oxford.*

KINGSTON BLOUNT *Oxon. – see Chinnor.*

KINGSTONE *Herefordshire* 503 L 27 *– see Hereford.*

KINGSTON-UPON-HULL *Kingston-upon-Hull* 502 S 22 *Great Britain G. – pop. 301 416.*

See : *The Deep*★ Y.
Exc. : *Burton Constable*★ *AC, NE : 9 m. by A 165 and B 1238* Z.
⛳18 *Springhead Park, Willerby Rd* ✆ *(01482) 656309* – ⛳18 *Sutton Park, Salthouse Rd* ✆ *(01482) 374242.*
Humber Bridge (toll).
✈ *Humberside Airport :* ✆ *(01652) 688456, S : 19 m. by A 63* – **Terminal :** *Coach Service.*
⛴ *to The Netherlands (Rotterdam) (P & O North Sea Ferries) daily (11 h) – to Belgium (Zeebrugge) (P & O North Sea Ferries) daily (13 h 45 mn).*
ℹ *1 Paragon St* ✆ *(01482) 223559 – King George Dock, Hedon Rd* ✆ *(01482) 702118.*
London 183 – Leeds 61 – Nottingham 94 – Sheffield 68.

Plan on next page

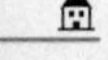

Premier Travel Inn, Kingswood Park, Ennerdale, HU7 4HS, North : 5 m. by A 1079 off A 1033 ✆ (01482) 820225, *Fax (01482) 820300* – |♦|, ⇔ rm, ▤ rest, ♿ P. MC AE D VISA
Rest (grill rest.) – **42 rm** ♠46.95/46.95 – ♠♠50.95/50.95.
◆ A consistent standard of trim, simply fitted accommodation in contemporary style which also serves as a useful location for cost-conscious travellers.

✕ **Boars Nest,** 22 Princes Ave, HU5 3QA, Northwest : 1 m. by Ferensway off West Spring Bank Rd ✆ (01482) 445577 – ⇔. MC D VISA
closed Tuesday – **Rest** (dinner only and Sunday lunch) a la carte 17.45/31.45.
◆ Early 20C butchers, with original tiles and carcass rails in situ. Comfy, cluttered first-floor lounge. Eat hearty English dishes downstairs at mismatched tables and chairs.

at Willerby *West : 5 m. by A 1079* – Z – *, Spring Bank and Willerby Rd* – ✉ *Kingston-upon-Hull.*

Willerby Manor, Well Lane (via Main St), HU10 6ER, ✆ (01482) 652616, *Fax (01482) 653901*, 🏞, Fá, ≘s, 🏊, 🎾 – ⇔ rm, P – 🎤 500. MC AE VISA. ✂
closed 2 weeks August, 1 Week January and 25-31 December – ***Icon :*** **Rest** *(closed Sunday)* (dinner only) 21.50/25.00 and a la carte 21.00/25.90 – ***Everglades :*** **Rest** a la carte 14.00/20.95 **s.** ♀ – ☕ 11.00 – **51 rm** ♠83.00/93.00 – ♠♠101.00/111.00.
◆ Modern hotel in residential area, with pleasantly laid-out landscaped grounds and rose gardens. Smart leisure facilities. Slightly functional bedrooms with colourful fabrics. Windowless Icon with contemporary menus. Everglades brasserie in hotel's lounge.

at Cottingham *Northwest : 5½ m. by A 1079* – Z – *on B 1233 (Cottingham Rd)* – ✉ *Kingston-upon-Hull.*

Lazaat, Woodhill Way, HU16 5SX, Northwest : 1 ½ m. by B 1233 on Skidby Lakes rd ✆ (01482) 847900, 🎾 – ⇔, ▤ rest, 📞 ♿ P – 🎤 100. MC D VISA
closed 25 December – **Rest** a la carte 18.95/23.00 **s.** – **13 rm** ☕ ♠95.00 – ♠♠100.00.
◆ Set in suburbs, this smart hotel boasts spacious public areas with a comfy lounge. Popular wedding venue. Bedrooms are a strong point: stylish, with high level of facilities. North African dishes - and themes - a speciality.

ENGLAND

KINGSTON-UPON-HULL

Street	Grid	No.
Bond St	X	3
Carr Lane	Y	
Commercial Rd	Y	8
County Rd North	Z	9
Dock Office Row	X	10
Dock St	X	12
Fairfax Ave	Z	13
Ferensway	XY	14
George St	X	
Grimston St	X	15
Humber Dock St	Y	16
Jameson St	Y	17
Jarratt St	X	18
King Edward St	Y	19
Kingston Retail Park	Y	
Lowgate	Y	23
Market Pl.	Y	24
Maybury Rd	Z	25
Paragon St	Y	29
Prince's Ave	Z	31
Prince's Dock St	Y	32
Princes Quay Shopping Centre	Y	
Prospect Shopping Centre	X	
Prospect St	X	
Queen's Dock Ave	X	36
Queen's Rd	Z	33
Queen St	Y	35
Reform St	X	37
Sculcoates Bridge	X	42
Southcoates Ave	Z	43
Southcoates Lane	Z	44
Waterhouse Lane	Y	47
Whitefriargate	Y	49
Wilberforce Drive	X	50
Worship St	X	52

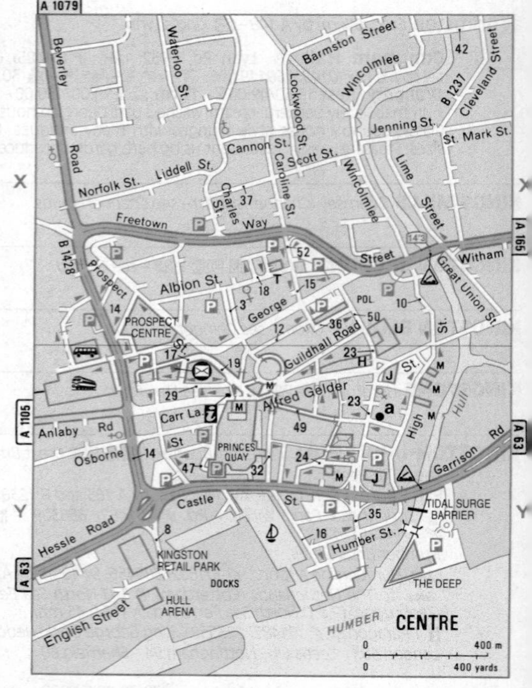

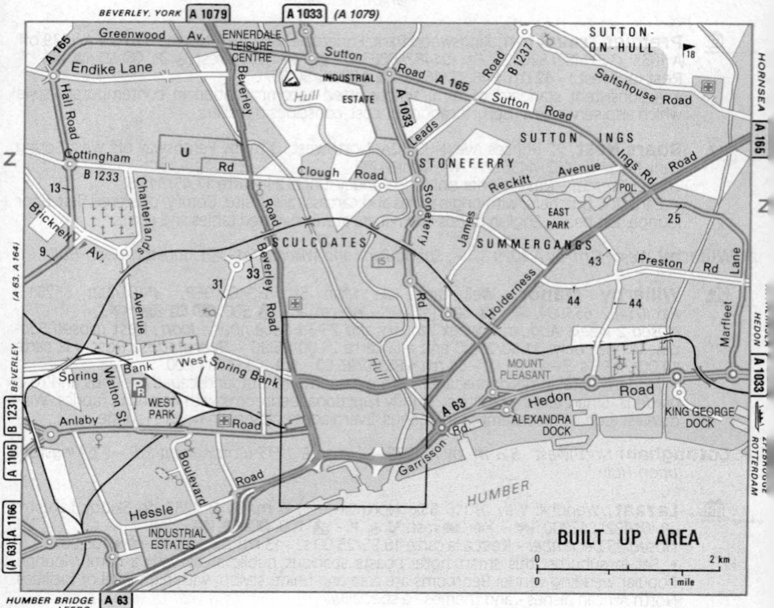

BEVERLEY, YORK A 1079 A 1033 (A 1079)

Greenwood Av. ENNERDALE LEISURE CENTRE SUTTON-ON-HULL 18

A 165 Endike Lane Sutton Road A 165 B 1237 Road Saltshouse Road HORNSEA

Hall Road INDUSTRIAL ESTATE Hull Beverley A 1033 Leads Sutton Road SUTTON INGS A 165

Z Cottingham Rd U B 1233 Clough Road STONEFERRY Reckitt Avenue Ings Rd Road

13 Chanterlands Stoneferry POL. EAST PARK 25 Z

Bricknell Av. 9 SCULCOATES James SUMMERGANGS 43 Preston Rd Lane

(A 63, A 164) 31 33 Beverley Road Avenue Rd Holderness 44 44 Marfleet HEDON

BEVERLEY Spring Bank West Spring Bank Hull MOUNT PLEASANT A 1033

B 1231 Walton St. WEST PARK A 63 Hedon Road KING GEORGE DOCK

A 1105 Anlaby Road Boulevard Garrison Rd. ALEXANDRA DOCK ZEEBRUGGE ROTTERDAM

A 1166 Hessle Road HUMBER

(A 63) INDUSTRIAL ESTATES BUILT UP AREA 0 2 km 0 1 mile

HUMBER BRIDGE LEEDS A 63

KINGSWEAR *Devon* 503 J 32 – *see Dartmouth.*

KINGTON *Herefordshire* 503 K 27 – *pop. 2 597.*
London 152 – Birmingham 61 – Hereford 19 – Shrewsbury 54.

at Titley *Northeast : 3½ m. on B 4355 – ✉ Kington.*

Stagg Inn (Reynolds) with rm, HR5 3RL, ✆ (01544) 230221, *reservations@thestagg.co.uk*, – rest, P. MO VISA
closed first 2 weeks November, 25-26 December and 1 January – **Rest** *(closed Sunday dinner and Monday except at Bank Holidays when closed Tuesday instead)* (booking essential) a la carte 17.50/25.00 ♀ – **6 rm** ☕ ♦50.00/70.00 – ♦♦120.00.
Spec. Seared scallops with celeriac purée and cumin. Venison with kummel and wild mushrooms. Bread and butter pudding.
• Modern pub cooking at its best in atmospheric inn; tasty, appealing dishes, full of local ingredients. Comfy rooms in the old vicarage or the inn where breakfast is served.

KIRKBY LONSDALE *Cumbria* 502 M 21 – *pop. 2 076* – ✉ *Carnforth (Lancs.).*
18 Scaleber Lane, Barbon ✆ (015242) 76365 – 9 Casterton, Sedbergh Rd ✆ (015242) 71592.
24 Main St ✆ (015242) 71437.
London 259 – Carlisle 62 – Kendal 13 – Lancaster 17 – Leeds 58.

at Casterton *Northeast : 1¼ m. by A 65 on A 683 – ✉ Carnforth (Lancs.).*

Pheasant Inn with rm, LA6 2RX, ✆ (015242) 71230, *pheasantinn@fsbdial.co.uk, Fax (015242) 74267*, – rest, P. MO VISA.
closed 25 December – **Rest** a la carte 14.00/26.00 ♀ – **10 rm** ☕ ♦38.00 – ♦♦90.00.
• 18C inn nestling beneath Fells. Bags of charm: open fire in bar, three sitting rooms, rural artefacts. Full menus with grills and hearty stews. Warm, welcoming bedrooms.

at Tunstall *South : 3½ m. by A 65 on A 683 – ✉ Kirkby Lonsdale.*

Lunesdale Arms, LA6 2QN, ✆ (015242) 74203, *Fax (015242) 74229*, – P. MO VISA
closed 25-26 December and Monday except Bank Holidays – **Rest** a la carte 15.50/21.45 ♀.
• Stone-built 18C pub; now a modern dining establishment.with bright, airy interior that includes a vast fireplace and squashy sofas. Locally sourced dishes to fore.

at Hutton Roof *West : 4½ m. by A 65 – ✉ Kirkby Lonsdale.*

Pickle Farm without rest., LA6 2PH, North : ¼ m. ✆ (015242) 72104, *stay@picklefarm.co.uk*, – P.
3 rm ☕ ♦44.00/48.00 – ♦♦68.00/76.00.
• Attractive, renovated part 18C farmhouse in a tranquil location. Pleasant sitting room opens onto walled garden. Organic breakfast. Simple but stylishly furnished rooms.

KIRKBYMOORSIDE *N. Yorks.* 502 R 21 – *pop. 2 650.*
18 Manor Vale ✆ (01751) 431525.
London 244 – Leeds 61 – Scarborough 26 – York 33.

Brickfields Farm, Kirby Mills, YO62 6NS, East : ¾ m. by A 170 on Kirby Mills Industrial Estate rd ✆ (01751) 433074, *janet@brickfieldsfarm.co.uk*, – P.
Rest (by arrangement) – **3 rm** ☕ ♦38.00/45.00 – ♦♦68.00/80.00.
• Personally run 1850s red-brick former farmhouse set down private driveway. Rooms are very comfortably appointed in rustic style with thoughtful extra touches. Homecooked meals in pleasant conservatory overlooking gardens and fields.

The Cornmill, Kirby Mills, YO62 6NP, East : ½ m. by A 170 ✆ (01751) 432000, *cornmill@kirbymills.demon.co.uk, Fax (01751) 432300*, – P. MO VISA.
Rest (by arrangement) 30.00 **s.** – **5 rm** ☕ ♦55.00 – ♦♦75.00/105.00.
• Converted 18C cornmill, its millrace still visible through the glass floor of a beamed and flagged dining room. Individually decorated bedrooms in the Victorian farmhouse.

at Fadmoor *Northwest : 2¼ m. – ✉ Kirkbymoorside.*

The Plough Inn, YO62 7HY, ✆ (01751) 431515, *Fax (01757) 431515*, – P. MO VISA
closed 25-26 December and 1 January – **Rest** a la carte 17.00/25.00 ♀.
• Pleasant rural pub with original tiled floor, rustic walls, scrubbed tables and real ales. Blackboard menu changes daily: traditional cooking with a modern twist.

KIRKBY STEPHEN *Cumbria* 502 M 20 – *pop. 2 209.*
London 296 – Carlisle 46 – Darlington 37 – Kendal 28.

Augill Castle, CA17 4DE, Northeast : 4 ½ m. by A 685 ☎ (01768) 341937, *enquiries@augillcastle.co.uk*, ←, ⚘, ♨, ✕ – ⇔ P. MO VISA.
Rest *(weekends only)* (dinner only) (set menu only) (communal dining) (residents only) 35.00 – **10 rm** ☕ ★70.00/90.00 – ★★140.00/160.00.
• Carefully restored Victorian folly in neo-Gothic style with extensive gardens; fine antiques and curios abound. Comfy music room and library. Individually decorated rooms. Expansive dining room with ornate ceiling and Spode tableware.

KIRKCAMBECK *Cumbria* 501 502 L 18 – *see Brampton.*

KIRKHAM *Lancs.* 502 L 22 – *pop. 10 372* – ✉ *Preston.*
London 240 – Blackpool 9 – Preston 7.

The Cromwellian, 16 Poulton St, PR4 2AB, ☎ (01772) 685680, *Fax (01772) 685680* – MO VISA
closed 1 week June, 1 week September – **Rest** (dinner only) 22.50.
• Narrow 17C townhouse with three dining rooms on two floors, characterised by uneven flooring and low beams. Home cooked dishes and an impressive wine list.

at Wrea Green *Southwest : 3 m. on B 5259* – ✉ *Kirkham.*

The Villa, Moss Side Lane, PR4 2PE, Southwest : ½ m. on B 5259 ☎ (01772) 684347, *info@villah.tel-wreagreen.co.uk, Fax (01772) 687647*, ⚘ – ⇔, ▤ rm, P – 🎭 25. MO AE ⓓ VISA.
Rest 19.95 and dinner a la carte 19.95/30.00 – **25 rm** ☕ ★65.00/95.00 – ★★75.00/110.00.
• Imposing red brick manor house with sympathetic extensions. Original house with bar and lounge, open fire, objets d'art. Purpose-built block has smart, well-furnished rooms. Dining room made up of many snugs, small rooms and conservatory; themed style.

Good food without spending a fortune? Look out for the Bib Gourmand

KIRKWHELPINGTON *Northd.* 501 502 N/O 18 *Great Britain G.* – ✉ *Morpeth.*
Env. : *Wallington House★ AC, E : 3½ m. by A 696 and B 6342.*
London 305 – Carlisle 46 – Newcastle upon Tyne 20.

Shieldhall, Wallington, NE61 4AQ, Southeast : 2 ½ m. by A 696 on B 6342 ☎ (01830) 540387, *robinson.gay@btinternet.com, Fax (01830) 540490*, ⚘ – P. MO VISA.
closed Christmas and New Year – **Rest** (by arrangement) 22.50 – **4 rm** ☕ ★45.00/55.00 – ★★80.00.
• Converted 18C farm buildings with gardens. Well-furnished, characterful lounge. Spotless rooms in former stable block: furniture constructed by cabinet-making owner!

KNAPTON *Norfolk* 504 Y 25 – *see North Walsham.*

KNARESBOROUGH *N. Yorks.* 502 P 21 – *pop. 13 380.*
Boroughbridge Rd ☎ (01423) 862690.
9 Castle Court, Market Pl ☎ (01423) 866886 (summer only).
London 217 – Bradford 21 – Harrogate 3 – Leeds 18 – York 18.

Dower House, Bond End, HG5 9AL, ☎ (01423) 863302, *enquiries@bwdowerhouse.co.uk, Fax (01423) 867665*, ⚘ – ⇔ ✆ ♿ P – 🎭 65. MO AE ⓓ VISA
Rest a la carte 15.95/31.85 – **31 rm** ☕ ★60.00/120.00 – ★★115.00/140.00.
• Part 15C, ivy clad, red brick house near town centre. Stone-floored reception and cosy bar. Small, well-equipped leisure centre. Good-sized, traditional bedrooms. Warmly toned restaurant overlooks the garden.

Off the Rails, The Station, Station Rd, HG5 9AA, ☎ (01423) 866587, *Fax (01423) 866163* – ⇔. MO VISA
closed 2 weeks August, Sunday dinner and Monday – **Rest** (booking essential) (dinner only and Sunday lunch/dinner) a la carte 17.90/26.45.
• Smart, cosy, wine bottle-strewn bistro; in a past life was Knaresborough station's ticket office. Sit at red gingham clad tables and enjoy well-executed modern bistro cooking.

at Ferrensby *Northeast : 3 m. on A 6055.*

The General Tarleton Inn with rm, Boroughbridge Rd, HG5 0PZ, (01423) 340284, *gti@generaltarleton.co.uk, Fax (01423) 340288* – P – 40. MC AE VISA
Rest (dinner only and Sunday lunch)/dinner 29.50 – (see also below) – **14 rm** 85.00 – 97.00/120.00.
◆ Attractive stone building, an extension to original 18C coaching inn; surrounded by North Yorkshire countryside. Comfy rooms and dining room full of rustic style and ambience.

The General Tarleton Inn, Boroughbridge Rd, HG5 0QB, (01423) 340284, *gti@generaltarleton.co.uk, Fax (01423) 340288,* – P. MC AE VISA
Rest a la carte 20.00/32.00 ♀.
◆ Characterful, well run 18C coaching inn with stone décor, open fires and various snugs and seating areas. Robust British dishes with northern influence: excellent value.

KNIPTON *Leics..*

London 125 – Leicester 28.5 – Melton Mowbray 10.5.

Manners Arms, Croxton Rd, NG32 1RH, (01476) 879222, *info@mannersarms.com, Fax (01476) 879228,* , – P. MC VISA
Rest a la carte 15.00/26.00 – **10 rm** 65.00/80.00 – 120.00.
◆ Refurbished former hunting lodge originally built for sixth Duke of Rutland; a relaxing feel pervades. Locals gather round bar's roaring fire. Individually styled bedrooms. Spacious dining room offers hearty rustic cooking.

KNOSSINGTON *Rutland* 502 504 R 25 – *see Oakham.*

KNOWLE GREEN *Lancs. – see Longridge.*

KNOWL HILL *Windsor & Maidenhead* 504 R 29 – ✉ *Twyford.*

9, Hennerton, Crazies Hill Rd, Wargrave (0118) 940 1000.
London 38 – Maidenhead 5 – Reading 8.

Bird in Hand, Bath Rd, RG10 9UP, (01628) 826622, *sthebirdinhand@aol.com, Fax (01628) 826748,* , – rest, rest, P. MC AE VISA
Rest a la carte 19.15/30.65 **s.** ♀ – **15 rm** 90.00 – 110.00.
◆ This red brick, black beamed former coaching inn of 14C origins counts George III as an 18C visitor! Characterful timbered bar and cosy residents' lounge. Cottagey rooms. Restaurant overlooks small garden and terrace.

KNOWSLEY INDUSTRIAL PARK *Mersey. – see Liverpool.*

KNOWSTONE *Devon – see South Molton.*

KNUTSFORD *Ches.* 502 503 504 M 24 – *pop. 12 656.*

Council Offices, Toft Rd (01565) 632611.
London 187 – Chester 25 – Liverpool 33 – Manchester 18 – Stoke-on-Trent 30.

Cottons, Manchester Rd, WA16 0SU, Northwest : 1 ½ m. on A 50 (01565) 650333, *cottons@shirehotels.com, Fax (01565) 755351,* , , , – – P – 200. MC AE VISA.
***Magnolia* : Rest** *(closed Saturday-Sunday)* (dinner only) a la carte 28.50/45.00 **s.** ♀ – **109 rm** 140.00 – 160.00.
◆ Large purpose-built hotel aimed at business travellers. Two good-sized country house style lounges and clubby bar. Smart leisure complex; comfortable, up-to-date bedrooms. French New Orleans themed dining room.

Longview, 55 Manchester Rd, WA16 0LX, on A 50 (01565) 632119, *enquiries@longviewhotel.com, Fax (01565) 652402* – rest, P. MC AE VISA
closed Christmas-New Year – **Rest** *(closed Sunday)* (dinner only) a la carte 17.95/30.45 **s.** ♀ – **28 rm** 83.00/86.00 – 110.00, 3 suites.
◆ Bay-windowed Victorian house, family run. Open log fire in reception. At foot of stone staircase lies cellar bar with soft lighting and low ceiling. Pleasant, comfy bedrooms. Mahogany furniture and chandeliers make for relaxed dining.

XX **Belle Epoque Brasserie** with rm, 60 King St, WA16 6DT, ✆ (01565) 633060, *info@thebelleepoque.com, Fax (01565) 634150*, – . VISA.
closed December and Bank Holidays – **Rest** *(closed Sunday dinner)* (dinner only and Sunday lunch) a la carte 18.20/33.20 – **6 rm** ★89.00 – ★★89.00.
◆ Bustling brasserie with Art Nouveau décor. Traditional and modern dishes with international touches using local produce. Contemporary style bedrooms with modern facilities.

at Mobberley *Northeast : 2½ m. by A 537 on B 5085 – ✉ Knutsford.*

Laburnum Cottage, Knutsford Rd, WA16 7PU, West : ¾ m. on B 5085 ✆ (01565) 872464, *Fax (01565) 872464*, – P. VISA
Rest (by arrangement) 15.00 – **5 rm** ★44.00 – ★★57.00.
◆ Red-brick two storey cottage guesthouse with large garden. Homely ambience, with velvet furnishings in lounge and small conservatory to rear. Good sized, individual rooms. Home cooking proudly undertaken.

Hinton, Town Lane, WA16 7HH, on B 5085 ✆ (01565) 873484, *the.hinton@virgin.net, Fax (01565) 873484*, – P. VISA.
Rest (by arrangement) 15.00 – **6 rm** ★44.00 – ★★58.00.
◆ Bay-windowed guesthouse with rear garden. Homely lounge where you can play the organ if you wish! Simple, uncluttered bedrooms with floral theme. Local produce used in meals.

at Hoo Green *Northwest : 3½ m. on A 50 – ✉ Knutsford.*

Mere Court, Warrington Rd, WA16 0RW, Northwest : 1 m. on A 50 ✆ (01565) 831000, *sales@merecourt.co.uk, Fax (01565) 831001*, – P – 75. VISA.
***Arboreum :* Rest** *(closed Saturday lunch)* 14.95/24.95 and a la carte – 11.95 – **34 rm** ★120.00 – ★★135.00/185.00.
◆ Immaculate looking part Edwardian manor house with attractive gardens. Pleasant country house feel with large, comfy, well-equipped, individually decorated bedrooms. Elegant oak-beamed, panelled dining room with lake and garden vistas.

KYNASTON *Herefordshire – see Ledbury.*

LACOCK *Wilts.* 503 504 N 29 *The West Country G.* – ✉ *Chippenham.*
See : *Village★★ - Lacock Abbey★ AC – High St★, St Cyriac★, Fox Talbot Museum of Photography★ AC.*
London 109 – Bath 16 – Bristol 30 – Chippenham 3.

At The Sign of the Angel, 6 Church St, SN15 2LB, ✆ (01249) 730230, *angel@lacock.co.uk, Fax (01249) 730527*, , – rm, P. VISA
closed 23-31 December – **Rest** *(closed Monday lunch except Bank Holidays)* a la carte 23.70/33.25 – **10 rm** ★72.00/105.00 – ★★155.00.
◆ Part 14C and 15C former wool merchant's house in charming National Trust village. Relaxed and historic atmosphere. Antique furnished rooms, four in the garden cottage. Tremendously characterful dining room of hotel's vintage: traditional English dishes served.

LADOCK *Cornwall* 503 F 33.
London 268 – Exeter 84 – Newquay 12 – Penzance 37 – Plymouth 51 – Truro 13.

Bissick Old Mill without rest., TR2 4PG, off B 3275 ✆ (01726) 882557, *sonia.v@bissickoldmill.ndo.co.uk, Fax (01726) 884057* – P. VISA.
February-November – **4 rm** ★54.00 – ★★75.00/84.00.
◆ Charming stone-built 17C former mill. Much historic character with low beamed ceilings and stone fireplaces. Comfortable bedrooms. Breakfast room has much period charm.

LAMBOURN WOODLANDS *Berks. – see Hungerford.*

LANCASTER *Lancs.* 502 L 21 *Great Britain G. – pop. 45 952.*
See : *Castle★ AC.*
Ashton Hall, Ashton-with-Stodday ✆ (01524) 752090 – Lansil, Caton Rd ✆ (01524) 39269.
29 Castle Hill ✆ (01524) 32878, tourism@lancaster.gov.uk.
London 252 – Blackpool 26 – Bradford 62 – Burnley 44 – Leeds 71 – Middlesbrough 97 – Preston 26.

Lancaster House, Green Lane, Ellel, LA1 4GJ, South : 3 ¼ m. by A 6 ✆ (01524) 844822, *lancaster@elhmail.co.uk, Fax (01524) 844766,* – 120. VISA
***The Gressingham* :** **Rest** 24.95 s. – 12.50 – **99 rm** 105.00/111.00 – 105.00/111.00.
◆ A purpose-built hotel set amidst lawned grounds and adjacent to Lancaster University, whose conference facilities can be used. Comfortable modern decor and country views. Split-level restaurant with views towards Morecambe Bay.

Edenbreck House without rest., Sunnyside Lane, off Ashfield Ave, LA1 5ED, by Westbourne Rd, near the station ✆ (01524) 32464, *han2312@aol.com*, –
3 rm 40.00 – 60.00.
◆ Large detached house on a short private drive in a peaceful residential area of the city. Inviting garden and homely, individual bedrooms.

at Carnforth *North : 6¼ m. on A 6.*

New Capernwray Farm without rest., Capernwray, LA6 1AD, Northeast : 3 m. by B 6254 ✆ (01524) 734284, *newcapfarm@aol.com, Fax (01524) 734284,* – VISA
March-September – **3 rm** 53.00/58.00 – 86.00.
◆ Grade II listed 17C former farmhouse in quiet countryside. Attractive lounge with fire. Breakfast at antique table. Cosy, comfortably furnished bedrooms.

LANCING *W. Sussex* 504 S 31 – *pop. 30 360 (inc. Sompting).*

London 59 – Brighton 4 – Southampton 53.

Sussex Pad, Old Shoreham Rd, BN15 0RH, East : 1 m. off A 27 ✆ (01273) 454647, *reception@sussexpadhotel.co.uk, Fax (01273) 453010,* – VISA
closed 25 December-5 January – **Rest** a la carte 20.65/38.25 – **18 rm** 72.00/85.00 – 100.00.
◆ Pubby modern hotel against the formidable backdrop of Lancing College. Co-ordinated rooms named after grand marque Champagnes: their namesakes in plentiful supply in the bar. Dine on seafood from nearby Brighton market.

LANGAR *Notts.* 502 R 25.

London 132 – Boston 45 – Leicester 25 – Lincoln 37 – Nottingham 14.

Langar Hall , NG13 9HG, ✆ (01949) 860559, *imogen@langarhall.co.uk, Fax (01949) 861045,* – rm, VISA
Rest 20.00/35.00 and dinner a la carte 28.00/40.00 s. – **11 rm** 90.00/110.00 – 210.00, 1 suite.
◆ Georgian manor in pastoral setting, next to early English church; overlooks park, medieval fishponds. Antique filled rooms named after people featuring in house's history. Elegant, candle-lit, pillared dining room.

LANGHO *Lancs.* 502 M 22 – *see Blackburn.*

LANGTHWAITE *N. Yorks.* 502 O 20 – *see Reeth.*

LAPWORTH *Warks.* – *see Hockley Heath.*

LASKILL *N. Yorks.* – *see Helmsley.*

LASTINGHAM *N. Yorks.* 502 R 21 – *pop. 87* – ✉ *York.*

London 244 – Scarborough 26 – York 32.

Lastingham Grange , YO62 6TH, ✆ (01751) 417345, *reservations@lastinghamgrange.com, Fax (01751) 417358,* – rest, VISA
March-November – **Rest** (light lunch Monday-Saturday)/dinner 26.50/37.50 – **11 rm** (dinner included) 105.00/140.00 – 250.00.
◆ A delightfully traditional country house atmosphere prevails throughout this extended, pleasantly old-fashioned, 17C farmhouse. Lovely gardens; well-appointed bedrooms. Dining room with rustic fare and rose garden view.

Look out for red symbols, indicating particularly pleasant establishments.

LAVENHAM *Suffolk* 504 W 27 *Great Britain G.* – ✉ *Sudbury.*
See : *Town*★★ – *Church of St Peter and St Paul*★.
ℹ *Lady St* ☎ *(01787) 248207.*
London 66 – Cambridge 39 – Colchester 22 – Ipswich 19.

Swan, High St, CO10 9QA, ☎ (01787) 247477, *info@theswanatlavenham.co.uk, Fax (01787) 248286,* – P – 35. VISA
Rest (bar lunch Monday-Saturday)/dinner 29.00 ♀ – **47 rm** ★90.00/100.00 – ★★150.00, 2 suites.
◆ Well-restored, part 14C, half timbered house with an engaging historical ambience. Each atmospheric bedroom is individually and stylishly decorated. Dining room has impressive timbered ceiling verging on the cavernous.

Lavenham Priory without rest., Water St, CO10 9RW, ☎ (01787) 247404, *mail@lavenhampriory.co.uk, Fax (01787) 248472,* – P. VISA.
closed Christmas-New Year – **6 rm** ★70.00 – ★★115.00/135.00.
◆ A Jacobean oak staircase and Elizabethan wall paintings are just two elements of this captivating part 13C former priory. Bedrooms stylishly furnished with antiques.

The Great House with rm, Market Pl, CO10 9QZ, ☎ (01787) 247431, *info@greathouse.co.uk, Fax (01787) 248007,* VISA
closed January – **Rest** - French - *(closed Sunday dinner and Monday)* 24.95 (lunch) and a la carte 20.95/34.70 ♀ – 9.50 – **3 rm** ★70.00/90.00 – ★★96.00/150.00, 2 suites 96.00/150.00.
◆ Timbered house with Georgian façade in town centre, dating from 14C. Rustic-style restaurant serves good range of French dishes. Comfortable, antique furnished bedrooms.

Angel with rm, Market Pl, CO10 9QZ, ☎ (01787) 247388, *angellav@aol.com, Fax (01787) 248344,* P. VISA
closed 25-26 December – **Rest** a la carte 15.00/20.00 ♀ – **8 rm** ★55.00 – ★★80.00.
◆ 15C inn on the market square. Residents' lounge has original early 17C ceiling. Comfortable, well-kept rooms are individually furnished and some are heavily timbered.

LEAFIELD *Oxon.* 503 504 P 28 – *see Witney.*

LEAMINGTON SPA *Warks.* 503 504 P 27 – *see Royal Leamington Spa.*

LECHLADE *Glos.* 503 504 O 28 *Great Britain G.*
Env. : *Fairford : Church of St Mary*★ *(stained glass windows*★★*), W : 4½ m. on A 417.*
London 84 – Cirencester 13 – Oxford 25.

at Southrop *Northwest : 3 m. on Eastleach rd* – ✉ *Lechlade.*

The Swan, GL7 2NU, ☎ (01367) 850205, *Fax (01367) 850517* – VISA
closed 25-26 December – **Rest** a la carte 23.00/27.00 ♀.
◆ Ivy covered 14C Cotswold inn. Characterful bar, popular with locals. Main dining room boasts low beamed ceiling and log fires. Modern menus with subtle Mediterranean twist.

LEDBURY *Herefordshire* 503 504 M 27 – *pop. 8 491.*
London 119 – Hereford 14 – Newport 46 – Worcester 16.

The Feathers, High St, HR8 1DS, ☎ (01531) 635266, *mary@feathers-ledbury.co.uk, Fax (01531) 638955,* – P – 120. VISA
Quills : **Rest** a la carte 15.75/29.50 ♀ – ***Fuggles :*** **Rest** a la carte 15.75/29.50 ♀ – **19 rm** ★79.50/85.00 – ★★135.00/175.00.
◆ Impressive timbered 16C inn in centre of town. Much character with open fires and antique furnishings. Rooms vary in design, though they all lay claim to a stylish modernity. Fuggles is decorated with hops.

The Barn House without rest., New St, HR8 2DX, ☎ (01531) 632825, *barnhouseledbury@lineone.net,* – P – 60. VISA.
closed Christmas-New Year – **3 rm** ★55.00 – ★★80.00.
◆ Parts date from 18C and the ancient "Barn Room", used for functions, from early 17C. Homely traditional style throughout the communal areas and accommodation.

The Malthouse, Church Lane, HR8 1DW, ☎ (01531) 634443, VISA
closed 2 weeks spring, 1 January, 24-25 December, Sunday and Monday – **Rest** (dinner only and Saturday lunch)/dinner 23.00 (midweek) and a la carte 23.20/31.75 ♀.
◆ Tucked away behind the butter market; rustic décor and attractive courtyard lend a classic country cottage aura. Monthly menu of carefully prepared dishes using local produce.

at Much Marcle *Southwest : 4¼ m. on A 449 – ✉ Ledbury.*

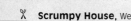

Scrumpy House, Westons Cider, The Bounds, HR8 2NQ, West : ¾ m. on Woolhope rd (01531) 660626, *matt@scrumpyhouse.co.uk,* – P. MO AE VISA
closed 26 December, 1 January and dinner Sunday-Wednesday – **Rest** a la carte 17.90/32.45.
◆ Charmingly simple eatery boasting rafters and exposed stone: the essence of rusticity. Local ingredients, like Marcle beef or home-made ice-cream, feature prominently.

at Kynaston *West : 6½ m. by A 449, A 4172, Aylton Rd, on Fownhope Rd – ✉ Ledbury.*

Hall End, HR8 2PD, (01531) 670225, *khjefferson@hallend91.freeserve.co.uk, Fax (01531) 670747,* – P.
closed Christmas and New Year – **Rest** (booking essential) (communal dining) (by arrangement) 27.50 – **3 rm** 55.00/62.50 – 95.00.
◆ Lovingly restored, personally run, part Georgian home and livery stable in the countryside. Relax in the orangery and, suitably reposed, retire to lavishly furnished bedrooms.

at Trumpet *Northwest : 3¼ m. on A 38 – ✉ Ledbury.*

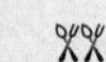

The Verzon with rm, Hereford Rd, HR8 2PZ, (01531) 670381, *info@theverzon.co.uk, Fax (01531) 670830,* – P. MO AE VISA.
Rest 18.50 (lunch) and dinner a la carte 19.95/30.00 – **8 rm** 65.00 – 98.00.
◆ Extended Georgian redbrick house with cool bar-brasserie interior. Relax in deep leather sofas; tuck into original dishes sourced from local ingredients. Airy, stylish rooms.

Undecided between two equivalent establishments? Within each category, establishments are classified in our order of preference.

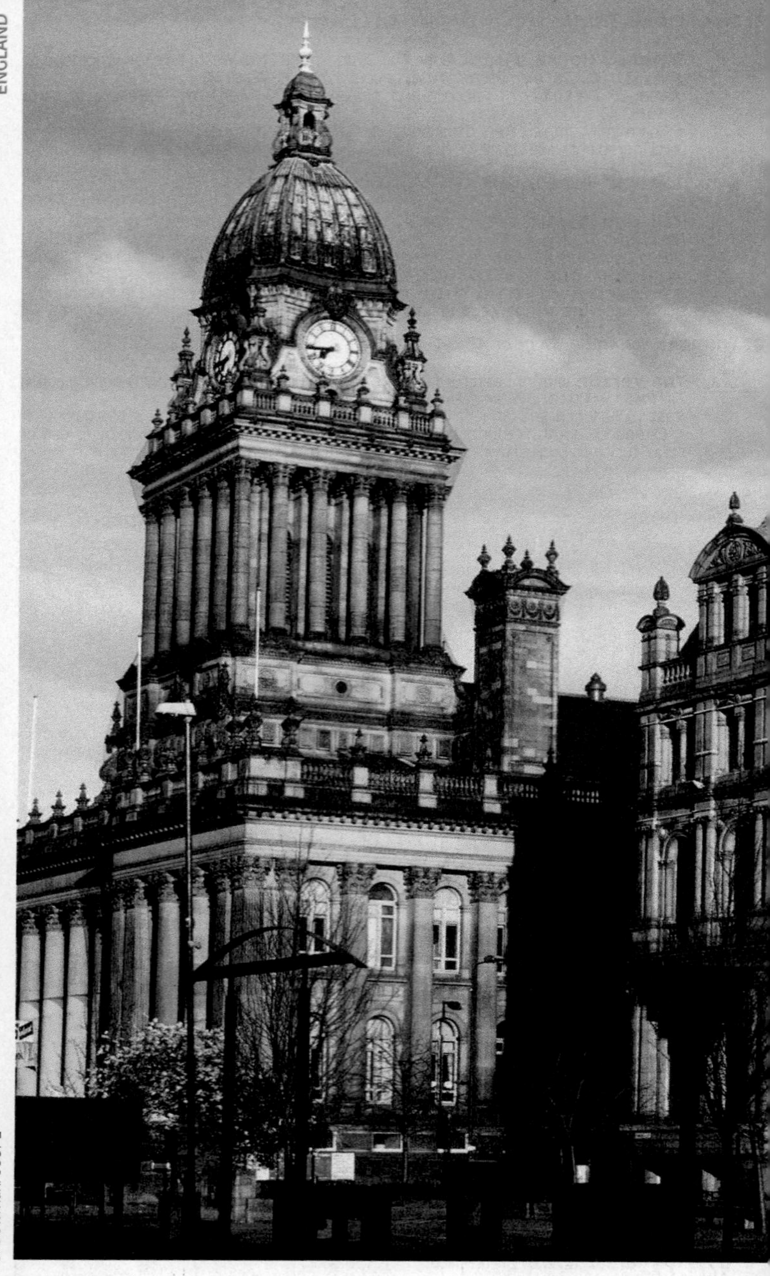

Leeds: Town Hall

LEEDS

W. Yorks. 502 P 22 *Great Britain G. – pop. 443 247.*

London 204 – Liverpool 75 – Manchester 43 – Newcastle upon Tyne 95 – Nottingham 74.

TOURIST INFORMATION

The Arcade, City Station ☎ (0113) 242 5242; tourinfo@leeds.golf.uk

PRACTICAL INFORMATION

18, 18 *Temple Newsam, Temple Newsam Rd, Halton ☎ (0113) 264 5624,* **CT**.
18 *Gotts Park, Armley Ridge Rd, Armley ☎ (0113) 234 2019,* **BT**.
18 *Middleton Park, Ring Rd, Beeston Park, Middleton ☎ (0113) 270 9506,* **CU**.
18, 9 *Moor Allerton, Coal Rd, Wike ☎ (0113) 266 1154.*
18 *Howley Hall, Scotchman Lane, Morley ☎ (01924) 350100.*
9 *Roundhay, Park Lane ☎ (0113) 266 2695* **CT**.
✈ *Leeds – Bradford Airport : ☎ (0113) 250 9696, NW : 8 m. by A 65 and A 658* **BT**.

SIGHTS

See : *City★ - Royal Armouries Museum★★★* **GZ** *– City Art Gallery★ AC* **GY M**.

Env. : *Kirkstall Abbey★ AC, NW : 3 m. by A 65* **GY** *– Temple Newsam★ (decorative arts★) AC, E : 5 m. by A 64 and A 63* **CU D**.

Exc. : *Harewood House★★ (The Gallery★) AC, N : 8 m. by A 61* **CT** *– Nostell Priory★, SE : 18 m. by A 61 and A 638 – Yorkshire Sculpture Park★, S : 20 m. by M 1 to junction 38 and 1 m. north off A 637 – Brodsworth Hall★, SE : 25 m. by M 1 to junction 40, A 638 and minor rd (right) in Upton.*

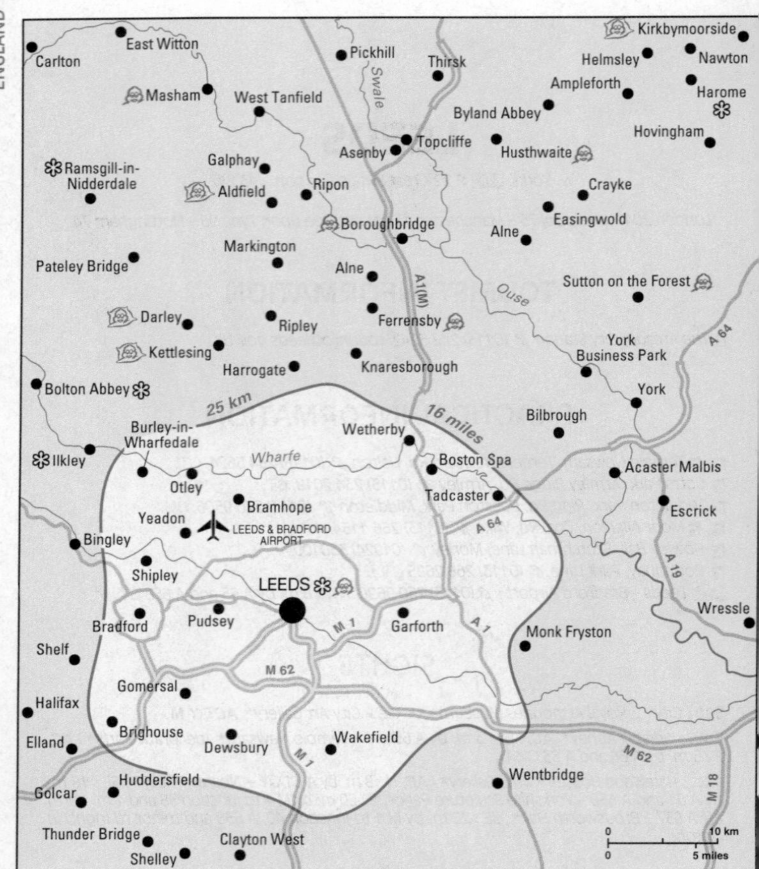

De Vere Oulton Hall, Rothwell Lane, Oulton, LS26 8HN, Southeast : 5½ m. by A 61 and A 639 on A 654 ☎ (0113) 282 1000, *oulton.hall@devere-hotels.com, Fax (0113) 282 8066,* ≤, Ⓦ, Lδ, ≘s, ⊡, ⛳9 (x3), ⇗, ♙ – |‡| ⇹ ▤ ✆ ♿ ⚹ Ⓟ – ⚐ 330. MC AE ⓓ VISA.
⚹ **CU a**

Bronte : **Rest** a la carte 28.00/40.00 s. ♀ – **150 rm** ⊒ ☨160.00 – ☨☨170.00, 2 suites.

◆ Once home to Leeds' Calverley family; neo-Classical mansion set in woodland with PGA standard golf course. The drawing room and main house bedrooms exemplify elegant style. Pictures of the famous family adorn walls of Bronte restaurant.

Thorpe Park H. and Spa, 1150 Century Way, Thorpe Park, LS15 8ZB, East : 6 m. by A 64 and A 63 on B 6120 ☎ (0113) 264 1000, *thorpepark@shirehotels.co.uk, Fax (0113) 264 1010,* ⛱, Ⓦ, Lδ, ≘s, ⊡ – |‡| ⇹ ▤ ✆ ♿ Ⓟ – ⚐ 200. MC AE VISA
⚹

closed 24-30 December – **Rest** 14.50/17.00 (lunch) and dinner a la carte approx 29.50 ♀ – **123 rm** ⊒ ☨155.00 – ☨☨175.00/220.00.

◆ Smart, modish hotel, close to motorways. Open-fired reception and richly toned central atrium. Fully equipped leisure centre with spa. Immaculate rooms with host of extras. Spacious, modern restaurant.

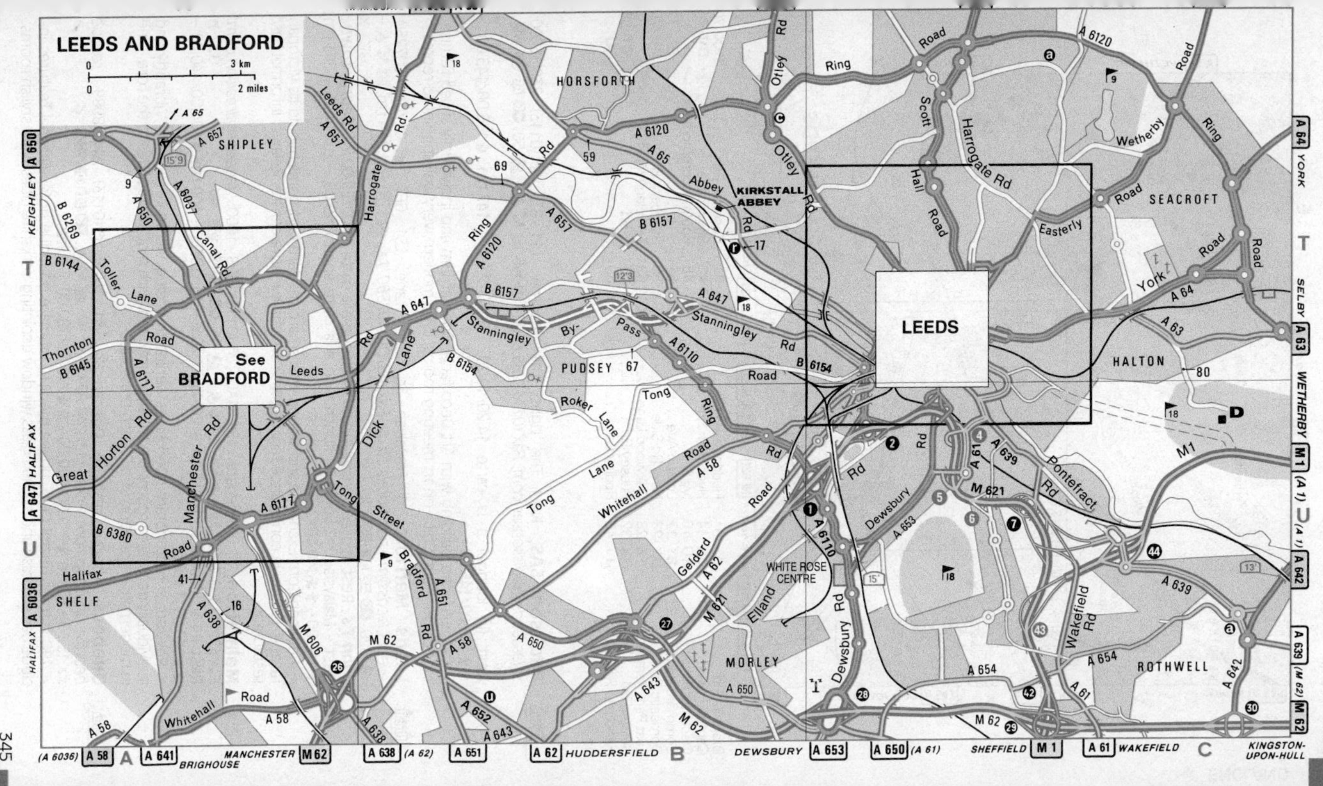
LEEDS AND BRADFORD
0 3 km
0 2 miles
LEEDS
See BRADFORD
HORSFORTH
SHIPLEY
SEACROFT
HALTON
PUDSEY
MORLEY
ROTHWELL
SHELF
KIRKSTALL ABBEY
WHITE ROSE CENTRE
A 64 YORK
SELBY A 63
WETHERBY M 1 (A 1)
(A 1) A 642
A 639 (M 62) M 62
KINGSTON-UPON-HULL
A 61 WAKEFIELD
SHEFFIELD M 1
A 650 (A 61)
DEWSBURY A 653
A 62 HUDDERSFIELD
A 651
A 638 (A 62)
MANCHESTER M 62
A 641 BRIGHOUSE
(A 6036) A 58
HALIFAX A 6036
HALIFAX A 647
KEIGHLEY A 650

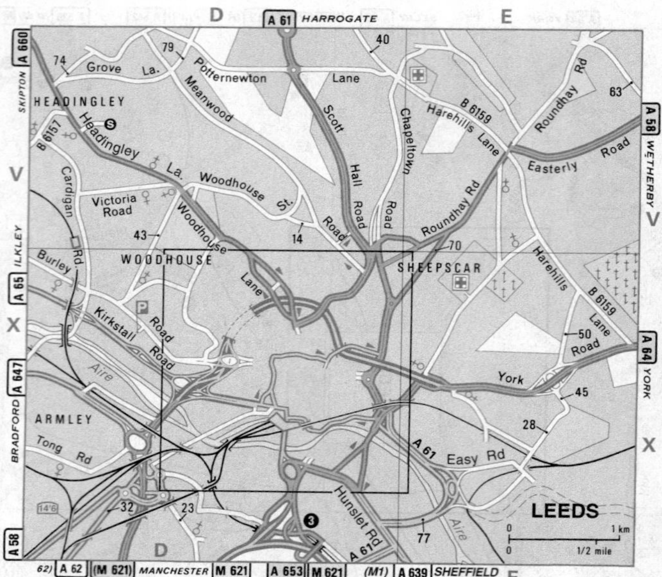

Bradford Rd . . . . . AT 9	Huddersfield Rd . . . . . AU 41	Roseville Rd . . . . . EVX 70
Cambridge Rd . . . . . DV 14	Hyde Park Rd . . . . . AV 43	Shaw Lane . . . . . DV 74
Cleckheaton Rd . . . . . AU 16	Ivy St . . . . . EX 45	South Accommodation Rd . . . . . EX 77
Commercial Rd . . . . . BT 17	Lupton Ave . . . . . EX 51	Stainbeck Rd . . . . . DV 79
Domestic St . . . . . DX 23	New Rd Side . . . . . BT 59	Templenewsam Rd . . . . . CT 80
East Park Parade . . . . . EX 28	Oakwood Lane . . . . . EV 63	White Rose Centre . . . . . CU
Gelderd Rd . . . . . DX 32	Pudsey Rd . . . . . BT 67	
Harrogate Rd . . . . . DV 40	Rodley Lane . . . . . BV 69	

Radisson SAS, No.1 The Light, The Headrow, LS1 8TL, ☎ (0113) 236 6000, *sales.leeds@radissonsas.com, Fax (0113) 236 6100* – 50. MO AE VISA. GY a

Rest (in lounge) a la carte 14.20/16.20 – 12.95 – **147 rm** 135.00/145.00 – 135.00/145.00.

◆ Grade II listed building with Art Deco facia. Open atrium and individually styled furnishings throughout. State-of-art meeting rooms. Ultra modern, very well appointed rooms.

Leeds Marriott, 4 Trevelyan Sq, Boar Lane, LS1 6ET, ☎ (0870) 4007260, *events.leeds@marriotthotels.co.uk, Fax (0870) 4007360,* – rm, – 320. MO AE VISA. GZ x

***John T's :* Rest** *(closed Sunday lunch)* 24.00 and a la carte 23.00/29.00 – ***Georgetown :* Rest** - Malaysian - 7.50/10.00 (lunch) and a la carte approx 19.00 – 14.95 – **243 rm** 140.00 – 140.00/240.00, 1 suite.

◆ Between Corn Exchange and station with smart, modern bedrooms behind its Victorian façade. Extensive conference facilities with an ample leisure centre. Relax in informal bar/restaurant.

Malmaison, 1 Swinegate, LS1 4AG, ☎ (0113) 398 1000, *leeds@malmaison.com, Fax (0113) 398 1002,* – 45. MO AE VISA. GZ n

Rest 14.50 (lunch) and a la carte 26.45/37.70 – 12.95 – **100 rm** 104.00/140.00 – 140.00, 1 suite.

◆ Relaxed, contemporary hotel hides behind imposing Victorian exterior. Vibrantly and individually decorated rooms are stylishly furnished, with modern facilities to the fore. Dine in modern interpretation of a French brasserie.

Quebecs without rest., 9 Quebec St, LS1 2HA, ☎ (0113) 244 8989, *resquebecs@etongroup.com, Fax (0113) 244 9090* – MO AE VISA. FZ a

15.50 – **43 rm** 115.00/180.00 – 145.00/180.00, 2 suites.

◆ 19C former Liberal Club, now a modish, intimate boutique hotel. Original features include oak staircase and stained glass window depicting Yorkshire cities. Very stylish rooms.

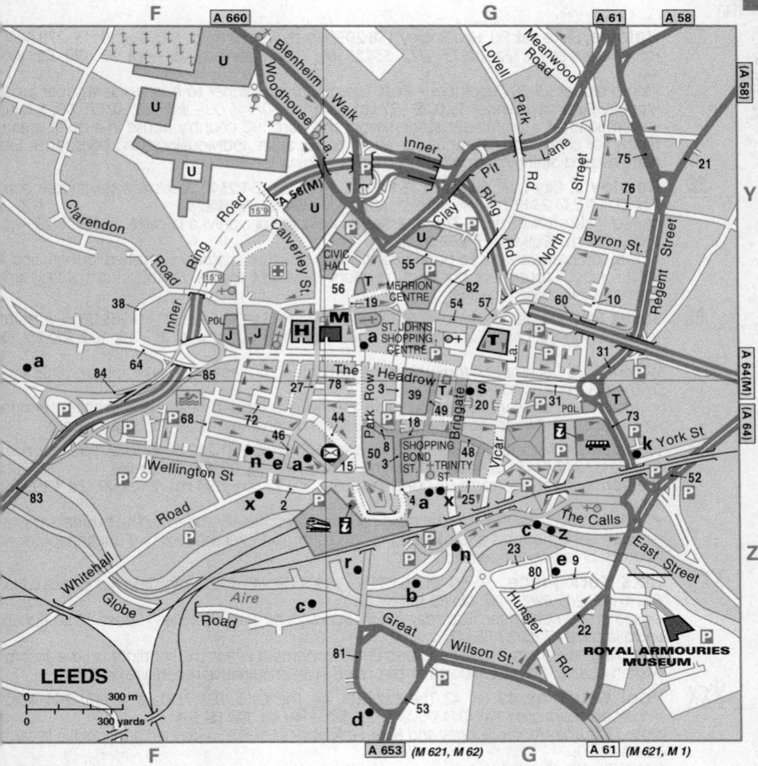

Street	Grid	No.	Street	Grid	No.	Street	Grid	No.
Aire St.	FZ	2	Eastgate	GZ	31	New York Rd.	GY	60
Albion St	GZ	3	Hanover Way	FY	38	Park Lane	FY	64
Boar Lane	GZ	4	Headrow (The)	GY		Queen St	FZ	68
Bond St	GZ	8	Headrow Centre	GZ	39	St John's Centre	GY	
Bowman Lane	GZ	9	Infirmary St	GZ	44	St Paul's St	FZ	72
Bridge St	GY	10	King St	FZ	46	St Peter's St	GZ	73
Briggate	GZ		Kirkgate	GZ	48	Sheepscar St South	GY	75
City Square	GZ	15	Lands Lane	GZ	49	Skinner Lane	GY	76
Commercial St	GZ	18	Leeds Shopping Plaza	GZ	50	South Parade	FGZ	78
Cookridge St	GY	19	Marsh Lane	GZ	52	Trinity St Shopping Centre	GZ	
County Arcade	GZ	20	Meadow Lane	GZ	53	Victoria Rd	GZ	81
Cross Stamford St	GY	21	Merrion Centre	GY		Wade Lane	GY	82
Crown Point Rd	GZ	22	Merrion St	GY	54	Waterloo St	GZ	80
Dock St	GZ	23	Merrion Way	GY	55	Wellington Rd	FZ	83
Duncan St	GZ	25	Millennium Square	GY	56	West St	FZ	84
East Parade	FGZ	27	New Briggate	GY	57	Westgate	FZ	85

42 The Calls, 42 The Calls, LS2 7EW, ✆ (0113) 244 0099, *hotel@42thecalls.co.uk, Fax (0113) 234 4100,* ⇐ – 🅿 ✆ ♿ – 🏛 70. 🅒🅒 AE ⓓ VISA GZ z
closed 4 days Christmas – **Rest** – (see ***Pool Court at 42*** and ***Brasserie Forty Four*** below) – ☕ 14.00 – **38 rm** ✝120.00/180.00 – ✝✝225.00/295.00, 3 suites.
◆ Stylish, contemporary converted quayside grain mill retaining many of the original workings. Rooms facing river have best views; all well equipped with a host of extras.

Hilton Leeds City, Neville St, LS1 4BX, ✆ (0113) 244 2000, *Fax (0113) 243 3577,* ⇐, 🏋, ⌂s, 🏊 – 🅿 ⇔, ▤ rm, ✆ ♿ 🅿 – 🏛 400. 🅒🅒 AE ⓓ VISA GZ r
***New World*:** **Rest** (bar lunch)/dinner a la carte 21.95/34.25 ♀ – ☕ 17.95 – **186 rm** ✝101.00/157.00 – ✝✝101.00/157.00, 20 suites.
◆ Proximity to station, business and commercial districts make this 1970s tower block a favourite for the corporate traveller. Neat rooms have views of city. Extensive brasserie menus with dishes from around the globe.

ENGLAND

Haley's, Shire Oak Rd, Headingley, LS6 2DE, Northwest : 2 m. by A 660 ✆ (0113) 278 4446 *info@haleys.co.uk, Fax (0113) 275 3342,* – , rest, – 25. VISA. DV s
closed dinner 25-30 December – **Rest** *(closed Sunday dinner to non-residents)* (bar lunch Monday-Saturday)/dinner 35.00 – **27 rm** 120.00/145.00 – 165.00/175.00, 1 suite.
• Named after a prominent stonemason, this part 19C country house in a quiet area is handy for cricket fans. Antique furnished public areas. Individually styled bedrooms. Elegant, relaxed dining room with collection of original local artwork.

Bewley's, City Walk, Sweet St, LS11 9AT, ✆ (0113) 234 2340, *leeds@bewleyshotels.com, Fax (0113) 234 2349* – , rest, . VISA. GZ d
closed 4 days Christmas – ***The Brasserie :*** **Rest** (dinner only) a la carte 16.95/26.20 – 6.95 – **334 rm** 69.00 – 69.00.
• This competitively priced hotel boasts a very spacious, stylishly furnished lounge, and is ideal for both tourists or business travellers. Well-kept rooms. Bright, informal brasserie with classically based menus.

Jurys Inn, Kendell St, Brewery Pl, Brewery Wharf, LS10 1NE, ✆ (0113) 283 8800, *jurysinn leeds@jurysdoyal.com, Fax (0113) 283 8880* – , rm, – 100. VISA GZ e
closed 24-26 December – ***Innfusion :*** **Rest** (bar lunch)/dinner a la carte approx 18.65 – 9.50 – **248 rm** 85.00 – 85.00.
• Adjacent to brewery, this good value 21C hotel is located near the Millennium Bridge. Airy, modern public areas. Well-equipped, stylish bedrooms. Informal, bright eatery.

Novotel, 4 Whitehall, Whitehall Quay, LS1 4HR, ✆ (0113) 242 6446, *h3270@accor.com, Fax (0113) 242 6445,* , – , rm, – 90. VISA FZ x
Elements : **Rest** a la carte 24.00/30.00 **s.** – 12.50 – **194 rm** 109.00 – 109.00, 1 suite.
• Just a minute's walk from the main railway station. Ideally suited to the business traveller, with desk modems and meeting rooms. Compact exercise facility. Functional rooms. Informal brasserie adjacent to lobby.

XXX **No.3 York Place,** 3 York Pl, LS1 2DR, ✆ (0113) 245 9922, *dine@no3yorkplace.co.uk, Fax (0113) 245 9965* – . VISA FZ e
closed 25-30 December, Saturday lunch, Sunday and Bank Holidays – **Rest** 18.50 (lunch) and a la carte 27.85/37.85.
• Striking, stylish, minimalist and discreet environment keeps the spotlight on the accomplished cuisine. Classic flavours reinterpreted in an imaginative repertoire of dishes.

XXX **Pool Court at 42** (at 42 The Calls H.), 44 The Calls, LS2 7EW, ✆ (0113) 244 4242, *info@poolcourt.com, Fax (0113) 234 3332,* – . VISA GZ z
closed Saturday lunch, Sunday and Bank Holidays – **Rest** 47.50 (dinner) and lunch a la carte 35.00/43.00.
Spec. Risotto of oxtail and winter vegetables, truffle and thyme. New season lamb roasted with garlic, ratatouille with anchovy. Lemon thyme brûlée, chocolate and lavender millefeuille, elderflower ice cream.
• Book early for the small terrace overlooking the Aire. Sophisticated, modern menus with seasonal dishes and attentive service make for formal yet intimate armchair dining.

XXX **Anthony's,** 19 Boar Lane, LS1 6EA, ✆ (0113) 245 5922, *reservations@anthonysrestaurant.co.uk* – . VISA GZ a
closed first week September, 1 January, 25-26 December, Sunday, Monday and Tuesdays after Bank Holidays. – **Rest** (booking essential) 22.95 (lunch) and a la carte 36.65/49.45.
• Converted 19C property; ground floor lounge with red leather Chesterfields; minimalist basement dining room offers innovative menus with some intriguing combinations.

XX **Leodis,** Victoria Mill, Sovereign St, LS1 4BA, ✆ (0113) 242 1010, *Fax (0113) 243 0432,* – VISA GZ b
closed 25-26 December, 1 January, Sunday and lunch on Saturday and Bank Holidays – **Rest** 16.95 and a la carte 27.40/30.40.
• Appealing converted riverside storehouse offers hearty roasts, carving trolley and other generous British-style favourites in a bustling atmosphere. Friendly service.

XX **Simply Heathcotes,** Canal Wharf, Water Lane, LS11 5PS, ✆ (0113) 244 6611, *leeds@heathcotes.co.uk, Fax (0113) 244 0736,* – . VISA FZ c
closed 25-26 December and Bank Holidays except Good Friday – **Rest** a la carte 24.40/29.25.
• Converted grain warehouse by the canal. Distinctive modern feel with rich black banquettes. Effective contemporary cooking with prominent "northern" slant.

XX **Aagrah Leeds City,** St Peter's Sq, Quarry Hill, LS9 8AH, ✆ (0113) 245 5667 – 40. VISA GZ k
closed 25 December, Saturday and Sunday lunch – **Rest** - Indian (Kashmiri) - (booking essential) a la carte 13.55/19.90.
• On ground floor of BBC building in city centre, this stylish, open-plan restaurant gets very busy, but service invariably runs smoothly. Extensive, authentic Kashmiri menus.

XX **Plush**, 10 York Pl, LS1 2DS, ☎ (0113) 234 3344, *plushrestaurant@hotmail.com, Fax (0113) 242 7051* – ▤ ⇔ 16. MO AE VISA FZ n
closed 25-26 December, 1 January, Sunday, Saturday lunch and Bank Holidays – **Rest** 14.95 (lunch) and a la carte 20.40/30.35 ♀.
◆ Based in the heart of Leeds: a modern, vibrant gathering place. Contemporary basement restaurant with fish tank containing lion fish. Eclectic menus invite close attention.

XX **Fourth Floor** (at Harvey Nichols), 107-111 Briggate, LS1 6AZ, ☎ (0113) 204 8000, *Fax (0113) 204 8080*, – ⇕ ▤. MO AE ⓓ VISA GZ s
closed 25-26 December, 1 January, Easter Sunday and dinner Sunday-Wednesday – **Rest** (lunch bookings not accepted on Saturday) 18.00 (lunch) and a la carte 27.00/29.00 ♀.
◆ Watch the chefs prepare the modern food with world-wide influences in these bright, stylish, buzzy, contemporary surroundings. Advisable to get here early at lunch.

XX **Maxi's**, 6 Bingley St, LS3 1LX, off Kirkstall Rd ☎ (0113) 244 0552, *info@maxi-s.co.uk, Fax (0113) 234 3902* – ▤ P. MO AE ⓓ VISA FY a
closed 25-26 December – **Rest** - Chinese (Canton, Peking) - 17.80/24.00 and a la carte 15.40/29.40 s..
◆ Savour the taste of the Orient in this ornately decorated and busy pagoda style restaurant. Specialises in the rich flavours of Canton and hot and spicy Peking dishes.

XX **Quantro**, 62 Street Lane, LS8 2DQ, ☎ (0113) 288 8063, *info@quantro.co.uk, Fax (0113) 288 8008*, – ⅍ ▤. MO AE VISA CT a
closed 25-26 December, 1 January and Sunday – **Rest** 12.95 (lunch) and a la carte 22.40/29.00 ♀.
◆ Modern restaurant in suburban parade. Stylish décor: the smart atmosphere is augmented by friendly service. Excellent value lunches; modern dishes with international twists.

XX **Brasserie Forty Four** (at 42 The Calls H.), 44 The Calls, LS2 7EW, ☎ (0113) 234 3232, *info@brasserie44.com, Fax (0113) 234 3332* – ▤. MO VISA GZ z
closed Sunday, Saturday lunch and Bank Holidays – **Rest** a la carte 22.95/32.50.
◆ Former riverside warehouse with stylish bar; exudes atmosphere of buzzy informality. Smokehouse and char-grilled options in an eclectic range of menu dishes.

X **The Calls Grill**, Calls Landing, 38 The Calls, LS2 7EW, ☎ (0113) 245 3870, *info@callsgrill.co.uk, Fax (0113) 243 9035* – ⅍ ▤. MO AE ⓓ VISA GZ c
closed 1 week Christmas-New Year, Sunday and lunch Saturday and Monday – **Rest** 18.50 and a la carte 20.95/34.95 ♀.
◆ Restored Aireside textile mill with rustic ambience: exposed brickwork and timbers. Well-priced modern British cooking; bustling informality. Steaks a speciality.

X **The Mill Race**, 2-4 Commercial Rd, Kirkstall, LS5 3AQ, ☎ (0113) 275 7555, *enquiries@themillrace-organic.com, Fax (0113) 275 0222* – ⅍. MO VISA BT r
closed 25-26 December – **Rest** - Organic - (dinner only) a la carte 15.00/25.85 ♀.
◆ Former neighbourhood smithy offering an intimate, comfortable dining experience, personally run by friendly owners. All meals are totally organic.

at Garforth *East : 7 m. by A 63* – **CT** – ✉ *Leeds.*

XX **Aagrah**, Aberford Rd, LS25 1BA, on A 642 (Garforth rd) ☎ (0113) 287 6606 – ▤ P. MO AE VISA
closed 25 December – **Rest** - Indian (Kashmiri) - (booking essential) (dinner only) 14.00/15.00 and a la carte 14.95/21.05 **s.**
◆ Part of a family owned and personally run expanding group. Classic regional Indian cooking, specialising in the fragrant and subtly spiced dishes of the Kashmir region.

at Pudsey *West : 5¾ m. by A 647* – ✉ *Leeds.*

XX **Aagrah**, 483 Bradford Rd, LS28 8ED, on A 647 ☎ (01274) 668818 – ▤ P. MO AE VISA BT e
closed 25 December – **Rest** - Indian (Kashmiri) - (booking essential) (dinner only) 14.00/15.00 and a la carte 14.95/21.05 **s.**
◆ Advance booking most definitely required here; a bustling Indian restaurant with modish styling. Offers an extensive range of carefully prepared authentic dishes.

at Bramhope *Northwest : 8 m. on A 660* – **BT** – ✉ *Leeds.*

⌂ **The Cottages** without rest., Moor Rd, LS16 9HH, South : ¼ m. on Cookridge rd ☎ (0113) 284 2754, *Fax (0113) 203 7496*, – ⅍ P. ⅍
closed Christmas – **5 rm** ☕ ✝40.00 – ✝✝55.00.
◆ A warm welcome awaits at this converted row of 18C stone cottages. Comfortable lounge with open fire. Cosy, homely rooms are individually decorated. Good value accommodation.

at Yeadon *Northwest : 8 m. by A 65 on A 658* – **BT** – ✉ *Leeds.*

Premier Travel Inn, Victoria Ave, LS19 7AW, on A 658 ☎ (0113) 250 4284, *Fax (0113) 250 5838* – ⇔ rm, ▤ rest, ♿ P. MO AE ⓓ VISA. ⛌
Rest (grill rest.) – **40 rm** ★52.95 – ★★52.95.
◆ Convenient for the airport. Well proportioned modern bedrooms suitable for business and family stopovers. Relaxed pub adjacent offering popular dishes.

LEICESTER *Leicester* 502 503 504 Q 26 *Great Britain G. – pop. 330 574.*
See : *Guildhall*★ **BY B** – *Museum and Art Gallery*★ **CY M3** – *St Mary de Castro Church*★ **BY D.**
Env. : *National Space Centre*★, *N : 2 m. by A 6* – **AX** –, *turning east into Corporation Rd and right into Exploration Drive.*
Leicestershire, Evington Lane ☎ (0116) 273 8825 **AY** – *Western Park, Scudamore Rd ☎ (0116) 287 6158* – *Humberstone Heights, Gipsy Lane ☎ (0116) 299 5570* **AX** – *Oadby, Leicester Road Racecourse ☎ (0116) 270 0215* **AY** – *Lutterworth Rd, Blaby ☎ (0116) 278 4804.*
East Midlands Airport, Castle Donington : ☎ (0871) 9199000 NW : 22 m. by A 50 – **AX** – *and M 1.*
7-9 Every St, Town Hall Sq ☎ (0116) 299 8888, info@goleicestershire.com.
London 107 – Birmingham 43 – Coventry 24 – Nottingham 26.

Plans on following pages

Holiday Inn Leicester City, 129 St Nicholas Circle, LE1 5LX, ☎ (0870) 4009048, *leicestercity.reservations@ichotelsgroup.com, Fax (0116) 251 3169,* 🏋, ≋, ▣ – |♦|, ⇔ rm, ▤ P. – 🏛 250. MO AE ⓓ VISA **BY c**
***Vermont* :** **Rest** a la carte 21.00/28.70 ♀ – ☕ 13.95 – **187 rm** ★109.00 – ★★149.00, 1 suite.
◆ Centrally located, imposing modern hotel convenient for the ring road. Comfortable brand style bedrooms with fitted furniture and particularly good Executive rooms. Stylish, modern restaurant and bar with American style menus.

Belmont House, De Montfort St, LE1 7GR, ☎ (0116) 254 4773, *info@belmonthotel.co.uk, Fax (0116) 247 0804* – |♦|, ⇔ rm, P. – 🏛 160. MO AE ⓓ VISA **CY c**
closed 24-30 December – ***Cherry's* :** **Rest** *(closed Saturday lunch, Sunday dinner and weekends in August* 15.95/22.95 – ☕ 10.95 – **77 rm** ★70.00/115.00 – ★★100.00/140.00.
◆ Privately owned, centrally located and adjacent to a conservation area. Enlarged to provide a large bar and several function rooms. Spacious, comfortable bedrooms. Conservatory restaurant with formal air.

The Regency, 360 London Rd, LE2 2PL, Southeast : 2 m. on A 6 ☎ (0116) 270 9634, *info@the-regency-hotel.com, Fax (0116) 270 1375* – ⇔ rest, P. MO AE VISA. ⛌ **AY z**
(accommodation closed 25 December) **Rest** *(closed Saturday lunch and Bank Holidays)* a la carte 15.95/21.70 ♀ – **32 rm** ☕ ★48.00/55.00 – ★★70.00.
◆ Attractive Victorian town house, formerly a convent. Character and historical notes in décor, especially in the individual bedrooms. Range of themed dinner-dance events. Restaurant or brasserie dining options.

Premier Travel Inn, Leicester Rd, Glenfield, LE3 8HB, Northwest : 3 ½ m. on A 50 ☎ (0870) 7001416, *Fax (0870) 7001417,* 🐕 – ⇔ rm, ♿ P. MO AE ⓓ VISA. ⛌ **AX a**
Rest (grill rest.) – **43 rm** ★49.95/49.95 – ★★52.95/52.95.
◆ Maintains the group's reputation for affordable accommodation and simple contemporary styling. Sofa beds and convenient work surfaces are useful features. Pub-style restaurant with an informal and friendly atmosphere.

Watsons, 5-9 Upper Brown St, LE1 5TE, ☎ (0116) 222 7770, *watsons.restaurant@virgin.net, Fax (0116) 222 7771* – ▤. MO AE VISA **BY x**
closed 10 days at Christmas-New Year, Sunday and Bank Holidays – **Rest** 12.95 (lunch) and a la carte 22.00/28.00 ♀.
◆ Converted Victorian cotton mill in the centre of town. Vivid modern interior replete with chrome, glass and a cosmopolitan ambience. Wide ranging, competent, modern menu.

Entropy, 3 Dover St, LE1 6PW, ☎ (0116) 254 8530, *mail@entropylife.com* – ⇔ ▤. MO AE ⓓ VISA **CY a**
closed 25 December-5 January, Sunday and Bank Holidays – **Rest** 15.95 (lunch) and a la carte 26.95/42.85 ♀.
◆ Smart, cream-painted restaurant with full-length front windows. Sip champagne or cocktails in bar before enjoying confident cooking with bold flavours on a fine dining menu.

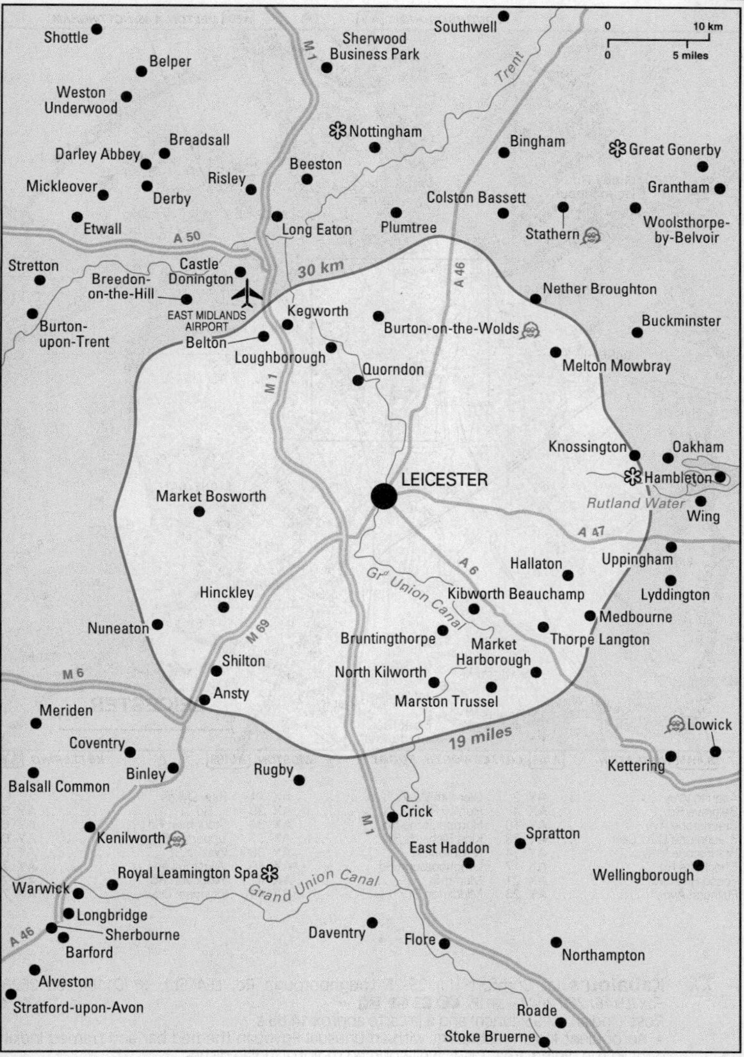

Undecided between two equivalent establishments? Within each category, establishments are classified in our order of preference.

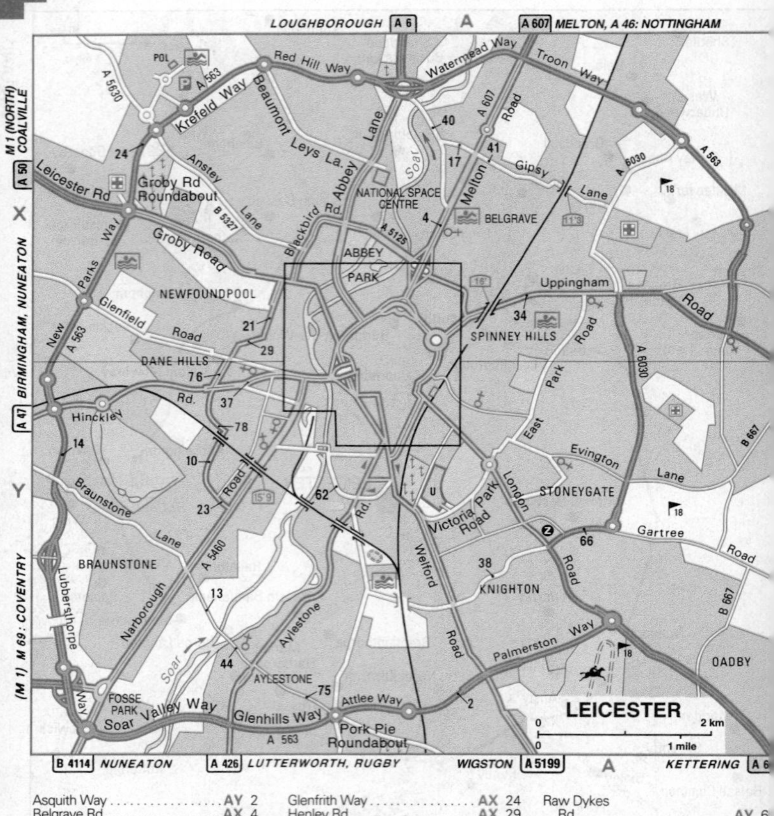

Asquith Way ..... AY 2	Glenfrith Way ..... AX 24	Raw Dykes Rd ..... AY 6
Belgrave Rd ..... AX 4	Henley Rd ..... AX 29	Stoughton Rd ..... AY 6
Braunstone Ave ..... AY 10	Humberstone Rd ..... AX 34	Upperton Rd ..... AY 6
Braunstone Lane East ..... AY 13	King Richards Rd ..... AY 37	Walnut St ..... AY 6
Braunstone Way ..... AY 14	Knighton Rd ..... AY 38	Wigston Lane ..... AY 7
Checketts Rd ..... AX 17	Loughborough Rd ..... AX 40	Woodville Rd ..... AY 7
Fosse Rd North ..... AX 21	Marfitt St ..... AX 41	Wyngate Drive ..... AY 7
Fullhurst Ave ..... AY 23	Middleton St ..... AY 44	

XX **Kabalou's** (at Comfort H.), 23-25 Loughborough Rd, LE4 5LJ, ✆ (0116) 268 2626, *Fax (0116) 268 2641* – ▤ P. MC AE ⓓ VISA AX c
Rest - Indian - 7.95 (lunch) and a la carte approx 14.85 s.
◆ An opulent Indian restaurant with an unusual Egyptian themed bar and framed Indian gods in the dining area. Tasty, well-sourced regional Indian dishes.

XX **The Opera House,** 10 Guildhall Lane, LE1 5FQ, ✆ (0116) 223 6666, *theopera house@hotmail.com, Fax (0116) 223 4704* – ⇋. MC AE VISA BY a
closed 24 December-4 January, Sunday and Bank Holidays – **Rest** 13.50 (lunch) and dinner a la carte 24.50/39.00 ♀.
◆ 17C building in city centre, so called because of proximity to former Opera House. Menu is a roll call of the classics; includes Opera "Variations" (a dessert selection).

XX **The Tiffin,** 1 De Montfort St, LE1 7GE, ✆ (0116) 247 0420, *thetiffin@msn.com, Fax (0116) 255 3737* – ⇋ ▤. MC AE ⓓ VISA CY r
closed 24-26 December, Saturday and Sunday – **Rest** - Indian - (booking essential) 12.00/25.00 and a la carte 15.15/28.15.
◆ Busy, spacious and comfortable with a gentle Eastern theme to the décor. Tasty, authentic flavour in carefully prepared Indian dishes.

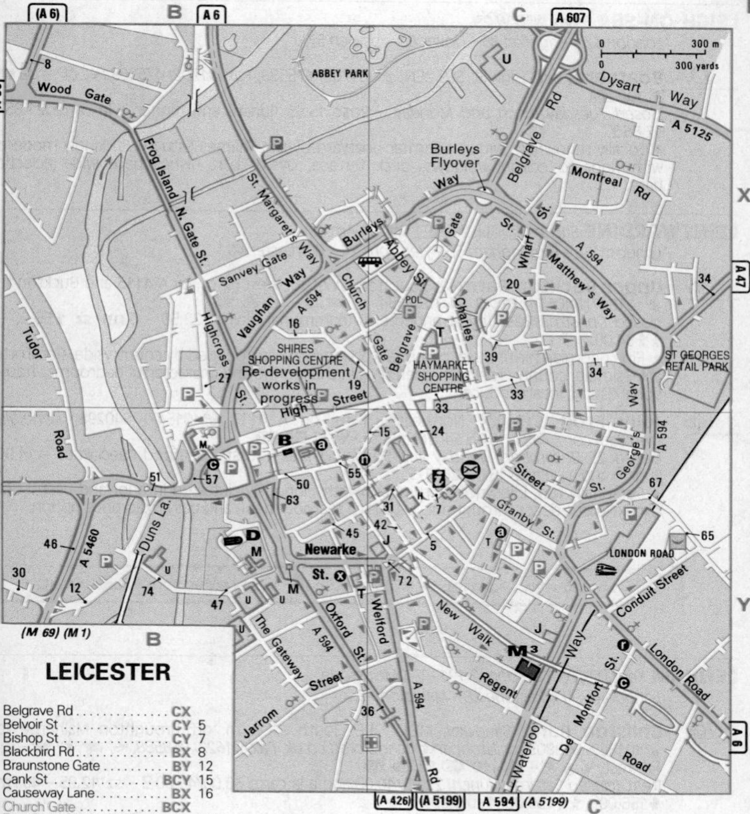

LEICESTER

The Case, 4-6 Hotel St, St Martin's, LE1 5AW, ✆ (0116) 251 7675, *Fax (0116) 251 7675* – MC AE Ⓓ VISA **BY n**

closed 24-30 December, Sunday and Bank Holidays – **Rest** a la carte 21.25/29.55 ♀.

◆ Stylish modern restaurant in a converted Victorian luggage factory. Open main dining area and a small bar. Large, modern, seasonal menu. Champagne bar adjacent.

at Blaby *South : 4¼ m. on A 426 – AY – ✉ Leicester.*

Corus H. Leicester, Enderby Rd, LE8 4GD, ✆ (0870) 609 6106, *reservations.leicester@corushotels.com, Fax (01162) 781974,* – rm, rest, – 70. MC AE Ⓓ VISA

Rest *(closed Saturday lunch)* 19.95 and dinner a la carte 22.00/28.50 **s.** ♀ – ☕ 11.50 – **48 rm** 45.00/95.00 – 45.00/95.00.

◆ Distinctly modern atmosphere in this hotel based around a Victorian house. Smart, elegant rooms in contemporary style with co-ordinated soft furnishings. Smart bar/brasserie with stylish ambience.

LEIGH-ON-SEA *Essex* 504 W 29.
London 37 – Brighton 85 – Dover 86 – Ipswich 57.

Boatyard, 8-13 High St, SS9 2EN, ✆ (01702) 475588, *Fax (01702) 475588*, ≤, – P. VISA
closed Tuesday lunch and Monday – **Rest** 15.95 (lunch) and dinner a la carte 21.85/37.85 ♀.
◆ Locally renowned, within a former boatyard by the Thames Estuary. Strikingly modern with floor to ceiling windows, deck terrace, oyster bar. Dishes have wide eclectic base.

LEINTWARDINE *Shrops.* 503 L 26 – ✉ *Craven Arms.*
London 156 – Birmingham 55 – Hereford 24 – Worcester 40.

Upper Buckton Farm ≫, Buckton, SY7 0JU, West : 2 m. by A 4113 and Buckton rd ✆ (01547) 540634, *Fax (01547) 540634*, ≤, – P.
*closed Christmas***Rest** (by arrangement) (communal dining) 22.50 – **3 rm** ☕ ★50.00 – ★★84.00.
◆ Fine Georgian farmhouse, part of a working farm, surrounded by countryside. Comfortable, simple, country feel with open fires in the lounge and characterful bedrooms. Traditional dining; local produce.

Jolly Frog, SY7 0LX, Northeast : 1 m. on A 4113 ✆ (01547) 540298, *jaynejollyfrog@aol.com, Fax (01547) 540105*, – P. VISA
closed 25 December, Monday and Sunday dinner – **Rest** - Seafood specialities - 14.00 (lunch) and a la carte 16.00/26.30 ♀.
◆ Personally run, idiosyncratic rural pub with gloriously cluttered interior and useful deli annex! Rustic decor throughout. Extensive seafood menu and daily fixed price option.

Look out for red symbols, indicating particularly pleasant establishments.

LENHAM *Kent* 504 W 30 – *pop. 2 191* – ✉ *Maidstone.*
London 45 – Folkestone 28 – Maidstone 9.

Chilston Park, Sandway, ME17 2BE, South : 1 ¾ m. off Broughton Malherbe rd ✆ (01622) 859803, *chilstonpark@handpicked.co.uk, Fax (01622) 858588*, ≤, – rest, P – 110. VISA
Rest *(closed Saturday lunch)* 22.95/40.00 and a la carte 30.00/40.00 ♀ – ☕ 12.95 – **49 rm** ★155.00 – ★★155.00, 4 suites.
◆ Part 17C mansion, set in parkland and furnished with antiques. Bedrooms are very individual and comfortable. Old stable conference facilities retain original stalls! Smart dining room and well-appointed sitting room.

LEOMINSTER *Herefordshire* 503 L 27 *Great Britain G.* – *pop. 10 440.*
Env. : *Berrington Hall★ AC, N : 3 m. by A 49.*
Ford Bridge ✆ (01568) 612863.
1 Corn Sq ✆ (01568) 616460.
London 141 – Birmingham 47 – Hereford 13 – Worcester 26.

at Kimbolton *Northeast : 3 m. by A 49 on A 4112.*

Lower Bache House ≫, HR6 0ER, East : 1 ¾ m. by A 4112 ✆ (01568) 750304, *leslie.wiles@care4free.net*, – P.
Rest (by arrangement) 23.50 – **4 rm** ☕ ★44.50 – ★★69.00.
◆ A fine 17C farmhouse in a very quiet rural setting. Spacious, characterful, open feel throughout: bedrooms located in a charming converted granary. Converted cider barn dining room features original mill and press.

at Leysters *Northeast : 5 m. by A 49 on A 4112* – ✉ *Leominster.*

The Hills Farm ≫ without rest., HR6 0HP, ✆ (01568) 750205, *conolly@bigwig.net*, ≤, – P. VISA
closed November-February and 3 weeks June – **5 rm** ☕ ★35.00/45.00 – ★★70.00.
◆ An attractive ivy-clad farmhouse on a working farm. The interior is delightfully comfortable, from the cosy lounge to the country-cottage rooms, three in the converted barns. Extensive country views from conservatory dining room.

at Pudleston *East : 5 m. by A 49 off A 44 – ✉ Leominster.*

Ford Abbey ⛶, HR6 0RZ, South : 1 m. on Pudleston rd ✆ (01568) 760700, *info@fordabbey.co.uk, Fax (01568) 760264,* ≤, ⛶, ⛶, ⛶, ⛶ – ⛶ ⛶ ⛶. ⛶ AE VISA ⛶
Rest (booking essential to non-residents) (dinner only) (set menu only) 35.00/42.50 **s.** – **5 rm** ⛶ ★85.00/150.00 – ★★125.00/225.00, 1 suite.
◆ Sumptuous, splendid isolation: a wonderful collection of medieval and 19C farmhouses and barns. Very characterful throughout. Luxurious rooms with low beams and hideaways.. Dining room exudes appeal: 15C window frame still intact.

LETCHWORTH *Herts.* 504 T 28.
London 39.5 – Luton 18 – Stevenage 7.5.

at Willian *South : 1¾ m. by A 6141 – ✉ Letchworth.*

The Fox, SG6 2AE, ✆ (01462) 480233, *restaurant@foxatwillian.co.uk, Fax (01462) 676966,* ⛶ – ⛶. ⛶ VISA
Rest *(closed 26 December, 1 January, Monday and Sunday dinner)* a la carte 20.85/35.85.
◆ Refurbished pub in a pretty little village. Attractive pitched ceiling windows make restaurant feel like a conservatory. Interesting menus with emphasis on fish and shellfish.

LEVINGTON *Suffolk Great Britain G.*
Exc. : *Ipswich : Christchurch Mansion (collection of paintings★), NW : 9 m. on A 1189, A 12, A 137 and A 1022.*
London 75 – Ipswich 5 – Woodbridge 8.

Ship Inn, Church Lane, IP10 0LQ, ✆ (01473) 659573, ⛶ – ⛶. ⛶ VISA. ⛶
closed 25-26 December, 1 January and Sunday dinner – **Rest** a la carte 15.00/24.00.
◆ Characterful, part 14C thatched and beamed pub with plenty of maritime curios and rustic charm. Fish a key element of dishes which range from traditional to rather innovative.

LEVISHAM *N. Yorks.* 502 R 21 – *see Pickering.*

LEWDOWN *Devon* 503 H 32 *The West Country G.*
Env. : *Lydford★★, E : 4 m.*
Exc. : *Launceston★ - Castle★ (≤★) St Mary Magdalene★, W : 8 m. by A 30 and A 388.*
London 238 – Exeter 37 – Plymouth 29.

Lewtrenchard Manor ⛶, EX20 4PN, South : ¾ m. by Lewtrenchard rd ✆ (01566) 783222, *info@lewtrenchard.co.uk, Fax (01566) 783332,* ≤, ⛶, ⛶ – ⛶ rest, ⛶ – ⛶ 50. ⛶ AE ⛶ VISA
Rest *(closed Monday lunch)* (booking essential to non-residents) 20.00/39.50 – **10 rm** ⛶ ★95.00/120.00 – ★★150.00/250.00, 4 suite.
◆ A grand historical atmosphere pervades this delightfully secluded 17C manor house. Plenty of personality with antiques, artworks, ornate ceilings and panelling throughout. Two elegant dining rooms with stained glass windows.

LEWES *E. Sussex* 504 U 31 *Great Britain G. – pop. 15 988.*
See : *Town★ (High St★, Keere St★) – Castle (≤★) AC.*
Exc. : *Sheffield Park Garden★ AC, N : 9½ m. by A 275.*
⛳18 *Chapel Hill ✆ (01273) 473245.*
ℹ *187 High St ✆ (01273) 483448.*
London 53 – Brighton 8 – Hastings 29 – Maidstone 43.

Shelleys, High St, BN7 1XS, ✆ (01273) 472361, *info@shelleys-hotel-lewes.com, Fax (01273) 483152,* ⛶, ⛶ – ⛶ ⛶ ⛶ – ⛶ 50. ⛶ AE ⛶ VISA
Rest 15.00/30.00 and a la carte 28.50/34.50 ♀ – ⛶ 13.50 – **18 rm** ★85.00/145.00 – ★★150.00/185.00, 1 suite.
◆ The great poet's family once owned this Georgian former inn. It has spacious bedrooms which are furnished and decorated in keeping with its historical connections.. Smart restaurant exudes Georgian panache.

ENGLAND

Millers without rest., 134 High St, BN7 1XS, ✆ (01273) 475631, *millers134@aol.com, Fax (01273) 486226,* – .
closed 4-6 November and 21 December - 5 January – **3 rm** ☕ ★68.00 – ★★75.00.
◆ Characterful, small family home in a row of 16C houses that lead to the high street. Appealing personal feel in the individual bedrooms with books, trinkets and knick-knacks.

Circa, 145 High St, BN7 1XT, ✆ (01273) 471777, *eat@circacirca.com* – . MO AE VISA
Rest - Asian influences - a la carte 27.00/34.45 ♀.
◆ Near the castle gate; partly frosted glass frontage. Modern ambience pertains, large circular banquettes a feature. Highly original cooking with an elaborate, eclectic scope.

The Long Room, 18 Cliffe High St, BN7 2AJ, ✆ (01273) 472444, *mail@thelongroom.com, Fax (01273) 488539,* – . MO AE VISA
closed 25 December and Sunday dinner – **Rest** a la carte 17.75/27.45 ♀.
◆ Grade II listed building with original wood flooring in situ. All-day service, including breakfast and plates to share. Home-made dishes; ingredients from local suppliers.

at East Chiltington *Northwest : 5½ m. by A 275 and B 2116 off Novington Lane* – ✉ *Lewes.*

Jolly Sportsman, Chapel Lane, BN7 3BA, ✆ (01273) 890400, *jollysportsman@mistral.co.uk, Fax (01273) 890400,* – P. MO VISA
closed 24-27 December, Sunday dinner and Monday except Bank Holidays – **Rest** 15.75 (lunch) and a la carte 19.50/29.00 ♀.
◆ Brick and clapboard country pub with an open and uncluttered interior and interesting contemporary dishes on a regularly changing menu.

LEYBURN *N. Yorks.* 502 O 21 – *pop. 1 844.*
4 Central Chambers, Market Pl ✆ (01969) 623069.
London 251 – Darlington 25 – Kendal 43 – Leeds 53 – Newcastle upon Tyne 62 – York 49.

The Haven without rest., Market Pl, DL8 5BJ, ✆ (01969) 623814, *warmwelcome@havenguesthouse.co.uk* – P. MO VISA.
closed 1 week February, 24-26 December – **6 rm** ☕ ★38.00/40.00 – ★★60.00.
◆ Neat and tidy house in village centre. Pleasant rural views from breakfast room, which also displays artwork from local gallery. Colourful rooms include DVD and CD players.

Clyde House without rest., Railway St, DL8 5AY, ✆ (01969) 623941, *info@clydehouseleyburn.co.uk, Fax (01969) 623941* – MO VISA
5 rm ☕ ★32.00/37.00 – ★★50.00/60.00.
◆ Former coaching inn dating from mid-18C: one of the oldest buildings in town. Two of the bedrooms are in the converted hayloft. Hearty Yorkshire breakfasts to start the day.

Sandpiper Inn with rm, Market Place, DL8 5AT, ✆ (01969) 622206, *hsandpiper.99@aol.com, Fax (01969) 625367,* – P. MO VISA
Rest *(closed Monday)* a la carte 21.25/29.00 ♀ – **3 rm** ☕ ★60.00/80.00 – ★★70.00/90.00.
◆ Converted 16C stone house off market square. Rustic and simple with daily changing blackboard menu of tasty Yorkshire fare; good local ales. Pleasant pine furnished rooms.

at Constable Burton *East : 3½ m. on A 684* – ✉ *Leyburn.*

Park Gate House, Constable Burton, DL8 5RG, ✆ (01677) 450466, *parkgatehouse@freenet.co.uk, Fax (01677) 450466,* – P. MO AE VISA.
Rest (by arrangement) 15.50 – **4 rm** ☕ ★45.00 – ★★75.00.
◆ Stone-built 18C cottage at the entrance to Constable Burton House. Snug and intimate cottage atmosphere throughout with open fires and antique pine furnished rooms. Cosy cottage style dining room.

Wyvill Arms with rm, DL8 5LH, ✆ (01677) 450581, , – rest, P. MO AE VISA
*closed Monday except lunch on Bank Holidays*Rest a la carte 20.00/29.00 ♀ – **3 rm** ☕ ★40.00 – ★★66.00.
◆ A classic Yorkshire pub with stone bar area and good choice of ales. Seasonally changing menu with steaks a speciality: eat in bar or formal dining room. Neat, tidy bedrooms.

LEYSTERS *Herefordshire* 503 504 M 27 – *see Leominster.*

Good food without spending a fortune? Look out for the Bib Gourmand

LICHFIELD *Staffs.* 502 503 504 O 25 *Great Britain G. – pop. 28 435.*
See : *City★ - Cathedral★★ AC.*
18, 9 *Seedy Mill, Elmhurst* ☎ *(01543) 417333.*
Donegal House, Bore St ☎ *(01543) 308209.*
London 128 – Birmingham 16 – Derby 23 – Stoke-on-Trent 30.

Swinfen Hall, WS14 9RE, Southeast : 2 ¼ m. by A 5206 on A 38 ☎ (01543) 481494, *info@swinfenhallhotel.co.uk, Fax (01543) 480341,* – rest, P – 160. MC AE VISA.
Four Seasons *:* Rest *(closed Saturday lunch and Sunday dinner to non-residents)* 22.50/37.50 s. – 5.00 – **16 rm** 115.00/120.00 – 140.00/150.00, 1 suite.
◆ Very fine 18C house in 100 acres with beautiful façade, impressive stucco ceilings and elegant lounges furnished with taste and style. Bedrooms offer high levels of comfort. Modern menus served in superb oak-panelled restaurant with Grinling Gibbons carvings.

Express By Holiday Inn, Wall Island, Birmingham Rd, Shenstone, WS14 0QP, South : 2 ¼ m. on A 5127 ☎ (0870) 7201078, *lichfield@morethanhotels.com, Fax (0870) 7201079* – P – 30. MC AE VISA.
Rest (light dinners Monday-Thursday only) a la carte approx 12.00 – **102 rm** 60.00 – 72.50.
◆ A standard lodge with simply furnished rooms. Well placed for Lichfield Cathedral and Alton Towers. Strategically placed close to A5 and M6.

Thrales, 40-44 Tamworth St, WS13 6JJ, (corner of Backcester Lane) ☎ (01543) 255091, *Fax (01543) 415352* – . MC AE VISA
closed Sunday dinner, Monday and Saturday lunch – **Rest** a la carte 22.00/32.00.
◆ Busy, popular restaurant with a rustic style; building has 16C origins. Wide-ranging menu of simple homely dishes using mainly local produce.

Chandlers Grande Brasserie, Corn Exchange, Conduit St, WS13 6JU, ☎ (01543) 416688, *Fax (01543) 417887* – . MC AE VISA
closed 26 December, 1 week January, Easter Monday and spring Bank Holiday – **Rest** 11.95/16.95 and a la carte 21.70/29.50.
◆ On two floors in old cornmarket building. Tiled floors, prints and pin lights; a pleasant, relaxed atmosphere in which to enjoy a brasserie menu with good value lunch options.

For a pleasant stay in a charming hotel, look for the red ... symbols.

LICKFOLD *W. Sussex* – *see Petworth.*

LIDGATE *Suffolk* 504 V 27 – *see Newmarket.*

LIFTON *Devon* 503 H 32 *The West Country G. – pop. 964.*
Env. : *Launceston★ – Castle★ (★) St Mary Magdalene★, W : 4½ m. by A 30 and A 388.*
London 238 – Bude 24 – Exeter 37 – Launceston 4 – Plymouth 26.

Arundell Arms, Fore St, PL16 0AA, ☎ (01566) 784666, *reservations@arundellarms.com, Fax (01566) 784494,* – rest, P – 100. MC AE VISA
closed 24-25 December – **Rest** – (see ***The Restaurant*** below) – **21 rm** 95.00/110.00 – 150.00/180.00.
◆ Coaching inn, in a valley of five rivers, dating back to Saxon times. True English sporting hotel - popular with shooting parties and fishermen. Good country lodge style.

The Restaurant (at Arundell Arms H.), Fore St, PL16 0AA, ☎ (01566) 784666, *arundel larms@btinternet.com, Fax (01566) 784494* – P. MC AE VISA
closed dinner 24-25 December – **Rest** 25.50/35.00.
◆ A grand dining room with high ceiling, large windows and an opulent feel. Local produce, including fish caught by guests, contribute to a menu of English and French cuisine.

Tinhay Mill with rm, Tinhay, PL16 0AJ, ☎ (01566) 784201, *tinhay.mill@talk21.com, Fax (01566) 784201* – P. MC VISA
closed 2 weeks November and 2 weeks May/June – **Rest** (dinner only) 28.00 and a la carte 21.95/33.00 – **3 rm** 48.00/50.00 – 72.50/75.00.
◆ Small converted mill near hamlet: furnishings a mix of rustic and traditional, creating a cosy atmosphere. Locally based, tasty cuisine. Cottagey bedrooms.

LINCOLN *Lincs.* **502** **504** S 24 *Great Britain G.* – *pop. 85 963.*

See : *City★★ – Cathedral and Precincts★★★* AC **Y** – *High Bridge★★* **Z 9** – *Usher Gallery★* AC **YZ M1** – *Jew's House★* **Y** – *Castle★* AC **Y**.

Env. : *Doddington Hall★* AC, W : 6 m. by B 1003 – **Z** – and B 1190.

Exc. : *Gainsborough Old Hall★* AC, NW : 19 m. by A 57 – **Z** – and A 156.

Carholme, Carholme Rd ☎ (01522) 523725.

Humberside Airport : ☎ (01652) 688456, N : 32 m. by A 15 – Y – M 180 and A 18.

9 Castle Hill ☎ (01522) 873213.

London 140 – Bradford 81 – Cambridge 94 – Kingston-upon-Hull 44 – Leeds 73 – Leicester 53 – Norwich 104 – Nottingham 38 – Sheffield 48 – York 82.

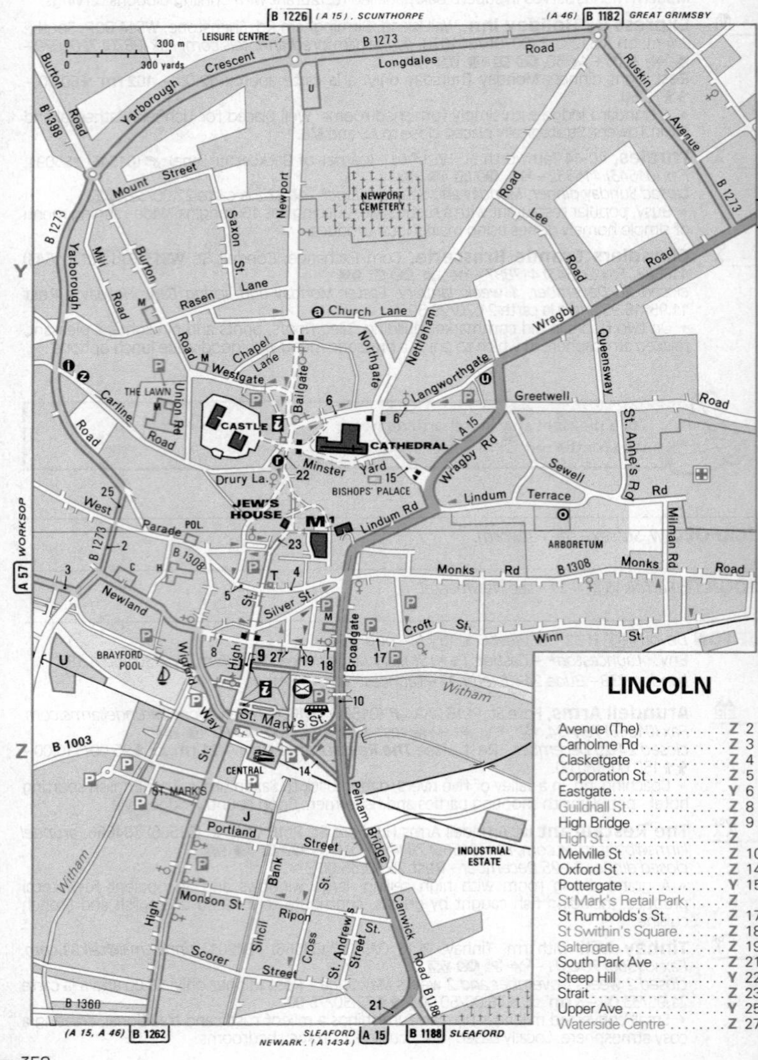

Bentley, Newark Rd, South Hykeham, LN6 9NH, Southwest : 5 ¾ m. by A 15 on B 1434 at junction with A 46 ☎ (01522) 878000, *infothebentleyhotel@btconnect.com, Fax (01522) 878001,* ⑦, Ls, ≘s, ▢ – ▯ ⇔, ▤ rest, ♿ P – 🏛 300. MC AE VISA. ✈
Rest (carvery lunch)/dinner 18.50/20.00 **s.** and a la carte – **80 rm** ☕ ✝83.00/93.00 – ✝✝98.00/130.00.
◆ New purpose-built hotel. Smart, modern feel with traditional touches throughout. Well kept bedrooms including Executive and more traditional styles. Well-run leisure club. Formal or relaxed dining alternatives.

Hillcrest, 15 Lindum Terrace, LN2 5RT, ☎ (01522) 510182, *reservations@hillcrest-hotel.com, Fax (01522) 538009,* <, ⇌ – ⇔ P. MC AE VISA Y o
closed 23 December-5 January – **Rest** *(closed Sunday)* (bar lunch Saturday)/dinner 22.00/28.00 and a la carte 22.00/24.90 – **14 rm** ☕ ✝56.00/79.00 – ✝✝87.00/97.00.
◆ Victorian former rectory in a tranquil part of town. Adjacent to an arboretum which can be seen from most of the traditionally appointed bedrooms - one with four-poster bed. Large conservatory dining room overlooks garden.

Premier Travel Inn, Lincoln Rd, Canwick Hill, LN4 2RF, Southeast : 1 ¾ m. by B 1188 on B 1131 ☎ (01522) 525216, *Fax (01522) 542521,* ⇌ – ⇔ rm, ♿ P. MC AE ⓓ VISA. ✈
Rest (grill rest.) – **40 rm** ✝50.95 – ✝✝50.95.
◆ Simply furnished and brightly decorated bedrooms with ample work space. Family rooms with sofa beds. Ideal for corporate or leisure travel.

Minster Lodge without rest., 3 Church Lane, LN2 1QJ, ☎ (01522) 513220, *info@minsterlodge.co.uk, Fax (01522) 513220* – ⇔ ☎ P. MC AE VISA. ✈ Y a
6 rm ☕ ✝60.00/75.00 – ✝✝85.00/90.00.
◆ Converted house, close to the cathedral and castle, just by 3C Newport Arch with good access to the ring road. Immaculately kept throughout and run with a professional touch.

St Clements Lodge without rest., 21 Langworthgate, LN2 4AD, ☎ (01522) 521532, *Fax (01522) 521532* – ⇔ P. ✈ Y u
– **3 rm** ☕ ✝40.00 – ✝✝56.00.
◆ A good value house in a convenient location, a short walk from the sights. Run by hospitable owners who keep three large, pleasantly decorated bedrooms.

Carline without rest., 1-3 Carline Rd, LN1 1HL, ☎ (01522) 530422, *sales@carlineguesthouse.co.uk, Fax (01522) 530422* – ⇔ P. ✈ Y i
closed Christmas and New Year – **9 rm** ☕ ✝40.00 – ✝✝55.00.
◆ Double fronted Edwardian house a short walk from the city centre. Homely, traditional décor and style. Large sitting room with plenty of tourism literature.

Tennyson without rest., 7 South Park, LN5 8EN, South : 1 ¼ m. on A 15 ☎ (01522) 521624, *tennyson.hotel@virgin.net, Fax (01522) 521355* – P. MC AE VISA. ✈
8 rm ☕ ✝35.00/40.00 – ✝✝50.00.
◆ Located at the southern end of the city, adjacent to large public park. Welcoming ambience and traditional feel. Delightful Art Deco tiled fireplace in sitting room.

Abbottsford House without rest., 5 Yarborough Terr, LN1 1HN, ☎ (01522) 826696, *abbottsfordhouse@ntl.world.co.uk, Fax (01522) 826696* – ⇔ P. ✈ Y z
closed Christmas-New Year – **3 rm** ☕ ✝35.00/40.00 – ✝✝50.00.
◆ Snug Victorian house in a residential area. Cottage-style bedrooms with a pleasant, homely feel. Agreeable rear courtyard with Koi pond and free range chickens.

Wig & Mitre, First Floor, 30-32 Steep Hill, LN2 1TL, ☎ (01522) 535190, *email@wigandmitre.com, Fax (01522) 532402* – ⇔. MC AE ⓓ VISA Y r
Rest 13.95 (lunch) and a la carte 22.00/34.00 ♀.
◆ First floor dining area, with characterful almost medieval decor, in a building which dates back to 14C. Skilfully prepared, confident, classic cooking.

INDALE *Cumbria* 502 L 21 – *see Grange-over-Sands.*

The red ✈ symbol? This denotes the very essence of peace – only the sound of birdsong first thing in the morning ...

LISKEARD *Cornwall* 503 G 32 *The West Country G.* – *pop. 8 478.*
See : *Church*★.
Exc. : *Lanhydrock*★★, *W : 11½ m. by A 38 and A 390* – *NW : Bodmin Moor*★★ - *St Endellio Church*★★ - *Altarnun Church*★ - *St Breward Church*★ - *Blisland*★ *(church*★*)* - *Camelford*★ *Cardinham Church*★ - *Michaelstow Church*★ - *St Kew*★ *(church*★*)* - *St Mabyn Church*★ – *S Neot*★ *(Parish Church*★★*)* - *St Sidwell's, Laneast*★ - *St Teath Church*★ - *St Tudy*★ – *Launces ton*★ – *Castle*★ *(≤*★*) St Mary Magdalene*★, *NE : 19 m. by A 390 and A 388.*
London 261 – Exeter 59 – Plymouth 19 – Truro 37.

The Well House, St Keyne, PL14 4RN, South : 3½ m. by B 3254 on St Keyne Well r (01579) 342001, *enquiries@wellhouse.co.uk, Fax (01579) 343891,* ≤, heated, , – rest, P. VISA
closed 1 week January – **Rest** (booking essential to non-residents) 23.50/32.50 – **9 rm** ★85.00 – ★★180.00.
◆ Large 19C country house surrounded by extensive grounds; personally run b friendly owner. Individual rooms have winning outlooks; those by the garden hav private patios. Stylish, modern country house restaurant looks out over the country side.

Pencubitt Country House, Station Rd, PL14 4EB, South : ½ m. by B 3254 o Lamellion rd (01579) 342694, *hotel@pencubitt.com, Fax (01579) 342694,* – P VISA.
closed 20 December-15 January – **Rest** (booking essential) (dinner only) 24.00 **s.** – **9 rm** ★50.00/75.00 – ★★105.00/115.00.
◆ Late Victorian mansion, with fine views of East Looe Valley. Spacious drawing room wit open fire, plus sitting room, bar and veranda. Comfy rooms, most with rural views. Attrac tive, candlelit dining room.

Red = Pleasant. Look for the red and symbols.

LITTLE BARROW *Ches.* – *see Chester.*

LITTLE BEDWYN *Newbury* 503 504 P 29 – *see Hungerford.*

LITTLE BOLLINGTON *Gtr Manchester* – *see Altrincham.*

LITTLEBOROUGH *Gtr Manchester* 502 504 N 23 – *see Rochdale.*

LITTLEBURY GREEN *Essex* – *see Saffron Walden.*

LITTLEHAMPTON *W. Sussex* 504 S 31 – *pop. 55 716.*
The Look and Sea Centre, 63-65 Surrey St (01903) 721866.
London 64 – Brighton 18 – Portsmouth 31.

Bailiffscourt & Spa, Climping St, Climping, BN17 5RW, West : 2¾ m. by A 25 (01903) 723511, *bailiffscourt@hshotels.co.uk, Fax (01903) 723107,* , , , , heated, , , , – rest, P – 35. VISA
Rest 16.00/43.50 ♀ – **39 rm** (dinner included) ★250.00/290.00 – ★★330.00/385.00.
◆ Alluring reconstructed medieval house basking in acres of utterly peaceful grounds. Ric antiques and fine period features in an enchanting medieval ambience. Superb spa. Spli room dining area nestling amidst warmly tapestried walls.

Amberley Court without rest., Crookthorn Lane, Climping, BN17 5SN, Wes 1¾ m. by B 2187 off A 259 (01903) 725131, *Fax (01903) 725131,* – P. VISA.
9 rm ★40.00/50.00 – ★★75.00.
◆ Converted farm barn with a tidy, homely atmosphere. Exposed beams, flourishin plants and a warm welcome. Simply decorated rooms, some in grounds, with tradition chintz.

ITTLE LANGDALE *Cumbria* 502 K 20 – *see Ambleside.*

ITTLE LANGFORD *Wilts. – see Salisbury.*

ITTLE PETHERICK *Cornwall* 503 F 32 – *see Padstow.*

ITTLE SHELFORD *Cambs.* 504 U 27 – *see Cambridge.*

ITTLE THETFORD *Cambs. – see Ely.*

ITTLETON *Hants.* 503 504 P 30 – *see Winchester.*

ITTLEWORTH *Oxon.* 503 504 P 28 – *see Faringdon.*

C. Bowman/SCOPE

On the docks of Liverpool

LIVERPOOL

Mersey. 502 503 L 23 *Great Britain G. – pop. 469 017.*

London 219 – Birmingham 103 – Leeds 75 – Manchester 35.

TOURIST INFORMATION

Queens Square ☎ (0906) 680 6886; askme@visitliverpool.com – Atlantic Pavilion, Albert Dock ☎ (0906) 680 6886.

PRACTICAL INFORMATION

18, 9 Allerton Municipal, Allerton Rd ☎ (0151) 428 1046.
18 Liverpool Municipal, Ingoe Lane, Kirkby ☎ (0151) 546 5435, **BV**.
9 Bowring, Bowring Park, Roby Rd ☎ (0151) 489 1901.
Mersey Tunnels (toll) **AX**.

Liverpool Airport : ☎ (0870) 7508484, SE : 6 m. by A 561 **BX**.
Terminal : *Pier Head.*

to Isle of Man (Douglas) (Isle of Man Steam Packet Co. Ltd) (2 h 30 mn/4 h) – to Northern Ireland (Belfast) (NorseMerchant Ferries Ltd) 1-2 daily (11 h) – to Dublin (Norse Merchant Ferries Ltd) 2 daily (approx. 7 h 45 mn) – to Dublin (P & O Irish Sea) daily (8 h) – to Dublin (Seacat) daily February-November (3 h 45 mn).

to Birkenhead and Wallasey (Mersey Ferries) frequent services daily.

SIGHTS

See: *City★ – Walker Art Gallery★★* **DY M3** *– Liverpool Cathedral★★ (Lady Chapel★)* **EZ** *– Metropolitan Cathedral of Christ the King★★* **EY** *– Albert Dock★* **CZ** *(Merseyside Maritime Museum★* **AC M2** *- Tate Liverpool★).*

Exc. : *Speke Hall★* **AC**, *SE : 8 m. by A 561* **BX**.

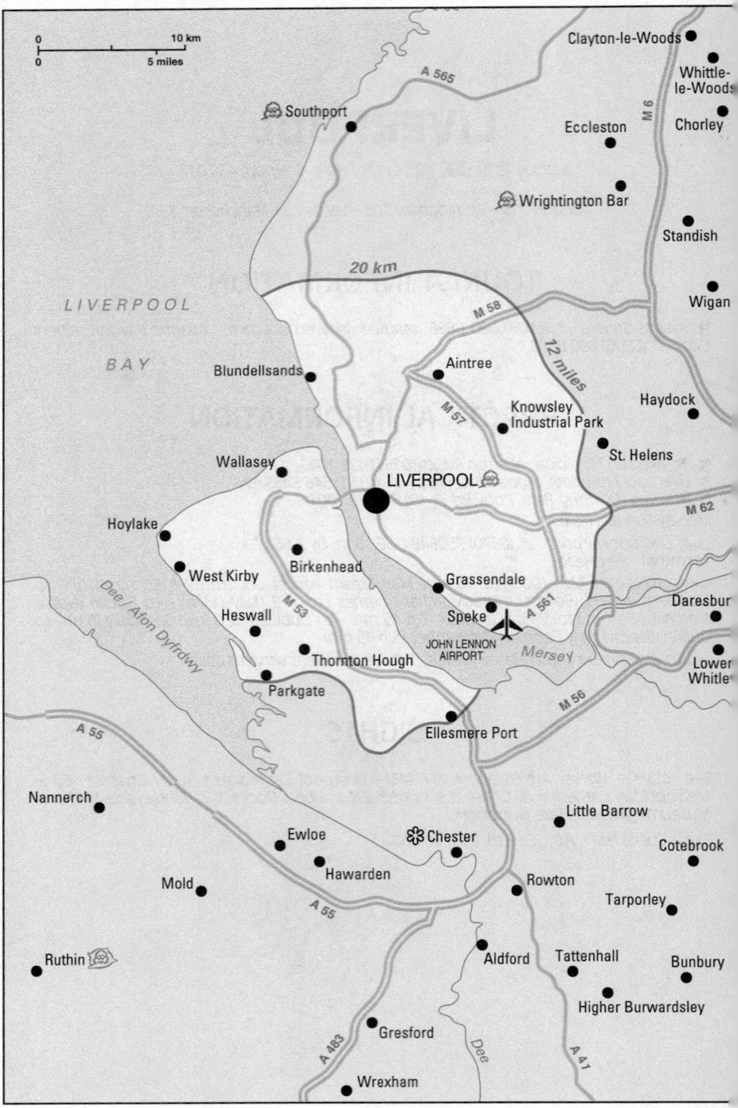

0 10 km
0 5 miles

A 565
Southport
Clayton-le-Woods
Whittle-le-Woods
M 6
Chorley
Eccleston
Wrightington Bar
Standish
20 km
Wigan
LIVERPOOL BAY
M 58
12 miles
Aintree
Blundellsands
Haydock
M 57
Knowsley Industrial Park
St. Helens
Wallasey
LIVERPOOL
M 62
Hoylake
Birkenhead
West Kirby
Grassendale
Dee / Afon Dyfrdwy
M 53
A 561
Daresbur
Heswall
Speke
JOHN LENNON AIRPORT
Mersey
Thornton Hough
Lower Whitle
Parkgate
M 56
A 55
Ellesmere Port
Nannerch
Little Barrow
Ewloe
Chester
Cotebrook
Hawarden
Rowton
Mold
Tarporley
A 55
Ruthin
Aldford
Tattenhall
Bunbury
Higher Burwardsley
Gresford
A 483
Dee
A 41
Wrexham

Undecided between two equivalent establishments? Within each category, establishments are classified in our order of preference.

INDEX OF STREET NAMES IN LIVERPOOL

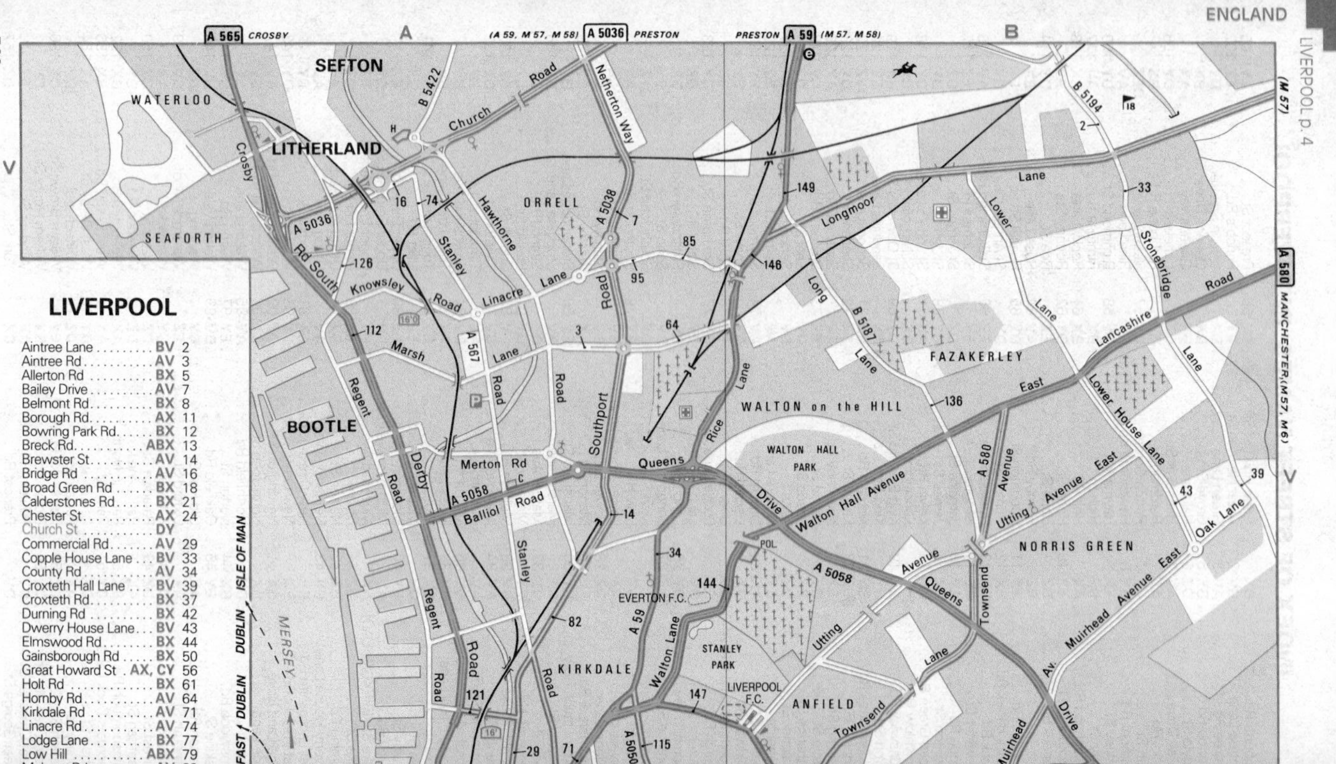

LIVERPOOL

Aintree Lane . . . . BV 2
Aintree Rd . . . . AV 3
Allerton Rd . . . . BX 5
Bailey Drive . . . . AV 7
Belmont Rd . . . . BX 8
Borough Rd . . . . AX 11
Bowring Park Rd . . . . . BX 12
Breck Rd . . . . ABX 13
Brewster St . . . . AV 14
Bridge Rd . . . . AV 16
Broad Green Rd . . . . . . BX 18
Calderstones Rd . . . . . . BX 21
Chester St . . . . AX 24
Church St . . . . DY
Commercial Rd . . . . AV 29
Copple House Lane . . . BV 33
County Rd . . . . AV 34
Croxteth Hall Lane . . . . BV 39
Croxteth Rd . . . . BX 37
Durning Rd . . . . BX 42
Dwerry House Lane . . . BV 43
Elmswood Rd . . . . BX 44
Gainsborough Rd . . . . . BX 50
Great Howard St . AX, CY 56
Holt Rd . . . . BX 61
Hornby Rd . . . . AV 64
Kirkdale Rd . . . . AV 71
Linacre Rd . . . . AV 74
Lodge Lane . . . . BX 77
Low Hill . . . . ABX 79

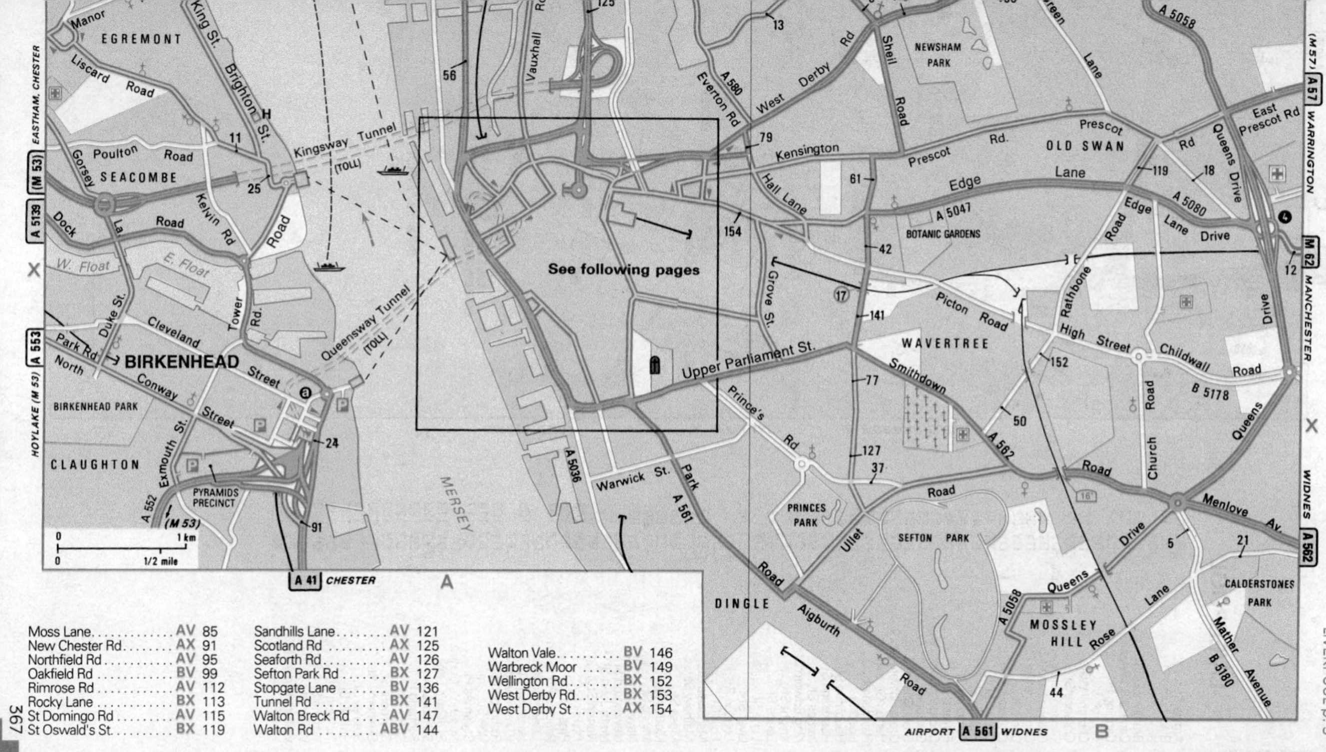
(M 57) A 57 WARRINGTON
M 62 MANCHESTER
WIDNES A 562
AIRPORT A 561 WIDNES
A 41 CHESTER
HOYLAKE (M 53) A 553
EASTHAM, CHESTER (M 53) A 5139
See following pages
EGREMONT
SEACOMBE
BIRKENHEAD
BIRKENHEAD PARK
CLAUGHTON
PYRAMIDS PRECINCT
OLD SWAN
NEWSHAM PARK
BOTANIC GARDENS
WAVERTREE
PRINCES PARK
SEFTON PARK
DINGLE
MOSSLEY HILL
CALDERSTONES PARK
MERSEY
Kingsway Tunnel (TOLL)
Queensway Tunnel (TOLL)
Upper Parliament St.
Smithdown Road
Picton Road
High Street
Childwall Road
Edge Lane Drive
Prescot Rd.
Queens Drive
Menlove Av.
Aigburth Road
Park Road
Warwick St.
Prince's Rd
Ullet Road
Grove St.
Hall Lane
Kensington
West Derby Rd
Everton Rd
Sheil Road
Vauxhall Rd
Mather Avenue
Rose Lane
Church Road
Rathbone Road
Liscard Road
Poulton Road
Brighton St.
King St.
Kelvin Rd
Dock Road
Gorsey La.
Cleveland Street
Conway Street
Exmouth St.
Duke St.
Park Rd North
Tower Rd.
W. Float
E. Float
A 5058
A 5080
A 5047
A 580
A 562
A 561
A 5036
A 552
B 5178
B 5180
0 1 km
0 1/2 mile
A
B

LIVERPOOL

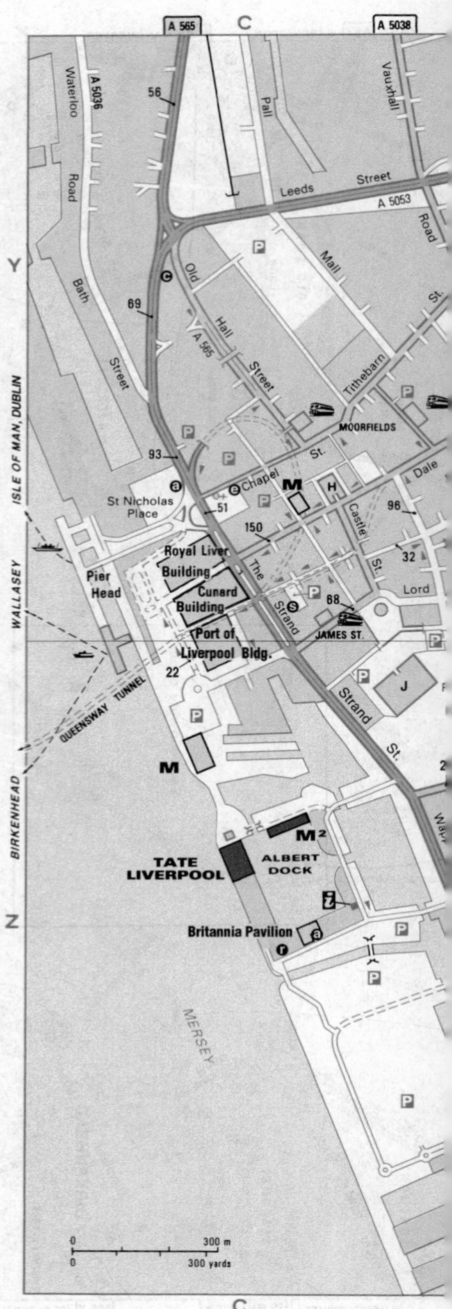

A 565
C
A 5038
Y
Z
Waterloo
A 5036
Road
56
Pall
Vauxhall
Leeds
Street
A 5053
Road
Bath
Old
Mall
69
Hall
A 565
Street
Tithebarn
St.
Street
MOORFIELDS
93
St.
Chapel
Dale
St Nicholas Place
M
H
51
Castle
96
150
Royal Liver Building
St.
32
Pier Head
Cunard Building
The
Strand
68
Lord
JAMES ST.
Port of Liverpool Bldg.
ISLE OF MAN, DUBLIN
WALLASEY
BIRKENHEAD
22
QUEENSWAY TUNNEL
J
Strand
St.
M
M2
TATE LIVERPOOL
ALBERT DOCK
Britannia Pavilion
MERSEY
0
300 m
0
300 yards
C

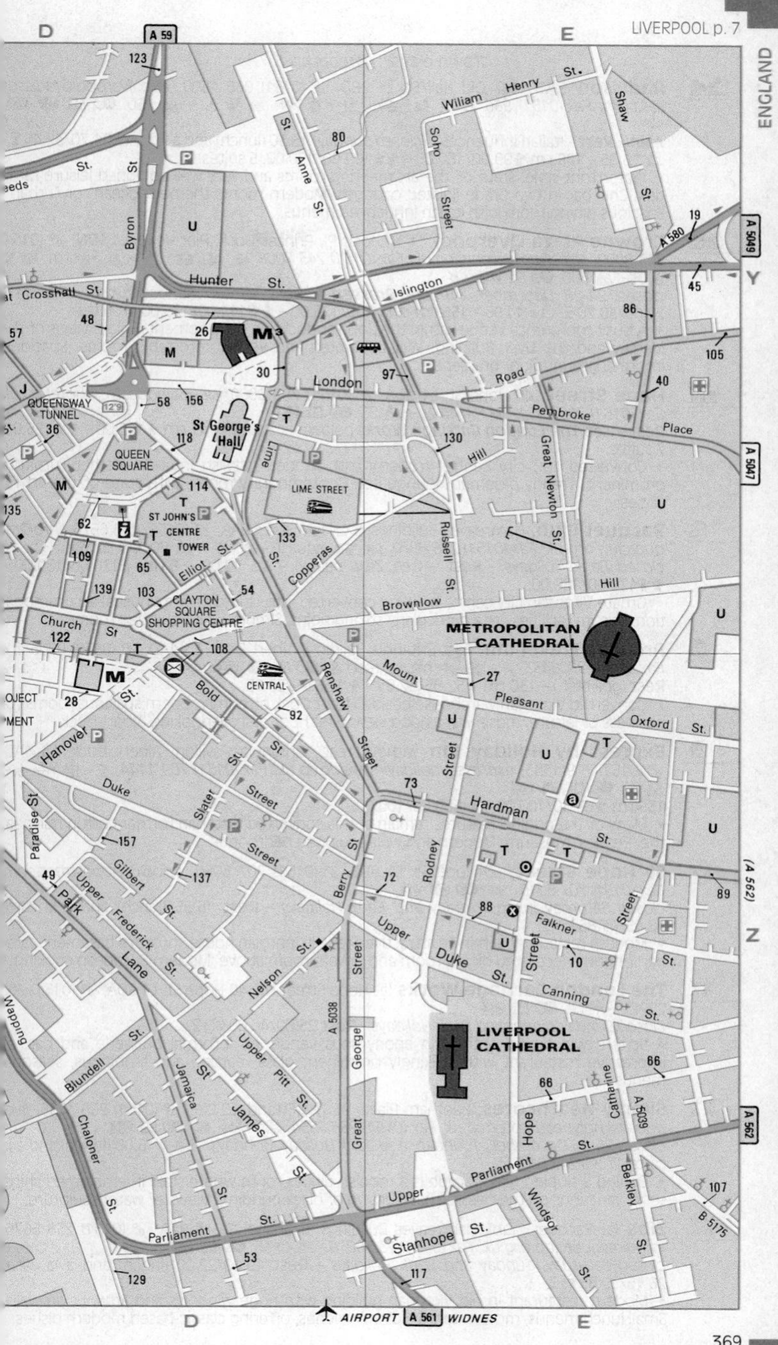

ENGLAND
METROPOLITAN CATHEDRAL
LIVERPOOL CATHEDRAL
St George's Hall
LIME STREET
CENTRAL
QUEEN SQUARE
ST JOHN'S CENTRE
TOWER
CLAYTON SQUARE SHOPPING CENTRE
QUEENSWAY TUNNEL
AIRPORT
A 561
WIDNES

ENGLAND

Town plans: Liverpool pp. 3-7

Radisson SAS, 107 Old Hall St, L3 9BD, (0151) 966 1500, *info.liverpool@radissonsas.com, Fax (0151) 966 1501,* – 160. CY c
Filini : **Rest** - Italian influences - *(closed Sunday)* 13.50 (lunch) and a la carte 21.70/32.45 – 15.95 – **189 rm** 99.00/180.00 – 109.00/190.00, 5 suites.
• Waterfront style: state-of-the-art meeting rooms and very well equipped leisure facilities. Chic bar in two Grade II listed cottages. Modern rooms themed "ocean" or "urban". Spacious dining room with Italian influenced menus.

Crowne Plaza Liverpool, St Nicholas Pl, Princes Dock, Pier Head, L3 1QN, (0151) 243 8000, *sales@cpliverpool.co.uk, Fax (0151) 243 8008,* – rm, – 500. CY a
closed 24-26 December – ***Plaza Brasserie :*** **Rest** *(closed Sunday lunch)* a la carte 22.60/30.70 – 14.95 – **155 rm** 114.00/125.00 – 114.00/125.00, 4 suites.
• A busy conference venue within the popular dockside development. Enjoys views of the Mersey and the Liver Building. Well-appointed and very comfortable rooms. Spacious, informal ground floor brasserie.

Hope Street, 40 Hope St, L1 9DA, (0151) 709 3000, *sleep@hopestreethotel.co.uk Fax (0151) 709 2454* – – 25. EZ c
Rest – (see ***The London Carriage Works*** below) – 14.50 – **41 rm** 125.00 – 125.00, 7 suites.
• Converted 19C city centre property with modern, stylish interior: leather furniture prominent. Trendy basement lounge bar. Contemporary rooms with state-of-the-art facilities.

Racquet Club, Hargreaves Buildings, 5 Chapel St, L3 9AA, (0151) 236 6676, *info@racquetclub.org.uk, Fax (0151) 236 6870,* squash – – 80. CY e
closed Bank Holidays – **Rest** – (see ***Ziba*** below) – 12.00 – **8 rm** 120.00/180.00 – 120.00/180.00.
• Ornate Victorian city centre building converted into club offering unusual accommodation. Leisure facilities are a particularly strong point. Simple, well-equipped rooms.

Premier Travel Inn, East Britannia Building, Albert Dock, L3 4AD, (0870) 9906432, *Fax (0870) 9906433,* – rm, rest, . CZ a
Rest (grill rest.) – **130 rm** 52.95/52.95 – 55.95/55.95.
• Converted Victorian warehouse beside Albert Dock offering modern spacious rooms for business or leisure, most with a good view. First floor grill overlooking Albert Dock.

Express by Holiday Inn without rest., Britannia Pavilion, Albert Dock, L3 4AD (0151) 709 1133, *expressbyholidayinn@cidc.co.uk, Fax (0151) 709 1144,* – 35. CZ r
135 rm 69.50/100.00 – 69.50/100.00.
• Many of the original features remain at this converted Victorian former cotton mill near the 'Beatles' museum. Modern and well-equipped bedrooms.

60 Hope Street, 60 Hope St, L1 9BZ, (0151) 707 6060, *info@60hopestreet.com Fax (0151) 707 6016* – . EZ x
closed Saturday lunch, Sunday and Bank Holidays – **Rest** 15.95 (lunch) and a la carte 28.85/41.85 .
• Modern restaurant within an attractive Grade II Georgian house. Informal basement café-bar, brightly decorated dining room and private room above. Modern European cooking.

The London Carriage Works (at Hope Street H.), 40 Hope St, L1 9DA, (0151) 705 2222 – . EZ c
closed Sunday dinner and Bank Holidays – **Rest** 25.00/40.00 .
• Stylish twin dining options in eponymous venue: an informal brasserie and bar, or impressive restaurant with strikingly prominent glass feature, and ambitious, seasonal menus.

Simply Heathcotes, Beetham Plaza, 25 The Strand, L2 0XL, (0151) 236 3536, *liverpool@simplyheathcotes.co.uk, Fax (0151) 236 3534,* – . CY s
closed 25-26 December, 1 January and Bank Holiday Mondays – **Rest** 16.00 (lunch) and a la carte 17.25/24.00 .
• Behind a sloping glass façade is a modish dining room where staff in emblemed shirts serve variations on the classics: hash brown of black pudding. Views of water sculpture.

Ziba (at Racquet Club), Hargreaves Buildings, 5 Chapel St, L3 9AA, (0151) 236 6676 *info@racquetclub.org.uk, Fax (0151) 236 6870* – 35. CY e
closed Saturday, Sunday and Bank Holidays – **Rest** 19.00/22.00 (lunch) and a la carte 26.15/30.85 **s.** .
• Modern restaurant in old Victorian building with huge windows and artwork on walls. Small lunch menus, more extensive dinner menus, offering classic-based modern dishes.

ENGLAND

The Side Door, 29a Hope St, L1 9BQ, ☎ (0151) 707 7888, *Fax (0151) 707 7888* – MC VISA EZ a
closed 24-26 and 31 December, 1 January, Sunday and Monday – **Rest** 14.95 (dinner) and a la carte 13.15/26.85 ♀.
◆ Victorian end of terrace ground floor and basement eatery with green painted brick and wood floors. Good value dishes are supplemented by a concise wine list.

Floor One @ The Baltic Fleet, 33A Wapping, L1 8DQ, ☎ (0151) 708 4545, *Fax (0151) 643 8304* – MC VISA.
Rest *(closed dinner Sunday and Monday)* a la carte 12.00/23.00.
◆ One of the city's most famous hostelries: a basement micro brewery does sterling work. First floor dining room serves fresh, unfussy fare: check out the wild boar sausages.

at Aintree *North : 6 m. by A 59* – ✉ *Liverpool.*

Premier Travel Inn, Ormskirk Rd, L9 5AS, on A 59 ☎ (0151) 530 3700, *Fax (0151) 525 8696* – rm, rest, P. MC AE VISA. BV e
Rest (grill rest.) – **40 rm** 48.95 – 48.95.
◆ A modern lodge adjacent to the Aintree racecourse, in the shadow of the Princess Royal stand.Rooms are bright, neat and of good value.

at Blundellsands *North : 7½ m. by A 565* – **CY** – ✉ *Liverpool.*

The Blundellsands without rest., 9 Elton Ave, L23 8UN, ☎ (0151) 924 6947, *bsbb@blueyonder.co.uk, Fax (0151) 287 4113* – P. MC AE VISA.
4 rm 39.00/55.00 – 75.00.
◆ Large semi-detached guesthouse with residential setting. Comfortable guests' lounge; the bedrooms, chintz in style, are clean, well-kept and have lots of extra touches.

at Knowsley Industrial Park *Northeast : 8 m. by A 580* – **BV** – ✉ *Liverpool.*

Suites H., Ribblers Lane, L34 9HA, ☎ (0151) 549 2222, *enquiries@suiteshotelgroup.com, Fax (0151) 549 1116,* – P – 300. MC AE VISA
Rest *(closed lunch Saturday and Sunday)* a la carte 17.75/25.75 s. –, **80 suites** 72.00/109.00.
◆ Adjoins a business park, with smartly designed work areas. A well-equipped, privately owned hotel, ideal for corporate clients. All rooms are comfortably furnished suites. Upbeat, vibrantly decorated dining room.

at Grassendale *Southeast : 4½ m. on A 561* – **BX** – ✉ *Liverpool.*

Gulshan, 544-548 Aigburth Rd, L19 3QG, on A 561 ☎ (0151) 427 2273, *Fax (0151) 427 2111* – MC AE VISA
Rest - Indian - (dinner only) a la carte 17.15/22.75.
◆ A richly decorated and comfortable traditional Indian restaurant within a parade of shops. Smart and efficient service of an extensive menu of authentic dishes.

at Speke *Southeast : 8¾ m. by A 561* – **BX** – ✉ *Liverpool.*

Liverpool Marriott H. South, Speke Aerodrome, Speke Rd, L24 8QD, West : 1 ¾ m. on A 561 ☎ (0870) 4007269, *events.liverpoolsouth@marriotthotels.co.uk, Fax (0870) 4007369,* , squash – P – 350. MC AE VISA.
Starways : **Rest** a la carte 22.00/31.00 ♀ – 13.95 – **163 rm** 89.00/109.00 – 195.00/300.00, 1 suite.
◆ Converted Art Deco airport terminal building, built 1937. Aviation and 1930s era the prevailing themes throughout. The modern, well-equipped bedrooms have a stylish appeal. Smart brasserie within original airport terminal; in keeping with hotel's style.

LIZARD *Cornwall* 503 E 34 *The West Country G.*

Env. : *Lizard Peninsula★ - Mullion Cove★★ (Church★) - Kynance Cove★★ - Cadgwith★ - Coverack★ – Cury★ (Church★) - Gunwalloe Fishing Cove★ - St Keverne (Church★) - Landewednack★ (Church★) – Mawgan-in-Meneage (Church★) - Ruan Minor (Church★) - St Anthony-in-Meneage★.*

London 326 – Penzance 24 – Truro 29.

Housel Bay, Housel Bay, TR12 7PG, ☎ (01326) 290417, *info@houselbay.com, Fax (01326) 290359,* ≤ Housel Cove, – P. MC AE VISA.
Rest (bar lunch Monday-Saturday)/dinner a la carte 18.40/19.40 – **21 rm** 30.00/42.00 – 60.00/130.00.
◆ Britain's most southerly mainland hotel, with spectacular views of Atlantic and Channel: the Cornish coastal path runs through its gardens. Comfortable bedrooms. Dining room affords dramatic sea and lighthouse views.

ENGLAND

Landewednack House, Church Cove, TR12 7PQ, East : 1 m. by A 3083 (01326) 290877, *luxurybandb@landewednackhouse.com, Fax (01326) 290192*, heated, rm, [P]. AE VISA
Rest (by arrangement) (communal dining) 33.00/45.00 – **6 rm** 60.00/90.00 120.00/150.00.
• Part 17C former rectory and garden, overlooking Church Cove. Smart interiors stylish furnished with antiques. Diners encouraged to discuss menus: best local produce to han

Tregullas House without rest., Housel Bay, TR12 7PF, (01326) 290351, [P]
restricted opening in winter – **3 rm** 32.00/48.00 – 56.00.
• Simple guesthouse in a charming location with mature garden and sea vista. Spotless kept with a cottagey style. Uncluttered bedrooms. At breakfast, take in the garden view.

LLANGARRON *Herefordshire* 503 504 L 28 – *see Ross-on-Wye.*

LLANYMYNECH *Shrops.* 502 503 K 25 – *see Oswestry.*

We try to be as accurate as possible when giving room rates. But prices are susceptible to change, so please check rates when booking.

- *Discover the best restaurant ?*
- *Find the nearest hotel ?*
- *Find your bearings using our maps and guides ?*
- *Understand the symbols used in the guide...*

Follow the red Bibs !

Advice on restaurants from Chef Bib.

Advice on hotels from Bellboy Bib.

Tips and advice from Clever Bib on finding your way around the guide and on the road.

B. Pérousse/MICHELIN

London: Big Ben

LONDON

504 *folds* S 29 *to* U 29 – *London G.* – *pop.* 6679699

SIGHTS

HISTORIC BUILDINGS AND MONUMENTS

Palace of Westminster★★★ : *House of Lords*★★, *Westminster Hall*★★ *(hammerbeam roof*★★★*), Robing Room*★, *Central Lobby*★, *House of Commons*★, *Big Ben*★, *Victoria Tower*★, **39** ALX – *Tower of London*★★★ *(Crown Jewels*★★★, *White Tower or Keep*★★★, *St. John's Chapel*★★, *Beauchamp Tower*★, *Tower Hill Pageant*★*)* **34** ASU – *British Airways London Eye (views*★★★*)* **32** AMV.

Banqueting House★★ **31** ALV – *Buckingham Palace*★★ *(Changing of the Guard*★★, *Royal Mews*★★*)* **38** AIX – *Kensington Palace*★★ **27** ABV – *Lincoln's Inn*★★ **32** AMT – *London Bridge*★ **34** ARV – *Royal Hospital Chelsea*★★ **37** AGZ – *St. James's Palace*★★ **30** AJV – *Somerset House*★★ **32** AMU – *South Bank Arts Centre*★★ *(Royal Festival Hall*★, *National Theatre*★, *County Hall*★*)* **32** AMV – *The Temple*★★ *(Middle Temple Hall*★*)* **32** ANU – *Tower Bridge*★★ **34** ASV.

Albert Memorial★ **36** ADX – *Apsley House*★ **30** AHV – *Burlington House*★ **30** AIV – *Charterhouse*★ **19** UZD – *George Inn*★, *Southwark* **33** AQV – *Gray's Inn*★ **32** AMV – *Guildhall*★ *(Lord Mayor's Show*★★*)* **33** AQT – *International Shakespeare Globe Centre*★ **33** APV – *Dr Johnson's House*★ **32** ANT – *Lancaster House*★ **30** AIV – *Leighton House*★ **35** AAX – *Linley Sambourne House*★ **35** AAX – *Lloyds Building*★★ **34** ARU – *Mansion House*★ *(plate and insignia*★★*)* **33** AQV – *The Monument*★ *(✳★)* **34** ARU – *Old Admiralty*★ **31** AKV – *Royal Albert Hall*★ **36** ADX – *Royal Exchange*★ **34** ARU – *Royal Opera House*★ *(Covent Garden)* **31** ALU – *Spencer House*★★ **30** AIV – *Staple Inn*★ **32** ANT – *Theatre Royal*★ *(Haymarket),* **31** AKV – *Westminster Bridge*★ **39** ALX.

CHURCHES

The City Churches

St. Paul's Cathedral★★★ (Dome ←★★★) **33** APU.

St. Bartholomew the Great★★ (choir★) **33** APT – *St. Dunstan-in-the-East★★* **34** ARU – *St. Mary-at-Hill★★ (woodwork★★, plan★)* **34** ARU – *Temple Church★★* **32** ANU.

All Hallows-by-the-Tower (font cover★★, brasses★) **34** ARU – *Christ Church★* **33** APT – *St. Andrew Undershaft (monuments★)* **34** ARU – *St. Bride★ (steeple★★)* **32** ANU – *St. Clement Eastcheap (panelled interior★★)* **34** ARU – *St. Edmund the King and Martyr (tower and spire★)* **34** ARU – *St-Giles Cripplegate★* **33** AQT – *St. Helen Bishopsgate★ (monuments★★)* **34** ART – *St. James Garlickhythe (tower and spire★, sword rests★)* **33** AQU – *St. Magnus the Martyr (tower★, sword rest★)* **34** ARU – *St. Margaret Lothbury★ (tower and spire★, woodwork★, screen★, font★)* **33** AQT – *St. Margaret Pattens (spire★, woodwork★)* **34** ARU – *St. Martin-within-Ludgate (tower and spire★, door cases★)* **33** APU – *St. Mary Abchurch★ (reredos★★, tower and spire★, dome★)* **33** AQU – *St. Mary-le-Bow (tower and steeple★★)* **33** AQU – *St. Michael Paternoster Royal (tower and spire★)* **35** AQU – *St. Nicholas Cole Abbey (tower and spire★)* **33** APU – *St. Olave★* **34** ARU – *St. Peter upon Cornhill (screen★)* **34** ARU – *St. Stephen Walbrook★ (tower and steeple★, dome★)* **33** AQU – *St. Vedast (tower and spire★ ceiling★),* **33** APT.

Other Churches

Westminster Abbey★★★ (Henry VII Chapel★★★, Chapel of Edward the Confessor★★, Chapter House★★, Poets' Corner★) **39** ALX.

Southwark Cathedral★★ **33** AQV.

Queen's Chapel★ **30** AJV – *St. Clement Danes★* **32** AMU – *St. James's★* **30** AJV – *St. Margaret's★* **39** ALX – *St. Martin-in-the-Fields★* **31** ALV – *St. Paul's★ (Covent Garden)* **31** ALU – *Westminster Roman Catholic Cathedral★* **39** ALX.

PARKS

Regent's Park★★★ **11** QZC *(terraces★★, Zoo★★).*

Hyde Park **29** AFV – *Kensington Gardens★★* **28** ACV *(Orangery★)* **27** ABV – *St. James's Park★★* **31** AKV.

STREETS AND SQUARES

The City★★★ **33** AQT.

Bedford Square★★ **31** AKT – *Belgrave Square★★* **37** AGX – *Burlington Arcade★★* **30** AIV – *Covent Garden★★ (The Piazza★★)* **31** ALU – *The Mall★★* **31** AKV – *Piccadilly★* **30** AIV – *The Thames★★* **32** ANU – *Trafalgar Square★★* **31** AKV – *Whitehall★★ (Horse Guards★)* **31** ALV.

Barbican★ **33** AQT – *Bond Street★* **30** AIU – *Canonbury Square★* **13** UZB – *Carlton House Terrace★* **31** AKV – *Cheyne Walk★* **23** PZG – *Fitzroy Square★* **18** RZD – *Jermyn Street★* **30** AJV – *Leicester Square★* **31** AKU – *Merrick Square★* **19** VZE – *Montpelier Square★* **37** AFX – *Neal's Yard★* **31** ALU – *Piccadilly Arcade★* **30** AIV – *Portman Square★* **29** AGT – *Queen Anne's Gate★* **39** AKX – *Regent Street★* **30** AIU – *Royal Opera Arcade★* **31** AKV – *Piccadilly Circus★* **31** AKU – *St. James's Square★* **31** AJV – *St. James's Street★* **30** AIV – *Shepherd Market★* **30** AHV – *Soho★* **31** AKU – *Trinity Church Square★* **19** VZE – *Victoria Embankment gardens★* **31** ALV – *Waterloo Place★* **31** AKV.

MUSEUMS

British Museum★★★ **31** AKL – *National Gallery★★★* **31** AKV – *Science Museum★★★* **36** ADX – *Tate Britain★★★* **39** ALY – *Victoria and Albert Museum★★★* **36** ADY – *Wallace Collection★★★* **29** AGT.

Courtauld Institute Galleries★★ (Somerset House) **32** AMU – *Gilbert Collection★★ (Somerset House)* **32** AMU – *Museum of London★★* **33** APT – *National Portrait Gallery★★* **31** AKU – *Natural History Museum★★* **36** ADY – *Sir John Soane's Museum★★* **32** AMT – *Tate Modern★★ (views★★★ from top floors)* **33** APV.

Clock Museum★ (Guildhall) **33** AQT – *Imperial War Museum★* **40** ANY – *London's Transport Museum★* **31** ALU – *Madame Tussaud's★* **17** QZD – *Museum of Mankind★* **33** DM – *National Army Museum★* **37** AGZ – *Percival David Foundation of Chinese Art★* **18** SZD – *Planetarium★* **15** HVL – *Wellington Museum★ (Apsley House)* **30** AHV.

OUTER LONDON

Blackheath 8 HX *terraces and houses*★, *Eltham Palace*★ **A**
Brentford 5 BX *Syon Park*★★, *gardens*★
Bromley 7 GXY *The Crystal Palace Park*★
Chiswick 6 CV *Chiswick Mall*★★, *Chiswick House*★ **D**, *Hogarth's House*★ **E**
Dulwich 11 *Picture Gallery*★ FX **X**
Greenwich 7 *and* 8 GHV *Cutty Sark*★★ GV **F**, *Footway Tunnel* (⋞ ★★), *Fan Museum*★ **10** GV **A**, *National Maritime Museum*★★ (*Queen's House*★★) GV **M**[2] *Royal Naval College*★★ (*Painted Hall*★, *the Chapel*★) GV **G**, *The Park and Old Royal Observatory*★ (*Meridian Building : collection*★★) HV **K**, *Ranger's House*★ GX **N**
Hampstead *Kenwood House*★★ (*Adam Library*★★, *paintings*★★) **2** EU **P**, *Fenton House*★★ **11** PZA
Hampton Court 5 BY (*The Palace*★★★, *gardens*★★★, *Fountain Court*★, *The Great Vine*★)
Kew 6 CX *Royal Botanic Gardens*★★★ : *Palm House*★★, *Temperate House*★, *Kew Palace or Dutch House*★★, *Orangery*★, *Pagoda*★, *Japanese Gateway*★
Hendon★ 2 *Royal Air Force Museum*★★ CT **M**[3]
Hounslow 5 BV *Osterley Park*★★
Lewisham 7 GX *Horniman Museum*★ **M**[4]
Richmond 5 *and* 6 CX *Richmond Park*★★, ⁕★★★ CX, *Richmond Hill*⁕★★ CX, *Richmond Bridge*★★ BX **R**, *Richmond Green*★★ BX **S**, (*Maids of Honour Row*★★, *Trumpeter's House*★), *Asgill House*★ BX **B**, *Ham House*★★ BX **V**
Shoreditch 14 XZ *Beffrye Museum*★ **M**
Tower Hamlets 7 GV *Canary Wharf*★★ B, *Isle of Dogs*★ *St. Katharine Dock*★ **34** ASV
Twickenham 5 BX *Marble Hill House*★ **Z**, *Strawberry Hill*★ **A** .

PRACTICAL INFORMATION

Britain Visitor Centre, 1 Regent St, W1 ☎ (020) 8846 9000

Airports

✈ *Heathrow ☎ 08700 000123* **12 AX** *Terminal: Airbus (A1) from Victoria, Airbus (A2) from Paddington Underground (Piccadilly line) frequent service daily.*
✈ *Gatwick ☎ 08700 002468* **13**: *by A23* **EZ** *and M23* – Terminal: *Coach service from Victoria Coach Station (Flightline 777, hourly service) - Railink (Gatwick Express) from Victoria (24 h service).*
✈ *London City Airport ☎ (020) 7646 0000* **11 HV**
✈ *Stansted, at Bishop's Stortford ☎ 08700 000303, NE: 34m* **11** *by M11* **JT** *and A120.*
British Airways, Ticket sales and reservations Paddington Station London W2 ☎ 0870 85098500 **36 BX**

Banks

Open, generally 9.30 am to 4.30 pm weekdays (except public holidays). Most have cash dispensers. You need ID (passport) for cashing cheques. Banks levy smaller commissions than hotels.
Many 'Bureaux de Change' around Piccadilly open 7 days.

Medical Emergencies

To contact a doctor for first aid, emergency medical advice and chemists night service: 07000 372255.
Accident & Emergency: dial 999 for Ambulance, Police or Fire Services.

Post Offices

Open Monday to Friday 9 am to 5.30 pm. Late collections made from Leicester Square.

Shopping

Most stores are found in Oxford Street (Selfridges, M & S), Regent Street (Hamleys, Libertys) and Knightsbridge (Harrods, Harvey Nichols). Open usually Monday to Saturday 9 am to 6 pm. Some open later (8 pm) once a week; Knightsbridge Wednesday, Oxford Street and Regent Street Thursday. Other areas worth visiting include Jermyn Street and Savile Row (mens outfitters), Bond Street (jewellers and haute couture).

Theatres

The "West End" has many major theatre performances and can generally be found around Shaftesbury Avenue. Most daily newspapers give details of performances. A half-price ticket booth is located in Leicester Square and is open Monday-Saturday 1 - 6.30 pm, Sunday and matinée days 12 noon - 6.30 pm. Restrictions apply.

Tipping

When a service charge is included in a bill it is not necessary to tip extra. If service is not included a discretionary 10% is normal.

Travel

As driving in London is difficult, it is advisable to take the Underground, a bus or taxi. Taxis can be hailed when the amber light is illuminated.

Congestion Charging

The congestion charge is £8 per day on all vehicles (except motor cycles and exempt vehicles) entering the central zone between 7.00 am and 6.30 pm - Monday to Friday except on Bank Holidays.

Payment can be made in advance, on the day, by post, on the Internet, by telephone (0845 900 1234) or at retail outlets.

A charge of up to £80 will be made for non-payment.

Further information is available on the Transport for London website - www.cclondon.com.

Localities outside the Greater London limits are listed alphabetically throughout the guide.

Les localités situées en dehors des limites de Greater London se trouvent à leur place alphabetique dans le guide.

Alle Städte und Gemeinden außerhalb von Greater London sind in alphabetischer Reihenfolge aufgelistet.

Le località situate al di fuori dei confini della Greater London sono ordinate alfabeticamente all'interno della Guida.

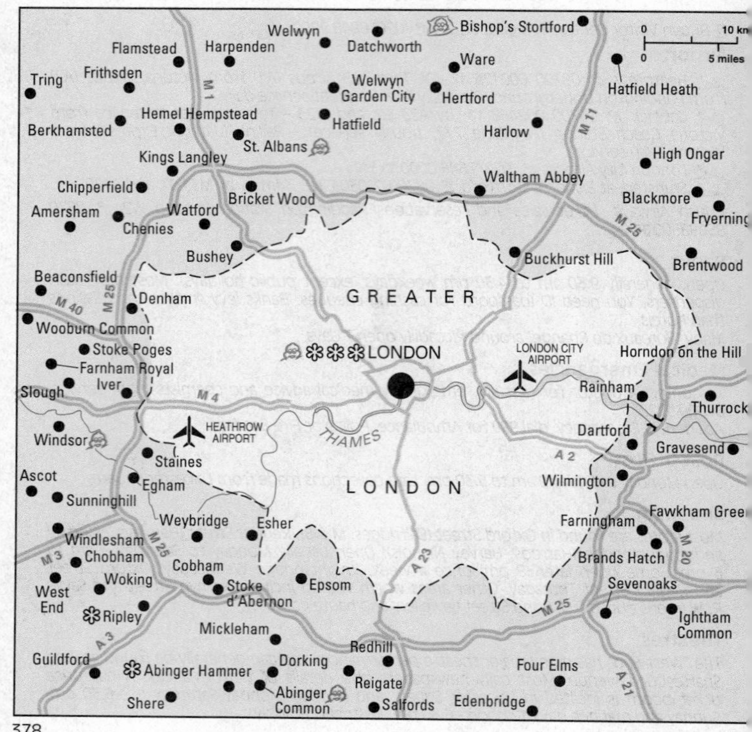

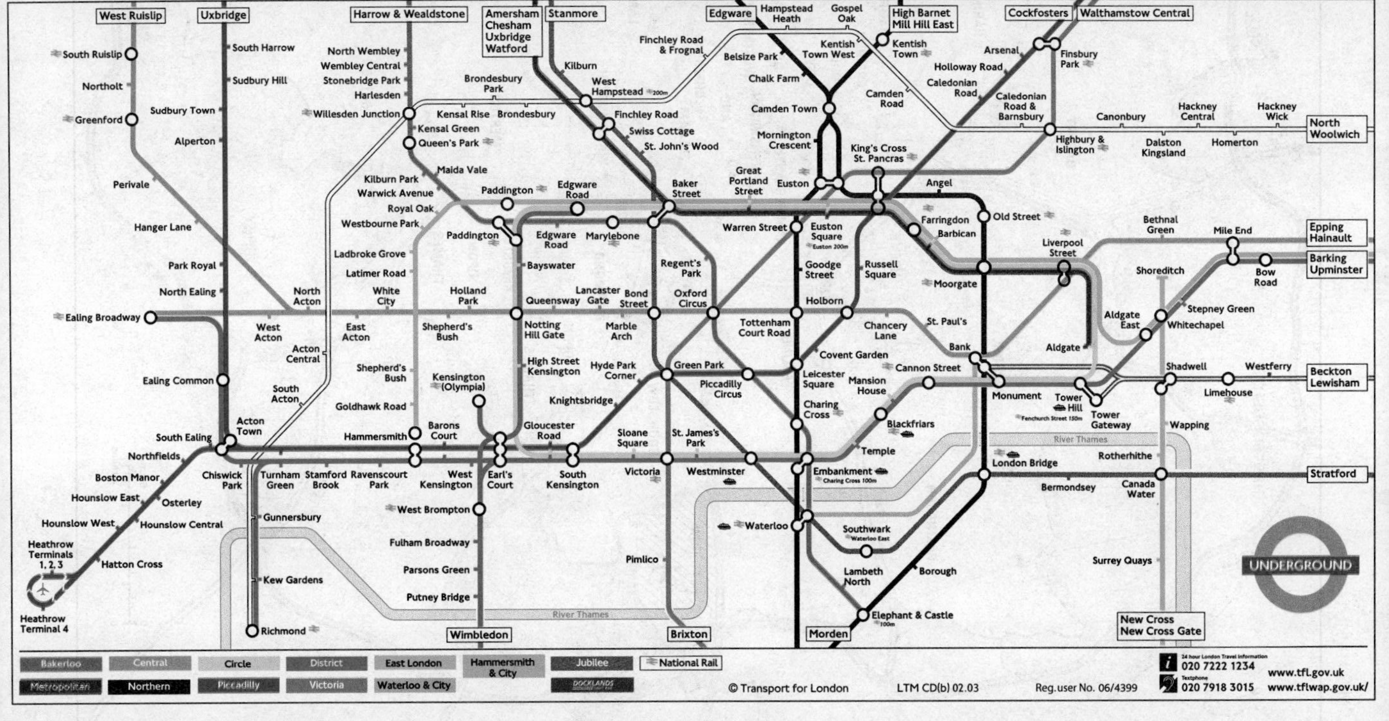
West Ruislip
Uxbridge
Harrow & Wealdstone
Amersham
Chesham
Uxbridge
Watford
Stanmore
Edgware
Hampstead Heath
Gospel Oak
High Barnet
Mill Hill East
Cockfosters
Walthamstow Central
South Ruislip
Northolt
Greenford
South Harrow
Sudbury Hill
Sudbury Town
Alperton
Perivale
Hanger Lane
Park Royal
North Ealing
Ealing Broadway
Ealing Common
North Wembley
Wembley Central
Stonebridge Park
Harlesden
Willesden Junction
Kensal Green
Queen's Park
Kensal Rise
Brondesbury Park
Brondesbury
Kilburn
West Hampstead
Finchley Road & Frognal
Finchley Road
Swiss Cottage
St. John's Wood
Belsize Park
Chalk Farm
Kentish Town West
Kentish Town
Camden Town
Camden Road
Mornington Crescent
Holloway Road
Caledonian Road
Arsenal
Finsbury Park
Caledonian Road & Barnsbury
Canonbury
Hackney Central
Hackney Wick
North Woolwich
Highbury & Islington
Dalston Kingsland
Homerton
King's Cross St. Pancras
Euston
Great Portland Street
Baker Street
Maida Vale
Kilburn Park
Warwick Avenue
Royal Oak
Westbourne Park
Paddington
Edgware Road
Marylebone
Ladbroke Grove
Latimer Road
Bayswater
North Acton
White City
Holland Park
Queensway
Lancaster Gate
Bond Street
Oxford Circus
Regent's Park
Warren Street
Euston Square
Euston 200m
Goodge Street
Russell Square
Angel
Old Street
Farringdon
Barbican
Moorgate
Liverpool Street
Bethnal Green
Mile End
Bow Road
Epping
Hainault
Barking
Upminster
Shoreditch
Stepney Green
Whitechapel
Aldgate East
Aldgate
West Acton
East Acton
Acton Central
Shepherd's Bush
Notting Hill Gate
Marble Arch
Tottenham Court Road
Holborn
Chancery Lane
St. Paul's
Bank
South Acton
Shepherd's Bush
Kensington (Olympia)
High Street Kensington
Hyde Park Corner
Green Park
Piccadilly Circus
Leicester Square
Covent Garden
Mansion House
Cannon Street
Monument
Tower Hill
Fenchurch Street 150m
Tower Gateway
Shadwell
Westferry
Limehouse
Beckton
Lewisham
Wapping
Goldhawk Road
Acton Town
South Ealing
Northfields
Boston Manor
Hounslow East
Osterley
Hounslow West
Hounslow Central
Hatton Cross
Heathrow Terminals 1, 2, 3
Heathrow Terminal 4
Chiswick Park
Turnham Green
Stamford Brook
Ravenscourt Park
Hammersmith
Barons Court
West Kensington
Earl's Court
Gloucester Road
Knightsbridge
South Kensington
Sloane Square
Victoria
St. James's Park
Westminster
Charing Cross
Embankment
Charing Cross 100m
Blackfriars
Temple
London Bridge
River Thames
Rotherhithe
Canada Water
Bermondsey
Stratford
West Brompton
Gunnersbury
Fulham Broadway
Parsons Green
Putney Bridge
Kew Gardens
Richmond
Wimbledon
Pimlico
Brixton
Waterloo
Southwark
Waterloo East
Lambeth North
Borough
Elephant & Castle
100m
Morden
Surrey Quays
New Cross
New Cross Gate
UNDERGROUND
Bakerloo
Central
Circle
District
East London
Hammersmith & City
Jubilee
National Rail
Metropolitan
Northern
Piccadilly
Victoria
Waterloo & City
DOCKLANDS
© Transport for London
LTM CD(b) 02.03
Reg.user No. 06/4399
24 hour London Travel Information
020 7222 1234
Textphone
020 7918 3015
www.tfl.gov.uk
www.tflwap.gov.uk/

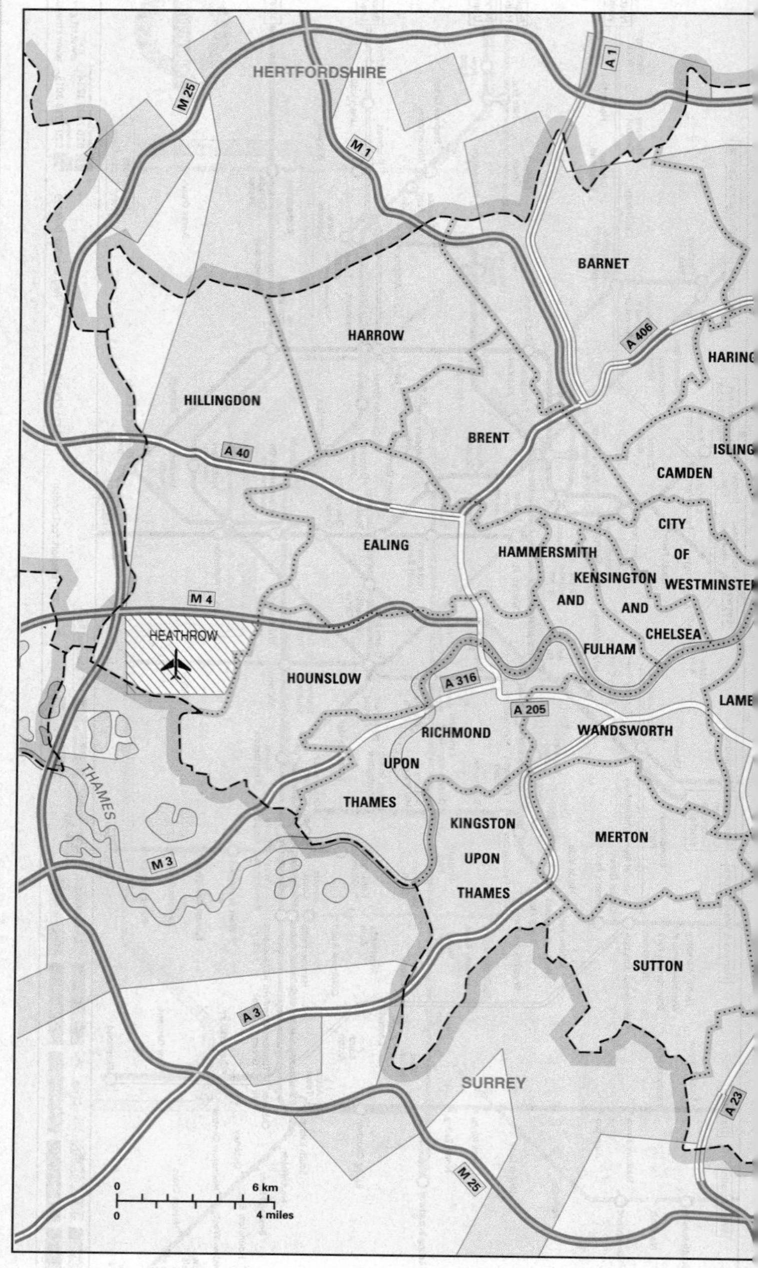
HERTFORDSHIRE
M 25
M 1
A 1
BARNET
HARROW
A 406
HARING
HILLINGDON
BRENT
A 40
ISLING
CAMDEN
CITY
OF
WESTMINSTE
EALING
HAMMERSMITH
AND
FULHAM
KENSINGTON
AND
CHELSEA
M 4
HEATHROW
HOUNSLOW
A 316
A 205
LAMB
RICHMOND
UPON
THAMES
WANDSWORTH
THAMES
KINGSTON
UPON
THAMES
MERTON
M 3
SUTTON
A 3
SURREY
A 23
M 25
0
6 km
0
4 miles

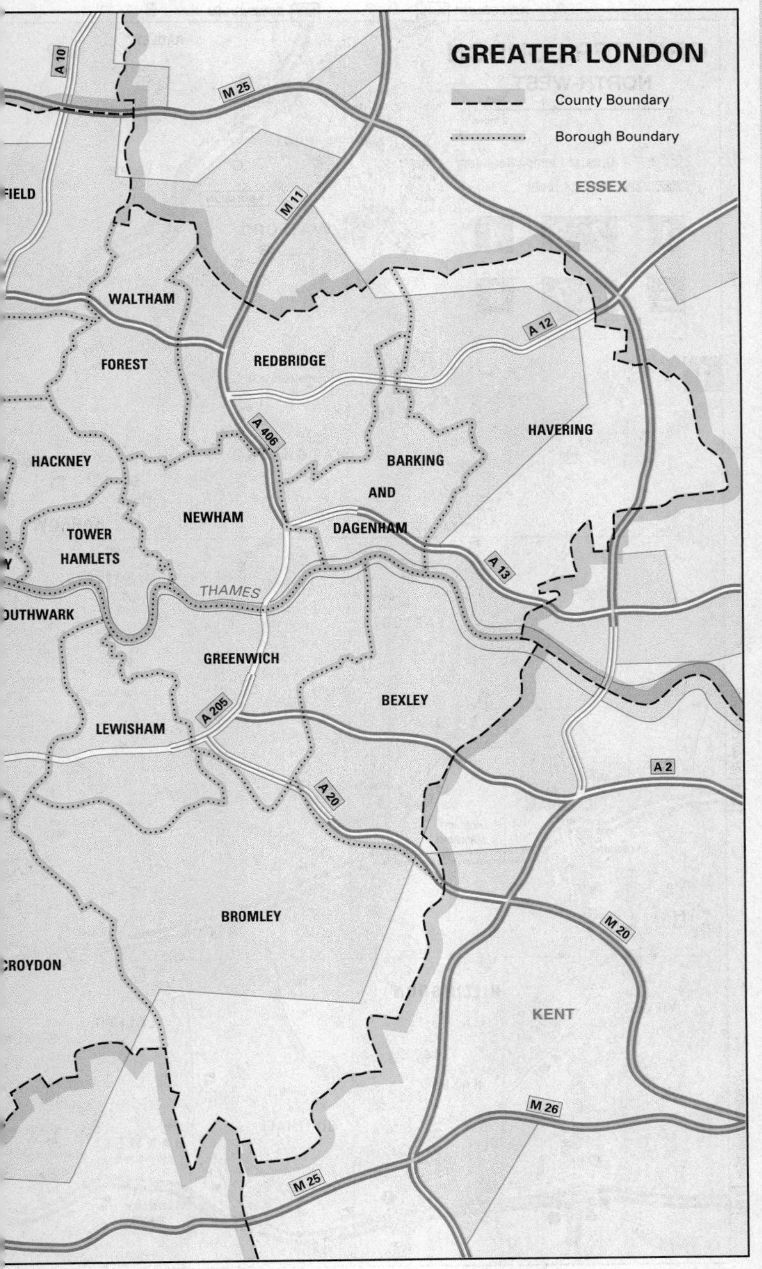
GREATER LONDON
County Boundary
Borough Boundary
ESSEX
M 25
A 10
M 11
A 12
A 406
A 13
A 205
A 20
A 2
M 20
M 26
M 25
FIELD
WALTHAM
FOREST
REDBRIDGE
HAVERING
HACKNEY
BARKING
AND
DAGENHAM
NEWHAM
TOWER
HAMLETS
THAMES
OUTHWARK
GREENWICH
BEXLEY
LEWISHAM
BROMLEY
CROYDON
KENT

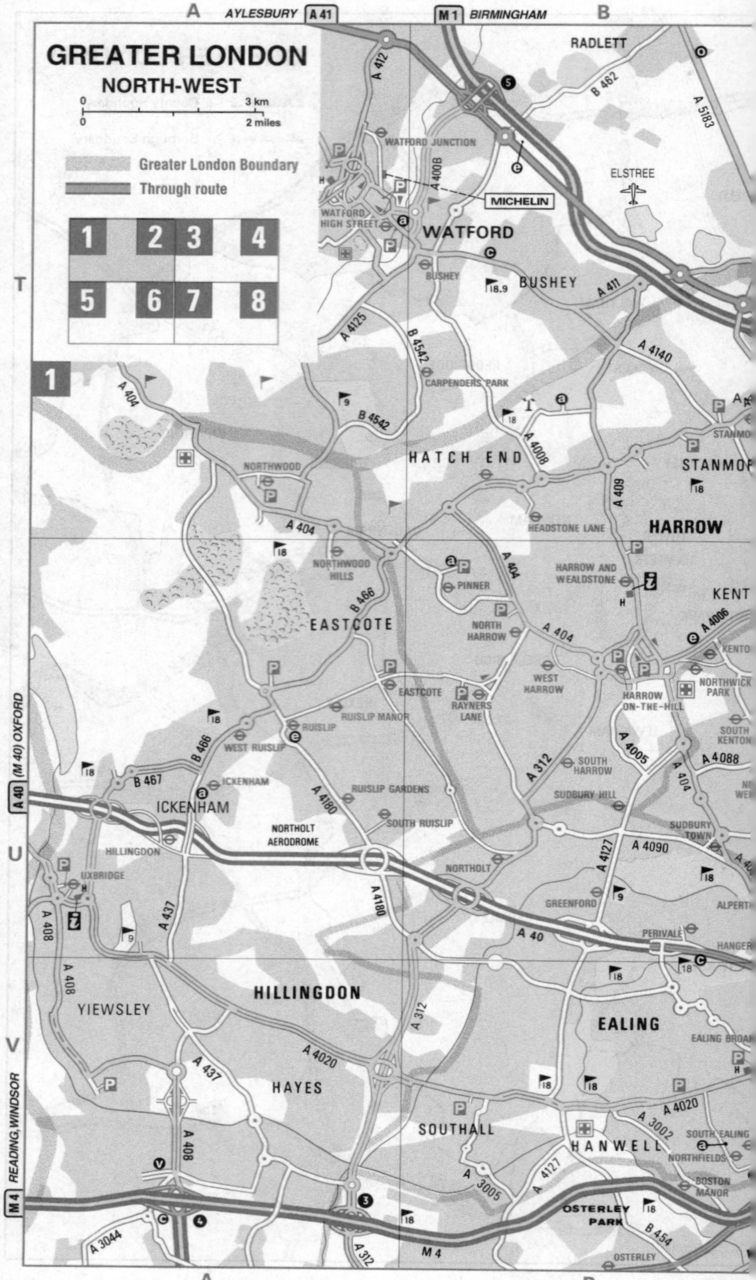

GREATER LONDON

NORTH-WEST

0 3 km
0 2 miles

Greater London Boundary
Through route

1 2 3 4
5 6 7 8

A
AYLESBURY A 41
M 1 BIRMINGHAM
B
RADLETT
B 462
A 5183
A 412
WATFORD JUNCTION
A 4008
ELSTREE
MICHELIN
WATFORD HIGH STREET
WATFORD
BUSHEY
18.9
BUSHEY
A 411
A 4125
B 4542
A 4140
T
1
A 404
CARPENDERS PARK
9
B 4542
18
HATCH END
A 4008
STANMORE
NORTHWOOD
A 409
18
A 404
HEADSTONE LANE
HARROW
18
NORTHWOOD HILLS
PINNER
A 404
HARROW AND WEALDSTONE
KENT
B 466
EASTCOTE
NORTH HARROW
A 404
A 4006
KENTON
EASTCOTE
RAYNERS LANE
WEST HARROW
NORTHWICK PARK
HARROW ON-THE-HILL
RUISLIP MANOR
18
RUISLIP
WEST RUISLIP
A 4005
SOUTH KENTON
B 466
A 312
SOUTH HARROW
A 4088
18
B 467
ICKENHAM
A 4180
RUISLIP GARDENS
A 404
SUDBURY HILL
A 40 (M 40) OXFORD
ICKENHAM
SOUTH RUISLIP
NORTHOLT AERODROME
SUDBURY TOWN
U
HILLINGDON
A 4127
A 4090
UXBRIDGE
NORTHOLT
18
A 4180
GREENFORD
9
ALPERTON
A 408
A 437
9
A 40
PERIVALE
HANGER
18
A 408
18
YIEWSLEY
HILLINGDON
A 312
EALING
V
EALING BROADWAY
A 4020
READING, WINDSOR
A 437
HAYES
18
18
A 4020
A 3002
SOUTHALL
SOUTH EALING
A 408
HANWELL
NORTHFIELDS
A 3005
A 4127
BOSTON MANOR
M 4
OSTERLEY PARK
18
18
B 454
A 3044
A 312
M 4
OSTERLEY
A
B

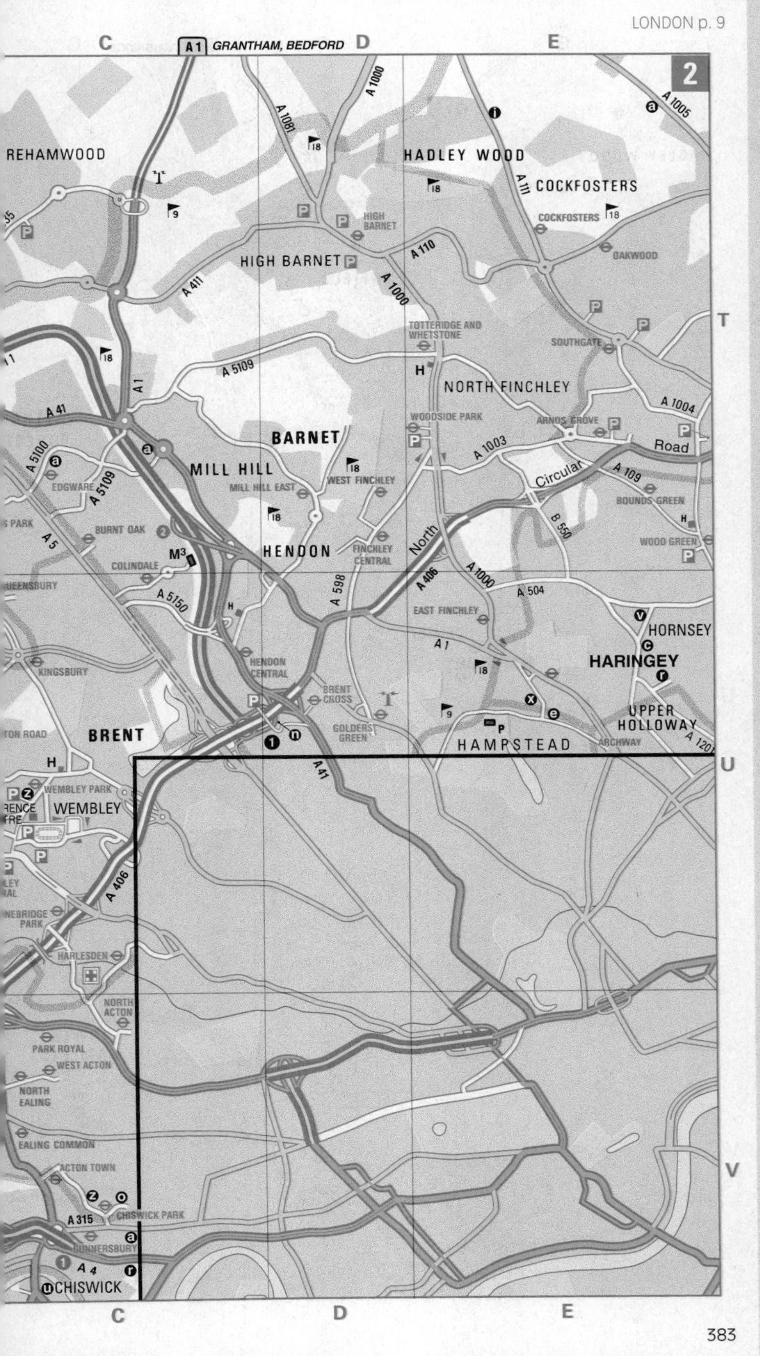

A1 GRANTHAM, BEDFORD
REHAMWOOD
HADLEY WOOD
COCKFOSTERS
HIGH BARNET
OAKWOOD
TOTTERIDGE AND WHETSTONE
SOUTHGATE
NORTH FINCHLEY
WOODSIDE PARK
ARNOS GROVE
BARNET
MILL HILL
MILL HILL EAST
WEST FINCHLEY
EDGWARE
BURNT OAK
BOUNDS GREEN
WOOD GREEN
HENDON
FINCHLEY CENTRAL
COLINDALE
EAST FINCHLEY
HORNSEY
HARINGEY
KINGSBURY
HENDON CENTRAL
BRENT CROSS
GOLDERS GREEN
UPPER HOLLOWAY
BRENT
HAMPSTEAD
ARCHWAY
WEMBLEY PARK
WEMBLEY
HARLESDEN
NORTH ACTON
PARK ROYAL
WEST ACTON
NORTH EALING
EALING COMMON
ACTON TOWN
CHISWICK PARK
GUNNERSBURY
CHISWICK
North Circular Road

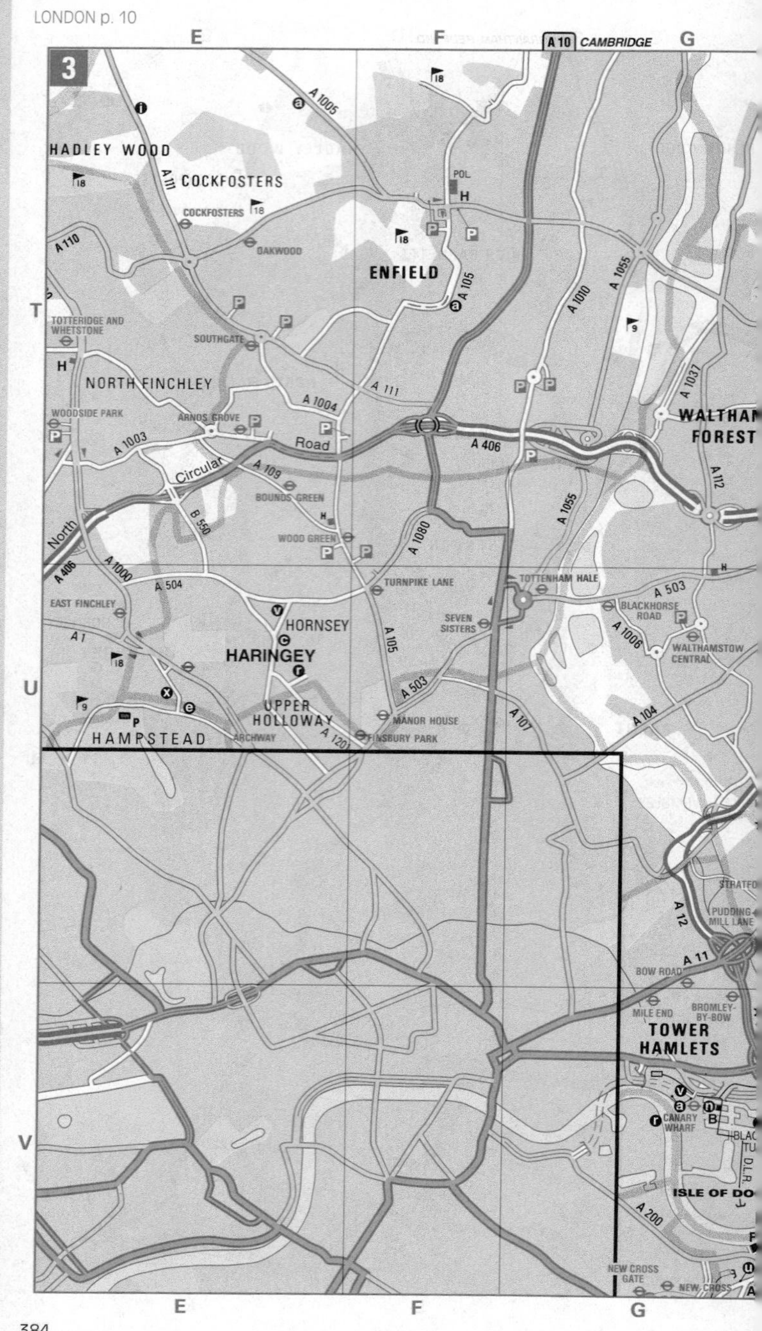
E
F
G
A 10 CAMBRIDGE
3
A 1005
HADLEY WOOD
A 111
COCKFOSTERS
COCKFOSTERS
POL.
H
A 110
OAKWOOD
ENFIELD
A 105
A 1010
A 1055
T
TOTTERIDGE AND WHETSTONE
SOUTHGATE
H
NORTH FINCHLEY
A 111
A 1004
A 1037
WOODSIDE PARK
ARNOS GROVE
WALTHAM FOREST
A 1003
Road
A 406
Circular
A 109
BOUNDS GREEN
A 112
B 550
A 1055
North
WOOD GREEN
A 1080
A 406
A 1000
A 504
TURNPIKE LANE
TOTTENHAM HALE
A 503
EAST FINCHLEY
BLACKHORSE ROAD
HORNSEY
SEVEN SISTERS
A 1
A 105
A 1006
WALTHAMSTOW CENTRAL
HARINGEY
U
A 503
UPPER HOLLOWAY
MANOR HOUSE
A 107
A 104
HAMPSTEAD
ARCHWAY
A 1201
FINSBURY PARK
A 12
PUDDING MILL LANE
A 11
BOW ROAD
MILE END
BROMLEY-BY-BOW
TOWER HAMLETS
CANARY WHARF
B
V
D.L.R.
ISLE OF DO
A 200
NEW CROSS GATE
NEW CROSS
E
F
G

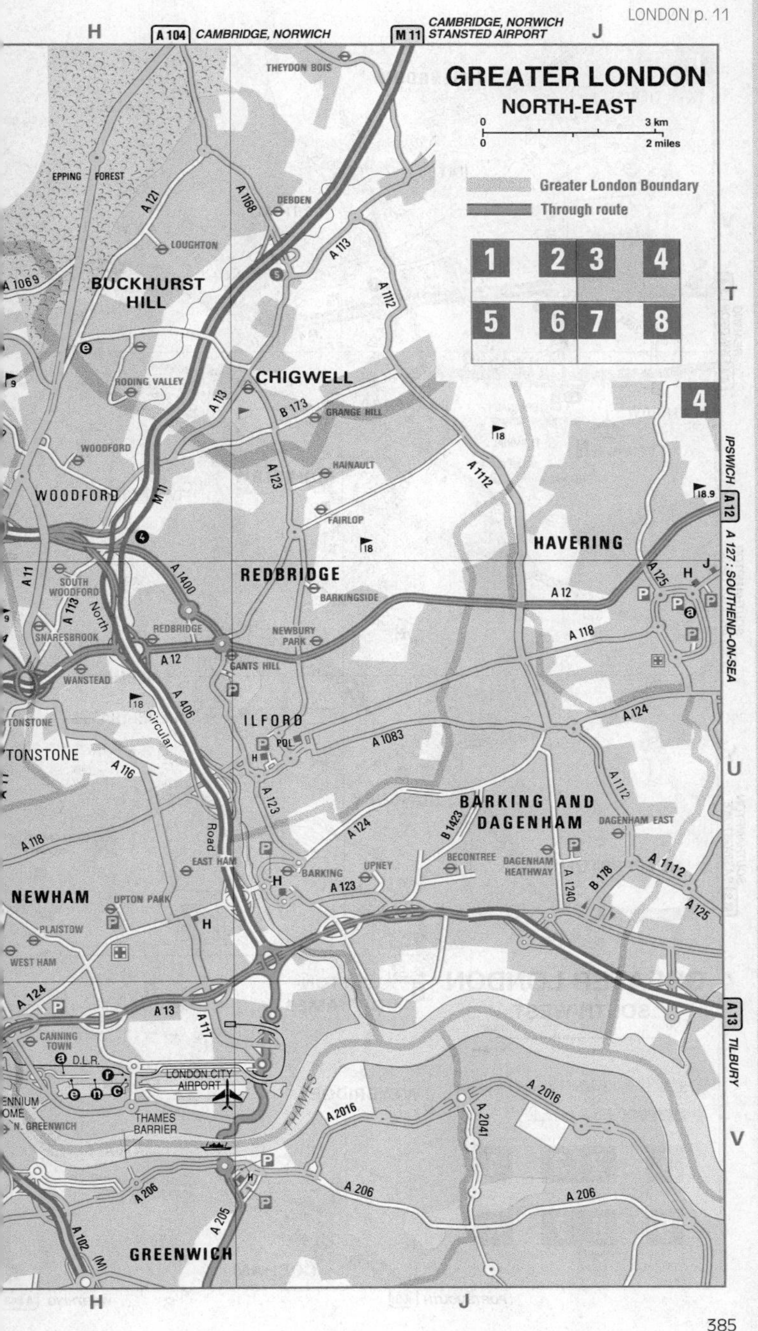
GREATER LONDON
NORTH-EAST
0 3 km
0 2 miles
Greater London Boundary
Through route
A 104 CAMBRIDGE, NORWICH
M 11 CAMBRIDGE, NORWICH STANSTED AIRPORT
THEYDON BOIS
EPPING FOREST
DEBDEN
LOUGHTON
BUCKHURST HILL
RODING VALLEY
CHIGWELL
GRANGE HILL
WOODFORD
HAINAULT
FAIRLOP
HAVERING
REDBRIDGE
SOUTH WOODFORD
SNARESBROOK
BARKINGSIDE
NEWBURY PARK
GANTS HILL
WANSTEAD
North Circular Road
ILFORD
BARKING AND DAGENHAM
DAGENHAM EAST
BECONTREE
DAGENHAM HEATHWAY
EAST HAM
BARKING
UPNEY
NEWHAM
UPTON PARK
PLAISTOW
WEST HAM
CANNING TOWN
D.L.R.
LONDON CITY AIRPORT
THAMES BARRIER
N. GREENWICH
THAMES
GREENWICH
IPSWICH A 12
A 127 : SOUTHEND-ON-SEA
A 13 TILBURY
A 12
A 118
A 124
A 1083
A 1112
A 125
A 123
A 113
A 1400
A 406
A 116
A 2016
A 2041
A 206
A 205
A 102 (M)
A 117
B 173
B 1423
B 178
A 1240
A 1168
A 121
A 1069
A 11
M 11

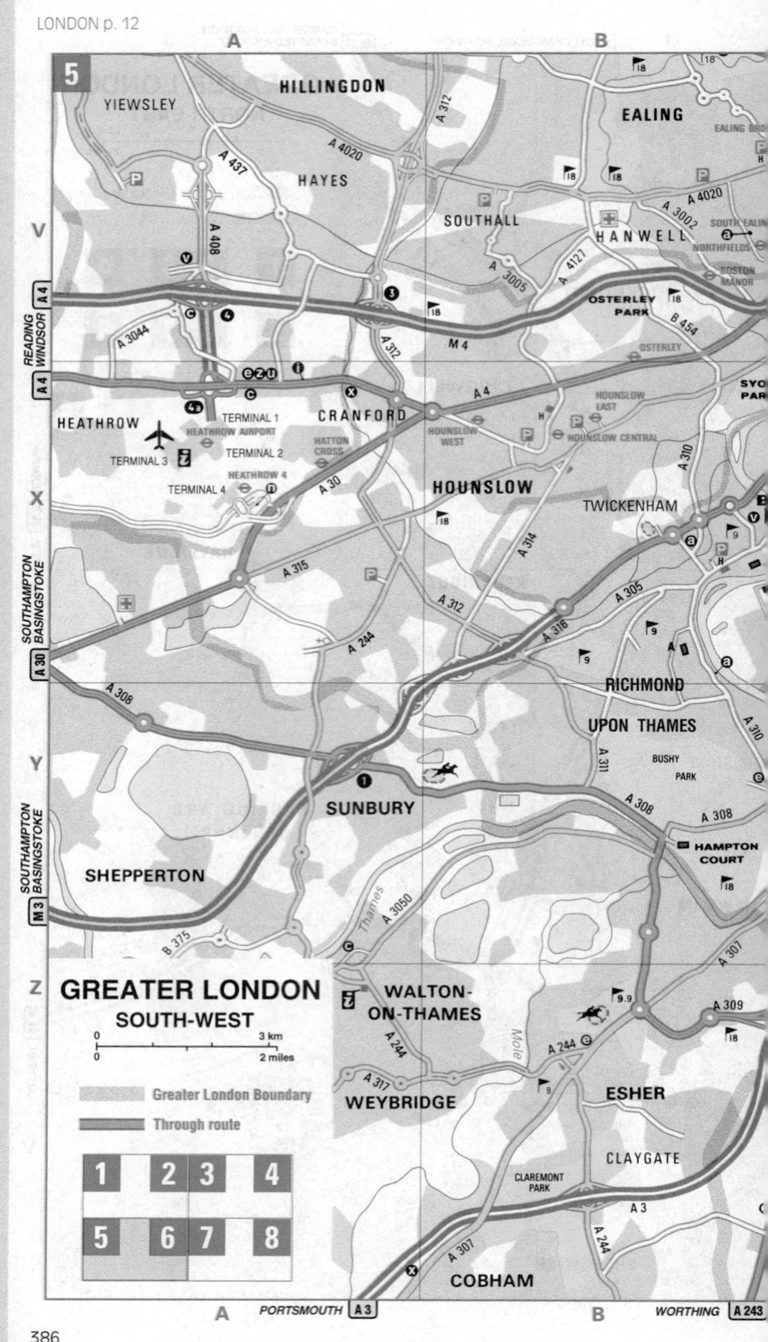

5
HILLINGDON
YIEWSLEY
EALING
HAYES
SOUTHALL
HANWELL
OSTERLEY PARK
M 4
HEATHROW
HEATHROW AIRPORT
TERMINAL 1
TERMINAL 2
TERMINAL 3
TERMINAL 4
CRANFORD
HOUNSLOW
TWICKENHAM
RICHMOND
UPON THAMES
BUSHY PARK
SUNBURY
SHEPPERTON
HAMPTON COURT
WALTON-ON-THAMES
WEYBRIDGE
ESHER
CLAYGATE
CLAREMONT PARK
COBHAM
READING WINDSOR
SOUTHAMPTON BASINGSTOKE
PORTSMOUTH A 3
WORTHING A 243
GREATER LONDON
SOUTH-WEST
0 3 km
0 2 miles
Greater London Boundary
Through route
1 2 3 4
5 6 7 8

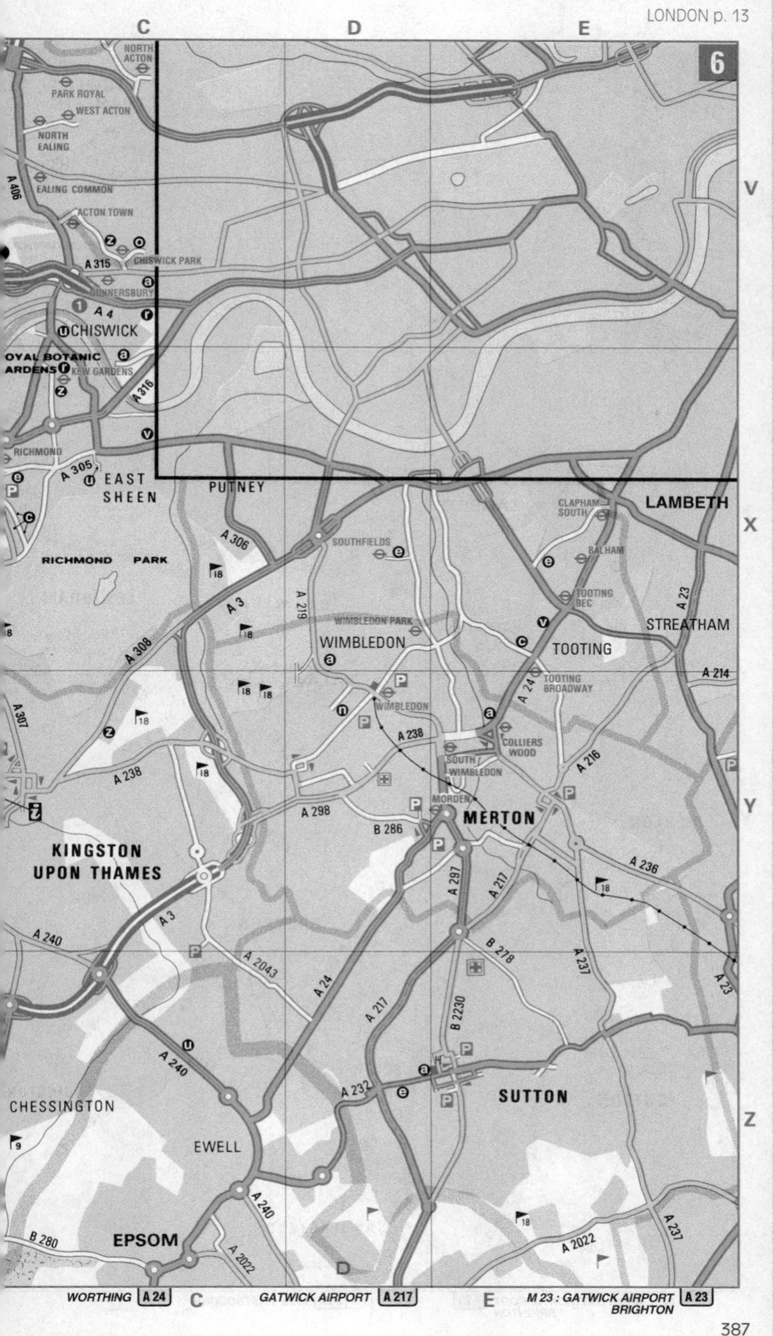
C
D
E
6
V
X
Y
Z
NORTH ACTON
PARK ROYAL
WEST ACTON
NORTH EALING
A 406
EALING COMMON
ACTON TOWN
A 315
CHISWICK PARK
GUNNERSBURY
A 4
CHISWICK
OYAL BOTANIC
ARDENS
KEW GARDENS
A 316
RICHMOND
A 305
EAST
SHEEN
PUTNEY
A 306
SOUTHFIELDS
RICHMOND PARK
A 3
A 219
WIMBLEDON PARK
WIMBLEDON
A 308
A 307
WIMBLEDON
A 238
SOUTH WIMBLEDON
MORDEN
A 298
B 286
MERTON
KINGSTON
UPON THAMES
A 297
A 217
A 240
A 2043
A 24
B 278
A 237
CHESSINGTON
A 232
SUTTON
B 2230
EWELL
EPSOM
B 280
A 2022
LAMBETH
CLAPHAM SOUTH
BALHAM
TOOTING BEC
A 23
STREATHAM
TOOTING
A 214
TOOTING BROADWAY
COLLIERS WOOD
A 216
A 236
WORTHING A 24
GATWICK AIRPORT A 217
M 23 : GATWICK AIRPORT A 23
BRIGHTON

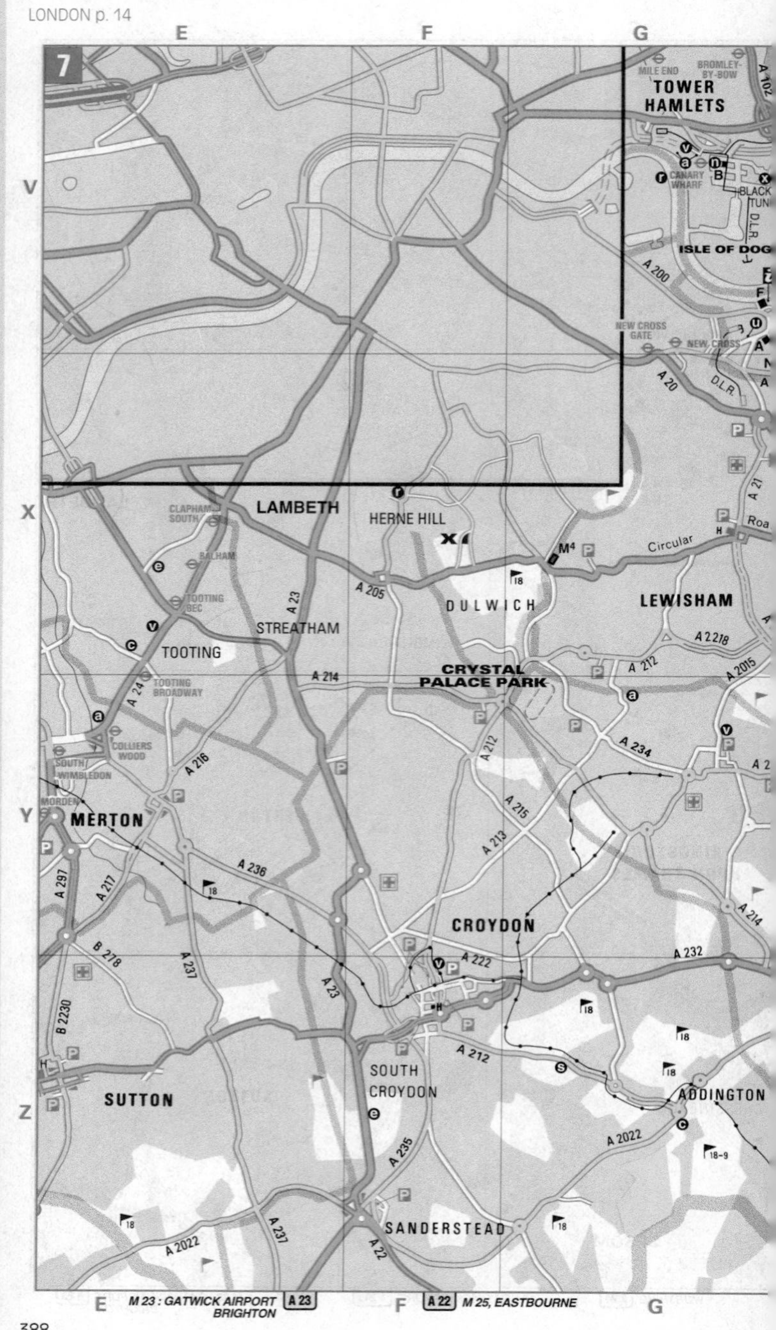
E
F
G
7
V
X
Y
Z
MILE END
BROMLEY-BY-BOW
TOWER HAMLETS
CANARY WHARF
ISLE OF DOGS
A 200
NEW CROSS GATE
NEW CROSS
A 20
D.L.R.
CLAPHAM SOUTH
LAMBETH
HERNE HILL
BALHAM
TOOTING BEC
A 23
A 205
DULWICH
LEWISHAM
Circular
STREATHAM
TOOTING
A 2218
CRYSTAL PALACE PARK
A 212
A 2015
A 214
TOOTING BROADWAY
A 24
COLLIERS WOOD
SOUTH WIMBLEDON
A 216
A 234
A 215
A 213
MORDEN
MERTON
A 236
A 297
A 217
CROYDON
A 214
B 278
A 237
A 222
A 232
B 2230
A 212
SOUTH CROYDON
SUTTON
ADDINGTON
A 2022
A 235
SANDERSTEAD
A 2022
A 237
A 22
M 23 : GATWICK AIRPORT BRIGHTON
A 23
A 22
M 25, EASTBOURNE

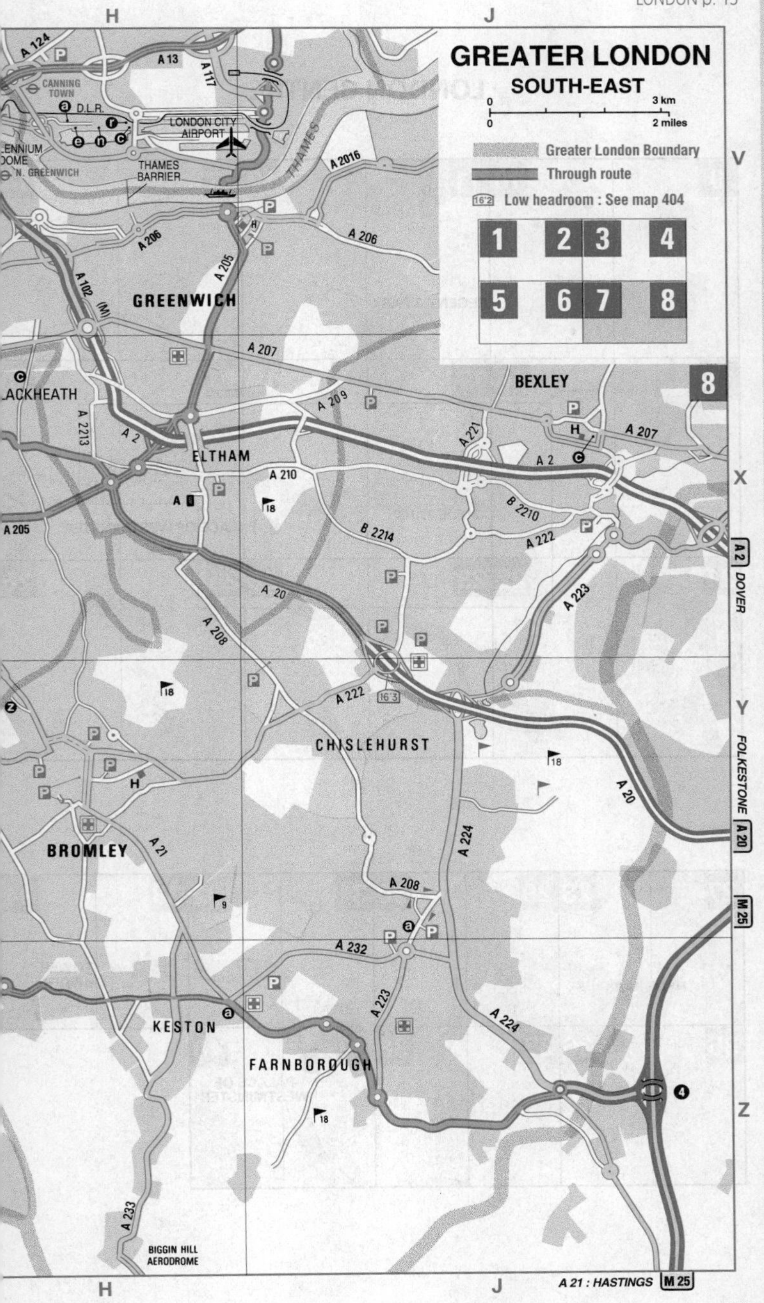
GREATER LONDON
SOUTH-EAST
0
3 km
0
2 miles
Greater London Boundary
Through route
16'2 Low headroom : See map 404
1 2 3 4
5 6 7 8
H
J
V
X
Y
Z
GREENWICH
ELTHAM
BEXLEY
CHISLEHURST
BROMLEY
KESTON
FARNBOROUGH
CANNING TOWN
D.L.R.
LONDON CITY AIRPORT
THAMES BARRIER
THAMES
N. GREENWICH
BIGGIN HILL AERODROME
A 2 DOVER
FOLKESTONE A 20
M 25
A 21 : HASTINGS M 25

LONDON CENTRE

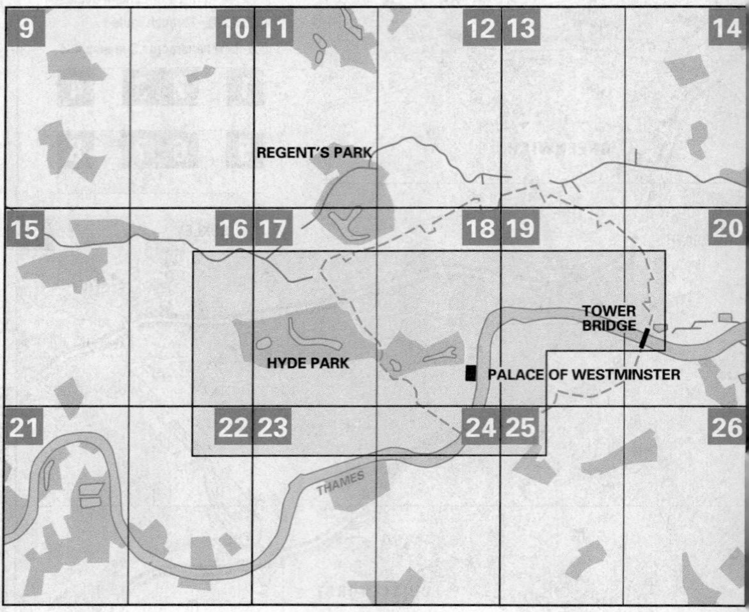

9
10
11
12
13
14
REGENT'S PARK
15
16
17
18
19
20
TOWER BRIDGE
HYDE PARK
PALACE OF WESTMINSTER
21
22
23
24
25
26
THAMES

27
28
29
30
31
32
33
34
HYDE PARK
THAMES
TOWER BRIDGE
35
36
37
38
39
40
PALACE OF WESTMINSTER

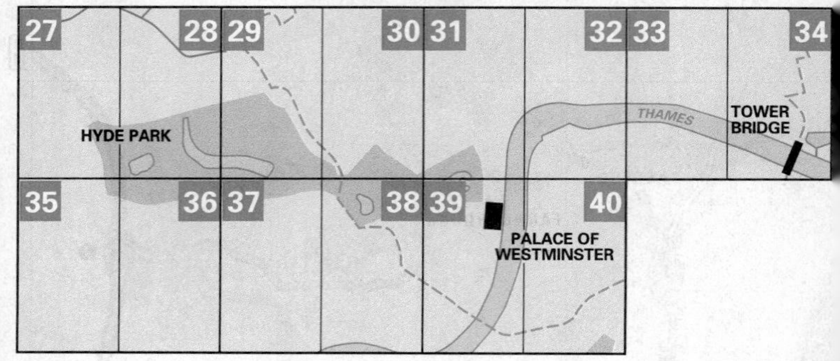

INDEX OF STREET NAMES IN LONDON CENTRE

Oxford Gardens . . . . 16 MZD
Royal Crescent . . . . . 16 MZE 371
St Ann's Rd. . . . . 16 MZE
St Mark's Rd. . . . . 16 MZD
Shirland Rd . . . . 16 NZD
Sinclair Rd . . . . 16 MZE
Sixth Ave. . . . . 16 MZC
Sutherland Ave . . . . . 16 NZD
Walterton Rd. . . . . . . 16 NZD 347
Warwick Ave. . . . . . . 16 OZD
West Cross Route . . 16 MZE

PLAN 17

Allsop Pl. . . . . 17 OZD 4
Blomfield Rd . . . . 17 OZD
Broadley St . . . . 17 PZD
Clifton Gardens. . . . . 17 PZD
Frampton St . . . . 17 PZD
Hall Rd. . . . . 17 PZC
Lisson Grove. . . . . 17 PZD
Maida Ave. . . . . 17 PZD
North Carriage Drive. 17 PZE
Park Rd . . . . 17 QZD
Rossmore Rd . . . . 17 QZD
St John's Wood Rd . . 17 PZD
Warrington Crescent 17 OZD 348

PLAN 18

Bernard St. . . . . 18 SZD 25
Chester Rd . . . . 18 RZC
Euston Rd. . . . . 18 RZD
Fitzroy Square . . . . . . 18 RZD
Great Ormond St . . . . 18 SZD
Guilford St. . . . . 18 SZD
Herbrand St. . . . . 18 SZD 218
Hunter St. . . . . 18 SZD 233
Judd St . . . . 18 SZC
Park Crescent . . . . . . 18 RZD 28
Robert St. . . . . 18 RZC
Russell Square . . . . . 18 SZD
Sidmouth St . . . . 18 SZD 385
Tavistock Pl. . . . . 18 SZD
Tavistock Square. . . . 18 SZD 409
Upper Woburn Pl. . . . 18 SZD 432
Woburn Pl. . . . . 18 SZD

PLAN 19

Bath St . . . . 19 VZC
Beech St . . . . 19 VZD
Borough Rd. . . . . 19 UZE
Bowling Green Lane 19 UZD 43
Bunhill Row. . . . . 19 VZD
Calthorpe St . . . . 19 TZD 65
Central St . . . . 19 VZC
Chiswell St . . . . 19 VZD
City Rd. . . . . 19 VZC
Clerkenwell Rd . . . . . 19 UZD 474
Corporation Row . . . 19 UZD 110
Dufferin St. . . . . 19 VZD 141
Elephant and Castle
Shopping Centre. . . 19 UZF
Falmouth Rd . . . . 19 VZE
Fann St . . . . 19 VZD 166
Goswell Rd . . . . 19 UZC
Great Dover St . . . . . 19 VZE
Harper Rd . . . . 19 VZE
King's Cross Rd . . . . 19 TZC
Lever St. . . . . 19 VZC
Lloyd Baker St . . . . . 19 UZC 265
Long Lane
SOUTHWARK. . . . 19 VZE
Merrick Square . . . . . 19 VZE
Moreland St . . . . 19 VZC 293
Myddelton St . . . . . . 19 UZC 296
New Kent Rd . . . . . . 19 VZF
Newington
Causeway . . . . 19 VZE 307
Old St . . . . 19 VZD
Paul St. . . . . 19 VZD
Percival St . . . . 19 UZD
Pilgrimage St. . . . . . . 19 VZE 349
Rosebery Ave . . . . . . 19 UZD
St John St . . . . 19 UZC
Suffolk St. . . . . 19 VZE
Tabard St. . . . . 19 VZE 408
Trinity Church Square 19 VZE
Trinity St. . . . . 19 VZE
Whitecross St . . . . . . 19 VZD
Worship St . . . . 19 VZD

PLAN 20

Abbey St . . . . 20 XZE
Appold St . . . . 20 XZD 5
Back Church Rd . . . . 20 XZD
Bermondsey St. . . . . 20 XZE
Bethnal Green Rd. . . 20 XZD
Bigland St . . . . 20 YZD
Brady St. . . . . 20 YZD
Brick Lane . . . . 20 XZD
Brunel Rd . . . . 20 YZE
Cable St. . . . . 20 YZD
Cambridge Heath Rd 20 YZD
Cannon Street Rd. . . . 20 YZD
Cavell St . . . . 20 YZD
Cephas St . . . . 20 YZD
Cheshire St . . . . 20 XZD
Christian St . . . . 20 YZD
Clements Rd. . . . . 20 YZE
Club Row . . . . 20 XZD
Commercial Rd. . . . . 20 YZD
Curtain Rd . . . . 20 XZD 126
Dock St . . . . 20 XZD
Drummond Rd . . . . . 20 YZE
Fielgate St . . . . 20 XZD
Globe Rd . . . . 20 YZC
Grange Rd. . . . . 20 XZE
Great Eastern St . . . . 20 XZD 192
Highway (The). . . . . . 20 YZE
Jamaica Rd . . . . 20 XZE
Jublilee St . . . . 20 YZD
Lower Rd . . . . 20 YZE
Luke St . . . . 20 XZD
Mile End Rd . . . . 20 YZD
New Rd. . . . . 20 YZD
Old Montague St . . . 20 XZD
Pages Walk. . . . . 20 XZF
Redman's Rd . . . . . . 20 YZD
Roman Rd. . . . . 20 YZC
Rovel Rd . . . . 20 XZE 75
Salter Rd . . . . 20 YZE
Sclater St. . . . . 20 XZD 470
Shoreditch High St . . 20 XZD 384
Sidney St. . . . . 20 YZD
Spa Rd. . . . . 20 XZE
Stepney Way . . . . 20 YZD
Surrey Quay's Rd . . . 20 YZE 377
Tarling St . . . . 20 YZD
Thomas Moore St . . 20 XZE 365
Turin St . . . . 20 XZC
Vallance Rd . . . . 20 YZD
Vaughan Way . . . . . . 20 XZE
Wapping High St . . . 20 YZE
Wapping Lane . . . . . 20 YZE
Wapping Wall . . . . . . 20 YZE
Whitechapel Rd . . . . 20 XZD

PLAN 21

Banin St. . . . . 21 LZF
Barnes High St . . . . . 21 KZH 404
Bath Rd . . . . 21 KZF
Brook Green . . . . 21 LZF
Burlington Lane . . . . 21 KZG
Castelnau . . . . 21 LZG
Chancellor's Rd. . . . . 21 LZG 21
Chiswick High Rd . . . 21 KZG
Chiswick Lane . . . . . 21 KZG
Chiswick Mall . . . . . . 21 KZG
Church Rd RICHMOND
UPON THAMES . . . . 21 KZH
Dailing Rd . . . . 21 LZF 13
Devonshire Rd . . . . . 21 KZG
Dorchester Grove . . . 21 KZG 402
Dover House Rd. . . . 21 LZH
Erpingham Rd . . . . . . 21 LZH
Ferry Rd. . . . . 21 KZG
Glenthorne Rd . . . . . 21 LZF
Great West Rd . . . . . 21 KZG
Gwendolen Ave . . . . 21 LZH
Hammersmith Bridge
Rd . . . . 21 LZG 431
Hammersmith
Bridge . . . . 21 LZG
Hertford Ave . . . . 21 KZH
Hotham Rd . . . . 21 LZH
Howards Lane . . . . . 21 LZH
King St
HAMMERSMITH . 21 KZG
Lonsdale Rd . . . . 21 KZG
Lower Richmond Rd 21 LZH
Mill Hill Rd. . . . . 21 KZH
Prebend Gardens . . . 21 KZF
Priory Lane . . . . 21 KZH
Queen's Ride Lower 21 LZH
Rainville Rd . . . . 21 LZG
Rannoch Rd . . . . 21 LZG
Rocks Lane . . . . 21 LZH
Roehampton Lane . . 21 KZH
Station Rd . . . . 21 KZH
Stevenage Rd . . . . . . 21 LZG
Suffolk Rd . . . . 21 KZG
Talgarth Rd . . . . 21 LZG
Terrace (The). . . . . . 21 KZH
Turnham Green
Terrace. . . . . 21 KZG 389
Upper Richmond Rd
West . . . . 21 KZH
Upper Richmond Rd 21 LZH
Verdun Rd . . . . 21 KZG
Vine Rd . . . . 21 KZH
White Hart Lane . . . . 21 KZH

PLAN 22

Armoury Way . . . . . . 22 NZH 7
Bagley's Lane . . . . . . 22 OZH
Baron's Court Rd . . . 22 MZG
Bishop's Park Rd. . . . 22 MZH
Bishops Rd . . . . 22 NZG
Broomhouse Lane . . 22 NZH
Carnwath Rd. . . . . . . 22 NZH
Charlwood Rd. . . . . . 22 MZH
Clancarty Rd . . . . . . 22 NZH
Crabtree Lane . . . . . 22 MZG 164
Dawes Rd . . . . 22 MZG
Disraeli Rd . . . . 22 MZH
Edith Rd. . . . . 22 MZG
Estcourt Rd . . . . 22 MZG 203
Fairfield St . . . . 22 OZH 165
Fawe Park Rd . . . . . . 22 MZH
Filmer Rd. . . . . 22 MZG
Finlay St. . . . . 22 MZH
Fulham High St. . . . . 22 MZH 172
Fulham Palace Rd. . . 22 MZG
Gliddon Rd . . . . 22 MZG 182
Greyhound Rd . . . . . 22 MZG
Gunterstone Rd . . . . 22 MZG
Halford Rd. . . . . 22 NZG
Hammersmith Rd. . . 22 MZG
Harwood Rd . . . . 22 NZG
Hugon Rd . . . . 22 NZH
Hurlingham Rd . . . . 22 NZH
Munster Rd. . . . . 22 MZG
Musard Rd . . . . 22 MZG
New King's Rd . . . . . 22 NZH
Oakhill Rd . . . . 22 NZH

PLAN 33

PLAN 34

PLAN 35

PLAN 36

Gloucester Rd . . . . . . 36 **ACX**
Grenville Pl. . . . . 36 **ACY**
Harcourt Terrace . . . . 36 **ACZ** 477
Harrington Gardens . 36 **ACY**
Harrington Rd . . . . . . 36 **ADY**
Hollywood Rd . . . . . . 36 **ACZ**
Hyde Park Gate . . . . 36 **ACX**
Kensington Gore . . . . 36 **ACX**
King's Rd . . . . 36 **ADZ**
Launceston Pl. . . . . . 36 **ACX** 259
Little Boltons (The) . . 36 **ACZ**
Manresa Rd . . . . 36 **ADZ**
Neville Terrace . . . . . 36 **ADZ** 300
Old Church St . . . . . . 36 **ADZ**
Onslow Gardens . . . 36 **ADZ**
Onslow Square . . . . . 36 **ADY**
Palace Gate . . . . 36 **ACX**
Park Walk . . . . 36 **ACZ**
Pelham St . . . . 36 **ADY**
Prince Consort Rd . . 36 **ADX**
Prince's Gardens. . . . 36 **ADX** 356
Queen's Gate
Gardens . . . . 36 **ACY** 198
Queen's Gate Pl. . . . . 36 **ACY** 363
Queen's Gate
Terrace. . . . . 36 **ACX**
Queen's Gate . . . . . . 36 **ACX**
Queensberry Pl. . . . . 36 **ADY** 360
Redcliffe Rd . . . . 36 **ACZ**
Roland Gardens . . . . 36 **ACZ**
South Parade . . . . . . 36 **ADZ**
Stanhope Gardens . . 36 **ACY**
Sumner Pl. . . . . 36 **ADY**
Sydney Pl. . . . . 36 **ADY** 405
Thurloe Pl. . . . . 36 **ADY**
Thurloe Square . . . . . 36 **ADY**
Tregunter Rd . . . . . . 36 **ACZ**
Vale (The) . . . . 36 **ADZ**
Victoria Grove . . . . . . 36 **ACX**
Victoria Rd
KENSINGTON. . . . . 36 **ACX**
Wetherby Gardens . . 36 **ACY**

PLAN 37

Basil St . . . . 37 **AFX**
Beauchamp Pl. . . . . . 37 **AFX**
Belgrave Square . . . . 37 **AGX**
Bourne St . . . . 37 **AGY**
Bray Pl. . . . . 37 **AFY** 45
Britten St . . . . 37 **AEZ**
Brompton Rd . . . . . . 37 **AFX**
Cadogan Gardens . . . 37 **AGY** 23
Cadogan Gate . . . . . . 37 **AGY** 220
Cadogan Pl. . . . . 37 **AGY**
Cadogan Square . . . . 37 **AGY**
Cadogan St . . . . 37 **AFY**
Carriage Rd (The) . . . 37 **AFX**
Chelsea Bridge Rd . . 37 **AGZ**
Chelsea
Embankment . . . . 37 **AGZ**
Chelsea Manor St. . . 37 **AFZ**
Cheltenham Terrace. 37 **AGZ**
Chesham Pl. . . . . 37 **AGX**
Chesham St . . . . 37 **AGY**
Chester Row . . . . 37 **AGY**
Cheval Pl. . . . . 37 **AFX**
Christchurch St . . . . . 37 **AFZ**
Draycott Ave . . . . 37 **AFY**
Draycott Pl. . . . . 37 **AFY**
Eaton Pl. . . . . 37 **AGY**
Egerton Gardens
Mews . . . . 37 **AFY** 162
Egerton Gardens . . . 37 **AFY** 160
Egerton Terrace . . . . 37 **AFY** 161
Elystan Pl. . . . . 37 **AFZ**
Elystan St . . . . 37 **AEY**
Ennismore Gardens . 37 **AEX**
Flood St . . . . 37 **AFZ**
Franklin's Row . . . . . 37 **AGZ**

Glebe Pl. . . . . 37 **AEZ**
Grosvenor Crescent . 37 **AGX**
Hans Crescent . . . . . 37 **AFX**
Hans Pl. . . . . 37 **AFX**
Hans Rd . . . . 37 **AFX**
Harriet St . . . . 37 **AGX** 214
Hasker St . . . . 37 **AFY**
Holbein Mews . . . . . 37 **AGZ** 223
Holbein Pl. . . . . 37 **AGY**
Ixworth Pl. . . . . 37 **AEY**
Jubilee Pl. . . . . 37 **AFZ**
Knightsbridge . . . . . . 37 **AFX**
Lennox Gardens
Mews . . . . 37 **AFY** 263
Lennox Gardens . . . . 37 **AFY**
Lower Sloane St . . . . 37 **AGY**
Lowndes Square . . . 37 **AGX**
Lowndes St . . . . 37 **AGX**
Lyall St . . . . 37 **AGY**
Markham St . . . . 37 **AFZ**
Milner St . . . . 37 **AFY**
Montpelier Square . . 37 **AFX**
Montpelier St . . . . . . 37 **AFX**
Moore St . . . . 37 **AFY**
Mossop St . . . . 37 **AFY**
Oakley St. . . . . 37 **AEZ**
Ormonde Gate . . . . . 37 **AGZ** 329
Pimlico Rd . . . . 37 **AGZ**
Pont St . . . . 37 **AFY**
Radnor Walk . . . . 37 **AFZ**
Rawlings St . . . . 37 **AFY**
Redesdale St . . . . . . 37 **AFZ** 367
Royal Hospital Rd . . . 37 **AFZ**
Rutland Gate . . . . 37 **AEX**
St Leonard's Terrace. 37 **AGZ**
Shawfield St . . . . 37 **AFZ**
Sloane Ave . . . . 37 **AFY**
Sloane Square . . . . . 37 **AGY**
Sloane St . . . . 37 **AGX**
Smith St . . . . 37 **AFZ**
South Terrace . . . . . . 37 **AEY**
Sydney St . . . . 37 **AEZ**
Symons St . . . . 37 **AGY** 407
Tedworth Square . . . 37 **AFZ**
Tite St . . . . 37 **AFZ**
Trevor Pl. . . . . 37 **AFX**
Trevor Square . . . . . 37 **AFX**
Walton St . . . . 37 **AFY**
West Halkin St . . . . . 37 **AGX**
Whiteheads . . . . 37 **AFY**
William St . . . . 37 **AGX** 468
Wilton Pl. . . . . 37 **AGX**

PLAN 38

Alderney St . . . . 38 **AIY**
Belgrave Pl. . . . . 38 **AHX**
Belgrave Rd . . . . 38 **AIY**
Birdcage Walk . . . . . . 38 **AIX**
Bressenden Pl. . . . . . 38 **AIX**
Buckingham Gate . . . 38 **AIX**
Buckingham Palace
Rd . . . . 38 **AHY**
Carlisle Pl. . . . . 38 **AIY**
Castle Lane . . . . 38 **AIX**
Chapel St
BELGRAVIA . . . . . 38 **AHX**
Charlwood St . . . . . . 38 **AIZ**
Chelsea Bridge . . . . . 38 **AHZ**
Chester Square . . . . . 38 **AHY**
Chester St . . . . 38 **AHX**
Churchill Gardens Rd 38 **AIZ**
Clarendon St . . . . 38 **AIZ**
Constitution Hill . . . . 38 **AHX**
Cumberland St . . . . . 38 **AIZ**
Denbigh St . . . . 38 **AIZ**
Duke
of Wellington Pl. . . 38 **AHX** 142
Eaton Square . . . . . . 38 **AHY**
Ebury Bridge Rd . . . . 38 **AHZ**

Ebury Bridge . . . . 38 **AHZ**
Ebury St . . . . 38 **AHY**
Eccleston Bridge . . . . 38 **AHY** 157
Eccleston Square . . . 38 **AIY**
Eccleston St . . . . 38 **AHY**
Elizabeth St . . . . 38 **AHY**
Francis St . . . . 38 **AIY**
Gillingham St . . . . 38 **AIY**
Gloucester St . . . . . . 38 **AIZ**
Grosvenor Gardens . 38 **AHX**
Grosvenor Pl. . . . . . . 38 **AHX**
Grosvenor Rd . . . . . . 38 **AHZ**
Guildhouse St . . . . . . 38 **AIY** 201
Halkin St . . . . 38 **AHX**
Hobart Pl. . . . . 38 **AHX**
Hudson's Pl. . . . . 38 **AIY**
Hugh St . . . . 38 **AIY**
Lower Belgrave St . . 38 **AHY**
Lower Grosvenor Pl. 38 **AIX** 274
Lupus St . . . . 38 **AIZ**
Palace St . . . . 38 **AIX**
St George's Drive . . . 38 **AIY**
South Eaton Pl. . . . . . 38 **AHY**
Sutherland St . . . . . . 38 **AHZ**
Terminus Pl. . . . . 38 **AIY** 412
Upper Belgrave St . . 38 **AHX**
Vauxhall Bridge Rd . . 38 **AIY**
Victoria St . . . . 38 **AIX**
Warwick Square . . . . 38 **AIY**
Warwick Way . . . . . . 38 **AHZ**
Wilton Rd . . . . 38 **AIY**
Wilton St . . . . 38 **AHX**

PLAN 39

Abingdon St . . . . 39 **AKY**
Albert Embankment . 39 **ALY**
Artillery Row . . . . 39 **AKX** 8
Atterbury St. . . . . 39 **ALZ**
Aylesford St . . . . 39 **AKZ**
Bessborough
Gardens . . . . 39 **AKZ**
Bessborough St . . . . 39 **AKZ** 30
Bridge St . . . . 39 **ALX**
Broad Sanctuary . . . . 39 **ALX** 52
Caxton St . . . . 39 **AKX**
Chichester St . . . . . . 39 **AJZ**
Claverton St . . . . 39 **AJZ**
Dolphin Square . . . . . 39 **AJZ**
Douglas St . . . . 39 **AKY**
Erasmus St . . . . 39 **AKY**
Glasshouse St
LAMBETH . . . . 39 **ALZ** 108
Great College St . . . . 39 **ALX**
Great George St . . . . 39 **AKX** 193
Great Peter St . . . . . . 39 **AKY**
Great Smith St . . . . . 39 **AKX**
Greencoat Pl. . . . . . . 39 **AJY**
Greycoat Pl. . . . . 39 **AKY** 200
Greycoat St . . . . 39 **AKY**
Horseferry Rd . . . . . . 39 **AKY**
Howick Pl. . . . . 39 **AJY**
John Islip St . . . . 39 **AKZ**
King Charles St . . . . . 39 **AKX**
Lambeth Bridge . . . . . 39 **ALY**
Marsham St . . . . 39 **AKY**
Millbank . . . . 39 **ALZ**
Monck St. . . . . 39 **AKY**
Montpelier Walk . . . . 37 **AFX**
Moreton St . . . . 39 **AJZ**
Nine Elms Lane . . . . 39 **AKZ**
Old Pye St . . . . 39 **AKX**
Page St . . . . 39 **AKY**
Palmer St . . . . 39 **AKX**
Parlament Square . . . 39 **ALX**
Parliament St . . . . . . 39 **ALX**
Parry St . . . . 39 **ALZ** 341
Petty France . . . . 39 **AJX**
Ponsonby Pl. . . . . 39 **AKZ**
Rampayne St . . . . . . 39 **AKZ**

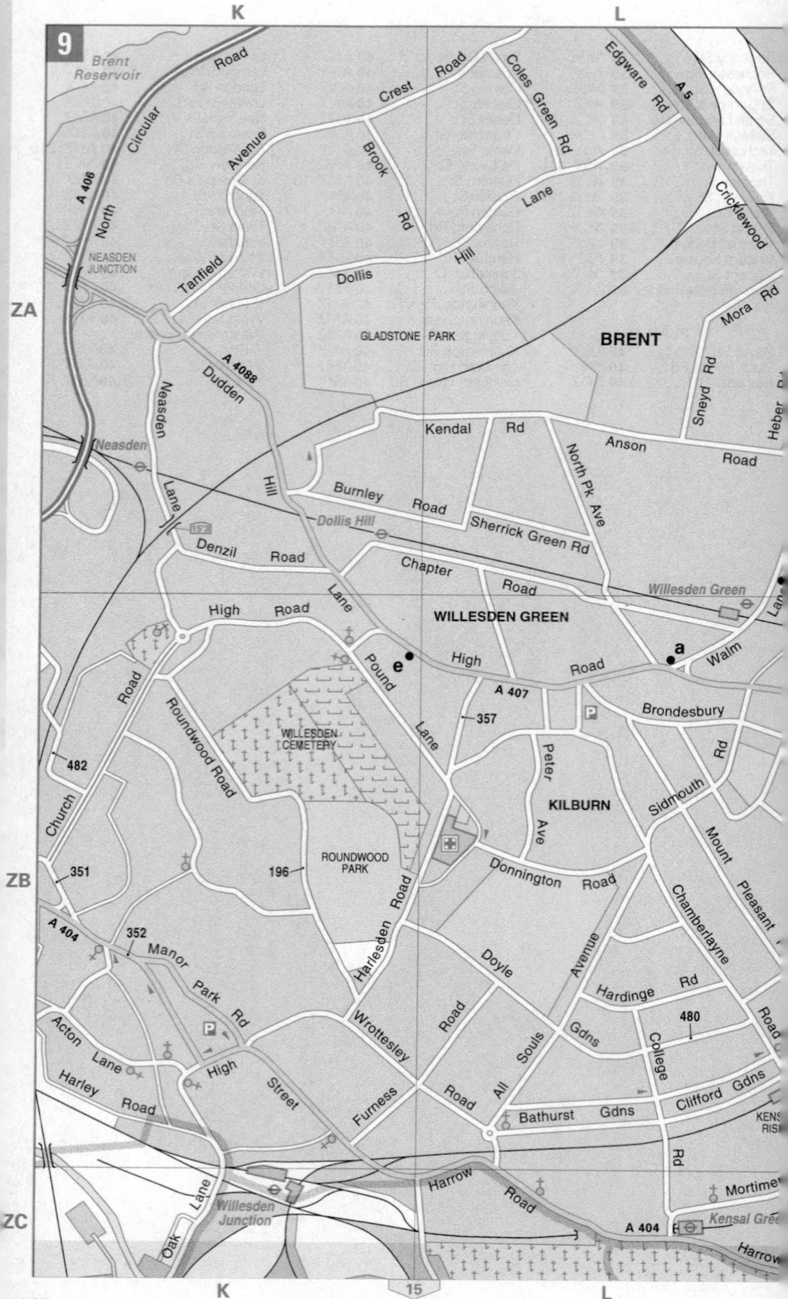

K
L
9
Brent Reservoir
North Circular Road
A 406
Crest Road
Coles Green Rd
Edgware Rd
A 5
Avenue
Brook Rd
Lane
Hill
Dollis
Tanfield
NEASDEN JUNCTION
Cricklewood
ZA
Mora Rd
GLADSTONE PARK
BRENT
A 4088
Dudden
Neasden
Sneyd Rd
Heber
Kendal Rd
Anson Road
North Pk Ave
Neasden
Burnley Road
Lane
Dollis Hill
Sherrick Green Rd
Denzil Road
Chapter Road
Willesden Green
High Road
Lane
WILLESDEN GREEN
a
Walm
e
High Road
Pound
A 407
Brondesbury
357
Road
Roundwood Road
WILLESDEN CEMETERY
Lane
Peter
Rd
482
KILBURN
Sidmouth
Church
Ave
Mount
ROUNDWOOD PARK
Donnington Road
ZB
351
196
Chamberlayne
Pleasant
Harlesden Road
A 404
352
Manor Park Rd
Doyle
Avenue
Hardinge Rd
Wrottesley
Road
480
Road
Gdns
College
Acton Lane
Souls
All
High
Street
Clifford Gdns
Harley Road
Furness
Road
Bathurst Gdns
KENS RISE
Rd
Harrow
Road
Mortimer
Lane
Willesden Junction
ZC
Oak
A 404
Kensal Gre
Harrow
K
15
L

M
N
O
10
0
500 m
0
500 yards
CHILD'S HILL
BARNET
475
476
477
478
479
335
336
Hendon Way
A 41
Finchley Rd
Claremont Road
The Vale
Cricklewood La.
Hermitage La.
West Heath Road
Lyndale Ave
Platt's La.
Redington Road
FENTON HOUS
Lower
CRICKLEWOOD
Cricklewood Lane
Lichfield Rd
Finchley Road
U
Heath Drive
Frognal
ZA
A 407
Anson Rd
Westbere Rd
West End Lane
Frognal Lane
Shoot Up Hill
Mill Lane
Crediton Hill
Finchley Road
A 41
Arkwrig
Lane
gnmouth Road
FINCHLEY ROAD AND FROGNAL
Road
WEST HAMPSTEAD
Rd
Chatsworth Road
Kilburn
Iverson
West Hampstead
Finchley Road
11
Broadhurst Gdns
Willesden Lane
A 4003
Park
Mapesbury Avenue
Cavendish Ave
14'9
15'9
BRONDESBURY
West End Lane
Road
Fairhazel
Canfield
Greencroft
Gdns
Dyne Rd
Kilburn
A 5
Gascony Ave
FINCHLEY ROAD
Avenue
Christchurch
Willesden Lane
High Road
Abbey Road
Road
ZB
The
BRONDESBURY PARK
PADDINGTON CEMETERY
Quex Rd
Priory
Belsize
Bounda
Salusbury Rd
Kingswood Ave
Road
Tiverton Rd
Road
KILBURN HIGH ROAD
a
Abb
Brondesbury Road
Brondesbury Villas
c
Greville Pl.
Carlton
QUEEN'S PARK
Milman Rd
Kilburn Park
Road
Road
Hamilton
Chevening
POL
Queen's Park
Randolph
Maida Vale
Harvist
Lane
Carlton
Vale
Chamberlayne Rd
Kilburn
Bravington
Fernhead
Ave
Avenue
Kilburn Park
Ave
Avenue
ZC
Maida Vale
Elgin
Randol
16

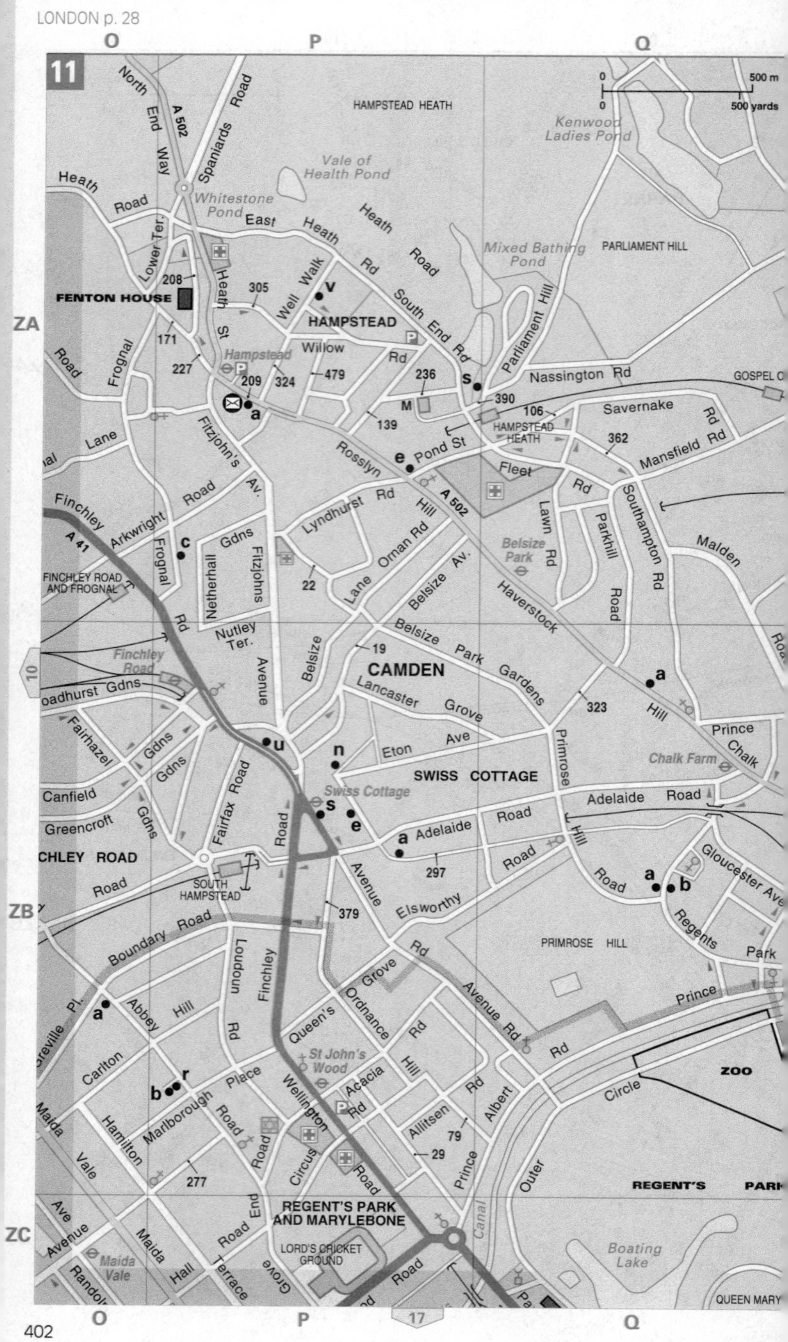
11
HAMPSTEAD HEATH
Kenwood Ladies Pond
Vale of Health Pond
Whitestone Pond
Mixed Bathing Pond
PARLIAMENT HILL
FENTON HOUSE
HAMPSTEAD
Hampstead
Belsize Park
CAMDEN
SWISS COTTAGE
Swiss Cottage
Chalk Farm
Finchley Road
FINCHLEY ROAD AND FROGNAL
SOUTH HAMPSTEAD
PRIMROSE HILL
St John's Wood
ZOO
REGENT'S PARK
REGENT'S PARK AND MARYLEBONE
LORD'S CRICKET GROUND
Maida Vale
Boating Lake
QUEEN MARY
HAMPSTEAD HEATH
GOSPEL O
500 m
500 yards

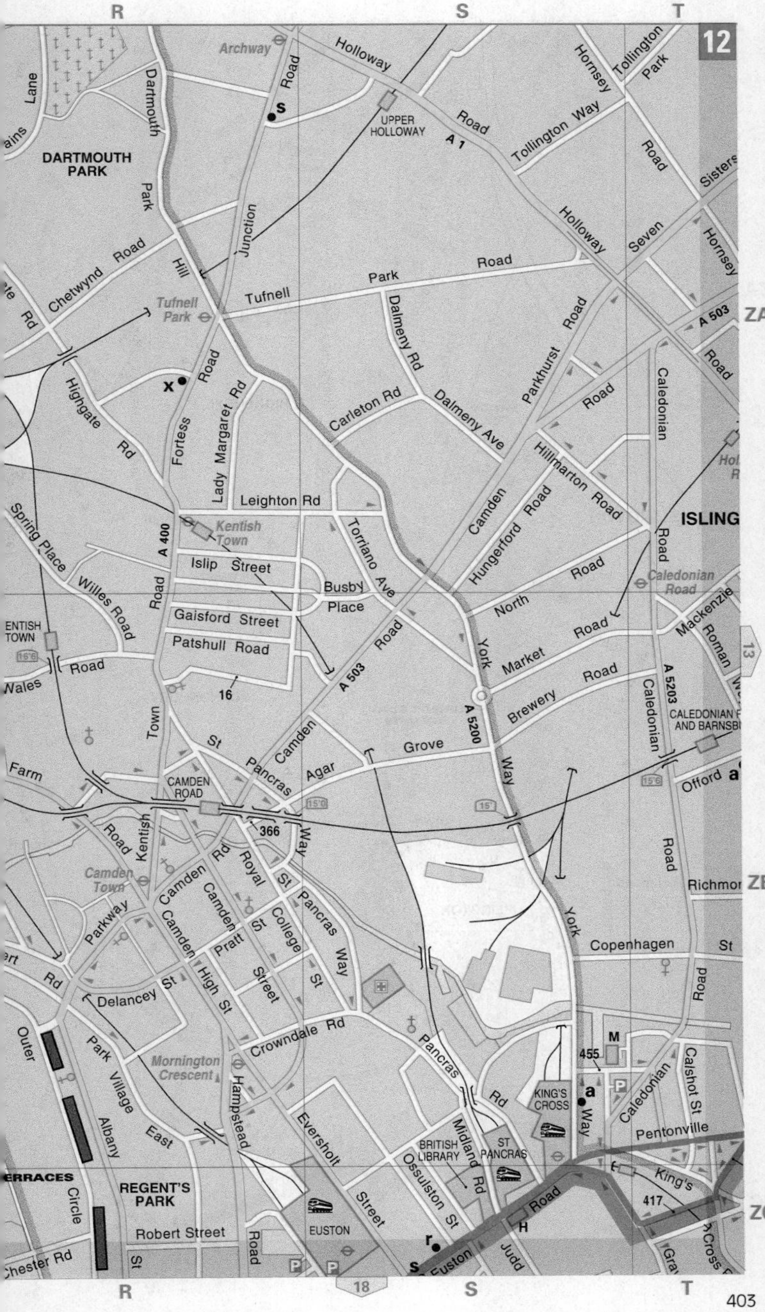

R S T

12

Archway
Holloway Road
UPPER HOLLOWAY
A 1
Hornsey Road
Tollington Park
Tollington Way
Junction Road
Dartmouth Park Hill
DARTMOUTH PARK
Lane
Chetwynd Road
Tufnell Park
Tufnell Park Road
Dalmeny Rd
Dalmeny Ave
Parkhurst Road
Seven Sisters Road
Hornsey Road
Holloway Road
A 503
ZA
Caledonian Road
Highgate Rd
Fortess Road
Lady Margaret Rd
Carleton Rd
Hillmarton Road
Leighton Rd
Kentish Town
Torriano Ave
Camden Road
Hungerford Road
ISLING
Spring Place
A 400
Islip Street
Busby Place
Caledonian Road
Willes Road
Gaisford Street
North Road
Mackenzie
Roman
KENTISH TOWN
Patshull Road
Market Road
York Way
A 503
13
Wales Road
16
Brewery Road
A 5203
A 5200
CALEDONIAN AND BARNSB
Kentish Town Road
St Pancras Way
Agar Grove
Farm
CAMDEN ROAD
Offord
366
Camden Town
Camden Rd
Royal College St
Richmon
ZB
Parkway
Camden High St
Pratt St
Copenhagen St
Delancey St
Crowndale Rd
Outer Circle
Park Village East
Mornington Crescent
Hampstead Road
Pancras Rd
455
M
KING'S CROSS
Caledonian Road
Calshot St
Pentonville Road
Albany Street
Eversholt Street
Midland Rd
BRITISH LIBRARY
ST PANCRAS
Ossulston St
King's Cross
417
ZC
REGENT'S PARK
TERRACES
Robert Street
EUSTON
Euston Road
Judd
Gray
Chester Rd
18

R S T

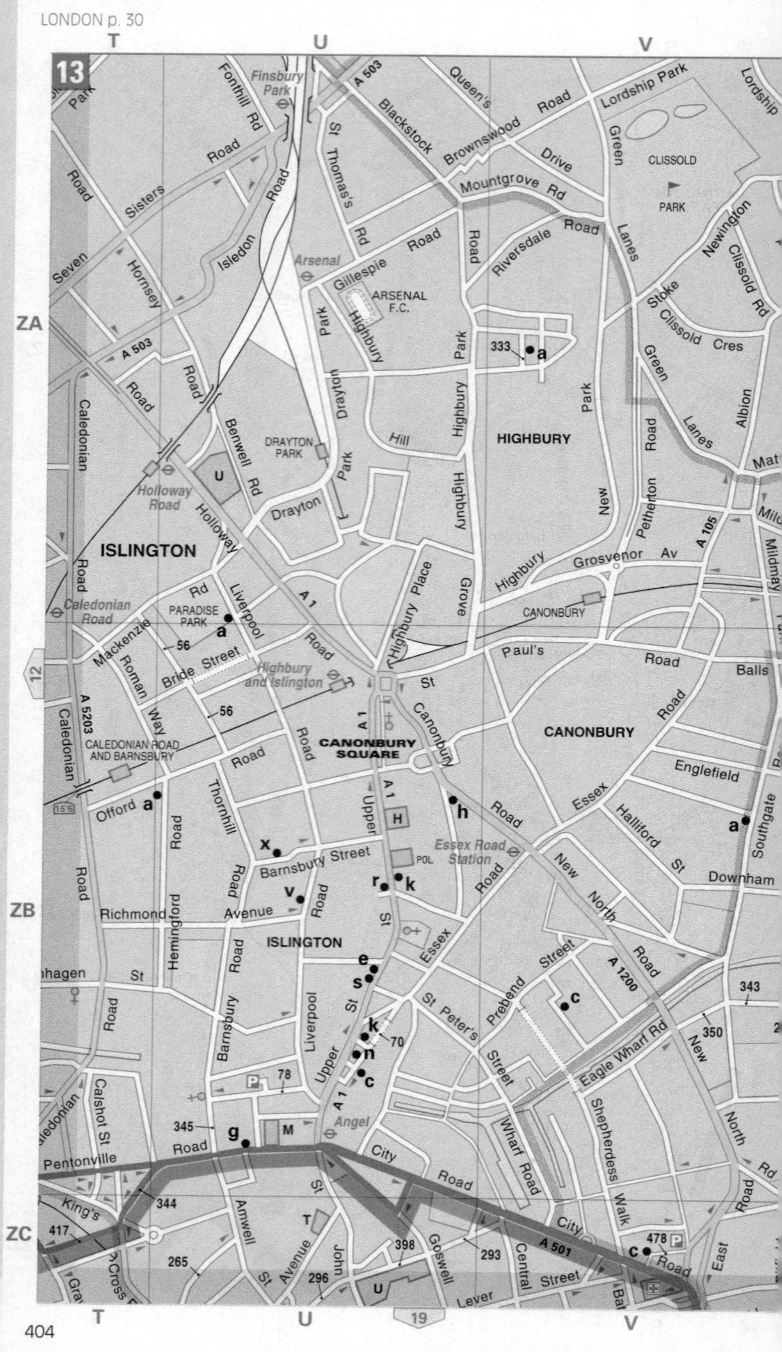
13
T
U
V
ZA
ZB
ZC
ISLINGTON
HIGHBURY
CANONBURY
CANONBURY SQUARE
ARSENAL F.C.
CLISSOLD PARK
DRAYTON PARK
PARADISE PARK
CALEDONIAN ROAD AND BARNSBURY
Finsbury Park
Arsenal
Holloway Road
Caledonian Road
Highbury and Islington
Essex Road Station
Angel
Seven Sisters Road
Hornsey Road
Isledon Road
Fonthill Rd
St Thomas's Rd
Blackstock Road
Queen's Drive
Brownswood Road
Lordship Park
Mountgrove Rd
Riversdale Road
Gillespie Road
Highbury Park
Highbury Hill
Highbury Grove
Highbury Place
Drayton Park
Benwell Rd
Holloway Road
Caledonian Road
Liverpool Road
Mackenzie Rd
Roman Way
Bride Street
Offord Road
Thornhill Road
Barnsbury Street
Richmond Avenue
Hemingford Road
Barnsbury Road
Upper St
Essex Road
New North Road
St Paul's Road
Grosvenor Av
Petherton Road
New Park
Green Lanes
Stoke Newington
Clissold Rd
Clissold Cres
Albion
Englefield
Halliford St
Essex Road
Downham
Southgate
Balls
Prebend Street
St Peter's Street
Eagle Wharf Rd
Wharf Road
Shepherdess Walk
City Road
Pentonville Road
King's Cross
Calshot St
Amwell St
St John St
Goswell
Central Street
Lever
East Road
New North Rd
A 503
A 1
A 5203
A 105
A 1200
A 501
12
19
333
56
343
350
70
78
345
344
417
265
296
398
293
478

X
Y
14
STOKE NEWINGTON
Kyverdale Road
Northwold Road
Upper Clapton Road
A 107
Mount Pleasant Hill
500 m
500 yards
Cleveleys Road
Lea Bridge Road
A 104
Chatsworth Road
Rectory Road
Maury Road
Brooke Road
Evering Rd
Kenninghall Road
RECTORY ROAD
Clapton Way
Lower Clapton
Millfields Road
High Street
A 10
Amhurst
Downs Rd
Nevill Road
Walford Rd
HACKNEY
HACKNEY DOWNS
378
Powerscroft Road
Prince George Rd
Barretts Grv
Newington
Shacklewell La
Cecilia
Downs Park Road
Pembury Rd
Clifden Rd
Median
Boleyn
Amhurst
Sandringham Road
Dalston Lane
Lower Clapton Rd
A 102
Homerton High Street
DALSTON KINGSLAND
Ridley Rd
HACKNEY DOWNS
HACKNEY CENTRAL
337
Stoke
Morning Lane
Dalston Lane
Graham Road
Forest Road
Richmond Road
Mare Street
A 107
Well Street
Frampton Park Rd
Cassland Rd
Richmond Road
Lansdowne Drive
LONDON FIELDS
Middleton Road
Queensbridge Road
Albion Drive
Kingsland Road
Well Street
ZA
ZB
ZC
DALSTON
Pownall Rd
Sheep Lane
Mare
Victoria Park Road
464
Nuttall St
Whiston Road
Pritchard's Rd
VICTORIA PARK
Sewardstone Rd
Bishop's Way
Bonner Rd
HAGGERSTON PARK
GEFFRYE MUSEUM
Hackney Road
CAMBRIDGE HEATH
Ford Rd
Old Road
Warner Pl.
Hoxton
Columbia
Green
Canrobert St
B 119
Road
Old Bethnal Green Road
M
Roman Road
Bethnal Green
Globe
Turin
A 1209
20

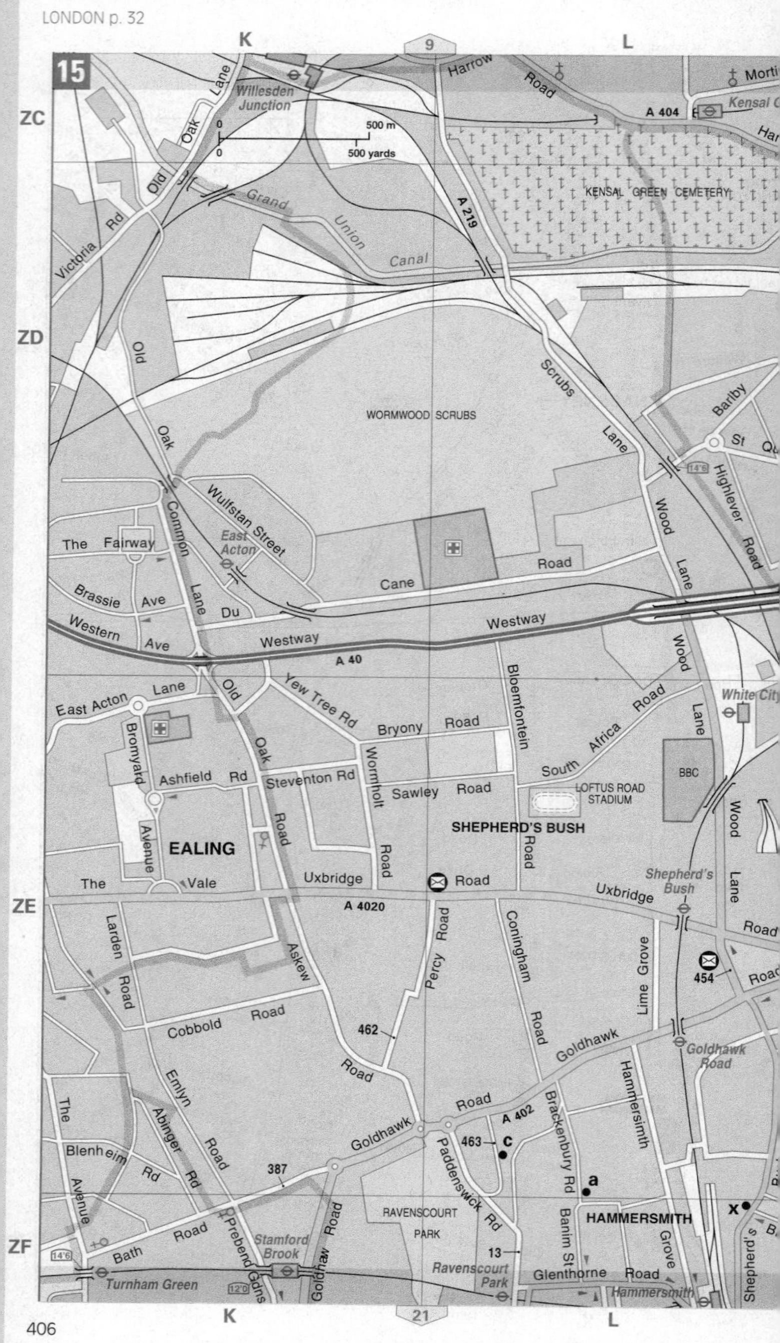
K
9
L
15
ZC
ZD
ZE
ZF
Harrow Road
A 404
Kensal Green Cemetery
Willesden Junction
Old Oak Lane
Victoria Rd
Grand Union Canal
A 219
500 m
500 yards
Old Oak Common Lane
Scrubs Lane
Wormwood Scrubs
Barlby
St
Highlever Road
Wood Lane
Wulfstan Street
East Acton
The Fairway
Brassie Ave
Du Cane Road
Western Ave
Westway
A 40
East Acton Lane
Yew Tree Rd
Bryony Road
Bloemfontein Road
South Africa Road
White City
BBC
Loftus Road Stadium
Bromyard Avenue
Ashfield Rd
Steventon Rd
Wormholt Road
Sawley Road
Shepherd's Bush
Ealing
The Vale
Uxbridge Road
A 4020
Larden Road
Askew Road
Percy Road
Coningham Road
Lime Grove
454
Cobbold Road
462
Goldhawk Road
A 402
Emlyn Road
Abinger Rd
The Avenue
Blenheim Rd
387
463
c
Paddenswick Rd
Brackenbury Rd
a
Hammersmith Grove
Hammersmith
x
Shepherd's Bush
Ravenscourt Park
Bath Road
Prebend Gdns
Stamford Brook
Goldhawk Road
13
Banim St
Glenthorne Road
Turnham Green
Hammersmith
21

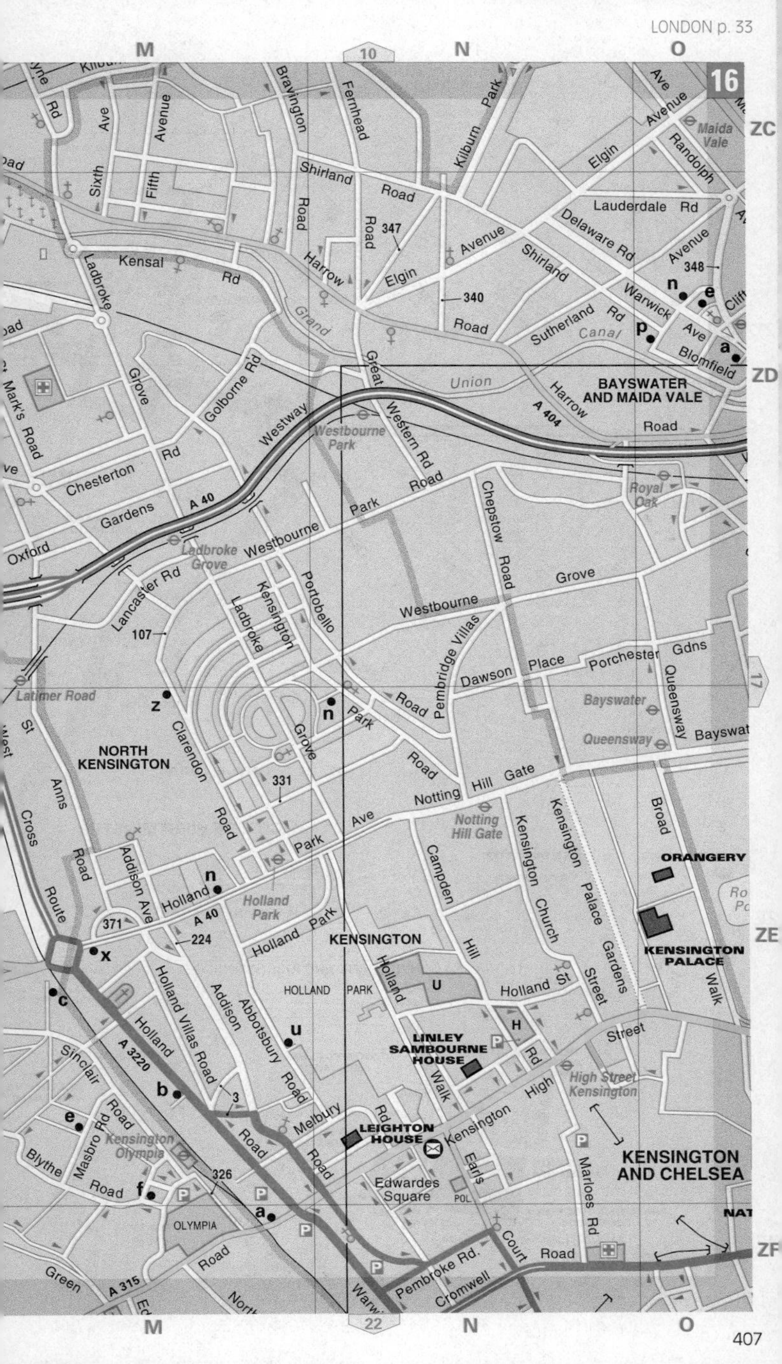
M
10
N
O
16
ZC
ZD
ZE
ZF
17
22
Maida Vale
Randolph
Elgin
Avenue
Kilburn
Park
Bravington
Fernhead
Shirland
Road
Sixth
Ave
Fifth
Avenue
Rd
Lauderdale Rd
Delaware Rd
Avenue
348
Kensal
Rd
Ladbroke
Harrow
Road
347
Elgin
Avenue
Shirland
Warwick
Ave
340
Road
Sutherland
Rd
Canal
Grand
Union
Blomfield
Great
Western Rd
BAYSWATER
AND MAIDA VALE
Harrow
A 404
Road
Grove
Golborne Rd
Westway
Westbourne
Park
Mark's Road
Chesterton
Rd
Gardens
A 40
Park
Road
Royal
Oak
Chepstow
Road
Oxford
Ladbroke
Grove
Westbourne
Lancaster Rd
Kensington
Ladbroke
Portobello
Grove
Westbourne
107
Pembridge Villas
Dawson
Place
Porchester
Gdns
Queensway
Bayswater
Queensway
Latimer Road
St
NORTH
KENSINGTON
Clarendon
Road
Grove
Park
Road
331
Notting
Hill
Gate
Notting
Hill Gate
Kensington
Church
Kensington
Palace
Gardens
Broad
Walk
ORANGERY
KENSINGTON
PALACE
Anns
Cross
Road
Route
Addison Ave
Holland
Park
Ave
Holland
Park
A 40
371
224
Holland
Park
KENSINGTON
Campden
Hill
HOLLAND
PARK
Holland
Holland
St
Street
Holland Villas Road
Holland
A 3220
Addison
Abbotsbury
Road
Sinclair
Road
LINLEY
SAMBOURNE
HOUSE
Walk
Rd
Street
High
High Street
Kensington
Kensington
Masbro Rd
Blythe
Road
Kensington
Olympia
Road
Melbury
Road
Rd
LEIGHTON
HOUSE
Edwardes
Square
POL
Earls
Court
Marloes Rd
KENSINGTON
AND CHELSEA
326
OLYMPIA
Road
Road
Pembroke Rd.
Cromwell
Green
A 315
North
Warwi
NAT

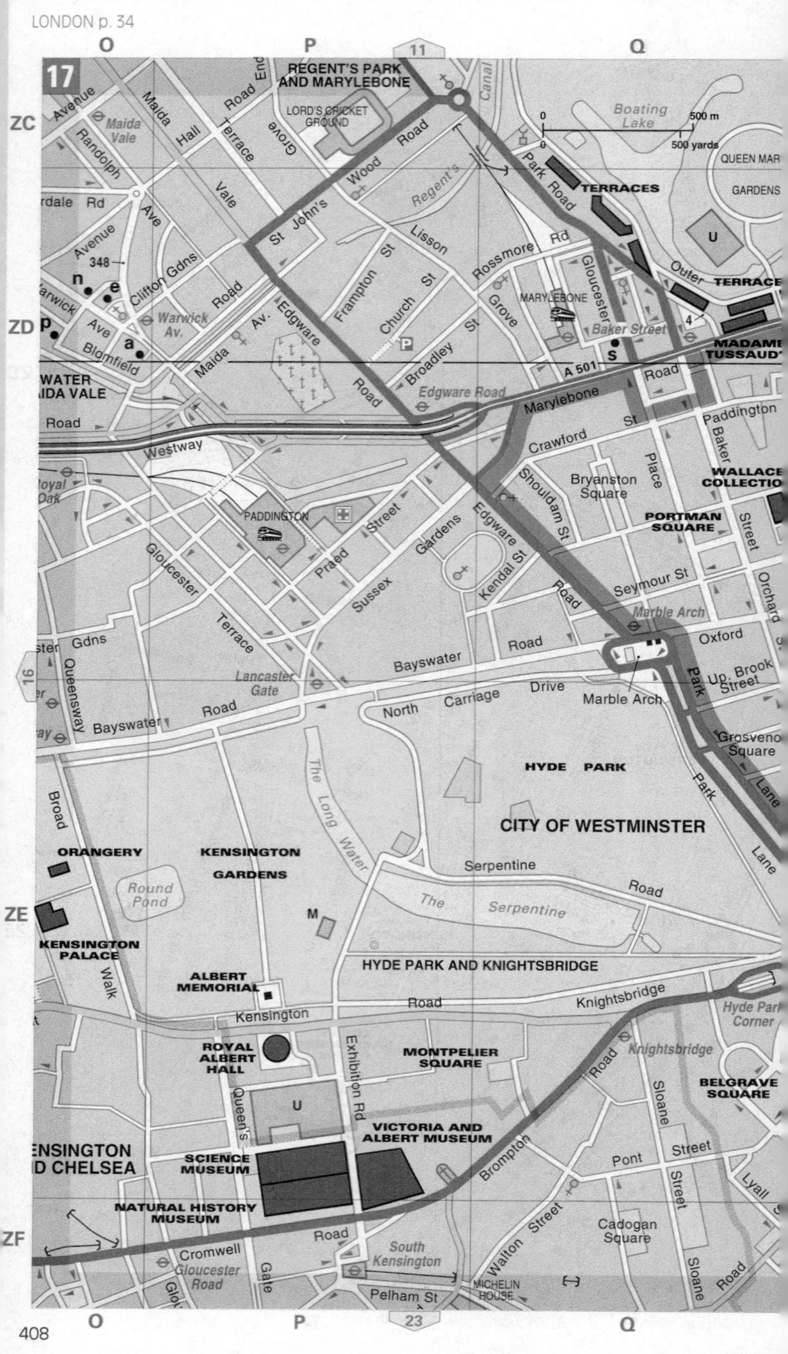
17
REGENT'S PARK AND MARYLEBONE
LORD'S CRICKET GROUND
Boating Lake
QUEEN MARY'S GARDENS
TERRACES
MARYLEBONE
Baker Street
MADAME TUSSAUD'S
PADDINGTON
Edgware Road
Marble Arch
WALLACE COLLECTION
PORTMAN SQUARE
Bryanston Square
Grosvenor Square
Lancaster Gate
HYDE PARK
CITY OF WESTMINSTER
The Serpentine
The Long Water
KENSINGTON GARDENS
ORANGERY
Round Pond
KENSINGTON PALACE
ALBERT MEMORIAL
ROYAL ALBERT HALL
HYDE PARK AND KNIGHTSBRIDGE
MONTPELIER SQUARE
Knightsbridge
Hyde Park Corner
BELGRAVE SQUARE
VICTORIA AND ALBERT MUSEUM
SCIENCE MUSEUM
NATURAL HISTORY MUSEUM
KENSINGTON AND CHELSEA
Cadogan Square
South Kensington
Gloucester Road
MICHELIN HOUSE
A 501
500 m
500 yards

R
12
S
T
18
REGENT'S PARK
Robert Street
EUSTON
Euston Square
A 501
Euston Road
PERCIVAL DAVID FOUNDATION OF CHINESE ART
Tavistock Pl.
CORAM'S FIELDS PLAYGROUND
Great Portland Street
Warren Street
FITZROY SQUARE
BRITISH TELECOM TOWER
Russell Square
Guilford St
Great Ormond St
ZC
ZD
BLOOMSBURY
Theobald's Rd
Red Lion Street
BRITISH MUSEUM
BEDFORD SQUARE
Goodge Street
Tottenham Court Rd
Gower St
Bloomsbury St
Cleveland St
Cavendish Place
Mortimer St
Wells St
Newman St
Percy St
New Oxford St
Holborn
SIR JOHN SOANE'S MUSEUM
Kingsway
Lincoln's Inn Fields
Wigmore Street
Cavendish Square
Oxford Circus
Oxford Street
Tottenham Court Rd
High Holborn
Drury Lane
Great Queen St
Bond Street
NEW BOND STREET
Hannover Square
Great Marlborough Street
Wardour St
Charing Cross Rd
Shaftesbury Ave
ROYAL OPERA HOUSE
Covent Garden
Long Acre
Bow St
Aldwych
SOHO
REGENT STREET
Davies St
Burton St
PICCADILLY CIRCUS
LEICESTER SQUARE
ST PAUL'S
NATIONAL PORTRAIT GALLERY
NATIONAL GALLERY
STRAND
Embankment
Bedford Street
CHARING CROSS
BURLINGTON HOUSE
Berkeley Square
Berkeley Street
Piccadilly
ST JAMES'S
Regent St
TRAFALGAR SQUARE
MAYFAIR
Curzon St
Green Park
ST JAMES'S STREET
Pall Mall
CARLTON HOUSE TERRACE
Northumberland Ave
WHITEHALL
Victoria
SPENCER HOUSE
OLD ADMIRALTY
BRITISH AIRWAYS LONDON EYE
ST JAMES'S PALACE
THE MALL
Horse Guards
HORSE GUARDS
BANQUETING HOUSE
ZE
LANCASTER HOUSE
Constitution Hill
ST JAMES'S PARK
COUNTY HALL
Westminster
WESTMINSTER BRIDGE
Belvedere Road
York
Grosvenor Place
BUCKINGHAM PALACE
Birdcage Walk
ST MARGARET'S
Petty France
St James's Park
Tothill St
PALACE OF WESTMINSTER
ROYAL MEWS
Buckingham Gate
WESTMINSTER ABBEY
NEW SCOTLAND YARD
BELGRAVIA
Bressenden Place
THAMES
Lambeth Palace Rd
Victoria Street
Great Peter street
Millbank
LAMBETH PALACE
WESTMINSTER CATHEDRAL
Rochester Row
Horseferry Road
Lambeth Bridge
Lambeth High St
ZF
VICTORIA
Vauxhall Bridge Road
Regency
Wilton Rd
24

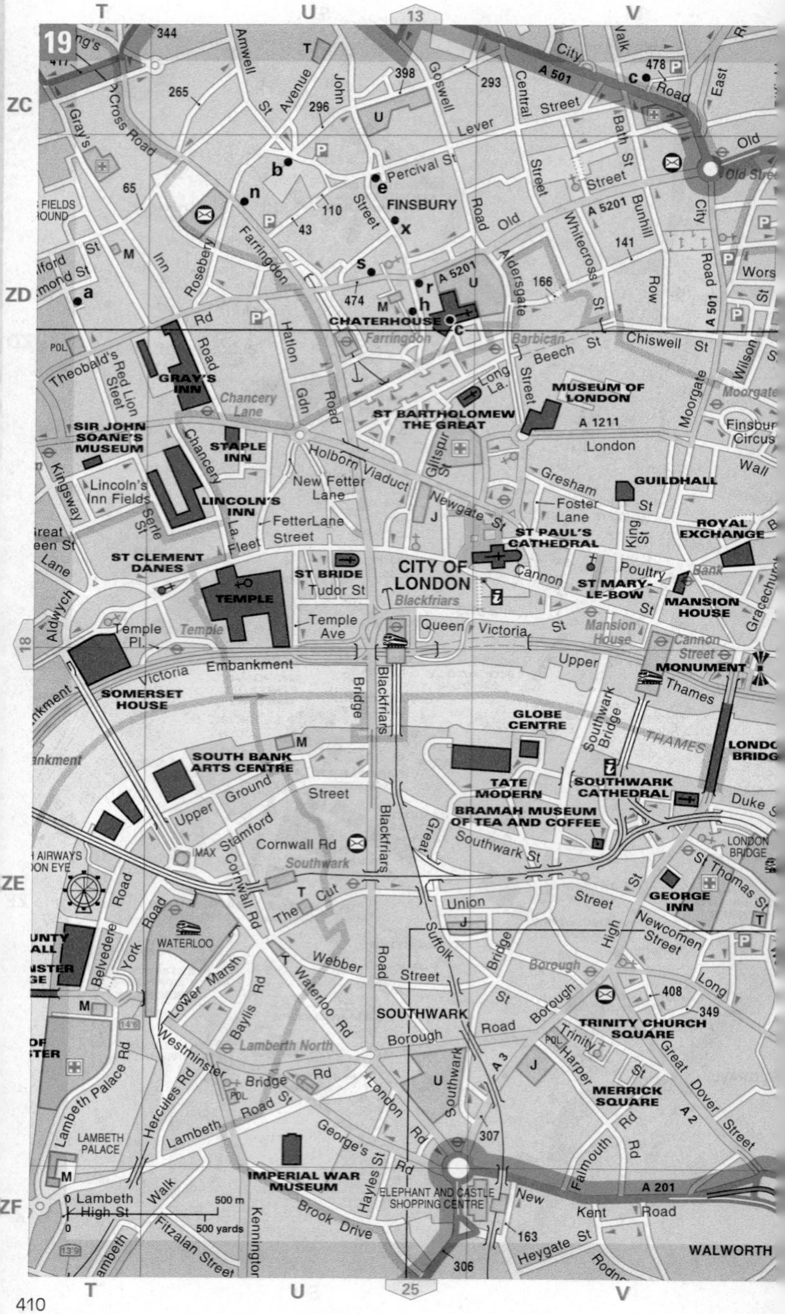
19
FINSBURY
CHATERHOUSE
Farringdon
Barbican
GRAY'S INN
Chancery Lane
MUSEUM OF LONDON
ST BARTHOLOMEW THE GREAT
Moorgate
Finsbury Circus
SIR JOHN SOANE'S MUSEUM
STAPLE INN
Lincoln's Inn Fields
LINCOLN'S INN
GUILDHALL
ROYAL EXCHANGE
ST PAUL'S CATHEDRAL
ST CLEMENT DANES
ST BRIDE
CITY OF LONDON
Blackfriars
ST MARY-LE-BOW
Bank
MANSION HOUSE
Mansion House
TEMPLE
Temple
Cannon Street
MONUMENT
SOMERSET HOUSE
GLOBE CENTRE
THAMES
LONDON BRIDGE
SOUTH BANK ARTS CENTRE
TATE MODERN
SOUTHWARK CATHEDRAL
BRAMAH MUSEUM OF TEA AND COFFEE
IMAX
Southwark
GEORGE INN
WATERLOO
Borough
SOUTHWARK
Lamberth North
TRINITY CHURCH SQUARE
MERRICK SQUARE
LAMBETH PALACE
IMPERIAL WAR MUSEUM
ELEPHANT AND CASTLE SHOPPING CENTRE
WALWORTH
A 501
A 5201
A 1211
A 3
A 2
A 201
500 m
500 yards
Amwell St
Avenue
John
Goswell Road
Central Street
City Road
Lever Street
Percival St
Old Street
Bath St
Bunhill Row
Whitecross St
Aldersgate Street
Farringdon Road
Rosebery Ave
Gray's Inn Road
Theobald's Rd
Red Lion Steet
Hatton Gdn
Chiswell St
Beech St
Long La.
Holborn Viaduct
New Fetter Lane
Fetter Lane
Fleet Street
Newgate St
Giltspur St
Gresham St
Foster Lane
King St
London Wall
Cannon St
Poultry
Queen Victoria St
Upper Thames St
Tudor St
Temple Ave
Temple Pl.
Victoria Embankment
Kingsway
Aldwych
Serle St
Chancery La.
Blackfriars Bridge
Blackfriars Road
Southwark Bridge
Upper Ground
Stamford Street
Cornwall Rd
The Cut
Union Street
Great Suffolk Street
Southwark St
Borough High St
St Thomas St
Newcomen Street
Long Lane
Webber Street
Waterloo Rd
Baylis Rd
Lower Marsh
York Road
Belvedere Road
Westminster Bridge Rd
Lambeth Palace Rd
Hercules Rd
Lambeth Road
Lambeth Walk
Lambeth High St
Fitzalan Street
Kennington
Brook Drive
Hayles St
St George's Rd
London Rd
Southwark Bridge Rd
Borough Road
Trinity St
Harper Rd
Falmouth Rd
Great Dover Street
New Kent Road
Heygate St
Duke St
Gracechurch
Wilson St
Worship St
Old St
East Road
Aldwych
Lincoln's Inn Fields
13
25
18
T
U
V
ZC
ZD
ZE
ZF

X
14
Y
20
ZC
Hoxton
Hackney
Columbia
Old
Bethnal
Green
Canrobert
St
Road
Road
B 119
Roa
M
Roman
Bethnal
Green
Globe
Turin St
Green
A 1209
Vallance
k
384
126
A 10
Club Row
Bethnal
Brick
BETHNAL
GREEN
15'0
Heath
A 107
16'3
Road
St
St
Cheshire
Street
470
P
12'6
Brady
Cambridge
Cephas
Stepney
Green
Commercial
A 1202
14'0
Shoreditch
P
k
Lane
TOWER
HAMLETS
Road
Street
Mile
End
Road
ZD
Bishopsgate
Brushfield St
Brick
Whitechapel
Road
Redman's
Road
St
P
Old Montague St
Whitechapel
A 11
New
Cavell
Sidney
Street
Middlesex
Lane
Stepney
Way
Stepney
Way
Liverpool
Street
Wentworth
St
Fieldgate St
Road
Street
Street
Houndsditch
St
Street
A 13
P
Jubilee
Aldgate East
Commercial
Road
Cannon
Commercial
Road
LLOYD'S
BUILDING
Aldgate
Brahm
Street
Back Church La.
Christian St
Tarling St
Leadenhall St
Minories
Mansell St
Prescot
St
Dock
Bigland St
Street
FENCHURCH
STREET
Shadwell
St
Cable
Street
Cable
Street
MARY
HILL
Tower Hill
Royal Mint
Road
Street
The
Highway
Road
The
Highway
ST DUNSTAN-
IN-THE-EAST
Approach
East Smithfield
Vaughan
TOBACCO
DOCK
Wapping
Garnet
15'9
TOWER OF
LONDON
Tower Bridge
365
Wall
Lower Thames
Street
ST KATHARINE
DOCK
n
St
Wapping
HAY'S GALLERIA
SHOPPING CENTRE
Lane
Way
Street
Wapping
H.M.S. BELFAST
18
TOWER
BRIDGE
Wapping
J
CITY HALL
Shad Thames
High
Tooley
Druid
St
Road
Gainford St
M
Gainford
Street
THAMES
ZE
Rd
Salter
B 205
J
P
Rotherhithe
Street
x
Brunel Rd
Bermondsey
a
Druid
Street
A 200
Bermondsey
Canada Water
Bridge
Abbey Street
Jamaica
St
Road
Drummond
Southwark
Lower
St
A 200
377
CALEDONIAN
MARKET
Grange
H
Road
75
James
Road
Tower
c
Walk
Spa
Clements
Rd
Park
369
Road
Road
Surrey
Quays
ZF
Pages
Willow
Road
Road
Road
Mandela
Walk
Southwark
Park
Road
Raymouth Rd
Rotherhithe
New Rd
Way
X
26
Y

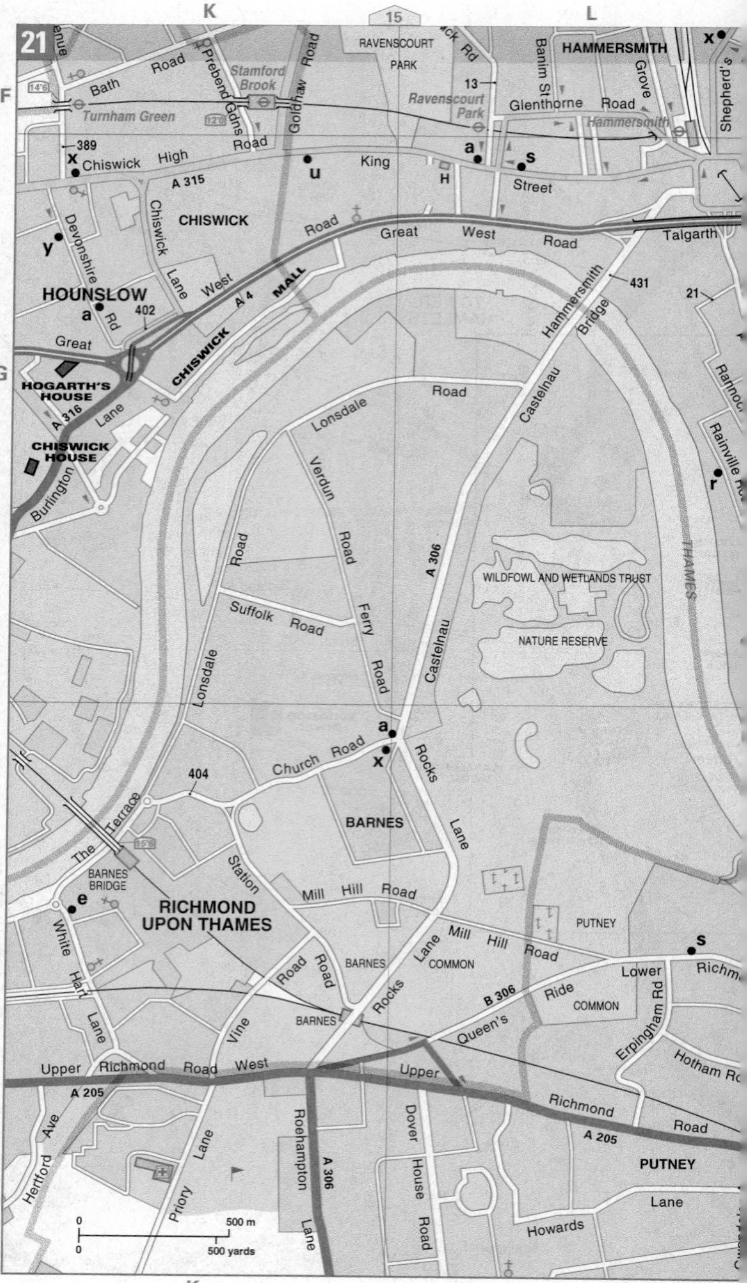

K 15 L

21

ZF ZG ZH

HAMMERSMITH
RAVENSCOURT PARK
Ravenscourt Park
Stamford Brook
Turnham Green
Hammersmith
Bath Road
Prebend Gdns
Goldhawk Road
Glenthorne Road
Banim St
Grove
Shepherd's
Chiswick High Road
King Street
A 315
CHISWICK
Chiswick Lane
Devonshire Rd
HOUNSLOW
Great West Road
A 4
CHISWICK MALL
Talgarth
Hammersmith Bridge
HOGARTH'S HOUSE
CHISWICK HOUSE
A 316
Burlington Lane
Lonsdale Road
Verdun Road
Suffolk Road
Ferry Road
Castelnau
A 306
WILDFOWL AND WETLANDS TRUST
NATURE RESERVE
THAMES
Rainville Rd
Church Road
Rocks Lane
BARNES
The Terrace
BARNES BRIDGE
Station Road
Mill Hill Road
RICHMOND UPON THAMES
White Hart Lane
Vine Road
BARNES COMMON
PUTNEY
Lower Richmond
Queen's Ride
B 306
COMMON
Erpingham Rd
Hotham Rd
Upper Richmond Road West
A 205
Upper Richmond Road
Hertford Ave
Priory Lane
Roehampton Lane
Dover House Road
PUTNEY
Lane
Howards

0 500 m
0 500 yards

K L

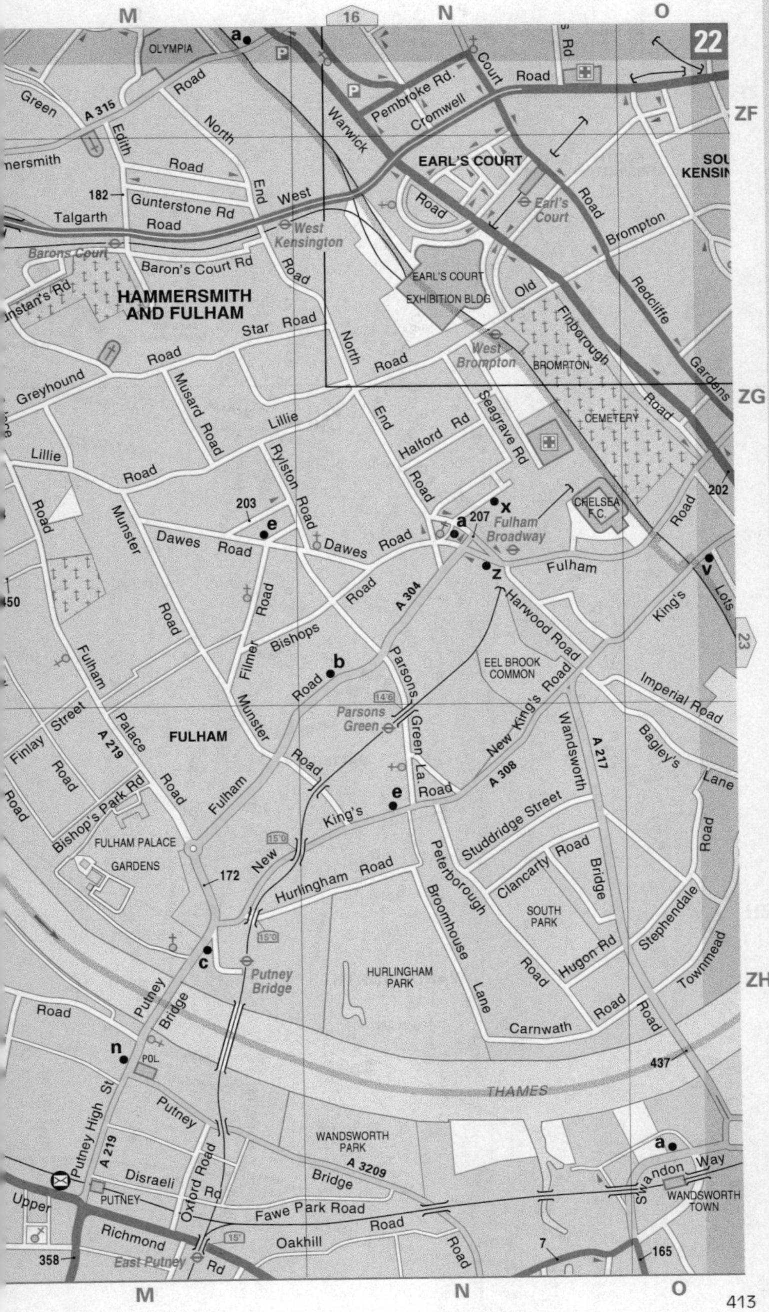

M
16
N
O
22
ZF
ZG
ZH
23
OLYMPIA
EARL'S COURT
Earl's Court
West Kensington
Barons Court
HAMMERSMITH AND FULHAM
EARL'S COURT EXHIBITION BLDG
West Brompton
BROMPTON CEMETERY
CHELSEA F.C.
Fulham Broadway
EEL BROOK COMMON
Parsons Green
FULHAM
FULHAM PALACE GARDENS
Putney Bridge
HURLINGHAM PARK
SOUTH PARK
THAMES
WANDSWORTH PARK
PUTNEY
East Putney
WANDSWORTH TOWN
SOUTH KENSINGTON
A 315
A 304
A 219
A 308
A 217
A 3209
Cromwell Road
Pembroke Rd.
Warwick Road
Earl's Court Road
North End Road
West Cromwell Road
Talgarth Road
Hammersmith Road
Gunterstone Rd
Edith Road
Baron's Court Rd
Star Road
Greyhound Road
Lillie Road
Musard Road
Rylston Road
Dawes Road
Munster Road
Filmer Road
Bishops Road
Fulham Road
Fulham Palace Road
Finlay Street
Bishop's Park Rd
Parsons Green La.
New King's Road
Harwood Road
Halford Rd
Seagrave Rd
Old Brompton Road
Finborough Road
Redcliffe Gardens
King's Road
Lots Road
Imperial Road
Bagley's Lane
Wandsworth Bridge Road
Studdridge Street
Clancarty Road
Peterborough Road
Broomhouse Lane
Hurlingham Road
Hugon Rd
Stephendale Road
Townmead Road
Carnwath Road
Putney Bridge Road
Putney High St
Upper Richmond Rd
Disraeli Rd
Oxford Road
Fawe Park Road
Oakhill Road
Swandon Way
POL.
182
203
207
172
202
437
358
7
165
450
a
b
c
e
n
v
x
z
14'6
15'0
15'

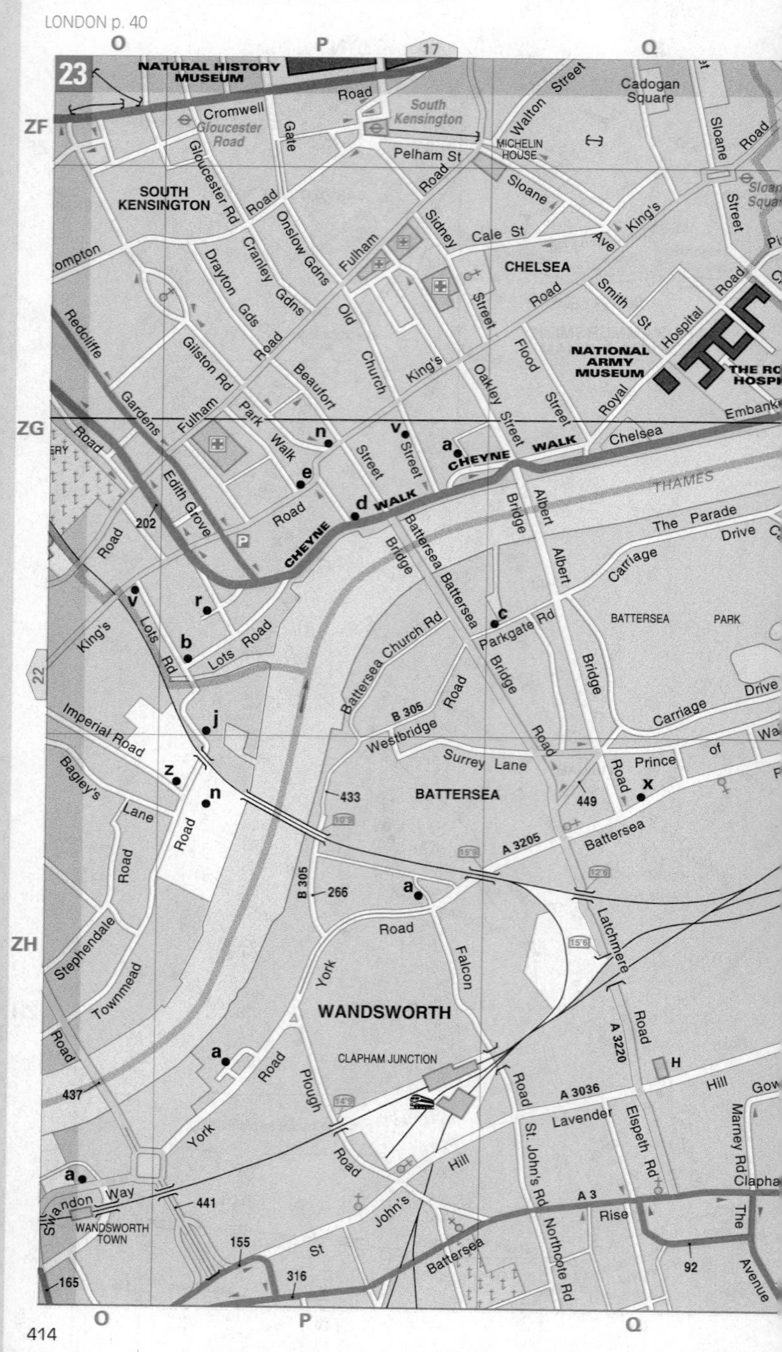

NATURAL HISTORY MUSEUM
Cromwell Road
Gloucester Road
South Kensington
Pelham St
Walton Street
MICHELIN HOUSE
Cadogan Square
Sloane Street
SOUTH KENSINGTON
Gloucester Rd
Onslow Gdns
Cranley Gdns
Drayton Gds
Fulham Road
Sidney Street
Cale St
Sloane Ave
King's Road
CHELSEA
Smith St
Hospital Road
NATIONAL ARMY MUSEUM
THE ROYAL HOSPITAL
Royal Hospital Road
Redcliffe Gardens
Gilston Rd
Old Church Street
Beaufort Street
Oakley Street
Flood Street
Chelsea Embankment
Park Walk
Edith Grove
CHEYNE WALK
THAMES
Battersea Bridge
Albert Bridge
The Parade
Carriage Drive
BATTERSEA PARK
Lots Road
King's Road
Battersea Church Rd
Parkgate Rd
Battersea Bridge Road
Albert Bridge Road
Imperial Road
Bagley's Lane
B 305
Westbridge Road
Surrey Lane
Prince of Wales Drive
BATTERSEA
A 3205
Battersea Park Road
Latchmere Road
Stephendale Road
Townmead Road
York Road
Falcon Road
WANDSWORTH
CLAPHAM JUNCTION
Plough Road
A 3220
A 3036
Lavender Hill
St. John's Rd
Elspeth Rd
Marney Rd
Clapham Common
St John's Hill
Swandon Way
WANDSWORTH TOWN
A 3
Rise
Northcote Rd
Battersea Rise
The Avenue

24
WESTMINSTER CATHEDRAL
VICTORIA
TATE BRITAIN
Pimlico
Vauxhall
NEW COVENT GARDEN MARKET
SOUTH LAMBETH
BATTERSEA PARK
QUEENSTOWN ROAD
WANDSWORTH ROAD
Stockwell
CLAPHAM HIGH ST.
Clapham North
Clapham Common
CLAPHAM COMMON
Vauxhall Bridge Road
Grosvenor Road
Nine Elms Lane
Wandsworth Road
Clapham High St
Queenstown Road
South Lambeth Road
Landsdowne Way
Clapham Road
Stockwell Road
Harleyford Rd
Lambeth Bridge
Albert Embankment
Millbank
Fentiman Road
Dorset Rd
500 m
500 yards

25
IMPERIAL WAR MUSEUM
ELEPHANT AND CASTLE SHOPPING CENTRE
A 201
WALWORTH
KENNINGTON
THE OVAL
KENNINGTON PARK
Oval
Kennington
BURGESS PARK
LAMBETH
A 3204
A 23
A 3
A 202
A 2217
A 215
DENMARK HILL
LOUGHBOROUGH JUNCTION
RUSKIN PARK
Brixton
Champion Park
Lambeth High St
Walk
Fitzalan Street
Kennington Road
Brook Drive
Hayles
New Kent Road
Heygate St
Rodney Rd
Flint St
Black
Vauxhall Walk
Prince
Road
Newburn St
Tyers St
Vauxhall
Chester Way
Kennington Lane
Penton Place
Walworth Road
Pl.
East Street
Portland Street
Braganza St
Manor
Kennington Lane
Clayton St.
Kennington Str.
Harleyford Rd
Chapter Rd
Albany
Street
Ruskin
Camberwell
New Church Rd
Edmund St
Southampton
Oval
Kennington
Camberwell
Road
Dorset Rd
John
New Wyndham Rd
Foxley Rd
Road
Vassall
Comber Gro.
Lomond Gro.
Road
Elmington
Benhill Road
Caldwell St
Lothian Rd
Flodden Rd
Road
Church Street
Camberwell
Way
Stockwell
Clapham
Groveway
Brixton
Calais St
Road
Mostyn Road
Road
Warner Road
Denmark Hill
Grove
Lane
Park Rd
Road
Akerman
Knatchbull
Carew St
Denmark Rd
Lilford
Loughborough Rd
Minet Rd
Loughborough
Road
Stockwell
Sidney Rd
Coldharbour
Lane
St
A 23
Angell Dr.
Road
Brixton
Road
Rd
Barrington Rd
Wiltshire
Lane
Coldharbour
Road
Road
Herne Hill
Ferndene Rd
Denmark Hill
Atlantic Rd
Hill
Lane
Acre
Kellett Rd
Effra Rd
Brixton
Railton
Road
Shakespeare
Milkwood
Fawnbrake Avenue
Road
Herne Hill
Red Post Hill
Sunray Avenue
19
24
T
U
V
ZF
ZG
ZH
163
306
211
420

X
Y
20
26
ZF
ZG
ZH
SOUTHWARK
BURGESS PARK
SOUTH BERMONDSEY
QUEENS ROAD PECKHAM
PECKHAM RYE
NUNHEAD
EAST DULWICH
PECKHAM RYE PARK
A 2
A 202
A 2214
A 2216
Old Kent Road
Peckham Road
Peckham High Street
Queens Road
Commercial Way
Rotherhithe New Road
Ilderton Road
Surrey Canal Rd
Verney Road
Lynton Road
Rolls Road
Southwark Park Road
Raymouth Rd
Galleywall Road
Catlin St
St James Road
Peckham Park Road
Bird in Bush Road
Peckham Hill St
Asylum Road
Meeting House Lane
Clifton Way
Kender Street
Pomeroy Street
Avonley Rd
Lausanne Rd
Hollydale Road
Evelina Road
Nunhead Lane
Nunhead Grove
Linden Grove
Peckham Rye
East Dulwich Rd
Crystal Palace Rd
Lordship Lane
Dog Kennel Hill
Grove Vale
Melbourne Grove
Avondale Rise
Bellenden Road
Oglander Rd
Ady's Road
Barry Rd
Heaton Rd
Copeland Rd
Consort Road
Rye Lane
Lyndhurst Grove
Lyndhurst Way
Shenley Road
Dalwood St
Sumner Road
Trafalgar Ave
Glengall Road
Willowbrook Rd
Coopers Rd
Marlborough Gro.
Cobourg Road
Neate Street
St George's Way
Mandela Way
Willow Walk
Dunton Road
Reverdy Rd
Naylor Rd
Carlton Gro.
Clayton Rd
Hanover Pk
Pytchley Rd
Grove Hill Rd
Cheltenham Rd
Stuart Rd
500 m
500 yards
X
Y

AA
AB
27
0
200 m
0
200 yards
Grand Union Canal
A 40
Westway
Harrow Road
Bourne Terrace
BAYSWATER AND MAIDA VALE
Harrow
Westbourne Park
Great Western Road
Tavistock Rd
St Luke's Rd
Westbourne Park Road
Westbourne Park Villas
Royal Oak
Porchester Rd
Gloucester
Westbourne Park Road
Chepstow Rd
Talbot Rd
Ledbury Road
Westbourne Gdns
197
Hereford Road
Talbot
a
NORTH KENSINGTON
Newton Rd
Bishop's Bridge
Colville Ter.
Artesian Road
Westbourne Grove
Queensway
Inverness
Colville Rd
Ledbury
v
a
Garway
b
Grove x Villas
Kensington Gdns Sq.
Porchester
Gdns
Queensborough
Road
Westbourne
Chepstow
c
Hereford
Leinster Sq.
Road
Chepstow Villas
Pembridge
84
Pl.
Road
Bayswater
Portobello Road
a
Dawson
Place
Road
Moscow
Pembridge Cres.
Bark Place
Queensway
Terrace
Kensington Park Road
Pembridge Square
Ossington St
Palace Court
St Petersburgh Pl.
Pembridge
Pembridge Gdns
Gdns
Linden
Queensway
328
c
Ladbroke Square
u
Gate
Bayswater Road
Road
Hill
Rd
Ladbroke
r
Palace
Kensington
Broad Walk
Notting
Ave
Notting Hill Gate
Holland Park
e
Uxbridge St
z
Kensington
Campden Hill Square
Campden
Place
Kensington
Gardens
Kensington Palace Gardens
Walk
Aubrey
Hill
Bedford Gardens
c
Terrace
ORANGERY
Sheffield Terrace
Church
Rd
KENSINGTON AND CHELSEA
U
Holland
Campden Gro.
St
KENSINGTON PALACE
Campden Hill
Palace
T
U
V
35

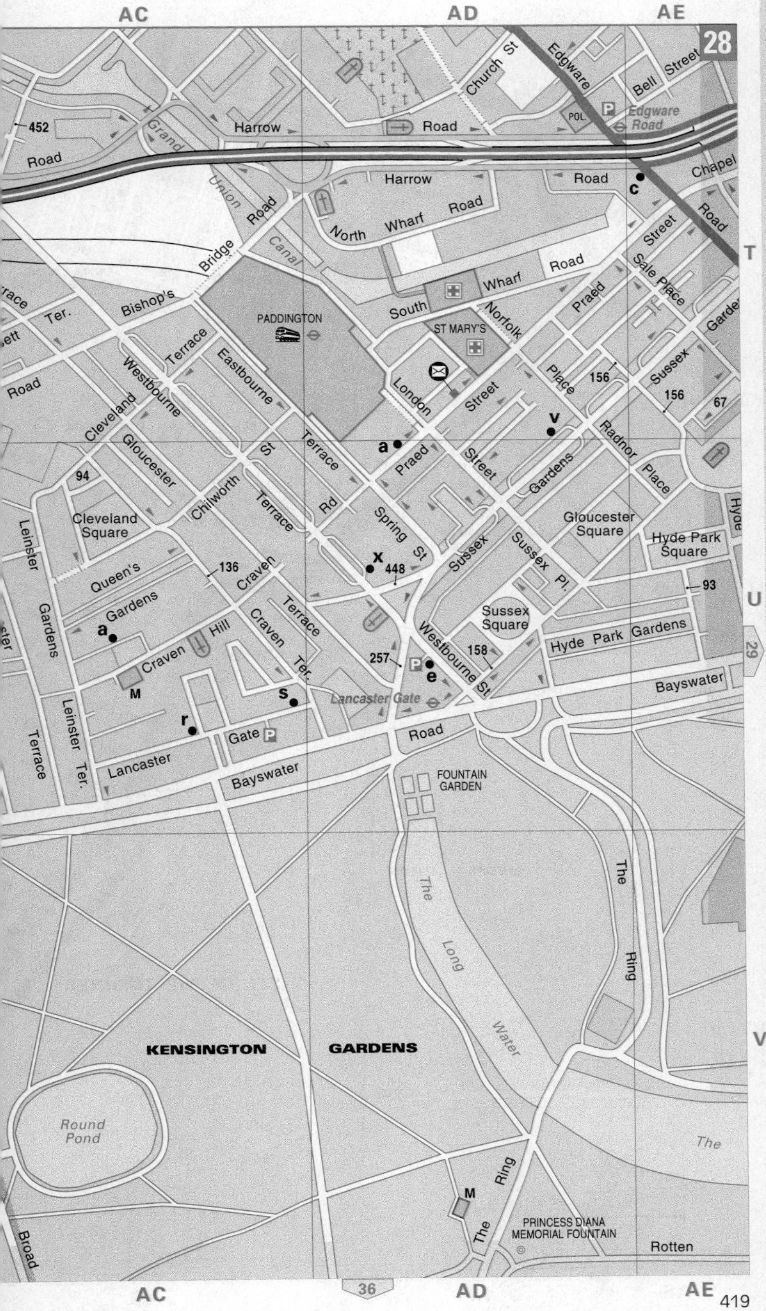

AC AD AE

28

KENSINGTON GARDENS

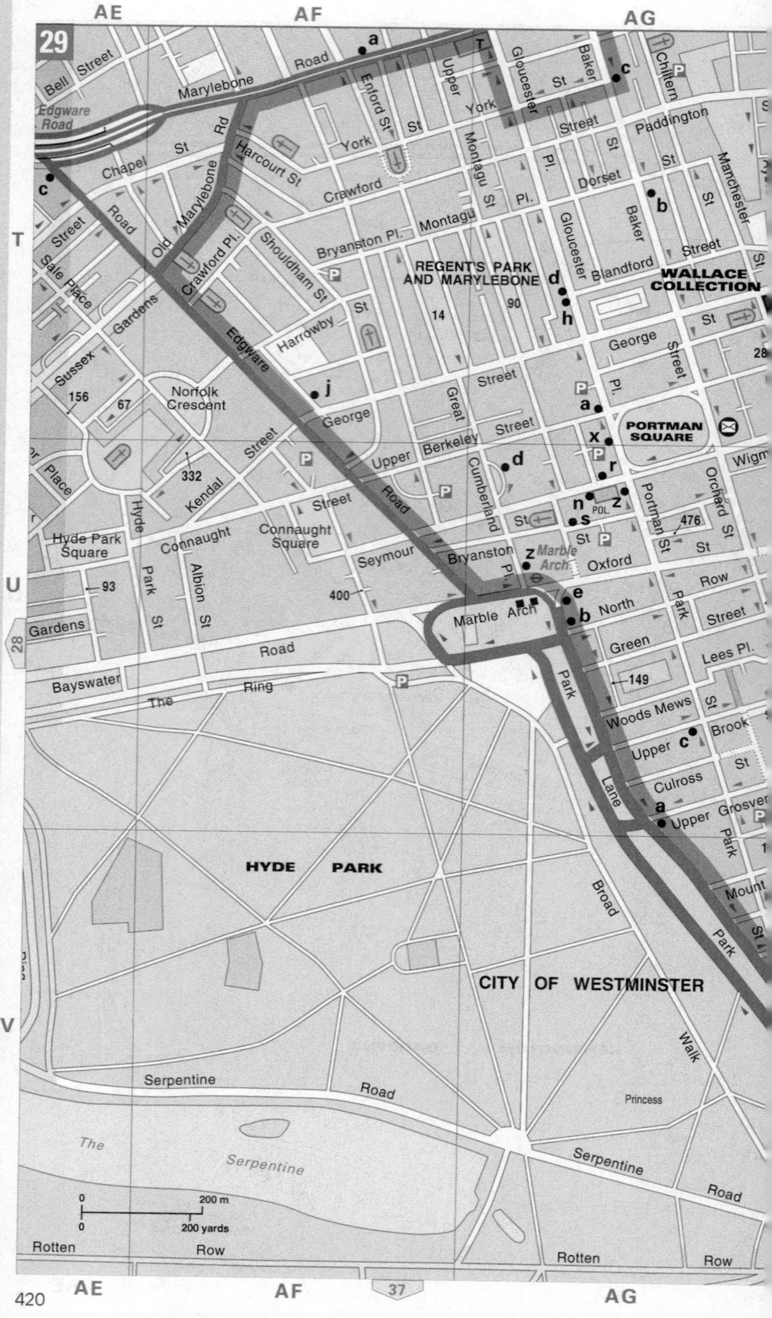

AE AF AG

29

T

U

V

28

REGENT'S PARK AND MARYLEBONE

WALLACE COLLECTION

PORTMAN SQUARE

Marble Arch

HYDE PARK

CITY OF WESTMINSTER

Bell Street
Marylebone Road
Edgware Road
Chapel St
Old Marylebone Rd
Harcourt St
Crawford St
Crawford Pl.
Enford St
York St
Upper Montagu St
Montagu Pl.
Gloucester Pl.
Baker St
York Street
Paddington St
Dorset St
Chiltern
Manchester St
Blandford Street
Bryanston Pl.
Shouldham St
Harrowby St
Sale Place
Sussex Gardens
Norfolk Crescent
Kendal Street
George Street
Great Cumberland Pl.
Upper Berkeley Street
Seymour Street
Bryanston St
Connaught Square
Connaught St
Hyde Park Square
Hyde Park Gardens
Hyde Park St
Albion St
Portman St
Orchard St
Oxford St
North Row
Park Street
Green St
Lees Pl.
Wigmore
Upper Brook St
Woods Mews
Culross St
Upper Grosvenor St
Mount St
Park Lane
Bayswater Road
The Ring
Broad Walk
Serpentine Road
The Serpentine
Princess
Rotten Row

a c b d h j a x r z n s z e b c a

14 90 156 67 332 93 400 476 149 28

POL

0 200 m
0 200 yards

37

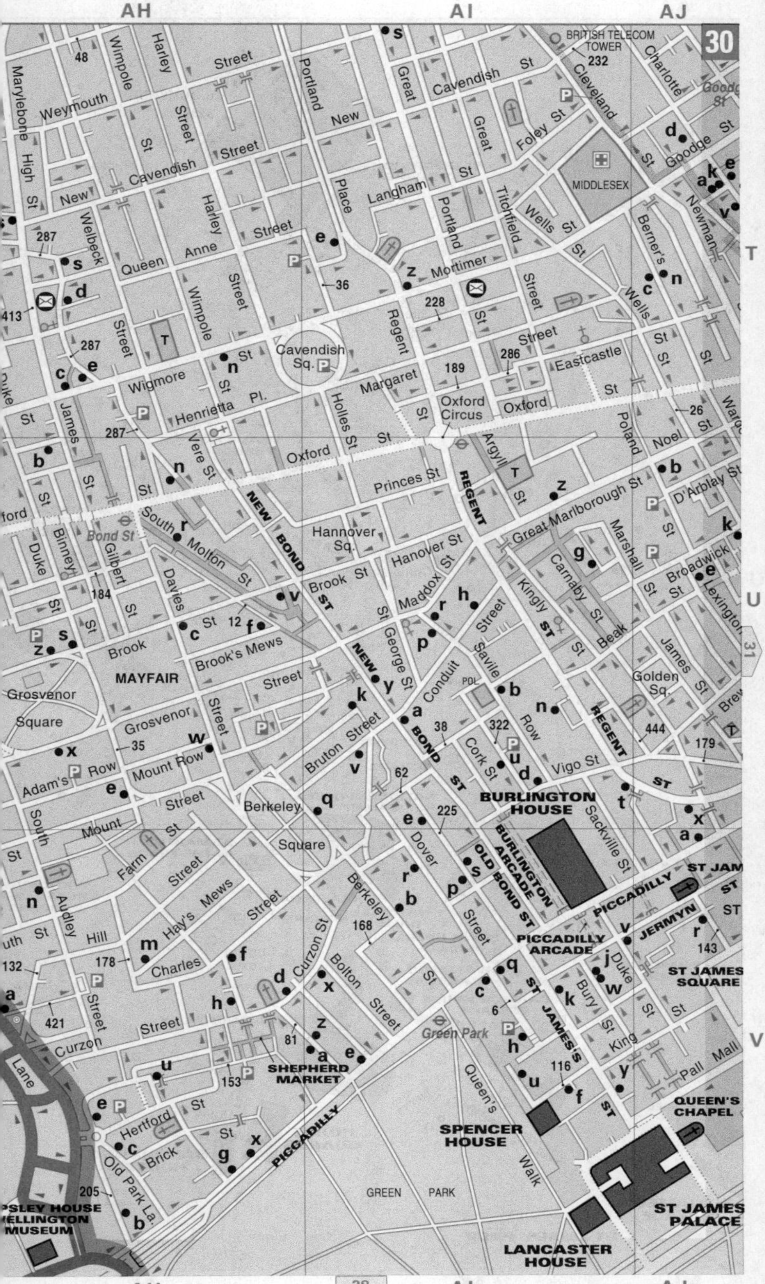
AH
AI
AJ
30
31
38
T
U
V
BRITISH TELECOM TOWER
MIDDLESEX
Marylebone High St
Weymouth
Wimpole
Harley
Street
Portland
New Cavendish Street
Great Portland St
Cleveland
Charlotte
Goodge St
Foley St
Langham
Place
Welbeck
Queen Anne Street
Mortimer
Titchfield
Wells St
Berner's
Newman
Regent
Cavendish Sq.
Wigmore
Henrietta Pl.
Margaret
Eastcastle
Oxford Circus
Oxford
Holles St
Vere St
James
Argyll
Poland
Noel
D'Arblay St
Princes St
REGENT
NEW BOND
Hannover Sq.
Hanover St
Great Marlborough St
Marshall
Carnaby
Kingly
Broadwick
Lexington
South Molton
Bond St
Gilbert
Binney
Duke
Davies
Brook St
Maddox St
George St
Savile Row
Conduit
Beak
Golden Sq.
Brook's Mews
Brook
MAYFAIR
Grosvenor Square
Grosvenor
Mount Row
Adam's Row
Bruton Street
Cork St
Vigo St
BURLINGTON HOUSE
BURLINGTON ARCADE
OLD BOND ST
Sackville St
Berkeley Square
Dover
South
Mount
Farm
Audley
Hill
Hay's Mews
Charles
Berkeley
Curzon St
Bolton Street
PICCADILLY
JERMYN
PICCADILLY ARCADE
Duke
Bury
ST JAMES'S ST
ST JAMES SQUARE
King
Pall Mall
Curzon
Lane
Shepherd Market
SHEPHERD MARKET
Green Park
Queen's Walk
SPENCER HOUSE
QUEEN'S CHAPEL
Hertford
Brick
Old Park La.
GREEN PARK
LANCASTER HOUSE
ST JAMES PALACE
APSLEY HOUSE WELLINGTON MUSEUM

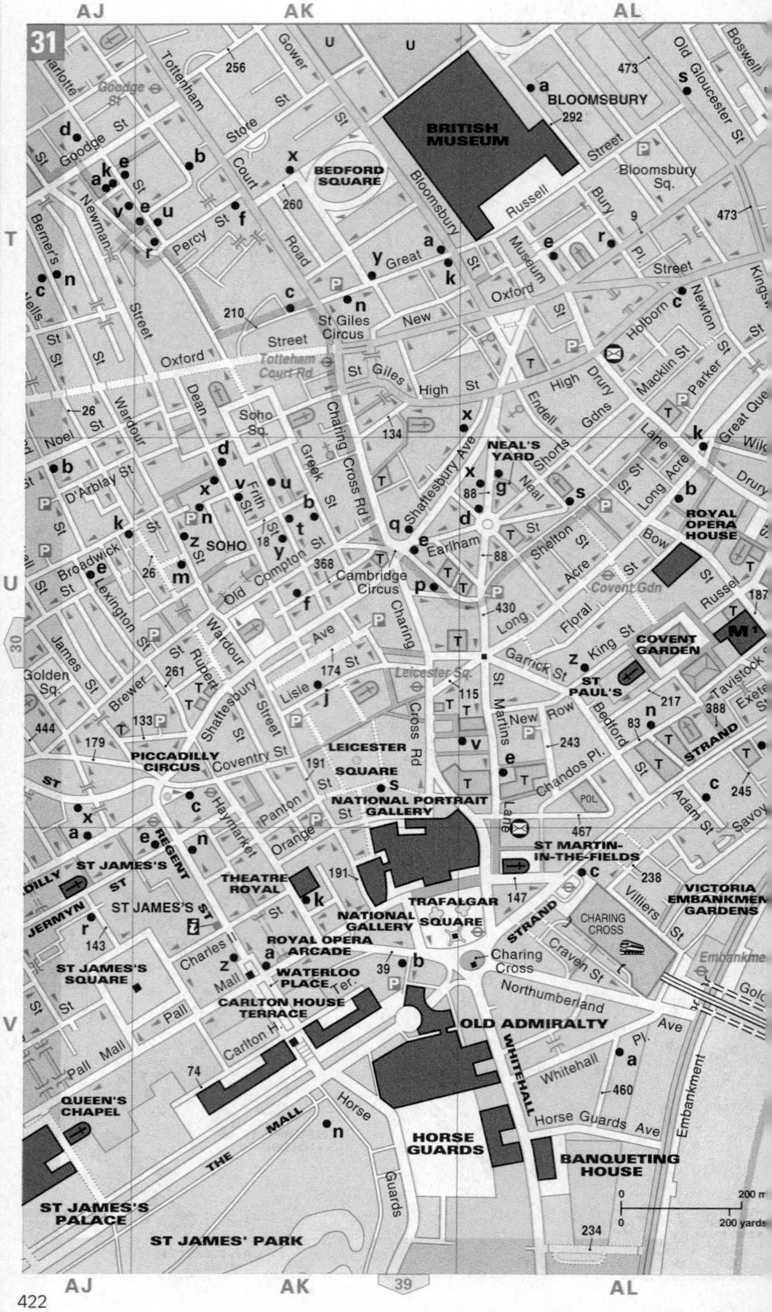

AJ AK AL

31

BRITISH MUSEUM
BLOOMSBURY
BEDFORD SQUARE
Bloomsbury Sq.
Goodge St
Tottenham Court Rd
St Giles Circus
Oxford Street
New Oxford St
St Giles High St
High Holborn
Soho Sq.
SOHO
NEAL'S YARD
ROYAL OPERA HOUSE
Covent Gdn
COVENT GARDEN
ST PAUL'S
Cambridge Circus
Shaftesbury Ave
Charing Cross Rd
Leicester Sq.
LEICESTER SQUARE
NATIONAL PORTRAIT GALLERY
PICCADILLY CIRCUS
Coventry St
Haymarket
REGENT ST
ST JAMES'S
JERMYN ST
ST JAMES'S ST
THEATRE ROYAL
ROYAL OPERA ARCADE
WATERLOO PLACE
CARLTON HOUSE TERRACE
NATIONAL GALLERY
TRAFALGAR SQUARE
ST MARTIN-IN-THE-FIELDS
STRAND
CHARING CROSS
Charing Cross
VICTORIA EMBANKMENT GARDENS
Embankment
Northumberland Ave
OLD ADMIRALTY
WHITEHALL
Whitehall Pl.
Horse Guards Ave
HORSE GUARDS
BANQUETING HOUSE
ST JAMES'S SQUARE
Pall Mall
QUEEN'S CHAPEL
THE MALL
ST JAMES'S PALACE
ST JAMES' PARK
Horse Guards

T U V

0 200 m
0 200 yards

AJ AK 39 AL

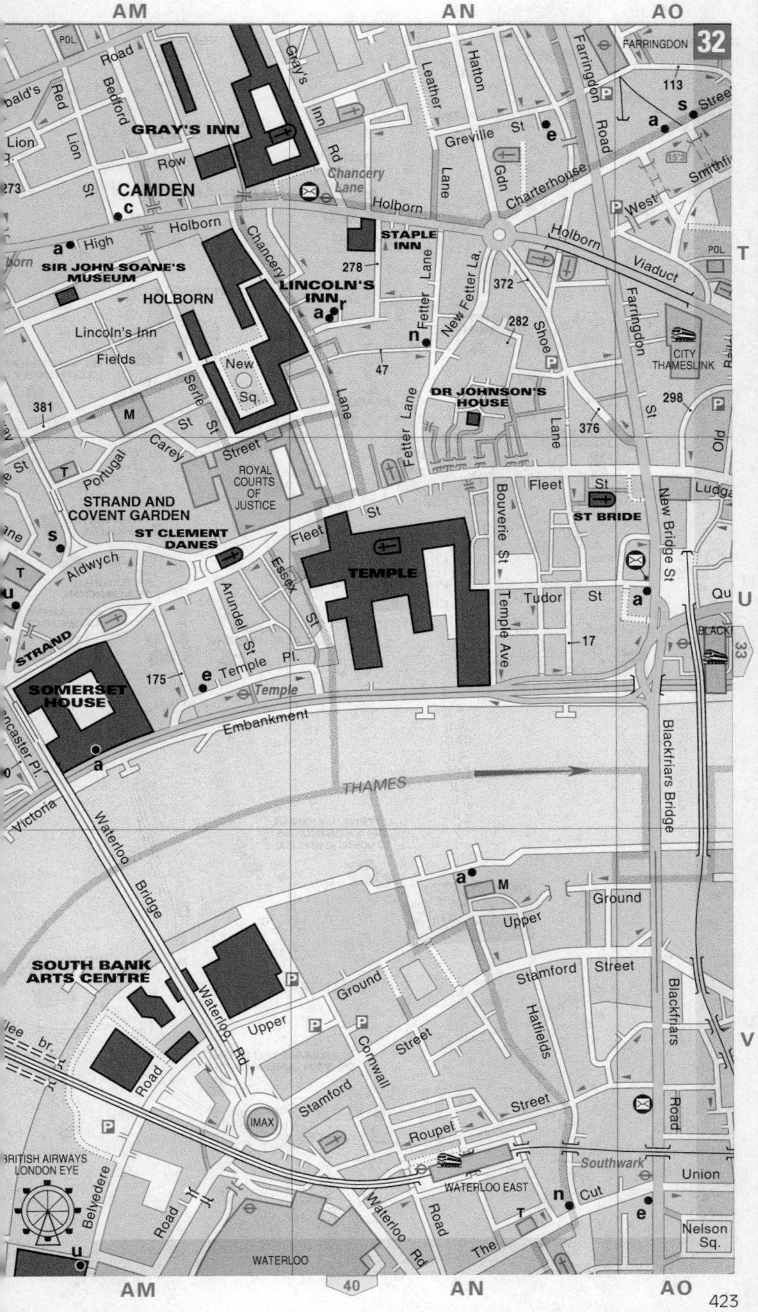
AM
AN
AO
32
FARRINGDON
113
POL
Road
Bedford
Red
Lion
GRAY'S INN
Gray's
Inn
Rd
Chancery
Lane
Row
CAMDEN
St
273
Holborn
High
SIR JOHN SOANE'S
MUSEUM
HOLBORN
Chancery
Lane
LINCOLN'S
INN
Lincoln's Inn
Fields
New
Sq.
Serle
St
381
M
Carey
Street
Portugal
St
ROYAL
COURTS
OF
JUSTICE
STRAND AND
COVENT GARDEN
ST CLEMENT
DANES
Aldwych
Fleet
St
Essex
St
Arundel
St
STRAND
SOMERSET
HOUSE
175
Temple
Pl.
Temple
Embankment
Victoria
THAMES
Leather
Hatton
Greville
St
Lane
Gdn
Charterhouse
Holborn
STAPLE
INN
278
Fetter
Lane
New Fetter La.
47
372
282
Shoe
Lane
DR JOHNSON'S
HOUSE
Fetter
Lane
376
Fleet
St
ST BRIDE
TEMPLE
Bouverie
St
Tudor
St
Temple
Ave
17
Farringdon
Road
Street
Smithfield
West
Holborn
Viaduct
Farringdon
St
CITY
THAMESLINK
298
Old
Ludgate
New Bridge St
BLACKFRIARS
33
Qu
Blackfriars Bridge
T
U
V
Waterloo
Bridge
SOUTH BANK
ARTS CENTRE
Waterloo
Rd
Upper
Ground
Road
Cornwall
Street
Stamford
Street
IMAX
Roupell
St
M
Upper
Ground
Stamford
Street
Hatfields
Street
Blackfriars
Road
Jubilee br.
BRITISH AIRWAYS
LONDON EYE
Belvedere
Road
WATERLOO
WATERLOO EAST
Southwark
Waterloo
Road
Rd
The
Cut
Union
Nelson
Sq.
Lancaster Pl.
40
AM
AN
AO

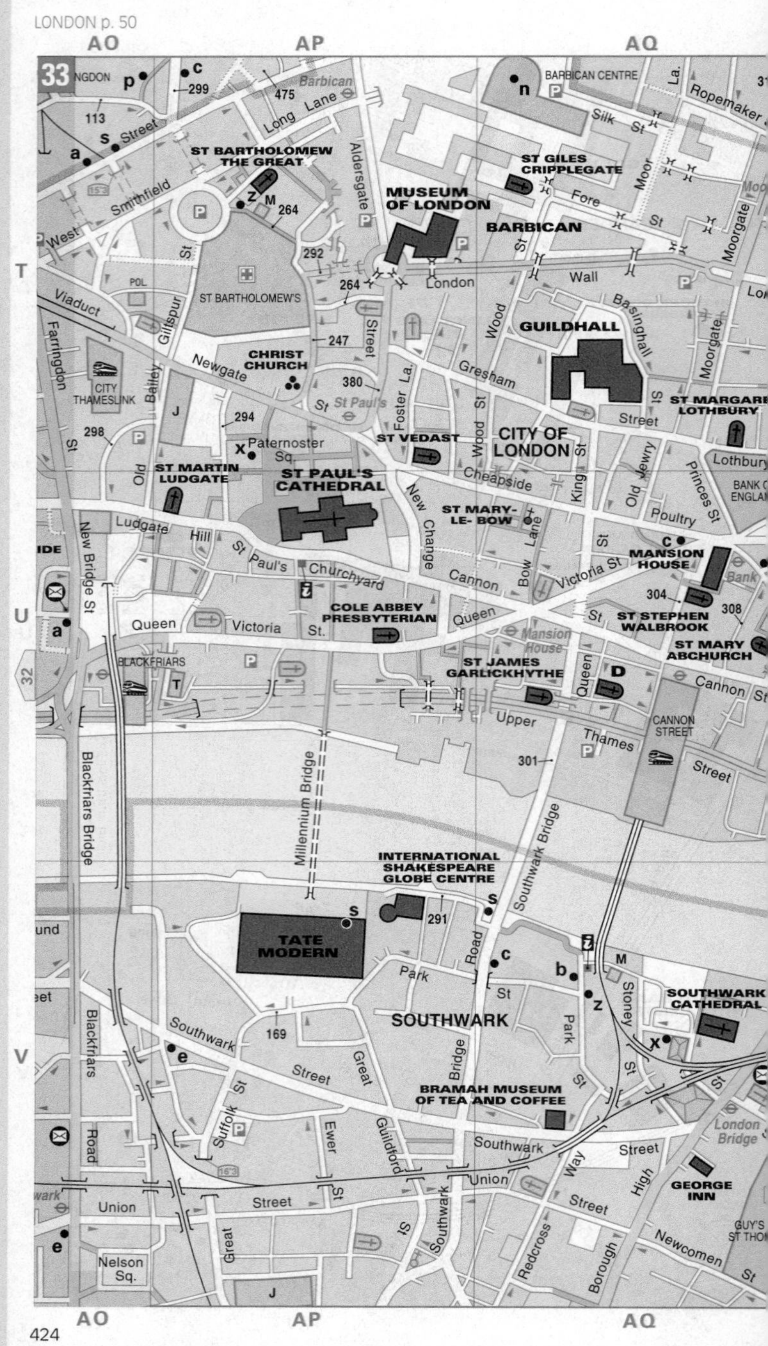
AO
AP
AQ
33
ST BARTHOLOMEW THE GREAT
MUSEUM OF LONDON
BARBICAN
BARBICAN CENTRE
ST GILES CRIPPLEGATE
ST BARTHOLOMEW'S
CHRIST CHURCH
GUILDHALL
CITY THAMESLINK
ST MARTIN LUDGATE
ST PAUL'S CATHEDRAL
ST VEDAST
CITY OF LONDON
ST MARGARET LOTHBURY
BANK OF ENGLAND
ST MARY-LE-BOW
MANSION HOUSE
COLE ABBEY PRESBYTERIAN
ST STEPHEN WALBROOK
ST MARY ABCHURCH
ST JAMES GARLICKHYTHE
BLACKFRIARS
CANNON STREET
INTERNATIONAL SHAKESPEARE GLOBE CENTRE
TATE MODERN
SOUTHWARK
SOUTHWARK CATHEDRAL
BRAMAH MUSEUM OF TEA AND COFFEE
GEORGE INN
Millennium Bridge
Blackfriars Bridge
Southwark Bridge
London Bridge
Newgate St
Cheapside
Queen Victoria St.
Upper Thames Street
Southwark Street
Union Street
T
U
V

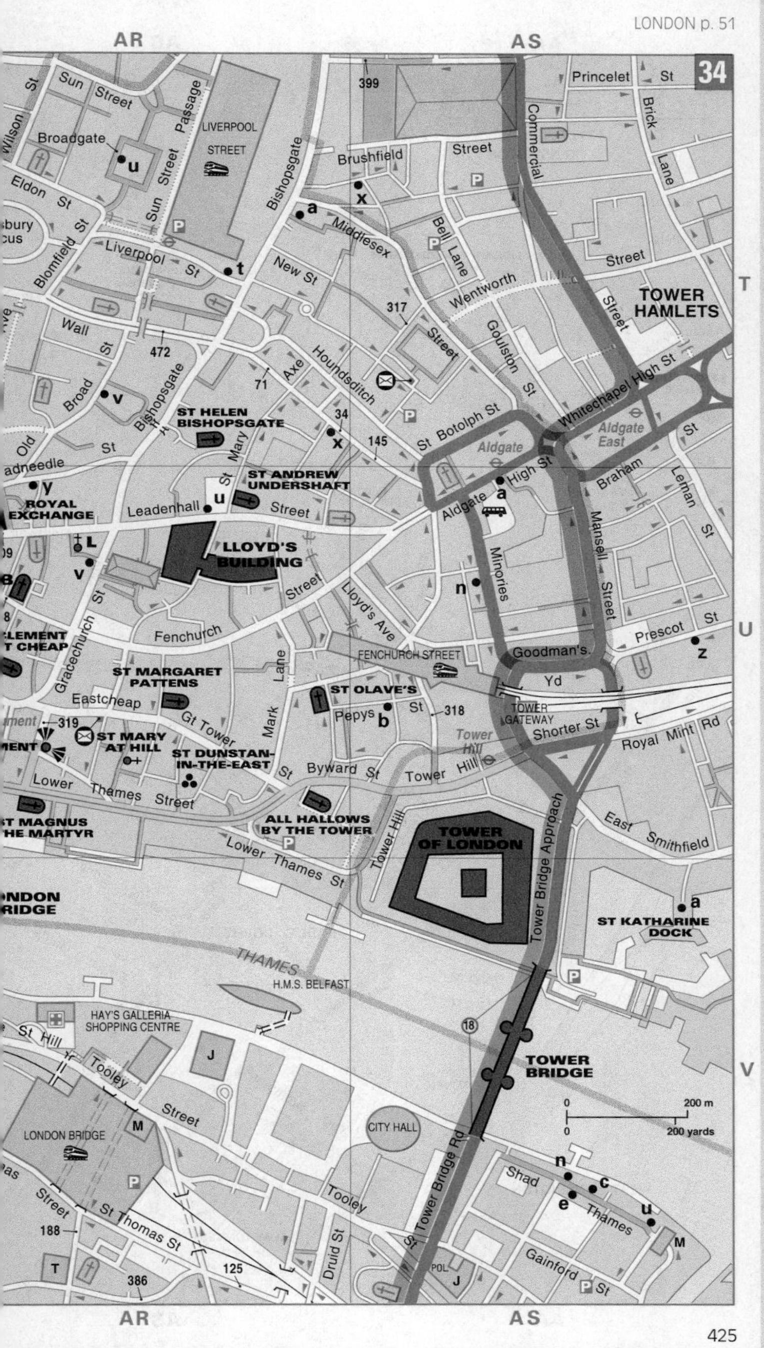
AR
AS
34
T
U
V
LIVERPOOL STREET
TOWER HAMLETS
ST HELEN BISHOPSGATE
ST ANDREW UNDERSHAFT
ROYAL EXCHANGE
LLOYD'S BUILDING
FENCHURCH STREET
ST MARGARET PATTENS
ST OLAVE'S
ST MARY AT HILL
ST DUNSTAN-IN-THE-EAST
ALL HALLOWS BY THE TOWER
TOWER GATEWAY
TOWER OF LONDON
ST KATHARINE DOCK
THAMES
H.M.S. BELFAST
HAY'S GALLERIA SHOPPING CENTRE
CITY HALL
TOWER BRIDGE
LONDON BRIDGE
Aldgate
Aldgate East
Tower Hill
Bishopsgate
Commercial
Whitechapel High St
Houndsditch
Minories
Mansell Street
Leadenhall Street
Fenchurch Street
Eastcheap
Lower Thames Street
Tower Bridge Approach
Tower Bridge Rd
Tooley Street
East Smithfield
Royal Mint Rd
0 200 m
0 200 yards

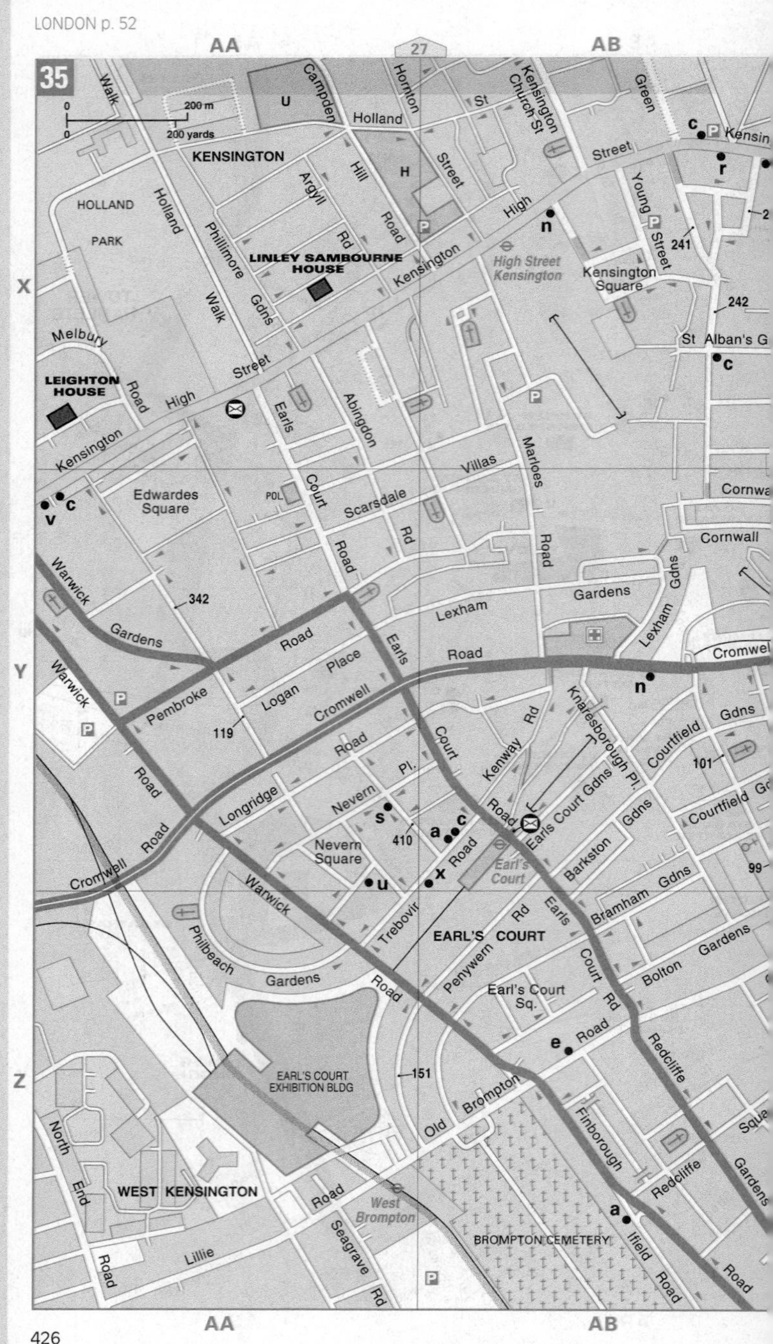
AA
27
AB
35
0
200 m
0
200 yards
KENSINGTON
HOLLAND
PARK
LINLEY SAMBOURNE
HOUSE
LEIGHTON
HOUSE
High Street
Kensington
Kensington
Square
Edwardes
Square
Nevern
Square
EARL'S COURT
Earl's
Court
Earl's Court
Sq.
EARL'S COURT
EXHIBITION BLDG
West
Brompton
WEST KENSINGTON
BROMPTON CEMETERY
X
Y
Z
AA
AB

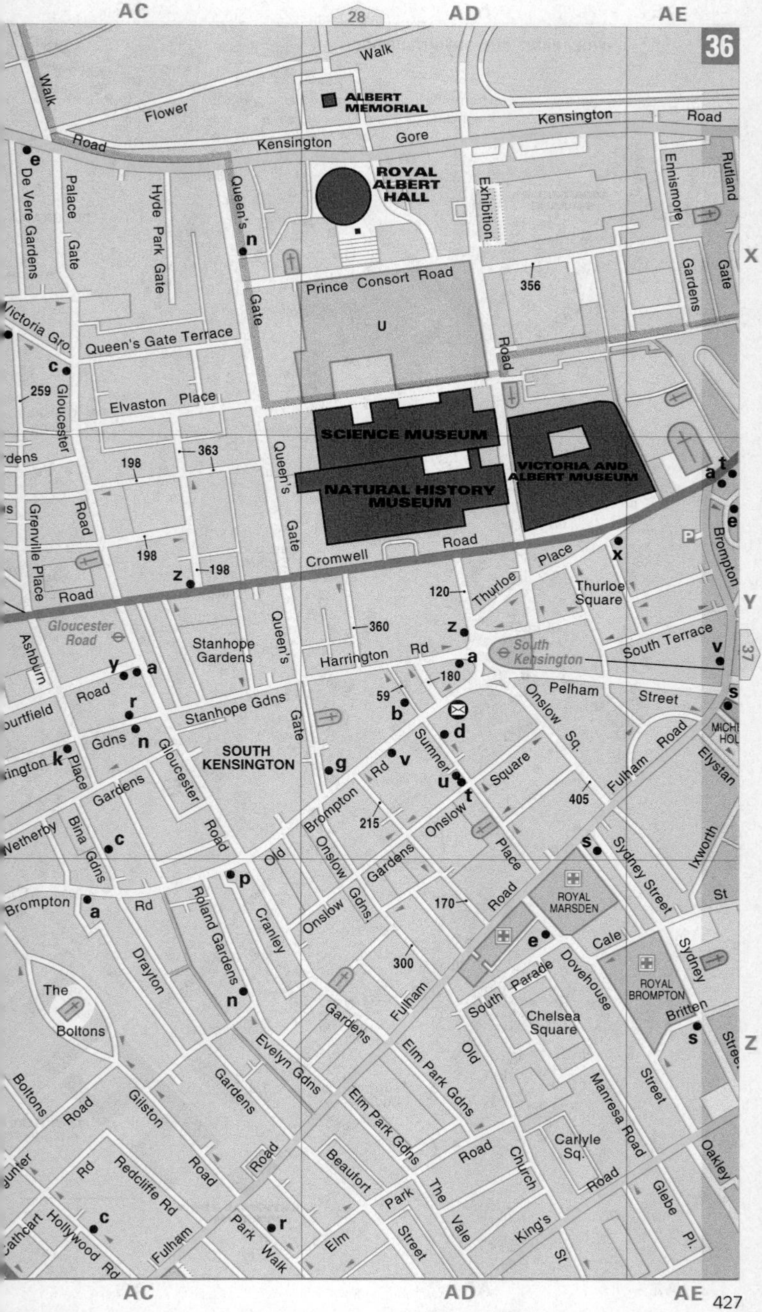

AC 28 AD AE 36

ALBERT MEMORIAL
ROYAL ALBERT HALL
SCIENCE MUSEUM
NATURAL HISTORY MUSEUM
VICTORIA AND ALBERT MUSEUM
SOUTH KENSINGTON
ROYAL MARSDEN
ROYAL BROMPTON

Kensington Road, Kensington Gore, Flower Walk, Queen's Gate, Prince Consort Road, Exhibition Road, Queen's Gate Terrace, Elvaston Place, Cromwell Road, Thurloe Place, Thurloe Square, Harrington Rd, Stanhope Gardens, Stanhope Gdns, Pelham Street, South Terrace, Onslow Sq., Sumner Place, Brompton Road, Fulham Road, Old Brompton Rd, Onslow Gardens, Cranley Gardens, Roland Gardens, Drayton Gardens, The Boltons, Evelyn Gdns, Elm Park Gdns, Sydney Street, Chelsea Square, Carlyle Sq., Manresa Road, King's Road, Oakley Street, Glebe Pl., Beaufort Street, Park Walk, Redcliffe Rd, Hollywood Rd, Gloucester Road, Ennismore Gardens, Rutland Gate, De Vere Gardens, Palace Gate, Hyde Park Gate, Grenville Place, Ashburn Place, Bina Gdns, Wetherby Gardens, Gilston Road, Elystan Street, Ixworth Pl., Cale St, Dovehouse Street, Britten Street, The Vale, Church Street

X Y Z

AC AD AE

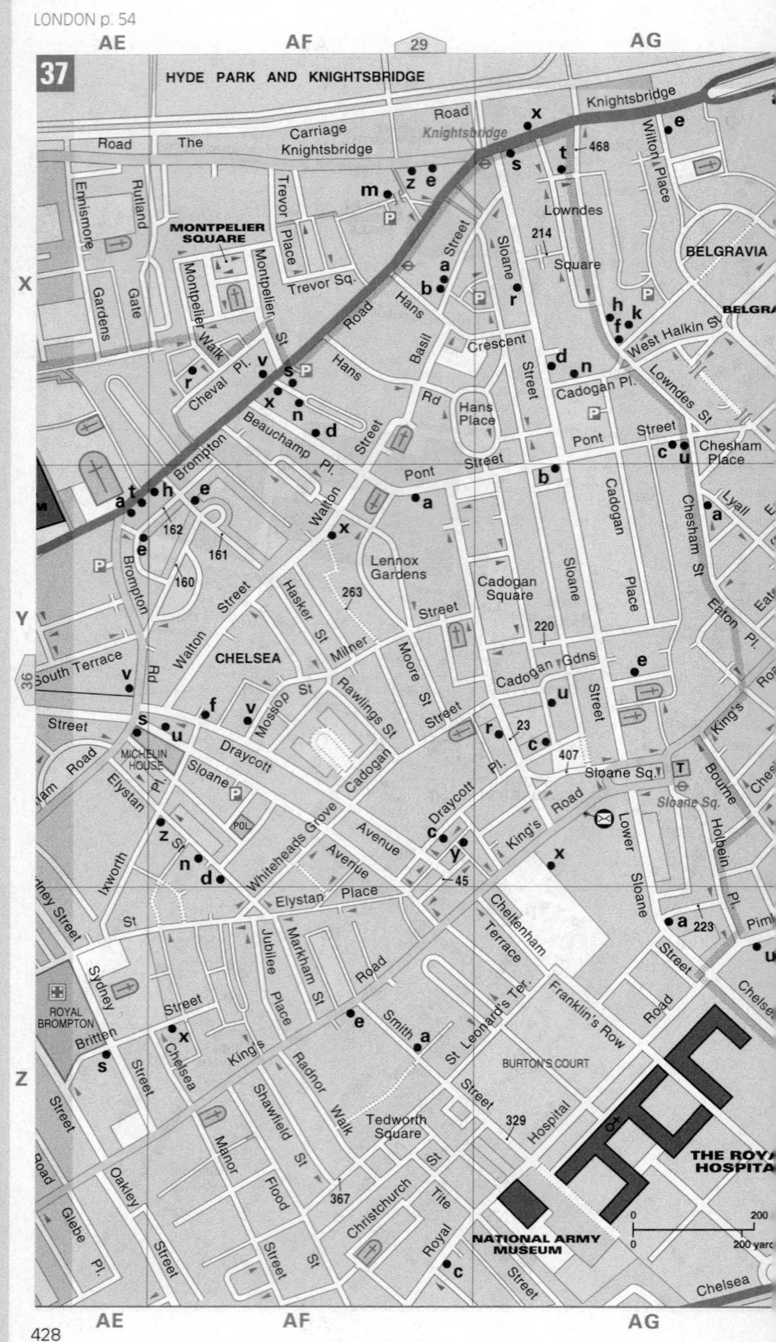
AE
AF
29
AG
37
HYDE PARK AND KNIGHTSBRIDGE
Road
The
Carriage
Knightsbridge
Road
Knightsbridge
Knightsbridge
468
Wilton Place
Ennismore
Gardens
Rutland
Gate
MONTPELIER
SQUARE
Montpelier Walk
Montpelier St
Trevor Place
Trevor Sq.
Hans Road
Hans
Basil Street
Sloane Street
Lowndes
214
Square
BELGRAVIA
West Halkin St
Hans Crescent
Cadogan Pl.
Lowndes St
Cheval Pl.
Brompton
Beauchamp Pl.
Hans Rd
Hans Place
Pont Street
Chesham Place
Walton Street
162
161
160
Brompton Rd
Lennox Gardens
263
Cadogan Square
Cadogan Place
Sloane Street
Chesham St
Lyall
Hasker St
Milner Street
Moore St
220
Cadogan Gdns
Eaton Pl.
X
Y
Z
36
South Terrace
CHELSEA
Mossop St
Rawlings St
Street
King's
Street
Draycott
MICHELIN HOUSE
Sloane Ave
Cadogan
23
407
Sloane Sq.
Sloane Sq.
Bourne
Elystan Pl.
Whiteheads Grove
Avenue
Draycott
King's Road
Lower Sloane
Holbein Pl.
Ixworth
St
Elystan Place
45
Sydney Street
Jubilee Place
Markham St
Road
Cheltenham Terrace
223
Pimlico
ROYAL BROMPTON
Britten Street
Chelsea
King's
Radnor Walk
Smith St
St Leonard's Ter.
Franklin's Row
Road
BURTON'S COURT
Street
Shawfield St
Tedworth Square
Street
329
Hospital
THE ROYAL HOSPITAL
Oakley Street
Glebe Pl.
Manor
Flood Street
367
Christchurch St
Tite St
Royal
NATIONAL ARMY MUSEUM
0
200
200 yards
Chelsea

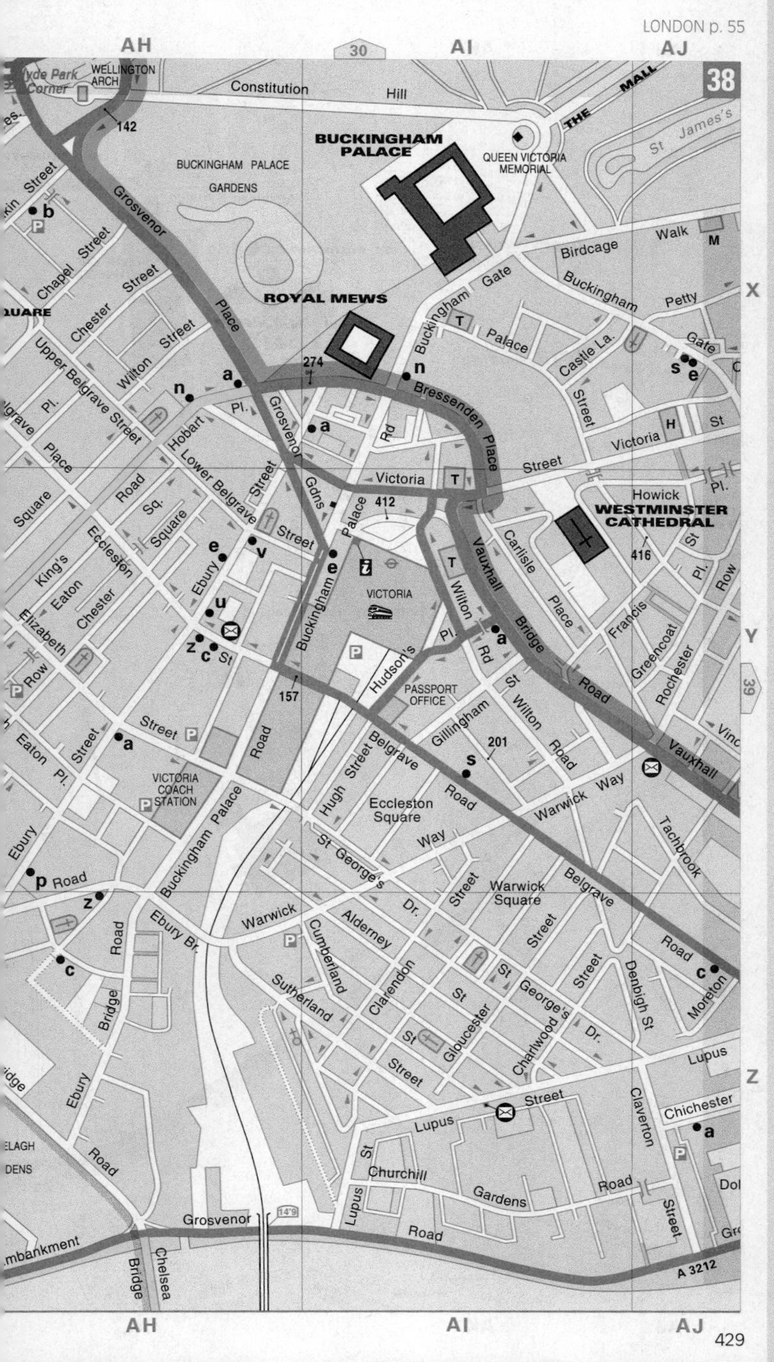
AH
30
AI
AJ
38
X
Y
Z
39
WELLINGTON ARCH
Hyde Park Corner
Constitution Hill
THE MALL
BUCKINGHAM PALACE
QUEEN VICTORIA MEMORIAL
BUCKINGHAM PALACE GARDENS
St James's
Grosvenor Place
Birdcage Walk
ROYAL MEWS
Buckingham Gate
Petty
Buckingham Palace
Castle La.
Bressenden Place
Victoria Street
WESTMINSTER CATHEDRAL
Howick Pl.
VICTORIA
PASSPORT OFFICE
Vauxhall Bridge Road
VICTORIA COACH STATION
Eccleston Square
Warwick Way
Warwick Square
Belgrave Road
St George's Dr.
Tachbrook
Lupus Street
Churchill Gardens Road
Grosvenor Road
Chelsea Bridge
A 3212
142
274
412
416
157
201
14'9
AH
AI
AJ

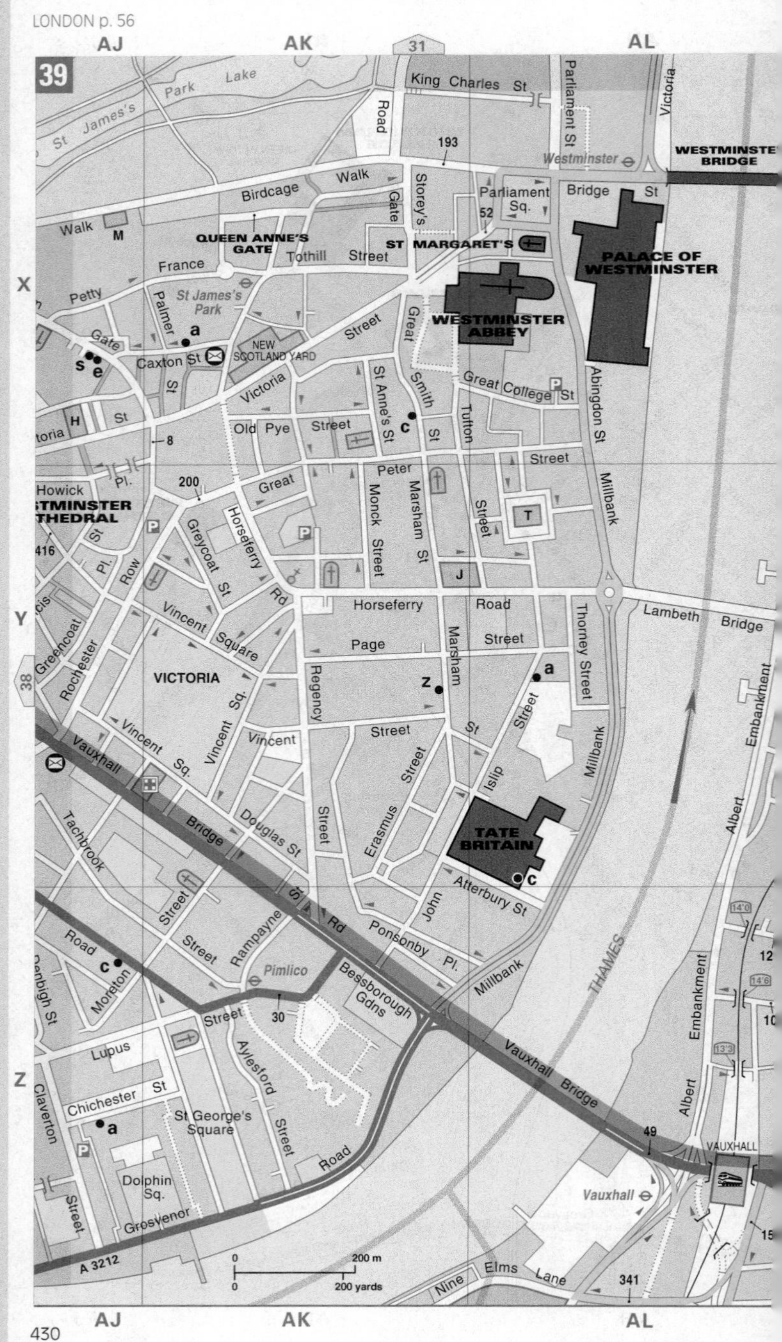
AJ
AK
AL
31
39
King Charles St
Parliament St
Victoria
Road
193
Westminster
WESTMINSTER BRIDGE
St James's Park Lake
Birdcage Walk
Walk
M
Gate
Storey's
Parliament Sq.
52
Bridge St
QUEEN ANNE'S GATE
Tothill Street
ST MARGARET'S
PALACE OF WESTMINSTER
X
France
Petty
Palmer
St James's Park
Great
WESTMINSTER ABBEY
Gate
a
Caxton St
NEW SCOTLAND YARD
Street
Victoria
s
e
St
Smith
Great College St
Abingdon St
H
St
Old Pye Street
St Anne's St
c
St
Tufton
Street
8
Peter
Pl.
Great
200
Howick
Millbank
Horseferry
Greycoat
Moncck Street
Marsham St
Street
T
J
416
Row
St
Horseferry Rd
Horseferry Road
Lambeth Bridge
Y
Vincent Square
Page Street
Thorney Street
38
Greencoat
Rochester
VICTORIA
Regency
z
Marsham
a
Street
Vincent Sq.
Vincent Sq.
Vincent
Street
St
Embankment
Vauxhall
Street
Islip
Millbank
Street
Tachbrook
Bridge
Douglas St
Erasmus
Albert
TATE BRITAIN
c
Atterbury St
John
St
Rd
Street
Ponsonby Pl.
Road
Street
Rampayne
Millbank
THAMES
c
Moreton
Pimlico
Bessborough Gdns
Embankment
Street
30
Vauxhall Bridge
Lupus
Aylesford
Z
Chichester St
a
St George's Square
Street
Albert
49
Claverton
Road
VAUXHALL
Dolphin Sq.
Street
Vauxhall
Grosvenor
A 3212
0
200 m
0
200 yards
Nine Elms Lane
341
AJ
AK
AL

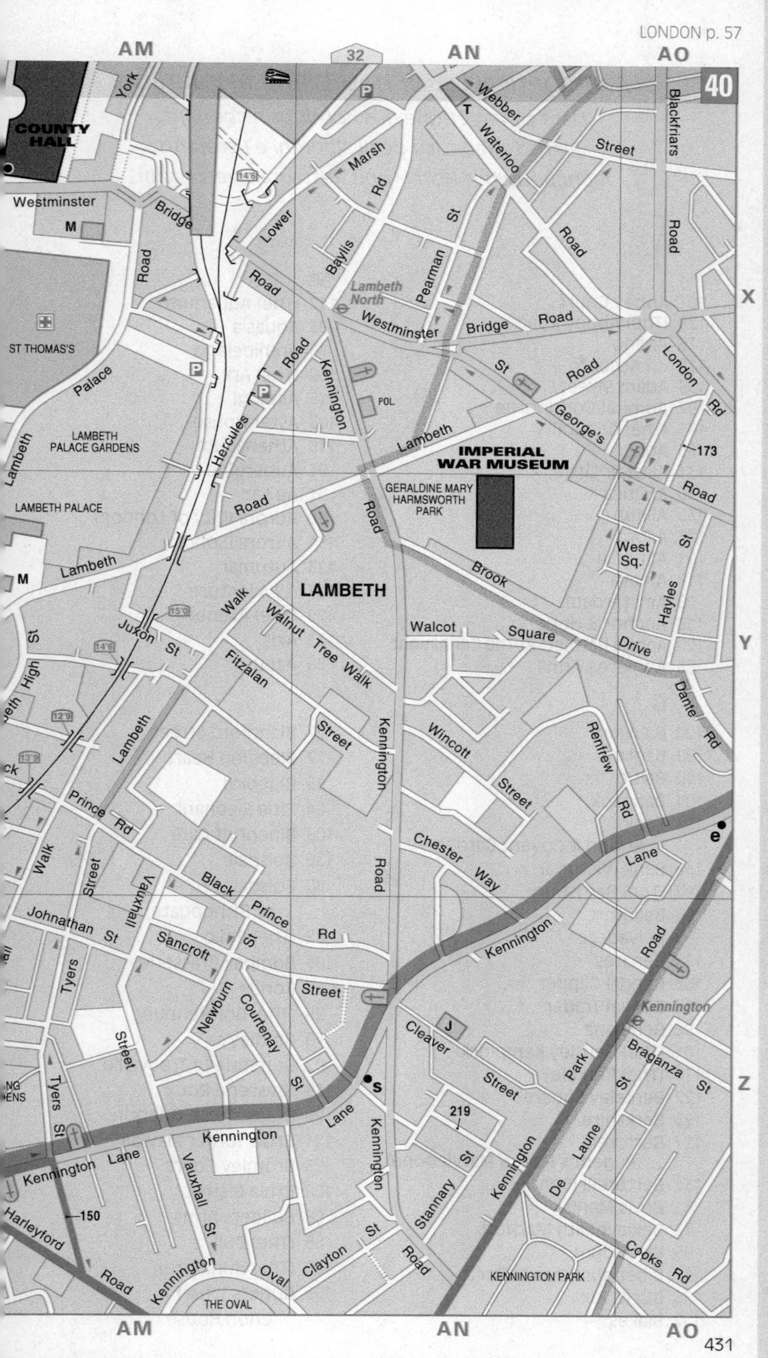
AM
AN
AO
32
40
X
Y
Z
COUNTY HALL
Westminster
Bridge
Road
ST THOMAS'S
Palace
LAMBETH PALACE GARDENS
LAMBETH PALACE
Lambeth
Lower
Marsh
Rd
Baylis
Lambeth North
Pearman
St
Webber
Waterloo
Street
Blackfriars
Road
Westminster
Bridge
Road
London
Rd
St
George's
Road
Kennington
POL.
Hercules
Lambeth
IMPERIAL WAR MUSEUM
GERALDINE MARY HARMSWORTH PARK
173
West Sq.
Hayles
Brook
Drive
LAMBETH
Walk
Walnut Tree Walk
Walcot
Square
Juxon
St
High
Fitzalan
Street
Kennington
Wincott
Street
Renfrew
Rd
Dante
Rd
Prince
Rd
Chester
Way
Lane
Black
Prince
Rd
Johnathan St
Vauxhall
Sancroft
Street
Tyers
Newburn
Courtenay
St
Cleaver
Street
Park
Kennington
Braganza
St
219
Stannary
St
De Laune
Kennington Lane
Harleyford
Road
150
Oval
Clayton
THE OVAL
KENNINGTON PARK
Cooks
Rd

Alphabetical list of hotels and restaurants

Liste alphabétique des hôtels et restaurants

Elenco alfabetico degli alberghi e ristoranti

Alphabetisches Hotel- und Restaurantverzeichnis

A

B

C

D

E

F

G

H

I

J

K

L

M

U - V - W

X - Y - Z

Starred establishments in London

Les établissements à étoiles de Londres
Gli esercizi con stelle a Londra
Die Stern-Restaurants in London

✿✿✿

✿✿

✿

page			
20	*Mayfair*	XXXX	Angela Hartnett at The Connaught
16	*Belgravia*	XXXX	Pétrus (at The Berkeley H.)
32	*Strand and Covent Garden*	XXXX	The Savoy Grill
20	*Mayfair*	XXXX	Sketch (The Lecture Room)
25	*Regent's Park & Marylebone*	XXX	Orrery
16	*Belgravia*	XXX	Amaya
95	*Chelsea*	XXX	Aubergine
73	*Farnborough*	XXX	Chapter One
30	*Soho*	XXX	L'Escargot
17	*Hyde Park & Knightsbridge*	XXX	Foliage
20	*Mayfair*	XXX	Gordon Ramsay at Claridge's
21	*Mayfair*	XXX	The Greenhouse
01	*North Kesington*	XXX	The Ledbury
25	*Regent's Park & Marylebone*	XXX	Locanda Locatelli
21	*Mayfair*	XXX	Maze
21	*Mayfair*	XXX	Mirabelle
30	*City of London*	XXX	1 Lombard Street (Restaurant)

page			
80	*City of London*	XXX	Rhodes Twenty Four
135	*Victoria*	XXX	Roussillon
121	*Mayfair*	XXX	Tamarind
95	*Chelsea*	XXX	Tom Aikens
116	*Belgravia*	XXX	Zafferano
113	*Wandsworth*	XX	Chez Bruce
80	*City of London*	XX	Club Gascon
107	*Kew*	XX	The Glasshouse
76	*Bloomsbury*	XX	Hakkasan
117	*Belgravia*	XX	Nahm
122	*Mayfair*	XX	Nobu
123	*Mayfair*	XX	Nobu Berkeley
96	*Chelsea*	XX	Rasoi Vineet Bhatia
131	*Soho*	XX	Richard Corrigan at Lindsay House
85	*Hammersmith*	XX	River Café
122	*Mayfair*	XX	Umu
115	*Bayswater & Maida Vale*	X	Assaggi
131	*Soho*	X	Yauatcha

Good food at moderate prices

Repas soignés à prix modérés

Pasti accurati a prezzi contenuti

Sorgfältig zubereitete, preiswerte Mahlzeiten

"Bib Gourmand"

page			
29	*St James's*	XX	Brasserie Roux
2	*Whitechapel*	XX	Café Spice Namaste
5	*Greenwich*	XX	Chapter Two
6	*Olympia*	XX	Cotto
6	*Regent's Park & Marylebone*	XX	Galvin
3	*Beckenham*	XX	Mello
2	*Islington*	XX	Metrogusto
6	*Chelsea*	XX	Racine
3	*Southfields*	XX	Sarkhel's
5	*Bayswater & Maida Vale*	X	L'Accento
5	*Hammersmith*	X	Agni

page			
130	*St. James's*	X	Al Duca
92	*Islington*	X	Brasserie La Trouvaille
108	*Twickenham*	X	Brula Bistrot
90	*City of London*	X	Comptoir Gascon
100	*Kensington*	X	Malabar
107	*Kew*	X	Ma Cuisine
108	*Twickenham*	X	Ma Cuisine
89	*Archway*	X	The Parsee
112	*Battersea*	X	Le Petit Max
76	*Bloomsbury*	X	Salt Yard
110	*Southwark*		Anchor & Hope

Particularly pleasant hotels and restaurants

Hôtels et restaurants agréables

Alberghi e ristoranti ameni

Angenehme Hotels und Restaurants

[5 pavilions]

page			page		
116	*Belgravia*	The Berkeley	117	*Hyde Park & Knightsbridge*	Mandarin Oriental Hyde Park
118	*Mayfair*	Claridge's	128	*St James's*	Ritz
117	*Mayfair*	Dorchester	132	*Strand & Covent Garden*	Savoy

[4 pavilions]

page			page		
101	*South Kensington*	The Bentley Kempinski	118	*Belgravia*	Connaught
			133	*Victoria*	The Goring
			130	*Soho*	The Soho

[3 pavilions]

page			page		
102	*South Kensington*	Blakes	116	*Belgravia*	The Halkin
93	*Chelsea*	Capital	99	*Kensington*	The Milestone
124	*Regent's Park & Marylebone*	Charlotte Street	132	*Strand & Covent Garden*	One Aldwych
74	*Bloomsbury*	Covent Garden	102	*South Kensington*	The Pelham
93	*Chelsea*	Draycott			

[2 pavilions]

page			page		
93	*Chelsea*	Knightsbridge	102	*South Kensington*	Number Sixteen

XXXXX

page		
128	*St. James's*	The Restaurant (at Ritz H.)

XXXX

page			page		
120	*Mayfair*	Angela Hartnett at The Connaught	116	*Belgravia*	Pétrus (at The Berkeley H.)
103	*South Kensington*	1880 (at The Bentley Kempinski)	132	*Strand & Covent Garden*	The Savoy Grill
120	*Mayfair*	Grill Room (at Dorchester H.)			

XXX

page			page		
95	*Chelsea*	Bibendum	125	*Regent's Park & Marylebone*	Orrery
94	*Chelsea*	The Capital Restaurant	110	*Southwark*	Oxo Tower
121	*Mayfair*	Mirabelle	108	*Bermondsey*	Le Pont de la Tour
			129	*St. James's*	The Wolseley

XX

page			page		
129	*St. James's*	Le Caprice	76	Camden	Mon Plaisir
133	*Strand & Covent Garden*	J. Sheekey	133	*Strand & Covent Garden*	Rules

X

page			page		
130	*St. James's*	Al Duca	110	*Southwark*	Oxo Tower Brasser
109	*Bermondsey*	Blueprint Café			

Restaurants classified according to type

Restaurants classés suivant leur genre
Ristoranti classificati secondo il loro genere
Restaurants nach Art und Einrichtung geordnet

merican

ge

3 *Mayfair*	X	Automat	

sian

5	*Chelsea*	XXX	Pengelley's	97	*Chelsea*	XX	Eight over Eight
3	*Mayfair*	XX	Cocoon	123	*Mayfair*	XX	Taman Gang
6	*Bloomsbury*	XX	Crazy Bear				

angladeshi

5	*Bayswater & Maida Vale*	X	Ginger

hinese

0	*Mayfair*	XXXX	China Tang	82	*Ealing*	XX	Maxim
2	*Mayfair*	XXX	Kai	100	*Kensington*	XX	Memories of China
7	*Chelsea*	XX	Good Earth	117	*Hyde Park & Knightsbridge*	XX	Mr Chow
2	*Mill Hill*	XX	Good Earth	78	*Holborn*	XX	Shangai Blues
6	*Bloomsbury*	XX	✿ Hakkasan	73	*Orpington*	XX	Xian
6	*Victoria*	XX	Ken Lo's Memories of China	77	*Hampstead*	XX	ZeNW3
6	*Chelsea*	XX	Mao Tai	132	*Soho*	X	Fung Shing
4	*Fulham*	XX	Mao Tai	131	*Soho*	X	✿ Yauatcha

anish

3	*South Kensington*	XX	Lundum's

astern European

0	*Southwark*	XX	Baltic	100	*Kensington*	XX	Wodka

nglish

0	*Mayfair*	XXXX	Grill Room (at Dorchester H.)	133	*Strand & Covent Garden*	XX	Rules
1	*Mayfair*	XXX	Brian Turner Mayfair	81	*City of London*	X	Paternoster Chop House
5	*Victoria*	XXX	Shepherd's				

rench

0	*Mayfair*	XXXX	✿✿ (Le) Gavroche	127	*Regent's Park & Marylebone*	XX	L'Aventure
0	*City of London*	XXX	Coq d'Argent	129	*St. James's*	XX	Bib Brasserie Roux
5	*Victoria*	XXX	✿ Roussillon				
1	*Islington*	XX	Almeida				

96	*Chelsea*	XX	(Le) Cercle
80	*City of London*	XX	✿ Club Gascon
96	*Chelsea*	XX	(Le) Colombier
81	*City of London*	XX	Dine
112	*Battersea*	XX	(The) Food Room
104	*Surbiton*	XX	(The) French Table
76	*Bloomsbury*	XX	Mon Plaisir
96	*Chelsea*	XX	Poissonnerie de l'Avenue (Seafood)
96	*Chelsea*	XX	☺ Racine
131	*Soho*	XX	(La) Trouvaille
92	*Islington*	X	☺ Brasserie La Trouvaille
108	*Twickenham*	X	☺ Brula Bistrot
90	*Clerkenwell*	X	☺ Comptoir Gascon
104	*Kennington*	X	Lobster Pot (Seafood)
107	*Kew*	X	☺ Ma Cuisin
108	*Twickenham*	X	☺ Ma Cuisin
112	*Battersea*	X	☺ (Le) Petit M
136	*Victoria*	X	(La) Poule au Pot

Greek

83	*Hoxton*	XX	Real Greek
84	*Hoxton*	X	Mezedopolio
110	*Southwark*	X	Souvlaki and Bar

Indian

116	*Belgravia*	XXX	✿ Amaya
121	*Mayfair*	XXX	Benares
103	*South Kensington*	XXX	Bombay Brasserie
95	*Chelsea*	XXX	Chutney Mary
135	*Victoria*	XXX	(The) Cinnamon Club
135	*Victoria*	XXX	Quilon
130	*Soho*	XXX	Red Fort
121	*Mayfair*	XXX	✿ Tamarind
108	*Bermondsey*	XX	Bengal Clipper
112	*Spitalfields*	XX	Bengal Trader
131	*Soho*	XX	Café Lazeez
112	*Whitechapel*	XX	☺ Café Spice Namaste
123	*Mayfair*	XX	Chor Bizarre
126	*Regent's Park & Marylebone*	XX	Deya
79	*Swiss Cottage*	XX	Eriki
97	*Chelsea*	XX	Haandi
72	*Edgware*	XX	Haandi
85	*Hammersmith*	XX	Indian Zing
81	*City of London*	XX	Kasturi
103	*South Kensington*	XX	Khan's of Kensington
76	*Bloomsbury*	XX	Malabar Junction
129	*St James's*	XX	Mint Leaf
78	*Holborn*	XX	Moti Mahal
96	*Chelsea*	XX	Painted Hero
104	*Kennington*	XX	Painted Hero
81	*Addington*	XX	Planet Spice
126	*Regent's Park & Marylebone*	XX	(La) Porte des Indes
127	*Regent's Park & Marylebone*	XX	Rasa Samudr (Seafood) (Vegetarian)
96	*Chelsea*	XX	✿ Rasoi Vinee Bhatia
113	*Southfields*	XX	☺ Sarkhel's
104	*Herne Hill*	XX	3 Monkeys
97	*Chelsea*	XX	Vama
100	*Kensington*	XX	Zaika
85	*Hammersmith*	X	☺ Agni
104	*South Kensington*	X	Café Lazeez
113	*Southfields*	X	Calcutta Notebook
113	*Tooting*	X	Kastoori (Vegetarian)
100	*Kensington*	X	☺ Malabar
76	*Bloomsbury*	X	Mela
89	*Archway*	X	☺ (The) Pars
84	*Stoke Newington*	X	Rasa (Vegetarian)
73	*Willesden Green*	X	Sabras (Vegetarian)
123	*Mayfair*	X	Veeraswamy

Italian

121	*Mayfair*	XXX	Cecconi's
129	*St James's*	XXX	Fiore
133	*Victoria*	XXX	(L') Incontro
126	*Regent's Park & Marylebone*	XXX	Latium
125	*Regent's Park & Marylebone*	XXX	✿ Locanda Locatelli
130	*Soho*	XXX	Quo Vadis
135	*Victoria*	XXX	Santini

1	*Mayfair*	XXX	Sartoria
5	*Chelsea*	XXX	Toto's
6	*Belgravia*	XXX	✪ Zafferano
2	*Mayfair*	XX	Alloro
0	*Kensington*	XX	(The) Ark
7	*Regent's Park & Marylebone*	XX	Bertorelli
7	*Regent's Park & Marylebone*	XX	Caldesi
6	*Chelsea*	XX	Caraffini
6	*Victoria*	XX	(Il) Convivio
5	*Chelsea*	XX	Daphne's
1	*North Kensington*	XX	Edera
3	*Putney*	XX	Enoteca Turi
2	*Mayfair*	XX	Giardinetto
2	*Islington*	XX	☺ Metrogusto
5	*Bloomsbury*	XX	Neal Street
6	*Chelsea*	XX	Pellicano
1	*Canary Wharf*	XX	Quadrato
5	*Hammersmith*	XX	✪ River Café
6	*Regent's Park & Marylebone*	XX	Rosmarino
5	*Bloomsbury*	XX	Sardo
78	*Primrose Hill*	XX	Sardo Canale
122	*Mayfair*	XX	Teca
109	*Bermondsey*	XX	Tentazioni
100	*Kensington*	XX	Timo
131	*Soho*	XX	Vasco and Piero's Pavillion
115	*Bayswater & Maida Vale*	X	☺ (L') Accento
130	*St. James's*	X	☺ Al Duca
115	*Bayswater & Maida Vale*	X	✪ Assaggi
131	*Soho*	X	Bertorelli
127	*Regent's Park & Marylebone*	X	Caffè Caldesi
76	*Bloomsbury*	X	Camerino
109	*Bermondsey*	X	Cantina Del Ponte
100	*Kensington*	X	Cibo
86	*Crouch End*	X	Florians
115	*Bayswater & Maida Vale*	X	Green Olive
97	*Chelsea*	X	Manicomio
136	*Victoria*	X	Olivo
76	*Bloomsbury*	X	Passione
106	*Barnes*	X	Riva

panese

6	*Chelsea*	XX	Benihana
8	*Holborn*	XX	Matsuri-High Holborn
9	*St James's*	XX	Matsuri-St James
2	*Mayfair*	XX	✪ Nobu
3	*Mayfair*	XX	✪ Nobu Berkeley
6	*Chelsea*	XX	Nozomi
6	*Regent's Park & Marylebone*	XX	Roka
123	*Mayfair*	XX	Sumosan
81	*City of London*	XX	Tatsuso
111	*Canary Wharf*	XX	Ubon by Nobu
122	*Mayfair*	XX	✪ Umu
117	*Hyde Park & Knightsbridge*	XX	Zuma
76	*Bloomsbury*	X	Abeno
131	*Soho*	X	itsu
73	*Willesden Green*	X	Sushi-Say
104	*Clapham*	X	Tsunami

orean

4	*Fulham*	X	Wizzy

osher

1	*Bloomsbury*	XX	Bevis Marks
126	*Regent's Park & Marylebone*	XX	Six 13

tin American

1	*Soho*	XX	Floridita

ebanese

2	*Mayfair*	XX	Fakhreldine
7	*Regent's Park & Marylebone*	XX	Levant
117	*Belgravia*	XX	Noura Brasserie
129	*St James's*	XX	Noura Central

Moroccan

123	*Mayfair*	XX	Momo

North African

85	*Hammersmith & Fulham*	X	Azou

Pubs

128	*Regent's Park & Marylebone*	(The) Abbey Road
97	*Chelsea*	Admiral Codrington
110	*Southwark*	Anchor & Hope
85	*Hammersmith*	Anglesea Arms
92	*Islington*	(The) Barnsbury
82	*Acton Green*	(The) Bollo
98	*Chelsea*	Builders Arms
86	*Highgate*	(The) Bull
83	*Hackney*	Cat and Mutton
97	*Chelsea*	Chelsea Ram
98	*Chelsea*	Cross Keys
89	*Chiswick*	(The) Devonshire House
92	*Islington*	Drapers Arms
82	*South Ealing*	Ealing Park Tavern
78	*Primrose Hill*	(The) Engineer
85	*Fulham*	(The) Farm
105	*Wimbledon*	(The) Fire Stables
73	*Willesden Green*	(The) Green
113	*Battersea*	(The) Greyhound
72	*Kensal Rise*	(The) Greyhound
111	*Canary Wharf*	(The) Gun
109	*Bermondsey*	(The) Hartley
74	*Belsize Park*	(The) Hill
99	*Earl's Court*	Hollywood Arr
90	*Canonbury*	(The) House
79	*Tufnell Park*	Junction Tave
98	*Chelsea*	Lots Road Pub & Dining Roo
77	*Hampstead*	(The) Magdala
92	*Islington*	(The) Northga
91	*Finsbury*	(The) Peasant
98	*Chelsea*	(The) Phoenix
98	*Chelsea*	(The) Pig's Ea
84	*Shoreditch*	(The) Princess
78	*Primrose Hill*	(The) Queens
86	*Highgate*	Rose & Crown
89	*Archway*	St John's
85	*Fulham*	(The) Salisbur
92	*Islington*	(The) Social
98	*Chelsea*	Swag and Tails
107	*East Sheen*	(The) Victoria
115	*Bayswater & Maida Vale*	(The) Waterwa
91	*Finsbury*	(The) Well
77	*Hampstead*	(The) Wells

Scottish

136	*Victoria*	XX	Boisdale
80	*City of London*	XX	Boisdale of Bishopgate

Seafood

95	*Chelsea*	XXX	One-O-One
112	*St. Katherine's Dock*	XX	(The) Aquarium
81	*City of London*	XX	Chamberlain's
84	*Fulham*	XX	Deep
133	*Strand & Covent Garden*	XX	J. Sheekey
96	*Chelsea*	XX	Poissonnerie de l'Avenue (French)
127	*Regent's Park & Marylebone*	XX	Rasa Samudr (Indian) (Vegetarian)
89	*Chiswick*	X	Fishworks
128	*Regent's Park & Marylebone*	X	Fishworks
104	*Kennington*	X	Lobster Pot (French)

Spanish

103	*South Kensington*	XX	Cambio De Tercio
76	*Bloomsbury*	XX	Fino
76	*Bloomsbury*	X	Cigala

wedish

hai

urkish

egetarian

ietnamese

Boroughs and areas

Greater London *is divided, for administrative purposes, into 32 boroughs plus the City : the sub-divide naturally into minor areas, usually grouped around former villages or quarters, whi often maintain a distinctive character.*

BARNET *Gtr London.*

Brent Cross *Gtr London – ✉ NW2.*

Holiday Inn London Brent Cross, Tilling Rd, NW2 1LP, ✆ (020) 8201 868 *Fax (020) 8455 4660* – 🛗 ⇌ ▤ ♿ 🅿 – 🏛 70. MC AE VISA. ✗ 2 DU
Rest *(closed Sunday)* a la carte 25.00/32.00 – ☕ 13.95 – **153 rm** 🚹117.50/211.50 🚹🚹117.50/223.25.
◆ A ten storey purpose-built group hotel, usefully located at the foot of the M1. We equipped bedrooms are triple-glazed and business rooms are available. Informal resta rant and all-day open bar.

Child's Hill *Gtr London – ✉ NW2.*

Philpott's Mezzaluna, 424 Finchley Rd, NW2 2HY, ✆ (020) 7794 045 *Fax (020) 7794 0452*, 🏠 – ▤. MC VISA 10 NZA
closed 25-26 December, 1 January, Good Friday, Saturday lunch and Monday – **Rest** - Itali influences - 20.00/29.50.
◆ Homely Italian restaurant, affably run by patrons. Huge lunar artefacts complement t plain walls. Weekly changing menus offer tasty, modern cuisine at moderate prices.

Edgware *Gtr London – ✉ HA8.*

Haandi, 301-303 Hale Lane, HA8 7AX ⊖ *Edgware*, ✆ (020) 8905 4433, *haandiresta ant@btconnect.com, Fax (020) 8905 4646* – ▤. MC AE ⓓ VISA 2 CT
closed lunch Monday and Tuesday – **Rest** - Indian - a la carte 14.35/27.00.
◆ In the middle of a busy high street, this brightly lit restaurant boasts skylight, sm central fountain, vivid colours and flavoursome dishes from North India.

Mill Hill *Gtr London – ✉ NW7.*

⛳18 *100 Barnet Way, Mill Hill* ✆ *(020) 8959 2339* **CT.**

Good Earth, 143 The Broadway, NW7 4RN, ✆ (020) 8959 7011, *Fax (020) 8959 1464* – ▤ MC AE VISA 2 CT
closed 23-30 December – **Rest** - Chinese - 25.00/35.00 (dinner) and a la carte 23.50/50.0
◆ Smart, well-kept Chinese restaurant set slightly back from the busy A1 outside. Spacio and comfortable with efficient staff. Authentic menu; extensive vegetarian choice.

BEXLEY *Gtr London.*

Bexleyheath *Kent – ✉ Kent.*

Bexleyheath Marriott, 1 Broadway, DA6 7JZ, ✆ (020) 8298 1000, *bexleyheath@m riotthotels.co.uk, Fax (020) 8298 1234*, Fö, 🏊 – 🛗, ⇌ rm, ▤ ♿ 🅿 – 🏛 250. MC AE VISA. ✗ 8 JX
***Copper*:** **Rest** *(closed Sunday)* a la carte 17.50/37.50 s. 🍷 – ☕ 14.95 – **142 r** 🚹114.00/119.00 – 🚹🚹114.00/119.00.
◆ A group hotel offering extensive conference facilities as well as a leisure club in a Graec Roman theme. Comfortable and spacious bedrooms with marble bathrooms. Popul carvery restaurant..

BRENT *Gtr London.*

Kensal Rise *Middx – ✉ Middx.*

The Greyhound, 64-66 Chamberlayne Rd, NW10 3JJ ⊖ *Kensal Green*, ✆ (020) 896 8080, *thegreyhoundnw10@aol.com, Fax (020) 8969 8081*, 🏠 – ▤. MC VISA 10 MZB
closed 25-26 December, 1 January and Monday lunch – **Rest** a la carte 18.00/28.50 🍷.
◆ Trendy gastropub, opened in late 2003. On one side: bar with leather sofas; on othe restaurant with reclaimed furniture, black oak floors and modern British cooking.

Wembley Middx – ✉ Middx.

Premier Travel Inn Metro, 151 Wembley Park Drive, HA9 8HQ ⊖ *Wembley Park,* ✆ (0870) 7001446, *Fax (0870) 7001447* – |♦|, ⇔ ▤ ♿ P. MC AE ◑ VISA. ✂ 2 **CU** z
Rest (grill rest.) – **153 rm** 59.95 – 59.95.
◆ Lodge offering good value accommodation. All of the spacious modern bedrooms are carefully planned and feature king size beds. Bright, colourful restaurant.

Willesden Green Middx – ✉ Middx.

Sabras, 263 High Rd, NW10 2RX ⊖ *Dollis Hill,* ✆ (020) 8459 0340, *Fax (020) 8459 0541* – ⇔. MC VISA 9 **KZB** e
closed 25-26 December and Monday – **Rest** - Indian Vegetarian - (dinner only) a la carte approx 12.00.
◆ Tasty Indian vegetarian food served in modest, but friendly, surroundings. Framed awards and write-ups garnered since opening in 1973 bear testament to its popularity.

Sushi-Say, 33B Walm Lane, NW2 5SH ⊖ *Willesden Green,* ✆ (020) 8459 2971, *Fax (020) 8907 3229* – MC AE VISA 9 **LZB** a
closed 25-26 December, 1 January, Easter, 1 week August and Monday – **Rest** - Japanese - (dinner only and lunch Saturday and Sunday)/dinner 13.50/30.30 and a la carte 12.45/37.30.
◆ Friendly service provided by the owner in traditional dress. From bare wooden tables, watch her husband in the open-plan kitchen carefully prepare authentic Japanese food.

The Green, 110a Walm Lane, NW2 4RS ⊖ *Willesden Green,* ✆ (020) 8452 0171, *info@thegreennw2.com, Fax (020) 8452 0774,* ☂ – MC VISA 9 **LZA** a
closed 25 December – **Rest** a la carte 15.00/25.00.
◆ Large bustling bar with high ceiling conveying airy feel: light menus served here. Rear dining room: chef adds subtle Caribbean twists to modern dishes in generous portions.

BROMLEY Gtr London.

18, 9 *Cray Valley, Sandy Lane, St Paul's Cray, Orpington* ✆ *(01689) 837909* **JY**.

Beckenham Kent – ✉ Kent.

Mello, 2 Southend Rd, BR3 1SD, ✆ (020) 8663 0994, *info@mello.uk.com, Fax (020) 8663 3674* – ▤ P – 35. MC AE VISA 7 **GY** v
closed 2-9 January, 17 August-1 September and Sunday dinner – **Rest** a la carte 22.50/32.00.
◆ Unassuming and welcomingly run neighbourhood restaurant; walls hung with multi-coloured modern oils. Good value, seasonally sensitive dishes enhanced by precise execution.

Bromley Kent – ✉ Kent.

9 *Magpie Hall Lane* ✆ *(020) 8462 7014* **HY**.

Bromley Court, Bromley Hill, BR1 4JD, ✆ (020) 8461 8600, *enquiries@bromleycourthotel.co.uk, Fax (020) 8460 0899,* ☂, Fб, ♣ – |♦|, ⇔ rm, ▤ ✆ P – 150. MC AE ◑ VISA 8 **HY** z
Rest *(closed Saturday lunch)* 15.95/19.95 – **112 rm** ☐ 89.00/109.00 – 105.00/120.00, 2 suites.
◆ A grand neo-Gothic mansion in three acres of well-tended garden. Popular with corporate guests for the large conference space, and the bedrooms with modems and voicemail. Conservatory or terrace dining available.

Farnborough Kent – ✉ Kent.

Chapter One, Farnborough Common, Locksbottom, BR6 8NF, ✆ (01689) 854848, *info@chaptersrestaurants.com, Fax (01689) 858439* – ⇔ ▤ P. MC AE ◑ VISA 8 **HZ** a
closed first week January – **Rest** 19.95/26.95 ♀.
Spec. Ravioli of lobster, cauliflower purée and a lobster and Cognac sauce. Canon of lamb, roast shoulder, gnocchi and barigoule sauce. Lemon tart, passion fruit millefeuille.
◆ The mock Tudor exterior belies the stylish, light and contemporary interior. Precise and well executed modern European menu. West End sophistication without the prices.

Orpington Kent – ✉ Kent.

18 *High Elms, High Elms Rd, Downe, Orpington* ✆ *(01689) 858175.*

Xian, 324 High St, BR6 0NG, ✆ (01689) 871881 – ▤. MC AE ◑ VISA 8 **JY** a
closed Christmas, 1 week August and Sunday lunch – **Rest** - Chinese (Peking, Szechuan) - 11.10/17.50 and a la carte 11.10/17.50.
◆ Modern, marbled interior with oriental artefacts make this personally run Chinese restaurant a firm favourite with locals. Specialises in the hotter dishes of Peking.

Penge *Gtr London* – ✉ *SE20.*

Melrose House without rest., 89 Lennard Rd, SE20 7LY, ✆ (020) 8776 8884, *m... rose.hotel@virgin.net, Fax (020) 8778 6366,* – ⇹ ✆ ♿ P. VISA. ⚹ 7 GY
closed 22 December-2 January – **6 rm** 35.00/50.00 – 60.00/65.00.
◆ An imposing Victorian house with a conservatory sitting room. Breakfast is taken "e... famille" and the older bedrooms still have their original fireplaces.

CAMDEN *Gtr London.*

Belsize Park *Gtr London* – ✉ *NW3.*

The Hill, 94 Haverstock Hill, NW3 2BD ⊖ *Chalk Farm,* ✆ (020) 7267 0033 – ... VISA 11 QZB
closed 25-26 December and 1 January – **Rest** a la carte 16.00/24.00 ♀.
◆ Large 19C pub; lively main bar with twinkling fairy lights, old sofas, deep red walls an... dining tables. Menus offer a good choice with a Mediterranean or Asian influence.

Bloomsbury *Gtr London* – ✉ *NW1/W1/WC1/WC2.*

Russell, Russell Sq, WC1B 5BE ⊖ *Russell Square,* ✆ (020) 7837 6470, *sales.russell@prin... pal-hotels.com, Fax (020) 7837 2857* – |♦|, ⇹ rm, ▤ ✆ – 🏛 400. ⓜⓒ AE VIS... ⚹ 18 SZC
Rest a la carte approx 31.00 ♀ – ☕ 19.50 – **371 rm** 185.00 – 215.00, 2 suites.
◆ An impressive Victorian building dominating Russell Square. Boasts many original fea... tures including the imposing marbled lobby and staircase. Traditional or modern room... Restaurant has noticeable feel of grandeur.

Covent Garden, 10 Monmouth St, WC2H 9HB ⊖ *Covent Garden,* ✆ (020) 7806 100... *covent@firmdale.com, Fax (020) 7806 1100,* ⚒ – |♦| ▤ ✆ – 🏛 50. ⓜⓒ AE VIS... ⚹ 31 ALU
Brasserie Max **: Rest** (booking essential) a la carte 32.50/47.50 ♀ – ☕ 18.00 – **56 r...** 246.00/300.00 – 358.00, 2 suites.
◆ Individually designed and stylish bedrooms, with CDs and VCRs discreetly conceale... Boasts a very relaxing first floor oak-panelled drawing room with its own honesty ba... Informal restaurant.

Marlborough, 9-14 Bloomsbury St, WC1B 3QD ⊖ *Tottenham Court Road,* ✆ (02... 7636 5601, *resmarl@radisson.com, Fax (020) 7636 0532* – |♦|, ⇹ rm, ▤ rest, ✆ ♿ – 🏛 25... ⓜⓒ AE ⓓ VISA. ⚹ 31 AKT
Glass **: Rest** *(closed Saturday-Sunday)* a la carte 25.00/30.00 – ☕ 15.00 – **171 rm** 171.50... 238.50, 2 suites.
◆ A Victorian building around the corner from the British Museum. The lobby has bee... restored to its original marbled splendour and the bedrooms offer good comforts. Brigh... breezy restaurant with suitably modish cooking.

Mountbatten, 20 Monmouth St, WC2H 9HD ⊖ *Covent Garden,* ✆ (020) 7836 430... *Fax (020) 7240 3540,* ⚒ – |♦|, ⇹ rm, ▤ ✆ – 🏛 90. ⓜⓒ AE ⓓ VISA. ⚹ 31 ALU
Dial **: Rest** *(closed lunch Friday-Sunday)* a la carte 25.00/45.00 – ☕ 15.00 – **149 rm** 240.8... – 297.00, 2 suites.
◆ Photographs and memorabilia of the eponymous Lord Louis adorn the walls and corr... dors. Ideally located in the heart of Covent Garden. Compact but comfortable bedroom... Bright, stylish restaurant.

Grafton, 130 Tottenham Court Rd, W1P 9HP ⊖ *Warren Street,* ✆ (020) 7388 413... *resgraf@radisson.com, Fax (020) 7387 7394,* ⚒ – |♦|, ⇹ rm, ▤ ✆ ♿ – 🏛 100. ⓜⓒ AE ⓓ VISA. ⚹ 18 RZC
Aston's **: Rest** *(closed lunch Friday-Sunday)* a la carte 25.00/45.00 – ☕ 15.00 – **326 r...** 171.50 – 238.50, 4 suites.
◆ Just yards from Warren Street tube. Discreet Edwardian charm that belies its location i... one of London's busier streets. Bedrooms to becalm in soft beige tones. Open-plan res... taurant and bar.

Kenilworth, 97 Great Russell St, WC1B 3BL ⊖ *Tottenham Court Road,* ✆ (020) 763... 3477, *resmarl@radisson.com, Fax (020) 7631 3133,* ⚒ – |♦|, ⇹ rm, ▤ ♿ – 🏛 100. ⓜⓒ A... ⓓ VISA. ⚹ 31 AKT
Rest *(closed lunch Saturday-Sunday)* 19.50 (lunch) and a la carte 29.50/33.50 – ☕ 15.00 **186 rm** 171.50 – 238.50.
◆ Usefully placed for the shops of Oxford Street. Stylish interiors and modern designe... hi-tech bedrooms, equipped to meet the needs of the corporate traveller. Smart dinin... room with a modern style.

Jurys Gt Russell St, 16-22 Gt Russell St, WC1B 3NN ⊖ *Tottenham Court Road,* ✆ (020) 7347 1000, *gtrussellstreet@jurysdoyle.com, Fax (020) 7347 1001* – |♦|, ⇹ rm, ▤ ✆ ♿ – 220. MC AE ◑ VISA. 31 **AKT** n
Lutyens : **Rest** (bar lunch)/dinner a la carte 26.30/36.25 **s** – 16.00 – **169 rm** ✦240.00 – ✦✦240.00, 1 suite.
◆ Neo-Georgian building by Edward Lutyens, built for YMCA in 1929. Smart comfortable interior decoration from the lounge to the bedrooms. Facilities include a business centre. Restaurant has understated traditional style.

Montague on the Gardens, 15 Montague St, WC1B 5BJ ⊖ *Holborn,* ✆ (020) 7637 1001, *bookmt@rchmail.com, Fax (020) 7637 2516,* – |♦|, ⇹ rm, ▤ ✆ ♿ – 100. MC AE ◑ VISA 31 **ALT** a
The Chef's Table : **Rest** a la carte 26.85/41.00 ♀ – 16.50 – **93 rm** ✦159.00/246.00 – ✦✦176.00/246.00, 6 suites.
◆ A period townhouse with pretty hanging baskets outside. The hushed conservatory overlooks a secluded garden. The clubby bar has a Scottish golfing theme. Rich bedroom décor. Restaurant divided into two small, pretty rooms.

Holiday Inn Bloomsbury, Coram St, WC1N 1HT ⊖ *Russell Square,* ✆ (0870) 4009222, *reservation-bloomsbury@ichotelsgroup.com, Fax (020) 7713 5954* – |♦|, ⇹ rm, ▤ ♿ – 300. MC AE ◑ VISA. 18 **SZD** c
Rest 16.95/20.00 and dinner a la carte 24.00/30.85 – 14.95 – **315 rm** ✦99.00/115.00 – ✦✦105.00/120.00.
◆ Bright, modern bedrooms in warm, neutral tones. Have a drink in either the stylish bar with leather chairs or Callaghans Irish themed bar. Relaxed and contemporary dining.

Myhotel Bloomsbury, 11-13 Bayley St, Bedford Sq, WC1B 3HD ⊖ *Tottenham Court Road,* ✆ (020) 7667 6000, *res@myhotels.co.uk, Fax (020) 7667 6001,* – |♦| ⇹ ▤ ✆ – 40. MC AE VISA. 31 **AKT** x
Yo! Sushi : **Rest** - Japanese - a la carte 17.50/22.50 – 18.00 – **77 rm** ✦155.00/230.00 – ✦✦340.00/360.00.
◆ The minimalist interior is designed on the principles of feng shui; even the smaller bedrooms are stylish and uncluttered. Mybar is a fashionable meeting point. Diners can enjoy Japanese food from conveyor belt.

Pied à Terre (Osborn), 34 Charlotte St, W1T 2NH ⊖ *Goodge Street,* ✆ (020) 7636 1178, *p-a-t@dircon.co.uk, Fax (020) 7916 1171* – ⇹ ▤ 12. MC AE ◑ VISA 31 **AJT** e
closed 10 days Christmas, Saturday lunch, Sunday and Bank Holidays – **Rest** 28.50/60.00 ♀.
Spec. Ceviche of scallops, avocado and crème fraîche, basil jelly. Assiette of rabbit with pistachios, baby carrots and mustard sauce. Chocolate tart with stout ice cream and macadamia mousse.
◆ Understated, discreet exterior; intimate, stylish interior, incorporating sleek first floor lounge. Elaborate yet refined modern cuisine complemented by accomplished service.

Mon Plaisir, 21 Monmouth St, WC2H 9DD ⊖ *Covent Garden,* ✆ (020) 7836 7243, *eatafrog@mail.com, Fax (020) 7240 4774* – MC AE VISA 31 **ALU** g
closed Christmas, Saturday lunch, Sunday and Bank Holidays – **Rest** - French - 15.95 (lunch) and a la carte 26.20/37.85 ♀.
◆ London's oldest French restaurant and family-run for over fifty years. Divided into four rooms, all with a different feel but all proudly Gallic in their decoration.

Incognico, 117 Shaftesbury Ave, WC2H 8AD ⊖ *Tottenham Court Road,* ✆ (020) 7836 8866, *Fax (020) 7240 9525* – ▤. MC AE ◑ VISA 31 **AKU** q
closed 1 week Christmas, Sunday and Bank Holidays – **Rest** a la carte 20.50/32.00 ♀.
◆ Opened in 2000 with its robust décor of wood panelling and brown leather chairs. Downstairs bar has a window into the kitchen, from where French and English classics derive.

Neal Street, 26 Neal St, WC2H 9QW ⊖ *Covent Garden,* ✆ (020) 7836 8368, *Fax (020) 7240 3964* – MC AE ◑ VISA 31 **ALU** s
closed 24 December-2 January, Sunday and Bank Holidays – **Rest** - Italian - 25.00 (lunch) and a la carte 28.00/44.50 ♀.
◆ Light, bright and airy; tiled flooring and colourful pictures. Dishes range from the simple to the more complex. Mushrooms a speciality. Has its own shop next door.

Sardo, 45 Grafton Way, W1T 5DQ ⊖ *Warren Street,* ✆ (020) 7387 2521, *info@sardo-restaurant.com, Fax (020) 7387 2559.* MC AE ◑ VISA 18 **RZD** c
closed Saturday lunch and Sunday – **Rest** - Italian (Sardinian specialities) - a la carte 24.90/34.00.
◆ Simple, stylish interior run in a very warm and welcoming manner with very efficient service. Rustic Italian cooking with a Sardinian character and a modern tone.

Hakkasan, 8 Hanway Pl, W1T 1HD ⊖ *Tottenham Court Road,* ✆ (020) 7927 700(
mail@hakkasan.com, Fax (020) 7907 1889 – ▤. MC AE VISA 31 AKT
closed 24-25 December – **Rest** - Chinese (Canton) - a la carte 29.00/78.00 ♀.
Spec. Roast sesame chicken in Malay sauce. Stir-fry black pepper rib-eye beef. Pan-frie silver cod in XO sauce.
◆ A distinctive, modern interpretation of Cantonese cooking in an appropriately cor temporary and cavernous basement. The lively, bustling bar is an equally popular night spot.

Fino, 33 Charlotte St (entrance on Rathbone St), W1T 1RR ⊖ *Goodge Street,* ✆ (020) 781 8010, *info@finorestaurant.com, Fax (020) 7813 8011* – MC AE VISA 31 AJT
closed 25 December, Sunday and Bank Holidays – **Rest** - Spanish - a la cart 16.50/49.50 **s.** ♀.
◆ Spanish-run basement bar with modern style décor and banquette seating. Wide-rang ing menu of authentic dishes; 2 set-price selections offering an introduction to tapas.

Crazy Bear, 26-28 Whitfield St, W1T 2RG ⊖ *Goodge Street,* ✆ (020) 7631 0088, *enq ries@crazybeargroup.co.uk, Fax (020) 7631 1188* – ▤. MC AE VISA 31 AKT
closed 1 week Christmas, Saturday lunch and Sunday – **Rest** - South East Asian - a la cart 23.00/32.00.
◆ Exotic destination: downstairs bar geared to fashionable set; ground floor dining roor is art deco inspired. Asian flavoured menus, with predominance towards Thai dishes.

Archipelago, 110 Whitfield St, W1T 5ED ⊖ *Goodge Street,* ✆ (020) 7383 3346, *archip lago@onetel.com, Fax (020) 7383 7181* – ✂. MC AE DC VISA 18 RZD
closed 25 December, Saturday lunch, Sunday and Bank Holiday Mondays – **Rest** a la cart 26.00/37.00.
◆ Eccentric in both menu and décor and not for the faint hearted. Crammed with knick knacks from cages to Buddhas. Menu an eclectic mix of influences from around the worl

Malabar Junction, 107 Great Russell St, WC1B 3NA ⊖ *Tottenham Court Road,* ✆ (02(7580 5230, *Fax (020) 7436 9942* – ▤. MC AE VISA 31 AKT
closed 25-27 December – **Rest** - South Indian - a la carte 15.00/23.50 🎭.
◆ Specialising in dishes from southern India. Bright restaurant with a small fountain in th centre of the room below a large skylight. Helpful and attentive service.

Passione, 10 Charlotte St, W1T 2LT ⊖ *Tottenham Court Road,* ✆ (020) 7636 283 *Liz@passione.co.uk, Fax (020) 7636 2889* – MC AE DC VISA 31 AKT
closed Saturday lunch and Sunday – **Rest** - Italian - (booking essential) a la cart 40.50/45.50.
◆ Compact but light and airy. Modern Italian cooking served in informal surroundings, wit friendly and affable service. Particularly busy at lunchtime.

Cigala, 54 Lamb's Conduit St, WC1N 3LW ⊖ *Holborn,* ✆ (020) 7405 1717, *tasty@ gala.co.uk, Fax (020) 7242 9949* – MC AE DC VISA 19 TZD
closed 25-26 December, 1 January and Easter Sunday – **Rest** - Spanish - 18.00 (lunch) and la carte 18.50/34.50 🎭 ♀.
◆ Spanish restaurant on the corner of attractive street. Simply furnished with large win dows and open-plan kitchen. Robust Iberian cooking. Informal tapas bar downstairs.

Camerino, 16 Percy St, W1T 1DT ⊖ *Tottenham Court Road,* ✆ (020) 7637 990(*info@camerinorestaurant.com, Fax (020) 7637 9696* – ▤. MC AE DC VISA 31 AKT
closed 25-26 December, 1 January, Saturday lunch and Sunday – **Rest** - Italian - 21.50/26.5 🎭 ♀.
◆ Personally run, wood floored restaurant where bold red drapes contrast with crisp whit linen-clad tables. Menus take the authentic taste of Italy's regions for inspiration.

Mela, 152-156 Shaftesbury Ave, WC2H 8HL ⊖ *Leicester Square,* ✆ (020) 7836 863 *info@melarestaurant.co.uk, Fax (020) 7379 0527* – ▤. MC AE DC VISA 31 AKU
closed 25-26 December – **Rest** - Indian - 12.50/18.00 and a la carte 13.50/26.95 **s.**.
◆ Vibrantly decorated dining room with a simple style in a useful location close to Theatre land. Enjoy thoroughly tasty Indian food in a bustling, buzzy environment.

Abeno, 47 Museum St, WC1A 1LY ⊖ *Tottenham Court Road,* ✆ (020) 7405 3211, *ok nomi@abeno.co.uk, Fax (020) 7405 3212* – ▤. MC AE DC VISA 31 ALT
closed 24-26 and 31 December and 1 January – **Rest** - Japanese (Okonomi-Yaki) 7.50/19.80 (lunch) and a la carte 15.20/29.50.
◆ Specialises in Okonomi-yaki: little Japanese "pancakes" cooked on a hotplate on eac table. Choose your own filling and the size of your pancake.

Salt Yard, 54 Goodge St, W1T 4NA, ✆ (020) 7637 0657, *info@saltyard.co.u Fax (020) 7580 7435* – ▤. MC AE VISA 31 AJT
closed 2 weeks Christmas-New Year, Sunday, Saturday lunch and Bank Holidays – **Res** -Spanish and Italian tapas - a la carte 15.00/30.00.
◆ Vogue destination with buzzy downstairs restaurant specialising in inexpensive sharin plates of tasty Italian and Spanish dishes: try the freshly cut hams. Super wine list.

uston *Gtr London – ✉ NW1/WC1.*

Novotel London Euston, 100-110 Euston Rd, NW1 2AJ ⊖ *Euston,* ✆ (020) 7666 9000, *h5309@accor.com, Fax (020) 7666 9001,* ≤, Fø, ≘s – |¢|, ⇔ rm, ▤ ♿ – 🏠 450. MC AE ⓓ VISA. ✂ 18 SZC r
Mirrors : Rest *(closed Saturday-Sunday)* 17.95 (lunch) and dinner a la carte 23.95/31.90 s. ♀ – ▭ 14.50 – **311 rm** ★165.00 – ★★165.00, 1 suite.
◆ Extensive conference facilities that include the redeveloped Shaw theatre. Large marbled lobby. Modern bedrooms that offer views of London's rooftops from the higher floors. Lobby-based restaurant and bar look onto busy street.

Hilton London Euston, 17-18 Upper Woburn Pl, WC1H 0HT ⊖ *Euston,* ✆ (020) 7943 4500, *euston.reservations@hilton.com, Fax (020) 7943 4501,* Fø, ≘s – |¢|, ⇔ rm, ▤ ♿ – 🏠 120. MC AE ⓓ VISA. ✂ 18 SZC e
Woburn Place : Rest 19.95 (dinner) and a la carte 20.40/29.50 ♀ – ▭ 15.95 – **150 rm** ★217.00 – ★★264.00.
◆ Nearby transport links make this a useful location. Scandinavian styled bedrooms. Executive rooms are particularly well-equipped. Lighter fare in Woburn Place conservatory.

Premier Travel Inn Metro, 1 Dukes Rd, WC1H 9PJ ⊖ *Euston,* ✆ (0870) 2383301, *Fax (020) 7554 3419* – |¢|, ⇔ rm, ▤ rest, ♿. MC AE ⓓ VISA. ✂ 18 SZC s
Rest (grill rest.) – **220 rm** ★74.95/74.95 – ★★84.95/84.95.
◆ Budget accommodation with clean and spacious bedrooms, all with a large workspace. Double glazed but still ask for a quieter room at the back.

ampstead *Gtr London – ✉ NW3.*

Winnington Rd, Hampstead ✆ (020) 8455 0203.

The House without rest., 2 Rosslyn Hill, NW3 1PH, ✆ (020) 7431 8000, *reception@thehousehotel.co.uk, Fax (020) 7433 1775* – ⇔. MC AE ⓓ 11 PZA e
▭ 8.00 – **23 rm** ★70.00/120.00 – ★★180.00/220.00.
◆ Large Victorian house close to the shops and not far from Hampstead Heath. Pleasant breakfast room/bar. Individually styled, well appointed rooms; smart marbled bathrooms.

Langorf without rest., 20 Frognal, NW3 6AG ⊖ *Finchley Road,* ✆ (020) 7794 4483, *info@langorfhotel.com, Fax (020) 7435 9055* – |¢|. MC AE ⓓ VISA. ✂ 11 PZA c
41 rm ★82.00/98.00 – ★★98.00, 5 suites.
◆ Converted Edwardian house in a quiet residential area. Bright breakfast room overlooks secluded walled garden. Fresh bedrooms, many of which have high ceilings.

ZeNW3, 83-84 Hampstead High St, NW3 1RE ⊖ *Hampstead Heath,* ✆ (020) 7794 7863, *info@zenw3.com, Fax (020) 7794 6956* – ▤. MC ⓓ 11 PZA a
closed 24-25 December – **Rest** - Chinese - 14.80/26.00 and a la carte 22.00/32.50.
◆ Contemporary interior provided by the glass topped tables and small waterfall feature on the stairs. Professional service. Carefully prepared Chinese food.

The Wells, 30 Well Walk, NW3 1BX ⊖ *Hampstead Heath,* ✆ (020) 7794 3785, *info@thewellshampstead.co.uk, Fax (020) 7794 6817,* 🏠 – ▤. MC VISA 11 PZA v
closed 25-26 December – **Rest** 13.95/29.50 ♀.
◆ Attractive 18C inn with modern interior. Ground floor bar and a few tables next to open-plan kitchen; upstairs more formal dining rooms. Classically-based French cooking.

The Magdala, 2A South Hill Park, NW3 2SB ⊖ *Belsize Park,* ✆ (020) 7435 2503, *Fax (020) 7435 6167,* 🏠 – MC VISA 11 PZA s
closed 25 December – **Rest** a la carte 17.50/26.00 ♀.
◆ Located on the edge of the Heath. Two bars popular with locals, one with open-plan kitchen. Upstairs dining room, open at weekends, offers robust cooking. Simpler lunch menu.

atton Garden *Gtr London – ✉ EC1.*

Bleeding Heart, Bleeding Heart Yard, EC1N 8SJ, off Greville St ⊖ *Farringdon,* ✆ (020) 7242 8238, *bookings@bleedingheart.co.uk, Fax (020) 7831 1402,* 🏠 – MC AE ⓓ VISA 32 ANT e
closed 24 December-3 January, Saturday, Sunday and Bank Holidays – **Rest** a la carte 24.85/36.40 ♀ 🍇.
◆ Wood panelling, candlelight and a heart motif; a popular romantic dinner spot. By contrast, a busy City restaurant at lunchtime. French influenced menu. Weighty wine list.

Holborn Gtr London – ✉ WC1/WC2.

Renaissance Chancery Court, 252 High Holborn, WC1V 7EN ⊖ Holborn, ✆ (020) 7829 9888, sales.chancerycourt@renaissancehotels.com, Fax (020) 7829 9889, Fš, ≘s, ♯, ⇤ rm, ▤ ✆ ♿ – 🏰 400. MC AE ⓓ VISA. ✗ 32 AMT
Rest – (see *Pearl* below) – ☕ 21.50 – **354 rm** ✝300.00 – ✝✝300.00, 2 suites.
◆ Striking building built in 1914, converted to a hotel in 2000. Impressive marbled lob and grand central courtyard. Very large bedrooms with comprehensive modern facilitie

Kingsway Hall, Great Queen St, WC2B 5BX ⊖ Holborn, ✆ (020) 7309 0909, reservations@kingswayhall.co.uk, Fax (020) 7309 9129, Fš – ♯, ⇤ rm, ▤ ✆ ♿ – 🏰 150. MC ⓓ VISA. ✗ 31 ALT
Harlequin : Rest 16.00/35.00 and a la carte 16.00/32.00 – ☕ 15.50 – **168 rm** ✝300.0 ✝✝346.00, 2 suites.
◆ Large, corporate-minded hotel. Striking glass-framed and marbled lobby. Stylish grou floor bar. Well-appointed bedrooms with an extensive array of mod cons.

XXX **Pearl** (at Renaissance Chancery Court H.), 252 High Holborn, WC1V 7EN ⊖ Holbo ✆ (020) 7829 7000, Fax (020) 7829 9889 – ⇔ 10. MC AE ⓓ VISA 32 AMT
closed Saturday lunch and Sunday – **Rest** 24.50/26.50 and a la carte 50.00/90.00 ♀ ✗.
◆ Impressive dining room with walls clad in Italian marble; Corinthian columns. Waite provide efficient service at well-spaced tables ; original menus.

XX **Moti Mahal,** 45 Great Queen St, WC2B 5AA ⊖ Covent Garden, ✆ (020) 7240 932 reservations@motimahal-uk.com, Fax (020) 7836 0790 – ▤ ⇔ 35. MC AE VISA 31 ALU
closed 25-26 December and 1 January – **Rest** - Indian - 15.95/19.95 and a la ca 24.00/30.00.
◆ Elegant stone fronted restaurant. Bar with huge whisky selection; cool contempora dining room where concise, modern Indian dishes using well prepared ingredients a served.

XX **Matsuri - High Holborn,** Mid City Pl, 71 High Holborn, WC1V 6EA ⊖ Holborn, ✆ (02 7430 1970, eat@matsuri-restaurant.com, Fax (020) 7430 1971 – MC AE ⓓ VISA 32 AMT
closed 25 December, 1 January, Sunday and Bank Holidays – **Rest** - Japanese - 22.00/35. and a la carte 22.00/40.50 ♀.
◆ Spacious, airy Japanese restaurant. Authentic menu served in main dining room, basement teppan-yaki bar and at large sushi counter, where chefs demonstrate their ski

XX **Shanghai Blues,** 193-197 High Holborn, WC1V 7BD ⊖ Holborn, ✆ (020) 7404 166 info@shanghaiblues.co.uk, Fax (020) 7404 1448 – ▤ ⇔ 28. MC AE VISA 31 ALT
closed 25 December – **Rest** - Chinese - a la carte 22.00/35.00.
◆ Set in Grade II listed former St Giles Library, this spacious, moody Chinese restaurant offset by cool bar and mezzanine lounge. Wide range of specialities to choose from.

Primrose Hill Gtr London – ✉ NW1.

XX **Odette's,** 130 Regent's Park Rd, NW1 8XL ⊖ Chalk Farm, ✆ (020) 7586 5486, odettesrestaurant@yahoo.co.uk, Fax (020) 7722 5388 – MC AE VISA 11 QZB
closed 25 December, Sunday dinner, Monday lunch and Bank Holidays – **Rest** 20.00 (lunc and a la carte approx 42.50.
◆ Identified by the pretty hanging baskets outside. A charming interior with mirrors various sizes covering the walls. Detailed service. Contemporary cuisine.

XX **Sardo Canale,** 42 Gloucester Ave, NW1 8JD ⊖ Chalk Farm, ✆ (020) 7722 280 info@sardocanale.com, Fax (020) 7722 0802, 余 – ⇤ ▤. MC AE ⓓ VISA 12 RZB
closed Monday lunch – **Rest** - Italian (Sardinian specialities) - a la carte 22.90/32.90.
◆ A series of five snug but individual dining rooms in conservatory style; delightful terra with 200 year old olive tree. Appealing Italian menus with strong Sardinian accent.

🍺 **The Queens,** 49 Regent's Park Rd, NW1 8XD ⊖ Chalk Farm, ✆ (020) 7586 040 mail@thequeens49.fsnet.co.uk, Fax (020) 7586 5677, 余 – MC VISA 11 QZB
Rest a la carte 25.00/35.00 ♀.
◆ One of the original "gastropubs". Very popular balcony overlooking Primrose Hill and th high street. Robust and traditional cooking from the blackboard menu.

🍺 **The Engineer,** 65 Gloucester Ave, NW1 8JH ⊖ Chalk Farm, ✆ (020) 7722 095 Fax (020) 7483 0592, 余 – MC VISA 11 QZB
closed 25 December – **Rest** a la carte 23.00/28.75 ♀.
◆ Busy pub that boasts a warm, neighbourhood feel. Dining room, decorated with mod ern pictures, has modish appeal. Informal, chatty service. Modern cuisine.

Swiss Cottage Gtr London – ✉ NW3.

Marriott Regents Park, 128 King Henry's Rd, NW3 3ST ⊖ Swiss Cottage, ✆ (02 7722 7711, Fax (020) 7586 5822, Fš, ≘s, ⛝ – ♯, ⇤ rm, ▤ ✆ ♿ P – 🏰 300. MC AE ⓓ VISA. ✗ 11 PZB
Meditterano : Rest (dinner only) a la carte 18.45/32.15 s. ♀ – ☕ 16.45 – **298 rm** ✝163.30 ✝✝163.30, 5 suites.
◆ Large writing desks and technological extras attract the corporate market to this purpose-built group hotel. The impressive leisure facilities appeal to weekend guests. Larg open-plan restaurant and bar.

Swiss Cottage without rest., 4 Adamson Rd, NW3 3HP ⊖ *Swiss Cottage*, ✆ (020) 7722 2281, *reservations@swisscottagehotel.co.uk, Fax (020) 7483 4588* – 35. 11 PZB n
5.95 **53 rm** 59.50/99.50 – 69.50/130.00, 6 suites.
◆ Made up of four Victorian houses in a residential conservation area. Bedrooms vary in size and shape, reflecting the age of the house. Basement breakfast room.

Bradley's, 25 Winchester Rd, NW3 3NR ⊖ *Swiss Cottage*, ✆ (020) 7722 3457, *ssjbradleys@aol.com, Fax (020) 7435 1392* – 11 PZB e
closed 1 week Christmas, Monday, Sunday dinner and Saturday lunch – **Rest** 16.00/22.00 and a la carte 26.50/37.00
◆ Warm pastel colours and modern artwork add a Mediterranean touch to this neighbourhood restaurant. The theme is complemented by the cooking of the chef patron.

Eriki, 4-6 Northways Parade, Finchley Rd, NW3 5EN ⊖ *Swiss Cottage*, ✆ (020) 7722 0606, *info@eriki.co.uk, Fax (020) 7722 8866* – 11 PZB u
closed 25-26 December and lunch Saturday and Bank Holidays – **Rest** - Indian - a la carte 17.35/27.80.
◆ A calm and relaxing venue, in spite of the bright interior set off by vivid red walls. Obliging service of carefully presented, flavoursome dishes from southern India.

ufnell Park *Gtr London* – ✉ *NW5*.

Junction Tavern, 101 Fortess Rd, NW5 1AG ⊖ *Tufnell Park*, ✆ (020) 7485 9400, *Fax (020) 7485 9401*, – 12 RZA x
closed 24-26 December and 1 January – **Rest** a la carte 20.00/27.00.
◆ Typical Victorian pub with wood panelling. Eat in the bar or in view of the open plan kitchen. Robust cooking using good fresh ingredients, served in generous portions.

ITY OF LONDON *Gtr London* – ✉ *E1/EC1/EC2/EC3/EC4*.

Great Eastern, Liverpool St, EC2M 7QN ⊖ *Liverpool Street*, ✆ (020) 7618 5000, *info@great-eastern-hotel.co.uk, Fax (020) 7618 5001*, – rm, – 250. 34 ART t
Fishmarket **: Rest** - Seafood - *(closed Saturday-Sunday)* a la carte 31.00/49.00 – ***Miyabi*** **: Rest** - Japanese - *(closed Easter, Christmas, Saturday and Sunday)* (booking essential) 17.50 (lunch) and a la carte 15.00/25.00 – (see also ***Aurora*** below) – 22.00 – **264 rm** 287.00/346.00 – 405.00, 3 suites.
◆ A contemporary and stylish interior hides behind the classic Victorian façade of this railway hotel. Bright and spacious bedrooms with state-of-the-art facilities. Fishmarket based within original hotel lobby. Miyabi is compact Japanese restaurant.

Crowne Plaza London - The City, 19 New Bridge St, EC4V 6DB ⊖ *Blackfriars*, ✆ (0870) 4009190, *loncy.info@ichotelsgroup.com, Fax (020) 7438 8080*, – rm, – 180. 32 AOU a
Refettorio **: Rest** - Italian - *(closed Sunday and Saturday lunch)* a la carte 26.00/36.00 – ***Benugo*** **: Rest** a la carte 25.00/30.00 – 17.00 – **201 rm** 358.00 – 358.00, 2 suites.
◆ Art deco façade by the river; interior enhanced by funky chocolate, cream and brown palette. Compact meeting room; well equipped fitness centre. Sizable, stylish rooms. Modish Refettorio for Italian cuisine. Informal, all-day dining at Benugo.

Threadneedles, 5 Threadneedle St, EC2R 8AY ⊖ *Bank*, ✆ (020) 7657 8080, *resthreadneedles@theetongroup.com, Fax (020) 7657 8100* – 35. 34 ARU y
Rest – (see ***Bonds*** below) – 19.50 – **68 rm** 288.00/317.00 – 288.00/487.00, 1 suite.
◆ A converted bank, dating from 1856, with a stunning stained-glass cupola in the lounge. Rooms are very stylish and individual featuring CD players and Egyptian cotton sheets.

The Chamberlain, 130-135 Minories, EC3N 1NU ⊖ *Aldgate*, ✆ (020) 7680 1500, *thechamberlain@fullers.co.uk, Fax (020) 7702 2500* – 50. 34 ASU n
closed Christmas – **Rest** (in bar Saturday and Sunday) a la carte 10.85/19.85 – 12.95 – **64 rm** 195.00 – 195.00.
◆ Modern hotel aimed at business traveller, two minutes from the Tower of London. Warmly decorated bedrooms with writing desks. All bathrooms have inbuilt plasma TVs. Popular range of dishes.

Novotel London Tower Bridge, 10 Pepys St, EC3N 2NR ⊖ *Tower Hill*, ✆ (020) 7265 6000, *h3107@accor.com, Fax (020) 7265 6060*, – rm, rest, – 100. 34 ASU b
The Garden Brasserie **: Rest** (bar lunch Saturday-Sunday) (buffet lunch)/dinner a la carte 23.95/29.50 s. – 13.50 – **199 rm** 175.00 – 195.00, 4 suites.
◆ Modern, purpose-built hotel with carefully planned, comfortable bedrooms. Useful City location and close to Tower of London which is visible from some of the higher rooms. Informally styled brasserie.

XXX **Aurora** (at Great Eastern H.), Liverpool St, EC2M 7QN ⊖ *Liverpool Street*, ✆ (020) 76 7000, *restaurants@great-eastern-hotel.co.uk*, *Fax (020) 7618 5035* – ▤. MC AE (VISA 34 ART
closed Saturday-Sunday – **Rest** 28.00 (lunch) and a la carte 33.50/52.50 ♀.
• Vast columns, ornate plasterwork and a striking glass dome feature in this imposi dining room. Polished and attentive service of an elaborate and modern menu.

XXX ✿ **Rhodes Twenty Four,** 24th floor, Tower 42, 25 Old Broad St, EC2N 1HQ ⊖ *Liverpc Street*, ✆ (020) 7877 7703, *reservations@rhodes24.co.uk, Fax (020) 7877 7788*, ≤ Londor |‡| ▤. MC AE ⓞ VISA 34 ART
closed Christmas-New Year, Saturday, Sunday and Bank Holidays – **Rest** a la car 26.90/33.20 ♀.
Spec. Seared scallops with mashed potato and shallot mustard sauce. Truffled macarc cheese with chestnut mushroom, watercress and rocket salad. Bread and butter puddin
• Modern restaurant on the 24th floor of the former Natwest building with panoran views of the city. Modern, refined cooking of classic British recipes. Booking advised.

XXX **Coq d'Argent,** No.1 Poultry, EC2R 8EJ ⊖ *Bank*, ✆ (020) 7395 5000, *coqdargent@c ran-restaurants.co.uk, Fax (020) 7395 5050*, 斎 – |‡| ▤. MC AE ⓞ VISA 33 AQU
closed Saturday lunch, Sunday dinner and Bank Holidays – **Rest** - French - (booking esse tial) 27.00 (lunch) and a la carte 37.00/44.25 ♀.
• Take the dedicated lift to the top of this modern office block. Tables on the rooftc terrace have city views; busy bar. Gallic menus highlighted by popular shellfish dishes.

XXX ✿ **1 Lombard Street (Restaurant),** 1 Lombard St, EC3V 9AA ⊖ *Bank*, ✆ (020) 79 6611, *hb@1lombardstreet.com, Fax (020) 7929 6622* – ⇹ ▤ ⇔ 25. MC AE (VISA 33 AQU
closed Saturday, Sunday and Bank Holidays – **Rest** (lunch booking essential) 39.00/45. and a la carte 52.50/61.50 ♀.
Spec. Carpaccio of tuna with Oriental spices, ginger and lime vinaigrette. Beef tourned with wild mushrooms, parsley purée and oxtail sauce. Feuillantine of apple, Guinness i cream and glazed hazelnuts.
• A haven of tranquillity behind the forever busy brasserie. Former bank provides tl modern and very comfortable surroundings in which to savour the accomplished cuisine

XXX **Prism,** 147 Leadenhall, EC3V 4QT ⊖ *Aldgate*, ✆ (020) 7256 3875, *Fax (020) 7256 387* ▤. MC AE ⓞ VISA 34 ARU
closed 23 December-2 January, Saturday, Sunday and Bank Holidays – **Rest** a la car 33.00/42.50 ♀.
• Enormous Corinthian pillars and a busy bar feature in this capacious and modern resta rant. Efficient service of an eclectic menu. Quieter tables in covered courtyard.

XXX **Bonds** (at Threadneedles H.), 5 Threadneedle St, EC2R 8AY ⊖ *Bank*, ✆ (020) 7657 808 *bonds@theetongroup.com, Fax (020) 7657 8089* – ⇹ ▤ ⇔ 16. MC AE (VISA 34 ARU
closed 2 weeks Christmas-New Year, Saturday, Sunday and Bank Holidays – Re 20.00/25.00 and a la carte 30.00/47.50 ♀.
• Modern interior juxtaposed with the grandeur of a listed city building. Vast dining roo with high ceiling and tall pillars. Attentive service of hearty, contemporary food.

XX ✿ **Club Gascon** (Aussignac), 57 West Smithfield, EC1A 9DS ⊖ *Barbican*, ✆ (020) 7796 060 *Fax (020) 7796 0601* – ▤. MC AE VISA 33 APT
closed 22-31 December, Sunday, Saturday lunch and Bank Holidays – **Rest** - French (Ga cony specialities) - (booking essential) 38.00/60.00 and a la carte 32.50/78.50 ♀.
Spec. Foie gras "Rose Sangria". Glazed black cod with almonds and smoked grapes. Ste of "confit" snails, mousserons, Aligot and ventrèche.
• Intimate restaurant on the edge of Smithfield Market. Specialises in both the food ar wines of Southwest France. Renowned for its tapas-sized dishes.

XX **The Chancery,** 9 Cursitor St, EC4A 1LL ⊖ *Chancery Lane*, ✆ (020) 7831 4000, *reser tions@thechancery.co.uk, Fax (020) 7831 4002* – ▤. MC AE ⓞ VISA 32 ANT
closed 24-December-1 January and Saturday-Sunday – **Rest** 19.50/32.00 ♀.
• Near Law Courts, a small restaurant with basement bar. Contemporary interior wi intimate style. Quality ingredients put to good use in accomplished, modern dishes.

XX **Boisdale of Bishopgate,** Swedeland Court, 202 Bishopgate, EC2M 4NR ⊖ *Liverpc Street*, ✆ (020) 7283 1763, *Fax (020) 7283 1664* – ▤. MC AE VISA 34 ART
closed 25 December-2 January, Saturday, Sunday and Bank Holidays – **Rest** - Scottish 27.50/36.00 and a la carte 22.95/39.90 ♀.
• Through ground floor bar, serving oysters and champagne, to brick vaulted baseme with red and tartan décor. Menu featuring Scottish produce. Live jazz most evenings.

XX **Bevis Marks,** Bevis Marks, EC3 5DQ ⊖ *Aldgate,* ✆ (020) 7283 2220, *enquiries@bevismarkstherestaurant.com, Fax (020) 7283 2221,* – . MC AE VISA 34 ART x
closed Saturday, Sunday, Friday dinner and Jewish Holidays – **Rest** - Kosher - a la carte 23.00/33.90 ♀.
◆ Glass-roofed extension to city's oldest synagogue: limestone flooring, modern murals on wall. Regularly changing Kosher menus; influences from Mediterranean and Middle East.

XX **Searcy's,** Barbican Centre, Level 2, Silk St, EC2Y 8DS ⊖ *Barbican,* ✆ (020) 7588 3008, *searcys@barbican.org.uk, Fax (028) 7382 7247* – . MC AE VISA 33 AQT n
closed 25-26 December, Sunday and Saturday lunch – **Rest** 22.50/26.50 ♀.
◆ Stylish modern surroundings, smooth effective service and seasonal modern British cooking. Unique location ideal for visitors to Barbican's multi-arts events.

XX **Kasturi,** 57 Aldgate High St, EC3N 1AL ⊖ *Aldgate,* ✆ (020) 7480 7402, *reservation@kasturi-restaurant.co.uk, Fax (020) 7702 0256* – . MC AE VISA 34 ASU a
closed Sunday – **Rest** - Indian - 15.95 (lunch) and a la carte 16.85/23.85.
◆ Spacious wooden floored restaurant enhanced by mirrors; modern art on walls. Good service. Varied menu with original and authentic dishes.

XX **Chamberlain's,** 23-25 Leadenhall Market, EC3V 1LR ⊖ *Bank,* ✆ (020) 7648 8690, *info@chamberlains.org, Fax (020) 7648 8691* – . MC AE VISA 34 ARU v
closed Saturday, Sunday and Bank Holidays – **Rest** - Seafood - 16.95 (dinner) and a la carte 28.95/52.75 s. ♀.
◆ Bright, modern restaurant in ornate Victorian indoor market. Top quality seafood from fish and chips to mousse of lobster. There's even a fish tank in the lavatories!

XX **Tatsuso,** 32 Broadgate Circle, EC2M 2QS, ✆ (020) 7638 5863, *info.tatsuso@btinternet.com, Fax (020) 7638 5864* – . MC AE VISA 34 ART u
closed Saturday, Sunday and Bank Holidays – **Rest** - Japanese - (booking essential) a la carte 25.00/58.00 s..
◆ Dine in the busy teppan-yaki bar or in the more formal restaurant. Approachable staff in traditional costume provide attentive service of authentic and precise dishes.

XX **The White Swan,** 1st Floor, 108 Fetter Lane, EC4A 1ES ⊖ *Temple,* ✆ (020) 7242 9696, *info@thewhiteswanlondon.com, Fax (020) 7242 9122* – . MC AE VISA. 32 ANT n
closed 25-26 December, 1 January, Saturday, Sunday and Bank Holidays – **Rest** 24.00 (lunch) and dinner a la carte 22.00/30.00 ♀.
◆ Smart dining room above pub just off Fleet Street: mirrored ceilings, colourful paintings on wall. Modern, daily changing menus, are good value for the heart of London.

XX **Dine,** 17-18 Tooks Court, EC4A 1LB ⊖ *Chancery Lane,* ✆ (020) 7404 1818, *manager@dine-restaurant.co.uk, Fax (020) 7404 3838* – . MC AE VISA 32 ANT r
closed 2 weeks Christmas, Saturday, Sunday and Bank Holidays – **Rest** - French - 19.00/30.00 ♀.
◆ Cosy neighbourhood feel pervades with simple tables and bistro style informality. Real variety of artwork on the walls. Seasonal dishes with French base and modern touches.

X **Paternoster Chop House,** Warwick Court, Paternoster Square, EC4N 7DX ⊖ *St Paul's,* ✆ (020) 7029 9400, *Fax (020) 7029 9409,* – . MC AE VISA 33 APT x
closed 23 December-3 January, Saturday and Sunday – **Rest** - English - a la carte 30.50/35.50 ♀.
◆ A bistro ambience holds sway, while there's a reassuringly resolute British classic style to the dishes. Back to basics menu relies on seasonality and sourcing of ingredients.

ROYDON *Gtr London.*

Addington – ✉ *Surrey.*

18, 18, 9 Addington Court, Featherbed Lane ✆ *(020) 8657 0281* GZ – *18 The Addington, 205 Shirley Church Rd* ✆ *(020) 8777 1055* GZ.

XX **Planet Spice,** 88 Selsdon Park Rd, CR2 8JT, ✆ (020) 8651 3300, *emdad@planet-spice.com, Fax (020) 8651 4400* – P. MC AE VISA 7 GZ c
closed dinner 25-26 December – **Rest** - Indian - 11.95/16.95 and a la carte 12.20/20.40 ♀.
◆ Brasserie style Indian restaurant with fresh, vibrant décor and a modern feel. Attentive and helpful service. Traditional cooking with some innovative touches.

Coulsdon Surrey – ✉ Surrey.

Coulsdon Manor ⑤, Coulsdon Court Rd, via Stoats Nest Rd (B 2030), CR5 2LL, ☎ (020) 8668 0414, *swallow.coulsdon@swallowhotels.com, Fax (020) 8668 3118*, <, Ⓕ, ☰s, 18, squash – |‡| ⇔ & P – 🏛 180. MC AE ① VISA. ✗
Manor House : **Rest** 17.50/34.00 s. ♀ – **35 rm** ☐ ★131.00 – ★★168.00.
◆ A secluded Victorian country house, extended over the years. Set in 140 acres, much of which is taken up by the popular golf course. Smart bedrooms, restful sitting room. Softly-lit dining room with cocktail bar.

Croydon Surrey – ✉ Surrey.

Croydon Clocktower, Katharine St ☎ (020) 8253 1009.

Hilton Croydon, Waddon Way, Purley Way, CR9 4HH, ☎ (020) 8680 3000, *reservations.croydon@hilton.com, Fax (020) 8681 6171*, Ⓕ, ☰, ⊡ – |‡| ⇔ ▤ & P – 🏛 400. MC AE ① VISA. ✗ 7 FZ
closed 1-3 January – **Rest** *(closed Sunday)* (dinner only) a la carte 20.00/30.00 s. ♀ – ☐ 15.50 – **168 rm** ★215.00 – ★★215.00.
◆ A modern hotel where the relaxing café in the open-plan lobby is open all day. Internet access is available in all bedrooms, which are decorated to a good standard. Open-plan dining room; informal char-grill concept.

Jurys Inn, Wellesley Road, CR0 9XY, ☎ (020) 8448 6000, *jurysinncroydon@jurysdoyle.com, Fax (020) 8448 6111* – |‡|, ⇔ rm, ▤ ✆ & – 🏛 120. MC AE ① VISA ✗ 7 FZ
Rest (bar lunch)/dinner 16.95 s. – ☐ 9.50 – **240 rm** ★49.00/89.00 – ★★49.00/89.00.
◆ Along main dual carriageway in town centre. Informal coffee bar in foyer. Conference facilities on first and second floors. Bright, modern rooms with good facilities. Restaurant near foyer; very relaxed informality.

Premier Travel Inn Metro, 104 Coombe Rd, CR0 5RB, on A 212 ☎ (0870) 1977068, *Fax (020) 8686 6435*, ☞ – ⇔ rm, & P. MC AE ① VISA. ✗ 7 GZ
Rest (grill rest.) – **39 rm** ★59.95/59.95 – ★★64.95/64.95.
◆ Surprisingly pleasant country setting for this purpose-built lodge-style hotel; surrounded by woodland with an adjacent mock-rustic pub serving traditional cuisine.

EALING Gtr London.

Acton Green Gtr London – ✉ W4.

The Bollo, 13-15 Bollo Lane, W4 5LS ⊖ *Chiswick Park*, ☎ (020) 8994 6037, *thebollopub@btinternet.com, Fax (020) 8743 5810*, ☞ – MC AE ① VISA 6 CV
closed 25-26 December – **Rest** a la carte 19.00/22.00 ♀.
◆ Attractive redbrick pub with dining area under a domed glass rotunda. Daily changing menu - mixture of traditional and eclectic dishes - served throughout the pub.

Ealing Gtr London – ✉ UB6/W13.

18 *West Middlesex, Greenford Rd, Southall ☎ (020) 8574 3450* **BV** – 9 *Horsenden Hill, Woodland Rise, Greenford ☎ (020) 8902 4555* **BU**.

Premier Travel Inn Metro, Myllet Arns, Western Ave, Greenford, UB6 8TR, off A 40 ⊖ *Perivale*, ☎ (08701) 977119, *Fax (020) 8998 8823* – ⇔ rm, ▤ rest, & P. MC AE ① VISA ✗ 1 BU
Rest (grill rest.) – **39 rm** ★59.95/59.95 – ★★69.95/69.95.
◆ Modern, purpose-built lodge offering good value accommodation with bright and carefully planned bedrooms. Children's play area and popular grill restaurant adjacent.

Maxim, 153-155 Northfield Ave, W13 9QT ⊖ *Northfields*, ☎ (020) 8567 171[illegible] *Fax (020) 8932 0717* – ▤. MC AE VISA 1 BV
closed 25-28 December and Sunday lunch – **Rest** - Chinese (Peking) - 15.00/35.00 and a la carte 17.00/30.00.
◆ Decorated with assorted oriental ornaments and pictures. Well-organised service from smartly attired staff. Authentic Chinese cooking from the extensive menu.

South Ealing Gtr London – ✉ W5.

Ealing Park Tavern, 222 South Ealing Rd, W5 4RL ⊖ *South Ealing*, ☎ (020) 8758 187[illegible] *Fax (020) 8560 5269*, ☞ – MC AE VISA 1 BV
closed Monday lunch – **Rest** a la carte approx 22.00 ♀.
◆ Victorian building with an atmospheric, cavernous interior. Characterful beamed dining room and an open-plan kitchen serving modern dishes from a daily changing menu.

ENFIELD Gtr London.

Lee Valley Leisure, Picketts Lock Lane, Edmonton (020) 8803 3611 GT.

Enfield Middx – Middx.

Whitewebbs, Beggars Hollow, Clay Hill (020) 8363 2951, N : 1 m. FT.

Oak Lodge without rest., 80 Village Rd, Bush Hill Park, EN1 2EU, (020) 8360 7082, *oaklodge@fsmail.net*, – . MC AE VISA 3 FT a
6 rm 79.50/99.50 – 99.50.
◆ An Edwardian house personally run by the hospitable owner and located in a residential area. Individually decorated bedrooms are compact but well equipped.

Hadley Wood Herts. – Herts.

West Lodge Park , off Cockfosters Rd, EN4 0PY, (020) 8216 3900, *westlodge park@bealeshotel.co.uk, Fax (020) 8216 3937*, – – 80. MC AE VISA. 3 ET i
The Cedar : **Rest** *(closed Saturday lunch)* a la carte 31.25/41.75 – 13.50 – **59 rm** 110.00/130.00 – 150.00.
◆ Family owned for over half a century, a country house in sweeping grounds with arboretum. Comfortable sitting rooms; neat, spacious bedrooms. Use of nearby leisure centre. Dining room boasts large windows and exposed brick walls.

GREENWICH Gtr London.

Greenwich Gtr London – SE10.

North Pole, 131 Greenwich High Rd, SE10 8JA, (020) 8853 3020, *north-pole@btconnect.com, Fax (020) 8853 3501* – MC AE VISA 7 GV u
closed 25 December – **Rest** (bar lunch Monday-Saturday)/dinner 17.50/25.00 and a la carte 23.50/29.00 ♀.
◆ Rat-pack themed former pub with popular bar: piano played most evenings. Upstairs dining room benefits from large windows and bright colours. Relaxed service; robust cooking.

Spread Eagle, 1-2 Stockwell St, SE10 9JN, (020) 8853 2333, *goodfood@spreadeagle.org, Fax (020) 8305 0447* – . MC VISA 7 GV c
closed January – **Rest** a la carte 25.00/30.00 ♀.
◆ This converted pub is something of an institution. Cosy booth seating, wood panelling and a further upstairs room. Traditional French-influenced menu with attentive service.

HACKNEY Gtr London.

Hackney Gtr London – E8.

Cat & Mutton, 76 Broadway Market, E8 4QJ ⊖ *Bethnal Green*, (020) 7254 5599, *info@catandmutton.co.uk* – MC AE VISA 14 YZB a
closed 25-26 December, Sunday dinner and Monday lunch – **Rest** a la carte 18.00/30.00 ♀.
◆ 19C corner pub with vast windows, school chairs and wood-panelled ceiling. Menu on a slate board: robust gastro pub fare with ingredients from the Saturday farmers' market.

Hoxton Gtr London – E1/EC1/N1.

Saint Gregory, 100 Shoreditch High St, E1 6JQ ⊖ *Shoreditch*, (020) 7613 9800, *sales@saintgregoryhotel.com, Fax (020) 7613 9811*, – – 110. MC AE VISA. 20 XZD k
Rest a la carte 29.70/33.40 s. – 13.95 – **200 rm** 199.00/299.00 – 299.00.
◆ Purpose-built hotel on the edge of the Square Mile. Clean-lined, co-ordinated rooms with smart mod cons and king-size beds. Stylish 'Saints' bar. The Globe bar and restaurant has great views over The City.

Express by Holiday Inn without rest., 275 Old St, EC1V 9LN ⊖ *Old Street*, (020) 7300 4300, *reservationsfc@holidayinnlondon.com, Fax (020) 7300 4555* – – 80. MC AE VISA. 20 XZC a
224 rm 119.00 – 119.00.
◆ Large purpose-built property close to the tube and the financial district. Brightly decorated bedrooms are all generously sized and offer good value accommodation.

Real Greek, 15 Hoxton Market, N1 6HG ⊖ *Old Street*, (020) 7739 8212, *admin@therealgreek.co.uk, Fax (020) 7739 4910*, – MC VISA 20 XZC v
closed 24-27 December, Sunday and Bank Holidays – **Rest** - Greek - a la carte 18.45/30.10 ♀.
◆ A former Victorian pub in a pleasant square. Plain wooden tables with open-plan kitchen. Very tasty, wholly Greek menu and wine list with unaffected and pleasant service.

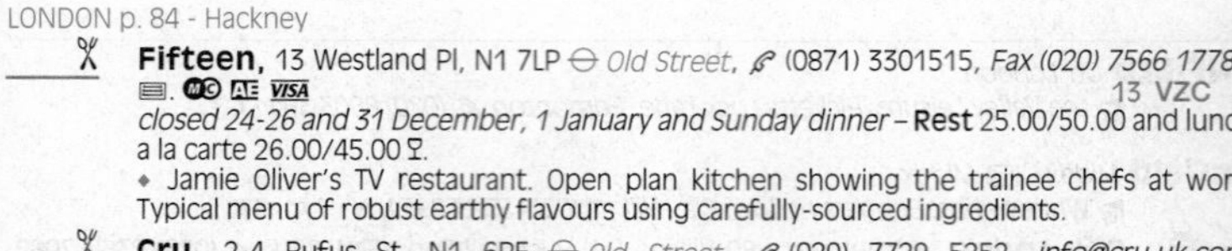

Fifteen, 13 Westland Pl, N1 7LP ⊖ *Old Street*, ✆ (0871) 3301515, *Fax (020) 7566 1778*
. MC AE VISA 13 VZC
closed 24-26 and 31 December, 1 January and Sunday dinner – **Rest** 25.00/50.00 and lunc a la carte 26.00/45.00 ♀.
◆ Jamie Oliver's TV restaurant. Open plan kitchen showing the trainee chefs at wor Typical menu of robust earthy flavours using carefully-sourced ingredients.

Cru, 2-4 Rufus St, N1 6PE ⊖ *Old Street*, ✆ (020) 7729 5252, *info@cru.uk.cor*, *Fax (020) 7729 1070* – . MC AE VISA 20 XZC r
closed 25 December-2 January and Monday – **Rest** 18.00 (lunch) and dinner a la cart 25.50/33.50 ♀.
◆ Converted 19C warehouse trendily located with artwork for sale. Bar and delicatesse leading past open kitchen to restaurant. Modern menu with Asian influences. Good value

Mezedopolio, 15 Hoxton Market, N1 6HG ⊖ *Old Street*, ✆ (020) 7739 8212, *a min@therealgreek.demon.co.uk, Fax (020) 7739 4910* – MC VISA 20 XZC
closed 24-27 December, Sunday and Bank Holidays – **Rest** - Greek meze - (bookings nc accepted) a la carte 10.00/16.70.
◆ Greek meze bar, part of The Real Greek, though with a more informal style. High ceiling marble memorials. Large menu of authentic dishes from Greece and the Aegean.

Shoreditch *Gtr London* – ✉ *EC2.*

The Princess (first floor), 76 Paul St, EC2A 4NE ⊖ *Old Street*, ✆ (020) 7729 9270
MC AE VISA 19 VZD
closed 25 December, Saturday lunch and Sunday dinner – **Rest** a la carte 21.85/28.40 ♀.
◆ Traditional corner pub given a gastro makeover. Dining room, above busy bar, has stylish appeal matched by interesting international dishes underpinned by strong cooking

Stoke Newington *Gtr London* – ✉ *N16.*

Rasa, 55 Stoke Newington Church St, N16 0AR, ✆ (020) 7249 0344, *Fax (02) 7637 0224*
. MC AE VISA 14 XZA
closed 24-26 December and 1 January – **Rest** - Indian Vegetarian - (booking essentia (dinner only and Saturday and Sunday lunch) 15.50 and a la carte 8.00/11.00.
◆ Busy Indian restaurant, an unpretentious environment in which to sample authenti sometimes unusual, dishes. The "Feast" offers a taste of the range of foods on offer.

HAMMERSMITH and FULHAM *Gtr London.*

Fulham *Gtr London* – ✉ *SW6.*

Premier Travel Inn Metro, 3 Putney Bridge Approach, SW6 3JD ⊖ *Putney Bridge* ✆ (0870) 2383302, *Fax (020) 7471 8315* – , rm, rest, . MC AE VIS 22 MZH
Rest (grill rest.) (dinner only) – **154 rm** 72.95/72.95 – 79.95/79.95.
◆ Converted office block offering clean, well-priced accommodation. All rooms have sof beds and large worktops.

Deep, The Boulevard, Imperial Wharf, SW6 2UB ⊖ *Fulham Broadway*, ✆ (020) 7736 333 *info@deeplondon.co.uk, Fax (020) 7736 7578,* – . MC AE VISA 23 PZH
closed 1 week Christmas, Monday, Sunday dinner and Saturday lunch – **Rest** - Seafood 19.50 (lunch) and a la carte 23.00/35.50 ♀.
◆ Slick, modern restaurant on rejuvenated riverside wharf. Linen-clad tables; floor-to ceiling windows. Modern seafood dishes with Scandinavian feel; large aquavit selection.

Blue Elephant, 4-6 Fulham Broadway, SW6 1AA ⊖ *Fulham Broadway*, ✆ (020) 738 6595, *london@blueelephant.com, Fax (020) 7386 7665* – . MC AE VISA 22 NZG
closed 1 January and Saturday lunch – **Rest** - Thai - (booking essential) 15.00/35.00 and a carte 25.00/38.00.
◆ Elaborately ornate, unrestrained décor: fountains, bridges, orchids and ponds with carp Authentic Thai food served by attentive staff in national costumes.

Mao Tai, 58 New Kings Rd, Parsons Green, SW6 4LS ⊖ *Parsons Green*, ✆ (020) 7731 252 *info@maotai.co.uk, Fax (020) 7471 8994* – . MC AE VISA 22 NZH
closed 25-26 December – **Rest** - Chinese (Szechuan) - a la carte 21.50/31.00 s ♀.
◆ A light and modern interior with wood flooring and framed artwork with an easter theme. Well organised service. Chinese cuisine with Szechuan specialities.

Wizzy, 616 Fulham Rd, SW6 5RP ⊖ *Parsons Green*, ✆ (020) 7736 9171, *wizzy838@y hoo.co.uk* – 24. MC AE VISA 22 NZG
Rest - Korean - 10.00/30.00 and a la carte 20.50/25.50 ♀.
◆ Minimalist restaurant where the cooking takes centre stage: concise, appealin contemporary Korean dishes calculated on nutritional balance: herbs and flavour to th fore.

Zinc Bar and Grill, 11 Jerdan Pl, Fulham Island, SW6 1BE *Fulham Broadway,* (020) 7386 2250, *zincfulham-reservations@conran-restaurants.co.uk, Fax (020) 7386 2260,* – . VISA 22 **NZG** a
closed 25 December – **Rest** a la carte 15.00/32.00.
◆ Bright modern bar; informal chic restaurant. Grills, seafood and modern international fare. No bookings accepted for the heated terrace so arrive early for a table.

The Farm, 18 Farm Lane, SW6 1PP *Fulham Broadway,* (020) 7381 3331, *info@thefarmfulham.co.uk* – . VISA . 22 **NZG** x
Rest a la carte 21.00/27.00.
◆ Red brick pub with leather sofas and contemporary fireplaces. Rear dining room is ultra stylish, and the menus are suitably modern British with a French accent.

The Salisbury, 21 Sherbrooke Rd, SW6 7HX *Fulham Broadway,* (020) 7381 4005, *thesalisburytavern@longshotplc.co.uk, Fax (020) 7381 1002* – . VISA 22 **MZG** e
– **Rest** (live jazz Monday evening) a la carte 19.45/26.15.
◆ Its residential location attracts a local crowd to the stylish bar. Separate, and equally à la mode, dining room with pleasant young staff. Wide ranging traditional menu.

Hammersmith *Gtr London – W6.*

River Café (Ruth Rogers/Rose Gray), Thames Wharf, Rainville Rd, W6 9HA *Barons Court,* (020) 7386 4200, *info@rivercafe.co.uk, Fax (020) 7386 4201,* – . VISA 21 **LZG** r
closed Christmas-New Year, Sunday dinner and Bank Holidays – **Rest** - Italian - (booking essential) a la carte 42.00/55.00.
Spec. Chargrilled squid with rocket, red chilli and lemon. Roast fillet of wild sea bass with cherry vine tomatoes and salsa verde. "Chocolate nemesis".
◆ Warehouse conversion with full length windows on one side, open plan kitchen the other. Canteen-style atmosphere. Accomplished rustic Italian cooking, uses the finest produce.

Indian Zing, 236 King St, W6 0RF *Ravenscourt Park,* (020) 8748 5959, *indianzing@aol.com, Fax (020) 8748 2332,* – . VISA 21 **LZG** a
closed 25 December – **Rest** - Indian - a la carte 20.60/26.00.
◆ Sophisticated, modern restaurant with crisp white walls adorned with photos of life on the subcontinent. Traditional Indian menus are jettisoned for modish, original dishes.

Snows on the Green, 166 Shepherd's Bush Rd, Brook Green, W6 7PB *Hammersmith,* (020) 7603 2142, *sebastian@snowsonthegreen.freeserve.co.uk, Fax (020) 7602 7553* – . VISA 15 **LZF** x
closed 24-29 December, Saturday lunch, Sunday and Bank Holiday Mondays – **Rest** 17.50 (lunch) and a la carte 24.00/28.00.
◆ Name refers to the chef patron, not the inclement weather found in west London. Mediterranean influenced decoration matched by the style of the cooking.

The Brackenbury, 129-131 Brackenbury Rd, W6 0BQ *Ravenscourt Park,* (020) 8748 0107, *Fax (020) 8748 6159,* – 15 **LZE** a
closed August Bank Holiday, 25-26 December, 1 January, Saturday lunch and Sunday dinner – **Rest** 14.50 (lunch) and a la carte 17.00/29.50.
◆ The closely set wooden tables, pavement terrace and relaxed service add to the cosy, neighbourhood feel. Cooking is equally unfussy; modern yet robust.

Azou, 375 King St, W6 9NJ *Stamford Brook,* (020) 8563 7266, *azourestaurant@artserve.net, Fax (020) 8748 1009* – . VISA 21 **KZG** u
closed lunch Saturday and Sunday and Bank Holidays – **Rest** - North African - (lunch booking essential) a la carte 15.35/24.05.
◆ The North African theme is not confined to the menu; the room is decorated with hanging lanterns, screens and assorted knick-knacks. Friendly service and well priced dishes.

Agni, 160 King St, W6 0QU *Ravenscourt Park,* (020) 8846 9191, *info@agnirestaurant.com, Fax (0870) 1996940* – . VISA 21 **LZG** s
closed 24-31 December and Saturday lunch – **Rest** - Indian - 12.50/22.50 and a la carte 15.95/24.00.
◆ Modest façade hides a clean, bright interior. Dishes are 'home' style from Hyderabad and the Indian interior, with biryani to the fore, and are notably good value.

Anglesea Arms, 35 Wingate Rd, W6 0UR *Ravenscourt Park,* (020) 8749 1291, *Fax (020) 8749 1254* – VISA 15 **LZE** c
closed 1 week Christmas-New Year – **Rest** (bookings not accepted) 12.95 (lunch) and a la carte 22.00/31.00.
◆ The laid-back atmosphere and local feel make this pub a popular venue. Worth arriving early as bookings are not taken. Modern cooking from blackboard menu.

Olympia *Gtr London* – ✉ *W14.*

XX **Cotto,** 44 Blythe Rd, W14 0HA ⊖ *Kensington Olympia,* ☎ (020) 7602 9333, *bookings@cottorestaurant.co.uk, Fax (020) 7602 5003* – ▤. MC AE VISA 16 MZE
closed 1 week Christmas, Saturday lunch, Sunday and Bank Holidays – **Rest** 17.50/20.50 s. ♀.
◆ On two floors, with vivid abstract paintings on white walls, chrome-framed chairs and music. Efficient service from black-clad staff. Modern cooking with some originality.

Shepherd's Bush *Gtr London* – ✉ *W14.*

K West, Richmond Way, W14 0AX ⊖ *Kensington Olympia,* ☎ (020) 7674 1000, *bookit@kwest.co.uk, Fax (020) 7674 1050,* – – ▤ – 50. MC AE VISA 16 MZE
Kanteen **:** **Rest** a la carte 25.50/37.50 – ☕ 19.50 – **214 rm** ✝128.00/240.90 ✝✝175.10/358.40, 6 suites.
◆ Former BBC offices, the interior is decorated in a smart, contemporary fashion. Bedrooms in understated modern style, deluxe rooms with work desks and DVD and CD facilities. Modish menus in trendy dining room.

HARINGEY *Gtr London.*

Crouch End *Gtr London* – ✉ *N4/N8.*

Mountview without rest., 31 Mount View Rd, N4 4SS, ☎ (020) 8340 9222, *mountviewbb@aol.com,* – . MC VISA. 3 EU
3 rm ☕ ✝40.00 – ✝✝80.00.
◆ Redbrick Victorian house with a warm and stylish ambience engendered by the homely décor. One bedroom features an original fireplace and two overlook the quiet rear garden.

X **Florians,** 4 Topsfield Parade, Middle Lane, N8 8RP, ☎ (020) 8348 8348, *Fax (020) 8292 2092,* – ▤. MC VISA 3 EU
closed 25-26 December – **Rest** - Italian - a la carte 20.40/25.80 ♀.
◆ Light room with tiled flooring and large paintings, nestling behind a busy front bar. Italian menu with blackboard daily specials. Efficient and obliging service.

X **Bistro Aix,** 54 Topsfield Parade, Tottenham Lane, N8 8PT, ☎ (020) 8340 6346, *Fax (020) 8348 7236* – MC AE VISA 3 EU
closed 26 December, 1 January and Monday – **Rest** a la carte 20.40/35.40.
◆ The simple wood furniture is complemented by plants and pictures. The owner chef's experience in France is reflected in the menu and the robust and hearty cooking.

Highgate *Gtr London* – ✉ *N6.*

The Bull, 13 North Hill, N6 4AB ⊖ *Highgate,* ☎ (0845) 4565053, *Fax (0845) 4565034,* – 20. MC VISA 2 EU
closed 25-26 December – **Rest** *(closed Monday lunch)* 17.95 and a la carte ♀.
◆ Grade II listed pub with spacious terrace and cavernous contemporary interior. Appealing dishes - some for two sharing - offer plenty of choice and are reliant on the seasons.

Rose and Crown, 86 Highgate High St, N6 5HX ⊖ *Highgate,* ☎ (020) 8340 6712, *johnkrimsonbars@aol.com, Fax (020) 9340 0770,* – MC VISA. 2 EU
closed Monday lunch – **Rest** a la carte 13.95/23.50 ♀.
◆ Small pub with neighbourhood feel; decorated in reds and creams. Two steps up from bar is restaurant and secluded rear terrace. Menu's roots are in classic French dishes.

HARROW *Gtr London.*

Harrow Weald *Middx* – ✉ *Middx.*

Grim's Dyke , Old Redding, HA3 6SH, ☎ (020) 8385 3100, *reservations@grimsdyke.com, Fax (020) 8954 4560,* – rm, – 100. MC AE VISA 1 BT
closed 24-30 December ***Gilberts*** **:** **Rest** *closed Saturday lunch* 19.95/29.00 and a la carte 27.70/37.50 ♀ – **46 rm** ☕ ✝125.00/135.00 – ✝✝152.00.
◆ Victorian mansion, former country residence of W.S.Gilbert. Rooms divided between main house and lodge, the former more characterful. Over 40 acres of garden and woodland. Restaurant with ornately carved fireplace.

Kenton *Middx* – ✉ *Middx.*

Premier Travel Inn Metro, Kenton Rd, HA3 8AT ⊖ *Kenton,* ☎ (020) 8907 4069, *Fax (020) 8909 1604* – |♦|, ⇔ rm, ♿ P. MC AE ⊙ VISA. ✈ 1 BU e
Rest (grill rest.) – **70 rm** ★49.95/49.95 – ★★59.95/59.95.
◆ Lodge hotel providing clean, comfortable and affordable accommodation. Adjacent Beefeater pub offers a menu specialising in popular grill-based dishes.

Pinner *Middx* – ✉ *Middx.*

XX **Friends,** 11 High St, HA5 5PJ ⊖ *Pinner,* ☎ (020) 8866 0286, *info@friendsrestaurant.co.uk, Fax (020) 8866 0286* – ⇔ ▤. MC AE ⊙ VISA 1 BU a
closed 25 December, Monday, Sunday dinner and Bank Holidays – **Rest** 19.50/27.50 and a la carte 31.50/42.00 ♀.
◆ Pretty beamed cottage, with some parts dating back 400 years. Inside, a welcoming glow from the log fire; personal service from owners and a fresh, regularly-changing menu.

HAVERING *Gtr London.*

Romford *Essex* – ✉ *Essex.*

⛳18, ⛳9 *Risebridge, Risebridge Chase, Lower Bedfords Rd ☎ (01708) 741429,* **JT** .

Premier Travel Inn, Mercury Gdns, RM1 3EN, ☎ (01708) 760548, *Fax (01708) 760456* – |♦|, ⇔ rm, ♿ P. MC AE ⊙ VISA 4 JU a
Rest (grill rest.) – **40 rm** ★57.95/57.95 – ★★62.95/62.95.
◆ Clean and well-maintained lodge-style accommodation, with the nearby M25 providing easy road links. Adjacent pub-restaurant specialises in popular, grilled dishes.

HILLINGDON *Gtr London.*

⛳18 *Haste Hill, The Drive, Northwood ☎ (01923) 825224* **AU** .

Heathrow Airport *Middx.*

London Heathrow Marriott, Bath Rd, Hayes, UB3 5AN, ☎ (020) 8990 1100, *reservations.heathrow@marriotthotels.co.uk, Fax (020) 8990 1110,* Fā, ≘s, ▣ – |♦|, ⇔ rm, ▤ ☎ ♿ P – 🏛 540. MC AE ⊙ VISA. ✈ 5 AX z
Tuscany : **Rest** - Italian - (dinner only) a la carte 32.40/39.40 ♀ – ***Allie's grille :*** **Rest** a la carte 19.25/30.25 ♀ – ☕ 14.95 – **391 rm** ★163.00 – ★★163.00, 2 suites.
◆ Built at the end of 20C, this modern, comfortable hotel is centred around a large atrium, with comprehensive business facilities: there is an exclusive Executive floor. Tuscany is bright and convivial.

Crowne Plaza London - Heathrow, Stockley Rd, West Drayton, UB7 9NA, ☎ (0870) 400 9140, *reservations.cplhr@ichotelsgroup.com, Fax (01895) 445122,* Fā, ≘s, ▣, ⛳9 – |♦|, ⇔ rm, ▤ ♿ P – 🏛 200. MC AE ⊙ VISA. ✈ 1 AV v
Concha Grill : **Rest** 18.50 (lunch) and dinner a la carte approx 23.00 ♀ – (see also ***Simply Nico Heathrow*** below) – ☕ 17.50 – **457 rm** ★229.00 – ★★229.00, 1 suite.
◆ Extensive leisure, aromatherapy and beauty salons make this large hotel a popular stopover for travellers. Club bedrooms are particularly well-equipped. Bright, breezy Concha Grill with juice bar.

Radisson Edwardian, 140 Bath Rd, Hayes, UB3 5AW, ☎ (020) 8759 6311, *resreh@radisson.com, Fax (020) 8759 4559,* Fā, ≘s – |♦|, ⇔ rm, ▤ ☎ P – 🏛 550. MC AE ⊙ VISA. ✈ 5 AX e
Henleys : **Rest** a la carte 22.00/36.50 – ***Brasserie :*** **Rest** 18.00 (lunch) and a la carte 19.00/27.50 – ☕ 15.00 – **442 rm** ★185.65 – ★★237.40, 17 suites.
◆ Capacious group hotel with a huge atrium over the leisure facilities. Plenty of comfortable lounges, well-appointed bedrooms and attentive service. Henleys boasts oil paintings and cocktail bar.

Sheraton Skyline, Bath Rd, Hayes, UB3 5BP, ☎ (020) 8759 2535, *res268-skyline@sheraton.com, Fax (020) 8750 9150,* Fā, ▣ – |♦| ⇔ ▤ ☎ ♿ P – 🏛 500. MC AE ⊙ VISA 5 AX u
Sage : **Rest** a la carte 15.00/25.00 ♀ – ☕ 17.00 – **348 rm** ★209.20 – ★★209.20, 2 suites.
◆ Well known for its unique indoor swimming pool surrounded by a tropical garden which is overlooked by many of the bedrooms. Business centre available. Classically decorated dining room.

Hilton London Heathrow Airport, Terminal 4, TW6 3AF, ✆ (020) 8759 775 gm–heathrow@hilton.com, Fax (020) 8759 7579, ⚡, ≘s, ▣ – |♣|, ⇔ rm, ▤ ✆ ♿ P – 🎓 250. MC AE ⓓ VISA. ✂ 5 AX

Brasserie : Rest *(closed lunch Saturday and Sunday)* (buffet lunch) 26.50/32.50 and dinne a la carte 25.00/51.00 s ♀

Zen Oriental : Rest - Chinese - 28.80 and a la carte 20.30/55.50 – ☕ 19.95 – **390 r** ☆209.00 – ☆☆209.00/255.56, 5 suites.

◆ Group hotel with a striking modern exterior and linked to Terminal 4 by a covere walkway. Good sized bedrooms, with contemporary styled suites. Spacious Brasserie in vas atrium. Zen Oriental offers formal Chinese experience.

Holiday Inn London Heathrow, Sipson Rd, West Drayton, UB7 0JU, (M 4 junctio 4) ✆ (0870) 4008595, *reservations-heathrowm4@ichotelsgroup.com, Fax (020) 8897 865.* ⚡ – |♣|, ⇔ rm, ▤ ✆ ♿ P – 🎓 140. MC AE ⓓ VISA. ✂ 1 AV

Sampans : Rest - Asian - (dinner only) a la carte 17.00/27.00

Rotisserie : Rest (buffet meals) 17.95/19.95 – ☕ 14.95 – **604 rm** ☆210.00 – ☆☆210.0 4 suites.

◆ Busy group hotel where the Academy conference suite attracts the business commun ity. Bedrooms come in a variety of styles. Popular Irish bar. Sampans offers regional Ch nese dishes. Spacious Rotisserie with chef carving to order.

Renaissance London Heathrow, Bath Rd, TW6 2AQ, ✆ (020) 8897 6363, *lhrrena sance@aol.com, Fax (020) 8897 1113,* ⚡, ≘s – |♣|, ⇔ rm, ▤ ♿ P – 🎓 400. MC AE ⓓ VISA ✂ 5 AX

Rest 19.50/23.50 and a la carte 28.50/37.50 ♀ – ☕ 16.00 – **643 rm** ☆163.00 – ☆☆163.0 6 suites.

◆ Low level façade belies the size of this easily accessible hotel. Large lounge and assorte shops in the lobby. Some of the soundproofed bedrooms have views of the runwa Open-plan restaurant with buffet or à la carte.

Holiday Inn Heathrow Ariel, 118 Bath Rd, Hayes, UB3 5AJ, ✆ (0870) 400904 *reservations-heathrow@ichotelsgroup.com, Fax (020) 8564 9265* – |♣|, ⇔ rm, ▤ rest, P 🎓 55. MC AE ⓓ VISA. ✂ 5 AX

Rest (bar lunch) 20.00 – ☕ 14.95 – **184 rm** ☆59.00/184.00 – ☆☆59.00/184.00.

◆ Usefully located hotel in a cylindrical shape. Modern bedrooms with warm colours. Thir floor executive rooms particularly impressive. Conference rooms available. Subtly-lit, relax ing restaurant.

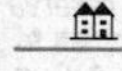

Premier Travel Inn Metro, 15 Bath Rd, TW3 3BQ, ✆ (0870) 6075075 *Fax (0870) 2419000* – |♣|, ⇔ rm, ▤ ♿ P – 🎓 30. MC AE ⓓ VISA. ✂ 5 AX

Rest (grill rest.) – **590 rm** ☆52.95/52.95 – ☆☆74.95/74.95.

◆ Well-priced Travel Inn with modern, wood-panelled exterior and huge atrium. Well equipped meeting rooms. Bedrooms are of good quality with triple glazing. Bright, airy informal grill restaurant.

Simply Nico Heathrow (at Crowne Plaza London-Heathrow H.), Stockley Rd, Wes Drayton, UB7 9NA, ✆ (01895) 437564, *heathrow.simplynico@corushotels.com Fax (01895) 437565* – ▤ P. MC AE ⓓ VISA 5 AV

closed Sunday – **Rest** (dinner only) 19.50 and a la carte 29.40/44.15 ♀.

◆ Located within the hotel but with its own personality. Mixes modern with more classi cally French dishes. Professional service in comfortable surroundings.

Ickenham *Middx.*

Jospens, 15 Long Lane, UB10 8QU ⊖ *Ickenham,* ✆ (01895) 632519, *Fax (01895) 272284* ▤. MC AE ⓓ VISA 1 AU

closed 1 week Christmas, 2 weeks summer and Monday – **Rest** 12.50 (lunch) and a la cart 22.00/28.50.

◆ Neighbourhood restaurant with window boxes. Smart interior boasts deep lilac ceiling Simple, well executed dishes with modern influences.

Ruislip *Middx.*

Hawtrey's (at The Barn H.), West End Rd, HA4 6JB, ✆ (01895) 679999, *info@thebarnh tel.co.uk, Fax (01895) 638379,* 🌳 – ⇔ ▤ P ⇔ 30. MC AE ⓓ VISA 1 AU

closed Saturday lunch – **Rest** 19.50/29.95 ♀.

◆ Jacobean styled baronial hall: an extension to 16C Barn Hotel. Cloth clad tables, brigh chandeliers. Fine dining - modern cooking that's confident and assured.

HOUNSLOW *Gtr London.*

Wyke Green, Syon Lane, Isleworth ✆ (020) 8560 8777 **BV** – *Airlinks, Southall Lane ✆ (020) 8561 1418* **ABV** – *Hounslow Heath, Staines Rd ✆ (020) 8570 5271* **BX**.
24 The Treaty Centre, High St ✆ (020) 8572 8279 (closed Sunday).

Chiswick *Middx* – ✉ *W4.*

XX **La Trompette,** 5-7 Devonshire Rd, W4 2EU ⊖ *Turnham Green,* ✆ (020) 8747 1836, *latrompette@btconnect.com, Fax (020) 8995 8097,* – . MC AE VISA 21 KZG y
closed 25 December – **Rest** 23.50/35.00 ♀.
◆ Terraced property on smart residential street. Open-plan restaurant with linen laid tables and a bustling atmosphere. Daily menus of French influenced robust modern dishes.

XX **The Burlington,** 1 Station Parade, Burlington Lane, W4 3HD ⊖ *Gunnersbury,* ✆ (020) 8995 3344, *pippa@theburlington.org.uk,* – . MC VISA 6 CX a
closed Christmas, Bank Holidays, Sunday dinner and lunch Saturday and Monday – **Rest** 15.50 (lunch) and a la carte 20.45/28.25 ♀.
◆ Relaxed, simply styled neighbourhood bistro, run by a husband and wife. Bold, tasty cuisine mixes modern British and classic French styles. Well-priced early evening menu.

X **Sam's Brasserie,** 11 Barley Mow Passage, W4 4PH ⊖ *Turnham Green,* ✆ (020) 8987 0555, *info@samsbrasserie.co.uk, Fax (020) 8987 7389* – . MC AE VISA 2 CV a
closed Christmas – **Rest** a la carte 19.05/32.50 ♀.
◆ Former paper mill by Turnham Green. 'Industrial', open plan feel with concrete and stainless steel. Robust brasserie dishes seem to be in keeping with the surroundings.

X **Fishworks,** 6 Turnham Green Terrace, W4 1QP, ✆ (020) 8994 0086, *chiswick@fishworks.co.uk, Fax (020) 8994 0778,* – . MC AE VISA 21 KZG x
closed 25-26 December, 1 January, Monday and dinner Sunday – **Rest** - Seafood - (booking essential) a la carte 20.00/40.00 ♀.
◆ Well-run branded restaurant opening onto delightful rear terrace with olive trees. Daily blackboard menu of grills and popular seafood dishes.

The Devonshire House, 126 Devonshire Rd, W4 2JJ, ✆ (020) 8987 2626, *info@thedevonshirehouse.co.uk, Fax (020) 8995 0152,* – MC AE VISA 21 KZG a
closed 24-26 December, 1 January and Monday – **Rest** a la carte 20.85/33.90 ♀.
◆ Period pub conversion retaining original features. Leather banquettes and chairs; bare tables. Daily menu of modern cooking, slightly simpler at lunchtime. Attentive service.

ISLINGTON *Gtr London.*

Archway – ✉ *N19.*

X **The Parsee,** 34 Highgate Hill, N19 5NL ⊖ *Archway,* ✆ (020) 7272 9091, *dining@theparsee.co.uk, Fax (020) 7687 1139* – . MC AE VISA 3 EU a
closed Christmas-New Year, Sunday and Bank Holidays – **Rest** - Indian (Parsee) - (dinner only) a la carte 16.50/23.95 ♀.
◆ Two brightly painted rooms, one non smoking and featuring a painting of a Parsee Angel. Good value, interesting, carefully spiced cuisine, Persian and Indian in inspiration.

St John's, 91 Junction Rd, N19 5QU ⊖ *Archway,* ✆ (020) 7272 1587, *Fax (020) 7687 2247* – MC AE VISA 12 RZA s
closed 25-26 December, 1 January and Monday lunch – **Rest** a la carte 18.00/25.00 ♀.
◆ Busy front bar enjoys a lively atmosphere; dining room in a large rear room. Log fire at one end, open hatch into kitchen the other. Blackboard menu; rustic cooking.

Barnsbury *Gtr London* – ✉ *N1/N7.*

XX **Morgan M,** 489 Liverpool Rd, N7 8NS ⊖ *Highbury and Islington,* ✆ (020) 7609 3560, *Fax (020) 8292 5699* – . MC VISA 13 UZA a
closed 24-30 December, lunch Tuesday and Saturday, Sunday dinner and Monday – **Rest** 23.50/32.00 ♀.
◆ Simple restaurant in a converted pub. Smartly-laid tables complemented by formal service. Modern dishes based on classical French combinations.

X **Fig,** 169 Hemingford Rd, N1 1DA, ✆ (020) 7609 3009, – MC VISA 13 UZB a
closed 24 December- 3 January, 21 August-5 September, Sunday dinner, Tuesday lunch and Monday – **Rest** a la carte 21.60/28.30 ♀.
◆ Simple, attractive and cosy neighbourhood restaurant with fawn colours and mirrors. Open hatch into kitchen. Asian-influenced cooking at a fair price.

Canonbury Gtr London – ✉ N1.

The House, 63-69 Canonbury Rd, N1 2DG ⊖ *Highbury and Islington,* ☎ (020) 7704 7410, *info@inthehouse.biz, Fax (020) 7704 9388,* – AE VISA 13 UZB h
closed 24-26 December and Monday lunch – **Rest** 17.95 (lunch) and a la carte 30.00/50.00 ♀.
◆ This pleasant pub, on a street corner and popular with locals, has a restaurant with linen-covered tables, ceiling fans, art for sale, and modern menus with a classical base.

Clerkenwell Gtr London – ✉ EC1.

Malmaison, Charterhouse Sq, EC1M 6AH ⊖ *Barbican,* ☎ (020) 7012 3700, *london@malmaison.com, Fax (020) 7012 3702,* – – rm, – 30. MO AE VISA 19 UZD o
Brasserie: Rest 12.50/17.95 and a la carte 24.75/44.50 ♀ – 16.95 – **97 rm** 205.00/229.00 – 252.00/305.00.
◆ Striking early 20C redbrick building overlooking pleasant square. Stylish, comfy public areas. Bedrooms in vivid, bold colours, with extras such as stereo and free broadband. Modern brasserie employing meats from Smithfield.

The Rookery without rest., 12 Peters Lane, Cowcross St, EC1M 6DS ⊖ *Barbican,* ☎ (020) 7336 0931, *reservations@rookery.co.uk, Fax (020) 7336 0932* – . MO AE VISA. 33 AOT p
closed 24-27 December – – 9.75 **32 rm** 205.00/240.00 – 300.00, 1 suite.
◆ A row of charmingly restored 18C houses. Wood panelling, stone-flagged flooring, open fires and antique furniture. Highly individual bedrooms, with Victorian bathrooms.

Smiths of Smithfield, Top Floor, 67-77 Charterhouse St, EC1M 6HJ ⊖ *Barbican,* ☎ (020) 7251 7950, *reservations@smithsofsmithfield.co.uk, Fax (020) 7236 5666,* –. MO AE VISA 33 AOT s
closed 25-26 December, 1 January and Saturday lunch – **Rest** a la carte approx 35.00 ♀ –
The Dining Room : **Rest** *(closed Saturday lunch and Sunday)* a la carte approx 23.00 ♀.
◆ On three floors where the higher you go the more formal it becomes. Busy, bustling atmosphere and modern menu. Good views of the market from the top floor terrace. The Dining Room with mirrors and dark blue walls.

St John, 26 St John St, EC1M 4AY ⊖ *Barbican,* ☎ (020) 7251 0848, *reservations@stjohnrestaurant.com, Fax (020) 7251 4090* – 18. MO AE VISA 33 APT c
closed 2 weeks Christmas-New Year, Easter, Saturday lunch and Sunday – **Rest** a la carte 26.60/43.90 ♀.
◆ Deservedly busy converted 19C former smokehouse. Popular bar, simple comforts. Menu specialises in offal and an original mix of traditional and rediscovered English dishes.

Comptoir Gascon, 61-63 Charterhouse St, EC1M 6HJ ⊖ *Barbican,* ☎ (020) 7608 0851, *Fax (020) 7608 0871* – . MO AE VISA 33 AOT a
closed 2 weeks Christmas-New Year, Sunday, Monday and Bank Holidays – **Rest** - French - a la carte 19.50/27.00 ♀.
◆ Half restaurant, half deli, situated opposite Smithfield. Rustic notions enhanced by exposed brick. Well priced, French based dishes form the mainstay of a simple restaurant.

Finsbury Gtr London – ✉ EC1.

The Zetter, 86-88 Clerkenwell Rd, EC1M 5RJ ⊖ *Farringdon,* ☎ (020) 7324 4444, *info@thezetter.com, Fax (020) 7324 4445* – rm, – 50. MO AE VISA. 19 UZD s
Rest a la carte 22.00/27.50 ♀ – 15.00 – **59 rm** 158.50 – 188.00/229.00.
◆ Discreetly trendy modern design in the well-equipped bedrooms and rooftop studios of a converted 19C warehouse:pleasant extras from old paperbacks to flat-screen TV/DVDs. Light, informal restaurant serves modern Mediterranean dishes and weekend brunches.

The Clerkenwell Dining Room, 69-73 St John St, EC1M 4AN ⊖ *Farringdon,* ☎ (020) 7253 9000, *zak@theclerkenwell.com, Fax (020) 7253 3322* – . MO AE VISA 19 UZD h
closed 23 December-2 January and Saturday lunch – **Rest** 19.50 (lunch) and a la carte 30.50/40.00 ♀.
◆ Former pub, now a stylish modern restaurant with etched glass façade. Three adjoining dining areas with bar provide setting for contemporary British cooking.

Portal, 88 St John St, EC1M 4EH ⊖ *Farringdon,* ☎ (020) 7253 6950 – 12. MO AE VISA 19 UZD r
closed Christmas-New Year, Easter, Sunday and Saturday lunch – **Rest** a la carte 21.50/35.50 ♀.
◆ Set in Grade II listed building with entrance to the 'industrial chic' restaurant via busy, bustling bar. The influence of Spain and Portugal highlighted in interesting menus.

Quality Chop House, 94 Farringdon Rd, EC1R 3EA ⊖ *Farringdon*, ✆ (020) 7837 5093, *enquiries@qualitychophouse.co.uk, Fax (020) 7833 8748* – ▤. MC AE VISA 19 UZD n
closed 24-27 December and Saturday lunch – **Rest** a la carte 16.00/29.40.
◆ On the window is etched "Progressive working class caterers". This is borne out with the individual café-style booths and a menu ranging from jellied eels to caviar.

Moro, 34-36 Exmouth Market, EC1R 4QE ⊖ *Farringdon*, ✆ (020) 7833 8336, *info@moro.co.uk, Fax (020) 7833 9338* – ▤. MC AE VISA 19 UZD b
closed Christmas, New Year, Sunday and Bank Holidays – **Rest** (booking essential) a la carte 20.00/29.00 ₹.
◆ Daily changing menu an eclectic mix of Mediterranean, Moroccan and Spanish. Friendly T-shirted staff. Informal surroundings with bare tables and a large zinc bar.

The Peasant, 240 St John St, EC1V 4PH ⊖ *Farringdon*, ✆ (020) 7336 7726, *Fax (020) 7490 1089* – MC AE VISA 19 UZD e
closed 24 December- 2 January – **Rest** (booking essential) a la carte 24.00/30.00 ₹.
◆ Large, busy pub with half of the ground floor given over as a bar. Dining continues in the high-ceilinged room upstairs. Robust and rustic cooking with generous portions.

The Well, 180 St John St, EC1V 4JY ⊖ *Farringdon*, ✆ (021) 7251 9363, *drinks@downthewell.co.uk, Fax (020) 7404 2250* – MC AE VISA 19 UZD x
closed 25-26 December and 1 January – **Rest** a la carte 20.00/28.00 ₹.
◆ Rather predictable looking pub distinguished by big black canopies. Food lifts it above the average: everything from 'pie of the week' to sophisticated modern British dishes.

Highbury *Gtr London* – ✉ *N5.*

Au Lac, 82 Highbury Park, N5 2XE ⊖ *Arsenal*, ✆ (020) 7704 9187, *Fax (020) 7704 9187* – ▤. MC VISA 13 VZA a
closed lunch Saturday, Sunday and Bank Holidays – **Rest** - Vietnamese - 16.00 and a la carte 8.20/20.00.
◆ Cosy Vietnamese restaurant, with brightly coloured walls and painted fans. Large menus with authentic dishes usefully highlighted. Fresh flavours; good value.

Islington *Gtr London* – ✉ *N1.*

Hilton London Islington, 53 Upper St, N1 0UY ⊖ *Angel*, ✆ (020) 7354 7700, *reservations.islington@hilton.com, Fax (020) 7354 7711*, ▤ – 35. MC AE VISA. 13 UZB s
Rest a la carte approx 18.00 ₹ – ☕ 17.50 – **178 rm** 157.45/216.20 – 157.45/216.20, 6 suites.
◆ Benefits from its location adjacent to the Business Design Centre. A purpose-built hotel with all bedrooms enjoying the appropriate creature comforts. Open-plan brasserie with small bar.

Jurys Inn Islington, 60 Pentonville Rd, N1 9LA ⊖ *Angel*, ✆ (020) 7282 5500, *jurysinnislington@jurysdoyle.com, Fax (020) 7282 5511* – rm, ▤ – 60. MC AE VISA. 13 UZB g
closed 24-26 December – **Rest** (bar lunch)/dinner 17.95 – ☕ 10.50 – **229 rm** 135.00 – 135.00.
◆ A corporate group hotel with good local transport links. Large lobby leads off to the characterful Irish themed pub. Uniform-sized bedrooms, all well-equipped. Popular dishes in restaurant.

Lola's, The Mall, 359 Upper St, N1 0PD ⊖ *Angel*, ✆ (020) 7359 1932, *lolas@lolas.co.uk, Fax (020) 7359 2209* – ▤ 12. MC AE VISA 13 UZB n
closed 25-26 December. 1 January and Sunday dinner – **Rest** 16.75 (lunch) and a la carte 26.75/40.25 ₹.
◆ On the first floor of a converted tram shed above the antique shops. Bright and airy, with glass ceiling and assorted artwork: an ideal setting to enjoy modern British dishes.

Frederick's, Camden Passage, N1 8EC ⊖ *Angel*, ✆ (020) 7359 2888, *eat@fredericks.co.uk, Fax (020) 7359 5173*, – ▤. MC VISA 13 UZB c
closed 25 December, Sunday and Bank Holidays – **Rest** 17.00 (lunch) and a la carte 30.50/36.00 ₹.
◆ Long-standing restaurant among the antique shops of Camden Passage. Attractive garden and al fresco dining; main room with large, plant-filled conservatory.

Almeida, 30 Almeida St, N1 1AD ⊖ *Old Street*, ✆ (020) 7354 4777, *oliviere@conran-restaurants.co.uk, Fax (020) 7354 2777* – ▤. MC AE VISA 13 UZB r
closed Christmas – **Rest** - French - 17.50 (lunch) and a la carte 26.00/36.50 ₹.
◆ Spacious, open plan restaurant with pleasant contemporary styling adjacent to Almeida Theatre. Large à la carte: a collection of classic French dishes.

Metrogusto, 13 Theberton St, N1 0QY ⊖ *Angel,* ✆ (020) 7226 9400, *Fax (020) 7226 9400* – ✈ ▤. MO AE VISA 13 UZB e
closed 25 December, 1 January, Sunday and Easter Monday – **Rest** - Italian - 24.50/25.00 and a la carte 24.45/30.50 ♀.
◆ Stylish and smart with a contemporary feel. Dining in two rooms with striking modern art on the walls and a relaxed atmosphere. Modern, carefully prepared Italian food.

Brasserie La Trouvaille, 353 Upper St, N1 0PD ⊖ *Angel,* ✆ (020) 7704 8323, *brasserielatrouvaille@hotmail.co.uk, Fax (020) 7359 6671* – MO AE VISA 13 UZB k
closed 24-26 December, Monday and Bank Holidays – **Rest** (dinner only and lunch Saturday and Sunday) a la carte 21.75/28.45 ♀.
◆ Around the corner from Camden Passage, this appealing brasserie's two rooms have warm yellow walls and simple tables. Classic French cooking ranges from cassoulet to snails.

Ottolenghi, 287 Upper St, N1 2TZ ⊖ *Highbury and Islington,* ✆ (020) 7288 1454, *upper@ottolenghi.co.uk, Fax (020) 7704 1456* – ▤. MO VISA 13 UZB k
closed Christmas-New Year – **Rest** a la carte 22.50/34.00.
◆ Cool, contemporary restaurant behind a smart deli. Two long tables accommodate most diners. Grazing style dishes are fresh, vibrant and tasty with a subtle Eastern spicing.

Drapers Arms, 44 Barnsbury St, N1 1ER ⊖ *Highbury and Islington,* ✆ (020) 7619 0348, *info@thedrapersarms.co.uk, Fax (020) 7619 0413,* 🏠 – MO AE VISA 13 UZB x
closed 25-26 December and 1-2 January – **Rest** a la carte 23.00/30.00 ♀.
◆ Real presence to the façade of this Georgian pub tucked away in a quiet residential area. Spacious modern interior where competent, contemporary dishes are served.

The Northgate, 113 Southgate Rd, N1 3JS, ✆ (020) 7359 7392, *thenorthgate@hppubs.co.uk, Fax (020) 7359 7393,* 🏠 – MO VISA 13 VZB a
closed 25-26 December and 1 January – **Rest** (dinner only and lunch Saturday and Sunday) a la carte 18.00/25.00 ♀.
◆ Corner pub with wood flooring and modern art on display. Rear dining area with a large blackboard menu offering a cross section of internationally influenced modern dishes.

The Social, 33 Linton St, N1 7DU, ✆ (020) 7354 5809, *managers@thesocialn1.com, Fax (020) 7354 8087* – MO ⓓ VISA 13 VZB c
closed 25-30 December and lunch Monday-Friday – **Rest** (booking essential) a la carte 17.50/24.50 ♀.
◆ The former Hanbury Arms has a youthful clientele attracted by the DJ and music in the bar. The open plan kitchen and restaurant serve from a modern, sensibly priced menu.

The Barnsbury, 209-211 Liverpool Rd, N1 1LX ⊖ *Highbury and Islington,* ✆ (020) 7607 5519, *info@thebarnsbury.co.uk, Fax (020) 7607 3256,* 🏠 – MO AE VISA. ✗ 13 UZB v
closed 25-26 December and 1 January – **Rest** a la carte 19.00/26.50 ♀.
◆ Former public house with pine tables and chairs arranged round central counter bar; art work for sale on the walls. Robust and hearty food in generous portions.

King's Cross *Gtr London* – ✉ *N1.*

Premier Travel Inn Metro, 26-30 York Way, King's Cross, N1 9AA ⊖ *King's Cross St Pancras,* ✆ (0870) 9906414 – |‡|, ✈ rm, ▤ rest, ♿ – 🪑 60. MO AE ⓓ VISA. ✗
Rest (grill rest.) ♀ – **282 rm** ☨74.95/74.95 – ☨☨84.95/84.95. 12 SZB a
◆ Modern purpose-built lodge in perfect location for King's Cross; very good value accommodation for visitors to London on a budget. Ask for room on top floor: they're quieter. Grill restaurant available.

KENSINGTON and CHELSEA (Royal Borough of) *Gtr London.*

Chelsea *Gtr London* – ✉ *SW1/SW3/SW7/SW10.*

Jumeirah Carlton Tower, Cadogan Pl, SW1X 9PY ⊖ *Knightsbridge,* ✆ (020) 7235 1234, *jctinfo@jumeirah.com, Fax (020) 7235 9129,* ←, ⊘, F₆, ≘s, ▣, ⛶, ✂ – |‡|, ✈ rm, ▤ ✆ ♿ 🚗 – 🪑 400. MO AE ⓓ VISA. ✗ 37 AGX n
Rib Room : Rest *(closed Sunday lunch)* 28.00 (lunch) and a la carte 24.00/44.00 ♀ – ☕ 28.00 – **190 rm** ☨393.00 – ☨☨393.00, 30 suites.
◆ Imposing international hotel overlooking a leafy square. Well-equipped roof-top health club has funky views. Generously proportioned rooms boast every conceivable facility. Rib Room restaurant has a clubby atmosphere.

Conrad London, Chelsea Harbour, SW10 0XG, ✆ (020) 7823 3000, *lonch-rs@hilton.com, Fax (020) 7351 6525,* ←, ⊘, F₆, ≘s, ▣ – |‡|, ✈ rm, ▤ ✆ ♿ 🚗 – 🪑 250. MO AE ⓓ VISA 23 PZG j
Rest – (see ***Aquasia*** below) – ☕ 22.50, **160 suites** 411.25.
◆ Modern, all-suite hotel within an exclusive marina and retail development. Many of the spacious and well-appointed rooms have balconies and views across the Thames.

Sheraton Park Tower, 101 Knightsbridge, SW1X 7RN ⊖ *Knightsbridge,* (020) 7235 8050, *central.london.reservations@sheraton.com, Fax (020) 7235 8231,* rm, – 100. 37 AGX t
Rest – (see ***One-O-One*** below) – 21.95 – **258 rm** 446.50 – 517.00, 22 suites.
◆ Built in the 1970s in a unique cylindrical shape. Well-equipped bedrooms are all identical in size. Top floor executive rooms have commanding views of Hyde Park and City.

Capital, 22-24 Basil St, SW3 1AT ⊖ *Knightsbridge,* (020) 7589 5171, *reservations@capitalhotel.co.uk, Fax (020) 7225 0011* – – 25. 37 AFX a
Rest (see **The Capital Restaurant** below) – 16.50 – **49 rm** 229.00/323.00 – 417.00/500.00.
◆ Discreet and privately owned town house with distinct English charm. Individually decorated rooms with plenty of thoughtful touches.

Draycott, 26 Cadogan Gdns, SW3 2RP ⊖ *Sloane Square,* (020) 7730 6466, *reservations@draycotthotel.com, Fax (020) 7730 0236,* – rm, 37 AGY c
Rest (room service only) – 18.50 – **31 rm** 141.00/229.00 – 376.00, 4 suites.
◆ Charmingly discreet 19C house in exclusive residential area. Elegant sitting room overlooks tranquil communal garden. Individually decorated rooms in a country house style.

The Cadogan, 75 Sloane St, SW1X 9SG ⊖ *Knightsbridge,* (020) 7235 7141, *reservations@cadogan.com, Fax (020) 7245 0994,* – – 40. 37 AGY b
Mes'anges : Rest (dinner only in August) 18.00 (lunch) and a la carte 28.00/45.00 – 19.50 – **61 rm** 223.25/323.00 – 382.00, 4 suites.
◆ An Edwardian town house, where Oscar Wilde was arrested; modernised and refurbished with a French accent. Contemporary drawing room. Stylish bedrooms; latest facilities. Discreet, stylish restaurant.

Millennium Knightsbridge, 17-25 Sloane St, SW1X 9NU ⊖ *Knightsbridge,* (020) 7235 4377, *reservations.knightsbridge@mill-cop.com, Fax (020) 7235 7125* – – 120. 37 AGX r
Mju : Rest *(closed Saturday lunch and Sunday)* 19.50/38.00 – 18.00 – **218 rm** 258.00/282.00 – 282.00, 4 suites.
◆ Modern, corporate hotel in the heart of London's most fashionable shopping district. Executive bedrooms are well-appointed and equipped with the latest technology.

Franklin, 22-28 Egerton Gdns, SW3 2DB ⊖ *South Kensington,* (020) 7584 5533, *bookings@franklinhotel.co.uk, Fax (020) 7584 5449,* – rest, 37 AEY e
Rest a la carte 29.50/37.50 **s.** – 17.50 – **47 rm** 152.75/246.75 – 346.60/464.00.
◆ Attractive Victorian town house in an exclusive residential area. Charming drawing room overlooks a tranquil communal garden. Well-furnished rooms in a country house style. Elegantly appointed dining room offering traditional meals.

Knightsbridge, 10 Beaufort Gdns, SW3 1PT ⊖ *Knightsbridge,* (020) 7584 6300, *knightsbridge@firmdale.com, Fax (020) 7584 6355* – 37 AFX s
Rest (room service only) – **44 rm** 176.25/211.50 – 305.50.
◆ Attractively furnished town house with a very stylish, discreet feel. Every bedroom is immaculately appointed and has an individuality of its own; fine detailing throughout.

San Domenico House, 29-31 Draycott Pl, SW3 2SH ⊖ *Sloane Square,* (020) 7581 5757, *info@sandomenicohouse.com, Fax (020) 7584 1348* – rm, 37 AFY c
Rest (room service only) – 11.00 – **18 rm** 207.00 – 329.00.
◆ Intimate and discreet Victorian town house with an attractive rooftop terrace. Individually styled and generally spacious rooms with antique furniture and rich fabrics.

Parkes without rest., 41 Beaufort Gdns, SW3 1PW ⊖ *Knightsbridge,* (020) 7581 9944, *info@parkeshotel.com, Fax (020) 7581 1999* – 37 AFX x
15.20 – **19 rm** 229.00/382.00 – 282.00/382.00, 14 suites 382.00/488.00.
◆ Behind the portico entrance one finds a well-kept private hotel. The generally spacious and high ceilinged rooms are pleasantly decorated. Friendly and personally run.

The London Outpost of Bovey Castle without rest., 69 Cadogan Gdns, SW3 2RB ⊖ *Sloane Square,* (020) 7589 7333, *info@londonoutpost.co.uk, Fax (020) 7581 4958,* – 37 AGY r
closed 24-26 December – 16.95 – **11 rm** 200.00 – 329.00.
◆ Classic town house in a most fashionable area. Relaxed and comfy lounges full of English charm. Bedrooms, named after local artists and writers, full of thoughtful touches.

Egerton House, 17-19 Egerton Terrace, SW3 2BX ⊖ *South Kensington,* ✆ (020) 758 2412, *bookings@egertonhousehotel.co.uk, Fax (020) 7584 6540* – . 37 **AFY**
Rest (room service only) – 17.00 – **29 rm** 135.00/211.00 – 170.00/294.00.
◆ Stylish redbrick Victorian town house close to the exclusive shops. Relaxed drawing room. Antique furnished and individually decorated rooms.

Beaufort without rest., 33 Beaufort Gdns, SW3 1PP ⊖ *Knightsbridge,* ✆ (020) 758 5252, *reservations@thebeaufort.co.uk, Fax (020) 7589 2834* – – 17.50 **29 rm** 176.25/223.25 – 200.00/317.25. 37 **AFX**
◆ World's largest collection of English floral watercolours adorn this 19C town house. Modern and co-ordinated rooms. Tariff includes all drinks and continental breakfast.

Jurys Inn, Imperial Rd, SW6 2GA ⊖ *Fulham Broadway,* ✆ (020) 7411 2201 *Fax (020) 7411 2211* – . 23 **PZH**
Rest a la carte 16.85/25.65 – 9.50 – **172 rm** 92.00/95.00 – 92.00/95.00.
◆ Six-storey hotel offering smart, superior lodge quality. Appealing coffee shop. Good value bedrooms: those on top floor are Executive rooms with top quality floral fabrics. Airy dining room offering international favourites.

Myhotel Chelsea, 35 Ixworth Pl, SW3 3QX ⊖ *South Kensington,* ✆ (020) 7225 7500 *chelsea@myhotel.com, Fax (020) 7225 7555,* – – 60. 37 **AFY**
Rest a la carte 14.00/22.00 – 18.00 – **44 rm** 242.00/294.00 – 294.00/305.00, 1 suite.
◆ Restored Victorian property in a fairly quiet and smart side street. Conservatory breakfast room. Modern and well-equipped rooms are ideal for the corporate traveller. Smart dining room for modern menus.

Eleven Cadogan Gardens, 11 Cadogan Gdns, SW3 2RJ ⊖ *Sloane Square,* ✆ (020) 7730 7000, *reservations@number-eleven.co.uk, Fax (020) 7730 5217,* , , – . 37 **AGY**
Rest (residents only) a la carte 26.00/44.00 **s** – 14.00 – **55 rm** 182.00/229.00 – 276.00/382.00, 4 suites.
◆ Occupying four Victorian houses, one of London's first private town house hotels. Traditionally appointed bedrooms vary considerably in size. Genteel atmosphere. Light and airy basement dining room exclusively for residents.

Sydney House, 9-11 Sydney St, SW3 6PU ⊖ *South Kensington,* ✆ (020) 7376 7711 *info@sydneyhousechelsea.com, Fax (020) 7376 4233* – . *closed 25-26 December* – **Rest** (room service only) – 9.95 – **21 rm** 125.00/175.00 – 145.00/210.00. 36 **ADY**
◆ Two usefully located Victorian town houses. Basement breakfast room; small lounge near entrance. Compact contemporary style bedrooms; one on top floor with own roof terrace.

The Lennox without rest., 57 Pont St, SW1X 0BD ⊖ *Knightsbridge,* ✆ (020) 7590 1090 *info@thelennox.com, Fax (020) 7590 1099* – – 30. . 12.00 – **20 rm** 123.00/159.00 – 217.00/294.00. 37 **AFY**
◆ Small, friendly, modern townhouse with discreet plaque at the end of Pont Street, in a neat Victorian terrace. Contemporary bedrooms.

L'Hotel, 28 Basil St, SW3 1AS ⊖ *Knightsbridge,* ✆ (020) 7589 6286, *reservations@lhotel.co.uk, Fax (020) 7823 7826* – , rm, rest, . . 37 **AFX**
Le Metro **: Rest** a la carte 19.00/22.00 – **12 rm** 182.00 – 211.50.
◆ Discreet town house a short walk from Harrods. Wooden shutters, pine furniture and stencilled walls provide a subtle rural theme. Well-appointed, comfy and informally run. Basement bistro dining.

Gordon Ramsay, 68-69 Royal Hospital Rd, SW3 4HP ⊖ *Sloane Square,* ✆ (020) 7352 4441, *reservations@gordonramsay.com, Fax (020) 7352 3334* – . *closed 2 weeks Christmas-New Year, Saturday and Sunday* – **Rest** (booking essential) 40.00/70.00 . 37 **AFZ**
Spec. Beef tartare with caviar, peppers and deep-fried onions rings. Roast pigeon with foie gras, braised cabbage and creamed potatoes. Chocolate cylinder with coffee granité and ginger mousse.
◆ Elegant and sophisticated room. The eponymous chef creates some of Britain's finest, classically inspired cooking. Detailed and attentive service. Book one month in advance.

The Capital Restaurant (at Capital H.), 22-24 Basil St, SW3 1AT ⊖ *Knightsbridge* ✆ (020) 7589 5171, *caprest@capitalhotel.co.uk, Fax (020) 7225 0011* – . 37 **AFX**
Rest(booking essential) 29.50/55.00 .
Spec. Langoustine with pork belly and sweet spice. Saddle of rabbit with calamari and tomato risotto. Coffee parfait with chocolate fondant.
◆ A hotel restaurant known for its understated elegance, discretion and graceful service. Cooking blends the innovative with the classic to create carefully crafted dishes.

XXX **Bibendum,** Michelin House, 81 Fulham Rd, SW3 6RD ⊖ *South Kensington,* ☎ (020) 7581 5817, *manager@bibendum.co.uk, Fax (020) 7823 7925* – ▤. MC AE ① VISA 37 AEY s
closed 25-26 December and 1 January – **Rest** 28.50 (lunch) and dinner a la carte 31.50/60.25 ♀.
◆ A fine example of Art Nouveau architecture; a London landmark. 1st floor restaurant with striking stained glass 'Michelin Man'. Attentive service of modern British cooking.

XXX ✿ **Tom Aikens,** 43 Elystan St, SW3 3NT ⊖ *South Kensington,* ☎ (020) 7584 2003, *info@tomaikens.co.uk, Fax (020) 7584 2001* – ⇹ ▤. MC AE VISA 37 AFY n
closed last two weeks August, 2 weeks Christmas-New Year, Saturday and Sunday – **Rest** 29.00/60.00 ♀.
Spec. Ballottine of foie gras with apple jelly and foie gras mousse. Loin of lamb with fennel risotto, anchovy tart and almonds. Chocolate marquise with grapefruit and chocolate mousses.
◆ Smart restaurant; minimalist style decor with chic tableware. Highly original menu of individual and inventive dishes; smooth service. Book one month in advance.

XXX ✿ **Aubergine,** 11 Park Walk, SW10 0AJ ⊖ *South Kensington,* ☎ (020) 7352 3449, *Fax (020) 7351 1770* – ⇹ ▤. MC AE ① VISA 36 ACZ r
closed 23 December-3 January, Sunday, Saturday lunch and Bank Holidays – **Rest** (booking essential) 34.00/60.00 ♀.
Spec. Carpaccio of scallops, artichoke and truffle vinaigrette. Best end of lamb with garlic purée. Assiette of sorbets.
◆ Intimate, refined restaurant where the keen staff provide well drilled service. French influenced menu uses top quality ingredients with skill and flair. Extensive wine list.

XXX **One-O-One** (at Sheraton Park Tower H.), William St, SW1X 7RN ⊖ *Knightsbridge,* ☎ (020) 7290 7101, *Fax (020) 7235 6196* – ▤. MC AE ① VISA 37 AGX t
Rest - Seafood - 25.00 (lunch) and a la carte approx 54.00 ♀.
◆ Modern and very comfortable restaurant overlooking Knightsbridge decorated in cool blue tones. Predominantly seafood menu offers traditional and more adventurous dishes.

XXX **Aquasia** (at Conrad London H.), Chelsea Harbour, SW10 0XG, ☎ (020) 7300 8443, *Fax (020) 7351 6525,* ⩤, ⛱ – ▤ P. MC AE ① VISA 23 PZG j
Rest a la carte 28.00/43.00 ♀.
◆ Modern restaurant located within Conrad International hotel. Views over Chelsea Harbour. Cuisine captures the essence of the Mediterranean and Asia.

XXX **Drones,** 1 Pont St, SW1X 9EJ ⊖ *Knightsbridge,* ☎ (020) 7235 9555, *sales@whitestarline.org.uk, Fax (020) 7235 9566* – ▤ ⇔ 40. MC AE ① VISA 37 AGX c
closed 26 December, 1 January, Saturday lunch and Sunday dinner – **Rest** 17.95 (lunch) and a la carte 27.50/43.50 ♀.
◆ Smart exterior with etched plate-glass window. U-shaped interior with moody film star photos on walls. French and classically inspired tone to dishes.

XXX **Fifth Floor** (at Harvey Nichols), Knightsbridge, SW1X 7RJ ⊖ *Knightsbridge,* ☎ (020) 7235 5250, *Fax (020) 7235 7856* – |‡| ▤. MC AE ① VISA 37 AGX s
closed Christmas, Sunday dinner and Monday – **Rest** 19.50/39.50 and a la carte 30.00/48.00 ♀.
◆ On Harvey Nichols' top floor; elevated style sporting a pink-hued oval shaped interior with green frosted glass. Chic surroundings with food to match and smooth service.

XXX **Toto's,** Walton House, Walton St, SW3 2JH ⊖ *Knightsbridge,* ☎ (020) 7589 0075, *Fax (020) 7581 9668* – MC AE ① VISA 37 AFY x
closed 3 days Christmas – **Rest** - Italian - 23.00 (lunch) and a la carte 34.00/46.00 ♀.
◆ Converted mews house in tucked away location. Ornately decorated and bright restaurant with additional balcony area. Professional service of an extensive Italian menu.

XXX **Chutney Mary,** 535 King's Rd, SW10 0SZ ⊖ *Fulham Broadway,* ☎ (020) 7351 3113, *chutneymary@realindianfood.com, Fax (020) 7351 7694* – ▤. MC AE ① VISA 22 OZG v
Rest - Indian - (dinner only and lunch Saturday and Sunday) 16.50 (lunch) and dinner a la carte 25.25/46.50 ♀.
◆ Soft lighting and sepia etchings hold sway at this forever popular restaurant. Extensive menu of specialities from all corners of India. Complementary wine list.

XXX **Pengelley's,** 164 Sloane St, SW1X 9QB ⊖ *Knightsbridge,* ☎ (020) 7750 5000, *reservations@pengelleys.com, Fax (020) 7750 5001* – ⇹ ▤. MC AE VISA 37 AGX d
closed 1 week Christmas and Bank Holidays – **Rest** - Asian - 15.00 (lunch) and a la carte 19.00/38.00.
◆ There's a vibrant second floor bar where the champage corks pop and the cocktail glasses clink; equally funky first floor Asian restaurant with dim sum and original twists.

XX **Daphne's,** 112 Draycott Ave, SW3 3AE ⊖ *South Kensington,* ☎ (020) 7589 4257, *office@daphnes-restaurant.co.uk, Fax (020) 7225 2766* – ▤. MC AE ① VISA 37 AFY j
closed 25-26 December, 1 January and August Bank Holiday – **Rest** - Italian - (booking essential) a la carte 27.00/43.00 ♀.
◆ Positively buzzes in the evening, the Chelsea set gelling smoothly and seamlessly with the welcoming Tuscan interior ambience. A modern twist updates classic Italian dishes.

XXX **Rasoi Vineet Bhatia,** 10 Lincoln St, SW3 2TS ⊖ *Sloane Square*, ☎ (020) 7225 1881, *Fax (020) 7581 0220* – ✈ ▤. MC AE Ⓓ VISA 37 **AFY** y
closed Saturday lunch, Sunday and Bank Holidays – **Rest** - Indian - 24.00 (lunch) and a la carte 46.00/61.00 ♀.
Spec. Tandoori salmon, masala crab cake and spring onion khichdi. Grilled spiced duck, tamarind chutney, crispy onion fritters. Chocolate and almond samosa, Indian tea ice cream.
◆ Elegant mid-19C townhouse off Kings Road with L-shaped dining room and attractive friezes. Seamlessly crafted mix of classic and contemporary Indian flavour combinations.

XX **Racine,** 239 Brompton Rd, SW3 2EP ⊖ *South Kensington*, ☎ (020) 7584 4477, *Fax (020) 7584 4900* – ✈ ▤. MC AE Ⓓ VISA 37 **AEY** t
closed 25 December – **Rest** - French - 17.50 (lunch) and a la carte 24.50/38.00 ♀.
◆ Dark leather banquettes, large mirrors and wood floors create the atmosphere of a genuine Parisienne brasserie. Good value, well crafted, regional French fare.

XX **Nozomi,** 15 Beauchamp Pl, SW3 1NQ ⊖ *Knightsbridge*, ☎ (020) 7838 1500, *Fax (020) 7838 1001* – ▤ ⇔ 24. MC AE Ⓓ VISA 37 **AFX** d
closed 2 weeks January, 2 weeks August and Sunday – **Rest** - Japanese - a la carte 27.00/42.00 ♀.
◆ DJ mixes lounge music at the front bar; up the stairs in the restaurant the feeling is minimal with soft lighting. Innovative Japanese menus provide an interesting choice.

XX **Bluebird,** 350 King's Rd, SW3 5UU, ☎ (020) 7559 1000, *Fax (020) 7559 1111* – |♦| ▤. MC AE Ⓓ VISA 23 **ZGP** e
Rest a la carte 21.50/37.25 ♀.
◆ A foodstore, café and homeware shop also feature at this impressive skylit restaurant. Much of the modern British food is cooked in wood-fired ovens. Lively atmosphere.

XX **Poissonnerie de l'Avenue,** 82 Sloane Ave, SW3 3DZ ⊖ *South Kensington*, ☎ (020) 7589 2457, *info@poissonnerie.co.uk, Fax (020) 7581 3360* – ▤. MC AE Ⓓ VISA 37 **AFY** u
closed dinner 24 December, 25 December, Sunday and Bank Holidays – **Rest** - French Seafood - 22.00 (lunch) and a la carte 24.50/35.50.
◆ Long-established and under the same ownership since 1965. Spacious and traditional French restaurant offering an extensive seafood menu. An institution favoured by locals.

XX **Le Cercle,** 1 Wilbraham Pl, SW1X 9AE ⊖ *Sloane Square*, ☎ (020) 7901 9999, *info@lecercle.co.uk, Fax (020) 7901 9111* – ▤. MC AE VISA 37 **AGY** e
closed Sunday-Monday – **Rest** - French - 19.50 (lunch) and a la carte 12.20/48.00 ♀.
◆ Discreetly signed basement restaurant down residential side street. High, spacious room with chocolate banquettes. Tapas style French menus; accomplished cooking.

XX **Le Colombier,** 145 Dovehouse St, SW3 6LB ⊖ *South Kensington*, ☎ (020) 7351 1155, *Fax (020) 7351 5124*, 🏠 – MC AE VISA 36 **ADZ** e
Rest - French - 14.50 (lunch) and a la carte 26.80/33.80 ♀.
◆ Proudly Gallic corner restaurant in an affluent residential area. Attractive enclosed terrace. Bright and cheerful surroundings and service of traditional French cooking.

XX **Mao Tai,** 96 Draycott Ave, SW3 3AD ⊖ *South Kensington*, ☎ (020) 7225 2500, *info@maotai.co.uk* – ▤. MC AE Ⓓ VISA 37 **AFY** f
closed 24-25 December – **Rest** - Chinese (Szechuan) - a la carte 23.70/41.00 s. ♀.
◆ Spacious Chinese restaurant in the heart of Chelsea. Modern, stylish décor with distinctive Eastern feel. Unique Szechuan menus, boasting some highly original dishes.

XX **Painted Heron,** 112 Cheyne Walk, SW10 0DJ ⊖ *Gloucester Road*, ☎ (020) 7351 5232, *Fax (020) 7351 5313*, 🏠 – ▤. MC AE VISA 23 **PZG** d
closed Saturday lunch – **Rest** - Indian - a la carte 24.00/31.00 ♀.
◆ Just off Cheyne Walk near the river. Contemporary in style, exemplified by oil paintings. Modern Indian dishes with eclectic ingredients drawn from around the sub-continent.

XX **Pellicano,** 19-21 Elystan St, SW3 3NT ⊖ *South Kensington*, ☎ (020) 7589 3718, *pellicanor@aol.com, Fax (020) 7584 1789*, 🏠 – ▤. MC AE Ⓓ VISA 37 **AFY** d
closed 24 December-2 January – **Rest** - Italian - 16.50 (lunch) and a la carte 20.00/33.50 ♀.
◆ Attractive neighbourhood restaurant with dark blue canopy over pavement terrace. Contemporary interior with wood floors. Tasty and interesting modern Italian dishes.

XX **Brasserie St Quentin,** 243 Brompton Rd, SW3 2EP ⊖ *South Kensington*, ☎ (020) 7589 8005, *reservations@brasseriestquentin.co.uk, Fax (020) 7584 6064* – ▤. MC AE Ⓓ VISA 37 **AEY** a
closed 1 week Christmas – **Rest** 17.50 (lunch) and a la carte 25.50/31.65 ♀.
◆ Authentic Parisien brasserie, with rows of closely set tables, banquettes and ornate chandeliers. Attentive service and a lively atmosphere. French classics aplenty.

XX **Benihana,** 77 King's Rd, SW3 4NX ⊖ *Sloane Square*, ☎ (020) 7376 7799, *info@benihana.co.uk, Fax (020) 7376 7377* – ▤. MC AE Ⓓ VISA 37 **AFZ** e
closed 25 December – **Rest** - Japanese (Teppan-Yaki) - 33.00/45.00 s..
◆ Vast basement restaurant. Be prepared to share your table with other guests; teppan-yakis sit up to eight. Theatrical preparation and service of modern Japanese cooking.

XX **Caraffini,** 61-63 Lower Sloane St, SW1W 8DH ⊖ *Sloane Square,* ✆ (020) 7259 0235, *info@caraffini.co.uk, Fax (020) 7259 0236,* – ▤. MO AE VISA 37 **AGZ** a
closed 25 December, Easter, Sunday and Bank Holidays – **Rest** - Italian - a la carte 24.20/32.00.
◆ The omnipresent and ebullient owner oversees the friendly service in this attractive neighbourhood restaurant. Authentic and robust Italian cooking; informal atmosphere.

XX **Vama,** 438 King's Rd, SW10 0LJ ⊖ *Sloane Square,* ✆ (020) 7351 4118, *andy@vama.co.uk, Fax (020) 7565 8501* – MO AE ⓓ VISA 23 **PZG** e
closed 25-26 December and 1 January – **Rest** - Indian - (booking essential) 14.95 (lunch) and a la carte 21.20/30.95 ♀.
◆ Adorned with traditional artefacts, a modern and bright restaurant. Keen and eager service of an elaborate and seasonally changing menu of Northwest Indian specialities.

XX **The Collection,** 264 Brompton Rd, SW3 2AS ⊖ *South Kensington,* ✆ (020) 7225 1212, *office@thecollection.co.uk, Fax (020) 7225 1050* – ▤. MO AE VISA 37 **AEY** v
closed 25-26 December, 1 January and Bank Holidays – **Rest** (dinner only) 40.00 and a la carte 29.00/41.00 ♀.
◆ Beyond the impressive catwalk entrance one will find a chic bar and a vast split level, lively restaurant. The eclectic and global modern menu is enjoyed by the young crowd.

XX **Eight over Eight,** 392 King's Rd, SW3 5UZ ⊖ *Gloucester Road,* ✆ (020) 7349 9934, *Fax (020) 7351 5157* – ▤. MO AE ⓓ VISA 23 **PZG** n
closed 25-26 December and lunch Sunday and Bank Holidays – **Rest** - South East Asian - a la carte 21.50/42.00 ♀.
◆ Lively modern restaurant in converted theatre pub; bar in front and dining room at rear. Enthusiastic service. Eclectic Asian menu: strong flavours and unusual combinations.

XX **Good Earth,** 233 Brompton Rd, SW3 2EP ⊖ *Knightsbridge,* ✆ (020) 7584 3658, *goodearthgroup@aol.com, Fax (020) 7823 8769* – ▤. MO AE VISA 37 **AFY** h
closed 22-30 December – **Rest** - Chinese - 21.00/35.00 (dinner) and a la carte 20.00/33.50 ♀.
◆ Ornately decorated, long-established and comfortable restaurant. Polite and efficient service. Extensive and traditional Chinese menu.

XX **Dan's,** 119 Sydney St, SW3 6NR ⊖ *South Kensington,* ✆ (020) 7352 2718, *Fax (020) 7352 3265,* – MO AE VISA 37 **AEZ** s
closed 24 December-1 January and Bank Holidays – **Rest** 20.50 (lunch) and a la carte 28.00/33.00.
◆ The eponymous owner oversees the operation in this long established neighbourhood restaurant. Eclectic menu with global influences. Private dining available.

XX **Haandi,** 136 Brompton Rd, SW3 1HY ⊖ *Knightsbridge,* ✆ (020) 7823 7373, *haandirestaurant@btconnect.com, Fax (020) 7823 9696* – ▤. MO AE ⓓ VISA 37 **AFX** v
closed 25 December – **Rest** - Indian - a la carte 12.95/29.70 ♀.
◆ Spacious basement restaurant, though with natural light in some sections. Live jazz in the bar and chefs very much on display. Flavoursome, succulent north Indian food.

X **Bibendum Oyster Bar,** Michelin House, 81 Fulham Rd, SW3 6RD ⊖ *South Kensington,* ✆ (020) 7589 1480, *manager@bibendum.co.uk, Fax (020) 7823 7148* – MO AE ⓓ VISA 37 **AEY** s
closed 25-26 December and 1 January – **Rest** - Seafood specialities - (bookings not accepted) a la carte 20.50/46.75.
◆ Dine in either the busy bar, or in the light and relaxed foyer of this striking landmark. Concise menu of mainly cold dishes focusing on fresh seafood and shellfish.

X **Manicomio,** 85 Duke of York Sq, King's Rd, SW3 4LY ⊖ *Sloane Square,* ✆ (020) 7730 3366, *Fax (020) 7730 3377,* – ▤. MO AE VISA 37 **AGY** x
closed 25-26 December and 1 January – **Rest** - Italian - a la carte 23.00/40.50.
◆ Outside, a delightful terrace overlooks the trendy Square. Inside, a clean, modern, informal style prevails. Rustic Italian menus. Next door, a café and superbly stocked deli.

Admiral Codrington, 17 Mossop St, SW3 2LY ⊖ *South Kensington,* ✆ (020) 7581 0005, *admiralcodrington@longshotplc.com, Fax (020) 7589 2452* – ▤. MO AE VISA 37 **AFY** v
– **Rest** a la carte 20.00/35.00 ♀.
◆ Aproned staff offer attentive, relaxed service in this busy gastropub. A retractable roof provides alfresco dining in the modern back room. Cosmopolitan menu of modern dishes.

Chelsea Ram, 32 Burnaby St, SW10 0PL ⊖ *Gloucester Road,* ✆ (020) 7351 4008, *pint@chelsearam.com, Fax (020) 7349 0885* – MO VISA 23 **PZG** r
Rest a la carte 18.00/21.00 ♀.
◆ Wooden floors, modern artwork and books galore feature in this forever popular pub. Concise menu of modern British cooking with daily changing specials. Friendly atmosphere.

Swag and Tails, 10-11 Fairholt St, SW7 1EG ⊖ *Knightsbridge*, ✆ (020) 7584 6926, *theswag@swagandtails.com, Fax (020) 7581 9935* – MC AE VISA 37 AFX r
closed Saturday, Sunday and Bank Holidays – **Rest** a la carte 24.00/32.00 ♀.
◆ Attractive Victorian pub close to Harrods and the fashionable Knightsbridge shops. Polite and approachable service of a blackboard menu of light snacks and seasonal dishes.

Builders Arms, 13 Britten St, SW3 3TY ⊖ *South Kensington*, ✆ (020) 7349 9040 – ▤. MC VISA 37 AFZ x
closed 25-26 December and 1 January – **Rest** (bookings not accepted) a la carte 17.00/26.00 ♀.
◆ Extremely busy modern 'gastropub' favoured by the locals. Eclectic menu of contemporary dishes with blackboard specials. Polite service from a young and eager team.

The Pig's Ear, 35 Old Church St, SW3 5BS, ✆ (020) 7352 2908, *hello@thepigsear.co.uk, Fax (020) 7352 9321* – ⇹. MC AE VISA 23 PZG v
Rest a la carte 16.00/22.00 ♀.
◆ Corner pub that gets very busy, particularly for downstairs bar dining. Upstairs, more sedate wood panelled dining room. Both menus are rustic, robust and seasonal in nature.

The Phoenix, 23 Smith St, SW3 4EE ⊖ *Sloane Square*, ✆ (020) 7730 9182, *mail@geronimo-phoenix.fsnet.co.uk*, 帀 – ⇹ ▤. MC VISA 37 AFZ a
closed 25-26 December – **Rest** a la carte 15.00/28.00 ♀.
◆ Tile-fronted pub with al fresco seating area, very popular in summer. Shabby chic décor that's been modernised but feels retro. Modern British repertoire on extensive menus.

Cross Keys, 1 Lawrence St, SW3 5NB ⊖ *South Kensington*, ✆ (020) 7349 9111, *crosskeys@fsmail-net, Fax (020) 7349 9333* – ▤. MC AE VISA. ⛌ 23 PZG a
closed 23-28 December, and Bank Holidays – **Rest** 24.50/28.00 ♀.
◆ Hidden away near the Embankment, this 18C pub has period furniture and impressive carved stone fireplaces. Interesting, modern menus include blackboard of daily specials.

Lots Road Pub and Dining Room, 114 Lots Rd, SW10 0RJ ⊖ *Gloucester Road*, ✆ (020) 7352 6645, *lotsroad@thespiritgroup.com, Fax (020) 7376 4975* – ▤. MC VISA 23 PZG b
Rest a la carte 18.00/26.00 ♀.
◆ Traditional corner pub with an open-plan kitchen, flowers at each table and large modern pictures on the walls. Contemporary menus change daily.

Earl's Court *Gtr London* – ✉ *SW5/SW10.*

K + K George, 1-15 Templeton Pl, SW5 9NB ⊖ *Earl's Court*, ✆ (020) 7598 8700, *hotelgeorge@kkhotels.co.uk, Fax (020) 7370 2285*, 帀 – 🛗 ⇹ ▤ ✆ P – 🏛 30. MC AE ⓓ VISA 35 AAY s
Rest (in bar) a la carte 18.40/28.50 **s.** ♀ – **154 rm** ☕ ★182.00 – ★★217.00.
◆ Five converted 19C houses overlooking large rear garden. Scandinavian style to rooms with low beds, white walls and light wood furniture. Breakfast room has the garden view. Informal dining in the bar.

Twenty Nevern Square without rest., Nevern Sq, SW5 9PD ⊖ *Earl's Court*, ✆ (020) 7565 9555, *hotel@twentynevernsquare.co.uk, Fax (020) 7565 9444* – 🛗 ⇹ ✆ P. MC AE ⓓ VISA. ⛌ 35 AAY u
☕ 9.00 – **19 rm** ★79.00/99.00 – ★★95.00/109.00.
◆ In an attractive Victorian garden square, an individually designed, privately owned town house. Original pieces of furniture and some rooms with their own terrace.

Mayflower without rest., 26-28 Trebovir Rd, SW5 9NJ ⊖ *Earl's Court*, ✆ (020) 7370 0991, *info@mayflower-group.co.uk, Fax (020) 7370 0994* – 🛗 ⇹ ✆. MC AE ⓓ VISA. ⛌ 35 ABY x
☕ 7.00 – **47 rm** ★69.00/85.00 – ★★95.00/99.00.
◆ Conveniently placed, stylish establishment with a secluded rear breakfast terrace, juice bar and basement breakfast room. Individualistic rooms have Indian/ Asian influence.

Amsterdam without rest., 7 and 9 Trebovir Rd, SW5 9LS ⊖ *Earl's Court*, ✆ (020) 7370 2814, *reservations@amsterdam-hotel.com, Fax (020) 7244 7608*, 帀 – 🛗 ⇹ ✆. MC AE ⓓ VISA. ⛌ 35 ABY c
☕ 2.75 **19 rm** ★72.00/86.00 – ★★87.00/92.00, 8 suites.
◆ Basement breakfast room and a small secluded garden. The brightly decorated bedrooms are light and airy. Some have smart wood floors; some boast their own balcony.

Rushmore without rest., 11 Trebovir Rd, SW5 9LS ⊖ *Earl's Court*, ✆ (020) 7370 3839, *rushmore-reservations@london.com, Fax (020) 7370 0274* – ⇹. MC AE ⓓ VISA. ⛌ 35 ABY a
22 rm ★55.00/69.00 – ★★69.00/97.00.
◆ Behind its Victorian façade lies an hotel popular with tourists. Individually decorated bedrooms in a variety of shapes and sizes. Piazza-styled conservatory breakfast room.

Langan's Coq d'Or, 254-260 Old Brompton Rd, SW5 9HR ⊖ *Earl's Court*, ✆ (020) 7259 2599, *admin@langansrestaurant.co.uk, Fax (020) 7370 7735* – ▤. MO AE ① VISA 35 ABZ e
closed 25-26 December and 1 January – **Rest** 20.50.
◆ Classic, buzzy brasserie and excellent-value menu to match. Walls adorned with pictures of celebrities: look out for more from the enclosed pavement terrace. Smooth service.

Hollywood Arms, 45 Hollywood Rd, SW10 9HX ⊖ *Earl's Court*, ✆ (020) 7349 7840, *Fax (020) 7349 7841* – ▤. MO AE VISA. 36 ACZ c
closed 25 December – **Rest** a la carte 17.00/24.00 ♀.
◆ Period pub in smart residential area with stylish interior furnished in rich autumnal colours. Efficient service. Concise menu with Mediterranean influences and flavours.

Kensington *Gtr London* – ✉ *SW7/W8/W11/W14.*

Royal Garden, 2-24 Kensington High St, W8 4PT ⊖ *High Street Kensington*, ✆ (020) 7937 8000, *sales@royalgarden.co.uk, Fax (020) 7361 1991*, ←, ₣₅, ≘s – |‡|, ⇹ rm, ▤ ✆ ♿ P – 🏠 550. MO AE ① VISA. 35 ABX c
Park Terrace : **Rest** a la carte 23.75/33.00 **s** – (see also ***The Tenth*** below) – ☕ 18.00 – **376 rm** ☆317.00/388.00 – ☆☆388.00, 20 suites.
◆ A tall, modern hotel with many of its rooms enjoying enviable views over the adjacent Kensington Gardens. All the modern amenities and services, with well-drilled staff. Bright, spacious, large-windowed restaurant.

The Milestone, 1-2 Kensington Court, W8 5DL ⊖ *High Street Kensington*, ✆ (020) 7917 1000, *bookms@rchmail.com, Fax (020) 7917 1010*, ₣₅, ≘s – |‡| ⇹ ▤ ✆. MO AE ① VISA 35 ABX u
Rest (booking essential to non-residents) 18.50 and a la carte 27.50/50.00 ♀ – ☕ 21.50 – **52 rm** ☆352.00/376.00 – ☆☆382.50/405.00, 5 suites.
◆ Elegant 'boutique' hotel with decorative Victorian façade and English feel. Charming oak panelled lounge and snug bar. Meticulously decorated bedrooms with period detail. Panelled dining room with charming little oratory for privacy seekers.

Baglioni, 60 Hyde Park Gate, SW7 5BB ⊖ *High Street Kensington*, ✆ (020) 7368 5700, *info@baglionihotellondon.com, Fax (020) 7368 5701*, 🏛, ₣₅, ≘s – |‡|, ⇹ rm, ▤ ✆ – 🏠 80. MO AE ① VISA. 36 ACX e
Brunello : **Rest** - Italian - 24.00 (lunch) and a la carte 47.00/72.00 – ☕ 25.00 – **53 rm** ☆352.00 – ☆☆423.00, 15 suites.
◆ Opposite Kensington Palace: ornate interior, trendy basement bar. Impressively high levels of service. Small gym/sauna. Superb rooms in cool shades boast striking facilities. Restaurant specialises in rustic Italian cooking.

Hilton London Kensington, 179-199 Holland Park Ave, W11 4UL ⊖ *Holland Park*, ✆ (020) 7603 3355, *rm.kensington@hilton.com, Fax (020) 7602 9397*, ₣₅, ≘s – |‡|, ⇹ rm, ▤ ✆ ♿ P – 🏠 250. MO AE ① VISA. 16 MZE x
Rest 24.95 and a la carte 22.40/61.90 – ☕ 19.95 – **602 rm** ☆75.00/175.00 – ☆☆198.00.
◆ The executive bedrooms and the nearby exhibition centres make this a popular business hotel. Equally useful spot for tourists; it has all the necessary amenities. Warm, pastel coloured Imbue.

Hilton London Olympia, 380 Kensington High St, W14 8NL ⊖ *Kensington Olympia*, ✆ (020) 7603 3333, *Fax (020) 7603 4846*, ₣₅ – |‡|, ⇹ rm, ▤ ✆ ♿ P – 🏠 250. MO AE ① VISA 16 MZF a
Rest (bar lunch Saturday) 15.00/20.00 and a la carte 17.95/31.95 ♀ – ☕ 17.95 – **395 rm** ☆104.00/194.00 – ☆☆116.00/216.00, 10 suites.
◆ Busy, corporate hotel, benefiting from being within walking distance of Olympia. Bedrooms of a good size, with light wood furniture and fully tiled bathrooms. Bright dining room with large windows.

The Tenth (at Royal Garden H.), 2-24 Kensington High St, W8 4PT ⊖ *High Street Kensington*, ✆ (020) 7361 1910, *tenthrestaurant@royalgardenhotel.co.uk, Fax (020) 7361 1921*, ← Kensington Palace and Gardens, London skyline – ▤ P. MO AE ① VISA 35 ABX c
closed Saturday lunch, Sunday and Bank Holidays – **Rest** (live music Saturday) 23.00 (lunch) and a la carte 33.50/47.00 **s** ♀.
◆ Named after the hotel's top floor where this stylish yet relaxed room is situated. Commanding views of Kensington Palace and the Park. Well-structured service; modern menu.

Belvedere, Holland House, off Abbotsbury Rd, W8 6LU ⊖ *Holland Park*, ✆ (020) 7602 1238, *sales@whitestarline.org.uk, Fax (020) 7610 4382*, 🏛, – ▤ ⇔ 70. MO AE ① VISA 16 MZE u
closed 26 December, 1 January and Sunday dinner – **Rest** 17.95/22.50 (lunch) and a la carte 25.50/36.00 ♀.
◆ Former 19C orangery in a delightful position in the middle of the Park. On two floors with a bar and balcony terrace. Huge vases of flowers. Modern take on classic dishes.

XX **Zaika,** 1 Kensington High St, W8 5NP ⊖ *High Street Kensington,* ✆ (020) 7795 6533, *info@zaika-restaurant.co.uk, Fax (020) 7937 8854* – ▤. MC AE ⊙ VISA 35 ABX r
closed 25-26 December and Saturday lunch – **Rest** - Indian - 18.00 (lunch) and a la carte 27.20/41.50 ♀.
◆ A converted bank, sympathetically restored, with original features and Indian artefacts. Well organised service of modern Indian dishes.

XX **Clarke's,** 124 Kensington Church St, W8 4BH ⊖ *Notting Hill,* ✆ (020) 7221 9225, *restaurant@sallyclarke.com, Fax (020) 7229 4564* – ⇆ ▤. MC AE ⊙ VISA 27 ABV c
closed 10 days Christmas-New Year, Monday dinner, Sunday and Bank Holidays – **Rest** (set menu only at dinner) 44.00 (dinner) and lunch a la carte 26.50/31.50 **s** ♀.
◆ Open-plan kitchen, personally overseen by the owner, provides modern British cooking. No choice, set menu at dinner. Comfortable and bright, with a neighbourhood feel.

XX **Babylon** (at The Roof Gardens), 99 Kensington High St (entrance on Derry St), W8 5SA ⊖ *High Street Kensington,* ✆ (020) 7368 3993, *babylon@roofgardens.virgin.co.uk, Fax (020) 7938 2774,* ≤, 常 – ▤. MC AE VISA 35 ABX n
closed Christmas, New Year and Sunday dinner – **Rest** 21.00 (lunch) and a la carte 28.00/48.50 ♀.
◆ Situated on the roof of this pleasant London building affording attractive views of the London skyline. Stylish modern décor in keeping with the contemporary, British cooking.

XX **Launceston Place,** 1a Launceston Pl, W8 5RL ⊖ *Gloucester Road,* ✆ (020) 7937 6912, *Fax (020) 7938 2412* – ▤. MC AE ⊙ VISA 35 ACX a
closed 24-28 December, 1 January, Saturday lunch and August Bank Holiday – **Rest** 18.50 (lunch) and a la carte 30.75/37.50 ♀.
◆ Divided into a number of rooms, this corner restaurant is lent a bright feel by its large windows and gilded mirrors. Chatty service and contemporary cooking.

XX **Memories of China,** 353 Kensington High St, W8 6NW ⊖ *High Street Kensington,* ✆ (020) 7603 6951, *Fax (020) 7603 0848* – ▤. MC AE VISA 35 AAY v
closed Easter and Christmas – **Rest** - Chinese - (booking essential) 15.00/38.00 and a la carte 29.40/32.15 ♀.
◆ Subtle lighting and brightly coloured high-back chairs add to the modern feel of this Chinese restaurant. Screens separate the tables. Plenty of choice from extensive menu.

XX **Timo,** 343 Kensington High St, W8 6NW ⊖ *High Street Kensington,* ✆ (020) 7603 3888, *timorestaurant@fsmail.net, Fax (020) 7603 8111* – ▤. MC AE VISA 35 AAY c
closed 24 December-7 January and Saturday lunch – **Rest** - Italian - a la carte 22.00/32.00 ♀.
◆ Modern, personally run restaurant with unadorned walls and comfortable seating in brown suede banquettes. Italian menus of contemporary dishes and daily changing specials.

XX **The Ark,** 122 Palace Gardens Terr, W8 4RT ⊖ *Notting Hill Gate,* ✆ (020) 7229 4024, *mail@thearkrestaurant.co.uk, Fax (020) 7792 8787,* 常 – ▤. MC AE VISA 27 ABV r
closed Sunday, Monday lunch and Bank Holidays – **Rest** - Italian - a la carte 23.00/34.00 ♀.
◆ The hut-like external appearance belies the contemporary interior of this Italian restaurant. Comfortable, bright feel with bar and lounge. Smoothly run, rustic cooking.

X **Kensington Place,** 201 Kensington Church St, W8 7LX ⊖ *Notting Hill Gate,* ✆ (020) 7727 3184, *kpr@egami.co.uk, Fax (020) 7229 2025* – ▤. MC AE ⊙ VISA 27 AAV z
closed 24-26 December – **Rest** (booking essential) 18.50/24.50 and a la carte 28.50/46.00 ♀.
◆ A cosmopolitan crowd still head for this establishment that set the trend for large, bustling and informal restaurants. Professionally run with skilled modern cooking.

X **Cibo,** 3 Russell Gdns, W14 8EZ ⊖ *Kensington Olympia,* ✆ (020) 7371 6271, *Fax (020) 7602 1371* – MC AE ⊙ VISA 16 MZE b
closed Easter, Christmas, Saturday lunch and Sunday dinner – **Rest** - Italian - a la carte 24.00/37.95.
◆ Smoothly run Italian restaurant that combines style with the atmosphere of a neighbourhood favourite. Unaffected service with robust and tasty food.

X **Malabar,** 27 Uxbridge St, W8 7TQ ⊖ *Notting Hill Gate,* ✆ (020) 7727 8800, *feedback@malabar-restaurant.co.uk* – MC AE VISA 27 AAV e
closed 1 week Christmas and last week August – **Rest** - Indian - (booking essential) (buffet lunch Sunday) 21.00 and a la carte 17.05/31.15 **s**.
◆ Indian restaurant in a residential street. Three rooms with individual personalities and informal service. Extensive range of good value dishes, particularly vegetarian.

X **Wódka,** 12 St Albans Grove, W8 5PN ⊖ *High Street Kensington,* ✆ (020) 7937 6513, *info@wodka.co.uk, Fax (020) 7937 8621* – MC AE ⊙ VISA 35 ABX c
closed lunch Saturday and Sunday – **Rest** - Polish - 14.50 (lunch) and dinner a la carte 21.50/43.00 ♀.
◆ Unpretentious Polish restaurant with rustic, authentic menu. Assorted blinis and flavoured vodkas a speciality. Simply decorated, with wooden tables and paper napkins.

North Kensington - ✉ W2/W11.

The Portobello without rest., 22 Stanley Gdns, W11 2NG ⊖ *Notting Hill Gate*, ✆ (020) 7727 2777, *info@portobello-hotel.co.uk, Fax (020) 7792 9641* – 🛗 ✆. MO AE VISA
16 NZE n
closed 24-29 December – ☕ 12.50 **24 rm** 130.00/160.00 – 170.00/285.00.
◆ An attractive Victorian town house in an elegant terrace. Original and theatrical décor. Circular beds, half-testers, Victorian baths: no two bedrooms are the same.

Abbey Court without rest., 20 Pembridge Gdns, W2 4DU ⊖ *Notting Hill Gate*, ✆ (020) 7221 7518, *info@abbeycourthotel.co.uk, Fax (020) 7792 0858* – ⇔. MO AE ① VISA.
27 AAV u
☕ 8.00 **22 rm** 99.00/125.00 – 130.00/279.00.
◆ Five-storey Victorian town house with individually decorated bedrooms, with many thoughtful touches. Breakfast served in a pleasant conservatory. Friendly service.

Guesthouse West, 163-165 Westbourne Grove, W11 2RS ⊖ *Notting Hill Gate*, ✆ (020) 7792 9800, *reception@guesthousewest.com, Fax (020) 7792 9797*, – ⇔ rm, ▤ ✆. MO AE VISA.
27 AAU x
Rest *(closed lunch Monday-Wednesday)* a la carte 10.50/19.00 – ☕ 10.00 – **20 rm** 170.00/200.00 – 170.00/200.00.
◆ Attractive Edwardian house in the heart of Notting Hill, close to its shops and restaurants. Contemporary bedrooms boast the latest in audio visual gadgetry. Chic Parlour Bar for all-day light dishes in a tapas style.

The Ledbury, 127 Ledbury Rd, W11 2AQ ⊖ *Notting Hill Gate*, ✆ (020) 7792 9090, *info@theledbury.com, Fax (020) 7792 9191*, – ⇔ ▤. MO AE ① VISA
27 AAT a
closed 25-26 December, 1 January and August Bank Holiday – **Rest** 24.50/45.00 ♀.
Spec. Lasagne of rabbit and girolles, thyme velouté. Assiette of lamb with garlic, borlotti beans and rosemary. Vanilla yoghurt parfait.
◆ Converted pub whose cool décor fits seamlessly into the neighbourhood it serves. Confident, highly accomplished cooking using first-rate ingredients; portions are generous.

Notting Hill Brasserie, 92 Kensington Park Rd, W11 2PN ⊖ *Notting Hill Gate*, ✆ (020) 7229 4481, *enquiries@nottinghillbrasserie.com, Fax (020) 7221 1246* – ▤ ⇔ 44. MO AE VISA
27 AAU a
closed Sunday dinner – **Rest** 19.50 (lunch) and dinner a la carte 30.00/40.00 ♀.
◆ Modern, comfortable restaurant with quiet, formal atmosphere set over four small rooms. Authentic African artwork on walls. Contemporary dishes with European influence.

Edera, 148 Holland Park Ave, W11 4UE ⊖ *Holland Park*, ✆ (020) 7221 6090, *Fax (020) 7313 9700* – ▤. MO AE VISA
16 MZE n
Rest - Italian - a la carte 23.00/35.00 ♀.
◆ Split level restaurant with 4 outdoor tables. Attentive service by all staff. Interesting menus of modern Italian cooking with some unusual ingredients and combinations.

Notting Grill, 123A Clarendon Rd, W11 4JG ⊖ *Holland Park*, ✆ (020) 7229 1500, *nottinggrill@aol.com, Fax (020) 7229 8889*, – MO AE ① VISA
16 MZE z
closed 24 December-3 January, 27-28 August and Monday lunch – **Rest** - Steak specialities - a la carte 23.15/38.75 ♀.
◆ Converted pub that retains a rustic feel, with bare brick walls and wooden tables. Specialises in well sourced, quality meats.

South Kensington *Gtr London* – ✉ *SW5/SW7.*

The Bentley Kempinski, 27-33 Harrington Gdns, SW7 4JX ⊖ *Gloucester Road*, ✆ (020) 7244 5555, *info@thebentley-hotel.com, Fax (020) 7244 5566*, Ⅰ₅, ≘s – 🛗 ⇔ ▤ ✆ – 🎪 80. MO AE ① VISA
36 ACY k
Peridot*:** **Rest** (lunch only) 26.00 – (see also ***1880 below) – ☕ 18.50 – **52 rm** 340.00 – 616.00, 12 suites.
◆ A number of 19C houses have been joined to create this opulent, lavish, hidden gem, decorated with marble, mosaics and ornate gold leaf. Bedrooms with gorgeous silk fabrics. Airy, intimate Peridot offers brasserie menus.

Millennium Gloucester, 4-18 Harrington Gdns, SW7 4LH ⊖ *Gloucester Road*, ✆ (020) 7373 6030, *sales.gloucester@mill-cop.com, Fax (020) 7373 0409*, Ⅰ₅ – 🛗 ⇔ ▤ ♿ P – 🎪 500. MO AE ① VISA.
36 ACY r
***Bugis Street*:** **Rest** - Chinese (Singaporean) - 15.50 and a la carte – ***South West 7*:** **Rest** (dinner only) (buffet only) 21.00 – ☕ 17.50 – **604 rm** 252.00 – 252.00, 6 suites.
◆ A large international group hotel. Busy marbled lobby and vast conference facilities. Smart and well-equipped bedrooms are generously sized, especially the 'Club' rooms. Dinner or buffet at South West 7. Informal, compact Bugis Street.

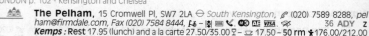

The Pelham, 15 Cromwell Pl, SW7 2LA ⊖ *South Kensington,* ✆ (020) 7589 8288, *pelham@firmdale.com, Fax (020) 7584 8444,* – . VISA. 36 **ADY** z
Kemps : Rest 17.95 (lunch) and a la carte 27.50/35.00 – 17.50 – **50 rm** 176.00/212.00 – 294.00, 2 suites.
◆ Attractive Victorian town house with a discreet and comfortable feel. Wood panelled drawing room and individually decorated bedrooms with marble bathrooms. Detailed service. Warm basement dining room.

Blakes, 33 Roland Gdns, SW7 3PF ⊖ *Gloucester Road,* ✆ (020) 7370 6701, *blakes@blakeshotels.com, Fax (020) 7373 0442,* – , rest, . VISA. 36 **ACZ** n
Rest *(closed 25-26 December and 1 January)* a la carte 62.75/123.75 – 25.00 – **45 rm** 153.00/200.00 – 305.00/323.00, 3 suites.
◆ Behind the Victorian façade lies one of London's first 'boutique' hotels. Dramatic, bold and eclectic décor, with oriental influences and antiques from around the globe. Fashionable restaurant with bamboo and black walls.

Harrington Hall, 5-25 Harrington Gdns, SW7 4JW ⊖ *Gloucester Road,* ✆ (020) 7396 9696, *sales@harringtonhall.co.uk, Fax (020) 7396 9090,* , – – 200. VISA. 36 **ACY** n
Wetherby's : Rest *(closed lunch Saturday and Sunday)* 18.95 and a la carte 21.55/36.45 – 15.50 – **200 rm** 195.00 – 195.00.
◆ A series of adjoined terraced houses, with an attractive period façade that belies the size. Tastefully furnished bedrooms, with an extensive array of facilities. Classically decorated dining room.

Vanderbilt, 68-86 Cromwell Rd, SW7 5BT ⊖ *Gloucester Road,* ✆ (020) 7761 9000, *Fax (020) 7761 9001,* – – 100. VISA. 36 **ACY** z
6886 : Rest 25.00 and a la carte 25.00/33.50 – 15.00 – **215 rm** 171.50 – 238.50.
◆ A Victorian town house, once home to the Vanderbilt family. Retains many original features such as stained glass windows and fireplaces. Now a modern, group hotel. Restaurant has unusual objets d'art and striking cracked glass bar.

London Marriott Kensington, 147 Cromwell Rd, SW5 0TH ⊖ *Gloucester Road,* ✆ (020) 7973 1000, *Fax (020) 7370 1685,* , , – – 200. VISA. 35 **ABY** n
Fratelli : Rest - Italian - a la carte 20.00/36.50 – 16.95 – **215 rm** 145.70/198.60 – 198.60/257.30, 1 suite.
◆ Modern seven-storey hotel around atrium with good leisure centre. Coffee bar and Spanish tapas bar. Spacious, comfortable, well-equipped bedrooms with many extras. Informal Italian restaurant with open kitchen and wide ranging menu.

Rembrandt, 11 Thurloe Pl, SW7 2RS ⊖ *South Kensington,* ✆ (020) 7589 8100, *rembrandt@sarova.co.uk, Fax (020) 7225 3476,* , , – , rm, rest, – 200. VISA. 36 **ADY** x
Rest (carving lunch) 19.95 and a la carte approx 25.00 **s.** – **195 rm** 200.00/220.00 – 220.00.
◆ Built originally as apartments in the 19C, now a well-equipped hotel opposite the Victoria and Albert museum. Comfortable lounge, adjacent leisure club, well appointed rooms. Spacious dining room.

Millennium Bailey's, 140 Gloucester Rd, SW7 4QH ⊖ *Gloucester Road,* ✆ (020) 7373 6000, *baileys@mill-cop.com, Fax (020) 7370 3760* – . VISA. 36 **ACY** a
Olives : Rest (bar lunch)/dinner 19.95/24.95 and a la carte 25.50/35.00 – 16.50 – **211 rm** 188.00/264.00 – 264.00.
◆ Elegant lobby, restored to its origins dating from 1876, with elaborate plasterwork and a striking grand staircase. Victorian feel continues through into the bedrooms. Modern, pastel shaded restaurant.

Jurys Kensington, 109-113 Queen's Gate, SW7 5LR ⊖ *South Kensington,* ✆ (020) 7589 6300, *kensington@jurydoyle.com, Fax (020) 7581 1492* – – 80. VISA. 36 **ADY** g
Rest (dinner only) 15.00 – 16.00 – **174 rm** 190.00 – 190.00.
◆ A row of 18C town houses that were converted into a hotel in the 1920s. Spacious lobby lounge and busy basement Irish pub. Well-equipped, comfortable bedrooms. Dining room exudes a traditional appeal.

Number Sixteen, 16 Sumner Pl, SW7 3EG ⊖ *South Kensington,* ✆ (020) 7589 5232, *sixteen@firmdale.com, Fax (020) 7584 8615,* – . VISA. 36 **ADY** d
Rest (room service only) – 13.00 – **42 rm** 112.00/200.00 – 294.00.
◆ Enticingly refurbished 19C town houses in smart area. Discreet entrance, comfy sitting room and charming breakfast terrace. Bedrooms in English country house style.

The Cranley, 10 Bina Gdns, SW5 0LA ⊖ *Gloucester Road*, ✆ (020) 7373 0123, *info@thecranley.com, Fax (020) 7373 9497* – MC AE VISA. 36 ACY c
Rest (room service only) – 9.95 – **38 rm** 141.00/164.00 – 164.00/235.00, 1 suite.
◆ Delightful Regency town house that artfully combines charm and period details with modern comforts and technology. Individually styled bedrooms; some with four-posters.

The Gore, 190 Queen's Gate, SW7 5EX ⊖ *Gloucester Road*, ✆ (020) 7584 6601, *reservations@gorehotel.com, Fax (020) 7589 8127* – rm, rest, – 70. MC AE VISA. 36 ACX n
Bistrot 190 **:** **Rest** (booking essential) 20.00/30.00 and a la carte 24.00/30.50 ♀ – 16.95 – **49 rm** 176.25/223.75 – 329.00.
◆ Opened its doors in 1892; has retained its individual charm. Richly decorated with antiques, rugs and over 4,000 pictures that cover every inch of wall. Bistrot 190 boasts French-inspired décor.

Aster House without rest., 3 Sumner Pl, SW7 3EE ⊖ *South Kensington*, ✆ (020) 7581 5888, *asterhouse@btinternet.com, Fax (020) 7584 4925*, – MC VISA. 36 ADY t
13 rm 105.75/152.75 – 152.75/170.00.
◆ End of terrace Victorian house with a pretty little rear garden and first floor conservatory. Ground floor rooms available. A wholly non-smoking establishment.

Five Sumner Place without rest., 5 Sumner Pl, SW7 3EE ⊖ *South Kensington*, ✆ (020) 7584 7586, *reservations@sumnerplace.com, Fax (020) 7823 9962* – MC AE VISA. 36 ADY u
13 rm 85.00 – 150.00.
◆ Part of a striking white terrace built in 1848 in this fashionable part of town. Breakfast served in bright conservatory. Good sized bedrooms.

Premier Travel Inn Metro, 11 Knaresborough Place, SW5 0TJ ⊖ *Earl's Court*, ✆ (0870) 2383304, *Fax (020) 7370 9292* – MC AE VISA.
Rest (dinner only) – **184 rm** 74.95/74.95 – 79.95/79.95.
◆ Lodge hotel providing clean, comfortable, well-priced accommodation for visitors to the museums who find themselves on a budget. Well situated for local restaurants.

1880 (at The Bentley Kempinski H.), 27-33 Harrington Gdns, SW7 4JX ⊖ *Gloucester Road*, ✆ (020) 7244 5555, *info@thebentley-hotel.com, Fax (020) 7244 5566* – MC AE VISA. 36 ACY k
closed Sunday and Monday – **Rest** (dinner only) 45.00.
◆ Luxurious, opulently decorated room in Bentley basement: silk panels, gold leaf, Italian marble, chandeliers. Choose à la carte or extensive "grazing" menu up to 10 courses.

Bombay Brasserie, Courtfield Rd, SW7 4QH ⊖ *Gloucester Road*, ✆ (020) 7370 4040, *bombay1brasserie@aol.com, Fax (020) 7835 1669* – MC AE VISA. 36 ACY y
closed 25-26 December – **Rest** - Indian - (buffet lunch) 18.95 and dinner a la carte 27.75/36.00 ♀.
◆ Something of a London institution: an ever busy Indian restaurant with Raj-style décor. Ask to sit in the brighter plant-filled conservatory. Popular lunchtime buffet.

Lundum's, 119 Old Brompton Rd, SW7 3RN ⊖ *Gloucester Road*, ✆ (020) 7373 7774, *Fax (020) 7373 4472*, – MC AE VISA. 36 ACZ p
closed Sunday dinner – **Rest** - Danish - 19.25/24.50 and a la carte 26.50/48.50.
◆ A family run Danish restaurant offering an authentic, traditional lunch with a more expansive dinner menu. Comfortable room, with large windows. Charming service.

L'Etranger, 36 Gloucester Rd, SW7 4QT ⊖ *Gloucester Road*, ✆ (020) 7584 1118, *sasha@etranger.co.uk, Fax (020) 7584 8886* – 12. MC AE VISA. 35 ACX c
closed lunch Saturday and Sunday – **Rest** (booking essential) 16.50 (lunch) and a la carte 31.00/54.00.
◆ Corner restaurant with mosaic entrance floor and bay window. Modern décor. Tables extend into adjoining wine shop. French based cooking with Asian influences.

Khan's of Kensington, 3 Harrington Rd, SW7 3ES ⊖ *South Kensington*, ✆ (020) 7584 4114, *Fax (020) 7581 2900* – MC AE VISA. 36 ADY a
closed 25 December – **Rest** - Indian - 8.95/16.50 and a la carte 15.70/28.25 ♀.
◆ Bright room with wood flooring and a large mural depicting scenes from old India. Basement bar in a colonial style. Authentic Indian cooking with attentive service.

Cambio de Tercio, 163 Old Brompton Rd, SW5 0LJ ⊖ *Gloucester Road*, ✆ (020) 7244 8970, *Fax (020) 7373 8817* – 18. MC AE VISA. 36 ACZ a
closed 10 days Christmas – **Rest** - Spanish - a la carte 25.75/32.75.
◆ The keen young owners have created a vibrant destination offering a mix of traditional and sophisticated Spanish cooking complemented by a well-sourced regional wine list.

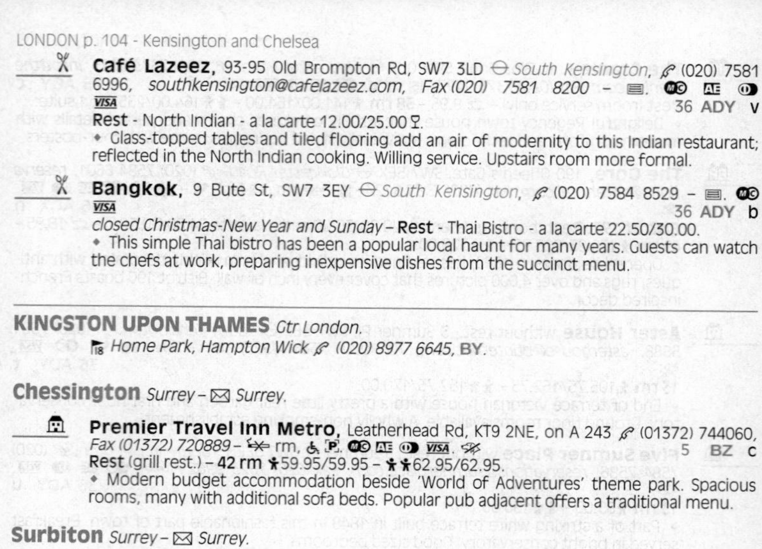

Café Lazeez, 93-95 Old Brompton Rd, SW7 3LD ⊖ *South Kensington,* ☏ (020) 7581 6996, *southkensington@cafelazeez.com, Fax (020) 7581 8200* – ▤. MC AE ⓓ VISA 36 ADY v

Rest - North Indian - a la carte 12.00/25.00 ♀.

◆ Glass-topped tables and tiled flooring add an air of modernity to this Indian restaurant; reflected in the North Indian cooking. Willing service. Upstairs room more formal.

Bangkok, 9 Bute St, SW7 3EY ⊖ *South Kensington,* ☏ (020) 7584 8529 – ▤. MC VISA 36 ADY b

closed Christmas-New Year and Sunday – **Rest** - Thai Bistro - a la carte 22.50/30.00.

◆ This simple Thai bistro has been a popular local haunt for many years. Guests can watch the chefs at work, preparing inexpensive dishes from the succinct menu.

KINGSTON UPON THAMES *Gtr London.*

Home Park, Hampton Wick ☏ (020) 8977 6645, **BY.**

Chessington *Surrey* – ✉ *Surrey.*

Premier Travel Inn Metro, Leatherhead Rd, KT9 2NE, on A 243 ☏ (01372) 744060, *Fax (01372) 720889* – rm, ♿ P. MC AE ⓓ VISA. 5 BZ c

Rest (grill rest.) – **42 rm** 59.95/59.95 – 62.95/62.95.

◆ Modern budget accommodation beside 'World of Adventures' theme park. Spacious rooms, many with additional sofa beds. Popular pub adjacent offers a traditional menu.

Surbiton *Surrey* – ✉ *Surrey.*

The French Table, 85 Maple Rd, KT6 4AW, ☏ (020) 8399 2365, *Fax (020) 8390 5353* – ▤. MC VISA 6 CY a

Closed 25-26 December, 1 week January, last 2 weeks in August, Monday, Sunday dinner and lunch Saturday – **Rest** - French-Mediterranean - 16.50 (lunch) and dinner a la carte 26.70/33.75 ♀.

◆ The lively atmosphere makes this narrow room with wooden tables and modern art a popular local. Attentive and relaxed service of a concise French-Mediterranean menu.

LAMBETH *Gtr London.*

Clapham Common *Gtr London* – ✉ *SW4.*

Tsunami, Unit 3, 1-7 Voltaire Rd, SW4 6DQ ⊖ *Clapham North,* ☏ (020) 7978 1610, *Fax (020) 7978 1591* – MC AE VISA 24 SZH a

closed 25 December - 2 January and Sunday – **Rest** - Japanese - (dinner only and Saturday lunch) a la carte 17.70/49.50 ♀.

◆ Trendy, mininalist-style restaurant. Interesting Japanese menu with many dishes designed for sharing and plenty of original options. Good Sushi and Sashimi selection.

Herne Hill *Gtr London* – ✉ *SE24.*

3 Monkeys, 136-140 Herne Hill, SE24 9QH, ☏ (020) 7738 5500, *info@3monkeysrestaurant.com, Fax (020) 7738 5505* – ▤. MC AE ⓓ VISA 7 FX r

Rest - Indian - 9.95/14.95 and a la carte 14.40/18.90 ♀.

◆ 'New wave' Indian restaurant in a converted bank. Dining room in bright white reached via a bridge over the bar and kitchen. Menu uses influences from all over India.

Kennington *Gtr London* – ✉ *SE11.*

Painted Heron, 205-209 Kennington Lane, SE11 5QS ⊖ *Kennington,* ☏ (020) 7793 8313, *Fax (020) 7793 8323,* – ▤. MC AE VISA 40 ANZ s

Rest - Indian - a la carte 24.00/31.00 ♀.

◆ Attractive, predominantly glass-fronted restaurant with pleasant courtyard terrace. Linen-clad tables and an interesting modern Indian menu with touches of invention.

Lobster Pot, 3 Kennington Lane, SE11 4RG ⊖ *Kennington,* ☏ (020) 7582 5556 – ▤. MC AE VISA 40 AOY e

closed Christmas-New Year, Sunday and Monday – **Rest** - French Seafood - 14.50/39.50 and a la carte 26.30/39.30.

◆ A nautical theme so bold you'll need your sea legs: fishing nets, shells, aquariums, portholes, even the sound of seagulls. Classic French seafood menu is more restrained.

Waterloo *Gtr London – ✉ SE1.*

Channel Tunnel : Eurostar information and reservations ✆ (08705) 186186.

London Marriott H. County Hall, Westminster Bridge Rd, SE1 7PB ⊖ *Westminster,* ✆ (020) 7928 5200, *salesadmin.countyhall@marriotthotels.co.uk, Fax (020) 7928 5300,* ←, ⓟ, ƒ₆, ≘s, ⊡ – |ǂ|, ⇹ rm, ▤ ✆ ♿ – 🏔 70. ⓂⒸ AE ⓓ VISA. ✈ 40 AMX a
County Hall : **Rest** 26.50 and a la carte 25.50/50.50 ♀ – ☕ 21.50 – **195 rm** ★292.50 – ★★292.50, 5 suites.
◆ Occupying the historic County Hall building. Many of the spacious and comfortable bedrooms enjoy river and Parliament outlook. Impressive leisure facilities. Famously impressive views from restaurant.

Premier Travel Inn Metro, Belvedere Rd, SE1 7PB ⊖ *Waterloo,* ✆ (0870) 2383300, *london.county.hall.mti.@whitbread.com, Fax (020) 7902 1619* – |ǂ| ⇹, ▤ rest, ♿. ⓂⒸ AE ⓓ VISA. ✈ 32 AMV u
Rest (grill rest.) (dinner only) – **314 rm** ★86.95/86.95 – ★★89.95/89.95.
◆ Adjacent to the London Eye and within the County Hall building. Budget accommodation in a central London location that is the envy of many, more expensive, hotels.

LEWISHAM *Gtr London.*

Blackheath *Gtr London – ✉ SE3.*

Chapter Two, 43-45 Montpelier Vale, SE3 0TJ, ✆ (020) 8333 2666, *fiona.chapter2@talk21.com, Fax (020) 8355 8399* – ⇹ ▤. ⓂⒸ AE ⓓ VISA 8 HX c
closed 2-5 January – **Rest** 18.50/23.50 ♀.
◆ Smart and contemporary interior. Decorated in primary colours, with pine flooring. Formal service of a well-priced, well-judged European-influenced modern menu.

LONDON HEATHROW AIRPORT *– see Hillingdon, London p. 87.*

MERTON *Gtr London.*

Colliers Wood *Gtr London – ✉ SW19.*

Express by Holiday Inn without rest., 200 High St, SW19 2BH, on A 24 ⊖ *Colliers Wood,* ✆ (020) 8545 7300, *Fax (020) 8545 7301* – |ǂ| ⇹ ✆ ♿ 🚗 – 🏔 50. ⓂⒸ AE ⓓ VISA. ✈ 7 EY a
83 rm ★82.00 – ★★82.00.
◆ Modern, corporate budget hotel. Spacious and well-equipped bedrooms; power showers in en suite bathrooms. Ideal for the business traveller. Continental breakfast included.

Wimbledon *Gtr London – ✉ SW19.*

Cannizaro House 🐎, West Side, Wimbledon Common, SW19 4UE ⊖ *Wimbledon,* ✆ (0870) 333 9124, *info@cannizarohouse.com, Fax (0870) 3339224,* ←, 🌳, 🏛 – |ǂ|, ⇹ rm, P – 🏔 120. ⓂⒸ AE ⓓ VISA. ✈ 6 DXY x
Rest 16.00/34.50 and a la carte ♀ – ☕ 14.50 – **43 rm** ★100.00/297.00 – ★★100.00/297.00, 2 suites.
◆ Part Georgian mansion in a charming spot on the Common. Appealing drawing room popular for afternoon tea. Rooms in original house are antique furnished, some with balconies. Refined restaurant overlooks splendid formal garden.

Light House, 75-77 Ridgway, SW19 4ST ⊖ *Wimbledon,* ✆ (020) 8944 6338, *lightrest@aol.com, Fax (020) 8946 4440* – ⓂⒸ AE VISA 6 DY n
closed 25-26 December, Easter Monday and Sunday dinner – **Rest** - Italian influences - 16.50 (lunch) and a la carte 22.20/31.20 ♀.
◆ Bright and modern neighbourhood restaurant with open plan kitchen. Informal service of a weekly changing and diverse menu of progressive Italian/fusion dishes.

The Fire Stables, 27-29 Church Rd, SW19 5DQ ⊖ *Wimbledon,* ✆ (020) 8946 3197, *thefirestables@thespiritgroup.com, Fax (020) 8946 1101* – ▤. ⓂⒸ VISA 6 DX a
Rest 15.50 (lunch) and a la carte 24.00/30.00 ♀.
◆ Modern gastropub in village centre. Open-plan kitchen. Polished wood tables and banquettes. Varied modern British dishes. Expect fishcakes, duck confit salad or risotto.

NEWHAM Gtr London.

ExCel Gtr London – ✉ E16.

Crowne Plaza Docklands, Royal Victoria Dock, Western Gateway, E16 1AL ⊖ *Royal Victoria*, ✆ (0870) 9909692, *sales@crowneplazadocklands.co.uk, Fax (0870) 9909693*, – 275. 8 HV a
Terra : **Rest** a la carte 20.15/31.70 – 14.50 – **199 rm** 95.00/140.00 – 105.00/150.00, 11 suites.
◆ Spacious and stylish hotel with emphasis on the business traveller. State-of-the-art meeting rooms; snazzy, compact leisure centre. Ultra-smart, well-equipped rooms. Modish dining room with funky bar.

Ramada H. & Suites - London Docklands, 2 Festoon Way, Royal Victoria Dock, E16 1RH ⊖ *Prince Regent*, ✆ (0870) 1118779, *Fax (0870) 1118789*, – – 25. 8 HV c
The Waterfront : **Rest** a la carte 14.00/28.00 – **153 rm** 140.00/150.00 – 140.00/150.00, 71 suites.
◆ Plush, purpose-built hotel five minutes from City Airport and ExCel. Two small, well-equipped meeting rooms. The bedrooms are a strong point with impressive facilities. Modern dining room with al fresco option for fine weather.

Novotel London ExCel, 7 Western Gateway, Royal Victoria Dock, E16 1AA ⊖ *Royal Victoria*, ✆ (020) 7540 9700, *h3656@accor.com, Fax (020) 7540 9710*, – – 70. 8 HV e
The Upper Deck : **Rest** a la carte approx 25.00 – 13.50 – **250 rm** 79.00 – 255.00, 7 suites.
◆ Capacious purpose-built hotel adjacent to ExCel Centre. Ultra modish bar and coffee area exudes minimalism. Up-to-date meeting facilities. Well-appointed, comfortable rooms. Formal dining room with menus influenced by the seasons.

Sunborn Yacht H., Royal Victoria Dock, E16 1SL ⊖ *Prince Regent*, ✆ (020) 7059 9100, *reservations.london@sunbornhotels.com, Fax (020) 7059 9432*, – – 90. 8 HV n
Rest (bar lunch)/dinner a la carte 35.00/47.00 – 13.50 – **102 rm** 160.00/190.00 – 160.00/190.00, 2 suites.
◆ Permanently moored next to ExCel, this glitzy yacht hotel offers unique, water-borne accommodation. The sizable rooms have a distinct 'cabin' feel: two suites boast a sauna. European menus in the formal, airy dining room.

Premier Travel Inn Metro, Royal Victoria Dock, E16 1SL, ✆ (0870) 2383322, *Fax (020) 7540 2250* – 8 HV r
Rest (grill rest.) – **202 rm** 59.95/59.95 – 72.95/72.95.
◆ Good value lodge accommodation two minutes from ExCel, and five from City Airport. Bedrooms are of uniform design, shape and shade. Grill based eatery.

RICHMOND-UPON-THAMES Gtr London.

Barnes Gtr London – ✉ SW13.

Sonny's, 94 Church Rd, SW13 0DQ, ✆ (020) 8748 0393, *barnes@sonnys.co.uk, Fax (020) 8748 2698* – 20. 21 KZH x
closed 25-26 December, Sunday dinner and Bank Holidays – **Rest** 16.50/19.50 and a la carte 23.50/31.50.
◆ Dine in the bright, modern and informal restaurant or the equally relaxed café-bar. Attentive service of imaginative modern dishes.

MVH, 5 White Hart Lane, SW13 0PX, ✆ (020) 8392 1111, *Fax (020) 8878 1919* – 21 KZH e
closed 2 weeks after Christmas and lunch Monday-Wednesday – **Rest** 22.00/29.00.
◆ Restaurant exuding individuality, Bohemian-style bar area and a dining room that mixes a Louis XIV style and modern elements. Unique food in keeping with the mood.

Riva, 169 Church Rd, SW13 9HR, ✆ (020) 8748 0434, *Fax (020) 8748 0434* – 21 LZH a
closed last 2 weeks July, 1 week Easter and 24 December-4 January – **Rest** - Italian - a la carte 27.00/39.00.
◆ The eponymous owner manages the polite service in this unassuming restaurant. Rustic and robust cooking uses some of Italy's finest produce. Extensive all-Italian wine list.

East Sheen Gtr London – ✉ SW14.

XX **Redmond's,** 170 Upper Richmond Road West, SW14 8AW, ✆ (020) 8878 1922, *pippa@redmonds.org.uk* – ✈ ▤. MO VISA 6 CX v
closed 3 days Christmas, Sunday dinner and Bank Holidays – **Rest** (dinner only and Sunday lunch)/dinner 15.50/32.00.
◆ Bright, spacious and relaxed restaurant. Friendly and approachable service of modern British cooking prepared with care. Mid-week set-price menu is good value.

The Victoria, 10 West Temple Sheen, SW14 7RT, ✆ (020) 8876 4238, *reservations@thevictoria.net, Fax (020) 8878 3464,* – ✈ P. MO AE VISA. ✂ 6 CX u
closed Christmas – **Rest** a la carte 18.00/28.00 ♀.
◆ Traditional pub near Richmond Park with bright modern décor. Large conservatory, terrace and children's play area. Daily menu of interesting modern and traditional dishes.

Hampton Wick Surrey – ✉ Surrey.

Chase Lodge, 10 Park Rd, KT1 4AS, ✆ (020) 8943 1862, *info@chaselodgehotel.com, Fax (020) 8943 9363* – MO AE ① VISA 5 BY e
Rest (dinner only) 15.00/25.00 – **12 rm** ✝55.00/85.00 – ✝✝105.00/145.00.
◆ Personally-run small hotel in mid-terrace Victorian property in an area of outstanding architectural and historical interest. Individually furnished, comfortable rooms. Bright, airy conservatory restaurant.

Kew Surrey – ✉ Surrey.

XX ✿ **The Glasshouse,** 14 Station Parade, TW9 3PZ ⊖ *Kew Gardens,* ✆ (020) 8940 6777, *info@glasshouserestaurant.co.uk, Fax (020) 8940 3833* – ✈ ▤. MO AE VISA 6 CX z
closed 24-26 December – **Rest** 23.50/35.00 ♀.
Spec. Roast scallops and prawns with onion purée, pea shoot and garlic wafers. Slow roast pork belly with apple tart, choucroute and crispy ham. Vanilla yoghurt with melon, mango and passion fruit.
◆ Light pours in through the glass façade of this forever busy and contemporary restaurant. Assured service of original modern British cooking.

XX **Kew Grill,** 10b Kew Green, TW9 3BH ⊖ *Kew Gardens,* ✆ (020) 8948 4433, *kewgrill@aol.com, Fax (020) 8605 3532* – ▤. MO AE ① VISA 6 CX u
closed 25-26 December and Monday lunch – **Rest** - Beef specialities - (booking essential) a la carte 23.90/40.15 ♀.
◆ Just off Kew Green, this long, narrow restaurant has a Mediterranean style and feel. Grilled specialities employing top-rate ingredients: the beef is hung for 35 days.

X **Ma Cuisine,** The Old Post Office, 9 Station Approach, TW9 3QB ⊖ *Kew Gardens,* ✆ (020) 8332 1923, – MO VISA 6 CX r
Rest - French - 18.00 (lunch) and a la carte 18.10/25.15 ♀.
◆ Formerly Kew's post office building; features tables on the pavement, arched roof and red gingham tablecloths. Good value, classic French dishes. Truly, "le petit bistrot".

Richmond Surrey – ✉ Surrey.

18, 18 Richmond Park, Roehampton Gate ✆ (020) 8876 3205 **CX** – *18 Sudbrook Park ✆ (020) 8940 1463* **CX**.
Old Town Hall, Whittaker Ave ✆ (020) 8940 9125.

Petersham, Nightingale Lane, TW10 6UZ, ✆ (020) 8940 7471, *enq@petershamhotel.co.uk, Fax (020) 8939 1002,* ←, – |‡| ✆ P – 🎤 30. MO AE ① VISA. ✂ 6 CX c
Rest – (see ***Restaurant*** below) – **60 rm** ☕ ✝135.00/160.00 – ✝✝170.00/285.00, 1 suite.
◆ Extended over the years, a fine example of Victorian Gothic architecture. Impressive Portland stone, self-supporting staircase. Most comfortable rooms overlook the Thames.

Richmond Gate, 158 Richmond Hill, TW10 6RP, ✆ (020) 8940 0061, *richmondgate@foliohotels.com, Fax (020) 8332 0354,* Fö, ≘s, ▢, – ✈ ✆ ✝ P – 🎤 45. MO AE VISA. ✂ 6 CX c
***Gates On The Park* : Rest** *(closed lunch Saturday and Bank Holidays)* 18.50/31.00 ♀ – ☕ 14.50 – **67 rm** ✝160.00 – ✝✝160.00/180.00, 1 suite.
◆ Originally four elegant Georgian town houses and now a very comfortable corporate hotel. Cosy lounges have a period charm. Well-appointed deluxe rooms have thoughtful extras. Comfortable restaurant has intimate feel.

Doughty Cottage without rest., 142A Richmond Hill, TW10 6RN, ✆ (020) 8332 9434, *deniseoneill425@aol.co.uk, Fax (020) 8948 3716,* – ✈ P. MO VISA 6 CX c
closed 25-26 December – **3 rm** ✝68.00/90.00 – ✝✝105.00.
◆ Positioned high above the river, this attractive 18C Regency house is discreetly set behind a picturesque walled garden. Thoughtfully equipped rooms, two with patio gardens.

Chalon House without rest., 8 Spring Terrace, Paradise Rd, TW9 1LW ⊖ *Richmond*, ✆ (020) 8332 1121, *chalonhouse@hotmail.com*, *Fax (020) 8332 1131*, – [P]. 6 CX e
closed March – **3 rm** 70.00 – 85.00.
◆ Carefully renovated Georgian house a couple of minutes from town centre. Comfy, well furnished lounge; organic breakfasts shared with fellow guests. Individually styled rooms.

XXX **Restaurant** (at Petersham H.), Nightingale Lane, TW10 6UZ, ✆ (020) 8939 1084, *Fax (020) 8939 1002*, <, – [P] 16. MC AE VISA 6 CX c
closed 25-26 December – **Rest** 24.00 (lunch) and a la carte 31.50/42.00.
◆ Tables by the window have spectacular views across royal parkland and the winding Thames. Formal surroundings in which to enjoy classic and modern cooking. See the cellars.

Teddington *Middx* – ✉ *Middx.*

XX **The Wharf,** 22 Manor Rd, TW11 8BG, ✆ (020) 8977 6333, *the.wharf@walk-on-water.co.uk*, *Fax (020) 8977 9444*, <, – [P]. MC AE VISA 5 BX a
closed 25-26 December, first week January and Sunday dinner – **Rest** 16.00/19.00 and a la carte 25.00/35.00.
◆ Riverside restaurant with large heated terrace opposite Teddington lock. Modern menu of good value dishes; fixed price menu in the week; modern music.

Twickenham *Middx* – ✉ *Middx.*

XX **McClements,** 2 Whitton Rd, TW1 1BJ, ✆ (020) 8744 9610, *johnmac21@aol.com*, *Fax (020) 8744 9598* – 6. MC AE VISA 5 BX a
closed 2 weeks January, 1 week Easter, 1 week August, Sunday and Monday – **Rest** 25.00/38.00.
◆ An intimate neighbourhood restaurant not far from rugby stadium offering polished service of modern cooking. 'Degustation' menu includes wines.

X **Brula Bistrot,** 43 Crown Rd, St Margarets, TW1 3EJ, ✆ (020) 8892 0602, *info@brulabistrot.com*, *Fax (020) 8892 7727* – 25. MC VISA 5 BX v
closed 25-26 December and 1 January – **Rest** - French - (booking essential) 13.50 (lunch) and a la carte 20.75/33.75.
◆ Behind the stained glass windows and the rose arched entrance, you'll find an intimate and cosy bistro. Friendly and relaxed service of a weekly changing, rustic menu.

X **Ma Cuisine,** 6 Whitton Rd, TW1 1BJ, ✆ (020) 8607 9849 – MC VISA 5 BX a
Rest - French - 18.00 (lunch) and a la carte 18.10/25.15.
◆ Small neighbourhood bistro style restaurant offering good value. Classic French country cooking with blackboard specials; concise wine list.

SOUTHWARK *Gtr London.*

Vinopolis, 1 Bank End ✆ (020) 7357 9168, tourisminfo@southwark.gov.uk.

Bermondsey *Gtr London* – ✉ *SE1.*

London Bridge, 8-18 London Bridge St, SE1 9SG ⊖ *London Bridge*, ✆ (020) 7855 2200, *sales@london-bridge-hotel.co.uk*, *Fax (020) 7855 2233*, – , rm, 100. MC AE VISA. 33 AQV a
Georgetown **: Rest** 25.00/30.00 (lunch) and a la carte 19.25/28.70 – 14.95 – **135 rm** 199.00 – 199.00, 3 suites.
◆ In one of the oldest parts of London, independently owned with an ornate façade dating from 1915. Modern interior with classically decorated bedrooms and an impressive gym. Restaurant echoing the colonial style serving Malaysian dishes.

XXX **Le Pont de la Tour,** 36d Shad Thames, Butlers Wharf, SE1 2YE ⊖ *London Bridge*, ✆ (020) 7403 8403, *lepontres@conran-restaurants.co.uk*, *Fax (020) 7403 0267*, <, – 24. MC AE VISA 34 ASV c
Rest 29.50 (lunch) and dinner a la carte 40.50/82.50.
◆ Elegant and stylish room commanding spectacular views of the Thames and Tower Bridge. Formal and detailed service. Modern menu with an informal bar attached.

XX **Bengal Clipper,** Cardamom Building, Shad Thames, Butlers Wharf, SE1 2YR ⊖ *London Bridge*, ✆ (020) 7357 9001, *mail@bengalclipper.co.uk*, *Fax (020) 7357 9002* – . MC AE VISA 34 ASV e
Rest - Indian - a la carte 16.60/26.95.
◆ Housed in a Thames-side converted warehouse, a smart Indian restaurant with original brickwork and steel supports. Menu features Bengali and Goan dishes. Evening pianist.

XX **Tentazioni,** 2 Mill St, Lloyds Wharf, SE1 2BD ⊖ *Bermondsey,* ✆ (020) 7237 1100, *tentazioni@aol.com, Fax (020) 7237 1100* – MC AE VISA 20 **XZE** x
closed 23 December - 3 January, Easter, Sunday and lunch Saturday and Monday – **Rest** - Italian - 19.00 (lunch) and a la carte 30.00/36.00 ♀.
◆ Former warehouse provides a bright and lively environment. Open staircase between the two floors. Keenly run, with a menu offering simple, carefully prepared Italian food.

X **Blueprint Café,** Design Museum, Shad Thames, Butlers Wharf, SE1 2YD ⊖ *London Bridge,* ✆ (020) 7378 7031, *Fax (020) 7357 8810,* < Tower Bridge – MC AE ⓓ VISA 34 **ASV** u
closed 25-28 December, 1-2 January and Sunday dinner – **Rest** a la carte 24.00/37.50 ♀.
◆ Above the Design Museum, with impressive views of the river and bridge: handy binoculars on tables. Eager and energetic service, modern British menus: robust and rustic.

X **Cantina Del Ponte,** 36c Shad Thames, Butlers Wharf, SE1 2YE ⊖ *London Bridge,* ✆ (020) 7403 5403, *Fax (020) 7403 4432,* <, 😊 – MC AE ⓓ VISA 34 **ASV** c
closed 25-26 December – **Rest** - Italian - a la carte 15.85/27.95 ♀.
◆ Quayside setting with a large canopied terrace. Terracotta flooring; modern rustic style décor, simple and unfussy. Tasty, refreshing Mediterranean-influenced cooking.

X **Butlers Wharf Chop House,** 36e Shad Thames, Butlers Wharf, SE1 2YE ⊖ *London Bridge,* ✆ (020) 7403 3403, *Fax (020) 7403 3414,* < Tower Bridge, 😊 – MC AE ⓓ VISA 34 **ASV** n
closed 25-26 December, 1-3 January and Sunday dinner – **Rest** 26.00 (lunch) and dinner a la carte 24.50/37.50 ♀.
◆ Book the terrace in summer and dine in the shadow of Tower Bridge. Rustic feel to the interior, with obliging service. Menu focuses on traditional English dishes.

🍺 **The Hartley,** 64 Tower Bridge Rd, SE1 4TR ⊖ *Borough,* ✆ (020) 7394 7023, *enquiries@thehartley.com* – MC AE ⓓ VISA 20 **XZE** c
closed 25-26 December – **Rest** a la carte 16.00/27.00 ♀.
◆ Classic 19C red brick pub, named after former Hartley jam factory opposite: jam jars even adorn the walls! Interesting menus offer five daily changing blackboard specials.

Rotherhithe *Gtr London* – ✉ *SE16.*

Hilton London Docklands, 265 Rotherhithe St, Nelson Dock, SE16 5HW, ✆ (020) 7231 1001, *sales-docklands@hilton.com, Fax (020) 7231 0599,* <, 😊, Ⅰ5, ≘s, ▣ – |◆|, ⚓, ⇝ rm, ▤ ♿ P – 🏛 350. MC AE ⓓ VISA 7 **GV** r
closed 22-30 December – ***Traders Bistro :*** **Rest** *(closed Sunday)* (dinner only) 25.00 ♀ – **361 rm** ☕ ★110.00/200.00 – ★★110.00/200.00, 4 suites.
◆ Redbrick group hotel with glass façade. River-taxi from the hotel's own pier. Extensive leisure facilities. Standard size rooms with all mod cons. Eat on board Traders Bistro, a reconstructed galleon moored in dry dock.

Southwark *Gtr London* – ✉ *SE1.*

Novotel London City South, 53-61 Southwark Bridge Rd, SE1 9HH ⊖ *London Bridge,* ✆ (020) 7089 0400, *h3269@accor.com, Fax (020) 7089 0410,* Ⅰ5, ≘s – |◆|, ⇝ rm, ▤ ✆ ♿ – 🏛 100. MC AE ⓓ VISA 34 **AQV** c
The Garden Brasserie : **Rest** a la carte 16.70/31.85 **s.** ♀ – ☕ 13.50 – **178 rm** ★170.00/250.00 – ★★190.00/280.00, 4 suites.
◆ The new style of Novotel with good business facilities. Triple glazed bedrooms, furnished in the Scandinavian style with keyboard and high speed internet. Brasserie style dining room with windows all down one side.

Premier Travel Inn Metro, Bankside, 34 Park St, SE1 9EF ⊖ *London Bridge,* ✆ (0870) 7001456, *Fax (0870) 7001457* – |◆|, ⇝ rm, ♿. MC AE ⓓ VISA. ✂ 33 **AQV** b
Rest (grill rest.) – **56 rm** ★82.95/82.95 – ★★84.95/84.95.
◆ A good value lodge with modern, well-equipped bedrooms which include a spacious desk area, ideal for the corporate and leisure traveller. Popular, tried-and-tested menus.

Express by Holiday Inn without rest., 103-109 Southwark St, SE1 0JQ ⊖ *Southwark,* ✆ (020) 7401 2525, *stay@expresssouthwark.co.uk, Fax (020) 7401 3322* – |◆| ⇝ ▤ ♿ P. MC AE ⓓ VISA. ✂ 33 **APV** e
88 rm ★93.00/125.00 – ★★110.00/128.00.
◆ Useful location, just ten minutes from Waterloo. Purpose-built hotel with modern bedrooms in warm pastel shades. Fully equipped business centre.

Southwark Rose, 43-47 Southwark Bridge Rd, SE1 9HH ⊖ *London Bridge,* ✆ (020) 7015 1480, *info@southwarkrosehotel.co.uk, Fax (020) 7015 1481* – |◆| ⇝ ▤ ✆ ♿ P – 🏛 80. MC AE VISA. ✂ 34 **AQV** c
Rest *(dinner only)* a la carte 12.00/21.00 – ☕ 9.95 – **78 rm** ★115.00 – ★★115.00, 6 suites.
◆ Purpose built budget hotel south of the City, near the Globe Theatre. Top floor breakfast room with bar. Uniform style, reasonably spacious bedrooms with writing desks.

XXX **Oxo Tower,** (8th floor), Oxo Tower Wharf, Barge House St, SE1 9PH ⊖ *Southwark*, ☎ (020) 7803 3888, *oxo.reservations@harveynichols.co.uk, Fax (020) 7803 3838*, ≤ London skyline and River Thames, – |‡| ▤. MC AE ⓓ VISA 32 ANV a
closed 25-26 December – **Rest** 29.50 (lunch) and dinner a la carte 42.00/56.75 ♀ – (see also ***Oxo Tower Brasserie*** below).
◆ Top of a converted factory, providing stunning views of the Thames and beyond. Stylish, minimalist interior with huge windows. Smooth service of modern cuisine.

XX **Baltic,** 74 Blackfriars Rd, SE1 8HA ⊖ *Southwark*, ☎ (020) 7928 1111, *info@balticrestaurant.co.uk, Fax (020) 7928 8487* – MC AE ⓓ VISA 33 AOV e
Rest - East European with Baltic influences - 13.50 (lunch) and a la carte 23.00/27.50 ♀.
◆ Set in a Grade II listed 18C former coach house. Enjoy authentic and hearty east European and Baltic influenced food. Interesting vodka selection and live jazz on Sundays.

X **Oxo Tower Brasserie,** (8th floor), Oxo Tower Wharf, Barge House St, SE1 9PH ⊖ *Southwark*, ☎ (020) 7803 3888, *Fax (020) 7803 3838*, ≤ London skyline and River Thames, – |‡| ▤. MC AE ⓓ VISA 32 ANV a
closed 25-26 December – **Rest** 21.50 (lunch) and a la carte 30.00/40.50 ♀.
◆ Same views but less formal than the restaurant. Open-plan kitchen, relaxed service, the modern menu is slightly lighter. In summer, try to secure a table on the terrace.

X **Cantina Vinopolis,** No.1 Bank End, SE1 9BU ⊖ *London Bridge*, ☎ (020) 7940 8333, *cantina@vinopolis.co.uk, Fax (020) 7940 8334* – ▤. MC AE ⓓ VISA 33 AQV z
closed 24 December-2 January and Sunday dinner – **Rest** 17.50 (lunch) and a la carte 19.50/28.30 ♀.
◆ Large, solid brick vaulted room under Victorian railway arches, with an adjacent wine museum. Modern menu with a huge selection of wines by the glass.

X **Glas,** 3 Park St, SE1 9AB ⊖ *London Bridge*, ☎ (020) 7357 6060, *glas@glasrestaurant.com, Fax (020) 7357 6061* – ⇔ ▤. MC AE VISA 33 AQV x
closed 23 December-5 January, 1 week August, Sunday and Monday – **Rest** - Swedish - a la carte 21.00/27.00 ♀.
◆ Hidden away in Borough Market area, this intimate restaurant has a distinct Scandinavian feel, and serves good value, authentic Swedish grazing dishes in a relaxed atmosphere.

X **Tate Cafe (7th Floor),** Tate Modern, Bankside, SE1 9TG ⊖ *Southwark*, ☎ (020) 7401 5020, *Fax (020) 7401 5171*, ≤ London skyline and River Thames – ⇔. MC AE ⓓ VISA 33 APV s
closed 24-26 December – **Rest** (lunch only and dinner Friday-Saturday) a la carte 19.50/32.15 ♀.
◆ Modernity to match the museum, with vast murals and huge windows affording stunning views. Canteen-style menu at a sensible price with obliging service.

X **Souvlaki & Bar (Bankside),** Units 1-2, Riverside House, 2A Southwark Bridge Rd, SE1 9HA ⊖ *Southwark*, ☎ (020) 7620 0162, *Fax (020) 7620 0262*, ≤, – ▤. MC VISA 33 AQV s
Rest - Greek - a la carte 14.00/25.00.
◆ Overlooking the Thames, two minutes from Globe Theatre: a casual, modern restaurant with excellent value menus featuring totally authentic Greek dishes and beers.

Anchor and Hope, 36 The Cut, SE1 8LP ⊖ *Southwark*, ☎ (020) 7928 9898, *Fax (020) 7928 4595* – MC VISA 32 ANV n
closed Christmas-New Year, last 2 weeks August, Sunday, Monday lunch and Bank Holidays – **Rest** (bookings not accepted) a la carte 20.00/30.00 ♀.
◆ Close to Waterloo, the distinctive dark green exterior lures visitors in droves. Bare floorboards, simple wooden furniture. Seriously original cooking with rustic French base.

SUTTON *Gtr London.*

Sutton *Surrey* – ✉ *Surrey.*

18, 9 *Oak Sports Centre, Woodmansterne Rd, Carshalton* ☎ *(020) 8643 8363.*

Holiday Inn, Gibson Rd, SM1 2RF, ☎ (0870) 4009113, *sales-sutton@ichotelsgroup.com, Fax (020) 8770 1995*, – |‡|, ⇔ rm, ▤ ♿ P – 🔬 180. MC AE ⓓ VISA. 6 DZ a
Rest 20.00/27.00 s. – ☕ 14.95 – **115 rm** ✝165.00 – ✝✝165.00, 1 suite.
◆ Centrally located and modern. Offers comprehensive conference facilities. Spacious and well-equipped bedrooms. An ideal base for both corporate and leisure guests. Bright, modern, relaxed bar and restaurant.

Thatched House, 135-141 Cheam Rd, SM1 2BN, ☎ (020) 8642 3131, *thatched house@btconnect.com, Fax (020) 8770 0684,* – rest, – 50. VISA. 6 DZ e
closed 23 December-2 January – **Rest** *(closed Friday-Sunday)* (bar lunch)/dinner a la carte 13.50/23.25 – **32 rm** 65.00/75.00 – 75.00/90.00.
◆ Part thatched and gabled private hotel on busy main road just out of the town centre. Most comfortable and quietest rooms overlook the pretty gardens. Rustic-styled dining room.

TOWER HAMLETS *Gtr London.*

Canary Wharf *Gtr London* – ✉ *E14.*

Four Seasons, Westferry Circus, E14 8RS ⊖ *Canary Wharf (DLR),* ☎ (020) 7510 1999, *Fax (020) 7510 1998,* – – 200. VISA 3 GV a
Rest – (see ***Quadrato*** below) – 21.00 – **128 rm** 376.00 – 399.50, 14 suites.
◆ Stylish hotel opened in 2000, with striking river and city views. Atrium lobby leading to modern bedrooms boasting every conceivable extra. Detailed service.

Marriott London West India Quay, 22 Hertsmere Rd, E14 4ED ⊖ *West India Quay (DLR),* ☎ (020) 7093 1000, *reservations@marriott.com, Fax (020) 7093 1001,* – – 300. VISA. 7 GV v
Curve: **Rest** a la carte 21.00/40.00 – 18.00 – **294 rm** 274.00/327.00 – 274.00/327.00, 7 suites.
◆ Spacious, very well-equipped bedrooms, classic or modern, plus a 24-hour business centre in this glass-fronted high-rise hotel on the quay. Champagne and oyster bar and informal, American-style seafood inn serving fish from nearby Billingsgate market.

Circus Apartments without rest., 39 Westferry Circus, E14 8RW ⊖ *Canary Wharf,* ☎ (020) 7719 7000, *res@circusapartments.co.uk, Fax (020) 7719 7001,* – . VISA. 7 GV a
45 suites 217.00/240.00.
◆ Smart, contemporary, fully serviced apartment block close to Canary Wharf: rooms, comfortable and spacious, can be taken from one day to one year.

Plateau (Restaurant), Canada Place, Canada Square, E14 5ER ⊖ *Canary Wharf,* ☎ (020) 7715 7100, *Fax (020) 7715 7110* – . VISA 3 GV n
closed 25 December, 1 January, Saturday lunch and Sunday – **Rest** 24.75 (dinner) and a la carte 39.75/50.50.
◆ Fourth floor restaurant overlooking Canada Square and The Big Blue art installation. Glass-sided kitchen; well-spaced, uncluttered tables. Modern menus with classical base.

Ubon by Nobu, 34 Westferry Circus, E14 8RR ⊖ *Canary Wharf,* ☎ (020) 7719 7800, *ubon@noburestaurants.com, Fax (020) 7719 7801,* ≤ River Thames and city skyline – . VISA 7 GV a
closed Saturday lunch, Sunday and Bank Holidays – **Rest** - Japanese - 45.00/70.00.
◆ Light, airy, open-plan restaurant, with floor to ceiling glass and great Thames views. Informal atmosphere. Large menu with wide selection of modern Japanese dishes.

Quadrato (at Four Seasons H.), Westferry Circus, E14 8RS ⊖ *Canary Wharf (DLR),* ☎ (020) 7510 1999, *Fax (020) 7510 1998,* – . VISA 3 GV a
Rest - Italian - 27.00/33.00 and a la carte 27.00/41.00.
◆ Striking, modern restaurant with terrace overlooking river. Sleek, stylish dining room with glass-fronted open-plan kitchen. Menu of northern Italian dishes; swift service.

Plateau (Grill), Canada Place, Canada Square, E14 5ER ⊖ *Canary Wharf,* ☎ (020) 7715 7100, *Fax (020) 7715 7110* – . VISA 3 GV n
closed 25 December, 1 January and Sunday dinner – **Rest** 20.00/35.00 and a la carte 24.25/34.50.
◆ Situated on fourth floor of 21C building; adjacent to Plateau Restaurant, with simpler table settings. Classical dishes, with seasonal base, employing grill specialities.

The Gun, 27 Coldharbour, E14 9NS ⊖ *Blackwall (DLR),* ☎ (020) 7515 5222, *info@thegun docklands.com,* – VISA. 7 GV x
closed 25-26 December and 1 January – **Rest** a la carte 20.00/33.00.
◆ Restored historic pub with a terrace facing the Dome: tasty dishes, including Billingsgate market fish, balance bold simplicity and a bit of French finesse. Efficient service.

St Katherine's Dock *Gtr London* – ✉ *E1.*

XX **The Aquarium,** Ivory House, E1W 1AT ⊖ *Tower Hill,* ✆ (020) 7480 6116, *info@theaquarium.co.uk, Fax (020) 7480 5973,* ←, – MC AE ⊙ VISA 34 ASV a
closed 2 weeks Christmas, Saturday lunch, Sunday and Monday dinner and Bank Holidays – **Rest** - Seafood - a la carte 30.00/70.00 ♀.
◆ Seafood restaurant in a pleasant marina setting with views of the boats from some tables. Simple, smart modern décor. Menu of market-fresh, seafood dishes.

Spitalfields *Gtr London* – ✉ *E1.*

XX **Bengal Trader,** 44 Artillery Lane, E1 7NA ⊖ *Liverpool Street,* ✆ (020) 7375 0072, *mail@bengalclipper.co.uk, Fax (020) 7247 1002* – ▤. MC AE VISA 34 AST x
Rest - Indian - a la carte 13.00/25.00.
◆ Contemporary Indian paintings feature in this stylish basement room beneath a ground floor bar. Menu provides ample choice of Indian dishes.

X **St John Bread and Wine,** 94-96 Commercial St, E1 6LZ ⊖ *Shoreditch,* ✆ (020) 7247 8724, *Fax (020) 7247 8924* – ▤. MC AE VISA 20 XZD k
closed 24 December-2 January, Sunday dinner and Bank Holiday Mondays – **Rest** a la carte 25.20/29.20.
◆ Very popular neighbourhood bakery providing wide variety of home-made breads. Appealing, intimate dining section: all day menus that offer continually changing dishes.

Wapping *Gtr London* – ✉ *E1.*

X **Wapping Food,** Wapping Wall, E1W 3ST ⊖ *Wapping,* ✆ (020) 7680 2080, *info@wapping-wpt.com,* – P. MC AE VISA 20 YZE n
closed 24 December-2 January and Sunday dinner – **Rest** a la carte 25.50/42.00.
◆ Something a little unusual; a combination of restaurant and gallery in a converted hydraulic power station. Enjoy the modern menu surrounded by turbines and TV screens.

Whitechapel *Gtr London* – ✉ *E1.*

XX **Cafe Spice Namaste,** 16 Prescot St, E1 8AZ ⊖ *Tower Hill,* ✆ (020) 7488 9242, *info@cafespice.co.uk, Fax (020) 7481 0508* – ▤. MC AE ⊙ VISA 34 ASU z
closed Christmas-New Year, Sunday and Bank Holidays – **Rest** - Indian - 30.00 and a la carte 17.25/28.95 ♀.
◆ A riot of colour from the brightly painted walls to the flowing drapes. Sweet-natured service adds to the engaging feel. Fragrant and competitively priced Indian cooking.

WANDSWORTH *Gtr London.*

Battersea *Gtr London* – ✉ *SW8/SW11/SW18.*

Express by Holiday Inn without rest., Smugglers Way, SW18 1EG, ✆ (0870) 7201298, *wandsworth@morethanhotels.com, Fax (0870) 7201299* – |‡| ⇔ ▤ ✆ ♿ P – 🏃 35. MC AE ⊙ VISA 22 OZH a
148 rm ✝92.00 – ✝✝92.00.
◆ Modern, purpose-built hotel on major roundabout, very much designed for the cost-conscious business guest or traveller. Adjacent steak house. Sizeable, well-kept bedrooms.

XX **The Food Room,** 123 Queenstown Rd, SW8 3RH, ✆ (020) 7622 0555, *Fax (020) 7627 5440* – ▤. MC VISA 24 RZH c
closed 1-7 January, 25-26 December, 2 weeks August, Sunday, Monday, and lunch Tuesday and Saturday – **Rest** - French - 16.50/24.50.
◆ Attractive eatery with a relaxed feel and attentive service. Concise French/Mediterranean menus with Italian and North African flavours, utilising very good quality produce.

XX **Chada,** 208-210 Battersea Park Rd, SW11 4ND, ✆ (020) 7622 2209, *enquiry@chadathai.com, Fax (020) 7924 2178* – ▤. MC AE ⊙ VISA 23 QZH x
closed Sunday and Bank Holidays – **Rest** - Thai - (dinner only) a la carte 11.20/37.95 ♀.
◆ Weather notwithstanding, the Thai ornaments and charming staff in traditional silk costumes transport you to Bangkok. Carefully prepared and authentic dishes.

X **Le Petit Max,** Chatfield Rd, by Battersea Reach, SW11 3SE, ✆ (020) 7223 0999, *Fax (020) 7223 2558,* – ▤. MC VISA 23 PZH a
closed Sunday dinner and Bank Holidays – **Rest** - French - 18.50 and a la carte 18.50/31.00 ♀.
◆ Set on ground floor of Thames side apartment with outside decked terrace. Walls feature display case of French Michelin Red Guides. Good value, rustic, robust Gallic menus.

Ransome's Dock, 35-37 Parkgate Rd, SW11 4NP, ✆ (020) 7223 1611, *chef@ransomesdock.co.uk, Fax (020) 7924 2614,* – MC AE VISA 23 QZG c
closed 25-26 December, August Bank Holiday and Sunday dinner – **Rest** a la carte 21.00/37.00.
◆ Secreted in a warehouse development, with a dock-side terrace in summer. Vivid blue interior, crowded with pictures. Chef patron produces reliable brasserie-style cuisine.

The Greyhound, 136 Battersea High St, SW11 3JR, ✆ (020) 7978 7021, *eat@thegreyhoundatbattersea.co.uk,* – 25. MC AE VISA 23 PZH a
closed 24-27 December, 31 December-3 January, Sunday dinner and Monday – **Rest** 15.00/31.00.
◆ Attractive tile-and-glass fronted pub with superb wine list and range of beers. Leather pouffes in stylish bar. Cosy restaurant serves concise, organically inspired menus.

Putney – *SW15.*

Enoteca Turi, 28 Putney High St, SW15 1SQ *Putney Bridge,* ✆ (020) 8785 4449, *enoteca@aol.com, Fax (020) 8780 5409* – MC AE VISA 22 MZH n
closed 25-26 December, 1 January and Sunday – **Rest** - Italian - 16.50 (lunch) and a la carte 25.75/32.50.
◆ A friendly neighbourhood Italian restaurant, overseen by the owner. Rustic cooking, with daily changing specials. Good selection of wine by the glass.

The Phoenix, Pentlow St, SW15 1LY, ✆ (020) 8780 3131, *phoenix@sonnys.co.uk, Fax (020) 8780 1114,* – MC AE VISA 21 LZH s
closed Bank Holidays – **Rest** - Italian influences - 19.50 (lunch) and a la carte 18.50/32.50.
◆ Light and bright interior with French windows leading out on to a spacious terrace. Unfussy and considerate service. An eclectic element to the modern Mediterranean menu.

Southfields *Gtr London* – *SW18.*

Sarkhel's, 199 Replingham Rd, SW18 5LY *Southfields,* ✆ (020) 8870 1483, *veronica@sarkhels.co.uk* – MC VISA 6 DX e
closed 25-26 December and Monday – **Rest** - Indian - 9.95 (lunch) and a la carte 15.65/28.45.
◆ Recently expanded Indian restaurant with a large local following. Authentic, carefully prepared and well-priced dishes from many different Indian regions. Obliging service.

Calcutta Notebook, 201 Replingham Rd, SW18 5LY *Southfields,* ✆ (020) 8874 6603, *info@sarkhels.com* – MC VISA 6 DX e
closed 25-26 December and Monday – **Rest** - Indian (Bengali) - 18.00 and a la carte 14.70/27.35.
◆ Simple little eatery next to Sarkhel's, from whose kitchen the meals are served. East Indian cooking reflecting three generations of Sarkhel family; also several street foods.

Tooting *Gtr London* – *SW17.*

Kastoori, 188 Upper Tooting Rd, SW17 7EJ *Tooting Bec,* ✆ (020) 8767 7027 – MC VISA 6 EX v
closed 25-26 December and lunch Monday and Tuesday – **Rest** - Indian Vegetarian - a la carte 12.75/15.50.
◆ Specialising in Indian vegetarian cooking with a subtle East African influence. Family-run for many years, a warm and welcoming establishment with helpful service.

Oh Boy, 843 Garratt Lane, SW17 0PG *Broadway,* ✆ (020) 8947 9760, *Fax (020) 8879 7867* – MC AE VISA 6 EX c
closed 1 week Christmas and Monday – **Rest** - Thai - (dinner only) 22.00 and a la carte 12.25/26.65 s.
◆ Long-standing neighbourhood Thai restaurant. Extensive menu offers authentic and carefully prepared dishes, in simple but friendly surroundings.

Wandsworth *Gtr London* – *SW17.*

Chez Bruce (Poole), 2 Bellevue Rd, SW17 7EG *Tooting Bec,* ✆ (020) 8672 0114, *enquiries@chezbruce.co.uk, Fax (020) 8767 6648* – MC AE VISA 6 EX e
closed 24-26 December – **Rest** (booking essential) 23.50/35.00.
Spec. Foie gras and chicken liver parfait, toasted brioche. Roast cod with olive oil mash and grilled courgette. Strawberry and Champagne trifle.
◆ An ever-popular restaurant, overlooking the Common. Simple yet considered modern British cooking. Convivial and informal, with enthusiastic service.

WESTMINSTER (City of) *Gtr London.*

Bayswater and Maida Vale *Gtr London – ✉ NW6/W2/W9.*

Hilton London Paddington, 146 Praed St, W2 1EE ⊖ *Paddington,* ☎ (020) 7850 0500, *paddington@hilton.com, Fax (020) 7850 0600,* – rm, – 350. VISA. 28 **ADU** a
The Brasserie : Rest 15.00/30.00 and a la carte 20.00/51.00 s. – 19.95 – **335 rm** 282.00 – 282.00, 20 suites.
◆ Early Victorian railway hotel, sympathetically restored in contemporary style with Art Deco details. Co-ordinated bedrooms with high tech facilities continue the modern style. Contemporarily styled brasserie offering a modern menu.

Hilton London Metropole, Edgware Rd, W2 1JU ⊖ *Edgware Road,* ☎ (020) 7402 4141, *cbs-londonmet@hilton.com, Fax (020) 7724 8866,* – rm, – 2000. VISA. 28 **AET** c
Nippon Tuk : Rest - South East Asian - 13.50/35.00 and a la carte 32.25/42.75 – ***Fiamma :*** Rest a la carte 17.95/29.40 – 17.95 – **1033 rm** 100.00/229.00 – 100.00/229.00, 25 suites.
◆ One of London's most popular convention venues by virtue of both its size and transport links. Well-appointed and modern rooms have state-of-the-art facilities. Vibrant restaurant and bar.

Royal Lancaster, Lancaster Terrace, W2 2TY ⊖ *Lancaster Gate,* ☎ (020) 7262 6737, *sales@royallancaster.com, Fax (020) 7724 3191,* – 1200. VISA. 28 **ADU** e
Rest – (see ***Island*** and ***Nipa*** below) – 18.00 – **394 rm** 290.00 – 378.00, 22 suites.
◆ Imposing 1960s purpose-built hotel overlooking Hyde Park. Some of London's most extensive conference facilities. Well-equipped bedrooms are decorated in traditional style.

The Hempel , 31-35 Craven Hill Gdns, W2 3EA ⊖ *Queensway,* ☎ (020) 7298 9000, *hotel@the-hempel.co.uk, Fax (020) 7402 4666,* – VISA. 28 **ACU** a
I-Thai : Rest - Italian-Japanese-Thai - *(closed Sunday)* a la carte 31.95/41.50 – 15.00 – **37 rm** 311.00 – 311.00, 9 suites.
◆ A striking example of minimalist design. Individually appointed bedrooms are understated yet very comfortable. Relaxed ambience. Modern basement restaurant.

Marriott, Plaza Parade, NW6 5RP ⊖ *Kilburn Park,* ☎ (020) 7543 6000, *reservations.maidavale@marriotthotels.co.uk, Fax (020) 7543 2100,* – – 200. VISA. 10 **NZB** c
Fratelli : Rest - Italian - (dinner only) a la carte 22.00/31.00 – 16.45 – **226 rm** 135.00/163.00 – 135.00/163.00, 11 suites.
◆ A capacious hotel, away from the busier city centre streets. Well equipped with both business and leisure facilities including 12m pool. Suites have small kitchens. Informal restaurant and brasserie.

The Royal Park, 3 Westbourne Terrace, Lancaster Gate, W2 3UL ⊖ *Lancaster Gate,* ☎ (020) 7479 6600, *info@theroyalpark.com, Fax (020) 7479 6601* – VISA. 28 **ADU** x
Rest (room service only) – **45 rm** 141.00/223.00 – 176.00/246.75, 3 suites.
◆ Three superbly restored Grade II listed Victorian houses. Comfy, period styled drawing rooms exude townhouse style. A minimalist air pervades the understated bedrooms.

Colonnade Town House without rest., 2 Warrington Crescent, W9 1ER ⊖ *Warwick Avenue,* ☎ (020) 7286 1052, *rescolonnade@theetongroup.com, Fax (020) 7286 1057* – VISA. 17 **OZD** e
15.00 – **43 rm** 152.75/164.50 – 164.50/188.00.
◆ Two Victorian townhouses with comfortable well-furnished communal rooms decorated with fresh flowers. Stylish and comfortable bedrooms with many extra touches.

Commodore, 50 Lancaster Gate, Hyde Park, W2 3NA ⊖ *Lancaster Gate,* ☎ (020) 7402 5291, *reservations@commodore-hotel.com, Fax (020) 7262 1088,* – rm, rest, VISA. 28 **ACU** r
Rest *(closed Sunday)* (dinner only) a la carte 24.50/30.50 s. – 7.50 – **78 rm** 125.00/165.00 – 145.00/165.00, 2 suites.
◆ Three converted Georgian town houses in a leafy residential area. Bedrooms vary considerably in size and style. Largest rooms decorated with a Victorian theme. Relaxed, casual bistro.

Mornington without rest., 12 Lancaster Gate, W2 3LG ⊖ *Lancaster Gate*, ☎ (020) 7262 7361, *london@mornington.co.uk*, *Fax (020) 7706 1028* – lift. MC AE DC VISA. 28 ACU s
closed Christmas – **66 rm** ☕ ★85.00/105.00 – ★★89.00/109.00.
◆ The classic portico facade belies the cool and modern Scandinavian influenced interior. Modern bedrooms are well-equipped and generally spacious. Duplex rooms available.

Delmere, 130 Sussex Gdns, W2 1UB ⊖ *Paddington*, ☎ (020) 7706 3344, *delmerehotel@compuserve.com*, *Fax (020) 7262 1863* – lift, rm, MC AE DC VISA. 28 ADT v
Rest *(closed Christmas, Sunday and Bank Holidays)* (dinner only) 19.00 and a la carte 14.95/23.95 – ☕ 9.00 – **36 rm** ★75.00/109.00 – ★★95.00/121.00.
◆ Attractive stucco fronted and porticoed Victorian property. Now a friendly private hotel. Compact bedrooms are both well-equipped and kept. Modest prices. Bright, relaxed restaurant and adjacent bar.

Miller's without rest., 111A Westbourne Grove, W2 4UW ⊖ *Bayswater*, ☎ (020) 7243 1024, *enquiries@millersuk.com*, *Fax (020) 7243 1064* – MC AE VISA. 27 ABU a
7 rm ☕ ★176.25 – ★★217.40/270.25.
◆ Victorian house brimming with antiques and knick-knacks. Charming sitting room provides the setting for a relaxed breakfast. Individual, theatrical rooms named after poets.

Island (at Royal Lancaster H.), Lancaster Terrace, W2 2TY ⊖ *Lancaster Gate*, ☎ (020) 7551 6070, *eat@islandrestaurant.co.uk*, *Fax (020) 7551 6071* – MC AE DC VISA 28 ADU e
Rest 15.00 (lunch) and a la carte 25.00/35.50 ♀.
◆ Modern, stylish restaurant with buzzy open kitchen. Full length windows allow good views of adjacent Hyde Park. Seasonally based, modern menus with wide range of dishes.

Nipa (at Royal Lancaster H.), Lancaster Terrace, W2 2TY ⊖ *Lancaster Gate*, ☎ (020) 7262 6737, *Fax (020) 7724 3191* – P. MC AE DC VISA 28 ADU e
closed Saturday lunch, Sunday and Bank Holidays – **Rest** - Thai - 14.90 (lunch) and a la carte 29.40/41.90 s.
◆ On the 1st floor and overlooking Hyde Park. Authentic and ornately decorated restaurant offers subtly spiced Thai cuisine. Keen to please staff in traditional silk costumes.

Green Olive, 5 Warwick Pl, W9 2PX ⊖ *Warwick Avenue*, ☎ (020) 7289 2469, *Fax (020) 7289 2463* – MC AE VISA 17 OZD a
closed 1 week Christmas, Sunday dinner and Saturday lunch – **Rest** - Italian - (booking essential) a la carte approx 35.00 ♀.
◆ Attractive neighbourhood restaurant in a smart residential area. Modern Italian food served in the bright street level room or the more intimate basement.

Assaggi (Sassu), 39 Chepstow Pl, (above Chepstow pub), W2 4TS ⊖ *Bayswater*, ☎ (020) 7792 5501, *nipi@assaggi.demon.co.uk* – MC DC VISA 27 AAU c
closed 2 weeks Christmas and Sunday – **Rest** - Italian - (booking essential) a la carte 36.50/38.90 ♀.
Spec. Pecorino con carpegna & rucola. Tagliolini alle erbe. Fegato di vitello.
◆ Polished wood flooring, tall windows and modern artwork provide the bright surroundings for this forever busy restaurant. Concise menu of robust Italian dishes.

Ginger, 115 Westbourne Grove, W2 4UP ⊖ *Bayswater*, ☎ (020) 7908 1990, *info@gingerrestaurant.co.uk*, *Fax (020) 7908 1991* – MC AE VISA 27 ABU v
closed 25 December – **Rest** - Bangladeshi - (dinner only and lunch Saturday and Sunday) a la carte 14.70/25.40.
◆ Bengali specialities served in contemporary styled dining room. True to its name, ginger is a key flavouring; dishes range from mild to spicy and are graded accordingly.

L'Accento, 16 Garway Rd, W2 4NH ⊖ *Bayswater*, ☎ (020) 7243 2201, *laccentorest@aol.com*, *Fax (020) 7243 2201* – MC AE VISA 27 ABU b
closed 25-26 December and Sunday – **Rest** - Italian - 18.50 and a la carte 25.50/30.50.
◆ Rustic surroundings and provincial, well priced, Italian cooking. Menu specialises in tasty pasta, made on the premises, and shellfish. Rear conservatory for the summer.

Formosa Dining Room (at Prince Alfred), 5A Formosa St, W9 1EE ⊖ *Warwick Avenue*, ☎ (020) 7286 3287, *theprincealfred@thespiritgroup.com*, *Fax (020) 7286 3383* – MC AE VISA 17 OZD n
Rest a la carte 21.50/33.00 ♀.
◆ Traditional pub appearance and a relaxed dining experience on offer behind the elegant main bar. Contemporary style of cooking.

The Waterway, 54 Formosa St, W9 2JU ⊖ *Warwick Avenue*, ☎ (020) 7266 3557, *info@thewaterway.co.uk*, *Fax (020) 7266 3547*, – MC AE VISA 17 OZD p
Rest a la carte 19.00/27.00 ♀.
◆ Pub with a thoroughly modern, metropolitan ambience. Spacious bar and large decked terrace overlooking canal. Concise, well-balanced menu served in open plan dining room.

Belgravia Gtr London – ✉ SW1.

The Berkeley, Wilton Pl, SW1X 7RL ⊖ *Knightsbridge,* ✆ (020) 7235 6000, *info@the-berkeley.co.uk, Fax (020) 7235 4330,* – rm, – 250. MC AE VISA 37 AGX e
Boxwood Café *(✆ (020) 7235 1010)* **: Rest** 21.00 (lunch) and a la carte 28.00/35.50 ♀ – (see also ***Pétrus*** below) – ☕ 23.50 – **189 rm** ★433.00/480.00 – ★★492.00/539.00, 25 suites.
◆ A gracious and discreet hotel. Relax in the gilded and panelled Lutyens lounge or enjoy a swim in the roof-top pool with its retracting roof. Opulent bedrooms. Split-level basement restaurant, divided by bar, with modern stylish décor; New York-style dining.

The Lanesborough, Hyde Park Corner, SW1X 7TA ⊖ *Hyde Park Corner,* ✆ (020) 7259 5599, *info@lanesborough.com, Fax (020) 7259 5606,* – rm, P – 90. MC AE VISA 37 AGX a
The Conservatory : **Rest** 24.00/48.00 and a la carte 56.50/78.00 s. ♀ – ☕ 26.00 – **86 rm** ★347.00/464.00 – ★★582.00, 9 suites.
◆ Converted in the 1990s from 18C St George's Hospital. A grand and traditional atmosphere prevails. Butler service offered. Regency-era decorated, lavishly appointed rooms . Ornate, glass-roofed dining room with palm trees and fountains.

The Halkin, 5 Halkin St, SW1X 7DJ ⊖ *Hyde Park Corner,* ✆ (020) 7333 1000, *res@halkin.como.bz, Fax (020) 7333 1100* – MC AE VISA 38 AHX b
closed 25-26 December and 1 January – **Rest** – (see ***Nahm*** below) – ☕ 23.00 – **35 rm** ★387.75 – ★★387.75, 6 suites.
◆ One of London's first minimalist hotels. The cool, marbled reception and bar have an understated charm. Spacious rooms have every conceivable facility.

Sheraton Belgravia, 20 Chesham Pl, SW1X 8HQ ⊖ *Knightsbridge,* ✆ (020) 7235 6040, *reservations.sheratonbelgravia@sheraton.com, Fax (020) 7259 6243* – rm, P – 25. MC AE VISA 37 AGX u
The Dining Room : **Rest** a la carte 26.00/33.00 ♀ – ☕ 19.50 – **82 rm** ★329.00 – ★★329.00, 7 suites.
◆ Modern corporate hotel overlooking Chesham Place. Comfortable and well-equipped for the tourist and business traveller alike. A few minutes' walk from Harrods. Modern, international menus.

The Lowndes, 21 Lowndes St, SW1X 9ES *(closing during 2006 for refurbishment)* ⊖ *Knightsbridge,* ✆ (020) 7823 1234, *contact@lowndeshotel.com, Fax (020) 7235 1154,* – rm, P – 25. MC AE VISA 37 AGX h
Citronelle : **Rest** *(closed 25 December)* 18.95 and a la carte 30.50/40.50 ♀ – ☕ 17.50 – **77 rm** ★329.00 – ★★329.00/470.00, 1 suite.
◆ Compact yet friendly modern corporate hotel within this exclusive residential area. Good levels of personal service offered. Close to the famous shops of Knightsbridge. Modern restaurant opens onto street terrace.

Diplomat without rest., 2 Chesham St, SW1X 8DT ⊖ *Sloane Square,* ✆ (020) 7235 1544, *diplomat.hotel@btinternet.com, Fax (020) 7259 6153* – MC AE VISA 37 AGY a
26 rm ☕ ★90.00/115.00 – ★★150.00/175.00.
◆ Imposing Victorian corner house built in 1882 by Thomas Cubitt. Attractive glass-domed stairwell and sweeping staircase. Spacious and well-appointed bedrooms.

XXXX ✿ **Pétrus** (Wareing) (at The Berkeley H.), Wilton Pl, SW1X 7RL ⊖ *Knightsbridge,* ✆ (020) 7235 1200, *petrus@marcuswareing.com, Fax (020) 7235 1266* – 14. MC AE VISA 37 AGX e
closed 1 week Christmas, Sunday, Saturday lunch and Bank Holidays – **Rest** 30.00/80.00 ♀
Spec. Tuna Rossini with chicory salad, Madeira and truffle dressing. Glazed beef fillet with sautéed foie gras and braised leeks. Baked meringue and cherry sauce, coconut cream.
◆ Elegantly appointed restaurant named after one of the 40 Pétrus vintages on the wine list. One table in the kitchen to watch the chefs at work. Accomplished modern cooking.

XXX ✿ **Amaya,** Halkin Arcade, 19 Motcomb St, SW1X 8JT ⊖ *Knightsbridge,* ✆ (020) 7823 1166, *info@realindianfood.com, Fax (020) 7259 6464* – 14. MC AE VISA 37 AGX k
Rest - Indian - 18.50 (lunch) and a la carte 24.75/49.75.
Spec. Minced chicken lettuce parcels with coconut and mustard dressing. Tandoori tiger prawns with tomato and ginger. Biryani of fenugreek and cauliflower.
◆ Light, piquant and aromatic Indian cooking specialising in kebabs from a tawa skillet, sigri grill or tandoor oven. Chic comfortable surroundings, modern and subtly exotic.

XXX ✿ **Zafferano,** 15 Lowndes St, SW1X 9EY ⊖ *Knightsbridge,* ✆ (020) 7235 5800, *Fax (020) 7235 1971* – 18. MC AE VISA 37 AGX f
closed 1 week Christmas and Bank Holidays – **Rest** - Italian - 29.50/39.50 ♀
Spec. Slow baked onion with fonduta and white truffle. Potato and rosemary filled parcels with porcini mushrooms. Lobster and langoustine skewer with artichokes.
◆ Forever busy and relaxed. No frills, robust and gutsy Italian cooking, where the quality of the produce shines through. Wholly Italian wine list has some hidden treasures.

XX **Nahm** (at The Halkin H.), 5 Halkin St, SW1X 7DJ ⊖ *Hyde Park Corner*, ✆ (020) 7333 1234, *Fax (020) 7333 1100* – ▤ ⇔ 30. MC AE ⓓ VISA 38 **AHX** b
✿ *closed lunch Saturday and Sunday and Bank Holidays* – **Rest** - Thai - (booking essential) 26.00/49.50 and a la carte 30.50/41.00 ♀.
Spec. Lemongrass salad of prawns, squid and shredded chicken with peanuts and mint. Relish of dried prawns with sweet pork, Thai herb omelette and turmeric. Curry of beef with santol, peanuts and shallots.
◆ Brown marble floored restaurant with uncovered tables and understated decor. Menu offers the best of Thai cooking with modern interpretations and original use of ingredients.

XX **Mango Tree,** 46 Grosvenor Pl, SW1X 7EQ ⊖ *Victoria*, ✆ (020) 7823 1888, *mango tree@mangotree.org.uk, Fax (020) 7838 9275* – ▤. MC AE ⓓ VISA 38 **AHX** a
closed 25 December, 1 January and Saturday lunch – **Rest** - Thai - 30.00/45.00 and a la carte 26.20/27.25 ♀.
◆ Thai staff in regional dress in contemporarily styled dining room of refined yet minimalist furnishings sums up the cuisine: authentic Thai dishes with modern presentation.

XX **Noura Brasserie,** 16 Hobart Pl, SW1W 0HH ⊖ *Victoria*, ✆ (020) 7235 9444, *noura@noura.co.uk, Fax (020) 7235 9244* – ▤. MC AE ⓓ VISA 38 **AHX** n
Rest - Lebanese - 14.50/25.00 and a la carte approx 23.00.
◆ Dine in either the bright bar or the comfortable, contemporary restaurant. Authentic, modern Lebanese cooking specialises in char-grilled meats and mezzes.

Hyde Park and Knightsbridge *Gtr London* – ✉ *SW1/SW7.*

Mandarin Oriental Hyde Park, 66 Knightsbridge, SW1X 7LA ⊖ *Knightsbridge*, ✆ (020) 7235 2000, *molon-reservations@mohg.com, Fax (020) 7235 2001*, ←, ⓦ, Fø, ≘s – |‡|, ⇔ rm, ▤ ✆ ♿ – 🏛 220. MC AE ⓓ VISA. ✗ 37 **AGX** x
The Park **:** **Rest** 31.00 (lunch) and a la carte 25.00/35.00 – (see also ***Foliage*** below) – ☕ 25.00 – **177 rm** ✝429.00/440.00 – ✝✝646.00/705.00, 23 suites.
◆ Built in 1889 this classic hotel, with striking façade, remains one of London's grandest. Many of the luxurious bedrooms enjoy Park views. Immaculate and detailed service. Smart ambience in The Park.

Knightsbridge Green without rest., 159 Knightsbridge, SW1X 7PD ⊖ *Knightsbridge*, ✆ (020) 7584 6274, *reservations@thekghotel.com, Fax (020) 7225 1635* – |‡| ⇔ ▤. MC AE ⓓ VISA. ✗ 37 **AFX** z
☕ 12.00 – **16 rm** ✝117.50/170.00 – ✝✝152.75/170.00, 12 suites.
◆ Privately owned hotel, boasting peaceful sitting room with writing desk. Breakfast - sausage and bacon from Harrods! - served in the generously proportioned bedrooms.

XXX **Foliage** (at Mandarin Oriental Hyde Park H.), 66 Knightsbridge, SW1X 7LA ⊖ *Knightsbridge*, ✆ (020) 7201 3723, *Fax (020) 7235 4552* – ▤. MC AE ⓓ VISA 37 **AGX** x
✿ **Rest** 25.00 (lunch) and a la carte 47.50/50.00 ♀.
Spec. Duo of foie gras with caramelised endive tarte Tatin. Roast turbot with pork, langoustine and horseradish cream. Pear and almond tart with malted milk ice cream.
◆ Reached via a glass-enclosed walkway that houses the cellar. Hyde Park outside the window reflected in the foliage-themed décor. Gracious service, skilled modern cooking.

XX **Zuma,** 5 Raphael St, SW7 1DL ⊖ *Knightsbridge*, ✆ (020) 7584 1010, *info@zumarestaurant.com, Fax (020) 7584 5005* – ▤. MC AE VISA 37 **AFX** m
Rest - Japanese - a la carte 27.40/45.60 ♀.
◆ Strong modern feel with exposed pipes, modern lighting and granite flooring. A theatrical atmosphere around the Sushi bar and a varied and interesting modern Japanese menu.

XX **Mr Chow,** 151 Knightsbridge, SW1X 7PA ⊖ *Knightsbridge*, ✆ (020) 7589 7347, *mrchow@aol.com, Fax (020) 7584 5780* – ▤. MC AE ⓓ VISA 37 **AFX** e
closed 24-26 December, 1 January and Easter Monday – **Rest** - Chinese - 22.00 (lunch) and a la carte 44.00/51.00 ♀.
◆ Cosmopolitan Chinese restaurant with branches in New York and L.A. Well established ambience. Walls covered with mirrors and modern art. House specialities worth opting for.

Mayfair *Gtr London* – ✉ *W1.*

Dorchester, Park Lane, W1A 2HJ ⊖ *Hyde Park Corner*, ✆ (020) 7629 8888, *info@thedorchester.com, Fax (020) 7409 0114*, ⓦ, Fø, ≘s – |‡|, ⇔ rm, ▤ ✆ ♿ 🚗 – 🏛 500. MC AE ⓓ VISA. ✗ 30 **AHV** a
Rest – (see ***Grill Room*** and ***China Tang*** below) – ☕ 25.50 – **200 rm** ✝423.00/522.00 – ✝✝522.00, 49 suites 816.00/2937.00.
◆ A sumptuously decorated, luxury hotel offering every possible facility. Impressive marbled and pillared promenade. Rooms quintessentially English in style. Faultless service.

Claridge's, Brook St, W1A 2JQ ⊖ *Bond Street*, ✆ (020) 7629 8860, *info@claridges.co.uk*, *Fax (020) 7499 2210*, – rm, – 200. VISA. 30 **AHU** c
Rest 32.00/35.00 and a la carte – (see also ***Gordon Ramsay at Claridge's*** below) – 24.50 – **143 rm** 480.00/504.00 – 610.00/633.00, 60 suites.
◆ The epitome of English grandeur, celebrated for its Art Deco. Exceptionally well-appointed and sumptuous bedrooms, all with butler service. Magnificently restored foyer. Relaxed, elegant restaurant.

Grosvenor House, Park Lane, W1K 7TN ⊖ *Marble Arch*, ✆ (020) 7499 6363, *Fax (020) 7493 8512*, – rm, – 1500. VISA. 29 **AGU** a
La Terrazza : Rest - Italian influences - 25.50 and a la carte 27.00/41.00 – 21.50 – **378 rm** 257.00/280.00 – 257.00/280.00, 74 suites.
◆ Over 70 years old and occupying an enviable position by the Park. Edwardian style décor. The Great Room, an ice rink in the 1920s, is Europe's largest banqueting room. Bright, relaxing dining room with contemporary feel.

Four Seasons, Hamilton Pl, Park Lane, W1A 1AZ ⊖ *Hyde Park Corner*, ✆ (020) 7499 0888, *fsh.london@fourseasons.com*, *Fax (020) 7493 1895*, – rm, – 500. VISA. 30 **AHV** b
Lanes : Rest 29.00/36.00 and a la carte 43.00/63.00 s. – 25.00 – **185 rm** 393.00/428.00 – 458.00, 35 suites.
◆ Set back from Park Lane so shielded from the traffic. Large, marbled lobby; its lounge a popular spot for light meals. Spacious rooms, some with their own conservatory. Restaurant's vivid blue and stained glass give modern, yet relaxing, feel.

Le Meridien Piccadilly, 21 Piccadilly, W1J 0BH ⊖ *Piccadilly Circus*, ✆ (020) 7734 8000, *piccadilly.reservations@lemeridien.com*, *Fax (020) 7437 3574*, squash – rm, – 250. VISA. 31 **AJV** a
Terrace : Rest 22.50 and a la carte 36.50/54.50 – 22.50 – **248 rm** 164.00/211.50 – 211.50, 18 suites.
◆ Comfortable international hotel, in a central location. Boasts one of the finest leisure clubs in London. Individually decorated bedrooms, with first class facilities. Modern cuisine in comfortable surroundings.

London Hilton, 22 Park Lane, W1K 1BE ⊖ *Hyde Park Corner*, ✆ (020) 7493 8000, *reservations.parklane@hilton.com*, *Fax (020) 7208 4142*, ≤ London, – rm, – 1000. VISA. 30 **AHV** e
Trader Vics (✆ *(020) 7208 4113)* **: Rest** *(closed lunch Saturday and Sunday)* 19.50 (lunch) and a la carte 34.00/50.00 – ***Park Brasserie :*** **Rest** 22.00 (lunch) and a la carte 27.50/43.25 – (see also ***Windows*** below) – 22.00 – **395 rm** 200.00/394.00 – 247.00/488.00, 55 suites.
◆ This 28 storey tower is one of the city's tallest hotels, providing impressive views from the upper floors. Club floor bedrooms are particularly comfortable. Exotic Trader Vics with bamboo and plants. A harpist adds to the relaxed feel of Park Brasserie.

Connaught, 16 Carlos Pl, W1K 2AL ⊖ *Bond Street*, ✆ (020) 7499 7070, *info@the-connaught.co.uk*, *Fax (020) 7495 3262*, VISA. 30 **AHU** e
Rest – (see ***Angela Hartnett at The connaught*** below) – 26.50 – **68 rm** 352.00/458.00 – 500.00, 24 suites.
◆ 19C quintessentially English hotel, with country house feel. The grand mahogany staircase leads up to antique furnished rooms. One of the capital's most exclusive addresses.

Park Lane, Piccadilly, W1J 7BX ⊖ *Green Park*, ✆ (020) 7499 6321, *reservations.theparklane@sheraton.com*, *Fax (020) 7499 1965*, – rm, – 500. VISA. 30 **AHV** x
Citrus (✆ *(020) 7290 7364)* **: Rest** a la carte 28.00/35.00 – 19.95 – **285 rm** 305.50 – 305.50, 20 suites.
◆ The history of the hotel is reflected in the elegant 'Palm Court' lounge and ballroom, both restored to their Art Deco origins. Bedrooms vary in shape and size. Summer pavement tables in restaurant opposite Green Park.

London Marriott Park Lane, 140 Park Lane, W1K 7AA ⊖ *Marble Arch*, ✆ (020) 7493 7000, *mhrs.parklane@marriotthotels.com*, *Fax (020) 7493 8333*, – – 75. VISA. 29 **AGU** b
140 Park Lane : **Rest** (bar lunch Saturday) 18.50 (lunch) and a la carte 26.50/34.50 – 20.95 – **148 rm** 311.00/358.00 – 311.00/358.00, 9 suites.
◆ Superbly located 'boutique' style hotel at intersection of Park Lane and Oxford Street. Attractive basement health club. Spacious, well-equipped rooms with luxurious elements. Attractive restaurant overlooking Marble Arch.

Westbury, Bond St, W1S 2YF ⊖ *Bond Street,* ☎ (020) 7629 7755, *sales@westburymayfair.com, Fax (020) 7495 1163,* – |‡|, ⇋ rm, ▤ ☎ ♿ – 🏛 120. MC AE ◑ VISA. ✈ 30 **AIU** a

Rest *(closed Sunday and Saturday lunch)* 24.50 and a la carte 39.50/55.50 – ☐ 23.00 – **233 rm** ★327.00/351.00 – ★★351.00, 21 suites.

◆ Surrounded by London's most fashionable shops; the renowned Polo bar and lounge provide soothing sanctuary. Some suites have their own terrace. Bright, fresh restaurant enhanced by modern art.

The Metropolitan, Old Park Lane, W1Y 1LB ⊖ *Hyde Park Corner,* ☎ (020) 7447 1000, *res.lon@metropolitan.como.bz, Fax (020) 7447 1100,* ≤, – |‡|, ⇋ rm, ▤ ☎ 🚗. MC AE ◑ VISA. ✈ 30 **AHV** c

Rest – (see ***Nobu*** below) – ☐ 24.00 – **147 rm** ★376.00 – ★★376.00, 3 suites.

◆ Minimalist interior and a voguish reputation make this the favoured hotel of pop stars and celebrities. Innovative design and fashionably attired staff set it apart.

Athenaeum, 116 Piccadilly, W1J 7BS ⊖ *Hyde Park Corner,* ☎ (020) 7499 3464, *info@athenaeumhotel.com, Fax (020) 7493 1860,* – |‡|, ⇋ rm, ▤ ☎ – 🏛 55. MC AE ◑ VISA 30 **AHV** g

Bulloch's at 116 : **Rest** *(closed lunch Saturday and Sunday)* 15.00 (lunch) and a la carte approx 54.00 **s.** ♀ – ☐ 21.00 – **124 rm** ★323.00 – ★★323.00, 33 suites.

◆ Built in 1925 as a luxury apartment block. Comfortable bedrooms with video and CD players. Individually designed suites are in an adjacent Edwardian townhouse. Conservatory roofed dining room renowned for its mosaics and malt whiskies.

Chesterfield, 35 Charles St, W1J 5EB ⊖ *Green Park,* ☎ (020) 7491 2622, *bookch@rchmail.com, Fax (020) 7491 4793* |‡|, ⇋ rm, ▤ ☎ – 🏛 110. MC AE ◑ VISA 30 **AHV** f

Rest 24.95 and a la carte 29.70/40.00 ♀ – ☐ 19.00 – **106 rm** ★264.00/346.00 – ★★381.00, 4 suites.

◆ An assuredly English feel to this Georgian house. Discreet lobby leads to a clubby bar and wood panelled library. Individually decorated bedrooms, with some antique pieces. Classically decorated restaurant.

Washington Mayfair, 5-7 Curzon St, W1J 5HE ⊖ *Green Park,* ☎ (020) 7499 7000, *info@washington-mayfair.co.uk, Fax (020) 7495 6172,* – |‡|, ⇋ rm, ▤ ☎ – 🏛 90. MC AE ◑ VISA. ✈ 30 **AHV** d

Rest 18.95 and a la carte 24.85/37.90 **s.** ♀ – ☐ 18.95 – **166 rm** ★264.00 – ★★264.00, 5 suites.

◆ Successfully blends a classical style with modern amenities. Relaxing lounge with traditional English furniture and bedrooms with polished, burred oak. Piano bar annex to formal dining room.

London Marriott Grosvenor Square, Grosvenor Sq, W1K 6JP ⊖ *Bond Street,* ☎ (020) 7514 1540, *Fax (020) 7514 1528,* – |‡|, ⇋ rm, ▤ ☎ ♿ – 🏛 600. MC AE ◑ VISA. ✈ 30 **AHU** s

Rest 23.00 and a la carte 23.00/30.00 ♀ – ☐ 22.50 – **209 rm** ★264.00/311.00 – ★★276.00/311.00, 12 suites.

◆ A well-appointed international group hotel that benefits from an excellent location. Many of the bedrooms specifically equipped for the business traveller. Formal dining room with its own cocktail bar.

Hilton London Green Park, Half Moon St, W1J 7BN ⊖ *Green Park,* ☎ (020) 7629 7522, *reservations.greenpark@hilton.com, Fax (020) 7491 8971* – |‡| ⇋ ☎ ♿ – 🏛 130. MC AE ◑ VISA. ✈ 30 **AIV** a

Rest (bar lunch)/dinner 24.00 and a la carte 23.65/35.50 ♀ – ☐ 19.95 – **162 rm** ★182.00/245.50 – ★★194.00/245.00.

◆ A row of sympathetically adjoined townhouses, dating from the 1730s. Discreet marble lobby. Bedrooms share the same décor but vary in size and shape. Monet prints decorate light, airy dining room.

Flemings, Half Moon St, W1J 7BH ⊖ *Green Park,* ☎ (020) 7499 2964, *sales@flemings-mayfair.co.uk, Fax (020) 7491 8866* – |‡|, ⇋ rm, ▤ ☎ ♿ – 🏛 55. MC AE ◑ VISA. ✈ 30 **AIV** z

Rest *(closed Saturday lunch)* 25.00 and a la carte ♀ – ☐ 18.00 – **121 rm** ★205.00/247.00 – ★★247.00, 10 suites.

◆ A Georgian town house where the oil paintings and English furniture add to the charm. Apartments located in adjoining house, once home to noted polymath Henry Wagner. Candlelit basement restaurant with oil paintings.

Hilton London Mews, 2 Stanhope Row, W1J 7BS ⊖ *Hyde Park Corner,* ✆ (020) 7493 7222, *reservations.mews@hilton.com, Fax (020) 7629 9423* – 50. VISA. 30 AHV u
closed 23-28 December – **Rest** (dinner only) 21.95 and a la carte 22.15/29.25 – 17.95 – **72 rm** 171.50/229.00 – 183.00/229.00.
◆ Tucked away in a discreet corner of Mayfair. This modern, group hotel manages to retain a cosy and intimate feel. Well-equipped bedrooms to meet corporate needs. Meals in cosy dining room or lounge.

Grill Room (at Dorchester H.), Park Lane, W1A 2HJ ⊖ *Hyde Park Corner,* ✆ (020) 7317 6336, *Fax (020) 7317 6464* – VISA 30 AHV a
Rest - English - 25.00 (lunch) and a la carte 35.00/58.00 **s.**
◆ Ornate Spanish influenced, baroque decoration with gilded ceiling, tapestries and highly polished oak tables. Formal and immaculate service. Traditional English cooking.

Le Gavroche (Roux), 43 Upper Brook St, W1K 7QR ⊖ *Marble Arch,* ✆ (020) 7408 0881, *bookings@le-gavroche.com, Fax (020) 7491 4387* – VISA 29 AGU c
closed Christmas-New Year, Sunday, Saturday lunch and Bank Holidays – **Rest** - French - (booking essential) 46.00 (lunch) and a la carte 59.60/117.20
Spec. Foie gras chaud et pastilla de canard à la cannelle. Râble de lapin et galette au parmesan. Le palet au chocolat amer et praline croustillant.
◆ Long-standing, renowned restaurant with a clubby, formal atmosphere. Accomplished classical French cuisine, served by smartly attired and well-drilled staff.

Angela Hartnett at The Connaught, 16 Carlos Pl, W1K 2AL ⊖ *Bond Street,* ✆ (020) 7592 1222, *reservations@angelahartnett.com, Fax (020) 7592 1223* – VISA 30 AHU e
Rest (booking essential) 30.00/70.00
Spec. Mosaic of pressed tomatoes with feta cheese and balsamic vinegar. Roast rabbit, confit of shoulder and loin, girolles and truffle vinaigrette. Apricot soufflé, almond and amaretto ice cream.
◆ Refined Italian influenced cooking can be enjoyed in the elegantly panelled 'Menu'. Meanwhile, the more intimate 'Grill' offers a selection of traditional British favourites.

Gordon Ramsay at Claridge's, Brook St, W1A 2JQ ⊖ *Bond Street,* ✆ (020) 7499 0099, *reservations@gordonramsay.com, Fax (020) 7499 3099* – VISA 30 AHU c
Rest (booking essential) 30.00/70.00
Spec. Salad of crab and carrot à la Grecque, ginger and carrot vinaigrette. Pork cheeks cooked in honey and cloves, spring vegetables, braising juices. Banana and passion fruit parfait with coconut tuile.
◆ A thoroughly comfortable dining room with a charming and gracious atmosphere. Serves classically inspired food executed with a high degree of finesse.

The Square (Howard), 6-10 Bruton St, W1J 6PU ⊖ *Green Park,* ✆ (020) 7495 7100, *info@squarerestaurant.com, Fax (020) 7495 7150* – 18. VISA 30 AIU v
closed 24-26 December, 1 January and lunch Saturday, Sunday and Bank Holidays – **Rest** 30.00/60.00
Spec. Lasagne of crab with shellfish and basil cappuccino. Langoustines with parmesan gnocchi, wild mushrooms and truffle emulsion. Assiette of chocolate.
◆ Varnished wood and bold abstract canvasses add an air of modernity. Extensive menus offer French influenced cooking of the highest order. Prompt and efficient service.

Sketch (The Lecture Room), First Floor, 9 Conduit St, W1S 2XG ⊖ *Oxford Street,* ✆ (0870) 7774488, *Fax (0870) 7774400* – VISA 30 AIU h
closed 25 December, 1 January, Sunday, Monday, Saturday lunch and Bank Holidays – **Rest** (booking essential) 35.00 (lunch) and a la carte 39.00/90.00
Spec. Langoustine four ways. Sea bass with apple purée, ratte potatoes amd sweet whisky sauce. Cumin roasted lamb with baby carrots, sweet onions and watercress.
◆ Stunning venue, combining art and food, creating an experience of true sensory stimulation. Vibrant dining options: Lecture Room or Library. Highly original, complex cooking.

China Tang (at Dorchester H.), Park Lane, W1A 2HJ, ✆ (020) 7629 9988, *Fax (020) 7629 9595* – 16. VISA 30 AHV a
closed 25 December – **Rest** - Chinese (Cantonese) - a la carte 35.00/70.00.
◆ A striking mix of Art Deco, Oriental motifs, hand-painted fabrics, mirrors and marbled table tops. Carefully prepared, traditional Cantonese dishes using quality ingredients.

Windows (at London Hilton H.), 22 Park Lane, W1Y 1BE ⊖ *Hyde Park Corner,* ✆ (020) 7208 4021, *windows.parklane@hilton.com, Fax (020) 7208 4142,* London – VISA 30 AHV e
closed Saturday lunch and Sunday dinner – **Rest** 39.50/59.50 and a la carte 37.00/64.75
◆ Enjoys some of the city's best views. The lunchtime buffet provides a popular alternative to the international menu. Formal service and a busy adjoining piano bar.

XXX ✿ **The Greenhouse,** 27a Hay's Mews, W1X 7RJ ⊖ *Hyde Park Corner*, ✆ (020) 7499 3331, *reservations@greenhouserestaurant.co.uk, Fax (020) 7499 5368* – ✈ ▤ ⇔ 12. MC AE ◑ VISA 30 **AHV** m
closed Christmas-New Year, Sunday, Saturday lunch and Bank Holidays – **Rest** 32.00/60.00 ♀.
Spec. Seared foie gras, espresso syrup, amaretto foam. Quail galantine with plum carpaccio and microcress salad. Poached halibut, sweet pea sabayon and liquorice.
◆ A pleasant courtyard, off a quiet mews, leads to this stylish, discreet restaurant where an elaborate, innovative blend of flavours is much in evidence on inventive menus.

XXX ✿ **Mirabelle,** 56 Curzon St, W1J 8PA ⊖ *Green Park*, ✆ (020) 7499 4636, *sales@whitestarline.org.uk, Fax (020) 7499 5449*, – ▤ ⇔ 48. MC AE ◑ VISA 30 **AIV** x
closed 26 December and 1 January – **Rest** 21.00 (lunch) and a la carte 33.00/50.00 ♀.
Spec. Omelette Arnold Bennett, Mornay sauce. Braised pig's trotter with morels and pomme purée, Périgueux sauce. Raspberry soufflé, cardinal sauce.
◆ As celebrated now as it was in the 1950s. Stylish bar with screens and mirrors, leather banquettes and rows of windows. Modern interpretation of some classic dishes.

XXX ✿ **Maze,** 10-13 Grosvenor Sq, W1K 6JP ⊖ *Bond Street*, ✆ (020) 7107 0000, *maze@gordonramsay.com, Fax (020) 7107 0001* – ✈ ▤ ⇔ 10. MC AE VISA 30 **AHU** z
Rest a la carte 23.50/35.00.
Spec. Wild sea trout with lime, peas, caper and raisin purée. Grilled spring lamb with cinnamon sweetbreads, lettuce with bacon and onion. Aged beef with foie gras, parsley, snail and garlic.
◆ Part of the Gordon Ramsay empire; a stylish, sleek restaurant. Kitchen eschews usual three-course menus by offering a number of small dishes of variety, precision and flair.

XXX **Benares,** 12 Berkeley House, Berkeley Sq, W1J 6BS ⊖ *Green Park*, ✆ (020) 7629 8886, *enquiries@benaresrestaurant.com, Fax (020) 7491 8883* – ▤ ⇔ 22. MC AE ◑ VISA 30 **AIU** q
closed 25-26 December, 1 January, lunch Saturday and Sunday – **Rest** - Indian - a la carte 30.00/44.00 ♀.
◆ Indian restaurant where pools of water scattered with petals and candles compensate for lack of natural light. Original Indian dishes; particularly good value at lunch.

XXX **Embassy,** 29 Old Burlington St, W1S 3AN ⊖ *Green Park*, ✆ (020) 7851 0956, *embassy@embassylondon.com, Fax (020) 7734 3224*, – ▤. MC AE VISA 30 **AIU** u
closed 25 December, 1 January, Sunday, Monday and Saturday lunch – **Rest** 22.50 (lunch) and dinner a la carte 27.25/48.95 ♀.
◆ Marble floors, ornate cornicing and a long bar create a characterful, moody dining room. Tables are smartly laid and menus offer accomplished, classic dishes.

XXX ✿ **Tamarind,** 20 Queen St, W1J 5PR ⊖ *Green Park*, ✆ (020) 7629 3561, *manager@tamarindrestaurant.com, Fax (020) 7499 5034* – ▤. MC AE ◑ VISA 30 **AHV** h
closed 25-26 December, 1 January and lunch Saturday and Bank Holidays – **Rest** - Indian - 18.95 (lunch) and a la carte 37.70/54.95 ♀.
Spec. Ground lamb with cinnamon, red chillies and garlic. Grilled monkfish with coriander, mint and pickling spices. Chicken grilled in tandoor with tomatoes, ginger, honey and fenugreek.
◆ Gold coloured pillars add to the opulence of this basement room. Windows allow diners the chance to watch the kitchen prepare original and accomplished Indian dishes.

XXX **Sartoria,** 20 Savile Row, W1X 1AE ⊖ *Green Park*, ✆ (020) 7534 7000, *sartoriareservations@conran-restaurants.co.uk, Fax (020) 7534 7070* – ▤. MC AE VISA 30 **AIU** b
closed 25-27 December, Sunday, Saturday lunch and Bank Holidays – **Rest** - Italian - 21.50 and a la carte 29.50/43.00 **s.** ♀.
◆ In the street renowned for English tailoring, a coolly sophisticated restaurant to suit those looking for classic Italian cooking with modern touches.

XXX **Brian Turner Mayfair** (at Millennium Mayfair H.), 44 Grosvenor Sq, W1K 2HP ⊖ *Bond Street*, ✆ (020) 7596 3444, *turner.mayfair@mill-cop.com, Fax (020) 7596 3443* – ✈. MC AE ◑ VISA 30 **AHU** x
closed 1 week Christmas, Sunday, Saturday lunch and Bank Holidays – **Rest** - English - 25.50 (lunch) and a la carte 36.75/52.50 ♀.
◆ Located within the Millennium Mayfair overlooking Grosvenor Square. Restaurant on several levels with sharp modern décor. Good English dishes with modern twist.

XXX **Cecconi's,** 5a Burlington Gdns, W1S 3EP ⊖ *Green Park*, ✆ (020) 7434 1500, *Fax (020) 7434 2020* – ▤. MC AE ◑ VISA 30 **AIU** d
closed 25 December and 1 January – **Rest** - Italian - a la carte 25.00/40.00 ♀.
◆ A chic bar and a stylish, modern dining venue, invariably busy; the menus call on the Italian classics with unusual touches.

XXX **Berkeley Square,** 7 Davies St, W1K 3DD ⊖ *Bond Street,* ✆ (020) 7629 6993, *info@theberkeleysquare.com, Fax (020) 7491 9719,* 🏠 – MO AE ① VISA 30 AHU w
closed 24-30 December, Saturday, Sunday and Bank Holidays – **Rest** 21.95/49.95 ♀.
◆ Smart contemporary restaurant with pavement terrace and recordings of famous novels in the loos! Modern British food with original touches.

XXX **Kai,** 65 South Audley St, W1K 2QU ⊖ *Hyde Park Corner,* ✆ (020) 7493 8988, *kai@kaimayfair.com, Fax (020) 7493 1456* – ▤. MO AE ① VISA 30 AHV n
closed 25-26 December and 1 January – **Rest** - Chinese - 23.00/40.00 and a la carte 31.50/54.00 ♀.
◆ Marble flooring and mirrors add to the opulent feel of this smoothly run Chinese restaurant. Extensive menu offers dishes ranging from the luxury to the more familiar.

XX ✿ **Umu,** 14-16 Bruton Pl, W1J 6LX ⊖ *Bond Street,* ✆ (020) 7499 8881, *enquiries@umurestaurant.com* – ⇐ ▤. MO AE ① VISA 30 AIU k
closed between Christmas and New Year, Sunday and Bank Holidays – **Rest** - Japanese - 22.00/60.00 and a la carte 50.00/70.00 ✿.
Spec. Sesame tofu with wasabi and nori seaweed. Eel kabayaki with kinone pepper. Sake flavoured soup with fish of the day.
◆ Exclusive neighbourhood location: stylish, discreet interior with central sushi bar. Japanese dishes, specialising in Kyoto cuisine, employing highest quality ingredients.

XX **Giardinetto,** 39-40 Albemarle St, W1S 4TE ⊖ *Green Park,* ✆ (020) 7493 7091, *info@giardinetto.co.uk, Fax (020) 7493 7096* – ▤. MO AE ① VISA 30 AIV p
closed Saturday lunch – **Rest** - Italian - 22.00 (lunch) and a la carte 33.00/45.50 ♀.
◆ Manages to mix a smart, stylish interior with a neighbourhood intimacy. Three dining areas, front being largest. Genoese chef/owner conjures up well-presented Ligurian dishes.

XX **Patterson's,** 4 Mill St, W1S 2AX ⊖ *Oxford Street,* ✆ (020) 7499 1308, *pattersonmayfair@btconnect.com, Fax (020) 7491 2122* – ▤ ⇔ 30. MO AE VISA 30 AIU p
closed Sunday and Saturday lunch – **Rest** 20.00/35.00 ♀.
◆ Stylish modern interior in black and white. Elegant tables and attentive service. Modern British cooking with concise wine list and sensible prices.

XX **Teca,** 54 Brooks Mews, W1Y 2NY ⊖ *Bond Street,* ✆ (020) 7495 4774, *Fax (020) 7491 3545* – ▤. MO AE VISA 30 AHU f
closed 1 week January, Sunday and Saturday lunch – **Rest** - Italian - 34.00 (dinner) and lunch a la carte 30.00/49.00 ♀.
◆ A glass-enclosed cellar is one of the features of this modern, slick Italian restaurant. Set price menu, with the emphasis on fresh, seasonal produce.

XX **Alloro,** 19-20 Dover St, W1S 4LU ⊖ *Green Park,* ✆ (020) 7495 4768, *Fax (020) 7629 5348* – ▤ ⇔ 16. MO AE ① VISA 30 AIV r
closed 25 December-2 January, Saturday lunch, Sunday and Bank Holidays – **Rest** - Italian - 26.00/36.00 ♀.
◆ One of the new breed of stylish Italian restaurants, with contemporary art and leather seating. A separate, bustling bar. Smoothly run, with modern cooking.

XX **Le Club at hush,** 8 Lancashire Court, Brook St, W1S 1EY ⊖ *Bond Street,* ✆ (020) 7659 1500, *info@hush.co.uk, Fax (020) 7659 1501* – |‡| ▤. MO AE ① VISA 30 AHU v
closed 24-26 December, 31 December-3 January, Sunday and Saturday lunch – **Rest** (booking essential) 26.50 (lunch) and a la carte 30.00/50.00 ♀ – ***Brasserie*** 🏠 : **Rest** a la carte approx 32.00 ♀.
◆ Tucked away down a side street. Spacious, informal hush down brasserie with a secluded courtyard terrace. Serves tasty modern classics. Join the fashionable set in the busy bar or settle down on the banquettes at hush up. Serves robust, satisfying dishes.

XX **Fakhreldine,** 85 Piccadilly, W1J 7NB ⊖ *Green Park,* ✆ (020) 7493 3424, *info@fakhreldine.co.uk, Fax (020) 7495 1977* – ▤. MO AE ① VISA 30 AIV e
closed 25 December and 1 January – **Rest** - Lebanese - 22.00 (lunch) and a la carte 25.50/37.00 ♀.
◆ Long standing Lebanese restaurant with great view of Green Park. Large selection of classic mezze dishes and more modern European styled menu of original Lebanese dishes.

XX ✿ **Nobu** (at The Metropolitan H.), 19 Old Park Lane, W1Y 4LB ⊖ *Hyde Park Corner,* ✆ (020) 7447 4747, *confirmations@noburestaurants.com, Fax (020) 7447 4749,* ≤ – ▤ ⇔ 40. MO AE ① VISA 30 AHV c
closed 25 December – **Rest** - Japanese with South American influences - (booking essential) 30.00/70.00 and a la carte 33.50/40.00 ♀.
Spec. Yellowtail with jalapeño. Black cod with miso. Sashimi salad.
◆ Its celebrity clientele has made this one of the most glamorous spots. Staff are fully conversant in the unique menu that adds South American influences to Japanese cooking.

XX **Taman Gang,** 141 Park Lane, W1K 7AA ⊖ *Marble Arch,* ☎ (020) 7518 3160, *info@tamangang.com, Fax (020) 7518 3161* – ▤. MC AE ⓘ VISA 29 AGU e
Rest - South East Asian - (dinner only and Sunday lunch) a la carte 26.00/87.00 ♀.
◆ Basement restaurant with largish bar and lounge area. Stylish but intimate décor. Informal and intelligent service. Pan-Asian dishes presented in exciting modern manner.

XX **Sumosan,** 26 Albemarle St, W1S 4HY ⊖ *Green Park,* ☎ (020) 7495 5999, *info@sumosan.co.uk, Fax (020) 7355 1247* – ▤. MC AE ⓘ VISA 30 AIU e
closed 25-26 December and lunch Saturday and Sunday – **Rest** - Japanese - 19.50/45.00 and a la carte 21.50/44.50 **s.** ♀.
◆ A very smart interior in which diners sit in comfy banquettes and armchairs. Sushi bar to the rear with some semi-private booths. Extensive menus of Sushi and Sashimi.

XX **Chor Bizarre,** 16 Albemarle St, W1S 4HW ⊖ *Green Park,* ☎ (020) 7629 9802, *chorbizarrelondon@oldworldhospitality.com, Fax (020) 7493 7756* – ▤. MC AE ⓘ VISA 30 AIV s
closed 25-26 December, 1 January, Sunday lunch and Bank Holidays – **Rest** - Indian - 16.50 (lunch) and a la carte 19.00/38.00.
◆ Translates as 'thieves market' and the décor is equally vibrant; antiques, curios, carvings and ornaments abound. Cooking and recipes chiefly from north India and Kashmir.

XX **Sketch (The Gallery),** 9 Conduit St, W1S 2XG ⊖ *Oxford Street,* ☎ (0870) 7774488, *info@sketch.uk.com, Fax (0870) 7774400* – ▤. MC AE ⓘ VISA 30 AIU h
closed 25 December, 1 January, Sunday and Bank Holidays – **Rest** (booking essential) (dinner only) a la carte 29.50/47.50.
◆ On the ground floor of the Sketch building: daytime video art gallery metamorphoses into evening brasserie with ambient wall projections and light menus with eclectic range.

XX **Cocoon,** 65 Regent St, W1B 4EA ⊖ *Piccadilly Circus,* ☎ (020) 7494 7600, *reservations@cocoon-restaurants.com, Fax (020) 7494 7601* – ⊁ ▤ ⇔ 12. MC AE VISA 30 AJU x
closed lunch Saturday and Sunday – **Rest** - Asian - a la carte 28.00/85.00 ☺ ♀.
◆ Trendy restaurant, based on a prime Regent Street site. Silk nets cleverly divide long, winding room. Bold, eclectic menus cover a wide spectrum of Asian dishes.

XX ✿ **Nobu Berkeley,** 15 Berkeley St, W1J 8DY ⊖ *Green Park,* ☎ (020) 7290 9222, *nobuberkeley@noburestaurants.com, Fax (020) 7290 9223* – ⊁ ▤. MC AE VISA 30 AIV b
closed Sunday and Bank Holidays – **Rest** - Japanese with South American influences - (bookings not accepted) (dinner only) a la carte 39.00/76.00 ♀.
Spec. Crispy pork belly with spicy miso. Yellowtail sashimi with jalapeño. Rib-eye anticucho.
◆ In a prime position off Berkeley Square: downstairs 'destination' bar and, above, a top quality, minimal restaurant. Innovative Japanese dishes with original combinations.

XX **Momo,** 25 Heddon St, W1B 4BH ⊖ *Oxford Circus,* ☎ (020) 7434 4040, *reservations@momoresto.com, Fax (020) 7287 0404,* ☂ – ▤. MC AE ⓘ VISA 30 AIU n
closed 24-26 and 31 December, 1 January and Sunday lunch – **Rest** - Moroccan - 14.00 (lunch) and a la carte 27.00/39.50.
◆ Elaborate adornment of rugs, drapes and ornaments mixed with Arabic music lend an authentic feel to this busy Moroccan restaurant. Helpful service. Popular basement bar.

X **Veeraswamy,** Victory House, 99 Regent St, W1B 4RS, entrance on Swallow St ⊖ *Piccadilly Circus,* ☎ (020) 7734 1401, *veeraswamy@realindianfood.com, Fax (020) 7439 8434* – ▤. MC AE ⓘ VISA 30 AIU t
Rest - Indian - 17.50 (lunch) and a la carte 22.50/40.50 ☺ ♀.
◆ The country's oldest Indian restaurant boasts a new look with vivid coloured walls and glass screens. The menu also combines the familiar with some modern twists.

X **Automat,** 33 Dover St, W1S 4NF ⊖ *Green Park,* ☎ (020) 7499 3033, *info@automat-london.com, Fax (020) 7499 2682* – ▤. MC AE VISA 30 AIV r
Rest - American - a la carte 26.00/40.00 ♀.
◆ Buzzing New York style brasserie in three areas: a café, a 'dining car' with deep leather banquettes, and actual brasserie itself. Classic dishes from burgers to cheesecake.

X **The Cafe** (at Sotheby's), 34-35 New Bond St, W1A 2AA ⊖ *Bond Street,* ☎ (020) 7293 5077, *Fax (020) 7293 5920* – ⊁. MC AE ⓘ VISA 30 AIU y
closed last 2 weeks August, 22 December-3 January, Saturday, Sunday and Bank Holidays – **Rest** (booking essential) (lunch only) a la carte 19.95/30.50 ♀.
◆ A velvet rope separates this simple room from the main lobby of this famous auction house. Pleasant service from staff in aprons. Menu is short but well-chosen and light.

Regent's Park and Marylebone *Gtr London* – ✉ *NW1/NW8/W1.*

Landmark London, 222 Marylebone Rd, NW1 6JQ ⊖ *Edgware Rd,* ☎ (020) 7631 8000, *reservations@thelandmark.co.uk, Fax (020) 7631 8080,* – 350. MC AE DC VISA. 29 AFT a
Winter Garden **:** Rest a la carte 35.85/55.40 – 25.00 – **290 rm** 238.00/288.00 – 288.00, 9 suites.
◆ Imposing Victorian Gothic building with a vast glass enclosed atrium, overlooked by many of the modern, well-equipped bedrooms. Winter Garden popular for afternoon tea.

Langham, 1c Portland Pl, Regent St, W1B 1JA ⊖ *Oxford Circus,* ☎ (020) 7636 1000, *info@langhamhotels.com, Fax (020) 7323 2340,* rm, – 250. MC AE DC VISA. 30 AIT e
Memories **:** Rest 24.00/45.00 – 23.00 – **409 rm** 220.00/257.00 – 320.00/364.00, 20 suites.
◆ Opposite the BBC, with Colonial inspired décor. Polo themed bar and barrel vaulted Palm Court. Concierge Club rooms offer superior comfort and butler service. Memories is a bright, elegant dining room.

The Cumberland, Great Cumberland Pl, W1A 4RF ⊖ *Marble Arch,* ☎ (0870) 3339280, *enquiries@thecumberland.co.uk, Fax (0870) 3339281* – – 300. MC AE DC VISA 29 AGU z
Rest – (see ***Rhodes W1*** below) – 16.95 – **1019 rm** 140.00/315.00 – 150.00/315.00.
◆ Fully refurbished, conference oriented hotel whose vast lobby boasts modern art, sculpture and running water panels. Distinctive bedrooms with a host of impressive extras.

Hyatt Regency London-The Churchill, 30 Portman Sq, W1A 4ZX ⊖ *Marble Arch,* ☎ (020) 7486 5800, *london.churchill@hyattintl.com, Fax (020) 7486 1255,* rm, – 250. MC AE DC VISA. 29 AGT x
The Montagu **:** Rest a la carte 32.50/46.00 – 20.75 – **405 rm** 282.00 – 305.00, 40 suites.
◆ Modern property overlooking attractive square. Elegant marbled lobby .Cigar bar open until 2am for members. Well-appointed rooms have the international traveller in mind. Restaurant provides popular Sunday brunch entertainment.

Charlotte Street, 15 Charlotte St, W1T 1RJ ⊖ *Goodge Street,* ☎ (020) 7806 2000, *charlotte@firmdale.com, Fax (020) 7806 2002,* – – 65. MC AE VISA. 31 AKT e
Rest – (see ***Oscar*** below) – 18.50 – **44 rm** 230.00/240.00 – 335.00, 8 suites.
◆ Interior designed with a charming and understated English feel. Welcoming lobby laden with floral displays. Individually decorated rooms with CDs and mobile phones.

Sanderson, 50 Berners St, W1T 3NG ⊖ *Oxford Circus,* ☎ (020) 7300 1400, *sanderson@morganshotelgroup.com, Fax (020) 7300 1401,* – rm, MC AE DC VISA. 31 AJT c
Spoon+ **:** Rest a la carte 55.00/135.00 – 25.00 – **150 rm** 376.00 – 376.00/750.00.
◆ Designed by Philipe Starck: the height of contemporary design. Bar is the place to see and be seen. Bedrooms with minimalistic white décor have DVDs and striking bathrooms. Stylish Spoon+ allows diners to construct own dishes.

The Leonard, 15 Seymour St, W1H 7JW ⊖ *Marble Arch,* ☎ (020) 7935 2010, *reservations@theleonard.com, Fax (020) 7935 6700,* – MC AE DC VISA. 29 AGU n
Rest (room service only) – 19.50 – **24 rm** 276.00 – 276.00, **20 suites** 234.00/999.00.
◆ Around the corner from Selfridges, an attractive Georgian townhouse: antiques and oil paintings abound. Informal, stylish café bar offers light snacks. Well-appointed rooms.

Radisson SAS Portman, 22 Portman Sq, W1H 7BG ⊖ *Marble Arch,* ☎ (020) 7208 6000, *sales.london@radissonsas.com, Fax (020) 7208 6001,* rm, – 650. MC AE DC VISA. 29 AGT a
Talavera **:** Rest *(closed lunch Saturday, Sunday and Bank Holidays)* (buffet lunch)/dinner a la carte 27.50/38.00 – 17.50 – **265 rm** 163.35/186.83 – 211.50/245.60, 7 suites.
◆ This modern, corporate hotel offers check-in for both British Midland and SAS airlines. Rooms in attached towers decorated in Scandinavian, Chinese and Italian styles. Restaurant renowned for its elaborate buffet lunch.

Montcalm, Great Cumberland Pl, W1H 7TW ⊖ *Marble Arch,* ☎ (020) 7402 4288, *montcalm@montcalm.co.uk, Fax (020) 7724 9180* – rm, – 80. MC AE DC VISA. 29 AGU d
Rest – (see ***The Crescent*** below) – 15.95 – **110 rm** 270.25/293.75 – 293.75, 10 suites.
◆ Named after the 18C French general, the Marquis de Montcalm. In a charming crescent a short walk from Hyde Park. Spacious bedrooms with a subtle oriental feel.

London Marriott Marble Arch, 134 George St, W1H 5DN ⊖ *Marble Arch,* ✆ (0870) 4007255, *salesadmin.marblearch@marriott.co.uk, Fax (020) 7402 0666,* – 150. VISA. 29 AFT j
Mediterrano : Rest (dinner only) a la carte approx 20.00 – 18.95 – **240 rm** 210.00 – 210.00.
◆ Centrally located and modern. Offers comprehensive conference facilities. Leisure centre underground. An ideal base for both corporate and leisure guests. Mediterranean-influenced cooking.

Berkshire, 350 Oxford St, W1N 0BY ⊖ *Bond Street,* ✆ (020) 7629 7474, *Fax (020) 7629 8156* – rm, – 40. VISA. 30 AHU n
Ascots : Rest *(closed lunch Friday-Sunday)* a la carte 25.00/45.00 – 15.00 – **146 rm** 231.50 – 297.25, 2 suites.
◆ Above the shops of Oxford St. Reception areas have a pleasant traditional charm. Comfortably appointed modern bedrooms have plenty of style. Personable staff. Stylish, relaxed dining room.

Durrants, 26-32 George St, W1H 5BJ ⊖ *Bond Street,* ✆ (020) 7935 8131, *enquiries@durrantshotel.co.uk, Fax (020) 7487 3510* – rest – 55. VISA. 29 AGT e
Rest 19.50/22.00 (lunch) and a la carte 27.50/38.75 – 13.50 – **88 rm** 99.00/145.00 – 165.00, 4 suites.
◆ First opened in 1790 and family owned since 1921. Traditionally English feel with the charm of a bygone era. Cosy wood panelled bar. Attractive rooms vary somewhat in size. Semi-private booths in quintessentially British dining room.

Dorset Square, 39-40 Dorset Sq, NW1 6QN ⊖ *Marylebone,* ✆ (020) 7723 7874, *reservations@dorsetsquare.co.uk, Fax (020) 7724 3328,* – VISA. 17 QZD s
closed 25-26 December – ***The Potting Shed :*** Rest (booking essential) 19.50/24.50 and a la carte 24.95/34.90 – 14.00 – **37 rm** 258.00/305.50 – 305.50.
◆ Converted Regency townhouses in a charming square and the site of the original Lord's cricket ground. A relaxed country house in the city. Individually decorated rooms. The Potting Shed features modern cuisine and a set business menu.

Sherlock Holmes, 108 Baker St, W1U 6LJ ⊖ *Baker Street,* ✆ (020) 7486 6161, *info@sherlockholmeshotel.com, Fax (020) 7958 5211,* – 45. VISA 29 AGT c
Rest 16.50 (lunch) and a la carte 25.00/44.00 – 16.50 – **116 rm** 235.00 – 235.00, 3 suites.
◆ A stylish building with a relaxed contemporary feel. Comfortable guests' lounge with Holmes pictures on the walls. Bedrooms welcoming and smart, some with wood floors. Brasserie style dining.

Hart House without rest., 51 Gloucester Pl, W1U 8JF ⊖ *Marble Arch,* ✆ (020) 7935 2288, *reservations@harthouse.co.uk, Fax (020) 7935 8516* – VISA. 29 AGT d
15 rm 65.00/95.00 – 95.00/110.00.
◆ Once home to French nobility escaping the 1789 Revolution. Now an attractive Georgian, mid-terraced private hotel. Warm and welcoming service. Well kept bedrooms.

St George without rest., 49 Gloucester Pl, W1U 8JE ⊖ *Marble Arch,* ✆ (020) 7486 8586, *reservations@stgeorge-hotel.net, Fax (020) 7486 6567* – VISA. 29 AGT h
5.00 **19 rm** 75.00/110.00 – 100.00/140.00.
◆ Terraced house on a busy street, usefully located within walking distance of many attractions. Offers a warm welcome and comfortable bedrooms which are spotlessly maintained.

Orrery, 55 Marylebone High St, W1U 5RB ⊖ *Regent's Park,* ✆ (020) 7616 8000, *Fax (020) 7616 8080* – VISA 18 RZD a
closed Christmas and New Year – **Rest** (booking essential) 25.00 (lunch) and a la carte 37.00/53.50 .
Spec. Langoustine and ceps, sherry jelly, shellfish velouté. Poached and roasted pigeon, confit of leg, creamed spinach and date purée. Apricot soufflé, pistachio ice cream.
◆ Contemporary elegance: a smoothly run 1st floor restaurant in converted 19C stables, with a Conran shop below. Accomplished modern British cooking.

Locanda Locatelli, 8 Seymour St, W1H 7JZ ⊖ *Marble Arch,* ✆ (020) 7935 9088, *info@locandalocatelli.com, Fax (020) 7935 1149* – VISA 29 AGU r
closed Bank Holidays – **Rest** - Italian - a la carte 32.50/51.50 .
Spec. Roast rabbit wrapped in Parma ham with polenta. Scallops with saffron vinaigrette. Tagliatelle with kid goat ragu.
◆ Very stylishly appointed restaurant with banquettes and cherry wood or glass dividers which contribute to an intimate and relaxing ambience. Accomplished Italian cooking.

XXX **Latium,** 21 Berners St, Fitzrovia, W1T 3LP ⊖ *Oxford Circus,* ✆ (020) 7323 9123, *info@latiumrestaurant.com, Fax (020) 7323 3205* – ▤. MO AE VISA 31 AJT
closed Easter, 25 December, Sunday, Saturday lunch and Bank Holidays – **Rest** - Italian 28.50 ♀.
◆ Welcoming restaurant owned by affable chef. Smart feel with well-spaced linen-cla tables, tiled floors and rural pictures. Italian country cooking in the heart of town.

XX **Deya,** 34 Portman Sq, W1H 7BY ⊖ *Marble Arch,* ✆ (020) 7224 0028, *reservations@deyarestaurant.co.uk, Fax (020) 7224 0411* – ▤. MO AE VISA 29 AGU
closed 25-26 December, 1 January, Sunday and Saturday lunch – **Rest** - Indian - 20.0 (lunch) and a la carte 22.50/31.94 ♀.
◆ Has its own pillared entrance, though part of Mostyn hotel. Grand 18C Grade II liste room with ornate ceiling. Modern, stylish makeover. Interesting, original Indian menus.

XX **The Crescent** (at Montcalm H.), Great Cumberland Pl, W1H 7TW ⊖ *Marble Arch,* ✆ (020) 7402 4288, *reservations@montcalm.co.uk, Fax (020) 7724 9180* – ▤. MO AE VISA 29 AGU
closed lunch Saturday and Sunday – **Rest** 26.00/29.50 **s.** ♀.
◆ Discreetly appointed room favoured by local residents. Best tables overlook a prett square. Frequently changing fixed price modern menu includes half bottle of house wine

XX **Rhodes W1** (at The Cumberland H.), Great Cumberland Pl, W1A 4RF ⊖ *Marble Arc* ✆ (020) 7479 3838, *rhodesw1@thecumberland.co.uk, Fax (020) 7479 3888* – ▤. MO AE VISA 29 AGU
Rest 21.75 (lunch) and a la carte 20.15/42.25 ♀.
◆ In the heart of the Cumberland Hotel, a very stylish dining experience with impressive high ceiling and classical Gary Rhodes dishes bringing out the best of the seasons.

XX **Galvin,** 66 Baker St, W14 7DH ⊖ *Baker Street,* ✆ (020) 7935 4007, *info@galvinbistrotoluxe.co.uk, Fax (020) 7486 1735* – ▤. MO AE VISA 29 AGT
closed 25-26 December and 1 January – **Rest** 15.50 (lunch) and a la carte 19.70/32.25 ♀.
◆ A modern take on the classic Gallic bistro with ceiling fans, globe lights, rich woo panelled walls and French influenced dishes where precision and good value are paramount.

XX **Six13,** 19 Wigmore St, W1H 9UA ⊖ *Bond Street,* ✆ (020) 7629 6133, *jay@six13.com Fax (020) 7629 6135* – ▤. MO AE VISA 30 AHT
closed Jewish Holidays, Friday dinner and Saturday – **Rest** - Kosher - 24.50 (lunch) and a carte 29.00/41.00 ♀.
◆ Stylish and immaculate with banquette seating. Strictly kosher menu supervised by th Shama offering interesting cooking with a modern slant.

XX **Oscar** (at Charlotte Street H.), 15 Charlotte St, W1T 1RJ ⊖ *Goodge Street,* ✆ (020) 790 4005, *charlotte@firmdale.com, Fax (020) 7806 2002* – ▤. MO AE VISA 31 AKT
closed Sunday lunch – **Rest** (booking essential) a la carte 33.00/48.50 ♀.
◆ Adjacent to hotel lobby and dominated by a large, vivid mural of contemporary Londo life. Sophisticated dishes served by attentive staff: oysters, wasabi and soya dressing.

XX **The Providores,** 109 Marylebone High St, W1U 4RX ⊖ *Bond Street,* ✆ (020) 7935 6175 *anyone@theprovidores.co.uk, Fax (020) 7935 6877* – ⇹ ▤. MO AE VISA 30 AHT
closed 25-26 and 31 December and 1 January – **Rest** a la carte 29.80/43.20 ♀.
◆ Swish, stylish restaurant on first floor; unusual dishes with New World base and fusio of Asian, Mediterranean influences. Tapas and light meals in downstairs Tapa Room.

XX **La Porte des Indes,** 32 Bryanston St, W1H 7EG ⊖ *Marble Arch,* ✆ (020) 7224 0055 *london.reservation@laportedesindes.com, Fax (020) 7224 1144* – ▤ ⇔ 14. MO AE VISA 29 AGU
closed 25-27 December and Saturday lunch – **Rest** - Indian - a la carte 22.30/45.00 ♀.
◆ Don't be fooled by the discreet entrance: inside there is a spectacularly unrestraine display of palm trees, murals and waterfalls. French influenced Indian cuisine.

XX **Rosmarino,** 1 Blenheim Terrace, NW8 0EH ⊖ *St John's Wood,* ✆ (020) 7328 5014 *Fax (020) 7625 2639,* 🏠 – ▤. MO AE VISA 11 PZB
closed Easter Monday, 25 December and 1 January – **Rest** - Italian - 24.50/29.50 ♀.
◆ Modern, understated and relaxed. Friendly and approachable service of robust an rustic Italian dishes. Set priced menu is carefully balanced.

XX **Ozer,** 4-5 Langham Pl, Regent St, W1B 3DG ⊖ *Oxford Circus,* ✆ (020) 7323 0505, *info@sofra.co.uk, Fax (020) 7323 0111* – ▤. MO AE VISA 30 AIT
Rest - Turkish - 17.45/22.45 and a la carte 16.85/34.65 ♀.
◆ Behind the busy and vibrantly decorated bar you'll find a smart modern restaurant Lively atmosphere and efficient service of modern, light and aromatic Turkish cooking.

XX **Roka,** 37 Charlotte St, W1T 1RR ⊖ *Tottenham Court Road,* ✆ (020) 7580 6464, *info@rokarestaurant.com, Fax (020) 7580 0220* – ⇹ ▤. MO AE VISA 31 AJT
closed Sunday lunch – **Rest** - Japanese - a la carte 35.50/78.50 ♀.
◆ Striking glass and steel frontage. Airy, atmospheric interior of teak, oak and paper wa screens. Authentic, flavoursome Japanese cuisine with variety of grill dishes.

XX **Rasa Samudra,** 5 Charlotte St, W1T 1RE ⊖ *Goodge Street,* ✆ (020) 7637 0222, *Fax (020) 7637 0224* – ⇔. MC AE VISA 31 AKT r
closed 24-30 December, 1 January and Sunday lunch – **Rest** - Indian Seafood and Vegetarian - 22.50/30.00.
◆ Comfortably appointed, richly decorated and modern Indian restaurant. Authentic Keralan (south Indian) cooking with seafood and vegetarian specialities.

XX **Levant,** Jason Court, 76 Wigmore St, W1U 2SJ ⊖ *Bond Street,* ✆ (020) 7224 1111, *Fax (020) 7486 1216* – ▤. MC AE ◑ VISA 30 AHT c
Rest - Lebanese - 15.00/26.50 and a la carte 20.00/35.00 ♀.
◆ The somewhat unpromising entrance leads down to a vibrantly decorated basement. Modern Lebanese cooking featuring subtly spiced dishes.

XX **Caldesi,** 15-17 Marylebone Lane, W1U 2NE ⊖ *Bond Street,* ✆ (020) 7935 9226, *tuscan@caldesi.com, Fax (020) 7935 9228* – ▤. MC AE ◑ VISA 30 AHT e
closed Sunday, Saturday lunch and Bank Holidays – **Rest** - Italian - a la carte 30.00/37.00.
◆ A traditional Italian restaurant that continues to attract a loyal clientele. Robust and authentic dishes with Tuscan specialities. Attentive service by established team.

XX **Villandry,** 170 Great Portland St, W1W 5QB ⊖ *Regent's Park,* ✆ (020) 7631 3131, *bookatable@villandry.com, Fax (020) 7631 3030* – ⇔ ▤. MC AE ◑ VISA 30 AIT s
closed Sunday dinner and Bank Holidays – **Rest** a la carte 22.75/38.25 ♀.
◆ The senses are heightened by passing through the well-stocked deli to the dining room behind. Bare walls, wooden tables and a menu offering simple, tasty dishes.

XX **Bertorelli,** 19-23 Charlotte St, W1T 1RL ⊖ *Goodge Street,* ✆ (020) 7636 4174, *bertorellisc@groupechezgerard.co.uk, Fax (020) 7467 8902* – ▤. MC AE ◑ VISA 31 AJT v
closed 25-26 December and Sunday – **Rest** - Italian - 18.50 (lunch) and a la carte 16.50/40.85 ☺ ♀.
◆ Above the informal and busy bar/café. Bright and airy room with vibrant décor and informal atmosphere. Extensive menu combines traditional and new wave Italian dishes.

XX **Blandford Street,** 5-7 Blandford St, W1U 3DB ⊖ *Bond Street,* ✆ (020) 7486 9696, *info@blandford-street.co.uk, Fax (020) 7486 5067* – ▤. MC AE VISA 30 AHT v
closed Sunday, Saturday lunch and Bank Holidays – **Rest** a la carte 21.85/36.85 ☺ ♀.
◆ Understated interior with plain walls hung with modern pictures and subtle spot-lighting. Contemporary menu with a notably European character.

XX **L'Aventure,** 3 Blenheim Terrace, NW8 0EH ⊖ *St John's Wood,* ✆ (020) 7624 6232, *Fax (020) 7625 5548,* 🏠 – MC AE VISA 11 PZB b
closed Easter, Sunday, Saturday lunch and Bank Holidays – **Rest** - French - 18.50/32.50.
◆ Behind the pretty tree lined entrance you'll find a charming neighbourhood restaurant. Relaxed atmosphere and service by personable owner. Authentic French cuisine.

X **Union Café,** 96 Marylebone Lane, W1U 2QA ⊖ *Bond Street,* ✆ (020) 7486 4860, *unioncafe@brinkleys.com, Fax (020) 7486 4860* – MC AE VISA 30 AHT d
closed 25-26 December, 1 January, Sunday and August Bank Holiday – **Rest** a la carte 25.00/30.00 ♀.
◆ No standing on ceremony at this bright, relaxed restaurant. The open kitchen at one end produces modern Mediterranean cuisine. Ideal for visitors to the Wallace Collection.

X **Caffè Caldesi,** 1st Floor, 118 Marylebone Lane, W1U 2QF ⊖ *Bond Street,* ✆ (020) 7935 1144, *people@caldesi.com, Fax (020) 7935 8832* – ▤. MC AE ◑ VISA 30 AHT s
closed Sunday dinner – **Rest** - Italian - a la carte 23.00/33.00 ♀.
◆ Converted pub with a simple modern interior in which to enjoy tasty, uncomplicated Italian dishes. Downstairs is a lively bar with a deli counter serving pizzas and pastas.

X **Chada Chada,** 16-17 Picton Pl, W1M 5DE ⊖ *Bond Street,* ✆ (020) 7935 8212, *enquiry@chadathai.com, Fax (020) 7924 2178* – ▤. MC AE ◑ VISA 30 AHU b
closed Sunday and Bank Holidays – **Rest** - Thai - a la carte 11.20/37.95 ♀.
◆ Authentic and fragrant Thai cooking; the good value menu offers some interesting departures from the norm. Service is eager to please in the compact and cosy rooms.

X **No.6,** 6 George St, W1U 3QX ⊖ *Bond Street,* ✆ (020) 7935 1910, *Fax (020) 7935 6036* – ⇔ ▤. MC VISA 30 AHT a
closed 2 weeks August, 2 weeks Christmas, Saturday and Sunday – **Rest** (lunch only) a la carte 23.95/28.95.
◆ To the front is a charming delicatessen offering fresh produce and behind is a simple, well-kept dining room. Daily changing menu with good use of fresh ingredients.

Fishworks, 89 Marylebone High St, W1V 4QW ⊖ *Baker Street*, ✆ (020) 7935 9796, *marylebone@fishworks.co.uk* – ⇹ ▤. MO AE VISA 30 AHT
closed Monday – **Rest** - Seafood - (booking essential) a la carte 20.00/40.00 ♀.
◆ Go through the fish shop to bright, unfussy restaurant where a blackboard lists the daily specials. Extensive menus offer simply prepared seafood straight from front-of-house!

The Abbey Road, 63 Abbey Rd, NW8 0AE ⊖ *St John's Wood*, ✆ (020) 7328 6626 *theabbeyroadpub@btconnect.com, Fax (020) 7625 9168*, – MO AE VISA 11 OZB
closed 25 and 31 December – **Rest** *(closed Monday lunch)* a la carte 20.00/25.00 ♀.
◆ Grand Victorian pub appearance in bottle green. Busy bar at the front; main dining room, in calm duck egg blue, to the rear. Modern menus boast a distinct Mediterranean style.

St James's *Gtr London* – ✉ *W1/SW1.*

The Ritz, 150 Piccadilly, W1J 9BR ⊖ *Green Park*, ✆ (020) 7493 8181, *enquire@theritzlondon.com, Fax (020) 7493 2687*, – ⇹ rm, ▤ – 50. MO AE VISA 30 AIV
Rest – (see ***The Restaurant*** below) – ☕ 30.00 – **116 rm** ★388.00 – ★★588.00, 17 suites.
◆ Opened 1906, a fine example of Louis XVI architecture and decoration. Elegant Palm Court famed for afternoon tea. Many of the lavishly appointed rooms overlook the park.

Sofitel St James London, 6 Waterloo Pl, SW1Y 4AN ⊖ *Piccadilly Circus*, ✆ (020) 7747 2200, *h3144@accor-hotels.com, Fax (020) 7747 2210*, – ⇹ rm, ▤ – 180. MO AE VISA 31 AKV
Rest – (see ***Brasserie Roux*** below) – ☕ 21.00 – **179 rm** ★350.00 – ★★350.00, 7 suites.
◆ Grade II listed building in smart Pall Mall location. Classically English interiors include floral Rose Lounge and club-style St. James bar. Comfortable, well-fitted bedrooms.

Stafford, 16-18 St James's Pl, SW1A 1NJ ⊖ *Green Park*, ✆ (020) 7493 0111 *info@thestaffordhotel.co.uk, Fax (020) 7493 7121* – ▤ – 40. MO AE VISA 30 AIV
Rest *(closed lunch Saturday and Bank Holidays)* 29.50 (lunch) and a la carte 53.50/67.50 **s.** – ☕ 19.50 – **75 rm** ★252.00/293.00 – ★★323.00/393.00, 6 suites.
◆ A genteel atmosphere prevails in this elegant and discreet country house in the city. Do not miss the famed American bar. Well-appointed rooms created from 18C stables. Refined, elegant, intimate dining room.

Dukes, 35 St James's Pl, SW1A 1NY ⊖ *Green Park*, ✆ (020) 7491 4840, *bookings@dukeshotel.com, Fax (020) 7493 1264*, – ⇹ rest, ▤ – 50. MO AE VISA 30 AIV
Rest a la carte 34.50/42.50 ♀ – ☕ 19.50 – **82 rm** ★188.00/364.00 – ★★217.00/429.00, 7 suites.
◆ Privately owned, discreet and quiet hotel. Traditional bar, famous for its martinis and Cognac collection. Well-kept spacious rooms in a country house style. Refined dining.

Trafalgar Hilton, 2 Spring Gdns, SW1A 2TS ⊖ *Charing Cross*, ✆ (020) 7870 2900 *sales.trafalgar@hilton.com, Fax (020) 7870 2911* – ⇹ rm, ▤ – 50. MO AE VISA 31 AKV
Rockwell : **Rest** *(closed Saturday lunch and Sunday)* 18.00/45.00 and a la carte 30.00/42.00 ♀ – ☕ 17.50 – **127 rm** ★340.00 – ★★398.00, 2 suites.
◆ Enjoys a commanding position on the square of which the deluxe rooms, some split level, have views. Bedrooms are in pastel shades with leather armchairs or stools; mod cons. Low-lit restaurant with open-plan kitchen.

De Vere Cavendish, 81 Jermyn St, SW1Y 6JF ⊖ *Piccadilly Circus*, ✆ (020) 7930 2111 *cavendish.reservations@devere-hotels.com, Fax (020) 7839 2125* – ⇹ rm, ▤ – 100. MO AE VISA 30 AIV
Rest a la carte 18.00/31.75 **s.** ♀ – ☕ 19.95 – **227 rm** ★288.00 – ★★311.00, 3 suites.
◆ Modern hotel in heart of Piccadilly. Contemporary, minimalist style of rooms with moody prints of London; top five floors offer far-reaching views over and beyond the city. Classic styled restaurant overlooks Jermyn Street.

22 Jermyn Street, 22 Jermyn St, SW1Y 6HL ⊖ *Piccadilly Circus*, ✆ (020) 7734 2353 *office@22jermyn.com, Fax (020) 7734 0750* – ▤. MO AE VISA. 31 AKV
closed 24-25 December – **Rest** (room service only) – ☕ 12.65 – **5 rm** ★246.00 – ★★246.00, **13 suites** 346.00/393.00.
◆ Discreet entrance amid famous shirt-makers' shops leads to this exclusive boutique hotel. Stylishly decorated bedrooms more than compensate for the lack of lounge space.

The Restaurant (at The Ritz H.), 150 Piccadilly, W1V 9DG ⊖ *Green Park*, ✆ (020) 7493 8181, *Fax (020) 7493 2687*, – ▤. MO AE VISA 30 AIV
Rest (dancing Friday and Saturday evenings) 45.00/65.00 and a la carte 52.00/89.00 **s.** ♀.
◆ The height of opulence: magnificent Louis XVI décor with trompe l'oeil and ornate gilding. Delightful terrace over Green Park. Refined service, classic and modern menu.

XXX **The Wolseley,** 160 Piccadilly, W1J 9EB ⊖ *Green Park,* ✆ (020) 7499 6996, *Fax (020) 7499 6888* – ▤. MO AE ⓓ VISA 30 AIV q
closed dinner 24-25 December, 1 January and August Bank Holiday – **Rest** (booking essential) a la carte 27.75/53.75 ♀.
◆ Has the feel of a grand European coffee house: pillars, high vaulted ceiling, mezzanine tables. Menus range from caviar to a hot dog. Also open for breakfasts and tea.

XXX **W'Sens,** 12 Waterloo Pl, SW1Y 4AU ⊖ *Piccadilly Circus,* ✆ (020) 7484 1355, *info@wsens.co.uk, Fax (020) 7484 1366* – ▤ ⇔ 12. MO AE VISA 31 AKV x
closed Saturday lunch and Sunday – **Rest** 22.50/30.00 and a la carte 26.50/49.50 ☺ ♀.
◆ Impressive 19C façade; contrastingly cool interior: dive bar is a destination in its own right and the wildly eclectic restaurant is matched by three intriguing menu sections.

XXX **Fiore,** 33 St James's St, SW1A 1HD ⊖ *Green Park,* ✆ (020) 7930 7100, *info@fiore-restaurant.co.uk, Fax (020) 7930 4070* – ▤. MO AE ⓓ VISA 30 AIV k
closed 25 December and 1 January – **Rest** - Italian - 22.00/45.00 and a la carte 25.50/37.00.
◆ Formal restaurant with affluent feel appropriate to its setting: full linen cover and smart banquettes. Traditional Italian regional cooking with contemporary embellishments.

XX **Le Caprice,** Arlington House, Arlington St, SW1A 1RT ⊖ *Green Park,* ✆ (020) 7629 2239, *Fax (020) 7493 9040* – ▤. MO AE ⓓ VISA 30 AIV h
closed 25-26 December, 1 January and August Bank Holiday – **Rest** (Sunday brunch) a la carte 22.25/54.00 ♀.
◆ Still attracting a fashionable clientele and as busy as ever. Dine at the bar or in the smoothly run restaurant. Food combines timeless classics with modern dishes.

XX **Quaglino's,** 16 Bury St, SW1Y 6AL ⊖ *Green Park,* ✆ (020) 7930 6767, *Fax (020) 7839 2866* – ▤ ⇔ 45. MO AE ⓓ VISA 30 AIV j
closed 25 December and 1 January – **Rest** (booking essential) 19.00 (lunch) and a la carte 21.50/38.00 ☺ ♀.
◆ Descend the sweeping staircase into the capacious room where a busy and buzzy atmosphere prevails. Watch the chefs prepare everything from osso bucco to fish and chips.

XX **Mint Leaf,** Suffolk Pl, SW1Y 4HX ⊖ *Piccadilly Circus,* ✆ (020) 7930 9020, *reservations@mintleafrestaurant.com, Fax (020) 7930 6205* – ▤. MO AE ⓓ VISA 31 AKV k
closed Bank Holidays and lunch Saturday and Sunday – **Rest** - Indian - a la carte 25.00/45.00 ☺ ♀.
◆ Basement restaurant in theatreland. Cavernous dining room incorporating busy, trendy bar with unique cocktail list and loud music. Helpful service. Contemporary Indian dishes.

XX **Criterion Grill Marco Pierre White,** 224 Piccadilly, W1J 9HP ⊖ *Piccadilly Circus,* ✆ (020) 7930 0488, *sales@whitestarline.org.uk, Fax (020) 7930 8380* – ▤. MO AE ⓓ VISA 31 AKU c
closed 24-26 December, 1 January and Sunday – **Rest** 17.95 (lunch) and a la carte 27.00/56.00 ☺ ♀.
◆ A stunning modern brasserie behind the revolving doors. Ornate gilding, columns and mirrors aplenty. Bustling, characterful atmosphere, Pre and post-theatre menus.

XX **Brasserie Roux,** 8 Pall Mall, SW1Y 5NG ⊖ *Piccadilly Circus,* ✆ (020) 7968 2900, *h3144-fb4@accor-hotels.com, Fax (020) 7747 2242* – ▤. MO AE ⓓ VISA 31 AKV a
Rest - French - 24.50 and a la carte 22.50/31.50 ☺ ♀.
◆ Informal, smart, classic brasserie style with large windows making the most of the location. Large menu of French classics with many daily specials; comprehensive wine list.

XX **The Avenue,** 7-9 St James's St, SW1A 1EE ⊖ *Green Park,* ✆ (020) 7321 2111, *avenue@egami.co.uk, Fax (020) 7321 2500* – ▤. MO AE ⓓ VISA 30 AIV y
closed 25-26 December – **Rest** 19.95 and a la carte 25.50/46.00 ☺ ♀.
◆ The attractive and stylish bar is a local favourite. Behind is a striking, modern and busy restaurant. Appealing and contemporary food. Pre-theatre menu available.

XX **Matsuri - St James's,** 15 Bury St, SW1Y 6AL ⊖ *Green Park,* ✆ (020) 7839 1101, *dine@matsuri-restaurant.com, Fax (020) 7930 7010* – ▤ ⇔ 20. MO AE ⓓ VISA 30 AIV w
Rest - Japanese (Teppan-Yaki, Sushi) - 15.00/35.00 and a la carte 24.00/54.00 ☺ ♀.
◆ Specialising in theatrical and precise teppan-yaki cooking. Separate restaurant offers sushi delicacies. Charming service by traditionally dressed staff.

XX **Noura Central,** 22 Lower Regent St, SW1Y 4UJ ⊖ *Piccadilly Circus,* ✆ (020) 7839 2020, *Fax (020) 7839 7700* – ▤. MO AE ⓓ VISA 31 AKV n
Rest - Lebanese - 14.50/34.00 and a la carte 15.00/35.00.
◆ Eye-catching Lebanese façade, matched by sleek interior design. Buzzy atmosphere enhanced by amplified background music. Large menus cover all aspects of Lebanese cuisine.

Al Duca, 4-5 Duke of York St, SW1Y 6LA *Piccadilly Circus,* (020) 7839 3090, *info@aduca-restaurants.co.uk, Fax (020) 7839 4050* – . VISA 31 AJV
closed 23 December-4 January, Sunday and Bank Holidays – **Rest** - Italian - 20.50/24.00.
◆ Relaxed, modern, stylish restaurant. Friendly and approachable service of robust and rustic Italian dishes. Set priced menu is good value.

Inn the Park, St James's Park, SW1A 2BJ *Charing Cross,* (020) 7451 9999, *info@innthepark.co.uk, Fax (020) 7451 9998,* – VISA 31 AKV
closed 25 December – **Rest** a la carte 22.50/39.50.
◆ Eco-friendly restaurant with grass covered roof; pleasant views across park and lakes. Super-heated dining terrace. Modern British menus of tasty, wholesome dishes.

Soho *Gtr London* – *W1/WC2.*

The Soho, 4 Richmond Mews, W1D 3DH *Tottenham Court Road,* (020) 7559 3000, *soho@firmdale.com, Fax (020) 7559 3003,* – – 100. VISA 31 AKU
Refuel **:** Rest 19.95 (lunch) and a la carte 26.50/34.50 – 18.50 – **83 rm** 276.00 – 346.00, 2 suites.
◆ Opened in autumn 2004: stylish hotel with two screening rooms, comfy drawing room and up-to-the-minute bedrooms, some vivid, others more muted, all boasting hi-tec extras. Contemporary bar and restaurant.

Hampshire, Leicester Sq, WC2H 7LH *Leicester Square,* (020) 7839 9399, *Fax (020) 7930 8122,* , – , rm, – 100. VISA. 31 AKU
The Apex **:** Rest (dinner only) a la carte 25.00/45.00 – 16.50 – **119 rm** 309.00 – 405.40, 5 suites.
◆ The bright lights of the city are literally outside and many rooms overlook the bustling Square. Inside, it is tranquil and comfortable, with well-appointed bedrooms. Formal yet relaxing dining room with immaculately dressed tables.

Courthouse Kempinski, 19-21 Great Marlborough St, W1F 7HL *Oxford Circus,* (020) 7297 5555, *info@courthouse-hotel.com, Fax (020) 7297 5566,* , , – rm, – 180. VISA 30 AIU
The Carnaby **:** Rest a la carte approx 22.50 – (see also ***Silk*** below) – 22.50 – **107 rm** 317.25 – 317.25, 5 suites.
◆ Striking Grade II listed ex magistrates' court: interior fused imaginatively with original features: for example, the bar incorporates three former cells. Ultra stylish rooms. Informal Carnaby offers extensive French, modern and British menu.

Hazlitt's without rest., 6 Frith St, W1D 3JA *Tottenham Court Road,* (020) 7434 1771, *reservations@hazlitts.co.uk, Fax (020) 7439 1524* – . VISA 31 AKU
22 rm 206.00/240.00 – 240.00, 1 suite.
◆ A row of three adjoining early 18c town houses and former home of the eponymous essayist. Individual and charming bedrooms, many with antique furniture and Victorian baths.

L'Escargot, 48 Greek St, W1D 5EF *Tottenham Court Road,* (020) 7437 2679, *sales@whitestarline.org.uk, Fax (020) 7437 0790* – 60. VISA 31 AKU
Rest *(closed 25-26 December, 1 January, Sunday and Saturday lunch)* 18.00 (lunch) and a la carte 26.50/28.95 – ***Picasso Room*** **:** Rest *(closed August, Sunday, Monday and Saturday lunch)* 25.50/42.00.
Spec. Escargots en coquille Bordelaise. Roast pork cutlet, stuffed pig's trotter and fondant potato. Hot chocolate fondant, iced crème fraîche.
◆ Soho institution. Ground Floor is chic, vibrant brasserie with early-evening buzz of theatre-goers. Finely judged modern dishes. Intimate and more formal upstairs Picasso Room famed for its limited edition art.

Quo Vadis, 26-29 Dean St, W1D 3LL *Tottenham Court Road,* (020) 7437 9585, *whitestarline@org.uk, Fax (020) 7734 7593* – . VISA 31 AKU
closed 24-25 December, 1 January, Sunday and Saturday lunch – **Rest** - Italian - 19.95 (lunch) and a la carte 22.00/36.00.
◆ Stained glass windows and a neon sign hint at the smooth modernity of the interior. Modern artwork abounds. Contemporary cooking and a serious wine list.

Red Fort, 77 Dean St, W1D 3SH *Tottenham Court Road,* (020) 7437 2525, *info@redfort.co.uk, Fax (020) 7434 0721* – . VISA 31 AKU
closed lunch Saturday, Sunday and Bank Holidays – **Rest** - Indian - a la carte 25.50/46.00.
◆ Smart, stylish restaurant with modern water feature and glass ceiling to rear. Seasonally changing menus of authentic dishes handed down over generations.

XX **Richard Corrigan at Lindsay House,** 21 Romilly St, W1D 5AF ⊖ *Leicester Square,* ☎ (020) 7439 0450, *richardcorrigan@lindsayhouse.co.uk, Fax (020) 7437 7349* – ▤. MC AE ① VISA 31 AKU f
closed Christmas, Sunday, Saturday lunch and Bank Holidays – **Rest** 27.00/52.00 ♀.
Spec. Ravioli of chorizo and feta with onion and lime velouté. Tea roasted veal sweetbreads with cauliflower. Compote of rhubarb, mango, nutmeg and vanilla ice cream.
◆ One rings the doorbell before being welcomed into this handsome 18C town house, retaining many original features. Skilled and individual cooking with a subtle Irish hint.

XX **Floridita,** 100 Wardour St, W1F 0TN ⊖ *Tottenham Court Road,* ☎ (020) 7314 4000, *Fax (020) 7314 4040* – ▤ ⇔ 8. MC AE ① VISA 31 AKU z
closed Sunday – **Rest** - Latin American - (live music and dancing) (dinner only and lunch mid November-December) a la carte 33.25/39.00 **s.** ♀.
◆ Buzzy destination where the Latino cuisine is a fiery accompaniment to the vivacious Cuban dancing. Slightly less frenetic upstairs in the Spanish tapas and cocktail bar.

XX **Silk** (at Courthouse Kempinksi H.), 19-21 Great Marlborough St, W1F 7HL ⊖ *Oxford Circus,* ☎ (020) 7297 5555, *Fax (020) 7297 5566* – ▤. MC AE VISA 30 AIU z
closed Sunday – **Rest** (dinner only) 45.00 and a la carte 40.00/52.00.
◆ Stunningly unique former courtroom with original panelling, court benches and glass roof. Menu follows the journey of the Silk Route with Asian, Indian and Italian influences.

XX **Café Lazeez,** 21 Dean St, W1V 5AH ⊖ *Tottenham Court Road,* ☎ (020) 7434 9393, *soho@cafelazeez.com, Fax (020) 7434 0022* – ▤ MC AE ① VISA 31 AKU d
closed 25 December, Sunday and Bank Holidays – **Rest** - North Indian - 17.50 (lunch) and a la carte 27.15/41.65 ♀.
◆ In the same building as Soho Theatre; the bar hums before shows, restaurant is popular for pre- and post-theatre meals of modern Indian fare. Refined décor; private booths.

XX **Vasco and Piero's Pavilion,** 15 Poland St, W1F 8QE ⊖ *Tottenham Court Road,* ☎ (020) 7437 8774, *vascosfood@hotmail.com, Fax (020) 7437 0467* – ▤ ⇔ 30. MC AE ① VISA 31 AJU b
closed Sunday and Bank Holidays – **Rest** - Italian - (lunch booking essential) 26.00 (dinner) and lunch a la carte 23.50/30.50.
◆ A long standing, family run Italian restaurant with a loyal local following. Pleasant service under the owners' guidance. Warm décor and traditional cooking.

XX **La Trouvaille,** 12A Newburgh St, W1F 7RR ⊖ *Piccadilly Circus,* ☎ (020) 7287 8488, *Fax (020) 7434 4170,* – MC AE VISA 30 AIU g
closed 25-26 December, Sunday dinner and Bank Holidays – **Rest** - French - 18.75/29.50.
◆ Atmospheric restaurant located just off Carnaby Street. Hearty, robust French cooking with a rustic character. French wine list with the emphasis on southern regions.

X **Yauatcha,** 15 Broadwick St, W1F 0DL ⊖ *Tottenham Court Road,* ☎ (020) 7494 8888, *mail@yauatcha.com, Fax (020) 7494 8889* – ▤. MC AE VISA 31 AJU k
closed 25-26 December – **Rest** - Chinese (Dim Sum) a la carte 17.80/45.50.
Spec. Venison puff. Scallop shumai. Prawn and beancurd cheung fun.
◆ Converted 1960s post office in heart of Soho. Below smart, cool tea room is spacious restaurant serving Chinese cuisine that's original, refined, authentic and flavoursome.

X **Bertorelli,** 11-13 Frith St, W1D 4RB ⊖ *Tottenham Court Road,* ☎ (020) 7494 3491, *bertorelli-soho@groupechezgerard.co.uk, Fax (020) 7439 9431,* – ▤. MC AE VISA 31 AKU t
closed 25-26 December and 1 January – **Rest** - Italian - 18.50 (lunch) and a la carte 15.85/30.00 ♀.
◆ A haven of tranquillity from the bustling street below. Discreet and professionally run first floor restaurant with Italian menu. Popular ground floor café.

X **Alastair Little,** 49 Frith St, W1D 5SG ⊖ *Tottenham Court Road,* ☎ (020) 7734 5183, *Fax (020) 7734 5206* – ▤. MC AE ① VISA 31 AKU y
closed Sunday, Saturday lunch and Bank Holidays – **Rest** (booking essential) 31.00/38.00.
◆ The eponymous owner was at the vanguard of Soho's culinary renaissance. Tasty, daily changing British based cuisine; the compact room is rustic and simple.

X **itsu,** 103 Wardour St, W1F 0UQ ⊖ *Piccadilly Circus,* ☎ (020) 7479 4790, *Fax (020) 7479 4795* – ▤. MC AE VISA 31 AKU m
closed 25 December – **Rest** - Japanese - (bookings not accepted) a la carte approx 18.00.
◆ Japanese dishes of Sushi, Sashimi, handrolls and miso soup turn on a conveyor belt in a pleasingly hypnotic fashion. Hot bowls of chicken and coconut soup also appear.

X **Aurora,** 49 Lexington St, W1F 9AP ⊖ *Piccadilly Circus,* ☎ (020) 7494 0514, – ⇔ 18. MC AE VISA 31 AJU e
closed 24 December-3 January, Sunday and Bank Holidays – **Rest** (booking essential) a la carte approx 23.50.
◆ An informal, no-nonsense, bohemian style bistro with a small, but pretty, walled garden terrace. Short but balanced menu; simple fresh food. Pleasant, languid atmosphere.

Fung Shing, 15 Lisle St, WC2H 7BE *Leicester Square,* (020) 7437 153
Fax (020) 7734 0284 – 50. VISA 31 AKU
closed 24-26 December and lunch Bank Holidays – **Rest** - Chinese (Canton) - 17.00/35.0 and a la carte 13.00/24.00.
• A long-standing Chinese restaurant on the edge of Chinatown. Chatty and pleasa service. A mix of authentic, rustic dishes and the more adventurous chef's specials.

Strand and Covent Garden *Gtr London* – WC2.

Savoy, Strand, WC2R 0EU *Charing Cross,* (020) 7836 4343, *info@the-savoy.co.u Fax (020) 7240 6040,* – rm, – 500. VISA 31 ALU
Banquette : Rest a la carte approx 30.00 – (see also ***The Savoy Grill*** below) – 24.50 – **236 rm** 422.00/516.00 – 539.00/656.00, 27 suites.
• Famous the world over, since 1889, as the epitome of English elegance and styl Celebrated for its Art Deco features and luxurious bedrooms. Banquette is bright, air upmarket American diner.

Swissôtel The Howard, Temple Pl, WC2R 2PR *Temple,* (020) 7836 3555, *res vations.london@swissotel.com, Fax (020) 7379 4547,* – rm, 120. VISA. 32 AMU
Rest – (see ***Jaan*** below) – 23.50 – **177 rm** 358.00 – 358.00, 12 suites.
• Cool elegance is the order of the day at this handsomely appointed hotel. Many of th comfortable rooms enjoy balcony views of the Thames. Attentive service.

The Waldorf Hilton, Aldwych, WC2B 4DD *Covent Garden,* (020) 7836 2400, *w dorflondon@hilton.com, Fax (020) 7836 7244,* – rm, – 40 VISA. 32 AMU
Homage : Rest *(closed lunch Saturday and Sunday and Bank Holidays)* 16.50 (lunch) and la carte 26.00/37.50 – 22.00 – **290 rm** 233.00/329.00 – 233.00/329.00, 10 suites.
• Impressive curved and columned façade: an Edwardian landmark. Basement leisure clu Ornate meeting rooms. Two bedroom styles: one contemporary, one more tradition Large, modish brasserie with extensive range of modern menus.

One Aldwych, 1 Aldwych, WC2B 4RH *Covent Garden,* (020) 7300 1000, *reser tions@onealdwych.com, Fax (020) 7300 1001,* – rm, – 5 VISA. 32 AMU
Indigo : Rest a la carte 28.75/38.20 – (see also ***Axis*** below) – 21.25 – **96 rm** 370.00 476.00, 9 suites.
• Decorative Edwardian building, former home to the Morning Post newspaper. Now stylish and contemporary address with modern artwork, a screening room and hi-te bedrooms. All-day restaurant looks down on fashionable bar.

St Martins Lane, 45 St Martin's Lane, WC2N 4HX *Trafalgar Square,* (020) 73 5500, *sml@morganshotelgroup.com, Fax (020) 7300 5501,* – rm, – 40. VISA. 31 ALU
Asia de Cuba : Rest - Asian - a la carte 48.50/84.00 – 20.50 – **202 rm** 370.00 394.00, 2 suites.
• The unmistakable hand of Philippe Starck evident at this most contemporary of hote Unique and stylish, from the starkly modern lobby to the state-of-the-art rooms. 3 varieties of rum at fashionable Asia de Cuba.

Thistle Charing Cross, Strand, WC2N 5HX *Charing Cross,* (0870) 333910 *Fax (0870) 3339205* – rm, – 150. VISA. 31 ALV
Rest a la carte approx 32.00 **s.** – 17.50 – **239 rm** 305.00/349.00 – 349.00.
• Classic Victorian hotel built above the station. In keeping with its origins, rooms in t Buckingham wing are traditionally styled whilst others have contemporary décor. Wat the world go by from restaurant's pleasant vantage point.

The Savoy Grill (at Savoy H.), Strand, WC2R 0EU *Charing Cross,* (020) 7592 16 *savoygrill@marcuswareing.com, Fax (020) 7592 1601* – 55. VISA
Rest 30.00/65.00. 31 ALU
Spec. Smoked salmon and gravadlax carved from the trolley. Roast rack of lamb w confit of shoulder, celery leaf gnocchi. Vanilla parfait with passion fruit curd, blood oran sorbet.
• Redesigned in 2003 to conserve its best traditions, the Grill buzzes at midday and in t evening. Formal service; menu of modern European dishes and the Savoy classics.

Ivy, 1 West St, WC2H 9NQ *Leicester Square,* (020) 7836 4751, *Fax (020) 7240 933* . VISA 31 AKU
closed 25-26 December, 1 January and August Bank Holiday – **Rest** a la carte 24.25/53.75
• Wood panelling and stained glass combine with an unpretentious menu to create veritable institution. A favourite of 'celebrities', so securing a table can be challenging.

XXX **Axis,** 1 Aldwych, WC2B 4RH ⊖ *Covent Garden,* ✆ (020) 7300 0300, *axis@onealdwych.com, Fax (020) 7300 0301* – ▤. MC AE ① VISA 31 AMU r
closed 24 December-4 January, Easter, Sunday, Saturday lunch and Bank Holidays – **Rest** (live jazz at dinner Tuesday and Wednesday) 19.75 (lunch) and a la carte 24.40/40.40 ♀.
◆ Lower-level room overlooked by gallery bar. Muted tones, black leather chairs and vast futuristic mural appeal to the fashion cognoscenti. Globally-influenced menu.

XXX **Jaan** (at Swissôtel The Howard), Temple Pl, WC2R 2PR ⊖ *Temple,* ✆ (020) 7300 1700, *jaan.london@swissotel.com, Fax (020) 7240 7816,* – ▤. MC AE ① VISA 32 AMU e
closed lunch Saturday and Sunday – **Rest** 33.00 ♀.
◆ Bright room on the ground floor of the hotel with large windows overlooking an attractive terrace. Original cooking - modern French with Cambodian flavours and ingredients.

XX **J. Sheekey,** 28-32 St Martin's Court, WC2N 4AL ⊖ *Leicester Square,* ✆ (020) 7240 2565, *Fax (020) 7240 8114* – ▤. MC AE ① VISA 31 ALU v
closed 25-26 December, 1 January and August Bank Holiday – **Rest** - Seafood - (booking essential) a la carte 24.50/47.75 ♀.
◆ Festooned with photographs of actors and linked to the theatrical world since opening in 1890. Wood panels and alcove tables add famed intimacy. Accomplished seafood cooking.

XX **Rules,** 35 Maiden Lane, WC2E 7LB ⊖ *Leicester Square,* ✆ (020) 7836 5314, *info@rules.co.uk, Fax (020) 7497 1081* – ▤. MC AE ① VISA 31 ALU n
closed 4 days Christmas – **Rest** - English - (booking essential) a la carte 29.15/39.85 ♀.
◆ London's oldest restaurant boasts a fine collection of antique cartoons, drawings and paintings. Tradition continues in the menu, specialising in game from its own estate.

XX **Maggiore's,** 33 King St, WC2 8JD ⊖ *Leicester Square,* ✆ (020) 7379 9696, *enquiries@maggiores.uk.com, Fax (020) 7379 6767* – ▤ ⇔ 20. MC AE VISA 31 ALU z
closed 24-26 December and 1 January – **Rest** 17.50 (lunch) and a la carte 31.90/42.60 ♀.
◆ Walls covered with flowering branches create delightful woodland feel to rear dining area with retractable glass roof. Seriously accomplished, original, rustic French cooking.

XX **Adam Street,** 9 Adam St, WC2N 6AA ⊖ *Charing Cross,* ✆ (020) 7379 8000, *info@adamstreet.co.uk, Fax (020) 7379 1444* – ▤. MC AE ① VISA 31 ALU c
closed 25 December, Saturday, Sunday and Bank Holidays – **Rest** (lunch only) 19.50 and a la carte 28.00/38.00 ♀.
◆ Set in the striking vaults of a private members club just off the Strand. Sumptuous suede banquettes and elegantly laid tables. Well executed classic and modern English food.

XX **The Admiralty,** Somerset House, The Strand, WC2R 1LA ⊖ *Temple,* ✆ (020) 7845 4646, *Fax (020) 7845 4658* – MC AE ① VISA 32 AMU a
closed 23-26 December and dinner Sunday and Bank Holidays – **Rest** a la carte 37.00/42.40 ♀.
◆ Interconnecting rooms with bold colours and informal service contrast with its setting within the restored Georgian splendour of Somerset House. 'Cuisine de terroir'.

XX **Bank,** 1 Kingsway, Aldwych, WC2B 6XF ⊖ *Covent Garden,* ✆ (020) 7379 9797, *aldres@bankrestaurants.com, Fax (020) 7379 5070* – ▤. MC AE ① VISA 32 AMU s
closed 25 December, 1-2 January and Sunday dinner – **Rest** 16.00 (lunch) and a la carte 23.95/45.40 ♀.
◆ Ceiling decoration of hanging glass shards creates a high level of interest in this bustling converted bank. Open-plan kitchen provides an extensive array of modern dishes.

XX **Le Deuxième,** 65a Long Acre, WC2E 9JH ⊖ *Covent Garden,* ✆ (020) 7379 0033, *Fax (020) 7379 0066* – ▤. MC AE VISA 31 ALU b
closed 25-26 December – **Rest** 14.50 (lunch) and a la carte 24.00/29.50 ♀.
◆ Caters well for theatregoers: opens early, closes late. Buzzy eatery, quietly decorated in white with subtle lighting. Varied International menu: Japanese to Mediterranean.

X **Le Café du Jardin,** 28 Wellington St, WC2E 7BD ⊖ *Covent Garden,* ✆ (020) 7836 8769, *Fax (020) 7836 4123* – ▤. MC AE ① VISA 31 ALU f
closed 25-26 December – **Rest** 14.50 (lunch) and a la carte 24.00/28.50 ♀.
◆ Divided into two floors with the downstairs slightly more comfortable. Light and contemporary interior with European-influenced cooking. Ideally placed for the Opera House.

Victoria *Gtr London* – ✉ *SW1.*

ℹ *Victoria Station Forecourt.*

The Goring, 15 Beeston Pl, Grosvenor Gdns, SW1W 0JW ⊖ *Victoria,* ✆ (020) 7396 9000, *reception@goringhotel.co.uk, Fax (020) 7834 4393,* – |‡| ▤ – 50. MC AE ① VISA. 38 AIX a
Rest - British - *(closed Saturday lunch)* 28.00/42.00 ♀ – ☕ 19.00 – **65 rm** ✝211.50/340.75 – ✝✝258.50/382.00, 6 suites.
◆ Opened in 1910 as a quintessentially English hotel. The fourth generation of Goring is now at the helm. Many of the attractive rooms overlook a peaceful garden. Elegantly appointed restaurant provides memorable dining experience.

Crowne Plaza London - St James, 45 Buckingham Gate, SW1E 6AF ⊖ *St James'*
(020) 7834 6655, *sales@cplonsj.co.uk, Fax (020) 7630 7587,* – , rm,
180. *VISA*. 39 AJX
Bistro 51 : Rest 15.00/18.50 and a la carte 20.75/40.25 – (see also ***Quilon*** and ***Ban***
below) – 16.00 – **323 rm** 294.00 – 294.00, 19 suites.
◆ Built in 1897 as serviced accommodation for visiting aristocrats. Behind the impressiv
Edwardian façade lies an equally elegant interior. Quietest rooms overlook courtyar
Bright and informal café style restaurant.

Royal Horseguards, 2 Whitehall Court, SW1A 2EJ ⊖ *Charing Cross,* (020) 783
3400, *royalhorseguards@thistle.co.uk, Fax (020) 7925 2263,* , – , rm,
200. *VISA*. 31 ALV
One Twenty One Two : Rest *(closed lunch Saturday and Sunday)* 25.50 and a la cart
25.50/37.50 – 17.50 – **276 rm** 309.00 – 329.00/372.00, 4 suites.
◆ Imposing Grade I listed property in Whitehall overlooking the Thames and close to Lor
don Eye. Impressive meeting rooms. Some of the well-appointed bedrooms have rive
views. Stylish restaurant, sub-divided into intimate rooms.

51 Buckingham Gate, 51 Buckingham Gate, SW1E 6AF ⊖ *St James's,* (020) 776
7766, *info@51-buckinghamgate.co.uk, Fax (020) 7828 5909,* , – .
VISA. 39 AJX
Rest – (see ***Quilon*** and ***Bank*** below) – 17.75 –, **82 suites** 382.00/999.00.
◆ Canopied entrance leads to luxurious suites: every detail considered, every mod co
provided. Colour schemes echoed in plants and paintings. Butler and nanny service.

41 without rest., 41 Buckingham Palace Rd, SW1W 0PS ⊖ *Victoria,* (020) 7300 004
book41@rchmail.com, Fax (020) 7300 0141 – . *VISA* 38 AIX
19 rm 346.00 – 346.00/370.00, 1 suite.
◆ Discreet appearance; exudes exclusive air. Leather armchairs; bookcases line the wall
Intimate service. State-of-the-art rooms where hi-tec and fireplace merge appealingly.

The Rubens at The Palace, 39 Buckingham Palace Rd, SW1W 0PS ⊖ *Victori*
(020) 7834 6600, *bookrb@rchmail.com, Fax (020) 7828 5401* – – 90.
VISA 38 AIX
Rest *(closed lunch Saturday and Sunday)* (carvery) 19.50 – 15.00 – **170 r**
217.00/287.00 – 264.00/287.00, 2 suites.
◆ Traditional hotel with an air of understated elegance. Tastefully furnished rooms: th
Royal Wing, themed after Kings and Queens, features TVs in bathrooms. Smart carve
restaurant. Intimate, richly decorated Library restaurant has sumptuous armchairs.

Victoria Park Plaza, 239 Vauxhall Bridge Rd, SW1V 1EQ ⊖ *Victoria,* (020) 776
9999, *vppsales@parkplazahotels.co.uk, Fax (020) 7769 9998,* , –
750. *VISA*. 38 AIY
J.B.'s : Rest *(closed Sunday)* 15.00/19.00 – 16.00 – **299 rm** 215.00 – 215.00.
◆ Conveniently located for Victoria station. Spacious modern interior filled with modis
artwork. State-of-the-art meeting rooms. Well-equipped rooms boast a host of faciliti
Appealing dining room offers modern European cuisine.

Dolphin Square, Dolphin Sq, Chichester St, SW1V 3LX ⊖ *Pimlico,* (020) 7834 380
reservations@dolphinsquarehotel.co.uk, Fax (020) 7798 8735, , , , , , squas
– , rest, – 85. *VISA*. 39 AJZ
The Brasserie : Rest 16.00 and a la carte 21.95/26.20 – (see also ***Allium*** below) – 13.5
– **30 rm** 195.00 – 195.00, **118 suites** 215.00/450.00.
◆ Built in 1935 and shared with residential apartments. Art Deco influence remains in th
Clipper bar overlooking the leisure club. Spacious suites with contemporary styling. Bra
serie overlooks the swimming pool.

Jolly St Ermin's, Caxton St, SW1H 0QW ⊖ *St James's,* (020) 7222 7888, *sterm*
suk@jollyhotels.com, Fax (020) 7222 6914 – , rm, rm – 150. *VIS*
39 AKX
Cloisters Brasserie : Rest *(closed lunch Saturday and Sunday)* 22.50/26.50 and a la car
37.00/45.80 – 16.00 – **282 rm** 198.00/280.00 – 222.00/280.00, 8 suites.
◆ Ornate plasterwork to both the lobby and the balconied former ballroom are particular
striking features. Club rooms have both air conditioning and a private lounge. Grand bra
serie with ornate ceiling.

Thistle Victoria, 101 Buckingham Palace Rd, SW1W 0SJ ⊖ *Victoria,* (0870) 333912
victoria@thistle.co.uk, Fax (0870) 3339220 – , rm, – 200. *VIS*
38 AIY
Harvard Bar & Grill : Rest 15.75 and a la carte – 15.00 – **354 rm** 221.00/263.00
284.00, 3 suites.
◆ Former Victorian railway hotel with ornate front entrance and grand reception. Harva
bar particularly noteworthy. Well-furnished rooms are generally spacious. Elegantly a
pointed dining room.

City Inn, 30 John Islip St, SW1P 4DD ⊖ *Pimlico,* ✆ (020) 7630 1000, *westminster.res@cityinn.com, Fax (020) 7233 7575,* – |‡| ⇔ ▤ ✆ ♿ – 🏛 150. MO AE ⓓ VISA 39 ALY a
City Cafe : Rest 17.00 and a la carte 23.25/35.70 ♀ – ☕ 19.00 – **444 rm** ✝264.00 – ✝✝264.00, 16 suites.
• Modern hotel five minutes' walk from Westminster Abbey and Tate Britain. Well-appointed bedrooms with high-tech equipment and some with pleasant views of London. Brasserie serving modern style food next to a glass covered terrace with artwork feature.

Tophams Belgravia without rest., 28 Ebury St, SW1W 0LU ⊖ *Victoria,* ✆ (020) 7730 8147, *tophams@zolahotels.com, Fax (020) 7823 5966* – |‡| – 🏛 30. MO AE VISA. 38 AHY e
37 rm ☕ ✝85.00/130.00 – ✝✝100.00/150.00.
• Five adjoining houses creating a hotel which has a certain traditional charm. Cosy lounges, roaring fires and antique furniture aplenty. Individually decorated bedrooms. Homely basement dining room.

Winchester without rest., 17 Belgrave Rd, SW1V 1RB ⊖ *Victoria,* ✆ (020) 7828 2972, *winchesterhotel17@hotmail.com, Fax (020) 7828 5191* – 38 AIY s
18 rm ☕ ✝70.00/85.00 – ✝✝85.00/140.00.
• Behind the portico entrance one finds a friendly, well-kept private hotel. The generally spacious rooms are pleasantly appointed. Comprehensive English breakfast offered.

Express by Holiday Inn without rest., 106-110 Belgrave Rd, SW1V 2BJ ⊖ *Pimlico,* ✆ (020) 7630 8888, *info@hiexpressvictoria.co.uk, Fax (020) 7828 0441* – |‡| ⇔ ♿. MO AE ⓓ VISA. 39 AJZ c
52 rm ✝119.00 – ✝✝119.00.
• Converted Georgian terraced houses a short walk from station. Despite property's age, all rooms are stylish and modern with good range of facilities including TV movies.

XXX **Allium** (at Dolphin Square H.), Dolphin Sq, Chichester St, SW1V 3LX ⊖ *Pimlico,* ✆ (020) 7798 6888, *info@allium.co.uk, Fax (020) 7798 5685* – ▤. MO AE ⓓ VISA 39 AJZ a
closed Monday and Saturday lunch – **Rest** 23.50/29.50 and a la carte 32.20/45.70 ♀.
• A calm atmosphere prevails in this richly decorated room. Raised tables to rear with sumptuous banquettes for more privacy. Interesting and assured modern British cooking.

XXX **The Cinnamon Club,** Great Smith St, SW1P 3BU ⊖ *St James's,* ✆ (020) 7222 2555, *info@cinnamonclub.com, Fax (020) 7222 1333* – ▤ P ⇔ 50. MO AE ⓓ VISA 39 AKX c
closed Saturday lunch, Sunday and Bank Holidays – **Rest** - Indian - 22.00 (lunch) and a la carte 25.50/49.00 ♀.
• Housed in former Westminster Library: exterior has ornate detail, interior is stylish and modern. Walls are lined with books. New Wave Indian cooking with plenty of choice.

XXX **Quilon** (at Crowne Plaza London - St James H.), 45 Buckingham Gate, SW1 6AF ⊖ *St James's,* ✆ (020) 7821 1899, *Fax (020) 7828 5802* – ▤. MO AE ⓓ VISA 39 AJX e
closed Sunday and Saturday lunch – **Rest** - Indian - 15.95 (lunch) and a la carte 17.95/36.20 ♀.
• A selection of Eastern pictures adorn the walls in this smart, modern and busy restaurant. Specialising in progressive south coastal Indian cooking.

XXX **L'Incontro,** 87 Pimlico Rd, SW1W 8PH ⊖ *Sloane Square,* ✆ (020) 7730 6327, *cristiano@lincontro-restaurant.com, Fax (020) 7730 5062* – ▤. MO AE ⓓ VISA 37 AGZ u
closed Easter, 25-26 December, 1 January and Sunday lunch – **Rest** - Italian - 19.50 (lunch) and a la carte 28.50/47.50.
• Cool, understated and comfortable with attentive service. Simple, unfussy, traditional Italian cooking; set lunch good value. Private dining downstairs for 30 people.

XXX **Santini,** 29 Ebury St, SW1W 0NZ ⊖ *Victoria,* ✆ (020) 7730 4094, *info@santini-restaurant.com, Fax (020) 7730 0544* – ▤. MO AE ⓓ VISA 38 AHY v
closed 25 December, lunch Saturday, Sunday and Bank Holidays – **Rest** - Italian - 19.50 (lunch) and a la carte 34.24/56.25 ♀.
• Discreet, refined and elegant modern Italian restaurant. Assured and professional service. Extensive selection of modern dishes and a more affordable set lunch menu.

XXX **Shepherd's,** Marsham Court, Marsham St, SW1P 4LA ⊖ *Pimlico,* ✆ (020) 7834 9552, *admin@langansrestaurants.co.uk, Fax (020) 7233 6047* – ▤. MO AE ⓓ VISA 39 AKY z
closed Saturday, Sunday and Bank Holidays – **Rest** - English - (booking essential) 29.50.
• A truly English restaurant where game and traditional puddings are a highlight. Popular with those from Westminster - the booths offer a degree of privacy.

XXX ✿ **Roussillon,** 16 St Barnabas St, SW1W 8PE ⊖ *Sloane Square,* ✆ (020) 7730 5550, *alexis@roussillon.co.uk, Fax (020) 7824 8617* – ▤. MO AE VISA 38 AHZ c
closed 27 August-4 September, 25 December-3 January, Sunday and lunch Saturday-Tuesday – **Rest** - French - 30.00/45.00 ♀.
Spec. Chestnut and pheasant soup, ceps and marrow ravioli. Venison with pear, truffle and celeriac purée. Spicy soufflé of duck eggs with a maple infusion.
• Tucked away in a smart residential area. Cooking clearly focuses on the quality of the ingredients. Seasonal menu with inventive elements and a French base.

XX **The Ebury (Dining Room),** 1st Floor, 11 Pimlico Rd, SW1W 8NA ⊖ *Sloane Square* ℘ (020) 7730 6784, *info@theebury.co.uk, Fax (020) 7730 6149* – ▤. MO AE VISA 38 AHZ
closed Christmas, Sunday and Monday – **Rest** (dinner only) a la carte 24.50/33.50 ♀.
◆ Mount the spiral stair to the formal restaurant with tall windows overlooking the street. Open-plan kitchen provides set gastronomic style menu using first-class ingredients.

XX **Il Convivio,** 143 Ebury St, SW1W 9QN ⊖ *Sloane Square,* ℘ (020) 7730 4099, *comments@etruscarestaurants.com, Fax (020) 7730 4103,* 余 – ▤ ⇔14. MO AE VISA 38 AHY
closed Sunday and Bank Holidays – **Rest** - Italian - 19.50/32.50 ♀.
◆ A retractable roof provides alfresco dining to part of this comfortable and modern restaurant. Contemporary and traditional Italian menu, with home-made pasta specialities.

XX **Bank,** 45 Buckingham Gate, SW1E 6BS ⊖ *St James's,* ℘ (020) 7379 9797, *info@bankrestaurants.com, Fax (020) 7379 5070,* 余 – ▤. MO AE ⓓ VISA 39 AJX
closed Sunday and Saturday lunch – **Rest** 16.00 (lunch) and a la carte 24.75/38.40 ♀.
◆ The understated entrance belies the vibrant contemporary interior. One of Europe's longest bars has a lively atmosphere. Conservatory restaurant, modern European cooking.

XX **Boisdale,** 15 Eccleston St, SW1W 9LX ⊖ *Victoria,* ℘ (020) 7730 6922, *info@boisdale.co.uk, Fax (020) 7730 0548,* 余 – ▤. MO AE ⓓ VISA 38 AHY
closed Christmas and Sunday – **Rest** - Scottish - (live jazz at dinner) 20.50/24.30 and a la carte 28.95/47.95 ♀.
◆ Popular haunt of politicians; dark green, lacquer red panelled interior. Run by a Scot of Clanranald, hence modern British dishes with Scottish flavour: Crofter's pie.

XX **Tate Britain,** Tate Britain, Millbank, SW1P 4RG ⊖ *Pimlico,* ℘ (020) 7887 8825, *tate.restaurant@tate.org.uk, Fax (020) 7887 8902* – ▤. MO AE ⓓ VISA 39 ALY
closed 24-26 December – **Rest** (booking essential) (lunch only) 26.75 ♀.
◆ Continue your appreciation of art when lunching in this basement room decorated with original Rex Whistler murals. Forever busy, it offers modern British fare.

XX **Ken Lo's Memories of China,** 65-69 Ebury St, SW1W 0NZ ⊖ *Victoria,* ℘ (020) 7730 7734, *Fax (020) 7730 2992* – ▤. MO AE ⓓ VISA 38 AHY
closed Sunday lunch – **Rest** - Chinese - a la carte approx 28.00 ♀.
◆ An air of tranquillity pervades this traditionally furnished room. Lattice screens add extra privacy. Extensive Chinese menu: bold flavours with a clean, fresh style..

X **The Ebury (Brasserie),** Ground Floor, 11 Pimlico Rd, SW1W 8NA ⊖ *Sloane Square* ℘ (020) 7730 6784, *info@theebury.co.uk, Fax (020) 7730 6149* – ▤. MO AE VISA 38 AHZ
closed 24-26 December and 1 January – **Rest** a la carte 21.00/34.00 ♀.
◆ Victorian corner pub restaurant with walnut bar, simple tables and large seafood bar. Friendly service. Wide-ranging menu from snacks to full meals.

X **Olivo,** 21 Eccleston St, SW1W 9LX ⊖ *Victoria,* ℘ (020) 7730 2505, *maurosanna@oliveto.fsnet.co.uk, Fax (020) 7823 5377* – ▤. MO AE ⓓ VISA 39 AHY
closed lunch Saturday and Sunday and Bank Holidays – **Rest** - Italian - 19.00 (lunch) and a la carte 27.00/30.50.
◆ Rustic, informal Italian restaurant. Relaxed atmosphere provided by the friendly staff. Simple, non-fussy cuisine with emphasis on best available fresh produce.

X **La Poule au Pot,** 231 Ebury St, SW1W 8UT ⊖ *Sloane Square,* ℘ (020) 7730 7763, *Fax (020) 7259 9651,* 余 – ▤. MO AE ⓓ VISA 38 AHY
closed 25 December – **Rest** - French - 16.50 (lunch) and a la carte 25.50/41.00.
◆ The subdued lighting and friendly informality make this one of London's more romantic restaurants. Classic French menu with extensive plats du jour.

**We try to be as accurate as possible when giving room rates.
But prices are susceptible to change,
so please check rates when booking.**

ONGBRIDGE *Warks. – see Warwick.*

ONG CRENDON *Bucks.* 503 504 R 28 – *pop.* 2 383 – ✉ *Aylesbury.*
London 50 – Aylesbury 11 – Oxford 15.

Angel with rm, Bicester Rd, HP18 9EE, ☎ (01844) 208268, *Fax (01844) 202497*, – rm, P. MC VISA.
closed 1 January – **Rest** *(closed Sunday dinner)* 17.95 (lunch) and a la carte 25.00/35.00 ♀ – **3 rm** ☐ ✝65.00 – ✝✝85.00.
◆ Part 16C building with a pubby feel - leather furnished lounge bar, tiled floors and low ceilings. Seasonally changing menus with fresh seafood a speciality. Stylish rooms.

ONGHORSLEY *Northd.* 501 502 O 18 – *see Morpeth.*

ONG MELFORD *Suffolk* 504 W 27 *Great Britain G.* – *pop.* 2 734.
See : *Melford Hall★ AC.*
London 62 – Cambridge 34 – Colchester 18 – Ipswich 24.

Black Lion, The Green, CO10 9DN, ☎ (01787) 312356, *enquiries@blacklionhotel.net*, *Fax (01787) 374557*, – P. MC AE VISA
Rest a la carte 22.70/27.20 ♀ – **9 rm** ☐ ✝90.50/113.50 – ✝✝170.00, 1 suite.
◆ 17C inn overlooking the village green and beyond to the Tudor Melford Hall. Individual rooms have a mix of furnishings with much use of antique pine. Stylish restaurant with walled garden terrace.

Chimneys, Hall St, CO10 9JR, ☎ (01787) 379806, *sam.chalmers@chimneyslongmelford.co.uk*, *Fax (01787) 312294* – MC AE VISA
closed 25 December and Sunday – **Rest** (lunch booking essential) 18.50 and a la carte 30.15/40.25 **s.** ♀.
◆ Part 16C timbered cottage in village centre. Something of a quaint country atmosphere amidst exposed beams. British and Continental food with international touches.

Scutchers, Westgate St, CO10 9DP, on A 1092 ☎ (01787) 310200, *Fax (01787) 375700* – MC AE VISA
closed Christmas, 10 days March, 10 days August, Sunday and Monday – **Rest** a la carte 23.00/34.00 ♀.
◆ Former medieval Hall House now contains an informal and unpretentious restaurant serving a range of creative modern dishes using good quality ingredients.

ONGRIDGE *Lancs.* 502 M 22 – *pop.* 7 491.
London 241 – Blackburn 12 – Burnley 18.

The Longridge Restaurant, 104-106 Higher Rd, PR3 3SY, Northeast : ½ m. by B 5269 following signs for Jeffrey Hill ☎ (01772) 784969, *longridge@heathcotes.co.uk*, *Fax (01772) 785713* – 18. MC AE VISA
closed 1-2 January, Saturday lunch and Monday – **Rest** 17.00 (lunch) and a la carte 21.50/34.50 ♀.
Spec. Black pudding and blue cheese fritters, apple and air-dried bacon. Breast of duck with buttered kale, fondant potato, glazed plums and sage. Bread and butter pudding, clotted cream and apricots.
◆ Contemporary styling in a former pub with precise, modern cooking that proudly and winningly boasts a decidedly Lancastrian bias throughout the menus.

Thyme, 1-3 Inglewhite Rd, PR3 3SR, ☎ (01772) 786888, *Fax (01772) 786888* – . MC AE VISA
closed first week January and Monday – **Rest** 9.95 (lunch) and a la carte 21.95/26.85 **s.** ♀.
◆ Modern restaurant near roundabout; wooden floors and modern lighting; artwork on the walls. Locally sourced produce used as much as possible. Good value, especially at lunch.

at Knowle Green *East : 2¼ m. by A 5269 on B 6243 – ✉ Longridge.*

Oak Lea without rest., Clitheroe Rd, PR3 2YS, East : ½ m. on B 6243 ☎ (01254) 878486, *tandm.mellor@amserve.com*, *Fax (01254) 878486*, – P.
closed 25 and 31 December – **3 rm** ☐ ✝25.00/35.00 – ✝✝50.00.
◆ Neat little guesthouse in the heart of the Ribble Valley with fine all-round views. Conservatory with access to mature garden. Pleasantly furnished bedrooms.

LONG SUTTON *Somerset* 503 L 30 – ✉ *Langport.*
London 132.5 – Bridgwater 16 – Yeovil 10.

The Devonshire Arms with rm, TA10 9LP, ✆ (01458) 241271, *mail@thedevonsh earms.com, Fax (01458) 241037,* , – P. VISA
Rest *(closed 25 December)* a la carte 18.40/25.00 – **9 rm** ♀55.00/70.00 – ♀♀70.00/120.00.
◆ 17C ivy-clad ex-hunting lodge on the green. Sun-trap terrace and walled garden. Modern sofa-strewn interior in tune with refined, flavoursome menus. Boldly appointed rooms.

LONGTOWN *Cumbria* 501 502 L 18.
London 326 – Carlisle 9 – Newcastle upon Tyne 61.

Bessiestown Farm, Catlowdy, CA6 5QP, Northeast : 8 m. by Netherby St on B 63 ✆ (01228) 577219, *info@bessiestown.co.uk, Fax (01228) 577019,* , – P. VISA.
closed 25 December – **Rest** (by arrangement) 16.00 – **6 rm** ♀42.50 – ♀♀65.00/120.00
◆ Comfortable, warm accommodation in homely, modern farmhouse conversion in rural location on a working farm. Décor has a traditional British tone, well-kept throughout. Home-cooked food served in airy dining room.

Undecided between two equivalent establishments?
Within each category, establishments are classified
in our order of preference.

LOOE *Cornwall* 503 G 32 *The West Country G. – pop. 5 280.*
See : Town★ – Monkey Sanctuary★ AC.
Bin Down ✆ (01503) 240239 – Whitsand Bay Hotel, Portwrinkle, Torpoint ✆ (0150 230276.
The Guildhall, Fore St ✆ (01503) 262072.
London 264 – Plymouth 23 – Truro 39.

Barclay House, St Martins Rd, East Looe, PL13 1LP, East : ½ m. by A 387 on B 32 ✆ (01503) 262929, *info@barclayhouse.co.uk, Fax (01503) 262632,* ←, – P. AE VISA.
closed Christmas and 2 weeks mid January – **Rest** – (see ***The Restaurant*** below) – **10 r** ♀40.00/97.50 – ♀♀100.00/150.00.
◆ Smart but relaxed and welcoming hotel near harbour. Gardens overlooking estua Snug sitting room and bar. Individually decorated bedrooms.

Bucklawren Farm without rest., St Martin-by-Looe, PL13 1NZ, Northeast : 3½ by A 387 and B 3253 turning right onto single track road signposted to Monkey Sanctua ✆ (01503) 240738, *bucklawren@btopenworld.com, Fax (01503) 240481,* ←, , – VISA.
March-October – **6 rm** ♀26.00/40.00 – ♀♀52.00/59.00.
◆ Characterful farmhouse within 500 acre working farm. Large conservatory overloo pleasant garden. Spotlessly kept interior with simple, country house-style bedrooms.

St Aubyn's without rest., Marine Drive, Hannafore, West Looe, PL13 2DH, by Quay ✆ (01503) 264351, *welcome@staubyns.co.uk, Fax (01503) 263670,* ←, – P. VISA
Easter-October – **7 rm** ♀35.00 – ♀♀82.00/90.00.
◆ Victorian house set out from the town centre in a location which affords many views Looe Bay and English Channel. Personally run with spacious bedrooms.

The Restaurant (at Barclay House), St Martin's Rd, East Looe, PL13 1LP, East : ½ m. A 387 on B 3253 ✆ (01503) 262929, *Fax (01503) 262632,* ←, – P. AE VISA
closed Christmas, 2 weeks mid January and Sunday – **Rest** (dinner only) 30.00 ♀.
◆ Extensive views of estuary. Matching mustard coloured walls and table cloths. Attenti well-informed service. Eclectic menu using fresh local produce, particularly seafood.

Bucklawren Granary, St Martin-by-Looe, PL13 1NZ, Northeast : 3½ m. by A 387 a B 3253 turning right onto single track road signposted to Monkey Sanctuary ✆ (0150 240778, *bucklawren@onetel.com, Fax (01503) 240898* – P. VISA
closed 2 weeks January and Wednesday – **Rest** (dinner only and Sunday lunch)/dinner a carte 20.95/27.40 ♀.
◆ Converted barn with central stairs leading up from spacious restaurant to the bar. Me of modern and classic dishes using fresh local produce.

Trawlers on the Quay, The Quay, East Looe, PL13 1AH, (01503) 263593, *info@trawlersrestaurant.co.uk* – . VISA
closed Sunday and Monday – **Rest** (dinner only) 26.00.
◆ Personally run restaurant in a pretty setting on the quay. Faux marble table tops; clean, neutral décor. Balanced menu of local seafood and meat dishes. Home-made bread, too.

at Talland Bay *Southwest : 4 m. by A 387 – Looe.*

Talland Bay, PL13 2JB, (01503) 272667, *reception@tallandbayhotel.co.uk, Fax (01503) 272940*, <, heated, – rest, P. VISA
Terrace : **Rest** (bar lunch)/dinner 32.50 **s.** – **20 rm** (dinner included) 105.00/155.00 – 190.00/230.00, 2 suite.
◆ 16C house in secluded position with lovely gardens. Well chosen fabrics and furniture create a warm and comfortable environment. Many rooms with sea views. Modern fine dining from interesting menu.

ORTON *Cumbria* 502 K 20 – *see Cockermouth.*

OUGHBOROUGH *Leics.* 502 503 504 Q 25 – *pop. 55 258.*
Lingdale, Joe Moore's Lane, Woodhouse Eaves (01509) 890703.
Town Hall, Market Pl (01509) 218113.
London 117 – Birmingham 41 – Leicester 11 – Nottingham 15.

The Old Manor without rest., 11-14 Sparrow Hill, LE11 1BT, off Baxter Gate (01509) 211228, *bookings@oldmanor.com, Fax (01509) 211128* – . AE VISA.
10.50 – **8 rm** 92.00 – 120.00.
◆ Charming part 15C house close to a church and away from the town centre. Spacious breakfast room with Hispanic feel and characterful bedrooms.

at Burton-on-the-Wolds *East : 3¾ m. by A 60 on B 676 – Loughborough.*

Lang's, Horse Leys Farm, LE12 5TQ, East : 1 m. on B 676 (01509) 880980, *langsrestaurant@amserve.net, Fax (01509) 889018* – P. VISA
closed Sunday dinner and Monday – **Rest** 15.50 (lunch) and a la carte 21.00/30.00.
◆ Converted barn in a rural location. Snug, simple and homely rustic feel. Good, tasty and unpretentious menu built around a strong seasonal foundation.

at Quorndon *Southeast : 3 m. by A 6 – Loughborough.*

Quorn Country H., 66 Leicester Rd, LE12 8BB, (01509) 415050, *Fax (01509) 405557*, – rm, rm, P – 300. AE VISA.
Shires : **Rest** *(closed Saturday lunch)* 23.50 and a la carte 22.00/39.70 – ***Orangery :*** **Rest** *(closed Saturday lunch)* 23.50 and a la carte 22.50/39.20 – 10.95 – **28 rm** 110.00/135.00 – 125.00/135.00, 2 suites.
◆ Personally run hotel based around a listed 17C building, once a private club. Very comfortable and appealingly traditional, individually decorated bedrooms. Classic, intimate, traditionally styled Shires. Spacious Orangery features hanging plants and rural art

Quorn Grange, 88 Wood Lane, LE12 8DB, Southeast : ¾ m. (01509) 412167, *mail@quorngrangehotel.co.uk, Fax (01509) 415621*, – P – 100. AE VISA.
closed 1 week Christmas – **Rest** (bar lunch)/dinner 23.00 and a la carte 25.75/27.20 **s.** – **38 rm** 85.00 – 105.00.
◆ Spacious 18th century building in landscaped garden. Owned by a media union and used, though not exclusively, for union business. Agreeable, uniformly decorated bedrooms. Bright conservatory dining room with pleasant garden views.

at Belton *West : 6 m. by A 6 on B 5324 – Loughborough.*

The Queen's Head, 2 Long St, LE12 9TP, (01530) 222359, *enquiries@thequeenshead.org, Fax (01530) 224860*, , – P 24. VISA
Rest (residents only Sunday and Monday dinner, restricted menu) 15.00 and a la carte 15.00/30.00 – **6 rm** 60.00 – 100.00.
◆ Early 19C pub, with extension, now embraces a sleek modernity. Restaurant boasts chocolate suede chairs. Serious dining menus evolve constantly. Modish, bright, airy rooms.

The award is the crème de la crème. This is awarded to restaurants which are really worth travelling miles for!

LOUTH *Lincs.* 502 504 U 23 – *pop. 15 930.*
The New Market Hall, off Cornmarket ☏ (01507) 609289.
London 156 – Boston 34 – Great Grimsby 17 – Lincoln 26.

Kenwick Park, LN11 8NR, Southeast : 2 ¼ m. by B 1520 on A 157 ☏ (0150 608806, *enquiries@kenwick-park.co.uk, Fax (01507) 608027*, squash – 250. MO AE VISA
Rest 24.95 – **34 rm** ☕ ★95.00/105.00 – ★★100.00/120.00.
◆ Privately owned Victorian house in rural location. Focus is on very comprehensive a up-to-date leisure facilities. Uniform rooms to a high standard. Popular for weddin Conservatory dining room filled with natural light.

Brackenborough Arms, Cordeaux Corner, Brackenborough, LN11 0SZ, North : 2 by A 16 ☏ (01507) 609169, *info@brackenborough.co.uk, Fax (01507) 609413* – rm, P – 35. MO AE VISA.
closed 25-26 December – ***Signature :*** Rest a la carte 18.95/27.95 – **24 rm** ★58.95/70.00 – ★★70.00/77.00.
◆ Family owned hotel run with a warm and personal style. Public areas have a relaxed fe and bedrooms are spacious, individually designed and boast a host of extras. Home dining.

The Beaumont, 66 Victoria Rd, LN11 0BX, by Eastgate off Ramsgate Rd ☏ (0150 605005, *beaumonthotel@aol.com, Fax (01507) 607768* – P. MO AE VISA
Rest *(closed Sunday)* 16.95 and a la carte 16.85/28.40 s. – **16 rm** ☕ ★58.00/78.00 ★★88.00.
◆ Conveniently located close to the town centre. A comfy, settled atmosphere in t public areas and especially the bar. Uniformly fitted, comfortable bedrooms. Cosy dini room.

The sun's out – let's eat al fresco! Look for a terrace:

LOVINGTON *Somerset* 503 M 30 – *see Castle Cary.*

LOWER HARDRES *Kent* 504 X 30 – *see Canterbury.*

LOWER ODDINGTON *Glos. – see Stow-on-the-Wold.*

LOWER QUINTON *Warks. – see Stratford-upon-Avon.*

LOWER SHIPLAKE *Oxon. – see Henley-on-Thames.*

LOWER SLAUGHTER *Glos.* 503 504 O 28 – *see Bourton-on-the-Water.*

LOWER SWELL *Glos. – see Stow-on-the-Wold.*

LOWER WHITLEY *Ches.* 502 M 24.
London 199 – Liverpool 25 – Manchester 24 – Warrington 7.

Chetwode Arms, Street Lane, WA4 4EN, ☏ (01925) 730203, – P. MO VISA
closed 25 December and 1 January – **Rest** a la carte 20.00/35.00.
◆ Redbrick 17C coaching inn with lawned garden. Variety of rooms and snugs with br and panelling. Large menus and blackboard specials of classic British dishes.

LOWESTOFT *Suffolk* 504 Z 26 *Great Britain G. – pop. 62 907.*
Env. : *The Broads*★.
18, 9 *Rookery Park, Carlton Colville ☏ (01502) 509190.*
East Point Pavillion, Royal Plain ☏ (01502) 533600, touristinfo@wavernly.gov.uk.
London 116 – Ipswich 43 – Norwich 30.

Premier Travel Inn, 249 Yarmouth Rd, NR32 4AA, North : 2½ m. on A 12 ☎ (01502) 572441 – rm, P. VISA.
Rest (grill rest.) – **41 rm** 48.95 – 48.95.
◆ Simply furnished and brightly decorated bedrooms with ample work space. Family rooms with sofa beds. Ideal for corporate or leisure travel.

at Oulton Broad *West : 2 m. by A 146 – ✉ Lowestoft.*

Ivy House, Ivy Lane, NR33 8HY, Southwest : 1½ m. by A 146 ☎ (01502) 501353, *micheline@ivyhousecountryhotel.co.uk, Fax (01502) 501539,* – P – 50. VISA
closed 22 December-5 January – **Rest** – (see ***The Crooked Barn*** below) – **19 rm** 89.00/92.00 – 119.00/159.00.
◆ Converted farm in rural seclusion down an unmade lane. Well kept gardens and grounds. Spacious bedrooms, in converted barns, have bright, fresh décor.

The Crooked Barn (at Ivy House), Ivy Lane, NR33 8HY, Southwest : 1½ m. by A 146 ☎ (01502) 501353, *micheline@ivyhousecountryhotel.co.uk, Fax (01502) 501539* – P. VISA
closed 22 December-5 January – **Rest** 12.95/25.00 and a la carte 24.85/38.85 **s.**
◆ Thatched part 18C former hay loft, the focus of Ivy House Farm's characterful setting. Delightful crooked beamed interior. Modern British fare using fresh, local produce.

"Rest" appears in red for establishments with a ✿ (star) or (Bib Gourmand).

LOW FELL *Tyne and Wear – see Gateshead.*

LOWICK *Northants.*
London 92 – Leicester 39 – Peterborough 23.

Snooty Fox, Main St, NN14 3BH, ☎ (01832) 733434, *thesnootyfox@btinternet.com, Fax (01832) 733931* – P. VISA
closed dinner 25-26 December and 1 January – **Rest** 13.95 (lunch) and a la carte 18.50/30.00 ♀.
◆ Locally renowned stone-built village inn. Main bar with appealing blackboard menu and elegant dining room. Noteworthy, accomplished rotisserie.

LUDLOW *Shrops.* 503 L 26 *Great Britain G.* – *pop. 9 548.*
See : *Town★* **Z** – *Castle★ AC – Feathers Hotel★ – St Laurence's Parish Church★ (Misericords★)* **S.**
Exc. : *Stokesay Castle★ AC, NW : 6½ m. by A 49.*
Castle St ☎ (01584) 875053.
London 162 – Birmingham 39 – Hereford 24 – Shrewsbury 29.

Plan on next page

Overton Grange, Hereford Rd, SY8 4AD, South : 1¾ m. by B 4361 ☎ (01584) 873500, *info@overtongrangehotel.com, Fax (01584) 873524,* – P – 100. VISA.
Rest (booking essential for non-residents) (lunch by arrangement) 29.50/39.50 ♀ – **14 rm** 95.00/130.00 – 130.00/190.00.
◆ Edwardian country house with good views of the surrounding countryside. Comfortable lounges. Attentive service and well-kept, individual rooms. Accomplished, inventive modern cuisine with a French base.

Dinham Hall, Dinham, SY8 1EJ, ☎ (01584) 876464, *info@dinhamhall.co.uk, Fax (01584) 876019,* – rest, P – 40. VISA Z b
Rest *(closed Monday lunch)* 35.00 ♀ – **12 rm** 110.00/210.00 – 140.00/240.00.
◆ 18C manor house, with pretty walled garden, situated by Ludlow Castle in the heart of charming medieval town. Period furnishings and individual rooms. Crisp, bright décor and creative menu.

Bromley Court without rest., 73-74 Lower Broad St, SY8 1PH, ☎ (0845) 0656192, – . VISA Z e
minimum stay 2 nights at weekend – **3 rm** 95.00 – 115.00.
◆ Delightful Tudor cottage converted to provide three well-furnished suites of bed and living room: high quality comfort. Breakfast and check-in opposite at 73 Lower Broad St.

LUDLOW

Stokesay Castle B 4361 *SHREWSBURY, (A 49)*

HEREFORD B 4361 (A 49)

XXX ✿✿ **Hibiscus** (Bosi), 17 Corve St, SY8 1DA, ℘ (01584) 872325, *Fax (01584) 874024* – ⇝ P. C
VISA
closed 23 December-16 January, first 2 weeks August, Sunday, Monday and lunch Tuesd
– **Rest** (booking essential) 25.00/45.00 s. ♀.
Spec. Beetroot and orange tart, feta cheese sorbet and girolles. Roast rack of veal, cou gette and coriander purée, black olive & gherkin sauce. Iced sweet olive oil parfait, cor pote of cherries.
◆ Two dining rooms, one with 17C oak panelling and the other with exposed stone wa
Precise cooking with some original and innovative touches; attentive formal service.

ENGLAND

Mr Underhill's at Dinham Weir (Bradley) with rm, Dinham Bridge, SY8 1EH, (01584) 874431, ... – ... Z f
closed 1 week January and 1 week July – **Rest** *(closed Monday-Tuesday)* (booking essential) (set menu only) (dinner only) 40.00 – **7 rm** 100.00/150.00 – 120.00/170.00, 2 suites.

Spec. Foie gras custard with sweetcorn cream and sesame jelly. Monkfish with cep noodles, cep and beef glaze. Caramelised oatmeal parfait with Drambuie syrup, flapjack wafer.

◆ Period house on riverside, away from town centre. Daily set menu: unfussy, simple cooking with good flavours, prepared with skill. Smart bedrooms with wood and inlay décor.

Koo, 127 Old St, SY8 1NU, (01584) 878462, *Fax (01584) 878 462* – VISA Z a
closed 25-26 December, 1 January, Sunday and Monday – **Rest** - Japanese - (light lunch)/dinner 18.95/22.95.

◆ Friendly atmosphere in a simply styled interior decorated with banners and artefacts. Good value meals from a regularly changing menu of authentic and tasty Japanese dishes.

Cleedownton *Northeast : 6¾ m. by A 4117 – Y – on B 4364 – Ludlow.*

Lower House Farm, SY8 3EH, (01584) 823648, *gsblack@talk21.com*, – ...
Rest (by arrangement) 20.00 – **3 rm** 70.00 – 70.00.

◆ Early 17C farmhouse with bags of rustic character: a peaceful retreat with comfy, timbered lounge. Flagstoned dining room offers home-cooked menus. Characterful rooms.

Woofferton *South : 4 m. by B 4361 – Z – and A 49 – Ludlow.*

Ravenscourt Manor without rest., SY8 4AL, on A 49 (01584) 711905, *ravenscourt manor@amserve.com, Fax (01584) 711905*, – ...
closed 25-26 December and mid January-mid March – **3 rm** 45.00/50.00 – 65.00/70.00.

◆ Characterful black and white timbered 16C manor house in two and a half acres of lawned gardens. Friendly welcome; comfy lounge. Individually decorated, period style rooms.

Brimfield *South : 4½ m. by B 4361 – Z – and A 49 – Ludlow.*

The Marcle without rest., SY8 4NE, (01584) 711459, *marcle@supanet.com, Fax (01584) 711459*, – ...
March - November – **3 rm** 50.00/70.00 – 70.00.

◆ 16C cottage with attractive gardens in the heart of the village. Characterful feel to the interior with its beams and open fires. Compact, comfortable bedrooms. Period dining room; home-grown herbs to the fore.

Roebuck Inn with rm, SY8 4NE, (01584) 711230, *Fax (01584) 711654*, – ... VISA.
Rest a la carte 19.00/31.50 – **3 rm** 50.00 – 80.00.

◆ Country pub filled with rustic objects and curios. Well prepared, locally sourced, traditional-style food in bar and formal dining room. Warm, homely bedrooms.

Orleton *South : 5½ m. by B 4361 – Y – Ludlow.*

Line Farm without rest., Tunnel Lane, SY8 4HY, Southeast : ¾ m. (01568) 780400, *linefarm@lineone.net, Fax (01568) 780995*, – ...
closed Christmas and New Year – **3 rm** 60.00 – 60.00/65.00.

◆ Purpose-built house in a relaxing location on a working farm. Pleasant views across a pretty garden to open countryside from each of the comfortable bedrooms.

Bromfield *Northwest : 2½ m. on A 49 – Y – Ludlow.*

The Clive with rm, SY8 2JR, (01584) 856565, *info@theclive.co.uk, Fax (01584) 856661*, – ... – 40. VISA
closed 25-26 December – **Rest** 25.00 and a la carte 24.15/29.40 – **15 rm** 50.00 – 100.00.

◆ Large converted pub with modern décor in vivid colours. Restaurant, bar, café and bistro areas. Menu of internationally inspired traditional dishes. Very good modern bedrooms.

LUTON

Luton 504 S 28 Great Britain G. – pop. 185 543.

See : *Luton Hoo★ (Wernher Collection★★) ACX.*

Exc. : *Whipsnade Wild Animal Park★, West : 8 m. by B 489, signed from M 1 (junction 9) and M 25 (junction 21)X.*

Stockwood Park, London Rd (01582) 413704, X – South Beds, Warden Hill Rd (01582) 575201.

Luton International Airport : (01582) 405100, E : 1½ m. X – **Terminal** : Luton Bus Station.

Central Library, St George's Sq (01582) 401579.

London 35 – Cambridge 36 – Ipswich 93 – Oxford 45 – Southend-on-Sea 63.

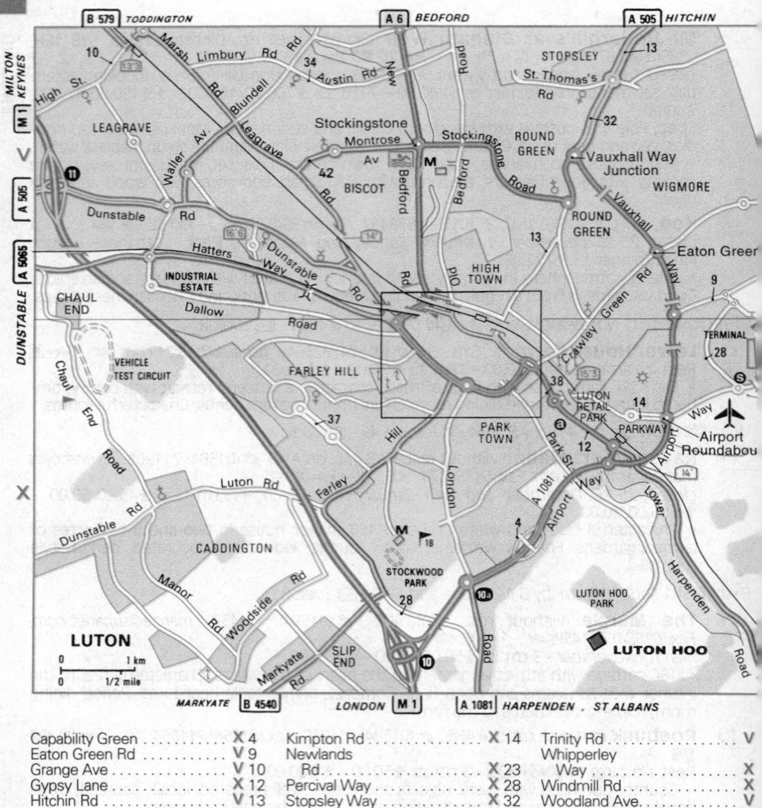

Capability Green . . . . . . X 4	Kimpton Rd . . . . . . X 14	Trinity Rd V
Eaton Green Rd . . . . . . V 9	Newlands Rd. . . . . . X 23	Whipperley Way X
Grange Ave . . . . . . V 10	Percival Way . . . . . . X 28	Windmill Rd. X
Gypsy Lane . . . . . . X 12	Stopsley Way . . . . . . X 32	Woodland Ave. V
Hitchin Rd . . . . . . V 13		

St Lawrence, 40A Guildford St, LU1 2PA, ℘ (01582) 482119, *reservations@hotelstlawrence.co.uk, Fax (01582) 482818* – ⇔, ▤ rest, ✆. MO AE ◑ VISA. ✂ Y
closed 24 December-2 January
Fields **: Rest** *(closed Sunday, lunch Saturday and Bank Holidays)* a la carte 21.00/26.00 ♀
28 rm ☕ ✝72.00/77.00 – ✝✝82.00.
◆ Red-brick hotel next to the station. A former hat factory; some decorate the lounge wall. Elsewhere, modern leather prevails. Refurbished bedrooms completed early in 2005.. Informal restaurant boasts vivid colours and modern, Mediterranean inspired dishes.

Premier Travel Inn, Osborne Rd, LU1 3HJ, Southeast : ½ m. on A 505 ℘ (01582) 417654, *Fax (01582) 421900* – |‡|, ⇔ rm, ▤ rest, ♿ P – 🔺 80. MO AE ◑ VISA. ✂ X
Rest (grill rest.) – **129 rm** ✝53.95/53.95 – ✝✝59.95/59.95.
◆ Well-proportioned modern bedrooms, suitable for business and family stopovers, designed with practicality and price in mind. Grill restaurant adjacent.

at Luton Airport *East : 2 m. by A 505 –* ✉ *Luton.*

Express by Holiday Inn without rest., 2 Percival Way, LU2 9GP, ℘ (0870) 4448920, *lutonairport@expressbyholidayinn.net, Fax (0870) 4448930* – |‡| ⇔ ▤ ♿ P – 🔺 50. MO AE ◑ VISA X
147 rm ✝89.95 – ✝✝89.95.
◆ Purpose-built hotel handily placed beside the airport. Inclusive contenental breakfast plus 24 hour snack menus. Rooms are modern and well-equipped.

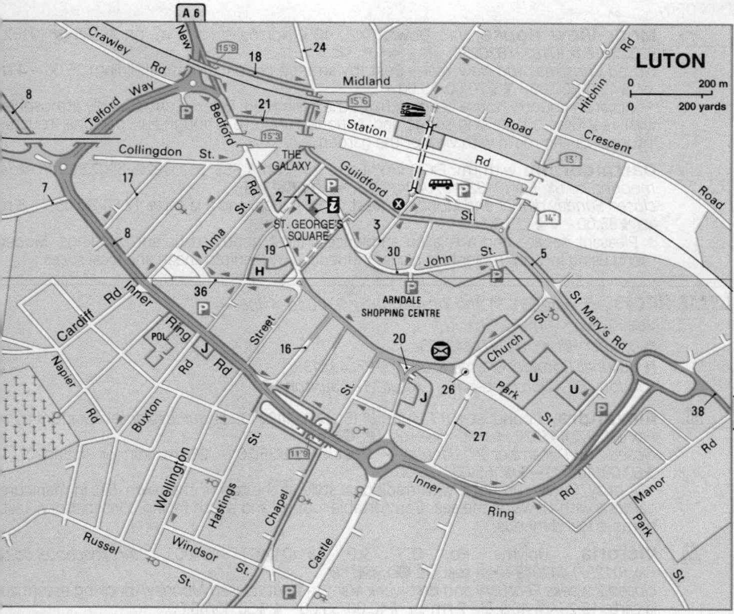

LUTON

Y

Z

The red symbol? This denotes the very essence of peace – only the sound of birdsong first thing in the morning ...

LUTON AIRPORT *Luton* 504 S 28 – *see Luton.*

LUXBOROUGH *Somerset* 503 J 30 – ✉ *Watchet.*

London 205 – Exeter 42 – Minehead 9 – Taunton 25.

Royal Oak Inn of Luxborough with rm, Exmoor National Park, TA23 0SH, ✆ (01984) 640319, *info@theroyaloakinnluxborough.co.uk, Fax (01984) 641561*, – P. MC VISA

closed 25 December – **Rest** a la carte 15.00/25.00 – **12 rm** ★55.00/65.00 – ★★85.00.

◆ Rural inn with bags of character and lots of real ale. Home-cooked food, including fresh fish and game, served in numerous beamed rooms. Tastefully furnished bedrooms.

LYDDINGTON *Rutland – see Uppingham.*

LYDFORD *Devon* 503 H 32 *The West Country G.* – *pop. 1 734* – ✉ *Okehampton.*

See : *Village*★★.

Env. : *Dartmoor National Park*★★.

London 234 – Exeter 33 – Plymouth 25.

ENGLAND

Moor View House, Vale Down, EX20 4BB, Northeast : 1 ½ m. on A 386 ✆ (0182 820220, *Fax (01822) 820220*, – [P].
closed Christmas and New Year – **Rest** (by arrangement) (communal dining) 25.00 – **4 r** ☕ ★45.00/50.00 – ★★70.00/75.00.
◆ Victorian country house set back from the main road. Relaxed and friendly atmosphe with real fires, piano sing-songs and antique furniture. Thoughtful, personal touche Informal dining room with view of the garden.

Dartmoor Inn with rm, EX20 4AY, East : 1 m. on A 386 ✆ (01822) 820221, *info@da moorinn.co.uk, Fax (01822) 820494*, – [P]. VISA
closed Sunday dinner and Monday – **Rest** 17.50 (lunch) and a la carte 17.50/30.00 – **3 r** ☕ ★85.00 – ★★125.00.
◆ Pleasant service and a relaxed ambience amidst gently rustic surroundings. Mode menu using local ingredients in dishes influenced by Mediterranean and local styles.

LYME REGIS *Dorset* 503 L 31 *The West Country G.* – *pop. 4 406.*
See : *Town*★ – *The Cobb*★.
Timber Hill ✆ *(01297) 442963.*
Guildhall Cottage, Church St ✆ *(01297) 442138.*
London 160 – Dorchester 25 – Exeter 31 – Taunton 27.

Alexandra, Pound St, DT7 3HZ, ✆ (01297) 442010, *enquiries@hotelalexandra.co.u Fax (01297) 443229*, ≤, – rest, [P]. VISA
closed 18 December-27 January – **Rest** 16.50/26.50 – **26 rm** (dinner included) ★60.00/100.00 – ★★165.00/175.00.
◆ A busy, family run hotel with traditional style at the top of the town. Set in manicur gardens with views of the sea. Comfortable lounge and south facing conservatory. Tast home-cooked menus.

Victoria, Uplyme Rd, DT7 3LP, ✆ (01297) 444801, *info@vichotel.co.u Fax (01297) 442949* – rest, [P]. VISA.
closed 2 weeks February and first week March – **Rest** *(closed Monday)* (booking essential la carte 15.25/24.40 **s.** – **7 rm** ☕ ★40.00/55.00 – ★★50.00/65.00.
◆ Former Victorian pub on the outskirts of town. Still something of a pubby feel to t public areas. Comfortable rooms; some have views over Lyme Bay and the town. Form dining room and brightly coloured bar.

LYMINGTON *Hants.* 503 504 P 31 – *pop. 14 227.*
to the Isle of Wight (Yarmouth) (Wightlink Ltd) frequent services daily (30 mn).
St Barb Museum & Visitor Centre, New St ✆ *(01590) 689000.*
London 103 – Bournemouth 18 – Southampton 19 – Winchester 32.

Passford House, Mount Pleasant Lane, Mount Pleasant, SO41 8LS, Northwes 2 m. by A 337 and Sway Rd ✆ (01590) 682398, *sales@passfordhousehotel.co.u Fax (01590) 683494*, ≤, , , heated, , , , – [P] – 80. VISA
Rest 32.50 (dinner) and lunch a la carte 34.00/42.50 **s.** – **50 rm** ☕ ★85.00/120.00 ★★350.00.
◆ Classically decorated mansion on edge of New Forest in 10 acres of peaceful groun accommodating various leisure activities. Smart, comfortable bedrooms with garde views. Elegant dining with pleasant vista.

Stanwell House, 15 High St, SO41 9AA, ✆ (01590) 677123, *sales@stanwellhouse tel.co.uk, Fax (01590) 677756*, – rm, – 40. VISA
Bistro : **Rest** a la carte 20.85/29.85 – **23 rm** ☕ ★55.00/85.00 – ★★85.00/170.00, 5 suite
◆ Privately owned hotel with individual style in Georgian building. Rich décor verges on t gothic with sumptuous silks, crushed velvets and an eclectic mix of furniture. Atmospher Bistro in dramatic, rich colours.

The Mill at Gordleton, Silver St, Hordle, SO41 6DJ, Northwest : 3 ½ m. by A 337 an Sway Rd ✆ (01590) 682219, *info@themillatgordleton.co.uk, Fax (01590) 683073*, – rest, [P]. VISA.
closed 25 December – **Rest** *(closed Sunday dinner)* a la carte 23.25/34.90 – **6 rm** ★85.00 – ★★120.00, 1 suite.
◆ Delightfully located part 17C water mill on edge of New Forest, in well-kept garden Comfortable, traditionally styled interior with a pubby bar and clean-lined rooms. Terra available for alfresco dining.

Efford Cottage without rest., Everton, SO41 0JD, West : 2 m. on A 337 ✆ (0159 642315, *effordcottage@aol.com, Fax (01590) 641030* – [P]
3 rm ☕ ★60.00 – ★★80.00.
◆ Family run guesthouse in Georgian cottage with garden. Traditional-style interiors in clude a spacious drawing room with large windows and well-equipped bedrooms.

XX **Wistaria** with rm, 32 St Thomas St, SO41 9NE, ✆ (01590) 688090, *enquiries@wistaria.org.uk, Fax (01590) 677010* – ⇔ ✆ P. MC AE ◑ VISA
Rest 10.50/13.50 (lunch) and a la carte 21.20/30.90 – **3 rm** ☕ ☨60.00/75.00 – ☨☨80.00/95.00.
◆ Elegant Grade II listed Georgian town house with wisteria clad walls. Many original features in situ. Intimate dining room serving tasty, modish dishes. Luxurious bedrooms.

X **Egan's,** 24 Gosport St, SO41 9BG, ✆ (01590) 676165, *Fax (01590) 670133* – ⇔. MC VISA
closed 26 December-5 January, Monday and Sunday except Sunday dinner before Bank Holiday – **Rest** - Bistro - (booking essential) 12.95 (lunch) and dinner a la carte 22.45/30.85.
◆ Bustling bistro style restaurant near the High Street. Warm yellow walls give it a Mediterranean feel. Pleasant, efficient service. Fresh, simple cooking with modern elements.

t Downton *West : 3 m. on A 337* – ✉ *Lymington.*

⌂ **The Olde Barn** without rest., Christchurch Rd, SO41 0LA, East : ½ m. on A 337 ✆ (01590) 644939, *julie@theoldbarn.co.uk, Fax (01590) 644939* – ⇔ P. MC VISA. ⚔
3 rm ☕ ☨45.00/60.00 – ☨☨60.00.
◆ Unsurprisingly, a converted 17C barn with large, chintzy lounge and wood burner. Some bedrooms in barn annex: a mix of modern style and exposed brick, all spotlessly clean.

YNDHURST *Hants.* 503 504 P 31 *Great Britain G.*

Env. : *New Forest★★ (Bolderwood Ornamental Drive★★, Rhinefield Ornamental Drive★★).*

18, 9 Dibden Golf Centre, Main Rd ✆ (023) 8084 5596 – 18 New Forest, Southampton Rd ✆ (023) 8028 2752.

ℹ New Forest Museum & Visitor Centre, Main Car Park ✆ (023) 8028 2269.

London 95 – Bournemouth 20 – Southampton 10 – Winchester 23.

Crown, 9 High St, SO43 7NF, ✆ (023) 8028 2922, *reception@crownhotel-lyndhurst.co.uk, Fax (023) 8028 2751,* – |‡| ⇔ ✆ P – 🏛 70. MC AE ◑ VISA
Rest (bar lunch Monday-Saturday)/dinner 23.00 **s.** ♀ – **37 rm** ☕ ☨77.50/87.50 – ☨☨145.00, 1 suite.
◆ Extended house with 19C façade in the middle of town - a classically English hotel. Spacious public areas include a wood panelled bar. Bedrooms vary in shapes and sizes. "Decidedly fattening" puddings a dining room speciality.

Beaulieu, Beaulieu Rd, SO42 7YQ, Southeast : 3 ½ m. on B 3056 ✆ (023) 8029 3344, *beaulieu@newforesthotels.co.uk, Fax (023) 8029 2729,* , – ⇔ rest, P – 🏛 40. MC AE VISA
March-December – **Rest** (dinner only) 21.50 – **18 rm** ☕ ☨70.00/75.00 – ☨☨120.00/155.00.
◆ Small country hotel in terrific location deep in New Forest, giving some rooms great views. Traditional interior and well-equipped rooms. Dining room is divided into partitioned areas.

Ormonde House, Southampton Rd, SO43 7BT, ✆ (023) 8028 2806, *enquiries@ormondehouse.co.uk, Fax (023) 8028 2004,* – ⇔ P. MC VISA
closed 1 week Christmas – **Rest** (by arrangement) (residents only) (dinner only) 19.00/24.00 **s.** – **23 rm** ☕ ☨35.00/60.00 – ☨☨80.00/120.00.
◆ Privately owned hotel on edge of the New Forest. Decorated in warm pastel colours throughout, including the well-kept bedrooms. Public areas include conservatory lounge.

⌂ **Whitemoor House** without rest., Southampton Rd, SO43 7BU, ✆ (023) 8028 2186, *whitemoor@aol.com* – ⇔ P. MC VISA. ⚔
closed 1 week Christmas – **7 rm** ☕ ☨35.00/50.00 – ☨☨70.00/80.00.
◆ Detached house overlooking the New Forest, a short walk from town. Bright, modern drawing room. Simple, sunny, spacious bedrooms.

YNMOUTH *Devon* 503 I 30 – *see Lynton.*

YNTON *Devon* 503 I 30 *The West Country G.*

See : *Town★ (≤★).*

Env. : *Valley of the Rocks★, W : 1 m. – Watersmeet★, E : 1½ m. by A 39.*

Exc. : *Exmoor National Park★★ – Doone Valley★, SE : 7½ m. by A 39 (access from Oare on foot).*

ℹ Town Hall, Lee Rd ✆ (0845) 6603232, info@lyntourism.co.uk.

London 206 – Exeter 59 – Taunton 44.

Lynton Cottage , North Walk Hill, EX35 6ED, ✆ (01598) 752342, *enquiries@lynton-cottage.com, Fax (01598) 754016,* ≤ bay and Countisbury Hill, , – ⇔ P. MC VISA
closed December-January – **Rest** a la carte 26.00/35.00 – **16 rm** ☕ ☨45.00/60.00 – ☨☨112.00/150.00.
◆ Stunning vistas of the bay and Countisbury Hill from this large, informal, cottage-style hotel. All bedrooms to a good standard - superior rooms command the best views. Admire the scenery from bright, modern restaurant.

ENGLAND

Hewitt's, North Walk, EX35 6HJ, (01598) 752293, *hewitts.hotel@talk21.cor* *Fax (01598) 752489*, bay and Countisbury Hill, , , – P. VISA
closed 15 December-15 February – **Rest** *(closed Tuesday)* (booking essential) 30.00/38.5 and a la carte 24.00/38.50 s. – **12 rm** 60.00/70.00 – 140.00/210.00.
◆ Splendid Victorian house in tranquil wooded cliffside setting. Stained glass window b Burne Jones and library filled with antiques. Stylish rooms with sea views. Oak panelle dining room; charming service.

Victoria Lodge without rest., 30-31 Lee Rd, EX35 6BS, (01598) 753203, *info@vict ialodge.co.uk, Fax (01598) 753203*, – P. VISA.
March-November – **9 rm** 45.00/72.00 – 60.00/90.00.
◆ Large Victorian house decorated with period photographs and prints. Traditional déc in communal areas and bedrooms which are comfortable and inviting. In keeping with th overall tone of the house the breakfast room is hung with old-fashioned country maps.

Highcliffe House, Sinai Hill, EX35 6AR, (01598) 752235, *info@highcliffehouse.co.u* *Fax (01598) 753815*, bay and Countisbury Hill, – P. VISA.
closed December-January – **Rest** *(closed Monday-Thursday)* (residents only) (dinner onl 28.00 – **6 rm** 60.00 – 96.00.
◆ Intimate, friendly atmosphere in former Victorian gentleman's residence. Authentic pe riod-style rooms with panoramic views and ornate antique beds.

Seawood, North Walk, EX35 6HJ, (01598) 752272, *gllnjnk@aol.com*, bay ar headland – P. VISA
April-October – **Rest** (dinner only) 22.50 – **12 rm** 42.50 – 90.00.
◆ Victorian house with marvellous views of bay and headland. Spacious lounges wi tranquil, comfy feel. Immaculate rooms in floral and pastel shades with four-poster bed Neatly kept dining room overlooking the sea.

Rockvale, Lee Rd, EX35 6HW, off Lee Rd (01598) 752279, *judithwoodland@ro vale.fsbusiness.co.uk*, – P. VISA.
March-October – **Rest** (by arrangement) 19.00 s. – **8 rm** 24.00/38.00 – 52.00/56.00.
◆ South facing Victorian house in elevated position. Homely ambience. Guests' lounge with books and games. Simple, traditional rooms; some with views to Watersmeet Valle Home-cooked meals proudly served.

St Vincent, Castle Hill, EX35 6JA, (01598) 752244, *welcome@st-vincent-hotel.co.u* *Fax (01598) 752244*, – . VISA.
closed January and first 2 weeks February – **Rest** *(closed Monday)* (booking essential non-residents) (dinner only) 24.00 – **6 rm** 40.00 – 60.00.
◆ Grade II listed building 200 metres from Coastal Path and close to famous funicul railway. Lovely Edwardian lounge with crackling fire. Neat, simple, clean bedrooms. Clot clad dining room: owners proud of French/Mediterranean menus.

at Lynmouth.

Tors, EX35 6NA, (01598) 753236, *torshotel@torslynmouth.co.u* *Fax (01598) 752544*, Lynmouth and bay, heated, – , rest, P – 80. VISA
closed 4 January-March except weekends – **Rest** (bar lunch)/dinner 30.00 and a la cart 30.00/39.00 s. – **31 rm** 75.00/180.00 – 110.00/220.00.
◆ Perched above Lynmouth and the bay, affording splendid views. Spacious lounges and traditional bar. Well-appointed, bright rooms in light tones. Traditional restaurant; te served on the terrace.

Rising Sun, Harbourside, EX35 6EG, (01598) 753223, *risingsunlynmouth@eas net.co.uk, Fax (01598) 753480*, , – . VISA
Rest (bar lunch)/dinner a la carte 26.85/39.15 s. – **15 rm** 54.00/79.00 – 148.0 1 suite.
◆ Part 14C thatched and whitewashed harbourside smuggler's inn. Warm, intimate styl Pubby bar with tiled floor and exposed beams. Well furnished, individually styled room Balanced modern meals making good use of local game and seafood.

Shelley's without rest., 8 Watersmeet Rd, EX35 6EP, (01598) 753219, *info@shelle shotel.co.uk, Fax (01598) 753219*, – . VISA.
March-November – **11 rm** 60.00/75.00 – 69.50/109.50.
◆ Centrally located hotel named after eponymous poet who honeymooned here in 181 Stylish public areas. Very comfortable bedrooms with good views of picturesque locale.

Bonnicott House, Watersmeet Rd, EX35 6EP, (01598) 753346, *bonnicott@aol.cor* *Fax (01598) 753724*, , – . VISA.
Rest (by arrangement) 26.00 – **8 rm** 28.00/42.00 – 84.00/96.00.
◆ Former 19C rectory in elevated setting. Spacious lounge with log fire: large window offer good views to sea. Bright rooms, two with four poster, all with sherry decante Fresh, traditional meals cooked on the Aga.

Heatherville , Tors Park, EX35 6NB, by Tors Rd (01598) 752327, *Fax (01598) 752634*, – P. VISA
closed December-January – **Rest** (by arrangement) 23.00 – **6 rm** 80.00 – 80.00.
◆ Victorian house perched above the town. Well kept throughout with bright, warm décor. Rooms with bold fabrics and woodland views: room 6 has the best outlook. Home-cooked meals employ fresh, local produce.

at Martinhoe *West : 4¼ m. via Coast rd (toll) – Barnstaple.*

Old Rectory , EX31 4QT, (01598) 763368, *reception@oldrectoryhotel.co.uk, Fax (01598) 763567*, – P. VISA.
March-October – **Rest** (residents only) (dinner only) 32.00 **s.** – **9 rm** (dinner included) 67.00/87.00 – 104.00/134.00.
◆ Built in 19C for rector of Martinhoe's 11C church. Quiet country retreat in charming three acre garden with cascading brook. Bright and co-ordinated bedrooms. Classic country house dining room.

LYTHAM ST ANNE'S *Lancs. 502 L 22 – pop. 41 327.*

Fairhaven, Lytham Hall Park, Ansdell (01253) 736741 – St Annes Old Links, Highbury Rd (01253) 723597.

67 St Annes Rd West (01253) 725610, touristinfo@flyde.gov.uk.
London 237 – Blackpool 7 – Liverpool 44 – Preston 13.

at Lytham.

Clifton Arms, West Beach, FY8 5QJ, (01253) 739898, *welcome@cliftonarms-lytham.com, Fax (01253) 730657*, – P – 200. VISA.
Rest 25.00 (dinner) and a la carte 21.40/29.45 – **45 rm** 65.00/130.00 – 105.00/160.00, 3 suites.
◆ Former coaching inn with strong associations with local championship golf course. Traditional country house public areas. Cottage-style rooms, front ones with great views. Restaurant's popular window tables overlook Lytham Green.

at St Anne's.

The Grand, South Promenade, FY8 1NB, (01253) 721288, *book@the-grand.co.uk, Fax (01253) 714459*, , , , – P – 140. VISA.
closed 24-26 December – ***The Bay :*** **Rest** (bar lunch Monday-Saturday)/dinner a la carte 22.95/30.25 – **53 rm** 75.00 – 160.00, 2 suites.
◆ Impressive, turreted Victorian hotel on promenade. Warm, country house-style décor. Spacious rooms, most with good views, turret rooms have particularly good aspect. Rich crimson restaurant overlooks the sea.

Dalmeny, 19-33 South Promenade, FY8 1LX, (01253) 712236, *info@dalmenyhotel.com, Fax (01253) 724447*, , , , , , squash – P – 200. VISA.
closed 24-26 December – **Rest** – (see ***Atrium*** below) – **128 rm** 62.90/87.00 – 85.80/174.00.
◆ 1970s building with most rooms overlooking sea. Range of lounges, games rooms, and three restaurants to suit a range of styles and pockets. Well geared up for children.

Glendower, North Promenade, FY8 2NQ, (01253) 723241, *glendower@bestwestern.co.uk, Fax (01253) 640069*, , , , – P – 150. VISA.
closed 24-26 December – ***The Clifton :*** **Rest** (bar lunch)/dinner 19.50 – **61 rm** 46.00/60.00 – 120.00/130.00.
◆ Family owned hotel consisting of 19C buildings overlooking the beach and Irish Sea. Comfortable, traditional style throughout. Choose the west facing rooms for best views. Comfortable, welcoming restaurant.

Bedford, 307-313 Clifton Drive South, FY8 1HN, (01253) 724636, *reservations@bedford-hotel.com, Fax (01253) 729244*, – P – 120. VISA.
Rest 22.50 (dinner) and a la carte 19.40/30.40 – **45 rm** 50.00/70.00 – 80.00/110.00.
◆ Privately owned traditional hotel in town centre. Large, comfy public areas include a basement pub with live music most days. Well-kept, simple rooms; those to rear quieter. Daily, fresh, local produce used in restaurant.

Atrium (at Dalmeny H.), 19-33 South Promenade, FY8 1LX, (01253) 716009, *Fax (01253) 724447* – P. VISA
closed 24-26 December – **Rest** (dinner only) 17.50 and a la carte 25.85/36.40 **s.**
◆ Contemporarily styled open-plan restaurant: bright décor and modern fitted bar. Bustling atmosphere with informality and piped jazz. Regularly changing British menu.

XX **Greens Bistro,** 3-9 St Andrews Road South - Lower Ground Floor, FY8 1SX, ☎ (0125 789990, *info@greensbistro.co.uk* – MO VISA
closed 25 December, 1 week spring, 1 week autumn, Sunday and Monday – **Rest** (dinn only) 15.50 and a la carte 22.40/27.45 ♀.
◆ Worth the effort to find, this simple, pleasant bistro, hidden beneath some shops, h linen clad tables, friendly service, and good value, well executed modern British menus.

MACCLESFIELD *Ches.* 502 503 504 N 24 – *pop. 50 688.*

The Tytherington Club ☎ (01625) 506000 – Shrigley Hall, Shrigley Park, Pott Shrig ☎ (01625) 575757.

Town Hall ☎ (01625) 504114.

London 186 – Chester 38 – Manchester 18 – Stoke-on-Trent 21.

Chadwick House, 55 Beech Lane, SK10 2DS, North : ¼ m. on A 538 ☎ (01625) 6155 *chadwickhouse@aol.com, Fax (01625) 610265* – MO VISA.
Rest (booking essential) (dinner only) (residents only) 25.00 **s.** – **14 rm** ☕ ✝30.00/40.0 ✝✝55.00.
◆ Two converted terraced houses away from the town centre. Bedrooms vary in shap and sizes and all are traditionally decorated and pine furnished.

Premier Travel Inn, Tytherington Business Park, Springwood Way, Tytherington, SK 2XA, Northeast : 2½ m. by A 523 ☎ (01625) 427809, *Fax (01625) 422874* – rm, re P. MO AE ⓓ VISA
Rest (grill rest.) – **40 rm** ✝46.95/46.95 – ✝✝48.95/48.95.
◆ Well-proportioned modern bedrooms, suitable for family and business stopovers, d signed with practicality and price in mind. A useful addresss for cost-conscious travellers

at Pott Shrigley *Northeast : 4¾ m. by A 523 on B 5090 – ✉ Macclesfield.*

Shrigley Hall, Shrigley Park, SK10 5SB, North : ¼ m. ☎ (01625) 575757, *shrigle servations@paramount-hotels.co.uk, Fax (01625) 573323*, P. – 250. MO AE ⓓ VISA
Oakridge : **Rest** (dinner only) 25.00 – **148 rm** ☕ ✝150.00/180.00 – ✝✝200.00.
◆ Peaceful setting for impressive part Edwardian country house with grand staircase a plush lounges. Conference facilities and leisure centre. Rooms with quality décor. Ne classically styled restaurant.

MADINGLEY *Cambs.* 504 U 27 – *see Cambridge.*

MAGHAM DOWN *E. Sussex – see Hailsham.*

MAIDENCOMBE *Devon* 503 J 32 – *see Torquay.*

MAIDENHEAD *Windsor & Maidenhead* 504 R 29 – *pop. 58 848.*

Bird Hills, Drift Rd, Hawthorn Hill ☎ (01628) 771030 – Shoppenhangers Rd ☎ (0162 624693 X.

to Marlow, Cookham and Windsor (Salter Bros. Ltd) (summer only) (3 h 45 mn).

The Library, St Ives Rd ☎ (01628) 796502.

London 33 – Oxford 32 – Reading 13.

Plan opposite

Holiday Inn Maidenhead, Manor Lane, SL6 2RA, off Shoppenhangers Rd ☎ (087 400 9053, *reservations-maidenhead@ichotelsgroup.com, Fax (01628) 506001,* , squash – P. – 400. MO AE ⓓ VISA. X
Rest *(closed Saturday lunch)* a la carte 22.85/30.85 **s.** – **193 rm** ☕ ✝70.00/180.00 ✝✝70.00/180.00.
◆ 1970s purpose-built hotel. Convenient for M4 motorway. Ideal for business guests wi extensive conference facilities and spacious, well-equipped leisure centre.

Fredrick's, Shoppenhangers Rd, SL6 2PZ, ☎ (01628) 581000, *reservations@fredrick hotel.co.uk, Fax (01628) 771054,* heated, P. – 15 MO AE ⓓ VISA. X
closed Christmas and New Year – **Rest** – (see ***Fredrick's*** below) – **33 rm** ☕ ✝215.00 ✝✝285.00, 1 suite.
◆ Redbrick, part beamed former inn. Ornate, marble floored reception with smoked m rors. Conservatory with wicker chairs. Very comfortable, individually styled bedrooms.

MAIDENHEAD

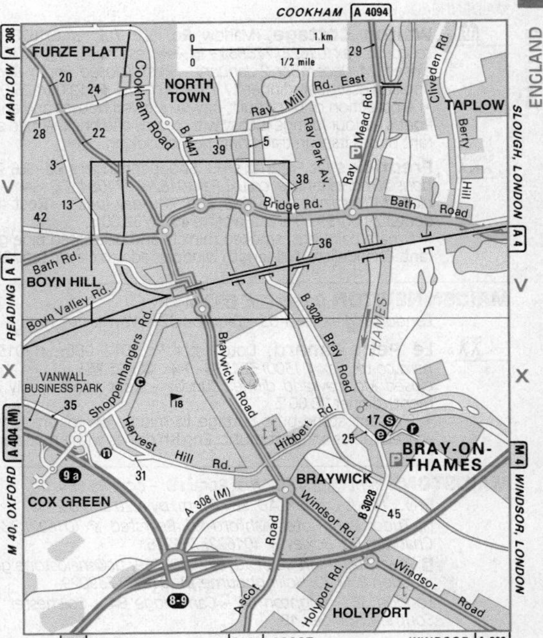

COOKHAM
A 4094
0
1 km
0
1/2 mile
A 308
MARLOW
FURZE PLATT
Cookham Road
NORTH TOWN
Ray Mill Rd. East
Ray Mead Rd.
Cliveden Rd
TAPLOW
Berry Hill
SLOUGH, LONDON
ENGLAND
B 4447
Ray Park Av.
Bridge Rd.
Bath Road
A 4
Bath Rd.
BOYN HILL
READING
Boyn Valley Rd.
Shoppenhangers Rd.
B 3028
Bray Road
THAMES
V
X
VANWALL BUSINESS PARK
Braywick Road
Harvest Hill Rd.
Hibbert Rd.
BRAY-ON-THAMES
M 4
A 404 (M)
M 40, OXFORD
COX GREEN
A 308 (M)
BRAYWICK
Windsor Rd.
WINDSOR, LONDON
Road
Ascot
Holyport Rd.
Windsor Road
HOLYPORT
M 4
READING
A 330
ASCOT
WINDSOR
A 308

A 308
Av.
Norfolk
Rd
Rd.
Kennet Rd
B 4447
Craufurd Rise
St Luke's
LEISURE CENTRE
College
Marlow Rd
KIDWELLS PARK
St Cloud Way
J
POL.
Y
A 4
Bridge Road
College Av.
West St.
High Street
Castle Hill
NICHOLSON'S CENTRE
St.
H
Bridge Av.
Forlease Road
Grenfell Rd
King
Broadway
York Road
South Rd
Queen St.
GRENFELL PARK
Grenfell Road
TOWER
Z
INDUSTRIAL ESTATE
Boyn Valley Rd.
Shoppenhangers Road
0
200 m
0
200 yards
A 308

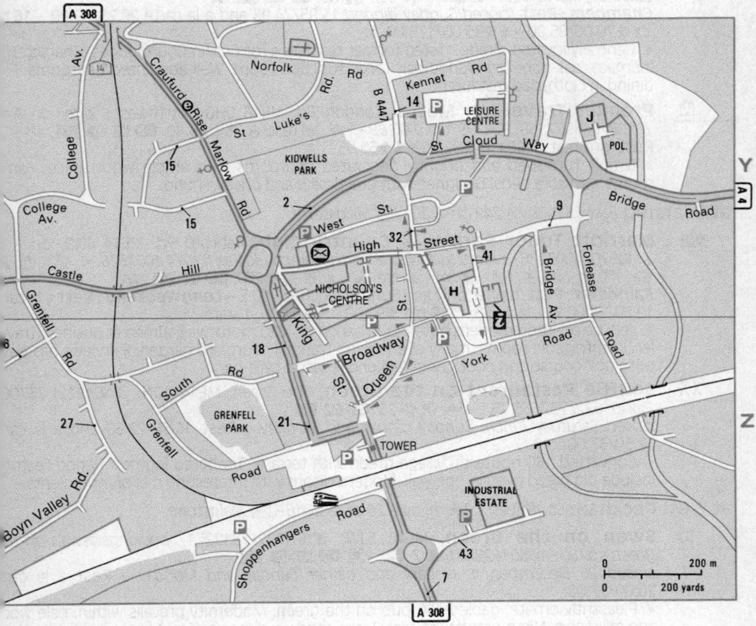

ENGLAND

Walton Cottage, Marlow Rd, SL6 7LT, ✆ (01628) 624394, *res@waltoncottage-tel.co.uk, Fax (01628) 773851* – |$|, ⇔ rest, ✆ [P] – 60. MC AE VISA. *closed 24 December-2 January* – **Rest** *(closed Friday-Sunday and Bank Holidays)* (lunch booking essential)/dinner 17.75 – **69 rm** ☕ ★119.00/125.00 – ★★160.00/185.00, 3 suites.
• A collection of brick built, bay-windowed houses and annexed blocks near town centre. Poet's Parlour lounge is cosy with beams and brick. Aimed at the business traveller. Restaurant prides itself in traditional home cooking.

XXX **Fredrick's** (at Fredrick's H.), Shoppenhangers Rd, SL6 2PZ, ✆ (01628) 581000, *reservations@fredricks-hotel.co.uk, Fax (01628) 771054*, – [P]. MC AE VISA
closed Christmas, New Year and Saturday lunch – **Rest** (booking essential for non-residents) 29.50/39.50 and a la carte 49.50/62.00 ♀.
• Ornate paintings, smoked mirrors and distressed pine greet diners in this large restaurant. Chandeliers, full-length windows add to classic feel. Elaborate British menus.

MAIDEN NEWTON *Dorset* 503 504 M 31.
London 144 – Exeter 55 – Taunton 37 – Weymouth 16.

XX **Le Petit Canard,** Dorchester Rd, DT2 0BE, ✆ (01300) 320536, *craigs@le-petit-canard.co.uk, Fax (01300) 321286* – ⇔. MC AE VISA
closed Monday and dinner Sunday – **Rest** (dinner only and Sunday lunch by arrangement)/dinner 28.00 ♀.
• Pleasant stone-built cottage in middle of charming village. Plenty of candles, well spaced tables and soft music. English dishes with French and Oriental touches.

MAIDSTONE *Kent* 504 V 30 *Great Britain G.* – *pop. 89 684.*
Env. : *Leeds Castle★ AC, SE : 4½ m. by A 20 and B 2163.*
Tudor Park Hotel, Ashford Rd, Bearsted ✆ (01622) 734334 – Cobtree Manor Park, Chatham Rd, Boxley ✆ (01622) 753276.
Town Hall, High St ✆ (01622) 602169, tic@maidstone.gov.uk – Motorway Service Area, junction 8, M 20, Hollingbourne ✆ (01622) 739029.
London 36 – Brighton 64 – Cambridge 84 – Colchester 72 – Croydon 36 – Dover 45 – Southend-on-Sea 49.

Stone Court, 28 Lower Stone St, ME15 6LX, ✆ (01622) 769769, *sales@stonecourt-tel.co.uk, Fax (01622) 769888* – ⇔ [P] – 80. MC AE VISA.
Chambers : **Rest** *(closed Sunday dinner)* 13.95/24.95 and a la carte 29.25/39.20 – **16 rm** ☕ ★70.00/85.00 – ★★95.00/175.00.
• Centrally located, Grade II listed former residence for Crown Court judges. Characterful intimate, oak-panelled lounge bar. Large function room. Well-appointed bedrooms. Fine dining in cloth-clad restaurant.

Premier Travel Inn Metro, London Rd, ME16 0HG, Northwest : 2 m. on A ✆ (08701) 977168, *Fax (08701) 977168* – ⇔, rest, ♿ [P] – 40. MC AE VISA.
Rest (grill rest.) – **40 rm** ★52.95 – ★★52.95.
• Simply furnished and brightly decorated bedrooms with ample work space. Family rooms with sofa beds. Designed with practicality and price in mind.

at Bearsted *East : 3 m. by A 249 off A 20 – ✉ Maidstone.*

Marriott Tudor Park H. & Country Club, Ashford Rd, ME14 4NQ, on A ✆ (0870) 4007226, *events.tudor@marriotthotels.co.uk, Fax (0870) 4007326*, – |$| ⇔, rm, ♿ [P] – 250. MC AE VISA.
Fairviews : **Rest** (dinner only and Sunday lunch) 25.00 ♀ – ***LongWeekend*** : **Rest** a la carte 19.50/24.00 ♀ – ☕ 14.95 – **119 rm** ★97.00 – ★★97.00, 1 suite.
• Leisure oriented modern hotel set in park near M20 motorway. Aimed at business traveller. Comfortable rooms, many overlooking tranquil courtyard garden. Fairviews has views onto golf course and pool. LongWeekend is casual café-bar.

XX **Soufflé Restaurant on the Green,** The Green, ME14 4DN, ✆ (01622) 73706 *Fax (01622) 737065*, – ⇔ [P] 25. MC AE VISA
closed Saturday lunch, Sunday dinner and Monday – **Rest** 16.50/22.50 and a la carte 32.50/37.00.
• Converted 16C house on village green with terrace. Timbered interior. Period features include old bread oven in one wall. Modern dishes with interesting mix of ingredients.

at West Peckham *Southwest : 7¾ m. by A 26 off B 2016 – ✉ Maidstone.*

Swan on the Green, ME18 5JW, ✆ (01622) 812271, *bookings@swan-on-the-green.co.uk, Fax 301622) 814977*, – [P]. MC AE VISA
closed 25 December, 1 January and dinner Sunday and Monday – **Rest** a la carte 20.00/27.00.
• Pleasantly ornate, gabled 16C pub on the green. Modernity prevails within: pale wood and tall stools. Micro brewery to rear. Tasty, modern dishes on frequently changing menu.

MALDON Essex 504 W 28 – pop. 20 731.

Forrester Park, Beckingham Rd, Great Totham ☎ (01621) 891406 – , Bunsay Downs, Little Baddow Rd, Woodham Walter ☎ (01245) 412648.

Coach Lane ☎ (01621) 856503.

London 42 – Chelmsford 9 – Colchester 17.

Five Lakes Resort, Colchester Rd, Tolleshunt Knights, CM9 8HX, Northeast : 8 ¼ m. by B 1026 ☎ (01621) 868888, *enquiries@fivelakes.co.uk, Fax (01621) 869696*, squash – 400. VISA.
Camelot : **Rest** *(closed Sunday-Monday)* (dinner only) 24.00 and a la carte 23.50/36.50 ♀ –
Bejerano's Brasserie : **Rest** a la carte 14.90/25.50 ♀ – 13.95 – **190 rm** 146.00/215.00 – 264.00, 4 suites.

◆ Massive, purpose-built hotel in 320 acres with two golf courses, imposing lobby with fountain and extensive leisure and conference facilities. Modern, well-equipped rooms. Relax in fine dining Camelot. Informal Bejerano's with adjoining Sports Bar and terrace.

MALMESBURY Wilts. 503 504 N 29 The West Country G. – pop. 5 094.

See : *Town*★ – *Market Cross*★★ – *Abbey*★.

Town Hall, Market Lane ☎ (01666) 823748.

London 108 – Bristol 28 – Gloucester 24 – Swindon 19.

Whatley Manor, Easton Grey, SN12 0RB, West : 2 ¼ m. on B 4040 ☎ (01666) 822888, *reservations@whatleymanor.com, Fax (01666) 826120*, – 40. VISA
The Dining Room : **Rest** *(closed Monday-Tuesday)* (booking essential to non-residents) (dinner only) 60.00/75.00 **s.** ♀ – (see also ***Le Mazot*** below) – **15 rm** 275.00/450.00 – 275.00/450.00, 8 suites.
Spec. Snails in garlic with red wine sauce infused with veal kidneys, parsley purée. Roast loin of venison with cauliflower purée. Selection of summer fruits.

◆ Extended Cotswold stone manor in its own grounds. Luxurious décor; superb hydrotherapy treatment spa. Elegant, well-appointed, stylish bedrooms in varying sizes. Refined, well-judged and accomplished cooking in The Dining Room overlooking terrace and gardens.

The Old Bell, Abbey Row, SN16 0BW, ☎ (01666) 822344, *info@oldbellhotel.com, Fax (01666) 825145*, – 55. VISA
Rest – (see ***The Restaurant*** below) – **31 rm** 85.00/95.00 – 125.00.

◆ Part 13C former abbots hostel with gardens. Elegant public areas with hugely characterful bar and lounge. Handsome, well-kept rooms in coach-house or inn.

Le Mazot (at Whatley Manor), Easton Grey, SN12 0RB, West : 2 ¼ m. on B 4040 ☎ (01666) 822888, *lemazot@whatleymanor.com, Fax (01666) 826120* – VISA
Rest 21.50 (lunch) and a la carte 26.00/32.00 **s.** ♀.

◆ Wood carving and alpine tones recreate a Swiss ambience. Interesting modern menus prevail. Disarmingly relaxed and intimate with assured, friendly service.

The Restaurant (at The Old Bell), Abbey Row, SN16 0BW, ☎ (01666) 822344, *info@oldbellhotel.com, Fax (01666) 825145* – VISA
Rest a la carte 26.50/35.50.

◆ Charming restaurant with accomplished modern cooking; local ingredients are very much to the fore. Outside terrace with peaceful garden allows for relaxed summer dining.

at Crudwell *North : 4 m. on A 429 – ✉ Malmesbury.*

The Rectory, SN16 9EP, ☎ (01666) 577194, *info@therectoryhotel.com, Fax (01666) 577853*, – VISA
Rest a la carte approx 28.50 – **11 rm** 85.00 – 120.00, 1 suite.

◆ 17C stone-built former Rectory with formal garden and mature trees. Personally run. Comfortable, individually-styled bedrooms with many modern extras, some with spa baths. Airy oak-panelled dining room; modern seasonal cooking.

MALPAS Ches. 502 503 L 24.

London 177 – Birmingham 60 – Chester 15 – Shrewsbury 26 – Stoke-on-Trent 30.

Tilston Lodge without rest., Tilston, SY14 7DR, Northwest : 3 m. on Tilston Rd ☎ (01829) 250223, *Fax (01829) 250223*, –
closed 24-25 December – **3 rm** 45.00/50.00 – 78.00.

◆ A former Victorian hunting lodge with pleasant gardens and grounds, the latter occupied by various rare breeds of sheep. Cosy, individually decorated bedrooms.

MALVERN Worcs. 503 504 N 27 – *see Great Malvern.*

MALVERN WELLS Worcs. 503 504 N 27 – *see Great Malvern.*

P. Desclos/SCOPE

Douglas: on the seafront

MAN (Isle of)

502 F/G 21 *Great Britain G. – pop. 76 315.*

PRACTICAL INFORMATION

from Douglas to Belfast (Isle of Man Steam Packet Co. Ltd) (summer only) (2 h 45 mn) – from Douglas to Republic of Ireland (Dublin) (Isle of Man Steam Packet Co. Ltd) (2 h 45 mn/ 4 h) – from Douglas to Heysham (Isle of Man Steam Packet Co.) (2 h 30 mn) – from Douglas to Liverpool (Isle of Man Steam Packet Co. Ltd) (2 h 30 mn/4 h).

SIGHTS

See : *Laxey Wheel★★ – Snaefell★ (✳★★★) – Cregneash Folk Museum★.*

Douglas *I.O.M. – pop. 25 347.*

Douglas Municipal, Pulrose Park (01624) 675952.
King Edward Bay, Groudle Rd, Onchan (01624) 620430.
Ronaldsway Airport : (01624) 821600, SW : 7 m.
Terminal : *Coach service from Lord St.*
Sea Terminal Building (01624) 686801.

Sefton, Harris Promenade, IM1 2RW, (01624) 645500, *info@seftonhotel.com* *Fax (01624) 676004,* – 80. *VISA.*
The Gallery : **Rest** (lunch residents only) a la carte 15.00/40.00 – 9.95 – **89 rm** 80.00/90.00 – 160.00, 3 suites.
◆ Enviable promenade position: behind the 19C façade lies a stunning atrium with water features and flora; marble reception. The well-appointed bedrooms overlook the bay. Modish, bright eatery with modern Manx art on the walls.

The Regency, Queens Promenade, IM2 4NN, (01624) 680680, *regency@iom-1.net* *Fax (01624) 680690,* rm, – 30. *VISA.*
Five Continents : **Rest** 21.50 and a la carte 28.30/41.80 **s.** – 8.90 – **42 rm** 80.00/105.00 – 113.00, 3 suites.
◆ Grand-looking, four storey hotel with appealing traditional style. Sea front position with good views over Douglas Bay. Rooms equipped with latest technology. Wood-panelled restaurant with sea outlook.

Mount Murray H. & Country Club, Santon, IM4 2HT, Southwest : 4 ¾ m. by A (01624) 661111, *hotel@mountmurray.com, Fax (01624) 611116,* squash – – 300. *VISA.*
Murray's : **Rest** (dinner only and Sunday lunch) a la carte 20.00/30.00 **s.** – ***Charlotte Bistro :*** **Rest** *(closed Sunday lunch)* 14.50/22.95 and a la carte 16.40/29.70 – **90 rm** 98.00 – 144.00.
◆ Surrounded by vast grounds and golf course. Large sports bar and two lounges. Extensive leisure and conference facilities. Comfortable, modern rooms. Large formal Murray's overlooks golf course. Charlotte's Bistro offers monthly themed cuisine.

Admirals House, 12 Loch Promenade, IM1 2LX, (01624) 629551, *enquiries@admirals house.com, Fax (01624) 675021* – rm, – 40. *VISA.*
Rest *(closed Sunday)* a la carte 30.95/46.50 – **26 rm** 75.00/99.00 – 90.00/125.00.
◆ Impressively situated Victorian building on promenade and only two minutes from ferry terminal. Split-level café-bar. Particularly large, modern bedrooms. Local produce to the fore in restaurant dishes.

Empress, Central Promenade, IM2 4RA, (01624) 661155, *gm@theempresshotel.net* *Fax (01624) 6735543,* rest, – 150. *VISA.*
La Brasserie : **Rest** (bar lunch Monday-Saturday)/dinner 19.95 and a la carte 14.95/23.40 8.95 – **100 rm** 70.00/75.00 – 80.00/130.00.
◆ Large Victorian hotel in prominent position on promenade overlooking Douglas Bay. Lounge and bar with jazz style pianist at weekends. Small leisure centre. Modern rooms. Informal, colourful basement brasserie.

Penta without rest., Queens Promenade, IM9 4NE, (01624) 680680, *penta@iom-1.net, Fax (01624) 680690* – *VISA.* – **22 rm** 49.00 – 57.00/65.00.
◆ Victorian property with bay windows on the town's main promenade. By way of contrast, spacious and up-to-date bedrooms which include a computer in each room.

The Lodge without rest., Oak Hill, Port Soderick, IM4 1AS, Southeast : 2 ¼ m. on A 2 (01624) 614949, *thelodge@manx.net, Fax (01624) 614949* –
closed Christmas and New Year – **3 rm** 50.00 – 90.00.
◆ Series of converted stables and outbuildings a few minutes' walk from coastline. Some individually styled bedrooms boast a spa or sauna. All rooms have a pleasant view.

Port Erin *I.O.M. – pop. 3 369.*

Rowany Cottier without rest., Spaldrick, IM9 6PE, (01624) 832287, *rowanycottier@manx.net, Fax (01624) 835685,* Port Erin Bay, –
5 rm 34.00/46.00 – 64.00/72.00.
◆ Detached house with spectacular views over Port Erin Bay. Homely lounge with open fires. Oak floor and pine tables in breakfast room. Bright, colourful bedrooms.

Port St Mary *I.O.M. – pop. 1 941.*

Aaron House without rest., The Promenade, IM9 5DE, ✆ (01624) 835702 –
closed Christmas-New Year – **5 rm** ☕ ★49.00/59.00 – ★★70.00/98.00.
◆ High degree of hospitality guaranteed in this imposing 19C property - owner wears Victorian dresses. Substantial breakfasts. Very comfortable rooms with winning touches.

Ramsey *I.O.M. – pop. 7 322.*

The River House without rest., IM8 3DA, North : ¼ m. turning left after bridge before Bridge Inn on Bowring Rd ✆ (01624) 816412, *Fax (01624) 816412*, ←, – P
closed February – **3 rm** ☕ ★49.50/75.00 – ★★95.00.
◆ Part Georgian house in delightful location along riverside. Peaceful ambience. Country house style lounge. Scrubbed wood breakfast room. Individually styled bedrooms.

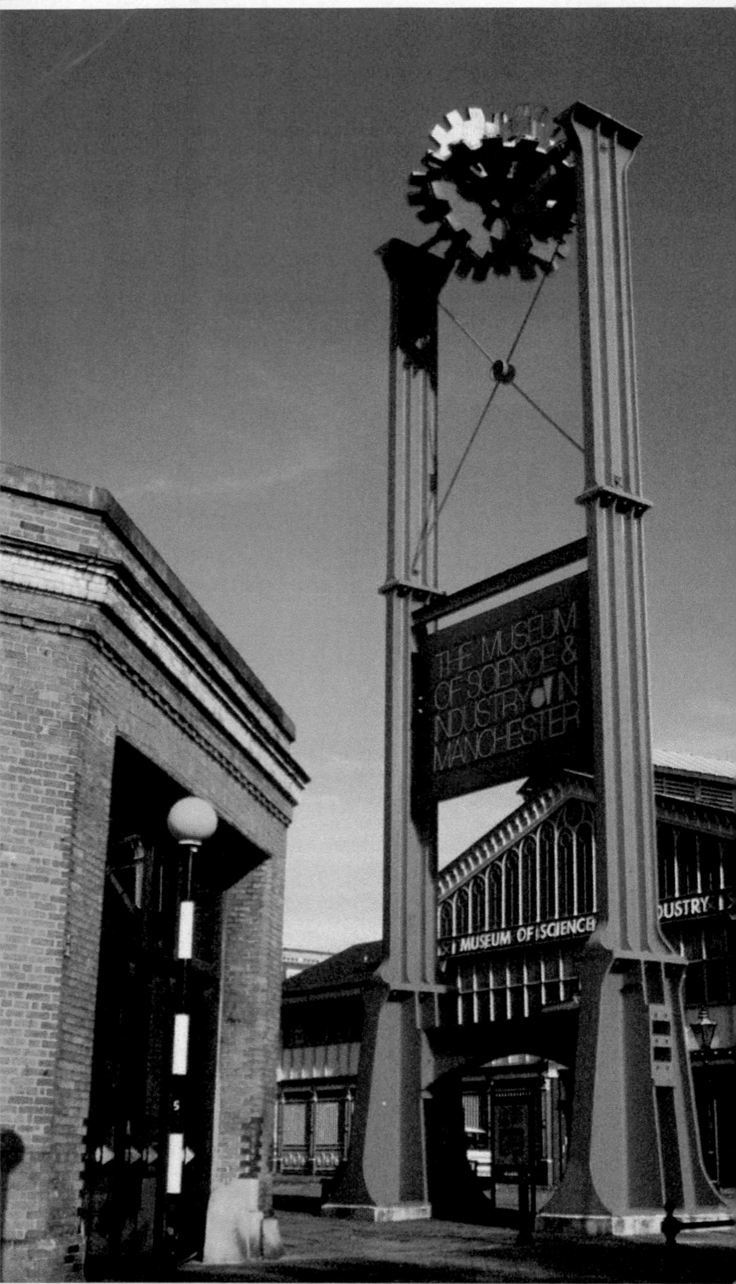

N. Boyd/Robert HARDING

Manchester, the Museum of Science and Industry

MANCHESTER

Gtr Manchester 502 503 504 N 23 *Great Britain G. – pop. 394 269.*

London 202 – Birmingham 86 – Glasgow 221 – Leeds 43 – Liverpool 35 – Nottingham 72.

TOURIST INFORMATION

Manchester Visitor Centre, Town Hall Extension, Lloyd St ☎ (0161) 234 3157; manchester_visitor_centre@notes.manchester.gov.uk

Manchester Airport, International Arrivals Hall, Terminal 1 ☎ (0161) 436 3344 – Manchester Airport, International Arrivals Hall, Terminal 2 ☎ (061) 489 6412 – Salford T.I.C., 1 The Quays, Salford ☎ (0161) 848 8601.

PRACTICAL INFORMATION

Heaton Park, Prestwich ☎ (0161) 654 9899, ABV.

Houldsworth Park, Houldsworth St, Reddish, Stockport ☎ (0161) 442 1712.

Chorlton-cum-Hardy, Barlow Hall, Barlow Hall Rd ☎ (0161) 881 3139.

William Wroe, Pennybridge Lane, Flixton ☎ (0161) 748 8680.

Manchester International Airport : ☎ (0161) 489 3000, S : 10 m. by A 5103 – AX *– and M 56.*

Terminal : *Coach service from Victoria Station.*

SIGHTS

See : *City★ - Castlefield Heritage Park★* CZ *– Town Hall★* CZ *– Manchester Art Gallery★* CZ **M2** *– Cathedral★ (stalls and canopies★)* CY *– Museum of Science and Industry★* CZ M. *– Urbis★* CY *– National War Museum North★, Trafford Park* AX **M**.

Env. : *Whitworth Art Gallery★, S : 1½ m.*

Exc. : *Quarry Bank Mill★, S : 10 m. off B 5166, exit 5 from M 56 - Bramall Hall★, SE : 13 m by A6* BX *and A5102.*

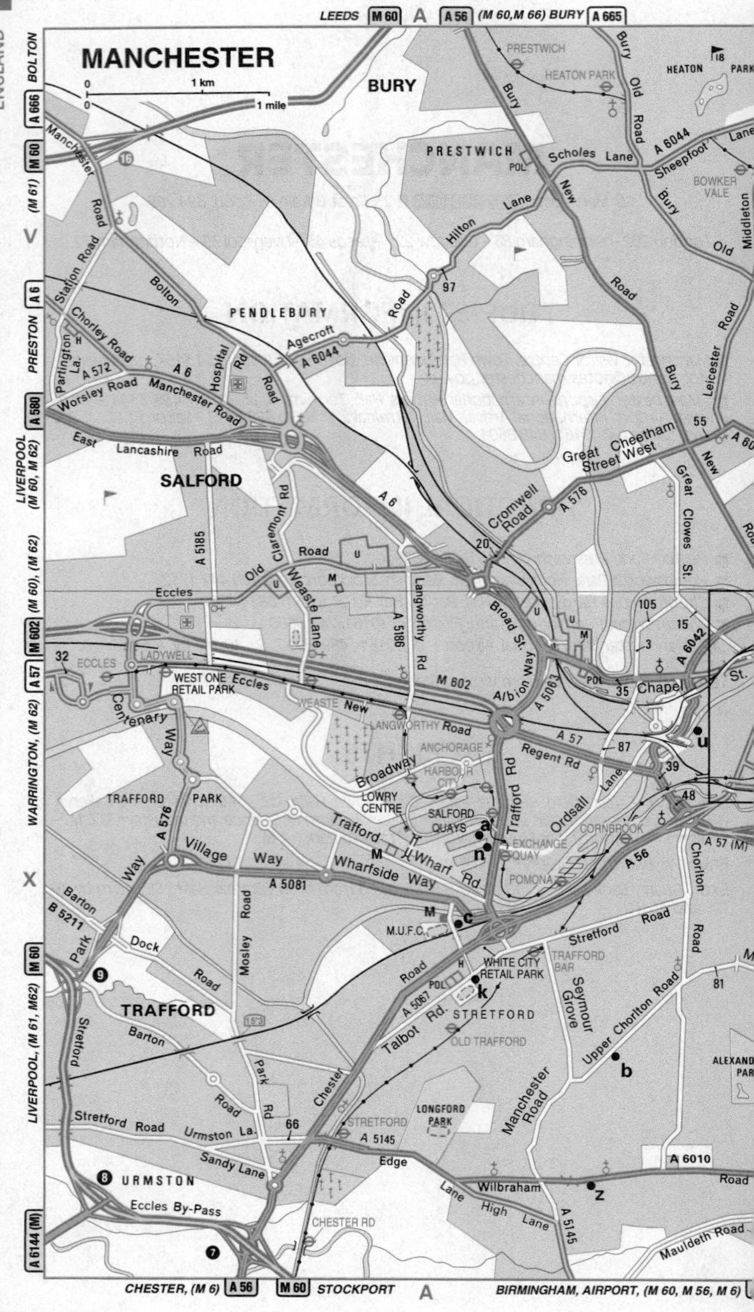
MANCHESTER
LEEDS M 60 A A 56 (M 60, M 66) BURY A 665
BOLTON A 666
M 60
(M 61)
PRESTON A 6
LIVERPOOL (M 60, M 62) A 580
(M 60), (M 62) M 602
WARRINGTON, (M 62) A 57
LIVERPOOL, (M 61, M62) M 60
A 6144 (M)
CHESTER, (M 6) A 56 M 60 STOCKPORT A BIRMINGHAM, AIRPORT, (M 60, M 56, M 6)
BURY
PRESTWICH
HEATON PARK
HEATON PARK
BOWKER VALE
PENDLEBURY
SALFORD
TRAFFORD PARK
TRAFFORD
URMSTON
STRETFORD
LOWRY CENTRE
SALFORD QUAYS
M.U.F.C.
WHITE CITY RETAIL PARK
WEST ONE RETAIL PARK
LONGFORD PARK
ALEXANDRA PARK
Scholes Lane
Hilton Lane
Agecroft Road
Bolton Road
Manchester Road
Station Road
Chorley Road
Worsley Road
Manchester Road
East Lancashire Road
Great Cheetham Street West
Cromwell Road
Old Road
Claremont Rd
Weaste Lane
Langworthy Rd
Broad St.
Albion Way
Eccles New Road
Langworthy Road
Regent Rd
Trafford Rd
Ordsall Lane
Chapel St.
Great Clowes St.
Centenary Way
Broadway
Trafford Road
Wharf Rd
Wharfside Way
Village Way
Mosley Road
Barton Dock Road
Stretford Road
Talbot Rd.
Seymour Grove
Upper Chorlton Road
Chorlton Road
Manchester Road
Chester Road
Urmston La.
Sandy Lane
Eccles By-Pass
Edge Lane
Wilbraham Road
High Lane
Mauldeth Road
A 6044
A 576
A 5063
A 5081
A 5067
A 5145
A 6010
A 5185
A 5186
B 5211
A 6042
A 57 (M)
Leicester Road
Middleton Old Road
1 km
1 mile
534

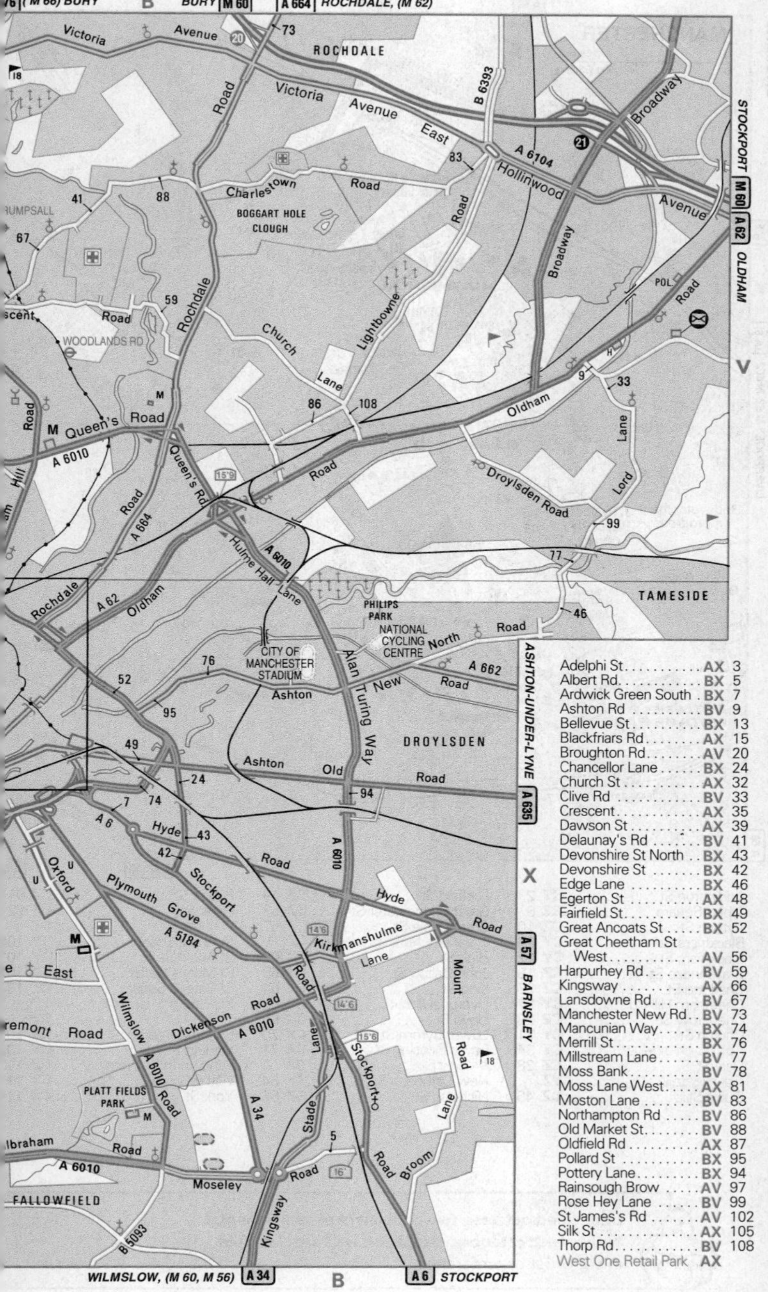
(M 66) BURY
B
BURY M 60
A 664 ROCHDALE, (M 62)
ROCHDALE
Victoria Avenue
Victoria Avenue East
B 6393
Broadway
21
A 6104
Hollinwood Avenue
STOCKPORT M 60 A 62 OLDHAM
Charlestown Road
BOGGART HOLE CLOUGH
Rochdale Road
Moston Lane
Road
Broadway
POL.
Road
Church Lane
Lightbowne
WOODLANDS RD
Queen's Road
A 6010
Queen's Rd
Oldham Road
Droylsden Road
Lord Lane
Hill
Road
A 664
Hulme Hall Lane
A 6010
TAMESIDE
Rochdale
A 62
Oldham
PHILIPS PARK
NATIONAL CYCLING CENTRE
North Road
CITY OF MANCHESTER STADIUM
Ashton New Road
A 662
Alan Turing Way
DROYLSDEN
Ashton Old Road
ASHTON-UNDER-LYNE A 635
A 6
Hyde Road
Stockport
Oxford
Plymouth Grove
A 5184
A 6010
Hyde Road
Kirkmanshulme Lane
A 57 BARNSLEY
X
V
Mount Road
East
Wilmslow
A 6010 Road
Dickenson Road
A 6010
Lane
Stockport
PLATT FIELDS PARK
A 34
Stade
Broom Lane
Road
A 6010
Moseley Road
FALLOWFIELD
B 5093
Kingsway
WILMSLOW, (M 60, M 56) A 34
B
A 6 STOCKPORT
ENGLAND

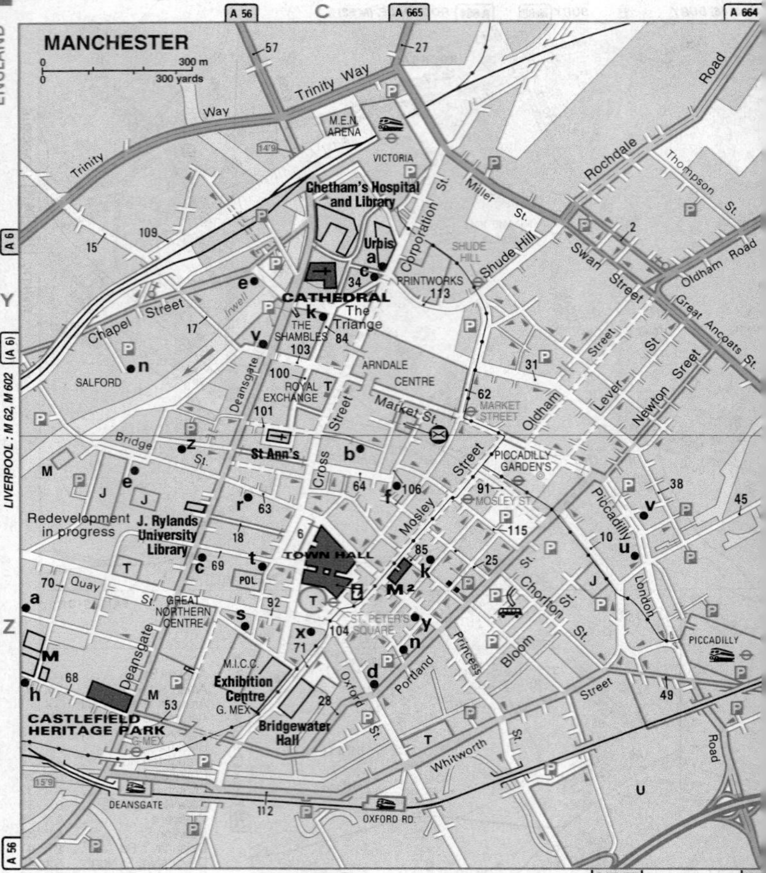

MANCHESTER

Addington St .... CY 2
Albert Square .... CZ 6
Aytoun St .... CZ 10
Blackfriars Rd .... CY 15
Blackfriars St .... CY 17
Brazennoze St .... CZ 18
Charlotte St .... CZ 25
Cheetham Hill Rd .... CY 27
Chepstow St .... CZ 28
Church St .... CY 31
Corn Exchange .... CY 34
Dale St .... CZ 38
Deansgate .... CYZ
Ducie St .... CZ 45
Fairfield St .... CZ 49
Great Bridgewater St .... CZ 53
Great Ducie St .... CY 57
Great Northern centre .... CZ
High St .... CY 62
John Dalton St .... CZ 63
King St .... CZ 64
Liverpool Rd .... CZ 68
Lloyd St .... CZ 69
Lower Byrom St .... CZ 70
Lower Mosley St .... CZ 71
Mosley St .... CZ
New Cathedral St .... CY 84
Nicholas St .... CZ 85
Parker St .... CZ 91
Peter St .... CZ 92
Princess St .... CZ
St Ann's Square .... CY 10
St Ann's St .... CY 10
St Mary's Gate .... CY 10
St Peter's Square .... CZ 10
Shambles Shopping Centre (The) .... CY
Spring Gardens .... CZ 10
Viaduct St .... CY 10
Whitworth St West .... CZ 11
Withy Grove .... CY 11
York St .... CZ 11

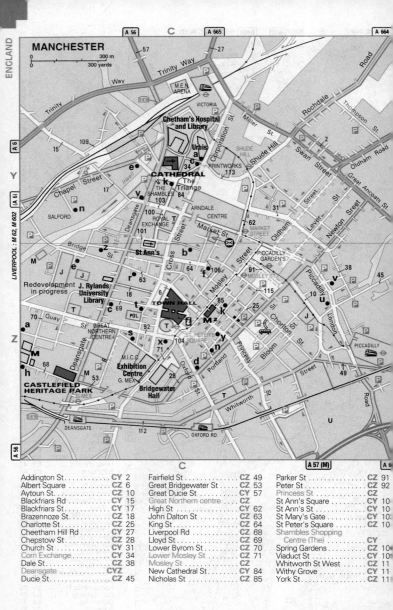

**Undecided between two equivalent establishments?
Within each category, establishments are classified
in our order of preference.**

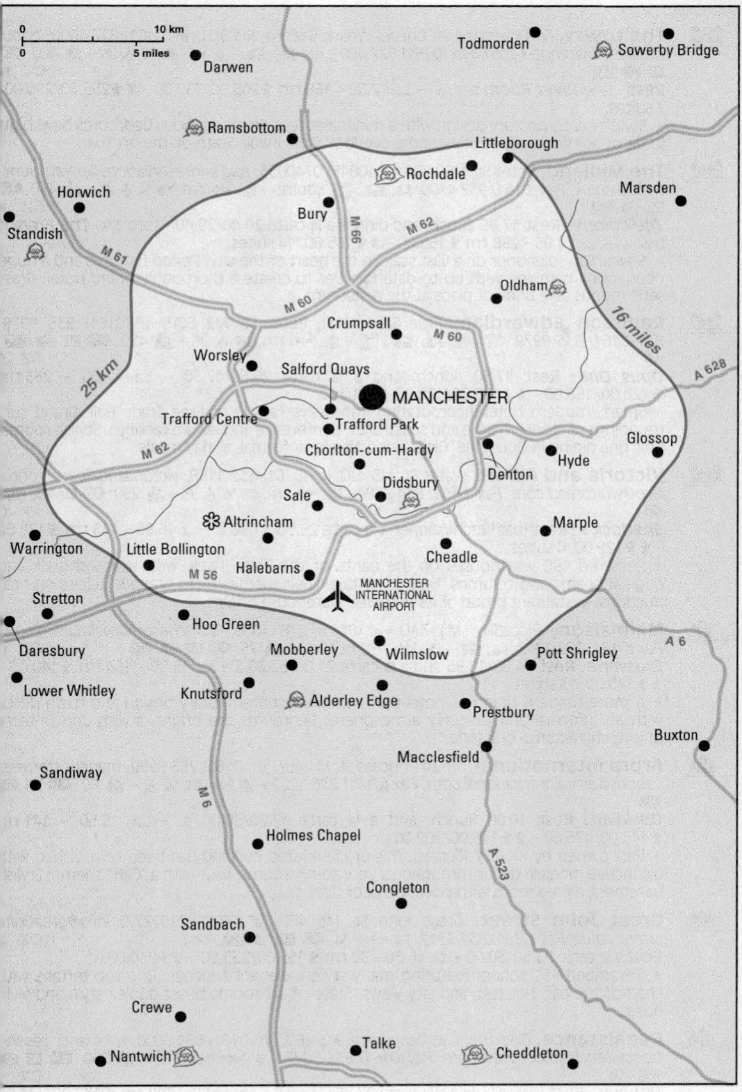

0 10 km
0 5 miles
Darwen
Todmorden
Sowerby Bridge
Ramsbottom
Littleborough
Rochdale
Horwich
Marsden
Standish
Bury
M 66
M 62
M 61
Oldham
M 60
Crumpsall
16 miles
M 60
Worsley
Salford Quays
A 628
25 km
MANCHESTER
Trafford Centre
Trafford Park
M 62
Chorlton-cum-Hardy
Glossop
Hyde
Denton
Didsbury
Sale
Altrincham
Marple
Warrington
Little Bollington
Cheadle
M 56
Halebarns
MANCHESTER INTERNATIONAL AIRPORT
Stretton
Hoo Green
A 6
Daresbury
Mobberley
Wilmslow
Pott Shrigley
Lower Whitley
Knutsford
Alderley Edge
Prestbury
Buxton
Macclesfield
Sandiway
M 6
Holmes Chapel
A 523
Congleton
Sandbach
Crewe
Talke
Nantwich
Cheddleton

We try to be as accurate as possible when giving room rates.
But prices are susceptible to change,
so please check rates when booking.

ENGLAND

The Lowry, 50 Dearmans Pl, Chapel Wharf, Salford, M3 5LH, ✆ (0161) 827 4000, *enquiries@thelowryhotel.com, Fax (0161) 827 4001,* – 400. AE VISA CY n
Rest – (see ***River Room*** below) – 17.50 – **158 rm** 205.00/230.00 – 255.00/290.00, 7 suites.
• Stylish contemporary design with a minimalist feel. Smart spacious bedrooms have high levels of comfort and facilities; some overlook River Irwell. State-of-the-art spa.

The Midland, Peter St, M60 2DS, ✆ (0845) 0740053, *midlandreservations@paramount-hotels.co.uk, Fax (0161) 932 4100,* squash – rm, – 450. AE VISA CZ x
The Colony **:** Rest 17.95 (lunch) and dinner a la carte 20.40/29.40 – (see also ***The French*** below) – 14.95 – **298 rm** 165.00 – 165.00, 14 suites.
• Edwardian splendour on a vast scale in the heart of the city. Period features and a huge open lobby combine with up-to-date facilities to create a thoroughly grand hotel. Brasserie menus take pride of place at the restaurant.

Radisson Edwardian, Free Trade Hall, Peter St, M2 5GP, ✆ (0161) 835 9929, *Fax (0161) 835 9979,* – rm, – 425. AE VISA. CZ s
Opus One **:** Rest 17.50 (lunch) and a la carte 26.50/47.50 – 17.00 – **233 rm** 128.00/158.00 – 128.00/198.00, 30 suites.
• Smart, modern hotel incorporating impressive façade of Free Trade Hall. Grand surroundings of stone, marble and sculptures. Conference and leisure facilities. Stylish rooms. Chic fine dining in Opus One. Glass-sided Alto for informal, all day meals.

Victoria and Albert, Water St, M3 4JQ, ✆ (0161) 832 1188, *victoriaandalbert.frontoffice@whitbread.com, Fax (0161) 834 2484* – rm, – 250. AE VISA. AX u
Sherlock's **:** Rest (bar lunch)/dinner a la carte 26.50/31.90 – 16.95 – **143 rm** 129.00 – 129.00, 4 suites.
• Restored 19C warehouses on the banks of the River Irwell, with exposed brick and original beams and columns. Bedrooms take their themes from Granada Television productions. Restaurant proud of its timbered warehouse origins.

Malmaison, Piccadilly, M1 3AQ, ✆ (0161) 278 1000, *manchester@malmaison.com, Fax (0161) 278 1002,* – rm, – 75. AE VISA CZ u
Brasserie **:** Rest 14.50/15.95 and a la carte 21.00/32.00 – 12.95 – **154 rm** 140.00 – 140.00, 13 suites.
• A more modern brand of hotel that combines contemporary design and fresh décor with an informal and unstuffy atmosphere. Bedrooms are bright, stylish and hi-tech. Bright, characterful brasserie.

Arora International, 18-24 Princess St, M1 4LY, ✆ (0161) 236 8999, *manchesterreservations@arorainternational.com, Fax (0161) 236 3222* – – 80. AE VISA
Obsidian **:** Rest 16.00 (lunch) and a la carte 17.00/30.00 s. – 13.50 – **141 rm** 145.00/175.00 – 145.00/209.00.
• Part owned by Sir Cliff Richard, this Grade II listed building has been refurbished with distinctive modern décor throughout. Very comfy rooms, four with a "Cliff" theme! Stylish basement dining room with eclectic mix of dishes.

Great John Street, Great John St, M3 4FD, ✆ (0870) 2202277, *info@greatjohnstreet.co.uk, Fax (0161) 831 3212,* – . AE VISA. CZ a
Rest a la carte 23.50/30.00 – 16.50 – **30 rm** 155.00/235.00 – 235.00.
• Revamped 19C school featuring many stylish, elegant touches. Rooftop terrace with champagne bar, hot tub, and city views. State-of-art rooms boast duplex style and vivid hues.

Renaissance, Blackfriars St, Deansgate, M3 2EQ, ✆ (0161) 831 6000, *rhi.manbr.reservations@renaissancehotels.com, Fax (0161) 835 3077* – – 250. AE VISA. CY v
Robbies **:** Rest (dinner only) a la carte 27.35/31.90 – 14.50 – **199 rm** 133.00/139.00 – 189.00, 4 suites.
• Converted 15-storey office block with large, marbled lobby well sited at top of Deansgate. Spacious, well-equipped bedrooms, most enjoying city skyline views. Airy dining room with adjacent bar.

Rossetti, 107 Piccadilly, M1 2DB, ✆ (0161) 247 7744, *info@aliasrossetti.com, Fax (0161) 247 7747* – . AE VISA CZ
Cafe Paradiso **:** Rest a la carte 19.75/24.50 – 12.00 – **57 rm** 110.00 – 110.00, 4 suites.
• Former 19C textile factory with original features: tiled staircases, cast iron pillars. Staff by contrast, in casual attire. Chic basement bar. Rooms exude designer style. Informal restaurant with wood-burning stove and rotisserie dishes.

Novotel, 21 Dickinson St, M1 4LX, ☎ (0161) 235 2200, *h3145@accor.com, Fax (0161) 235 2210,* – rm, – 90. MO AE VISA CZ n
Rest a la carte 22.50/28.90 ♀ – 12.50 – **164 rm** 119.00 – 119.00.

◆ The open-plan lobby boasts a spacious, stylish bar and residents can take advantage of an exclusive exercise area. Decently equipped, tidily appointed bedrooms. Compact dining room with grill-style menus.

Premier Travel Inn, North Tower, Victoria Bridge St, Salford, M3 5AS, ☎ (0870) 7001488, *Fax (0870) 7001489* – , rest, P – 35. MO AE VISA. CY e
Rest (grill rest.) – **170 rm** 55.95 – 55.95.

◆ Modern accommodation with bright, well-planned rooms. Convenient city centre location close to Deansgate and Victoria station. The higher the room the better the view. Popular dishes in airy restaurant.

Premier Travel Inn, The Circus, 112-114 Portland St, M1 4WB, ☎ (0870) 2383315, *Fax (0161) 233 5299* – , rest, P. MO AE VISA. CZ d
Rest (grill rest.) – **225 rm** 55.95 – 55.95.

◆ Maintains the group's reputation for affordable accommodation and simple contemporary styling. Neat, bright rooms, spacious and carefully designed.

XXXX **The French** (at The Midland H.), Peter St, M60 2DS, ☎ (0845) 074 0053, *Fax (0161) 932 4100* – P. MO AE VISA CZ x
closed Sunday and Bank Holidays – **Rest** (dinner only) a la carte 34.00/68.00 ♀.

◆ As grand as the hotel in which it is housed, with gilded paintings, large mirrors and heavy drapes. Attentively formal service, classically French-based cooking.

XXX **Le Mont,** Urbis, Levels 5 and 6, Cathedral Gardens, M4 3BG, ☎ (0161) 605 8282, *robert@urbis.org.uk, Fax (0161) 605 8283,* – . MO AE VISA CY a
closed 24 December-6 January, Saturday lunch, Sunday and Bank Holidays – **Rest** 24.00 (lunch) and a la carte 33.40/39.95 ♀.

◆ Set on top of the Urbis Museum, boasting spectacular views of the city: formal dining in dramatic surroundings. Imaginative modern cuisine based around a classic French style.

XXX **River Room** (at The Lowry H.), 50 Dearmans Pl, Chapel Wharf, Salford, M3 5LH, ☎ (0161) 827 4003, *enquiries@thelowryhotel.com, Fax (0161) 827 4001,* – P. MO AE VISA CY n
Rest 14.50 (lunch) and a la carte 40.85/46.20 ♀.

◆ Matching its surroundings, this is a stylish modern restaurant serving, in a precise manner, classic dishes that have stood the test of time. Irwell views, for good measure.

XXX **Cotton House,** Ducie St, M1 2TP, ☎ (0161) 237 5052, *info@thecottonhouse.com, Fax (0161) 237 5072* – . MO AE VISA
closed 25 December, 1 January and Sunday dinner – **Rest** a la carte 23.70/33.20.

◆ Situated on ground floor of 19C warehouse; separate, stylish Champagne bar. Huge dining room with exposed brickwork, tables clad in black linen. Well executed modern menus.

XX **Establishment,** 43-45 Spring Gdns, M2 2BG, ☎ (0161) 839 6300, *Fax (0161) 839 6353* – . MO AE VISA CZ f
closed 1 week Christmas, Saturday lunch, Sunday, Monday and Bank Holidays – **Rest** a la carte 31.85/44.70 ♀.

◆ Converted Victorian building in city centre: marble columns, ornate glass domed ceilings. Precise, modern dishes, with a classical base, cooked in accomplished fashion.

XX **Second Floor - Restaurant** (at Harvey Nichols), 21 New Cathedral St, M1 1AD, ☎ (0161) 828 8898, *Fax (0161) 828 8570* – . MO AE VISA CY k
closed 25 December, Easter Sunday and dinner Sunday and Monday – **Rest** a la carte 24.50/35.50 ♀.

◆ Central location on second floor of a department store. Well-designed restaurant with immaculate linen-clad tables. Brasserie style cooking.

XX **Yang Sing,** 34 Princess St, M1 4JY, ☎ (0161) 236 2200, *info@yang-sing.com, Fax (0161) 236 5934* – . MO AE VISA CZ y
closed 25 December – **Rest** - Chinese - a la carte 8.00/40.00.

◆ This most renowned of Chinese restaurants continues to provide some of the most authentic, carefully prepared and varied cooking of its kind to be found in the country.

XX **Pacific,** 58-60 George St, M1 4HF, ☎ (0161) 228 6668, *enquiries@pacificrestaurant.co.uk, Fax (0161) 236 0191* – . MO AE VISA CZ k
Rest - Chinese and Thai - 9.50/25.00 and a la carte 19.00/41.00.

◆ Located in Chinatown: Chinese cuisine on first floor, Thai on the second; modern décor incorporating subtle Asian influences. Large menus boast high levels of authenticity.

ENGLAND

Simply Heathcotes, Jackson Row, M2 5WD, ☎ (0161) 835 3536, *manchester@simply heathcotes.co.uk, Fax (0161) 835 3534* – . CZ
closed 25-26 December and Bank Holidays – **Rest** a la carte 16.95/24.00 ♀.
◆ Contemporary interior, with live jazz in the wine bar, contrasts with the original oak panels of this Victorian former register office. Robust menu is equally à la mode.

Koreana, Kings House, 40a King St West, M3 2WY, ☎ (0161) 832 4330, *alexkoreana@aol.com, Fax (0161) 832 2293* – CZ
closed 25-26 December, 1 January, Sunday, lunch Saturday and Bank Holidays – **Rest** Korean - 12.40 and a la carte 11.00/26.50.
◆ Family run basement restaurant, bustling yet still relaxed, offers authentic, balanced Korean cuisine. Novices are guided gently through the menu by staff in national dress.

The Restaurant Bar and Grill, 14 John Dalton St, M2 6JR, ☎ (0161) 839 1999, *manchester@rbgltd.co.uk, Fax (0161) 835 1886* – . CZ
closed 25-26 December – **Rest** a la carte 19.90/37.15 ♀.
◆ Stylish ground floor lounge bar and lively first floor eatery. Extensive international repertoire from an open kitchen. Very busy with business community at lunch.

Second Floor - Brasserie (at Harvey Nichols), 21 New Cathedral St, M1 1AH, ☎ (0161) 828 8898, *secondfloor.reservations@harveynichols.com, Fax (0161) 828 8815* – . CY
closed 25 December, Easter Sunday and dinner Sunday and Monday – **Rest** a la carte 19.00/28.25 ♀.
◆ Open and lively restaurant with minimalist décor. Wide range of cocktails available at the large bar. Attractive menu with a European eclectic mix of dishes.

Le Petit Blanc, 55 King St, M2 4LQ, ☎ (0161) 832 1000, *manchester@lepetitblanc.co.uk, Fax (0161) 832 1001* – . CZ
Rest 14.50 (lunch) and a la carte 21.25/36.70 ♀.
◆ Busy, group-owned brasserie with large bar and polished tables. Extensive menus of classic and modern British dishes as well as regional French options. Attentive service.

Palmiro, 197 Upper Chorlton Rd, M16 0BH, South : 2 m. by A 56 off Chorlton Rd ☎ (0161) 860 7330, *bookings@palmiro.net, Fax (0161) 861 7464,* – AX
closed 1-5 January – **Rest** - Italian - (dinner only and Sunday lunch)/dinner a la carte 19.75/25.50 s..
◆ Spartan interior with grey mottled walls and halogen lighting: a highly regarded neighbourhood Italian eatery boasting good value rustic dishes cooked with maximum simplicity.

Livebait, 22 Lloyd St, Albert Sq, M2 5WA, ☎ (0161) 817 4110, *lbmanchester@groupechezgerard.co.uk, Fax (0161) 817 4111* – . CZ
closed 25 December and 1 January – **Rest** - Seafood - 16.50 (lunch) and a la carte approx. 17.95 ♀.
◆ A friendly atmosphere in which to dine at linen-clad tables amid Art Deco styling. Plenty of choice from seafood oriented menus; indeed, crustacea are on display.

Shimla Pinks, Dolefield Crown Sq, M3 3HA, ☎ (0161) 831 7099, *enquiries@shimlapinksmanchester.com, Fax (0161) 832 2202* – . CZ
closed 25-26 December, lunch Saturday and Sunday and Bank Holidays – **Rest** - Indian - 8.95/19.95 and a la carte 18.65/27.45.
◆ Centrally located Indian restaurant. Colourful artwork and murals and a bustling modern ambience. Extensive menus of authentic Indian dishes and regional specialities.

Zinc Bar and Grill, The Triangle, Hanging Ditch, M4 3ES, ☎ (0161) 827 4200, *zincmanchester-reservations@conran-restaurants.co.uk, Fax (0161) 827 4212,* – CY
Rest 13.00 (lunch) and a la carte 16.50/25.00 ♀.
◆ Converted 19C corn exchange with bustling atmosphere, background jazz and a late night bar. Tables available on pavement and in shopping centre. Modern international menu.

The Ox, 71 Liverpool Rd, Castlefield, M3 4NQ, ☎ (0161) 839 7740, *gmtheox@barbar.co.uk* CZ
Rest a la carte 21.85/26.00.
◆ Central, homely pub, ideal after local museum trip. Cooking style is eclectic, featuring many well-tried or original dishes. Spot a celebrity from nearby Granada TV studios!

at Crumpsall *North : 3½ m. on A 576 – ✉ Manchester.*

Premier Travel Inn, Middleton Rd, M8 6NB, ☎ (0161) 720 6171, *Fax (0161) 740 9142* – , rm, rest, . AV
Rest (grill rest.) – **45 rm** 47.95/47.95 – 50.95/50.95.
◆ Good value, group owned, purpose-built lodge set on a main road in the city's suburbs. Bedrooms decorated in a uniform fitted modern style. Rear rooms quietest.

at Didsbury *South : 5½ m. by 5103 –* **AX** *– on A 5145 – ✉ Manchester.*

Didsbury House, Didsbury Park, M20 5LJ, South : 1½ m. on A 5145 ✆ (0161) 448 2200, *enquiries@didsburyhouse.co.uk, Fax (0161) 448 2525,* – ✈ P. MC AE VISA.
Rest (room service only) – 14.95 – **23 rm** ★88.00 – ★★135.00, 4 suites.
◆ Grade II listed 19C house: grand wooden staircase, superb stained glass window. Otherwise, stylish and modern with roof-top hot tubs. Spacious, individually designed rooms.

Eleven Didsbury Park, 11 Didsbury Park, M20 5LH, South : ½ m. by A 5145 ✆ (0161) 448 7711, *enquiries@elevendidsburypark.com, Fax (0161) 448 8282,* – P. MC AE VISA.
Rest (room service only) – 13.50 – **20 rm** ★88.00 – ★★135.00.
◆ The cool contemporary design in this Victorian town house creates a serene and relaxing atmosphere. Good-sized bedrooms decorated with flair and style. Personally run.

Café Jem&I, 1c School Lane, M20 6SA, ✆ (0161) 445 3996, *jemosullivan@aol.com* – MC AE VISA
closed 25 December, Monday lunch and Bank Holidays – **Rest** a la carte 18.20/27.95 s.
◆ Simple, unpretentious cream coloured building tucked away off the high street. Open-plan kitchen; homely, bistro feel. Good value, tasty modern classics.

at Manchester Airport *South : 9 m. by A 5103 –* **AX** *– off M 56 – ✉ Manchester.*

Radisson SAS Manchester Airport, Chicago Ave, M90 3RA, ✆ (0161) 490 5000, *sales.airport.manchester@radissonsas.com, Fax (0161) 490 5100,* – rm, P – 250. MC AE VISA.
***Phileas Fogg :* Rest** (dinner only) a la carte 31.50/40.50 s. – ***Runway Brasserie :* Rest** a la carte 17.20/26.65 s. – 16.95 – **354 rm** ★135.00/145.00 – ★★135.00/145.00, 6 suites.
◆ Vast, modern hotel linked to airport passenger walkway. Four room styles with many extras. Ideal for business clients or travellers. Phileas Fogg is curved restaurant with eclectic menus and runway views. All-day Runway with arrivals/departures info.

Hilton Manchester Airport, Outwood Lane (Terminal One), M90 4WP, ✆ (0161) 435 3000, *reservations.manchester@hilton.com, Fax (0161) 435 3040,* – rm, P – 300. MC AE VISA
***Lowry's :* Rest** *(closed lunch Saturday and Sunday)* 14.95/27.95 and dinner a la carte 29.85/36.85 s. – 17.95 – **224 rm** ★110.00/175.00 – ★★110.00/175.00, 1 suite.
◆ Popular with corporate travellers for its business centre and location 200 metres from the airport terminal. Comfortable, soundproofed bedrooms. Restaurant exudes pleasant, modern style. Open-plan bar leads to informal Lowry's.

Etrop Grange, Thorley Lane, M90 4EG, ✆ (0161) 499 0500, *etropgrange@corushotels.com, Fax (0161) 499 0790* – P – 80. MC AE VISA
Rest a la carte 30.00/42.00 s. – 13.50 – **62 rm** ★129.00/169.00 – ★★129.00/189.00, 2 suites.
◆ Sympathetically extended Georgian house that retains a period feel. Rooms vary in size; all are pleasantly decorated with some boasting four-posters, others cast-iron beds. Intimate, traditionally styled dining room.

Bewley's, Outwood Lane, (Terminal One), M90 4HL, ✆ (0161) 498 0333, *man@bewleyshotels.com, Fax (0161) 498 0222* – rm, rest, P – 90. MC AE VISA.
Rest (bar lunch)/dinner a la carte 13.85/25.65 – 6.95 – **365 rm** ★69.00 – ★★69.00.
◆ Good value, four-storey, purpose-built group hotel with modern, open lobby. Brightly decorated bedrooms that all have either one double bed and sofa or two double beds. Main restaurant or lobby café dining options.

Moss Nook, Ringway Rd, Moss Nook, M22 5WD, East : 1¼ m. on Cheadle rd ✆ (0161) 437 4778, *Fax (0161) 498 8089,* – P. MC AE VISA
closed 2 weeks Christmas, Saturday lunch, Sunday and Monday – **Rest** 19.50/36.50 and a la carte 32.50/43.75.
◆ Decorated in a combination of Art Nouveau, lace and panelling. Long-standing owners provide polished and ceremonial service; cooking is robust and classically based.

at Trafford Park *Southwest : 2 m. by A 56 and A 5081 – ✉ Manchester.*

Golden Tulip, Waters Reach, M17 1WS, ✆ (0161) 873 8899, *info@goldentulipmanchester.co.uk, Fax (0161) 872 6556* – P – 180. MC AE VISA. **AX c**
Rest – (see ***Watersreach*** below) – 12.00 – **157 rm** ★140.00 – ★★140.00, 3 suites.
◆ Manchester United fans will not only appreciate the proximity to the ground but also the football paraphernalia in the lobby. Uniformly decorated bedrooms are a good size.

Old Trafford Lodge without rest., Lancashire County Cricket Club, Talbot Rd, Old Trafford, M16 0PX, ☎ (0161) 874 3333, *lodge@lccc.co.uk, Fax (0161) 874 3399*, ← – 🛗 ⇍ 🅿. MC AE VISA. ✈ AX k
closed 23 December-3 January – **68 rm** ♀49.00/74.00 – ♀♀54.00/74.00.
◆ Purpose-built lodge within Lancashire County Cricket Club; half the rooms have balconies overlooking the ground. Good value accommodation in smart, colourful bedrooms.

Watersreach, Waters Reach, M17 1WS, ☎ (0161) 868 1900, *watersreach@goldentulipmanchester.co.uk, Fax (0161) 868 1901* – ⇍ ▤ 🅿. MC AE ◑ VISA AX c
closed lunch Saturday, Sunday and Bank Holidays – **Rest** a la carte 21.00/31.95 ♀.
◆ Modern, stylish, David Collins designed restaurant, adjacent to Old Trafford. Smart bar area has comfortable seating. Good, eclectic mix of precisely cooked dishes.

at Salford Quays *Southwest : 2¼ m. by A 56 off A 5063 – ✉ Manchester.*

Copthorne Manchester, Clippers Quay, M50 3SN, ☎ (0161) 873 7321, *roomsales.manchester@mill-cop.com, Fax (0161) 877 1639* – 🛗, ⇍ rm, ▤ rest, ♿ 🅿 – 🏛 150. MC AE ◑ VISA. ✈ AX n
Chandlers : Rest *(closed Saturday lunch and Sunday)* (dinner only) 37.50/42.50 and a la carte ♀ – ***Clippers :*** Rest *(carving rest.)* (bar lunch Saturday) a la carte 18.35/33.20 ♀ – ☕ 15.75 – **166 rm** ♀175.00 – ♀♀175.00.
◆ Part of the redeveloped Quays, overlooking the waterfront, with a Metrolink to the City. Connoisseur bedrooms are particularly well-appointed. Chandlers offers diners enjoyable waterfront views. Informal, pleasantly busy Clippers with open kitchen.

Express by Holiday Inn without rest., Waterfront Quay, M5 2XW, ☎ (0161) 868 1000, *managersalfordquays@expressholidayinn.co.uk, Fax (0161) 868 1068*, ← – 🛗 ⇍ 📞 ♿ 🅿 – 🏛 25. MC AE ◑ VISA AX a
120 rm ♀85.00/95.00 – ♀♀85.00/95.00.
◆ Its pleasant quayside position and modern, well-equipped bedrooms make it a popular choice with both business and leisure travellers. Complimentary breakfast provided.

at Chorlton-Cum-Hardy *Southwest : 5 m. by A 5103 on A 6010 – ✉ Manchester.*

Abbey Lodge without rest., 501 Wilbraham Rd, M21 0UJ, ☎ (0161) 862 9266, *info@abbey-lodge.co.uk, Fax (0161) 862 9266*, 🌳 – ⇍ 🅿. MC AE VISA. ✈ AX z
☕ 6.00 **4 rm** ♀35.00/40.00 – ♀♀55.00/60.00.
◆ Attractive Edwardian house boasting many original features including stained glass windows. Owners provide charming hospitality and pine fitted rooms are immaculately kept.

at Trafford Centre *Southwest : 5¼ m. by A 56 –* **AX** *– and A 5081 – ✉ Manchester.*

Tulip Inn, Old Park Lane, M17 8PG, on B 5214 ☎ (0161) 755 3355, *info@tulipinnmanchester.co.uk, Fax (0161) 755 3344* – 🛗, ⇍ rm, ▤ rest, ♿ 🅿 – 🏛 30. MC AE ◑ VISA. ✈
Rest (dinner only) a la carte approx 15.00 s. – ☕ 7.95 – **160 rm** ♀85.00 – ♀♀85.00.
◆ Large, modern hotel within a stone's throw of the Trafford Centre and M60. Good value accommodation. Bedrooms are notably spacious, well-equipped and up-to-date. Relaxed, informal bistro.

at Worsley *West : 7¼ m. by M 602 –* **AV** *– and M 60 (eastbound) on A 572 – ✉ Manchester.*

Marriott Worsley Park Hotel & Country Club, Worsley Park, M28 2QT, on A 575 ☎ (0161) 975 2000, *events.worsley@marriotthotels.co.uk, Fax (0161) 975 2033*, 🏊, Lб, ≘s, 🏊, 🏌18, 🌳 – 🛗, ⇍ rm, ▤ rest, ♿ 🅿 – 🏛 250. MC AE ◑ VISA
Brindley's : Rest *(closed Saturday lunch)* (carving lunch)/dinner 25.00 and a la carte 29.00/35.50 ♀ – ☕ 14.95 – **153 rm** ♀125.00 – ♀♀125.00, 5 suites.
◆ Built around restored Victorian farm buildings in over 200 acres. Excellent leisure facilities including a championship standard golf course. Large, well-equipped bedrooms. Restaurant is former farm building with high beamed ceiling.

MANCHESTER AIRPORT *Gtr Manchester* 502 503 504 N 23 – *see Manchester.*

MANNINGTREE *Essex* 504 X 28 – *pop. 5 628 – ✉ Colchester.*
London 67 – Colchester 10 – Ipswich 12.

Stour Bay Café, 39-43 High St, CO11 1AH, ☎ (01206) 396687, *jaynewarner@btconnect.com, Fax (01206) 395462* – ⇍. MC VISA
closed Sunday dinner and Monday-Tuesday – **Rest** - Seafood - a la carte 20.00/29.00 ♀.
◆ Rustic and unpretentious bistro with good value, modern, filling dishes. Daily changing menus. Simple, beamed interior and friendly service of prominently seafood menus.

MANSFIELD *Notts.* 502 503 504 Q 24.
London 143 – Chesterfield 12.5 – Worksop 14.5.

No.4 Wood Street, No.4 Wood St, NG18 1QA, ☎ (01623) 424824 – ⇹ ▤ P. MC AE VISA
closed 26 December, 1 January, Monday, Sunday dinner and Saturday lunch – **Rest** a la carte 22.70/37.95.
◆ Solid brick restaurant hidden away in town centre. Relax in lounge bar with comfy armchairs before enjoying well-executed, modern, seasonal dishes in rustic dining room.

MARAZION *Cornwall* 503 D 33 *The West Country G.* – ✉ *Penzance.*
Env. : *St Michael's Mount★★ (≤★★) – Ludgvan★ (Church★) N : 2 m. by A 30 – Chysauster Village★, N : 2 m. by A 30 – Gulval★ (Church★) W : 2½ m – Prussia Cove★, SE : 5½ m. by A 30 and minor rd.*
Praa Sands, Penzance ☎ (01736) 763445.
London 318 – Penzance 3 – Truro 26.

Mount Haven, Turnpike Rd, TR17 0DQ, East : ¼ m. ☎ (01736) 710249, *reception@mounthaven.co.uk, Fax (01736) 711658,* ≤ St Michael's Mount and bay, – ⇹ P. MC VISA
closed week before Christmas-first weekend in February – **Rest** (bar lunch)/dinner a la carte 25.45/30.50 **s.** – **18 rm** ☐ ★60.00/80.00 – ★★84.00/150.00.
◆ Small hotel overlooking St Michael's Bay. Spacious bar and lounge featuring Indian crafts and fabrics. Contemporary rooms with modern amenities, some with balcony and view. Bright attractive dining room; menu mixes modern and traditional.

Ennys without rest., Trewhella Lane, St Hilary, TR20 9BZ, East : 2½ m. by Turnpike Rd, on B 3280 ☎ (01736) 740262, *ennys@ennys.co.uk, Fax (01736) 740055,* heated, – ⇹ P. MC VISA.
mid March-October – **5 rm** ☐ ★50.00/85.00 – ★★85.00/105.00.
◆ Blissful 17C manor house on working farm. Spacious breakfast room and large farmhouse kitchen for afternoon tea. Modern country house style lounge. Elegant, classical rooms.

at Perranuthnoe *Southeast : 1¾ m. by A 394 – ✉ Penzance.*

Ednovean Farm without rest., TR20 9LZ, ☎ (01736) 711883, *info@ednoveanfarm.co.uk, Fax (01736) 710480,* ≤ St Michaels Mount and Bay, – ⇹ P. MC VISA
closed Christmas and New Year – **3 rm** ☐ ★70.00/95.00 – ★★80.00/95.00.
◆ Very spacious, characterful converted 17C granite barn offering peace, tranquillity and Mounts Bay views. Fine choice at breakfast on oak table. Charming, individual rooms.

MARDEN *Wilts.* – *see Devizes.*

MARGATE *Kent* 504 Y 29.
12-13 The Parade ☎ (01843) 583334.
London 74 – Canterbury 17 – Dover 21 – Maidstone 43.

Premier Travel Inn, Station Green, Station Rd, CT9 5AF, ☎ (08701) 977182, *Fax (01843) 221101* – ⇹ rm, ▤ rest, P. MC AE VISA.
Rest (grill rest.) – **44 rm** ★49.95 – ★★49.95.
◆ Simply furnished and brightly decorated bedrooms with ample work space. Suitable for business and family stopovers. Conveniently located next to Brewers Fayre.

Bruno Delamare @ The Art Room, 6 Market Pl, CT9 1EN, ☎ (01843) 295603, *brunomalou@hotmail.com* – ⇹. MC AE VISA
closed 3-25 January, 6-13 August and Sunday-Monday – **Rest** - French - 18.50 (lunch) and a la carte 34.00/45.50 ♀.
◆ 17C former butchers' in old market place. Spacious main dining area with original butchers' hook, beams and vivid artwork. Impressive presentation of classical French menus.

MARKET BOSWORTH *Leics.* 502 503 504 P 26 – *pop. 1 906* – ✉ *Nuneaton.*
London 109 – Birmingham 30 – Coventry 23 – Leicester 22.

Softleys, Market Pl, CV13 OLE, ☎ (01455) 290464, *softleysrestaurant@tiscali.co.uk, Fax (01455) 292532* – ⇹. MC VISA.
closed 25-26 December and Bank Holidays – **Rest** *(closed Monday lunch, Sunday and Bank Holidays)* 10.95 (lunch) and a la carte 25.50/32.15 ♀ – **3 rm** ☐ ★60.00 – ★★70.00.
◆ Solid stone hotel in centre of historic town close to famous battlefield. Snug bar area; first floor dining room used for parties. Good-sized bedrooms exude homely charm. Pleasantly spacious dining room; good use of appealing seasonal ingredients.

MARKET DRAYTON *Shrops.* 502 503 504 M 25.

London 159.5 – Nantwich 13.5 – Shrewsbury 21.

Goldstone Hall, TF9 2NA, South : 4 ½ m. on A 529 ☎ (01630) 661202, *info@goldstonehall.com, Fax (01630) 661585,* ←, – ⇔ **P.** MC VISA
Rest 20.00/29.00 – **11 rm** ☕ ★78.00/95.00 – ★★105.00/760.
• 16C red-brick country house that's been extensively added to over the ages. Five acres of formal garden: PG Wodehouse enjoyed its shade! Modern rooms with huge beds. Contemporary twists on daily changing menus.

MARKET HARBOROUGH *Leics.* 504 R 26 – *pop. 20 127.*

Great Oxendon Rd ☎ (01858) 463684.
Council Offices, Adam and Eve St ☎ (01858) 821270.
London 88 – Birmingham 47 – Leicester 15 – Northampton 17.

The Angel, 37 High St, LE16 7AF, ☎ (01858) 462702, *theangel@theangelhotel.net, Fax (01858) 410464* – ⇔ **P.** – 25. MC AE VISA.
The Brasserie : **Rest** (dinner only and Sunday lunch) a la carte 15.70/24.70 **s.** – ☕ 9.95 – **16 rm** ★48.00/62.50 – ★★58.00/80.00.
• Centrally located former coaching inn dating from 1746. Sophisticated yet informal feel throughout. Ostlers lounge bar has open fire. Good-sized, comfortable bedrooms. A rustic feel permeates French style Brasserie.

at Thorpe Langton *North : 3¾ m. by A 4304 via Great Bowden – ✉ Market Harborough.*

Bakers Arms, Main St, LE16 7TS, ☎ (01858) 545201, *thebakersarms@tiscali.co.uk, Fax (01858) 545924* – MC VISA.
closed Sunday dinner and Monday – **Rest** (booking essential) (dinner only and lunch Saturday and Sunday) a la carte 18.00/30.00.
• Atmospheric thatched pub with deep red walls, exposed timbers and pew seats. Scrubbed wooden tables add to the relaxed feel. Tasty, well-priced, tried-and-tested dishes.

at Marston Trussell *(Northants.) West : 3½ m. by A 4304 – ✉ Market Harborough.*

The Sun Inn, Main St, LE16 9TY, ☎ (01858) 465531, *manager@suninn.com, Fax (01858) 433155* – ⇔ rest, **P.** – 70. MC AE VISA.
closed 25-26 December and 1 January – **Rest** *(closed Sunday dinner)* a la carte 15.00/25.00 – **20 rm** ☕ ★59.00 – ★★69.00.
• Spacious, 17C red-brick former coaching inn in village centre. Distinctly formal dining areas in which to enjoy original, ambitious cooking. Simple, comfortable bedrooms.

MARKET RASEN *Lincs.* 502 504 T 23 – *pop. 3 491.*

London 156 – Boston 41 – Great Grimsby 19 – Lincoln 16.

Bleasby House without rest., Legsby, LN8 3QN, Southeast : 4 ¼ m. by B 1202 ☎ (01673) 842383, *janet@bleasbyhouse.com, Fax (01673) 844808,* – ⇔ **P.**
closed Christmas-New Year – **3 rm** ☕ ★25.00 – ★★50.00.
• Victorian guesthouse close to racecouse and Cadwell Park motor racing circuit. Very pretty garden. Sun lounge with flowers and comfortable rooms with an old English flavour.

MARKINGTON *N. Yorks.* 502 P 21 – *see Ripon.*

MARLBOROUGH *Wilts.* 503 504 O 29 *The West Country G. – pop. 7 713.*

See : *Town*★.
Env. : *Savernake Forest*★★ *(Grand Avenue*★★★*), SE : 2 m. by A 4 – Whitehorse (←★), NW : 5 m – West Kennett Long Barrow*★*, Silbury Hill*★*, W : 6 m. by A 4.*
Exc. : *Ridgeway Path*★★ *– Avebury*★★ *(The Stones*★*, Church*★*), W : 7 m. by A 4 – Crofton Beam Engines*★ *AC, SE : 9 m. by A 346 – Wilton Windmill*★ *AC, SE : 9 m. by A 346, A 338 and minor rd.*
The Common ☎ (01672) 512147.
The Library, High St ☎ (01672) 513989.
London 84 – Bristol 47 – Southampton 40 – Swindon 12.

Coles, 27 Kingsbury Hill, SN8 1JA, ☎ (01672) 515004, *Fax (01672) 512069,* – ⇔. MC VISA
closed 25-26 December, Sunday and Bank Holiday Mondays – **Rest** a la carte 23.45/30.00 ♀.
• Shots of 70s film stars adorn a busy, bay-windowed former pub which retains its firelit bar. Friendly staff and elaborate but robust cuisine with an array of daily specials.

MARLOW Bucks. 504 R 29 – pop. 17 552.

to Henley-on-Thames (Salter Bros. Ltd) (summer only) (2 h 45 mn) – to Maidenhead, Cookham and Windsor (Salter Bros. Ltd) (summer only).

31 High St (01628) 483597.

London 35 – Aylesbury 22 – Oxford 29 – Reading 14.

Danesfield House, Henley Rd, SL7 2EY, Southwest : 2 ½ m. on A 4155 (01628) 891010, *sales@danesfieldhouse.co.uk, Fax (01628) 890408*, ≤ Terraced gardens and River Thames, – rest, rest, – 100. VISA.

Oak Room : Rest 24.50/49.00 and a la carte 49.00/55.00 – ***Orangery :*** Rest 24.50/30.00 – **86 rm** 215.00/220.00 – 260.00, 1 suite.

◆ Stunning house and gardens in Italian Renaissance style with breathtaking views of Thames. Grand lounge with country house feel. Comfy rooms; state-of-art health spa. Intimate Oak Room restaurant. Orangery is a charming terrace brasserie.

Crowne Plaza Marlow, Fieldhouse Lane, SL7 1GJ, East : 2 m. by A 4155 off Parkway Rd (0870) 4448940, *enquiries@crowneplazamarlow.co.uk, Fax (0870) 4448950*, – rm, – 350. VISA.

Glaze : Rest *(closed lunch Saturday and Sunday)* 25.00 and a la carte 18.70/28.20 – ***Agua :*** Rest a la carte 11.75/20.00 – 15.95 – **162 rm** 215.00 – 235.00, 6 suites.

◆ Purpose built hotel near business park. Spacious lobby, leisure club and meeting rooms. Bedrooms well equipped with large desk. Glaze with conservatory overlooking the artificial lake. More informal Agua.

Compleat Angler, Marlow Bridge, Bisham Rd, SL7 1RG, (0870) 4008100, *general.compleatangler@macdonald-hotels.co.uk, Fax (01628) 486388*, ≤ River Thames, – rm, – 120. VISA

Riverside : Rest 27.50/37.50 – ***Alfresco :*** Rest *(closed Sunday dinner)* a la carte 22.45/32.50 – 16.50 – **61 rm** 220.00/260.00 – 220.00/450.00, 3 suites.

◆ Picturesque riverside hotel; spectacular view of Marlow weir. Well-furnished lounges. Rooms are very comfortable; those on river side have four-poster beds and balcony. Formal Riverside restaurant; fine views. Alfresco is a relaxed conservatory brasserie.

The Vanilla Pod, 31 West St, SL7 2LS, (01628) 898101, *info@thevanillapod.co.uk, Fax (01628) 898108* – VISA

closed 1 week Easter, 1 week September, 1 week Christmas, New Year, Sunday and Monday – **Rest** (booking essential) 19.50/40.00.

◆ Distinctly comfy restaurant in town centre. Richly hued dining room with snug, intimate feel and courteous service. Modern cooking, classically underpinned.

The Market, Market Sq, SL7 3HH, (01628) 487661 – 10. VISA

closed 25 December and 1 January – **Rest** 12.00 (lunch) and a la carte 23.25/28.75.

◆ Prominent Georgian building in heart of town. Rich, bohemian style first floor lounge. Casual brasserie dining on ground floor: classic French meets modern Mediterranean.

The Hand & Flowers (Kerridge), West St, SL7 3BP, (01628) 482277, – VISA

closed 26-30 December and 2-8 January – **Rest** *(closed Sunday dinner and Monday)* a la carte 23.50/37.00.

Spec. Potted Dorset crab with brown bread. Rump of new season lamb with aubergine purée. Pistachio cheesecake with banana ice cream.

◆ Series of 19C cottages with timbered exterior. Unspoilt within: original bar and adjacent chunky wood tables for diners. Appealing dishes use only best quality local produce.

Royal Oak, Frieth Rd, Bovingdon Green, SL7 2JF, West : 1 ¼ m. by A 4155 (01628) 488611, *info@royaloakpub.co.uk, Fax (01628) 478680*, – VISA

closed 25-26 December – **Rest** a la carte 17.75/27.25.

◆ Characterful pub with redbrick exterior and smart interior. Full-length window area at back faces spacious garden terrace. Modern menus plus specials board.

MARPLE Gtr Manchester 502 503 504 N 23 – pop. 18 475.

London 190 – Chesterfield 35 – Manchester 11.

Springfield without rest., 99 Station Rd, SK6 6PA, (0161) 449 0721, *Fax (0161) 449 0766*, – VISA.

8 rm 50.00 – 65.00.

◆ Part Victorian house with sympathetic extensions. Useful for visits to Peak District. Two homely lounges, one with good views to Derbyshire hills. Individually styled rooms.

For a pleasant stay in a charming hotel, look for the red ... symbols.

MARSDEN *W. Yorks.* 502 504 O 23 – *pop. 3 499* – ✉ *Huddersfield.*
London 195 – Leeds 22 – Manchester 18 – Sheffield 30.

Olive Branch with rm, Manchester Rd, HD7 6LU, Northeast : 1 m. on A 62 ☎ (01484) 844487, *reservations@olivebranch.uk.com*, – P. MO VISA.
closed 25 December and first 2 weeks January – **Rest** - Seafood specialities - *(closed Monday and lunch Tuesday and Saturday)* 13.95/18.50 and a la carte 24.65/34.95 ♀ – 10.50 – **3 rm** ★50.00 – ★★65.00.
◆ In a secluded valley, a part 16C drovers inn, run with real warmth. Open fire and wide-ranging menus in smart restaurant with outside decking; seafood specials. Modern rooms.

MARSH BENHAM *West Berks.* – *see Newbury.*

MARSTON MONTGOMERY *Derbs.* – *see Ashbourne.*

MARSTON TRUSSELL *Northants.* 504 R 26 – *see Market Harborough.*

MARTEN *Wilts.*
London 77 – Marlborough 9 – Southampton 48.

XX **The Windmill,** Salisbury Rd, SN8 3SH, on A 338 ☎ (01264) 731372, *thewindmill@whsmith.net.co.uk, Fax (01264) 731284*, – P. MO VISA
closed 25 December, Sunday dinner and Monday – **Rest** 19.50 and a la carte 28.95/35.95 ♀.
◆ Former roadside pub with informal but serious attitude to food. Delightful terrace with views to the windmill. Attractive interiors boast antique tables. Very good wine list.

MARTINHOE *Devon* – *see Lynton.*

MARTOCK *Somerset* 503 L 31 *The West Country G.* – *pop. 4 309.*
See : *Village*★ – *All Saints*★★.
Env. : *Montacute House*★★ *AC, SE : 4 m. – Muchelney*★★ *(Parish Church*★★*), NW : 4½ m. by B 3165 – Ham Hill (≤★★), S : 2 m. by minor roads.*
Exc. : *Martock*★ – *Barrington Court*★ *AC, SW : 7½ m. by B 3165 and A 303.*
London 148 – Taunton 19 – Yeovil 6.

The Hollies, Bower Hinton, TA12 6LG, South : 1 m. on B 3165 ☎ (01935) 822232, *enquiries@theholliesshotel.com, Fax (01935) 822249*, – P – 100. MO AE VISA.
Rest *(closed Sunday)* (dinner only) a la carte 16.85/24.85 ♀ – **30 rm** ★80.00 – ★★95.00/125.00, 3 suites.
◆ Impressive former 17C farmhouse in small village near grand Montacute House. Separate annex has large, well-equipped, up-to-date bedrooms with good comforts and facilities. Characterful oak beamed, boothed restaurant and lounge in the farmhouse.

MARTON *Lincs.* 502 504 R 24 – *pop. 508.*
London 155 – Doncaster 27 – Lincoln 14 – Nottingham 40.

Black Swan without rest., 21 High St, DN21 5AH, ☎ (01427) 718878, *reservations@blackswan-marton.co.uk, Fax (01427) 718878*, – P. MO AE VISA.
10 rm ★35.00/40.00 – ★★75.00.
◆ Village centre coaching inn. Homely lounge has velvet furniture; breakfast room with pine table. Six rooms in main house, two in converted stables: all individually styled.

MARTON *N. Yorks.* 502 R 21 – *see Pickering.*

MARTON *Shrops. Great Britain G.*
Env. : *Montgomery*★, *SW : 6 m. by B 4386.*
Exc. : *Powis Castle*★★★, *NW : 7 m. by B 4386 and A 490.*
London 174 – Birmingham 57 – Shrewsbury 16.

The Sun Inn, SY21 8JP, ☎ (01938) 561211 – P. MO VISA
closed Tuesday lunch, Sunday dinner and Monday – **Rest** a la carte 12.00/29.00.
◆ Rural pub where keen young owners serve good value, tasty, traditional dishes heavily influenced by local ingredients. Choose to eat in bar or pine-furnished dining room.

MASHAM *N. Yorks.* 502 P 21 – ✉ *Ripon.*
London 231 – Leeds 38 – Middlesbrough 37 – York 32.

Swinton Park, Swinton, HG4 4JH, Southwest : 1 m ✆ (01765) 680900, *enquiries@swintonpark.com, Fax (01765) 680901*, – 120. AE VISA
Samuels : Rest 18.00/40.00 – **26 rm** 140.00/270.00 – 140.00/270.00, 4 suites.
◆ 17C castle with Georgian and Victorian additions, on a 20,000 acre estate and deer park. Luxurious, antique filled lounges. Very comfortable, individually styled bedrooms. Grand dining room with ornate gold leaf ceiling and garden views.

King's Head, Market Pl, HG4 4EF, ✆ (01765) 689295, *masham.kingshead@snr.co.uk, Fax (01765) 689070*, – rest, – 50. AE VISA.
Rest a la carte 16.45/29.85 – 6.95 – **23 rm** 50.00/55.00 – 85.00.
◆ Dominant Georgian building on main market square. Atmospheric bar with old church pews, beams and vivid walls. Individually styled, well furnished rooms, some in smart annex. Characterful dining room with oak panelling.

Bank Villa, HG4 4DB, on A 6108 ✆ (01765) 689605, *bankvilla@btopenworld.com*, – VISA.
Rest (by arrangement) a la carte 17.50/22.95 – **6 rm** 45.00/55.00 – 55.00/85.00.
◆ Stone-built Georgian villa with Victorian additions. Two lounges and conservatory; delightful, "sun-trap" stepped garden. Cosy, cottagey rooms: some are in the eaves! Home-cooked menus in pastel dining room/tea room.

Vennell's, 7 Silver St, HG4 4DX, ✆ (01765) 689000, *info@vennellsrestaurant.co.uk* – . VISA
closed 1-14 January, 26-30 December, Sunday, Monday and lunch Tuesday-Thursday – Rest 23.00 s.
◆ Smart restaurant with comfy basement bar; linen-clad dining room enhanced by local artwork. Warm service of good value, seasonal dishes prepared with flair and a flourish.

MATFEN *Northd.* 501 502 O 18.
London 309 – Carlisle 42 – Newcastle upon Tyne 24.

Matfen Hall, NE20 0RH, ✆ (01661) 886500, *info@matfenhall.com, Fax (01661) 886055*, – 100. AE VISA
Library and Print Room : Rest (dinner only and Sunday lunch)/dinner 25.00 and a la carte 32.95/37.45 – **53 rm** 125.00/135.00 – 155.00.
◆ 19C country mansion built by Thomas Ruckman, master of Gothic design. Set in 500 acres with superb Grand Hall, fine paintings, plush drawing room and grand bedrooms. Characterful Library dining room displays original books.

MATLOCK *Derbs.* 502 503 504 P 24 *Great Britain G. – pop. 11 265.*
Exc. : *Hardwick Hall★★ AC, E : 12½ m. by A 615 and B 6014.*
Crown Sq ✆ (01629) 583388 – The Pavilion, Matlock Bath ✆ (01629) 55082.
London 153 – Derby 17 – Manchester 46 – Nottingham 24 – Sheffield 24.

Riber Hall, Riber Village, DE4 5JU, Southeast : 3 m. by A 615 ✆ (01629) 582795, *info@riber-hall.co.uk, Fax (01629) 580475*, – AE VISA
closed 25 December – Rest 19.00/37.00 – 8.00 – **14 rm** 85.00/95.00 – 110.00/136.00.
◆ Part Elizabethan manor house on hilltop hamlet. Wonderfully peaceful setting. Leaded windows, Elizabethan styling, exposed beams, stone walls. Four posters in rooms. Period style restaurant with gold drapes.

at Birchover *Northeast : 7½ m. by A 6 – ✉ Matlock.*

Druid Inn, DE4 2BL, ✆ (01629) 650302, – VISA
closed Sunday dinner – Rest a la carte 20.00/29.00 .
◆ Early 19C stone-built pub in Peak District, providing Derbyshire tradition in contemporary style. Huge menus offer a vast choice of sensibly priced modern dishes.

MAULDS MEABURN *Cumbria* – *see Appleby-in-Westmorland.*

MAWNAN SMITH *Cornwall* 503 E 33 – *see Falmouth.*

Good food and accommodation at moderate prices? Look for the Bib symbols: red Bib Gourmand for food, blue Bib Hotel for hotels

MEDBOURNE *Leics.* 504 R 26.
London 93 – Corby 9 – Leicester 16.

XX **Horse & Trumpet** with rm, Old Green, LE16 8DX, ✆ (01858) 565000, *info@horseandtrumpet.com, Fax (01858) 565551,* – . VISA
closed 1 week January, Sunday dinner and Monday – **Rest** 20.00 (lunch) and dinner a la carte 32.00/46.00 ♀ – **4 rm** ☐ ★75.00 – ★★75.00.
◆ 18C thatched inn with bowling green. Stylish well-furnished bedrooms. Linen clad tables in the dining rooms; al fresco eating in courtyard. Modern menu using local produce.

MELBOURN *Cambs.* 504 U 27 – *pop. 4 298* – ✉ *Royston (Herts.).*
London 44 – Cambridge 10.

Melbourn Bury, Royston Rd, SG8 6DE, Southwest : ¾ m. ✆ (01763) 261151, *melbournbury@biztobiz.co.uk, Fax (01763) 262375,* <, , – P. VISA.
closed Easter and 24 December-2 January – **Rest** (by arrangement) (communal dining) 26.00 – **3 rm** ☐ ★85.00 – ★★130.00.
◆ Country house of Tudor origins with good views of surrounding countryside. Drawing room with antiques and lovely oil paintings. Spacious rooms have period furnishings. Dine communally at antique table.

XX **Pink Geranium,** 25 Station Rd, SG8 6DX, ✆ (01763) 260215, *info@pinkgeranium.co.uk, Fax (01763) 262110,* – P. AE VISA
closed 26-30 December, 1 January, Sunday dinner and Monday – **Rest** 24.50/27.50 and a la carte 31.95/47.95 ♀.
◆ Converted 16C thatched cottages. Chintzy, rustic interior. Timbered ceiling and floral drapes. French inspired cooking is the basis of the wide-ranging menus.

XX **Sheene Mill** with rm, Station Rd, SG8 6DX, ✆ (01763) 261393, *info@sheenemill.co.uk, Fax (01763) 261376,* <, , – , rest, P. AE VISA.
closed 26 December and 1 January – **Rest** *(closed Sunday dinner)* 18.00/35.00 ♀ – **9 rm** ☐ ★95.00 – ★★120.00.
◆ Restored 17C watermill with gardens, terraces and good views of millpond. Log fire and flagstones; friendly service. Modern à la carte menu. Designer themed bedrooms.

MELKSHAM *Wilts.* 503 504 N 29 *The West Country G.* – *pop. 14 372.*
Env. : *Corsham Court★★ AC, NW : 4½ m. by A 365 and B 3353 – Lacock★★ (Lacock Abbey★ AC, High Street★, St Cyriac★, Fox Talbot Museum of Photography★ AC) N : 3 ½ m. by A 350.*
Church St ✆ (01225) 707424.
London 113 – Bristol 25 – Salisbury 35 – Swindon 28.

at Whitley *Northwest : 2 m. by A 365 on B 3353 –* ✉ *Melksham.*

Pear Tree Inn with rm, Top Lane, SN12 8QX, by First Lane ✆ (01225) 709131, *sales@peartreeinn.co.uk, Fax (01225) 702276,* , – P. VISA.
closed 25-26 December and 1 January – **Rest** 16.50 (lunch) and a la carte 20.95/29.50 ♀ – **8 rm** ☐ ★75.00 – ★★110.00.
◆ Characterful Bath stone pub with lovely gardens and terrace. Modish restaurant to rear: assured, tasty cooking. Very smart, modern, stylish bedrooms in house and conversion.

MELLOR *Lancs.* – *see Blackburn.*

MELTON MOWBRAY *Leics.* 502 504 R 25 – *pop. 25 554.*
Waltham Rd, Thorpe Arnold ✆ (01664) 562118.
Windsor House, Windsor St ✆ (01664) 480992.
London 113 – Leicester 15 – Northampton 45 – Nottingham 18.

Stapleford Park , LE14 2EF, East : 5 m. by B 676 on Stapleford rd ✆ (01572) 787000, *reservations@stapleford.co.uk, Fax (01572) 787001,* <, , , , , , , , – P – 200. AE VISA
Grinling Gibbons Dining Room : **Rest** (booking essential) (dinner only and Sunday lunch) 44.00 and a la carte 46.50/56.50 – ***Pavilion Brasserie :*** **Rest** a la carte 19.50/26.50 – **53 rm** ☐ ★195.00/250.00 – ★★465.00, 2 suites.
◆ Astoundingly beautiful stately home in 500 glorious acres, exuding a grandeur rarely surpassed. Extensive leisure facilities; uniquely designed rooms of sumptuous elegance. Ornate rococo dining room a superb example of master craftsman's work. Smart brasserie.

Quorn Lodge, 46 Asfordby Rd, LE13 0HR, West : ½ m. on A 6006 ✆ (01664) 566660, *quornlodge@aol.com, Fax (01664) 480660* – ⇔ ✆ P – 🏛 80. MC VISA. ✂
closed 26 December-2 January – ***The Laurels :*** **Rest** a la carte 16.55/25.85 ♀ – **19 rm** ☕ ★62.50/71.00 – ★★77.00/80.00.
◆ Former hunting lodge, privately owned, situated just outside town centre. Spacious sitting room and bar leads on to small conference room. Spacious, neatly kept rooms. Homely restaurant with pretty garden to rear.

at Stathern *North : 8 m. by A 607 – ✉ Melton Mowbray.*

Red Lion Inn, 2 Red Lion St, LE14 4HS, ✆ (01949) 860868, *info@theredlioninn.co.uk, Fax (01949) 861579,* ☂ – P. MC VISA
closed 1 January and Sunday dinner – **Rest** (booking essential) 15.50 (lunch) and a la carte 19.50/28.00 ♀.
◆ Rural pub with a predominant "country" feel: solid stone floors, wooden antiques, rustic ornaments, solid fireplaces, skittle alley. Daily changing, modern menus.

at Nether Broughton *Northwest : 5¾ m. on A 606 – ✉ Melton Mowbray.*

The Red house, 23 Main St, LE14 3HB, ✆ (01664) 822429, *bookings@the-redhouse.com, Fax (01664) 823805,* ☂ – ⇔ P. MC AE ⓓ VISA
closed 25 December – **Rest** a la carte 24.50/36.50 ♀ – **8 rm** ☕ ★65.00 – ★★130.00.
◆ Stylish, smart bedrooms with plenty of extras are the highlight of this 15C former coaching inn. Brightly painted, modern public areas. Delightful terrace and bar. Popular favourites to fore in dining room; local produce much in evidence.

MEMBURY *Devon – see Axminster.*

MERIDEN *W. Mids.* 503 504 P 26 – *see Coventry.*

MEVAGISSEY *Cornwall* 503 F 33 *The West Country G.* – *pop. 2 221.*

See : *Town*★★.
Env. : *NW : Lost Gardens of Heligan*★.
London 287 – Newquay 21 – Plymouth 44 – Truro 20.

Trevalsa Court, School Hill, PL26 6TH, East : ½ m. on B 3273 (St Austell rd) ✆ (01726) 842468, *stay@cornwall-hotel.net, Fax (01726) 844482,* ←, 🌳 – ⇔ ✆ P. MC AE VISA. ✂
closed 15 November-12 February – **Rest** (dinner only) 29.00 and a la carte 23.00/38.00 ♀ – **14 rm** ☕ ★55.00/94.00 – ★★78.00/148.00.
◆ Charming 1930s building with lovely garden which has access to Polstreath Beach. Homely morning room; quirky, 'Continental'-style bar. Autumnal shades enhance tasteful rooms. Oak-panelled dining room with daily menu, devised using best available produce.

Kerryanna 🐴 without rest., Treleaven Farm, PL26 6RZ, ✆ (01726) 843558, *enquiries@kerryanna.co.uk, Fax (01726) 843558,* 🏊 heated, 🌳, 🎾 – ⇔ P. MC VISA. ✂
March-November – **6 rm** ☕ ★40.00/50.00 – ★★70.00/76.00.
◆ Purpose-built bungalow within farm providing pleasant ambience. Useful for Lost Gardens of Heligan. Spacious front sitting room. Immaculately kept, sizeable, chintz bedrooms.

MICKLEHAM *Surrey* 504 T 30.

London 21 – Brighton 32 – Guildford 14 – Worthing 34.

The King William IV, Byttom Hill, RH5 6EL, North : ½ m. by A 24 ✆ (01372) 372590, ☂ – MC ⓓ VISA. ✂
closed 25 December and Sunday dinner – **Rest** a la carte 16.40/22.75.
◆ Once a beer house for Lord Beaverbrook's staff, this part 19C hillside pub looks over Mole Valley from lounge and terrace. Large blackboard menu: wholesome and homely.

MICKLEOVER *Derbs.* 502 503 504 P 25 – *see Derby.*

MICKLETON *Glos.* 503 504 O 27 – *see Chipping Campden.*

Do not confuse ✗ with ✿! ✗ defines comfort, while stars are awarded for the best cuisine, across all categories of comfort.

MIDDLEHAM *N. Yorks.* 502 O 21.

London 233 – Kendal 45 – Leeds 47 – Newcastle upon Tyne 63 – York 45.

Waterford House, 19 Kirkgate, DL8 4PC, ✆ (01969) 622090, *info@waterfordhousehotel.co.uk, Fax (01969) 624020,* – P. VISA

closed 23 December-3 January – **Rest** *(closed Sunday-Monday)* (residents only) (dinner only) 32.00 s. – **5 rm** ☕ ★65.00/70.00 – ★★105.00/115.00.

◆ Elegant Georgian house, just off cobbled market square, with neat walled garden. Drawing room boasts cluttered charm. Individually appointed rooms with thoughtful touches. Formal restaurant: home cooked menus use much local produce.

Middleham Grange without rest., Market Pl, DL8 4NR, ✆ (01969) 622630, *Fax (01969) 625437,* – P

3 rm ☕ ★60.00 – ★★80.00.

◆ Beautifully restored part-Georgian manor house. Comfy period style lounge; bright breakfast room in conservatory overlooking garden. Snug bedrooms exude a classical style.

White Swan with rm, Market Pl, DL8 4PE, ✆ (01969) 622093, *whiteswan@easynet.co.uk, Fax (01969) 624551,* – P. VISA

Rest *(closed 25 December)* 13.95 (lunch) and a la carte 16.50/23.50 – **19 rm** ☕ ★47.50 – ★★90.00.

◆ Former coaching inn in the market place. Traditional flagged floor bar with wood-burning stove and inglenook. Hearty English dishes with local ingredients. Comfy rooms.

at Carlton-in-Coverdale *Southwest : 4½ m. by Coverham rd – ✉ Leyburn.*

Abbots Thorn, DL8 4AY, ✆ (01969) 640620, *abbots.thorn@virgin.net, Fax (01969) 640304,*

closed 23 December-6 January – **Rest** (by arrangement) (communal dining) 17.00 – **3 rm** ☕ ★40.00/50.00 – ★★50.00.

◆ Well priced, comfortable, quiet guesthouse in attractive rural village. Handy for visits to Moors. Cosy sitting room. Sizeable bedrooms which are homely and well-kept. Fresh, local produce to fore at dinner.

Forester's Arms with rm, DL8 4BB, ✆ (01969) 640272, *Fax (01969) 640272,* – P. VISA

closed 1 week February, Monday, Sunday dinner and Tuesday lunch – **Rest** a la carte 16.00/25.00 – **3 rm** ☕ ★65.00 – ★★79.00.

◆ Compact 17C stone-built inn. Flagged floor bar with beams and open fire. Timbered restaurant where modern dishes utilise fresh, local produce. Pleasant, cottagey rooms.

Undecided between two equivalent establishments?
Within each category, establishments are classified in our order of preference.

MIDDLESBROUGH *Middlesbrough* 502 Q 20 – *pop. 142 691.*

Middlesbrough Municipal, Ladgate Lane ✆ (01642) 315533 – Brass Castle Lane, Marton ✆ (01642) 311515.

Cleveland Transporter Bridge (toll) **BY**.

Teesside Airport : ✆ (01325) 332811, SW : 13 m. by A 66 – **AZ** *– and A 19 on A 67.*

The Town Hall, Albert Rd ✆ (01642) 729700.

London 246 – Kingston-upon-Hull 89 – Leeds 66 – Newcastle upon Tyne 41.

Plan opposite

Thistle, Fry St, TS1 1JH, ✆ (0870) 3339141, *middlesbrough@thistle.co.uk, Fax (0870) 3339241,* rest, P – 350. VISA **BY e**

Gengis : **Rest** 17.00/24.00 (dinner) and a la carte approx 23.95 s. – ☕ 11.50 – **132 rm** ★150.00 – ★★150.00.

◆ Tower block hotel in a convenient central location. Well-planned modern style and décor throughout public areas and well-equipped bedrooms. East meets west cuisine in bright, informal restaurant.

Express by Holiday Inn without rest., Marton Rd, TS4 3BS, ✆ (01642) 814444, *Fax (01642) 829999* – P – 30. VISA **BZ a**

74 rm ★55.00 – ★★55.00.

◆ Purpose-built lodge on main road into city opposite South Cleveland Hospital. Smart modern rooms decorated in bright, well-ordered style. Well suited to business travellers.

MIDDLESBROUGH

Street	Grid	No.
Albert Rd	BY	2
Ayresome Green Lane	AZ	3
Bridge St West	AY	4
Bright St	BY	5
Captain Cook Square	AY	43
Clairville Rd	BZ	6
Cleveland Centre	ABY	
Cleveland St	BY	7
Corporation Rd	BY	8
Devonshire Rd	AZ	10
Dundas St	ABY	12
Eastbourne Rd	AZ	14
Ferry Rd	BY	15
Finsbury St	AZ	16
Grange Rd	ABY	17
Gresham Rd	AZ	18
Hartington Rd	AY	19
Hill St Centre	AY	
Linthorpe Rd	AY	
Longford St	AZ	22
Newport Rd	AY	
Ormesby Rd	BZ	24
Princes Rd	AZ	26
St Barnabas Rd	AZ	27
Saltersgill Ave	BZ	28
Sussex St	AY	30
Tees Bridge Approach Rd	AZ	34
West Terrace	BZ	35
Westbourne Grove	BZ	36
Wilson St	AY	38
Woodlands Rd	BZ	39
Zetland St	ABY	41

⌂ **Grey House** without rest., 79 Cambridge Rd, TS5 5NL, ✆ (01642) 817485, *dwattis@fsmail.net, Fax (01642) 817485,* – ⚟ P. MC VISA AZ n
8 rm ☕ ★45.00/50.00 – ★★60.00.
◆ Large, detached hotel with pleasant garden providing good value accommodation. Personally run. Nicely furnished traditional lounge. Clean, well-kept bedrooms.

Hotels and restaurants change every year,
so change your Michelin guide every year!

MIDDLETON *N.Yorks. – see Pickering.*

MIDDLETON-IN-TEESDALE *Durham* 502 N 20 – *pop. 1 143* – *Market Pl* ✆ *(01833) 641001.*
London 447 – Carlisle 91 – Leeds 124 – Middlesbrough 70 – Newcastle upon Tyne *65.*

Grove Lodge, Hude, DL12 0QW, Northwest : ½ m. on B 6277 ✆ (01833) 640798, ≤, – – **Rest** a la carte 16.15/28.95 ♀ – **3 rm** ☐ ★36.00 – ★★58.00.
◆ Victorian former shooting lodge perched on a hill where the two front facing rooms have the best views. Neat and friendly house, traditionally decorated. Home-cooked dinners are proudly served.

MIDDLETON STONEY *Oxon.* 503 504 Q 28.
London 66 – Northampton 30 – Oxford *12.*

Jersey Arms, OX25 4AD, ✆ (01869) 343234, *jerseyarms@bestwestern.co.uk, Fax (01869) 343565,* – VISA.
Rest a la carte 16.20/26.40 ♀ – **17 rm** ☐ ★75.00/89.00 – ★★99.00/125.00, 3 suites.
◆ Characterful hotel on site of old coaching inn. Comfortable, beamed lounge and bar. Modern rooms in courtyard have rust and cream décor; older rooms exude traditional style. Small dining room with beams.

MIDDLEWICH *Ches.* 502 503 504 M 24.
London 176.5 – Crewe 13 – Northwich 7.5.

Kinderton's with rm, Kinderton St, CW10 0JE, ✆ (01606) 834325, *Fax (01606) 832323,* , – , rest, 10. VISA
closed 4 days Christmas and New Year – **Rest** a la carte 20.60/29.35 – **12 rm** ☐ ★55.00 – ★★55.00.
◆ Personally run restaurant in pleasantly refurbished hotel with garden and terrace. The simple, modern style is complemented by good value, appealing menus. Comfy bedrooms.

MIDDLE WINTERSLOW *Wilts. – see Salisbury.*

MIDHURST *W. Sussex* 504 R 31 – *pop. 6 120* – *North St* ✆ *(01730) 817322.*
London 57 – Brighton 38 – Chichester 12 – Southampton *41.*

Spread Eagle, South St, GU29 9NH, ✆ (01730) 816911, *spreadeagle@hshotels.co.uk, Fax (01730) 815668,* , , – – 80. VISA
Rest 18.50/35.00 ♀ – **37 rm** ☐ ★85.00/190.00 – ★★99.00/228.00, 2 suites.
◆ 15C hostelry boasting lovely characterful bar with uneven oak flooring and roaring fire. Many antiques. Good leisure facilities. Rooms have country house décor and style. A very traditional ambience pervades restaurant.

Angel, North St, GU29 9DN, ✆ (01730) 812421, *info@theangelmidhurst.co.uk, Fax (01730) 815928,* – – 60. VISA
Brasserie : **Rest** (lunch booking essential)/dinner a la carte 19.85/26.85 ♀ – **28 rm** ☐ ★80.00/90.00 – ★★150.00.
◆ 16C coaching inn with a country house feel on main road in town centre. Georgian façade and Tudor origins. Neatly furnished lounge. Well kept, chintz bedrooms. Informal brasserie with distinctive mahogany furniture.

at Bepton *Southwest : 2½ m. by A 286 on Bepton rd – ✉ Midhurst.*

Park House , Bepton, GU29 0JB, ✆ (01730) 819000, *reservations@parkhousehotel.com, Fax (01730) 819099,* heated, , , – – 70. VISA
Rest (booking essential) 25.00/32.00 – **14 rm** ☐ ★85.00/125.00 – ★★125.00/290.00, 1 suite.
◆ Comfortable, privately owned country house. Charming lounge with chintz armchairs, antique paintings, heavy drapes. Bar with honesty policy. Rooms are bright and colourful. Classical dining room with antique tables and chairs.

at Elsted *Southwest : 5 m. by A 272 on Elsted rd – ✉ Midhurst.*

Three Horseshoes, GU29 0JY, ✆ (01730) 825746, – . VISA
Rest a la carte 20.00/27.00.
◆ Lovely, informal 16C drovers inn with wood burners, stone floors and low ceiling. Honest pub cooking, fresh and tasty. Expect cottage or fish pie with a little extra twist.

at Stedham *West : 2 m. by A 272 – ✉ Midhurst.*

Nava Thai at Hamilton Arms, School Lane, GU29 0NZ, ✆ (01730) 812555, *hamiltonarms@hotmail.com, Fax (01730) 817459* – . VISA
closed 1 week January and Monday except Bank Holidays – **Rest** - Thai - 19.50 and a la carte 15.00/25.00 ♀.
◆ Busy Thai restaurant in bustling pub. Mahogany tables, wicker chairs. Thai royalty adorns the walls. Lanterns lighten your way. Colourful cooking, fragrant and flavoursome.

MIDSOMER NORTON *Somerset* 503 504 M 30.
London 125 – Bath 11 – Wells 12.

The Moody Goose at the Old Priory (Shore) with rm, Church Sq, BA3 2HX, ✆ (01761) 416784, *info@theoldpriory.co.uk, Fax (01761) 417851*, – P. MO AE VISA
closed Sunday and Bank Holidays except Good Friday – **Rest** 17.50/25.50 and dinner a la carte 29.00/36.00 – **7 rm** 80.00 – 135.00.
Spec. Parfait of foie gras with brioche and roast apricots. Braised belly of pork with apple, lentils and white onion sauce. Assiette of banana.
◆ 12C former priory, by a chuch, with enviable walled garden. Flagged floors, beams and vast fireplaces create impressive interior. Accomplished modern cooking. Comfy rooms.

MILFORD-ON-SEA *Hants.* 503 504 P 31 – *pop. 4 229* – ✉ *Lymington.*
London 109 – Bournemouth 15 – Southampton 24 – Winchester 37.

Westover Hall, Park Lane, SO41 0PT, ✆ (01590) 643044, *info@westoverhallhotel.com, Fax (01590) 644490*, ≤ Christchurch Bay, Isle of Wight and The Needles, , – P. MO AE VISA
Rest 25.00/38.50 **s.** – **11 rm** (dinner included) 115.00/200.00 – 230.00/330.00, 1 suite.
◆ Characterful 19C mansion in peaceful, stunning spot overlooking Christchurch Bay. Very comfortable sitting room. Magnificent hall and minstrels gallery. Sumptuous rooms. Ornate dining room: decorative ceiling, stained glass, panelling.

MILLOM *Cumbria* 502 K 21 *Great Britain G.* – *pop. 6 103.*
Exc.: *Hard Knott Pass★★, N : 23 m. by A 595 and minor rd (eastbound).*
London 299 – Barrow-in-Furness 22 – Ulverston 17.

Underwood, The Hill, LA18 5EZ, North : 2 m. on A 5093 ✆ (01229) 771116, *andrew.miller@aggregate.com, Fax (01229) 719900*, ≤, , , – P. MO VISA.
closed 2 weeks in winter and 1 week in autumn – **Rest** (booking essential) (dinner only) 25.00 – **7 rm** 50.00 – 110.00.
◆ Built in classic Lakeland grey, a Victorian former vicarage boasting two comfortable lounges and a large indoor pool. Well-kept, spacious double rooms with countryside views. Pleasant dining room overlooks gardens; tasty home cooking.

MILTON ABBOT *Devon* 503 H 32 – *see Tavistock.*

MILTON ERNEST *Beds.* 504 S 27 – *see Bedford.*

MILTON KEYNES *Milton Keynes* 504 R 27 – *pop. 184 506.*
18 Abbey Hill, Monks Way, Two Mile Ash ✆ (01908) 563845 **AV** – *18 Windmill Hill, Tattenhoe Lane, Bletchley ✆ (01908) 631113* **BX** – *18, 9 Wavendon Golf Centre, Lower End Rd, Wavendon ✆ (01908) 281811* **CV**.
890 Midsummer Boulevard ✆ (0870) 120 1269/(01908) 558300 **FY**, *askvic@powernet.com.*
London 56 – Bedford 16 – Birmingham 72 – Northampton 18 – Oxford 37.

Plans on following pages

Holiday Inn Milton Keynes, 500 Saxon Gate West, Central Milton Keynes, MK9 2HQ, ✆ (0870) 400 9057, *reservations-miltonkeynes@ichotelsgroup.com, Fax (01908) 698693*, , , – , rm, P – 100. MO AE VISA. **EYZ a**
Rest 20.00/31.85 and dinner a la carte 15.00/25.00 – 14.95 – **164 rm** 170.00 – 170.00, 2 suites.
◆ Commercial business hotel, with public areas set in modern atrium. Opposite main shopping area. Good leisure club with above average sized pool. Well-kept, clean rooms. Informal, family-friendly restaurant.

Hilton Milton Keynes, Timbold Drive, Kents Hill Park, MK6 7AH, Southeast : 4 m. by B 4034 and A 421 off Brickhill St. (V10) ✆ (01908) 694433, *Fax (01908) 695533*, , , – , rest, P – 300. MO AE VISA **CVX d**
Britisserie **: Rest** *(closed Saturday lunch)* 12.75/19.50 and dinner a la carte 25.00/35.00 **s.** – 14.95 – **138 rm** 136.00/240.00 – 146.00/260.00.
◆ Modern, commercial group hotel with comprehensive business facilities. Large lounge and bar. Comfortable rooms in three different grades varying slightly by size. Informal dining room aimed at business traveller.

HORIZONTAL ROADS

Bletcham Way (H10) CX
Chaffron Way (H7) .... BX, CV
Childs Way (H6) .... BX, CV
Dansteed Way (H4) .... ABV
Groveway (H9) CVX
Millers Way (H2) .... AV
Monks Way (H3) .... ABV
Portway (H5) .... BCV
Ridgeway (H1) .... AV
Standing Way (H8) .... BX, CV

MILTON KEYNES

Buckingham Rd .... BX
London Rd .... CUV
Manor Rd CX
Marsh End Rd .... CU
Newport Rd .... BV
Northampton Rd .... AU
Stoke Rd CX
Stratford Rd .... AV
Whaddon Way .... BX
Wolverton Rd .... BU

VERTICAL ROADS

Brickhill St (V10) .... BU, CX
Fulmer St (V3) .... ABX
Grafton St (V6) .... BVX
Great Monks St (V5) .... AV
Marlborough St (V8) .... BV, CX
Overstreet (V9) .... BV
Saxon St (V7) .... BVX
Snelshall St (V1) .... BX
Tattenhoe St (V2) .... ABX
Tongwell St (V11) CVX
Watling St (V4) .... AV, BX

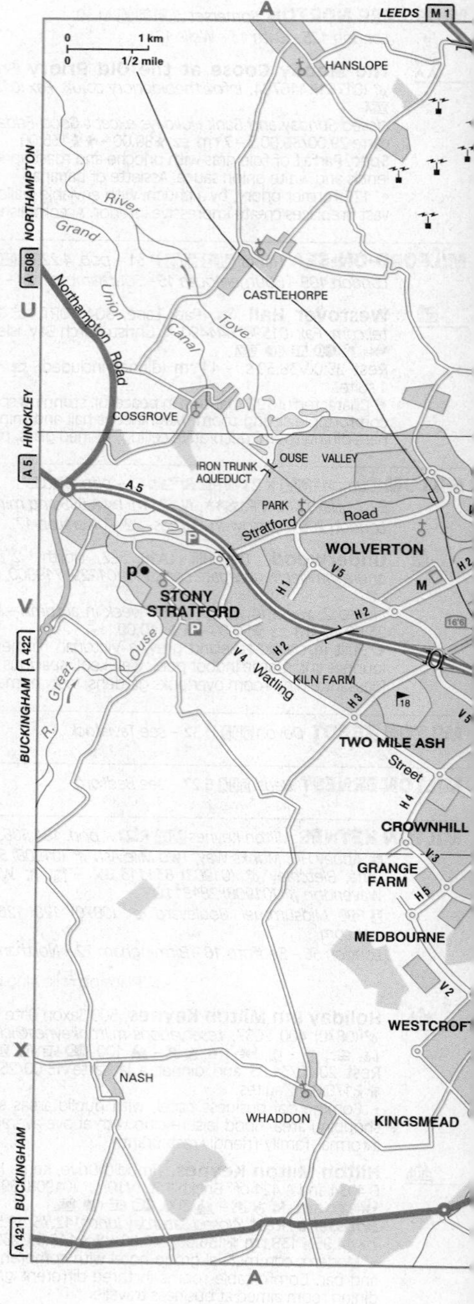

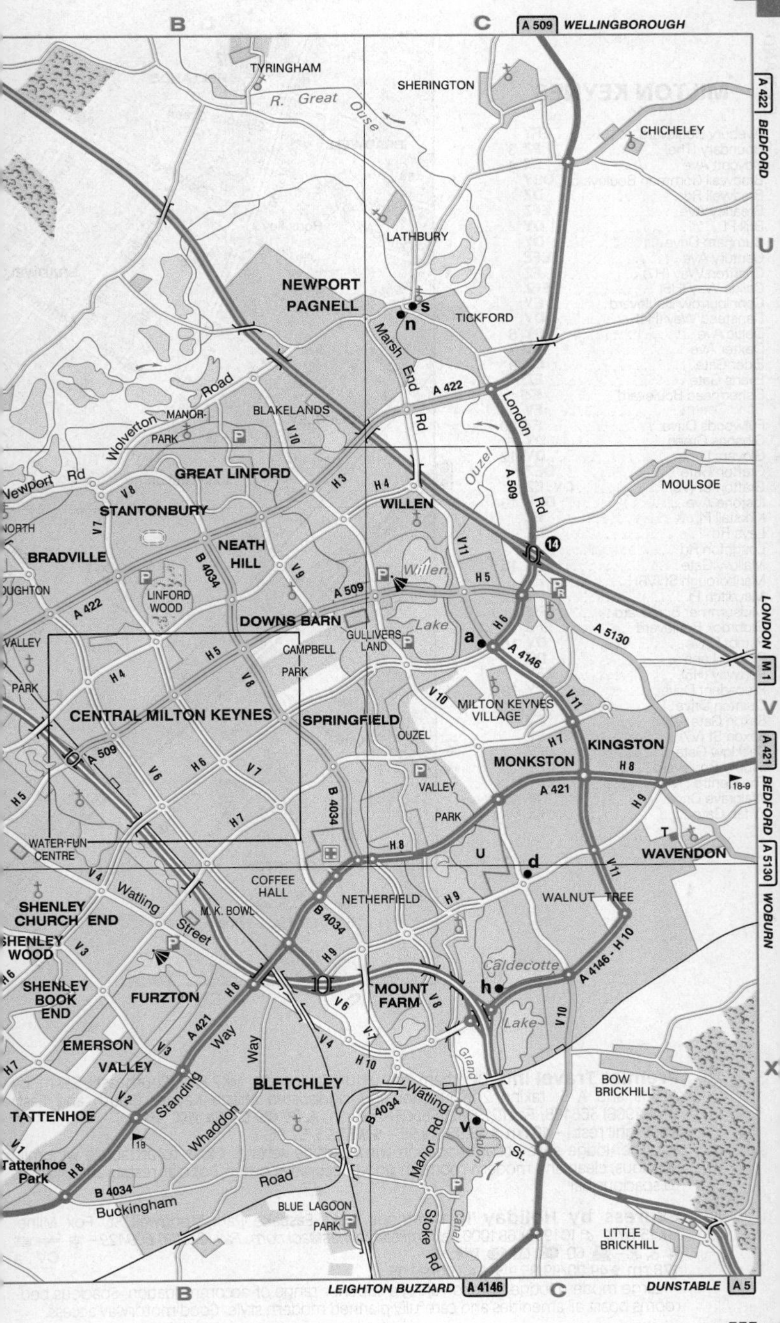
A 509 WELLINGBOROUGH
A 422 BEDFORD
TYRINGHAM
SHERINGTON
CHICHELEY
R. Great Ouse
LATHBURY
NEWPORT PAGNELL
TICKFORD
Marsh End Rd
A 422
London Rd
Wolverton Road
MANOR-PARK
BLAKELANDS
GREAT LINFORD
Newport Rd
STANTONBURY
WILLEN
MOULSOE
A 509
Ouzel
BRADVILLE
NEATH HILL
B 4034
Willen Lake
LINFORD WOOD
DOWNS BARN
GULLIVERS LAND
CAMPBELL PARK
A 5130
A 4146
LONDON
M 1
CENTRAL MILTON KEYNES
SPRINGFIELD
MILTON KEYNES VILLAGE
OUZEL
KINGSTON
MONKSTON
A 421
A 421 BEDFORD
VALLEY PARK
WAVENDON
WATER·FUN CENTRE
COFFEE HALL
NETHERFIELD
WALNUT TREE
A 5130 WOBURN
SHENLEY CHURCH END
SHENLEY WOOD
Watling Street
M.K. BOWL
Caldecotte Lake
A 4146 - H 10
SHENLEY BOOK END
FURZTON
MOUNT FARM
EMERSON VALLEY
Standing Way
BLETCHLEY
BOW BRICKHILL
TATTENHOE
Whaddon Way
Manor Rd
Grand Union Canal
Tattenhoe Park
B 4034
Buckingham Road
BLUE LAGOON PARK
Stoke Rd
LITTLE BRICKHILL
LEIGHTON BUZZARD
A 4146
DUNSTABLE
A 5

MILTON KEYNES

Avebury Boulevard. . . . . EFY
Boundary (The) . . . . FZ 3
Boycott Ave . . . . EZ 4
Bradwell Common Boulevard . DEY
Bradwell Rd . . . . DZ
Brearley Ave . . . . EFZ
Brill Pl. DY
Burnham Drive . . . . DY
Century Ave . . . . EFZ
Chaffron Way (H7) . . . . FZ
Childs Way (H6) . . . . EFZ
Conniburrow Boulevard . . . . EY
Dansteed Way (H4) . . . . DY
Deltic Ave . . . . DY 6
Dexter Ave . . . . FZ 7
Elder Gate . . . . DZ 9
Evans Gate . . . . EZ
Fishermead Boulevard . . . . FZ
Food Centre . . . . FY
Fulwoods Drive . . . . FZ 10
Gibsons Green . . . . DY
Glovers Lane . . . . DY 12
Grafton Gate . . . . DEZ
Grafton St (V6) . . . . DY, EZ
Ibstone Ave . . . . DEY 13
Kirkstall Pl. . . . . EZ
Leys Rd. . . . . DZ
Loughton Rd . . . . DY
Mallow Gate . . . . EY 15
Marlborough St (V8) . . . . FY
Maydlitch Pl. . . . . DY
Midsummer Boulevard . . . . EFY
Oldbrook Boulevard . . . . EFZ
Patriot Drive . . . . DY 16
Pitcher Lane . . . . DZ
Portway (H5). . . . . EFY
Precedent Drive . . . . DY 18
Quinton Drive . . . . DY
Saxon Gate (V7) . . . . EY
Saxon St (V7) . . . . EY, FZ
Secklow Gate . . . . FY
Silbury Boulevard . . . . EFY
The Centre : MK. . . . . EFY
Walgrave Drive. . . . . DY 19
Witan Gate . . . . EZ

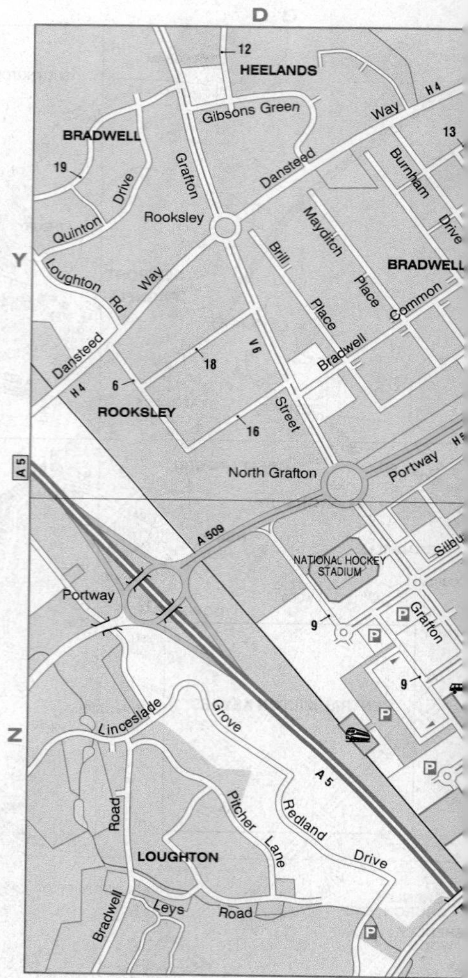

Premier Travel Inn, Bletcham Way (H10), Caldecotte, MK7 8HP, Southeast : 5 ½ m. by A 509 and A 5, taking 2nd junction left signposted Milton Keynes (South and East) (01908) 366188, *Fax (01908) 366603* – rm, (P). MC AE DC VISA. CX h
Rest (grill rest.) – **40 rm** 49.95/49.95 – 52.95/52.95.
◆ Large, lodge style accommodation with lakeside setting. Close to attractive windmill. Spacious, clean and modern rooms in good decorative order. Popular restaurant adjacent to spacious bar.

Express by Holiday Inn without rest., Eastlake Park, Tongwell St, Fox Milne, MK15 0YA, (01908) 681000, *exhimiltonkeynes@aol.com, Fax (01908) 609429* – (P) – 60. MC AE DC VISA. CV a
178 rm 49.00/99.95 – 49.00/99.95.
◆ Large modern lodge hotel offering a superior range of accommodation. Spacious bedrooms boast all amenities and carefully planned modern style. Good motorway access.

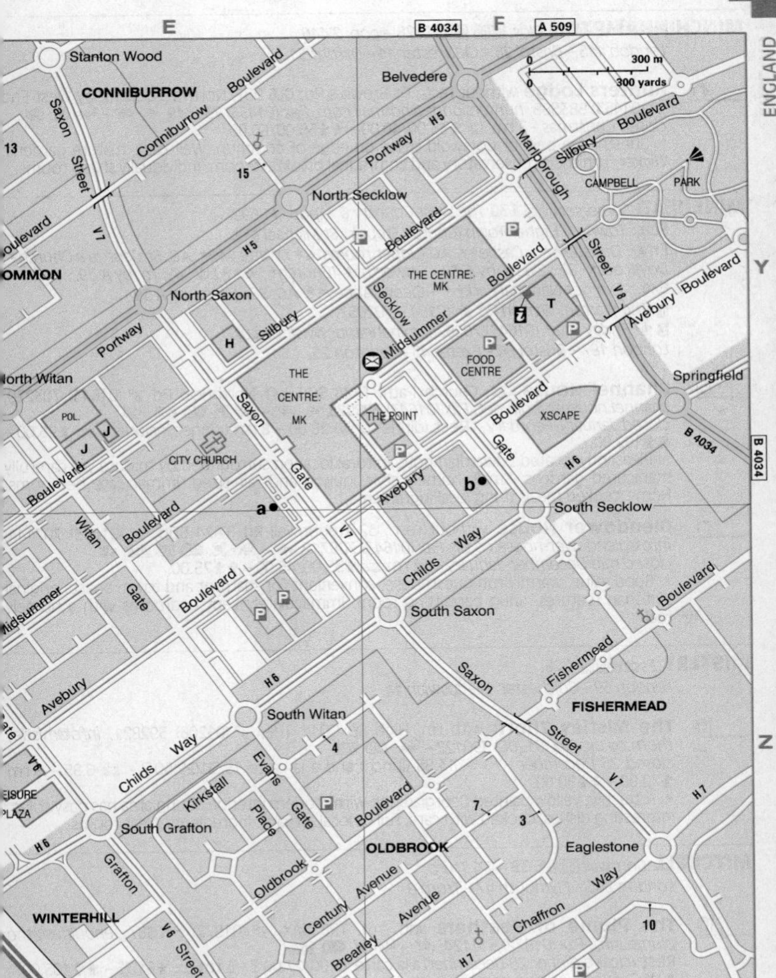

JSA **Premier Travel Inn,** Secklow Gate West, Central Milton Keynes, MK9 3BZ, (01908) 663388, *Fax (01908) 607481* – rest, – 50. FY b
Rest (grill rest.) – **38 rm** 55.95/55.95 – 57.95/57.95.
◆ A consistent standard of trim, simply fitted accommodation in contemporary style. Family rooms with sofa beds. Useful address for cost-conscious travellers.

at Newton Longville *Southwest : 6 m. by A 421 – AX – Milton Keynes.*

Crooked Billet, MK17 0DF, (01908) 373936, *john@thebillet.co.uk, Fax (01908) 631979,* –
closed 25-26 December, 1 January, Sunday dinner and Monday lunch – **Rest** a la carte 25.00/50.00.
◆ A pretty, thatched exterior and large front garden greet visitors to this village pub. Dining in two areas on scrubbed pine and mahogany tables. Tasty, modern English menus.

MINCHINHAMPTON *Glos.* 503 504 N 28 – *pop. 2 446.*
London 115 – Bristol 26 – Gloucester 11 – Oxford 51.

Hunters Lodge without rest., Dr Brown's Rd, GL6 9BT, Northwest : ½ m. by West End
(01453) 883588, *hunterslodge@hotmail.com, Fax (01453) 731449*, ←, – P.
closed Christmas – **3 rm** ★35.00/40.00 – ★★55.00/60.00.
◆ Guesthouse built of Cotswold stone on edge of common. Well-kept, mature gardens. Wicker furnished conservatory and communal breakfast room. Individually styled rooms.

MINEHEAD *Somerset* 503 J 30 *The West Country G.* – *pop. 11 699.*
See : *Town★ - Higher Town (Church Steps★, St Michael's★).*
Env. : *Dunster★★ - Castle★★ AC (upper rooms ←★) Water Mill★ AC, St George's Church★, Dovecote★, SE : 2½ m. by A 39 – Selworthy★ (Church★, ←★★) W : 4½ m. by A 39.*
Exc. : *Exmoor National Park★★ – Cleeve Abbey★★ AC, SE : 6½ m. by A 39.*
The Warren, Warren Rd (01643) 702057.
17 Friday St (01643) 702624, mineheadtic@visit.org.uk.
London 187 – Bristol 64 – Exeter 43 – Taunton 25.

Channel House, Church Path, TA24 5QG, off Northfield Rd (01643) 703229, *channel.house@virgin.net, Fax (01643) 708925*, ←, – P. VISA.
closed January-February – **Rest** (dinner only) 26.00 – **8 rm** (dinner included) ★96.00 – ★★162.00.
◆ Pleasantly located Edwardian hotel in rural location surrounded by mature yet carefully manicured gardens. Small, homely style lounge and fair sized, immaculate bedrooms. Home-cooked meals using local ingredients.

Glendower House without rest., 32 Tregonwell Rd, TA24 5DU, (01643) 707144, *info@glendower-house.co.uk, Fax (01643) 708719*, – P. AE VISA.
closed mid December-January – **12 rm** ★35.00/45.00 – ★★75.00.
◆ Good value, warmly run guesthouse, convenient for seafront and town; boasts original Victorian features. Snug bar/sitting room. Immaculately kept bedrooms with a homely feel.

MISTLEY *Essex* 504 X 28.
London 69 – Colchester 11 – Ipswich 14.

The Mistley Thorn with rm, High St, CO11 1HE, (01206) 392821, *info@mistleythorn.co.uk, Fax (01206) 390122* – . VISA
closed 25 December – **Rest** 13.95 (lunch) and a la carte 15.50/22.50 ♀ – 6.95 – **5 rm** ★70.00 – ★★90.00.
◆ Attractive yellow painted Georgian pub with modern interior: sitting area has cosy sofas. Interesting dishes, cooked with care, full of local, organic ingredients. Neat rooms.

MITCHELL *Cornwall* 503 E 32 – *Truro.*
London 265 – Plymouth 47 – Truro 9.

The Plume of Feathers with rm, TR8 5AX, (01872) 510387, *enquiries@theplume.info, Fax (01872) 511124*, – P. VISA
Rest *(closed dinner 25 December)* a la carte 16.00/27.00 ♀ – **5 rm** ★63.75 – ★★105.00.
◆ 16C pub in village centre. Rustic, beamed interior. Pleasant dining area with fresh flowers and small candles. Modern food with fine Cornish ingredients. Airy, modish rooms.

MITTON *Lancs.* – *see Whalley.*

MOBBERLEY *Ches.* 502 503 504 N 24 – *see Knutsford.*

MONK FRYSTON *N. Yorks.* 502 Q 22 – *Lumby.*
London 190 – Kingston-upon-Hull 42 – Leeds 13 – York 20.

Monk Fryston Hall, LS25 5DU, (01977) 682369, *reception@monkfryston-hotel.co.uk, Fax (01977) 683544*, , , – P – 50. AE VISA
Rest (lunch by arrangement)/dinner 35.00 ♀ – **29 rm** ★95.00/105.00 – ★★140.00.
◆ Very characterful, possibly haunted, manor house dating from the 1300s with many later additions. Spacious grounds. Baronial style hall with antiques. Imposing rooms. Comfortable dining room with baronial touches.

MONKS ELEIGH *Suffolk* 504 W 27.
London 72 – Cambridge 47 – Colchester 17 – Ipswich 16 – Norwich 49.

Swan Inn, The Street, IP7 7AU, ✆ (01449) 741391, – P. MC VISA
closed 25-26 December, 1 January, Monday and Tuesday – **Rest** a la carte 16.75/37.50 ♀.
◆ 16C whitewashed inn with thatched roof in centre of rural village. Daily changing blackboard menus of modern British pub food using fresh local produce.

MONKTON COMBE *Bath & North East Somerset – see Bath.*

MONKTON FARLEIGH *Wilts.* 503 504 N 29 – *see Bradford-on-Avon.*

MONTACUTE *Somerset* 503 504 L 31 – *see Yeovil.*

MORETONHAMPSTEAD *Devon* 503 I 32 *The West Country G.* – ✉ *Newton Abbot.*
Env. : *Dartmoor National Park*★★.
18 *Manor House Hotel* ✆ *(01647) 440998.*
London 213 – Exeter 13 – Plymouth 30.

The White Hart, The Square, TQ13 8NF, ✆ (01647) 441340, *enquiries@whitehartdartmoor.co.uk, Fax (01647) 441341* – – 60. MC AE VISA
Rest a la carte approx 19.00 – **20 rm** ☕ ★45.00/60.00 – ★★110.00.
◆ 17C Grade II listed house near Bovey Castle. Charming, country furnished guest lounge. Pleasant bar frequented by locals. Attractively refurbished rooms are strong point. Clothed dining room with Glorious Devon posters on the wall.

Moorcote without rest., TQ13 8LS, Northwest : ¼ m. on A 382 ✆ (01647) 440966, *moorcote@smartone.co.uk,* ←, – P.
March-October – **4 rm** ☕ ★30.00/35.00 – ★★48.00/52.00.
◆ Perched on hill above Moretonhampstead, this Victorian guesthouse has mature gardens and well-kept bedrooms with stunning views of Dartmoor. Cosy breakfast room and lounge.

Great Wooston Farm without rest., TQ13 8QA, North : 2 m. by Lime St on Clifford Bridge rd ✆ (01647) 440367, *info@greatwoostonfarm.com, Fax (01647) 440367,* ←, – P. MC VISA.
3 rm ☕ ★28.00/35.00 – ★★60.00/62.00.
◆ A beef and sheep farm in a secluded setting above the town. Lounge with wood-burning stove. Cottagey breakfast room. Pretty bedrooms overlooking surrounding fields.

Great Sloncombe Farm without rest., TQ13 8QF, Northwest : 1 ½ m. by A 382 ✆ (01647) 440595, *hmerchant@sloncombe.freeserve.co.uk, Fax (01647) 440595,* – P
3 rm ☕ ★35.00 – ★★56.00/64.00.
◆ Cottagey farmhouse on vast working farm. Atmospheric beamed lounge with wood-burning stove. Spacious, comfy, pine furnished rooms. Pleasant breakfast room with rustic feel.

The ✿ award is the crème de la crème. This is awarded to restaurants which are really worth travelling miles for!

MORETON-IN-MARSH *Glos.* 503 504 O 28 *Great Britain G.* – *pop. 3 198.*
Env. : *Chastleton House*★★, *SE : 5 m. by A 44.*
London 86 – Birmingham 40 – Gloucester 31 – Oxford 29.

Manor House, High St, GL56 0LJ, ✆ (01608) 650501, *info@manorhousehotel.info, Fax (01608) 651481,* – , rest, P – 90. MC AE VISA
***Mulberry* :** **Rest** 14.95/34.95 – **36 rm** ☕ ★69.00/155.00 – ★★135.00/175.00, 2 suites.
◆ Part 16C manor house in town centre. Walled lawns to rear. Two country house style low-beamed lounges with open fires. Sympathetically styled rooms; luxurious fabrics. Pretty dining room.

MORPETH *Northd.* 501 502 O 18 – *pop. 13 555.*
18 *The Common* ✆ *(01670) 504942.*
The Chantry, Bridge St ✆ *(01670) 500700.*
London 301 – Edinburgh 93 – Newcastle upon Tyne 15.

ENGLAND

at Longhorsley *Northwest : 6½ m. by A 192 on A 697 – ✉ Morpeth.*

Linden Hall ⛺, NE65 8XF, North : 1 m. on A 697 ✆ (01670) 500000, *lindenhall@macdonald-hotels.co.uk, Fax (01670) 500001,* ≤, ... 300. MC AE VISA
Dobson : **Rest** 15.00/32.50 s. ♀ – **50 rm** ☕ ★110.00/120.00 – ★★190.00/210.00.
◆ Imposing, ivy clad Georgian house in extensive grounds. Chintz drawing room with real fire. Conference facilities. Pub with conservatory. Well-kept rooms. Formal dining in very comfortable surroundings.

Thistleyhaugh Farm ⛺, NE65 8RG, Northwest : 3 ¾ m. by A 697 and Todburn road taking first right turn ✆ (01665) 570629, *stay@thistleyhaugh.com, Fax (01665) 570629,* ... P.
closed Christmas-New Year – **Rest** (by arrangement) (communal dining) 17.50 – **5 rm** ☕ ★42.50 – ★★65.00.
◆ Attractive little Georgian farmhouse on working farm in a pleasant rural area. The River Coquet flows through the grounds. Comfortable, cosy bedrooms in traditional style. Communal dining overlooking garden.

MORSTON *Norfolk – see Blakeney.*

MORTEHOE *Devon* 503 H 30 – *see Woolacombe.*

MOTCOMBE *Dorset* 503 504 N 30 – *see Shaftesbury.*

MOULSFORD *Oxon.*
London 53.5 – Newbury 16 – Reading 13.5.

The Boathouse, Ferry Lane, OX10 9JF, ✆ (01491) 651381, *Fax (01491) 651376,* ≤, ... P. MC AE VISA
Rest (booking essential) a la carte 26.50/33.00.
◆ Beautifully located by the Thames and enhanced by lovely terrace. Two dining options: bare-brick char-grill or conservatory dining room. Daily changing, wide-ranging menus.

MOULTON *N. Yorks.* 502 P 20 – ✉ *Richmond.*
London 243 – Leeds 53 – Middlesbrough 25 – Newcastle upon Tyne 43.

Black Bull Inn, DL10 6QJ, ✆ (01325) 377289, *sarah@blackbullinn.demon.co.uk, Fax (01325) 377422* – P. MC AE VISA
closed 24-26 December and Sunday – **Rest** - Seafood specialities - 19.95 (lunch) and a la carte 35.00/45.00.
◆ Old country pub with variety of dining areas, including an original Brighton Belle Pullman carriage from 1932 and conservatory with huge grapevine. Seafood a speciality.

MOUSEHOLE *Cornwall* 503 D 33 *The West Country G.* – ✉ *Penzance.*
See : *Village*★.
Env. : *Penwith*★★ – *Lamorna (The Merry Maidens and The Pipers Standing Stone*★*) SW : 3 m. by B 3315.*
Exc. : *Land's End*★ *(cliff scenery*★★★*) W : 9 m. by B 3315.*
London 321 – Penzance 3 – Truro 29.

The Old Coastguard, The Parade, TR19 6PR, ✆ (01736) 731222, *bookings@oldcoastguardhotel.co.uk, Fax (01736) 731720,* ≤, ... P. MC AE VISA.
Rest *(closed 25 December)* a la carte 26.00/36.00 ♀ – **20 rm** ☕ ★40.00/90.00 – ★★90.00/130.00.
◆ Creamwash hotel in unspoilt village with good views of Mounts Bay. Spacious lounge has sun terrace overlooking water. Modern rooms: Premier variety are best for the vista. Watch the bay as you eat freshly caught seafood.

Cornish Range with rm, 6 Chapel St, TR19 6SB, ✆ (01736) 731488, *info@cornishrange.co.uk* – rm. MC VISA
closed 25 December, Sunday and Monday-Tuesday in winter – **Rest** - Seafood - (booking essential) (dinner only) a la carte 25.00/37.50 ♀ – **3 rm** ☕ ★75.00/95.00 – ★★75.00/95.00.
◆ Converted 18C pilchard processing cottage hidden away in narrow street. Cottagey inner filled with Cornish artwork. Excellent local seafood dishes. Very comfortable rooms.

MUCH MARCLE *Herefordshire* 503 504 M 28 – *see Ledbury.*

MUCH WENLOCK *Shrops.* 502 503 M26 *Great Britain G. – pop. 1 959.*
See : *Priory★ AC.*
Env. : *Ironbridge Gorge Museum★★ AC (The Iron Bridge★★ - Coalport China Museum★★ - Blists Hill Open Air Museum★★ – Museum of the River and Visitor Centre★) NE : 4½ m. by A 4169 and B 4380.*
The Museum, The Square, High St ☎ (01952) 727679 (summer only).
London 154 – Birmingham 34 – Shrewsbury 12 – Worcester 37.

Raven, Barrow St, TF13 6EN, ☎ (01952) 727251, *enquiry@ravenhotel.com, Fax (01952) 728416,* – rest, P. MC AE VISA.
closed 25 December – ***The Restaurant :*** **Rest** 25.00 and a la carte 13.95/25.70 – **14 rm** ★75.00 – ★★110.00.
◆ Hotel spread across range of historic buildings with 17C coaching inn at its heart. Pleasant inner courtyard and conservatory. Good sized bedrooms with chintz fabrics. Dining room exudes homely rustic charm.

at Brockton *Southwest : 5 m. on B 4378 – ✉ Much Wenlock.*

The Feathers, TF13 6JR, ☎ (01746) 785202, *Fax (01746) 785202,* – P. MC AE VISA.
closed 25-26 December, Monday and lunch Tuesday and Wednesday – **Rest** a la carte 20.00/27.00.
◆ Characterful part 16C pub near Wenlock Edge: whitewashed stone walls, beams and vast inglenooks. Constantly changing blackboard menus provide plethora of interesting dishes.

MUDEFORD *Dorset* 503 504 O 31 – *see Christchurch.*

MULLION *Cornwall* 503 E 33 *The West Country G. – pop. 1 834 – ✉ Helston.*
See : *Mullion Cove★★ (Church★) – Lizard Peninsula★.*
Env. : *Kynance Cove★★, S : 5 m. – Cury★ (Church★), N : 2 m. by minor roads.*
Exc. : *Helston (The Flora Day Furry Dance★★) (May), N : 7 ½ m. by A 3083 – Culdrose (Flambards Village Theme Park★) AC, N : 6 m. by A 3083 – Wendron (Poldark Mine★), N : 9½ m. by A 3083 and B 3297.*
London 323 – Falmouth 21 – Penzance 21 – Truro 26.

Mullion Cove, TR12 7EP, Southwest : 1 m. by B 3296 ☎ (01326) 240328, *mullion.cove@btinternet.com, Fax (01326) 240998,* ≤ Mullion Cove and Mount's Bay, , , – rest, P. MC AE VISA
Atlantic View : **Rest** (dinner only and Sunday lunch) 26.95 **s.** – ***Bistro :*** **Rest** a la carte 14.00/38.20 **s.** – **30 rm** (dinner included) ★77.50/211.50 – ★★170.00/230.00.
◆ Dramatic Victorian hotel, personally run, standing in spectacular position on cliffs above Mullion Cove. Terrific views along coastline. Comfortable, modern rooms. Cream painted, welcoming Atlantic View. Bistro with terrace perfect for lunch.

MUNSLOW *Shrops.* 503 L 26.
London 166 – Ludlow 10 – Shrewsbury 21.

The Crown Country Inn with rm, SY7 9ET, on B 4378 ☎ (01584) 841205, *info@crowncountryinn.co.uk, Fax (01584) 841255,* , – P. MC AE .
closed 25 December – **Rest** *(closed Monday)* a la carte 19.25/29.95 – **3 rm** ★40.00 – ★★70.00.
◆ Hugely characterful, heavily beamed bar, crackling fire and hops hanging from the rafters. Well executed dishes served here or in linen clad restaurant. Simple, comfy rooms.

MYLOR BRIDGE *Cornwall* 503 E 33 – *see Falmouth.*

NAILSWORTH *Glos.* 503 504 N 28 – *pop. 5 276.*
London 110 – Bristol 30 – Swindon 28.

Egypt Mill, GL6 0AE, ☎ (01453) 833449, *reception@egyptmill.com, Fax (01453) 839919,* , – P – 100. MC VISA.
Rest a la carte 19.95/27.00 – **28 rm** ★65.00/75.00 – ★★80.00/95.00.
◆ A colourful history: former 16C mill on Frome used for cloth manufacture, later dyes for soldier's tunics. Rooms in two blocks; some with original features and river views. Comfortable restaurant with river views from window tables.

NANTITHET *Cornwall – see Helston.*

NANTWICH *Ches.* 502 503 504 M 24 – *pop. 13 447.*

Alvaston Hall, Middlewich Rd ✆ (01270) 628473.

Church House, Church Walk ✆ (01270) 610983.

London 176 – Chester 20 – Liverpool 45 – Manchester 40 – Stoke-on-Trent 17.

Rookery Hall, Worleston, CW5 6DQ, North : 2½ m. by A 51 on B 5074 ✆ (01270) 610016, *rookery@handpicked.co.uk, Fax (01270) 626027,* ≤, – , rest, – 70. VISA

Rest *(closed Saturday lunch)* (booking essential) 19.50/29.50 and dinner a la carte 32.50/47.00 – 12.50 – **44 rm** 180.00 – 280.00, 2 suites.

◆ Originally built in 1816 in Georgian style; enjoys a peacefully set, smart country house ambience. The individually decorated bedrooms offer a very good level of comfort. Wood panelled restaurant with polished tables.

The Limes without rest., 5 Park Rd, CW5 7AQ, on A 530 (Whitchurch rd) ✆ (01270) 624081, *thelimesparkroad@aol.com, Fax (01270) 624081,* –

April-October – **3** rm 45.00/50.00 – 55.00/58.00.

◆ Redbrick Victorian house in Queen Anne style. The large bedrooms have been individually decorated and benefit from a warm personality. Friendly and personally run.

Oakland House without rest., 252 Newcastle Rd, Blakelow, Shavington, CW5 7ET, East : 2½ m. by A 51 on A 500 ✆ (01270) 567134, *enquiries@oaklandhouseonline.co.uk,* – VISA

9 rm 39.00 – 54.00.

◆ Private guesthouse with family photos adding personal touch. Homely lounge, warmly decorated breakfast room and conservatory. Comfy rooms in house and converted outbuildings.

Curshaws at the Cat with rm, 26 Welsh Row, CW5 5ED, ✆ (01270) 623020, *enquiries@curshaws.com, Fax (01270) 613350,* – , rest, VISA.

closed 25 and 31 December – **Rest** a la carte 9.50/20.00 – **11 rm** 85.00 – 105.00.

◆ Heavily beamed 16C inn which has been dramatically modernised: imposing glass and steel conservatory to rear. Flexible, modern dishes. Stylish rooms with plasma screen TVs.

NATIONAL EXHIBITION CENTRE *W. Mids.* 503 504 O 26 – *see Birmingham.*

NAWTON *N. Yorks.* – *see Helmsley.*

NAYLAND *Suffolk* 504 W 28.

London 64 – Bury St Edmunds 24 – Cambridge 54 – Colchester 6 – Ipswich 19.

White Hart Inn with rm, High St, CO6 4JF, ✆ (01206) 263382, *nayhart@aol.com, Fax (01206) 263638,* – rm, VISA.

closed 26 December-9 January and Monday – **Rest** (booking essential) 14.95 (lunch) and a la carte 19.50/28.50 – **6 rm** 74.00/80.00 – 92.00/105.00.

◆ Accomplished food served in terracotta tiled dining room of part 15C coaching inn. Floodlit cellars and comfortable beamed bedrooms.

NEAR SAWREY *Cumbria* 502 L 20 – *see Hawkshead.*

NETHER BROUGHTON *Leics.* 502 504 R 25 – *see Melton Mowbray.*

NETHER WASDALE *Cumbria.*

London 309 – Ambleside 24 – Blackpool 85 – Carlisle 52 – Whitehaven 17.

Low Wood Hall with rm, CA20 1ET, ✆ (019467) 26100, *reservations@lowwoodhall.co.uk, Fax (019467) 26111,* ≤, – VISA

closed Sunday and restricted opening in winter – **Rest** (dinner only) 22.50 **s.** – **6 rm** 100.00 – 100.00.

◆ Split-level dining room with garden views within fine Victorian country house boasting tiled floor and stained glass. Tasty, fresh, well-cooked modern menus. Homely rooms.

NETTLEBED *Oxon.* 504 R 29.
London 44 – Oxford 20 – Reading 10.

White Hart, 28 High St, RG9 5DD, ✆ (01491) 641245, *info@whitehartnettlebed.com, Fax (01491) 649018* – ⅏ 30. MC AE VISA.
Bistro : **Rest** 15.25 and a la carte 24.50/28.95 **s.** ♀ – ***The Nettlebed*** (dinner only Friday and Saturday) 35.00/55.00 – **12 rm** ☐ ★105.00 – ★★105.00.
◆ Part 17C inn boasting modern bedrooms, all uniquely styled with Minimalist Bistro "designer" appeal, some in original hotel, others in new block. Nettlebed for contemporary cooking.

NETTLETON SHRUB *Wilts.* 503 504 N 29 – *see Castle Combe.*

NEWARK-ON-TRENT *Notts.* 502 504 R 24 *Great Britain G.* – *pop. 35 454.*
See : *St Mary Magdalene*★.
Kelwick, Coddington ✆ (01636) 626241.
London 127 – Lincoln 16 – Nottingham 20 – Sheffield 42.

Grange, 73 London Rd, NG24 1RZ, South : ½ m. on Grantham rd (B 6326) ✆ (01636) 703399, *info@grangenewark.co.uk, Fax (01636) 702328,* – P. MC AE VISA
closed 24 December-3 January – ***Cutlers :*** **Rest** (bar lunch Monday-Saturday)/dinner 21.95 and a la carte 21.40/27.70 – **19 rm** ☐ ★72.00/100.00 – ★★96.00/150.00.
◆ Situated in a residential area but not far from town centre, this small hotel is fitted with functional, simply decorated bedrooms and miniature pulpit-style bar. Compact dining room boasts cadlelit dinners.

Premier Travel Inn, Lincoln Rd, NG24 2DB, Northwest : 1½ m. at A1/A46 roundabout ✆ (01636) 640690, *Fax (01636) 605135* – rm, P. MC AE VISA.
Rest (grill rest.) – **40 rm** ★49.95 – ★★49.95.
◆ A two storey redbrick inn next to Brewers Fayre and close to supermarkets, leisure centre and Caesar's Palace nightclub. Simply furnished bedrooms.

Reeds, 13-15 Castlegate, NG24 1AL, ✆ (01636) 704500, *food@reedrestaurants.com, Fax (01636) 611139* – MC AE VISA
closed Sunday dinner – **Rest** a la carte 16.95/26.75.
◆ Intimate, brick vaulted, Georgian house cellar with original ceiling meat hooks in situ. Mix of linen-clad and plain tables. Seasonal ingredients to the fore in varied menus.

at Caunton *Northwest : 4½ m. by A 616 – ✉ Newark-on-Trent.*

Caunton Beck, Main St, NG23 6AB, ✆ (01636) 636793, *email@wigandmitre.com, Fax (01636) 636828,* – P. MC AE VISA
Rest 13.95 (lunch) and a la carte 22.00/32.00 ♀.
◆ Period pub by stream; sparkling menus singing with flavour: modern with oriental, Mediterranean touches. Sample elderflower blancmange with shortbread and rose petal syrup.

NEWBIGGIN *Cumbria* 502 L 19 – *see Penrith.*

NEWBURY *Newbury* 503 504 Q 29 – *pop. 33 273.*
Newbury and Crookham, Bury's Bank Rd, Greenham Common ✆ (01635) 40035 **AX** – *Donnington Valley, Old Oxford Rd ✆ (01635) 568140* **AV**.
The Wharf ✆ (01635) 30267, tourism@westberks.gov.uk.
London 67 – Bristol 66 – Oxford 28 – Reading 17 – Southampton 38.

Plans on following pages

Vineyard, Stockcross, RG20 8JU, Northwest : 2 m. by A 4 on B 4000 ✆ (01635) 528770, *general@the-vineyard.co.uk, Fax (01635) 528398,* rm, P – 100. MC AE VISA. **AV b**
Rest 30.00/63.00 ♀ – **34 rm** ☐ ★190.00 – ★★285.00, 15 suites ☐ 365.00/705.00.
Spec. Organic salmon mi-cuit with spiced lentils and foie gras. Slow cooked beef with Tatin of onion, horseradish emulsion. Strawberry brûlée with black olives and Pedro Ximenez jelly.
◆ Outside, a pool bearing bowls of fire encapsulates bright art-filled interiors. Luxurious suites with woven fabrics. Spa treatments; swimming pool with sculpture. Indulge in accomplished original cuisine and range of fine wines.

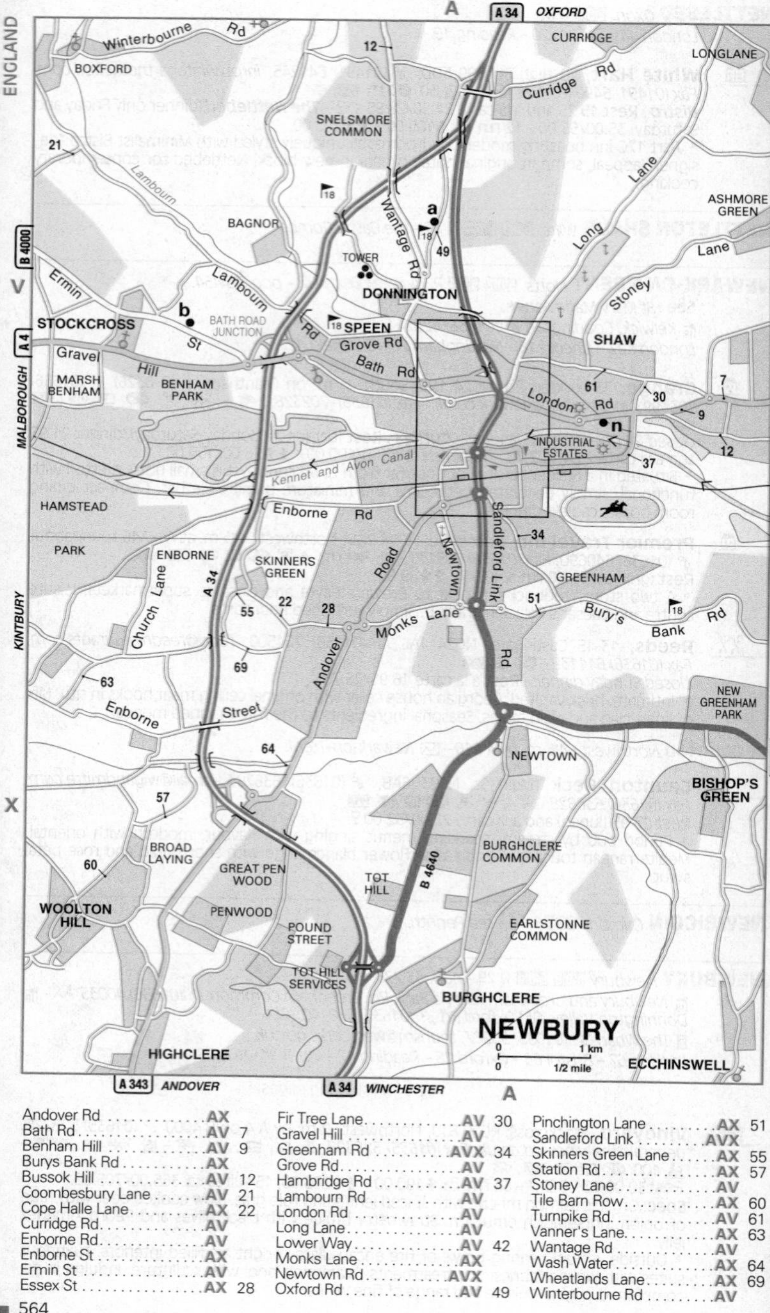

Andover Rd . . . . AX
Bath Rd . . . . AV 7
Benham Hill . . . . AV 9
Burys Bank Rd . . . . AX
Bussok Hill . . . . AV 12
Coombesbury Lane . . . . AV 21
Cope Halle Lane . . . . AX 22
Curridge Rd . . . . AV
Enborne Rd . . . . AV
Enborne St . . . . AX
Ermin St . . . . AV
Essex St . . . . AX 28
Fir Tree Lane . . . . AV 30
Gravel Hill . . . . AV
Greenham Rd . . . . AVX 34
Grove Rd . . . . AV
Hambridge Rd . . . . AV 37
Lambourn Rd . . . . AV
London Rd . . . . AV
Long Lane . . . . AV
Lower Way . . . . AV 42
Monks Lane . . . . AX
Newtown Rd . . . . AVX
Oxford Rd . . . . AV 49
Pinchington Lane . . . . AX 51
Sandleford Link . . . . AVX
Skinners Green Lane . . . . AX 55
Station Rd . . . . AX 57
Stoney Lane . . . . AV
Tile Barn Row . . . . AX 60
Turnpike Rd . . . . AV 61
Vanner's Lane . . . . AX 63
Wantage Rd . . . . AV
Wash Water . . . . AX 64
Wheatlands Lane . . . . AX 69
Winterbourne Rd . . . . AV

NEWBURY

Street	Grid	No.
Almond Ave	BY	3
Andover Rd	BZ	4
Bartholomew St	BZ	6
Bone Lane	BZ	10
Carnegie Rd	BZ	13
Castle Grove	BY	15
Cheap St	BZ	16
Chesterfield Rd	BZ	18
Craven Rd	BZ	24
Dolman Rd	BY	25
Donnington Link	BY	27
Greenham Hill	BZ	31
Greenham Rd	BZ	33
Hambridge Rd	BZ	36
Kennett Shopping Centre	BZ	
Kiln Rd	BY	40
Kings Rd	BZ	
London Rd	BY	
Love Lane	BY	
Maple Crescent	BY	43
Market St	BZ	45
Mill Lane	BZ	
New Rd	BZ	46
Newtown Rd	BZ	48
Northbrook St	BYZ	
Northcroft Lane	BZ	
Old Bath Rd	BY	
Oxford Rd	BY	
Park Way	BYZ	50
Pound St	BZ	
Queens Rd	BZ	
Racecourse Rd	BZ	
Rockingham Rd	BZ	52
St Johns Rd	BZ	
Sandleford Link	BZ	54
Shaw Hill	BY	
Shaw Rd	BY	
Station Rd	BZ	
Strawberry Hill	BY	58
West St	BZ	66
Western Ave	BY	
Wharf St	BZ	67

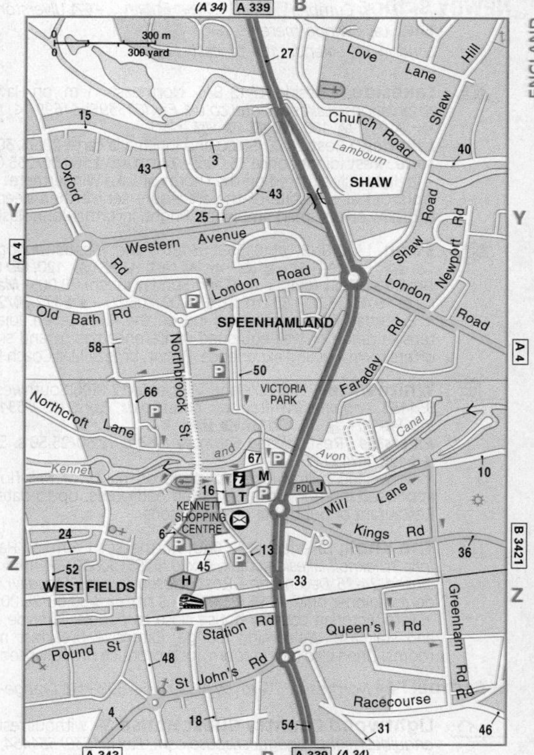

Donnington Valley H. & Golf Course, Old Oxford Rd, Donnington, RG14 3AG, North : 1 ¾ m. by A 4 off B 4494 ☎ (01635) 551199, *general@donningtonvalley.co.uk, Fax (01635) 551123,* 18, – ✈, rest, ♿ P – 140. MC AE VISA. AV a
Winepress : Rest 21.00/29.50 and a la carte – 14.00 – **58 rm** 160.00 – 200.00.
◆ Smart executive and family rooms in purpose-built country hotel with 18-hole golf course. Artwork abounds: sculptures and paintings as well as concerts and other events. Dine in conservatory or gallery.

Newbury Manor , London Rd, RG14 2BY, ☎ (01635) 528838, *enquiries@newbury-manor-hotel.co.uk, Fax (01635) 523406,* , , – , rest, ♿ P – 80. MC AE VISA AV n
Rest *(closed Saturday lunch, Sunday dinner and Bank Holidays)* 22.50 (lunch) and dinner a la carte 23.45/28.45 s – **32 rm** 140.00/160.00 – 150.00/170.00, 1 suite.
◆ Close to Newbury racecourse and on banks of river Kennett, this listed building boasts soft furnished rooms, some with balconies. Deep sofas in conservatory to relax in. Restaurant has glass wall which opens for alfresco dining.

at Marsh Benham *West : 3½ m. by A 4 – AV – ✉ Newbury.*

The Red House, RG20 8LY, ☎ (01635) 582017, *Fax (01635) 581621,* , – P. MC AE VISA.
closed 25 and 31 December, 1 January and dinner Sunday – **Rest** 16.95 (lunch) and a la carte 25.50/32.95.
◆ Redbrick thatched house, once an inn. Interior comprises tiled, beamed pub and adjacent dining room with modern fabrics and furnishings. Lively hubub, French influenced food.

NEWBY BRIDGE *Cumbria* 502 L 21 *Great Britain G.* – ✉ *Ulverston.*
Env. : *Lake Windermere★★.*
London 270 – Kendal 16 – Lancaster 27.

Lakeside, Lakeside, LA12 8AT, Northeast : 1 m. on Hawkshead rd ✆ (015395) 30001, *reservations@Lakesidehotel.co.uk, Fax (015395) 31699,* ←, ⓘ, Fō, ⛆, ☐, ↷, ⛏ – |‡| ⚓ ⇜ ♿ P – 🏛 100. ⓜⓒ AE ⓓ VISA. ✂
Lakeview : Rest 28.00/50.00 and lunch a la carte 20.95/30.95 s. ♀ – ***John Ruskins Brasserie :*** Rest (dinner only) 33.00 ♀ – **74 rm** ☕ ★160.00/235.00 – ★★275.00, 3 suites.
◆ Delightfully situated on the shores of Lake Windermere. Plenty of charm and character. Work out at the state-of-the-art leisure centre then sleep in fitted, modern bedrooms. Lakeview offers smart ambience. Bright, informal John Ruskins Brasserie.

Swan, LA12 8NB, ✆ (01539) 531681, *enquiries@swanhotel.com, Fax (01539) 531917,* ←, Fō, ⛆, ☐, ↷, ⛏ – |‡| ⚓ ⇜, ≡ rest, ♿ P – 🏛 120. ⓜⓒ AE VISA. ✂
Revell's : Rest (dinner only and Sunday lunch) 28.00 – ***Mail Coach Brasserie :*** Rest a la carte 16.45/26.30 – **55 rm** ☕ ★86.00/106.00 – ★★172.00/212.00.
◆ Extended former coaching inn on the River Leven adjacent to Lake Windermere. Extensive range of well-equipped conference rooms and smart, fitted bedrooms. Revell's offers formal dining experience. Bright, breezy Mail Coach Brasserie.

Whitewater, The Lakeland Village, LA12 8PX, Southwest : 1 ½ m. by A 590 ✆ (01539) 531133, *enquiries@whitewater-hotel.co.uk, Fax (01539) 531881,* ⓘ, Fō, ⛆, ☐, ✂, squash – |‡| ⇜ P – 🏛 70. ⓜⓒ AE ⓓ VISA. ✂
Riverside : Rest *(closed Saturday lunch)* 12.50/25.50 s. ♀ – **35 rm** ☕ ★92.50/115.00 – ★★120.00/132.00.
◆ Converted mill of lakeland stone on banks of fast-flowing River Leven. Traditionally appointed interior with good sized bedrooms. Up-to-date leisure and treatment rooms. Restaurant or pubby bar dining options.

The Knoll, Lakeside, LA12 8AU, Northeast : 1 ¼ m. on Hawkshead rd ✆ (015395) 31347, *info@theknoll-lakeside.co.uk, Fax (015395) 30850,* ⛏ – ⇜ P. ⓜⓒ VISA. ✂
closed 24-26 December – **Rest** *(closed Sunday-Monday)* (booking essential to non-residents) (dinner only) 19.95/23.95 s. – **8 rm** ☕ ★50.00/78.00 – ★★96.00/108.00.
◆ Late Victorian country house close to popular lakeside. Original stained glass, cornices and staircase. Welcoming lounge. Extensive breakfast menu. Cosy, comfortable bedrooms. Linen clad dining room; local produce proudly used.

at Cartmel Fell *Northeast : 3¼ m. by A 590 off A 592* – ✉ *Grange-over-Sands.*

Lightwood Country Guest House ⛟ without rest., LA11 6NP, ✆ (01539) 531454, *enquiries@lightwoodguesthouse.com, Fax (01539) 531454,* ←, ⛏ – ⇜ P. ⓜⓒ VISA. ✂
closed January and 25 December – **5 rm** ☕ ★40.00/50.00 – ★★60.00/70.00.
◆ 17C farmhouse charmingly set in picturesque valley. Characterful interior with exposed beams and open fires. Cottage-style bedrooms. Sunny conservatory overlooking gardens. Breakfast room boasts warm, homely style.

"Rest" appears in red for establishments with a ✿ (star) or ☺ (Bib Gourmand).

NEWBY WISKE *N. Yorks.* 502 P 21 – *see Northallerton.*

NEWCASTLE AIRPORT *Tyne and Wear* 501 502 O 19 – *see Newcastle upon Tyne.*

NEWCASTLE-UNDER-LYME *Staffs.* 502 503 504 N 24 *Great Britain G.* – *pop. 74 247.*
Exc. : *Wedgwood Visitor's Centre★ AC, SE : 6½ m. by A 34 Z.*
⛳18 *Keele Golf Centre, Keele Rd* ✆ *(01782) 627596.*
ℹ *Newcastle Library, Ironmarket* ✆ *(01782) 297313, tic.newcastle@staffordshire.gov.uk.*
London 161 – Birmingham 46 – Liverpool 56 – Manchester 43.
Plan of Built up Area : see Stoke-on-Trent

NEWCASTLE-UNDER-LYME

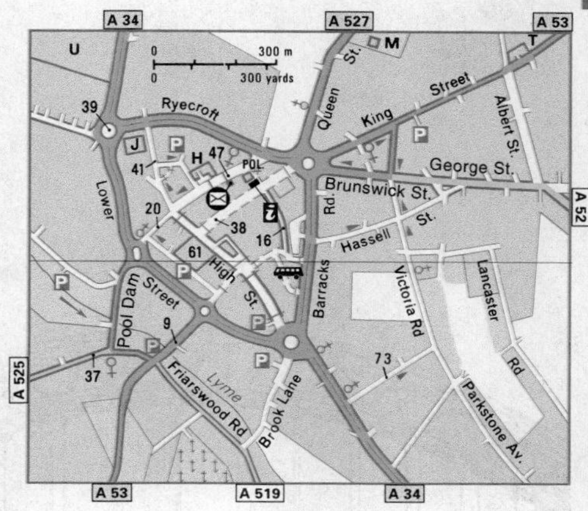

Number One King Street, 1 King St, ST5 1EN, ☎ (01782) 715885, *Fax (01782) 715886* – 14. MC AE VISA

closed 25-26 December, 1 January, Saturday lunch, Sunday and Monday – **Rest** 11.00/19.00 and a la carte 31.00/36.50 **s.**.

◆ 18C redbrick house in terrace of similar properties in heart of town. Comfy bar and lounge for pre- and post-prandials. Up-to-date restaurant with good value, modern menus.

C. Bowman/SCOPE

Newcastle upon Tyne, Northumbria

NEWCASTLE UPON TYNE

Tyne and Wear 501 502 O 19 *Great Britain G.* – *pop. 189 863.*

London 276 – Edinburgh 105 – Leeds 95.

TOURIST INFORMATION

132 Grainger St ☎ (0191) 277 8000; tourist.info@newcastle.gov.uk.
Main Concourse, Central Station ☎ (0191) 230 0030;
Newcastle International Airport ☎ (0191) 214 4422.

PRACTICAL INFORMATION

Broadway East, Gosforth ☎ (0191) 285 6710, **BV**.
City of Newcastle, Three Mile Bridge, Gosforth ☎ (0191) 285 1775.
Wallsend, Rheydt Ave, Bigges Main ☎ (0191) 262 1973, NE : by A 1058 **BV**.
Whickham, Hollinside Park, Fellside Rd ☎ (0191) 488 7309.
Tyne Tunnel (toll).

Newcastle Airport : ☎ (0191) 286 0966, NW : 5 m. by A 696 **AV**.

Terminal : *Bus Assembly : Central Station Forecourt.*

to Norway (Bergen, Haugesund and Stavanger) (Fjord Line) (approx. 26 h) – to Sweden (Gothenburg) (via Kristiansand, Norway) (Scandinavian Seaways) (summer only) 2 weekly (approx. 22 h) – to The Netherlands (Amsterdam) (DFDS Seaways A/S) daily (15 h).

SIGHTS

See : *City★★ – Grey Street★* **CZ** – *Quayside★* **CZ** : *Composition★, All Saints Church★ (interior★) – Castle Keep★ AC* **CZ** – *Laing Art Gallery and Museum★ AC* **CY M1** – *Museum of Antiquities★* **CY M2** – *LIFE Interactive World★* **CZ** – *Gateshead Millennium Bridge★* **CZ**.

Env. : *Hadrian's Wall★★, W : by A 69* **AV**.

Exc. : *Beamish : North of England Open-Air Museum★★ AC, SW : 7 m. by A 692 and A 6076* **AX** – *Seaton Delaval Hall★ AC, NE : 11 m. by A 189 –* **BV** *– and A 190.*

NEWCASTLE-UPON-TYNE

Street	Grid	No.
Adelaide Terrace	AX	2
Atkinson Rd	AX	3
Bath St	BX	4
Bensham Rd	AX	6
Benton Bank	BV	8
Buddle St	BV	13
Byker Bridge	BV	15
Church Ave	AV	16
Church Rd	AV	18
Clayton Rd	BV	21
Coldwell Lane	BX	22
Coldwell St	BX	24
Condercum Rd	AX	26
Fossway	BV	31
Haddrick's Mill Rd	BV	36
High St West	BV	37
Jesmond Dene Rd	BV	39
Killingworth Rd	BV	42
Lobley Hill Rd	AX	45
Matthew Bank	BV	49
Neptune Rd	BV	51
Red Hall Drive	BV	61
Redheugh Bridge	AX	62
Saltwell Rd	BX	69
Shipdon Rd	AX	71
Springfield Rd	AV	72
Station Rd	BX	73
Stephenson Rd	BV	74
Sunderland Rd	BX	76
Sutton St	BV	77
Swalwell Bank	ABX	79
Waverdale Ave	BV	83
West Farm Ave	BV	87
Whickham Bank	AX	89
Windy Nook Rd	BX	91

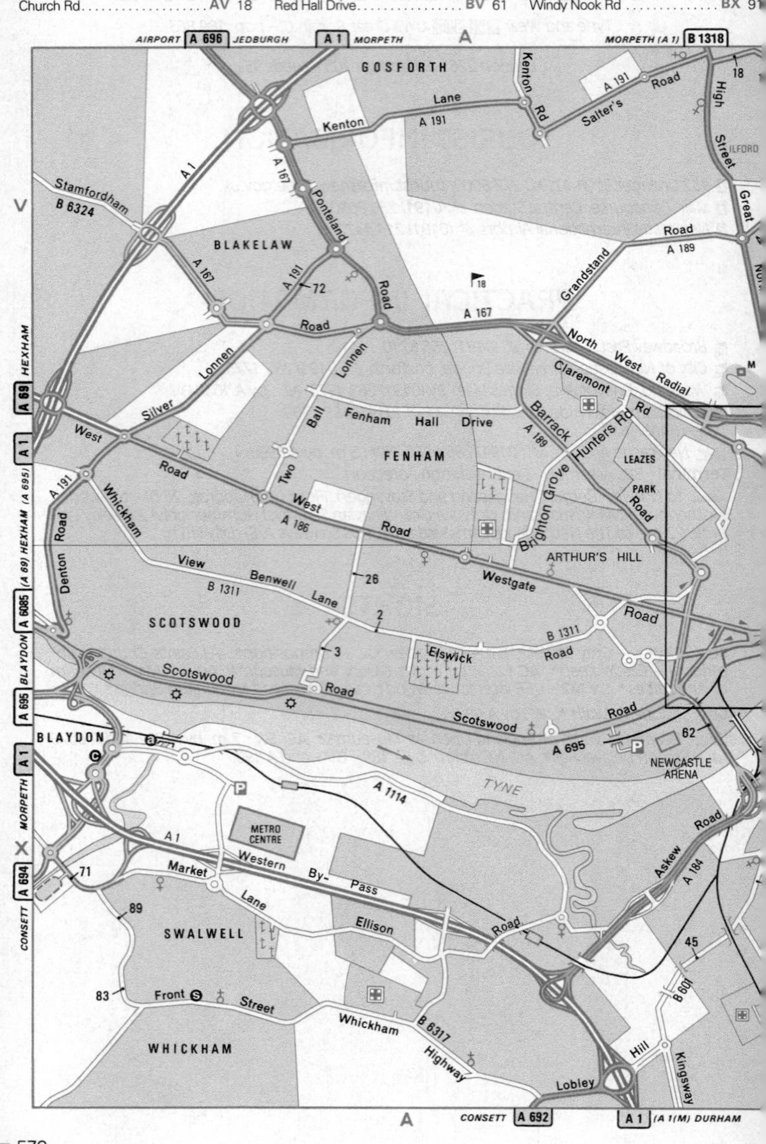

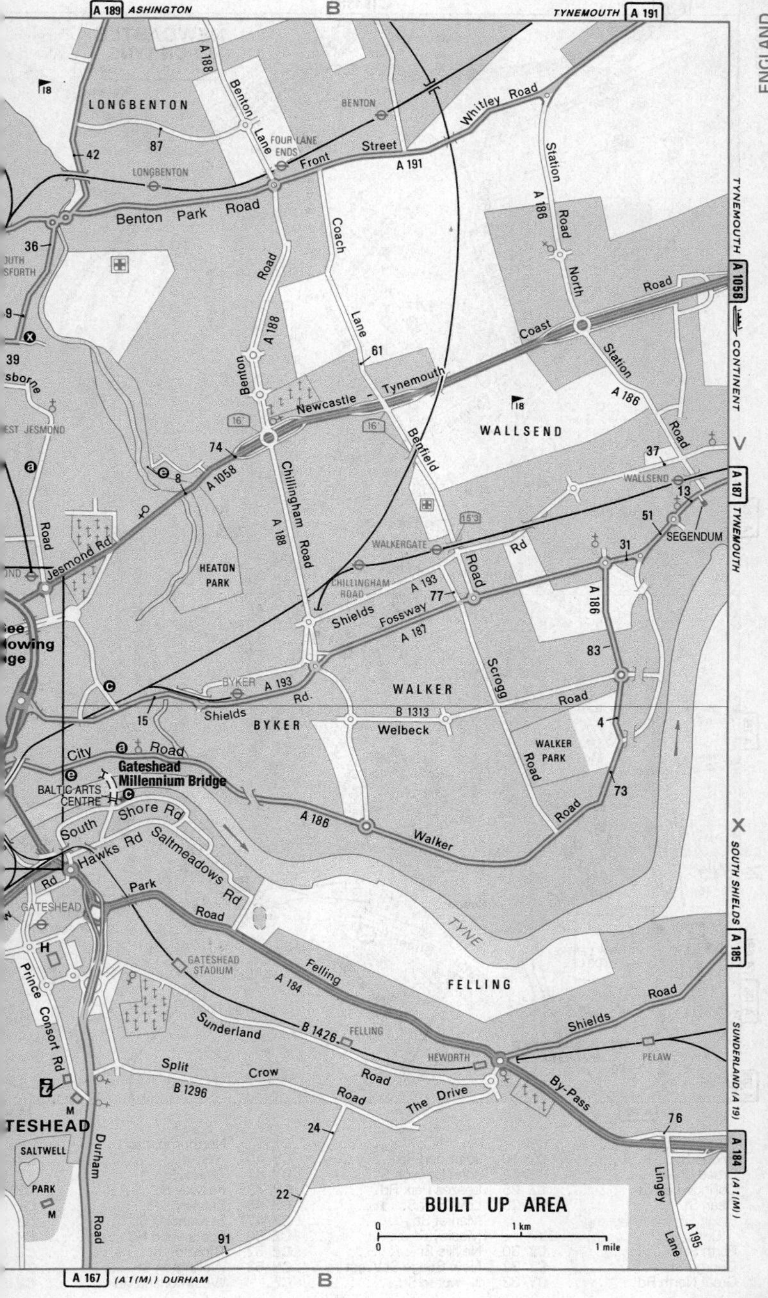

A 189 ASHINGTON
B
TYNEMOUTH A 191
ENGLAND
LONGBENTON
BENTON
FOUR LANE ENDS
Front Street
A 191
Whitley Road
Benton Lane
A 188
Benton Park Road
Coach Lane
Station Road
A 186
North Road
Coast Road
TYNEMOUTH
A 1058
CONTINENT
Newcastle - Tynemouth
Benton Road
A 188
Station Road
A 186
WALLSEND
Benfield Road
Chillingham Road
A 188
A 1058
Jesmond Rd
HEATON PARK
WALKERGATE
CHILLINGHAM ROAD
Shields Road
A 193
Fossway
A 187
A 187
TYNEMOUTH
SEGENDUM
WALLSEND
WALKER
Scrogg Road
BYKER
A 193
Shields Rd.
B 1313
Welbeck Road
WALKER PARK
City Road
Gateshead Millennium Bridge
BALTIC ARTS CENTRE
South Shore Rd
A 186
Walker Road
Hawks Rd
Saltmeadows Rd
Park Road
GATESHEAD
TYNE
GATESHEAD STADIUM
Felling
A 184
FELLING
Prince Consort Rd
Sunderland Road
B 1426
FELLING
HEWORTH
Split Crow Road
B 1296
The Drive
Shields Road
PELAW
By-Pass
SOUTH SHIELDS
A 185
SUNDERLAND (A 19)
A 184
(A 1(M))
GATESHEAD
SALTWELL PARK
Durham Road
Lingey Lane
A 195
BUILT UP AREA
1 km
1 mile
A 167 (A 1(M)) DURHAM
B

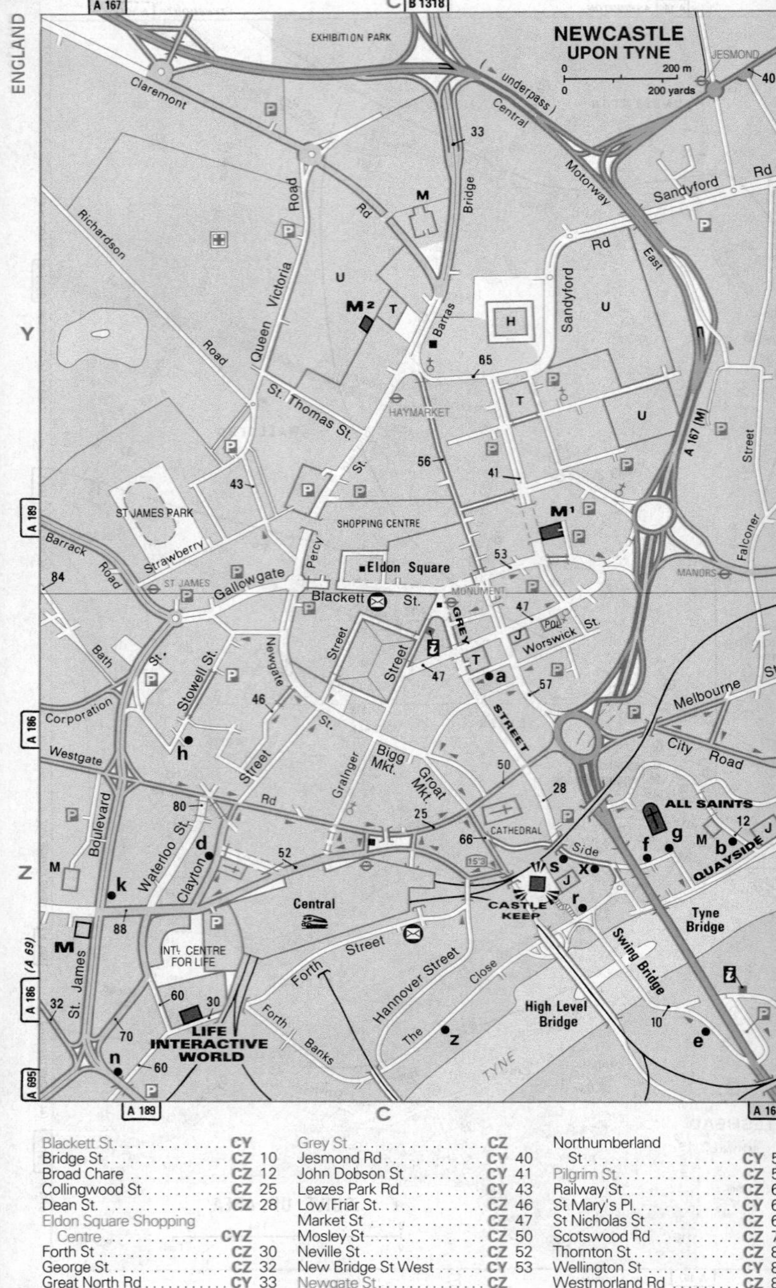

Blackett St. . . . . CY
Bridge St . . . . CZ 10
Broad Chare . . . . CZ 12
Collingwood St . . . . CZ 25
Dean St. . . . . CZ 28
Eldon Square Shopping
Centre . . . . CYZ
Forth St . . . . CZ 30
George St . . . . CZ 32
Great North Rd . . . . CY 33

Grey St . . . . CZ
Jesmond Rd . . . . CY 40
John Dobson St . . . . CY 41
Leazes Park Rd . . . . CY 43
Low Friar St . . . . CZ 46
Market St . . . . CZ 47
Mosley St . . . . CZ 50
Neville St . . . . CZ 52
New Bridge St West . . . . . . CY 53
Newgate St . . . . CZ

Northumberland
St . . . . CY 5
Pilgrim St . . . . CZ 5
Railway St . . . . CZ 6
St Mary's Pl. . . . . CY 6
St Nicholas St . . . . CZ 6
Scotswood Rd . . . . CZ 7
Thornton St . . . . CZ 8
Wellington St . . . . CY 8
Westmorland Rd . . . . CZ 8

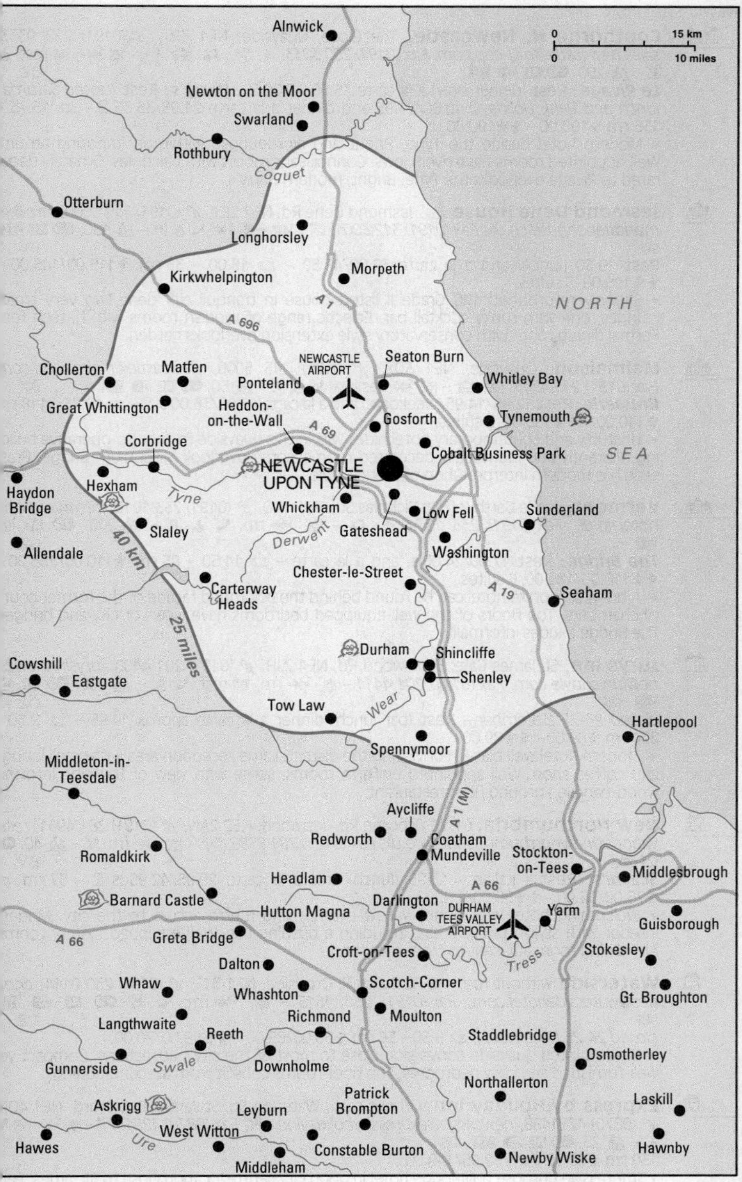

Alnwick
0 15 km
0 10 miles
Newton on the Moor
Swarland
Rothbury
Coquet
Otterburn
Longhorsley
Morpeth
Kirkwhelpington
A 1
NORTH
A 696
NEWCASTLE AIRPORT
Seaton Burn
Chollerton
Matfen
Ponteland
Whitley Bay
Great Whittington
Heddon-on-the-Wall
Tynemouth
Gosforth
A 69
Corbridge
Cobalt Business Park
SEA
NEWCASTLE UPON TYNE
Haydon Bridge
Hexham
Tyne
Whickham
Low Fell
Sunderland
Slaley
Derwent
Gateshead
Allendale
40 km
Washington
Chester-le-Street
A 19
Carterway Heads
Seaham
25 miles
Durham
Shincliffe
Cowshill
Eastgate
Shenley
Tow Law
Wear
Hartlepool
Spennymoor
Middleton-in-Teesdale
A 1 (M)
Aycliffe
Redworth
Coatham Mundeville
Romaldkirk
Stockton-on-Tees
Middlesbrough
Headlam
A 66
Barnard Castle
Darlington
DURHAM TEES VALLEY AIRPORT
Yarm
Hutton Magna
Guisborough
A 66
Greta Bridge
Croft-on-Tees
Stokesley
Dalton
Tees
Scotch-Corner
Whaw
Whashton
Gt. Broughton
Moulton
Langthwaite
Richmond
Reeth
Staddlebridge
Osmotherley
Gunnerside
Swale
Downholme
Northallerton
Patrick Brompton
Laskill
Askrigg
Leyburn
West Witton
Hawes
Ure
Constable Burton
Hawnby
Newby Wiske
Middleham

Look out for red symbols, indicating particularly pleasant establishments.

ENGLAND

Copthorne H. Newcastle, The Close, Quayside, NE1 3RT, (0191) 222 0333 *sales.newcastle@mill-cop.com, Fax (0191) 260 3033,* rest, – 200. CZ
Le Rivage : **Rest** (dinner only) a la carte 35.00/75.00 – ***Harry's :*** **Rest** *(closed Saturday lunch and Bank Holidays)* 10.00/21.95 and dinner a la carte 21.95/35.35 – 15.75 – **156 rm** ☆190.00 – ☆☆190.00.
• Modern hotel beside the Tyne. Bright and airy lounges within an imposing atrium. Well-appointed rooms have river views. Connoisseur rooms with balconies. Ornately decorated Le Rivage overlooks the Tyne. Bright, modern Harry's.

Jesmond Dene House, Jesmond Dene Rd, NE2 2EY, (0191) 212 3000, *info@jesmonddenehouse.co.uk, Fax (0191) 312 3001,* – 130. BV
Rest 19.50 (lunch) and a la carte 32.00/48.50 – 15.00 – **35 rm** ☆115.00/145.00 – ☆☆195.00, 5 suites.
• Stylishly refurbished 19C Grade II listed house in tranquil city dene. Two very smart lounges, one with funky cocktail bar. Eclectic range of modish rooms with hi-tech feel. Formal dining room with conservatory style extension overlooks garden.

Malmaison, Quayside, NE1 3DX, (0191) 245 5000, *newcastle@malmaison.com, Fax (0191) 245 4545,* rest, – 50. BX
Brasserie : **Rest** 12.95/14.95 (weekdays) and a la carte 16.00/36.00 **s.** – 12.75 – **118 rm** ☆140.00 – ☆☆160.00, 2 suites.
• Unstuffy and contemporary hotel hides within this quayside former Co-operative building. Vibrantly and individually decorated rooms; some overlook Millennium Bridge. Brasserie has modern interpretation of French style.

Vermont, Castle Garth (off St Nicholas St), NE1 1RQ, (0191) 233 1010, *info@vermont-hotel.co.uk, Fax (0191) 233 1234,* rm, – 200. CZ
The Bridge : **Rest** 17.00/24.00 **s.** and a la carte – 14.50 – **95 rm** ☆110.00/185.00 – ☆☆110.00/185.00, 6 suites.
• A busy, corporate hotel can be found behind the columned façade of the former council chambers. Top floors of the well-equipped bedrooms have views of city and bridges. The Bridge exudes informality.

Jurys Inn, St James Gate, Scotswood Rd, NE4 7JH, (0191) 201 4400, *jurysinnnewcastle@jurysdoyle.com, Fax (0191) 201 4411* – rm, rest, – 100. CZ
closed 23-27 December – **Rest** (bar lunch)/dinner a la carte approx 14.95 – 9.50 – **274 rm** ☆89.00 – ☆☆89.00.
• Modern hotel well placed for visiting the district. Large reception area with small lounge and coffee shop. Well-appointed uniform rooms, some with view of the city. Informal wood-panelled ground floor restaurant.

New Northumbria, 61-73 Osborne Rd, Jesmond, NE2 2AN, (0191) 281 4961, *reservations@newnorthumbriahotel.co.uk, Fax (0191) 281 8588,* – rm, – 40. BV
Scalini's : **Rest** - Italian - 13.95 (lunch) and a la carte 20.85/42.95 **s** – **57 rm** ☆75.00/95.00 – ☆☆95.00/115.00.
• Welcoming hotel with bright yellow exterior and metro access to the city. Modern interior with stylish public areas, including a bustling bar. Well-equipped, comfy rooms. Airy dining room adjacent to front reception.

Waterside without rest., 48-52 Sandhill, Quayside, NE1 3JF, (0191) 230 0111, *enquiries@watersidehotel.com, Fax (0191) 230 1615* – rm, CZ
closed 24-26 December – 9.50 – **36 rm** ☆50.00/65.00 – ☆☆68.00/70.00.
• Grade II listed quayside conversion close to most of the city's attractions. Compact yet well-furnished and cosy bedrooms. Top floor rooms benefit from air-conditioning.

Express by Holiday Inn without rest., Waterloo Sq, St James Boulevard, NE1 4DN, (0870) 4281488, *newcastle@expressbyholidayinn.net, Fax (0870) 4281477* – – 25. CZ
130 rm ☆89.95 – ☆☆89.95/149.00.
• Impressive purpose built lodge hotel in good city centre location close to St James' Park and Arena. Rich, warm rooms are inviting for leisure or business travellers.

Premier Travel Inn, City Rd, Quayside, NE1 2AN, (0191) 232 6533, *Fax (0191) 232 6557* – rm, rest, BX
Rest (grill rest.) – **81 rm** ☆59.95/59.95 – ☆☆61.95/61.95.
• Only a short walk into city centre and with a good location beside the Tyne. Comfy spacious and modern bedrooms, designed with ample work space.

XXX **Fisherman's Lodge,** Jesmond Dene, Jesmond, NE7 7BQ, (0191) 281 3281, *enquiries@fishermanslodge.co.uk, Fax (0191) 281 6410,* – P. VISA BV e
closed Sunday and Bank Holidays – **Rest** - Seafood - 17.50/50.00 ♀.
◆ Attractive Victorian house secreted in a narrow wooded valley yet close to city centre. Series of well-appointed, stylish rooms. Modern British cooking with seafood bias.

XXX **Charley's,** 2-6 Shakespeare St, NE1 6AQ, (0191) 261 8177, *Fax (0191) 221 1551* – . VISA CZ a
closed 24-26 December, 1 January, Saturday lunch, Sunday and Monday – **Rest** 13.95 (lunch) and a la carte 27.85/36.45 ♀.
◆ The former bank vault is a fine setting for a pre or post theatre meal. Bar and lounge and separate cigar lounge with leather Chesterfield. Good value modern British cooking.

XXX **Black Door,** 32 Clayton Street West, NE1 5DZ, (0191) 261 6295, *Fax (0191) 261 6295* – . AE VISA CZ d
closed 1 week January, 25-26 December, Sunday and Monday – **Rest** 16.50/39.50 ♀.
◆ Set in Georgian terrace, with smart and contemporary interior. There's a wood floored lounge with leather sofas and a cosy dining room serving intriguing modern combinations.

XX **Treacle Moon,** 5-7 The Side, Quayside, NE1 3JE, (0191) 232 5537, *Fax (0191) 221 1745* – . AE VISA CZ x
closed 25 December, 1 January, Sunday and Bank Holidays – **Rest** (booking essential) (dinner only) a la carte 30.00/36.00.
◆ Split-level, brightly decorated cosmopolitan restaurant with a lively atmosphere. Polite and relaxed service of a regularly changing menu of modern International dishes.

XX **Vujon,** 29 Queen St, Quayside, NE1 3UG, (0191) 221 0601, *matab@vujon.demon.co.uk, Fax (0191) 221 0602* – . AE VISA CZ g
closed 25 December and Sunday lunch – **Rest** - Indian - a la carte 20.90/36.80.
◆ A friendly and authentic Indian restaurant can be found behind the striking Victorian façade with modern etched windows. Menu of traditional and more contemporary dishes.

XX **Café 21,** 19-21 Queen St, Princes Wharf, Quayside, NE1 3UG, (0191) 222 0755, *Fax (0191) 221 0761* – . AE VISA CZ f
closed 25-26 December, Sunday and Bank Holidays – **Rest** (booking essential) 16.50 (lunch) and a la carte 25.50/38.50 ♀.
◆ Relaxed bistro-style restaurant with an informal atmosphere in the heart of the lively quayside area. Extensive selection of rustic and sensibly priced dishes.

X **Barn @ The Biscuit,** The Biscuit Factory, Stoddart St, NE2 1AN, (0191) 230 3338, *Fax (0191) 232 7909* – . AE VISA BV c
closed 25-26 December, Sunday and dinner Bank Holiday Mondays – **Rest** a la carte 18.00/31.00.
◆ Separated by stretched hide walls from art gallery in 30's biscuit factory. Featuring rustic furniture from North America. Asian influenced dishes with unusual combinations.

X **Café Live, Bar and Bistro,** 27 Broad Chare, Quayside, NE1 3DQ, (0191) 232 1331, *Fax (0191) 261 1577* – . AE VISA CZ b
closed Sunday – **Rest** (booking essential) 12.50 (lunch) and dinner a la carte 21.00/27.00.
◆ Converted warehouse near the quay, the Millennium Bridge and the Baltic Arts Centre. Ground floor café for snacks; upstairs for classic British cooking.

X **Blackfriars,** Friars St, NE1 4XN, (0191) 261 5945, *info@blackfriarscafebar.co.uk, Fax (0191) 261 9432,* – . AE VISA CZ h
closed 25-26 December, Sunday lunch and Monday – **Rest** 15.00 (lunch) and a la carte 20.00/31.00 ♀.
◆ Late 13C stone built monks' refectory still serving food in a split level beamed restaurant. Relaxed atmosphere with friendly informal service. Interesting and original menu.

at Gosforth *North : 2½ m. by B 1318* – **AV** – ✉ *Newcastle upon Tyne.*

Newcastle Marriott H. Gosforth Park, High Gosforth Park, NE3 5HN, North : 2 m. on B 1318 at junction with A 1056 0870 400 7288, *events.gosforth@marriotthotels.com, Fax (0191) 236 8192,* squash – , rm, rest, P – 800. AE VISA.
Chats : **Rest** (dinner only and Sunday lunch) a la carte 16.85/27.85 **s.** ♀ – ***Park :*** **Rest** (dinner only and Sunday lunch)/dinner 27.60/28.00 and a la carte 27.60/36.65 ♀ – 14.95 – **174 rm** 165.00/170.00 – 199.00, 4 suites.
◆ Ideal for both corporate and leisure guests. Extensive conference and leisure facilities. Well-equipped bedrooms with up-to-date décor. Close to the racecourse and the A1. Informal Chats for light snacks. Relaxed Park overlooks the grounds.

at Seaton Burn *North : 8 m. by B 1318 – AV – ✉ Newcastle upon Tyne.*

Horton Grange, NE13 6BU, Northwest : 3 ½ m. by Blagdon rd on Ponteland rd ✆ (01661) 860686, *enquiries@horton-grange.co.uk, Fax (01661) 860308,* – rest, P. MC AE VISA.
closed 25-26 December – **Rest** *(closed Sunday dinner)* (booking essential) a la carte 11.85/37.85 ♀ – 9.95 – **9 rm** 95.00 – 105.00.
◆ Attractive, personally run Edwardian country house. Rooms in main house have more character and space than those in annexe. Dine in the pleasant conservatory overlooking the manicured gardens.

at Cobalt Business Park *Northeast : 8 m. by A 1058 – BV –, A 19 off A 191 – ✉ Newcastle upon Tyne.*

Village H. and Leisure Club, NE27 0BY, ✆ (0191) 270 1414, *village.newcastle@village-hotels.com, Fax (0191) 270 1515,* – rest, P – 250. MC AE VISA
Rest (grill rest.) 8.95 (lunch) and a la carte 17.65/21.75 ♀ – 9.95 – **127 rm** 99.00 – 109.00.
◆ A modern hotel, well placed local attractions, with an excellent, extensive and well-equipped leisure club. Bright, light and airy modern bedrooms. Popular menus in the grill restaurant, the village pub or the cafe in the leisure club.

at Newcastle Airport *Northwest : 6¾ m. by A 167 off A 696 – AV – ✉ Newcastle upon Tyne.*

Premier Travel Inn, Ponteland Rd, Prestwick, NE20 9DB, ✆ (01661) 825040, *Fax (01661) 824940* – , rest, P – 30. MC AE VISA.
Rest (grill rest.) – **86 rm** 53.95 – 53.95.
◆ Bright and modern functional lodge accommodation directly adjacent to the main airport entrance. Aeronautical themed restaurant.

at Ponteland *Northwest : 8¼ m. by A 167 on A 696 – AV – ✉ Newcastle upon Tyne.*

New Rendezvous, 3-5 Broadway, NE20 9PW, Southwest : 1½ m. by B 6323 and Darras Hall Estate rd ✆ (01661) 821775 – MC AE VISA
Rest - Chinese - (dinner only and lunch Friday and Saturday) 25.00 and a la carte approx 17.00.
◆ Situated in a shopping parade. Family run restaurant specialising in Peking and Cantonese cuisine; extensive menu. Tables with revolving centres for large parties.

Cafe Lowrey, 35 Broadway, Darras Hall Estate, NE20 9PW, Southwest : 1½ m. by B 6323 and Darras Hall Estate rd ✆ (01661) 820357, *Fax (01661) 820357* – MC AE VISA
closed 25-26 December, Sunday and Bank Holidays – **Rest** (booking essential) (dinner only and Saturday lunch) a la carte 20.50/35.00 ♀.
◆ Small restaurant in shopping parade with wooden chairs and cloth-laid tables. Blackboard menus offering modern British cooking using local produce.

NEWENT *Glos. 503 504 M 28 – pop. 4 247.*

7 Church St ✆ (01531) 822468.
London 109 – Gloucester 10 – Hereford 22 – Newport 44.

at Clifford's Mesne *Southwest : 3 m. by B 4216 – ✉ Newent.*

Yew Tree with rm, GL18 1JS, on Glasshouse rd ✆ (01531) 820719, *paul@yewtreemahill.freeserve.co.uk, Fax (01531) 820912,* – P. MC VISA
closed 2-22 January – **Rest** *(closed Monday and dinner Sunday)* 28.50 ♀ – **2 rm** 55.00 – 70.00.
◆ Former cider press dating back to 19C, now serving ambitious dishes using ingredients with emphasis on local produce: dinner in the dining room and lunches in the bar.

NEWHAVEN *E. Sussex 504 U 31 – pop. 12 276.*

to France (Dieppe) (Hoverspeed Ltd) 2-6 daily (2 h).
London 63 – Brighton 9 – Eastbourne 14 – Lewes 7.

Premier Travel Inn, Avis Rd, BN9 0AG, East : ½ m. on A 259 ✆ (01273) 612356 *Fax (01273) 612359* – , rest, P. MC AE VISA
Rest (grill rest.) – **40 rm** 51.95 – 51.95.
◆ A consistent standard of trim accommodation in contemporary style; a useful address for cost-conscious travellers. Next to Drove Brewsters and handy for ferry users.

Also in the Michelin Guide collection

Benelux
Deutschland
España & Portugal
France
Great Britain & Ireland
Italia
Österreich
Portugal
Suisse

Pari
London
Main Cities of Europe
New York City

EWICK *E. Sussex* 504 U 31 – *pop. 2 129.*
London 57 – Brighton 14 – Eastbourne 20 – Hastings 34 – Maidstone 30.

Newick Park, BN8 4SB, Southeast : 1 ½ m. following signs for Newick Park (01825) 723633, *bookings@newickpark.co.uk, Fax (01825) 723969,* heated, VISA
closed 31 December – **Rest** (booking essential to non-residents) 18.00/25.00 (lunch) and dinner a la carte 36.00/50.00 – **15 rm** 125.00 – 165.00/285.00, 1 suite.
◆ Georgian manor in 200 acres; views of Longford river and South Downs. Stately hallway and lounge. Unique rooms, some with original fireplaces, all with Egyptian cotton sheets. Dine in relaxed formality on high-back crimson chairs.

272, 20-22 High St, BN8 4LQ, (01825) 721272, *twoseventwo@hotmail.co.uk, Fax (01825) 724698* – VISA
closed 25-27 December, 1-3 January, Monday, Sunday dinner and Tuesday lunch – **Rest** 17.50/19.95 and a la carte 22.40/31.70.
◆ Well-run restaurant with an easy-going, relaxed feel. Chairs from Italy, modern art on walls. Frequently changing menus offer a winning blend of British and European flavours.

EWMARKET *Suffolk* 504 V 27 – *pop. 16 947.*
Links, Cambridge Rd (01638) 663000.
Palace House, Palace St (01638) 667200.
London 64 – Cambridge 13 – Ipswich 40 – Norwich 48.

Bedford Lodge, Bury Rd, CB8 7BX, Northeast : ½ m. on A 1304 (01638) 663175, *info@bedfordlodgehotel.co.uk, Fax (01638) 667391,* – 200. VISA.
Orangery : Rest *(closed Saturday lunch)* a la carte 27.00/42.00 s. – **55 rm** 125.00/140.00 – 150.00/225.00.
◆ Extended Georgian hunting lodge built for Duke of Bedford, set in three acres of secluded gardens, close to racecourse. Racing theme pursued in stylish contemporary rooms. Characterful dining room with chandelier and large windows.

Rutland Arms, High St, CB8 8NB, (01638) 664251, *gapleisure@rutlandarmshotel.com, Fax (01638) 666298,* – rm, – 80. VISA.
Rest 17.50/19.95 and a la carte 25.40/33.95 – 12.00 – **46 rm** 78.00/83.00 – 90.00.
◆ Constructed round a central courtyard, this Georgian coaching inn has warm interiors of patterned carpets and wallpapers. Bedrooms are similarly traditional. Rustic dining room with racing theme.

t Lidgate *Southeast : 7 m. on B 1063 – Newmarket.*

The Star, CB8 9PP, (01638) 500275, – VISA.
closed 25-26 December, 1 January and Sunday dinner – **Rest** - Spanish - a la carte 24.95/29.35.
◆ Pink washed part 16C inn, oozing charm with beams and inglenooks, in pretty village. Original, predominantly Iberian menus: local game cooked in a hearty, fresh Spanish style.

t Six Mile Bottom *(Cambs.) Southwest : 6 m. on A 1304 – Newmarket.*

Swynford Paddocks, CB8 0UE, (01638) 570234, *sales@swynfordpaddocks.com, Fax (01638) 570283,* – rest, – 25. VISA
Rest 16.95/22.95 and a la carte 16.95/30.45 – **15 rm** 90.00/135.00 – 110.00/165.00.
◆ Hotel in pastures with a past: Lord Byron stayed here, penning poetry and having an affair with half-sister: their portraits on stairs. Elegant rooms. Softly lit, oak-panelled restaurant.

EW MILTON *Hants.* 503 504 P 31 – *pop. 26 681 (inc. Barton-on-Sea).*
Barton-on-Sea, Milford Rd (01425) 615308.
London 106 – Bournemouth 12 – Southampton 21 – Winchester 34.

Chewton Glen, Christchurch Rd, BH25 6QS, West : 2 m. by A 337 and Ringwood Rd on Chewton Farm Rd (01425) 275341, *reservations@chewtonglen.com, Fax (01425) 272310,* heated, indoor/outdoor – rest, – 120. VISA.
Marryat Room and Conservatory : **Rest** 22.50/59.50 and a la carte 41.75 s. – 25.00 – **36 rm** 235.00/315.00 – 325.00/435.00, 22 suites 535.00/775.00.
◆ A byword in luxury: 19C house where Captain Marryat wrote novels. Sherry and shortbread await in huge rooms of jewel colours; balconies overlook grounds. Scented steam room. Accomplished cooking in cool smooth conservatory and bright dining room.

EWPORT *Isle of Wight – see Wight (Isle of).*

NEWPORT Shrops. 502 503 504 M 25.
London 148 – Stafford 12.5 – Telford 9.5.

The Fox, Chetwynd Aston, TF10 9LQ, South : 1 ½ m. by Wolverhampton rd (A 4 ℘ (01952) 815940, *fox@brunningandprice.co.uk, Fax (01952) 815941*, , – P. VISA
closed 25-26 December – **Rest** a la carte 12.85/27.15 ♀.
◆ Updated pub with lawned garden and terrace. Light, airy interior: walls filled with o pictures and posters. Big tables predominate for family get-togethers. Modern menus.

NEWPORT PAGNELL *Milton Keynes* 504 R 27 – *pop. 14 739.*
London 57 – Bedford 13 – Luton 21 – Northampton 15 – Oxford 46.

Plan : see Milton Keynes

Swan Revived, High St, MK16 8AR, ℘ (01908) 610565, *info@swanrevived.co.u Fax (01908) 210995* – , rest, rest, P – 70. AE VISA CU
Rest (dinner only and Sunday lunch) a la carte 16.95/29.95 ♀ – **40 rm** ★83.95/88.95 ★★93.95, 2 suites.
◆ You no longer need a horse to stay at this 15C coaching inn, known for its stablin Rooms are welcoming, many in pine, one has four-poster. A naturopathic clinic is nearb Oak-panelled dining room enhanced by soft lighting.

Robinsons, 18-20 St John St, MK16 8HJ, ℘ (01908) 611400, *info@robinsonsresta ant.co.uk, Fax (01908) 216900* – . AE VISA CU
closed Sunday and Bank Holidays – **Rest** 6.50/17.95 and a la carte 29.35/33.55.
◆ A bright façade defines sunny nature of Mediterranean style cuisine. An upbeat eate in which to sample an eclectic blend of dishes which range from modern to traditional.

NEWQUAY *Cornwall* 503 E 32 *The West Country G.* – *pop. 19 562.*
Env. : *Penhale Point and Kelsey Head*★ (≤★★), *SW : by A 3075 Y – Trerice*★ *AC, SE : 3½ r by A 392 – Y – and A 3058.*
Exc. : *St Agnes – St Agnes Beacon*★★ (※★★), *SW : 12½ m. by A 3075 – Y – and B 3285.*
18 *Tower Rd* ℘ *(01637) 872091*, Z – 9 *Treloy* ℘ *(01637) 878554* – 18 *Merlin, Mawgan Por ℘ (01841) 540222.*
Newquay Airport : ℘ *(01637) 860600 Y.*
Municipal Offices, Marcus Hill ℘ *(01637) 854020, info@newquay.co.uk.*
London 291 – Exeter 83 – Penzance 34 – Plymouth 48 – Truro 14.

Plan opposite

Trebarwith, Trebarwith Crescent, TR7 1BZ, ℘ (01637) 872288, *enquiry@trebarwith-h tel.co.uk, Fax (01637) 875431*, ≤ bay and coast, , , – P. VISA. Z
April-October – **Rest** (bar lunch)/dinner 18.00/30.00 **s.** ♀ – **42 rm** (dinner included) ★35.00/70.00 – ★★70.00/140.00.
◆ Superb bay and coastline views from this renowned seaside hotel. Has its own cinem plus evening discos and dances. You'll get the stunning vistas from traditional bedroom Dine by the sea beneath Wedgewood-style ceiling.

The Bristol, Narrowcliff, TR7 2PQ, ℘ (01637) 870275, *info@hotelbristol.co.u Fax (01637) 879347*, ≤, , – , rest, P – 200. AE VISA Z
Rest *(dinner only and Sunday lunch)* (bar lunch Monday-Saturday)/dinner 21.00 and a carte 25.00/32.50 ♀ – 11.00 – **73 rm** ★57.00/87.00 – ★★104.00/114.00, 1 suite.
◆ Classic Victorian seaside hotel, well established and family run. Wide range of bedroom from singles to family suites. Extensive conference facilities. Large windowed dining roo overlooks Atlantic.

Trenance Lodge, 83 Trenance Rd, TR7 2HW, ℘ (01637) 876702, *info@trenanc lodge.co.uk, Fax (01637) 878772*, – P. VISA Z
closed 25 December and 2 weeks January and 1 week November – **Rest** (booking essentia (dinner only) a la carte 21.95/29.00 – **5 rm** ★40.00/50.00 – ★★60.00/65.00.
◆ Purpose-built, personally run hotel. Modern feel to the interior with well-maintained an comfortable guest areas. Provides neat accommodation. Wide-ranging menu with stror Cornish flavour.

Corisande Manor , Riverside Ave, Pentire, TR7 1PL, ℘ (01637) 872042, *relax@cc sande.com, Fax (01637) 874557*, ≤ Gannel Estuary, – rest, P. VISA Y
April-December – **Rest** (dinner only) (set menu only) 25.00 **s.** – **9 rm** ★89.00/99.00 ★★169.00/179.00.
◆ Attractive manor house, built for an Austrian count, perched above, and with suprem views of, Gannel Estuary. Bedrooms with a fine, co-ordinated, modern elegance. Dinin room boasts historic beamed ceiling.

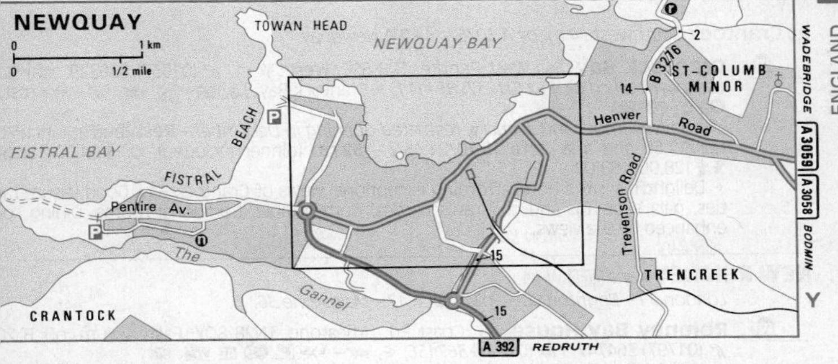

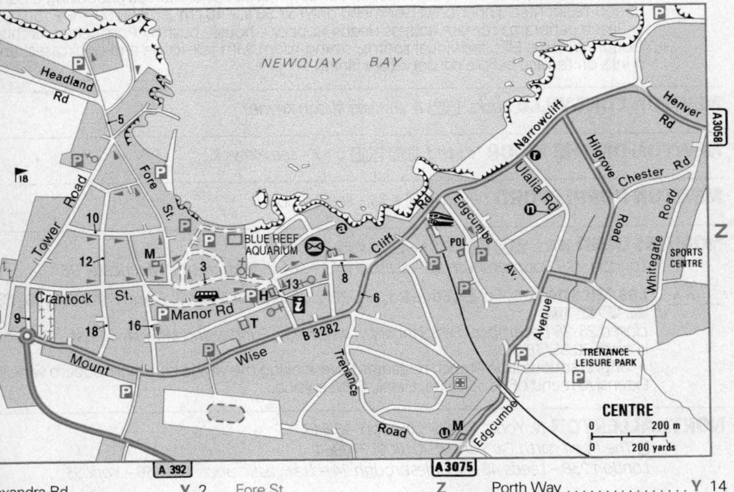

...exandra Rd . . . . Y 2
...nk St. . . . . Z 3
...acon Rd . . . . Z 5
...rry Rd . . . . Z 6
...st St . . . . Z 8
Fore St . . . . Z
Higher Tower Rd . . . . Z 9
Hope Terrace . . . . Z 10
Jubilee St . . . . Z 12
Marcus Hill . . . . Z 13
Porth Way . . . . Y 14
St George Rd . . . . Z 16
St John's Rd . . . . Z 18
Trevemper Rd . . . . Y 15

Whipsiderry, Trevelgue Rd, Porth, TR7 3LY, Northeast : 2 m. by A 392 off B 3276 ✆ (01637) 874777, *info@whipsiderry.co.uk, Fax (01637) 874777,* ≤, heated, – P. MC VISA
closed January, February and November – **Rest** (bar lunch)/dinner 17.50 – **20 rm** (dinner included) ☕ ★49.00/62.00 – ★★98.00/124.00.
◆ Simple, whitewashed building; family run, in a residential area. Communal areas include two lounges with a small bar and panoramic views. Pine furnished bedrooms. Tried-and-tested menus.

The Windward without rest., Alexandra Rd, Porth Bay, TR7 3NB, ✆ (01637) 873185, *enquiries@windwardhotel.co.uk, Fax (01637) 851400* – P. MC VISA. Y r
Easter-October – **12 rm** ☕ ★50.00/70.00 – ★★70.00/90.00.
◆ Small hotel with large windows overlooking the sea; a super place to have breakfast. Simply appointed, pine furnished bedrooms, some with large balconies.

Philadelphia without rest., 19 Eliot Gdns, TR7 2QE, ✆ (01637) 877747, *stay@thephiladelphia.co.uk* – P. MC AE VISA. Z n
7 rm ☕ ★30.00/45.00 – ★★50.00/66.00.
◆ In a tree-lined avenue, close to seafront. Cosy breakfast room serves full English breakfast. Themed bedrooms are very well kept. Hot tub available. Non smoking.

ENGLAND

at Crantock *Southwest : 4 m. by A 3075 – Y – ✉ Newquay.*

Crantock Bay ⛰, West Pentire, TR8 5SE, West : ¾ m. ☎ (01637) 830229, *stay@crantockbayhotel.co.uk, Fax (01637) 831111,* ← Crantock Bay, ⛾, ≘s, ▢, ⛸, ⛹ – ⛔ rest, P. MC AE ⓓ VISA
closed November and January, restricted opening in December – **Rest** (buffet lunch)/dinner 22.50 and a la carte 16.70/21.45 ⛽ – **32 rm** (dinner included) ⛼ ★64.00/136.50 ★★128.00/182.00.
• Delightfully sited hotel affording exceptional views of Crantock Bay. Good leisure facilities, gala evenings and children's parties. Comfortable, traditional rooms. Dining room enhanced by the views.

NEW ROMNEY *Kent* 504 W 31.
London 71 – Brighton 60 – Folkestone 17 – Maidstone 36.

Romney Bay House ⛰, Coast Rd, Littlestone, TN28 8QY, East : 2 ¼ m. off B 207 ☎ (01797) 364747, *Fax (01797) 367156,* ←, ⛸ – ⛔ P. MC AE VISA. ⛔
closed 1 week Christmas – **Rest** *(closed Sunday, Monday and Thursday)* (booking essential to non-residents) (dinner only) (set menu only) 37.50 **s.** – **10 rm** ⛼ ★60.00 – ★★150.00.
• Beach panorama for late actress Hedda Hopper's house, built by Portmeirion architect Clough Williams-Ellis. Individual rooms; sitting room with telescope and bookcases. Enjoy drinks on terrace before conservatory dining.

NEWTON LONGVILLE *Bucks.* 504 R 28 – *see Milton Keynes.*

NEWTON ON THE MOOR *Northd.* 501 502 O 17 – *see Alnwick.*

NEWTON POPPLEFORD *Devon* 503 K 31 – *see Sidmouth.*

NOMANSLAND *Wilts.* 503 504 P 31 – ✉ *Salisbury.*
London 96 – Bournemouth 26 – Salisbury 13 – Southampton 14 – Winchester 25.

XX **Les Mirabelles,** Forest Edge Rd, SP5 2BN, ☎ (01794) 390205, *Fax (01794) 390106,* ⛱ ▤. MC AE VISA
closed 25-26 December, 1-18 January, 1 week May, Sunday and Monday – **Rest** - French - a la carte 20.55/36.00 ⛽.
• Unpretentious little French restaurant overlooking the village common. Superb wine list. Extensive menu of good value, classic Gallic cuisine.

NORTHALLERTON *N. Yorks.* 502 P 20 – *pop. 15 517.*
ℹ *The Applegarth Car Park ☎ (01609) 776864.*
London 238 – Leeds 48 – Middlesbrough 24 – Newcastle upon Tyne 56 – York 33.

at Staddlebridge *Northeast : 7½ m. by A 684 on A 19 at junction with A 172 – ✉ Northallerton.*

X **McCoys Bistro at The Tontine** with rm, DL6 3JB, on southbound carriageway (A 19 ☎ (01609) 882671, *enquiries@mccoysatthetontine.co.uk, Fax (01609) 882660* – ▤ rm, P. MC AE ⓓ VISA
closed 25-26 December and 1-2 January – **Rest** (booking essential) 14.95/39.00 and a la carte 23.75/40.20 – **6 rm** ⛼ ★85.00 – ★★110.00.
• Yorkshire meets France in long standing restaurant with mirrors, wood panelling framed memorabilia. Snug bar to plot coups in. Large bedrooms, unique in decorative style.

at Newby Wiske *South : 2½ m. by A 167 – ✉ Northallerton.*

Solberge Hall ⛰, DL7 9ER, Northwest : 1 ¼ m. on Warlaby rd ☎ (01609) 779191 *reservations@solbergehall.co.uk, Fax (01609) 780472,* ←, ⛸, ⛳ – ⛔ P – ⛺ 80. MC AE VISA
Rest 20.95/24.50 – **23 rm** ⛼ ★75.00/85.00 – ★★100.00, 1 suite.
• Tranquil grounds surround this graceful Georgian house, situated in the heart of the countryside. Popular for weddings; bedrooms in main house or stable block. Local ingredients well employed in flavoursome menus.

NORTHAMPTON *Northants.* 504 R 27 *Great Britain G.* – *pop. 189 474.*
Exc. : *All Saints, Brixworth*★, *N : 7 m. on A 508 Y.*
⛳18, ⛳9 *Delapre, Eagle Drive, Nene Valley Way ☎ (01604) 764036 Z* – ⛳18 *Collingtree Park Windingbrook Lane ☎ (01604) 700000.*
ℹ *The Guildhall, St Giles Square ☎ (01604) 838800, tic@northampton.gov.uk.*
London 69 – Cambridge 53 – Coventry 34 – Leicester 42 – Luton 35 – Oxford 41.

NORTHAMPTON

Street	Zone	No.
Abington Square	X	2
Abington St	X	
Bewick Rd	Y	4
Billing Rd	X	5
Bridge St	X	6
Campbell St	X	7
Castillian St	X	8
Charnwood Ave.	Y	10
Church Lane	X	12
Cliftonville Rd	Z	13
College St	X	14
Derngate	X	15
Drapery	X	18
Gold St	X	
Greyfriars	X	23
Grosvenor Centre	X	
Guildhall Rd	X	24
Hazelwood Rd	X	25
Horse Shoe St	X	28
Kettering Rd	X	30
Kingsthorpe Grove	Y	34
Lower Mounts	X	35
Oaklands Drive	Y	38
Overstone Rd	X	39
Park Ave North	Y	40
Park Ave South	Z	43
Rushmere Rd	Z	44
St Andrew's Rd	Y	45
St Edmund's Rd	X	48
St Edmund's St	Z	49
St James's Rd	Z	50
St John's St	X	51
St Leonard's Rd	Z	52
St Michael's Rd	X	53
St Peters Way Centre	X	
St James Retail Park	X	
Sheep St	X	54
Silver St	X	55
Spencer Bridge Rd	X, Z	57
Towcester Rd	Z	58
Upper Mounts	X	59
Waveney Way	Y	60
West Bridge	X	62
Weston Favell Centre	Y	
Windrush Way	Y	63

A 5095 (A 508)
A 508
A 4500
A 5123
A 4500
A 428 (A 45)
A 5123
A 508
A 428
X
Grafton St.
Robert St.
Earl St.
Broad St.
Andrew's Rd
St.
Horse Market
Lady's Lane
GROSVENOR CENTRE
Abington St.
St. Giles' St.
York Rd
Cheyne Walk
Bedford Rd
Mare Fair
SOL CENTRAL
Gold St.
ST-PETERS CENTRE
Peter's Way
St.
Victoria Promenade
ST-JAMES RETAIL PARK
POL
0 200 m
0 200 yards

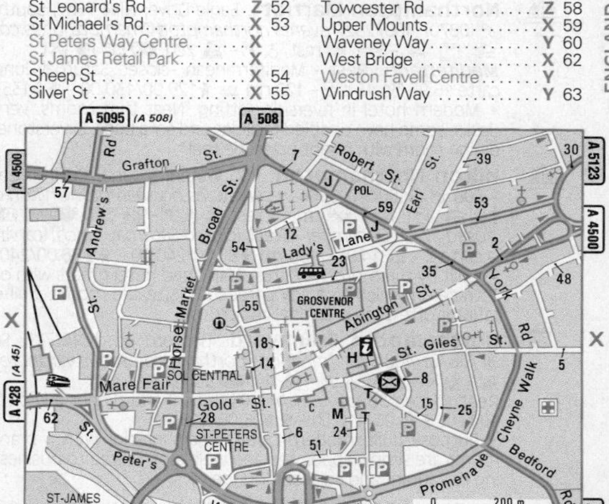

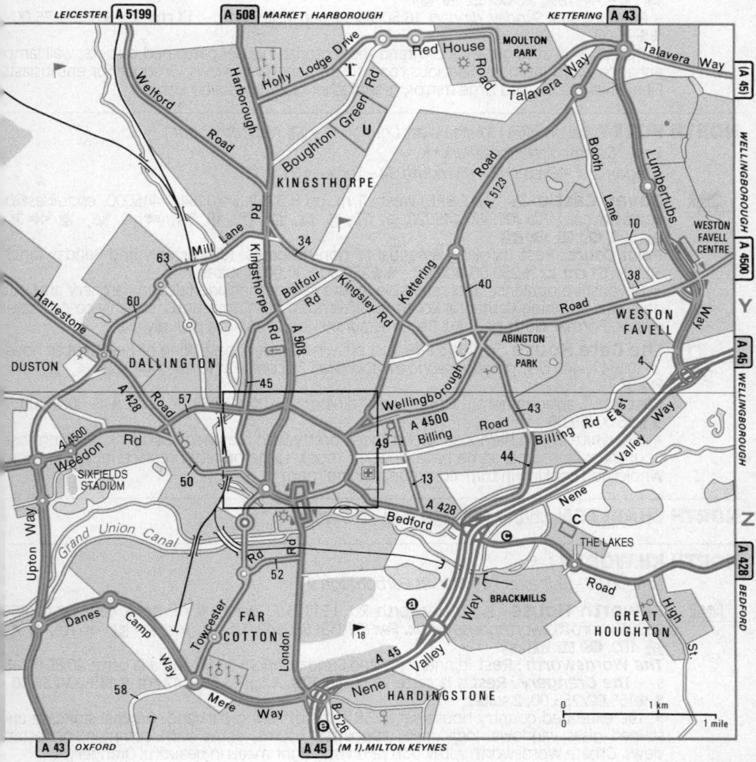

LEICESTER A 5199
A 508 MARKET HARBOROUGH
KETTERING A 43
(A 45)
WELLINGBOROUGH
A 4500
A 45 WELLINGBOROUGH
A 428 BEDFORD
A 43 OXFORD
A 45 (M 1), MILTON KEYNES
Y
Z
Welford Road
Harborough Rd
Holly Lodge Drive
Red House Road
MOULTON PARK
Talavera Way
Boughton Green Rd
KINGSTHORPE
Kettering Road
A 5123
Booth Lane
Lumbertubs
WESTON FAVELL CENTRE
Mill Lane
Kingsthorpe Rd
Balfour Rd
Kingsley Rd
Harlestone
DUSTON
DALLINGTON
A 508
WESTON FAVELL
ABINGTON PARK
A 428 Road
Wellingborough
A 4500 Billing Road
Billing Rd East
Valley Way
A 4500 Weedon Rd
SIXFIELDS STADIUM
Grand Union Canal
Bedford
A 428
Nene
THE LAKES
Road
Upton Way
Danes Camp Way
Towcester Rd
FAR COTTON
London Rd
BRACKMILLS
Way
GREAT HOUGHTON
High St.
A 45
Valley
Nene
HARDINGSTONE
B 526
Mere Way
0 1 km
0 1 mile

ENGLAND

Northampton Marriott, Eagle Drive, NN4 7HW, Southeast : 2 m. by A 428 off A 4 ☎ (0870) 4007252, *events.northampton@marriotthotels.co.uk, Fax (0870) 4007352,* ⇌s, ▣, – ✗, ▤ rest, ♿ P – 220. MC AE VISA Z

Mediterrano : **Rest** - Mediterranean -closed Saturday lunch (buffet lunch)/dinner a la carte 16.95/31.15 **s.** ♀ – **120 rm** ☕ ✝125.00/130.00 – ✝✝135.00/140.00.

◆ Modern hotel in riverside setting. Neat trim rooms, very practical, with well-lit work desks, some have disabled facilities and sofa beds. Silverstone race track is nearby. Pleasing dining room with bright brasserie feel.

Hilton Northampton, 100 Watering Lane, Collingtree, NN4 0XW, South : 3 m. on A 508 ☎ (01604) 700666, *reservations.northampton@hilton.com, Fax (01604) 702850,* ⇌s, ▣, – ✗ rm, ▤ rest, ♿ P – 300. MC AE VISA

closed 27-30 December – **Rest** *(closed Saturday lunch)* (carving lunch) 12.50/21.75 **s.** and a la carte ♀ – ☕ 14.95 – **136 rm** ✝86.00/240.00 – ✝✝86.00/240.00, 3 suites.

◆ Built by the motorway, this clean-lined hotel greets with open-plan foyer and café area. Terrace on which to enjoy barbecues. Sizeable rooms; well-equipped leisure centre. Restaurant offers international choice.

Northampton Courtyard, Bedford Rd, NN4 7YF, Southeast : 1 ½ m. on A 428 ☎ (0870) 4007214, *meetings.northampton@courtyardhotels.co.uk, Fax (0870) 4007314* – ✗ ▤ ♿ P – 40. MC AE VISA. Z

Rest *(closed Sunday lunch)* 9.95 (lunch) and dinner a la carte 15.40/22.95 ♀ – ☕ 12.95 – **104 rm** ✝95.00/110.00 – ✝✝95.00/110.00.

◆ Purpose-built, modern hotel. Smart interior with a branded style. Comfortable bedrooms are simply appointed and well-kept. Suited to business and leisure travellers. Relaxing restaurant and adjacent lounge.

at Spratton *North : 7 m. by A 508 off A 5199 – Y – ✉ Northampton.*

Broomhill Country House ⛰, Holdenby Rd, NN6 8LD, Southwest : 1 m. on Holdenby rd ☎ (01604) 845959, *broomhillhotel@aol.com, Fax (01604) 845834,* ≤, heated, – ✗ rest, P. MC AE VISA

– **Rest** *(closed Sunday dinner)* 16.50/23.95 and a la carte – **13 rm** ☕ ✝50.00/75.00 – ✝✝95.00.

◆ Peacocks strut in grounds of grand red Victorian house; patterned carpets, wall lamps enhance warm interiors. Spacious rooms with panoramic views. Croquet for enthusiasts. Fine dining room with large mirror, grandfather clock and lovely vistas.

NORTH BOVEY *Devon* 503 I 32 *The West Country G.* – ✉ *Newton Abbot.*

Env. : *Dartmoor National Park*★★.

London 214 – Exeter 13 – Plymouth 34 – Torquay 21.

Bovey Castle ⛰, TQ13 8RE, West : 1 m. on B 3212 ☎ (01647) 445000, *enquiries@boveycastle.com, Fax (01647) 445020,* ≤, ⇌s, ▣, 18, – ✗ P – 120. MC AE VISA

Palm Court : **Rest** (booking essential to non-residents) (dinner only and Sunday lunch) 52.50 – **61 rm** ☕ ✝250.00/800.00 – ✝✝250.00/800.00, 4 suites.

◆ Devonshire opulence: incomparable leisure facilities include falconry, archery and outdoor spa. Stunning Cathedral Room for afternoon tea. Sumptuous, stylishly co-ordinated rooms. Formal, cloth-clad, Art Deco restaurant: local suppliers proudly used.

The Gate House ⛰, TQ13 8RB, just off village green, past "Ring of Bells" public house ☎ (01647) 440479, *gatehouseondartmoor@talk21.com, Fax (01647) 440479,* ≤, – ✗ P

Rest (by arrangement) (communal dining) 22.00 – **3 rm** ☕ ✝45.00/48.00 – ✝✝66.00/68.00.

◆ 15C white Devon hallhouse; picturebook pretty with thatched roof, pink climbing roses. Country style rooms; some have views of moor. Large granite fireplace in sitting room. Wholefood cooking in trim, communal dining room.

NORTH CHARLTON *Northd.* 501 502 O 17 – *see Alnwick.*

NORTH KILWORTH *Leics.*

London 95 – Leicester 20 – Market Harborough 9.

Kilworth House ⛰, Lutterworth Rd, LE17 6JE, West : ½ m. on A 4304 ☎ (01858) 880058, *info@kilworthhouse.co.uk, Fax (01858) 880349,* – ✗ rm, ♿ P – 100. MC AE VISA.

The Wordsworth : **Rest** (dinner only and Sunday lunch) 28.50 and a la carte 30.85/47.40 **s.** – ***The Orangery :*** **Rest** a la carte 22.50/30.40 **s.** – ☕ 13.50 – **42 rm** ✝135.00/235.00 – ✝✝155.00/255.00, 2 suites.

◆ 19C extended country house set in 38 acres of rolling parkland. Original staircase and stained glass windows. Individually appointed rooms, some with commanding estate views. Ornate Wordsworth with courtyard vista. Light meals in beautiful Orangery.

IORTH NEWINGTON *Oxon. – see Banbury.*

IORTHREPPS *Norfolk* 504 Y 25 – *see Cromer.*

IORTH STOKE *Oxon. – see Wallingford.*

IORTH WALSHAM *Norfolk* 503 504 Y 25 *Great Britain G.* – *pop. 11 845.*
Exc. : *Blicking Hall★★ AC, W : 8½ m. by B 1145, A 140 and B 1354.*
London 125 – Norwich 16.

Beechwood, 20 Cromer Rd, NR28 0HD, ✆ (01692) 403231, *enquiries@beechwood-hotel.co.uk, Fax (01692) 407284,* – P. MC VISA
Rest (dinner only and Sunday lunch)/dinner 34.00 – **17 rm** ☕ ★70.00 – ★★120.00/150.00.
◆ Privately owned, peacefully set, part 19C hotel where Agatha Christie once stayed. Attentive service, as typified by tea and biscuits on arrival. Thoughtfully appointed rooms. Handsome dining room with flowers.

t Knapton *Northeast : 3 m. on B 1145* – ✉ *North Walsham.*

White House Farm without rest., NR28 0RX, ✆ (01263) 721344, *mg@whitehousefarmnorfolk.co.uk,* – P. MC VISA.
3 rm ☕ ★40.00 – ★★60.00.
◆ 18C brick and flint farmhouse. Spacious lounge with many books. Breakfast of local produce. Comfortable, modern, well-kept bedrooms.

IORTON *Shrops. – see Telford.*

IORTON ST PHILIP *Somerset* 503 504 N 30 – ✉ *Bath.*
London 113 – Bristol 22 – Southampton 55 – Swindon 40.

George Inn, High St, BA2 7LH, ✆ (01373) 834224, *georgeinnsp@aol.com, Fax (01373) 834861,* – P. MC AE VISA
accommodation closed 24-25 December – **Rest** a la carte 18.85/26.85 – **8 rm** ☕ ★60.00 – ★★110.00.
◆ Spectacular timber framed medieval inn built for merchants attending wool fairs. Popular now as a film set. Unique rooms: wall paintings, 15C fireplaces and leaded windows. Rustic dining.

Bath Lodge without rest., BA2 7NH, East : 1¼ m. by A 366 on A 36 ✆ (01225) 723040, *info@bathlodge.com, Fax (01225) 723737,* – P. MC AE VISA.
7 rm ☕ ★40.00/65.00 – ★★110.00/120.00.
◆ Grade II listed lodge with a charming exterior of towers and battlements once served as a gatehouse to the Farleigh estate. Country house décor, spacious, comfortable rooms.

Monmouth Lodge without rest., BA2 7LH, on B 3110 ✆ (01373) 834367, – P. MC VISA.
closed mid December-February – **3 rm** ☕ ★65.00 – ★★75.00.
◆ Homely guesthouse in delightful gardens and orchard. Tea and biscuits on arrival. Shared breakfast room; antique-strewn lounge. Quality, individualistic rooms open to terrace.

The Plaine without rest., BA2 7LT, ✆ (01373) 834723, *theplaine@easynet.co.uk, Fax (01373) 834101* – P. MC VISA.
closed 24 December-1 January – **3 rm** ☕ ★45.00/52.00 – ★★65.00/80.00.
◆ 16C stone cottages opposite George Inn on site of original market place. Beams, stone walls denote historic origins. Four-posters, pine furnishings in bedrooms. Family run.

IORWICH *Norfolk* 504 Y 26 *Great Britain G.* – *pop. 174 047.*
See : *City★★ - Cathedral★★* Y – *Castle (Museum and Art Gallery★ AC)* Z – *Market Place★* Z.
Env. : *Sainsbury Centre for Visual Arts★ AC, W : 3 m. by B 1108* X.
Exc. : *Blicking Hall★★ AC, N : 11 m. by A 140* – V – *and B 1354 – NE : The Broads★.*
Royal Norwich, Drayton High Rd, Hellesdon ✆ (01603) 425712, V – *Marriott Sprowston Manor Hotel, Wroxham Rd ✆ (0870) 4007229 – Costessy Park, Costessey ✆ (01603) 746333 – Bawburgh, Glen Lodge, Marlingford Rd ✆ (01603) 740404.*
Norwich Airport : ✆ (01603) 411923, N : 3½ m. by A 140 V.
The Forum, Millennium Plain ✆ (01603) 727927.
London 109 – Kingston-upon-Hull 148 – Leicester 117 – Nottingham 120.

NORWICH BUILT UP AREA

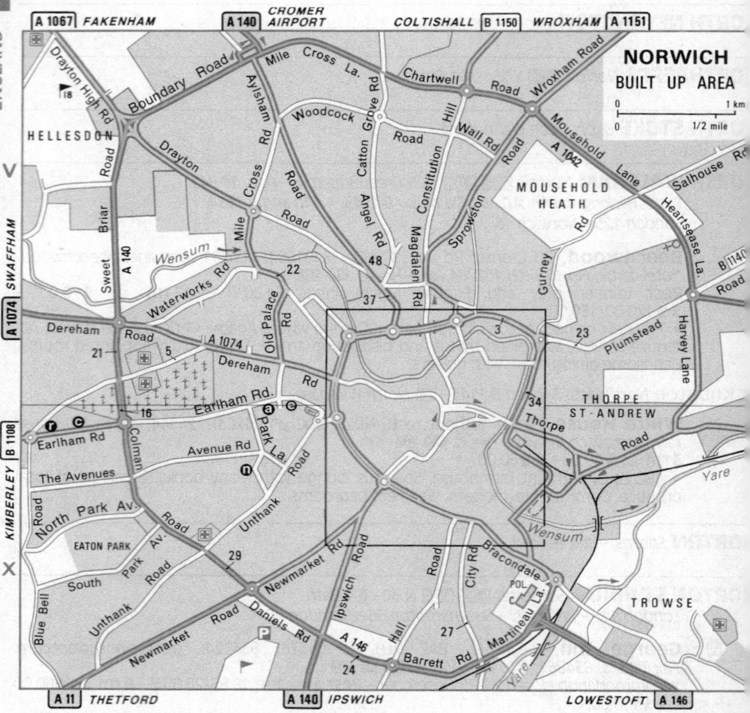

Barrack St	V 3	Heigham St	V 22	Mile End Rd	X
Bowthorpe Rd	V 5	Ketts Hill	V 23	Riverside Rd	V
Farrow Rd	V 16	Lakenham Rd	X 24	St Augustine's St	V
Guardian Rd	V 21	Long John Hill	X 27	Waterloo Rd	V

Marriott Sprowston Manor H. & Country Club, Wroxham Rd, NR7 8RP, North east : 3 ¼ m. on A 1151 ☏ (01603) 410871, *sprowstonmanor@marriotthotels.co.u Fax (01603) 423911,* ⓦ, Fö, ≘s, ⬚, ⚑18, ⛱, ⚘ – |‡| ⇹, ▤ rest, ♿ P – ⚠ 120. MC AE ⓘ VISA. ⚒

Manor : **Rest** *(closed Saturday lunch)* 31.50 and a la carte 17.00/39.00 ♀ – ☕ 14.95 – **93 rr** ☆115.00 – ☆☆115.00/140.00, 1 suite.

◆ Part Elizabethan manor house set in 10 acres of parkland and golf course. Pleasar lounge. Extensive leisure facilities. Many of the bedrooms overlook the picturesqu grounds. Restaurant with Gothic arched windows, ancient mahogany columns and c paintings.

Dunston Hall H. Golf & Country Club, Ipswich Rd, NR14 8PQ, South : 4 m. c A 140 ☏ (01508) 470444, *dhreception@devere-hotels.com, Fax (01508) 470689*
⛱, Fö, ≘s, ⬚, ⚑18, ⛱, ⚘, ⚔ – |‡| ⇹, ▤ rest, ♿ P – ⚠ 250. MC AE ⓘ VIS ⚒

Rest (carvery lunch) a la carte 15.45/29.95 **s.** ♀ – **127 rm** ☆130.00 – ☆☆160.00, 2 suites.

◆ Built in 1859, a wealth of original features remain in this imposing Elizabetha style country mansion. Most characterful rooms in the main house have golf cours views. Restaurant overlooks magnificent golf course.

Beeches, 2-6 Earlham Rd, NR2 3DB, ☏ (01603) 621167, *reception@beeches.co.u Fax (01603) 620151,* ⛱ – ⇹ P. MC AE ⓘ VISA. ⚒ VX

Rest (dinner only) 21.95 and a la carte 15.00/21.95 ♀ – **42 rm** ☕ ☆74.00/79.00 – ☆☆95.00 1 suite.

◆ Personally run series of Grade II listed properties overlooking terraced Victorian gardens Spacious rooms may have Cathedral views. Popular with business guests. Dining room wit Plantation Garden outlook.

ank Plain	Y 2	Elm Hill	Y	St George St	Y 38
ethel St	Z 4	Exchange St	YZ 15	St Stephen's St	Z
astle Mall Shopping Centre	Z	Gentleman's Walk	Z 17	Thorn Lane	Z 42
astle Meadow	Z 6	Grapes Hill	Y 19	Timber Hill	Z 43
attle Market St	Z 7	London St	YZ 26	Tombland	Y 45
hapel Field North	Z 9	Market Ave	Z 28	Upper King St	Y 46
haring Cross	Y 10	Rampant Horse St	Z 32	Wensum St	Y 49
oslany St	Y 14	Red Lion St	Z 33	Westlegate	Z 50
		St Andrew's St	Y 36	Whitefriars	Y 51

Annesley House, 6 Newmarket Rd, NR2 2LA, ✆ (01603) 624553, *annesleyhouse@bestwestern.co.uk, Fax (01603) 621577,* – [P]. MC AE VISA. Z c
closed 22 December-4 January – **Rest** (light lunch)/dinner 22.50 and a la carte 22.50/25.00 – **26 rm** 86.00/95.00 – 116.00.
◆ A relaxed atmosphere prevails at this established hotel set in a pair of Georgian houses. Some of the generously proportioned bedrooms overlook the feature water garden. Conservatory restaurant.

Catton Old Hall without rest., Lodge Lane, Old Catton, NR6 7HG, North : 3 ¼ m. by Catton Grove Rd and St Faiths Rd ✆ (01603) 419379, *enquiries@catton-hall.co.uk, Fax (01603) 400339,* – [P]. MC AE VISA
7 rm 70.00 – 120.00.
◆ 17C flint fronted farmhouse in a residential area. Antique furnished lounge with log fire. Individually and attractively furnished rooms have plenty of thoughtful extras.

Premier Travel Inn, Duke St, NR3 3AP, ✆ (0870) 9906632, *Fax (0870) 9906633* – ⇕ ⇆ ▤ ♿. MC AE ⓞ VISA. ⊁ Y
Rest (grill rest.) (dinner only) – **117 rm** ✱53.95 – ✱✱53.95.
◆ Purpose-built hotel occupying a useful city centre position. Good value up-to-date accommodation. Dine in the busy grill restaurant.

Premier Travel Inn, Longwater Interchange, Dereham Rd, New Costessey, NR5 0T Northwest : 5 ¼ m. on A 1074 (junction with A 47) ✆ (08701) 977197, *Fax (01603) 741219* ⇆ rm, ♿ P. MC AE ⓞ VISA
Rest (grill rest.) – **40 rm** ✱49.95/49.95 – ✱✱51.95/51.95.
◆ Suitable for both corporate travellers and families alike. Spacious, carefully designed bright and modern en suite bedrooms. Informal dining in adjacent pub.

The Gables without rest., 527 Earlham Rd, NR4 7HN, ✆ (01603) 45666 *Fax (01603) 250320,* ⇌ – ⇆ P. MC VISA. ⊁ X
closed 20 December - 2 January – **11 rm** ☕ ✱44.00 – ✱✱70.00.
◆ Modern detached house close to university Enjoy a game of snooker before retiring t the well-kept and homely bedrooms. Breakfast served in the conservatory.

Beaufort Lodge without rest., 62 Earlham Rd, NR2 3DF, ✆ (01603) 627928, *beaufortlodge@aol.com, Fax (01603) 440712,* ⇌ – ⇆ P. ⊁ VX
4 rm ☕ ✱50.00/60.00 – ✱✱65.00.
◆ Within easy walking distance of the Market Place, a pretty Victorian terraced house ru by a husband and wife team. Good-sized bedrooms in modern pine.

Arbor Linden Lodge without rest., 557 Earlham Rd, NR4 7HW, ✆ (01603) 45130 *info@guesthousenorwich.com, Fax (01603) 250641,* ⇌ – ⇆ ✆ P. MC VISA. ⊁ X
6 rm ☕ ✱38.00/45.00 – ✱✱55.00/60.00.
◆ Close to both university and hospitals. Friendly and family run guesthouse. Enjoy relaxed breakfast in the conservatory. A non smoking establishment.

Adlard's, 79 Upper St Giles St, NR2 1AB, ✆ (01603) 633522, *bookings@adlards.co.uk* – ▤ MC AE ⓞ VISA YZ
closed 1 week Christmas, Sunday and Monday – **Rest** 21.00 (lunch) and a la cart 36.00/44.00.
◆ Personally run, well-established restaurant - relaxed, classic style. Upper area also incorporates a bar. Refined dishes with a distinct French base.

By Appointment with rm, 25-29 St Georges St, NR3 1AB, ✆ (01603) 63073 *Fax (01603) 630730* – ⇆ P. MC VISA. ⊁ Y
closed 25 December – **Rest** *(closed Sunday-Monday)* (dinner only) a la carte 30.15/32.15
5 rm ☕ ✱70.00/85.00 – ✱✱110.00/130.00.
◆ Pretty, antique furnished restaurant. Interesting, traditional dishes off blackboard wit theatrical service. Characterful bedrooms include a host of thoughtful extras.

Tatler's, 21 Tombland, NR3 1RF, ✆ (01603) 766670, *info@tatlers.con* *Fax (01603) 766625* – ⇆. MC AE VISA Y
Rest 18.00 (lunch) and a la carte 23.45/32.50 ♀.
◆ Georgian townhouse near cathedral comprising small rooms on several floors set off b period detail. Relaxed atmosphere. Modern menu; inventive cooking using local produce.

St Benedicts, 9 St Benedicts St, NR2 4PE, ✆ (01603) 765377, *stbens@ukonline.co.u* *Fax (01603) 624541* – MC AE ⓞ VISA Y
closed 25 December-1 January, Sunday and Monday – **Rest** a la carte 19.50/25.10 ♀.
◆ Informal and personally run bistro. Interesting menus of both traditional British an adventurous heart-warming dishes. Booking advisable for dinner.

1 Up at The Mad Moose Arms, 2 Warwick St, NR2 3LD, off Dover St ✆ (0160 627687, *madmoose@animalinns.co.uk, Fax (01603) 633945* – ⇆. MC AE ⓞ VISA X
closed 25 December, 1 January and Sunday dinner – **Rest** (dinner only and Sunday lunch 16.50 and a la carte 23.50/26.50 ♀.
◆ Enjoy the relaxed atmosphere in this converted Victorian pub. Friendly service, occasional live music. Rustic and modern food guarantees great choice in the menus.

at Norwich Airport *North : 3½ m. by A 140 – V – ✉ Norwich.*

Holiday Inn Norwich City Airport, Cromer Rd, NR6 6JA, ✆ (01603) 410544 *sales@hinorwich.com, Fax (01603) 789935,* Fø, ≘s, ▢ – ⇕ ⇆, ▤ rest, ♿ P – 🏔 450. MC AE ⓞ VISA. ⊁
Rest (carvery) 15.50/21.50 and a la carte 18.40/34.40 **s.** – ☕ 13.95 – **121 rm** ✱89.00/129.0 – ✱✱89.00/129.00.
◆ Purpose built and benefits from easy access to terminal. Aimed at the corporate secto the well-proportioned rooms have ample work space. Extensive conference and leisure Informal carvery and lounge bar.

Premier Travel Inn Metro, Holt Rd, NR6 6JA, ✆ (08701) 977291, *Fax (01603) 428641*, – rest, P. MC AE VISA.
Rest (grill rest.) – **40 rm** 49.95/49.95 – 52.95/52.95.
◆ Handy, well-priced lodge accommodation, ideal for travellers arriving at the airport. Rooms have satellite TV and wireless access. Family rooms also available. Adjacent Brewers Fayre grill restaurant.

at Stoke Holy Cross *South : 5¾ m. by A 140 – X – ✉ Norwich.*

Wildebeest Arms, 82-86 Norwich Rd, NR14 8QJ, ✆ (01508) 492497, *wildebeestarms@animalinns.co.uk, Fax (01508) 494353*, – P. MC AE VISA.
closed 25-26 December – **Rest** (booking essential) 14.95/18.50 and a la carte 20.00/33.00 ♀.
◆ Modern-rustic pub in a pretty village. Inventive, seasonal, contemporary menus served at tree-trunk tables. Garden dining recommended. Attentive service from bright staff.

at Hethersett *Southwest : 6 m. by A 11 – X – ✉ Norwich.*

Park Farm, NR9 3DL, on B 1172 ✆ (01603) 810264, *enq@parkfarm-hotel.co.uk, Fax (01603) 812104*, – rest, P – 120. MC AE VISA.
Rest 16.45/21.95 ♀ – **42 rm** 95.00 – 165.00.
◆ Extended Georgian farmhouse set in 200 acres of gardens and parkland. Comprehensive leisure and conference facilities. Executive rooms in cottages are most comfortable. Well-appointed conservatory restaurant.

at Bawburgh *West : 5 m. by B 1108 – X – ✉ Norwich.*

Kings Head, Harts Lane, NR9 3LS, ✆ (01603) 744977, *anton@kingshead-bawburgh.co.uk, Fax (01603) 744990*, – P. MC AE VISA
closed dinner 25 December and dinner Sunday and Monday – **Rest** 21.00 (lunch) and a la carte 21.00/30.00 ♀.
◆ Family-owned pub with stylish interior, its timbered bar most inviting in winter. Modern menu with international influences: take a seat by the fire or in the dining room.

The red symbol? This denotes the very essence of peace – only the sound of birdsong first thing in the morning ...

NORWICH AIRPORT *Norfolk* 504 X 25 – *see Norwich.*

NOSS MAYO *Devon The West Country G.*

Exc. : *Saltram House★★, NW : 7 m. by B 3186 and A 379 – Plymouth★, NW : 9 m. by B 3186 and A 379.*
London 242 – Plymouth 12 – Yealmpton 3.

Ship Inn, PL8 1EW, ✆ (01752) 872387, *ship@nossmayo.com, Fax (01752) 873294*, – P. MC VISA
Rest 11.95 (lunch) and a la carte 15.00/25.00 ♀.
◆ On two floors with a terrific terrace; beside the water in delightful coastal village. Oldest part dates from 1700s. Extensive menus from the simple to the adventurous.

NOTTINGHAM *Nottingham* 502 503 504 Q 25 *Great Britain G. – pop. 249 584.*

See : *Castle Museum★ (alabasters★) AC,* CZ **M.**
Env. : *Wollaton Hall★ AC, W : 2½ m. by Ilkeston Rd, A 609* AZ **M.**
Exc. : *Southwell Minster★★, NE : 14 m. by A 612* BZ *– Newstead Abbey★ AC, N : 11 m. by A 60, A 611 -* AY *- and B 683 – Mr Straw's House★, Worksop, N : 20 m. signed from B 6045 (past Bassetlaw Hospital) – St Mary Magdalene★, Newark-on-Trent, NE : 20 m. by A 612* BZ.
18 Bulwell Forest, Hucknall Rd ✆ (0115) 977 0576, AY *– 18 Wollaton Park ✆ (0115) 978 7574,* AZ *– 18 Mapperley, Central Ave, Plains Rd ✆ (0115) 955 6672,* BY *– 18 Nottingham City, Lawton Drive, Bulwell ✆ (0115) 927 8021 – 18 Beeston Fields, Beeston ✆ (0115) 925 7062 – 18 Ruddington Grange, Wilford Rd, Ruddington ✆ (0115) 984 6141,* BZ *– 9, 9 Edwalton ✆ (0115) 923 4775,* BZ *– 9, 9, 9 Cotgrave Place G. & C.C., Stragglethorpe ✆ (0115) 933 3344.*
Nottingham East Midlands Airport, Castle Donington : ✆ (0871) 9199000 SW : 15 m. by A 453 AZ.
1-4 Smithy Row ✆ (0115) 915 5330, touristinfo@nottinghamcity.gov.uk – at West Bridgford : County Hall, Loughborough Rd ✆ (0115) 977 3558.
London 135 – Birmingham 50 – Leeds 74 – Leicester 27 – Manchester 72.

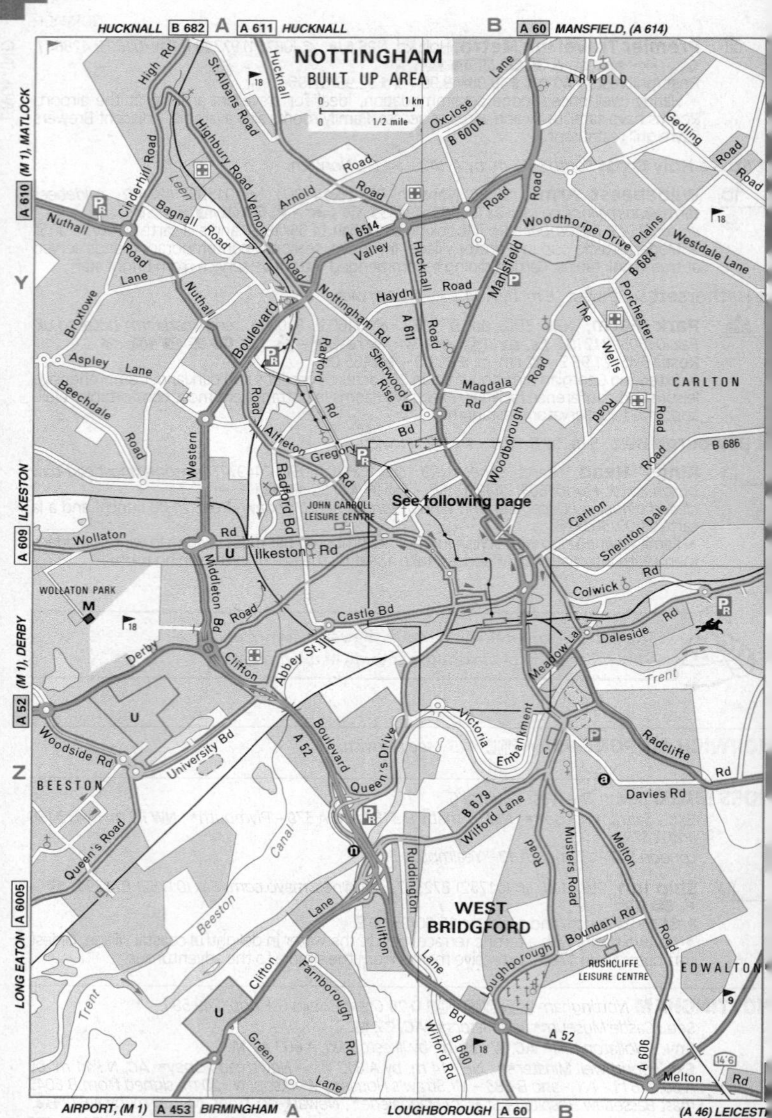

AIRPORT, (M 1) A 453 BIRMINGHAM A LOUGHBOROUGH A 60 B (A 46) LEICESTI MELTON MOWBRA

Park Plaza, 41 Maid Marian Way, NG1 6GD, ✆ (0115) 947 7200, *info@parkplazanotting ham.com, Fax (0115) 947 7300,* – , rm, – 175. VISA. CY *closed 25-26 December* – ***Chino Latino :*** Rest - Japanese influences - closed Sunday a la carte 24.00/37.00 – 9.95 – **172 rm** 145.00 – 145.00, 6 suites.

◆ Converted city centre office block with stylish and contemporary decor. Choice of meeting rooms. Spacious stylish bedrooms with many extras. Formal Chino Latino Japanese restaurant.

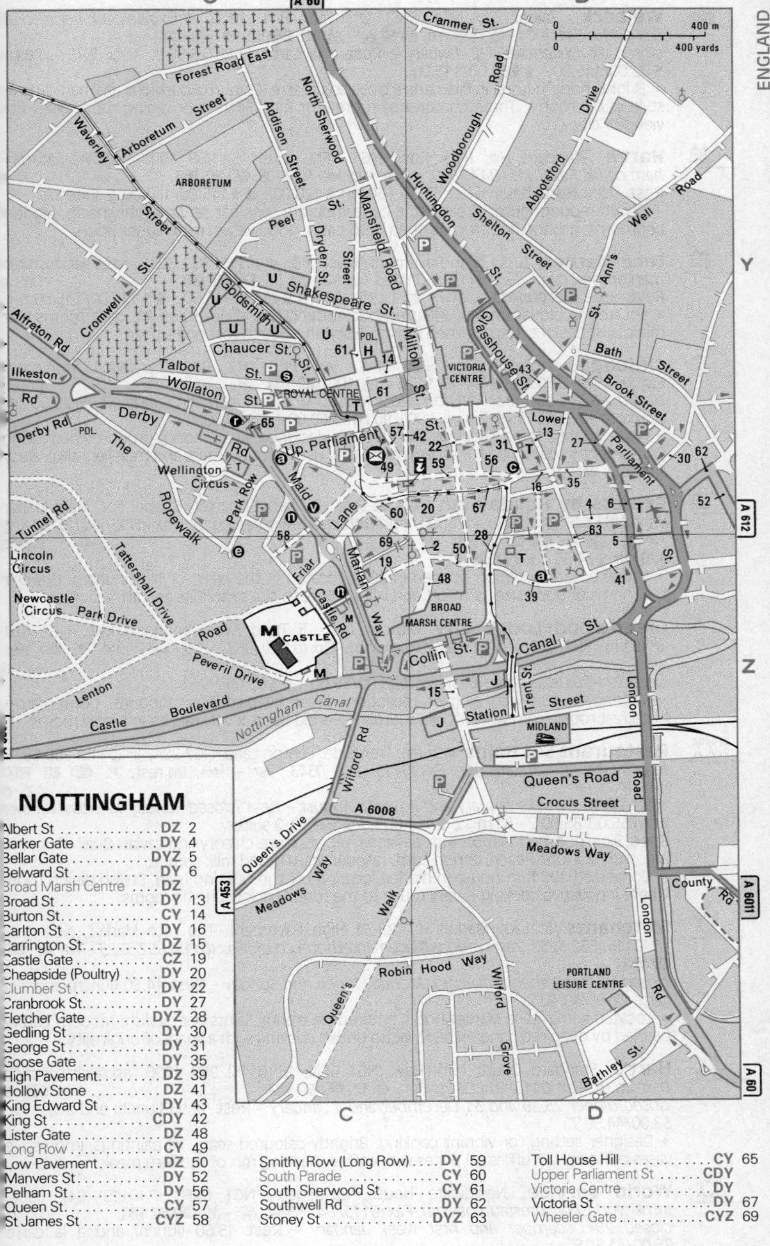
C
D
A 60
Y
Z
0
400 m
0
400 yards
Cranmer St.
Forest Road East
Arboretum Street
Waverley Street
ARBORETUM
Addison Street
North Sherwood St.
Peel St.
Dryden St.
Mansfield Road
Woodborough Road
Huntingdon St.
Shelton Street
Abbotsford Drive
Well Road
St. Ann's
Shakespeare St.
Goldsmith St.
Cromwell St.
Alfreton Rd
Ilkeston Rd
Derby Rd
Chaucer St.
Talbot St.
Wollaston St.
ROYAL CENTRE
Milton St.
VICTORIA CENTRE
Glasshouse St.
Bath Street
Brook Street
Lower Parliament St.
Up. Parliament
Derby Rd
The Ropewalk
Wellington Circus
Park Row
Maid Marian Way
Tunnel Rd
Lincoln Circus
Newcastle Circus
Park Drive
Tattershall Drive
Friar Lane
Castle Rd
CASTLE
BROAD MARSH CENTRE
Collin St.
Canal St
Peveril Drive
Lenton Road
Castle Boulevard
Nottingham Canal
Station Street
Trent St.
MIDLAND
London Road
Wilford Rd
A 6008
Queen's Road
Crocus Street
Meadows Way
Queen's Drive
A 453
Walk
County Rd
A 6011
A 612
Robin Hood Way
Wilford Grove
Queen's
PORTLAND LEISURE CENTRE
Bathley St.
A 60

NOTTINGHAM

ENGLAND

Welbeck, Talbot St, NG1 5GS, ✆ (0115) 841 1000, *info@welbeck-hotel.co.u... Fax (0115) 841 1001* – |‡|, ⊁ rm, ▤ ✆ ♿ – 🏫 60. MC AE ⓓ VISA. ⊁ CY
closed 24 December - 2 January – **Rest** a la carte 11.85/28.85 s. – ☕ 9.75 – **96 rm** ✝82.00/115.00 – ✝✝82.00/115.00.
◆ Bright modern hotel in city centre close to theatre. Colourful cushions and pared-dow... style in bedrooms. Three conference rooms for hire. Fifth floor dining room gives fin... views of city.

Hart's, Standard Hill, Park Row, NG1 6FN, ✆ (0115) 988 1900, *ask@hartsnottingham.co.uk, Fax (0115) 947 7600*, ≼, 🌳 – |‡| ⊁ ✆ ♿ P. MC AE VISA CZ
Rest – (see ***Harts*** below) – ☕ 13.50 – **30 rm** ✝120.00 – ✝✝145.00/160.00, 2 suites.
◆ Stylish modern hotel. Breakfast in contemporary style bar serving light snacks. Moder... bedrooms; ground floor rooms open onto patio; good views from higher floors.

Lace Market, 29-31 High Pavement, NG1 1HE, ✆ (0115) 852 3232, *reservations@lacemarkethotel.co.uk, Fax (0115) 852 3223* – |‡| ✆ – 🏫 35. MC AE VISA DZ
Rest – (see ***Merchants*** below) – ☕ 12.95 – **42 rm** ✝75.00/115.00 – ✝✝115.00/245.00.
◆ Located in old lacemaking quarter, but nothing lacy about interiors; crisp rooms wit... minimalist designs, unpatterned fabrics. A stylish place to rest one's head.

Citilodge, Wollaton St, NG1 5FW, ✆ (0115) 912 8000, *mail@citilodge.co.uk, Fax (0115) 912 8080* – |‡| ⊁ ▤ ✆ ♿ – 🏫 100. MC VISA. ⊁ CY
closed 24-28 December – ***Vision* :** **Rest** *(closed Monday lunch and Sunday)* 7.95/20.00 an... a la carte 13.85/27.95 s. ♀ – ☕ 7.00 – **90 rm** ✝60.00 – ✝✝60.00.
◆ Neat, bright rooms, spacious and carefully designed, in a modern group-owned lodge. Conveniently positioned for access to the city. Useful for business and travellers alike. Busy spacious eatery.

Express by Holiday Inn without rest., 7 Chapel Quarter, Chapel Bar, Maid Marian Way, NG1 6JS, ✆ (0870) 4176000, *nottingham@kewgreen.co.uk, Fax (0115) 941 5764* – |‡| ⊁ ♿ – 🏫 25. MC AE ⓓ VISA. ⊁ CY
120 rm ✝74.95 – ✝✝74.95.
◆ Lodge accommodation opened in 2004, located in the heart of Nottingham. Uniform bedrooms of good size, comfort and value. Close to city's facilities and attractions.

Greenwood Lodge City without rest., 5 Third Ave, Sherwood Rise, NG7 6JH ✆ (0115) 962 1206, *pdouglas71@aol.com, Fax (0115) 962 1206*, 🌳 – ⊁ P. MC VISA ⊁ AY
closed 24-28 December – **6 rm** ☕ ✝43.00/55.00 – ✝✝85.00.
◆ Regency house with elegant reception offset by paintings, antiques. Conservatory breakfast room from which to view birdlife. Period beds, lovely fabrics in pretty rooms.

Restaurant Sat Bains with rm, Trentside, Lenton Lane, NG7 2SA, ✆ (0115) 986 6566 *info@restaurantsatbains.net, Fax (0115) 986 0343*, 🌳 – ⊁, ▤ rest, P. MC AE VISA ⊁ AZ
closed first 2 weeks January and 2 weeks August – **Rest** *(closed Sunday-Monday)* (dinner only) 55.00/85.00 ♀ – **8 rm** ☕ ✝114.00 – ✝✝139.00, 2 suites.
Spec. Slow poached salmon with passion fruit, yoghurt, chicory and caviar. Quail cooked in hay, with shallots. Peach, lemon curd, raspberries, almond milk sorbet.
◆ Converted 19C farmhouse in hidden location off the city ring road. Stylish dining room where innovative cooking is very much to the fore. Spacious, rustic rooms.

Merchants (at Lace Market H.), 29-31 High Pavement, The Lace Market, NG1 1HE, ✆ (0115) 852 3232, *reservations@lacemarkethotel.co.uk, Fax (0115) 852 3223* – ⊁ ▤. MC AE VISA DZ
closed 26 December, 1 January, Monday lunch and Sunday – **Rest** 14.50 (lunch) and a la carte 27.50/40.40 ♀.
◆ Located within Lace Market hotel, entered via trendy Saints bar. Stylish, modern eatery typified by deep red banquettes. Modish British cooking with a spark of originality.

Hart's, Standard Court, Park Row, NG1 6GN, ✆ (0115) 988 1900, *ask@hartsnottingham.co.uk, Fax (0115) 911 0611*, 🌳 – ⇔ 12. MC AE VISA CZ
closed dinner 25,26 and 31 December and 1 January – **Rest** 15.95 (lunch) and a la carte 32.00/44.50 ♀.
◆ Designer setting for vibrant cooking. Brightly coloured seats, oil paintings, impressive vases of flowers. Truffles on plates with coffee. Dashing mix of modern meals.

World Service, Newdigate House, Castlegate, NG1 6AF, ✆ (0115) 847 5587, *info@worldservicerestaurant.com, Fax (0115) 847 5584*, 🌳 – P. MC AE VISA CZ
closed 25 December and first week January – **Rest** 15.50 (lunch) and a la carte 25.00/41.50 ♀.
◆ Spacious Georgian mansion close to castle, with chic glass tanks containing Eastern artefacts and huge ceiling squares with vivid silks. Effective, tasty fusion food.

XX **Sonny's,** 3 Carlton St, NG1 1NL, ☎ (0115) 947 3041, *nottingham@sonnys.co.uk, Fax (0115) 950 7776* – ▤. MC AE VISA DY c
closed 25-26 December, 1 January and Bank Holidays – **Rest** 13.50 (lunch) and a la carte 26.25/36.50 ♀.
◆ A sleek, streamlined, white restaurant; bare floorboards, mirrors, prints. Menu exhibits sophisticated layering of ingredients with Mediterranean feel. Very busy at lunch.

XX **4550 Miles from Delhi,** 41 Mount St, NG1 6HE, ☎ (0115) 947 5111, *Fax (0115) 947 4555* – ▤. MC AE VISA CY n
closed Saturday lunch and Sunday – **Rest** - Indian - a la carte 12.85/19.40.
◆ Stylish, up-to-date and very spacious restaurant incorporating a three storey glazed atrium and modish bar. Freshly prepared, skilfully cooked, authentic Indian cuisine.

XX **Mem-Saab,** 12-14 Maid Marian Way, NG1 6HS, ☎ (0115) 957 0009, *Fax (0115) 941 2724* – ▤. MC AE VISA CY n
Rest - Indian - 15.00/21.95 and a la carte 16.50/19.00.
◆ Large, spacious and relaxed restaurant away from town centre. Vivid oils on plain white walls. Authentic Indian cuisine: expect tasty, unusual regional dishes.

XX **The Monkey Tree,** 70 Bridgford Rd, West Bridgford, NG2 6AP, ☎ (0115) 981 1419, *info@themonkeytree.co.uk* – MC VISA BZ a
closed 25 December – **Rest** a la carte 18.85/29.00 ♀.
◆ Near Trent Bridge cricket ground; a relaxed, "neighbourhood" air prevails with very comfy leather-backed chairs. Freshly prepared dishes with distinctive Mediterranean base.

Cock and Hoop, 25 High Pavement, NG1 1HE, ☎ (0115) 852 3232, *Fax (0115) 852 3223* – ⚡ ▤. MC VISA DZ a
closed 25-26 December and 1 January – **Rest** (lunch only and Sunday dinner) a la carte 18.00/26.00 ♀.
◆ Set on cobbled street in redeveloped lace market area. Basement, now a large dining room, is a former cock fighting pit. Modern British cooking served in substantial portions.

at Plumtree *Southeast : 5¾ m. by A 60 – BZ – off A 606 – ✉ Nottingham.*

X **Perkins,** Old Railway Station, Station Rd, NG12 5NA, ☎ (0115) 937 3695, *info@perkinsrestaurant.co.uk, Fax (0115) 937 6405,* 🏖 – P. MC AE ◑ VISA
closed 25-26 December, 1 January and Sunday dinner – **Rest** 16.95 (lunch) and a la carte 23.00/31.45 ♀.
◆ Named after owners; once a railway station. Pot roast quails, pithivier of walnuts remove it from its origins. Dine in conservatory or relax in bar, a former waiting room.

at Beeston *Southwest : 4¼ m. on A 6005 – AZ – ✉ Nottingham.*

Village H. & Leisure Club, Brailsford Way, Chilwell Meadows, Chilwell Retail Park, NG9 6DL, Southwest : 2 ¾ m. by A 6005 ☎ (0115) 946 4422, *village.nottingham@village-hotels.com, Fax (0115) 946 4428,* ⑩, F₆, ≘s, ▢, squash – |♠|, ⚡, ▤ rest, ♿ P – 🏛 400. MC AE ◑ VISA
Rest (grill rest.) 15.00/30.00 and a la carte 14.85/23.95 ♀ – **94 rm** ☐ ✝75.00/120.00 – ✝✝75.00/100.00.
◆ Modern hotel with impressive leisure facilities: large pool, toning tables, cardio vascular area, gym, squash courts. After exercising, unwind in neat, comfortable rooms. A couple of traditionally based restaurant alternatives.

XX **La Toque,** 61 Wollaton Rd, NG9 2NG, ☎ (0115) 922 2268, *info@latoqueonline.co.uk, Fax (0115) 922 7979* – ⚡ ▤. MC AE VISA
closed 20 December - 8 January, 2 weeks August, Sunday, Monday and lunch Saturday – **Rest** - French - (lunch booking essential) 16.00 (lunch) and a la carte 33.50/39.50 ♀.
◆ Pleasantly spacious restaurant in centre of Beeston. On offer is a wide ranging and very tasty menu of classically based French cuisine with original twists.

at Risley *(Derbs.) Southwest : 7½ m. by A 52 – AZ – on B 5010 – ✉ Derby.*

Risley Hall, Derby Rd, DE72 3SS, ☎ (0115) 939 9000, *enquiries@risleyhallhotel.co.uk, Fax (0115) 939 7766,* ⑩, ≘s, ▢, 🐎 – |♠|, ⚡ rest, 📞 P – 🏛 110. MC AE ◑ VISA. ✂
Abbeys : **Rest** (dinner only) 28.00 and a la carte 27.40/43.85 – ***Orchid :*** **Rest** (dinner only) 28.00 – ☐ 11.95 – **16 rm** ✝119.00 – ✝✝119.00, 19 suites.
◆ Victorian country house with comfortable rooms fitted out with quality furnishings; some original features. Public rooms are also handsome: oak panelling, lovely fireplaces. Twin dining options: smart Abbeys. Informal Orchid.

at Sherwood Business Park *Northwest : 10 m. by A 611 – AY – off A 608 – ✉ Nottingham.*

Dakota, Lakeview Drive, NG15 0DA, ☎ (0870) 4422727, *enquiries@dakotahotels.co.uk, Fax (01623) 727677,* 🏖, F₆ – |♠|, ⚡ rm, ▤ ♿ P – 🏛 60. MC AE VISA. ✂
Grill : **Rest** a la carte approx 25.00 ♀ – ☐ 10.00 – **92 rm** ✝84.50/89.50 – ✝✝89.50/89.50.
◆ Hard-to-miss hotel just off the M1 - it's a big black cube! Lobby with plush sofas, bookshelves and Dakota aircraft montage. Spacious rooms with kingsize beds and plasma TVs. Modern British grill style menus.

NOTTINGHAM EAST MIDLANDS AIRPORT *Leics.* 502 503 504 P/Q 25 – ✉ *Derby.*

London 125 – Birmingham 40 – Derby 13 – Leicester 24 – Nottingham 15.

Hilton East Midlands Airport, Derby Rd, Lockington, DE74 2YW, Northeast : 2 ¾ m. by A 453 on A 50 at junction 24 of M 1 ☎ (01509) 674000, *Fax (01509) 672412,* – rm, – 300. VISA
Rest (carvery lunch)/dinner 25.00 and a la carte 24.00/33.00 **s.** – 15.95 – **150 rm** 76.00/146.00 – 76.00/146.00, 2 suites.
• Purpose-built hotel close to the airport and major motorway links, well suited to the business traveller. Comfortable, modern bedrooms and complimentary airport transport. Restaurant or café dining options.

Thistle East Midlands Airport, DE74 2SH, ☎ (0870) 333 9132, *east.midlandsairport@thistle.co.uk, Fax (0870) 333 9232,* – – 220. VISA
Rest (bar lunch Saturday) 14.95/24.95 and a la carte 20.00/45.00 **s.** – 13.95 – **164 rm** 197.00 – 254.00.
• Spacious and carefully designed modern, purpose-built hotel on the airport doorstep. Rooms are smart and bright with contemporary furnishings. Light, airy dining room; popular menu suiting all tastes.

NUNEATON *Warks.* 503 504 P 26 – *pop. 70 721.*

Purley Chase, Pipers Lane, Ridge Lane ☎ (024) 7639 3118.
Nuneaton Library, Church St ☎ (024) 7638 4027.
London 107 – Birmingham 25 – Coventry 10 – Leicester 18.

Premier Travel Inn, Coventry Rd, CV10 7PJ, South : 2½ m. by A 444 on B 4113 ☎ (024) 7634 3584, *Fax (024) 7632 7156,* – rm, rest, – 30. VISA
Rest (grill rest.) – **48 rm** 46.95/46.95 – 48.95/48.95.
• A consistent standard of trim accommodation in contemporary style. A Beefeater is on hand for meals. Well placed for visits to Arbury Hall and Nuneaton Museum and Gallery.

OAKHAM *Rutland* 502 504 R 25 – *pop. 9 620.*

Victoria Hall, 39 High St ☎ (01572) 724329.
London 103 – Leicester 26 – Northampton 35 – Nottingham 28.

Barnsdale Lodge, The Avenue, Rutland Water, LE15 8AH, East : 2 ½ m. on A 606 ☎ (01572) 724678, *reservations@barnsdalelodge.co.uk, Fax (01572) 724961,* – 300. VISA
Restaurant : Rest a la carte 18.25/26.90 – ***Conservatory :*** Rest a la carte 18.35/29.40 – **45 rm** 75.00/130.00 – 99.50/220.00.
• Privately owned, converted farmhouse with mature gardens. Ample, modern rooms, a large bar flagged in York stone and extensive meeting facilities in renovated stables. Flavours of the season to fore in the Restaurant. More informal Conservatory.

Lord Nelson's House H. and Nicks Restaurant with rm, Market Pl, LE15 6DT, ☎ (01572) 723199, *healeynelson@aol.com, Fax (01572) 723199* – rm. VISA
closed 1 week Christmas and 2 weeks August – **Rest** *(closed Sunday-Monday)* a la carte 17.95/34.40 – **4 rm** 65.00/75.00 – 90.00.
• Imaginative modern interiors in 17C town house: choose nautical dark wood, zebra-skin throws or an elegant chaise longue. Classic seasonal dishes with a flavourful flourish.

Whipper-In with rm, Market Pl, LE15 6DT, ☎ (01572) 756971, *whipperin@brook-hotels.co.uk, Fax (01572) 757759* – rest, – 60. VISA
No.5 *(☎ (01572) 740774)* **: Rest** a la carte 20.20/30.20 – 10.95 – **24 rm** 85.00/95.00 – 95.00/105.00.
• 17C inn on the Market Square has retained its coaching yard and much of its traditional feel. Rooms in understated country style and firelit lounge with inviting armchairs. No 5 is clean-lined brasserie.

at Hambleton *East : 3 m. by A 606 – ✉ Oakham.*

Hambleton Hall , LE15 8TH, ☎ (01572) 756991, *hotel@hambletonhall.com, Fax (01572) 724721,* ← Rutland Water, heated, – VISA
Rest 27.00/40.00 and a la carte 58.00/78.00 – 14.00 – **16 rm** 165.00/220.00 – 295.00/360.00, 1 suite.
Spec. Poached tails of langoustine with tomato essence and sorbet. Roast breast of pigeon with foie gras ravioli and Madeira sauce. Pavé of white and dark chocolate.
• Lovingly appointed period interiors in a peaceful and sumptuous Victorian manor. Drawing room with fine objets d'art. Antique filled bedrooms, immaculate in every respect. Confident, harmoniously balanced menus; abundant local produce..

Finch's Arms with rm, Oakham Rd, LE15 8TL, ✆ (01572) 756575, *finchsarms@talk21.com, Fax (01572) 771142,* ≤, ☂, ☗ – ⇔ P. MC VISA. ✂
closed 25 December – **Rest** 11.95 (lunch) and a la carte 15.00/25.00 ♀ – **6 rm** ☕ ✝65.00 – ✝✝75.00.
◆ Sandstone pub overlooking Rutland Water: rustic interior, flagged floors, rattan chairs. Real ales accompany tasty modern menus, brimming with Asian flavours. Cosy bedrooms.

at Wing *South : 5 m. by A 6003 – ✉ Oakham.*

Kings Arms with rm, Top St, LE15 8SE, ✆ (01572) 737634, *info@thekingsarms-wing.co.uk, Fax (01572) 737255,* ☗ – ⇔ rm, P. MC AE VISA. ✂
Rest a la carte 18.00/28.00 – **8 rm** ☕ ✝65.00 – ✝✝75.00.
◆ Cosy, rural 17C pub in pleasant hamlet near Rutland Water. Well furnished interior with flag floor, rafters and fire. Fresh, seasonally inspired dishes. Warm, welcoming rooms.

at Knossington *West : 4 m. by A 606 and Braunston rd – ✉ Oakham.*

The Fox and Hounds, 6 Somerby Rd, LE15 8LY, ✆ (01664) 454676, *bookings@foxandhounds.biz,* ☂ – ⇔ P. MC VISA. ✂
closed 25 December, Monday and Tuesday lunch – **Rest** (booking essential) a la carte 18.95/24.95.
◆ Welcoming 18C, ivy-clad former coaching inn set in pretty village. Low ceiling, beams and log fires enhance delightful ambience. Tasty dishes brimming with local fare.

OAKSEY *Wilts.* 503 N 29.

London 98 – Cirencester 8.5 – Stroud 20.

The Wheatsheaf at Oaksey, Wheatsheaf Lane, SN16 9TB, ✆ (01666) 577348, ☂ – ⇔ P. MC VISA
Rest a la carte 21.00/30.00 ♀.
◆ Rurally set traditional pub in the heart of the country. Rafters; exposed stone walls covered with farming implements above inglenook. Assured, ambitious, modern cooking.

OBORNE *Dorset* 503 504 M 31 – *see Sherborne.*

OCKLEY *Surrey* 504 S 30.

18 Gatton Manor Hotel G. & C.C., Standon Lane ✆ (01306) 627555.
London 31 – Brighton 32 – Guildford 23 – Lewes 36 – Worthing 29.

Bryce's, The Old School House, RH5 5TH, on A 29 ✆ (01306) 627430, *bryces.fish@virgin.net, Fax (01306) 628274* – P. MC VISA
closed 25-26 December, 1-2 January, Sunday dinner in January, February and November – **Rest** - Seafood - a la carte 18.40/24.40 ♀.
◆ Busy, redbrick former school, locally renowned for flavourful, home-smoked and market-fresh seafood from Thai fricassee to swordfish mille feuille. Attentive, dapper staff.

ODIHAM *Hants.* 504 R 30 – *pop. 2 908 – ✉ Hook.*

London 51 – Reading 16 – Southampton 37 – Winchester 25.

George, 100 High St, RG29 1LP, ✆ (01256) 702081, *reception@georgehotelodiham.com, Fax (01256) 704213* – ⇔ rm, P. MC AE ① VISA
closed 25-26 December – ***Cromwell's :*** **Rest** - Seafood specialities - *(closed Saturday lunch, Sunday dinner and Bank Holidays)* a la carte 25.95/32.95 ♀ – ***Next door at the George :*** **Rest** a la carte 15.70/26.40 ♀ – **28 rm** ☕ ✝85.00/100.00 – ✝✝95.00/115.00.
◆ 15C inn at the heart of the town; cosy lounge bar and comfortable rooms. Those in the main building have greater rural character than more recent, if smartly fitted ones. Cromwells is impressively oak-panelled. Informality rules Next door at the George.

St John, 83 High St, RG29 1UB, ✆ (01256) 702697, *reuben.evans@st-john-restaurant.co.uk, Fax (01256) 702697* – ⇔ ▤ ⇔ 12. MC AE VISA
closed 25 December and 1 January, Sunday dinner and Monday – **Rest** 18.95 (lunch) and dinner a la carte 21.40/37.90.
◆ Refurbished and stylish restaurant boasts vivid artwork, suspended arcs of wood from the ceiling and comfy leather banquettes. Eclectic menus with classical base.

Grapevine, 121 High St, RG29 1LA, ✆ (01256) 701122, *grapevine701122@tiscali.co.uk* – ▤. MC AE ① VISA
closed 1 week Christmas, Saturday lunch, Sunday and Bank Holiday Mondays – **Rest** 14.95 (lunch) and a la carte 20.85/30.15 ♀.
◆ Bright, airy, relaxed neighbourhood restaurant. Local produce used to good effect in generous modern British dishes, plus flavourful, more elaborate blackboard specialities.

OLD BURGHCLERE *Hants.* 504 Q 29 – ✉ *Newbury.*

London 77 – Bristol 76 – Newbury 10 – Reading 27 – Southampton 28.

XX **Dew Pond,** RG20 9LH, ✆ (01635) 278408, *Fax (01635) 278580,* ← – ⅍ P. MC VISA
closed 2 weeks August, 2 weeks Christmas, Sunday and Monday – **Rest** (dinner only) 28.00/32.00 ♀.
◆ This traditionally decorated cottage, set in fields and parkland, overlooks Watership Down and houses a collection of local art. Tasty Anglo-gallic menu.

OLDHAM *Gtr Manchester* 502 504 N 23 – *pop. 103 544.*

Crompton and Royton, High Barn, Royton ✆ (0161) 624 2154 – Werneth, Green Lane, Garden Suburb ✆ (0161) 624 1190 – Lees New Rd ✆ (0161) 624 4986.

12 Albion St ✆ (0161) 627 1024.

London 212 – Leeds 36 – Manchester 7 – Sheffield 38.

Plan : see Manchester

Smokies Park, Ashton Rd, Bardsley, OL8 3HX, South : 2 ¾ m. on A 627 ✆ (0161) 785 5000, *enquiries@smokies.co.uk, Fax (0161) 785 5010,* Ꞁ₆, ≘s – |‡|, ⅍ rm, ▤ rest, ✆ ♿ P. – 🎪 110. MC AE ⓓ VISA. ⅍
Cosi Fan Tutti : Rest - Italian - (dinner only) 21.00 and a la carte 17.40/28.50 **s.** ♀ – **72 rm** ☕ ✱65.00/90.00 – ✱✱65.00/100.00, 1 suite.
◆ Purpose-built hotel in the southern suburbs. Executive rooms in particular are modern and handsomely equipped. Regular music in the nightclub or more relaxing lounge bar. Trattoria styling in airy restaurant.

XX **White Hart Inn** with rm, 51 Stockport Rd, Lydgate, OL4 4JJ, East : 3 m. by A 669 on A 6050 ✆ (01457) 872566, *bookings@thewhitehart.co.uk, Fax (01457) 875190,* ← – ⅍, ▤ rest, P. MC AE VISA. ⅍
Rest *(closed Tuesday)* (dinner only and Sunday lunch)/dinner a la carte 24.00/31.00 ♀ – (see also ***Brasserie*** below) – **12 rm** ☕ ✱95.00 – ✱✱120.00.
◆ Hilltop inn with stylish, modern décor and attractive bedrooms, most with hearty views. Varied, robust, contemporary menus accompanied by seamless and personable service.

Brasserie (at White Hart Inn), 51 Stockport Rd, Lydgate, OL4 4JJ, East : 3 m. by A 669 on A 6050 ✆ (01457) 872566, *bookings@thewhitehart.co.uk, Fax (01457) 875190* – ⅍ P. MC AE VISA. ⅍
Rest (booking essential) 14.50 (lunch) and a la carte 24.00/31.00 ♀.
◆ Busy, yet laid-back pub with old timber and exposed brick. On the walls are sepia photos of Lydgate; open fires add to the rich, welcoming mix. Hearty modern dishes.

OLD WARDEN *Beds.* 504 S 27 – *see Biggleswade.*

OLTON *W. Mids.* 502 503 504 O 26 – *see Solihull.*

OMBERSLEY *Worcs.* 503 504 N 27 – *pop. 2 089.*

Bishopswood Rd ✆ (01905) 620747.

London 148 – Birmingham 42 – Leominster 33.

XX **The Venture In,** Main St, WR9 0EW, ✆ (01905) 620552, *Fax (01905) 620552* – ⅍ ▤ P. MC VISA
closed 25-31 December, 2 weeks February, 2 weeks July-August, Sunday dinner and Monday – **Rest** 17.95/31.50.
◆ Charming, restored Tudor inn, traditional from its broad inglenook to its fringed Victorian lights. Modern, flavourful menu, well judged and locally sourced. Friendly staff.

at Dunhampton *North : 1¾ m. by A 449 – ✉ Ombersley.*

XX **Epic,** Ombersley Rd, DY13 9SW, on A 449 (southbound) ✆ (01905) 620000, *Fax (01905) 621123,* 🏠, 🍽 – ⅍ ▤ P. MC AE VISA
closed Sunday dinner – **Rest** a la carte 30.00/40.00.
◆ Trendy bar/restaurant on main road with garden and decked area. Open-plan and modern interior, including comfy, stylish lounge with sofas. Good value menu of modern classics.

ORFORD *Suffolk* 504 Y 27 – ✉ *Woodbridge.*
London 103 – Ipswich 22 – Norwich 52.

Crown and Castle, IP12 2LJ, ☎ (01394) 450205, *info@crownandcastle.co.uk*, – P. VISA
closed 8-21 December – **Rest** – (see ***The Trinity*** below) – **18 rm** ★72.00/90.00 – ★★130.00/145.00.
◆ 19C redbrick hotel with garden and terrace standing proudly next to 12C Orford Castle. Cosy lounges with soft suites and sofas. Stylish modern rooms, some facing the Ness.

The Trinity (at Crown and Castle H.), IP12 2LJ, ☎ (01394) 450205, *info@crownandcastle.co.uk*, – P. VISA
closed 18-21 December and dinner 25-26 December – **Rest** (booking essential) a la carte 21.95/29.95 ♀.
◆ Stylish and relaxed - lovely al fresco dining on fine summer days. Full-flavoured dishes blend wide-ranging modern British cooking and Italian undertones. Well-chosen wines.

ORLETON *Shrops.* 503 L 23 – *see Ludlow.*

OSMOTHERLEY *N. Yorks.* 502 Q 20 – ✉ *Northallerton.*
London 245 – Darlington 25 – Leeds 49 – Middlesbrough 20 – Newcastle upon Tyne 54 – York 36.

Golden Lion, 6 West End, DL6 3AA, ☎ (01609) 883526, *Fax (01609) 884000* – . VISA
closed 25 December – **Rest** a la carte 15.00/25.00 ♀.
◆ Unpretentious, beamed, firelit alehouse; plant-filled upper dining room; large menu of satisfying, full-flavoured cooking, Yorkshire beers and sprightly, engaging service.

OSWESTRY *Shrops.* 502 503 K 25 – *pop. 16 660.*
18 *Aston Park* ☎ *(01691) 610221* – 18 *Llanymynech, Pant* ☎ *(01691) 830542.*
Mile End Services ☎ *(01691) 662488 – The Heritage Centre, 2 Church Terr* ☎ *(01691) 662753.*
London 182 – Chester 28 – Shrewsbury 18.

The Wynnstay, Church St, SY11 2SZ, ☎ (01691) 655261, *info@wynnstayhotel.com*, *Fax (01691) 670606*, , , – , rest, P – 250. AE VISA
Four Seasons : Rest *(closed Sunday dinner)* 21.00 and a la carte 21.00/29.40 ♀ – 12.00 – **28 rm** ★80.00/90.00 – ★★100.00, 1 suite.
◆ Town centre former posting inn with its own bowling green and a gym in the old stables. Behind a fine Georgian façade, sizeable rooms have kept traces of original character. Smart dining room for tasty, traditional dishes.

Lion Quays, Moreton, SY11 3EN, North : 4 m. on A 5 ☎ (01691) 684300, *sales@lionquays.co.uk*, *Fax (01691) 684313*, – , , rm, P – 400. AE VISA
Bridge 17 : Rest a la carte 16.85/26.20 s. – **79 rm** ★80.00/95.00 – ★★95.00/145.00, 3 suites.
◆ 21C hotel with two buildings in a tranquil canalside location: most public areas take in this view. There's a cosy little lounge bar and bedrooms which each boast a balcony. Conservatory restaurant beside the canal.

The Walls, Welsh Walls, SY11 1AW, ☎ (01691) 670970, *info@the-walls.co.uk*, *Fax (01691) 653820*, – P 40. AE VISA
closed 26-27 December, 1-3 January and Sunday dinner – **Rest** 17.00/22.00 and a la carte 18.50/32.00 ♀.
◆ Built in 1841 as a school; now a buzzy restaurant. High ceiling with wooden rafters; original wood flooring. Friendly atmosphere. Varied menu offers some adventurous options.

at Trefonen *Southwest : 2½ m. on Trefonen rd* – ✉ *Oswestry.*

The Pentre , SY10 9EE, Southwest : 1 ¾ m. by Treflach rd off New Well Lane ☎ (01691) 653952, *helen@thepentre.com*, ≤ Tanat Valley, , – P.
closed 1 week Christmas – **Rest** (communal dining) 17.00 – **3 rm** ★40.00 – ★★50.00/70.00.
◆ Restored 16C farmhouse with superb views over Tanat Valley. Heavily timbered inglenook and wood-burning stove in lounge. Sloping floors enhance rooms of tremendous character. Home-cooked dinners served with fellow guests.

at Llanymynech *Southwest : 7 m. on A 483 – ✉ Oswestry.*

Bradford Arms, SY22 6EJ, ✆ (01691) 830582, *info@bradfordarmshotel.com*, *Fax (01691) 830728* – P. MC AE VISA.
closed 25-26 December, 15-23 January and 1 week autumn – **Rest** *(closed Sunday-Monday)* 16.95 (lunch) and a la carte 19.45/29.45 – **5 rm** 40.00/50.00 – 75.00/90.00.
◆ Inside you're in England, outside the front door it's Wales! Pleasantly traditional ambience with cosy bar and conservatory. Smartly furnished rooms exude comfy character. Intimate dining room for interesting, modern dishes.

at Rhydycroesau *West : 3¼ m. on B 4580 – ✉ Oswestry.*

Pen-Y-Dyffryn Country H., SY10 7JD, ✆ (01691) 653700, *stay@peny.co.uk*, *Fax (01691) 650066*, – P. MC VISA
Rest (booking essential for non-residents) (dinner only) 32.00 – **12 rm** 79.00/82.00 – 100.00/150.00.
◆ Peaceful 19C listed rectory in five-acre informal gardens near Offa's Dyke. Cosy lounge, friendly ambience; good-sized, individually styled rooms, four in the coach house. Home-cooked dishes utilising organic ingredients.

OTLEY *W. Yorks.* 502 O 22 – *pop. 14 348.*
West Busk Lane ✆ (01943) 465329.
The Library, 4 Boroughgate ✆ (0113) 247 7707.
London 216 – Harrogate 14 – Leeds 12 – York 28.

Chevin Country Park H, York Gate, LS21 3NU, South : 2¼ m. by B 6451 off Chevin rd ✆ (01943) 467818, *reception@chevinhotel.com*, *Fax (01943) 850335*, – P – 120. MC AE VISA
Rest *(closed lunch Saturday and Monday)* 22.00/23.50 and dinner a la carte 25.85/37.85 s – **46 rm** 99.00 – 154.00, 3 suites.
◆ Pine lodge village in 50 acres of delightfully quiet woodland. Ample, usefully appointed rooms in wood, cane and bright fabrics, half linked to the main house by walkways. Two-level restaurant overlooks carp lake.

OTTERBURN *Northd.* 501 502 N 18 – ✉ *Hexham.*
London 330 – Carlisle 58 – Newcastle upon Tyne 32.

Otterburn Tower, NE19 1NS, ✆ (01830) 520620, *info@otterburntower.com*, *Fax (01830) 521504*, – P – 70. MC AE VISA
Rest (light lunch)/dinner 29.95 and a la carte 14.95/29.95 – **17 rm** 55.00/80.00 – 130.00, 1 suite.
◆ 14C and 17C castellated mansion, converted to characterful hotel, in small Northumbrian village. Superb wood panelling. Lounges with open fires.Tastefully furnished bedrooms. Restaurant in three rooms; good use of local produce.

OULTON BROAD *Suffolk* 504 Z 26 – *see Lowestoft.*

OUNDLE *Northants.* 504 S 26 – *pop. 5 219* – ✉ *Peterborough.*
Benefield Rd ✆ (01832) 273267.
14 West St ✆ (01832) 274333.
London 89 – Leicester 37 – Northampton 30.

Castle Farm without rest., Fotheringhay, PE8 5HZ, North : 3 ¾ m. by A 427 off A 605 ✆ (01832) 226200, *Fax (01832) 226200*, – P.
5 rm 37.00/40.00 – 60.00/65.00.
◆ Wisteria-clad, gabled 19C house in the Nene Valley; lawned gardens beside the river. Ample, pine furnished rooms, two in the adjacent wing; intimate lounge with open fire.

The Falcon Inn, Fotheringhay, PE8 5HZ, North : 3 ¾ m. by A 427 off A 605 ✆ (01832) 226254, *falcon@huntsbridge.co.uk*, *Fax (01832) 226046*, – P. MC AE VISA
Rest 16.50 (lunch) and a la carte 25.00/29.00.
◆ Popular village inn: pretty bouquets, framed prints and airy, spacious conservatory. Mediterranean flavours to the fore in robust dishes from the modern British menu.

OVERSTRAND *Norfolk* 504 Y 25 – *see Cromer.*

OVINGTON *Hants.* – *see Winchester.*

OXFORD *Oxon.* 503 504 Q 28 *Great Britain G. – pop. 143 016.*

See : *City*★★★ - *Christ Church*★★ *(Hall*★★ *AC, Tom Quad*★, *Tom Tower*★, *Cathedral*★ *AC - Choir Roof*★*)* BZ – *Merton College*★★ *AC* BZ - *Magdalen College*★★ BZ – *Ashmolean Museum*★★ BY **M1** – *Bodleian Library*★★ *(Ceiling*★★, *Lierne Vaulting*★*) AC* BZ **A1** – *St John's College*★ BY - *The Queen's College*★ BZ – *Lincoln College*★ BZ - *Trinity College (Chapel*★*)* BY – *New College (Chapel*★*) AC,* BZ – *Radcliffe Camera*★ BZ **P1** – *Sheldonian Theatre*★ *AC,* BZ **T** – *University Museum of National History*★ BY **M4** – *Pitt Rivers Museum*★ BY **M3**.

Env. : *Iffley Church*★ AZ **A**.

Exc. : *Woodstock : Blenheim Palace*★★★ *(The Grounds*★★★*) AC, NW : 8 m. by A 4144 and A 34* AY.

Swinford Bridge (toll).

to Abingdon Bridge (Salter Bros. Ltd) (summer only) daily (2 h).

15-16 Broad St (01865) 726871, tic@oxford.gov.uk.

London 59 – Birmingham 63 – Brighton 105 – Bristol 73 – Cardiff 107 – Coventry 54 – Southampton 64.

Plans on following pages

Randolph, Beaumont St, OX1 2LN, (0870) 4008200, *sales.randolph@macdonald-hotels.co.uk, Fax (01865) 791678* – – 250. VISA BY **n**
The Restaurant at the Randolph *((01865) 256410) :* **Rest** 14.00/45.00 and a la carte 19.50/36.50 **s.** – 14.95 – **146 rm** 120.00/150.00 – 150.00/180.00, 5 suites.
◆ Grand Victorian edifice. Lounge bar: deep burgundy, polished wood and chandeliers. Handsome rooms in a blend of rich fabrics; some, more spacious, have half-tester beds. Spacious, linen-clad Restaurant.

Old Bank, 92-94 High St, OX1 4BN, (01865) 799599, *info@oldbank-hotel.co.uk, Fax (01865) 799598,* – VISA. BZ **s**
closed 23-27 December – ***Quod :*** **Rest** 12.90 (lunch) and a la carte 18.00/28.00 – 14.00 – **41 rm** 150.00 – 165.00/240.00, 1 suite.
◆ Elegantly understated, clean-lined interiors and the neo-Classical façade of the city's first bank - an astute combination. Rooms in modern wood and leather with CD players. Lively Italian-influenced brasserie.

Oxford Spires, Abingdon Rd, OX1 4PS, (01865) 324324, *spires@four-pillars.co.uk, Fax (01865) 324325,* – – 230. VISA. AZ **e**
Deacons : **Rest** *(closed Saturday lunch)* (buffet lunch Monday-Friday) (carvery lunch Sunday) 12.95/25.95 **s.** – 12.95 – **136 rm** 119.00/149.00 – 149.00/169.00, 4 suites.
◆ Follow the river path to this imposing modern hotel; comprehensive gymnasium overlooks the pool; spacious rooms, some with iron-framed four-poster beds and parkland views. Pleasantly formal, spacious dining room.

Holiday Inn, Peartree Roundabout, OX2 8JD, (0870) 4009086, *oxford@ichotels.com, Fax (01865) 888333,* – , rm, rest, – 150. VISA. AY **n**
Rest 20.00 and dinner a la carte 19.85/27.85 – **154 rm** 98.00/195.00 – 98.00/195.00.
◆ Bright, well-soundproofed rooms, all with mini-bars and computer consoles, in a group hotel on the edge of the city. A useful address for the business traveller. The Junction Restaurant offers modern British cooking.

Old Parsonage, 1 Banbury Rd, OX2 6NN, (01865) 310210, *info@oldparsonage-hotel.co.uk, Fax (01865) 311262,* , – rm, VISA BY **e**
Rest 19.50/21.50 and a la carte 22.25/38.45 – 12.00 – **30 rm** 140.00 – 185.00.
◆ Part 17C house, creeper-clad and typically Oxfordian; dedicated staff; pristine rooms: antiques, modern and traditional fabrics and, in some cases, views of the roof garden. Meals in cosy lounge bar with antique prints and paintings.

Cotswold Lodge, 66a Banbury Rd, OX2 6JP, (01865) 512121, *info@cotswoldlodgehotel.co.uk, Fax (01865) 512490,* – – 80. VISA. AY **x**
Rest 15.00/30.00 and a la carte 19.00/38.00 – **48 rm** 85.00/150.00 – 125.00/175.00, 1 suite.
◆ Large 19C house in a quiet suburb. Relaxing, handsomely furnished drawing room with log fire; comfortable rooms, all individually styled, are named after colleges. Gallic influenced cuisine; immaculate layout.

Eastgate, High St, OX1 4BE, (0870) 4008201, *sales.eastgate@macdonald-hotels.co.uk, Fax (01865) 791681* – , rm, VISA. BZ **c**
mertonsbar : **Rest** - Grill rotisserie - a la carte 18.40/26.85 – 14.95 – **63 rm** 140.00/150.00 – 160.00.
◆ Near the botanical gardens and the Boathouse's punt moorings, a former coaching inn offering comfortable, traditionally styled rooms decorated in plaid and floral patterns. Grill rotisserie dining.

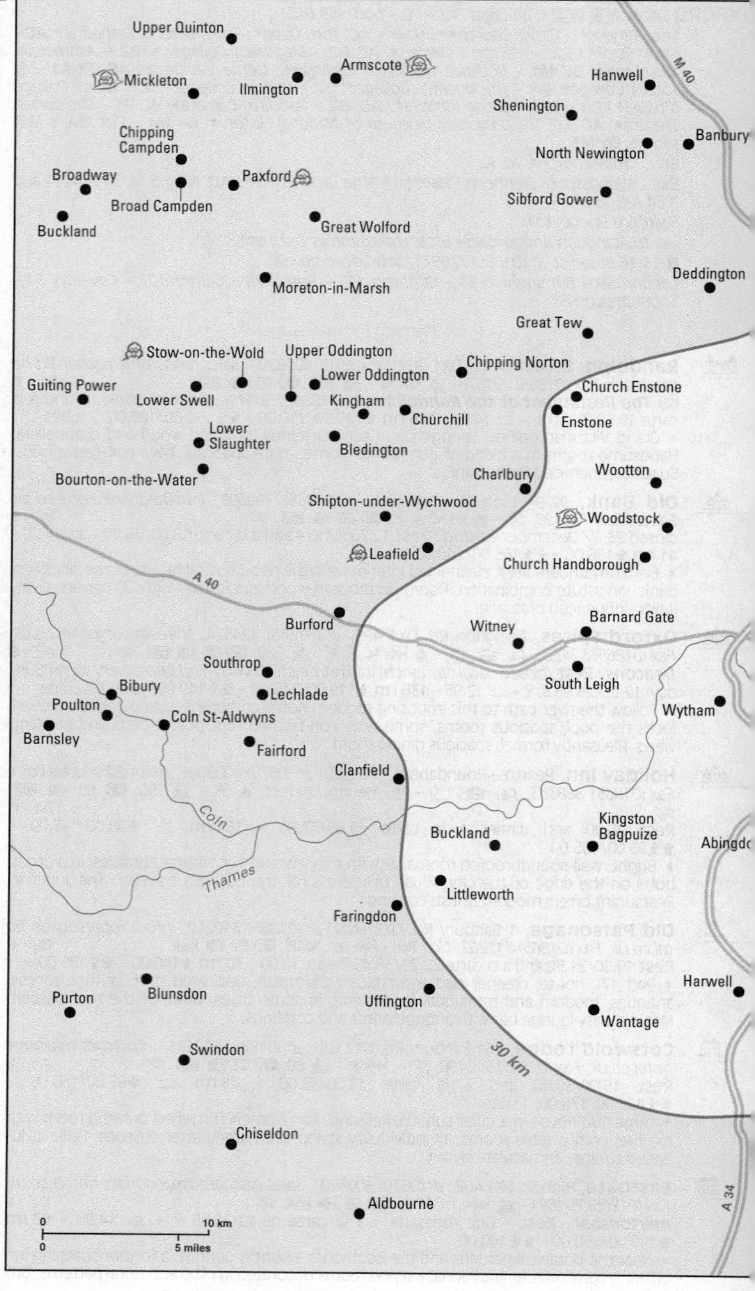

Upper Quinton
Armscote
Mickleton
Ilmington
Hanwell
M 40
Shenington
Chipping Campden
North Newington
Banbury
Broadway
Paxford
Broad Campden
Sibford Gower
Buckland
Great Wolford
Deddington
Moreton-in-Marsh
Great Tew
Stow-on-the-Wold
Upper Oddington
Chipping Norton
Guiting Power
Lower Oddington
Church Enstone
Lower Swell
Kingham
Churchill
Enstone
Lower Slaughter
Bledington
Bourton-on-the-Water
Charlbury
Wootton
Shipton-under-Wychwood
Woodstock
Leafield
Church Handborough
A 40
Burford
Witney
Barnard Gate
Southrop
South Leigh
Bibury
Lechlade
Poulton
Coln St-Aldwyns
Wytham
Barnsley
Fairford
Clanfield
Coln
Kingston Bagpuize
Buckland
Abingdo
Thames
Littleworth
Faringdon
Harwell
Blunsdon
Purton
Uffington
Wantage
Swindon
30 km
Chiseldon
A 34
Aldbourne
0
10 km
0
5 miles

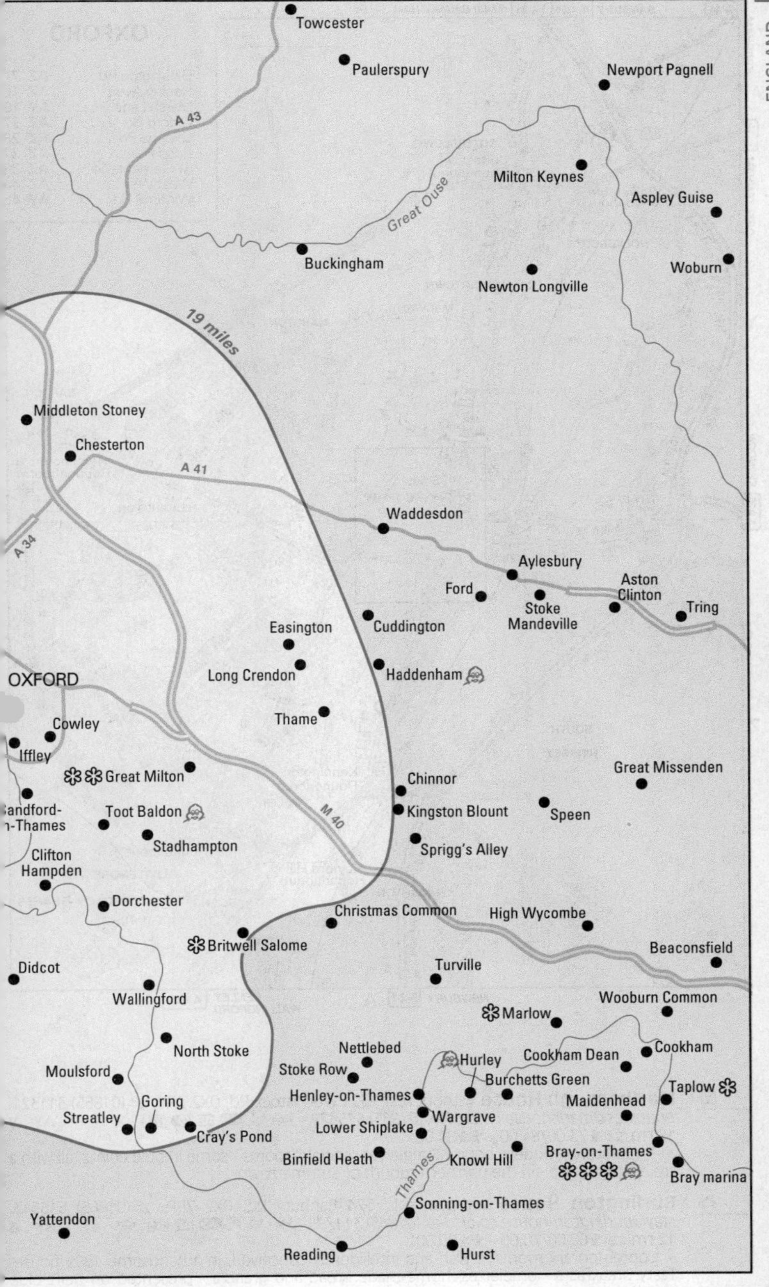
Towcester
Paulerspury
Newport Pagnell
A 43
Milton Keynes
Great Ouse
Aspley Guise
Buckingham
Woburn
Newton Longville
19 miles
Middleton Stoney
Chesterton
A 41
A 34
Waddesdon
Aylesbury
Ford
Aston Clinton
Stoke Mandeville
Tring
Easington
Cuddington
Long Crendon
Haddenham
OXFORD
Thame
Cowley
Iffley
Great Milton
Chinnor
Great Missenden
andford-
n-Thames
Toot Baldon
Kingston Blount
Speen
M 40
Stadhampton
Sprigg's Alley
Clifton Hampden
Dorchester
Christmas Common
High Wycombe
Britwell Salome
Beaconsfield
Didcot
Turville
Wallingford
Wooburn Common
Marlow
North Stoke
Nettlebed
Cookham
Hurley
Cookham Dean
Moulsford
Stoke Row
Burchetts Green
Taplow
Henley-on-Thames
Maidenhead
Goring
Wargrave
Streatley
Lower Shiplake
Cray's Pond
Knowl Hill
Bray-on-Thames
Binfield Heath
Thames
Bray marina
Sonning-on-Thames
Yattendon
Reading
Hurst

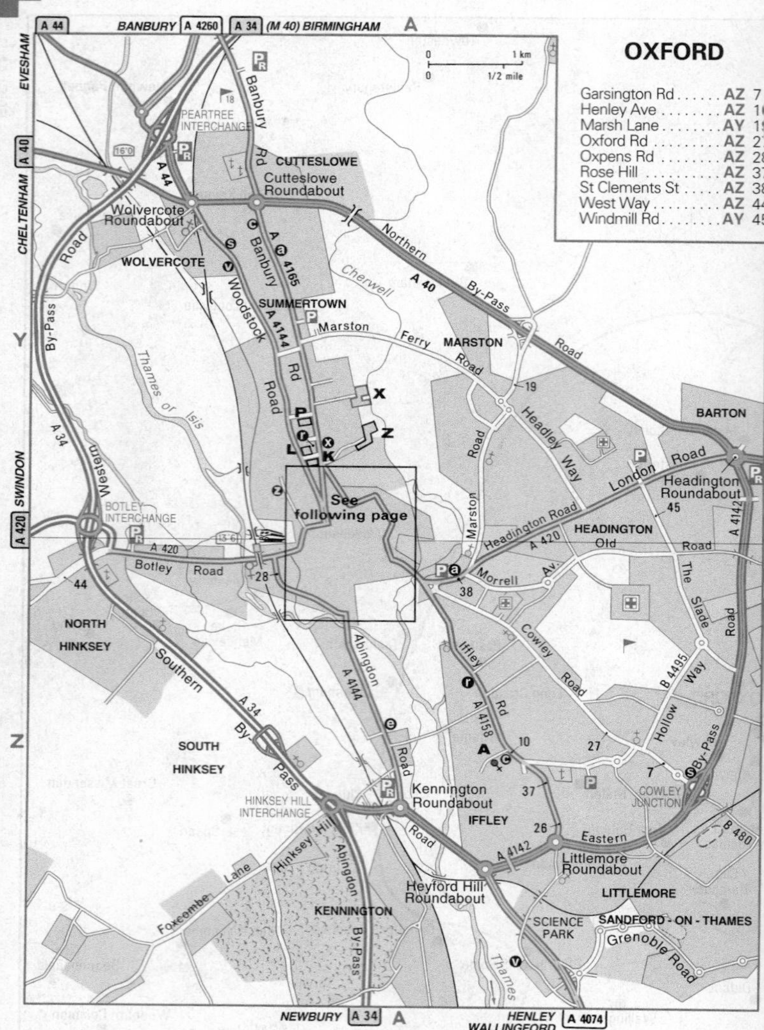

Marlborough House without rest., 321 Woodstock Rd, OX2 7NY, ☎ (01865) 311321, *enquiries@marlbhouse.co.uk, Fax (01865) 515329* – ⇔ ☎. MC AE D VISA. ⚘ AY v
16 rm ☐ ♦73.00/84.00 – ♦♦84.00.

◆ Three-storey modern house. Simple yet spacious rooms - some in bold chintz, all with a small kitchenette - in the northern suburb of Summertown.

Burlington House without rest., 374 Banbury Rd, OX2 7PP, ☎ (01865) 513513, *stay@burlington-house.co.uk, Fax (01865) 311785* – ⇔ ☎ P. MC AE VISA. ⚘ AY a
12 rm ☐ ♦60.00/70.00 – ♦♦90.00.

◆ Contemporary rooms, stylish and intelligently conceived, in a handsome 1889 house. Tasty breakfasts - omelettes, home-made bread and granola - presented on Delft-blue china.

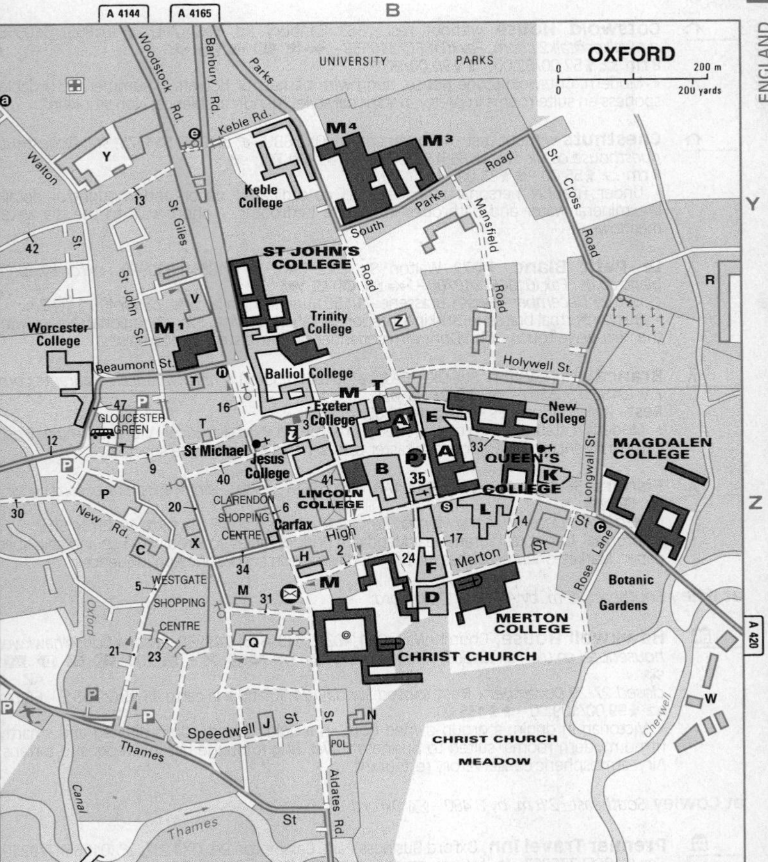

OXFORD

- Blue Boar St . . . . BY 2
- Broad St . . . . BZ 3
- Castle St . . . . BZ 5
- Clarendon Shopping Centre . . . BZ
- Cornmarket St . . . . BZ 6
- George St . . . . BZ 9
- High St . . . . BZ
- Hythe Bridge St . . . . BZ 12
- Little Clarendon St . . . . BY 13
- Logic Lane . . . . BZ 14
- Magdalen St . . . . BYZ 16
- Magpie Lane . . . . BZ 17
- New Inn Hall St . . . . BZ 20
- Norfolk St . . . . BZ 21
- Old Greyfriars St . . . . BZ 23
- Oriel Square . . . . BZ 24
- Park End St . . . . BZ 30
- Pembroke St . . . . BZ 31
- Queen's Lane . . . . BZ 33
- Queen St . . . . BZ 34
- Radcliffe Square . . . . BZ 35
- St Michael St . . . . BZ 40
- Turl St . . . . BZ 41
- Walton Crescent . . . . BY 42
- Westgate Shopping Centre . . . . BZ
- Worcester St . . . . BZ 47

COLLEGES

- All Souls . . . . BZ **A**
- Balliol . . . . BY
- Brasenose . . . . BZ **B**
- Christ Church . . . . BZ
- Corpus Christi . . . . BZ **D**
- Exeter . . . . BZ
- Hertford . . . . BZ **E**
- Jesus . . . . BZ
- Keble . . . . BY
- Lady Margaret Hall . . . . AY **Z**
- Linacre . . . . BZ **N**
- Lincoln . . . . BZ
- Magdalen . . . . BZ
- Merton . . . . BZ
- New . . . . BZ
- Nuffield . . . . BZ **P**
- Oriel . . . . BZ **F**
- Pembroke . . . . BZ **Q**
- Queen's . . . . BZ
- St Anne's . . . . AY **K**
- St Anthony's . . . . AY **L**
- St Catherine's . . . . BY **R**
- St Cross . . . . BY **V**
- St Edmund Hall . . . . BZ **K**
- St Hilda's . . . . BZ **W**
- St Hugh's . . . . AY **P**
- St John's . . . . BY
- St Peter's . . . . BZ **X**
- Sommerville . . . . BY **Y**
- Trinity . . . . BY
- University . . . . BZ **L**
- Wadham . . . . BY **Z**
- Wolfson . . . . AY **X**
- Worcester . . . . BY

ENGLAND

Cotswold House without rest., 363 Banbury Rd, OX2 7PL, ☎ (01865) 310558, *d.r.walker@talk21.com, Fax (01865) 310558* – ⇔ P. MC ① VISA. ✂ AY c
8 rm ☐ ✝52.00/62.00 – ✝✝80.00/90.00.
◆ Modern, Cotswold stone house, hung with baskets of flowers in summer. Affordable, spotless en suite rooms in pretty, traditional style; friendly ambience. Non smoking.

Chestnuts without rest., 45 Davenant Rd, OX2 8BU, ☎ (01865) 553375, *stay@chestnuts guesthouse.co.uk, Fax (01865) 553375* – ⇔ P. MC VISA. ✂ AY s
6 rm ☐ ✝55.00 – ✝✝85.00.
◆ Under friendly personal management; co-ordinated décor and thoughtful details like mineral water and bathrobes in ensuite bedrooms. A short walk to the Isis water meadows.

Le Petit Blanc, 71-72 Walton St, OX2 6AG, ☎ (01865) 510999, *oxford@lepetit blanc.co.uk, Fax (01865) 510700* – ⇔ ▤. MC AE VISA AY z
closed 25 December – **Rest** - Brasserie - 14.50 (lunch) and a la carte 22.50/40.75 ☺ ♀.
◆ Busy, informal brasserie; striking interior and sharp service; French regional recipes with the new-wave touch: John Dory with coriander or ribeye steak in béarnaise.

Branca, 111 Walton St, OX2 6AJ, ☎ (01865) 556111, *info@brancarestaurants.com, Fax (01865) 556501* – ▤. MC AE ① VISA BY a
Rest - Italian influences - a la carte 19.95/25.95 ♀.
◆ Modern restaurant with casual, friendly feel and minimalist décor. Vibrant, simple, fresh Italian influenced dishes: antipasti taster plates, pasta and pizza are specialities.

Fishers, 36-37 St Clements, OX4 1AB, ☎ (01865) 243003, *dining@fishers-oxford.co.uk* – ▤. MC VISA AZ a
closed 24-26 December and Monday lunch – **Rest** - Seafood - a la carte 19.15/34.50 ♀.
◆ Informal, bright restaurant near Magdalen Bridge. Tables covered with fish and chip style paper. Market-oriented dishes include Mediterranean and Pacific Rim influences.

at Iffley *Southeast : 2 m. by A 4158 – ✉ Oxford.*

Hawkwell House, Church Way, OX4 4DZ, ☎ (01865) 749988, *reservations@hawkwell househotel.co.uk, Fax (01865) 748525,* ⇌ – |♦| ⇔ ✆ ♿ P – 🏛 200. MC AE ① VISA. ✂ AZ c
closed 27-29 December – **Rest** *(closed Sunday)* 21.50 and a la carte 13.95/29.95 ♀ – **66 rm** ☐ ✝99.00/109.00 – ✝✝135.00.
◆ Victorian in origin, a group-owned hotel in a quiet suburb. Co-ordinated and smartly fitted modern rooms, suited to business travel. Bright lounge bar in checks and tartans. Airy, atmospheric conservatory restaurant.

at Cowley *Southeast : 2½ m. by B 480 – ✉ Oxford.*

Premier Travel Inn, Oxford Business Park, Garsington Rd, OX4 2JZ, ☎ (01865) 779230, *Fax (01865) 775887* – |♦|, ⇔ rm, ▤ rest, ♿ P. MC AE ① VISA. ✂ AZ s
Rest (grill rest.) – **121 rm** ✝57.95/57.95 – ✝✝62.95/62.95.
◆ A consistent standard of trim, simply fitted accommodation in modern style. Ideally situated for the Oxford Business Park. Meals may be taken in the adjacent Beefeater.

at Sandford-on-Thames *Southeast : 5 m. by A 4158 – ✉ Oxford.*

Oxford Thames Four Pillars, Henley Rd, OX4 4GX, ☎ (01865) 334444, *thames@four-pillars.co.uk, Fax (01865) 334400,* ⚓, ≘s, ▢, ⇌, ♧, ✂ – ⚓ ⇔, ▤ rest, ✆ ♿ P – 🏛 150. MC AE ① VISA. ✂ AZ v
The River Room : **Rest** 12.50/36.00 **s.** ♀ – ☐ 13.45 – **60 rm** ☐ ✝139.00/164.00 – ✝✝172.00/245.00.
◆ Modern sandstone hotel around a 13C barn, though the pool is more reminiscent of a Roman bath; spacious lounge with medieval style chandelier, spotless, comfortable rooms. Restaurant overlooks lawned grounds and river.

at Toot Baldon *Southeast : 5½ m. by B 480 – AZ – ✉ Oxford.*

Mole Inn, OX44 9NG, ☎ (01865) 340001, *info@themoleinn.com, Fax (01865) 343011* – P. MC AE VISA. ✂
closed 25 December and 1 January – **Rest** a la carte 20.00/25.00.
◆ Much refurbished pub in tiny hamlet. Beams galore, stone tiles, cosy lounge with leather sofas, pine/oak tables. Tasty, assured menus: rustic and earthy or appealingly modish.

at Great Milton *Southeast : 12 m. by A 40 off A 329 – AY – ✉ Oxford.*

Le Manoir aux Quat' Saisons (Blanc), Church Rd, OX44 7PD, ✆ (01844) 278881, *lemanoir@blanc.co.uk, Fax (01844) 278847*, ←, – rest, rest, P – 50. VISA.
Rest - French - 45.00 (lunch weekdays) and a la carte 84.00/98.00 s. – 16.00 – **25 rm** 360.00/895.00 – 360.00/895.00, 7 suites 530.00/895.00.
Spec. Confit of foie gras, soused cherries and spiced mango chutney. Corn-fed squab with coco beans and Madeira jus. Raspberry and chocolate tart.
◆ World famous and picture perfect, its beauty lies in its refinement. Sumptuous lounges and rooms, classic and modern, surrounded by Japanese, ornamental and kitchen gardens. Virtuoso classic French menu of precision and flair, inspired by the seasons.

at Kingston Bagpuize *Southwest : 10 m. by A 420 – AY – off A 415 – ✉ Oxford.*

Fallowfields Country House, Faringdon Rd, OX13 5BH, ✆ (01865) 820416, *stay@fallowfields.com, Fax (01865) 821275*, – P. VISA
closed 25-26 December – ***Wellingtonia :*** **Rest** 15.00 (lunch) and a la carte 27.25/35.75 – **10 rm** 80.00 – 90.00/140.00.
◆ Elephants are everywhere - in paintings, wood and china - in this privately run 19C manor. Cosy lounge, fireside chintz armchairs. Canopy beds in thoughtfully appointed rooms. Classically elegant restaurant views sweeping lawns.

at Wytham *Northwest : 3¼ m. by A 420 – AY – off A 34 (northbound carriageway) – ✉ Oxford.*

White Hart, OX2 8QA, ✆ (01865) 244372, *whitehartwytham@yahoo.co.uk, Fax (01865) 812950*, – P. VISA
Rest a la carte 18.00/30.00.
◆ Mellow 18C inn located in a pretty hamlet. Delightful courtyard terrace; inside are roaring fires, flagged floors, scrubbed pine tables. Menus mix classics with contemporary.

OXHILL *Warks.* 503 504 P 27.
London 90 – Banbury 11 – Birmingham 37.

Oxbourne House, CV35 0RA, ✆ (01295) 688202, *graememcdonald@msn.com*, ←, – P.
Rest (by arrangement) (communal dining) 25.00 – **3 rm** 39.00/45.00 – 65.00/70.00.
◆ Late 20C house oozing charm, individuality and fine rural views; splendid gardens. Antiques abound, complemented by the finest soft furnishings. Stylishly appointed bedrooms. Spacious dining room: plenty of ingredients grown in house grounds.

PADIHAM *Blackburn* 502 N 22.
London 230 – Burnley 6 – Clitheroe 8.5.

at Fence *Northeast : 3 m. by A 6068 – ✉ Padiham.*

The Forest Inn, Cuckstool Lane, BB12 9PA, Southwest : ½ m. on A 6248 ✆ (01282) 613641, *Fax (01282) 698140* – P. VISA
closed 1 week January and Monday – **Rest** a la carte 14.25/28.65.
◆ Rural pub with fine country views. Modish interior includes stripped wooden floors and comfy leather tub chairs. Main dining area serves hearty, seasonal, rustic dishes.

PADSTOW *Cornwall* 503 F 32 *The West Country G. – pop. 2 449.*
See : *Town★ – Prideaux Place★.*
Env. : *Trevone (Cornwall Coast Path★★) W : 3 m. by B 3276 – Trevose Head★ (←★★) W : 6 m. by B 3276.*
Exc. : *Bedruthan Steps★, SW : 7 m. by B 3276 – Pencarrow★, SE : 11 m. by A 389.*
18, 9, 9 *Trevose, Constantine Bay ✆ (01841) 520208.*
Red Brick Building, North Quay ✆ (01841) 533449, padstowtic@visit.org.uk.
London 288 – Exeter 78 – Plymouth 45 – Truro 23.

The Metropole, Station Rd, PL28 8DB, ✆ (01841) 532486, *info@the-metropole.co.uk, Fax (01841) 532867*, ← Camel Estuary, heated, – P. VISA
Rest (bar lunch Monday-Saturday)/dinner 27.95/37.95 – 12.95 – **50 rm** 90.00/130.00 – 130.00/170.00.
◆ Grand 19C hotel perched above this quaint fishing town. Exceptional views of Camel Estuary. Well-furnished sitting room. Comfortable bedrooms in smart, co-ordinated style. Traditional dining; local produce.

ENGLAND

Old Custom House Inn, South Quay, PL28 8BL, (01841) 532359, *oldcustom house@smallandfriendly.co.uk, Fax (01841) 533372,* ≤ Camel Estuary and harbour – rest. VISA.
Pescadou : Rest (booking essential) a la carte 29.00/34.50 – **24 rm** 63.00/82.00 – 170.00.
◆ Listed, slate-built former grain store and exciseman's house: spacious and comfortable throughout. Front and side rooms have views of the quayside and Camel Estuary. Seafood emphasis in bustling, glass-fronted restaurant.

Cross House without rest., Church St, PL28 8BG, (01841) 532391, *info@cross house.co.uk, Fax (01841) 533633* – . VISA.
11 rm 70.00/90.00 – 70.00/125.00.
◆ Charming, centrally located, Grade II listed Georgian house. Two lounges with real fires and a comfortable feel. Varying room sizes, all with co-ordinated fabrics.

Tregea, 16-18 High St, PL28 8BB, (0871) 871 2686, *tim@tregea.co.uk Fax (01841) 533542* – P. VISA.
The Estuary : Rest (booking essential) (dinner only) 24.00 – **13 rm** 86.00/115.00 – 86.00/115.00.
◆ Unusually quiet, considering the location; early 17C house with contrastingly cool, modern lounge. Clean, contemporary rooms in pale blue shades: a languid feel pervades. Popular restaurant.

Woodlands Country House without rest., Treator, PL28 8RU, West : 1 ¼ m. on B 3276 (01841) 532426, *info@woodlands-padstow.co.uk, Fax (01841) 533353,* ≤, – P. VISA
closed 18 December-27 January – **9 rm** 54.00/61.00 – 104.00/132.00.
◆ Personally run Victorian country house with well-kept garden. Large lounge in classic traditional style; views sweeping down to Trevone Bay. Co-ordinated bedrooms.

Treverbyn House without rest., Station Rd, PL28 8DA, (01841) 532855, *Fax (01841) 532855,* ≤, – P.
closed 1 week Christmas – **5 rm** 50.00/60.00 – 90.00/100.00.
◆ Something of a grand style with views of the Camel Estuary. Large rooms retain open fireplaces and have comfortable, uncluttered décor: Turret rooms are the ones to ask for.

Althea Library without rest., 27 High St, PL28 8BB, (01841) 532717, *beare27@tiscali.co.uk, Fax (01841) 532717* – P. VISA.
closed 22-26 December – **3 rm** 50.00 – 82.00.
◆ Grade II listed former school library with very friendly feel. Neat terrace; homely breakfast room/lounge with food cooked on the Aga. Cosy, individually styled beamed rooms.

The Seafood with rm, Riverside, PL28 8BY, (01841) 532700, *reservations@rick stein.com, Fax (01841) 532942* – , rest, P. VISA
closed 24-26 December and 1 May – **Rest** - Seafood - (booking essential) a la carte 35.50/59.50 – **20 rm** 115.00 – 245.00.
◆ Bold artwork and a buzz of enthusiasm animate Rick Stein's converted granary and conservatory. Flavourful Cornish seafood. Stylish rooms in a cool modern palette.

St Petroc's with rm, 4 New St, PL28 8EA, (01841) 532700, *reservations@rick stein.com, Fax (01841) 532942,* – P. VISA
closed 24-26 December and 1 May – **Rest** (booking essential) a la carte 27.95/31.95 – **10 rm** 115.00 – 185.00.
◆ Handsome white-fronted house on a steep hill, where confidently prepared modern dishes with local, seasonal produce take centre stage. Stylish, individual bedrooms.

The Ebb, 1a The Strand, PL28 8BS, (01841) 532565, *Fax (01841) 532565* – . VISA
early March - November – **Rest** - Seafood - *(closed Tuesday)* (dinner only) 26.00/34.00.
◆ First floor restaurant in busy fishing port. Lightwood furniture against neutral décor. Eclectic cooking using local ingredients spiced up with international influences.

Rick Stein's Café with rm, 10 Middle St, PL28 8AP, (01841) 532700, *reservations@rickstein.com, Fax (01841) 532942* – . VISA
closed 24-26 December, 1 May and dinner Sunday and Monday November-February – **Rest** (booking essential) 19.95 (dinner) and a la carte 22.25/29.70 – **3 rm** 85.00 – 105.00.
◆ Contemporary, unfussy bistro with modern, well-priced Mediterranean influenced cuisine employing the best local and seasonal ingredients. Well-appointed bedrooms.

Margot's, 11 Duke St, PL28 8AB, (01841) 533441, *enquiries@margots.co.uk* – . VISA
closed December, January, Sunday, Monday and lunch Tuesday – **Rest** (dinner booking essential) 25.95 (dinner) and lunch a la carte 20.95/29.20 s.
◆ Informal bistro-style restaurant with a friendly welcoming atmosphere. Varied menu capitalises on finest, fresh, local ingredients and bold, characterful flavours.

at Little Petherick *South : 3 m. on A 389 – ✉ Wadebridge.*

Molesworth Manor without rest., PL27 7QT, ✆ (01841) 540292, *molesworthmanor@aol.com,* ←, – ⇔ P. ✻
February-October – **10 rm** ☕ ★56.00/61.00 – ★★84.00/92.00.
◆ Part 17C and 19C former rectory. Charming individual establishment with inviting country house atmosphere amid antique furniture and curios. Rooms furnished in period style.

Old Mill House, PL27 7QT, ✆ (01841) 540388, *enquiries@theoldmill.com, Fax (01841) 540406,* – ⇔. MO VISA. ✻
February - October – **Rest** (by arrangement) 29.50 – **7 rm** ☕ ★80.00/85.00 – ★★105.00/110.00.
◆ Rural curios on display in a listed, family owned 16C cornmill with working water wheel. Homely, individually decorated rooms, some overlooking the millrace and neat garden.

at St Issey *South : 3½ m. on A 389 – ✉ Wadebridge.*

Olde Tredore House without rest., PL27 7QS, North : ¼ m. off A 389 ✆ (01841) 540291, ←, – ⇔ P. ✻
closed Christmas and New Year – **3 rm** ☕ ★58.00 – ★★60.00.
◆ Large, grand house in a tranquil and secluded location. Well-furnished guest areas and bedrooms all in traditional country house style.

at St Ervan *Southwest : 4 m. by A 398 off B 3274 – ✉ Padstow.*

St Ervan Manor , The Old Rectory, PL27 7TA, ✆ (01841) 540255, *info@stervanmanor.co.uk,* – ⇔ P. MO VISA. ✻
closed 8-31 January and 18-28 December – **Rest** *(closed Monday-Tuesday)* (booking essential) (dinner only) (2 Tasting menus only) 45.00/75.00 ♀ – **5 rm** ☕ ★100.00/135.00 – ★★140.00/180.00, 1 suite.
Spec. Lobster risotto with tarragon and orange. Pigeon and foie gras, fig and port with rocket leaves. Lemon curd with cherry sorbet and shortbread.
◆ Stone built 19C house in serene spot. Especially warm service from hands-on owners. Brightly co-ordinated bedrooms, including striking Garden Suite in rich red. Gourmet dining: two tasting menus on offer in local and French style. Fine, delicate cooking.

at St Merryn *West : 2½ m. on B 3276 – ✉ Padstow.*

Ripleys, PL28 8NQ, ✆ (01841) 520179, *chefripley@aol.com* – ⇔. MO VISA
closed 2 weeks Christmas, Sunday and Monday – **Rest** (booking essential) a la carte 25.50/36.50.
Spec. Pan-fried monkfish livers with leek fondue, sweet and sour dressing. Roast rump of spring lamb, garlic potatoes and sauce paloise. Summer pudding with Cornish double cream.
◆ Obeys the first rule of cooking: don't over-elaborate when you have great ingredients. Exposed beams and brickwork provide the ideal backdrop.

at Constantine Bay *West : 4 m. by B 3276 – ✉ Padstow.*

Treglos , PL28 8JH, ✆ (01841) 520727, *stay@tregloshotel.com, Fax (01841) 521163,* ←, , , – ⇔, rest, ✆ P. MO VISA
March-November – **Rest** 14.00/45.00 ♀ – **39 rm** (dinner included) ☕ ★67.75/144.75 – ★★135.50/193.00, 3 suites.
◆ An extensive, family run building surrounded by garden. Facilities include games rooms, children's play area and a lounge bar. Consistently decorated, bright, neat bedrooms. Smart attire the code in very comfortable dining room.

PADWORTH *Newbury* 503 504 Q 29 – ✉ *Reading.*

London 58 – Basingstoke 12 – Reading 10 – Southampton 37.

Courtyard by Marriott Reading, Bath Rd, RG7 5HT, on A 4 ✆ (0870) 400 7234, *Fax (0870) 400 7334,* , – ⇔ ✆ P – 200. MO AE VISA. ✻
Rest a la carte 15.15/29.40 **s.** ♀ – **50 rm** ★125.00 – ★★135.00/150.00.
◆ Purpose-built group hotel just off the main road; a peaceful gallery lounge overlooks the lobby. Rooms, quieter at the rear, are well equipped for the business traveller. Informal, split-level brasserie overlooks wooden pagoda.

Do not confuse X with ✿! X defines comfort, while stars are awarded for the best cuisine, across all categories of comfort.

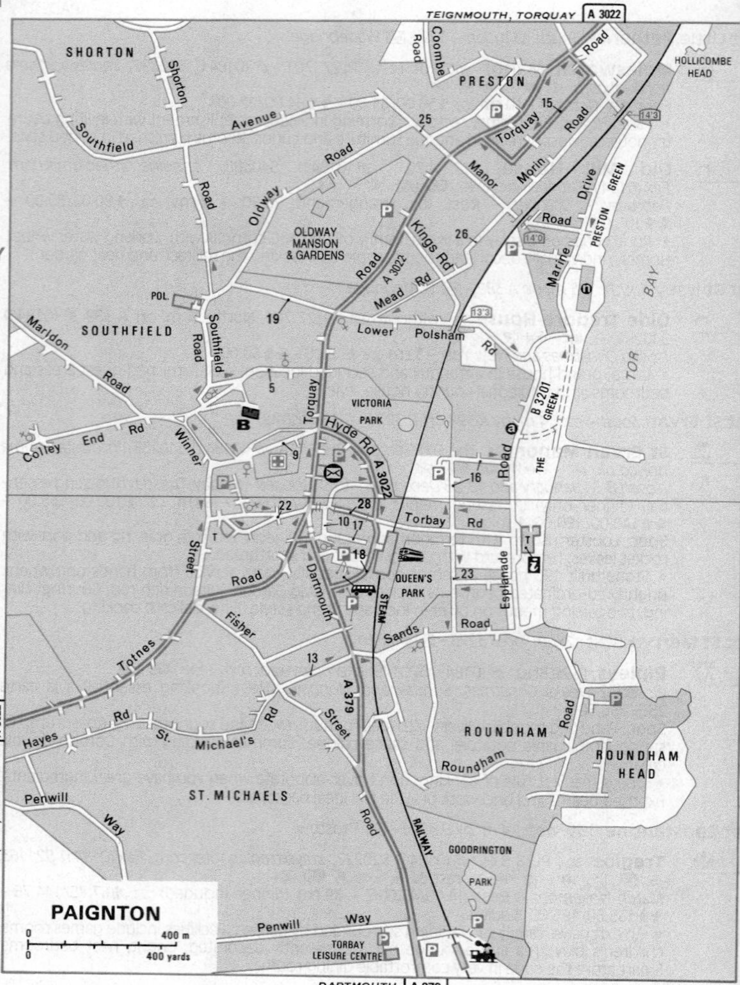

PAIGNTON

Street	Square	No.
Cecil Rd	Y	5
Church St	Y	9
Commercial Rd	Z	10
Elmsleigh Rd	Z	13
Eugene Rd	Y	15
Garfield Rd	Y	16
Gerston Rd	Z	17
Great Western Way	Z	18
Higher Polsham Rd	Y	19
Hyde Rd	Y	
Palace Ave	Z	22
Queen's Rd	Z	23
Torbay Rd	Z	
Torquay Rd	Y	
Upper Manor Rd	Y	25
Upper Morin Rd	Y	26
Victoria Rd	Z	28

Do not confuse X with ✿! X defines comfort, while stars are awarded for the best cuisine, across all categories of comfort.

PAIGNTON *Torbay* 503 J 32 *The West Country G. – pop. 47 398.*
See : *Torbay★ - Kirkham House★* **AC Y B.**
Env. : *Paignton Zoo★★ AC, SW : ½ m. by A 3022* **AY** *(see Plan of Torbay) – Cockington★, N : 3 m. by A 3022 and minor roads.*
The Esplanade, tourist.board@torbay.gov.uk.
London 226 – Exeter 26 – Plymouth 29.

Plan of Built up Area : see Torbay

Plan opposite

Redcliffe, 4 Marine Drive, TQ3 2NL, (01803) 526397, *redclfe@aol.com, Fax (01803) 528030,* < Torbay, heated, – , rest, – 200. VISA. **Y n**
Rest (bar lunch Monday-Saturday)/dinner 17.50 and a la carte 19.00/25.00 – **68 rm** ★55.00/108.00 – ★★110.00/120.00.
◆ Airy, pine furnished rooms in a well-run family hotel, home to a colonel of Engineers in the days of the Raj. Leisure options include putting green and children's play area. Admire the sea views from spacious, neat restaurant.

Palace, Esplanade Rd, TQ4 6BJ, (01803) 555121, *info@palacepaignton.com, Fax (01803) 527974,* <, – . AE VISA. **Y a**
Rest 15.00/16.75 – **54 rm** ★40.00/66.00 – ★★96.00/132.00.
◆ Mid-19C hotel: its white façade dominates the esplanade. Large public areas: comfy sun lounge has bay views. Smart, up-to-date leisure facilities. Well-equipped bedrooms. Comfortable dining room with traditional appeal.

Hotels and restaurants change every year, so change your Michelin guide every year!

PAINSWICK *Glos.* 503 504 N 28 *Great Britain G. – pop. 1 666.*
See : *Town★.*
London 107 – Bristol 35 – Cheltenham 10 – Gloucester 7.

Painswick , Kemps Lane, GL6 6YB, Southeast : ½ m. by Bisley St, St Marys St, The Cross and Tibbiwell Lane (01452) 812160, *reservations@painswickhotel.com, Fax (01452) 814059,* – . AE VISA.
Rest 22.50/25.00 – **19 rm** (dinner included) ★95.00/105.00 – ★★275.00/285.00.
◆ Tranquil, extended Palladian rectory in pretty village. Well-appointed rooms, most charming in the old house, mix modern and period furniture; good views from upper floors. Panelled dining room; terrace by croquet lawn.

Cardynham House without rest., The Cross, GL6 6XX, by Bisley St and St Marys St (01452) 814006, *info@cardynham.co.uk, Fax (01452) 812321* – AE VISA.
9 rm ★50.00/59.00 – ★★69.00/150.00.
◆ Part 15C house with a stylish, relaxed, even Bohemian feel to its elegant, firelit lounge. Themed, uniquely styled rooms: eight have four-poster beds, one a private pool.

PARKGATE *Mersey.* 502 503 K 24.
London 212 – Birkenhead 10 – Chester 16 – Liverpool 12.

Marsh Cat, 1 Mostyn Sq, CH64 6SL, (0151) 336 1963, *info@marshcat.com, Fax (0151) 336 4998,* < – . AE VISA
Rest (booking essential) 12.75/15.20 and a la carte 19.45/28.70 .
◆ Brightly painted, lively village bistro overlooking Wirral marshes. British, Cajun, French, Jamaican and Oriental flavours in worldwide repertoire - ask about set menus.

PARKHAM *Devon* 503 H 31 – *Bideford.*
London 229 – Barnstaple 14 – Exeter 87 – Plymouth 58.

Penhaven Country House , Rectory Lane, EX39 5PL, (01237) 451711, *restaurant@penhaven.co.uk, Fax (01237) 451878,* , – rest, . VISA
Rest (dinner only and Sunday lunch)/dinner 22.00 and a la carte 28.50/35.00 **s.** – **12 rm** (dinner included) ★78.00/150.00 – ★★156.00/170.00.
◆ Ducks potter around the grounds of this old rectory, traditional from the cosy chintz chairs and stone fireplace in the lounge to well-kept rooms, seven in cottage annexes. Dining room's tall arched windows overlook gardens and woods.

PARRACOMBE *Devon* 503 I 30 *The West Country G.*

Env. : *Arlington Court*★★, *S : 6 m. by A 39.*

Exc. : *Linton*★, *NE : 9 m. by A 39 – Barnstaple*★, *S : 14 m. by A 39.*

London 214 – Barnstaple 14 – Lynton 6.

Fox & Goose with rm, EX31 4PE, ℰ (01598) 763239, *Fax (01598) 763621*, – rm, P.

closed 25 December – **Rest** (booking essential) a la carte 20.00/25.00 – **2 rm** ★30.00 – ★★50.00.

◆ Placidly set by a stream in a pleasant little village with narrow streets. Trophies, books, plants and pictures abound. Good, honest, local dishes. Simple, bright bedrooms.

PARTRIDGE GREEN *W. Sussex* 504 T 31 – ✉ *Horsham.*

London 47 – Horsham 9.5 – Worthing 16.

Green Man Inn, Church Rd, Jolesfield, RH13 8JT, on B 2135 ℰ (01403) 710250, *Fax (01403) 713212*, – P.

closed 26-31 December, Sunday dinner and Monday except Bank Holidays – **Rest** 14.95 (lunch) and a la carte 20.00/32.00.

◆ Appealing 19C roadside pub with pleasant terrace. Stylish interior: rustic overtones and many Sussex prints. Locally sourced produce: fresh cooking with renowned tapas option.

PATCHWAY *South Gloucestershire* 503 504 M 29 – *see Bristol.*

PATELEY BRIDGE *N. Yorks.* 502 O 21 *Great Britain G. – pop. 2 504 –* ✉ *Harrogate.*

Exc. : *Fountains Abbey*★★★ *AC - Studley Royal*★★ *AC (<★ from Anne Boleyn's Seat) - Fountains Hall (Façade*★*), NE : 8½ m. by B 6265.*

18 High St ℰ *(01423) 711147.*

London 225 – Leeds 28 – Middlesbrough 46 – York 32.

at Ramsgill-in-Nidderdale *Northwest : 5 m. by Low Wath Rd –* ✉ *Harrogate.*

✻ **Yorke Arms** (Frances Atkins) with rm, HG3 5RL, ℰ (01423) 755243, *enquiries@yorke-arms.co.uk*, *Fax (01423) 755330*, – P.

Rest 17.50/29.00 (lunch) and a la carte 22.95/44.50 – **13 rm** (dinner included) ★120.00/200.00 – ★★320.00/380.00.

Spec. Potted beef, ham hock and foie gras terrine, asparagus velouté. Cheese soufflé, seared scallops, vanilla and salsify. Blanquette of mutton, black pudding, cider and apples.

◆ Part 17C former shooting lodge, now a quintessentially English Inn by Gouthwaite reservoir. Classically based seasonal dishes with a modern touch. Lavishly furnished bedrooms.

PATRICK BROMPTON *N. Yorks.* 502 P 21 – ✉ *Bedale.*

London 242 – Newcastle upon Tyne 58 – York 43.

Elmfield House, Arrathorne, DL8 1NE, Northwest : 2¼ m. by A 684 on Richmond rd ℰ (01677) 450558, *stay@elmfieldhouse.co.uk*, *Fax (01677) 450557*, – P.

closed 23 December-2January – **Rest** (booking essential) (residents only) (dinner only) 15.00 – **7 rm** ★45.00/59.00 – ★★80.00.

◆ Spacious, neatly fitted accommodation in a peaceful, personally run hotel, set in acres of gardens and open countryside. Try your luck at the adjacent fishing lake.

PAULERSPURY *Northants.* 503 504 R 27 – *see Towcester.*

PAXFORD *Glos.* 503 504 O 27 – *see Chipping Campden.*

PAYHEMBURY *Devon – see Honiton.*

PEASMARSH *E. Sussex* 504 W 31 – *see Rye.*

PEMBRIDGE *Herefordshire* 503 L 27.
London 162 – Hereford 15.5 – Leominster 7.5.

Lowe Farm, HR6 9JD, West : 3 ¼ m. by A 44 following signs through Marston village ℘ (01544) 388395, *wiliams-family@lineone.net, Fax (01544) 388395,* ≤, ⊞, ⊞ – ⊞ P.
closed 25-26 December and 1 week June – **Rest** (by arrangement) 18.00 – **5 rm** ☐ ★35.00 – ★★65.00.
◆ Working farm: farmhouse dates from 13C; renovated barn from 14C with pleasant lounge and countryside views. Rooms in house and barn are cosy, comfortable and of a good size. Dining room boasts chunky pine tables, exposed brick and beams.

PEMBURY *Kent* 504 U 30 – *see Royal Tunbridge Wells.*

PENRITH *Cumbria* 501 502 L 19 – *pop. 14 471.*
Salkeld Rd ℘ *(01768) 891919.*
Robinsons School, Middlegate ℘ *(01768) 867466, pen.tic@eden.gov.uk – Rheged, Redhills, Penrith* ℘ *(01768) 860034.*
London 290 – Carlisle 24 – Kendal 31 – Lancaster 48.

North Lakes, Ullswater Rd, CA11 8QT, South : 1 m. by A 592 at junction 40 of M 6 ℘ (01768) 868111, *nlakes@shirehotels.com, Fax (01768) 868291,* – P – 200. MC AE VISA.
***The Martindale :* Rest** (bar lunch Saturday and Sunday) 18.50 (lunch) and dinner a la carte 28.00/35.00 s. ♀ – **84 rm** ☐ ★115.00 – ★★160.00.
◆ Comprehensive leisure club, up-to-date meeting suites and comfortable, usefully appointed rooms in this group hotel; practically located and ideal for the working traveller. Medieval tapestry reproduction is restaurant's focal point.

Brooklands without rest., 2 Portland Pl, CA11 7QN, ℘ (01768) 863395, *enquiries@brooklandsguesthouse.com* – MC VISA.
7 rm ☐ ★30.00/55.00 – ★★60.00/70.00.
◆ Traditonal Victorian terraced house a minute's walk from the shops: many original features restored. Pleasantly furnished breakfast room. Locally made pine enhances bedrooms.

at Temple Sowerby *East : 6¾ m. on A 66 – ✉ Penrith.*

Temple Sowerby House, CA10 1RZ, ℘ (01768) 361578, *stay@templesowerby.com, Fax (01768) 361958,* – P. MC AE VISA
closed Christmas – **Rest** (dinner only) a la carte 25.00/35.00 – **12 rm** ☐ ★80.00/90.00 – ★★125.00/160.00.
◆ Part 16C, part 18C listed building with Georgian frontage and walled garden, run with enthusiasm and charm. Individually styled rooms exude either a period or rustic ambience. Elegant dining in 18C part of the house.

at Yanwath *Southwest : 2½ m. by A 6 and B 5320 – ✉ Penrith.*

The Gate Inn, CA10 2LF, ℘ (01768) 862386, *enquiries@yanwathgate.com, Fax (01768) 899892* – P. MC AE VISA
Rest a la carte 21.00/32.00.
◆ Charming, characterful 17C inn with intimate, open-fired interior. Adjacent dining room with panelled walls. Locally sourced dishes full of organic and free-range ingredients.

at Tirril *Southwest : 3 m. by A 6 on B 5320 – ✉ Penrith.*

Queens Head Inn with rm, CA10 2JF, ℘ (01768) 863219 – P. MC VISA
Rest *(closed dinner 25-26 December)* a la carte 17.50/25.00 – **7 rm** ☐ ★40.00 – ★★70.00.
◆ Characterful 18C inn once owned by the Wordsworth family; open fires, heavily beamed. Local produce features prominently on tried-and-tested menus. Cosy bedrooms.

at Newbiggin *West : 3½ m. by A 66 – ✉ Penrith.*

The Old School, CA11 0HT, ℘ (01768) 483709, *info@theold-school.com, Fax (01768) 483709,* – P. MC VISA
closed 18-28 December – **Rest** (by arrangement) 20.00 – **3 rm** ☐ ★30.00/50.00 – ★★60.00.
◆ Well sited off two major roads, this 19C former school house has been tastefully converted with an open-fired lounge and rooms individually decorated to a high standard.

PENZANCE *Cornwall* 503 D 33 *The West Country G. – pop. 20 255.*

See : *Town*★ - *Outlook*★★★ – *Western Promenade* (<★★★) **YZ** – *National Lighthouse Centre*★ *AC* **Y** – *Chapel St*★ **Y** – *Maritime Museum*★ *AC* **Y M1**.

Env. : *St Buryan*★★ (*church tower*★★), *SW* : *5 m. by A 30 and B 3283* – *Penwith*★★ – *Trengwainton Garden*★★, *NW* : *2 m.* – *Sancreed - Church*★★ (*Celtic Crosses*★★) - *Carn Euny*★, *W* : *3½ m. by A 30* **Z** – *St Michael's Mount*★★ (<★★), *E* : *4 m. by B 3311* – **Y** – *and A 30* – *Gulval*★ (*Church*★), *NE* : *1 m.* – *Ludgvan*★ (*Church*★), *NE* : *3½ m. by A 30* – *Chysauster Village*★, *N* : *3½ m. by A 30, B 3311 and minor rd* – *Newlyn*★ - *Pilchard Works*★, *SW* : *1½ m. by B 3315* **Z** – *Lanyon Quoit*★, *NW* : *3½ m. by St Clare Street* – *Men-an-Tol*★, *NW* : *5 m. by B 3312* – *Madron Church*★, *NW* : *1½ m. by St Clare Street* **Y**.

Exc. : *Morvah* (<★★), *NW* : *6½ m. by St Clare Street* **Y** – *Zennor* (*Church*★), *NW* : *6 m. by B 3311* **Y** – *Prussia Cove*★, *E* : *8 m. by B 3311* – **Y** – *and A 394* – *Land's End*★ (*cliff scenery*★★★), *SW* : *10 m. by A 30* **Z** – *Porthcurno*★, *SW* : *8½ m. by A 30, B 3283 and minor rd.*

Access to the Isles of Scilly by helicopter, British International Heliport (01736) 364296, Fax (01736) 332253.

to the Isles of Scilly (Hugh Town) (Isles of Scilly Steamship Co. Ltd) (summer only) (approx. 2 h 40 mn).

Station Rd (01736) 362207.

London 319 – Exeter 113 – Plymouth 77 – Taunton 155.

Plan opposite

Mount Prospect, Britons Hill, TR18 3AE, (01736) 363117, *enquiries@hotelpenzance.com, Fax (01736) 350970,* <, , heated, – , rest, P. VISA — Y c

Bay : **Rest** (booking essential to non-residents) (dinner only and lunch in summer) a la carte 25.00/39.00 **s.** – **24 rm** ★65.00/110.00 – ★★115.00/140.00.

◆ Well-established hotel with modern interior in elevated spot with views to St. Michaels Mount. Comfortable lounge. Bedrooms are immaculately kept and equipped with mod cons. Bright, modern restaurant with local artwork and bar.

The Abbey without rest., Abbey St, TR18 4AR, (01736) 366906, *hotel@theabbeyonline.com, Fax (01736) 351163,* – P. VISA — Y u

6 rm ★75.00/95.00 – ★★150.00/190.00, 1 suite.

◆ Powder blue painted 17C house with lovely Victorian gardens. Attractive antique furnishings include historical pictures. Country house atmosphere and characterful bedrooms.

Beachfield, The Promenade, TR18 4NW, (01736) 362067, *office@beachfield.co.uk, Fax (01736) 331100,* < – . VISA — Z a

closed Christmas-New Year – **Rest** (dinner only) 21.95 and a la carte 18.65/30.85 **s.** – **18 rm** ★54.50/74.50 – ★★119.00/129.00.

◆ Classic seaside hotel with good views. Well-kept public areas include traditional lounge. Comfy bedrooms are well maintained and have a neat, bright feel. Traditional, varied menus, featuring fish specials.

Chy-An-Mor without rest., 15 Regent Terrace, TR18 4DW, (01736) 363441, *info@chyanmor.co.uk, Fax (01736) 363441,* <, – P. VISA. — Y e

mid February-October – **10 rm** ★34.00/66.00 – ★★64.00/72.00.

◆ Located on a terrace of houses overlooking the promenade. Thoroughly well kept throughout. Comfy, well-furnished bedrooms. Wake up to a good choice at breakfast.

Estoril, 46 Morrab Rd, TR18 4EX, (01736) 362468, *enquiries@estorilhotel.co.uk, Fax (01736) 367471* – . VISA. — Y o

closed 8-20 January – **Rest** (by arrangement) 14.95 – **9 rm** ★32.00/45.00 – ★★64.00/70.00.

◆ In a quiet suburb near Morrab and Penlee Gardens, a characterful bay windowed Victorian house with a comfortable, traditional lounge and spotless rooms at modest rates.

Harris's, 46 New St, TR18 2LZ, (01736) 364408, *contact@harrissrestaurant.co.uk, Fax (01736) 333273* – . VISA — Y a

closed 3 weeks in winter, 25 December, 1 January, Monday in winter and Sunday – **Rest** a la carte 29.70/41.50 ♀.

◆ Friendly and well-established restaurant, tucked away on a cobbled street. Brightly decorated interior with smart linen clothed tables. Cornish menu with a French overlay.

The Summer House with rm, Cornwall Terrace, TR18 4HL, (01736) 363744, *reception@summerhouse-cornwall.com, Fax (01736) 360959,* , – P. VISA. — Z s

March-October – **Rest** (*closed Monday-Wednesday*) (dinner only) 26.00 – **5 rm** ★75.00/95.00 – ★★80.00/95.00.

◆ Listed Regency rooms and restaurant in bright blues and yellows. Relaxed, friendly ambience. Mediterranean influenced seafood; modern and flavourful. Leafy patio garden.

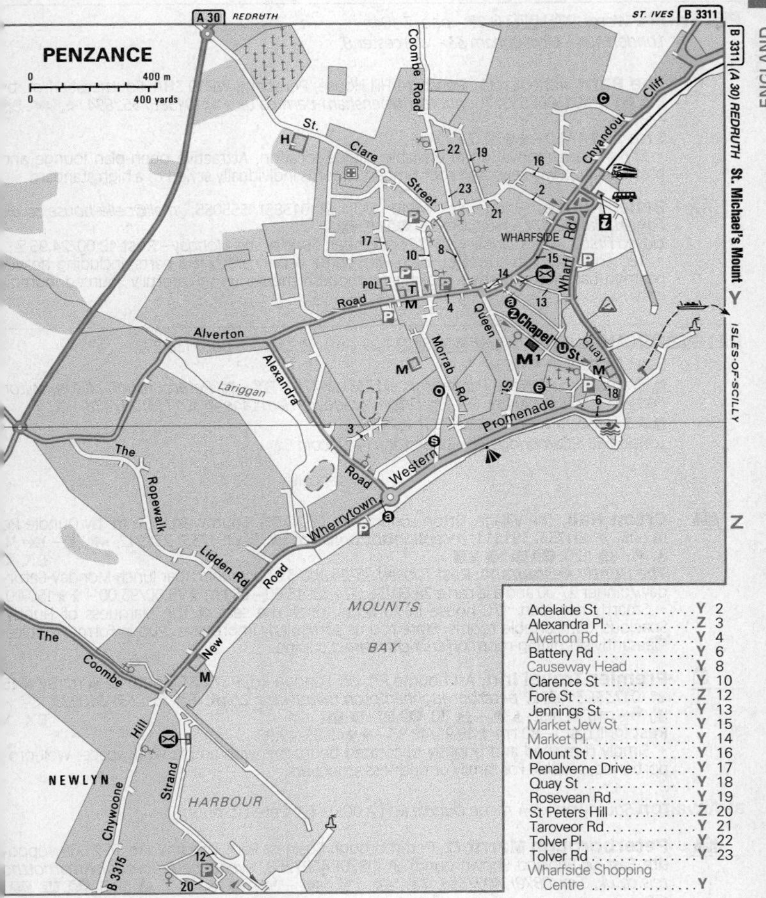

Bakehouse, Old Bakehouse Lane, Chapel St, TR18 4AE, ✆ (01736) 331331, *info@bakehouse-penzance.co.uk* – ✂. MC VISA Y Z

closed 25-26 December and Sunday – **Rest** a la carte 24.45/28.45 ♀.

◆ Penzance's original bakery, now a stylish restaurant on two floors, with old bakers oven in situ downstairs. Modern menus boast good choice of local seafood and produce.

at Drift *Southwest : 2½ m. on A 30 – Z – ✉ Penzance.*

Rose Farm without rest., Chyenhal, Buryas Bridge, TR19 6AN, Southwest : ¾ m. on Chyenhal rd ✆ (01736) 731808, *penny@rosefarmcornwall.co.uk, Fax (01736) 731808,* – P. MC VISA

closed 25-26 December – **3 rm** ☕ ★40.00 – ★★65.00.

◆ In the heart of the countryside, a tranquil working farm. Cosy, rustic farmhouse ambience with neatly kept bedrooms including large barn room.

PERRANUTHNOE Cornwall 503 D 33 – *see Marazion.*

PERSHORE *Worcs.* 503 504 N 27 – *pop. 7 104.*
London 106 – Birmingham 33 – Worcester 8.

The Barn without rest., Pensham Hill House, Pensham, WR10 3HA, Southeast : 1 m. by B 4084 ☎ (01386) 555270, *ghorton@pensham-barn.co.uk, Fax (01386) 552894*, ≤, – 🅿
3 rm ★47.50 – ★★70.00/80.00.
◆ Stylish barn renovation in enviable hillside location. Attractive open-plan lounge and breakfast area with exposed roof timbers. Rooms individually styled to a high standard.

Belle House, Bridge St, WR10 1AJ, ☎ (01386) 555055, *mail@belle-house.co.uk, Fax (01386) 555377* – ⇔ 36. MC AE VISA
closed first 2 weeks January, 25-26 December, Sunday and Monday – **Rest** 18.00/24.95 ♀.
◆ 16C and 18C high street building with some very characterful parts, including heavily beamed bar. Accomplished cooking on modern menus using carefully sourced ingredients.

PETERBOROUGH *Peterborough* 502 504 T 26 *Great Britain G.* – *pop. 136 292.*
See : *Cathedral★★ AC* Y.
Thorpe Wood, Nene Parkway ☎ (01733) 267701, BX – *Peterborough Milton, Milton Ferry ☎ (01733) 380489,* BX – *Orton Meadows, Ham Lane ☎ (01733) 237478,* BX.
3-5 Minster Precinct ☎ (01733) 452336.
London 85 – Cambridge 35 – Leicester 41 – Lincoln 51.

Plan opposite

Orton Hall, The Village, Orton Longueville, PE2 7DN, Southwest : 2 ½ m. by Oundle Rd (A 605) ☎ (01733) 391111, *reception@ortonhall.co.uk, Fax (01733) 231912*, – 🅿 – 120. MC AE VISA BX c
***The Huntly Restaurant* :** Rest *(closed 25-26 and 31 December)* (bar lunch Monday-Saturday)/dinner 27.00 and a la carte 28.00/36.00 – 13.00 – **65 rm** ★75.00/95.00 – ★★150.00.
◆ Smartly run, part 17C house in 20 acres, once the seat of the Marquess of Huntly. Spacious, comfortable rooms: State rooms particularly impressive. Pub in former stables. Pleasantly set dining room offers richly varied cuisine.

Premier Travel Inn, Ashbourne Rd, off London Rd, PE7 8BT, South : 2 ¾ m. by A 15 ☎ (01733) 310772, *peterboroughhampton.ti@travelinn.co.uk, Fax (01733) 310923*, – rm, rest, 🅿 – 30. MC AE VISA. BX x
Rest (grill rest.) – **80 rm** ★46.95/46.95 – ★★49.95/49.95.
◆ Simply furnished and brightly decorated bedrooms with ample work space. Well-proportioned; suitable for family or business stopovers.

at Alwalton *Southwest : 5¾ m. on Oundle Rd (A 605) – ✉ Peterborough.*

Peterborough Marriott, Peterborough Business Park, Lynch Wood, PE2 6GB, (opposite East of England Showground) ☎ (0870) 4007258, *events.peterborough@marriotthotels.co.uk, Fax (0870) 4007358*, – 🅿 – 300. MC AE VISA. AX u
Rest (buffet lunch)/dinner 22.00 and a la carte 27.20/32.20 **s.** ♀ – 14.95 – **155 rm** ★105.00 – ★★105.00, 2 suites.
◆ Modern group hotel located opposite the East of England Showground providing well-equipped bedrooms, smart leisure club and plenty of up-to-date conference space. Formal dining with international range.

Express by Holiday Inn without rest., East of England Way, PE2 6HE, ☎ (01733) 284450, *peterborough@oriel-leisure.co.uk, Fax (01733) 284451* – 🅿 – 25. MC AE VISA AX n
80 rm ★69.00 – ★★69.00.
◆ Purpose-built hotel under group management, providing trim, bright rooms, spacious and practically designed. A popular choice for East of England Show.

at Wansford *West : 8½ m. by A 47 – ✉ Peterborough.*

Haycock, PE8 6JA, ☎ (01780) 782223, *sales@thehaycock.co.uk, Fax (01780) 783031*, – 🅿 – 250. MC AE VISA AX e
***Orchards* :** Rest a la carte approx 26.00 ♀ – ***Bentley* :** Rest *(closed Sunday-Monday)* 15.95/55.00 – **48 rm** ★85.00/106.00 – ★★175.00.
◆ Extended part 17C coaching inn with neat gardens by the River Nene. Traditionally cosy, flagged lounge. Bedrooms, in a stylish theme, exude a good feeling of comfort. Orchards is breezy conservatory dining room. More formal dining in Bentley.

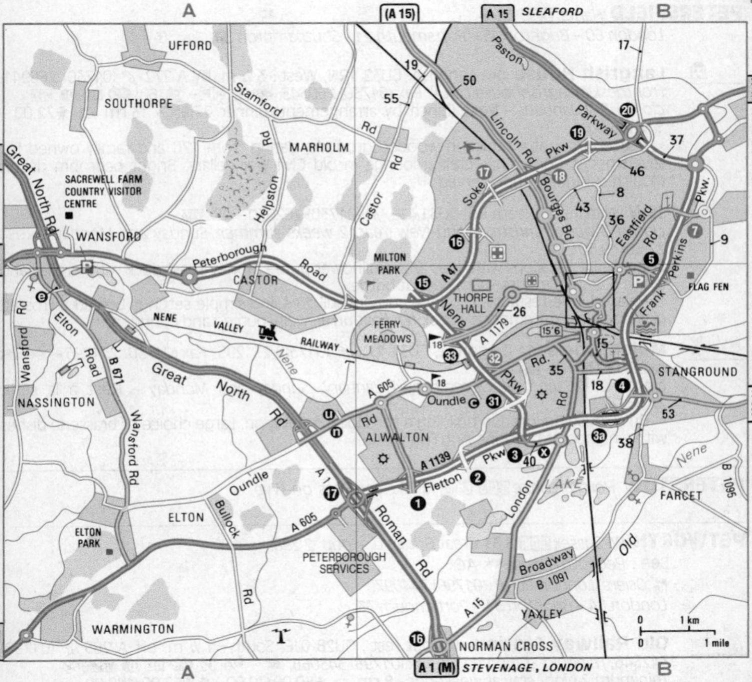

A B

(A 15) A 15 SLEAFORD

UFFORD
SOUTHORPE
MARHOLM
SACREWELL FARM COUNTRY VISITOR CENTRE
WANSFORD
CASTOR
MILTON PARK
THORPE HALL
FERRY MEADOWS
NENE VALLEY RAILWAY
ALWALTON
ELTON
ELTON PARK
NASSINGTON
PETERBOROUGH SERVICES
WARMINGTON
NORMAN CROSS
YAXLEY
FARCET
STANGROUND
FLAG FEN
A 47 WISBECH
WHITTLESEY A 605
A 1 (M) STEVENAGE, LONDON

PETERBOROUGH

Bridge St . . . . Z
Cattle Market Rd . . . . Y 2
Church St . . . . YZ
City Rd . . . . Y 3
Cowgate . . . . Y 5
Cross St. . . . . Z 6
Dogsthorpe Rd . . . . BV 8
Edgerley Drain Rd . . . . . . BV 9
Embankment Rd . . . . Z 12
Exchange St . . . . Y 13
Fletton Ave . . . . BX 15
Geneva St . . . . Y 16
Guntons Rd . . . . BV 17
High St . . . . BX 18
Hurn Rd . . . . BV 19
Long Causeway . . . . Y 25
Longthorpe Parkway . . . . . BX 26
Market Way . . . . Y 28
Midgate . . . . Y 29
New Rd . . . . BX 35
Park Rd. . . . . BV 36
Paston Parkway . . . . BV 37
Peterborough Rd . . . . BX 38
Phorpres Way . . . . BX 40
Queensgate Shopping Centre . . . . Y
Rivergate Shopping Centre . . . . Z
Rivergate . . . . Z 42
St Paul's Rd . . . . BV 43
Thorpe Rd . . . . Y 45
Welland Rd . . . . BV 46
Wentworth St. . . . . Z 48
Werrington Parkway . . . . . BV 50
Wheelyard . . . . Y 52
Whittlesey Rd . . . . BX 53
Woodcroft Rd . . . . BV 55

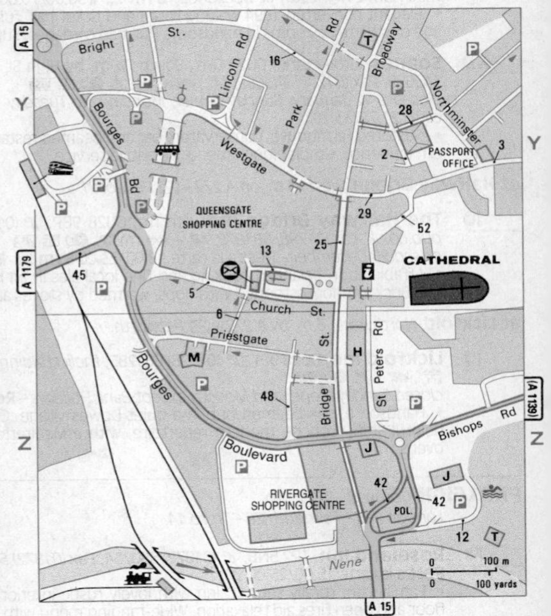

PETERSFIELD *Hants.* 504 R 30.

London 60 – Brighton 45 – Portsmouth 21 – Southampton 34.

Langrish House, Langrish, GU32 1RN, West : 3 ½ m. by A 272 (01730) 266941, *frontdesk@langrishhouse.co.uk, Fax (01730) 260543*, – P. – 60. MC AE VISA
closed 2-9 January – **Rest** (lunch by arrangement)/dinner 27.95 – **13 rm** 72.00 – 145.00.
◆ Peaceful country house in wooded grounds, dating from 17C and family owned for seven generations. Characterful lounge in old Civil War cellars. Bright bedroom décor. Modish cuisine, proudly served.

JSW (Watkins), 1 Heath Rd, GU31 4JE, (01730) 262030 – MC VISA
closed 2 weeks Christmas and New Year, 2 weeks summer, Sunday and Monday – **Rest** 22.50/39.50 .
Spec. Seared scallops with ceps and cauliflower purée. Honey-roast duck with girolles and lentils. Caramel mousse with peanut brittle.
◆ Relaxed little restaurant: prints, culinary still-lifes and simple settings behind a frosted glass façade. Contemporary cooking: flavourful, well-sourced and confident.

Mulchrone's, 14 Dragon St, GU31 4JJ, (01730) 231295, *Fax (01730) 231295* – 25. MC AE VISA
closed 25-26 and 31 December, 1 January, Sunday and Monday – **Rest** a la carte 22.65/27.95 .
◆ Busy, bustling location building a solid local reputation. Large choice of brasserie dishes with a highpoint the appealing fish menu.

PETERSTOW *Herefordshire* 503 504 M 28 – *see Ross-on-Wye.*

PETWORTH *W. Sussex* 504 S 31 *Great Britain G.* – *pop. 2 298.*

See : *Petworth House** AC.*
Osiers, London Rd (01798) 344097.
London 54 – Brighton 31 – Portsmouth 33.

Old Railway Station without rest., GU28 0JF, South : 1 ½ m. off A 285 (01798) 342346, *mlr@old-station.co.uk, Fax (01798) 343066*, – P. MC AE VISA.
minimum 2 night stay at weekends – **8 rm** 50.00/70.00 – 62.00/140.00.
◆ Elegant converted 1894 waiting room and ticket hall, full of charming details from the age of steam. Six rooms in handsome Pullman carriages. Summer breakfast on platform.

Soanes, Grove Lane, GU28 0HY, South : ½ m. by High St and Pulborough rd (01798) 343659, *Fax (01798) 343659*, , – P. MC AE VISA
closed 2-12 January, Sunday dinner, Monday and Tuesday – **Rest** (light lunch)/dinner a la carte 21.75/33.70.
◆ Restored farmhouse: conservatory bar and beamed restaurant. Dinner menu with modern influence, simpler lunch menu. Attentive service.

at Halfway Bridge *West : 3 m. on A 272 – Petworth.*

The Halfway Bridge Inn with rm, GU28 9BP, (01798) 861281, *hwb@thesussexpub.co.uk, Fax (01798) 861878*, – rm, P. MC AE VISA
closed 25 December – **Rest** a la carte 18.00/23.00 **8 rm** 55.00 – 120.00.
◆ Affable staff, balanced cooking and fine local ales in an instantly likeable 17C coaching inn. Brick interior festooned with hops, warmed by stoves and log fires. Comfy rooms.

at Lickfold *Northwest : 6 m. by A 272 – Petworth.*

Lickfold Inn, GU28 9EY, (01798) 861285, *thelickfoldinn@aol.com, Fax (01798) 861342*, , – P. MC VISA
closed Sunday dinner and Monday except Bank Holidays – **Rest** a la carte 19.95/29.95 .
◆ Handsome, oak-beamed pub in a quiet Downs village. Cosy ambience and easygoing, helpful staff. Concise modern repertoire, with a Mediterranean twist, from wood-fired ovens.

PHILLEIGH *Cornwall – Truro.*

London 273 – Falmouth 26 – Truro 14.

Roseland Inn, TR2 5NB, (01872) 580254, *Fax (01872) 580966* – P. MC VISA
Rest a la carte 15.00/25.00 .
◆ Family run, rurally set 16C inn with lovely rustic interior. Exposed beams, solid stone floor and open fires aid relaxation. Wide-ranging menu with Cornish base.

PICKERING *N. Yorks.* 502 R 21 – *pop. 6 616.*

The Ropery ☏ *(01751) 473791.*

London 237 – Middlesbrough 43 – Scarborough 19 – York 25.

White Swan Inn, Market Pl, YO18 7AA, ☏ (01751) 472288, *welcome@white-swan.co.uk, Fax (01751) 475554* – P. MC AE VISA

Rest – (see ***The Restaurant*** below) – **18 rm** ☐ ★79.00/119.00 – ★★129.00/159.00, 3 suites.

◆ Personally run former coaching halt in a popular market town. Welcoming, antique filled sitting room and comfortable, stylish bedrooms full of individual details.

Bramwood, 19 Hall Garth, YO18 7AW, ☏ (01751) 474066, *bramwood@fsbdial.co.uk,* – P. MC VISA.

Rest (by arrangement) 17.50 – **8 rm** ☐ ★30.00/45.00 – ★★60.00.

◆ Georgian town house with sheltered garden. Personally run with curios of rural life dotted around a firelit lounge. Cosy bedrooms in homely, cottagey style.

Old Manse, Middleton Rd, YO18 8AL, ☏ (01751) 476484, *info@oldmansepickering.co.uk, Fax (01751) 477124,* – P. MC VISA

Rest 18.75 ♀ – **10 rm** ☐ ★40.00/55.00 – ★★70.00/90.00.

◆ A welcoming ambience and modestly priced rooms, spacious and spotless, make this personally run house an ideal base for touring the moors. Secluded rear garden and orchard. Informal conservatory dining room.

The Restaurant (at White Swan Inn), Market Pl, YO18 7AA, ☏ (01751) 472288, *welcome@white-swan.co.uk, Fax (01751) 475554,* – P. MC AE VISA

Rest a la carte 21.85/30.85.

◆ Set in the coaching inn, with comfy lounge for pre-prandials. Restaurant boasts roaring fire, tapestry screens, modern décor, and modish menus with local produce to the fore.

at Levisham *Northeast : 6½ m. by A 169 – ✉ Pickering.*

The Moorlands Country House, YO18 7NL, ☏ (01751) 460229, *ronaldoleonardo@aol.com, Fax (01751) 460470,* – P. MC VISA.

March-mid November (minimum stay two nights) – **Rest** (by arrangement) 25.00 – **7 rm** ☐ ★50.00/120.00 – ★★100.00/140.00.

◆ Restored 19C house with attractive gardens in the heart of the North York Moors National Park. There are fine views to be enjoyed here. Rooms furnished to high standard. Traditional, home-cooked meals in pretty dining room.

at Marton *West : 5¼ m. by A 170 – ✉ Pickering.*

The Appletree Country Inn, YO62 6RD, ☏ (01751) 431457, *appletreeinn@supanet.com,* – P. MC VISA

closed 25 December, 2 weeks January, Monday and Tuesday – **Rest** a la carte 17.00/33.00 ♀.

◆ Large, part 18C inn in quiet village. Plenty of recently added beams. Small, comfy, sofa-strewn lounge. The modern British cooking provides originality and interest.

at Middleton *Northwest : 1½ m. on A 170 – ✉ Pickering.*

The Leas, Nova Lane, YO18 8PN, North : 1 m. via Church Lane ☏ (01751) 472129, *enquiries@cottageleashotel.co.uk, Fax (01751) 474930,* – P. MC AE VISA

Rest (lunch by arrangement)/dinner a la carte 19.95/25.40 – **17 rm** ☐ ★48.00/55.00 – ★★68.00/78.00.

◆ Get away from it all to an extended period house in the hills above Middleton. Large lounge with open fire. Simple, sizeable rooms looking to quiet, unspoilt fields. Bistro menus in heavily wood-furnished restaurant.

at Sinnington *Northwest : 4 m. by A 170 – ✉ York.*

Fox and Hounds with rm, Main St, YO62 6SQ, ☏ (01751) 431577, *foxhoundsinn@easynet.co.uk, Fax (01751) 432791,* – P. MC AE VISA

closed 25 December – **Rest** a la carte 15.90/25.00 ♀ – **10 rm** ☐ ★69.00 – ★★120.00.

◆ At the heart of this sleepy village on the river Seven, an extended coaching house, beamed and panelled in ancient oak. Well-proportioned, cottagey rooms; hearty breakfasts. Modern restaurant or rustic bar offer dining options.

at Cropton *Northwest : 4¾ m. by A 170 – ✉ Pickering.*

Burr Bank without rest., YO18 8HL, North : ¼ m. ☏ (01751) 417777, *bandb@burrbank.com.,* – P.

3 rm ☐ ★30.00 – ★★60.00.

◆ Homely, pine-beamed cottage, secluded and peaceful, run by a welcoming husband and wife team. Rooms in pretty modern décor. Two-acre garden looks north to sweeping dales.

PICKHILL *N. Yorks.* 502 P 21 – ✉ *Thirsk.*
London 229 – Leeds 41 – Middlesbrough 30 – York 34.

Nags Head Country Inn, YO7 4JG, ✆ (01845) 567391, *reservations@nagsheadpickhill.freeserve.co.uk, Fax (01845) 567212,* , – rest, P – 30. MC VISA
Rest a la carte 17.95/25.90 ♀ – **14 rm** ☐ ★55.00/60.00 – ★★80.00, 1 suite.
◆ Atmospheric 300 year old inn in an ancient hamlet, an easy drive to Thirsk and Ripon races. Neat rooms in soft floral fabrics. Over 800 ties on display in the rustic bar. Rural restaurant adorned with bookshelves and patterned rugs.

PILLERTON HERSEY *Warks.*
London 91 – Birmingham 33 – Stratford-upon-Avon 8.

Dockers Barn Farm without rest., Oxhill Bridle Rd, CV35 0QB, Southeast : 1 m. ✆ (01926) 640475, *jwhoward@onetel.com, Fax (01926) 641747* – P
closed 24-27 December – **3 rm** ☐ ★36.00/39.00 – ★★54.00/60.00.
◆ Restored 18C barn in charmingly rural location close to Stratford. Stone floors and hop vines enhance rustic character. Attractive rooms: four-poster in former threshing barn.

PILLING *Lancs.* 502 L 22 – *pop. 2 204* – ✉ *Preston.*
London 243 – Blackpool 11 – Burnley 43 – Manchester 49.

Springfield House, Wheel Lane, PR3 6HL, ✆ (01253) 790301, *recep@springfieldhousehotel.co.uk, Fax (01253) 790907,* ←, – rest, P. MC AE VISA
Rest *(closed Monday lunch)* 10.95/15.95 and a la carte 20.45/30.85 – **8 rm** ☐ ★55.00 – ★★95.00.
◆ 1840s house surrounded by tranquil walled gardens. Handsome façade in Georgian style, period inspired rooms and country house interiors make it a popular wedding venue. Traditionally inspired dining room.

PLUCKLEY *Kent* 504 W 30.
London 53 – Folkestone 25 – Maidstone 18.

Dering Arms, Station Rd, TN27 0RR, South : 1½ m. on Bethersden rd ✆ (01233) 840371, *jim@deringarms.com, Fax (01233) 840498,* – P. MC AE VISA
closed 26-27 December, 1 January, Sunday dinner and Monday – **Rest** - seafood specialities - a la carte 18.00/34.00 ♀.
◆ Well-established, personally run 19C gabled lodge; informal, flagged bar hung with hunting trophies. Robust dishes, seafood specials, farm ciders and a real "local" feel.

PLUMTREE *Notts. – see Nottingham.*

PLUSH *Dorset* 503 M 31.
London 142 – Bournemouth 35 – Salisbury 44 – Taunton 52 – Weymouth 15 – Yeovil 23.

Brace of Pheasants, DT2 7RQ, ✆ (01300) 348357, , – P. MC VISA
closed 25 December and Monday except Bank Holidays – **Rest** a la carte 22.45/29.25 ♀.
◆ Secluded 16C inn, once two thatched cottages and smithy; Robust modern and classic dishes in a spacious bar or more formal parlour. Rear garden, woods and bridleways beyond.

PLYMOUTH *Plymouth* 503 H 32 *The West Country G. – pop. 243 795.*
See : *Town*★ – *Smeaton's Tower (*≤★★*)* AC **BZ T1** – *Plymouth Dome*★ AC **BZ** – *Royal Citadel (ramparts* ≤★★*)* AC **BZ** – *City Museum and Art Gallery*★ **BZ M1**.
Env. : *Saltram House*★★ *AC, E : 3½ m.* **BY A** – *Tamar River*★★ – *Anthony House*★ *AC, W : 5 m. by A 374 – Mount Edgcumbe (*≤★*) AC, SW : 2 m. by passenger ferry from Stonehouse* **AZ**.
Exc. : *NE : Dartmoor National Park*★★ – *Buckland Abbey*★★ *AC, N : 7½ m. by A 386* **ABY**.
18 *Staddon Heights, Plymstock* ✆ *(01752) 402475* – 9 *Elfordleigh Hotel G. & C.C., Colebrook, Plympton* ✆ *(01752) 336428.*
Tamar Bridge (toll) **AY**.
✈ *Plymouth City (Roborough) Airport :* ✆ *(01752) 204090, N : 3½ m. by A 386* **ABY**.
⛴ *to France (Roscoff) (Brittany Ferries) 1-3 daily (6 h) – to Spain (Santander) (Brittany Ferries) 2 weekly (approx. 24 h).*
ℹ *Island House, 9 The Barbican* ✆ *(01752) 304849 – Plymouth Discovery Centre, Crabtree* ✆ *(01752) 266030.*
London 242 – Bristol 124 – Southampton 161.

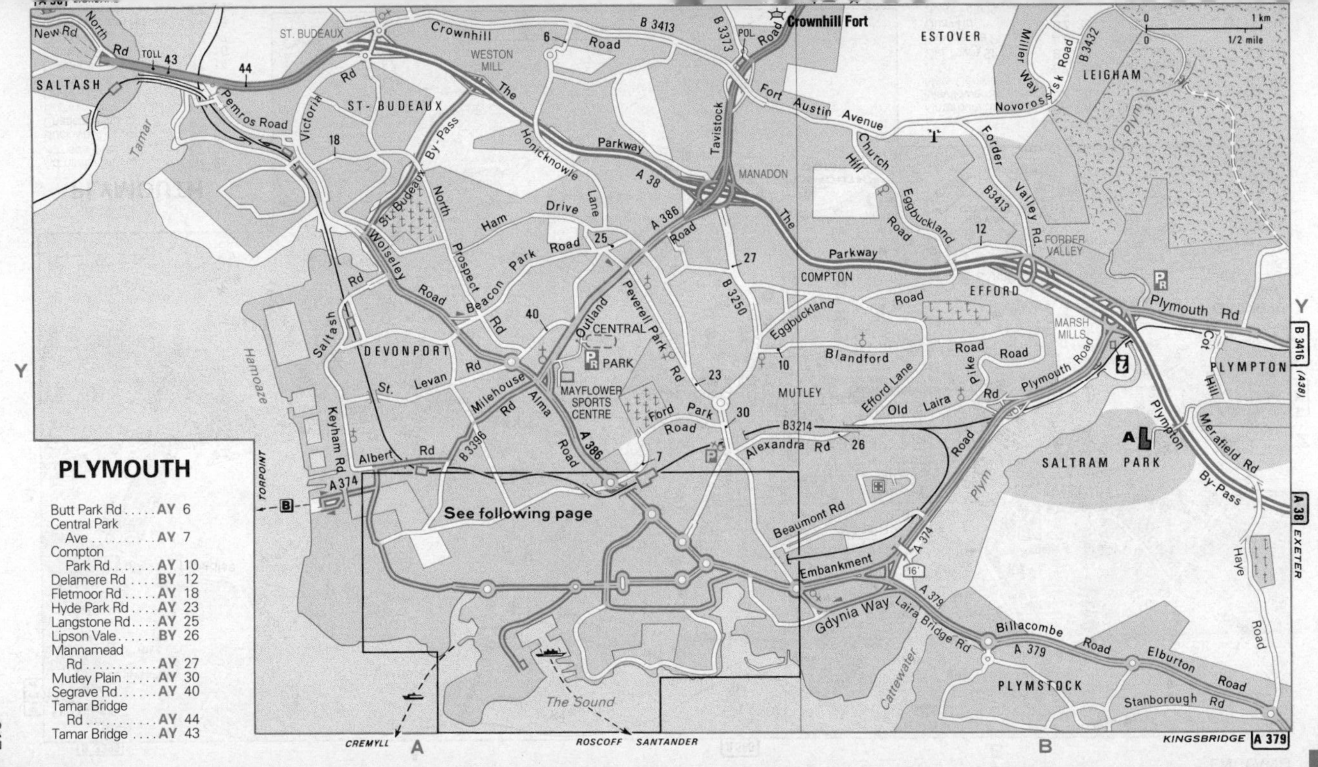

PLYMOUTH

Butt Park Rd . . . . . AY 6
Central Park Ave . . . . AY 7
Compton Park Rd . . . . AY 10
Delamere Rd . . . . BY 12
Fletmoor Rd . . . . . AY 18
Hyde Park Rd . . . . AY 23
Langstone Rd . . . . AY 25
Lipson Vale . . . . . . BY 26
Mannamead Rd . . . . AY 27
Mutley Plain . . . . . AY 30
Segrave Rd . . . . . . AY 40
Tamar Bridge Rd . . . . AY 44
Tamar Bridge . . . . AY 43

PLYMOUTH

Plymouth Hoe Moat House, Armada Way, PL1 2HJ, ☎ (01752) 639988, *reservations.plymouth@moathousehotels.com, Fax (01752) 673816,* ≤ city and Plymouth Sound, rest, 425. BZ s
Elliotts : **Rest** (bar lunch)/dinner 18.95 – 11.50 – **211 rm** 68.00/117.00 – 68.00/125.00.
◆ Substantial purpose-built hotel enjoys a panorama of the city skyline and the Plymouth Sound. Neatly laid-out, well-equipped bedrooms; extensive leisure club. Modern restaurant on top floor to make most of view.

Copthorne H. Plymouth, Armada Centre, Armada Way, PL1 1AR, (via Western Approach southbound) ☎ (01752) 224161, *sales.plymouth@mill-cop.com, Fax (01752) 670688,* – rm, rest, – 150. BZ e
Bentley's : **Rest** 20.00 (dinner) and a la carte 22.75/32.50 **s.** – 15.75 – **135 rm** 150.00 – 160.00.
◆ Popular with business travellers, a group-owned hotel in easy reach of the station. Smartly kept accommodation - quieter corner rooms look across the gardens or the city. Bentley's offers spacious, modern comforts.

The Duke of Cornwall, Millbay Rd, PL1 3LG, ☎ (01752) 275850, *info@thedukeofcornwallhotel.com, Fax (01752) 275854* – – 300. AZ c
closed 26-30 December – **Rest** (bar lunch)/dinner a la carte 26.40/30.50 **s.** – **69 rm** 90.00/150.00 – 120.00/160.00, 3 suites.
◆ Panelled bar with deep sofas and a relaxing atmosphere and individually styled rooms - some modern, some traditional - behind a locally famous, listed Victorian façade. Dining room centred on high-domed ceiling and sparkling chandelier.

Premier Travel Inn, 28 Sutton Rd, PL4 0HT, ☎ (0870) 9906458, *Fax (0870) 9906459* – rm, . BZ o
Rest (grill rest.) – **107 rm** 55.95/55.95 – 59.95/59.95.
◆ Opened in 2004 in a pleasant situation, close to the Aquarium, overlooking Sutton Harbour. Standard fitted bedrooms with desk. Popular grill dishes in dining room.

Premier Travel Inn, 1 Lockyers Quay, Coxside, PL4 0DX, ☎ (01752) 254180, *Fax (01752) 663872,* – rm, rest, – 20. BZ c
Rest (grill rest.) – **60 rm** 55.95/55.95 – 59.95/59.95.
◆ Near the Aquarium, a group-owned hotel offering trim, simply fitted accommodation in contemporary style. Family friendly dining, with some tables on a sheltered terrace.

Bowling Green without rest., 9-10 Osborne Pl, Lockyer St, The Hoe, PL1 2PU, ☎ (01752) 209090, *info@bowlingreenhotel.com, Fax (01752) 209092* – . BZ r
12 rm 42.00/54.00 – 58.00/62.00.
◆ A friendly couple run this fine Georgian house near the site of Sir Francis Drake's legendary game. High-ceilinged rooms in pine and modern fabrics; some have power showers.

Ashgrove without rest., 218 Citadel Rd, The Hoe, PL1 3BB, ☎ (01752) 664046, *ashgroveho@aol.com, Fax (01752) 252112* – . AZ l
closed 2 weeks Christmas-New Year – **9 rm** 32.00/47.00 – 50.00/60.00.
◆ Cream coloured 19C terraced house, with hanging baskets, on the Hoe. Hospitable owners. Bright, well-kept combined lounge and breakfast room. Immaculately appointed rooms.

Athenaeum Lodge without rest., 4 Athenaeum St, The Hoe, PL1 2RQ, ☎ (01752) 665005, *mi@athenaeumlodge.com, Fax (01752) 665005* – . BZ u
closed Christmas and New Year – **9 rm** 28.00/37.00 – 52.00/54.00.
◆ Trim bedrooms, all affordable, in a welcoming, invariably spotless, listed house, which is well run and family owned. A short walk from the historic Barbican district.

Berkeley's of St James without rest., 4 St James Place East, The Hoe, PL1 3AS, ☎ (01752) 221654, *Fax (01752) 221654* – . AZ n
closed 1 week Christmas – **5 rm** 35.00/45.00 – 55.00/60.00.
◆ Pristine, Victorian terraced house in a quiet street. Compact rooms in bright floral prints. The hearty, carefully sourced and all-organic breakfasts are a point of pride.

Tanners, Prysten House, Finewell St, PL1 2AE, ☎ (01752) 252001, *goodfood@tannersrestaurant.co.uk, Fax (01752) 252105,* – . BZ n
closed 25-26 and 31 December, first week January and Sunday – **Rest** (booking essential) 15.00/35.00.
◆ Characterful 15C house, reputedly Plymouth's oldest building: mullioned windows, tapestries, exposed stone and an illuminated water well. Modern, Mediterranean style cooking.

Artillery Tower, Firestone Bay, PL1 3QR, ☎ (01752) 257610, ≤ – . AZ a
closed Christmas-New Year, 2 weeks September, Sunday and Monday – **Rest** 23.50/31.00.
◆ Uniquely located in 500 year-old circular tower, built to defend the city. Courteous service of mostly well executed local dishes: blackboard fish specialities.

at Plympton *Northeast : 5 m. by A 374 on B 3416 – BY – ✉ Plymouth.*

Windwhistle Farm , Hemerdon, PL7 5BU, Northeast : 2 ½ m. by Glen Rd following signs for Newnham industrial estate then Hemerdon, turning left beside telephone box after Miners Arms in Hemerdon ☎ (01752) 340600, *rosemarie@windwhistlefarm.f9.co.uk, Fax (01752) 340600*, – P.
Rest (by arrangement) (communal dining) 15.00 – **3 rm** ★36.00 – ★★60.00.
◆ Bordered by woods, a peaceful guest house beside a two-acre garden and duckpond. Simple, modestly priced, cottage style bedrooms. Roaring log fire warms an intimate lounge. Meals in snug lounge using fresh ingredients.

PLYMPTON *Plymouth* 503 H 32 – *see Plymouth.*

POLPERRO *Cornwall* 503 G 33 *The West Country G.* – ✉ *Looe.*
See : *Village*★.
London 271 – Plymouth 28.

Trenderway Farm without rest., PL13 2LY, Northeast : 2 m. by A 387 ☎ (01503) 272214, *trenderwayfarm@hotmail.com, Fax (01503) 272991*, ≤, – P. MC VISA.
closed Christmas – **6 rm** ★50.00/80.00 – ★★70.00/90.00.
◆ Charming 16C farmhouse on working farm with converted outbuildings: modish ambience in a traditional setting. Breakfast over the lake. Stylish rooms with modern fabrics.

PONTELAND *Tyne and Wear* 501 502 O 19 – *see Newcastle upon Tyne.*

POOLE *Poole* 503 504 O 31 *The West Country G.* – *pop. 144 800.*
See : *Town*★ *(Waterfront* **M1** *, Scaplen's Court* **M2** *).*
Env. : *Compton Acres*★★, *(English Garden* ≤★★★*) AC, SE : 3 m. by B 3369* **BX** *(on Bournemouth town plan) – Brownsea Island*★ *(Baden-Powell Stone* ≤★★*) AC, by boat from Poole Quay or Sandbanks* **BX** *(on Bournemouth town plan).*
18 *Parkstone, Links Rd ☎ (01202) 707138 –* 18 *The Bulbury Club, Bulberry Lane, Lytchett Matravers ☎ (01929) 459574.*
to France (Cherbourg) (Brittany Ferries) 1-2 daily May-September (4 h 15 mn) day (5 h 45 mn) night – to France (St Malo) (Brittany Ferries) 4/7 weekly (8 h) – to France (St Malo) (Condor Ferries Ltd).
Welcome Centre, Enefco House, Poole Quay ☎ (01202) 262533.
London 116 – Bournemouth 4 – Dorchester 23 – Southampton 36 – Weymouth 28.

Plan of Built up Area : see Bournemouth

Haven, 161 Banks Rd, Sandbanks, BH13 7QL, Southeast : 4 ¼ m. on B 3369 ☎ (01202) 707333, *enquiries@havenhotel.co.uk, Fax (01202) 708796*, ≤ Ferry, Old Harry Rocks and Poole Bay, heated, – rest, rest, P – 160. MC AE VISA.
on Bournemouth town plan **BX c**
Seaview **: Rest** 17.50/24.50 (lunch) and a la carte 23.45/27.95 s. – (see ***La Roche*** below) – **76 rm** ★99.50/159.50 – ★★230.00/310.00, 2 suites.
◆ Sweeping white façade and heated seawater pool. Smart modern rooms. Lounge on site of Marconi's laboratory has fireside leather wing chairs. Candlelit Seaview overlooks bay.

Harbour Heights, Haven Rd, Sandbanks, BH13 7LW, Southeast : 3 m. by B 3369 ☎ (01202) 707272, *enquiries@harbourheights.net, Fax (01202) 708594*, ≤ Poole Harbour, – P – 50. MC AE VISA.
harbar bistro **: Rest** 21.00 (lunch) and a la carte 19.75/36.50 – **38 rm** ★145.00/155.00 – ★★240.00/270.00.
on Bournemouth town plan **BX n**
◆ 1920s hotel stylishly updated in 2003; walls decorated with vibrant modern art. Swanky, smart bedrooms boast modern interiors and all mod cons: request room with a sea view. Bistro-styled restaurant with very popular terrace.

Mansion House, 7-11 Thames St, BH15 1JN, off Poole Quay ☎ (01202) 685666, *enquiries@themansionhouse.co.uk, Fax (01202) 665709* – rest, P – 40. MC AE VISA.
a
closed 28-30 December – ***The Restaurant*** **: Rest** *(closed Sunday dinner and lunch Saturday and Bank Holidays)* 19.25/28.95 – ***Bistro*** **: Rest** *(closed Sunday lunch and Monday)* (residents only) 16.00/18.00 – **32 rm** ★75.00/105.00 – ★★130.00/145.00.
◆ Attractive, ivy-covered 18C town house in a narrow cobbled mews near the quay. An impressive staircase leads to Georgian-styled rooms, some with antique lamps and bedsteads. Cosy cherrywood-panelled Restaurant has paintings and naval prints. Informal Bistro.

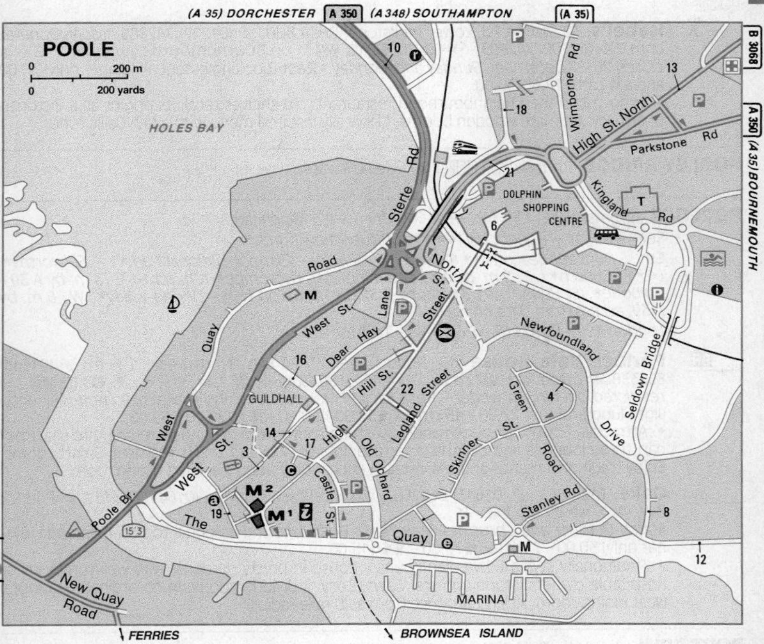

POOLE

Church St	3	Furnell Rd	8	New Orchard	16
Dolphin Quay Shopping Centre		High St		New St	17
Emerson Rd	4	Holes Bay Rd	10	Serpentine Rd	18
Falkland Square	6	Labrador Drive	12	Thames St	19
Fishermans Rd	7	Longfleet Rd	13	Towngate Bridge	21
		Market St	14	Westons Lane	22

Thistle Poole, The Quay, BH15 1HD, ✆ (0870) 333 9143, *poole@thistle.co.uk, Fax (0870) 333 9243,* ≤ – |≑| ⋟ P – 🏂 60. MC AE ⊙ VISA e
Rest (bar lunch Monday-Saturday) a la carte 18.40/30.40 s. – **70 rm** ☕ ★71.00/148.00 – ★★88.00/158.00.
◆ Purpose-built, redbrick, group hotel on the quay; informal bar; neatly laid-out rooms - half of which have views over the water - in sober blue fabrics and pine furniture. Fine outlook from wide-windowed restaurant.

Express Holiday Inn without rest., Walking Field Lane, BH15 1RZ, ✆ (01202) 649222, *poole@khl.uk.com, Fax (01202) 649666* – |≑| ⋟ ✆ ♿ P – 🏂 30. MC AE ⊙ VISA. ⋟ i
85 rm ★66.00/79.00 – ★★66.00/79.00.
◆ Modern lodge accommodation in central location within walking distance of shops and restaurants. Complimentary continental breakfast. Well appointed, comfy rooms.

Premier Travel Inn, Holes Bay Rd, BH15 2BD, ✆ (01202) 669944, *Fax (01202) 669954* – ⋟ rm, ♿ P. MC AE ⊙ VISA. ⋟ r
Rest (grill rest.) – **40 rm** ★55.95 – ★★55.95.
◆ A consistent standard of trim, simply fitted rooms in modern style, ideal for business stopovers and not far from the station. Informal pub dining at adjacent Brewers Fayre.

La Roche (at Haven H.), 161 Banks Rd, Sandbanks, BH13 7QL, Southeast : 4 ¼ m. on B 3369 ✆ (01202) 707333, *Fax (01202) 708796,* ≤ Ferry, Old Harry Rocks and Poole Bay, 🏖 – ⋟ P. MC AE ⊙ VISA
on Bournemouth town plan BX c
closed Sunday dinner and Monday – **Rest** a la carte 28.95/35.45 s. ♀.
◆ Perched at the side of the Haven, overlooking the bay. Watch the fishing boats from wonderful adjacent terrace. Eclectic menus with seafood base and tasty local ingredients.

Isabel's, 32 Station Rd, Lower Parkstone, BH14 8UD, ✆ (01202) 747885, *isabels@onetel.com, Fax (01202) 747885* – ⇔ 20. MC AE VISA on Bournemouth town plan BX a
closed 26-27 December, Sunday and Monday – **Rest** (booking essential) (dinner only) 30.00 and a la carte 24.60/30.60.
◆ Long-established neighbourhood restaurant; old shelves recall its origins as a Victorian pharmacy. Intimate wooden booths. Classically inspired menu with a rich Gallic tone.

POOLEY BRIDGE *Cumbria* 501 502 L 20 – *see Ullswater.*

PORLOCK *Somerset* 503 J 30 *The West Country G.* – ✉ *Minehead.*
See : *Village*★ – *Porlock Hill* (≤★★) – *St Dubricius Church*★.
Env. : *Dunkery Beacon*★★★ (≤★★★), *S : 5½ m.* – *Exmoor National Park*★★ – *Selworthy*★ (≤★★, *Church*★), *E : 2 m. by A 39 and minor rd* – *Luccombe*★ (*Church*★), *E : 3 m. by A 39* – *Culbone*★ (*St Beuno*), *W : 3½ m. by B 3225, 1½ m. on foot* – *Doone Valley*★, *W : 6 m. by A 39, access from Oare on foot.*
London 190 – Bristol 67 – Exeter 46 – Taunton 28.

Porlock Vale House, Porlock Weir, TA24 8NY, Northwest : 1¼ m. ✆ (01643) 862338, *info@porlockvale.co.uk, Fax (01643) 863338,* ≤, – P. MC AE VISA
restricted opening in winter – **Rest** *(closed Monday)* (booking essential to non-residents) (light lunch)/dinner 27.00 – **15 rm** ★55.00/110.00 – ★★120.00/160.00.
◆ Attractive Edwardian house and equestrian centre with grounds stretching to sea. Cosy bar, three lounges and delightful terrace; lots of Arts and Crafts features. Smart rooms. Enjoy traditional menus and sea vistas in enchanting wood-panelled dining room.

Oaks, TA24 8ES, ✆ (01643) 862265, *oakshotel@aol.com, Fax (01643) 863131,* ≤ Porlock Bay, – P. MC VISA.
March-October and Christmas-New Year – **Rest** (booking essential to non-residents) (dinner only) 30.00 – **7 rm** ★77.00 – ★★115.00.
◆ Traditionally styled Edwardian country house in pretty gardens, very well run by most hospitable owners. Stunning rural views. Cosy, individual rooms in co-ordinated colours. Neat dining room: all land produce from a 20 mile radius.

PORT ERIN *Isle of Man* 502 F 21 – *see Man (Isle of).*

PORTHLEVEN *Cornwall.*
London 284.5 – Helston 3 – Penzance 12.5.

The Smoke House, TR13 9JS, ✆ (01326) 563223, *thesmokehouse@btconnect.com, Fax (01326) 563223,* – MC VISA
restricted opening in winter – **Rest** a la carte 19.25/29.15 ♀.
◆ Small boats bob around this pretty fishing port; watch them from the terrace. Inside, sit at cosy leather chairs and enjoy friendly service of eclectic, Asian inspired menus.

PORTINSCALE *Cumbria* – *see Keswick.*

PORTISHEAD *Bristol* 503 504 M 28.
London 132 – Bristol 9 – Weston-super-Mare 20.

Premier Travel Inn, Wyndham Way, BS20 7GA, East : ½ m. by A 369 ✆ (0870) 1977212, *Fax (01275) 846534* – rest, P. MC AE VISA.
Rest (grill rest.) – **58 rm** ★49.95 – ★★49.95.
◆ Good value, purpose-built lodge accommodation handily situated just outside busy town. Modern, well-proportioned rooms. Bright, bustling grill restaurant for meals.

PORTLOE *Cornwall* 503 F 33 – ✉ *Truro.*
London 296 – St Austell 15 – Truro 15.

Lugger, TR2 5RD, ✆ (01872) 501322, *office@luggerhotel.com, Fax (01872) 501691,* ≤, – P. MC AE VISA.
Rest (light lunch)/dinner 37.50 ♀ – **22 rm** (dinner included) ★140.00/180.00 – ★★200.00/250.00.
◆ Former inn in a beautiful location within pretty Cornish cove. Stylish public areas. The bedrooms are created with a tasteful palette in strikingly contemporary vein. Restaurant enjoys blissful outlook over the cove.

PORT ST MARY *I.O.M.* 502 F/G 21 – *see Man (Isle of).*

PORTSCATHO *Cornwall* 503 F 33 *The West Country G.* – ✉ *Truro.*

Env. : *St Just-in-Roseland Church*★★, *W : 4 m. by A 3078 – St Anthony-in-Roseland* (≤★★) *S : 3½ m.*

London 298 – Plymouth 55 – Truro 16.

Rosevine, Rosevine, TR2 5EW, North : 2 m. by A 3078 ☎ (01872) 580206, *info@rosevine.co.uk, Fax (01872) 580230,* ≤, , , , – ⇌ P. MC AE VISA
7 February-5 November – **Rest** (bar lunch)/dinner 38.00 **s.** ♀ – **17 rm** ☕ ★128.00 – ★★226.00.
◆ Surrounded by attractive gardens, this family owned hotel offers traditional, homely comforts. Rooms are well looked after and a friendly air prevails. Pretty restaurant makes use of local ingredients.

Driftwood , Rosevine, TR2 5EW, North : 2 m. by A 3078 ☎ (01872) 580644, *info@driftwoodhotel.co.uk, Fax (01872) 580801,* ≤ Gerrans Bay, – ⇌ P. MC AE VISA.
closed Christmas-February – **Rest** *(closed Sunday dinner to non-residents)* (booking essential) (dinner only) 38.00 ♀ – **15 rm** ☕ ★135.00/142.50 – ★★200.00/210.00.
◆ Stylish décor and a neutral, contemporary feel make this an enviable spot to lay one's head. Attractive decking affords fine sea views. Smart bedrooms with pristine style. Distinctive modern dining room with fine vistas.

PORTSMOUTH and SOUTHSEA *Portsmouth* 503 504 Q 31 *Great Britain G.* – *pop. 187 056.*

See : *City*★ – *Naval Portsmouth* BY : *H.M.S. Victory*★★★ *AC, The Mary Rose*★★, *Royal Naval Museum*★★ *AC – Old Portsmouth*★ BYZ : *The Point* (≤★★) - *St Thomas Cathedral*★ – *Southsea (Castle*★ *AC)* AZ – *Royal Marines Museum, Eastney*★ *AC,* AZ **M1.**

Env. : *Portchester Castle*★ *AC, NW : 5½ m. by A 3 and A 27* AY.

18 *Great Salterns, Portsmouth Golf Centre, Burrfields Rd* ☎ *(023) 9266 4549* AY – 18 *Crookhorn Lane, Widley, Waterlooville* ☎ *(023) 9237 2210* – 18 *Southwick Park, Pinsley Drive, Southwick* ☎ *(023) 9238 0131.*

to France (St Malo) (Brittany Ferries) daily (8 h 45 mn) day (10 h 45 mn) night – to France (Caen) (Brittany Ferries) 2-3 daily (6 h) day (6 h 45 mn) night – to France (Cherbourg) (P & O Portsmouth) 3-4 daily (5 h) day, (7 h) night – to France (Le Havre) (P & O Portsmouth) 3 daily (5 h 30 mn/7 h 30 mn) – to France (Cherbourg) (Brittany Ferries) 2-3 daily (2 h 45 mn) – to France (Caen) (Brittany Ferries) 2-3 daily (3 h 25 mn) – to Spain (Bilbao) (P & O European Ferries Ltd) 1-2 weekly (35 h) – to Guernsey (St Peter Port) and Jersey (St Helier) (Condor Ferries Ltd) daily except Sunday (10 hrs) – to the Isle of Wight (Fishbourne) (Wightlink Ltd) frequent services daily (35 mn).

to the Isle of Wight (Ryde) (Wightlink Ltd) frequent services daily (15 mn) – from Southsea to the Isle of Wight (Ryde) (Hovertravel Ltd) frequent services daily (10 mn).

The Hard ☎ *(023) 9282 6722, tic@portsmouthcc.gov.uk – Clarence Esplanade* ☎ *(023) 9282 6722.*

London 78 – Brighton 48 – Salisbury 44 – Southampton *21.*

Plans on following pages

Beaufort, 71 Festing Rd, Southsea, PO4 0NQ, ☎ (023) 9282 3707, *enq@beaufortho tel.co.uk, Fax (023) 9287 0270* – ⇌ P. MC AE VISA. AZ n
closed 25-26 December – **Rest** (dinner only) 19.50 **s.** ♀ – **20 rm** ☕ ★40.00/70.00 – ★★70.00/90.00.
◆ Privately owned Southsea hotel, a few minutes from the water. Sizeable and well-kept bedrooms in smart modern décor. Cosy sitting room with leather chesterfields. Sprays of flowers brighten traditional dining room.

Upper Mount House without rest., The Vale, Clarendon Rd, PO5 2EQ, ☎ (023) 9282 0456, *Fax (023) 9282 0456* – ⇌ P. MC VISA. CZ e
closed 1 week Christmas – **16 rm** ☕ ★34.00/42.00 – ★★56.00.
◆ Privately managed, gabled Victorian villa, set in a quiet suburb. Handsomely sized rooms in varying styles, some with four poster beds, all simply appointed.

Premier Travel Inn, Long Curtain Rd, Southsea, PO4 3AA, ☎ (023) 9273 4622, *Fax (023) 9273 5048* – ⇌ rm, ♿ P. MC AE VISA. BZ r
Rest (grill rest.) – **40 rm** ★52.95 – ★★52.95.
◆ Purpose-built lodge hotel by the waterfront amusement arcade. Trim, simply fitted accommodation in bright modern décor. Family rooms, ideal for short breaks.

Fortitude Cottage without rest., 51 Broad St, Old Portsmouth, PO1 2JD, ☎ (023) 9282 3748, *fortcott@aol.com, Fax (023) 9282 3748* – ⇌. MC VISA. BY c
closed Christmas – **4 rm** ☕ ★45.00/70.00 – ★★70.00.
◆ Pretty little quayside townhouse named after an 18C battleship. Watch yachts rounding the Point from a cosy bow windowed lounge. Simple, well-priced rooms, charming owners.

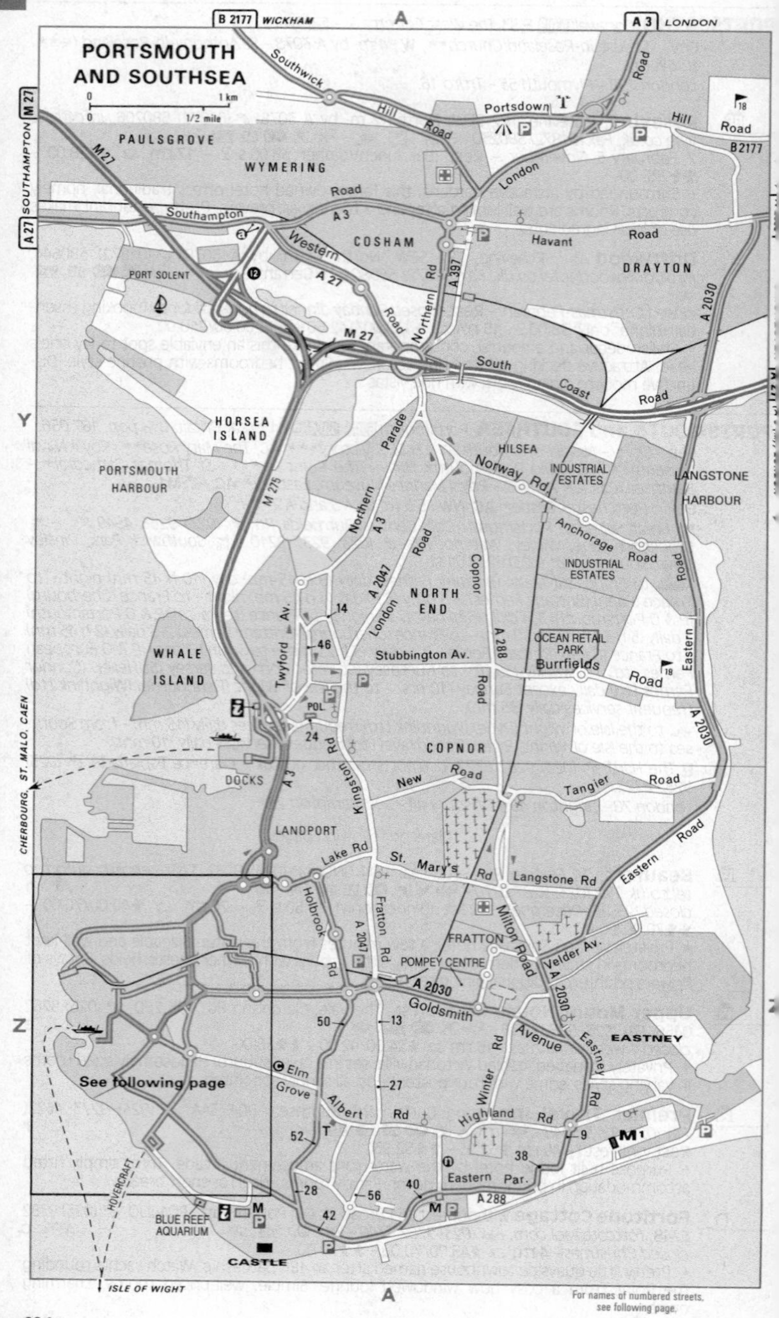
PORTSMOUTH AND SOUTHSEA
0
1 km
1/2 mile
B 2177 WICKHAM
A
A 3 LONDON
M 27
SOUTHAMPTON
A 27
PAULSGROVE
WYMERING
Southwick
Hill
Road
Portsdown
Hill
Road
B2177
London
Road
Southampton
Road
A 3
Western
A 27
Road
COSHAM
Havant
Road
DRAYTON
PORT SOLENT
Northern
Rd
A 397
M 27
South
Coast
Road
A 2030
HORSEA ISLAND
Y
PORTSMOUTH HARBOUR
HILSEA
Norway Rd.
INDUSTRIAL ESTATES
LANGSTONE HARBOUR
Northern
Parade
A 3
M 275
Anchorage
Road
INDUSTRIAL ESTATES
London
Road
A 2047
Copnor
Road
NORTH END
Eastern
Road
Twyford Av.
14
46
Stubbington Av.
OCEAN RETAIL PARK
Burrfields
Road
18
WHALE ISLAND
POL
24
Kingston
Rd
COPNOR
A 288
A 2030
CHERBOURG, ST. MALO, CAEN
DOCKS
New
Road
Tangier
Road
A 3
LANDPORT
Lake Rd
St.
Mary's
Rd
Langstone Rd
Eastern
Road
Holbrook
Rd
Fratton
Rd
A 2047
Milton Road
FRATTON
Velder Av.
A 2030
POMPEY CENTRE
A 2030
Goldsmith
Avenue
Z
50
13
Eastney
Rd
EASTNEY
Elm
Grove
See following page
27
Albert
Rd
Winter
Rd
Highland
Rd
52
T
9
M1
38
Eastern
Par.
A 288
HOVERCRAFT
28
56
40
42
M
BLUE REEF AQUARIUM
M
CASTLE
ISLE OF WIGHT
A
For names of numbered streets,
see following page.

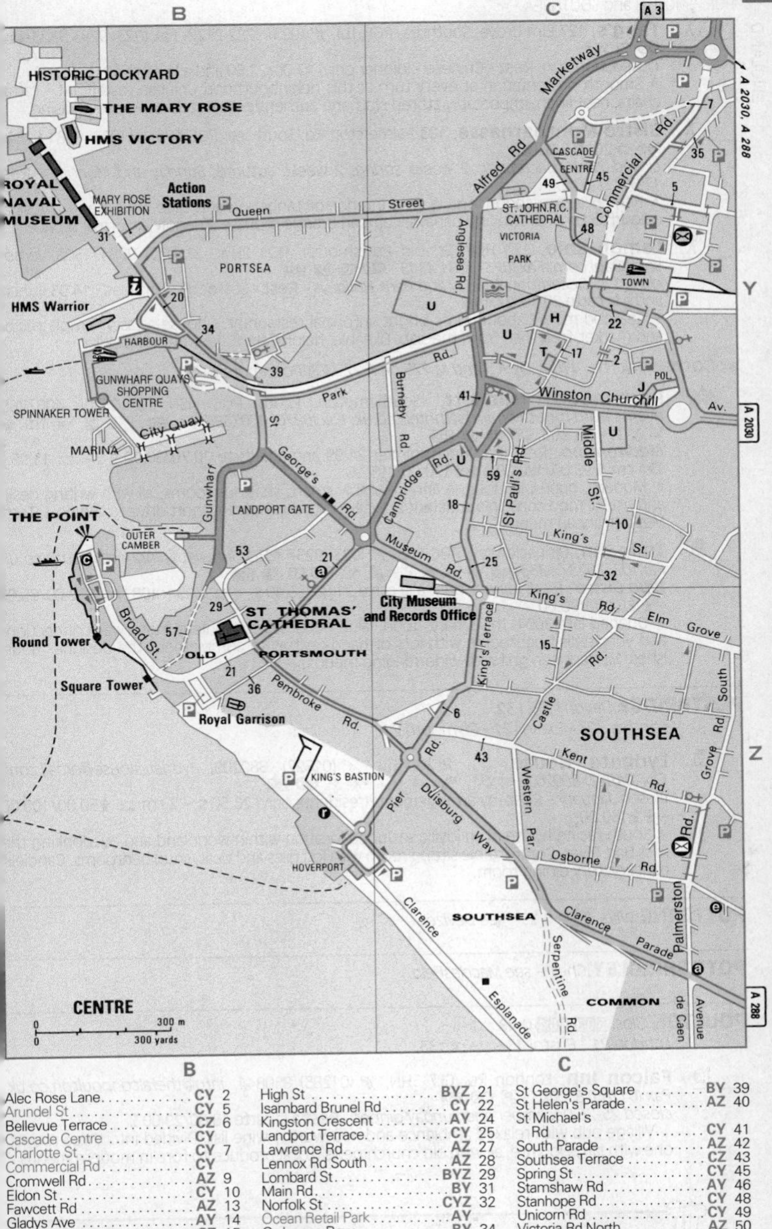

B
C
A 3
HISTORIC DOCKYARD
THE MARY ROSE
HMS VICTORY
ROYAL NAVAL MUSEUM
MARY ROSE EXHIBITION
Action Stations
Queen
Street
Marketway
Alfred Rd
CASCADE CENTRE
Commercial Rd.
A 2030. A 288
ST. JOHN.R.C. CATHEDRAL
VICTORIA PARK
Anglesea Rd.
PORTSEA
HMS Warrior
HARBOUR
GUNWHARF QUAYS SHOPPING CENTRE
SPINNAKER TOWER
City Quay
MARINA
TOWN
Y
Park
Rd.
Burnaby Rd.
Winston Churchill Av.
A 2030
St
George's Rd.
Gunwharf
LANDPORT GATE
Cambridge Rd.
St Paul's Rd.
Middle St.
King's St.
THE POINT
OUTER CAMBER
Museum Rd.
King's Rd.
Elm Grove
Round Tower
Broad St.
ST THOMAS' CATHEDRAL
City Museum and Records Office
OLD PORTSMOUTH
King's Terrace
Square Tower
Pembroke Rd.
Royal Garrison
Castle Rd.
SOUTHSEA
South Rd.
Z
KING'S BASTION
Pier Rd.
Duisburg Way
Western Par.
Kent Rd.
Grove Rd.
Osborne Rd.
HOVERPORT
Clarence
Clarence Parade
SOUTHSEA
Serpentine Rd.
Palmerston Rd.
Esplanade
COMMON
de Caen Avenue
A 288
CENTRE
300 m
300 yards

ENGLAND

Tang's, 127 Elm Grove, Southsea, PO5 1LJ, (023) 9282 2722, *Fax (023) 9283 8323* – AE VISA AZ c
closed Monday – **Rest** - Chinese - (dinner only) 17.00/22.50 and a la carte 12.00/19.00.
• Smooth presentation at every turn at this neighbourhood Chinese restaurant - rattan chairs, neat linen, impeccably attired staff and authentic, delicately composed cuisine.

Bistro Montparnasse, 103 Palmerston Rd, Southsea, PO5 3PS, (023) 9281 6754 – 20. AE VISA CZ a
closed 25-26 December, 2 weeks spring, 2 weeks autumn, Sunday and Monday – **Rest** 17.50/27.50.
• Behind a trim shop front, a vivid interior of tangerine and blue. The menu is just as colourful: tuna, prawn and papaya, Campari orange mousse. Friendly, informal service.

Lemon Sole, 123 High St, Old Portsmouth, PO1 2HW, (023) 9281 1303, *lemonsoles@aol.com, Fax (023) 9281 1345* – AE VISA BY a
closed 25 December, Sunday and Bank Holidays – **Rest** - Seafood specialities - 14.95 (lunch) and a la carte 20.15/27.15.
• Seafood motifs abound in a bright, informal restaurant. Choose a tasty, simple recipe and market-fresh fish from the slab. Likeable, helpful staff. Part 14C wine cellar.

at Cosham *North : 4½ m. by A 3 and M 275 on A 27 – Portsmouth.*

Portsmouth Marriott, Southampton Road, PO6 4SH, (0870) 4007285, *events.portsmouth@marriotthotels.co.uk, Fax (0870) 4007385,* – rm, – 300. AE VISA AY a
Mediterrano : **Rest** (bar lunch)/dinner 21.95 and a la carte 20.70/30.90 **s** – 13.95 – **174 rm** 98.00/180.00 – 120.00/195.00.
• Modern, open-plan lounge and invariably smart, spacious rooms, all with writing desks and useful mod cons, in a substantial, well-run group hotel. A short drive to the port. Tasty Mediterranean menus.

Tulip Inn, Binnacle Way, PO6 4FB, (023) 9237 3333, *info@tulipinnportsmouth.co.uk, Fax (023) 9237 3335* – – 30. AE VISA
Bibo Bistro : **Rest** *(dinner only)* a la carte 21.85/26.40 **s.** – 7.95 – **108 rm** 62.00/85.00 – 67.00/90.00.
• Opened late 2004, this smart, good value hotel has convenient motorway connections and very stylish bedrooms with lots of handy extras to complement the designer flourishes. Modern bar/grill with wide-ranging menus.

POSTBRIDGE *Devon* 503 I 32.
London 207 – Exeter 21 – Plymouth 21.

Lydgate House , PL20 6TJ, (01822) 880209, *lydgatehouse@email.com, Fax (01822) 880202,* – VISA
closed January – **Rest** (by arrangement) (residents only) 26.50 **s.** – **7 rm** 50.00/100.00 – 130.00.
• South facing house in an idyllic secluded location within woodland and overlooking the East Dart River. Comfortable sitting room with log fires and neat, snug bedrooms. Candlelit conservatory dining room.

POTTERNE *Wilts.* 503 O 29 – *see Devizes.*

POTT SHRIGLEY *Ches.* – *see Macclesfield.*

POULTON *Glos.* 503 504 O 28.
London 91 – Bristol 43 – Oxford 33.

Falcon Inn, London Rd, GL7 5HN, (01285) 850844, *info@thefalconpoulton.co.uk, Fax (01285) 850403* – VISA
closed 25-26 December and Sunday dinner – **Rest** a la carte 18.00/29.00.
• Village pub with relaxed ambience and noteworthy wine list. Divided into three rooms, one with large log fire, all with old church pews. Local produce to fore in modern menus.

The award is the crème de la crème. This is awarded to restaurants which are really worth travelling miles for!

PRESTBURY *Ches.* 502 503 504 N 24 – *pop. 3 269.*

De Vere Mottram Hall, Wilmslow Rd, Mottram St Andrews (01625) 828135.

London 184 – Liverpool 43 – Manchester 17 – Stoke-on-Trent 25.

De Vere Mottram Hall, Wilmslow Rd, Mottram St Andrew, SK10 4QT, Northwest : 2 ¼ m. on A 538 (01625) 828135, *dmh.sales@devere-hotels.com, Fax (01625) 828950*, squash – 200. VISA. ***Nathaniel's*** **:** **Rest** *(closed Saturday lunch)* (live music Saturday evenings) a la carte 22.85/37.90 **s.** – **128 rm** 140.00 – 150.00, 3 suites.
◆ Imposing part 18C mansion. Traditional rooms are larger in the manor. Lovely cocktail bar. Championship golf course crosses wooded parkland. Classically decorated dining room named after the original owner of the house; modern cooking.

White House Manor, The Village, SK10 4HP, (01625) 829376, *mail@thewhitehouse.uk.com, Fax (01625) 828627*, – VISA. *closed 25-26 December* – **Rest** – (room service or see ***White House*** below) – 9.50 – **11 rm** 75.00/90.00 – 140.00.
◆ Privately run 18C redbrick house with stylish, unique and individually decorated rooms which provide every luxury. Breakfast in your room or in the conservatory.

The Bridge, The Village, SK10 4DQ, (01625) 829326, *reception@bridge-hotel.co.uk, Fax (01625) 827557*, – rm, – 100. VISA. **Rest** 12.50/17.95 and a la carte 27.00/42.45 – 9.75 – **23 rm** 50.00/60.00 – 87.00/130.00.
◆ Dating back to the 1600s, a sympathetically extended hotel on the river Bollin. Classic, subtly co-ordinated décor in rooms, more characterful in the old timbered house. Live music at weekends in the beamed, galleried hall of the restaurant.

XX **White House,** The Village, SK10 4DG, (01625) 829376, *mail@thewhitehouse.uk.com, Fax (01625) 828627* – VISA. *closed 25 December, Monday lunch and Sunday dinner* – **Rest** 18.95 (lunch) and a la carte 26.65/34.20.
◆ 18c whitewashed farmhouse, a striking high street conversion: chic, modern and stylish. Informal bar lunches, or eat at linen-clad tables from menu of interesting dishes.

PRESTON 502 L 22 – *pop. 184 836.*

Fulwood Hall Lane, Fulwood (01772) 700011 – Ingol, Tanterton Hall Rd (01772) 734556 – Aston & Lea, Tudor Ave, Blackpool Rd (01772) 735282 – Penwortham, Blundell Lane (01772) 744630.

The Guildhall, Lancaster Rd (01772) 253731.

London 226 – Blackpool 18 – Burnley 22 – Liverpool 30 – Manchester 34 – Stoke-on-Trent 65.

The Park, 209 Tulketh Rd, PR2 1ES, Northwest : 2 ¼ m. by A 6 off (01772) 726250, *parkrestauranthotel@hotmail.com, Fax (01772) 723743* – VISA. *closed 25 December* – **Rest** (dinner only) a la carte approx 26.00 **s.** – **14 rm** 45.00/55.00 – 75.00/90.00.
◆ Built in 1903, a turreted, redbrick villa in a quiet suburb. Original hall - antique tiling and stained glass. Traditional rooms with greater personality in the old house. Light dining room dominated by black marble fireplace.

Premier Travel Inn, Bluebell Way, Preston East Link Rd, Fulwood, PR2 3RU, Northeast : 3 ¼ by B 6243 (Longridge rd) off B 6242 (Preston East) (01772) 651580, *Fax (01772) 651619* – rest, – 30. VISA. **Rest** (grill rest.) – **65 rm** 46.95/46.95 – 48.95/48.95.
◆ Simply furnished and brightly decorated bedrooms with ample work space; useful for business stopovers. Adjacent grill restaurant.

XX **Winckley Square Chop House,** 23 Winckley Sq, PR1 3JJ, (01772) 252732, *chophouse@heathcotes.co.uk, Fax (01772) 203433* – VISA. **Rest** a la carte 24.50/36.00 – ***Olive Press*** **:** **Rest** *(closed Bank Holidays)* a la carte 16.50/27.00.
◆ Chic and contemporary restaurant with a cuisine style that handsomely matches the surroundings. Robust, balanced, classic British cooking with some regional input. Spacious basement bar-bistro serving pizzas and pastas.

XX **Inside Out,** 100 Higher Walton Rd, Walton-le-Dale, PR5 4HR, Southeast : 1 ¾ m. by A 6 on A 675 (01772) 251366, *Fax (01772) 258918*, – VISA. *closed 25-26 December, 2 weeks January, Saturday lunch and Monday* – **Rest** 12.00/15.00 and a la carte 18.50/28.00.
◆ Inside - a chic and stylish restaurant; 'out' - a lovely decked terrace with heaters overlooking a garden. Well sourced, quality ingredients assembled with love and flair.

ENGLAND

at Broughton *North : 3 m. on A 6 – ✉ Preston.*

Preston Marriott, 418 Garstang Rd, PR3 5JB, ☎ (0870) 4007231, *frontdesk.preston@marriotthotels.co.uk, Fax (0870) 4007331,* – 🅿 – 200. VISA.

Rest (bar lunch Monday-Saturday)/dinner 23.50 and a la carte 22.90/35.85 s. –
***Broughton Brasserie*: Rest** (dinner only and Sunday lunch) a la carte 22.90/35.85 –
149 rm 118.00 – 128.00, 1 suite.

◆ Sympathetically extended 19C redbrick house in wooded grounds offers airy modern accommodation: more traditional comfort in original house rooms. Up-to-date leisure club. Easy-going lounge/restaurant. Formal, linen-clad Broughton Brasserie.

Ibis without rest., Garstang Rd, PR3 5JE, South : ¾ m. off A 6 ☎ (01772) 861800, *h3162@accor.com, Fax (01772) 861900* – 🅿 – 40. VISA
82 rm 45.95 – 45.95.

◆ Excellent motorway connections from this purpose-built lodge. Neatly laid-out and simply fitted accommodation in contemporary style: the rear-facing bedrooms are quieter.

PUCKRUP *Glos. – see Tewkesbury.*

PUDLESTON *Herefordshire – see Leominster.*

PUDSEY *W. Yorks.* 502 P 22 – *see Leeds.*

LA PULENTE *Jersey (Channel Islands)* 503 P 33 and 517 ⑪ – *see Channel Islands.*

PULHAM MARKET *Norfolk* 504 X 26 – *pop. 919* – ✉ *Diss.*
London 106 – Cambridge 58 – Ipswich 29 – Norwich 16.

Old Bakery without rest., Church Walk, IP21 4SL, ☎ (01379) 676492, *jean@theoldbakery.net, Fax (01379) 676492,* – 🅿.
Closed Christmas – **3 rm** 45.00/55.00 – 64.00/68.00.

◆ Characterful Elizabethan house on village green: spacious timbered rooms hold antiques or comfy armchairs; toiletries by local herbalist. Pretty garden with summer house.

PURTON *Wilts.* 503 504 O 29 – *pop. 3 328* – ✉ *Swindon.*
London 94 – Bristol 41 – Gloucester 31 – Oxford 38 – Swindon 5.

Pear Tree at Purton, Church End, SN5 4ED, South : ½ m. by Church St on Lydiard Millicent rd ☎ (01793) 772100, *stay@peartreepurton.co.uk, Fax (01793) 772369,* – 🅿 – 50. VISA
closed 26-30 December – **Rest** *(closed lunch Saturday and Bank Holidays)* 18.50/32.50 –
15 rm 110.00/140.00 – 110.00/140.00, 2 suites.

◆ Personally run, extended 16C sandstone vicarage in mature seven-acre garden. Spacious flower-filled lounge. Rooms with traditional comforts and thoughtful extras. Conservatory restaurant overlooks wild flower borders.

QUORNDON *Leics.* 502 503 504 Q 25 – *see Loughborough.*

RAINHAM *Essex* 504 U 29.
London 14 – Basildon 16 – Dartford 9.

The Manor, Berwick Pond Rd, RM13 9EL, North : ¾ m. ☎ (01708) 555586, *info@themanoressex.co.uk, Fax (01708) 630055,* – rest, 🅿 – 100. VISA.

Rest *(closed Saturday lunch and Sunday dinner)* a la carte 21.60/37.75 s – **14 rm** 99.00 – 99.00/129.00.

◆ This ultra stylish hotel, opened in 2004, has a distinctive, contemporary feel and a lovely rear garden; smart, compact conference facility. Elegant and modish bedrooms. Appealing menus with wide-ranging modern dishes.

The sun's out – let's eat al fresco! Look for a terrace:

RAMSBOTTOM *Gtr Manchester* 502 N 23 – *pop. 17 352.*
London 223 – Blackpool 39 – Burnley 12 – Leeds 46 – Manchester 13 – Liverpool 39.

Ramsons, 18 Market Pl, BL0 9HT, (01706) 825070 – . MO VISA
closed Sunday dinner, Monday and Tuesday – **Rest** - Italian influences - 25.00 and a la carte 28.50/43.50 s.
◆ Passionately run and slightly quirky, this well-regarded eatery offers mostly Italian influenced cooking utilising refined ingredients. Accompanying fine wine list.

RAMSEY *Isle of Man* 502 G 21 – *see Man (Isle of).*

RAMSGILL-IN-NIDDERDALE *N. Yorks.* 502 O 21 – *see Pateley Bridge.*

RAYLEIGH *Essex* 504 V 29 – *pop. 30 629.*
London 35 – Chelmsford 13 – Southend-on-Sea 6.

Express by Holiday Inn without rest., Rayleigh Weir, Arterial Rd, SS6 7SP, South : ½ m. by A 129 at junction with A 127 (01268) 775001, *express-rayleigh@btconnect.com, Fax (01268) 777505* – – 30. MO AE VISA.
49 rm 59.95 – 59.95.
◆ Compact, purpose-built hotel in a useful location near major road junction; complimentary continental buffet breakfast. Comfortable family rooms with all mod cons.

READING *Reading* 503 504 Q 29 – *pop. 232 662.*
Calcot Park, Bath Rd, Calcot (0118) 942 7124.
Whitchurch Bridge (toll).
to Henley-on-Thames (Salter Bros. Ltd) (summer only).
Church House, Chain St (0118) 956 6226.
London 43 – Brighton 79 – Bristol 78 – Croydon 47 – Luton 62 – Oxford 28 – Portsmouth 67 – Southampton 46.

Plan on next page

Holiday Inn Reading, Caversham Bridge, Richfield Ave, RG1 8BD, (0118) 925 9988, *reservations@readingholidayinn.co.uk, Fax (0118) 939 1665,* , , , , – , rest, – 200. MO AE VISA. X e
Rest *(closed Saturday lunch)* 18.00 and a la carte 23.00/30.50 **s** – 13.95 – **120.00** 130.00/155.00 – 130.00/155.00, 2 suites.
◆ Modern purpose-built hotel just out of centre on banks of Thames. Spacious public areas with large windows which look towards river. Executive rooms boast extra touches. Bright restaurant.

Renaissance Reading, Oxford Rd, RG1 7RH, (0118) 958 6222, *Fax (0118) 959 7842,* , , – , rm, – 220. MO AE VISA. Z i
Rest 13.50/21.50 and a la carte approx 24.50 – 12.50 – **195 rm** 142.00 – 157.00, 1 suite.
◆ Bustling, centrally located hotel, adjacent to Hexagon Theatre. Views improve with altitude. Business emphasis; leisure facilities a highlight. Comfortable, uniform rooms. Restaurant has comfortable, well organised air.

Millennium Madejski, Madejski Stadium, RG2 0FL, South : 1 ½ m. by A 33 (0118) 925 3500, *sales.reading@mill-cop.com, Fax (0118) 925 3501,* , , , – , rm, – 600. MO AE VISA X v
Cilantro : **Rest** (dinner only) 49.50 **s.** – ***Le Café :*** **Rest** *(closed Saturday lunch)* a la carte 26.50/31.00 **s.** – 15.75 – **132 rm** 200.00 – 200.00, 8 suites.
◆ Purpose-built hotel, in modern retail park, adjacent to Madejski sports stadium. Imposing Atrium lounge-bar and marble floored lobby. Stylish, inviting rooms. Impressively smart Cilantro. Informal Le Café is open plan to Atrium lounge.

Holiday Inn, 500 Basingstoke Rd, RG2 0SL, South : 2 ½ m. by A 33 (0870) 4009067, *reading@ichotelsgroup.com, Fax (0118) 931 1958,* , , – rm, – 110. MO AE VISA. X a
Rest 13.50 **s.** and a la carte – 14.95 – **202 rm** 50.00/135.00 – 50.00/135.00.
◆ Large purpose-built hotel out of the city centre in residential area. Smart, modern furniture and fittings. Well suited to business travellers; also family rooms available. Informal, family oriented restaurant.

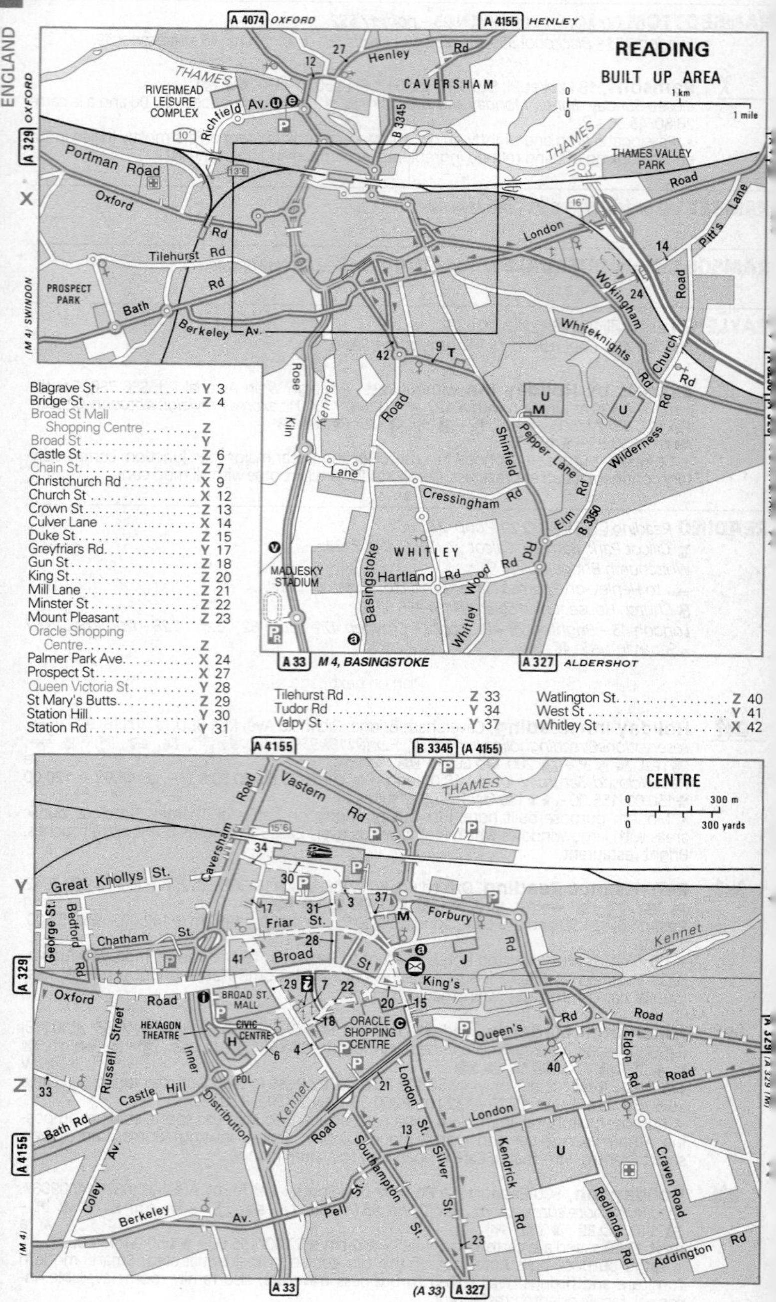

Street	Grid	No.
Blagrave St	Y	3
Bridge St	Z	4
Broad St Mall Shopping Centre	Z	
Broad St	Y	
Castle St	Z	6
Chain St	Z	7
Christchurch Rd	X	9
Church St	X	12
Crown St	Z	13
Culver Lane	X	14
Duke St	Z	15
Greyfriars Rd	Y	17
Gun St	Z	18
King St	Z	20
Mill Lane	Z	21
Minster St	Z	22
Mount Pleasant	Z	23
Oracle Shopping Centre	Z	
Palmer Park Ave	X	24
Prospect St	X	27
Queen Victoria St	Y	28
St Mary's Butts	Z	29
Station Hill	Y	30
Station Rd	Y	31
Tilehurst Rd	Z	33
Tudor Rd	Y	34
Valpy St	Y	37
Watlington St	Z	40
West St	Y	41
Whitley St	X	42

Express by Holiday Inn without rest., Richfield Ave, RG1 8EQ, ☎ (0118) 958 2558, *ebhi-reading@btconnect.com, Fax (0118) 958 2858* – 25. X u
74 rm ★69.95 – ★★69.95.
◆ Conveniently located next to Holiday Inn. The modern, well-equipped accommodation is ideal for business travellers. Good weekend rates and complimentary continental breakfast.

Forbury's, 1 Forbury Sq, The Forbury, RG1 3BB, ☎ (0118) 957 4044, *forburys@btconnect.com, Fax (0118) 956 9191* – VISA Y a
closed 26-28 December and Sunday dinner – **Rest** 18.95/21.00 a la carte 29.85/36.50.
◆ Modern eatery near law courts. Relaxing area of comfy leather seats. Spacious dining room enhanced by bold prints of wine labels. Eclectic menus with Gallic starting point.

London Street Brasserie, 2-4 London St, RG1 4SE, ☎ (0118) 950 5036, *Fax (0118) 950 5031,* – VISA Z c
Rest (booking essential) 18.50 lunch and a la carte 24.00/34.00.
◆ Lively and modern: a polite, friendly team serve appetising British classics and international dishes. Deck terrace and first-floor window tables overlook the river Kennett.

at Hurst *East : 5 m. by A 329 – X – on B 3030 – ✉ Reading.*

Castle Brasserie, Church Hill, RG10 0SJ, ☎ (0118) 934 0034, *info@castlerestaurant.co.uk, Fax (0118) 934 0334,* – 40. VISA
closed 26-30 December and Monday – **Rest** (booking essential) a la carte 18.85/34.15.
◆ Charming 16C monk's wash-house. Part panelled dining room with wattle and daub on display and a cosy snug. Modern dishes with traditional and international influences.

at Shinfield *South : 4¼ m. on A 327 – X – ✉ Reading.*

L'Ortolan (Murchison), Church Lane, RG2 9BY, ☎ (0118) 988 8500, *info@lortolan.com, Fax (0118) 988 9338,* – 18. VISA
closed Christmas-New Year, Monday except December and Sunday – **Rest** 21.00 (lunch) and a la carte approx 52.00.
Spec. Lobster cannelloni, langoustines, artichokes and truffle cream. Roast loin and braised shoulder of suckling pig, sage gnocchi and apple purée. Kalamansi soufflé with coconut sorbet.
◆ The ivy-clad exterior of this former vicarage contrasts with the contemporary interior. Service is detailed; cooking is classically based overlaid with modern influences.

at Grazeley Green *Southwest : 5½ m. by A 33 – X – ✉ Reading.*

Premier Travel Inn, Grazeley Green Rd, RG7 1LS, ☎ (0870) 9906454, *Fax (0870) 9906455,* – rm, VISA.
Rest (grill rest.) – **32 rm** ★53.95/53.95 – ★★59.95/59.95.
◆ Rural location outside small village but only three miles from the M4. Neat, bright rooms, spacious and carefully designed. Ideal for business or leisure stopovers. Popular restaurant with traditional pub theme.

Hotels and restaurants change every year,
so change your Michelin guide every year!

REDDITCH *Worcs.* 503 504 O 27 – *pop. 74 803.*
Abbey Park G. & C.C., Dagnell End Rd ☎ (01527) 406600 – Lower Grinsty, Green Lane, Callow Hill ☎ (01527) 543309 – Pitcheroak, Plymouth Rd ☎ (01527) 541054.
Civic Square, Alcester St ☎ (01527) 60806.
London 111 – Birmingham 15 – Cheltenham 33 – Stratford-upon-Avon 15.

Old Rectory, Ipsley Lane, Ipsley, B98 0AP, ☎ (01527) 523000, *ipsleyoldrectory@aol.com, Fax (01527) 517003,* – VISA
closed 25 December – **Rest** (booking essential to non-residents) 18.00/23.50 – **10 rm** ★91.00/97.00 – ★★133.00.
◆ Converted early Georgian rectory surrounded by pleasant mature gardens creating a quiet and secluded haven. Smart, traditional interior décor and individually styled rooms. Charming Georgian style conservatory restaurant.

REDHILL *Surrey* 504 T 30 – *pop. 50 436 (inc. Reigate).*
Redhill & Reigate, Clarence Lodge, Pendleton Rd ☎ (01737) 770204 – Canada Ave ☎ (01737) 770204.
London 22 – Brighton 31 – Guildford 20 – Maidstone 34.

ENGLAND

Nutfield Priory, Nutfield, RH1 4EL, East : 2 m. on A 25 ✆ (01737) 824400, *nutfield priory@handpicked.co.uk, Fax (01737) 824410,* ≤, squash – |‡ P – 🔑 80. MC AE VISA
Cloisters : Rest *(closed Saturday lunch)* 25.00/35.00 and a la carte 27.50/43.50 – ☕ 14.50 – **59 rm** ★160.00/195.00 – ★★225.00, 1 suite.
◆ Restored Victorian mansion boasting intricate stonework, stained glass and neo-Gothic cloisters. Tasteful country house décor throughout including the comfortable rooms. Characterful dining room with stained glass and views across countryside.

at Salfords *South : 2½ m. on A 23 – ✉ Redhill.*

Premier Travel Inn, Brighton Rd, RH1 5BT, ✆ (01737) 767277, *Fax (01737) 778099* – rm, rest, P. MC AE VISA.
Rest (grill rest.) – **48 rm** ★47.95/47.95 – ★★50.95/50.95.
◆ A consistent standard of trim, simply fitted and well-planned accommodation in contemporary style; a useful address for cost-conscious travellers.

REDWORTH *Durham – see Darlington.*

REETH *N. Yorks.* 502 O 20 – ✉ *Richmond.*
The Literary Institute, The Green ✆ (01748) 884059.
London 253 – Leeds 53 – Middlesbrough 36 – Newcsatle upon Tyne 61.

The Burgoyne, On The Green, DL11 6SN, ✆ (01748) 884292, *enquiries@theburgoyne.co.uk, Fax (01748) 884292,* ≤, – P. MC VISA
closed 2 January-14 February – **Rest** (booking essential to non-residents) (dinner only) 27.50 ♀ – **8 rm** ☕ ★92.50/125.00 – ★★112.50/135.00.
◆ Late Georgian hotel overlooking the green with views of the Dales. A charming, personally run, traditionally furnished house with well-appointed, individually styled rooms. Deep green dining room complements surrounding fells.

Arkleside, DL11 6SG, Northeast corner of the green ✆ (01748) 884200, *info@arklesidehotel.co.uk, Fax (01748) 884200,* ≤, – P. MC VISA
– **Rest** (booking essential to non-residents) (dinner only) 24.00 – **6 rm** ☕ ★55.00/60.00 – ★★80.00/85.00.
◆ Just off Reeth's village green, a row of modernised former lead miners' cottages. Comfortable décor throughout with a conservatory and bar area. Simple, traditional rooms. Dining room has vivid stone walls.

at Langthwaite *Northwest : 3¼ m. on Langthwaite rd – ✉ Reeth.*

Charles Bathurst Inn with rm, DL11 6EN, ✆ (01748) 884567, *info@cbinn.co.uk, Fax (01748) 884599,* ≤, – P. MC VISA
closed 25 December – **Rest** a la carte 17.50/25.00 – **18 rm** ☕ ★80.00 – ★★105.00.
◆ 18C inn sited high in the hills. Open fires provide appealing atmosphere. Fresh, locally sourced menus mixing classic with modern. Large, timbered rooms with country views.

at Whaw *Northwest : 5¼ m. by Langthwaite rd on Tan Hill rd – ✉ Reeth.*

Chapel Farm , DL11 6RT, ✆ (01748) 884062, *chapelfarmbb@aol.com,* ≤, – P. MC VISA.
Rest (by arrangement) (communal dining) 13.25 – **3 rm** ☕ ★38.50 – ★★55.00.
◆ Restored, peaceful 18C lead miners' cottages in remote hamlet: dales are literally outside the front door. Beamed lounge with open fire. Attractive rural styled bedrooms.

REIGATE *Surrey* 504 T 30 – *pop. 50 436 (inc. Redhill).*
London 26 – Brighton 33 – Guildford 20 – Maidstone 38.

Tony Tobin @ The Dining Room, 59a High St, RH2 9AE, ✆ (01737) 226650, *Fax (01737) 226650* – MC AE VISA
closed 24 December-3 January, Saturday lunch and Sunday dinner – **Rest** 19.50/36.50.
◆ Top floor of a building on the High Street with a smart modern interior. Busy, bustling atmosphere. International menus with a modern style of cooking.

La Barbe, 71 Bell St, RH2 7AN, ✆ (01737) 241966, *restaurant@labarbe.co.uk, Fax (01737) 226387* – MC AE VISA
closed Saturday lunch, Sunday and Bank Holidays – **Rest** - French - 21.95/29.95.
◆ Friendly bistro with Gallic atmosphere and welcoming ambience. Regularly changing menus offer good choice of traditional French cuisine - classical and provincial in style.

RETFORD *Notts.* 502 503 504 R 24 – *pop. 21 314.*
40 Grove St (01777) 860780.
London 148 – Lincoln 23 – Nottingham 31 – Sheffield 27.

The Barns without rest., Morton Farm, Babworth, DN22 8HA, Southwest : 2 ¼ m. by A 6420 (01777) 706336, *enquiries@thebarns.co.uk*, – P. MC AE VISA
Closed Christmas and New Year – **6 rm** 35.00/45.00 – 56.00.
◆ Privately owned and run converted part 18C farmhouse on a quiet country road. Informal, old-fashioned, cottage décor throughout. Beams within and lawned gardens without.

RHYDYCROESAU *Shrops.* 502 503 K 25 – *see Oswestry.*

RICHMOND *N. Yorks.* 502 O 20 *Great Britain G.* – *pop. 8 178.*
See : *Town★ – Castle★ AC – Georgian Theatre Royal and Museum★.*
Exc. : *Josephine and John Bowes Museum★, Barnard Castle, NW : 15 m. by B 6274, A 66 and minor rd (right) – Raby Castle★, NE : 6 m. of Barnard Castle by A 688.*
Bend Hagg (01748) 825319 – Catterick, Leyburn Rd (01748) 833268.
Friary Gardens, Victoria Rd (01748) 850252.
London 243 – Leeds 53 – Middlesbrough 26 – Newcastle upon Tyne 44.

The King's Head, Market Pl, DL10 4HS, (01748) 850220, *res@kingsheadrichmond.co.uk, Fax (01748) 850635* – P – 150. MC AE VISA
Rest (bar lunch Monday-Saturday)/dinner 12.50 (lunch) and dinner a la carte 14.85/24.85 s. – **30 rm** 87.00/97.00 – 110.00.
◆ Built in 1718, later to become a coaching inn, located on the main square. Classic, traditional style; a lounge with carriage and case clocks and simple, elegant bedrooms. Restaurant has views across square to Norman castle.

Millgate House without rest., 3 Millgate, DL10 4JN, (01748) 823571, *oztim@millgatehouse.demon.co.uk, Fax (01748) 850701*, – P
3 rm 65.00/85.00 – 85.00.
◆ Georgian townhouse with fine elevated views of river Swale and Richmond Castle. Award winning terraced garden. Antique furnished interior. Bedrooms are tastefully restrained.

West End without rest., 45 Reeth Rd, DL10 4EX, West : ½ m. on A 6108 (01748) 824783, *westend@richmond.org*, – P.
closed December-January – **5 rm** 27.00/35.00 – 54.00.
◆ Fine mid 19C house, away from town centre, with gardens. Homely lounge with plenty of maps and walking guides. Simple, neat and tidy rooms. Adjacent self-catering cottages.

at Downholme *Southwest : 5½ m. on A 6108 – Richmond.*

Walburn Hall without rest., DL11 6AF, South : 1 ½ m. on A 6108 (01748) 822152, *walburnhall@farmersweekly.net, Fax (01748) 822152*, – P. MC VISA.
closed December-January – **3 rm** 40.00 – 75.00.
◆ Mary Queen of Scots reputedly stayed in this part 14C fortified farmhouse. Cottage-style lounge; dining room serves traditional Yorkshire breakfasts. Beamed bedrooms.

at Whashton *Northwest : 4½ m. by Ravensworth rd – Richmond.*

Whashton Springs Farm without rest., DL11 7JS, South : 1 ½ m. on Richmond rd (01748) 822884, *whashtonsprings@btconnect.com, Fax (01748) 826285*, – P. MC VISA.
closed Christmas-New Year – **8 rm** 35.00/37.00 – 56.00/60.00.
◆ A working farm with a spacious, pleasantly converted, period farmhouse; surrounded by attractive countryside. Cottagey rooms, some in converted stable block.

at Dalton *Northwest : 6¾ m. by Ravensworth rd and Cayles rd – Richmond.*

The Travellers Rest, DL11 7HU, (01833) 621225, *daltontravellers@aol.com* – P. MC VISA
closed 25-26 December, January, Sunday and Monday – **Rest** (dinner only) a la carte 17.50/25.00 .
◆ Characterful country inn in tiny hamlet. Blackboard menu offers a wide-ranging menu where traditional meets the up-to-date. Linen-laid restaurant also available.

RIDGEWAY *Derbs.* – *see Sheffield (S. Yorks.).*

RILLA MILL *Cornwall* – *see Callington.*

RINGSTEAD *Norfolk* 504 V 25 – *see Hunstanton.*

RINGWOOD *Hants.* 503 504 O 31 – *pop. 13 387.*
The Furlong ☎ (01425) 470896.
London 102 – Bournemouth 11 – Salisbury 17 – Southampton 20.

Moortown Lodge without rest., 244 Christchurch Rd, BH24 3AS, South : 1 m. c B 3347 ☎ (01425) 471404, *hotel@moortownlodge.co.uk, Fax (01425) 476527* – MC AE VISA.
7 rm ☕ ♰64.00 – ♰♰64.00.
◆ House dating from the 1760s, located on the edge of the New Forest. Family ru traditional atmosphere with a cosy lounge and chintz-furnished rooms of varying sizes.

RIPLEY *N. Yorks.* 502 P 21 – ✉ *Harrogate.*
London 213 – Bradford 21 – Leeds 18 – Newcastle upon Tyne 79.

The Boar's Head, HG3 3AY, ☎ (01423) 771888, *reservations@boarsheadripley.co.u Fax (01423) 771509,* – P. MC AE VISA
The Restaurant : Rest 15.00/35.00 ♀ – ***The Bistro :*** Rest a la carte 11.50/21.00 ♀ – **25 rn** ☕ ♰105.00 – ♰♰125.00/150.00.
◆ 18C coaching inn within estate village of Ripley Castle, reputedly furnished from castle attics. Comfy, unique rooms, some in courtyard or adjacent house. The Restaurant, i deep burgundy, has period paintings. The Bistro boasts impressive flagged floors.

RIPLEY *Surrey* 504 S 30 – *pop. 1 697.*
London 28 – Guildford 6.

Drake's (Drake), The Clock House, High St, GU23 6AQ, ☎ (01483) 224777 *Fax (01483) 222940,* – 10. MC VISA
closed Christmas-New Year, 2 weeks August, Saturday lunch, Sunday and Monday – **Res** 22.00/39.50 ♀.
Spec. Roast sweetbreads with poached duck egg and sweetcorn sauce. Roast monkfis with saffron potatoes, baby leeks and crispy langoustine. Strawberry tart, basil and wil strawberry sorbet.
◆ Large illuminated clock announces this smart restaurant of Georgian red brick. Loca gallery art nestles on walls. Refined cooking on a classical base; good value lunches.

RIPON *N. Yorks.* 502 P 21 *Great Britain G.* – *pop. 16 468.*
See : *Town★ - Cathedral★ (Saxon Crypt★★) AC.*
Env. : *Fountains Abbey★★★ AC :- Studley Royal★★ AC (<★ from Anne Boleyn's Seat) Fountains Hall (Façade★), SW : 2½ m. by B 6265 – Newby Hall (Tapestries★) AC, SE : 3½ m by B 6265.*
18 Ripon City, Palace Rd ☎ (01765) 603640.
Minster Rd ☎ (01765) 604625.
London 222 – Leeds 26 – Middlesbrough 35 – York 23.

The Old Deanery, Minster Rd, HG4 1QS, ☎ (01765) 600003, *reception@theoldde nery.co.uk, Fax (01765) 600027,* – P. – 50. MC VISA
closed 25 December – **Rest** *(closed Sunday dinner)* a la carte 25.35/33.45 s ♀ – **11 rm** ☕ ♰80.00/100.00 – ♰♰125.00.
◆ Eponymously named hotel opposite cathedral. Stylish interior blends seamlessly with older charms. Afternoon tea in secluded garden. 18C oak staircase leads to modern rooms Appealing seasonal cooking in spacious dining room.

Sharow Cross House, Dishforth Rd, Sharow, HG4 5BQ, Northeast : 1 ¾ m. by A 61 on Sharow rd ☎ (01765) 609866, *sharowcrosshouse@btinternet.com,* – P.
closed Christmas and New Year – **Rest** (by arrangement) 19.00 – **3 rm** ☕ ♰50.00/60.00 – ♰♰60.00/70.00.
◆ Idyllically set 19C house, built for mill owner. Capacious hall with welcoming fire. Spacious bedrooms: the master room is huge and offers Cathedral views on clear days.

at Aldfield *Southwest : 3¾ m. by B 6265* – ✉ *Ripon.*

Bay Tree Farm , HG4 3BE, ☎ (01765) 620394, *btfarm@ppc.mail.co.uk, Fax (01765) 620394,* – P. MC VISA
restricted opening in winter – **Rest** (by arrangement) (communal dining) 15.00 – **6** rm ☕ ♰35.00/50.00 – ♰♰70.00/85.00.
◆ Comfortable and characterful farmhouse conversion with pleasant gardens. Homely rooms, some beamed, in 17C stone barn; all accommodation boasts serene views over pasture.

ENGLAND

at Markington *Southwest : 5 m. by A 61 – ✉ Harrogate.*

Hob Green , HG3 3PJ, Southwest : ½ m. ✆ (01423) 770031, *info@hobgreen.com, Fax (01423) 771589,* ≤, , – P. MO AE VISA
Rest 15.95/26.50 – **11 rm** ☕ ✝90.00/105.00 – ✝✝110.00/115.00, 1 suite.
◆ 18C country house in a rural position surrounded by extensive parkland. A true country house hotel furnished with antiques and curios. Each room unique and characterful. Dining room with country views; garden produce prominently used.

at Galphay *West : 4½ m. by B 6265 – ✉ Ripon.*

Galphay Inn, HG4 3NJ, ✆ (01765) 650133, *www.galphayinn.co.uk* – P. MO AE VISA
closed Tuesday and Sunday dinner – **Rest** a la carte 19.00/26.00.
◆ Pleasantly set in charming rural spot; a distinctive, homely feel prevails. Snug interior with open fire. Tasty, accomplished cooking propelled by a taste of the seasons.

RISLEY *Notts. – see Nottingham.*

ROADE *Northants.* 504 R 27 – *pop. 2 254.*
London 66 – Coventry 36 – Leicester 42 – Northampton 5.5.

Roade House with rm, 16 High St, NN7 2NW, ✆ (01604) 863372, *info@roadehouseho tel.co.uk, Fax (01604) 862421* – , rest, P. MO AE VISA.
closed 25 December-2 January and 1 week August – **Rest** *(closed Sunday and lunch Saturday)* 25.00/35.00 – **10 rm** ☕ ✝75.00 – ✝✝83.00.
◆ Personally run converted schoolhouse with comfortable bedrooms. Uncluttered, beamed dining room. Classic, seasonally based dishes with modern international elements.

ROCHDALE *Gtr Manchester* 502 N 23 – *pop. 95 796.*
18 Edenfield Rd, Bagslate ✆ (01706) 646024 – 18 Marland, Springfield Park, Bolton Rd ✆ (01706) 649801 – 18, 9 Castle Hawk, Chadwick Lane, Castleton ✆ (01706) 640841.
Touchstones, The Esplanade ✆ (01706) 864928.
London 224 – Blackpool 40 – Burnley 11 – Leeds 45 – Liverpool 40 – Manchester 12.

Hindle Pastures , Highgate Lane, Whitworth, OL12 0TS, North : 2½ m. by A 671 off Tonacliffe Rd ✆ (01706) 643310, *hindlepastures@tiscali.co.uk, Fax (01706) 653846,* ≤, , , – P.
Rest (by arrangement) (communal dining) 15.00 – **3 rm** ☕ ✝30.00/40.00 – ✝✝60.00.
◆ Superbly located barn high in the Pennines with views over four counties. Special attention paid to extensive breakfasts with freshly laid eggs. Brightly decorated rooms. Open plan dining room; imaginative meals served with fellow guests.

Nutters, Edenfield Rd, Norden, OL12 7TT, West : 5 m. on A 680 ✆ (01706) 650167, *Fax (01706) 650167,* ≤ – P 40. MO AE VISA
closed Monday – **Rest** 15.95/34.00 and a la carte 24.70/33.90.
◆ Views of the lyrical gardens contrast with a menu of often complex modern British dishes with international twists and influences. Best views at either end of the room.

After Eight, 2 Edenfield Rd, OL11 5AA, West : 1 m. on A 680 ✆ (01706) 646432, *ataylor@aftereight.uk.com, Fax (01706) 646432,* – . MO AE VISA
closed 25 December, 1 January, 1 week spring, 1 week summer, Sunday dinner and Monday-Wednesday – **Rest** (dinner only and Sunday lunch) a la carte 19.50/27.40.
◆ Substantial 19C house, personally run, offering a relaxed neighbourhood ambience. Concise menu offers a broad range of traditional dishes with vegetarians well catered for.

at Littleborough *Northeast : 4½ m. by A 58 on B 6225 – ✉ Rochdale.*

Hollingworth Lake without rest., 164 Smithybridge Rd, OL15 0DB, ✆ (01706) 376583, – P. MO VISA
5 rm ☕ ✝32.50/37.50 – ✝✝50.00.
◆ A short distance from country park, lake and the moors. A comfortable, friendly, good value house with well equipped, attractively furnished bedrooms.

ROCHESTER *Medway* 504 V 29 *Great Britain G. – pop. 17 125 – ✉ Chatham.*
See : *Castle★ AC – Cathedral★ AC.*
Env. : *The Historic Dockyard★, Chatham, NE : 2 m. of the Cathedral.*
Exc. : *Leeds Castle★, SE : 11 m. by A 229 and M 20.*
95 High St ✆ (01634) 843666, visitor.centre@medway.gov.uk.
London 30 – Dover 45 – Maidstone 8 – Margate 46.

ENGLAND

 **Bridgewood Manor,** Bridgewood Roundabout, ME5 9AX, Southeast : 3 m. by A 2 and A 229 on Walderslade rd ✆ (01634) 201333, *bridgewoodmanor@marstonhotels.com, Fax (01634) 201330,* – 🅿 – 250. VISA.
Squires : Rest *(closed Saturday lunch)* 19.95/25.00 **s.** and a la carte – **96 rm** 129.00 – 166.00, 4 suites.
♦ Purpose-built hotel with central courtyard and fitted modern interior. Bedrooms have a well-kept, comfortable feel. Geared to business travellers. Imposingly formal Squires.

ROCK *Cornwall* 503 F 32 *The West Country G. – pop. 3 433 –* ✉ *Wadebridge.*
Exc. : *Pencarrow★, SE : 8½ m. by B 3314 and A 389.*
London 266 – Newquay 24 – Tintagel 14 – Truro 32.

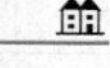 **St Enodoc,** PL27 6LA, ✆ (01208) 863394, *enodochotel@aol.com, Fax (01208) 863970,* heated, – rm, 🅿. VISA.
closed 10 December-9 February except New Year – ***Restaurant :*** Rest (light lunch) 22.50 (lunch) and a la carte 27.45/35.25 – **16 rm** 85.00/160.00 – 110.00/220.00, 4 suites.
♦ A refreshingly modern take on the seaside hotel; neutral fabrics, sandwashed pine and contemporary oil paintings in stylish rooms, many facing the Camel Estuary. Split-level bar-brasserie with terrace.

ROCKBEARE *Devon – see Exeter.*

LA ROCQUE *Jersey (Channel Islands)* 517 ⑪ *– see Channel Islands.*

ROGATE *W. Sussex* 504 R 30 – ✉ *Petersfield (Hants.).*
London 63 – Brighton 42 – Guildford 29 – Portsmouth 23 – Southampton 36.

Mizzards Farm without rest., GU31 5HS, Southwest : 1 m. by Harting rd ✆ (01730) 821656, *julian.francis@hemscott.net, Fax (01730) 821655,* heated, – 🅿.
closed Christmas and New Year – **3 rm** 50.00/55.00 – 80.00/82.00.
♦ 17C farmhouse with delightful landscaped gardens, which include a lake, bordered by river Rother. Views of woods and farmland. Fine fabrics and antiques in appealing rooms.

ROMALDKIRK *Durham* 502 N 20 *– see Barnard Castle.*

ROMSEY *Hants.* 503 504 P 31 *Great Britain G. – pop. 17 386.*
See : *Abbey★ (interior★★).*
Env. : *Broadlands★ AC, S : 1 m.*
Dunwood Manor, Danes Rd, Awbridge ✆ (01794) 340549 – Nursling ✆ (023) 8073 2218 – , Wellow, Ryedown Lane, East Wellow ✆ (01794) 322872.
13 Church St ✆ (01794) 512987.
London 82 – Bournemouth 28 – Salisbury 16 – Southampton 8 – Winchester 10.

Ranvilles Farm House without rest., Ower, SO51 6AA, Southwest : 2 m. on A 3090 (southbound carriageway) ✆ (023) 8081 4481, *info@ranvilles.com, Fax (023) 8081 4481,* – 🅿
4 rm 30.00/40.00 – 55.00/70.00.
♦ Attractive part 16C farmhouse set within five acres of garden and fields. Welcoming country style décor and furniture throughout, including the well-kept bedrooms.

Highfield House, Newtown Rd, Awbridge, SO51 0GG, Northwest : 3½ m. by A 3090 (old A 31) and A 27 ✆ (01794) 340727, *highfieldhouse@aol.com, Fax (01794) 341450,* – 🅿
Rest (by arrangement) (communal dining) 17.50 – **3 rm** 45.00 – 60.00.
♦ Modern house with gardens, in a tranquil location just out of Awbridge village. Accommodation is comfortable with good facilities. Real fires in the guest lounge. Communal dining with garden views.

Three Tuns, 58 Middlebridge St, SO51 8HL, ✆ (01794) 512639, *thethreetunsromsey@aol.com, Fax (01794) 514524* – 🅿. VISA
closed Sunday dinner – **Rest** a la carte 25.00/33.00.
♦ 18C town centre pub with period feel supplied by beams and log fire, though rest of interior is understated. Modern, well-judged cooking using first-rate ingredients.

ROSEDALE ABBEY *N. Yorks.* 502 R 20 *Great Britain G.* – ✉ *Pickering.*
Env. : ≤★ *on road to Hutton-le-Hole.*
London 247 – Middlesbrough 27 – Scarborough 25 – York 36.

Milburn Arms, YO18 8RA, ✆ (01751) 417312, *info@milburnarms.co.uk, Fax (01751) 417541,* – P. MO AE VISA
closed 1 week Christmas – ***Priory :*** **Rest** *(closed Monday lunch)* 18.00 and a la carte 18.70/31.85 – **13 rm** ☐ ★47.50 – ★★90.00.
◆ Neatly kept, comfy bedrooms in pastel shades, cosy little sitting room and traditional real ale bar in a well-run village inn: a good base for walking the North York Moors. Split-level dining room with subtle country styling.

ROSS-ON-WYE *Herefordshire* 503 504 M 28 *Great Britain G.* – *pop. 10 085.*
See : *Market House★ – Yat Rock (≤★).*
Env. : *SW : Wye Valley★ – Goodrich Castle★ AC, SW : 3½ m. by A 40.*
Swan House, Edde Cross St ✆ (01989) 562768.
London 118 – Gloucester 15 – Hereford 15 – Newport 35.

The Chase, Gloucester Rd, HR9 5LH, ✆ (01989) 763161, *res@chasehotel.co.uk, Fax (01989) 768330,* – P – 300. MO AE VISA.
closed 24-29 December – **Rest** 15.00/22.50 and a la carte 24.45/35.90 ♀ – **36 rm** ☐ ★79.00/109.00 – ★★89.00/155.00.
◆ Elegant Georgian country house, close to town centre. Original architectural features such as impressive tiled reception area. Range of room styles with traditional décor. Restaurant exudes airy, period feel.

Wilton Court, Wilton Lane, HR9 6AQ, West : ¾ m. by B 4260 (A 49 Hereford) ✆ (01989) 562569, *info@wiltoncourthotel.com, Fax (01989) 768460,* , – P. MO AE VISA
Mulberry : **Rest** *closed Sunday dinner* 25.00 (dinner) a la carte 19.15/31.90 – **10 rm** ☐ ★65.00/110.00 – ★★85.00/125.00.
◆ Attractive, part-Elizabethan house on the banks of the river Wye. 16C wood panelling in situ in bar and two of the bedrooms: others have a distinctly William Morris influence. Light, airy conservatory restaurant boasts Lloyd Loom furniture and garden views.

The Lough Pool Inn, Sellack, HR9 6LX, Northwest : 3 ¼ m. by B 4260 and A 49 on Hoarwithy rd ✆ (01989) 730236, *Fax (01432 886055),* , – P. MO VISA
closed 25 December, 1 week January, Sunday dinner and Monday in winter – **Rest** a la carte 19.00/30.50 ♀.
◆ Ancient beams and wattle walls in this personally run 16C inn. Seasonal cooking, served at scrubbed farmhouse tables, is well-priced, unfussy and full of local flavour.

at Kerne Bridge *South : 3¾ m. on B 4234* – ✉ *Ross-on-Wye.*

Lumleys without rest., HR9 5QT, ✆ (01600) 890040, *helen@lumleys.force9.co.uk,* – P
3 rm ☐ ★55.00 – ★★65.00.
◆ Welcoming and personally run guesthouse in sympathetically converted Victorian house. Ideally located for Wye valley and Forest of Dean. Pine decorated cottage style rooms.

at Glewstone *Southwest : 3¼ m. by A 40* – ✉ *Ross-on-Wye.*

Glewstone Court, HR9 6AW, ✆ (01989) 770367, *glewstone@aol.com, Fax (01989) 770282,* ≤, – rest, P. MO AE VISA
closed 25-26 December – **Rest** a la carte 26.15/30.15 s. – **8 rm** ☐ ★52.00/72.00 – ★★126.00.
◆ Part Georgian and Victorian country house with impressive cedar of Lebanon in grounds. Sweeping staircase leads to uncluttered rooms. Family run with charming eccentricity. Antique-strewn dining room.

at Llangarron *Southwest : 5½ m. by A 40* – ✉ *Ross-on-Wye.*

Trecilla Farm without rest., HR9 6NQ, ✆ (01989) 770647, *info@trecillafarm.co.uk,* , , – P
closed Christmas and New Year – **3 rm** ☐ ★45.00 – ★★60.00/80.00.
◆ 16C farmhouse with babbling brook. Beautiful lounge typifies smart, country house style. Breakfast locations dependent on time of year. Book the four-poster room if possible!

at Peterstow *West : 2½ m. on A 49 – ✉ Ross-on-Wye.*

Pengethley Manor ⛏, HR9 6LL, Northwest : 1 ½ m. on A 49 ☎ (01989) 730211 *reservations@pengethleymanor.co.uk, Fax (01989) 730238,* ≤, heated, ⛟, – ⇍ [P] 50. MC AE ◑ VISA

Georgian Restaurant : Rest 18.00 (lunch) and a la carte 22.50/40.00 ♀ – **22 rm** ☕ ✶75.00/90.00 – ✶✶120.00, 3 suites.

◆ Fine period house set in a prominent position affording country views. Grounds includ vineyard and giant chess set. Rooms vary in size and all are comfy and characterful. Spa cious dining room with country house feel.

ROSTHWAITE *Cumbria* 502 K 20 – *see Keswick.*

ROTHBURY *Northd.* 501 502 O 18 *Great Britain G. – pop. 1 963 – ✉ Morpeth.*

See : *Cragside House★ (interior★) AC.*

ℹ *National Park Centre, Church House, Church St ☎ (01669) 620887.*

London 311 – Edinburgh 84 – Newcastle upon Tyne 29.

Thropton Demesne Farmhouse ⛏ without rest., Thropton, NE65 7LT, West 2 ¼ m. on B 6341 ☎ (01669) 620196, *thropton-demesne@yahoo.co.uk,* ≤, ⛟ – ⇍ [P]

closed Christmas-New Year – **3 rm** ☕ ✶50.00 – ✶✶56.00/60.00.

◆ Early 19C stone-built former farmhouse; unbroken Coquet Valley views. Lounge define by quality décor. Artwork on walls by owner. Individually styled rooms with lovely vistas.

Lee Farm ⛏ without rest., NE65 8JQ, South : 3 ¼ m. by B 6342 on The Lee rd ☎ (01665 570257, *enqs@leefarm.co.uk, Fax (01665) 570257,* ≤, ⛟ – ⇍ [P].

closed Christmas-New Year – **3 rm** ☕ ✶42.00/45.00 – ✶✶60.00/64.00.

◆ Family-run house in a peaceful valley; firelit lounge, trim, pretty rooms in pastel tones breakfasts at a communal table. Guests are free to explore the livestock farm.

ROTHERHAM *S. Yorks.* 502 503 504 P 23 – *pop. 117 262.*

⛳18 *Thrybergh Park ☎ (01709) 850466 – ⛳18 Grange Park, Upper Wortley Rd, Kimberwort ☎ (01709) 558884 – ⛳18 Phoenix, Pavilion Lane, Brinsworth ☎ (01709) 363788.*

ℹ *40 Bridgegate ☎ (01709) 835904.*

London 166 – Kingston-upon-Hull 61 – Leeds 36 – Sheffield 6.

Courtyard by Marriott, West Bawtry Rd, S60 4NA, South : 2 ¼ m. on A 630 ☎ (087 400 7235, *reservations.rotherham@courtyardhotels.co.uk, Fax (0870) 400 7335,* ⛹, – ⇍, ▤ rest, ✆ ♿ [P] – 300. MC AE ◑ VISA.

Capistrano : Rest (bar lunch Saturday) (carving lunch)/dinner 19.95 and a la cart 17.15/28.15 ♀ – **102 rm** ☕ ✶98.00 – ✶✶108.00, 2 suites.

◆ Modern purpose-built hotel out of town centre. Uniform rooms have a bright tone Features, such as work desks and ergonomic chairs, are well suited to business traveller Restaurant boasts smoked glass conservatory extension.

Elton, Main St, Bramley, S66 2SF, East : 4 ¼ m. by A 6021, A 631 and Cross St. ☎ (0170 545681, *bestwestern.eltonhotel@btinternet.com, Fax (01709) 549100* – ⇍, ▤ rest, ♿ [P] 50. MC AE ◑ VISA

Rest 12.95/22.50 and a la carte 22.15/28.75 s. ♀ – **29 rm** ☕ ✶55.00/86.00 ✶✶76.00/95.00.

◆ Solid stone house with extensions, in the centre of village. Traditionally styled publi areas include conservatory lounge. Extension rooms have a more modern style. Richl styled dining room with warm burgundy walls.

Premier Travel Inn, Bawtry Rd, S65 3JB, East : 2 m. by A 6021 on A 631 ☎ (0170 543216, *Fax (01709) 531546* – ⇍ rm, ▤ rest, ♿ [P]. MC AE ◑ VISA.

Rest (grill rest.) – **37 rm** ✶46.95/46.95 – ✶✶48.95/48.95.

◆ A consistent standard of trim, simply fitted accommodation in contemporary style; useful address for cost-conscious travellers. Well located for major motorway links.

ROTHERWICK *Hants. – see Hook.*

ROUGHAM GREEN *Suffolk – see Bury St Edmunds.*

ROWDE *Wilts.* 503 504 N 29 – *see Devizes*

ROWSLEY *Derbs.* 502 503 504 P 24 *Great Britain G.* – ✉ *Matlock.*
Env. : *Chatsworth★★★ (Park and Garden★★★) AC, N : by B 6012.*
London 157 – Derby 23 – Manchester 40 – Nottingham 30.

East Lodge ⛢, DE4 2EF, ✆ (01629) 734474, *info@eastlodge.com, Fax (01629) 733949,* ... – ⇔ ♿ P. MC AE VISA. ⛝
Rest 16.00/35.00 and a la carte 20.00/37.00 – **14 rm** ☐ ♦110.00/130.00 – ♦♦120.00/150.00.
◆ Elegant 17C country house set in ten acres of well kept grounds, once the lodge to Haddon Hall. Rooms are each individually decorated and superior rooms have garden views. Simple dining room with terrace.

The Peacock, Bakewell Rd, DE4 2EB, ✆ (01629) 733518, *reception@thepeacockatrowsley.com, Fax (01629) 732671,* ... – ⇔ rest, P. MC AE VISA
Rest 21.50 (lunch) and a la carte 33.50/44.00 ♀ – ☐ 5.95 – **16 rm** ♦75.00/95.00 – ♦♦145.00/175.00.
◆ Characterful, antique furnished, 17C house with gardens leading down to the river Derwent. Rooms, a variety of shapes and sizes, are antique or reproduction furnished. Restaurant divided between three smart rooms.

ROWTON *Ches.* 502 503 L 24 – *see Chester.*

"Rest" appears in red for establishments with a ✿ (star) or ☺ (Bib Gourmand).

ROYAL LEAMINGTON SPA *Warks.* 503 504 P 27 – *pop. 61 595.*
Leamington and County, Golf Lane, Whitnash ✆ (01926) 425961 (on plan of Warwick).
The Royal Pump Rooms, The Parade ✆ (01926) 742762.
London 99 – Birmingham 23 – Coventry 9 – Leicester 33 – Warwick 3.

ROYAL LEAMINGTON SPA

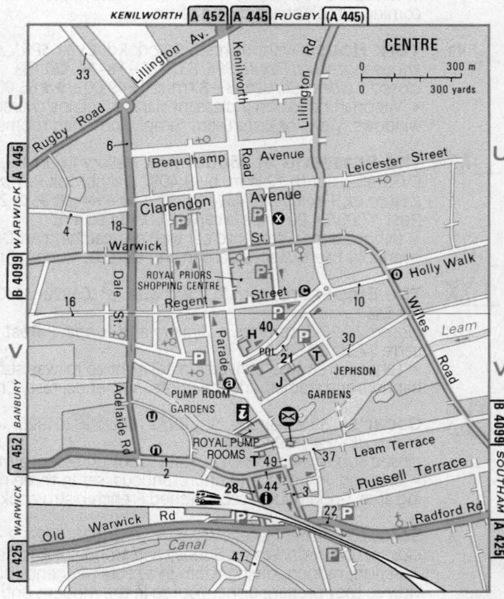

ENGLAND

Mallory Court, Harbury Lane, Bishop's Tachbrook, CV33 9QB, South : 2 ¼ m. by B 4087 (Tachbrook Rd) (01926) 330214, *reception@mallory.co.uk, Fax (01926) 451714*, <, , , - , rest, - 160.
Rest (booking essential) 25.00/49.50 s. - (see also ***The Brasserie at Mallory*** below)
27 rm 225.00/265.00 - 305.00/345.00, 2 suites.
Spec. Salad of foie gras, apples, sweet wine jelly and smoked duck breast. Fillet of beef with braised oxtail and cherry tomatoes. Raspberry soufflé.
♦ Part Edwardian country house in Lutyens style; extensive landscaped gardens. Finest quality antiques and furnishings throughout public areas and individually styled bedrooms. Refined dining in elegant, comfortable restaurant.

Courtyard by Marriott, Olympus Ave, Tachbrook Park, CV34 6RJ, Southwest : 1 ½ m by A 452 (01926) 425522, *res-lspcourtyard@kewgreen.co.uk, Fax (01926) 881322* - rm, rest, - 70. on Warwick town plan Z
Rest (bar lunch)/dinner 22.00 - **91 rm** 95.00/115.00 - 95.00/125.00.
♦ Modern hotel in the conveniently located Tachbrook business park. Smart modern fixtures and fittings provide good levels of comfort. Well suited to business travellers. Bright brasserie-style restaurant.

The Angel, 143 Regent St, CV32 4NZ, (01926) 881296, *angelhotel143@hotmail.com, Fax (01926) 313853* - - 40. U
closed 25-26 December - ***The Print Room :*** **Rest** (bar lunch Monday-Saturday)/dinner 15.00/18.00 - **47 rm** 70.00 - 80.00.
♦ Centrally located Regency hotel which once provided stabling for a hundred horses. Traditional public areas. Rooms have an uncluttered air with simple, elegant furnishings. Classic ambience defines restaurant.

Royal Leamington, 64 Upper Holly Walk, CV32 3JL, (01926) 883777, *royal.leamington@pageant.co.uk, Fax (01926) 330467*, - rest, - 40. U
Rest 14.95/18.00 - **31 rm** 80.00/85.00 - 90.00/100.00.
♦ Characterful Victorian house with spacious and well-decorated interior featuring high ceilings and parquet flooring. Good comfort levels in the sizeable bedrooms. Bistro dining room has smart, elegant, period feel.

Adams, 22 Avenue Rd, CV31 3PQ, (01926) 450742, *booking@adams-hotel.co.uk, Fax (01926) 313110*, - . V
Rest (bar lunch)/dinner a la carte 24.50/34.50 - **14 rm** 68.00/85.00 - 80.00/90.00.
♦ Delightful house of the Regency period with plenty of charm and character: original features include ceiling mouldings. Immaculate and similarly attractive bedrooms. Welcoming, simply styled dining room.

York House without rest., 9 York Rd, CV31 3PR, (01926) 424671, *reservations@yorkhousehotel.biz, Fax (01926) 832272* - . V
closed 2 weeks Christmas - **8 rm** 49.00 - 65.00.
♦ Victorian house on a pleasant parade, retains characterful fittings such as stained glass windows. Views of River Leam. Simply furnished rooms in period style.

The Brasserie at Mallory (at Mallory Court H.), Harbury Lane, Bishop's Tachbrook, CV33 9QB, South : 2 ¼ m. by B 4087 (Tachbrook Rd) (01926) 453939, *thebrasserie@mallory.co.uk, Fax (01926) 451714*, , - 25.
Rest 17.00/24.00 and a la carte 21.00/31.00 s.
♦ In hotel annex; step into bar with eye-catching Art Deco style. Conservatory dining room overlooks pretty walled garden and terrace. Modern British cooking in a buzzy setting.

The Emperors, Bath Pl, CV31 3BP, (01926) 313030, *Fax (01926) 435966* - . V
closed 25-26 December, 1 January and Sunday - **Rest** - Chinese (Canton and Peking) - a la carte 17.50/28.50.
♦ Large warehouse conversion adjacent to railway station. Decorated with traditional wall banners and framed oriental prints. Authentic, tasty Chinese cuisine.

Oscar's, 39 Chandos St, CV32 4RL, (01926) 452807, *enquiries@oscarsfrenchbistro.co.uk* - . U
closed Sunday and Monday - **Rest** (booking essential) 15.00/22.00.
♦ Bustling, informal and unpretentious, set in three rooms on two floors; upstairs smoking area. Good value, accomplished French bistro cooking; notable steak specialities.

Solo, 23 Dormer Place, CV32 5AA, (01926) 422422 - . V
closed 1 week Christmas, Sunday and Monday - **Rest** (dinner only) 22.00 s.
♦ Stylish, modern dining room in a rebuilt Regency building, in town centre. Chefs in full view as they prepare dishes rooted in the modern British style.

ROYAL TUNBRIDGE WELLS *Kent* 504 U 30 *Great Britain G. – pop. 60 095.*

See : *The Pantiles*★ **B 26** – *Calverley Park*★ **B**.

Langton Rd ☏ *(01892) 523034* **A**.

The Old Fish Market, The Pantiles ☏ *(01892) 515675.*

London 36 – Brighton 33 – Folkestone 46 – Hastings 27 – Maidstone 18.

ROYAL TUNRIDGE WELLS

enhall Mill Rd . . . . A 3
ishop's Down . . . . A 4
alverley Rd . . . . B
rescent Rd . . . . B 9
ir Tree Rd . . . . A 10
rosvenor Rd . . . . B 12
Hall's Hole Rd . . . . A 13
High Rocks Lane . . . . A 16
High St . . . . B 14
Hungershall Park Rd . . . . A 17
Lansdowne Rd . . . . B 18
Lower Green Rd . . . . A 20
Major York's Rd . . . . A 21
Monson Rd . . . . B 22
Mount Ephraim Rd . . . . B 24
Mount Ephraim . . . . A, B 23
Mount Pleasant Rd . . . . B 25
Pantiles (The) . . . . B 26
Prospect Rd . . . . A 27
Royal Victoria Pl. Shopping Centre . . . . B
Rusthall Rd . . . . A 28
St John's Rd . . . . B 29
Tea Garden Lane . . . . A 30
Vale Rd . . . . B 33
Victoria Rd . . . . B 34
Warwick Park . . . . B 35

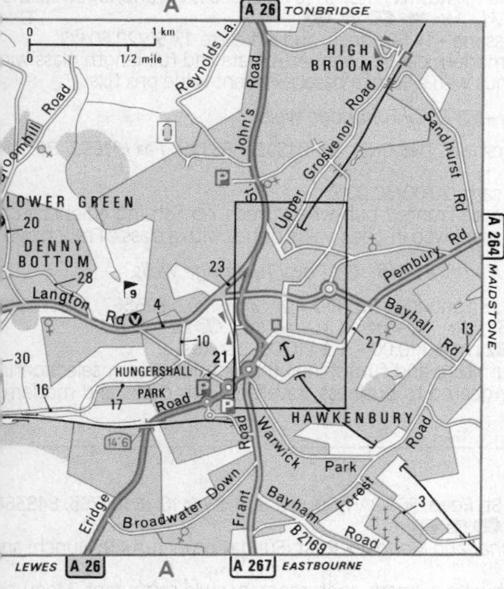

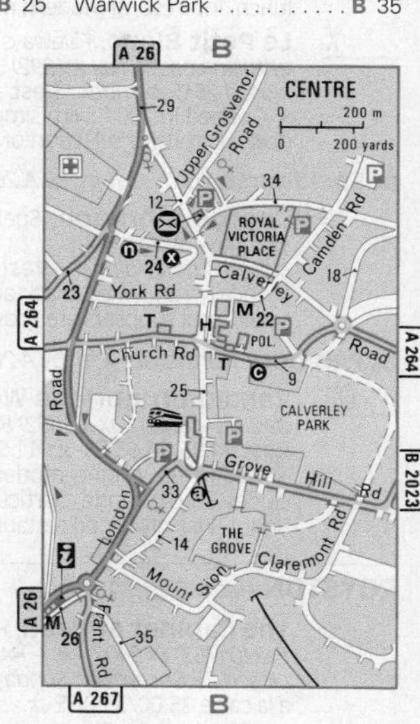

Hotel du Vin, Crescent Rd, TN1 2LY, ☏ (01892) 526455, *info@tunbridgewells.hotelduvin.com, Fax (01892) 512044,* ← – 80. VISA **B c**

Rest – (see ***Bistro*** below) – 14.50 – **36 rm** 95.00 – 200.00.

◆ Delightful Georgian house with a contemporarily styled interior themed around wine; provides a stylish, comfortable feel throughout. Occasional wine-based events.

Spa, Mount Ephraim, TN4 8XJ, ☏ (01892) 520331, *reservations@spahotel.co.uk, Fax (01892) 510575,* – rest, – 350. VISA **A v**

Chandelier **:** Rest *(closed Saturday lunch)* 19.50/34.50 – 13.00 – **66 rm** 99.00/119.00 – 140.00/150.00, 3 suites.

◆ Classic Georgian mansion set in 14 acres of gardens and parkland with lakes. An old-fashioned, English style of hospitality. Comfortable, well-furnished bedrooms. Dining options in formal restaurant or lounge.

Danehurst without rest., 41 Lower Green Rd, Rusthall, TN4 8TW, West : 1 ¾ m. by A 264 ☏ (01892) 527739, *info@danehurst.net, Fax (01892) 514804,* – . VISA. **A e**

closed 1-14 February, last week August, Christmas and New Year – **4 rm** 50.00/70.00 – 90.00.

◆ Victorian family home, with koi carp in the garden, located in residential area of town. Mix of homely furniture and furnishings and a conservatory breakfast room.

ENGLAND

XX **Thackeray's,** 85 London Rd, TN1 1EA, ✆ (01892) 511921, *reservations@thackeraysrestaurant.co.uk, Fax (01892) 527561,* – ⇔ 14. MC AE ◑ VISA B
closed Sunday dinner and Monday except in December – **Rest** 14.95 (lunch) and a la carte 38.20/45.40 ♀.
◆ Grade II listed 17C house with handsome Oriental terrace. Modern interior contrasts pleasingly with façade. The classically based cooking employs first rate ingredients.

XX **Signor Franco,** 5a High St, TN1 1UL, ✆ (01892) 549199, *Fax (01892) 541378* – ▤. MC ◑ VISA B
closed Sunday and Bank Holidays – **Rest** - Italian - a la carte 21.00/31.30.
◆ On first floor in high street. Several dining areas with good-sized, well-spaced tables. Classic Italian feel in the broad range of dishes and the welcoming ambience.

XX **Bistro** (at Hotel du Vin), TN1 2LY, ✆ (01892) 526455, *Fax (01892) 512044,* – ⇔ 14. MC AE ◑ VISA B
Rest (booking essential) a la carte approx 28.00 ♀.
◆ Classically styled with dark wood floors and furniture and wine memorabilia. Terrace for lunch. Interesting modern menu. Informal and efficient service.

X **Le Petit Blanc,** Fiveways, Lime Hill Rd, TN1 1LJ, ✆ (01892) 559170, *tunbridgewells@lepetitblanc.co.uk, Fax (01892) 559171* – ▤. MC AE VISA B
closed 25 December – **Rest** - Brasserie - 14.50 (lunch) and a la carte 17.50/29.50.
◆ Opened in 2004, with simple, modern décor: banquette seats and full-length glass windows. Extensive selection of menus with a French base: excellent value prix fixe.

at Speldhurst *North : 3½ m. by A 26 – A – ✉ Royal Tunbridge Wells.*

George & Dragon, Speldhurst Hill, TN3 0NN, ✆ (01892) 863125, *Fax (01892) 86321(* – P. MC VISA
closed Sunday dinner – **Rest** a la carte 20.00/30.00 ♀.
◆ Locally renowned black-and-white fronted pub where fresh Kentish ingredients from small, local suppliers are proudly employed in good value dishes with a classic French base.

at Pembury *Northeast : 4 m. by A 264 – A – off B 2015 – ✉ Royal Tunbridge Wells.*

Ramada Tunbridge Wells, 8 Tonbridge Rd, TN2 4QL, ✆ (01892) 823567, *sales@ramdajarvis .co.uk, Fax (01892) 823931,* – ⇔ P – 180. MC AE ◑ VISA
Rest 14.95/21.95 ♀ – 11.95 – **82 rm** 110.00 – 110.00, 2 suites.
◆ Well-fitted, bright, modern furniture and furnishings throughout. Room selection includes Studio range, particularly geared to business travellers, with desks and modems. Bright, warmly toned restaurant.

ROYSTON *Herts.* 504 T 27.

The Cabinet at Reed, High St, Reed, SG8 8AH, South : 3 m. by A 10 ✆ (01763) 84836(
Fax (01763) 849407, – ⇔ P. MC AE VISA
closed 25 December, Sunday dinner and Monday – **Rest** (Sunday brunch) 14.95 (lunch) and a la carte 25.00/35.00 ♀.
◆ 16C clapperboard country pub with a smart, contemporary style restaurant. Menu offers an interesting choice of modern British dishes; good wine list, many by the glass.

ROZEL BAY *Jersey (Channel Islands)* 503 P 33 and 517 ⑪ – *see Channel Islands.*

RUAN-HIGH-LANES *Cornwall* 503 F 33 – *see Veryan.*

RUCKHALL *Herefordshire – see Hereford.*

RUGBY *Warks.* 503 504 Q 26 – *pop. 61 988.*

18 Whitefields H., Coventry Rd, Thurlaston ✆ (01788) 815555 – 18 Clifton Rd ✆ (0178(544637.
The Home of Rugby Football Visitor Centre, 4 Lawrence Sheriff St ✆ (01788) 53497(visitor.centre@rugby.gov.uk.
London 88 – Birmingham 33 – Leicester 21 – Northampton 20 – Warwick 17.

Brownsover Hall, Brownsover Lane, CV21 1HU, North : 2 m. by A 426 and Brownsover Rd ✆ (0870) 6096104, *brownsoverhall@corushotels.com, Fax (01788) 535367,* – ⇔ P – 70. MC AE ◑ VISA.
Rest *(closed Saturday lunch)* (buffet lunch)/dinner 21.00 and a la carte 26.45/34.45 **s.**
45 rm 88.00/138.00 – 138.00/158.00, 2 suites.
◆ 19C Gothic building designed by Gilbert Scott. Interiors include a main hall of dramatic proportions and vast ornate fireplaces. Newer courtyard rooms particularly smart. Tall Gothic windows define dining room on a grand scale.

at Crick *Southeast : 6 m. on A 428.*

Ibis without rest., Parklands, NN6 7EX, West : 1 ¼ m. on A 428 ☎ (01788) 824331, *H3588@accor.com, Fax (01788) 824332* – **111 rm** 48.95 – 48.95.

• Simply furnished and brightly decorated with well-proportioned modern bedrooms. Conveniently located lodge hotel suited to business and family stopovers.

RUNSWICK BAY *N. Yorks. – ✉ Whitby.*

London 285 – Middlesbrough 24 – Whitby 9.

Cliffemount, TS13 5HU, ☎ (01947) 840103, *cliffemount@runswickbay.fsnet.co.uk, Fax (01947) 841025,* – rest, VISA

Rest a la carte 15.00/36.50 – **20 rm** 35.00/65.00 – 122.00.

• Well-run hotel, perched on the clifftops overlooking picturesque Runswick Bay. Neatly appointed rooms, most enjoying the excellent view, some with balcony. Bright, airy restaurant with fine sea outlook.

RUSHLAKE GREEN *E. Sussex* 504 U 31 – ✉ *Heathfield.*

London 54 – Brighton 26 – Eastbourne 13.

Stone House, TN21 9QJ, Northeast corner of the green ☎ (01435) 830553, *Fax (01435) 830726,* VISA

closed 24 December-1 January – **Rest** (residents only) (dinner only and lunch May-August) 24.95 s. – **5 rm** 85.00/120.00 – 195.00/245.00, 1 suite.

• Charming part 15C, part Georgian country house surrounded by parkland. All interiors delightfully furnished with antiques and fine art. Garden produce features on menu.

The Horse and Groom, The Green, TN21 9QE, ☎ (01435) 830320, *chappellhatpeg@aol.com, Fax (01435) 830310,* VISA

closed dinner 25-26 December – **Rest** a la carte 20.00/35.00 ♀.

• A warm country feel pervades: low beams, dried hops, copper kettles over fireplace. Two cosy dining rooms serving robust home-made fare, including best market fish.

RYDE *I.O.W.* 503 504 Q 31 – *see Wight (Isle of).*

RYE *E. Sussex* 504 W 31 *Great Britain G.* – *pop. 4 195.*

See : *Old Town★★ : Mermaid Street★, St Mary's Church (★).*

The Heritage Centre, Strand Quay ☎ (01797) 226696, ryetic@rother.gov.uk.

London 61 – Brighton 49 – Folkestone 27 – Maidstone 33.

Mermaid Inn, Mermaid St, TN31 7EY, ☎ (01797) 223065, *mermaidinnrye@btconnect.com, Fax (01797) 225069* – rest, VISA.

Rest 23.00/36.50 and a la carte 35.00/47.50 ♀ – **31 rm** (dinner included) 115.00 – 230.00.

• Historic inn dating from 15C. Immense character from the timbered exterior on a cobbled street to the heavily beamed, antique furnished interior warmed by roaring log fires. Two dining options: both exude age and character.

Rye Lodge, Hilders Cliff, TN31 7LD, ☎ (01797) 223838, *info@ryelodge.co.uk, Fax (01797) 223585,* – rest, VISA

Rest (dinner only) 29.50 and a la carte 22.50/32.00 ♀ – **18 rm** 75.00/110.00 – 100.00/200.00.

• Family run house located close to historic town centre yet with Romney Marsh in sight. Welcoming guest areas and comfortable, smartly fitted rooms, three in the courtyard. Enjoy dining in candlelight.

Jeake's House without rest., Mermaid St, TN31 7ET, ☎ (01797) 222828, *stay@jeakeshouse.com, Fax (01797) 222623* – VISA

11 rm 39.00/75.00 – 96.00/120.00.

• Down a cobbled lane, a part 17C house, once a wool store and a Quaker meeting place. Welcoming atmosphere amid antiques, sloping floors and beams. Pretty, traditional rooms.

Old Vicarage without rest., 66 Church Sq, TN31 7HF, ☎ (01797) 222119, *info@oldvicaragerye.co.uk, Fax (01797) 227466* –

closed Christmas – **4 rm** 70.00/85.00 – 90.00/110.00.

• Former vicarage dating from 14C with Georgian façade, surrounded by medieval houses. Floral fabrics and period furniture in bedrooms. Home baking and preserves at breakfast.

ENGLAND

Durrant House without rest., 2 Market St, TN31 7LA, (01797) 223182, info@durrant-house.com, Fax (01797) 226940, – . VISA
closed 5 January-12 February – **6 rm** ☐ ★55.00/78.00 – ★★75.00/98.00.
• Grade I listed house of unknown age. Neat breakfast room with daily breakfast specials. Bright lounge looks down East Street. Carefully appointed, immaculate modern rooms.

Little Orchard House without rest., West St, TN31 7ES, (01797) 223831, info@littleorchardhouse.com, Fax (01797) 223831, – . VISA.
minimum stay two nights at weekends – **3 rm** ☐ ★50.00/70.00 – ★★90.00/100.00.
• Charming cottage in quiet street, rebuilt 1745. Surrounded by peaceful garden. Pleasantly cluttered atmosphere with paintings and objets d'art in communal areas and rooms.

The Benson without rest., 15 East St, TN31 7JY, (01797) 225131, info@bensonhotel.co.uk, Fax (01797) 225512, ← – . VISA.
weekends only December-February – **3 rm** ★65.00 – ★★104.00.
• Former wool merchant's house and vicarage, built in 1707. Comfortable sitting room. Rooms have four-posters or half-testers: two have views of Romney Marsh and River Rother.

Flushing Inn, 4 Market St, TN31 7LA, (01797) 223292, j.e.flynn@talk21.com – .
VISA
closed first 2 weeks January, first 2 weeks June, Monday dinner and Tuesday – **Rest** Seafood - 18.50/26.50 and lunch a la carte 17.00/25.50.
• A neighbourhood institution, this 15C inn with heavily timbered and panelled dining area features a superb 16C fresco. The seafood oriented menu has a local, traditional tone.

The Fish Café, 17 Tower St, TN31 7AT, (01797) 222226, info@thefishcafe.com, Fax (01797) 229260 – 65. AE VISA
closed 25 December and 2-9 January – **Rest** - Seafood - (dinner booking essential) a la carte 18.00/28.00 ♀.
• Large converted warehouse: terracotta painted ground floor for seafood lunches and eclectic options. Dinner upstairs features more serious piscine menus. Tangible buzziness.

Landgate Bistro, 5-6 Landgate, TN31 7LH, (01797) 222829 – VISA
closed 1 week Christmas, 1 week summer, 1 week autumn, Sunday and Monday – **Rest** (dinner only) a la carte 19.60/28.10 **s.** ♀.
• Well established, personally run, unpretentious bistro: a local favourite. Classic and modern cooking is fresh and tasty with good choice seafood reassuringly to the fore.

at Camber Southeast : 4¼ m. by A 259 – ✉ Rye.

The Place, New Lydd Rd, Camber Sands, TN31 7RB, (01797) 225057, enquiries@theplacecambersands.co.uk, Fax (01797) 227003, , – rm, rest, – 50.
AE VISA.
closed 25-26 December – **Rest** a la carte 22.00/29.00 ♀ – **18 rm** ★75.00/90.00 ★★120.00/125.00.
• Immaculately whitewashed, converted former seaside motel located over the dunes. Smart, stylish rooms with a good level of facilities and charming extra touches. Informal brasserie style restaurant with emphasis on local ingredients.

at Peasmarsh Northwest : 4 m. on A 268 – ✉ Rye.

Flackley Ash, London Rd, TN31 6YH, on A 268 (01797) 230651, enquiries@flackleyashhotel.co.uk, Fax (01797) 230510, , , , – rest, – 100.
VISA
Rest (bar lunch Monday-Saturday)/dinner 24.50 ♀ – **41 rm** ☐ ★86.00/91.00 ★★156.00/166.00, 4 suites.
• Extended Georgian country house of red brick. Traditional style throughout with comfortable lounge and bar areas. Each well-equipped bedroom is of a unique size and shape. Dining room has sunny conservatory extension.

SAFFRON WALDEN Essex 504 U 27 – pop. 14 313.

London 43 – Bishop's Stortford 12 – Cambridge 18.

the restaurant, Victoria House, 2 Church St, CB10 1JW, (01799) 526444 –
VISA
closed 2 weeks January, Sunday and Monday – **Rest** (dinner only) a la carte 20.85/30.85 ♀.
• Stylishly converted cellar with an informal feel: candles light the brick and flint walls and etched glass tables. Original, contemporary menu; relaxed style and service.

Dish, 13a King St, CB10 1HE, (01799) 513300, sales@dishrestaurant.co.uk, Fax (01799) 531699 – . AE VISA
closed 25-26 December, 1 January and Sunday dinner – **Rest** 13.50 (lunch) and dinner a la carte 21.90/28.50 ♀.
• First floor restaurant within characterful beamed house in town centre. Modern paintings exude jazzy theme. Classically based dishes take on adventurous note at dinner.

Maze, 9 Market Pl, CB10 1HR, (01799) 529255, *Fax (01799) 520362* – . VISA
closed 25 December-5 January, Sunday and Monday – **Rest** (dinner only) a la carte 24.85/29.40.
◆ Well established eatery, a mix of old and new, tucked away in corner of market place. Coffee shop during the day; evening menu has a traditional base with French influences.

t Littlebury Green *West : 4½ m. by B 1383 – Saffron Walden.*

Chaff House, Ash Grove Barns, CB11 4XB, (01763) 836278, *dianaduke@btopenworld.com, Fax (01763) 837340,* , – rest, P. VISA.
closed 25 December and 13 January-6 February – **Rest** (by arrangement) (communal dining) 25.00/30.00 – **3 rm** ☆37.00/40.00 – ☆☆70.00/80.00.
◆ Lovely barn conversion on 900 acre estate. Excellent craftsmanship: exposed beams, well appointed lounge. Very smart rooms, two with their own stable doors, all with rafters. Communal dining room is full of rustic character.

T AGNES *Cornwall* 503 E 33 *The West Country G. – pop. 2 759.*
See : *St Agnes Beacon★★ (※★★).*
Env. : *Portreath★, SW : 5½ m.*
Perranporth, Budnic Hill (01872) 572454.
London 302 – Newquay 12 – Penzance 26 – Truro 9.

Rose-in-Vale Country House, Mithian, TR5 0QD, East : 2 m. by B 3285 (01872) 552202, *reception@rose-in-vale-hotel.co.uk, Fax (01872) 552700,* heated, – P. VISA
closed 3 January-20 February – ***The Valley :*** **Rest** (light lunch Monday-Saturday)/dinner 32.00 **s.** – **18 rm** ☆68.00/120.00 – ☆☆120.00/180.00.
◆ Handsome Georgian manor clad in climbing roses; outdoor pool and peaceful gardens with summer house and dovecote. Classically styled lounge bar and library; well-kept rooms. Neat, formal dining room with local specials.

T ALBANS *Herts.* 504 T 28 *Great Britain G. – pop. 82 429.*
See : *City★ - Cathedral★* BZ – *Verulamium★ (Museum★ AC AY).*
Env. : *Hatfield House★★ AC, E : 6 m. by A 1057.*
Batchwood Hall, Batchwood Drive (01727) 833349 – , Redbourn, Kinsbourne Green Lane (01582) 793493.
Town Hall, Market Pl (01727) 864511.
London 27 – Cambridge 41 – Luton 10.

Plans on following pages

Sopwell House, Cottonmill Lane, AL1 2HQ, Southeast : 1 ½ m. by A 1081 and Mile House Lane (01727) 864477, *enquiries@sopwellhouse.co.uk, Fax (01727) 844741,* , , , , , , – P – 450. VISA.
Magnolia : **Rest** *(closed Saturday and Monday lunch)* 17.50/25.95 and a la carte 27.20/41.85 – ***Bejerano's Brasserie :*** **Rest** a la carte 14.90/25.50 – 14.00 – **127 rm** ☆99.00/169.00 – ☆☆169.00/185.00, 2 suites.
◆ Everything denotes peace and seclusion: pretty gardens, leather furnished lounge, modern spa with Japanese treatments, pool and gym. Modern rooms and apartments. Magnolia features eponymous 100 year-old trees. Bejerano's Brasserie with swimming pool views.

St Michael's Manor; 'St Michael's Village', Fishpool St, AL3 4RY, (01727) 864444, *reservations@stmichaelsmanor.com, Fax (01727) 848909,* , – rest, P. VISA
AY d
Rest a la carte 26.90/45.30 – **29 rm** ☆145.00 – ☆☆250.00/250.00, 1 suite.
◆ This part 16C, part William and Mary manor house overlooks a lake. Elegant bedrooms are named after trees; some are suites with sitting rooms, all are luxurious and stylish. Conservatory dining room with splendid vistas.

Thistle St Albans, Watford Rd, AL2 3DS, Southwest : 2 ½ m. at junction of A 405 with B 4630 (0870) 3339144, *reservations.stalbans@thistle.co.uk, Fax (0870) 3339244,* , , – , rest, P – 50. VISA
Noke : **Rest** *(closed Sunday dinner and Monday)* 18.00/26.95 **s.** and a la carte – 11.50 – **109 rm** ☆160.00 – ☆☆160.00, 2 suites.
◆ A busy, business hotel with country house charm. Leisure facilities include pool, jacuzzi and fitness centre. Rooms are solidly stylish with wall lamps and patterned fabrics. Restaurant with conservatory and floral drapes.

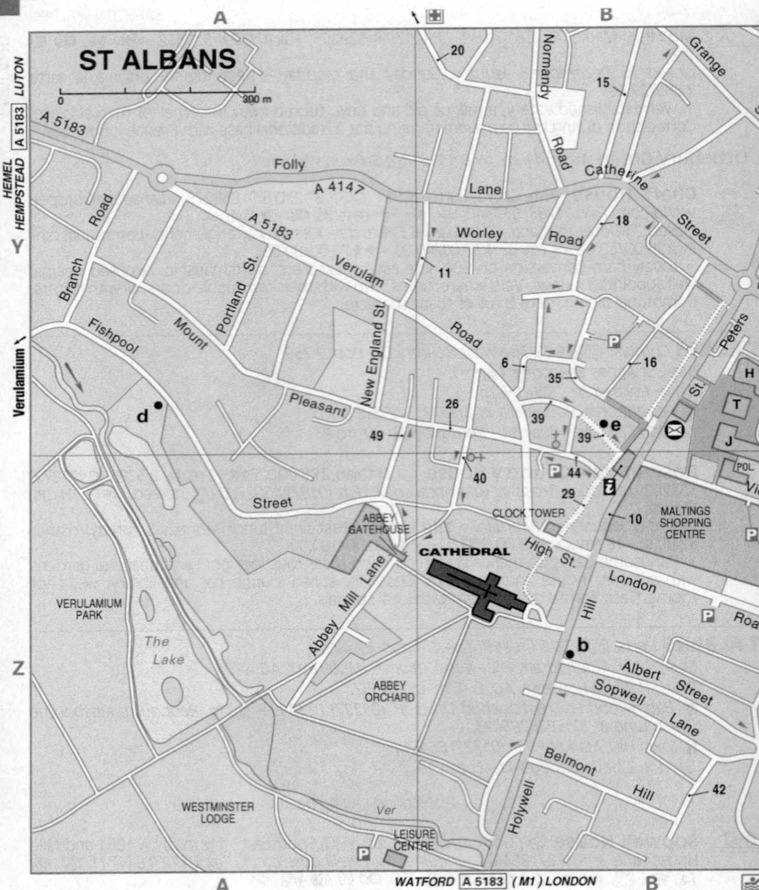

Comfort, Ryder House, Holywell Hill, AL1 1HG, ✆ (01727) 848849, *admin@gb055.net.com, Fax (01727) 812210* – ⇕, ⇆, ▤ rest, ♿ P – 35. MC AE ◑ VISA. BZ
Rest (dinner only) 18.95 and a la carte 18.00/22.00 s. – ☕ 8.95 – **60 rm** ☆75.00/79.00 ☆☆75.00/79.00.
◆ Built by Samuel Ryder, donor of golf's Ryder cup. Defined by Edwardian feature stained glass dome and carved fireplace. The bedrooms, though, are of practical ber Meals served in restaurant or your room.

Ardmore House, 54 Lemsford Rd, AL1 3PR, ✆ (01727) 859313, *info@ardmorehou hotel.co.uk, Fax (01727) 859313,* – ⇆ P. MC AE VISA. CY
Rest *(closed Saturday, Sunday and Bank Holidays)* (dinner only) a la carte 18.25/25.00 s.
40 rm ☕ ☆60.00/85.00 – ☆☆75.00/125.00.
◆ Edwardian residence with Victorian annex: this is a traditional, family owned hote Homely bedrooms have the feel of a lounge, boasting sofas and wall lamps. Tradition dining room with menu to match.

Sukiyaki, 6 Spencer St, AL3 5EG, ✆ (01727) 865009 – MC AE ◑ VISA BY
closed 2 weeks in summer, 1 week Christmas, Sunday and Monday – **Rest** - Japanese 9.50/25.00 and a la carte 14.25/19.50.
◆ A pared-down style, minimally decorated restaurant with simple, precise helpin of Japanese food. No noodles or sushi, expect instead sukiyaki (a beef dish), ar tempura.

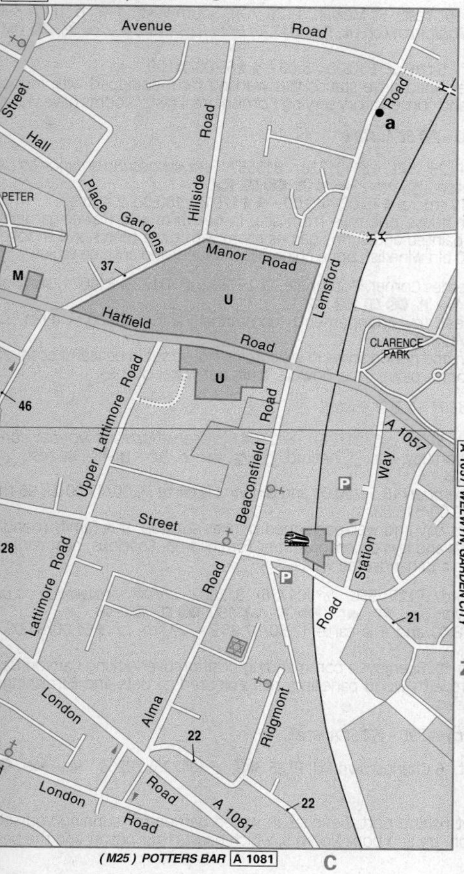

Abbey Mill Lane . . . . . AZ
Albert St . . . . . BZ
Alma Rd . . . . . CZ
Avenue Rd . . . . . CY
Beaconsfield Rd . . . . . CYZ
Belmont Hill . . . . . BZ
Branch Rd . . . . . AY
Bricket Rd . . . . . BCYZ 5
Britton Ave . . . . . BY 6
Carlisle Ave . . . . . BCY 8
Catherine St . . . . . BY
Chequer St . . . . . BZ 10
Church Crescent . . . . . ABY 11
Cottonmill Lane . . . . . BCZ 13
Dalton St . . . . . BY 15
Drovers Way . . . . . BY 16
Etna Rd . . . . . BY 18
Fishpool St . . . . . AYZ
Folly Ave . . . . . BY 20
Folly Lane . . . . . ABY
Grange St . . . . . BY
Grimston Rd . . . . . CZ 21
Grosvenor Rd . . . . . CZ 22
Hall Pl. Gardens . . . . . CY
Hatfield Rd . . . . . CY
High St . . . . . BZ
Hillside Rd . . . . . CY
Holywell Hill . . . . . BZ
Lattimore Rd . . . . . CZ
Lemsford Rd . . . . . CY
London Rd . . . . . BCZ
Lower Dagnall St . . . . . BYZ 26
Maltings Shopping Centre . . . . . BZ
Manor Rd . . . . . CY
Market Pl . . . . . BZ 29
Marlborough Rd . . . . . CZ 28
Mount Pleasant . . . . . AY
New England St . . . . . AY
Normandy Rd . . . . . BY
Old London Rd . . . . . CZ
Portland St . . . . . AY
Ridgemont Rd . . . . . CZ
Russell Ave . . . . . BY 35
St Peter's Rd . . . . . CY 37
St Peter's St . . . . . BCY
Sopwell Lane . . . . . BZ
Spencer St . . . . . BY 39
Spicer St College . . . . . BYZ 40
Station Way . . . . . CZ
Thorpe Rd . . . . . BZ 42
Upper Dagnall St . . . . . BYZ 44
Upper Lattimore Rd . . . . . CYZ
Upper Marlborough Rd . . . . . CYZ 46
Verulam Rd . . . . . ABY
Victoria St . . . . . BCZ
Watson's Walk . . . . . CZ 48
Welclose St . . . . . AYZ 49
Worley Rd . . . . . BY

ST ANNE *Alderney (Channel Islands)* 503 Q 33 and 517 ⑨ – *see Channel Islands.*

ST ANNE'S *Lancs.* 502 K 22 – *see Lytham St Anne's.*

ST AUBIN *Jersey (Channel Islands)* 503 P 33 and 517 ⑪ – *see Channel Islands.*

ST AUSTELL *Cornwall* 503 F 32 *The West Country G. – pop. 22 658.*

See : *Holy Trinity Church*★.

Env. : *St Austell Bay*★★ *(Gribbin Head*★★*) E : by A 390 and A 3082 – Carthew : Wheal Martyn China Clay Heritage Centre*★★ *AC, N : 2 m. by A 391 – Mevagissey*★★ *- Lost Gardens of Heligan*★*, S : 5 m. by B 3273 – Charlestown*★*, SE : 2 m. by A 390 – Eden Project*★★*, NE : 3 m. by A 390 at St Blazey Gate.*

Exc. : *Trewithen*★★★ *AC, NE : 7 m. by A 390 – Lanhydrock*★★*, NE : 11 m. by A 390 and B 3269 – Polkerris*★*, E : 7 m. by A 390 and A 3082.*

18 *Carlyon Bay* ☏ *(01726) 814250.*

London 281 – Newquay 16 – Plymouth 38 – Truro 14.

Poltarrow Farm without rest., St Mewan, PL26 7DR, Southwest : 1 ¾ m. by A 390 ✆ (01726) 67111, *enquire@poltarrow.co.uk, Fax (01726) 67111,* ⊠, ⌂, ⚘ – ⇎ P. MO VISA ✗
closed Christmas-New Year – **5 rm** ☐ ✝40.00/45.00 – ✝✝65.00/70.00.
◆ Tucked away down a tree-lined drive stands this working farm equipped with indoor pool, elegant sitting room and conservatory serving Cornish breakfasts. Rooms have views.

at Tregrehan *East : 2½ m. by A 390 – ⊠ St Austell.*

Boscundle Manor, PL25 3RL, ✆ (01726) 813557, *stay@boscundlemanor.co.uk Fax (01726) 814997,* ⚲ heated, ⊠, ⌂ – ⇎ ✆ P. MO AE VISA
Rest (dinner only) 35.00 – **12 rm** ☐ ✝75.00/140.00 – ✝✝170.00/180.00, 2 suites.
◆ A converted 18C manor house one mile from sea, in beautiful wild flower gardens. Clean-lined rooms; simply painted and sunny games room with table tennis and snooker table. Dining room with 170 bin wine list, bone china, silver cutlery and antique tables.

Anchorage House, Nettles Corner, Boscundle, PL25 3RH, ✆ (01726) 814071, *stay@anchoragehouse.co.uk,* ⌂ – ⇎ P. MO AE VISA. ✗
March-14 November – **Rest** (by arrangement) (communal dining) 35.00 – **4 rm** ☐ ✝80.00/85.00 – ✝✝118.00/128.00.
◆ Intriguing mix of modern and period styles in welcoming house set in peaceful position. Antique beds in spacious rooms plus extras: flowers, fruit, hot water bottles.

at Carlyon Bay *East : 2½ m. by A 3601 – ⊠ St Austell.*

Carlyon Bay, PL25 3RD, ✆ (01726) 812304, *reservations@carlyonbay.com Fax (01726) 814938,* ≤ Carlyon Bay, ≋, ⚲ heated, ⊠, 18, ⌂, ⚘, ✗ – |‡| ⇎, ▤ rest, ✝ P – ⚑ 65. MO AE ⓓ VISA. ✗
Rest *(closed 25 and 31 December)* 16.50/30.00 and dinner a la carte 30.00/47.00 ♀ – **86 rm** ☐ ✝70.00/152.50 – ✝✝210.00/316.00.
◆ With superb views across bay and well-positioned pool as suntrap, this family friendly hotel has golf course access and lays on programmes for children. Spacious, neat rooms. Dining room with live music and handsome vistas.

Porth Avallen, Sea Rd, PL25 3SG, ✆ (01726) 812802, *info@porthavallen.co.uk Fax (01726) 817097,* ≤ Carlyon Bay, ⛱, ⌂ – ⇎ P – ⚑ 100. MO AE VISA. ✗
Rest (bar lunch)/dinner 38.00 and a la carte 17.50/37.95 ♀ – **27 rm** ☐ ✝61.00/85.00 ✝✝102.00/120.00.
◆ Built as a family home in 1928; enjoys a commanding position overlooking Carlyon Bay. Warmly decorated interiors with wood panelling, rich coloured carpets and furnishings. Restaurant with fine sea views.

at Charlestown *Southeast : 2 m. by A 390 – ⊠ St Austell.*

T' Gallants without rest., 6 Charlestown Rd, PL25 3NJ, ✆ (01726) 70203, ⌂ – ⇎. MO VISA. ✗
8 rm ✝45.00 – ✝✝65.00.
◆ Georgian house in quiet fishing port. Benches in walled garden for sunning yourself. Good value accommodation: try and book Room 5, which boasts four poster and the best view.

Revival, PL25 3NJ, ✆ (01726) 879053, ⛱ – ⇎. MO VISA
closed Sunday dinner and Monday – **Rest** a la carte 26.15/39.85 ♀.
◆ Once a cooperage; reputedly Charlestown's second oldest building, it overlooks 19C tall ships in the harbour. Local, seasonal ingredients used to good effect on all-day menus.

ST BLAZEY *Cornwall* 503 F 32 *The West Country G. – pop. 9 256 (inc. Par).*

Env. : *Eden Project★★, NW ; 1½ m. by A 390 and minor roads.*
London 276 – Newquay 21 – Plymouth 33 – Truro 19.

Nanscawen Manor House ✗ without rest., Prideaux Rd, PL24 2SR, West : ¾ m. by Luxulyan rd ✆ (01726) 814488, *keith@nanscawen.com,* ≤, ⚲ heated, ⌂ – ⇎ P. MO VISA ✗
3 rm ☐ ✝82.00 – ✝✝92.00/110.00.
◆ Sumptuous country house, until 1520 the home of Nanscawen family. Conservatory breakfast room set in fragrant gardens. Welcoming bedrooms; outdoor spa bath. No smoking.

ST BRELADE'S BAY *Jersey (Channel Islands)* 503 P 33 and 517 ⑪ – *see Channel Islands.*

ST ERVAN *Cornwall* – *see Padstow.*

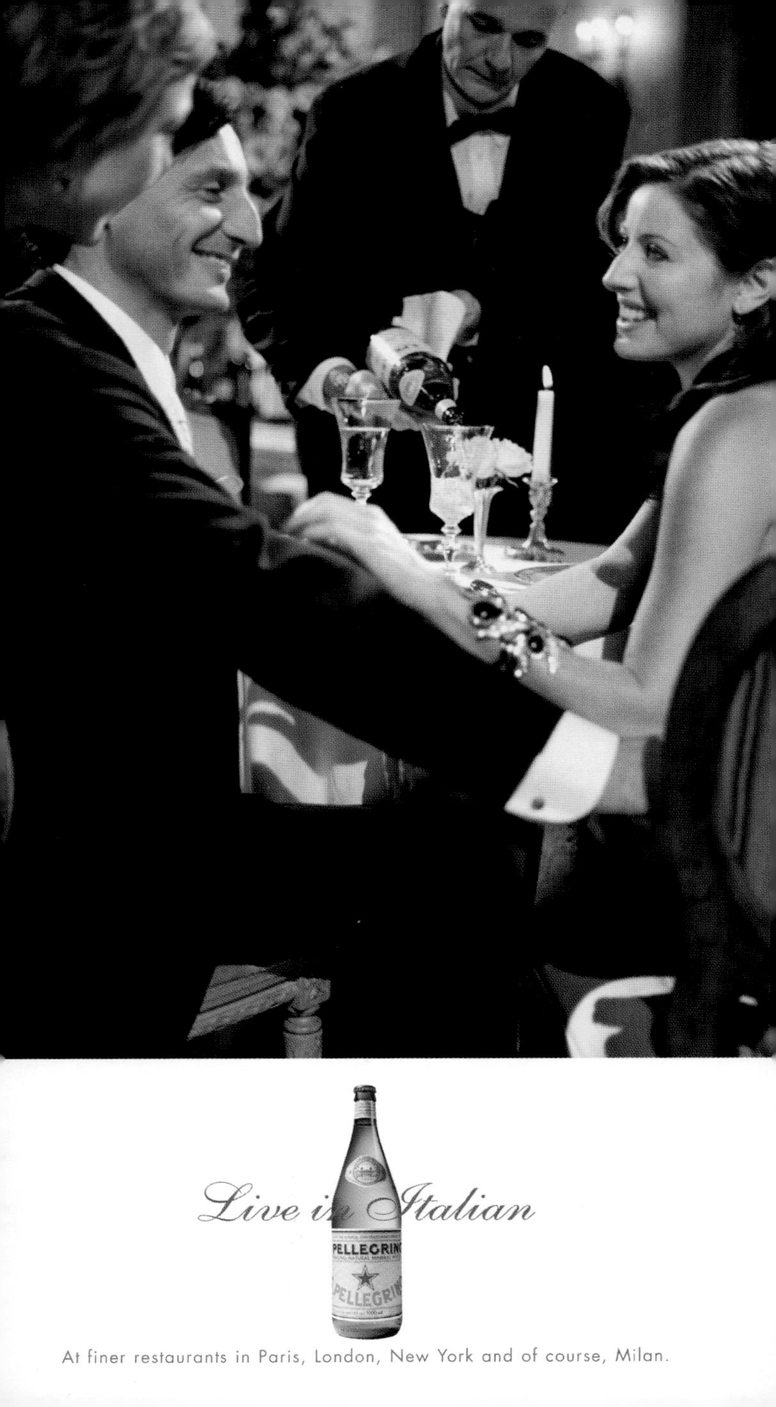

Live in Italian
At finer restaurants in Paris, London, New York and of course, Milan.

ST HELENS *Mersey.* 502 503 L 23 – *pop. 106 293.*

Sherdley Park Municipal, Sherdley Park ☎ (01744) 813149.

London 207 – Liverpool 16 – Manchester 27.

Hilton St Helens, Linkway West, WA10 1NG, ☎ (01744) 453444, *reservations.sthelens@hilton.com, Fax (01744) 454655,* ... 250. MC AE VISA

***Britisserie :* Rest** (bar lunch)/dinner 16.95 and a la carte 21.70/28.70 **s.** – 14.50 – **81 rm** 80.00/150.00 – 80.00/150.00, 3 suites.

• Built by Pilkington Glass, hence many glass features to the hotel, such as the atrium, and the consequent light ambience. Comfortable, unfussy rooms with air conditioning. Modern restaurant with glass pyramid ceiling.

Premier Travel Inn, Eurolink, Lea Green, WA9 4TT, South : 3 m. off A 570 ☎ (01744) 818971, *Fax (01744) 851427* – rm, rest, MC AE VISA.

Rest (grill rest.) – **40 rm** 46.95/46.95 – 48.95/48.95.

• Easy motorway access from this purpose-built lodge near the Europark business park. Practical, modern accommodation; informal, family friendly pub dining nearby.

ST HELIER *Jersey (Channel Islands)* 503 P 33 and 517 ⑪ – *see Channel Islands.*

ST ISSEY *Cornwall* 503 F 32 – *see Padstow.*

ST IVES *Cambs.* 504 T 27 – *pop. 9 866* – ✉ *Huntingdon.*

London 75 – Cambridge 14 – Huntingdon 6.

Slepe Hall, Ramsey Rd, PE27 5RB, ☎ (01480) 463122, *mail@slepehall.co.uk, Fax (01480) 300706,* – rest, – 200. MC AE VISA

closed 26-30 December – **Rest** 15.00 (lunch) and a la carte 16.45/22.95 – **16 rm** 80.00/90.00 – 100.00/125.00.

• Constructed in 1848 as girls' boarding school. Rooms are far from institutional: simple décor, brightly emulsioned walls, canopy beds. The four-poster room is very popular. Restaurant boasts garden views.

ST IVES *Cornwall* 503 D 33 *The West Country G.*

See : *Town★★ - Barbara Hepworth Museum★★* AC Y **M1** – *Tate St Ives★★ (≤★★) - St Nicholas Chapel (≤★★)* Y – *Parish Church★* Y **A.**

Env. : *S : Penwith★★* Y.

Exc. : *St Michael's Mount★★ (≤★★) S : 10 m. by B 3306 – Y – B 3311, B 3309 and A 30.*

Tregenna Castle H. ☎ (01736) 795254 ext: 121 Y – *West Cornwall, Lelant ☎ (01736) 753401.*

The Guildhall, Street-an-Pol ☎ (01736) 796297, ivtic@penwith.gov.uk.

London 319 – Penzance 10 – Truro 25.

Plan on next page

The Garrack, Burthallan Lane, TR26 3AA, ☎ (01736) 796199, *mich@garrack.com, Fax (01736) 798955,* ≤, – MC AE VISA Y a

closed Christmas – ***The Restaurant :*** **Rest** (dinner only) 18.50/25.50 and a la carte 16.95/29.20 – **18 rm** 68.00/140.00 – 162.00/170.00.

• Well-established hotel with pleasant gardens close to Tate. Plenty of homely touches. Spacious pool and sauna. Individually designed bedrooms, many with feature beds. Very popular dining room serves Cornish specialities.

Pedn-Olva, West Porthminster Beach, TR26 2EA, ☎ (01736) 796222, *pednolva@smallandfriendly.co.uk, Fax (01736) 797710,* ≤ Harbour and bay, – MC AE VISA. Y c

The Lookout : **Rest** (bar lunch)/dinner 30.00 – **31 rm** 60.00/93.00 – 120.00/146.00.

• Meaning "lookout on the headland" in Cornish; boasts commanding views of harbour and bay. Sheltered sun terrace and pool. Neutral décor typified by simple bedrooms. Restaurant offers diners splendid outlook.

Blue Hayes without rest., Trelyon Ave, TR26 2AD, ☎ (01736) 797129, *info@bluehayes.co.uk, Fax (01736) 799098,* ≤, MC AE VISA. Y u

closed December-January – **6 rm** 115.00/125.00 – 170.00/190.00.

• 19C house with super view from terrace over the harbour; access to coast path from garden. Hi-tech interior. Single course supper available. Well-appointed bedrooms.

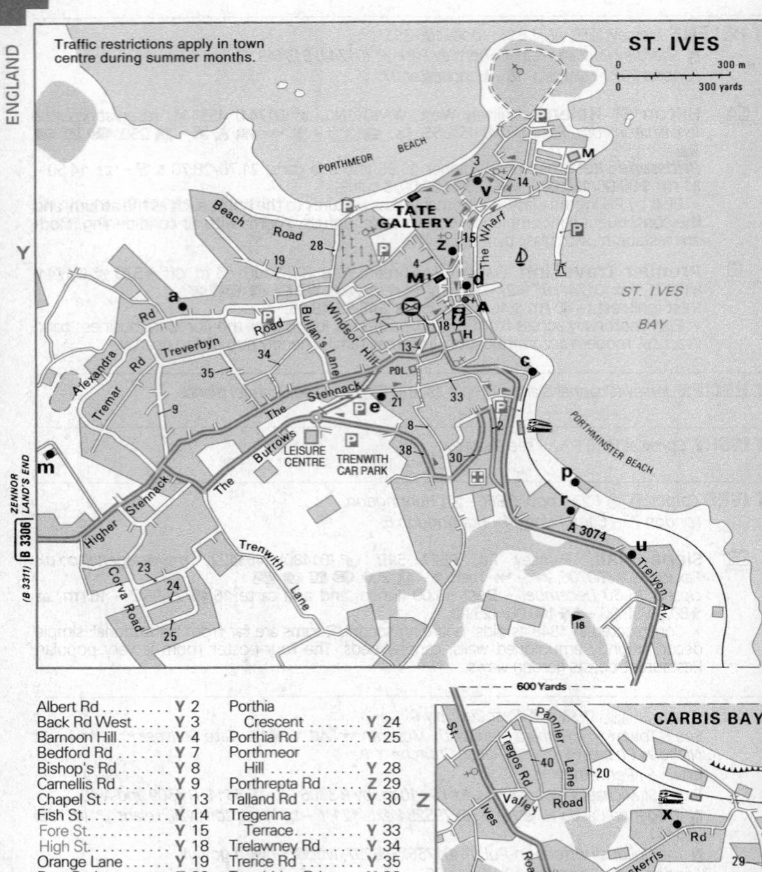

Albert Rd	Y 2	Porthia Crescent	Y 24
Back Rd West	Y 3	Porthia Rd	Y 25
Barnoon Hill	Y 4	Porthmeor Hill	Y 28
Bedford Rd	Y 7	Porthrepta Rd	Z 29
Bishop's Rd	Y 8	Talland Rd	Y 30
Carnellis Rd	Y 9	Tregenna Terrace	Y 33
Chapel St	Y 13	Trelawney Rd	Y 34
Fish St	Y 14	Trerice Rd	Y 35
Fore St	Y 15	Trewidden Rd	Y 38
High St	Y 18	Wheal Whidden	Z 40
Orange Lane	Y 19		
Parc Owles	Z 20		
Park Ave	Y 21		
Penwith Rd	Y 23		

Primrose Valley, Porthminster Beach, TR26 2ED, ✆ (01736) 794939, *info@primroseonline.co.uk, Fax (01736) 794939,* ← – ⇤ P. MC VISA. ⊁ Y
closed 20-27 December and January – **Rest** (by arrangement in summer only) 19.00 – **8 rm** ☖ 🚹63.00/80.00 – 🚹🚹100.00/760.00.
◆ Edwardian villa with unrivalled proximity to beach. Stylish café bar and lounge; relaxing front patio. Local suppliers ensure good breakfast choice. Individually styled rooms. Summer-time meals arranged with the owners.

Old Vicarage without rest., Parc-an-Creet, TR26 2ES, ✆ (01736) 796124, *holidays@oldvicaragehotel.com, Fax (01736) 796343,* – ⇤ P. MC VISA Y
March-October – **7 rm** ☖ 🚹52.00 – 🚹🚹68.00.
◆ Former vicarage built of granite and slate retains Victorian charm and character especially in bar lounge furnished in red velvet, gilt and mahogany. Rooms in uniform style.

Pebble without rest., 4 Parc Ave, TR26 2DN, ✆ (01736) 794168, *info@pebble-hotel.co.uk* Y
← – ⇤ ✆ P. MC VISA. ⊁
closed 20-28 December and January – **7 rm** ☖ 🚹30.00/90.00 – 🚹🚹60.00/100.00.
◆ Small family run hotel; superb views of harbour and bay. Make yourself at home in lounge stocked with local information books. Simply furnished bedrooms in cottage style.

XX **Alba,** Old Lifeboat House, The Wharf, TR26 1LF, ✆ (01736) 797222, *Fax (01736) 798937*, ≤ – ⊁ ▤. MC AE VISA Y d
restricted opening in winter – **Rest** - Seafood - a la carte 24.85/29.85 ♀.
◆ Ideally situated in centre of town, on both floors of Old Lifeboat House; good harbour views. Modern feel; artwork on walls. Tasty, extensive menus with a modern slant.

XX **Russets,** 18a Fore St, TR26 1AB, ✆ (01736) 794700, *info@russets.co.uk, Fax (01736) 794700* – ⊁. MC AE ⓓ VISA Y z
closed January – **Rest** - Seafood specialities - (light lunch)/dinner a la carte 22.45/28.65 ♀.
◆ Steamed monkfish wrapped in banana leaf sums up the seafood bias of the menus in a spacious town centre restaurant. Also boasts comfortable bar furnished with Chesterfields.

X **Porthminster Cafe,** Porthminster Beach, TR26 2EB, ✆ (01736) 795352, *p.minster@btopenworld.com, Fax (01736) 795352*, ≤ St Ives Bay and town, 🏖 – ⊁. MC VISA Y p
April-October – **Rest** - Seafood - a la carte 17.00/32.50 ♀.
◆ 1930s beach house on Porthminster sands. Super views: large terrace for al fresco dining. Colourful local artwork on walls. Seafood oriented dishes plus eclectic dinner menus.

X **Blue Fish,** Norway Lane, TR26 1LZ, ✆ (01736) 794204, *Fax (01736) 794204*, ≤, 🏖 – MC VISA Y v
Rest - Seafood - a la carte 20.85/47.90.
◆ Welcoming, family run eatery in the centre of town with a charming sunny terrace affording views of the town. Local and Mediterranean seafood in a simple, relaxed style.

at Carbis Bay *South : 1¾ m. on A 3074 – ✉ St Ives.*

🏨 **Boskerris,** Boskerris Rd, TR26 2NQ, ✆ (01736) 795295, *reservations@boskerrishotel.co.uk*, ≤, 🌳 – ⊁ 📞 P. MC AE VISA. ✂ Z x
closed January and Christmas – **Rest** *(closed Sunday)* (dinner only) a la carte 20.00/38.00 ♀ – **16 rm** ☕ ✝60.00/101.00 – ✝✝80.00/140.00.
◆ Hotel with panoramic views of Carbis Bay and coastline. Lounge, separate TV room and bar serving light lunches. Outdoor pool overlooking the sea. Restaurant serving local fish, produce and herbs from hotel garden.

ST JUST *Cornwall 503 C 33 The West Country G. – pop. 1 890.*

See : *Church★.*

Env. : *Penwith★★ – Sancreed – Church★★ (Celtic Crosses★★), SE : 3 m. by A 3071 – St Buryan★★ (Church Tower★★), SE : 5½ m. by B 3306 and A 30 – Land's End★ (cliff scenery★★★), S : 5½ m. by B 3306 and A 30 – Cape Cornwall★ (≤★★), W : 1½ m. – Morvah (≤★★), NE : 4½ m. by B 3306 – Geevor Tin Mine★ AC, N : 3 m. by B 3306 – Carn Euny★, SE : 3 m. by A 3071 – Wayside Cross★ – Sennen Cove★ (≤★), S : 5½ m. by B 3306 and A 30.*

Exc. : *Porthcurno★, S : 9½ m. by B 3306, A 30 and B 3315.*

⛳18 *Cape Cornwall G. & C.C. ✆ (01736) 788611.*

London 325 – Penzance 7.5 – Truro 35.

🏠 **Boscean Country** 🐦, TR19 7QP, Northwest : ½ m. by Boswedden Rd ✆ (01736) 788748, *boscean@aol.com, Fax (01736) 788748*, ≤, 🌳 – ⊁ P. MC VISA. ✂
Rest (dinner only) (residents only) 14.00 – **12 rm** ☕ ✝35.00/39.00 – ✝✝50.00/56.00.
◆ Originally a doctor's residence; this Edwardian house is surrounded by 3 acres of walled gardens, a haven for wildlife. Wealth of oak panelling indoors; most rooms have views.

ST KEVERNE *Cornwall 503 E 33.*

London 302 – Penzance 26 – Truro 28.

🏠 **Old Temperance House** without rest., The Square, TR12 6NA, ✆ (01326) 280986, *julianpeyser@hotmail.co.uk, Fax (01326) 280986* – ⊁ P.
3 rm ☕ ✝45.00/60.00 – ✝✝76.00/110.00.
◆ 'Roses round the door' charm, in idyllic spot on pretty square. Spotlessly neat lounge. Excellent, out-of-the-ordinary breakfasts. Fresh, bright, carefully co-ordinated rooms.

ST LAWRENCE *Channel Islands – see Jersey.*

ST LAWRENCE *I.O.W. 503 504 Q 32 – see Wight (Isle of).*

ST LEONARDS *E. Sussex 504 V 31 – see Hastings and St Leonards.*

ST MARGARET'S AT CLIFFE *Kent 504 Y 30 – see Dover.*

ST MARTIN *Guernsey (Channel Islands)* 503 P 33 and 517 ⑩ – *see Channel Islands.*

ST MARTIN'S *Cornwall* 503 B 34 – *see Scilly (Isles of).*

ST MARY'S *Cornwall* 503 B 34 – *see Scilly (Isles of).*

ST MAWES *Cornwall* 503 E 33 *The West Country G.* – ✉ *Truro.*

See : *Town★ - Castle★ AC (≤★).*

Env. : *St Just-in-Roseland Church★★, N : 2½ m. by A 3078.*

London 299 – Plymouth 56 – Truro 18.

Tresanton ⛵, 27 Lower Castle Rd, TR2 5DR, ☎ (01326) 270055, *info@tresanton.com* *Fax (01326) 270053,* ≤ St Mawes bay, St Anthony's Head and lighthouse, – P – 50. MC AE VISA.
Rest - Seafood specialities - (booking essential to non-residents) 26.00/38.00 ♀ – **27 rm** ☕ ★148.00/198.00 – ★★210.00/280.00, 2 suites.
◆ Enduringly trendy former 1940s yachtsman's club with cinema. Watercolours on pale walls; gleaming crisp rooms with views; contemporary lounge and attentive service. Dining room boasts open terrace with harbour views and modern seafood dishes.

Idle Rocks, Harbourside, 1 Tredenham Rd, TR2 5AN, ☎ (01326) 270771, *reception@idlerocks.co.uk, Fax (01326) 270062,* ≤ harbour and estuary – ⇔. MC AE VISA
The Water's Edge : Rest (light lunch)/dinner 35.00 – **33 rm** ☕ ★49.00/94.00 – ★★179.00/258.00.
◆ Fine waterfront hotel with splendid views of the harbour and fishermen's cottages. Deep comfortable chairs in lounge and bright bedrooms, many with sea views. Restaurant with terrace overlooks the sea.

Rising Sun, The Square, TR2 5DJ, ☎ (01326) 270233, *info@risingsunstmawes.co.uk* *Fax (01326) 270198* – ⇔ rest. MC VISA
Rest (bar lunch Monday-Saturday)/dinner 30.00 ♀ – **8 rm** ☕ ★55.00/120.00 – ★★110.00/150.00.
◆ Renovated 17C house on harbour. Immaculately furnished bedrooms with a stylish feel. Lively, open-fired bar. A friendly place to rest your head. Buzzy conservatory restaurant with seascapes on the walls.

ST MAWGAN *Cornwall* 503 F 32 – ✉ *Newquay.*

London 262 – Plymouth 41 – St Austell 3.

The Falcon Inn, TR8 4EP, ☎ (01637) 860225, *Fax (01637) 860884,* , – ⇔. MC VISA
Rest a la carte 12.00/20.00 – **3 rm** ☕ ★26.00 – ★★68.00/74.00.
◆ Characterful 16C pub with cosy terrace. Warm interior in keeping with age of property well maintained rustic décor. Popular menus, with seafood the highlight. Comfy rooms.

ST MERRYN *Cornwall* 503 F 32 – *see Padstow.*

ST MICHAELS-ON-WYRE *Lancs.* 502 L 22.

London 235 – Blackpool 24 – Burnley 35 – Manchester 43.

Compton House without rest., Garstang Rd, PR3 0TE, ☎ (01995) 679378, *dave@compton-hs.co.uk, Fax (01995) 679378,* – ⇔ P. MC VISA.
April-November – **3 rm** ☕ ★25.00/30.00 – ★★40.00/50.00.
◆ Redbrick house on busy road. Attractive garden; abundance of flowers in hanging baskets. Village location; riverside walks. Cottage style rooms; one to rear is quieter.

ST PETER *Jersey (Channel Islands)* 503 P 33 and 517 ⑪ – *see Channel Islands.*

ST PETER PORT *Guernsey (Channel Islands)* 503 P 33 and 517 ⑩ – *see Channel Islands.*

ST SAVIOUR *Guernsey (Channel Islands)* 503 P 33 and 517 ⑨ – *see Channel Islands.*

ST SAVIOUR *Jersey (Channel Islands)* 503 P 33 and 517 ⑪ – *see Channel Islands.*

SALCOMBE *Devon* 503 I 33 *The West Country G. – pop. 1 893.*

Env. : *Sharpitor (Overbecks Museum and Garden★) (≤★★) AC, S : 2 m. by South Sands* **Z**.

Exc. : *Prawle Point (≤★★★) E : 16 m. around coast by A 381 –* **Y** *– and A 379.*

Council Hall, Market St ✆ (01548) 843927, info@salcombeinformation.co.uk.

London 243 – Exeter 43 – Plymouth 27 – Torquay 28.

SALCOMBE

Street	Square	No.
Allenhayes Rd	Y	2
Bonaventure Rd	Y	3
Buckley St	Y	4
Camperdown Rd	Y	7
Church St	Y	8
Coronation Rd	Y	9
Devon Rd	Y	13
Fore St	Y	
Fortescue Rd	Z	14
Grenville Rd	Y	15
Herbert Rd	Z	18
Knowle Rd	Y	19
Moult Rd	Z	20
Newton Rd	Y	23
Sandhills Rd	Z	24
Shadycombe Rd	Y	25

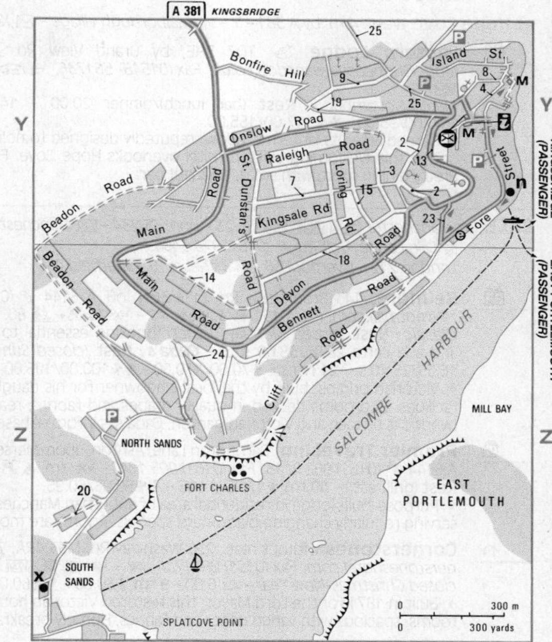

Tides Reach, South Sands, TQ8 8LJ, ✆ (01548) 843466, *enquire@tidesreach.com, Fax (01548) 843954,* ≤ estuary, squash – MC AE VISA **Z x**

closed December-January – **Rest** (dinner only) 35.00 s. – **35 rm** (dinner included) ★66.00/125.00 – ★★130.00/250.00.

◆ Set in sandy cove on Salcombe Estuary. South facing indoor pool with glass roof, plants. Lilac and green rooms boast floral fabrics and flowers; many have balconies. Stylish restaurant overlooks duck pond.

Marine, Cliff Rd, TQ8 8JH, ✆ (01548) 844444, *marine@menzies-hotels.co.uk, Fax (01548) 843109,* ≤ estuary, – MC AE VISA **Y e**

Rest 15.95/37.50 – **52 rm** (dinner included) ★55.00/225.00 – ★★110.00/300.00, 1 suite.

◆ Spectacular position on water's edge overlooking the estuary. Hotel makes the most of this; many bedrooms have balconies whilst centrally located rooms share the best views. Bright, roomy restaurant looks onto the water.

Restaurant 42, Fore St, TQ8 8JG, ✆ (01548) 843408, *jane@restaurant42.demon.co.uk, Fax (01548) 842854,* ≤ – MC VISA **Y n**

closed 4 January-10 February and Monday – **Rest** (dinner only and lunch Saturday-Sunday in July) a la carte 28.40/35.60.

◆ Things you may not know about 42: it has a delightful terrace/garden; fabulous views of the estuary; comfy lounge with squashy sofas; and interesting use of local ingredients.

ENGLAND

at Soar Mill Cove *Southwest : 4¼ m. by A 381 – Y – via Malborough village* – ✉ *Salcombe.*

Soar Mill Cove ⛰, TQ7 3DS, ☎ (01548) 561566, *info@soarmillcove.co.uk*
Fax (01548) 561223, <, ⛰, heated, ▢, ⛉, ✂ – ⇔ P. MC VISA
Rest (booking essential to non-residents) 25.00/38.00 and lunch a la carte 20.00/28.00 s. – **22 rm** (dinner included) ☕ ★80.00/160.00 – ★★150.00/250.00.
◆ Local stone and slate hotel on one level so that all guests can pass from bedroom to garden; rooms have terraces and chintz furnishings. A lovely secluded position. Classically styled dining room.

at Hope Cove *West : 4 m. by A 381 – Y – via Malborough village* – ✉ *Kingsbridge.*

Lantern Lodge ⛰, TQ7 3HE, by Grand View Rd ☎ (01548) 561280, *lantern-lodge@hopecove.wanadoo.co.uk, Fax (01548) 561736*, <, ⛰, ▢, ⛉ – ⇔ rest, P. MC VISA. ✗
March-November – **Rest** (bar lunch)/dinner 20.00 – **14 rm** (dinner included) ☕ ★70.00/93.00 – ★★117.00/155.00.
◆ Named after its lantern window, reputedly designed to hold a lantern and guide sailors home, this welcoming clifftop hotel overlooks Hope Cove. Front bedrooms have views. Pretty dining room with small, adjacent bar.

SALE *Gtr Manchester* 502 503 504 *N 23 – pop. 55 234* – ✉ *Manchester.*
18 Sale Lodge, Golf Rd ☎ (0161) 973 3404.
London 212 – Liverpool 36 – Manchester 6 – Sheffield 43.

Belmore, 143 Brooklands Rd, M33 3QN, off A 6144 ☎ (0161) 973 2538, *belmore-hotel@hotmail.com, Fax (0161) 973 2665*, ⛉ – ⇔ ☏ P – 🏛 80. MC AE ⓓ VISA
***Classic :* Rest** *(closed Monday dinner)* (booking essential to non-residents) 11.50/26.50 and a la carte 28.95/38.00 **s.** ♀ – ***Cada's :* Rest** *(closed Sunday)* (dinner only) a la carte 16.55/25.70 **s.** – **21 rm** ☕ ★70.00/170.00 – ★★100.00/195.00, 2 suites.
◆ Victorian origins: built by the local landowner for his daughter. Impressive conference facilities. Bedrooms decked in quality drapes and fabrics; rear rooms are quieter. Classic overlooks terrace and Victorian garden. Cada's is informal basement brasserie.

Premier Travel Inn, Carrington Lane, Ashton-upon-Mersey, M33 5BL, West : 1½ m. on A 6144 ☎ (0161) 962 8113, *Fax (0161) 905 1742* – ⇔ rm, ♿ P – 🏛 40. MC AE ⓓ VISA. ✗
Rest (grill rest.) – **40 rm** ★47.95/47.95 – ★★50.95/50.95.
◆ Purpose-built lodge in residential area of suburban Manchester, adjacent to popular grill serving regularly changing blackboard specials. Rooms are modern and good value.

Cornerstones without rest., 230 Washway Rd, M33 4RA, ☎ (0161) 283 6909, *info@cornerstoneshotel.com, Fax (0161) 2831754*, ⛉ – ⇔ P. MC VISA. ✗
closed Christmas-New Year – ☕ 6.00 – **9 rm** ★30.00 – ★★60.00.
◆ Built in 1871 for the Lord Mayor, this restored Victorian house is family run. A medley of rooms: spacious with varied décor and fabrics. Homely breakfast room.

Look out for red symbols, indicating particularly pleasant establishments.

SALFORD QUAYS *Gtr. Manchester* – *see Manchester.*

SALFORDS *Surrey* 504 *T 30* – *see Redhill.*

SALISBURY *Wilts.* 503 504 *O 30 The West Country G. – pop. 43 355.*
See : *City★★ – Cathedral★★★ AC* **Z** – *Salisbury and South Wiltshire Museum★ AC* **Z M2** – *Close★* **Z** *: Mompesson House★ AC* **Z A** – *Sarum St Thomas Church★* **Y B** – *Royal Gloucestershire, Berkshire and Wiltshire Regiment Museum★* **Z M1**.
Env. : *Wilton Village★ (Wilton House★★ AC, Wilton Carpet Factory★ AC), W : 3 m. by A 30* **Y** – *Old Sarum★ AC, N : 2 m. by A 345* **Y** – *Woodford (Heale House Garden★) AC, NW : 4½ m. by Stratford Rd* **Y**.
Exc. : *Stonehenge★★★ AC, NW : 10 m. by A 345 –* **Y** *– and A 303 – Wardour Castle★ AC, W : 15 m. by A 30* **Y**.
18, 9 Salisbury & South Wilts., Netherhampton ☎ (01722) 742645 – 18 High Post, Great Durnford ☎ (01722) 782356.
Fish Row ☎ (01722) 334956.
London 91 – Bournemouth 28 – Bristol 53 – Southampton 23.

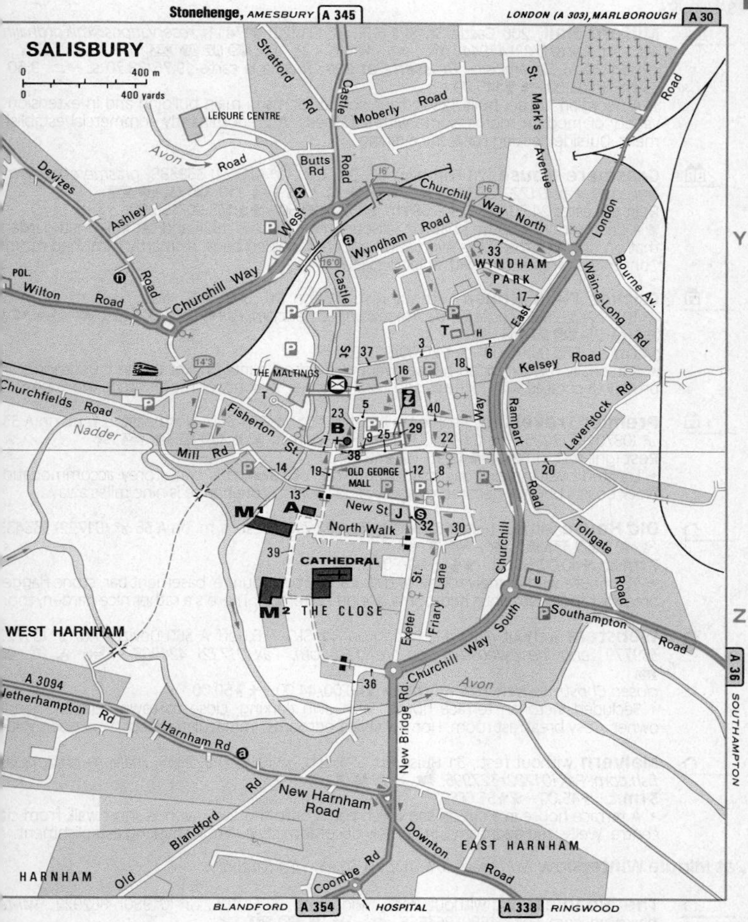

SALISBURY

edwin St . . . . . . Y 3	Greencroft St . . . . . . Y 18	Queen St . . . . . . Y 29
lue Boar Row . . . . . . Y 5	High St . . . . . . Z 19	St Ann St . . . . . . Z 30
ourne Hill . . . . . . Y 6	Maltings Shopping Centre (The) . . . . . . Y	St John St . . . . . . Z 32
ridge St . . . . . . YZ 7	Milford Hill . . . . . . Z 20	St Mark's Rd . . . . . . Y 33
rown St . . . . . . Z 8	Milford St . . . . . . Y 22	St Nicholas Rd . . . . . . Z 36
utcher Row . . . . . . Y 9	Minster St . . . . . . Y 23	Scots Lane . . . . . . Y 37
atherine St . . . . . . Z 12	New Canal . . . . . . Z 25	Silver St . . . . . . YZ 38
rane Bridge Rd . . . . . . Z 14	Old George Mall Shopping Centre . . . . . . Z	West Walk . . . . . . Z 39
rane St . . . . . . Z 13		Winchester St . . . . . . Y 40
ndless St . . . . . . Y 16		
stcourt Rd . . . . . . Y 17		

White Hart, 1 St John's St, SP1 2SD, ☎ (01722) 327476, *whitehartsalisbury@macdonald-hotels.co.uk, Fax (01722) 412761,* – – – 100. Z s

Squire's : **Rest** *(closed lunch Saturday and Bank Holidays)* 15.95/25.00 and dinner a la carte 22.95/30.95 **s.** – **68 rm** 125.00/135.00 – 135.00/145.00.

◆ The elegant portico façade of this 17C hotel hints at formality whilst interior is relaxed and comfortable with plenty of sofas and armchairs in lounge and plush bedrooms. Dine al fresco on foliage-filled terrace.

ENGLAND

Milford Hall, 206 Castle St, SP1 3TE, (01722) 417411, *reservations@milfordhallh tel.com, Fax (01722) 419444*, – P – 100. VISA Y
closed 25-26 December – ***Brasserie at 206 :*** **Rest** a la carte 19.75/28.70 **s.** – 9.50
35 rm 105.00 – 115.00.
• A Georgian house, built 1780s; four period rooms in main building and in extension variety of modern rooms, some with sofa beds. A predominantly commercial establish ment. Outside decking for terrace dining.

Grasmere House, 70 Harnham Rd, SP2 8JN, (01722) 338388, *grasmerehotel@m tral.co.uk, Fax (01722) 333710*, – P – 110. VISA Z
Rest a la carte 24.50/28.75 **s.** – **38 rm** 85.50/99.50 – 135.00/155.00.
• A deep redbrick house built for Salisbury merchants in 1896 and set in lawned garden that go down to the rivers Avon and Nadder. Canopied beds in smartly furnished room Conservatory restaurant with splendid views.

Cricket Field House without rest., Wilton Rd, SP2 9NS, West : 1 ¼ m. on A 3 (01722) 322595, *cricketfieldcottage@btinternet.com, Fax (01722) 322595*, – P – 25. VISA.
14 rm 50.00/75.00 – 70.00/90.00.
• Personally run extended house overlooking the County Cricket Ground. Bedrooms ar prettily decorated with pictures and floral touches; majority of rooms are in the annex.

Premier Travel Inn, Pearce Way, Bishopsdown, SP1 3GU, Northeast : 2 ½ m. on A 33 (08701) 977225, *Fax (01722) 337889* – , rest, P. VISA.
Rest (grill rest.) – **62 rm** 49.95 – 49.95.
• Located over a main road roundabout out of town, this two storey accommodatio block boasts brightly decorated, good value rooms. Stonehenge is nine miles away.

Old House without rest., 161 Wilton Rd, SP2 7JQ, West : 1 m. on A 36 (01722) 33343 *Fax (01722) 335551*, – P.
7 rm 40.00/55.00 – 55.00/80.00.
• 17C house with homely rooms and character: cosy lounge, basement bar, stone flagge breakfast room, spacious bedrooms, antique artefacts. There's a rather nice garden, too.

Websters without rest., 11 Hartington Rd, SP2 7LG, (off A 360 Devizes Rd) (0172 339779, *enquiries@websters-bed-breakfast.com, Fax (01722) 421903* – P. VISA Y
closed Christmas-New Year – **5 rm** 40.00/44.00 – 50.00.
• Secluded Victorian terrace house, with own parking, close to town centre. Friendl owner. Cosy breakfast room. Homely style bedrooms, immaculately kept; very good valu

Malvern without rest., 31 Hulse Rd, SP1 3LU, (01722) 327995, *malvern-gh@madas fish.com, Fax (01722) 327995*, – P. Y
3 rm 45.00 – 55.00.
• A terrace house in a cul-de-sac which backs onto the river Avon, a short walk from cit centre. Well-sized bedrooms, in homely decorative style. A non smoking establishment.

at Middle Winterslow *Northeast : 6½ m. by A 30 – Y – Salisbury.*

The Beadles without rest., Middleton, SP5 1QS, (01980) 862922, *winte bead@aol.com, Fax (01980) 863565*, – P. VISA.
March-December – – **3 rm** 40.00/50.00 – 65.00/70.00.
• Recently built from 100-year old bricks and Georgian in style; geese clack in garder Flower-filled rooms with extra touches: pictures, reading lamps, comfortable chairs. Cele bration breakfasts served on antique table.

at Whiteparish *Southeast : 7½ m. by A 36 – Z – on A 27 – Salisbury.*

Newton Farmhouse without rest., Southampton Rd, SP5 2QL, Southwest : 1½ m. o A 36 (01794) 884416, *reservations@newtonfarmhouse.co.uk*, – P.
closed Christmas – **8 rm** 40.00 – 90.00.
• Step back in time in this 16C farmhouse, gifted to Nelson's family after Battle of Trafa gar. Original bread oven in inglenook fireplace, oak beams and well. Cottagey rooms. Fi and fruit trees grow in conservatory breakfast room.

at Broad Chalke *Southwest : 7 m. by A 354 – Z – and Stratford Tony rd – Salisbury.*

Ebblesway Courtyard without rest., High Rd, SP5 5EF, East : ¾ m. (0172 780182, *enquiries@ebblesway courtyard.co.uk*, – P. VISA.
closed Christmas-New Year – **4 rm** 48.00/60.00 – 78.00.
• Peacefully located, stone-built, tastefully converted 19C stables in pretty grass court yard. Flag floored breakfast room with communal table. Exposed beams in all bedrooms.

at Burcombe *West : 5¼ m. by A 36 – Y – off A 30 – ✉ Salisbury.*

The Ship Inn, Burcombe Lane, SP2 0EJ, ☎ (01722) 743182, *theshipburcombe@mail.com, Fax (01722) 743182,* ☂, 🚗 – P. MC AE VISA
closed 5-20 January – **Rest** a la carte 18.20/26.45.
◆ Attractive part 17C pub: a tributary of river Nadder gurgles along at garden's end. Beams, open fires, plus sprinkling of modernity. Ample choice menus with seasonal variety.

at Teffont *West : 10¼ m. by A 36 – Y – and A 30 on B 3089 – ✉ Salisbury.*

Howard's House ⛵, Teffont Evias, SP3 5RJ, ☎ (01722) 716392, *enq@howardshousehotel.com, Fax (01722) 716820,* 🚗 – ⊭ rest, ☎ P. MC AE VISA
closed 5 days Christmas, last week February and first week March – **Rest** *(closed lunch Monday and Friday)* (booking essential to non-residents) 25.00/25.95 and dinner a la carte 37.85/40.15 ♀ – **9 rm** ☕ ★95.00 – ★★165.00.
◆ Personally run, part 17C dower house boasting fine gardens in a quaint, quiet village. Comfortable lounge and pleasant bedrooms with village/ garden vistas. Garden herbs and vegetables grace accomplished cooking.

at Stapleford *Northwest : 7 m. by A 36 – Y – on B 3083 – ✉ Salisbury.*

Elm Tree Cottage without rest., Chain Hill, SP3 4LH, ☎ (01722) 790507, *jaw.sykes@virgin.net,* 🚗 – ⊭ P
3 rm ☕ ★35.00/40.00 – ★★55.00/60.00.
◆ Pretty, redbrick, quintessentially English cottage; the lounge boasts inglenook fireplace. Conservatory overlooks garden. Self-contained, chintz rooms with cottagey décor.

at Little Langford *Northwest : 8 m. by A 36 – Y – and Great Wishford rd – ✉ Salisbury.*

Little Langford Farmhouse without rest., SP3 4NP, ☎ (01722) 790205, *bandb@littlelangford.co.uk, Fax (01722) 790086,* ≤, 🚗, 🐎 – ⊭ P. MC VISA. ✂
restricted opening in winter – **3 rm** ☕ ★50.00/60.00 – ★★65.00/70.00.
◆ An unusual Victorian Gothic farmhouse with turret, crenellations and lancet windows. Period style interiors throughout. Spacious, well-furnished bedrooms with rural views.

SANDBACH *Ches.* 502 503 504 M 24 – *pop. 17 630.*

⛳18 *Malkins Bank* ☎ *(01270) 765931.*
London 177 – Liverpool 44 – Manchester 28 – Stoke-on-Trent 16.

Chimney House, Congleton Rd, CW11 4ST, East : 1 ½ m. on A 534 ☎ 0870 609 6164, *chimneyhouse@corushotels.com, Fax (01270) 768916,* 🚗 – ⊭ P – 🎪 100. MC AE ⓓ VISA. ✂
Rest a la carte 21.95/28.90 ♀ – ☕ 10.75 – **48 rm** ★79.00 – ★★79.00.
◆ A mock-Tudor hotel in the wooded Cheshire countryside. Practical, well-kept bedrooms with modern facilities. Also a sauna and bar for relaxing. Fixed price menu of classic dishes in the restaurant with a view of the grounds or a 'casual' menu in the lounge.

Curshaws at the Mill, Town Mill, High St, CW11 1AH, ☎ (01270) 753009, *enquiries@curshaws.com, Fax (01270) 750305,* ☂ – ⊭. MC AE ⓓ VISA
closed 25 December and 1 January – **Rest** a la carte 9.50/20.00 ♀.
◆ Located in a former mill alongside an antique shop off the town square. Lively, informal dining with an extensive menu of popular modern dishes.

SANDFORD-ON-THAMES *Oxon. – see Oxford.*

SANDGATE *Kent* 504 X 30 – *see Folkestone.*

SANDIWAY *Ches.* 502 503 504 M 24 – ✉ *Northwich.*

London 191 – Liverpool 34 – Manchester 22 – Stoke-on-Trent 26.

Nunsmere Hall, Tarporley Rd, CW8 2ES, Southwest : 1½ m. by A 556 on A 49 ☎ (01606) 889100, *reservations@nunsmere.co.uk, Fax (01606) 889055,* ☂, 🚗, 🐎 – 🛗 ⊭ P – 🎪 50. MC AE ⓓ VISA. ✂
***Crystal* : Rest** 26.50 (lunch) and a la carte 32.50/48.75 **s.** ♀ – **36 rm** ☕ ★140.00/170.00 – ★★195.00/360.00.
◆ Secluded, on a wooded peninsular, originally built in 1900. Deep-seated sofas and sumptuous drawing rooms. Tasteful, individually furnished bedrooms exude quality and comfort. Dine in the classical style on imaginative and accomplished cuisine.

SANDWICH *Kent* 504 Y 30 *Great Britain G. – pop. 4 398.*
See : *Town*★.
Guildhall ✆ *(01304) 613565.*
London 72.5 – Canterbury 13 – Dover 12.

The Bell at Sandwich, The Quay, CT13 9EF, ✆ (01304) 613388, *reservations@bellhotelsandwich.co.uk, Fax (01304) 615308* – 🚭 P – 150. MC AE VISA. *closed 24-26 December* – ***The Place Brasserie :*** Rest a la carte 23.40/31.90 – **34 rm** ☕ ★75.00/100.00 – ★★100.00/155.00.
◆ Situated by River Stour with original Victorian fittings in situ. Refurbishment has resulted in stunning transformation of bedrooms: now cool, elegant, stylish and welcoming. Pleasant brasserie with strong seafood base.

SANDY *Beds.* 504 T 27 – *pop. 10 887.*
5 Shannon Court, High St ✆ *(01767) 682728.*
London 49 – Bedford 8 – Cambridge 24 – Peterborough 35.

Holiday Inn Garden Court, Girtford Bridge, London Rd, SG19 1DH, West : ¾ m. by B 1042 at junction of A 1 with A 603 ✆ (01767) 692220, *Fax (01767) 680452* – 🚭 rm rest, P – 150. MC AE VISA.
Rest *(closed Saturday lunch)* (dinner only) 15.00/20.00 s. – ☕ 10.95 – **57 rm** ★72.00/88.00 – ★★72.00/88.00.
◆ Located on A1; Bedford museums are among local attractions. Comfortable rooms of uniform shape and size accommodating up to three people (sofa beds available). Well staffed. Pleasant, family-friendly dining room.

Highfield Farm without rest., Great North Rd, SG19 2AQ, North : 2 m. by B 1042 on A 1 (southbound carriageway) ✆ (01767) 682332, *margaret@highfield-farm.co.uk, Fax (01767) 692503,* – 🚭 P. MC VISA
6 rm ☕ ★58.00/68.00 – ★★70.00/75.00.
◆ Working arable farm with gardens and 300 acres of land. Light, airy breakfast room, homely lounge and immaculately kept bedrooms, three of which are outside in coach house.

SANDYPARK *Devon* 503 I 31 – *see Chagford.*

SAPPERTON *Glos.* 503 504 N 28 – *see Cirencester.*

SARK *C.I.* 503 P 33 and 517 ⑩ – *see Channel Islands.*

SAUNTON *Devon* 503 H 30 *The West Country G.* – ✉ *Braunton.*
Env. : *Braunton*★ – *St Brannock's Church*★, *E : 2½ m. on B 3231* – *Braunton Burrows*★, *E : ½ m. on B 3231.*
⛳, ⛳ *Saunton, Braunton* ✆ *(01271) 812436.*
London 230 – Barnstaple 8 – Exeter 48.

Saunton Sands, EX33 1LQ, ✆ (01271) 890212, *info@sauntonsands.com, Fax (01271) 890145,* ≤ Saunton Sands, heated, squash – 🚭 rest, P – 175. MC AE VISA.
Rest 17.50/30.00 s. – ☕ 5.00 – **92 rm** ★74.00/175.00 – ★★270.00/325.00.
◆ Seaside hotel with terrace lounge for cream teas and cocktail bar. Airy, spacious deluxe rooms have sea vistas. Families are well catered for; staffed crèche available.. Dining room has sweeping sea views.

SAWLEY *Lancs.* 502 M 22.
London 242 – Blackpool 39 – Leeds 44 – Liverpool 54.

Spread Eagle, BB7 4NH, ✆ (01200) 441202, *Fax (01200) 441973* – 🚭 P. MC VISA
closed 2-5 January, Sunday dinner and Monday – **Rest** 15.75 (lunch) and a la carte 18.50/26.50 ♀.
◆ Former pub overlooking the Ribble and surrounding countryside; now a busy restaurant serving well-priced dishes with a modern twist.

SAXMUNDHAM *Suffolk* 504 Y 27 – *pop. 2 712* – ✉ *Ipswich.*
London 95 – Aldeburgh 7 – Ipswich 20.

The Bell, 31 High St, IP17 1AF, ✆ (01728) 602331, *thebell@saxhighstreet.fsnet.co.uk, Fax (01728) 602331* – 🚭. MC VISA
Rest *(closed 1 week in spring, 1 week in autumn, Sunday and Monday except Bank Holidays)* 14.00/17.50 and a la carte 24.10/28.50 s. ♀ – ☕ 5.95 – **10 rm** ★40.00 – ★★70.00.
◆ 17C former coaching inn, retaining much original visual character. Striking wall mural in hall. Local ale flows in cosy public bar. Spacious bedrooms offer stylish comforts. Dining room sparkles in crisp green and white; unadulterated, accomplished cooking.

SCALBY *N. Yorks.* 502 S 21 – *see Scarborough.*

SCARBOROUGH *N. Yorks.* 502 S 21 *Great Britain G. – pop. 38 364.*

Exc. : Robin Hood's Bay★, N : 16 m. on A 171 and minor rd to the right (signposted) – Whitby Abbey★, N : 21 m. on A 171 – Sledmere House★, S : 21 m. on A 645, B 1249 and B 1253 (right).

18 Scarborough North Cliff, North Cliff Ave, Burniston Rd ☎ (01723) 360786, NW : 2 m. by A 165 Y – 18 Scarborough South Cliff, Deepdale Ave, off Filey Rd ☎ (01723) 374737, S : 1 m. by A 165 Z.

Unit 15A, Brunswick Shopping Centre, Westborough ☎ (01723) 383636 – Harbourside, Sandside ☎ (01723) 383637 (except November-Easter Sunday only).

London 253 – Kingston-upon-Hull 47 – Leeds 67 – Middlesbrough 52.

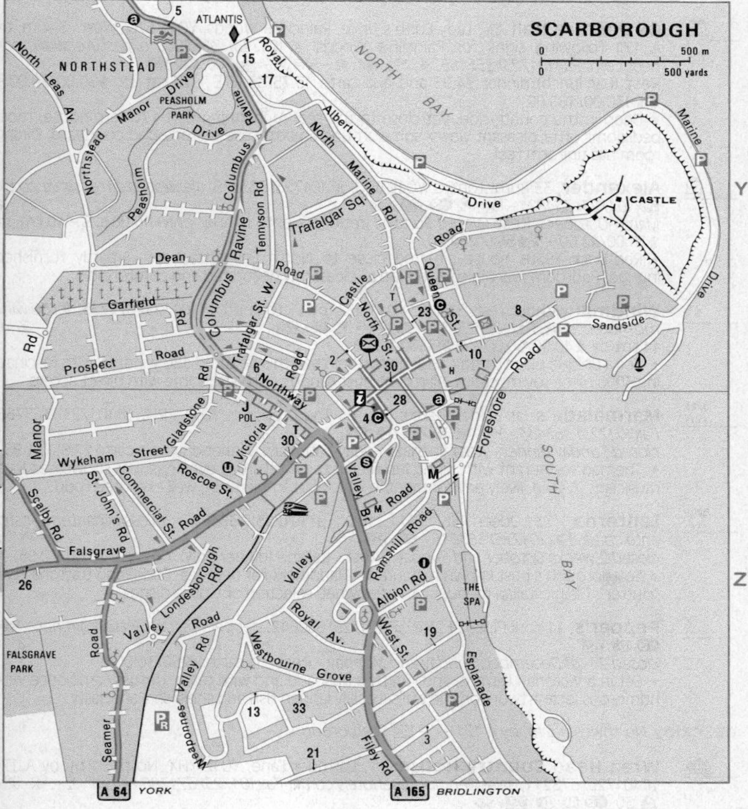

Beiderbecke's, 1-3 The Crescent, YO11 2PW, ☎ (01723) 365766, *info@beiderbeckes.com, Fax (01723) 367433* – MO AE VISA Z s
Rest – (see ***Marmalade's*** below) – **26 rm** ★60.00/80.00 – ★★100.00/120.00, 1 suite.
◆ Named after the jazz musician. Although housed in a restored Georgian building, the rooms' décor is balanced between period style and contemporary feel with bright colours.

ENGLAND

The Royal, St Nicholas St, YO11 2HE, ✆ (01723) 364333, *royalhotel@englishrosehotels.co.uk, Fax (01723) 500618,* – 275. VISA Z
Rest 15.95/40.00 – **118 rm** 65.00/75.00 – 125.00/200.00.
◆ Make-up recently re-applied to one of the town's grand old ladies; 1830s elegance exemplified by unforgettable main staircase. Mix of original or contemporary bedroom styles. Formal ambience in grand dining room.

The Crown Spa H., 7-11 Esplanade, YO11 2AG, ✆ (01723) 357400, *info@crownspahotel.com, Fax (01723) 362271,* – 200. VISA Z
Sharpins : Rest (dinner only) 19.95 s. – ***Spice Traders Brasserie :*** Rest a la carte approx. 12.95 s. – **85 rm** 45.00/120.00 – 70.00/130.00, 1 suite.
◆ 19C landmark - the town's first resort hotel, on the esplanade overlooking the bay. Spacious lounges in the classic style. Large bedrooms, many with fine sea views. Popular Sharpins serves family favourites. Select your cut of meat in Spice Traders Brasserie.

Ox Pasture Hall, Lady Edith's Drive, Raincliffe Woods, YO12 5TD, West : 3 ¼ m. by A 171 following signs for Raincliffe Woods ✆ (01723) 365295, *oxpasturehall@btconnect.com, Fax (01723) 355156,* – 200. VISA
Rest (bar lunch)/dinner 24.95 and a la carte 13.75/33.95 – **23 rm** 50.00/70.00 – 130.00/160.00.
◆ Deep in the countryside, yet close to the sea. A charming part-17C farmhouse: most bedrooms offer pleasant views, some around an attractive wisteria-clad courtyard. Dining room has uniform feel.

Alexander, 33 Burniston Rd, YO12 6PG, ✆ (01723) 363178, *alex@atesto.freeserve.co.uk, Fax (01723) 354821* – VISA. Y
March-October – **Rest** *(closed Sunday)* (residents only) (dinner only) 16.00 s. – **10 rm** 28.00/42.00 – 56.00/64.00.
◆ Red-brick 1930s house situated close to North Bay attractions. Smartly furnished lounge. Bedrooms vary in size and are all pleasantly decorated and comfortable.

Windmill without rest., Mill St, YO11 1SZ, by Victoria Rd ✆ (01723) 372735, *info@windmill-hotel.co.uk, Fax (01723) 372735* – VISA Z
11 rm 40.00/90.00 – 80.00/90.00.
◆ For a unique place to stay, look no further than this restored 18C windmill with fascinating 3000 piece toy museum. All rooms built round courtyard; some with direct access.

Marmalade's (at Beiderbecke's H.), 1-3 The Crescent, YO11 2PN, ✆ (01723) 365766, *Fax (01723) 367433* – VISA Z
closed Sunday dinner – **Rest** (live jazz Friday-Saturday) (dinner only) a la carte 22.85/31.85.
◆ Themed restaurant with nightclub feel: jazz on Saturday evenings; bar showcases local musicians. A vivid, lively environment in which to sample tasty, well executed food.

Lanterna, 33 Queen St, YO11 1HQ, ✆ (01723) 363616, *ralessio@lanterna-ristorante.co.uk, Fax (01723) 363616* – VISA Y
closed 2 weeks October and Sunday – **Rest** - Italian - (dinner only) a la carte 23.50/70.95.
◆ Scarborough's best known restaurant: a landmark for decades. Endearing trattoria style "clutter". Classic Italian menu, plus a renowned selection of truffle dishes.

Pepper's, 11 York Pl, YO11 2NP, ✆ (01723) 500642, *peppers.restaurant@virgin.net* – VISA Z
closed 24-28 December, Sunday and Monday – **Rest** a la carte 23.50/30.00.
◆ Set in a Victorian terrace, and run by a husband and wife team. Unfussy ambience with humorous local artwork on the walls. Locally landed fish and shellfish a speciality.

at Scalby *Northwest : 3 m. by A 171 – Z – ✉ Scarborough.*

Wrea Head Country House, Barmoor Lane, YO12 7HX, North : 1 m. by A 171 ✆ (01723) 378211, *sales@englishrosehotels.co.uk, Fax (01723) 371780,* – 30. VISA.
Rest 16.50/35.00 – **19 rm** 49.50/97.50 – 90.00/155.00, 1 suite.
◆ Close to North York Moors National Park and flanked by gardens, this Victorian manor promises a peaceful stay: oak panelling, stained glass, spacious rooms. Elegant dining room renowned for its local produce.

at Hackness *Northwest : 7 m. by A 171 – Z – ✉ Scarborough.*

Hackness Grange, YO13 0JW, ✆ (01723) 882345, *hacknessgrange@englishrosehotels.co.uk, Fax (01723) 882391,* – VISA.
Rest (bar lunch)/dinner 25.00 s. – **31 rm** 77.50/87.50 – 125.00, 1 suite.
◆ A grand 18C house, part of Lord Derwent's estate, set in attractive grounds. Indoor pool with floor to ceiling windows; bedrooms in main house have good views. Restaurant diners can contemplate views of lake.

SCILLY (Isles of) Cornwall 503 A/B 34 *The West Country G.*

See : Islands★ - The Archipelago (≤★★★).
Env. : St Agnes : Horsepoint★.
Helicopter service from St Mary's and Tresco to Penzance : ☎ (01736) 363871.
St Mary's Airport : ☎ (01720) 422677, E : 1½ m. from Hugh Town.
from Hugh Town to Penzance (Isles of Scilly Steamship Co. Ltd) (summer only) (2 h 40 mn).
Hugh Town, St Mary's ☎ (01720) (Scillonia) 422536.

Bryher Cornwall *The West Country G.* – pop. 78 – ✉ Scillonia.

See : Watch Hill (≤★) – Hell Bay★.

Hell Bay, TR23 0PR, ☎ (01720) 422947, *contactus@hellbay.co.uk, Fax (01720) 423004*, heated, – rest. VISA
closed January and February – **Rest** (bar lunch)/dinner 35.00 – **4 rm** (dinner included) ★138.00/275.00 – ★★300.00/440.00, **21 suites** 300.00/400.00.
◆ Quiet, former farmhouse with quadrangle of chalet-style rooms. Garden suites are each decorated using island flowers as a theme. Tropical plants; pleasant pool. Cheerful dining room with lovely garden views.

Bank Cottage without rest., TR23 0PR, ☎ (01720) 422612, *macmace@patrol.i-way.co.uk, Fax (01720) 422612*, ≤, –
March-October – **4 rm** (dinner included) ★80.00 – ★★90.00.
◆ A modern guesthouse in lush sub-tropical gardens, complete with koi fish pond. A peaceful haven: floral bedrooms and cosy breakfast room enhance the tranquil feel.

St Martin's Cornwall *The West Country G.* – pop. 113.

See : St Martin's Head (≤★★).

St Martin's on the Isle, TR25 0QW, ☎ (01720) 422092, *stay@stmartinshotel.co.uk, Fax (01720) 422298*, ≤ Tean Sound and islands, – rest. AE VISA
April-October – ***Tean*** **: Rest** (bar lunch)/dinner 44.50 **s.** – **28 rm** (dinner included) ★130.00/240.00 – ★★260.00/400.00, 2 suites.
◆ Set on the quayside with unrivalled views of white beaches and blue sea; a truly idyllic island setting. Snooze extremely peacefully in snug and cosy rooms. Dining room offers views out to the Sound.

St Mary's Cornwall *The West Country G.* – pop. 1 607.

See : Gig racing★★ – Garrison Walk★ (≤★★) – Peninnis Head★ – Hugh Town - Museum★.
9 ☎ (01720) 422692.

Star Castle, The Garrison, TR21 0JA, ☎ (01720) 422317, *Fax (01720) 422343*, ≤, – rest. AE VISA
closed 1 January-10 February – **Rest** (bar lunch)/dinner 30.00 **s.** – **34 rm** (dinner included) ★67.00/150.00 – ★★208.00/280.00, 4 suites.
◆ Elizabethan castle built in 1593 in the shape of an eight pointed star, surrounded by dry moat. There are harbour views; palms, echiums in garden. Airy rooms; subtle colours. Dining room has beams, stone walls and granite fireplace.

Atlantic, Hugh St, Hugh Town, TR21 0PL, ☎ (01720) 422417, *atlantichotel@smallandfriendly.co.uk, Fax (01720) 423009*, ≤ St Mary's Harbour – . AE VISA
closed 2 January-5 February – **Rest** (dinner only) a la carte 17.50/22.85 – **24 rm** (dinner included) ★75.00/89.00 – ★★198.00/220.00.
◆ A cruise liner style white hotel with views of St Mary's harbour and bobbing boats. Cottage charm in older rooms - low ceilings, floral fabrics; modern rooms in extension. Scillonian ingredients in dining room with harbour views.

Evergreen Cottage without rest., Parade, High Town, TR21 0LP, ☎ (01720) 422711 –
5 rm ★33.00/60.00 – ★★67.00/71.00.
◆ A 300-year old captain's cottage; very pleasant, with window boxes, a few minutes walk from the quay. Plenty of local literature in low beamed lounge. Compact, tidy rooms.

Tresco Cornwall *The West Country G.* – pop. 167 – ✉ New Grimsby.

See : Island★ - Abbey Gardens★★ AC (Lighthouse Way ≤★★).

The Island, Old Grimsby, TR24 0PU, ☎ (01720) 422883, *islandhotel@tresco.co.uk, Fax (01720) 423008*, ≤ St Martin's and islands, heated, – rest. VISA
13 February-October – **Rest** (bar lunch)/dinner 35.00 **s.** – **46 rm** (dinner included) ★133.00/353.00 – ★★272.00/470.00, 2 suites.
◆ A heated pool, sub-tropical gardens, panoramic views to be had at this peaceful hotel. Enthusiastic owners collect art for interiors. Very comfortable, well appointed rooms. Enjoy sea vistas from warm, welcoming dining room.

ENGLAND

New Inn, TR24 0QQ, ✆ (01720) 422844, *newinn@tresco.co.uk, Fax (01720) 423200,* ←, heated, – rest. VISA.
Rest (booking essential to non-residents) a la carte 15.00/29.00 – **15 rm** (dinner included) 218.00 – 218.00.
◆ This stone built former inn makes a hospitable stopping off point. Friendly, bustling ambience in lounges and bars where the locals congregate. Comfortable bedrooms. Striking orange and blue bistro-style dining room.

SCUNTHORPE *North Lincolnshire* 502 S 23 – *pop. 72 669.*
Ashby Decoy, Burringham Rd ✆ (01724) 842913 – Kingsway ✆ (01724) 840945 – Grange Park, Butterwick Rd, Messingham ✆ (01724) 762945.
Humberside Airport : ✆ (01652) 688456, E : 15 m. by A 18.
London 167 – Leeds 54 – Lincoln 30 – Sheffield 45.

Forest Pines, Ermine St, Broughton, DN20 0AQ, Southeast : 5 m. by A 1029 off A 18 ✆ (01652) 650770, *forestpines@qhotels.co.uk, Fax (01652) 650495,* , – , rest, – 250. VISA.
Beechtree : Rest 19.95/39.95 s. – ***Garden Room :*** Rest 12.90/14.90 – **112 rm** 99.00/119.00 – 109.00/129.00, 2 suites.
◆ A luxury hotel in woodland with 27 hole golf course and smart, well-equipped leisure complex; includes beauty treatments. Bedrooms are all spacious with modern facilities. Fine dining at the Beech Tree. The Garden Room features a lovely decked terrace.

Premier Travel Inn, Lakeside Retail Park, Lakeside Parkway, DN16 3UA, Southeast : 2½ m. by A 1029 off junction with A 18 ✆ (01724) 870030, *Fax (01724) 851809* – rm, rest, VISA.
Rest (grill rest.) – **40 rm** 46.95/46.95 – 49.95/49.95.
◆ Modern rooms suitable for business and family stopovers, designed with practicality and price in mind. Next to Anchor Brewsters; near Normanby Hall and Scunthorpe Museum.

SEAHAM *Durham* 501 502 P/Q 19 – *pop. 21 153.*
London 284 – Carlisle 77 – Leeds 84 – Middlesbrough 24 – Newcastle upon Tyne 17.

Seaham Hall, Lord Byron's Walk, SR7 7AG, North : 1¼ m. by B 1287 ✆ (0191) 516 1400, *reservations@seaham-hall.com, Fax (0191) 516 1410,* ←, – – 120. VISA.
Rest (booking essential to non-residents) 17.50 (lunch) and a la carte 40.00/63.00 s. – **16 rm** 195.00/245.00 – 325.00/355.00, 3 suites.
◆ Imposing 17C and 19C mansion with ultra-modern technology in spacious rooms. Contemporary sculpture and décor. Unique Oriental spa has relaxing, Far Eastern ambience. Crisp linen and fine china define restaurant.

SEAHOUSES *Northd.* 501 502 P 17 *Great Britain G.*
Env. : *Farne Islands★ (by boat from harbour).*
Beadnell Rd ✆ (01665) 720794.
Car Park, Seafield Rd ✆ (01665) 720884 (Easter-October).
London 328 – Edinburgh 80 – Newcastle upon Tyne 46.

Olde Ship, 9 Main St, NE68 7RD, ✆ (01665) 720200, *theoldeship@seahouses.co.uk Fax (01665) 721383* – rest, VISA.
closed December and January – **Rest** (bar lunch)/dinner 20.00 and a la carte 18.25/19.75 – **18 rm** 45.00/104.00 – 90.00/104.00.
◆ Built in 1745 as a farmhouse but has left origins far behind, proudly proclaiming nautical links. Harbour views and marine artefacts throughout. Cosy, comfortable rooms. Spoilt for choice with several eating areas.

SEASALTER *Kent* 504 X 29 – *see Whitstable.*

SEATON BURN *Tyne and Wear* 502 P 18 – *see Newcastle upon Tyne.*

SEAVIEW *I.O.W.* 503 504 Q 31 – *see Wight (Isle of).*

Your opinions are important to us:
please write and let us know about your discoveries and experiences – good and bad!

SEDLESCOMBE *E. Sussex* 504 V 31 – ✉ *Battle.*
London 56 – Hastings 7 – Lewes 26 – Maidstone 27.

Brickwall, The Green, TN33 0QA, ✆ (01424) 870253, *info@brickwallhotel.com, Fax (01424) 870785,* , heated, – – P. MC AE VISA
Rest 13.50/28.00 – **25 rm** 60.00/75.00 – 80.00/106.00.
◆ Part Tudor mansion at top of village green, built for local ironmaster in 1597. Well placed for beauty spots. Range of rooms include family, four-poster and ground floor. Dining room boasts characterful low beamed ceiling.

SEMINGTON *Wilts.* 503 504 N 29 – *see Trowbridge.*

SETTLE *N. Yorks.* 502 N 21 – *pop. 3 621.*
Giggleswick ✆ (01729) 825288.
Town Hall, Cheapside ✆ (01729) 825192.
London 238 – Bradford 34 – Kendal 30 – Leeds 41.

Falcon Manor, Skipton Rd, BD24 9BD, ✆ (01729) 823814, *enquiries@thefalconmanor.com, Fax (01729) 822087,* – – P – 100. MC VISA.
Ingfield : **Rest** (dinner only and Sunday lunch) 24.95 **s.** – **18 rm** 90.00 – 90.00.
◆ Built in 1842 as a rectory; sits on the fringe of Dales National Park. A grand hall with chandelier and sweeping wooden staircase leads to traditionally furnished rooms. Elegant dining room: ornate ceiling, large leaded window.

Husband's Barn without rest., Stainforth, BD24 9PB, North : 2 m. on B 6479 ✆ (01729) 822240, *Fax (01729) 822240* – P.
closed January, February and 25 December – **3 rm** 40.00/45.00 – 55.00/60.00.
◆ Recently converted barn, surrounded by attractive dales scenery. Comfy beamed lounge with open fire. Light, airy breakfast room with views. Bedrooms have exposed rafters.

Little House, 17 Duke St, BD24 9DJ, ✆ (01729) 823963 – . MC VISA
Rest (booking essential) (dinner only Wednesday-Saturday and Sunday May-September) a la carte 19.40/25.40.
◆ Former 19C gate house, a 'little house' of stone that was once a cobblers. Well-kept, rustic style within a compact space. Traditional and classic styles of cooking prevail.

SEVENOAKS *Kent* 504 U 30 *Great Britain G.* – *pop. 26 699.*
Env. : *Knole★★ AC, SE : ½ m. – Ightham Mote★ AC, E : 5 m. by A 25.*
Woodlands Manor, Tinkerpot Lane ✆ (01959) 523806 – Darenth Valley, Station Rd, Shoreham ✆ (01959) 522944.
Buckhurst Lane ✆ (01732) 450305, tic@sevenoakstown.gov.uk.
London 26 – Guildford 40 – Maidstone 17.

Sun Do, 61 High St, TN13 1JF, ✆ (01732) 453299, *Fax (01732) 741991* – . MC AE VISA
closed 25-26 December – **Rest** - Chinese - a la carte 18.00/27.00.
◆ Meaning "Happiness", with attentive staff and oriental setting, you can expect authentic Chinese food here. Extensive choice, including various set menus.

at Ightham Common *Southeast : 5 m. by A 25 on Common Rd* – ✉ *Sevenoaks.*

Harrow Inn, Common Rd, TN15 9EB, ✆ (01732) 885912, *Fax (01732) 885912,* – P. MC VISA.
closed 26 December, 1 January, Sunday dinner and Monday – **Rest** a la carte 18.00/30.00.
◆ Attractive 17C stone and brick inn on sleepy narrow lane. Oozing character: flags, beams, open fire. Appealing and inventive dishes are enhanced by honest, rustic cooking.

SHAFTESBURY *Dorset* 503 504 N 30 *The West Country G.* – *pop. 6 665.*
See : *Gold Hill★ (≤★) – Local History Museum★ AC.*
Env. : *Wardour Castle★ AC, NE : 5 m.*
8 Bell St ✆ (01747) 853514.
London 115 – Bournemouth 31 – Bristol 47 – Dorchester 29 – Salisbury 20.

Royal Chase, Royal Chase Roundabout, SP7 8DB, Southeast : at junction of A 30 with A 350 ✆ (01747) 853355, *theroyalchasehotel@btinternet.com, Fax (01747) 851969,* , – – P – 180. MC AE VISA
Byzant : **Rest** 14.95 (lunch) and a la carte 21.45/30.25 – 8.50 – **33 rm** 95.00 – 120.00/185.00.
◆ Located in "Thomas Hardy" country and once a training school for the Order of Missionary Priests. Possesses a Turkish steam room, indoor pool. Individually styled bedrooms. Cosy, atmospheric dining room.

ENGLAND

The Retreat without rest., 47 Bell St, SP7 8AE, ☎ (01747) 850372, *Fax (01747) 850372* – P.
closed January – **10 rm** ☕ ★35.00/55.00 – ★★70.00.
◆ Georgian townhouse in good location - central but not noisy. Spotlessly clean throughout. Individually decorated bedrooms; several overlook the rear, so particularly quiet.

La Fleur de Lys with rm, Bleke St, SP7 8AW, ☎ (01747) 853717, *info@lafleurdelys.co.uk Fax (01747) 853130*, – P. MO AE VISA
closed Sunday dinner and Monday and Tuesday lunch – **Rest** 27.50 (dinner) and a la carte 27.50/38.00 ♀ – **7 rm** ☕ ★65.00/75.00 – ★★85.00/105.00.
◆ Owners relocated to this address in 2003: smart restaurant in an 1870s ivy-covered house. Comfy bar with plenty of sofas. Well-kept bedrooms, named after grape varieties.

Wayfarers, Sherborne Causeway, SP7 9PX, West : 2½ m. on A 30 ☎ (01747) 852821 – P. MO VISA
closed 26 December-17 January, 10 days June, Monday, Tuesday lunch, Saturday lunch and Sunday dinner – **Rest** (lunch booking essential) 21.00/34.00 ♀.
◆ A 200-year old cottage with an Old England interior of exposed stone walls, beams hung with china plates and a lovely log fire. Broad à la carte with simpler lunch menus.

at Donhead St Andrew *East : 5 m. by A 30 – ✉ Shaftesbury.*

Forester Inn with rm, Lower St, SP7 9EE, ☎ (01747) 828038, *enquiries@foresterinndonheadstandrew.co.uk, Fax (01747) 828050*, – P. MO AE VISA
closed dinner 25 December – **Rest** a la carte 20.00/30.00 ♀ – ☕ 6.00 – **2 rm** ★57.50 – ★★95.00.
◆ Attractive thatched pub with 13C origins. Lovely rustic bar with beams and inglenooks. Dine in barn style extension where much locally sourced produce enhances modern dishes.

at Compton Abbas *South : 4 m. on A 350 – ✉ Shaftesbury.*

Old Forge without rest., Chapel Hill, SP7 0NQ, ☎ (01747) 811881, *theoldforge@hotmail.com, Fax (01747) 811881*, – P.
3 rm ☕ ★40.00/50.00 – ★★60.00/65.00.
◆ Thatched cottage dating from 1700; once a wheelwright, carriage builder. Tradition continues in car restoration business. Rooms all slightly different; pretty, characterful.

at Motcombe *Northwest : 2½ m. by B 3081 – ✉ Shaftesbury.*

Coppleridge Inn, SP7 9HW, North : 1 m. on Mere rd ☎ (01747) 851980, *thecoppleridgeinn@btinternet.com, Fax (01747) 851858*, – P – 🏛 50. MO AE VISA
Rest a la carte 14.50/23.00 ♀ – **10 rm** ☕ ★45.00 – ★★80.00.
◆ A converted 18C farmhouse in 15 acres of meadow. Bedrooms, in a separate courtyard, with views, are a particular strength - bright and airy. Magnificent barn for functions.

SHANKLIN *I.O.W.* 503 504 Q 32 – *see Wight (Isle of).*

SHEDFIELD *Hants.* 503 504 Q 31 – *pop. 3 558* – ✉ *Southampton.*
Marriott Meon Valley H. & C.C., Sandy Lane, off A 334 ☎ *(01329) 833455.*
London 75 – Portsmouth 13 – Southampton 10.

Marriott Meon Valley H. & Country Club, Sandy Lane, SO32 2HQ, off A 334 ☎ (0870) 4007228, *events.meon@marriotthotels.co.uk, Fax (0870) 4007328*, – rest, P – 🏛 80. MO AE VISA
***Treetops*:** Rest (dinner only and Sunday lunch) 32.00 and a la carte ♀ – ***The Long Weekend*:** Rest a la carte 16.00/32.00 ♀ – ☕ 14.95 – **113 rm** ★103.00/109.00 – ★★103.00/119.00.
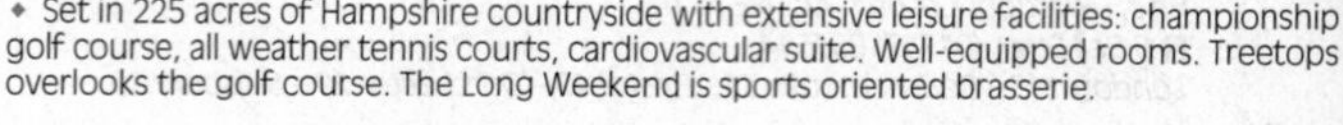
◆ Set in 225 acres of Hampshire countryside with extensive leisure facilities: championship golf course, all weather tennis courts, cardiovascular suite. Well-equipped rooms. Treetops overlooks the golf course. The Long Weekend is sports oriented brasserie.

Do not confuse X with ✿! X defines comfort, while stars are awarded for the best cuisine, across all categories of comfort.

SHEFFIELD *S. Yorks.* 502 503 504 P 23 *Great Britain G. – pop. 439 866.*

See : *Cutlers' Hall*★ **CZ A** – *Cathedral Church of SS. Peter and Paul* **CZ B** : *Shrewsbury Chapel (Tomb*★*).*

Env. : *Magna*★, *Northeast : 3 m. by A 6178* – **BY** – *and Bessemer Way.*

Tinsley Park, High Hazel Park, Darnall ☎ *(0114) 203 7435* **BY** – *Beauchief Municipal, Abbey Lane* ☎ *(0114) 236 7274* **AZ** – *Birley Wood, Birley Lane* ☎ *(0114) 264 7262* **BZ** – *Concord Park, Shiregreen Lane* ☎ *(0114) 257 7378* **BY** – *Abbeydale, Twentywell Lane, Dore* ☎ *(0114) 236 0763* **AZ** – *Lees Hall, Hemsworth Rd, Norton* ☎ *(0114) 255 4402* **AZ**.

Winter Garden ☎ *(0114) 221 1900.*

London 174 – Leeds 36 – Liverpool 80 – Manchester 41 – Nottingham 44.

Plans on following pages

Sheffield Marriott, Kenwood Rd, S7 1NQ, ☎ (0870) 4007261, *events.sheffield@marriotthotels.co.uk, Fax (0870) 4007361,* – rest, – 200. VISA AZ r

18/10: **Rest** (bar lunch Monday-Saturday)/dinner 25.00 s. – **114 rm** 132.00 – 152.00.

◆ Refurbished part Victorian mansion in quiet suburb. Whilst rooms in original house have character, the more modern rooms overlook the landscaped gardens and ornamental lake. Relaxing views a feature of the restaurant.

Westbourne House without rest., 25 Westbourne Rd, S10 2QQ, ☎ (0114) 266 0109, *guests@westbournehousehotel.com, Fax (0114) 266 7778,* – . VISA AZ c

closed 16-31 August – – **10 rm** 50.00/70.00 – 85.00/95.00.

◆ 19C former gentleman's residence full of character. Overlooks tree-lined garden. Friendly, personal service by affable owners. Individually decorated, well-appointed rooms.

Premier Travel Inn Metro, Angel St, S3 8LN, ☎ (0870) 2383324, *Fax (0114) 2502802* – , rest, – 30. VISA. DY c

Rest (grill rest.) – **160 rm** 53.95 – 53.95.

◆ Modern purpose-built hotel on busy road in central location. Designed for cost-conscious families or business travellers. Bright, spacious bedrooms with ample work space.

Premier Travel Inn, Attercliffe Common Rd, S9 2LU, ☎ (0114) 242 2802, *Fax (0114) 242 3703* – , rm, rest, . VISA. BY a

Rest (grill rest.) – **61 rm** 49.95/49.95 – 52.95/52.95.

◆ Suitable for both corporate and leisure travellers, as well as being convenient for Sheffield Arena. Bright, modern bedrooms. Adjacent grill food diner.

Quarry House without rest., Rivelin Glen Quarry, Rivelin Valley Rd, S6 5SE, Northwest : 4½ m. by A 61 on A 6101 ☎ (0114) 234 0382, *penelopeslack@aol.com, Fax (0114) 234 7630,* –

4 rm 40.00/80.00 – 80.00.

◆ Sited in a disused 19C quarry - check out the local stonemason! Bohemian style prevails; thespians stay regularly. Individually styled rooms with plenty of hospitable touches. Supper tray available.

Rafters, 220 Oakbrook Rd, Nether Green, S11 7ED, Southwest : 2 ½ m. by A 625 and Fulwood rd, turning left at mini roundabout, on right at traffic lights ☎ (0114) 230 4819, *Fax (0114) 230 4819* – . VISA

closed 25-26 December, 1 week January, 1 week August, Sunday, Tuesday and Bank Holiday Mondays – **Rest** (dinner only) 28.00.

◆ Discreetly located above a parade of shops and definitely worth seeking out. Friendly and approachable service of a classically influenced modern British menu.

Bluefin, 85 Junction Rd, Hunters Bar, S11 8XA, ☎ (0114) 266 0805 – . VISA AZ n

closed first week January, Sunday and Monday – **Rest** - Seafood - 8.95 (lunch) and a la carte 26.00/35.00 s..

◆ Suburban twin level restaurant: downstairs dining in the bar, upstairs includes local artists' work for sale on walls. Eclectic seafood menus: modern and Asian influences.

Delhi Junction, The Old Station, Abbeydale Road South, S17 3LB, Southwest : 4 m. on A 621 ☎ (0114) 262 0675 – . VISA

closed 25-26 December, 1 January and Sunday – **Rest** - Indian - (dinner only) a la carte 14.90/21.85 s..

◆ Pleasantly converted Victorian railway station. Spacious, open dining rooms with Easten feel; proceedings orchestrated by larger-than-life owner. Tasty Indian menus.

Thyme, 32-34 Sandygate Rd, S10 5RY, West : 2 ¼ m. by A 57, turning left at Crosspool Tavern ☎ (0114) 266 6096, *Fax (0114) 2660279* – . VISA

Rest 16.00/24.00 and a la carte 22.00/34.00.

◆ Relaxed neighbourhood eatery with frequent midweek themed evenings. Robust, good value menus featuring British seafood, organic meats and influences from around the globe.

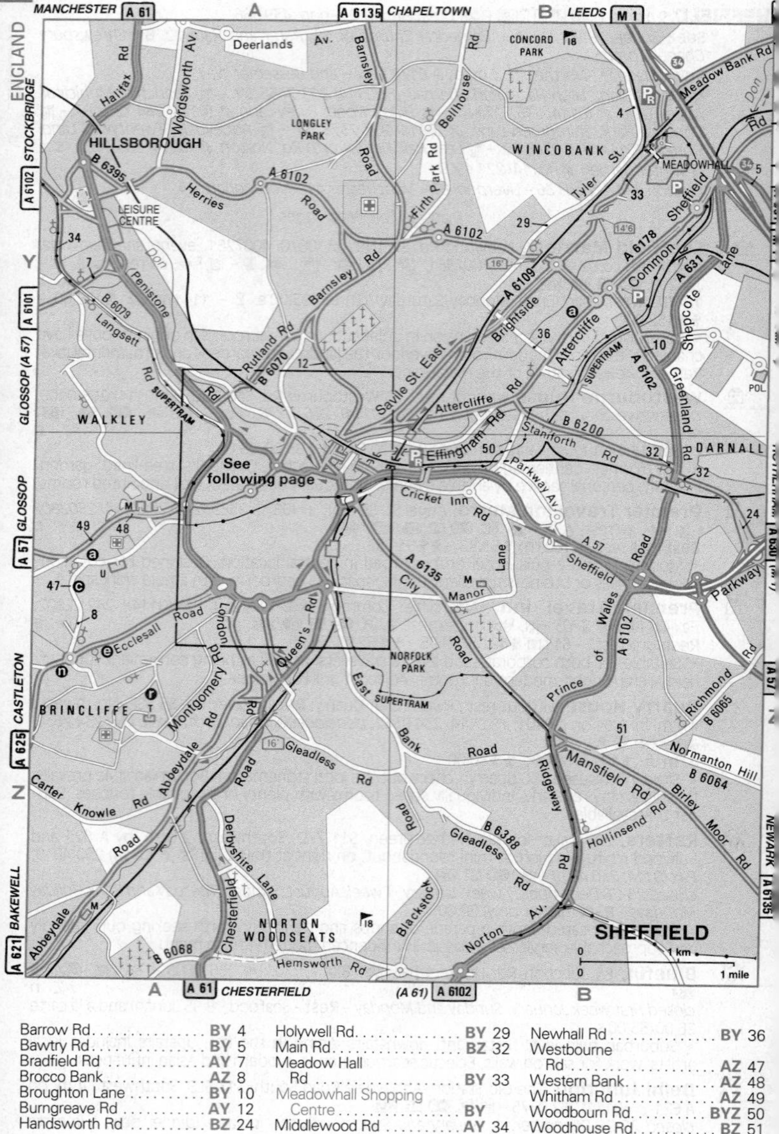

Barrow Rd . . . . BY 4	Holywell Rd . . . . BY 29	Newhall Rd . . . . BY 36
Bawtry Rd . . . . BY 5	Main Rd . . . . BZ 32	Westbourne Rd . . . . AZ 47
Bradfield Rd . . . . AY 7	Meadow Hall Rd . . . . BY 33	Western Bank . . . . AZ 48
Brocco Bank . . . . AZ 8	Meadowhall Shopping Centre . . . . BY	Whitham Rd . . . . AZ 49
Broughton Lane . . . . BY 10	Middlewood Rd . . . . AY 34	Woodbourn Rd . . . . BYZ 50
Burngreave Rd . . . . AY 12		Woodhouse Rd . . . . BZ 51
Handsworth Rd . . . . BZ 24		

Thyme Cafe, 490 Glossop Rd, S10 2QA, ☎ (0114) 267 0735, – . VISA AZ a
closed 25-26 December, 1 January, Sunday dinner and Bank Holiday Mondays – **Rest** (bookings not accepted) a la carte 19.00/25.00 ♀.
◆ Snug, though bustling, bistro located outside city centre. Rustic interior with wooden school chairs and church pews. Appealing range of hearty dishes, ordered from the bar.

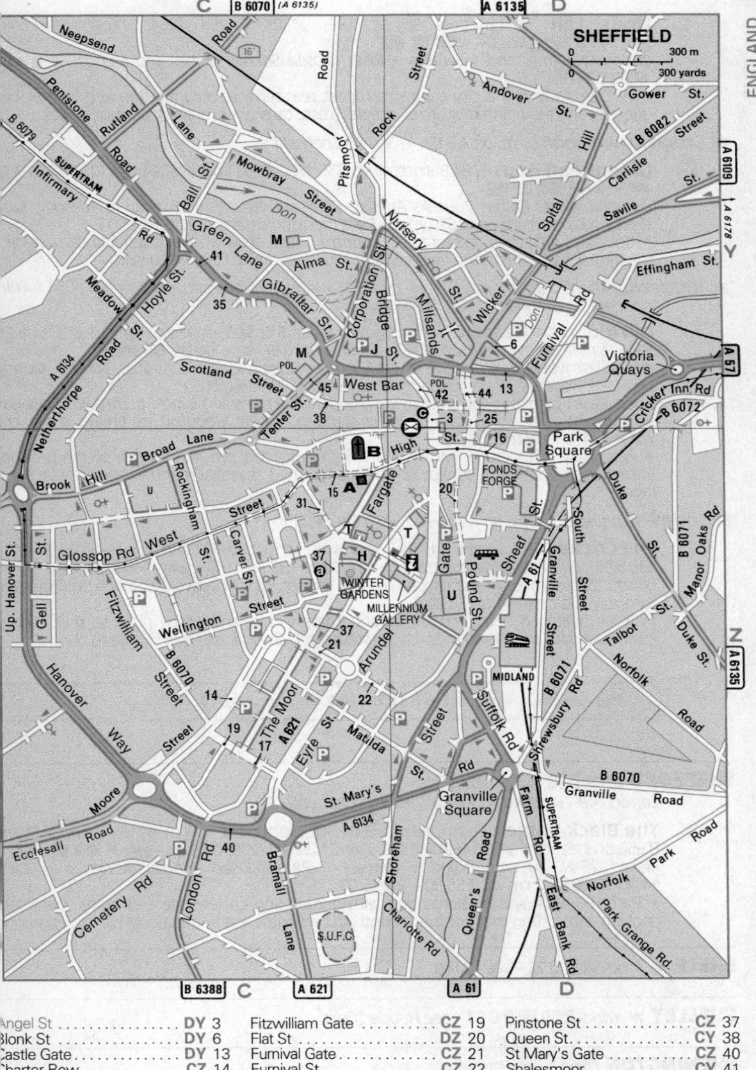

Street	Grid	No.
Angel St	DY	3
Blonk St	DY	6
Castle Gate	DY	13
Charter Row	CZ	14
Church St	CZ	15
Commercial St	DZ	16
Cumberland St	CZ	17
Fargate	CZ	
Fitzwilliam Gate	CZ	19
Flat St	DZ	20
Furnival Gate	CZ	21
Furnival St	CZ	22
Haymarket	DY	25
High St	DZ	
Leopold St	CZ	31
Moorfields	CY	35
Pinstone St	CZ	37
Queen St	CY	38
St Mary's Gate	CZ	40
Shalesmoor	CY	41
Snig Hill	DY	42
Waingate	DY	44
West Bar Green	CY	45
West St	CZ	

Nonna's, 535-541 Ecclesall Rd, S11 8PR, ☎ (0114) 268 6166, *enquiries@nonnas.co.uk,*
Fax (0114) 266 6122 – MC VISA AZ e
Rest - Italian - a la carte 16.00/30.00 ♀.
◆ Take a walk through the deli before sitting down to savour the robust and authentic Italian dishes in busy surroundings. Speciality home-made pastas.

ENGLAND

Lions Lair, 31 Burgess St, S1 2HF, ☎ (0114) 263 4264, *info@lionslair.co.u* *Fax (0114) 263 4265,* – MC AE VISA CZ
closed Christmas and 1 January – **Rest** *(closed Sunday dinner and Monday)* a la cart 17.00/22.00.
◆ Hidden away in the city centre; compact rear terrace, cosy interior with leather bar quettes, and a winning mixture of simple, fresh, carefully prepared, popular dishes.

at Chapeltown *North : 6 m. on A 6135 –* **AY** *– ✉ Sheffield.*

XX **Greenhead House,** 84 Burncross Rd, S35 1SF, ☎ (0114) 246 9004, *Fax (0114) 246 900* – P. MC AE VISA
closed 2 weeks Easter, 2 weeks August, Christmas-New Year, Sunday to Tuesday, lunc Wednesday, Thursday and Saturday – **Rest** (booking essential) 22.00/39.00 ♀.
◆ Cosy and attractive restaurant in country house style where hospitable owners offe traditional, tasty and home-cooked fare. A local favourite for many a year.

at Ridgeway *(Derbs.) Southeast : 6¾ m. by A 6135 (signed Hyde Park) –* **BZ** *– on B 6054 turnin right at Ridgeway Arms – ✉ Sheffield.*

XXX **Old Vicarage** (Tessa Bramley), Ridgeway Moor, S12 3XW, on Marsh Lane rd ☎ (0114) 24 5814, *eat@theoldvicarage.co.uk, Fax (0114) 247 7079,* – P. MC VISA
closed last week December, first week January, first two weeks August, Sunday, Monda and Bank Holidays – **Rest** (lunch by arrangement) 40.00/60.00 ♀.
Spec. Roast partridge with forcemeat, fondant potatoes and winter greens. Wild sea bas with potato galette and salad of cod and mango. Sweet woodruff ice cream in pistachi wafer with sherry trifle.
◆ Personally run Victorian vicarage, its kitchen garden providing much of the produce Formal yet unobtrusive service of an accomplished seasonal menu in elegant surroundings.

at Totley *Southwest : 5½ m. on A 621 –* **AZ** *– ✉ Sheffield.*

The Cricket, Penny Lane, S17 3AZ, Southwest : 1 m. by A 621 and Lane Head Rd ☎ (0114 236 5256, *enquiries@the.cricket.com, Fax (0114) 235 6582,* – P. MC VISA
closed 25 December – **Rest** *(closed Monday except Bank Holidays)* (bar lunch only Tuesday Saturday) a la carte 14.00/30.00 ♀.
◆ Stone built pub boasts cricket paraphernalia within, and village pitch to rear. Dine at pubby bar with pews or in linen-clad restaurant. Dishes range from simple to classic.

The sun's out – let's eat al fresco! Look for a terrace:

SHEFFORD *Beds.* 504 S 27 – *pop. 3 319.*
London 48 – Bedford 10 – Luton 16 – Northampton 37.

The Black Horse with rm, Ireland, SG17 5QL, Northwest : 1 ¾ m. by Northbridge St and B 658 on Ireland rd ☎ (01462) 811398, *Fax (01462) 817238,* – P. MC VISA.
closed 25-26 December and 1 January – **Rest** *(closed Sunday dinner)* a la carte 14.00/22.00 ♀ – **2 rm** ★55.00 – ★★55.00.
◆ Part 18C brick and timbered pub with garden and chalet-style bedrooms. Confident cooking, interesting menus based round old favourites. Eat in traditional bar or restaurant.

SHELF *W. Yorks.* 502 O 22 – *see Halifax.*

SHELLEY *W. Yorks.* 502 504 O 23 – *see Huddersfield.*

SHENINGTON *Oxon. – see Banbury.*

SHEPTON MALLET *Somerset* 503 504 M 30 *The West Country G. – pop. 8 830.*
See : *Town★ - SS. Peter and Paul's Church★.*
Env. : *Downside Abbey★ (Abbey Church★) N : 5½ m. by A 37 and A 367.*
Exc. : *Longleat House★★★ AC, E : 15 m. by A 361 and B 3092 – Wells★★ - Cathedral★★★, Vicars' Close★, Bishop's Palace★ AC (≤★★) W : 6 m. by A 371 – Wookey Hole★ (Caves★ AC, Papermill★) W : 6 ½ m. by B 371 – Glastonbury★★ - Abbey★★ (Abbot's Kitchen★) AC, St John the Baptist★★, Somerset Rural Life Museum★ AC – Glastonbury Tor★ (≤★★★) SW : 9 m. by B 3136 and A 361 - Nunney★, E : 8½ m. by A 361.*
18 *The Mendip, Gurney Slade ☎ (01749) 840570.*
London 127 – Bristol 20 – Southampton 63 – Taunton 31.

Charlton House, BA4 4PR, East : 1 m. on A 361 (Frome rd) ✆ (01749) 342008, *enquiry@charltonhouse.com, Fax (01749) 346362*, – 100. VISA.
Rest 32.50/49.50 – **25 rm** 130.00 – 325.00.
◆ Grand 17C house owned by founders of Mulberry Company; a smart, boutique style prevails touched by informality. Antiques in luxury bedrooms: Adam and Eve carved four-poster. Well used local produce to the fore in conservatory dining room.

SHERBORNE *Dorset 503 504 M 31 The West Country G. – pop. 7 606.*

See : *Town★ - Abbey★★ – Castle★ AC.*
Env. : *Sandford Orcas Manor House★ AC, NW : 4 m. by B 3148 – Purse Caundle Manor★ AC, NE : 5 m. by A 30.*
Exc. : *Cadbury Castle (≤★★) N : 8 m. by A 30 – Parish Church★, Crewkerne, W : 14 m. on A 30.*
Higher Clatcombe ✆ (01935) 812274.
3 Tilton Court, Digby Rd ✆ (01935) 815341.
London 128 – Bournemouth 39 – Dorchester 19 – Salisbury 36 – Taunton 31.

Eastbury, Long St, DT9 3BY, ✆ (01935) 813131, *enquiries@theeastbury.co.uk, Fax (01935) 817296*, – 60. VISA.
Rest 15.00/28.00 and dinner a la carte 29.50/37.00 – **21 rm** 58.00/80.00 – 98.00/140.00.
◆ Traditional town house, a former gentleman's residence, built in 1740 with peaceful walled garden. Well-kept rooms named after country flowers. 15C abbey is nearby. Bright restaurant looking onto garden.

The Green, On The Green, DT9 3HY, ✆ (01935) 813821 – 20. VISA
closed 2 weeks January-February, 1 week June, 1 week September, 24-25 December, Sunday and Monday – **Rest** 23.50/28.95 (dinner) and lunch a la carte 14.95/22.45.
◆ Pretty Grade II listing at the top of the hill in town centre with stone floor and inglenook. A bistro feel predominates; dishes are traditional with a strong seasonal base.

at Corton Denham *North : 3¾ m. by B 3145 – ✉ Sherborne.*

The Queens Arms with rm, DT9 4LR, ✆ (01963) 220317, *relax@thequeens-arms.co.uk*, – VISA
Rest a la carte 15.00/19.00 – **5 rm** 70.00 – 120.00.
◆ The essence of this pub is relaxed informality, engendered by sofas and armchairs inside, and an attractively sunny rear terrace. Locally inspired dishes; luxurious bedrooms.

at Oborne *Northeast : 2 m. by A 30 – ✉ Sherborne.*

The Grange, DT9 4LA, ✆ (01935) 813463, *reception@thegrange.co.uk, Fax (01935) 817464*, – VISA.
Rest *(closed Sunday dinner)* (light lunch)/dinner 29.50 – **18 rm** 85.00 – 120.00/140.00.
◆ A 200-year old country house in floodlit gardens. Rooms are a treat: some modern, some traditional, all large; some have patio access; some have balconies. Friendly owner. Dorset and Somerset ingredients zealously used in dining room.

at Hermitage *South : 7½ m. by A 352 – ✉ Sherborne.*

Almshouse Farm without rest., DT9 6HA, ✆ (01963) 210296, *Fax (01963) 210296*, ≤, –
February-October – **3 rm** 30.00/40.00 – 60.00/65.00.
◆ Part 16C former monastery, now a working farm, surrounded by rural landscape. Original features include inglenook fireplace in cosy breakfast room. Pretty, neat bedrooms.

at Alweston *Southeast : 2½ m. by A 352 A 3030 – ✉ Sherborne.*

Munden House without rest., Munden Lane, DT9 5HU, ✆ (01963) 23150, *admin@mundenhouse.demon.co.uk, Fax (01963) 23153*, – VISA
7 rm 49.00/55.00 – 70.00/100.00.
◆ Peacefully located guesthouse: originally a small complex of stone cottages. Modern country house furnishings. Breakfast room with 300 year old fireplace. Elegant bedrooms.

SHERE *Surrey 504 S 30 – see Guildford.*

Undecided between two equivalent establishments?
Within each category, establishments are classified in our order of preference.

SHERINGHAM *Norfolk* 504 X 25 – *pop. 7 143.*
London 136 – Cromer 5 – Norwich 27.

The Dales Country House , Lodge Hill, Upper Sheringham, NR26 8TJ, South west : 1 ¼ m. by A 149 on B 1157 ℘ (01263) 824555, *dales@mackenziehotels.com Fax (01263) 822647*, – – P – 60. VISA.
Upchers : Rest 13.95/15.50 (lunch) and a la carte 24.05/31.85 – **17 rm** ★82.00/124.00 – ★★124.00/146.00.
• Substantial 19C country house whose rich décor affords much comfort. Famous gardens conveniently adjacent. Original oak staircase in situ. Smart bedrooms overlook the grounds. Wood-panelled restaurant with superb oak-carved inglenook.

Willow Lodge without rest., 6 Vicarage Rd, NR26 8NH, off B 1157 ℘ (01263) 822204, *Fax (01263) 824424*, – P. VISA.
5 rm ★38.00/40.00 – ★★56.00/60.00.
• Late 19C house in quiet residential area not far from town. Comfy lounge overlooking garden. Attractively decorated, spacious bedrooms with handmade pine furniture.

SHERWOOD BUSINESS PARK *Nottingham – see Nottingham.*

SHILTON *W. Mids.* 503 504 P 26 – *see Coventry.*

SHINCLIFFE *Durham – see Durham.*

SHINFIELD *Reading* 504 R 29 – *see Reading.*

SHIPLEY *W. Yorks.* 502 O 22 – *pop. 28 162.*
Northcliffe, High Bank Lane ℘ (01274) 584085 – Beckfoot Lane, Cottingley Bridge Bingley ℘ (01274) 568652.
London 216 – Bradford 4 – Leeds 12.

Marriott Hollins Hall H. and Country Club , Hollins Hill, Baildon, BD17 7QW Northeast : 2 ½ m. on A 6038 ℘ (0870) 4007227, *events.hollins@marriotthotels.co.uk Fax (0870) 4007327*, , , , , , , – , rest, P – 170. AE VISA.
Heathcliffe's : Rest (bar lunch) 27.50 and a la carte 18.20/29.70 – **121 rm** ★117.00 – ★★129.00, 1 suite.
• In the heart of Yorkshire with excellent leisure facilities including 20m pool and 18 hole golf course overlooking Aire Valley. Sandstone façade conceals restful rooms. Roomy, modern restaurant; good views over gardens.

Beeties Gallery with rm, 7 Victoria Rd, Saltaire Village, BD18 3LA, ℘ (01274) 595988, *jayne@beeties.co.uk, Fax (01274) 582118* – rm, . AE VISA
closed 1 January – **Rest** (dinner only) 16.95 and a la carte 20.40/28.85 – **5 rm** ★45.00/60.00 – ★★60.00/70.00.
• Grade II listed Victorian building with regularly changing art on walls: 50 yards from Hockney collection at Salt Mills. Well executed modern British cuisine. Cottagey rooms.

Aagrah, 4 Saltaire Rd, BD18 3HN, ℘ (01274) 530880, *Fax (01274) 599105* – P. AE VISA.
closed lunch Saturday and Sunday – **Rest** - Indian (Kashmiri) - 15.00 and a la carte 14.95/21.05 s.
• Another member of this growing chain of Indian restaurants, refurbished to modern standard. Cuisine includes Dahi dishes from Kashmir, made with yoghurt and chilli sauce.

SHIPTON GORGE *Dorset – see Bridport.*

SHIPTON-UNDER-WYCHWOOD *Oxon.* 503 504 P 28.
London 81 – Birmingham 50 – Gloucester 37 – Oxford 25.

Shipton Grange House without rest., OX7 6DG, ℘ (01993) 831298, *veronica@shiptongrangehouse.com, Fax (01993) 832082*, – P.
3 rm ★55.00 – ★★75.00.
• An arched gateway leads to a charming walled garden, converted Georgian coach house and stables. Handsomely furnished sitting room, spotless bedrooms, welcoming atmosphere.

SHOBDON *Herefordshire* 503 L 27 – ✉ *Leominster.*
London 158 – Birmingham 55 – Hereford 18 – Shrewsbury 37 – Worcester 33.

The Paddock, HR6 9NQ, ✆ (01568) 708176, *thepaddock@talk21.com, Fax (01568) 708829* – ⇔ P. ✂
Rest (by arrangement) 19.00 – **4 rm** ☕ ✝35.00/38.00 – ✝✝48.00/52.00.
◆ Well-priced, ground floor accommodation in this pleasant, village centre bungalow. All rooms are comfy and immaculately kept. Well run by hospitable owner.

SHOTTLE *Derbs. – see Belper.*

SHREWSBURY *Shrops.* 502 503 L 25 *Great Britain G. – pop. 67 126.*
See : *Abbey*★ **D.**
Exc. : *Ironbridge Gorge Museum*★★ *AC (The Iron Bridge*★★ *- Coalport China Museum*★★ *- Blists Hill Open Air Museum*★★ *– Museum of the River and Visitor Centre*★ *) SE : 12 m. by A 5 and B 4380.*
18 *Condover* ✆ *(01743) 872976* – 9 *Meole Brace* ✆ *(01743) 364050.*
ℹ *The Music Hall, The Square* ✆ *(01743) 281200, tic@shrewsburytourism.co.uk.*
London 164 – Birmingham 48 – Chester 43 – Derby 67 – Gloucester 93 – Manchester 68 – Stoke-on-Trent 39 – Swansea 124.

Plan on next page

Prince Rupert, Butcher Row, SY1 1UQ, ✆ (01743) 499955, *post@prince-rupert-hotel.co.uk, Fax (01743) 357306,* Fб, ≘s – ⎮ ⇔, ▤ rest, ♿ P – 🎓 120. MC AE ⦿ VISA n
Royalist : **Rest** *(closed Sunday dinner and Monday)* 25.00 and a la carte 26.70/33.15 ♀ – ***Chambers :*** **Rest** a la carte 19.90/26.90 – ☕ 10.50 – **68 rm** ✝85.00/95.00 – ✝✝105.00, 2 suites.
◆ 12C home of Prince Rupert, in the shadow of the cathedral. A collection of old buildings, some 15C, affords tremendous character. Rooms vary in age: the oldest are the best. Baronial style Royalist. Olde Worlde atmosphere of Chambers.

Pinewood House without rest., Shelton Park, The Mount, SY3 8BL, Northwest : 1 ½ m. on A 458 ✆ (01743) 364200, ⛰ – P
closed 25-26 December and 25 March-11 April – **4 rm** ☕ ✝46.00/54.00 – ✝✝54.00/62.00.
◆ A Regency house surrounded by wooded gardens. A homely, intimate atmosphere pervades the drawing room with its sofas, fresh flowers whilst bedrooms are charmingly decorated.

Tudor House without rest., 2 Fish St, SY1 1UR, ✆ (01743) 351735, *enquire@tudorhouseshrewsbury.co.uk, Fax (01743) 351735* – ⇔. ✂ e
4 rm ☕ ✝59.00/89.00 – ✝✝79.00/120.00.
◆ On a picturesque medieval street in a historic part of Shrewsbury, this compact 15C house retains its antiquated charm in its cosy sitting room and simple bedrooms.

The Armoury, Victoria Quay, Welsh Bridge, SY1 1HH, ✆ (01743) 340525, *armoury@brunningandprice.co.uk, Fax (01743) 340526* – MC AE VISA c
closed 25-26 December – **Rest** a la carte 19.00/30.00 ♀.
◆ Former 18C riverside warehouse with huge open-plan interior; sturdy brick walls full of old pictures and bookshelves. Daily changing menus offer an eclectic range of dishes.

at Albrighton *North : 3 m. on A 528 –* ✉ *Shrewsbury.*

Albrighton Hall, Ellesmere Rd, SY4 3AG, ✆ (0870) 1942129, *albrighton@macdonald-hotels.co.uk, Fax (01939) 291123,* ⊕, Fб, ≘s, ⛳, ⛰, 🎾, squash – ⎮ ⇔ ✆ ♿ P – 🎓 400. MC AE ⦿ VISA
Oak Room : **Rest** 14.95/25.00 and dinner a la carte 25.00/35.00 ♀ – **86 rm** ☕ ✝70.00/90.00 – ✝✝120.00/140.00.
◆ Extended 17C manor house with ornamental lake and lovely gardens. Impressive spa. Characterful panelled lounge. Individualistic rooms in old house; spacious and modern in new. Dine in oak-panelled formality.

Albright Hussey ⛰, Ellesmere Rd, SY4 3AF, ✆ (01939) 290571, *info@albrighthussey.co.uk, Fax (01939) 291143,* <, ⛰ – ⇔ ✆ ♿ P – 🎓 200. MC AE ⦿ VISA
Rest 15.00/35.00 and a la carte 25.95/35.45 – **25 rm** ☕ ✝79.00/99.00 – ✝✝160.00/180.00, 1 suite.
◆ Most impressive part 16C moated manor house. Fountains, stone walls and bridge in lawned gardens. The five rooms in the original house have oak panelling and huge fireplaces. Hugely characterful, heavily beamed 16C dining room.

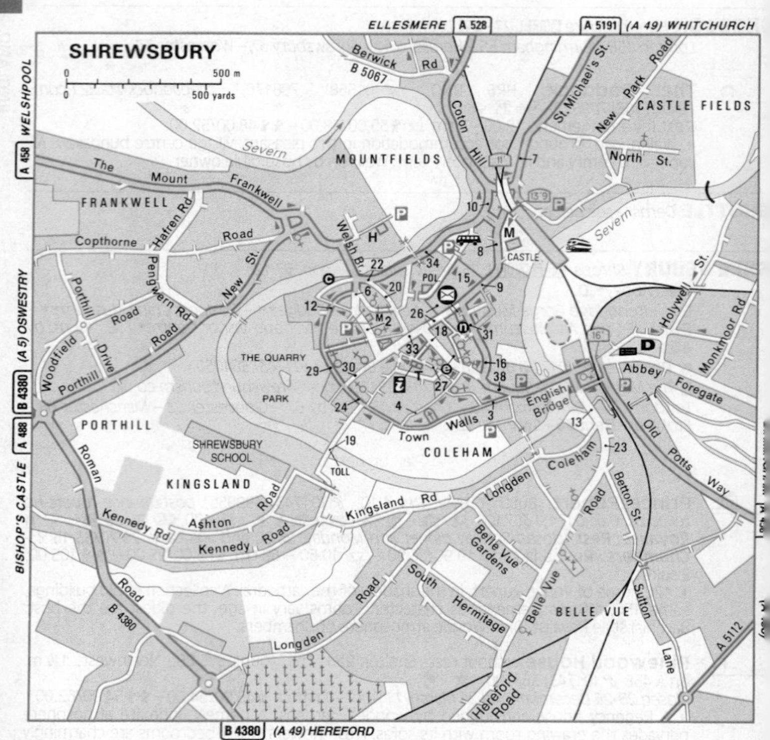

Barker St.	2	Coleham Head	13	Pride Hill	26
Beeches Lane	3	Darwin Centre	15	Princess St	27
Belmont	4	Dogpole	16	St Chad's Terrace	29
Bridge St.	6	High St	18	St John's Hill	30
Castle Foregate	7	Kingsland Bridge	19	St Mary's St	31
Castle Gates	8	Mardol Quay	22	Shoplatch	33
Castle St	9	Mardol	20	Smithfield Rd	34
Chester St	10	Moreton Crescent	23	Wyle Cop	38
Claremont Bank	12	Murivance	24		

at Grinshill *North : 7¾ m. by A 49 – ✉ Shrewsbury.*

XX **The Inn at Grinshill** with rm, The High St, SY4 3BL, ✆ (01939) 220410, *info@theinnatgrinshill.co.uk, Fax (01939) 220327,* – ✈ ✆ P. MO VISA. ✂
closed Sunday dinner – **Rest** 9.95 (lunch) and a la carte 19.00/33.00 ♀ – ☕ 10.00 – **6 rm** ★75.00/95.00 – ★★100.00/120.00.
◆ 18C stable block in small village: a cosy bar with sofas awaits, while beyond a light and airy, modern restaurant serves a wide range of menus. Spacious, stylish bedrooms.

at Atcham *Southeast : 3 m. by A 5064 on B 4380 – ✉ Shrewsbury.*

Mytton and Mermaid, SY5 6QG, ✆ (01743) 761220, *info@myttonandmermaid.co.uk, Fax (01743) 761292,* – ✈ P – 50. MO AE O VISA. ✂
closed 25 December – **Rest** a la carte 20.00/35.00 ♀ – **18 rm** ☕ ★70.00 – ★★150.00.
◆ Impressive, ivy clad18C house on the banks of the Severn. Quirky bar with log fire and sofas. Riverside drawing room. Smart rooms divided between main house and courtyard. Informal restaurant dining: seasonal menus.

at Acton Burnell *Southeast : 7½ m. by A 458 – ✉ Shrewsbury.*

Acton Pigot, Acton Pigot, SY5 7PH, Northeast : 1 ¾ m. by Kenley rd ☎ (01694) 731209, *acton@farmline.com, Fax (01694) 731399*, heated, , , – P
closed 25 December – **Rest** (by arrangement) (communal dining) 18.00/24.00 – **3 rm** ☕ 40.00 – 65.00.
◆ 17C farmhouse on working farm. Wealth of pursuits includes heated pool, fishing lake and tennis court. Age of house handsomely apparent in guest areas. Pleasant, cosy rooms. Huge oak dining table for dinner with fellow guests; adventurous cooking.

at Dorrington *South : 7 m. on A 49 – ✉ Shrewsbury.*

Country Friends, SY5 7JD, ☎ (01743) 718707, *countryfriends@ukonline.co.uk, Fax (01743) 718707*, – P. MO AE VISA
closed 2 weeks late February, 1 week August, Christmas-New Year, Sunday dinner and Monday – **Rest** 19.50/34.50.
◆ Quaint, old fashioned, beamed restaurant: fringed lamps, velour seats, framed photographs. Homespun cooking with rustic touch. Local produce well to the fore.

SHURDINGTON *Glos.* 503 504 N 28 – *see Cheltenham.*

SIBFORD GOWER *Oxon. – see Banbury.*

SIDFORD *Devon* 503 K 31 – *see Sidmouth.*

SIDMOUTH *Devon* 503 K 31 *The West Country G. – pop. 12 066.*
Env. : *Bicton★ (Gardens★) AC, SW : 5 m.*
18 *Cotmaton Rd ☎ (01395) 513023.*
Ham Lane ☎ (01395) 516441.
London 176 – Exeter 14 – Taunton 27 – Weymouth 45.

Victoria, The Esplanade, EX10 8RY, ☎ (01395) 512651, *info@victoriahotel.co.uk, Fax (01395) 579154*, ←, , , heated, , , – , rest, P. MO AE VISA.
Rest (dancing Saturday evening) 18.00/32.00 **s.** – ☕ 15.00 – **58 rm** 90.00/230.00 – 130.00/230.00, 3 suites.
◆ An imposing Edwardian house on Esplanade; most rooms are south facing with coastal views. Sun lounge, games room, dancing every Saturday night are among its attractions. Menus run on traditional lines.

Riviera, The Esplanade, EX10 8AY, ☎ (01395) 515201, *enquiries@hotelriviera.co.uk, Fax (01395) 577775*, ←, – , rest, – 85. MO AE VISA
Rest 22.00/34.00 and a la carte 40.00/44.95 – **27 rm** (dinner included) ☕ 99.00/150.00 – 198.00/318.00.
◆ An established seafront hotel with fine Regency façade and bow fronted windows. Peach and pink bedrooms with floral touches and friendly staff make for a comfortable stay. Formal dining salon affords views across Lyme Bay.

Belmont, The Esplanade, EX10 8RX, ☎ (01395) 512555, *reservations@belmont-hotel.co.uk, Fax (01395) 579101*, ←, – , rest, rest, P. MO AE VISA.
Rest (dancing Saturday evening) 17.50/32.00 and a la carte 40.00/47.00 **s.** – ☕ 13.00 – **50 rm** 80.00/120.00 – 160.00/180.00.
◆ A former Victorian family summer residence situated on seafront with attendant views. Spacious lounge; modern bedrooms. Guests can use leisure facilities at Victoria hotel. Stylish dining room with resident pianist.

Hunters Moon, Sid Rd, EX10 9AA, ☎ (01395) 513380, *huntersmoon.hotel@virgin.net, Fax (01395) 514270*, – P. MO VISA
closed January-February – **Rest** (booking essential to non-residents) (dinner only and Sunday lunch) 19.95 – **21 rm** (dinner included) ☕ 62.00/68.00 – 116.00/122.00.
◆ A fine, creeper-clad Georgian hotel in wooded grounds. Take in the garden views from the deep seated sofa in the lounge. Tall, sash windows in highly floral bedrooms. Period-style dining room with ornate ceiling.

ENGLAND

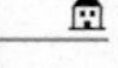

Woodlands, Station Rd, Cotmaton Cross, EX10 8HG, ✆ (01395) 513120, *info@woodlands-hotel.com, Fax (01395) 513348,* – P. VISA.
closed 21 December-18 January – **Rest** 16.50/28.00 (dinner) and a la carte 16.50/29.00 s. – **20 rm** ☐ ✝35.00/80.00 – ✝✝80.00/110.00.
◆ Historic country house in seaside garden with babbling stream. One-handed clock made in 1704 still stands in hall; piano, dance floor in the Sun Room. Fresh, neat bedrooms. Crystal chandeliered dining room; windows look out to garden stream.

at Sidford *North : 2 m. – ✉ Sidmouth.*

Salty Monk, Church St, EX10 9QP, on A 3052 ✆ (01395) 513174, *saltymonk@btconnect.com,* – P. VISA
closed 2 weeks November and 2 weeks January – **Rest** (booking essential) (lunch by arrangement) 20.00/28.50 – **5 rm** ☐ ✝65.00 – ✝✝95.00/115.00.
◆ Former 16C salt house where salt trading monks stayed en route to Exeter Cathedral. Fine lounge with deep leather armchairs; cottage-style rooms. Has a hydro massage shower. Restaurant converted from garden room.

at Newton Poppleford *Northwest : 4 m. by B 3176 on A 3052 – ✉ Sidmouth.*

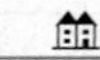

Moore's, 6 Greenbank, High St, EX10 0EB, ✆ (01395) 568100, *mooresrestaurant@aol.com, Fax (01395) 568092* – . VISA
closed Christmas, 2 weeks January, Sunday dinner, Monday and Bank Holidays – **Rest** 12.50/24.50 ♀.
◆ Two pretty 18C cottages set back from main road; pleasant ambience highlighted by candlelit evening meals. Conservatory extension. Modern, locally sourced dishes.

SILCHESTER *Hants.* 503 504 Q 29 – ✉ *Reading (Berks.).*
London 62 – Basingstoke 8 – Reading 14 – Southampton 37 – Winchester 26.

Romans, Little London Rd, RG7 2PN, ✆ (0118) 970 0421, *romanhotel@hotmail.com, Fax (0118) 970 0691,* , , , heated, , – rest, P – 80. VISA
Rest 21.95/24.95 and a la carte 34.00/43.00 ♀ – **25 rm** ☐ ✝95.00 – ✝✝155.00.
◆ A Lutyens-style manor set in well-kept gardens, close to the historic village. Boasts strong leisure and conference facilities. Rooms divided between main house and annex. Dining room, adjacent to garden, is hung with century old oil painting.

SINGLETON *Lancs.* 502 L 22 – *see Blackpool.*

SINNINGTON *N. Yorks.* 502 R 21 – *see Pickering.*

SISSINGHURST *Kent* 504 V 30 – *see Cranbrook.*

SITTINGBOURNE *Kent* 504 W 29.
London 44 – Canterbury 18 – Maidstone 15 – Sheerness 9.

Hempstead House, London Rd, Bapchild, ME9 9PP, East : 2 m. on A 2 ✆ (01795) 428020, *info@hempsteadhouse.co.uk, Fax (01795) 436362,* , heated, – P – 150. VISA
Lakes : **Rest** (Sunday dinner residents only) 16.50/24.50 and a la carte 25.75/33.75 ♀ – **27 rm** ☐ ✝75.00 – ✝✝120.00.
◆ Part Victorian manor, a former estate house for surrounding farmland. Original sitting room in situ; outdoor heated pool. Cheerful, individually designed, modern bedrooms. Sunny restaurant with terrace.

SIX MILE BOTTOM *Cambs. – see Newmarket (Suffolk).*

SKELWITH BRIDGE *Cumbria* 502 K 20 – *see Ambleside.*

SKIPTON *N. Yorks.* 502 N 22 *Great Britain G. – pop. 14 313.*
See : *Castle*★ *AC.*
off NW Bypass (01756) 793922.
35 Coach St (01756) 792809.
London 217 – Kendal 45 – Leeds 26 – Preston 36 – York 43.

Carlton House without rest., 46 Keighley Rd, BD23 2NB, (01756) 700921, *carlton house@rapidial.co.uk, Fax (01756) 700921* – . VISA.
5 rm ★25.00/40.00 – ★★50.00.
◆ Victorian terraced house near centre of town. Pleasantly furnished in sympathetic style. Attractive dining room serves full English breakfast. Individually decorated bedrooms.

The Bull, Broughton, BD23 3AE, West : 3 m. on A 59 (01756) 792065, *janeneil@thebullatbroughton.co.uk, Fax (01756) 792065,* – P. AE VISA
closed Bank Holiday Monday and Sunday dinner – **Rest** a la carte 18.10/25.95 ♀.
◆ Set on busy main road, this delightful country pub has open log fire and its own specially brewed beer. Intimate dining room serving varied, tasty menus full of local produce.

at Hetton *North : 5¾ m. by B 6265 – Skipton.*

Angel Inn and Barn Lodgings with rm, BD23 6LT, (01756) 730263, *info@angelhetton.co.uk, Fax (01756) 730363* – P. AE VISA
closed 25 December, 1 week January and Sunday dinner – **Rest** (booking essential) (dinner only and Sunday lunch)/dinner a la carte 20.70/30.40 ♀ – (see also below) – **5 rm** ★120.00 – ★★145.00/170.00.
◆ Well regarded restaurant with stone walls, beams and roaring log fire. Fine quality, locally sourced produce. Bedrooms with antique furniture and modern appointments.

Angel Inn, BD23 6LT, (01756) 730263, *info@angelhetton.co.uk, Fax (01756) 730363,* – P. AE VISA
closed 25 December and 1 week January – **Rest** (booking essential) a la carte 23.00/30.00 ♀.
◆ Ancient beams and inglenooks in hugely characterful pubby part of renowned 18C inn. Fine modern British cooking. Shares rooms with restaurant in converted farmbuildings.

SLALEY *Northd.* 501 502 N 19 – *see Hexham.*

SLAPTON *Devon* 503 J 33 *The West Country G.*
Exc. : *Dartmouth*★★, *N : 7 m. by A 379 – Kingsbridge*★, *W : 7 m. by A 379.*
London 223 – Dartmouth 7 – Plymouth 29.

Tower Inn with rm, Church Rd, TQ7 2PN, (01548) 580216, *towerinn@slapton.org,* – rm. AE VISA
closed 25 December, Sunday dinner and Monday in winter. – **Rest** a la carte 20.00/25.00 ♀ – **3 rm** ★40.00 – ★★60.00.
◆ Built in 1347 as cottages for men working on local chantry. Beams, flag floors, stone walls: all very characterful. Surprisingly modern menus. Simple annex bedrooms.

SLEAFORD *Lincs.* 502 504 S 25 – *pop. 15 219.*
Willoughby Rd, South Rauceby (01529) 488273.
Money's Yard, Carre St (01529) 414294.
London 119 – Leicester 45 – Lincoln 17 – Nottingham 39.

Lincolnshire Oak, East Rd, NG34 7EH, Northeast : ¾ m. on B 1517 (01529) 413807, *reception@lincolnshire-oak.co.uk, Fax (01529) 413710,* – P – 140. AE VISA.
Rest (booking essential) 17.95 – **17 rm** ★59.50/65.00 – ★★75.00/90.00.
◆ A hospitable Victorian house on the edge of town, once used as an officer's mess. Outside are small, pleasant gardens; inside are amply sized, comfortably furnished rooms. Homely dining room.

SLINFOLD *W. Sussex* – *see Horsham.*

The ✿ award is the crème de la crème. This is awarded to restaurants which are really worth travelling miles for!

SLOUGH *Slough* 504 S 29 – *pop. 126 276.*
London 29 – Oxford 39 – Reading 19.

Slough/Windsor Marriott, Ditton Rd, Langley, SL3 8PT, Southeast : 2 ½ m. on A 4 ✆ (0870) 4007244, *events.sloughwindsor@marriotthotels.co.uk, Fax (0870) 4007344,* – rm, – 400. VISA.
Rest a la carte 19.45/31.35 **s.** – 14.95 – **381 rm** 165.00 – 165.00, 1 suite.
◆ A five-storey hotel, 15 minutes from Heathrow airport, with well-equipped leisure club Bedrooms are furnished with good quality fabrics; Executive rooms have private lounge All-day restaurant option.

Copthorne, 400 Cippenham Lane, SL1 2YE, Southwest : 1 ¼ m. by A 4 on A 355 off M 4 junction 6 ✆ (01753) 516222, *Fax (01753) 516237,* – rm, – 250. VISA.
Veranda : **Rest** *(closed Saturday lunch)* a la carte 21.00/34.50 **s.** – 15.75 – **217 rm** 180.00 – 210.00, 2 suites.
◆ The marble floored reception leads to split-level lounge, bar, leisure club. Rooms with mini-bars; some overlook Windsor Castle. Good business facilities in Executive rooms. Bright, modern brasserie; views to Windsor Castle.

Courtyard by Marriott Slough/Windsor, Church St, Chalvey, SL1 2NH, Southwest : 1 ¼ m. by A 4 on A 355 off M 4 junction 6 ✆ (0870) 4007215, *events.slcourtyard@kewgreen.co.uk, Fax (0870) 4007315,* – rm, – 40. VISA.
Rest (bar lunch)/dinner a la carte 17.00/24.65 – 12.00 – **150 rm** 125.00/140.00 – 125.00/140.00.
◆ Modern hotel, ideal for leisure and business travellers, close to Windsor Castle. All mod cons and services readily available. Executive rooms have work area. Smart mezzanine level restaurant.

SNAINTON *N. Yorks.* 502 S 21.
London 241 – Pickering 8.5 – Scarborough 10.

Coachman Inn with rm, Pickering Road West, YO13 9PL, West : ½ m. by A 170 on B 1258 ✆ (01723) 859231, *Fax (01723) 850008,* – 10. VISA
closed Wednesday – **Rest** a la carte 19.00/25.00 – **4 rm** 66.00 – 85.00.
◆ Classically Georgian former coaching inn. Eat in the cosy bar with fire or the modern dining room. Prominent Yorkshire produce on modern British menus. Individual bedrooms.

SNAPE *Suffolk* 504 Y 27.
London 113 – Ipswich 19 – Norwich 50.

Crown Inn with rm, Bridge Rd, IP17 1SL, ✆ (01728) 688324, – rm, VISA.
closed 25 December and dinner 26 December – **Rest** a la carte 18.00/28.00 – **3 rm** 70.00 – 80.00.
◆ 15C inn with antique settle, log fire and exposed rafters. Agricultural artefacts and paintings fill the small dining room where simple dishes are served. Comfortable rooms.

SNETTISHAM *Norfolk* 504 V 25 – *pop. 2 145.*
London 113 – King's Lynn 13 – Norwich 44.

The Rose and Crown with rm, Old Church Rd, PE31 7LX, ✆ (01485) 541382, *info@roseandcrownsnettisham.co.uk, Fax (01485) 543172,* – rm. VISA
Rest a la carte 16.00/25.00 – **16 rm** 60.00 – 100.00.
◆ Cosy, rustic pub in centre of town: open fires, antique furniture, bustling ambience. Original menus with Asiatic and Italian influences. Vibrant, well-maintained rooms.

SOAR MILL COVE *Devon* – *see Salcombe.*

We try to be as accurate as possible when giving room rates. But prices are susceptible to change, so please check rates when booking.

SOLIHULL *W. Mids.* 503 504 O 26 – *pop. 94 753.*
Central Library, Homer Rd ℰ (0121) 704 6130.
London 109 – Birmingham 7 – Coventry 13 – Warwick 13.

Renaissance Solihull, 651 Warwick Rd, B91 1AT, ℰ (0121) 711 3000, *reservations.solihull@marriotthotels.co.uk, Fax (0121) 705 6629,* – 700.
MC AE VISA
651 **:** Rest 16.00/21.95 and a la carte 23.00/28.00 **s.** – 14.95 – **176 rm** 140.00/199.00 – 150.00/209.00, 4 suites.
◆ Well placed for road and rail links and the airport. Behind an unpromising façade, modern rooms are usefully equipped and extensive conference facilities are much in demand. Restaurant with garden outlook.

The Town House, 727 Warwick Rd, B91 3DA, ℰ (0121) 704 1567, *hospitalityengineers@btinternet.com, Fax (0121) 713 2189* – P. MC AE VISA
Rest 15.00 (lunch) and a la carte 19.25/25.25.
◆ Once a salubrious nightclub with town centre location. Stylish open-plan interior boasts large dining area with leather banquettes. Soundly prepared modern dishes.

Shimla Pinks, 44 Station Rd, B91 3RX, ℰ (0121) 704 0344, *Fax (0121) 643 3325* – . MC AE VISA
Rest - Indian - (dinner only) 14.95/20.95 and a la carte 10.40/16.40.
◆ Well regarded Indian cuisine in distinctly modern surroundings. A popular venue: regulars return for the original, interesting cooking that ventures away from the traditional.

Metro Bar and Grill, 680-684 Warwick Rd, B91 3DX, ℰ (0121) 705 9495, *Fax (0121) 705 4754* – . MC AE VISA
closed 25-26 December, 1 January and Sunday – **Rest** 11.95/14.95 (lunch) and a la carte 19.70/26.85.
◆ Locally renowned town centre bar/restaurant that combines buzzy informality with appealing range of brasserie dishes. Dine alongside busy bar: don't expect a quiet night out!

at Olton *Northwest : 2½ m. on A 41 – ✉ Solihull.*

Rajnagar, 256 Lyndon Rd, B92 7QW, ℰ (0121) 742 8140, *info@rajnagar.com, Fax (0121) 743 3147* – . MC AE VISA
– **Rest** - Indian - (dinner only) a la carte 11.00/16.40.
◆ A busy, modern neighbourhood favourite, privately owned, offering authentic, regional specialities of Indian cuisine. Service is flexible and friendly.

SOMERTON *Somerset* 503 L 30 *The West Country G. – pop. 4 133.*
See : *Town★ - Market Place★ (cross★) – St Michael's Church★.*
Env. : *Long Sutton★ (Church★★) SW : 2½ m. by B 3165 – Huish Episcopi (St Mary's Church Tower★★) SW : 4½ m. by B 3153 – Lytes Cary★, SE : 3½ m. by B 3151 – Street - The Shoe Museum★, N : 5 m. by B 3151.*
Exc. : *Muchelney★★ (Parish Church★★) SW : 6½ m. by B 3153 and A 372 – High Ham (≤★★, St Andrew's Church★), NW : 9 m. by B 3153, A 372 and minor rd – Midelney Manor★ AC, SW : 9 m. by B 3153 and A 378.*
London 138 – Bristol 32 – Taunton 17.

Lynch Country House without rest., 4 Behind Berry, TA11 7PD, ℰ (01458) 272316, *the-lynch@talk21.com, Fax (01458) 272590,* ≤, – P. MC AE VISA.
9 rm 50.00/65.00 – 95.00.
◆ Stands on a crest overlooking the Cary Valley. The grounds of this Regency house are equally rich with unusual shrubs, trees and lake. Antique four-poster; spotless rooms.

at Kingsdon *Southeast : 2½ m. by B 3151 – ✉ Somerton.*

Kingsdon Inn, TA11 7LG, ℰ (01935) 840543, *Fax (01935) 840916,* – P. MC VISA
closed 25-26 December and 1 January – **Rest** a la carte 15.00/23.20.
◆ Thatched inn with bags of character. Modernised interior retains beams, wood-burning stove, colourful scatter cushions. Daily changing menus full of traditional favourites.

SONNING-ON-THAMES *Wokingham* 504 R 29.
London 48 – Reading 4.

French Horn with rm, RG4 6TN, ℰ (01189) 692204, *info@thefrenchhorn.co.uk, Fax (01189) 442210,* ≤ River Thames and gardens – P. MC AE VISA.
closed Christmas-New Year – **Rest** (booking essential) 28.50/40.00 and a la carte 48.00/85.00 **s.** – **17 rm** 130.00 – 170.00, 4 suites.
◆ A retreat from the world on the banks of the Thames. Cove ceilinged lounge; open fire used to roast ducks. Dining room with garden views. Classic cuisine. Spacious rooms.

SOUTHAMPTON *Southampton* 503 504 P 31 *Great Britain G. – pop. 234 224.*

See : *Old Southampton* AZ : *Bargate*★ B - *Tudor House Museum*★ M1.

18, 9 Southampton Municipal, Golf Course Rd, Bassett ☎ (023) 8076 8407, AY *– 18 Stoneham, Monks Wood Close, Bassett ☎ (023) 8076 9272,* AY *– 18 Chilworth Golf Centre, Main Rd, Chilworth ☎ (023) 8074 0544,* AY.

Itchen Bridge (toll) AZ.

Southampton/Eastleigh Airport : ☎ (0870) 0001000, N : 4 m. BY.

to France (Cherbourg) (Stena Line) 1-2 daily (5 h) – to the Isle of Wight (East Cowes) (Red Funnel Ferries) frequent services daily (55 mn).

to Hythe (White Horse Ferries Ltd) frequent services daily (12 mn) – to the Isle of Wight (Cowes) (Red Funnel Ferries) frequent services daily (approx. 22 mn).

9 Civic Centre Rd ☎ (023) 8083 3333, city.information@southampton.gov.uk.

London 87 – Bristol 79 – Plymouth 161.

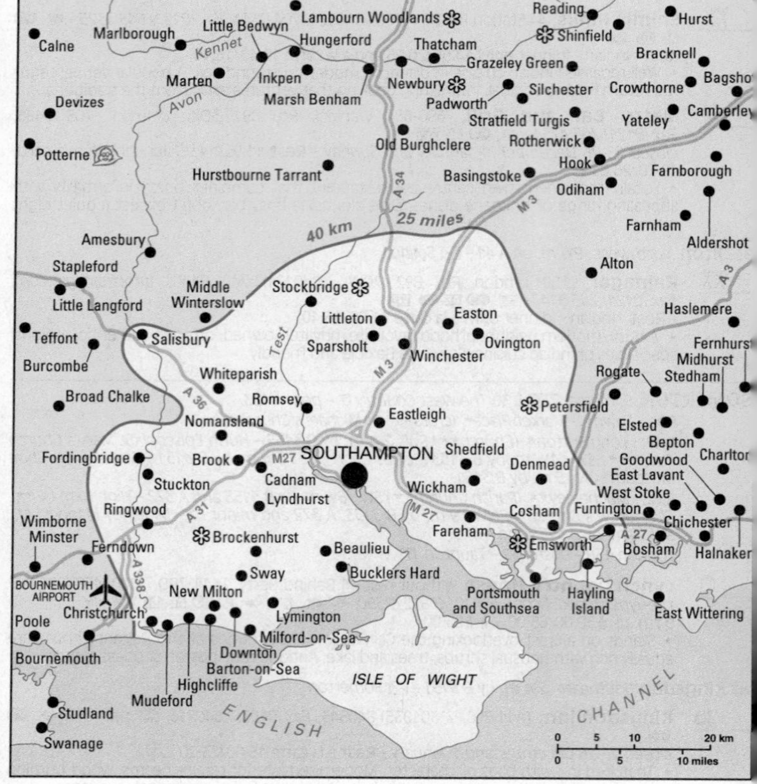

De Vere Grand Harbour, West Quay Rd, SO15 1AG, ☎ (023) 8063 3033, *grandharbour@devere-hotels.com, Fax (023) 8063 3066,* – rest, – 500. VISA. AZ a

Allerton's : Rest *(closed Sunday-Monday)* (booking essential) 39.50 ♀ – ***Number 5 :*** Rest a la carte 13.95/33.45 **s.** ♀ – **168 rm** ★118.00/150.00 – ★★128.00/160.00, 4 suites.

◆ Modern and stylish. The split-level pavilion leisure club boasts a Finnish sauna, Turkish steam room and bar. Well furnished rooms; some with balconies and king-size beds. Allerton's is arcaded, with screens. Chic, informal Number 5.

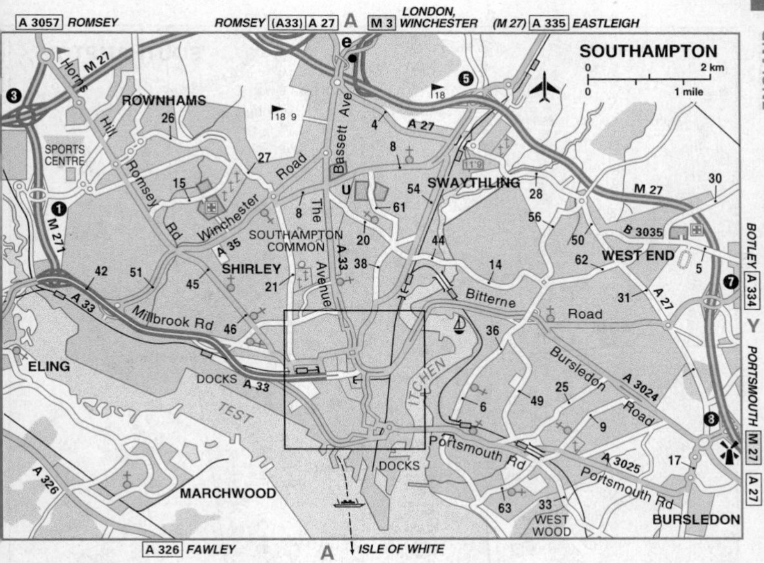

Basset Green Rd	AY	4
Botley Rd	AY	5
Bridge Rd	AY	6
Burgess Rd	AY	8
Butts Rd	AY	9
Cobden Ave	AY	14
Coxford Rd	AY	15
Hamble Lane	AY	17
Highfield Lane	AY	20
Hill Lane	AY	21
Kane's Hill	AY	24
Kathleen Rd	AY	25
Lords Hill Way	AY	26
Lordswood Rd	AY	27
Mansbridge Rd	AY	28
Moor Hill	AY	31
Moorgreen Rd	AY	30
Newtown Rd	AY	33
Peartree Ave	AY	36
Portswood Rd	AY	38
Redbridge Rd	AY	42
St Denys Rd	AY	44
Shirley High Rd	AY	45
Shirley Rd	AY	46
Spring Rd	AY	49
Swaythling Rd	AY	50
Tebourba Way	AY	51
Thomas Lewis Way	AY	54
Townhill Way	AY	56
Welbeck Ave	AY	61
Westend Rd	AY	62
Weston Lane	AY	63

Hilton Southampton, Bracken Pl, Chilworth, SO16 3RB, ☎ (023) 8070 2700, *Fax (023) 8076 7233,* – 200. **AY e**
Rest *(closed Saturday lunch)* 13.50/25.95 and dinner a la carte 19.50/36.15 – 15.95 – **133 rm** 99.00/104.00 – 144.00/170.00, 2 suites.
◆ A purpose-built hotel with smart marbled lobby and individual reception desks. Extensive leisure facilities and good size bedrooms, well furnished to a high standard. Informal, family-oriented restaurant.

Jurys Inn, 1 Charlotte Pl, SO14 0JB, ☎ (023) 8037 1111, *jurysinnsouthampton@jurysdoyle.com, Fax (023) 8037 1100* – 120. **AZ c**
Innfusion : **Rest** (bar lunch)/dinner a la carte 18.55/25.40 s. – 9.50 – **270 rm** 79.00 – 79.00.
◆ Up-to-date hotel, handily placed close to city centre. Well-equipped conference facilities; spacious coffee shop/bar. Good value, ample sized accommodation. Modern dining room with modish menus.

Premier Travel Inn, 6 Dials, New Rd, SO14 0AB, ☎ (0870) 2383308, *Fax (023) 8033 8395* – **AZ e**
Rest (grill rest.) – **172 rm** 55.95/55.95 – 59.95/59.95.
◆ This spacious lodge hotel is situated on main arterial road into the city, five minutes' walk from Southampton's St Marys football stadium. Good value accommodation.

Dockgate 4, 1 South Western House, SO14 3AS, ☎ (023) 8033 9303, *info@dockgate4.com, Fax (023) 8033 6999* – 12. **AZ n**
Rest a la carte 22.95/35.95.
◆ Set in elegantly apportioned Wedgwood ballroom with beautifully ornate ceiling. Smart, well-spaced tables mirror surroundings. Tasty, appealing menus boast plenty of choice.

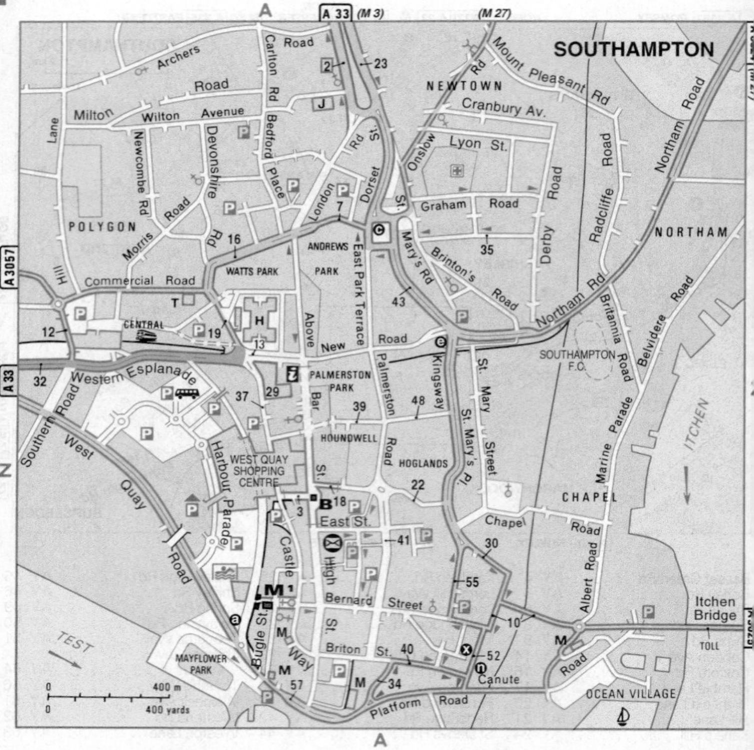

SOUTHAMPTON

Above Bar St. . . . . AZ
Avenue (The). . . . . AZ 2
Bargate St. . . . . AZ 3
Brunswick Pl. . . . . AZ 7
Central Bridge. . . . . AZ 10
Central Station Bridge . . . . . . AZ 12
Civic Centre Rd. . . . . AZ 13
Cumberland Pl. . . . . AZ 16
Hanover Buildings . . . . AZ 18
Havelock Rd . . . . AZ 19
High St . . . . AZ
Houndwell Pl. . . . . AZ 22
Inner Ave. . . . . AZ 23
Marlands Shopping Centre . . . . AZ 29
Marsh Lane. . . . . AZ 30
Mountbatten Way . . . . AZ 32
Orchard Pl. . . . . AZ 34
Oxford Ave . . . . AZ 35
Portland Terrace . . . . AZ 37
Pound Tree Rd . . . . AZ 39
Queen's Terrace. . . . . AZ 40
Queen's Way . . . . AZ 41
St Andrew's Rd . . . . AZ 43
South Front. . . . . AZ 48
Terminus Terrace . . . . AZ 52
Threefield Lane. . . . . AZ 55
Town Quay . . . . AZ 57
West Quay Shopping Centre . . . . AZ

Oxfords, 35-36 Oxford St, SO14 3DS, ✆ (023) 8022 4444, *bookings@oxfordsrestaurant.com, Fax (023) 8022 2284* – MC AE VISA AZ x
Rest 12.95 and a la carte 25.00/30.00 ♀.
◆ Well-run, modern eatery in lively part of town. Entrance bar has impressively vast wall of wines. Restaurant features bold, fresh brasserie cuisine with extensive choice.

White Star Dining Rooms, 28 Oxford St, SO14 3DJ, ✆ (023) 8082 1990, *manager@whitestartavern.co.uk, Fax 023 8090 4982* – ▤. MC AE VISA AZ x
closed 25-26 December and 1 January – **Rest** 14.95 (lunch) and a la carte 19.00/35.00 ♀.
◆ Recently revamped town centre pub. Spacious, comfortable premises with antique tables. Small lounge with leather armchairs. Good range of contemporary cuisine.

SOUTH CADBURY *Somerset* 503 M 30 – *see Castle Cary.*

If breakfast is included the ☕ symbol appears after the number of rooms.

SOUTHEND-ON-SEA *Southend* 504 W 29 – *pop. 160 257.*

Belfairs, Eastwood Road North, Leigh-on-Sea (01702) 525345 – Ballards Gore G. & C.C., Gore Rd, Canewdon, Rochford (01702) 258917 – The Essex Golf Complex, Garon Park, Eastern Ave (01702) 601701.

Southend-on-Sea Airport : (01702) 608100, N : 2 m.

19 High St (01702) 215120.

London 39 – Cambridge 69 – Croydon 46 – Dover 85.

Camelia, 178 Eastern Esplanade, Thorpe Bay, SS1 3AA, (01702) 587917, *enquiries@cameliahotel.com, Fax (01702) 585704* – , rest. MO AE VISA.
Rest (residents only Sunday dinner)(dinner only and Sunday lunch) 14.95 and a la carte 22.15/26.15 s – **34 rm** ★55.00/65.00 – ★★100.00.
◆ A white hotel on the seafront at Thorpe Bay with good views of the Thames Estuary. Comfortable, well-kept bedrooms, particularly Superior rooms in the new extension. Popular menus in front dining room.

Beaches without rest., 192 Eastern Esplanade, Thorpe Bay, SS1 3AA, (01702) 586124, *Fax (01702) 587793,* ← – . MO AE VISA.
7 rm ★25.00/35.00 – ★★75.00.
◆ A sunny guesthouse on Thorpe Bay with panorama of Thames Estuary. Continental buffet breakfast. Individually styled rooms: four have sea views; two have balconies.

Pebbles without rest., 190 Eastern Esplanade, Thorpe Bay, SS1 3AA, (01702) 582329, *pebbles-guesthouse@yahoo.co.uk, Fax (01702) 582329,* ← – . MO VISA.
5 rm ★35.00/45.00 – ★★55.00/60.00.
◆ Friendly guesthouse on the Esplanade overlooking estuary; away from bustle of town but within easy walking distance. Rooftop garden and sea views from most bedrooms.

Atlantis without rest., 63 Alexandra Rd, SS1 1EY, (01702) 332538, *atlantisguesthouse@eurotelbroadband.com, Fax (01702) 392736* – P. MO VISA.
closed 25-26 December – **8 rm** ★35.00 – ★★65.00.
◆ Centrally located Victorian terraced house; pretty cloth-clad dining room with good traditional breakfast choice. Thoughtfully decorated bedrooms are all very well maintained.

The Bay without rest., 187 Eastern Esplanade, Thorpe Bay, SS1 3AA, (01702) 588415, *thebayguesthouse@hotmail.com* – . MO AE VISA.
4 rm ★35.00 – ★★55.00.
◆ Spruce Edwardian house on seafront; a flint wall and pretty tiled path leads to roomy interiors. Generous breakfasts served in light, mirrored breakfast room. Neat bedrooms.

Moorings without rest., 172 Eastern Esplanade,, SS1 3AA, (01702) 587575, *Fax (01702) 586791* – .
3 rm ★35.00/40.00 – ★★50.00/55.00.
◆ An Edwardian terraced house overlooking the sea; one room with a view. Well-kept and comfortable with affable owner. Simple, modern breakfast room.

Fleur de Provence, 52 Alexandra St, SS1 1BJ, (01702) 352987, *marcel@fleurdeprovence.co.uk, Fax (01702) 431123* – MO AE VISA
closed Saturday lunch and Sunday – **Rest** 15.00 and a la carte 32.85/38.85 ♀.
◆ Personally run restaurant, a classical French inspiration with a modern edge underpinning flavourful menus. Friendly service and continental style; well regarded in the area.

Paris, 719 London Rd, Westcliff-on-Sea, SS0 9ST, (01702) 344077, *info@parisrestaurant.net, Fax (01702) 349238* – . MO AE VISA
closed Saturday lunch, Sunday dinner and Monday – **Rest** (lunch booking essential) 18.95 and dinner a la carte 29.85/35.85 ♀.
◆ Unprepossessing façade conceals a modern restaurant with well-spaced, well-sized tables waited on by attentive staff. Ambitious cooking on good choice of daily changing menus.

SOUTH LEIGH *Oxon.* 503 504 P 28 – *see Witney.*

SOUTH MOLTON *Devon* 503 I 30.

London 197 – Barnstaple 11 – Bristol 81.

at Knowstone *Southeast : 9½ m. by A 361 – South Molton.*

The Masons Arms (Dodson), EX36 4RY, (01398) 341231, *dodsonmasonsarms@aol.com,* , – P. AE VISA
Rest *(closed Monday lunch)* (booking essential) a la carte 23.00/30.00.
Spec. Ham hock terrine, grain mustard dressing. Medallions of monkfish wrapped in Parma ham, scallop and caramelised orange. Chocolate parfait, caramelised pistachio nuts.
◆ Delightful, thatched 13C inn, with beams, vast fireplace and superb ceiling mural in restaurant. Classically based menus, full of flavour, employ quality seasonal ingredients.

SOUTH NORMANTON *Derbs.* 502 503 504 Q 24 – *pop. 14 044 (inc. Pinxton).*
London 130 – Derby 17 – Nottingham 15 – Sheffield 31.

Renaissance Derby/Nottingham, Carter Lane East, DE55 2EH, on A 38 ✆ (01773) 812000, *Fax (01773) 580032,* – 220. VISA
Rest *(closed Saturday lunch)* 17.95/22.50 and dinner a la carte approx 22.50 **s.** – **158 rm** 64.00/116.00 – 78.00/128.00.
◆ Located close to M1; a modern hotel offering comfortable, well-equipped rooms; those away from motorway are quieter. Usefully, newspapers, toiletries available at reception. Capacious restaurant.

Premier Travel Inn, Carter Lane East, DE55 2EH, on A 38 ✆ (01773) 862899, *Fax (01773) 861155* – rm, rest, VISA.
Rest (grill rest.) – **82 rm** 46.95/46.95 – 49.95/49.95.
◆ Modern lodge next to Castlewood Brewsters. Well-proportioned bedrooms suitable for business and family stopovers. Hardwick Hall and Midland Railway Centre are close by.

SOUTHPORT *Mersey.* 502 K 23 – *pop. 91 404.*
Southport Municipal, Park Road West ✆ (01704) 535286.
112 Lord St ✆ (01704) 533333.
London 221 – Liverpool 25 – Manchester 38 – Preston 19.

Cambridge House, 4 Cambridge Rd, PR9 9NG, Northeast : 1½ m. on A 565 ✆ (01704) 538372, *info@cambridgehousehotel.co.uk, Fax (01704) 547183,* – VISA.
Rest (dinner only and Sunday lunch)/dinner 24.95 – **16 rm** 55.00/65.00 – 88.00.
◆ Personally run Victorian town house; lavishly furnished lounge and cosy bar. Very comfortably appointed period rooms in original house; large, more modern style in extension. Regency-style dining room with elegant chairs.

The Waterford without rest., 37 Leicester St, PR9 0EX, ✆ (01704) 530559, *reception@waterford-hotel.co.uk, Fax (01704) 542630* – VISA.
March-October – **8 rm** 45.00 – 75.00.
◆ Pleasantly located close to the promenade, this personally run seaside hotel features a cosy bar for residents and decently sized, neatly decorated bedrooms.

Lynwood without rest., 11A Leicester St, PR9 0ER, ✆ (01704) 540794, *info@lynwoodhotel.com, Fax (01704) 500724* – VISA.
closed 1 week Christmas – **10 rm** 35.00/39.50 – 65.00/85.00.
◆ Only a couple of minutes' walk from busy Lord Street, this 19C terraced house retains period style in its lounge and neat breakfast room. Pleasantly individual bedrooms.

Warehouse Brasserie, 30 West St, PR8 1QN, ✆ (01704) 544662, *info@warehousebrasserie.co.uk, Fax (01704) 500074* – VISA
closed 25 December, 1 January and Sunday – **Rest** 12.95 (lunch) and a la carte 17.40/31.85.
◆ Former warehouse, now a sleek modern restaurant with Salvador Dali prints and buzzy atmosphere. The open-plan kitchen offers modern cooking with interesting daily specials.

SOUTHROP *Glos.* 503 504 O 28 – *see Lechlade.*

SOUTHSEA *Portsmouth* 503 504 Q 31 – *see Portsmouth and Southsea.*

SOUTHWELL *Notts.* 502 504 R 24 *Great Britain G.* – *pop. 6 285.*
See : *Minster*★★ *AC.*
London 135 – Leicester 35 – Lincoln 24 – Nottingham 14 – Sheffield 34.

Old Forge without rest., 2 Burgage Lane, NG25 0ER, ✆ (01636) 812809, *Fax (01636) 816302,* – VISA
4 rm 45.00 – 75.00.
◆ Quaint, converted forge with stable looks out to rear Minster. Sunny conservatory leads off from breakfast room. Relax on patio with tiny pond. Homely, well-sized rooms.

"Rest" appears in red for establishments with a ✿ (star) or (Bib Gourmand).

SOUTHWOLD *Suffolk* 504 Z 27 – *pop. 3 858.*
The Common ☎ *(01502) 723234.*
69 High St ☎ *(01502) 724729.*
London 108 – Great Yarmouth 24 – Ipswich 35 – Norwich 34.

Swan, Market Pl, IP18 6EG, ☎ (01502) 722186, *swan.hotel@adnams.co.uk, Fax (01502) 724800,* – rest, P – 40. MC VISA.
Rest 23.00/30.00 – **40 rm** 80.00/115.00 – 140.00/160.00, 2 suites.
◆ Restored coaching inn by Adnams Brewery. Antique filled interiors: 17C portrait of local heiress in hallway. Vintage rooms in main house; garden rooms built round the green. Tall windows define elegant restaurant.

The Crown, 90 High St, IP18 6DP, ☎ (01502) 722275, *crown.hotel@adnams.co.uk, Fax (01502) 727263* – P. MC VISA.
Rest a la carte 20.00/35.00 – **13 rm** 83.00 – 122.00, 1 suite.
◆ Whitewashed inn combines a smart bar with buzzy dining area and a locally popular real ale pub. Unfussy rooms are furnished in contemporary style. Smart, elegant restaurant with impressive wine list.

Northcliffe without rest., 20 North Parade, IP18 6LT, ☎ (01502) 724074, *northcliffe.southwold@virgin.net,* ←.
closed January – **6 rm** 55.00/80.00 – 90.00.
◆ Keenly run 19C house commands fine clifftop views; contemporary en suite rooms: ask for one facing the sea. Model boats and nautical curios decorate a cosy, firelit lounge.

The Randolph with rm, Wangford Rd, Reydon, IP18 6PZ, Northwest : 1 m. by A 1095 on B 1126 ☎ (01502) 723603, *reception@therandolph.co.uk, Fax (01502) 722194,* – rest, P. MC VISA
Rest a la carte 18.00/26.00 – **10 rm** 55.00 – 100.00.
◆ Renovated in bright contemporary style, a substantial turn of 20C inn named in honour of Randolph Churchill. Spacious bedrooms, each with distinctive décor.

SOWERBY BRIDGE *W. Yorks.* 502 O 22 – *pop. 9 901* – ✉ *Halifax.*
London 211 – Bradford 10 – Burnley 35 – Manchester 32 – Sheffield 40.

The Millbank, Mill Bank, HX6 3DY, Southwest : 2 ¼ m. by A 58 ☎ (01422) 825588, *themillbank@yahoo.co.uk,* MC VISA
closed first 2 weeks October, first 2 weeks January and Monday lunch – **Rest** (booking essential) a la carte 19.95/34.95.
◆ A stone inn, now a modernised dining pub with wooden and flagstone floors. Smart conservatory from which views of valley can be savoured over interesting modern cooking.

SPALDWICK *Cambs.* 504 S 26 – *see Huntingdon.*

SPARSHOLT *Hants.* 503 504 P 30 – *see Winchester.*

SPEEN *Bucks.* 504 R 28 – ✉ *Princes Risborough.*
London 41 – Aylesbury 15 – Oxford 33 – Reading 25.

Old Plow (Restaurant), Flowers Bottom, HP27 0PZ, West : ½ m. by Chapel Hill and Highwood Bottom ☎ (01494) 488300, *Fax (01494) 488702,* – P. MC AE VISA
closed Christmas-New Year, August, Monday, Saturday lunch, Sunday dinner and Bank Holidays except Good Friday – **Rest** 25.95/29.95 – (see also ***Bistro*** below).
◆ A fine, oak beamed restaurant at back of the bistro; more formal in style with linen table cover and high-back chairs. Set menus show French influence with classic sauces.

Bistro (at Old Plow), Flowers Bottom, HP27 0PZ, West : ½ m. by Chapel Hill and Highwood Bottom ☎ (01494) 488300, *Fax (01494) 488702,* – P. MC AE VISA
closed Christmas-New Year, August, Monday, Saturday lunch Sunday dinner and Bank Holidays except Good Friday – **Rest** (booking essential) a la carte 26.85/34.85.
◆ A cosy little bistro: low ceiling, tiled floors; log fire in the lounge. Blackboards announce simple à la carte menus; includes separate Brixham fish board. Affable owners.

SPEKE *Mersey.* 502 503 L 23 – *see Liverpool.*

SPELDHURST *Kent* 504 U 30 – *see Royal Tunbridge Wells.*

SPENNYMOOR Durham 501 502 P 19 – pop. 17 207 – ✉ Darlington.

London 275 – Durham 6 – Leeds 75 – Newcastle upon Tyne 24.

Whitworth Hall Country Park H., DL16 7QX, Northwest : 1 ½ m. by Middlestone Moor rd on Brancepeth rd ✆ (01388) 811772, *enquiries@whitworthhall.co.uk, Fax (01388) 818669*, ≤, – ✗ P – 150. VISA.
Four Seasons : Rest *(closed Sunday dinner)* (dinner only and Sunday lunch) 25.00 s. – ***Silver Buckles Brasserie :*** **Rest** *(closed Sunday lunch)* 11.75 (lunch) and dinner a la carte 19.70/25.40 s. – **29 rm** ☕ ★125.00 – ★★165.00.
◆ Part 19C country house, sympathetically converted; fine views over deer park and vineyard. Orangery lounge and spacious rooms with mod cons for business travellers. Four Seasons handsomely set in old library. Silver Buckles Brasserie set in conservatory.

SPRATTON Northants. 504 R 27 – see Northampton.

SPRIGG'S ALLEY Oxon. – see Chinnor.

STADDLEBRIDGE N. Yorks. – see Northallerton.

STADHAMPTON Oxon. 503 504 Q 28.

London 53 – Aylesbury 18 – Oxford 10.

Crazy Bear with rm, Bear Lane, OX44 7UR, off Wallingford rd ✆ (01865) 890714, *enquiries@crazybear-oxford.co.uk, Fax (01865) 400481*, – P ⇔ 20. VISA.
Rest a la carte 24.50/35.00 ♀ – ***Thai Thai :*** **Rest** *(closed Sunday lunch)* (booking essential) a la carte 22.00/29.50 ♀ – **18 rm** ☕ ★65.00/140.00 – ★★120.00/265.00.
◆ Behind unassuming stone pub exterior are wacky rooms to hit you between the eyes: zebra striped carpets, walls of peacock blue and purple. Vibrant, contemporary bedrooms. Either modern British or Thai cuisine where exotic fish swim in tanks.

STAFFORD Staffs. 502 503 504 N 25 – pop. 63 681.

Stafford Castle, Newport Rd ✆ (01785) 223821.
Market St ✆ (01785) 619619.
London 142 – Birmingham 26 – Derby 32 – Shrewsbury 31 – Stoke-on-Trent 17.

Moat House, Lower Penkridge Rd, Acton Trussell, ST17 0RJ, South : 3 ¾ m. by A 449 ✆ (01785) 712217, *info@moathouse.co.uk, Fax (01785) 715344*, – ✗, rest, P – 200. VISA.
closed 25 December – ***The Conservatory :*** **Rest** 15.00/38.00 and a la carte 28.00/38.00 s. ♀ – **31 rm** ☕ ★130.00/140.00 – ★★140.00, 1 suite.
◆ Timbered 15C moated manor house with modern extensions and lawned gardens, within sight of the M6. Characterful rustic bar. Colourful rooms with individual style. Bright, airy conservatory restaurant overlooks canal.

The Swan, 46-46A Greengate St, ST16 2JA, ✆ (01785) 258142, *info@theswanstafford.co.uk, Fax (01785) 225372*, – ✗, rest, P. VISA.
closed 25 December – ***The Brasserie at The Swan :*** **Rest** 8.95 (lunch) and a la carte 19.70/30.75 s. ♀ – **31 rm** ☕ ★80.00/90.00 – ★★95.00/130.00.
◆ Part 17C coaching inn with modern décor throughout. Convenient central location. Stylish reception. Well-equipped bedrooms with good facilities. Light, airy brasserie is open all day.

Express by Holiday Inn without rest., Acton Court, Acton Gate, ST18 9AR, South : 3 m. on A 449 ✆ (01785) 212244, *exhi-stafford@foremosthotels.co.uk, Fax (01785) 212377* – ✗ P – 40. VISA
103 rm ★39.00/69.00 – ★★39.00/69.00.
◆ A good value hotel, ideal as a stopover for those travelling both North and South and close to the famous Staffordshire Potteries. Comfortable bedrooms.

The Sun, 7 Lichfield Rd, ST17 4JX, ✆ (01785) 229700, *admin@thesunstafford.co.uk, Fax (01785) 215015*, – ✗ P ⇔ 25. VISA.
closed Sunday and Monday – **Rest** 13.95 and a la carte 15.50/29.40.
◆ Early 19C pub in town centre. Plain exterior; modern interior with trendy bar featuring pop art. Gastro pub ambience prevails: modern dishes offer interest and originality.

Your opinions are important to us:
please write and let us know about your discoveries and experiences – good and bad!

STAINES *Middx.* 504 S 29 – *pop. 50 538.*
London 26 – Reading 25.

Thames Lodge, Thames St, TW18 4SF, ✆ (0870) 4008121, *sales.thameslodge@macdonald-hotels.co.uk, Fax (01784) 454858,* ← – ⇹, ▤ rest, ✆ ♿ P – 🏛 50. MC AE ① VISA
The Brasserie : **Rest** 18.00/20.00 and a la carte 21.00/29.00 **s.** ♀ – ☕ 14.95 – **78 rm** ✝100.00/160.00 – ✝✝110.00/180.00.
◆ Once used as a stopover for horse-pulled barges, this riverside hotel has moorings on the Thames. A mix of rooms: some with traditional décor, some more modern in style. Terrace brasserie overlooks river.

STAITHES *N. Yorks.* 502 R 20 – ✉ *Saltburn (Cleveland).*
London 269 – Middlesbrough 22 – Scarborough 31.

Endeavour with rm, 1 High St, TS13 5BH, ✆ (01947) 840825, *theendeavour@ntlworld.com* – ⇹ P. MC AE ① VISA
closed 25-26 December, 1 January, Sunday and Monday – **Rest** - Seafood - (dinner only) a la carte 22.75/31.85 – **3 rm** ☕ ✝65.00/80.00 – ✝✝80.00.
◆ Named after Captain Cook's sailing ship: a compact former fisherman's cottage serving tasty menus, with emphasis on locally caught fish. Neat, well-appointed bedrooms.

STAMFORD *Lincs.* 502 504 S 26 *Great Britain G.* – *pop. 19 525.*
See : *Town*★★ - *St Martin's Church*★ – *Lord Burghley's Hospital*★ – *Browne's Hospital*★ *AC.*
Env. : *Burghley House*★★ *AC, SE : 1½ m. by B 1443.*
ℹ *The Arts Centre, 27 St Mary's St* ✆ *(01780) 755611.*
London 92 – Leicester 31 – Lincoln 50 – Nottingham 45.

The George of Stamford, 71 St Martin's, PE9 2LB, ✆ (01780) 750750, *reservations@georgehotelofstamford.com, Fax (01780) 750701,* 🏡, 🌳 – P – 🏛 50. MC AE ① VISA
The George : **Rest** 17.50 (lunch) and a la carte 32.50/49.75 **s.** ♀ – ***Garden Lounge :*** **Rest** - Seafood specialities - a la carte 21.85/44.45 **s.** ♀ – **46 rm** ☕ ✝78.00/98.00 – ✝✝225.00, 1 suite.
◆ Historic inn, over 900 years old. Crusading knights stayed here en route to Jerusalem. Walled garden and courtyard with 17C mulberry tree. Original bedrooms; designer décor. Oak panelled dining room exudes elegance. Garden Lounge with leafy courtyard.

Garden House, 42 High St, St Martin's, PE9 2LP, ✆ (01780) 763359, *enquiries@gardenhousehotel.com, Fax (01780) 763339,* 🏡, 🌳 – ⇹ rest, P. MC AE VISA
closed 26-30 December and 1-7 January – **Rest** *(closed Sunday dinner)* a la carte 22.70/28.20 – **20 rm** ☕ ✝65.00/79.00 – ✝✝80.00/95.00.
◆ Next to Burghley Park, dating from 1796, this fine hotel with garden and conservatory makes a good base for exploring Stamford. Variety of rooms; includes large family ones. Dining room with graceful chairs and Belgian tapestries.

Oakhouse, 11 All Saints Pl, PE9 2AR, ✆ (01780) 756565, *info@oakhouserestaurant.com,* 🏡 – ⇹. MC AE VISA
closed 1 week January and Sunday dinner – **Rest** 14.50 (lunch) and a la carte 25.00/36.00 ♀.
◆ Unsurprisingly, oak is a mainstay of this modern restaurant, which also boasts a delightful rear terrace and stylish dining areas set over two floors. Modish dishes prevail.

at Stretton *(Rutland) Northwest : 8 m. by B 1081 off A 1* – ✉ *Stamford.*

The Jackson Stops Inn, Rookery Rd, LE15 7RA, ✆ (01780) 410237, *james@jacksonstops-inn.fsnet.co.uk, Fax (01780) 410280,* 🏡, 🌳 – ⇹ P. MC VISA
closed Sunday dinner, Monday, 27 December-3 January – **Rest** a la carte 20.00/25.95 ♀.
◆ 17C stone inn with thatched roof and garden and rural decor. Low wood bar and four eating areas. Daily menu of good British cooking with blackboard specials.

at Clipsham *(Rutland) Northwest : 9½ m. by B 1081 off A 1* – ✉ *Stamford.*

The Olive Branch (Hope), Main St, LE15 7SH, ✆ (01780) 410355, *info@theolivebranchpub.com, Fax (01780) 410000,* 🏡 – ⇹ P. MC VISA
closed 26 December and 1 January – **Rest** (booking essential) 17.00 (lunch) and a la carte 20.50/32.50 ♀.
Spec. Tiger prawn tempura, sweet chilli mayonnaise. Braised shoulder of lamb, rosemary butter beans and artichokes. Tiramisu with espresso ice cream.
◆ Simple pews and scrubbed tables in a cosy firelit pub; cookery books and sepia prints on display. Varied, seasonal modern cooking, intelligently judged and full of flavour.

STANDISH *Gtr Manchester* 502 504 M 23 – *pop. 14 350* – ✉ *Wigan.*
London 210 – Liverpool 25 – Manchester 21 – Preston 15.

Premier Travel Inn, Almond Brook Rd, WN6 0SS, West : 1 m. on A 5209 ℘ (0870) 7001574, *Fax (01257) 473768* – ⇔ rm, ▤ rest, ♿ P. MC AE VISA. ⚘
Rest (grill rest.) – **36 rm** ★46.95/46.95 – ★★48.95/48.95.
◆ Purpose-built lodge suited to families and the business traveller. Variety of bedrooms catering for all needs; includes spacious desk areas and free newspaper. Pub restaurant next to the lodge.

Simply Heathcotes (at The Wrightington H. & Country Club), Moss Lane, Wrightington, WN6 9PB, West : 2 m. on A 5209 ℘ (01257) 478244, *wrightington@heathcotes.co.uk, Fax (01257) 424212* – ▤ P. MC AE VISA
closed Bank Holidays – **Rest** a la carte 14.25/27.45.
◆ Stylish restaurant on first floor of Wrightington Hotel. The split-level main dining room has a conservatory style roof. Appealing menus with strong use of regional produce.

at Wrightington Bar *Northwest : 3½ m. by A 5209 on B 5250* – ✉ *Wigan.*

The Mulberry Tree, 9 Wood Lane, WN6 9SE, ℘ (01257) 451400, *Fax (01257) 451400* – ⇔ P. MC VISA
closed 26 December – **Rest** a la carte 25.00/28.00.
◆ Foody-themed modern pub with warm, buzzy atmosphere. Modern cooking, generous portions and plenty of blackboard specials. Eat in the bar or more formal dining room.

STANNERSBURN *Northd.* 501 502 M 18 – ✉ *Hexham.*
London 363 – Carlisle 56 – Newcastle upon Tyne 46.

Pheasant Inn ⛯ with rm, Falstone, NE48 1DD, ℘ (01434) 240382, *enquiries@thepheasantinn.com, Fax (01434) 240382* – ⇔ P. MC VISA. ⚘
closed 25-26 December and Monday and Tuesday November-March – **Rest** a la carte 14.45/21.20 ♀ – **8 rm** ☐ ★40.00 – ★★75.00.
◆ Set in Northumberland National Park, near Kielder reservoir; epitome of a traditional inn. Pine dining room serves homecooked local fare. Cottagey rooms in converted stables.

STANSTED AIRPORT *Essex* 504 U 28 – ✉ *Stansted Mountfitchet.*
✈ *Stansted International Airport* : ℘ *(0870) 0000303* – **Terminal** : to Liverpool St Station, London.
London 37 – Cambridge 29 – Chelmsford 18 – Colchester 29.

Radisson SAS, Waltham Close, CM24 1PP, ℘ (01279) 661012, *info.stansted@radissonsas.com, Fax (01279) 661013,* ⓢ, Fō, ≘s, ⛆ – |♦|, ⇔ ▤ ♿ P – 🔬 400. MC AE VISA. ⚘
New York Grill Bar **:** Rest a la carte 23.40/31.40 s. – ***Wine Tower*** **:** Rest a la carte 10.70/13.00 s. – ***Filini*** **:** Rest - Italian - a la carte 15.70/24.95 s. – ☐ 12.95 – **484 rm** ★125.00 – ★★125.00, 16 suites.
◆ Impressive hotel just two minutes from main terminal; vast open atrium housing 40 foot wine cellar. Extensive meeting facilities. Very stylish bedrooms in three themes. Small, formal New York Grill Bar. Impressive Wine Tower. Filini for Italian dishes.

Hilton London Stansted Airport, Round Coppice Rd, CM24 1SF, ℘ (01279) 680800, *reservations.stansted@hilton.com, Fax (01279) 680890,* Fō, ≘s, ⛆ – |♦|, ⇔ rm, ▤ rest, ♿ P – 🔬 250. MC AE ⓓ VISA. ⚘
Rest *(closed lunch Saturday, Sunday and Bank Holidays)* a la carte 28.90/35.35 ♀ – ☐ 17.95 – **237 rm** ★89.50/145.50 – ★★89.50/145.50, 2 suites.
◆ Bustling hotel whose facilities include leisure club, hairdressers and beauty salon. Modern rooms, with two of executive style. Transport can be arranged to and from terminal. Restaurant/bar has popular menu; sometimes carvery lunch as well.

Express by Holiday Inn without rest., Thremhall Ave, CM24 1PY, ℘ (01279) 680015, *stansted@kewgreen.co.uk, Fax (01279) 680838* – |♦| ⇔ ♿ P – 🔬 60. MC AE ⓓ. ⚘
183 rm ★79.95 – ★★79.95.
◆ Adjacent to the airport and medium term parking facilities, so useful for leisure and business travellers. Functional rooms provide good value accommodation.

STANSTED MOUNTFITCHET *Essex* 504 U 28 – *see Bishop's Stortford (Herts.).*

Do not confuse X with ✿! X defines comfort, while stars are awarded for the best cuisine, across all categories of comfort.

STANTON *Suffolk* 504 W 27 – *pop. 2 073.*
London 88 – Cambridge 38 – Ipswich 40 – King's Lynn 38 – Norwich 39.

Leaping Hare, Wyken Vineyards, IP31 2DW, South : 1 ¼ m. by Wyken Rd ☏ (01359) 250287, *Fax (01359) 253022*, – P. MC VISA
closed 25 December-5 January – **Rest** (booking essential) (lunch only and dinner Friday and Saturday) a la carte 21.20/31.40 ♀.
◆ 17C long barn in working farm and vineyard. Hare-themed pictures and tapestries decorate a beamed restaurant and café. Tasty dishes underpinned by local, organic produce.

STANTON SAINT QUINTIN *Wilts.* 503 504 N 29 – *see Chippenham.*

STANTON WICK *Bath & North East Somerset* 503 504 M 29 – *see Bristol.*

STAPLEFORD *Wilts.* 503 504 O 30 – *see Salisbury.*

STATHERN *Leics.* – *see Melton Mowbray.*

For a pleasant stay in a charming hotel, look for the red … symbols.

STAVERTON *Devon* 503 I 32 – *pop. 682* – ✉ *Totnes.*
London 220 – Exeter 20 – Torquay 33.

Kingston House , TQ9 6AR, Northwest : 1 m. on Kingston rd ☏ (01803) 762235, *info@kingston-estate.com, Fax (01803) 762444*, – P. MC VISA.
closed 22 December-3 January – **Rest** (set menu only) (residents only) (dinner only) 32.50 s. – **3 rm** 100.00/110.00 – 160.00/180.00.
◆ A spectacular Georgian mansion in sweeping moorland. Unique period details include painted china closet, marquetry staircase, authentic wallpapers. Variety of antique beds.

STAVERTON *Northants.* 504 Q 27 – *see Daventry.*

STEDHAM *W. Sussex* 504 R 31 – *see Midhurst.*

STEPPINGLEY *Beds.*
London 44.5 – Luton 12.5 – Milton Keynes 13.5.

The French Horn, MK45 5AU, ☏ (01525) 712051, *paul@thefrenchhorn.com, Fax (01525) 714067*, – P. MC VISA
closed Sunday dinner – **Rest** (booking essential) a la carte 26.40/31.40 ♀.
◆ Refurbished late 18C pub with restaurant in pretty hamlet. Characterful front bar and smart restaurant where contemporary style and well-regarded seasonal menus hold sway.

STEVENAGE *Herts.* 504 T 28 *Great Britain G.* – *pop. 81 482.*
Env. : *Knebworth House* AC, S : 2½ m.*
18, 9 *Aston Lane* ☏ *(01438) 880424* – 18, 9 *Chesfield Downs, Jack's Hill, Graveley* ☏ *(01462) 482929.*
London 36 – Bedford 25 – Cambridge 27.

Novotel Stevenage, Knebworth Park, SG1 2AX, Southwest : 1 ½ m. by A 602 at junction 7 of A 1(M) ☏ (01438) 346100, *h0992@accor-hotels.com, Fax (01438) 723872*, heated – , rm, rest, P – 120. MC AE VISA
Rest 19.00 (dinner) and a la carte 18.40/28.15 s. ♀ – 12.00 – **100 rm** 69.00/99.00 – 69.00/99.00.
◆ Modern hotel not far from Knebworth Park and Hatfield House. Large rooms with family facilities, some with sofa beds. Outdoor playground available and babysitting on request. Dining room with open kitchen area.

Premier Travel Inn, Corey's Mill Lane, SG1 4AA, Northwest : 2 m. on A 602 ☏ (01438) 351318, *Fax (01438) 721609* – , rm, rest, P. MC AE VISA.
Rest (grill rest.) – **40 rm** 47.95/47.95 – 50.95/50.95.
◆ A consistent standard of trim, simply fitted accommodation in contemporary style; a useful address for cost-conscious travellers. The Beefeater is close by for grilled snacks.

STEYNING W. Sussex 504 T 31 – pop. 9 501 (inc. Upper Beeding).

London 52 – Brighton 12 – Worthing 10.

The Old Tollgate, The Street, Bramber, BN44 3WE, Southwest : 1 m. ✆ (01903) 879494, *info@oldtollgatehotel.com, Fax (01903) 813399,* – P. VISA.

Rest (carvery) 16.25/23.95 – 9.95 – **30 rm** 82.00 – 82.00.

◆ Once travellers had to stop here to pay toll; now it is a pleasant hotel offering hospitality and resting place. Spic and span rooms; pine furnishings. Renowned three-roomed carvery restaurant.

Springwells without rest., 9 High St, BN44 3GG, ✆ (01903) 812446, *contact@springwells.co.uk, Fax (01903) 879823,* , heated, – P. VISA

closed 2 weeks Christmas-New Year – **11 rm** 38.00/58.00 – 66.00/90.00.

◆ Built in 1772, a picturesque former merchant's house in the heart of town. Tidy accommodation in pretty chintz; four-poster rooms on the first floor face the High Street.

at Ashurst North : 3½ m. on B 2135 – ✉ Steyning.

Fountain Inn, BN44 3AP, ✆ (01403) 710219, – P. VISA

closed Sunday dinner – **Rest** a la carte 20.00/25.00.

◆ Former farmhouse dating from 1572, now an attractive pub with garden and pond. Interior oozes charm with low ceilings and beams galore. Freshly prepared traditional fare.

STILTON Cambs. 504 T 26 – pop. 2 500 – ✉ Peterborough.

London 76 – Cambridge 30 – Northampton 43 – Peterborough 6.

Bell Inn, Great North Rd, PE7 3RA, ✆ (01733) 241066, *reception@thebellstilton.co.uk, Fax (01733) 245173,* – P – 100. VISA.

closed 25 December and Bank Holidays – **Rest** *(closed Saturday lunch)* 25.95 – (see also ***Village Bar*** below) – **22 rm** 72.50/79.50 – 129.50.

◆ A swinging red bell pub sign hangs outside this part 16C inn with garden. Deluxe bedrooms are individually styled; some retain original rafters and stonework. Nook-and-cranny galleried dining room with exposed stone walls.

Village Bar (at Bell Inn), Great North Rd, PE7 3RA, ✆ (01733) 241066, *reception@thebellstilton.co.uk,* – P. VISA

closed 25 December – **Rest** 10.95/25.95.

◆ As one would expect, Stilton cheese is used to full effect in this rustic bar, appearing in soups, dumplings, quiche and dressings. Blackboard specials to tickle tastebuds.

STOCK Essex 504 V 29.

London 38.5 – Brentwood 12 – Chelmsford 8.

Bear, 16 The Square, CM4 9LH, ✆ (01277) 829100, *info@thebearinn.biz, Fax (01277) 841300,* – P. VISA

closed 25 December, Sunday dinner and Monday – **Rest** 13.95/24.00 and a la carte 37.50/60.00.

◆ 16C former inn, featuring a noteworthy duck pond and terrace. Thick walls enhance rustic interior. Frequently changing modern menus in ground and first floor restaurants.

STOCKBRIDGE Hants. 503 504 P 30.

London 75 – Salisbury 14 – Southampton 19 – Winchester 9.

The Greyhound, 31 High St, SO20 6EY, ✆ (01264) 810833, *Fax (01264) 811184,* – P. VISA

closed 25-26 December, 1 January and Sunday dinner – **Rest** a la carte 25.00/39.00.

Spec. Gravadlax with new potato and fennel salad, caper vinaigrette. Fillet of beef, smoked bacon dumplings and cep consommé. Vanilla and raspberry rice pudding.

◆ Yellow brick pub beside River Test on pleasant high street. Low beamed ceiling; aged wooden tables and lots of character; contemporary dishes of carefully sourced ingredients.

STOCKTON-ON-TEES Stockton-on-Tees 502 P 20 – pop. 80 060.

Eaglescliffe, Yarm Rd ✆ (01642) 780098 – Knotty Hill Golf Centre, Sedgefield ✆ (01740) 620320 – Norton, Junction Rd ✆ (01642) 676385.

Teesside Airport : ✆ (01325) 332811, SW : 6 m. by A 1027, A 135 and A 67.

Stockton Central Library, Church Road ✆ (01642) 528130.

London 251 – Leeds 61 – Middlesbrough 4 – Newcastle upon Tyne 39.

Premier Travel Inn, Yarm Rd, TS18 3RT, Southwest : 1 ¾ m. on A 135 ✆ (01642) 633354, *Fax (01642) 633339* – rm, rest, P. VISA.
Rest (grill rest.) – **40 rm** 46.95/46.95 – 49.95/49.95.
◆ Located next to Preston Farm Brewsters; not far from Preston Hall Museum and the Green Dragon Museum. Simply furnished and brightly decorated bedrooms; ideal for stopovers.

at Eaglescliffe *South : 3½ m. on A 135 – ✉ Stockton-on-Tees.*

Parkmore, 636 Yarm Rd, TS16 0DH, ✆ (01642) 786815, *enquiries@parkmorehotel.co.uk, Fax (01642) 790485,* – P – 120. VISA
Reeds at Six Three Six : **Rest** 13.00/19.00 and dinner a la carte 17.50/28.45 **s.** – 10.00 – **54 rm** 69.00/80.00 – 85.00/110.00, 1 suite.
◆ Built in 1896 for shipbuilding family; combines a sense of the old and new. Rooms are furnished in modern style; impressive leisure and conference facilities. Dining room specialises in steak options.

STOKE BRUERNE *Northants.* 504 R 27 – ✉ *Towcester.*

London 69 – Coventry 33 – Leicester 44 – Northampton 9 – Oxford 33.

XX **Bruerne's Lock,** 5 The Canalside, NN12 7SB, ✆ (01604) 863654, *Fax (01604) 863330,* – VISA.
closed 2 weeks Christmas-New Year, Monday, Sunday dinner and Saturday lunch – **Rest** 18.50 (lunch) and a la carte 22.20/27.45 ♀.
◆ Georgian house overlooking the busy Grand Union Canal. Restaurant is modern in style with well-spaced tables. Flexible menus with Mediterranean base; themed gourmet evenings.

STOKE BY NAYLAND *Suffolk* 504 W 28.

London 70 – Bury St Edmunds 24 – Cambridge 54 – Colchester 11 – Ipswich 14.

The Stoke by Nayland, Keepers Lane, Leavenheath, CO6 4PZ, Northwest : 1 ½ m. on B 1068 ✆ (01206) 262836, *sales@stokebynayland.com, Fax (01206) 263356,* 18, – P – 500. VISA.
Rest (bar lunch Monday-Saturday) (carvery lunch Sunday)/dinner 19.95 – **30 rm** 99.00 – 129.00.
◆ Golfers will be in their element with a pro-shop, driving range and two courses tacking through 300 acres of woods and lakes. Neat, modern rooms; well-equipped spa and gym. Dining room overlooks the fairway.

Ryegate House without rest., CO6 4RA, ✆ (01206) 263679, <, – P.
closed Christmas, New Year, 1 week spring and 1 week autumn – **3 rm** 45.50 – 65.00.
◆ Congenial modern guesthouse on edge of the village; a comfortable base from which to explore Dedham Vale and surrounding countryside. Neat rooms with traditional furnishings.

The Crown, CO6 4SE, ✆ (01206) 262001, *crown.eoinns@btopenworld.com, Fax (01206) 264026,* – P. VISA
closed 25-26 December – **Rest** (booking essential) a la carte 17.00/27.00 ♀.
◆ 16C pub with 21C style: spacious rooms offer variety of cool dining options. Splendid wine selection. Locally renowned menus: a seasonal, modern take on classic dishes.

Angel Inn with rm, Polstead St, CO6 4SA, ✆ (01206) 263245, *the.angel@tiscali.co.uk, Fax (01206) 263373,* – P. VISA.
closed 25-26 December – **Rest** a la carte 16.50/25.00 ♀ – **6 rm** 60.00/70.00 – 75.00/85.00.
◆ 16C timbered inn, its original well is the dining room centrepiece; Speciality griddle dishes are well worth tucking into. Traditional rooms available.

STOKE CANON *Devon* 503 J 31 – *see Exeter.*

STOKE D'ABERNON *Surrey* 504 S 30 – *see Cobham.*

STOKE GABRIEL *Devon* 503 J 32 – *see Totnes.*

STOKE HOLY CROSS *Norfolk* 504 X 26 – *see Norwich.*

STOKE MANDEVILLE *Bucks.* 504 R 28.

London 41 – Aylesbury 4 – Oxford 26.

The Wool Pack, 21 Risborough Rd, HP22 5UP, ℘ (01296) 615970, *Fax (01296) 615971* – P. MC AE VISA

Rest a la carte 17.00/36.00 ♀.

• Attractive, part-thatched pub with pretty terrace. Low beams, roaring fire in front bar, airy rear restaurant serves appealing, well-priced menus with subtle Italian twists.

STOKENHAM *Devon* 503 I 33 *The West Country G.* – ✉ *Kingsbridge.*

Env. : *Kingsbridge*★, *W : 5 m. by A 379.*

Exc. : *Dartmouth*★★, *N : 9 m. by A 379.*

London 225 – Plymouth 26 – Salcombe 11.

Tradesman's Arms, TQ7 2SZ, ℘ (01548) 580313, *Fax (01548) 580657,* – P. MC VISA

Rest (booking essential) a la carte 14.15/26.15 ♀.

• Charming 14C thatched inn in delightful coastal village. Divided into two areas: a beamed bar with stone fireplace, and a non-smoking room. Fresh, local fish and game feature.

STOKE-ON-TRENT *Stoke-on-Trent* 502 503 504 N 24 *Great Britain G.* – *pop. 259 252.*

See : *The Potteries Museum and Art Gallery*★ Y **M** – *Gladstone Pottery Museum*★ *AC* V.

Env. : *Wedgwood Visitor Centre*★ *AC, S : 7 m. on A 500, A 34 and minor rd* V.

Exc. : *Little Moreton Hall*★★ *AC, N : 10 m. by A 500 on A 34* U – *Biddulph Grange Garden*★, *N : 7 m. by A 52, A 50 and A 527* U.

Greenway Hall, Stockton Brook ℘ (01782) 503158, U – *Parkhall, Hulme Rd, Weston Coyney ℘ (01782) 599584,* V.

Quadrant Rd, Hanley ℘ (01782) 236000, stoke.tic@virgin.net.

London 162 – Birmingham 46 – Leicester 59 – Liverpool 58 – Manchester 41 – Sheffield 53.

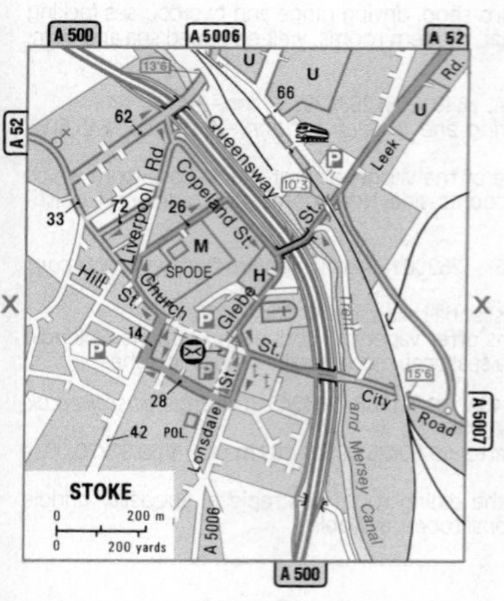

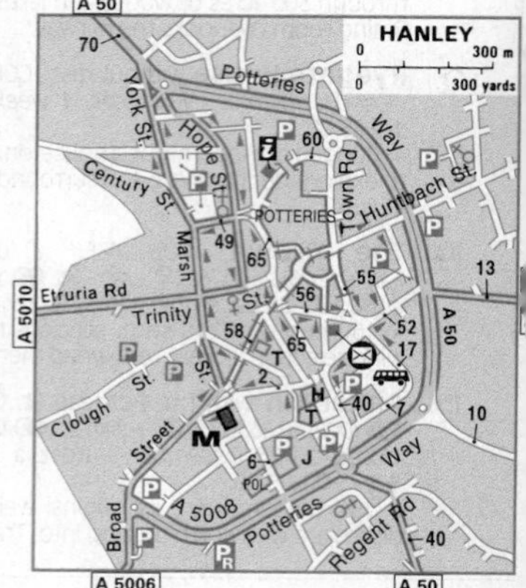

HANLEY

Albion St . . . . . Y 2
Bethesda St . . . . . Y 6
Birch Terrace . . . . . Y 7
Botteslow St . . . . . Y 10
Bucknall New Rd . . . . . Y 13
Charles St . . . . . Y 17
Lichfield St . . . . . Y 40
New Hall St . . . . . Y 49
Old Hall St . . . . . Y 52
Parliament Row . . . . . Y 55
Percy St . . . . . Y 56
Piccadilly . . . . . Y 58
Potteries Shopping Centre . . . . . Y
Quadrant Rd . . . . . Y 60
Stafford St . . . . . Y 65
Vale Pl. . . . . . Y 70

STOKE-ON-TRENT

Campbell Pl. . . . . . X 14
Church St X
Elenora St . . . . . X 26
Fleming Rd . . . . . X 28
Hartshill Rd . . . . . X 33
London Rd . . . . . X 42
Shelton Old Rd . . . . . X 62
Station Rd . . . . . X 66
Vale St . . . . . X 72

STOKE-ON-TRENT NEWCASTLE-UNDER-LYME

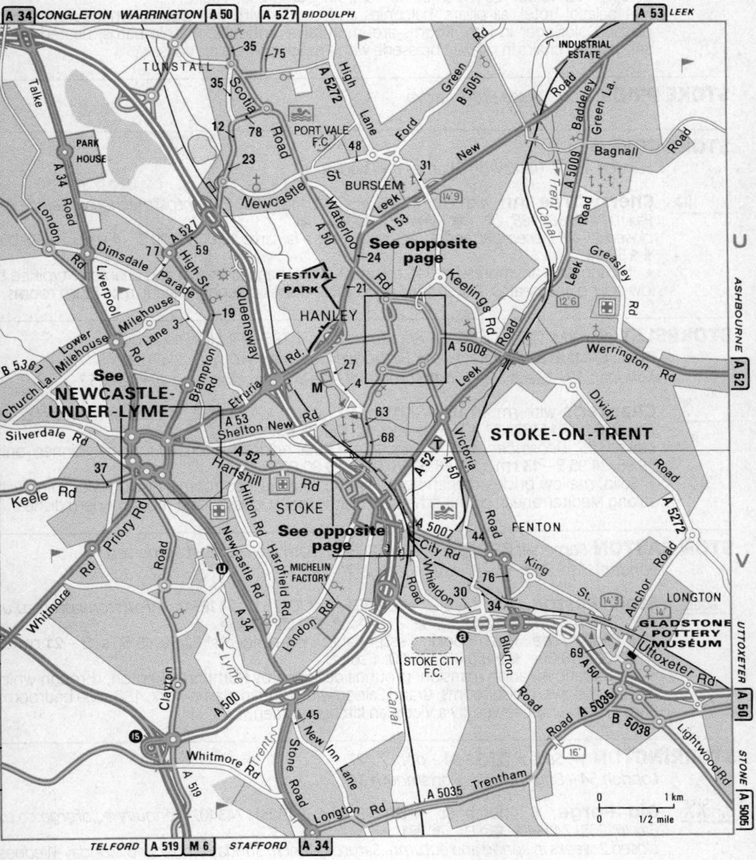

Express by Holiday Inn without rest., Sir Stanley Matthews Way, Trentham Lakes, ST4 4EG, ☎ (01782) 377000, *stokeontrent@expressholidayinn.co.uk, Fax (01782) 377037* – V a
– 30. MC AE VISA
123 rm 71.00 – 71.00.

◆ Purpose-built lodge in outskirts and next to Britannia Stadium. Fitted modern style throughout and a good level of facilities in the bedrooms.

STOKE POGES *Bucks.* 504 S 29 – *pop. 4 112.*
18, 9 Park Rd ☏ *(01753) 643332.*
London 30 – Aylesbury 28 – Oxford 44.

Stoke Park Club, Park Rd, SL2 4PG, ☏ (01753) 717171, *info@stokeparkclub.com, Fax (01753) 717181*, – rest, rest, P – 70. MC AE VISA.
closed 25 December and 2-6 January – ***Park :*** **Rest** (dinner only and Sunday lunch)/dinner 36.00 ♀ – 18.50 – **20 rm** 282.00 – 347.00/394.00, 1 suite.
◆ A palatial hotel, all pillars, balconies and cupola with golf course where James Bond played Goldfinger in film. Rooms are impressive: antiques, marble baths, heated floors. Snug, plush chairs in relaxed brasserie with French posters on walls.

STOKE PRIOR *Worcs. – see Bromsgrove.*

STOKE ROW *Oxon.*
London 45.5 – Henley-on-Thames 6 – Reading 10.

Cherry Tree Inn with rm, RG9 5QA, ☏ (01491) 680430, *info@thecherrytreeinn.com, Fax (01491) 682168*, – P. MC VISA.
closed 25-26 December and 1 January – **Rest** a la carte 19.00/26.00 ♀ – **4 rm** 85.00 – 85.00.
◆ 17C inn with an impressive 21C refurbishment: bags of charm and character typified by low ceiling and beams. Platefuls of good value dishes offering eclectic mix. Plush rooms.

STOKESLEY *N. Yorks.* 502 Q 20 *Great Britain G. – pop. 4 725 – ✉ Middlesbrough.*
Env. : *Great Ayton (Captain Cook Birthplace Museum★ AC), NE : 2½ m. on A 173.*
London 239 – Leeds 59 – Middlesbrough 8 – Newcastle upon Tyne 49 – York 52.

Chapter's with rm, 27 High St, TS9 5AD, ☏ (01642) 711888, *info@chaptershotel.co.uk, Fax (01642) 713387*, – , rest, . MC AE VISA
closed 25 December and 1 January – **Rest** *(closed Sunday-Monday)* (dinner only) 19.95/24.95 ♀ – **13 rm** 66.00/70.00 – 80.00.
◆ Solid, mellow brick Victorian house with colour washed rooms. Bistro style dining with strong Mediterranean colour scheme. Eclectic menu: classics and more modern dishes.

STON EASTON *Somerset* 503 504 M 30 – *✉ Bath (Bath & North East Somerset).*
London 131 – Bath 12 – Bristol 11 – Wells 7.

Ston Easton Park, BA3 4DF, ☏ (01761) 241631, *info@stoneaston.co.uk, Fax (01761) 241377*, – P. MC AE VISA
The Cedar Tree : **Rest** (booking essential to non-residents) 22.50/45.50 **s.** ♀ – **21 rm** 120.00/340.00 – 150.00/395.00, 1 suite.
◆ Aristocratic Palladian mansion; grounds designed by Humphrey Repton, through which river Norr flows. Lavish rooms: Grand Saloon with Kentian plasterwork. 18C style bedrooms. Formal restaurant served by a Victorian kitchen garden.

STORRINGTON *W. Sussex* 504 S 31 – *pop. 7 727.*
London 54 – Brighton 20 – Portsmouth 36.

Old Forge, 6 Church St, RH20 4LA, ☏ (01903) 743402, *enquiry@oldforge.co.uk, Fax (01903) 742540* – MC AE VISA
closed 2 weeks in spring and autumn, Saturday lunch, Sunday dinner and Monday-Wednesday – **Rest** 16.00/33.00 ♀.
◆ Appealing whitewashed and brick cottages with three dining rooms bearing all hallmarks of flavoursome traditional cuisine. Array of cheeses; fine wine from small producers.

STOURPORT-ON-SEVERN *Worcs.* 503 504 N 26 – *pop. 18 899.*
London 137 – Birmingham 21 – Worcester 12.

Stourport Manor, Hartlebury Rd, DY13 9JA, East : 1¼ m. on B 4193 ☏ (01299) 289955, *stourport@menzies-hotels.co.uk, Fax (01299) 878520*, squash – P – 350. MC AE VISA.
The Brasserie : **Rest** 12.95/24.95 and a la carte 24.85/33.15 ♀ – 14.95 – **66 rm** 119.00 – 119.00, 2 suites.
◆ Gracious country house, once home to former prime minister, Stanley Baldwin. Lovely, warm-hued lounge; wide-ranging indoor leisure facilities. Bedrooms are nicely spacious. Brasserie overlooks the garden; wide ranging menus.

STOURTON Wilts.

London 112 – Shaftesbury 12 – Wincanton 10.

The Spread Eagle Inn with rm, Church Lawn, BA12 6QE, ✆ (01747) 840587, *enquiries@spreadeagleinn.com, Fax (01747) 840954*, – ⇔ P. MO VISA. ✻
closed 25 December – **Rest** a la carte 16.50/22.25 – **5 rm** ☐ ✝60.00 – ✝✝90.00.
◆ Located within the stunning grounds of Stourhead House, this 18C pub has a front bar and two rear burgundy rooms, serving locally sourced menus. Simple, well-kept rooms.

STOW-ON-THE-WOLD Glos. 503 504 O 28 *Great Britain G. – pop. 2 074.*

Exc. : *Chastleton House★★, NE : 6½ m. by A 436 and A 44.*
Hollis House, The Square ✆ (01451) 831082.
London 86 – Birmingham 44 – Gloucester 27 – Oxford 30.

Wyck Hill House ⟡, GL54 1HY, South : 2 ¼ m. by A 429 on A 424 ✆ (01451) 831936, *enquiries@wyckhillhouse.com, Fax (01451) 832243*, ≤, , – ⇔, ▤ rest, P – 60. MO AE VISA
Rest 14.50/36.50 – **31 rm** ☐ ✝128.75 – ✝✝180.25, 1 suite.
◆ Handsome 18C mansion set in 100-acre grounds above Windrush Valley. Panelled drawing rooms; quiet and characterful rooms in the old wing, coach house and modern orangery. Conservatory restaurant with wold views.

The Royalist, Digbeth St, GL54 1BN, ✆ (01451) 830670, *info@theroyalisthotel.co.uk, Fax (01451) 870048* – ⇔ P. MO AE VISA. ✻
947 AD : **Rest** 24.00/36.00 and a la carte 24.00/32.00 ♀ – (see also ***Eagle & Child*** below) – **8 rm** ☐ ✝85.00/125.00 – ✝✝125.00/195.00.
◆ Historic, privately owned inn - reputedly England's oldest. Comfortable, stylish rooms, individual in shape and décor and quieter at the rear. Two-room bar in exposed stone. Intimate, beamed restaurant offers fine dining: inglenook fireplace.

Grapevine, Sheep St, GL54 1AU, ✆ (01451) 830344, *enquiries@vines.co.uk, Fax (01451) 832278* – ⇔ P – 25. MO AE VISA
Rest 15.00/28.00 ♀ – **22 rm** ☐ ✝80.00/95.00 – ✝✝130.00/160.00.
◆ Among the antique shops, two extended 17C houses. Rooms in bright, modern décor with a nod to tradition, half with beams and bare stone. Timbered bar; sepia photos of Stow. Glass-roofed restaurant: black grapes hang from spreading vine.

Fosse Manor, Fosse Way, GL54 1JX, South : 1 ¼ m. on A 429 ✆ (01451) 830354, *enquiries@fossemanor.co.uk, Fax (01451) 832486*, , – ⇔ P – 60. MO AE VISA
Rest 14.50 (lunch) and a la carte 22.25/33.75 ♀ – **20 rm** ☐ ✝76.00/95.00 – ✝✝104.00/130.00, 1 suite.
◆ Former coaching inn on the main road. Contemporary public areas with informal feel. Up-to-date bedrooms, some of which are set in the coach house. Lunch available in bar. Classically proportioned dining room with menu of Mediterranean favourites.

Stow Lodge, The Square, GL54 1AB, ✆ (01451) 830485, *enquiries@stowlodge.com, Fax (01451) 831671*, – ⇔ P. MO VISA. ✻
closed Christmas-early January – **Rest** (bar lunch) (residents only Monday-Friday)/dinner 21.50 ♀ – **20 rm** ☐ ✝55.00/130.00 – ✝✝75.00/140.00.
◆ Part 17C house next to St Edward's church; shrub-filled garden. Intrigue of bygone days signalled by lounge bookcase concealing old priest hole. Sizeable rooms. Beamed, panelled restaurant.

Crestow House without rest., GL54 1JX, at junction of A 429 on B 4068 Lower Swell rd ✆ (01451) 830969, *fsimonetti@btinternet.com*, ≤, , heated, – ⇔ P. MO VISA. ✻
closed 25-26 December and 1 January – **4 rm** ☐ ✝50.00 – ✝✝75.00.
◆ Victorian manor house with conservatory, garden and pool. Breakfast served in family style. Well-appointed rooms larger at front or smaller at rear overlooking the garden.

Number Nine without rest., 9 Park St, GL54 1AQ, ✆ (01451) 870333, *enquiries@number-nine.info* – ⇔. MO VISA. ✻
3 rm ☐ ✝45.00/55.00 – ✝✝60.00/70.00.
◆ Ivy-clad 18C Cotswold stone house. Winding staircase leads to rooms, each decorated in simple fabrics plus nuts and sherry extras. Cosy; the very top room is notably compact.

The Old Butchers, 7 Park St, GL54 1AQ, ✆ (01451) 831700, *louise@theoldbutchers.com, Fax (01451) 831388*, – ▤. MO AE VISA
closed 3 days mid May and 3 days mid October – **Rest** a la carte 18.45/24.95 **s.** ♀.
◆ Former butcher's shop of Cotswold stone: closely set tables define a cosy, modern restaurant. Daily changing, affordable, modish menus feature prominent use of local produce.

Eagle & Child (at The Royalist H.), Digbeth St, GL54 1BN, (01451) 830670, *info@theroyalisthotel.co.uk, Fax (01451) 870048*, – rm, P. VISA
Rest a la carte 19.00/41.50 ♀.
• Stone pub attached to an inn; conservatory to the rear. Atmospheric dining room: soft lighting, flagstones, beams. Robust cooking: plenty of choice.

at Upper Oddington *East : 2 m. by A 436 – ✉ Stow-on-the-Wold.*

Horse and Groom with rm, GL56 0XH, (01451) 830584, *info@horseandgroom.uk.com, Fax (01451) 831496*, – rm, P. VISA.
Rest a la carte 18.00/27.00 – **7 rm** ☐ ★55.00/64.00 – ★★69.00.
• Part 16C former coaching inn in rural hamlet. Long narrow interior with beams and open fires. Traditional pub food from a regularly changing menu. Cottage-style bedrooms.

at Lower Oddington *East : 3 m. by A 436 – ✉ Stow-on-the-Wold.*

Fox Inn with rm, GL56 0UR, (01451) 870555, *info@foxinn.net, Fax (01451) 870666*, – rm, P. VISA
closed 25 December and Sunday dinner December-February – **Rest** a la carte 17.95/27.65 – **3 rm** ☐ ★68.00 – ★★85.00/95.00.
• 16C ivy dressed pub in a charming village. Flag floors, beams, fireplaces, nooks, crannies, books and candlelight. Hearty English fare. Sumptuously decorated rooms.

at Bledington *Southeast : 4 m. by A 436 on B 4450 – ✉ Kingham.*

Kings Head Inn, OX7 6XQ, (01608) 658365, *kingshead@orr-ewing.com, Fax (01608) 658902* – rm, P. AE VISA
closed 25-26 December – **Rest** a la carte 20.00/30.00 ♀ – **12 rm** ☐ ★55.00/60.00 – ★★95.00/125.00.
• 15C inn on the green where Morris dancers perform Bledington Dances in summer. Timbered bedrooms in original building; modern annex rooms are quieter.

at Lower Swell *West : 1¼ m. on B 4068 – ✉ Stow-on-the-Wold.*

Rectory Farmhouse without rest., GL54 1LH, by Rectory Barns Rd (01451) 832351, *rectory.farmhouse@cw-warwick.co.uk*, – P.
closed Christmas and New Year – **3 rm** ☐ ★55.00 – ★★86.00.
• 17C former farmhouse of Cotswold stone. Bedrooms are very comfortable and decorated in distinctive cottage style. Family breakfast table, secluded location.

STRATFIELD TURGIS *Hants.* 503 504 Q 29 – ✉ *Basingstoke.*

London 46 – Basingstoke 8 – Reading 11 – Southampton 37.

Wellington Arms, RG27 0AS, on A 33 (01256) 882214, *wellington.arms@virgin.net, Fax (01256) 882934*, – P. – 200. AE VISA
Rest *(closed Saturday lunch and Sunday dinner)* a la carte 16.70/29.95 ♀ – **29 rm** ☐ ★95.00/120.00 – ★★130.00.
• 17C farmhouse on the Duke of Wellington Estate. The "pièce de résistance" is the lounge-bar with log fire and sofas. Bedrooms are pine furnished in quiet colour schemes. Homely dining room; window seats are particularly popular.

STRATFORD-UPON-AVON *Warks.* 503 504 P 27 *Great Britain G. – pop. 22 187.*

See : *Town★ - Shakespeare's Birthplace★ AC, AB.*
Env. : *Mary Arden's House★ AC, NW : 4 m. by A 3400 A.*
Exc. : *Ragley Hall★ AC, W : 9 m. by A 422 A.*
Tiddington Rd (01789) 205749, **B** – *Welcombe Hotel, Warwick Rd (01789) 413800*, **B** – *Stratford Oaks, Bearley Rd, Snitterfield (01789) 731980*, **B**.
Bridgefoot (0870) 1607930, stratfordtic@shakespeare-country.co.uk.
London 96 – Birmingham 23 – Coventry 18 – Leicester 44 – Oxford 40.

Plan opposite

Ettington Park , Alderminster, CV37 8BU, Southeast : 6 ¼ m. on A 3400 (01789) 450123, *ettingtonpark@handpicked.co.uk, Fax (01789) 450472*, – rest, P. – 100. AE VISA
Rest *(dinner only and Sunday lunch)* 35.00 and a la carte 38.50/47.45 ♀ – **43 rm** ☐ ★135.00/190.00 – ★★147.00/210.00, 5 suites.
• Imposing, corporate friendly, Gothic mansion with sympathetic extensions in attractive grounds. Ornate ceilings, classic country house feel. Comfy, well-equipped bedrooms. Oak-panelled dining room with medieval feel.

STRATFORD-UPON-AVON

Banbury Rd	B	2
Benson Rd.	B	3
Bridge Foot	B	6
Bridge St	B	8
Chapel Lane	A	13
Chapel St.	A	14
Church St	A	16
Clopton Bridge	B	18
College Lane	A	19
Ely St	A	22
Evesham Pl.	A	24
Great William St	A	25
Greenhill St	A	27
Guild St	A	28
Henley St.	A	29
High St.	A	31
Rother St.	A	32
Scholars Lane	A	33
Sheep St	AB	35
Tiddington Rd	B	38
Town Square Shopping Centre	A	39
Trinity St.	A	40
Warwick Rd.	B	42
Waterside	B	43
Windsor St	A	45
Wood St	A	47

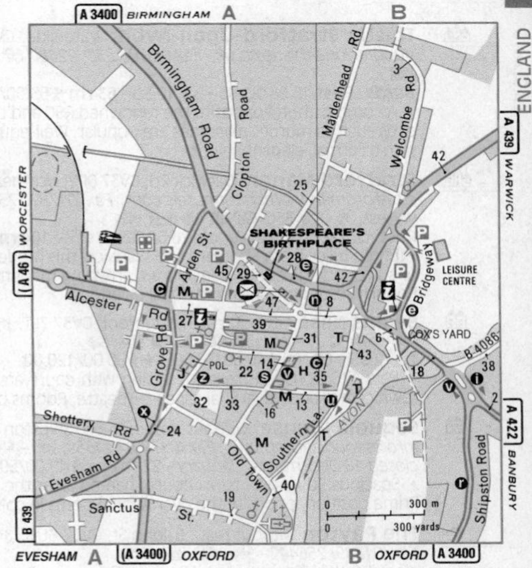

Welcombe H. & Golf Course, Warwick Rd, CV37 0NR, Northeast : 1½ m. on A 439 (01789) 295252, *welcombe@menzies-hotels.co.uk, Fax (01789) 414666*, – 100.
Trevelyan : Rest 19.50/45.00 – **73 rm** 169.00/319.00 – 189.00/209.00, 5 suites.
◆ Jacobean house built 1869; sweeping Italian gardens and gracious, oak panelled interiors. Grand rooms in main house with many antique features. Golf course overlooks Avon. Savour views of gardens, fountain and waterfall from restaurant.

Alveston Manor, Clopton Bridge, CV37 7HP, (0870) 4008181, *alvestonmanor@macdonald-hotels.co.uk, Fax (01789) 414095*, – 120. B i
The Manor Grill : Rest 16.50/25.00 and dinner a la carte 25.00/39.00 s. – **109 rm** 143.00 – 153.00, 4 suites.
◆ Part Elizabethan manor where "A Midsummer's Night Dream" was first performed beneath the cedar tree in the grounds. Richly decorated period rooms; modern rooms in extension. Seasoned oak panelling in medieval dining room.

Holiday Inn, Bridgefoot, CV37 6YR, (01789) 279988, *Fax (01789) 298589*, – rm, – 600. B e
The Riverside : Rest (carving rest.) 17.50 – 11.50 – **249 rm** 82.00/142.00 – 90.00/150.00, 2 suites.
◆ Overlooking the river Avon with imposing open reception area. Close to all sights, including Warwick Castle, for which discounts are available. Spacious, comfortable rooms. Spacious informality at The Riverside.

Stratford Victoria, Arden St, CV37 6QQ, (01789) 271000, *stratfordvictoria@marstonhotels.com, Fax (01789) 271001*, – rest, – 140. A c
Rest (carvery lunch Sunday) 14.50 and a la carte 24.50/25.50 s. – **101 rm** 79.00/105.00 – 85.00/130.00, 1 suite.
◆ Situated near a train station; built on site of a former 19C hospital and designed in Victorian style. Retains original gardens; modern, nicely decorated rooms. Discreet dining room where British classics play centre stage.

The Shakespeare, Chapel St, CV37 6ER, (0870) 400 8182, *sales.shakespeare@macdonald-hotels.co.uk, Fax (01789) 415411* – – 100. A V
David Garrick : Rest (dinner only and Sunday lunch) a la carte 30.00/42.00 – **73 rm** 70.00/125.00 – 140.00, 1 suite.
◆ Exudes atmosphere with gabled façade, leaded windows; this 18C inn was once a writers' watering hole. Afternoon tea served in vintage lounge; rooms with modern furnishings. Medieval styled restaurant; abundance of tried-and-tested dishes.

ENGLAND

Thistle Stratford-Upon-Avon, Waterside, CV37 6BA, ✆ (01789) 294949, *stratforduponavon@thistle.co.uk, Fax (0870) 333 9246,* – – 60. VISA B u
Bards : Rest 15.95/21.95 – 10.50 – **63 rm** 53.00/170.00 – 89.00/170.00.
◆ A compact hotel opposite the renowned RSC and birthplace of the bard. Themed weekends such as murder mysteries are popular. Well-equipped bedrooms. Bustling restaurant with a formal, elegant style.

Stratford Manor, Warwick Rd, CV37 0PY, Northeast : 3 m. on A 439 ✆ (01789) 731173, *stratfordmanor@marstonhotels.com, Fax (01789) 731131,* , , , , – rest, – 350. VISA.
Rest *(closed Saturday lunch)* 26.50/33.50 s. – **104 rm** 129.00 – 166.00.
◆ Three miles from Stratford and Warwick, this modern, well located hotel enjoys 21 acres of surrounding countryside. Murals, arresting meeting room and ample bedrooms within. Popular restaurant with traditional palette.

Swans Nest without rest., Bridgefoot, CV37 7LT, ✆ (01789) 266804, *Fax (01789) 414547,* – – 150. VISA. B v
12.95 – **67 rm** 40.00/70.00 – 80.00/120.00.
◆ Part 17C house in pleasant setting with courtyard garden and river frontage close to town centre and Royal Shakespeare Theatre. Rooms boast minibar, interactive television.

Sequoia House without rest., 51-53 Shipston Rd, CV37 7LN, ✆ (01789) 268852, *info@sequoiahotel.co.uk, Fax (01789) 414559,* – – 40. VISA. B r
closed 18 December-2 January – **22 rm** 49.00/59.00 – 89.00/99.00.
◆ Spacious Edwardian town house, named after the 175-year old sequoia tree in garden. Prime position, opposite the river Avon. Rooms in co-ordinated fabrics; restful lounge.

The Payton without rest., 6 John St, CV37 6UB, ✆ (01789) 266442, *info@payton.co.uk, Fax (01789) 266442* – . VISA. A e
closed 1 week Christmas and 2 weeks February – **5 rm** 50.00/60.00 – 50.00/68.00.
◆ Pretty, white Grade II listed Georgian town house built in 1832 in quiet conservation area. Pale, pastel coloured bedrooms and small neat breakfast room.

Victoria Spa Lodge without rest., Bishopton Lane, CV37 9QY, Northwest : 2 m. by A 3400 on Bishopton Lane turning left at roundabout with A 46 ✆ (01789) 267985, *ptozer@victoriaspalodge.demon.co.uk, Fax (01789) 204728,* – . VISA.
closed 25-26 and 31 December and 1 January – **7 rm** 50.00 – 65.00.
◆ Built as spa, hotel and pump room; Queen Victoria stayed as one of its many guests, testified by the gables which bear her coat of arms. Pristine rooms are among its charms.

Virginia Lodge without rest., 12 Evesham Pl, CV37 6HT, ✆ (01789) 292157, *Fax (01789) 292157,* – . VISA. A x
closed 24-25 December – **7 rm** 20.00/48.00 – 40.00/50.00.
◆ Family friendly Victorian house; pretty lounge in cottage style; individually decorated rooms named after furnishings: Laura Ashley and Country Manor.

Malbec, 6 Union St, CV37 6QT, ✆ (01789) 269106, *eatmalbec@aol.com, Fax (01789) 269106* – . VISA A n
closed 1 week April, 1 week Christmas, Sunday, Monday and Bank Holidays – **Rest** a la carte 26.00/30.50 s. .
◆ Pleasant modern restaurant with atmospheric barrel ceiling in intimate basement. Good value set menus: accomplished à la carte with season's larder bolstering a classic base.

Lambs, 12 Sheep St, CV37 6EF, ✆ (01789) 292554, *eat@lambsrestaurant.co.uk* – VISA B c
closed 25-26 December – **Rest** 20.00 and a la carte 23.95/30.15 .
◆ 16C town house with zesty bistro-style cooking in old-world surrounds of white wattle walls, rafters and well-spaced wooden tables.

at Alveston *East : 2 m. by B 4086* – **B** – ✉ *Stratford-upon-Avon.*

Baraset Barn, 1 Pimlico Lane, CV37 7RF, on B 4086 ✆ (01789) 295510, *Fax (01789) 292961,* – 14. VISA.
closed 25 December and Sunday dinner – **Rest** a la carte 23.00/35.00 .
◆ 200 year-old pub given a sumptuous contemporary makeover. Decked terrace; stylish lounge conservatory; Main dining in barn or mezzanine: bold, freshly prepared modern cooking.

at Lower Quinton *Southwest : 6½ m. by A 3400* – **B** – *and B 4632* – ✉ *Stratford-upon-Avon.*

The College Arms with rm, CV37 8SG, ✆ (01789) 720342, *mail@collegearms.co.uk, Fax (01789) 720392,* , – 12. VISA.
Rest 18.00/30.00 – **4 rm** 40.00 – 80.00.
◆ Part 16C pub with beams, inglenook and solid stone surrounds. Ideal watering hole for those on the tourist trail. Menus offer plenty of choice. Cosy, well maintained bedrooms.

at Ardens Grafton *Southwest : 5 m. by A 46 – A – ✉ Stratford-upon-Avon.*

Golden Cross, Wixford Rd, B50 4LG, South : ¼ m. ✆ (01789) 772420, *Fax (01789) 773697*, – P. MO VISA
closed Sunday dinner – **Rest** 12.95 (lunch) and a la carte 17.95/27.00.
◆ Solid stone floor, exposed beams, open fire, scrubbed wooden furnishing: all the winning ingredients for a welcoming pub. Freshly prepared dishes with tasty seasonal base.

at Billesley *West : 4½ m. by A 422 – A – off A 46 – ✉ Stratford-upon-Avon.*

Billesley Manor , B49 6NF, ✆ (01789) 279955, *info@billesleymanor.co.uk*, *Fax (01789) 764145*, ≤, , , , , , , – – P – 120. MO AE VISA
The Stuart **:** Rest 24.95/27.95 and dinner a la carte 33.20/42.50 – **70 rm** ★95.00/105.00 – ★★150.00/190.00, 2 suites.
◆ Topiary garden and ornamental pond complements lovely 16C manor. The oak panelled interior evokes its past: Shakespeare reputedly used the library. Modern and period rooms. Original 16C oak panelling in restaurant.

at Wilmcote *Northwest : 3½ m. by A 3400 – A – ✉ Stratford-upon-Avon.*

Pear Tree Cottage without rest., 7 Church Rd, CV37 9UX, ✆ (01789) 205889, *mander@peartreecot.co.uk*, *Fax (01789) 262862*, – P.
closed 24 December-2 January – **3 rm** ★40.00 – ★★60.00.
◆ Built in 1600, once owned by Shakespeare's parents; originally a yeoman farmer's cottage, overlooking village green. Fresh flowers, flagstone floors, beams and pretty rooms.

STREATLEY *Newbury* 503 504 Q 29 *Great Britain G. – pop. 3 924 (inc. Goring) – ✉ Goring.*
Env. : *Basildon Park★ AC, SE : 2½ m. by A 329 – Mapledurham★ AC, E : 6 m. by A 329, B 471 and B 4526.*
Exc. : *Ridgeway Path★★.*
Goring & Streatley, Rectory Rd ✆ (01491) 873229.
London 56 – Oxford 16 – Reading 11.

The Swan at Streatley, High St, RG8 9HR, ✆ (01491) 878800, *sales@swan-at-streatley.co.uk*, *Fax (01491) 872554*, ≤ River Thames, , , , , – – P – 140. MO AE VISA
Cygnetures **:** Rest a la carte 31.15/39.85 – **44 rm** ★110.00/140.00 – ★★140.00/150.00, 1 suite.
◆ Spectacular riverside views to be savoured from large windows of most bedrooms which also have patios and balconies. Hotel owns a barge for special occasions. Nautically themed restaurant overlooking Thames; alfresco dining on terrace.

STRETE *Devon – see Dartmouth.*

STRETTON *Ches.* 502 503 504 M 23 *– see Warrington.*

STRETTON *Rutland – see Stamford.*

STRETTON *Staffs.* 502 503 504 P 25 *– see Burton-upon-Trent.*

STROUD *Glos.* 503 504 N 28 *– pop. 32 052.*
, , *Minchinhampton ✆ (01453) 832642 (old course) (01453) 833840 (new course) –* *Painswick ✆ (01452) 812180.*
Subscription Rooms, George St ✆ (01453) 760960.
London 113 – Bristol 30 – Gloucester 9.

at Brimscombe *Southeast : 2¼ m. on A 419 – ✉ Stroud.*

Burleigh Court , Burleigh Lane, GL5 2PF, South : ½ m. by Burleigh rd via The Roundabouts ✆ (01453) 883804, *info@burleighcourthotel.co.uk*, *Fax (01453) 886870*, ≤, , – rest, P. MO VISA
Rest 15.95/33.00 and a la carte 27.50/40.00 s. – **18 rm** ★85.00/105.00 – ★★115.00/155.00.
◆ 18C manor house on edge of a steep hill overlooking Golden Valley. Victorian swimming pool in closeted garden of hidden pathways and stone walls. Homely bedrooms with views. Regency style dining room overlooks terraced gardens.

STUCKTON *Hants. – see Fordingbridge.*

STUDLAND Dorset 503 504 O 32.

London 135 – Bournemouth 25 – Southampton 53 – Weymouth 29.

X **Shell Bay,** Ferry Rd, BH19 3BA, North : 3 m. or via car ferry from Sandbanks ℘ (01929) 450363, *Fax (01929) 450570,* ≤ Poole Harbour and Brownsea Island, – . VISA
closed January and weekends only in winter – **Rest** - Seafood - a la carte 22.25/42.00.
◆ Hut-like appearance, but in a spectacular location with views of Poole Harbour and Brownsea Island. Inside, large windows and mirrors make the most of this. Seafood emphasis.

STUDLEY Warks. 503 504 O 27 – pop. 6 257 – ✉ Redditch.

London 109 – Birmingham 15 – Coventry 33 – Gloucester 39.

XX **Peppers,** 45 High St, B80 7HN, ℘ (01527) 853183 – . VISA
closed 25 December – **Rest** - Indian - (dinner only) 28.50 and a la carte approx 20.00.
◆ Fresh, authentic Indian food served by committed, friendly staff. Balance of flavour and spice in "something for everyone" dishes. Speciality cocktails.

STURMINSTER NEWTON Dorset 503 504 N 31 The West Country G. – pop. 2 317.

See : *Mill★ AC.*

London 123 – Bournemouth 30 – Bristol 49 – Salisbury 28 – Taunton 41.

Stourcastle Lodge, Gough's Close, DT10 1BU, (off the Market Place) ℘ (01258) 472320, *enquiries@stourcastle-lodge.co.uk, Fax (01258) 473381,* – P. VISA.
Rest 21.00 – **5 rm** ★48.00/55.00 – ★★78.00/92.00.
◆ 18C cottage with slate roof and whitewashed walls. Cosy, pastel-toned rooms, named after former owners, the Dashwood family, have brass bedsteads and views of the garden. Herbs and vegetables from garden cooked on owner's Aga.

XXX **Plumber Manor** with rm, DT10 2AF, Southwest : 1 ¾ m. by A 357 on Hazelbury Bryan rd ℘ (01258) 472507, *book@plumbermanor.com, Fax (01258) 473370,* ≤, – P – 25. VISA
closed February – **Rest** (dinner only and Sunday lunch)/dinner 26.00 **s.** – **16 rm** ★95.00/115.00 – ★★170.00.
◆ Secluded 18C manor house owned by the same family since it was first built. Three dining rooms where assured, popular dishes are served. Well-kept rooms, some with antiques.

SUMMERCOURT Cornwall 503 F 32 – ✉ Newquay.

London 263 – Newquay 9 – Plymouth 45.

X **Viners,** Carvynick (Golf & Country Club), TR8 5AF, Northwest : 1 ½ m. of the junction of A 30 and A 3058 ℘ (01872) 510544, *Fax (01872) 510468,* – 25. VISA
closed Monday except July-September – **Rest** (dinner only and Sunday lunch)/dinner a la carte 21.70/30.00 ♀.
◆ 17C pub with grey stone exterior and rustic interior boasting original beams. Welcoming ambience. Buzzy restaurant offers a creative, but very affordable, style of cooking.

SUNDERLAND Tyne and Wear 501 502 P 19 – pop. 177 739.

See : *National Glass Centre★ A.*

Whitburn, Lizard Lane, South Shields ℘ (0191) 529 2144.

50 Fawcett St ℘ (0191) 553 2000, tourist.info@sunderland.gov.uk.

London 272 – Leeds 92 – Middlesbrough 29 – Newcastle upon Tyne 12.

Plan opposite

Sunderland Marriott, Queens Parade, Seaburn, SR6 8DB, ℘ (0870) 4007287, *events.sunderland@marriotthotels.co.uk, Fax (0870) 4007387,* ≤, , , – – P – 300. VISA A e
The Promenade : Rest (dinner only and Sunday lunch)/dinner 30.00 and a la carte 22.40/28.85 **s.** ♀ – **82 rm** ★119.00 – ★★139.00.
◆ Overlooks Whitburn Sands. Smart reception and lounge; brightly patterned carpets, bold coloured cushions and chairs. Equally cheerful bedrooms with up-to-date facilities. Restaurant and bar dining alternatives.

SUNDERLAND

Street	Grid	No.
Albion Pl.	B	2
Barnes Park Rd	A	3
Bedford St	B	4
Borough Rd	B	5
Bridge St	B	6
Charlton Rd	A	8
Chester Rd	B	10
Crowtree Rd	B	11
Dame Dorothy St	A	12
Derwent St	B	13
Fawcett St	B	
Harbour View	A	14
High St West	B	15
Holmeside	B	
John St	B	16
Kayll Rd	A	17
Livingstone Rd	B	18
New Durham Rd	B	19
Ormonde St	A	21
Pallion Rd	A	22
Park Lane	B	23
Queens Rd	A	24
Roker Terrace	A	25
St Luke's Terrace	A	26
St Mary's Way	B	27
Shields Rd	A	29
Southwick Rd	B	30
Station Rd	A	32
The Bridges	B	
Trimdon St	A	35
Vine Pl.	B	36
Wessington Way	A	38

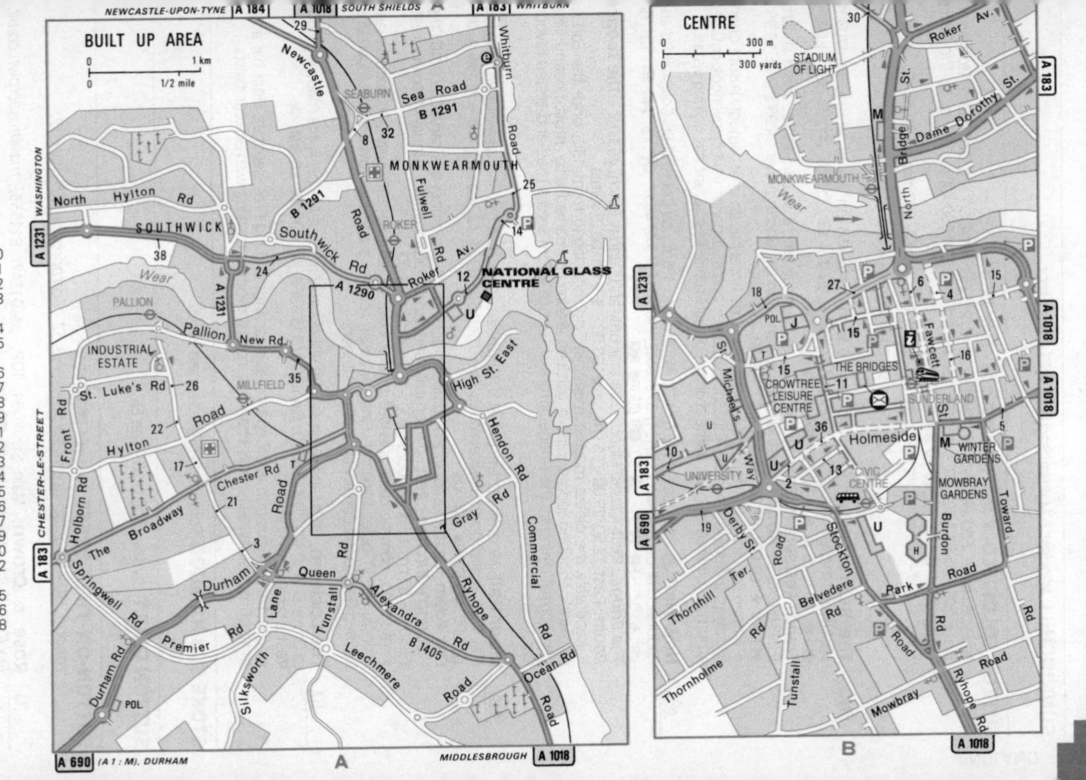

SUNNINGHILL *Windsor & Maidenhead* 504 S 29 – *see Ascot.*

SUTTON COLDFIELD *W. Mids.* 503 504 O 26 – *pop. 105 452.*

Pype Hayes, Eachelhurst Rd, Walmley (0121) 351 1014, DT – Boldmere, Monmouth Dr. (0121) 354 3379, DT – 110 Thornhill Rd (0121) 580 7878, DT – , The Belfry, Lichfield Rd, Wishaw (01675) 470301 DT.

London 124 – Birmingham 8 – Coventry 29 – Nottingham 47 – Stoke-on-Trent 40.

Plan : see Birmingham pp. 4 and 5

The Belfry, Wishaw, B76 9PR, East : 6 ½ m. by A 453 on A 446 (01675) 470301, *enquiries@thebelfry.com, Fax (01675) 470256,* ←, , , , , 27, , , , squash – , rest, , – 450. AE VISA.
French Restaurant : **Rest** (dinner only and Sunday lunch) 34.95/54.95 **s.** and a la carte 35.95/60.40 – ***Atrium :*** **Rest** (dinner only and Sunday lunch)/dinner 24.95 – 13.95 – **311 rm** 169.00/189.00 – 169.00/189.00, 13 suites.
◆ Famed for championship golf course, this large hotel has an unashamedly leisure oriented slant, including a superb AquaSpa. Sizeable rooms; superior variety overlook courses. Atrium dominated by glass dome ceiling. Formal French Restaurant has golfing vistas.

New Hall , Walmley Rd, B76 1QX, Southeast : 1 ½ m. by Coleshill St, Coleshill Rd and Reddicap Hill on B 4148 (0121) 378 2442, *Fax (0121) 378 4637,* , , , , , 9, , , – , – 50. AE VISA DT i
The Bridge : **Rest** *(closed Monday)* (dinner only and Sunday lunch) 45.00 – ***The Terrace Room :*** **Rest** 12.50/25.00 – **55 rm** 150.00 – 175.00, 5 suites.
◆ Reputedly the oldest moated manor in England, dating from 13C; once the Earl of Warwick's shooting lodge. Superb gardens. Bedrooms named after moat-floating lilies. Very formal dining at The Bridge. Informal Terrace Room serves tried-and-tested favourites.

Moor Hall, Moor Hall Drive, B75 6LN, Northeast : 2 m. by A 453 and Weeford Rd (0121) 308 3751, *mail@moorhallhotel.co.uk, Fax (0121) 308 8974,* , , , – , – 200. AE VISA. DT r
Oak Room : **Rest** *(closed Sunday dinner)* 10.95/20.00 and dinner a la carte 20.00/40.00 **s.** – ***Country Kitchen :*** **Rest** (dinner only and lunch Saturday and Sunday) (carvery rest.) 13.50 **s.** – **82 rm** 128.00/148.00 – 148.00/168.00.
◆ Imposing, commercially oriented manor house featuring 19C/early 20C fixtures and fittings, set in quiet parkland. Fine range of rooms: some look over sunken gardens. Refined Oak Room. Carvery at Country Kitchen.

The Cock Inn, Bulls Lane, Wishaw, B76 9QL, East : 7 m. by A 453 off A 446 following signs to Grove End (0121) 313 3960, *Fax (0121) 313 3964,* – . AE VISA.
Rest a la carte 16.00/29.00.
◆ Modern, spacious pub adorned by wood carvings and log fires; separate cigar bar adds an air of exclusivity. Seasonally changing, robust modern cooking with eclectic twists.

STOKE SUB HAMDON *Somerset* 503 L 31 – *see Yeovil.*

SUTTON GAULT *Cambs.* 504 U 26 – *see Ely.*

SUTTON-ON-THE-FOREST *N. Yorks.* 502 P 21.

London 230 – Kingston-upon-Hull 50 – Leeds 52 – Scarborough 40 – York 12.

Rose & Crown, Main St, YO61 1DP, (01347) 811333, *mail@rosecrown.co.uk, Fax (01347) 811444,* – . VISA
closed first week January, Sunday dinner and Monday – **Rest** (booking essential) 9.95 (lunch) and a la carte 25.00/35.00 .
◆ Lovely enclosed rear terrace and garden. Rustic bar ambience made all the warmer by roaring fires. Modern menu plus blackboard specials with imaginative, stylish twists.

**Undecided between two equivalent establishments?
Within each category, establishments are classified
in our order of preference.**

SWANAGE *Dorset* 503 504 O 32 *The West Country G. – pop. 11 097.*

See : *Town★.*

Env. : *St Aldhelm's Head★★ (≤★★★), SW : 4 m. by B 3069 – Durlston Country Park (≤★★), S : 1 m. – Studland (Old Harry Rocks★★, Studland Beach (≤★), St Nicholas Church★), N : 3 m. – Worth Matravers (Anvil Point Lighthouse ≤★★), S : 2 m. – Great Globe★, S : 1¼ m.*

Exc. : *Corfe Castle★ (≤★★) AC, NW : 6 m. by A 351 – Blue Pool★, NW : 9 m. by A 351 and minor roads – Lulworth Cove★, W : 18 m. by A 351 and B 3070.*

18, 9 Isle of Purbeck, Studland ☎ (01929) 450361.

The White House, Shore Rd ☎ (01929) 422885.

London 130 – Bournemouth 22 – Dorchester 26 – Southampton 52.

Cauldron Bistro, 5 High St, BH19 2LN, ☎ (01929) 422671 – VISA
closed 2 weeks December, 2 weeks January and Monday-Wednesday – **Rest** (light lunch) a la carte 23.20/29.20.
◆ Quaint and cosy; boothed tables, mix and match furniture. Quality ingredients, local fish, generous portions cooked with care. Unusual vegetarian dishes.

SWARLAND *Northd.* 501 502 O 18 – *see Alnwick.*

SWAY *Hants.* 503 504 P 31 – *see Brockenhurst.*

The red symbol? This denotes the very essence of peace – only the sound of birdsong first thing in the morning ...

SWINDON *Swindon* 503 504 O 29 *The West Country G. – pop. 155 432.*

See : *Great Western Railway Museum★ AC – Railway Village Museum★ AC* Y **M.**

Env. : *Lydiard Park (St Mary's★) W : 4 m.* U.

Exc. : *Ridgeway Path★★, S : 8½ m. by A 4361 – Whitehorse (≤★)E : 7½ m. by A 4312, A 420 and B 400 off B 4057.*

18, 9 Broome Manor, Pipers Way ☎ (01793) 532403 – 18 Shrivenham Park, Penny Hooks, Shrivenham ☎ (01793) 783853 – 18 The Wiltshire, Vastern, Wootton Bassett ☎ (01793) 849999 – 18 Wrag Barn G & C.C., Shrivenham Rd, Highworth ☎ (01793) 861327.

37 Regent St ☎ (01793) 530328.

London 83 – Bournemouth 69 – Bristol 40 – Coventry 66 – Oxford 29 – Reading 40 – Southampton 65.

Plans on following pages

Swindon Marriott, Pipers Way, SN3 1SH, South : 1 ½ m. by Marlborough Road off B 4006 ☎ (0870) 4007281, *events.swindon@marriotthotels.co.uk, Fax (0870) 4007381,* – 250. AE VISA. V s
***Mediterrano* :** Rest 16.00/21.00 and a la carte 17.95/30.15 **s.** – 14.95 – **156 rm** ★119.00 – ★★119.00.
◆ A modern, four storey business hotel in woodland yet close to the business park. Double beds in standard rooms; king size in executives: all have up-to-date mod cons. Restaurant exudes Mediterranean ambience.

De Vere, Shaw Ridge Leisure Park, Whitehill Way, SN5 7DW, West : 2 ¾ m. by A 3102 off B 4553 ☎ (01793) 878785, *dvs.sales@devere-hotels.com, Fax (01793) 877822,* – rest, – 400. AE VISA U e
***The Park Brasserie* :** Rest 14.95/24.00 – 12.95 – **148 rm** ★105.00 – ★★105.00, 4 suites.
◆ Large, corporate, well-equipped hotel on out-of-town leisure site ; a good range of well-equipped, up-to-date rooms, from suites and four-posters to family rooms. Brasserie with theatre kitchen, walk-in cellar and fish tanks.

Hilton Swindon, Lydiard Fields, Great Western Way, SN5 8UZ, West : 3 ½ m. by A 3102 at junction 16 of M 4 ☎ (01793) 881777, *reservations.swindon@hilton.com, Fax (01793) 881881,* – 350. AE VISA. V a
***Minsky's* :** Rest *(closed 24-26 December, lunch Saturday and Bank Holidays)* (buffet lunch) (carving dinner) 19.95/22.95 **s.** – **171 rm** ★65.00/200.00 – ★★75.00/200.00.
◆ Corporate hotel usefully located to west of town, making an excellent base from which to explore the West Country. The Living Well health club is also on hand. Spacious rooms. Dining options: buffet lunch, carvery dinner.

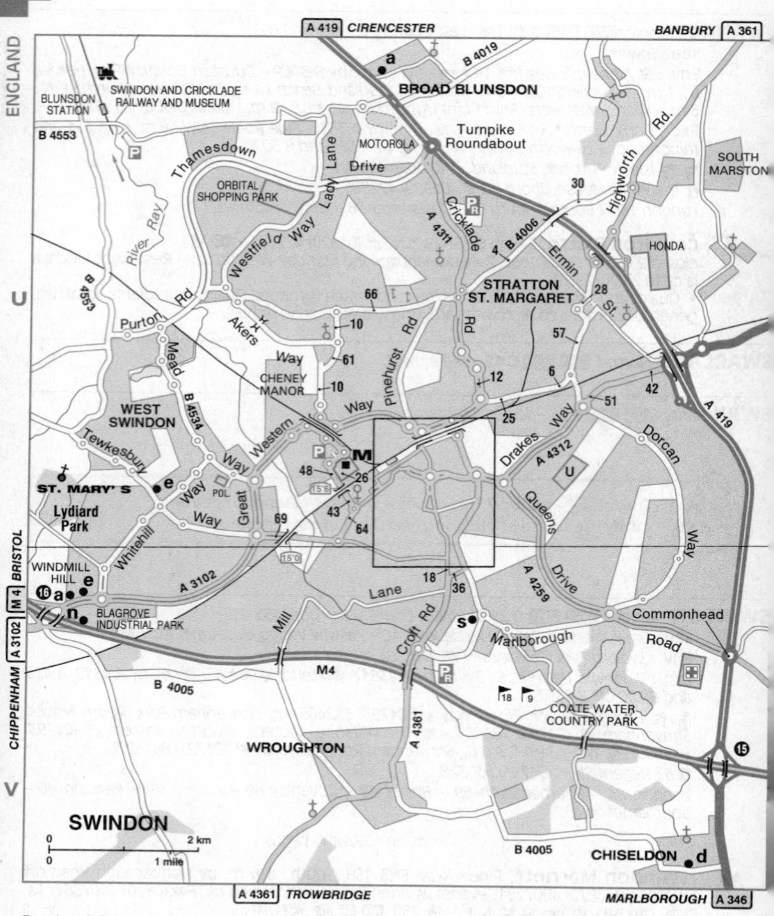

Beechcroft Rd . . . . U 4
Bridge End Rd. . . . . U 6
Cheney Manor Rd. . . . . U 10
Cirencester Way . . . . U 12
Devises Rd . . . . V 18
Gipsy Lane . . . . U 25
Great Western Retail Outlet. . . . . U 26
Hobley Drive . . . . U 28
Kingsdown Rd . . . . U 30
Newport St . . . . V 36
Oxford Rd . . . . U 42
Park Lane . . . . U 43
Rodbourne Rd. . . . . U 48
Slade Drive . . . . U 51
Swindon Rd . . . . U 57
Vicarage Rd . . . . U 61
Westcott Pl. . . . . U 64
Whitworth Rd . . . . U 66
Wootton Basset Rd . . . . . . U 69

Express by Holiday Inn without rest., Frankland Rd, Blagrove, SN5 8UD, West : 3 ½ m. by A 3102 at junction 16 of M 4 ✆ (01793) 818800, *swindon@expressbyholidayinn.net, Fax (01793) 818888* – |☰| ⇔ ✆ ♿ P – 🏛 45. MO AE ◑ VISA V n
121 rm ☕ ✝82.50 – ✝✝82.50.
◆ Modern purpose-built lodge accommodation in handy position next to M4 motorway. Smart, contemporary rooms for business or leisure customers.

Premier Travel Inn, Great Western Way, SN5 8UY, West : 3 ½ m. by A 3102 at junction 16 of M 4 ✆ (0870) 1977247, *Fax (01793) 886890* – |☰| ⇔, ▤ rest, ✆ ♿ P – 🏛 65. MO AE ◑ VISA V e
Rest (grill rest.) – **63 rm** ✝46.95/46.95 – ✝✝49.95/49.95.
◆ Conveniently positioned lodge hotel next to a Beefeater. Swindon Museum nearby. Impressive annex conference suite. Rooms are modern; uniformly fitted with worktops, sofa beds.

SWINDON

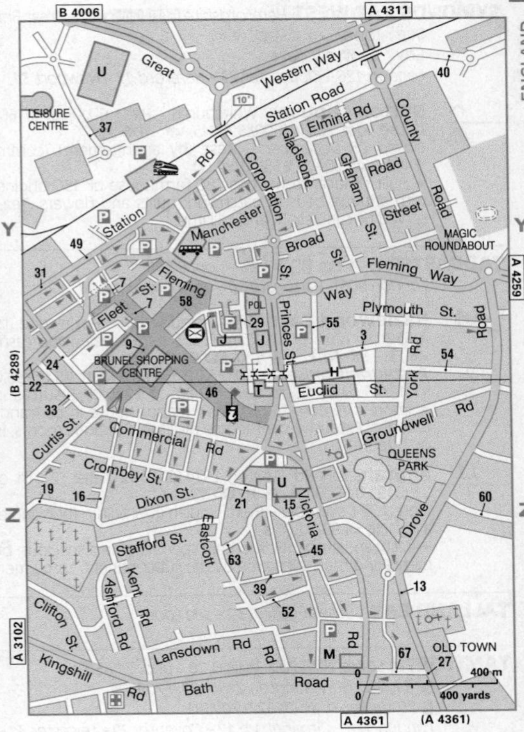

at Blunsdon *North : 4½ m. by A 4311 on A 419 – ✉ Swindon.*

Blunsdon House, SN26 7AS, ☎ (01793) 721701, *info@blunsdonhouse.co.uk, Fax (01793) 721056*, squash – |¶|, ⇔ rest, ☎ & [P] – 300. MC AE (D) VISA, JCB
U a

The Ridge : **Rest** (dinner only and Sunday lunch)/dinner 29.00/33.50 **s.** ♀ – ***Christophers :*** **Rest** (carving lunch) 15.00/16.50 **s.** ♀ – **114 rm** ☕ ✝120.00 – ✝✝130.00, 3 suites.

◆ Built as a farmhouse, this vast family-owned establishment now offers conference rooms and excellent leisure facilities. Large bedrooms with patios or balconies are popular. The Ridge is elegant and stylish. Christophers offers lively carvery - and discos!

at Chiseldon *South : 6¼ m. by A 4259, A 419 and A 346 on B 4005 – ✉ Swindon.*

Chiseldon House, New Rd, SN4 0NE, ☎ (01793) 741010, *chishoho@hotmail.com, Fax (01793) 741059*, – ⇔ rm, ☎ [P] – 50. MC AE (D) VISA
V d

Orangery : **Rest** 14.95/35.00 and a la carte 22.15/31.40 **s.** ♀ – **21 rm** ☕ ✝90.00/110.00 – ✝✝130.00.

◆ The gardens are one of the strongest aspects of this extended Georgian house. Rooms are a particularly good size with all mod cons. Close to motorway and easily accessible. Ornate, split-level restaurant decorated with murals.

We try to be as accurate as possible when giving room rates. But prices are susceptible to change, so please check rates when booking.

SYMONDS YAT WEST *Herefordshire* 503 504 M 28 *Great Britain G.* – ✉ *Ross-on-Wye.*

See : *Town★ – Yat Rock (≤★).*
Env. : *S : Wye Valley★.*
London 126 – Gloucester 23 – Hereford 17 – Newport 31.

Norton House, Whitchurch, HR9 6DJ, ℘ (01600) 890046, *enquiries@nortonhouse.com, Fax (01600) 890045,* – P
closed 25 December – **Rest** (by arrangement) (communal dining) 17.50 – **3 rm** ★40.00/45.00 – ★★55.00/60.00.
♦ Built of local stone, this 18C farmhouse of 15C origins boasts quaint interiors. Room with antique beds in patchwork quilts and flowers. Tea, cake on arrival. Evening mea served by candlelight and oil lamp.

TADCASTER *N. Yorks.* 502 Q 22 – *pop. 6 548.*

London 206 – Harrogate 16 – Leeds 14 – York 11.

Hazlewood Castle , Paradise Lane, Hazlewood, LS24 9NJ, Southwest : 2 ¾ m. b A 659 off A 64 ℘ (01937) 535353, *info@hazlewood-castle.co.uk, Fax (01937) 530630,* ≤ , – P – 120. MC AE VISA.
Restaurant Anise *(℘ (01937) 535317)* **: Rest** 25.00/30.00 (dinner) and lunch a la cart 17.40/23.40 ♀ – **12 rm** ★140.00 – ★★220.00, **9 suites** 280.00/300.00.
♦ Impressive part 13C fortified manor house in parkland. Panelled entrance hall, ornat lounges. Extensive conference facilities. Spacious rooms, individually styled. Dine informe orangery.

Aagrah, York Rd, Steeton, LS24 8EG, Northeast : 2½ m. on A 64 (westbound carriageway ℘ (01937) 530888 – P. MC AE VISA
closed 25 December – **Rest** - Indian (Kashmiri) - (booking essential) (dinner only) 15.00 an a la carte 14.95/21.05 **s.**
♦ Tasty and authentic Kashmiri specialities in a spacious, busy Indian restaurant with ornaments and friezes inspired by the subcontinent. Large menus and quality ingredients.

TALLAND BAY *Cornwall* 503 G 32 – *see Looe.*

TAMWORTH *Staffs.* 502 503 504 O 26 – *pop. 71 650.*

Eagle Drive, Amington ℘ (01827) 709303.
29 Market St ℘ (01827) 709581.
London 128 – Birmingham 12 – Coventry 29 – Leicester 31 – Stoke-on-Trent 37.

Premier Travel Inn, Bonehill Rd, Bitterscote, B78 3HQ, on A 51 ℘ (08701) 977248, *Fax (01827) 310420* – , rest, P – 50. MC AE VISA.
Rest (grill rest.) – **58 rm** ★46.95/46.95 – ★★49.95/49.95.
♦ A consistent standard of trim, simply fitted accommodation in contemporary style situated near canal and busy retail/leisure park. Useful for cost-conscious travellers.

TANWORTH-IN-ARDEN *Warks.* 503 504 O 26/27 – *see Henley-in-Arden.*

TAPLOW *Windsor & Maidenhead* 504 R 29.

London 33 – Maidenhead 2 – Oxford 36 – Reading 12.

Cliveden , SL6 0JF, North : 2 m. by Berry Hill ℘ (01628) 668561, *info@clivedenhouse.co.uk, Fax (01628) 661837,* ≤ National Trust Gardens, parterre and River Thames, , , heated, , , , , indoor/outdoor, squash – P – 40. MC AE VISA.
Terrace : **Rest** 29.50/53.00 **s.** – (see also ***Waldo's*** below) – **32 rm** ★230.00/345.00 – ★★295.00/410.00, 7 suites 495.00/610.00.
♦ Breathtakingly stunning 19C stately home in National Trust gardens. Ornate, sumptuous public areas, filled with antiques. Exquisitely appointed rooms the last word in luxury. View parterre and Thames in top class style from Terrace.

Taplow House, Berry Hill, SL6 0DA, ℘ (01628) 670056, *reception@taplow.wrensgroup.com, Fax (01628) 773625,* , – P – 100. MC AE VISA.
Rest *(closed Saturday lunch)* 18.95 (lunch) and dinner a la carte 30.40/46.85 **s.** ♀ – 12.00 – **31 rm** ★135.00/145.00 – ★★145.00, 1 suite.
♦ Part 16C mansion with Europe's tallest tulip tree, planted by Elizabeth I. Set in mature woodland. Warm, cosy décor throughout. Plush suites and sofas. Well-equipped rooms. Intimate dining room, overlooking lawned gardens.

XXXX **Waldo's** (at Cliveden H.), SL6 0JF, North : 2 m. by Berry Hill ✆ (01628) 668561, *info@clivedenhouse.co.uk, Fax (01628) 661837* – ⇔ ▤ P. MO AE ⊕ VISA
closed, 2 weeks Christmas-New Year, first week January, two weeks August, Sunday and Monday – **Rest** (booking essential) (dinner only) 65.00 s.
Spec. Pressed terrine of foie gras, compote of apricot and chilli. Fillet of John Dory with niçoise vegetables, essence of crab. Bitter chocolate box with caramel mousse, hazelnut and caramel ice cream.
◆ Exquisitely upholstered restaurant, seamlessly weaving into the grand tapestry of Cliveden. Superbly prepared ingredients contribute to seasonal menus served with flair.

ENGLAND

TARPORLEY *Ches.* 502 503 504 L/M 24 – *pop. 2 634.*

Portal G & C.C., Cobblers Cross Lane ✆ (01829) 733933 – Portal Premier, Forest Rd ✆ (01829) 733884.
London 186 – Chester 11 – Liverpool 27 – Shrewsbury 36.

The Swan, 50 High St, CW6 0AG, ✆ (01829) 733838, *Fax (01829) 732932,* – ⇔ P – 60. MO AE VISA
Rest a la carte 10.95/29.00 ♀ – **16 rm** ☐ ★62.00/77.50 – ★★86.00/130.00.
◆ 16C former coaching inn with hanging baskets, located in pleasant village. Original beams, open fires and oak panelling adorn guest areas. Bedrooms retain period feel of inn. Informality the key to relaxed dining room.

at Cotebrook *Northeast : 2½ m. on A 49 – ✉ Tarporley.*

Fox and Barrel, CW6 9DZ, ✆ (01829) 760529, *info@thefoxandbarrel.com, Fax (01829) 760529,* – ⇔ P. MO AE VISA
closed 25 December – **Rest** (live jazz Monday evening) a la carte 15.00/25.00 ♀.
◆ Wood floors, beamed ceiling and character aplenty. Busy and friendly pub offers an extensive menu of hearty traditional fare. Book early for the Monday live Jazz evenings.

at Bunbury *South : 3¼ m. by A 49 – ✉ Tarporley.*

Dysart Arms, Bowes Gate Rd, CW6 9PH, by Bunbury Mill rd ✆ (01829) 260183, *dysart.arms@brunningandprice.co.uk, Fax (01829) 261286,* – P. MO VISA
closed 25 December – **Rest** a la carte 15.40/27.70 ♀.
◆ Characterful village pub, in the shadow of impressive Bunbury Church. Open fire, beams and lots of clutter. Interesting, original, hearty British food.

at Willington *Northwest : 3½ m. by A 51 – ✉ Tarporley.*

Willington Hall ⛰, CW6 0NB, ✆ (01829) 752321, *enquiries@willingtonhall.co.uk, Fax (01829) 752596,* ≤, – ⇔ rest, P – 150. MO AE VISA
closed 25-26 December – **Rest** *(closed Sunday dinner)* 15.00/24.00 and dinner a la carte 21.80/28.70 – **10 rm** ☐ ★70.00 – ★★120.00.
◆ Imposing 19C country house with ornate façade in mature grounds; many original features remain, including vast hall and impressive staircase. Most rooms have rural outlook. Intimate dinners served in classically proportioned surroundings.

Luxury pad or humble abode? X and ⌂ denote categories of comfort.

TARR STEPS *Somerset* 503 J 30.

London 191.5 – Taunton 31 – Tiverton 20.

Tarr Farm Inn with rm, TA22 9PY, ✆ (01643) 851507, *enquiries@tarrfarm.co.uk, Fax (01643) 851111,* – ⇔ P. MO VISA
Rest a la carte 14.50/29.75 ♀ – **9 rm** ☐ ★60.00 – ★★120.00.
◆ On beautiful Exmoor, overlooking ancient clapper bridge. Hugely characterful, beamed interior. Accomplished, modish menus in intimate restaurant. Bedrooms exude luxury.

TATTENHALL *Ches.* 502 503 504 L 24 – *pop. 1 860.*

London 200 – Birmingham 71 – Chester 10 – Liverpool 29 – Manchester 38 – Stoke-on-Trent 30.

Higher Huxley Hall ⛰, CH3 9BZ, North : 2 ¼ m. on Huxley rd ✆ (01829) 781484, *info@huxleyhall.co.uk,* ≤, – ⇔ P. MO AE VISA.
booking essential – **Rest** (by arrangement) (communal dining) 30.00 – **5 rm** ☐ ★50.00/70.00 – ★★88.00/95.00.
◆ This historic manor house, sited on a former farm, dates from 13C and is attractively furnished with antiques. Bedrooms are comfortable and well equipped. Homely, communal dining room serving local produce.

ENGLAND

at Higher Burwardsley *Southeast : 1 m. – ✉ Tattenhall.*

The Pheasant with rm, CH3 9PF, ✆ (01829) 770434, *info@thepheasantinn.co.u* *Fax (01829) 771097,* ≤ Cheshire plain, – P. MC AE VISA.
Rest a la carte 20.00/28.00 – **10 rm** ☐ 65.00 – 80.00.
◆ Appealing part-timber pub with superb views over Cheshire Plain. Accomplished, orig nal food on offer. Attractively stylish rooms in adjacent, converted sandstone barn.

TAUNTON *Somerset* 503 K 30 *The West Country G. – pop. 58 241.*
See : *Town★ – St Mary Magdalene★* V – *Somerset County Museum★* AC V **M** – *St James'* U – *Hammett St★* V **25** – *The Crescent★* V – *Bath Place★* V **3**.
Env. : *Trull (Church★), S : 2½ m. by A 38 – Hestercombe Gardens★, N : 5 m. by A 3259 B and minor roads to Cheddon Fitzpaine.*
Exc. : *Bishops Lydeard★ (Church★), NW : 6 m. – Wellington : Church★, Wellington Monu ment (≤★★), SW : 7½ m. by A 38 – Combe Florey★, NW : 8 m. – Gaulden Manor★ AC, NW 10 m. by A 358 and B 3227.*
18, 9 *Taunton Vale, Creech Heathfield ✆ (01823) 412220 –* 18 *Vivary, Vivary Park ✆ (01823 289274 –* 18 *Taunton and Pickeridge, Corfe ✆ (01823) 421537.*
Paul St ✆ (01823) 336344.
London 168 – Bournemouth 69 – Bristol 50 – Exeter 37 – Plymouth 78 – Southampton 93 Weymouth 50.

Plan opposite

The Castle, Castle Green, TA1 1NF, ✆ (01823) 272671, *reception@the-castle-hotel.com* *Fax (01823) 336066,* , – P – 100. MC AE VISA V a
Rest *(closed Sunday dinner)* 25.00/45.00 – **43 rm** ☐ 110.00/125.00 – 180.00/255.00.
Spec. Scrambled duck egg with smoked eel and spiced oil. "A celebration" of British beef Seared scallops with a fine bean and tomato salad.
◆ Traditionally renowned, family owned British hotel: afternoon tea a speciality. 12C origins with Norman garden. Wisteria-clad and castellated. Individually styled rooms. Top quality West Country produce underpins inventive cuisine.

Meryan House, Bishop's Hull Rd, TA1 5EG, West : ¾ m. by A 38 ✆ (01823) 337445 *meryanhouse@btclick.com, Fax (01823) 322355,* – P. MC VISA AZ c
Rest (booking essential to non-residents) (dinner only) 21.00 s. – **12 rm** ☐ 50.00/55.00 – 65.00/80.00.
◆ Privately owned extended house on town outskirts. Comfortable sitting room has adjacent patio garden and small bar with jukebox. Well-kept, individually styled rooms. Intimate dining room with large inglenook.

Express by Holiday Inn without rest., Blackbrook Business Park, TA1 2PX, ✆ (01823) 624000, *tauntondutymanager@somerstonhotels.co.uk, Fax (01823) 624024* – P – 30. MC AE VISA BY a
92 rm 75.00 – 75.00.
◆ Purpose-built hotel with cosy bar. Bedrooms have a Scandinavian feel and boast good extras. Next door is a Harvester restaurant.

Premier Travel Inn, 81 Bridgwater Rd, TA1 2DU, East : 1 ¾ m. by A 358 ✆ (0870) 1977249, *Fax (01823) 322054* – , rest, P. MC AE VISA. BY e
Rest (grill rest.) – **40 rm** 49.95 – 49.95.
◆ A consistent standard of trim, simply fitted accommodation in contemporary style: a useful address for cost-conscious travellers. Family rooms with sofa beds.

The Willow Tree, 3 Tower Lane, TA1 4AR, ✆ (01823) 352835 – . MC VISA V c
closed Christmas, early January, Sunday and Monday – **Rest** (dinner only) a la carte 23.40/30.40.
◆ Converted 17C town house in central location. Exposed beams and large inglenook fireplaces. Friendly service. Appealing menu of modern seasonal cooking with a classical base.

Brazz, Castle Bow, TA1 1NF, ✆ (01823) 252000, *taunton@brazz.co.uk, Fax (01823) 336066* – P. MC AE VISA V e
closed dinner 25 December – **Rest** a la carte 16.50/26.25 .
◆ Bright and breezy bistro style eatery to rear of The Castle hotel. Large, bustling bar area. Main restaurant has large aquarium, concave ceiling and brasserie favourites.

The Sanctuary, Middle St, TA1 1SJ, ✆ (01823) 257788, *Fax (01823) 257788,* – . MC VISA U a
closed 24-26 December, Saturday lunch, Sunday and Bank Holidays – **Rest** a la carte 19.00/29.00 .
◆ Longstanding, popular eatery of exposed brick and beams tucked away down a side street. Search out charming little landscaped roof terrace. Simple and eclectic modern menus.

TAUNTON

ath Pl.	V	3
illet St.	V	4
illetfield	V	6
irch Grove	U	7
ishop's Hull Rd	AZ	9
ridge (The)	U	10
ridge St	U	12
urton Pl.	V	13
ann St	V	15
leveland St	U	16
omeytrowe Lane	AZ	18
orporation St	V	19
County Walk Shopping Centre	V	
uke St	V	21
ast St	V	
ore St	V	22
lamilton Rd	BZ	24
lammet St	V	25
ligh St.	V	
lurdle Way	V	27
minster Rd.	BZ	28
Magdalene St	V	30
Middleway	AZ	31
North St	V	33
Obridge Viaduct	BY	34
Old Market Shopping Centre	V	
Portland St.	U	36
Priory Ave	U	37
Shoreditch Rd	BZ	39
Shuttern	V	40
Silver St South	V, Z	42
Upper High St	V	43
Upper Wood St	U	44
Victoria Parkway	BYZ	45
Wellington New Rd	AZ	46
Wilton St	V	48
Winchester St	U	49
Wood St	U	51

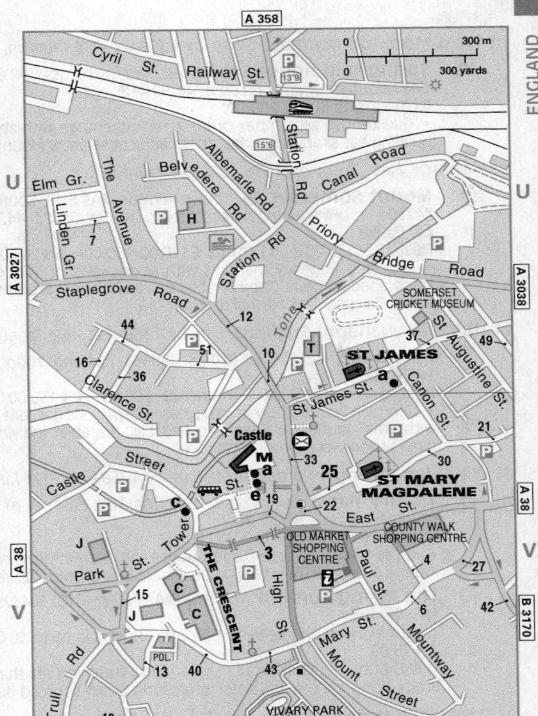

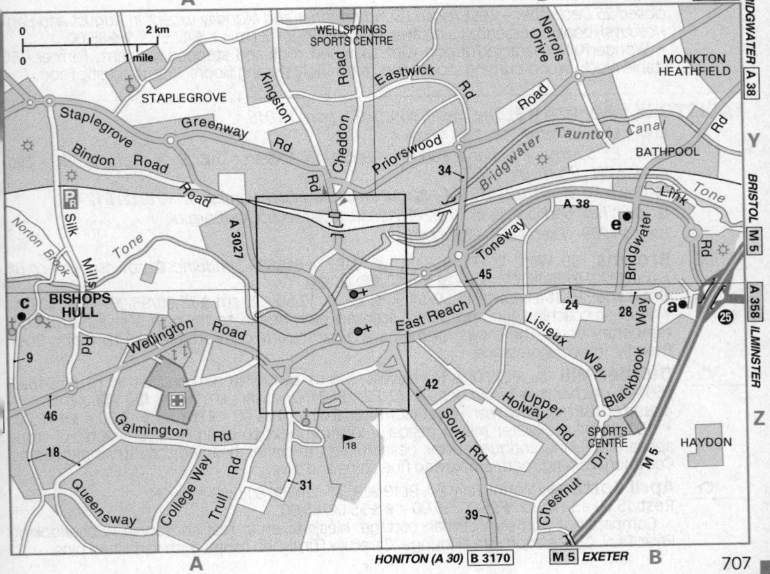

(A 38) A 3259

2 km
1 mile
WELLSPRINGS SPORTS CENTRE
Nerrols Drive
Eastwick Rd
Road
MONKTON HEATHFIELD
BRIDGWATER A 38
STAPLEGROVE
Staplegrove Road
Greenway
Kingston Rd
Cheddon Road
Bindon Road
Priorswood Rd
Bridgwater Taunton Canal
BATHPOOL
Y
BRISTOL M 5
A 3027
Silk Mills
Norton Brook
Tone
A 38
Link Rd
Toneway
Bridgwater Rd
BISHOPS HULL
Wellington Road
East Reach
Lisieux Way
Way
A 358 ILMINSTER
Rd
Upper Holway Rd
Blackbrook
SPORTS CENTRE
Galmington Rd
Queensway
College Way
Trull Rd
South Rd
Chestnut Dr.
M 5
HAYDON
Z
A
HONITON (A 30) B 3170
M 5 EXETER
B

at West Monkton *Northeast : 3½ m. by A 38 – BY – ✉ Taunton.*

Springfield House without rest., Walford Cross, TA2 8QW, on A 38 ☎ (01823) 41211 *tina.ridout@btopenworld.com,* – **P**.
5 rm ☕ ★35.00 – ★★55.00.
◆ Guesthouse with annex of quite recent vintage with attractive, spacious gardens. Ma building has simple breakfast room and conservatory lounge. Cottage style bedrooms.

at Henlade *East : 3½ m. on A 358 – BZ – ✉ Taunton.*

Mount Somerset , Lower Henlade, TA3 5NB, South : ½ m. by Stoke Rd ☎ (0182 442500, *info@mountsomersethotel.co.uk, Fax (01823) 442900,* ←, – **P** – 5
MC AE VISA
Rest 18.50/36.00 ♀ – **11 rm** ☕ ★110.00/130.00 – ★★205.00/225.00.
◆ Imposing Regency mansion with good views of Vale of Taunton. Exotic peacocks i landscaped gardens. Comfortable, spacious drawing rooms. Elegant bedrooms, most wit views. Oak panelled, formal dining room.

at Hatch Beauchamp *Southeast : 6 m. by A 358 – BZ – ✉ Taunton.*

Farthings, TA3 6SG, ☎ (01823) 480664, *farthings1@aol.com, Fax (01823) 481118,*
P. MC AE VISA
Rest (dinner only) 28.50 ♀ – **10 rm** ☕ ★80.00 – ★★135.00/155.00.
◆ Georgian country house with pleasant, spacious gardens in pretty village. Personally rur with small lounge and well-stocked bar. Sizeable, individually decorated rooms. Smar dining room; local produce to fore.

at West Bagborough *Northwest : 10½ m. by A 358 – AY – ✉ Taunton.*

Tilbury Farm without rest., TA4 3DY, East : ¾ m. ☎ (01823) 432391, ← Vale o Taunton, – **P**.
3 rm ☕ ★40.00 – ★★55.00/60.00.
◆ Impressively characterful 18C house with terrific views of Vale of Taunton. Characterfu lounge boasts log fire. Well- kept, spacious bedrooms all with beams and good views.

The Rising Sun Inn with rm, TA4 3EF, ☎ (01823) 432575, *enquiries@theriser.co.uk* – . MC VISA
closed Monday except Bank Holidays – **Rest** a la carte 18.00/26.00 ♀ – **2 rm** ☕ ★45.00 – ★★75.00.
◆ 16C pub, rebuilt after a fire, seemingly tumbling off the edge of the Quantocks! Modernity alongside oak and slate; interesting locally sourced dishes. Two stylish bedrooms.

at Triscombe *Northwest : 11 m. by A 358 – AY – ✉ Taunton.*

Blue Ball Inn with rm, TA4 3HE, ☎ (01984) 618242, *Fax (01984) 618371,* , –
P. MC VISA.
closed 25 December – **Rest** *(closed Sunday dinner and Monday except in August and Bank Holidays)* (booking essential) a la carte 23.00/29.95 ♀ – **2 rm** ☕ ★42.50 – ★★85.00.
◆ Wonderfully characterful pub with thatched roof and stepped gardens: former 15C stable block. Wood burning stoves and charmingly sloping floors. Robust, rustic food.

TAVISTOCK *Devon* 503 H 32 *The West Country G. – pop. 11 018.*
Env. : *Morwellham★ AC, SW : 4½ m.*
Exc. : *E : Dartmoor National Park★★ – Buckland Abbey★★ AC, S : 7 m. by A 386 – Lydford★★, N : 8½ m. by A 386.*
18 *Down Rd ☎ (01822) 612344* – 18 *Hurdwick, Tavistock Hamlets ☎ (01822) 612746.*
Town Hall, Bedford Sq ☎ (01822) 612938, tavistocktic@visit.org.uk.
London 239 – Exeter 38 – Plymouth 16.

Browns, 80 West St, PL19 8AQ, ☎ (01822) 618686, *enquiries@brownsdevon.co.uk, Fax (01822) 618646,* , – . MC AE VISA
Brasserie : **Rest** a la carte 18.50/34.50 **s.** ♀ – ☕ 12.50 – **20 rm** ★75.00/95.00 – ★★140.00.
◆ Former coaching inn and oldest licensed premises in town; now a stylish and contemporary hotel. The mews rooms have a particularly comfortable feel to them. Busy, friendly, informal brasserie.

Quither Mill , PL19 0PZ, Northwest : 5 ¾ m. by Chillaton rd on Quither rd ☎ (01822) 860160, *quither.mill@virgin.net, Fax (01822) 860160,* ←, , – **P**. MC VISA.
closed Christmas-New Year – **Rest** (communal dining) 25.00 – **3 rm** ☕ ★45.00 – ★★76.00.
◆ 18C converted water mill in peaceful location next to open field. Characterful stone appearance. Fine antiques. Utter peacefulness pervades beamed, country style rooms. Communal dining room employing fine china and silver.

April Cottage, Mount Tavy Rd, PL19 9JB, ☎ (01822) 613280 – **P**
Rest 15.00 – **3 rm** ☕ ★35.00/50.00 – ★★55.00/60.00.
◆ Compact but homely Victorian cottage. Meals taken in rear conservatory overlooking River Tavy. Curios adorn small lounge. Carefully furnished rooms with varnished pine.

Colcharton Farm without rest., Gulworthy, PL19 8HU, West : 2½ m. by A 390 on Colcharton rd (01822) 616435, *colchartonfarm@agriplus.net, Fax (01822) 616435,* , – P.
3 rm ☕ 30.00/40.00 – 60.00.
◆ Modern farmhouse in 150 acres of farmland enjoying panoramic views: wander in the fields with sheep and ponies. Front conservatory. Homely lounge. Modern, pretty rooms. Communal breakfast room with fine country views.

at Gulworthy *West : 3 m. on A 390 – ✉ Tavistock.*

Horn of Plenty with rm, PL19 8JD, Northwest : 1 m. by Chipshop rd (01822) 832528, *enquiries@thehornofplenty.co.uk, Fax (01822) 834390,* ≤ Tamar Valley and Bodmin Moor, , – P. MC AE VISA
closed 25-26 December – **Rest** *(closed Monday lunch)* 25.00/42.00 ♀ – **10 rm** ☕ 110.00 – 230.00.
Spec. Sautéed scallops with salmon tartare and sushi rice salad. Roast Devonshire lamb, twice baked garlic soufflé, red wine sauce. Cassis vacherin with pecan shortbread biscuits.
◆ Smart, individually styled bedrooms enhance enchanting creeper-clad Tamar Valley country house. Confident, sharp, imaginative cooking served with great charm in restaurant.

at Milton Abbot *Northwest : 6 m. on B 3362 – ✉ Tavistock.*

Hotel Endsleigh , PL19 0PQ, Southwest : 1 m. (01822) 870000, *mail@hotelendsleigh.com, Fax (01822) 870578,* ≤, , , – rest, P. MC AE VISA
closed 5-31 January – **Rest** 27.00/38.00 – **13 rm** ☕ 210.00/250.00 – 275.00, 2 suites.
◆ Painstakingly restored Regency lodge in magnificent Devonian gardens and grounds. Stylish lounge and refined bedrooms are imbued with an engaging, understated elegance. Interesting, traditionally based dishes served in two minimalist dining rooms.

at Chillaton *Northwest : 6¼ m. by Chillaton rd – ✉ Tavistock.*

Tor Cottage without rest., PL16 0JE, Southwest : ¼ m. by Tavistock rd, turning right at bridle path sign, down unmarked track for ½ m. (01822) 860248, *info@torcottage.co.uk, Fax (01822) 860126,* ≤, heated, , – P. MC VISA.
closed mid December-6 January – **5 rm** ☕ 94.00 – 140.00/150.00.
◆ Peace reigns in the 18 hillside acres surrounding this lovely cottage and gardens. Terrace or conservatory breakfast. Individual rooms with tremendous attention to detail.

TEFFONT *Wilts. – see Salisbury.*

TEIGNMOUTH *Devon 503 J 32 – pop. 14 799.*
The Den, Sea Front (01626) 215666.
London 216 – Exeter 16 – Torquay 8.

Thomas Luny House without rest., Teign St, TQ14 8EG, follow signs for the Quays, off the A 381 (01626) 772976, *alisonandjohn@thomas-luny-house.co.uk,* – P. MC VISA.
4 rm ☕ 52.00/62.00 – 70.00/88.00.
◆ Georgian house in old quarter. Sheltered walled garden. Smart breakfast room with antique pieces. Well furnished drawing room. Stylish, individually decorated bedrooms.

TELFORD *Wrekin 502 503 504 M 25 Great Britain G. – pop. 138 241.*
Env. : *Ironbridge Gorge Museum★★ AC (The Iron Bridge★★, Coalport China Museum★★, Blists Hill Open Air Museum★★, Museum of the River and Visitor Centre★) S : 5 m. by B 4373.*
Exc. : *Weston Park★★ AC, E : 7 m. by A 5.*
18, 9 Telford, Great Hay, Sutton Heights (01952) 429977 – 18 Wrekin, Wellington (01952) 244032 – 9, 9, 9 The Shropshire, Muxton Grange, Muxton (01952) 677866.
Management Suite, The Telford Centre (01952) 238008.
London 152 – Birmingham 33 – Shrewsbury 12 – Stoke-on-Trent 29.

Hadley Park House, Hadley, TF1 6QS, North : 3 ¼ m. by A 442 (01952) 677269, *info@hadleypark.co.uk, Fax (01952) 676938,* , – rest, rest, P. MC AE VISA
The Conservatory : **Rest** *(closed Sunday dinner and Bank Holidays)* a la carte 19.95/30.00 s. – **12 rm** ☕ 85.00/95.00 – 105.00/125.00.
◆ Georgian house with good communications if you're coming by road. Cosy bar lounge with an attractive "English" style. Bedrooms on two floors are comfortable and up-to-date. Very appealing conservatory restaurant with its own summer terrace.

ENGLAND

at Norton *South : 7 m. on A 442 – ✉ Shifnal.*

Hundred House with rm, Bridgnorth Rd, TF11 9EE, ☎ (01952) 730353, *reservations@hundredhouse.co.uk, Fax (01952) 730355,* – P. MC VISA
Rest a la carte 24.00/34.00 – **10 rm** ☕ ★69.00/85.00 – ★★135.00.
◆ Characterful, family run redbrick inn with herb garden. Carefully sourced dishes, robust and original. Sizable rooms in 19C style, some with canopied beds and swings.

at Bratton *Northwest : 6¾ m. by A 442 and B 5063 (following signs for Admaston) off the B 4394 ✉ Telford.*

Dovecote Grange without rest., Bratton Rd, TF5 0BT, ☎ (01952) 243739, *mandy@dovecotegrange.co.uk, Fax (01952) 243739,* – P. MC VISA.
5 rm ☕ ★45.00/60.00 – ★★70.00.
◆ Attractive guesthouse, garden and terrace enjoying views over the local fields. Combined lounge and breakfast area with modern leather furniture. Large, comfy, modish rooms.

TEMPLE SOWERBY *Cumbria 502 M 20 – see Penrith.*

TENBURY WELLS *Worcs. 503 504 M 27 – pop. 3 316.*

London 144 – Birmingham 36 – Hereford 20 – Shrewsbury 37 – Worcester 28.

Cadmore Lodge, St Michaels, WR15 8TQ, Southwest : 2 ¾ m. by A 4112 ☎ (01584) 810044, *info@cadmorelodge.co.uk, Fax (01584) 810044,* – P 100. MC VISA.
closed 25 December – **Rest** (bar lunch Monday) 14.00/22.50 and a la carte 14.50/24.00
14 rm ☕ ★47.50/56.00 – ★★85.00/125.00.
◆ Family run hotel in pleasant location. Lakeside setting. Plenty of outdoor activities, including golf and fishing. Well-planned rooms: some larger ones have antique furniture. Restaurant overlooks the lake.

TENTERDEN *Kent 504 W 30 – pop. 6 977.*

Town Hall, High St ☎ (01580) 763572 (summer only).
London 57 – Folkestone 26 – Hastings 21 – Maidstone 19.

Little Silver Country H., Ashford Rd, St Michaels, TN30 6SP, North : 2 m. on A 28 ☎ (01233) 850321, *enquiries@little-silver.co.uk, Fax (01233) 850647,* – P. – 120. MC AE VISA.
Rest (light lunch)/dinner a la carte 24.40/32.50 – **16 rm** ☕ ★60.00 – ★★125.00/175.00.
◆ Extended mock-Tudor country house hotel with smart gardens. Large function room ideal for weddings. Cosy conservatory breakfast room. Clean and spacious bedrooms. Dining room with table lamps, candelabra and Kentish watercolours.

Collina House, 5 East Hill (via Oaks Rd), TN30 6RL, ☎ (01580) 764852, *enquiries@collinahousehotel.co.uk, Fax (01580) 762224* – P. MC VISA.
closed 22 December-10 January – **Rest** (dinner only) 21.50 and a la carte 23.00/30.00 s.
15 rm ☕ ★45.00/75.00 – ★★50.00/85.00.
◆ Family run detached house with annex. In good position for visits to Sissinghurst and Leeds Castle. Small, cosy bar and very spacious rooms with neat, simple style. Cosy, family friendly restaurant.

TETBURY *Glos. 503 504 N 29 Great Britain G. – pop. 5 250.*

Env. : *Westonbirt Arboretum★ AC, SW : 2½ m. by A 433.*
Westonbirt ☎ (01666) 880242.
33 Church St ☎ (01666) 503552, tourism@tetbury.com.
London 113 – Bristol 27 – Gloucester 19 – Swindon 24.

Snooty Fox, Market Pl, GL8 8DD, ☎ (01666) 502436, *res@snooty-fox.co.uk, Fax (01666) 503479* – rest, MC AE VISA
Rest (bar lunch)/dinner a la carte 17.50/30.00 – **12 rm** ☕ ★69.00/73.00 – ★★199.00.
◆ Stone built former 17C wool factory, with extensions, opposite Tudor market place. Characterful wood panelled bar. Individualistic rooms with superior drapes and fabrics. Cosy but elegant wood panelled restaurant.

The Trouble House (Bedford), GL8 8SG, Northeast : 2 m. on A 433 ☎ (01666) 502206, *enquiries@troublehouse.co.uk, Fax (01666) 504508,* – P. MC AE VISA
closed 25 December-5 January, Sunday dinner, Monday and Bank Holidays – **Rest** a la carte 28.50/39.00.
Spec. Roast scallops with crayfish, Parma ham and mixed leaves. Cassoulet. Dessert plate.
◆ Traditional pub with characterful low beamed ceiling and stone walls. Robust, hearty classics cooked with care and fine local ingredients in a proper pubby atmosphere.

at Willesley *Southwest : 4 m. on A 433 – ✉ Tetbury.*

Tavern House, GL8 8QU, ☎ (01666) 880444, *robertson@tavernhouse.co.uk,* – P.
Rest (by arrangement) a la carte 15.00/18.00 **4 rm** 50.00/70.00 – 60.00/90.00.
◆ Part 17C former inn and staging post with an attractive and secluded rear garden, which is overlooked by lounge and little breakfast room. Pretty, cottagey bedrooms.

at Calcot *West : 3½ m. on A 4135 – ✉ Tetbury.*

Calcot Manor , GL8 8YJ, ☎ (01666) 890391, *reception@calcotmanor.co.uk, Fax (01666) 890394,* , , , , heated, , , , – rest, P – 80. MC AE VISA
Conservatory : Rest (booking essential) a la carte 26.50/41.50 – (see also ***The Gumstool Inn*** below) – **26 rm** 170.00 – 225.00, 4 suites.
◆ Impressive Cotswold farmhouse with converted ancient barns and stables. Surrounded by meadows and gardens. Country house style lounge and very comfortable, beamed rooms. Stylish restaurant with weeping fig, lawn views.

The Gumstool Inn (at Calcot Manor H.), GL8 8YJ, ☎ (01666) 890391, *reception@calcotmanor.com, Fax (01666) 890394,* , – P. MC AE VISA
Rest (booking essential) a la carte 20.95/25.60 .
◆ Cheerful, flagstoned pub incorporated into Calcot Manor. Low ceiling creates atmosphere. Large menus with daily blackboard specials. Classic pub dishes.

TEWKESBURY *Glos.* 503 504 N 28 *Great Britain G. – pop. 9 978.*
See : *Town★ – Abbey★★ (Nave★★, vault★).*
Env. : *St Mary's, Deerhurst★, SW : 4 m. by A 38 and B 4213.*
Tewkesbury Park Hotel, Lincoln Green Lane ☎ (01684) 295405.
64 Barton St ☎ (01684) 295027.
London 108 – Birmingham 39 – Gloucester 11.

Jessop House without rest., 65 Church St, GL20 5RZ, ☎ (01684) 292017, *jessophousehotel@aol.com, Fax (01684) 273076* – P. MC AE VISA.
closed Christmas-New Year – **8 rm** 55.00/59.00 – 75.00/79.00.
◆ Grade II listed, three storey town house with restrained façade opposite Norman Abbey. Georgian origins. Velvet furnished bar. Simple, spacious, individually styled rooms.

Alstone Fields Farm without rest., Stow Rd, Teddington Hands, GL20 8NG, East : 5 m. by A 438 and A 46 on B 4077 ☎ (01242) 620592, *alstone.fields@freeuk.com,* , , – P.
closed 25 December – **6 rm** 45.00 – 60.00.
◆ Farmhouse in well-tended garden. Communal breakfast room with view; local ingredients and fruit from the garden. Bright, clean, chintzy rooms, two on the ground floor.

Evington Hill Farm without rest., Tewkesbury Rd, The Leigh, GL19 4AQ, South : 5 m. on A 38 ☎ (01242) 680255, *evingtonfarm@gmail.com,* , – P.
6 rm 55.00 – 90.00/100.00.
◆ Converted farmhouse with 16C origins and small conservatory extension. Set in four acres. Characterful, low beamed lounge with real fire. Antique and pine furnished rooms.

at Puckrup *North : 2½ m. by A 38 – ✉ Tewkesbury.*

Hilton Puckrup Hall, GL20 6EL, ☎ (01684) 296200, *events-tewkesbury@hilton.com, Fax (01684) 850788,* , , , , – , rest, P – 200. MC AE VISA
Rest *(closed Saturday lunch)* (buffet lunch)/dinner 22.95 and a la carte 25.85/34.85 – 13.95 – **110 rm** 75.00/140.00 – 75.00/140.00, 2 suites.
◆ Vast, modern hotel with emphasis on business traveller. 17C annex has the best rooms. Strong leisure facilities. Rooms in main hotel offer all that the business guest needs. Restaurant offers good views across golf course.

at Corse Lawn *Southwest : 6 m. by A 38 and A 438 on B 4211 – ✉ Gloucester.*

Corse Lawn House , GL19 4LZ, ☎ (01452) 780771, *enquiries@corselawn.com, Fax (01452) 780840,* , , – P – 40. MC AE VISA
closed 24-26 December – ***Bistro :*** Rest a la carte 16.40/34.85 **s.** – (see also ***The Restaurant*** below) – **17 rm** 87.50 – 135.00, 2 suites.
◆ Elegant Queen Anne Grade II listed house, set back from village green and fronted by former "coach wash". Two comfortable lounges and classic country house style rooms. Informal brasserie style eatery in atmospheric bar.

The Restaurant (at Corse Lawn House H.), GL19 4LZ, ☎ (01452) 780771, *Fax (01452) 780840,* – P. MC AE VISA
Rest 22.50/29.50 and a la carte 23.80/39.35 **s.** .
◆ Formal, L-shaped restaurant with period décor and framed prints. Traditional, robust food, extensive a la carte and set menu. Classic style of dishes.

THAME *Oxon.* 504 R 28 *Great Britain G. – pop. 10 886.*
Exc. : *Ridgeway Path★★.*
Market House, North St ☎ (01844) 212834.
London 48 – Aylesbury 9 – Oxford 13.

Spread Eagle, 16 Cornmarket, OX9 2BW, ☎ (01844) 213661, *enquiries@spreadeagle thame.co.uk, Fax (01844) 261380* – rest, P – 250. MC AE VISA.
Rest 20.45 and a la carte 25.85/34.00 – **31 rm** ★97.95/120.50 – ★★115.95/134.95 2 suites.
◆ Well established market town hotel. In use since 16C and host to writers and politicians over the years. Immaculate lounge bar. Pink and green rooms with antique pine. Informal relaxed restaurant.

The Old Trout with rm, 29-30 Lower High St, OX9 2AA, ☎ (01844) 212146, *info@theold trouthotel.co.uk, Fax (01844) 212614,* – P. MC AE VISA.
Rest a la carte 23.85/34.85 – **6 rm** ★55.00/75.00 – ★★75.00/105.00.
◆ Pair of characterful 16C thatched houses. Stone floor and beams. Elaborate dishes on lengthy, modern menus. Compact, interesting rooms with low ceilings and sloped floors.

THATCHAM *Newbury* 503 504 Q 29 – *pop. 22 989* – ✉ *Newbury.*
London 69 – Bristol 68 – Oxford 30 – Reading 15 – Southampton 40.

Premier Travel Inn, Bath Rd, Midgham, RG7 5UX, East : 2 m. on A 4 ☎ (0870) 7001498 *Fax (0870) 7001499,* – rm, P – 20. MC AE VISA.
Rest (grill rest.) – **49 rm** ★53.95/53.95 – ★★57.95/57.95.
◆ Purpose-built lodge on busy main road close to town centre. Convenient for visits to Reading and Newbury. Comfortable rooms with modern facilities. Adjacent restaurant specialising in grills.

THAXTED *Essex* 504 V 28 – *pop. 2 066.*
London 44 – Cambridge 24 – Colchester 31 – Chelmsford 20.

Crossways without rest., 32 Town St, CM6 2LA, ☎ (01371) 830348, *info@crosswaystha ted.co.uk,* – .
3 rm ★38.00 – ★★58.00.
◆ 16C house in picturesque, largely timbered village. Breakfast room is tea room during day. Small lounge with fireplace and beams. Rooms in keeping with age of property.

THIRSK *N. Yorks.* 502 P 21 – *pop. 9 099.*
Thornton-Le-Street ☎ (01845) 522170.
49 Market Pl ☎ (01845) 522755.
London 227 – Leeds 37 – Middlesbrough 24 – York 24.

Golden Fleece, 42 Market Pl, YO7 1LL, ☎ (01845) 523108, *reservations@goldenfleece hotel.com, Fax (01845) 523996* – P – 70. MC AE VISA
Rest (bar lunch Monday-Saturday)/dinner 17.50 and a la carte 13.45/23.20 – **23 rm** ★65.00 – ★★105.00.
◆ Sizeable Grade II listed 16C coaching inn located in centre of market town. Dick Turpin was a regular visitor. Spacious, comfortable lounge. Well-kept, inviting rooms. Yorkshire flavours are a staple of restaurant.

Spital Hill, York Rd, YO7 3AE, Southeast : 1 ¾ m. on A 19, entrance between 2 white posts ☎ (01845) 522273, *spitalhill@amserve.net, Fax (01845) 524970,* – P. MC AE VISA.
Rest (by arrangement) (communal dining) 28.00 – **3 rm** ★61.00/64.00 ★★82.00/98.00.
◆ Expansive early Victorian house surrounded by nearly two acres of secluded gardens. Fully tiled entrance hall and comfortable sitting room. Spacious rooms, warmly furnished. Communal dining at mealtimes.

Laburnum House without rest., 31 Topcliffe Rd, YO7 1RX, Southwest : ¾ m. by A 61 on Wetherby rd ☎ (01845) 524120, – P.
mid March-October – **3 rm** ★50.00 – ★★50.00.
◆ Modern house on the road into this busy market town, famous for its connection with vet and author James Herriot. Spacious, well-maintained bedrooms at affordable rates.

Oswalds with rm, Church Farm, Front St, Sowerby, YO7 1JF, South : ¾ m. by A 61 Wetherby rd on Sowerby Rd ☎ (01845) 523655, *bookings@oswaldsrestaurantwith rooms.co.uk, Fax (01845) 524720,* – P 22. MC VISA
closed 25 December and Monday lunch – **Rest** 12.00 (lunch) and a la carte 17.65/27.85
8 rm ★65.00 – ★★85.00.
◆ Collection of red-brick former farm buildings. Characterful rusticity prevails within both dining rooms. Traditionally based cooking with an old-fashioned feel. Comfy rooms.

at Topcliffe *Southwest : 4½ m. by A 168 – ✉ Thirsk.*

Angel Inn, Long St, YO7 3RW, ☎ (01845) 577237, *res@angelinn.co.uk, Fax (01845) 578000,* – rest, P – 150. MC AE VISA
Rest a la carte 23.00/30.25 ♀ – **15 rm** ☐ ★55.00/60.00 – ★★75.00.
◆ Enlarged hostelry dating back to early 17C in tiny village. Spacious lounge and character-ful bar. Popular with business travellers. Sizeable bedrooms have pine furniture. Bright décor enlivens dining room.

at Asenby *Southwest : 5¼ m. by A 168 – ✉ Thirsk.*

Crab Manor, Dishforth Rd, YO7 3QL, ☎ (01845) 577286, *info@crabandlobster.co.uk, Fax (01845) 577109,* – P. MC AE VISA.
Rest – (see ***Crab and Lobster*** below) – **14 rm** ☐ ★200.00 – ★★200.00, 2 suites.
◆ Part Georgian manor filled with quality objects and Victoriana. Highly individual bed-rooms, themed around world famous hotels. Some rooms have outdoor hot tubs.

Crab and Lobster, Dishforth Rd, YO7 3QL, ☎ (01845) 577286, *info@crabandlobster.co.uk, Fax (01845) 577109,* – P. MC AE VISA
Rest - Seafood - a la carte 25.00/50.00 ♀.
◆ Atmospheric and individual eating place filled with memorabilia. Choose the informal bar or formal Pavilion restaurant. Seafood oriented menus with blackboard specials.

The ✿ award is the crème de la crème. This is awarded to restaurants which are really worth travelling miles for!

THORNBURY *South Gloucestershire* 503 504 *M 29 – pop. 11 969 – ✉ Bristol.*
London 128 – Bristol 12 – Gloucester 23 – Swindon 43.

Thornbury Castle , Castle St, BS35 1HH, ☎ (01454) 281182, *info@thornburycastle.co.uk, Fax (01454) 416188,* – rest, P – 60. MC AE VISA
Rest 22.50/42.50 ♀ – **22 rm** ☐ ★80.00/110.00 – ★★375.00, 3 suites.
◆ 16C castle built by Henry VIII with gardens and vineyard. Two lounges boast plenty of antiques. Rooms of stately comfort; several bathrooms resplendent in marble. Restaurant exudes formal aura.

THORNHAM MAGNA *Suffolk* 504 *X 27 – ✉ Eye.*
London 96 – Cambridge 47 – Ipswich 20 – Norwich 30.

Thornham Hall , IP23 8HA, ☎ (01379) 783314, *lhenniker@aol.com, Fax (01379) 788347,* – P. MC AE VISA
Rest (by arrangement) (communal dining) 25.00 – **3 rm** ☐ ★55.00/80.00 – ★★90.00.
◆ 20C incarnation of former Tudor, Georgian and Victorian homes. House party atmos-phere. Lovely paintings throughout. Comfortable, welcoming rooms. Dining room of char-acter in converted coach house.

at Yaxley *West : 2 m. on A 140 – ✉ Eye.*

The Bull Auberge with rm, Ipswich Rd, IP23 8BZ, ☎ (01379) 783604, *Fax (01379) 788486* – P. MC AE VISA.
closed 25-26 December, Saturday lunch, Sunday, Monday and Bank Holidays – **Rest** (dinner only) a la carte 20.70/31.75 – **4 rm** ☐ ★60.00/80.00 – ★★80.00/100.00.
◆ 15C inn by busy road; rustic origins enhanced by brick walls, beams and open fire. Original, well presented, modern menus prepared with care. Cosy rooms are adjacent.

THORNTON *Lancs* 502 *K 22 –see Blackpool.*

THORNTON HOUGH *Mersey.* 502 503 *K 24 – ✉ Wirral.*
London 215 – Birkenhead 12 – Chester 17 – Liverpool 12.

Thornton Hall, CH63 1JF, on B 5136 ☎ (0151) 336 3938, *reservations@thorntonhallhotel.com, Fax (0151) 336 7864,* – rm, P – 200. MC AE VISA
The Italian Room : **Rest** (bar lunch Saturday) 9.95/28.50 and a la carte 31.40/41.95 **s.** ♀ – ☐ 13.50 – **62 rm** ★117.00 – ★★117.00, 1 suite.
◆ Family owned, extended manor house with lawned gardens in rural location. Atmos-pheric wood panelled lounges with heavy drapes. Excellent leisure club. Spacious bed-rooms. Rich, warmly decorated dining room with chandelier.

THORPE *Derbs.* 502 503 504 O 24 *Great Britain G.* – ✉ *Ashbourne.*
See : *Dovedale*★★ *(Ilam Rock*★*).*
London 151 – Birmingham 50 – Sheffield 33 – Stoke-on-Trent 26.

Peveril of the Peak , DE6 2AW, ✆ (01335) 350396, *frontdesk@peverilofthepeak.co.uk, Fax (01335) 350507,* ≤, , – ✆ P – 150. MC AE VISA
Rest 9.00/20.00 – **45 rm** ☐ ★65.00 – ★★130.00.
◆ Charming Peak District inn hotel at foot of Thorpe Cloud in Dovedale Valley. Set in its own farmland and country gardens. Rustic lounge. Rooms richly hued with heavy drapes. Local ingredients to fore in spacious dining room.

THORPE LANGTON *Leics. – see Market Harborough.*

THORPE MARKET *Norfolk* 504 X 25 – ✉ *North Walsham.*
London 130 – Norwich 21.

Elderton Lodge , Gunton Park, NR11 8TZ, South : 1 m. on A 149 ✆ (01263) 833547, *enquiries@eldertonlodge.co.uk, Fax (01263) 834673,* ≤, – ✆ P. MC AE VISA
Rest 15.00/27.00 – **11 rm** ☐ ★65.00 – ★★100.00/120.00.
◆ Late 18C former shooting lodge on large estate and deer park. Tranquil air. Favoured retreat of Lillie Langtry. Modern bedrooms are individually styled and comfortable. Local ingredients used widely in restaurant; particularly good value lunches.

THRELKELD *Cumbria* 502 K 20 – *see Keswick.*

THUNDER BRIDGE *W. Yorks. – see Huddersfield.*

THURROCK *Essex* 504 U 29 – *pop. 127 819.*
London 21 – Cambridge 60 – Dover 69 – Southend-on-Sea 20.

Premier Travel Inn, Stonehouse Lane, West Thurrock, RM19 1NS, on A 1090 at junction 31 of M 25 ✆ (0870) 9906490, *Fax (0870) 9906491* – , rm, P. MC AE VISA
Rest (grill rest.) – **161 rm** ★53.95/53.95 – ★★57.95/57.95.
◆ Close to Lakeside Shopping Centre and Brands Hatch with good motorway access and road links. Smart modern rooms with expansive, six feet wide beds in all rooms. Grill-style restaurant with popular menus.

THURSFORD GREEN *Norfolk.*
London 120 – Fakenham 7 – Norwich 29.

Holly Lodge without rest., The Street, NR21 0AS (01328) 878465, ✆ (01328) 878465, *info@hollylodgeguesthouse.co.uk,* – P.
closed January, February and October, minimum 2 night stay in summer – **3 rm** ☐ ★90.00/120.00 – ★★100.00/130.00.
◆ Stylishly furnished 18C house set in delightful garden. Welcome includes Pimms by the pond or afternoon tea. Excellent breakfast. Well appointed bedrooms in converted stables.

TICEHURST *E. Sussex* 504 V 30 – *pop. 3 118* – ✉ *Wadhurst.*
18, 18 *Dale Hill* ✆ *(01580) 200112.*
London 49 – Brighton 44 – Folkestone 38 – Hastings 15 – Maidstone 24.

King John's Lodge , Sheepstreet Lane, Etchingham, TN19 7AZ, South : 2 m. by Church St ✆ (01580) 819232, *kingjohnslodge@aol.com, Fax (01580) 819562,* ≤, heated, , – rm, P.
closed 25-26 December – **Rest** (by arrangement) (communal dining) 25.00 – **3 rm** ☐ ★45.00/50.00 – ★★80.00.
◆ Part Tudor hunting lodge with Jacobean additions and stunning gardens. King John imprisoned here in 1350. Cosy sitting rooms with log fire. Cottagey bedrooms. Communal dining room exudes great rustic charm.

TIRRIL *Cumbria – see Penrith.*

TITLEY *Herefordshire* 503 L 27 – *see Kington.*

TIVERTON *Devon* 503 J 31 – *pop. 16 772.*
London 191 – Bristol 64 – Exeter 15 – Plymouth 63.

Hornhill without rest., Exeter Hill, EX16 4PL, East : ½ m. by A 396 and Butterleigh rd (01884) 253352, *hornhill@tinyworld.co.uk, Fax (01884) 253352,* ←, , – P.
closed Christmas-New Year – **3 rm** ☐ ★32.00 – ★★55.00.
◆ Georgian house on hilltop boasting panoramic views of the Exe Valley. Well-furnished drawing room with real fire. Attractively styled bedrooms with antiques.

TODMORDEN *W. Yorks.* 502 N 22.
London 217 – Burnley 10 – Leeds 35 – Manchester 22.

The Old Hall, Hall St, OL14 7AD, off A 6033 (01706) 815998, *Fax (01706) 810669,* , – . VISA
closed 25 December, first week January, Sunday, Monday, lunch Tuesday-Wednesday and Saturday – **Rest** a la carte 21.95/27.40 ♀.
◆ Impressive example of an Elizabethan manor house. Three rooms in which to dine: one boasts a vast fireplace and period grandeur. Sound cooking with global twists.

TOOT BALDON *Oxon.* – *see Oxford.*

Good food without spending a fortune? Look out for the Bib Gourmand

TOPCLIFFE *N. Yorks.* 502 P 21 – *see Thirsk.*

TORQUAY *Torbay* 503 J 32 *The West Country G.* – *pop. 62 968.*
See : *Torbay★ – Kent's Cavern★* AC CX A.
Env. : *Paignton Zoo★★ AC, SE : 3 m. by A 3022 – Cockington★, W : 1 m.* AX.
18 *Petitor Rd, St Marychurch (01803) 327471,* CX.
Vaughan Parade, torquay.tic@torbay.gov.uk.
London 223 – Exeter 23 – Plymouth 32.

Plans on following pages

Imperial, Park Hill Rd, TQ1 2DG, (01803) 294301, *imperialtorquay@paramounthotels.co.uk, Fax (01803) 298293,* ← Torbay, , , , heated, , , , squash – , rest, , P – 350. AE VISA CZ a
Regatta : **Rest** (dinner only) 25.00/35.00 and a la carte 33.50/49.50 ♀ – ***TQ1 :*** **Rest** a la carte 32.50/39.50 ♀ – ☐ 12.50 – **134 rm** ★105.00/180.00 – ★★180.00, 17 suites.
◆ Landmark hotel is part of Torquay skyline. Clifftop position at end of bay. Palm Court lounge has classic style. Excellent leisure facilities. Rooms of top class comfort. Regatta's style emulates cruise liner luxury. TQ1 brasserie in conservatory.

Palace, Babbacombe Rd, TQ1 3TG, (01803) 200200, *info@palacetorquay.co.uk, Fax (01803) 299899,* ←, , , , heated, , 9, , , indoor/outdoor, squash – , P – 350. AE VISA. CX u
Rest (dinner only) 26.00 and a la carte 27.25/38.50 – **135 rm** ☐ ★65.00/90.00 – ★★160.00, 6 suites.
◆ Large, traditional hotel in 25 acres of gardens with sub-tropical woodland and charming terraces. Well-furnished lounge. Excellent leisure facilities. Comfortable rooms. Spacious restaurant exudes air of fine dining.

Grand, Sea Front, TQ2 6NT, (01803) 296677, *reservations@grandtorquay.co.uk, Fax (01803) 213462,* ←, , , heated, , – , – 300. AE VISA. BZ z
Rest (bar lunch Monday-Saturday)/dinner 27.95 – **123 rm** ☐ ★65.00/95.00 – ★★90.00/150.00, 7 suites.
◆ All-time classic seaside hotel with famously imposing blue and white exterior. Resident manicurist available. Riviera bar, sunny terrace, comfortable rooms. Resplendent restaurant with heavy drapes, crisp white tablecloths.

Osborne, Hesketh Crescent, Meadfoot, TQ1 2LL, (01803) 213311, *enq@osborne-torquay.co.uk, Fax (01803) 296788,* ←, , , , heated, , , – , rest, P – 80. AE VISA. CX n
Langtry's : **Rest** (dinner only) a la carte 19.70/29.50 – ***The Brasserie :*** **Rest** a la carte 13.20/19.40 ♀ – **32 rm** ☐ ★57.00/97.00 – ★★114.00/164.00.
◆ Smart hotel situated within elegant Regency crescent. Charming terrace and garden with views over Torbay. Well-appointed rooms: those facing sea have telescope and balcony. Langtry's has classic deep green décor. Informal Brasserie with terrace.

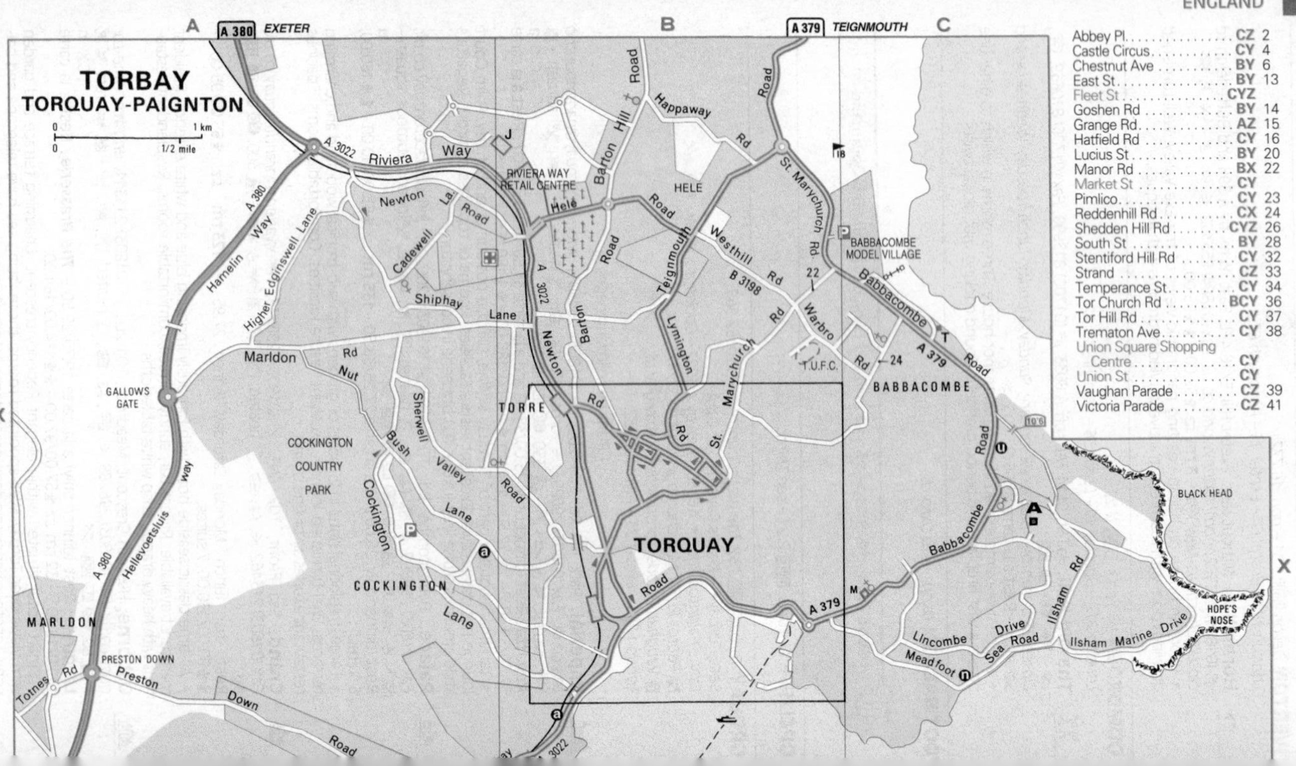
TORBAY
TORQUAY-PAIGNTON
0 1 km
0 1/2 mile
A 380 EXETER
A 379 TEIGNMOUTH
A
B
C
X
Abbey Pl. CZ 2
Castle Circus CY 4
Chestnut Ave BY 6
East St BY 13
Fleet St CYZ
Goshen Rd BY 14
Grange Rd AZ 15
Hatfield Rd CY 16
Lucius St BY 20
Manor Rd BX 22
Market St CY
Pimlico CY 23
Reddenhill Rd CX 24
Shedden Hill Rd CYZ 26
South St BY 28
Stentiford Hill Rd CY 32
Strand CZ 33
Temperance St CY 34
Tor Church Rd BCY 36
Tor Hill Rd CY 37
Trematon Ave CY 38
Union Square Shopping Centre CY
Union St CY
Vaughan Parade CZ 39
Victoria Parade CZ 41
TORQUAY
BABBACOMBE
BABBACOMBE MODEL VILLAGE
HELE
TORRE
COCKINGTON
COCKINGTON COUNTRY PARK
MARLDON
GALLOWS GATE
PRESTON DOWN
RIVIERA WAY RETAIL CENTRE
T.U.F.C.
BLACK HEAD
HOPE'S NOSE
Riviera Way
Hamelin Way
Hellevoetsluis Way
Higher Edginswell Lane
Newton Road
Cadewell La.
Shiphay Lane
Hele Road
Barton Hill Road
Happaway Rd
Barton Road
Teignmouth Road
Westhill Rd
B 3198
St. Marychurch Rd
Warbro Rd
Lymington Rd
St. Marychurch Rd
Babbacombe Road
Marldon Rd
Nut Rd
Sherwell Valley Road
Bush Cockington Lane
Cockington Lane
Lincombe Drive
Meadfoot Sea Road
Ilsham Rd
Ilsham Marine Drive
Totnes Rd
Preston Down Road
A 3022
A 379
A 380

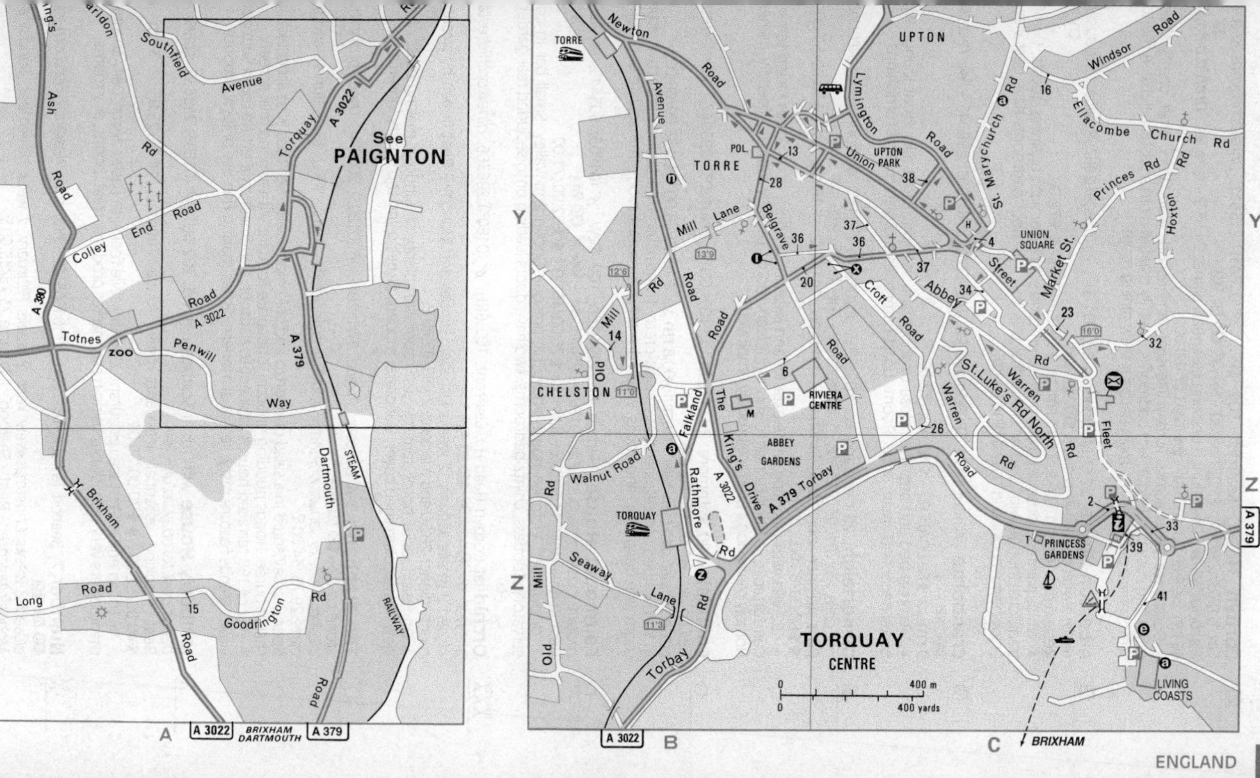
TORQUAY
CENTRE
See
PAIGNTON
UPTON
TORRE
CHELSTON
UPTON PARK
UNION SQUARE
RIVIERA CENTRE
ABBEY GARDENS
PRINCESS GARDENS
LIVING COASTS
Newton Road
Avenue
Lymington Road
Union
St. Marychurch Rd
Windsor Road
Ellacombe Church Rd
Princes Rd
Hoxton Rd
Market St.
Union Street
Abbey Road
Croft Road
Belgrave Road
Mill Lane
Old Mill Rd
Falkland Road
The King's Drive
A 3022
A 379 Torbay Road
Rathmore Rd
Walnut Road
Seaway Lane
Torbay Rd
St.Luke's Rd North
Warren Rd
Fleet
Southfield Avenue
Torquay Road
A 3022
Colley End Road
Totnes Road
ZOO
Penwill Way
A 379
Dartmouth Road
STEAM RAILWAY
Brixham Road
Long Road
Goodrington Rd
Ash Road
A 380
PLYMOUTH
A 385
BRIXHAM
DARTMOUTH
A 3022
A 379
400 m
400 yards
ENGLAND

ENGLAND

Corbyn Head, Seafront, TQ2 6RH, ☎ (01803) 213611, *info@corbynhead.cor*
Fax (01803) 296152, ≤, heated – ⇔ P. MC AE VISA BX
Harbour View*: Rest** (lunch booking essential)/dinner 24.95 ♀ – (see also ***Orchid below)
45 rm ☕ ★60.00/100.00 – ★★120.00/180.00.
• Boasts sea views across Torbay. Pleasant, enthusiastic staff. Very large, comfy sittir room and cosy bar. Bright, airy bedrooms, prettily created from a pastel palette. A friend atmosphere pervades the main Harbour View dining room.

Albaston House, 27 St Marychurch Rd, TQ1 3JF, ☎ (01803) 296758, *albastonhouseh tel@hotmail.com* – ⇔ rest, P. MC VISA. ✗ CY
Rest (dinner only) 15.00 **s.** ♀ – **13 rm** ☕ ★36.00/46.00 – ★★72.00.
• White painted house set away from town centre, popular with business guests. Comf traditional lounge with leather Chesterfields in bar. Top floor bedrooms have best view Enjoy home cooking in cosy dining room.

Cranborne without rest., 58 Belgrave Rd, TQ2 5HY, ☎ (01803) 298046 – ⇔ rest. M VISA. ✗ BY
9 rm ☕ ★60.00/65.00 – ★★60.00/72.00.
• Victorian bed and breakfast close to shops and seafront. Light, airy front lounge wi pastel décor and cream sofas. Rooms boast bathrobes and tasteful soft furnishings.

Glenorleigh, 26 Cleveland Rd, TQ2 5BE, ☎ (01803) 292135, *glenorleighhotel@btint net.com, Fax (01803) 213717*, heated, – ⇔ P. MC VISA. ✗ BY
Rest (dinner only and lunch in summer) 14.00 **s.** – **15 rm** ☕ ★30.00/50.00 ★★60.00/80.00.
• 19C villa with gleaming white exterior and pleasant outdoor pool. South facing terrac Comfortable, leather furnished lounge. Clean rooms proudly kept by friendly owner Homely meals; local produce proudly employed.

Colindale, 20 Rathmore Rd, Chelston, TQ2 6NY, ☎ (01803) 293947, *bronte@eu bell.co.uk* – ⇔ P. MC AE VISA. ✗ BZ
closed Christmas-New Year – **Rest** 15.00 **8 rm** ☕ ★29.00/45.00 – ★★58.00/68.00.
• Yellow hued 19C terraced house with pretty front garden. Particularly attractive sittir room with deep sofas and books. Welsh dresser in breakfast room. Immaculate bedroom

Fairmount House, Herbert Rd, Chelston, TQ2 6RW, ☎ (01803) 605446, *stay@f mounthousehotel.co.uk, Fax (01803) 605446*, – ⇔ P. MC VISA AX
Rest (dinner only) 13.50 **s.** ♀ – **8 rm** ☕ ★26.00/43.00 – ★★52.00/71.00.
• Yellow-hued Victorian house above picturesque Cockington Valley. Small bar in co servatory. Spotless, chintz bedrooms: two have doors leading onto secluded rear garden

Orchid (at Corbyn Head H.), Seafront, TQ2 6RH, ☎ (01803) 296366, *dine@orchidresta ant.net*, ≤ – ⇔ ▤ P. MC AE VISA BX
closed 2 weeks January, 2 weeks October, Sunday and Monday – **Rest** (lunch by arrang ment)/dinner 28.50 and a la carte 29.85/42.40 ♀.
• On first floor of hotel: semi-circular room with plenty of windows making most of s view. Immaculate linen cover. Elaborate, modern dishes using top quality ingredients.

The Elephant, 3-4 Beacon Terrace, TQ1 2BH, ☎ (01803) 200044, *theelephant@c stone.co.uk* – MC AE VISA CZ
closed 2 weeks January, Sunday and Tuesday October-April – **Rest** 16.75 (lunch) and a carte 29.75/34.00 ♀.
Spec. Torbay squid in a salad of chorizo and chilli marmalade. Sea bass with artichoke a shallot purée, Hoggs pudding gnocchi. Chocolate fondant with almond milk sorbet.
• Pair of 19C terraced houses adjacent to harbour. Bohemian style sitting room with goo views. Menus feature tasty, seasonal modern dishes making fine use of local produce.

Mulberry House with rm, 1 Scarborough Rd, TQ2 5UJ, ☎ (01803) 213639, *stay@m berryhousetorquay.co.uk* – ⇔ CY
Rest (booking essential) (residents only Monday-Tuesday) 14.95/25.95 – **3 rm** ★40.00/52.00 – ★★70.00/80.00.
• Victorian end-of-terrace restaurant. Country style feel with pastel décor. Daily changir menu offers very tasty dishes using fresh market produce. Neat, bright, airy rooms.

Number 7, Beacon Terrace, TQ1 2BH, ☎ (01803) 295055, *enquiries@no7-fish.com* – MC AE VISA CZ
closed 2 weeks Christmas-New Year, 2 weeks February, 1 week November, Sunday a Monday in winter – **Rest** - Seafood - a la carte 23.75/33.00 ♀.
• On harbour front in centre of town: modest, friendly, family run restaurant specialisir in simply prepared fresh fish, mostly from Brixham. Fishing themes enhance ambience.

at Maidencombe *North : 3½ m. by A 379 – BX – ✉ Torquay.*

Orestone Manor, Rockhouse Lane, TQ1 4SX, ☎ (01803) 328098, *enquiries@orestonemanor.com, Fax (01803) 328336*, ≤, heated, – rest, P. MC AE VISA
Rest 17.95 (lunch) and a la carte 32.95/45.25 ♀ – **12 rm** ☐ ★89.00/109.00 – ★★135.00/170.00.
Spec. Tian of crab and avocado, tomato vinaigrette. Breast of duck with confit duck croquettes, rocket and parmesan. Assiette of peach and apricot.
◆ Yellow painted, country house hotel in wooded location. Terrace overlooks mature gardens. Conservatory exudes exotic charm. Individual rooms. Spacious dining room: stylish, inspired cooking with strong use of seasonal produce from the kitchen garden.

TORTWORTH *South Glos.* 503 M 29.
London 128 – Bristol 19 – Stroud 18.

Tortworth Court, Wotton-under-Edge, GL12 8HH, ☎ (01454) 263000, *tortworth@fourpillars.co.uk, Fax (01454) 263001*, – P – 400. MC AE VISA.
Moretons : Rest *(closed Saturday lunch)* (carvery lunch) 25.95 **s.** ♀ – ***Orangery :*** Rest *(closed Sunday dinner and Monday)* a la carte 17.25/24.20 **s.** ♀ – **188 rm** ☐ ★69.00/139.00 – ★★139.00/159.00, 1 suite.
◆ 19C hotel built in the Gothic style with arboretum and sculptured gardens. Country house lounges abound. Glass ceilinged atrium bar. Comfy rooms with lovely views. Inspiring outlook to lake from Moretons. Superbly restored stand-alone Orangery in the grounds.

TORVER *Cumbria* 502 K 20 – *see Coniston.*

TOTLAND *I.O.W.* 503 504 P 31 – *see Wight (Isle of).*

TOTLEY *S. Yorks.* 502 503 504 P 24 – *see Sheffield.*

TOTNES *Devon* 503 I 32 *The West Country G. – pop. 7 929.*
See : *Town★ – Elizabethan Museum★ – St Mary's★ – Butterwalk★ – Castle (≤★★★) AC.*
Env. : *Paignton Zoo★★ AC, E : 4½ m. by A 385 and A 3022 – British Photographic Museum, Bowden House★ AC, S : 1 m. by A 381 – Dartington Hall (High Cross House★), NW : 2 m. on A 385 and A 384.*
Exc. : *Dartmouth★★ (Castle ≤★★★) SE : 12 m. by A 381 and A 3122.*
18, 9 *Dartmouth G & C.C., Blackawton ☎ (01803) 712686.*
The Town Mill, Coronation Rd ☎ (01803) 863168.
London 224 – Exeter 24 – Plymouth 23 – Torquay 9.

XX **Wills,** 2-3 The Plains, TQ9 5DR, ☎ (01803) 865192, *philsil@btconnect.com* – MC AE VISA
closed 25 December, 1 January, Sunday and Monday – **Rest** (dinner only) a la carte 19.30/37.85 ♀.
◆ Smart Regency townhouse restaurant, named after local explorer William Wills. Bold Georgian décor and antique chairs for dining. Classic cuisine from the Gallic repertoire.

at Stoke Gabriel *Southeast : 4 m. by A 385 – ✉ Totnes.*

Gabriel Court, Stoke Hill, TQ9 6SF, ☎ (01803) 782206, *reservations@gabrielcourthotel.co.uk, Fax (01803) 782333*, heated, – P. MC AE VISA
Rest 12.50/28.50 and dinner a la carte 23.70/37.95 – **16 rm** ☐ ★73.00 – ★★175.00.
◆ 15C manor house in terraced Elizabethan garden with yew, box and magnolia. Tranquil setting. Swim in the pool or relax in the welcoming lounge. Country house rooms. Ornate dining room using fruit and vegetables from garden.

TOWCESTER *Northants.* 503 504 R 27 – *pop. 8 073.*
18, 18 *Whittelbury Park G. & C.C., Whittlebury ☎ (01327) 858092 –* 18 *Farthingstone Hotel, Farthingstone ☎ (01327) 361291.*
London 70 – Birmingham 50 – Northampton 9 – Oxford 36.

at Paulerspury *Southeast : 3¼ m. by A 5 – ✉ Towcester.*

XX **Vine House,** 100 High St, NN12 7NA, ☎ (01327) 811267, *info@vinehousehotel.com, Fax (01327) 811309*, – P. MC VISA.
closed lunch Monday and Sunday – **Rest** 29.95.
◆ Converted 17C stone building with cottage garden in old village. Pleasantly rustic sitting room, bar with log fire. Quality cooking with traditional base.

TRAFFORD CENTRE *Gtr Manchester – see Manchester.*

TRAFFORD PARK *Gtr Manchester – see Manchester.*

TREFONEN *Shrops.* 502 503 K 25 – *see Oswestry.*

TREGREHAN *Cornwall* 503 F 32 – *see St Austell.*

TRELOWARREN *Cornwall – see Helston.*

TRESCO *Cornwall* 503 B 34 – *see Scilly (Isles of).*

TRING *Herts.* 504 S 28 – *pop. 11 835.*
London 38 – Aylesbury 7 – Luton 14 – Oxford 31.

Pendley Manor, Cow Lane, HP23 5QY, East : 1½ m. by B 4635 off B 4251 ☎ (01442 891891, *info@pendley-manor.co.uk, Fax (01442) 890687,* ≤, ⅃, ≘, ⊡, ⇁, ♔, ✗ – ⅠⅠ ⇹ rest, ♿, P – ⛺ 350. MC AE ◑ VISA
Rest 25.00/35.00 and a la carte 26.00/37.00 s. – **73 rm** ⊏ ☦90.00/110.00 ☦☦90.00/150.00.
◆ Attractive manor house in 35 acres of parkland. Good outdoor leisure facilities. Charm ing, wicker furnished lounge in the modern conservatory. Spacious, functional room Smart, comfy air pervades dining room.

Premier Travel Inn, Tring Hill, HP23 4LD, West : 1½ m. by A 41 on B 4009 ☎ (087 1977254, *Fax (01442) 890787* – ⇹ rm, ▤ rest, ♿, P. MC AE ◑ VISA. ✗
Rest (grill rest.) – **30 rm** ☦46.95/46.95 – ☦☦50.95/50.95.
◆ Simply furnished and brightly decorated bedrooms with ample work space. Located i position off busy main road. A useful address for cost-conscious travellers.

TRINITY *Jersey (Channel Islands)* 503 P 33 and 517 ⑪ – *see Channel Islands.*

TRISCOMBE *Somerset* 503 K 30 – *see Taunton.*

TROUTBECK *Cumbria* 502 L 20 – *see Windermere.*

TROWBRIDGE *Wilts.* 503 504 N 30 *The West Country G. – pop. 34 401.*
Env. : *Westwood Manor★, NW : 3 m. by A 363 – Farleigh Hungerford★ (St Leonard's Chap el★) AC, W : 4 m.*
Exc. : *Longleat House★★★ AC, SW : 12 m. by A 363, A 350 and A 362 - Bratton Castle (≤★★ SE : 7½ m. by A 363 and B 3098 – Steeple Ashton★ (The Green★) E : 6 m. – Edington (Mary, St Katherine and All Saints★) SE : 7½ m.*
🅘 *St Stephen's Pl ☎ (01225) 777054, visittrowbridge@westwiltshire.gov.uk.*
London 115 – Bristol 27 – Southampton 55 – Swindon 32.

Old Manor, Trowle Common, BA14 9BL, Northwest : 1 m. on A 363 ☎ (01225) 77739 *romanticbeds@oldmanorhotel.com, Fax (01225) 765443,* ⇁ – ⇹ ♿ P. MC AE VISA
closed 23-30 December – **Rest** *(closed Sunday dinner)* (dinner only and Sunday lunch) 21.0 – **19 rm** ⊏ ☦70.00 – ☦☦130.00.
◆ Attractive Grade II listed Queen Anne house with 15C origins. Lovely gardens and plea ant lounges: wealth of beams adds to charm. Most bedrooms - some four poster - annex. Spacious restaurant with welcoming ambience.

Red or White, Evolution House, 46 Castle St, BA14 8AY, ☎ (01225) 781666, *info@red white.biz, Fax (01225) 776505* – ⇹ ▤ P ⟡ 25. MC VISA
closed Sunday and Bank Holidays – **Rest** a la carte 18.00/29.00 ♀ ❀.
◆ Modern personally-run restaurant at the rear of wine shop where you choose what t drink with your meal. Seasonal food cooked with flair; good value for lunch.

at Semington *Northeast : 2½ m. by A 361 – ✉ Trowbridge.*

The Lamb on the Strand, 99 The Strand, BA14 6LL, East : 1½ m. on A 361 ☎ (0138 870263, *Fax (01380) 871203,* ⛱, ⇁ – ⇹ P. MC AE VISA
closed 25-26 December and Sunday dinner – **Rest** (booking essential) a la car 15.50/19.50 ♀.
◆ Attractive ivy-clad pub with 18C origins. Spacious bar affords plenty of seating whi dining area has exposed bricks and tasty, original dishes on blackboard menu.

RUMPET *Herefordshire – see Ledbury.*

RURO *Cornwall 503 E 33 The West Country G. – pop. 20 920.*
See : *Royal Cornwall Museum★★ AC.*
Env. : *Trelissick Garden★★ (≤★★) AC, S : 4 m. by A 39 – Feock (Church★) S : 5 m. by A 39 and B 3289.*
Exc. : *Trewithen★★★, NE : 7½ m. by A 39 and A 390 – Probus★ (tower★ - garden★) NE : 9 m. by A 39 and A 390.*
Treliske ☎ (01872) 272640 – Killiow Park, Killiow, Kea ☎ (01872) 270246.
Municipal Buildings, Boscawen St ☎ (01872) 274555.
London 295 – Exeter 87 – Penzance 26 – Plymouth 52.

Royal, Lemon St, TR1 2QB, ☎ (01872) 270345, *reception@royalhotelcornwall.co.uk, Fax (01872) 242453* – ⇔ ♿ P. MO AE ① VISA. ✗
closed 4 days Christmas – ***Mannings :*** **Rest** *(closed Sunday lunch)* a la carte 17.25/32.00 ♀ – **26 rm** ☐ ★65.00/85.00 – ★★100.00, 9 suites.
◆ The name came after Prince Albert stayed in 1846: the Royal Arms stands proudly above the entrance. Comfortable, stylish lounges; modern bedrooms. Cuisine with global influences.

Saffron, 5 Quay St, TR1 2HB, ☎ (01872) 263771, *saffronrestaurant@btconnect.com* – ⇔. MO VISA
closed 25-26 December, Bank Holidays, Sunday and Monday dinner in winter – **Rest** a la carte 24.00/31.00 ♀.
◆ Bright exterior with colourful hanging baskets and attractive brightly coloured interior with a rustic tone. Varied Cornish menus to be enjoyed at any hour of the day.

Carnon Downs *Southwest : 3¼ m. by A 39 – ✉ Truro.*

Premier Travel Inn, Old Carnon Hill, TR3 6JT, ☎ (0870) 1977255, *Fax (01872) 865620,* – ⇔, ▤ rest, ♿ P. MO AE ① VISA. ✗
Rest (grill rest.) – **62 rm** ★52.95 – ★★52.95.
◆ Well-proportioned modern bedrooms, suitable for family and business stopovers, designed with price in mind. Useful for visitors moving on to visit the Eden Project.

UNBRIDGE WELLS *Kent 504 U 30 – see Royal Tunbridge Wells.*

UNSTALL *Cumbria – see Kirkby Lonsdale.*

URNERS HILL *W. Sussex 504 T 30 – pop. 1 534.*
London 33 – Brighton 24 – Crawley 7.

Alexander House ⛭, East St, RH10 4QD, East : 1 m. on B 2110 ☎ (01342) 714914, *info@alexanderhouse.co.uk, Fax (01342) 717328,* ≤, ⛭, ⛭, ✂ – |‡|, ⇔ rest, ☎ P – 🏛 120. MO AE ① VISA. ✗
Rest (booking essential to non-residents) 17.50/39.50 and a la carte 49.50 – ☐ 15.00 – **14 rm** ★125.00/145.00 – ★★155.00, 4 suites.
◆ Set in extensive gardens, a stunning, classically comfortable country house, once owned by the family of poet Percy Shelley. Luxuriously appointed rooms in rich chintz. Sumptuous dining room.

URVILLE *Bucks. – ✉ Henley-on-Thames.*
London 45 – Oxford 22 – Reading 17.

Bull & Butcher, RG9 6QU, ☎ (01491) 638283, *info@thebullandbutcher.com, Fax (01491) 638836,* ⛭ – ⇔ P. MO VISA
Rest a la carte 23.00/27.00 ♀.
◆ Small pub in charming 'Vicar of Dibley' village. Flagstone flooring, log fires and scrubbed pine. Slightly different modern and traditional menus served in all dining areas.

We try to be as accurate as possible when giving room rates. But prices are susceptible to change, so please check rates when booking.

TWO BRIDGES *Devon* 503 I 32 *The West Country G.* – ✉ *Yelverton.*
Env. : *Dartmoor National Park*★★.
London 226 – Exeter 25 – Plymouth 17.

Prince Hall ⛰, PL20 6SA, East : 1 m. on B 3357 ☎ (01822) 890403, *info@prin hall.co.uk, Fax (01822) 890676*, ≤, ⛰, ⛰ – ⛰ P. MO AE VISA
closed 2 January-12 February – **Rest** (booking essential to non-residents) (dinner or 40.00 and a la carte 23.70/35.40 s. – **9 rm** (dinner included) ⛰ ★85.00/135.00 ★★200.00/230.00.
◆ Unique 18C country house set alone in heart of Dartmoor. Magnificent view over W Dart River to rolling hills. Exposed beams add character to individually styled rooms. Lo dishes and open log fire in rustic restaurant.

TYNEMOUTH *Tyne and Wear* 501 502 P 18 – *pop. 17 056.*
London 290 – Newcastle upon Tyne 8 – Sunderland 7.

Grand, Grand Parade, NE30 4ER, ☎ (0191) 293 6666, *info@grandhotel-uk.co Fax (0191) 293 6665*, ≤ – |≑|, ⛰ rest, P – ⛰ 130. MO AE O VISA. ⛰
Rest *(closed Sunday dinner)* 13.00/23.00 and a la carte 25.95/32.00 – **45 rm** ⛰ ★65.0 ★★160.00.
◆ Impressive Victorian hotel built as home for Duchess of Northumberland. Commandi views over coastline. Atmospheric lounges and bars. Well-equipped rooms with fine view Classical dining room with imposing drapes, floral displays and ceiling cornices.

Martineau Guest House without rest., 57 Front St, NE30 4BX, ☎ (0191) 296 07 *martineau.house@ukgateway.net*, ⛰ – ⛰. ⛰
3 rm ⛰ ★45.00/55.00 – ★★65.00.
◆ 18C Georgian stone terraced house in main street, named after Harriet Martinea Breakfast in open plan kitchen. Homely spacious individually styled rooms, two with view

Sidney's, 3-5 Percy Park Rd, NE30 4LZ, ☎ (0191) 257 8500, *bookings@sidneys.co. Fax (0191) 257 9800* – ⛰. MO AE VISA
closed 25-26 December and Sunday – **Rest** (booking essential) 12.00 (lunch) and a la car 20.00/31.00 ♀.
◆ Fine painted, wood floored, busy little restaurant with two dining areas. The mode British cooking is interesting with plenty of variety and choice.

UCKFIELD *E. Sussex* 504 U 31 – *pop. 15 374.*
London 45 – Brighton 17 – Eastbourne 20 – Maidstone 34.

Horsted Place ⛰, Little Horsted, TN22 5TS, South : 2½ m. by B 2102 and A 22 on A ☎ (01825) 750581, *hotel@horstedplace.co.uk, Fax (01825) 750459*, ≤, ⛰, ⛰18, ⛰, ⛰, ⛰ |≑|, ⛰ rest, P – ⛰ 80. MO AE O VISA. ⛰
closed first week January – **Rest** *(closed Saturday lunch)* 18.95 (lunch) and a la car 32.10/40.00 ♀ – **15 rm** ⛰ ★165.00 – ★★165.00, 5 suites.
◆ Imposing country house from the height of the Victorian Gothic revival; handsor Pugin-inspired drawing rooms and luxurious bedrooms overlook formal gardens and pa land. Pristine restaurant with tall 19C archways and windows.

Buxted Park ⛰, Buxted, TN22 4AY, Northeast : 2 m. on A 272 ☎ (01825) 7333 *buxtedpark@handpicked.co.uk, Fax (01825) 732770*, ≤, ⛰, ⛰, ⛰, ⛰, ⛰, ⛰ – ⛰ P – ⛰ 130. MO AE O VISA
Orangery : **Rest** *(closed Saturday lunch)* 16.95/35.00 and a la carte approx 38.50 s. – **43 r** ⛰ ★60.00/140.00 – ★★60.00/180.00, 1 suite.
◆ 18C Palladian mansion in 300 acres with ornate public areas exuding much char spacious, period lounges. Rooms, modern in style, in original house or garden wing. Bea tiful all-glass Orangery restaurant with large terrace.

UFFINGTON *Oxon.* 503 504 P 29.
London 75 – Oxford 29 – Reading 32 – Swindon 17.

Craven ⛰, Fernham Rd, SN7 7RD, ☎ (01367) 820449, *carol@thecraven.co. Fax (01367) 820351*, ⛰ – ⛰ P. MO O VISA. ⛰
Rest (by arrangement) (communal dining) 27.00 – **5 rm** ⛰ ★50.00/55.00 ★★75.00/95.00.
◆ 17C thatched hostelry; some rooms in brewhouse, stables. Quaint features: windi passageways, antique weighing machine in bathroom, four-poster with Victorian pillo slips. Dine in huge scarlet-walled kitchen with pretty china on dresser.

LLINGSWICK *Herefordshire* 503 504 M 27 – ✉ *Hereford.*
London 134 – Hereford 12 – Shrewsbury 52 – Worcester 19.

Three Crowns Inn, Bleak Acre, HR1 3JQ, East : 1 ¼ m. ☎ (01432) 820279, *info@threecrownsinn.com, Fax (01432) 820911,* – P. MC VISA.
closed 2 weeks Christmas and Monday – **Rest** a la carte 16.75/24.75 ♀.
◆ Pleasant part-timbered pub on a quiet country road: hops hang from the beams. Eclectic assortment of benches and pews. Rustic, robust dishes on daily changing menus.

LLSWATER *Cumbria* 502 L 20 – ✉ *Penrith.*
Main Car Park, Glenridding, Penrith ☎ (017684) 82414.
London 296 – Carlisle 25 – Kendal 31 – Penrith 6.

Pooley Bridge *on B 5320* – ✉ *Penrith.*

Sharrow Bay Country House, CA10 2LZ, South : 2 m. on Howtown rd ☎ (017684) 86301, *info@sharrowbay.co.uk, Fax (017684) 86349,* ≤ Ullswater and fells, – , rest, P. MC AE VISA.
Rest (booking essential) 39.50/52.50 ♀ – **20 rm** (dinner included) ☕ ★128.00/210.00 – ★★336.00/420.00, 4 suites.
Spec. Seared foie gras with sweetbread, black pudding and glazed apple. Best end and braised shoulder of lamb with black olive and basil crust. Goat's cheese cheesecake with blueberries.
◆ Quintessential country house on the shores of Ullswater: marvellous lake views. Traditional rooms, some in grounds and formal gardens, retain a charming, very English feel. Antique-filled restaurant plus tables overlooking the water. Refined classical cooking.

Watermillock *on A 592* – ✉ *Penrith.*

Rampsbeck Country House, CA11 0LP, ☎ (017684) 86442, *enquiries@rampsbeck.fsnet.co.uk, Fax (017684) 86688,* ≤ Ullswater and fells, – rest, P. MC VISA
closed early January-mid February – **Rest** – (see ***The Restaurant*** below) – **18 rm** ☕ ★75.00/125.00 – ★★140.00/250.00, 1 suite.
◆ Classically proportioned 18C country house with attractive terraced gardens and spectacular views across Lake Ullswater; some rooms have balconies to make the most of this.

Leeming House, CA11 0JJ, on A 592 ☎ (017684) 86622, *leeminghouse@macdonald-hotels.co.uk, Fax (017684) 86443,* ≤, – P – 35. MC AE VISA
Regency : **Rest** (dinner only) 34.00 ♀ – **41 rm** ☕ ★140.00/170.00 – ★★180.00/240.00.
◆ Built as private residence in 19C for local family; in stepped gardens leading down to Lake Ullswater. A rural retreat with croquet lawn; appropriately styled country rooms. Georgian dining room brightened by mirrors and chandelier.

Old Church, CA11 0JN, ☎ (017684) 86204, *info@oldchurch.co.uk, Fax (017684) 86368,* ≤ Ullswater and fells, – P. MC AE VISA.
March-October – **Rest** *(closed Sunday)* (booking essential) (dinner only) 30.00 **s.** – **10 rm** ☕ ★75.00/79.00 – ★★95.00/180.00.
◆ Beautifully located Georgian house looks out on austere fells the shores of Ullswater. Charming, traditionally appointed lounge and cosy rooms in tasteful fabrics. Polished wood tables and simple, locally sourced cooking in the dining room.

The Restaurant (at Rampsbeck Country House H.), CA11 0LP, ☎ (017684) 86442, *Fax (017684) 86688,* ≤ Ullswater and fells, – P. MC VISA
closed early January-mid February – **Rest** (booking essential) (lunch by arrangement Monday-Saturday)/dinner 39.00/44.50.
◆ Choose from classic staples - salmon and spinach - to more creative options - beef fillet with roast veal sweetbreads, kumquat soufflé. Savour the flavour; admire the view.

Brackenrigg Inn with rm, CA11 0LP, ☎ (017684) 86206, *enquiries@brackenrigginn.co.uk, Fax (017684) 86945,* ≤ Ullswater and fells, – P. MC VISA
Rest a la carte 16.85/24.95 ♀ – **17 rm** ☕ ★33.00/38.00 – ★★56.00/99.00.
◆ 18C coaching inn in prime position overlooking lake and fells. Tasty, traditional cooking served in the bar or the restaurant. Fine selection of ales. Cosy rooms.

Glenridding *on A 592* – ✉ *Penrith.*

The Inn on the Lake, CA11 0PE, ☎ (017684) 82444, *info@innonthelakeullswater.co.uk, Fax (017684) 82303,* ≤ Ullswater and fells, – P – 50. MC AE VISA
Rest *(closed Saturday lunch)* 15.95/31.95 **s.** ♀ – **46 rm** (dinner included) ☕ ★91.00 – ★★168.00.
◆ This busy Lakeland hotel on the shores of Ullswater is popular with families. Pleasant terrace. Sizeable bedrooms, most with grand views. Ramblers Bar pub. Restaurant takes in lovely vistas of lake and fells.

ULVERSTON *Cumbria 502 K 21 – pop. 11 210.*

Coronation Hall, County Sq ☎ (01229) 587120.
London 278 – Kendal 25 – Lancaster 36.

Church Walk House without rest., Church Walk, LA12 7EW, ☎ (01229) 58221 *churchwalk@mchadderton.freeserve.co.uk* –
closed 2 weeks Christmas – **3 rm** ☕ ★25.00/35.00 – ★★60.00.
• Converted, privately owned Georgian town house; bedrooms and sitting room alike a spacious and comfortably furnished. A short walk from the Laurel and Hardy Museum.

Bay Horse with rm, Canal Foot, LA12 9EL, East : 2 ¼ m. by A 5087, turning left Morecambe Tavern B&B and beyond Industrial area, on the coast ☎ (01229) 583972, *res vations@thebayhorsehotel.co.uk, Fax (01229) 580502,* ≤ Morecambe bay – rest, P. AE VISA
Rest *(closed Monday lunch)* (booking essential) 29.00 (dinner) and a la carte 27.20/38.95 **9 rm** ☕ ★80.00 – ★★90.00/110.00.
• Well-established inn by Ulverston Sands. Smart conservatory, flavourful seasonal me and friendly staff. Cosy rooms, some equipped with binoculars and birdwatching guides

UPPER HARBLEDOWN SERVICE AREA *Kent – see Canterbury.*

UPPER ODDINGTON *Glos. – see Stow-on-the-Wold.*

UPPER QUINTON *Warks. – ✉ Stratford-upon-Avon.*

London 95 – Cheltenham 24 – Oxford 43 – Stratford-upon-Avon 6.

Winton House without rest., The Green, CV37 8SX, ☎ (01789) 720500, *gail@wint house.com,* – P.
3 rm ☕ ★75.00 – ★★75.00.
• 1856 brick farmhouse, half hidden by ivy and a row of evergreens. Antique pine, parqu floors and individually styled rooms. Tasty breakfast: home-made jam, orchard fruits.

UPPINGHAM *Rutland 504 R 26 – pop. 3 947.*

London 101 – Leicester 19 – Northampton 28 – Nottingham 35.

Lake Isle with rm, 16 High St East, LE15 9PZ, ☎ (01572) 822951, *info@lakeislehotel.co Fax (01572) 824400* – rest, P. MO AE VISA
Rest *(closed Sunday dinner and Monday lunch)* a la carte 19.95/27.70 – **10 rm** ☕ ★60. – ★★100.00, 2 suites.
• Converted 18C shop; old scales, pine dresser and tables. Simple, well-judged seasor menu, fine half-bottle cellar. Rooms in pretty cottage style, named after wine regions.

at Lyddington *South : 2 m. by A 6003 – ✉ Uppingham.*

Old White Hart with rm, 51 Main St, LE15 9LR, ☎ (01572) 821703, *mail@oldwh hart.co.uk, Fax (01572) 821965,* – rest, P. MO VISA.
closed 25 December – **Rest** *(closed Sunday dinner)* 12.95 (lunch) and a la carte 18.00/38. – **5 rm** ☕ ★55.00/60.00 – ★★80.00/85.00.
• Very pleasant 17C pub in pretty village; rural memorabilia within and huge petanq court without. Tasty, carefully prepared dishes. Welcoming rooms with a country feel.

UPTON SCUDAMORE *Wilts. 503 N 30 – see Warminster.*

UPTON-UPON-SEVERN *Worcs. 503 504 N 27 – pop. 1 789.*

4 High St ☎ (01684) 594200, upton.tic@malvernhills.gov.uk.
London 116 – Hereford 25 – Stratford-upon-Avon 29 – Worcester 11.

Tiltridge Farm and Vineyard without rest., Upper Hook Rd, WR8 0SA, Wes 1 ½ m. by A 4104 and Greenfields Rd following B&B signs ☎ (01684) 592906, *info@ tridge.com, Fax (01684) 594142,* – P. MO VISA
closed 24 December-1 January – **3 rm** ☕ ★40.00 – ★★60.00.
• Extended 17C farmhouse at the entrance to a small vineyard. Homely lounge, domin ted by a broad inglenook fireplace, and spacious bedrooms, one with original timbers.

at Hanley Swan *Northwest : 3 m. by B 4211 on B 4209 – ✉ Upton-upon-Severn.*

Yew Tree House without rest., WR8 0DN, ☎ (01684) 310736, *info@yewtr house.co.uk, Fax (01684) 311709,* – P. MO VISA.
3 rm ☕ ★45.00 – ★★70.00.
• Imposing cream coloured Georgian guesthouse, built in 1780, in centre of pleasa village. One mile from Three Counties Showground. Cosy lounge; individually styled room

TTOXETER *Staffs.* 503 504 O 25 – *pop. 12 023.*
London 150 – Birmingham 41 – Stafford 16.

t Beamhurst *Northwest : 3 m. on A 522 –* ✉ *Uttoxeter.*

Gilmore at Strine's Farm, ST14 5DZ, ☎ (01889) 507100, *paul@restaurantgilmore.com, Fax (01889) 507238,* – P. MC AE VISA
closed 1 week January, 1 week Easter, 2 weeks August, Monday, Tuesday, Saturday lunch and Sunday dinner – **Rest** (booking essential) 16.50/29.50.
◆ Personally run converted farmhouse in classic rural setting. Three separate, beamed, cottage style dining rooms. New approach to classic dishes: fine local ingredients used.

AZON BAY *Guernsey (Channel Islands)* 503 P 33 and 517 ⑨ – *see Channel Islands.*

ENTNOR *I.O.W.* 503 504 Q 32 – *see Wight (Isle of).*

ERYAN *Cornwall* 503 F 33 *The West Country G.* – ✉ *Truro.*
See : *Village*★.
London 291 – St. Austell 13 – Truro 13.

Nare, Carne Beach, TR2 5PF, Southwest : 1 ¼ m. ☎ (01872) 501111, *office@narehotel.co.uk, Fax (01872) 501856,* ≤ Carne Bay, , , , heated, , , – , rest, rest, P. MC VISA
The Dining Room : **Rest** (dinner only and Sunday lunch) 39.00 – ***Quarterdeck :*** **Rest** a la carte 16.00/41.00 – **36 rm** ★95.00/210.00 – ★★270.00/340.00, 4 suites.
◆ On the curve of Carne Bay, surrounded by National Trust land; superb beach. Inside, owner's Cornish art collection in evidence. Most rooms have patios and balconies. The Dining Room boasts high windows and sea views; dinner dress code. Informal Quarterdeck.

Crugsillick Manor, TR2 5LJ, West : 1 m. on St Mawes rd ☎ (01872) 501214, *barstow@adtel.co.uk, Fax (01872) 501874,* – rm, P. MC VISA
Rest (by arrangement) (communal dining) 27.50 – **3 rm** ★70.00/75.00 – ★★110.00.
◆ Personally run Queen Anne manor; drawing room with decorative friezes, antiques and period-style furniture. Large rooms overlook lawned gardens of hydrangeas and camelias. Beamed, flagstoned dining room with antique table.

t Ruan High Lanes *West : 1¼ m. on A 3078 –* ✉ *Truro.*

The Hundred House, TR2 5JR, ☎ (01872) 501336, *enquiries@hundredhousehotel.co.uk, Fax (01872) 501151,* – P. MC AE VISA.
Fish in the Fountain : **Rest** (booking essential to non-residents) (dinner only) 28.50 – **10 rm** (dinner included) ★82.00/123.00 – ★★164.00/172.00.
◆ Personally run small hotel: its period furnished hallway with fine staircase, ornate wallpaper sets tone of care and attention to detail. Mirrors, flowers, fine china abound. Comfortable dining room serves West Country fare.

The sun's out – let's eat al fresco! Look for a terrace:

IRGINSTOW *Devon* 503 H 31.
London 227 – Bideford 25 – Exeter 41 – Launceston 11 – Plymouth 33.

Percy's, Coombeshead Estate, EX21 5EA, Southwest : 1 ¼ m. on Tower Hill rd ☎ (01409) 211236, *info@percys.co.uk, Fax (01409) 211460,* ≤, , – P. MC VISA.
Rest – (see below) – **11 rm** ★90.00 – ★★150.00/210.00.
◆ Rural location surrounded by 90 acres of land and forest which include woodland trails. Spacious, modern bedrooms with an unfussy style and a range of charming extras.

Percy's, Coombeshead Estate, EX21 5EA, Southwest : 1 ¼ m. on Tower Hill rd ☎ (01409) 211236, *info@percys.co.uk, Fax (01409) 211460,* – P. MC VISA
Rest (dinner only) 40.00.
◆ Converted longhouse; chic ash and zinc bar by deep sofas; restaurant, like the rooms, is stylish but understated. Locally-sourced, organic produce and homegrown vegetables.

ADDESDON *Bucks.* 504 R 28 *Great Britain G.* – *pop. 1 865* – ✉ *Aylesbury.*
See : *Chiltern Hills*★.
Env. : *Waddesdon Manor*★★*, S : ½ m. by a 41 and minor rd – Claydon House*★*, N : by minor rd.*
London 51 – Aylesbury 5 – Northampton 32 – Oxford 31.

ENGLAND

Five Arrows with rm, High St, HP18 0JE, ✆ (01296) 651727, *bookings@thefivearro shotel.fsnet.co.uk, Fax (01296) 658596,* – P. MO AE VISA.
closed 26 and dinner 31 December, 1 January and Sunday dinner – **Rest** a la car 23.85/32.40 ♀ – **11 rm** ☕ 70.00 – 90.00/150.00.
• 19C inn on the Rothschild estate, an influence apparent in pub crest and wine cella Stylish dining, relaxed ambience, Anglo-Mediterranean menu. Classic rooms.

WAKEFIELD *W. Yorks.* 502 P 22 *Great Britain G. – pop. 76 886.*

Env. : *Nostell Priory★ AC, SE : 4½ m. by A 638.*

City of Wakefield, Lupset Park, Horbury Rd ✆ (01924) 367442 – 28 Woodthorpe Lan Sandal ✆ (01924) 255104 – Painthorpe House, Painthorpe Lane, Crigglestone ✆ (0192 255083.

9 The Bull Ring ✆ (0845) 6018353, tic@wakefield.gov.uk.

London 188 – Leeds 9 – Manchester 38 – Sheffield 23.

Express By Holiday Inn without rest., Denby Dale Rd, WF4 3BB, Southwest : 2 m. c A 636 at junction with M 1 ✆ (01924) 257555, *exhi-wakefield@btconnect.cor Fax (01924) 249888* – P – 30. MO AE VISA.
74 rm 59.95 – 59.95.
• A short distance from the M1, and 10 minutes' drive from centre of town. Good valu up-to-date budget accommodation for the business traveller with well-equipped rooms

Premier Travel Inn, Thornes Park, Denby Dale Rd, WF2 8DY, Southwest : ½ m. c A 636 ✆ (01924) 367901, *Fax (01924) 373620,* – rm, rest, P – 60. MO AE VISA.
Rest (grill rest.) – **42 rm** 49.95 – 49.95.
• In neat gardens on the edge of the town centre, a purpose-built lodge providing we proportioned modern bedrooms, suitable for business travel or family stopovers.

Aagrah, 108 Barnsley Rd, Sandal, WF1 5NX, South : 1¼ m. on A 61 ✆ (01924) 24222 *Fax (01924) 240562* – P. MO AE VISA
closed 25 December – **Rest** - Indian (Kashmiri) - (booking essential) (dinner only) 15.00 ar a la carte 14.95/21.05 s..
• Ornate Eastern curios and furnishings catch the eye in this ever-lively restaurant; goc choice of genuine Indian dishes; friendly service from a smartly dressed team.

WALBERTON *W. Sussex – see Arundel.*

WALCOTT *Norfolk – ✉ Norwich.*

London 134 – Cromer 12 – Norwich 23.

Holly Tree Cottage without rest., Walcott Green, NR12 0NS, South : 2 m. B 1159 and Stalham rd taking 2nd left after Lighthouse Inn ✆ (01692) 650721, –
May-September – **3 rm** ☕ 37.00 – 54.00.
• A hospitable couple keep this traditional Norfolk flint cottage in excellent order. Snu lounge with wood-fired stove and neat rooms overlooking fields. Good breakfasts.

WALLASEY *Mersey.* 502 503 K 23 – *pop. 58 710 – ✉ Wirral.*

Wallasey, Bayswater Rd ✆ (0151) 691 1024.

London 222 – Birkenhead 3 – Liverpool 4.

Grove House, Grove Rd, CH45 3HF, ✆ (0151) 639 3947, *reception@thegro house.co.uk, Fax (0151) 639 0028,* – rest, P – 100. MO AE VISA.
Rest *(closed Bank Holidays)* 15.95/16.95 (lunch) and a la carte – ☕ 7.95 – **14 rm** 64.75 69.75.
• Part Victorian house in a residential street. Meeting room with conservatory. Bedroon in different shapes and sizes: quieter rear accommodation overlooks garden. Oak-panelle dining room.

WALLINGFORD *Oxon.* 503 504 Q 29 *Great Britain G. – pop. 8 019.*

Exc. : *Ridgeway Path★★.*

Town Hall, Market Pl ✆ (01491) 826972.

London 54 – Oxford 12 – Reading 16.

George, High St, OX10 0BS, ✆ (01491) 836665, *info@george-hotel-wallingford.co Fax (01491) 825359* – P – 140. MO AE VISA.
Rest 13.95/29.50 and a la carte ♀ – ☕ 11.50 – **39 rm** 115.00/140.00 – 130.00/145.0
• Part 16C coaching inn with well-run ambience in market town centre. Bustling beame public bar with real fire. Cosy, well-kept lounge. Characterful, stylish bedrooms. Appealir restaurant with memorable pink décor.

at North Stoke *South : 2¾ m. by A 4130 and A 4074 on B 4009 – ✉ Wallingford.*

The Springs, Wallingford Rd, OX10 6BE, ✆ (01491) 836687, *info@thespringshotel.com, Fax (01491) 836877,* ≤, ▢, ▢, ▢, ▢, ▢, ▢, ▢ – ▢ ▢ ▢ – ▢ 70. ▢ ▢ ▢ VISA
Rest (carving lunch Sunday) 16.50/25.00 and dinner a la carte 32.00/40.00 s. ♀ – **30 rm** ▢ ✝95.00 – ✝✝110.00, 2 suites.
◆ Sympathetically extended Victorian mock-Tudor house incorporates spacious bedrooms, oak-panelled front lounge with fireside leather armchairs and several meeting rooms. Ducks bob past restaurant on lake fed by local spring.

WALTHAM ABBEY *Essex 504 U 28 – pop. 17 675.*

▢ 4 Highbridge St ✆ (01992) 652295.
London 15 – Cambridge 44 – Ipswich 66 – Luton 30 – Southend-on-Sea 35.

Waltham Abbey Marriott, Old Shire Lane, EN9 3LX, Southeast : 1½ m. on A 121 ✆ (01992) 717170, *events.waltham@marriotthotels.co.uk, Fax (01992) 711841,* ▢, ▢, ▢ – ▢ ▢ ▢ ▢ – ▢ 280. ▢ ▢ ▢ VISA
Rest a la carte 25.85/37.40 s. – ▢ 14.95 – **162 rm** ✝129.00 – ✝✝129.00/209.00.
◆ Useful motorway links from this group hotel, a few minutes' drive from the town centre; Well-equipped bedrooms, designed for business travel, plus modern meeting rooms. Capacious restaurant conveniently open all day.

Premier Travel Inn, The Grange, Sewardstone Rd, EN9 3QF, South : 1½ m. on A 112 ✆ (0870) 7001458, *Fax (0870) 7001459* – ▢, ▢ rm, ▢ rest, ▢ ▢ – ▢ 30. ▢ ▢ ▢ VISA. ▢
Rest (grill rest.) – **93 rm** ✝53.95/53.95 – ✝✝62.95/62.95.
◆ Good value lodge accommodation, convenient for M11 and M25, and just two miles from Epping Forest. Rooms are comfortable, modern and smart. Grill-style restaurant is adjacent to main building.

WANSFORD *Peterborough 504 S 26 – see Peterborough.*

WANTAGE *Oxon. 503 504 P 29 – pop. 17 913.*

▢ Vale and Downland Museum, 19 Church St ✆ (01235) 760176.
London 71 – Oxford 16 – Reading 24 – Swindon 21.

Boar's Head with rm, Church St, Ardington, OX12 8QA, East : 2½ m. by A 417 ✆ (01235) 833254, *info@boarsheadardington.co.uk, Fax (01235) 833254,* ▢ – ▢ rm, ▢. ▢ ▢ VISA. ▢
Rest a la carte 24.00/40.00 ♀ – **3 rm** ▢ ✝75.00/105.00 – ✝✝85.00/130.00.
◆ Pretty, timbered pub: pine tables, hunting curios and rural magazines. Locally-grown salad, modern British dishes, good wine and ale draw the locals. Bright modern bedrooms.

WARE *Herts. 504 T 28 – pop. 17 193.*

▢ Whitehill, Dane End ✆ (01920) 438495.
London 24 – Cambridge 30 – Luton 22.

Marriott Hanbury Manor H. & Country Club, Thundridge, SG12 0SD, North : 1¾ m. by A 1170 on A 10 ✆ (01920) 487722, *reservations.hanburymanor@marriotthotels.co.uk, Fax (01920) 487692,* ≤, ▢, ▢, ▢, ▢, ▢, ▢, ▢, ▢, ▢ – ▢ ▢, ▢ rest, ▢ ▢ ▢ – ▢ 120. ▢ ▢ ▢ VISA
Zodiac : **Rest** *(closed first 2 weeks January, Sunday dinner and Monday)* a la carte 50.45/62.40 s. – ***Oakes*** : **Rest** a la carte 27.75/51.70 s. – ▢ 17.50 – **156 rm** ✝149.00 – ✝✝149.00, 5 suites.
◆ 1890s neo-Jacobean mansion, a former convent, in 220 acres. Tea in firelit, oak-beamed hall. Classically luxurious rooms; many overlook golf course and lake. Walled garden. Formal, fine dining Zodiac. Mediterranean menus in spacious Oakes.

Jacoby's, Churchgate House, 15 West St, SG12 9EE, ✆ (01920) 469181, *info@jacobys.co.uk, Fax (01920) 469182,* ▢ – ▢ ▢. ▢ ▢ VISA
closed 24 December-3 January, Monday lunch and Sunday – **Rest** a la carte 24.50/32.00.
◆ Carefully renovated 15C Grade II listed timber framed house with tremendous character. Front bar with leather armchairs. Twin level dining: British or Mediterranean classics.

WAREHAM *Dorset* 503 504 N 31 *The West Country G. – pop. 2 568.*

See : Town★ – St Martin's★★.

Env. : Blue Pool★ AC, S : 3½ m. by A 351 – Bovington Tank Museum★ AC, Woolbridg Manor★, W : 5 m. by A 352.

Exc. : Moreton Church★★, W : 9½ m. by A 352 – Corfe Castle★ (≤★★) AC, SE : 6 m. by A 35 – Lulworth Cove★, SW : 10 m. by A 352 and B 3070 – Bere Regis★ (St John the Bapti Church★), NW : 6½ m. by minor rd.

Holy Trinity Church, South St ℘ (01929) 552740.

London 123 – Bournemouth 13 – Weymouth 19.

Springfield Country H., Grange Rd, BH20 5AL, South : 1¼ m. by South St and Wes Lane ℘ (01929) 552177, *enquiries@springfield-country-hotel.co.uk, Fax (01929) 55186* , heated, , , , squash – , rest, – 200. VISA
Millview : **Rest** (bar lunch)/dinner 23.50 and a la carte 17.95/26.45 – ***Springers :*** **Res** *(closed Friday-Sunday)* (dinner only) a la carte 16.70/26.45 – **50 rm** ★83.00/99.00 ★★120.00/160.00.
◆ Privately owned hotel in sight of the Purbeck Hills. Neatly laid-out rooms; landscape gardens. Comprehensive spa treatments and a state-of-the-art gym. Regional flavou abound in Millview. Informal, unfussy Springers.

Priory, Church Green, BH20 4ND, ℘ (01929) 551666, *reservations@theprioryh tel.co.uk, Fax (01929) 554519*, ≤, , , – , rest, . VISA.
Rest 35.00 (dinner) and lunch a la carte 25.70/30.95 – **16 rm** ★110.00/184.00 ★★170.00/230.00, 2 suites.
◆ Charming, privately run part 16C priory, friendly and discreetly cosy. Well-equippe rooms. Manicured four-acre gardens lead down to River Frome: luxury suites in boat house. Charming restaurant beneath stone vaults of undercroft.

Gold Court House, St John's Hill, BH20 4LZ, ℘ (01929) 553320, *Fax (01929) 553320*, – .
closed Christmas-New Year – **Rest** *(winter only)* (by arrangement) (communal dining) 15.0 – **3 rm** ★40.00 – ★★60.00.
◆ Affable hosts are justly proud of this pretty 1760s house on a quiet square. Classical charming sitting room and bedrooms; well-chosen books and antiques. Dine communal while viewing delightful courtyard garden.

WAREN MILL *Northd.* 501 502 O 17 – *see Bamburgh.*

WARGRAVE *Windsor & Maidenhead* 504 R 29 – *pop. 2 876.*

London 37 – Henley-on-Thames 4 – Oxford 27.

St George & Dragon, High St, RG10 8HY, ℘ (0118) 940 5021, *stgeorgeandd gon@hotmail.com, Fax (0118) 940 5024*, ≤, , – . VISA.
closed Sunday dinner – **Rest** a la carte 18.50/34.35.
◆ Stunning cream-washed pub with lovely decked terrace overlooking Thames. Text-boo modern interior. Stone-fired oven provides spit roasts, grills, pastas and modern dishes.

WARMINSTER *Wilts.* 503 504 N 30 *The West Country G. – pop. 17 486.*

Env. : Longleat House★★★ AC, SW : 3 m.

Exc. : Stonehenge★★★ AC, E : 18 m. by A 36 and A 303 – Bratton Castle (≤★★) NE : 6 m. b A 350 and B 3098.

Central Car Park ℘ (01985) 218548.

London 111 – Bristol 29 – Exeter 74 – Southampton 47.

Bishopstrow House, BA12 9HH, Southeast : 1½ m. on B 3414 ℘ (01985) 21231 *enquiries@bishopstrow.co.uk, Fax (01985) 216769*, ≤, , , , , heated, , , , indoor/outdoor – rest, – 60. VISA
The Mulberry : **Rest** 18.00/38.00 – **29 rm** ★99.00 – ★★199.00, 3 suites.
◆ Dignified, ivy-clad Georgian manor; 22-acre gardens along the river Wylye. Large moder rooms. Clubby, panelled bar with log fire; popular leisure club for the more active. Wa lanterns lend a warm feel to restaurant, which overlooks the garden.

at Upton Scudamore *North : 2½ m. by A 350 – ✉ Warminster.*

Angel Inn with rm, BA12 0AG, ℘ (01985) 213225, *theangelinn.uptonscudamore@bt penworld.com, Fax (01985) 218182*, – . VISA.
closed 25-26 December and 1 January – **Rest** a la carte 16.00/30.00 – **10 rm** ★70.00 ★★80.00.
◆ Refurbished 16C inn with a warm personal style. Sunny rear terrace. Rustic interior c scrubbed wood and pine. Fish specials highlight of appealing menus. Immaculate rooms.

t Heytesbury *Southeast : 3¾ m. by B 3414 – ✉ Warminster.*

Angel Inn with rm, High St, BA12 0ED, ✆ (01985) 840330, *admin@theangelheytesbury.co.uk, Fax (01985) 840931,* – P. MC AE VISA
Rest - Steak specialities - a la carte 12.00/35.00 – **8 rm** 60.00 – 75.00.
◆ 17C village inn with a delightful courtyard terrace. Dine at well-spaced tables in an elegant restaurant or the friendly real-ale bar. Cosy, well-appointed bedrooms.

t Corsley *Northwest : 5 m. by A 362 – ✉ Warminster.*

Cross Keys, Lyes Green, BA12 7PB, ✆ (01373) 832406, *Fax (01373) 832934,* – P 50. VISA
closed 25-26 December and 1 January – **Rest** a la carte 10.50/27.75.
◆ Very personally run rural pub with large garden; local pictures and prints adorn walls. Extensive, freshly prepared menus utilise local suppliers: try renowned fish specials.

WARRINGTON *Warrington* 502 503 504 M 23 – *pop. 80 661.*

Hill Warren, Appleton ✆ (01925) 261620 – Walton Hall, Warrington Rd, Higher Walton ✆ (01925) 266775 – Birchwood, Kelvin Close ✆ (01925) 818819 – Leigh, Kenyon Hall, Broseley Lane, Culcheth ✆ (01925) 762943 – Alder Root, Alder Root Lane, Winwick ✆ (01925) 291919.
The Market Hall, Academy Way ✆ (01925) 632571.
London 195 – Chester 20 – Liverpool 18 – Manchester 21 – Preston 28.

Village H. and Leisure Club, Centre Park, WA1 1QA, South : ¾ m. by A 49 ✆ (01925) 240000, *village.warrington@village-hotels.com, Fax (01925) 445240,* , squash – rm, rest, P – 250. MC AE VISA.
Rest 8.95/9.95 and a la carte 16.15/23.15 s. – 9.95 **116 rm** 119.00 – 139.00.
◆ Located just outside the town centre and consistently busy, a substantial redbrick hotel offering a state-of-the-art health and leisure complex. Smartly fitted modern rooms. Spacious, wood-furnished restaurant.

Premier Travel Inn, 1430 Centre Park, Park Boulevard, WA1 1PR, South : ¾ m. by A 49 ✆ (01925) 242692, *Fax (01925) 244259* – rm, rest, P. MC AE VISA.
Rest (grill rest.) – **42 rm** 49.95/49.95 – 52.95/52.95.
◆ Excellent motorway connections from this group lodge, located in a business park on the southern outskirts. Modern accommodation for the cost-conscious traveller.

t Stretton *South : 3½ m. by A 49 on B 5356 – ✉ Warrington.*

Park Royal, Stretton Rd, WA4 4NS, ✆ (01925) 730706, *parkroyalreservations@qhotels.co.uk, Fax (01925) 730740,* – rest, P – 400. MC AE VISA.
***The Harlequin :* Rest** (bar lunch)/dinner a la carte 27.75/45.45 s. – 11.65 – **139 rm** 70.00/115.00 – 140.00/185.00, 3 suites.
◆ Busy, well-equipped business hotel with motorway access. Well-appointed rooms in co-ordinated patterns, facing open countryside at rear. Excellent leisure centre and café-bar. Traditionally formal restaurant.

t Daresbury *Southwest : 4 m. on A 56 – ✉ Warrington.*

Daresbury Park, Chester Rd, WA4 4BB, Southwest : 1½ m. by A 56 ✆ (01925) 267331, *reservations.daresbury@devere-hotels.com, Fax (01925) 265615,* , squash – rest, P – 300. MC AE VISA
***The Looking Glass :* Rest** (carving lunch Sunday) 14.50/24.95 s. – 11.95 – **171 rm** 69.00/119.00 – 79.00/129.00, 12 suites.
◆ In a modern business park near Lewis Carroll's birthplace. An impressively modish entrance leads into this well-equipped and up-to-date business and leisure hotel. Informal styling at The Looking Glass.

WARTLING *E. Sussex* 504 V 31 – *see Herstmonceux.*

"Rest" appears in red for establishments with a ✿ (star) or (Bib Gourmand).

WARWICK *Warks.* 503 504 P 27 *Great Britain G. – pop. 23 350.*

See : *Town★ – Castle★★* AC Y – *Leycester Hospital★* AC Y B – *Collegiate Church of St Mary (Tomb★)* Y A.

Warwick Racecourse ✆ *(01926) 494316* Y.

The Court House, Jury St ✆ *(01926) 492212.*

London 96 – Birmingham 20 – Coventry 11 – Leicester 34 – Oxford 43.

WARWICK-ROYAL LEAMINGTON SPA

Birmingham Rd	Z	7
Bowling Green St	Y	9
Brook St	Y	12
Butts (The)	Y	13
Castle Hill	Y	15
Church St	Y	17
High St	Y	23
Jury St	Y	
Lakin Rd	Y	25
Linen St	Y	26
Market Pl.	Y	29
Old Square	Y	35
Old Warwick Rd	Z	36
Radford Rd	Z	39
Rock (The)	Y	32
St John's Rd	Y	42
St Nicholas Church St	Y	43
Shires Retail Park	Z	
Smith St	Y	
Swan St	Y	46
Theatre St	Y	48
West St	Y	50

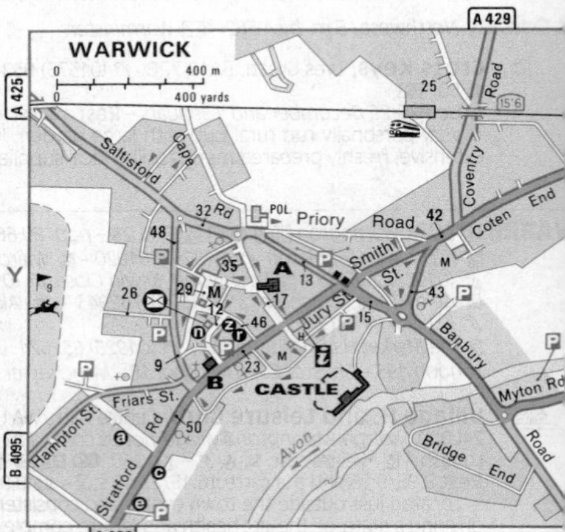

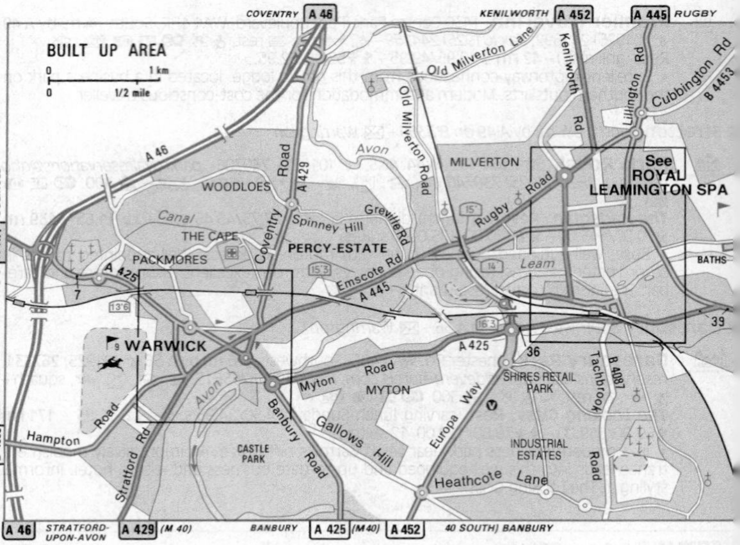

Old Fourpenny Shop, 27-29 Crompton St, CV34 6HJ, ✆ (01926) 491360, *fourpenny shop@aol.com, Fax (01926) 411892* – P. VISA Y

closed 25-26 December and 1 January – **Rest** *(closed Sunday dinner)* a la carte 19.00/29.95 s. – **11 rm** ☐ ★47.50/70.00 – ★★85.00/90.00.

◆ One-time pub has retained its inn sign and local reputation for real ale. Simple yet comfortable and neatly kept bedrooms, some in the rear courtyard extension. Smart bar and dining room.

Charter House without rest., 87 West St, CV34 6AH, ☎ (01926) 496965, – [P]. MC VISA. Y c
closed 24-25 December – **3 rm** ☕ ★56.00/65.00 – ★★85.00/95.00.
◆ Timbered 15C house not far from the castle. Comfortable, delicately ordered rooms with a personal touch: pretty counterpanes and posies of dried flowers. Tasty breakfasts.

Park Cottage without rest., 113 West St, CV34 6AH, ☎ (01926) 410319, *janet@parkcottagewarwick.co.uk, Fax (01926) 497994* – [P]. MC AE VISA. Y e
5 rm ☕ ★50.00/57.00 – ★★95.00/80.00.
◆ Between the shops and restaurants of West Street and the River Avon, a listed part Tudor house offering a homely lounge and sizeable, traditionally appointed bedrooms.

Saffron, Unit 1, Westgate House, Market St, CV34 4DE, ☎ (01926) 402061 – MC AE VISA Y n
closed 25 December – **Rest** - Indian - (dinner only) a la carte 9.95/20.65.
◆ Split-level dining room hung with sitars and prints from the subcontinent. Piquant seafood and Goan dishes are the specialities of a freshly prepared Indian repertoire.

Jury's, 3 Swan St, CV34 4BJ, ☎ (01926) 403833, *booking@jurys-restaurant.co.uk, Fax (01926) 403833* – MC VISA Y r
closed 26 December, 1 January and Sunday dinner – **Rest** a la carte 26.85/30.85.
◆ Boasts a welcoming bistro style in the centre of town. Rustic style décor with Mediterranean touches. Flavoursome, well executed dishes with good use of seasonal produce.

Prym's, 48 Brook St, CV34 4BL, ☎ (01926) 493504, *Fax (01926) 493322* – MC AE VISA Y z
closed 25 December, 1 week spring, 1 week October, Sunday and Monday – **Rest** a la carte 23.85/30.85.
◆ Bright, modern restaurant in the heart of the city. Stripped wooden floor, exposed beams, lots of wrought iron. Simple, tasty and well-cooked British fare on offer.

Art Kitchen, 7 Swan St, CV34 4BJ, ☎ (01926) 494303, *reservations@theartkitchen.com, Fax (01926) 494304* – MC AE VISA Y r
closed 25 December-14 January – **Rest** - Thai - 12.95 (lunch) and a la carte 16.45/29.70.
◆ Unpretentious town centre restaurant with upstairs dining area featuring artwork for sale by owners' daughter. Authentic Thai cooking with attention paid to originality.

t Barford *South : 3½ m. on A 429* – **Z** – ✉ *Warwick.*

Glebe, Church St, CV35 8BS, on B 4462 ☎ (01926) 624218, *sales@glebehotel.co.uk, Fax (01926) 624625*, – , rest, [P] – 120. MC AE VISA
Rest a la carte 25.95/32.90 – **38 rm** ☕ ★105.00 – ★★125.00, 1 suite.
◆ On the edge of a quiet hamlet by St. Peter's church, a classically proportioned manor in late Georgian redbrick. Neatly-equipped bedrooms in smart co-ordinated prints. Arch-roofed conservatory restaurant with views of evergreen borders.

t Longbridge *Southwest : 2 m. on A 429* – **Z** – ✉ *Warwick.*

Hilton Warwick, Stratford Rd, CV34 6RE, on A 429 at junction 15 of M 40 ☎ (01926) 499555, *Fax (01926) 410020*, – , rest, [P] – 250. MC AE VISA
Rest 12.95/21.95 **s.** – ☕ 15.50 – **181 rm** ★98.00/151.00 – ★★98.00/151.00.
◆ Substantial group hotel, outside the city centre. Handsomely equipped, contemporary rooms; open-plan foyer and popular conference rooms. Restaurant or café-bar dining alternatives.

Express by Holiday Inn without rest., Stratford Rd, CV34 6TW, on A 429 at junction 15 of M 40 ☎ (01926) 483000, *warwick@expressholidayinn.co.uk, Fax (01926) 483033* – [P] – 25. MC AE VISA
138 rm ★85.00 – ★★85.00.
◆ Purpose-built lodge with useful motorway links. Trim, modern rooms with work desks and power showers; low-fat and take-away light breakfasts - ideal for business stopovers.

WASHINGTON *Tyne and Wear* 501 502 P 19 – *pop. 53 388.*

Washington Moat House, Stone Cellar Rd, Usworth ☎ (0191) 402 9988.
London 278 – Durham 13 – Middlesbrough 32 – Newcastle upon Tyne 7.

Holiday Inn, Emerson, District 5, NE37 1LB, at junction of A 1(M) with A 195 ☎ (0870) 4009084, *reservations-washington@ichotelsgroup.com, Fax (0191) 415 3371* – rm, [P] – 80. MC AE VISA
Rest (bar lunch Monday-Saturday)/dinner 15.00/20.00 and a la carte 18.00/26.00 – ☕ 12.95 – **136 rm** ★79.00 – ★★79.00.
◆ Neat rooms, well fitted with mod cons and worktops, in a modern hotel; from Durham Cricket Ground to the Angel of the North, Tyne and Wear's sights are a short drive away. Light, contemporary dining.

Express by Holiday Inn without rest., Emerson Rd, District 5, NE37 1LB, ☎ (0191) 416 9416, *ebhi-washington@btconnect.com, Fax (0191) 416 3123* – |♦|, ⇔ ♿ P – 🔥 30. MC AE ⊙ VISA. ✂
74 rm 49.95/55.00 – 49.95/55.00.
◆ Recently built, comfortable lodge accommodation in a useful location close to A1 motorway and Angel of the North. An ideal stop-over address for business travellers.

WATERMILLOCK *Cumbria* 502 L 20 – *see Ullswater.*

WATFORD *Herts.* 504 S 29 – *pop. 120 960.*
West Herts., Cassiobury Park ☎ (01923) 236484 – Oxhey Park, Prestwick Rd, South Oxhey ☎ (01923) 248213, AT.
London 21 – Aylesbury 23.
Plan : see Greater London (North-West) 2

The Grove, Chandler's Cross, WD3 4TG, Northwest : 2 m. on A 411 ☎ (01923) 80780... *info@thegrove.co.uk, Fax (01923) 221008,* heated, – ⇔ rm, rest, ♿ P – 🔥 500. MC AE ⊙ VISA. ✂
Glasshouse : **Rest** (buffet) 27.50/37.50 ♀ – ***Stables*** *(☎ (01923) 296015)* : **Rest** *(closed 25 December)* a la carte 24.50/34.50 ♀ – (see also ***Colette's*** below) – ☕ 19.50 – **215 rm** 240.00 – 240.00, 12 suites.
◆ Converted country house with walled garden and golf course. Modern décor in public rooms. Extensive new spa facility. Hi-tech bedrooms and suites in modern extension. Glasshouse for stylish buffet meals. Informal dining in golfer-friendly Stables.

Hilton Watford, Elton Way, WD25 8HA, Watford Bypass, East : 3 ½ m. on A 41 at junction with B 462 ☎ (01923) 235881, *rm-watford@hilton.com, Fax (01923) 220836,* – |♦| ⇔, rest, ♿ P – 🔥 375. MC AE ⊙ VISA. ✂ BT
Patio : **Rest** *(closed Saturday lunch)* (carvery rest.) (live music and dancing Saturday) 15.50/19.95 – ☕ 14.95 – **199 rm** 140.00 – 140.00, 2 suites.
◆ Behind the austere façade of this group-owned block are rooms with work spaces, internet access and contemporary minimalist décor. Comfortable if busy first-floor lounge. Spacious Patio rest. has jazz Sunday lunch.

Premier Travel Inn, Timms Meadow, Water Lane, WD17 2NU, ☎ (0870) 9906620, *Fax (0870) 9906621* – |♦|, ⇔ rm, rest, ♿ P. MC AE ⊙ VISA AT
Rest (grill rest.) – **105 rm** 55.95/55.95 – 59.95/59.95.
◆ A bright and modern hotel situated near town centre. Rooms are carefully designed and include useful desk areas. Well suited to business and leisure travellers alike. Family friendly-style restaurant.

Premier Travel Inn, 2 Ascot Rd, WD18 8AP, Southwest : 1 ½ m. by A 412 ☎ (0870) 8500328, *Fax (0870) 8500343* – |♦| ⇔ ♿ P. MC AE ⊙ VISA. ✂
Rest (grill rest.) – **121 rm** 55.95/55.95 – 59.95/59.95.
◆ Sizeable lodge accommodation, adjacent to a busy industrial estate. Good value, uniform rooms at a very affordable price. Spacious grill restaurant.

Colette's (at The Grove), WD3 4TG, Northwest : 2 m. on A 411 ☎ (01923) 296015, *restaurants@thegrove.co.uk, Fax (01923) 221008* – ⇔ P. MC AE ⊙ VISA
closed 2 weeks January, 2 weeks August, Sunday dinner and Bank Holiday Mondays – **Rest** (dinner only and Sunday lunch) 35.00/65.00 and a la carte 46.50/65.50 **s.** ♀.
◆ Delightful terrace for relaxing pre-prandials. Intimate bar with sofas. Elegant dining room lit by stylish chandeliers. Menus boast luxury ingredients and original touches.

If breakfast is included the ☕ symbol appears after the number of rooms.

WATTON *Norfolk* 504 W 26.
London 95 – Norwich 22 – Swaffham 10.

The Café at Brovey Lair with rm, Carbrooke Rd, Ovington, IP25 6SD, Northeast : 1 ¾ m. by A 1075 ☎ (01953) 882706, *champagne@broveylair.com, Fax (01953) 885365,* heated, – ⇔, rest, P. MC AE VISA. ✂
closed 25 December – **Rest** - Seafood - (booking essential) (set menu only) 35.00/42.50
2 rm ☕ 120.00 – 135.00.
◆ Unique dining experience, within chef's own house: you're encouraged to watch her cook an accomplished four-course, no choice set seafood menu. Personally run. Smart rooms.

WEDMORE *Somerset* 503 L 30.
London 155.5 – Cheddar 4.5 – Glastonbury 9.5.

The Sexey's Arms, Sexey's Rd, Blackford, BS28 4NT, West : 1 ¾ m. on B 3139 ℘ (01934) 712487, *enquiries@thesexeysarms.co.uk, Fax (01934) 712447,* – P. AE VISA
closed 25 December, 1 January and Monday January-May – **Rest** a la carte 17.00/26.00.
◆ A cider house that evolved into a pub, with a locals snug and a dining room featuring tiled floor, beams and inglenook. French owner/chef serves accomplished modern classics.

WELLINGBOROUGH *Northants.* 504 R 27 – *pop. 46 959.*
Library, Pebble Lane ℘ (01933) 276412.
London 73 – Cambridge 43 – Leicester 34 – Northampton 10.

Ibis without rest., Enstone Court, NN8 2DR, Southwest : 2 ½ m. by A 5128 (Northampton rd) on A 509 at junction with A 45 ℘ (01933) 228333, *h3164@accor-hotels.com, Fax (01933) 228444* – P – 25. AE VISA
– **78 rm** 52.95 – 52.95.
◆ Modern purpose-built hotel offering simple and well-maintained lodge accommodation. Good value and convenient for business and leisure travellers.

WELLINGHAM *Norfolk.*
London 120 – King's Lynn 29 – Norwich 28.

Manor House Farm without rest., PE32 2TH, ℘ (01328) 838227, *Fax (01328) 838348,* – P. – **3 rm** 45.00/60.00 – 70.00/85.00.
◆ Idyllic setting beside church, surrounded by gardens and working farm. Family style breakfast; home grown bacon and sausage. Charming rooms in the house or comfortable annexe.

WELLINGTON *Somerset* 503 K 31 – *pop. 10 599.*
London 176 – Barnstaple 42 – Exeter 32 – Taunton 10.

Bindon Country House, Langford Budville, TA21 0RU, Northwest : 4 ½ m. by B 3187 via Langford Budville village following signs for Wiveliscombe ℘ (01823) 400070, *stay@bindon.com, Fax (01823) 400071,* heated, – P – 45. AE VISA
The Wellesley : **Rest** a la carte 16.95/39.95 – **12 rm** 95.00/115.00 – 215.00.
◆ A rural idyll; splendid part 17C house with distinctive Flemish gables, rose garden; personally run with tasteful style. Individually designed rooms in refined, quiet colours. Fine views from restaurant; accomplished cooking in modern style.

WELLS *Somerset* 503 504 M 30 *The West Country G. – pop. 10 406.*
See : *City★★ – Cathedral★★★ – Vicars' Close★ – Bishop's Palace★ (★★) AC – St Cuthbert★.*
Env. : *Glastonbury★★ – Abbey★★ (Abbot's Kitchen★) AC, St John the Baptist★★, Somerset Rural Life Museum★ AC, Glastonbury Tor★ (★★★), SW : 5½ m. by A 39 – Wookey Hole★ (Caves★ AC, Papermill★), NW : 2 m –* **Exc. :** *Cheddar Gorge★★ (Gorge★★, Caves★, Jacob's Ladder ★) – St Andrew's Church★, NW : 7 m. by A 371 – Axbridge★★ (King John's Hunting Lodge★, St John the Baptist Church★), NW : 8½ m. by A 371.*
18 East Horrington Rd ℘ (01749) 675005.
Town Hall, Market Pl ℘ (01749) 672552, wells.tic@ukonline.co.uk.
London 132 – Bristol 20 – Southampton 68 – Taunton 28.

The Swan, 11 Sadler St, BA5 2RX, ℘ (01749) 836300, *swan@bhere.co.uk, Fax (01749) 836301,* – P – 120. AE VISA.
Rest 26.50 (dinner) and a la carte 31.75/37.70 – **50 rm** 90.00/98.00 – 165.00.
◆ Refurbished to a very good standard, this friendly former posting inn faces the Cathedral's west front. Two relaxing, firelit lounges; stylish individually decorated rooms. Restaurant boasts framed antique clothing and oak panelling.

Beryl without rest., BA5 3JP, East : 1 ¼ m. by B 3139 off Hawkers Lane ℘ (01749) 678738, *stay@beryl-wells.co.uk, Fax (01749) 670508,* heated, – P. VISA
closed 24-26 December – **8 rm** 55.00/65.00 – 120.00.
◆ Neo-gothic former hunting lodge in formal gardens run in idiosyncratic style. Impeccable antique-filled drawing room. Traditional rooms, larger on first floor. Charming hosts.

Littlewell Farm without rest., Coxley, BA5 1QP, Southwest : 1 ½ m. on A 39 ℘ (01749) 677914, *enquiries@littlewellfarm.co.uk,* – P.
4 rm 30.00/35.00 – 54.00.
◆ Restored 18C farmhouse set in a broad lawned garden. Cosy, attractively furnished sitting room and pristine, individually decorated bedrooms. Breakfasts at communal table.

ENGLAND

at Wookey Hole *Northwest : 1¾ m. by A 371 – ✉ Wells.*

Glencot House ⓢ, Glencot Lane, BA5 1BH, ☎ (01749) 677160, *relax@glencothouse.co.uk, Fax (01749) 670210,* ≘s, ⚐, ⚐– ⚐ P. MO AE VISA
closed Christmas-New Year – **Rest** (booking essential to non-residents) (dinner only) 26.5 – **13 rm** ☐ ★75.00 – ★★134.00.
◆ Set in mature gardens by the river Axe, a 19C mansion in Jacobean style. Preserved walnut panelling, carved ceilings and comfortable rooms with decorative touches. Dining room with mullioned windows, chandelier, river views.

at Easton *Northwest : 3 m. on A 371 – ✉ Wells.*

Beaconsfield Farm without rest., BA5 1DU, on A 371 ☎ (01749) 870308, *carol@beaconsfieldfarm.co.uk,* ⚐ – ⚐ P. ⚐
closed 4 weeks Christmas – **3** rm ☐ ★58.00 – ★★65.00.
◆ In the foothills of the Mendips, a renovated farmhouse offering well-fitted, cottage style rooms. Generous breakfasts in the parlour overlooking the four-acre grounds.

WELLS-NEXT-THE-SEA *Norfolk* 504 W 25 – *pop. 2 451.*
London 122 – Cromer 22 – Norwich 38.

The Crown, The Buttlands, NR23 1EX, ☎ (01328) 710209, *reception@thecrownhotelwells.co.uk, Fax (01328) 711432,* ⚐ – ⚐ ⚐. MO VISA. ⚐
Restaurant : Rest (dinner only) 29.95 – ***Bar :*** Rest (bookings not accepted) a la carte 17.15/22.25 ♀ – **12 rm** ☐ ★100.00 – ★★150.00.
◆ 16C coaching inn with smart Georgian façade, overlooking the village green. Bedrooms are contemporary in style; service is informal and friendly. Light, airy Restaurant with bright décor. Modern conservatory Bar with terrace.

WELWYN *Herts.* 504 T 28 – *pop. 10 700 (inc. Codicote).*
London 31 – Bedford 31 – Cambridge 31.

Tewin Bury Farm, AL6 0JB, Southeast : 3½ m. by A 1000 on B 1000 ☎ (01438) 71779 *hotel@tewinbury.co.uk, Fax (01438) 840440,* ⚐, ⚐ – ⚐ rest, ⚐ rest, P – ⚐ 150. MO ⚐ VISA. ⚐
closed 25-26 December and 1 January – **Rest** a la carte 21.60/25.10 – **29 rm** ☐ ★108.00 ★★115.00.
◆ Consisting of a range of converted farm buildings on 400-acre working farm. 17C tythe barn used as function room located next to river. Individual rooms have beamed ceilings. Restaurant located in timbered farm building.

WELWYN GARDEN CITY *Herts.* 504 T 28.
⚐18, ⚐9 *Panshanger Golf Complex, Old Herns Lane ☎ (01707) 333312.*
London 22 – Luton 21.

Premier Travel Inn, Stanborough Rd, AL8 6DQ, South : ¾ m. on A 6129 ☎ (01707) 391345, *Fax (01707) 393789* – ⚐, ⚐ rm, ⚐ rest, ⚐ P. MO AE ⚐ VISA. ⚐
Rest (grill rest.) – **60 rm** ★47.95/47.95 – ★★50.95/50.95.
◆ Simply furnished and brightly decorated bedrooms with ample work space. Family rooms with sofa beds. A useful address for cost-conscious travellers.

XXX **Auberge du Lac** ⓢ, Brocket Hall, AL8 7XG, West : 3 m. by A 6129 on B 653 ☎ (01707) 368888, *auberge@brocket-hall.co.uk, Fax (01707) 368898,* ⚐, ⚐ – ⚐ P. MO AE ⚐ VISA
closed 27 December-5 January and Monday – **Rest** 28.50/45.00 and a la carte 35.00/59.00 ⚐.
◆ Part 18C former hunting lodge with lakeside terrace in the grounds of Brocket Hall - an idyllic setting for confident, classic cooking with a firm French base.

WENDLING *Norfolk* 504 W 25 – *see East Dereham.*

WENTBRIDGE *W. Yorks.* 502 504 Q 23 – ✉ *Pontefract.*
London 183 – Leeds 19 – Nottingham 55 – Sheffield 28.

Wentbridge House, Old Great North Rd, WF8 3JJ, ☎ (01977) 620444, *info@wentbridgehouse.co.uk, Fax (01977) 620148,* ⚐, ⚐ – P – ⚐ 120. MO AE ⚐ VISA. ⚐
closed 25 December – ***Fleur de Lys :*** Rest *(closed Sunday dinner)* 16.50/28.00 and a la carte 28.95/39.45 – ***Wentbridge Brasserie :*** Rest *(closed Sunday lunch)* a la carte 16.95/29.95 ♀ – **18 rm** ☐ ★84.00 – ★★150.00.
◆ Once owned by the late Queen Mother's family, a part 18C bay-windowed house decorated in traditional colours. Sizeable rooms, some overlooking the lawned grounds. Fleur de Lys adjacent to smart firelit bar. Informal Wentbridge Brasserie.

WEOBLEY Herefordshire 503 L 27 – ✉ Hereford.

London 145 – Brecon 30 – Hereford 12 – Leominster 9.

Broxwood Court, Broxwood, HR6 9JJ, Northwest : 3¼ m. by A 4112, Broxwood rd on Lyonshall rd ✆ (01544) 340245, *mikeanne@broxwood.kc3.co.uk, Fax (01544) 340573,* ≤, heated, , , – , rm, P. MC VISA.
closed Christmas and New Year – **Rest** (by arrangement) (communal dining) 25.00 ♀ – **3 rm** ☕ ☆40.00/60.00 – ☆☆90.00.
◆ 1950s house set in wonderfully tranquil location: vast grounds and formally laid-out gardens. Spacious drawing room, cosy library. Individually styled rooms with views.

The Salutation Inn with rm, Market Pitch, HR4 8SJ, ✆ (01544) 318443, *salutationinn@btinternet.com, Fax (01544) 318405,* – P. MC AE VISA.
closed 25 December – **Rest** a la carte 15.20/25.35 ♀ – **4 rm** ☕ ☆52.00/57.00 – ☆☆78.00/84.00.
◆ In the heart of this pretty village, a charming, part 16C former cider house with a rustic real ale bar. Traditionally decorated bedrooms, two in the next-door cottage. Attractive dining room.

WEST BAGBOROUGH Somerset 503 K 30 – see Taunton.

WEST BEXINGTON Dorset 503 504 M 31 – ✉ Dorchester.

London 150 – Bournemouth 43 – Bridport 6 – Weymouth 13.

Manor, Beach Rd, DT2 9DF, ✆ (01308) 897616, *themanorhotel@btconnect.com, Fax (01308) 897704,* ≤, – P. MC AE VISA.
Rest 19.50/26.50 – **13 rm** ☕ ☆75.00/100.00 – ☆☆120.00/155.00.
◆ A short walk from the beach, a personally run and pleasantly unfussy country house of 11C origin. Neat, traditional rooms and a convivial cellar bar popular with the locals. Pretty flag-floored dining room decorated with rural curios.

WEST BURTON N. Yorks. 502 O 21 – ✉ Leyburn.

London 260 – Carlisle 81 – Darlington 34 – Kendal 40 – Leeds 62 – York 58.

The Grange, DL8 4JR, ✆ (01969) 663348, *ashfordpaul5@aol.com,* , – P. MC VISA
Rest 20.00 – **3 rm** ☕ ☆40.00 – ☆☆65.00/70.00.
◆ 19C house: preserved tiling, staircase and antiques. Well-proportioned bedrooms, firelit drawing room. Mature riverside gardens. Impressive mahogany breakfast table.

WESTBURY Wilts. 503 N 30.

London 111 – Trowbridge 5.5 – Warminster 4.5.

XX **Garden House** with rm, 26 Edward St, BA13 3BD, North : 4 m. by A 350 ✆ (01373) 859995, *reception@thegardenhouse-hotel.co.uk, Fax (01373) 858586,* , – , rest, MC AE VISA
closed 25-26 December and 1 January – **Rest** *(closed Saturday lunch, Sunday dinner and Bank Holidays)* (light lunch)/dinner a la carte 15.95/31.45 **s.** – **8 rm** ☕ ☆70.00/95.00 – ☆☆95.00/110.00.
◆ Very personally run former post office in centre of town, with lovely enclosed rear garden. Modern, tasty menus with strong seasonal base. Cosy bedrooms.

WEST END Surrey 504 S 29 – pop. 4 135 – ✉ Guildford.

London 37 – Bracknell 7 – Camberley 5 – Guildford 8 – Woking 6.

The Inn @ West End, 42 Guildford Rd, GU24 9PW, on A 322 ✆ (01276) 858652, *greatfood@the-inn.co.uk, Fax (01276) 485842,* – P. MC AE VISA
Rest 19.75/27.50 ♀.
◆ Well-prepared modern British standards and good-value lunches in this smartly renovated Victorian roadside pub; occasional wine tastings from a diverse cellar.

WESTFIELD E. Sussex 504 V 31 – pop. 1 509.

London 66 – Brighton 38 – Folkestone 45 – Maidstone 30.

XX **The Wild Mushroom,** Woodgate House, Westfield Lane, TN35 4SB, Southwest : ½ m. on A 28 ✆ (01424) 751137, *info@wildmushroom.co.uk, Fax (01424) 753405,* – P. MC AE VISA
closed 25 December-10 January, 2 weeks August, Monday, Saturday lunch and Sunday dinner – **Rest** (booking essential) 16.95 (lunch) and dinner a la carte 22.00/30.50 ♀.
◆ Bustling and hospitable with modern interior and conservatory lounge. Flavourful, well-priced dishes from a varied, interesting menu. Loyal local following: be sure to book.

WEST KIRBY *Wirral* 502 504 K 23 *Great Britain G.*
Exc. : *Liverpool★ - Cathedrals★★, Walker Art Gallery★★, Merseyside Maritime Museum and Albert Dock★, E : 13½ m. by A 553.*
London 219 – Chester 19 – Liverpool 12.

Peel Hey, Frankby Rd, Frankby, CH48 1PP, East : 2¼ m. by A 540 on B 5139 ℘ (0151) 677 9077, *enquiries@peelhey.com, Fax (0151) 604 1999,* – ⇔ & P. MC VISA. ⅏
Rest 17.50 – 5.75 – **9 rm** ★55.00/75.00 – ★★75.00/95.00.
◆ Modernised 19C house that offers a good standard of accommodation. Smart breakfast room with linen-clad tables and chunky wooden chairs. Attractive, comfortable rooms.

WESTLETON *Suffolk* 504 Y 27 – ✉ *Saxmundham.*
London 97 – Cambridge 72 – Ipswich 28 – Norwich 31.

Pond House without rest., The Hill, IP17 3AN, ℘ (01728) 648773, – ⇔ P. ⅏
closed 1 week Christmas – **3 rm** ★32.00 – ★★54.00.
◆ A welcoming atmosphere prevails in this neatly maintained 1700s cottage beside the village green. Simple, pine furnished bedrooms. Convenient for Minsmere Nature Reserve.

WEST LULWORTH *Dorset* 503 504 N 32 *The West Country G.* – ✉ *Wareham.*
See : *Lulworth Cove★.*
London 129 – Bournemouth 21 – Dorchester 17 – Weymouth 19.

Gatton House without rest., Main Rd, BH20 5RL, ℘ (01929) 400252, *avril@gatton house.co.uk, Fax (01929) 400252,* – ⇔ P. MC VISA. ⅏
April-late September – **8 rm** ★60.00 – ★★94.00.
◆ Follow the winding garden path to a smart gabled house in the middle of this pleasant village. Comfy accommodation in co-ordinated décor; neat front-facing breakfast room.

Red = Pleasant. Look for the red ✗ and symbols.

WEST MALLING *Kent* 504 V 30 – *pop. 2 144.*
18, 18 *Addington, Maidstone ℘ (01732) 844785.*
London 35 – Maidstone 7 – Royal Tunbridge Wells 14.

Premier Travel Inn, Castle Way, Leybourne, ME19 5TR, Northeast : 1 m. on A 228 ℘ (08701) 977170, *Fax (01732) 844474* – ⇔ rm, ▤ rest, & P. MC AE VISA. ⅏
Rest (grill rest.) – **40 rm** ★49.95 – ★★49.95.
◆ Group-owned lodge with convenient road links to the Medway towns and Kent coast. Competitively priced rooms in trim modern style, useful for business and family stopovers.

Scott House without rest., 37 High St, ME19 6QH, ℘ (01732) 841380, *mail@scott house.co.uk, Fax (01732) 522367* – ⇔ ✆. MC AE VISA. ⅏
closed Christmas-New Year – **5 rm** ★59.00 – ★★79.00.
◆ Comfy rooms in period style and a relaxing first-floor lounge share this part Georgian town house with a fine interior décor shop, run by the same warm husband and wife team.

The Swan, 35 Swan St, ME19 6JU, ℘ (01732) 521910, *info@theswanwestmalling.co.uk, Fax (01732) 522898,* – ⇔ ▤ ⇔ 28. MC AE VISA
closed 26 December, 1 January and lunch 31 December and 2 January – **Rest** a la carte 22.00/30.00 ♀.
◆ Radically renovated 16C pub in modern pine. Stylish lounge: leopard-print carpet, purple cushions. Modish menu at sensible prices; informal, very efficient service.

WEST MONKTON *Somerset* 503 K 30 – *see Taunton.*

WESTON-SUPER-MARE *North Somerset* 503 K 29 *The West Country G.* – *pop. 78 044.*
See : *Seafront (≤★★) BZ.*
Exc. : *Axbridge★★ (King John's Hunting Lodge★, St John the Baptist Church★) SE : 9 m. by A 371 – BY – and A 38 – Cheddar Gorge★★ (Gorge★★, Caves★, Jacob's Ladder ✵★) – Clevedon★ (≤★★, Clevedon Court★), NE : 10 m. by A 370 and M 5 – St Andrew's Church★, SE : 10½ m. by A 371.*
18 *Worlebury, Monks Hill ℘ (01934) 625789* **BY.**
i *Beach Lawns ℘ (01934) 888800.*
London 147 – Bristol 24 – Taunton 32.

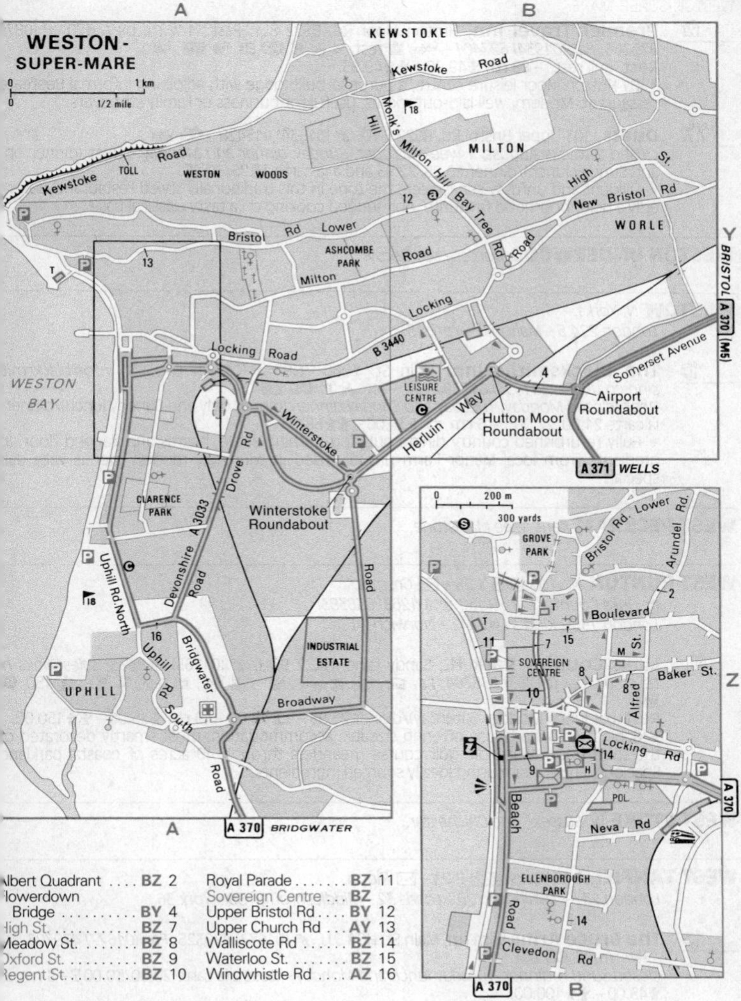

lbert Quadrant	BZ 2	Royal Parade	BZ 11
lowerdown Bridge	BY 4	Sovereign Centre	BZ
High St.	BZ 7	Upper Bristol Rd	BY 12
Meadow St.	BZ 8	Upper Church Rd	AY 13
Oxford St.	BZ 9	Walliscote Rd	BZ 14
Regent St.	BZ 10	Waterloo St.	BZ 15
		Windwhistle Rd	AZ 16

The Beachlands, 17 Uphill Road North, BS23 4NG, ✆ (01934) 621401, *info@beachlandshotel.com, Fax (01934) 621966,* ≘s, ▣, 🛋 – ⇸ ♿ P – 🏊 40. 🅜🅒 AE ⓓ VISA. ✂ **AZ c**
closed 24 December-2 January – **Rest** (bar lunch Monday-Saturday)/dinner 21.00 **s.** – **23 rm** ☕ ✝55.00/79.50 – ✝✝107.00/109.00.
◆ Well-established and family run, convenient for beach and golf course. Rooms in traditional prints; some, south-facing, have veranda doors giving on to a secluded garden. Formal dining room overlooks pleasant gardens.

Queenswood, Victoria Park, BS23 2HZ, off Upper Church Rd ✆ (01934) 416141, *Fax (01934) 621759* – ⇸, ▤ rest. 🅜🅒 AE VISA **BZ s**
closed Christmas and New Year – **Rest** *(closed Sunday dinner)* (bar lunch)/dinner 20.00 **s.** 🍷 – **19 rm** ☕ ✝50.00/65.00 – ✝✝75.00/100.00.
◆ Sizeable, 19C-style house, well kept by friendly, long-standing owners. Red velour lounge sofas and neat rooms in the time-honoured tradition of the British seaside holiday. Tried-and-tested menus.

ENGLAND

Premier Travel Inn, Hutton Moor Rd, BS22 8LY, East : 1 ½ m. by A 370 ℘ (087(977266, *Fax (01934) 627401* – ⇔, ▤ rest, ℃ ♿ 🅿. MO AE ⓓ VISA. ⚡ BY
Rest (grill rest.) – **88 rm** ☆49.95 – ☆☆49.95.
◆ By Hutton Moor leisure centre, a purpose-built lodge with adjoining informal Beefeate restaurant. Modern, well laid-out rooms, useful for business or family stopovers.

Duets, 103 Upper Bristol Rd, BS22 8ND, ℘ (01934) 413428 – MO VISA BY
closed 2 weeks August, 1 week October, Sunday dinner and Monday – **Rest** (dinner onl and Sunday lunch)/dinner 19.95/22.95 and a la carte 17.95/30.85.
◆ Diligent and unfussy service sets the tone in this traditionally styled restaurant, deserv edly a neighbourhood favourite. Ably judged cooking on a tasty classical base.

WESTON UNDERWOOD *Derbs. – see Derby.*

WESTOW *N. Yorks.*

London 224.5 – Malton 8 – York 15.

The Blacksmiths Inn, Main St, YO60 7NE, ℘ (01653) 618365, *info@blacksmit sinn.co.uk, Fax (01653) 618394,* ☂ – ⇔ ♿ 🅿. MO VISA
Rest *(closed Monday, Tuesday and Sunday dinner)* (dinner only and Sunday lunch)/dinner la carte 21.00/27.00 ♀ – **6 rm** ☕ ☆34.00 – ☆☆68.00.
◆ Fully refurbished country dining pub; log-burning stove, beams and flagged floor. In gredients from local Manor Farm proudly used in winningly modish menus with dail specials.

WEST PECKHAM *Kent – see Maidstone.*

WEST RUNTON *Norfolk* 504 X 25 – ✉ *Cromer.*

Links Country Park Hotel ℘ (01263) 838383.
London 135 – King's Lynn 42 – Norwich 24.

Links Country Park H., Sandy Lane, NR27 9QH, ℘ (01263) 838383, *sales@links-h tel.co.uk, Fax (01263) 838264,* Ɫ6, ≘s, ▧, 9, ⛱, ⚔ – ▮ ⇔, ▤ rest, ℃ 🅿 – 🏛 150. MO VISA
Rest (bar lunch Monday-Saturday)/dinner 25.95 – ☕ 15.00 – **49 rm** ☆75.00 – ☆☆150.00.
◆ Gabled Victorian house offering sizeable accommodation, most smartly decorated o the third floor. Nine-hole golf course meanders through 40 acres of coastal parklanc Spacious dining room using locally sourced ingredients.

WEST STOKE *W. Sussex – see Chichester.*

WEST TANFIELD *N. Yorks.* 502 P 21 – ✉ *Ripon.*

London 237 – Darlington 29 – Leeds 32 – Middlesbrough 39 – York 36.

The Bruce Arms with rm, Main St, HG4 5JJ, ℘ (01677) 470325, *Fax (01677) 470796,* ☂ – ⇔ rm, 🅿. MO VISA. ⚡
closed Sunday dinner, Tuesday lunch and Monday – **Rest** a la carte 20.00/30.00 ♀ – **3 rm** ☕ ☆45.00 – ☆☆100.00.
◆ Stone-built village pub: log fire, local ales, leather sofas. Vine covered, decked terrace Well-spaced candlelit pub tables. Satisfying blackboard menu.. Rustic bedrooms.

WEST WITTON *N. Yorks.* 502 O 21 – ✉ *Leyburn.*

London 241 – Kendal 39 – Leeds 60 – Newcastle upon Tyne 65 – York 53.

Ivy Dene, DL8 4LP, ℘ (01969) 622785, *info@ivydeneguesthouse.co.uk Fax (01969) 622785* – ⇔ 🅿. ⚡
closed 23 December - 6 January – **Rest** (by arrangement) 16.00 – **4 rm** ☕ ☆35.00/40.00 – ☆☆54.00/56.00.
◆ Cosy, cottage-style rooms, one with four-poster bed, others with brass bedsteads, in this 300-year-old house. Firelit sitting room with a collection of clocks and antiques. Dining room offers renowned sticky toffee pudding.

WETHERAL *Cumbria* 501 502 L 19 – *see Carlisle.*

WETHERBY *W. Yorks.* 502 P 22 *Great Britain G. – pop. 10 562.*

Env. : *Harewood House★★ (The Gallery★) AC, SW : 5½ m. by A 58 and A 659.*

Linton Lane, Linton ☎ (01937) 580089.

The Library, 17 Westgate ☎ (01937) 582151.

London 208 – Harrogate 8 – Leeds 13 – York 14.

Wood Hall, Trip Lane, Linton, LS22 4JA, Southwest : 3 m. by A 61 and Linton Rd ☎ (01937) 587271, *woodhall@handpicked.co.uk, Fax (01937) 584353,* ≤, – rest, P – 140. MO AE VISA.
Rest (bar lunch Monday-Saturday)/dinner 32.50 – **44 rm** 144.00/185.00 – 189.00/235.00.
◆ Peacefully set part Jacobean and Georgian manor in 100 acres of woods and gardens. Refurbished contemporary public areas; well-appointed bedrooms. Popular wedding venue. Elegant dining room with candelabras and tall sash windows.

WEYBRIDGE *Surrey* 504 S 29 *– pop. 52 890 (inc. Walton).*

London 23 – Crawley 27 – Guildford 17 – Reading 33.

The Ship, Monument Green, High St, KT13 8BQ, off A 317 ☎ (01932) 848364, *info@shiphotel.co.uk, Fax (01932) 857153* – , rest, P – 150. MO AE VISA
Rest (bar lunch Monday-Saturday)/dinner a la carte 18.70/26.50 – **77 rm** 92.50/135.00 – 135.00/165.00.
◆ This former coaching inn is pleasingly decorated throughout: pictures and plates on walls, floral furnishings, soft lighting, welcoming fire in lounge. Rooms in quiet hues. Dining room defined by flowers and mellow tones.

WEYMOUTH *Dorset* 503 504 M 32 *The West Country G. – pop. 48 279.*

See : *Town★ – Timewalk★ AC – Nothe Fort (≤★) AC – Boat Trip★ (Weymouth Bay and Portland Harbour) AC.*

Env. : *Chesil Beach★★ – Portland★ - Portland Bill (★★) S : 2½ m. by A 354.*

Exc. : *Maiden Castle★★ (≤★) N : 6½ m. by A 354 – Abbotsbury★★ (Swannery★ AC, Sub-Tropical Gardens★ AC, St Catherine's Chapel★) NW : 9 m. by B 3157.*

Links Rd ☎ (01305) 773981.

to Guernsey (St Peter Port) and Jersey (St Helier) (Condor Ferries Ltd).

The King's Statue, The Esplanade ☎ (01305) 785747, tic@weymouth.gov.uk.

London 142 – Bournemouth 35 – Bristol 68 – Exeter 59 – Swindon 94.

Moonfleet Manor, DT3 4ED, Northwest : 4½ m. by B 3157 ☎ (01305) 786948, *info@moonfleetmanor.com, Fax (01305) 774395,* ≤, , squash – rest, P – 60. MO AE VISA
Rest (bar lunch Monday-Saturday)/dinner 28.00/34.00 – **36 rm** (dinner included) 126.00/160.00 – 230.00/340.00, 2 suites.
◆ Georgian in origin, an extended country house with stunning coastal views. Well equipped rooms, cosy lounges hung with oils. Games room and special facilities for families. Subtle Mediterranean styling imbues restaurant.

Premier Travel Inn, Green Hill, DT4 7SX, East : ½ m. on A 353 ☎ (01303) 767964, *Fax (01303) 768113* – rm, P. MO AE VISA.
Rest (grill rest.) – **40 rm** 51.95 – 51.95.
◆ Purpose-built, two-storey lodge on the outskirts of the town. Trim, modern bedrooms with ample work space. Meals may be taken at the adjacent Brewers Fayre restaurant.

Chatsworth, 14 The Esplanade, DT4 8EB, ☎ (01305) 785012, *david@thechatsworth.co.uk, Fax (01305) 766342,* ≤, – . MO VISA.
Rest (by arrangement) 22.50 – **8 rm** 30.00/50.00 – 80.00/100.00.
◆ Seafront terraced house; brightly coloured bedrooms, modern and well-maintained. A pretty terrace, facing south over the quay, overflows with hanging baskets in summer. Combined bay-windowed dining room and fire-lit lounge.

Bay View without rest., 35 The Esplanade, DT4 8DH, ☎ (01305) 782083, *Fax (01305) 782083,* ≤ – P. MO VISA.
closed December – **8 rm** 45.00/50.00 – 60.00/70.00.
◆ Generously sized en suite rooms, many with four-poster beds or broad bay windows, in a sizeable townhouse with views over the bay. Neatly kept basement lounge.

Perry's, 4 Trinity Rd, The Old Harbour, DT4 8TJ, ☎ (01305) 785799, *enquiries@perrysrestaurant.co.uk, Fax (01305) 787002* – . MO AE VISA
closed 25-26 December, 1 January, lunch Monday and Saturday and Sunday dinner in winter – **Rest** a la carte 19.85/27.85.
◆ Simple, family-run local favourite by the old harbour. Friendly staff, tasty cooking and plenty of seafood specials: shellfish soup, Portland crab, citrus-dressed bass.

WHALLEY *Lancs.* 502 M 22 – *pop. 3 230* – ✉ *Blackburn.*

Long Leese Barn, Clerkhill ☎ (01254) 822236.

London 233 – Blackpool 32 – Burnley 12 – Manchester 28 – Preston 15.

Clarion H. Foxfields, Whalley Rd, Billington, BB7 9HY, Southwest : 1 ¼ m. ☎ (01254 822556, *enquiries@hotels-blackburn.com, Fax (01254) 823156,* – rest, – 180. MC AE VISA
Foxfields : **Rest** (bar lunch Saturday) (dancing Saturday evening) a la carte 16.85/27.85 – 12.95 – **18 rm** 105.00/125.00 – 115.00/135.00, **26 suites** 115.00/135.00.
◆ Group run hotel with suites and lounges in the original building and modern, wood furnished rooms in the annex: most overlook the countryside, some have balconies. Spacious restaurant plays host to regular live music.

at Mitton *Northwest : 2½ m. on B 6246* – ✉ *Whalley.*

The Three Fishes, Mitton Rd, BB7 9PQ, ☎ (01254) 826888, *Fax (01254) 826026,* MC AE VISA
closed 25 December – **Rest** (bookings not accepted) a la carte 15.00/19.50.
◆ Huge, 140 cover modern dining pub, once a coaching inn. Lancashire and north-west England regional specialities dominate the menu. Perenially busy: remember, you can't book!

WHASHTON *N. Yorks. – see Richmond.*

WHAW *N. Yorks.* 502 O 20 – *see Reeth.*

WHICKHAM *Tyne and Wear* 501 502 O/P 19 – *see Gateshead.*

WHITBY *N. Yorks.* 502 S 20 *Great Britain G.* – *pop. 13 594.*

See : *Abbey★.*

Sandsend Rd, Low Straggleton ☎ (01947) 600660.

Langborne Rd ☎ (01723) 383637.

London 257 – Middlesbrough 31 – Scarborough 21 – York 45.

Bagdale Hall, 1 Bagdale, YO21 1QL, ☎ (01947) 602958, *Fax (01947) 820714* – rest P. MC AE VISA.
Rest (dinner only and Sunday lunch)/dinner a la carte 17.70/29.70 – **14 rm** 70.00 – 118.00.
◆ Tudor manor with fine fireplaces in carved wood and 19C Delft tiles; panelled rooms with mullioned windows; four-posters in period style bedrooms. Annex for more modern rooms. Dining room boasts timbered ceiling and massive wooden fireplace.

Cross Butts Stable, Guisborough Rd, YO21 1TL, West : 1 ¾ m. on A 171 (Teeside rd ☎ (01947) 820986, *Fax (01947) 825665,* P. MC VISA.
Rest a la carte 15.50/27.00 – **9 rm** 45.00/70.00 – 65.00/145.00.
◆ Extended farmhouse on working farm personally run by a welcoming family. Superb bedrooms, set round courtyard with water feature, have flag floors and warm, sumptuous aura. Smart, informal restaurant areas over two floors: a mix of suites, sofas and tables.

Greens, 13 Bridge St, YO22 4BG, ☎ (01947) 600284 – MC VISA
closed 25-26 December and 1 January – **Rest** - Seafood specialities - (booking essential) (dinner only and lunch Friday-Sunday) a la carte 21.75/32.75.
◆ Set in town centre, close to quayside, with a rustic, informal ambience. Constantly changing seafood menus are simply cooked and employ much produce freshly landed at Whitby.

at Briggswath *Southwest : 3½ m. by A 171 (Teesdie rd), A 169 on B 1410* – ✉ *Whitby.*

The Lawns, 73 Carr Hill Lane, YO21 1RS, ☎ (01947) 810310, *lorton@onetel.com Fax (01947) 810310,* P.
closed January-February – **Rest** (by arrangement) 19.00 – **3** rm 58.00 – 64.00.
◆ Sizeable, converted house above a south-facing garden and verge of evergreens. Stripped wooden floors, understated décor. Spotless rooms. Fine views of moors and Esk valley.

The Olde Ford, 1 Briggswath, YO21 1RU, ☎ (01947) 810704, *gray.theoldeford@btinternet.com,* P. MC AE VISA
closed 22-28 December, 2 weeks June and 2 weeks spring – **Rest** (by arrangement) 15.00 – **3 rm** 40.00 – 55.00.
◆ Appealing little stone cottage on the banks of the river Esk: former village post office. Traditional Yorkshire breakfasts. All rooms look out over garden and river.

at Dunsley *West : 3¼ m. by A 171 – ✉ Whitby.*

Dunsley Hall Country House, YO22 5PW, ☎ (01947) 893437, *reception@dunsleyhall.com, Fax (01947) 893505*, ←, 🏋, ≘s, ▣, 🌳, ✗ – ⇹ 🅿 – 🏠 100. 🅜🅒 🅐🅔 VISA
Rest (bar lunch Monday-Saturday)/dinner 27.95 ♀ – **18 rm** ☕ ✝82.50/105.00 – ✝✝135.00/177.00.
◆ Behind pillared gates, a personally run late Victorian house: intricately oak panelled lounge with leather furnished bar. Comfortable, period styled rooms with country views. Dining room boasts Whitby seafood.

WHITCHURCH *Shrops.* 502 503 L 25.
London 168.5 – Nantwich 11 – Wrexham 15.5.

at Burleydam *East : 4¼ m. on A 525 – ✉ Whitchurch.*

The Combermere Arms, SY13 4AT, ☎ (01948) 871223, *combermere.arms@brunningandprice.co.uk, Fax (01948) 661371*, 🏠, 🌳 – ⇹ 🅿. 🅜🅒 VISA
Rest a la carte 16.50/26.40 ♀.
◆ Rurally located pub with smart terrace ideal for al fresco refreshment. Interior skylights lend an open, airy feel. Informal, eclectic menus. Some vast tables for big parties.

Hotels and restaurants change every year, so change your Michelin guide every year!

WHITEHAVEN *Cumbria* 502 J 20.
London 332 – Carlisle 39 – Keswick 28 – Penrith 47.

Premier Travel Inn, Howgate, CA28 6PL, Northeast : 3 m. by A 5094 on A 595 ☎ (01946) 66286, *Fax (01946) 63407* – ⇹, ▤ rest, ♿ 🅿. 🅜🅒 🅐🅔 🅓 VISA. ✗
Rest (grill rest.) – **38 rm** ✝46.95/46.95 – ✝✝48.95/48.95.
◆ Well-proportioned modern bedrooms, suitable for business and family stopovers, designed with practicality and price in mind. Adjacent grill restaurant.

Zest, Low Rd, CA28 9HS, South : ½ m. on B 5345 (St Bees) ☎ (01946) 692848, *Fax (01946) 66984* – 🅿. 🅜🅒 🅓 VISA
closed Sunday-Tuesday – **Rest** (dinner only) a la carte 16.50/28.00 s. ♀.
◆ Don't be put off by the unprepossessing exterior: inside is a smart, stylish eatery and bar with brown leather sofas. Eclectic range of modern menus with numerous influences.

WHITEPARISH *Wilts.* 503 504 P 30 – *see Salisbury.*

WHITEWELL *Lancs.* 502 M 22 – ✉ *Clitheroe.*
London 281 – Lancaster 31 – Leeds 55 – Manchester 41 – Preston 13.

Inn at Whitewell, Forest of Bowland, BB7 3AT, ☎ (01200) 448222, *Fax (01200) 448298*, ←, 🐟, 🌳 – 🅿. 🅜🅒 VISA
Rest (bar lunch)/dinner a la carte 18.00/41.00 ♀ – **23 rm** ☕ ✝70.00/114.00 – ✝✝96.00/150.00, 1 suite.
◆ Once home to the Royal Keeper of the Forest, a popular inn with considerable charm, full of eyecatching curios. Stylish rooms with CD players; some have real peat fires. Intimate dining room overlooks river Hodder and Trough of Bowland.

WHITLEY *Wilts. – see Melksham.*

WHITLEY BAY *Tyne and Wear* 501 502 P 18 – *pop. 36 544.*
🅘 Park Rd ☎ *(0191) 200 8535.*
London 295 – Newcastle upon Tyne 10 – Sunderland 10.

Windsor, South Parade, NE26 2RF, ☎ (0191) 251 8888, *reservations@windsorhotel-uk.com, Fax (0191) 297 0272* – |♦|, ▤ rest, 🅿 – 🏠 80. 🅜🅒 🅐🅔 🅓 VISA. ✗
Bazil *:* Rest *(closed Sunday)* (dinner only) a la carte 20.40/28.70 s. ♀ – **69 rm** ☕ ✝69.00/85.00 – ✝✝75.00/95.00.
◆ Close to the seafront on the Northumbrian coast; a family owned hotel with spacious, neatly decorated, up-to-date bedrooms. Bar Zync for night owls. Bright, modern contemporary brasserie.

WHITSTABLE *Kent* 504 X 29 – *pop. 30 195.*

7 Oxford St (01227) 275482, whitstableinformation@canterbury.gov.uk.
London 68 – Dover 24 – Maidstone 37 – Margate 12.

Continental, 29 Beach Walk, CT5 2BP, East : ½ m. by Sea St and Harbour St (01227 280280, *jamie@hotelcontinental.co.uk, Fax (01227) 284114*, ←, – MO VISA.
closed 1 week Christmas – **Rest** *(bar lunch)/dinner* 24.95 and a la carte 24.15/45.90 – **24 r** 52.00/72.00 – 100.00/135.00.
• Laid-back, privately owned hotel with an unadorned 30s-style façade overlooking th sea; simply furnished, plain-walled rooms - picture windows and warm colours. Split-lev bistro with "no frills" approach.

Premier Travel Inn, Thanet Way, CT5 3DB, Southwest : 2 m. by A 290 (0870 977269, *Fax (01227) 263151* – , rest, P. MO AE VISA.
Rest (grill rest.) – **40 rm** 48.95 – 48.95.
• Purpose-built group hotel on the outskirts of town. Neat modern rooms with wo desks and sofa beds. Meals may be taken at the adjacent Brewers Fayre.

Whitstable Oyster Fishery Co., Royal Native Oyster Stores, The Horsebridge, CT 1BU, (01227) 276856, *Fax (01227) 770829*, ← – MO AE VISA
closed 25-26 December, Monday except Bank Holidays and Tuesday-Thursday dinner winter – **Rest** - Seafood - (booking essential in winter) a la carte 25.45/40.95 ♀.
• Relaxed and unfussy converted beach warehouse; seafood on display in open kitche oysters and moules-frites draw a trendy young set at weekends. Arthouse cinema upstair

Jo Jo's, 209 Tankerton Rd, CT5 2AT, East : 1 ½ m. by Sea St and Harbour St (0122 274891, –
closed Monday-Tuesday and Sunday dinner – **Rest** (booking essential) a la car 12.00/14.00.
• Charmingly laid back eatery with snug interior and mix of bar stools and rustic woode tables. There's a simple terrace, too. Appealing mix of tapas and meze to graze over.

at Seasalter *Southwest : 2 m. by B 2205 – Whitstable.*

The Sportsman, Faversham Rd, CT5 4BP, Southwest : 2 m. following coast r (01227) 273370, *Fax (01227) 281564*, – P. MO VISA
closed 25 December, Sunday dinner and Monday – **Rest** a la carte 23.00/30.00 ♀.
• Set along the coast road with shingle and beach to one side, acres of marshland to th other. Tasty classic and modern menus. Local farmer supplies best seasonal ingredients.

WHITTLE-LE-WOODS *Lancs.* 502 M 23 – *see Chorley.*

WHITTLESFORD *Cambs.* 504 U 27.

London 50 – Cambridge 11 – Peterborough 46.

The Tickell Arms, 1 North Rd, CB2 4NZ, (01223) 833128, *Fax (01223) 835907*, P. MO AE
closed Sunday dinner and Monday – **Rest** 25.50/34.50 ♀.
• Richly ornate 300 year-old exterior with conservatory and terrace. Quirky feel pervade emerald green walls, yellow ceiling. Rich, classic meals from the Gallic repertoire.

WHITWELL-ON-THE-HILL *N. Yorks.* 502 R 21 – *York.*

London 240 – Kingston-upon-Hull 47 – Scarborough 29 – York 13.

The Stone Trough Inn, Kirkham Abbey, YO60 7JS, East : 1 ¾ m. by A 64 on Kirkha Priory rd (01653) 618713, *info@stonetroughinn.co.uk, Fax (01653) 618819*, – P MO VISA
closed 25 December, Sunday dinner and Monday except Bank Holidays – **Rest** a la cart 20.00/25.00 ♀.
• Friendly rustic pub, two minutes from the striking ruins of Kirkham Abbey. Wide-rangin menu on a sound local base: satisfying and full of flavour. Warm, attentive service.

WICKFORD *Essex* 504 V 29 – *see Basildon.*

WICKHAM *Hants.* 503 504 Q 31 – *pop. 1 915.*

London 74 – Portsmouth 12 – Southampton 11 – Winchester 16.

The Old House with rm, The Square, PO17 5JG, (01329) 833049, *oldhouseh tel@aol.com, Fax (01329) 833672*, , – P. MO AE VISA.
Rest *(closed Sunday dinner)* a la carte 22.65/39.40 ♀ – 10.00 – **15 rm** 65.00/75.00 150.00.
• Handsome Queen Anne house in town centre. Eat in pretty conservatory or on delightfu terrace. Unfussy, accomplished, seasonal cooking. Smarter bedrooms in the garden wing.

WIGAN *Gtr Manchester* 502 M 23 – *pop. 81 203.*
Trencherfield Mill, Wallgate (01942) 825677, tic@wiganbc.gov.uk.
London 203 – Liverpool 22 – Manchester 24 – Preston 18.

Premier Travel Inn, Warrington Rd, Marus Bridge, WN3 6XB, South : 2 ¾ m. on A 49 (0870) 1977270, *Fax (01942) 498679* – rm, rest, P. MC AE VISA
Rest (grill rest.) – **40 rm** 46.95/46.95 – 48.95/48.95.
◆ Useful motorway connections from this group-owned lodge. Bright, modern and competitively priced rooms. Family-friendly grill restaurant.

WIGHT (Isle of) *I.O.W.* 503 504 P/Q 31 32 *Great Britain G. – pop. 124 577.*
See : *Island★★.*
Env. : *Osborne House, East Cowes★★ AC – Carisbrooke Castle, Newport★★ AC (Keep ≤★) – Brading★ (Roman Villa★ AC, St Mary's Church★, Nunwell House★ AC) – Shorwell : St Peter's Church★ (wall paintings★).*
from East Cowes to Southampton (Red Funnel Ferries) frequent services daily (1 h) – from Yarmouth to Lymington (Wightlink Ltd) frequent services daily (30 mn) – from Fishbourne to Portsmouth (Wightlink Ltd) frequent services daily (35 mn).
from Ryde to Portsmouth (Hovertravel Ltd) frequent services daily (10 mn) – from Ryde to Portsmouth (Wightlink Ltd) frequent services daily (15 mn) – from East Cowes to Southampton (Red Funnel Ferries) frequent services daily (22 mn).

Brighstone.

The Lodge without rest., Main Rd, PO30 4DJ, (01983) 741272, *paul@thelodgebrighstone.com, Fax (01983) 741272,* – P.
March-October – **7 rm** 40.00 – 60.00.
◆ Victorian country house set in two and a half acres: quiet location. Real fire centrepiece of large sitting room. Completely co-ordinated rooms of varnished pine.

Freshwater *I.O.W. – pop. 7 317 (inc. Totland) – Isle of Wight.*
Newport 13.

Sandpipers, Coastguard Lane (via public car park), Freshwater Bay, PO40 9QX, South : 1 ½ m. by A 3055 (01983) 758500, *fatcat@btconnect.com, Fax (01983) 754364,* – P. MC VISA
Rest (bar lunch Monday-Saturday)/dinner a la carte 26.50/36.00 – **26 rm** 30.00/60.00 – 60.00/120.00.
◆ Detached Victorian house with a friendly, family run atmosphere. Close to the cliffs, beach and Afton nature reserve. Good sized, modern-style rooms. Garden conservatory restaurant set around variety of water features.

Rockstone Cottage without rest., Colwell Chine Rd, PO40 9NR, Northwest : ¾ m. by A 3055 off A 3054 (01983) 753723, *enquiries@rockstonecottage.co.uk, Fax (01983) 753721,* – P.
5 rm 35.00/39.00 – 50.00/58.00.
◆ Simple, pretty cottage, with small garden, dating from the 1790s. Well-kept domestic feel with a traditional and homely standard of décor.

Red Lion, Church Pl, PO40 9BP, via Hooke Hill (01983) 754925, *info@redlionwight.co.uk, Fax (01983) 754925,* – P. MC VISA
closed 25 December – **Rest** a la carte 16.00/25.00.
◆ Bustling part 14C pub with much charm. Located at the top of a hill and next to the church. Stone floors, open fires and a couple of sofas. Blackboard menu of seasonal fare.

Newport.

Premier Travel Inn, Seaclose Quay, Newport Quay, PO30 2DN, North : 1 ¼ m. on A 3054 (01983) 825082, *Fax (01983) 824111* – rm, P. MC AE VISA.
Rest (grill rest.) – **42 rm** 49.95 – 49.95.
◆ The first of its kind to appear on the Island. Views over working shipyard. The comfortable, purpose-built rooms are all spacious and bright.

Ryde *I.O.W. – Isle of Wight.*
Binstead Rd (01983) 614809.
81-83 Union St (01983) 813818.
Newport 7.

Beijing Palace, Appley Rise, PO33 1LE, (01983) 811888, *Fax (01983) 562888* – MC AE VISA
closed 25-26 December – **Rest** - Chinese - a la carte approx 19.00.
◆ Sizable thatched roofed façade belied by narrow interior with simple décor that's highlighted by life-sized central Buddha. Good value menus, full of tasty, regional dishes.

ENGLAND

St Lawrence *I.O.W. – ✉ Isle of Wight.*
Newport 16.

Little Orchard without rest., Undercliffe Drive, PO38 1YA, West : 1 m. on A 305 ✆ (01983) 731106, – P.
3 rm ★38.00 – ★★60.00.
◆ A pretty, detached stone cottage with secluded rear garden and some views of the sea. Large, welcoming lounge with piano. Simple, comfortable bedrooms.

Seaview *I.O.W. – pop. 2 181 – ✉ Isle of Wight.*

Priory Bay, Priory Drive, PO34 5BU, Southeast : 1½ m. by B 3330 ✆ (01983) 613146 *enquiries@priorybay.co.uk, Fax (01983) 616539*, , , , , – rest, P. VISA
The Restaurant : Rest 27.50 (dinner) and a la carte approx 22.40 – **18 rm** ★65.00/130.00 – ★★150.00/200.00, 2 suites.
◆ Medieval priory with Georgian additions, surrounded by woodland. High ceilinged drawing room and bar area with leaded windows. Characterful rooms. Main Restaurant has views of the garden.

Seaview, High St, PO34 5EX, ✆ (01983) 612711, *reception@seaviewhotel.co.uk Fax (01983) 613729*, – , rest, P. AE VISA
closed 24-26 December – ***The Restaurant and Sunshine Room :*** **Rest** (booking essential) (in bar Sunday dinner except Bank Holidays) a la carte 18.00/26.00 – **15 rm** ★58.00/177.00 – ★★137.00/188.00, 2 suites.
◆ Victorian hotel with smart genuine style. Integral part of the community, on street leading to seafront. Bold modern bedrooms and nautically styled, welcoming public areas. Twin eateries, full of clocks and rare model ship collection.

Shanklin *I.O.W. – pop. 17 305 (inc. Sandown) – ✉ Isle of Wight.*
18 The Fairway, Lake Sandown ✆ (01983) 403217.
67 High St ✆ (01983) 813818.
Newport 9.

Rylstone Manor, Rylstone Gdns, PO37 6RG, ✆ (01983) 862806, *rylstonemanor@btinternet.com, Fax (01983) 862806*, – P. AE VISA.
mid March-early October – **Rest** (dinner only) 20.00 – **9 rm** (dinner included) ★66.00/119.00 – ★★147.00.
◆ Part 19C former gentleman's residence set in the town's cliff-top gardens. Interior has a comfortable period feel. Well furnished, individually styled bedrooms. Characterful Victorian hued dining room.

Foxhills without rest., 30 Victoria Ave, PO37 6LS, ✆ (01983) 862329, *info@foxhillshotel.co.uk, Fax (01983) 866666*, – P. VISA.
closed 3-31 January – **8 rm** ★45.00/90.00 – ★★90.00.
◆ Attractive house in leafy avenue with woodland to the rear. Bright lounge with fireplace. Bedrooms in pastel shades. Unusual jacuzzi, spa and beauty treatments. Breakfast room opens onto terrace.

Grange Bank, Grange Rd, PO37 6NN, ✆ (01983) 862337, *grangebank@btinternet.com* – P. VISA.
Easter-October – **Rest** (booking essential) (residents only) (dinner only) (unlicensed) 9.50 – **9 rm** ★26.00/29.00 – ★★104.00/116.00.
◆ Extended Victorian house near high street. Comfortable, simple and immaculately kept with friendly, domestic ambience. Good value accommodation.

Totland *I.O.W. – pop. 7 317 (inc. Freshwater) – ✉ Isle of Wight.*
Newport 13.

Sentry Mead, Madeira Rd, PO39 0BJ, ✆ (01983) 753212, *brochure@sentrymead.co.uk Fax (01983) 753212*, – P. AE VISA
Rest (bar lunch)/dinner 19.50 – **14 rm** ★40.00/70.00 – ★★80.00/120.00.
◆ Detached Victorian house with quiet garden 100 yards from beach. Traditional interiors include bar area and conservatory lounge. Comfortable rooms furnished with light wood. Popular menus in dining room.

Ventnor *I.O.W. – pop. 5 978 – ✉ Isle of Wight.*
9 Steephill Down Rd ✆ (01983) 853326.
Coastal Visitors Centre, Salisbury Gdns, Dudley Rd ✆ (01983) 813818 (summer only).
Newport 10.

Royal, Belgrave Rd, PO38 1JJ, ✆ (01983) 852186, *enquiries@royalhoteliow.co.uk Fax (01983) 855395*, , – P – 40. AE VISA
closed 4-19 January – **Rest** (bar lunch Monday-Saturday)/dinner 32.50/42.50 s. – **55 rm** ★75.00/135.00 – ★★130.00/150.00.
◆ Largest hotel on the island, a Victorian property, in the classic style of English seaside hotels. Traditional décor throughout the public areas and comfortable bedrooms. Light lunches in conservatory; classic meals in capacious dining room.

Wellington, Belgrave Rd, PO38 1JH, ✆ (01983) 856600, *enquiries@thewellingtonhotel.net, Fax (01983) 856611,* ≤ Ventnor and English Channel, 🏠 – ⇆ rest, ✆ [P]. MC AE VISA. 🚫

Rest (dinner only) a la carte 21.20/27.50 – **28 rm** ☐ ✝80.00/88.00 – ✝✝110.00/118.00.

◆ Totally refurbished Victorian hotel with commanding town and sea views. Modish lines throughout. Most rooms have a balcony; all are imbued with a stunning sense of modernity. Spacious dining room with dramatic views and beautiful decked terrace.

Lake 🐦, Shore Rd, Bonchurch, PO38 1RF, ✆ (01983) 852613, *mich@lakehotel.co.uk*, 🌳 – ⇆ [P]

February-November – **Rest** (dinner only) 12.00 **s.** – **20 rm** ☐ ✝38.00/68.00 – ✝✝74.00.

◆ 19C private residence, run as hotel by one family since 1960s. South facing public rooms in traditional style. Bedrooms in annex and main house have simple country feel. Garden views from dining room.

Hambrough with rm, Hambrough Rd, PO38 1SQ, ✆ (01983) 856333, *info@thehambrough.com, Fax (01983) 857260,* ≤, 🌳 – ⇆, ▤ rest, [P] ⇔ 25. MC AE ⊙ VISA. 🚫

Rest 18.00/50.00 and a la carte 23.00/40.00 – **7 rm** ☐ ✝100.00/160.00 – ✝✝130.00/200.00.

◆ Victorian house with contrastingly modish bar and avant-garde restaurant. Well-conceived menus enjoy contemporary starting point. State-of-the-art rooms with neutral hues.

The Pond Café, Bonchurch, PO38 1RG, ✆ (01983) 855666, *info@thepondcafe.com*, 🏠 – ⇆. MC AE ⊙ VISA

closed 2 weeks November, Monday and lunch Tuesday-Thursday October-1 April – **Rest** 20.00/25.00 and a la carte 23.00/40.00.

◆ Intimate restaurant, with duck pond, in sleepy hamlet. Cosy sunlit terrace. Island's larder utilised to the full for seasonal dishes in unfussy, halogen lit surroundings.

Yarmouth *I.O.W.* – ✉ *Isle of Wight.*

Newport 10.

The George, Quay St, PO41 0PE, ✆ (01983) 760331, *res@thegeorge.co.uk, Fax (01983) 760425,* ≤, 🌳 – ⇆ rm, ▤ rest. MC AE VISA

The Restaurant : Rest *(closed Sunday-Monday)* (booking essential) (dinner only) 46.50 ♀ – (see also ***The Brasserie*** below) – **16 rm** ☐ ✝95.00/150.00 – ✝✝245.00/265.00, 1 suite.

Spec. Courgette flower with lobster mousse and pineapple tapioca. Breast of duck with nougatine, endive and Jasmine tea sauce. Rhubarb and cardamom trifle.

◆ Splendid 17C quayside hotel. Relaxed, intimate style engendered by gracious comfort and attentive service. Superb individually decorated rooms. Memorable cooking: highly competent and inventive skills; fine traditional ingredients.

The Brasserie (at The George H.), Quay St, PO41 0PE, ✆ (01983) 760331, *Fax (01983) 760425,* 🏠 – MC AE VISA

Rest a la carte 27.25/32.00 ♀.

◆ French bistro-style restaurant. Warm yellow walls, wood furniture and views of the garden create a sunny ambience. Modern menu offers exciting choice of eclectic dishes.

WILLERBY *East Riding* 502 S 22 – *see Kingston-upon-Hull.*

WILLESLEY *Glos.* 503 504 N 29 – *see Tetbury.*

WILLIAN *Herts.* – *see Letchworth.*

WILLINGTON *Ches.* – *see Tarporley.*

WILMCOTE *Warks.* 503 504 O 27 – *see Stratford-upon-Avon.*

WILMINGTON *Devon* 503 K 31 – *see Honiton.*

WILMINGTON *E. Sussex* 504 U 31 – *see Eastbourne.*

WILMINGTON *Kent* 504 V 29 – *see Dartford.*

WILMSLOW *Ches.* 502 503 504 N 24 – *pop. 34 087.*
Great Warford, Mobberley (01565) 872148.
London 189 – Liverpool 38 – Manchester 12 – Stoke-on-Trent 27.

Holiday Inn Manchester Airport, Oversley Ford, Altrincham Rd, SK9 4LR, North-west : 2 ¾ m. on A 538 (01625) 889988, *Fax (01625) 531876*, squash – rm, P – 300.
The Terrace : **Rest** 12.95/15.95 and a la carte 18.20/30.45 – 11.50 – **126 rm** 85.00/115.00 – 85.00/115.00.
◆ Group hotel, at first sight suggestive of a large cream-painted villa. Bright rooms, busy meeting suites plus coffee shop and extensive leisure club for relaxing time-outs. Bright modern décor. Extensive menu of popular dishes to suit all tastes.

Stanneylands, Stanneylands Rd, SK9 4EY, North : 1 m. by A 34 (01625) 525225, *enquiries@stanneylandshotel.co.uk, Fax (01625) 537282*, – rm, P – 100.
The Restaurant : **Rest** (residents only Sunday dinner) 17.50/27.50 and a la carte 37.00/44.20 – 11.50 – **30 rm** 105.00/110.00 – 125.00, 1 suite.
◆ Attractive 19C redbrick hotel standing in mature grounds; exudes pleasant, country house style. Two characterful lounges and comfortable, traditional bedrooms. Comfy oak-panelled surroundings for diners.

Premier Travel Inn, Racecourse Rd, SK9 5LR, West : 1 m. by A 538 (01625) 525849, *Fax (01625) 548382* – , rest, P – 50.
Rest (grill rest.) – **37 rm** 53.95/53.95 – 55.95/55.95.
◆ Affordable, group-owned hotel in a residential area just outside the town centre. Wood-furnished bedrooms are simple yet comfortable and contemporary. Informal dining in spacious restaurant. Modern popular cookery.

Marigold House without rest., 132 Knutsford Rd, SK9 6JH, Southwest : 1 m. on B 5086 (01625) 584414, – P
closed 1 week Christmas – **3 rm** 38.00 – 50.00.
◆ 18C former farmhouse, 10 minutes from Manchester Airport; flagged floors throughout with log fires and antiques. Oak beams in bedrooms. Communal breakfast at superb oak table.

WIMBORNE MINSTER *Dorset* 503 504 O 31 *The West Country G.* – *pop. 14 884.*
See : *Town★ – Minster★ – Priest's House Museum★ AC.*
Env. : *Kingston Lacy★★ AC, NW : 3 m. by B 3082.*
29 High St (01202) 886116, wimbornetic@eastdorsetdc.gov.uk.
London 112 – Bournemouth 10 – Dorchester 23 – Salisbury 27 – Southampton 30.

Les Bouviers, Oakley Hill, Merley, BH21 1RJ, South : 1¼ m. on A 349 (01202) 886633, *info@lesbouviers.co.uk, Fax (01202) 886633* – P 30.
Rest a la carte 22.85/24.65.
◆ Classically decorated and family run; culinary style is enthusiastic, elaborate and indebted to the Gallic tradition. Planned relaunch in 2006; all-day brasserie.

WINCANTON *Somerset* 503 504 M 30.
London 118 – Bruton 5 – Glastonbury 20.

Holbrook House , BA9 8BS, West : 2 ¼ m. on A 371 (01963) 824466, *enquiries@holbrookhouse.co.uk, Fax (01963) 32681*, – rest, P – 220.
The Cedar : **Rest** *(closed Sunday dinner)* 14.95/29.95 – **19 rm** 135.00/175.00 – 135.00/175.00, 2 suites.
◆ Substantial 19C country house in mature grounds. Dramatic proportions prevail, but intimate spaces - like the wood-panelled bar - gel seamlessly. Smart spa; individual rooms. Classic dining room overlooks gardens.

WINCHCOMBE *Glos.* 503 504 O 28 – *pop. 3 682.*
Town Hall, High St (01242) 602925.
London 100 – Birmingham 43 – Gloucester 26 – Oxford 43.

Westward without rest., Sudeley Lodge, GL54 5JB, East : 1 ½ m. by Castle St on Sudeley Lodge/Parks/Farm rd (01242) 604372, *jimw@haldon.co.uk, Fax (01242) 604640*, – rm, P.
March-November – **3 rm** 55.00 – 100.00.
◆ Secluded, personally run 18C farmhouse: elegant, wood-floored drawing room and charming sitting room, bedrooms share fine views of 550-acre estate and mature gardens.

Isbourne Manor House without rest., Castle St, GL54 5JA, (01242) 602281, *felicity@isbourne-manor.co.uk, Fax (01242) 602281*, – [P].
closed Christmas – **3 rm** 55.00/75.00 – 85.00/90.00.
◆ Wisteria-clad Georgian and Elizabethan manor. Cosy drawing room: antique furniture and open fire. One room has a four-poster bed, one a roof top terrace. Riverside garden.

Sudeley Hill Farm without rest., GL54 5JB, East : 1 m. by Castle St (01242) 602344, *scudamore4@aol.com, Fax (01242) 602344*, , – [P].
closed Christmas – **3 rm** 30.00 – 60.00.
◆ Simple homely details and rural ornaments throughout this part 15C house on a working farm. Beamed lounge with fireside armchairs and comfortable rooms in cottage style.

Wesley House with rm, High St, GL54 5LJ, (01242) 602366, *enquiries@wesleyhouse.co.uk, Fax (01242) 609046*, – . MC AE VISA
closed 25-26 December – **Rest** *(closed Sunday dinner)* 15.00/39.50 and lunch a la carte 28.95/37.25 – **5 rm** (dinner included) 110.00/130.00 – 150.00/200.00.
◆ Part 15C house: cosy rooms, flag-floored, firelit lounge and split-level timbered restaurant. Engaging, chatty owner; flavourful, original menu with a classical tenor.

5 North St (Ashenford), 5 North St, GL54 5LH, (01242) 604566, *marcusashenford@yahoo.co.uk, Fax (01242) 603788* – . MC AE VISA
closed 2 weeks January, 1 week August, Sunday dinner, Tuesday lunch and Monday – **Rest** 21.50 (lunch) and dinner 26.00/36.00.
Spec. Sautéed langoustine, chicken wings, gingered carrot and leek, shellfish bisque. Squab pigeon with pear, baby onions and grand veneur sauce. Chocolate and banana mousse, Guinness ice cream.
◆ Personally run, cosy, 17C timbered restaurant with low-beamed ceiling and a pleasantly relaxed, friendly atmosphere. Good value menus offer flavoursome and refined cooking.

White Hart Inn with rm, High St, GL54 5LJ, (01242) 602359, *enquiries@the-white-hart-inn.com, Fax (01242) 602703* – rm, [P]. MC AE VISA
closed 25 December – **Rest** - Swedish specialities - a la carte 20.00/30.00 – **8 rm** 55.00/85.00 – 65.00/125.00.
◆ Very characterful 16C coaching inn in picturesque Cotswold town. Personally run by Swedish owners: authentic Scandinavian menus. Stylish, individually themed rooms.

WINCHELSEA *E. Sussex* 504 W 31 *Great Britain G.*

See : *Town★ – St Thomas Church (effigies★).*
London 64 – Brighton 46 – Folkestone 30.

Strand House without rest., Tanyard's Lane, TN36 4JT, East : ¼ m. on A 259 (01797) 226276, *info@thestrandhouse.co.uk, Fax (01797) 224806*, – [P]. MC AE VISA.
closed 24-26 December – **10 rm** 45.00/50.00 – 80.00.
◆ 14C and 15C half-timbered house of low beams and inglenook fireplaces: carefully tended rear garden shaded by tall trees, snug lounge; well-kept rooms in traditional style.

WINCHESTER *Hants.* 503 504 P 30 *Great Britain G. – pop. 41 420.*

See : *City★★ - Cathedral★★★ AC* B – *Winchester College★ AC* B B – *Castle Great Hall★* B D – *God Begot House★* B A.
Env. : *St Cross Hospital★★ AC* A.
Guildhall, The Broadway (01962) 840500, tourism@winchester.gov.uk.
London 72 – Bristol 76 – Oxford 52 – Southampton 12.

Plan on next page

Wessex, Paternoster Row, SO23 9LQ, (0870) 400 8126, *wessex@macdonald-hotels.co.uk, Fax (01962) 849617*, – , rest, [P] – 100. MC AE VISA. B c
Walkers **: Rest** 18.50/25.00 and dinner a la carte 29.50/34.50 – **93 rm** 75.00/160.00 – 120.00/180.00, 1 suite.
◆ Smartly run group hotel. Enviable cathedral view from the lounge - a pleasant spot for tea - and many of the rooms, all well appointed and decorated in traditional patterns. Wide windowed restaurant with floodlit views of cathedral by night.

Hotel du Vin, 14 Southgate St, SO23 9EF, (01962) 841414, *info@winchester.hotelduvin.com, Fax (01962) 842458*, – [P] – 30. MC AE VISA. B i
Rest – (see ***Bistro*** below) – 13.50 – **24 rm** 120.00 – 175.00.
◆ Elegant bedrooms, each with CD player, mini bar and distinct décor reflecting its wine house sponsors, in a 1715 redbrick house. Smart Champagne bar with inviting sofas.

Giffard House without rest., 50 Christchurch Rd, SO23 9SU, (01962) 852628, *giffardhotel@aol.com, Fax (01962) 856722*, – [P]. MC AE VISA. B s
closed 24 December-2 January – **13 rm** 67.00/88.00 – 101.00.
◆ Imposing part Victorian, part Edwardian house. Spacious breakfast room and comfortable sitting room with large fireplace. Immaculate rooms with good facilities.

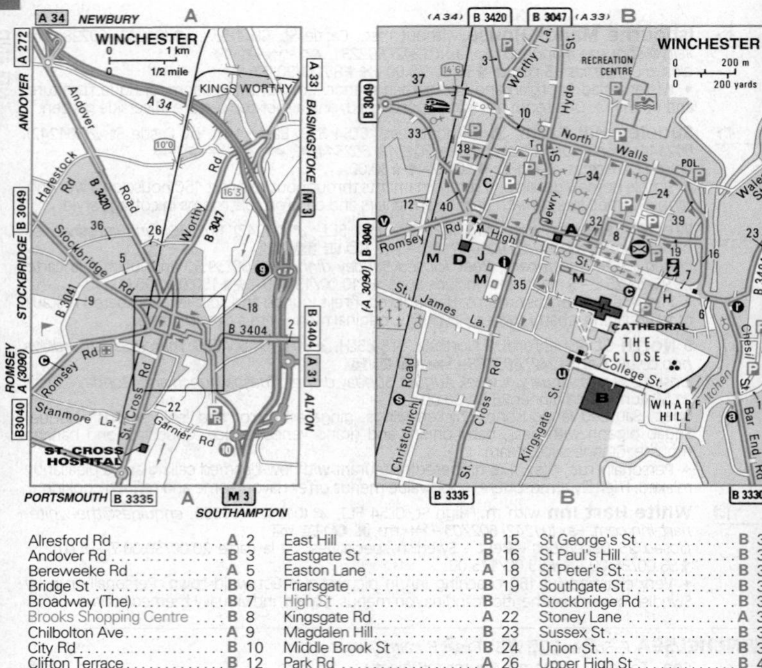

Alresford Rd	A 2	East Hill	B 15	St George's St	B 3
Andover Rd	B 3	Eastgate St	B 16	St Paul's Hill	B 3
Bereweeke Rd	A 5	Easton Lane	A 18	St Peter's St	B 3
Bridge St	B 6	Friarsgate	B 19	Southgate St	B 3
Broadway (The)	B 7	High St	B	Stockbridge Rd	B 3
Brooks Shopping Centre	B 8	Kingsgate Rd	A 22	Stoney Lane	A 3
Chilbolton Ave	A 9	Magdalen Hill	B 23	Sussex St	B 3
City Rd	B 10	Middle Brook St	B 24	Union St	B 3
Clifton Terrace	B 12	Park Rd	A 26	Upper High St	B 4

Dawn Cottage without rest., Romsey Rd, SO22 5PQ, ☎ (01962) 869956, *dawncottage@hotmail.com, Fax (01962) 869956*, ≤, 🌳 – ⇔ **P**. ✗ A c
closed 1 week Christmas – **3 rm** ☕ ✝55.00 – ✝✝65.00.

◆ Attractive, spotlessly kept cottage; friendly hosts. Simply decorated rooms; all have views across the Itchen Valley. Secluded rear garden flanked by tall trees.

Chesil Rectory, Chesil St, SO23 0HU, ☎ (01962) 851555, *Fax (01962) 869704* – MC AE ⊙ VISA B
closed 2 weeks Christmas, 2 weeks August, Sunday and Monday – **Rest** (dinner only and Saturday lunch)/dinner 30.00/45.00 ♀.

◆ Formal white linen blends well with a part 15C interior of low beams and leaded windows. Attentive service; modern cooking in marked contrast with the surroundings.

Bistro (at Hotel du Vin), 14 Southgate St, SO23 9EF, ☎ (01962) 841414 *Fax (01962) 842458*, 🌳, 🌳 – **P**. MC AE ⊙ VISA B
Rest (booking essential) 28.00 ♀.

◆ Oenophile memorabilia covers panelled cream walls; hops crown tall sash windows Terrace under broad sunshades. Classic modern flavours set off the carefully chosen wines.

Wykeham Arms with rm, 75 Kingsgate St, SO23 9PE, ☎ (01962) 853834, *wykeharms@accommodating-inns.co.uk, Fax (01962) 854411*, 🌳, 🌳 – ⇔ rm, **P**. MC AE ⊙ VISA. ✗ B
closed 25 December – **Rest** *(closed Sunday dinner)* (booking essential) a la carte 19.75/30.50 ♀ – **14 rm** ☕ ✝57.00/85.00 – ✝✝135.00.

◆ 18C inn; cosy snugs off a bar crammed with tankards, sporting curios and old school desks. Full-flavoured cooking. Cottage-style rooms, larger in annex: a city institution.

The Black Boy, 1 Wharf Hill, SO23 9NQ, ☎ (01962) 861754, 🌳 – MC VISA B
closed 2 weeks September and 2 weeks Christmas-New Year – **Rest** *(closed Sunday dinner-Tuesday lunch)* (booking essential) (light lunch) a la carte 24.25/29.40.

◆ Gloriously quirky pub: feast your eyes on a multitude of disparate items. Loaf around in intimate nooks, one boasting an Aga. In evening, dine on cutting-edge concoctions.

at Easton *Northeast : 4 m. by A 3090 – A – off B 3047 – ✉ Winchester.*

The Chestnut Horse, SO21 1EG, ✆ (01962) 779257, *Fax (01962) 779037,* – P. MO VISA
closed 25 December and Sunday dinner – **Rest** a la carte 24.00/30.00 ♀.
◆ Characterful 16C pub in rural village near M3. Welcoming interior with log fires, beams and hanging pots and jugs. Two dining rooms serve tasty, classic pub favourites.

at Ovington *East : 5¾ m. by B 3404 and A 31 – ✉ Winchester.*

Bush Inn, SO24 0RE, ✆ (01962) 732764, *thebushinn@wadworth.co.uk, Fax (01962) 735130,* – P. MO AE VISA
closed 25 December – **Rest** *(closed Sunday dinner)* a la carte 22.00/35.00.
◆ 17C country inn, hidden down winding country road along river Itchen, with delightful garden and engaging rural décor. Four intimate dining rooms serve tasty country dishes.

at Littleton *Northwest : 2½ m. by B 3049 – A – ✉ Winchester.*

The Running Horse, 88 Main Rd, SO22 6QS, ✆ (01962) 880218, *runninghorse@btconnect.com, Fax (01962) 886596,* – P. MO VISA
closed first 2 weeks January and 25-26 December – **Rest** *(closed Monday and Sunday lunch)* a la carte 27.00/33.00 ♀.
◆ Refurbished in 2004, this yellow hued hostelry boasts a rear restaurant with stone floors, wicker chairs and a sophisticated range of dishes. Two terraces for summer dining.

at Sparsholt *Northwest : 3½ m. by B 3049 – A – ✉ Winchester.*

Lainston House, SO21 2LT, ✆ (01962) 863588, *enquiries@lainstonhouse.com, Fax (01962) 776672,* – rest, P – 80. MO AE VISA
Avenue : **Rest** 22.00/36.50 and a la carte 39.80/49.20 **s.** ♀ – 17.50 – **48 rm** 120.00/180.00 – 275.00, 2 suites.
◆ Charming 17C manor with pretty grounds, parks and old herb garden. Traditionally styled lounge, cedar-panelled bar and up-to-date gym. Rooms, some more modern, vary in size. Dark wood dining room overlooks lawn.

Plough Inn, SO21 2NW, ✆ (01962) 776353, *Fax (01962) 776400,* – P. MO VISA
closed 25 December – **Rest** (booking essential) a la carte 18.00/25.00 ♀.
◆ Friendly, unassuming pub - book early for a varied blackboard menu combining the modern and traditional, all served at pine tables. Real ales.

WINDERMERE *Cumbria* 502 L 20 *Great Britain G. – pop. 7 941.*
Env. : *Lake Windermere★★ – Brockhole National Park Centre★ AC, NW : 2 m. by A 591.*
Victoria St ✆ (015394) 46499.
London 274 – Blackpool 55 – Carlisle 46 – Kendal 10.

Plan on next page

Langdale Chase, LA23 1LW, Northwest : 3 m. on A 591 ✆ (015394) 32201, *sales@langdalechase.co.uk, Fax (015394) 32604,* Lake Windermere and mountains, – rest, rest, P. MO AE VISA
Rest 16.95/34.00 ♀ – **26 rm** 80.00/101.00 – 150.00/198.00, 1 suite.
◆ Substantial 19C house with beautiful gardens and wonderful lakeside setting boasting a wealth of ornate Victoriana and superbly preserved carvings. Pleasantly styled rooms. Formal dining in a classic room; sweeping views across the lake.

Holbeck Ghyll, Holbeck Lane, LA23 1LU, Northwest : 3 ¼ m. by A 591 ✆ (015394) 32375, *stay@holbeckghyll.com, Fax (015394) 34743,* Lake Windermere and mountains, – P. MO AE VISA
Rest (lunch booking essential) 25.00/45.00 ♀ – **20 rm** (dinner included) 150.00/275.00 – 260.00/350.00, 1 suite.
Spec. Veal sweetbread ravioli with asparagus and morels. Breast and confit of duckling with smoked bacon and foie gras cassoulet. Assiette of strawberry and vanilla.
◆ In lovely gardens; breathtaking mountain vistas. A Victorian hunting lodge formerly owned by Lord Lonsdale; exudes luxury from oak panelled hall to fine fabrics in rooms. Refined dining: exquisite flavours in opulent surroundings, complete with mountain views.

Cedar Manor, Ambleside Rd, LA23 1AX, ✆ (015394) 43192, *info@cedarmanor.co.uk, Fax (015394) 45970,* – P. MO VISA
closed 1 week January – **Rest** (dinner only) 22.50 and a la carte 25.40/29.40 **s. 10 rm** 70.00/74.00 – 110.00/120.00, 1 suite.
◆ 1860s house, its mature garden shaded by an ancient cedar. Sizeable bedrooms, including the Coniston Room with views of Langdale Pike, and lounge with ornate stained glass.

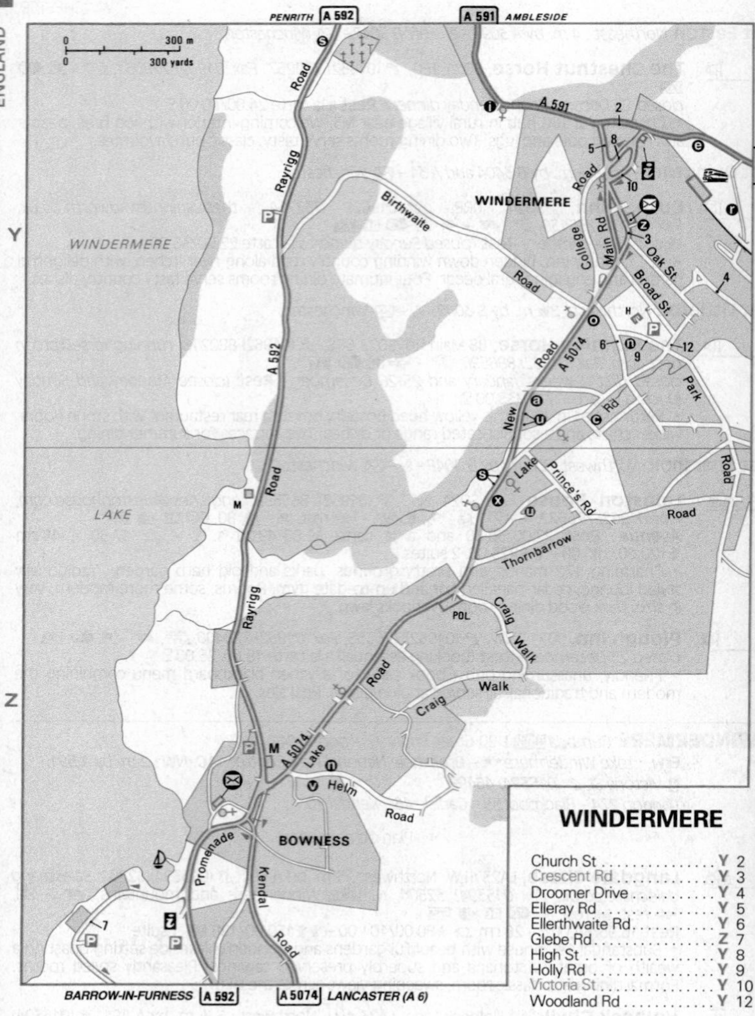

Glenburn, New Rd, LA23 2EE, ℘ (015394) 42649, *glen.burn@virgin.net, Fax (015394) 88998* – ⇔ P. MC AE VISA. ✂ Y u
closed 10-28 December – **Rest** (dinner only) 18.50/21.00 **s. – 16 rm** ☐ ✝49.50/54.50 – ✝✝69.00/79.00.
◆ Well-placed for exploring the central Lakes, a privately run hotel offering homely rooms in soft-toned décor plus a small bar and lounge with an open fire. Neatly set dining room with peach and white linen.

Woodlands, New Rd, LA23 2EE, ℘ (015394) 43915, *enquiries@woodlands-windermere.co.uk, Fax (015394) 43915* – ⇔ ℡ P. MC AE ① VISA. ✂ Y u
Rest (dinner only) 15.00 ♀ **15 rm** ☐ ✝36.00 – ✝✝60.00.
◆ Personally run hotel with spacious sitting room centred on the fireplace and affordable bedrooms - homely and immaculate - in cheerful floral décor. Neat dining room; fresh local produce served.

Boston House without rest., The Terrace, LA23 1AJ, (015394) 43654, *stay@bostonhouse.co.uk* – P. MC VISA. Y e
closed Christmas – **5 rm** 35.00/45.00 – 84.00.
◆ Personally run Victorian house: a tasteful style prevails throughout. Nicely appointed lounge and breakfast room. Individually decorated rooms exhibit quality furnishings.

Beaumont without rest., Holly Rd, LA23 2AF, (015394) 47075, *thebeaumonthotel@btinternet.com, Fax (015394) 88311* – P. MC VISA. Y n
11 rm 40.00/70.00 – 80.00/120.00.
◆ Substantial Victorian house, its period stained glass and tiling still intact. Good-sized en suite bedrooms, comfortably furnished with a traditional feel.

Glencree without rest., Lake Rd, LA23 2EQ, (015394) 45822, *h.butterworth@btinternet.com* – P. MC VISA. Z s
6 rm 30.00/40.00 – 60.00/70.00.
◆ Personally managed, detached guesthouse built of local slate. Spotless, individually decorated - and affordable - rooms in co-ordinated fabrics offer a good level of comfort.

Newstead without rest., New Rd, LA23 2EE, (015394) 44485, *info@newstead-guesthouse.co.uk, Fax (015394) 88904* – P. Y a
closed 1 week Christmas – **7 rm** 45.00/65.00 – 50.00/90.00.
◆ A warm welcome is assured at this restored Victorian residence. Original features aplenty; fireplaces in all the cosy, spotless bedrooms. Hearty breakfasts a speciality.

The Howbeck, New Rd, LA23 2LA, (015394) 44739, *relax@howbeck.co.uk* – P. MC VISA. Y o
Rest (by arrangement) 24.95 – **10 rm** 47.25/83.00 – 63.00/143.00.
◆ Victorian slate house on the outskirts. Well appointed lounge with maritime theme. Spacious bedrooms, some boasting four-posters, stylishly painted in up-to-date palette. Attractive dining room with well-laid tables: home-cooked, daily changing dinners.

Fir Trees without rest., Lake Rd, LA23 2EQ, (015394) 42272, *enquiries@fir-trees.com, Fax (015394) 42512*, – P. MC VISA. Z x
9 rm 40.00/90.00 – 40.00/90.00.
◆ Built in 1888 as a gentleman's residence and retains its original pine staircase. Contrastingly modern bedrooms. Broad-windowed breakfast room surveyed by a grandfather clock.

The Coach House without rest., Lake Rd, LA23 2EQ, (015394) 44494, *enquiries@lakedistrictbandb.com* – P. MC VISA. Z s
closed 24-26 December – **5 rm** 37.00/52.00 – 50.00/70.00.
◆ Converted 19C coach house with modern twists: in the compact, individually decorated bedrooms, bright, vivid colours predominate. Outside is a weather vane and roof clock.

Braemount House without rest., Sunny Bank Rd, LA23 2EN, by Queens Drive (015394) 45967, *enquiries@braemount-house.co.uk, Fax (015394) 45967* – P. MC VISA Z u
closed 24-25 December – **9 rm** 40.00/50.00 – 60.00/90.00.
◆ Extended 1870s bay-windowed house: original tiles and decorative glasswork add period character. Homely bedrooms; simple breakfast room with slate fireplace.

Oldfield House without rest., Oldfield Rd, LA23 2BY, (015394) 88445, *info@oldfieldhouse.co.uk* – P. MC VISA. Y c
closed January and weekends only November-December except Christmas-New Year – **8 rm** 32.00/49.00 – 64.00/70.00.
◆ Located in a quiet residential area; pretty, well-priced rooms - one with a four poster bed, all neatly kept - in a lakeland stone house run by a husband and wife team.

Miller Howe with rm, Rayrigg Rd, LA23 1EY, (015394) 42536, *lakeview@millerhowe.com, Fax (015394) 45664*, ≤ Lake Windermere and mountains, – rest, rest, P. MC AE VISA Y s
Rest (booking essential) 21.50/42.50 – **13 rm** (dinner included) 260.00 – 260.00/290.00, 2 suites.
◆ Renowned, elegantly furnished lakeside villa with handsomely fitted rooms. Modern Italianate restaurant; distinct Northern character to classic, seasonal dishes.

Jerichos, Birch St, LA23 1EG, (015394) 42522, *enquiries@jerichos.co.uk, Fax (015394) 42522* – . MC VISA Y z
closed last 2 weeks November, first week December, 24-26 December, 1 January and Monday – **Rest** (dinner only) a la carte 25.45/31.45 ♀.
◆ Personally run restaurant with open kitchen; well-spaced tables, elegant glassware and framed Beryl Cook prints. Local produce enhances rich, complex blend of modern flavours.

ENGLAND

First Floor Cafe (at Lakeland Ltd), Alexandra Buildings, Station Precinct, LA23 1BQ
(015394) 88200, *email@firstfloorcafe.co.uk* – **P**. VISA
closed 25 December, 1 January and Easter Sunday – **Rest** (bookings not accepted) (lunch only) a la carte 12.10/19.45 **s.**
◆ Modern, airy and stylish cafe/restaurant on first floor of Lakeland Ltd's new store. A smart setting for coffee, cake or good value, well prepared hot dishes.

at Bowness-on-Windermere *South : 1 m. – Z – Windermere.*

Gilpin Lodge, Crook Rd, LA23 3NE, Southeast : 2 ½ m. by A 5074 on B 5284
(015394) 88818, *hotel@gilpinlodge.com, Fax (015394) 88058*, ≤, , , – **P**. AE VISA.
Rest (booking essential to non-residents) 27.50/47.50 and lunch a la carte 17.75/25.25 **s.**
– **14 rm** (dinner included) 175.00 – 300.00.
Spec. Lasagne of scallops with ginger cream and fennel purée. Roast fillet of veal with asparagus and wild mushrooms. Vanilla cream with strawberry soup.
◆ Friendly, family run Edwardian country house rightly proud of its luxuriously appointed rooms. Firelit lounges awash with autumnal shades, deep sofas and welcoming bouquets. Carefully cooked modern British dishes using prime Lakeland ingredients.

Storrs Hall, LA23 3LG, South : 2 m. on A 592 (015394) 47111, *storrshall@email.co.uk, Fax (015394) 47555*, ≤, , , – **P** – 40. AE VISA.
The Terrace : **Rest** 19.75/39.50 – **29 rm** 147.50 – 370.00, 1 suite.
◆ Oils, antiques and fine fabrics fill an elegant Georgian mansion. Traditional orangery, 19C bar in dark wood and stained glass and comfortable, individually decorated rooms. Ornate dining room overlooks lawns and lake.

Linthwaite House, Crook Rd, LA23 3JA, South : ¾ m. by A 5074 on B 5284
(015394) 88600, *stayn@linthwaite.com, Fax (015394) 88601*, ≤ Lake Windermere and fells, , , – **P**. VISA.
Rest (light lunch Monday-Saturday)/dinner 44.00 **s.** – **27 rm** (dinner included) 120.00/135.00 – 280.00.
◆ Set in superb elevated position with stunning views of Lake Windermere. Chic, modern rooms. Cane chairs and louvred blinds give conservatory teas an almost colonial feel. Refined modern cooking in restaurant boasting vast mirror collection!

Lindeth Howe, Storrs Park, LA23 3JF, South : 1 ¼ m. by A 592 off B 5284 (015394) 45759, *hotel@lindeth-howe.co.uk, Fax (015394) 46368*, ≤, , , – **P**. AE VISA.
The Dining Room : **Rest** (light lunch Monday-Saturday)/dinner 34.95 **s.** – **36 rm** 48.00/60.00 – 188.00/210.00.
◆ Once owned by Beatrix Potter, this extended and updated house surveys a broad sweep of Lakeland scenery. Smart, spacious rooms in traditional style, some with useful extras. Spacious dining room with wonderful fell views.

Fayrer Garden House, Lyth Valley Rd, LA23 3JP, South : 1 m. on A 5074
(015394) 88195, *lakescene@fayrergarden.com, Fax (015394) 45986*, ≤, – rest, **P**. VISA.
closed 3-16 January – ***The Terrace :*** **Rest** (booking essential for non-residents) (dinner only) 35.00 – **29 rm** (dinner included) 70.00/94.00 – 178.00/198.00.
◆ Extensive house with five acres of grounds and beautiful gardens. Clubby bar and pleasantly homely lounge. Cosy rooms show the owners' feel for thoughtful detail. Wonderful views to be gained from The Terrace.

Lindeth Fell, Lyth Valley Rd, LA23 3JP, South : 1 m. on A 5074 (015394) 43286, *kennedy@lindethfell.co.uk, Fax (015394) 47455*, ≤ Lake Windermere and mountains, , – rest, **P**. VISA.
closed 3 weeks January – **Rest** 16.50/30.00 – **14 rm** 40.00/75.00 – 100.00/150.00.
◆ In landscaped gardens with bowls and croquet lawns, a privately owned 1907 house with neat, bright rooms, oak-panelled hall and curios and watercolours in the drawing room. Elegantly set dining room with superb Lakeland views.

Angel Inn, Helm Rd, LA23 3BU, (015394) 44080, – **P**. AE VISA
Rest (dinner only) a la carte 17.40/25.45 – **11 rm** 45.00/90.00 – 55.00/140.00.
◆ Homely, good-sized rooms in an enlarged early 18C cottage, set in a secluded spot yet close to town. Cosy, unpretentious bar, its armchairs centred on an open fire. Dining room has columned archway and landscape murals.

Oakbank House without rest., Helm Rd, LA23 3BU, (015394) 43386, *enquiries@oakbankhousehotel.co.uk, Fax (015394) 47965*, ≤ – **P**. AE VISA.
12 rm 50.00/90.00 – 100.00.
◆ Privately run house off the main street. Affordable bedrooms, stylish and individually decorated. Ferns and chandeliers lend grandeur to substantial Cumbrian breakfasts.

Fair Rigg without rest., Ferry View, LA23 3JB, South : ½ m. on A 5074 ☎ (015394) 43941, *stay@fairrigg.co.uk,* ≤ – ⇔ P. ✻
closed 24-25 December – **6 rm** ☐ ✝42.00/70.00 – ✝✝70.00/80.00.
◆ 19C property with pleasing views over the lake to the hills. Hearty Cumbrian breakfasts guaranteed, accompanied by the fine vista. Original fireplaces enhance comfy rooms.

at Troutbeck *North : 4 m. by A 592 – Y – ✉ Windermere.*

Broadoaks ⛯, Bridge Lane, LA23 1LA, South : 1 m. on Windermere rd ☎ (015394) 45566, *trev@broadoaksf9.co.uk, Fax (015394) 88766,* ≤, ⛬ – ⇔ P. MC AE VISA
Rest 14.95/55.00 and a la carte 15.00/48.00 **s.** ♀ – **14 rm** ☐ ✝59.50/75.00 – ✝✝140.00/160.00.
◆ Extended 19C manor in mature 10-acre garden. Victoriana fills the panelled hall and a handsome Music Room with Bechstein piano. Individual rooms, many with four-poster beds. Imposing period fireplace is dining room's focal point.

Queens Head with rm, LA23 1PW, North : ¾ m. on A 592 ☎ (015394) 32174, *enquiries@queensheadhotel.com, Fax (015394) 31938,* ≤, ⛬ – ⇔ P. MC VISA. ✻
closed 25 December – **Rest** 15.50 and a la carte 15.50/28.95 ♀ – **14 rm** ☐ ✝77.50 – ✝✝120.00.
◆ 17C posting inn with charm to spare: beamed, panelled interior, unique four-poster bar. Tasty blackboard menu; real ale. Cosy rooms, many have antique beds and furniture.

Do not confuse ✗ with ✿! ✗ defines comfort, while stars are awarded for the best cuisine, across all categories of comfort.

WINDLESHAM *Surrey* 504 S 29 – *pop. 4 103.*

London 40 – Reading 18 – Southampton 53.

The Brickmakers, Chertsey Rd, GU20 6HT, East : 1 m. on B 386 ☎ (01276) 472267, *thebrickmakers@4cinns.co.uk, Fax (01276) 451014,* ⛬ – P. MC AE VISA
Rest 25.95 (dinner) and a la carte 19.50/31.50 ♀.
◆ Appropriately redbrick pub with bright, modern dining room and conservatory. Tasty menu with a new-British slant plus daily fish specials. Friendly staff; good ale.

WINDSOR *Windsor & Maidenhead* 504 S 29 *Great Britain G. – pop. 30 568 (inc. Eton).*

See : *Town★ – Castle★★★ : St George's Chapel★★★ AC (stalls★★★), State Apartments★★ AC, North Terrace (≤★★) Z – Eton College★★ AC (College Chapel★★, Wall paintings★) Z.*
Env. : *Windsor Park★ AC Y – Legoland★, SW : 1 m. on A 332 Y.*
⛴ *to Marlow, Maidenhead and Cookham (Salter Bros. Ltd) (summer only).*
ℹ *24 High St ☎ (01753) 743900, windsor.tic@86wm.gov.uk.*
London 28 – Reading 19 – Southampton 59.

Plan on next page

Oakley Court, Windsor Rd, Water Oakley, SL4 5UR, West : 3 m. on A 308 ☎ (01753) 609988, *reservations.oakleycourt@moathousehotels.com, Fax (01628) 637011,* ≤, Fö, ≘s, ⬚, 🏌9, ⛬, ⛬, ⛬, ✗ – ⚓ ⇔ ▤ ☎ ♿ P – 🏛 160. MC AE ⊙ VISA. ✻
The Oakleaf **: Rest** *(closed Saturday lunch)* 24.50/29.50 and a la carte 34.50/47.50 **s.** ♀ – ☐ 14.95 – **118 rm** ✝155.00/185.00 – ✝✝165.00/195.00.
◆ Impressive part Gothic mansion on banks of river Thames. Spacious public areas in classic country house style. Many bedrooms in annex, most characterful ones in main house. Large dining room provides pleasant views of gardens and river.

Castle, High St, SL4 1LJ, ☎ (0870) 4008300, *castle@macdonald-hotels.co.uk, Fax (01753) 856930* – |‡| ⇔ ☎ P – 🏛 400. MC AE ⊙ VISA. ✻ Z c
Castle restaurant **: Rest** (dinner only and Sunday lunch) a la carte 16.00/35.00 ♀ – ***Freshfields*** **: Rest** (lunch only) a la carte 16.00/22.00 ♀ – ☐ 14.95 – **105 rm** ✝192.00 – ✝✝262.00, 3 suites.
◆ Former inn built by monks, now a terraced property with Georgian façade. Décor in traditional style. Modern rooms in converted stables, more characterful ones in old building. Very comfortable Castle restaurant. Bright, modern Freshfields brasserie.

WINDSOR

Street	Grid	No.
Bexley St	Z	2
Bolton Rd	Y	3
Castle Hill	Z	4
Charles St	Z	5
Claremont Rd	Z	6
Clarence Crescent	Z	7
Clewer Crescent Rd	Z	8
Datchet Rd	Z	9
Goswell Rd	Z	10
Grove Rd	Z	12
High St DATCHET	Y	14
High St	Z	13
Horton Rd	Y	16
Keats Lane	Z	17
King Edward Court Centre	Z	
Peascod St	Z	19
Ragstone Rd	Y	20
River St	Z	21
Sheet St Rd	Y	22
Stovell Rd	Z	23
Thames Ave	Z	24
Thames St	Z	25
Trinity Pl	Z	27
Windsor Bridge	Z	28
Windsor Rd	Y	29

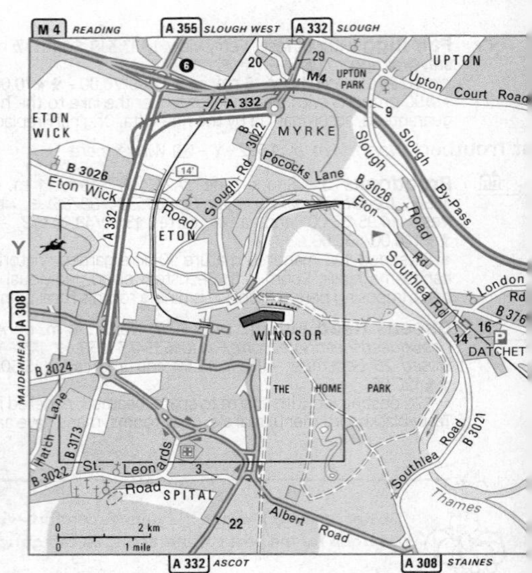

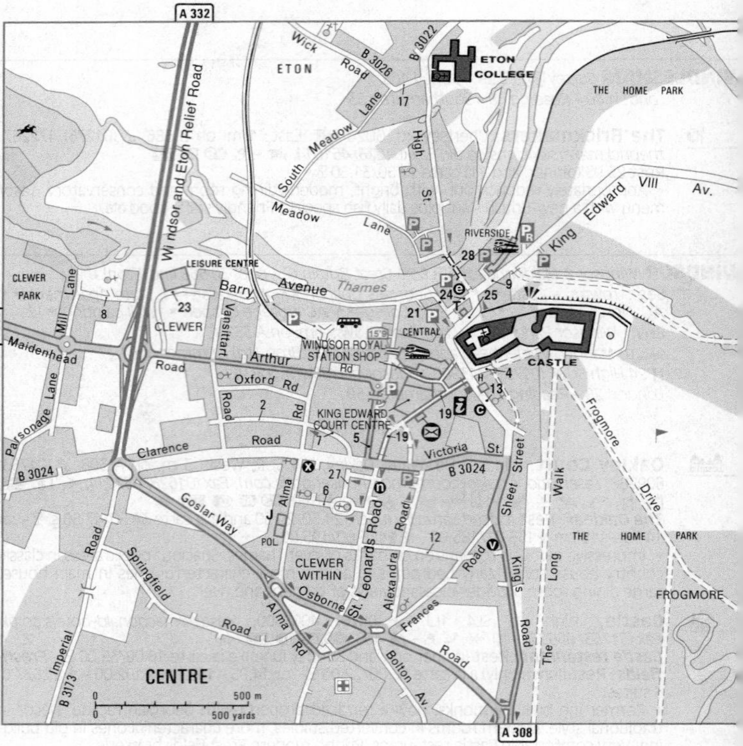

Sir Christopher Wren's House, Thames St, SL4 1PX, ☎ (01753) 861354, *reservations@wrensgroup.com, Fax (01753) 860172,* – rest, – 90. MC AE VISA. Z e
Strok's : Rest 18.00/22.50 (dinner) and a la carte 30.50/40.50 – **85 rm** 129.00/246.00 – 219.00/246.00, 5 suites.
◆ Built by Wren as his family home in 1676, he supposedly haunts his old rooms. On banks of Thames close to station and Windsor Castle. Antique furnished in original building. Restaurant has views of Thames and elegant dining terrace.

Royal Adelaide, 46 Kings Rd, SL4 2AG, ☎ (01753) 863916, *royaladelaide@meridianleisure.com, Fax (01753) 830682* – P – 120. MC AE VISA Z v
Rest (dinner only) 19.95 and a la carte 17.00/23.70 – **42 rm** 69.00/115.00 – 89.00/125.00.
◆ Three adjoining Georgian houses with light blue painted façade. Just outside town centre. Rooms vary in shapes and sizes, all in individual traditional style. Dining room offers daily changing, international menus.

The Dorset without rest., 4 Dorset Rd, SL4 3BA, ☎ (01753) 852669, *Fax (01753) 852669* – P. MC VISA. Z x
closed 22 December-4 January – **4 rm** 60.00/65.00 – 80.00.
◆ Bay windowed, late Victorian detached house on quiet residential street, just out of town centre. Traditional décor with large and comfortable bedrooms.

Al Fassia, 27 St Leonards Rd, SL4 3BP, ☎ (01753) 855370, *Fax (01753) 855370* – MC AE VISA Z n
closed 25 December, 1 January and last 2 weeks August – **Rest** - Moroccan - (booking essential) 12.95/19.95 and a la carte 16.95/21.95.
◆ The name means "a lady from Fez" and the food has an authentic fresh Moroccan flavour with subtle spicing and fragrant flavours. Friendly and well run.

WINEHAM *W. Sussex* 504 T 31 – *see Henfield.*

WINFORTON *Herefordshire* 503 K 27 – ✉ *Hereford.*
London 155 – Birmingham 71 – Cardiff 66 – Hereford 15.

Winforton Court without rest., HR3 6EA, ☎ (01544) 328498, *Fax (01544) 328498,* – P
closed 24-28 December – **3 rm** 64.00 – 76.00/84.00.
◆ Wonderfully characterful 16C house used as a circuit court by "Hanging" Judge Jeffries. Exudes personality with exposed beams, thick walls and uneven floors. Rustic rooms.

WING *Rutland* 504 R 28 – *see Oakham.*

WINSFORD *Somerset* 503 J 30 *The West Country G.* – ✉ *Minehead.*
See : *Village*★.
Env. : *Exmoor National Park*★★.
London 194 – Exeter 31 – Minehead 10 – Taunton 32.

Royal Oak Inn, TA24 7JE, ☎ (01643) 851455, *enquiries@royaloak-somerset.co.uk, Fax (01643) 851009,* , – rest, P. MC AE VISA
Rest (in bar Monday-Saturday lunch and Sunday dinner)/dinner a la carte 20.20/25.95 – **10 rm** 75.00 – 116.00/136.00.
◆ Attractive part 12C thatched inn overlooking the village green. Quaint cottage atmosphere, especially in those rooms in the main house; annex rooms of more recent vintage. Out-and-out English cooking prevails.

Karslake House, Halse Lane, TA24 7JE, ☎ (01643) 851242, *enquiries@karslakehouse.co.uk, Fax (01643) 851242,* – P. MC VISA
closed February-March and 1 week Christmas – **Rest** *(closed Sunday-Monday and Tuesday-Thursday to non-residents)* (dinner only) 29.50 – **6 rm** 63.00 – 108.00.
◆ Personally run 15C malthouse with lovely gardens. Good home-cooked fare on varied menus with fine use of local produce. Welcoming accommodation including four-poster comfort.

WINSLEY *Wilts.* 503 504 N 29 – *see Bradford-on-Avon.*

WINTERBOURNE STEEPLETON *Dorset* 503 504 M 31 – *see Dorchester.*

WINTERINGHAM *North Lincolnshire* 502 S 22 – ✉ *Scunthorpe.*
London 176 – Kingston-upon-Hull 16 – Sheffield 67.

XXXX **Winteringham Fields** with rm, Silver St, DN15 9PF, ✆ (01724) 733096, *wir fields@aol.com, Fax (01724) 733898* – ⇔ ✆ P ⇔ 10. MC AE ① VISA
✿ *closed 24 December-7 January, 12 days August, first 4 days October and last wee March* – **Rest** *(closed Sunday-Monday)* (booking essential to non-residents) 34.00 72.00 and dinner a la carte 60.00/76.00 ♀ – ☕ 12.00 – **8 rm** ✝140.00 – ✝✝210.00 2 suites.
Spec. Bouillabaisse with panaché of vegetables and saffron butter. Seared scallops wit pig's trotter and sautéed ceps. Ravioli of poached egg yolk, black truffle and veal sweet breads.
◆ 16C house with beamed ceilings, and original range with fire. Cosy, cottagey atmos phere. Carefully executed menu, served in choice of dining rooms. Characterful bed rooms.

WITNEY *Oxon.* 503 504 P 28 – *pop. 22 765.*
26A Market Sq ✆ (01993) 775802.
London 69 – Gloucester 39 – Oxford 13.

Witney Four Pillars, Ducklington Lane, OX8 7TJ, South : 1½ m. on A 415 ✆ (01993 779777, *witney@fourpillars.co.uk, Fax (01993) 703467,* – ⇔ rm, ▤ rest, ✆ ♿ P – 🏛 160. MC AE ① VISA. ✗
Rest 9.95/19.95 and a la carte approx 19.50 ♀ – ☕ 9.25 – **87 rm** ✝79.00/105.00 – ✝✝95.00/120.00.
◆ Situated at the edge of the Cotswolds. Built in traditional style, accommodating busines and leisure visitors. Modern rooms with, in the deluxe category, extra comforts. Convivial popular restaurant.

at Barnard Gate *East : 3¼ m. by B 4022 off A 40 – ✉ Eynsham.*

The Boot Inn, OX8 6XE, ✆ (01865) 881231, *info@theboot-inn.com, Fax (01865) 88211* – P. MC VISA. ✗
closed 26 December – **Rest** a la carte 18.75/25.95 ♀.
◆ Friendly pub in Cotswold stone. Snug interior with memorabilia and boot collection including footwear from Bee Gees and Stanley Matthews. Traditional menu, informal serv ice.

at South Leigh *Southeast : 3 m. by B 4022 – ✉ Witney.*

X **Mason Arms** with rm, OX29 6XN, ✆ (01993) 702485, – P. AE. ✗
closed 21-31 December, 1 week in spring, 2 weeks August, Sunday dinner and Monday – **Rest** a la carte 45.00/65.00 – **2 rm** ✝35.00 – ✝✝65.00.
◆ Privately owned 15C thatched inn with unique style and much individuality. Comfor table rooms and public areas. French influenced traditional cooking and extensive wine list.

at Leafield *Northwest : 5¾ m. by B 4022 (Charlbury Rd) – ✉ Witney.*

The Navy Oak, Lower End, OX29 9QQ, ✆ (01993) 878496, *thenavyoak@aol.com Fax (01993) 878496,* – ⇔ P. MC VISA
closed 2 weeks January, Monday and Sunday dinner – **Rest** a la carte 18.00/30.00.
◆ Refurbished solid stone pub in rural village; pleasant outside seating and cosy ba with open fire. Good value, appealing, modern menus in rustic or formal dining areas.

"Rest" appears in red for establishments with a ✿ (star) or ☺ (Bib Gourmand).

WIX *Essex* 504 X 28 – ✉ *Manningtree.*
London 70 – Colchester 10 – Harwich 7 – Ipswich 16.

Dairy House Farm without rest., Bradfield Rd, CO11 2SR, Northwest : 1 m. ☎ (01255) 870322, *bridgetwhitworth@hotmail.com, Fax (01255) 870186,* ≤, P.
3 rm ★35.00/38.00 – ★★55.00/58.00.
◆ Victorian farmhouse, delightfully secluded in 700 acres of working arable and fruit farmland. Friendly and welcoming. Simple, comfortable style and well-kept throughout.

WOBURN *Beds.* 504 S 28 *Great Britain G.* – ✉ *Milton Keynes.*
See : *Woburn Abbey*★★.
London 49 – Bedford 13 – Luton 13 – Northampton 24 – Oxford 47.

Inn at Woburn, George St, MK17 9PX, ☎ (01525) 290441, *enquiries@theinnatwoburn.com, Fax (01525) 290432* – rest, P – 60. VISA
Rest 12.50 (lunch) and a la carte 20.45/31.65 – 11.00 – **52 rm** ★110.00/125.00 – ★★130.00, 5 suites.
◆ 18C coaching inn, part of Woburn Estate with its abbey and 3000 acre park. Pleasant modern furnishings and interior décor. Tastefully decorated rooms: book a Cottage suite. Brasserie open throughout the day.

Paris House, Woburn Park, MK17 9QP, Southeast : 2 ¼ m. on A 4012 ☎ (01525) 290692, *info@parishouse.co.uk, Fax (01525) 290471,* – P. VISA
closed Sunday dinner and Monday – **Rest** 22.00/55.00.
◆ Built 1878 for Paris Exhibition, dismantled and rebuilt on Woburn Estate, this striking timbered house provides an august setting for classic French-inspired cuisine.

The Birch, 20 Newport Rd, MK17 9HX, North : ½ m. on A 5130 ☎ (01525) 290295, *Fax (01525) 290899,* – P. VISA
closed 25-26 December, 1 January and Sunday dinner – **Rest** (booking essential) a la carte 18.95/27.95.
◆ Established modern dining pub. Stylish décor in the smart restaurant and bar. Modern menu specialising in meat and fish from an open grill. Attentive service.

Luxury pad or humble abode? and denote categories of comfort.

WOKING *Surrey* 504 S 30.
London 34 – Guildford 7 – Farnborough 14.

Holiday Inn, Victoria Way (A 320), GU21 8EW, ☎ (01483) 221000, *f&b@wokingholiday-inn.com, Fax (01483) 221021,* – rm, P – 90. VISA
Rest *(closed Saturday lunch, Sunday and Bank Holidays)* 12.95/15.25 and a la carte 17.45/29.15 – 13.50 – **161 rm** ★150.00/169.00 – ★★150.00/169.00.
◆ Two minutes from the high street, a modern group hotel in redbrick and glass, geared to the corporate market. Usefully equiped bedrooms with bright fabrics and work desks. Tried-and-tested menus.

Premier Travel Inn, Bridge Barn Lane, Horsell, GU21 1NL, West : ¾ m. by Church St West off Goldsworth Rd ☎ (01483) 763642, *Fax (01483) 771735* – rm, P. VISA.
Rest (grill rest.) – **34 rm** ★57.95/57.95 – ★★59.95/59.95.
◆ Modern purpose built lodge pleasantly situated by canal. Offers simply furnished, brightly decorated rooms with ample work space. Adjacent Out and Out restaurant.

WOLD NEWTON *East Riding.*
London 229.5 – Bridlington 25 – Scarborough 13.5.

Wold Cottage, YO25 3HL, South : ½ m. on Thwing rd ☎ (01262) 470696, *katrina@woldcottage.com, Fax (01262) 470696,* ≤, P. VISA
Rest (by arrangement) 17.50 – **5 rm** ★40.00/55.00 – ★★90.00/110.00.
◆ Georgian former farmhouse set in many rural acres; a country house style prevails with antique furniture in all areas. Spacious, individually named rooms: two in barn annex. Home-cooked dishes in two-roomed dining area.

WOLVERHAMPTON *W. Mids.* 502 503 504 N 26 – *pop. 254 623.*

18 Queen Sq ✆ (01902) 556110, wolverhampton.tic@dial.pipex.com.
London 132 – Birmingham 15 – Liverpool 89 – Shrewsbury 30.
Plan of Enlarged Area : see Birmingham pp. 4 and 5

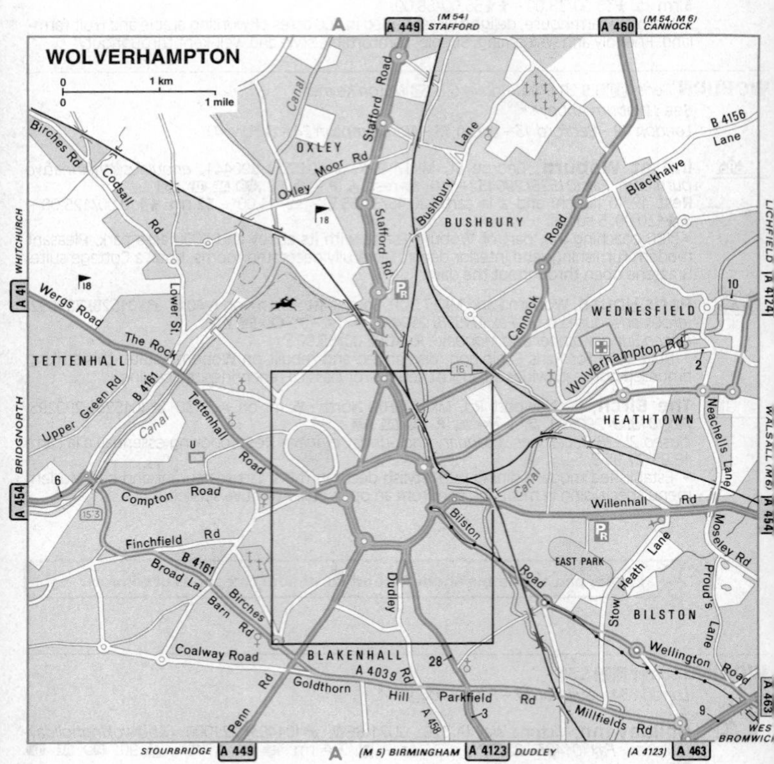

Novotel, Union St, WV1 3JN, ✆ (01902) 871100, *h1188@accor.com, Fax (01902) 870054,* heated – |≡|, ⇔ rm, ✆ ♿ P – 🏛 200. MC AE ◐ VISA B a
The Garden Brasserie : **Rest** *(closed Sunday lunch)* a la carte 21.00/27.00 **s.** ♀ – ☕ 11.00 – **132 rm** ★89.00 – ★★89.00.
◆ Conveniently located in the centre of town near to train station. Purpose-built lodge hotel with well fitted modern furnishings. Suitable for business and leisure stopovers. Large windows give bright feel to restaurant.

Premier Travel Inn, Wolverhampton Business Park, Greenfield Lane, Stafford Rd, WV10 6TA, North : 3 ½ m. by A 449 at junction with M 54 ✆ (0870) 1977277, *Fax (01902) 785260* – |≡| ⇔, ▤ rest, ♿ P – 🏛 50. MC AE ◐ VISA. ✂
Rest (grill rest.) – **56 rm** ★47.95/47.95 – ★★50.95/50.95.
◆ A consistent standard of trim, simply fitted accommodation in contemporary style; a useful address for cost-conscious travellers. Popular grill restaurant adjacent.

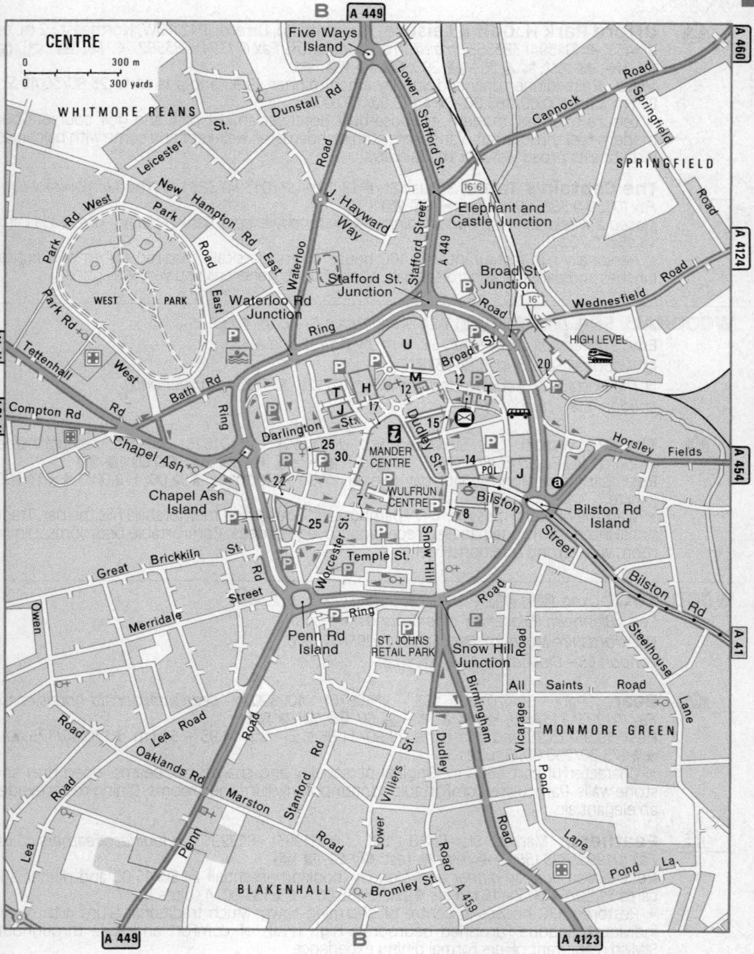

WOOBURN COMMON *Bucks.* – *see Beaconsfield.*

WOODBRIDGE *Suffolk* 504 X 27 – *pop. 10 965.*

9 Cretingham, Grove Farm ✆ (01728) 685275 – 18 Seckford, Seckford Hall Rd, Great Bealings ✆ (01394) 388000.

London 81 – Great Yarmouth 45 – Ipswich 8 – Norwich 47.

Seckford Hall, IP13 6NU, Southwest : 1 ¼ m. by A 12 ✆ (01394) 385678, *reception@seckford.co.uk, Fax (01394) 380610,* ≤, 18, – rest, – 120. VISA

closed 25 December – **Rest** *(closed Monday lunch)* a la carte 27.50/37.50 **s.** – **25 rm** 85.00/105.00 – 200.00, 7 suites.

◆ Reputedly once visited by Elizabeth I, a part Tudor country house set in attractive gardens. Charming traditionally panelled public areas. Comfortable bedrooms. Local lobster proudly served in smart dining room.

ENGLAND

Ufford Park H. Golf & Leisure, Yarmouth Rd, Ufford, IP12 1QW, Northeast : 2 m. on B 1438 ☎ (01394) 383555, *mail@uffordpark.co.uk, Fax (01394) 383582*, ←, ₺, ≘s, ⬚, ⛳18, ♔ – ⇆, ▤ rest, ✆ ♿ 🅿 – 🏠 200. MC ⓘ VISA. ✂
Vista : **Rest** (dinner only and Sunday lunch)/dinner 19.95 and a la carte 23.80/30.40 ♀ – **87 rm** ☕ ✝100.00/165.00 – ✝✝120.00/170.00.
◆ Leisure oriented, modern, purpose-built hotel set amidst park and golf course. Good modern feel throughout. Variety of room standards, all well-kept and some with balconies. Vista boasts broad views of the fairways.

The Captain's Table, 3 Quay St, IP12 1BX, ☎ (01394) 383145, *food2enjoy@aol.com, Fax (01394) 388508*, ⛱ – ⇆. MC VISA
closed 2 weeks January, Sunday dinner and Monday except Bank Holidays – **Rest** a la carte 15.15/23.70 **s.**
◆ Personally run restaurant in a 16C house offers classically inspired dishes plus lighter lunches and daily blackboard specials, all confident, generous and very well priced.

WOODHALL SPA *Lincs.* 502 504 T 24 *Great Britain G. – pop. 4 133.*

Env. : *Tattershall Castle★ AC, SE : 4 m. by B 1192 and A 153.*
⛳18 *Woodhall Spa ☎ (01526) 351835.*
ℹ *The Cottage Museum, Iddesleigh Rd ☎ (01526) 353775 (summer only).*
London 138 – Lincoln 18.

The Petwood ⛰, Stixwould Rd, LN10 6QF, ☎ (01526) 352411, *reception@petwood.co.uk, Fax (01526) 353473*, ←, ⛳18, ♔ – ⇅ ⇆ ♿ 🅿 – 🏠 200. MC AE ⓘ VISA
Rest (bar lunch Monday-Saturday)/dinner 22.50 – **52 rm** ☕ ✝92.00/112.00 – ✝✝136.00, 1 suite.
◆ Wartime officers' mess for 617 "Dambusters" Squadron - memorabilia fills the bar. Traditional interiors include panelled reception. Lovely gardens. Comfortable bedrooms. Dining room with strong traditional feel.

WOODSTOCK *Oxon.* 503 504 P 28 *Great Britain G. – pop. 2 589.*

See : *Blenheim Palace★★★ (The Grounds★★★) AC.*
ℹ *Oxfordshire Museum, Park St ☎ (01993) 813276.*
London 65 – Gloucester 47 – Oxford 8.

Bear, Park St, OX20 1SZ, ☎ (0870) 4008202, *bear@macdonald-hotels.co.uk, Fax (01993) 813380* – ⇆ ✆ ♿ 🅿 – 🏠 60. MC AE ⓘ VISA
Rest 19.95/25.95 and a la carte 29.90/41.85 **s.** ♀ – ☕ 14.95 – **51 rm** ✝170.00/175.00 – ✝✝175.00/250.00, 3 suites.
◆ Characterful part 16C inn. Original personality and charm; oak beams, open fires and stone walls. Particularly comfortable contemporarily furnished rooms. Dining room exudes an elegant air.

Feathers, Market St, OX20 1SX, ☎ (01993) 812291, *enquiries@feathers.co.uk, Fax (01993) 813158* – ⇆ rest, ▤ rest. MC AE ⓘ VISA
Rest *closed Sunday dinner and Monday* (booking essential) 24.50/45.00 and dinner a la carte 31.50/54.00 ♀ – **16 rm** ☕ ✝99.00/155.00 – ✝✝185.00, 4 suites.
◆ Restored 17C houses in centre of charming town. Much traditional allure with highly individual, antique furnished bedrooms. High levels of comfort and style throughout. Stylish restaurant offers formal dining experience.

The Townhouse without rest., 15 High St, OX20 1TE, ☎ (01993) 810843, *info@woodstock-townhouse.com, Fax (01993) 810864* – ⇆. MC AE VISA. ✂
5 rm ☕ ✝55.00 – ✝✝80.00.
◆ Charming town house in the centre of this attractive market town. Friendly owner and bright bedrooms with all amenities. Breakfast is served in the garden conservatory.

The Laurels without rest., Hensington Rd, OX20 1JL, ☎ (01993) 812583, *stay@laurelsguesthouse.co.uk, Fax (01993) 810041* – ⇆. MC VISA. ✂
closed 15 December-2 January – **3 rm** ☕ ✝55.00/65.00 – ✝✝65.00/75.00.
◆ Fine Victorian house just off the town centre. Personally run home with pretty guest rooms and private room facilities.

at Church Hanborough *Southwest : 4¼ m. by A 44 off A 4095 – ✉ Woodstock.*

Hand & Shears, OX29 8AB, ☎ (01993) 883337, *handandshears@tiscali.co.uk, Fax (01993) 881392* – ⇆. MC VISA
closed Sunday dinnerand Monday – **Rest** a la carte 20.00/30.00 ♀.
◆ Mellow sandstone 17/18C pub opposite church in pretty village. Delightful, richly decorated front bar. Beamed restaurant for modern British dishes and re-invented classics.

at Wootton *North : 2½ m. by A 44 – ✉ Woodstock.*

Kings Head with rm, Chapel Hill, OX20 1DX, ✆ (01993) 811340, *t.fay@kings-head.co.uk* – P. MC VISA
closed 25 December, Sunday dinner and Monday except Bank Holidays – **Rest** a la carte 18.00/28.00 ♀ – **3 rm** ☕ ♀65.00 – ♀♀85.00.
◆ Pubby appearance in quaint village. Personally run and a traditional ambience. Cooking has a varied and eclectic style with several fish specials. Tidy, simple bedrooms.

WOOFFERTON *Shrops. – see Ludlow.*

WOOKEY HOLE *Somerset* 503 L 30 – *see Wells.*

WOOLACOMBE *Devon* 503 H 30 *The West Country G.*

Env. : *Exmoor National Park★★ – Mortehoe★★ (St Mary's Church★, Morte Point – vantage point★) N : ½ m. – Ilfracombe : Hillsborough (≤★★) AC, Capstone Hill★ (≤★), St Nicholas' Chapel (≤★) AC, NE : 5½ m. by B 3343 and A 361.*
Exc. : *Braunton★ (St Braunton's Church★, Braunton Burrows★), S : 8 m. by B 3343 and A 361.*
ℹ *The Esplanade ✆ (01271) 870553.*
London 237 – Barnstaple 15 – Exeter 55.

Woolacombe Bay, South St, EX34 7BN, ✆ (01271) 870388, *contact@woolacombe-bay-hotel.co.uk, Fax (01271) 870613,* ≤, ₺, ≘s, heated, , , squash – |‡| ⇸, rest, P – 200. MC AE VISA.
closed 2 January-10 February – ***Doyles :*** **Rest** (dinner only) 29.00 ♀ – ***Maxwell's :*** **Rest** (lunch only) a la carte approx 15.00 ♀ – **64 rm** (dinner included) ☕ ♀92.00/125.00 – ♀♀142.00/250.00.
◆ Large, traditional, Victorian seaside hotel in the centre of town offering coastal or inland views. Activities from board games to health suite. Well-kept, bright bedrooms. Elegantly styled Doyles dining room. Informal Maxwell's bistro.

at Mortehoe *North : ½ m. – ✉ Woolacombe.*

Watersmeet, The Esplanade, EX34 7EB, ✆ (01271) 870333, *info@watersmeethotel.co.uk, Fax (01271) 870890,* ≤ Morte Bay, heated, , – ⇸ rest, P. MC VISA.
Rest 15.95/33.00 **s.** ♀ – **25 rm** (dinner included) ☕ ♀80.00/210.00 – ♀♀160.00/260.00.
◆ Edwardian house on the National Trust's rugged North Atlantic coastline. Superb views of Morte Bay. Smart country house style, large lounges and steps to the beach. Stylish restaurant offers tremendous sea views.

Cleeve House, EX34 7ED, ✆ (01271) 870719, *info@cleevehouse.co.uk, Fax (01271) 870719,* – ⇸ ♿ P. MC VISA.
April-October – **Rest** (by arrangement) (dinner only) 19.00 and a la carte 17.00/26.50 **s.** – **6 rm** ☕ ♀51.00/53.00 – ♀♀72.00/76.00.
◆ Bright and welcoming feel in décor and atmosphere. Very comfortable lounge and individually styled bedrooms with co-ordinated fabrics. Rear rooms with great country views. Neat dining room; walls hung with local artwork.

WOOLAVINGTON *Somerset* 503 L 30 – *see Bridgwater.*

WOOLHAMPTON *Berks.* 503 504 Q 29 *Great Britain G.*

Exc. : *Basildon Park★, NE : 10 m. by A 4, A 340 and A 417.*
London 56 – Newbury 8 – Thatcham 4.

The Angel, Bath Rd, RG7 5RT, ✆ (0118) 971 3307, *mail@a4angel.com* – P. MC VISA
closed 1 week Christmas, Sunday dinner and Monday – **Rest** (booking essential) a la carte 18.00/32.00 **s.** ♀.
◆ Technicolored interior, vividly dressed with elaborate vases and rows of bottles. Fireplaces divide rooms. Well-spaced tables. Interesting dishes from modern British range.

WOOLSTHORPE-BY-BELVOIR *Lincs.* 502 504 R 25 – *see Grantham.*

WOOTTON *Oxon.* 503 504 P 28 – *see Woodstock.*

WORCESTER *Worcs.* 503 504 N 27 *Great Britain G.* – *pop. 94 029.*

See : *City★ – Cathedral★★ – Royal Worcester Porcelain Works★ (Dyson Perrins Museum★)* M.

Exc. : *The Elgar Trail★.*

Perdiswell Park, Bilford Rd ☎ (01905) 754668.

The Guildhall, High St ☎ (01905) 726311.

London 124 – Birmingham 26 – Bristol 61 – Cardiff 74.

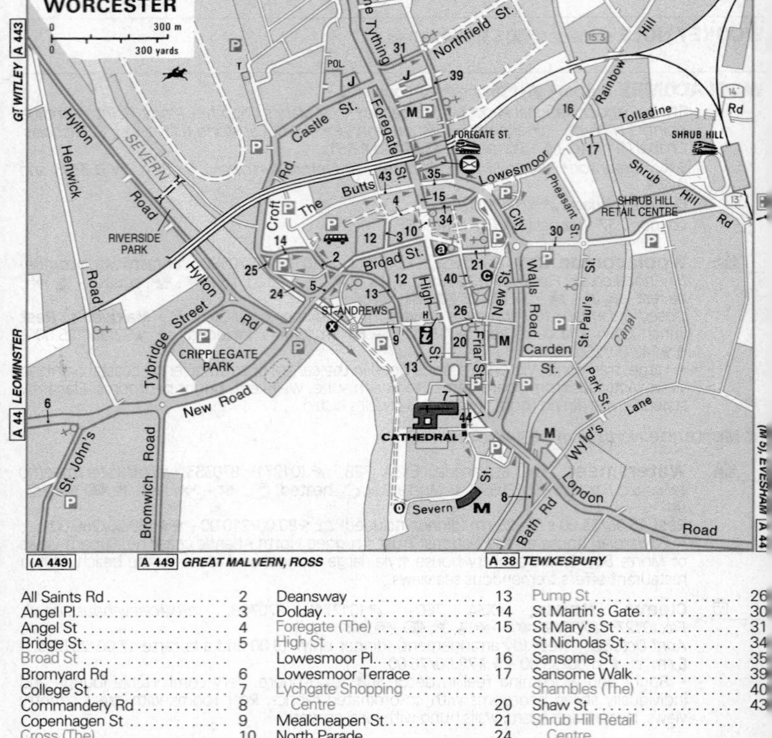

All Saints Rd 2
Angel Pl. 3
Angel St 4
Bridge St. 5
Broad St . . . .
Bromyard Rd 6
College St 7
Commandery Rd 8
Copenhagen St 9
Cross (The) 10
Crown Gate Centre 12
Deansway 13
Dolday 14
Foregate (The) 15
High St . . . .
Lowesmoor Pl. 16
Lowesmoor Terrace 17
Lychgate Shopping Centre 20
Mealcheapen St. 21
North Parade 24
North Quay 25
Pump St 26
St Martin's Gate. 30
St Mary's St 31
St Nicholas St. 34
Sansome St 35
Sansome Walk. 39
Shambles (The) 40
Shaw St 43
Shrub Hill Retail Centre . . . .
Sidbury 44

Diglis House, Severn St, WR1 2NF, ☎ (01905) 353518, *diglishouse@yahoo.com, Fax (01905) 767772,* <, ..., ... – ... P – 50. MC AE D VISA. ... O
closed 26 December-3 January – **Rest** (bar lunch)/dinner 24.50 **s.** – **25 rm** ... ★90.00 – ★★100.00, 1 suite.
◆ Georgian house on banks of river Severn. Close to Royal Worcester factory. Attractive bar terrace. Characterful rooms in main house, those in annex more modern. Conservatory dining room with river outlook.

Premier Travel Inn, Wainwright Way, Warndon, WR4 9FA, Northeast : 6 ¾ m. by A 449 on A 4440 (at junction 6 of M 5) ☎ (08701) 977278, *Fax (01905) 756601* – ..., ... rest, ... P – 50. MC AE D VISA. ...
Rest (grill rest.) – **60 rm** ★50.95 – ★★50.95.
◆ Simply furnished and brightly decorated bedrooms with ample work space. Family rooms with sofa beds. Ideal for corporate or leisure travel.

XX **Brown's,** 24 Quay St, WR1 2JJ, ✆ (01905) 26263 – ⇔. MO AE VISA x
closed 26-31 December, Saturday lunch, Sunday dinner and Monday – **Rest** 29.50/39.50 and a la carte 20.40/33.40 ♀.
◆ Converted riverside corn mill. Spacious, open interior as befits the building's origins. Impressive collection of modern artwork. Mainly British dishes are renowned locally.

XX **Glass House,** Church St, WR1 2RH, ✆ (01905) 611120, *eat@theglasshouse.co.uk, Fax (01905) 616510* – ⇔ ▤. MO AE VISA a
closed 25-27 December, first 2 weeks January and Sunday – **Rest** 13.95 (lunch) and a la carte 23.50/32.95 ♀.
◆ Former 16C grammar school with vaulted cellar bar and terrace for alfresco dining. Name comes from restaurant's colourful stained glass windows. Eclectic menus.

X **Epic,** 15A Reindeer Court, New St, WR1 2DS, ✆ (01905) 745625, *epic.worcester@virgin.co.uk, Fax (01905) 739174* – ⇔ ▤. MO AE VISA c
closed 25-26 December and Sunday-Monday – **Rest** 12.95 (lunch) and a la carte 20.95/33.40 **s.** ♀.
◆ Modern bar/brasserie in attractive area of city centre. Restaurant, separated from busy bar by glass doors, offers classics old and new in informal, contemporary surroundings.

at Bransford *West : 4 m. by A 44 on A 4103 – ✉ Worcester.*

Bear and Ragged Staff, Station Rd, WR6 5JH, Southeast : ½ m. on Powick rd ✆ (01886) 833399, *enquiries@bear.uk.com, Fax (01886) 833106,* , – ⇔ P. MO AE ① VISA
Rest a la carte 18.70/31.25.
◆ Two oak trees dominate the front of this traditional pub in quiet country lane. Huge blackboard menus offer plenty of interest: vegetables travel from rear garden to kitchen.

WORFIELD *Shrops. – see Bridgnorth.*

WORSLEY *Gtr Manchester* 502 503 504 **M/N 23** – *see Manchester.*

WORTHING *W. Sussex* 504 **S 31** – *pop. 96 964.*

Hill Barn, Hill Barn Lane ✆ (01903) 237301 **BY** – 18, *Links Rd ✆ (01903) 260801* **AY**.
Shoreham Airport : ✆ (01273) 296900, E : 4 m. by A 27 **BY**.
Chapel Rd ✆ (01903) 221307, tic@worthing.gov.uk – Marine Parade ✆ (01903) 221307.
London 59 – Brighton 11 – Southampton 50.

Plan on next page

Beach, Marine Parade, BN11 3QJ, ✆ (01903) 234001, *info@thebeachhotel.co.uk, Fax (01903) 234567,* ← – ⇔ & P – 100. MO AE ① VISA. **AZ** e
Rest (light lunch) /dinner 19.95 – **75 rm** ☐ ★52.00/79.50 – ★★95.00/106.00, 4 suites.
◆ On town's marine parade with front rooms all boasting clear Channel views. Large public areas decorated in Art Deco style. Bedrooms of a good size and well kept. Popular, family-friendly restaurant.

The Windsor, 14-20 Windsor Rd, BN11 2LX, ✆ (01903) 239655, Reservations (Freephone) 0800 9804242, *reception@thewindsor.co.uk, Fax (01903) 210763,* – ⇔ ▤ P – 120. MO AE ① VISA. **BY** i
closed 24-30 December – **Rest** (bar lunch Monday-Saturday) (carvery Saturday)/dinner 17.95 and a la carte 20.50/28.80 – ☐ 10.00 – **35 rm** ★80.00 – ★★130.00.
◆ At eastern entrance to town in quiet residential area. Well suited to business or leisure traveller with a wide range of rooms. Front rooms particularly spacious and bright. Large dining room with welcoming atmosphere.

Berkeley, 86-95 Marine Parade, BN11 3QD, ✆ (01903) 820000, *reservations@berkeleyhotel-worthing.co.uk, Fax (01903) 821333,* ← – ⇔, ▤ rest, & P – 100. MO AE ① VISA. **BZ** a
Rest (bar lunch Monday-Saturday)/dinner 21.95 – **80 rm** ☐ ★86.00/99.00 – ★★126.00.
◆ Overlooking the Channel and well located for visiting the famous South Downs. First floor rooms boast original Victorian splendour of high ceilings and larger windows. Dining room boasts pleasant sea views.

Chatsworth, Steyne, BN11 3DU, ✆ (01903) 236103, *hotel@chatsworthworthing.co.uk, Fax (01903) 823726* – , ⇔ rest, ▤ rest, & – 150. MO AE ① VISA **BZ** x
Rest (dinner only) 20.95 and a la carte 19.95/26.95 – **98 rm** ☐ ★75.00 – ★★109.00.
◆ In a Georgian terrace overlooking Steyne Gardens and ideally located for a range of the town's resort activities. Attentive service and good sized bedrooms. Simple, uncluttered dining room.

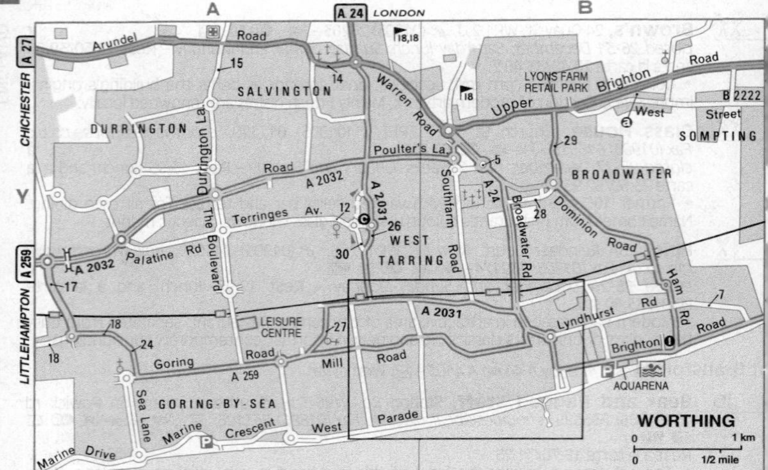
A
B
Y
A 24
LONDON
A 27
CHICHESTER
A 259
LITTLEHAMPTON
Arundel
Road
SALVINGTON
DURRINGTON
Durrington La.
Warren Road
LYONS FARM RETAIL PARK
Upper Brighton Road
West Street
B 2222
SOMPTING
Poulter's La.
Southfarm Road
A 24
Broadwater Rd
BROADWATER
Dominion Road
Road
A 2032
Terringes Av.
WEST TARRING
A 2031
Palatine Rd
The Boulevard
A 2032
LEISURE CENTRE
A 2031
Lyndhurst Rd
Ham Rd
Road
Brighton
Goring Road
A 259
Mill Road
Sea Lane
GORING-BY-SEA
AQUARENA
Marine Crescent
West Parade
Marine Drive
WORTHING
0 1 km
0 1/2 mile

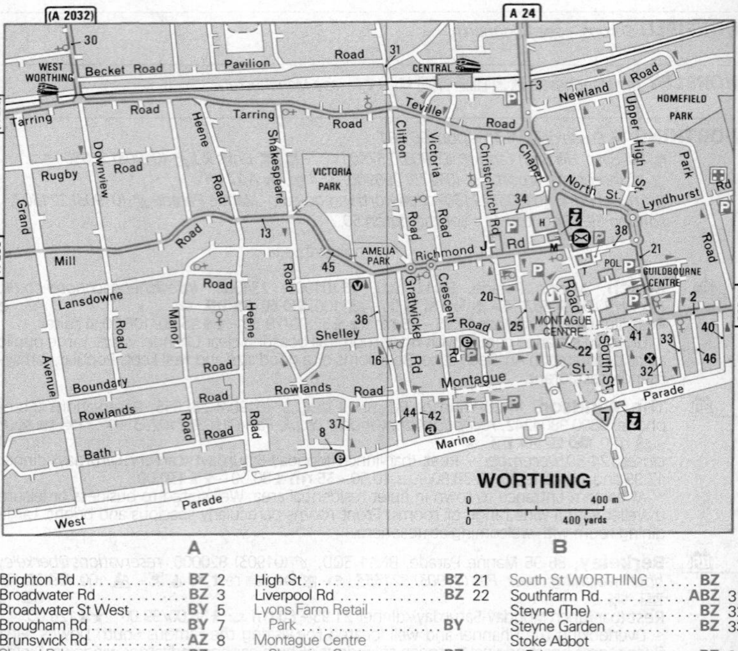

Beacons without rest., 18 Shelley Rd, BN11 1TU, ✆ (01903) 230948, *beaconshotel@amserve.net* – ⇔ 🅿. MC VISA BZ e
8 rm ☕ ★36.00/40.00 – ★★64.00/70.00.
◆ Friendly traditional home providing classic English seaside accommodation. In the centre of town close to parks. Ideal base for visiting historic Arundel and Chichester.

Bonchurch House without rest., 1 Winchester Rd, BN11 4DJ, ✆ (01903) 202492, *bonchurch@enta.net* – 🅿. MC AE VISA. ✗ AZ v
6 rm ☕ ★34.50 – ★★75.00.
◆ Simple, bright accommodation with neat and traditional atmosphere. In quiet, residential area convenient for local amenities. Plenty of information leaflets in lounge area.

The Parsonage, 6-10 High St, Tarring, BN14 7NN, ✆ (01903) 820140, *parsonage.bookings@ntlworld.com, Fax (01903) 523233*, 🍽 – ⚭ 18. MC AE VISA AY c
closed 26 December-3 January, Sunday and Bank Holidays – **Rest** 20.00 and a la carte 24.50/30.95 ♀.
◆ Within one of Tarring high street's original 15C cottages. Exposed beams and framed photographs. Good international cuisine and a friendly, comfortable atmosphere.

WREA GREEN *Lancs.* 502 L 22 – *see Kirkham.*

WRESSLE *East Riding* 502 R 22 *Great Britain G.* – ✉ *Selby (N. Yorks.).*
Env. : *Selby (Abbey Church★), W : 5 m. by minor road and A 63.*
London 208 – Kingston-upon-Hull 31 – Leeds 31 – York 19.

Loftsome Bridge Coaching House, YO8 6EN, South : ½ m. ✆ (01757) 630070, *reception@loftsomebridge-hotel.co.uk, Fax (01757) 633900*, 🌳 – ⇔, ▤ rest, 🅿. MC AE VISA. ✗
closed 25 December – **Rest** *closed Sunday dinner* (dinner only and Sunday lunch)/dinner 22.95 **s.** – **17 rm** ☕ ★50.00 – ★★67.50/79.50, 1 suite.
◆ One-time coaching inn from 1782, with converted former farm outbuildings and lawned garden. Adjacent to River Derwent. Comfortable rooms in main house and annexes. Smart dining room echoing house's light style.

WRIGHTINGTON BAR *Gtr Manchester* 502 504 L 23 – *see Standish.*

WROXHAM *Norfolk* 504 Y 25 *Great Britain G.*
Env. : *The Broads★.*
London 118 – Great Yarmouth 21 – Norwich 7.

Coach House without rest., 96 Norwich Rd, NR12 8RY, ✆ (01603) 784376, *bishop@worldonline.co.uk, Fax (01603) 783734* – ⇔ 🅿. MC AE VISA. ✗
closed 25-26 December – **3 rm** ☕ ★35.00/50.00 – ★★50.00/60.00.
◆ Converted Georgian coach house. Interior décor retains an English country feel with a snug lounge and good-sized, well-kept bedrooms.

WYCH CROSS *E. Sussex* 504 U 30 – *see Forest Row.*

WYE *Kent* 504 W 30 – *pop. 11 420* – ✉ *Ashford.*
London 60 – Canterbury 10 – Dover 28 – Hastings 34.

Wife of Bath with rm, 4 Upper Bridge St, TN25 5AF, ✆ (01233) 812540, *reservations@wifeofbath.com, Fax (01233) 813033*, 🌳 – ⇔ 🅿. MC AE VISA. ✗
closed 2 weeks Christmas and 2 weeks August – **Rest** *(closed Sunday-Monday)* 22.50/24.50 and a la carte 30.00/43.00 – ☕ 7.50 – **5 rm** ★55.00 – ★★75.00.
◆ A lovely timber-framed house built in 1760. Fine cloth tables. Well chosen menu of satisfying dishes. Full or Continental breakfast after staying in comfy, soft-toned rooms.

WYMONDHAM *Norfolk* 504 X 26.
London 102 – Cambridge 55 – King's Lynn 49 – Norwich 12.

Wymondham Consort, 28 Market St, NR18 0BB, ✆ (01953) 606721, *wymondham@bestwestern.co.uk, Fax (01953) 601361*, 🍽, 🌳 – ⇔ 🅿. MC AE ① VISA
closed 24 December-1 January – **Rest** 11.00/15.00 and a la carte approx 24.00 ♀ – **20 rm** ☕ ★60.00/65.00 – ★★85.00.
◆ 18C town house in heart of historic, pretty town. Classic traditional style of décor throughout with well-kept bedrooms decorated in cosy cottage style. Restaurant and café which doubles up as wine bar in the evening.

Old Thorn Barn without rest., Corporation Farm, Wymondham Rd, Hethel, NR14 8EU, Southeast : 3 ½ m. on B 1135 (following signs to Mulbarton) ☎ (01953) 607785, *enquiries@oldthornbarn.co.uk, Fax (01953) 601909* – P. VISA
7 rm ★31.00/40.00 – ★★48.00/52.00.
◆ Simple, rural guesthouse sited on farm and utilising former outbuildings as bedrooms with hand-built wood furniture. Rustic lounge and breakfast area with wood-burning stove.

WYTHAM *Oxon. – see Oxford.*

YANWATH *Cumbria – see Penrith.*

YARCOMBE *Devon 503 K 31 – see Honiton.*

YARM *Stockton-on-Tees 502 P 20 – pop. 8 929.*
London 242 – Middlesbrough 8 – Newcastle upon Tyne 47.

Crathorne Hall, Crathorne, TS15 0AR, South : 3 ½ m. by A 67 ☎ (01642) 700398, *crathornehall@handpicked.co.uk, Fax (01642) 700814*, – P – 140. VISA
Leven **:** Rest 22.50/37.50 and a la carte 30.00/36.40 – **36 rm** ★85.00/140.00 – ★★99.00/180.00, 1 suite.
◆ One of the last stately homes of the Edwardian period. Plenty of original features such as wood panelling and ornate fireplaces. Antique furnished bedrooms and public areas. Formal dining room with an air of classic elegance and tables clothed in crisp linen.

Judges Country House, Kirklevington Hall, Kirklevington, TS15 9LW, South : 1½ m. on A 67 ☎ (01642) 789000, *enquiries@judgeshotel.co.uk, Fax (01642) 787692*, – rest, P – 220. VISA.
Rest 14.95/32.50 – **21 rm** ★120.00/153.00 – ★★164.00/179.00.
◆ Former Victorian judge's residence surrounded by gardens. Welcoming panelled bar and spacious lounge filled with antiques and curios. Attractive rooms with a host of extras. Conservatory dining room overlooks the gardens.

The ✿ award is the crème de la crème. This is awarded to restaurants which are really worth travelling miles for!

YARMOUTH *I.O.W. 503 504 P 31 – see Wight (Isle of).*

YATELEY *Hants. 504 R 29 – pop. 15 395 – ✉ Camberley.*
London 37 – Reading 12 – Southampton 58.

Casa Dei Cesari, Handford Lane, Cricket Hill, GU46 6BT, ☎ (01252) 873275, *reservations@casadeicesari.co.uk, Fax (01252) 870614*, – P. VISA.
Rest - Italian - a la carte 21.55/35.80 – **42 rm** ★60.00/108.50 – ★★65.00/115.00, 2 suites.
◆ An attractive extended 17C house with surrounding gardens. Offers well-run, uncomplicated, uncluttered accommodation with few frills. Beamed ceilings adorn cosy restaurant.

YATTENDON *Newbury 503 504 Q 29 – ✉ Newbury.*
London 61 – Oxford 23 – Reading 12.

Royal Oak with rm, The Square, RG18 0UG, ☎ (01635) 201325, *info@royaloakyattendon.com, Fax (01635) 201926*, – P. VISA
closed 1 January – **Rest** (booking essential) 15.00 (lunch) and a la carte 28.00/33.00 – **5 rm** ★110.00 – ★★130.00.
◆ Part 17C former coaching inn. Country house-style lounge next to smart, intimate restaurant. Classic or modern dishes: worldwide palette. Rear bedrooms overlook garden.

YAXLEY *Suffolk – see Thornham Magna.*

YEADON *W. Yorks. 502 O 22 – see Leeds.*

YELVERTON *Devon* 503 H 32 *The West Country G. – pop. 3 647 (inc. Horrabridge).*

See : *Yelverton Paperweight Centre★.*

Env. : *Buckland Abbey★★ AC, SW : 2 m.*

Exc. : *E : Dartmoor National Park★★.*

Golf Links Rd ✆ (01822) 852824.

London 234 – Exeter 33 – Plymouth 10.

Moorland Links, PL20 6DA, South : 2 m. on A 386 ✆ (01822) 852245, *moorland.links@forestdale.com, Fax (01822) 855004*, ≤, – ★ 200. MO AE VISA

Rest (bar lunch Saturday) a la carte 12.95/22.25 **s.** – **44 rm** ★70.00/110.00 – ★★120.00/140.00, 1 suite.

◆ Quiet location on Dartmoor - views of Tamar Valley. Bright, comfy, modern lounge bar. Bedrooms blend modern and traditional styles, those to front make the most of the view. Restaurant with views over lawns fringed with gnarled oaks.

YEOVIL *Somerset* 503 504 M 31 *The West Country G. – pop. 41 871.*

See : *St John the Baptist★.*

Env. : *Monacute House★★ AC, W : 4 m. on A 3088 – Fleet Air Arm Museum, Yeovilton★★ AC, NW : 5 m. by A 37 – Tintinhull House Garden★ AC, NW: 5½ m. – Ham Hill (≤★★) W : 5½ m. by A 3088 – Stoke sub-Hamdon (parish church★) W : 5¼ m. by A 3088.*

Exc. : *Muchelney★★ (Parish Church★★) NW : 14 m. by A 3088, A 303 and B 3165 – Lytes Cary★, N : 7½ m. by A 37, B 3151 and A 372 – Sandford Orcas Manor House★, NW : 8 m. by A 359 – Cadbury Castle (≤★★) NE : 10½ m. by A 359 – East Lambrook Manor★ AC, W : 12 m. by A 3088 and A 303.*

Sherborne Rd ✆ (01935) 475949.

Hendford ✆ (01935) 845946, yeoviltic@southsomerset.gov.uk – at Cart Gate : Picnic Site ✆ (01935) 829333.

London 136 – Exeter 48 – Southampton 72 – Taunton 26.

Lanes, West Coker, BA22 9AJ, Southwest : 3 m. on A 30 ✆ (01935) 862555, *Fax (01935) 864260*, – rest, – 45. MO AE VISA

Rest a la carte 14.50/23.25 – **10 rm** ★80.00 – ★★100.00.

◆ 18C stone former rectory in walled grounds. Stylish modern interior with chocolate and red leather predominant. Stretch out in relaxed lounge. Airy, modish bedrooms. Modern classics and lots of glass in the Brasserie.

at Barwick *South : 2 m. by A 30 off A 37 – ✉ Yeovil.*

Little Barwick House with rm, BA22 9TD, ✆ (01935) 423902, *reservations@barwick7.fsnet.co.uk, Fax (01935) 420908*, – , rest, MO AE VISA

closed 2 weeks Christmas – **Rest** *(closed Sunday dinner, Tuesday lunch and Monday)* (booking essential) 18.95/32.95 – **6 rm** ★70.00 – ★★130.00.

◆ Dignified Georgian dower house in a secluded spot. Though cosy rooms are available, the focus is on the restaurant with its menu of satisfying regionally based menus.

at Montacute *Northwest : 5 m. by A 3088 – ✉ Yeovil.*

Phelips Arms, The Borough, TA15 6XB, ✆ (01935) 822557, *infophelipsarms@aol.com, Fax (01935) 822557*, – MO AE VISA

closed 25 December – **Rest** a la carte 20.25/31.75.

◆ Sand coloured 17C pub with traditional décor and furnishings. Modern, interesting menus, underpinned by accomplished cooking, have an eclectic range.

at Stoke sub Hamdon *Northwest : 5½ m. by A 3088 – ✉ Yeovil.*

The Priory House, 1 High St, TA14 6PP, ✆ (01935) 822826, *reservations@thepriory houserestaurant.co.uk, Fax (01935) 825822* – . MO VISA

closed last week May, first week June, first 2 weeks November, Sunday and Monday – **Rest** (dinner only and Saturday lunch) a la carte 26.50/36.00 **s.**

◆ Village centre restaurant that sticks firmly to traditions with tried and tested classics to the fore: a quiet and relaxing experience. Swallow a cider brandy after dinner!

YETTINGTON *Devon – see Budleigh Salterton.*

We try to be as accurate as possible when giving room rates. But prices are susceptible to change, so please check rates when booking.

YORK *N. Yorks.* 502 Q 22 *Great Britain G.* – *pop. 137 505.*

See : *City*★★★ – *Minster*★★★ *(Stained Glass*★★★, *Chapter House*★★, *Choir Screen*★★*)* **CDY** – *National Railway Museum*★★★ **CY** – *The Walls*★★ **CDXYZ** – *Castle Museum*★ *AC* **DZ M2** – *Jorvik Viking Centre*★ *AC* **DY M1** – *Fairfax House*★ *AC* **DY A** – *The Shambles*★ **DY 54.**

18 *Lords Moor Lane, Strensall* ✆ *(01904) 491840* **BY** – 9 *Heworth, Muncaster House, Muncastergate* ✆ *(01904) 424618* **BY**.

The De Grey Rooms, Exhibition Sq ✆ *(01904) 621756, tic@york.tourism.co.uk* – *York Railway Station, Outer Concourse* ✆ *(01904) 621756.*

London 203 – *Kingston-upon-Hull 38* – *Leeds 26* – *Middlesbrough 51* – *Nottingham 88* – *Sheffield 62.*

Plan opposite

Middlethorpe Hall, Bishopthorpe Rd, YO23 2GB, South : 1 ¾ m. ✆ (01904) 641241, *info@middlethorpe.com, Fax (01904) 620176,* – 50. MO AE VISA.
Rest (booking essential to non-residents) 23.00/39.00 **s.** – 6.95 – **21 rm** ★115.00/175.00 – ★★175.00/305.00, 8 suites.
◆ Impressive William and Mary country house dating from 1699. Elegantly and carefully restored; abundantly furnished with antiques. Most characterful rooms in main house. Wood-panelled, three-roomed restaurant with period feel.

The Grange, Clifton, YO30 6AA, ✆ (01904) 644744, *info@grangehotel.co.uk, Fax (01904) 612453* – rest, 16 – 50. MO AE VISA **CX u**
The Ivy **:** Rest *(closed Sunday dinner)* (dinner only and Sunday lunch) a la carte 28.00/39.45 – ***The Brasserie*** **:** Rest *(closed Sunday lunch)* a la carte 21.25/26.50 – **29 rm** ★135.00 – ★★165.00, 1 suite.
◆ Elegant Regency town house with stylish period furniture throughout. Comfortable lounges and marble columned entrance hall. Excellently kept rooms vary in shapes and sizes. The Ivy boasts grand ceiling mural. Basement brasserie exudes much character.

Marriott, Tadcaster Rd, YO24 1QQ, ✆ (01904) 701000, *york@marriotthotels.co.uk, Fax (01904) 702308,* – – 170. MO AE VISA. **AZ a**
Ridings **:** Rest *(closed Sunday lunch)* 15.00/25.00 and dinner a la carte 27.70/38.60 **s.** – **148 rm** ★130.00 – ★★140.00, 3 suites.
◆ Large, group owned property on the edge of the racecourse with purpose-built extensions. Grandstand rooms, featuring large balconies and terraces, overlook course. Dining room with racecourse outlook.

York Pavilion, 45 Main St, Fulford, YO10 4PJ, South : 1½ m. on A 19 ✆ (01904) 622099, *help@yorkpavilionhotel.com, Fax (01904) 626939,* – – 150. MO AE VISA.
Langtons Brasserie **:** Rest 16.95 (lunch) and dinner a la carte 22.85/32.65 **s.** – **57 rm** ★100.00/110.00 – ★★130.00/150.00.
◆ Georgian house on main road in suburbs. Wood panelled reception and period-style lounge. Older, more individual rooms in main house and uniform, chintzy style in extension. Informal dining.

Dean Court, Duncombe Pl, YO1 7EF, ✆ (01904) 625082, *info@deancourt-york.co.uk, Fax (01904) 620305* – rest, – 50. MO AE VISA. **CY c**
DCH **:** Rest 16.75 (lunch) and dinner a la carte 26.00/32.00 – **36 rm** ★75.00/99.00 – ★★120.00/230.00, 1 suite.
◆ Built in the 1850s to house clerics visiting the Minster, visible from most rooms. Now a very modern feel pervades the public areas. Aforementioned rooms more traditional. Minster outlook from smart restaurant.

Monkbar, St Maurice's Rd, YO31 7JA, ✆ (01904) 638086, *sales@monkbarhotel.co.uk, Fax (01904) 629195* – – 160. MO AE VISA **DX a**
Rest (bar lunch)/dinner 25.00 and a la carte 26.00/32.50 **s.** – **99 rm** ★105.00/125.00 – ★★140.00/175.00.
◆ Purpose-built and close to impressive Monkbar Gate. Modern décor throughout. Two room types: traditional, cottage-style in annex and uniform, modern rooms in main building. Restaurant exudes medieval atmosphere.

Four High Petergate, 2-4 High Petergate, YO1 7EH, ✆ (01904) 658516, *enquiries@fourhighpetergate.co.uk, Fax (01904) 634573,* – . MO AE VISA. **CX e**
Rest – (see also ***The Bistro*** below) – **14 rm** ★60.00/80.00 – ★★120.00.
◆ Early 18C house, just inside old city walls. Antiques and racing pictures in all areas. Tranquil enclosed garden to rear. Bedrooms are sleek, minimalist and modern.

Holmwood House without rest., 114 Holgate Rd, YO24 4BB, ✆ (01904) 626183, *holmwood.house@dial.pipex.com, Fax (01904) 670899* – . MO VISA. **AZ x**
14 rm ★50.00/70.00 – ★★80.00/110.00.
◆ Informal atmosphere in well-kept terraced Victorian property. Individually decorated bedrooms include William Morris styling. Bright basement breakfast room.

YORK

Street	Grid	No.
Bishopgate St.	CZ	3
Bishophill Senior	CZ	4
Blake St.	CY	5
Campleshon Rd	AZ	7
Church St.	DY	8
Clifford St.	DY	10
Colliergate	DY	12
Coney St.	CY	13
Cromwell Rd.	CZ	15
Davygate	CY	16
Deangate	DY	18
Duncombe Pl.	CY	20
Fawcett St	DZ	21
Fetter Lane	CY	22
Goodramgate	DY	25
High Ousegate	DY	26
High Petergate	CY	28
Knavesmire Rd	AZ	29
Leeman Rd.	AY, CY	30
Lendal	CY	32
Lord Mayor's Walk	DX	33
Low Petergate	DY	35
Melrosegate	BY	36
Museum St	CY	39
Parliament St	DY	42
Pavement	DY	43
Peasholme Green	DY	45
Penley's Grove St	DX	46
Queen St	CZ	49
St Helen's Rd	AZ	50
St Leonard's Pl.	CY	52
St Maurice's Rd.	DXY	53
Shambles (The)	DY	54
Station Rd.	CY	55
Stonebow (The)	DY	56
Stonegate	CY	58
Tower St.	DZ	59
University Rd	BZ	60

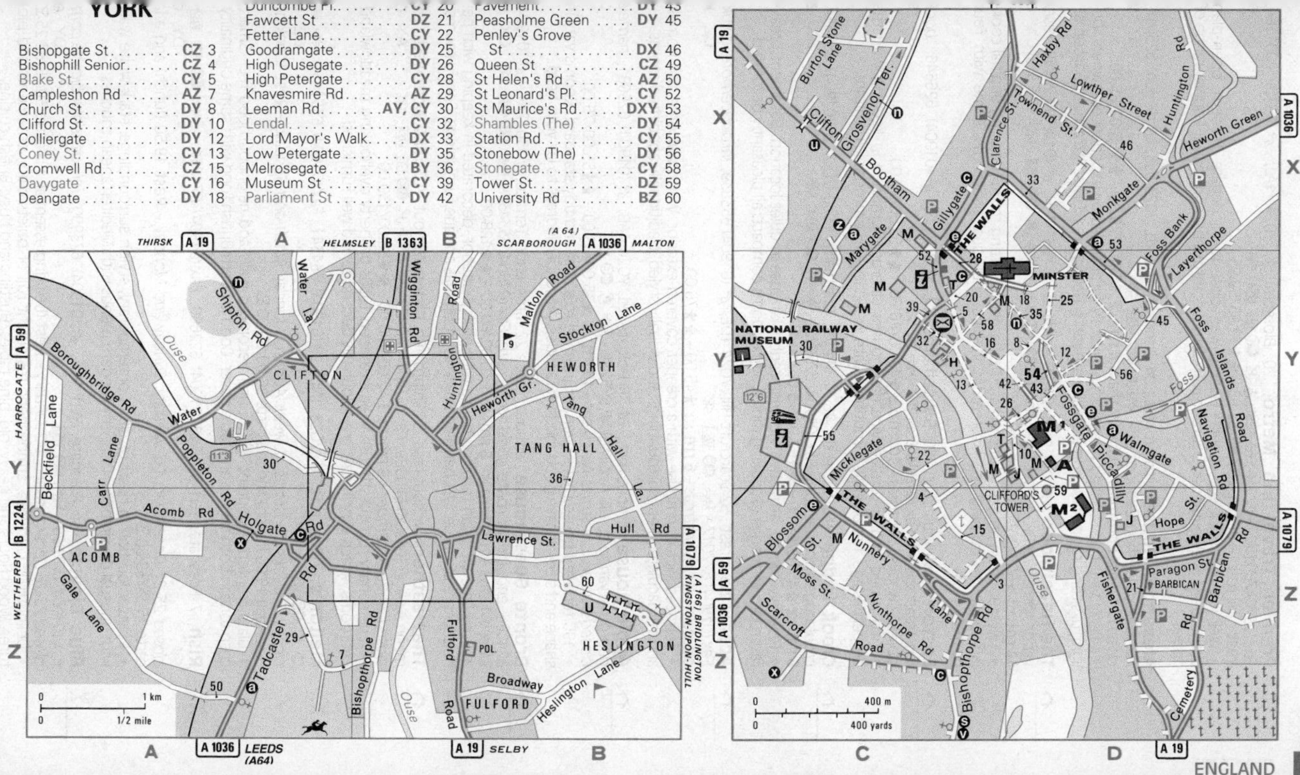

Premier Travel Inn Metro, 20 Blossom St, YO24 1AJ, ✆ (0870) 7001584 *Fax (0870) 7001585* – |‡|, ⇔, ▤ rest, ♿ P. MC AE VISA. ✂ CZ e
Rest (grill rest.) – **86 rm** ☆57.95/57.95 – ☆☆59.95/59.95.
◆ Well located, brick edifice with clock tower, close to Micklegate. Modern, open-plan public areas. Well-equipped bedrooms are large, comfortable and stylish. Popular range of dishes.

Alexander House without rest., 94 Bishopthorpe Rd, YO23 1JS, ✆ (01904) 625016, *info@alexanderhouseyork.co.uk* – ⇔ P. MC VISA. ✂ CZ v
closed 2 weeks Christmas and New Year – **4 rm** ☕ ☆59.00/79.00 – ☆☆65.00/85.00.
◆ Classic Victorian terraced house, immaculately refurbished by experienced owners. Delightful sitting room with porcelain and artworks. Hearty breakfasts. Attractive bedrooms.

The Hazelwood without rest., 24-25 Portland St, YO31 7EH, ✆ (01904) 626548, *reservations@thehazelwoodyork.com, Fax (01904) 628032* – ⇔ P. MC VISA. ✂ CX c
14 rm ☕ ☆50.00/95.00 – ☆☆110.00.
◆ Two 19C town houses with characterful basement sitting room featuring original cooking range. Welcoming breakfast room in blue. Individual bedrooms, some with four posters.

Easton's without rest., 90 Bishopthorpe Rd, YO23 1JS, ✆ (01904) 626646, *bookings@eastons.ws, Fax (01904) 626646* – ⇔ P. ✂ CZ s
closed 2 weeks Christmas – **10 rm** ☕ ☆42.00/46.00 – ☆☆52.00/76.00.
◆ Two joined end-of-terrace Victorian houses carefully furnished in keeping with the property's age. Period style throughout with well-chosen, comfortable furniture.

Crook Lodge without rest., 26 St Mary's, Bootham, YO30 7DD, ✆ (01904) 655614, *crooklodge@hotmail.com, Fax (01904) 625915* – ⇔ P. MC VISA. ✂ CX z
6 rm ☕ ☆45.00/65.00 – ☆☆62.00/75.00.
◆ Privately owned, attractive Victorian redbrick house in quiet location. Basement breakfast room with original cooking range. Some rooms compact, all pleasantly decorated.

Acer without rest., 52 Scarcroft Hill, YO24 1DE, ✆ (01904) 653839, *info@acerhotel.co.uk, Fax (01904) 677017* – ⇔. MC VISA. ✂ CZ x
closed 1 week Christmas – **6 rm** ☕ ☆45.00 – ☆☆76.00.
◆ Terraced Victorian house with a creeper covered exterior. Warm welcome into homely and immaculately kept surroundings. Individually styled, traditionally appointed rooms.

Apple House without rest., 74-76 Holgate Rd, YO24 4AB, ✆ (01904) 625081, *pamelageorge1@yahoo.co.uk, Fax (01904) 673239* – ⇔ P. MC VISA AZ c
closed 2 weeks Christmas-New Year – **10 rm** ☕ ☆35.00/65.00 – ☆☆55.00/75.00.
◆ 19C terraced house that's been refurbished to a neat and tidy standard. Rooms vary in shape and size; all have good modern facilities. A friendly address to lay your head.

Bronte Guesthouse without rest., 22 Grosvenor Terrace, YO30 7AG, ✆ (01904) 621066, *enquiries@bronte-guesthouse.com, Fax (01904) 653434* – ⇔. MC VISA. ✂ CX n
closed 4 days at Christmas – **6 rm** ☕ ☆36.00/60.00 – ☆☆128.00.
◆ Cosy little Victorian terraced house with pretty exterior, decorated in keeping with period nature of property. Charming breakfast room has antique furnishings. Comfy rooms.

The Heathers without rest., 54 Shipton Rd, Clifton-Without, YO30 5RQ, Northwest : 1½ m. on A 19 ✆ (01904) 640989, *Fax (01904) 640989*, ⇐ – ⇔ P. MC AE VISA. ✂ AY n
closed 24-26 December – **6 rm** ☕ ☆42.00/126.00 – ☆☆80.00/130.00.
◆ A personally run guesthouse in an extended 1930s property overlooking meadowland. Bedrooms, which vary in size, are colourfully decorated and well furnished.

Melton's, 7 Scarcroft Rd, YO23 1ND, ✆ (01904) 634341, *Fax (01904) 635115* – ⇔ ▤ ⇔ 20. MC VISA CZ c
closed 3 weeks Christmas, 1 week August, Monday lunch and Sunday – **Rest** (booking essential) 19.00 (lunch) and a la carte 26.00/39.00 ♀.
◆ Glass fronted restaurant with mural decorated walls and neighbourhood feel. Smart, crisp tone in both service and table cover. Good modern British food with some originality.

Rish, 7 Fossgate, YO1 9TA, ✆ (01904) 622688, *Fax (01904) 671931* – ⇔. MC AE VISA. ✂ DY c
closed 25-27 December, 1-3 January, Sunday and Monday – **Rest** 19.50 (lunch) and a la carte 25.35/39.50 ♀.
◆ Popular location in heart of city. Contemporary, stylish surroundings: stark white walls with unusual decorations. Distinctly modern menus with Mediterranean touches.

Blue Bicycle, 34 Fossgate, YO1 9TA, ✆ (01904) 673990, *info@thebluebicycle.com, Fax (01904) 677688* – ⇔. MC VISA DY e
closed 25-26 December and 1-2 January – **Rest** (booking essential) a la carte 30.75/38.25 ♀.
◆ Delightfully cluttered, atmospheric restaurant full of objets d'art, ornaments and pictures. Wood floors and heavy, old, pine tables. Bustling and busy; British cuisine.

X **The Bistro** (at Four High Petergate H.), 2-4 High Petergate, YO1 7EH, ✆ (01904) 658516, *enquiries@fourhighpetergate.co.uk, Fax (01904) 634573* – . CX e
Rest (booking essential) a la carte 24.00/30.00.
• Set in a former doll's house repair shop, this smart, compact bistro has a friendly, welcoming ambience. Modern cooking strikes the right chord after a visit to the sights.

X **The Tasting Room,** 13a Swinegate Court East, YO1 8AJ, ✆ (01904) 627879, *bookings@thetastingroom.co.uk* – . DY n
closed 25 December, 1 week January, Bank Holidays and dinner Sunday and Monday – **Rest** 16.95 (lunch) and a la carte 22.00/34.50.
• Near the Minster with outdoor tables in good weather. Refurbished in 2005: smart fabrics and mood lighting. Simple, tasty, approachable cooking based upon a few good flavours.

X **Melton's Too,** 25 Walmgate, YO1 9TX, ✆ (01904) 629222, *Fax (01904) 636677* – . DY a
closed 25-26 and dinner 31 December and 1 January – **Rest** a la carte 13.30/24.30.
• Café-bistro 'descendant' of Melton's restaurant. Located in former saddlers shop with oak beams and exposed brick walls. Good value eclectic dishes, with tapas a speciality.

at Acaster Malbis *South : 4¾ m. by Bishopthorpe Rd* – **BZ** – ✉ *York.*

The Manor Country House without rest., Mill Lane, YO23 2UL, ✆ (01904) 706723, *manorhouse@selcom.co.uk, Fax (01904) 700737*, – .
closed Christmas-New Year – **10 rm** 45.00/50.00 – 72.00/80.00.
• A quiet location in picturesque village on River Ouse, 15 minutes from city centre. River bus in summer. Parts date from 1700s. Snug, elegant country house atmosphere.

at Escrick *South : 5¾ m. on A 19* – **BZ** – ✉ *York.*

Parsonage Country House, Main St, YO19 6LF, ✆ (01904) 728111, *reservations@parsonagehotel.co.uk, Fax (01904) 728151*, – – 150.
Rest *(closed Saturday lunch)* 25.00 (dinner) and a la carte 24.95/38.45 – **48 rm** 85.00/95.00 – 110.00/140.00.
• Ivy-clad former parsonage with gardens; dating from 1848 and located adjacent to the parish church of St. Helen. Main house rooms most characterful, all are well appointed. Dining room with palpable country house feel.

at York Business Park *Northwest : 3¾ m. by A 59* – **AY** – *on A 1237* – ✉ *York.*

XX **Maxi's,** Ings Lane, Nether Poppleton, YO26 6RA, ✆ (01904) 783898, *info@maxi-s.co.uk, Fax (01904) 783818* – .
Rest - Chinese (Canton, Peking) - a la carte 17.80/24.00.
• Purpose-built property with an ornate exterior. Chinese theme throughout including a feature pagoda in the dining room. Authentic food and attentive, friendly service.

M.P. Renier/MICHELIN

Castle of Scotland: flowers and towers

Towns
from A to Z

Villes
de A à Z

Città
de A a Z

Städte
von A bis Z

Scotland

Place with at least

a hotel or restaurant ● Tongue
a pleasant hotel or restaurant 🏨, 🏠, ✗
Good accommodation at moderate prices
a quiet, secluded hotel
a restaurant with ✿, ✿✿, ✿✿✿, Rest
Town with a local map ●

La località possiede come minimo

una risorsa alberghiera ● Tongue
Albergo o ristorante ameno 🏨, 🏠,
Buona sistemazione a prezzi contenuti
un albergo molto tranquillo, isolato
un'ottima tavola con ✿, ✿✿, ✿✿✿, Res
Città con carta dei dintorni ●

Localité offrant au moins

une ressource hôtelière ● Tongue
un hôtel ou restaurant agréable 🏨, 🏠, ✗
Bonnes nuits à petits prix
un hôtel très tranquille, isolé
une bonne table à ✿, ✿✿, ✿✿✿, Rest
Carte de voisinage : voir à la ville choisie ●

Ort mit mindestens

einem Hotel oder Restaurant ● Tongue
einem angenehmen Hotel oder Restaurant 🏨, 🏠,
Hier übernachten Sie gut und preiswert
einem sehr ruhigen und abgelegenen Hotel
einem Restaurant mit ✿, ✿✿, ✿✿✿, Res
Stadt mit Umgebungskarte ●

Galson
Rhiconich
Scourie
Aird Uig
Breasclete
Stornoway
ISLE OF LEWIS
Drumbeg
Kyles
Lochinver
Ardhasaig
Tarbert
Achiltibuie
Ullapool
Scarista
Leverburgh
ISLE OF HARRIS
Dundonnell
Flodigarry
Gairloch
Lochmaddy
NORTH UIST
Culnaknock
Talladale
Waternish
Torridon
Grimsay
BENBECULA
Liniclate
Shieldaig
Dunvegan
Portree
Lochcarron
SOUTH UIST
ISLE OF SKYE
Erbusaig
Plockton
Kyle of Lochalsh
Dornie
Broadford
Lochboisdale
Elgol
Isleornsay
Castlebay
ISLE OF BARRA
Invergarry

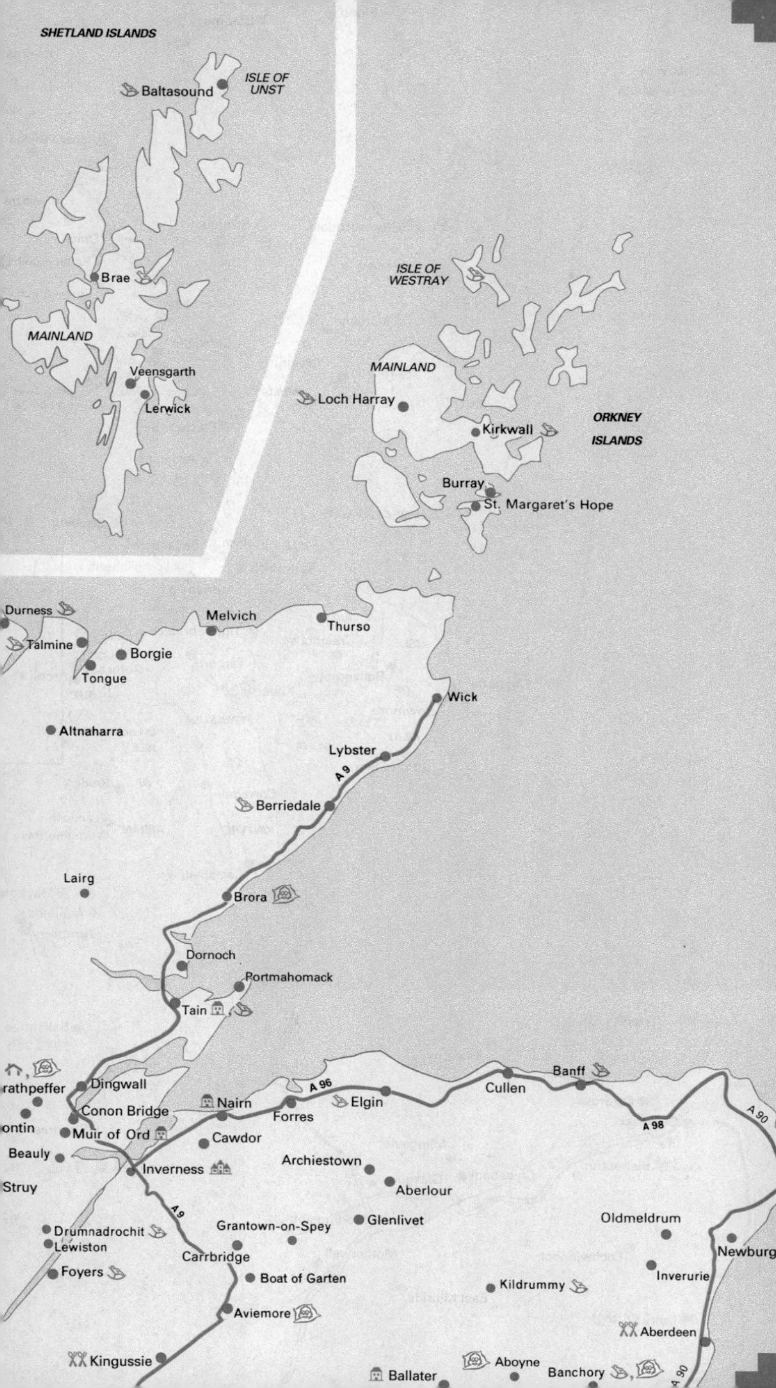
SHETLAND ISLANDS
Baltasound
ISLE OF UNST
Brae
MAINLAND
Veensgarth
Lerwick
ISLE OF WESTRAY
MAINLAND
Loch Harray
Kirkwall
ORKNEY ISLANDS
Burray
St. Margaret's Hope
Durness
Melvich
Thurso
Talmine
Borgie
Tongue
Wick
Altnaharra
Lybster
A 9
Berriedale
Lairg
Brora
Dornoch
Portmahomack
Tain
rathpeffer
Dingwall
Nairn
A 96
Elgin
Cullen
Banff
A 98
A 90
Conon Bridge
Forres
ontin
Muir of Ord
Cawdor
Beauly
Inverness
Archiestown
Aberlour
Struy
A 9
Glenlivet
Oldmeldrum
Drumnadrochit
Lewiston
Grantown-on-Spey
Carrbridge
Newburg
Foyers
Boat of Garten
Kildrummy
Inverurie
Aviemore
Aberdeen
Kingussie
Aboyne
Ballater
Banchory
A 90

Elgol
Isleornsay
Invergar
Castlebay
ISLE OF BARRA
Spean Bridge
Fort William
Glenborrodale
Strontian
Onich
Ballachulish
Tobermory
Fasnacloich
ISLE
Port Appin
Gruline
Eriska
OF
Barcaldine
Craignure
Connel
Tiroran
A 85
MULL
Oban
IONA
Kilchrenan
SEIL
Clachan Seil
Arduaine
Strachur
ISLE OF COLONSAY
Scalasaig
ISLE
Crinan
Bellanoch
Tayvallich
Lochgilphead
OF
Ardrishaig
JURA
Tighnabruaich
ISLE
ISLE
Craighouse
OF
Tarbert
Rothesay
Ballygrant
Ascog
Port Charlotte
OF
Kilberry
BUTE
Bowmore
ISLE
PENINSULA
OF
Lochranza
ISLAY
GIGHA
ISLE
Port Ellen
OF
OF
Brodick
Carradale
Lamlash
KINTYRE
ARRAN
Whiting Bay
Campbeltown
Maybole
Maidens
Turnberry
Ballantrae
Luss
Killearn
unoon
Balloch
Cardross
Greenock
A 8
M 8
Milngavie
Bishopton
Clydebank
Glasgow
Uddingston
Lochwinnoch
Motherwell
Fairlie
A78
East Kilbride
Dalry
Stranraer
Portpatrick

Aviemore
Aberdeen
Kingussie
Aboyne
Ballater
Banchory
A 90
Braemar
Stonehaven
Spittal of Glenshee
A 9
Blair Atholl
Edzell
Kirkton of Glenisla
Kirkmichael
Bridgend of Lintrathen
St. Cyrus
Kinloch Rannoch
Pitlochry
Montrose
Kirriemuir
Alyth
Rannoch Station
Aberfeldy
Inverkeilor
Blairgowrie
Glamis
Kenmore
A 92
Dunkeld
Arbroath
Killin
Kinclaven
A 90
Carnoustie
Dundee
St. Fillans
Lochearnhead
Comrie
Perth
Wormit
Strathyre
Crieff
Cupar
St. Andrews
Auchterarder
Glendevon
Ladybank
Callander
A 9
A 84
Kinross
Lundin Links
Anstruther
Aberfoyle
Dunblane
M 90
Leslie
Glenrothes
St. Monans
Elie
Kippen
Tillicoultry
Stirling
Dunfermline
North Berwick
Gullane
A 80
Falkirk
M 7
Edinburgh
Linlithgow
Uphall
Haddington
Glasgow
Bathgate
Livingston
Bonnyrigg
M 8
A 68
Chirnside
Lauder
New Lanark
Swinton
Peebles
Kilmarnock
Quothquan
Innerleithen
M 74
Kelso
Gatehead
Skirling
Biggar
Walkerburn
Melrose
Sorn
St. Boswells
Prestwick
Annbank
Selkirk
Jedburgh
A 74
Hawick
Kirkmichael
Moffat
Eskdalemuir
Thornhill
Lockerbie
Dumfries
Crocketford
Castle Douglas
Kirkbean
Gatehouse of Fleet
Kirkcudbright
Auchencairn

ABERDEEN *Aberdeen* **501** N 12 *Scotland G. – pop. 184 788.*

See : *City★★ – Old Aberdeen★★* X – *St Machar's Cathedral★★ (West Front★★★, Heraldic Ceiling★★★)* X **A** – *Art Gallery★★ (Macdonald Collection★★)* Y **M** – *Mercat Cross★★* Y **B** – *King's College Chapel★ (Crown Spire★★★, medieval fittings★★★)* X **D** – *Provost Skene's House★ (painted ceilings★★)* Y **E** – *Maritime Museum★* Z **M1** – *Marischal College★* Y **U**.

Env. : *Brig o' Balgownie★, by Don St* X.

Exc. : *SW : Deeside★★ – Crathes Castle★★ (Gardens★★★) AC, SW : 16 m. by A 93* X – *Dunnottar Castle★★ AC (site★★★), S : 18 m. by A 90* X – *Pitmedden Garden★★, N : 14 m. by A 90 or B 999* X – *Castle Fraser★ (exterior★★) AC, W : 16 m. by A 944* X – *Fyvie Castle★, NW : 26½ m. on A 947.*

18, 18, 9 *Hazelhead, Hazelhead Park* ☎ *(01224) 321830*
18, 18 *Royal Aberdeen, Balgownie, Bridge of Don* ☎ *(01224) 702571*, X
18 *Balnagask, St Fitticks Rd* ☎ *(01224) 871286*, X
18 *King's Links, Golf Rd* ☎ *(01224) 632269*, X
18 *Portlethen, Badentoy Rd* ☎ *(01224) 781090*, X
18, 9 *Murcar, Bridge of Don* ☎ *(01224) 704354*, X
18 *Auchmill, Bomyview Rd, West Heatheryfold* ☎ *(01224) 704354*, X.
✈ *Aberdeen Airport, Dyce :* ☎ *(0870) 0400006, NW : 7 m. by A 96* X
Terminal : *Bus Station, Guild St (adjacent to Railway Station).*
⛴ *to Shetland Islands (Lerwick) and via Orkney Islands (Stromness) (P & O Scottish Ferries) 1-2 weekly.*
ℹ *23 Union St* ☎ *(01224) 288828.*
Edinburgh 130 – Dundee 67.

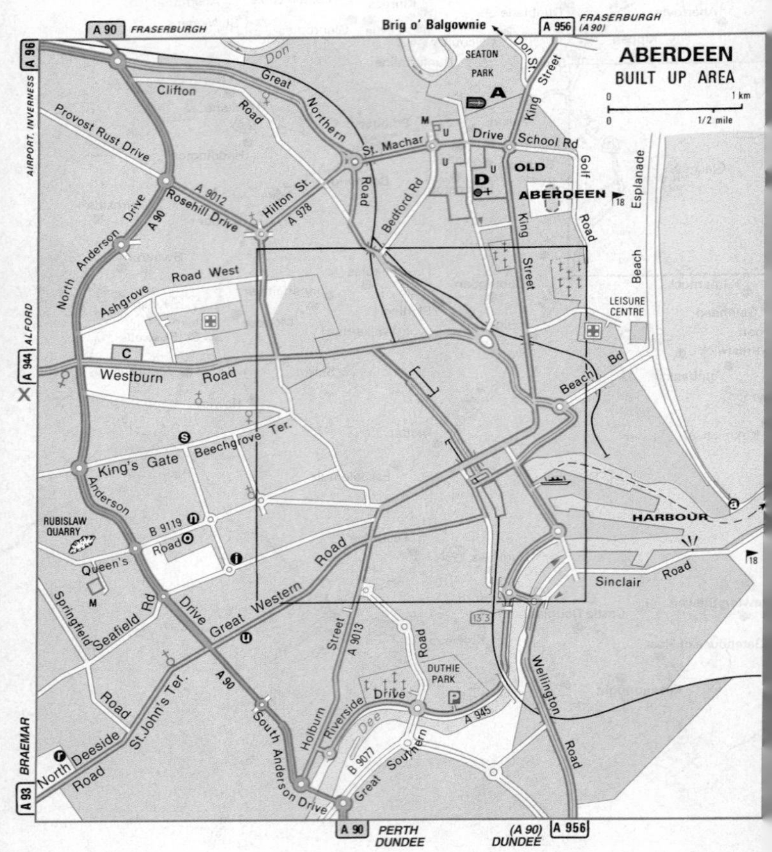

The Marcliffe at Pitfodels, North Deeside Rd, AB15 9YA, (01224) 861000, *enquiries@marcliffe.com, Fax (01224) 868860,* – rest, – 400. X r
Conservatory: **Rest** a la carte 26.70/43.70 **s.** – **40 rm** 135.00/165.00 – 155.00/215.00, 2 suites.
◆ Family owned and professionally run modern country house set amidst 8 acres of pleasant grounds. Spacious, individually decorated rooms with antique furniture. Light, airy conservatory dining.

Ardoe House, South Deeside Rd, Blairs, AB12 5YP, Southwest: 5 m. on B 9077 (01224) 860600, *ardoe@macdonald-hotels.co.uk, Fax (01224) 860644,* – – 500.
Blairs: **Rest** (dinner only) 29.50 and a la carte 27.85/43.95 **s.** – ***Soapies:*** **Rest** (dinner only) a la carte 21.40/31.40 **s.** – 14.95 – **107 rm** 180.00 – 180.00, 2 suites.
◆ Imposing 18C Scottish baronial style mansion. Country house character aligned to excellent leisure facilities. Comfortable bedrooms, many overlooking the grounds. Formal, wood-panelled Blairs. Soapies is cosy, traditional Scottish lounge.

Thistle Aberdeen Caledonian, 10-14 Union Terr, AB10 1WE, (01224) 640233, *reservations.aberdeencaledonian@thistle.co.uk, Fax (01224) 641627* – – 45. Z i
The Restaurant On The Terrace: **Rest** (dinner only) 20.00 and a la carte 17.00/29.00 **s.** – ***Caley Café Bar:*** **Rest** a la carte 13.75/25.00 **s.** – 12.95 – **75 rm** 158.00 – 190.00, 2 suites.
◆ Victorian property overlooking Union Terrace Gardens. Traditional hotel ideal for both the corporate and leisure traveller. Well-appointed and generously proportioned rooms. Classical dining at the Restaurant on the Terrace. Eat informally at Caley Café Bar.

Copthorne, 122 Huntly St, AB10 1SU, (01224) 630404, *reservations.aberdeen@millcop.com, Fax (01224) 640573* – rm, rest, – 220. Z a
Poachers: **Rest** (dinner only) a la carte 17.00/33.00 **s.** – 16.00 – **89 rm** 180.00 – 180.00.
◆ Behind the granite façade you will find a traditional corporate hotel. A 5-minute walk from the main shopping and entertainment area. "Connoisseur" rooms offer extra comfort. Traditional and spacious dining room offering a comprehensive Scottish menu.

Simpson's, 59 Queen's Rd, AB15 4YP, (01224) 327777, *reservations@simpsonshotel.co.uk, Fax (01224) 327700* – X o
closed 24 December-3 January – **Rest** – (see ***Brasserie*** below) – **48 rm** 75.00/135.00 – 90.00/155.00, 2 suites.
◆ The period granite façade belies the vibrantly decorated and contemporary interior. Family owned and relaxed "boutique" hotel. Stylish and modern bedrooms with CD players.

Skene House Holburn without rest., 6 Union Grove, AB10 6SY, (01224) 580000, *holburn@skene-house.co.uk, Fax (01224) 585193* – Z v
8.25, **39 suites** 149.00/192.00.
◆ Row of five granite town houses. Not your conventional hotel, but well-appointed serviced apartments. Each suite benefits from its own kitchen. Ideal for long stays.

Atholl, 54 King's Gate, AB15 4YN, (01224) 323505, *info@atholl-aberdeen.co.uk, Fax (01224) 321555* – – 60. X s
closed 1 January – **Rest** a la carte 13.10/27.90 – **34 rm** 75.00/95.00 – 120.00.
◆ Baronial style hotel set in leafy suburbs; well run by friendly staff. Traditional lounge bar; well-priced, up-to-date rooms. A useful address for visitors to the city. Dining room specialises in tried-and-tested Scottish cooking.

The Mariner, 349 Great Western Rd, AB10 6NW, (01224) 588901, *info@themarinerhotel.co.uk, Fax (01224) 571621* – rm, X u
Atlantis: **Rest** - Seafood - (bar lunch Saturday) 17.00 and a la carte 22.25/42.25 – **25 rm** 70.00/80.00 – 95.00/120.00.
◆ A nautical theme prevails through the ground floor of this commercial hotel. Spacious, colourfully decorated bedrooms with extensive facilities. More seclusion in annex rooms. Long established restaurant with wood panelling and maritime themed décor.

Express By Holiday Inn without rest., Chapel St, AB10 1SQ, (01224) 623500, *info@hieaberdeen.co.uk, Fax (01224) 623523* – – 35. Z u
155 rm 72.00 – 72.00.
◆ Located in the heart of the city; well-equipped, up-to-date bedrooms for the business traveller. Plenty of restaurants are located nearby.

Penny Meadow without rest., 189 Great Western Rd, AB10 6PS, (01224) 588037, *frances@pennymeadow.freeserve.co.uk, Fax (01224) 573639,* – Z x
3 rm 35.00/50.00 – 50.00/80.00.
◆ Attractive period house built of local granite. Welcoming service by owners. Light and airy bedrooms have some thoughtful touches and are well-appointed.

ABERDEEN

Street	Grid	No.
Bon Accord Centre	Y	
Broad St	Y	6
Castle St	Y	7
College St	Z	9
Craigie Loanings	Y	12
Denburn Rd	YZ	14
East North St	Y	16
George St	Y	
Great Southern Rd	Z	18
Guild St	Z	19
Justice St	Y	21
Millburn St	Z	23
Rosemount Terrace	Y	25
Rosemount Viaduct	Y	26
St Andrew St	Y	28
St Nicholas Centre	Y	29
St Nicholas St	YZ	30
School Hill	YZ	32
South Esplanade West	Z	33
South Mount St	Y	34
Spring Garden	Y	36
Springbank Terrace	Z	35
Trinity Centre	Z	
Trinity Quay	Z	37
Union St	Z	
Union Terrace	Z	39
Upperkirkgate	Y	40
Victoria St	Z	42
Waverley Pl	Z	43
Wellington Pl	Z	45
Woolmanhill	Y	48

Silver Darling, Pocra Quay, North Pier, AB11 5DQ, (01224) 576229, *Fax (01224) 588119,* < Aberdeen Harbour and Bay, – . X a
closed 2 weeks Christmas-New Year, Saturday lunch and Sunday – **Rest** - Seafood - a la carte 34.75/43.00.

◆ Former customs house attractively set at port entrance; panoramic views across harbour and coastline. Attentive service of superb quality seafood prepared in imaginative ways.

Olive Tree, 32-34 Queens Rd, AB15 6YF, (01224) 208877, *info@olive-tree.co.uk, Fax (01224) 314255* – 50. X n
closed 1-2 January, 25-26 December, Saturday lunch and Sunday – **Rest** a la carte 19.85/34.50 – (see also ***Black Olive Brasserie*** below).

◆ Modern Mediterranean influences, allied to contemporary British cooking, feature in this former tollhouse. Moderately priced lunch and supper menu available.

Nargile, 77-79 Skene St, AB10 1QD, (01224) 636093, *nargile@freeserve.co.uk, Fax (01224) 647919* – . VISA Y a
closed 25-26 December, 1-2 January and Sunday – **Rest** - Turkish - (dinner only and lunch in December) 16.95/21.75.
◆ Traditionally decorated Turkish restaurant with subdued lighting from Turkish lamps. Open-plan kitchen allows the diner to watch the chefs prepare the authentic dishes.

Brasserie (at Simpson's H.), 59 Queens Rd, AB15 4YP, (01224) 327799, – VISA X o
closed 24 December-3 January – **Rest** a la carte 19.85/29.75.
◆ Behind the bustling bar you'll find this striking and vibrantly decorated restaurant. Designed on a Roman bath house theme with columns and palm trees. Modern cooking.

Black Olive Brasserie, 32-34 Queens Rd, AB15 6YF, (01224) 208877, *info@olivetree.co.uk, Fax (01224) 314255* – 30. VISA X n
closed 25-26 December and 1-2 January – **Rest** - Brasserie - a la carte 14.50/34.50 – (see also ***Olive Tree*** above).
◆ Situated on the edge of the city in a modern conservatory with tinted glass and white ceiling blinds. Open all day for breakfast, mid-morning refreshments, lunch and dinner.

Rendezvous at Nargile, 106-108 Forest Ave, AB15 4UP, (01224) 323700, *nargile@freeserve.co.uk, Fax (01224) 647919* – . VISA X I
closed 25-26 December and 1-2 January – **Rest** - Turkish/Mediterranean - 17.95/22.95 and a la carte (dinner) 19.40/29.70 **s.**
◆ Corner restaurant with contemporary décor. Mediterranean - predominantly Turkish - menu from snacks to a full a la carte meal; fixed price menu between 5-7pm.

t Kirkton of Maryculter *(Aberdeenshire) Southwest : 8 m. by B 9077* – X – *Aberdeen.*

Maryculter House, South Deeside Rd, AB12 5GB, Southwest : 1 ½ m. on B 9077 (01224) 732124, *info@maryculterhousehotel.com, Fax (01224) 733510*, , – – 220. VISA
Priory : Rest *(closed Sunday)* (dinner only) a la carte 23.00/26.40 – ***Poachers Pocket :*** Rest a la carte 14.70/20.45 – **40 rm** 65.00/110.00 – 85.00/150.00.
◆ Restored and extended country house on banks of River Dee. Built in 1225 for the Knights Templars; many features remain. Brightly decorated, modern rooms. Intimate and candlelit Priory restaurant. Relaxed and popular bar overlooking the River Dee.

t Aberdeen Airport *(Aberdeenshire) Northwest : 6 m. by A 96* – X – *Aberdeen.*

Thistle Aberdeen Airport, Argyll Rd, AB21 0AF, (0870) 3339149, *aberdeenairport@thistle.co.uk, Fax (0870) 3339249*, – – 600. VISA
Osprey : Rest *(closed Saturday and Sunday lunch)* 13.95/22.00 and dinner a la carte 20.50/29.75 – 11.00 – **146 rm** 150.00 – 175.00, 1 suite.
◆ Busy commercial hotel within walking distance of the terminal. Extensive conference and banqueting facilities. Well-appointed and boldly decorated modern bedrooms. Restaurant combines international cuisine with traditional Scottish dishes.

BERDEEN AIRPORT *Aberdeenshire* 501 N 12 – *see Aberdeen.*

BERFELDY *Perth and Kinross* 501 I 14.
Edinburgh 75 – Dunkeld 17.5 – Pitlochry 14.5.

Guinach House without rest., Urlar Rd, PH15 2ET, South : ½ m. by A 826 (01887) 820251, *info@guinachhouse.co.uk, Fax (01887) 829607*, – .
3 rm 75.00 – 105.00.
◆ Personally run Edwardian house in mature grounds. Dressers on landing house DVD library, books and games. Modish, individually appointed rooms. Continental breakfast in bed.

BERFOYLE *Stirling* 501 G 15.
Trossachs Discovery Centre, Main St (08707) 200604, info@aberfoylevisitscotland.com.
Edinburgh 57 – Glasgow 30 – Perth 49.

Forest Hills , Kinlochard, FK8 3TL, West : 4 ¼ m. on B 829 (0870) 1942105, *forest-hills@macdonald-hotels.co.uk, Fax (01877) 387307*, Loch Ard, , , , , , – 150. VISA.
Garden : Rest (dinner only) 26.95/35.95 **s.** – ***Rafters :*** Rest a la carte 13.00/25.00 **s.** – **49 rm** (dinner included) 130.00/160.00 – 180.00/240.00, 1 suite.
◆ Lovely location overlooking Loch Ard. Country house ambience with open fires and pleasant views. Extensive leisure club: haggis hurling on offer too. Well-furnished rooms. Glorious views from Garden restaurant. Informal Rafters.

ABERLOUR *Aberdeenshire* 501 K 11 *Scotland G.*
Env. : *Dufftown (Glenfiddich Distillery★), SE : 6 m. by A 95 and A 941.*
Rothes, Blackhall ✆ (01340) 831443.
Edinburgh 192 – Aberdeen 60 – Elgin 15 – Inverness 55.

Dowans, AB38 9LS, Southwest : ¾ m. by A 95 ✆ (01340) 871488, *enquiries@dowanshotel.com, Fax (01340) 871038,* – rest, P. MC VISA
Rest a la carte 16.45/26.00 **s.** – **19 rm** ☕ ★54.00/79.00 – ★★98.00/103.00.
◆ Comfortable and informal establishment with classic Scottish country house style. Inviting public areas with a fishing theme. Best views from second floor bedrooms. Two roomed restaurant.

ABOYNE *Aberdeenshire* 501 L 12 *Scotland G. – pop. 2 202 (inc. Cromar).*
Exc. : *Craigievar Castle★ AC, NE : 12 m. by B 9094, B 9119 and A 980.*
Formanston Park ✆ (013398) 86328.
Edinburgh 131 – Aberdeen 30 – Dundee 68.

Arbor Lodge without rest., Ballater Rd, AB34 5HY, ✆ (013398) 86951, *arborlodge@aol.com, Fax (013398) 86951,* – P. MC VISA.
April-September – **3 rm** ☕ ★35.00 – ★★70.00.
◆ Immaculately kept modern house: one is unlikely to find a more spotless guesthouse in Scotland. French windows lead to beautiful garden. Very comfortable bedrooms.

Struan Hall without rest., Ballater Rd, AB34 5HY, ✆ (013398) 87241, *struanhall@zetnet.co.uk, Fax (013398) 87241,* – P. MC VISA.
April-September – **3 rm** ☕ ★35.00/42.00 – ★★70.00.
◆ An agreeable and welcoming guesthouse with attractive garden. Well kept throughout. Large sitting room and antique breakfast table. Simple, comfy bedrooms.

The Candlestick-Maker, Charleston Rd, AB34 5EJ, ✆ (013398) 86060, *jude@thecandle.com* – . MC VISA
closed 24-26 December, 1-2 January, Monday and Tuesday – **Rest** (dinner only) a la carte 21.00/30.00.
◆ From butcher to baker to a pleasantly informal, personally run restaurant with rustic feel on the village green. Traditional dishes using locally sourced produce; good value.

ACHILTIBUIE *Highland* 501 D 9.
Edinburgh 243 – Inverness 84 – Ullapool 25.

Summer Isles , IV26 2YG, ✆ (01854) 622282, *info@summerisleshotel.co.uk, Fax (01854) 622251,* < Summer Isles, – P. MC VISA
4 April-16 October – **Rest** (booking essential) (set menu at dinner) (light seafood lunch)/dinner 48.00 ♀ – (see also ***Summer Isles Bar*** below) – **10 rm** ☕ ★75.00 – ★★185.00, 3 suites.
Spec. Saddle of rabbit with rosemary risotto on a bed of leeks. Goujons of monkfish and langoustine tails with lime, ginger and coriander. Roast rib of beef with mushrooms and red onion.
◆ Exceedingly well run with a picturesque setting and fantastic views of Summer Isles. Very comfortable lounges and real fire. Superb duplex suite and cosy log cabin rooms. Very pleasant restaurant boasts exacting cooking to a very high standard.

Summer Isles Bar (at Summer Isles H.), IV26 2YG, ✆ (01854) 622282, *bar@summerisleshotel.co.uk, Fax (01854) 622251,* – P. MC VISA.
22 March-16 October – **Rest** - Seafood - (bookings not accepted) a la carte 14.25/22.50 **s.**
◆ Simple, informal bar with outside seating for sunny days and snug interior for more bracing weather. Seafood oriented blackboard menu and puddings from the restaurant.

AIRD UIG *Western Isles (Outer Hebrides) – see Lewis and Harris (Isle of).*

ALLOWAY *South Ayrshire* 501 502 G 17 – *see Ayr.*

ALTNAHARRA *Highland* 501 G 9 *Scotland G.* – ✉ *Lairg.*
Exc. : *Ben Loyal★★, N : 10 m. by A 836 – Ben Hope★ (<★★★) NW : 14 m.*
Edinburgh 239 – Inverness 83 – Thurso 61.

Altnaharra , IV27 4UE, ✆ (01549) 411222, *office@altnaharra.co.uk, Fax (01549) 411233,* <, – P. MC AE VISA
Rest 30.00/35.00 – **14 rm** (dinner included) ☕ ★105.00/125.00 – ★★210.00/250.00.
◆ Refurbished rural hunting lodge with abundance of local wildlife. Stylishly decorated cosy interiors include a cocktail bar and library. Simple, good-sized bedrooms. Local, seasonal menus in smart, formally set restaurant oozing charm and character.

ALYTH *Perthshire and Kinross* 501 J 14 – *pop. 2 301.*
Pitcrocknie ✆ *(01828) 632268.*
Edinburgh 63 – Aberdeen 69 – Dundee 16 – Perth 21.

Lands of Loyal, Loyal Rd, PH11 8JQ, North : ½ m. by B 952 ✆ (01828) 633151, *enq@landsofloyal.com, Fax (01828) 633313*, ≤, – P. VISA
Rest a la carte 19.95/30.50 **s.** – **16 rm** ☕ ★79.00 – ★★176.00.
◆ Victorian mansion with an impressive reproduction salon from the SS Mauritania. Individually decorated bedrooms blend a pleasant traditional style with antiques. Appealing restaurant spans three different rooms.

ANNBANK *South Ayrshire* 501 G 17.
Edinburgh 84 – Glasgow 38 – Ayr 6 – Dumfries 54.

Enterkine, KA6 5AL, Southeast : ½ m. on B 742 (Coylton rd) ✆ (01292) 520580, *mail@enterkine.com, Fax (01292) 521582*, ≤, – rest, P. VISA
Rest (booking essential) 16.50/37.50 – **6 rm** (dinner included) ☕ ★70.00/110.00 – ★★140.00/160.00.
◆ 1930s country house in utterly peaceful location surrounded by extensive gardens and woodlands. Log fires and a charming library. Excellent bedrooms with a luxurious feel. Crystal glassware embodies style of attractive dining room.

ANSTRUTHER *Fife* 501 L 15 *Scotland G. – pop. 3 442.*
See : *Scottish Fisheries Museum★★ AC.*
Env. : *The East Neuk★★ – Crail★★ (Old Centre★★, Upper Crail★) NE : 4 m. by A 917.*
Exc. : *Kellie Castle★ AC, NW : 7 m. by B 9171, B 942 and A 917.*
Marsfield Shore Rd ✆ *(01333) 310956.*
Scottish Fisheries Museum,Harbourhead ✆ *(01333) 311073 (April-October).*
Edinburgh 46 – Dundee 23 – Dunfermline 34.

The Spindrift, Pittenweem Rd, KY10 3DT, ✆ (01333) 310573, *info@thespindrift.co.uk, Fax (01333) 310573* – P. VISA
closed 5-23 January, 2 weeks November and Christmas – **Rest** (by arrangement) 18.00 – 8 rm ☕ ★38.00/48.00 – ★★56.00/76.00.
◆ Victorian house originally owned by tea clipper captain whose bedroom replicates a master's cabin. Comfortable period style throughout and local kippers for breakfast. 19C style dining room reflects house's age.

The Grange without rest., 45 Pittenweem Rd, KY10 3DT, ✆ (01333) 310842, *pamela@thegrangeanstruther.fsnet.co.uk, Fax (01333) 310842*, – P. VISA.
4 rm ☕ ★27.00/50.00 – ★★60.00/70.00.
◆ Spacious Edwardian house on main road into this delightful coastal village. Snug lounges including charming sun room. Neatly kept, traditional bedrooms.

Cellar, 24 East Green, KY10 3AA, ✆ (01333) 310378, *Fax (01333) 312544* – . VISA
closed Christmas, Sunday, Monday and Tuesday lunch in winter – **Rest** - Seafood - (booking essential) 35.00 (dinner) and lunch a la carte 17.95/32.00 ♀.
◆ Located through an archway on quiet back streets. Warm ambience with fires and exposed brick and stone. Bold, original cooking, more elaborate at dinner.

ARBROATH *Angus* 501 M 14.
Edinburgh 72.5 – Dundee 17.5 – Montrose 12.

The Old Vicarage without rest., 2 Seaton Rd, DD11 5DX, Northeast : ¾ m. by A 92 and Hayshead Rd ✆ (01241) 430475, *theoldvicaragebandb@tiscali.co.uk*, – P.
3 rm ☕ ★35.00/45.00 – ★★50.00/65.00.
◆ Detached 19C house, of large proportions, clothed in Victorian style throughout. Eye-catching dolls house in lounge. Antique furnished rooms: ask for view of Arbroath Abbey.

ARCHIESTOWN *Moray* 501 K 11 – ✉ *Aberlour (Aberdeenshire).*
Edinburgh 194 – Aberdeen 62 – Inverness 49.

Archiestown, AB38 7QL, ✆ (01340) 810218, *jah@archiestownhotel.co.uk, Fax (01340) 810239*, – rest, P. VISA
closed 3 January-3 February and 23-27 December – ***Bistro* :** **Rest** a la carte 25.50/34.45 – **11 rm** ☕ ★40.00/60.00 – ★★80.00/100.00.
◆ Very much geared to the fisherman but appealing to all with its characterful, cluttered lounge and nearby golf and distilleries. Comfy rooms, simple and prettily decorated. Informal bistro with daily changing menu.

ARDEONAIG *Perth and Kinross* 501 H 14 – *see Killin (Stirling).*

ARDHASAIG *Western Isles (Outer Hebrides)* 501 Z 10 – *see Lewis and Harris (Isle of).*

ARDRISHAIG *Argyll and Bute* 501 D 15 – ✉ *Lochgilphead.*
Edinburgh 132 – Glasgow 86 – Oban 40.

Allt-na-Craig, Tarbert Rd, PA30 8EP, on A 83 ✆ (01546) 603245, *information@allt-na-craig.co.uk, Fax (01546) 603255,* ←, – P. VISA
closed Christmas – **Rest** (by arrangement) 17.50/25.00 – **5 rm** ☕ ✝35.00/55.55 – ✝✝70.00/75.00.
• Spacious, modernised Victorian house with lovely gardens, once the childhood home of author Kenneth Grahame. Front bedrooms have good views over loch. Simple, traditional dining room where breakfasts and evening meals are served.

ARDUAINE *Argyll and Bute* 501 D 15 *Scotland G.* – ✉ *Oban.*
Exc. : *Loch Awe*★★*, E : 12 m. by A 816 and B 840.*
Edinburgh 142 – Oban 20.

Loch Melfort , PA34 4XG, ✆ (01852) 200233, *reception@lochmelfort.co.uk, Fax (01852) 200214,* ← Asknish bay and Islands of Jura, Shuna and Scarba, , – rest, P – 45. AE VISA
closed 3 January-9 February – **Rest** - Seafood specialities - (bar lunch)/dinner 31.50/36.00 – **26 rm** ☕ ✝79.00 – ✝✝118.00.
• Next to Arduaine Gardens and with glorious, captivating views of the Sound of Jura, this hotel has spacious public areas including a bistro bar. Largest rooms in main house. Formal atmosphere in the main restaurant with a focus on quality local seafood.

Undecided between two equivalent establishments?
Within each category, establishments are classified
in our order of preference.

ARRAN (Isle of) *North Ayrshire* 501 502 DE 16 17 *Scotland G.*
See : *Island*★★ - *Brodick Castle*★★ AC.
from Brodick to Ardrossan (Caledonian MacBrayne Ltd) 4-6 daily (55 mn) – from Lochranza to Kintyre Peninsula (Claonaig) (Caledonian MacBrayne Ltd) frequent services daily (30 mn) – from Brodick to Isle of Bute (Rothesay) (Caledonian MacBrayne Ltd) 3 weekly (2 h 5 mn).

Brodick *North Ayrshire – pop. 822.*
18 *Brodick* ✆ *(01770) 302349* – 9 *Machrie Bay* ✆ *(01770) 850232.*
The Pier ✆ *(0845) 2255121.*

Kilmichael Country House , Glen Cloy, KA27 8BY, West : 1 m. by Shore Rd, taking left turn opposite Golf Club ✆ (01770) 302219, *enquiries@kilmichael.com, Fax (01770) 302068,* – P. VISA
mid March-October – **Rest** *(closed Tuesday)* (booking essential) (dinner only) 38.50 – **4 rm** ☕ ✝95.00 – ✝✝120.00/190.00, 3 suites.
• Arran's oldest building in its delightfully tranquil country setting creates a very fine small hotel. Individually styled, antique furnished rooms. Cosy elegance throughout. Daily changing menus in conservatory extension to main house.

Dunvegan House, Shore Rd, KA27 8AJ, ✆ (01770) 302811, *dunveganhouse@hotmail.com, Fax (01770) 302811,* ←, – P
closed Christmas – **Rest** 18.00/20.00 – **9 rm** ☕ ✝30.00/35.00 – ✝✝60.00/66.00.
• Located on the Brodick seafront with a pleasant outlook over the bay. Lawned garden area and comfortable lounge. Bedrooms are modern and well kept.

Lamlash *North Ayrshire – pop. 900* – ✉ *Brodick.*
18 *Lamlash* ✆ *(01770) 600296.*

Lilybank without rest., Shore Rd, KA27 8LS, ✆ (01770) 600230, *colin369.richardson@virgin.net, Fax (01770) 600230,* ←, – P.
March-October – **7 rm** ☕ ✝25.00/40.00 – ✝✝60.00.
• Whitewashed late 18C cottage on shores of Lamlash Bay overlooking Holy Island. Tidy, snug bedrooms and atmosphere throughout. A good value base for touring the island.

ochranza *North Ayrshire.*

Lochranza (0177083) 0273.

Apple Lodge, KA27 8HJ, Southeast : ½ m. on Brodick rd (01770) 830229, *Fax (01770) 830229,* ←, – P.
closed Christmas and New Year, minimum stay 3 nights – **Rest** (by arrangement) 22.00 – **4 rm** 48.00 – 74.00/80.00.
◆ Extended period house with small garden and pleasing views, in centre of quiet village. Homely cottage-style decor with antique furniture and a welcoming atmosphere. Food is home-cooked and uses island and home produce in good, hearty, varied dishes.

/hiting Bay *North Ayrshire* – ✉.

Whiting Bay, Golf Course Rd (01770) 700775.

Royal Arran, Shore Rd, KA27 8PZ, (01770) 700286, *royalarran@aol.com, Fax (01770) 700286,* ←, – P. VISA
March-October – **Rest** (by arrangement) 19.50 – **6 rm** 35.00 – 70.00.
◆ Large sandstone Victorian house, almost on the seashore, with fine views to the mainland. Welcoming interiors with open fires. Comfy bedrooms with pleasant aspects. The spacious dining room is decorated in the traditional style of the rest of the house.

SCOG *Argyll and Bute* 501 E 16 – *see Bute (Isle of).*

UCHENCAIRN *Dumfries and Galloway* 501 502 I 19 – ✉ *Castle Douglas.*
Edinburgh 94 – Dumfries 21 – Stranraer 60.

Balcary Bay, DG7 1QZ, Southeast : 2 m. on Balcary rd (01556) 640217, *reservations@balcary-bay-hotel.co.uk, Fax (01556) 640272,* ← Auchencairn Bay and Solway Firth, – rest, P. VISA
closed 5 December-10 February – **Rest** (bar lunch Monday-Saturday)/dinner 30.25 and a la carte 25.30/32.20 – **20 rm** 60.00/89.00 – 114.00/136.00.
◆ Perched on the eponymous bay with magnificent views of Auchencairn Bay and Solway Firth. Comfortable, family run hotel. Bedrooms have bay or garden views. Restaurant decorated in keeping with the hotel's traditional style; window tables much in request.

UCHTERARDER *Perth and Kinross* 501 I 15 *Scotland G.* – *pop. 3 945.*
Env. : *Tullibardine Chapel*★, *NW : 2 m.*
Ochil Rd (01764) 662804 – Dunning, Rollo Park (01764) 684747.
90 High St (01764) 663450 (closed half day Wednesday October-March), auchterardertic@perthshire.co.uk.
Edinburgh 55 – Glasgow 45 – Perth 14.

Gleneagles, PH3 1NF, Southwest : 2 m. by A 824 on A 823 (01764) 662231, *resort.sales@gleneagles.com, Fax (01764) 662134,* ←, , , , , , , , , , , squash – , rm, P. – 360. AE VISA
Strathearn : **Rest** (dinner only and Sunday lunch)/dinner 47.00 – ***The Club :*** **Rest** a la carte 20.00/34.00 – (see also ***Andrew Fairlie at Gleneagles*** below) – **256 rm** 380.00/500.00 – 380.00/500.00, 13 suites.
◆ World renowned hotel. Graceful Art Deco and country house décor within impressive grandeur of early 20C mansion. Championship golf courses and extensive leisure facilities. Strathearn is elegant Art Deco dining room. The Club offers informal dining.

Coll Earn House, PH3 1DF, (01764) 663553, *reservations@collearnhousehotel.co.uk, Fax (01764) 662376,* – P. – 50. AE VISA.
closed 24 December-5 January – **Rest** a la carte 18.20/27.00 – **8 rm** 75.00/85.00 – 120.00.
◆ Striking Victorian country house with large lawned gardens, just off town's main street. Bedrooms are capacious and well furnished with antique and reproduction furniture. The restaurant has a light ambience with plain walls with light wood half-panelling.

Andrew Fairlie at Gleneagles, PH3 1NF, Southwest : 2 m. by A 824 on A 823 (01764) 694267, *andrew.fairlie@gleneagles.com, Fax (01764) 694163* – P. AE VISA
closed 3 weeks January, 24-25 December and Sunday – **Rest** (dinner only) 60.00.
Spec. Home-smoked lobster, lime and herb butter sauce. Roast fillet of lamb, slow roast shoulder, peas and beans. Chocolate "biscuit", milk ice cream.
◆ Stylish dining room with a discreet, contemporary feel on the ground floor of this world renowned hotel. Accomplished modern style applied to excellent Scottish ingredients.

AVIEMORE *Highland* 501 I 12 *Scotland G. – pop. 2 397 – Winter sports.*

See : *Town*★.

Exc. : *The Cairngorms*★★ (<★★★) – ✳★★★ *from Cairn Gorm, SE : 11 m. by B 970 – Landmark Visitor Centre (The Highlander*★*) AC, N : 7 m. by A 9 – Highland Wildlife Park*★ *AC, SW : 7 m. by A 9.*

Grampian Rd ✆ (0845) 2255121, aviemoretic@host.co.uk.

Edinburgh 129 – Inverness 29 – Perth 85.

Corrour House, Inverdruie, PH22 1QH, Southeast : 1 m. on B 970 ✆ (01479) 810220, *enquiries@corrourhousehotel.co.uk, Fax (01479) 811500*, <, –, – rest, P. MC VISA

closed mid November-29 December – **Rest** (booking essential to non-residents) (dinner only) 20.00/28.50 s. – **8 rm** ★35.00/50.00 – ★★70.00/100.00.

◆ Victorian dower house in charming setting surrounded by neat lawned garden. Rooms are comfortably furnished with reproduction furniture - those on top floor have best views. Good sized dining room with a slightly more modern feel than the rest of the house.

The Old Minister's Guest House without rest., Rothiemurchus, PH22 1QH, Southeast : 1 m. on B 970 ✆ (01479) 812181, *theoldministershouse@btinternet.com, Fax (01479) 812181*, – P. MC VISA.

closed 23-27 December – **4 rm** ★35.00/40.00 – ★★70.00/80.00.

◆ Early 20C house on outskirts of town, recently vacated by minister. River at bottom of pretty garden. Nicely-laid breakfast room. Spacious bedrooms, finished to high standard.

Lynwilg House, Lynwilg, PH22 1PZ, South : 2 m. by B 9152 on A 9 ✆ (01479) 811685, *marge@lynwilg.co.uk, Fax (01479) 811685*, <, – P. MC VISA

closed November-December – **Rest** (by arrangement) 30.00 – **3 rm** ★30.00/45.00 – ★★65.00/75.00.

◆ Cream painted 1930s house amidst large, tidy gardens. Personally run with a quiet, relaxed atmosphere. Cottagey décor includes open fires. Comfortable, individual rooms. Dining room with spacious, comfortable feel and a view of the Cairngorms.

AYR *South Ayrshire* 501 502 G 17 *Scotland G. – pop. 46 431.*

Env. : *Alloway*★ *(Burns Cottage and Museum*★ *AC) S : 3 m. by B 7024* BZ.

Exc. : *Culzean Castle*★ *AC (setting*★★★*, Oval Staircase*★★*) SW : 13 m. by A 719* BZ.

18 Belleisle, Bellisle Park, Doonfoot Rd ✆ (01292) 441258, BZ – *18 Dalmilling, Westwood Ave ✆ (01292) 263893,* BZ – *9 Doon Valley, Hillside, Patna ✆ (01292) 531607,* BZ.

22 Sandgate ✆ (0845) 2255121.

Edinburgh 81 – Glasgow 35.

Plan opposite

Fairfield House, 12 Fairfield Rd, KA7 2AS, ✆ (01292) 267461, *reservations@fairfieldhotel.co.uk, Fax (01292) 261456*, – P – 140. MC AE VISA. AY

Martins Bar & Grill : **Rest** 15.00/35.00 and a la carte 20.85/28.85 s. – **44 rm** ★79.00/169.00 – ★★99.00/169.00.

◆ Extended Victorian house on seafront, well equipped with leisure and function facilities. Newer bedrooms with a fitted modern feel and older rooms more traditional in tone. Popular favourites at Martin's Bar & Grill.

Western House, Ayr Racecourse, 2 Whitletts Rd, KA8 0JE, ✆ (0870) 0555510, *info@westernhousehotel.co.uk, Fax (0870) 0555515*, – P – 180. MC VISA BZ

The Jockey Club : **Rest** (dinner only) a la carte 16.50/31.00 s. – 9.50 – **48 rm** ★100.00/140.00 – ★★100.00/140.00, 1 suite.

◆ Charm and luxury - all within 60 metres of Ayr racecourse! Stylish, 21C interior harmonises with 18C/19C period detail. Bedrooms offer a high degree of space and luxury. Small restaurant offers traditional Scottish cuisine.

No.26 The Crescent without rest., 26 Bellevue Crescent, KA7 2DR, ✆ (01292) 287329, *carrie@26crescent.freeserve.co.uk, Fax (01292) 286779* – . MC VISA. BZ

restricted opening in winter – **5 rm** ★40.00/45.00 – ★★60.00/65.00.

◆ Located in a smart Victorian terrace in a quiet residential area. Tastefully and comfortably furnished and decorated throughout. Bedrooms finished to a high standard.

Coila without rest., 10 Holmston Rd, KA7 3BB, ✆ (01292) 262642, *hazel@coila.co.uk* – P. MC VISA. AY

closed Christmas and New Year – **4 rm** ★35.00/40.00 – ★★50.00/60.00.

◆ Friendly family home within walking distance of town centre. Simple, comfortably styled interior with golfing memorabilia. Good sized bedrooms, all with en suite facilities.

Fouters, 2a Academy St, KA7 1HS, ✆ (01292) 261391, *qualityfood@fouters.co.uk, Fax (01292) 619323* – . MC VISA AY

closed Sunday and Monday – **Rest** a la carte 24.50/34.00 s..

◆ Down a little alleyway is a modern entrance leading to the vaulted basements of this 18C building. Modern British cooking with good use of locally sourced ingredients.

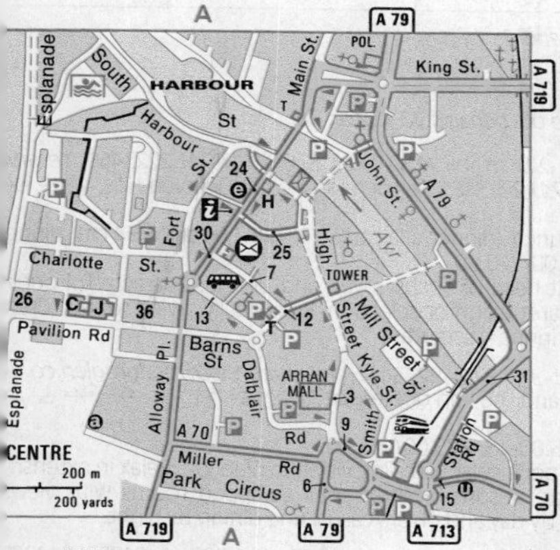

AYR AND PRESTWICK

son St	BZ	2
oway St	AY	3
an Mall	AY	
resford Terrace	AY	6
swell Park	AY	7
rns' Statue Square	AY	9
rick Rd	BZ	10
rick St	AY	12
larton St	AY	13
athfield Retail Park	BY	
gh Rd	BYZ	14
gh St	AY	
lmston Rd	AY	15
c Call's Ave	BZ	20
w Bridge St	AY	24
wmarket St	AY	25
Germain-en-Laye (Pl. de)	AY	26
Leonard's Rd	BZ	27
Quivox Rd	BY	28
ndgate	AY	30
toria Bridge	AY	31
gon Rd	BZ	33
lker Rd	BZ	34
ellington Square	AY	36

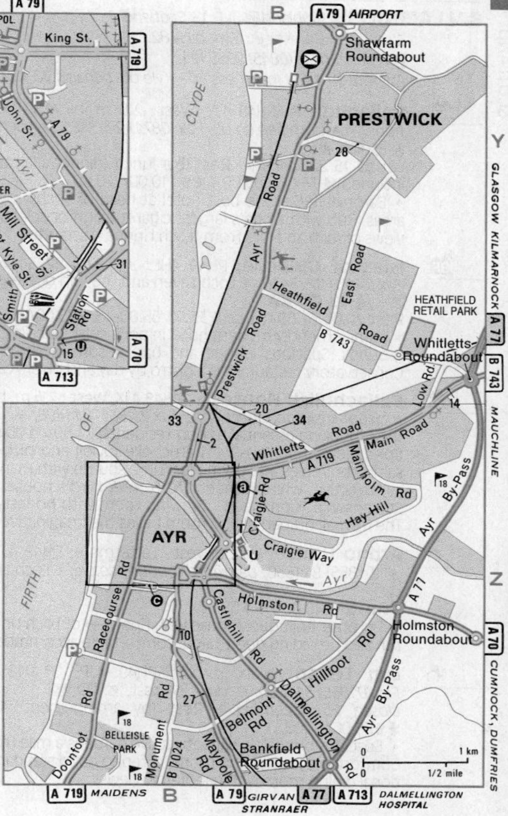

t Alloway *South : 3 m. on B 7024 – BZ – ✉ Ayr.*

Brig O'Doon House, KA7 4PQ, ✆ (01292) 442466, *brigodoon@costleyhotels.co.uk, Fax (01292) 441999,* – – 220. MC AE VISA.
Rest a la carte 17.15/31.15 – **5 rm** ☕ ✝85.00 – ✝✝120.00.
◆ Attractive 19C inn in the pretty village where Robbie Burns was born. Cosy, warm atmosphere amidst tartan and timbers. Atmospheric bedrooms with dark wood furnishings. Heavily timbered, open fired restaurant.

t Dunfoot/Doonfoot *Southwest : 2½ m. on A 719 – BZ – ✉ Ayr.*

Greenan Lodge without rest., 39 Dunure Rd, Doonfoot, KA7 4HR, on A 719 ✆ (01292) 443939, *helen@greenanlodge.com* – P.
closed Christmas and New Year – **3 rm** ☕ ✝40.00/45.00 – ✝✝60.00/64.00.
◆ The birthplace of Robert Burns is just five minutes away from this personally run, homely guesthouse. Sitting room with open fire. Immaculately kept bedrooms.

The ✿ award is the crème de la crème. This is awarded to restaurants which are really worth travelling miles for!

BALLACHULISH *Highland* 501 E 13 *Scotland G.*

Exc. : *Glen Coe★★, E : 6 m. by A 82.*

Albert Rd ✆ (0845) 2255121.

Edinburgh 117 – Inverness 80 – Kyle of Lochalsh 90 – Oban 38.

Ballachulish, PH49 4JY, West : 2 ¼ m. by A 82 on A 828 ✆ (0871) 2223460, *reservations@freedomglen.co.uk, Fax (0871) 2223461,* ≤ Loch Linnhe and Morven Hills, – P. VISA
closed 15-22 January – **Rest** (bar lunch)/dinner a la carte 19.00/31.00 **s.** – **54 rm** (dinner included) ★75.00/105.00 – ★★110.00/220.00.
◆ Baronial 19C stone built hotel at head of Lochs Leven and Linnhe. Characterful public areas. Pub with world's largest cigarette lighter selection. Individually styled rooms. Great views of loch and hills from "Loch Linnhe" restaurant.

Isles of Glencoe, PH49 4HL, ✆ (0871) 2223417, *reservations@freedomglen.co.uk, Fax (0871) 2223418,* ≤ Loch Leven and the Pap of Glencoe, P. – 40. VISA
Rest 20.00 – **59 rm** ★35.00/65.00 – ★★75.00/115.00.
◆ Family-friendly modern hotel in peninsular with fine views to Glencoe. Relax in extensive grounds. Spacious lounge and bar. Leisure facilities. Well-equipped rooms with views. Conservatory restaurant is a bistro by day and offers casual fine dining by night.

Ballachulish House, PH49 4JX, West : 2½ m. by A 82 off A 828 ✆ (01855) 811266 *mclaughlins@btconnect.com, Fax (01855) 811498,* ≤, – P. AE VISA.
Rest (booking essential to non-residents) 21.50/44.00 **s.** – **8 rm** ★75.00 – ★★188.00.
Spec. Seared scallops with artichoke ravioli and pickled chanterelles. Roast grouse with salsify, brambles and thyme jus. Lime soufflé with mango sorbet and coconut sauce.
◆ Attractive, whitewashed, 17C former laird's house with colourful history that inspired Stevenson's "Kidnapped". Drawing room with honesty bar. Large rooms with loch views. The formal, draped dining room belies the imaginative cooking on offer.

Ardno House without rest., Lettermore, PH49 4JD, West : 3 ½ m. by A 82 on A 828 ✆ (01855) 811830, *pam@ardnohouse.co.uk,* ≤ Loch Linnhe and Morven Hills, – P.
3 rm ★48.00 – ★★58.00.
◆ Purpose-built guesthouse with fine view of Loch Linnhe and the Morven Hills. Personally run and providing good value, comfortable accommodation. Spacious bedrooms.

Lyn Leven, West Laroch, PH49 4JP, ✆ (01855) 811392, *macleodcilla@aol.com, Fax (01855) 811600,* ≤, – rest, P. VISA
closed 25 December – **Rest** (by arrangement) 10.00 – **8 rm** ★26.00/30.00 ★★55.00/60.00.
◆ Spacious bungalow with attractive gardens a mile from Glencoe overlooking Loch Leven. Comfortable lounge and rooms offering good standard of homely accommodation. Traditional dining room with panoramic views.

BALLANTRAE *South Ayrshire* 501 502 E 18 – ✉ *Girvan.*

Edinburgh 115 – Ayr 33 – Stranraer 18.

Glenapp Castle, KA26 0NZ, South : 1 m. by A 77 taking first right turn after bridge ✆ (01465) 831212, *enquiries@glenappcastle.com, Fax (01465) 831000,* ≤, – P. AE VISA
April-October and New Year – **Rest** (booking essential for non residents) (set menu only) (light lunch)/dinner 55.00 – **14 rm** (dinner included) ★255.00/275.00 – ★★385.00/405.00, 3 suites.
◆ Stunning Victorian Baronial castle in extensive gardens and woodland. Grand sitting rooms with rich fabrics and fine antiques. Peaceful library. Luxuriously furnished rooms. Elaborate, refined dining.

Cosses Country House, KA26 0LR, East : 2 ¼ m. by A 77 (south) taking first turn left after bridge ✆ (01465) 831363, *info@cossescountryhouse.com, Fax (01465) 83159[…]*, – P. VISA
March-November – **Rest** (by arrangement) (communal dining) 27.50 – **3 rm** ★55.00 ★★80.00.
◆ Part 16C former shooting lodge with most agreeable rural ambience. Wood-floored hall and well-furnished country house style drawing room. Bedrooms of taste and quality. Own garden produce in elegant dining room.

Good food without spending a fortune? Look out for the Bib Gourmand

BALLATER Aberdeenshire 501 K 12 – pop. 1 446.

Victoria Rd ☎ (013397) 55567.
The Old Royal Station ☎ (013397) 55306, ballater@agtb.org.
Edinburgh 111 – Aberdeen 41 – Inverness 70 – Perth 67.

Hilton Craigendarroch, Braemar Rd, AB35 5XA, on A 93 ☎ (013397) 55858, *reservations.craigendarroch@hilton.com, Fax (013397) 55447,* ≤ Dee Valley and Grampians, squash – 110. MC AE VISA.
***Oaks*: Rest** *(closed Monday-Tuesday)* (dinner only) 27.95/32.95 **s.** – ***The Club House*:** Rest (dinner only) a la carte approx 15.00 **s.** – **40 rm** (dinner included) 72.00/126.00 – 102.00/212.00, 5 suites.
◆ Substantial leisure based hotel in a superb location. Extensive spa facilities. Comfortable bedrooms: some enhanced to notable degree with balconies. Formal Oaks restaurant with smart wood furnishing. Club House Grill is informal with a popular menu.

Darroch Learg, Braemar Rd, AB35 5UX, ☎ (013397) 55443, *info@darrochlearg.co.uk, Fax (013397) 55252,* ≤ Dee Valley and Grampians, – P. MC AE VISA
closed last 3 weeks January and Christmas – **Rest** – (see ***The Conservatory*** below) – **17 rm** (dinner included) 85.00/130.00 – 140.00/230.00.
◆ Country house hotel: enjoy superb views from its elevated position. Plush lounges with soft suites, open fires and antiques. Enticing bedrooms: upper floors have best outlook.

Balgonie Country House, Braemar Pl, AB35 5NQ, ☎ (013397) 55482, *balgoniech@aol.com, Fax (013397) 55497,* ≤, – rest, P. MC AE VISA.
closed 6 January-28 February – **Rest** (booking essential to non-residents) (lunch by arrangement)/dinner 37.50/40.00 – **9 rm** 77.50/87.50 – 135.00/145.00.
◆ Personally run, peaceful Edwardian country house with relaxed atmosphere in mature gardens with fine hill views. Individually furnished bedrooms boast admirable outlook. Restaurant renowned for its use of fine Scottish produce and accomplished cooking.

Auld Kirk, Braemar Rd, AB35 5RX, ☎ (013397) 55762, *info@auldkirkhotel.com, Fax (013397) 55762* – P. MC VISA
closed 1-3 January, 25-27 December – ***Johnson's*:** **Rest** *(closed Sunday)* (bar lunch)/dinner 27.50 – **6 rm** 50.00/53.00 – 70.00/80.00.
◆ Former 19C church handily located on main road. An interesting and unusual conversion, with simply furnished and brightly decorated bedrooms. Church origins most visible in dining room.

Morvada House without rest., 28 Braemar Rd, AB35 5RL, ☎ (013397) 56334, *morvada@aol.com, Fax (013397) 56092* – P. MC VISA.
closed December and January – **6 rm** 50.00 – 55.00.
◆ Attractive stone built house. Personally run. Notable for its collection of Russel Flint pictures. Immaculately kept, individually decorated rooms, some with mountain views.

Moorside House without rest., 26 Braemar Rd, AB35 5RL, ☎ (013397) 55492, *info@moorsidehouse.co.uk, Fax (013397) 55492,* – P. MC VISA.
April-October – **9 rm** 40.00 – 55.00.
◆ Detached Victorian pink stone guesthouse on main road just outside town centre. Neat garden. Vividly coloured breakfast room. Sizeable, well-furnished rooms.

The Conservatory (at Darroch Learg H.), Braemar Rd, AB35 5UX, ☎ (013397) 55443, *info@darrochlearg.co.uk, Fax (013397) 55252,* ≤, – P. MC AE VISA
closed Christmas and last 3 weeks January – **Rest** (light lunch Monday-Saturday)/dinner 38.50/45.00.
◆ Attractive conservatory restaurant with a fine view from its garden location: comfortable dining enhanced by attentive service. Notably impressive wine list.

The Green Inn with rm, 9 Victoria Rd, AB35 5QQ, ☎ (013397) 55701, *info@green-inn.com* – rest. MC AE VISA
closed 2 weeks February, 25 December, Monday in winter and Sunday – **Rest** (dinner only) 28.50/33.50 – **2 rm** 35.00/40.00 – 50.00/60.00.
◆ Former temperance hall, opposite village green, boasting pleasant conservatory. Fine tableware. Interesting, well sourced and accomplished modern British cooking. Cosy rooms.

BALLOCH West Dunbartonshire 501 G 15 *Scotland G.* – ✉ *Alexandria.*

Env.: *N : Loch Lomond**.*
The Old Station Building, Balloch Rd ☎ (08707) 200607 (April-October), info@balloch.visitscotland.com.
Edinburgh 72 – Glasgow 20 – Stirling 30.

De Vere Cameron House , Loch Lomond, G83 8QZ, Northwest : 1½ m. by A 81 on A 82 ✆ (01389) 755565, *reservations@cameronhouse.co.uk, Fax (01389) 759522*, ≤ Loch Lomond, , , , , , , , , , squash – , , , rest, , , 300. MC AE VISA.

Smolletts : **Rest** (dinner only) a la carte 25.15/39.40 **s.** – ***Marina :*** **Rest** - Mediterranean a la carte 17.85/35.65 **s.** – (see also ***Georgian Room*** below) – **89 rm** ☕ ★120.00/200.00 – ★★150.00/290.00, 7 suites.

◆ Extensive Victorian house superbly situated on shores of Loch Lomond. Impressive leisure facilities. Luxurious rooms with four posters and panoramic views. Stylish Smolletts with superb views. Delightfully set Marina for Mediterranean cuisine.

XXXX **Georgian Room** (at De Vere Cameron House H.), Loch Lomond, G83 8QZ, Northwest : 1½ m. by A 811 on A 82 ✆ (01389) 755565, *reservations@cameronhouse.co.uk, Fax (01389) 759522,* ≤ Loch Lomond, – . MC AE VISA

closed Monday-Tuesday – **Rest** (booking essential) (dinner only and Sunday lunch) 55.00/65.00 **s.**

◆ Elegant refurbishment guarantees a refined and formal dining experience that utilises notably fine ingredients in a well-executed, precisely prepared style.

BALLYGRANT *Argyll and Bute* 501 B 16 – *see Islay (Isle of).*

BALTASOUND *Shetland Islands* 501 R 1 – *see Shetland Islands (Island of Unst).*

BANAVIE *Highland* 501 E 13 – *see Fort William.*

BANCHORY *Aberdeenshire* 501 M 12 *Scotland G.* – *pop. 6 034.*

Env. : *Crathes Castle★★ (Gardens★★★) AC, E : 3 m. by A 93 – Cairn o'Mount Road★ (≤★★) S : by B 974.*

Exc. : *Dunnottar Castle★★ (site★★★) AC, SW : 15½ m. by A 93 and A 957 – Aberdeen★★, NE : 17 m. by A 93.*

Kinneskie ✆ (01330) 822365 – Torphins ✆ (013398) 82115.

Bridge St ✆ (01330) 822000 (Easter-October).

Edinburgh 118 – Aberdeen 17 – Dundee 55 – Inverness 94.

Raemoir House , AB31 4ED, North : 2½ m. on A 980 ✆ (01330) 824884, *relax@raemoir.com, Fax (01330) 822171,* ≤, , , – rest, – 50. MC VISA

closed 25-29 December – **Rest** 20.00/35.00 – **20 rm** ☕ ★66.00/85.00 – ★★138.00.

◆ Impressive, enviably located 18C Highland mansion with 16C "ha-hoose" (hall house) and popular annex. Country house ambience: antiques abound. Very comfortable rooms. The "Oval" dining room luxuriates with Victorian tapestry walls.

Banchory Lodge , Dee St, AB31 5HS, ✆ (01330) 822625, *enquiries@bancholodge.co.uk, Fax (01330) 825019,* ≤, , – – 30. MC AE VISA

Rest a la carte 14.00/27.00 – **22 rm** ☕ ★65.00/85.00 – ★★130.00/180.00.

◆ Part 16C former coaching inn delightfully situated on River Dee. Country house style accentuated by antiques and china. Individually decorated bedrooms. Dee views and floral displays enhance the attraction of the dining room.

The Old West Manse without rest., 71 Station Rd, AB31 5YD, ✆ (01330) 82220 *westmanse@btinternet.com, Fax (01330) 822202,* – . MC VISA

3 rm ☕ ★35.00/45.00 – ★★55.00/65.00.

◆ Immaculately distinctive guesthouse just outside village. Bright yellow exterior, lovely gardens and homely lounge with warm décor. Spotlessly kept, bright bedrooms.

XX **The Milton,** Milton of Crathes, North Deeside Rd, Crathes, AB31 5QH, East : 3 m. on A ✆ (01330) 844566, *reservations@themilton.co.uk, Fax (01330) 844353* – . MC AE VISA

closed 25-26 December, 1-2 January and dinner Sunday and Monday – **Rest** a la carte 22.25/37.25 .

◆ An attractively styled converted stone barn with a modern feel, part of a 'craft village' and adjacent to Crathes Castle. An appealing range of eclectic contemporary dishes.

BANFF *Aberdeenshire* 501 M 10 *Scotland G.* – *pop. 3 991.*

See : *Town★ – Duff House★★ (baroque exterior★) AC – Mercat Cross★.*

Royal Tarlair, Buchan St, Macduff ✆ (01261) 832897 – Duff House Royal, The Barnyards ✆ (01261) 812062.

Collie Lodge ✆ (01261) 812419 (Easter-October).

Edinburgh 177 – Aberdeen 47 – Fraserburgh 26 – Inverness 74.

The Orchard without rest., Duff House, AB45 3TA, by Duff House rd and Wrack Wood rd ☎ (01261) 812146, *orchardbanff@aol.com, Fax (01261) 812146*, – P.
5 rm ☕ 27.50/37.50 – 55.00.
◆ Good value, purpose-built guesthouse in tranquil, wooded location in grounds of Duff House Gallery and Country House. Cosy lounge and breakfast room. Simple, spotless rooms.

Morayhill without rest., Bellevue Rd, AB45 1BJ, South : ¼ m. by A 97 ☎ (01261) 815956, *morayhill@aol.com, Fax (01261) 818717*, – P
3 rm ☕ 29.00 – 48.00.
◆ Victorian house with garden in residential road, not far from the golf course and town. Lounge and separate breakfast room. Comfortable bedrooms, individually decorated.

BARCALDINE *Argyll and Bute* 501 E 14 – ✉ *Oban.*

Edinburgh 128 – Dundee 122 – Glasgow 105 – Inverness 103 – Oban 13.

Barcaldine House without rest., PA37 1SG, ☎ (01631) 720219, *info@barcaldinehousehotel.com*, – P. MC VISA.
8 rm ☕ 80.00 – 96.00.
◆ Fine 18C country house in quiet location. Communal areas include two spacious lounges, one in Louis XVI-style, and a billiard room. Comfortable, traditional bedrooms.

BARRA (Isle of) *Western Isles* 501 X 12/13 – ✉ *Castlebay.*

from Castlebay to Oban, South Uist (Lochboisdale) and Mallaig (Caledonian MacBrayne Ltd) (summer only) Sunday-Thursday.

Castlebay *Western Isles.*

Castlebay, HS9 5XD, ☎ (01871) 810223, *castlebayhotel@aol.com, Fax (01871) 810455,* ≤ Kisimul Castle and Island of Vatersay – rest, P. MC VISA
closed Christmas-February – **Rest** a la carte 14.65/25.95 s. – **10 rm** ☕ 45.00/85.00 – 78.00/76.00.
◆ Personally run, early 20C hotel situated in prominent position overlooking Kisimul Castle and Isle of Vatersay. Cosy sitting room and spacious bar. Homely, well-kept rooms. Welcoming, linen-clad dining room with homely fare on offer.

Grianamul without rest., HS9 5XD, ☎ (01871) 810416, *macneilronnie@aol.com, Fax (01871) 810319*, – P. MC.
closed 20 December-5 January – **3 rm** ☕ 30.00/40.00 – 50.00.
◆ Purpose-built guesthouse, convenient for local amenities; adjacent to heritage centre. Comfortable, homely lounge. Very sunny breakfast room. Sizeable, well-kept rooms.

Tigh na Mara without rest., HS9 5XD, ☎ (01871) 810304, *tighnamara@aol.com, Fax (01871) 810858*, ≤ – P. MC VISA.
5 rm ☕ 25.00 – 50.00.
◆ Aptly named "Shelter By The Sea", this pleasantly located guesthouse has extensive views of Castlebay Harbour. Map-strewn, homely lounge. Cosy rooms, most with castle views.

BATHGATE *West Lothian* 501 J 16 – *pop. 15 068.*

Edinburgh 24 – Dundee 62 – Glasgow 29 – Perth 50.

Express by Holiday Inn without rest., Starlaw Rd, EH48 1LQ, ☎ (0800) 434040, *Fax (01506) 650651* – – 20. MC AE VISA.
74 rm 59.00/70.00 – 59.00/70.00.
◆ Purpose-built corporate hotel close to motorway junction providing good standard of accommodation at fair price. Open plan breakfast-cum-bar area. Sizeable, modern rooms.

BEAULY *Highland* 501 G 11 – *pop. 1 164.*

Edinburgh 169 – Inverness 13 – Wick 125.

Lovat Arms, High St, IV4 7BS, ☎ (01463) 782313, *lovatarms@cali.co.uk, Fax (01463) 782862* – rest, P – 60. MC VISA
Rest a la carte 9.50/26.70 – **28 rm** ☕ 30.00/50.00 – 60.00/110.00.
◆ Stylish, family owned hotel in village centre with distinctive Scottish feel: full tartan décor abounds. Spacious sitting room, busy bar. Smart rooms with clan influence. All-enveloping tartan curtains dominate warmly hued dining room.

Priory, The Square, IV4 7BX, ℘ (01463) 782309, *reservations@priory-hotel.com* *Fax (01463) 782531* – ▯ ✆ . MC AE ⓓ VISA
Rest 19.95 (dinner) and a la carte 7.00/20.00 ♀ – **34 rm** ☕ ✝45.00/52.50 – ✝✝70.00/95.00
◆ Popular hotel located in centre of village, particularly well suited to the business or leisure traveller. Very busy bar with pool tables. Good sized, comfortable rooms. Spacious open dining room with pink linen-clad tables.

BELLANOCH *Argyll and Bute* 501 D 15 *Scotland G.*
Env. : *Crinan*★, *W : 2 m. by B 841.*
Exc. : *Auchindrain Folklife Museum*★, *E : 25 m. by B 841 and A 83.*
Edinburgh 134 – Arduaine 16 – Oban 34.

Bellanoch House, Bellanoch Bay, Crinan Canal, PA31 8SN, ℘ (01546) 830149 *stay@bellanochhouse.co.uk,* ←, – ⚓ ✆ P.
closed 1 week autumn and 25 December – **Rest** (by arrangement) 35.00 – **4 rm** ☕ ✝35.00/45.00 – ✝✝70.00/80.00.
◆ Former church and school-house with gardens. Stylish lounge boasts stone fireplace from Italy. Owners' family paintings on walls. Airy rooms; front two with good views. Home-cooked food served in dining area.

BENBECULA *Western Isles* 501 X/Y 11 – *see Uist (Isles of).*

BERRIEDALE *Highland* 501 J 9.
Edinburgh 251 – Inverness 94 – Thurso 28 – Wick 14.

The Factor's House , Langwell, KW7 6HD, take private road to Langwell House 2.9 m. ℘ (01593) 751280, *robert@welbeck2.freeserve.co.uk, Fax (01593) 751251,* ←, – rm, P
closed Christmas and New Year – **Rest** (communal dining) 25.00 – **3 rm** ☕ ✝40.00/50.00 ✝✝70.00.
◆ Enviably sited lodge accommodation set in many glorious acres. Extremely peaceful situation. Simple, pleasant drawing room and bedrooms with mix of antique furnishings. Home-cooked dishes and good Highland views.

BIGGAR *South Lanarkshire* 501 J 17 – *pop. 2 098.*
The Park, Broughton Rd ℘ (01899) 220319.
155 High St ℘ (01899) 221066 (Easter-September).
Edinburgh 31 – Dumfries 49 – Glasgow 40.

Lindsaylands , Lindsaylands Rd, ML12 6NR, Southwest : ¾ m. via Park Place and The Wynd ℘ (01899) 220033, *elspeth@lindsaylands.co.uk, Fax (01899) 221009,* ←, , , P.
March-October – **Rest** (by arrangement) 16.50 – **3 rm** ☕ ✝35.00 – ✝✝60.00.
◆ Attractive baronial style Victorian country house set in six acres of mature gardens. Comfortable lounge and tidy, well-kept bedrooms, two with huge, private bathrooms. Elegant, spacious dining room with neatly laid pine tables.

BIRNAM *Perth and Kinross* 501 J 14 – *see Dunkeld.*

BISHOPTON *Renfrewshire* 501 G 16.
Edinburgh 59 – Dumbarton 9 – Glasgow 13.

Mar Hall , Earl of Mar Estate, PA7 5NW, Northeast : 1 m. on B 815 ℘ (0141) 812 9999 *sales@marhall.com, Fax (0141) 812 9997,* ←, , , , , , , – ▯ ✆ ♿ P
400. MC AE VISA
***Cristal* :** **Rest** (dinner only and Sunday lunch) a la carte 33.50/39.50 ♀ – ☕ 15.50 – **50 rm** ✝135.00 – ✝✝475.00, 3 suites.
◆ Impressive Gothic mansion, overlooking Clyde and Kilpatrick Hills. Excellent leisure club incorporating Asian influenced spa. Period and contemporary mix to bedrooms. Formal fine dining in The Cristal.

We try to be as accurate as possible when giving room rates. But prices are susceptible to change, so please check rates when booking.

LAIR ATHOLL *Perth and Kinross* 501 I 13.

Blair Atholl, Invertilt Rd (01796) 481407.
Edinburgh 79 – Inverness 83 – Perth 35.

The Loft, Golf Course Rd, PH18 5TE, (01796) 481377, *daniel@theloftrestaurant.co.uk, Fax (01796) 481511* – VISA
closed 8 January-8 February – **Rest** (dinner only Thursday-Saturday and Sunday lunch) a la carte approx 25.00.
• Modern restaurant set on first floor of former hayloft, with beamed ceilings in situ. Bright décor; lots of natural light. Good value, freshly prepared modern menus.

LAIRGOWRIE *Perth and Kinross* 501 J 14 *Scotland G. – pop. 7 965.*

Exc. : *Scone Palace★★ AC, S : 12 m. by A 93.*
26 Wellmeadow (01250) 872960, blairgowrietic@perthshire.co.uk.
Edinburgh 60 – Dundee 19 – Perth 16.

Kinloch House, PH10 6SG, West : 3 m. on A 923 (01250) 884237, *reception@kinlochhouse.com, Fax (01250) 884333,* – VISA.
closed 2 weeks Christmas – **Rest** 39.00/45.00 (dinner) and lunch a la carte 21.00/32.50 – **17 rm** (dinner included) 100.00/250.00 – 240.00/300.00, 1 suite.
• Wonderfully tranquil, ivy-clad 19C country house set in its own grounds. Appealingly traditional lounges. Conservatory and leisure centre. Large, smart, well-furnished rooms. Restaurant with bright yellow décor and Scottish influenced cooking.

Heathpark House without rest., Coupar Angus Rd, Rosemount, PH10 6JT, Southeast : ¾ m. on A 923 (01250) 870700, *lori@forsyth12.freeserve.co.uk, Fax (01250) 870700,* – VISA.
closed 1 week September and October and 25-26 December – **3 rm** 35.00/40.00 – 60.00/70.00.
• Substantial Victorian guesthouse in a quiet residential spot with mature gardens. Spacious lounge; breakfasts taken in welcoming dining room. Large, individually styled rooms.

Gilmore House without rest., Perth Rd, PH10 6EJ, Southwest : ½ m. on A 93 (01250) 872791, *jill@gilmorehouse.co.uk, Fax (01250) 872791* –
closed 24-26 December – **3 rm** 19.50/35.00 – 39.00/50.00.
• Traditional stone-built guesthouse only a few minutes' walk from town, keenly run by owners. Comfortable front lounge and breakfast room. Cosy bedrooms with tartan flourishes.

Laurels, Golf Course Rd, PH10 6LH, Southwest : 1 ¼ m. on A 93 (01250) 874920, *laurel-blairgowrie@talk21.com, Fax (01250) 874920,* – VISA.
closed mid November-mid January – **Rest** (by arrangement) 13.00 – **6 rm** 22.00/30.00 – 44.00.
• Stone built extended cottage just out of town centre and useful base for touring Perthshire. Comfortable, homely lounge with soft velvet suites. Simple, spotless rooms.

OAT OF GARTEN *Highland* 501 I 12.

Boat of Garten (01479) 831282.
Edinburgh 133 – Inverness 28 – Perth 89.

The Boat, PH24 3BH, (01479) 831258, *holidays@boathotel.co.uk, Fax (01479) 831414,* – 60. VISA
closed last 3 weeks January – ***The Capercaillie :*** **Rest** (bar lunch)/dinner 34.50/38.50 – **22 rm** 64.50/89.50 – 80.00/149.00.
• An evocative hiss of steam from adjacent Strathspey railway line adds character to this Victorian hotel. Modern, bright décor, wood panelled bar and chintz rooms. Comfortable dining room with modern wood and traditional menu.

ONNYRIGG *Lothian* 501 K 16.

Edinburgh 8 – Galashiels 27 – Glasgow 50.

Dalhousie Castle, EH19 3JB, Southeast : 1 ¼ m. on B 704 (01875) 820153, *info@dalhousiecastle.co.uk, Fax (01875) 821936,* – – 120. VISA
Dungeon : **Rest** (booking essential to non-residents) (dinner only) 38.00 – ***The Orangery :*** **Rest** a la carte 19.95/28.25 – **35 rm** 130.00 – 290.00.
• 13C castle in woodland on the South Esk. Period-style furnishing in the spacious rooms, eclipsed by the library's 19C panelling and rococo ceiling. Falconry centre in grounds. Classic menus in characterful Dungeon. Orangery overlooks river and parkland.

BORGIE *Highland* 501 H 8.
Edinburgh 262 – Inverness 93 – Thurso 31.

Borgie Lodge , KW14 7TH, ☎ (01641) 521332, *info@borgielodgehotel.co.u*
Fax (01641) 521332, ←, , – , P. VISA
March-October – **Rest** (bar lunch)/dinner 32.00 **s.** ♀ – **8 rm** ☐ ✝50.00/65.00 – ✝✝95.00.
◆ Small, detached hotel in peaceful Highland setting. Simple "locals" bar and residen lounge with coal fire and deep sofas. Rooms with characterful older style furnishings. Co dining room.

BOWMORE *Argyll and Bute* 501 B 16 – *see Islay (Isle of).*

BRAE *Shetland Islands* 501 P 2 – *see Shetland Islands (Mainland).*

BRAEMAR *Aberdeenshire* 501 J 12 *Scotland G.*
Env. : *Lin O'Dee*★, *W : 5 m.*
18 *Cluniebank Rd* ☎ *(013397) 41618.*
The Mews, Mar Rd ☎ *(013397) 41600.*
Edinburgh 85 – Aberdeen 58 – Dundee 51 – Perth 51.

Braemar Lodge, Glenshee Rd, AB35 5YQ, ☎ (013397) 41627, *info@braem lodge.co.uk, Fax (013397) 41627,* , P. VISA
closed 25 December – **Rest** (dinner only) a la carte 14.85/29.85 **s.** ♀ – **7 rm** ☐ ✝20.00/65.(– ✝✝40.00/100.00.
◆ Victorian granite former shooting lodge renowned for its sporting origins. Set in e tensive grounds. Wood panelled bar with large whisky selection. Smart, clean rooms. E tensive dining room and conservatory with light, airy feel.

Callater Lodge Guest House without rest., 9 Glenshee Rd, AB35 5YQ, ☎ (01339 41275, *hampsons@hotel-braemar.co.uk, Fax (013397) 41345,* – P. VISA.
closed November and December – **6 rm** ☐ ✝28.00/45.00 – ✝✝52.00/56.00.
◆ Stone house in large garden on the road to Glenshee. Lounge with leather chairs ar library with inglenook. Pleasant spacious bedrooms, some with view across the valley.

BREASCLETE *Western Isles (Outer Hebrides)* 501 Z 9 – *see Lewis and Harris (Isle of).*

BRIDGEND OF LINTRATHEN *Angus* 501 K 13 – ✉ *Kirriemuir.*
Edinburgh 70 – Dundee 20 – Pitlochry 37.

Lochside Lodge and Roundhouse Restaurant with rm, DD8 5JJ, ☎ (0157 560340, *enquiries@lochsidelodge.com, Fax (01575) 560202,* – rest, P. VISA
closed 25-27 December, 1-21 January and 1 week October – **Rest** *(closed Monday exce August and Sunday dinner)* 16.00/32.00 – **6 rm** ☐ ✝50.00 – ✝✝80.00/100.00.
◆ Converted farmstead in tiny hamlet at gateway to Angus Glens by Loch Lintrathe Elaborate modern cooking in former grain grinding room. Comfy rooms in hayloft co version.

BROADFORD *Highland* 501 C 12 – *see Skye (Isle of).*

BRODICK *North Ayrshire* 501 502 E 17 – *see Arran (Isle of).*

BRORA *Highland* 501 I 9 – *pop. 1 140.*
18 *Golf Rd* ☎ *(01408) 621417.*
Edinburgh 234 – Inverness 78 – Wick 49.

Royal Marine, Golf Rd, KW9 6QS, ☎ (01408) 621252, *info@highlandescape.co Fax (01408) 621181,* , , , , – rest, , P – 70. AE VISA
Rest a la carte 14.00/27.50 ♀ – **22 rm** ☐ ✝79.00/99.00 – ✝✝120.00/150.00.
◆ Originally a laird's home. Traditional lounge with log fire. Good leisure facilities p snooker room and unlimited golf. Spacious bedrooms with antique furnishings. Cuisi reflects Highland location.

Glenaveron without rest., Golf Rd, KW9 6QS, ☎ (01408) 621601, *glenaveron@ mail.com,* – , P. VISA.
closed 2 weeks mid October, Christmas and New Year – **3 rm** ☐ ✝30.00/48.0 ✝✝60.00/64.00.
◆ Agreeable looking, detached, stone guesthouse with gardens. Spick and span loun Pleasant communal breakfast room. Very spacious rooms with superior pine furnishings

The Quiet Piggy, Station Sq, KW9 6QJ, ✆ (01408) 622011, *info@thequietpiggy.com* – ⇜ P. MC VISA
closed Monday – **Rest** a la carte 16.20/29.40.
◆ Personally run by buzzy owner, her liveliness matched by vivid, frequently changing artwork on the walls. Good value, home-made dishes employing quality local ingredients.

ROUGHTY FERRY *Dundee City* 501 L 14 – *see Dundee.*

UNCHREW *Highland* – *see Inverness.*

URRAY *Orkney Islands* 501 L 7 – *see Orkney Islands.*

UTE (Isle of) *Argyll and Bute* 501 502 E 16 – *pop. 7 354.*
from Rothesay to Wemyss Bay (Mainland) (Caledonian MacBrayne Ltd) frequent services daily (35 mn) – from Rhubodach to Colintraive (Mainland) (Caledonian MacBrayne Ltd) frequent services daily (5 mn).

scog *Argyll and Bute.*

Balmory Hall without rest., Balmory Rd, PA20 9LL, ✆ (01700) 500669, *enquiries@balmoryhall.com, Fax (01700) 500669,* ≤, , – ⇜ P. MC VISA.
closed Christmas – **4 rm** ☕ ★75.00 – ★★150.00.
◆ Impressive, carefully restored mid 19C Italianate mansion. Columned hall and well-furnished lounge. Tastefully furnished bedrooms. Breakfast at an antique table.

othesay *Argyll and Bute.*
18 Canada Hill ✆ (01700) 503554 – 9 Sithean, Academy Rd ✆ (01700) 503091 – 9 Port Bannatyne, Bannatyne Mains Rd ✆ (01700) 504544.
Isle of Bute Discovery Centre, Winter Garden ✆ (08707) 200619, info@rothesay.visitscotland.com.

Cannon House, 5 Battery Pl, PA20 9DP, ✆ (01700) 502819, *cannon.house@btinternet.com, Fax (01700) 505725,* ≤, – ⇜. MC VISA.
closed February and 25 December – **Rest** (booking essential to non-residents) (dinner only) a la carte 15.75/21.00 – **7 rm** ☕ ★45.00/70.00 – ★★70.00/100.00.
◆ Attractive late Georgian house on Rothesay promenade with panoramic view of bay and harbour. Furnished in keeping with house's age. Individually styled rooms. Elegant, clean-lined dining room with daily changing menu of Scottish based dishes.

ADBOLL *Highland* – *see Tain.*

AIRNBAAN *Argyll and Bute* 501 D 15 – *see Lochgilphead.*

ALLANDER *Stirling* 501 H 15 *Scotland G.* – *pop. 2 754.*
See : *Town*★.
Exc. : *The Trossachs*★★★ *(Loch Katrine*★★*) – Hilltop Viewpoint*★★★ *(★★★) W : 10 m. by A 821.*
18 Aveland Rd ✆ (01877) 330090.
Rob Roy & Trossachs Visitor Centre, Ancaster Sq ✆ (01877) 330342, robroyandt@eillst.ossian.net.
Edinburgh 52 – Glasgow 43 – Oban 71 – Perth 41.

Roman Camp, Main St, FK17 8BG, ✆ (01877) 330003, *mail@roman-camp-hotel.co.uk, Fax (01877) 331533,* ≤, , , – ♿ P. MC AE VISA
Rest – (see ***The Restaurant*** below) – **10 rm** ☕ ★75.00/125.00 – ★★165.00, 4 suites.
◆ Part 17C hunting lodge in extensive gardens. Replete with antiques and fine objets d'art. Public rooms include a hidden chapel. Comfortable, country house-style bedrooms.

Lubnaig without rest., Leny Feus, FK17 8AS, ✆ (01877) 330376, *info@lubnaighouse.co.uk, Fax (01877) 330376,* – ⇜ P. MC VISA.
May-October – **8 rm** ☕ ★50.00/60.00 – ★★60.00/76.00.
◆ Built in 1864, a characterful Victorian house on the outskirts of town. Well-kept mature gardens visible from communal rooms. Homely bedrooms, two in converted stables.

SCOTLAND

Leny House without rest., FK17 8HA, West : 1 m. on A 84 (01877) 331078, *res@nyestate.com, Fax (01877) 331335,* <, P. MC VISA.
May-September – **4 rm** ★110.00 – ★★120.00.
◆ Located in Victorian mansion, surrounded by lawns and animal paddocks. Country hous style interior: antiques in all areas. Individually styled rooms boast splendid views.

Priory without rest., Bracklinn Rd, FK17 8EH, on Golf Club rd (01877) 33000 *judith@bracklinnroad.fsnet.co.uk, Fax (01877) 339200,* – P. MC VISA
April-September – **8 rm** ★45.00/60.00 – ★★80.00.
◆ Spacious Victorian house within walled garden, in a residential area. Elegantly furnishe sitting room with antique and reproduction pieces. Homely, welcoming bedrooms.

Dunmor House without rest., Leny Rd, FK17 8AL, (01877) 330756, *reservations@dunmorhouse.co.uk, Fax (01877) 339558* – P
closed 18 December-7 January – **4 rm** ★30.00/40.00 – ★★50.00/70.00.
◆ Large Victorian house conveniently situated on Callander's high street. Good sized sitting room and bedrooms. Decorated in comfortable, homely style throughout.

Brook Linn without rest., Leny Feus, FK17 8AU, (01877) 33010 *derek@blinn.freeserve.co.uk, Fax (01877) 330103,* <, – P. MC VISA
Easter-mid October – **6 rm** ★25.00/28.00 – ★★50.00/56.00.
◆ Victorian house in a fairly secluded rural location. Homely style lounge and wood furnished dining room for breakfast. Traditional, well-kept bedrooms.

XXX **The Restaurant** (at Roman Camp H.), Main St, FK19 8BG, (01877) 330003, *mail@roman-camp-hotel-co.uk, Fax (01877) 331533* – P. MC AE VISA
Rest 24.00/45.00 and dinner a la carte 40.00/60.00 ♀.
◆ Crisp linen covered tables with simple, elegant place settings in vibrant modern room Attentive staff serve carefully and skilfully prepared modern Scottish cuisine.

CAMPBELTOWN *Argyll and Bute* 501 D 17 – *see Kintyre (Peninsula).*

CARDROSS *Argyll and Bute* 501 G 16 *Scotland G.*
Env. : *The Clyde Estuary*★.
Edinburgh 63 – Glasgow 17 – Helensburgh 5.

Kirkton House without rest., Darleith Rd, G82 5EZ, (01389) 841951, *mich@kirktonhouse.co.uk, Fax (01389) 841868,* <, – P. MC AE VISA
closed December-January – **6 rm** ★40.00 – ★★60.00.
◆ Former farmhouse with origins in 18C; quiet, elevated spot overlooking North Clyd Ideal stop-off between Glasgow airport and Highlands. Bedrooms all have country view Traditional breakfast room with oil lamps at the tables.

CARNOUSTIE *Angus* 501 L 14 – *pop. 10 561.*
18, 18 *Monifieth Golf Links, Medal Starter's Box, Princes St, Monifieth (01382) 532767* 18 *Burnside, Links Par (01241) 855344* – 18 *Panmure, Barry (01241) 853120* – *Buddon Links, Links Par (01241) 853249.*
1B High St (01241) 852258 (Easter-September).
Edinburgh 68 – Aberdeen 59 – Dundee 12.

The Carnoustie Golf Course H., The Links, DD7 7JE, (01241) 411999, *enquiries@carnoustie-hotel.com, Fax (01241) 411998,* <, 18, – res P – 220. MC AE VISA.
closed 1-4 January – ***Dalhousie* : Rest** (dinner only) 34.50 – **81 rm** ★200.00 – ★★210.0 4 suites.
◆ Purpose-built property set on the championship golf course which, with the sea as backdrop, can be seen from most rooms. Well-equipped rooms decorated with golfi pictures. Dining room with views of the courses.

The Old Manor without rest., Panbride, DD7 6JP, Northeast : 1 ¼ m. by A 930 Panbride Rd (01241) 854804, *stay@oldmanorcarnoustie.com, Fax (01241) 855327,* – P. MC VISA.
closed Christmas and New Year – **5 rm** ★45.00 – ★★60.00/70.00.
◆ Substantial 18C house five minutes' drive from championship golf course. Good view of Tay Estuary. Hearty Scottish breakfast guaranteed. Smart rooms, some with brass bed

XX **11 Park Avenue,** 11 Park Ave, DD7 7JA, (01241) 853336, *Fax (01241) 853336* – MC VISA
closed Sunday and Monday – **Rest** (lunch by arrangement)/dinner) a la carte 24.95/38.75
◆ A former Masonic hall tucked away off the High Street. Comfortable, traditional surroundings and accomplished modern cooking from classic Scottish ingredients.

CARRADALE *Argyll and Bute* 501 D 17 – *see Kintyre Peninsula.*

CARRBRIDGE *Highland* 501 I 12.
Carrbridge (01479) 841623.
Edinburgh 135 – Aberdeen 92 – Inverness 23.

Fairwinds, PH23 3AA, (01479) 841240, *enquiries@fairwindshotel.com, Fax (01479) 841240,* – P. VISA.
closed mid November-mid December and 25 December – ***Conservatory*** **: Rest** *(closed Monday to non-residents)* (booking essential) (dinner only) a la carte 19.70/26.40 – **5 rm** 40.00/60.00 – 80.00/100.00.
◆ Modernised and extended former manse in woodland, dating from the Victorian era. Attractive gardens and a bar open to guests only. Comfortable, well-kept bedrooms. Large conservatory lounge which doubles as the restaurant.

Feith Mho'r Lodge without rest., Station Rd, PH23 3AP, West : 1 ¼ m. (01479) 841621, *feith.mhor@btinternet.com,* – P. VISA
closed Christmas and New Year – **6 rm** 20.00/25.00 – 40.00/56.00.
◆ A pleasant little house surrounded by green fields. Communal areas include a large lounge and separate breakfast room. Spotless, traditionally styled bedrooms.

CASTLEBAY *Western Isles* 501 X 12/13 – *see Barra (Isle of).*

Hotels and restaurants change every year, so change your Michelin guide every year!

CASTLE DOUGLAS *Dumfries and Galloway* 501 502 I 19 *Scotland G. – pop. 3 671.*
Env. : *Threave Garden★★ AC, SW : 2½ m. by A 75 – Threave Castle★ AC, W : 1 m.*
Abercromby Rd (01556) 502801.
Market Hill (01556) 502611 *(Easter-October).*
Edinburgh 98 – Ayr 49 – Dumfries 18 – Stranraer 57.

Douglas House without rest., 63 Queen St, DG7 1HS, (01556) 503262, *chris@douglas-house.com* – . VISA.
4 rm 27.00/50.00 – 70.00/77.00.
◆ Attractive stone built house (1880) with some original features near the high street. Communal breakfast table in guest lounge. Comfortable individually decorated bedrooms.

Smithy House without rest., The Buchan, DG7 1TH, Southwest : 1 ½ m. on B 736 (01556) 503841, *enquiries@smithyhouse.co.uk,* – P. VISA.
3 rm 45.00/55.00 – 60.00/70.00.
◆ Converted 14C smithy in large garden 10 minutes walk from town. Communal breakfast table. Guests' lounge featuring original forge. Pleasant bedrooms facing garden or loch.

at Kirkpatrick Durham *Northeast : 5½ m. by A 75 and B 794 – Castle Douglas.*

Chipperkyle without rest., DG7 3EY, (01556) 650223, *Fax (01556) 650223,* – P.
closed Christmas – **3 rm** 60.00/76.00 – 80.00.
◆ Georgian manor house in rural location. Interior with antiques and curios which engender charming country house atmosphere. Comfortable rooms.

at Crossmichael *Northwest : 3¾ m. on A 713 – Castle Douglas.*

Plumed Horse (Borthwick), Main St, DG7 3AU, (01556) 670333, *plumedhorse@aol.com, Fax (01556) 670333* – 16. VISA
closed 2 weeks September, 2 weeks January, 25-26 December, 1 January, Sunday dinner and Monday – **Rest** (booking essential) 22.00/25.00 (lunch) and a la carte 35.00/40.50 **s.**
Spec. Ballottine of lobster, oyster with rhubarb, seafood and fennel velouté. Roast loin of pork with braised belly stuffed with prunes. Passion fruit délice, white chocolate ice cream.
◆ Bright contemporary décor and a snug ambience in this tiny personally run restaurant. Modern dishes, using seasonal local produce, prepared with much skill and understanding.

CAWDOR *Highland* 501 I 11 – *Inverness.*
Edinburgh 170 – Aberdeen 100 – Inverness 14.

Cawdor Tavern, The Lane, IV12 5XP, (01667) 404777, *cawdortavern@btopenworld.com, Fax (01667) 404777,* – P. AE VISA
closed 1-2 January and 25-26 December – **Rest** (booking essential Saturday-Sunday) a la carte 15.50/26.00.
◆ Country inn at the end of a lane. Well run with an emphasis on the food. Friendly staff serve dishes from blackboard menu which offers traditional and more adventurous fare.

CHIRNSIDE *Borders* 501 N 16 – *pop. 1 204* – ✉ *Duns.*
Edinburgh 52 – Berwick-upon-Tweed 8 – Glasgow 95 – Newcastle upon Tyne 70.

Chirnside Hall ⛰, TD11 3LD, East : 1 ¼ m. on A 6105 ☎ (01890) 818219, *chirnside hall@globalnet.co.uk, Fax (01890) 818231*, ≤, ⅉ, ♨, ♣ – ⇹ rest, ☎ P. MC AE VISA
closed March – **Rest** (booking essential to non-residents) (dinner only) 28.50 – **10 rm** ☕ ✝85.00/145.00 – ✝✝145.00/160.00.
◆ Large, imposing, Victorian country house in a very rural location. Well appointed interior with good quality period atmosphere. Individually decorated bedrooms. Smart place settings in a traditionally appointed dining room with open fires.

CLACHAN SEIL *Argyll and Bute* 501 D 15 – *see Seil (Isle of).*

CLYDEBANK *West Dunbartonshire* 501 G 16 – *pop. 29 858.*
18 *Clydebank Municipal, Overtoun Rd, Dalmuir* ☎ *(0141) 952 8698.*
Edinburgh 52 – Glasgow 6.

The Beardmore, Beardmore St, G81 4SA, off A 814 ☎ (0141) 951 6000, *info@beardmore.scot.nhs.uk, Fax (0141) 951 6019*, ⓘ, ⅉ, ≘s, ⬜, ♣ – |‡| ⇹ ▤ ♿ P. – ⚑ 170. MC AE ⓓ VISA. ✂
Arcoona : **Rest** *(closed Sunday)* (dinner only) a la carte 23.15/35.15 s. ♀ – ***B bar cafe :*** **Rest** a la carte 17.85/24.65 s. ♀ – ☕ 14.95 – **160 rm** ✝99.00 – ✝✝99.00, 6 suites.
◆ Large purpose-built building immediately adjacent to Clydebank hospital. Good leisure and beauty facility and open-plan lounge. Smart, well-equipped, large bedrooms. Arcoona offers smart formality. B bar café provides bright setting in open-plan lounge bar.

COLONSAY (Isle of) *Argyll and Bute* 501 B 15.
18 *Isle of Colonsay* ☎ *(019512) 316.*
⛴ – *from Scalasaig to Oban (Caledonian MacBrayne Ltd) 3 weekly (2 h) – from Scalasaig to Kintyre Peninsula (Kennacraig) via Isle of Islay (Port Askaig) (Caledonian MacBrayne Ltd) weekly.*

Scalasaig *Argyll and Bute* – ✉ *Colonsay.*

Isle of Colonsay ⛰, PA61 7YP, ☎ (01951) 200316, *reception@thecolonsay.com, Fax (01951) 200353*, ≤, ♣ – ⇹ rest, P. MC VISA
March-October – **Rest** (bar lunch)/dinner a la carte 17.50/23.50 ♀ – **9 rm** ☕ ✝80.00 – ✝✝120.00.
◆ Listed building from mid- 18C; a thoroughly rural, remote setting. Public areas include excellent photos of local scenes and the only bar on the island. Bright, modern rooms. Welcoming, informal dining room.

COMRIE *Perthshire* 501 I 14 – *pop. 1 839.*
9 *Comrie, Laggan Braes* ☎ *(01764) 670055.*
Edinburgh 66 – Glasgow 56 – Oban 70 – Perth 24.

The Royal, Melville Sq, PH6 2DN, ☎ (01764) 679200, *reception@royalhotel.co.uk, Fax (01764) 679219*, ♨, ♣ – ⇹ ☎ P. MC AE ⓓ VISA
Royal : **Rest** 26.50 (dinner) and a la carte 16.75/26.50 – **13 rm** ☕ ✝75.00 – ✝✝120.00.
◆ 18C coaching inn in centre of town: Queen Victoria once stayed here. Stylish, contemporary feel, especially individually decorated bedrooms, with four posters and antiques. Restaurant with two rooms: conservatory brasserie or intimate dining room.

CONNEL *Argyll and Bute* 501 D 14 – ✉ *Oban.*
Edinburgh 118 – Glasgow 88 – Inverness 113 – Oban 5.

Ards House without rest., PA37 1PT, on A 85 ☎ (01631) 710255, *ardsconnel@aol.com, Fax (01631) 710857*, ≤, ♣ – ⇹ P. MC VISA
closed Christmas and early January – **4 rm** ☕ ✝50.00/60.00 – ✝✝70.00/80.00.
◆ Victorian house overlooking Loch Etive. Well run with a smart and elegant atmosphere. Traditional décor and appointments throughout communal areas and bedrooms. Conservatory breakfast room.

Ronebhal without rest., PA37 1PJ, on A 85 ☎ (01631) 710310, *ronebhal@btinternet.com, Fax (01631) 710310*, ≤, ♣ – ⇹ P. MC VISA. ✂
March-October – **6 rm** ☕ ✝22.00/50.00 – ✝✝50.00/80.00.
◆ Victorian house built in granite, with fine views over Loch Etive. Attractive guests' lounge with plenty of local information. Individually decorated bedrooms.

CONON BRIDGE *Highland* 501 G 11.
Edinburgh 168 – Inverness 12.

Kinkell House, Easter Kinkell, IV7 8HY, Southeast : 3 m. by B 9163 and A 835 on B 9169 ℘ (01349) 861270, *info@kinkellhousehotel.com, Fax (01349) 867240,* <, – P. VISA
closed 18 December-9 January – **Rest** (booking essential) (dinner only and Sunday lunch) 22.00 ♀ – **9 rm** ☐ ✝60.00/80.00 – ✝✝80.00/100.00.
◆ Peacefully located house in a rural location. Personally run with a welcoming country house atmosphere. Homely bedrooms and cooking using local produce. Locally inspired dishes like haggis-stuffed chicken or hot smoked salmon.

CONTIN *Highland* 501 G 11 – ✉ *Strathpeffer.*
Edinburgh 175 – Inverness 19.

Coul House, IV14 9ES, ℘ (01997) 421487, *stay@coulhousehotel.com, Fax (01997) 421945,* <, – rest, P. AE VISA
The Dining Room **:** Rest a la carte 21.45/33.95 s. – **20 rm** ☐ ✝55.00/95.00 – ✝✝90.00/138.00, 1 suite.
◆ Family run country house in a quiet, rural location. Log fired communal areas decorated in traditional style. Comfortable bedrooms, individually decorated. The Dining Room has a country house feel.

Achilty, IV14 9EG, Northwest : ¾ m. on A 835 ℘ (01997) 421355, *info@achiltyhotel.co.uk, Fax (01997) 421923* – P. VISA.
closed 25 December – **Rest** *(closed lunch Monday-Tuesday September-Easter)* a la carte 21.40/28.35 ♀ – **11 rm** ☐ ✝65.50/89.00 – ✝✝78.50/101.50.
◆ Roadside coaching inn dating from 18C. Run with a real personal touch. Traditionally appointed interior with open fired communal areas. Simple, comfortable bedrooms. Pub atmosphere and style in the restaurant.

CRAIGHOUSE *Argyll and Bute* 501 C 16 – *see Jura (Isle of).*

CRAIGNURE *Argyll and Bute* 501 C 14 – *see Mull (Isle of).*

CRAILING *Borders* 501 502 M 17 – *see Jedburgh.*

CRIEFF *Perth and Kinross* 501 I 14 *Scotland G.* – *pop. 6 579.*
See : *Town★.*
Env. : *Drummond Castle Gardens★ AC, S : 2 m. by A 822 – Comrie (Scottish Tartans Museum★) W : 6 m. by A 85.*
Exc. : *Scone Palace★★ AC, E : 16 m. by A 85 and A 93.*
18, 9 *Perth Rd ℘ (01764) 652909 –* 9 *Muthill, Peat Rd ℘ (01764) 681523.*
Town Hall, High St ℘ (01764) 652578, criefftic@perthshire.co.uk.
Edinburgh 60 – Glasgow 50 – Oban 76 – Perth 18.

Merlindale, Perth Rd, PH7 3EQ, on A 85 ℘ (01764) 655205, *merlin.dale@virgin.net, Fax (01764) 655205,* – P.
closed 19 December-12 January – **Rest** (by arrangement) (communal dining) 27.00 – **3 rm** ☐ ✝35.00/60.00 – ✝✝60.00/80.00.
◆ Traditional, stone-built house close to the town. Well-equipped bedrooms are individually decorated and very comfortable. Accomplished evening meals at a communal table.

Glenearn House without rest., Perth Rd, PH7 3EQ, on A 85 ℘ (01764) 650000, *bookings@glenearnhouse.f9.co.uk,* – P. VISA.
closed 20 December-15 January – **5 rm** ☐ ✝35.00/56.00 – ✝✝60.00/80.00.
◆ Personally run former school house, built in Victorian times. Extremely comfy, modern lounge. Neat and tidy garden complements the immaculate nature of the accommodation.

The Bank, 32 High St, PH7 3BS, ℘ (01764) 656575, *mail@thebankrestaurant.co.uk, Fax (01764) 656575* – . AE VISA
closed 1 week January, 1 week July, Sunday and Monday – **Rest** a la carte 17.25/24.60 **s.** ♀.
◆ Impressive, Gothic, former bank dating from 1901 which dominates the high street. Traditional, good value cooking using fine ingredients and an informal, friendly atmosphere.

CRINAN *Argyll and Bute* 501 D 15 *Scotland G.* – ✉ *Lochgilphead.*
See : *Hamlet*★.
Exc. : *Kilmory Knap (Macmillan's Cross*★ *) SW : 14 m.*
Edinburgh 137 – Glasgow 91 – Oban 36.

Crinan, PA31 8SR, ☎ (01546) 830261, *nryan@crinanhotel.com, Fax (01546) 830292,* Loch Crinan and Sound of Jura, – – P. VISA
closed 19 December-1 February – **Rest** (bar lunch)/dinner a la carte 20.00/40.00 – **18 r** (dinner included) ★95.00 – ★★310.00.
◆ Superbly located in a commanding setting with exceptional views of Loch Crinan ar Sound of Jura. Cosy, wood panelled, nautically themed bar. Bright, pleasant bedroom Restaurant provides wonderful views and interesting cuisine with seafood predominance

CROCKETFORD *Dumfries and Galloway* 501 502 I 18 *Scotland G.* – ✉ *Castle Douglas.*
Exc. : *Sweetheart Abbey*★, *SE : 10 m. by minor rd – Threave Garden*★★ *and Threave Ca tle*★, *S : 10 m. by A 75.*
Edinburgh 89 – Dumfries 9 – Kirkcudbright 18.

Craigadam, DG7 3HU, West : 2 m. on A 712 ☎ (01556) 650233, *inquiry@crai dam.com, Fax (01556) 650233,* – P. VISA
closed 24 December-6 January – **Rest** (communal dining) 20.00 – **10 rm** ★50.00/76.00 ★★76.00.
◆ 18C country house on sporting estate. Comfortable and elegant rooms with sout facing view. Communal meals. Distinctively themed bedrooms in house or rear courtyar

CROSSFORD *Fife* 501 J 15 – *see Dunfermline.*

CROSSMICHAEL *Dumfries and Galloway* 501 502 I 19 – *see Castle Douglas.*

CULLEN *Moray* 501 L 10 *Scotland G.* – *pop. 1 327.*
See : *Auld Kirk*★.
Env. : *Portsoy*★, *E : 5 m. by A 98.*
Exc. : *Banff*★ *- Duff House*★★, *E : 10 m. by A 98.*
Edinburgh 179 – Aberdeen 56 – Fraserburgh 41.

The Restaurant (at The Seafield H.), AB56 4SG, ☎ (01542) 840791, *info@theseafieldh tel.com, Fax (01542) 840736,* – P. VISA
Rest a la carte 19.40/31.95 ♀.
◆ Formal dining room in red and green and tartan. Classic menu emphasizing seasor produce, game and local fish; extensive wine list.

CULLODEN *Highland* 501 H 11 – *see Inverness.*

CULNAKNOCK *Highland* 501 B 11 – *see Skye (Isle of).*

CUPAR *Fife* 501 K 15 – *pop. 8 506.*
Edinburgh 45 – Dundee 15 – Perth 23.

Westfield House without rest., Westfield Rd, KY15 5AR, West : ½ m. by A 91 c Westfield Ave ☎ (1334) 655699, *westfieldhouse@standrews4.freeserve.co.u Fax (01334) 650075,* – P.
3 rm ★55.00 – ★★90.00.
◆ Georgian house with the feeling of a comfy private home. Extensive gardens. Traditio ally decorated communal areas and great care taken over details in the well-kept be rooms.

Ostler's Close, 25 Bonnygate, KY15 4BU, ☎ (01334) 655574, *Fax (01334) 654036* – VISA
closed 1-2 January, 2 weeks Easter, 2 weeks October, 25-26 December, Sunday, Mond and lunch Tuesday-Friday – **Rest** a la carte 20.75/36.50 ♀.
◆ Welcoming restaurant with snug atmosphere and low ceilings. Very personally run, wit cottage feel throughout. Particular attention to prime Scottish meat and local fish.

For a pleasant stay in a charming hotel, look for the red ... symbols.

DALRY *North Ayrshire* 501 502 F 16.
Edinburgh 70 – Ayr 21 – Glasgow 25.

Langside Farm, KA24 5JZ, North : 2 m. by B 780 (Kilbirnie rd) on B 784 (Largs rd) ℘ (01294) 834402, *mail@langsidefarm.co.uk, Fax (0870) 0569380,* ≤, – P. MC AE VISA
restricted opening in winter – **Rest** (by arrangement) (communal dining) 24.50 – **4 rm** ★33.00 – ★★70.00.
◆ Converted farmhouse, dating from 1745, set on hillside affording panoramic views. Classic furnishings throughout. Comfortable bedrooms exude a homely, relaxing ambience.

Lochwood Farm Steading without rest., KA21 6NG, Southwest : 5 m. by A 737 on Saltcoats rd ℘ (01294) 552529, *info@lochwoodfarm.co.uk,* ≤ – P. MC VISA.
February-November – **8 rm** ★40.00 – ★★60.00.
◆ Excellent hospitality at a good value farmhouse on one hundred acres of dairy farm. Fine views of country and coast from outside hot tub. Pleasant, well-kept little bedrooms.

Braidwoods, Drumastle Mill Cottage, KA24 4LN, Southwest : 1 ½ m. by A 737 on Saltcoats rd ℘ (01294) 833544, *keithbraidwood@btconnect.com, Fax (01294) 833553* – P. MC AE VISA
closed first 3 weeks January, first 2 weeks September, 25-26 December, Monday, Tuesday lunch and Sunday except lunch October-April – **Rest** (booking essential) 20.00/38.00.
Spec. Grilled John Dory with new potato, tomato, olive and basil salad. Roast loin of lamb, braised stew of neck fillet. Honey wafers filled with poached nectarines, vanilla cream and raspberries.
◆ Personally run, cosy, cottagey restaurant off the beaten track. Chef patron prides himself on use of local produce: prime ingredients used with care. Well-flavoured dishes.

Look out for red symbols, indicating particularly pleasant establishments.

DINGWALL *Highland* 501 G 11 – *pop. 5 026.*
Edinburgh 172 – Inverness 14.

Cafe India Brasserie, Lockhart House, Tulloch St, IV15 9JZ, ℘ (01349) 862552 – MC AE VISA
closed 25 December – **Rest** - Indian - 28.00 and a la carte 16.55/29.90 s.
◆ Bustling, highly renowned Indian restaurant, handily located in pleasant town centre. Authentically prepared, tasty regional Indian food. Welcoming, friendly owners.

DOONFOOT *Sth Ayrshire* 501 502 G 17 – *see Ayr.*

DORNIE *Highland* 501 D 12 *Scotland G.* – ✉ *Kyle of Lochalsh.*
See : *Eilean Donan Castle★ AC (site★★).*
Env. : *Glen Shiel★, SE : 4 m. on A 87.*
Edinburgh 212 – Inverness 74 – Kyle of Lochalsh 8.

Conchra House, Sallachy Rd, Ardelve, IV40 8DZ, North : 1 ¾ m. by A 87 on Conchra rd ℘ (01599) 555233, *reservations@conchrahouse.co.uk, Fax (01599) 555433,* ≤ Loch Long, – P – 40. MC VISA
closed Christmas and New year – **Rest** *(closed Monday)* (booking essential to non-residents) (dinner only) 20.00 – **6 rm** ★31.00/39.00 – ★★58.00/72.00.
◆ Part Georgian country house in inspiringly elevated position overlooking Loch Long. Handy for exploring Skye. Impressive carved fireplace in lounge. Compact, cosy rooms. Simple, lacy dining room with good views.

DORNOCH *Highland* 501 H 10 *Scotland G.* – *pop. 1 206.*
See : *Town★.*
18, 18 *Royal Dornoch, Golf Rd* ℘ *(01862) 810219.*
The Coffee Shop, The Square ℘ *(0845) 2255121.*
Edinburgh 219 – Inverness 63 – Wick 65.

Highfield House without rest., Evelix Rd, IV25 3HR, ℘ (01862) 810909, *enquiries@highfieldhouse.co.uk, Fax (01862) 811605,* ≤, – P
March-October – **3 rm** ★50.00 – ★★70.00.
◆ Purpose-built guesthouse with garden and fine Highland views. Small, spruce lounge; neat and tidy breakfast room. Bedrooms offer ample comforts: one has whirlpool bath.

XX **2 Quail** with rm, Castle St, IV25 3SN, ✆ (01862) 811811, *bookings@2quail.com* – ⇔ rm MC AE VISA
closed 2 weeks spring, Christmas and restricted opening October-April – **Rest** *(closed Sunday-Monday)* (dinner only) 37.00 ♀ – **3 rm** ☕ ✝85.00 – ✝✝95.00.
◆ Elegant, book-lined restaurant in town house. Interesting dishes with high levels of skill and sensitivity brought to tasty, well-prepared ingredients. Pleasant guest rooms.

DRUMBEG *Highland* 501 E 9 – ✉ *Lairg.*
Edinburgh 262 – Inverness 105 – Ullapool 48.

XX **Drumbeg** with rm, Assynt, IV27 4NW, ✆ (01571) 833236, *cu@drumbeghotel.com* *Fax (01571) 833353*, ←, – ⇔ P. MC VISA
closed 2 weeks mid January and 2 weeks early December – **Rest** *(closed Wednesday lunch)* (booking essential to non-residents) a la carte 19.80/28.40 s. ♀ – **6 rm** ☕ ✝34.00 ✝✝96.00.
◆ Remotely located Highland restaurant with views of Drumbeg Loch. The French owner makes good use of local seafood. Comfortable lounge; simple rooms.

DRUMNADROCHIT *Highland* 501 G 11 *Scotland G.* – ✉ *Milton.*
Env. : *Loch Ness★★ – Loch Ness Monster Exhibition★ AC – The Great Glen★.*
Edinburgh 172 – Inverness 16 – Kyle of Lochalsh 66.

Drumbuie Farm without rest., Drumbuie, IV63 6XP, East : ¾ m. by A 82 ✆ (01456) 450634, *drumbuie@amserve.net, Fax (01456) 450595*, ←, – ⇔ P. MC VISA.
3 rm ☕ ✝28.00 – ✝✝52.00.
◆ Immaculate guesthouse on working farm with Highland cattle. Splendid views of Loch Ness from conservatory breakfast room. Elegant reading room. Spacious bedrooms.

DUFFUS *Moray* 501 K 11 – *see Elgin.*

DULNAIN BRIDGE *Highland* 501 J 12 – *see Grantown-on-Spey.*

DUMFRIES *Dumfries and Galloway* 501 502 J 18 *Scotland G. – pop. 31 146.*
See : *Town★ – Midsteeple★* A A.
Env. : *Lincluden College (Tomb★) AC, N : 1½ m. by College St* A.
Exc. : *Drumlanrig Castle★★ (cabinets★) AC, NW : 16½ m. by A 76* A – *Shambellie House Museum of Costume (Costume Collection★) S : 7¼ m. by A 710* A – *Sweetheart Abbey★ AC, S : 8 m. by A 710* A – *Caerlaverock Castle★ (Renaissance façade★★) AC, SE : 9 m. by B 725* B – *Glenkiln (Sculptures★) W : 9 m. by A 780 – A – and A 75 – Ruthwell Cross★, SE : 12 m. by A 780 – B – A 75 and B 724.*
18 *Dumfries & Galloway, 2 Laurieston Ave, Maxwelltown* ✆ *(01387) 253582* A – 18 *Dumfries & County, Nuffield, Edinburgh Rd* ✆ *(01387) 253585* – 9 *Crichton, Bankend Rd* ✆ *(01387) 247894*, B.
64 Whitesands ✆ *(01387) 253862*, A.
Edinburgh 80 – Ayr 59 – Carlisle 34 – Glasgow 79 – Manchester 155 – Newcastle upon Tyne 91.

Plan opposite

Cairndale, English St, DG1 2DF, ✆ (01387) 254111, *sales@cairndale.fsnet.co.uk* *Fax (01387) 250555*, – ⇔ rm, rest, P – 300. MC AE VISA B
Reivers **: Rest** (dinner only) 20.00/25.00 and a la carte 22.90/27.90 s. ♀ – ***Sawney Beans*** : **Rest** *(closed Sunday-Monday)* (dinner only) 17.50/22.50 and a la carte 17.15/21.15 s.
89 rm ☕ ✝59.00/99.00 – ✝✝109.00/149.00, 2 suites.
◆ Extended Victorian hotel with extensive conference and leisure facilities. Popular with business people. Up-to-date bedrooms. Formal, linen-clad dining room with adjacent cocktail bar. Informal basement bistro with grill style menu.

Station, 49 Lovers Walk, DG1 1LT, ✆ (01387) 254316, *info@stationhotel.co.uk* *Fax (01387) 250388* – ⇔ P – 120. MC AE VISA. B
The Bistro **: Rest** (bar lunch Monday-Saturday)/dinner 16.25 and a la carte 19.50/30.50
32 rm ☕ ✝65.00/85.00 – ✝✝120.00.
◆ Characterful 19C hotel by railway station. Grandiose high ceilings give the feeling of immense space. Bustling bar. Huge open corridors; adjacent rooms of varied styles. A simple relaxed style informs this rustic bistro.

DUMFRIES

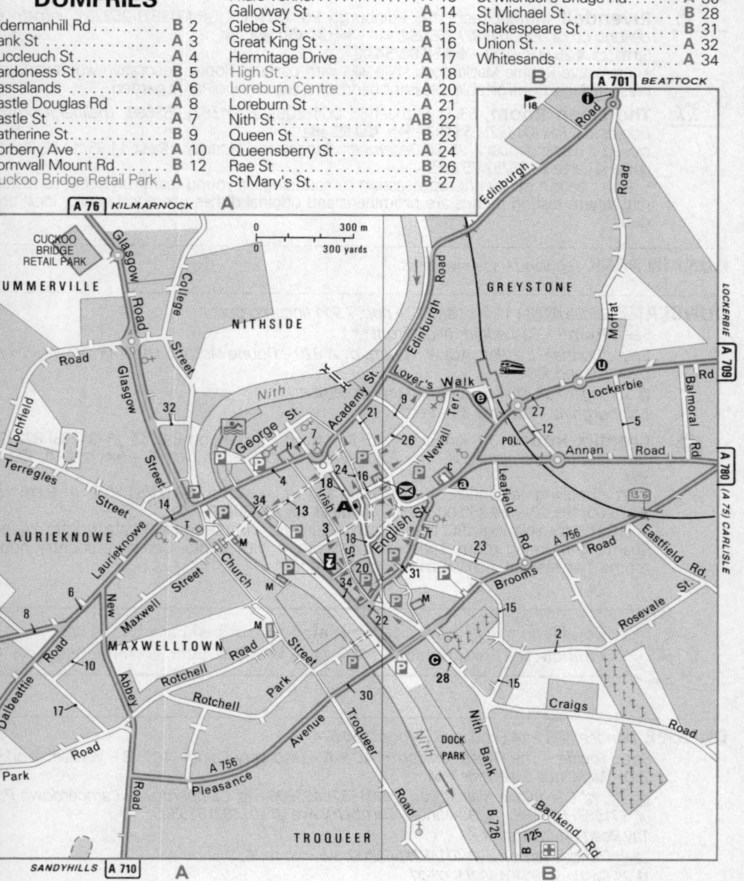

🏠 **Premier Travel Inn,** Annan Rd, Collin, DG1 3JX, East : 2 m. on A 780 (Carlisle rd) at junction with A 75 ✆ (08701) 977078, *Fax (01387) 266475* – rm, rest, P. MC AE VISA.
Rest (grill rest.) – **40 rm** 48.95 – 48.95.
◆ A consistent standard of trim, simply fitted accommodation in contemporary style. Simply furnished and brightly decorated bedrooms. Accessible for Borders and Carlisle.

Redbank House without rest., New Abbey Rd, DG2 8EW, South : 1 ½ m. by A 711 (Stranraer rd) on A 710 ✆ (01387) 247034, *redbankhouse@talk21.com, Fax (01387) 266220,* – P. MC AE VISA.
5 rm 35.00/40.00 – 55.00.
◆ Spacious Victorian villa with formally laid, mature gardens. Large sitting room with adjacent conservatory. Sizeable breakfast room. Homely rooms with floral furnishings.

Hazeldean House without rest., 4 Moffat Rd, DG1 1NJ, ✆ (01387) 266178, *info@hazeldeanhouse.com, Fax (01387) 266178,* – P. MC VISA. B u
closed Christmas – **6 rm** 30.00/35.00 – 50.00/52.00.
◆ Interestingly furnished 19C villa. Entrance door has original stained glass. Characterful antiques and Victoriana in lounge. Conservatory breakfast room. Spacious bedrooms.

Rivendell without rest., 105 Edinburgh Rd, DG1 1JX, ☎ (01387) 252251, *info@rivendellbnb.co.uk, Fax (01387) 263084*, – P. VISA. B
5 rm ★25.00/50.00 – ★★50.00/54.00.
◆ Attractive Rennie Mackintosh style villa with parquet floors, decorative woodwork an brass fittings. Comfortable, pleasant bedrooms with view of large garden.

The Linen Room, 53 St Michael St, DG1 2QB, ☎ (01387) 255689, *thelinenroom@yahoo.co.uk, Fax (01387) 253387* – . AE VISA B
closed 2 weeks January, 25-26 December, Sunday and Monday – **Rest** 11.95/14.95 (lunch and a la carte 28.25/32.75 **s.** ♀.
◆ Don't be put off by unprepossessing surroundings: a young team run a serious restaurant where tasting menus are prominent and original dishes use good quality local produce.

DUNAIN PARK *Highland – see Inverness.*

DUNBLANE *Stirling* 501 I 15 *Scotland G. – pop. 7 911 (inc. Lecropt).*
See : *Town★ – Cathedral★ (west front★★).*
Env. : *Doune★ (castle★ AC) W : 4½ m. by A 820 – Doune Motor Museum★ AC, W : 5½ m by A 820 and A 84.*
Stirling Rd ☎ (08707) 200613 (May-September).
Edinburgh 42 – Glasgow 33 – Perth 29.

Cromlix House , Kinbuck, FK15 9JT, North : 3 ½ m. on B 8033 ☎ (01786) 822125 *reservations@cromlixhouse.com, Fax (01786) 825450*, ←, , , – rest, P. VISA
Rest (booking essential) 39.00/49.00 and a la carte 38.50/51.50 ♀ – **6 rm** ★175.00/195.00 – ★★250.00/280.00, **8 suites** 250.00/390.00.
◆ Effortlessly relaxing 19C mansion in extensive grounds with ornate private chape Charming morning room; spacious conservatory with plants. Definitive country hous rooms. Two elegant, richly furnished dining rooms.

Good food and accommodation at moderate prices? Look for the Bib symbols: red Bib Gourmand for food, blue Bib Hotel for hotels

DUNDEE *Dundee* 501 L 14 *Scotland G. – pop. 154 674.*
See : *Town★ – The Frigate Unicorn★* **AC Y A** – *Discovery Point★* **AC Y B** – *Verdant Works* **Z D** – *McManus Galleries★* **Y M.**
18, 9, 9 *Caird Park, Mains Loan ☎ (01382) 453606 –* 18 *Camperdown, Camperdown Pa ☎ (01382) 623398 –* 18 *Downfield, Turnberry Ave ☎ (01382) 825595.*
Tay Road Bridge (toll) **Y.**
Dundee Airport : ☎ (01382) 662200, SW : 1½ m. **Z.**
21 Castle St ☎ (01382) 527527.
Edinburgh 63 – Aberdeen 67 – Glasgow 83.

Plan opposite

Premier Travel Inn, Discovery Quay, Riverside Drive, DD1 4XA, ☎ (01382) 20324 *Fax (01382) 203237*, ← – rm, rest, P. AE VISA. Z
Rest (grill rest.) – **40 rm** ★55.95 – ★★55.95.
◆ Bright and modern budget lodge beside Discovery Point and H.M.S. Discovery. Quiete rooms have Tay views. Adjacent pub.

at Broughty Ferry *East : 4½ m. by A 930 – Z – ✉ Dundee.*

Broughty Ferry, 16 West Queen St, DD5 1AR, ☎ (01382) 480027, *enquiries@hot broughtyferry.co.uk, Fax (01382) 739426*, , , – P. AE VISA.
Bombay Brasserie : **Rest** - Indian - a la carte 16.00/26.00 **s.** – **16 rm** ★68.00/80.00 ★★88.00.
◆ Family owned and friendly modern hotel beside the main road. The spacious, individual decorated bedrooms are furnished to a high standard. Brasserie serves elaborate, authen tic Indian menus.

Invermark House without rest., 23 Monifieth Rd, DD5 2RN, ☎ (01382) 739430, *enq ries@invermarkhotel.co.uk*, – P. AE VISA.
5 rm ★30.00 – ★★50.00.
◆ Imposing, detached Victorian house retains a period charm. Welcoming owners ar relaxed atmosphere. Individually decorated rooms with thoughtful touches.

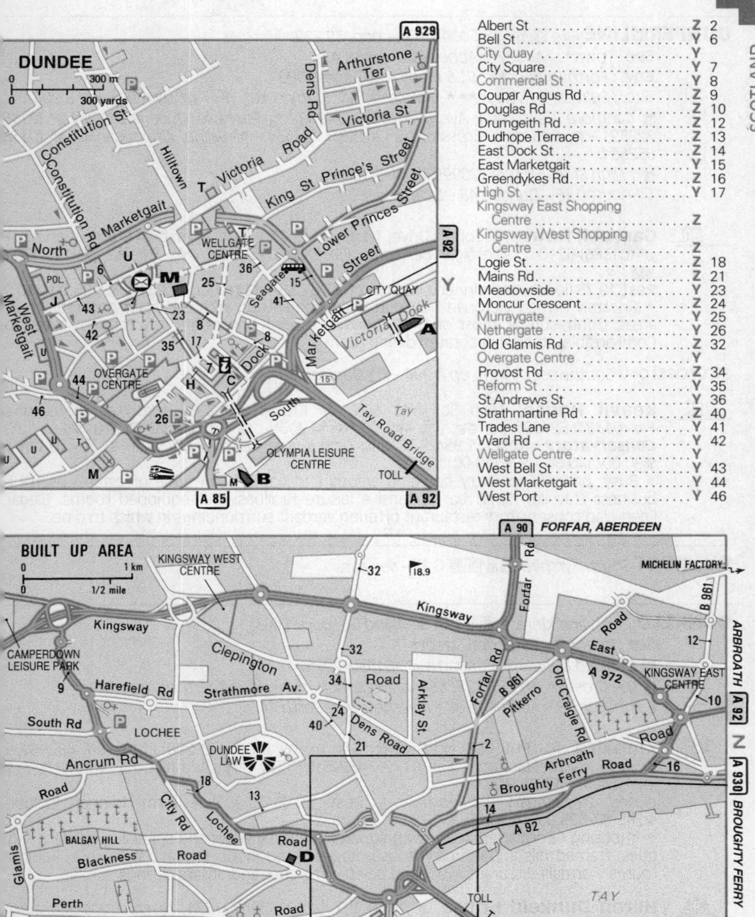

DUNDONNELL *Highland* 501 E 10 *Scotland G.* – ✉ *Garve.*

Env. : *Wester Ross*★★★ – *Loch Broom*★★, *N : 4½ m. via Allt na h-Airbhe.*

Exc. : *Falls of Measach*★★, *SE : 10 m. by A 832 – Corrieshalloch Gorge*★, *SE : 11½ m. by A 832 and A 835.*

Edinburgh 215 – Inverness 59.

Dundonnell, Little Loch Broom, IV23 2QR, ✆ (01854) 633204, *enquiries@dundonnellhotel.co.uk, Fax (01854) 633366,* ≤ Dundonnell Valley – ✻ ♿ P – 🏋 90. MO VISA
closed 2 January-14 April and 14 November-29 December – **Rest** (booking essential in winter) (bar lunch)/dinner 19.50/27.50 **s.** – **32 rm** (dinner included) ☕ ★65.00/100.00 – ★★130.00/170.00.
◆ Up-to-date, comfortable hotel where the mountains meet the sea with views over Dundonnell Valley. Bustling bar and two well-furnished lounges. Clean, spruce rooms. Home baking makes use of finest local produce.

DUNFERMLINE *Fife* 501 J 15 *Scotland G. – pop. 39 229.*

See : *Town★ – Abbey★ (Abbey Church★★) AC.*

Env. : *Forth Bridges★★, S : 5 m. by A 823 and B 980.*

Exc. : *Culross★★ (Village★★★, Palace★★ AC, Study★ AC), W : 7 m. by A 994 and B 9037.*

18 Canmore, Venturefair Ave (01383) 724969 – 18 Pitreavie, Queensferry Rd (0138 722591 – 18 Pitfirrane, Crossford (01383) 723534 – 9 Saline, Kinneddar Hill (0138 852591.

1 High St (01383) 720999 (April-October).

Edinburgh 16 – Dundee 48 – Motherwell 39.

Garvock House, St John's Drive, Transy, KY12 7TU, East : ¾ m. by A 907 off Garvock H (01383) 621067, *sales@garvock.co.uk, Fax (01383) 621168,* – – P – 150. VISA

Rest 19.75 (lunch) and dinner a la carte 21.95/32.35 – **12 rm** 79.50 – 95.00/130.0

◆ Privately owned Victorian house in woodland setting with classically decorated pub areas. Contrastingly, most of the attractive, modish rooms are in a modern extensio Comfortable, smartly decorated dining room.

at Crossford *Southwest : 1¾ m. on A 994 – ✉ Dunfermline.*

Keavil House, Main St, KY12 8QW, (01383) 736258, *sales@keavilhouse.co.u Fax (01383) 621600,* , , , , – P – 300. AE VISA.

Conservatory : **Rest** 11.95/27.50 and dinner a la carte 19.00/32.00 **s.** – **47 rm** 90.00/140.00 – 140.00/180.00.

◆ Busy, part 16C country house in woods and gardens on edge of estate. Useful f business traveller. Small bar, extensive leisure facilities. Well-equipped rooms. Elegar linen-clad conservatory restaurant offering verdant surroundings in which to dine.

DUNFOOT *South Ayrshire* 501 502 G 17 – *see Ayr.*

DUNKELD *Perth and Kinross* 501 J 14 *Scotland G. – pop. 1 005.*

See : *Village★ – Cathedral Street★.*

9 Dunkeld & Birnam, Fungarth (01350) 727524.

The Cross (01350) 727688 (April-October), dunkeldtic@perthshire.co.uk.

Edinburgh 58 – Aberdeen 88 – Inverness 98 – Perth 14.

Kinnaird , PH8 0LB, Northwest : 6 ¾ m. by A 9 on B 898 (01796) 482440, e *quiry@kinnairdestate.com, Fax (01796) 482289,* ≤ Tay valley and hills, , , , – rest, P. AE VISA.

closed 22 January-10 February – **Rest** 30.00/50.00 – **8 rm** (dinner include 245.00/525.00 – 295.00/575.00, 1 suite.

◆ Imposing Georgian mansion with superb Tay Valley views and sprawling gardens. Ant ques, framed oils and country house drapes throughout. Immaculately kept, luxuriou rooms. Formal restaurant with hand painted frescoes and ornate ceilings.

Hilton Dunkeld House , PH8 0HT, (01350) 727771, *reservations.dunkeld@ ton.com, Fax (01350) 728924,* ≤, , , , , , , , – P – 80. AE VISA.

The Garden : **Rest** (bar lunch)/dinner 29.00 and a la carte 20.00/35.00 **s.** – **90 rm** (dinn included) 142.00/199.00 – 162.00/219.00, 6 suites.

◆ Edwardian country house on banks of Tay. Two good sized drawing rooms with Scottis décor. Modern leisure centre. Warmly inviting rooms, with lush fabrics and soft suite Rich, Scottish themed restaurant overlooking river.

Letter Farm without rest., Loch of the Lowes, PH8 0HH, Northeast : 3 m. by A 92 on Loch of Lowes rd (01350) 724254, *letterlowe@aol.com, Fax (01350) 724341,* – P. VISA.

May-October – **3 rm** 35.00 – 60.00.

◆ Attractive, traditional farm house close to the Loch of Lowes Nature Reserve. Welcon ing, homely atmosphere and comfortable bedrooms.

at Birnam *Southeast : ¾ m. – ✉ Dunkeld.*

Birnam Wood House without rest., Perth Rd, PH8 0BH, (01350) 727782, *bob@b namwoodhouse.co.uk, Fax (01350) 727196,* – P. VISA.

closed January-February and first 2 weeks October – **4 rm** 40.00/60.00 50.00/70.00.

◆ Off-white painted house in quiet little hamlet. Homely bedrooms are comfortably fu nished and a welcoming lounge is available to guests. Dine in conservatory extension.

UNOON *Argyll and Bute* 501 F 16 *Scotland G. – pop. 8 251.*

Env. : *The Clyde Estuary*★.

Cowal, Ardenslate Rd ☎ (01369) 705673 – Innellan, Knockamillie Rd ☎ (01369) 830242.

from Dunoon Pier to Gourock Railway Pier (Caledonian MacBrayne Ltd) frequent services daily (20 mn) – from Hunters Quay to McInroy's Point, Gourock (Western Ferries (Clyde) Ltd) frequent services daily (20 mn).

7 Alexandra Parade ☎ (08707) 200629, info@dunoon.visitscotland.com.

Edinburgh 73 – Glasgow 27 – Oban 77.

Enmore, Marine Parade, Kirn, PA23 8HH, North : 1 ¼ m. on A 815 ☎ (01369) 702230, *enmorehotel@btinternet.com, Fax (01369) 702148,* ← Firth of Clyde, , squash – P. MC AE VISA

Rest (lunch booking essential)/dinner 20.00/29.00 **s.** and a la carte ♀ – **8 rm** ☕ ★65.00/69.00 – ★★75.00, 2 suites.

◆ Neat and tidy little hotel on the shores of Holy Loch with fine views down the Firth of Clyde. Filled with interesting antiques and curios. Individually decorated rooms. Traditionally styled restaurant serves dishes well endowed with Scottish ingredients.

Dhailling Lodge, 155 Alexandra Parade, PA23 8AW, North : ¾ m. on A 815 ☎ (01369) 701253, *donald@dhaillinglodge.com,* – P. MC VISA

March-October – **Rest** (booking essential to non-residents) (dinner only) 20.00 – **7 rm** ☕ ★36.00 – ★★68.00.

◆ Victorian villa with neat and tidy gardens, overlooking Firth of Clyde. Homely lounge boasts books and local guides. Individually decorated rooms with welcoming extra touches. Smart dining room with good views from all tables.

UNVEGAN *Highland* 501 A 11 – *see Skye (Isle of).*

URNESS *Highland* 501 F 8 – ✉ *Lairg.*

Durness, Balnakeil ☎ (01971) 511364.

Durine ☎ (0845) 2255121 (April-October).

Edinburgh 266 – Thurso 78 – Ullapool 71.

Port-na-Con House , Loch Eribol, IV27 4UN, Southeast : 6 m. on A 838 ☎ (01971) 511367, *portnacon70@hotmail.com, Fax (01971) 511367,* ← Loch Eribol – P. MC AE VISA

mid February-mid October – **Rest** (by arrangement) 14.00 and a la carte 11.65/19.10 – **3 rm** ☕ ★32.00 – ★★46.00.

◆ Converted house with tranquil lochside setting and good views of Loch Eribol. Relaxing conservatory lounge. Rooms offer simple guesthouse comforts and spotless maintenance. Homely dining room plays host to fine views.

YKE *Moray* 501 J 11 – *see Forres.*

AST KILBRIDE *South Lanarkshire* 501 502 H 16 – *pop. 73 796.*

Torrance House, Strathaven Rd ☎ (01355) 248638.

Edinburgh 46 – Ayr 35 – Glasgow 10.

Crutherland House, Strathaven Rd, G75 0QZ, Southeast : 2 m. on A 726 ☎ (01355) 577000, *crutherland@macdonald-hotels.co.uk, Fax (01355) 220855,* , , , , – P – 500. MC AE VISA

The Restaurant : **Rest** *(closed Saturday lunch)* 26.50 (dinner) and a la carte 27.25/41.95 ♀ – **75 rm** ☕ ★135.00/145.00 – ★★155.00.

◆ Recently extended country house amidst woodland. Business traveller oriented. Comfortable furnishings and décor throughout. Impressive meeting facilities and well run leisure. Elegant, comfortable dining room: fresh, local produce in tried-and-tested dishes.

Hilton East Kilbride, Stewartfield Way, G74 5LA, Northwest : 2 ¼ m. on A 726 ☎ (01355) 236300, *reservations@hieastkilbride.com, Fax (01355) 233552,* , , – , rest, P – 350. MC AE VISA.

Rest 11.50 (lunch) and a la carte 23.85/30.25 ♀ – ☕ 13.95 – **99 rm** ★110.00/145.00 – ★★120.00/155.00, 2 suites.

◆ Modern purpose-built hotel with extensive leisure facilities. Conveniently located for the Clyde Valley. Well-presented, modern bedrooms have a smart, comfortable style. Restaurant with an informal bustling atmosphere.

Premier Travel Inn, Brunel Way, The Murray, G75 0JY, ☎ (0870) 1977110, *Fax (01355) 230517* – rm, rest, P. MC AE VISA.

Rest (grill rest.) – **40 rm** ★46.95/46.95 – ★★49.95/49.95.

◆ Simply furnished and brightly decorated bedrooms with ample work space. Family rooms with sofa beds. Ideal for corporate or leisure travel.

J.P. Renier/MICHELIN

Edinburgh: old building on the Royal Mile

EDINBURGH

501 K 16 *Scotland G.* – *pop. 430 082.*

Glasgow 46 – Newcastle upon Tyne 105.

TOURIST INFORMATION

Edinburgh & Scotland Information Centre, 3 Princes St ☎ (0845) 2255121; info@visitscotland.co.uk

Edinburgh Airport, Tourist Information Desk ☎ (0845) 2255121.

PRACTICAL INFORMATION

18, 18 *Braid Hills, Braid Hills Rd ☎ (0131) 447 6666,* **BX**.

18 *Carrick Knowe, Glendevon Park ☎ (0131) 337 1096,* **AX**.

18 *Duddingston, Duddingston Road West ☎ (0131) 661 7688,* **BV**.

18 *Silverknowes, Parkway ☎ (0131) 336 3843,* **AV**.

18 *Liberton, 297 Gilmerton Rd ☎ (0131) 664 3009,* **BX**.

18, 18 *Marriott Dalmahoy Hotel & C.C., Kirknewton ☎ (0131) 335 8010,* **AX**.

9 *Portobello, Stanley St ☎ (0131) 669 4361,* **BV**.

Edinburgh Airport : ☎ (0870) 040 0007, W : 6 m. by A 8 **AV**.
Terminal : *Waverley Bridge.*

SIGHTS

See : *City★★★ – Edinburgh International Festival★★★ (August) – Royal Museum of Scotland★★★* **EZ M2** *– National Gallery of Scotland★★* **DY M4** *– Royal Botanic Garden★★★* **AV** *– The Castle★★ AC* **DYZ** *: Site★★★ – Palace Block (Honours of Scotland★★★) – St Margaret's Chapel (※★★★) – Great Hall (Hammerbeam Roof★★) – ≤★★ from Argyle and Mill's Mount* **DZ** *– Abbey and Palace of Holyroodhouse★★ AC (Plasterwork Ceilings★★★, ※★★ from Arthur's Seat)* **BV** *– Royal Mile★★ : St Giles' Cathedral★★ (Crown Spire★★★)* **EYZ** *– Gladstone's Land★ AC* **EYZ A** *– Canongate Talbooth★* **EY B** *– New Town★★ (Charlotte Square★★★* **CY 14** *– The Georgian House★ AC* **CY D** *– Scottish National Portrait Gallery★* **EY M6** *– Dundas House★* **EY E**) *– Scottish National Gallery of Modern Art★* **AV M1** *– Victoria Street★* **EZ 84** *– Scott Monument★ (≤★) AC* **EY F** *– Craigmillar Castle★ AC, SE: 3 m by A7* **BX** *– Calton Hill (※★★★ AC from Nelson's Monument)* **EY** *– Dean Gallery★* **AV** *opposite* **M1** *– Royal Yacht Britannia★* **BV**.

Env. : *Edinburgh Zoo★★ AC* **AV** *– Hill End Ski Centre (※★★) AC, S : 5½ m. by A 702* **BX** *– The Royal Observatory (West Tower ≤★) AC* **BX** *– Ingleston, Scottish Agricultural Museum★, W : 6½ m. by A 8* **AV**.

Exc. : *Rosslyn Chapel★★ AC (Apprentice Pillar★★★) S : 7½ m. by A 701* **BX** *and B 7006 – Forth Bridges★★, NW : 9½ m. by A 90* **AV** *– Hopetoun House★★ AC, NW : 11½ m. by A 90* **AV** *– and A 904 – Dalmeny★ – Dalmeny House★ AC, St Cuthbert's Church★ (Norman South Doorway★★) NW: 7 m. by A 90* **AV** *– Crichton Castle (Italianate courtyard range★) AC, SE : 10 m. by A 7* **X** *and B 6372.*

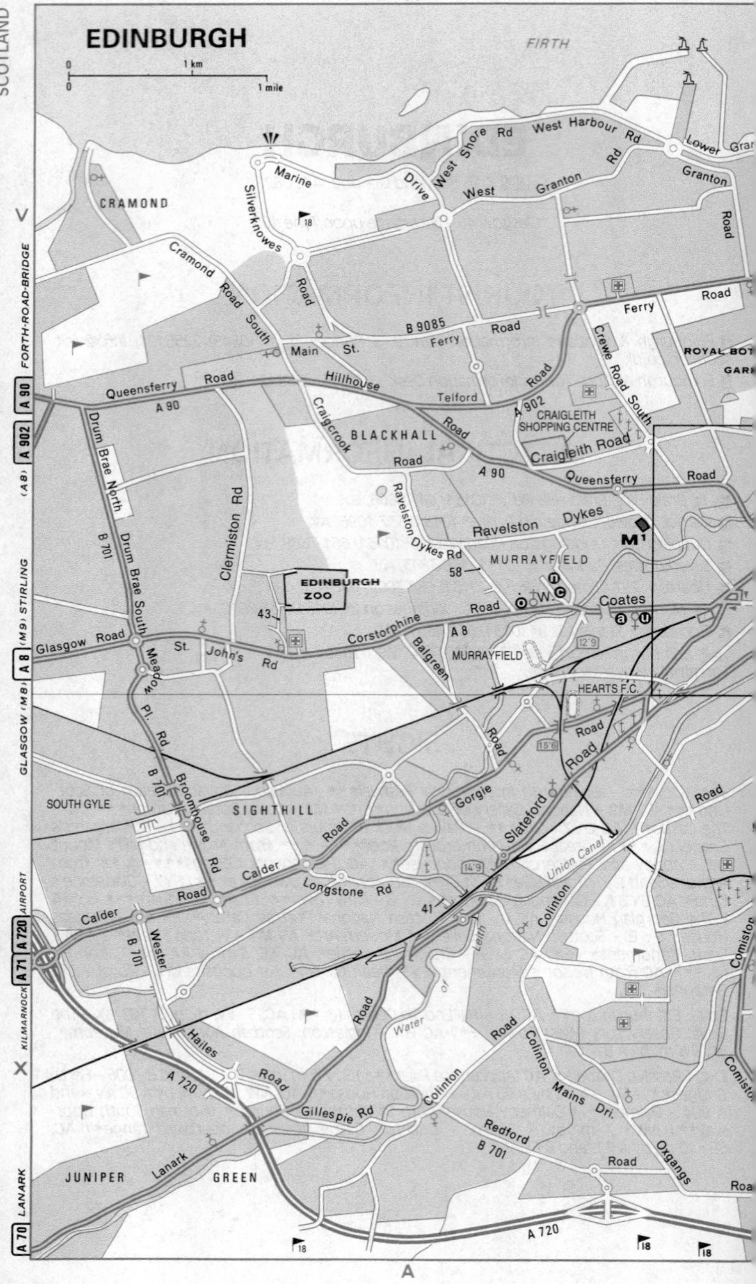
EDINBURGH
0 1 km
0 1 mile
A
FIRTH
West Shore Rd
West Harbour Rd
Lower Granton
West Granton Rd
Granton Road
Marine Drive
Silverknowes Road
CRAMOND
Cramond Road South
Main St.
B 9085
Ferry Road
Ferry Road
ROYAL BOT GAR
Crewe Road South
Hillhouse Road
Telford Road
A 902
CRAIGLEITH SHOPPING CENTRE
Craigleith Road
Queensferry Road
A 90
Craigcrook Road
BLACKHALL
Queensferry Road
A 90
Drum Brae North
B 701
Drum Brae South
Clermiston Rd
Ravelston Dykes Rd
Ravelston Dykes
M1
MURRAYFIELD
58
EDINBURGH ZOO
43
Coates
Glasgow Road
St. John's Rd
Corstorphine Road
A 8
Balgreen Road
MURRAYFIELD
12'9
HEARTS F.C.
Meadow Pl. Rd
B 701
Broomhouse Rd
SOUTH GYLE
SIGHTHILL
Gorgie Road
Slateford Road
15'6
Road
Calder Road
Longstone Rd
14'9
Union Canal
Colinton Road
41
Calder Road
B 701
Wester Hailes Road
Water of Leith
Road
A 720
Colinton Road
Colinton Mains Dri.
Comiston
Gillespie Rd
Redford Road
B 701
Oxgangs Road
JUNIPER GREEN
Lanark
A 720
V
X
FORTH-ROAD-BRIDGE
A 90
A 902
(A8)
(M9) STIRLING
A 8
GLASGOW (M8)
AIRPORT
A 720
A 71
KILMARNOCK
LANARK
A 70

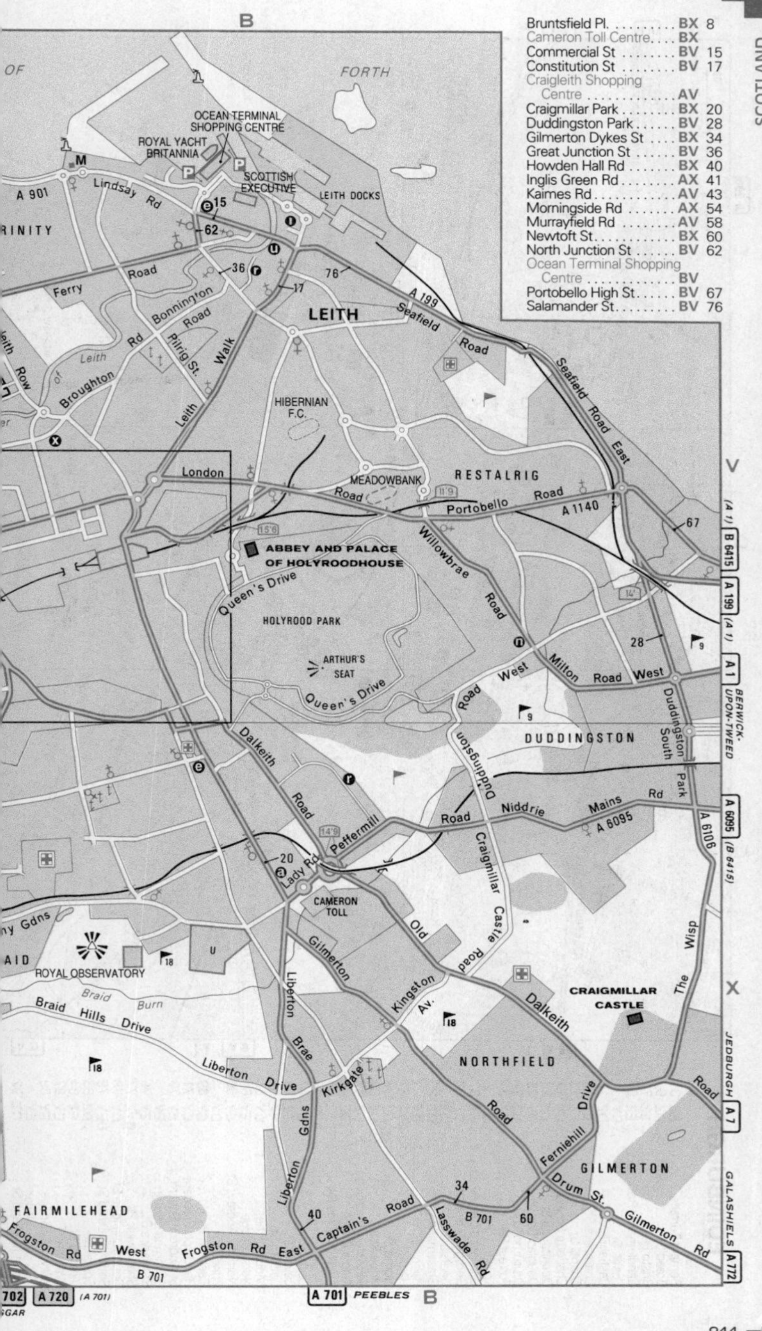
Bruntsfield Pl. .... BX 8
Cameron Toll Centre.... BX
Commercial St .... BV 15
Constitution St .... BV 17
Craigleith Shopping Centre .... AV
Craigmillar Park .... BX 20
Duddingston Park ...... BV 28
Gilmerton Dykes St .... BX 34
Great Junction St ...... BV 36
Howden Hall Rd .... BX 40
Inglis Green Rd .... AX 41
Kaimes Rd .... AV 43
Morningside Rd .... AX 54
Murrayfield Rd .... AV 58
Newtoft St............ BX 60
North Junction St ...... BV 62
Ocean Terminal Shopping Centre .... BV
Portobello High St...... BV 67
Salamander St.......... BV 76
B
FORTH
OCEAN TERMINAL SHOPPING CENTRE
ROYAL YACHT BRITANNIA
SCOTTISH EXECUTIVE
LEITH DOCKS
A 901
Lindsay Rd
Ferry Road
Bonnington Road
Pilrig St.
Leith Walk
Broughton
LEITH
A 199
Seafield Road
Seafield Road East
HIBERNIAN F.C.
MEADOWBANK
RESTALRIG
London Road
Portobello Road
A 1140
ABBEY AND PALACE OF HOLYROODHOUSE
Queen's Drive
HOLYROOD PARK
ARTHUR'S SEAT
Willowbrae Road
Milton Road West
Duddingston South Park
DUDDINGSTON
Dalkeith Road
Duddingston
Niddrie Mains Rd
A 6095
Peffermill Road
Craigmillar Castle Road
Lady Rd
CAMERON TOLL
Old Dalkeith Road
Gilmerton
Liberton Brae
Kingston Av.
CRAIGMILLAR CASTLE
The Wisp
A 6106
ROYAL OBSERVATORY
Braid Burn
Braid Hills Drive
Liberton Drive
Kirkgate
NORTHFIELD
Ferniehill Drive
GILMERTON
Drum St.
Gilmerton Rd
Liberton Gdns
Captain's Road
Lasswade Rd
B 701
FAIRMILEHEAD
Frogston Rd West
Frogston Rd East
V
X
B 6415
A 199
A 1
BERWICK-UPON-TWEED
A 6095
(B 6415)
JEDBURGH
A 7
GALASHIELS
A 772
A 720
(A 701)
A 701
PEEBLES

EDINBURGH

Street	Grid	No.
Bernard Terrace	EZ	3
Bread St	DZ	6
Bristo Pl.	EZ	7
Candlemaker Row	EZ	9
Castle St	DY	
Castlehill	DZ	10
Chambers St	EZ	12
Chapel St	EZ	13
Charlotte Square	CY	14
Deanhaugh St	CY	23
Douglas Gardens	CY	25
Drummond St	EZ	27
Forrest Rd	EZ	31
Frederick St	DY	
Gardner's Crescent	CZ	32
George IV Bridge	EZ	33
George St	DY	
Grassmarket	DZ	35
Hanover St	DY	
High St	EYZ	37
Home St	DZ	38
Hope St	CY	39
Johnston Terrace	DZ	42
King's Bridge	DZ	44
King's Stables Rd	DZ	45
Lawnmarket	EYZ	46
Leith St	EY	47
Leven St	DZ	48
Lothian St	EZ	51
Mound (The)	DY	55
North Bridge	EY	61
North St Andrew St	EY	66
Princes St	DY	
Raeburn Pl.	CY	69
Randolph Crescent	CY	71
St Andrew Square	EY	73
St James Centre	EY	
St Mary's St	EY	75
Shandwick Pl.	CYZ	77
South Charlotte St	DY	78
South St David St	DEY	79
Spittal St	DZ	83
Victoria St	EZ	84
Waterloo Pl.	EY	87
Waverley Bridge	EY	89
Waverley Market	EY	
West Maitland St	CZ	92

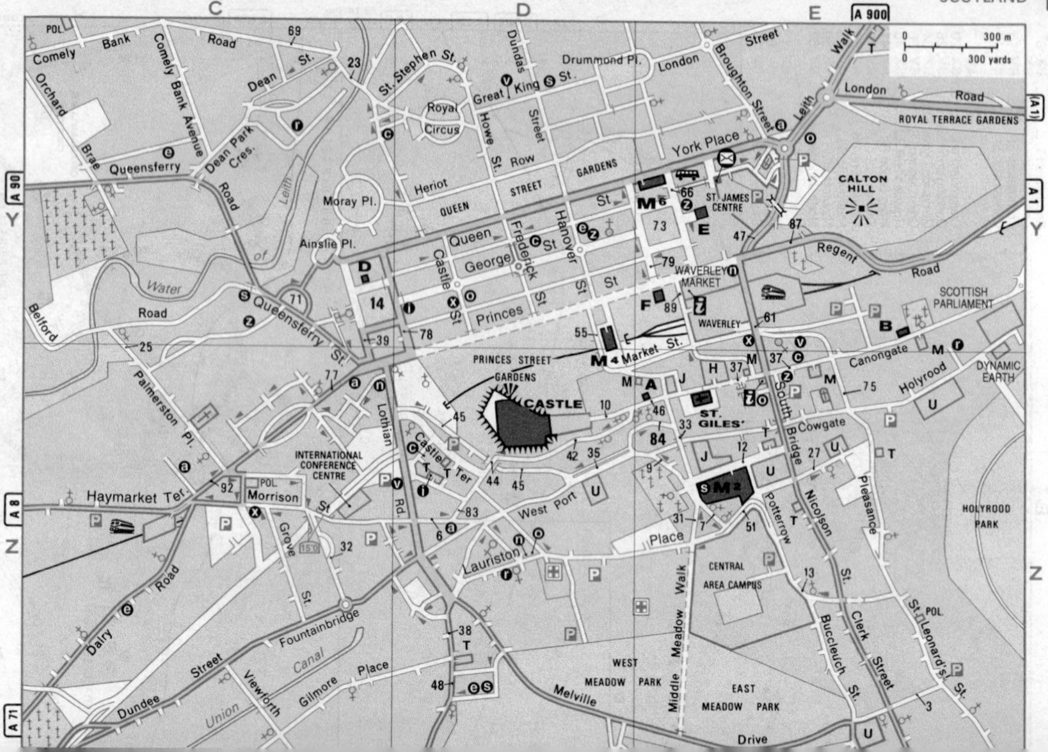

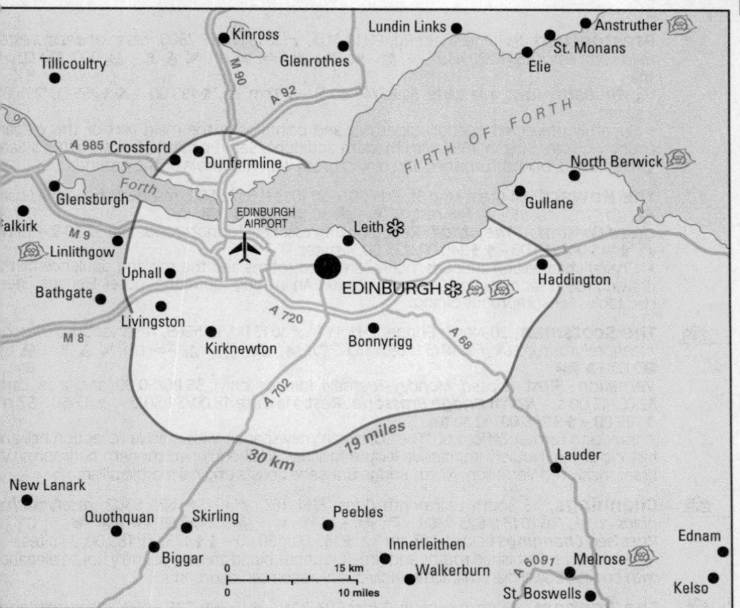

Balmoral, 1 Princes St, EH2 2EQ, ✆ (0131) 556 2414, *reservations@thebalmoralhotel.com, Fax (0131) 557 8740,* Ꮀ, ⌂, ⊡ – ⧆ ⇹ ▤ ✆ ♿ ⇔ – 🏛 350. MC AE ⓓ VISA. ✈ EY n

Rest – (see ***Number One*** and ***Hadrian's*** below) – ☕ 18.50 – **167 rm** ✝270.00/470.00 – ✝✝320.00/470.00, 21 suites.

◆ Richly furnished rooms in grand baronial style complemented by contemporary furnishings in the Palm Court exemplify this de luxe Edwardian railway hotel and city landmark.

Caledonian Hilton, Princes St, EH1 2AB, ✆ (0131) 222 8888, *guest.caledonian@hilton.com, Fax (0131) 222 8889,* Ꮀ, ⌂, ⊡ – ⧆, ⇹ rm, ▤ rest, ✆ ♿ 🅿 – 🏛 250. MC AE ⓓ VISA. ✈ CY n

The Pompadour : Rest *(closed Saturday lunch, Sunday and Monday)* 16.95 (lunch) and a la carte 33.85/43.85 ♀ – ***Chisholms :*** Rest 19.95 (dinner) and a la carte 22.85/33.40 ♀ – ☕ 19.50 – **238 rm** ✝150.00/245.00 – ✝✝180.00/275.00, 13 suites.

◆ A city landmark, affectionately known locally as "The Cally". Overlooked by the castle, with handsomely appointed rooms and wood-panelled halls behind an imposing 19C façade. The Pompadour boasts elegant dining. Informal Chisholms serves popular brasserie fare.

Sheraton Grand, 1 Festival Sq, EH3 9SR, ✆ (0131) 229 9131, *grandedinburgh.sheraton@sheraton.com, Fax (0131) 229 9631,* ⓓ, Ꮀ, ⌂, ⊡ – ⧆, ⇹ rm, ▤ ✆ ♿ 🅿 – 🏛 500. MC AE ⓓ VISA. ✈ CDZ v

Terrace : Rest (buffet only) 19.95/20.95 ♀ – (see also ***Grill Room*** and ***Santini*** below) – ☕ 17.00 – **244 rm** ✝225.00 – ✝✝265.00, 16 suites.

◆ A modern, centrally located and smartly run hotel. A popular choice for the working traveller, as it boasts Europe's most advanced urban spa. Comfy, well-kept rooms. Glass expanse of Terrace restaurant overlooks Festival Square.

The George, 19-21 George St, EH2 2PB, ✆ (0131) 225 1251, *Fax (0131) 226 5644* – ⧆, ⇹ rm – 🏛 200. MC AE ⓓ VISA. ✈ DY z

Le Chambertin *(✆ (0131) 240 7178)* **:** Rest *(closed Saturday lunch and Sunday)* a la carte 28.50/42.45 **s.** ♀ – ***Carvers*** *(✆ (0131) 459 2305)* **:** Rest a la carte 17.25/28.75 **s.** ♀ – ☕ 16.00 – **192 rm** ✝134.00/184.00 – ✝✝149.00/199.00, 3 suites.

◆ An established classic that makes the most of Robert Adam's listed 18C design. Welcoming marble-floored lobby, convivial Clans bar and well-proportioned bedrooms. Le Chambertin is light, spacious and stylish. Carvers is set in magnificent glass-domed room.

Prestonfield, Priestfield Rd, EH16 5UT, (0131) 225 7800, *reservations@prestonfield.com, Fax (0131) 220 4392*, ←, 18, – rm, – 900. VISA BX

Rhubarb : Rest a la carte 31.85/49.40 – **20 rm** ★195.00 – ★★255.00/295.00, 2 suites.

• Superbly preserved interior, tapestries and paintings in the main part of this elegant country house, built in 1687 with modern additions. Set in parkland below Arthur's Seat. Two-roomed, period-furnished 18C dining room with fine views of the grounds.

The Howard, 34 Great King St, EH3 6QH, (0131) 557 3500, *reserve@thehoward.com, Fax (0131) 557 6515* – rest, – 30. VISA. DY

closed Christmas – ***The Atholl :*** Rest (booking essential for non-residents) 32.50 – **13 rm** ★145.00/210.00 – ★★240.00/275.00, 4 suites.

• Crystal chandeliers, antiques, richly furnished rooms and the relaxing opulence of the drawing room set off a fine Georgian interior. An inviting "boutique" hotel. Elegant, linen clad tables for sumptuous dining.

The Scotsman, 20 North Bridge, EH1 1YT, (0131) 556 5565, *reservations@thescotsmanhotelgroup.co.uk, Fax (0131) 652 3652*, – rm, – 80. VISA EY

Vermilion : Rest *(closed Monday-Tuesday)* (dinner only) 35.00/50.00 and a la carte 32.00/45.00 s. – ***North Bridge Brasserie :*** Rest a la carte 18.00/31.50 – 17.50 – **57 rm** ★295.00 – ★★295.00, 12 suites.

• Imposing former offices of "The Scotsman" newspaper, with marble reception hall and historic prints. Notably impressive leisure facilities. Well-equipped modern bedrooms. Vibrant, richly red Vermilion. North Bridge Brasserie boasts original marble pillars.

Channings, 15 South Learmonth Gdns, EH4 1EZ, (0131) 623 9302, *reserve@channings.co.uk, Fax (0131) 623 9306*, – 35. VISA. CY

Rest (see ***Channings*** below) – **43 rm** ★135.00/160.00 – ★★175.00/185.00, 3 suites.

• Sensitively refurbished rooms and fire-lit lounges blend an easy country house elegance with original Edwardian character. Individually appointed bedrooms.

The Bonham, 35 Drumsheugh Gdns, EH3 7RN, (0131) 226 6050, *reserve@thebonham.com, Fax (0131) 226 6080* – – 50. VISA. CY

Rest 16.00 (lunch) and dinner a la carte 29.00/32.80 – **46 rm** ★145.00/165.00 ★★195.00, 2 suites.

• A striking synthesis of Victorian architecture, eclectic fittings and bold, rich colours of contemporary décor. Numerous pictures by "up-and-coming" local artists. Chic dining room with massive mirrors and "catwalk" in spotlights.

The Glasshouse without rest., 2 Greenside Pl, EH1 3AA, (0131) 525 8200, *resglasshouse@theetongroup.com, Fax (0131) 525 8205*, ←, – – 70. VISA. EY

16.50 – **65 rm** ★230.00 – ★★270.00.

• Glass themes dominate the discreet style. Modern bedrooms, with floor to ceiling windows, have views of spacious roof garden or the city below. Breakfast room to the rear.

The Roxburghe, 38 Charlotte Sq, EH2 4HG, (0131) 240 5500, *roxburghe@macdonald-hotels.co.uk, Fax (0131) 240 5555*, – rest, – 350. VISA. DY

The Melrose : Rest *(closed Saturday lunch)* (dinner only and Sunday lunch) 18.95/24.50 and a la carte 19.40/29.45 – 14.50 – **197 rm** ★65.00/210.00 – ★★90.00/290.00, 1 suite.

• Attentive service, understated period-inspired charm and individuality in the British style. Part modern, part Georgian but roomy throughout; welcoming bar. Restaurant reflects the grandeur of architect Robert Adam's exterior.

Radisson SAS, 80 High St, EH1 1TH, (0131) 557 9797, *reservations.edinburgh@radissonsas.com, Fax (0131) 557 9789*, – rm, – 250. VISA. EY

closed 24-26 December – **Rest** a la carte approx 16.00 s. – 14.50 – **228 rm** ★105.00/180.00 – ★★105.00/180.00, 10 suites.

• Recreates the look of a baronial Great House. Rooms are pleasantly spacious, some looking down on the Royal Mile. Compact leisure centre with jet stream swimming pool. Basement restaurant flaunts eye-catching suspended lighting.

Hilton Edinburgh Grosvenor, Grosvenor St, EH12 5EF, (0131) 226 6001, *Fax (0131) 220 2387* – rest – 300. VISA. CZ

Rest (bar lunch)/dinner 22.45 – 15.50 – **187 rm** ★93.00/225.00 – ★★93.00/225.00, 2 suites.

• Company hotel in an attractive 19C row, with some rooms in the annex across the road. Relax in the welcoming lounge and bar after a day in the main shopping streets nearby. Scottish themed restaurant.

Edinburgh Marriott, 111 Glasgow Rd, EH12 8NF, West : 4½ m. on A 8 ☎ (0870) 400 7293, *edinburgh@marriotthotels.co.uk, Fax (0870) 400 7393,* – 250.
Mediterrano : Rest (lunch booking essential) 25.00/30.00 and a la carte 20.75/33.25 **s.** – 14.95 – **241 rm** 105.00/175.00 – 105.00/175.00, 4 suites.
◆ Excellent road connections for the airport and Glasgow and well-equipped rooms make this large, group-operated hotel a practical choice for business travel. Modern restaurant with Mediterranean twist.

Point, 34 Bread St, EH3 9AF, ☎ (0131) 221 5555, *Fax (0131) 221 9929* – rm, – 100. DZ a
Rest 11.90/18.00 – 10.00 – **134 rm** 145.00 – 165.00, 4 suites.
◆ Formerly the Co-operative offices, converted in daring minimalist style. Boldly toned lobby and light, clean-lined rooms. Castle views over the rooftops from the upper floors. Strikingly lit avant-garde restaurant.

Holyrood Aparthotel without rest., 1 Nether Bakehouse (via Gentles entry), EH8 8PE, ☎ (0131) 524 3200, *mail@holyroodaparthotel.com, Fax (0131) 524 3210* – . EY r
, **41 suites** 100.00/300.00.
◆ These two-bedroomed apartments are neat and up-to-date with well-stocked kitchens. Located in a booming area of the city, not far from the Palace of Holyrood.

Christopher North House, 6 Gloucester Pl, EH3 6EF, ☎ (0131) 225 2720, *reservations@christophernorth.co.uk, Fax (0131) 220 4706* – rm, . CY c
Rest (dinner only) a la carte 15.50/25.50 **s.** – **32 rm** 98.00/140.00 – 140.00/240.00.
◆ Georgian house on cobbled street in quiet residential area; a chintzy feel overlays the contemporary interior. Eclectically styled bedrooms feature homely extra touches. Classic Scottish cooking in formally styled dining room.

Novotel Edinburgh Centre, 80 Lauriston Pl, EH3 9DE, ☎ (0131) 656 3500, *h3271@accor.com, Fax (0131) 656 3510,* – rm, . DZ o
Rest (bar lunch)/dinner 18.50 and a la carte 23.25/31.85 **s.** – 12.00 – **180 rm** 85.00 – 169.00.
◆ 21C hotel in a smart, contemporary style. Well-equipped leisure club. Modern bedrooms: two top-floor suites have private balconies, while 40 rooms look towards the castle. Informal dining room, open 18 hours a day.

Clarendon without rest., 25 Shandwick Pl, EH2 4RG, ☎ (0131) 229 1467, *res@clarendonhoteledi.com, Fax (0131) 229 7549* – . CZ a
66 rm 70.00/120.00 – 90.00/160.00.
◆ Two minutes' walk from Princes Street, and completely refurbished in 2004, this smart hotel boasts bright, vivid colours, a cosy, contemporary bar and well-presented rooms.

Edinburgh City, 79 Lauriston Pl, EH3 9HZ, ☎ (0131) 622 7979, *reservations@bestwesternedinburghcity.co.uk, Fax (0131) 622 7900* – rest, . DZ r
closed 24-27 December – **Rest** (bar lunch)/dinner a la carte 20.00/29.00 – 6.95 – **51 rm** 70.00/160.00 – 95.00/190.00, 1 suite.
◆ Tidily run hotel, converted from Scotland's first maternity hospital, an easy stroll from the centre. A listed Victorian building, it boasts bright, good-sized bedrooms. Smart, comfortable restaurant.

The Lodge, 6 Hampton Terrace, West Coates, EH12 5JD, ☎ (0131) 337 3682, *info@thelodgehotel.co.uk, Fax (0131) 313 1700,* – . AV u
Rest (booking essential) (residents only) (dinner only) a la carte 23.00/35.00 **s.** – **10 rm** 60.00/95.00 – 80.00/135.00.
◆ A converted Georgian manse, family owned and immaculately kept. Individually designed bedrooms and lounge decorated with taste and care; close to Murrayfield rugby stadium.

Kildonan Lodge without rest., 27 Craigmillar Park, EH16 5PE, ☎ (0131) 667 2793, *info@kildonanlodgehotel.co.uk, Fax (0131) 667 9777* – . BX a
closed 23-26 December – **12 rm** 56.00/89.00 – 70.00/145.00.
◆ Privately managed, with a cosy, firelit drawing room which feels true to the Lodge's origins as a 19C family house. One room has a four-poster bed and a fine bay window. Classical breakfast room; parquet floor spread with rugs.

Greenside without rest., 9 Royal Terrace, EH7 5AB, ☎ (0131) 557 0022, *greensidehotel@ednet.co.uk, Fax (0131) 557 0022,* – . EY i
16 rm 30.00 – 90.00.
◆ Situated in one of the city's most prestigious terraces, looking towards the Firth of Forth and over the rear gardens. Good value bedrooms, some with pronounced charm.

Express by Holiday Inn without rest., Picardy Pl, EH1 3JT, (0131) 558 2300, *info@hieedinburgh.co.uk, Fax (0131) 558 2323* – 30. EY
161 rm 95.00 – 95.00.
• Converted Georgian house offering trim, bright, reasonably priced accommodation. Great position for Princes Street and the other central city tourist attractions.

Premier Travel Inn, 1 Morrison Link, EH3 8DN, (0131) 228 9819, *Fax (0131) 228 983* – , rest, . CZ
Rest (grill rest.) – **281 rm** 74.95 – 74.95.
• Large hotel provides a consistent standard of modern budget accommodation. Between the conference centre and Haymarket station - a real plus for business travellers.

Premier Travel Inn, Lauriston Pl, Lady Lawson St, EH3 9HZ, (0870) 9906610, *Fax (0870) 9906611* – , rm, rest, . DZ
Rest (grill rest.) – **117 rm** 74.95 – 74.95.
• Good value, centrally located accommodation, an ideal resting place for tourists to the city. Modern, spacious, well-equipped bedrooms. Grill restaurant features tried-and-tested favourites.

Ibis without rest., 6 Hunter Sq, EH1 1QW, (0131) 240 7000, *h2039@accor.com, Fax (0131) 240 7007* – . EZ
4.95 **99 rm** 54.95/76.95 – 54.95/76.95.
• Interior design reflects the group's ethos - compact and functional, yet comfortable. super position just off the High Street will appeal to tourists throughout the year.

Kingsburgh House without rest., 2 Corstorphine Rd, EH12 6HN, (0131) 313 1679, *enquiries@thekingsburgh.co.uk, Fax (0131) 346 0554,* – . AV
5 rm 70.00/120.00 – 100.00/150.00.
• Personally run Victorian villa with leather furnished lounge and wood floors throughout. Hearty breakfasts. Individually styled bedrooms boast numerous homely touches.

22 Murrayfield Gardens without rest, 22 Murrayfield Gdns, EH12 6DF, (0131) 33 3569, *mac@number22.co.uk, Fax (0131) 337 3803,* – . AV
– **3 rm** 50.00/60.00 – 80.00/90.00.
• Inviting fireside sofas and light, comfortable accommodation in a handsome Victorian house, managed with enthusiasm and care. Ideally located for Murrayfield Stadium.

Kew House without rest., 1 Kew Terr, Murrayfield, EH12 5JE, (0131) 313 0700, *info@kewhouse.com, Fax (0131) 313 0747* – . AV
6 rm 70.00/75.00 – 75.00/110.00.
• Secure private parking and good road access for the city or Murrayfield Stadium. Neat carefully kept rooms which are modern and well-proportioned.

The Stuarts without rest., 17 Glengyle Terrace, EH3 9LN, (0131) 229 9559, *red@thestuarts.com, Fax (0131) 477 6073* – . DZ
closed 22-29 December – **4 rm** 60.00/90.00 – 80.00/110.00.
• Each room in this smartly kept guest house boasts a contemporary look and an impressive range of modern conveniences. Faces a 36-hole short golf course.

Elmview without rest., 15 Glengyle Terrace, EH3 9LN, (0131) 228 1973, *nici@elmview.co.uk* – . DZ
February-November – **3 rm** 70.00/90.00 – 90.00/110.00.
• Basement of a Victorian house in pretty terrace overlooking The Meadows. Bedrooms are spotlessly kept and feature a host of extras: videos, fridges, sherry and more.

Davenport House without rest., 58 Great King St, EH3 6QY, (0131) 558 8495, *davenporthouse@btinternet.com, Fax (0131) 558 8496* – . DY
closed Christmas – **6 rm** 55.00/85.00 – 85.00/95.00.
• Three-storey Georgian townhouse on cobbled street. Welcoming period style lounge chintzy breakfast room. The bedrooms are of varying styles and sizes; all are well equipped.

The Beverley without rest., 40 Murrayfield Ave, EH12 6AY, (0131) 337 1128, *enquiries@thebeverley.com, Fax (0131) 313 3275* – . AV
closed 24-28 December – **8 rm** 35.00/80.00 – 60.00/90.00.
• Elegant 19C bay windowed house in quiet, tree-lined avenue close to the rugby stadium. Good value, individually appointed rooms with modern facilties and thoughtful extras.

16 Lynedoch Place without rest., 16 Lynedoch Pl, EH3 7PY, (0131) 225 5507, *susie.lynedoch@btinternet.com, Fax (0131) 226 4185* – . CY
closed Christmas – **3 rm** 35.00/55.00 – 70.00/110.00.
• Under charming family management for over 20 years, a listed Georgian residence close to the West End with cosy and well maintained en suite rooms.

Seven Danube Street without rest., 7 Danube St, EH4 1NN, (0131) 332 2755, *seven.danubestreet@virgin.net, Fax (0131) 343 3648,* – . CY
closed Christmas – **3 rm** 50.00/85.00 – 95.00/130.00.
• Bright, traditionally styled rooms with antique furnishings in a residential street. Breakfasts taken around one large table add to a feeling of engaging hospitality.

Castle View without rest., 30 Castle St, EH2 3HT, ☎ (0131) 226 5784, *coranne@castleviewgh.co.uk, Fax (0131) 226 1603* – ⇔. MO VISA. ✈ DY x
closed 24-26 December – **8 rm** ☕ ✶45.00/100.00 – ✶✶70.00/100.00.
• As name implies, set in great position for tourists. Lounge with comfy sofas. Well-kept, individual rooms in a terraced house; those at front have castle views.

Number One (at Balmoral H.), 1 Princes St, EH2 2EQ, ☎ (0131) 622 8831, *Fax (0131) 557 8740* – ▤. MO AE ① VISA EY n
closed first 2 weeks January – **Rest** (dinner only) a la carte 46.40/62.40 ♀.
Spec. Isle of Skye crab with melon, cucumber and tomato jus. Roast fillet of beef, onion purée, girolles and Madeira jus. Raspberry soufflé with raspberry sorbet in dark chocolate.
• Edinburgh's nonpareil for polished fine dining and immaculate service; spacious basement setting. Original dishes with a well-balanced flair showcase Scottish produce.

Oloroso, 33 Castle St, EH2 3DN, ☎ (0131) 226 7614, *info@oloroso.co.uk, Fax (0131) 226 7608,* <, 余 – ▤ ⇔ 14. MO AE VISA DY o
Rest a la carte 26.00/34.50 ♀.
• Modish third floor restaurant in heart of city. Busy, atmospheric bar. Lovely terrace with good castle views to the west. Stylish, modern cooking with Asian influence.

Grill Room (at Sheraton Grand H.), 1 Festival Sq, EH3 9SR, ☎ (0131) 221 6422, *Fax (0131) 229 6254* – ⇔ ▤ P. MO AE ① VISA CDZ v
closed Saturday lunch, Sunday and Monday – **Rest** a la carte 29.00/47.00 ♀.
• Ornate ceilings, wood panels and modern glass make an ideal setting for imaginative, well presented cooking. Local ingredients with a few European and Pacific Rim elements.

Santini (at Sheraton Grand H.), 8 Conference Sq, EH3 8AN, ☎ (0131) 221 7788, *Fax (0131) 221 7789* – ▤ P. MO AE ① VISA CDZ v
closed Saturday lunch and Sunday – **Rest** - Italian - a la carte 27.00/37.50.
• The personal touch is predominant in this stylish restaurant appealingly situated under a superb spa. Charming service heightens the enjoyment of tasty, modern Italian food.

Off The Wall, 105 High St, EH1 1SG, ☎ (0131) 558 1497, *otwedinburgh@aol.com* – MO AE VISA EY c
closed 25-26 December, 1-2 January, Monday lunch January-May and Sunday except during Edinburgh Festival – **Rest** 16.50/19.95 (lunch) and dinner a la carte 36.85/41.85 ♀.
• Located on the Royal Mile, though hidden on first floor away from bustling crowds. Vividly coloured dining room. Modern menus underpinned by a seasonal Scottish base.

Channings (at Channings H.), 12-16 South Learmonth Gdns, EH4 1EZ, ☎ (0131) 623 9302, *Fax (0131) 623 9306,* 余 – ⇔. MO AE ① VISA CY e
closed Sunday – **Rest** 16.00 (lunch) and a la carte 27.50/32.50 ♀.
• A warm, contemporary design doesn't detract from the formal ambience pervading this basement restaurant in which classic Gallic flavours hold sway.

Forth Floor (at Harvey Nichols), 30-34 St Andrew Sq, EH2 2AD, ☎ (0131) 524 8350, *Fax (0131) 524 8351,* < Castle and city skyline, 余 – |‡| ▤. MO AE ① VISA EY z
closed 25 December, 1 January and dinner Sunday-Monday – **Rest** 14.00/24.50 and a la carte 22.25/38.00 ☺ ♀.
• Stylish restaurant with delightful outside terrace affording views over the city. Half the room in informal brasserie-style and the other more formal. Modern, Scottish menus.

Atrium, 10 Cambridge St, EH1 2ED, ☎ (0131) 228 8882, *eat@atriumrestaurant.co.uk, Fax (0131) 228 8808* – ▤. MO AE ① VISA DZ c
closed 25-26 December, 1-2 January, Sunday and Saturday lunch except during Edinburgh Festival – **Rest** 17.50/25.00 and a la carte 30.50/40.50 ♀ 🍇.
• Located inside the Traverse Theatre, an adventurous repertoire enjoyed on tables made of wooden railway sleepers. Twisted copper lamps subtly light the ultra-modern interior.

Duck's at Le Marche Noir, 2-4 Eyre Pl, EH3 5EP, ☎ (0131) 558 1608, *enquiries@ducks.co.uk, Fax (0131) 556 0798* – ⇔ ⇔ 24. MO AE ① VISA BV x
closed 25-26 December and lunch Saturday-Monday – **Rest** a la carte 25.90/36.90 ♀.
• Confident, inventive cuisine with a modern, discreetly French character, served with friendly efficiency in bistro-style surroundings - intimate and very personally run.

Hadrian's (at Balmoral H.), 2 North Bridge, EH1 1TR, ☎ (0131) 557 5000, *Fax (0131) 557 3747* – ▤. MO AE ① VISA EY n
Rest 14.95/18.95 and a la carte 18.95/29.20 **s.** ☺ ♀.
• Drawing on light, clean-lined styling, reminiscent of Art Deco, and a "British new wave" approach; an extensive range of contemporary brasserie classics and smart service.

Marque Central, 30b Grindley St, EH3 9AX, ☎ (0131) 229 9859, *Fax (0131) 221 9515* – MO AE VISA DZ i
closed first week September, Christmas, 1-2 January, Sunday and Monday – **Rest** 16.00 (lunch) and a la carte 19.40/27.75 ☺ ♀.
• Modern restaurant, incorporated into the Lyceum Theatre. Generous, reasonably priced dishes which draw on contemporary Scottish and Italian traditions with equal facility.

XX **La Garrigue,** 31 Jeffrey St, EH1 1DH, ☎ (0131) 557 3032, *jeanmichel@lagarrigue.co.uk*
Fax (0131) 5573032 – MC AE VISA EY
closed Sunday except July-September – **Rest** - French - 14.50/18.50 and a la carte 15.50/29.50.
◆ Very pleasant restaurant near the Royal Mile: beautiful handmade wood tables add warmth to rustic décor. Authentic French regional cooking with classical touches.

XX **The Tower,** Museum of Scotland (fifth floor), Chambers St, EH1 1JF, ☎ (0131) 225 3003 *mail@tower-restaurant.com, Fax (0131) 220 4392,* ←, – MC AE VISA EZ
closed 25-26 December – **Rest** a la carte 24.00/41.50 ♀.
◆ Game, grills and seafood feature in a popular, contemporary brasserie style menu. On the fifth floor of the Museum of Scotland - ask for a terrace table and admire the view.

X **Le Café Saint-Honoré,** 34 North West Thistle Street Lane, EH2 1EA, ☎ (0131) 226 2211 – MC AE VISA DY
closed 3 days Christmas and 3 days New Year – **Rest** (booking essential) 19.95 and a la carte 19.70/34.90 ♀.
◆ Tucked away off Frederick St., a bustling, personally run bistro furnished in the classic French style of a century ago. Good-value cuisine with a pronounced Gallic flavour.

X **First Coast,** 99-101 Dalry Rd, EH11 2AB, ☎ (0131) 313 4404, *info@first-coast.co.uk Fax (0131) 346 7811* – MC AE VISA CZ
closed Sunday, 25-26 December and 1-2 January – **Rest** a la carte 17.85/26.40.
◆ Informal restaurant near Haymarket station. The exposed stone walls in one of the rooms lend a rustic aspect. Sizeable menus boast a classic base with modern twists.

X **Fenwicks,** 15 Salisbury Pl, EH9 1SL, ☎ (0131) 667 4265, *enquiries@fenwicks-restaurant.co.uk, Fax (0131) 667 4285.* MC AE VISA BX
Rest 12.50/20.00 and a la carte 20.40/23.40.
◆ Cosy and unpretentious with a neighbourhood feel. Colourful French posters on the walls. Good value menus: the cooking is rustic Scottish with dashes of French inspiration.

X **Nargile,** 73 Hanover St, EH2 1EE, ☎ (0131) 225 5755, *info@nargile.co.uk* – MC AE VISA DY
closed 2 weeks September, 25-27 December, 1-3 January and Sunday – **Rest** - Turkish - a la carte 19.15/25.15.
◆ Unpretentious and welcoming restaurant with simple décor and enthusiastic service. A la carte, set menus and lunch time mezes of tasty, well-prepared Turkish cuisine.

X **Blue,** 10 Cambridge St, EH1 2ED, ☎ (0131) 221 1222, *eat@bluebarcafe.com Fax (0131) 228 8808* – MC AE VISA DZ
closed 25-26 December, 1-2 January and Sunday except during Edinburgh Festival – **Rest** 13.95 (lunch) and a la carte 15.40/24.50 ♀.
◆ Strikes a modern note with bright, curving walls, glass and simple settings. A café-bar with a light, concise and affordable menu drawing a young clientele. Bustling feel.

Leith *Edinburgh.*

Malmaison, 1 Tower Pl, EH6 7DB, ☎ (0131) 468 5000, *edinburgh@malmaison.com Fax (0131) 468 5002,* rm, – 70. MC AE VISA BV
Brasserie : **Rest** 14.50/13.95 and a la carte 22.40/35.75 ♀ – 12.75 – **95 rm** 135.00 – 135.00, 5 suites.
◆ Imposing quayside sailors' mission converted in strikingly elegant style. Good-sized rooms, thoughtfully appointed, combine more traditional comfort with up-to-date overtones. Sophisticated brasserie with finely wrought iron.

Express by Holiday Inn without rest., Britannia Way, Ocean Drive, EH6 6JJ, ☎ (0131) 555 4422, *info@hiex-edinburgh.com, Fax (0131) 555 4646* – 25. MC AE VISA BV
145 rm 95.00 – 95.00.
◆ Modern, purpose-built hotel offering trim, bright, reasonably-priced accommodation. Convenient for Leith centre restaurants and a short walk from the Ocean Terminal.

XXX **Martin Wishart,** 54 The Shore, EH6 6RA, ☎ (0131) 553 3557, *info@martin-wishart.co.uk, Fax (0131) 467 7091* – MC AE VISA BV
closed 25-26 December, 1 January, 1 week February, Sunday, Monday and Saturday lunch – **Rest** (booking essential) 20.50 (lunch) and a la carte 47.00/52.00 **s.** ♀.
Spec. Lobster and smoked haddock soufflé. Roast halibut, glazed pig's trotter and braised endive. Caramel mousseline, chocolate croustillant and milk sorbet.
◆ Simply decorated dockside conversion with a growing reputation. Modern French-accented menus characterised by clear, intelligently combined flavours.

XX **The Vintners Rooms,** The Vaults, 87 Giles St, EH6 6BZ, ☎ (0131) 554 6767, *enquiries@thevintnersrooms.com, Fax (0131) 555 5653* – MC AE VISA BV
closed 1-15 January, Sunday dinner and Monday – **Rest** 18.00 (lunch) and a la carte 32.50/38.00 ♀.
◆ Atmospheric 18C bonded spirits warehouse with high ceilings, stone floor, rug-covered walls and candlelit side-room with ornate plasterwork. French/Mediterranean cooking.

at Kirknewton *Southwest : 7 m. on A 71 – AX – ✉ Edinburgh.*

Dalmahoy H. & Country Club, EH27 8EB, ☎ (0870) 400 7299, *reservations.dalmahoy@marriotthotels.co.uk, Fax (0870) 400 7399*, ≤, ®, Fø, ≘s, ⊠, ⚑18, ⚑, ⚑, ⚑ – |‡| ⇎, ▤ rest, ♿ P – 🏛 300. 🅜🅒 🅐🅔 ⓓ 𝐕𝐈𝐒𝐀. ✗

Pentland **:** Rest (dinner only) a la carte 34.00/45.00 ♀ – ***The Long Weekend*** **:** Rest *(closed Christmas and New Year)* (grill rest.) a la carte 19.00/31.00 ♀ – ☐ 14.95 – **212 rm** ☐ ✶110.00/160.00 – ✶✶110.00/160.00, 3 suites.

◆ Extended Georgian mansion in 1000 acres with 2 Championship golf courses. Comprehensive leisure club, smart rooms and a clubby cocktail lounge. Tranquil atmosphere with elegant comfort in Pentland restaurant. Informal modern dining at The Long Weekend.

at Edinburgh International Airport *West : 7½ m. by A 8 – AV – ✉ Edinburgh.*

Hilton Edinburgh Airport, 100 Eastfield Rd, EH28 8LL, ☎ (0131) 519 4400, *Fax (0131) 519 4422*, Fø, ≘s, ⊠ – |‡| ⇎, ▤ rest, ✆ ♿ P – 🏛 240. 🅜🅒 🅐🅔 ⓓ 𝐕𝐈𝐒𝐀

Rest (carvery lunch)/dinner 26.00/32.00 and a la carte approx 26.00 **s.** ♀ – ☐ 17.95 – **150 rm** ✶101.00/210.00 – ✶✶101.00/210.00.

◆ Busy, purpose-built hotel offering large, well-equipped rooms designed with working travellers in mind. Shuttle service to the terminal and excellent road links to the city. A large modern restaurant, comfortable and informal.

"Rest" appears in red for establishments with a ✿ (star) or ☺ (Bib Gourmand).

EDINBURGH INTERNATIONAL AIRPORT *Edinburgh City* 501 J 16 – *see Edinburgh.*

EDNAM *Borders* 501 502 M 17 – *see Kelso.*

EDZELL *Angus* 501 M 13 *Scotland G. – pop. 783.*

Env. : *Castle★ AC (The Pleasance★★★) W : 2 m.*

Exc. : *Glen Esk★, NW : 7 m.*

Edinburgh 94 – Aberdeen 36 – Dundee 31.

Glenesk, High St, DD9 7TF, ☎ (01356) 648319, *gleneskhotel@btconnect.com, Fax (01356) 647333*, Fø, ≘s, ⊠, ⚑ – ⇎ rest, P – 🏛 150. 🅜🅒 🅐🅔 𝐕𝐈𝐒𝐀

closed first week January – **Rest** (bar lunch)/dinner 22.50 **s.** – **24 rm** ☐ ✶65.00 – ✶✶110.00.

◆ Well run and family owned, a substantial 19C hotel with the pleasant village on its doorstep. Friendly atmosphere prevails; simple rooms of varying shapes and sizes. Restaurant overlooks golf course and gardens.

ELGIN *Moray* 501 K 11 *Scotland G. – pop. 20 829.*

See : *Town★ – Cathedral★ (Chapter house★★) AC.*

Exc. : *Glenfiddich Distillery★, SE : 10 m. by A 941.*

⚑18, ⚑18 *Moray, Stotfield Rd, Lossiemouth ☎ (01343) 812018 – ⚑18 Hardhillock, Birnie Rd ☎ (01343) 542338 – ⚑18 Hopeman, Moray ☎ (01343) 830578.*

ℹ *17 High St ☎ (01343) 542666.*

Edinburgh 198 – Aberdeen 68 – Fraserburgh 61 – Inverness 39.

Mansion House, The Haugh, IV30 1AW, via Haugh Rd and Murdocks Wynd ☎ (01343) 548811, *reception@mhelgin.co.uk, Fax (01343) 547916*, Fø, ≘s, ⊠, ⚑ – ⇎ rest, P – 🏛 200. 🅜🅒 🅐🅔 𝐕𝐈𝐒𝐀. ✗

Rest 17.50/29.95 and a la carte 19.55/32.15 **s.** – **23 rm** ☐ ✶90.00/97.00 – ✶✶175.00.

◆ 19C Baronial mansion surrounded by lawned gardens. Country house-style interior. Rooms in main house most characterful, those in purpose-built annex more modern. The formal restaurant is decorated in warm yellows and blues.

Mansefield, Mayne Rd, IV30 1NY, ☎ (01343) 540883, *reception@themansfield.com, Fax (01343) 552491* – |‡| ⇎ ♿ P – 🏛 230. 🅜🅒 🅐🅔 𝐕𝐈𝐒𝐀. ✗

closed 25-26 December – ***The Restaurant*** **:** Rest a la carte 17.75/27.75 ♀ – ***Mezzo*** **:** Rest *(closed Sunday lunch)* a la carte approx 15.45 ♀ – **39 rm** ☐ ✶65.00/85.00 – ✶✶110.00/140.00, 1 suite.

◆ Extended Victorian manse in the town centre. Comfortable public areas including a "whisky lounge". Traditional or spacious, comfortable, modern bedrooms. Stylish modern eatery with bright menu. Mezzo is a stylish eating place adjacent to the conference suite.

The Pines without rest., East Rd, IV30 1XG, East : ½ m. on A 96 ✆ (01343) 552495
thepines@dsl.pipex.com, Fax (01343) 552495, – P. VISA.
6 rm ★40.00/45.00 – ★★54.00/58.00.
• Detached Victorian house with a friendly and warm ambience amidst comfy, homel décor. Bedrooms are of a good size and furnished with colourful, modern fabrics.

The Croft without rest., 10 Institution Rd, IV30 1QX, via Duff Ave ✆ (01343) 546004
thecroftelgin@hotmail.com, Fax (01343) 546004, – P.
closed 10 December-January – **3 rm** ★30.00/50.00 – ★★56.00/60.00.
• Victorian family home with delightful garden. Large, comfortable, library-style loung and a breakfast room with fine dining suite. Comfy, pine furnished rooms.

The Lodge, 20 Duff Ave, IV30 1QS, ✆ (01343) 549981, *info@thelodge-elgin.com*
Fax (01343) 540527, – P. VISA.
Rest (by arrangement) a la carte 15.65/21.75 **8 rm** ★30.00/45.00 – ★★48.00/56.00.
• Victorian house with a distinctive facade. Antique furnished hall and homely lounge with open fires. Comfortable bedrooms with dark wood furniture. Tasty home-cooked meals.

at Urquhart *East : 5 m. by A 96 – ✉ Elgin.*

Parrandier, The Old Church of Urquhart, Meft Rd, IV30 8NH, Northwest : ¼ m. b Meft Rd ✆ (01343) 843063, *parrandier@freeuk.com, Fax (01343) 843063,* ←, – P
VISA
closed 24-26 December – **Rest** (by arrangement) 11.00 – **3 rm** ★36.00 – ★★52.00.
• Former 19C church in quiet rural location converted to provide open plan lounge and split level dining area. Comfortable bedrooms with original church features.

at Duffus *Northwest : 5½ m. by A 941 on B 9012 – ✉ Elgin.*

Burnside House without rest., IV30 5QS, Northwest : 1 ¾ m. by B 9012 on B 904
✆ (01343) 835165, *burnside@begga.fsnet.co.uk, Fax (01343) 835165,* ←, – P
3 rm ★28.00 – ★★50.00.
• 19C house with garden; the residence of the founder of Gordonstoun School nearby Attractive rooms with view; snooker table. Large bedrooms with tartan themes.

ELGOL *Highland* 501 B 12 – *see Skye (Isle of).*

ELIE *Fife* 501 L 15.
Edinburgh 44 – Dundee 24 – St Andrews 13.

Sangster's, 51 High St, KY9 1BZ, ✆ (01333) 331001, *bruce@sangster.co.uk*
Fax (01333) 331001 – . VISA
closed first 3 weeks January, 1 week November, 25-26 December, Saturday and Tuesday lunch, Sunday dinner and Monday – **Rest** (booking essential) 17.50/32.50.
• Husband and wife team run this homely, modern restaurant with local artwork for sale on the walls. The classical style of cooking employs notable use of good, local produce.

ERBUSAIG *Highland* 501 C 12 *Scotland G.* – ✉ *Kyle of Lochalsh.*
Env. : *Wester Ross*★★★.
Skye Bridge (toll).
Edinburgh 206 – Dundee 184 – Inverness 84 – Oban 127.

Old Schoolhouse, IV40 8BB, ✆ (01599) 534369, *joanne@oldschoolhouse87.co.uk*
Fax (01599) 534369, – rest, P. VISA
closed 2 weeks October and 20 December-10 January – **Rest** (by arrangement) 22.00 –
3 rm ★40.00/45.00 – ★★58.00/62.00.
• Converted schoolhouse with rustic feel, on edge of sleepy hamlet close to Skye Bridge. Homely, traditional décor matches simple, Caledonian menus. Spacious bedrooms.

Your opinions are important to us:
please write and let us know about your discoveries and experiences – good and bad!

ERISKA (Isle of) *Argyll and Bute* 501 D 14 – ✉ *Oban.*
Edinburgh 127 – Glasgow 104 – Oban 12.

Isle of Eriska, Benderloch, PA37 1SD, ☎ (01631) 720371, *office@eriska-hotel.co.uk, Fax (01631) 720531,* ← Lismore and mountains, 🏊, Fö, ≘s, 🏊, 9, ⇐, ⚘, ✂ – ⇸ rest, ▤ rest, 📞 ♿ P. 🅜 AE VISA
closed January – **Rest** (booking essential) (light lunch residents only)/dinner 38.50 **s.** – **18 rm** ☕ ✝205.00 – ✝✝320.00, 4 suites.
◆ On a private island, a wonderfully secluded 19C Scottish Baronial mansion with dramatic views of Lismore and mountains. Highest levels of country house comfort and style. Elegant dining.

ESKDALEMUIR *Dumfries and Galloway* 501 K 18.
Edinburgh 71 – Dumfries 27 – Hawick 32.

Hart Manor, DG13 0QO, Southeast : 1 m. on B 709 ☎ (01387) 373217, *visit@hartmanor.co.uk,* ←, ⇐ – ⇸ P. 🅜 VISA. ⚘
closed Christmas and New Year – **Rest** (booking essential to non-residents) (dinner only) 28.00 – **5 rm** (dinner included) ☕ ✝82.50 – ✝✝145.00.
◆ Former shooting lodge in an attractive rural location and dating from the 19C. Most of the comfortable bedrooms have countryside views, superior rooms are notably larger. Cosy restaurant offers daily changing, home-made, traditional fare.

ETTRICKBRIDGE *Borders* 501 502 L 17 – *see Selkirk.*

FAIRLIE *North Ayrshire* 501 502 F 16.
Edinburgh 75 – Ayr 50 – Glasgow 36.

Fins, Fencebay Fisheries, Fencefoot Farm, KA29 0EG, South : 1 ½ m. on A 78 ☎ (01475) 568989, *fencebay@aol.com, Fax (01475) 568921* – ⇸ P. 🅜 VISA
closed 25-26 December and 1-2 January – **Rest** - Seafood - (booking essential) a la carte 23.00/34.00.
◆ Converted farm buildings house a simple, flag-floored restaurant, craft shops and a traditional beech smokery. Friendly service and fresh seasonal seafood.

FALKIRK *Falkirk* 501 I 16 – *pop. 32 379.*
18 *Grangemouth, Polmonthill ☎ (01324) 711500* – 9 *Polmont, Manuel Rigg, Maddiston ☎ (01324) 711277* – 18 *Stirling Rd, Camelon ☎ (01324) 611061* – 18 *Falkirk Tryst, 86 Burnhead Rd, Larbet ☎ (01324) 562415.*
i *2-4 Glebe St ☎ (08707) 200614, info@falkirk.visitscotland.com.*
Edinburgh 26 – Dunfermline 18 – Glasgow 25 – Motherwell 27 – Perth 43.

Inchyra Grange, Grange Rd, Polmont, FK2 0YB, Southeast : 3 m. by A 803 and Kirk Entry Bo'ness Rd ☎ (01324) 711911, *general.inchyra@macdonald-hotels.co.uk, Fax (01324) 716134,* Fö, ≘s, 🏊, ⇐, ⚘, ✂ – |✿|, ⇸ rm, ▤ rest, 📞 ♿ P – 🎤 700. 🅜 AE ⓓ VISA
Opus 504 : **Rest** 12.95/23.50 and a la carte 25.85/39.40 **s.** ♀ – **100 rm** ☕ ✝85.00/105.00 – ✝✝90.00/115.00, 1 suite.
◆ Extended Victorian manor house. Business orientated, being close to motorway and industrial areas, with good conference and leisure facilities. Well-equipped bedrooms. Opus 504 boasts cocktail bar area.

Premier Travel Inn, Beancross Rd, Polmont, FK2 0YS, East : 3 m. by A 904 on A 9 ☎ (01324) 720726, *Fax (01324) 716801* – |✿| ⇸, ▤ rest, ♿ P. 🅜 AE ⓓ VISA. ⚘
Rest (grill rest.) – **40 rm** ✝46.95/46.95 – ✝✝48.95/48.95.
◆ Simply furnished and brightly decorated bedrooms with ample work space. Family rooms with sofa beds. Ideal for corporate or leisure travel.

at Glensburgh *Northeast : 2 m. by A 904 on A 905 – ✉ Falkirk.*

Grange Manor, FK3 8XJ, ☎ (01324) 474836, *info@grangemanor.co.uk, Fax (01324) 665861,* ⇐ – |✿| ⇸ ♿ P – 🎤 200. 🅜 AE ⓓ VISA. ⚘
closed 26 December and 1-2 January – ***Le Chardon :*** **Rest** *(closed Saturday lunch and Sunday)* 15.95 (lunch) and dinner a la carte 27.00/36.00 – ***Wallace's :*** **Rest** a la carte 17.00/28.00 **s.** – **36 rm** ☕ ✝105.00 – ✝✝132.00.
◆ Renovated Georgian manor house with sympathetic modern additions. Rooms have a smart, comfortable feel and those in the main house a more traditional air. Buzzing, contemporary Le Chardon. Bistro-style Wallace's retains stone walls and beamed ceiling.

FASNACLOICH *Argyll and Bute* – ✉ *Appin.*
Edinburgh 133 – Fort William 34 – Oban 19.

Lochside Cottage ⛨, PA38 4BJ, ✆ (01631) 730216, *broadbent@lochsidecottage.fsnet.co.uk, Fax (01631) 730216,* ≤ Loch Baile Mhic Chailen and mountains, – P
Rest (by arrangement) (communal dining) 25.00 – **3 rm** ☐ ✶35.00 – ✶✶70.00.
◆ Captivating views of surrounding mountains and Loch Baile Mhic Chailen, on whose shore it stands in idyllic seclusion. Log fires in the lounge and inviting, cosy bedrooms. Dinners take place with a house party atmosphere as guests dine together at one table.

FIONNPHORT *Argyll and Bute* 501 A 15 – *Shipping Services : see Mull (Isle of).*

FLODIGARRY *Highland* 501 B 11 – *see Skye (Isle of).*

FORGANDENNY *Perth* 501 J 14 – *see Perth.*

FORRES *Moray* 501 J 11 *Scotland G. – pop. 8 967.*
Env. : *Sueno's Stone★★, N : ½ m. by A 940 on A 96 – Brodie Castle★ AC, W : 3 m. by A 96.*
Exc. : *Elgin★ (Cathedral★, chapter house★★ AC), E : 10¼ m. by A 96.*
Muiryshade ✆ (01309) 672949.
116 High St ✆ (01309) 672938 (Easter-October).
Edinburgh 165 – Aberdeen 80 – Inverness 27.

Knockomie ⛨, Grantown Rd, IV36 2SG, South : 1 ½ m. on A 940 ✆ (01309) 673146, *stay@knockomie.co.uk, Fax (01309) 673290,* – P – 40. MO AE VISA
The Grill Room : Rest (dinner only) a la carte 20.00/35.00 ♀ – **14 rm** ☐ ✶108.00/135.00 – ✶✶200.00, 1 suite.
◆ Extended stone-built house in comfortable seclusion off a country road. Country house atmosphere. Bedrooms in main house older and more characterful. The Grill baronial style restaurant specializes in Scottish beef.

Ramnee, Victoria Rd, IV36 3BN, ✆ (01309) 672410, *ramneehotel@btconnect.com, Fax (01309) 673392,* – P – 80. MO AE VISA
closed 25-26 December and 1-3 January – ***Hamlyns :*** Rest (bar lunch)/dinner a la carte 14.50/21.25 ♀ – **19 rm** ☐ ✶80.00/90.00 – ✶✶95.00/105.00, 1 suite.
◆ Family owned Edwardian building in town centre with extensive lawned grounds. Welcoming public areas include panelled reception and pubby bar. Warmly traditional bedrooms. Formal dining room in traditional style.

Cluny Bank, St Leonard's Rd, IV36 1DW, ✆ (01309) 674304, *mtb@clunybankhotel.co.uk, Fax (01309) 671400,* – P. MO AE VISA.
closed January – ***The Restaurant :*** Rest (dinner only) (residents only Monday-Tuesday) 31.00 s. – **10 rm** ☐ ✶70.00/85.00 – ✶✶120.00/130.00.
◆ Personally run 19C listed house, nestling beneath Cluny Hill. Extended in 1910, it boasts antiques, oak staircase, original floor tiling and simple, pleasant, airy bedrooms. Dining room features much work by local artist.

at Dyke *West : 3¾ m. by A 96 –* ✉ *Forres.*

The Old Kirk ⛨ without rest., IV36 2TL, ✆ (01309) 641414, *oldkirk@gmx.net, Fax (01309) 641144* – P. MO VISA
3 rm ☐ ✶30.00/35.00 – ✶✶60.00.
◆ Former 19C church in country location. Stained glass window in first floor lounge; pine furnished breakfast room. Pleasantly furnished bedrooms with original stonework.

FORT WILLIAM *Highland* 501 E 13 *Scotland G. – pop. 9 908.*
See : *Town★.*
Exc. : *The Road to the Isles★★ (Neptune's Staircase (≤★★), Glenfinnan★ ≤★, Arisaig★, Silver Sands of Morar★, Mallaig★), NW : 46 m. by A 830 – Ardnamurchan Peninsula★★ – Ardnamurchan Point (≤★★), NW : 65 m. by A 830, A 861 and B 8007 – SE : Ben Nevis★★ (≤★★) - Glen Nevis★.*
North Rd ✆ (01397) 704464.
Cameron Sq ✆ (0845) 2255121.
Edinburgh 133 – Glasgow 104 – Inverness 68 – Oban 50.

Inverlochy Castle, Torlundy, PH33 6SN, Northeast : 3 m. on A 82 (01397) 702177, *info@inverlochy.co.uk, Fax (01397) 702953*, ≤ loch and mountains, – P. MO AE VISA
Rest (dinner booking essential to non-residents) 28.50/58.00 – **17 rm** 220.00/410.00 – 410.00/495.00, 1 suite.
Spec. Home smoked tuna with avocado, focaccia, sesame and curried mayonnaise. Poached duck with crusted foie gras and apricot foam. Rhubarb crème brûlée with macaroons and its own soufflé.
◆ A world renowned hotel set in a Victorian castle with extensive parkland and stunning views of the loch and mountains. Impressive luxury and detailed yet friendly service. Three classic dining rooms ensure that meals are a special experience.

Distillery House without rest., Nevis Bridge, North Rd, PH33 6LR, (01397) 700103, *disthouse@aol.com, Fax (01397) 702980*, – P. MO AE VISA.
10 rm 38.00/45.00 – 50.00/76.00.
◆ Conveniently located a short walk from the centre of town, formerly part of Glenlochy distillery. Cosy guests' lounge and comfortable rooms, some with views of Ben Nevis.

Premier Travel Inn, Loch Iall, An Aird, PH33 6AN, Northwest : ½ m. by A 82 (08701) 977104, *Fax (01397) 703618* – , rm, rest, P. MO AE VISA
Rest (grill rest.) – **40 rm** 52.95 – 52.95.
◆ Simply furnished and brightly decorated bedrooms with ample work space. Family rooms with sofa beds. Ideal for corporate or leisure travel.

The Grange without rest., Grange Rd, PH33 6JF, South : ¾ m. by A 82 and Ashburn Lane (01397) 705516, *info@grangefortwilliam.com, Fax (01397) 701595*, ≤, – P. MO VISA.
March-October – **4 rm** 85.00/99.00 – 95.00/110.00.
◆ Large Victorian house with attractive garden, in an elevated position in a quiet residential part of town. Very comfortable and tastefully furnished with many antiques.

Crolinnhe without rest., Grange Rd, PH33 6JF, South : ¾ m. by A 82 and Ashburn Lane (01397) 702709, *crolinnhe@yahoo.com, Fax (01397) 700506*, ≤, – P. MO VISA.
Easter-October – **3 rm** 110.00 – 125.00.
◆ Very comfortably and attractively furnished Victorian house, run with a real personal touch. Relaxing guests' sitting room and well furnished bedrooms.

Lochan Cottage without rest., Lochyside, PH33 7NX, North : 2½ m. by A 82, A 830 on B 8006 (01397) 702695, *lochanco@btopenworld.com*, – P. MO VISA.
closed Christmas – **6 rm** 30.00/56.00 – 44.00/56.00.
◆ Spotlessly kept, whitewashed cottage with homely public areas. Breakfast taken in conservatory overlooking delightfully landscaped gardens. Neat, well-kept rooms.

Ashburn House without rest., 18 Achintore Rd, PH33 6RQ, South : ½ m. on A 82 (01397) 706000, *christine@no-1.fsworld.co.uk, Fax (01397) 702024*, – P. MO VISA.
7 rm 40.00/50.00 – 80.00/100.00.
◆ Attractive Victorian house overlooking Loch Linnhe, on the main road into town which is a short walk away. Well furnished bedrooms and a comfortable conservatory lounge.

Lawriestone Guest House without rest., Achintore Rd, PH33 6RQ, South : ½ m. on A 82 (01397) 700777, *susan@lawriestone.co.uk, Fax (01397) 700777*, ≤, – P. MO VISA.
closed 25-26 December and 1-2 January – **4 rm** 60.00/80.00 – 60.00/80.00.
◆ Victorian house overlooking Loch Linnhe; not far from town centre, ideal for touring Western Highlands. Especially proud of Scottish breakfasts. Airy rooms; some with views.

Crannog, The Underwater Centre, An Aird, PH33 6AN, (01397) 705589, *enquiries@crannog.net, Fax (01397) 705026*, ≤ Loch Linnhe – . MO VISA
closed dinner 24-25 and 31 December and 1 January – **Rest** - Seafood - (booking essential) a la carte 17.85/30.95.
◆ Name reflects philosophy of catching and preparing local seafood. The owner, a former fisherman, has converted a bait store into a lochside restaurant; wonderful views.

at Banavie *North : 3 m. by A 82 and A 830 on B 8004 – ✉ Fort William.*

Moorings, PH33 7LY, (01397) 772797, *reservations@moorings-fortwilliam.co.uk, Fax (01397) 772441*, ≤, – P – 100. MO AE VISA
closed 25-26 December – **Rest** (bar lunch)/dinner 26.00 and a la carte 18.35/31.85 s. – **28 rm** 55.00/85.00 – 86.00/134.00.
◆ Modern accommodation in traditional style. Adjacent to Caledonian Canal and at start of "Road to the Isles". Most rooms boast views of mountains and Neptune's Staircase. Meals served in panelled lounge bar with views of Ben Nevis.

FOYERS *Highland* 501 G 12 *Scotland G.* – ✉ *Loch Ness.*
Env. : *Loch Ness*★★ – *The Great Glen*★.
Edinburgh 175 – Inverness 19 – Kyle of Lochalsh 63 – Oban 96.

Craigdarroch House, IV2 6XU, North : ¼ m. on B 852 ℘ (01456) 48640C *munro@hotel-loch-ness.co.uk, Fax (01456) 486444,* ≤ Loch Ness and mountains, P. MC AE VISA.
closed 25-26 December – **Rest** 22.50/27.50 (dinner) and a la carte 16.50/27.50 – **10 rm** ★80.00/95.00 – ★★110.00/160.00.
◆ Spacious hotel with extensive parkland. In a very rural location with exceptional views c Loch Ness and mountains. Run with personal style. Alluring comfort throughout. Half panelled dining room with a light colour scheme and tall bay window.

Foyers Bay House, Lower Foyers, IV2 6YB, West : 1 ¼ m. by B 852 on Lower Foyer rd ℘ (01456) 486624, *carol@foyersbay.co.uk, Fax (01456) 486337,* ≤, – rm, P. MC AE VISA.
closed 6-20 January – **Rest** (dinner only) 11.50/18.50 and a la carte 12.95/24.95 – **6 rm** ★33.00/48.00 – ★★54.00/66.00.
◆ Victorian house surrounded by lawned garden, close to the banks of Loch Ness an ideally located for touring the Highlands. Homely, welcoming bedrooms. The main dinin room is in a spacious conservatory with views of Loch Ness.

The red symbol? This denotes the very essence of peace – only the sound of birdsong first thing in the morning ...

GAIRLOCH *Highland* 501 C 10 *Scotland G.*
Env. : *Wester Ross*★★★ – *Loch Maree*★★★, *E : 5½ m. by A 832.*
Exc. : *Inverewe Gardens*★★★ *AC, NE : 8 m. by A 832 – Victoria Falls*★, *SE : 8 m. by A 832.*
Gairloch ℘ *(01445) 712407.*
Auchtercairn ℘ *(0845) 2255121 (April-October).*
Edinburgh 228 – Inverness 72 – Kyle of Lochalsh 68.

Gairloch Highland Lodge, Charleston, IV21 2AH, South : 1 ¾ m. on A 832 ℘ (01445 712068, *enquiries@gairlochhighlandlodge.net, Fax (01445) 712044,* ≤, – rest, P MC VISA
closed mid January-mid February and 25 December – **Rest** a la carte 19.25/27.25 ♀ – 5.50 – **17 rm** ★27.50/42.00 – ★★49.00/65.00, 1 suite.
◆ Large purpose-built hotel in dominant position overlooking Wester Ross coastal trai Spacious sitting room with pleasant views. Comfortable, colour co-ordinated rooms. Com fortable dining room specialises in Scottish cuisine.

GALSON *Western Isles (Outer Hebrides)* 501 A 8 – *see Lewis and Harris (Isle of).*

GATEHEAD *East Ayrshire* 501 502 G 17 – ✉ *Kilmarnock.*
Edinburgh 72 – Ayr 10 – Glasgow 25 – Kilmarnock 5.

Cochrane Inn, 45 Main Rd, KA2 0AP, ℘ (01563) 570122 – P. MC VISA.
Rest (booking essential) a la carte 16.00/20.00 ♀.
◆ Neat and tidy pub in tiny hamlet near Kilmarnock. Traditional establishment with beam and open fire. Mixture of popular and modern dishes. Perennially busy.

GATEHOUSE OF FLEET *Dumfries and Galloway* 501 502 H 19 – *pop. 919.*
Gatehouse, Innisfree, Lauriestown, Castle Douglas ℘ *(01557) 814766.*
Car Park ℘ *(01557) 814212 (Easter-October).*
Edinburgh 113 – Dumfries 33 – Stranraer 42.

Cally Palace, DG7 2DL, East : ½ m. on B 727 ℘ (01557) 814341, *info@callyp lace.co.uk, Fax (01557) 814522,* ≤, 18, – rest, P – 40. MC AE VISA.
closed 3 January-mid February – **Rest** 28.00 (dinner) and lunch a la carte 20.20/21.95 **s.** ♀ – **50 rm** (dinner included) ★99.00/138.00 – ★★208.00/220.00, 5 suites.
◆ Highly impressive 18C mansion with golf course. Sitting room with fantastically ornate ceiling of original gilding. Small leisure centre. Large rooms with delightful views. Elegant dining room serving Galloway produce. Pianist in attendance.

GATTONSIDE *Borders* – *see Melrose.*

GIGHA (Isle of) *Argyll and Bute* 501 C 16.

to Tayinloan (Caledonian MacBrayne Ltd) 8-10 daily (20 mn).
Edinburgh 168.

Gigha, PA41 7AA, (01583) 505254, *hotel@gigha.org.uk, Fax (01583) 505244*, < Sound of Gigha and Kintyre Peninsula, , – , rest, P. *closed Christmas* – **Rest** (booking essential to non-residents) (bar lunch)/dinner 26.00 and a la carte – **13 rm** ★39.95/70.95 – ★★79.90/125.90.

◆ 18C whitewashed house on island owned by residents; views over Ardminish Bay to Kintyre. Cosy pine-panelled bar. Elegant lounge. Simple, clean and tidy rooms. Inviting restaurant with exposed stone walls and pine tables.

GLAMIS *Angus* 501 K/L 14 – ✉ *Forfar.*

Edinburgh 69 – Dundee 13 – Forfar 7.

Castleton House, DD8 1SJ, West : 3 ¼ m. on A 94 (01307) 840340, *hotel@castletonglamis.co.uk, Fax (01307) 840506*, , – rest, P. AE VISA
***The Conservatory*: Rest** 30.00/35.00 and a la carte 21.50/32.25 – **6 rm** ★120.00/140.00 – ★★200.00.

◆ Moat still visible in gardens of this 20C country house built on site of medieval fortress. Appealing lounges, cosy bar. Individually designed, attractively appointed rooms. Stylish conservatory restaurant looks out to garden.

B. Pérousse/MICHELIN

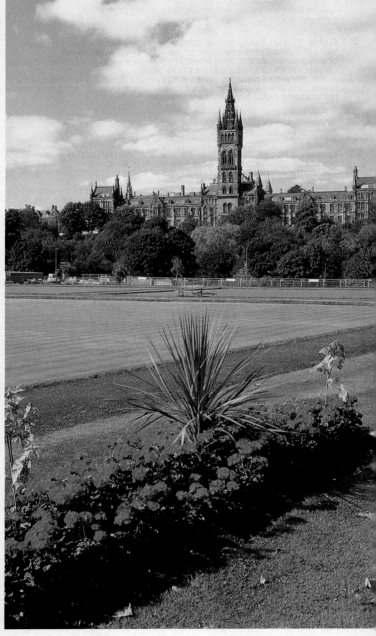

Glasgow: Scotland University

GLASGOW

501 502 H 16 *Scotland G. – pop. 624 501.*

Edinburgh 46 – Manchester 221.

TOURIST INFORMATION

11 George Sq ☎ (0141) 204 4400; enquiries@seeglasgow.com
Glasgow Airport, Tourist Information Desk, ☎ (0141) 848 4440.

PRACTICAL INFORMATION

18 *Littlehill, Auchinairn Rd ☎ (0141) 772 1916.*
18 *Rouken Glen, Stewarton Rd, Thornliebank ☎ (0141) 638 7044* **AX**.
18 *Linn Park, Simshill Rd ☎ (0141) 633 0377,* **BX**.
18 *Lethamhill, Cumbernauld Rd ☎ (0141) 770 6220,* **BV**.
9 *Alexandra Park, Dennistoun ☎ (0141) 556 1294* **BV**.
9 *King's Park, 150a Croftpark Ave, Croftfoot ☎ (0141) 630 1597,* **BX**.
9 *Knightswood, Lincoln Ave ☎ (0141) 959 6358* **AV**.
9 *Ruchill Park, Brassey St ☎ (0141) 946 7676.*
Access to Oban by helicopter.
Erskine Bridge (toll) **AV**.
Glasgow Airport : ☎ (0870) 0400008, W : 8 m. by M 8 **AV**.
Terminal : *Coach service from Glasgow Central and Queen Street main line Railway Stations and from Anderston Cross and Buchanan Bus Stations.*
see also Prestwick.

SIGHTS

See : *City★★★ – Cathedral★★★ (≤★)* **DZ** *– The Burrell Collection★★★* **AX M1** *– Hunterian Art Gallery★★ (Whistler Collection★★★ – Mackintosh Wing★★★)* **AC CY M4** *– Museum of Transport★★ (Scottish Built Cars★★★, The Clyde Room of Ship Models★★★)* **AV M6** *– Art Gallery and Museum Kelvingrove★★* **CY** *– Pollok House★ (The Paintings★★)* **AX D** *– Tolbooth Steeple★* **DZ** *– Hunterian Museum (Coin and Medal Collection★)* **CY M5** *– City Chambers★* **DZ C** *– Glasgow School of Art★* **AC CY M3** *– Necropolis (≤★ of Cathedral)* **DYZ** *– Gallery of Modern Art★ – Glasgow (National) Science Centre★, Pacific Quay* **AV**.

Env. : *Paisley Museum and Art Gallery (Paisley Shawl Section★), W : 4 m. by M 8* **AV**.

Exc. : *The Trossachs★★★, N : 31 m. by A 879* **BV**, *A 81 and A 821 – Loch Lomond★★, NW : 19 m. by A 82* **AV** *– New Lanark★★, SE : 20 m. by M 74 and A 72* **BX**.

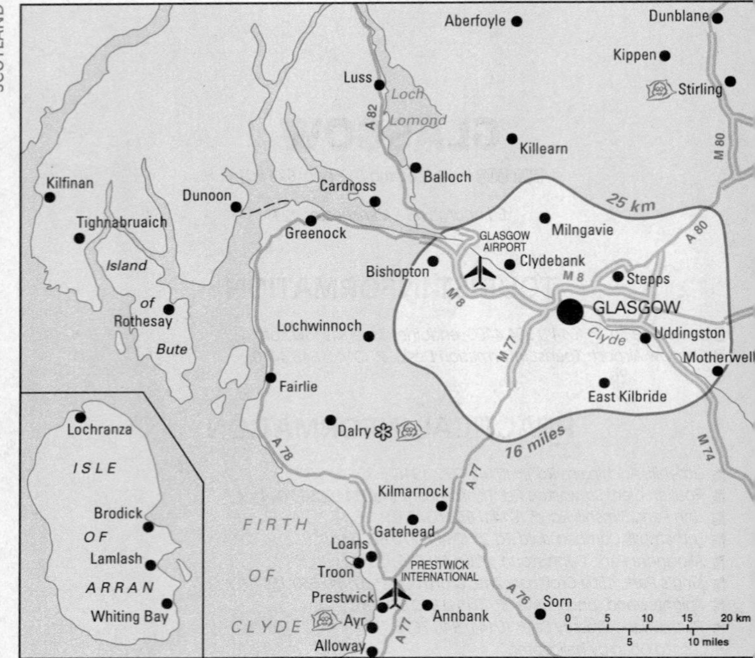

Hilton Glasgow, 1 William St, G3 8HT, ✆ (0141) 204 5555, *reservations.glasgow@hilton.com, Fax (0141) 204 5004*, ≤, Ⓛ, ≘s, ⊠ – |⧫|, ⇹ ▤ ✆ ♿ ⇔ Ⓟ – 🏛 1000. ⓂⒸ ⒶⒺ ⓓ VISA. ✂ CZ
Minsky's **:** Rest 18.95/24.95 and a la carte 27.40/36.85 ♀ – (see also ***Camerons*** below) – ⊏ 17.95 – **315 rm** ✝170.00/190.00 – ✝✝170.00/190.00, 4 suites.
◆ A city centre tower with impressive views on every side. Comfortable, comprehensively fitted rooms. Extensive leisure and conference facilities. Spacious, modern Minsky's has the style of a New York deli.

Radisson SAS, 301 Argyle St, G2 8DL, ✆ (0141) 204 3333, *reservations.glasgow@radissonsas.com, Fax (0141) 204 3344*, Ⓛ, ≘s, ⊠ – |⧫|, ⇹ rm, ▤ ✆ ♿ Ⓟ – 🏛 800. ⓂⒸ ⒶⒺ ⓓ VISA. ✂ DZ
Collage **:** Rest - Mediterranean - 11.95/15.00 and a la carte 20.65/35.40 ♀ – ***TaPaell'Ya*** **:** Rest - Tapas - *(closed Saturday lunch and Sunday)* a la carte 17.40/26.90 ♀ – ⊏ 13.75 – **246 rm** ✝190.00 – ✝✝190.00, 1 suite.
◆ A stunning, angular, modish exterior greets visitors to this consummate, modern commercial hotel. Large, stylish, eclectically furnished bedrooms. Collage is a bright modern restaurant. TaPaell'Ya serves tapas.

One Devonshire Gardens, 1 Devonshire Gdns, G12 0UX, ✆ (0141) 339 2001, *reservations@onedevonshiregardens.com, Fax (0141) 337 1663*, Ⓛ – ⇹ ✆ – 🏛 50. ⓂⒸ ⒶⒺ ⓓ VISA AV
No.5 **:** Rest (dinner only) 39.00 – (see also ***Room*** below) – ⊏ 17.00 – **32 rm** ✝135.00/495.00 – ✝✝135.00/495.00, 3 suites.
◆ Collection of adjoining 19C houses in terrace, furnished with attention to detail. Elegantly convivial drawing room, comfortable bedrooms and unobtrusive service. Smart No. 5.

Malmaison, 278 West George St, G2 4LL, ✆ (0141) 572 1000, *glasgow@malmaison.com, Fax (0141) 572 1002*, Ⓛ – |⧫|, ⇹ rm, ✆ ♿ – 🏛 25. ⓂⒸ ⒶⒺ ⓓ VISA CY
🎭 ***The Brasserie*** *(✆ (0141) 572 1001)* **:** Rest 14.50 (lunch) and a la carte 25.00/40.00 ♀ – ⊏ 12.75 – **64 rm** ✝135.00 – ✝✝135.00, 8 suites.
◆ Visually arresting former Masonic chapel. Comfortable, well-proportioned rooms seem effortlessly stylish with bold patterns and colours and thoughtful extra attentions. Informal Brasserie with French themed menu and Champagne bar.

Thistle Glasgow, 36 Cambridge St, G2 3HN, ✆ (0141) 332 3311, *moria.gilchrist@thistle.co.uk, Fax (0141) 332 4050,* – rm, – 1300. DY z
Gengis **:** **Rest** 10.50/18.00 and a la carte 16.50/23.50 **s.** – 12.95 – **297 rm** 210.00 – 210.00, 3 suites.
• Purpose-built hotel just north of the centre, geared to the corporate market. Smartly-appointed rooms and excellent inter-city road connections. Extensive meeting facilities. Grills meet tandoori in themed restaurant.

Glasgow Marriott, 500 Argyle St, Anderston, G3 8RR, ✆ (0141) 226 5577, *frontdesk.glasgow@marriotthotels.co.uk, Fax (0141) 221 9202,* – – 600. CZ a
Mediterrano **:** **Rest** - Mediterranean - 21.00 (dinner) and a la carte 22.00/30.00 **s.** – 14.95 – **300 rm** 145.00 – 185.00.
• Internationally owned city centre hotel with every necessary convenience for working travellers and an extensive lounge and café-bar. Upper floors have views of the city. Strong Mediterranean feel infuses restaurant.

ArtHouse, 129 Bath St, G2 2SZ, ✆ (0141) 221 6789, *info@arthousehotel.com, Fax (0141) 221 6777* – , rm, rest, – 70. DY v
Grill **:** **Rest** 12.50/16.50 and a la carte 24.40/33.40 **s.** – 14.50 – **60 rm** 115.00 – 125.00/155.00.
• Near Mackintosh's School of Art, an early 20C building decorated with a daring modern palette: striking colour schemes and lighting in the spacious, elegantly fitted rooms. Basement grill restaurant, plus seafood and Teppan-Yaki bar.

Millennium Glasgow, 40 George Sq, G2 1DS, ✆ (0141) 332 6711, *reservations.glasgow@mill-cop.com, Fax (0141) 332 4264* – – 60. DZ v
Brasserie on George Square **:** **Rest** *(closed lunch Sunday and Bank Holidays)* a la carte 18.50/34.70 **s.** – 15.75 – **112 rm** 185.00 – 185.00, 5 suites.
• Group-owned hotel aimed at business travellers, nicely located overlooking George Square and adjacent to main railway station. Contemporary interior in a Victorian building. Brasserie with airy, columned interior and views to Square.

Carlton George, 44 West George St, G2 1DH, ✆ (0141) 353 6373, *salesgeorge@carltonhotels.co.uk, Fax (0141) 353 6263* – . DZ a
closed 25-26 December and 1-2 January – ***Windows*** **:** **Rest** 16.00 (lunch) and a la carte 22.00/30.00 **s.** – 14.00 – **64 rm** 165.00/185.00 – 165.00/185.00.
• A quiet oasis away from the city bustle. Attractive tartan decorated bedrooms bestow warm tidings. Comfortable 7th floor business lounge. An overall traditional ambience. Ask for restaurant table with excellent view across city's rooftops.

Langs, 2 Port Dundas Pl, G2 3LD, ✆ (0141) 333 1500, *reservations@langshotel.co.uk, Fax (0141) 333 5700,* – , rest, . DY n
closed 24-26 December – ***Aurora*** **:** **Rest** (dinner only) a la carte 17.25/32.25 **s.** – ***Oshi*** **:** **Rest** - Asian - 13.50 (lunch) and a la carte 15.75/26.50 **s.** – 11.95 – **100 rm** 100.00/110.00 – 210.00.
• Opposite the Royal Concert Hall. Themed loft suites and stylish Japanese or Californian inspired rooms, all with CD players and computer game systems. Cool and contemporary. Scottish ingredients to fore at Aurora. Stunning water feature enhances Oshi.

Sherbrooke Castle, 11 Sherbrooke Ave, Pollokshields, G41 4PG, ✆ (0141) 427 4227, *mail@sherbrooke.co.uk, Fax (0141) 427 5685,* – , rest, – 300. AX r
Morrisons **:** **Rest** a la carte 15.00/35.00 – **16 rm** 75.00/140.00 – 95.00/160.00, 2 suites.
• Late 19C baronial Romanticism given free rein inside and out. The hall is richly furnished and imposing; rooms in the old castle have a comfortable country house refinement. Panelled Victorian dining room with open fire.

City Inn, Finnieston Quay, G3 8HN, ✆ (0141) 240 1002, *glasgow.reservations@cityinn.com, Fax (0141) 248 2754,* – – 50. CZ u
closed 26-28 December – ***City Café*** **:** **Rest** 14.95/16.50 and a la carte 18.25/34.15 – 12.50 – **164 rm** 129.00 – 129.00.
• Quayside location and views of the Clyde. Well priced hotel with a "business-friendly" ethos; neatly maintained modern rooms with sofas and en suite power showers. Restaurant fronts waterside terrace.

Jurys Inn, 80 Jamaica St, G1 4QE, ✆ (0141) 314 4800, *jurysinnglasgow@jurydoyle.com, Fax (0141) 314 4888* – , rm, – 100. DZ s
closed 24-26 December – **Rest** 19.50/24.00 (dinner) and a la carte 18.55/28.60 – 9.50 – **321 rm** 79.00/89.00 – 79.00/89.00.
• Attractive modern hotel on the riverside with excellent access to main shopping areas. Spacious interior with all day coffee bar. Good value, up-to-date, comfy bedrooms. Informal eatery serves breakfast as well as eclectic range of dinners.

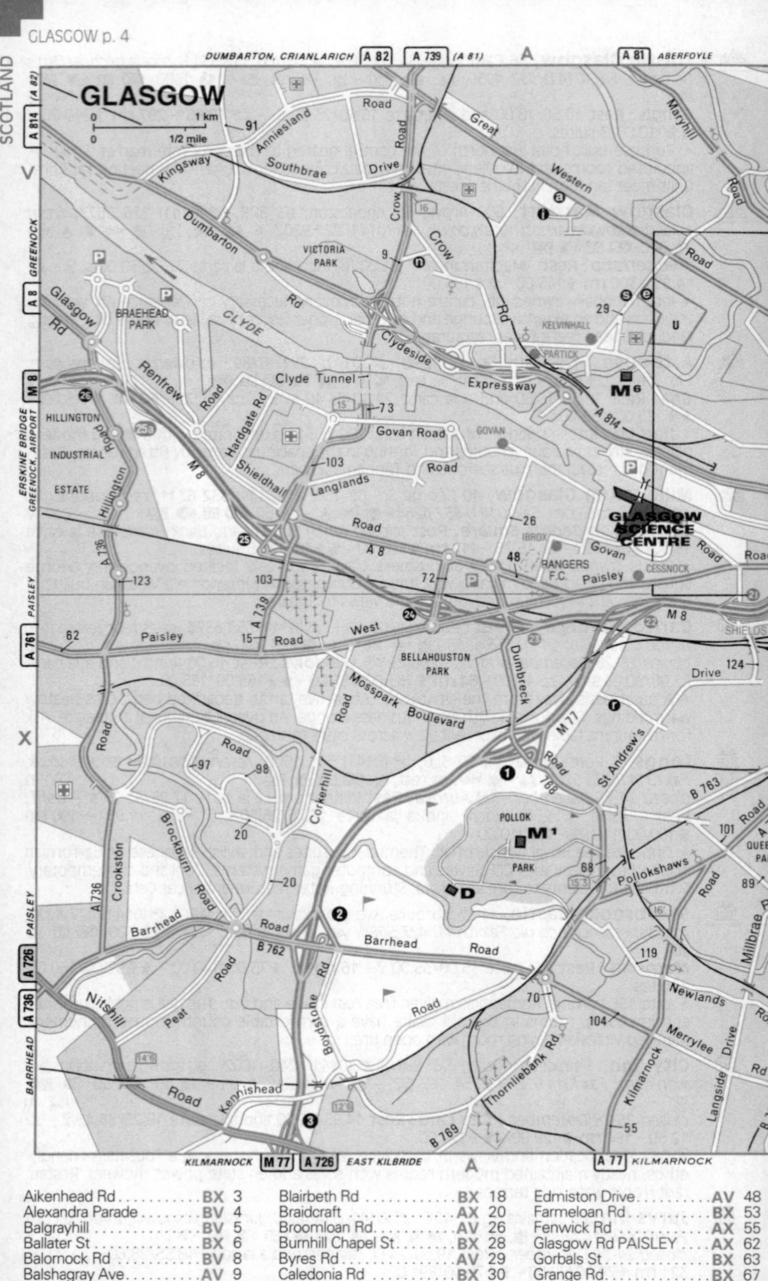
GLASGOW
0 1 km
0 1/2 mile
DUMBARTON, CRIANLARICH
A 82
A 739
(A 81)
A
A 81
ABERFOYLE
A 814
(A 82)
V
GREENOCK
A 8
M 8
ERSKINE BRIDGE
GREENOCK, AIRPORT
PAISLEY
A 761
X
PAISLEY
A 726
A 736
BARRHEAD
KILMARNOCK
M 77
A 726
EAST KILBRIDE
A
A 77
KILMARNOCK
Anniesland
Road
Southbrae
Drive
Kingsway
Great
Western
Road
Maryhill
Road
Dumbarton
Rd
Crow
Road
Crow
Rd
VICTORIA
PARK
Glasgow
Rd
BRAEHEAD
PARK
CLYDE
Clydeside
Expressway
KELVINHALL
PARTICK
A 814
Renfrew
Road
Clyde Tunnel
Hardgate Rd
Govan Road
GOVAN
HILLINGTON
INDUSTRIAL
ESTATE
Hillington
Road
A 736
M 8
Shieldhall
Langlands
Road
Road
A 8
GLASGOW
SCIENCE
CENTRE
IBROX
RANGERS
F.C.
Govan
Road
Paisley
CESSNOCK
Road
A 739
Paisley
Road
West
BELLAHOUSTON
PARK
Dumbreck
M 8
SHIELDS
Drive
Mosspark
Boulevard
Road
M 77
Road
St Andrew's
B 768
B 763
Road
Corkerhill
POLLOK
M1
PARK
D
Road
Brockburn
Road
Crookston
A736
Barrhead
Road
B 762
Barrhead
Road
Pollokshaws
Road
QUEEN'S
PARK
Millbrae
Road
Nitshill
Peat
Road
Boydstone
Rd
Road
Thornliebank Rd
Newlands
Merrylee
Drive
Rd
Kilmarnock
Langside
Road
Kennishead
Road
B 769

A 803 KIRKINTILLOCH
B
BISHOPBRIGGS
A 879
Balmore Road
SPRINGBURN PARK
Wallacewell Rd
B 765
Saughs Rd
M 80
(A 80) M 80 STIRLING
A 80
Broomfield Rd
Keppochhill Rd
Pinkston Rd
Springburn Road
Petershill Road
Royston Road
Road
V
EDINBURGH
B 765
Ring Road
Royston
See following pages
M 8
ALEXANDRA PARK
A 8
Edinburgh Road
A 8 (M 74, M 8)
Duke Street
Carntyne Road
Carntynehall Rd
Cardowan Rd
THE FORGE SHOPPING CENTRE
A 89
Gallowgate
London Road
B 763
GLASGOW GREEN
Shettleston Road
A 89
CELTIC F.C.
A 74 Rd
POL.
Tollcross
TOLLCROSS PARK
WEST ST.
Eglinton St.
A 74
Main St.
Dalmarnock
A 749
Springfield Road
London Rd
Victoria Rd
Road
Rutherglen Road
RICHMOND PARK
Glasgow Rd
A 730
A 749
Road
CARLISLE
A 74
M 74
Calder St.
Allison St.
A 728
CLYDE
Cambuslang Road
Cathcart
B 768
Main Street
Rd
Stonelaw Road
Mill Street
HAMPDEN PARK (M)
RUTHERGLEN
King's Park Avenue
B 762
X
Duke's Road
B 762
Glasgow Rd
A 724
Brownside Road
HAMILTON
KING'S PARK
B 766
Croftfoot Road
A 730
East Kilbride Road
EAST-KILBRIDE A 749
B

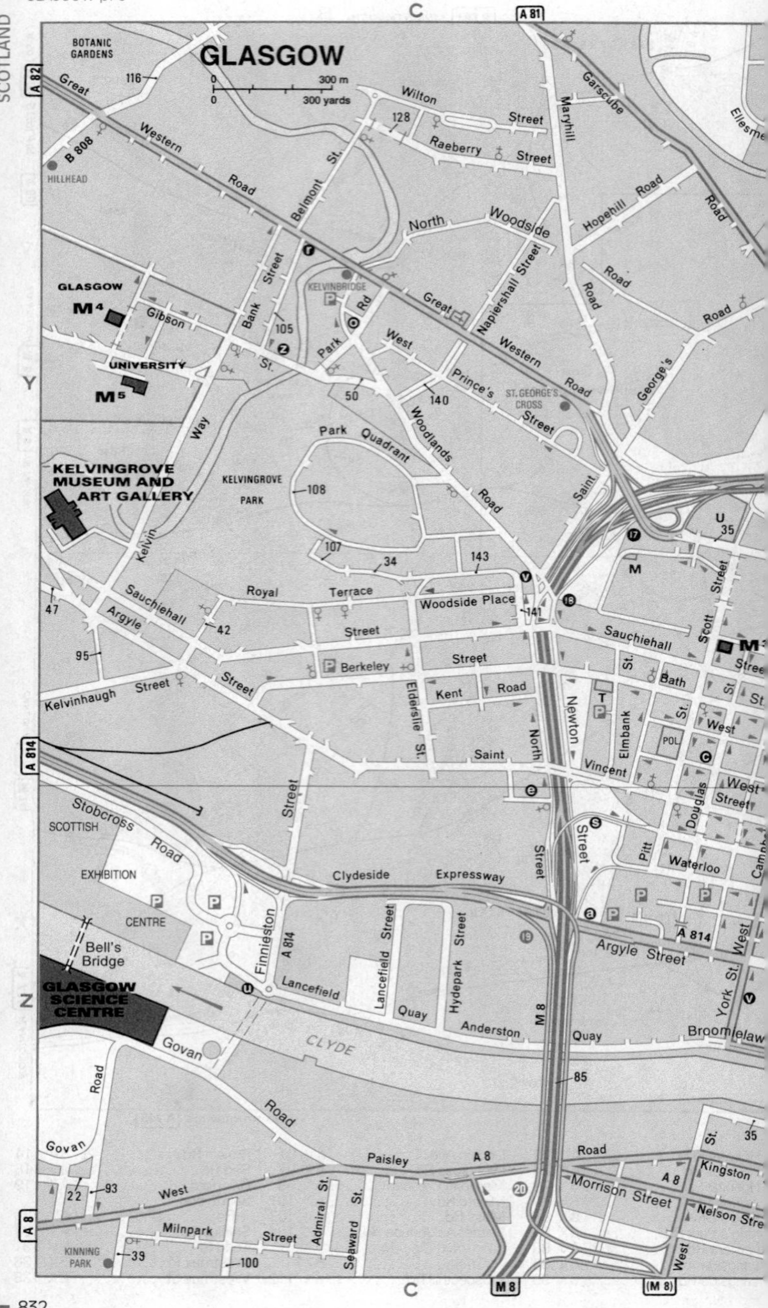
GLASGOW
0 300 m
0 300 yards
C
Y
Z
BOTANIC GARDENS
HILLHEAD
Great Western Road
B 808
A 82
A 81
Wilton Street
Raeberry Street
Belmont St.
Maryhill Road
Garscube Road
Hopehill Road
North Woodside Road
Napiershall Street
KELVINBRIDGE
Park Rd
Bank Street
GLASGOW UNIVERSITY
M 4
M 5
Gibson St.
University Way
West Prince's Street
St. George's Road
ST. GEORGE'S CROSS
Saint George's Road
Park Quadrant
Woodlands Road
KELVINGROVE MUSEUM AND ART GALLERY
KELVINGROVE PARK
Kelvin Way
Royal Terrace
Woodside Place
Sauchiehall Street
Argyle Street
Kelvinhaugh Street
Berkeley Street
Kent Road
Elderslie St.
Saint Vincent Street
North Street
Newton Street
Elmbank St.
Bath St.
Scott Street
West Regent St.
West George Street
Douglas St.
Pitt St.
Waterloo St.
POL
A 814
Stobcross Road
SCOTTISH EXHIBITION CENTRE
Clydeside Expressway
Finnieston Street
Lancefield Street
Lancefield Quay
Hydepark Street
Anderston Quay
Bell's Bridge
GLASGOW SCIENCE CENTRE
CLYDE
Broomielaw
York St.
Govan Road
Paisley Road West
A 8
Kingston St.
Morrison Street
Nelson Street
West St.
Milnpark Street
Admiral St.
Seaward St.
KINNING PARK
M 8
(M 8)

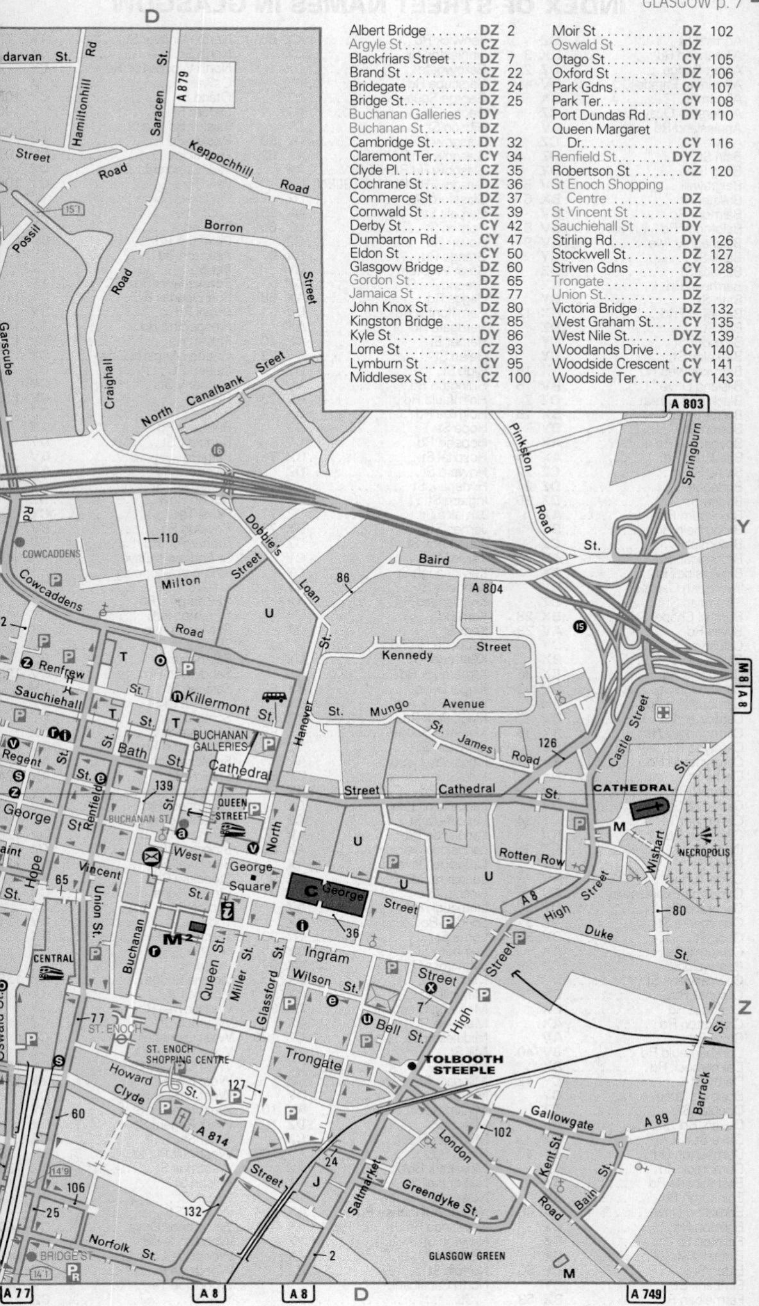
Albert Bridge DZ 2
Argyle St CZ
Blackfriars Street DZ 7
Brand St CZ 22
Bridegate DZ 24
Bridge St. DZ 25
Buchanan Galleries DY
Buchanan St. DZ
Cambridge St. DY 32
Claremont Ter. CY 34
Clyde Pl. CZ 35
Cochrane St DZ 36
Commerce St DZ 37
Cornwald St CZ 39
Derby St CY 42
Dumbarton Rd CY 47
Eldon St CY 50
Glasgow Bridge DZ 60
Gordon St DZ 65
Jamaica St DZ 77
John Knox St DZ 80
Kingston Bridge CZ 85
Kyle St DY 86
Lorne St CZ 93
Lymburn St CY 95
Middlesex St CZ 100
Moir St DZ 102
Oswald St DZ
Otago St CY 105
Oxford St DZ 106
Park Gdns CY 107
Park Ter. CY 108
Port Dundas Rd DY 110
Queen Margaret Dr. CY 116
Renfield St DYZ
Robertson St CZ 120
St Enoch Shopping Centre DZ
St Vincent St DZ
Sauchiehall St DY
Stirling Rd. DY 126
Stockwell St DZ 127
Striven Gdns CY 128
Trongate DZ
Union St. DZ
Victoria Bridge DZ 132
West Graham St. CY 135
West Nile St. DYZ 139
Woodlands Drive CY 140
Woodside Crescent CY 141
Woodside Ter. CY 143
D
Y
Z
A 879
A 803
A 804
A 8
M 8
A 77
A 814
A 89
A 749
Saracen St.
Hamiltonhill Rd
Keppochhill Road
Possil Road
Borron Street
Craighall Road
Garscube Rd
North Canalbank Street
Pinkston Road
Springburn
Baird St.
Dobbie's Loan
Milton Street
Cowcaddens Road
COWCADDENS
Kennedy Street
St. Mungo Avenue
St. James Road
Castle Street
CATHEDRAL
Cathedral Street
Renfrew St.
Sauchiehall St.
Killermont St.
BUCHANAN GALLERIES
Bath St.
Regent St.
Hanover St.
North
QUEEN STREET
BUCHANAN ST
George St.
West George St.
George Square
Vincent St.
Hope St.
Union St.
Buchanan
Queen St.
Miller St.
Glassford St.
Ingram Street
Wilson St.
Bell St.
High Street
Rotten Row
Wishart
NECROPOLIS
Duke St.
CENTRAL
ST. ENOCH
ST. ENOCH SHOPPING CENTRE
Trongate
TOLBOOTH STEEPLE
Howard St.
Clyde Street
Gallowgate
Barrack St.
Saltmarket
London Road
Kent St.
Bain St.
Greendyke St.
Norfolk St.
BRIDGE ST
GLASGOW GREEN

INDEX OF STREET NAMES IN GLASGOW

Bewley's, 110 Bath St, G2 2EN, (0141) 353 0800, *gla@bewleyshotels.com, Fax (0141) 353 0900* – rm, rest, – DY i
closed 25-27 December – ***Loop*** **: Rest** a la carte 18.00/25.00 – 6.95 – **103 rm** 69.00 – 69.00/99.00.
◆ A well-run group hotel, relaxed but professional in approach, in the middle of Glasgow's shopping streets. Upper rooms boast rooftop views and duplex apartments. People-watch from glass-walled eatery.

Tulip Inn, 80 Ballater St, G5 0TW, (0141) 429 4233, *info@tulipinnglasgow.co.uk, Fax (0141) 429 4244* – , rest, – 180. BX a
Bibo Bar and Bistro **: Rest** (dinner only) a la carte 18.45/21.85 – 7.95 – **114 rm** 59.50/85.00 – 59.50/85.00.
◆ Sensibly priced hotel appealing to cost-conscious business travellers. Good access to motorway and city centre. Bedrooms have working space and most modern conveniences. Informal, bright eatery serves a varied menu.

Express by Holiday Inn without rest., Theatreland, 165 West Nile St, G1 2RL, (0141) 331 6800, *express@higlasgow.com, Fax (0141) 331 6828* – . DY o
closed 25-26 December – **118 rm** 75.00/89.00 – 75.00/89.00.
◆ Modern accommodation - simple and well arranged with adequate amenities. Equally suitable for business travel or leisure tourism.

Park House, 13 Victoria Park Gardens South, G11 7BX, (0141) 339 1559, *mail@parkhouseglasgow.co.uk, Fax (0141) 576 0915* – . AV n
closed 2 weeks spring, Christmas and New Year – **Rest** (by arrangement) 25.00 – **3 rm** 35.00/60.00 – 60.00/80.00.
◆ An extensive, smartly kept suburban house retaining much of its Victorian character. Comfortable, classically stylish bedrooms combine period furniture with CD systems. Dining room with neatly set 19C ambience.

The Town House without rest., 4 Hughenden Terrace, G12 9XR, (0141) 357 0862, *hospitality@thetownhouseglasgow.com, Fax (0141) 339 9605* – . AV i
10 rm 60.00 – 72.00.
◆ Elegant, personally run town house with fine Victorian plasterwork: spacious, pleasantly decorated rooms and an inviting firelit lounge. Hearty breakfasts.

Camerons (at Hilton Glasgow H.), 1 William St, G3 8HT, (0141) 204 5511, *Fax (0141) 204 5004* – CZ s
closed Saturday lunch, Sunday and Bank Holidays – **Rest** 19.50 (lunch) and dinner a la carte 29.85/44.85.
◆ Carefully prepared and full-flavoured modern cuisine with strong Scottish character. Very formal, neo-classical styling and smart staff have advanced its local reputation.

Buttery, 652 Argyle St, G3 8UF, (0141) 221 8188, *ia.fleming@btopenworld.com, Fax (0141) 204 4639* – CZ e
closed first week January, Sunday, Monday and Saturday lunch – **Rest** 38.00 and lunch a la carte 24.00/27.50.
◆ Established, comfortable restaurant away from the bright lights; red velour and ageing bric-a-brac reveal its past as a pub. Ambitiously composed modern Scottish repertoire.

étain, The Glass House, Springfield Court, G1 3JN, (0141) 225 5630, *etain@conran.com, Fax (0141) 225 5640* – DZ r
closed 25 December, 1 January, Saturday lunch and Sunday dinner – **Rest** 29.00/32.00.
◆ Comfortable, contemporary restaurant in unusual glass extension to Princes Square Centre. Well-sourced Scottish ingredients prepared in a modern, interesting way.

Rococo, 202 West George St, G2 2NR, (0141) 221 5004, *info@rococoglasgow.co.uk, Fax (0141) 221 5006* – DYZ z
closed 26 December and 1 January – **Rest** 18.00/36.50 and lunch a la carte 32.45/42.75.
◆ In style, more like studied avant-garde: stark, white-walled cellar with vibrant modern art and high-backed leather chairs. Accomplished, fully flavoured contemporary menu.

Lux, 1051 Great Western Rd, G12 0XP, (0141) 576 7576, *luxstazione@btconnect.com, Fax (0141) 576 0162* – AV o
closed 25-26 December, 1-2 January and Sunday – **Rest** (dinner only) 29.50/33.50.
◆ 19C railway station converted with clean-lined elegance: dark wood, subtle lighting and vivid blue banquettes. Fine service and flavourful, well-prepared modern menus.

Brian Maule at Chardon d'Or, 176 West Regent St, G2 4RL, (0141) 248 3801, *info@brianmaule.com, Fax (0141) 248 3901* – CY i
closed 2 weeks January, 2 weeks summer, 25-26 December, 1-2 January, Saturday lunch, Sunday and Bank Holidays – **Rest** 15.50/18.50 (lunch) and a la carte 29.00/40.00.
◆ Large pillared Georgian building. Airy interior with ornate carved ceiling and hung with modern art. Modern dishes with fine Scottish produce; substantial wine list.

SCOTLAND

XX **Gamba,** 225a West George St, G2 2ND, ✆ (0141) 572 0899, *info@gamba.co.uk* DZ
Fax (0141) 572 0896 – ⋟⋞. MO AE VISA
closed 25-26 December, 1-2 January and Sunday – **Rest** - Seafood - 15.95/18.95 (lunch) and a la carte 18.00/32.85.
◆ Seafood specialists: an enterprising diversity of influences and well-priced lunches. Compact, brightly decorated basement in hot terracotta with a pleasant cosy bar.

XX **La Parmigiana,** 447 Great Western Rd, Kelvinbridge, G12 8HH, ✆ (0141) 334 0686 CY
s.giovanazzi@btclick.com, Fax (0141) 357 5595 – ▤. MO AE ⓓ VISA
closed 25-26 December, 1-2 January and Sunday – **Rest** - Italian - 10.50 (lunch) and a la carte 24.20/36.10 s.
◆ Compact, pleasantly decorated traditional eatery with a lively atmosphere and good local reputation. Obliging, professional service and a sound, authentic Italian repertoire.

XX **Papingo,** 104 Bath St, G2 2EN, ✆ (0141) 332 6678, *info@papingo.co.uk* DY
Fax (0141) 332 6549 – MO AE VISA
closed 25-26 December, 1-2 January and Sunday lunch – **Rest** 10.95 (lunch) and a la carte 23.85/32.85 ♀.
◆ Parrot motifs recur everywhere, even on the door handles! Well-spaced tables and mirrored walls add a sense of space to the basement. A free-ranging fusion style prevails.

XX **Room,** 1 Devonshire Gardens, G12 0UX, ✆ (0141) 341 0000, *glasgow.reservations@roomrestaurants.com* – ⋟⋞ ⇔ 16. MO AE ⓓ VISA AV
Rest 12.75/19.00 and a la carte approx 28.00 ♀.
◆ Victorian façade hides trendy interior with cool, comfy bar and stylish eating area with bold colour schemes and modern art. Good value dishes are exciting and original.

XX **Zinc Bar and Grill,** Princes Sq, G1 3JN, ✆ (0141) 225 5620, *zincglasgow@conran.com* DZ
Fax (0141) 225 5640 – |‡| ⋟⋞ ▤. MO AE ⓓ VISA
closed 25 December, 1 January and Sunday dinner – **Rest** a la carte 16.95/29.00 ♀.
◆ Contemporary dining on second floor atrium of Princes Square Centre. Stylish décor and tableware. Modern menu offering popular dishes; good value lunches.

XX **Ho Wong,** 82 York St, G2 8LE, ✆ (0141) 221 3550, *ho.wong@amserve.com* CZ
Fax (0141) 248 5330 – ▤. MO AE ⓓ VISA
closed Sunday lunch – **Rest** - Chinese (Peking) - 9.50/38.00 (dinner) and a la carte 22.50/36.00.
◆ In an up-and-coming part of town, a long-established restaurant with a modern style. Authentic Chinese cuisine with the emphasis on Peking dishes.

XX **Amber Regent,** 50 West Regent St, G2 2QZ, ✆ (0141) 331 1655, *Fax (0141) 353 3398* – ▤. MO AE ⓓ VISA DY
closed Chinese New Year and Sunday – **Rest** - Chinese - 9.95/38.95 and a la carte 22.25/42.90.
◆ Traditional Chinese dishes served by conscientious staff. Comfy, personally managed restaurant in a 19C office building in the heart of the city. Good value lunch.

XX **Bouzy Rouge Seafood and Grill,** 71 Renfield St, G2 1LP, ✆ (0141) 333 9725 DY
info@seafoodandgrill.co.uk, Fax (0141) 354 0453 – MO AE VISA
closed 25 December and 1 January – **Rest** 12.95 (lunch) and a la carte 22.85/29.85.
◆ Wonderfully atmospheric former bank with original tiled interior reflecting a superb Moorish style. Fresh Scottish seafood and fish with carefully sourced Aberdeen Angus beef.

XX **Shish Mahal,** 60-68 Park Rd, G4 9JF, ✆ (0141) 3398256, *reservations@shishmahal.co.uk* CY
Fax (0141) 572 0800 – ▤. MO AE VISA
Rest - Indian - 5.50/11.95 and a la carte 12.85/22.40.
◆ Tandoori specialities in a varied pan-Indian menu, attentive service and an evocative modern interior of etched glass, oak and Moorish tiles have won city-wide recognition.

X **The Ubiquitous Chip,** 12 Ashton Lane, G12 8SJ, off Byres Rd ✆ (0141) 334 5007 AV
mail@ubiquitouschip.co.uk, Fax (0141) 337 1302 – ▤. MO AE ⓓ VISA
closed 25 December and 1 January – **Rest** 22.80/38.95 and a la carte 17.15/28.60 ♀.
◆ A long standing favourite, "The Chip" mixes Scottish and fusion styles. Well known for its glass-roofed courtyard, with a more formal but equally lively warehouse interior.

X **Stravaigin,** 28 Gibson St, (basement), G12 8NX, ✆ (0141) 334 2665, *stravaigin@btinternet.com, Fax (0141) 334 4099* – ⋟⋞ ▤. MO AE ⓓ VISA CY
closed 25-26 December, 1 January and Monday – **Rest** (dinner only and lunch Friday-Sunday) a la carte 17.25/27.85 ♀.
◆ Basement restaurant with bright murals. A refined instinct for genuinely global cuisine produces surprising but well-prepared combinations - ask about pre-theatre menus.

Stravaigin 2, 8 Ruthven Lane, G12 9BG, off Byres Rd, (0141) 334 7165, *stravaigin@btinternet.com, Fax (0141) 357 4785* – . AV s
closed 25-26 December dinner and 1 January – **Rest** 12.95 (lunch) and a la carte 18.35/32.35.
◆ Lilac painted cottage tucked away in an alley off Byres Road. Simple, unfussy, modern bistro-style interior. Contemporary menu offering eclectic range of original dishes.

Cafe Ostra, The Italian Centre, 15 John St, G1 1HP, (0141) 552 4433, *info@cafeostra.com, Fax (0141) 552 1500,* – . DZ i
closed 25-26 December and 1-2 January – **Rest** - Seafood - a la carte 16.85/28.85.
◆ City centre setting. The large outside terrace leads into a smart art deco interior, set on two levels. Smoothly run service. Tasty seafood oriented dishes.

The Dhabba, 44 Candleriggs, G1 1LE, (0141) 553 1249, *info@thedhabba.com, Fax (0141) 553 1730* – . DZ u
closed 25 December and 1 January – **Rest** - North Indian - 9.95 (lunch) and a la carte 15.00/30.00.
◆ In the heart of the Merchant City, this large, modern restaurant boasts bold colours and huge wall photos. Concentrates on authentic, accomplished North Indian cooking.

Mao, 84 Brunswick St, G1 1ZZ, (0141) 564 5161, *glasgow@cafemao.com, Fax (0141) 564 5163* – . DZ e
closed 24-26 December – **Rest** - South East Asian - a la carte 10.00/16.50 **s.**
◆ Eatery located on two floors, decorated in bright, funky style with vivid, modern colours; centrally located, buzzy atmosphere. Thoroughly tasty South East Asian food.

Bouzy Rouge, 111 West Regent St, G2 2RU, (0141) 221 8804, *info@bouzyrouge.co.uk, Fax (0141) 221 6941* – . DY s
closed 26 December and 1 January – **Rest** a la carte 18.40/28.40.
◆ Informal dining in a popular basement restaurant serving modern, Mediterranean-inspired cuisine: candlelit booths and vivid burgundy interior with elaborate metalwork.

Babbity Bowster, 16-18 Blackfriars St, G1 1PE, (0141) 552 5055, *fraser@babbity.com, Fax (0141) 552 7774,* – . DZ x
closed 25 December – **Rest** a la carte 12.95/25.85.
◆ Well regarded pub of Georgian origins with columned façade. Paradoxically simple ambience: gingham-clothed tables, hearty Scottish dishes, slightly more formal in evenings.

at Glasgow Airport *(Renfrewshire) West : 8 m. by M 8 - AV -* ✉ *Paisley.*

Ramada, Marchburn Drive, PA3 2SJ, (0141) 840 2200, *sales.glasgowairport@ramadajarvis.co.uk, Fax (0141) 889 6830* – , rest, – 30.
Bagio **: Rest** - Mediterranean - a la carte 19.95/26.40 **s.** – 11.95 – **108 rm** 85.00 – 85.00.
◆ Within walking distance of the terminal building and with facilities for long-term parking; modern style throughout, with well-equipped, generously proportioned bedrooms. Casual Mediterranean eatery: emphasis on pizzas and pastas.

Express by Holiday Inn, St Andrews Drive, PA3 2TJ, (0141) 842 1100, *info@hiex-glasgow.com, Fax (0141) 842 1122* – , rest, – 75.
Rest (dinner only) a la carte 16.00/21.50 – **143 rm** 99.00/109.00 – 99.00/109.00.
◆ Ideal for both business travellers and families. Spacious, carefully designed, bright and modern bedrooms with plenty of work space. Complimentary continental breakfast. Traditional and busy buffet-style restaurant.

GLASGOW AIRPORT *Renfrewshire* 501 502 G 16 – *see Glasgow.*

GLENBORRODALE *Highland* 501 C 13 – ✉ *Acharacle.*
Edinburgh 190 – Inverness 116 – Oban 106.

Feorag House, PH36 4JP, (01972) 500248, *admin@feorag.co.uk, Fax (01972) 500285,* ≤ Loch Sunart, , – .
3 rm (dinner included) 115.00 – 150.00.
◆ Modern house in superb location overlooking Loch Sunart. Regular wildlife visitors in the grounds. Sitting room with open fire; comfortable, well-kept bedrooms.

GLENDEVON *Perth and Kinross* 501 I/J 15.
Edinburgh 37 – Perth 26 – Stirling 19.

The Tormaukin Country Inn with rm, FK14 7JY, (01259) 781252, *enquiries@tormaukin.co.uk, Fax (01259) 781526,* , rest, .
closed 1 week January and 25 December – **Rest** a la carte 20.00/45.00 – **12 rm** 60.00 – 90.00.
◆ Extended 18C drovers' inn tucked away in this picturesque glen. Traditional Scottish fare is served in the atmospheric bar or in the cosy restaurant. Comfortable bedrooms.

GLENLIVET *Moray* 501 J 11 – ✉ *Ballindalloch.*
Edinburgh 180 – Aberdeen 59 – Elgin 27 – Inverness 49.

Minmore House, AB37 9DB, South : ¾ m. on Glenlivet Distillery rd (01807 590378, *minmorehouse@ukonline.co.uk, Fax (01807) 590472*, ←, – P. MC AE VISA
closed 1-28 December – **Rest** (booking essential to non-residents) (set menu only) 35.00/37.50 – **10 rm** 55.00/70.00 – 90.00/160.00.
◆ Country house built for the original owner of Glenlivet Distillery on Glenlivet estate. Oak panelled bar with over 105 malts and open log fire. Light, airy, spacious rooms. Traditional dining room with fine views; set menus using local ingredients.

GLENROTHES *Fife* 501 K 15 *Scotland G. – pop. 38 679.*
Env. : *Falkland★ (Village★, Palace of Falkland★ AC, Gardens★ AC) N : 5½ m. by A 92 and A 912.*
18 *Thornton, Station Rd (01592) 771173* – 18 *Golf Course Rd (01592) 758686* – 18 *Balbirnie Park, Markinch (01592) 612095* – 9 *Auchterderran, Woodend Rd, Cardenden (01592) 721579* – 9 *Leslie, Balsillie Laws (01592) 620040.*
Edinburgh 33 – Dundee 25 – Stirling 36.

Balbirnie House, Markinch, KY7 6NE, Northeast : 1 ¾ m. by A 911 and A 92 on B 9130 (01592) 610066, *info@balbirnie.co.uk, Fax (01592) 610529*, 18, – rest, P – 250. MC AE VISA
Orangery : Rest 14.50/32.50 and lunch a la carte approx 15.00/18.95 – **28 rm** 130.00/160.00 – 250.00, 2 suites.
◆ Highly imposing part Georgian mansion in Capability Brown-styled grounds. Several lounges and library bar with period style and individually furnished country house rooms. Glass-roofed restaurant; friendly service from kilted staff.

Express by Holiday Inn without rest., Leslie Roundabout, Leslie Rd, KY7 3EP, West 2 m. on A 911 (0800) 434040, *ebhi-glenrothes@btconnect.com, Fax (01592) 743377* – P – 30. MC AE VISA.
49 rm 62.00 – 62.00.
◆ Modern lodge accommodation in the heart of Fife within close proximity of Dundee, Perth and St. Andrews. Ideal for business travellers.

GLENSBURGH *Falkirk* – *see Falkirk.*

GRANTOWN-ON-SPEY *Highland* 501 J 12 – *pop. 2 166.*
18 *Golf Course Rd (01479) 872079* – 9 *Abernethy, Nethy Bridge (01479) 821305.*
54 High St (0845) 2255121 (April-October).
Edinburgh 143 – Inverness 34 – Perth 99.

Culdearn House, Woodlands Terrace, PH26 3JU, (01479) 872106, *enquiries@culdearn.com, Fax (01479) 873641*, – P. MC VISA.
closed December-January – **Rest** (booking essential to non-residents) (dinner only) 30.00 s. – **7 rm** (dinner included) 85.00 – 170.00.
◆ Personally run Victorian granite stone hotel with wood panelling and fine moulded ceilings. Spacious, cream and pink lounge. Very tastefully furnished, luxurious bedrooms. Formally attired dining room with pink linen and chintz drapes.

Ravenscourt House, Seafield Ave, PH26 3JG, (01479) 872286, *Fax (01479) 873260*, – P. MC VISA.
Rest (residents only) (dinner only) a la carte 18.70/23.75 **s.** – **8 rm** 38.00/60.00 – 82.00/98.00.
◆ 19C former manse. Solid stone exterior. Interiors designed to enhance original house. Oil and watercolours enrich lounges, as do log fires in winter. Elegantly smart rooms.

at Dulnain Bridge *Southwest : 3 m. by A 95 on A 938* – ✉ *Grantown-on-Spey.*

Muckrach Lodge, PH26 3LY, West : ½ m. on A 938 (01479) 851257, *info@muckrach.co.uk, Fax (01479) 851325*, ←, – P – 35. MC AE VISA
closed 24-26 December, 2-18 January and Monday and Tuesday in winter – ***Finlarig*** : Rest (dinner only) 35.00 **s.** – ***Conservatory Bistro*** : Rest 15.50/21.00 (lunch) and dinner a la carte 18.20/27.50 **s.** – **12 rm** 65.00/150.00 – 130.00/150.00, 2 suites.
◆ 19C country house whose name translates as "haunt of the wild boar". Log fires and soft sofas in lounges. Bedrooms with fresh flowers and old books. Formal dining in Finlaig from a traditional menu. Less formal Gingham-clad tables in the Conservatory bistro.

Auchendean Lodge, PH26 3LU, South : 1 m. on A 95 ☎ (01479) 851347, *hotel@auchendean.com,* ≤ Spey Valley and Cairngorms, ⌂ – ⇔ rest, P. MC VISA
Easter-October – **Rest** (dinner only) 33.00 s. – **5 rm** ☕ ★53.00/65.00 – ★★122.00.
◆ Early 20C lodge with Arts and Crafts style architecture. Soaring views over Spey Valley to Cairngorms. Log-fired drawing room. Comfortable rooms with elegant pine furniture. Enviably located restaurant facing the mountains.

GREENOCK *Inverclyde* 501 F 16 – *pop. 45 467.*
18, 9 *Forsyth St* ☎ *(01475) 720793.*
Edinburgh 70 – Ayr 48 – Glasgow 24.

Express by Holiday Inn without rest., Cartsburn, PA15 4RT, East : ¾ m. off A 8 ☎ (01475) 786666, *greenock@expressbyholidayinn.net, Fax (01475) 786777* – ⇔ ♿ P – 80. MC AE VISA
71 rm ★39.95/69.95 – ★★39.95/69.95.
◆ Large, purpose-built hotel aimed at business traveller. Reception with multi-purpose bar and breakfast room. Light snacks in evening. Spacious, modern, lodge style rooms.

GRIMSAY *Western Isles (Outer Hebrides)* 501 Y 11 – *see Uist (Isles of).*

GRULINE *Argyll and Bute – see Mull (Isle of).*

GULLANE *East Lothian* 501 L 15 *Scotland G. – pop. 2 172.*
Env. : *Dirleton★ (Castle★) NE : 2 m. by A 198.*
Edinburgh 19 – North Berwick 5.

Greywalls , Duncur Rd, Muirfield, EH31 2EG, ☎ (01620) 842144, *hotel@greywalls.co.uk, Fax (01620) 842241,* ≤ Gardens and Muirfield golf course, ⌂, – ⇔ rest, P – 30. MC AE VISA
April-October – **Rest** (booking essential to non-residents) (dinner only) 45.00 – **23 rm** ☕ ★135.00/180.00 – ★★270.00.
◆ Crescent shaped Edwardian country house by Lutyens; formal gardens by Jekyll. Superb views of Muirfield golf course. Beautifully kept sitting room. Charming, stylish rooms. Inviting dining room with warm, pretty country house style, view of golf course.

Faussetthill House without rest., Main St, EH31 2DR, ☎ (01620) 842396, *faussetthill@talk21.com, Fax (01620) 842396,* ⌂ – ⇔ P. MC VISA.
March-October – **3 rm** ☕ ★48.00/50.00 – ★★68.00/72.00.
◆ Large Edwardian house in corner of town. Ideally located for local golf courses. Spacious lounge and welcoming breakfast room. Very comfortably appointed bedrooms.

Hopefield House without rest., Main St, EH31 2DP, ☎ (01620) 842191, *info@hopefieldhouse.co.uk, Fax (01620) 842191,* ⌂ – ⇔ P.
April-September – **3 rm** ☕ ★45.00/50.00 – ★★56.00.
◆ Detached Victorian house on main road with large, attractive rear garden. Communal breakfast room. Well-decorated lounge. Comfortable bedrooms have thoughtful touches.

HADDINGTON *East Lothian* 501 L 16 *Scotland G. – pop. 8 851.*
See : *Town★ - High Street★.*
Env. : *Lennoxlove★ AC, S : 1 m – Gifford★, SE : 5 m. by B 6369.*
Exc. : *Tantallon Castle★★ (clifftop site★★★) AC, NE : 12 m. by A 1 and A 198 – Northern foothills of the Lammermuir Hills★★, S : 14 m. by A 6137 and B 6368 – Stenton★, E : 7 m.*
18 *Amisfield Park* ☎ *(01620) 823627.*
Edinburgh 17 – Hawick 53 – Newcastle upon Tyne 101.

Brown's, 1 West Rd, EH41 3RD, ☎ (01620) 822254, *info@browns-hotel.com, Fax (01620) 822254,* ⌂ – ⇔ rest, P. MC AE VISA.
Rest (dinner only and Sunday lunch) 30.50 – **5 rm** ☕ ★65.00/70.00 – ★★70.00/100.00.
◆ Personally run and traditionally styled Georgian house, full of antiques. Drawing room and large bedrooms decorated along country house lines. Small restaurant.

Bonars, Poldrate, Tyne House, EH41 4DA, South : ¼ m. on B 6368 ☎ (01620) 822100, *dabonar@aol.com* – ⇔. MC VISA
closed 26 December, 1 January and Monday – **Rest** a la carte 18.35/32.65 ♀.
◆ In charming surroundings adjacent to burn and 18C mill. Interior in warm Mediterranean style. Regularly changing menus of elaborate dishes using Scottish produce.

HARRIS (Isle of) *Western Isles (Outer Hebrides)* 501 Z 10 – *see Lewis and Harris (Isle of).*

HAWICK *Borders* 501 502 L 17 *Scotland G. – pop. 14 573.*
Exc. : *Jedburgh★ - Abbey★★, Mary Queen of Scots Visitor Centre★, NE : 11 m. by A 698 and B 6358 – Bowhill★★, N : 15 m. by A 7, B 7009 and B 7039.*
Edinburgh 51 – Galashiels 18 – Jedburgh 12.

Glenteviot Park, Hassendeanburn, TD9 8RU, Northeast : 3 ¾ m. by A 698 taking first left after Trowmill Woollen Mill on Hassendean Burn rd (01450) 870660, *info@glenteviotpark.com, Fax (01450) 870154,* P. MO AE VISA
Rest (dinner only) (residents only) 29.00 **s.** – **5 rm** 65.00/75.00 – 95.00/125.00.
◆ Imposing hotel idyllically sited overlooking River Teviot and surrounding hills. Rustic bar/lounge, sauna and snooker room. Individually furnished, well-equipped rooms. Cosy dining room overlooking the garden.

INNERLEITHEN *Borders* 501 502 K 17 – *pop. 2 586 – ✉ Peebles.*
Edinburgh 31 – Dumfries 57 – Glasgow 60.

Caddon View without rest., 14 Pirn Rd, EH44 6HH, (01896) 830208, *contact-us@caddonview.co.uk, Fax (01896) 831807,* P. MO VISA.
8 rm 47.00/75.00 – 110.00.
◆ Personally run Victorian house with charming gardens near the centre of the village. Cosy lounge with log fire. Individually decorated, well-furnished bedrooms.

INVERGARRY *Highland* 501 F 12 *Scotland G. – ✉ Inverness.*
Env. : *The Great Glen★.*
Edinburgh 159 – Fort William 25 – Inverness 43 – Kyle of Lochalsh 50.

Glengarry Castle, PH35 4HW, on A 82 (01809) 501254, *castle@glengarry.net Fax (01809) 501207,* P. MO VISA
17 March-12 November – **Rest** (light lunch Monday-Saturday)/dinner 28.00 **s.** ♀ – **26 rm** 58.00/85.00 – 146.00/160.00.
◆ Victorian castle in rural location on shores of Loch Oich, surrounded by parkland and gardens. Warm country house feel throughout and many bedrooms retain original fittings. Dining room shares the warm, country house style of the hotel.

INVERKEILOR *Angus* 501 M 14 – *✉ Arbroath.*
Edinburgh 85 – Aberdeen 32 – Dundee 22.

Gordon's with rm, 32 Main St, DD11 5RN, (01241) 830364, *gordonsrest@aol.com Fax (01241) 830364* – P. MO VISA.
closed 2 weeks January – **Rest** *(closed Monday and Sunday dinner to non-residents)* (booking essential) 22.00/37.00 – **3 rm** 60.00 – 80.00/90.00.
◆ Family owned restaurant in small village. Welcoming atmosphere, beams, open fires and rugs on the wood floors. Classic cooking with modern twists. Pleasant, pine fitted rooms.

INVERNESS *Highland* 501 H 11 *Scotland G. – pop. 40 949.*
See : *Town★ – Museum and Art Gallery★* Y **M.**
Exc. : *Loch Ness★★, SW : by A 82* Z *– Clava Cairns★, E : 9 m. by Culcabock Rd, B 9006 and B 851* Z *– Cawdor Castle★* **AC**, *NE : 14 m. by A 96 and B 9090* Y.
Culcabock Rd (01463) 239882 Z *– Torvean, Glenurquhart Rd (01463) 711434.*
Inverness Airport, Dalcross : (01667) 464000, NE : 8 m. by A 96 Y.
Castle Wynd (0845) 2255121 Y, *invernesstic@host.co.uk.*
Edinburgh 156 – Aberdeen 107 – Dundee 134.

Plan opposite

Glenmoriston Town House, 20 Ness Bank, IV2 4SF, (01463) 223777, *reception@glenmoristontownhouse.com, Fax (01463) 712378* – P. – 80. MO AE VISA. Z x
Rest (see ***Abstract*** below) – **30 rm** 95.00/115.00 – 130.00/170.00.
◆ Privately owned, stylish and contemporary town house. Bedrooms are modern and individual, those on the front enjoy river views, those at the rear are quieter.

Glen Mhor, 9-12 Ness Bank, IV2 4SG, (01463) 234308, *glenmhor@btconnect.com, Fax (01463) 713170* – rm, P. MO AE VISA. Z r
closed 30 December-4 January – ***Nico's :*** **Rest** a la carte 16.35/28.35 ♀ – **41 rm** 59.00/79.00 – 90.00/120.00, 1 suite.
◆ Personally run stone-built house. Bedrooms are traditionally decorated with additional rooms in adjacent riverside properties; those in main house more characterful. Nico's has the feel of a Victorian inn.

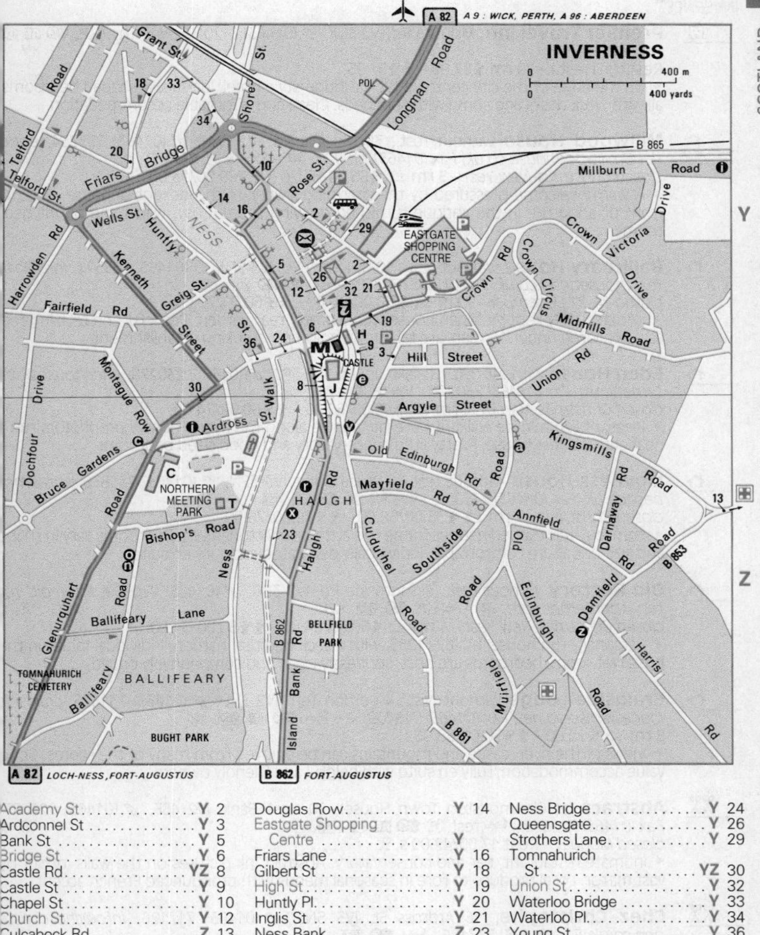

Academy St	Y 2	Douglas Row	Y 14	Ness Bridge	Y 24		
Ardconnel St	Y 3	Eastgate Shopping Centre	Y	Queensgate	Y 26		
Bank St	Y 5	Friars Lane	Y 16	Strothers Lane	Y 29		
Bridge St	Y 6	Gilbert St	Y 18	Tomnahurich St	YZ 30		
Castle Rd	YZ 8	High St	Y 19	Union St	Y 32		
Castle St	Y 9	Huntly Pl	Y 20	Waterloo Bridge	Y 33		
Chapel St	Y 10	Inglis St	Y 21	Waterloo Pl	Y 34		
Church St	Y 12	Ness Bank	Z 23	Young St	Y 36		
Culcabock Rd	Z 13						

Glendruidh House ⛰, Old Edinburgh Rd South, IV2 6AR, Southeast : 2 m. ✆ (01463) 226499, *michael@cozzee-nessie-bed.co.uk, Fax (01463) 710745*, – ⇔ P. MO AE O VISA.
closed 24-26 December – **Rest** (booking essential) (residents only) (dinner only) 33.00 ♀ – **5 rm** ☕ ♂69.00/110.00 – ♂♂99.00/139.00.
◆ Peaceful countryside setting with pretty garden. Some parts of the house over 200 years old; unusual circular shaped drawing room. Additional bedrooms in a modern annexe.

Express by Holiday Inn without rest., Stoneyfield, IV2 7PA, East : 1½ m. by A 865 on A 96 (eastbound carriageway) ✆ (01463) 732700, *managerinverness@expressholidayinn.co.uk, Fax (01463) 732732* – ⇔ ♿ P – 30. MO AE O VISA
94 rm ♂79.00/83.00 – ♂♂79.00/83.00.
◆ Purpose-built lodge-style accommodation at an out-of-town retail park. Fully equipped bedrooms, ideal for the business traveller.

Premier Travel Inn, Millburn Rd, IV2 3QX, ✆ (01463) 712010 – ⇔ rm, ♿ P. MC AE ⊙ VISA. ✻ Y
Rest (grill rest.) – **79 rm** ✝57.95 – ✝✝57.95.
◆ On the edge of the city centre, a typical lodge-style hotel. Identically shaped bedrooms all with work desks and some with sofa beds. Clean and affordable accommodation.

Millwood House without rest., 36 Old Mill Rd, IV2 3HR, ✆ (01463) 237254, *enquries@millwoodhouse.co.uk, Fax (01463) 719400,* – ⇔ ✆ P. MC VISA. ✻ Z
closed Christmas-New Year – **3 rm** ✝60.00/83.70 – ✝✝89.00/93.00.
◆ A warm welcome is assured by the charming owner of this delightful house. Relax in front of a log fire in the antique furnished drawing room. Cosy, warm and bright bedrooms.

Ballifeary House without rest., 10 Ballifeary Rd, IV3 5PJ, ✆ (01463) 235572, *info@ballifearyhousehotel.co.uk, Fax (01463) 717583* – ⇔ P. MC VISA. ✻ Z
closed 24-27 December – **7 rm** ✝30.00/70.00 – ✝✝60.00/70.00.
◆ Immaculately kept Victorian house with a pretty rear garden. Peaceful and relaxing fee as no children under 15 years are taken. A wholly non-smoking establishment.

Eden House without rest., 8 Ballifeary Rd, IV3 5PJ, ✆ (01463) 230278, *edenhouse@btinternet.com, Fax (01463) 230278* – ⇔ P. MC VISA. ✻ Z
closed Christmas-March – **4 rm** ✝40.00/60.00 – ✝✝60.00/74.00.
◆ Pleasant ten minute walk into the city centre along the river. Friendly proprietors run a neat and spotless house. Pretty little conservatory and good sized bedrooms.

Moyness House without rest., 6 Bruce Gdns, IV3 5EN, ✆ (01463) 233836, *stay@moyness.co.uk, Fax (01463) 233836,* – ⇔ P. MC AE VISA Z
closed Christmas – **7 rm** ✝35.00/58.00 – ✝✝70.00/76.00.
◆ Immaculately clipped hedges frame this attractive Victorian villa. Bedrooms vary in shape and size but all are comfortable, individually decorated and fully en suite.

Old Rectory without rest., 9 Southside Rd, IV2 3BG, ✆ (01463) 220969, *lister-old-rectory@btinternet.com,* – ⇔ P. MC VISA. ✻ Z
closed Christmas-New Year – **4 rm** ✝50.00/54.00 – ✝✝50.00/54.00.
◆ Personally run house, built in 1855, with a secluded rear garden. Individual tables in the breakfast room; bedrooms are neat, spotlessly clean and competitively priced.

Craigside Lodge without rest., 4 Gordon Terr, IV2 3HD, ✆ (01463) 231576, *craigsidelodge@amserve.net, Fax (01463) 713409,* ← – ⇔. MC ⊙ VISA. ✻ Z
5 rm ✝25.00 – ✝✝50.00/55.00.
◆ Views of the river, castle and mountains can be enjoyed from many of the rooms. Good value accommodation, fully en suite with helpful and friendly owners.

Abstract (at Glenmoriston Town House), 20 Ness Bank, IV2 4SF, ✆ (01463) 223777 *Fax (01463) 712378* – ⇔ rest, P. MC AE ⊙ VISA Z
closed Monday – **Rest** 17.00/42.00 s. ♀.
◆ Intimate restaurant, bar and conservatory. Abstract ink pictures on the walls, offset by vast mirror. Local produce to fore in seasonal menus with pronounced French accent.

Chez Christophe, 16 Ardross St, IV3 5NS, ✆ (01463) 717126, *info@chezchristophe.co.uk, Fax (01463) 717126* – ⇔. MC VISA Z
closed 25 December, 1 January, Sunday and Monday – **Rest** (booking essential) (dinner only) 23.95/39.50.
◆ Restaurant set within guesthouse, comprising two small dining rooms with a few tables in each. Very good quality Scottish and French ingredients combine most agreeably.

Café 1, Castle St, IV2 3EA, ✆ (01463) 226200, *info@cafe1.net, Fax (01463) 716363* – MC AE VISA Y
closed 25 December, New Year and Sunday – **Rest** a la carte 15.25/27.85 ♀.
◆ Local ingredients feature in the short, regularly changing modern menu with daily specials. Has an informal and contemporary feel, with tiled flooring and modern chairs.

at Culloden *East : 3 m. by A 96 – Y – ✉ Inverness.*

Culloden House ⟡, IV2 7BZ, ✆ (01463) 790461, *info@cullodenhouse.co.uk, Fax (01463) 792181,* ←, ≘s, ⛶, ⛶ – ⇔ P. MC AE ⊙ VISA
closed Christmas and 10-27 January – ***Adams Dining Room :*** **Rest** a la carte 28.85/38.45 ♀ – **22 rm** ✝95.00/155.00 – ✝✝140.00/260.00, 6 suites.
◆ Imposing Georgian mansion in 40 acres, requisitioned by Bonnie Prince Charlie in 1746 before the battle. Small bar and open sitting room. Antique-furnished bedrooms. Adam's plaster reliefs adorn the walls and ceiling of the grand dining room; traditional menu.

at Dunain Park *Southwest : 2½ m. on A 82 – Z – ✉ Inverness.*

Dunain Park , IV3 8JN, ☎ (01463) 230512, *dunainparkhotel@btinternet.com, Fax (01463) 224532,* <, , , – ⇔ P. MO ⓓ VISA
closed 4-20 January – **Rest** (dinner only) a la carte 26.40/32.85 – **5 rm** ☐ ★138.00/198.00 – ★★138.00/198.00, **8 suites** ☐ 178.00/218.00.
◆ Secluded Georgian country house, surrounded by gardens and woodland and personally run by the owners. Marbled bathrooms and spacious bedrooms, some with four-poster beds. Dining room is warmly decorated and the tables highly polished.

at Bunchrew *West : 3 m. on A 862 – Y – ✉ Inverness.*

Bunchrew House , IV3 8TA, ☎ (01463) 234917, *welcome@bunchrew-inverness.co.uk, Fax (01463) 710620,* <, , , – ⇔ rest, P. MO AE VISA
closed 4 days Christmas – **Rest** 25.50/35.50 s. – **16 rm** ☐ ★95.00/135.00 – ★★140.00/220.00.
◆ Unhurried relaxation is assured at this 17C Scottish mansion nestling in a tranquil spot on the shores of Bealy Firth. Drawing room is wood panelled; bedrooms restful. Gardens seen through the windows provide a pleasant backdrop to spacious dining room.

Hotels and restaurants change every year, so change your Michelin guide every year!

INVERURIE *Aberdeenshire* 501 M 12 *Scotland G. – pop. 10 882.*
EXC. : *Castle Fraser★ (exterior★★) AC, SW : 6 m. by B 993 – Pitmedden Gardens★★, NE : 10 m. by B 9170 and A 920 – Haddo House★, N : 14 m. by B 9170 and B 9005 – Fyvie Castle★, N : 13 m. by B 9170 and A 947.*
18 Blackhall Rd ☎ (01467) 624080 – 18 Kintore, Balbithan Rd ☎ (01467) 632631 – 18 Kemnay, Monymusk Rd ☎ (01467) 642060.
18 High St ☎ (01467) 625800.
Edinburgh 147 – Aberdeen 17 – Inverness 90.

Thainstone House H. & Country Club , AB51 5NT, South : 2 m. by B 993 off A 96 ☎ (01467) 621643, *swallow.thainstone@swallowhotels.com, Fax (01467) 625084,* , , , , – ⇔ P. – 250. MO AE VISA
Simpson's : **Rest** a la carte 16.15/28.90 s. – **47 rm** ☐ ★115.00/125.00 – ★★135.00, 1 suite.
◆ Impressive 19C house by Archibald Simpson, now a group owned hotel in parkland setting. Attentive staffing and well-provided rooms, those in main house most characterful. The country house feel of the public areas is carried through to the stylish restaurant.

Strathburn, Burghmuir Drive, AB51 4GY, Northwest : 1 ¼ m. by Inverness rd (A 96) ☎ (01467) 624422, *strathburn@btconnect.com, Fax (01467) 625133,* – ⇔, rest, P. – 30. MO AE ⓓ VISA
closed 25-26 December and 1-2 January – **Rest** a la carte 15.25/30.75 s. – **25 rm** ☐ ★60.00/75.00 – ★★80.00/105.00.
◆ Uncluttered purpose-built hotel in a residential area of town and conveniently located for A96. Well-planned modern interiors. Rooms in uniform fitted style. Dining available in the comfortable lounge-bar area or the adjacent dining room.

ISLAY (Isle of) *Argyll and Bute* 501 B 16.
18 25 Charlotte St, Port Ellen ☎ (01496) 300094.
Port Ellen Airport : ☎ (01496) 302022.
from Port Askaig to Isle of Jura (Feolin) (Serco Denholm Ltd) frequent services daily (approx. 4 mn) – from Port Ellen or Port Askaig to Kintyre Peninsula (Kennacraig) (Caledonian MacBrayne Ltd) 1-2 daily – from Port Askaig to Oban via Isle of Colonsay (Scalasaig) (Caledonian MacBrayne Ltd) weekly – from Port Askaig to Isle of Colonsay (Scalasaig) and Kintyre Peninsula (Kennacraig) (Caledonian MacBrayne Ltd) weekly.
The Square, Main St, Bowmore ☎ (08707) 200617.

Ballygrant *Argyll and Bute.*

Kilmeny Country Guest House , PA45 7QW, Southwest : ½ m. on A 846 ☎ (01496) 840668, *info@kilmeny.co.uk, Fax (01496) 840668,* <, , – ⇔ P.
closed Christmas and New Year – **Rest** (by arrangement) (communal dining) 28.00 – **3 rm** ☐ ★70.00 – ★★100.00.
◆ 19C converted farmhouse on a working farm. Its elevated position affords far reaching countryside views. Best of Scottish hospitality, home-cooking and comfort.

Bowmore *Argyll and Bute.*

XX **Harbour Inn** with rm, The Square, PA43 7JR, ☎ (01496) 810330, *info@harbour-inn.com*
Fax (01496) 810990, ← – ⇔. MO VISA. ✗
Rest a la carte 26.40/42.20 ♀ – **7 rm** ☐ ★79.00 – ★★109.00/130.00.
◆ Attractive whitewashed inn in busy little town, short walk from distillery. Panelled bar and a dining room with bay views. Menus centre on Islay produce. Bright bedrooms.

Port Charlotte *Argyll and Bute.*

Port Charlotte, Main St, PA48 7TU, ☎ (01496) 850360, *info@portcharlottehotel.co.uk*
Fax (01496) 850361, ←, – ⇔ P. MO VISA
closed 24-26 December – **Rest** (bar lunch)/dinner a la carte 17.00/31.00 **s.** – **10 rm** ☐ ★70.00 – ★★115.00.
◆ Simple, well-modernised, Victorian building in attractive conservation village. Pine panelled bar and relaxing lounge with open fires. Rooms furnished with fine old pieces. Attractive wood furnished restaurant with stone walls and views over the bay.

Port Ellen *Argyll and Bute.*

Glenmachrie Farmhouse, PA42 7AQ, Northwest : 4 ½ m. on A 846 ☎ (01496) 302560, *glenmachrie@lineone.net, Fax (01496) 302560,* , , – ⇔ P.
Rest (by arrangement) 30.00 – **5 rm** ☐ ★60.00 – ★★80.00.
◆ Modern farmhouse on a working farm a short drive from a number of Islay's distilleries and Duich Nature Reserve. Run on "green" low-impact policies. Warm welcoming rooms. Dinner by candlelight is something of an event.

ISLEORNSAY *Highland* 501 C 12 – *see Skye (Isle of).*

JEDBURGH *Borders* 501 502 M 17 *Scotland G. – pop. 4 090.*
See : *Town★ - Abbey★★ AC – Mary Queen of Scots House Visitor Centre★ AC – The Canongate Bridge★.*
Env. : *Waterloo Monument (※★★) N : 4 m. by A 68 and B 6400.*
Jedburgh, Dunion Rd ☎ (01835) 863587.
Murray's Green ☎ (0870) 608 0404.
Edinburgh 48 – Carlisle 54 – Newcastle upon Tyne 57.

Jedforest, Camptown, TD8 6PJ, South : 4 m. on A 68 ☎ (01835) 840222, *info@jedforesthotel.com, Fax (01835) 840226,* , , – ⇔ P. MO AE VISA
Rest light lunch/dinner 18.75/21.05 – **12 rm** ☐ ★65.00/100.00 – ★★140.00/160.00.
◆ Extended period house with outbuildings and attractive views. Public areas include spacious lounge, bar and brasserie. Bedrooms in varying co-ordinated styles and sizes. Formal dining room decorated to have an intimate feel with alcoves and low lighting.

The Spinney without rest., Langlee, TD8 6PB, South : 2 m. on A 68 ☎ (01835) 863525, *thespinney@btinternet.com, Fax (01835) 864883,* – ⇔ P. MO VISA. ✗
March-October – **3 rm** ☐ ★52.00/55.00 – ★★52.00/55.00.
◆ Good value accommodation with homely atmosphere and ambience. Traditional feel from the gardens to the lounge. Bedrooms of a good size overlooking the attractive gardens.

Hundalee House without rest., TD8 6PA, South : 1½ m. by A 68 ☎ (01835) 863011, *sheila.whittaker@btinternet.com, Fax (01835) 863011,* ←, , – ⇔ P. ✗
March-October – **5 rm** ☐ ★28.00/40.00 – ★★44.00/60.00.
◆ 18C country lodge in a very rural location, with good gardens featuring mature topiary. County house feel and a warm welcome. Distinctive period décor and some antiques.

at Crailing *Northeast : 4 m. by A 68 and A 698 on B 6400 – ✉ Jedburgh.*

Crailing Old School, TD8 6TL, ☎ (01835) 850382, *info@crailingoldschool.co.uk*
Fax (01835) 850382, – ⇔ P. MO VISA. ✗
closed Christmas-New Year, 2 weeks February and 2 weeks November – **Rest** (by arrangement) (communal dining) 25.00 – **4 rm** ☐ ★28.50/35.00 – ★★55.00/70.00.
◆ Former village school well sited for touring and golfing. Attractive guests' lounge also used for communal breakfast. Comfortable bedrooms in the house and the garden lodge. Home-cooked dinners.

JOHN O'GROATS *Highland* 501 K 8 – *Shipping Services : see Orkney Islands.*

URA (Isle of) *Argyll and Bute* 501 C 15.

from Feolin to Isle of Islay (Port Askaig) (Serco Denholm Ltd) frequent services daily (approx. 4 mn).

Craighouse *Argyll and Bute* – *Jura.*

Jura, PA60 7XU, (01496) 820243, *jurahotel@aol.com, Fax (01496) 820249,* Small Isles Bay, – rest, P. VISA
closed 15 December-10 January – **Rest** (bar lunch)/dinner a la carte 12.95/24.90 **s.** – **16 rm** 36.00/46.00 – 100.00, 1 suite.
◆ The only hotel on one of the wildest and quietest of the Scottish islands. Next door to the distillery. Relaxed, traditional and simple in style. Many rooms with fine views. Dining room shares the feel of the establishment with wooden chairs and fine views.

KELSO *Borders* 501 502 M 17 *Scotland G.* – *pop. 5 116.*

See : *Town★ – The Square★★ – ≤★ from Kelso Bridge.*
Env. : *Tweed Valley★★ – Floors Castle★ AC, NW : 1½ m. by A 6089.*
Exc. : *Mellerstain★★ (Ceilings★★★, Library★★★) AC, NW : 6 m. by A 6089 – Waterloo Monument (★★), SW : 7 m. by A 698 and B 6400 – Jedburgh Abbey★★ AC, SW : 8½ m. by A 698 – Dryburgh Abbey★★ AC (setting★★★), SW : 10½ m. by A 6089, B 6397 and B 6404 – Scott's View★★, W : 11 m. by A 6089, B 6397, B 6404 and B 6356 – Smailholm Tower★ (★★), NW : 6 m. by A 6089 and B 6397 – Lady Kirk (Kirk o'Steil★), NE : 16 m. by A 698, A 697, A 6112 and B 6437.*
Berrymoss Racecourse Rd (01573) 23009.
Town House, The Square (0870) 608 0404 (Easter-October).
Edinburgh 44 – Hawick 21 – Newcastle upon Tyne 68.

The Roxburghe, Heiton, TD5 8JZ, Southwest : 3 ½ m. by A 698 (01573) 450331, *hotel@roxburghe.net, Fax (01573) 450611,* ≤, 18, – P – 60. VISA
Rest 27.00/32.00 (dinner) and lunch a la carte approx 16.95 **s.** – **21 rm** 130.00/150.00 – 240.00, 1 suite.
◆ Wonderfully characterful Jacobean style mansion built in 1853. Sitting rooms with log fires and fresh flowers. Lovely conservatory, attractive library bar. Luxurious rooms. Warmly hued, formal restaurant with collection of horse racing pictures.

Ednam House, Bridge St, TD5 7HT, (01573) 224168, *contact@ednamhouse.com, Fax (01573) 226319,* ≤, – rm, P – 200. VISA
closed Christmas and New Year – **Rest** (bar lunch Monday-Friday)/dinner a la carte approx 23.50 – **32 rm** 53.50/74.00 – 92.00/94.00.
◆ Dominant Georgian mansion on Tweed. Distinctive décor exudes period appeal. Three impressively ornate lounges. Bar with fishing theme. Traditional rooms. Spacious dining room with relaxed atmosphere, overlooking gardens and river.

Bellevue House without rest., Bowmont St, TD5 7DZ, North : ½ m. on A 6089 (01573) 224588, *bellevuekelso@aol.com* – P. VISA
closed 2 weeks November and 24 December-2 January – **6 rm** 35.00/37.50 – 54.00/60.00.
◆ Victorian house 5 minutes from the Market Square. Individually decorated bedrooms. Good hospitality and range of breakfast dishes.

Queens Bistro, Queens Head Hotel, 24 Bridge St, TD5 7JD, (0870) 2424453, *info@garymoorsrestaurant.com, Fax (01573) 228869* – . VISA
closed 25 December – **Rest** a la carte approx 21.00.
◆ On the ground floor of the Queens Head Hotel. Modern décor with interesting pieces of art and sculpture. Popular dishes at lunchtime; dinner in the traditional style.

at Ednam *North : 2¼ m. on B 6461* – *Kelso.*

Edenwater House, TD5 7QL, off Stichill rd (01573) 224070, *relax@edenwaterhouse.co.uk, Fax (01573) 226615,* ≤, – P. VISA.
closed first 2 weeks January, 2 weeks October, Christmas and New Year – **Rest** *(closed Sunday-Tuesday)* (booking essential) (dinner only) (non-residents Friday and Saturday only) 35.00/40.00 **s.** – **4 rm** 50.00/65.00 – 80.00/95.00.
◆ Charming house in rural location next to 17C kirk. Beautiful gardens with stream and meadows beyond. Antique filled lounges. Rooms boast fine quality furnishings. Elegant dining room serving traditionally based meals using local produce.

Do not confuse X with ✿! X defines comfort, while stars are awarded for the best cuisine, across all categories of comfort.

KENMORE *Perth and Kinross* 501 I 14 *Scotland G.*

See : *Village*★.

Env. : *Loch Tay*★★.

Exc. : *Ben Lawers*★★, *SW : 8 m. by A 827.*

Taymouth Castle, Aberfeldy ✆ *(01887) 830228 –* , *Mains of Taymouth* ✆ *(0188 830226.*

Edinburgh 82 – Dundee 60 – Oban 71 – Perth 38.

Kenmore, The Square, PH15 2NU, ✆ (01887) 830205, *reception@kenmorehotel.co.u Fax (01887) 830262,* , , – , , rest, – 70. MC AE VISA

Taymouth : **Rest** a la carte 20.15/30.85 **s. – 40 rm** ★50.00/67.00 – ★★70.00/104.00.

◆ Scotland's oldest inn. Standing on the Tay, it is now a smart, white-fronted hotel wit Poet's Parlour featuring original pencilled verse by Burns. Cosy, well-kept rooms. Restau rant with panoramic river views.

KILBERRY *Argyll and Bute* 501 D 16 – *see Kintyre (Peninsula).*

KILCHRENAN *Argyll and Bute* 501 E 14 *Scotland G.* – ✉ *Taynuilt.*

Env. : *Loch Awe*★★, *E : 1¼ m.*

Edinburgh 117 – Glasgow 87 – Oban 18.

Ardanaiseig , PA35 1HE, Northeast : 4 m. ✆ (01866) 833333, *ardanaiseig@clara.ne Fax (01866) 833222,* ≤ gardens and Loch Awe, , , , – rest, . MC AE VISA

closed 2 January-10 February – **Rest** (booking essential to non-residents) (light lunch)/dir ner 42.00 – **16 rm** ★80.00/180.00 – ★★200.00/300.00.

◆ Substantial country house in extensive informal gardens beside Loch Awe. Undisturbe peace. Impressively elegant interior; antiques to the fore. Tasteful bedrooms. Dining roor boasts views to loch; classic country house cooking.

Taychreggan , PA35 1HQ, Southeast : 1 ¼ m. ✆ (01866) 833211, *info@taychregga hotel.co.uk, Fax (01866) 833244,* ≤ Loch Awe and mountains, , , – – 3(MC AE VISA

closed Christmas – **Rest** (booking essential to non-residents) (bar lunch)/dinner 37.50 **18 rm** ★117.50/135.00 – ★★175.00/180.00, 2 suites.

◆ Former cattle drovers' inn superbly sited with its own grounds on shores of Loch Awe Cosy feel: lounges with open fires. Well-equipped bedrooms, most with excellent views Light, airy dining room with large window making the most of stunning outlook.

Roineabhal , PA35 1HD, ✆ (01866) 833207, *maria@roinbhal.com Fax (01866) 833477,* – , . MC VISA

closed 25-26 December – **Rest** (by arrangement) (communal dining) 30.00 – **3 rm** ★50.00 – ★★75.00.

◆ Large stone house, built by the owners, enviably located by rushing stream and close to Loch Awe. Rusticity prevails in welcoming interior; spacious rooms with homely extras. B arrangement five-course communal dinner, home-cooked using local produce.

KILDRUMMY *Aberdeenshire* 501 L 12 *Scotland G.* – ✉ *Alford.*

See : *Castle*★ *AC.*

Exc. : *Huntly Castle (Heraldic carvings*★★★*) N : 15 m. by A 97 – Craigievar Castle*★, *SE : 13 m by A 97, A 944 and A 980.*

Edinburgh 137 – Aberdeen 35.

Kildrummy Castle , AB33 8RA, South : 1 ¼ m. on A 97 ✆ (019755) 71288, *boo ings@kildrummycastlehotel.co.uk, Fax (019755) 71345,* ≤ gardens and Kildrummy Castle , , – rest, . MC VISA

closed 3 January-2 February – ***The Dining Room :*** **Rest** 21.00/36.00 and dinner a la carte 26.50/34.25 – **16 rm** ★83.00/170.00 – ★★160.00/190.00.

◆ Imposing, stone built 19C mansion in superb grounds with fine view of original 13C castle. Baronial, country house style abounds: lounges flaunt antiques. Sizeable rooms Delightfully wood-panelled dining room; homely Scottish cooking.

KILLEARN *Stirling* 501 G 15 – ✉ *Glasgow.*

Edinburgh 60 – Glasgow 19 – Perth 55 – Stirling 22.

Black Bull, 2 The Square, G63 9NG, ✆ (01360) 550215, *sales@blackbullhotel.com Fax (01360) 550143,* , – . MC AE VISA

The Grill : Rest 14.95/29.50 and a la carte 15.00/29.50 ♀ – **11 rm** ★70.00/95.00 – ★★95.00, 1 suite.

◆ Pleasant little inn in centre of small village close to Campsie Fells. Local artwork is on display in all areas. Contemporary bar and rooms that offer neat and tidy comforts. Trendy modern brasserie.

KILLIECRANKIE *Perth and Kinross* 501 I 13 – *see Pitlochry.*

KILLIN *Stirling* 501 H 14 *Scotland G.* – *pop. 666.*

Exc. : *Loch Tay★★, Ben Lawers★★, NE : 8 m. by A 827 – Loch Earn★★, SE : 7 m. by A 827 and A 85.*

Killin ℘ *(01567) 820312.*

Breadalbane Folklore Centre, Falls of Dochart ℘ *(0870) 200627.*

Edinburgh 72 – Dundee 65 – Perth 43 – Oban 54.

Dall Lodge Country House without rest., Main St, FK21 8TN, on A 827 ℘ (01567) 820217, *connor@dallodge.co.uk, Fax (01567) 820726,* P. VISA
Easter-October – **9 rm** 27.50/35.00 – 70.00.
◆ Victorian hotel of stone, proudly overlooking river Lochay. Walls adorned by foreign artefacts and local oils. Conservatory with exotic plants. Stylish, halogen lit rooms.

Breadalbane House, Main St, FK21 8UT, ℘ (01567) 820134, *info@breadalbanehouse.com, Fax (01567) 820798* – P. VISA.
Rest (by arrangement) 15.00 – **5 rm** 35.00/40.00 – 55.00/60.00.
◆ Surrounded by Ben Lawers, Loch Tay, Glen Lochay and the Falls of Dochart, this cosy guesthouse offers simple, homely comforts. Clean, well-kept rooms with good views. Evening meals available by prior arrangement in the simple, pine furnished dining room.

at Ardeonaig *(Perth and Kinross) Northeast : 6¾ m. –* ✉ *Killin (Stirling).*

Ardeonaig, South Loch Tay Side, FK21 8SU, ℘ (01567) 820400, *info@ardeonaighotel.co.uk, Fax (01567) 820282,* P. VISA
Rest – (see ***The Restaurant*** below) – **20 rm** (dinner included) 62.50/75.00 – 125.00/150.00.
◆ Family run 17C inn, set in wooded meadows on south shore of Loch Tay. Cheery bar with good choice of malts. Cosy sitting room. Library with fine views. Smart rooms.

The Restaurant (at Ardeonaig H.), South Loch Tay Side, FK21 8SU, ℘ (01567) 820400, *info@ardeonaighotel.co.uk, Fax (01567) 820282,* P. VISA
Rest 21.50/35.00 and a la carte 21.00/30.50.
◆ Located in Ardeonaig hotel extension. Rennie Mackintosh style chairs, white linen-clad tables. Good value dishes: South African influences merge well with local ingredients.

KILMARNOCK *East Ayrshire* 501 502 G 17 *Scotland G.*

See : *Dean Castle (arms and armour★, musical instruments★).*

62 Bank St ℘ *(01563) 539090.*

Edinburgh 64 – Ayr 13 – Glasgow 25.

The Park, Kilmarnock Football Club, Rugby Park, KA1 2DP, off Dundonald Rd ℘ (01563) 545999, *enquiries@theparkhotel.uk.com, Fax (01563) 545322,* P – 600. AE VISA.
Blues : Rest a la carte 16.75/30.00 – **50 rm** 65.00/120.00 – 75.00/132.00.
◆ Adjacent to Kilmarnock Football Club, who are its owners, this stylish, glass structured hotel offers up-to-date facilities. Spacious, well-equipped and comfortable bedrooms. Mezzanine-level restaurant boasts tables with views of the pitch.

Premier Travel Inn, Moorfield Roundabout, Annadale, KA1 2RS, Southwest : 2 m. by A 759 at junction with A 71 ℘ (01563) 570534, *Fax (01563) 570536* – rest, P. AE VISA.
Rest (grill rest.) – **40 rm** 46.95/46.95 – 48.95/48.95.
◆ Well-proportioned modern bedrooms, suitable for business and family stopovers. Located on busy road junction. Simply fitted accommodation in contemporary style.

KINCLAVEN *Perth and Kinross* 501 J 14 – *pop. 394* – ✉ *Stanley.*

Edinburgh 56 – Perth 12.

Ballathie House, Stanley, PH1 4QN, ℘ (01250) 883268, *email@ballathiehousehotel.com, Fax (01250) 883396,* P – 50. AE VISA
Rest 19.50/39.00 – **39 rm** 82.50/112.50 – 165.00/185.00, 3 suites.
◆ Imposing mid 19C former shooting lodge on banks of Tay, imbued with tranquil, charming atmosphere. Elegant, individually furnished bedrooms with a floral theme. Richly alluring restaurant overlooking river.

KINFAUNS *Perth and Kinross* 501 J 14 – *see Perth.*

KINGUSSIE *Highland* 501 H 12 *Scotland G. – pop. 1 410.*
Env. : Highland Wildlife Park★ AC, NE : 4 m. by A 9.
Exc. : Aviemore★, NE : 11 m. by A 9 – The Cairngorms★★ (<★★★) – ★★★ from Cair Gorm, NE : 18 m. by B 970.
Gynack Rd (01540) 661600.
Edinburgh 117 – Inverness 41 – Perth 73.

Columba House, Manse Rd, PH21 1JF, (01540) 661402, *reservations@columbahosehotel.com, Fax (01540) 661652,* – P. VISA
closed 24-26 December – **Rest** (dinner only) a la carte 23.05/28.40 – **11 rm** ★60.00/75.00 – ★★100.00/110.00.
◆ Former 19C church manse of rugged stone with lawned, walled garden on threshold of Cairngorms. Small, homely lounge with traditional décor. Spotless, pastel shaded rooms. Intimate, lacy dining room serving local fare.

Hermitage, Spey St, PH21 1HN, (01540) 662137, *thehermitage@clara.net Fax (01540) 662177,* – P. VISA.
Rest (by arrangement) 17.00 – **5 rm** ★30.00/45.00 – ★★50.00/60.00.
◆ Pleasant Victorian detached house with uninterrupted views of Cairngorms. Attractive lawned garden. Homely, welcoming lounge with log fire. Colourful, floral rooms. Wood furnished dining room with chintz décor.

Homewood Lodge, Newtonmore Rd, PH21 1HD, (01540) 661507, *enquiries@homewood-lodge-kingussie.co.uk,* <, – P.
Rest (by arrangement) 13.00 **4 rm** ★25.00 – ★★50.00.
◆ An immaculate whitewashed exterior and a prominent hilltop position attract the visitor's eye to this Victorian villa guesthouse with its uncluttered feel and simple rooms.

The Cross with rm, Tweed Mill Brae, Ardbroilach Rd, PH21 1LB, (01540) 661166 *relax@thecross.co.uk, Fax (01540) 661080* – P. VISA.
restricted opening in winter – **Rest** *(closed Sunday-Monday)* (booking essential) (dinner only) 37.00/44.00 – **8 rm** (dinner included) ★115.00/130.00 – ★★170.00/200.00.
◆ Converted tweed mill restaurant in four acres of waterside grounds with beamed ceilings and modern artwork. Scottish cuisine with worldwide influences. Comfortable rooms.

KINLOCH RANNOCH 501 H 13.
Edinburgh 94 – Blair Atholl 19 – Pitlochry 22.

Finnart Lodge, PH17 2QF, West : 9 ½ m. on South Loch Rannoch rd (01882) 633366, *aandaboyd@aol.com, Fax (01882) 633232,* < Loch Rannoch, – P
closed Christmas and New Year, 3 weeks February-March – **Rest** (communal dining) (by arrangement) 25.00 – **3 rm** ★40.00 – ★★80.00.
◆ 19C country house with charming owners, beautifully located on shores of Loch Rannoch. Traditional drawing room and conservatory. Cosy accommodation in rooms with loch views. Communal fine dining on antique table.

KINROSS *Perth and Kinross* 501 J 15 *– pop. 4 681.*
Green Hotel, 2 The Muirs (01577) 863407 – Milnathort, South St (01577) 864069 – Bishopshire, Kinnesswood (01592) 780203.
Heart of Scotland Visitor Centre, junction 6, M 90 (01577) 863680 (closed weekends October-April).
Edinburgh 28 – Dunfermline 13 – Perth 18 – Stirling 25.

The Green, 2 Muirs, KY13 8AS, (01577) 863467, *reservations@green-hotel.com, Fax (01577) 863180,* squash – P – 130. VISA
accommodation closed 22-29 December – ***Basil's :*** **Rest** 34.50 – **46 rm** ★85.00/95.00 – ★★160.00/170.00.
◆ 18C former coaching inn in neat grounds off village high street. Spacious, welcoming lounge. Leisure complex includes curling rink. Comfortable, modern rooms. Bright, airy modern restaurant with modish menus to match.

Burnbank without rest., 79 Muirs, KY13 8AZ, North : ¾ m. on A 922 (01577) 861931, *bandb@burnbank-kinross.co.uk,* – P. VISA.
3 rm ★35.00/38.00 – ★★60.00.
◆ Well-kept, proudly run guesthouse: cosy reception room full of maps and local info. Owners make their own breakfast bread and preserves. Lomond Hills vistas from smart rooms.

For a pleasant stay in a charming hotel, look for the red ... symbols.

KINTYRE (Peninsula) *Argyll and Bute* 501 D 16 *Scotland G.*

See : *Carradale★ – Saddell (Collection of grave slabs★).*

Machrihanish, Campbeltown ℘ (01586) 810213 – Dunaverty, Southend, Campbeltown ℘ (01586) 830677 – Gigha, Isle of Gigha ℘ (01583) 505247.

Campbeltown Airport : ℘ (01586) 553797.

from Claonaig to Isle of Arran (Lochranza) (Caledonian MacBrayne Ltd) frequent services daily (30 mn) – from Kennacraig to Isle of Islay (Port Ellen or Port Askaig) (Caledonian MacBrayne Ltd) 1-3 daily – from Kennacraig to Oban via Isle of Colonsay (Scalasaig) and Isle of Islay (Port Askaig) 3 weekly.

Campbeltown *Argyll and Bute.*

Mackinnon House, The Pier ℘ (01586) 552056, info@campbeltown.visitscotland.com.
Edinburgh 176.

Craigard House, Low Askomil, PA28 6EP, East : ¾ m. by B 842 on no through rd ℘ (01586) 554242, *info@craigard-house.co.uk, Fax (01586) 551137,* – rest, P. MC AE VISA
Rest (booking essential to non-residents) a la carte 18.50/28.50 – **14 rm** ★45.00/55.00 – ★★120.00.
◆ Built 1882 by distillery owner on shores of Campbeltown Loch. Fine hallway with stained -glass window. Individually decorated rooms named after local geographical features. Tables at bow window looking out to loch are popular in period styled dining room.

Seafield, Kilkerran Rd, PA28 6JL, ℘ (01586) 554385, *seafield.hotel@btconnect.com, Fax (01586) 552741* – P. MC AE VISA
Rest a la carte 13.05/29.90 – **8 rm** ★45.00/55.00 – ★★60.00/75.00.
◆ Victorian seafront hotel overlooking harbour and bay. Traditionally furnished bar with maritime pictures. Some rooms have good sea views: others in rear annex are quieter. Spacious dining room classically decorated in green with wheel backed chairs.

Carradale *Argyll and Bute.*

Dunvalanree, Port Righ Bay, PA28 6SE, ℘ (01583) 431226, *eat@dunvalanree.com,* – P. MC VISA
closed January-February – **Rest** 24.00 – **7 rm** (dinner included) ★55.00/75.00 – ★★130.00.
◆ 1930s house on the bay facing Arran and Kilbrannan Sound. Comfortable firelit lounge, "Arts and Crafts" stained glass entrance and well-fitted rooms, one in Mackintosh style. Intimate dining room takes up the period style.

Kilberry *Argyll and Bute.*

Edinburgh 165 – Glasgow 121 – Oban 75.

Kilberry Inn with rm, PA29 6YD, ℘ (01880) 770223, *relax@kilberryinn.com, Fax (01880) 770223* – P. MC VISA
closed January-February – **Rest** *(closed Monday and Tuesday-Thursday November-December and March)* a la carte 17.95/26.25 – **3 rm** ★39.50 – ★★79.00.
◆ Characterful, cosy, red tin-roofed cottage incorporating open fires, beams, exposed stone. Walls hung with local artists' work. Well-priced dishes. Stylish, modern bedrooms.

Tarbert *Argyll and Bute.*

Kilberry Rd, Tarbert ℘ (01880) 820565.
Harbour St ℘ (01880) 820429 (April-October), info@tarbet.visitscotland.com.

Columba, East Pier Rd, PA29 6UF, East : ¾ m. ℘ (01880) 820808, *columbahotel@fsdial.co.uk, Fax (01880) 821129,* – P. MC VISA
closed January – **Rest** (bar lunch)/dinner 26.00 – **7 rm** ★40.00/50.00 – ★★80.00/100.00, 3 suites.
◆ Victorian hotel, built to provide accommodation for visitors arriving by steamer at nearby dock. Cosy bar has simple, interesting menus. Rooms with a view, three with sauna. Formal dining room with super view over Loch Fyne.

KIPPEN *Stirlingshire* 501 H 15 *Scotland G. – pop. 934.*

Exc. : *Doune★ - Castle★, NE : 8 m. by A 811, B 8075 and A 84 – Dunblane★ - Cathedral★★, NE : 13 m. by A 811 and M 9 – Stirling★★ - Castle★★, Argyll and Sutherland Highlanders Regimental Museum★, Argyll's Lodging★, Church of the Holy Rude★, E : 9 m. by A 811.*
Edinburgh 75 – Glasgow 62 – Stirling 16.

The Inn at Kippen with rm, Fore Rd, FK8 3DT, ℘ (01786) 871010, *info@theinnatkippen.co.uk, Fax (01786) 871011,* – P. MC VISA
closed 1 January – **Rest** a la carte 15.40/28.90 – **4 rm** ★40.00 – ★★70.00.
◆ Village inn with modern interior and photos of former village life. Large lunch and dinner menu of popular pub and restaurant style dishes. Simple wood-furnished bedrooms.

KIRKBEAN *Dumfries and Galloway* 501 502 J 19 *Scotland G.*

Env. : *Sweetheart Abbey★, N : 5 m. by A 710.*

Exc. : *Threave Garden★★ and Threave Castle★, W : 20 m. by A 710 and A 745.*

Edinburgh 92 – Dumfries 13 – Kirkcudbright 29.

Cavens, DG2 8AA, (01387) 880234, *enquiries@cavens.com, Fax (01387) 880467,* – P. MO AE VISA
closed January-12 February – **Rest** (dinner only) 25.00 s. – **7 rm** ★80.00/90.00 – ★★125.00/160.00.
◆ 18C house with extensions set in mature gardens. Very comfortable lounges opening onto terrace. Spacious well furnished bedrooms. Simple refreshing meals using local produce.

KIRKCOLM *Dumfries and Galloway* 501 502 E 19 – *see Stranraer.*

KIRKCUDBRIGHT *Dumfries and Galloway* 501 502 H 19 *Scotland G. – pop. 3 447.*

See : *Town★.*

Env. : *Dundrennan Abbey★ AC, SE : 5 m. by A 711.*

18 *Stirling Crescent (01557) 330314.*

Harbour Sq (01557) 330494 (Easter-October).

Edinburgh 108 – Dumfries 28 – Stranraer 50.

Selkirk Arms, High St, DG6 4JG, (01557) 330402, *reception@selkirkarmshotel.co.uk, Fax (01557) 331639,* – P. MO AE VISA
Rest (bar lunch)/dinner a la carte 14.15/27.25 – **16 rm** ★64.00/88.00 – ★★95.00/99.50.
◆ Traditional coaching inn in centre of quaint harbour town; Burns reputedly wrote "The Selkirk Grace" here. Rustic interior. Large bar serving simple food. Good sized rooms. Comfortable dining room with seasonal, classically based menu.

Baytree House without rest., 110 High St, DG6 4JQ, (01557) 330824, *jackie@baytreekirkcudbright.co.uk, Fax (01557) 330824,* –
3 rm ★42.00 – ★★60.00/76.00.
◆ 18C house with original first floor drawing room. Breakfast at individual tables overlooking the garden or on the sundeck. Large comfortably furnished bedrooms.

Gladstone House, 48 High St, DG6 4JX, (01557) 331734, *hilarygladstone@aol.com, Fax (01557) 331734,* – . MO VISA.
Rest (by arrangement) 18.00 **3 rm** ★41.00 – ★★64.00.
◆ Attractive Georgian house. Spacious, comfortably furnished sitting room and breakfast room. Evening meals offered. Traditional rooms with stripped wooden furnishings.

KIRKMICHAEL *Perth and Kinross* 501 J 13.

Edinburgh 73 – Aberdeen 85 – Inverness 102 – Perth 29.

Cruachan Country Cottage, PH10 7NZ, on A 924 (01250) 881226, *cruachan@kirkmichael.net,* – P. MO VISA
Rest (by arrangement) a la carte 16.55/24.95 – **3 rm** ★29.50/33.50 – ★★51.00/59.00.
◆ Extended stone cottage with neat garden, overlooking River Ardle. Homely lounge with open fire and interesting, local prints. Individually decorated bedrooms. Dinners home-cooked proudly by owners.

KIRKNEWTON *Edinburgh* 501 J 16 – *see Edinburgh.*

KIRKPATRICK DURHAM *Dumfries and Galloway* 501 502 I 18 – *see Castle Douglas.*

KIRKTON OF GLENISLA *Perthshire* 501 K 13 – ✉ *Blairgowrie.*

Edinburgh 73 – Forfar 19 – Pitlochry 24.

Glenmarkie Guest House Health Spa and Riding Centre, PH11 8QB, East : 3 ¾ m. by B 951 (01575) 582295, *holidays@glenmarkie.freeserve.co.uk, Fax (01575) 582295,* ←, , – P.
Rest (by arrangement) 20.00 – **3 rm** ★40.00 – ★★56.00.
◆ Stunningly located, cosy little farmhouse in beautiful glen. Horse riding and massages available, not necessarily in that order. Simple, individually decorated bedrooms.

KIRKTON OF MARYCULTER *Aberdeenshire* 501 N 12 – *see Aberdeen.*

KIRKWALL *Orkney Islands* 501 L 7 – *see Orkney Islands (Mainland).*

KIRRIEMUIR *Angus* 501 K 13 – *pop. 5 963.*

1 Cumberland Close ☎ (01575) 574097 (Easter-September).
Edinburgh 65 – Aberdeen 50 – Dundee 16 – Perth 30.

Purgavie Farm, Lintrathen, DD8 5HZ, West : 5 ½ m. on B 951 ☎ (01575) 560213, *purgavie@aol.com, Fax (01575) 560213*, ≤, – P. VISA
Rest (by arrangement) (communal dining) 15.00 – **3 rm** ★30.00 – ★★50.00.
◆ Farmhouse on working farm at foot of Glen Isla, part of lovely Glens of Angus. Homely lounge with open fire. Large, comfortable rooms with panoramic views. Meals are taken communally in the comfortable dining room.

KYLE OF LOCHALSH *Highland* 501 C 12 – *pop. 739.*

Car park ☎ (01599) 534276 (April-October).
Edinburgh 207 – Dundee 177 – Inverness 81 – Oban 123.

The Seafood, Railway Station, IV40 8AE, ☎ (01599) 534813, *jann@the-seafood-restau rant.co.uk, Fax (01599) 577230*, – rest. VISA
April-October – **Rest** - Seafood - *(closed Sunday except summer)* (dinner only) a la carte 16.25/25.25 s.
◆ Popular restaurant on main platform of railway station. Light, airy dining room with fishy prints. Wide ranging menus, very strong on local seafood. Fresh, unfussy cooking.

Undecided between two equivalent establishments?
Within each category, establishments are classified
in our order of preference.

KYLESKU *Highland* 501 E 9 *Scotland G.*

Env. : *Loch Assynt★★, S : 6 m. by A 894.*
Edinburgh 256 – Inverness 100 – Ullapool 34.

Kylesku with rm, IV27 4HW, ☎ (01971) 502231, *info@kyleskuhotel.co.uk, Fax (01971) 502313*, ≤ Loch Glencoul and mountains, – rest. VISA
March-15 October – **Rest** (in bar Monday dinner and lunch)/dinner 28.50 and a la carte 14.85/24.20 – **8 rm** ★50.00 – ★★80.00.
◆ Stunningly located inn, at the end of the pier overlooking loch, mountain and countryside. Spacious establishment with interesting, intriguing, individual rooms. Restaurant in superb spot with great views: local, seasonal ingredients with strong seafood slant.

LADYBANK *Fife* 501 K 15 *Scotland G.* – *pop. 1 487.*

Env. : *Falkland★ – Palace of Falkland★ – Gardens★ – Village★, S : ½ m. by A 914 on A 912.*
18 Ladybank, Annsmuir ☎ (01337) 830814.
Edinburgh 38 – Dundee 20 – Stirling 40.

Redlands Country Lodge without rest., Pitlessie Rd, KY15 7SH, East : ¾ m. by Kingskettle rd taking first left after railway bridge ☎ (01337) 831091, – P. VISA
4 rm ★35.00 – ★★50.00.
◆ Detached cottage on a quiet country lane in a rural location. Bedrooms, which have a simple snug air, are located in an adjacent pine lodge. Breakfast in the main cottage and with a sun terrace for warmer days.

LAIRG *Highland* 501 G9 – *pop. 857.*

Ferrycroft Countryside Centre, Sutherland ☎ (01549) 402160 (April-October).
Edinburgh 218 – Inverness 61 – Wick 72.

Park House, IV27 4AU, ☎ (01549) 402208, *david-walker@park-house@freeserve.co.uk, Fax (01549) 402693*, ≤, , – rest, P. VISA
closed Christmas and New Year – **Rest** (by arrangement) 18.00 – **3 rm** ★32.50/47.00 – ★★54.00/70.00.
◆ Victorian house on the banks of Loch Shin, comfortable and well furnished with high ceilings and views of the loch. Good spacious bedrooms. Country pursuits organised. Hunting and fishing activities of the establishment reflected in the home-cooked menus.

LAMLASH *North Ayrshire* 501 E 17 – *see Arran (Isle of).*

LAUDER *Berwickshire* 501 L 16 – *pop. 1 108.*

Galashiels Rd (01578) 722526.

Edinburgh 27 – Berwick-upon-Tweed 34 – Carlisle 74 – Newcastle upon Tyne 77.

The Lodge, Carfraemill, TD2 6RA, Northwest : 4 m. by A 68 on A 697 (01578) 750750, *enquiries@carfraemill.co.uk, Fax (01578) 750751,* – P – 150. MO AE VISA.
***Jo's Kitchen* : Rest** (grill rest.) a la carte 16.00/26.50 – **10 rm** 60.00 – 90.00.
◆ Family run hotel, once a coaching inn, just off the Newcastle-Edinburgh road. Warmly traditional style of décor and a welcoming ambience. Well-equipped bedrooms. A choice of informal eating areas with a traditional farmhouse feel.

LEITH *Edinburgh* 501 K 16 – *see Edinburgh.*

LERWICK *Shetland Islands* 501 Q 3 – *see Shetland Islands (Mainland).*

LESLIE *Fife* 501 K 15 – *pop. 2 998.*

Edinburgh 35 – Dundee 26 – Perth 25 – Stirling 33.

Rescobie House, 6 Valley Drive, KY6 3BQ, (01592) 749555, *rescobiehotel@compuserve.com, Fax (01592) 620231,* – P. MO AE VISA
closed 1 week January and 1 week December – **Rest** (dinner only and Sunday lunch)/dinner (booking essential) 24.95 **s.** – **10 rm** 49.50/74.50 – 87.50/99.50.
◆ Listed house, dating from 1930s, in extensive gardens. Smart, uncluttered feel throughout. Rooms in soft creams and browns; spacious and comfortable with a simple elegance Bay-windowed dining room, intimate and formally set.

LEVERBURGH *Western Isles (Outer Hebrides)* 501 Y 10 – *see Lewis and Harris (Isle of).*

LEWIS and HARRIS (Isle of) *Western Isles (Outer Hebrides)* 501 A 9 *Scotland G.*

See : *Callanish Standing Stones★★ – Carloway Broch★ – St Clement's Church, Rodel (tomb★).*

from Stornoway to Ullapool (Mainland) (Caledonian MacBrayne Ltd) 2 daily (2 h 40 mn) – from Kyles Scalpay to the Isle of Scalpay (Caledonian MacBrayne Ltd) (10 mn) – from Tarbert to Isle of Skye (Uig) (Caledonian MacBrayne Ltd) 1-2 daily (1 h 45 mn) – from Tarbert to Portavadie (Caledonian MacBrayne Ltd) (summer only) frequent services daily (25 mn) – from Leverburgh to North Uist (Otternish) (Caledonian MacBrayne Ltd) (3-4 daily) (1 h 10 mn).

LEWIS *Western Isles.*

Aird Uig *Western Isles.*

Bonaventure with rm, HS2 9JA, (01851) 672474, *jo@bonaventurelewis.co.uk, Fax (01851) 672474* – P
closed February – **Rest** (booking essential) (residents only Sunday-Monday) (dinner only) 28.95 – **5 rm** 35.00 – 50.00.
◆ A 1950s RAF radar station in remote setting converted to spacious bistro style dining room with Scottish/French menu serving local produce. Simple homely bedrooms.

Breasclete *Western Isles.*

Eshcol , 21 Breasclete, HS2 9ED, (01851) 621357, *neil@eshcol.com, Fax (01851) 621357,* ←, – P
March-September – **Rest** (by arrangement) 22.00 – **3 rm** 60.00 – 70.00.
◆ Modern house in a very rural location, set against a backdrop of delightful scenery. Immaculately kept throughout with a homely atmosphere and views from most rooms. Simple dining room hung with a selection of old photos.

Loch Roag , 22A Breasclete, HS2 9EF, (01851) 621357, *donald@lochroag.com, Fax (01851) 621357,* – P.
March-September **Rest** (by arrangement) 22.00 – **4 rm** 30.00/35.00 – 60.00/70.00.
◆ Charming rural location with classic Hebridean views all around. Bedrooms are decorated in traditional style and the house as a whole has a snug welcoming atmosphere. Simple uncluttered dining room with patio windows opening into the garden.

Galson Western Isles.

Galson Farm, South Galson, HS2 0SH, (01851) 850492, *galsonfarm@yahoo.com, Fax (01851) 850492*, ≤, – P. MC VISA
Rest (by arrangement) (communal dining) 25.00 – **4 rm** 42.00 – 74.00/80.00.
◆ Characterful working farm in a very remote location. Close to the ocean and ideally placed for exploring the north of the island. Very comfortable, well-kept bedrooms. Traditionally styled dining room where meals are taken communally at a large central table.

Stornoway Western Isles.

Lady Lever Park (01851) 702240.
26 Cromwell St (01851) 703088, witb@visitthehebrides.co.uk.

Cabarfeidh, Manor Park, HS1 2EU, North : ½ m. on A 859 (01851) 702604, *cabarfeidh@calahotels.com, Fax (01851) 705572* – , rest, P – 300. MC AE VISA
Rest 15.00/25.50 (dinner) and a la carte 26.15/31.85 **s.** – **46 rm** 88.00/98.00 – 118.00/128.00.
◆ Modern purpose-built hotel surrounded by gardens and close to golf course. Simply furnished, well-equipped bedrooms. Range of banqueting and conference facilities. Restaurant is divided into four areas including conservatory, bistro and garden rooms.

HARRIS Western Isles.

Ardhasaig Western Isles.

Ardhasaig House, HS3 3AJ, (01859) 502066, *accommodation@ardhasaig.co.uk, Fax (01859) 502077*, ≤ Ardhasaig bay and North Harris mountains – P. MC AE VISA
March-October – **Rest** 30.00/45.00 – **6 rm** 55.00/75.00 – 110.00/150.00.
◆ Dramatic views of bay and mountains in this remote location. Modern bar and sitting room. Well-kept bedrooms. Smart dining room with daily changing menu featuring seasonal island produce.

Leverburgh Western Isles.

Carminish, 1a Strond, HS5 3UD, South : 1 m. on Srandda rd (01859) 520400, *info@carminish.com, Fax (01859) 520307*, ≤ Carminish Islands and Sound of Harris, – P
restricted opening in winter – **Rest** (by arrangement) (communal dining) 18.00 – **3 rm** 22.00/44.00 – 44.00/54.00.
◆ Idyllically located guesthouse with spectacular views of the Carminish Islands and Sound of Harris. Pleasant public areas. Well-kept rooms. Hearty meals in communal setting.

Scarista Western Isles.

9 (01859) 520331.

Scarista House, HS3 3HX, (01859) 550238, *timandpatricia@scaristahouse.com, Fax (01859) 550277*, ≤ Scarista Bay, – P. MC VISA
booking essential in winter – **Rest** (booking essential for non-residents) (dinner only) (set menu only) 39.50/47.00 – **5 rm** 110.00/125.00 – 160.00/180.00.
◆ Sympathetically restored part 18C former manse, commanding position affords delightful views of Scarista Bay. Elegant library and inviting antique furnished bedrooms. Strong local flavour to the daily changing menu.

Tarbert Western Isles – *pop. 795* – Harris.

Hillcrest without rest., HS3 3AH, Northwest : 1 ¾ m. on A 859 (01859) 502119, *angusahillcrest@tiscali.co.uk, Fax (01859) 502119*, ≤, – P. MC AE VISA.
3 rm 35.00 – 50.00.
◆ A private house, family run, in a commanding position overlooking Loch Tarbert. Small cosy sitting room and spacious bedrooms, most enjoying sea views. Simply appointed breakfast room.

LEWISTON Highland 501 G 12 Scotland G.

Env. : *Loch Ness★★ – The Great Glen★.*
Edinburgh 173 – Inverness 17.

Woodlands without rest., East Lewiston, IV63 6UJ, (01456) 450356, *woodlands2004@btinternet.com, Fax (01456) 459343*, – P. MC VISA.
February-October and New Year – **5 rm** 30.00/37.00 – 40.00/56.00.
◆ With a large garden and welcoming owner this guesthouse has a friendly, homely atmosphere. Situated just away from the town. Immaculately kept, comfortable bedrooms.

Glen Rowan without rest., West Lewiston, IV63 6UW, ☏ (01456) 450235, *info@glenrowan.co.uk, Fax (01456) 450817*, – P. MC AE VISA.
3 rm ★22.00/37.50 – ★★44.00/55.00.
◆ Good value accommodation in quiet village near Loch Ness. High levels of comfort in a rooms. Good traditional and vegetarian breakfast.

LINICLATE *Western Isles (Outer Hebrides)* 501 X/Y 11 – *see Uist (Isles of).*

LINLITHGOW *West Lothian* 501 J 16 *Scotland G. – pop. 13 370.*
See : *Town★★ – Palace★★ AC : Courtyard (fountain★★), Great Hall (Hooded Fireplace★★), Gateway★ – Old Town★ – St Michaels★.*
Env. : *Cairnpapple Hill★ AC, SW : 5 m. by A 706 – House of the Binns (plasterwork ceilings★) AC, NE : 4½ m. by A 803 and A 904.*
Exc. : *Hopetoun House★★ AC, E : 7 m. by A 706 and A 904 – Abercorn Parish Church (Hopetoun Loft★★) NE : 7 m. by A 803 and A 904.*
Braehead ☏ (01506) 842585 – West Lothian, Airngath Hill ☏ (01506) 826030.
Burgh Hall, The Cross ☏ (01506) 844600 (April-October).
Edinburgh 19 – Falkirk 9 – Glasgow 35.

Champany Inn, Champany, EH49 7LU, Northeast : 2 m. on A 803 at junction with A 904 ☏ (01506) 834532, *reception@champany.com, Fax (01506) 834302*, – P. MC AE VISA.
closed 24-26 December and 1-2 January – ***The Chop and Ale House :*** **Rest** (grill rest.) a la carte 16.85/30.50 – (see also ***The Restaurant*** below) – **16 rm** ★105.00 – ★★125.00.
◆ A recent addition to the restaurant; comfortable lounges, a rustic breakfast room with kitchen range and handsomely equipped rooms themed around tartan colour schemes. The Chop and Ale House is set in inn's original bar.

Arden House without rest., Belsyde, EH49 6QE, Southwest : 2 ¼ m. on A 706 ☏ (01506) 670172, *info@ardencountryhouse.com, Fax (01506) 670172*, – P. MC AE VISA.
closed 25 December – **3 rm** ★45.00/80.00 – ★★70.00/90.00.
◆ Charmingly run guesthouse set in peaceful location with lovely rural views. Thoughtful extras include scones and shortbread on arrival. Rooms boast a luxurious style.

The Restaurant (at Champany Inn), Champany, EH49 7LU, Northeast : 2 m. on A 803 at junction with A 904 ☏ (01506) 834532, *Fax (01506) 834302*, – P. MC AE VISA
closed 25 December, 1 January, Saturday lunch and Sunday – **Rest** - Beef specialities - a la carte 46.40/48.90.
◆ Personally run converted horse mill. Superb South African wines in a charming cellar, fine china and twinkling glass in the roundhouse restaurant, specialising in prime beef.

Livingston's, 52 High St, EH49 7AE, ☏ (01506) 846565, *contact@livingstons-restaurant.co.uk*, – MC AE VISA
closed first 2 weeks January, 1 week June, Sunday and Monday – **Rest** 17.95/32.95.
◆ Friendly restaurant tucked away off high street. Menus offer good value meals using fresh regional produce; comfortable dining room, conservatory and summer terrace.

LIVINGSTON *West Lothian* 501 J 16 – *pop. 50 826.*
Bathgate, Edinburgh Rd ☏ (01506) 652232 – Deer Park C.C., Knightsridge ☏ (01506) 446699.
Edinburgh 16 – Falkirk 23 – Glasgow 32.

Premier Travel Inn, Deer Park Ave, Deer Park, Knightsridge, EH54 8AD, Northwest : 2 ¾ m. by A 899 at junction 3 of M 8 ☏ (01506) 439202, *Fax (01506) 438912* – rm rest, P. MC AE VISA.
Rest (grill rest.) – **83 rm** ★46.95/46.95 – ★★48.95/48.95.
◆ Simply furnished and brightly decorated bedrooms with ample work space. Family rooms with sofa beds. Ideal for corporate or leisure travel.

LOANS *South Ayrshire* 501 502 G 17 – *see Troon.*

LOCHBOISDALE *Western Isles (Outer Hebrides)* 501 Y 12 – *see Uist (Isles of).*

LOCHCARRON *Highland* 501 D 11 *Scotland G. – pop. 870.*

Env. : *Wester Ross*★★★ *– Loch Earn*★★.

☐ *Main St* ✆ *(01520) 722357 (April-October).*

Edinburgh 221 – Inverness 65 – Kyle of Lochalsh 23.

Rockvilla, Main St, IV54 8YB, ✆ (01520) 722379, *enquiries@rockvilla-hotel.co.uk, Fax (01520) 722844,* ← Loch Carron – ⋟. MC VISA
Rest (booking essential in winter) (bar lunch)/dinner a la carte 12.00/18.95 – **4 rm** ☐ ★40.00 – ★★65.00.

◆ Cosy, private hotel with enchanting views of Loch Carron, on whose shore it stands. Ideally situated for Highland touring. Bedrooms with good homely comforts. Meals taken in simply decorated dining room.

LOCHEARNHEAD *Stirling* 501 H 14 *Scotland G.*

Env. : *Loch Earn*★★.

Edinburgh 65 – Glasgow 56 – Oban 57 – Perth 36.

Mansewood Country House, FK19 8NS, South : ½ m. on A 84 ✆ (01567) 830213, *stay@mansewoodcountryhouse.co.uk, Fax (01567) 830485,* – ⋟ P. MC VISA
February-November – **Rest** (residents only) (dinner only) 17.50 **s.** – **5 rm** ☐ ★40.00 – ★★60.00.

◆ An attractive stone building, once a toll house and later a manse. Comfortable lounge and a bar area, well stocked with whiskies. Bedrooms have a cosy snug feel.

LOCHGILPHEAD *Argyll and Bute* 501 D 15 *Scotland G. – pop. 2 326.*

Env. : *Loch Fyne*★★, *E : 3½ m. by A 83.*

Blarbuie Rd ✆ *(01546) 602340.*

☐ *Lochnell St* ✆ *(01546) 602344 (April-October), info@lochgilphead.visitscotland.org.*

Edinburgh 130 – Glasgow 84 – Oban 38.

Empire Travel Lodge, Union St, PA31 8JS, ✆ (01546) 602381, *enquiries@empirelodge.co.uk, Fax (01546) 606606* – ⋟ rest, ♿ P. MC ⓓ VISA. ⋟
closed 1 January and 25 December – **Rest** *(closed Monday)* a la carte 11.20/21.75 **s.** – **9 rm** ☐ ★32.00/35.00 – ★★52.00/55.00.

◆ Former cinema whose interior walls are decorated with classic posters of screen stars. Provides simple, spacious, good value accommodation. Booth seating available in popular dining room.

at Cairnbaan *Northwest : 2¼ m. by A 816 on B 841 – ✉ Lochgilphead.*

Cairnbaan, PA31 8SJ, ✆ (01546) 603668, *info@cairnbaan.com, Fax (01546) 606045,* – ⋟ P – 100. MC VISA
closed Christmas **Rest** (bar lunch)/dinner a la carte 15.00/33.50 – **12 rm** ☐ ★72.50/79.50 – ★★92.00/145.00.

◆ 18C former coaching inn overlooking the Crinan Canal. Comfortable lounges and panelled bar. Well-equipped, individually decorated rooms, some in attractive contemporary style. Light, airy restaurant with modern art decorating the walls.

LOCH HARRAY *Orkney Islands* 501 K 6 – *see Orkney Islands (Mainland).*

LOCHINVER *Highland* 501 E 9 *Scotland G. – ✉ Lairg.*

See : *Village*★.

Env. : *Loch Assynt*★★, *E : 6 m. by A 837.*

☐ *Assynt Visitor Centre, Main St* ✆ *(01571) 844330 (April-October).*

Edinburgh 251 – Inverness 95 – Wick 105.

Inver Lodge, Iolaire Rd, IV27 4LU, ✆ (01571) 844496, *stay@inverlodge.com, Fax (01571) 844395,* ← Loch Inver Bay, Suilven and Canisp mountains, – ⋟ rest, P. MC AE ⓓ VISA
14 April-October – **Rest** (bar lunch)/dinner a la carte 19.90/23.95 **s.** – **20 rm** ☐ ★80.00 – ★★150.00.

◆ Comfy, modern hotel set in hillside above the village, surrounded by unspoilt wilderness. Choice of spacious lounges. Superior bedrooms with ocean views are particularly good. Restaurant boasts wonderful outlook.

Veyatie without rest., 66 Baddidarroch, IV27 4LP, West : 1 ¼ m. by Baddidarroch rd ✆ (01571) 844424, *veyatie-lochinver@tiscali.co.uk, Fax (01571) 844424,* ← Loch Inver Bay, Suilven and Canisp mountains, – ⋟ P. ⋟
closed 15 December - 15 January – **3 rm** ☐ ★30.00/46.00 – ★★48.00/54.00.

◆ An idyllic secluded haven with stunning views of Loch Inver Bay and mountains. Lovely conservatory. Friendly welcome, relaxing gardens and simple, snug bedrooms.

Davar without rest., Baddidarroch Rd, IV27 4LJ, West : ½ m. on Baddidarroch r
☎ (01571) 844501, *jean@davar36.fsnet.co.uk*, ≤ Loch Inver Bay and Suilven – ⇔ P. ⚡
March-November – **3 rm** ☕ ✦30.00/35.00 – ✦✦50.00.
◆ Modern guesthouse in an excellent position which affords wonderful views of Loch Inve Bay and Suilven. Homely and simple with well-kept bedrooms and communal breakfast.

The Albannach with rm, Baddidarroch, IV27 4LP, West : 1 m. by Baddidarroch r ☎ (01571) 844407, *the.albannach@virgin.net, Fax (01571) 844285*, ≤ Loch Inver Bay Suilven and Canisp mountains, ⚑, – ⇔ P. MO VISA. ⚡
closed mid November-March – **Rest** *(closed Monday)* (booking essential to non-residents (dinner only) (set menu only) 45.00 ♀ – **5 rm** ☕ ✦120.00/160.00 – ✦✦240.00/250.00.
◆ Pleasant restaurant and conservatory with predominantly Scottish feel and exceptiona views. Daily changing menu makes fine use of Highland produce. Warm inviting bedrooms

LOCHMADDY *Western Isles (Outer Hebrides)* 501 Y 11 – *see Uist (Isles of).*

LOCHRANZA *North Ayrshire* 501 502 E 16 – *see Arran (Isle of).*

LOCHWINNOCH *Renfrewshire* 501 502 G 16 – *pop. 2 570* – ✉ *Paisley.*
Edinburgh 61 – Ayr 37 – Glasgow 15 – Greenock 20.

East Lochhead Country House without rest., Largs Rd, PA12 4DX, Southwest 1 ¼ m. on A 760 ☎ (01505) 842610, *admin@eastlochhead.co.uk, Fax (01505) 842610*, ⚑,
– ⇔ ☎ P. MO AE VISA
closed January and Christmas – **3 rm** ☕ ✦45.00/55.00 – ✦✦75.00/85.00.
◆ Within striking distance of Glasgow airport yet firmly rural with views of Barr Loch an Renfrewshire hills. Comfy rooms in the farmhouse and outbuildings; lovely rear garden.

LOCKERBIE *Dumfries and Galloway* 501 502 J 18 – *pop. 4 009.*
18 Corrie Rd ☎ (01576) 203363 – 18 Lochmaben, Castlehill Gate ☎ (01387) 810552.
Edinburgh 74 – Carlisle 27 – Dumfries 13 – Glasgow 73.

Dryfesdale Country House, DG11 2SF, Northwest : 1 m. by Glasgow rd off B 707 ☎ (01576) 202427, *reception@dryfesdalehotel.co.uk, Fax (01576) 204187*, ≤, ⚑ – ⇔
P. MO AE VISA
Rest 25.00 (dinner) and a la carte 17.65/25.95 ♀ – **16 rm** (dinner included) ☕ ✦75.00/85.0 – ✦✦160.00, 1 suite.
◆ Extended, family-run 17C house in a rural setting with pleasant countryside views. Larg bar with fine selection of malts. Garden suites offer the most comfort. Comfortabl traditional dining room with large dance floor.

LUNDIN LINKS *Fife* 501 L 15.
Edinburgh 38 – Dundee 29 – Perth 31 – Stirling 46.

Swallow Old Manor, Leven Rd, KY8 6AJ, ☎ (01333) 320368, *swallow.lundinlinks@swallowhotels.co.uk, Fax (01333) 320911*, ≤, ⚑ – ⇔, ▤ rest, ☎ P – 🏛 150. MO AE ⓓ VISA
closed 26 December – ***Terrace Brasserie :*** **Rest** a la carte 24.65/32.40 ♀ – ***Coachman's*** **Rest** a la carte 14.20/23.95 ♀ – **26 rm** ☕ ✦75.00/110.00 – ✦✦115.00/155.00.
◆ 19C house with grand outlook over the Firth of Forth. Ideal golfing base, having man courses nearby. All bedrooms well kept, superior bedrooms have best views. Terrace Brasserie offers an excellent vista. Coachman's offers bistro-style ambience.

LUSS *Argyll and Bute* 501 G 15 *Scotland G.* – *pop. 402.*
See : *Village*★.
Env. : *E : Loch Lomond*★★.
Edinburgh 89 – Glasgow 26 – Oban 65.

Lodge on Loch Lomond, G83 8PA, ☎ (01436) 860201, *res@loch-lomond.co.u Fax (01436) 860203*, ≤ Loch Lomond, ≘s, ⚓ – ⇔ ♿ P – 🏛 175. MO AE VISA
Rest (light lunch Monday-Saturday)/dinner a la carte 29.00/39.45 ♀ – **46 rm** (dinner included) ✦134.00/181.00 – ✦✦161.00/214.00, 1 suite.
◆ Busy family run establishment in a superb spot on the shores of Loch Lomond. Most c the cosy pine panelled rooms have balconies; all of them can boast a sauna.. Restaurar and bar lounge carefully designed on two levels, opening the view to every table.

LYBSTER *Highland* 501 K 9 *Scotland G.*

Env. : The Hill o'Many Stanes★, NE : 3½ m. by A 9 – Grey Cairns of Camster★, N : 6 m. by A 9 and minor rd.

Edinburgh 251 – Inverness 94 – Thurso 28 – Wick 14.

Portland Arms, Main St, KW3 6BS, on A 9 ☎ (01593) 721721, *info@portlandarms.co.uk, Fax (01593) 721722* – P – 200. VISA
closed 1-2 January **Rest** (bar lunch Monday-Saturday)/dinner a la carte 16.50/25.20 – **22 rm** ★55.00/65.00 – ★★80.00.

◆ Former coaching inn dating from mid-19C. Informal atmosphere: spacious country house style lounge. Bedrooms are modern, comfortable and brightly decorated. Library dining room.

MAIDENS *South Ayrshire* 501 502 F 18.

Edinburgh 99 – Glasgow 53 – Maybole 7.

Wildings with rm, 21 Harbour Rd, KA26 9NR, ☎ (01655) 331401, *Fax (01655) 331330*, ← – P. VISA
closed 25-26 December and 1-2 January – **Rest** - Seafood specialities - 11.50/21.50 ♀ – **10 rm** ★45.00 – ★★75.00/120.00.

◆ Adjacent to harbour in coastal hamlet, visible from many bedrooms. Very hearty robust food from extensive menus which include excellent seafood. Simple rooms available.

MAYBOLE *South Ayrshire* 501 402 F 17 *Scotland G. – pop. 4 552.*

Env. : Culzean Castle★ AC (setting★★★, Oval Staircase★★) W : 5 m. by B 7023 and A 719.

Memorial Park ☎ (01655) 889770.

Edinburgh 93 – Ayr 10 – New Galloway 35 – Stranraer 42.

Ladyburn, KA19 7SG, South : 5 ½ m. by B 7023 off B 741 (Girvan rd) ☎ (01655) 740585, *jh@ladyburn.co.uk, Fax (01655) 740580*, ←, – P. VISA
closed Christmas-New Year and restricted opening in winter – **Rest** *(closed Sunday-Wednesday)* (booking essential to non-residents) (light lunch)/dinner 32.50/40.00 – **5 rm** ★60.00/90.00 – ★★160.00/200.00.

◆ Friendly and relaxed family run dower house in beautiful rose gardens. Elegant, bay windowed drawing room, firelit library, charming rooms with antique furniture and prints. Richly flavoured Scottish or Gallic dishes served at candlelit tables.

MELROSE *Borders* 501 502 L 17 *Scotland G. – pop. 11 656.*

See : Town★ - Abbey★★ (decorative sculpture★★★) AC.

Env. : Eildon Hills (★★★) – Scott's View★★ – Abbotsford★★ AC, W : 4½ m. by A 6091 and B 6360 – Dryburgh Abbey★★ AC (setting★★★), SE : 4 m. by A 6091 – Tweed Valley★★.

Exc. : Bowhill★★ AC, SW : 11½ m. by A 6091, A 7 and A 708 – Thirlestane Castle (plasterwork ceilings★★) AC, NE : 21 m. by A 6091 and A 68.

Melrose, Dingleton ☎ (01896) 822855.

Abbey House, Abbey St ☎ (08706) 080404 (Easter-October).

Edinburgh 38 – Hawick 19 – Newcastle upon Tyne 70.

Burts, Market Sq, TD6 9PL, ☎ (01896) 822285, *burtshotel@aol.com, Fax (01896) 822870* – P – 30. VISA
closed 25-27 December – **Rest** – (see ***The Restaurant*** below) – **20 rm** ★54.00/85.00 – ★★100.00/120.00.

◆ One-time coaching inn on main square - traditionally appointed and family run. Unpretentious rooms behind a neat black and white façade, brightened by pretty window boxes.

The Restaurant (at Burts H.), Market Sq, TD6 9PL, ☎ (01896) 822285, *Fax (01896) 822870* – P. VISA
closed 26 December – **Rest** 23.75/33.50 ♀.

◆ Cosy, clubby milieu of hunting scenes and rich tartans. Well-sourced local produce features extensively in elaborate modern variations on classic Scottish themes.

at Gattonside *North : 2 m. by B 6374 on B 6360 – ✉ Melrose.*

Fauhope House without rest., TD6 9LU, East : ¼ m. by B 6360 taking unmarked lane to the right of Monkswood Rd at edge of village ☎ (01896) 823184, *fauhope@border net.co.uk, Fax (01896) 823184*, ←, – P. VISA
3 rm ★50.00 – ★★70.00.

◆ Melrose Abbey just visible through the trees of this charming 19C country house with its antiques and fine furniture. Valley views at breakfast. Flower strewn, stylish rooms.

MELVICH *Highland* 501 I 8 *Scotland G. – ✉ Thurso.*
Env. : *Strathy Point★ (<★★★, Ben Loyal★★), NW : 5 m. by A 836 and minor rd.*
Edinburgh 267 – Inverness 110 – Thurso 18 – Wick 40.

The Sheiling without rest., KW14 7YJ, on A 836 ☎ (01641) 531256, *thesheiling@btinternet.com, Fax (01641) 531256,* <, – . VISA.
May-September – **3 rm** ★64.00/70.00 – ★★64.00/70.00.
◆ Pebble-dashed 1950s house run by husband and wife team. Spotless, thoughtfully furnished rooms overlook countryside. Extensive breakfast choice at family style table.

METHVEN *Perth and Kinross* 501 J 14 – *see Perth.*

MILNGAVIE *East Dunbarton* 501 H 16.
Edinburgh 52 – Glasgow 8 – Dumfries 83 – Stirling 28.

Premier Travel Inn, West Highland Gate, Main St, G62 6JJ, ☎ (0141) 956 7835, *Fax (0141) 956 7839* – rm, rest, . VISA.
Rest (grill rest.) – **60 rm** ★46.95/46.95 – ★★48.95/48.95.
◆ Modern, good value lodge accommodation north of town on main roundabout. Simply furnished and brightly decorated bedrooms with ample work space.

The Wild Bergamot, 1 Hillhead St, G62 8AF, ☎ (0141) 956 6515, *info@thewildbergamot.co.uk* – . VISA
closed first 3 weeks January, Monday and Tuesday – **Rest** (dinner only and lunch Friday and Saturday) 18.95/30.00 ♀.
◆ Compact, unfussy first-floor restaurant on a pedestrianised town centre street. Friendly service adds to the enjoyment of well executed dishes with pronounced Scottish accent.

MOFFAT *Dumfries and Galloway* 501 502 J 17 *Scotland G. – pop. 2 135.*
Exc. : *Grey Mare's Tail★★, NE : 9 m. by A 708.*
Coatshill ☎ (01683) 220020.
Churchgate ☎ (01683) 220620 (Easter-October).
Edinburgh 61 – Carlisle 43 – Dumfries 22 – Glasgow 60.

Craigie Lodge, Ballplay Rd, DG10 9JU, East : ¾ m. by Selkirk rd (A 708) ☎ (01683) 221769, *craigielodge@aol.com, Fax (01683) 221769,* – . VISA.
closed 25-26 December and 1-2 January – **Rest** 17.00 – **3 rm** ★37.50 – ★★55.00.
◆ Detached Victorian house in large garden about 10 minutes' walk from town centre. Original features in public rooms. Spacious, comfortable bedrooms, one on the ground floor. Choice of good home-cooked dishes for dinner prepared with local produce.

Well View with rm, Ballplay Rd, DG10 9JU, East : ¾ m. by Selkirk rd (A 708) ☎ (01683) 220184, *info@wellview.co.uk, Fax (01683) 220088,* – . VISA.
closed 2 weeks May and 25-26 December – **Rest** (booking essential) (set menu only) (dinner only and Sunday lunch)/dinner 32.00 – **3 rm** ★70.00 – ★★110.00.
◆ Well-established 19C house, run by family. Amply-sized, traditionally-furnished, comfortable bedrooms. Sample the seasonal dishes: generous, tasty and locally sourced.

The Limetree, High St, DG10 9HG, ☎ (01683) 221654, *Fax (01683) 221721* – . VISA
closed 2 weeks October, Sunday dinner and Monday – **Rest** (booking essential) (dinner only and Sunday lunch) 16.95/21.00.
◆ Simple, informal but busy restaurant in a little High Street cottage. Popular with locals and visitors. Small constantly-changing menus using local produce. Good value.

MONTROSE *Angus* 501 M 13 *Scotland G. – pop. 10 845.*
Exc. : *Edzell Castle★ (The Pleasance★★★) AC, NW : 17 m. by A 935 and B 966 – Cairn O'Mount Road★ (<★★) N : 17 m. by B 966 and B 974 – Brechin (Round Tower★) W : 7 m. by A 935 – Aberlemno (Aberlemno Stones★, Pictish sculptured stones★) W : 13 m. by A 935 and B 9134.*
Traill Drive ☎ (01674) 672932.
Bridge St ☎ (01674) 672000 (Easter-September).
Edinburgh 92 – Aberdeen 39 – Dundee 29.

36 The Mall without rest., 36 The Mall, DD10 8SS, North : ½ m. by A 92 at junction with North Esk Road ☎ (01674) 673646, *enquiries@36themall.co.uk, Fax (01674) 673646,* . VISA
3 rm ★35.00/45.00 – ★★50.00/70.00.
◆ Bay windowed 19C former manse with pleasant conservatory lounge to rear. Impressive plate collection the talking point of communal breakfast room. Sizable, well-kept rooms.

MOTHERWELL *North Lanarkshire* 501 I 16.
Edinburgh 38 – Glasgow 12.

Hilton Strathclyde, Phoenix Crescent, Bellshill, ML4 3JQ, Northwest : 4 m. by A 721 on A 725 ✆ (01698) 395500, *reservations.strathclyde@hilton.com, Fax (01698) 395511,* ⑩, Fö, ≘s, ▣ – |‡| ⇹, ▤ rest, ✆ ♿ 🅿 – 🏛 400. MC AE VISA. ✈
Rest *(closed lunch Saturday and Bank Holidays)* 9.50/22.95 and dinner a la carte ♀ – ☐ 15.95 – **107 rm** ✝63.00/145.00 – ✝✝63.00/145.00.
◆ Group owned and smoothly run; a regular choice for business travellers, drawn by smartly laid-out modern rooms, open-plan lounge and coffee shop and superb leisure complex. Restaurant sets out to put a subtle new spin on classic dishes.

Alona, Strathclyde Country Park, ML1 3RT, Northwest : 4 ½ m. by A 721 and B 7070 off A 725 ✆ (01698) 333888, *julian@alonahotel.co.uk, Fax (01698) 338720* – |‡|, ⇹ rm, ▤ rest, ✆ ♿ 🅿. MC AE ⓓ VISA
Rest (carving lunch)/dinner 19.95 and a la carte 19.25/31.15 – **51 rm** ☐ ✝84.00/120.00 – ✝✝89.00/130.00.
◆ Attractively set modern hotel in 1500 acres of Strathclyde Country Park. Conservatory atrium with open-plan lounge and bar. Good-sized bedrooms exuding contemporary taste. Restaurant affords pleasant lakeside views.

Express by Holiday Inn without rest., Strathclyde Country Park, Hamilton Rd, ML1 3RB, Northwest : 4 ¼ m. by A 721 and B 7070 off A 725 ✆ (01698) 858585, *Fax (01698) 852375* – |‡| ⇹ ♿ 🅿 – 🏛 30. MC AE ⓓ VISA
120 rm ✝65.00 – ✝✝65.00.
◆ Good motorway connections from this purpose-built hotel offering trim rooms in contemporary style plus a small lounge and bar: a useful address for business stopovers.

MUIR OF ORD *Highland* 501 G 11 – *pop. 1 812.*
⛳18 Great North Rd ✆ (01463) 870825.
Edinburgh 173 – Inverness 10 – Wick 121.

Dower House 🐎, Highfield, IV6 7XN, North : 1 m. on A 862 ✆ (01463) 870090, *enquiries@thedowerhouse.co.uk, Fax (01463) 870090,* 🌳 – ⇹ ✆ 🅿. MC VISA
closed 2 weeks November and 25 December – **Rest** (booking essential to non-residents) (set menu only) (lunch by arrangement)/dinner 38.00 s. – **4 rm** ☐ ✝65.00/85.00 – ✝✝115.00/135.00, 1 suite.
◆ Personally run, part 17C house in mature garden. Stacked bookshelves, soft fireside armchairs, cosy bedrooms and fresh flowers: a relaxed but well-ordered country home. Fine glassware, glossy hardwood tables and a sofa by the fire for a post-prandial dram.

MULL (Isle of) *Argyll and Bute* 501 B/C 14/15 *Scotland G. – pop. 2 838.*
See : *Island★ - Calgary Bay★★ – Torosay Castle AC (Gardens★ ≤★).*
Env. : *Isle of Iona★ (Maclean's Cross★, St Oran's Chapel★, St Martin's High Cross★, Infirmary Museum★ AC (Cross of St John★)).*
⛳9 Craignure, Scallastle ✆ (01680) 302517.
⛴ from Craignure to Oban (Caledonian MacBrayne Ltd) frequent services daily (45 mn) – from Fishnish to Lochaline (Mainland) (Caledonian MacBrayne Ltd) frequent services daily (15 mn) – from Tobermory to Isle of Tiree (Scarinish) via Isle of Coll (Arinagour) (Caledonian MacBrayne Ltd) 3 weekly (2 h 30 mn) – from Tobermory to Kilchoan (Caledonian MacBrayne Ltd) 4 daily (summer only) (35 mn).
⛴ from Fionnphort to Isle of Iona (Caledonian MacBrayne Ltd) frequent services daily (10 mn) – from Pierowall to Papa Westray (Orkney Ferries Ltd) (summer only) (25 mn).
ℹ The Pier, Craignure ✆ (01680) 812377 – Main Street, Tobermory ✆ (01688) 302182 (April-October).

Craignure *Argyll and Bute.*

Birchgrove 🐎 without rest., Lochdon, PA64 6AP, Southeast : 3 m. on A 849 ✆ (01680) 812364, *birchgrove@isle-of-mull.demon.co.uk,* ≤, 🌳 – ⇹ 🅿. MC VISA. ✈
mid March - mid October – **3 rm** ☐ ✝42.00/45.00 – ✝✝54.00/56.00.
◆ Modern guesthouse with landscaped gardens in peaceful setting with good views. Close to ferry pier. Clean, well-kept rooms, all boasting pleasant island outlook.

Gruline *Argyll and Bute.*

Gruline Home Farm 🐎, PA71 6HR, ✆ (01680) 300581, *boo@gruline.com, Fax (01680) 300573,* ≤, 🌳 – ⇹ 🅿. MC VISA
Rest (by arrangement) (communal dining) 30.00 – **3 rm** ☐ ✝100.00 – ✝✝100.00.
◆ Former farmhouse with both 17C and 18C origins, located off the beaten track with fine views over surrounding mountains. Sitting room and conservatory. Well-furnished rooms. Traditional dining room with guests seated together.

SCOTLAND

Tiroran *Argyll and Bute.*

Tiroran House, PA69 6ES, (01681) 705232, *info@tiroran.com* *Fax (01681) 705240*, ≤ Loch Scridain, – P. VISA.
Rest (booking essential) (residents only) (dinner only) 30.00 **s.** – **5 rm** 104.00/124.00 – 104.00/124.00.
◆ Attractive whitewashed hotel sited in remote location with superb views across Loch Scridain. Well-decorated lounges with country house style. Individually appointed rooms. Home-cooked dinners in vine-covered dining room or conservatory.

Tobermory *Argyll and Bute – pop. 2 708.*

Erray Rd (01688) 302140.

Tobermory, 53 Main St, PA75 6NT, (01688) 302091, *tobhotel@tinyworld.co.uk* *Fax (01688) 302254*, ≤ – VISA
closed 8 January - 4 February and 1 week Christmas – ***Waters Edge :* Rest** (booking essential to non-residents) (dinner only) 27.00 – **16 rm** 36.00/86.00 – 80.00/110.00.
◆ Pink-painted, converted fishing cottages - cosy, well-run and informal - on the pretty quayside. Soft toned bedrooms in cottage style, most overlooking the bay. Intimate setting: linen-clad tables and subtly nautical décor.

Brockville without rest., Raeric Rd, PA75 6RS, by Back Brae (01688) 302741, *helen@brockville-tobermory.co.uk, Fax (01688) 302741*, ≤, – P.
3 rm 30.00/40.00 – 50.00/60.00.
◆ Modern guesthouse in the residential part of town. The communal breakfast room has good views over the sea. Cottagey rooms have extra touches including videos and CDs.

Highland Cottage with rm, Breadalbane St, PA75 6PD, via B 8073 (01688) 302030, *davidandjo@highlandcottage.co.uk* – P. VISA
closed November - December – **Rest** (booking essential to non-residents) (dinner only) 35.00 ♀ – **6 rm** 96.00 – 155.00.
◆ Modern cottage near the harbour. Prettily set dining room shows the same care and attention as the locally sourced menu. Individually styled rooms with good views.

NAIRN *Highland 501 I 11 Scotland G. – pop. 8 418.*

Env. : *Forres (Sueno's Stone★★) E : 11 m. by A 96 and B 9011 – Cawdor Castle★ AC, S : 5½ m. by B 9090 – Brodie Castle★ AC, E : 6 m. by A 96.*
Exc. : *Fort George★, W : 8 m. by A 96, B 9092 and B 9006.*
18, 9 Seabank Rd (01667) 453208 – 18 Nairn Dunbar, Lochloy Rd (01667) 452741.
Edinburgh 172 – Aberdeen 91 – Inverness 16.

Golf View, The Seafront, IV12 4HD, (01667) 458800, *reservations.golfview@swallowhotels.com, Fax (01667) 458818*, ≤, – rest, P – 120. VISA
***Restaurant :* Rest** (dinner only) 27.00 **s.** – ***Conservatory :* Rest** a la carte 18.05/33.30 **s.** – **41 rm** 95.00/118.00 – 159.00/217.00, 1 suite.
◆ Non-golfers may prefer the vista of the Moray Firth from one of the sea-view rooms or a poolside lounger. Smart, traditional accommodation, up-to-date gym and beauty salon. Half-panelled dining room. Stylish, spacious conservatory restaurant.

Swallow Newton, Inverness Rd, IV12 4RX, (01667) 453144, *swallow.newton@swallowhotels.com, Fax (01667) 454026*, – P – 400. VISA
Rest (bar lunch)/dinner a la carte 19.00/30.00 ♀ – **52 rm** 92.00/166.00 – 117.00/200.00, 4 suites.
◆ Enlarged mansion bounded by woods. Traditional lounge in velvet and paisley; state-of-the-art conference centre. Period styled rooms in the old house have greater character. Formally set restaurant, its windows give on to a lawn edged with rhododendrons.

Claymore House, 45 Seabank Rd, IV12 4EY, (01667) 453731, *claymorehouse@btconnect.com, Fax (01667) 455290*, – P. VISA
Rest (bar lunch)/dinner a la carte 15.10/26.45 **s.** – **12 rm** 47.50/70.00 – 95.00, 1 suite.
◆ A privately-run, extended 19C house in a residential area. Comfortable lounge and conservatory. Modern rooms in warm colours are quieter at the rear. Neatly laid-out dining room: choose from a range of traditional Scottish favourites.

Boath House, Auldearn, IV12 5TE, East : 2 m. on A 96 (01667) 454896, *wendy@boathhouse.demon.co.uk, Fax (01667) 455469*, ≤, – P. VISA
closed 1 week Christmas – **Rest** *(closed to non-residents Monday-Wednesday lunch)* (booking essential) 18.95/45.00 ♀ – **6 rm** 120.00 – 170.00/280.00.
◆ 1820s neo-classical mansion, owned by a charming couple, hosts modern Highland art collections. Intimate, elegant rooms may have half-tester beds or views of the trout lake. Dining room with 18C garden views: precise, accomplished cooking in a modern style.

Sunny Brae, Marine Rd, IV12 4EA, ☎ (01667) 452309, *Fax (01667) 454860,* ≤, – ⇔ [P]. MC VISA.
Rest (booking essential to non-residents) (lunch residents only)/dinner 14.00/31.00 ♀ – **8 rm** ⊒ ✝39.00/109.00 – ✝✝59.00/109.00.
◆ Behind an unassuming façade, this family-owned hotel offers sizeable, neatly kept bedrooms in cheerful patterns - many, like the terrace, have views of the shore.

The Classroom, 1 Cawdor St, IV12 4QD, ☎ (01667) 455999, *Fax (01667) 455999* – ⇔.
MC AE D VISA
closed 25 December and 1-2 January – **Rest** a la carte 17.40/25.95 ♀.
◆ Extended former school house in town centre. Split level wood-floored restaurant with L-shaped bar and pictures of pupils on the walls. Extensive menu with daily specials.

NETHERLEY *Aberdeenshire* 501 N 13 – *see Stonehaven.*

NEWBURGH *Aberdeenshire* 501 N 12 *Scotland G.*

Exc. : *Pitmedden Gardens★★ AC, W : 6½ m. by B 9000 – Haddo House★ AC, NW : 14 m. by B 900, A 92 and B 9005.*
McDonald, Hospital Rd, Ellon ☎ (01358) 720576 – Newburgh-on-Ythan, Ellon ☎ (01358) 789058.
Edinburgh 144 – Aberdeen 14 – Fraserburgh 33.

Udny Arms, Main St, AB41 6BL, ☎ (01358) 789444, *enquiry@udny.demon.co.uk., Fax (01358) 789012,* – ⇔ [P] – 45. MC AE D VISA
Rest – (see ***The Bistro*** below) – **27 rm** ⊒ ✝55.00/90.00 – ✝✝75.00/110.00, 1 suite.
◆ Fishing, shooting and sporting memorabilia on display in an extended, family-run hotel on the river Ython. Bedrooms in traditional colours and fabrics, quieter at the rear.

The Bistro (at Udny Arms H.), Main St, AB41 6BL, ☎ (01358) 789444, *Fax (01358) 789012* – ⇔ [P]. MC AE D VISA
Rest (booking essential) a la carte 14.85/30.90.
◆ A pleasant coastal outlook dominates this cosily informal eatery with its mismatched wooden tables and chairs. Well-regarded dishes, using quality, locally sourced produce.

NEW LANARK *Lanarkshire* 501 I 17.

Edinburgh 44 – Dumfries 55 – Glasgow 31.

New Lanark Mill, Mill One, New Lanark Mills, ML11 9DB, ☎ (01555) 667200, *hotel@newlanark.org, Fax (01555) 667222,* ≤ – |‡| ⇔ & [P] – 150. MC AE D VISA
Mill One : **Rest** (carving lunch Sunday) (bar lunch Monday-Saturday)/dinner 23.50 **s.** – **38 rm** ⊒ ✝69.50 – ✝✝109.00/134.00.
◆ Converted Clydeside cotton mill on the riverside in this superbly restored Georgian village, a World Heritage site. Usefully equipped, modern accommodation. Formal restaurant overlooking the river.

NEWTON STEWART *Dumfries and Galloway* 501 502 G 19 *Scotland G.* – *pop. 3 573.*

Env. : *Galloway Forest Park★, Queen's Way★ (Newton Stewart to New Galloway) N : 19 m. by A 712.*
Kirroughtree Ave, Minnigaff ☎ (01671) 402172 – Wigtownshire County, Mains of Park, Glenluce ☎ (01581) 300420.
Dashwood Sq ☎ (01671) 402431 (Easter-October).
Edinburgh 131 – Dumfries 51 – Glasgow 87 – Stranraer 24.

Kirroughtree House, DG8 6AN, Northeast : 1½ m. by A 75 on A 712 ☎ (01671) 402141, *info@kirroughtreehouse.co.uk, Fax (01671) 402425,* ≤ woodland and Wigtown Bay, – ⇔ rest, [P]. MC AE VISA
closed 2 January-9 February – **Rest** (booking essential to non-residents) 32.50 (dinner) and lunch a la carte 17.25/24.25 **s.** – **15 rm** ⊒ ✝85.00/105.00 – ✝✝190.00/230.00, 2 suites.
◆ Grand 1719 mansion dominates acres of sculpted garden. Well-proportioned bedrooms; firelit lounge with antiques, period oils and French windows leading to the croquet lawn. Elegant fine dining, in keeping with formal grandeur of the house.

Rowallan without rest., Corsbie Rd, via Jubilee Rd off Dashwood Sq, DG8 6JB, ☎ (01671) 402520, *enquiries@rowallan.co.uk, Fax (01671) 402520,* – ⇔ [P].
5 rm ⊒ ✝32.50 – ✝✝60.00.
◆ Victorian house in attractive large garden not far from town centre. Large lounge with bar; breakfast served in conservatory. Brightly decorated bedrooms.

NORTH BERWICK *East Lothian* 501 L 15 *Scotland G. – pop. 5 871.*

Env. : *North Berwick Law (※★★★) S : 1 m. - Tantallon Castle★★ (clifftop site★★★) AC E : 3½ m. by A 198 – Dirleton★ (Castle★ AC) SW : 2½ m. by A 198.*

Exc. : *Museum of Flight★, S : 6 m. by B 1347 – Preston Mill★, S : 8½ m. by A 198 and B 104 – Tyninghame★, S : 7 m. by A 198 – Coastal road from North Berwick to Portseton★, SW 13 m. by A 198 and B 1348.*

North Berwick, West Links, Beach Rd ☎ (01620) 895040 – The Glen, East Link ☎ (01620) 892726.

Quality St ☎ (01620) 892197.

Edinburgh 24 – Newcastle upon Tyne 102.

Glebe House without rest., Law Rd, EH39 4PL, ☎ (01620) 892608, *gwenscott@glebehouse-nb.co.uk, Fax (01620) 893588,* – P.
closed 25-26 December – **3 rm** – ★★70.00/90.00.
◆ Owned by a likeable couple, a classically charming 1780s manse in secluded gardens. E suite rooms are pleasantly unfussy and well-kept. Breakfasts at a long communal table.

Beach Lodge without rest., 5 Beach Rd, EH39 4AB, ☎ (01620) 892257, ≤ –.
3 rm ★35.00/40.00 – ★★70.00.
◆ Friendly and well-run: breakfast room and compact, modern bedrooms share an appealing, clean-lined style. All rooms have fridges and videos, one overlooks the sea.

NORTH UIST *Western Isles (Outer Hebrides)* 501 X/Y 10/11 – *see Uist (Isles of).*

OBAN *Argyll and Bute* 501 D 14 *Scotland G. – pop. 8 120.*

Exc. : *Loch Awe★★, SE : 17 m. by A 85 – Bonawe Furnace★, E : 12 m. by A 85 – Cruacha Power Station★ AC, E : 16 m. by A 85 – Sea Life Centre★ AC, N : 14 m. by A 828.*

Glencruitten, Glencruitten Rd ☎ (01631) 562868.

Access to Glasgow by helicopter.

to Isle of Mull (Craignure) (Caledonian MacBrayne Ltd) (45 mn) – to South Uist (Lochboisdale) via Isle of Barra (Castlebay) (Caledonian MacBrayne Ltd) (summer only) – to Isle of Tiree (Scarinish) via Isle of Mull (Tobermory) and Isle of Coll (Arinagour) (Caledonian MacBrayne Ltd) – to Isle of Islay (Port Askaig) and Kintyre Peninsula (Kennacraig) via Isle of Colonsay (Scalasaig) (Caledonian MacBrayne Ltd) (summer only) – to Isle of Lismore (Achnacroish) (Caledonian MacBrayne Ltd) 2-3 daily (except Sunday) (55 mn) – to Isle of Colonsay (Scalasaig) (Caledonian MacBrayne Ltd) 3 weekly (2 h).

Church Building, Argyll Sq ☎ (01631) 563122, info@oban.org.uk.

Edinburgh 123 – Dundee 116 – Glasgow 93 – Inverness 118.

Manor House, Gallanach Rd, PA34 4LS, ☎ (01631) 562087, *info@manorhouseoban.com, Fax (01631) 563053,* ≤ Oban harbour and bay, – P. MC AE VISA
closed 25-26 December – **Rest** (lunch by arrangement)/dinner 29.50 – **11 rm** (dinner included) ★88.00/147.00 – ★★136.00/204.00.
◆ Period furniture and colour schemes bring out the character of this 18C dower house once part of the Argyll ducal estate. Individual rooms, most with fine views of the bay. Green and tartan restaurant warmed by an ancient range.

Knipoch House, PA34 4QT, Southwest : 6 m. on A 816 ☎ (01852) 316251, *reception@knipochhotel.co.uk, Fax (01852) 316249,* ≤, – rest, P. MC AE VISA
Rest (bar lunch) /dinner a la carte 24.50/36.75 – **19 rm** ★76.00/83.00 ★★152.00/166.00, 1 suite.
◆ Between wooded hills and Loch Feochan, a relaxing, traditional environment of wood panelling and roaring fires. Comfortable, well-equipped rooms; most look on to the water. Unpretentious Scottish cooking and lake views in three separate rooms.

Lerags House, Lerags, PA34 4SE, Southwest : 4 ½ m. by A 816 on Lerags ☎ (01631) 563381, *stay@leragshouse.com,* ≤, – P. MC VISA.
restricted opening in winter – **Rest** (booking essential) (dinner only) 28.00 **s.** – **6 rm** (dinner included) ★95.00 – ★★150.00/170.00.
◆ Peacefully located, characterful Georgian house with extensions in mature gardens near Loch Feochan. Comfortable, welcoming lounge. Sizeable rooms boasting homely extras. Simple dining room with garden aspect.

The Barriemore without rest., Corran Esplanade, PA34 5AQ, ☎ (01631) 566356, *reception@barriemore-hotel.co.uk, Fax (01631) 571084,* ≤ Oban bay, Kerrera and Isle of Mull P. MC VISA
closed 3 weeks January, 1 week November and Christmas – **13 rm** ★32.00/50.00 ★★80.00/84.00.
◆ Gabled 1890s house overlooking town and islands. A comfortable blend of modern and period styling - front bedrooms are larger and look towards Oban Bay, Kerrera and Mull.

Glenburnie House without rest., Corran Esplanade, PA34 5AQ, ☎ (01631) 562089, *graeme.strachan@btinternet.com, Fax (01631) 562089,* ≤ Oban bay, Kerrera and Isle of Mull – ⇔ P. MC VISA. ✈
mid March-mid November – **11 rm** ☐ ★37.00/70.00 – ★★70.00/95.00, 1 suite.
◆ Bay-windowed Victorian house has enviable views over the bay. Pleasant lounge with a hint of homely informality and usefully equipped rooms, one with a four-poster bed.

Alltavona without rest., Corran Esplanade, PA34 5AQ, ☎ (01631) 565067, *carol@alltavona.co.uk, Fax (01631) 565067,* ≤ Oban bay, Kerrera and Isle of Mull – ⇔ P. MC VISA. ✈
closed Christmas-New Year and restricted opening in winter – **6 rm** ☐ ★35.00/75.00 – ★★60.00/80.00.
◆ 19C villa on smart esplanade with fine views of Oban Bay. Attractively furnished interiors in keeping with the house's age. Fine oak staircase and individually styled rooms.

The Old Manse without rest., Dalriach Rd, PA34 5JE, via A 85 (Fort William) and Deanery Brae ☎ (01631) 564886, *oldmanse@obanguesthouse.co.uk,* ⛰ – ⇔ P. MC VISA
closed December-January – **6 rm** ☐ ★46.00/57.00 – ★★52.00/72.00.
◆ Victorian former manse perched on hill with views out to sea. Neat breakfast room also boasts impressive outlook; gardens with wood decking. Large but homely rooms.

Coast, 104 George St, PA34 5NT, ☎ (01631) 569900, *coastoban@yahoo.co.uk, Fax (01631) 569901* – ⇔. MC VISA
closed 2 weeks January and 25 December – **Rest** 10.00 (lunch) and a la carte 18.65/28.70.
◆ Former bank building in town centre. Contemporary interior of stripped wood floors and khaki coloured walls. Appealing modern menus including plenty of fish and shellfish.

Ee-usk at The North Pier, The North Pier, PA34 5DQ, ☎ (01631) 565666, *eeusk.fishcafe@virgin.net, Fax (01631) 570282,* ≤ Oban harbour and bay, ☎ – MC VISA
closed 5-19 January – **Rest** - Seafood - a la carte 17.85/32.90.
◆ A smart addition to the pier with its harbour proximity; excellent views of the bay add a relaxing charm. Fresh seafood menus with daily specials.

The Waterfront, No 1, The Pier, PA34 4LW, ☎ (01631) 563110, *Fax (01631) 563110,* ≤ Oban harbour and bay – MC AE VISA
closed 20 December-14 February – **Rest** - Seafood - a la carte 17.15/29.45.
◆ Converted quayside mission with fine views of harbour and bay; airy, open-plan interior. Flavourful but simple seafood: blackboard specials feature the day's fresh catch.

OLDMELDRUM *Aberdeenshire* 501 N 11 *Scotland G.*

Exc. : *Haddo House★, NE : 9 m. by B 9170 on B 9005.*
🏌 *Oldmeldrum, Kirkbrae ☎ (01651) 872648.*
Edinburgh 140 – Aberdeen 17 – Inverness 87.

Cromlet Hill without rest., South Rd, AB51 0AB, ☎ (01651) 872315, *johnpage@cromlethill.co.uk, Fax (01651) 872164,* ⛰ – ⇔ P. ✈
3 rm ☐ ★30.00/37.00 – ★★56.00/70.00.
◆ Half Georgian, half Victorian house with attractive front garden. Characterful sitting room, smart, spacious bedrooms, all well-equipped. Breakfast at antique dining table.

ONICH *Highland* 501 E 13 – ✉ *Fort William.*

Edinburgh 123 – Glasgow 93 – Inverness 79 – Oban 39.

Lodge on the Loch, PH33 6RY, on A 82 ☎ (01855) 821238, *info@lodgeontheloch.com, Fax (01855) 821190,* ≤ Loch Linnhe and mountains, ⛰ – ⇔ ☎ P. MC VISA
mid March-mid November and Christmas-New Year – **Rest** (dinner only) 30.00 ♀ – **14 rm** (dinner included) ☐ ★70.00/100.00 – ★★130.00/180.00, 1 suite.
◆ Steam shower or sleigh bed, Shaker or Art Nouveau styling: carefully composed bijou rooms in a Victorian hotel above Loch Linnhe - classically cosy lounges have fine views. Formally set tables in the dining room and a great view south across the water.

The ✿ award is the crème de la crème. This is awarded to restaurants which are really worth travelling miles for!

ORKNEY ISLANDS *Orkney Islands* 501 *K/L 6/7 Scotland G. – pop. 19 612.*

See : *Old Man of Hoy*★★★ – *Islands*★★ – *Maes Howe*★★ *AC* – *Skara Brae*★★ *AC* – *Corriga Farm Museum*★ *AC* – *Brough of Birsay*★ *AC* – *Birsay* (≤★) – *Ring of Brodgar*★ – *Unstar Cairn*★.

see Kirkwall.

service between Isle of Hoy (Longhope), Isle of Hoy (Lyness), Isle of Flotta and Hou ton (Orkney Ferries Ltd) – from Stromness to Scrabster (P & O Scottish Ferries) (1-3 daily (2 h) – from Stromness to Shetland Islands (Lerwick) and Aberdeen (P & O Scottish Ferries 2 weekly – from Kirkwall to Westray, Stronsay via Eday and Sanday (Orkney Ferries Ltd) - from Tingwall to Wyre via Egilsay and Rousay (Orkney Ferries Ltd) – from Kirkwall to Shapin say (Orkney Ferries Ltd) (25 mn) – from Stromness to Isle of Hoy (Moness) and Graemsa (Orkney Ferries Ltd) – from Kirkwall to North Ronaldsay (Orkney Ferries Ltd) weekl (2 h 40 mn) – from Kirkwall to Invergordon (Orcargo Ltd) daily (8 h 30 mn) – from Houton to Isle of Hoy (Lyness), Flotta and Longhope (Orkney Ferries Ltd) – from Stromness to Graem say via Isle of Hoy (Orkney Ferries Ltd).

from Burwick (South Ronaldsay) to John O'Groats (John O'Groats Ferries) 2-4 dail (40 mn).

MAINLAND *Orkney Islands.*

Burray *Orkney Islands.*

Sands, KW17 2SS, ℘ (01856) 731298, *info@thesandshotel.co.uk, Fax (01856) 731303,* ≤ P. MO AE VISA.
Rest (bar lunch) /dinner a la carte 14.00/25.00 s. – **6 rm** ☕ ★30.00/60.00 ★★50.00/75.00.
◆ Former fish store, just 20 yards' walk from main pier. Totally modern interior with plent of space and lots of seafaring knick-knacks. Popular bar. Sizeable, modish bedrooms Spacious dining room with views of bay: light or formal choice of menus.

Kirkwall *Orkney Islands Scotland G. – pop. 5 952.*

See : *Kirkwall*★★ – *St Magnus Cathedral*★★ – *Western Mainland*★★, *Eastern Mainland (Italia Chapel*★) – *Earl's Palace*★ *AC* – *Tankerness House Museum*★ *AC* – *Orkney Farm and Fo Museum*★.

18 *Grainbank* ℘ *(01856) 872457.*

Kirkwall Airport : ℘ *(01856) 886210, S : 3½ m.*

6 Broad St ℘ *(01856) 872856.*

Ayre, Ayre Rd, KW15 1QX, ℘ (01856) 873001, *ayrehotel@btconnect.con Fax (01856) 876289* – rm, P – 200. MO AE VISA
closed 24-25 and 31 December and 1 January – **Rest** a la carte 14.95/27.50 – **32 rm** ☕ ★72.00/82.00 – ★★110.00.
◆ Smoothly run by an experienced family team, this hotel by the harbour offers moderr practically fitted bedrooms and one of the island's most spacious conference rooms Dining room decorated in simple, modern style.

St Ola without rest., Harbour St, KW15 1LE, ℘ (01856) 875090, *enquiries@stolah tel.co.uk, Fax (01856) 875090* – MO VISA.
closed 20 December-5 January – **6 rm** ☕ ★37.00/40.00 – ★★52.00/54.00.
◆ Practically furnished, converted town house facing the harbour and convenient for th ferry terminal. Neat bedrooms in co-ordinating fabrics. Simple public bar.

Lav'rockha, Inganess Rd, KW15 1SP, Southeast : 1 ¼ m. by A 960 ℘ (01856) 87610 *lavrockha@orkney.com, Fax (01856) 876103,* – P. MO VISA.
closed February – **Rest** (by arrangement) 14.95 – **5 rm** ☕ ★35.00 – ★★52.00.
◆ Personally run in an enthusiastic spirit. Spotless en suite rooms in floral fabrics or dar tartans. Homely, uncluttered lounge with useful tourist information. Popular, tradition menu, served in the simplest of settings.

Polrudden without rest., Peerie Sea Loan, KW15 1UH, West : 1 m. by Pickaquoy R ℘ (01856) 874761, *linda@polrudden.com, Fax (01856) 870950* – P. MO VISA.
closed 24 December - 3 January – **7 rm** ☕ ★40.00 – ★★52.00.
◆ Well-kept en suite accommodation - over two floors - with matching fabrics and va nished pine in a sizeable converted house just outside the town centre. Friendly owne Dining room: picture windows give on to quiet fields.

Brekk-Ness without rest., Muddisdale Rd, KW15 1RS, West : ¾ m. by Pickaquoy R ℘ (01856) 874317, *sandrabews@aol.com, Fax (01856) 874317* – P. MO AE VISA
closed 1 week Christmas – **11 rm** ☕ ★35.00/40.00 – ★★50.00/55.00.
◆ In the fields on the edge of the town, an unassuming guesthouse, neatly maintained b a likeable couple. Bedrooms are practically fitted and en suite.

Foveran with rm, St Ola, KW15 1SF, Southwest : 3 m. on A 964 (01856) 872389, *foveranhotel@aol.com, Fax (01856) 876430*, – P. MC VISA. *restricted opening in winter* – **Rest** (dinner only) a la carte 17.90/31.70 – **8 rm** 60.00/80.00 – 100.00.

◆ Modern hotel enjoys a beautiful view of Scapa Flow. Simple, soft-toned bedrooms, furnished in warm wood and a firelit lounge, in the same style, where apéritifs are served. Orkney fudge cheesecake a dining room regular.

och Harray *Orkney Islands.*

Merkister , KW17 2LF, off A 986 (01856) 771366, *merkister-hotel@ecosse.net, Fax (01856) 771515*, ≤ Loch Harray, , – , rest, P. MC AE VISA *closed 22 December-4 January* – **Rest** *(booking essential in winter)* (bar lunch Monday-Saturday)/dinner 22.50/31.25 and a la carte 20.00/35.25 – **16 rm** 25.00/60.00 – 60.00/110.00.

◆ In a peaceful spot above Loch Harray, a popular angling base, family run with friendly efficiency. Trim bedrooms; public bar with a quiet buzz of far-fetched fishing tales. Restaurant offers an extensive menu on a distinctly Scottish base.

t Margaret's Hope *Orkney Islands.*

Shoreside, KW17 2TQ, Northeast : 1 ½ m. on A 961 (01856) 831560, *tracey@shellfish.co.uk, Fax (01856) 831436*, ≤ West Sound, – P. MC AE VISA *closed Christmas* – **Rest** (by arrangement) (communal dining) 25.00 – **3 rm** 35.00 – 70.00.

◆ Superbly positioned guesthouse with fine views of West Sound. Refurbished in a pleasant fashion with stylish, well executed, individually styled bedrooms. Dine communally on top quality local shellfish.

Creel with rm, Front Rd, KW17 2SL, (01856) 831311, *alan@thecreel.freeserve.co.uk*, ≤ – P. MC VISA. *April-October* – **Rest** - Seafood specialities - *(closed Monday except June-August)* (dinner only) 31.00/42.00 – **3 rm** 60.00/70.00 – 90.00/100.00.

◆ Smart, family run restaurant; flavourful local dishes without culinary curlicues: menu devised daily based upon the best seasonal produce. Friendly staff. Neat, homely rooms.

'estray (Island of).

Cleaton House , KW17 2DB, (01857) 677508, *cleaton@orkney.com, Fax (01857) 677442*, ≤ Papa Westray, – P. MC VISA *closed November and 25-26 December* – **Rest** (booking essential to non-residents) (bar lunch)/dinner 26.00 – **6 rm** 49.00 – 76.00/90.00.

◆ Originally built as mansion for Laird of Cleat in 1850, this charming guesthouse is idyllically situated halfway up the island. Charming lounge. Individually appointed rooms. Country house dining room overlooks garden.

EEBLES *Borders* 501 502 K 17 *Scotland G. – pop. 8 065.*

Env. : *Tweed Valley★★.*

Exc. : *Traquair House★★ AC, SE : 7 m. by B 7062 – Rosslyn Chapel★★ AC, N : 16½ m. by A 703, A 6094, B 7026 and B 7003.*

Kirkland St (01721) 720197.

High St (0870) 608 0404.

Edinburgh 24 – Glasgow 53 – Hawick 31.

Cringletie House , Edinburgh Rd, EH45 8PL, North : 3 m. on A 703 (01721) 725750, *enquiries@cringletie.com, Fax (01721) 725751*, ≤, , – P. MC AE VISA *closed 2 January-3 February* – ***Restaurant :*** Rest 19.50/37.50 – **14 rm** 100.00/120.00 – 240.00/280.00.

◆ Smoothly run and handsomely furnished Victorian country house in Baronial style. 20-acre grounds and open-air theatre. Rooms are tasteful, well-equipped and peaceful. Spacious, formal restaurant with a trompe l'oeil ceiling.

Peebles Hydro, Innerleithen Rd, EH45 8LX, (01721) 720602, *info@peebleshydro.com, Fax (01721) 722999*, ≤, , , , , , , – P – 450. MC VISA. **Rest** 19.50/29.00 – **126 rm** (dinner included) 124.00/152.00 – 302.50/325.50, 2 suites.

◆ Grand Edwardian spa hotel, now offering everything from aromatherapy to reflexology plus a crèche and supervised activities to keep children busy. Modern, soft-toned bedrooms. High ceilinged, classically styled restaurant.

Castle Venlaw ⚘, Edinburgh Road, EH45 8QG, North : 1 ¼ m. by A 703 ✆ (01721) 720384, *stay@venlaw.co.uk, Fax (01721) 724066*, ≤, ⌂ – ⇹ [P] – 🏛 35. MC VISA
Rest (booking essential to non-residents) (bar lunch)/dinner 30.00/40.00 ♀ – **12 rm** ⊐ ✝70.00/90.00 – ✝✝140.00/200.00, 1 suite.
◆ Renovated 18C Scottish baronial style house in wooded gardens: friendly and privately run. Well-appointed rooms; family suite in tower. Afternoon tea in firelit Library bar. Parquet-floored dining room with pleasant views through the trees.

Park, Innerleithen Rd, EH45 8BA, ✆ (01721) 720451, *reserve@parkpeebles.co.uk, Fax (01721) 723510*, ⌂ – |‡| ⇹ [P]. MC VISA
Rest 25.50 (dinner) and lunch a la carte 12.85/22.15 **s.** – **24 rm** (dinner included) ✝78.00/86.00 – ✝✝142.00/195.00.
◆ Extended town-centre hotel - tidy and unpretentious - overlooks a well-tended lawn. Simple bar with tartan sofas, neatly kept rooms: a good address for the mature traveller. Wood-panelled restaurant continues the traditional décor and atmosphere of the hotel.

Rowanbrae without rest., 103 Northgate, EH45 8BU, ✆ (01721) 721630, *john@rowanbrae.freeserve.co.uk, Fax (01721) 723324* – ⇹. ✗
closed December-mid January – **3 rm** ⊐ ✝30.00/48.00 – ✝✝48.00.
◆ Built for the manager of a 19C woollen mill. Pleasant, affordable rooms, well kept by cheerful couple. Fortifying breakfasts with posies of garden flowers on each table.

PERTH *Perth and Kinross* 501 J 14 *Scotland G. – pop. 43 450.*

See : *City★ – Black Watch Regimental Museum★* Y **M1** – *Georgian Terraces★* Y – *Museum and Art Gallery★* Y **M2.**

Env. : *Scone Palace★★ AC, N : 2 m. by A 93* Y – *Branklyn Garden★ AC, SE : 1 m. by A 85* Z – *Kinnoull Hill (≤★) SE : 1¼ m. by A 85* Z – *Huntingtower Castle★ AC, NW : 3 m. by A 85* Y – *Elcho Castle★ AC, SE : 4 m. by A 912* – Z – *and Rhynd rd.*

Exc. : *Abernethy (11C Round Tower★), SE : 8 m. by A 912* – Z – *and A 913.*

18 *Craigie Hill, Cherrybank ✆ (01738) 620829* Z – 18 *King James VI, Moncreiffe Island ✆ (01738) 625170* Z – 18 *Murrayshall, New Scone ✆ (01738) 554804* Y – 18 *North Inch, c/o Perth & Kinross Council, 5 High St ✆ (01738) 636481* Y.

ℹ *Lower City Mills, West Mill St ✆ (01738) 450600, perthtic@perthshire.co.uk.*

Edinburgh 44 – Aberdeen 86 – Dundee 22 – Dunfermline 29 – Glasgow 64 – Inverness 112 – Oban 94.

Plan opposite

Huntingtower ⚘, Crieff Rd, PH1 3JT, West : 3 ½ m. by A 85 ✆ (01738) 583771, *reservations@huntingtowerhotel.co.uk, Fax (01738) 583777*, ⌂, ⌂ – |‡| ⇹ ♿ [P] – 🏛 250. MC AE ① VISA
Oak Room : **Rest** (bar lunch)/dinner 21.95 and a la carte 15.15/23.45 ♀ – **34 rm** ⊐ ✝79.00/89.00 – ✝✝125.00.
◆ Late Victorian half-timbered country house named after nearby castle. Choose between rooms in the more traditional old house or modern, executive rooms. Restaurant with views towards lawn and stream.

Parklands, 2 St Leonard's Bank, PH2 8EB, ✆ (01738) 622451, *info@theparklandshotel.com, Fax (01738) 622046*, ⌂, ⌂ – ⇹ ✆ [P]. MC VISA Z
Rest 14.45/36.25 and a la carte approx 17.30 – ***Ancanthus :*** **Rest** *(closed Sunday-Monday)* (dinner only) 27.50/34.25 – ***No.1 The Bank :*** **Rest** 14.45/19.95 (lunch) and a la carte 17.30/27.10 – **14 rm** ⊐ ✝79.00/119.00 – ✝✝99.00/169.00.
◆ Privately run, these two well-kept houses are handily positioned opposite railway station. Rooms, in co-ordinated patterns, are named after local places: most face garden. New British dishes in contemporary Acanthus. Conservatory bistro fare at No 1 The Bank.

Express by Holiday Inn without rest., 200 Dunkeld Rd, Inveralmond, PH1 3AQ, Northwest : 2 m. on A 912 ✆ (01738) 636666, *info@hiexpressperth.co.uk, Fax (01738) 633363* – |‡| ⇹ ✆ ♿ [P] – 🏛 40. MC AE ① VISA
81 rm ✝65.00/80.00 – ✝✝65.00/80.00.
◆ Outside the city centre, a group-owned lodge, modern in style, providing practical, simply planned accommodation in cheerful colours. Excellent road connections.

Beechgrove without rest., Dundee Rd, PH2 7AQ, ✆ (01738) 636147, *beechgrove.h@sol.co.uk, Fax (01738) 636147*, ⌂ – ⇹ [P]. MC VISA. ✗ Z
8 rm ⊐ ✝50.00/60.00 – ✝✝60.00/70.00.
◆ Virginia creeper clad Georgian manse, immaculately kept. Bedrooms with mahogany furniture and a few added extras; comfy firelit lounge in traditional décor. Friendly hosts.

Taythorpe without rest., Isla Rd, PH2 7HQ, North : 1 m. on A 93 ✆ (01738) 447994, *stay@taythorpe.co.uk, Fax (01738) 447994* – ⇹ [P]. ✗ Y
3 rm ⊐ ✝42.00 – ✝✝70.00.
◆ Immaculately kept, modern guesthouse close to Scone Palace. Good value accommodation. Welcoming, homely lounge. Cosy, communal breakfasts. Warmly inviting, well-kept bedrooms.

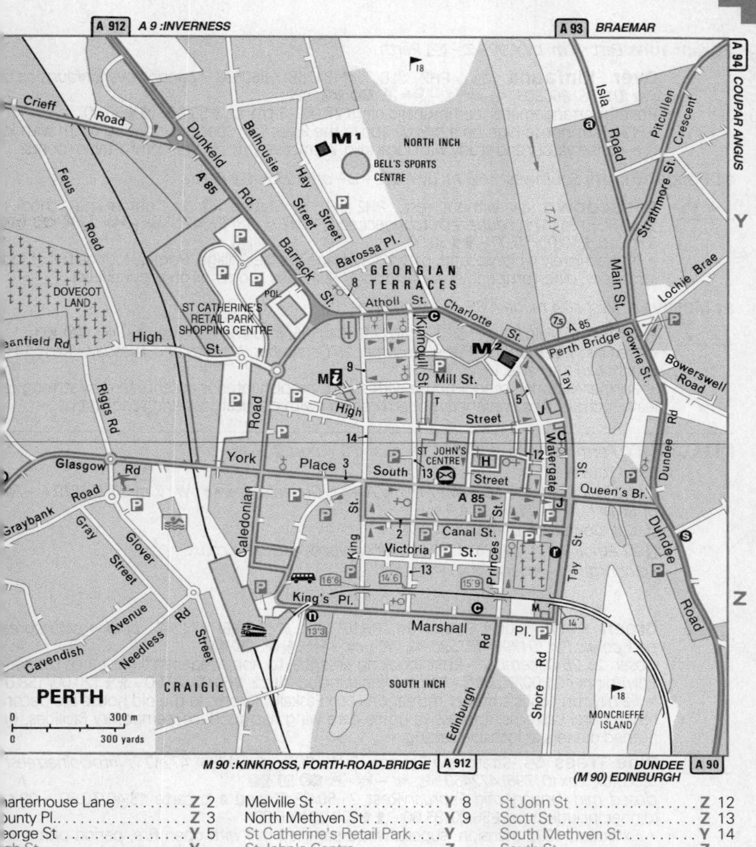

harterhouse Lane	Z 2	Melville St	Y 8	St John St	Z 12
ounty Pl..	Z 3	North Methven St	Y 9	Scott St	Z 13
eorge St	Y 5	St Catherine's Retail Park	Y	South Methven St.	Y 14
gh St.	Y	St John's Centre	Z	South St	Z

Kinnaird without rest., 5 Marshall Pl, PH2 8AH, ✆ (01738) 628021, *info@kinnaird-guesthouse.co.uk, Fax (01738) 444056*, – ⇔. P. VISA — Z c
closed 24 December-3 January – **7 rm** ☕ ★30.00/40.00 – ★★50.00/60.00.
◆ Neatly kept Georgian town house behind a tidy front lawn edged with flowers. Traditional sitting room with a touch of period style. Individual rooms, thoughtfully appointed.

63 Tay Street, 63 Tay St, PH2 8NN, ✆ (01738) 441451, *Fax (01738) 441461* – ⇔. AE VISA — Z r
closed 2 weeks late December, last week June, first week July, Sunday and Monday – **Rest** 19.40/27.40 ♀.
◆ Contemporary style restaurant close to the riverside. Subtle décor with bright sea-blue chairs. Well-priced modern cuisine with penchant for seasonal ingredients.

Let's Eat, 77-79 Kinnoull St, PH1 5EZ, ✆ (01738) 643377, *enquiries@letseatperth.co.uk, Fax (01738) 621464* – ⇔. AE VISA — Y c
closed 2 weeks July, 2 weeks January, 25-26 December, Sunday and Monday – **Rest** a la carte 18.95/30.95 ♀.
◆ Polite, unflustered service and relaxed, warm-toned setting combine in a strong neighbourhood favourite. Robust, varied modern dishes at a good price.

SCOTLAND

at Kinfauns *East : 4 m. by A 90 – Z – ✉ Perth.*

Over Kinfauns ⛰, PH2 7LD, ✆ (01738) 860538, *bandb@overkinfauns.co.u* *Fax (01738) 860803,* ←, 🌳, – ⛔ P. MC VISA. ✂
Rest (by arrangement) (communal dining) 27.00 – **3 rm** ☕ ✝55.00 – ✝✝80.00.
◆ 19C farmhouse high on a hillside above the River Tay. Spacious drawing room with lo fire; conservatory and study with local info. Attractively furnished, comfortable rooms.

at Forgandenny *Southwest : 6½ m. by A 912 – Z – on B 935 – ✉ Perth.*

Battledown ⛰ without rest., PH2 9EL, by Station Rd on Church and School r ✆ (01738) 812471, *i.dunsire@btconnect.com, Fax (01738) 812471,* 🌳 – ⛔ ♿ P. MC VISA
3 rm ☕ ✝30.00/35.00 – ✝✝50.00.
◆ Immaculately whitewashed, part 18C cottage in quiet village. Homely lounge full of loc info. Cosy, pine-furnished breakfast room. Neat, tidy rooms, all on ground level.

at Methven *West : 6½ m. on A 85 – Y – ✉ Perth.*

Hamish's, Main St, PH1 3PU, ✆ (01738) 840505, *info@hamishs.co.uk* – ⛔. MC VISA
closed last week spring, 1 week autumn, 25 December, Monday and Tuesday – **Rest** 14.9 (lunch) and a la carte 16.15/30.90 **s.**
◆ Former Victorian school-house with smart, modish interior accentuated by striking re leather chairs. Accomplished modern cooking with classical base and Scottish bias.

PITLOCHRY *Perth and Kinross* 501 I 13 *Scotland G. – pop. 2 564.*
See : *Town*★.
Exc. : *Blair Castle*★★ *AC, NW : 7 m. by A 9 A – Queen's View*★★, *W : 7 m. by B 8019 A – Fal of Bruar*★, *NW : 11 m. by A 9 A.*
18 *Golf Course Rd* ✆ *(01796) 472792.*
ℹ *22 Atholl Rd* ✆ *(01796) 472215, pitlochrytic@perthshire.co.uk.*
Edinburgh 71 – Inverness 85 – Perth 27.

Plan opposite

Green Park, Clunie Bridge Rd, PH16 5JY, ✆ (01796) 473248, *bookings@thegree park.co.uk, Fax (01796) 473520,* ←, 🏛, 🌳 – ⛔ ♿ P. MC VISA A
closed 25-26 December – **Rest** (booking essential to non-residents) (light lunch resident only)/dinner 21.00/25.00 🍷 – **51 rm** (dinner included) ☕ ✝60.00/79.00 – ✝✝120.00/158.0
◆ Family run 1860s summer retreat on Loch Faskally. Rooms in the old house are decora ted in floral patterns; impressive up-to-date wing has good, contemporary facilities. Ur hurried dinners at lochside setting.

Pine Trees ⛰, Strathview Terrace, PH16 5QR, ✆ (01796) 472121, *info@pinetreesh tel.co.uk, Fax (01796) 472460,* ←, 🌳 – ⛔ P. MC AE VISA A
closed mid January-mid February **Rest** 21.50/25.50 and a la carte 13.40/30.50 – **20 rr** (dinner included) ☕ ✝56.00/83.00 – ✝✝128.00/166.00.
◆ Extended 1892 mansion: superb wood-panelled hall with open fire, period prints an antiques. Modern rooms in warm décor; those at front have best views of 8-acre garden Two eating alternatives: dining room or bistro area.

Craigatin House and Courtyard without rest., 165 Atholl Rd, PH16 5QL, ✆ (0179 472478, *enquiries@craigatinhouse.co.uk,* 🌳 – ⛔ ♿ P. MC VISA. ✂ A
closed 16-28 December – **12 rm** ☕ ✝30.00/55.00 – ✝✝70.00/80.00, 1 suite.
◆ 19C detached house with converted stables. Smart, stylish décor, including comfy cor servatory lounge and breakfast room. Eye-catchingly inviting rooms, some in the annexe

Knockendarroch House, 2 Higher Oakfield, PH16 5HT, ✆ (01796) 47347 *info@knockendarroch.co.uk, Fax (01796) 474068,* ←, 🌳 – ⛔ P. MC VISA. ✂ B r
March-October – **Rest** (dinner only) 26.00 – **12 rm** (dinner included) ☕ ✝81.00/99.00 ✝✝124.00/152.00.
◆ A handsome late Victorian house in a neat garden. Most of the large, light bedroor have good views; comfortably furnished, bright, airy, two-room lounge. Cosy, home dining room.

Balrobin, Higher Oakfield, PH16 5HT, ✆ (01796) 472901, *info@balrobin.co.u Fax (01796) 474200,* ←, 🌳 – ⛔ P. MC VISA B
April-October – **Rest** (residents only) (dinner only) 18.75 – **14 rm** ☕ ✝39.50/45.50 ✝✝68.00/80.00.
◆ Affordable, simply furnished, spacious bedrooms - with good town views from front in a local stone house of late 19C origin. Impressive range of whiskies in residents' bar.

Torrdarach without rest., Golf Course Rd, PH16 5AU, ✆ (01796) 472136, *torrd ach@msn.com, Fax (01796) 473733,* 🌳 – ⛔ P. MC AE ◐ VISA. ✂ A
7 rm ☕ ✝20.00/48.00 – ✝✝40.00/58.00.
◆ Pleasant, well-priced rooms in bright colours and traditionally cosy sitting room behin the deep red façade of this Edwardian country house. Beautifully kept, ornate gardens.

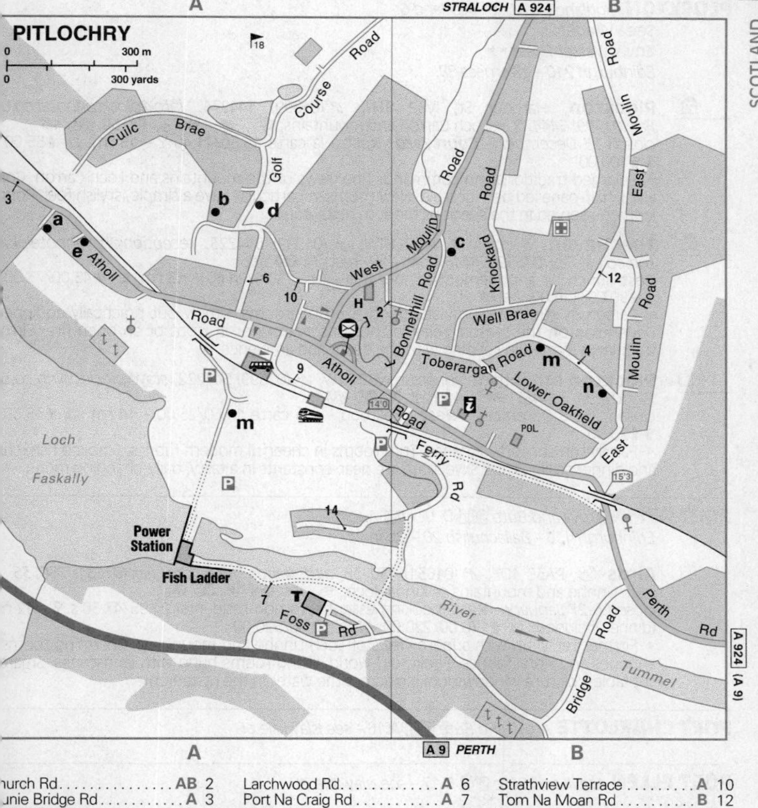

hurch Rd . . . . AB 2	Larchwood Rd. . . . . A 6	Strathview Terrace . . . . A 10
unie Bridge Rd . . . . A 3	Port Na Craig Rd . . . . A 7	Tom Na Moan Rd . . . . B 12
gher Oakfield . . . . B 4	Station Rd . . . . A 9	Tummel Crescent . . . . A 14

Dunmurray Lodge without rest., 72 Bonnethill Rd, PH16 5ED, (01796) 473624, *tony@dunmurray.co.uk, Fax (01796) 473624,* – P. B c
closed 25-26 December and 5 January-5 February – **4 rm** 32.00/50.00 – 48.00/64.00.
◆ Pretty, immaculately kept 19C cottage, once a doctor's surgery. Relax in homely sitting room's squashy sofas. Bedrooms are small and cosy with soothing cream colour scheme.

Old Armoury, Armoury Rd, PH16 5AP, (01796) 474281, *info@theoldarmouryrestaurant.com, Fax (01796) 473157,* , – P. MC VISA A m
weekends only in winter – **Rest** 18.25/26.25 (lunch) and dinner a la carte 23.15/32.15.
◆ 18C former Black Watch armoury. Smart al fresco dining area and wishing well. Inside: a bright lounge, three dining rooms and traditional menus with distinct Scottish accent.

t Killiecrankie *Northwest : 4 m. by A 924 – A – and B 8019 on B 8079 – Pitlochry.*

Killiecrankie House , PH16 5LG, (01796) 473220, *enquiries@killiecrankiehotel.co.uk, Fax (01796) 472451,* , – P. MC VISA
April-December – **Rest** (bar lunch)/dinner a la carte 16.00/28.00 **s.** – **9 rm** (dinner included) 79.00/168.00 – 158.00/198.00, 1 suite.
◆ Quiet and privately run, a converted 1840 vicarage with a distinct rural feel. Mahogany panelled bar; sizeable rooms in co-ordinated patterns overlook pleasant countryside. Warm, red dining room; garden produce prominent on menus.

PLOCKTON *Highland* 501 D 11 *Scotland G.*

See : *Village*★.
Env. : *Wester Ross*★★★.
Edinburgh 210 – Inverness 88.

Plockton, Harbour St, IV52 8TN, ✆ (01599) 544274, *info@plocktonhotel.co.u* *Fax (01599) 544475,* ≤ Loch Carron and mountains, – ⇔ ♿. MC AE VISA.
closed 25 December – ***Courtyard* : Rest** a la carte 15.50/41.40 ♀ – **15 rm** ☐ ★55.00 ★★100.00.
◆ Enlarged traditional inn commands fine views of the mountains and Loch Carron. Cor vivial, half-panelled bar; local ale. New rooms in particular have a simple, stylish feel. Pop lar menu served in the spacious modern restaurant.

The Haven, 3 Innes St, IV52 8TW, ✆ (01599) 544223, *reception@havenhotelplo ton.co.uk, Fax (01599) 544467,* – ⇔ rest, P. MC VISA
Rest (lunch by arrangement)/dinner a la carte 13.25/24.60 – **13 rm** ☐ ★45.00/73.00 ★★90.00/116.00, 2 suites.
◆ Personally run hotel provides good-sized bedrooms, simply but practically equippe Depending on the season, relax in the conservatory or in front of an open fire. Firm traditional menu - in keeping with the décor and ambience.

Plockton Inn with rm, Innes St, IV52 8TW, ✆ (01599) 544222, *stay@plocktoninn.co.u* *Fax (01599) 544487,* – ⇔ rest, P. MC VISA
closed 25-26 December – **Rest** - Seafood - a la carte 14.00/25.00 – **14 rm** ☐ ★35.00 ★★70.00.
◆ Family run converted manse. Trim rooms in cheerful modern fabrics. Smoked fish, ch and ginger scallops and Skye skate are near-constants in a tasty, daily-changing menu.

PORT APPIN *Argyll and Bute* 501 D 14 – ✉ *Appin.*

Edinburgh 136 – Ballachulish 20 – Oban 24.

Airds, PA38 4DF, ✆ (01631) 730236, *airds@airds-hotel.com, Fax (01631) 730535,* Loch Linnhe and mountains of Kingairloch, , – ⇔ P. MC VISA
closed 5-27 January – **Rest** (booking essential to non-residents) 21.95/47.50 **s.** ♀ – **12 r** (dinner included) ☐ ★170.00/220.00 – ★★250.00/320.00.
◆ Former ferry inn with superb views of Loch Linnhe and mountains. Charming rooms antiques and floral fabrics. Firelit, old-world sitting rooms hung with landscapes. Smart set tables, picture windows looking across the water in the restaurant.

PORT CHARLOTTE *Argyll and Bute* 501 A 16 – *see Islay (Isle of).*

PORT ELLEN *Argyll and Bute* 501 B 17 – *see Islay (Isle of).*

PORTMAHOMACK *Highland* 501 I 10.

Edinburgh 194.5 – Dornoch 21 – Tain 12.5.

The Oystercatcher with rm, Main St, IV20 1YB, ✆ (01862) 871560, *gordon@burton bertson.fsnet.co.uk, Fax (01862) 871777* – ⇔ P. MC AE VISA
restricted opening in Winter – **Rest** - Seafood - (booking essential) a la carte 24.50/56.00 – **2 rm** ☐ ★70.00 – ★★95.00.
◆ Personally run bistro and piscatorially themed main dining room in a lovely setting, ide for sunsets. Enjoyable local fish dishes, with lobster a speciality. Homely rooms.

PORTPATRICK *Dumfries and Galloway* 501 502 E 19 – *pop. 585* – ✉ *Stranraer.*

18, 9 *Golf Course Rd* ✆ *(01776) 810273.*
Edinburgh 141 – Ayr 60 – Dumfries 80 – Stranraer 9.

Knockinaam Lodge, DG9 9AD, Southeast : 5 m. by A 77 off B 7042 ✆ (0177 810471, *reservations@knockinaamlodge.com, Fax (01776) 810435,* ≤, , , – ⇔ res P. MC AE VISA
Rest (booking essential for non-residents) (set menu only) 35.00/45.00 ♀ – **9 rm** (dinn included) ☐ ★130.00/170.00 – ★★260.00/340.00.
Spec. Roast courgette flower with Bouton Doc and gazpacho dressing. Steamed turb with baby leeks, truffle and bonne femme sauce. Blackcurrant soufflé, honey and Calvad ice cream.
◆ 19C shooting lodge, housing fine china and oils, in a picturesque coastal setting. Pane led bar with superb rare single malts. Thoughtfully equipped rooms. Personally manage Ornate ceilings, pristine tables and warm service in the restaurant.

Fernhill, Heugh Rd, DG9 8TD, ☎ (01776) 810220, *info@fernhillhotel.co.uk, Fax (01776) 810596,* ≤ Portpatrick and the North Channel, – *closed 3 January-mid February* – **Rest** 16.00/32.50 – **34 rm** (dinner included) ☕ 75.00/102.00 – 164.00.
◆ Family owned hotel in an elevated position; comfortable lounge and bar with fine view of the harbour and sea. Rooms vary in size; the more luxurious have balconies. Unpretentious restaurant and conservatory with menu which changes with the seasons.

The Waterfront, North Crescent, DG9 8SX, ☎ (01776) 810800, *waterfronthotel@aol.com, Fax (01776) 810850,* ≤, – , rest, . AE VISA
Rest (bar lunch)/dinner 22.00 and a la carte 12.25/24.40 – **8 rm** ☕ 55.00/65.00 – 90.00/96.00.
◆ 18C harbourside hotel with pleasant views and comfortable terraced seating. Modern, stylish décor with a light, arty Contemporary styled bedrooms overlooking the harbour. Pleasant, pine-panelled dining room with extensive menu.

Blinkbonnie without rest., School Brae, DG9 8LG, ☎ (01776) 810282, *info@blinkbonnieguesthouse.co.uk, Fax (01776) 810792,* ≤, – P.
5 rm ☕ 35.00 – 50.00.
◆ Good hospitality is assured here on a hill above the harbour. Bedrooms are compact and simple but comfortable and undeniably well priced.

Campbells, 1 South Cres, DG9 8JR, ☎ (01776) 810314, *Fax (01776) 810361,* ≤ Portpatrick harbour, – VISA
closed 2 weeks February, 25 December and 1 January – **Rest** - Seafood specialities - a la carte 17.50/29.25.
◆ Personally run attractive harbourside restaurant with modern rustic feel throughout. Tasty, appealing menus, full of seafood specialities and Scottish ingredients.

ORTREE *Highland* 501 B 11 – *see Skye (Isle of).*

RESTWICK *South Ayrshire* 501 502 G 17 – *pop. 14 934.*
18 2 Links Rd ☎ (01292) 477404 – 18 Prestwick St Nicholas, Grangemuir Rd ☎ (01292) 477608.
Prestwick International Airport : ☎ (01292) 511000 – **BY** – **Terminal :** *Buchanan Bus Station.*
see also Glasgow.
Edinburgh 78 – Ayr 2 – Glasgow 32.

Plan of Built up Area : see Ayr

Premier Travel Inn, Kilmarnock Rd, Monkton, KA9 2RJ, Northeast : 3 m. by A 79 and A 78 at junction with A 77 ☎ (01292) 678262, *Fax (01292) 678248* – rm, rest, P. AE VISA.
Rest (grill rest.) – **58 rm** 50.95 – 50.95.
◆ Excellent road links from this group-owned lodge. Neat modern rooms fitted with work desks and sofa beds. Meals may be taken at the adjacent family friendly pub.

UOTHQUAN *South Lanarkshire* 501 J 27 *Scotland G.* – ✉ *Biggar.*
Env. : *Biggar★ (Gladstone Court Museum★ AC – Greenhill Covenanting Museum★ AC) SE : 4½ m. by B 7016.*
Edinburgh 32 – Dumfries 50 – Glasgow 36.

Shieldhill Castle , ML12 6NA, Northeast : ¾ m. ☎ (01899) 220035, *enquiries@shieldhill.co.uk, Fax (01899) 221092,* ≤, – P – 250. VISA
Chancellors : **Rest** 17.95 and a la carte 22.85/43.35 – **16 rm** ☕ 50.00/90.00 – 99.00/198.00.
◆ Part 12C fortified manor with 16C additions and invitingly comfortable panelled lounge. Large rooms, individually furnished, some with vast sunken baths. Popular for weddings. Accomplished cooking in 16C dining room with high carved ceilings.

ANNOCH STATION *Perth and Kinross* 501 G 13.
Edinburgh 108 – Kinloch Rannoch 17 – Pitlochry 36.5.

Moor of Rannoch , PH17 2QA, ☎ (01882) 633238, *bookings@moorofrannoch.co.uk,* ≤ Rannoch Moor, – P. VISA
10 February-5 November – **Rest** *(closed Monday to non-residents)* (booking essential for non-residents) a la carte 14.25/23.75 **s.** – **5 rm** ☕ 48.00 – 80.00.
◆ Immaculately whitewashed 19C property "in the middle of nowhere", next to railway station with link to London! Comfy, sofa-strewn lounges. Rustic rooms with antiques. Home-cooked menus in characterful dining room with conservatory.

RHICONICH *Highland* 501 *F 8 Scotland G.* – ✉ *Lairg.*

Exc. : *Cape Wrath*★★★ *(≤★★) AC, N : 21 m. (including ferry crossing) by A 838 and minor rd.*

Edinburgh 249 – Thurso 87 – Ullapool 57.

Rhiconich, IV27 4RN, ☎ (01971) 521224, *rhiconichhotel@aol.com, Fax (01971) 52173*

≤ Loch Inchard, – ⚭ rest, P. MO VISA

closed Christmas and New Year – **Rest** (bar lunch)/dinner a la carte 13.00/23.35 – **11 rm**

★40.00/50.00 – ★★79.00.

◆ White-fronted hotel sitting majestically at the head of Loch Inchard. Stylish rooms offer loch views; larger, well located superior rooms feature pastel co-ordinated décor. Dining room, with stunning views and serving local produce.

ROTHESAY *Argyll and Bute* 501 502 *E 16* – *see Bute (Isle of).*

ROYBRIDGE *Highland* 501 *F 13* – *see Spean Bridge.*

Luxury pad or humble abode? ✗ and ⌂ denote categories of comfort.

ST ANDREWS *Fife* 501 *L 14 Scotland G.* – *pop. 14 209.*

See : *City*★★ – *Cathedral*★ *(✳★★) AC* **B** – *West Port*★ **A**.

Env. : *Leuchars (parish church*★*), NW : 6 m. by A 91 and A 919.*

Exc. : *The East Neuk*★★*, SE : 9 m. by A 917 and B 9131* **B** – *Crail*★★ *(Old Centre*★★*, Upper Crail*★*) SE : 9 m. by A 917* **B** – *Kellie Castle*★ *AC, S : 9 m. by B 9131 and B 9171* **B** – *Ceres SW : 9 m. by B 939 - E : Inland Fife*★ **A**.

⛳18 *(x4), Eden, Jubilee, New, Strathtyrum and* ⛳9 *Balgove Course* ☎ *(01334) 466666 – Duke's, Craigtoun Park* ☎ *(01334) 474371.*

ℹ *70 Market St* ☎ *(01334) 472021.*

Edinburgh 51 – Dundee 14 – Stirling 51.

ST ANDREWS

Street	Grid	No.
Abbey St.	B	2
Abbey Walk	B	3
Alexandra Pl.	A	5
Alfred Pl.	A	6
Bridge St.	A	7
Butts Wynd	B	9
Castle St	B	10
Church St	AB	13
Ellice Pl.	A	15
Gibson Pl.	A	17
Gillespie Terrace	A	18
Greenside Pl.	B	20
Gregory Lane	B	21
Gregory Pl.	B	22
Greyfriars Garden	A	24
Hepburn Gardens	A	25
Link Crescent	A	27
Murray Park	A	
Murray Pl.	A	
Pilmour Links	A	
Pilmour Pl.	A	
Playfair Terrace	A	
Queen's Gardens	A	
Queen's Terrace	B	
St Mary's Pl.	A	
Union St	B	

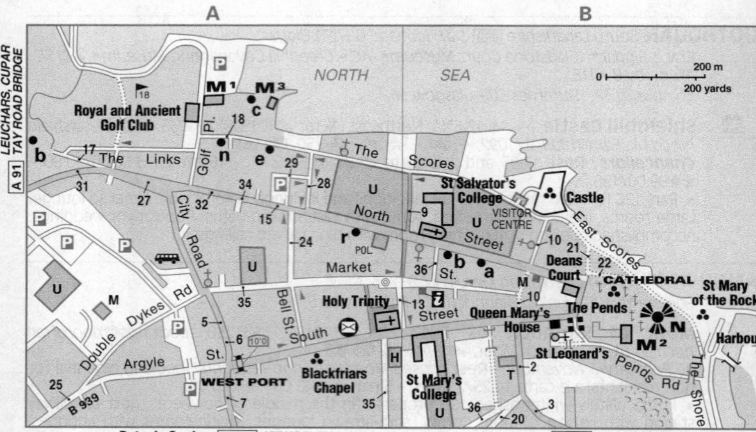

The Old Course H. Golf Resort and Spa, Old Station Rd, KY16 9SP, (01334) 474371, *reservations@oldcoursehotel.co.uk, Fax (01334) 477668,* < Championship golf course and St Andrews Bay, – rm, – 300. VISA A b
Road Hole Grill : Rest (dinner only) 40.00 and a la carte 41.00/50.50 – ***Sands :*** Rest a la carte approx 31.00 – **116 rm** 230.00/314.00 – 246.00/330.00, 28 suites 330.00/714.00.
• Relax into richly composed formal interiors and comprehensive luxury with a fine malt or a spa mudpack. Bright, stylish rooms. Unrivalled views of the bay and Old Course. Road Hole Grill has a fine view of the 17th hole. Worldwide flavours at Sands brasserie.

St Andrews Bay, KY16 8PN, Southeast : 3 m. on A 917 (01334) 837000, *info@standrewsbay.com, Fax (01334) 471115,* <, – rm, – 700. VISA
The Squire : Rest (dinner only) 27.00/44.00 **s.** – ***Esperante :*** Rest *(closed Monday-Tuesday)* (dinner only) 39.50 **s.** – **192 rm** 270.00/310.00 – 270.00/310.00, 17 suites.
• Golf oriented modern, purpose-built hotel on clifftop site with wonderful Tayside views and pristine fairways. Extensive conference facilities. Stylish, modern rooms. Golf chat to the "fore" in informal Squire. Mediterranean influenced Esperante.

Rufflets Country House, Strathkinness Low Rd, KY16 9TX, West : 1½ m. on B 939 (01334) 472594, *reservations@rufflets.co.uk, Fax (01334) 478703,* <, – – 25. VISA.
closed 2 weeks January-February – ***Garden :*** Rest (dinner only and Sunday lunch) 36.00 – ***Music Room :*** Rest (lunch only) 12.95 a la carte 16.00/25.15 – **22 rm** 125.00/188.00 – 199.00, 1 suite.
• Handsome 1920s house set in ornamental gardens. Traditional drawing room with cosy fireside sofas, thoughtfully appointed rooms are pristine and characterful. Garden restaurant offers fine vantage point to view the lawns. Informal Music Room for lunch.

St Andrews Golf, 40 The Scores, KY16 9AS, (01334) 472611, *reception@standrewsgolf.co.uk, Fax (01334) 472188,* < – rest, – 200. VISA A e
closed 24-28 December – **Rest** 12.50/28.50 – **21 rm** 60.00/190.00 – 100.00/240.00.
• Two converted 19C town houses: well-established and family run. Cellar bar is a local favourite. Traditional, pastel-toned rooms vary in size, with sea views from the front. Oak panelled, firelit dining room.

The Scores, 76 The Scores, KY16 9BB, (01334) 472451, *reception@scoreshotel.co.uk, Fax (01334) 473947,* <, – rest, – 160. VISA. A n
Alexanders : Rest (dinner only) 22.95 – **29 rm** 88.00/134.00 – 118.00/177.00, 1 suite.
• Practically equipped rooms in a handsome 1880s terrace by the Old Course and facing the bay. Bar celebrates Scots heroes and the filming of "Chariots of Fire" on the beach. Formal, classic restaurant; views out to sea.

Albany without rest., 56-58 North St, KY16 9AH, (01334) 477737, *enq@standrewsalbany.co.uk, Fax (01334) 477742,* – . VISA. B a
22 rm 45.00/95.00 – 90.00/120.00.
• Well-kept, pleasingly unfussy rooms - quieter at the rear - in a family run 1790s house. Homely, firelit lounge with stacked bookshelves, antique sideboards and deep sofas.

Aslar House without rest., 120 North St, KY16 9AF, (01334) 473460, *enquiries@aslar.com, Fax (01334) 477540,* – . VISA. A r
restricted opening December-January – **6 rm** 38.00/65.00 – 76.00/82.00.
• Victorian house, privately run in a welcoming spirit. Homely, pine furnished rooms, all en suite, are larger on the top floor; most overlook a quiet rear garden. Good value.

18 Queens Terrace, 18 Queens Terrace, KY16 9QF, by Queens Gardens (01334) 478849, *dtay@18queensterrace.com, Fax (01334) 470283,* – . VISA
Rest (by arrangement) 35.00 – **4 rm** 50.00/65.00 – 70.00/85.00.
• Characterful Victorian guesthouse in smart street next to one of the colleges. Very well-furnished lounge with antiques. Stunning rooms in period and sympathetic style.

Deveron House without rest., 64 North St, KY16 9AH, (01334) 473513, *angela@deveron-house.co.uk, Fax (01334) 473513* – . VISA. B b
6 rm 45.00 – 75.00.
• Centrally located Victorian guesthouse. Cosy, clean lounge. Sunny, bright and modern breakfast room with smart wicker chairs. Flowery bedrooms with varnished pine.

The Seafood, The Scores, KY16 9AB, (01334) 479475, *info@theseafoodrestaurant.com, Fax (01334) 479476,* < West Sands and St Andrews Bay – . VISA A c
closed 25-26 December and 1 January – **Rest** - Seafood - (booking essential) 24.00/38.50.
• Super views as restaurant's four sides are of glass. A very pleasant attitude and attention to detail accompanies agreeable, top quality, regularly changing seafood menus.

ST BOSWELLS Borders 501 502 L 17 *Scotland G. – pop. 2 092 – ✉ Melrose.*

Env. : *Dryburgh Abbey★★ AC (setting★★★), NW : 4 m. by B 6404 and B 6356 – Twee Valley★★.*

Exc. : *Bowhill★★ AC, SW : 11½ m. by A 699 and A 708.*

St Boswells ☎ (01835) 823527.

Edinburgh 39 – Glasgow 79 – Hawick 17 – Newcastle upon Tyne 66.

Dryburgh Abbey, TD6 0RQ, North : 3 ½ m. by B 6404 on B 6356 ☎ (0183 822261, *enquiries@dryburgh.co.uk, Fax (01835) 823945*, ≤, – rest, – 110. VISA.

Tweed : Rest (bar lunch Monday-Saturday)/dinner 32.50 ♀ – **37 rm** ★55.00/95.00 ★★95.00/95.00, 2 suites.

◆ With the dramatic ruins of the abbey in its grounds, a restored country house near th river Tweed. Comfortable, well-equipped bedrooms, named after salmon-fishing flie Spacious, soft-toned setting for armchair dining.

Clint Lodge, TD6 0DZ, North : 2 ¼ m. by B 6404 on B 6356 ☎ (01835) 822027, *c tlodge@aol.com, Fax (01835) 822656*, ≤ River Tweed and Cheviot Hills, – P. AE VISA

Rest 25.00 – **5 rm** ★45.00/60.00 – ★★90.00.

◆ Personally run Victorian shooting lodge with sweeping prospects of the Tweed Valle and Cheviots. Antiques, open fires, fishing memorabilia and comfortable, spotless room A choice of tables allows for private or communal dining.

ST CYRUS Aberdeenshire 501 M 13 *Scotland G. – pop. 1 365.*

Exc. : *Dunnottar Castle★★, N : 15 m. by A 92.*

Edinburgh 93 – Aberdeen 32 – Montrose 5.

Woodston Fishing Station, DD10 0DG, Northeast : 1 m. by A 92 ☎ (0167 850226, *info@woodstonfishingstation.co.uk, Fax (01674) 850343*, ≤ St Cyrus Bay, – P. VISA

Rest a la carte 20.00/27.00 – **5 rm** ★40.00/80.00 – ★★60.00/80.00.

◆ Superbly sited on an isolated wind-swept cliff top. High degree of comfort. Simp Victorian style rooms with fine views of bay and nature reserve. Honest evening mea including fish and shellfish caught by owner.

ST FILLANS Perth & Kinross 501 H 14.

Edinburgh 65 – Lochearnhead 8 – Perth 29.

Achray House, PH6 2NF, ☎ (01764) 685231, *info@achray-house.co.u Fax (01764) 685320*, ≤ Loch Earn, – P. VISA

closed first 2 weeks January – **Rest** a la carte 17.85/28.05 – **9 rm** ★60.00/75.00 ★★110.00/160.00.

◆ Well run, former Edwardian villa with a stunning Loch Earn view. A homely warmt pervades all areas. Bedrooms are clean and simple; some are suitable for families. Fresh prepared seafood a feature of dining room menus.

ST MARGARET'S HOPE Orkney Islands 501 K 6 – *see Orkney Islands.*

ST MONANS Fife 501 L 15 – *pop. 3 965 (inc. Elie and Pinttenweem).*

Edinburgh 47 – Dundee 26 – Perth 40 – Stirling 56.

The Seafood, 16 West End, KY10 2BX, ☎ (01333) 730327, *info@theseafoodrestau ant.com, Fax (01333) 730508*, ≤, – . AE VISA

closed 25-26 December, first 2 weeks January, Monday - Tuesday in winter – **Rest** - Sea food - (booking essential) 24.00/35.00 ♀.

◆ Informal former pub in a quiet fishing village; nautical memorabilia abounds. Sma lounge bar leads into a neatly set restaurant with sea views. Tasty, locally caught dishes.

SCALASAIG Argyll and Bute 501 B 15 – *see Colonsay (Isle of).*

SCARISTA Western Isles (Outer Hebrides) 501 Y 10 – *see Lewis and Harris (Isle of).*

SCOURIE *Highland* 501 E 8 *Scotland G.* – ✉ *Lairg.*

Exc. : *Cape Wrath★★★ (≤★★) AC, N : 31 m. (including ferry crossing) by A 894 and A 838 – Loch Assynt★★, S : 17 m. by A 894.*

Edinburgh 263 – Inverness 107.

Eddrachilles ⛰, Badcall Bay, IV27 4TH, South : 2 ½ m. on A 894 ☎ (01971) 502080, *enq@eddrachilles.com, Fax (01971) 502477,* ≤ Badcall Bay and islands, ⛵, ⛑, ⛳ – 🅿. MC VISA. ✗
mid March-mid October – **Rest** (bar lunch)/dinner 25.00/40.00 – **11 rm** ☕ ★58.90/61.95 – ★★87.80/93.90.

◆ Isolated hotel, converted from small part 19C building, magnificently set at the head of Badcall Bay and its islands. Conservatory lounge. Traditional, well-kept rooms. Dining room with stone walls and flagstone floors.

SEIL (Isle of) *Argyll and Bute* 501 D 15 – ✉ *Oban.*

Clachan Seil *Argyll and Bute* – ✉ *Oban.*

Willowburn ⛰, PA34 4TJ, ☎ (01852) 300276, *willowburn.hotel@virgin.net,* ≤, ⛑ – ✗ 🅿. MC VISA
March-November – **Rest** (booking essential for non-residents) (dinner only) 35.00 – **7 rm** (dinner included) ☕ ★80.00/110.00 – ★★160.00.

◆ Simple, white-painted hotel overlooking Clachan Sound. Comfortable lounge with bird-watching telescope. Cosy bedrooms show an individual, personal touch. Airy dining room overlooks the water.

We try to be as accurate as possible when giving room rates.
But prices are susceptible to change,
so please check rates when booking.

SELKIRK *Borders* 501 502 L 17 *Scotland G.* – *pop. 5 772.*

Env. : *Bowhill★★ AC, W : 3½ m. by A 708 – Abbotsford★★ AC, NE : 5½ m. by A 7 and B 6360 – Tweed Valley★★.*

Exc. : *Melrose Abbey★★ (decorative sculpture★★★) AC, NE : 8½ m. by A 7 and A 6091 – Eildon Hills (✳★★★) NE : 7½ m. by A 699 and B 6359.*

The Hill ☎ (01750) 20621.

Halliwell's House ☎ (0870) 6080404 (Easter-October), selkirk@scot-borders.co.uk.

Edinburgh 48 – Hawick 11 – Newcastle upon Tyne 77.

at Ettrickbridge *Southwest : 7 m. by A 707 on B 7009* – ✉ *Selkirk.*

Ettrickshaws Country House ⛰, TD7 5HW, Southwest : 1 m. on B 7009 ☎ (01750) 52229, *jenny@ettrickshaws.co.uk, Fax (01750) 52377,* ≤, ⛵, ⛑, ⛳ – ✗ 🅿. MC VISA. ✗
Rest (booking essential for non-residents) (dinner only) 27.50 **s.** 🍷 – **5 rm** ☕ ★65.00 – ★★100.00.

◆ Traditionally decorated Victorian lodge in isolated spot: old wooden floors, peat fires, comfortable rooms overlooking meadows and fir woods. Trout fishing on Ettrick Water. Bay windowed dining room with high-backed wickerwork chairs at neatly set tables.

SHETLAND ISLANDS *Shetland Islands* 501 P/Q 3 *Scotland G.* – *pop. 22 522.*

See : *Islands★ - Up Helly Aa★★ (last Tuesday in January) – Mousa Broch★★★ AC (Mousa Island) – Jarlshof★★ - Lerwick to Jarlshof★ (≤★) – Shetland Croft House Museum★ AC.*

✈ *Tingwall Airport : ☎ (01595) 840306, NW : 6½ m. of Lerwick by A 971.*

⛴ *from Lerwick (Mainland) to Aberdeen and via Orkney Islands (Stromness) (P & O Scottish Ferries) – from Vidlin to Skerries (Shetland Islands Council) booking essential 3-4 weekly (1 h 30 mn) – from Lerwick (Mainland) to Skerries (Shetland Islands Council) 2 weekly (booking essential) (2 h 30 mn) – from Lerwick (Mainland) to Bressay (Shetland Islands Council) frequent services daily (7 mn) – from Laxo (Mainland) to Isle of Whalsay (Symbister) (Shetland Islands Council) frequent services daily (30 mn) – from Toft (Mainland) to Isle of Yell (Ulsta) (Shetland Islands Council) frequent services daily (20 mn) – from Isle of Yell (Gutcher) to Isle of Fetlar (Oddsta) and via Isle of Unst (Belmont) (Shetland Islands Council) – from Fair Isle to Sumburgh (Mainland) (Shetland Islands Council) 3 weekly (2 h 40 mn).*

⛴ *from Foula to Walls (Shetland Islands Council) 3 weekly (2 h 30 mn) – from Fair Isle to Sumburgh (Shetland Islands Council) 3 weekly (2 h 40 mn).*

SCOTLAND

MAINLAND *Shetland Islands*

Brae *Shetland Islands.*

Busta House, ZE2 9QN, Southwest : 1 ½ m. by A 970 ℘ (01806) 522506, *reservations@bustahouse.com, Fax (01806) 522588*, ←, – , rest, P. MC AE ⓘ VISA
closed 23 December-5 January – **Rest** (bar lunch Monday-Saturday)/dinner 30.00 and a la carte 13.00/23.90 s. ♀ – **22 rm** ☕ ★75.00/80.00 – ★★100.00/110.00.
◆ Part 16C and 18C house on Busta Voe. Good-sized traditional rooms, some have canopy beds. Elegant "long room" with ancestral portraits. House of Commons gargoyles in garden. Garden views add balance to sober dining room.

Lerwick *Shetland Islands Scotland G. – pop. 7 590.*

See : *Clickhimin Broch★.*
Env. : *Gulber Wick (←★), S : 2 m. by A 970.*
Shetland, Dale, Gott ℘ (01595) 840369.
The Market Cross, Lerwick ℘ (01595) 693434.

Kveldsro House, Greenfield Pl, ZE1 0AQ, ℘ (01595) 692195, *reception@kveldsrohotel.co.uk, Fax (01595) 696595* – P. MC AE ⓘ VISA.
Rest (carving lunch Sunday) (bar lunch Monday-Saturday)/dinner a la carte 15.95/26.45 s. **17 rm** ☕ ★89.00 – ★★110.00.
◆ Neat, modern style in evidence throughout this smoothly run hotel - its name comes from the Norse for "evening peace". Tidy rooms, well-equipped and furnished in pale wood. Classically smart and formally set restaurant.

Grand, 149 Commercial St, ZE1 0EX, ℘ (01595) 692826, *info@kgqhotels.co.uk, Fax (01595) 694048* – MC AE ⓘ VISA.
closed 25 December-4 January – **Rest** (bar lunch)/dinner 17.75 and a la carte approx. 13.25 s. – **24 rm** ☕ ★69.00/85.00 – ★★95.00.
◆ Handsome period hotel with turret and stepped gables. Above the row of ground-floor shops are neatly kept rooms with modern fittings, a simple lounge bar and a night-club. Comfortably furnished dining room with a formal atmosphere.

Shetland, Holmsgarth Rd, ZE1 0PW, ℘ (01595) 695515, *reception@shetlandhotel.co.uk, Fax (01595) 695828*, ← – , P – 250. MC AE ⓘ VISA.
closed 25-26 December and 1-2 January – **Rest** (bar lunch)/dinner a la carte 15.45/25.35 s. ♀ – **63 rm** ☕ ★79.00 – ★★97.50, 1 suite.
◆ Purpose-built hotel near the harbourside. Mahogany furnished bar, a choice of modern conference rooms and usefully fitted rooms in co-ordinated fabrics. Simply but formally arranged dining room.

Glen Orchy House, 20 Knab Rd, ZE1 0AX, ℘ (01595) 692031, *glenorchy.house@virgin.net, Fax (01595) 692031* – P. MC VISA
Rest - Thai - (booking essential) (residents only) (dinner only) 17.00 s. – **24 rm** ☕ ★42.50 – ★★69.00.
◆ Built as a convent in the 1900s and sympathetically extended. Colourful public areas. Bright honesty bar. Spotless bedrooms with neat modern fabrics and fittings. Restaurant offers authentic Thai menus.

Veensgarth *Shetland Islands.*

Herrislea House, ZE2 9SB, ℘ (01595) 840208, *herrislea.house@zetnet.co.uk, Fax (01595) 840630*, – P. MC ⓘ VISA
closed 23 December-6 January – **Rest** *(closed Sunday)* (booking essential to non-residents) (bar lunch)/dinner a la carte 12.25/27.75 s. ♀ – **13 rm** ☕ ★70.00/80.00 – ★★110.00.
◆ Purpose-built hotel run by native islanders; a homely hall, with mounted antlers, leads to tidy bedrooms, pleasantly furnished in solid pine, and an angling themed bar. Neatly laid out but fairly informal restaurant.

ISLAND OF UNST *Shetland Islands*

Baltasound *Shetland Islands.*

Buness House, ZE2 9DS, East : ½ m. by A 968 and Springpark Rd ℘ (01957) 711315, *buness-house@zetnet.co.uk, Fax (01957) 711815*, ← Balta Sound, – , P. MC VISA
restricted opening in January-February – **Rest** (by arrangement) (communal dining) 30.00 – **3 rm** ☕ ★55.50 – ★★90.00.
◆ Whitewashed house of 16C origin. Cosy, well-stocked library. Comfortable rooms facing Balta Sound, one decorated with Victorian prints and découpages. Nearby nature reserve. Willow-pattern china and sea views from the conservatory dining room.

HIELDAIG *Highland* 501 D 11 *Scotland G.* – ✉ *Strathcarron.*
Env. : *Wester Ross*★★★.
Edinburgh 226 – Inverness 70 – Kyle of Lochalsh 36.

Tigh An Eilean, IV54 8XN, ☎ (01520) 755251, *tighaneileanhotel@shieldaig.fsnet.co.uk, Fax (01520) 755321,* ≤ Shieldaig Islands and Loch – ⇔ rest. MC VISA
mid March-October – **Rest** (booking essential to non-residents) (bar lunch)/dinner 37.50 – **11 rm** ☕ ★62.50 – ★★130.00.
◆ In a sleepy lochside village, an attractive Victorian inn with fine views of the Shieldaig Islands. Sizeable, well-kept bedrooms and a comfortable lounge with a homely feel. Linen-clad dining room with simply set tables.

KIRLING *Peebleshire* 501 502 J 17 *Scotland G.* – ✉ *Biggar.*
Env. : *Biggar*★ - *Gladstone Court Museum*★, *Greenhill Covenanting Museum*★, *S : 3 m. by A 72 and A 702.*
Exc. : *New Lanark*★★, *NW : 16 m. by A 72 and A 73.*
Edinburgh 29 – Glasgow 45 – Peebles 16.

Skirling House, ML12 6HD, ☎ (01899) 860274, *enquiry@skirlinghouse.com, Fax (01899) 860255,* ⛳, ⚘, ⚔ – ⇔ P. MC VISA
closed January-February – **Rest** 27.50 – **5 rm** ☕ ★55.00 – ★★90.00.
◆ Attractive Arts and Crafts house (1908). 16C Florentine carved ceiling in drawing room. Comfortable bedrooms with modern conveniences. Daily dinner menu using fresh produce.

KYE (Isle of) *Highland* 501 B 11 /12 *Scotland G.* – *pop. 8 868.*
See : *Island*★★ – *The Cuillins*★★★ – *Skye Museum of Island Life*★ *AC.*
Env. : *N : Trotternish Peninsula*★★ – *W : Duirinish Peninsula*★ – *Portree*★.
Skye Bridge (toll).
⛴ – *from Mallaig to Armadale (Caledonian MacBrayne Ltd) 1-5 daily (30 mn) – from Uig to North Uist (Lochmaddy) or Isle of Harris (Tarbert) (Caledonian MacBrayne Ltd) 1-3 daily (1 h 50 mn) – from Sconser to Isle of Raasay (Caledonian MacBrayne Ltd) 9-10 daily (except Sunday) (15 mn).*
⛴ *from Mallaig to Isles of Eigg, Muck, Rhum and Canna (Caledonian MacBrayne Ltd) (summer only) – from Mallaig to Armadale (Caledonian MacBrayne Ltd) (summer only) 1-2 weekly (30 mn).*

roadford *Highland.*

Corry Lodge ⛱ without rest., Liveras, IV49 9AA, North : 1 m. by An Acarsaid rd ☎ (01471) 822235, *Fax (01471) 822318,* ≤, ⛳, ⚘ – ⇔ P. MC VISA. ✗
April-September – **4 rm** ☕ ★35.00/55.00 – ★★65.00.
◆ Fine part 18C house in quiet countryside. Firelit library, antique furniture and a baby grand in a tasteful sitting room; unfussy bedrooms overlooking gardens or the bay.

Earsary without rest., 7-8 Harrapool, IV49 9AQ, East : ¾ m. on A 87 ☎ (01471) 822697, *earsary@isleofskye.net, Fax (01471) 822781,* ≤, ⛳, ⚘ – ⇔ P. ✗
3 rm ☕ ★25.00/35.00 – ★★46.00/50.00.
◆ Highland cattle and sheep wander past the broad windows of this purpose-built house, kept spotless by a friendly owner. Well-equipped, good-value rooms. Hearty breakfasts.

ulnaknock *Highland* – ✉ *Portree*

Glenview Inn, IV51 9JH, ☎ (01470) 562248, *enquiries@glenviewskye.co.uk, Fax (01470) 562211,* ≤ – ⇔ P. MC VISA
Rest (dinner only) 22.50 – **5 rm** ☕ ★40.00/80.00 – ★★60.00/85.00.
◆ Traditional stone-built croft house, sympathetically extended and personally run. Comfortable little sitting room and public bar; simple, spotless rooms. Cottage-style dining room.

unvegan *Highland.*

Dunorin House ⛱, Herebost, IV55 8GZ, Southeast : 2 ½ m. by A 863 on Roag rd ☎ (01470) 521488, *stay@dunorin.freeserve.co.uk, Fax (01470) 521488,* ≤, ⛳ – ⇔ P. MC VISA. ✗
February-November – **Rest** (booking essential) (dinner only) 25.00 s. – **10 rm** ☕ ★46.00/70.00 – ★★70.00/100.00.
◆ Run by a husband and wife team, a simple, modern hotel in unspoilt countryside with views of the Cuillin hills. Good-sized, practical bedrooms in co-ordinated colours. Simply furnished dining room; ladder back chairs at individual wooden tables.

Kinlochfollart ⛰, IV55 8WQ, South : ¾ m. on Glendale rd ✆ (01470) 52147
klfskye@tiscali.co.uk, Fax (01470) 521740, ≤, – ⅹ P. MC AE VISA
closed 23 December-2 January – **Rest** (by arrangement) (communal dining) 25.00 – **3 rm** ☐ ☆40.00/52.00 – ☆☆76.00.
◆ Early Victorian house retains its marble fireplaces and family heirlooms. Stylish, comfortable rooms with fresh flowers and views of the lake, hills and extensive grounds. Handsomely decorated dining room has an air of agreeable, old-world gentility.

Roskhill House, Roskhill, IV55 8ZD, Southeast : 2 ½ m. by A 863 ✆ (01470) 52131
stay@roskhillhouse.co.uk, Fax (01470) 521827 – ⅹ P. MC VISA.
restricted opening in October – **Rest** (by arrangement) 12.95 – **4 rm** ☐ ☆35.00/45.00 ☆☆70.00.
◆ In friendly personal ownership, an extended, traditional 19C croft house which preserve its exposed brick walls and peat fires. Bedrooms are homely and unpretentious. Once th island's post office, a beamed, stone-walled dining room with simple wooden tables.

Three Chimneys & The House Over-By ⛰ with rm, Colbost, IV55 8ZT, Northwest : 5 ¾ m. by A 863 on B 884 (Glendale) ✆ (01470) 511258, *eatandstay@threechimneys.co.uk, Fax (01470) 511358*, ≤ – ⅹ ♿ P. MC AE VISA
closed 3 weeks January and 1 week December – **Rest** - Seafood specialities - *(closed Sunday lunch)* (booking essential) (dinner only in winter) 25.00/45.00 ♀ – **6 rm** ☐ – ☆☆240.00.
◆ Locally renowned crofter's cottage restaurant on Loch Dunvegan's shores. Accomplished Skye seafood dishes, plus Highland lamb, beef and game. Sumptuous rooms available.

Elgol *Highland.*

Rowan Cottage ⛰, 9 Glasnakille, IV49 9BQ, Southeast : 2 m. ✆ (01471) 86628
rown@rowancottage-skye.co.uk, Fax (01471) 866287, ≤ Loch Slapin and Sleat peninsul – ⅹ P. MC VISA.
March-October – **Rest** (by arrangement) 25.00 – **3 rm** ☐ ☆30.00 – ☆☆70.00.
◆ Converted crofter's cottage offering spectacular views of Loch Slapin and the Sleat Peninsula. Little firelit lounge and cosy, immaculate rooms. Friendly owner. Cottage-style dining room with old pewter plates.

Flodigarry *Highland* – ✉ *Staffin.*

Flodigarry Country House ⛰, IV51 9HZ, ✆ (01470) 552203, *info@flodigarry.co.uk, Fax (01470) 552301*, ≤ Staffin Island and coastline, – ⅹ ♿ P. MC AE VISA
Rest (bar lunch Monday-Saturday)/dinner 30.00/36.00 and a la carte 14.15/25.45 – **18 rm** ☐ – ☆☆150.00/190.00.
◆ With views of Staffin and the coast, a curio-filled country house once home to Flora Macdonald. Traditional down to its old-world rooms, peat fire and 19C conservatory. Semi panelled candlelit restaurant.

Isleornsay *Highland* – ✉ *Sleat*

Kinloch Lodge ⛰, IV43 8QY, North : 3½ m. by A 851 ✆ (01471) 833214, *bookings@kinloch-lodge.co.uk, Fax (01471) 833277*, ≤ Loch Na Dal, , , – ⅹ P. MC AE VISA
closed 22-28 December – **Rest** (booking essential to non-residents) (dinner only) 40.00 ♀
14 rm (dinner included) ☐ ☆100.00/140.00 – ☆☆200.00/280.00.
◆ Historic 17C hunting lodge on Loch Na Dal run by Lord and Lady Macdonald. Handsome comfortable drawing room with family antiques; sizeable rooms, some of great characte Gilt-framed ancestral oils and candlelit wooden dining tables with fine silverware.

Duisdale Country House ⛰, IV43 8QW, North : 1¼ m. on A 851 ✆ (01471) 83320
info@duisdale.com, Fax (01471) 833404, ≤ Sound of Sleat and mountains, – ⅹ rest, P MC AE VISA.
Rest *(closed Sunday dinner)* (booking essential to non-residents) a la carte 18.95/30.20 **s.** – **17 rm** ☐ ☆50.00/85.00 – ☆☆90.00/140.00.
◆ Restored Clan Mackinnon hunting lodge in beautiful Victorian gardens. Fine period curios and paintings. Traditional rooms in floral prints; views of the Sound and mountains. collection of Spode china and tartan trimmed tables in the dining room.

Portree *Highland* – *pop. 2 126.*

ℹ *Bayfield House, Bayfield Rd* ✆ *(01478) 612137.*

Cuillin Hills ⛰, IV51 9QU, Northeast : ¾ m. by A 855 ✆ (01478) 612003, *info@cuillinhills-hotel-skye.co.uk, Fax (01478) 613092*, ≤, , – ⅹ rest, P – 140. MC AE VISA.
Rest (bar lunch Monday-Saturday) (buffet lunch Sunday)/dinner 31.50/34.00 **s.** – **27 rm** ☐ ☆55.00/130.00 – ☆☆140.00/230.00.
◆ Set in 15-acre grounds, an enlarged early Victorian hunting lodge: well-proportione drawing room with broad chesterfields; usefully equipped bedrooms which vary in size Smart and spacious dining room with views of Portree Bay.

Bosville, Bosville Terrace, IV51 9DG, ✆ (01478) 612846, *bosville@macleodhotels.co.uk, Fax (01478) 613434,* ≤ – ⇔ ✆. MC AE ⊕ VISA
***Chandlery :* Rest** - Seafood - (booking essential) (dinner only) 28.00/37.00 **s.** ♀ – **19 rm** ☐ ★55.00/110.00 – ★★70.00/110.00.
◆ Well-established, family run hotel overlooking the town, its harbour and the hills. First-floor sitting room and tidy, modern accommodation in co-ordinated décor. Formal dining from an original menu.

Rosedale, Beaumont Cres, IV51 9DB, ✆ (01478) 613131, *Fax (01478) 612531,* ≤ harbour, – ⇔. MC VISA
March-October – **Rest** (dinner only) 26.00 ♀ – **18 rm** ☐ ★35.00/80.00 – ★★60.00/130.00.
◆ Converted quayside terrace of fishermen's houses with fine views over the water. Small coffee shop, lounge and compact but immaculately kept bedrooms in floral prints. First-floor, linen-clad restaurant with a traditionally based, seasonal menu.

Almondbank without rest., Viewfield Rd, IV51 9EU, Southwest : ¾ m. on A 87 ✆ (01478) 612696, *jansvans@aol.com, Fax (01478) 613114,* ≤ Portree Bay, – P. MC VISA
4 rm ☐ ★45.00/49.00 – ★★60.00/65.00.
◆ Situated away from the town centre, a converted modern house, well maintained by the friendly owner. Spotless bedrooms; superb views across Portree Bay.

Waternish *Highland.*

Stein Inn, MacLeod Terrace, Stein, IV55 8GA, ✆ (01470) 592362, *angus.teresa@steininn.co.uk,* ≤ Loch bay – ⇔ P. MC VISA
closed 25 December and 1 January – **Rest** - Seafood specialities - (residents only Monday dinner except Bank Holidays) a la carte 10.65/21.65 – **5 rm** ☐ ★25.00 – ★★68.00.
◆ The oldest inn on Skye with dramatic waterfront views. Charming friendly place serving locally brewed ale and over 90 malt whiskies. Comfy well-kept rooms with seaview. Solid traditional fare in the dining room.

Loch Bay Seafood, 1 MacLeod Terrace, Stein, IV55 8GA, ✆ (01470) 592235, *david@lochbay-seafood-restaurant.co.uk, Fax (01470) 592235* – ⇔ P. MC VISA. ⚹
Easter-October and New Year – **Rest** - Seafood - *(closed Saturday lunch and Sunday)* a la carte 16.00/27.00 ♀.
◆ Converted white cottage restaurant in charming loch-side hamlet. Tiny, atmospheric room. Seafood menus, featuring locally caught halibut, sole and turbot.

SORN *East Ayrshire* 501 H 17.
Edinburgh 67 – Ayr 15 – Glasgow 35.

Sorn Inn with rm, 35 Main St, KA5 6HU, ✆ (01290) 551305, *craig@sorninn.com, Fax (01290) 553470* – ⇔ P. MC VISA
Rest *(closed Monday)* 13.95/23.50 and a la carte 14.00/23.50 **s.** – **4 rm** ☐ ★40.00 – ★★90.00.
◆ Family run, traditional pub in small village. Its hub is the dining room, where good value, locally sourced modern dishes are cooked in an accomplished way. Comfy rooms.

SOUTH UIST *Western Isles (Outer Hebrides)* 501 X/Y 11/12 – *see Uist (Isles of).*

SPEAN BRIDGE *Highland* 501 F 13.
✆ *(01397) 703907.*
✆ *(01397) 712576 (April-October).*
Edinburgh 143 – Fort William 10 – Glasgow 94 – Inverness 58 – Oban 60.

Corriegour Lodge, Loch Lochy, PH34 4EA, North : 8 ¾ m. on A 82 ✆ (01397) 712685, *info@corriegour-lodge-hotel.com, Fax (01397) 712696,* ≤, – ⚓ ⇔ P. MC AE VISA. ⚹
closed December-January except New Year – **Rest** *(weekends only February and November)* (booking essential to non-residents) (dinner only) 46.50 – ☐ 17.50 – **12 rm** (dinner included) ★79.50/99.50 – ★★159.00/199.00.
◆ Enthusiastically run 19C hunting lodge in woods and gardens above Loch Lochy. Bright, individually decorated rooms and a cosy bar and lounge share a warm, traditional feel. Formally set dining room with wide picture windows.

Corriechoille Lodge, PH34 4EY, East : 2 ¾ m. on Corriechoille rd ✆ (01397) 712002, ≤, – ⇔ ♿ P. MC VISA. ⚹
closed November-Easter, Monday and Tuesday – **Rest** (by arrangement) 20.00 – **4 rm** ☐ ★42.00 – ★★64.00.
◆ Off the beaten track in quiet estate land, a part 18C lodge: stylishly modern lounge, spacious en suite rooms: those facing south have fine views of the Grey Corries.

SCOTLAND

Smiddy House, Roybridge Road, PH34 4EU, Tel. (01397) 712335, *enquiry@smidd house.co.uk, Fax (01397) 712043* – P. VISA
Russell's Bistro : Rest (booking essential) (dinner only) 19.95/24.95 – **4 rm** ✩45.00/65.00 – ✩✩55.00/75.00.
◆ Large Victorian house with colourful history as a blacksmith's, church manse an butcher's; set in heart of village. Good facilities in the cosy, pine-furnished bedroom Bustling bistro restaurant with popular menus.

Old Pines with rm, PH34 4EG, Northwest : 1 ½ m. by A 82 on B 8004 Tel. (0139 712324, *enquiries@oldpines.co.uk*, – P. VISA
February-October – **Rest** (booking essential for non-residents) (set menu only) (ligh lunch)/dinner 20.00/35.00 – **8 rm** ✩40.00/70.00 – ✩✩80.00/110.00.
◆ You're encouraged to share tables in this restaurant which favours a dinner party atmos phere. Emphasis on the seasonal and the organic. Friendly staff. Well-kept rooms.

at Roybridge *East : 3 m. on A 86.*

Glenspean Lodge, PH31 4AW, East : 2 m. on A 86 Tel. (01397) 712223, *reser tions@glenspeanlodge.com, Fax (01397) 712660*, – P. AE VISA
Rest (bar lunch)/dinner a la carte 16.40/24.00 s. – **15 rm** ✩55.00/80.00 ✩✩140.00/160.00.
◆ Elevated, extensively updated 1880s hunting lodge commanding valley views. Comfor able modern rooms, wood-fitted bar with banquettes and one or two Highland huntin trophies. Formal restaurant with superb Nevis range views.

SPITTAL OF GLENSHEE *Perth and Kinross* 501 J 13 *Scotland G.* – *Blairgowrie.*

Env. : *Glenshee (✩✩) (chairlift AC).*
Edinburgh 69 – Aberdeen 74 – Dundee 35.

Dalmunzie House, PH10 7QG, Tel. (01250) 885224, *reservations@dalmunzie.com Fax (01250) 885225*, – P. VISA
closed 1-28 December – **Rest** (bar lunch)/dinner 29.00/32.00 – **16 rm** ✩70.00/119.00 ✩✩100.00/170.00.
◆ Edwardian hunting lodge in a magnificent spot, encircled by mountains. Tradition rooms mix antique and pine furniture. Bar with cosy panelled alcove and leather chair Modern dining room with views down the valley.

STIRLING *Stirling* 501 I 15 *Scotland G. – pop. 32 673.*

See : *Town*✩✩ – *Castle*✩✩ *AC (Site*✩✩✩*, external elevations*✩✩✩*, Stirling Heads*✩✩*, Argy and Sutherland Highlanders Regimental Museum*✩*)* B – *Argyll's Lodging*✩ *(Renaissanc decoration*✩*)* B A – *Church of the Holy Rude*✩ B B.
Env. : *Wallace Monument (✩✩) NE : 2½ m. by A 9 – A – and B 998.*
Exc. : *Dunblane*✩ *(Cathedral*✩✩*, West Front*✩✩*), N : 6½ m. by A 9 A.*
Dumbarton Rd Tel. (01786) 475019, stirlingtic@aillst.ossian.net – Royal Burgh Stirling Vis tor Centre Tel. (01786) 479901 – Pirnhall, Motorway Service Area, junction 9, M 9 Tel. (0178 814111 (April-October).
Edinburgh 37 – Dunfermline 23 – Falkirk 14 – Glasgow 28 – Greenock 52 – Motherwell 30 Oban 87 – Perth 35.

Plan opposite

Park Lodge, 32 Park Terrace, FK8 2JS, Tel. (01786) 474862, *info@parklodge.ne Fax (01786) 449748*, – P. – 50. AE VISA B
closed Christmas and New Year – **Rest** *(closed Sunday)* 16.00/28.00 and a la cart 13.00/25.50 – **9 rm** ✩65.00/90.00 – ✩✩90.00/110.00.
◆ Creeper-clad Georgian and Victorian house, still in private hands and furnished with a enviable collection of antiques. Compact but well-equipped rooms with a stylish fee Intimate dining room overlooking a pretty garden.

Express by Holiday Inn without rest., Springkerse Business Park, FK7 7XH, East : 2 m by A 905 off A 91 Tel. (01786) 449922, *info@hiex-stirling.com, Fax (01786) 449932* – rm, P. – 30. AE VISA
78 rm – ✩✩75.00.
◆ Purpose-built hotel on the periphery of the town. Neat, contemporary bedrooms, simple but up-to-date meeting room and buffet breakfast bar: useful for business stop overs.

Premier Travel Inn, Whins of Milton, Glasgow Rd, FK7 8EX, South : 3 m. by A 9 o A 872 Tel. (01786) 811256, *Fax (01786) 816415* – rm, rest, P. AE VISA
Rest (grill rest.) – **60 rm** ✩46.95/46.95 – ✩✩48.95/48.95.
◆ Excellent motorway connections from this group-owned lodge. Competitively price modern bedrooms with ample work space. Informal dining at the family-friendly pu nearby.

STIRLING

arnton St. . . . . B 2
orestone Crescent . . . . . . A 3
ausewayhead Rd . . . . . . A, B 4
orn Exchange Rd . . . . B 5
ornton Rd . . . . A 7
oxithill Rd . . . . A 8
rummond Pl. . . . . B 9
Dumbarton Rd . . . . B 10
Goosecroft Rd . . . . B 12
King St . . . . B 13
Leisure Centre . . . . B
Murray Pl. . . . . B 15
Newhouse . . . . A 16
Park Pl. . . . . A 18
Port St. . . . . B
Queen St . . . . B 20
Randolph Terrace . . . . A 22
St John St. . . . . B 23
St Mary's Wynd . . . . B 24
Seaforth Pl. . . . . B 25
Shirra's Brae Rd . . . . A 26
Spittal St . . . . B 27
Thistle Centre . . . . B
Union St . . . . B 28
Upper Craigs . . . . B 29
Weaver Row. . . . . A 31

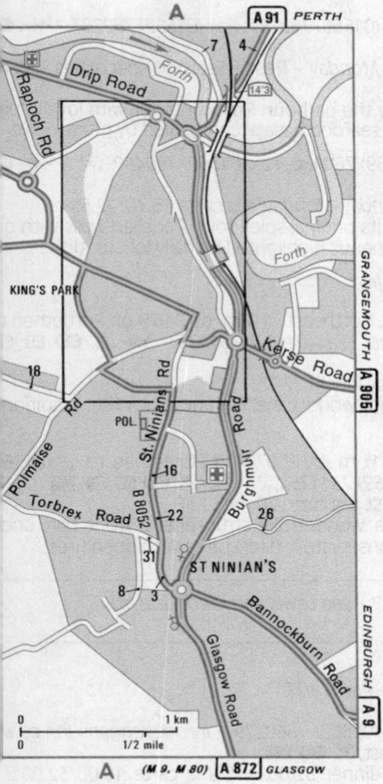

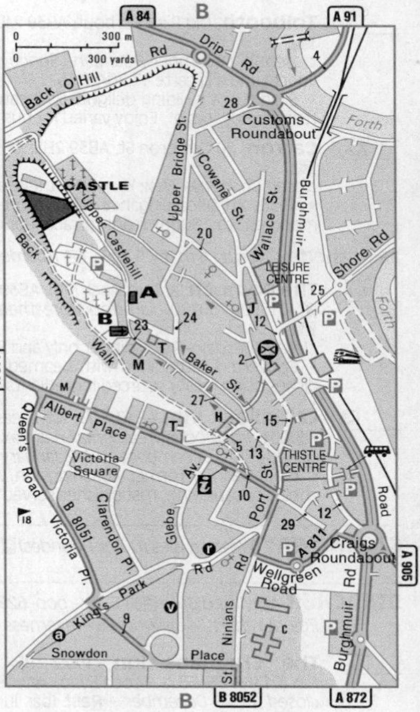

Ashgrove House without rest., 2 Park Ave, FK8 2LX, ☎ (01786) 472640, *ashgrovehouse@strayduck.com, Fax (01786) 472640*, – ⊭ P. MO VISA. ⌘ B r
April-16 October – **3 rm** ☕ ★50.00/60.00 – ★★80.00.
• Smart, centrally located 19C town house; spacious rooms furnished in traditional style, two with four-poster beds. Two lounges, one on first floor. Good breakfast choices.

Number 10 without rest., Gladstone Pl, FK8 2NN, ☎ (01786) 472681, *cameron-10@tinyonline.co.uk, Fax (01786) 472681*, – ⊭. ⌘ B v
3 rm ☕ ★40.00/45.00 – ★★50.00.
• Surprisingly spacious 19C terrace house in a pleasant suburb. Pine furnished en suite bedrooms are characteristically well kept and comfortable. Friendly owner.

West Plean House without rest., FK7 8HA, South : 3 ½ m. on A 872 (Denny rd) ☎ (01786) 812208, *moira@westpleanhouse.com, Fax (01786) 480550*, – ⊭ P. MO VISA. ⌘
February-November – **3 rm** ☕ ★40.00/50.00 – ★★56.00/60.00.
• Dating back to the 1800s, a homely and traditional house under pleasant personal ownership. Simple en suite accommodation. Neat gardens, duckpond and working farm close by.

Red = Pleasant. Look for the red ✗ and ⌂ symbols.

STONEHAVEN *Aberdeenshire* 501 N 13 *Scotland G.*
Env. : *Dunnottar Castle★★, S : 1½ m. by A 92.*
Edinburgh 109 – Aberdeen 16 – Montrose 22.

Arduthie Guest House without rest., 28 Ann St, AB39 2DA, ☎ (01569) 762381, *ma tin@arduthieguesthouse.com*, – . VISA.
6 rm ★24.00/54.00 – ★★54.00.
◆ Victorian house in an attractive coastal town. Personally run with comfortable lounge Individually decorated rooms, some with sea view, and your own whisky decanter.

Tolbooth, Old Pier, Harbour, AB39 2JU, ☎ (01569) 762287, *Fax (01569) 762287* – . VISA
closed 25 December-6 January, Sunday and Monday – **Rest** - Seafood specialities - 15.0 (lunch) and a la carte 17.70/29.65.
◆ Solid stone building delightfully located by the harbour. Rustic interior with lovely "pic ture window table". Enjoy varied menus with seafood base accompanied by great views.

Carron, 20 Cameron St, AB39 2HS, ☎ (01569) 760460, *Fax (01569) 760460*, – . VISA
closed Christmas-New Year – **Rest** *(closed Sunday-Monday)* a la carte 15.70/22.55.
◆ 1930s Art Deco elegance fully restored to its original splendour. Panelled walls with ol mono photos. Sunny front terrace. Popular menus highlighted by daily lobster dishes.

at Netherley *North : 6 m. by B 979 – ✉ Aberdeenshire.*

The Crynoch (at Lairhillock Inn), AB39 3QS, Northeast : 1½ m. by B 979 on Portlethen r ☎ (01569) 730220, *lairhillock@breathemail.net, Fax (01569) 731175* – P. AE VISA
closed Tuesday – **Rest** (dinner only and Sunday lunch) 22.75.
◆ Converted cattle shed with beamed ceiling, wood panelling and open fire. Traditiona dishes using locally sourced ingredients.

Lairhillock Inn, AB39 3QS, Northeast : 1½ m. by B 979 on Portlethen rd ☎ (0156 730001, *lairhillock@breathemail.net, Fax (01569) 731175*, – P. AE VISA
closed 25-26 December and 1-2 January – **Rest** a la carte 20.45/31.30.
◆ Whitewashed former coaching inn with a wonderfully atmospheric front bar. Goo choice of satisfying, rustic dishes served in conservatory dining area with open fires.

STORNOWAY *Western Isles (Outer Hebrides)* 501 A 9 – *see Lewis and Harris (Isle of).*

STRACHUR *Argyll and Bute* 501 E 15 – *pop. 628.*
Edinburgh 112 – Glasgow 66 – Inverness 162 – Perth 101.

The Creggans Inn, PA27 8BX, ☎ (01369) 860279, *info@creggans-inn.co.u Fax (01369) 860637*, ≤ Loch Fyne, – rest, P. VISA
closed 25-26 December – **Rest** (bar lunch)/dinner 32.00 and a la carte 15.00/32.00
13 rm ★70.00 – ★★120.00, 1 suite.
◆ Locally renowned inn, with splendid views over Loch Fyne. Cosy bar with busy pub dinin trade and two lounges, one with fine outlook. Individually styled, comfy rooms. Larg dining room with wood floor and warm colour scheme.

Inver Cottage, Strathlaclan, PA27 8BU, Southwest : 6½ m. by A 886 on B 800 ☎ (01369) 860537, ≤ Loch Fyne and mountains, – P 20
April-September lunch only except Thursday-Saturday July, August and October – **Res** *(closed Monday except July, August and Bank Holidays)* a la carte 17.50/24.50.
◆ Wonderfully located former crofters' cottage with fine views over lake and mountains The simple little restaurant, with its own craft shop, serves tasty Scottish based menus.

STRANRAER *Dumfries and Galloway* 501 502 E 19 *Scotland G. – pop. 10 851.*
Exc. : *Logan Botanic Garden★ AC, S : 11 m. by A 77, A 716 and B 7065.*
18 *Creachmore, Leswalt ☎ (01776) 870245.*
to Northern Ireland (Belfast) (Stena Line) (1 h 45 mn) – to Northern Ireland (Belfas (Stena Line) 4-5 daily (1 h 45 mn/3 h 15 mn).
28 Harbour St ☎ (01776) 702595.
Edinburgh 132 – Ayr 51 – Dumfries 75.

Glenotter without rest., Leswalt Rd, DG9 0EP, Northwest : 1 m. on A 718 ☎ (0177 703199, *enquiries@glenotter.co.uk*, – P.
closed 25 December and 1 January – **3 rm** ★37.00 – ★★48.00/56.00.
◆ In a quiet street near the ferry terminal, a homely guesthouse run by a husband an wife team. Well-kept bedrooms in co-ordinated colours are simple and sensibly priced.

at Kirkcolm *Northwest : 6 m. by A 718 – ✉ Stranraer.*

Corsewall Lighthouse, Corsewall Point, DG9 0QG, Northwest : 4 ¼ m. by B 738 ℘ (01776) 853220, *lighthousehotel@btinternet.com, Fax (01776) 854231*, ←, – P. MO AE VISA
Rest a la carte 17.50/26.75 – **6 rm** (dinner included) ☕ 110.00/130.00 – 190.00/240.00, 3 suites.
◆ Sensitively converted and family run, a 19C working lighthouse at the mouth of Loch Ryan. Snug bedrooms in traditional fabrics - views of the sea or the windswept promontory. Simple, characterful restaurant with seascapes and old black beams.

STRATHPEFFER *Highland* 501 G 11 – *pop. 918.*

Strathpeffer Spa ℘ (01997) 421219.
The Square ℘ (01997) 421415 (April-October).
Edinburgh 174 – Inverness 18.

Craigvar without rest., The Square, IV14 9DL, ℘ (01997) 421622, *craigvar@talk21.com, Fax (01997) 421622*, – P. MO VISA.
closed Christmas and New Year – **3 rm** ☕ 30.00/40.00 – 58.00/64.00.
◆ Georgian house overlooking town square; an agreeable stay is guaranteed with sherry, fruit and biscuits on arrival. Bedrooms are crammed with antiques and original fittings.

"Rest" appears in red for establishments with a ✿ (star) or (Bib Gourmand).

STRATHYRE *Stirling* 501 H 15 *Scotland G.* – ✉ *Callander.*

EXC. : *The Trossachs★★★ (Loch Katherine★★) SW : 14 m. by A 84 and A 821 – Hilltop viewpoint★★★ (※★★★) SW : 16½ m. by A 84 and A 821.*
Edinburgh 62 – Glasgow 53 – Perth 42.

Ardoch Lodge, FK18 8NF, West : ¼ m. ℘ (01877) 384666, *ardoch@btinternet.com, Fax (01877) 384666*, ←, – rest, P. MO VISA
April-October – **Rest** (by arrangement) 24.00 – **3 rm** ☕ 45.00/54.00 – 66.00/86.00.
◆ Victorian in origin, a family-owned country house set in wooded hills above Strathyre's river. Simple accommodation and traditionally decorated sitting room. Home cooking prepared with pride.

Creagan House with rm, FK18 8ND, on A 84 ℘ (01877) 384638, *eatandstay@creaganhouse.co.uk, Fax (01877) 384319*, ← – P. MO AE VISA
closed February and 5-24 November – **Rest** *(closed Thursday)* (booking essential) (dinner only) 23.50/27.50 ♀ – **5 rm** ☕ 65.00 – 110.00.
◆ Surrounded by hills which inspired Sir Walter Scott; a feast for the eye to be enjoyed in baronial style dining room. French classics with Scottish overtones. Cosy rooms.

STRONTIAN *Highland* 501 D 13.

℘ *(01967) 402131 (April-October).*
Edinburgh 139 – Fort William 23 – Oban 66.

Kilcamb Lodge, PH36 4HY, ℘ (01967) 402257, *enquiries@kilcamblodge@aol.co.uk, Fax (01967) 402041*, ←, – P. MO AE VISA
closed 3-31 January – **Rest** *(closed Monday lunch)* (light lunch) (dinner booking essential for non-residents)/dinner 42.00 ♀ – **12 rm** ☕ 85.00/110.00 – 117.00/220.00.
◆ A spectacular location in 19 acres of lawn and woodland, leading down to a private shore on Loch Sunart. The idyll continues indoors: immaculate bedrooms; thoughtful extras. Savour views from large windows and tuck into roast grouse.

STRUY *Highland* 501 F 11.

Edinburgh 180 – Inverness 19 – Kyle of Lochalsh 82.

The Glass at the Struy Inn, IV4 7JS, ℘ (01463) 761219 – rest, P. MO VISA
closed Monday lunch and October-mid March except Christmas – **Rest** (booking essential) 17.95 (dinner) and a la carte 19.20/24.65.
◆ Converted inn retains a traditional, almost homely feel. Wide-ranging menu of wholesome, satisfying dishes, plus a blackboard listing daily specials and fresh seafood.

SWINTON *Borders* 501 502 N 16 – *pop. 472* – ✉ *Duns.*
Edinburgh 49 – Berwick-upon-Tweed 13 – Glasgow 93 – Newcastle upon Tyne 66.

The Wheatsheaf with rm, TD11 3JJ, ☎ (01890) 860257, *reception@wheatsheaf-swinton.co.uk, Fax (01890) 860688,* – P. VISA.
closed 25-27 December – **Rest** a la carte 22.00/35.00 – **7 rm** ★66.00 ★★99.00/128.00.
◆ A village inn with firelit real ale bar and comfortable, well-furnished rooms. Classic unfussy seasonal dishes bring out the distinctive flavour of local produce.

TAIN *Highland* 501 H 10.
Tain, Chapel Rd ☎ (01862) 892314 – Tarbat, Portmahomack ☎ (01862) 871486.
Edinburgh 191 – Inverness 35 – Wick 91.

Golf View House without rest., 13 Knockbreck Rd, IV19 1BN, ☎ (01862) 892856, *golfview@btinternet.com, Fax (01862) 892856,* ←, – P. VISA.
February-November – **5 rm** ★35.00/45.00 – ★★48.00/60.00.
◆ Built as a vicarage, a local sandstone house overlooking the Firth and the fairways. Simple rooms are well kept and tidy. Lawn and flowers shaded by beech trees.

at Cadboll *Southeast : 8½ m. by A 9 and B 9165 (Portmahomack rd) off Hilton rd* – ✉ *Tain.*

Glenmorangie House , Fearn, IV20 1XP, ☎ (01862) 871671, *relax@glenmorangieplc.co.uk, Fax (01862) 871625,* ←, – P. AE VISA
closed 4-26 January – **Rest** (booking essential to non-residents) (dinner only and Sunday lunch) (communal dining) (set menu only) 42.50 – **9 rm** (dinner included) ★170.00 ★★380.00.
◆ Restored part 17C house owned by the famous distillery. Tasteful, old-world morning room and more informal firelit lounge; house party ambience prevails. Smart, comfortable rooms. Imposing communal dining room: gilt-framed portraits, eastern rugs and a long table.

TALLADALE *Highland* 501 D 10 *Scotland G.* – ✉ *Achnasheen.*
Env. : *Wester Ross*★★★ – *Loch Maree*★★★ – *Victoria Falls*★, N : *2 m. by A 832.*
Edinburgh 218 – Inverness 62 – Kyle of Lochalsh 58.

Old Mill Highland Lodge , Loch Maree, IV22 2HL, ☎ (01445) 760271, *jo.powell@bosinternet.com,* – P
mid March-mid October – **Rest** – **6 rm** (dinner included) – ★★140.00/160.00.
◆ Enlarged guesthouse near Loch Maree; good-sized bedrooms in unfussy style. Welcoming owners. A useful base for exploring Talladale and the wilds of Wester Ross.

TALMINE *Highland* 501 G 8 – ✉ *Lairg.*
Edinburgh 245 – Inverness 86 – Thurso 48.

Cloisters without rest., Church Holme, IV27 4YP, ☎ (01847) 601286, *reception@cloistertal.demon.co.uk, Fax (01847) 601286,* ← Rabbit Islands and Tongue Bay, P
closed 25 December and 1 January – **3 rm** ★27.50/30.00 – ★★45.00/50.00.
◆ Purpose-built guesthouse, by a converted church, offers simple but trim and spotless rooms in bright fabrics and superb view of Rabbit Islands and Tongue Bay. Friendly host.

TARBERT *Argyll and Bute* 501 D 16 – *see Kintyre (Peninsula).*

TARBERT *Western Isles (Outer Hebrides)* 501 Z 10 – *see Lewis and Harris (Isle of).*

TARBET *Argyll and Bute* 501 F 15 – ✉ *Arrochar.*
Edinburgh 88 – Glasgow 42 – Inverness 138 – Perth 78.

Lomond View without rest., G83 7DG, on A 82 ☎ (01301) 702477, *lomondviewhouse@aol.com, Fax (01301) 702477,* ← Loch Lomond, – P. VISA.
3 rm ★55.00/65.00 – ★★70.00/80.00.
◆ Purpose-built guesthouse which lives up to its name: there are stunning loch views. Spacious sitting room. Light and airy breakfast room. Sizeable, modern bedrooms.

TAYVALLICH *Argyll and Bute* 501 D 15 – ✉ *Lochgilphead.*
Edinburgh 148 – Glasgow 103 – Inverness 157.

Tayvallich Inn, PA31 8PL, ☎ (01546) 870282, *Fax (01546) 870330,* ←, – P. AE VISA
closed Monday in winter – **Rest** a la carte 17.00/24.00.
◆ Well-regarded pub in little coastal hamlet close to the shores of Loch Sween. Interior of pine panelling and log fires. Simple or creative seafood dishes are the speciality.

THORNHILL *Dumfries and Galloway* 501 502 I 18 *Scotland G. – pop. 1 512.*
Env. : *Drumlanrig Castle★★ (cabinets★) AC, NW : 4 m. by A 76.*
Edinburgh 64 – Ayr 44 – Dumfries 15 – Glasgow 63.

Gillbank House without rest., 8 East Morton St, DG3 5LZ, ☎ (01848) 330597, *hanne@gillbank.co.uk, Fax (01848) 330597,* – P. MC VISA
6 rm ☕ ★35.00 – ★★55.00.
◆ Victorian stone built personally run house just off town square. Guests' sitting room and airy breakfast room. Spacious, well-furnished bedrooms with bright décor.

Trigony House with rm, Closeburn, DG3 5EZ, South : 1½ m. on A 76 ☎ (01848) 331211, *info@trigonyhotel.co.uk,* – rest, P. MC VISA
closed 21-27 December – **Rest** (dinner only) a la carte 14.65/22.50 **s.** 🍷 – **8 rm** (dinner included) ★72.50 – ★★135.00.
◆ Ivy-clad Victorian shooting lodge, family owned, mixes period décor and modern art. Cosy bar with an open fire. Traditional rooms overlook four acres of woodland and garden.

THURSO *Highland* 501 J 8 *Scotland G. – pop. 7 737.*
Exc. : *Strathy Point★ (< ★★★) W : 22 m. by A 836.*
18 *Newlands of Geise ☎ (01847) 893807.*
from Scrabster to Stromness (Orkney Islands) (P & O Scottish Ferries) (2 h).
Riverside ☎ (01847) 892371 (April-October).
Edinburgh 289 – Inverness 133 – Wick 21.

Forss House, Forss, KW14 7XY, West : 5½ m. on A 836 ☎ (01847) 861201, *anne@forsshousehotel.co.uk, Fax (01847) 861301,* – rest, P. MC AE O VISA
*closed 24 December - 3 January***Rest** (dinner only and Sunday lunch/dinner) a la carte 22.40/31.25 – **12 rm** ☕ ★65.00/80.00 – ★★125.00, 1 suite.
◆ Traditional décor sets off the interior of this 19C house, smoothly run in a friendly style. Good-sized, comfy rooms. Angling themed bar, drying room and warm atmosphere. Vast choice of malts in restaurant bar.

Station, 54 Princes St, KW14 7DH, ☎ (01847) 892003, *stationhotel@lineone.net, Fax (01847) 891820* – rest, P. MC AE VISA
Rest a la carte 14.90/23.45 🍷 – **38 rm** ☕ ★45.00/70.00 – ★★60.00/90.00.
◆ Personally run with care and immaculate housekeeping. Co-ordinated bedrooms are bright, attractive and well-appointed. Some rooms in Coach House annex are slightly larger. Simple, neat restaurant with traditional menus.

Murray House, 1 Campbell St, KW14 7HD, ☎ (01847) 895759, *angela@murrayhousebb.com* – P.
closed Christmas and New Year – **Rest** 15.00 – **5 rm** ☕ ★25.00/50.00 – ★★50.00.
◆ A centrally located and family owned Victorian town house. Pine furnished bedrooms, half en suite, are simple but carefully maintained. Modern dining room where home-cooked evening meals may be taken.

TIGHNABRUAICH *Argyll and Bute* 501 E 16.
Edinburgh 113 – Glasgow 63 – Oban 66.

Royal, PA21 2BE, ☎ (01700) 811239, *info@royalhotel.org.uk, Fax (01700) 811300,* < – P. MC VISA
closed Christmas – **Rest** (meals in bar lunch and Sunday-Tuesday dinner) 29.95 (dinner) and a la carte 18.85/34.90 🍷 – **11 rm** ☕ ★110.00 – ★★160.00.
◆ Privately owned 19C hotel in an unspoilt village overlooking the Kyles of Bute. Firelit shinty bar and bistro option. Well-equipped rooms in strong individual styles. Fine loch views and an interesting modern art collection in a pleasant formal dining room.

TILLICOULTRY *Clackmannanshire* 501 I 15 *– pop. 5 400.*
9 *Alva Rd ☎ (01259) 50124.*
Edinburgh 35 – Dundee 43 – Glasgow 38.

Harviestoun Country Inn, Dollar Rd, FK13 6PQ, East : ¼ m. by A 91 ☎ (01259) 752522, *harviestounhotel@aol.com, Fax (01259) 752523,* – P – 70. MC AE VISA.
Rest a la carte 16.25/26.25 – **11 rm** ☕ ★60.00 – ★★80.00.
◆ Converted Georgian stable block, now a smoothly run modern hotel. Neat, unfussy, pine furnished bedrooms, half facing the Ochil hills; coffees and home baking in the lounge. Beams and flagstones hint at the restaurant's rustic past.

TIRORAN *Argyll and Bute – see Mull (Isle of).*

TOBERMORY *Argyll and Bute* 501 B 14 – *see Mull (Isle of).*

TONGUE *Highland* 501 G 8 *Scotland G.* – ✉ *Lairg.*

Exc. : *Cape Wrath★★★ (≤★★) W : 44 m. (including ferry crossing) by A 838 – Ben Loyal★★ S : 8 m. by A 836 – Ben Hope★ (≤★★★) SW : 15 m. by A 838 – Strathy Point★ (≤★★★ E : 22 m. by A 836 – Torrisdale Bay★ (≤★★) NE : 8 m. by A 836.*

Edinburgh 257 – Inverness 101 – Thurso 43.

Tongue, Main St, IV27 4XD, ℘ (01847) 611206, *info@tonguehotel.co.uk* *Fax (01847) 611345,* ≤, – P. VISA
April-October – **Rest** (bar lunch)/dinner a la carte 15.95/26.90 – **19 rm** ☕ ★50.00/60.00 ★★110.00/120.00.
◆ Former hunting lodge of the Duke of Sutherland overlooking Kyle of Tongue. Smar interiors include intimate bar and beamed lounge. Individually styled rooms with antiques Restaurant with fireplace and antique dressers.

Ben Loyal, Main St, IV27 4XE, ℘ (01847) 611216, *benloyalhotel@btinternet.com* *Fax (01847) 611212,* ≤ Ben Loyal and Kyle of Tongue – P. VISA
closed 24 December - 1 March – **Rest** (bar lunch)/dinner a la carte 13.70/24.85 – **11 rm** ☕ ★35.00/50.00 – ★★70.00.
◆ Unassuming hotel in the village centre enjoys excellent views of Ben Loyal and the Kyle of Tongue - a useful hiking or fishing base. Rooms are unfussy, modern and well kept. Pine furnished restaurant overlooks the hills and sea.

TORRIDON *Highland* 501 D 11 *Scotland G.* – ✉ *Achnasheen.*

Env. : *Wester Ross★★★.*

Edinburgh 234 – Inverness 62 – Kyle of Lochalsh 44.

Loch Torridon ⛰, IV22 2EY, South : 1 ½ m. on A 896 ℘ (01445) 791242, *enquiries@lochtorridonhotel.com, Fax (01445) 712253,* ≤ Upper Loch Torridon and mountains, P. – 25. AE VISA.
closed 2-25 January – **Rest** (booking essential) (bar lunch)/dinner 40.00 ♀ – **18 rm** ☕ ★67.00/160.00 – ★★212.00/348.00, 1 suite.
◆ 19C hunting lodge; idyllic view of Loch Torridon and mountains. Ornate ceilings, pea fires and Highland curios add to a calm period feel shared by the more luxurious rooms Formal, pine-panelled restaurant uses fine local produce, some from the grounds.

Ben Damph Inn ⛰, IV22 2EY, South : 1 ½ m. on A 896 ℘ (01445) 791242, *bendamph@lochtorridonhotel.com, Fax (01445) 712253,* P. AE VISA.
April-October – **Rest** (grill rest.) 17.00 and a la carte 21.75/26.25 – **12 rm** ☕ ★49.00 ★★74.00.
◆ Simple, modern, affordable rooms - some sleeping up to six - in a converted stable block, set in a quiet rural spot and named after the mountain nearby. Spacious pubby bar Traditionally styled and informal restaurant.

TROON *South Ayrshire* 501 502 G 17 – *pop. 14 766.*

18, 18, 18 *Troon Municipal, Harling Drive ℘ (01292) 312464.*

to Northern Ireland (Larne) (P & O Irish Sea) 2 daily.

Edinburgh 77 – Ayr 7 – Glasgow 31.

Lochgreen House ⛰, Monktonhill Rd, Southwood, KA10 7EN, Southeast : 2 m. on B 749 ℘ (01292) 313343, *lochgreen@costley-hotels.co.uk, Fax (01292) 318661,* P. – 80. AE VISA.
Costley's Brasserie : **Rest** 35.00 and lunch a la carte 20.00/35.00 **s.** – (see also ***The Restaurant*** below) – **43 rm** ☕ ★99.00/110.00 – ★★170.00, 1 suite.
◆ Attractive, coastal Edwardian house in mature grounds. Lounges exude luxurious country house feel. Large rooms, modern or traditional, have a good eye for welcoming detail Brasserie overlooks garden: modern, informal dining.

Piersland House, 15 Craigend Rd, KA10 6HD, ℘ (01292) 314747, *reservations@piersland.co.uk, Fax (01292) 315613,* – rest, P – 70. AE VISA
Restaurant 1820 : **Rest** *(closed Monday)* (bar lunch Monday-Saturday)/dinner a la carte 21.40/27.40 **s.** – **15 rm** ☕ ★70.00/99.50 – ★★80.00/130.00, **15 suites** ☕ 100.00/147.00.
◆ Built for the family of Johnnie Walker; Jacobean and 19C in style: fine original panelling stonework and Arts and Crafts garden. Well-equipped rooms, 15 in courtyard annex. Tastefully replicated period dining room of dark wood and neat linen.

The Restaurant (at Lochgreen House H.), Monktonhill Rd, Southwood, KA10 7EN Southeast : 2 m. on B 749 ℘ (01292) 313343, *Fax (01292) 318661,* – P. AE VISA
Rest (dinner only and Sunday lunch) 35.00 and lunch a la carte 20.00/35.00 **s.** ♀.
◆ Spacious dining room with baronial feel. Elegant chandeliers; large pottery cockerels Classical, modern cooking, with a strong Scottish base.

X **Apple Inn,** 89 Portland St, KA10 6QU, ✆ (01292) 318819 – ⋟. MC AE ⊙ VISA
Rest a la carte 14.95/28.15.
◆ Former High Street bar, now a popular little eatery with pale green, cool and tidy décor; simple pine tables and chairs. Tasty, modish British menus.

t Loans *East : 2 m. on A 759 – ✉ Troon.*

XX **Highgrove House** with rm, Old Loans Rd, KA10 7HL, East : ¼ m. on Dundonald rd ✆ (01292) 312511, *highgrove@costleyhotels.co.uk, Fax (01292) 318228,* <, – ⋟ P. MC AE VISA. ⋟
Rest 19.95/25.95 and a la carte 16.00/32.00 – **9 rm** ☐ ✦69.00/75.00 – ✦✦110.00/120.00.
◆ Elevated position, offering superb coastal panorama. Open plan dining area with lounge and bar. Seafood, and local meat and game, to the fore. Comfy rooms with fine views.

'URNBERRY *South Ayrshire* 501 502 F 18 *Scotland G. – ✉ Girvan.*

Env. : *Culzean Castle★ AC (setting★★★, Oval Staircase★★) NE : 5 m. by A 719.*
Edinburgh 97 – Ayr 15 – Glasgow 51 – Stranraer 36.

The Westin Turnberry Resort ⋟, KA26 9LT, on A 719 ✆ (01655) 331000, *turnberry@westin.com, Fax (01655) 331706,* < golf courses, bay, Ailsa Craig and Mull of Kintyre, , , Ⅰ₆, , , 18, , – |‡|, ⋟ rest, ▤ rest, ♿ P – 🏛 275. MC AE ⊙ VISA
closed 24-26 December – ***Turnberry :*** Rest (dinner only) a la carte 42.00/69.00 ♀ – ***Terrace Brasserie :*** Rest 25.00 and a la carte 25.00/45.00 ♀ – ***Tappie Toorie Grill :*** Rest a la carte 17.25/24.25 ♀ – **193 rm** ☐ ✦175.00 – ✦✦220.00, 28 suites.
◆ Impeccably run part Edwardian hotel with panoramic views of coast and world famous golf courses. Much original charm intact. Superbly equipped with every conceivable facility. Fine diningTurnberry. Smart Terrace Brasserie. Informal Tappie Toorie Grill.

DDINGSTON *South Lanarkshire* 501 502 H 16 – *pop. 5 576 – ✉ Glasgow.*

18 *Coatbridge, Townhead Rd ✆ (01236) 28975.*
Edinburgh 41 – Glasgow 10.

Redstones, 8-10 Glasgow Rd, G71 7AS, ✆ (01698) 813774, *info@redstoneshotel.com, Fax (01698) 815319,* – ⋟ rm, ✆ P – 🏛 30. MC AE ⊙ VISA. ⋟
Rest 11.45/23.00 and a la carte 12.85/24.90 – **12 rm** ☐ ✦75.00/85.00 – ✦✦85.00.
◆ Renovated Victorian houses in distinctive red sandstone - the conservatory lounge is a later addition; usefully-equipped bedrooms feel stylish and modern. Formal dining room.

Premier Travel Inn, Glasgow Zoo, 601 Hamilton Rd, G71 7SA, Northwest : 2 m. by B 7071 and A 74 following signs for Glasgow Zoo park ✆ (0141) 773 1133, *Fax (0141) 771 8354,* – |‡|, ⋟ rm, ▤ rest, ♿ P. MC AE ⊙ VISA. ⋟
Rest (grill rest.) – **66 rm** ✦46.95/46.95 – ✦✦49.95/49.95.
◆ Adjacent to Glasgow Zoo: simply furnished bedrooms with ample workspace. Useful for corporate or leisure travel. Informal dining in the adjacent Beefeater.

IST (Isles of) *Western Isles (Outer Hebrides)* 501 X/Y 10 /11/12 – *pop. 3 510.*

✈ *see Liniclate.*
⛴ *from Lochboisdale to Oban via Isle of Barra (Castlebay) and Mallaig (Mainland) (Caledonian MacBrayne Ltd) (summer only) – from Lochmaddy to Isle of Skye (Uig) (Caledonian MacBrayne Ltd) 1-3 daily (1 h 50 mn) – from Otternish to Isle of Harris (Leverburgh) (Caledonian MacBrayne Ltd) (1 h 10 mn).*

NORTH UIST *Western Isles*

rimsay *Western Isles.*

Glendale ⋟ without rest., 7 Kallin, HS6 5HY, ✆ (01870) 602029, *glendale@ecosse.net,* < – ⋟ P. ⋟
closed Christmas and New Year – **3 rm** ☐ ✦25.00 – ✦✦40.00.
◆ Overlooking picturesque Kallin harbour, a simple converted house with a friendly atmosphere. Homely lounge and compact but pleasant and affordable bedrooms.

ochmaddy *Western Isles.*

Lochmaddy, HS6 5AA, ✆ (01876) 500331, *info@lochmaddyhotel.co.uk, Fax (01876) 500210,* <, – ⋟ rest, P. MC AE VISA
Rest (bar lunch)/dinner 25.50 and a la carte 16.00/30.00 **s.** – **15 rm** ☐ ✦25.00/60.00 – ✦✦60.00/90.00.
◆ A popular fishing base, this traditional, white-painted hotel offers good-sized rooms, all neat and homely. Parquet-floored sitting room and large pubby bar. Sea views. Unpretentious dining room, its tables clad in soft linen.

BENBECULA *Western Isles*

Liniclate *Western Isles.*

Benbecula Airport : (01870) 602051.

Dark Island, HS7 5PJ, (01870) 603030, *reservations@darkislandhotel.co.u* *Fax (01870) 602347* – P – 100. MC AE VISA
closed 25 December and 1 January – **Rest** (bar lunch)/dinner 25.00 and a la car 25.00/32.00 s. – **42 rm** 69.00/84.00 – 99.00.
◆ Purpose-built and privately owned hotel just off the main road, a popular choice f large groups. Modern, practically fitted bedrooms; large bar - occasional live music. Ca riages restaurant, compact and linen-clad, offers an extensive popular repertoire.

SOUTH UIST *Western Isles*

Lochboisdale *Western Isles.*

Brae Lea, Lasgair, HS8 5TH, Northwest : 1 m. by A 865 (01878) 700497, *braelea@s panet.com, Fax (01878) 700497* – rm, P.
Rest (by arrangement) 15.00 – **6 rm** 30.00/35.00 – 60.00/70.00.
◆ In a quiet spot yet convenient for the ferry, a purpose-built guesthouse, well-estab lished and family run. Neat, pine-fitted rooms, homely lounge with wide picture window Unpretentious home-cooked dinners in a suitably simple setting.

ULLAPOOL *Highland* 501 E 10 *Scotland G.* – *pop. 1 308.*

See : *Town*★.

Env. : *Wester Ross*★★★ – *Loch Broom*★★.

Exc. : *Falls of Measach*★★, *S : 11 m. by A 835 and A 832 - Corrieshalloch Gorge*★, *SE : 10 r by A 835 – Northwards to Lochinver*★★, *Morefield (*≤★★ *of Ullapool),* ≤★ *Loch Broom.*

to Isle of Lewis (Stornoway) (Caledonian MacBrayne Ltd) (2 h 40 mn).

Argyle St (01854) 612135.

Edinburgh 215 – Inverness 59.

Ardvreck without rest., Morefield Brae, IV26 2TH, Northwest : 2 m. by A 83 (01854) 612028, *ardvreck.guesthouse@btinternet.com, Fax (01854) 613000,* ≤ Loc Broom and mountains, – P. MC VISA.
February-November – **10 rm** 28.00/54.00 – 56.00/70.00.
◆ Peacefully located hotel boasting fine views of loch and mountains. Well appointe breakfast room with splendid vistas. Spacious rooms: some with particularly fine outlooks

Tanglewood House, IV26 2TB, on A 835 (01854) 612059, *tanglewoo house@ecosse.net,* ≤ Loch Broom, – P. MC VISA
closed Christmas and New Year – **Rest** (by arrangement) (communal dining) 30.00 – **3 r** 58.00/65.00 – 76.00/90.00.
◆ Blissfully located guesthouse on heather covered headland. Drawing room has a 20 foo window overlooking loch. Homely, pastel shaded rooms, all with vistas. Meals taken a communal table.

The Sheiling without rest., Garve Rd, IV26 2SX, (01854) 612947, *Fax (01854) 61294* ≤ Loch Broom, – P. MC VISA.
closed Christmas and New Year – **6 rm** 35.00/45.00 – 50.00/60.00.
◆ Welcoming guesthouse by the shores of Loch Broom. Renowned breakfasts include platter of locally smoked fish. Homely lounge and comfortable bedrooms.

Point Cottage without rest., West Shore St, IV26 2UR, (01854) 612494, *stay@poir cottage.co.uk,* ≤ Loch Broom, – P.
March-October – **3 rm** 25.00/50.00 – 44.00/56.00.
◆ Converted fisherman's cottage of 18C origin. Rooms in bright modern fabrics enjo beautiful views across Loch Broom to the hills. Substantial breakfasts.

Dromnan without rest., Garve Rd, IV26 2SX, (01854) 612333, *info@dromnan.con Fax (01854) 613364,* ≤, – P. MC VISA.
7 rm 40.00 – 54.00/60.00.
◆ Family run, modern house overlooking Loch Broom. Television lounge with deep leathe chairs. Practically equipped rooms vary in décor from patterned pastels to dark tartan.

UNST (Island of) *Shetland Islands* 501 R 1 – *see Shetland Islands.*

UPHALL *West Lothian* 501 J 16 – *pop. 14 600.*

Uphall, Houston Mains ☎ (01506) 856404.

Edinburgh 13 – Glasgow 32.

Houstoun House, EH52 6JS, ☎ (01506) 853831, *houstoun@macdonald-hotels.co.uk*, *Fax (01506) 854220*, – 400.
***The Great Dining Rooms* : Rest** *(closed Saturday lunch)* 25.20/25.95 (dinner) and a la carte 29.50/39.00 **s.** – ***The Steakhouse* : Rest** *(closed Sunday-Monday)* (dinner only and Saturday lunch) a la carte 18.40/32.95 **s.** – 12.95 – **71 rm** 145.00/195.00 – 165.00/195.00.
◆ Fortified house - now group owned - in acres of lawned gardens. Atmospheric cellar bar and comfortable rooms, some in converted outbuildings. Three dining rooms with panelled walls. The Steakhouse, an informal setting for Italian and traditional dishes.

URQUHART *Moray – see Elgin.*

VEENSGARTH *Shetland Islands – see Shetland Islands (Mainland).*

WALKERBURN *Borders.*

Edinburgh 30 – Galashiels 23.5 – Peebles 8.5.

Windlestraw Lodge, Tweed Valley, EH43 6AA, on A 72 ☎ (01896) 870636, *reception@windlestraw.co.uk, Fax (01896) 870639*, –
Rest (booking essential to non-residents) (residents only Sunday-Wednesday) (dinner only and lunch Wednesday and Sunday)/dinner 19.75/30.00 – **6 rm** 70.00 – 110.00/120.00.
◆ Edwardian country house in picturesque Tweed Valley: lovely views guaranteed. Period style lounges serviced by well-stocked bar. Half the good-sized rooms enjoy the vista. Cosy, linen-clad dining room.

WATERNISH *Highland – see Skye (Isle of).*

WESTRAY (Island of) *Orkney Islands* 501 K/L 6/7 – *see Orkney Islands.*

WHITING BAY *North Ayrshire* 501 502 E 17 – *see Arran (Isle of).*

WICK *Highland* 501 K 8 *Scotland G. – pop. 7 333.*

Exc. : *Duncansby Head★ (Stacks of Duncansby★★) N : 14 m. by A 9 – Grey Cairns of Camster★ (Long Cairn★★) S : 17 m. by A 9 – The Hill O'Many Stanes★, S : 10 m. by A 9.*

Reiss ☎ (01955) 602726.

Wick Airport : ☎ (01955) 602215, N : 1 m.

Whitechapel Rd ☎ (01955) 602596.

Edinburgh 282 – Inverness 126.

The Clachan without rest., South Rd, KW1 5NJ, South : ¾ m. on A 99 ☎ (01955) 605384, *enquiry@theclachan.co.uk*,
closed Christmas and New Year – **3 rm** 30.00/35.00 – 44.00/45.00.
◆ This detached 1930s house on the town's southern outskirts provides homely en suite accommodation in pastels and floral patterns. Charming owner.

Bord De L'Eau, 2 Market St (Riverside), KW1 4AR, ☎ (01955) 604400,
closed January, 25-26 December, Sunday lunch and Monday – **Rest** - French Bistro - a la carte 17.45/31.40.
◆ Totally relaxed little riverside eatery with French owner. Friendly, attentive service of an often-changing, distinctly Gallic repertoire. Keenly priced dishes.

WORMIT *Fife* 501 L 14 – ✉ *Newport-on-Tay.*

Scotscraig, Golf Rd, Tayport ☎ (01382) 552515.

Edinburgh 53 – Dundee 6 – St Andrews 12.

Sandford Country House, DD6 8RG, South : 2 m. on B 946 ☎ (01382) 541802, *sandford.hotel@btinternet.com, Fax (01382) 542136*, – 45.
Rest (bar lunch)/dinner 23.75 **s.** – **14 rm** 55.00/65.00 – 75.00/105.00.
◆ Designed by Baillie Scott, a 20C country house in wooded gardens. Comfy lounge with minstrels gallery; rooms, contrasting with exterior, are modern and minimalist in style. Restaurant boasts tall church candles and Mackintosh-style chairs.

P. Desclos/SCOPE

Caernarfon: the pier and the medieval walls of the castle

Towns
from A to Z

Villes
de A à Z

Città
de A a Z

Städte
von A bis Z

Wales

Place with at least

a hotel or restaurant	● Cardiff
a pleasant hotel or restaurant	🏨, ⌂, ✕
Good accommodation at moderate prices	Bib Hotel
a quiet, secluded hotel	🐴
a restaurant with	✿, ✿✿, ✿✿✿, Bib Gourmand Rest
Town with a local map	●

Localité offrant au moins

une ressource hôtelière	● Cardiff
un hôtel ou restaurant agréable	🏨, ⌂, ✕
Bonnes nuits à petits prix	Bib Hotel
un hôtel très tranquille, isolé	🐴
une bonne table à	✿, ✿✿, ✿✿✿, Bib Gourmand Rest
Carte de voisinage : voir à la ville choisie	●

La località possiede come minimo

una risorsa alberghiera	● Cardiff
Albergo o ristorante ameno	🏨, ⌂, ✕
Buona sistemazione a prezzi contenuti	Bib Hotel
un albergo molto tranquillo, isolato	🐴
un'ottima tavola con	✿, ✿✿, ✿✿✿, Bib Gourmand Rest
Città con carta dei dintorni	●

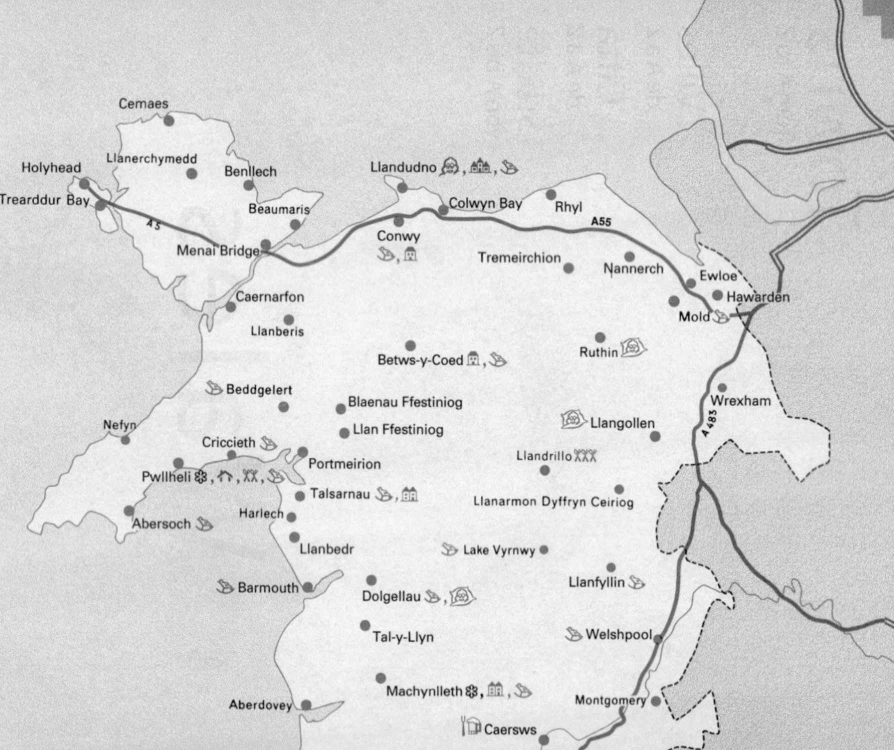

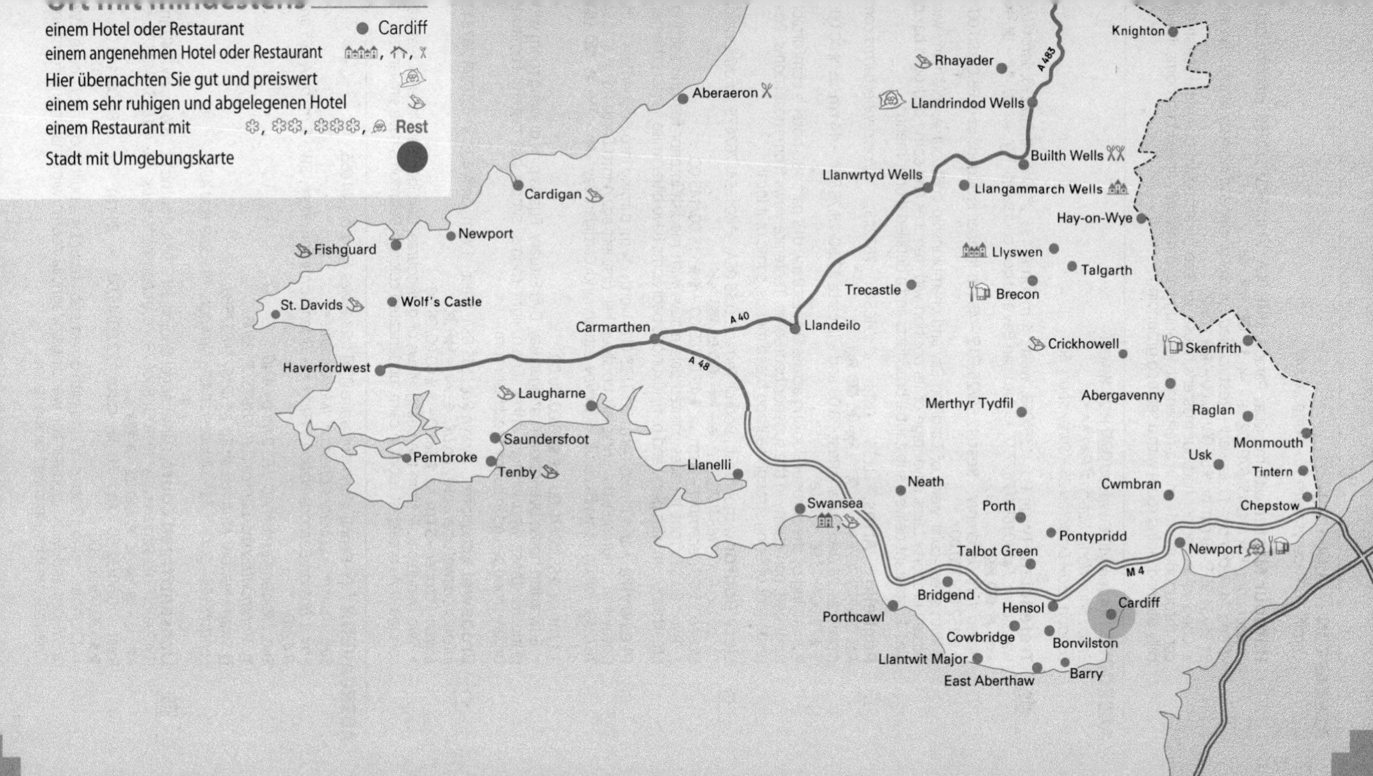

einem Hotel oder Restaurant Cardiff
einem angenehmen Hotel oder Restaurant
Hier übernachten Sie gut und preiswert
einem sehr ruhigen und abgelegenen Hotel
einem Restaurant mit Rest
Stadt mit Umgebungskarte
Knighton
Rhayader
A 483
Aberaeron
Llandrindod Wells
Builth Wells
Llanwrtyd Wells
Llangammarch Wells
Cardigan
Hay-on-Wye
Newport
Fishguard
Llyswen
Talgarth
Trecastle
Brecon
St. Davids
Wolf's Castle
A 40
Carmarthen
Llandeilo
Crickhowell
Skenfrith
Haverfordwest
A 48
Laugharne
Abergavenny
Merthyr Tydfil
Raglan
Saundersfoot
Monmouth
Pembroke
Usk
Tenby
Llanelli
Tintern
Neath
Cwmbran
Swansea
Porth
Chepstow
Pontypridd
Talbot Green
Newport
M 4
Bridgend
Cardiff
Hensol
Porthcawl
Cowbridge
Bonvilston
Llantwit Major
East Aberthaw
Barry

ABERAERON *Ceredigion* 503 H 27.

Cardiff 90 – Aberystwyth 16 – Fishguard 41.

Harbour Master with rm, Quay Parade, SA46 0BA, ✆ (01545) 570755, *info@harbourmaster.com, Fax (01545) 570762,* ≤ – ⇔ ✆. MC VISA. ⅌
closed 24 December-11 January – **Rest** *(closed Sunday dinner and Monday lunch)* a la carte 21.95/31.95 ♀ – **9 rm** ☕ ✝55.00/95.00 – ✝✝125.00.
◆ Good value, former harbour master's house, located on attractive quayside. Stylish décor throughout and run in a relaxing style. Snug bar; individually styled bedrooms. Nautically themed dining room with a seafood grounding.

ABERDOVEY (Aberdyfi) *Gwynedd* 503 H 26 *Wales G.*

Env. : *Snowdonia National Park*★★★.

London 230 – Dolgellau 25 – Shrewsbury 66.

Trefeddian, Tywyn Rd, LL35 0SB, West : 1 m. on A 493 ✆ (01654) 767213, *info@trefwales.com, Fax (01654) 767777,* ≤ Cardigan Bay and golf course, ⊛, ☐, ⚘, ⚑, ✂ – |♦| ⇔ 🚗 P. MC VISA
closed 1-14 December – **Rest** 12.50/25.50 ♀ – **45 rm** (dinner included) ☕ ✝66.00/90.00 – ✝✝132.00/180.00.
◆ With spectacular views of Cardigan Bay and championship golf course, this many windowed property takes advantage of its position with terraces and some bedroom balconies. Restaurant delivers substantial breakfasts and a detailed dinner menu.

Penhelig Arms, LL35 0LT, ✆ (01654) 767215, *info@penheligarms.com, Fax (01654) 767690,* ≤, ⛱ – ⇔ P. MC VISA
closed 25-26 December – **Rest** 28.00 and a la carte 17.50/25.75 ♀ ❀ – **14 rm** ☕ ✝40.00 – ✝✝79.00/140.00, 1 suite.
◆ Standing by the harbour, looking across Dyfi Estuary, this part 18C hotel is comfortably furnished, particularly in the superior bedrooms. There are views from most rooms. Cosy restaurant offering strongly seafood based menus, some of it local.

Llety Bodfor without rest., Bodfor Terrace, LL35 0EA, ✆ (01654) 767475, *info@lletybodfor.co.uk, Fax (01654) 767850,* ≤ – ⇔. MC AE VISA. ⅌
closed 23-29 December – **8 rm** ☕ ✝45.00/65.00 – ✝✝115.00/145.00.
◆ Two 19C seafront terraces painted pale mauve with modish interior featuring sitting/breakfast room with piano and hi-fi; luxurious bedrooms have blue/white seaside theme.

Preswylfa without rest, Garth Rd, LL35 0LE, North : ¼ m. turning into Copperfield St (by Dovey Inn), Church St then first left up steep hill, first left again into Garth Rd ✆ (01654) 767239, *info@preswylfa.co.uk,* ≤ Dovey estuary and Cardigan Bay, ⚘ – ⇔ P. MC VISA ⅌
– **3 rm** ☕ ✝65.00/70.00 – ✝✝70.00/80.00.
◆ Edwardian house overlooking Cardigan Bay, Dyfi Estuary. Fushia pink drawing room with piano for those who wish to tinker. Fresh, light rooms; simple but tasteful furniture. Organic food served in sunny breakfast room.

Brodawel without rest., Tywyn Rd, LL35 0SA, West : 1 ¼ m. on A 493 ✆ (01654) 767347 *info@brodawel-aberdovey.co.uk,* ≤, ⚘ – ⇔ P
March-October – **5 rm** ☕ ✝38.00 – ✝✝60.00/68.00.
◆ Two minutes walk from the beach; views of golf course, Cardigan Bay. Interior features cottage-style breakfast room in calm, understated colours. Bedrooms have similar feel.

ABERGAVENNY (Y-Fenni) *Monmouthshire* 503 L 28 *Wales G. – pop. 14 055.*

See : *Town*★ – *St Mary's Church*★ *(Monuments*★★*).*

Env. : *Brecon Beacons National Park*★★ – *Blaenavon Ironworks*★, *SW : 5 m. by A 465 and B 4246.*

Exc. : *Raglan Castle*★ *AC, SE : 9 m. by A 40.*

18 *Monmouthshire, Llanfoist* ✆ *(01873) 852606.*

ℹ *Swan Meadow, Monmouth Rd* ✆ *(01873) 857588.*

London 163 – Cardiff 31 – Gloucester 43 – Newport 19 – Swansea 49.

Llansantffraed Court, Llanvihangel Gobion, NP7 9BA, Southeast : 6 ½ m. by A 40 and B 4598 off old Raglan rd ✆ (01873) 840678, *reception@llch.co.uk, Fax (01873) 840674,* ≤, ⚘, ⚑ – |♦| ⇔ ✆ P. MC AE ⓓ VISA
Rest 16.50/32.50 and a la carte 22.00/43.00 – **21 rm** ☕ ✝80.00/112.00 – ✝✝120.00/160.00.
◆ 12C hotel, set in 19 acres of land with ornamental trout lake; built in country house style of William and Mary; popular for weddings. Magnolia rooms with mahogany furniture. Welsh seasonal fare in chintz dining room.

The Angel, 15 Cross St, NP7 5EN, ✆ (01873) 857121, *mail@angelhotelabergavenny.com, Fax (01873) 858059,* – **P** – 180. VISA
closed 25 December – **Rest** 13.80/25.00 and a la carte 22.40/31.20 – **30 rm** 60.00 – 85.00.
◆ Georgian building. refurbished in 2004. Warm and cosy bar has leather armchairs and real fire. Impressive public areas; afternoon tea is locally renowned. Functional rooms. Stylish restaurant offers classic French and British blend.

t Llandewi Skirrid *Northeast : 3¼ m. on B 4521 (Skenfrith rd) – Abergavenny.*

The Walnut Tree Inn, NP7 8AW, ✆ (01873) 852797, *francesco@thewalnuttreeinn.com, Fax (01873) 859764,* – **P**. VISA
closed Sunday dinner and Monday – **Rest** - Italian - (booking essential) a la carte 26.00/34.00.
◆ Renowned inn displays work by Welsh artists. Rustic Italian cooking, full-flavoured and seasonal, employing best local produce. Booking ahead is essential.

t Nant-y-Derry *Southeast : 6½ m. by A 40 off A 4042 – Abergavenny.*

The Foxhunter, NP7 9DN, ✆ (01873) 881101, *info@thefoxhunter.com, Fax (01873) 881377* – **P**. VISA
closed 25-26 December, 2 weeks February, Sunday and Monday – **Rest** 22.00 (lunch) and a la carte 22.00/40.00.
◆ Bright, contemporary feel within flint-stone former 19C ticket master's office. Light and airy in summer and cosy in the winter. Modern menus using fine local ingredients.

t Llanwenarth *Northwest : 3 m. on A 40 – Abergavenny.*

Llanwenarth, Brecon Rd, NP8 1EP, ✆ (01873) 810550, *info@llanwenarthhotel.com, Fax (01873) 811880,* ≤, – **P**. AE VISA.
closed 26 December – **Rest** *(closed dinner 25 December)* 12.95 (lunch) and a la carte 23.50/27.20 – **17 rm** 63.00 – 85.00/105.00.
◆ Part 16C inn; perches on banks of river Usk, famed for salmon, trout fishing. Most bedrooms have balconies from which to enjoy panoramas of Blorenge Mountain and Usk Valley. Tall-windowed dining room with fine valley views and home-made food.

ABERSOCH *Gwynedd* 502 503 G 25 *Wales G.* – Pwllheli.

Env. : *Lleyn Peninsula★★ – Plas-yn-Rhiw★ AC, W : 6 m. by minor roads.*
Exc. : *Bardsey Island★, SW : 15 m. by A 499 and B 4413 – Mynydd Mawr★, SW : 17 m. by A 499, B 4413 and minor roads.*
Golf Rd ✆ (01758) 712636.
London 265 – Caernarfon 28 – Shrewsbury 101.

Neigwl, Lon Sarn Bach, LL53 7DY, ✆ (01758) 712363, *relax@neigwl.com, Fax (01758) 712544,* ≤ Cardigan Bay – **P**. VISA.
closed January – **Rest** (booking essential) (dinner only) 26.00/32.00 s. – **9 rm** (dinner included) 95.00/110.00 – 165.00.
◆ A comfortable, family owned hotel close to town yet with fine sea vistas. Rooms are perfectly neat and individually decorated whilst the lounge is the ideal place to relax. The restaurant overlooks sea and mountains.

t Bwlchtocyn *South : 2 m. – Pwllheli.*

Porth Tocyn , LL53 7BU, ✆ (01758) 713303, *bookings@porthtocyn.fsnet.co.uk, Fax (01758) 713538,* ≤ Cardigan Bay and mountains, heated, – **P**. VISA
Easter-mid November – **Rest** (bar lunch Monday-Saturday) (buffet lunch Sunday)/dinner 37.00 – 5.50 – **17 rm** 62.00/81.00 – 114.00/154.00.
◆ Originally a row of miners' cottages; family run for three generations and family orientated. A pleasant headland location: panoramas of bay and mountains. Pretty bedrooms. Sunday buffet lunch, described as a family event. Interesting, varied menus.

ABERYSTWYTH *Ceredigion* 503 H 26 *Wales G. – pop. 15 935.*

See : *Town★★ – The Seafront★ – National Library of Wales★ (Permanent Exhibition★).*
Env. : *Vale of Rheidol★ (Railway★★ AC) – St. Padarn's Church★, SE : 1 m. by A 44.*
Exc. : *Devil's Bridge (Pontarfynach)★, E : 12 m. by A 4120 – Strata Florida Abbey★ AC (West Door★), SE : 15 m. by B 4340 and minor rd.*
Bryn-y-Mor ✆ (01970) 615104.
Terrace Rd ✆ (01970) 612125, aberystwythtic@ceredigion.gov.uk.
London 238 – Chester 98 – Fishguard 58 – Shrewsbury 74.

Four Seasons, 50-54 Portland St, SY23 2DX, ✆ (01970) 612120, *info@fourseasonsh tel.uk.com, Fax (01970) 627458* – ⇔ P. VISA. *closed 25 December* – **Rest** (dinner only) a la carte 16.95/22.00 – **16 rm** ☕ ★50.00/65.0 – ★★70.00/80.00.

◆ With a good local reputation, and enjoying a central position, this stalwart hotel make an ideal base to explore the Welsh countryside. Individually decorated bedrooms. Frequen ted by Aberyswythians, the cosy dining room offers broad menus.

Bodalwyn without rest., Queen's Ave, SY23 2EG, ✆ (01970) 612578, *hilary.d@lin one.net, Fax (01970) 639261* – ⇔. *closed 24 December-1 January* – **8 rm** ☕ ★35.00/40.00 – ★★55.00/65.00.

◆ Very well furnished house, converted from Victorian origins. Plenty of period charm and character, including beautiful tiled floor. Immaculate rooms, most with fireplaces.

at Chancery (Rhydgaled) *South : 4 m. on A 487 – ✉ Aberystwyth.*

Conrah Country House, SY23 4DF, ✆ (01970) 617941, *enquiries@conrah.co.uk Fax (01970) 624546*, ≤, – – , ⇔ rest, P – 50. AE VISA. *closed 1 week Christmas* – **Rest** *(closed Sunday October-April)* 30.00/35.00 (dinner) and lunch a la carte 19.00/30.00 – **17 rm** ☕ ★82.00/120.00 – ★★130.00/160.00.

◆ Part 18C mansion, elegant inside and out. Lovely grounds, kitchen garden, pleasan views. Airy country house rooms include three very smart new ones in converted outbuild ings. Scenic vistas greet restaurant diners.

BARMOUTH (Abermaw) *Gwynedd* 502 503 H 25 *Wales G. – pop. 2 251.*

See : *Town★ – Bridge★ AC.*

Env. : *Snowdonia National Park★★★.*

The Old Library, Station Rd ✆ (01341) 280787, barmouth.tic@gwynedd.gov.uk.

London 231 – Chester 74 – Dolgellau 10 – Shrewsbury 67.

Bae Abermaw, Panorama Rd, LL42 1DQ, ✆ (01341) 280550, *enquiries@baeabe maw.com, Fax (01341) 280346*, ≤ Mawddach estuary and Cardigan Bay, – ⇔ rm, P AE VISA

Rest *(closed Monday)* (dinner only) a la carte 30.00/37.00 – **14 rm** ☕ ★77.00/93.00 – ★★124.00/150.00.

◆ Victorian house with inspiring views over Cardigan Bay. Classic façade allied to minimalis interior, typified by an uncluttered, airy lounge. Brilliant white bedrooms. Pleasant, comf restaurant with appealing modern menus.

Llwyndû Farmhouse, LL42 1RR, Northwest : 2 ¼ m. on A 496 ✆ (01341) 28014 *intouch@llwyndu-farmhouse.co.uk, Fax (01341) 281236*, – ⇔ P. VISA *closed 25 December and restricted opening in winter* – **Rest** (by arrangement) 23.95/25.9 – **7 rm** ☕ ★76.00/80.00 – ★★76.00/80.00.

◆ Characterful part 17C farmhouse and 18C barn conversion on a hillside overlookin Cardigan Bay. Bunk beds and four-posters amidst stone walls and wood beams. An eclecti style of home-cooking using traditional regional ingredients.

BARRY (Barri) *Vale of Glamorgan* 503 K 29 *– pop. 50 661.*

RAF St Athan ✆ (01446) 751043.

The Promenade, The Triangle, Barry Island ✆ (01446) 747171, tourism@valeofglamo gan.gov.uk.

London 167 – Cardiff 10 – Swansea 39.

Egerton Grey Country House, CF62 3BZ, Southwest : 4 ½ m. by B 4226 and A 4226 and Porthkerry rd via Cardiff Airport ✆ (01446) 711666, *info@egertongrey.co.uk Fax (01446) 711690*, ≤, – ⇔ rest, P. AE VISA

Rest 15.00/30.00 and a la carte 15.00/30.00 – **10 rm** ☕ ★90.00 – ★★110.00/140.00.

◆ A secluded country house with a restful library and drawing room. Part Victorian rectory Bedrooms overlook gardens with views down to Porthkerry Park and the sea. Intimate dining room with paintings and antiques.

BEAUMARIS *Anglesey* 502 503 H 24 *Wales G. – pop. 1 513.*

See : *Town★ – Castle★★ AC.*

Env. : *Anglesey★★ – Penmon Priory★, NE : 4 m. by B 5109 and minor roads.*

Exc. : *Plas Newydd★ AC, SW : 7 m. by A 545 and A 4080.*

Baron Hill ✆ (01248) 810231.

London 253 – Birkenhead 74 – Holyhead 25.

WALES

Ye Olde Bull's Head Inn, Castle St, LL58 8AP, ☎ (01248) 810329, *info@bullsheadinn.co.uk, Fax (01248) 811294* – ⇔ rm – 🏋 25. MC AE VISA. ✂
closed 25-26 December and 1 January – ***The brasserie*: Rest** a la carte 12.25/20.65 ♀ – (see also ***The Restaurant*** below) – **13 rm** ☕ ★73.00 – ★★93.00.
◆ Part 17C inn on the high street. Cosy pubby bar area sets the tone with period charm, brasses and bric-a-brac. Well decorated bedrooms, named after Dickens characters. Less formal dining facility decorated in an attractive modern style.

Bishopsgate House, 54 Castle St, LL58 8BB, ☎ (01248) 810302, *hazel@johnson-ollier.freeserve.co.uk, Fax (01248) 810166* – ⇔ P. MC AE VISA
Rest (booking essential for non-residents) 16.95 and a la carte 20.95/24.70 – **9 rm** ☕ ★49.00/55.00 – ★★79.00/92.00.
◆ Georgian townhouse on the high street. Chesterfields in the lounge, a rare Chinese Chippendale staircase and a small bar area. Individually decorated bedrooms. Classically decorated dining room in keeping with the character of the establishment.

Mountfield without rest., LL58 8RA, ☎ (01248) 810380, ←, 🌳 – ⇔ P. ✂
March-October – **4 rm** ☕ – ★★60.00/65.00.
◆ Set prominently at north end of seafront. Lead lined windows and neat garden. Combined lounge/breakfast room. Very pleasant bedrooms with views to castle and coastline.

The Restaurant (at Ye Olde Bull's Head Inn H.), Castle St, LL58 8AP, ☎ (01248) 810329, *Fax (01248) 811294* – ⇔. MC AE VISA
closed Sunday – **Rest** (dinner only) 35.00 s.
◆ In contrast to the inn the restaurant has a contemporary feel and style engendered by subtle colours and modern lighting. A fresh approach to traditional ingredients.

BEDDGELERT *Gwynedd* 502 503 H 24 *Wales G. – pop. 535.*

Env. : *Snowdonia National Park*★★★ – *Aberglaslyn Pass*★, *S : 1½ m. on A 498.*
London 249 – Caernarfon 13 – Chester 73.

Sygun Fawr Country House 🐦, LL55 4NE, Northeast : ¾ m. by A 498 ☎ (01766) 890258, *sygunfawr@aol.com, Fax (01766) 890258,* ← Snowdon and Gwynant valley, 🌳, 🏠 – ⇔ P. MC VISA
closed January – **Rest** *(closed Tuesday)* (booking essential to non-residents) (dinner only) 20.00 – **11 rm** ☕ ★50.00 – ★★70.00/92.00.
◆ Part 16C stone built house in Gwynant Valley. Superbly located, an elevated spot which affords exceptional views of Snowdon, particularly from double deluxe rooms. Simple dining room decorated in country style.

BENLLECH *Anglesey* 502 503 H 24.

London 277 – Caernarfon 17 – Chester 76 – Holyhead 29.

Hafod without rest., Amlwch Rd, LL74 8SR, ☎ (01248) 853092, *hughastley@amserve.net,* 🌳 – ⇔ P. ✂
closed 25 December and 1 week October – **3 rm** ☕ ★40.00/50.00 – ★★60.00/62.00.
◆ Detached house with garden and some views of sea and bays. Well renovated and furnished to a good standard. Comfortably finished bedrooms well maintained by charming owner.

BETWS-Y-COED *Conwy* 502 503 I 24 *Wales G. – pop. 848.*

See : *Town*★.
Env. : *Snowdonia National Park*★★★.
Exc. : *Blaenau Ffestiniog*★ *(Llechwedd Slate Caverns*★ *AC), SW : 10½ m. by A 470 – The Glyders and Nant Ffrancon (Cwm Idwal*★*), W : 14 m. by A 5.*
⛳9 *Clubhouse ☎ (01690) 710556.*
ℹ *Royal Oak Stables ☎ (01690) 710426.*
London 226 – Holyhead 44 – Shrewsbury 62.

Tan-y-Foel Country House 🐦, LL26 0RE, East : 4 m. by A 5 and A 470 on Capel Garmon/Nebo rd ☎ (01690) 710507, *enquiries@tyfhotel.co.uk, Fax (01690) 710681,* ← Vale of Conwy and Snowdonia, 🌳 – ⇔ P. MC VISA. ✂
closed December and first week January – **Rest** (booking essential) (dinner only) 39.00 ♀ – **6 rm** ☕ ★90.00/120.00 – ★★145.00/165.00.
◆ Part 16C country house, stylishly decorated in modern vein. Stunning views of Vale of Conwy and Snowdonia. Lovely rooms revel in the quality and elegance of the establishment. Rear room and conservatory make up the restaurant.

Henllys The Old Courthouse without rest., Old Church Rd, LL24 0AL, ☎ (01690) 710534, *gillian.bidwell@btconnect.com, Fax (01690) 710884,* 🌳 – ⇔ P. MC VISA. ✂
restricted opening December-January – **9 rm** ☕ – ★★68.00/78.00.
◆ Former Victorian magistrates' court and police station overlooking the River Conwy. Comfortable rooms include a former cell. Police memorabilia all around.

Glyntwrog House without rest., LL24 0SG, Southeast : ¾ m. on A 5 ☎ (01690) 710930 *glyntwrog@betws-y-coed.org,* – P. VISA.
4 rm ☕ ★36.00/39.00 – ★★52.00/60.00.
• Victorian stone house set just off the road and surrounded by woodland. Pleasantly renovated to a homely and attractive standard. Comfortable bedrooms in varying sizes.

Bryn Bella without rest., Lôn Muriau, Llanrwst Rd, LL24 0HD, Northeast : 1 m. by A 5 on A 470 ☎ (01690) 710627, *welcome@bryn-bella.co.uk,* ← Vale of Conwy – P. VISA
– 5 rm ☕ ★40.00/45.00 – ★★50.00/56.00.
• Snug guesthouse in an elevated position with splendid views of the Vale of Conwy. Affordable accommodation; modern colours. Convenient base for touring the Snowdonia region.

Llannerch Goch without rest., Capel Garmon, LL26 0RL, East : 4 ½ m. by A 5 and A 470 on Nebo rd ☎ (01690) 710261, ←, – P.
February-November – **3 rm** ☕ ★45.00/60.00 – ★★54.00/70.00.
• Very peaceful 17C country house with original features. Pleasant sun lounge overlooking the garden. Set in four idyllic acres. Cosy sitting room, smart bedrooms.

at Penmachno *Southwest : 4¾ m. by A 5 on B 4406 – ✉ Betws-y-Coed.*

Penmachno Hall, LL24 0PU, ☎ (01690) 760410, *enquiries@penmachnohall.co.uk, Fax (01690) 760410,* ←, – P. VISA.
closed Christmas-New year – **Rest** (by arrangement) (communal dining) 25.00/28.00 – **3 rm** ☕ – ★★80.00.
• Former rectory built in 1862 with neat garden; super country setting. Sunny morning room where breakfast is served. Modern, bright bedrooms personally styled by the owners. Tasty home-cooking in deep burgundy communal dining room.

BLAENAU FFESTINIOG *Gwynedd* 502 503 I 25.
Unit 3, High St ☎ (01766) 830360.
London 237 – Bangor 32 – Caernarfon 32 – Chester 70 – Dolgellau 23.

Queen's, 1 High St, LL41 3ES, ☎ (01766) 830055, *cathy@queensffestiniog.freeserve.co.uk, Fax (01766) 830046* – P – 80. VISA.
closed 25 December – **Rest** a la carte approx 12.00 s. – **12 rm** ☕ ★45.00 – ★★90.00.
• Situated by the station in the centre of this industrial town famous for its slate mines. One of the town's original inns with a popular bar and comfortable rooms. All-day eatery with a relaxed and informal atmosphere.

BODUAN *Gwynedd* 502 503 G 25 – *see Pwllheli.*

BONT-NEWYDD *Gwynedd* 502 503 H 24 – *see Caernarfon.*

BONVILSTON (Tresimwn) *Vale of Glamorgan* 503 J 29.
London 164 – Cardiff 9 – Swansea 25.

The Great Barn without rest., Lillypot, CF5 6TR, Northwest : 1 m. by A 48 off Tre-Dodridge rd ☎ (01446) 781010, *nina@greatbarn.com, Fax (01446) 781185,* ←, – P
6 rm ☕ ★35.00/40.00 – ★★60.00/65.00.
• Converted corn barn in Vale of Glamorgan. Personally run in simple style of a country home. Pine and white furniture in rooms; some pleasant antiques. Great view at breakfast.

BRECON (Aberhonddu) *Powys* 503 J 28 *Wales G. – pop. 7 901.*
See : *Town★ – Cathedral★ AC – Penyclawdd Court★.*
Env. : *Brecon Beacons National Park★★.*
Exc. : *Llanthony Priory★★, S : 8 m. of Hay-on-Wye by B 4423 – Dan-yr-Ogof Showcaves★ AC, SW : 20 m. by A 40 and A 4067 – Pen-y-Fan★★, SW : by A 470.*
18 Cradoc, Penoyre Park ☎ (01874) 623658 – 9 Newton Park, Llanfaes ☎ (01874) 622004.
Cattle Market Car Park ☎ (01874) 622485, brectic@powys.gov.uk.
London 171 – Cardiff 40 – Carmarthen 31 – Gloucester 65.

Cantre Selyf without rest., 5 Lion St, LD3 7AU, ☎ (01874) 622904, *enquiries@cantreselyf.co.uk, Fax (01874) 622315,* – P.
closed December-January – **3 rm** ☕ ★48.00 – ★★70.00.
• An engaging 18C townhouse in town centre. Georgian fireplaces and beamed ceilings. Lovely quiet rooms with period feel. Attractive rear walled garden with sun house. Comfortable surroundings matching the smart period feel of the property.

Felin Fach Griffin with rm, Felin Fach, LD3 0UB, Northeast : 4¾ m. by B 4602 off A 470 ✆ (01874) 620111, *enquiries@eatdrinksleep.ltd.uk, Fax (01874) 620120*, rm, VISA
– **Rest** a la carte 24.00/32.00 – **7 rm** 67.50 – 92.50.
◆ Terracotta hued traditional pub, once a farmhouse. Characterful interior boasts log fire with sofas, antiques and reclaimed furniture. Modern menus and smart bedrooms.

at Llanfrynach *Southeast : 3½ m. by A 40 off B 4558 – ✉ Brecon.*

The White Swan, LD3 7BZ, ✆ (01874) 665276, *Fax (01874) 665362*, VISA.
closed 25-26 December, 1 January, Monday and Tuesday – **Rest** (light lunch)/dinner a la carte 19.50/27.50.
◆ Characterful village pub: open fires, brick and beams, cheerful service, real ales and a modern and classic menu: from chicken broth to pannacotta and balsamic strawberries.

at Talybont-on-Usk *Southeast : 6 m. by A 40 – ✉ Brecon.*

Usk Inn with rm, LD3 7JE, ✆ (01874) 676251, *stay@uskinn.co.uk, Fax (01874) 676392* – rm, AE VISA.
closed Christmas – **Rest** 14.95 (lunch) and a la carte 20.00/30.00 – **11 rm** 65.00 – 120.00.
◆ Country pub near the River Usk. Open fires in the spacious comfy sitting room. Large dining room serving seasonal dishes. Well-kept bedrooms.

BRIDGEND (Pen-y-Bont) *Bridgend* 503 J 29 – *pop. 39 427.*

McArthur Glen Design Outlet Village, The Derwen, junction 36, M 4 ✆ *(01656) 654906, bridgendtic@bridgend.gov.uk.*
London 177 – Cardiff 20 – Swansea 23.

at Coychurch (Llangrallo) *East : 2¼ m. by A 473 – ✉ Bridgend.*

Coed-y-Mwstwr, CF35 6AF, North : 1 m. by Bryn Rd ✆ (01656) 860621, *enquiries@coed-y-mwstwr.com, Fax (01656) 863122*, heated, – 175. AE VISA.
Eliots : **Rest** 12.95/26.95 and dinner a la carte 19.70/31.45 – **26 rm** 103.00 – 150.00, 2 suites.
◆ Meaning "whispering trees", this Victorian mansion overlooks Vale of Glamorgan and woodland. Local golf courses, well-equipped leisure centre. Sizeable country house rooms. Well-kept restaurant with a formal, traditional ambience.

at Southerndown *Southwest : 5½ m. by A 4265 on B 4524 – ✉ Bridgend.*

Frolics, Beach Rd, CF32 0RP, ✆ (01656) 880127, *dougwindsor34@aol.com* – . VISA
closed Sunday dinner and Monday – **Rest** 12.95 (lunch) and a la carte 20.40/30.95.
◆ Personally run restaurant named after 17C ship wrecked on nearby coast. Cosy neighbourhood style. Menus make full use of area's abundance of fresh fish and seafood.

at Laleston *West : 2 m. on A 473 – ✉ Bridgend.*

Great House, High St, CF32 0HP, on A 473 ✆ (01656) 657644, *enquiries@great-house-laleston.co.uk, Fax (01656) 668892*, AE VISA.
closed 25-26 December – (see ***Leicester's*** below) – **21 rm** 80.00/100.00 – 120.00/145.00.
◆ 15C Grade II listed building, believed to have been a gift from Elizabeth I to the Earl of Leicester. Personally run - attention to detail particularly evident in the rooms.

Leicester's (at Great House H.), High St, CF32 0HP, on A 473 ✆ (01656) 657644, *enquiries@great-house-laleston.co.uk, Fax (01656) 668892*, AE VISA.
closed 25-26 December and Sunday dinner – **Rest** a la carte 22.05/35.40.
◆ Peppermint green walls with exposed beams, fireplace and original windows. Imaginative modern style using finest local and Welsh produce. Bistro or à la carte menus.

BUILTH WELLS (Llanfair-ym-Muallt) *Powys* 503 J 27.

London 191.5 – Cardiff 63.5 – Brecon 20.5.

The Drawing Room with rm, Twixt Cwmbach, Newbridge-on-Wye, LD2 3RT, North : 3½ m. on A 470 ✆ (01982) 552493, *post@the-drawing-room.co.uk*, 8. AE VISA
closed 2 weeks January, 2 weeks September, Sunday dinner and Monday – **Rest** (booking essential) 22.50 (lunch) and a la carte 28.50/35.50 – **3 rm** 85.00 – 150.00.
◆ Delightful Georgian house with 19C additions: sumptuous country style at every turn. Carefully sourced seasonal menu with distinct French classic emphasis. Very stylish rooms.

BWLCHTOCYN *Gwynedd* 502 503 G 25 – *see Abersoch.*

CAERNARFON *Gwynedd* 502 503 H 24 *Wales G.* – *pop. 9 695.*

See : *Town*★★★ – *Castle*★★★ *AC* – *Town Walls*★.
Env. : *Snowdonia National Park*★★★.
Aberforeshore, Llanfaglan ☎ *(01286) 673783.*
Oriel Pendeitsh, Castle St. ☎ *(01286) 672232, caernarfon.tic@gwynedd.gov.uk.*
London 249 – Birkenhead 76 – Chester 68 – Holyhead 30 – Shrewsbury 85.

Celtic Royal, Bangor St, LL55 1AY, ☎ (01286) 674477, *admin@celtic-royal.co.uk* *Fax (01286) 674139,* – rest, P – 500. MO AE VISA.
Rest (bar lunch)/dinner 15.95 and a la carte 22.45/32.40 s. – **110 rm** ★68.00/73.00 – ★★100.00/110.00.
◆ Updated Victorian hotel which now caters primarily for the corporate market. Good access to Holyhead and Bangor. Strong leisure and conference facilities. Modern rooms. Comfortable, split-level restaurant with modern ambience.

at Llanrug *East : 3 m. on A 4086* – ✉ *Caernarfon.*

Plas Tirion Farm without rest., LL55 4PY, South : 1 m. by Ffordd Glanmoelyn Rd on Waenfawr rd ☎ (01286) 673190, *cerid@plastirion.plus.com, Fax (01286) 671883,* P.
April-October – **3 rm** ★30.00 – ★★60.00.
◆ Stone built farmhouse on dairy farm surrounded by 300 acres. Relaxing, homely sitting room. Generous portions served in airy breakfast room with log burner. Cottagey rooms.

at Bont-Newydd *South : 2 m. A 487* – ✉ *Caernarfon.*

Plas Dinas , LL54 7YF, on A 487 ☎ (01286) 830214, *info@plasdinas.co.uk* *Fax (01286) 830214,* – P. MO AE VISA
Rest (dinner only) 24.95/29.95 – **8 rm** ★69.00 – ★★120.00.
◆ Informally run hotel, family owned and their paintings and photos adorn walls. Attractive drawing room. Good sized bedrooms, many with antiques and rural views. Cosy restaurant looks onto pretty garden.

at Saron *Southwest : 3¼ m. by A 487 on Saron rd* – ✉ *Caernarfon.*

Pengwern , LL54 5UH, Southwest : ¼ m. ☎ (01286) 831500, *janepengwern@aol.com* *Fax (01286) 830741,* – P. MO AE VISA.
April-October – **Rest** (by arrangement) 22.50 – **3 rm** ★45.00 – ★★70.00.
◆ Charming, spacious farmhouse on working farm, picturesquely situated between mountains and sea. Snowdonia views. Neat and tidy sitting room. Bedrooms of luxurious quality. Owner serves fresh, robust farmhouse cuisine including home-reared beef and lamb.

CAERSWS *Powys* 502 503 J 26.

London 194 – Aberystwyth 39 – Chester 63 – Shrewsbury 42.

Maesmawr Hall , SY17 5SF, East : 1 m. on A 489 ☎ (01686) 688255, *reception@maesmawr.co.uk, Fax (01686) 688410,* – P – 120. MO VISA
closed 25 December - 1 January – **Rest** *(closed Sunday dinner)* (bar lunch Monday-Saturday)/dinner 16.95/26.00 and a la carte 24.00/30.00 – **17 rm** ★70.00/80.00 – ★★110.00.
◆ Grade II listed, part 16C timbered hunting lodge in Severn Valley. Peaceful atmosphere. Oak floors, beams and huge fireplaces adorn public areas. Traditionally styled rooms. Formal dining room with heavy drapes and ornately framed mirror.

at Pontdolgoch *Northwest : 1½ m. on A 470* – ✉ *Newtown.*

Talkhouse with rm, SY17 5JE, ☎ (01686) 688919, *info@talkhouse.co.uk,* – P. MO VISA.
closed first 2 weeks January and 25 December – **Rest** *(closed Monday, Tuesday lunch and Sunday dinner)* a la carte 21.00/29.00 – **3 rm** ★70.00 – ★★95.00.
◆ 17C coaching inn on Aberystwyth-Shrewsbury road. Ornate rustic bar. Dining room opening onto terrace and gardens. Wide ranging locally-based menu. Stylish well-kept bedrooms.

Your opinions are important to us:
please write and let us know about your discoveries and experiences – good and bad!

ARDIFF **(Caerdydd)** *Cardiff* 503 K 29 *Wales G. – pop. 292 150.*

See : *City★★★ – National Museum and Gallery★★★* **AC** *(Evolution of Wales★★, Picture galleries★★ (Galleries 12 and 13★★), Pottery and Porcelain★)* **BY** *– Castle★★* **AC BZ** *– Civic Centre★* **BY** *– Llandaff Cathedral★* **AV B** *– Cardiff Bay★ (Techniquest★* **AC***)* **AX**.

Env. : *Museum of Welsh Life★★★* **AC**, *St. Fagan's, W : 5 m. by A 4161* **AV** *– Castell Coch★★* **AC**, *NW : 5 m. by A 470* **AV**.

Exc. : *Caerphilly Castle★★* **AC**, *N : 7 m. by A 469* **AV** *– Dyffryn Gardens★* **AC**, *W : 8 m. by A 48* **AX**.

18 *Dinas Powis, Old Highwalls ☏ (029) 2051 2727,* **AX**.

✈ *Cardiff (Wales) Airport : ☏ (01446) 711111, SW : 8 m. by A 48* **AX** – **Terminal** : *Central Bus Station.*

ℹ *16 Wood St ☏ (029) 2022 7281.*

London 155 – Birmingham 110 – Bristol 46 – Coventry 124.

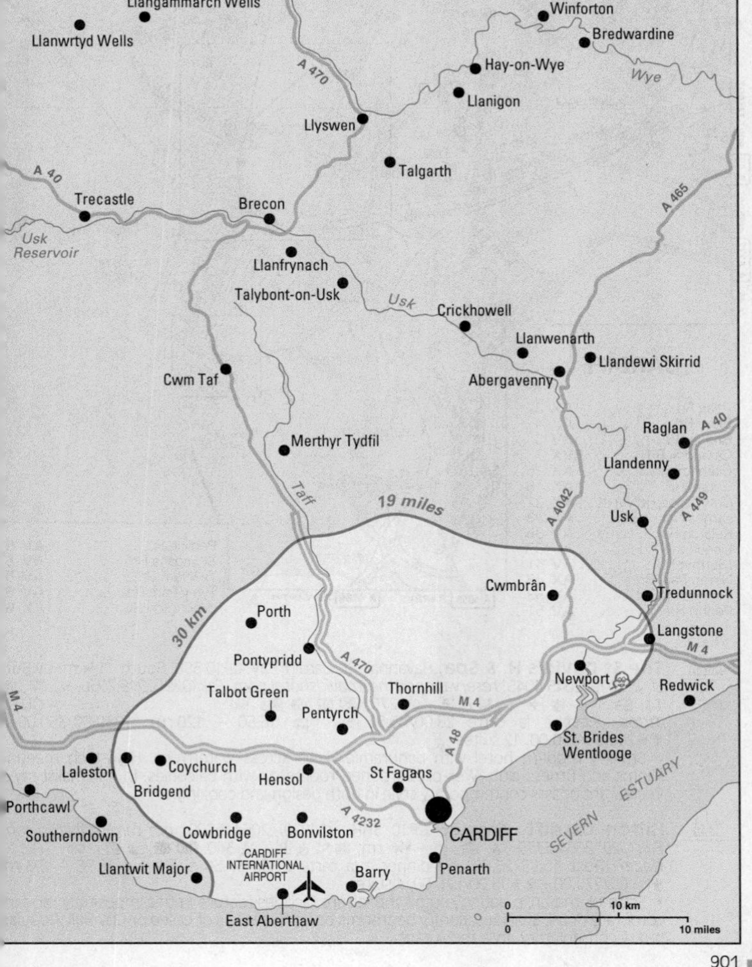

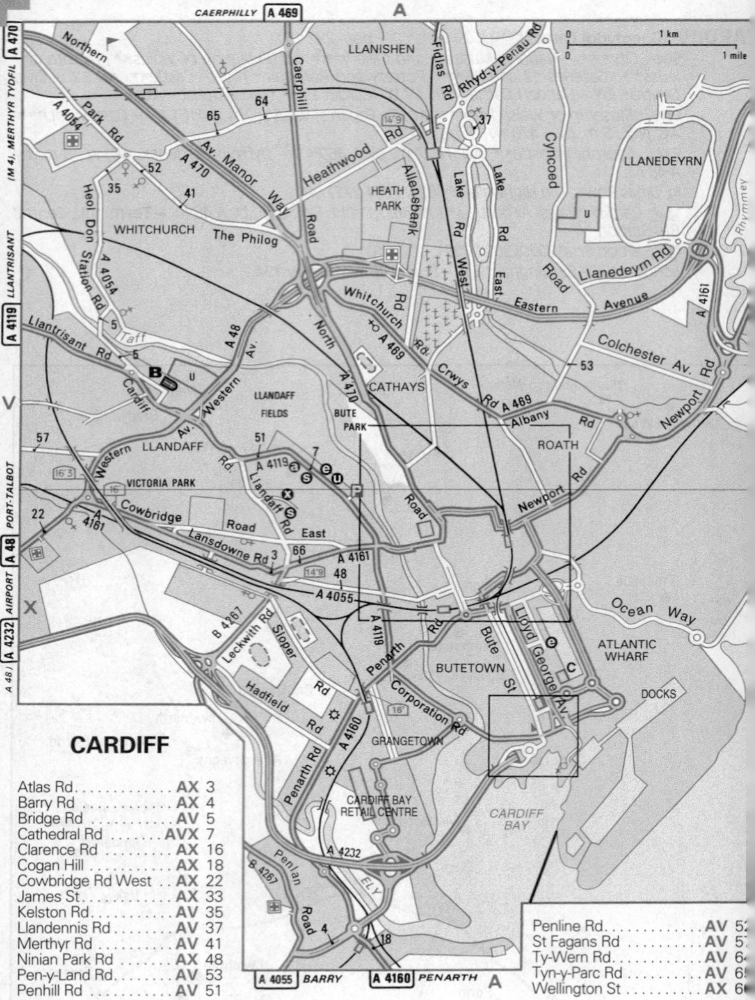

CARDIFF

The St David's H. & Spa, Havannah St, Cardiff Bay, CF10 5SD, South : 1 ¾ m. by Bute St ✆ (029) 2045 4045, *reservations@thestdavidshotel.com, Fax (029) 2048 7056,* ←, … – … 270. MC AE ⦶ VISA. CU a
Tides: Rest a la carte 28.00/45.50 ♀ – ☕ 16.50 – **120 rm** ★230.00/350.00 – ★★260.00/350.00, 12 suites.
◆ Striking modern hotel with panoramic views across waterfront. High-tech meeting rooms and fitness club. Well-proportioned rooms, all with balconies, in minimalist style. Restaurant boasts contemporary style in both design and cooking.

Hilton Cardiff, Kingsway, CF10 3HH, ✆ (029) 2064 6300, *gm-cardiff@hilton.com Fax (029) 2064 6333,* … rm, … 340. MC AE ⦶ VISA. BZ x
Razzi: Rest 16.95/26.50 and dinner a la carte 27.90/37.50 **s.** ♀ – ☕ 16.95 – **193 rm** ★85.00/270.00 – ★★95.00/270.00, 4 suites.
◆ State-of-the-art meeting rooms and leisure facilities feature in this imposingly modern corporate hotel. Spacious, comfy bedrooms boast fine views of castle or City Hall. Popular buzzy conservatory-style restaurant.

CARDIFF

Copthorne, Copthorne Way, Culverhouse Cross, CF5 6DH, West : 4 ¾ m. by A 4161 and A 48 at junction with A 4232 ✆ (029) 2059 9100, *sales.cardiff@mill-cop.com*, *Fax (029) 2059 9080*, – rest, – 300. MC AE VISA
Raglan's : Rest *(closed Saturday lunch)* 25.00/33.50 and a la carte approx 18.50 **s.** – 15.75 – **134 rm** 197.50 – 197.50, 1 suite.
◆ Large commercial hotel handy for both the airport and city centre. Many of the well-furnished rooms overlook a tranquil lake. "Connoisseur" rooms have extra facilities. Comfortable rear restaurant with lakeside views.

Park Plaza, Greyfriars Rd, CF10 3AL, ✆ (029) 2011 1111, *ppinfo@parkplazahotels.co.uk*, *Fax (029) 2011 1112*, – – 160. MC AE VISA **BY s**
Laguna : Rest 15.00 (lunch) and a la carte 19.00/28.50 – **129 rm** 79.50/160.00 – 89.00/200.00.
◆ Central hotel, opened early 2005. Vast leisure centre boasts stainless steel pool. Impressive meeting rooms. Spacious, white bedrooms, with good, up-to-date amenities. Restaurant, with its own street entrance, has a mix of local and international flavours.

CARDIFF BAY

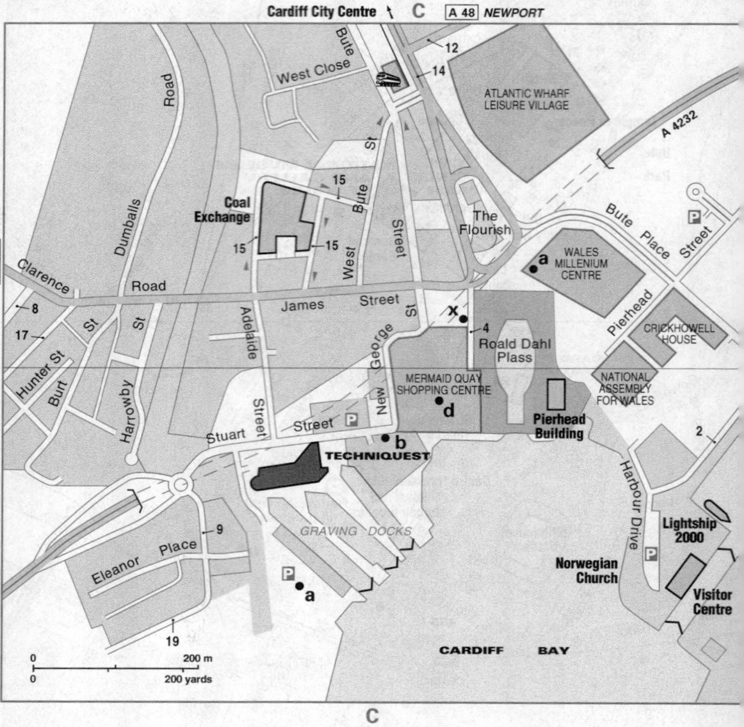

Holland House, 24-26 Newport Rd, CF24 0DD, (0870) 1220020, *ops.holland@macdonald-hotels.co.uk, Fax (029) 2048 8894*, – 700. MC AE D VISA. BY
Rest 20.00 and a la carte 23.00/36.50 – **160 rm** ★80.00/220.00 – ★★116.00/245.00, 5 suites.
◆ 14-storey converted office block that opened as an hotel in 2004. Large marbled lobby spacious busy bar. State-of-the-art gym and therapy rooms. Airy, well-equipped rooms Modern menus with local produce to fore in informal restaurant.

Angel, Castle St, CF10 1SZ, (029) 2064 9200, *angelreservations@paramount-hotels.co.uk, Fax (029) 2039 6212* – 300. MC AE D VISA. BZ a
Rest (bar lunch)/dinner a la carte 25.00/35.00 s. – **100 rm** ★140.00/160.00 – ★★170.00, 2 suites.
◆ Restored Victorian hotel near Millennium Stadium. Magnificent Waterford Crystal foyer chandelier and sweeping staircase. Some of the airy, well-equipped rooms overlook castle Elegant and intimate restaurant ideal for both social and business entertaining.

Village H. and Leisure Club, 29 Pendwyallt Rd, Coryton, CF14 7EF, Northwest : 5 m by A 470 on A 4054 at southern side of junction 32 of M 4 (029) 2052 4300, *village.cardiff@village-hotels.com, Fax (029) 2052 4302*, – 250. MC AE D VISA
Rest (grill rest.) 6.95 (lunch) and a la carte 16.85/21.85 s. – 9.95 – **118 rm** ★79.00/145.00 – ★★79.00/145.00.
◆ Modern, corporate hotel with unrivalled high-tech leisure facilities. A favourite with families at weekends. Spacious rooms are vibrantly decorated and well-equipped. Traditional British cooking and a selection from the Far East are offered in the restaurant.

Jurys Cardiff, Mary Ann St, CF10 2JH, (029) 2034 1441, *cardiff@jurysdoyle.com, Fax (029) 2022 3742* – rm, rest, – 300. AE VISA. BZ u
Rest (bar lunch Monday-Saturday)/dinner 19.95 and a la carte 20.45/27.40 s. – **143 rm** 105.00/175.00 – 105.00/175.00, 3 suites.
◆ Corporate hotel opposite the International Arena. Impressive Victorian-style lobby overlooked by many of the well-equipped bedrooms. Executive rooms have thoughtful extras. Snug, formal dining room with cosy, intimate feel.

Holiday Inn, Castle St, CF10 1XD, (0870) 4008140, *cardiffcity@ichotelsgroup.com, Fax (029) 2037 1495* – rm, rest, – 150. AE VISA. BZ e
closed 25-26 December – **Rest** *(closed Sunday lunch)* (bar lunch)/dinner a la carte 20.00/30.00 s. – 13.95 – **159 rm** 135.00 – 135.00.
◆ Modern corporate hotel with superb meeting facilities unrivalled in city. Bright, contemporary bedrooms have a Scandinavian feel. Superior rooms offer more workspace. Informal and lively restaurant.

Jolyon's without rest., 5 Bute Crescent, Cardiff Bay, CF10 5AN, (029) 2048 8775, *jolyons@btopenworld.com, Fax (029) 2048 8775* – . VISA CT x
5.95 – **7 rm** 78.00 – 165.00.
◆ Georgian townhouse within Cardiff Bay's oldest terrace. Boutique style prevails. Rustic, slate-floored bar with log stove, red leather sofas. Light, modern, stylish bedrooms.

Lincoln House without rest., 118 Cathedral Rd, CF11 9LQ, (029) 2039 5558, *reservations@lincolnhotel.co.uk, Fax (029) 2023 0537* – . AE VISA. AV e
23 rm 60.00/65.00 – 120.00.
◆ Sympathetically restored Victorian house close to the attractive Bute Gardens. Friendly service by eager-to-please owners. Four-poster room in period style most comfortable.

Express by Holiday Inn without rest., Longueil Close, Atlantic Wharf, CF10 4EE, (0800) 434040, *reservations@exhicardiff.co.uk, Fax (029) 20488922* – – 30. AE VISA. AX e
87 rm 72.00 – 72.00.
◆ Ideal for both corporate and leisure travellers and even meetings can be held here. Overlooking the waterfront and within the up-and-coming Bay area. Well-equipped rooms.

The Town House without rest., 70 Cathedral Rd, CF11 9LL, (029) 2023 9399, *thetownhouse@msn.com, Fax (029) 2022 3214* – . AE VISA AV u
8 rm 45.00/59.50 – 59.50/79.50.
◆ Carefully restored Victorian house with Gothic features. Welcoming service by owners. Light and airy bedrooms have some thoughtful touches and are well-appointed.

Georgian without rest., 179 Cathedral Rd, CF11 9PL, (029) 2023 2594, *gmenin@georgianhotelcardiff.co.uk, Fax (029) 2023 2594* – . AV a
closed 22 December-2 January – **8 rm** 37.00/45.00 – 70.00/75.00.
◆ Friendly, family run guesthouse a short walk from the city centre. Neat and well-kept traditional accommodation in a homely atmosphere. Italian and French spoken.

Annedd Lon without rest., 157 Cathedral Rd, CF11 9PL, (029) 2022 3349, *Fax (029) 2064 0885* – . VISA. AV s
closed 24-30 December – **6 rm** 35.00/45.00 – 60.00.
◆ Victorian house with Gothic influences located within a conservation area. Genuine Welsh hospitality in this a non-smoking establishment. Comfortable bedrooms.

Woods Brasserie, The Pilotage Building, Stuart St, Cardiff Bay, CF10 5BW, South : 1½ m. by Bute St (029) 2049 2400, *Fax (029) 2048 1998,* – . AE VISA CU b
closed 25 December, 1 January and Sunday dinner – **Rest** 12.50/15.50 (lunch) and dinner a la carte 20.40/33.90.
◆ Modern brasserie dishes and seafood specials from an open kitchen. Professionally run. Live evening music. Bay view from the first-floor terrace.

Da Venditto, 7-8 Park Pl, CF10 3DP, (029) 2023 0781, *toni@vendittogroup.co.uk, Fax (029) 2039 9949* – . AE VISA BZ b
closed 24-26 December, first week January, Sunday and Monday – **Rest** - Italian - a la carte 22.50/29.50.
◆ Italian restaurant in the basement of a town house. Stylish contemporary interior with wood floors and modern furnishings. Well-prepared, seasonal cuisine.

Le Gallois, 6-10 Romilly Cres, CF11 9NR, (029) 2034 1264, *info@legallois-ycymro.com, Fax (029) 2023 7911* – . VISA AX x
closed 1 week late August/September, Christmas-New Year, Sunday and Monday – **Rest** 19.95/35.00.
◆ Bright and relaxed restaurant where keen owners provide both the friendly service and the assured modern European cooking. Daily changing set price lunch menu available.

XX **Da Castaldo,** 5 Romilly Crescent, CF11 9NP, ✆ (029) 2022 1905, *Fax (029) 2022 1920* AX
– ⇔ ▤. MC VISA
closed 2 weeks August, Christmas, Sunday and Monday – **Rest** - Italian influences - 15.9 (lunch) and a la carte 19.40/30.40 ♀.
◆ Appealingly modern ambience in a residential setting; jolly owners add to the relaxed ai Tasty Italian influences enhance the classical cooking. Good value lunch.

X **Brazz,** Wales Millennium Centre, Bute Place, Cardiff Bay, CF10 5AL, ✆ (029) 2045 900 CT
cardiff@brazz.co.uk, Fax (029) 2044 0270 – ⇔ ▤. MC AE ⓓ VISA
closed 25 December, 1 January and Sunday dinner – **Rest** 12.95/15.95 and a la cart 24.00/31.45 ♀.
◆ Based in the stunning Wales Millennium Centre. In two sections: the intimate Club c more spacious Brasserie. Eclectic, daily changing menus offer a modern and classic blend

X **Armless Dragon,** 97 Wyeverne Rd, CF24 4BG, ✆ (029) 2038 2357, *paul@thearmle dragon.fsnet.co.uk, Fax (029) 2038 2055* – ⇔. MC AE ⓓ VISA BY
closed 1 week Easter, 2 weeks August, 1 week Christmas, Sunday, Monday and Saturda lunch – **Rest** 12.00 (lunch) and dinner a la carte 22.25/27.25 ♀.
◆ Well-established, homely restaurant with welcoming atmosphere and snug décor. Dai changing blackboard menus feature honest, no-nonsense cooking utilising Welsh ingredients.

X **Izakaya Japanese Tavern,** 1st Floor, Mermaid Quay, Cardiff Bay, CF10 5BZ, ✆ (02 2049 2939, *ayakazi@aol.com, Fax (029) 2049 2969* – ▤. MC AE ⓓ VISA CU
closed 25-26 December and 1-2 January – **Rest** - Japanese - 17.00 (dinner) and a la car 18.00/28.00.
◆ Smartly furnished restaurant in bay-side location: banners and paper lanterns predominate. Individual tables or counter service. Authentic, high quality Japanese menus.

at Thornhill *North : 5¼ m. by A 470 – AV – on A 469 – ✉ Cardiff.*

New House Country, Thornhill Rd, CF14 9UA, on A 469 ✆ (029) 2052 0280, *enq ries@newhousehotel.com, Fax (029) 2052 0324,* ≤, 🌳, 👤 – ⇔ rest, ✆ P – 🔔 200. MC ⓓ VISA. ⊗
Rest 23.00 ♀ – **33 rm** ☕ ★98.00 – ★★170.00, 3 suites.
◆ Extended Edwardian country house in secluded spot commanding views over Vale o Glamorgan. Popular for weddings, ideal for corporate or leisure guests. Spacious room Classically appointed, Regency-styled dining room.

Manor Parc, Thornhill Rd, CF14 9UA, on A 469 ✆ (029) 2069 3723, *enquiry@man parc.com, Fax (029) 2061 4624,* 🌳, ⚔ – ✆ P – 🔔 120. MC AE VISA. ⊗
closed 24 and 26 December - 2 January – **Rest** *(closed Sunday dinner)* a la carte 25.00/35.0 – **21 rm** ☕ ★47.50/72.00 – ★★95.00/130.00.
◆ Personally run country house set in attractive terraced gardens. Some of the wel appointed rooms have south facing balconies and views over the Bristol Channel. Brigh airy orangery restaurant with Italian-based menu.

at Penarth *South : 3 m. by A 4160 – AX – ✉ Cardiff.*

XX **The Olive Tree,** 21 Glebe St, CF64 1EE, ✆ (029) 2070 7077 – ⇔. MC VISA
closed Sunday dinner-Monday – **Rest** (dinner only and Sunday lunch) 19.75 and a la car 23.20/33.20 ☺.
◆ Rewarding discovery tucked away in the centre of town. Relaxing feel augmented b vivid artwork. Warm, friendly service of good value, seasonal, frequently changing dishes

at St Fagans *Northwest : 3½ m. by A 4119 – AV –, B 4258 and B 4488 – ✉ Cardiff.*

XX **The Old Post Office** with rm, Greenwood Lane, CF5 6EL, by Croft-y-Genau Rd ✆ (02 2056 5400, *heiditheoldpost@aol.com, Fax (029) 2056 3400* – ⇔, ▤ rest, P. MC AE ⓓ VISA
Rest *(closed Monday, Tuesday, Wednesday lunch and Sunday dinner)* 17.95/35.00 – ☕ 5.0 – **6 rm** ★70.00 – ★★80.00.
◆ The eponymous building in this pleasant hamlet is now a spacious, rustic restaurant wit stylish bar. Modern seasonal dishes with notable quality and balance. Excellent rooms.

at Pentyrch *Northwest : 7 m. by A 4119 – AV – ✉ Cardiff.*

XXXX **De Courcey's,** Tyla Morris Ave, CF15 9QN, South : 1 m. ✆ (029) 2089 2232, *dinedeco ceys@aol.com, Fax (029) 2089 1949,* 🌳 – P ⇔ 30 – 🔔 100. MC AE ⓓ VISA
closed 25-26 December, Sunday dinner, Monday and Tuesday and Bank Holidays – **Re** (dinner only and Sunday lunch) 29.95 and a la carte 30.50/43.50 ♀.
◆ Long-standing restaurant in an ornately decorated neo-Georgian house. Formal y homely atmosphere. Accomplished traditional cuisine, served by smartly attired staff.

CARDIGAN (Aberteifi) *Ceredigion* 503 G 27 *Wales G. – pop. 4 082.*
Env. : *Pembrokeshire Coast National Park★★.*
Gwbert-on-Sea (01239) 612035.
Theatr Mwldan, Bath House Rd (01239) 613230, cardigan.tic@ceredigion.gov.uk.
London 250 – Carmarthen 30 – Fishguard 19.

Penbontbren Farm, Glynarthen, SA44 6PE, Northeast : 9½ m. by A 487 (01239) 810248, *welcome@penbontbren.com, Fax (01239) 811129,* – rest, – 25. MC AE VISA.
closed Christmas-New Year – **Rest** (residents only Sunday) (dinner only) a la carte 20.10/25.35 – **10 rm** ★63.00 – ★★96.00.
◆ Hotel set in series of modern farmhouses in wonderfully secluded valley of River Dulais. Two lounges and farm museum. You can sleep in a granary, stable or thrashing barn. Pine furnished dining room which also houses a bar and lounge.

at St Dogmaels *West : 1½ m. by A 487 on B 4546 – Cardigan.*

Berwyn without rest., Cardigan Rd, SA43 3HS, (01239) 613555, <, – P.
closed Christmas and New Year – **3 rm** ★35.00 – ★★50.00.
◆ Modern guesthouse in tranquil location with views of River Teifi and 12C St Dogmaels Abbey ruins. Welcoming breakfast room and lounge. Clean, well maintained bedrooms.

at Gwbert on Sea *Northwest : 3 m. on B 4548 – Cardigan.*

Gwbert, SA43 1PP, on B 4548 (01239) 612638, *gwbert@enterprise.net, Fax (01239) 621474,* < Cardigan Bay – , rest, P. MC AE VISA
– **Rest** *(closed Sunday in winter)* (bar lunch)/dinner 16.95 and a la carte 12.70/24.70 – **17 rm** ★40.00 – ★★97.00.
◆ Traditional seaside hotel on banks of Teifi with inspiring views of Cardigan Bay. Bright pastel public areas and smart bar. Well-kept rooms with co-ordinated fabrics. Pink washed dining room with panoramic views of Pembroke National Park coastline.

Do not confuse X with ✿! X defines comfort, while stars are awarded for the best cuisine, across all categories of comfort.

CARMARTHEN (Caerfyrddin) *Carmarthenshire* 503 H 28 *Wales G. – pop. 14 648.*
See : *Kidwelly Castle★ – National Botanic Garden★.*
113 Lammas St (01267) 231557, tourism@carmarthenshire.gov.uk.
London 219 – Fishguard 47 – Haverfordwest 32 – Swansea 27.

at Nantgaredig *East : 5 m. on A 40 – Carmarthen.*

Y Polyn, SA32 7LH, South : 1 m. by B 4310 on B 4300 (01267) 290000, *ypolyn@hotmail.com,* , – P. MC VISA.
closed Monday, Saturday lunch and Sunday dinner – **Rest** a la carte 20.00/27.50.
◆ Roadside hostelry enhanced by pleasant summer terrace and stream. Bright, fresh interior with rich, rose-painted walls. Classic, rustic menus with Gallic/Welsh starting point.

CEMAES (Cemais) *Anglesey* 502 503 G 23 *Wales G.*
Env. : *Anglesey★★.*
London 272 – Bangor 25 – Caernarfon 32 – Holyhead 16.

Hafod Country House without rest., LL67 ODS, South : ½ m. on Llanfechell rd (01407) 711645, <, – P. MC VISA.
March-September – **3 rm** ★26.00/30.00 – ★★52.00.
◆ Pleasant Edwardian guesthouse with very welcoming owner on outskirts of picturesque fishing village. Comfortable sitting room. The bedrooms are in immaculately kept order.

CHANCERY (Rhydgaled) *Ceredigion* 503 H 26 – *see Aberystwyth.*

CHEPSTOW (Cas-gwent) *Monmouthshire* 503 504 M 29 *Wales G. – pop. 10 821.*
See : *Town★ – Castle★★ AC (Great Tower★★).*
Env. : *Wynd Cliff★, N : 2½ m. by A 466 – Caerwent★ (Roman Walls★), SW : 4 m. by A 48.*
Castle Car Park, Bridge St (01291) 623772.
London 131 – Bristol 17 – Cardiff 28 – Gloucester 34.

WALES

Marriott St Pierre H. & Country Club, St Pierre Park, NP16 6YA, Southwest 3 ½ m. on A 48 ☏ (01291) 625261, *reservations.stpierre@marriotthotels.co.uk* Fax (01291) 629975, ⊛, Ⅎ₅, ≘s, ⊡, 18, ♔, ✗ – ⟡ ♿ P – 🧑 240. MC AE VISA. ✗
***Orangery* : Rest** (booking essential) (dinner only and Sunday lunch)/dinner 25.00 and a la carte 27.95/42.70 ♀ – ***Zest* : Rest** a la carte 20.90/27.90 ♀ – **132 rm** ☐ ★109.00 – ★★119.00, 16 suites.
◆ Part 14C manor house with extensions. Business and leisure facilities. Own church in grounds, popular for weddings. Rich lounges; well-kept rooms. Orangery restaurant boasts distinctive Georgian feel. Informal Zest.

Castle View, 16 Bridge St, NP16 5EZ, ☏ (01291) 620349, *taciliaok@aol.com* Fax (01291) 627397, ⌂ – ⟡ rest, ☏. MC AE ⓓ VISA
closed 25-26 December and 1 January **Rest** (bar lunch Monday-Saturday) (Sunday dinner residents only)/dinner a la carte 13.50/21.25 **s.** – ☐ 3.00 – **14 rm** ★60.00/65.00 ★★83.00/110.00.
◆ Ivy-clad hotel built over 300 years ago as private residence. Its stones probably came from adjacent Chepstow Castle. Secluded garden, large bar, some rooms have castle views. Regional produce to the fore in the restaurant.

COLWYN BAY (Bae Colwyn) *Conwy* 502 503 I 24 *Wales G. – pop. 30 269.*

See : *Welsh Mountain Zoo★ AC (⋞★).*
Env. : *Bodnant Garden★★ AC, SW : 6 m. by A 55 and A 470.*
18 *Abergele, Tan-y-Coppa Rd ☏ (01745) 824034* – 9 *Old Colwyn, Woodland Ave ☏ (01492) 515581.*
ℹ *Imperial Buildings, Station Sq, Princes Drive ☏ (01492) 530478 – The Promenade, Rhos-on-Sea ☏ (01492) 548778 (summer only).*
London 237 – Birkenhead 50 – Chester 42 – Holyhead 41.

Rathlin Country House without rest., 48 Kings Rd, LL29 7YH, Southwest : 1 m. on B 5113 ☏ (01492) 532173, *enquiries@rathlincountryhouse.co.uk, Fax (01492) 532173,* ⊡ heated, ⌂ – ⟡ ☏ P. MC VISA. ✗

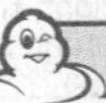

3 rm ☐ ★55.00 – ★★78.00.
◆ Surrounded by almost an acre of mature gardens, this personally run guesthouse has large summer pool, inglenook fireplace, oak panelling and highly individual, comfy rooms.

Pen-y-Bryn, Pen-y-Bryn Rd, Upper Colwyn Bay, LL29 6DD, Southwest : 1 m. by B 5113 ☏ (01492) 533360, *penybryn@brunningandprice.co.uk, Fax (01492) 535808,* ⌂ – ⟡ P. MC VISA
closed 25-26 December and dinner 1 January – **Rest** a la carte 16.00/23.45 ♀.
◆ Built in the 1970s, with sloped garden and bay view. Spacious interior with large, polished wood tables. Extensive menus feature Welsh dishes with eclectic influences.

at Rhos-on-Sea *Northwest : 1 m. – ✉ Colwyn Bay.*

Plas Rhos without rest., Cayley Promenade, LL28 4EP, ☏ (01492) 543698, *info@plasrhos.co.uk, Fax (01492) 540088,* ⋞, ⌂ – ⟡ ☏ P. MC VISA. ✗
closed 20 December-31 January – **8 rm** ☐ ★38.00/55.00 – ★★80.00/90.00.
◆ 19C house on the first promenade from Colwyn Bay. Homely front lounge with bay view and fresh flowers. Breakfasts feature local butcher's produce. Immaculately kept rooms.

Luxury pad or humble abode? ✗ and 🏠 denote categories of comfort.

CONWY *Conwy* 502 503 I 24 *Wales G. – pop. 3 847.*

See : *Town★★ – Castle★★★ AC – Town Walls★★ – Plas Mawr★★*
Env. : *Snowdonia National Park★★★ – Bodnant Garden★★ AC, S : 8 m. by A 55 and A 470 Conwy Crossing (suspension bridge★).*
9 *Penmaenmawr, Conway Old Rd ☏ (01492) 623330.*
ℹ *Conwy Castle Visitor Centre ☏ (01492) 592248.*
London 241 – Caernarfon 22 – Chester 46 – Holyhead 37.

Sychnant Pass House ⛰, Sychnant Pass Rd, LL32 8BJ, Southwest : 2 m. by A 547 and Sychnant rd, turning right at T junction ☏ (01492) 596868, *bre@sychnant-pass-house.co.uk, Fax (01492) 596868,* ⋞, Ⅎ₅, ≘s, ⊡, ⌂ – ⟡ P. MC VISA
closed 24-26 December **Rest** *(closed Monday)* (booking essential to non-residents) (dinner only) 27.50 – **8 rm** ☐ ★80.00/130.00 – ★★100.00/150.00, 2 suites.
◆ Country house with Snowdonia National Park providing utterly peaceful backdrop. Charming sitting room with attractive décor. Comfy rooms, named after cats from T.S. Elliott. Informal dining room with bright lighting and seasonal menus.

at Llansanffraid Glan Conwy *Southeast : 2½ m. A 547 and A 470 – ✉ Conwy.*

Old Rectory Country House, Llanrwst Rd, LL28 5LF, on A 470 ☎ (01492) 580611, *info@oldrectorycountryhouse.co.uk, Fax (01492) 584555,* ← Conwy estuary, – P. VISA
closed 11 December- 13 January – **Rest** *(closed Sunday except before Bank Holidays)* (booking essential to non-residents) (dinner only) (set menu only) 39.90 – **6 rm** 109.00/129.00 – 129.00/169.00.
◆ Enjoys fine position on Conwy Estuary; once home to parish rectors, renovated in Georgian style. House motto: "beautiful haven of peace"; antique beds, watercolours abound. Formal, antique furnished dining room serves accomplished set dinners.

at Tyn-y-Groes *(Gwynedd) South : 4 m. on B 5106 – ✉ Conwy.*

Groes Inn, LL32 8TN, North : 1½ m. on B 5106 ☎ (01492) 650545, *Fax (01492) 650855,* ←, – P. AE VISA.
Rest 28.00 and a la carte 15.00/25.00 – **14 rm** 79.00 – 146.00.
◆ Part 16C inn, Wales' first licensed house. Beamed ceilings, log fires and historic bric-a-brac. Immaculately sumptuous bedrooms, some with super rural views. Georgian-style dining room.

COWBRIDGE (Y Bont Faen) *Vale of Glamorgan* 503 *J 29 – pop. 3 616.*
London 170 – Cardiff 15 – Swansea 30.

Huddarts, 69 High St, CF71 7AF, ☎ (01446) 774645, *Fax (01446) 772215* – . VISA
closed 1 week spring, 1 week autumn, 26 December-8 January, Sunday dinner and Monday – **Rest** a la carte 26.85/31.85.
◆ Intimate, family run restaurant located on high street of this ancient market town. Welsh tapestries on wall. Skilfully executed traditional dishes with modern influences.

COYCHURCH (Llangrallo) *Bridgend* 503 *J 29 – see Bridgend.*

CRICCIETH *Gwynedd* 502 503 *H 25 Wales G. – pop. 1 826.*
Env. : *Lleyn Peninsula★★ – Ffestiniog Railway★★.*
Ednyfed Hill ☎ (01766) 522154.
London 249 – Caernarfon 17 – Shrewsbury 85.

Mynydd Ednyfed Country House, Caernarfon Rd, LL52 0PH, Northwest : ¾ m. on B 4411 ☎ (01766) 523269, *mynedd-ednyfed@criccieth.net, Fax (01766) 522929,* ←, , – rest, P. VISA
closed 22 December-4 January – **Rest** (dinner only and Sunday lunch)/dinner a la carte 16.70/26.00 **s.** – **9 rm** 50.00 – 105.00.
◆ Idyllically located 400 year old country house in seven acres of gardens and woods overlooking Tremadog Bay. Traditionally furnished lounge bar. Simply kept rooms. Small, cosy, comfortable dining room and spacious conservatory for meals.

CRICKHOWELL (Crucywel) *Powys* 503 *K 28 Wales G.*
Env. : *Brecon Beacons National Park★★.*
Exc. : *Llanthony Priory★★, NE : 10 m. by minor roads.*
Beaufort Chambers, Beaufort St ☎ (01873) 812105.
London 169 – Abergavenny 6 – Brecon 14 – Cardiff 40 – Newport 25.

Gliffaes Country House, NP8 1RH, West : 3 ¾ m. by A 40 ☎ (01874) 730371, *calls@gliffaeshotel.com, Fax (01874) 730463,* ←, , , – P – 40. AE VISA.
closed 3 weeks January – **Rest** (restricted lunch Monday-Saturday)/dinner 26.00/32.00 **s.** – **22 rm** 80.00/100.00 – 190.00.
◆ 19C country house and gardens on banks of Usk, offering great tranquillity. Welcoming bar, lounge and conservatory. Popular for outdoor pursuits. Modern, luxurious bedrooms. Bold, country house dining room has pleasant garden views.

Bear, High St, NP8 1BW, ☎ (01873) 810408, *bearhotel@aol.com, Fax (01873) 811696,* – P – 50. AE VISA
Rest (in bar) a la carte 16.00/29.00 – (see also ***The Restaurant*** below) – **33 rm** 58.00/110.00 – 144.00, 2 suites.
◆ Imposing, part 15C former coaching inn with maze of public areas. Bustling bar and lounges. Good conference facilities. Plush, spacious bedrooms with modern furnishings. Tried-and-tested, hearty bar menus.

Ty Croeso ⛾, The Dardy, NP8 1PU, West : 1½ m. by A 4077 off Llangynidr rd ☎ (01873 810573, *info@ty-croeso.co.uk, Fax (01873) 810573*, ≤, – ⇔ rest, P. MC AE VISA. ⛧
closed 9-31 January and 24-27 December – **Rest** (lunch booking essential)/dinner 18.0 and a la carte 18.00/25.00 ♀ – **8 rm** ☐ ♦40.00/50.00 – ♦♦80.00/85.00.
♦ Small hotel constructed from Welsh stone, originally part of a Victorian workhouse Cottagey atmosphere. Large bar with log fire. Chintz rooms with rewarding views. Strikingly pink dining room with rustic ambience.

Glangrwyney Court, NP8 1ES, South : 2 m. on A 40 ☎ (01873) 811288, *info@glacourt.co.uk, Fax (01873) 810317*, – ⇔ P. MC VISA
Rest (by arrangement) 25.00 – **5 rm** ☐ ♦50.00/70.00 – ♦♦65.00/90.00.
♦ Spacious Georgian house with sizeable garden and warm welcome. Large front lounge in chintz with antiques and trinkets. Pleasantly cluttered, well-kept rooms.

The Restaurant (at Bear H.), High St, NP2 1BN, ☎ (01873) 810408, *bearhotel@aol.com Fax (01873) 811696* – MC AE VISA
closed Monday – **Rest** (dinner only and Sunday lunch) a la carte 23.45/30.00 ♀.
♦ Charming dining rooms with antiques and curios. Open fire in the bar. Professional service. Wide-ranging menu with classical base using Welsh ingredients; daily specials.

Nantyffin Cider Mill Inn, Brecon Rd, NP8 1SG, West : 1 ½ m. on A 40 ☎ (01873 810775, *info@cidermill.co.uk*, – P. MC AE VISA
closed Sunday dinner and Monday except Bank Holidays – **Rest** 12.95 and a la cart 16.00/30.00 ♀.
♦ Converted 16C cider mill, its working parts still in situ. Rattan flooring and scrubbed pine tables. Varied menus featuring local fish and game. Also, unsurprisingly, cider.

CROSSGATES *Powys* 503 J 27 – *see Llandrindod Wells.*

CWMBRAN (Cwmbrân) *Torfaen* 503 K 29 – *pop. 47 254.*
London 149 – *Bristol 35* – *Cardiff 17* – *Newport 5.*

Parkway, Cwmbran Drive, NP44 3UW, South : 1 m. by A 4051 ☎ (01633) 871199, *enquiries@parkwayhotel.co.uk, Fax (01633) 869160*, – ⇔ rm, rest, P – 50 MC AE VISA
Ravello's **: Rest** (dinner only and Sunday lunch)/dinner 18.95/45.00 and a la car 18.85/30.90 **s.** – ☐ 12.95 – **69 rm** ☐ ♦105.00 – ♦♦120.00, 1 suite.
♦ Purpose-built hotel aimed at the business traveller with extensive conference facilitie Spacious lounge and coffee shop. Well-kept rooms with pine furniture and chintz. Sma comfortable restaurant with formal chairs and water fountain in centre.

CWM TAF *Merthyr Tydfil* 503 J 28 – *see Merthyr Tydfil.*

DEGANWY *Conwy* 502 503 I 24 – *see Llandudno.*

DOLGELLAU *Gwynedd* 502 503 I 25 *Wales G.* – *pop. 2 407.*
See : *Town*★.
Env. : *Snowdonia National Park*★★★ – *Cadair Idris*★★★ – *Precipice Walk*★, *NE : 3 m. minor roads.*
Hengwrt Estate, Pencefn Rd ☎ *(01341) 422603.*
Ty Meirion, Eldon Sq ☎ *(01341) 422888.*
London 221 – *Birkenhead 72* – *Chester 64* – *Shrewsbury 57.*

Penmaenuchaf Hall ⛾, Penmaenpool, LL40 1YB, West : 1 ¾ m. on A 493 (Tywyn R ☎ (01341) 422129, *relax@penhall.co.uk, Fax (01341) 422787*, ≤ Rhinog mountains a Mawddach estuary, – ⇔ P. MC VISA
Rest 17.95/34.00 and a la carte 34.20/41.50 – **14 rm** ☐ ♦75.00/135.00 ♦♦130.00/200.00.
♦ From a handsome drawing room, enjoy the enviable position of this Victorian mansi with its Rhinog Mountain and Mawddach Estuary vistas. Bedrooms are tastefully furnishe The panelled dining room offers lovely views of a sunken rose garden.

Tyddyn Mawr ⛾ without rest., Islawdref, Cader Rd, LL40 1TL, Southwest : (off top the Town Square) 3 m. on Cader Rd ☎ (01341) 422331, ≤ Cader Idris, – ⇔ ⛧
February-November – **3 rm** ☐ ♦60.00 – ♦♦60.00.
♦ Part 18C farmhouse with sympathetic extension: boasts spectacular views from breat taking position. Timbered breakfast room. Superb rooms: one with patio, one with b cony.

at Ganllwyd *North : 5½ m. on A 470 – ✉ Dolgellau.*

Plas Dolmelynllyn , LL40 2HP, ☎ (01341) 440273, *info@dolly-hotel.com, Fax (01341) 440640,* ←, , – ⇎ P. VISA.
closed 6 weeks January-February and 2 weeks November – **Rest** (booking essential to non-residents) (dinner only) 15.00/36.00 – **11 rm** (dinner included) 75.00/100.00 – 100.00/180.00.
◆ Down a beech-lined drive, imbued with aura of a bygone age, this part 17C manor has gardens where a stream flows into a lake; ideal for fishing enthusiasts. Bedroom views. Welsh dishes served in the part-panelled dining room.

EAST ABERTHAW **(Aberddawan)** *Vale of Glamorgan* 503 J 29 – ✉ *Barry.*
London 180 – Cardiff 20 – Swansea 33.

Blue Anchor Inn, CF62 3DD, ☎ (01446) 750329 – P. VISA
– **Rest** 17.95 (dinner) and a la carte 13.00/25.00.
◆ Characterful thatched and creeper covered inn, dating back to 1380. Nooks, crannies and warrens invoke charming atmosphere. Wide-ranging menus with creative dishes.

EWLOE *Flintshire* 502 503 K 24.
London 200 – Chester 8.5 – Liverpool 18 – Shrewsbury 48.

De Vere St David's Park, St David's Park, CH5 3YB, on B 5125 at junction with A 494 ☎ (01244) 520800, *reservations.stdavids@devere-hotels.com, Fax (01244) 520930,* , , , 18, , – ⇎, rest, P – 250. AE VISA.
Fountains : **Rest** (booking essential) 23.50/35.00 and a la carte 23.00/35.00 **s.** – **145 rm** 125.00 – 125.00/165.00.
◆ A large, modern, well-equipped business oriented hotel with its own golf course nearby. Bright modern style of décor throughout bedrooms and public areas. Large, smart, comfortable restaurant.

FISHGUARD **(Abergwaun)** *Pembrokeshire* 503 F 28 *Wales G. – pop. 3 193.*
Env. : *Pembrokeshire Coast National Park*★★.
to Republic of Ireland (Rosslare) (Stena Line) 2-4 daily (1 h 50 mn/3 h 30 mn).
Town Hall, The Square ☎ (01348) 873484 – Ocean Lab, The Parrog, Goodwick ☎ (01348) 872037.
London 265 – Cardiff 114 – Gloucester 176 – Holyhead 169 – Shrewsbury 136 – Swansea 76.

Manor Town House, 11 Main St, SA65 9HG, ☎ (01348) 873260, *enquiries@manortownhouse.com, Fax (01348) 873260,* ←, – ⇎. VISA
Rest (booking essential to non-residents) (dinner only) 17.00/22.00 **s.** – **6 rm** 35.00/40.00 – 70.00.
◆ Georgian Grade II listed house. Bedrooms are individually styled and furnished with antiques, choose from Victorian and Art Deco; some with harbour and sea views. Restaurant located in the beamed basement.

Three Main Street without rest., 3 Main St, SA65 9HG, ☎ (01348) 874275 – ⇎.
closed February and restricted opening in winter – **3 rm** 50.00 – 80.00.
◆ Well-established landmark, just off the market square. Simple, comfy bar, plenty of Welsh artwork on show. Comfortable, antique furnished bedrooms.

at Letterston *South : 5 m. on A 40.*

Heathfield Mansion , SA62 5EG, Northwest : 1½ m. by B 4331 ☎ (01348) 840263, *info@heathfieldaccommodation.co.uk, Fax (01348) 840263,* ←, , – ⇎ P
Rest (by arrangement) 15.00 – **3 rm** 35.00/40.00 – 54.00/70.00.
◆ Georgian house in 16 acres of pasture and woodland. Peaceful atmosphere and personal hospitality. Good bedrooms furnished with antiques. Outdoor pursuits can be arranged. Meals are taken at individual tables in the compact, pine fitted dining room.

at Welsh Hook *Southwest : 7½ m. by A 40 – ✉ Haverfordwest.*

Stone Hall with rm, SA62 5NS, ☎ (01348) 840212, *Fax (01348) 840815,* – P. AE VISA.
restricted opening in winter – **Rest** (booking essential) (dinner only) 25.90 and a la carte 26.70/32.35 – **5 rm** 70.00/80.00 – 100.00.
◆ Charming, characterful part 14C manor house with 17C additions. Tranquil setting and personal hospitality. Offers home-cooked, French-style menu and simple accommodation.

GANLLWYD *Gwynedd* 503 I 25 – *see Dolgellau.*

GELLILYDAN *Gwynedd – see Llan Ffestiniog.*

GLANWYDDEN *Conwy – see Llandudno.*

GRESFORD (Groes-ffordd) *Wrexham* 502 503 L 24 – *see Wrexham.*

GUILSFIELD (Cegidfa) *Powys* 502 503 K 26 – *see Welshpool.*

GWBERT ON SEA *Ceredigion* 503 F 27 – *see Cardigan.*

HARLECH *Gwynedd* 502 503 H 25 *Wales G.* – *pop. 1 233.*

See : *Castle★★ AC.*
Env. : *Snowdonia National Park★★★.*
Royal St. David's ℘ (01766) 780203.
Llys y Graig, High St ℘ (01766) 780658.
London 241 – Chester 72 – Dolgellau 21.

Hafod Wen, LL46 2RA, South : ¾ m. on A 496 ℘ (01766) 780356, *enquiries@harlec guesthouse.co.uk, Fax (01766) 780356,* ≤ Tremadoc bay and Snowdonia, – P. VISA
closed 3 weeks November – **Rest** (by arrangement) 26.00 – **6 rm** ★41.00/61.00 – ★★88.00.
◆ Unusual house with Dutch colonial architectural references. Superb views of Tremado Bay and Snowdonia from most of the antique and curio filled bedrooms. Footpath t beach. The dining room shares in the establishment's delightful views.

Gwrach Ynys without rest., LL47 6TS, North : 2 ¼ m. on A 496 ℘ (01766) 78074 *info@gwrachynys.co.uk, Fax (01766) 781199,* – P.
7 rm ★27.00/45.00 – ★★60.00/68.00.
◆ Edwardian house in good location for exploring Snowdonia and Cardigan Bay. Welcom ing owner. Traditional bedrooms, two of which are ideal for families.

Castle Cottage with rm, Pen Llech, LL46 2YL, off B 4573 ℘ (01766) 780479, *glyn@c tlecottageharlech.co.uk, Fax (01766) 781251* – . VISA.
closed 9 January-12 February – **Rest** (booking essential) (dinner only) 28.50 – **7 rm** (dinne included) ★90.00 – ★★170.00.
◆ A little cottage just a short distance from the imposing Harlech Castle. Snug, beame dining room where Welsh food with a modern twist is served. Smart contemporary be rooms.

HAVERFORDWEST (Hwlffordd) *Pembrokeshire* 503 F 28 *Wales G.* – *pop. 13 367.*

See : *Scolton Museum and Country Park★.*
Env. : *Pembrokeshire Coast National Park★★.*
Exc. : *Skomer Island and Skokholm Island★, SW : 14 m. by B 4327 and minor roads.*
Arnolds Down ℘ (01437) 763565.
Old Bridge ℘ (01437) 763110.
London 250 – Fishguard 15 – Swansea 57.

Wilton House, 6 Quay St, SA61 1BG, ℘ (01437) 760033, *wiltonhousehotel@h mail.com, Fax (01437) 760297,* heated – P. VISA
closed 24-27 December – **Rest** (dinner only) a la carte 15.40/25.50 s. – **10 rm** ★45.00/55.00 – ★★70.00.
◆ Georgian house conveniently located in the centre of town near shops and craft wor shops. Bedrooms, commensurate with the age of the building, are large with high ceiling The restaurant has something of an old-fashioned atmosphere and ambience.

Lower Haythog Farm, Spittal, SA62 5QL, Northeast : 5 m. on B 4329 ℘ (0143 731279, *nesta@lowerhaythogfarm.co.uk, Fax (01437) 731279,* – P.
Rest (by arrangement) 20.00 – **6 rm** ★35.00/45.00 – ★★55.00/75.00.
◆ Friendly atmosphere, traditional comforts and a warm welcome at this 250 acre workir dairy farm with accessible woodland walks. Well kept and comfortable throughout. Dinir room in homely, country style reflected in hearty, home-cooked food.

Undecided between two equivalent establishments?
Within each category, establishments are classified
in our order of preference.

AWARDEN (Penarlâg) *Flintshire* 502 K 24.
London 205 – Chester 9 – Liverpool 17 – Shrewsbury 45.

The Brasserie, 68 The Highway, CH5 3DH, ☎ (01244) 536353, *Fax (01244) 520888* – ▤. MC AE VISA
closed Saturday lunch – **Rest** (booking essential) a la carte 19.65/27.00 ♀.
◆ Neutral walls, wood floors and spot lighting contribute to the busy, modern ambience in this good value, small restaurant; well reputed locally. Cuisine with a Welsh tone.

AY-ON-WYE (Y Gelli) *Powys* 503 K 27 *Wales G. – pop. 1 846.*
See : *Town*★.
Env. : *Brecon Beacons National Park*★★.
Exc. : *Llanthony Priory*★★, *SE : 12 m. by minor roads.*
Rhosgoch, Builth Wells ☎ (01497) 851251.
Craft Centre, Oxford Rd ☎ (01497) 820144.
London 154 – Brecon 16 – Cardiff 59 – Hereford 21 – Newport 62.

York House without rest., Hardwick Rd, Cusop, HR3 5QX, East : ½ m. on B 4348 ☎ (01497) 820705, *roberts@yorkhouse59.fsnet.co.uk, Fax (01497) 820705,* – P. MC VISA
closed 24-26 December – **4 rm** ★32.00 – ★★60.00/64.00.
◆ On the east road into this town in the Brecon Beacons National Park. Late Victorian house with large, neatly lawned, south facing garden. Traditional, well-kept rooms. Home-cooked dishes proudly served in dining room.

Old Black Lion with rm, 26 Lion St, HR3 5AD, ☎ (01497) 820841, *info@oldblacklion.co.uk, Fax (01497) 822960* – P. MC VISA.
closed 2 weeks January and 24-26 December – **Rest** a la carte 20.00/28.00 ♀ – **10 rm** ★42.50/50.00 – ★★85.00.
◆ Inn with parts dating back to 13C and 17C when it reputedly hosted Oliver Cromwell. A friendly place with a traditional atmosphere, popular menu and comfortable bedrooms.

Llanigon *Southwest : 2½ m. by B 4350 – ✉ Hay-on-Wye.*

Old Post Office without rest., HR3 5QA, ☎ (01497) 820008 – P
3 rm ★35.00/50.00 – ★★50.00/70.00.
◆ Dating from 17C, a converted inn. Near the "book town" of Hay-on-Wye. Smart modern ambience blends with characterful charm. Pine furnished rooms with polished floors.

ENSOL *Rhondda Cynon Taff Wales G.*
Exc. : *Museum of Welsh Life*★★★, *E : 8 m. by minor rd north to Miskin, A 4119 and minor rd south.*
London 161 – Bridgend 10 – Cardiff 8 – Cowbridge 7.

Llanerch Vineyard without rest., CF72 8GG, ☎ (01443) 225877, *enquiries@llanerch-vineyard.co.uk, Fax (01443) 225546* – . MC VISA.
5 rm ★49.00/60.00 – ★★79.00.
◆ Rurally set, fully functioning vineyard in woodland with 20 acres of vines. The modern breakfast area is furnished with Welsh art. Immaculate, state of the art bedrooms.

OLYHEAD (Caergybi) *Anglesey* 502 503 G 24 *Wales G. – pop. 11 237.*
Env. : *South Stack Cliffs*★, *W : 3 m. by minor roads.*
to Republic of Ireland (Dun Laoghaire) (Stena Line) 4-5 daily (1 h 40 mn) – to Republic of Ireland (Dublin) (Irish Ferries) 2 daily (3 h 15 mn) – to Republic of Ireland (Dublin) (Stena Line) 1-2 daily (3 h 45 mn).
Terminal 1, Stena Line ☎ (01407) 762622.
London 269 – Birkenhead 94 – Cardiff 215 – Chester 88 – Shrewsbury 105 – Swansea 190.

Yr Hendre without rest., Porth-y-Felin Rd, LL65 1AH, Northwest : ¾ m. by Prince of Wales Rd off Walthew Ave ☎ (01407) 762929, *rita@yrhendre.freeserve.co.uk, Fax (01407) 765936,* – P.
3 rm ★60.00 – ★★60.00.
◆ Detached house dating from the 1920s in a pleasant, residential area of town and ideally located for the ferry terminus. Comfortable and well-furnished bedrooms. Breakfast overlooking the garden and with views of the sea.

OWEY *Powys – see Llandrindod Wells.*

KNIGHTON (Trefyclawdd) *Powys* 503 K 26 *Wales G. – pop. 2 743.*
See : *Town★.*
Exc. : *Offa's Dyke★, NW : 9½ m.*
Little Ffrydd Wood ℘ *(01547) 528646.*
Offa's Dyke Centre, West St ℘ *(01547) 528753.*
London 162 – Birmingham 59 – Hereford 31 – Shrewsbury 35.

Milebrook House, Ludlow Rd, Milebrook, LD7 1LT, East : 2 m. on A 4113 ℘ (0154 528632, *hotel@milebrook.kc3ltd.co.uk, Fax (01547) 520509,* – P. MC VISA
Rest *(closed Monday lunch)* (bar lunch)/dinner 28.00 and a la carte 12.95/27.40 s. – 10 r ★61.50/65.50 – ★★95.00/101.00.
◆ Located in the Teme Valley; good for exploring the Welsh Marches. Possesses a fin formal garden well stocked with exotic plants. Rooms are large and pleasingly decorate The kitchen garden provides most of the vegetables which appear in the restaurant.

LAKE VYRNWY *Powys* 502 503 J 25 *Wales G.* – ✉ *Llanwddyn.*
See : *Lake★.*
Unit 2, Vyrnwy Craft Workshops ℘ *(01691) 870346, laktic@powys.gov.uk.*
London 204 – Chester 52 – Llanfyllin 10 – Shrewsbury 40.

Lake Vyrnwy , SY10 OLY, ℘ (01691) 870692, *res@lakevyrnwy.cor Fax (01691) 870259,* ≤ Lake Vyrnwy, – rest, P – 120. MC AE VISA
Rest (bar lunch)/dinner 32.50 s. – **36 rm** ★75.00/175.00 – ★★170.00/205.00, 1 suite.
◆ Victorian country house built from locally quarried stone overlooking the lake; an RSP sanctuary and sporting estate, ideal for game enthusiasts. Rooms have timeless chi Spectacular lakeside views from the restaurant are matched by accomplished cooking.

LALESTON *Bridgend* 503 J 29 – *see Bridgend.*

LAMPHEY (Llandyfai) *Pembrokeshire* 503 F 28 – *see Pembroke.*

LANGSTONE *Newport* 503 L 29 – *see Newport.*

LAUGHARNE *Carmarthenshire* 503 G 28.
London 230 – Cardiff 80 – Carmarthen 13.

Hurst House , East Marsh, SA33 4RS, South : 3 m. by A 4066 taking left turn o unmarked road opposite Hill Crest house ℘ (01994) 427417, *Fax (01994) 427730,* P. MC AE VISA
Rest 16.95/42.00 s. – **7 rm** ★85.00/150.00 – ★★150.00.
◆ Converted farmhouse and outbuildings in Dylan Thomas country: epitomises new wa of trendy, informal country hotels. Rooms boast vivid colour schemes and up-to-da extras. Modish menus in restaurant with reclaimed tables and contemporary artwork.

LETTERSTON (Treletert) *Pembrokeshire* 503 F 28 – *see Fishguard.*

LLANARMON DYFFRYN CEIRIOG *Wrexham* 502 503 K 25 – ✉ *Llangollen (Denbighshire)*
London 196 – Chester 33 – Shrewsbury 32.

West Arms, LL20 7LD, ℘ (01691) 600665, *gowestarms@aol.com, Fax (01691) 60062* – rest, P – 30. MC VISA
Rest (bar lunch Monday-Saturday)/dinner 32.90 and a la carte 19.85/27.85 – **13 rm** ★53.50/69.50 – ★★174.00, 2 suites.
◆ Set in Ceiriog Valley; enjoys many original fixtures associated with a part 16C country i - slate-flagged floors, inglenooks, timberwork. Bedrooms with matching ambience. A co cise but well-balanced menu offered in atmospheric dining room.

LLANBEDR *Gwynedd* 502 503 H 25 *Wales G. – pop. 1 101.*
Env. : *Harlech Castle★★, N : 3 m. by A 496.*
Cardiff 150 – Dolgellau 18 – Harlech 3.

Pensarn Hall without rest., LL45 2HS, on A 496 ℘ (01341) 241236, *welcome@pensar hall.co.uk,* – P. MC VISA
7 rm ★60.00/80.00 – ★★60.00/80.00.
◆ Late 19C house on an estuary. Impressive staircase and entrance with orginal tiled flo Pleasant front conservatory. Breakfast room has good view. Large, well-kept rooms.

LLANBERIS *Gwynedd* 503 H 24 *Wales G. – pop. 1 842.*
See : *Town*★ – *Welsh Slate Museum*★ *AC – Power of Wales*★.
Env. : *Snowdonia National Park*★★★ *(Snowdon*★★★, *Snowdon Mountain Railway*★★ *AC – panorama*★★★*).*
41 High St (01286) 870765, llanberis.tic@gwynedd.gov.uk.
London 243 – Caernarfon 7 – Chester 65 – Shrewsbury 78.

Y Bistro, 43-45 High St, LL55 4EU, (01286) 871278, *ybistro@fsbdial.co.uk, Fax (01286) 871278* – . MO VISA
closed 2 weeks January – **Rest** *(closed Sunday and Monday in winter)* (booking essential) (dinner only) a la carte 26.00/34.50.
◆ Long established, in lakeside village at foot of Snowdonia. Brush up on your Welsh when perusing menus of Eidion Badell (beef flamed in Cognac), Cawl Tomato Ceiros, (soup).

LLANDEILO *Carmarthenshire* 503 I 28 *Wales G. – pop. 1 731.*
See : *Town*★ – *Dinefwr Park*★ *AC.*
Env. : *Brecon Beacons National Park*★★ – *Black Mountain*★, *SE : by minor roads – Carreg Cennen Castle*★ *AC, SE : 4 m. by A 483 and minor roads.*
London 218 – Brecon 34 – Carmarthen 15 – Swansea 25.

Plough Inn, Rhosmaen, SA19 6NP, North : 1 m. on A 40 (01558) 823431, *enquiries@ploughrhosmaen.co.uk, Fax (01558) 823969*, , , – rm, , P – 45. MO AE VISA.
Rest a la carte 15.75/24.15 – **14 rm** ★57.50 – ★★75.00.
◆ Once a farmhouse, the perfect base for country pursuits. Rooms, named after characters from Mabinogion, are well furnished with thick pile carpets, large windows for views. The Italian patron who is also chef uses local and Continental recipes.

at Salem *North : 3 m. by A 40 off Pen y banc rd – Llandeilo.*

Angel Inn, SA19 7LY, (01558) 823394, – P. MO VISA.
closed 1 week January – **Rest** *(closed Sunday-Monday)* a la carte 22.00/35.00.
◆ Cream coloured pub next to chapel in small village. Inviting bar lounge with chair and sofa assortment. Edwardian style dining room: elaborate cooking utilising local fare.

LLANDENNY *Monmouthshire* 503 L 28 – *see Usk.*

LLANDEWI SKIRRID *Monmouthshire – see Abergavenny.*

LLANDRILLO *Denbighshire* 502 503 J 25 – *Corwen.*
London 210 – Chester 40 – Dolgellau 26 – Shrewsbury 46.

Tyddyn Llan with rm, LL21 0ST, (01490) 440264, *tyddynllan@compuserve.com, Fax (01490) 440414*, – P. MO VISA
closed 17-28 January and 1 week November – **Rest** *(closed Monday-Thursday lunch)* (booking essential) 25.00/38.50 – **13 rm** (dinner included) ★95.00/115.00 – ★★180.00/240.00.
◆ Charming sitting areas for pre-dinner drinks. Two dining rooms with blue painted wood panels. Modern menus employing local produce. Fine selection of country house rooms.

LLANDRINDOD WELLS *Powys* 503 J 27 *Wales G. – pop. 5 024.*
Exc. : *Elan Valley*★★ *(Dol-y-Mynach and Claerwen Dam and Reservoir*★★, *Caban Coch Dam and Reservoir*★, *Garreg-ddu Viaduct*★, *Pen-y-Garreg Reservoir and Dam*★, *Craig Goch Dam and Reservoir*★*), NW : 12 m. by A 4081, A 470 and B 4518.*
Llandrindod Wells (01597) 823873.
Old Town Hall, Memorial Gardens (01597) 822600, llandtic@powys.gov.uk.
London 204 – Brecon 29 – Carmarthen 60 – Shrewsbury 58.

Metropole, Temple St, LD1 5DY, (01597) 823700, *info@metropole.co.uk, Fax (01597) 824828*, , , – , rest, , P – 300. MO AE VISA
Rest (lunch booking essential) 12.50/22.00 – **120 rm** ★79.00/94.00 – ★★104.00/124.00, 2 suites.
◆ Run by Baird-Murray family for 100 years and popular for hosting vintage car rallies. Leisure complex is in 19C style conservatory. Eight "Tower" rooms with adjoining lounge. Expect to find cuisine committed to using local ingredients.

WALES

at Crossgates *Northeast : 3½ m. on A 483 – ✉ Llandrindod Wells.*

Guidfa House, LD1 6RF, ☎ (01597) 851241, *guidfa@globalnet.co.uk* *Fax (01597) 851875,* – P. VISA.
Rest (by arrangement) 20.00 – **6 rm** ★40.00/48.00 – ★★70.00.
◆ Georgian house with white painted façade and pleasant garden to relax in. Indoors, find spacious, bright bedrooms. A friendly welcome is given with tips on local activities. Seasonally changing menu of zesty home cooking in traditionally decorated dining room.

at Howey *South : 1½ m. by A 483 – ✉ Llandrindod Wells.*

Acorn Court Country House without rest., Chapel Rd, LD1 5PB, Northeast ½ m. ☎ (01597) 823543, *info@acorncourt.co.uk, Fax (01597) 823543,* – P.
3 rm ★30.00/45.00 – ★★55.00/65.00.
◆ Chalet-style house in lovely countryside; guests can fish in the lake. Bedrooms are large with many extra touches: hairdryers, stationery, soft toys - homely and welcoming.

LLANDUDNO *Conwy* 502 503 I 24 *Wales G. – pop. 14 872.*
See : *Town★ – Seafront★ (Pier★)* **B** – *The Great Orme★ (panorama★★, Tramway★, Ancient Copper Mines★ AC)* **AB**.
Exc. : *Bodnant Garden★★ AC, S : 7 m. by A 470* **B**.
Rhos-on-Sea, Penrhyn Bay ☎ (01492) 549641 **A** – *72 Bryniau Rd, West Shore ☎ (01492) 875325* **A** – *Hospital Rd ☎ (01492) 876450* **B**.
1-2 Chapel St ☎ (01492) 876413.
London 243 – Birkenhead 55 – Chester 47 – Holyhead 43.

Plan opposite

Bodysgallen Hall, LL30 1RS, Southeast : 2 m. on A 470 ☎ (01492) 584466 *info@bodysgallen.com, Fax (01492) 582519,* ≤ gardens and mountains, – P – 40. AE VISA.
Rest (booking essential) 17.50/44.00 **s.** – 6.95 – **19 rm** ★125.00/175.00 – ★★295.00, 16 suites 210.00/235.00.
◆ Majestic and rare sums up this part 17C-18C hall with tower, once a soldier's lookout now a place to take in views of mountains and terraced gardens. Antique filled rooms. Elegant, gleaming dining room with tall windows; serves fine and distinctive dishes.

Osborne House, 17 North Parade, LL30 2LP, ☎ (01492) 860330, *sales@osbornehouse.com, Fax (01492) 860791,* ≤ – P. AE VISA. **A**
closed 1 week Christmas – **Rest** – (see ***Osborne's Cafe Grill*** below) – **6 rm** ★145.00/200.00 – ★★145.00/200.00.
◆ Unassuming exterior; sumptuous interior: the bedrooms epitomise Victorian luxury with original wood flooring, elaborate silk drapes, fine antiques. Lounge boasts rich décor.

The Empire, 73 Church Walks, LL30 2HE, (see also ***The Empire (No.72)*** below) ☎ (01492) 860555, *reservations@empirehotel.co.uk, Fax (01492) 860791,* heated, – rest, P – 40. AE VISA. **A**
closed 17-30 December – ***Watkins and Co. :*** **Rest** (dinner only and Sunday lunch)/dinner 19.95 – **43 rm** ★55.00/125.00 – ★★120.00/130.00, 7 suites.
◆ A porticoed façade sets the Victorian tone found in bedrooms with original cast iron beds, antiques and Russell Flint prints on walls. Bathrooms have Italian marble floors. Fine menus with a mix and match of the Celtic and the Continental.

The Empire (No.72) (at The Empire H.), 72 Church Walks, LL30 2HE, ☎ (01492) 860555 *reservations@empirehotel.co.uk, Fax (01492) 860791* – P. AE VISA. **A**
closed 17-30 December – **8 rm** ★75.00 – ★★120.00/125.00.
◆ Next to the Empire, once Llandudno's first bank, now a town house with "Victorian" furnishings, especially in the bedrooms: canopied beds, mirrors, reproduction baths.

St Tudno, North Parade, LL30 2LP, ☎ (01492) 874411, *sttudnohotel@btinternet.com* *Fax (01492) 860407,* ≤, – , rest, . AE VISA **A**
Rest – (see ***Terrace*** below) – **17 rm** ★75.00/95.00 – ★★180.00/240.00, 1 suite.
◆ Prime position on the promenade opposite a Victorian pier; boasts sitting room, lounge in charming period style with seafront vistas. Comfortable rooms with fine fabrics.

Dunoon, Gloddaeth St, LL30 2DW, ☎ (01492) 860787, *reservations@dunoonhotel.co.uk* *Fax (01492) 860031* – P. VISA **A**
11 March-26 December – **Rest** (bar lunch Monday-Saturday)/dinner 19.50 **s.** – **49 rm** (dinner included) ★60.00/128.00 – ★★120.00/128.00.
◆ A hospitable hotel; a panelled hallway leads to the "Welsh Dresser Bar" furnished with an antique cooking range. Bygone era ambience. Rooms are individually styled. Restaurant steeped in tradition with menu to match.

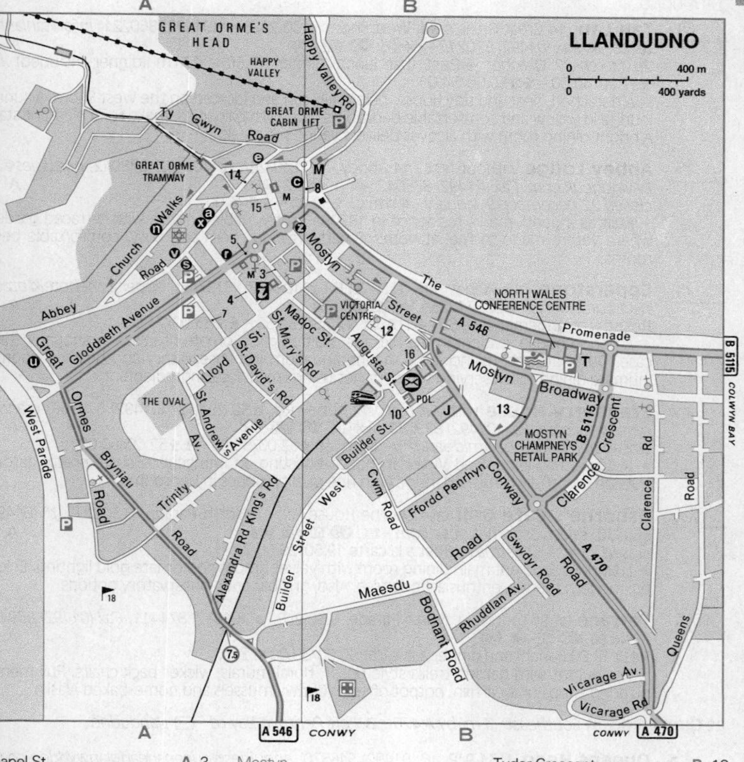

apel St . . . . A 3
eganwy Ave . . . . A 4
oddaeth St . . . . A 5
aelgwyn Rd . . . . A 7
ostyn Champneys Retail Park . . . . B
Mostyn St . . . . B
North Parade . . . . AB 8
Oxford Rd . . . . B 10
Trinity Square . . . . B 12
Tudno St . . . . A 14
Tudor Crescent . . . . B 13
Upper Mostyn St . . . . A 15
Vaughan St . . . . B 16
Victoria Centre . . . . B

Escape Boutique B & B without rest., 48 Church Walks, LL30 2HL, ☎ (01492) 877776, *info@escapebandb.co.uk, Fax (01492) 878777* – P. MC VISA. — A n
closed Christmas and restricted opening November-January – **9 rm** ☐ ♂65.00/85.00 – ♂♂75.00/95.00.
♦ Ornate, elevated Victorian villa with ultra contemporary furnishings. Modish breakfast room with fine choice. Cool beige/brown or 'French boudoir' rooms. B and B with style.

Bryn Derwen, 34 Abbey Rd, LL30 2EE, ☎ (01492) 876804, *brynderwen@fsmail.net, Fax (01492) 876804* – P. MC VISA. — A v
closed January – **Rest** *(closed Sunday)* (booking essential to non-residents) (dinner only) 19.00 **s.** – **9 rm** ☐ ♂46.00 – ♂♂90.00.
♦ Built in 1878 with welcoming owner. A beauty salon offering range of treatments is next door. Pine staircase leads to immaculate bedrooms. Quiet lounge to unwind in. A candlelit dining room in which to sample classic dishes.

The Wilton, 14 South Par, LL30 2LN, ☎ (01492) 878343, *info@wiltonhotel.com* – rest, P. MC AE VISA. — AB z
closed January-February – **Rest** (residents only) (dinner only) 12.50 ♀ – **14 rm** ☐ ♂28.00/42.00 – ♂♂52.00/60.00.
♦ Situated adjacent to the beach and pier. Lounge bar with interesting Victorian prints; the bedrooms, most of which have four-posters, are in bright, modern colour schemes.

Tan Lan, 14 Great Orme's Rd, West Shore, LL30 2AR, (01492) 860221, *info@tanlanh tel.co.uk, Fax (01492) 870219* – P. VISA. A
26 March-22 October – **Rest** (bar lunch)/dinner 17.50 – **17 rm** (dinner included) 37.00/40.00 – 50.00/54.00.
◆ A detached, neat and tidy house, personally run and located on the West Shore. A sunn lounge in yellow and comfortable bedrooms, two with balconies, make for a pleasant sta A bright dining room with alcoves delivers varied set meals.

Abbey Lodge without rest., 14 Abbey Rd, LL30 2EA, (01492) 878042, *enquiries@a beylodgeuk.com, Fax (01492) 878042,* – P. A
closed 22 December-9 January – **4 rm** 50.00 – 74.00.
◆ Built as a gentlemen's residence in 1870; a pretty, gabled house with terraced garde where you're made to feel at home. Smart drawing room and cosy, comfortable bec rooms.

Epperstone, 15 Abbey Rd, LL30 2EE, (01492) 878746, *epperstonehotel@btcc nect.com, Fax (01492) 871223* – P. VISA A
Rest (by arrangement) 18.50 – **8 rm** 26.50/36.50 – 53.00/73.00.
◆ A period house, evident in the fixtures: stained glass, ornate fireplace, mahogany stai case. Other attractions include a marine aquarium in conservatory and neat bedroom Intimate dining room serving varied dishes using fresh, local ingredients.

Cranberry House without rest., 12 Abbey Rd, LL30 2EA, (01492) 879760, *cranb ryhse@aol.com, Fax (01492) 879760* – P. VISA. A
closed mid December-mid January – **5 rm** 32.00/35.00 – 52.00/60.00.
◆ A white, bay windowed Victorian house boasting an immaculate style; pretty garde outside, tastefully furnished inside with fine quality fabrics in bedrooms.

Osborne's Cafe Grill (at Osborne House H.), 17 North Parade, LL30 2LP, (0149 860330, *sales@osbornehouse.com* – . AE VISA A
closed 1 week Christmas – **Rest** a la carte 19.50/29.50.
◆ Luxurious, opulent main dining room with velvet drapes and ornate gold lighting. Ecle tic, modern menus, enthusiastic service. Also, grill bar and conservatory options.

Terrace (at St Tudno H.), North Parade, LL30 2LP, (01492) 874411, *Fax (01492) 8604(* – . AE VISA A
Rest 18.00 (lunch) and dinner a la carte 30.00/38.00 **s.**
◆ Restaurant with garden trellis style décor, floral murals, wicker-back chairs. Full men offering soups of local fish, hotpot of spicy Conwy mussels and home-baked Alaska.

at Glanwydden *Southeast : 3 m. by A 470* – **B** – *off Penthyn Bay rd* – *Llandudno.*

Queens Head, LL31 9JP, (01492) 546570, *enquiries@queensheadglanwydden.co.u Fax (01492) 546487* – P. VISA.
closed 25 December – **Rest** a la carte 16.50/25.00.
◆ Popular pub which is renowned for its imaginative, weekly changing bar menus. Th creative dishes are served in a modern lounge of smart black tables.

at Deganwy *South : 2¾ m. on A 546* – **A** – *Llandudno.*

Nikki Ip's, 57 Station Rd, LL31 9DF, (01492) 596611, *Fax (01492) 596600* – . VISA
closed 25 December-1 January, Monday and Bank Holidays – **Rest** - Chinese - (bookir essential) (dinner only) 23.00/40.00 and a la carte 15.00/31.50.
◆ Good value, stylish and unconventional, but beware: no signage outside. Particula welcoming owners. Coral interior; Cantonese, Peking and Szechuan specialities are serve

Paysanne, Station Rd, LL31 9EJ, (01492) 582079, *Fax (01492) 583848* – . VISA
closed first week January, 25-26 December, 2 weeks September-October, Sunday ar Monday – **Rest** (booking essential) (dinner only) 21.00/25.00.
◆ Neat restaurant with a friendly ambience; Welsh and mainly French fare offered. The is a good selection of local fish and a carefully sourced French wine list.

LLANELLI *Carmarthenshire* 503 H 28.
London 202.5 – Cardiff 54.5 – Swansea 12.5.

Llwyn Hall, Llwynhendy, SA14 9LJ, East : 3 ½ m. by A 484 (01554) 777754, *llw hall@hotmail.com, Fax (01554) 744146,* – P. AE VISA
Rest (lunch by arrangement)/dinner 15.00/25.00 **s.** – **5 rm** 50.00/80.00 – 70.00/100.00.
◆ Pretty yellow-and-white 19C gabled house with extension. Country style soft furnis ings. Chintzy rooms of pleasant individuality: those at front face garden and North Gowe Cloth-clad dining room; traditional, well-priced menus.

Fairyhill Bar and Brasserie, Machynys Golf Club, Nicklaus Ave, Machynys, SA15 2DG, South : 3 m. by A 484 off Machynys rd ☎ (01554) 744944, *machynys@fairyhill.net*, ≤ golf course, Loughor estuary and Gower Peninsula, – ♿ ⇔. MC VISA
closed 25 December – **Rest** a la carte 15.05/28.20 s.
◆ On first floor of golf clubhouse with pleasant views of course and estuary. Choose between lounge bar with leather sofas or bustling brasserie for well prepared modern dishes.

LANERCHYMEDD *Anglesey* 502 503 G 24 *Wales G.*

Env. : *Anglesey★★*.
London 262 – Bangor 18 – Caernarfon 23 – Holyhead 15.

Llwydiarth Fawr without rest., LL71 8DF, North : 1 m. on B 5111 ☎ (01248) 470321, *llwydiarth@hotmail.com*, ≤, – ⇔ P. MC VISA.
closed Christmas – **4 rm** ☕ ★30.00/55.00 – ★★60.00/70.00.
◆ Part of a 1000-acre cattle and sheep farm, Georgian in style with picturesque country vistas. Guests can enjoy nature walks, fishing on lake; welcoming owner. Well-kept rooms.

Drws-Y-Coed without rest., LL71 8AD, East : 1 ½ m. by B 5111 on Benllech rd ☎ (01248) 470473, *drwsycoed2@hotmail.com*, ≤, – ⇔ P. MC VISA.
closed 25 December – **3 rm** ☕ ★35.00/40.00 – ★★60.00.
◆ Meaning "Door of the Wood"; run by Welsh speaking family in 550-acre farm of cattle and cereal crops. Original buildings have been preserved whilst bedrooms are trim, tidy.

LAN FFESTINIOG *Gwynedd.*

London 234 – Bangor 35 – Wrexham 52.

Cae'r Blaidd Country House, LL41 4PH, North : ¾ m. by A 470 on Blaenau Rd ☎ (01766) 762765, *info@caerblaidd.fsnet.co.uk, Fax (01766) 762765*, ≤ Vale of Ffestiniog and Moelwyn mountains, – ⇔ P. MC VISA.
closed January – **Rest** (communal dining) 17.50 – **3 rm** ☕ ★45.00 – ★★70.00.
◆ Spacious Victorian country house in wooded gardens; spectacular views of Ffestiniog and Moelwyn Mountains. Smart, uncluttered rooms. Guided tours and courses are organised. A huge dining room; large refectory table where communal dinners are served.

t Gellilydan *Southwest : 2¾ m. by A 470 off A 487 – ✉ Ffestiniog.*

Tyddyn du Farm, LL41 4RB, East : ½ m. by A 487 on A 470 ☎ (01766) 590281, *mich/paula@snowdoniafarm.com*, ≤, – ⇔ P
Rest (by arrangement) 17.50 – **4 rm** ☕ ★45.00/70.00 – ★★80.00/95.00.
◆ 400-year old farmhouse set against Moelwyn Mountains. Guests can participate in farming activities or visit Roman site. Bedrooms have large jacuzzis. Minimum two night stay. Cooking takes in free-range farm eggs; soups and rolls are home-made.

LANFIHANGEL *Powys* 502 503 J 25 – *see Llanfyllin.*

LANFRYNACH *Powys* 503 J 28 – *see Brecon.*

LANFYLLIN *Powys* 502 503 K 25 *Wales G.*

Exc. : *Pistyll Rhaeadr★, NW : 8 m. by A 490, B 4391, B 4580 and minor roads.*
London 188 – Chester 42 – Shrewsbury 24 – Welshpool 11.

Seeds, 5 Penybryn Cottages, High St, SY22 5AP, ☎ (01691) 648604 – ⇔. MC VISA
closed 1 week May, 2 weeks October, Monday, Tuesday, Wednesday and Sunday dinner – **Rest** *(restricted opening in winter)* 23.75 (dinner) and lunch a la carte 16.45/26.15.
◆ Converted 16C rustic cottages with eclectic décor: souvenirs from owner's travels. Blackboard menu offers modern or traditional dishes. Local seasonal ingredients to the fore.

: Llanfihangel *Southwest : 5 m. by A 490 and B 4393 on B 4382 – ✉ Llanfyllin.*

Cyfie Farm, SY22 5JE, South : 1 ½ m. by B 4382 ☎ (01691) 648451, *info@cyfiefarm.co.uk, Fax (01691) 648363*, ≤ Meifod valley, – ⇔ P. MC AE VISA.
Rest (by arrangement) (communal dining) 22.50 – **3 rm** ☕ ★72.00/95.00 – ★★72.00/95.00.
◆ 17C longhouse, now a sheep farm, with coveted views of Meifod Valley. Guests can enjoy seasonal activities: lambing, haymaking. Rooms with a distinctive cottage feel. Convivial, communal dining on a single table.

LLANGAMMARCH WELLS *Powys* 503 J 27.
London 200 – Brecon 17 – Builth Wells 8 – Cardiff 58.

Lake Country House, LD4 4BS, East : ¾ m. ℘ (01591) 620202, *info@lakecountryhouse.co.uk, Fax (01591) 620457*, ←, P. MC AE VISA
Rest (booking essential) 24.50/39.50 ♀ – **9 rm** ☕ ★110.00/135.00 – ★★160.00/170.00
22 suites ☕ 245.00.
◆ 19C country house set in mature grounds; speciality Welsh teas served in drawing room. Antiques, flowers and extravagant fabrics in individually furnished rooms. Candlelit dining; super wine list.

LLANGOLLEN *Denbighshire* 502 503 K 25 *Wales G. – pop. 2 930.*
See : *Town★ – Railway★ AC – Plas Newydd★ AC.*
Env. : *Pontcysyllte Aqueduct★★, E : 4 m. by A 539 – Castell Dinas Bran★, N : by footpath – Valle Crucis Abbey★ AC, N : 2 m. by A 542.*
Exc. : *Chirk Castle★★ AC (wrought iron gates★), SE : 7½ m. by A 5 – Rug Chapel★ AC, W : 11 m. by A 5 and A 494.*
18 *Vale of Llangollen, Holyhead Rd ℘ (01978) 860613.*
Y Chapel, Castle St ℘ (01978) 860828.
London 194 – Chester 23 – Holyhead 76 – Shrewsbury 30.

Bryn Howel, LL20 7UW, East : 2 ¾ m. by A 539 ℘ (01978) 860331, *hotel@brynhowel.co.uk, Fax (01978) 860119*, ←, – rest, P – 300. MC VISA
Cedar Tree : **Rest** 15.95/19.95 **s.** ♀ – **35 rm** ☕ ★69.95/73.50 – ★★99.90, 1 suite.
◆ Built 1896 for owner of Ruabon brick company, mock Jacobean in style with Vale of Llangollen views. Bar has unique "Anthem Fireplace". Rooms in main house and modern wing. Admire panoramas through mullioned windows and dine on classic Welsh cuisine.

Gales, 18 Bridge St, LL20 8PF, ℘ (01978) 860089, *richard@galesofllangollen.co.uk, Fax (01978) 861313*, – rm, P. MC AE VISA.
closed 25 December-2 January – **Rest** *(closed Sunday)* (in bar) a la carte 11.40/20.40 ♀
13 rm ☕ ★50.00 – ★★60.00, 2 suites.
◆ Part 17C and 18C town house; rooms are divided between two buildings and display many historic features: wattle and daub walls, brass and walnut beds, beams and inglenooks. A wooden floored dining room and bar with inn-like ambience.

Oakmere without rest., Regent St, LL20 8HS, on A 5 ℘ (01978) 861126, *oakmeregh@aol.com*, – P.
6 rm ☕ ★45.00/55.00 – ★★55.00/60.00.
◆ A restored Victorian house with terraced garden, all weather tennis court. Indoors are polished pitch pine furnishings and tidy bedrooms.

Hillcrest without rest, Hill St, LL20 8EU, ℘ (01978) 860208, *d-rayment@btconnect.com, Fax (01978) 860208*, – P. MC VISA
7 rm ☕ ★30.00/35.00 – ★★50.00/55.00.
◆ A semi-detached house with large garden, close to the town centre. Homely and tidy inside with nicely decorated bedrooms and some original features: a slate fireplace. Popular, traditional food served to the gentle tick of an antique grandfather clock.

The Corn Mill, Dee Lane, LL20 8PN, ℘ (01978) 869555, *cornmill@brunningandprice.co.uk, Fax (01978) 869930*, – rest. MC AE VISA
closed 25-26 December – **Rest** a la carte approx 20.00 ♀.
◆ Imposing corn mill on banks of the Dee with large decked seating area extending into the river. Inside are two restored water wheels, slate and brick rooms. Rustic cuisine.

LLANIGON *Powys* 503 K 27 – *see Hay-on-Wye.*

LLANRHIDIAN *Swansea* 503 H 29 – *see Swansea.*

LLANRUG *Gwynedd* 502 503 H 24 – *see Caernarfon.*

LLANSANFFRAID GLAN CONWY *Conwy* 502 503 I 24 – *see Conwy.*

The ✿ award is the crème de la crème. This is awarded to restaurants which are really worth travelling miles for!

LANTWIT MAJOR **(Llanilltud Fawr)** *Vale of Glamorgan* 503 J 29 – *pop. 13 366.*
London 175 – Cardiff 18 – Swansea 33.

West House Country, West St, CF61 1SP, ✆ (01446) 792406, *enq@westhouse-hotel.co.uk, Fax (01446) 796147,* – rest, P. MC AE VISA
Rest *(closed Sunday dinner)* (lunch booking essential) 12.50/15.50 and dinner a la carte 16.45/28.00 **s.** – **21 rm** ☕ ★52.00/60.50 – ★★68.00.
◆ 16C hotel in Vale of Glamorgan. After cliff top walks, relax in beautiful, coir carpeted conservatory for afternoon tea. Rooms vary in size and style; all are immaculate. Heritage restaurant is decorated in a cottage style with mahogany chairs.

LANWENARTH *Monmouthshire – see Abergavenny.*

LANWRTYD WELLS *Powys* 503 J 27 *Wales G.* – *pop. 649.*
Exc. : *Abergwesyn-Tregaron Mountain Road★, NW : 19 m. on minor roads.*
Ty Barcud, The Square ✆ (01591) 610666, tic@celt.rural.wales.org.
London 214 – Brecon 32 – Cardiff 68 – Carmarthen 39.

Lasswade Country House, Station Rd, LD5 4RW, ✆ (01591) 610515, *info@lasswadehotel.co.uk, Fax (01591) 610611,* ←, – P. MC VISA
Rest (dinner only) 26.50/29.00 **s.** – **8 rm** ☕ ★45.00/55.00 – ★★85.00.
◆ Smartly refurbished Edwardian country house, with fine views of mid-Wales countryside. Charming breakfast conservatory; cosy lounge. Bright, well-kept bedrooms. Proudly pro-organic meals the order of the day.

Carlton House with rm, Dolycoed Rd, LD5 4RA, ✆ (01591) 610248, *info@carltonrestaurant.co.uk* – rest. MC VISA
closed December – **Rest** *(closed Sunday)* (booking essential) (lunch by arrangement)/dinner a la carte 33.00/42.00 – **6 rm** ☕ ★45.00 – ★★90.00.
◆ Personally run, Victorian house; unpretentious and relaxing feel. Tasty seasonable dishes made with local ingredients. Comfortable rooms.

LYSWEN *Powys* 503 K 27 *Wales G.* – ✉ *Brecon.*
Env. : *Brecon Beacons National Park★★.*
London 188 – Brecon 8 – Cardiff 48 – Worcester 53.

Llangoed Hall, LD3 0YP, Northwest : 1 ¼ m. on A 470 ✆ (01874) 754525, *enquiries@llangoedhall.com, Fax (01874) 754545,* ←, – rest, P. MC AE VISA.
Rest (booking essential to non-residents) 25.00/43.00 – **20 rm** ☕ ★150.00/325.00 – ★★195.00/315.00, 3 suites.
◆ Set up by Sir Bernard Ashley of Laura Ashley group: rooms furnished accordingly. River Wye to rear. Tennis court, gardens, carved staircase; guests can arrive by helicopter. Dining room filled with Rex Whistler etchings.

ACHYNLLETH *Powys* 502 503 I 26 *Wales G.* – *pop. 2 147.*
See : *Town★ – Celtica★ AC.*
Env. : *Snowdonia National Park★★★ – Centre for Alternative Technology★★ AC, N : 3 m. by A 487.*
Ffordd Drenewydd ✆ (01654) 702000.
Canolfan Owain Glyndwr ✆ (01654) 702401, machtic@powys.gov.uk.
London 220 – Shrewsbury 56 – Welshpool 37.

Ynyshir Hall, Eglwysfach, SY20 8TA, Southwest : 6 m. on A 487 ✆ (01654) 781209, *info@ynyshir-hall.co.uk, Fax (01654) 781366,* ←, – P. MC AE VISA
closed January – **Rest** (booking essential) 30.00/65.00 **s.** – **6 rm** ☕ ★125.00/160.00 – ★★240.00/280.00, 3 suites.
Spec. Red mullet with spiced lentils, rhubarb purée and foie gras. Roast fillet of brill with peas, fèves and morels. Pistachio soufflé with chocolate sorbet.
◆ Part Georgian house set within 1000 acre RSPB reserve; bright, individually appointed bedrooms, classically cosy drawing room with art, antiques and Welsh pottery. Bold, modern cooking in classically appointed dining room featuring owner's vivid oils.

Wynnstay, Maengwyn St, SY20 8AE, ✆ (01654) 702941, *info@wynnstay-hotel.com, Fax (01654) 703884* – P. MC AE VISA
Rest 25.00 and a la carte 22.95/27.40 – **23 rm** ☕ ★55.00/95.00 – ★★110.00.
◆ Part-18C hotel with much local stone and slate used in refurbishment. Two-roomed lounge overlooks street; airy bar with reclaimed pine tables. Varied mix of bedrooms. Vivid yellow-hued dining room with rustic feel.

MENAI BRIDGE (Porthaethwy) *Anglesey* 502 503 H 24.

London 270 – Caernarfon 10 – Chester 69 – Holyhead 22.

Wern Farm without rest., Pentraeth Rd, LL59 5RR, North : 2 ¼ m. by B 5420 off A 502 ☎ (01248) 712421, *wernfarmanglesey@onetel.com, Fax (01248) 712421*, ←, 🚗, 🅿, MC VISA.
March-October – **3 rm** ☕ ★40.00/70.00 – ★★60.00/70.00.
• Attractive Georgian farmhouse run by a friendly couple. Bedrooms are spacious and comfortable. Enjoy countryside views in conservatory where vast breakfast is offered.

Ruby, Dale St, LL59 5AW, ☎ (01248) 714999, *rubymenai@aol.com, Fax (01248) 717888*. MC AE VISA
closed 26 December and 1 January – **Rest** (booking essential) (dinner only except December and Sunday lunch)/dinner 12.95/15.95 and a la carte 12.95/26.95 ♀.
• Former firestation and council offices; now a lively, bustling eatery on two floors with good local reputation. Eclectic, global menus employing flavoursome, vibrant cooking.

MERTHYR TYDFIL *Merthyr Tydfil* 503 J 28 *Wales G. – pop. 30 483.*

Env. : *Brecon Beacons National Park★★.*

Exc. : *Ystradfellte★, NW : 13 m. by A 4102, A 465, A 4059 and minor roads.*

Morlais Castle, Pant, Dowlais ☎ (01685) 722822 – Cilsanws Mountain, Cefn Coed ☎ (01685) 723308.

14a Glebeland St ☎ (01685) 379884.

London 179 – Cardiff 25 – Gloucester 59 – Swansea 33.

at Cwm Taf *Northwest : 6 m. on A 470 – ✉ Merthyr Tydfil.*

Nant Ddu Lodge, CF48 2HY, on A 470 ☎ (01685) 379111, *enquiries@nant-ddu-lodge.co.uk, Fax (01685) 377088*, 🅿, MC AE VISA
closed 25 December – **Rest** (in bar Monday to Saturday lunch) a la carte 19.85/24.85 s. ♀ ☕ 4.95 – **32 rm** ★69.50 – ★★89.50/125.00.
• Family run hotel, Georgian in origin, named after the nearby "black stream". Sizeable spotless rooms in an eye-catching blend of checks and plaids. Bustling, buzzy bar. Colourful bistro where blackboard specials complement a tasty and satisfying selection.

Look out for red symbols, indicating particularly pleasant establishments.

MOLD (Yr Wyddgrug) *Flintshire* 502 503 K 24 *Wales G. – pop. 9 586.*

See : *St Mary's Church★.*

Clicain Rd, Pantmywyn ☎ (01352) 740318 – Clicain Rd, Old Padeswood, Station Rd ☎ (01244) 547701 – Padeswood & Buckley, The Caia, Station Lane, Padeswood ☎ (01244) 550537 – Caerwys ☎ (01352) 721222.

Library, Museum and Art Gallery, Earl Rd ☎ (01352) 759331.

London 211 – Chester 12 – Liverpool 22 – Shrewsbury 45.

Soughton Hall, CH7 6AB, North : 2½ m. by A 5119 and Alltami rd ☎ (01352) 84081 *info@soughtonhall.co.uk, Fax (01352) 840382*, ←, 🚗, 🅿 – 50. MC AE VISA
Rest – (see ***The Stables*** below) – **15 rm** ☕ ★100.00 – ★★180.00.
• At the end of a tree-lined drive, an impressive 18C Italianate mansion; its collection of period antiques spreads through intimate drawing rooms and well-appointed bedrooms.

Tower without rest., Nercwys, CH7 4EW, South : 1 m. by B 5444 and Nercwys rd ☎ (01352) 700220, *Fax (01352) 700220*, ←, 🚗, 🅿. MC VISA.
3 rm ☕ ★50.00 – ★★80.00.
• Last of the Welsh fortified border houses, owned by the same family for 500 years. Vaulted breakfast room. Spacious, simply furnished bedrooms overlook private parkland.

The Stables (at Soughton Hall H.), CH7 6AB, North : 2 ½ m. by A 5119 and Alltami Rd ☎ (01352) 840577, *info@soughtonhall.co.uk, Fax (01352) 840382*, 🅿. MC VISA
Rest (booking essential) a la carte 20.00/29.00 ♀.
• Walk through the grounds to a 17C stable block; bar and first-floor brasserie in bare brick and scrubbed pine. Tasty classics from an open kitchen. Terrace for summer lunch.

Glas Fryn, Raikes Lane, Sychdyn, CH7 6LR, North : 1 m. by A 5119 on Civic Centre rd (Theatr Clwyd) ☎ (01352) 750500, *glasfryn@brunningandprice.co.uk, Fax (01352) 75192*, 🅿. MC AE VISA
closed 25-26 December – **Rest** a la carte 16.70/25.45 ♀.
• Informal and open-plan; sepia prints, crammed bookshelves and rows of old bottles surround wooden tables. Varied brasserie menu draws a lively young set.

MONMOUTH (Trefynwy) *Monmouthshire* 503 L 28 – *pop. 8 547.*
London 135 – Abergavenny 19 – Cardiff 40.

at Whitebrook *South : 8¼ m. by A 466 – ✉ Monmouth.*

XX **The Crown at Whitebrook** with rm, NP25 4TX, ✆ (01600) 860254, *info@crownatwhitebrook.co.uk, Fax (01600) 860607,* – P. VISA
closed 2 weeks December, Sunday dinner and Monday – **Rest** 25.00/37.50 s. – **8 rm** ★85.00 – ★★130.00.
◆ Personally run, with a vibrant, modern feel, in an area of outstanding natural beauty. Modern dishes; local ingredients. Very comfy, individual rooms with immense style.

at Rockfield *Northwest : 2½ m. on B 4233 – ✉ Monmouth.*

X **Stone Mill,** NP25 5SN, West : 1 m. on B 4233 ✆ (01600) 716273, *Fax (01600) 715257,* – P. VISA
closed 2 weeks January, Sunday dinner and Monday – **Rest** 11.95/15.95 and a la carte 26.95/31.95.
◆ Converted 16C stone cider mill with exposed timbers and stone walls. Leather sofa in sitting area. Warm and friendly service. Modern seasonal dishes; good value set menu.

MONTGOMERY (Trefaldwyn) *Powys* 503 K 26 *Wales G.*
See : *Town*★.
London 194 – Birmingham 71 – Chester 53 – Shrewsbury 30.

Dragon, Market Square, SY15 6PA, ✆ (01686) 668359, *reception@dragonhotel.com, Fax (0870) 011 8227,* – rm, P – 60. AE VISA
Rest (bar lunch Monday-Saturday)/dinner 20.75 and a la carte 19.00/30.00 – **20 rm** ★49.00/59.00 – ★★83.50.
◆ Neat, practically fitted rooms in a half timbered 17C coaching inn, not far from the Offa's Dyke path. Cosy, traditional public bar with Shropshire ale. Privately owned. Bay-windowed room with linen clad tables converted from the old bread oven.

Little Brompton Farm without rest., SY15 6HY, Southeast : 2 m. on B 4385 ✆ (01686) 668371, *gaynor.brompton@virgin.net, Fax (01686) 668371,* – P.
closed 25-26 December – **3 rm** ★30.00/36.00 – ★★50.00.
◆ Part 17C ivy-clad cottage on a working farm, run by an friendly couple. En suite rooms in traditional fabrics. Cosy beamed lounge with inglenook fireplace. Hearty breakfast.

MUMBLES (The) *Swansea* 503 I 29 – *see Swansea.*

NANNERCH *Flintshire* 502 503 K 24 – ✉ *Mold.*
London 218 – Chester 19 – Liverpool 29 – Shrewsbury 52.

Old Mill without rest., Melin-y-Wern, Denbigh Rd, CH7 5RH, Northwest : ¾ m. on A 541 ✆ (01352) 741542, *mail@old-mill.co.uk,* – P. AE VISA.
6 rm ★50.00 – ★★82.00.
◆ Set in simple gardens, a renovated Victorian corn mill and stables which also houses a craft studio. The beamed bedrooms are comfortable, modern and pine-fitted.

NANTGAREDIG *Carmarthenshire* 503 H 28 – *see Carmarthen.*

NANT-Y-DERRY *Monmouthshire – see Abergavenny.*

NEATH (Castell-Ned) *Neath Port Talbot* 503 I 29 *Wales G. – pop. 45 898.*
Env. : *Aberdulais Falls*★ *AC, NE : 2½ m. by B 4434 and A 4109.*
Swansea Bay, Jersey Marine ✆ (01792) 812198 – Cadoxton ✆ (01639) 643615.
London 188 – Cardiff 40 – Swansea 8.

Cwmbach Cottages without rest., Cwmbach Rd, Cadoxton, SA10 8AH, Northwest : 1 ¾ m. by A 474 ✆ (01639) 639825, *cwmbachcottages@guesthouse25.fsnet.co.uk,* – P.
5 rm ★32.00/38.00 – ★★48.00/58.00.
◆ Old miners' cottages in the wooded Vale of Neath. Homely rooms in soft chintz kept spotless by a friendly owner. Explore the hills or admire the view from a deep armchair.

NEFYN *Gwynedd* 502 503 G 25 *Wales G. – pop. 1 987.*
Env. : *Lleyn Peninsula★★ – Tre'r Ceiri★, NE : 5½ m. by B 4417 – Porth Dinllaen★, W : 1½ m by B 4417.*
18, 9 Nefyn & District, Morfa Nefyn ☎ (01758) 720218.
London 265 – Caernarfon 20.

Caeau Capel, Rhodfar Mor, LL53 6EB, ☎ (01758) 720240, *gwestycaeaucapel@hotmail.com, Fax (01758) 720750,* – rest, P. MC AE VISA
closed Christmas – **Rest** (booking essential to non-residents) (dinner only) 20.00 **s. – 18 rm** ★32.00/48.00 – ★★50.00/75.00.
◆ Dating from the late 1800s, a proudly traditional and privately owned hotel in an acre of neat garden. Tidy, good-sized bedrooms, sun lounge and snug little bar. Unpretentious dining room; high-backed pine chairs and neat tables.

NEWPORT (Casnewydd-Ar-Wysg) *Newport* 503 L 29 *Wales G. – pop. 116 143.*
See : *Museum and Art Gallery★* AX **M** – *Transporter Bridge★ AC* AY – *Civic Centre (murals★)* AX.
Env. : *Caerleon Roman Fortress★★ AC (Fortress Baths★ – Legionary Museum★ – Amphitheatre★), NE : 2½ m. by B 4596* AX *– Tredegar House★★ (Grounds★ – Stables★), SW : 2½ m. by A 48* AY.
Exc. : *Penhow Castle★, E : 8 m. by A 48* AX.
9 Caerleon, Broadway ☎ (01633) 420342 – 18 Parc, Church Lane, Coedkernew ☎ (01633) 680933.
Museum and Art Gallery, John Frost Sq ☎ (01633) 842962.
London 145 – Bristol 31 – Cardiff 12 – Gloucester 48.

Plan opposite

Celtic Manor Resort, Coldra Woods, NP18 1HQ, East : 3 m. on A 48 ☎ (01633) 413000, *postbox@celtic-manor.com, Fax (01633) 412910,* ⊛, 18, – |‡|, rm, P – 1500. MC AE VISA
Owens : Rest *(closed Sunday)* (dinner only) 45.00/60.00 **s.** ♀ – ***The Olive Tree*** : Rest (buffet lunch)/dinner 25.00 and a la carte 18.40/34.15 **s.** ♀ – 15.00 – **298 rm** ★225.00 ★★225.00, 32 suites 375.00/1500.00.
◆ Classical, Celtic and country house motifs on a grand modern scale. Smart contemporary rooms boast hi-tech mod cons. State-of-the-art gym, golf academy and spa. Elaborate Welsh-derived fusion food at Owens. Mediterranean classics in the Olive Tree bistro.

Newport Lodge, Brynglas Rd, NP20 5QN, North : ¾ m. by A 4042 off A 4051 ☎ (01633) 821818, *infor@newportlodgehotel.co.uk, Fax (01633) 856360* – rm, P. MC AE VISA
*closed 2 weeks Christmas*Rest *(closed Saturday-Sunday and Bank Holidays)* (booking essential) (dinner only) a la carte 16.00/21.00 **s.** ♀ – **27 rm** ★73.00/91.50 – ★★125.00.
◆ Modern rooms, furnished in dark wood and matching fabrics, in a privately owned lodge on the city's northern outskirts. Good motorway access. Neatly laid-out dining room with brasserie feel.

The Chandlery, 77-78 Lower Dock St, NP20 1EH, ☎ (01633) 256622, *Fax (01633) 256633* – MC VISA AY
closed 24 December-3 January, Saturday lunch, Sunday and Monday – **Rest** 12.95 (lunch) and a la carte 18.40/31.40 ♀.
◆ Converted 18C chandler's store by the River Usk. Spacious split-level restaurant with nautical theme. Enthusiastic service. Wide-ranging menu of freshly prepared dishes.

at Tredunnock *Northeast : 8¾ m. by A 4042 – AX –, B 4596 and B 4236, off Usk rd, turning right at Cwrt Bleddyn Hotel – ✉ Newport.*

The Newbridge with rm, NP15 1LY, East : ¼ m. ☎ (01633) 451000, *thenewbridge@tinyonline.co.uk, Fax (01633) 451001,* ←, – rm, P. MC AE VISA.
closed 26 December and 1 January – **Rest** a la carte 25.00/32.00 ♀ – **6 rm** ★90.00 ★★125.00.
◆ Bright, comfy pub idyllically set by bridge overlooking Usk. Modern and classical techniques applied to locally based dishes. Superb contemporary bedrooms exude immense style.

at Langstone *East : 4½ m. on A 48 – AX – ✉ Newport.*

Hilton Newport, Chepstow Rd, NP18 2LX, ☎ (01633) 413737, *reservations.newport@hilton.com, Fax (01633) 413713,* – rm, rest, P – 300. MC AE VISA
Rest (bar lunch Monday-Saturday)/dinner 22.95/24.50 ♀ – **146 rm** ★190.00 – ★★200.00, 2 suites.
◆ Redbrick hotel built around formal courtyard. Tall glass pillar marks centre of smart lounge. Choice of meeting rooms. Neatly fitted, modern bedrooms. Useful for motorway. Restaurant provides a comfortable dining environment.

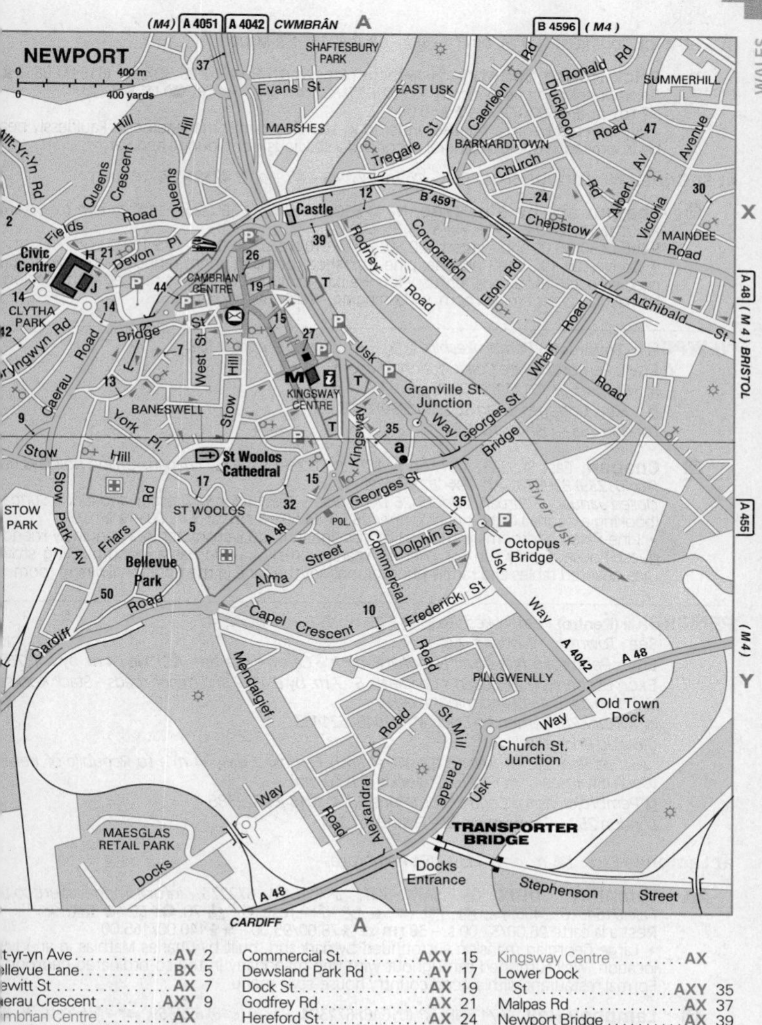

…t-yr-yn Ave . . . AY 2	Commercial St. . . . AXY 15	Kingsway Centre . . . AX
…ellevue Lane . . . BX 5	Dewsland Park Rd . . . AY 17	Lower Dock St . . . AXY 35
…ewitt St . . . AX 7	Dock St . . . AX 19	Malpas Rd . . . AX 37
…erau Crescent . . . AXY 9	Godfrey Rd . . . AX 21	Newport Bridge . . . AX 39
…mbrian Centre . . . AX	Hereford St . . . AX 24	Oakfield Rd . . . AX 42
…pel St . . . AY 10	High St . . . AX 26	Queensway . . . AX 44
…arence Pl . . . AX 12	John Frost Square . . . AX 27	Summerhill Ave . . . AX 47
…yffard Crescent . . . AX 13	Kensington Pl . . . AX 30	Waterloo Rd . . . AY 50
…ytha Park Rd . . . AX 14	Keynsham Ave . . . AY 32	

Premier Travel Inn, Coldra Junction, Chepstow Rd, NP18 2NX, on A 48 (westbound carriageway) ☎ (01633) 411390, *Fax (01633) 411376* – |♦|, ⇔ rm, ▤ rest, ♿ P. MC AE ◑ VISA. ✻

Rest (grill rest.) – **63 rm** ♦46.95/46.95 – ♦♦49.95/49.95.

◆ Trim, bright rooms, many with sofa beds, in a group-owned lodge. Useful for corporate travel or family stopovers. Informal dining at adjacent Beefeater.

WALES

at Redwick *Southeast : 9½ m. by M 4 – AY – off B 4245 – ✉ Magor.*

Brick House Country without rest., North Row, NP26 3DX, ☎ (01633) 880230
brickhouse@compuserve.com, Fax (01633) 882441, – P. MO AE VISA.
– **7 rm** ☐ 40.00/50.00 – 60.00.
• Ivy-covered Georgian house under long-standing family management. Faultlessly nea
bedrooms with traditional floral décor and a spacious front lounge and bar.

at St Brides Wentlooge *Southwest : 4½ m. by A 48 – AY – on B 4239 – ✉ Newport.*

The Inn at The Elm Tree, NP10 8SQ, ☎ (01633) 680225, *inn@the-elm-tree.co.uk*
Fax (01633) 681035, – P. MO VISA
Rest 12.50/30.00 and a la carte 20.50/35.00 – **10 rm** ☐ 80.00 – 130.00.
• Converted 19C barn; pristine, pine-furnished rooms in bright fabrics thoughtfully supplied with 21C mod cons. Unfussy lounge bar, its wicker armchairs padded with cushions. Immaculately set dining room; wide-ranging, Welsh-based dishes.

NEWPORT (Trefdraeth) *Pembrokeshire* 503 F 27 *Wales G. – pop. 1 162.*
Env. : *Pembrokeshire Coast National Park★★.*
Newport ☎ (01239) 820244.
2 Bank Cottages, Long St ☎ (01239) 820912.
London 258 – Fishguard 7.

Cnapan, East St, SA42 0SY, on A 487 ☎ (01239) 820575, *cnapan@online-holidays.ne*
Fax (01239) 820878, – P. MO VISA.
closed January-February and 25-26 December – **Rest** *(closed Tuesday and lunch Sunday)*
(booking essential) (light lunch)/dinner 26.50/34.50 – **5 rm** ☐ 45.00 – 76.00.
• Pine-fitted bedrooms with floral fabrics and individual character in a genuinely friendly guest house, family run for over 15 years. Homely lounge has a wood-burning stove. Lace-covered tables and family photographs set the tone in the traditional dining room.

PEMBROKE (Penfro) *Pembrokeshire* 503 F 28 *Wales G. – pop. 7 214.*
See : *Town★★ – Castle★★ AC.*
Env. : *Pembrokeshire Coast National Park★★ – Carew★ (Castle★ AC), NE : 4 m. by A 4075.*
Exc. : *Bosherston (St Govan's Chapel★), S : 7 m. by B 4319 and minor roads – Stack Rocks★ SW : 9 m. by B 4319 and minor roads.*
Military Rd, Pembroke Dock ☎ (01646) 621453.
Cleddau Bridge (toll).
to Republic of Ireland (Rosslare) (Irish Ferries) 2 daily (4 h) – to Republic of Ireland (Cork) (Swansea Cork Ferries) 2 weekly (8 h 30 mn).
Pembroke Visitor Centre, Commons Rd ☎ (01646) 622388.
London 252 – Carmarthen 32 – Fishguard 26.

at Lamphey *East : 1¾ m. on A 4139 – ✉ Pembroke.*

Lamphey Court, SA71 5NT, ☎ (01646) 672273, *info@lampheycourt.co.uk*
Fax (01646) 672480, – rest, P – 70. MO AE VISA.
Rest a la carte 26.00/32.00 **s.** – **38 rm** ☐ 78.00/95.00 – 140.00/165.00.
• Large Georgian mansion surrounded by parkland, built by Charles Mathias in an idyll location. Well furnished throughout with fine mahogany in the co-ordinated bedroom. Formal restaurant with a good country house-style menu.

Lamphey Hall, SA71 5NR, ☎ (01646) 672394, *Fax (01646) 672369,* – rest, P. MO AE VISA
Rest *(closed Monday lunch)* a la carte 15.40/30.15 – **12 rm** ☐ 50.00/65.00 – 75.00/85.00.
• Small country house with a neat garden and a traditional style of décor throughout. Bedrooms are a mix of shapes and sizes and all are well furnished and cared for. The main restaurant offers spacious, comfortable surroundings in which to enjoy Welsh produce.

at Stackpole *South : 5 m. by B 4319 – ✉ Pembroke.*

The Stackpole Inn, Jasons Corner, SA71 5DF, ☎ (01646) 672324, *Fax (01646) 67271*
– MO VISA
closed Sunday dinner in winter – **Rest** a la carte 16.00/26.00.
• Typical country pub with exposed beams and bunches of dried hops. Simple and unfussy pub good served at well-spaced wooden tables.

PENALLY (Penalun) *Pembrokeshire* 503 F 29 – *see Tenby.*

PENARTH *Cardiff* 503 K 29 – *see Cardiff.*

PENMACHNO *Conwy* 502 503 I 24 – *see Betws-y-Coed.*

PENTYRCH *Cardiff* 503 K 29 – *see Cardiff.*

PONTDOLGOCH *Powys* – *see Caersws.*

PONTYPRIDD *Rhondda Cynon Taff* 503 K 29 *Wales G. – pop. 29 781.*
Exc. : *Caerphilly Castle★★ AC, SE : 7 m. by A 470 and A 468 – Llancaiach Fawr Manor★ AC, NE : 6½ m. by A 4054, A 472, B 4255 and B 4254.*
Pontypridd Museum, Bridge St ☎ (01443) 490748.
London 164 – Cardiff 9 – Swansea 40.

Llechwen Hall, Llanfabon, CF37 4HP, Northeast : 4 ¼ m. by A 4223 off A 4054 ☎ (01443) 742050, *llechwen@aol.com, Fax (01443) 742189*, – rm, – 80. AE VISA
closed 24-29 December – **Rest** a la carte 20.65/28.65 **s.** – 8.95 – **20 rm** ★54.50/59.50 – ★★80.00/100.00.
◆ 17C house with Victorian frontage, overlooks the Aberdare and Merthyr Valleys. Smart country house style and comforts. Spotless bedrooms: large executive rooms in coach house. Two dining options, both decorated in similar traditional style.

PORTH *Rhondda Cynon Taff* 503 J 29 *Wales G. – pop. 6 225 – ✉ Pontypridd.*
Env. : *Trehafod (Rhondda Heritage Park★), E : 1½ m. by A 4058.*
London 168 – Cardiff 13 – Swansea 45.

Heritage Park, Coed Cae Rd, Trehafod, CF37 2NR, on A 4058 ☎ (01443) 687057, *heritageparkhotel@talk21.com, Fax (01443) 687060*, , , – , rest, – 200. AE VISA
closed 23-26 December and 1 January – ***The Loft*** : **Rest** a la carte 15.00/22.00 **s.** – **44 rm** ★83.00/93.00 – ★★105.00.
◆ Brick-built hotel in Rhondda Valley, adjacent to Heritage Park Centre; Museum of Mining close by. Countryside location, yet not far from Cardiff. Co-ordinated, modern rooms. Loft dining with verandah or conservatory options.

PORTHCAWL *Bridgend* 503 I 29 *Wales G. – pop. 15 640 –* **Env.** : *Glamorgan Heritage Coast★.*
The Old Police Station, John St ☎ (01656) 786639, porthcawltic@bridgend.gov.uk.
London 183 – Cardiff 28 – Swansea 18.

Atlantic, West Drive, CF36 3LT, ☎ (01656) 785011, *enquiries@atlantichotelporthcawl.co.uk, Fax (01656) 771877*, <, – . AE VISA.
Rest *(closed Sunday dinner)* (bar lunch)/dinner 14.50 and a la carte 18.40/30.40 ♀ – **18 rm** ★64.00/74.00 – ★★95.00.
◆ Midway between Cardiff and Swansea is this harbour side hotel offering traditional comfort and style and personal service. Simple bedrooms are spotlessly kept. The restaurant has a classic, traditional air with mahogany and burgundy décor.

PORTMEIRION *Gwynedd* 502 503 H 25 *Wales G* – **See** : *Village★★★ AC.*
Env. : *Snowdonia National Park★★★ – Lleyn Peninsula★★ – Ffestiniog Railway★★ AC.*
London 245 – Caernarfon 23 – Colwyn Bay 40 – Dolgellau 24.

Portmeirion, LL48 6ET, ☎ (01766) 770000, *hotel@portmeirion-village.com, Fax (01766) 771331*, < village and estuary, heated, – rest, – 120. AE VISA.
Rest (booking essential for non-residents) 18.50/39.00 ♀ – 13.50 – **35 rm** ★122.00 – ★★205.00, 16 suites.
◆ Private Italianate village in extensive gardens and woodland designed by Sir Clough Williams-Ellis. Delightful views of village and estuary. Antique furnished accommodation. Restaurant offers lovely views of the estuary and an open and light style of décor.

Castell Deudraeth, LL48 6EN, ☎ (01766) 772400, *hotel@portmeirion-village.com, Fax (01766) 771771*, <, , – , rest, rest, – 40. AE VISA.
closed 1 week January – ***Grill*** : **Rest** a la carte 19.00/33.85 **s.** ♀ – 12.50 – **8 rm** ★180.00/245.00 – ★★180.00/710.00, 3 suites.
◆ Crenellated 19C manor, its modern decor in harmony with the original Welsh oak, slate and stone. Superbly stylish rooms in blues, greys and pale wood. Restored walled garden. Victorian solarium, converted into a modish minimalist restaurant.

PWLLHELI *Gwynedd* 502 503 G 25 *Wales G. – pop. 3 861.*
Env. : *Lleyn Peninsula*★★.
18 *Golf Rd* ✆ *(01758) 701644.*
ℹ *MinyDon, Station Sq* ✆ *(01758) 613000, pwllheli.tic@gwynedd.gov.uk.*
London 261 – Aberystwyth 73 – Caernarfon 21.

Plas Bodegroes (Chown) with rm, LL53 5TH, Northwest : 1 ¾ m. on A 49 ✆ (01758) 612363, *gunna@bodegroes.co.uk, Fax (01758) 701247,* – P. MC VISA
mid March-mid November – **Rest** *(closed Sunday-Monday, except Bank Holidays)* (booking essential) (dinner only and Sunday lunch)/dinner 40.00 – **11 rm** ★50.00/80.00 ★★170.00.
Spec. Warm salad of monkfish, ham and mushrooms. Seared sea bass and scallops with chargrilled vegetables and harissa. Cinnamon biscuit of apple and rhubarb, elderflower custard.
◆ A Georgian mansion in secluded peace amidst charming gardens. Tasteful, attractive bedrooms. Spacious dining room with assorted artwork. Stylish, imaginative dishes.

at Boduan *Northwest : 3¾ m. on A 497 – ✉ Pwllheli.*

The Old Rectory, LL53 6DT, ✆ (01758) 721519, *thepollards@theoldrectory.net Fax (01758) 721519,* – P
closed 1 week Christmas – **Rest** (by arrangement) 25.00 – **4 rm** ★60.00/80.00 ★★85.00.
◆ Part Georgian house with garden and paddock, adjacent to church. Well restored providing comfortable, individually decorated bedrooms and attractive sitting room. Dining room decorated in keeping with the age and atmosphere of the house.

RAGLAN *Monmouthshire* 503 L 28 *Wales G. – ✉ Abergavenny.*
See : *Castle*★ AC.
London 154 – Cardiff 32 – Gloucester 34 – Newport 18 – Swansea 58.

Clytha Arms, NP7 9BW, West : 3 m. on Clytha rd (old Abergavenny Rd) ✆ (01873) 840206, *clythaarms@tiscali.co.uk, Fax (01873) 840209* – rest, P. MC AE VISA
closed 25 December – **Rest** *(closed Monday lunch)* 19.95 and a la carte 26.00/34.00 ♀.
◆ Personally run converted dower house close to Abergavenny. Welcoming, open fires, traditional games sprinkled around bar. Generous menus utilise the best of Welsh produce.

REDWICK *Newport* 503 L 29 – *see Newport (Newport).*

RHAYADER **(Rhaeadr)** *Powys* 503 J 27 – *pop. 1 783.*
ℹ *The Leisure Centre, North Street* ✆ *(01597) 810591.*
London 195 – Aberystwyth 39 – Carmarthen 67 – Shrewsbury 60.

Beili Neuadd without rest., LD6 5NS, Northeast : 2 m. by A 44 off Abbey-cwm-hir rd ✆ (01597) 810211, *ann-carl@thebeili.freeserve.co.uk, Fax (01597) 810211,* – P
closed Christmas and New Year – **3 rm** ★30.00 – ★★52.00.
◆ Part 16C stone-built farmhouse in a secluded rural setting with countryside views. Personally run with comfortable bedrooms. Close to Rhayader and the "Lakeland of Wales".

RHOS-ON-SEA **(Llandrillo-yn-Rhos)** *Conwy* 502 503 I 24 – *see Colwyn Bay.*

RHYL *Denbighshire* 502 503 J 24 *Wales G. – pop. 25 390.*
Exc. : *Rhuddlan Castle*★★, *S : 3 m. by A 525 – Bodelwyddan*★★, *S : 5 m. by A 525 and minor rd – St Asaph*★, *S : 5 m. by A 525.*
Exc. : *Llandudno*★, *W : 16 m. by A 548, A 55 and B 5115.*
Cardiff 154 – Chester 83 – Llandudno 131.

Barratt's at Ty'n Rhyl with rm, 167 Vale Rd, LL18 2PH, South : ½ m. on A 525 ✆ (01745) 344138, *barrat@freeserve.co.uk, Fax (01745) 344138,* – P. MC VISA.
Rest (booking essential) (dinner only and Sunday lunch) a la carte 20.00/26.50 – **3 rm** ★45.00 – ★★70.00.
◆ Rhyl's oldest house boasts characterful lounge with rich oak panelling. Dining room has chandelier, dressers and drapes. Ambitious cooking on classic base. Individual rooms.

ROCKFIELD *Monmouthshire* 503 L 28 – *see Monmouth.*

RUTHIN (Rhuthun) *Denbighshire* 502 503 K 24 *Wales G. – pop. 5 218.*

Env. : *Llandyrnog (St Dyfnog's Church★), Llanrhaeder-yng-Nghinmeirch (Jesse Window★★), N : 5½ m. by A 494 and B 5429.*

Exc. : *Denbigh★ (Castle★), NW : 7 m. on A 525.*

Ruthin-Pwllglas ☎ (01824) 702296.

Ruthin Craft Centre, Park Rd ☎ (01824) 703992.

London 210 – Birkenhead 31 – Chester 23 – Liverpool 34 – Shrewsbury 46.

Firgrove, Llanfwrog, LL15 2LL, West : 1 ¼ m. by A 494 on B 5105 ☎ (01824) 702677, *meadway@firgrovecountryhouse.co.uk, Fax (01824) 702677,* – P. VISA. *closed December-January* – **Rest** (by arrangement) (communal dinning) 28.00 – **3 rm** ★45.00 – ★★68.00.

◆ A well-furnished house with tasteful interiors set within attractive gardens. Bedrooms are comfortable and one is self-contained with a small kitchen. Close to the town. Traditionally furnished dining room with meals taken at a communal table.

Eyarth Station, Llanfair Dyffryn Clwyd, LL15 2EE, South : 1 ¾ m. by A 525 ☎ (01824) 703643, *stay@eyarthstation.com, Fax (01824) 707464,* heated, – P. VISA

March-October and December – **Rest** 16.00 – **6 rm** ★40.00 – ★★60.00.

◆ Former railway station with a fine collection of photographs of its previous life. Pleasant country location. Traditional décor in bedrooms, sitting room and a small bar. Views over the countryside and hearty home-cooked food in the dining room.

ST BRIDES WENTLOOGE *Newport* 503 K 29 – *see Newport.*

ST DAVIDS (Tyddewi) *Pembrokeshire* 503 E 28 *Wales G. – pop. 1 959 – ✉ Haverfordwest.*

See : *Town★★ – Cathedral★★ – Bishop's Palace★ AC.*

Env. : *Pembrokeshire Coast National Park★★.*

St Davids City, Whitesands Bay ☎ (01437) 721751.

National Park Visitor Centre, The Grove ☎ (01437) 720392, enquiries@stdavids.pembrokeshirecoast.org.uk.

London 266 – Carmarthen 46 – Fishguard 16.

Warpool Court, SA62 6BN, Southwest : ½ m. by Porth Clais rd ☎ (01437) 720300, *info@warpoolcourthotel.com, Fax (01437) 720676,* – rest, P. AE VISA

closed January – **Rest** (bar lunch Monday-Saturday) 29.00/49.00 – **25 rm** ★95.00/170.00 – ★★160.00/220.00.

◆ Over 3000 hand-painted tiles of Celtic or heraldic design decorate the interior of this 19C house. Modern bedrooms, some with views over neat lawned gardens to the sea. Classic menus served at simply set, dark wood tables.

Old Cross, Cross Sq, SA62 6SP, ☎ (01437) 720387, *enquiries@oldcrosshotel.co.uk, Fax (01437) 720394,* – rest, P. VISA

closed 22 December-1 February – **Rest** (bar lunch Monday-Saturday)/dinner a la carte 19.00/27.50 s. – **17 rm** ★45.00/85.00 – ★★75.00/110.00.

◆ Overlooking the old market square, a long-established, ivy-clad hotel: rooms are modern and simply decorated. Beamed lounge - club chairs grouped around a brick fireplace. Wheelback chairs and yellow linen-clad tables in an unassuming, traditional restaurant.

Ramsey House without rest., Lower Moor, SA62 6RP, Southeast : ½ m. on Porthclais rd ☎ (01437) 720321, *info@ramseyhouse.co.uk,* – P.

March-October – – **5 rm** ★35.00/40.00 – ★★60.00/70.00.

◆ Detached house just outside the town centre. Spotlessly kept, homely interior: welcoming lounge has comfy sofas; small bar overlooks gardens. Compact, neat and tidy rooms.

The Waterings without rest., Anchor Drive, High St, SA62 6QH, East : ¼ m. on A 487 ☎ (01437) 720876, *waterings@supanet.com, Fax (01437) 720876,* – P.

5 rm ★50.00/80.00 – ★★70.00/80.00.

◆ Set in peaceful landscaped gardens and named after a sheltered cove on Ramsey Island. Spacious rooms, furnished in solid pine, around a central courtyard. Likeable hosts.

Y-Gorlan without rest., 77 Nun St, SA62 6NU, ☎ (01437) 720837, *mikebohlen@aol.com, Fax (01437) 721148* – . VISA.

5 rm ★36.00 – ★★68.00.

◆ Run by a friendly couple, Y-Gorlan - "the fold" - offers comfortable, spotless modern rooms, all en suite. Homely lounge looks towards Whitesands Bay. Good breakfasts.

ST DOGMAELS (Llandudoch) *Ceredigion* 503 G 27 – *see Cardigan.*

ST FAGANS (Sain Ffagan) *Cardiff* 503 K 29 – *see Cardiff.*

SALEM *Carmarthenshire – see Llandeilo.*

SARON *Gwynedd – see Caernarfon.*

SAUNDERSFOOT *Pembrokeshire* 503 F 28.
London 241 – Cardiff 90 – Pembroke 12.

Gower, Milford Terrace, SA69 9EL, ☎ (01834) 813452, *tim.rowe@rotels.com*
Fax (01834) 813452 – MO VISA
Rest (bar lunch Monday-Saturday)/dinner 21.95/26.95 and a la carte 18.40/31.85 – **20 rm** ☐ ★50.00/56.00 – ★★88.00/92.00.
◆ Four-storey yellow hued hotel, refurbished in 2004, close to the beach. Leather chesterfields enhance wood-floored bar. Immaculate rooms, with free-standing pine furniture. Bright, spacious dining room with conservatory extension.

SKENFRITH *Monmouthshire.*
London 135 – Hereford 16 – Ross-on-Wye 11.

The Bell with rm, NP7 8UH, ☎ (01600) 750235, *enquiries@skenfrith.co.uk*
Fax (01600) 750525, – MO AE VISA
closed late January-early February and Mondays in winter – **Rest** (booking essential) a la carte 24.50/34.50 ♀ – **8 rm** ☐ ★70.00/110.00 – ★★100.00/180.00.
◆ 17C coaching inn retains much original charm with antiques and curios and open fires. Very comfortable bedrooms have state-of-the-art appointments. Daily changing modern menu.

The sun's out – let's eat al fresco! Look for a terrace:

SOUTHERNDOWN *Bridgend* 503 J 29 – *see Bridgend.*

STACKPOLE *Pembrokeshire – see Pembroke.*

SWANSEA (Abertawe) *Swansea* 503 I 29 *Wales G. – pop. 169 880.*
See : *Town★ – Maritime Quarter★* B – *Maritime and Industrial Museum★* B – *Glynn Vivian Art Gallery★* B – *Guildhall (British Empire Panels★* A H*).*
Env. : *Gower Peninsula★★ (Rhossili★★), W : by A 4067* A.
Exc. : *The Wildfowl and Wetlands Trust★, Llanelli, NW : 6½ m. by A 483 and A 484* A.
18 *Morriston, 160 Clasemont Rd ☎ (01792) 771079,* A – 18 *Clyne, 120 Owls Lodge Lane, Mayals ☎ (01792) 401989,* A – 18 *Langland Bay ☎ (01792) 366023,* A – 18 *Fairwood Park, Blackhills Lane, Upper Killay ☎ (01792) 297849,* A – 9 *Inco, Clydach ☎ (01792) 841257,* A – 9 *Allt-y-Graban, Allt-y-Graban Rd, Pontllin ☎ (01792) 885757* – 9 *Palleg, Lower Cwmtwrch, Swansea Valley ☎ (01639) 842193.*
to Republic of Ireland (Cork) (Swansea Cork Ferries) (10 h).
Plymouth St ☎ (01792) 468321, tourism@swansea.gov.uk.
London 191 – Birmingham 136 – Bristol 82 – Cardiff 40 – Liverpool 187 – Stoke-on-Trent 175.

Plan opposite

Morgans, Somerset Place, SA1 1RR, ☎ (01792) 484848, *info@morganshotel.co.uk*
Fax (01792) 484847 – MO AE VISA. B
Rest 15.00 (lunch) and dinner a la carte 25.45/30.45 ♀ – **40 rm** ☐ ★100.00/250.00 ★★100.00/250.00.
◆ Recently converted hotel near docks. Contemporary feel: neutral colours, leather sofas. Splendid original features include soaring cupola. Very stylish rooms. Modish cooking in sleek surroundings.

Swansea Marriott, Maritime Quarter, SA1 3SS, ☎ (0870) 4007282, *reservations.swansea@marriott.co.uk, Fax (0870) 4007382*, – – 300. MO AE

VISA. B
Rest (bar lunch)/dinner a la carte 20.45/29.00 **s.** – ☐ 14.95 – **122 rm** ☐ ★115.00/145.00 ★★115.00/145.00.
◆ Substantial group hotel in modern redbrick: smart leather furnished lounge and comfortable accommodation with all mod cons - ask for a room with a view over the marina. Small, bright, modern dining room.

SWANSEA

lase Rd. . . . . A 12
ʼlartin St . . . . A 24
en-y-Graig Rd. . . . . A 30
lasmarl By-Pass. . . . . . A 32
avenhill Rd. . . . . A 35
t Helen's Rd. . . . . A 40
tation Rd . . . . A 37
errace Rd . . . . A 45
'plands Crescent . . . . . A 49
Valter Rd. . . . . A 52
Voodfield St . . . . A 60

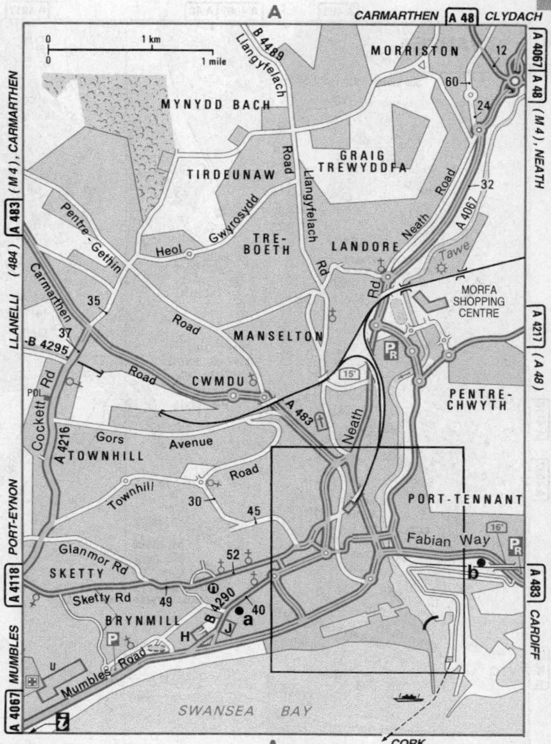

Beaumont, 72-73 Walter Rd, SA1 4QA, ✆ (01792) 643956, *info@beaumonthotel.co.uk, Fax (01792) 643044* – ☏ P. MC AE ⓓ VISA
A n
closed 31 December-2 January – **Rest** *(closed Sunday)* (dinner only) a la carte 12.50/17.50 **s.** – **16 rm** ☕ 🚶55.00/65.00 – 🚶🚶75.00.

◆ Traditional in spirit, a welcoming, family run, town house hotel in the western suburbs. Simple bedrooms - a few with sunken baths - combine modern and period furniture. Conservatory restaurant set in pink and white.

Ramada Encore without rest., Fabian Way, SA1 8LD, ✆ (0870) 4422825, *enquiries@encoreswanseabay.co.uk, Fax (0870) 4422826* – ⬍ ⇔ ☏ ♿ P – 🏫 30. MC AE ⓓ VISA.
A b
99 rm 🚶69.95 – 🚶🚶69.95.

◆ Colourful, light and modern hotel by Swansea's docks. Contemporary rooms with up-to-date amenities.

Didier & Stephanie's, 56 St Helens Rd, SA1 4BE, ✆ (01792) 655603, *Fax (01792) 470563* – MC VISA
A a
closed late December-mid January, Sunday and Monday – **Rest** - French - a la carte approx 24.30.

◆ Cosy, neighbourhood-styled restaurant with a strong Gallic influence. Welcoming owners provide tasty, good value, seasonally changing menus with lots of French ingredients.

Hanson's, Pilot House Wharf, Trawler Rd, Swansea Marina, SA1 1UN, ✆ (01792) 466200, *hansons1@btinternet.com, Fax (01792) 281528* – P. MC VISA
C a
closed 24-26 December, 1 January, Sunday, Monday lunch and Bank Holidays – **Rest** - Seafood specialities - (booking essential) 13.95 (lunch) and a la carte 20.85/35.40.

◆ Friendly, easygoing restaurant above a tackle shop and in sight of the harbour. Blackboard fish specials are the pick of a carefully sourced repertoire. Good value lunch.

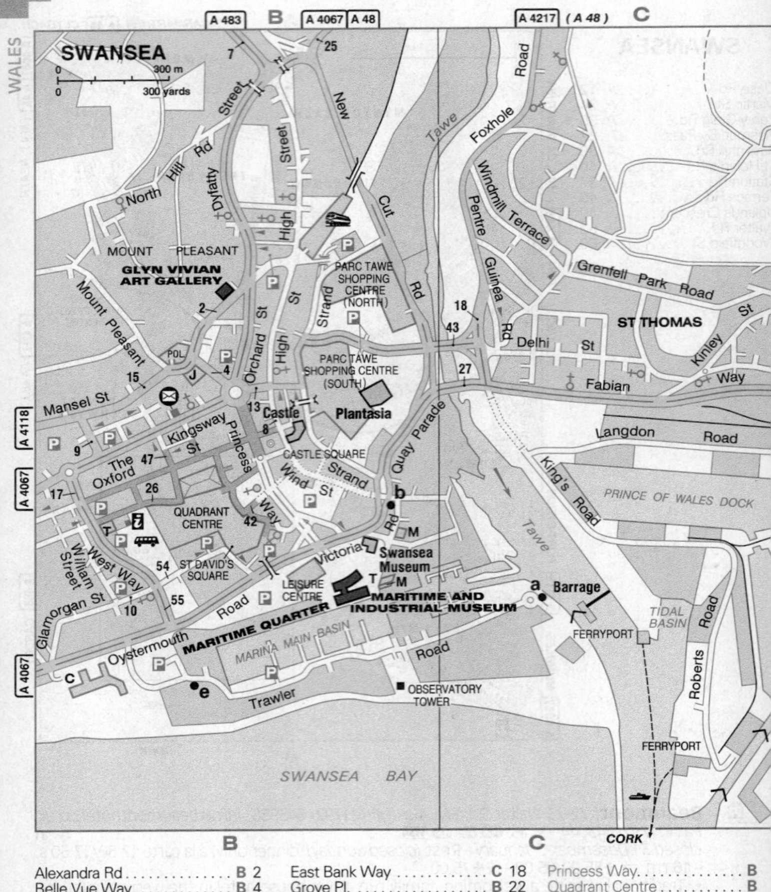

at The Mumbles *Southwest : 7¾ m. by A 4067 – A – ✉ Swansea.*

Norton House, 17 Norton Rd, SA3 5TQ, ✆ (01792) 404891, *nortonhouse@btcc nect.com, Fax (01792) 403210,* – rest, P – 25. *closed 22-29 December* – **Rest** (dinner only) a la carte 25.95/37.85 – **15 rm** ☕ 85.00 125.00.

◆ Georgian former master mariner's house, run with personable ease by a husband an wife team. Tidy rooms in traditional fabrics and furnishings - some have four-poster bed Elegant, classically proportioned dining room, offset by French etched glassware.

Hillcrest House without rest., 1 Higher Lane, SA3 4NS, West : ¾ m. on Langland r ✆ (01792) 363700, *stay@hillcresthousehotel.com, Fax (01792) 363768* – P. VISA

6 rm ☕ 65.00 – 85.00/95.00.

◆ Friendly and privately run; softly lit lounge with inviting sofas and armchairs; brigh bedrooms, each with a subtle national emblem like thistles or Canadian maple leave Prints and tall wine racks adorn dining room.

Claudes, 93 Newton Rd, SA3 4BN, (01792) 366006, *enquiries@claudes.org.uk*, *Fax (01792) 368931* – . MC AE VISA
closed 1 week September, 1 week Christmas, Sunday dinner and Monday – **Rest** 12.00/17.00 and a la carte 20.00/26.15 **s.**
◆ An intimate ambience prevails in this personally run restaurant.; vividly coloured prints enhance feel. Tasty, modish menus utilising local produce. Wide-ranging wine list.

at Llanrhidian *West : 10½ m. by A 4118 – A – and B 4271 – ✉ Reynoldston.*

Fairyhill, Reynoldston, SA3 1BS, West : 2½ m. by Llangennith Rd (01792) 390139, *postbox@fairyhill.net, Fax (01792) 391358*, – rest, P. MC VISA.
closed 1-25 January, Sunday dinner and Monday lunch in winter – **Rest** 19.95/37.50 and lunch a la carte 23.95/33.95 – **8 rm** 130.00 – 250.00.
◆ Georgian country house with modish ambience in extensive parkland and gardens. Contemporary lounge with fireside chairs. Bedrooms blend modern and traditional. Gower produce dominates seasonal menus.

The Welcome To Town, SA3 1EH, (01792) 390015, *Fax (01792) 390015* – P. MC VISA
closed 25-26 December, last 2 weeks February, 1 week October, Sunday dinner and Monday except Bank Holidays – **Rest** 15.95 (lunch) and a la carte 28.00/36.00.
◆ Converted pub set on picturesque peninsula. Rustic, characterful interior. Daily blackboard specials and good service of seasonal dishes cooked with real quality.

TALBOT GREEN (Tonysguborian) *Rhondda Cynon Taff – pop. 2 405.*
London 165 – Cardiff 17 – Swansea 60.

Brookes, 79-81 Talbot Rd, CF72 8AE, (01443) 239600, *Fax (01443) 239654* – MC AE VISA
closed 1-2 January, 24 and 26 December, Saturday lunch, Sunday dinner and Monday – **Rest** (booking essential) 15.95 (lunch) and a la carte 28.45/35.90 **s.**
◆ The bright blue canopied entrance sets the tone for this vibrant, modern restaurant in the centre of town. Wide-ranging menu offers an eclectic choice of modern food.

TALGARTH *Powys* 503 K 28 *Wales G.*
Env. : *Brecon Beacons National Park*★★.
London 182 – Brecon 10 – Cardiff 52 – Hereford 29 – Swansea 53.

Upper Trewalkin, Pengenffordd, LD3 0HA, South : 2 m. by A 479 (01874) 711349, *Fax (01874) 711349*, ←, – P.
Easter-September – **Rest** (communal dining) 15.00 – **3 rm** 27.00 – 54.00.
◆ Part Georgian farmhouse on a family run working farm in the eastern part of the Brecon Beacons National Park. Homely atmosphere, simple rooms and an attractive outlook. Meals are taken communally in the traditionally appointed dining room.

TALSARNAU *Gwynedd* 502 503 H 25 *Wales G. – pop. 647 – ✉ Harlech.*
Env. : *Snowdonia National Park*★★★.
London 236 – Caernafon 33 – Chester 67 – Dolgellau 25.

Maes-y-Neuadd, LL47 6YA, South : 1½ m. by A 496 off B 4573 (01766) 780200, *maes@neuadd.com, Fax (01766) 780211*, ←, – P. MC AE VISA
Rest 33.00/37.00 (dinner) and lunch a la carte 14.20/22.95 – **15 rm** (dinner included) 160.00/215.00 – 185.00/240.00, 1 suite.
◆ Part 14C country house with pleasant gardens in delightful rural seclusion. Furnished throughout with antiques and curios. Charming service. Individually styled bedrooms. Traditional dining room with linen-clad tables.

TALYBONT-ON-USK *Powys* 503 K 28 – *see Brecon.*

TAL-Y-LLYN *Gwynedd* 502 503 I 25 *Wales G. – ✉ Tywyn.*
Env. : *Snowdonia National Park*★★★ – *Cadair Idris*★★★.
London 224 – Dolgellau 9 – Shrewsbury 60.

Tynycornel, LL36 9AJ, on B 4405 (01654) 782282, *reception@tynycornel.co.uk, Fax (01654) 782679*, ← Tal-y-Llyn Lake and Cadair Idris, – P. MC VISA
Rest (bar lunch Monday-Saturday)/dinner a la carte 17.50/27.00 **s.** – **16 rm** 45.00/65.00 – 110.00/130.00, 2 suites.
◆ Extended former inn with fine views of Tal-y-Llyn Lake, renowned for its fishing, and Cadair Idris. Comfortable rooms with good facilities, some in converted outbuildings. Traditional style in décor and food in the comfortable dining room.

WALES

Minffordd, LL36 9AJ, Northeast : 2 ¼ m. by B 4405 on A 487 ✆ (01654) 761665, *h tel@minffordd.com, Fax (01654) 761517,* ←, – ⇔ P. MC VISA
closed 2-31 January – **Rest** (booking essential for non-residents) (bar lunch Monday-Saturday)/dinner 22.95 **s.** – **7 rm** ☕ ★45.00/56.00 – ★★90.00.
◆ A 17C former drovers' inn at the base of Cadair Idris; a good base for seeing this part of Snowdonia National Park. Traditional bedrooms, homely with characterful old beams. Simple country feel in the restaurant: uneven walls and crooked beams.

TENBY (Dinbych-Y-Pysgod) *Pembrokeshire* 503 F 28 *Wales G. – pop. 4 934.*
See : *Town★★ – Harbour and seafront★★.*
Env. : *Pembrokeshire Coast National Park★★ – Caldey Island★, S : by boat.*
18 *The Burrows ✆ (01834) 842978.*
The Croft ✆ (01834) 842402.
London 247 – Carmarthen 27 – Fishguard 36.

Broadmead, Heywood Lane, SA70 8DA, Northwest : ¾ m. ✆ (01834) 842641
Fax (01834) 845757, – ⇔ rest, P. MC AE VISA.
closed 20 December-1 March – **Rest** (dinner only) 13.00/21.00 – **20 rm** ☕ ★30.00/46.00 – ★★60.00/72.00.
◆ Privately owned country house hotel. Traditionally styled public rooms include conservatory overlooking gardens. Individually decorated rooms with modern amenities. Dining room in the traditional style common to the other parts of the house.

Fourcroft, North Beach, SA70 8AP, ✆ (01834) 842886, *staying@fourcroft-hotel.co.uk Fax (01834) 842888,* ←, heated – ⇔ – 80. MC AE VISA
Rest (bar lunch)/dinner 22.00/28.00 and a la carte 21.00/27.00 **s.** – **40 rm** ☕ ★45.00/130.00 – ★★90.00/140.00.
◆ Well-established, family owned hotel forming part of a Georgian terrace. Sea facing rooms benefit from large original windows. Attractions and water activities nearby. The dining room overlooks the sea and is decorated in traditional style.

Myrtle House without rest., St Marys St, SA70 7HW, ✆ (01834) 842508
Fax (01834) 842508 – ⇔. MC VISA
– **8 rm** ☕ ★26.00/50.00 – ★★52.00/64.00.
◆ House on main street within the medieval town walls. Close to beach, shopping and picturesque harbour. Simple, snug bedrooms. A non smoking establishment.

at Penally (Penalun) *Southwest : 2 m. by A 4139 – ✉ Tenby.*

Penally Abbey , SA70 7PY, ✆ (01834) 843033, *penally.abbey@btinternet.com Fax (01834) 844714,* ←, – ⇔ rest, P. MC AE VISA.
Rest 22.00/34.00 **s.** – **17 rm** ☕ ★125.00 – ★★164.00.
◆ Gothic style, stone built house with attractive views of Carmarthen Bay and surrounded by woodland. Calm, country house décor and atmosphere and individual rooms. Candlelit dinners in dining room which is decorated in the country style of the establishment.

THORNHILL *Cardiff* 503 K 29 – *see Cardiff.*

TINTERN (Tyndyrn) *Monmouthshire* 503 504 L 28 *Wales G. – ✉ Chepstow.*
See : *Abbey★★ AC.*
London 137 – Bristol 23 – Gloucester 40 – Newport 22.

Parva Farmhouse with rm, NP16 6SQ, on A 466 ✆ (01291) 689411, *parva-hotel-tintern@hotmail.com, Fax (01291) 689557* – ⇔ rest, P. MC AE VISA
Rest (dinner only) 22.50/25.00 **s.** – **9 rm** ☕ ★55.00/65.00 – ★★74.00/86.00.
◆ Mid 17C stone farmhouse adjacent to River Wye; refurbished to country standard. Traditional cooking, warm hospitality and a wide-ranging wine list. Comfortable rooms.

TREARDDUR BAY *Anglesey* 502 503 G 24 *Wales G. – ✉ Holyhead.*
Env. : *Anglesey★★.*
Exc. : *Barclodiad y Gawres Burial Chamber★, SE : 10 m. by B 4545, A 5 and A 4080.*
London 269 – Bangor 25 – Caernarfon 29 – Holyhead 3.

Trearddur Bay, LL65 2UN, ✆ (01407) 860301, *enquiries@trearddurbayhotel.co.uk Fax (01407) 861181,* – ⇔ P – 40. MC AE VISA.
closed Christmas – **Rest** (bar lunch)/dinner a la carte 22.40/28.40 – **42 rm** ☕ ★90.00 – ★★135.00/160.00.
◆ Situated next to "Blue Flag" beach. Well run with good facilities, including pool and bar and comfy, traditionally styled rooms: go for balcony rooms with bay window seating. Traditional dining room; drinks in cocktail lounge before dining.

TRECASTLE (Tregastell) *Powys* 503 J 28.
London 192 – Aberystwyth 60 – Cardiff 47 – Carmarthen 37 – Gloucester 81.

Castle Coaching Inn, LD3 8UH, ✆ (01874) 636354, *guest@castle-coaching-inn.co.uk, Fax (01874) 636457* – rest, P. VISA.
closed 2 weeks early January – **Rest** *(closed Monday-Friday lunch)* a la carte 11.80/22.85 ♀ – **9 rm** ☕ ★45.00 – ★★60.00/70.00.
◆ Family run Georgian coaching inn in a prominent position in this small village renowned for its surrounding landscape. Warm atmosphere and good home comforts in snug rooms. The main dining room has wood beams and is decorated in simple country style.

TREDUNNOCK *Newport* 503 L 29 – *see Newport.*

TREMEIRCHION *Denbighshire* 502 503 J 24 – ✉ *St. Asaph.*
London 225 – Chester 29 – Shrewsbury 59.

Bach-Y-Graig without rest., LL17 0UH, Southwest : 2 m. by B 5429 off Denbigh rd ✆ (01745) 730627, *anwen@bachygraig.co.uk, Fax (01745) 730971*, – P.
closed Christmas-New Year – **3 rm** ☕ ★35.00/45.00 – ★★68.00.
◆ Attractive brick-built farmhouse dating from 16C, on working farm. In quiet spot with woodland trails nearby. Large open fires and pine furnished rooms with cast iron beds.

TYN-Y-GROES *Gwynedd – see Conwy (Aberconwy and Colwyn).*

USK (Brynbuga) *Monmouthshire* 503 L 28 *Wales G. – pop. 2 318.*
Exc. : *Raglan Castle★ AC, NE : 7 m. by A 472, A 449 and A 40.*
18, 18 *Alice Springs, Bettws Newydd ✆ (01873) 880708.*
London 144 – Bristol 30 – Cardiff 26 – Gloucester 39 – Newport 10.

Glen-yr-Afon House, Pontypool Rd, NP15 1SY, ✆ (01291) 672302, *enquiries@glen-yr-afon.co.uk, Fax (01291) 672597*, – P – 200. AE VISA
Rest (Sunday dinner residents only) 12.00 and a la carte 24.65/33.00 ♀ – **28 rm** ☕ ★84.60 – ★★117.50.
◆ Across the bridge from the town is this warmly run 19C villa with a relaxing country house ambience. Several welcoming lounges and comfortable, warm, well-kept bedrooms.

at Llandenny *Northeast : 4¼ m. by A 472 off B 4235 – ✉ Usk.*

Raglan Arms, NP15 1DL, ✆ (01291) 690800, *raglan.arms@virgin.net, Fax (01291) 690155*, – P. VISA
closed Sunday dinner and Monday – **Rest** (booking essential) a la carte 20.50/29.75.
◆ Stone-faced pub in the middle of small village. Busy central bar: eating area includes big leather sofas in front of the fire, and good value dishes enhanced by sharp cooking.

WELSH HOOK *Pembrokeshire* 503 F 28 – *see Fishguard.*

WELSHPOOL (Trallwng) *Powys* 502 503 K 26 *Wales G. – pop. 5 539.*
See : *Town★.*
Env. : *Powis Castle★★★ AC, SW : 1½ m. by A 483.*
18 *Golfa Hill ✆ (01938) 850249.*
Vicarage Garden, Church St ✆ (01938) 552043, weltic@powys.gov.uk.
London 182 – Birmingham 64 – Chester 45 – Shrewsbury 19.

Buttington House, Buttington, SY21 8HD, Northeast : 2 m. by A 483 and A 458 on B 4388 ✆ (01938) 553351, *enquiries@buttingtonhouse.co.uk, Fax (01938) 553351*, – P.
closed 28 December-2 January – **Rest** (by arrangement) 25.00 – **3 rm** ☕ ★60.00 – ★★80.00.
◆ Comfortable, individually furnished rooms, some with old brass bedsteads, in an attractive Georgian house on classic lines. Two-acre gardens with pond and orchard. Neatly set dining room with a subtle nod to Regency styling.

Moat Farm without rest., SY21 8SE, South : 2 ¼ m. on A 483 ✆ (01938) 553179, *ewjones@freenetname.co.uk, Fax (01938) 553179*, – P.
closed December-January – **3 rm** ☕ ★30.00 – ★★50.00/54.00.
◆ Spacious 17C redbrick farmhouse and dairy farm near the river Severn. Affordable rooms, all en suite, are decorated in floral patterns and have views of quiet countryside. Homely and simple dining room with a broad dresser stacked with blue and white crockery.

WALES

at Guilsfield *North : 3 m. by A 490 on B 4392 – ✉ Welshpool.*

Lower Trelydan without rest., SY21 9PH, South : ¾ m. by B 4392 on unmarked road ☎ (01938) 553105, *stay@lowertrelydan.com, Fax (01938) 553105*, – P. VISA
closed Christmas and New Year – **3 rm** ★35.00 – ★★58.00.
◆ Sheep graze the quiet fields around this listed, 16C timbered farmhouse, run by likeable couple. Comfortable lounge and neatly kept, en suite rooms in traditional style. Nourishing farmhouse cooking, rooted in the Welsh tradition.

WHITEBROOK *Monmouthshire – see Monmouth.*

WOLF'S CASTLE (Cas-Blaidd) *Pembrokeshire* 503 F 28 *Wales G.* – ✉ *Haverfordwest.*
Env. : *Pembrokeshire Coast National Park*★★.
London 258 – Fishguard 7 – Haverfordwest 8.

Wolfscastle Country H., SA62 5LZ, ☎ (01437) 741225, *enquiries@wolfscastle.com Fax (01437) 741383*, – P – 150. AE VISA
closed 24-26 December – **Rest** (lunch by arrangement Monday-Saturday)/dinner a la carte 16.05/29.70 ♀ – **20 rm** ★59.00 – ★★115.00.
◆ Spacious, family run country house; tidy rooms in traditional soft chintz, modern conference room and simply styled bar with a mix of cushioned settles and old wooden chairs. Dining room with neatly laid tables in pink linens.

WREXHAM (Wrecsam) *Wrexham* 502 503 L 24 *Wales G. – pop. 42 576.*
See : *St Giles Church*★.
Env. : *Erddig*★★ *AC (Gardens*★★*), SW : 2 m – Gresford (All Saints Church*★*), N : 4 m. by A 5152 and B 5445.*
18, 9 *Chirk* ☎ *(01691) 774407* – 18 *Clays, Bryn Estyn Rd* ☎ *(01978) 661406* – 9 *Moss Valley Moss Rd* ☎ *(01978) 720518* – 9 *Pen-y-Cae, Ruabon Rd* ☎ *(01978) 810108* – 9 *The Plassey Eyton* ☎ *(01978) 780020.*
Lambpit St ☎ *(01978) 292015, tic@wrexham.gov.uk.*
London 192 – Chester 12 – Liverpool 35 – Shrewsbury 28.

Llwyn Onn Hall, Cefn Rd, LL13 0NY, Northeast : 2 ½ m. by A 534 off Cefn Rd ☎ (01978) 261225, *reception@llwynonnhallhotel.co.uk, Fax (01978) 363233*, P. AE VISA.
closed 26 December-3 January – **Rest** *(closed Sunday dinner and Bank Holidays to non residents)* 13.95/19.50 ♀ – **13 rm** ★79.00/87.00 – ★★120.00.
◆ Converted manor house on the town's outskirts - beams and old oak hint at its origin in the 1600s. Neat bedrooms in traditional style. Sun lounge overlooks the countryside. Spacious, high-ceilinged dining room with simply set, linen-clad tables.

Premier Travel Inn, Chester Rd, LL12 8PW, Northeast : 2 ½ m. by A 483 on B 5445 ☎ (01978) 853214, *Fax (01978) 856838* – rest, P. AE VISA.
Rest (grill rest.) – **38 rm** ★46.95/46.95 – ★★48.95/48.95.
◆ Purpose-built lodge on Wrexham's northern approaches. Rooms in simple, modern style, useful for business or leisure stopovers. Informal, family friendly pub dining nearby.

at Gresford *Northeast : 3 m. by A 483 on B 5445.*

Pant-yr-Ochain, Old Wrexham Rd, LL12 8TY, South : 1 m. ☎ (01978) 853525, *pantyrochain@brunningandprice.co.uk, Fax (01978) 853505*, – P. AE VISA.
closed 25-26 December – **Rest** (booking essential) a la carte 14.50/23.95 ♀.
◆ Bustling part 16C inn overlooking a lake with pleasant gardens and terrace. Open-plan dining rooms, bar and library. Blackboard menu and real ales.

Ireland

P. Desclos/SCOPE

Kilfenora: Celtic cross

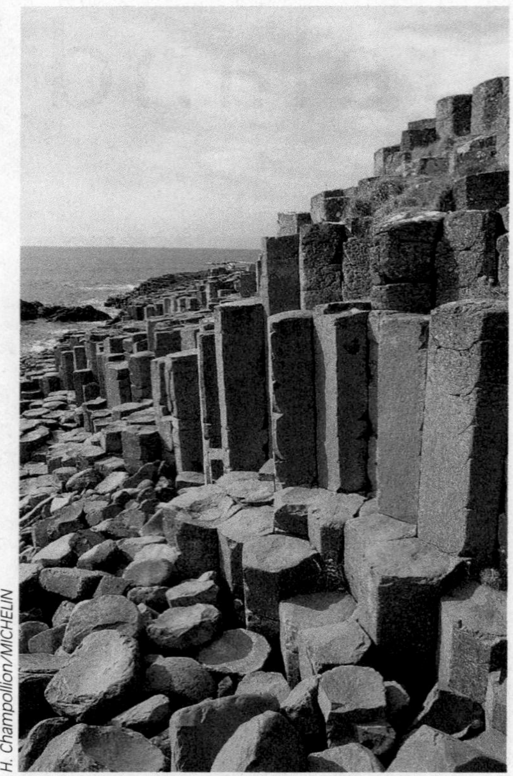
H. Champollion/MICHELIN
Giant's Causeway

Towns
from A to Z

Villes
de A à Z

Città
de A a Z

Städte
von A bis Z

Northern Ireland

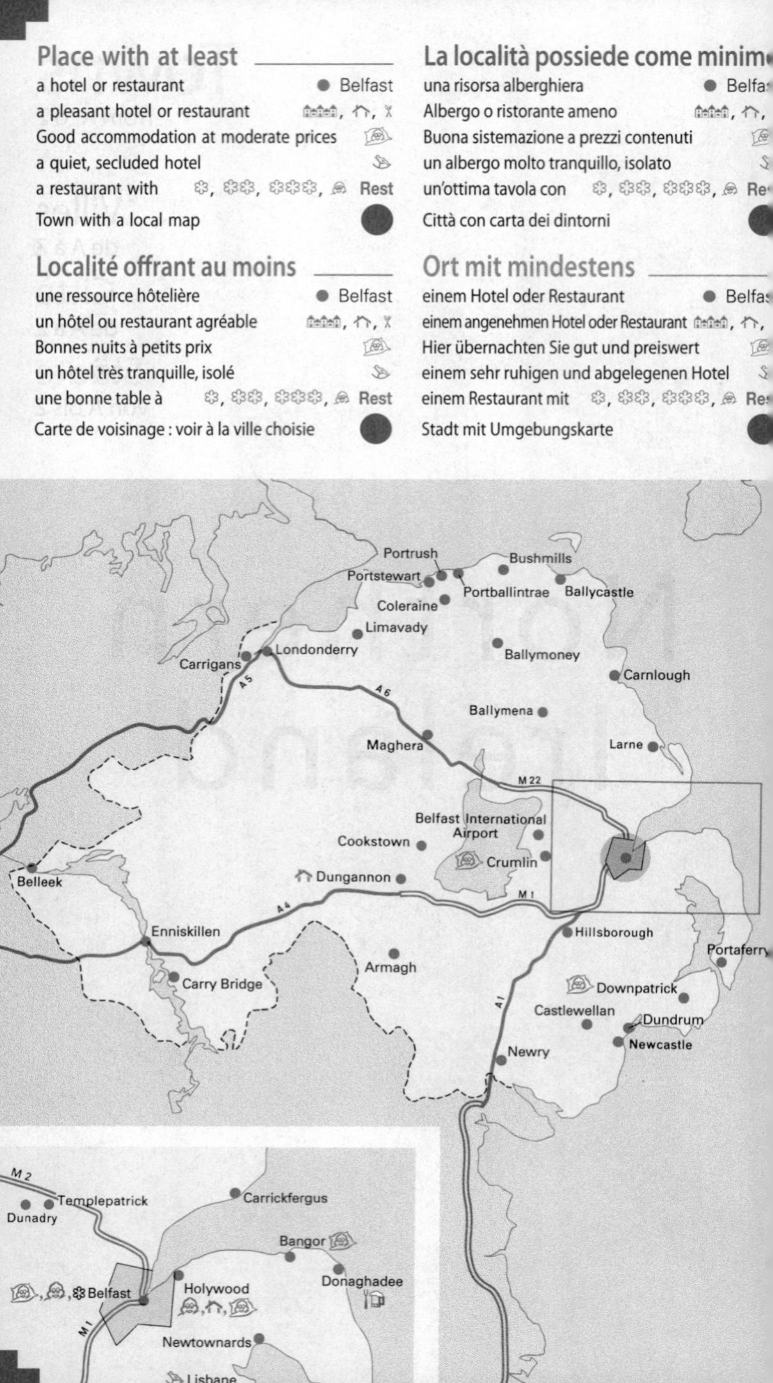
Place with at least
a hotel or restaurant ● Belfast
a pleasant hotel or restaurant
Good accommodation at moderate prices
a quiet, secluded hotel
a restaurant with Rest
Town with a local map
La località possiede come minim
una risorsa alberghiera ● Belfa
Albergo o ristorante ameno
Buona sistemazione a prezzi contenuti
un albergo molto tranquillo, isolato
un'ottima tavola con Re
Città con carta dei dintorni
Localité offrant au moins
une ressource hôtelière ● Belfast
un hôtel ou restaurant agréable
Bonnes nuits à petits prix
un hôtel très tranquille, isolé
une bonne table à Rest
Carte de voisinage : voir à la ville choisie
Ort mit mindestens
einem Hotel oder Restaurant ● Belfa
einem angenehmen Hotel oder Restaurant
Hier übernachten Sie gut und preiswert
einem sehr ruhigen und abgelegenen Hotel
einem Restaurant mit Re
Stadt mit Umgebungskarte
Portrush
Bushmills
Portstewart
Portballintrae
Ballycastle
Coleraine
Limavady
Ballymoney
Carrigans
Londonderry
Carnlough
A5
A6
Ballymena
Maghera
Larne
M 22
Belfast International Airport
Cookstown
Crumlin
Belleek
Dungannon
M 1
A4
Enniskillen
Hillsborough
Armagh
Portaferry
Carry Bridge
Downpatrick
Castlewellan
Dundrum
A1
Newcastle
Newry
M 2
Templepatrick
Dunadry
Carrickfergus
Bangor
Donaghadee
Belfast
Holywood
M1
Newtownards
Lisbane

ANNAHILT *Down* 712 N/O 4 – *see Hillsborough.*

ARMAGH *Armagh* 712 M 4.

Belfast 39 – Dungannon 13 – Portadown 11.

Armagh City H., 2 Friary Rd, BT60 4FR, ✆ (028) 3751 8888, *info@armaghcityhotel.com, Fax (028) 3751 2777,* – ♿ – 1200. MC AE VISA.
closed 24-25 December – **Rest** (dinner only and Sunday lunch) a la carte 19.00/25.00 s. – **82 rm** ☕ ✝79.00 – ✝✝92.00.
◆ Modern purpose-built hotel well geared-up to the business traveller. Stylish, wood furnished bedrooms, the city's two cathedrals visible from those to the front. Large, split-level restaurant serving traditional dishes.

BALLYMENA **(An Baile Meánach)** *Antrim* 712 N 3 *Ireland G. – pop. 58 610.*

Exc. : *Antrim Glens★★★ – Murlough Bay★★ (Fair Head ≤★★), Glengariff Forest Park★★ AC (Waterfall★★), Glengariff★, Glendun★ – Antrim (Round Tower★) S : 9½ m. by A 26.*
128 Raceview Rd ✆ (028) 2586 1207.
76 Church St ✆ (028) 2563 8494, ballymenatic@hotmail.com.
Belfast 27 – Dundalk 78 – Larne 21 – Londonderry 51 – Omagh 53.

Rosspark, 20 Doagh Rd, BT42 3LZ, Southeast : 6 m. by A 36 on B 59 ✆ (028) 2589 1663, *info@rosspark.com, Fax (028) 2589 1477,* – rest, ♿ – 300. MC AE VISA.
closed 25 December – ***The Restaurant :*** **Rest** 20.00/30.00 and a la carte 16.00/23.00 s. – **39 rm** ☕ ✝75.00 – ✝✝95.00, 1 suite.
◆ Off the beaten track, yet fully equipped with all mod cons. Rooms are smart and contemporarily styled with sofas, ironing centres. Executive rooms have large working areas. Restaurant in the heart of the hotel decorated in terracotta colours.

Marlagh Lodge, 71 Moorfields Rd, BT42 3BU, Southeast : 2¼ m. on A 36 ✆ (028) 2563 1505, *info@marlaghlodge.com, Fax (028) 2564 1590,* – MC VISA.
Rest (by arrangement) 30.50 – **3 rm** ☕ ✝35.00 – ✝✝70.00.
◆ Substantial 19C house dominated by vast monkey puzzle tree. Many original features restored; stained glass in front door and hall. Tasteful, individually furnished rooms. Guests treated to daily changing five course dinner.

Undecided between two equivalent establishments? Within each category, establishments are classified in our order of preference.

BALLYMONEY **(Baile Monaidh)** *Antrim* 712 M 2 – *pop. 26 894.*

Belfast 47 – Ballymena 19 – Coleraine 8.

Harmony Hill with rm, Balnamore, BT53 7PS, West : 2 m. on Balnamore rd ✆ (028) 2766 3459, *webmaster@harmonyhill.net, Fax (028) 2766 3740,* – MC VISA
Rest *(closed Sunday dinner)* (booking essential) (dinner only and Sunday lunch) a la carte 23.50/26.00 – **6 rm** ☕ ✝42.00 – ✝✝72.00.
◆ Pleasant Georgian house with individually designed bedrooms. Cosy, dining room with turf fire, beams and booths. Local meats, fish and home-grown produce, simply prepared.

BANGOR **(Beannchar)** *Down* 712 O/P 4 *Ireland G.*

See : *North Down Heritage Centre★.*
Exc. : *Priory (Cross Slabs★) – Mount Stewart★★★ AC, SE : 10 m. by A 2, A 21 and A 20 – Scrabo Tower (≤★★) S : 6½ m. by A 21 – Ballycopeland Windmill★, SE : 10 m. by B 21 and A 2, turning right at Millisle – Strangford Lough★ (Castle Espie Centre★ AC - Nendrum Monastery★) – Grey Abbey★ AC, SE : 20 m. by A 2, A 21 and A 20.*
34 Quay St ✆ (028) 9127 0069, bangor@nitic.net.
Belfast 15 – Newtownards 5.

Marine Court, The Marina, BT20 5ED, ✆ (028) 9145 1100, *marinecourt@btconnect.com, Fax (028) 9145 1200,* – rm, ♿ – 350. MC AE VISA.
closed 25 December – ***Nelson's :*** **Rest** a la carte 15.95/25.65 – **52 rm** ☕ ✝80.00/90.00 – ✝✝100.00.
◆ Close to harbour with rail connections to Dublin and Derry; only 15 minutes from Belfast airport. Practical, co-ordinated bedrooms; smart leisure club. Simple Nelson's has popular menus.

NORTHERN IRELAND

Clandeboye Lodge, 10 Estate Rd, Clandeboye, BT19 1UR, Southwest : 3 m. by A 2 an Dundonald rd following signs for Blackwood Golf Centre ✆ (028) 9185 2500, *info@clandeboyelodge.co.uk, Fax (028) 9185 2772*, 18, – |‡|, ⇹ rm, ✆ ♿ P – 🏫 400. MC AE VISA

closed 25-26 December – ***Lodge* : Rest** (bar lunch Monday-Saturday)/dinner a la cart 14.50/29.95 – **43 rm** ☕ ★85.00/95.00 – ★★95.00/105.00.

◆ On site of former estate school house, surrounded by 4 acres of woodland. Well place for country and coast. Meetings and weddings in separate extension. Comfy rooms. Restaurant boasts amiable, flexible approach to cooking.

Cairn Bay Lodge, 278 Seacliffe Rd, BT20 5HS, East : 1 ¼ m. by Quay St ✆ (028) 914 7636, *info@cairnbaylodge.com, Fax (028) 9145 7728*, ←, – ⇹ P. MC VISA

Rest 20.00 – **3 rm** ☕ ★35.00/60.00 – ★★65.00/70.00.

◆ Built in 1913 for councillor; expensive in its day. Lots of period charm: Dutch fireplaces stained glass, panelling. Beach views; trim bedrooms. Attractive rear garden.

Shelleven House, 59-61 Princetown Rd, BT20 3TA, ✆ (028) 9127 1777, *shelleven house@aol.com, Fax (028) 9127 1777* – ⇹ P. MC VISA.

Rest (by arrangement) 30.00 – **11 rm** ☕ ★33.00/45.00 – ★★56.00/60.00.

◆ End of terrace, double front Victorian house, personally run; stroll to marina and attractions. Large, uniformly decorated rooms with mahogany furniture. Homely, good value.

Coyle's (1st Floor), 44 High St, BT20 5AZ, ✆ (028) 9127 0362, *Fax (028) 9127 0362* – MC VISA

closed 25 December and Monday – **Rest** (dinner only) a la carte 15.00/24.70.

◆ Above a busy pub, this warm, cosy restaurant, in an interesting Art Deco style, offer precise, seasonal cooking which blends classic and modern dishes in harmonious ways.

- *Discover the best restaurant ?*
- *Find the nearest hotel ?*
- *Find your bearings using our maps and guides ?*
- *Understand the symbols used in the guide...*

Follow the red Bibs !

Advice on restaurants from Chef Bib.

Advice on hotels from Bellboy Bib.

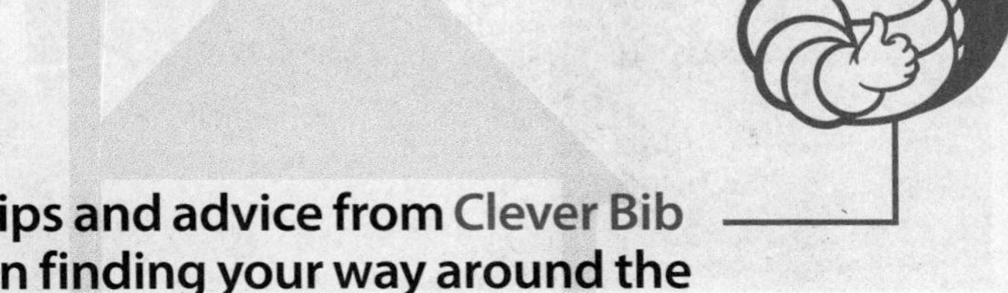

Tips and advice from Clever Bib on finding your way around the guide and on the road.

C. Bowman/SCOPE

Belfast: City Hall

BELFAST - (Béal Feirste)

Antrim 712 O 4 Ireland G. – pop. 277 391

Dublin 103 – Londonderry 70.

TOURIST INFORMATION

47 Donegal Pl ✆ (028) 9024 6609; info@nitic.com.
Belfast International Airport, Information desk ✆ (028) 9442 2888.
Belfast City Airport, Sydenham Bypass ✆ (028) 9093 9093.

PRACTICAL INFORMATION

18 *Balmoral, 518 Lisburn Rd ✆ (028) 9038 1514,* **AZ**.
18 *Belvoir Park, Church Rd, Newtonbreda ✆ (028) 9049 1693* **AZ**.
18 *Fortwilliam, Downview Ave ✆ (028) 9037 0770,* **AY**.
18 *The Knock Club, Summerfield, Dundonald ✆ (028) 9048 2249.*
18 *Shandon Park, 73 Shandon Park ✆ (028) 9079 3730.*
9 *Cliftonville, Westland Rd ✆ (028) 9074 4158,* **AY**.
9 *Ormeau, 50 Park Rd ✆ (028) 9064 1069,* **AZ**
Belfast International Airport, Aldergrove : ✆ (028) 9448 4848, W : 15½ m. by A 52 **AY** *– Belfast City Airport : ✆ (028) 9093 9093.*
Terminal : *Coach service (Ulsterbus Ltd.) from Great Victoria Street Station (40 mn).*
to Isle of Man (Douglas) (Isle of Man Steam Packet Co. Ltd) (summer only) (2 h 45 mn) – to Stranraer (Stena Line) 4-5 daily (1 h 30 mn/3 h 15 mn), (SeaCat Scotland) March-January (90 mn) – to Liverpool (NorseMerchant Ferries Ltd) daily (11 h) – to Troon (Sea Containers Ferries Scotland Ltd) 2 daily (2 h 30 mn) – to Heysham (Sea Containers Ferries Scotland Ltd) March-September (4 h).

SIGHTS

See : *City★ - Ulster Museum★★ (Spanish Armada Treasure★★, Shrine of St Patrick's Hand★)* **AZ M1** *– City Hall★* **BY** *– Donegall Square★* **BY 20** *– Botanic Gardens (Palm House★)* **AZ** *– St Anne's Cathedral★* **BX** *– Crown Liquor Saloon★* **BY** *– Sinclair Seamen's Church★* **BX** *– St Malachy's Church★* **BY**.
Env. : *Belfast Zoological Gardens★★ AC, N : 5 m. by A 6* **AY**.
Exc. : *Carrickfergus (Castle★★ AC, St Nicholas' Church★) NE : 9 ½ m. by A 2 – Talnotry Cottage Bird Garden, Crumlin★ AC, W : 13½ m. by A 52.*

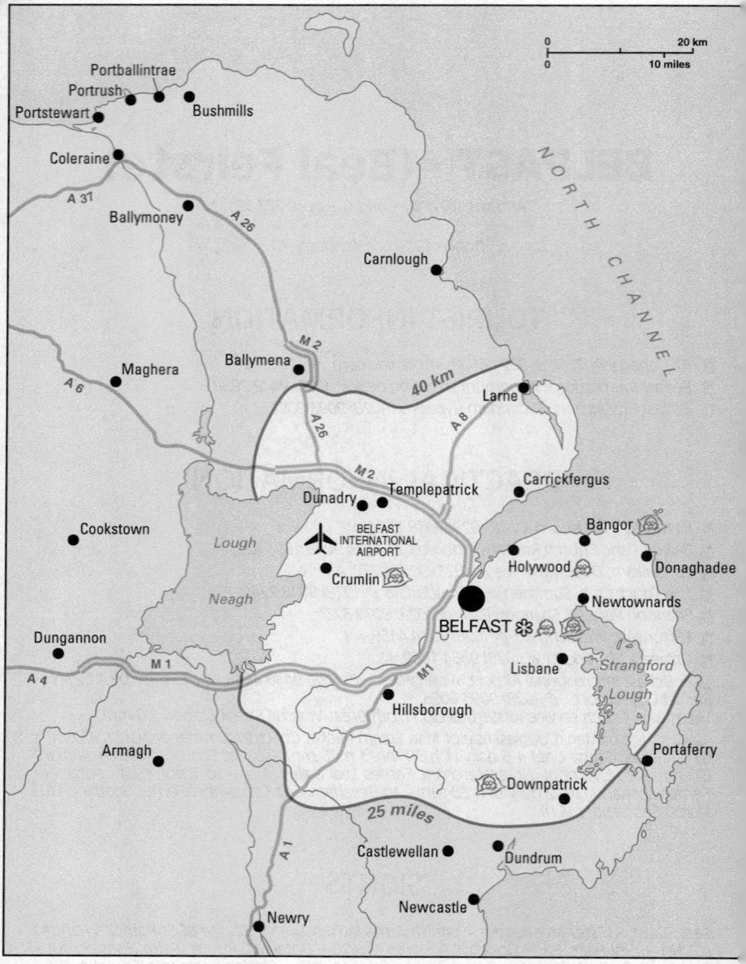

0 20 km
0 10 miles
NORTH CHANNEL
Portballintrae
Portrush
Portstewart
Bushmills
Coleraine
A 37
Ballymoney
A 26
Carnlough
M 2
Ballymena
Maghera
A 6
40 km
Larne
A 26
A 8
M 2
Templepatrick
Carrickfergus
Dunadry
Bangor
Cookstown
BELFAST INTERNATIONAL AIRPORT
Lough
Holywood
Donaghadee
Crumlin
Neagh
Newtownards
BELFAST
Dungannon
Lisbane
M 1
Strangford
A 4
M1
Lough
Hillsborough
Armagh
Portaferry
Downpatrick
25 miles
Castlewellan
Dundrum
A 1
Newcastle
Newry

Undecided between two equivalent establishments? Within each category, establishments are classified in our order of preference.

INDEX OF STREET NAMES IN BELFAST

In Northern Ireland traffic and parking are controlled in the town centres. No vehicle may be left unattended in a Control Zone.

delaïde St . . . . . BY
rport Rd . . . . . AY
bert Bridge Rd . . . . . AZ
bert Bridge . . . . . AZ 2
bert Square . . . . . BX 3
exandre Park Ave . . . . . AY
fred St . . . . . BY
nn St . . . . . BY 5
nnadale Ave . . . . . AZ
nnadale Embankment . . . . . AZ 4
ntrim Rd . . . . . AY
rdenlee Rd . . . . . AZ
almoral Ave . . . . . AZ
edford St . . . . . BY
eersdridge Rd . . . . . AZ
elmont Rd . . . . . BZ 7
otanic Ave . . . . . BZ
radbury Pl . . . . . BZ 9
ridge End . . . . . AZ 10
ridge St . . . . . BY 12
astle Pl . . . . . BY
astle St . . . . . BY
astlecourt Shopping Centre . . . . . BXY
astlereagh Rd . . . . . AZ
astlereagh St . . . . . AZ 14
avehill Rd . . . . . AY
hichester St . . . . . BX
ity Hospital St . . . . . BZ
lifton St . . . . . BX 15
liftonville Rd . . . . . AY
ollege Square . . . . . BY
orporation Square . . . . . BX 16
orporation St . . . . . BX
ranmore Park . . . . . AZ
regagh Rd . . . . . AZ
romac St . . . . . BY
rumlin Rd . . . . . AY, BX

Dargan Rd . . . . . AY
Divis St . . . . . BY
Donegall Park Ave . . . . . AY
Donegall Pass . . . . . BZ
Donegall Pl . . . . . BY
Donegall Quay . . . . . BXY 19
Donegall Rd . . . . . AZ, BZ
Donegall Square . . . . . BY 20
Donegall St . . . . . BX
Dublin Rd . . . . . BZ
Durham St . . . . . BY
East Bridge St . . . . . AZ 23
Falls Rd . . . . . AZ
Forestside Shopping Centre . AZ
Frederic St . . . . . BX
Galwally Rd . . . . . AZ
Garmoyle St . . . . . AY 24
Grand Parade . . . . . AZ 25
Gray's Lane . . . . . AY
Great George's St . . . . . BX
Great Victoria St . . . . . BY, BZ
Grosvenor Rd . . . . . AZ, BY
High St . . . . . BXY 28
Holywood Rd . . . . . AZ
Howard St . . . . . BY 29
James Street South . . . . . BY 30
Ladas Drive . . . . . BY 31
Lagan Bridge . . . . . BX 32
Lansdowne Rd . . . . . AY
Lisburn Rd . . . . . AZ, BZ
Malone Rd . . . . . AZ
May St . . . . . BX
Middlepath St . . . . . AZ 34
Millfield Carrick Hill . . . . . BXY
Mount Merrion Ave . . . . . AZ 35
Mountpottinger Rd . . . . . AZ 36
Nelson St . . . . . BX
Newtownards Rd . . . . . AZ 38

North Circular Rd . . . . . AY
North Queen St . . . . . AY
North St . . . . . BX
Oldpark Rd . . . . . AY
Ormeau Ave . . . . . BZ
Ormeau Embankment . . . . . AZ
Ormeau Rd . . . . . AZ, BZ
Oxford St . . . . . BY
Peters Hill . . . . . BX
Queen Elizabeth Bridge . . . . . BY 40
Queen's Bridge . . . . . BY 41
Queen's Square . . . . . BX 42
Queens Rd . . . . . AY
Ravenhill . . . . . AZ
Rosemary St . . . . . BY 44
Rosetta Park . . . . . AZ 45
Royal Ave . . . . . BXY
Saintfield Rd . . . . . AZ 47
Sandy Row . . . . . BZ
Shankill Rd . . . . . AZ
Shore Rd . . . . . AY
Short Strand . . . . . AZ 48
Springfiel Rd . . . . . AZ
Stranmillis Rd . . . . . AZ
Sydenham Rd . . . . . AZ 49
Townsend St . . . . . BX
University Rd . . . . . BZ
University Square . . . . . AZ 52
University St . . . . . BZ
Upper Knockbreda Rd . . . . . AZ
Victoria St . . . . . BY
Waring St . . . . . BX 54
Wellington Pl . . . . . BY 55
Westlink . . . . . BY
Woodstock Rd . . . . . AZ
Woodvalle Rd . . . . . AY
York Rd . . . . . AY
York St . . . . . BX

Hilton Belfast, 4 Lanyon Pl, BT1 3LP, ☎ (028) 9027 7000, *hilton.belfast@hilton.com, Fax (028) 9027 7277*, – |‡|, ⇔ rm, – 🏊 400. MC AE ① VISA BY s
Sonoma : Rest *(closed lunch Saturday and Sunday)* a la carte 25.15/34.25 **s.** ♀ – ***Cables :*** Rest a la carte 13.45/19.45 **s.** – ☕ 16.50 – **189 rm** ★165.00 – ★★165.00, 6 suites.
◆ Modern branded hotel overlooking river and close to concert hall. Spacious and brightly decorated rooms with all mod cons. Upper floors with good city views. Striking California-style décor and good city views from Sonoma. Contemporary Cables bar-restaurant.

Europa, Great Victoria St, BT2 7AP, ☎ (028) 9027 1066, *res@eur.hastingshotels.com, Fax (028) 9032 7800* – |‡|, ⇔ rm, – 🏊 750. MC AE ① VISA. ✂ BY e
closed 24-25 December – ***Gallery :*** Rest (dinner only) 22.00 and a la carte 24.90/27.90 ♀ – ***The Brasserie :*** Rest a la carte 21.00/30.90 ♀ – ☕ 16.00 – **235 rm** ★120.00/150.00 – ★★175.00, 5 suites.
◆ Busy hotel in the heart of the lively Golden Mile area. Extensive meeting facilities. Most executive rooms are well-equipped with hi-fis. Formal Gallery restaurant and immaculate bar. Pleasant feel suffuses Brasserie; fish and chips a favourite here.

Radisson SAS, 3 Cromac Pl, Cromac Wood, BT7 2JB, ☎ (028) 9043 4065, *info.belfast@radissonsas.com, Fax (028) 9043 4066*, ≤ – |‡|, ⇔ rm, – 🏊 150. MC AE ① VISA. ✂ BY z
Filini's : Rest *(closed Sunday)* 11.95/14.95 and a la carte 20.70/32.75 – ☕ 13.95 – **119 rm** ★140.00 – ★★140.00, 1 suite.
◆ Stylish, modern hotel on the site of former gasworks. Smart, up-to-date facilities.. Two room styles - Urban or Nordic; both boast fine views over city and waterfront. Restaurant/bar with floor-to-ceiling windows and part-open kitchen.

Stormont, Upper Newtownards Rd, BT4 3LP, East : 3½ m. on A 20 ☎ (028) 9065 1066, *res@stor.hastingshotels.com, Fax (028) 9048 0240* – |‡|, ⇔ rm, – 🏊 500. MC AE ① VISA. ✂
Shiraz : Rest *(closed Sunday)* (dinner only) a la carte 21.35/31.15 – ***La Scala Bistro :*** Rest a la carte 14.75/27.85 – **105 rm** ☕ ★118.00 – ★★148.00.
◆ In a suburb opposite the gardens of Stormont castle; an up-to-date conference and exhibition oriented hotel. Brightly decorated, modern bedrooms. Comfortable, split-level Shiraz. All-day La Scala has appealing ambience.

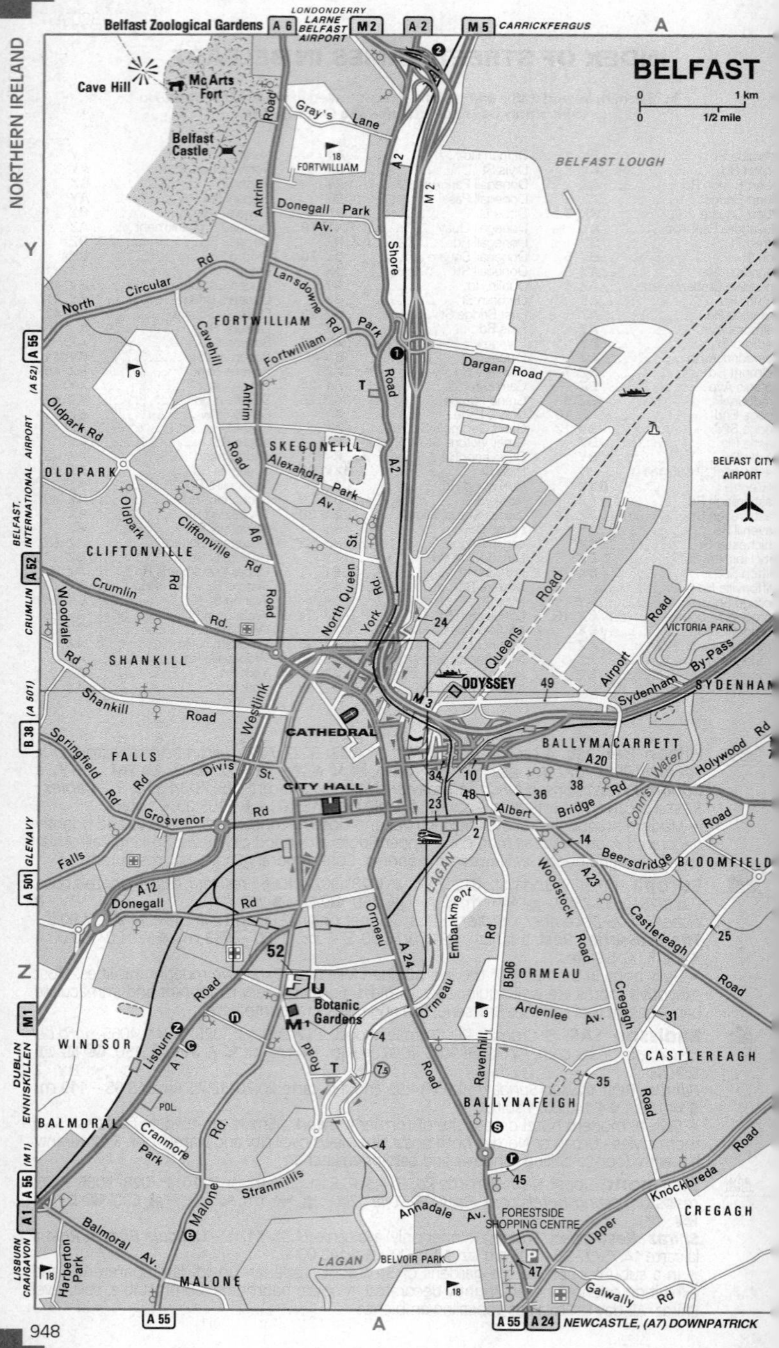
BELFAST
NORTHERN IRELAND
Belfast Zoological Gardens
LONDONDERRY
LARNE
BELFAST
AIRPORT
CARRICKFERGUS
Cave Hill
Mc Arts Fort
Belfast Castle
FORTWILLIAM
BELFAST LOUGH
FORTWILLIAM
SKEGONEILL
OLDPARK
CLIFTONVILLE
SHANKILL
FALLS
CATHEDRAL
CITY HALL
ODYSSEY
BALLYMACARRETT
SYDENHAM
VICTORIA PARK
BELFAST CITY AIRPORT
BLOOMFIELD
ORMEAU
CASTLEREAGH
BALLYNAFEIGH
WINDSOR
BALMORAL
MALONE
CREGAGH
Botanic Gardens
FORESTSIDE SHOPPING CENTRE
BELVOIR PARK
LAGAN
NEWCASTLE, (A7) DOWNPATRICK
BELFAST. INTERNATIONAL AIRPORT
CRUMLIN
GLENAVY
DUBLIN ENNISKILLEN
LISBURN CRAIGAVON

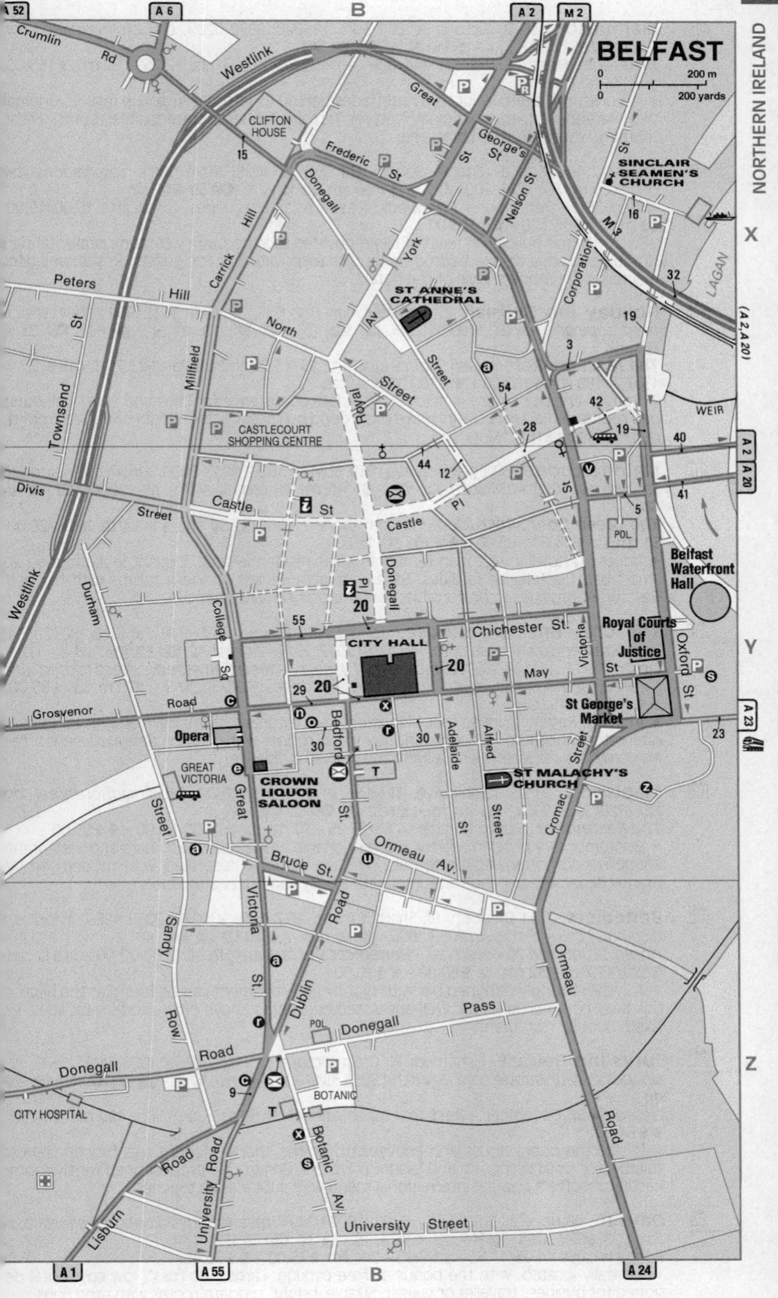
BELFAST
0 200 m
0 200 yards
A 52
A 6
B
A 2
M 2
Crumlin Rd
Westlink
CLIFTON HOUSE
Great George's St
Frederic St
Donegall St
York St
Nelson St
SINCLAIR SEAMEN'S CHURCH
M 3
X
LAGAN
Corporation St
Carrick Hill
Peters Hill
Townsend St
Millfield
North Street
ST ANNE'S CATHEDRAL
Royal Av
(A 2, A 20)
WEIR
CASTLECOURT SHOPPING CENTRE
Divis Street
Castle St
Castle Pl
Victoria St
A 2
A 20
POL
Belfast Waterfront Hall
Durham St
College Sq
Donegall Pl
Chichester St.
Royal Courts of Justice
CITY HALL
May St
Oxford St
Y
Grosvenor Road
St George's Market
A 23
Opera
GREAT VICTORIA
Great Victoria Street
CROWN LIQUOR SALOON
Bedford St.
Adelaide St
Alfred Street
ST MALACHY'S CHURCH
Cromac Street
Ormeau Av.
Bruce St.
Sandy Row
Dublin Road
Ormeau Road
Donegall Pass
Z
Donegall Road
CITY HOSPITAL
BOTANIC
Botanic Av.
Lisburn Road
University Road
University Street
A 1
A 55
A 24
15
16
32
19
3
54
42
28
19
40
44
12
41
5
20
55
20
29
20
30
30
23
9

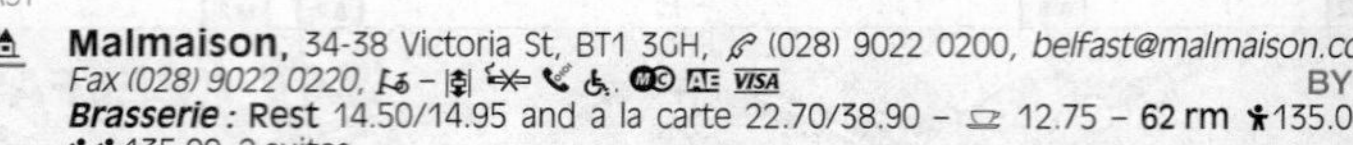

Malmaison, 34-38 Victoria St, BT1 3GH, ☎ (028) 9022 0200, *belfast@malmaison.co* *Fax (028) 9022 0220,* – – BY
Brasserie : **Rest** 14.50/14.95 and a la carte 22.70/38.90 – ☐ 12.75 – **62 rm** ✝135.00 ✝✝135.00, 2 suites.
◆ An unstuffy, centrally located hotel hides behind its intricate Victorian façade. Origina two warehouses, many original features remain. Modern, comfortable rooms. Frenc themed, wood-furnished brasserie.

Tensq, 10 Donegall Square South, BT1 5JD, ☎ (028) 9024 1001, *reservations@te quare.co.uk, Fax (028) 9024 3210* – , rm, . VISA. BY
closed 25-26 December – ***Porcelain :*** **Rest** - Asian specialities - a la carte 15.00/19.00 **22 rm** ☐ ✝160.00 – ✝✝160.00.
◆ Victorian mill building in heart of city renovated to a thoroughly contemporary standar Notably spacious deluxe bedrooms. Access to private bar for guests. Restaurant déc maintains the modern style of the hotel.

Holiday Inn Belfast, 22 Ormeau Ave, BT2 8HS, ☎ (028) 9032 8511, *belfast@ich telsgroup.com, Fax (028) 9062 6546,* , , – , rm, – 600. VISA. BY
The Junction : **Rest** *(closed Sunday lunch)* 11.95/15.00 and a la carte 21.70/25.15 **s.** ♀ – 13.95 – **168 rm** ✝160.00 – ✝✝160.00, 2 suites.
◆ Convenient city-centre location, up-to-date conference facilities and trim, well-equi ped rooms in modern colours make this a good business choice. Plenty of choice from th menu of modern cooking.

Malone Lodge, 60 Eglantine Ave, BT9 6DY, ☎ (028) 9038 8000, *info@malonelodgeh tel.com, Fax (028) 9038 8088,* , – , rm, rest, – 120. VISA AZ
The Green Door : **Rest** *(closed Sunday dinner)* 14.50/22.50 and a la carte 18.50/26.00 **51 rm** ☐ ✝95.00/105.00 – ✝✝109.00/119.00.
◆ Imposing hotel in Victorian terrace in quiet residential area. Elegant lobby lounge an smart bar. Conference facilities. Basement gym. Stylish, modern rooms with big bed Restaurant provides a comfortable, contemporary environment.

The Crescent Townhouse, 13 Lower Crescent, BT7 1NR, ☎ (028) 9032 334 *info@crescenttownhouse.com, Fax (028) 9032 0646* – rest, . VISA. BZ
closed 11-13 July, 25-26 December and 1 January – ***Metro Brasserie :*** **Rest** *(closed lunc Saturday and Sunday)* 14.50 (dinner) and a la carte 17.95/30.20 ♀ – **17 rm** ☐ ✝85.00 ✝✝125.00/145.00.
◆ Intimate Regency house that blends original features with modern amenities. Relaxe discreet atmosphere. Spacious and luxurious rooms with interior designed period fee Modern classic brasserie with a lively and relaxed ambience.

Madison's, 59-63 Botanic Ave, BT7 1JL, ☎ (028) 9050 9800, *info@madisonshotel.con Fax (028) 9050 9808* – , rm, rest, . VISA. BZ
The Restaurant : **Rest** a la carte 14.65/23.95 – **35 rm** ☐ ✝75.00/80.00 – ✝✝95.00.
◆ Contemporary hotel in a lively and fashionable area packed with bars and restaurant Spacious bedrooms with up-to-date facilities. Brightly decorated with modern art. V brantly decorated bar and restaurant with a busy and buzzy atmosphere.

Benedicts, 7-21 Bradbury Pl, Shaftsbury Sq, BT7 1RQ, ☎ (028) 9059 1999, *info@ben dictshotel.co.uk, Fax (028) 9059 1990* – , rest, . VISA. BZ
closed 12 July and 25 December – ***Benedicts Restaurant :*** **Rest** 12.00/22.00 and a la cart 12.20/23.70 ♀ – **32 rm** ☐ ✝60.00 – ✝✝70.00.
◆ A lively, strikingly designed bar with nightly entertainment can be found at the heart c this busy commercial hotel. Well-appointed bedrooms above offer modern facilities. Re laxed, popular restaurant.

Jurys Inn Belfast, Fisherwick Pl, Great Victoria St, BT2 7AP, ☎ (028) 9053 3500, *jur sinnbelfast@jurysdoyle.com, Fax (028) 9053 3511* – , rm, – 30. VISA BY
closed 24-26 December – **Rest** (bar lunch)/dinner 17.50 **s.** – ☐ 8.50 – **190 rm** ✝84.00 ✝✝84.00.
◆ Beside the opera house and convenient for the shops. Modern and functional hote suitable for both corporate and leisure travellers. Generously proportioned family room Restaurant offers popular international menu with subtle Asian touches.

Days H., 40 Hope St, BT12 5EE, ☎ (028) 9024 2494, *reservations@dayshotelbelfast.co.uk Fax (028) 9024 2495* – , rest, – 30. VISA. BY
Rest a la carte 14.95/17.85 – ☐ 7.95 – **244 rm** ✝75.00 – ✝✝75.00.
◆ Centrally located, with the bonus of free parking. Large, "no frills", low cost hotel de signed for business traveller or tourist. Sizable, bright, modern rooms with mod cons.

Ravenhill House without rest., 690 Ravenhill Rd, BT6 0BZ, ℘ (028) 9020 7444, *info@ravenhillhouse.com, Fax (028) 9028 2590* – P. VISA. AZ s
closed 1 week Christmas – **5 rm** 42.00/50.00 – 65.00.
◆ Personally run detached 19C house, attractively furnished in keeping with its age. The largely organic breakfast is a highlight. Good sized rooms with bold shades predominant.

Ash Rowan Town House, 12 Windsor Ave, BT9 6EE, ℘ (028) 9066 1758, *Fax (028) 9066 3227,* – P. VISA. AZ c
closed 22 December-4 January – **Rest** (by arrangement) 30.00 – **5 rm** 54.00/66.00 – 96.00.
◆ Late 19C house in quiet tree-lined avenue. Personally run; interestingly "cluttered" interior. Comfy conservatory sitting room. Well-judged bedrooms with thoughtful touches.

The Old Rectory, 148 Malone Rd, BT9 5LH, ℘ (028) 9066 7882, *info@anoldrectory.co.uk, Fax (028) 9068 3759,* – P. AZ e
closed Easter and Christmas-New Year – **Rest** (by arrangement) 18.50 – **5 rm** 36.00/45.00 – 65.00.
◆ Former Victorian rectory in residential area; period charm retained. Attractive drawing room. Traditionally furnished rooms. Hot Irish whiskey served as guests retire to bed.

Roseleigh House without rest., 19 Rosetta Park, BT6 0DL, South : 1 ½ m. by A 24 (Ormeau Rd) ℘ (028) 9064 4414, *info@roseleighhouse.co.uk* – P. VISA. AZ r
closed Christmas and New Year – **9 rm** 40.00/50.00 – 60.00.
◆ Imposing Victorian house close to the Belvoir Park golf course and in a fairly quiet residential suburb. Brightly decorated and well-kept bedrooms with modern amenities.

Restaurant Michael Deane, 34-40 Howard St, BT1 6PF, ℘ (028) 9033 1134, *info@michaeldeane.co.uk, Fax (028) 9056 0001* – . AE VISA BY n
closed 8-14 July, Christmas and Sunday-Tuesday – **Rest** (dinner only) 43.00 – (see also ***Deanes Brasserie*** below).
Spec. Pan-fried scallops with black pudding, potato bread and cauliflower purée. Beef fillet with foie gras, stuffed vine tomato with shin of beef stew. Chocolate fondant with vanilla ice cream and butterscotch sauce.
◆ Elegant 1st floor restaurant with rich, plush décor. Polished and professional service by approachable team. Concise menu of refined, classically based modern Irish dishes.

Roscoff Brasserie, 7-11 Linenhall St, BT2 8AA, ℘ (028) 9031 1150, *Fax (028) 9031 1151* – . AE VISA BY r
closed 12-13 July, 25 December, 1 January, Sunday and Saturday lunch – **Rest** 15.25/19.50 (lunch) and a la carte 27.50/39.00.
◆ Not your typical brasserie - more formal and a little quieter than most, but stylish and modern. Confidently prepared modish cooking with classic base. Good value lunches.

James Street South, 21 James Street South, BT2 7GA, ℘ (028) 9043 4310, *info@jamesstreetsouth.co.uk, Fax (028) 9043 4310* – . AE VISA BY o
closed 12-13 July, 25-26 December and Sunday lunch – **Rest** 15.50 (lunch) and a la carte 26.75/36.50.
◆ Tucked away down back alley in heart of the city. 19C façade hides distinctly modish interior. Good value menus; modern cooking based upon well-sourced, fine quality produce.

Aldens, 229 Upper Newtownards Rd, BT4 3JF, East : 2 m. on A 20 ℘ (028) 9065 0079, *info@aldensrestaurant.com, Fax (028) 9065 0032* – . AE VISA
closed 1 week July, Saturday lunch, Sunday and Bank Holidays – **Rest** (booking essential) 21.95 (dinner) and a la carte 16.00/21.00.
◆ Personally run, spacious and contemporary restaurant in "up-and-coming" suburb. Extensive selection of confident, modern dishes. Moderately priced midweek menu also offered.

Cayenne, 7 Ascot House, Shaftesbury Sq, BT2 7DB, ℘ (028) 9033 1532, *reservations@cayennerestaurant.com, Fax (028) 9026 1575* – . AE VISA BZ r
closed 25 December, 1 January, 12 July and lunch Saturday and Sunday – **Rest** (booking essential) 15.50 (lunch) and a la carte 19.95/36.45.
◆ Striking modern artwork and a lively atmosphere feature in this busy, relaxed and stylish restaurant. Carefully prepared selection of creative Asian influenced dishes.

Shu, 253 Lisburn Rd, BT9 7EN, ℘ (028) 9038 1655, *eat@shu-restaurant.com, Fax (028) 9068 1632* – 24. AE VISA AZ z
closed 1 January, 11-12 July, 24-25 December and Sunday – **Rest** a la carte 18.25/28.75.
◆ Trendy, modern restaurant on the Lisburn Road. Converted from terraced houses, it is spacious and uncluttered with neutral and black décor. Eclectic, contemporary dishes.

The Wok, 126 Great Victoria St, BT2 7BG, ℘ (028) 9023 3828 – . VISA BZ a
closed 25-26 December and lunch Saturday-Sunday – **Rest** - Chinese - 17.00/23.00 (dinner) and a la carte 15.00/21.50.
◆ Smart, modern Chinese restaurant with pleasant ambience. Menus feature classic interpretations and less well-known authentic dishes: most regions of China are represented.

Deanes Brasserie, 36-40 Howard St, BT1 6PF, ✆ (028) 9056 0000, *info@michaeldeane.co.uk, Fax (028) 9056 0001* – ▤. MC AE VISA BY
closed 8-14 July, Christmas and Sunday – **Rest** 15.00 (lunch) and a la carte 21.00/33.00 ♀.
◆ Ornately decorated, lively and modern street level brasserie continues to attract a loyal regular following. Robust and cosmopolitan cooking with a traditional Irish base.

Nick's Warehouse, 35-39 Hill St, BT1 2LB, ✆ (028) 9043 9690, *info@nickswarehouse.co.uk, Fax (028) 9023 0514* – ▤. MC AE ⓓ VISA BX
closed 2 days Easter, 1 May, 12 July, 1 January, Saturday lunch, Monday dinner and Sunday – **Rest** a la carte 15.80/32.25 ♀.
◆ Built in 1832 as a bonded whiskey store. On two floors, the ground floor Anix is relaxed and buzzy. Upstairs more formal. Well informed service of an eclectic menu.

at Belfast International Airport *West : 15½ m. by A 52* – **AY** – ✉ *Belfast.*

Park Plaza Belfast, Aldergrove, BT29 4ZY, ✆ (028) 9445 7000, *reception@parkplazabelfast.com, Fax (028) 9442 3500* – |♦|, ⇔ rm, ▤ ♿ P – 🏛 250. MC AE ⓓ VISA. ✻
Circles **: Rest** (booking essential) (buffet lunch)/dinner 20.00 s. – ☕ 12.00 – **106 rm** ☕ ✝105.00 – ✝✝120.00, 2 suites.
◆ Imposingly up-to-date hotel with sun-filled lobby, 50 metres from terminal entrance. Terrace, secluded garden, cocktail bar; conference facilities. Distinctively modern rooms. Formal restaurant with smart, cosmopolitan ambience.

The ✿ award is the crème de la crème. This is awarded to restaurants which are really worth travelling miles for!

BELFAST INTERNATIONAL AIRPORT (Aerphort Béal Feirste) *Antrim* 712 N 4 – *see Belfast.*

BELLEEK (Béal Leice) *Fermanagh* 712 H 4.
Belfast 117 – Londonderry 56.

Carlton, Main St, BT93 3FX, ✆ (028) 6865 8282, *reception@hotelcarlton.co.uk, Fax (028) 6865 9005* – ⇔ rm, P – 🏛 100. MC AE VISA. ✻
closed 24-25 December – **Rest** (bar lunch Monday-Saturday)/dinner a la carte 11.00/23.00 – **35 rm** ☕ ✝60.00 – ✝✝90.00.
◆ Located in the heart of Ireland's Lake District, bordering the river Erne and ideal for fishing enthusiasts. Bedrooms are in soft pastel colours and most have river views. Dine on fresh fish from Donegal at the Saimer, whilst admiring the river views.

BUSHMILLS (Muileann na Buaise) *Antrim* 712 M 2 *Ireland G.* – ✉ *Bushmills.*
Exc. : *Causeway Coast*** : *Giant's Causeway**** *(Hamilton's Seat ≤**), Carrick-a-rede Rope Bridge***, *Dunluce Castle*** *AC, Gortmore Viewpoint** – *Dunseverick Castle (≤**), Magilligan Strand**, *Downhill** *(Mussenden Temple***).*
⛳9 *Bushfoot, 50 Bushfoot Rd, Portballintrae ✆ (028) 2073 1317.*
Belfast 57 – Ballycastle 12 – Coleraine 10.

Bushmills Inn, 9 Dunluce Rd, BT57 8QG, ✆ (028) 2073 3000, *mail@bushmillsinn.com, Fax (028) 2073 2048* – ⇔ P – 🏛 40. MC AE VISA. ✻
closed 25 December – ***The Restaurant*** **: Rest** (carving lunch Sunday) (bar lunch Monday-Saturday)/dinner a la carte 25.00/31.00 ♀ – **32 rm** ☕ ✝68.00/148.00 – ✝✝138.00/158.00.
◆ Very characterful part 18C inn near famous whiskey distillery. Period features include turf fires, oil lamps, grand staircase and circular library. Rooms in house and mill. Try Irish coffee with Bushmills in restaurant overlooking courtyard.

Craig Park 🐦 without rest., 24 Carnbore Rd, BT57 8YF, Southeast : 2½ m. by B 66 and Ballycastle rd (B 17), off Billy rd ✆ (028) 2073 2496, *jan@craigpark.co.uk*, ≤, 🌳 – ⇔ P. MC VISA. ✻
closed Christmas and New Year – **3 rm** ☕ ✝35.00/40.00 – ✝✝65.00.
◆ Pleasant country house with views of Donegal mountains, Antrim Hills, dramatic coastal scenery. Communal breakfast room to start the day; immaculate bedrooms await at night.

Distillers Arms, 140 Main St, BT57 8QE, ✆ (028) 2073 1044, *simon@distillersarms.com, Fax (028) 2073 2843* – ⇔ P. MC VISA
closed 25-26 December – **Rest** *(closed lunch Monday-Friday in winter)* a la carte 15.00/25.00 ♀.
◆ Modern rusticity in village centre. Sit in squashy sofas in peat fired sitting area. Eat tasty dishes from frequently changing menus with a seasonal Irish base.

ARNLOUGH (Carnlach) *Antrim* 712 O 3.

Belfast 36 – *Ballymena* 16 – *Larne* 14.

Londonderry Arms, 20 Harbour Rd, BT44 0EU, ☎ (028) 2888 5255, *lda@glensofantrim.com, Fax (028) 2888 5263* – |♦|, ⇆ P – 🏃 120. MC AE ⊕ VISA. ⚒
closed 24-25 December – ***Tapestry Room :*** **Rest** *(booking essential in winter)* (bar lunch Monday-Saturday)/dinner a la carte 20.10/24.45 – **35 rm** ☐ ♦55.00 – ♦♦95.00.
◆ Built in 1848 as a coaching inn; the original architecture remains intact. Snug bar; pleasant meeting room. Paintings by local artists adorn the smartly furnished bedrooms. Cosy and traditional dining room.

ARRICKFERGUS (Carraig Fhearghais) *Antrim* 712 O 3.

18 35 North Rd ☎ (028) 9336 3713.
Heritage Plaza, Antrim Street ☎ (028) 9336 6455 (April-September), touristinfo@carrickfergus.org.
Belfast 11 – *Ballymena* 25.

Clarion, 75 Belfast Rd, BT38 8PH, on A 2 ☎ (028) 9336 4556, *info@choicehotelsireland.ie, Fax (028) 9335 1620* – |♦|, ⇆ rm, ▤ rest, ☎ ♿ P – 🏃 470. MC AE VISA. ⚒
closed 25 December – ***Camerons :*** **Rest** 21.00 and a la carte 12.40/22.90 **s.** ♀ – **64 rm** ☐ ♦67.50 – ♦♦82.50.
◆ A large, purpose-built hotel with trim, neatly furnished bedrooms; some suites have jacuzzis and views of Belfast Lough; the Scottish coastline can be seen on a clear day. Expect seafood specialities on à la carte menus.

ARRY BRIDGE *Fermanagh* 712 J 5 – ✉ *Lisbellaw.*

Belfast 80 – *Dundalk* 62 – *Londonderry* 60.

Aghnacarra House ✈, BT94 5HX, ☎ (028) 6638 7077, *normaensor@talk21.com, Fax (028) 6638 5811,* ✈, ⚘ – P. MC VISA. ⚒
mid March-mid October – **Rest** (by arrangement) 10.00 – **7 rm** ☐ ♦31.00 – ♦♦50.00.
◆ Overlooks the Erne; path leads to reed-fringed pool, ideal for fishing enthusiasts - bait and tackle room facilities available; photos of catches on the wall. Simple rooms. A neat, spacious dining room with views of gardens and lake.

ASTLEWELLAN *Down* 712 O 5 – *pop. 2 496.*

Belfast 32 – *Downpatrick* 12 – *Newcastle* 4.

Slieve Croob Inn ✈, 119 Clanvaraghan Rd, BT31 9LA, North : 5½ m. by A 25 off B 175 ☎ (028) 4377 1412, *info@slievecroobinn.com, Fax (028) 4377 1162,* ⩽, ⚘, ⚐ – ☎ P – 🏃 80. MC AE VISA. ⚒
– **Rest** *(closed Monday-Wednesday October-March)* (bar lunch Monday-Saturday)/dinner 22.95 and a la carte 11.65/22.15 **s** – **7 rm** ☐ ♦40.00 – ♦♦75.00.
◆ Pleasant inn in stunningly attractive mountainous area with panoramic sea views. Modern, rustic style. Appealing rooms with simple comforts. Peace and quiet aplenty. Roof timbers and exceptionally fine views in open, buzzy dining room.

OLERAINE (Cúil Raithin) *Londonderry* 712 L 2 *Ireland G. – pop. 56 315.*

Exc. : *Antrim Glens★★★ – Murlough Bay★★ (Fair Head ⩽★★), Glenariff Forest Park★★ AC (Waterfall★★), Glenariff★, Glendun★ – Causeway Coast★★ : Giant's Causeway★★★ (Hamilton's Seat ⩽★★) – Carrick-a-rede Rope Bridge★★ – Dunluce Castle★★ AC – Dunseverick Castle (⩽★★) – Gortmore Viewpoint★ – Magilligan Strand★ – Downhill★ (Mussenden Temple★).*
18, 9 Castlerock, Circular Rd ☎ (028) 7084 8314 – 9 Brown Trout, 209 Agivey Rd ☎ (028) 7086 8209.
Railway Rd ☎ (028) 7034 4723, colerainetic@btconnect.com.
Belfast 53 – *Ballymena* 25 – *Londonderry* 31 – *Omagh* 65.

Bushtown House, 283 Drumcroone Rd, BT51 3QT, South : 2½ m. on A 29 ☎ (028) 7035 8367, *reception@bushtownhotel.com, Fax (028) 7032 0909,* Fō, ⬚, ⚘ – ♿ P – 🏃 250. MC VISA
closed 26 December – **Rest** (bar lunch Monday-Saturday)/dinner and a la carte 14.15/21.50 **s.** – **39 rm** ☐ ♦55.00 – ♦♦80.00.
◆ Set in mature gardens on outskirts of university town. Indoors, comfortable and homely with impressive fitness suite. Rooms in co-ordinated patterned fabrics, muted colours. Intimately lit, cosy restaurant with farmhouse chairs and pine tables.

Brown Trout Golf and Country Inn, 209 Agivey Rd, Aghadowey, BT51 4A Southeast : 9 m. on A 54 ☎ (028) 7086 8209, *bill@browntroutinn.com, Fax (028) 7086 887* – rest, P – 40. MC AE VISA
Rest a la carte 15.00/20.00 – **19 rm** ☐ 55.00/70.00 – 70.00/90.00.
◆ A farm and blacksmith's forge was here in 1600s; now an inn well set up for those wit an active disposition - fishing, golf, horseriding are on hand. Modern rooms in annex Timbered roof in traditionally styled restaurant.

Greenhill House without rest., 24 Greenhill Rd, Aghadowey, BT51 4EU, South : 9 r by A 29 on B 66 ☎ (028) 7086 8241, *greenhill.house@btinternet.com, Fax (028) 7086 836* – P. MC AE VISA.
March-October – **6 rm** ☐ 35.00 – 55.00.
◆ An agreeably clean-lined Georgian house with large windows overlooking fields. Gam and course fishing available locally. Neat bedrooms replete with extra touches.

COOKSTOWN (An Chorr Chríochach) *Tyrone* 712 L 4 *Ireland G.*

Env. : *Ardboe Cross*★, *E : 4 m. by B 73.*
Killymoon, 200 Killymoon Rd ☎ (028) 8676 3762.
The Burnavon, Burn Rd ☎ (028) 8676 6727, tic@cookstown.gov.uk.
Belfast 45 – Ballymena 27 – Londonderry 49.

Tullylagan Country House, 40B Tullylagan Rd, BT80 8UP, South : 4 m. by A ☎ (028) 8676 5100, *reservations@tullylagan.fsnet.co.uk, Fax (028) 8676 1715*, P – 180. MC AE VISA.
closed 24-26 December – **Rest** a la carte 15.85/25.15 **s.** – **15 rm** ☐ 49.95 – 69.90.
◆ Late Georgian classic villa in vast grounds; Tullylagan river flows through them. Indoor a wood-floored hall with sweeping staircase leads to stylishly decorated rooms. A t windowed dining room with paintings from owner's travels on the walls.

CRUMLIN (Cromghlinn) *Antrim* 712 N 4 – *pop. 2 697.*

Belfast 14 – Ballymena 20.

Caldhame Lodge without rest., 102 Moira Rd, Nutts Corner, BT29 4HG, Southeas 1 ¼ m. on A 26 ☎ (028) 9442 3099, *info@caldhamelodge.co.uk, Fax (028) 9442 3099*, P. MC AE VISA.
8 rm ☐ 38.00/45.00 – 60.00/65.00.
◆ Spic and span, with thoroughly polished, wood furnished hall, complete with granc father clock. Immaculately kept rooms in yellow and ivory; one has its own sauna.

DONAGHADEE (Domhnach Daoi) *Down* 712 P 4.

Warren Rd ☎ (028) 9188 3624.
Belfast 18 – Ballymena 44.

Grace Neill's, 33 High St, BT21 0AH, ☎ (028) 9188 4595, *neil@graceneills.cor Fax (028) 9188 9631*, – P. MC AE VISA
closed 12 July and 25 December – **Rest** a la carte approx 22.00.
◆ Reputedly the oldest pub in Ireland; origins date from 1611. Thoroughly traditional ba restaurant is stylish and elegant. Well-priced modern dishes using fresh ingredients.

Pier 36, 36 The Parade, BT21 0HE, ☎ (028) 9188 4466, *info@pier36.co.u Fax (028) 9188 4636*, – . MC AE VISA
closed 25 December – **Rest** - Seafood specialities - a la carte 12.00/30.00.
◆ Spacious pub located right on the harbour's edge. Appealing rustic feel with stor flooring, curios and wood panelling. Good, extensive menus with an unfussy seafood bas

DOWNPATRICK (Dún Pádraig) *Down* 712 O 4/5.

Belfast 23 – Newtownards 22 – Newry 31.

The Mill at Ballydugan, Drumcullen Rd, BT30 8HZ, Southwest : 2 ¼ m. by A 2 ☎ (028) 4461 3654, *info@ballyduganmill.com, Fax (028) 4483 9754*, – rm, P – 80. MC AE VISA.
closed 25-26 December – **Rest** *(closed Monday)* (bar lunch)/dinner 14.95/25.00 and a carte 16.00/28.40 – **11 rm** ☐ 55.00/65.00 – 75.00.
◆ Grand looking converted mill hotel, built in 1792 and exuding much charm and chara ter. Stone-faced café on ground floor. Bedrooms boast exposed beams and stone wall Rugged, rustic style of restaurant in keeping with hotel; waterwheel in bar.

Pheasants' Hill Farm without rest., 37 Killyleagh Rd, BT30 9BL, North : 3 m. on A 22 ☎ (028) 4461 7246, *info@pheasantshill.com, Fax (028) 4461 7246*, – P. VISA.
March-October – **4 rm** ☕ ★47.00/50.00 – ★★70.00/72.00.
◆ Purpose-built house surrounded by an organic smallholding with livestock which provides many ingredients for hearty breakfasts. Homely, pine furnished bedrooms.

DUNADRY (Dún Eadradh) *Antrim* 712 N 3 *Ireland G.*

Env. : *Antrim (Round tower★) NW : 4 m. by A 6.*
Exc. : *Crumlin : Talnotry Cottage Bird Garden★ AC, SW : 10½ m. by A 5, A 26 and A 52.*
Belfast 16 – Larne 18 – Londonderry 56.

Dunadry H. and Country Club, 2 Islandreagh Drive, BT41 2HA, ☎ (028) 9443 4343, *info@dunadry.com, Fax (028) 9443 3389*, – P – 600. VISA.
closed 25-26 December – ***The Mill Race Bistro*** : **Rest** a la carte 19.00/23.00 ♀ – ☕ 10.00 – **83 rm** ★110.00 – ★★135.00.
◆ Large house with modern, co-ordinated décor; furnished with locally crafted pieces. Rooms vary in size and style and all are well kept and comfortable. Simple bistro overlooking the millstream.

Good food without spending a fortune? Look out for the Bib Gourmand

DUNDRUM *Down* 712 O 5.

Belfast 29 – Downpatrick 9 – Newcastle 4.

Buck's Head Inn, 77 Main St, BT33 0LU, ☎ (028) 4375 1868, *buckshead1@aol.com, Fax (028) 4481 1033*, – . VISA.
closed 24-25 December and Mondays October-March – **Rest** - Seafood specialities - 15.50/24.50 ♀.
◆ Traditional bar tucked away on village high street. Interesting and well-cooked dishes with strong seafood base are served in a large rear conservatory with terrace views.

DUNGANNON (Dún Geanainn) *Tyrone* 712 L 4 *Ireland G.*

Env. : *The Argory★, S : 5 m. by A 29 and east by minor rd.*
Exc. : *Armagh★★ (St Patrick's Cathedral★ (Anglican), St Patrick's Cathedral★ (Roman Catholic), The Mall★, Armagh County Museum★ – Regimental Museum of the Royal Irish Fusiliers★, Navan Fort★), S : 12 m. by A 29.*
Belfast 42 – Ballymena 37 – Dundalk 47 – Londonderry 60.

Stangmore Country House, 65 Moy Rd, BT71 7DT, South : 2 m. on A 29 ☎ (028) 8772) 5600, *info@stangmorecountryhouse.com, Fax (028) 8772 6644*, – rest, P. VISA.
closed 8-17 July and 24 December-2 January – **Rest** *(closed Sunday)* (booking essential to non-residents) (dinner only) 22.50/25.95 **s.** – **9 rm** ☕ ★60.00 – ★★90.00/100.00.
◆ Small, Georgian style hotel with rural views, though main road is close at hand. Tastefully furnished lounge. Individually decorated rooms, some in a quiet rear courtyard. Extravagantly furnished dining room in warm, deep burgundy.

Grange Lodge, 7 Grange Rd, Moy, BT71 7EJ, Southeast : 3 ½ m. by A 29 ☎ (028) 8778 4212, *grangelodge@nireland.com, Fax (028) 8778 4313*, – P. VISA.
closed 20 December-1 February – **Rest** (by arrangement) 26.00 – **5 rm** ☕ ★55.00/59.00 – ★★78.00.
◆ Attractive Georgian country house surrounded by well-kept mature gardens with a peaceful ambience. Fine hospitality and period furnishings. Tastefully decorated bedrooms. Large dining room furnished with elegant antiques and fine tableware.

ENNISKILLEN (Inis Ceithleann) *Fermanagh* 712 J 4 *Ireland G. – pop. 11 436.*

Env. : *Castle Coole★★★ AC, SE : 1 m.*
Exc. : *NW : Lough Erne★★ : Cliffs of Magho Viewpoint★★★ AC – Devenish Island★ AC – White Island★ – Janus Figure★ – Tully Castle★ AC – Florence Court★★ AC, SW : 8 m. by A 4 and A 32 – Marble Arch Caves and Forest Nature Reserve★ AC, SW : 10 m. by A 4 and A 32.*
18 *Castlecoole ☎ (028) 6632 5250.*
Wellington Rd ☎ (028) 6632 3110, tourism@fermanagh.gov.uk.
Belfast 87 – Londonderry 59.

Manor House , Killadeas, BT94 1NY, North : 7½ m. by A 32 on B 82 (028) 686 2200, *info@manor-house-hotel.com, Fax (028) 6862 1545*, rm, – 400.
The Belleck : Rest 13.95/25.00 – **81 rm** ☆95.00 – ☆☆110.00.
♦ In a commanding position overlooking Lough Erne. Noted for fine Italian plasterwo evident in guest areas. Excellent conference facilities. Spacious, comfortable bedroom Classically appointed dining room featuring chandeliers and ornate plasterwork.

Cedars, BT94 1PG, North : 10 m. by A 32 on B 82 (028) 6862 1493, *info@cedarsgue house.com, Fax (028) 6862 8335*, – .
closed Christmas – ***Rectory Bistro :*** Rest *(closed Monday and Tuesday in winter)* (dinn only and Sunday lunch)/dinner a la carte 18.00/27.00 – **10 rm** ☆48.00 – ☆☆75.00/85.0
♦ Good value, converted 19C former rectory with pleasant gardens. Exudes impression spaciousness; country style décor. Snug sitting room. Individually styled bedrooms. Cou try style bistro serves hearty cuisine.

Rossahilly House , BT94 2FP, North : 4½ m. by A 32 off B 82 (028) 6632 235 *info@rossahilly.com, Fax (028) 6632 0277*, Lower lough Erne, – .
Rest (by arrangement) 35.00 – **7 rm** ☆40.00 – ☆☆70.00.
♦ Superbly sited 1930s guesthouse, with supreme views of Lower Lough Erne. Comfort ble sitting room and conservatory. Individually styled rooms, one with its own sitting roor

Café Merlot (at Blake's of the Hollow), 6 Church St, BT74 7EJ, (028) 6632 0918, .
closed 25 December and dinner Monday-Tuesday – **Rest** 14.95/17.95 and a la car 17.95/25.50 **s.**
♦ Pleasant basement restaurant to the rear of Blake's of the Hollow pub. Vaulted ceilin and ornate stone work surroundings; dine on interesting menus with international scope

---

HILLSBOROUGH (Cromghlinn) *Down* 712 N 4 *Ireland G.*

See : *Town*★ – *Fort*★.
Exc. : *The Argory*★, *W : 25 m. by A 1 and M 1.*
Courthouse (028) 9268 9717, hillsborough@nitic.net.
Belfast 12.

The Plough Inn, 3 The Square, BT26 6AG, (028) 9268 2985, *Fax (028) 9268 2472* –
closed 25 December – **Rest** a la carte 15.00/25.00 – ***Bar Retro :*** **Rest** *(closed Monday)* a carte 18.00/26.00 .
♦ Characterful looking pub in lovely small town. Traditionally decorated bistro-style dinin in two rooms. Very large portions of good Irish pub cooking. Bar food available.

at Annahilt *Southeast : 4 m. on B 177 – Hillsborough.*

Fortwilliam without rest., 210 Ballynahinch Rd, BT26 6BH, Northwest : ¼ m. on B 17 (028) 9268 2255, *info@fortwilliamcountryhouse.com, Fax (028) 9268 9608*, –
4 rm ☆45.00 – ☆☆65.00.
♦ Large house on a working farm with attractive gardens. Charming hospitality amid traditional farmhouse surroundings. Characterful bedrooms with a range of extras.

The Pheasant, 410 Upper Ballynahinch Rd, BT26 6NR, North : 1 m. on Lisburn (028) 9263 8056, *Fax (028) 9263 8026* –
closed 12-13 July and 25-26 December – **Rest** a la carte 20.00/40.00 .
♦ Simple rustic feel with peat fires and wood floors. Extensive menu offers hearty portio of classic country dishes. Private dining room available. Popular with locals.

HOLYWOOD (Ard Mhic Nasca) *Down* 712 O 4 *Ireland G. – pop. 9 252.*

Env. : *Cultra : Ulster Folk and Transport Museum*★★ *AC, NE : 1 m. by A 2.*
Holywood, Nuns Walk, Demesne Rd (028) 9042 2138.
Belfast 7 – Bangor 6.

Culloden, Bangor Rd, BT18 0EX, East : 1½ m. on A 2 (028) 9042 1066, *res@cull.hastir shotel.com, Fax (028) 9042 6777*, rm, rest, – 100
Mitre : **Rest** (dinner only and Sunday lunch)/dinner 35.00/42.50 **s.** – (see also ***Cultra In*** below) – 18.00 – **76 rm** ☆170.00 – ☆☆210.00, 3 suites.
♦ Part Victorian Gothic manor, originally built as an official residence for the Bishops Down. Top class comfort amid characterful interiors. Smart, comfortable bedrooms. Th Mitre has a smart and well-kept air.

Rayanne House, 60 Demesne Rd, BT18 9EX, by High St and Downshire Rd ✆ (028) 9042 5859, *rayannehouse@hotmail.com, Fax (028) 9042 5859*, ≤, – ⇎ P. MC VISA.
closed 24 December-2 January – **Rest** (booking essential) 27.50/37.50 ♀ – **8 rm** ☕ ✝65.00/75.00 – ✝✝85.00/90.00.
◆ Redbrick house with attractive views of the town. Very personally run with smart, alluring interiors. Bedrooms are each individually styled and feature hand-painted murals. Warm, attentive service epitomises the family run restaurant.

Beech Hill without rest., 23 Ballymoney Rd, Craigantlet, BT23 4TG, Southeast : 4½ m. by A 2 on Craigantlet rd ✆ (028) 9042 5892, *info@beech-hill.net, Fax (028) 9042 5892*, ≤, – ⇎ P. MC VISA
3 rm ☕ ✝45.00/50.00 – ✝✝70.00/80.00.
◆ Country house in a rural location. Pleasant clutter of trinkets and antiques in communal areas which include a conservatory. Well-kept, traditionally styled bedrooms.

Fontana, 61A High St, BT18 9AE, ✆ (028) 9080 9908, *collenbennett@btopenworld.com, Fax (028) 9080 9912*, – MC VISA
closed 25-26 December, 1 January, 12 July, Monday, Sunday dinner and Saturday lunch – **Rest** (booking essential) 17.75 (lunch) and a la carte 21.85/32.85 ♀.
◆ Vividly coloured and contemporarily styled dining room. Friendly attentive staff. Tasty, unfussy, modern Irish food with refreshing Californian and Spanish influences.

Cultra Inn (at Culloden H.), Cultra Station Rd, BT18 0EX, East : 1½ m. on A 2 ✆ (028) 9042 5840, *Fax (028) 9042 6777*, – ⇎ P. MC AE ⊙ VISA.
closed 25 December – **Rest** a la carte 13.00/23.20.
◆ In the grounds of the Culloden Hotel, this whitewashed pub has a pleasant timbered roof and flagged floor. Enjoy well prepared, tasty Irish classics in front of the log fire.

ARNE (Latharna) *Antrim* 712 O 3 *Ireland G. – pop. 30 832.*
Env. : *SE : Island Magee (Ballylumford Dolmen★).*
Exc. : *NW : Antrim Glens★★★ – Murlough Bay★★ (Fair Head ≤★★), Glenariff Forest Park★★ AC (Waterfall★★), Glenariff★, Glendun★ – Carrickfergus (Castle★★ – St Nicholas' Church★), SW : 15 m. by A 2.*
18 *Cairndhu, 192 Coast Rd, Ballygally ✆ (028) 2858 3248.*
to Fleetwood (Stena Line) daily (8 h) – to Cairnryan (P & O Irish Sea) 3-5 daily (1 h/ 2 h 15 mn).
Narrow Gauge Rd ✆ (028) 2826 0088.
Belfast 23 – Ballymena 20.

Manor House without rest., 23 Olderfleet Rd, Harbour Highway, BT40 1AS, ✆ (028) 2827 3305, *welcome@themanorguesthouse.com, Fax (028) 2826 0505* – ⇎ P. MC VISA.
closed 25-26 December – **8 rm** ☕ ✝25.00 – ✝✝45.00.
◆ Spacious Victorian terraced house two minutes from ferry terminal. Well-furnished lounge with beautifully varnished wood floors. Small breakfast room. Cosy, homely bedrooms.

MAVADY (Léim an Mhadaidh) *Londonderry* 712 L 2.
9 *Benone Par Three, 53 Benone Ave, Benone ✆ (028) 7775 0555.*
Council Offices, 7 Connell St ✆ (028) 7776 0307, tourism@limavady.gov.uk.
Belfast 62 – Ballymena 39 – Coleraine 13 – Londonderry 17 – Omagh 50.

Radisson SAS Roe Park H. & Golf Resort, Roe Park, BT49 9LB, West : ½ m. on A 2 ✆ (028) 7772 2222, *reservations@radissonroepark.com, Fax (028) 7772 2313*, , , , 18, , – , ⇎ rm, , P – 440. MC AE ⊙ VISA.
Greens : **Rest** *(closed Sunday and Monday except Bank Holidays)* (dinner only and Sunday lunch) a la carte 21.95/28.95 **s.** ♀ – ***The Coach House*** : **Rest** a la carte 16.35/25.80 **s.** ♀ – **117 rm** ☕ ✝90.00/100.00 – ✝✝130.00/155.00, 1 suite.
◆ A golfer's idyll with academy and driving range in the grounds of Roe Park. Good leisure centre, plus creche and beauty salon. Modern bedrooms. Greens is formal in character with menu to match. Brasserie feel, plus beams and open fire, in The Coach House.

Lime Tree, 60 Catherine St, BT49 9DB, ✆ (028) 7776 4300, *info@limetreerest.com* – MC AE VISA
closed 2 weeks late February-early March, 12 July, Sunday and Monday – **Rest** (dinner only) 19.95 and a la carte 21.40/31.00.
◆ Simple eatery run by husband and wife. Local produce in satisfying staples: lamb casserole, Donegal fish crêpe, home-made cheesecake. Early dinners served.

LISBANE (An Lios Bán) *Down* 712 O 4 – ✉ *Comber.*
Belfast 14 – Newtownards 9 – Saintfield 7.

Anna's House without rest., Tullynagee, 35 Lisbarnett Rd, Comber, BT23 6AV West : ½ m. ☎ (028) 9754 1566, *anna@annashouse.com, Fax (028) 9754 1566*, ≤, ...
closed Christmas-New Year – **3 rm** ☐ ★45.00 – ★★70.00/80.00.
◆ 100 year old farmhouse with its own lake and panoramic rural views, particularly fro the huge lounge windows. Simple, comfortable bedrooms with lovely countryside vistas.

LONDONDERRY (Doire) *Londonderry* 712 K 2/3 *Ireland G. – pop. 72 334.*
See : *Town★ – City Walls and Gates★★ – Long Tower Church★ – Tower Museum★.*
Env. : *Grianan of Aileach★★ (≤★★) (Republic of Ireland) NW : 5 m. by A 2 and N 13.*
Exc. : *SE : by A 6 – Sperrin Mountains★ : Ulster-American Folk Park★★ – Glenshane Pass (※★★) – Sawel Mountain Drive★ (≤★★) – Roe Valley Country Park★ – Beaghmore Stor Circles★ – Ulster History Park★ – Oak Lough Scenic Road★.*
18, 9 *City of Derry, 49 Victoria Rd ☎ (01) 504 46369.*
Eglinton Airport : ☎ (028) 7181 0784, E : 6 m. by A 2.
44 Foyle St ☎ (028) 7126 7284, info@derry.visitor.com.
Belfast 70 – Dublin 146.

City, Queens Quay, BT48 7AS, ☎ (028) 7136 5800, *res@derry-gsh.cor Fax (028) 7136 5801*, ≤, ... rm, ... rest, ... – 250.
closed 24-26 December – ***Thompson's on the River :*** Rest (carving lunch)/dinner 21.5 and a la carte 20.00/28.40 **s.** – ☐ 10.00 – **144 rm** ★140.00 – ★★140.00, 1 suite.
◆ Hotel in purpose-built modern style. Well located, close to the city centre and the qua Smart rooms ordered for the business traveller. Useful conference facilities. Modern re taurant overlooks water; carvery lunch very popular.

Tower, Butcher St, BT48 6HL, ☎ (028) 7137 1000, *reservations@tnd.. Fax (028) 7137 1234*, ... rm, ... rest, ... – 250.
closed 25-27 December – ***Bistro at the Tower :*** Rest (dinner only) a la carte 17.00/22.0 **s.** – **90 rm** ☐ ★99.00 – ★★129.00, 3 suites.
◆ The only hotel within the city walls. Stylish lobby with conveniently adjacent gym f guests. Smart rooms decorated with bright colour schemes. All very comfortable. Groun floor bistro with modern art on the walls.

Hastings Everglades, Prehen Rd, BT47 2NH, South : 1½ m. on A 5 ☎ (028) 7132 106 *info@egh.hastingshotels.com, Fax (028) 7134 9200* – ... rm, ... rest, ... – 500.
Satchmo : Rest (dinner only and Sunday lunch) 28.00 and a la carte 20.95/28.50 **s.** – **64 rm** ☐ ★70/90 – ★★90/120.
◆ This modern hotel on the banks of the Foyle makes a useful base for exploring the 1 city of Derry. Golf facilities nearby. Uniformly decorated rooms. Vibrant painting of Lou Armstrong hangs in eponymous restaurant.

Beech Hill Country House , 32 Ardmore Rd, BT47 3QP, Southeast : 3½ m. by A ☎ (028) 7134 9279, *info@beech-hill.com, Fax (028) 7134 5366*, ... rest, ... – 80.
closed 24-25 December – ***The Ardmore :*** Rest 17.95/27.95 and a la carte 25.85/37.40 – **25 rm** ☐ ★80.00 – ★★130.00, 2 suites.
◆ 18C country house, now personally run but once a US marine camp; one lounge is fille with memorabilia. Accommodation varies from vast rooms to more traditional, rural one Restaurant housed within conservatory and old billiard room. Fine garden and lake view.

Waterfoot H. & Country Club, 14 Clooney Rd, Caw Roundabout, BT47 6TB, Nort east : 3 ¾ m. on A 2 at junction with A 55 ☎ (028) 7134 5500, *info@thewaterfoot tel.co.uk, Fax (028) 7131 1006*, ... rm, ... – 100.
closed 24-26 December – **Rest** (grill rest.) a la carte 12.95/25.00 – **46 rm** ☐ ★75.00 ★★85.00.
◆ Behind the unassuming exterior there is much to recommend: good facilities, hu bar-cum-lounge and particularly spacious bedrooms. Also, well located on city's ring roa Capacious dining room overlooks the Foyle. Excellent value early evening menus.

Ramada H. Da Vinci's, 15 Culmore Rd, BT48 8JB, North : 1 m. following signs f Foyle Bridge ☎ (028) 7127 9111, *info@davincishotel.com, Fax (028) 7127 9222* – ... r
closed 25 December – ***The Grill Room :*** Rest (bar lunch)/dinner a la carte 14.50/18.50 – 7.95 – **65 rm** ★65.00 – ★★65.00.
◆ Modern purpose-built hotel at northern end of city's quayside close to major throu routes. Stylish lobby area. Large, atmospheric bar. Good sized, well-equipped bedroon Spacious restaurant has an elegant ambience.

Mandarin Palace, Lower Clarendon St, BT48 7AW, ✆ (028) 7137 3656, *stanley.lee1@btinternet.com, Fax (028) 7137 3636* – ▤. MC AE VISA
closed 25-26 December – **Rest** - Chinese - (dinner only and Sunday lunch)/dinner a la carte 15.50/24.00 **s.**
◆ Oriental restaurant, with good views of Foyle river and bridge. Smart staff oversee the service of unfussy, well-executed Chinese cuisine, featuring good value set menus.

IAGHERA (Machaire Rátha) *Londonderry* 712 L 3.
Belfast 40 – Ballymena 19 – Coleraine 21 – Londonderry 32.

Ardtara Country House, 8 Gorteade Rd, Upperlands, BT46 5SA, North : 3 ¼ m. by A 29 off B 75 ✆ (028) 7964 4490, *Fax (028) 7964 5080*, – rest, P. MC AE VISA.
The Restaurant : Rest (booking essential to non-residents) (lunch by arrangement)/dinner 24.00/30.00 **s.** – **8 rm** ☕ ✝55.00/75.00 – ✝✝110.00/150.00.
◆ 19C house with a charming atmosphere. The interior features "objets trouvés" collected from owner's travels; original fireplaces set off the individually styled bedrooms. Restaurant set in former billiard room with hunting mural and panelled walls.

We try to be as accurate as possible when giving room rates.
But prices are susceptible to change,
so please check rates when booking.

EWCASTLE (An Caisleán Nua) *Down* 712 O 5 *Ireland G. – pop. 7 214.*
Env. : *Castlewellan Forest Park★★ AC, NW : 4 m. by A 50 – Dundrum Castle★ AC, NE : 4 m. by A 2 – Downpatrick (Down Cathedral★ – Down County Museum★), NE : by A 2.*
Exc. : *SW : Mourne Mountains★★ : Bryansford, Tollymore Forest Park★ AC – Silent Valley Reservoir★ (<★) – Spelga Pass and Dam★ – Kilbroney Forest Park (viewpoint★) – Struell Wells★, NE : 12 m. by A 2 – Ardglass★, NE : 18 m. by A 2.*
10-14 Central Promenade ✆ (028) 4372 2222, newcastletic@downdc.gov.uk.
Belfast 32 – Londonderry 101.

Slieve Donard, Downs Rd, BT33 0AH, ✆ (028) 4372 1066, *res@sdh.hastings.com, Fax (028) 4372 1166*, <, – P – 850. MC AE VISA
Oak : Rest 20.00/29.50 **s.** ♀ – ***Percy French :*** Rest a la carte 12.95/23.95 **s.** ♀ – **124 rm** ☕ ✝135.00/195.00 – ✝✝155.00/195.00.
◆ Victorian grand old lady with sea views. Domed lobby with an open fire, deep carpets and murals. Chaplins bar named after Charlie, who stayed here. Comfy rooms. Grand style dining in semi-panelled Oak. Percy French bar-restaurant in separate building.

Burrendale H. & Country Club, 51 Castlewellan Rd, BT33 0JY, North : 1 m. on A 50 ✆ (028) 4372 2599, *reservations@burrendale.com, Fax (028) 4372 2328*, – ▤ rest, P – 250. MC AE VISA.
Vine : Rest (dinner only and Sunday lunch) 25.50 ♀ – ***Cottage Kitchen :*** Rest a la carte 15.15/19.40 ♀ – **69 rm** ☕ ✝75.00 – ✝✝130.00, 1 suite.
◆ Set between the Mourne Mountains and Irish Sea, with the Royal Country Down Golf Course nearby. A well-maintained hotel with range of rooms from small to very spacious. Linen-clad Vine for traditional dining. Homely cooking to the fore at Cottage Kitchen.

EWRY (An tIúr) *Down* 712 M 5 *Ireland G. – pop. 87 058.*
See : *Bernish Rock Viewpoint★★.*
Town Hall, Bank Parade ✆ (028) 3026 8877.
Belfast 37 – Dundalk 16.

Canal Court, Merchants Quay, BT35 8HF, ✆ (028) 3025 1234, *manager@canalcourthotel.com, Fax (028) 3025 1177*, – ▤ rest, P – 500. MC AE VISA.
closed 25 December – ***Old Mill :*** Rest 16.00/32.00 and dinner a la carte – **50 rm** ☕ ✝65.00/80.00 – ✝✝130.00, 1 suite.
◆ Modern hotel in town centre overlooking canal. Dramatic lobby with huge stone staircase sweeping up to first floor. Characterful carvery pub. Large, well-equipped rooms. The Old Mill is a light and spacious fine dining restaurant overlooking the city.

Annahaia, Slieve Gullion Courtyard, Killeavy, BT35 8SW, Southwest : 6 ¼ m. by Dublin rd off B 113 ✆ (028) 3084 8084, *info@annahaia.com, Fax (028) 3084 8028* – P. MC AE VISA
closed January, 25 December, Monday-Wednesday and Sunday dinner – **Rest** (dinner only and Sunday lunch) 36.00.
◆ Former stable block with lovely courtyard. Modern restaurant has big windows, linen-clad tables and tasting menus balanced in terms of ingredients, flavours and combinations.

NEWTOWNARDS (Baile Nua na hArda) *Down* 712 O 4.

Belfast 10 – Bangor 144 – Downpatrick 22.

Edenvale House without rest., 130 Portaferry Rd, BT22 2AH, Southeast : 2 ¾ m. c A 20 ℘ (028) 9181 4881, *edenvalehouse@hotmail.com, Fax (028) 9182 6192*, ≤, – P. MO VISA
closed Christmas – **3 rm** ☕ ✝45.00/65.00 – ✝✝70.00.
◆ Attractive Georgian house with fine views of the Mourne Mountains. Elegant sittin room. Communal breakfasts featuring home-made bread and jams. Individually style rooms.

PORTAFERRY (Port an Pheire) *Down* 712 P 4 *Ireland G.*

See : *Aquarium*★.
Env. : *Castle Ward*★★ *AC, SW : 4 m. by boat and A 25.*
Exc. : *SE : Lecale Peninsula*★★ *– Struell Wells*★, *Quoile Pondage*★, *Ardglass*★, *Strangford*★ *Audley's Castle*★.
The Stables, Castle St ℘ *(028) 4272 9882 (Easter-September).*
Belfast 29 – Bangor 24.

Portaferry, 10 The Strand, BT22 1PE, ℘ (028) 4272 8231, *info@portaferryhotel.cor Fax (028) 4272 8999*, ≤ – MO AE VISA.
closed 24-25 December – **Rest** (bar lunch Monday-Saturday)/dinner a la carte 17.95/28.9 – **14 rm** ☕ ✝57.50/75.00 – ✝✝90.00/95.00.
◆ Formerly private dwellings, this personally run hotel dates from 18C. Located on Strang ford Lough, most rooms have waterside views. Lounge features Irish paintings. Simp dining room with strong emphasis on local produce.

The Narrows, 8 Shore Rd, BT22 1JY, ℘ (028) 4272 8148, *info@narrows.co.u Fax (028) 4272 8105*, ≤, – – 50. MO AE VISA.
Rest – (see ***The Restaurant*** below) – **13 rm** ☕ ✝45.00/90.00 – ✝✝90.00.
◆ At the mouth of Strangford Lough; two brothers have turned their father's home into stylish hotel. Outside, a walled garden, inside minimalist, hessian floored bedrooms.

The Restaurant (at The Narrows H.), 8 Shore Rd, BT22 1JY, ℘ (028) 4272 814 *Fax (028) 4272 8105*, ≤ – . MO AE VISA
restricted opening in winter – **Rest** a la carte 23.00/33.00 ♀.
◆ Seafood reigns supreme here, and this can be enjoyed while taking in the views of th Lough from the bistro-style, wooden floored dining room.

PORTBALLINTRAE (Port Bhaile an Trá) *Antrim* 712 M 2 *Ireland G.*

Env. : *Giant's Causeway*★★★, *E : 3 m. by A 2 – Benvarden*★, *S : 5 m. by B 66 – Dunlu Castle*★★, *W : 2 m. by A 2.*
Belfast 57 – Coleraine 11 – Portrush 5.

Bayview, 2 Bayhead Rd, BT57 8RZ, ℘ (028) 2073 4100, *info@bayviewhotelni.cor Fax (028) 2073 4330*, ≤ – P – 60. MO AE VISA.
Porthole : **Rest** a la carte approx 21.00 – **25 rm** ☕ ✝90.00/120.00 – ✝✝90.00/150.00.
◆ Situated in centre of pretty village and, as the name suggests, commanding good view of the bay. Well-equipped meeting room. Very comfy rooms, three in appealing 'turre Basement dining room with open, spacious feel.

PORTRUSH (Port Rois) *Antrim* 712 L 2 *Ireland G. – pop. 5 703.*

Exc. : *Causeway Coast*★★ : *Giant's Causeway*★★★ *(Hamilton's Seat* ≤★★*) – Carrick-a-ree Rope Bridge*★★ *– Dunluce Castle*★★ *AC – Dunseverick Castle (*≤★★*) – Gortmore Viewpoint – Magilligan Strand*★ *– Downhill*★ *(Mussenden Temple*★*).*
18, 18, 9 *Royal Portrush, Dunluce Rd* ℘ *(028) 7082 2311.*
Dunluce Centre, Sandhill Drive ℘ *(028) 7082 3333 (March-October), portrush@nitic.net*
Belfast 58 – Coleraine 4 – Londonderry 35.

Comfort, 73 Main St, BT56 8BN, ℘ (028) 7082 6100, *info@comforthotelportrush.cor Fax (028) 7082 6160*, ≤ – – 50. MO AE VISA.
closed 25 December – ***The Counties :*** **Rest** a la carte approx 21.00 – **50 rm** ☕ ✝80.00 ✝✝110.00.
◆ Located in the heart of town, but just two minutes' walk from blue flag beach. Plenty o small meeting rooms. Well-equipped bedrooms, many being useful for family group Simple, appealing cafe/restaurant serving popular menus.

Glenkeen without rest., 59 Coleraine Rd, BT56 8HR, ℘ (028) 7082 2279, *glenkeen@bt ternet.com, Fax (028) 7082 2279* – P. MO AE VISA.
closed 15 December-6 January – **10 rm** ☕ ✝32.00/40.00 – ✝✝50.00/55.00.
◆ Family owned guesthouse on the main road into town. Well-appointed, comfortab lounge. Separate breakfast room with linen-clad tables. Clean, tidy, spacious bedrooms.

The Harbour Bistro, 6 Harbour Rd, BT56 8DF, ✆ (028) 7082 2430, *Fax (028) 7082 3194* – MC VISA
closed 25 December – **Rest** (dinner only and Sunday lunch) a la carte 19.90/25.40 ♀.
◆ Buzzy bistro in the old part of town near to popular beach. Modern funky décor with banquette seating. Wide ranging, appealing menus providing excellent value.

ORTSTEWART (Port Stióbhaird) *Londonderry* 712 L 2.

Belfast 60 – Ballymena 32 – Coleraine 6.

Cromore Halt Inn, 158 Station Rd, BT55 7PU, East : ½ m. by A 2 (Portrush rd) on B 185 (Coleraine rd) ✆ (028) 7083 6888, *info@cromore.com, Fax (028) 7083 1910* – |♦|, ▤ rest, ✆, ♿, P – 🏛 30. MC ① VISA. ✂
closed 24-26 December – **Rest** a la carte 17.95/25.00 ♀ – **12 rm** ▭ ★45.00/55.00 – ★★75.00/85.00.
◆ Modern hotel sited on road into town. Bright, airy, open-plan bar and lounge area. Bedrooms are spacious and well-equipped with attractive, modern colour schemes. Pleasantly attired restaurant with a real bistro feel.

EMPLEPATRICK (Teampall Phádraig) *Antrim* 712 N 3 – ✉ *Ballyclare.*

Belfast 13 – Ballymena 16 – Dundalk 65 – Larne 16.

Hilton Templepatrick, Castle Upton Estate, BT39 0DD, North : 1 m. on B 95 (Parkgate rd) ✆ (028) 9443 5500, *hilton.templepatrick@hilton.com, Fax (028) 9443 5511,* Ꮀ, ≘s, ▣, ⛳18, 🎾, ✂ – |♦|, ⇔ rm, ▤ rest, ✆ ♿ P – 🏛 500. MC AE ① VISA
Treffner's : **Rest** a la carte 23.40/33.15 ♀ – ▭ 17.00 – **130 rm** ★135.00 – ★★135.00.
◆ Set on the Castle Upton Estate, where St Patrick (Ireland's patron saint) reputedly baptised converts in 450. Golf, conference facilities on hand; large, modern rooms. Classic cuisine with a popular carvery base.

Templeton, 882 Antrim Rd, BT39 0AH, ✆ (028) 9443 2984, *reception@templetonhotel.com, Fax (028) 9443 3406,* 🌳 – ⇔ rest, P – 🏛 350. MC AE ① VISA. ✂
closed 25-26 December – ***Raffles :*** **Rest** *(closed Monday-Tuesday)* (dinner only and Sunday lunch)/dinner a la carte 19.15/27.15 ♀ – ***Upton Grill :*** **Rest** (grill rest.) a la carte 10.95/22.65 ♀ – **24 rm** ▭ ★90.00 – ★★110.00.
◆ Large and distinctive pine "chalet" appearance. Inside, a swish atrium leads you to a pillared lounge; pine panelled rooms are warm and light. Very popular for weddings. Peaceful restaurant dining with garden and lake views. Buzzy Upton Grill with huge menu.

B. Pérousse/MICHELIN

Dingle peninsula

Towns
from A to Z

Villes
de A à Z

Città
de A a Z

Städte
von A bis Z

Republic of Ireland

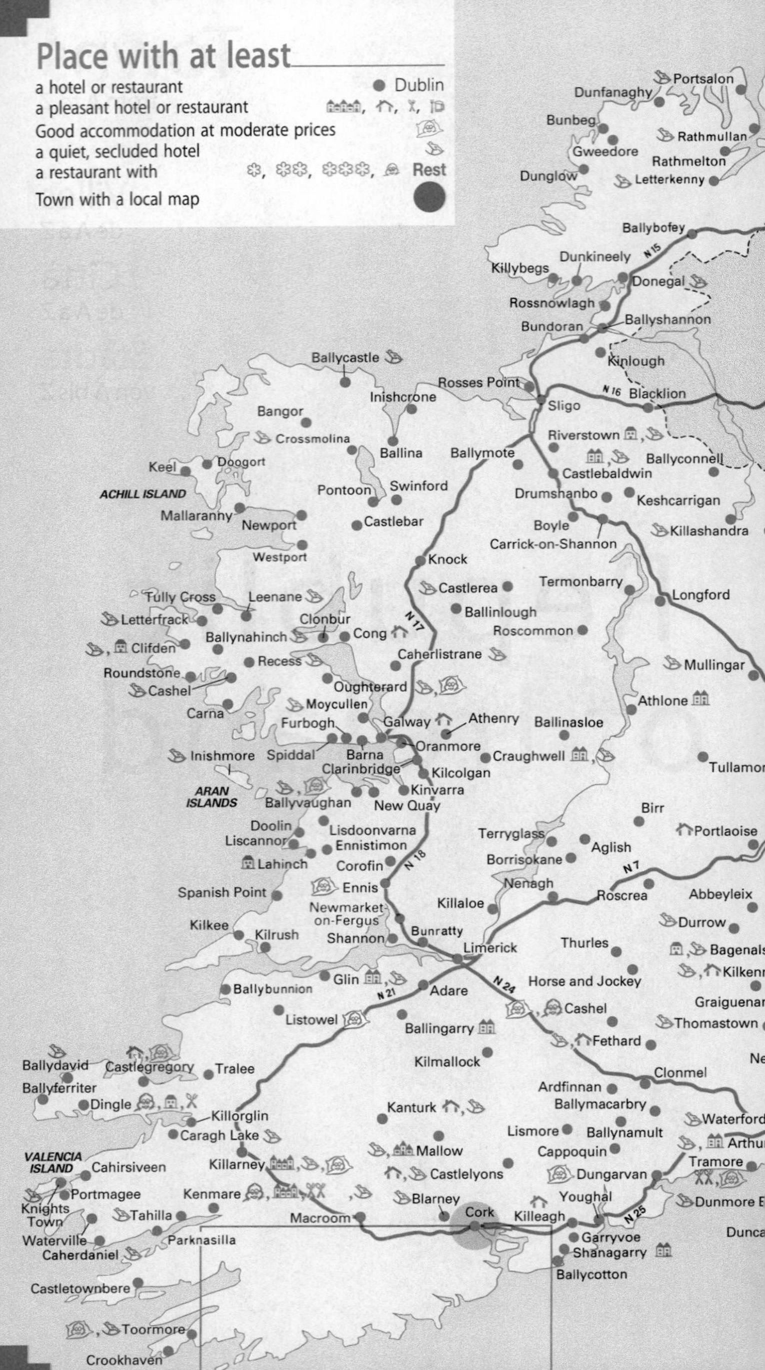

Place with at least
a hotel or restaurant
Dublin
a pleasant hotel or restaurant
Good accommodation at moderate prices
a quiet, secluded hotel
a restaurant with
Rest
Town with a local map
Portsalon
Dunfanaghy
Bunbeg
Rathmullan
Gweedore
Rathmelton
Dunglow
Letterkenny
Ballybofey
Dunkineely
N 15
Killybegs
Donegal
Rossnowlagh
Ballyshannon
Bundoran
Kinlough
Ballycastle
Rosses Point
Inishcrone
N 16
Blacklion
Sligo
Bangor
Crossmolina
Riverstown
Ballina
Ballymote
Ballyconnell
Keel
Doogort
Castlebaldwin
ACHILL ISLAND
Pontoon
Swinford
Drumshanbo
Keshcarrigan
Mallaranny
Newport
Castlebar
Boyle
Killashandra
Carrick-on-Shannon
Westport
Knock
Termonbarry
Castlerea
Longford
Tully Cross
Leenane
Ballinlough
Letterfrack
Clonbur
N 17
Ballynahinch
Cong
Roscommon
Clifden
Caherlistrane
Recess
Mullingar
Roundstone
Oughterard
Cashel
Athlone
Carna
Moycullen
Furbogh
Galway
Athenry
Ballinasloe
Oranmore
Inishmore
Spiddal
Barna
Craughwell
Tullamor
Clarinbridge
Kilcolgan
ARAN ISLANDS
Kinvarra
Ballyvaughan
New Quay
Birr
Doolin
Lisdoonvarna
Terryglass
Portlaoise
Liscannor
Ennistimon
Aglish
Lahinch
Corofin
N 18
Borrisokane
N 7
Ennis
Nenagh
Spanish Point
Roscrea
Abbeyleix
Newmarket-on-Fergus
Killaloe
Durrow
Kilkee
Kilrush
Shannon
Bunratty
Limerick
Thurles
Bagenals
Kilkenn
Glin
Horse and Jockey
Ballybunnion
N 21
Adare
N 24
Graiguenar
Cashel
Listowel
Ballingarry
Thomastown
Fethard
Ballydavid
Castlegregory
Tralee
Kilmallock
Ne
Clonmel
Ballyferriter
Ardfinnan
Dingle
Ballymacarbry
Kanturk
Killorglin
Waterford
Lismore
Ballynamult
Caragh Lake
Arthu
Mallow
Cappoquin
VALENCIA ISLAND
Tramore
Cahirsiveen
Killarney
Castlelyons
Dungarvan
Portmagee
Kenmare
Youghal
Blarney
Dunmore E
Knights Town
Tahilla
Cork
Killeagh
N 25
Macroom
Waterville
Parknasilla
Garryvoe
Dunca
Caherdaniel
Shanagarry
Ballycotton
Castletownbere
Toormore
Crookhaven

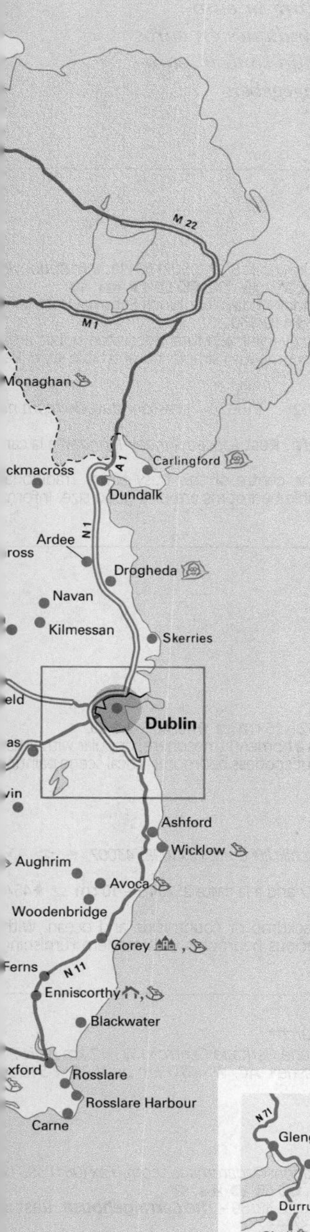

Localité offrant au moins

une ressource hôtelière — Dublin
un hôtel ou restaurant agréable
Bonnes nuits à petits prix
un hôtel très tranquille, isolé
une bonne table à — Rest
Carte de voisinage : voir à la ville choisie

La località possiede come minimo

una risorsa alberghiera — Dublin
Albergo o ristorante ameno
Buona sistemazione a prezzi contenuti
un albergo molto tranquillo, isolato
un'ottima tavola con — Rest
Città con carta dei dintorni

Ort mit mindestens

einem Hotel oder Restaurant — Dublin
einem angenehmen Hotel oder Restaurant
Hier übernachten Sie gut und preiswert
einem sehr ruhigen und abgelegenen Hotel
einem Restaurant mit — Rest
Stadt mit Umgebungskarte

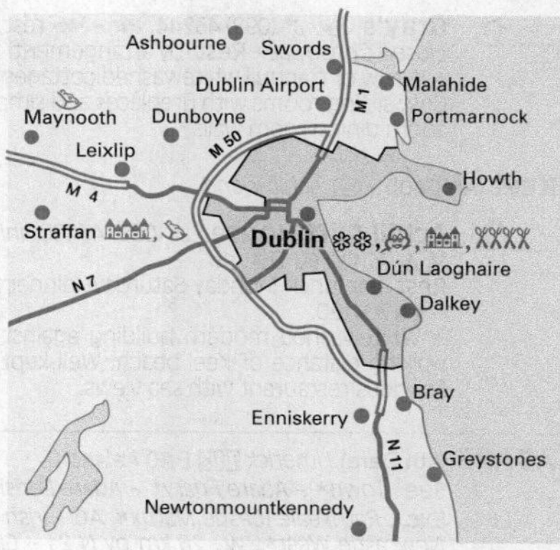

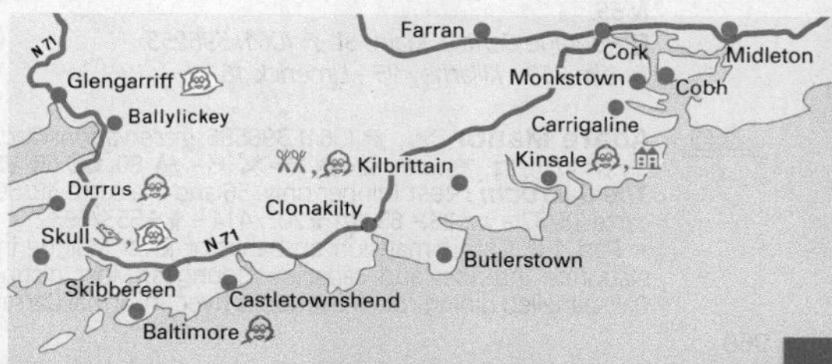

● *Prices quoted in this section of the guide are in euro*
● *Dans cette partie du guide, les prix sont indiqués en euros*
● *I prezzi indicati in questa parte della guida sono in euro*
● *Die Preise in diesem Teil sind in Euro angegeben*

ABBEYLEIX (Mainistir Laoise) *Laois* 712 J 9.
Abbeyleix, Rathmoyle ℘ (0502) 31450.
Dublin 96.5 – Kilkenny 35.5 – Limerick 108.

Abbeyleix Manor, Cork Rd, Southwest : ¾ km on N 8 ℘ (0502) 30111, *info@abbeyle manorhotel.com, Fax (0502) 30220* – ⇔ ▤ ✆ ♿ P – 🏛 400. MC AE ⓓ VISA. ✂
closed 25 December – **Rest** (carving lunch Monday-Friday) (bar lunch Saturday)/dinner and a la carte 20/34 **s.** ♀ – **23 rm** ☕ ✝65/75 – ✝✝110/130.
◆ Modern purpose-built hotel painted a distinctive yellow. Mural decorated public area Well-kept bar and a games room. Uniform bedrooms with simple, comfortable style. Restaurant has a bright modern feel.

Preston House, Main St, ℘ (0502) 31662, *prestonhouse@eircom.ne Fax (0502) 31432,* – ⇔ P. MC VISA. ✂
closed 10 days Christmas – ***Preston House Café :*** **Rest** *(closed Sunday-Monday)* a la car 24/33 – **4 rm** ☕ ✝70 – ✝✝120.
◆ Ivy-clad Georgian former schoolhouse in the centre of this busy town. Traditiona styled lounge features an open fire. Comfortable bedrooms are of a good size. Inform café with wrought iron fixtures and fittings.

ACHILL ISLAND (Acaill) *Mayo* 712 B 5/6 *Ireland G.*
See : *Island*★.
Achill Island, Keel ℘ (098) 43456.
Achill ℘ (098) 47353 (July-August).

Doogort (Dumha Goirt) – ✉ *Achill Island.*

Gray's ⛵, ℘ (098) 43244, – ⇔ rest, P
closed Christmas – **Rest** (by arrangement) 26/32 – **15 rm** ☕ ✝40/46 – ✝✝80.
◆ A row of tranquil whitewashed cottages with a homely atmosphere; popular with artist Cosy sitting rooms with fireplaces and simple but spotless bedrooms. Local scene paintin adorn dining room walls.

Keel (An Caol) – ✉ *Achill Island.*

Achill Cliff House, ℘ (098) 43400, *info@achillcliff.com, Fax (098) 43007,* ←, ≘s – ✆ ♿ P. MC AE VISA. ✂
Rest (bar lunch Monday-Saturday)/dinner 25/27 and a la carte 25/34 ♀ – **10 rm** ☕ ✝45/ – ✝✝70/120.
◆ Whitewashed modern building against a backdrop of countryside and ocean. With walking distance of Keel beach. Well-kept, spacious bedrooms with modern furnishing Spacious restaurant with sea views.

ADARE (Áth Dara) *Limerick* 712 F 10 *Ireland G.*
See : *Town*★ – *Adare Friary*★ – *Adare Parish Church*★.
Exc. : *Rathkeale (Castle Matrix*★ *AC – Irish Palatine Heritage Centre*★*) W : 12 km by N 21 Newcastle West*★, *W : 26 km by N 21 – Glin Castle*★ *AC, W : 46½ km by N 21, R 518 a N 69.*
Heritage Centre, Mains St ℘ (061) 396255.
Dublin 210 – Killarney 95 – Limerick 16.

Adare Manor ⛵, ℘ (061) 396566, *reservations@adaremanor.com, Fax (061) 39612* ←, , , 18, , , – | ⇔ ✆ P – 🏛 80. MC AE ⓓ VISA. ✂
The Oakroom : **Rest** (dinner only) 56 and a la carte 38/59 – ***The Carraigehouse :*** **Rest** a carte 25/37 – ☕ 23 – **63 rm** ✝283/414 – ✝✝553/663.
◆ Part 19C Gothic mansion on banks of River Maigue in extensive parkland. Impressive elaborate interiors and capacious lounges. Most distinctive rooms in the oldest part Oak-panelled dining room overlooks river. Informal Carraigehouse.

Dunraven Arms, Main St, ☎ (061) 396633, *reservations@dunravenhotel.com, Fax (061) 396541,* – 350. VISA.
The Inn Between : Rest *(closed January-April, Sunday and Monday)* (bar lunch) a la carte 25/34 – (see also ***Maigue*** below) – 20 – **86 rm** 135/180 – 155/200.
◆ Considerably extended 18C building opposite town's charming thatched cottages. Understated country house style. Comfortable bedrooms in bright magnolia. Well-equipped gym. Welcoming bistro in charming thatched cottage.

Carrabawn Guesthouse without rest., Killarney Rd, Southwest : ¾ km on N 21 ☎ (061) 396067, *carrabawnhouse@eircom.net, Fax (061) 396925,* – P. VISA.
8 rm 50/65 – 90.
◆ Well-established guesthouse with genuine homely style and large mature garden. Sitting room with games and books and comfortable sun lounge. Well-kept co-ordinated bedrooms.

Berkeley Lodge without rest., Station Rd, ☎ (061) 396857, *berlodge@iol.ie, Fax (061) 396857* – P. VISA.
6 rm 50/58 – 70.
◆ Good value accommodation with a friendly and well-run ambience. Hearty breakfast choices include pancakes and smoked salmon. Simply furnished traditional bedrooms.

The Wild Geese, Rose Cottage, ☎ (061) 396451, *wildgeese@indigo.ie, Fax (061) 396451* – . AE VISA
closed 3 weeks January, Monday in winter and Sunday – **Rest** (booking essential) (dinner only) 36 and a la carte approx 48.
◆ Traditional 18C cottage on main street. Friendly service and cosy welcoming atmosphere. Varied menu with classic and international influences uses much fresh local produce.

Maigue (at Dunraven Arms H.), Main St, ☎ (061) 396633, *Fax (061) 396541,* – P. AE VISA
Rest (dinner only and Sunday lunch) a la carte 33/39.
◆ Burgundy décor, antique chairs and historical paintings create a classic traditional air. Menus offer some eclectic choice on an Irish backbone. Formal yet friendly service.

Good food without spending a fortune? Look out for the Bib Gourmand

GLISH (An Eaglais) *Tipperary* 712 H 8 – ✉ *Borrisokane.*
Dublin 183.5 – Galway 85 – Limerick 69.

Ballycormac House, ☎ (067) 21129, *ballyc@indigo.ie,* – P. VISA
Rest (by arrangement) 35/45 – **12 rm** 45/50 – 90/120.
◆ Charming 17C cottage set amidst tranquil gardens and pasture. Specialises in equestrian activities. Homely country-style interiors; simple, comfy rooms, some in modern annex. Dining room offers dishes using home grown and local produce.

RAN ISLANDS (Oileáin Árann) *Galway* 712 CD 8 *Ireland G.*
See : *Islands★ – Inishmore (Dún Aonghasa★★★).*
Access by boat or aeroplane from Galway city or by boat from Kilkieran, Rossaveel or Fisherstreet (Clare) and by aeroplane from Inverin.
Aran Kilronan ☎ (099) 61263.

ishmore *Galway* – ✉ *Aran Islands.*

Pier House, Kilronan, ☎ (099) 61417, *pierh@iol.ie, Fax (099) 61122,* – P. VISA.
17 March-October – **Rest** – (see ***The Restaurant*** below) – **10 rm** 60/100 – 100/120.
◆ Purpose-built at the end of the pier with an attractive outlook. Spacious, planned interiors and spotlessly kept bedrooms furnished in a comfortable modern style.

Ard Einne Guesthouse, Killeany, ☎ (099) 61126, *ardeinne@eircom.net, Fax (099) 61388,* Killeany Bay – rest, P. VISA.
February-November – **Rest** (by arrangement) 25 – **14 rm** 55/70 – 80/90.
◆ Purpose-built chalet-style establishment in isolated spot with superb views of Killeany Bay. Homely atmosphere amidst traditional appointments. Simple, comfortable bedrooms. Spacious dining room provides home-cooked meals.

REPUBLIC OF IRELAND

Kilmurvey House, Kilmurvey, (099) 61218, *kilmurveyhouse@eircom.n*
Fax (099) 61397, – rest. VISA.
April-October – **Rest** (by arrangement) 26/30 – **12 rm** 60 – 110.
◆ Extended stone-built house in tranquil, secluded location with the remains of an ancie fort in grounds. Well-kept traditional style throughout. Simply decorated bedrooms. Tra tional dining room. Good use of fresh island produce.

The Restaurant (at Pier House H.), Kilronan, (099) 61417, *pierh@iol.*
Fax (099) 61122 – VISA
March-October – **Rest** - Seafood specialities - (light lunch) 25 and a la carte 20/45.
◆ Cosy, snug, cottagey restaurant, typified by its rustic, wooden tables. Light lunches a replaced by more serious dinner menus with strong selection of local fish dishes.

ARDEE (Baile Atha Fhirdhia) *Louth* 712 M 6 *Ireland G. – pop. 3 791.*
Exc. : *St Mochta's House★, N : 11 km by R 171 – Dún a'Rí Forest Park★, NW : 21 km by N and R 165 – Old Mellifont Abbey★, S : 21 km by N 2 and minor rd – Monasterboice★ S : 24 km by N 2, R 168 and minor rd.*
Dublin 66 – Drogheda 29 – Dundalk 27.

Rolf's Bistro, 52 Market St, (041) 685 7949, *rolfsbistro@eircom.n*
Fax (041) 685 7949 – VISA
closed Sunday – **Rest** (dinner only) a la carte 29/41 **s.**
◆ Georgian townhouse in main street. Bar and restaurant hung with local artists' work f sale. Early bird and main menu, a mixture of Irish, Swedish and Asian dishes.

ARDFINNAN (Ard Fhíonáin) *Tipperary* 712 I 11.
Dublin 185 – Caher 9.5 – Waterford 63.

Kilmaneen Farmhouse, East : 3 ¼ km by Goatenbridge rd (052) 36231, *kil neen@eircom.net, Fax (052) 36231*, – P. VISA
closed 20 December-10 January – **Rest** (communal dining) 25 – **4 rm** 45 – 80.
◆ Traditional farmhouse on dairy farm hidden away in the countryside. Cosy and neat, w a welcoming lounge. Comfortable bedrooms are well kept and individually furnished. Tas menus with a rural heart.

ARTHURSTOWN (Colmán) *Wexford* 712 L 11.
Dublin 166 – Cork 159 – Limerick 162.5 – Waterford 42.

Dunbrody Country House, (051) 389600, *dunbrody@indigo*
Fax (051) 389601, – rest, P. AE VISA.
closed 1 week Christmas – **Rest** (booking essential to non-residents) (residents only Sunc dinner) (bar lunch Monday-Saturday)/dinner 55 – **17 rm** 135/350 – 225/3 5 suites.
◆ A fine country house hotel with a pristine elegant style set within a part Georgian form hunting lodge, affording much peace. Smart comfortable bedrooms. Elegant dining roc in green damask and burgundy.

ASHBOURNE (Cill Dhéagláin) *Meath* 712 M 7.
Dublin 21 – Drogheda 26 – Navan 27.5.

Broadmeadow Country House without rest., Bullstown, Southeast : 4 km N 2 on R 125 (Swords rd) (01) 835 2823, *info@irishcountryhouse.com, Fax (01) 835 28*
– P. VISA.
closed 23 December-2 January – **8 rm** 50/80 – 100/120.
◆ Substantial ivy-clad guesthouse and equestrian centre in rural area yet close to airpc Light and airy breakfast room overlooks garden. Spacious rooms have country views.

ASHFORD (Ath na Fuinseoge) *Wicklow* 712 N 8 – *pop. 1 215.*
Dublin 43.5 – Rathdrum 17.5 – Wicklow 6.5.

Ballyknocken House, Glenealy, South : 4 ¾ km by N 11 (0404) 44627, *cfulvio@ lyknocken.com, Fax (0404) 44696*, – P. VISA.
February-14 December – **Rest** (by arrangement) 38 – **7 rm** 69/85 – 109/119.
◆ Part Victorian guesthouse on a working farm: the comfy bedrooms are furnished w antiques, and some have claw foot baths: most are in the new wing. Charming owr proud of home cooking.

THENRY (Baile Átha an Rí) *Galway* 712 F 8.
Dublin 202 – Ballinasloe 52 – Galway 26.

Raheen Woods, West : 1 ¼ km by R 348 ✆ (091) 875888, *raheenwoodshotel@eircom.net, Fax (091) 875444,* – rest, – 400.
closed 24-26 December – ***Blue Bayou:*** **Rest** (dinner only and Sunday lunch)/dinner a la carte 19/27 – ***McHales :*** **Rest** (lunch only) a la carte 19/27 – **50 rm** ★90/115 – ★★98/135.
◆ Spacious family owned hotel just outside historic village. Three comfy lounges; well-equipped leisure club and spa; modern conference rooms. Impressively appointed bedrooms. Linen-clad Blue Bayou for Irish based cooking. Popular dishes in informal McHales.

THLONE (Baile Átha Luain) *Westmeath* 712 I 7 *Ireland G.* – *pop. 15 544.*
Exc. : *Clonmacnois★★★ (Grave Slabs★, Cross of the Scriptures★) S : 21 km by N 6 and N 62 – N : Lough Ree (Ballykeeran Viewpoint★, Glassan★).*
Hodson Bay ✆ (0902) 92073.
Athlone Castle ✆ (090) 649 4630 (April-October).
Dublin 120.5 – Galway 92 – Limerick 120.5 – Roscommon 32 – Tullamore 38.5.

Radisson SAS, Northgate St, ✆ (090) 6442600, *info.athlone@radissonsas.com, Fax (090) 6442655,* – 700.
Rest (buffet lunch Monday-Saturday)/dinner 38 and a la carte 30/47 – **128 rm** ★110/130 – ★★145/175.
◆ Overlooks River Shannon, cathedral and marina. Quayside bar with super terrace. Impressive leisure and meeting facilities. Very modern rooms with hi-tech mod cons.. Modish restaurant serving buffet or à la carte.

Hodson Bay, Northwest : 7 ¾ km by N 61 ✆ (090) 6442000, *info@hodsonbayhotel.com, Fax (090) 6442020,* – 700.
L'Escale : **Rest** 20/40 and dinner a la carte 26/56 – **133 rm** ★180 – ★★280.
◆ Purpose-built hotel appealingly sited on shores of Lough Ree. Plenty of indoor and outdoor leisure activities; busy conference facility. Most bedrooms with views of the lough. Shoreside ambience is pleasant at breakfast.

Shelmalier House without rest., Retreat Rd, Cartrontroy, East : 2 ½ km by Dublin rd (N 6) ✆ (090) 6472245, *shelmalier@eircom.net, Fax (090) 6473190,*
closed 20 December-31 January – **7 rm** ★42/45 – ★★64/68.
◆ Modern house with large garden in a quiet residential area of town. Homely décor throughout, including comfortable bedrooms which are well kept.

Riverview House without rest., Summerhill, Galway Rd, West : 4 km on N 6 ✆ (090) 6494532, *riverviewhouse@hotmail.com, Fax (090) 6494596,*
March 18-December – **4 rm** ★45 – ★★64.
◆ Modern house with well-kept garden. Homely, comfortable lounge and wood furnished dining room. Uniformly styled fitted bedrooms. Good welcome.

Left Bank Bistro, Fry Pl, ✆ (090) 6494446, *info@leftbankbistro.com, Fax (090) 6494509* –
closed 25 December-6 January, Sunday and Monday – **Rest** (light lunch)/dinner a la carte 19/39.
◆ Glass-fronted with open-plan wine store and bright, modern bistro buzzing with regulars. Salads and foccacias, plus modern Irish dishes and fish specials in the evening.

Glassan *Northeast : 8 km on N 55 – ✉ Athlone.*

Wineport Lodge , Southwest : 1 ½ km ✆ (090) 6439010, *lodge@wineport.ie, Fax (090) 6485471,* Lough Ree, – 12.
closed 24-26 December – **Rest** *(closed Saturday lunch)* (restricted lunch)/dinner a la carte 39/66 – **21 rm** ★135 – ★★275/295.
◆ Beautifully located by Lough Ree. Come in from the delightful terrace and sip champagne in stylish bar. Superb rooms of limed oak and ash boast balconies and lough views. Smart restaurant with separate galleried area for private parties.

Glasson Golf H. & Country Club , West : 2 ¾ km ✆ (090) 6485120, *info@glassongolf.ie, Fax (090) 6485444,* Golf course and Lough Ree, – 80.
closed 25 December – **Rest** (bar lunch)/dinner 30/50 and a la carte 18/45 **s.** – **28 rm** ★80/210 – ★★120/400, 1 suite.
◆ Family owned hotel commands fine views of Lough Ree and its attractive golf course. Modern bedrooms are spacious with superior rooms making most of view. Original Georgian house restaurant with wonderful outlook.

Glasson Stone Lodge without rest., ☎ (090) 6485004, *glassonstonelodge@eircom.net*, – P. VISA.
April-November – **7 rm** ☐ ★45 – ★★66.
◆ A warm welcome and notable breakfasts with home-baked breads and locally sourced organic bacon. Bedrooms and communal areas are airy and tastefully furnished.

Harbour House without rest., Southwest : 2 km ☎ (090) 6485063, *ameade@indigo.ie., Fax (090) 6485933*, – P. VISA.
March-October – **6 rm** ☐ ★40/44 – ★★62.
◆ Sited in quiet rural spot a stone's throw from Lough Ree. Traditionally styled lounge with stone chimney breast; adjoining breakfast room. Comfy bedrooms overlook garden.

ATHY (Baile Átha Á) *Kildare* 712 L 9 *Ireland G. – pop. 5 306.*

Exc. : *Emo Court★★, N : 32 km by R 417 (L 18), west by N 7 (T 5) and north by R 422 – Stradbally★, NW : 14½ km by R 428 (L 109) – Castledermot High Crosses★, SE : 15¼ km by R 418 – Moone High Cross★, E : 19¼ km by Ballitore minor rd and south by N9 – Rock of Dunamase★ (≤★), NW : 19¼ km by R 428 (L109) and N80 (T16) – Timahoe Round Tower★, W : 16 km by R 428 (L 109) and N 80 (T 16).*
18 *Athy, Geraldine ☎ (0507) 31729.*
Dublin 64.5 – Kilkenny 46.5 – Wexford 95.

Clanard Court, Dublin Rd, Northeast : 2 km on N 78 ☎ (059) 8640666, *sales@clanardcourt.ie, Fax (059) 8640888*, – , rest, P – 350. AE VISA.
closed 25 December – ***Courtyard Bistro :*** Rest *(closed Sunday dinner and Monday)* 27/ and a la carte 38/59 – **38 rm** ☐ ★140/160 – ★★240/300.
◆ Commercially oriented modern hotel in bright yellow which opened in 2005. Well-equipped meeting rooms. Large bar to snack, sup and unwind. Comfy, smart bedrooms. Restaurant offers Mediterranean/North African style and menus.

AUGHRIM (Eachroim) *Wicklow* 712 N 9.

The Battle of Aughrim Visitors Centre, Ballinasloe ☎ (0909) 742604 (summer only).
Dublin 74 – Waterford 124 – Wexford 96.5.

Brooklodge, Macreddin Village, North : 3 ¼ km ☎ (0402) 36444, *brooklodge@macreddin.ie, Fax (0402) 36580*, , , , , – P – 220. AE VISA
Orchard Cafe : Rest (lunch only) a la carte 14/18 – ***Strawberry Tree :*** Rest (dinner only and Sunday lunch) 60 s. – **42 rm** ☐ ★115/270 – ★★390/430, 12 suites.
◆ Very individual hotel in idyllic parkland setting. Self-contained microbrewery, smokehouse and bakery. Well-appointed bedrooms and a friendly comfortable style throughout. Orchard Café is relaxed, informal eatery. Organic ingredients to the fore in Strawberry Tree.

AVOCA (Abhóca) *Wicklow* 712 N 9 *Ireland G.*

Exc. : *Meeting of the Waters★, N : by R 752 – Avondale★, N : by R 752.*
Dublin 75.5 – Waterford 116 – Wexford 88.5.

Keppel's Farmhouse without rest., Ballanagh, South : 3 ¼ km by unmarked rd ☎ (0402) 35168, *keppelsfarmhouse@eircom.net, Fax (0402) 30950*, ≤, , – P. VISA.
April-October – **5 rm** ☐ ★50/55 – ★★65/75.
◆ Farmhouse set in seclusion at end of long drive on working dairy farm. Attractive, simple modern and traditional bedrooms; those in front have far-reaching rural views.

BAGENALSTOWN (Muine Bheag) *Carlow* 712 L 9.

Dublin 101.5 – Carlow 16 – Kilkenny 21 – Wexford 59.5.

Kilgraney Country House, South : 6½ km by R 705 (Borris Rd) ☎ (059) 977528 *info@kilgraneyhouse.com, Fax (059) 9775595*, ≤, – P. AE VISA.
February-November – Rest *(closed Monday-Wednesday except July-August)* (booking essential) (residents only) (communal dining) (dinner only) 45/48 s. – **8 rm** ☐ ★85/120 ★★200/240.
◆ 18C house with individual interiors featuring Far Eastern artefacts from owners' travels. Sitting room in dramatic colours, paintings resting against wall. Stylish rooms. Communal dining in smart surroundings.

ALLINA (Béal an Átha) *Mayo* 712 E 5 *Ireland G. – pop. 8 762.*

Env. : *Mayo★ – Rosserk Abbey★, N : 6½ km by R 314.*

Exc. : *Moyne Abbey★, N : 11¼ km by R 314 – Pontoon Bridge View (≤★), S : 19¼ km by N 26 and R 310 – Downpatrick Head★, N : 32 km by R 314.*

Mossgrove, Shanaghy ☎ (096) 21050.

Cathedral Rd ☎ (096) 70848 (April-October).

Dublin 241.5 – Galway 117.5 – Roscommon 103 – Sligo 59.5.

Downhill Inn, Sligo Rd, East : 1 ½ km off N 59 ☎ (096) 73444, *thedownhillinn@eircom.net, Fax (096) 73411* – rest, P. MC AE VISA.
closed 21-28 December – **Rest** (bar lunch Monday-Saturday)/dinner 27/35 and a la carte 26/35 s. – **45 rm** 60/120 – 100/140.
◆ Purpose-built lodge-style hotel on Ballina outskirts in heart of Moy Valley, with superb salmon fishing nearby. Comfortable, warm interiors enhance the rooms. Simply decorated restaurant with a welcoming atmosphere.

ALLINADEE (Baile na Daidhche) *Cork* 712 G 12 – *see Kinsale.*

ALLINASLOE (Béal Átha na Sluaighe) *Galway* 712 H 8 *Ireland G. – pop. 5 723.*

Env. : *Clonfert Cathedral★ (west doorway★★), SW : by R 355 and minor roads.*

Exc. : *Turoe Stone, Bullaun★, SW : 29 km by R 348 and R 350 – Loughrea (St Brendan's Cathedral★), SW : 29 km by N 6.*

Rossgloss ☎ (0905) 42126 – Mountbellew ☎ (0905) 79259.

☎ (0909) 742604 (July-August).

Dublin 146.5 – Galway 66 – Limerick 106 – Roscommon 58 – Tullamore 55.

Tohers, 18 Dunlo St, ☎ (090) 9644848, *Fax (090) 9644844* – . MC VISA
closed 9-26 October and dinner Sunday and Monday – **Rest** (bar lunch)/dinner 38 and a la carte 25/40.
◆ Converted pub in a busy market town; simple restaurant and bustling lower bar. Tasty dishes. Charming, friendly service.

ALLINCLASHET (Baile na Claise) *Cork* 712 G 12 – *see Kinsale.*

ALLINGARRY (Baile an Gharraí) *Limerick* 712 F 10 *Ireland G.*

Exc. : *Kilmallock★ (Kilmallock Abbey★, Collegiate Church★), SE : 24 km by R 518 – Monasteranenagh Abbey★, NE : 24 km – Lough Gur Interpretive Centre★, NE : 38½ km.*

Dublin 227 – Killarney 90 – Limerick 29.

Mustard Seed at Echo Lodge , ☎ (069) 68508, *mustard@indigo.ie, Fax (069) 68511,* , – P. – 25. MC AE VISA.
closed first 2 weeks February and 24-26 December – **Rest** *(closed Sunday-Monday in winter)* (booking essential to non-residents) (dinner only) 52/55 – **16 rm** 110/145 – 300, 2 suites.
◆ Converted convent with very neat gardens and peaceful appeal. Cosy lounge with fireplace and beautiful fresh flowers. Individually furnished rooms with mix of antiques. Meals enlivened by home-grown herbs and organic farm produce.

ALLINLOUGH (Baile an Locha) *Roscommon* 712 G 6.

Dublin 183.5 – Galway 64.5 – Roscommon 38.5 – Sligo 82.

White House, ☎ (094) 9640112, *thewhitehousehotel@eircom.net, Fax (094) 9640993* – , rest, – 250. MC AE VISA.
closed 25 December – ***The Blue Room :*** **Rest** (carvery lunch) 16/35 and dinner a la carte 21/40 s. – **19 rm** 55/69 – 85/109.
◆ On the village square; popular bar with live music at weekends; conference room, lavishly decorated honeymoon suite and smartly furnished rooms. Intimate dining room with rich décor and antique furniture.

ALLSBRIDGE (Droichead na Dothra) *Dublin* 712 N 8 – *see Dublin.*

Undecided between two equivalent establishments? Within each category, establishments are classified in our order of preference.

BALLYBOFEY (Bealach Féich) *Donegal* 712 I 3 – *pop. 3 047 (inc. Stranorlar).*
Ballybofey & Stranorlar, The Glebe (074) 31093.
Dublin 238 – Londonderry 48 – Sligo 93.

Kee's, Main St, Stranorlar, Northeast : ¾ km on N 15 (074) 9131018, *info@keeshotel.i…* *Fax (074) 9131917,* – , rest, P. MC AE VISA.
Looking Glass : **Rest** (dinner only and Sunday lunch)/dinner 34/38 **s.** – ***Old Gallery :*** **Re…** a la carte 20/36 **s.** – **53 rm** 70/100 – 140/166.
♦ Very comfortable hotel established over 150 years ago. Smart lobby with plush sofa… Atmospheric bar and raised lounge area. Comfortable rooms. Intimate Looking Glass offe… ing international menus. Old Gallery is a simple, uncluttered bistro.

Villa Rose, Main St, (074) 32266, *villarose@oceanfree.net, Fax (074) 30666* – … MC AE VISA.
closed 25-26 December – **Rest** (bar lunch Monday-Saturday)/dinner a la carte 20/34 **s.** **16 rm** 60/75 – 90/120.
♦ Under private ownership, a modern hotel in the centre of the town. Neat, well-appoi… ted accommodation, furnished in co-ordinated colours and fabrics. Bright and airy dinir… room with ladder back pine chairs at simply set tables.

BALLYBUNNION (Baile an Bhuinneánaigh) *Kerry* 712 D 10 *Ireland G.*
Exc. : *Carrigafoyle Castle*★, *NE : 21 km by R 551 – Glin Castle*★ *AC, E : 30½ km by R 551 a… N 69.*
Ballybunnion, Sandhill Rd (068) 27146.
Dublin 283 – Limerick 90 – Tralee 42.

Iragh Ti Connor, Main St, (068) 27112, *iraghticonnor@eircom.net, Fax (068) 2778…* – P. MC AE VISA.
February-November – **Rest** (dinner only and Sunday lunch) a la carte 30/35 **s.** – **17 rm** 155 – 195.
♦ Locals gather in the cosy front bar of this rustic 19C inn with an ivy-clad modern win… Very spacious bedrooms in smart reproduction furnishings. Keen, friendly owner. Ba… grand piano accompanies diners.

Harty Costello Townhouse, Main St, (068) 27129, *hartycostello@eircom.n…* *Fax (068) 27489* – . MC AE VISA.
April-mid October – **Rest** *(closed Sunday)* (bar lunch)/dinner 22/30 and a la carte appr… 42 **s.** – **8 rm** 60/85 – 55/85.
♦ This personally run hotel, set around and above the pub downstairs, is smart, stylish ar… contemporary. A popular choice for visitors to this golfing town. Local fish in spruc… welcoming restaurant.

Teach de Broc Country House without rest., Link Rd, South : 2½ km on Golf Cl… rd (068) 27581, *teachdebroc@eircom.net, Fax (068) 27919* – P. MC VISA.
15 March-15 December – **14 rm** 90/130 – 120/180.
♦ Clean, tidy guesthouse with coastal proximity and great appeal to golfers as it's adjace… to the famous Ballybunion golf course. Cosy breakfast room. Neat, spacious rooms.

The 19th Lodge without rest., Golf Links Rd, South : 2 ¾ km by Golf Club rd (06… 27592, *the19thlodge@eircom.net, Fax (068) 27830,* – , rm, P. MC VISA.
closed 20 December-2 January – **12 rm** 70/120 – 105/170.
♦ Orange washed house aimed at golfers playing at adjacent course. First floor loun… with honesty bar and comfy sofas. Linen-clad breakfast room. Luxurious rooms.

Cashen Course House without rest., Golf Links Rd, South : 2 ¾ km by Golf Club (068) 27351, *golfstay@eircom.net, Fax (068) 28934,* – , rm, P. MC AE VIS…
March-October – **9 rm** 85/110 – 130/160.
♦ Overlooks first hole at the Cashen Course: clubhouse just one minute away. Brigh… breezy breakfast room; quality furnishings in comfy lounge. Spacious, colourful rooms.

BALLYCASTLE (Baile an Chaisil) *Mayo* 712 D 5.
Dublin 267 – Galway 140 – Sligo 88.5.

Stella Maris , Northwest : 3 km by R 314 (096) 43322, *info@stellamaris…* *land.com, Fax (096) 43965,* ≤ Bunatrahir Bay, – P. MC VISA.
April-September – **Rest** (lunch by arrangement)/dinner a la carte 32/43 – **12 rm** 14… 235.
♦ Former coastguard station and fort in a great spot overlooking the bay. Public are… include a long conservatory. Attractive rooms with antique and contemporary furnishing… Modern menus in stylish dining room.

BALLYCONNELL (Béal Atha Conaill) *Cavan* 712 J 5.
Slieve Russell ✆ *(049) 952 6458.*
Dublin 143 – Drogheda 122.5 – Enniskillen 37.

Slieve Russell, Southeast : 2 ¾ km on N 87 ✆ (049) 952 6444, *slieve-russell@quinn-hotels.com, Fax (049) 952 6474,* – rest, – 1200. AE VISA.
Conall Cearnach : **Rest** (dinner only and Sunday lunch) 27/43 – ***Setanta :*** **Rest** 17 (lunch) and dinner a la carte 30/47 – **217 rm** 140 – 270, 2 suites.
◆ Purpose-built hotel set in extensive gardens and golf course. Marbled entrance, large lounges, leisure and conference facilities. Spacious, modern rooms. Conall Cearnach has sophisticated appeal. Modern, informal, Mediterranean menu in Setanta.

Carnagh House without rest., Clinty, West : 3 km on N 87 ✆ (049) 952 3300, *caragh house@eircom.net, Fax (049) 952 3300,*
14 rm 45 – 65.
◆ Modern guesthouse with pleasant rural aspect. Warmly run by owners: tea and sandwiches await guests on arrival. Comfortable lounge with views. Good-sized bedrooms.

BALLYCOTTON (Baile Choitín) *Cork* 712 H 12 *Ireland G.*
Exc. : *Cloyne Cathedral★, NW : by R 629.*
Dublin 265.5 – Cork 43.5 – Waterford 106.

Bayview, ✆ (021) 4646746, *res@thebayviewhotel.com, Fax (021) 4646075,* ← Ballycotton Bay and harbour, AE VISA.
13 April-October – **Rest** (bar lunch Monday-Saturday)/dinner 47 and a la carte 44/54 – **33 rm** 118/137 – 172/210, 2 suites.
◆ A series of cottages in an elevated position with fine views of bay, harbour and island. Bar and lounge in library style with sofas. Spacious, comfy rooms with ocean views. Warm, inviting dining room.

BALLYDAVID (Baile na nGall) *Kerry* 712 A 11 – ✉ *Dingle.*
Dublin 362 – Dingle 11.5 – Tralee 58.

Gorman's Clifftop House, Glaise Bheag, North : 2 km ✆ (066) 9155162, *info@gormans-clifftophouse.com, Fax (066) 9155003,* ← Smerwick Harbour, Ballydavid Head and the Three Sisters, VISA.
restricted opening in winter – **Rest** *(closed Sunday)* (dinner only) 39 – **9 rm** 75/130 – 100/170.
◆ Fine views of Ballydavid Head and the Three Sisters from this peaceful modern house. Cosy sitting room with log fire; stylish, spacious rooms in vibrant colours and old pine. Bright restaurant invites diners to look out over the water.

Old Pier, An Fheothanach, North : 3 km ✆ (066) 9155242, *info@oldpier.com,* ← Smerwick Harbour, Ballydavid Head and the Three Sisters, – rest, VISA
mid March-mid November and New Year – **Rest** (by arrangement) 30/33 – **6 rm** 45/55 – 70/80.
◆ Run by the charming owner, a pretty clifftop house surveying the harbour and the Three Sisters. Immaculate rooms with bright bedspreads and cherrywood floors.

BALLYFERRITER (Baile an Fheirtéaraigh) *Kerry* 712 A 11 – ✉ *Dingle.*
Ceann Sibeal ✆ *(066) 9156255.*
Dublin 363.5 – Killarney 85.5 – Limerick 167.5.

Smerwick Harbour, Gallarus Cross, East : 4 ½ km on R 559 ✆ (066) 9156470, *info@smerwickhotel.com, Fax (066) 9156473,* ← AE VISA.
closed November-1 April – **Rest** 12/35 and a la carte 20/35 s. – **33 rm** 45/80 – 65/160.
◆ Purpose-built hotel in dramatic Dingle Peninsula, Ireland's most westerly point. Large, atmospheric oak tavern with local artefacts. Sizeable rooms have spectacular views. Inviting dining room has fire with large brick surround.

The ✿ award is the crème de la crème. This is awarded to restaurants which are really worth travelling miles for!

BALLYLICKEY (Béal Átha Leice) *Cork* 712 D 12 *Ireland G.* – ✉ *Bantry.*

Env. : *Bantry Bay★ – Bantry House★ AC, S : 5 km by R 584.*

Exc. : *Glengarriff★ (Garinish Island★★, access by boat) NW : 13 km by N 71 – Healy Pass★★ (≤★★) W : 37 km by N 71, R 572 and R 574 – Slieve Miskish Mountains (≤★★) W : 46¾ km by N 71 and R 572 – Lauragh (Derreen Gardens★ AC) NW : 44 km by N 71, R 572 and R 574 – Allihies (copper mines★) W : 66 ¾ km by N 71, R 572 and R 575 – Garnish Island (≤★) W : 70¾ km by N 71 and R 572.*

Bantry Bay, Donemark ✆ *(027) 50579.*

Dublin 347.5 – Cork 88.5 – Killarney 72.5.

Ballylickey Manor House, ✆ (027) 50071, *ballymh@eircom.net, Fax (027) 50124,* heated, rest, P. VISA.
late March-mid November – **Rest** *(residents only Wednesday March-April)* (dinner only) 40/60 s. – **5 rm** ★150/340 – ★★280/340, **8 suites** 260/340.
◆ Impressive hotel with attractive gardens set amongst Bantry Bay's ragged inlets. Well appointed sitting rooms with antiques. Rooms include luxurious garden cottage suites. Neatly set dining room has sideboard laden with china.

Seaview House, ✆ (027) 50462, *info@seaviewhousehotel.com, Fax (027) 51555,* P. VISA
mid March-mid November – **Rest** (dinner only and Sunday lunch)/dinner 45/50 and a la carte 25/45 ♀ – **25 rm** ★100/130 – ★★150/200.
◆ Tall, well-run, whitewashed Victorian house set amidst lush gardens which tumble down to Bantry Bay. Traditional lounges with bar and spacious, individually designed rooms. Warmly decorated dining room.

Ardnagashel Lodge without rest., Northwest : 4 km on N 71 ✆ (027) 51687, *ardnagashel@eircom.net,* – P.
May-September – **3 rm** ★45/50 – ★★70/80.
◆ Past the original gatehouse arch, a modern house with cottage style rooms and cosy drawing room. A walk though the woods rewards you with Bantry Bay view. Charming owners.

BALLYMACARBRY (Baile Mhac Cairbre) *Waterford* 712 I 11 *Ireland G.* – ✉ *Clonmel.*

Exc. : *W : Nier Valley Scenic Route★★.*

Dublin 190 – Cork 79 – Waterford 63.

Hanora's Cottage, Nire Valley, East : 6½ km by Nire Drive rd and Nire Valley Lakes rd ✆ (052) 36134, *hanorascottage@eircom.net, Fax (052) 36540,* ≤, – P. VISA
closed 1 week Christmas – **Rest** *(closed Sunday)* (booking essential for non-residents) (dinner only) a la carte 39/47 – **10 rm** ★100/180 – ★★250.
◆ Pleasant 19C farmhouse with purpose-built extensions in quiet location at foot of mountains. Very extensive and impressive breakfast buffet. Stylish rooms, all with jacuzzis. Locally renowned menus, brimming with fresh produce.

Cnoc-na-Ri without rest., Nire Valley, East : 6 km on Nire Drive rd ✆ (052) 3623[illegible] *richardharte@eircom.net,* ≤, – P. VISA.
February-October – **5 rm** ★40/45 – ★★70/80.
◆ Purpose-built guesthouse situated in the heart of the unspoilt Nire Valley, a perfect location for walking holidays. Immaculately kept, clean and spacious bedrooms. Comf[illegible] dining room doubles as lounge at other times of day.

Glasha Farmhouse, Northwest : 4 km by R 671 ✆ (052) 36108, *glasha@eircom.net, Fax (052) 36108,* ≤, – P. VISA.
closed 1-28 December – **Rest** (by arrangement) 35 – **8 rm** ★50/60 – ★★100/120.
◆ Immaculate farmhouse rurally set on working farm. Garden water feature is focal point. Spacious conservatory. Wonderful breakfasts with huge choice. Neat, tidy rooms.

BALLYMOTE (Baile an Mhóta) *Sligo* 712 G 5 – ✉ *Sligo.*

Ballymote, Ballinascarrow ✆ *(071) 83504.*

Dublin 199.5 – Longford 77 – Sligo 24.

Mill House without rest., Keenaghan, ✆ (071) 9183449, *millhousebb@eircom.net,* – P.
closed 18 December-10 January – **6 rm** ★31/45 – ★★62.
◆ Simple guesthouse situated on edge of busy market town. Very friendly welcome. Small comfortable sitting room. Light, airy breakfast room. Spacious, immaculate bedrooms.

BALLYNABOLA *Wexford* 712 L 10 – *see New Ross.*

BALLYNAGALL *Westmeath* – *see Mullingar.*

BALLYNAHINCH (Baile na hInse) *Galway* 712 C 7 – ✉ *Recess.*

Exc. : *Connemara*★★★ *– Roundstone*★, *S : by R 341 – Cashel*★, *SE : by R 341 and R 340.*
Dublin 225 – Galway 66 – Westport 79.

Ballynahinch Castle, (095) 31006, *bhinch@iol.ie, Fax (095) 31085,* ← Owenmore River and woods, rest, P. MC AE VISA.
closed February and 1 week Christmas – **Rest** (booking essential to non-residents) (bar lunch)/dinner 54 – **37 rm** ★125/145 – ★★240/310, 3 suites.
◆ Grey stone, part 17C castle in magnificent grounds with fine river views. Two large sitting rooms, characterful bar frequented by fishermen. Spacious rooms with antiques. Inviting dining room with stunning river views.

BALLYNAMULT (Béal na Molt) *Waterford.*
Dublin 194.5 – Clonmel 21 – Waterford 63.

Sliabh gCua without rest., Tooraneena, Southeast : 2 km (058) 47120, *breedaculin@sliabhgcua.com*, ←, – P.
April-October – **4 rm** ★45 – ★★80.
◆ Creeper clad early 20C house in quiet hamlet with rural views. Tea and scones on arrival. Comfy lounge with real fire. Individually decorated rooms boast period furniture.

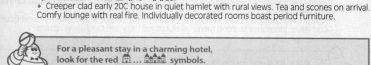

For a pleasant stay in a charming hotel,
look for the red ... symbols.

BALLYSHANNON (Béal Atha Seanaidh) *Donegal* 712 H 4 – *pop. 2 775.*
Dublin 53 – Donegal 272 – Letterkenny 283 – Sligo 215.5.

Dun Na Si without rest., Bundoran Rd, West : 1½ km on N 15 (071) 9852322, *dun-nasi@oceanfree.net*, – P. MC AE VISA.
7 rm ★38/42 – ★★64.
◆ Substantial, classically styled modern guesthouse: large, soft-toned rooms, some overlooking the estuary; breakfast room with neatly set pine tables and garden views.

BALLYVAUGHAN (Baile Uí Bheacháin) *Clare* 712 E 8 *Ireland G.* – *pop. 257.*

Env. : *The Burren*★★ *(Cliffs of Moher*★★★, *Scenic Routes*★★, *Poulnabrone Dolmen*★, *Aillwee Cave*★ *AC (Waterfall*★★*), Corcomroe Abbey*★, *Kilfenora Crosses*★*).*
Dublin 240 – Ennis 55 – Galway 46.5.

Gregans Castle, Southwest : 6 km on N 67 (065) 707 7005, *stay@gregans.ie, Fax (065) 707 7111,* ← countryside and Galway Bay, rest, P. MC AE VISA.
6 April-22 October – **Rest** (bar lunch)/dinner a la carte 45/55 **s.** – **17 rm** ★120/178 – ★★170/210, 4 suites.
◆ Idyllically positioned, family owned hotel with fine views to The Burren and Galway Bay. Relaxing sitting room, cosy bar lounge, country house-style bedrooms. Sizeable conservatory dining room specialising in seasonal, regional dishes.

Drumcreehy House without rest., Northeast : 2 km on N 67 (065) 7077377, *info@drumcreehyhouse.com, Fax (065) 7077379*, ←, – P. MC VISA
booking essential in winter – **10** rm ★51/90 – ★★70/100.
◆ Pristine house overlooking Galway Bay. Bedrooms are excellent value: spacious, comfortable and furnished in German stripped oak.

Rusheen Lodge without rest., Southwest : 1 km on N 67 (065) 7077092, *rusheen@iol.ie, Fax (065) 7077152*, – P. MC VISA.
3 February-mid November – **8 rm** ★57/68 – ★★76/96, 1 suite.
◆ Cheery yellow façade decked with flowers, lounge with fine sofas and rooms in pale woods and floral patterns. Pretty gardens complete the picture. Charming, welcoming owner.

Ballyvaughan Lodge without rest., (065) 7077292, *ballyvau@iol.ie, Fax (065) 7077287* – P. MC VISA.
closed 25-26 December – **11 rm** ★40/50 – ★★70/80.
◆ Red hued guesthouse, attractively furnished throughout. Light and airy sitting room with large windows. Home-made bread and jams for breakfast. Clean, tidy bedrooms.

Cappabhaile House without rest., Southwest : 1½ km on N 67 (065) 7077260, *cappabhaile@oceanfree.net*, ←, – P. MC VISA.
March-October – **8 rm** ★55/75 – ★★70/90.
◆ Stone clad bungalow with pleasant gardens and good views across the Burren. Spacious open-plan lounge-cum-breakfast room with central fireplace. Very large, spotless rooms.

BALTIMORE (Dún na Séad) *Cork* 712 D 13 *Ireland G.*
Exc. : Sherkin Island★ (by ferry).
Dublin 344.5 – Cork 95 – Killarney 124.

Casey's of Baltimore, East : ¾ km on R 595 ☎ (028) 20197, *info@caseysofbaltimore.com, Fax (028) 20509,* ← – rest, rest, P. *closed 20-27 December* – **Rest** 35/40 (dinner) and a la carte 29/44 – **14 rm** ☕ ★98/112 – ★★146/174.
◆ Popular hotel near sea-shore. Cosy bar with open fires and traditional music at weekends, with beer garden overlooking bay. Large, well-decorated rooms with pine furniture. Great sea views from dining room.

Slipway without rest., The Cove, East : ¾ km ☎ (028) 20134, *theslipway@hotmail.com, Fax (028) 20134,* ← Baltimore Harbour, – P.
March-October – **4 rm** ☕ ★55/70 – ★★68/75.
◆ Relaxed, informal guesthouse with yellow façade and lovely views of local harbour particularly from veranda outside breakfast room. Simple, individualistic, well-kept rooms.

Customs House, ☎ (028) 20200 –
closed October-Easter, Monday and Tuesday – **Rest** - Seafood - (booking essential) (dinner only) 28/38 s.
◆ Converted customs house, consisting of three small rooms with a painted wood floor. Good value, innovative seafood menu: all dishes are tasty and carefully prepared.

Good food and accommodation at moderate prices? Look for the Bib symbols: red Bib Gourmand for food, blue Bib Hotel for hotels

BANGOR (Baingear) *Mayo* 712 C 5.
Dublin 281.5 – Ballina 42 – Westport 63.

Teach Iorrais, Geesala, Southwest : 12 km on Geesala rd ☎ (097) 86888, *teachlor@iol.ie, Fax (097) 86855,* ← – , rest, P – 250.
An Neifin : Rest (bar lunch)/dinner 28 and a la carte 18/39 s. – **31 rm** ☕ ★50/55 – ★★92/120.
◆ Purpose-built hotel with views of Neifin mountains. Public bar with live music at weekends and quieter residents lounge. Bright bedrooms, those to the front with best views. Charming views from window tables of Gothic styled restaurant.

BARNA (Bearna) *Galway* 712 E 8.
Dublin 227 – Galway 9.5.

O'Grady's on the Pier, ☎ (091) 592223, *ogradysonthepier@hotmail.com, Fax (091) 590677,* ← Galway Bay – .
closed 1 week Christmas – **Rest** - Seafood - (booking essential) (dinner only and Sunday lunch) a la carte 27/48.
◆ Converted quayside pub on two floors with great views of Galway Bay. Cheerful, attentive staff and daily menus of simple, flavourful seafood have earned good local reputation.

BARRELLS CROSS *Cork* – *see Kinsale.*

BEAUFORT (Lios an Phúca) *Kerry* 712 D 11 – *see Killarney.*

BIRR (Biorra) *Offaly* 712 I 8 *Ireland G.* – *pop. 4 193.*
See : Town★ – Birr Castle Demesne★★ AC (Telescope★★).
Exc. : Roscrea★ (Damer House★ AC) S : 19 ¼ km by N 62 – Slieve Bloom Mountains★ E : 21 km by R 440 – Clonfert Cathedral★ (West doorway★★), NW : 24 km by R 439, R 356 and minor roads.
18 The Glenns ☎ (0509) 20082.
Castle St ☎ (0509) 20110.
Dublin 140 – Athlone 45 – Kilkenny 79 – Limerick 79.

County Arms, Railway Rd, South : ¾ km on N 62 ☎ (0509) 20791, *info@countyarmshotel.com, Fax (0509) 21234,* – P – 400.
Rest a la carte 19/29 s. ♀ – **70 rm** ☕ ★60/160 – ★★75/280.
◆ Sizeable, late Georgian hotel secluded in its own wooded grounds. Period furniture and old prints abound. Large conservatory bar. Flowery fabrics enrich the bedrooms. Dining room uses produce from its own gardens and greenhouse.

The Maltings, Castle St, (0509) 21345, *themaltingsbirr@eircom.net, Fax (0509) 22073* – P. VISA.
closed 24-27 December – **Rest** *(closed dinner in winter)* 30 (dinner) and a la carte – **13 rm** 50/60 – 70/80.
◆ Characterful 19C hotel on riverside near Birr Castle, originally built to store malt for Guinness. Cosy bar and lounge. Bedrooms enriched by flowery fabrics and drapes. Sizeable, bustling restaurant with chintz fabrics and spot lighting.

BLACKLION (An Blaic) *Cavan* 712 I 5.
Blacklion, Toam *(072) 53024.*
Dublin 194.5 – Drogheda 170.5 – Enniskillen 19.5.

Mac Nean House with rm, Main St, (071) 9853022, *Fax (071) 9853404* – rest. VISA
closed 1 week October and 2 weeks Christmas – **Rest** *(closed Monday-Wednesday in winter)* (dinner only and Sunday lunch)/dinner a la carte approx 44 **s.** – **5 rm** 45/50 – 70/80.
◆ Family run restaurant in the heart of border town. Antique chairs and fine tableware. Local produce to the fore in high quality, original menus. Homely rooms.

BLACKWATER *Wexford* 712 M 10.
Dublin 117.5 – Kilkenny 92 – Waterford 75.5 – Wexford 21.

Blackwater Lodge, The Square, (053) 27222, *blackwaterlodgeres@eircom.net, Fax (053) 27496* – P. VISA.
closed 24-25 December – **Rest** (bar lunch)/dinner a la carte 22/40 **s.** – **12 rm** 45/70 – 90/130.
◆ Colourful, competitively priced lodge accommodation in pretty village close to Wexford's coastal attractions. Pine decorated bar. Modern, pale wood rooms with all amenities. Local ingredients well used in menus.

BLARNEY (An Bhlarna) *Cork* 712 G 12 *Ireland G. – pop. 1 963 –* ✉ *Cork.*
See : *Blarney Castle★★ AC – Blarney House★ AC.*
(021) 4381624.
Dublin 268.5 – Cork 9.5.

Killarney House without rest., Station Rd, Northeast : 1 ½ km (021) 4381841, *info@killarneyhouseblarney.com, Fax (021) 4381841,* – P.
closed 25 December – **6 rm** 40/50 – 68/72.
◆ Spacious, modern guesthouse set above attractive village. Very comfortable lounge. Breakfast room equipped to high standard. Sizeable, immaculately kept rooms.

at **Tower** *West : 3¼ km on R 617 –* ✉ *Cork.*

Ashlee Lodge, (021) 4385346, *info@ashleelodge.com, Fax (021) 4385726,* – P. VISA
Rest *(closed Monday)* (dinner only) a la carte approx 38 **s.** – **10 rm** 85/95 – 130/200.
◆ Relaxing modern house, ideally located for Blarney Castle. Breakfast room with extensive menu. Outdoor Canadian hot tub. Very well-equipped rooms, some with whirlpool baths.

Maranatha Country House without rest., East : ¾ km on R 617 (021) 4385102, *info@maranathacountryhouse.com, Fax (021) 4382978,* , – P. VISA.
March-November – **6 rm** 50/90 – 68/120.
◆ Charming Victorian house in acres of peaceful grounds. Antique furnished drawing room. Relaxing, individual bedrooms, one lined with books, another with a large circular bath.

BORRISOKANE *Tipperary* 712 H 8/9 *– pop. 850.*
Dublin 162.5 – Galway 85.5 – Limerick 59.5.

Dancer Cottage , Curraghmore, West : 3 ¼ km by Ballinderry rd (067) 27414, *dcr@eircom.net, Fax (067) 27414,* , – P. VISA.
closed 4 December-8 January – **Rest** (by arrangement) (communal dining) 24 – **4 rm** 39 – 66/70.
◆ Modern guesthouse with spacious garden in wonderfully peaceful country location. Comfy lounge and extremely well-kept bedrooms with chintz fabrics; some four-posters.

BOYLE (Mainistir na Búille) *Roscommon* 712 H 6 – *pop. 1 690.*
Dublin 175 – Longford 53 – Sligo 45.

Rosdarrig House without rest., Dublin Rd, ☎ (071) 9662040, *rosdarrig@yahoo.co.uk* – P. VISA
April-October – **5 rm** ☐ ☆45/50 – ☆☆65/70.
◆ Comfortable, well-kept guesthouse with friendly owners. Attractive lounge and appealing wood-floored breakfast room. Good sized, smartly decorated rooms overlooking garden.

BRAY (Bré) *Wicklow* 712 N 8 *Ireland G.* – *pop. 27 923.*
Env. : *Powerscourt★★ (Waterfall★★ AC) W : 6½ km – Killruddery House and Gardens★ AC S : 3¼ km by R 761.*
Exc. : *Wicklow Mountains★★.*
18 *Woodbrook, Dublin Rd* ☎ *(01) 282 4799* – 18 *Old Conna, Ferndale Rd* ☎ *(01) 282 6055* – 9 *Ravenswell Rd* ☎ *(01) 286 2484.*
Dublin 21 – Wicklow 32.

Ramada Woodland Court, Southern Cross, South : 4 km by R 761 on Greystones rd ☎ (01) 276 0258, *info@woodlandcourthotel.com, Fax (01) 276 0298* – rest, rest, & P – 60. MC AE VISA.
closed 24-26 December – **Rest** (bar lunch)/dinner 25 and a la carte 15/29 **s.** – ☐ 10 – **61 rm** ☆69/99 – ☆☆79/109.
◆ Bright, yellow painted hotel and smart garden. Warm lounge and bar boasts burgundy and dark green sofas and chairs. Comfortable rooms with thick carpeting and rich décor. Afternoon tea a staple of airy restaurant.

BUNBEG (An Bun Beag) *Donegal* 712 H 2 *Ireland G.*
Exc. : *The Rosses★, S : by R 257.*
Dublin 314 – Donegal 106 – Londonderry 88.5.

Ostan Gweedore , ☎ (074) 9531177, *reservations@ostangweedore.com, Fax (074) 9531726,* ← Gweedore Bay, , , , – rest, P – 200. MC AE VISA.
Easter-October – ***Restaurant :*** **Rest** (dinner only) a la carte 37/44 ♀ – ***Sundowner :*** **Rest** Tapas - *(closed Monday-Wednesday and Thursday in winter)* (dinner only) a la carte 12/16 s ♀ – **36 rm** ☐ ☆88/96 – ☆☆154/169, 3 suites.
◆ Traditional hotel in a prominent position commanding spectacular views over Gweedore Bay. Large bar and pleasant sitting room. Good leisure club. Comfy, spacious rooms. Formal Restaurant with lovely window views of the bay. Tapas menus in informal Sundowner.

BUNDORAN (Bun Dobhráin) *Donegal* 712 H 4 – *pop. 1 796.*
The Bridge, Main St ☎ *(071) 9841350 (April-October).*
Dublin 259 – Donegal 27.5 – Sligo 37.

Allingham Arms, Main St, ☎ (071) 9841075, *allinghamarmshotel1@eircom.net, Fax (071) 9841171* – , & P – 400. MC AE VISA.
closed Christmas and weekends only December-February – **Rest** (bar lunch)/dinner 20/35 and a la carte 18/36 – **117 rm** ☐ ☆75/95 – ☆☆110/140.
◆ Sizeable hotel with pastel yellow frontage, named after poet William Allingham. Two bars, one housed in modern conservatory. Well-proportioned rooms with light wood décor. Restaurant is light and airy with spoke-back chairs and linen-clad tables.

Fitzgerald's, ☎ (071) 9841336, *info@fitzgeraldshotel.com, Fax (071) 9842121,* ← – rest, P. MC VISA.
restricted opening in winter – ***The Bistro :*** **Rest** (dinner only) a la carte 25/30 **s.** – **16 rm** ☐ ☆50/80 – ☆☆90/130.
◆ Stylish hotel in centre of popular seaside town overlooking Donegal Bay. Reception rooms warmed by wood-burning stove. Sumptuous sofas abound. Immaculate bedrooms. Stone-faced bistro-style restaurant with pleasant views onto the patio.

BUNRATTY (Bun Raite) *Clare* 712 F 9 *Ireland G.*
See : *Town★★ – Bunratty Castle★★.*
Dublin 207.5 – Ennis 24 – Limerick 13.

Bunratty Shannon Shamrock H., ☎ (061) 361177, *reservations@dunnehotels.com, Fax (061) 364863,* , , , – P – 1200. MC AE VISA.
closed 24-26 December – **Rest** (bar lunch Monday-Saturday)/dinner a la carte 29/37 – ☐ 13 – **115 rm** ☆170 – ☆☆215.
◆ Large, purpose-built hotel close to Limerick ideal for business travellers. Extensive conference and leisure facilities. Well-kept, contemporary rooms with mod cons. Dining room decorated with modern art, very popular at weekends.

Bunratty Manor, (061) 707984, *bunrattymanor@eircom.net, Fax (061) 360588*, – rest, P. VISA.
closed 22 December-6 January – **Rest** *(closed Sunday-Monday)* (dinner only) 35 and a la carte 29/40 – **14 rm** 69/92 – 110/135.
• Purpose-built, tourist-oriented hotel in village centre. Comfy lounge with chintz suites; Neat, modern rooms in colourful fabrics and drapes. Smart terrace fringed by pleasant garden.

The Courtyard without rest., (061) 361444, *info@bunrattycourtyard.com, Fax (061) 364498* – P. VISA.
closed January-February – **12 rm** 50/60 – 80/95.
• Smart, spotless guesthouse on main road in town. Very pleasant sitting room with beamed ceiling. Similar breakfast room. Immaculately kept bedrooms in soft colours.

Bunratty Grove without rest., Castle Rd, North : 2½ km (061) 369579, *bunratty grove@eircom.net, Fax (061) 369561*, – P. VISA.
9 rm 40/65 – 70/80.
• Pink painted guesthouse on country road with peaceful ambience. Large lounge-cum-library and pleasant, cottagey breakfast room. Immaculate rooms with polished wood floors.

Bunratty Lodge without rest., North : 2½ km (061) 369402, *reservations@bunratty lodge.com*, – P. VISA.
15 March-15 November – **5 rm** 72 – 72.
• Wedgwood painted neo-Georgian guesthouse with carefully kept gardens. Spacious sitting room. Traditionally styled breakfast room. Sizeable, spotless bedrooms.

Bunratty Woods without rest., Low Rd, North : 1½ km (061) 369689, *bun ratty@iol.ie, Fax (061) 369454*, ←, – P. VISA.
mid March-mid November – **14 rm** 50/65 – 90.
• Characterful guesthouse with large front garden. Owner collects and restores assorted items to decorate rooms, such as farmyard tools and old food tins. Sizeable bedrooms.

We try to be as accurate as possible when giving room rates. But prices are susceptible to change, so please check rates when booking.

UTLERSTOWN (Baile an Bhuitléaraigh) *Cork* 712 F 13 *Ireland G.* – *Bandon.*

Env. : *Courtmacsherry★, N : 5 km.*
Exc. : *Carbery Coast★.*
Dublin 310.5 – Cork 51.5.

Otto's Creative Catering with rm, Dunworley, South : 3¼ km (023) 40461, *ottokunze@eircom.net*, – rest, P. VISA
closed 16 January-8 March, Sunday dinner, Monday and Tuesday – **Rest** - Organic - (booking essential) (dinner only and Sunday lunch) 50 s. – **4 rm** 80 – 120.
• Quirky, highly individual restaurant built by owners and their son in remote location: amazing twisted wood staircase. Tremendously varied organic menus. Wood furnished rooms.

UTLERSTOWN (Baile an Bhuitléaraigh) *Waterford – see Waterford.*

AHERDANIEL (Cathair Dónall) *Kerry* 712 B 12 *Ireland G.* – *Killarney.*

Exc. : *Iveragh Peninsula★★ (Ring of Kerry★★) – Derrynane National Historic Park★★ – Staigue Fort★, E : 8 km by N 70 and minor rd – Sneem★, E : 19¼ km by N 70.*
Dublin 383 – Killarney 77.

Iskeroon without rest., West : 8 m. by N 70, Bunavalla Pier rd taking left turn at junction then turning left onto track immediately before pier (066) 9475119, *info@iske roon.com, Fax (066) 9475488*, ←, – P. VISA.
May-September, minimum stay 2 nights – **3 rm** 100 – 145.
• A "design icon", this low-lying house looking out to Derrynane Harbour was built in 1930s by the Earl of Dunraven. Lush gardens; boldly designed, vividly coloured bedrooms.

Derrynane Bay House without rest., West : ¾ km on N 70 (066) 9475404, *derryna nebayhouse@eircom.net, Fax (066) 9475436*, ←, – P. VISA.
15 March-October – **6 rm** 45 – 66/70.
• Purpose-built house on the Ring of Kerry with vast views over namesake bay. Stone Age monuments in the surrounding hills. Family-friendly; spacious bedrooms.

CAHERLISTRANE (Cathair Loistreáin) *Galway* 712 E 7.
Dublin 256 – Ballina 74 – Galway 42.

Lisdonagh House, Northwest : 2 ½ km by Shrule rd (093) 31163, *cooke@lisdonagh.com, Fax (093) 31528,* <, – rest, P. MC AE VISA.
29 April-October – **Rest** *(closed Monday except Bank Holidays)* (booking essential to non-residents) (dinner only) 45 – **10 rm** 98 – 240, 4 suites.
◆ Georgian house overlooking Lough Hacket; row across to island in the middle. A grand entrance hall with fine murals leads to antique filled rooms named after Irish artists. Locally caught fish predominant in dining room.

CAHERSIVEEN (Cathair Saidhbhín) *Kerry* 712 B 12.
Dublin 355.5 – Killarney 64.5.

The Point, Renard Point, Southwest : 2 ¾ km by N 70 (066) 947216 *Fax (066) 9472165,* < Valencia Harbour and Island, – P.
restricted opening in winter – **Rest** - Seafood - (bookings not accepted) (dinner only winter) a la carte approx 30.
◆ At the end of a road leading to Valencia Island ferry, this simply furnished pub offers concise menus of dishes, all seafood based, freshly prepared, unpretentiously served.

CAMPILE (Ceann Poill) *Wexford* 712 L 11 *Ireland G.*
Env. : *Dunbrody Abbey*★, *S : 3¼ km by R 733 – J F Kennedy Arboretum*★, *N : 3¼ km by R 733.*
Exc. : *Tintern Abbey*★, *SE : 12¾ km by R 733 – Duncannon*★, *S : 12¾ km by R 733.*
Dublin 154.5 – Waterford 35.5 – Wexford 37.

Kilmokea Country Manor, West : 8 km by R 733 and Great Island rd (051) 388109, *kilmokea@eircom.net, Fax (051) 388776,* <, – P. MC AE VISA
restricted opening in winter – **Rest** (booking essential to non-residents) (dinner only) 45/5 and lunch a la carte 20/29 – **6 rm** 120 – 260.
◆ Former Georgian rectory in large public gardens. Elegantly furnished. Games room, tennis and fishing. Comfortable bedrooms in house and converted stable block. Formal dining room with polished tables and period style; breakfast in conservatory.

CAPPOQUIN (Ceapach Choinn) *Waterford* 712 I 11 *Ireland G.*
Env. : *Lismore*★ *(Lismore Castle Gardens*★ *AC, St Carthage's Cathedral*★*), W : 6½ km by N 72 – Mount Melleray Abbey*★, *N : 6½ km by R 669.*
Exc. : *The Gap*★ *(<*★*) NW : 14½ km by R 669.*
Dublin 219 – Cork 56 – Waterford 64.5.

Richmond House with rm, Southeast : ¾ km on N 72 (058) 54278, *info@richmondhouse.net, Fax (058) 54988,* – P. MC AE VISA.
closed 22 December-14 January – **Rest** *(closed Sunday-Monday in winter)* (dinner only) 49 – **9 rm** 75/190 – 200.
◆ Built for Earl of Cork and Burlington in 1704; retains Georgian style with stately, coved ceilinged dining room: local produce to the fore. Individually decorated period rooms.

at Millstreet *East : 11¼ km by N 72 on R 671 – Cappoquin.*

Castle Country House, (058) 68049, *castlefm@iol.ie, Fax (058) 68099,* – P. MC VISA
March-October – **Rest** (by arrangement) 25/30 – **5 rm** 55/65 – 80/100.
◆ Extended farmhouse on working dairy and beef farm with 15C origins. Rural location and lovely gardens. Individual bedrooms with cottage style decor.

CARAGH LAKE (Loch Cárthaí) *Kerry* 712 C 11 *Ireland G.*
See : *Lough Caragh*★.
Exc. : *Iveragh Peninsula*★★ *(Ring of Kerry*★★*).*
Dooks, Glenbeigh (066) 9768205.
Dublin 341 – Killarney 35.5 – Tralee 40.

Caragh Lodge, (066) 9769115, *caraghl@iol.ie, Fax (066) 9769316,* <, – P. MC AE VISA.
late April-mid October – **Rest** (booking essential to non-residents) (dinner only) a la carte 35/49 – **14 rm** 140/195 – 250, 1 suite.
◆ McGillycuddy Reeks rises above this Victorian house on shores of Caragh Lough. Set in gardens with magnolias, camellias. Tastefully decorated rooms are spacious and classic. Ornate fireplace, elegant chairs lend restaurant a drawing room feel.

Ard-Na-Sidhe ⑤, ☎ (066) 9769105, *sales@kih.liebherr.com, Fax (066) 9769282*, ⑤, ⑤, ⑤ – ⑤ ⑤ P. ⑤ ⑤ ⑤ VISA
May-September – **Rest** *(closed Sunday)* (booking essential to non-residents) (dinner only) a la carte 31/56 **s.** – **18 rm** ☐ ★130/250 – ★★270.
◆ Built 1880 by an English Lady who called it "House of Fairies". Elizabethan in style; gardens lead down to lake. Possesses atmosphere of private home. Antique filled rooms. Tasteful dining room with intimate feel.

Carrig Country House ⑤, ☎ (066) 9769100, *info@carrighouse.com, Fax (066) 9769166*, ≤ Lough Caragh, ⑤, ⑤ – ⑤ ⑤ P. ⑤ ⑤ VISA. ⑤
4 March-26 November – **Rest** (booking essential to non-residents) (dinner only) a la carte 32/48 – **16 rm** ☐ ★115/130 – ★★130/160.
◆ Down a wooded drive, the yellow ochre façade of the house immediately strikes you. Its loughside setting assures good views. Ground floor rooms have their own private patio. Caragh Lough outlook from dining room windows.

ARLINGFORD (Cairlinn) *Louth* 712 N 5 *Ireland G.*

See : *Town*★.
Exc. : *Windy Gap*★, *NW : 12¾ km by R 173 – Proleek Dolmen*★, *SW : 14½ km by R 173.*
Dublin 106 – Dundalk 21.

Four Seasons, ☎ (042) 9373530, *info@fshc.ie, Fax (042) 9373531*, ≤, ⑤, ⑤, ⑤, ⑤ – ⑤ ⑤ ⑤ ⑤ P – ⑤ 800. ⑤ VISA. ⑤
closed 25 December – **Rest** 22/35 and dinner a la carte 29/39 **s.** – **59 rm** ☐ ★95/115 – ★★130/170.
◆ Impressive purpose-built hotel on outskirts of scenic market town. Extensive conference facilities; smart leisure centre. Spacious and well-equipped bedrooms. Popular bar leading to intimate dining room with Irish menus.

McKevitt's Village, Market Sq, ☎ (042) 9373116, *villagehotel@eircom.net, Fax (042) 9373144*, ⑤ – ⑤ rest, ⑤ rest. ⑤ ⑤ VISA. ⑤
Rest *(restricted opening in winter)* (bar lunch)/dinner 35/40 ♀ – **17 rm** ☐ ★60/105 – ★★120/160.
◆ Traditional inn occupying a central position in this medieval village, known for its ancient monuments. Modern style, yet retains Irish charm. Freshly decorated rooms. Part-panelled restaurant hosting range of maritime pictures.

Beaufort House ⑤ without rest., ☎ (042) 9373879, *michaelcaine@beauforthouse.net, Fax (042) 9373878*, ≤, ⑤ – ⑤ P. ⑤ VISA. ⑤
5 rm ☐ ★86 – ★★86.
◆ Modern house attractively sited on shores of Carlingford Lough. Very comfortable, spacious rooms with sea or mountain views. Substantial breakfasts served overlooking lough.

ARLOW (Ceatharlach) *Carlow* 712 L 9 – *pop. 14 979.*

⑤ *Carlow, Deer Park, Dublin Rd* ☎ *(0503) 31695.*
⑤ *Tullow St* ☎ *(059) 9131554.*
Dublin 80.5 – Kilkenny 37 – Wexford 75.5.

Seven Oaks, Athy Rd, ☎ (059) 9131308, *info@sevenoakshotel.com, Fax (059) 9132155*, ⑤, ⑤, ⑤, ⑤ – ⑤, ⑤ rest, P – ⑤ 300. ⑤ ⑤ ⑤ VISA. ⑤
closed 25-26 December – **Rest** (carving lunch Saturday) 25/40 and dinner a la carte 26/35 **s.** – **55 rm** ☐ ★85/90 – ★★140/150.
◆ Close to the sights of the River Barrow walk, this neat hotel in a residential area makes a good resting place. Well-kept rooms: ask for those on first or second floor. Intimate booths in tranquil dining room.

Barrowville Town House without rest., Kilkenny Rd, South : ¾ km on N 9 ☎ (059) 9143324, *barrowvilletownhouse@eircom.net, Fax (059) 9141953*, ⑤ – ⑤ P. ⑤ ⑤ VISA. ⑤
7 rm ☐ ★55/65 – ★★95/99.
◆ Regency townhouse professionally managed. Its conservatory breakfast room looks out over the garden containing ancient grape producing vine. Orthopaedic beds in all rooms.

Ballyvergal House without rest., Dublin Rd, North : 4 ¾ km on N 9 ☎ (059) 9143634, *ballyvergal@indigo.ie, Fax (059) 9140386*, ⑤ – ⑤ P. ⑤ VISA
10 rm ☐ ★55 – ★★80.
◆ Substantial redbrick house run in a friendly manner. Trim, en suite rooms at a good price; cheerful co-ordinated décor and tall Georgian style windows lend an airy feel.

CARNA *Galway* 712 C 8 *Ireland G.*
Exc. : *Connemara*★★★ – *Cashel*★, N : *by R 340.*
Dublin 299 – Cork 272 – Galway 77 – Limerick 180.

Carna Bay, (095) 32255, *carnabay@iol.ie, Fax (095) 32530,* ←, – VISA
closed 23-27 December – **Rest** (bar lunch Monday-Saturday)/dinner 28/34 – **25 rm**
70/110 – 90/140.
◆ A low-rise, purpose-built hotel in a quiet lobster fishing village overlooking bay and hill Walking, fishing, trekking available. Afterwards, recover in comfortable rooms. A fres looking dining room in which to sample fresh local produce.

CARNAROSS *Meath* 712 L 6 – ✉ *Kells.*
Dublin 69 – Cavan 43.5 – Drogheda 48.

The Forge with rm, Pottlereagh, Northwest : 5 ½ km by N 3 on Oldcastle rd (04 9245003, *theforgerest@eircom.net, Fax (046) 9245917* – P. VISA
closed 24-26 and 31 December and 1 January – **Rest** *(closed Sunday dinner and Monda* (dinner only and Sunday lunch) 30/35 and a la carte 36/51 – **2 rm** 50 – 70.
◆ Former forge tucked away in rural isolation. Family run, traditionally styled restaurar serving tried-and-tested dishes with modern twist: ample, good value choice.

CARNE *Wexford* 712 M 11.
Dublin 169 – Waterford 82 – Wexford 21.

Lobster Pot, (053) 31110, *Fax (053) 31401* – P. AE VISA.
closed January, 25 December, Good Friday and Monday except Bank Holidays – **Rest** Seafood - a la carte 29/50.
◆ Idiosyncratic pub crammed with engaging clutter: ornaments, pictures and metal sign Friendly staff serve fish orientated dishes against the background of Irish music.

CARRICKMACROSS **(Carraig Mhachaire Rois)** *Monaghan* 712 L 6 *Ireland G. – pop. 3 832.*
Env. : *Dún a' Rí Forest Park*★, *SW : 8 km by R 179.*
18 *Nuremore* *(042) 967 1368.*
Dublin 92 – Dundalk 22.5.

Nuremore, South : 1 ½ km on N 2 (042) 9661438, *nuremore@eircom.ne Fax (042) 9661853,* ←, 18, – P – 400. VISA.
Rest – (see ***The Restaurant*** below) – **72 rm** 175 – 300.
◆ Much extended Victorian house in attractive grounds; a rural retreat in which to swin ride or practice golf. Comfortable rooms, most with views over countryside.

The Restaurant (at Nuremore H.), South : 1 ½ km on N 2 (042) 966143 *Fax (042) 9661853* – P. AE VISA
closed Saturday lunch – **Rest** 30/80 s.
◆ Split-level dining room; tables laid with white linen, bone china and stylish glasswar Menu of seasonal dishes influenced by French fine dining. Attentive service.

CARRICK-ON-SHANNON **(Cora Droma Rúisc)** *Leitrim* 712 H 6 *Ireland G. – pop. 2 237.*
See : *Town*★.
Exc. : *Lough Rynn Demesne*★.
9 *Carrick-on-Shannon, Woodbrook* *(079) 67015.*
Old Barrel Store *(078) 20170 (April-October).*
Dublin 156 – Ballina 80.5 – Galway 119 – Roscommon 42 – Sligo 55.

The Landmark, on N 4 (071) 9622222, *landmarkhotel@eircom.ne Fax (071) 9622233,* ← – P – 500. AE VISA.
closed 24-25 December – ***Ferraris :*** Rest (dinner only) a la carte 30/40 – **60 rm**
119/160 – 178/260.
◆ Overlooks the Shannon; some areas reminiscent of a luxury liner: wooden floors, pane led ceiling. Marble fountain in lobby. Richly furnished rooms; water scenes on walls. Fer raris proudly boasts river views and and Niki Lauda F1 car on the wall.

Hollywell without rest., Liberty Hill, off N 4 (071) 9621124, *hollywell@esatbiz.con Fax (071) 9621124,* ←, – P. AE VISA.
restricted opening in winter – **4 rm** 65/75 – 120/140.
◆ A charming part 18C house in a peaceful spot by the river. Read up on area in a wel appointed lounge, take breakfast in dining room run by hospitable owner. Neat rooms.

Victoria Hall, Victoria Hall, Quay Rd, ✆ (071) 9620320, *info@victoriahall.ie, Fax (071) 9620320* – ⇔ ▤. MC VISA
closed 25 December and Good Friday – **Rest** - Asian - a la carte 30/39.
◆ Converted 19C church next to pretty quay. On two levels, with bright chairs and plush leather banquettes. Eclectic Asian menus are fresh, exciting, fragrant and original.

The Oarsman, Bridge St, ✆ (071) 9621733, *info@theoarsman.com, Fax (071) 9621734,* – ⇔. MC VISA
closed 25 December, Good Friday, Sunday and dinner Monday-Wednesday – **Rest** 35 and a la carte 18/41 ♀.
◆ Recently modernised bar, retaining its traditional charm and atmosphere. Flagged floors, exposed stone and beams, pubby bric-a-brac plus mezzanine. Menus with modern flavours.

CARRIGALINE (Carraig Uí Leighin) *Cork* 712 G 12 – *pop. 11 191.*

Fernhill ✆ (021) 372226.
Dublin 262 – Cork 14.5.

Carrigaline Court, Cork Rd, ✆ (021) 4852100, *reception@carrigcourt.com, Fax (021) 4371103,* , , , – ⇔, ▤ rest, ✆ & P – 350. MC AE VISA.
closed 25 December – ***The Bistro :*** **Rest** (carvery lunch Monday-Saturday)/dinner a la carte 30/40 s. ♀ – **89 rm** ☕ ★115 – ★★178, 2 suites.
◆ Modern hotel with airy interiors; rooms are spacious, with all mod cons, whilst leisure centre boasts a 20m pool, steam room, sauna. Corporate friendly with large ballroom. Local products to the fore in stylish restaurant.

Raffeen Lodge without rest., Ringaskiddy Rd, Monkstown, Northeast : 4 km by R 611 and N 28 off R 610 ✆ (021) 4371632, *info@raffeenlodge.com, Fax (021) 4371632,* – ⇔ P. MC VISA.
closed 20 December-3 January – **6 rm** ☕ ★40/50 – ★★70/80.
◆ A short drive from the fishing village of Ringaskiddy and Cork airport. A neat and tidy, good value house; rooms are uniformly decorated in pastel shades, simple in style.

Shannonpark House without rest., Cork Rd, North : 1 ½ km on R 611 ✆ (021) 437 2091, – P. VISA.
5 rm ☕ ★40/50 – ★★70/80.
◆ Breakfasts at the lace-topped communal table in this simple, homely guesthouse. Cosy little sitting room; bedrooms, always immaculate, furnished in dark wood.

Look out for red symbols, indicating particularly pleasant establishments.

CARRIGANS (An Carraigain) *Donegal* 712 J 3.

Dublin 225 – Donegal 66 – Letterkenny 230 – Sligo 124.

Mount Royd without rest., ✆ (074) 9140163, *jmartin@mountroyd.com, Fax (074) 9140400,* – ⇔ P.
closed January-February – **4 rm** ☕ ★35/40 – ★★60/65.
◆ Genuinely hospitable owners keep this creeper-clad period house in excellent order. En suite rooms are cosy and individually styled. Traditional, pleasantly cluttered lounge.

CASHEL (An Caiseal) *Galway* 712 C 7 *Ireland G.*

See : *Town*★.
Exc. : *Connemara*★★★.
Dublin 278 – Galway 66.

Cashel House , ✆ (095) 31001, *info@cashel-house-hotel.com, Fax (095) 31077,* <, , , , – ⇔ ✆ P. MC AE VISA
closed 5 January-5 February – **Rest** (booking essential to non-residents) (bar lunch Monday-Saturday)/dinner 49/57 and a la carte 30/50 – **32 rm** ☕ ★85/250 – ★★200/310.
◆ Built 1840; a very comfortable and restful country house, warmly decorated with delightful gardens. General de Gaulle stayed in one of the luxurious country house rooms. Dining room, with Queen Anne style chairs, opens into elegant conservatory.

Zetland Country House , ✆ (095) 31111, *zetland@iol.ie, Fax (095) 31117,* < Cashel Bay, , , – ⇔ rest, P. MC AE VISA
Rest (bar lunch)/dinner 50 – **20 rm** ☕ ★95/145 – ★★95/110.
◆ Lord Zetland's sporting lodge in 1800s; a splendid position in gardens sweeping down to Cashel Bay. Snooker, scuba diving, hunting organised. Pastel rooms. Dining room with silver cutlery, peerless views.

CASHEL (Caiseal) *Tipperary* 712 I 10 *Ireland G. – pop. 2 770.*
See : *Town★★★ – Rock of Cashel★★★ AC – Cormac's Chapel★★ – Round Tower★ – Museum★ – Cashel Palace Gardens★ – GPA Bolton Library★ AC.*
Env. : *Holy Cross Abbey★★, N : 14½ km by R 660 – Athassel Abbey★, W : 8 km by N 74.*
Heritage Centre, Town Hall, Main St ✆ (062) 61333 (April-September).
Dublin 162.5 – Cork 96.5 – Kilkenny 55 – Limerick 58 – Waterford 71.

Cashel Palace, Main St, ✆ (062) 62707, *reception@cashel-palace.ie, Fax (062) 6152*
– 80. VISA.
closed 24-25 December – ***Bishop's Buttery :*** **Rest** (carving lunch Monday-Saturday)/dinner 42 and a la carte 42/54 – **23 rm** ★150/200 – ★★225/375.
◆ A stately Queen Anne house, once home to an Archbishop, in walled gardens with path leading up to Cashel Rock. Inside, an extensive, pillared lounge and capacious rooms Harmonious dining room: vaulted ceilings, open fire and light, bright colours.

Aulber House without rest., Deerpark, West : ¾ km on N 74 ✆ (062) 63713, *berley@eircom.net, Fax (062) 63715,* VISA.
closed 23-30 December – **12** rm ★45/70 – ★★80/100.
◆ Modern house in Georgian style with lawned gardens; five minutes from town centre Comfy, leather furnished lounge. Smart, individually styled rooms.

Chez Hans, Rockside, Moor Lane St, ✆ (062) 61177, *Fax (062) 61177* – VISA
closed 25 December, Sunday and Monday – **Rest** (dinner only) a la carte 41/55 ♀.
◆ A converted synod hall with stained glass windows, near Cashel Rock: an unusual setting for a restaurant. Carefully prepared and cooked meals, using local ingredients.

Cafe Hans, Rockside, Moore Lane St, ✆ (062) 63660 –
closed last 3 weeks January, 25 December, Sunday and Monday – **Rest** (bookings not accepted) (lunch only) a la carte 19/29.
◆ Next door to Chez Hans; white emulsioned walls, open kitchen and glass roof. Simple tasty dishes are prepared with good, local ingredients. Come early as you can't book.

CASTLEBALDWIN (Béal Átha na gCarraigíní) *Sligo* 712 G 5 *Ireland G. – ✉ Boyle (Roscommon).*
Env. : *Carrowkeel Megalithic Cemetery (≤★★), S : 4¾ km.*
Exc. : *Arigna Scenic Drive★, N : 3¼ km by N 4 – Lough Key Forest Park★ AC, SE : 16 km by N 4 – View of Lough Allen★, N : 14½ km by N 4 on R 280 – Mountain Drive★, N : 9½ km on N 4 – Boyle Abbey★ AC, SE : 12¾ km by N 4 – King House★, SE : 12¾ km by N 4.*
Dublin 190 – Longford 67.5 – Sligo 24.

Cromleach Lodge, Ballindoon, Southeast : 5 ½ km ✆ (071) 9165155, *info@cromleach.com, Fax (071) 9165455,* ≤ Lough Arrow and Carrowkeel Cairns,
VISA
February-October – **Rest** (booking essential to non-residents) (dinner only) 65 ♀ – **10 rm**
★126/195 – ★★252/394.
◆ Contrasting with ancient Carrowkeel Cairns, overlooking Lough Arrow, this is a smart modern chalet with abundant local artwork indoors. Capacious rooms with large windows Modern dishes and attentive service.

CASTLEBAR (Caisléan an Bharraigh) *Mayo* 712 E 6 *Ireland G. – pop. 11 371.*
Env. : *Ballintubber Abbey★★, S : 13 km by N 84.*
Exc. : *Errew Abbey★, N : 35½ km by R 310, R 315 and minor rd.*
Castlebar, Hawthorn Ave, Rocklands ✆ (094) 21649.
Linenhall St ✆ (094) 9021207 (April-September).
Dublin 259 – Galway 79 – Sligo 75.5.

Breaffy House, Southeast : 4 ¾ km on N 60 ✆ (094) 9022033, *cro@lynchotels.com Fax (094) 9022276,* – 500. VISA.
Rest (bar lunch Monday-Saturday)/dinner 35/45 **s.** and a la carte – **125 rm** ★109/139 – ★★150/250.
◆ Baronial mansion with castellated façade in vast grounds. A wealth of activities in the area: fishing, golf, walking; summer cabarets laid on. Large, comfortable bedrooms Roomy, formal restaurant overlooking grounds.

CASTLEGREGORY (Caisleán Ghriaire) *Kerry* 712 B 11.
Dublin 330 – Dingle 24 – Killarney 54.5.

The Shores Country House, Conor Pass Rd, Kilcummin, Southwest : 6 km on Brandon rd ✆ (066) 7139196, *theshores@eircom.net, Fax (066) 7139196,* ≤,
VISA.
20 February-20 November – **Rest** (by arrangement) 35 – **6** rm ★40/80 – ★★60/80.
◆ Between Stradbally Mountain and a long sandy beach, a modern guest house run by the friendly longstanding owner. Immaculate, comfortable rooms, some with antique beds Dining room faces the Atlantic.

Strand View House without rest., Conor Pass Rd, Kilcummin, Southwest : 6 ¾ km on Brandon rd ✆ (066) 7138131, *strandview@eircom.net, Fax (066) 7138386*, ≤, – [P]. VISA.
closed 15 December-15 January – **5 rm** ☐ ✶50/70 – ✶✶70/80.
◆ Purpose-built guest house enjoys a fine view of the coast. Neatly set conservatory; mahogany furnished breakfast room and spotless bedrooms in pleasant traditional décor.

CASTLEKNOCK **(Caisleán Cnucha)** *Dublin* – *see Dublin*.

CASTLELYONS **(Caisleán Ó Liatháin)** *Cork* 712 H 11 – *pop. 164*.
Dublin 219 – Cork 30.5 – Killarney 104.5 – Limerick 64.5.

Ballyvolane House, Southeast : 5 ½ km by Midleton rd on Britway rd ✆ (025) 36349, *ballyvol@iol.ie, Fax (025) 36781*, ≤, – [P]. AE VISA
closed 24 December-1 January – **Rest** (by arrangement) (communal dining) 48 – **6 rm** ☐ ✶105/125 – ✶✶150/190.
◆ Stately 18C Italianate mansion mentioned in local legend, with lakes in parkland. Name means "place of springing heifers". Antique-filled rooms, some with Victorian baths. Dining room with silver candlesticks and balanced dishes.

CASTLEREA **(An Caisleán Riabhach)** *Roscommon* 712 G 6 *Ireland G.* – *pop. 1 788*.
Env. : *Clonalis House*★, *W : ¾ km by N 60*.
Castlerea, Clonalis ✆ (0907) 21214.
Dublin 174 – Galway 100 – Limerick 169.

Clonalis House, West : ¾ km on N 60 ✆ (094) 9620014, *clonalis@iol.ie, Fax (094) 9620014*, ≤, – [P]. VISA.
15 April-September – **Rest** (by arrangement) (communal dining) 40 ♀ – **4 rm** ☐ ✶95 – ✶✶170.
◆ Ancestral home to O'Conors, descendants of last kings of Ireland; inauguration stone, manuscripts, 18C harp displayed in this Victorian Italianate mansion. Opulent rooms. Historic and richly decorated restaurant offers sophisticated fare.

CASTLETOWNBERE **(Baile Chaisleáin Bhéarra)** *Cork* 712 C 13 *Ireland G.* – *pop. 926*.
Env. : *Beara Peninsula*★, *W : by R 572 (Allihies, mines*★ *- Garnish Bay* ≤★*) – Slieve Miskish Mountains (*≤★*)*.
Berehaven, Millcove ✆ (027) 70700.
Dublin 360 – Cork 130 – Killarney 93.5.

Rodeen without rest., East : 3 ¼ km by R 572 ✆ (027) 70158, ≤, – [P]. AE VISA.
17 March-17 October – **7 rm** ☐ ✶40/50 – ✶✶70/80.
◆ Owner used to run a horticulture business and this is evident in the variety of shrubs in the garden. Rooms are compact but nicely decorated; some look out to Bantry Bay.

CASTLETOWNSHEND **(Baile an Chaisleáin)** *Cork* 712 E 13.
Dublin 346 – Cork 95 – Killarney 116.

Mary Ann's, ✆ (028) 36146, *maryanns@eircom.net, Fax (028) 36920*, – . VISA.
closed 3 weeks January and 24-26 December – **Rest** (bookings not accepted) a la carte 19/45.
◆ A pleasant 19C pub in pretty village. Tempting dishes are distinguished by the fact that almost everything is homemade. Sunny terrace is popular for lunch.

CAVAN **(An Cabhán)** *Cavan* 712 J 6 *Ireland G.* – *pop. 6 098*.
Env. : *Killykeen Forest Park*★, *W : 9½ km by R 198*.
Farnham St ✆ (049) 4331942 (April-September), irelandnorthwest@eircom.net.
Dublin 114 – Drogheda 93.5 – Enniskillen 64.5.

Cavan Crystal, Dublin Rd, East : 1 ½ km on N 3 ✆ (049) 436 0600, *info@cavancrystalhotel.com, Fax (049) 436 0699*, – , rest, [P] – 650. AE VISA.
closed 24-25 December – ***Opus One*** : **Rest** a la carte 28/41 s. ♀ – **85 rm** ☐ ✶110/125 – ✶✶170/210.
◆ Modern hotel built next to the Cavan Crystal factory. Stylish contemporary public rooms. Well-appointed bedrooms with extra touches. Wood furnished restaurant offering modern contemporary menus.

REPUBLIC OF IRELAND

at Cloverhill *North : 12 km by N 3 on N 54 – ✉ Belturbet.*

Rockwood House without rest., ✆ (047) 55351, *jbmac@eircom.net, Fax (047) 5537.*
– [P]. MC VISA.
closed 10 December-1 February – **4 rm** ☕ ✝40 – ✝✝64.
◆ Stone-faced house with a charming garden located in a woodland clearing. Comfortab guests' lounge and a conservatory for breakfast. Simply appointed, comfortable bec rooms.

The Olde Post Inn with rm, ✆ (047) 55555, *gearoidlynch@eircom.net, Fax (047) 5511*
– [P]. MC AE VISA
closed 24-27 December and Monday – **Rest** (dinner only and Sunday lunch)/dinner a carte 35/46 – **6 rm** ☕ ✝40/50 – ✝✝80.
◆ Former village post office; now a restaurant with much character: exposed stone an brick, large rafters. A feel of genuine hospitality prevails. Fine dining with Gallic edge.

CLARINBRIDGE (Droichead an Chláirín) *Galway* 712 F 8.
Dublin 233.5 – Galway 17.5.

Clarinbridge Court, ✆ (091) 796988, *clarinbridgecourt@eircom.ne*
Fax (091) 796884, – [P] – 400. MC AE VISA.
closed 24-26 December – **Rest** (bar lunch)/dinner 26 and a la carte 19/31 **s.** – ☕ 10 – **51 rn**
✝69/199 – ✝✝69/199.
◆ Entrance on busy N18, but surrounded by woodland. Open plan lobby with leathe Chesterfields. Vivid rooms with red carpets, warm yellow walls. Good-value rates availabl Comfy, relaxing restaurant.

The Old Schoolhouse, ✆ (091) 796898, *kenc@iol.ie, Fax (091) 796117* – [P]. MC A
VISA
closed 24 December-3 January and Monday October-May – **Rest** (booking essential) (dinne only and Sunday lunch)/dinner a la carte 31/36.
◆ A converted school room is now the dining room and has been transformed by warr hued walls and elegant tableware. The speciality is the catch of the day and rock oysters.

CLIFDEN (An Clochán) *Galway* 712 B 7 *Ireland G.*
Exc. : *Connemara★★★, NE : by N 59 – Sky Road★★ (≤ ★★), NE : by N 59 – Connemar National Park★, NE : 1½ km by N 59.*
Galway Rd ✆ (095) 21163 (March-October).
Dublin 291 – Ballina 124 – Galway 79.

Rock Glen, South : 2 km by R 341 ✆ (095) 21035, *rockglen@iol.ie, Fax (095) 2173.*
≤, – rest, [P]. MC AE VISA
closed 5 January-4 March and 24-27 December – **Rest** (bar lunch)/dinner a la carte 30/52
27 rm ☕ ✝90/135 – ✝✝158/190.
◆ Former shooting lodge, built 1815, views of Ardbear Bay, the Twelve Bens. A handsom retreat; antique furnished, well-proportioned rooms. Aran Island boat trips available. Mem orable meals - fresh seafood straight from the boat - with memorable views.

Station House, ✆ (095) 21699, *reservations@clifdenstationhouse.con*
Fax (095) 21667, – [P] – 200. MC AE VISA.
closed 24-25 December – ***The Signal :*** **Rest** (bar lunch)/dinner 30/36 – **78 rm** ☕ ✝60/10 – ✝✝90/220.
◆ A modern hotel on site of the Galway-Clifden railway line closed in 1935. Now forms pa of a complex which includes a museum. Good sized rooms in cheerful colours. Rarefie ambience in which to dine on local delights, among them lamb and shellfish.

Ardagh, Ballyconneely rd, South : 2 ¾ km on R 341 ✆ (095) 21384, *ardaghhotel@e com.net, Fax (095) 21314,* ≤ Ardbear Bay – [P]. MC AE VISA
Easter-October – **Rest** (bar lunch)/dinner 50 and a la carte 31/58 **s.** – **16 rm** ☕ ✝108/120
✝✝155/180, 3 suites.
◆ Family run hotel on edge of Ardbear Bay. A welcoming, domestically furnished interic with turf fires, piano, pictures and plants. Bedrooms are large, especially superiors. Fresh pine dining room with views.

Dolphin Beach Country House, Lower Sky Rd, West : 5½ km by Sky Rd ✆ (095 21204, *dolphinbeach@iolfree.ie, Fax (095) 22935,* ≤ Clifden Bay, – [P]. MC VISA
closed 15 December-15 January – **Rest** (by arrangement) (residents only) 42 – **9 rm** ☕
✝85/100 – ✝✝160/180.
◆ Terracotta coloured former farmhouse, perched on side of hill with stunning views o bay. Delightful sitting room with huge windows to accommodate vista. Attractive rooms Tasty, home-cooked meals.

The Quay House without rest., Beach Rd, ☎ (095) 21369, *thequay@iol.ie, Fax (095) 21608*, ≤ – **MC** **VISA**.
mid March-October – **14 rm** ⊇ ★95/120 – ★★140/170.
◆ Once a harbour master's residence, then a Franciscan monastery. Rooms are divided between the main house: bohemian in style, and new annex: spacious with kitchenettes.

Byrne Mal Dua House without rest., Galway Rd, East : 1 ¼ km on N 59 ☎ (095) 21171, *info@maldua.com, Fax (095) 21739*, – **P**. **MC** **AE** **VISA**.
closed 22-26 December – **13 rm** ⊇ ★40/115 – ★★80/170.
◆ A white, detached house in well-tended gardens. Deep colours and subdued lighting indoors. Bedrooms are immaculately kept with fitted furniture. Neatly set dining room overlooks the garden.

Dún Rí without rest., Hulk St, ☎ (095) 21625, *dunri@anu.ie, Fax (095) 21635* – **P**. **MC** **VISA**.
closed 20-28 December – **13 rm** ⊇ ★50/60 – ★★80.
◆ A pleasant, cream-washed guesthouse overlooking Owenglin river with views of a pony showground and Dooneen hill. Good facilities including power showers in all rooms.

Benbaun without rest., Westport Rd, ☎ (095) 21462, *benbaunhouse@eircom.net, Fax (095) 21462*, – **P**. **MC** **VISA**.
May-September – **12 rm** ⊇ ★40/50 – ★★70/80.
◆ Family owned house to the north of the town: modern bedrooms - simple, spacious and decorated in cheerful patterned fabrics - represent very good value for money.

Buttermilk Lodge without rest., Westport Rd, ☎ (095) 21951, *buttermilklodge@eircom.net, Fax (095) 21953*, ≤, – **P**. **MC** **AE** **VISA**.
closed January-February – **11 rm** ⊇ ★45/65 – ★★70/110.
◆ Yellow painted, name refers to nearby lough, a theme which is continued indoors as each room bears the name of a lough. Daily breakfast specials; maps provided for exploring.

Joyce's Waterloo House, Galway Rd, East : 1 ½ km off N 59 ☎ (095) 21688, *pkp@joyces-waterloo.com, Fax (095) 22044*, – **P**. **MC** **AE** **VISA**.
closed 23-27 December – **Rest** (by arrangement) 30 – **8 rm** ⊇ ★45/100 – ★★90/114.
◆ Guesthouse announced by bright yellow exterior. Cosy, welcoming lounge. Smart bedrooms: owner puts national flag of guest outside each! All have VCRs and local art on walls.

Sea Mist House without rest., ☎ (095) 21441, *sgriffin@eircom.net*, – **P**. **MC** **VISA**.
closed 22-28 December – **4 rm** ⊇ ★90/120 – ★★90/120.
◆ 20C terraced stone house with sloping garden in town centre. Good choice at breakfast in cheerful room. Lounge at front and in conservatory. Spacious, modern bedrooms.

Connemara Country Lodge without rest., Westport Rd, ☎ (095) 22122, *connemara@unison.ie, Fax (095) 21122*, – **P**. **MC** **VISA**.
10 rm ⊇ ★45/75 – ★★70/90.
◆ Affordable accommodation in a personally run guest house. Breakfasts include home-baked raisin bread and scones: owner has tendency to break into song at this point!

"Rest" appears in red for establishments with a ✿ (star) or ☺ (Bib Gourmand).

CLONAKILTY (Cloich na Coillte) *Cork* 712 F 13 *Ireland G. – pop. 3 698.*

See : *West Cork Regional Museum★ AC – West Cork Model Railway Village★.*
Env. : *Timoleague★ (Franciscan Friary★, gardens★) E : 8 km by R 600.*
Exc. : *Carbery Coast★.*
Dunmore, Dunmore House, Muckross ☎ (023) 34644.
25 Ashe St ☎ (023) 33226.
Dublin 310.5 – Cork 51.5.

Inchydoney Island Lodge & Spa, South : 5 ¼ km by N 71 following signs for Inchydoney Beach ☎ (023) 33143, *reservations@inchydoneyisland.com, Fax (023) 35229*, ≤, , , **Ls**, , – , ▤ rest, , **P** – 350. **MC** **AE** **VISA**.
closed 23-27 December – ***The Gulfstream*** **:** **Rest** (dinner only) 49 – ***Dunes Bistro*** **: Rest** a la carte 19/30 – **63 rm** ⊇ ★190/210 – ★★310/350, 4 suites.
◆ Set on a headland looking out to sea. Range of leisure facilities; treatments - aquamarine spa, underwater massages - are especially good. Big, bright bedrooms with extras. The Gulfstream has fine sea views. The Dunes Bistro has a hearty, nautical theme.

REPUBLIC OF IRELAND

Quality, Clogheen, West : ¾ km by N 71 (Skibbereen rd) ✆ (023) 36400, *info@qualityhotelclonakility.com, Fax (023) 35404,* ⚲, ⛫, ▢ – ⧉ ⛔, ▤ rest, ♿, ⚲ Ⓟ – 🎪 160. Ⓜ ▢ VISA. ✂

closed 20-26 December – **Rest** (grill rest.) (carvery lunch Monday-Saturday)/dinner 26/3 and a la carte 20/41 **s.** ♀ – **68 rm** ☐ ★74/104 – ★★138/199, 12 suites.

◆ Modern hotel; rooms are uniformly decorated with matching fabrics. What distinguishe it is the three screen multiplex cinema, the "KidKamp" in summer, and leisure comple Menus feature popular favourites.

Randles, Wolfe Tone St, ✆ (023) 34749, *clonakilty@randleshotels.com, Fax (023) 35035* ⧉, ⛔ rest, ▤ rest, Ⓟ – 🎪 50. Ⓜ AE ⓓ VISA. ✂

closed 22-27 December – **Rest** (bar lunch)/dinner a la carte 19/32 – **30 rm** ☐ ★48/95 ★★60/120.

◆ Recently opened, family owned hotel close to town centre. Informal bar; well-equippe meeting room. Clean, fresh bedrooms in rich wood with modern drapes. Comfortab restaurant decorated in muted tones.

An Garrán Coir, Castlefreke, Rathbarry, West : 6½ km by N 71 ✆ (023) 48236, *angarracoir@eircom.net, Fax (023) 48236,* ⛰, ⚲, ✂ – ⛔ Ⓟ. VISA. ✂

Rest (by arrangement) 25/35 – **5 rm** ☐ ★45/50 – ★★75/80.

◆ Working farm overlooking rolling countryside: organic garden supplies ingredients f dinner. Homely lounge, well-kept rooms in bright, cheery colours. Good base for walking.

Gleesons, 3-4 Connolly St, ✆ (023) 21834, *gleesonsrestaurant@eircom.ne Fax (023) 21944* – ⛔. Ⓜ AE ⓓ VISA

closed 24-26 December, 3 weeks January-February, Monday and Sunday in winter – **Res** (dinner only except July-August) a la carte 31/55 **s.**

◆ Town centre restaurant with wood blinds. Low beamed interior with wood burnin stove. Classically based menus; dishes have individual twist and local produce is to the for

An Sugán, 41 Strand Rd, ✆ (023) 33719, *ansugan@eircom.net, Fax (023) 33825* – ⛔. Ⓜ VISA

closed 25-26 December and Good Friday – **Rest** a la carte 20/35 ♀.

◆ Situated in the old quays area of town. Homely wooden bar leads upstairs to restaura hung with old photographs. Known for lobster, baked crab and black pudding terrine.

CLONBUR (An Fhairche) *Galway* 712 D 7.

Dublin 260.5 – Ballina 79 – Galway 46.5.

John J. Burkes, ✆ (094) 9546175, *tibhurca@eircom.net, Fax (094) 9546290,* ⛱ – ⛔ Ⓜ VISA. ✂

restricted opening in winter – **Rest** (live music Saturday-Sunday) a la carte 23/39 ♀ – **5 rr** ☐ ★60 – ★★80.

◆ Family run for several generations; hearty food includes home-baked soda bread. Iris music at weekends. Simple exterior belies the vast interior.

CLONDALKIN *Dublin* 712 M 8 – *see Dublin.*

CLONMEL (Cluain Meala) *Tipperary* 712 I 10 *Ireland G. – pop. 16 910.*

See : *Town★ – County Museum★, St Mary's Church★.*

Env. : *Fethard★, N : 13 km by R 689.*

Exc. : *Nier Valley Scenic Route★★ – Ahenny High Crosses★, E : 30½ km by N 24 and R 697 Ormond Castle★, E : 33¾ km by N 24.*

⛳18 *Lyreanearla, Mountain Rd ✆ (052) 24050.*

ℹ *Community Office, Town Centre ✆ (052) 22960.*

Dublin 174 – Cork 95 – Kilkenny 50 – Limerick 77 – Waterford 46.5.

Minella, Coleville Rd, ✆ (052) 22388, *frontdesk@hotelminella.ie, Fax (052) 24381,* ⛱, ⚲ ⛫, ▢, ⚲, ⛰, ⚲, ✂ – ⛔, ▤ rest, ♿, Ⓟ – 🎪 550. Ⓜ AE ⓓ VISA. ✂

closed 23-28 December – **Rest** 28/40 and a la carte 35/43 – **70 rm** ☐ ★120 – ★★180.

◆ Heavily extended Georgian house on banks of River Suir. Excellent leisure facility. Bed rooms decorated in soft pinks and blues; garden rooms have pleasant views. Baseme restaurant has river vistas.

Clifford's, 29 Thomas St, ✆ (052) 70677, *Fax (052) 70676* – ⛔ ▤ Ⓟ. Ⓜ VISA

closed 24-27 December – **Rest** (dinner only and Sunday lunch) 22/52 and a la carte 25/50 ♀

◆ Attractive, renovated stone building with bright, modern, airy interior. White walls contrast with black linen. Modern art on walls. Local produce prominent on eclectic menus.

CLONTARF (Cluain Tarbh) *Dublin* 712 N 7 – *see Dublin.*

LOVERHILL *Cavan* 712 J 5 – *see Cavan.*

OBH **(An Cóbh)** *Cork* 712 H 12 *Ireland G. – pop. 9 811.*

See : *Town★ – St Colman's Cathedral★ – Lusitania Memorial★.*

Exc. : *Fota Island★ (Fota Wildlife Park★), N : 6½ km by R 624 – Cloyne Cathedral★, SE : 24 km by R 624/5, N 25, R 630 and R 629.*

Ballywilliam ℘ (021) 812399.

Dublin 264 – Cork 24 – Waterford 104.5.

WatersEdge, (next to Cobh Heritage Centre) ℘ (021) 481 5566, *info@watersedgehotel.ie, Fax (021) 481 2011,* ≤ Cork harbour, – , rest, . *closed 23-28 December and 1-10 January* – ***Jacob's Ladder*** **:** **Rest** (light lunch)/dinner a la carte 19/23 – **18 rm** 75/160 – 120/160, 1 suite.

◆ Next to the Heritage Centre, a converted salvage yard office overlooking Cork harbour. Some of the spacious, soft-toned rooms have French windows opening on to the veranda. Stylish restaurant with waterside setting.

ONG **(Conga)** *Mayo* 712 E 7 *Ireland G.*

See : *Town★.*

Env. : *Lough Corrib★★.*

Exc. : *Ross Abbey★ (Tower ≤★) – Joyce Country★★ (Lough Nafooey★) W : by R 345.*

℘ (094) 9546542 (March-October).

Dublin 257.5 – Ballina 79 – Galway 45.

Ashford Castle , ℘ (094) 9546003, *ashford@ashford.ie, Fax (094) 9546260,* ≤, – – 110. .

Connaught Room **:** **Rest** (dinner only) 80/160 – ***George V Room*** **:** **Rest** (residents only) 36/66 and dinner a la carte 63/75 – 25 – **79 rm** 225/417 – 225/417, 4 suites.

◆ Hugely imposing restored castle in formal grounds on Lough Corrib. Suits of armour and period antiques in a clubby lounge. Handsomely furnished country house rooms. Smart fine dining in Connaught Room. George V imbued with air of genteel formality.

Ballywarren House, East : 3½ km on R 346 ℘ (094) 9546989, *ballywarrenhouse@eircom.net, Fax (094) 9546989,* ≤, – .

closed 2 weeks spring and 2 weeks autumn – **Rest** (by arrangement) 38 – 8.50 – **3 rm** 98/136 – 148.

◆ Modern but 18C in style - open fires, galleried landing, oak staircase. Fresh colours: mint green, pink contrast pleasingly with woodwork. Carved pine beds; one four poster. Meals include own vegetables and daughter's farm eggs.

ORK **(Corcaigh)** *Cork* 712 G 12 *Ireland G. – pop. 186 239.*

See : *City★★ – Shandon Bells★★* **Y**, *St Fin Barre's Cathedral★★* **AC Z**, *Cork Public Museum★* **X M** – *Grand Parade★* **Z**, *South Mall★* **Z**, *St Patrick Street★* **Z**, *Crawford Art Gallery★* **Y** – *Christ the King Church★* **X D**, *Elizabethan Fort★* **Z**.

Env. : *Dunkathel House★* **AC**, *E : 9¼ km by N 8 and N 25* **X**.

Exc. : *Fota Island★ (Fota Wildlife Park★), E : 13 km by N 8 and N 25* **X** – *Cobh★ (St Colman's Cathedral★, Lusitania Memorial★) SE : 24 km by N 8, N 25 and R 624* **X**.

Douglas ℘ (021) 4891086, **X** – *Mahon, Cloverhill, Blackrock ℘ (021) 4292543* **X** – *Monkstown, Parkgarriffe ℘ (021) 4841376,* **X** – *Harbour Point, Clash, Little Island ℘ (021) 4353094,* **X**.

Cork Airport : ℘ (021) 4313131, S : 6½ km by L 42 **X** – **Terminal** : *Bus Station, Parnell Pl.*

to France (Roscoff) (Brittany Ferries and Irish Ferries) weekly (14 h/16 h) – to Pembroke (Swansea Cork Ferries) 2-6 weekly (8 h 30 mn) – to Swansea (Swansea Cork Ferries) (10 h).

Cork City, Grand Parade ℘ (021) 4255100 – Cork Airport, Freephone facility at Arrivals Terminal.

Dublin 248.

Plans on following pages

Hayfield Manor, Perrott Ave, College Rd, ℘ (021) 4845900, *enquiries@hayfieldmanor.ie, Fax (021) 4316839,* – – 120. . **X z**

closed 24-26 December – ***The Manor Room*** **:** **Rest** 32/65 – **83 rm** 380 – 380, 5 suites.

◆ Purpose-built yet Georgian in character. Stately interiors and harmoniously styled bedrooms with marble bathrooms and quality furniture - armchairs, coffee tables and desks. Restaurant with fine dining and professional service assured.

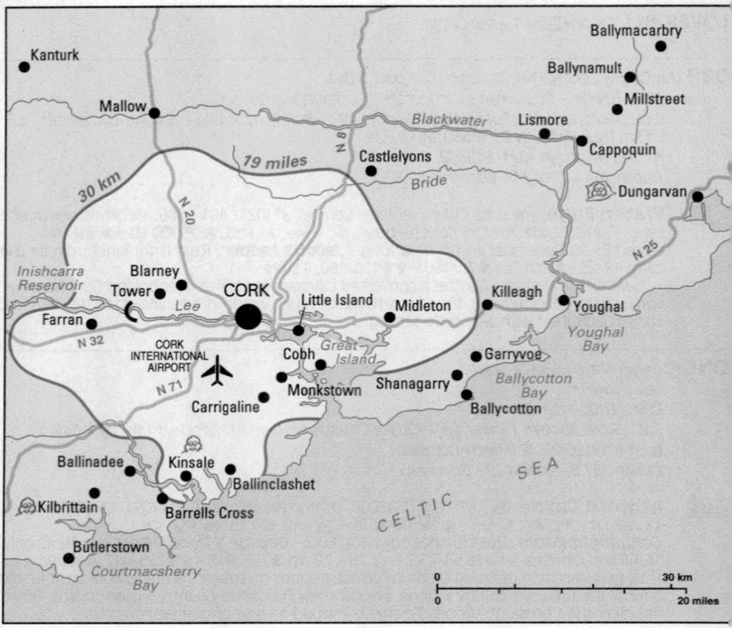

Maryborough House , Maryborough Hill, Douglas, Southeast : 4 ¾ km by R 60 and R 610 ☎ (021) 4365555, *info@maryborough.ie, Fax (021) 4365662*, , , , , – , , rest, , – 500. .
closed 24-26 December – ***Zing's :*** **Rest** 30/55 and dinner a la carte 40/50 **s.** – **74 rm** 145 – 198, 5 suites.
◆ Built as a home for a wealthy merchant, an extended Georgian house. Five very characterful bedrooms in original house; others are sleek, stylish and contemporary. Restaurant boasts walk-in wine cellar.

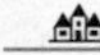

Clarion, Lapps Quay, ☎ (021) 4224900, *info@clarionhotelcorkcity.com, Fax (021) 4224901*, , , , , – , , , – 350.
Sinergie : **Rest** *(closed Saturday lunch)* 28/45 and a la carte 27/38 **s.** – ***Kudos :*** **Rest** - Asian - a la carte 21/33 – 18 – **188 rm** 220 – 220, 3 suites.
◆ Stylish hotel on the banks of the Lee. Well equipped spa and conference facilities. Modish bedrooms: some boast balconies and city views, others surround a stunning atrium. Modern classics at Sinergie. Informal Asian cooking in sleek Kudos.

The Kingsley, Victoria Cross, ☎ (021) 4800555, *resv@kingsleyhotel.com, Fax (021) 4800526*, , , , , – , , – 90. .
Otters *(☎ (021) 4800595)* **: Rest** 25 (lunch) and dinner a la carte 25/62 – **67 rm** (dinner included) 150/195 – 175/250, 2 suites.
◆ An inviting spot by river Lee, once site of Lee baths: outdoor hot tub and indoor pool takes their place. Relax in smart rooms or take tea in the lounge overlooking the weir. Airy restaurant has private booths and banquettes.

Silversprings Moran H., Tivoli, East : 4 km by N 8 ☎ (021) 4507533, *silversprings sinfo@moranhotels.com, Fax (021) 4507641*, , , , , , , squash – , rest, , – 700. .
closed 24-26 December – **Rest** 20/32 and a la carte 30/39 – **107 rm** 110/185 – 135/250, 2 suites.
◆ Conference oriented hotel surrounded by gardens and grounds. Smartly furnished public areas includes business and leisure centres. Comfortably appointed bedrooms. After dining, relax in smart, contemporary lounge.

X

X

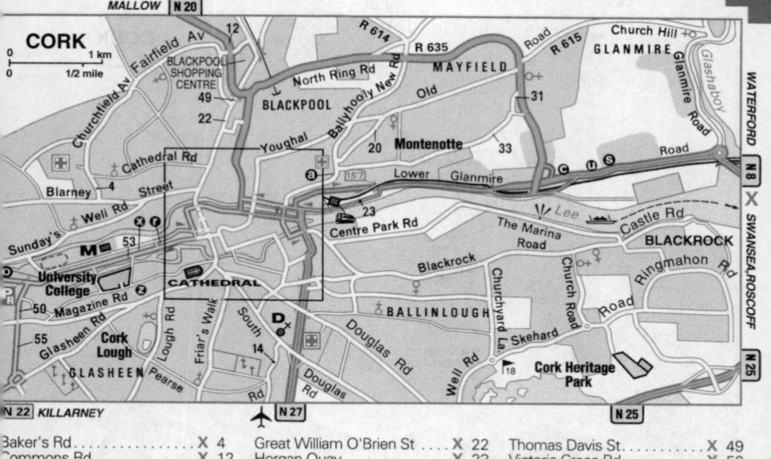

Baker's Rd . . . . X 4
Commons Rd . . . . X 12
Curragh Rd . . . . X 14
Gardiner's Hill . . . . X 20
Great William O'Brien St . . . . X 22
Horgan Quay . . . . X 23
Lower Mayfield Rd . . . . X 31
Middle Glanmire Rd . . . . X 33
Thomas Davis St. . . . . X 49
Victoria Cross Rd. . . . . X 50
Western Rd. . . . . X 53
Wilton Rd. . . . . X 55

The Ambassador, Military Hill, ☎ (021) 4551996, *reservations@ambassadorhotel.ie, Fax (021) 4551997,* ←, Fб, ≘s – |‡| ⇔ [P] – 🏔 220. MC AE ① VISA. ✂ X a
closed 24-26 December – **Rest** 22/42 and a la carte 30/42 **s.** ♀ – **57 rm** ☐ ♀99/120 – ♀♀115/150, 1 suite.
◆ Built as a military hospital; its high position affords city views from which most rooms benefit. All are furnished to a comfortable standard and most have a balcony. Home-made treats adorn dining room menus.

Jurys Inn Cork, Anderson's Quay, ☎ (021) 4943000, *jurysinncork@jurysdoyle.com, Fax (021) 4276144* – |‡| ⇔ ♿ – 🏔 30. MC AE VISA. ✂ Y c
closed 25-26 December – **Rest** (carving lunch)/dinner 25/28 and a la carte 25/39 **s.** – ☐ 11 – **133 rm** ♀75/89 – ♀♀75/89.
◆ Functional in its range of facilities: rooms fitted with 24-hour news channels, hairdryers, tea making facilities. Some rooms have the extra allure of overlooking the river. Buffet style breakfasts, lunchtime carvery and classic dinner menus.

Lancaster Lodge without rest., Lancaster Quay, Western Rd, ☎ (021) 4251125, *info@lancasterlodge.com, Fax (021) 4251126* – |‡| ☏ ♿ [P]. MC AE ① VISA. ✂ Z i
closed 23-25 December – **39 rm** ☐ ♀82/110 – ♀♀115/160.
◆ Purpose-built hotel with crisp, modern interior. Bedrooms are chintz-free, pleasingly and sparingly decorated. Largest rooms on the fourth floor; rear rooms are quieter.

Lotamore House without rest., Tivoli, East : 4 ¾ km on N 8 ☎ (021) 4822344, *lotamore@iol.ie, Fax (021) 4822219,* ←, 🌳 – ⇔ ☏ [P]. MC VISA. ✂ X s
closed 22 December-7 January – **20 rm** ☐ ♀70/95 – ♀♀110/160.
◆ Georgian house perched on hill with fine view over river and harbour. Country house style lounge with antiques. Individually styled rooms; relish vista from one at the front.

Crawford House without rest., Western Rd, ☎ (021) 4279000, *info@crawfordguesthouse.com, Fax (021) 4279927* – [P]. MC VISA. ✂ X x
closed 22 December-15 January – **12 rm** ☐ ♀65/100 – ♀♀100/120.
◆ Victorian-style building offering bright, airy and comfortable guesthouse accommodation. Modern interiors with a choice of wood floors or carpeting in guest rooms.

Garnish House without rest., Western Rd, ☎ (021) 4275111, *garnish@iol.ie, Fax (021) 4273872* – ⇔ [P]. MC AE ① VISA. ✂ X r
14 rm ☐ ♀75 – ♀♀150.
◆ Justifiably proud of gourmet breakfast: 30 options include pancakes and porridge. Guests are welcomed with home-made scones in cosy rooms; those at the rear have quiet aspect.

Achill House without rest., Western Rd, ☎ (021) 4279447, *info@achillhouse.com, Fax (021) 4279447* – ☏. MC VISA. ✂ Z e
closed 25 December – **6 rm** ☐ ♀60/100 – ♀♀90/130.
◆ Immaculate accommodation in a well run terrace house, five minutes from the centre; the two attic rooms, decorated in warm pastel tones, are the most cosy and characterful.

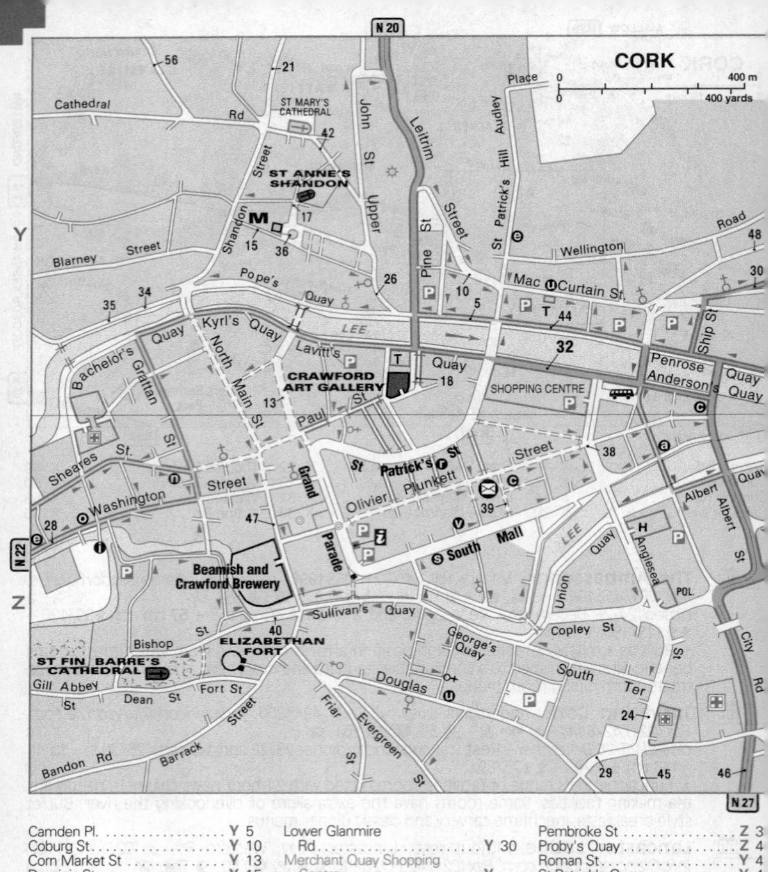

Camden Pl. .... Y 5
Coburg St .... Y 10
Corn Market St .... Y 13
Dominic St .... Y 15
Eason Hill .... Y 17
Emmet Pl. .... Y 18
Gerald Griffin St .... Y 21
Infirmary Rd .... Z 24
John Redmond St .... Y 26
Lancaster Quay .... Z 28
Langford Row .... Z 29
Lower Glanmire Rd .... Y 30
Merchant Quay Shopping Centre .... Y
Merchant's Quay .... Y 32
Newsom's Quay .... Y 34
North Main Street .... YZ
North Mall .... Y 35
O'Connell's Square .... Y 36
Olivier Plunkett St .... Z
Parnell Pl. .... Z 38
Pembroke St .... Z 3
Proby's Quay .... Z 4
Roman St .... Y 4
St Patrick's Quay .... Y 4
St Patrick's St .... Z
South Link .... Z 4
South Main St .... Z 4
Southern Rd .... Z 4
Summer Hill .... Y 4
Wolfe Tone St .... Y 5

Acorn House without rest., 14 St Patrick's Hill, ✆ (021) 4502474, *info@acornhouse cork.com, Fax (021) 4502474* – ⇔. MC VISA. ✂ Y 6
closed 14 December-18 January – **9 rm** ☕ ✝52/60 – ✝✝80/90.
◆ Behind Georgian façade, bright, high ceilinged en suite rooms and a pleasant lounge combine modern colours with period fireplaces and ornately framed pictures. Friendly hosts.

Flemings with rm, Silver Grange House, Tivoli, East : 4 ½ km on N 8 ✆ (021) 4821621 *flemings@iolfree.ie, Fax (021) 4821800*, – ⇔ rest, ✆ P. MC AE VISA. ✂ X u
closed 24-27 December – **Rest** 29 (lunch) and dinner a la carte 48/57 – **3 rm** ☕ ✝85/110 – ✝✝110.
◆ Classical cuisine, French bias; uses local produce, organically home-grown vegetables, herbs. Two dining rooms in keeping with Georgian character of house; extends to rooms.

XX **Jacobs on the Mall,** 30A South Mall, ✆ (021) 4251530, *info@jacobsonthemall.com, Fax (021) 4251531* – ⇔ ▤. MC AE ⓓ VISA Z s
closed Sunday – **Rest** (booking essential) 33/45 and a la carte 24/50 ♀.
◆ 19C former Turkish bath has retained its old steam windows and added contemporary Irish art. Modern dishes reveal a taste for bold, original combinations.

XX **Ambassador,** 3 Cook St, ✆ (021) 4273261, *Fax (021) 4272357* – ⇔ ▤. MC AE ⓓ VISA Z r
closed 25-26 December and Good Friday – **Rest** - Chinese - (dinner only) a la carte 30/37.
◆ Richly hued oak panelling and smoothly professional service add to the enjoyment of dishes prepared with care and fine ingredients in a long-established Chinese favourite.

XX **Jacques,** Phoenix St, ✆ (021) 4277387, *jacquesrestaurant@eircom.net, Fax (021) 4270634* – ⇔ ▤. MC AE VISA Z c
closed 25 December-2 January, Saturday lunch, Sunday and Bank Holidays – **Rest** a la carte approx 38.
◆ A long, warmly decorated room with modern tables on which old Irish classics are delivered. Farm ducks, wild game, fresh fish and organic vegetables are used in the cooking.

X **Les Gourmandises,** 17 Cook St, ✆ (021) 4251959, *Fax (021) 4899005* – ⇔. MC VISA Z v
closed 2 weeks Easter, 2 weeks August, Sunday and Monday – **Rest** - French - (booking essential) (dinner only and Friday lunch) 40 and a la carte 42/52 **s.**
◆ City centre restaurant boasting stained glass door and part-glass roof letting in lots of light. Irish produce employed on classic French menus in a relaxed atmosphere.

X **Isaacs,** 48 MacCurtain St, ✆ (021) 4503805, *isaacs@iol.ie, Fax (021) 4551348* – ⇔. MC AE ⓓ VISA Y u
closed 1 week Christmas, lunch Sunday and Bank Holidays – **Rest** (booking essential) a la carte 20/37.
◆ Tall brick arches and modern art in converted warehouse: buzzy, friendly and informal. Modern and traditional brasserie dishes plus home-made desserts and blackboard specials.

X **Cafe Paradiso,** 16 Lancaster Quay, Western Rd, ✆ (021) 4277939, *info@cafeparadiso.ie, Fax (021) 4274973* – ⇔. MC AE VISA Z o
closed 1 week Christmas, Sunday and Monday – **Rest** - Vegetarian - (booking essential) a la carte 27/44 ♀.
◆ A growing following means booking is essential at this relaxed vegetarian restaurant. Colourful and inventive international combinations; blackboard list of organic wines.

X **Fenn's Quay,** 5 Sheares St, ✆ (021) 4279527, *polary@eircom.net, Fax (021) 4279526* – ⇔ ▤. MC AE VISA Z n
closed 25 December, Sunday and Bank Holidays – **Rest** 20 (dinner) and a la carte 29/43 ♀.
◆ In a renovated 18C terrace in historic part of the city, this informal café-restaurant boasts modern art on display. Popular for mid-morning coffees and, light lunches.

The Douglas Hide, 63 Douglas St, ✆ (021) 4315695, *info@douglashide.com* – ⇔. MC VISA Z u
closed 25 December, Good Friday, Saturday lunch, Sunday and Monday – **Rest** a la carte 23/34.
◆ Friendly, personally run 19C pub close to town centre. Front bar leads onto dining area with heavy pine tables and chairs. Regularly changing menus have strong local accent.

at Little Island *East : 8½ km by N 25 – X – and R 623 – ✉ Cork.*

Radisson SAS, Ditchley House, ✆ (021) 4297000, *info.cork@radissonsas.com, Fax (021) 4297101,* – ⇔, ▤ rest, ♿ P – 600. MC AE ⓓ VISA.
The Island Grill Room : **Rest** (buffet lunch Monday-Saturday)/dinner a la carte 34/45 – **124 rm** ☕ 130 – 140, 5 suites.
◆ Opened in 2005 around the core of an 18C house: stylish and open-plan. Superbly equipped spa. Modish rooms in two themes: choose from Urban or highly individual Ocean! Island Grill Room serves an eclectic range of dishes.

Your opinions are important to us:
please write and let us know about your discoveries and experiences – good and bad!

CORROFIN (Cora Finne) *Clare* 712 E 9.
Dublin 228.5 – Gort 24 – Limerick 51.5.

Fergus View without rest., Kilnaboy, North : 3 ¼ km on R 476 ☎ (065) 6837606, *deckell@indigo.ie, Fax (065) 6837192,* ←, – ✈ P.
2 March-27 October – **6 rm** ☕ 51 – 72.
◆ Originally built for the owner's grandfather as a schoolhouse, with good countryside views. Conservatory entrance into cosy lounge with piles of books. Pristine bedrooms.

CRAUGHWELL (Creachmhaoil) *Galway* 712 F 8.
Dublin 194.5 – Galway 24 – Limerick 88.5.

St Clerans , Northeast : 5 ½ km off N 6 taking second turning left after 1 ½ km then veering left after a further 3 ¼ km ☎ (091) 846555, *stclerans@iol.ie, Fax (091) 846752,* ←, , – rest, P. MC AE VISA.
closed 25-26 December – **Rest** (booking essential for non-residents) (dinner only and Sunday lunch) 65 **s.** – **12 rm** ☕ 295/395 – 275/395.
◆ Grand, secluded 18C country house stands in rolling meadowland with fishing and hunting nearby. Former home of film director John Huston. Finely furnished and themed rooms. Great finesse in evidence in the elegant dining room.

The red symbol? This denotes the very essence of peace – only the sound of birdsong first thing in the morning ...

CROOKHAVEN (An Cruachán) *Cork* 712 C 13.
Dublin 373.5 – Bantry 40 – Cork 120.5.

Galley Cove House without rest., West : ¾ km on R 591 ☎ (028) 35137, *info@galleycovehouse.com, Fax (028) 35137,* ←, – P. MC VISA
10 March-October – **4 rm** ☕ 45/55 – 75/85.
◆ Perched overlooking eponymous bay and its pleasant harbour. Conservatory breakfast room has bamboo seating. Rooms are neat and tidy, and enhanced by colourful fabrics.

CROSSMOLINA (Crois Mhaoilíona) *Mayo* 712 E 5 *Ireland G. – pop. 1 103.*
Env. : *Errew Abbey★, SE : 9½ km by R 315.*
Exc. : *Broad Haven★, NW : 43½ km by N 59 and R 313.*
Dublin 252.5 – Ballina 10.5.

Enniscoe House , Castlehill, South : 3 ¼ km on R 315 ☎ (096) 31112, *dj@enniscoe.com, Fax (096) 31773,* ←, , , – P. MC VISA
April-October – **Rest** (booking essential to non-residents) (dinner only) 48 **s.** ♀ – **6 rm** ☕ 100/130 – 176/224.
◆ Georgian manor, overlooking Lough Conn, on Enniscoe estate with walled garden and heritage centre. Hallway boasts original family tree; antique beds in flower-filled rooms. Home cooked country dishes served in the dining room.

DALKEY (Deilginis) *Dublin* 712 N 8.
Dublin 13 – Bray 9.5.

Jaipur, 21 Castle St, ☎ (01) 285 0552, *dalkey@jaipur.ie, Fax (01) 284 0900* – . MC AE VISA
closed 25-26 December – **Rest** - Indian - (dinner only) 40 and a la carte 22/43.
◆ Central location and smart, lively, brightly coloured, modern décor. Well-spaced, linen-clad tables. Warm, friendly ambience. Contemporary Indian dishes.

DINGLE (An Daingean) *Kerry* 712 B 11 *Ireland G. – pop. 1 828.*
See : *Town★ – St Mary's Church★ (Presentation Convent Chapel★).*
Env. : *Gallarus Oratory★★, NW : 8 km by R 559 – NE : Connor Pass★★ – Kilmalkedar★, NW : 9 km by R 559.*
Exc. : *Dingle Peninsula★★★ – Stradbally Strand★★, NE : 17 km via Connor Pass – Mount Eagle (Beehive Huts★), W : 14½ km by R 559 – Corca Dhuibhne Regional Museum★ AC, NW : 13 km by R 559 – Blasket Islands★, W : 21 km by R 559 and ferry from Dunquin.*
The Quay ☎ (066) 9151188.
Dublin 347.5 – Killarney 82 – Limerick 153.

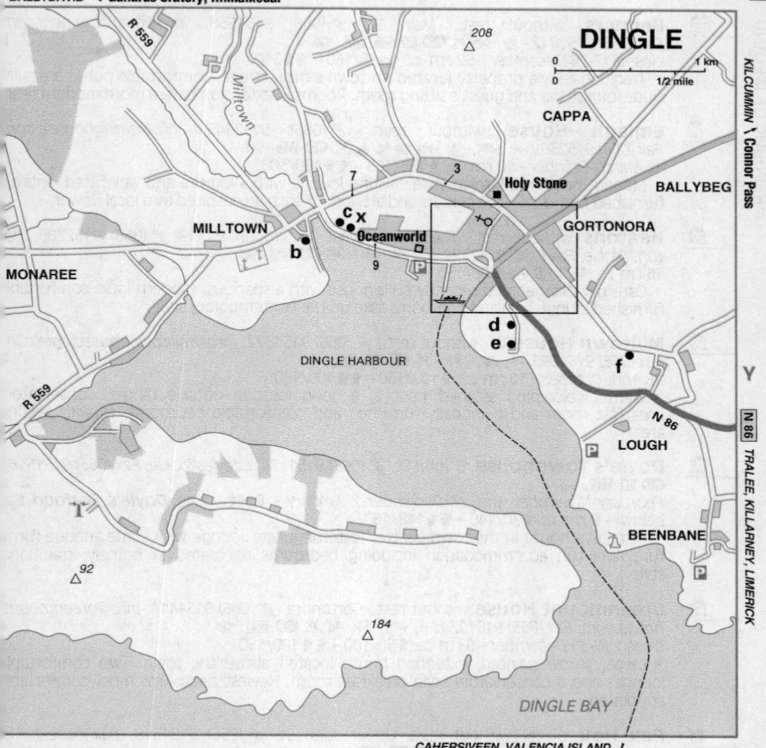

CONVENT
ST MARY'S CHURCH
Library
Green Street
Main Street
Spa Road
O'DONNELL PARK
Dykegate Lane
The Mall
John Street
Strand Street
POL
DINGLE MARINA
Cooleen
The Mall Road
N 86
DINGLE
0 200 m
0 200 yards

Street	Grid	No.
Avondale St	Z	2
Bridge St	Z	5
Goat St	Y, Z	3
Grey's Lane	Z	8
High Road (The)	Y	7
Holy Ground	Z	12
Orchard Lane	Z	14
Tracks (The)	Z	17
Wood (The)	Y	9

Dingle Skellig, ☎ (066) 9150200, *reservations@dingleskellig.com, Fax (066) 9151501*, – 250. Y e *weekends only November-December and restricted opening January-February* – **Rest** (bar lunch)/dinner 32/49 s. ♀ – **108 rm** ☕ 135 – 230, 2 suites.

◆ Large purpose-built hotel with views of Dingle Bay. Interior decorated in a modern style with good levels of comfort: the smartest executive rooms are on the third floor. Restaurant makes most of sea and harbour view.

REPUBLIC OF IRELAND

Benners without rest., Main St, ✆ (066) 9151638, *info@dinglebenners.com*
Fax (066) 9151412 – VISA.
closed 17-26 December – **52 rm** ☕ 115/160 – 210.
◆ Traditional-style property located on town's main street. Comfortable public areas include lounge bar and guest's sitting room. Rooms in extension have a more modern feel.

Emlagh House without rest., ✆ (066) 9152345, *info@emlaghhouse.com*
Fax (066) 9152369, ←, – VISA.
15 March-October – **10 rm** ☕ 125/165 – 180/300.
◆ Modern hotel in Georgian style. Inviting lounge with a log fire and well-fitted, antique furnished bedrooms: the colours and artwork of each are inspired by a local flower.

Heatons without rest., The Wood, West : ¾ km on R 559 ✆ (066) 9152288, *heatons@iol.ie, Fax (066) 9152324*, ←, – VISA.
16 rm ☕ 59/99 – 88/130.
◆ Carefully planned and recently built house with a spacious, modern look: comfortably furnished lounge area and bedrooms take up the contemporary style.

Milltown House without rest., ✆ (066) 9151372, *info@milltownhousedingle.com*
Fax (066) 9151095, ←, – VISA.
28 April-October – **10 rm** ☕ 100/130 – 100/150.
◆ Warm, welcoming establishment in a good location outside Dingle. Conservatory breakfast room and personally furnished and comfortable bedrooms, all with seating area.

Doyle's Townhouse, 5 John St, ✆ (066) 9151174, *cdoyles@iol.ie, Fax (066) 9151816*
VISA.
February-November and 27 December-7 January – **Rest** – (see ***Doyle's Seafood Bar*** below) – **8 rm** ☕ 70/140 – 148/160.
◆ Attractive house in the town centre. Tasteful guests' lounge with some antique furniture. Well-run accommodation including bedrooms decorated in homely, traditional style.

Greenmount House without rest., Gortonora, ✆ (066) 9151414, *info@greenmounthouse.com, Fax (066) 9151974*, ←, – VISA.
closed 10-31 December – **9 rm** ☕ 50/100 – 100/150.
◆ Large, yellow painted, extended house located above the town. Two comfortable lounges and a conservatory-style breakfast room. Newest bedrooms most comfortably appointed.

Pax House without rest., Upper John St, ✆ (066) 9151518, *paxhouse@iol.ie*
Fax (066) 9152461, ←, – VISA
April-October – **12 rm** ☕ 70 – 140.
◆ Family run guesthouse sited away from the town in an elevated position. Lounges are comfortable and traditionally appointed; bedrooms are colourful and personally designed.

Coastline without rest., The Wood, ✆ (066) 9152494, *coastlinedingle@eircom.net*
Fax (066) 9152493, ←, – VISA.
10 February-19 November – **6 rm** ☕ 40/90 – 60/90.
◆ Hard to miss modern guesthouse with bright pink façade. Comfy, homely interior with lots of local info. All rooms have pleasant view; those at the front face Dingle harbour.

Bambury's without rest., Mail Rd, ✆ (066) 9151244, *info@bamburysguesthouse.com*
Fax (066) 9151786, ← – VISA.
12 rm ☕ 35/70 – 70/120.
◆ Modern house located just on the edge of the town with garden and views over the sea. Large lounge and wood-floored breakfast room. Well-kept, comfortable bedrooms.

The Wild Bank's, Main St, ✆ (066) 9152888, *thewildbanks@eircom.net*
Fax (066) 9152888 – . VISA
closed Tuesday and restricted opening in winter – **Rest** (dinner only) 28 and a la carte 40/47.
◆ The bright blue exterior stands out in the busy high street. The interior is quieter. Local meat and fish dishes served by smart young people.

The Chart House, The Mall, ✆ (066) 9152255, *charthse@iol.ie, Fax (066) 9152255* – . VISA
closed Tuesday and restricted opening in winter – **Rest** (dinner only) 35 and a la carte 32/40.
◆ Attractive cottage close to a main route into town. Snug interior with exposed flint walls and wooden ceiling. Modern flourish applied to local ingredients.

Doyle's Seafood Bar, 4 John St, ✆ (066) 9151174, *cdoyles@iol.ie, Fax (066) 9151816* – ⇔ ▤. MC AE ◑ VISA
Z d
February-November and 27 December-7 January – **Rest** *(closed Sunday)* (dinner only) a la carte 35/46 ♀.
◆ Formerly a bar and retaining the traditional pubby interior with bric-a-brac and simple wooden tables. Offers a classic style menu with seafood as the backbone.

The Half Door, 3 John St, ✆ (066) 9151600, *halfdoor@iol.ie, Fax (066) 9151297* – ⇔ ▤. MC AE VISA
Z j
closed mid January-mid February and Sunday – **Rest** - Seafood - 30/37 and a la carte 34/70 ♀.
◆ A cosy atmosphere amid beams, wood and stone flooring. Menus offer a mix of dishes though the emphasis is on seafood in the classic French style. Lobsters from the tank.

Out of the Blue, Waterside, ✆ (066) 9150811, *info@outoftheblue.ie*, ☂ – ⇔. MC VISA
Z n
closed mid November-March and Wednesday – **Rest** - Seafood - (dinner booking essential) (lunch bookings not accepted) a la carte 27/56.
◆ Pleasingly unpretentious, this brightly painted shack with corrugated iron roof has fish on display at the front, and tasty seafood menus in the rustic restaurant to the rear.

Your opinions are important to us:
please write and let us know about your discoveries and experiences – good and bad!

DONEGAL (Dún na nGall) *Donegal* 712 H 4 *Ireland G. – pop. 2 453.*
See : *Donegal Castle★ AC.*
Exc. : *Donegal Coast★★ – Cliffs of Bunglass★★, W : 48¼ km by N 56 and R 263 – Glencolmcille Folk Village★★ AC, W : 53 km by N 56 and R 263 – Rossnowlagh Strand★★, S : 35½ km by N 15 and R 231 – Trabane Strand★, W : 58 km by N 56 and R 263.*
✈ *Donegal Airport* ✆ *(074) 954824.*
ℹ *The Quay* ✆ *(074) 9721148, irelandnorthwest@eircom.net.*
Dublin 264 – Londonderry 77 – Sligo 64.5.

Harvey's Point ⛰, Lough Eske, Northeast : 7 ¼ km by T 27 (Killybegs rd) ✆ (074) 9722208, *info@harveyspoint.com, Fax (074) 9722352*, ≤ Louch Eske, ⛴, ☘, ♣ – |♦| ⇔ ✆ ♿ 🅿 – 🎤 300. MC AE ◑ VISA
Rest – (see ***The Restaurant*** below) – **60 rm** ☕ ★195 – ★★290.
◆ Large hotel in tranquil setting on shores of Lough Eske and at foot of Blue Stack Mountains. Large, luxury bedrooms, some with Lough views.

Mill Park, The Mullans, Northwest : ¾ km by N 56 on Letterbarrow rd ✆ (074) 9722880, *info@millparkhotel.com, Fax (074) 9722640*, ⓒ, Fб, ▢, ☘ – |♦|, ⇔ rest, ♿ 🅿 – 🎤 400. MC AE VISA
closed 24-26 December – **Rest** 25/45 and a la carte 18/41 s. ♀ – **110 rm** ☕ ★105/170 – ★★140/210.
◆ Open-plan lounge in timber and stone leads to a well-equipped gym and large, comfortable bedrooms generously provided with mod cons - a useful family option. Spacious mezzanine restaurant; its tall pine trusses lend a rustic feel.

St Ernan's House ⛰, St Ernan's Island, Southwest : 3½ km by N 267 ✆ (074) 9721065, *res@sainternans.com, Fax (074) 9722098*, ≤ Donegal Bay, ☘, ♣ – ⇔ rest, 🅿. MC VISA. ⚔
mid April-October – **Rest** *(closed Sunday and Thursday)* (booking essential to non-residents) (dinner only) 52 – **4 rm** ☕ ★240/260 – ★★240/260, 2 suites.
◆ Very attractive Georgian house, enchantingly secluded on a wooded tidal island with delightful views of Donegal Bay. Country house-style interiors and individual bedrooms. Dining room with understated classic décor and views of the bay.

Ardeevin ⛰ without rest., Lough Eske, Barnesmore, Northeast : 9 km by N 15 following signs for Lough Eske Drive ✆ (074) 9721790, *seanmcginty@eircom.net, Fax (074) 9721790*, ≤ Lough Eske, ☘ – ⇔ 🅿. ⚔
17 March-November – **6 rm** ☕ ★40/45 – ★★60/65.
◆ Inviting, individual rooms, almost all with superb views of Lough Eske and the quiet countryside. Hearty Irish breakfasts with fresh bread baked by the long-standing owners.

Island View House without rest., Ballyshannon Rd, Southwest : 1 ¼ km on N 267 ✆ (074) 9722411, *dowds@indigo.ie*, ⇐, – P. ⁂
closed Christmas – **4 rm** ☐ ★40/45 – ★★60/66.
◆ Simple, homely establishment which overlooks Donegal Bay. Though a modern building it has a traditional appearance and style. Comfortable bedrooms.

The Restaurant (at Harvey's Point), Lough Eske, Northeast : 7 ¼ km by T 27 (Killybegs rd) ✆ (074) 9722208, *Fax (074) 9722352*, ⇐ Lough Eske, – P. MC AE VISA
closed Sunday dinner, Monday and Tuesday November-March – **Rest** 25/50 s. ♀.
◆ Wonderful views in a loughside setting. Very comfy, spacious cocktail lounge and bar. Huge restaurant: appealing menu uses regional ingredients and international elements.

at Laghy *South : 5½ km on N 15 – ✉ Donegal.*

Coxtown Manor, South : 2 m. on Ballintra rd ✆ (074) 973 4575, *coxtownmanor@oddpost.com, Fax (074) 973 4576*, – P. MC AE VISA
10 February-October – **Rest** *(closed Sunday-Monday)* (booking essential) (dinner only) a la carte 32/51 – **9 rm** ☐ ★113/123 – ★★192/232.
◆ Serenely located, this attractive, creeper-clad Georgian house boasts a comfy, country-house style sitting room and bedrooms which have a warm aura of luxury about them. Affable Belgian owner guarantees top-notch desserts using chocolate from his homeland!

DONNYBROOK (Domhnach Broc) *Dublin* 712 N 8 – *see Dublin.*

DOOGORT (Dumha Goirt) *Mayo* 712 B 5/6 – *see Achill Island.*

DOOLIN (Dúlainm) *Clare* 712 D 8 *Ireland G.*
Env. : *The Burren★★ (Cliffs of Moher★★★, Scenic Routes★★, Aillwee Cave★ AC (Waterfall★★), Corcomrow Abbey★, Kilfenora Crosses★).*
Dublin 275 – Galway 69 – Limerick 80.5.

Aran View House, Coast Rd, Northeast : ¾ km ✆ (065) 7074420, *bookings@aranview.com, Fax (065) 7074540*, ⇐, – P. MC AE VISA
Easter-October – **Rest** (dinner only) a la carte 31/36 – **19 rm** ☐ ★65/80 – ★★100/120.
◆ Georgian house set in 100 acres of working farmland, located on the main coastal road. Well-kept public areas and bedrooms, some in adjacent converted barn. Simply styled restaurant with a snug feel and traditional furnishings.

Ballyvara House, Southeast : 1 km ✆ (065) 7074467, *bvara@iol.ie, Fax (065) 7074868*, ⇐, – P. MC AE VISA. ⁂
closed 22-28 December and restricted opening in winter – **Rest** *(closed Sunday-Monday)* (dinner only) a la carte 30/38 – **9 rm** ☐ ★50/90 – ★★80/150, 2 suites.
◆ Pleasant rural views from this 19C former farm cottage, close to tourist village. Comfy lounge with squashy sofas; outside a smart decked courtyard. Bright, impressive rooms. Neatly laid dining room with Irish dishes predominant.

Cullinan's, ✆ (065) 7074183, *cullinans@eircom.net, Fax (065) 7074239*, – P. MC VISA. ⁂
closed 23-26 December – **Rest** – (see ***Restaurant*** below) – **8 rm** ☐ ★50/70 – ★★60/90.
◆ Friendly guesthouse in attractive village. Spotless facilities including small sitting room and pine-furnished bedrooms, some overlooking a little river.

Restaurant (at Cullinan's), ✆ (065) 7074183, *cullinans@eircom.net, Fax (065) 7074239* – P. MC VISA
April-October – **Rest** *(closed Wednesday)* (booking essential) (dinner only) 30 and a la carte 33/45.
◆ Simple wood floored dining room. Friendly service and charming setting with garden views and fresh flowers. Interesting contemporary menu uses local produce.

**We try to be as accurate as possible when giving room rates.
But prices are susceptible to change,
so please check rates when booking.**

DROGHEDA (Droichead Átha) *Louth* 712 M 6 *Ireland G. – pop. 31 020.*

See : *Town★ – Drogheda Museum★ – St Laurence Gate★.*

Env. : *Monasterboice★★, N : 10½ km by N 1 – Boyne Valley★★, on N 51 – Termonfeckin★, NE : 8 km by R 166.*

Exc. : *Newgrange★★★, W : 5 km by N 51 on N 2 – Old Mellifont★ – Knowth★.*

18 Seapoint, Termonfeckin ℘ (041) 9822333 – 9 Towneley Hall, Tullyallen ℘ (041) 42229.

Bus Eireann Station, Donore Rd ℘ (041) 9837070 (May-September).

Dublin 46.5 – Dundalk 35.5.

Boyne Valley H. and Country Club, Southeast : 2 km by N 1 ℘ (041) 9837737, *reservations@boyne-valley-hotel.ie, Fax (041) 9839188,* rest, – 500.

Rest 25/33 and dinner a la carte 31/45 **s.** – **72 rm** 90 – 225.

◆ Extended, ivy-clad house dating from the 1840s, with some character and set in pretty grounds. Well run and kept with well-proportioned bedrooms, the best have garden views. Basement bistro with original cast-iron range; intimate booths.

Boyne Haven House without rest., Dublin Rd, Southeast : 4 km on N 1 ℘ (041) 9836700, *taramcd@ireland.com, Fax (041) 9836700,* – .

4 rm 50/70 – 70/85.

◆ Whitewashed bungalow on the main road into town. Spotlessly kept accommodation with a homely atmosphere. Co-ordinated bedroom décor. Good breakfast menu.

DRUMSHANBO (Droim Seanbhó) *Leitrim* 712 H 5.

Dublin 166 – Carrick-on-Shannon 14.5 – Sligo 48.

Ramada H. and Suites at Lough Allen, on Keadew rd ℘ (071) 9640100, *info@loughallenhotel.com, Fax (071) 9640101,* – , rest, – 230.

Rushes : **Rest** *(closed Sunday dinner)* (dinner only and Sunday lunch) 33 **s.** – **64 rm** 75/95 – 128/160.

◆ Purpose-built hotel, beside Lough Allen, with part-stone exterior. Airy, up-to-the-minute bar. Pleasant terrace includes hot tub. Well-equipped spa. Minimalist, modern rooms. Dining room boasts stylish blond wood and seasonal menus.

Dublin, Georgian Doorways

DUBLIN - (Baile Átha Cliath)

712 N 7 *Ireland G. – pop. 1 004 614.*

Belfast 166 – Cork 248 – Londonderry 235.

TOURIST INFORMATION

Bord Failte Offices, Baggot Street Bridge, ✆ (01) 602 4000; information@dublintourism.ie – Suffolk St – Arrivals Hall, Dublin Airport – The Square, Shopping Centre, Tallaght.

PRACTICAL INFORMATION

18 *Elm Park, Nutley House, Donnybrook ✆ (01) 269 3438,* **GV**.
18 *Milltown, Lower Churchtown Rd ✆ (01) 497 6090.*
18 *Royal Dublin, North Bull Island, Dollymount ✆ (01) 833 6346.*
18 *Forrest Little, Cloghran ✆ (01) 840 1763.*
18 *Lucan, Celbridge Rd, Lucan ✆ (01) 628 2106.*
18 *Edmondstown, Rathfarnham ✆ (01) 493 2461.*
18 *Coldwinters, Newtown House, St Margaret's ✆ (01) 864 0324.*
Dublin Airport : ✆ (01) 814 1111, N : 9 Km. by N 1 **BS**.
Terminal : *Busaras (Central Bus Station) Store St.*
to Holyhead (Irish Ferries) 2 daily (3 h 15 mn) – to Holyhead (Stena Line) 1-2 daily (3 h 45 mn) – to the Isle of Man (Douglas) (Isle of Man Steam Packet Co. Ltd) (2 h 45 mn/ 4 h 45 mn) – to Liverpool (SeaCat) February-November (4 h) – to Liverpool (P & O Irish Sea) (8 h).

SIGHTS

See : *City★★★ Trinity College★★* **JY** *– Old Library★★★ (Treasury★★★, Long Room★★) – Dublin Castle★★ (Chester Beatty Library★★★)* **HY** *– Christ Church Cathedral★★* **HY** *– St Patrick's Cathedral★★* **HZ** *– Marsh's Library★★* **HZ** *– National Museum★★ (The Treasury★★)* **KZ** *– National Gallery★★* **KZ** *– Newman House★★* **JZ** *– Bank of Ireland★★* **JY** *– Custom House★★* **KX** *– Kilmainham Gaol Museum★★* **AT M6** *– Kilmainham Hospital★★* **AT** *– Phoenix Park★★ – National Botanic Gardens★★* **BS** *– Marino Casino★★* **CS** *– Tailors' Hall★* **HY** *– City Hall★* **HY** *– Temple Bar★* **HJY** *– Liffey Bridge★* **JY** *– Merrion Square★* **KZ** *– Number Twenty-Nine★* **KZ D** *– Grafton Street★* **JYZ** *– Powerscourt Centre★* **JY** *– Rotunda Hospital Chapel★* **JX** *– O'Connell Street★ (GPO Building★)* **JX** *– Hugh Lane Municipal Gallery of Modern Art★* **JX M4** *– Pro-Cathedral★* **JX** *– Bluecoat School★* **BS F** *– Guinness Museum★* **BT M7** *– Rathfarnham Castle★* **AT** *– Zoological Gardens★* **AS** *– Ceol★* **BS n**.

Env. : *The Ben of Howth★ (≤★), NE: 9½ Km. by R105* **CS**.

Exc. : *Powerscourt★★ (Waterfall★★* **AC***), S : 22½ Km. by N 11 and R 117* **EV** *– Russborough House★★★, SW : 35½ Km. by N 81* **BT**.

DUBLIN

Adelaïde Rd .... BT 3
Alfie Byrne Rd .... CS 5
Bath Ave .... CT 9
Benburb St .... BS 15
Berkeley Rd .... BS 16
Botanic Rd .... BS 19
Canal Rd .... BT 30
Clanbrassil St .... BT 40
Conyngham Rd .... AS 48
Denmark St .... BS 52
Donnybrook Rd .... CT 54
Dorset St .... BS 55
Drimnagh Rd .... AT 57
Eglinton Rd .... CT 63
Grand Parade .... BT 72
Inchicore Rd .... AT 79
Infirmary Rd .... AS 81
James St .... BT 84
Leeson St Upper .... BT 94
Macken St .... BST 99
Morehampton Rd .... BT 108
Mount St Upper .... BT 112
Palmerston Park .... BT 123
Phibsborough Rd .... BS 132
Rathmines Rd Upper .... BT 135
Ringsend Rd .... CT 139
St Agnes Rd .... AT 141
St Alphonsus Rd .... BS 144
St John's Rd West .... AS 147
Sandford Rd .... BT 151
Shelbourne Rd .... CT 157
Shrewsbury Rd .... CT 159
South Circular Rd .... AS 162
Suir Rd .... AT 168
Terenure Rd East .... BT 172
Thomas St West .... BT 174
Victoria Quay .... BS 178
Western Way .... BS 184
Wolfe Tone Quay .... BS 195

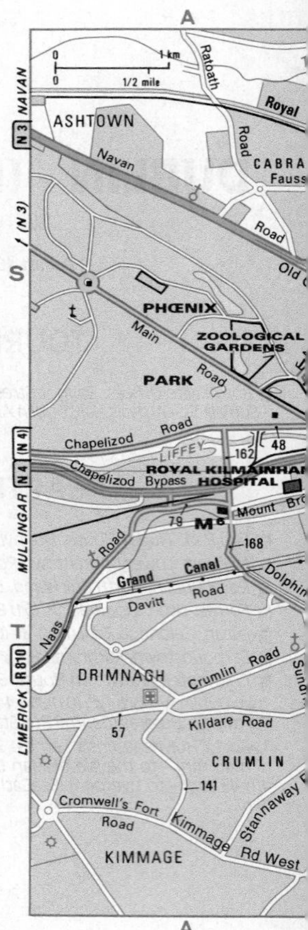

City Centre *Dublin.*

The Merrion, Upper Merrion St, D2, ✆ (01) 603 0600, *info@merrionhotel.com* *Fax (01) 603 0700,* – rm, – 50. AE VISA. KZ e
Rest – (see ***The Cellar*** and ***The Cellar Bar*** below) – 27 – **133 rm** 410 – 515, 10 suites.
◆ Classic hotel in series of elegantly restored Georgian town houses; many of the individually designed grand rooms overlook pleasant gardens. Irish art in opulent lounges.

The Westin, College Green, Westmoreland St, ✆ (01) 645 1000, *reservations.dublin@westin.com, Fax (01) 645 1234* – – 250. AE VISA. JY n
The Exchange : Rest *(closed Saturday lunch)* a la carte 33/51 – ***The Mint :*** Rest a la carte approx 26/60 s. – 25 – **150 rm** 190/410 – 190/410, 13 suites.
◆ Immaculately kept and consummately run hotel in a useful central location. Smart uniform interiors and an ornate period banking hall. Excellent bedrooms with marvellous beds. Elegant, Art Deco 1920s-style dining in Exchange. More informal fare at The Mint.

Conrad Dublin, Earlsfort Terrace, D2, ✆ (01) 602 8900, *dublininfo@conradhotels.com* *Fax (01) 676 5424,* – – 370. AE VISA. JZ w
Alex : Rest 32/39 s. and a la carte – 25 – **192 rm** 180/520 – 195/535.
◆ Smart, business oriented international hotel opposite the National Concert Hall. Popular pub-style bar. Spacious rooms with bright, modern décor and comprehensive facilities. Bright pastel and well-run brasserie.

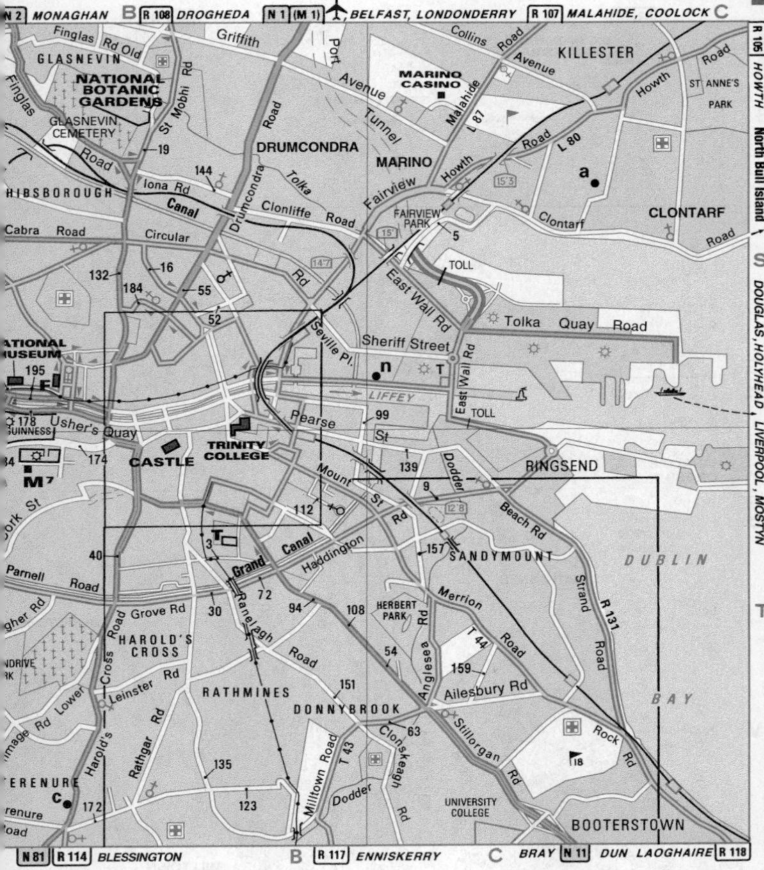

The Westbury, Grafton St, D2, ✆ (01) 679 1122, *westbury@jurysdoyle.com*, *Fax (01) 679 7078*, ⛹ – 🛗 ⋈ ▤ 📞 ♿ 🚗 – 🏛 220. MC AE ⦿ VISA. ⚟ JY b
Russell Room : Rest a la carte 34/62 s. – ***The Sandbank :*** Rest a la carte approx 21 s. – ☕ 24 – **196 rm** ✝401 – ✝✝441, 8 suites.
◆ Imposing marble foyer and stairs leading to lounge famous for afternoon teas. Huge luxurious bedrooms, most with air-conditioning, offer every conceivable facility. Russell Room has distinctive, formal feel. Informal, bistro-style Sandbank.

The Clarence, 6-8 Wellington Quay, D2, ✆ (01) 407 0800, *reservations@theclarence.ie*, *Fax (01) 407 0820*, ⋞, ⛹ – 🛗 ⋈ 📞 ♿ P – 🏛 60. MC AE ⦿ VISA. ⚟ HY a
Rest – (see ***The Tea Room*** below) – ☕ 28 – **43 rm** ✝340 – ✝✝340, 5 suites.
◆ A discreet, stylish warehouse conversion in Temple Bar overlooking river and boasting contemporary interior design. Small panelled library. Modern, distinctive bedrooms.

The Fitzwilliam, St Stephen's Green, D2, ✆ (01) 478 7000, *enq@fitzwilliamhotel.com*, *Fax (01) 478 7878*, ⋞ – 🛗 ⋈, ▤ rest, 📞 🚗 – 🏛 70. MC AE ⦿ VISA. ⚟ JZ d
Citron : Rest 30/40 and a la carte 30/45 – (see also ***Thornton's*** below) – ☕ 25 – **137 rm** ✝360 – ✝✝360, 2 suites.
◆ Rewardingly overlooks the Green and boasts a bright contemporary interior. Spacious, finely appointed rooms offer understated elegance. Largest hotel roof garden in Europe. Cheerful, informal brasserie.

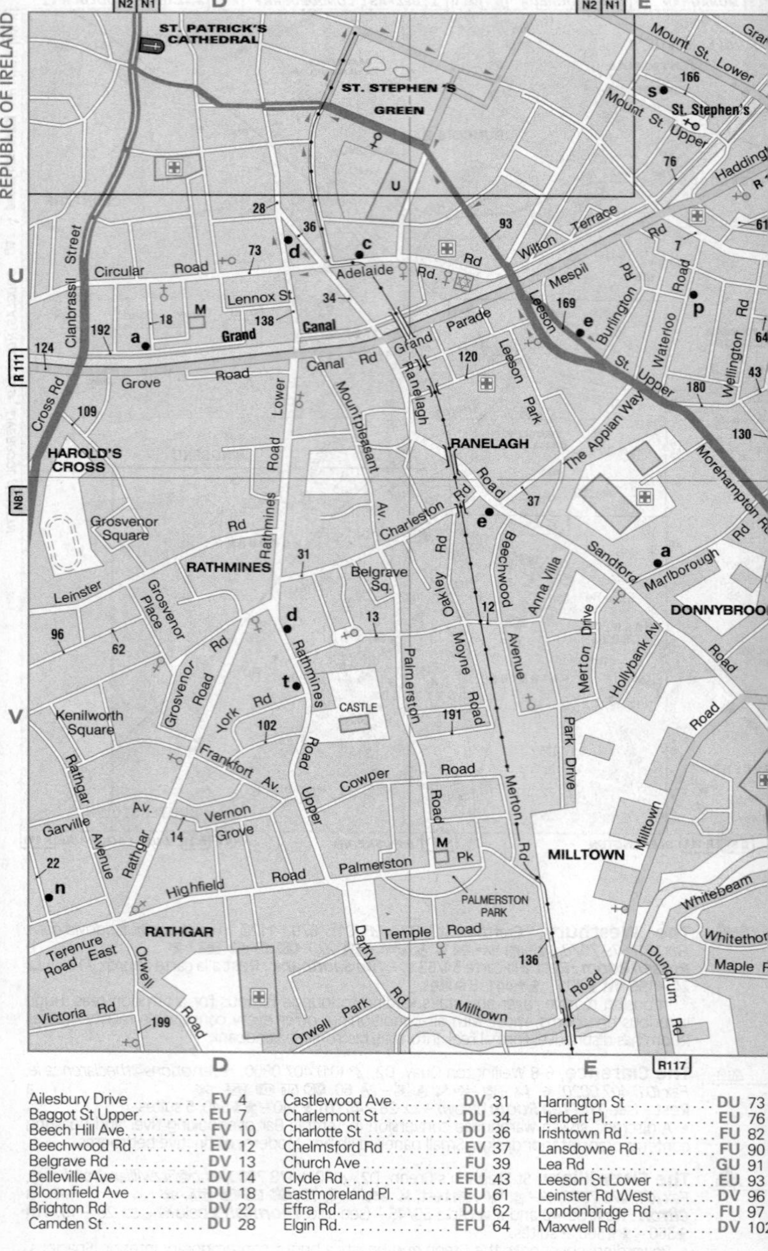

Ailesbury Drive	FV	4	Castlewood Ave	DV	31	Harrington St	DU	73
Baggot St Upper	EU	7	Charlemont St	DU	34	Herbert Pl.	EU	76
Beech Hill Ave.	FV	10	Charlotte St	DU	36	Irishtown Rd	FU	82
Beechwood Rd.	EV	12	Chelmsford Rd	EV	37	Lansdowne Rd	FU	90
Belgrave Rd	DV	13	Church Ave	FU	39	Lea Rd	GU	91
Belleville Ave	DV	14	Clyde Rd	EFU	43	Leeson St Lower	EU	93
Bloomfield Ave	DU	18	Eastmoreland Pl.	EU	61	Leinster Rd West	DV	96
Brighton Rd	DV	22	Effra Rd	DU	62	Londonbridge Rd	FU	97
Camden St	DU	28	Elgin Rd	EFU	64	Maxwell Rd	DV	102

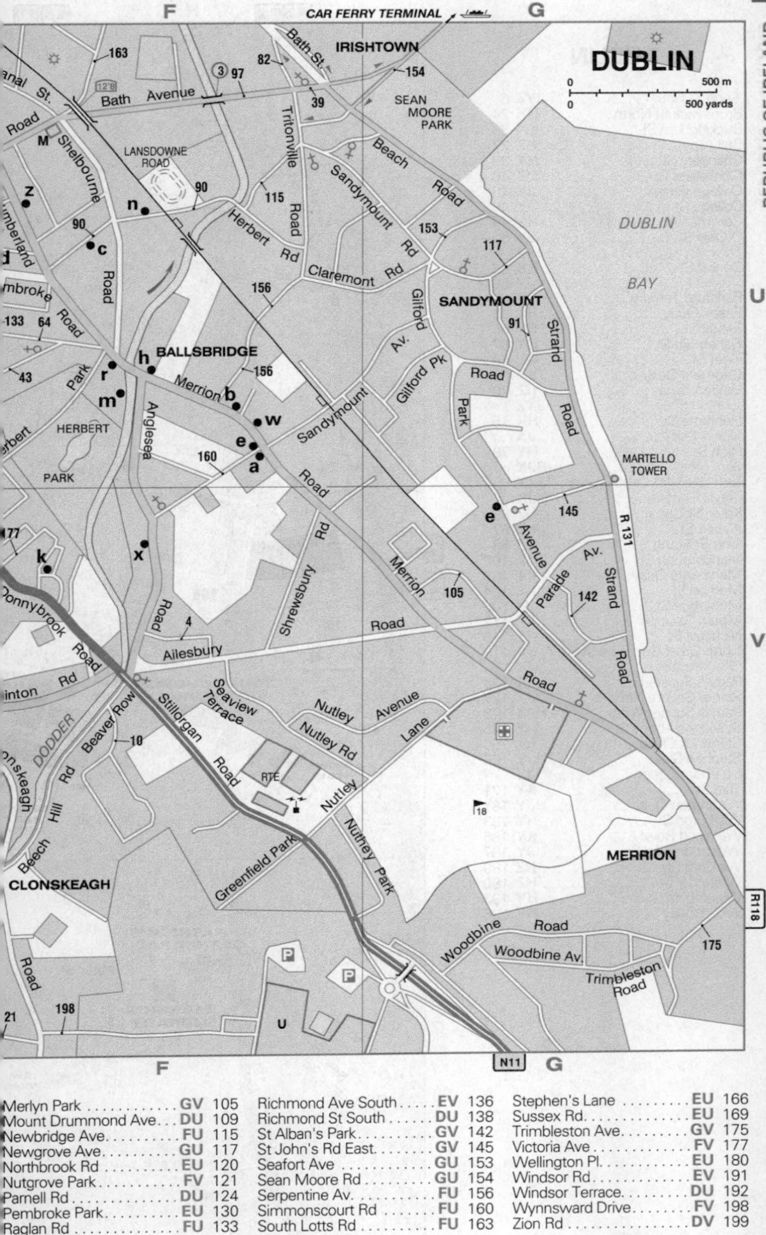

Merlyn Park . . . . GV 105
Mount Drummond Ave. . . DU 109
Newbridge Ave. . . . . FU 115
Newgrove Ave. . . . . GU 117
Northbrook Rd . . . . EU 120
Nutgrove Park . . . . FV 121
Parnell Rd . . . . DU 124
Pembroke Park. . . . . EU 130
Raglan Rd . . . . FU 133
Richmond Ave South . . . . . EV 136
Richmond St South . . . . . . DU 138
St Alban's Park . . . . GV 142
St John's Rd East. . . . . GV 145
Seafort Ave . . . . GU 153
Sean Moore Rd . . . . GU 154
Serpentine Av. . . . . FU 156
Simmonscourt Rd . . . . FU 160
South Lotts Rd . . . . FU 163
Stephen's Lane . . . . EU 166
Sussex Rd. . . . . EU 169
Trimbleston Ave. . . . . GV 175
Victoria Ave . . . . FV 177
Wellington Pl. . . . . EU 180
Windsor Rd. . . . . EV 191
Windsor Terrace. . . . . DU 192
Wynnsward Drive. . . . . FV 198
Zion Rd . . . . DV 199

DUBLIN

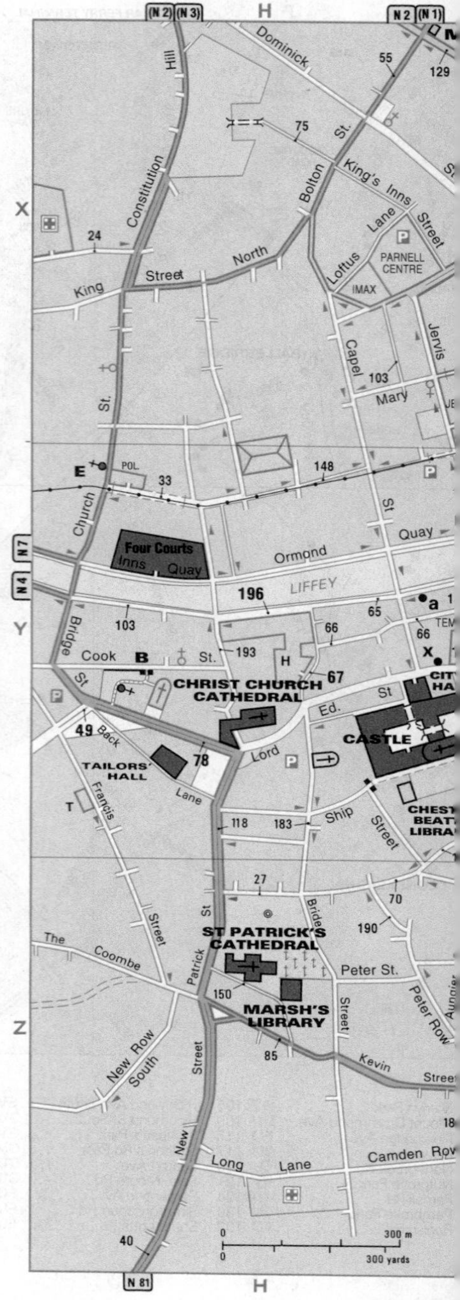

H
X
Y
Z
N 2
N 3
N 1
N 7
N 4
N 81
Dominick
Hill
Constitution
Bolton
St.
King's Inns
Street
Lane
Loftus
PARNELL CENTRE
IMAX
King
Street
North
Capel
Jervis
Mary
Church
St.
POL
Four Courts
Inns
Quay
Ormond
Quay
LIFFEY
Bridge
Cook
St.
CHRIST CHURCH CATHEDRAL
Ed.
St
CASTLE
Back
Lane
Lord
TAILORS' HALL
Francis
Ship
Street
Street
CHESTER BEATTY LIBRARY
Bride
ST PATRICK'S CATHEDRAL
MARSH'S LIBRARY
Patrick
St
The
Coombe
Peter St.
Peter Row
New Row South
Street
Kevin
Street
New
Long
Lane
Camden Row
0
300 m
300 yards

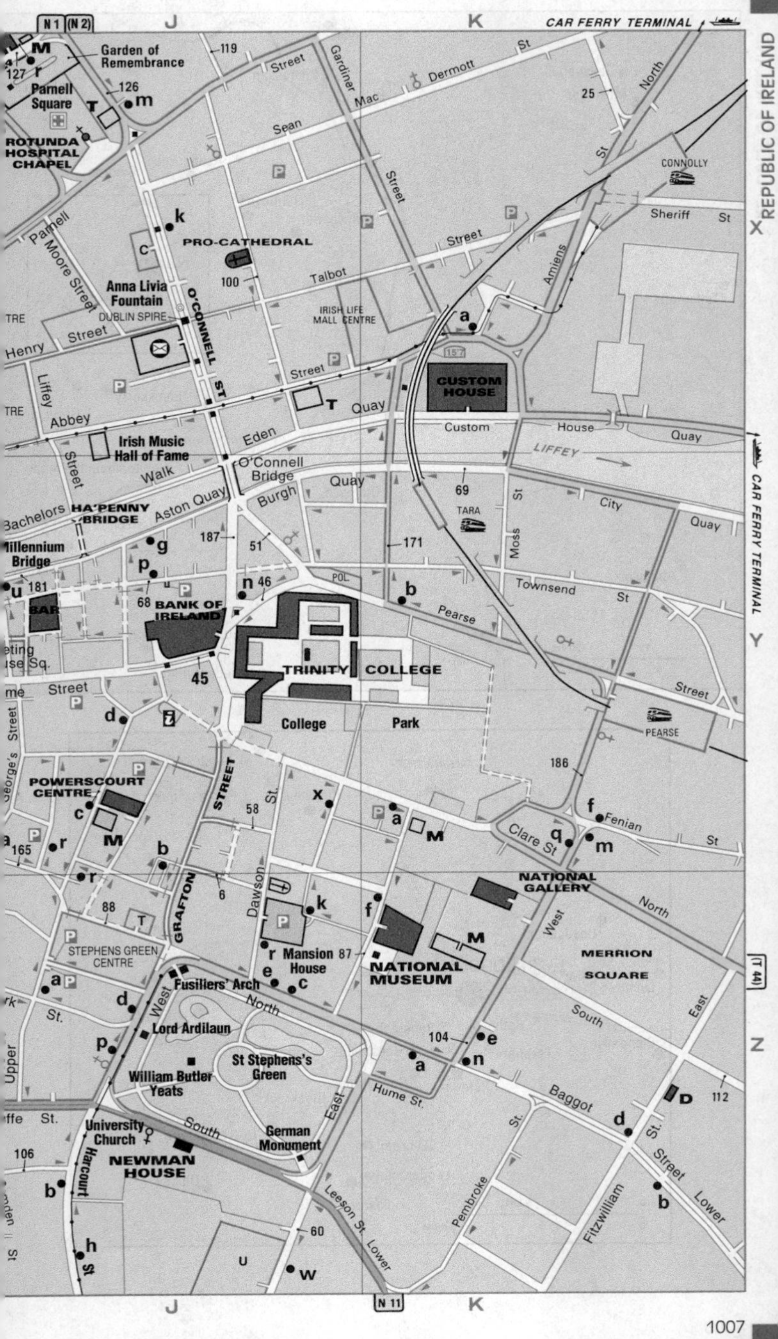

CAR FERRY TERMINAL
REPUBLIC OF IRELAND
Garden of Remembrance
Parnell Square
ROTUNDA HOSPITAL CHAPEL
PRO-CATHEDRAL
Anna Livia Fountain
DUBLIN SPIRE
O'CONNELL ST
IRISH LIFE MALL CENTRE
CUSTOM HOUSE
CONNOLLY
Irish Music Hall of Fame
O'Connell Bridge
HA'PENNY BRIDGE
Millennium Bridge
LIFFEY
TARA
BANK OF IRELAND
TRINITY COLLEGE
College Park
PEARSE
POWERSCOURT CENTRE
GRAFTON STREET
NATIONAL GALLERY
MERRION SQUARE
STEPHENS GREEN CENTRE
Mansion House
NATIONAL MUSEUM
Fusiliers' Arch
Lord Ardilaun
St Stephens's Green
William Butler Yeats
University Church
NEWMAN HOUSE
German Monument

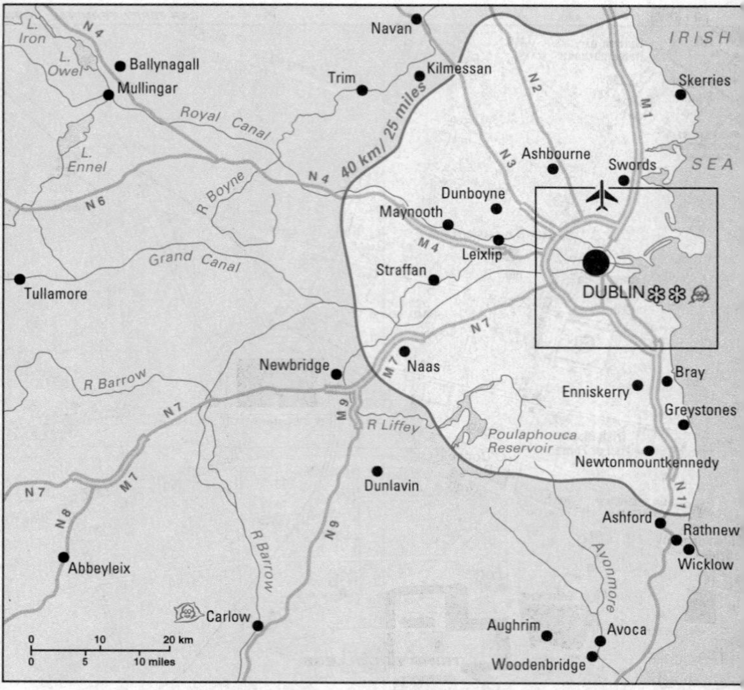

L. Iron
N 4
Navan
IRISH
L. Owel
Ballynagall
Kilmessan
Mullingar
Trim
40 km/ 25 miles
N 2
M 1
Skerries
Royal Canal
L. Ennel
N 3
Ashbourne
Swords
SEA
R Boyne
N 4
N 6
Dunboyne
Maynooth
M 4
Leixlip
Grand Canal
Straffan
Tullamore
DUBLIN
N 7
Newbridge
Naas
M 7
Bray
R Barrow
Enniskerry
N 7
M 9
R Liffey
Greystones
Poulaphouca Reservoir
Newtonmountkennedy
Dunlavin
N 7
M 7
N 11
N 8
R Barrow
N 9
Ashford
Rathnew
Avonmore
Wicklow
Abbeyleix
Carlow
Aughrim
Avoca
Woodenbridge
0 10 20 km
0 5 10 miles

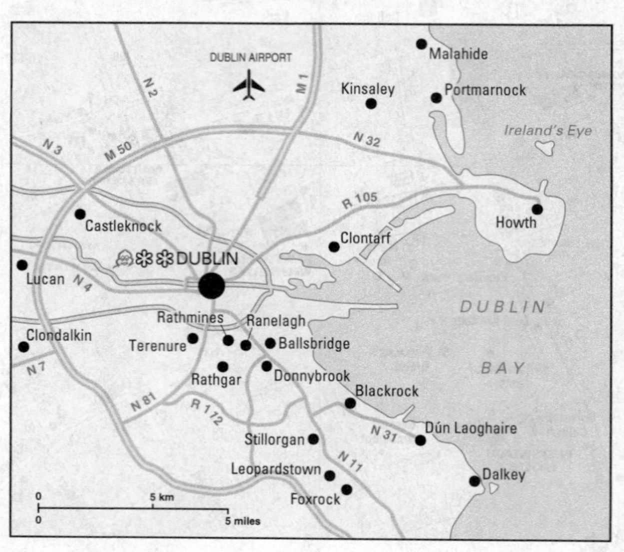

Stephen's Green, Cliffe St, off St Stephen's Green, D2, ☎ (01) 607 3600, *info@ocallaghanhotels.com, Fax (01) 661 5663,* – 50. JZ f
closed 25-27 December – ***The Pie Dish :*** **Rest** *(closed lunch Saturday and Sunday)* a la carte 35/60 **s.** – 14 – **64 rm** 325 – 325, 11 suites.
◆ This smart modern hotel housed in an originally Georgian property is popular with business clients. Bright, relatively compact bedrooms offer a good range of facilities. Bright and breezy bistro restaurant.

Brooks, Drury St, D2, ☎ (01) 670 4000, *sales@brookshotel.ie, Fax (01) 670 4455,* – 30. JY r
Francesca's : **Rest** (dinner only) a la carte 26/48 – **98 rm** 195/240 – 255/290.
◆ Commercial hotel in modern English town house style. Smart lounges and spacious rooms with tasteful feel and good facilities. Extras in top range rooms, at a supplement. Ground floor Francesca's restaurant with open kitchen for chef-watching.

The Alexander, Fienian St, Merrion Sq, D2, ☎ (01) 607 3700, *info@ocallaghanhotels.com, Fax (01) 661 5663,* – 400. KY f
closed 24-26 December – ***Caravaggio's :*** **Rest** (bar lunch Saturday and Sunday) a la carte 25/35 **s.** – 14 – **98 rm** 325 – 325, 4 suites.
◆ This bright corporate hotel, well placed for museums and Trinity College, has a stylish contemporary interior. Spacious comfortable rooms and suites with good facilities. Stylish contemporary restaurant with wide-ranging menus.

The Davenport, Lower Merrion St, off Merrion Sq, D2, ☎ (01) 607 3500, *info@ocallaghanhotels.com, Fax (01) 661 5663,* – 275. KY m
Lanyon : **Rest** a la carte 35/60 **s.** – 14 – **112 rm** 371 – 371, 2 suites.
◆ Sumptuous Victorian gospel hall façade heralds elegant hotel popular with business clientèle. Tastefully furnished, well-fitted rooms. Presidents bar honours past leaders. Dining room with formal, Georgian interior.

The Gresham, 23 Upper O'Connell St, D1, ☎ (01) 874 6881, *info@thegresham.com, Fax (01) 878 7175,* – rest, – 400. JX k
23 : **Rest** (dinner only) a la carte 33/52 – ***The Aberdeen :*** **Rest** 26/45 and a la carte 31/49 – 19 – **283 rm** 450 – 450, 6 suites.
◆ Long established restored 19C property in a famous street offers elegance tinged with luxury. Some penthouse suites. Well-equipped business centre, lounge and Toddy's bar. The Aberdeen boasts formal ambience. 23 is named after available wines by glass.

Clarion H. Dublin IFSC, Excise Walk, International Financial Services Centre, D1, ☎ (01) 433 8800, *info@clarionhotelifsc.com, Fax (01) 433 8811,* – 120. CS n
closed 25 December – ***Sinergie :*** **Rest** *(closed Saturday lunch)* 15/25 and a la carte 21/28 – ***Kudos :*** **Rest** - Asian - *(closed Sunday)* a la carte 19/34 **s.** – 21 – **154 rm** 265 – 265, 8 suites.
◆ In the heart of a modern financial district, a swish hotel for the business person: smart gym and light, spacious, contemporary rooms, some with balconies. Busy bar leads to clean-lined Sinergie with glass walls onto the kitchen. Kudos serves Asian menus.

Morrison, Lower Ormond Quay, D1, ☎ (01) 887 2400, *info@morrisonhotel.ie, Fax (01) 878 3185* – rm, – 240. HY r
closed 24-26 December – ***Halo :*** **Rest** a la carte 24/47 – 22 – **136 rm** 285 – 285, 4 suites.
◆ Modern riverside hotel with ultra-contemporary interior by acclaimed fashion designer John Rocha. Hi-tech amenities in rooms. "Lobo" late-night club and sushi bar.

brownes, 22 St Stephen's Green, D2, ☎ (01) 638 3939, *info@brownesdublin.com, Fax (01) 638 3900* – JZ c
closed 25-27 December – **Rest** – (see ***brownes brasserie*** below) – 21 – **11 rm** 200 – 270.
◆ Restored Georgian town house with original fittings in situ. Combines traditional charm with modern comfort.Bedrooms are well-appointed and stylish, some with view.

The Morgan without rest., 10 Fleet St, D2, ☎ (01) 679 3939, *reservations@themorgan.com, Fax (01) 679 3946* – , rest, JY p
closed 23-26 December – 18 – **106 rm** 130 – 130, 15 suites.
◆ Discreet designer contemporary hotel in vibrant area emphasises style. Simple elegant foyer contrasts with large, busy bar. Sleek minimalist décor in well-equipped bedrooms.

Mont Clare, Lower Merrion St, off Merrion Sq, D2, ☎ (01) 607 3800, *info@ocallaghanhotels.com* – , rest, – 120. KY q
closed 24-26 December – ***Goldsmiths :*** **Rest** *(closed lunch Saturday and Sunday)* a la carte 30/40 **s.** – 14 – **74 rm** 253 – 253.
◆ Classic property with elegant panelled reception and tasteful comfortable rooms at heart of Georgian Dublin. Corporate suites available. Traditional pub style Gallery bar. Formal restaurant with tried-and-tested menus.

Cassidys, Cavendish Row, Upper O'Connell St, D1, (01) 878 0555, *stay@cassidyshotel.com, Fax (01) 878 0687* – , rest, – 80. VISA. JX m
closed 24-26 December – ***Number Six :*** **Rest** (dinner only) 21/25 and a la carte 23/44 **s.** – **112 rm** 85/160 – 150/185, 1 suite.

◆ Classic Georgian redbrick town house makes an elegant backdrop for modern comfort. Cheerful room décor. Limited on-street guest parking. Popular Groomes bar open to public. Bright, stylish dining room sports a homely ambience.

The Mercer, Mercer Street Lower, D2, (01) 478 2179, *stay@mercerhotel.ie, Fax (01) 478 0328* – – 100. VISA. JZ a
closed 23-29 December – ***Cusack's :*** **Rest** *(closed Sunday)* a la carte approx 25 – 5 – **41 rm** 185/220 – 250.

◆ This modern boutique hotel, hidden away next to the Royal College of Surgeons, is pleasant and stylish. It offers comprehensive amenities including air conditioning. Smart yet relaxing restaurant.

Trinity Capital, Pearse St, D2, (01) 648 1000, *info@trinitycapital-hotel.com, Fax (01) 648 1010* – , rest, – 40. VISA. KY b
closed 24-26 December – ***Siena :*** **Rest** (bar lunch)/dinner 27 and a la carte 18/32 **s.** – 15 – **82 rm** 165/220 – 213/265.

◆ Spacious lobby with striking modern furnishings leads off to stylish, soft-toned bedrooms, generously supplied with mod cons. A few minutes walk from Trinity College. Relaxed and fashionably styled dining room filled with natural light.

Buswells, Molesworth St, D2, (01) 614 6500, *buswells@quinn-hotels.com, Fax (01) 676 2090,* – – 85. VISA. KZ
closed 24-26 December – ***Trumans :*** **Rest** (carvery lunch)/dinner 35/40 – **65 rm** 160/195 – 240/300, 2 suites.

◆ Elegant little hotel in quiet central location offering modern amenities while retaining its Georgian charm. Relax in cushioned lounge or cosy, pleasingly furnished rooms. Smart Trumans for formal dining.

Camden Court, Camden St, D2, (01) 475 9666, *sales@camdencourthotel.com, Fax (01) 475 9677,* , , – , rest, – 125. VISA. DU c
closed 23-28 December – ***The Court :*** **Rest** (dinner only and Sunday lunch) 24/32 and a la carte 28/37 – **246 rm** 220/290 – 220/290.

◆ A vaulted passageway leads to this smart, popular hotel in a thriving locality. Colourful soft furnishings in cosy, well-equipped rooms. Cheerful bar on an Irish myth theme. Open, informal restaurant with polished wood and popular menus.

Beresford Hall without rest., 2 Beresford Pl, D1, (01) 801 4500, *stay@beresfordhall.ie, Fax (01) 801 4501* – . VISA. KX a
closed 24 December-3 January – **16 rm** 80/90 – 110/160.

◆ Georgian townhouse on edge of city centre, exuding a stylish, discreet air. Comfy lounge with chintz décor. Especially impressive bedrooms: original features in most.

Longfield's, 10 Lower Fitzwilliam St, D2, (01) 676 1367, *info@longfields.ie, Fax (01) 676 1542* – , rest. VISA. KZ d
@Number 10 : **Rest** *(closed Saturday lunch, Sunday and Monday)* 25 (lunch) and dinner a la carte 26/42 – **26 rm** 90 – 235.

◆ Classic Georgian town house on reputedly Europe's longest Georgian road. Spacious lounge; stylish, individually furnished rooms of good size, all redolent of times gone by.

Harrington Hall without rest., 70 Harcourt St, D2, (01) 475 3497, *harringtonhall@eircom.net, Fax (01) 475 4544* – . VISA. JZ h
28 rm 115/173 – 173/240.

◆ Two usefully located mid-terrace Georgian town houses. Friendly and well-run. Bright, spacious bedrooms with soundproofing, ceiling fans, access to fax and internet.

Trinity Lodge without rest., 12 South Frederick St, D2, (01) 617 0900, *trinitylodge@eircom.net, Fax (01) 617 0999* – . VISA. JY x
closed 22-27 December – **12 rm** 110/180 – 150/190.

◆ Elegant Georgian town houses with local landmarks nearby. Spacious, well-furnished bedrooms with good level of comfort. Modern suites and de luxe rooms. Good value.

Eliza Lodge without rest., 23-24 Wellington Quay, D2, (01) 671 8044, *info@dublinlodge.com, Fax (01) 671 8362,* – . VISA. JY u
closed 22 December-2 January – **18 rm** 76/150 – 130/198.

◆ Ideally placed for Temple Bar nightlife. Lounge with video facilities and internet access; comfortable, practical rooms: the balconied penthouse floor has fine river views.

Kilronan House without rest., 70 Adelaide Rd, D2, (01) 475 5266, *info@dublinn.com, Fax (01) 478 2841* – . VISA. DU c
12 rm 45/120 – 90/170.

◆ In the heart of Georgian Dublin, a good value, well-kept town house run by knowledgeable, friendly couple. Individually styled rooms; sustaining breakfasts.

XXXX ✿✿ **Patrick Guilbaud,** 21 Upper Merrion St, D2, ✆ (01) 676 4192, *restaurantpatrickguilbaud@eircom.net, Fax (01) 661 0052* – ⇆ ▤ ⇔ 25. MC AE ① VISA KZ e
closed 1 week after Christmas, Sunday and Monday – **Rest** 45 (lunch) and a la carte 83/112 s. ♀.

Spec. Oysters and caviar. Calf's sweetbreads and liquorice, parsnip sauce, lemon confit. Assiette of chocolate.

◆ Top class restaurant run by consummate professional offering accomplished Irish influenced dishes in elegant Georgian town house. Contemporary Irish art collection.

XXXX ✿ **Thornton's** (at The Fitzwilliam H.), 128 St Stephen's Green, D2, ✆ (01) 478 7008, *thorntonsrestaurant@eircom.net, Fax (01) 478 7009* – ⇆ ▤ ⇔. MC AE ① VISA JZ d
closed 1 week Christmas, Good Friday, Sunday and Monday – **Rest** 30/40 (lunch) and a la carte 91/104 ♀.

Spec. Sautéed prawns with prawn bisque, truffle sabayon. Suckling pig with trotter, glazed turnip and poitin sauce. Orange soufflé with mandarin sorbet.

◆ Stylish modern restaurant on second floor offers interesting culinary ideas drawing on Irish, French and Italian cuisine, and fine views too. Good value lunch menus.

XXX **Shanahan's on the Green,** 119 St Stephen's Green, D2, ✆ (01) 407 0939, *sales@shanahans.ie, Fax (01) 407 0940* – ⇆ ▤. MC AE ① VISA JZ p
closed Christmas-New Year and Good Friday – **Rest** (booking essential) (dinner only and Friday lunch) a la carte 76/99 ♀.

◆ Sumptuous Georgian town house: upper floor window tables survey the Green. Supreme comfort enhances your enjoyment of strong seafood dishes and choice cuts of Irish beef.

XXX ✿ **L'Ecrivain** (Clarke), 109A Lower Baggot St, D2, ✆ (01) 661 1919, *enquiries@lecrivain.com, Fax (01) 661 0617,* ⛱ – ⇆ ▤ ⇔ 20. MC AE VISA KZ b
closed 23 December-4 January, Easter, Saturday lunch, Sunday and Bank Holidays – **Rest** (booking essential) 45/70 and dinner a la carte 74/98 ♀.

Spec. Loin of wild venison, candied pear, celeriac mousseline and beetroot jus. Assiette of Dublin Bay prawns. Roast turbot with pea purée, foie gras tart and girolles.

◆ Soft piano notes add to the welcoming ambience. Robust, well prepared, modern Irish food with emphasis on fish and game. Private dining room has agreeable wine selection.

XXX **Chapter One,** The Dublin Writers Museum, 18-19 Parnell Sq, D1, ✆ (01) 873 2266, *info@chapteronerestaurant.com, Fax (01) 873 2330* – ⇆ ▤ ⇔ 14. MC VISA JX r
closed first 2 weeks August, 24 December-8 January, Saturday lunch, Sunday and Monday – **Rest** 31 (lunch) and dinner a la carte 52/60 ♀.

◆ In basement of historic building, once home to whiskey baron. Comfortable restaurant with Irish art on walls. Interesting menus focus on good hearty food: sample the oysters.

XX **The Tea Room** (at The Clarence H.), 6-8 Wellington Quay, D2, ✆ (01) 407 0813, *tearoom@theclarence.ie, Fax (01) 407 0826* – ⇆. MC AE ① VISA HY a
closed 24-26 December and Saturday lunch – **Rest** (booking essential) 30/55 ♀.

◆ Spacious elegant ground floor room with soaring coved ceiling and stylish contemporary décor offers interesting modern Irish dishes with hint of continental influence.

XX **brownes brasserie** (at brownes H.), 22 St Stephen's Green, D2, ✆ (01) 638 3939, *info@brownesdublin.ie, Fax (01) 638 3900* – ⇆ ▤. MC AE ① VISA JZ c
closed Saturday lunch and Bank Holidays – **Rest** (booking essential) 30 (lunch) and a la carte 43/53 ♀.

◆ Smart, characterful, with a Belle Epoque feel. On the ground floor of the eponymous Georgian town house with interesting and appealing classic dishes. A good value location.

XX **The Cellar** (at The Merrion H.), Upper Merrion St, D2, ✆ (01) 603 0630, *Fax (01) 603 0700* – ⇆ ▤ ⇔. MC AE ① VISA KZ e
closed Saturday lunch – **Rest** 25 (lunch) and dinner a la carte 31/58 ♀.

◆ Smart open-plan basement restaurant with informal ambience offering well prepared formal style fare crossing Irish with Mediterranean influences. Good value lunch menu.

XX **One Pico,** 5-6 Molesworth Pl, D2, ✆ (01) 676 0300, *eamonnoreilly@ireland.com, Fax (01) 676 0411* – ⇆ ▤. MC AE ① VISA JZ k
closed 24-31 December, Sunday and Bank Holidays – **Rest** 25/35 and a la carte 40/55 s. ♀.

◆ Wide-ranging cuisine, classic and traditional by turns, always with an elaborate, eclectic edge. Décor and service share a pleasant formality, crisp, modern and stylish.

XX **Les Frères Jacques,** 74 Dame St, D2, ✆ (01) 679 4555, *info@lesfreresjacques.com, Fax (01) 679 4725* – ⇆ ▤. MC AE VISA HY x
closed 24 December-3 January, Saturday lunch, Sunday and Bank Holidays – **Rest** - French - 22/36 and a la carte 50/62 ♀.

◆ Smart popular family-run bistro offering well prepared simple classic French cuisine with fresh fish and seafood a speciality, served by efficient team of French staff.

XX **Peploe's,** 16 St Stephen's Green, D2, (01) 676 3144, *reservations@peploes.com, Fax (01) 676 3154* – . AE VISA JZ e
closed 25-29 December and Good Friday – **Rest** 33/45 and a la carte 29/49.
• Fashionable restaurant - a former bank vault - by the Green. Irish wall mural, Italian leather chairs, suede banquettes. Original dishes with pronounced Mediterranean accents.

XX **Saagar,** 16 Harcourt St, D2, (01) 475 5060, *info@saagarindianrestaurants.com, Fax (01) 475 5741* – . AE VISA JZ b
closed 25 December, 1 January, Sunday and Bank Holidays – **Rest** - Indian - a la carte 16/27 s.
• Well-run restaurant serving subtly toned, freshly prepared Indian fare in basement of Georgian terraced house. Main road setting. Ring bell at foot of stairs to enter.

XX **Locks,** 1 Windsor Terrace, Portobello, D8, (01) 4543391, *Fax (01) 4538352* – . AE VISA DU a
closed 1 week Easter, 1 week Christmas-New Year, Saturday lunch, Sunday and Bank Holidays – **Rest** (dinner booking essential) 29/49 and a la carte 59/75 ♀.
• Street corner mainstay for 20 years; watch the swans swimming by on adjacent canal. Offers wide range, from simple one course dishes to more elaborate classic French fare.

XX **Jacobs Ladder,** 4-5 Nassau St, D2, (01) 670 3865, *dining@jacobsladder.ie, Fax (01) 670 3868* – . AE VISA KY a
closed 1 week Christmas, 1 week August, 17 March, Sunday, Monday and Bank Holidays – **Rest** (booking essential) 37/45 (dinner) and a la carte 30/57 s. ♀.
• Up a narrow staircase, this popular small first floor restaurant with unfussy modern décor and a good view offers good value modern Irish fare and very personable service.

XX **Siam Thai,** 14-15 Andrew St, D2, (01) 677 3363, *siam@eircom.net, Fax (01) 670 7644* – . AE VISA JY d
closed 25-26 December and lunch Saturday and Sunday – **Rest** - Thai - 35 (dinner) and a la carte 26/35 s.
• Centrally located restaurant with a warm, homely feel, embodied by woven Thai prints. Basement room for parties. Daily specials; Thai menus with choice and originality.

XX **Jaipur,** 41 South Great George's St, D2, (01) 677 0999, *dublin@jaipur.ie, Fax (01) 677 0979* – . AE VISA JY a
closed 25-26 December – **Rest** - Indian - (dinner only) 40 and a la carte 23/43.
• Vivid modernity in the city centre; run by knowledgable team. Immaculately laid, linen-clad tables. Interesting, freshly prepared Indian dishes using unique variations.

XX **Bang Café,** 11 Merrion Row, D2, (01) 676 0898, *Fax (01) 676 0899* – . AE VISA KZ a
closed 1 week Christmas, Sunday and Bank Holidays – **Rest** (booking essential) a la carte 26/47.
• Stylish, mirror-lined lounge bar, closely set linen-topped tables and an open kitchen lend a lively, contemporary air. Flavourful menu balances the classical and the creative.

X **Bleu,** Joshua House, Dawson St, D2, (01) 676 7015, *Fax (01) 676 7027* – . AE VISA JZ r
closed 25-26 December – **Rest** 20/29 and a la carte 21/38 s. ♀.
• Distinctive modern interior serves as chic background to this friendly all-day diner. Appealing bistro fare, well executed and very tasty. Good selection of wines by glass.

X **Dobbin's,** 15 Stephen's Lane, off Lower Mount St, D2, (01) 676 4679, *dobbinswinebistro@eircom.net, Fax (01) 661 3331,* – . AE VISA EU s
closed 1 week Christmas-New Year, Sunday, Monday dinner, Saturday lunch and Bank Holidays – **Rest** - Bistro - (booking essential) 25/45 and a la carte 28/45 ♀.
• In the unlikely setting of a former Nissen hut in a residential part of town, this popular restaurant, something of a local landmark, offers good food to suit all tastes.

X **Pearl Brasserie,** 20 Merrion St Upper, D2, (01) 661 3572, *info@pearl-brasserie.com, Fax (01) 661 3629* – . AE VISA KZ n
closed first week January, and lunch Saturday-Monday – **Rest** - French - 25 (lunch) and dinner a la carte 29/52 ♀.
• A metal staircase leads down to this intimate, vaulted cellar brasserie and oyster bar. Franco-Irish dishes served at granite-topped tables. Amiable and helpful service.

X **The Bistro,** 4-5 Castlemarket, D2, (01) 671 5430, *info@thebistro.ie, Fax (01) 6703379,* – . AE VISA JY c
closed 25-26 December, 1 January and Good Friday – **Rest** a la carte 22/44 ♀.
• Friendly and buzzing in the heart of the city. Exposed floor boards, coir carpeting and vividly coloured walls. Additional terrace area. Interesting, modern dishes.

Eden, Meeting House Sq, Temple Bar, D2, (01) 670 5372, *Fax (01) 670 3330*, – . HY e
closed 25 December - 3 January and Bank Holidays – **Rest** 20/23 (lunch) and dinner a la carte 36/49.
◆ Modern minimalist restaurant with open plan kitchen serves good robust food. Terrace overlooks theatre square, at the heart of a busy arty district. Children welcome.

Mermaid Café, 69-70 Dame St, D2, (01) 670 8236, *info@mermaid.ie, Fax (01) 670 8205* – 25. HY d
closed 24-26 and 31 December, 1 January and Good Friday – **Rest** (booking essential) 24 (lunch) and a la carte 31/48.
◆ This small informal restaurant with unfussy décor and wood floors offers an interesting and well cooked selection of robust modern dishes. Good service.

Cafe Mao, 2-3 Chatham Row, D2, (01) 670 4899, *info@cafemao.com* – . JZ r
Rest - South East Asian - (bookings not accepted) a la carte 28/35.
◆ Well run trendy modern restaurant serving authentic southeast Asian fusion cuisine in an informal setting buzzing with action and atmosphere. Tasty food at tasty prices.

La Maison des Gourmets, 15 Castlemarket, D2, (01) 672 7258, *lamaison@indigo.ie, Fax (01) 864 5672* – . JY c
closed 25-28 December and Sunday – **Rest** (lunch only) a la carte 18.50/23.50 **s.**
◆ Simple, snug restaurant on the first floor above an excellent bakery offering high quality breads and pastries. Extremely good value meals using fine local ingredients.

The Cellar Bar (at The Merrion H.), Upper Merrion St, D2, (01) 603 0631, *info@merrionhotel.com, Fax (01) 603 0700* – . KZ e
closed Sunday – **Rest** (lunch only) (carving lunch) a la carte 22/30.
◆ Characterful stone and brick bar-restaurant in the original vaulted cellars with large wood bar. Popular with Dublin's social set. Offers wholesome Irish pub lunch fare.

Ballsbridge *Dublin.*

Dublin 6.5.

Four Seasons, Simmonscourt Rd, D4, (01) 665 4000, *sales.dublin@fourseasons.com, Fax (01) 665 4099*, – – 800. FU e
Seasons : **Rest** 28/72 and a la carte 28/38 – ***The Cafe :*** **Rest** a la carte 34/48 **s.** – 27 – **192 rm** 380/425 – 380/425, 67 suites 715.
◆ Every inch the epitome of international style - supremely comfortable rooms with every facility; richly furnished lounge; a warm mix of antiques, oils and soft piano études. Dining in Seasons guarantees luxury ingredients. Informal comforts in The Café.

The Berkeley Court, Lansdowne Rd, D4, (01) 6653200, *berkeleycourt@jurysdoyle.com, Fax (01) 6617238* – – 450. . FU c
Berkeley Room : **Rest** 30/60 **s.** – ***Palm Court Café :*** **Rest** a la carte 42/71 **s.** – 25 – **182 rm** 338/380 – 380, 4 suites.
◆ Luxurious international hotel in former botanical gardens; two minutes from the home of Irish rugby. Large amount of repeat business. Solidly formal feel throughout. Berkeley Room for elegant fine dining. Breakfast buffets a feature of Palm Court Café.

Herbert Park, D4, (01) 667 2200, *reservations@herbertparkhotel.ie, Fax (01) 667 2595*, – – 100. . FU m
The Pavilion : **Rest** *(closed dinner Sunday and Monday)* 24 (lunch) and dinner a la carte 36/53 – 19 – **150 rm** 230 – 275, 3 suites.
◆ Stylish contemporary hotel. Spacious, open, modern lobby and lounges. Excellent, well-designed rooms with tasteful décor. Some offer views of park. Good business facilities. French-windowed restaurant with al fresco potential; oyster/lobster specialities.

The Schoolhouse, 2-8 Northumberland Rd, D4, (01) 667 5014, *reservations@schoolhousehotel.com, Fax (01) 667 5015*, – . EU a
closed 24-26 December – ***The Canteen :*** **Rest** (bar lunch Saturday and Sunday) a la carte 26/51 – **31 rm** 99/199 – 199/300.
◆ Spacious converted 19C schoolhouse, close to canal, boasts modernity and charm. Rooms contain locally crafted furniture. Inkwell bar has impressive split-level seating area. Old classroom now a large restaurant with beamed ceilings.

Merrion Hall, 54-56 Merrion Rd, D4, (01) 668 1426, *merrionhall@iol.ie, Fax (01) 668 4280*, – – 40. . FU b
Rest (dinner only) a la carte 23/34 **s.** – **30 rm** 109 – 149, 4 suites.
◆ Extended ivy-clad house on main road in suburbs. Welcoming lounges with open fires and homely ornaments. Well-equipped, refurbished bedrooms are brightly lit and airy. Large, formal dining room overlooking patio/terrace.

Ariel House without rest., 50-54 Lansdowne Rd, D4, ☎ (01) 668 5512, *reservations@ariel-house.net, Fax (01) 668 5845* – ⇔ ☎ [P]. MC VISA. ✂ FU r
closed 23-28 December – **37 rm** ☕ ★69/99 – ★★170/210.
◆ Restored, listed Victorian mansion in smart suburb houses personally run, traditional small hotel. Rooms feature period décor and original antiques; some four poster beds.

Bewley's, Merrion Rd, D4, ☎ (01) 668 1111, *bb@bewleyshotels.com, Fax (01) 668 1999* – ⇔, ▤ rest, ☎ ♿ – 🏛 30. MC AE ⓓ VISA. ✂ FU a
closed 24-26 December – ***O'Connells*** (☎ *(01) 647 3400*) : **Rest** (carvery lunch)/dinner 28/33 and a la carte 27/39 **s.** Ⅰ – ☕ 9 – **220 rm** ★99 – ★★99.
◆ Huge hotel offers stylish modern accommodation behind sumptuous Victorian façade of former Masonic school. Location, facilities and value for money make this a good choice. Informal modern O'Connells restaurant, cleverly constructed with terrace in stairwell.

Aberdeen Lodge, 53-55 Park Ave, D4, ☎ (01) 283 8155, *aberdeen@iol.ie, Fax (01) 283 7877,* – ⇔ ☎ [P]. MC AE ⓓ VISA. ✂ GV e
Rest (light meals) (residents only) a la carte 23/34 **s.** Ⅰ – **17 rm** ☕ ★99 – ★★140/200.
◆ Neat red brick house in smart residential suburb. Comfortable rooms with Edwardian style décor in neutral tones, wood furniture and modern facilities. Some garden views. Comfortable, traditionally decorated dining room.

Pembroke Townhouse without rest., 90 Pembroke Rd, D4, ☎ (01) 660 0277, *info@pembroketownhouse.ie, Fax (01) 660 0291* – |♦| ⇔ ☎ [P]. MC AE ⓓ VISA. ✂ FU c
closed 22 December-3 January – **48 rm** ☕ ★88/165 – ★★120/260.
◆ Period-inspired décor adds to the appeal of a sensitively modernised, personally run Georgian terrace town house in the smart suburbs. Neat, up-to-date accommodation.

Waterloo House without rest., 8-10 Waterloo Rd, D4, ☎ (01) 660 1888, *waterloohouse@eircom.net, Fax (01) 667 1955,* – |♦| ⇔ ☎ [P]. MC VISA. ✂ EU p
closed 23-28 December – **17 rm** ☕ ★59/79 – ★★115/155.
◆ Pair of imposing Georgian town houses. Elegant breakfast room with conservatory. Large comfortable rooms with coordinated heavy drapes and fabrics in warm modern colours.

Glenogra House without rest., 64 Merrion Rd, D4, ☎ (01) 668 3661, *info@glenogra.com, Fax (01) 668 3698* – ⇔ ☎ [P]. MC AE ⓓ VISA. ✂ FU w
closed 23 December-5 January – **13 rm** ☕ ★79/89 – ★★109.
◆ Neat and tidy bay windowed house in smart suburb. Personally run guesthouse with bedrooms attractively decorated in keeping with a period property. Modern facilities.

Anglesea Town House without rest., 63 Anglesea Rd, D4, ☎ (01) 668 3877, *helen@63anglesea.com, Fax (01) 668 3461* – ⇔. MC AE VISA. ✂ FV x
closed 20 December-5 January – **7 rm** ☕ ★70/100 – ★★130/140.
◆ Red brick Edwardian residence in smart suburb with many pieces of fine period furniture. Individually styled rooms with good facilities. Parking can be a challenge.

66 Townhouse without rest., 66 Northumberland Rd, D4, ☎ (01) 660 0333, *Fax (01) 660 1051* – ⇔ [P]. MC VISA. ✂ FU z
closed 22 December-6 January – **8 rm** ☕ ★70/80 – ★★100/175.
◆ Attractive Victorian red brick house with extension in smart suburb. Comfortable homely atmosphere. Good size rooms with tasteful décor and modern facilities.

Siam Thai, Sweepstake Centre, D4, ☎ (01) 660 1722, *siam@eircom.net, Fax (01) 660 1537* – ⇔ ▤. MC AE ⓓ VISA FU h
closed 25-26 December, lunch Saturday and Sunday and Good Friday – **Rest** - Thai - 13/32 and a la carte 31/34 **s.**
◆ Unerringly busy restaurant that combines comfort with liveliness. Smart waiters serve authentic Thai cuisine, prepared with skill and understanding. Good value lunches.

Roly's Bistro, 7 Ballsbridge Terrace, D4, ☎ (01) 668 2611, *ireland@rolysbistro.ie, Fax (01) 660 8535* – ⇔ ▤. MC AE ⓓ VISA FU r
closed 25- 27 December – **Rest** (booking essential) 20/39 and a la carte 36/48 Ⅰ.
◆ A Dublin institution: this roadside bistro is very busy and well run, with a buzzy, fun atmosphere. Its two floors offer modern Irish dishes and a very good value lunch.

Bella Cuba, 11 Ballsbridge Terrace, D4, ☎ (01) 660 5539, *info@bella-cuba.com, Fax (01) 660 5539* – ⇔. MC AE VISA FU r
closed lunch Saturday and Sunday – **Rest** - Cuban - (booking essential) (dinner only and lunch Thursday-Friday) 20 (lunch) and a la carte 31/37 Ⅰ.
◆ Family-owned restaurant with an intimate feel. Cuban memoirs on walls, fine choice of cigars. Authentic Cuban dishes, employing many of the island's culinary influences.

Donnybrook *Dublin.*
Dublin 6.5.

Marble Hall without rest., 81 Marlborough Rd, D4, ✆ (01) 497 7350, *marblehall@eircom.net* – ⇔ P. ✻ EV a
closed 15 December-1 January – **3 rm** ☐ ✝60 – ✝✝90/100.
◆ Georgian townhouse with effusive welcome guaranteed. Individually styled throughout, with plenty of antiques and quality soft furnishings. Stylish, warmly decorated bedrooms.

Ernie's, Mulberry Gdns, off Morehampton Rd, D4, ✆ (01) 269 3300, *Fax (01) 269 3260* – ⇔ ▤. MC AE ⓓ VISA FV k
closed Easter, 1 week Christmas-New Year, Saturday lunch, Sunday and Monday – **Rest** 22/40 and a la carte 53/70 ♀.
◆ Discreet professionally run restaurant in tranquil location offering classic Irish fare. Bright room with garden aspect, modern feel and contemporary Irish art collection.

Ranelagh *Dublin.*

Mint, 47 Ranelagh, D6, ✆ (01) 497 8655, *info@mintrestaurant.ie, Fax (01) 497 9035* – ⇔ ▤. MC AE VISA EV e
closed Monday and Bank Holidays – **Rest** 29 (lunch) and dinner a la carte 37/52.
◆ Modern, minimalist restaurant south of city centre. Mix of banquettes and slim, beige leather chairs. Modern fine dining, with French influences to the fore.

Rathgar *Dublin.*
Dublin 9.5.

St Aiden's without rest., 32 Brighton Rd, D6, ✆ (01) 490 2011, *staidens@eircom.net, Fax (01) 492 0234* – ✆ P. MC VISA. ✻ DV n
closed 22 December-8 January – **8 rm** ☐ ✝49/75 – ✝✝100/110.
◆ Friendly, family run guesthouse in early Victorian mid-terrace. Comfortable lounge with tea, coffee and books. Ample rooms with simple décor and furniture. Good facilities.

Rathmines *Dublin.*
Dublin 9.5.

Uppercross House, 26-30 Upper Rathmines Rd, D6, ✆ (01) 4975486, *enquiries@uppercrosshousehotel.com, Fax (01) 4975361* – |✱| ⇔ ✆ P. MC AE VISA DV d
closed 24-31 December – ***The Restaurant :*** **Rest** (dinner only and lunch Friday-Sunday) 15/18 and a la carte 19/36 **s.** ♀ – **49 rm** ☐ ✝70/120 – ✝✝100/160.
◆ Privately run suburban hotel in three adjacent town houses with modern extension wing. Good size rooms and standard facilities. Live music midweek in traditional Irish bar. Restaurant offers a mellow and friendly setting with welcoming wood décor.

Zen, 89 Upper Rathmines Rd, D6, ✆ (01) 4979428, *Fax (01) 4979428* – ⇔ ▤. MC AE ⓓ VISA DV t
closed 25-27 December – **Rest** - Chinese (Szechuan) - (dinner only and lunch Friday) 15/20 and a la carte 24/35.
◆ Renowned Chinese restaurant in the unusual setting of an old church hall. Imaginative, authentic oriental cuisine with particular emphasis on spicy Szechuan dishes.

Terenure *Dublin.*
Dublin 9.5.

Vermilion, 1st Floor above Terenure Inn, 94-96 Terenure Road North, D6, South : 9½ km by N 81 ✆ (01) 499 1400, *mail@vermilion.ie, Fax (01) 499 1300* – ⇔. MC AE ⓓ VISA BT c
closed 25-26 December and Good Friday – **Rest** - Indian - (live jazz Thursday dinner) (dinner only) a la carte 29/46 ♀.
◆ Smart restaurant above a busy pub in a residential part of town. Vividly coloured dining room and efficient service. Well-balanced, modern Indian food with a Keralan base.

at Dublin Airport *North : 10½ km by N 1* – **BS** – *and M 1* – ✉ *Dublin.*

Crowne Plaza, Northwood Park, Santry Demesne, Santry, D9, South : 3¼ km on R 132 ✆ (01) 8628888, *info@crowneplazadublin.ie, Fax (01) 8628800,* ⚒ – |✱| ⇔ ▤ ✆ ♿ P – 🏛 240. MC AE ⓓ VISA. ✻
Touzai : **Rest** - Asian influences - *(closed Saturday and Bank Holidays)* (buffet lunch)/dinner a la carte 32/37 **s.** ♀ – ***Cinnabar :*** **Rest** a la carte 25/30 **s.** ♀ – ☐ 21 – **202 rm** ✝105/265 – ✝✝105/265, 2 suites.
◆ Next to Fingal Park, two miles from the airport. Hotel has predominant Oriental style, extensive meeting facilities, and modern, well-equipped rooms, some of Club standard. Touzai for Asian specialities. Stylish Cinnabar has extensive, eclectic menu range.

Hilton Dublin Airport, Northern Cross, Malahide Rd, D17, ✆ (01) 8661800, *dunb nairport@hilton.com, Fax (01) 8661866,* – |⇕| ⇔ ▤ ✆ ♿ P – 🏋 550. MO AE VISA.
Solas : **Rest** (dinner only and Sunday lunch)/dinner 31/39 – ☕ 20 – **162 rm** ★120/320 ★★120/320, 4 suites.
◆ Opened in 2005, just five minutes from the airport, adjacent to busy shopping centre Modish feel throughout. State-of-the-art meeting facilities. Airy, well-equipped rooms Spacious dining room serves tried-and-tested dishes.

Great Southern, ✆ (01) 8446000, *res@dubairport-gsh.com, Fax (01) 8446001* – |⇕| ⇔ ✆ ♿ P – 🏋 450. MO AE ⊕ VISA.
closed 23-27 December – ***Potters :*** **Rest** *(closed Sunday-Monday)* (dinner only) 35 – ***O'Dea Bar :*** **Rest** (carvery lunch)/dinner a la carte 23/37 – ☕ 15 – **227 rm** ★270 – ★★270, 2 suites
◆ Modern hotel catering for international and business travellers. Range of guest rooms all spacious and smartly furnished with wood furniture and colourful fabrics. Potters has spacious, formal feel. O'Deas Bar for intimate carvery menus.

Clarion H. Dublin Airport, ✆ (01) 8080500, *reservations@clarionhoteldublina port.com, Fax (01) 8446002* – ⇔, ▤ rest, ♿ P – 🏋 130. MO AE ⊕ VISA.
closed 24-26 December – ***Bistro :*** **Rest** *(closed Saturday lunch)* a la carte 18/29 **s.** ♀
Sampan's : **Rest** - Asian - *(closed Bank Holidays)* (dinner only) a la carte 18/29 **s.** ♀ – ☕ 19 – **247 rm** ★250 – ★★250.
◆ Modern commercial hotel offers standard or Millennium rooms, all with colourful fee and good facilities. Free use of leisure centre. Live music at weekends in Bodhran bar Informal Bistro restaurant with monthly themed menus. Oriental specials at Sampan's.

at Clontarf *Northeast : 5½ km by R 105 – ✉ Dublin.*

Clontarf Castle, Castle Ave, D3, ✆ (01) 833 2321, *info@clontarfcastle.ie Fax (01) 833 2279,* – |⇕| ⇔ ✆ ♿ P – 🏋 500. MO AE VISA CS
closed 25-26 December – ***Templars Bistro :*** **Rest** (carvery lunch Monday-Friday)/dinne 35/45 and a la carte 27/43 **s.** ♀ – **108 rm** ★115/185 – ★★295, 3 suites.
◆ Set in an historic castle, partly dating back to 1172. Striking medieval style entrance lobby. Modern rooms and characterful luxury suites, all with cutting edge facilities. Restau rant with grand medieval style décor reminiscent of a knights' banqueting hall.

at Stillorgan *Southeast : 8 km on N 11 – CT – ✉ Dublin.*

Radisson SAS St Helen's, Stillorgan Rd, D4, ✆ (01) 218 6000, *info.dublin@radisso sas.com, Fax (01) 218 6010,* – |⇕| ⇔ ▤ ✆ ♿ P – 🏋 350. MO AE ⊕ VISA.
Talavera : **Rest** - Italian - a la carte 26/53 **s.** ♀ – ☕ 22 – **130 rm** ★170/225 – ★★170/225 21 suites.
◆ Imposing part 18C mansion with substantial extensions and well laid out gardens. Wel run with good level of services. Smart modern rooms with warm feel and all facilities Delicious antipasti table at basement Talavera.

Stillorgan Park, Stillorgan Rd, ✆ (01) 288 1621, *sales@stillorganpark.com Fax (01) 283 1610,* – |⇕| ⇔ ▤ ✆ ♿ P – 🏋 600. MO AE VISA.
closed 25 December – ***Purple Sage :*** **Rest** (carvery lunch)/dinner 37/42 and a la carte 31/41 **s.** – **165 rm** ☕ ★85/130 – ★★130/196.
◆ Modern commercial hotel in southside city suburb. Spacious rooms with modern facili ties. Interesting horse theme décor in large stone floored bar with buffet. Purple Sage restaurant with mosaics, frescos and hidden alcoves.

at Foxrock *Southeast : 12 km by N 11 – CT – ✉ Dublin.*

XX **Bistro One,** 3 Brighton Rd, D18, ✆ (01) 289 7711, *bistroone@eircom.net Fax (01) 207 0742* – ⇔. MO VISA
closed 25 December-2 January, Sunday and Monday – **Rest** (booking essential) (dinne only) a la carte 27/41.
◆ Pleasantly set in residential area. Homely, with beams and walls of wine racks. Simple menu offers well-prepared classic Irish fare and Italian or Asian influenced dishes.

at Leopardstown *Southeast : 13 km by N 11 – GV – ✉ Dublin.*

Bewleys, Central Park, D18, ✆ (01) 293 5000, *leop@bewleyshotels.com Fax (01) 293 5099* – |⇕| ⇔, ▤ rest, ✆ ♿ – 🏋 30. MO AE ⊕ VISA.
closed 24-25 December – ***Brasserie :*** **Rest** (carvery lunch)/dinner 25/30 and a la carte 19/25 **s.** ♀ – ☕ 10 – **352 rm** ★89 – ★★89.
◆ Handily placed next to racecourse, this modern hotel boasts smart bar with leathe armchairs, decked terrace, and comfy, uniform bedrooms with good facilities. Informa brasserie with neutral, stylish tones.

at Clondalkin *Southwest : 13 km by N 7 on R 113 – AT – ✉ Dublin.*

Red Cow Moran, Naas Rd, D22, Southeast : 3¼ km on N 7 at junction with M 50 ✆ (01) 459 3650, *info@morangroup.ie, Fax (01) 459 1588* – ⎈ ⇝ ▤ ✆ ♿ P – 🏛 700. MC AE DC VISA. ⚘
closed 24-26 December – ***The Winter Garden :*** **Rest** 22/27 (lunch) and dinner a la carte 36/48 **s.** ♀ – **120 rm** ☕ ♂380 – ♂♂380, 3 suites.
◆ Splendid sweeping lobby staircase gives a foretaste of this smart commercial hotel's mix of traditional elegance and modern design. Landmark Red Cow inn and Diva nightclub. Large characterful Winter Garden restaurant with bare brick walls and warm wood floor.

Bewley's H. Newlands Cross, Newlands Cross, Naas Rd (N 7), D22, ✆ (01) 464 0140, *res@bewleyshotels.com, Fax (01) 464 0900* – ⎈ ⇝, ▤ rest, ✆ ♿ P. MC AE DC VISA. ⚘
closed 25-26 December – **Rest** (carving lunch)/dinner 25 and a la carte 28/33 **s.** – ☕ 7 – **258 rm** ♂89 – ♂♂89.
◆ Well run, busy, commercial hotel popular with business people. Spacious rooms with modern facilities can also accommodate families. Represents good value for money. Large, busy café-restaurant with traditional dark wood fittings and colourful décor.

at Lucan *West : 12 km by N 4 – AT – ✉ Dublin.*

Clarion H. Dublin Liffey Valley, Liffey Valley, D22, off N 4 at M 50 junction ✆ (01) 6258000, *info@clarionhotelliffeyvalley.com, Fax (01) 6258001,* Fá, ≘s, ⛶ – ⎈ ⇝, ▤ rest, ✆ ♿ 🚗 P – 🏛 390. MC AE DC VISA. ⚘
closed 24-25 December – ***Sinergie :*** **Rest** 16/26 (lunch) and dinner a la carte 31/38 – ***Kudos :*** **Rest** a la carte 19/25 – ☕ 18 – **254 rm** ♂99/240 – ♂♂99/240, 31 suites.
◆ U-shaped hotel opened in 2005; bright, open public areas. Well equipped conference facilities; smart leisure club. Sizable, up-to-date rooms with high quality furnishings. Irish dishes with a twist at Sinergie. Asian themed Kudos with on-view wok kitchen.

at Castleknock *Northwest : 13 km by N 3 (Caven Rd) – AS – and Auburn Ave – ✉ Dublin.*

Castleknock H. & Country Club, Porterstown Rd, D15, Southwest : 1½ km by Castleknock Rd and Porterstown Rd ✆ (01) 6406301, *Fax (01) 6406382,* Fá, ≘s, ⛶, 🏌18, ⛱, ⚘ – ⎈, ▤ rest, ✆ ♿ P – 🏛 500. MC AE VISA. ⚘
closed 25-26 December – ***The Park :*** **Rest** *(closed Sunday-Wednesday)* (dinner only) a la carte 32/53 – ***The Brasserie :*** **Rest** a la carte 25/42 – **142 rm** ☕ ♂190 – ♂♂240/290.
◆ Impressive corporate hotel incorporating golf course and 160 acres of grounds. Stylish, contemporary design; extensive business and leisure facilities; well equipped rooms. Formal Park restaurant with golf course views. Brasserie with popular menus.

DUBLIN AIRPORT *Dublin* 712 N 7 – *see Dublin.*

DUNBOYNE *Meath* 712 M 7.
Dublin 17.5 – Drogheda 45 – Newbridge 54.5.

Caldwell's, Summerhill Rd, ✆ (01) 8013866, *d-caldwell2002@yahoo.com,* 🏠 – ⇝ P. MC AE VISA
closed 1 week Christmas and Monday – **Rest** (dinner only and lunch Friday and Sunday)/dinner 28 and a la carte approx 47 ♀.
◆ Appealingly understated restaurant in village not far from Dublin. Simple glass façade, light wood floors create uncluttered feel. Neat, accomplished cooking of modern dishes.

DUNCANNON **(Dún Canann)** *Wexford* 712 L 11 – *pop. 318.*
Dublin 167.5 – New Ross 26 – Waterford 48.

Sqigl, Quay Rd, ✆ (051) 389188, *sqiglrestaurant@eircom.net, Fax (051) 389346* – ⇝. MC VISA
closed January-mid February, 24-26 December, Sunday and Monday – **Rest** (dinner only) 25/30 and a la carte 29/46.
◆ Stone-built restaurant; a converted barn standing behind a popular bar in this coastal village. Faux leopard skin banquettes. Modern European cuisine with amiable service.

Do not confuse ✕ with ✿! ✕ defines comfort, while stars are awarded for the best cuisine, across all categories of comfort.

REPUBLIC OF IRELAND

DUNDALK **(Dun Dealgan)** *Louth* 712 M 5/6 *Ireland G. – pop. 32 505.*

Exc. : *Dún a' Rí Forest Park★, W : 34 km by R 178 and R 179.*

18 *Killinbeg, Killin Park, Bridge a Chrin ☎ (042) 9339303.*

Dublin 82 – Drogheda 35.5.

Ballymascanlon, Northeast : 5 ¾ km by N 1 on R 173 ☎ (042) 9358200, *info@ballyma canlon.com, Fax (042) 9371598,* 18, – rest, 200. VISA.

Rest 29/45 and dinner a la carte 36/42 – **90 rm** ★108/110 – ★★160/170, 3 suites.

◆ Victorian house with modern extensions, surrounded by gardens and golf course. Goo size leisure club. Bedrooms and various lounges are in a modern style. Bright restaurar with stylish terrace bar.

Rosemount without rest., Dublin Rd, South : 2 ½ km on N 1 ☎ (042) 9335878, *m. sieb7@eircom.net, Fax (042) 9335878,* – P

9 rm ★45 – ★★65.

◆ A modern house a short drive from the town with good access to the M1. Well-appoin ted guests' lounge and attractive breakfast room. Comfortably furnished bedrooms.

DUNFANAGHY **(Dún Fionnachaidh)** *Donegal* 712 I 2 *Ireland G. – pop. 290 – ✉ Letterkenny.*

Env. : *Horn Head Scenic Route★, N : 4 km.*

Exc. : *Doe Castle★, SE : 11¼ km by N 56 – The Rosses★, SW : 40¼ km by N 56 and R 259.*

18 *Dunfanaghy, Letterkenny ☎ (074) 36335.*

Dublin 277 – Donegal 87 – Londonderry 69.

Arnolds, Main St, ☎ (074) 9136208, *enquiries@arnoldshotel.com, Fax (074) 9136352,* – P. VISA.

mid March-October – ***Tramore :*** **Rest** (dinner only and Sunday lunch)/dinner 39/44 ♀ – ***Garden Bistro :*** Rest (dinner only) a la carte 21/43 ♀ – **30 rm** ★59/99 – ★★140/160.

◆ Pleasant traditional coaching inn with a variety of extensions. Spacious lounge area an a charming bar with open fires. Family run with well-provided bedrooms. The Tramor serves traditional dishes in a more formal atmosphere. Relaxed and informal bistro.

The Mill with rm, Southwest : ¾ km on N 56 ☎ (074) 9136985, *themillrestaurant@ocea free.net, Fax (074) 9136985,* ≤ New Lake and Mount Muckish, – P. VISA.

mid March-mid December – **Rest** *(closed Monday)* (dinner only) 37/39 – **6 rm** ★60 – ★★90.

◆ Flax mill on New Lake with view of Mount Muckish. Linen-clad restaurant lined wit watercolours: modern Irish menu, well sourced and judged. Pleasant, uncluttered rooms.

Hotels and restaurants change every year, so change your Michelin guide every year!

DUNGARVAN **(Dún Garbháin)** *Waterford* 712 J 11 *Ireland G. – pop. 7 425.*

See : *East Bank (Augustinian priory, ≤★).*

Exc. : *Ringville (≤★), S : 13 km by N 25 and R 674 – Helvick Head★ (≤★), SE : 13 km by N 2. and R 674.*

18 *Knocknagrannagh ☎ (058) 41605 –* 9 *Gold Coast, Ballinacourty ☎ (058) 42249.*

The Courthouse ☎ (058) 41741.

Dublin 190 – Cork 71 – Waterford 48.5.

An Bohreen , Killineen West, Northeast : 8 km by N 25 ☎ (051) 291010, *mu gans@anbohreen.com, Fax (051) 291011,* – P. VISA.

16 March-October – **Rest** 34 – **4 rm** ★55/60 – ★★75/80.

◆ Very personally run bungalow with fine views over countryside and bay. Cosy sofa are within large open plan layout. Individually designed rooms are tastefully furnished. Dinne menu employs best local ingredients and is cooked with some passion.

Powersfield House, Ballinamuck West, Northwest : 2 ½ km on R 672 ☎ (058) 45594 *powersfieldhouse@cablesurf.com, Fax (058) 45550,* – P. VISA.

Rest (by arrangement) 37 – **6 rm** ★65 – ★★110/120.

◆ Set on main road just out of town. Georgian style exterior welcomes guests into a cos lounge. All bedrooms have individual style with warm feel and some antique furniture.

Gortnadiha Lodge without rest., South : 6½ km by N 25 off R 674 ☎ (058) 46142 *gortnadihalodge@eircom.net,* ≤, – P. VISA

3 rm ★40/45 – ★★70/80.

◆ Friendly guesthouse set in its own glen with fine bay views, a first floor terrace fo afternoon tea, homemade jams and breads for breakfast, and antique furnished bed rooms.

Barnawee Bridge without rest., Kilminion, East : 3 ¼ km by R 675 ✆ (058) 42074, *michelle@barnawee.com*, ≤, – ⅍ P. MC VISA. ⅍
6 rm ☐ ★45/75 – ★★70/80.
◆ Modern guesthouse and gardens lying just off coastal road with good views of Dungarvan Bay. Comfortable, homely lounge. Four of the warm, spacious rooms look out to sea.

Tannery with rm, 10 Quay St, via Parnell St ✆ (058) 45420, *tannery@cablesurf.com*, *Fax (058) 45814* – ⅍, ▤ rest, ✆ ⇔ 30. MC AE ⓞ VISA
closed late January-early February, 1 week September, Monday and Sunday dinner except summer and Bank Holidays – **Rest** a la carte 27/48 – **7 rm** ★70 – ★★100/140.
◆ Characterful 19C former tannery. Informal ambience and contemporary styling with high ceilings and wood floors. Imaginative modern menus. Stylish rooms in adjacent townhouse.

DUNGLOW (An Clochán Liath) *Donegal* 712 G 3 *Ireland G.*

Env. : *The Rosses*★.
Exc. : *Gweebarra Estuary*★, *S : by N 56.*
Cruit Island, Kincasslagh ✆ (075) 43296.
The Quay ✆ (074) 9521297 (June-August).
Dublin 278.5 – Londonderry 82 – Sligo 122.5.

Ostan na Rosann, Mill Rd, ✆ (074) 9522444, *info@ostannarosann.com*, *Fax (074) 9522400*, ≤, ⅍, ≘, ☐ – ⅍ P – 🏔 350. MC AE VISA. ⅍
Rest (bar lunch)/dinner 31/35 ♀ – **48 rm** ☐ ★67/79 – ★★114/138.
◆ Motel-style establishment with attractive views from the edge of the town centre. Modern décor with traditional references throughout and comfortable bedrooms. Main dining room with traditional menu and pub-style bar area serving a lighter alternative.

Undecided between two equivalent establishments?
Within each category, establishments are classified
in our order of preference.

DUNKINEELY *Donegal* 712 G 4.

Castle Murray House ⅍ with rm, ✆ (074) 9737022, *info@castlemurray.com*, *Fax (074) 9737330*, ≤ McSwyne's Bay – ⅍ P. MC VISA
closed January and 24-26 December – **Rest** - Seafood specialities - 26/56 ♀ – **10 rm** ☐ ★80/90 – ★★120/130.
◆ In delightful, picturesque position with view of sea and sunsets from the conservatory. Pleasant dining room. Good local seafood. Comfortable well furnished bedrooms.

DUN LAOGHAIRE (Dún Laoghaire) *Dublin* 712 N 8 *Ireland G.*

Env. : ≤★★ *of Killiney Bay from coast road south of Sorrento Point.*
Dun Laoghaire, Eglinton Park ✆ (01) 280 3916.
to Holyhead (Stena Line) 4-5 daily (1 h 40 mn).
Ferry Terminal ✆ (01) 602 4000.
Dublin 14.5.

Plan on next page

Rasam, 1st Floor (above Eagle House pub), 18-19 Glasthule Rd, ✆ (01) 230 0600, *info@rasam.ie, Fax (01) 230 1000* – ⅍. MC VISA e
closed 25-26 December, 1 January and Good Friday – **Rest** - Indian - (dinner only) a la carte 35/40.
◆ Located above Eagle House pub, this airy, modern, stylish restaurant shimmers with silky green wallpaper. Interesting, authentic dishes covering all regions of India.

Cavistons, 58-59 Glasthule Rd, ✆ (01) 280 9245, *info@cavistons.com, Fax (01) 284 4054* – ⅍. MC AE ⓞ VISA a
closed 22 December-3 January, Sunday and Monday – **Rest** - Seafood - (booking essential) (lunch only) a la carte 27/46 ♀.
◆ Simple, informal restaurant attached to the well-established deli which specialises in fine seafood. Mermaid friezes on walls hint at the quality crustacean cuisine.

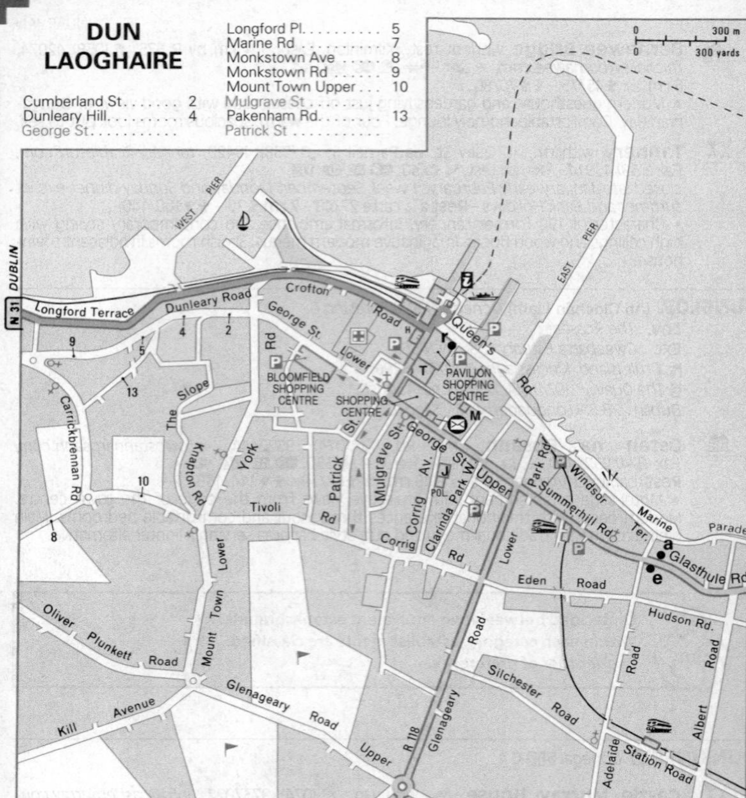

Mao Café, The Pavilion, ✆ (01) 214 8090, *info@cafemao.com, Fax (01) 214 7064* – ✈ ▤. MC AE VISA

Rest - South East Asian - (bookings not accepted) a la carte 24/38.

◆ Modern and informal with the background bustle of the Pavillion Centre and open kitchen. Quick, tasty meals find favour with hungry shoppers: try Vietnamese, Chinese or Thai.

DUNLAVIN (Dún Luáin) *Wicklow* 712 L 8.

⛳18 *Rathsallagh ✆ (045) 403316.*

Dublin 50 – Kilkenny 71 – Wexford 98.

Rathsallagh House ⚘, Southwest : 3 ¼ km on Grangecon Rd ✆ (045) 403112, *info@rathsallagh.com, Fax (045) 403343,* ←, ⛳18, ⚘, ⚘, ⚘, ⚘ – ✈ ♿ P – ⚘ 150. MC AE ⓓ VISA

Rest (dinner only) 60/75 ♀ – **28 rm** ⚘ ⚘175/250 – ⚘⚘250/300, 1 suite.

◆ 18C converted stables set in extensive grounds and golf course. Picturesque walled garden. Characterful, country house-style public areas and cosy, individual bedrooms. Kitchen garden provides ingredients for welcoming dining room.

DUNMORE EAST (Dún Mór) *Waterford* 712 L 11 *Ireland G. – pop. 1 750 – ✉ Waterford.*

See : *Village*★.

⛳18 *Dunmore East ✆ (051) 383151.*

Dublin 174 – Waterford 19.5.

The Beach without rest., 1 Lower Village, ☎ (051) 383316, *beachouse@eircom.net*, *Fax (051) 383319*, ←, – ✗ ☎ ♿ P. MC AE VISA. ✗
March-October – **7 rm** ☐ ♛40/60 – ♛♛70/90.
◆ Modern house close to the beach. Wonderful views from conservatory breakfast/lounge area. Very spacious bedrooms with pine furniture and modern facilities; some with balcony.

Ocean View without rest., ☎ (051) 383695, *Fax (051) 383695* – ✗. ✗
June-September – **9 rm** ☐ ♛45/50 – ♛♛60/70.
◆ Immaculate, whitewashed guesthouse of Victorian origins in pretty harbour village. Stands next to recommended pub, The Ship. Airy, period style, pine furnished bedrooms.

The Ship, Dock Rd, ☎ (051) 383141, *theshiprestaurant@eircom.net*, *Fax (051) 383144* – ✗. MC AE VISA
closed Sunday-Monday October-March and Christmas – **Rest** - Seafood - (dinner only October-March) a la carte 25/50.
◆ Small, stone-built pub in fishing village. Open fires and wood floor with cushioned furniture and old wood tables. Menus of seafood with blackboard specials.

DURROW (Darú) *Laois* 712 J 9.
Dublin 108 – Cork 141.5 – Kilkenny 27.5.

Castle Durrow ✗, ☎ (0502) 36555, *info@castledurrow.com*, *Fax (0502) 36559*, ←, ✗, ✗, ✗ – ✗ ✗ P – ✗ 300. MC AE VISA. ✗
closed 30 December-18 January – **Rest** (dinner only) 50 ♀ – **32 rm** ☐ ♛100 – ♛♛280.
◆ Imposing greystone early 18C country mansion set in carefully manicured gardens and 30 acres of parkland. Eye-catching stained glass. Modern, understated bedrooms. High, ornate ceilings and views across gardens from the dining room.

DURRUS (Dúras) *Cork* 712 D 13.
Dublin 338 – Cork 90 – Killarney 85.5.

Blairs Cove ✗ with rm, Southwest : 1 ½ km on R 591 ☎ (027) 61127, *blairscove@eircom.net*, *Fax (027) 61487*, ←, ✗ – ✗ rest, P. MC AE VISA. ✗
mid March-October – **Rest** *(closed Sunday-Monday)* (booking essential) (dinner only) 53 s. ♀ – **3 suites** ☐ 120/210.
◆ Fine Georgian house with outbuildings and sea views, set around a courtyard. Meals taken in converted 17C barn. Wood fired grill. Holiday apartments and bedrooms available.

Good Things Cafe, Ahakista Rd, West : ¾ km on Ahakista rd ☎ (027) 61426, *carmelsomers04@eircom.net*, *Fax (027) 62896*, ✗, ✗ – ✗ P. MC VISA
Easter-August – **Rest** *(closed Tuesday and dinner Wednesday)* a la carte 22/38.
◆ Simple and unpretentious. Walls filled with shelves full of books and foods of all kinds for sale. Open-plan kitchen serves accomplished dishes full of quality local produce.

ENFIELD/INNFIELD (An Bóthar Buí) *Meath* 712 L 7.
Dublin 40 – Drogheda 59.5 – Trim 19.5.

Marriott Johnstown House, Southwest : ¾ km on R 402 ☎ (046) 9540000, *info@johnstownhouse.com*, *Fax (046) 9540001*, ✗ – ✗ ✗, ✗ rest, ☎ ♿ P – ✗ 900. MC AE VISA. ✗
Pavilion : Rest 39 (dinner) and a la carte 33/47 – ***Atrium Brasserie :*** Rest (lunch only) a la carte 23/31 – **121 rm** ☐ ♛175 – ♛♛190, 5 suites.
◆ Reconstructed Georgian manor house at the centre of modern business and leisure hotel set in extensive grounds. Large, well-furnished bedrooms provide all mod cons. Formal, classic style in the Pavillion restaurant. Smart Atrium Brasserie serves a modern menu.

ENNIS (Inis) *Clare* 712 F 9 *Ireland G. – pop. 22 051.*

See : *Ennis Friary★ AC.*

Exc. : *Dysert O'Dea★, N : 9¾ km by N 85 and R 476, turning left after 6½ km and right after 1½ km – Quin Franciscan Friary★, SE : 10½ km by R 469 – Knappogue Castle★ AC, SE : 12¾ km by R 469 – Corrofin (Clare Heritage Centre★ AC), N : 13¾ km by N 85 and R 476 – Craggaunowen Centre★ AC, SE : 17¾ km by R 469 – Kilmacduagh Churches and Round Tower★, NE : 17¾ km by N 18 – Kilrush★ (Scattery Island★ by boat) SW : 43½ km by N 68 – Bridge of Ross, Kilkee★, SW : 57 km by N 68 and N 67.*

18 *Drumbiggle Rd* ☎ *(065) 6824074.*

Arthurs Row ☎ *(065) 6828366.*

Dublin 228.5 – Galway 67.5 – Limerick 35.5 – Roscommon 148 – Tullamore 149.5.

REPUBLIC OF IRELAND

Woodstock, Shanaway Rd, Northwest : 4½ km by N 85, turning left at One Mile In
(065) 6846600, *info@woodstockhotel.com, Fax (065) 6846611*, – rest, – 200.
closed 24-26 December – **Rest** (bar lunch Monday-Saturday)/dinner 35 and a la carte 31/42 s. – **67 rm** 130/240 – 200/240.
◆ Large purpose-built establishment surrounded by golf course. Bright modern style décor in the bedrooms and public areas. Well-equipped leisure complex. Watch the go from the smart brasserie.

Temple Gate, The Square, (065) 6823300, *info@templegatehotel.com Fax (065) 6823322* – – 220.
closed 25-26 December – **Rest** (carving lunch Monday-Saturday)/dinner a la carte 30/41 ***JM's bistro :*** **Rest** (dinner only and Sunday lunch) 25/35 and a la carte 30/41 – **68 rm** 100/124 – 145/178, 2 suites.
◆ A professional yet friendly mood prevails at this privately run hotel in modern, subtl neo-Gothic style. Panelled library and well-fitted rooms in traditional patterns. JM's Bistro serves popular, carefully presented modern dishes in informal surroundings.

West County, Clare Rd, Southeast : 1¼ km on N 18 (065) 6828421, Central reservations (065) 6823000, *cro@lynchotels.com, Fax (065) 6828801*, – rest – 1650.
Rest (carvery lunch Monday-Saturday in bar)/dinner 35 and a la carte 16/36 – **152 rm** 75/95 – 160/189.
◆ Modern gym and an impressive choice of function facilities are the main attractions a this group hotel just outside the town. Spacious wood fitted rooms with useful mod cons Meals served in either the Grill or Pine Rooms.

Old Ground, O'Connell St, (065) 6828127, *reservations@oldgroundhotel.ie Fax (065) 6828112*, – – 150.
closed 25 December – ***O'Brien's :*** **Rest** a la carte 21/33 s. – ***Town Hall :*** **Rest** a la carte 26/35 – **113 rm** 75/115 – 110/160.
◆ Handsome ivy-clad hotel. Firelit lounge and inviting panelled bar with paintings, curio and book-lined snugs. Traditional rooms in cream, burgundy and dark wood. Gilt-framed mirrors and white linen lend a formal aspect to the O'Brien Room. Informal Town Hall.

Fountain Court without rest., Northwest : 3 ½ km on N 85 (065) 682984 *kyran@fountain-court.com, Fax (065) 6845030*, – .
17 March-November – **12 rm** 45/60 – 76/86.
◆ Modern hotel, extensive and personally run. Well-proportioned, comfortably furnished rooms in spotless order with garden and countryside views to the front.

Cill Eoin House without rest., Killadysert Cross, Clare Rd, Southeast : 2½ km at junctio of N 18 with R 473 (065) 6841668, *cilleoin@iol.ie, Fax (065) 6841669*, –
closed 20-28 December – **14 rm** 40/50 – 70/80.
◆ Spotless en suite rooms in prints and pastels in this sizeable, purpose-built guesthouse Breakfasts served in a simple, pine-fitted dining room: good value.

Westbrook House without rest., Galway Rd, Northeast : ¾ km on N 18 (06 6840173, *westbrook.ennis@eircom.net, Fax (065) 6867777* –
closed 23-27 December – **10 rm** 35/45 – 70/90.
◆ Sensibly priced guesthouse on outskirts of town. Spacious entry hallway with tiled flooring and fireplace. Breakfast room has conservatory extension. Light, airy rooms.

Hal Pino's, 7 High St, (065) 684 0011, *halpinosrestaurant@eircom.ne Fax (065) 684 0022* – .
closed 25 December – **Rest** (booking essential) (dinner only) 26/32 and a la carte 23/41.
◆ Simple, colourful restaurant located on the main high street of the town. Busy atmosphere in which a distinctive, wide-ranging, modern menu served by efficient staff.

at Inch *Southwest : 6½ km on R 474 (Kilmaley rd)* – ✉ *Ennis.*

Magowna House, West : 1½ km by R 474 (065) 6839009, *info@magowna.com Fax (065) 6839258*, – rest, – 300.
closed 25-26 December – **Rest** (bar lunch Monday-Saturday)/dinner 25/35 and a la carte 26/35 s. – **10 rm** 55/65 – 100/110.
◆ Purpose-built hotel in primrose yellow stands in quiet countryside. The simple, woo furnished bar and good-sized rooms, named after local places, are agreeably unfuss Neatly set dining room overlooking the fields offers a traditionally based menu.

The award is the crème de la crème. This is awarded to restaurants which are really worth travelling miles for!

ENNISCORTHY **(Inis Córthaidh)** *Wexford* 712 M 10 *Ireland G. – pop. 8 964.*

See : *Enniscorthy Castle★ (County Museum★).*

Exc. : *Ferns★, NE : 13 km by N 11 – Mount Leinster★, N : 27¼ km by N 11.*

Knockmarshal ☎ (054) 33191.

1798 Rebellion Centre ☎ (054) 34699 (summer only).

Dublin 122.5 – Kilkenny 74 – Waterford 54.5 – Wexford 24.

Riverside Park, The Promenade, ☎ (054) 37800, *info@riversideparkhotel.com, Fax (054) 37900,* – rest, – 700. VISA. *closed 23-26 December* – ***The Moorings :*** **Rest** *(closed Sunday dinner and Monday)* (carving lunch Tuesday-Saturday)/dinner 29/40 and a la carte 22/35 – **59 rm** ★91/100 – ★★158/170, 1 suite.

◆ Purpose-built hotel just outside the town: a high, airy lobby leads into smart bedrooms in matching patterns, modern meeting rooms and a rustic, "no-frills" wood-fitted bar. Spacious, modern Moorings restaurant with light, soft tones.

Monfin House, St John's, South : 2½ km by N 30 turning onto Slaney Drive rd by Corn mill ☎ (054) 38582, *info@monfinhouse.com, Fax (054) 38583,* – . VISA

closed December and 1-20 January – **Rest** (by arrangement) (communal dining) 35 – **4 rm** – ★★85/150.

◆ Georgian country house in five acres of gardens and parkland with attractive views. Well furnished with antique furniture in bedrooms and public areas. Communal dining in charming, formal dining room.

Ballinkeele House, Ballymurn, Southeast : 10½ km by unmarked road on Curracloe rd ☎ (053) 38105, *john@ballinkeele.com, Fax (053) 38468,* – . VISA.

March-October – **Rest** (by arrangement) (communal dining) 40 – **5 rm** ★95/115 – ★★150/160.

◆ High ceilinged, firelit lounge plus sizeable rooms with period-style furniture and countryside views add to the charm of a quiet 1840 manor, well run by experienced owners. Dining room enriched by candlelight and period oils.

NNISKERRY **(Áth an Sceire)** *Wicklow* 712 N 8 *– pop. 1 904.*

Powerscourt, Powerscourt Estate ☎ (01) 204 6033.

Dublin 25.5 – Wicklow 32.

Summerhill House, Cookstown Rd, South : ¾ km ☎ (01) 286 7928, *info@summerhillhousehotel.com, Fax (01) 286 7929,* – rest, – 220. VISA.

closed 24-25 December – **Rest** (dinner only and Sunday lunch)/dinner 30 s. – **56 rm** ★79/99 – ★★198.

◆ Sizeable country hotel run with business guests in mind. Bright, modern rooms; spacious lounge with comfortable sofas and busy function rooms. Agreeable atmosphere enlivens dining room.

NNISTIMON **(Inis Díomáin)** *Clare* 712 E 9 *– pop. 920.*

Dublin 254 – Galway 83.5 – Limerick 63.

Grovemount House without rest., Lahinch Rd, West : ¾ km on N 67 ☎ (065) 7071431, *grovmnt@eircom.net, Fax (065) 7071823,* – . VISA.

May-October – **7 rm** ★45/55 – ★★64/84.

◆ Spotless bedrooms in warm oak and a homely lounge in this modern guesthouse, run by the friendly owner. A short drive to the sandy beach at Lahinch and the Cliffs of Moher.

ARRAN **(An Fearann)** *Cork* 712 F 12 *Ireland G.*

Exc. : *Blarney Castle★★, NE : 22½ km by N 22 and R 579 – Cork★★ – St Fin Barre's Cathedral★★, Shandon Bells★★ – Grand Parade★, South Mall★, St Patrick's St★, Crawford Art Gallery★, Cork Public Museum★, E : 17¾ km by N 22.*

Dublin 436 – Cork 21 – Mallow 48.5.

Farran House without rest., ☎ (021) 7331215, *info@farranhouse.com, Fax (021) 7331450,* – . VISA.

April-October – **4 rm** ★100/120 – ★★150/180.

◆ Italianate 18C-19C house in mature gardens overlooking Bride Valley. Spacious and elegantly furnished; rooms have fine views.

FERNS (Fearna) *Wexford* 712 M 10 *Ireland G.* – ✉ *Enniscorthy.*

See : *Town*★.

Exc. : *Mount Leinster*★, *NW : 27 ¼ km – Enniscorthy Castle*★ *(County Museum*★ *AC)*
S : 12¾ km by N 11.

Dublin 111 – Kilkenny 85.5 – Waterford 66 – Wexford 35.5.

Clone House without rest., South : 3 ¼ km by Boolavogue rd off Monageer rd
✆ (054) 66113, *tbreen@vodaphone.ie, Fax (054) 66113,* P.
April-October – **5 rm** ★50 – ★★90.

◆ Cream-painted, ivy-clad house on working farm with large grounds. Traditionally furnished communal breakfast room. Sizeable, individually designed rooms with stylish fabrics.

FETHARD (Fiodh Ard) *Tipperary* 712 I 10.

Dublin 161 – Cashel 16 – Clonmel 13.

Mobarnane House, North : 8 km by Cashel rd on Ballinure rd ✆ (052) 31962
info@mobarnanehouse.com, Fax (052) 31962, P. VISA
March-October – **Rest** (by arrangement) (communal dining) 45 – **4 rm** ★105
★★150/180.

◆ Very personally run classic Georgian house with mature gardens in quiet rural setting tastefully restored to reflect its age. Ask for a bedroom with its own sitting room. Beautiful dining room for menus agreed in advance.

An-Teach, Killusty, Southeast : 8 km by R 706 (Kilsheelan rd) ✆ (052) 32088, *anteach@an-teach.com, Fax (052) 32178,* P. VISA.
Rest (by arrangement) 22 – **11 rm** ★50/60 – ★★90.

◆ Extended family home against the backdrop of the Sliabh na Mban mountains. Airy en suite rooms in solid pine, two facing the hills. Carefully prepared wholesome meals.

FOXROCK (Carraig an tSionnaigh) *Dublin* 712 N 7 – *see Dublin.*

FURBO (Na Forbacha) *Calway* 712 E 8 – *see Furbogh.*

FURBOGH/FURBO (Na Forbacha) *Calway* 712 E 8.

Dublin 228.5 – Galway 11.5.

Connemara Coast, ✆ (091) 592108, *sinnott@iol.ie, Fax (091) 592065,* ≤ Galway Bay, P – 500. VISA.
Rest (bar lunch)/dinner 37 and a la carte 24/41 s. ♀ – **112 rm** ★115/170 – ★★160/260, 1 suite.

◆ Sprawling hotel with super views of Galway Bay, The Burren and Aran from the well-kept bedrooms. Marbled reception area. Characterful Players bar. Good leisure facilities. Two informal dining areas overlook the bay.

GALWAY (Gaillimh) *Galway* 712 E 8 *Ireland G. – pop. 66 163.*

See : *City*★★ – *Lynch's Castle*★ **BY** – *St Nicholas' Church*★ **BY** – *Roman Catholic Cathedral*★ **AY** – *Eyre Square : Bank of Ireland Building (sword and mace*★*)* **BY**.

Env. : *NW : Lough Corrib*★★.

Exc. : *W : by boat, Aran Islands (Inishmore – Dun Aenghus*★★★*)* **BZ** – *Thoor Ballylee*★, *SE : 33¾ km by N 6 and N 18* **D** – *Athenry*★, *E : 22½ km by N 6 and R 348* **D** – *Dunguaire Castle, Kinvarra*★ *AC, S : 25¾ km by N 6, N 18 and N 67* **D** – *Aughnanure Castle*★, *NW : 25¾ km by N 59 – Oughterard*★ *(≤★★), NW : 29 km by N 59 – Knockmoy Abbey*★, *NE : 30½ km by N 17 and N 63* **D** – *Coole Park (Autograph Tree*★*), SE : 33 ¾ km by N 6 and N 18* **D** – *St Mary's Cathedral, Tuam*★, *NE : 33 ¾ km by N 17* **D** – *Loughrea (St Brendan's Cathedral*★*), SE : 35½ km by N 6* **D** – *Turoe Stone*★, *SE : 35½ km by N 6 and north by R 350.*

Galway, Blackrock, Salthill ✆ (091) 522033.

Carnmore Airport : ✆ (091) 755569, NE : 6½ km.

Galway City Aeas Failte, Forster St ✆ (091) 537700, info@irelandwest.ie – Salthill Promenade ✆ (091) 520500 (May-August).

Dublin 217 – Limerick 103 – Sligo 145.

Plans on following pages

Radisson SAS, Lough Atalia Rd, ✆ (091) 538300, *sales.galway@radissonsas.com, Fax (091) 538380,* ≤, – 750. VISA **D**
Marinas : **Rest** (bar lunch Monday-Saturday)/dinner a la carte 40/57 s. ♀ – **214 rm** ★180/220 – ★★240, 3 suites.

◆ Striking atrium leads to ultra-modern meeting facilities and very comfortable accommodation: sumptuous 5th floor rooms have private glass balconies. Superb penthouse suites. Split-level dining in dark walnut wood.

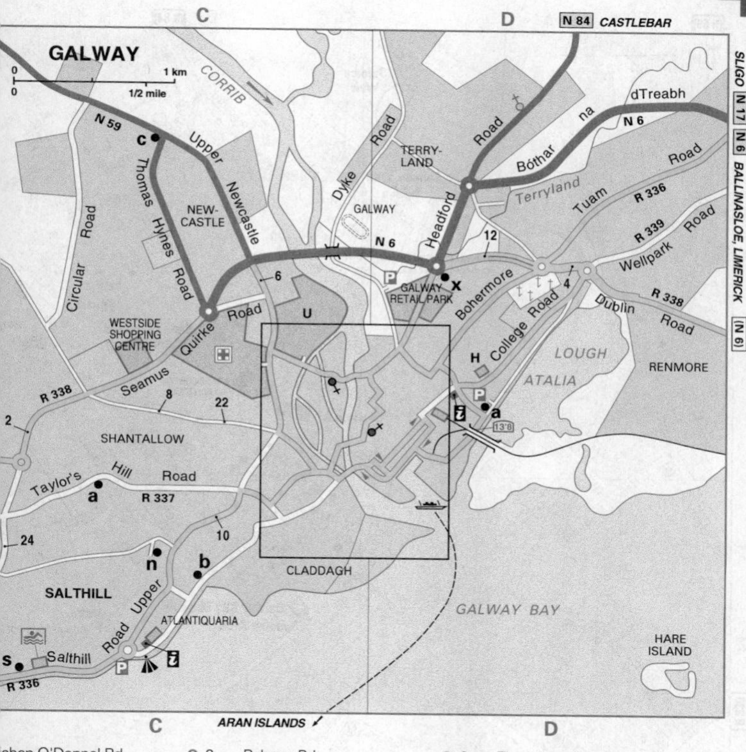

Glenlo Abbey, Bushypark, Northwest : 5 ¼ km on N 59 ☎ (091) 526666, *info@glenloabbey.ie, Fax (091) 527800*, ←, 9, – rest, – 200. MC AE VISA.
closed 24-26 December – ***River Room :*** Rest *(closed Sunday-Monday)* (dinner only) 45 and a la carte 47/80 – ***Pullman :*** Rest *(closed Tuesday-Wednesday)* (dinner only) 39 and a la carte 37/47 – 18 – **41 rm** 155/220 – 210/315, 5 suites.
◆ Imposing 18C greystone country house with adjacent church and bay views. Formal service. Very comfortable lounge, leading into chapel. Spacious, smart rooms. River Room boasts golfcourse views. Converted railway carriage offers modern dishes with an Asian base.

Great Southern, Eyre Sq, ☎ (091) 564041, *res@galway-gsh.com, Fax (091) 566704*, – rest, – 350. MC AE VISA. BY a
closed 24-26 December – ***The Oyster Room :*** Rest (carving lunch Monday-Saturday)/dinner 40/50 and a la carte 29/44 s. – 15 – **97 rm** 125/160 – 180/260, 2 suites.
◆ Imposing, greystone Victorian hotel in city centre. Relaxing, elegant interior. Strong conference facilities. Rooftop pool with great city views. Plush rooms. Restaurant exudes old world charm and elegance.

Westwood House, Dangan, Upper Newcastle, ☎ (091) 521442, *resmanager@westwoodhouse.com, Fax (091) 521400* – – 350. MC AE VISA. C c
closed 24-26 December – **Rest** (carving lunch Monday-Saturday)/dinner a la carte 29/38 s. – **58 rm** 110/140 – 150/199.
◆ Striking hotel with pastel orange painted exterior on outskirts of town. Impressive reception area and huge bar on two levels. Small conservatory. Modern, comfy rooms. Appealing carvery restaurant.

GALWAY

Street	Grid	No.
Bothar Ui Eithir	BY	2
Claddagh Bridge	AZ	3
Corrib Shopping Centre	BY	
Courthouse St.	BZ	4
Dominick St	AZ	5
Father Griffin Ave	AZ	6
Forster St	BY	7
High St	BY	8
Main Guard St.	BY	9
Market St	BY	10
Mary St	BY	11
New Dock St.	BZ	13
Newton Smith	BY	14
O'Brien Bridge	AY	15
Presentation St.	AY	
Quay St	BZ	
St Francis St	BY	
St Vincent's Ave	BY	
Shantalla Rd	AY	
Shop St	BY	
William St	BY	

Corrib Great Southern, Renmore, East : 2 ¾ km on R 338 ✆ (091) 755281, *res@corrib-gsh.com, Fax (091) 751390,* Fitness, ▢ – lift ✱, ▤ rest, ♿ P – 750. MC AE DC VISA
closed 25 December – **Rest** (carving lunch Monday-Saturday)/dinner 37 and a la carte approx 45 s. – ☕ 15 – **175 rm** 85/250 – 150/250, 4 suites.
◆ Purpose-built hotel on main road with colourful décor and comfortable public areas. Ideal for business guests. Atmospheric O'Malleys bar. Smart, modern rooms. Carvery restaurant.

Ardilaun House, Taylor's Hill, West : 2 ½ km on R 337 ✆ (091) 521433, *info@ardilaunhousehotel.ie, Fax (091) 521546,* – 450. **VISA** C a
closed December – **Rest** (bar lunch Saturday) 29/40 and dinner a la carte 34/42 – ***Camilaun :*** **Rest** 20/40 and dinner a la carte 34/42 – **88 rm** 110/140 – 150/280, 1 suite.
◆ Georgian style country house hotel in five acres of gardens and ancient trees. Informal bar. Extensive leisure facilities. Spacious rooms in dark woods with quilted fabrics. Seafood, including oysters, feature strongly in restaurant. Stylish, formal Camilaun.

Park House, Forster St, Eyre Sq, ✆ (091) 564924, *parkhousehotel@eircom.net, Fax (091) 569219* – rest, rest, – 35. **VISA**. BY c
closed 24-26 December – **Rest** 43 and a la carte 29/48 – **84 rm** 95/235 – 95/235.
◆ Popular greystone hotel in city centre. Marble reception and comfy seating areas. Boss Doyle's Bar is busy and spacious. Dark wood bedrooms with rich, soft fabrics. Strong international flavours define restaurant menus.

Courtyard by Marriott, Headford Point, Headford Rd, at junction of N 6 and N 84 ✆ (091) 513200, *galway.info@courtyard.com, Fax (091) 513201,* – 120. **VISA**. D x
Rest 15/35 and a la carte 20/43 – **86 rm** 99/350 – 200/600, 4 suites.
◆ Stylish, smart corporate hotel where the bedrooms are the strong point with a high level of modish facilities. Well-equipped gym. Excellent sound-proofing a bonus. Informal dining in modern, open-plan restaurant.

Jurys Inn Galway, Quay St, ✆ (091) 566444, *jurysinngalway@jurysdoyle.com, Fax (091) 568415,* – rest, – 25. **VISA**. BZ c
closed 24-27 December – **Rest** (carvery lunch in bar)/dinner a la carte approx 22 – 11 – **130 rm** 59/120 – 59/120.
◆ Lodge style hotel overlooking Galway Bay, with light, airy and expansive reception lobby. Popular Inn Pub is warm and friendly. Superior rooms, with bright, fresh feel. Popular favourites in dining room.

Brennan's Yard, Lower Merchants Rd, ✆ (091) 568166, *info@brennansyardhotel.com, Fax (091) 568262* – rest, rest, . **VISA**. BZ e
May-December – **Rest** (bar lunch)/dinner a la carte 13/24 **s.** – **45 rm** 75/105 – 100/130.
◆ Converted stone warehouse in heart of the city, adjacent to Spanish Arch. Lively Spanish Bar has evening entertainment. Bedrooms individually furnished with antique pine. Local produce well-used in dining room.

Spanish Arch, Quay St, ✆ (091) 569600, *info@spanisharchhotel.ie, Fax (091) 569191* – rest, . **VISA**. BZ u
closed 24-26 December – **Rest** – (see ***The Restaurant*** below) – **20 rm** 75/119 – 129/145.
◆ Part 18C Carmelite convent with discreet entrance, in the heart of pedestrianised area. Busy, populous bar. Individually furnished, compact rooms with rich, striking fabrics.

Killeen House without rest., Killeen Bushypark, Northwest : 6 ½ km on N 59 ✆ (091) 524179, *killeenhouse@ireland.com, Fax (091) 528065,* – . **VISA**.
closed 1 week Christmas – **6 rm** 100/140 – 140/180.
◆ Whitewashed mid 19C guesthouse with pleasant gardens. Cosy sitting room with Art Nouveau styled furniture. Very comfortable, individually furnished bedrooms.

Adare Guest House without rest., 9 Father Griffin Pl, ✆ (091) 582638, *adare@iol.ie, Fax (091) 583963* – . **VISA**. AZ n
closed 21-27 December – **12 rm** 40/65 – 80/104.
◆ Three storey guesthouse west of river Corrib in quiet residential area near Wolf Tone Bridge. Cheery breakfast room. Modern rooms with orthopaedic beds and pine furniture.

Vina Mara, 19 Middle St, ✆ (091) 561610, *info@vinamara.com, Fax (091) 562607* – . **VISA** BY n
closed 1 week Christmas – **Rest** (dinner only) a la carte 27/47.
◆ Spacious restaurant in warm welcoming colours - smart yet informal; attentive service. Mediterranean style dishes with Irish and other touches.

Kirwan's Lane, Kirwan's Lane, ✆ (091) 568266, *Fax (091) 561645,* – . **VISA** BZ s
closed Sunday lunch – **Rest** (dinner only except summer) a la carte 32/47.
◆ Modern restaurant in warm, autumnal shades. Adventurous menus. Welcoming atmosphere and a genuine neighbourhood feel.

The Restaurant (at Spanish Arch H.), Quay St, ✆ (091) 569600, *Fax (091) 569191* – . **VISA** BZ u
closed 24-26 December – **Rest** (bar lunch)/dinner a la carte 15/23.
◆ 16C Carmelite convent with original exposed brick walls, now a busy ground floor bar and first floor dining room. Appealing, distinctive and seasonal Irish based menus.

REPUBLIC OF IRELAND

Ard Bia (The Restaurant), First Floor, 2 Quay St, ✆ (087) 2368648, *Fax (091) 53989* BZ
– ⇔. MO VISA
closed 25-26 December and Sunday – **Rest** (dinner only) a la carte 28/45.
◆ Personally run neighbourhood restaurant with bohemian edge, located in the heart of the city. Good value, refreshingly simple, unfussy dishes utilising quality local produce.

at Salthill *Southwest : 3¼ km.*

Galway Bay, The Promenade, ✆ (091) 520520, *info@galwaybayhotel.net*, *Fax (091) 520530*, ≤ Galway Bay, ⅉ, ≘s, ⊡, ⇐ – |‡| ⇔, ▤ rest, ✆ ♿ P – 🔺 500. MO AE ⊙ VISA. ✻ C
***Lobster Pot* : Rest** (bar lunch Monday-Saturday)/dinner 28/36 and a la carte 29/49 s. ♀ – **149 rm** ☐ ★115/180 – ★★160/290, 4 suites.
◆ Imposing, yellow painted hotel on promenade with super views of the Aran Isles. Characterful public bar. Good leisure facilities. Very large rooms with armchairs and sofas. Dining room has bay views and floral displays.

West Winds without rest., 5 Ocean Wave, Dr Colohan Rd, ✆ (091) 520223, *westwinds@eircom.net, Fax (091) 520223* – ⇔ P. MO AE VISA. ✻ C
May-October – **8 rm** ☐ ★45/75 – ★★70/100.
◆ Detached guesthouse in an ideal spot for holiday makers: right on the seafront. Cosy sitting room; breakfast room has conservatory extension. Simple, spotlessly kept bedrooms.

Devondell without rest., 47 Devon Park, Lower Salthill, off Lower Salthill Rd ✆ (091) 528306, *devondell@iol.ie* – ⇔. ✻ C
March-October – **4 rm** ☐ ★45/50 – ★★90.
◆ 1950s semi-detached guesthouse on suburban estate. Warm and friendly owner. Homely breakfast room. Spotless rooms with pristine Irish linen.

GARRYVOE (Garraí Uí Bhuaigh) *Cork* 712 H 12 – ✉ *Castlemartyr.*

Dublin 259 – Cork 37 – Waterford 100.

Garryvoe, ✆ (021) 4646718, *res@garryvoehotel.com, Fax (021) 4646824*, ≤ – |‡| ⇔ rest, ♿ P – 🔺 300. MO AE ⊙ VISA. ✻
closed 24-25 December – **Rest** (bar lunch Monday-Saturday)/dinner 39 and dinner a la carte 39/49 – **47 rm** ☐ ★105/115 – ★★150/170, 1 suite.
◆ Traditionally styled hotel adjacent to the beach with good sea views, to be enjoyed in characterful locals bar. A purpose-built, up-to-date wing features smart, modern rooms. Bright, colourful, contemporary restaurant.

GLASLOUGH (Glasloch) *Monaghan* 712 L 5 – *see Monaghan.*

GLASSAN (Glasán) *Westmeath* 712 I 7 – *see Athlone.*

GLENGARRIFF (An Gleann Garbh) *Cork* 712 D 12 *Ireland G.*

See : *Town★ – Garinish Island★★.*
Env. : *Healy Pass★★ (≤★★), W : by R 572 – Derreen Gardens★, W : by R 572 and north by R 574 (Healy Pass).*
ℹ ✆ *(027) 63084 (seasonal).*
Dublin 343 – Cork 96.5 – Killarney 59.5.

Cois Coille ⛒ without rest., ✆ (027) 63202, *coiscoille@eircom.net*, ⇐ – ⇔ P. ✻
June-September – **6 rm** ☐ ★45/50 – ★★68.
◆ Purpose-built house in a peaceful setting: a lovely, steeply sloping garden leads to the river, with picnic areas on different levels. Cosy lounge, well-kept bedrooms.

GLIN (An Gleann) *Limerick* 712 E 10.

Dublin 244.5 – Limerick 51.5 – Tralee 51.5.

Glin Castle ⛒, ✆ (068) 34173, *knight@iol.ie, Fax (068) 34364*, ≤, ⇐, ⚘, ✂ – ⇔ P. MO AE ⊙ VISA. ✻
March-November – **Rest** (residents only) (dinner only) 50 ♀ – **15 rm** ☐ ★290 – ★★450.
◆ Crenellated Georgian country house, overlooking the Shannon estuary, with superb collection of antique furnishings, paintings and porcelain. Beautifully appointed rooms. Home cooked meals full of local produce.

OREY (Guaire) *Wexford* 712 N 9 *Ireland G. – pop. 5 282.*
Exc. : *Ferns*★, *SW : 17¾ km by N 11.*
Courtown, Kiltennel ✆ *(055) 25166.*
Main St ✆ *(055) 21248.*
Dublin 93.5 – Waterford 88.5 – Wexford 61.

Marlfield House, Courtown Rd, Southeast : 1 ½ km on R 742 ✆ (055) 21124, *info@marfieldhouse.ie, Fax (055) 21572*, – rest. MC AE VISA.
closed 1-30 January – **Rest** (booking essential to non-residents) (dinner only and Sunday lunch)/dinner 62 – **19 rm** ★125/145 – ★★230/255, 1 suite.
◆ Luxuriously comfortable Regency mansion, with extensive gardens and woods. Utterly charming public areas with fine antiques and splendid fabrics. Thoughtfully furnished rooms. Very comfortable conservatory restaurant utilising produce from the garden.

Ashdown Park, Coach Rd, ✆ (055) 80500, *info@ashdownparkhotel.com, Fax (055) 80777*, – 500. MC AE VISA.
Rowan Tree : **Rest** (dinner only and Sunday lunch) a la carte 23/39 – **79 rm** ★110/160 – ★★160/260.
◆ Imposing hotel for business traveller in heart of market town. Atrium with sumptuous sofas. State-of-art leisure centre. Very comfortable rooms boast rich velvet curtains. Fine dining in the Rowan Tree restaurant.

We try to be as accurate as possible when giving room rates.
But prices are susceptible to change,
so please check rates when booking.

RAIGUENAMANAGH (Gráig na Manach) *Kilkenny* 712 L 10.
Dublin 125.5 – Kilkenny 34 – Waterford 42 – Wexford 26.

Waterside with rm, The Quay, ✆ (059) 9724246, *info@watersideguesthouse.com, Fax (059) 9724733*, – rest. MC AE VISA.
closed January and 24-26 December – **Rest** (restricted opening in winter) (dinner only and Sunday lunch) a la carte 30/38 s. – **10 rm** ★55/63 – ★★78/95.
◆ Converted 19C cornstore on banks of river Barrow, at foot of Brandon Hill. Base for hill-walkers. Modern cooking with Mediterranean flourishes. Beamed rooms with river views.

REYSTONES (Na Clocha Liatha) *Wicklow* 712 N 8 – *pop. 11 913.*
Greystones ✆ *(01) 287 6624.*
Dublin 35.5.

Hungry Monk, Church Rd, ✆ (01) 287 5759, *info@thehungrymonk.ie, Fax (01) 287 7183* – MC AE VISA
closed 24-26 December – **Rest** (dinner only and Sunday lunch)/dinner a la carte 33/60.
◆ Busy, long-established, candlelit restaurant above a wine bar. Pictures of monks in all areas. Robust, traditional cooking including blackboard seafood specials.

WEEDORE (Gaoth Dobhair) *Donegal* 712 H 2.
Dublin 278.5 – Donegal 72.5 – Letterkenny 43.5 – Sligo 135.

Gweedore Court, on N 56 ✆ (074) 953 2900, *anchuirt@eircom.net, Fax (074) 953 2929*, – rest, – 80. MC VISA.
closed for refurbishment until June – **Rest** (dinner only and Sunday lunch) 25/40 and a la carte 31/41 – **19 rm** ★90/130 – ★★130/150.
◆ Rebuilt 19C house sharing grounds with a Gaelic heritage centre. Spacious accommodation in classic patterns; east-facing rooms enjoy superb views of Glenreagh National Park. Classic menu matched by traditional surroundings and period-inspired décor.

ORSE AND JOCKEY *Tipperary.*
Dublin 146.5 – Cashel 14.5 – Thurles 9.5.

The Horse and Jockey Inn, ✆ (0504) 44192, *horseandjockeyinn@eircom.net, Fax (0504) 44747* – – 70. MC AE VISA.
closed 25 December – **Rest** a la carte 20/40 s. – **29 rm** ★90 – ★★160, 1 suite.
◆ Set on main Cork to Dublin road; big, busy and informal former inn. Reception area with gift shop. Bar full of horse racing pictures on walls. Comfy, bright, modern rooms. Easy going dining room with traditional menus.

HOWTH (Binn Èadair) *Dublin* 712 N 7 *Ireland G.* – ✉ Dublin.
See : *Town*★ – *The Summit*★ (≤★).
18, 18, 9 *Deer Park Hotel, Howth Castle* ✆ *(01) 832 6039.*
Dublin 16.

Inisradharc without rest., Balkill Rd, D13, North : ¾ km ✆ (01) 8322306, *harbour-view@msn.com*, ≤, – P. MO AE VISA.
closed 12 December-7 January – **3 rm** ☐ ★66/68 – ★★72/76.
◆ High above the pretty fishing village with views of the harbour and Eye Island. Conservatory breakfast room and spacious en suite bedrooms share a homely style.

Aqua, 1 West Pier, ✆ (0832) 0690, *dine@aqua.ie, Fax (0832) 0687,* ≤ Ireland's Eye and coastline – . MO AE VISA
closed 25-26 December and Monday except Bank Holidays – **Rest** - Seafood - 30 (lunch) and a la carte 29/52.
◆ Glass sided, first floor restaurant affording super bay views. Intimate bar filled with local photos, whetting the appetite for accomplished dishes of freshly caught seafood.

King Sitric with rm, East Pier, ✆ (01) 832 5235, *info@kingsitric.ie, Fax (01) 839 2442,* ≤ , rest. MO AE VISA.
closed Christmas – **Rest** - Seafood - *(closed Saturday lunch, Sunday and Bank Holiday)* 29/52 and a la carte 40/72 – **8 rm** ☐ ★105 – ★★205.
◆ Well established for 50 years; one of Ireland's original seafood restaurants. Enjoy locally caught produce in first floor dining room with bay views. Modern, comfy bedrooms.

Deep, 12 West Pier, ✆ (01) 8063921, *Fax (01) 8063921* – . MO VISA
closed 25-26 December and Monday except Bank Holidays – **Rest** - Bistro - a la carte 27/5
◆ Personally run, intimate restaurant on busy pier. Deep brown leather banquettes accentuate stylish feel. Wide-ranging, freshly prepared menus underpinned by local seafood.

INCH (An Inis) *Clare – see Ennis.*

INISHCRONE (Inis Crabhann) *Sligo* 712 E 5.
Dublin 257.5 – Ballina 13 – Galway 127 – Sligo 55.

Ceol na Mara without rest., Main St, ✆ (096) 36351, *ceolnamara@eircom.net,* ≤ – P. MO VISA.
closed 1 week Christmas and restricted opening in winter – **9 rm** ☐ ★38/45 – ★★76.
◆ At the centre of town, a sizeable guest house kept spotless by the friendly longstanding owners. Simply appointed bedrooms are all en suite, with sea views to the rear.

INISHMORE (Inis Mór) *Galway* 712 C/D 8 – *see Aran Islands.*

INNFIELD *Meath* 712 L 7 – *see Enfield.*

KANTURK (Ceann Toirc) *Cork* 712 F 11 *Ireland G.* – *pop. 1 651.*
See : *Town*★ - *Castle*★.
9 *Fairy Hill* ✆ *(029) 50534.*
Dublin 259 – Cork 53 – Killarney 50 – Limerick 71.

Glenlohane without rest., East : 4 km by R 576 and Charlville rd on Cecilstown ✆ (029) 50014, *glenlohane@iol.ie, Fax (029) 51100,* ≤, , – P. MO AE VISA.
4 rm ☐ ★100/115 – ★★185/200.
◆ In the family for over 250 years, a Georgian country house at the centre of wood parkland and a working farm. Library and cosy, en suite rooms overlooking the fiel Friendly owners.

KEEL (An Caol) *Mayo* 712 B 5/6 – *see Achill Island.*

KENMARE (Neidín) *Kerry* 712 D 12 *Ireland G.* – *pop. 1 844.*
See : *Town*★.
Exc. : *Ring of Kerry*★★ – *Healy Pass*★★ (≤★★), *SW : 30½ km by R 571 and R 574* **AY** – *Mountain Road to Glengarriff* (≤★★) *S : by N 71* **AY** – *Slieve Miskish Mountains* (≤★★), *S 48¼ km by R 571* **AY** – *Gougane Barra Forest Park*★★, *SE : 16 km* **AY** – *Lauragh (Derreen Gardens*★ *AC), SW : 23½ km by R 571* **AY** – *Allihies (Copper Mines*★*), SW : 57 km by R 5 and R 575* **AY** – *Garnish Island* (≤★), *SW : 68½ km by R 571, R 575 and R 572* **AY**.
18 *Kenmare* ✆ *(064) 41291.*
Heritage Centre ✆ *(064) 41233 (April-October)* **AY**.
Dublin 338 – Cork 93.5 – Killarney 32.

KENMARE

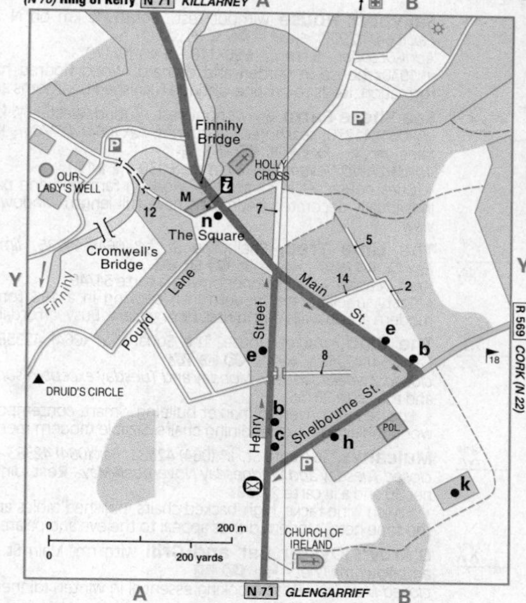

Park ⚘, ℘ (064) 41200, *info@parkkenmare.com, Fax (064) 41402*, < Kenmare Bay and hills, ⓪, Ⅎ5, ≘s, ⛳18, ♪, ⛫, ♔, ✗ – |♦| ⇹ ♿ [P]. ⓂⒸ AE VISA. ✕ **BY k**
closed 6 weeks January-February and 4 weeks November-December – **Rest** (dinner only) 72 s. – **46 rm** ☐ ☨206/256 – ☨☨412/552.
◆ Privately run country house boasts many paintings and antiques. Superb spa facilities. Inviting, classically tasteful rooms; many offer superb views of Kenmare Bay and hills. Grand, bay-windowed dining room; local produce to fore.

Sheen Falls Lodge ⚘, Southeast : 2 km by N 71 ℘ (064) 41600, *info@sheenfallslodge.ie, Fax (064) 41386*, < Sheen Falls, ⛱, Ⅎ5, ≘s, ⊡, ♪, ⛫, ♔, ✗ – |♦| ⇹ ☏ ♿ [P] – 🏛 120. ⓂⒸ AE Ⓓ VISA. ✕
closed January and first 2 weeks December – ***La Cascade*** **: Rest** (dinner only) 65 and a la carte 66/79 ♀ – ***Oscar's*** **: Rest** *(closed Monday-Tuesday in the season)* (dinner only and Sunday lunch in summer) a la carte 25/47 – ☐ 24 – **57 rm** ☨425 – ☨☨425, 9 suites 495/1835.
◆ On the banks of the Sheen; modern but classically inspired. Spacious rooms with stunning extras. Extensive spa, gym and stables. Attentive, formal service. Floodlit river views at La Cascade. Oscars, more informal, also overlooks the falls.

Davitt's, Henry St, ℘ (064) 42741, *davittskenmare@eircom.net, Fax (064) 42756*, ⛱ – ⇹, ▤ rest, ☏ [P]. ⓂⒸ AE VISA. ✕ **AY e**
closed 2 weeks November and 23-27 December – **Rest** a la carte 17/36 s. – **11 rm** ☐ ☨45/60 – ☨☨76/100.
◆ Behind a classically styled pub façade, hung with flower baskets, this personally run hotel offers trim, modern rooms furnished in warm wood and co-ordinated fabrics. Spacious brasserie dining.

The Rosegarden without rest., West : 1 ¼ km by N 71 on N 70 (Sneem rd) ℘ (064) 42288, *rosegard@iol.ie, Fax (064) 42305*, ⛫ – ⇹ ☏ [P]. ⓂⒸ AE VISA
8 rm ☐ ☨40/90 – ☨☨60/100.
◆ Bright, airy accommodation, practical and sensibly priced, in a purpose-built hotel outside the town; keenly run by a husband and wife team.

Shelburne Lodge without rest., East : ¾ km on R 569 (Cork Rd) ℘ (064) 41013, *shelburne@kenmare.com, Fax (064) 42135*, ⛫, ✗ – ⇹ [P]. ⓂⒸ VISA. ✕
10 March-10 December – **9 rm** ☐ ☨70/90 – ☨☨130/155.
◆ Georgian farmhouse with pleasant lawns and herb garden. Antiques stylishly combined with contemporary colours and modern art. Firelit lounge and cosy rooms. Affable hosts.

Sallyport House without rest., South : ½ km on N 71 (064) 42066, *port@iol.ie* *Fax (064) 42067,*
April-October – **5 rm** 90/110 – 140/170.
• 1930s house in garden and orchard. Wood floored hall, full of books and local information, leads to pristine, antique furnished bedrooms and a pretty front sitting room.

Sea Shore Farm without rest., Tubrid, West : 1 ½ km by N 71 off N 70 (Sneem rd) (064) 41270, *seashore@eircom.net, Fax (064) 41270,* Kenmare River and Caha mountains,
10 March-10 November – **6 rm** 130 – 130.
• Guesthouse set in 32 acres of working farmland and park with lovely views. All of the individually decorated bedrooms have full length windows which make the most of the view.

The Lime Tree, Shelburne St, (064) 41225, *limetree@limetreerestaurant.com,* *Fax (064) 41839* – BY
April-October – **Rest** (dinner only) a la carte 31/40.
• Tasty, unelaborate modern Irish cooking in a 19C former schoolhouse: stone walls, modern art on walls and in first-floor gallery. Busy, affordable and unfailingly friendly.

The Club, Market House, The Square, (064) 42958, *info@theclubrestaurant.com,* *Fax (064) 42958* – AY
closed 2 weeks January, Monday and Tuesday except in summer – **Rest** (dinner only) 20/4 and a la carte 26/36.
• Located in converted market building. Smart, contemporary interior enhanced by black wood tables and leather dining chairs. Sizable modern menus with Mediterranean accent.

Mulcahys, 36 Henry St, (064) 42383, *Fax (064) 42383* – AY
closed Tuesday and Wednesday November-May – **Rest** (dinner only and Sunday lunch)/dinner 30 and a la carte 27/39.
• Stylish wine racks, high-backed chairs, polished tables and friendly, attentive service set the tone here. Modern dishes appeal to the eye and palate alike.

D'Arcy's Oyster Bar and Grill with rm, Main St, (064) 41589, *keatingrestaurants@ownmail.net* – BY
closed Monday – **Rest** (booking essential in winter) (dinner only) a la carte 32/47 **s.** – **7 rm** 40/70 – 60/90.
• Restaurant set in striking, green-painted former bank. Pop in for oysters or fresh Kerry seafood at Oyster Bar or modern Irish menu in restaurant. Comfy, up-to-date bedrooms.

An Leath Phingin, 35 Main St, (064) 41559 – BY
closed mid November-mid January, Tuesday and Wednesday – **Rest** - Italian - (dinner only) a la carte 24/35 **s.**
• Simply styled, but cosy and welcoming. Unpretentious dishes, authentically prepared home-made pasta, pizzas and dishes from the wood grill. An affordable local favourite.

Packies, Henry St, (064) 41508 – AY
closed February-March, Sunday and restricted opening in winter – **Rest** (dinner only) a la carte 31/45.
• A locally popular, personally run little place an understated rustic feel. Handwritten menu of fresh modern Irish dishes prepared with care and simplicity. Personable staff.

KESHCARRIGAN (Ceis Charraigin) *Leitrim* 712 I 5 – *Carrick-on-Shannon.*
Dublin 162.5 – Carrick-on-Shannon 14.5 – Ballinamore 14.5.

Canal View House without rest., East : ½ km (071) 9642404, *canalviewcountryhouse@eircom.net, Fax (071) 9642261,*
closed 25 December – **6 rm** 40/42 – 60/70.
• Agreeably located, overlooking the Shannon/Erne waterway and countryside beyond: for hours watching the canal boats. Comfy conservatory lounge with view. Sizeable rooms.

KILBRITTAIN (Cill Briotáin) *Cork* 712 F 12.
Dublin 289.5 – Cork 38.5 – Killarney 96.5.

The Glen without rest., Southwest : 6 ½ km by un-marked rd off R 600 (023) 49862, *info@glencountryhouse.com, Fax (023) 49862,*
Easter-October – **5 rm** 60/75 – 120/130.
• 130 year-old family house, part of working farm close to beach. Delicious organic farmhouse breakfasts. Lovingly restored bedrooms elegantly furnished to a high standard.

Casino House, Coolmain Bay, Southeast : 3 ½ km by unmarked rd on R 600 (023) 49944, *chouse@eircom.net, Fax (023) 49945,*
closed January-17 March and Wednesday – **Rest** *(weekends only November-December)* (dinner only and Sunday lunch)/dinner a la carte 31/48 **s.**
• Whitewashed walls, Shaker style furniture and art on a culinary theme in this converted farmhouse run by a husband and wife. Locally sourced menu is balanced and flavourful.

LCOLGAN (Cill Cholgáin) *Galway* 712 F 8 – ✉ *Oranmore.*
Dublin 220.5 – Galway 17.5.

Moran's Oyster Cottage, The Weir, Northwest : 2 km by N 18 ☎ (091) 796113, *moranstheweir@eircom.net, Fax (091) 796503,* – 🚭 🅿. MC AE VISA
closed Christmas and Good Friday – **Rest** - Seafood - 32/45 a la carte 30/70.
◆ Likeable thatched pub in sleepy village. Settle down in one of the beamed snugs and parlours to enjoy prime local seafood - simple and fresh - or soups, salads and sandwiches.

LKEE (Cill Chaoi) *Clare* 712 D 9 *Ireland G.* – *pop. 1 331.*
Exc. : *Kilrush★ (Scattery Island★ by boat), SE : 16 m. by N 67 – SW : Loop Head Peninsula (Bridge of Ross★).*
Kilkee, East End ☎ (065) 9056048.
The Square ☎ (065) 9056112 (June-early September), tourisminfo@shannon-dev.ie.
Dublin 285 – Galway 124 – Limerick 93.5.

Kilkee Bay, ☎ (065) 9060060, *info@kilkee-bay.com, Fax (065) 9060062* – 🚭 rest, ▤ rest, ♿ 🅿 – 🏛 150. MC AE DC VISA. ✗
10 March-October – **Rest** (bar lunch)/dinner 28 and a la carte 25/36 – **40 rm** ☐ ★67/85 – ★★94/130, 1 suite.
◆ Purpose-built and competitively priced - useful for business or leisure travel; Plenty of conference space and pristine bedrooms, many with sofa beds, in modern blond wood. Informal restaurant serving an extensive menu.

Halpin's, Erin St, ☎ (065) 9056032, *halpinshotel@iol.ie, Fax (065) 9056317* – 🚭 rest, 🅿. MC AE DC VISA. ✗
15 March-October – **Rest** (bar lunch Monday-Saturday)/dinner 19/35 and a la carte 21/30 ♀ – **12 rm** ☐ ★75 – ★★120.
◆ Attractive terraced house offering good value accommodation and a warm welcome. Pub-style bar in the basement and uniform bedrooms with fitted furniture. Traditionally appointed ground floor restaurant.

Kilkee Thalassotherapy Centre and Guest House without rest., Grattan St, ☎ (065) 9056742, *info@kilkeethalasso.com, Fax (065) 9056762,* – 🚭 🅿. MC VISA. ✗
closed 24-28 December – **5 rm** ☐ ★38/70 – ★★76/90.
◆ Modern guest house with combined breakfast room and sitting room. Spacious well-equipped bedrooms. Preferential booking for guests in the adjoining thalassotherapy centre.

LKENNY (Cill Chainnigh) *Kilkenny* 712 K 10 *Ireland G.* – *pop. 20 735.*
See : *Town★★ – St Canice's Cathedral★★ – Kilkenny Castle and Grounds★★ AC – Cityscope★ AC – Black Abbey★ – Rothe House★.*
Exc. : *Jerpoint Abbey★★ AC, S : 19 ¼ km by R 700 and N 9 – Dunmore Cave★ AC, N : 11¼ km by N 77 and N 78 – Kells Priory★, S : 12½ km by R 697.*
Glendine ☎ (056) 65400 – Callan, Geraldine ☎ (056) 25136 – Castlecomer, Drumgoole ☎ (056) 41139.
Shee Alms House ☎ (056) 7751500.
Dublin 114 – Cork 138.5 – Killarney 185 – Limerick 111 – Tullamore 83.5 – Waterford 46.5.

Kilkenny River Court, The Bridge, John St, ☎ (056) 772 3388, *reservations@kilrivercourt.com, Fax (056) 772 3389,* ≤, 🏋, – 🛗 🚭, ▤ rest, ♿ 🅿 – 🏛 210. MC AE VISA. ✗
closed 24-25 December – **Rest** (bar lunch Monday-Saturday)/dinner a la carte 28/48 **s.** ♀ – **88 rm** ☐ ★90 – ★★180/210, 2 suites.
◆ Smart hotel opposite Kilkenny Castle. Modern rooms in traditional, co-ordinated colours. Bar boasts eye-catching fibre-optic lighting and a view of the River Nore. Candlelit dining room.

The Hibernian, 1 Ormonde St, ☎ (056) 7771888, *info@kilkennyhibernianhotel.com, Fax (056) 7771877* – 🛗, 🚭 rest, ▤ rest, ☎ ♿ 🅿 – 🏛 30. MC AE DC VISA. ✗
closed 24-26 December – **Rest** (bar lunch Monday-Friday)/dinner a la carte 31/45 **s.** – **43 rm** ☐ ★80/120 – ★★210/280, 3 suites.
◆ Part Georgian hotel, set in former bank, in sight of Kilkenny Castle: classically proportioned, understated modern bedrooms, spacious bar in dark wood with long tan sofas. Comfortable restaurant with traditional appeal.

Kilkenny, College Rd, Southwest : 1 ¼ km at junction with N 76 ☎ (056) 7762000, *kilkenny@griffingroup.ie, Fax (056) 7765984,* 🏋, 🏊, – 🚭, ▤ rest, ☎ ♿ 🅿 – 🏛 400. MC AE DC VISA. ✗
Brooms Bistro : **Rest** 22/35 and a la carte 25/40 – **103 rm** ☐ ★77 – ★★140/170.
◆ Busy modern hotel popular with business travellers. Up-to-date spa and gym, colourful, wood-fitted rooms and a tiled lounge and conservatory in subtle continental style. Open restaurant in terracotta, wicker and wrought iron.

REPUBLIC OF IRELAND

Newpark, Castlecomer Rd, North : 1½ km on N 77 ✆ (056) 7760500, *info@newpark-hotel.com, Fax (056) 7760555,* – rest, – 600.
Rest (carvery lunch Monday-Saturday)/dinner 25/39 **s.** and a la carte – 13 – **130 rm** ★79/99 – ★★99/160.
◆ Under experienced management, a purpose-built hotel on the edge of the town. Bright, stylish lobby leads off to soft-toned modern rooms and smart conference facilities. Modern bar and bistro style dining; grill-based menu in the evenings.

Langton's House, 69 John St, ✆ (056) 7765133, *reservations@langtons. Fax (056) 7763693,* – rest, rest,
closed 25 December and Good Friday – **Rest** 25/35 (dinner) and a la carte 19/35 – **30 rm** ★50/100 – ★★120/200.
◆ Traditional rooms furnished in mahogany plus 16 more in comfortable modern annexe. Firelit bar in wood and aged red leather is a convivial, locally popular evening venue. Wrought iron and trailing greenery in spacious dining room.

Butler House without rest., 15-16 Patrick St, ✆ (056) 7765707, *res@butler. Fax (056) 7765626,* – – 100.
closed 23-29 December – **12 rm** ★80/155 – ★★120/170, 1 suite.
◆ Substantial part Georgian house. Spacious accommodation with 1970s-style furnishings - superior bow-fronted bedrooms to the rear overlook neat, geometric lawned gardens.

Blanchville House without rest., Dunbell, Maddoxtown, Southeast : 10 ½ km N 10 turning right ¾ km after the Pike Inn ✆ (056) 7727197, *mail@blanchville Fax (056) 7727636,* –
March-October – **6 rm** ★60/70 – ★★110/120.
◆ Follow the tree-lined drive to this restored Georgian country house in quiet farmland. Firelit drawing room. Charming bedrooms furnished with antiques and family heirlooms.

Fanad House without rest., Castle Rd, South : ¾ km on R 700 ✆ (056) 7764126, *fanadhouse@hotmail.com, Fax (056) 7756001,* –
8 rm ★45/65 – ★★110/130.
◆ Modern, purpose-built, green painted house within the castle walls. A warm welcome and bright, well-appointed bedrooms await the visitor.

Shillogher House without rest., Callan Rd, Southwest : 1 ½ km on N 76 ✆ (056) 7763249, *shillogherhouse@eircom.net,* –
closed Christmas – **6 rm** ★40/50 – ★★80/90.
◆ More modern than its gables at first suggest, a redbrick guesthouse facing a neat landscaped lawn. Modern en suite bedrooms kept spotless by affable hosts.

Zuni with rm, 26 Patrick St, ✆ (056) 7723999, *info@zuni.ie, Fax (056) 7756400,* –
closed 23-27 December – **Rest** a la carte 33/42 – **13 rm** ★65/80 – ★★90/120.
◆ Chic modern design in leather and dark wood draws the smart set to this former theatre. Friendly service; bold, generous and eclectic cooking. Stylish, good-value rooms.

Lacken House with rm, Dublin rd, East : ½ km on N 10 ✆ (056) 7761085, *info@lackenhouse.ie, Fax (056) 7762435,* – rest,
closed 24-27 December – **Rest** *(closed Sunday except at Bank Holidays, June-September and Monday)* (dinner only) 43 and a la carte 45/56 – **10 rm** ★69/85 – ★★120/170.
◆ Yellow painted Victorian house with brightly decorated bedrooms. Smart dining room offers an interesting menu of both traditional Irish and modern European dishes.

Ristorante Rinuccini with rm, 1 The Parade, ✆ (056) 7761575, *info@rinuccini.com Fax (056) 7751288* – rest,
closed 25-26 December – **Rest** - Italian - 22/47 – **7 rm** ★75/85 – ★★100/120.
◆ Named after the 17C archbishop, "bon viveur" and papal nuncio to Ireland, a family owned restaurant with Italian classics served at closely set tables. Smart rooms available.

KILLALOE (Cill Dalua) *Clare* 712 G 9 *Ireland G.*

See : *Town★ – St Flannan's Cathedral★.*
Env. : *Graves of the Leinstermen (≤★), N : 7¼ km by R 494.*
Exc. : *Nenagh★ (Heritage Centre★ AC, Castle★), NE : 19¼ km by R 496 and N 7 – Holy Island★ AC, N : 25¾ km by R 463 and boat from Tuamgraney.*
The Bridge ✆ (061) 376866, tourisminfo@shannon-dev.ie.
Dublin 175.5 – Ennis 51.5 – Limerick 21 – Tullamore 93.5.

Cherry Tree, Lakeside, Ballina, following signs for Lakeside H. ✆ (061) 375688, *Fax (061) 375689,* ≤ –
closed 24-25 December, last week January, first week February, Sunday dinner and Monday – **Rest** (dinner only and Sunday lunch) 39 and a la carte 43/52.
◆ Contemporary, relaxing interior, polite staff and original, well-sourced modern Irish dishes from an open kitchen: asparagus fritters and aïoli, turbot on leek and bacon.

KILLARNEY (Cill Airne) *Kerry* 712 D 11 *Ireland G. – pop. 13 137.*

See : *Town*★★ – *St Mary's Cathedral*★ **CX**.

Env. : *Killarney National Park*★★★ *(Muckross Abbey*★, *Muckross House and Farms*★*)* **AZ** – *Gap of Dunloe*★★, *SW : 9½ km by R 562* **AZ** – *Ross Castle*★ **AC**, *S : 1½ km by N 71 and minor rd* – *Torc Waterfall*★, *S : 8 km by N 71* **BZ**.

Exc. : *Iveragh Peninsula*★★ *(Ring of Kerry*★★*)* – *Ladies View*★★, *SW : 19¼ km by N 71* **BZ** – *Moll's Gap*★, *SW : 25 km by N 71* **BZ**.

18, 18 *Mahoney's Point* ℘ *(064) 31034* **AZ**.

Kerry (Farranfore) Airport : ℘ (066) 976 4644, N : 15¼ km by N 22.

Beech Rd ℘ (064) 31633, user@cktourism.ie.

Dublin 304 – Cork 87 – Limerick 111 – Waterford 180.

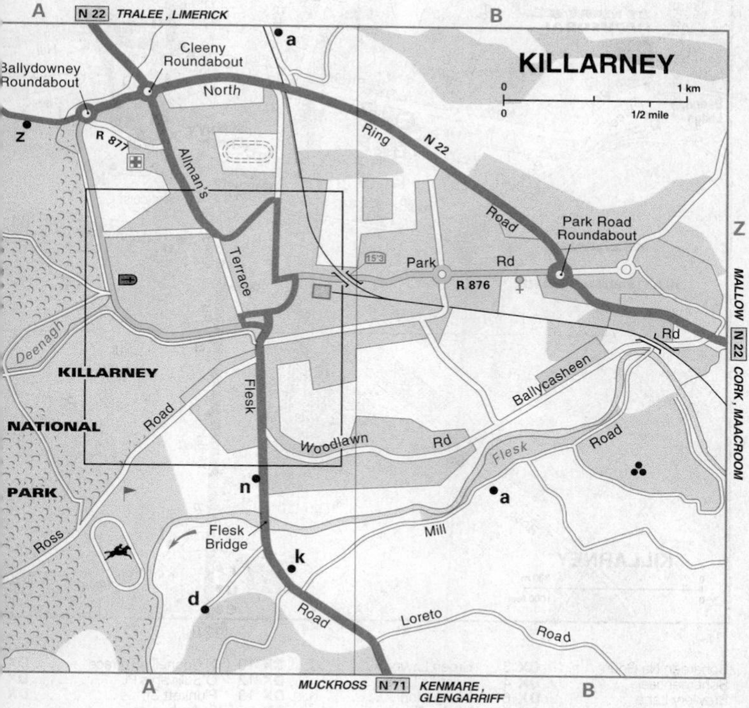

A N 22 TRALEE, LIMERICK B
KILLARNEY
0 1 km
0 1/2 mile
Ballydowney Roundabout
Cleeny Roundabout
North
Ring
N 22
Road
Park Road Roundabout
R 877
Allman's
Terrace
Park
Rd
R 876
Deenagh
KILLARNEY
NATIONAL
PARK
Flesk
Road
Woodlawn
Rd
Ballycasheen
Rd
Flesk
Road
Mill
Flesk Bridge
Ross
Road
Loreto
Road
a
z
n
a
k
d
Z
MALLOW N 22 CORK, MACROOM
A MUCKROSS N 71 KENMARE, GLENGARRIFF B

Killarney Park, ℘ (064) 35555, *info@killarneyparkhotel.ie, Fax (064) 35266,* – 150. **DX k**
closed 18-27 December – ***Park*** : **Rest** (bar lunch)/dinner 58 and a la carte approx 58 ♀ – **69 rm** ☕ ★385 – ★★385, 3 suites.
◆ Smart modern hotel. Firelit library, panelled billiard room and the bedrooms' décor and fine details balance old-world styling and contemporary convenience. Armchair dining beneath sparkling chandeliers and Corinthian capitals.

Aghadoe Heights , Northwest : 4 ½ km by N 22 ℘ (064) 31766, *info@aghadoeheights.com, Fax (064) 31345,* ≤ Lough Leane, Macgillycuddy's Reeks and countryside, – 100.
closed 28 December-10 March – ***Fredrick's*** : **Rest** (bar lunch Monday-Saturday)/dinner a la carte 29/62 **s.** – **71 rm** ☕ ★200/280 – ★★230/350, 2 suites.
◆ Striking glass-fronted hotel: stylish bar, modern health and fitness centre and contemporary rooms, many with sumptuous sofas. Balconied front rooms offer views of the lough. Picture-windowed restaurant with rural views.

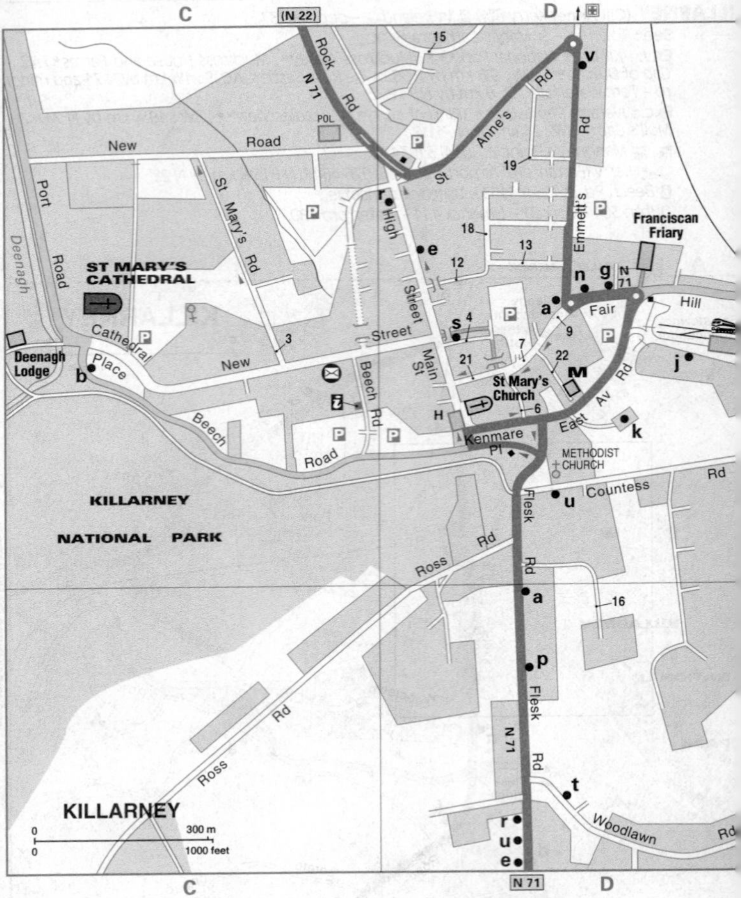

Bohereen Na Goun . . . . CX 3	Green Lawn . . . . CX 10	O'Connell's Terrace . . . . DX
Bohereencael . . . . DX 4	Hillard's Lane . . . . DX 12	O'Sullivan's Pl. . . . . DX
Brewery Lane . . . . DX 6	Mangerton . . . . DX 13	Plunkett St . . . . DX
College Square . . . . DX 7	Marian Terrace . . . . DX 15	St Anthony's Pl. . . . . DX
College St . . . . DX 9	Muckross Drive . . . . DXY 16	

Great Southern, ✆ (064) 38000, *res@killarney-gsh.com, Fax (064) 31642*, Ꝭ, ≘s, ◻, ⛝, 🌿, ✂ – |♯| ⇹ ♿ [P] – 🎓 800. ⓒ ⓐ ⓓ VISA. ✂ DX
Garden Room : Rest (dinner only) 38 s. – ***Peppers :*** Rest *(closed Sunday-Monday)* (dinner only) a la carte 31/41 s. – ☐ 18 – **170 rm** ✝270 – ✝✝270, 2 suites.
◆ Vast lobby sets the tone in this ivy-clad 19C landmark. Country house style accommodation in the original house, ultra-modern rooms in the new wing. Classical Garden Room has a fabulous domed ceiling. Peppers for Mediterranean themed menus.

Europe ⛵, Fossa, West : 4 ¾ km by R 562 on N 72 ✆ (064) 71350, *sales@kih.liebherr.com, Fax (064) 37900*, ≤ Lough Leane and Macgillycuddy's Reeks, Ꝭ, ≘s, ◻, 🐟, ⛝, 🌿, ✂indoor – |♯| ⚓ ⇹ ♿ [P] – 🎓 400. ⓒ ⓐ ⓓ VISA. ✂
17 March-October – **Rest** *(closed Sunday dinner)* (light lunch)/dinner a la carte 38/66 s.
202 rm ☐ ✝174/236 – ✝✝256, 3 suites.
◆ Spacious lounges and bedrooms plus excellent prospects of Macgillicuddy's Reeks and Lough Leane. Fully equipped modern comfort, even luxury, on a vast but well managed scale. Restaurant offers Lough views.

The Brehon, Muckross Rd, (064) 30700, *info@thebrehon.com, Fax (064) 30701,* – 250. AZ k
The Brehon : Rest (bar lunch)/dinner a la carte 34/45 **s.** – **120 rm** 120/180 – 180/280, 5 suites.
◆ Spacious hotel near Muckross Park with views to mountains. High standards of comfort. Basement Wellness Centre. Airy bedrooms are well equipped with latest mod cons. Stylish restaurant for formal, original dining.

Randles Court, Muckross Rd, (064) 35333, *info@randlescourt.com, Fax (064) 35206,* rest, – 80. DY p
closed January-February and 23-27 December – ***Checkers :*** Rest (bar lunch)/dinner 30/40 and a la carte 27/38 **s.** – **52 rm** 150/200 – 170/260.
◆ Family run hotel, centred on a rectory built in 1906. Good leisure facilities. Rooms, at their best in the modern extension, and comfy lounge subtly reflect the period style. Good choice of local produce in chequerboard floored restaurant.

Dromhall, Muckross Rd, (064) 39300, *info@dromhall.com, Fax (064) 39301,* rest, – 300. DY p
closed 22-27 December – ***Abbey :*** Rest (dinner only) 32/40 and a la carte 25/40 – ***Kayne's :*** Rest *(closed 22-27 December)* (dinner only) 25/35 and a la carte 26/40 – **72 rm** 75/210 – 90/240.
◆ Modern, marble-tiled lobby leads to sizeable rooms with reproduction furnishings and an unexpectedly homely lounge: ideal for business travel. Abbey restaurant offers a classic repertory. Kayne's bistro serves a wide-ranging modern menu.

Cahernane House, Muckross Rd, (064) 31895, *info@cahernane.com, Fax (064) 34340,* AZ d
February-November – ***The Herbert Room :*** Rest (bar lunch Monday-Saturday)/dinner 50/70 and a la carte 27/51 – **37 rm** 180/220 – 224/264, 1 suite.
◆ Peacefully located 19C house with pleasant mountain outlook. Array of lounges in sympathetic style. Rooms in main house or modern wing: all are large, comfy and well equipped. Restaurant offers formal dining with inspiring views.

Killarney Royal, College St, (064) 31853, *royalhot@iol.ie, Fax (064) 34001* – DX g
closed 24-26 December – **Rest** (bar lunch Monday-Saturday)/dinner 20/30 and a la carte 27/43 – **29 rm** 160/320 – 230/360.
◆ Smart yet cosy lounge with an open fire, spacious, individually decorated rooms and a traditional bar in a town house hotel, built at the turn of the 20th century. Classic, candlelit dining room with flowing white linen.

Holiday Inn, Muckross Rd, (064) 33000, *info@holidayinnkillarney.com, Fax (064) 33001,* rest, AZ n
closed 24-25 December – **Rest** (bar lunch)/dinner 30 **s.** – **86 rm** 60/149 – 220/360, 14 suites.
◆ Hotel on the town's southern outskirts. Comfortable, well-equipped bedrooms and a compact but modern gym will appeal to business travellers. Formula dining room.

Killeen House, Aghadoe, Northwest : 5 ¾ km by N 22 (064) 31711, *charming@indigo.ie, Fax (064) 31811,* –
April-October – **Rest** (dinner only) 50 – **23 rm** 75/115 – 150.
◆ Extended 19C rectory run by a friendly couple. Rooms in bright matching prints. Thousands of golf balls cover the walls of a cosy "bar"; deluxe rooms particularly comfy. Homely dining room with garden views.

McSweeney Arms, College St, (064) 31211, *mcsweeney@eircom.net, Fax (065) 34553* – rest, DX n
closed January – **Rest** 25/45 a la carte 24/48 **s.** – **26 rm** 130/150 – 150/180.
◆ The hotel's unusual corner tower provides extra seating areas in some rooms; the characterful bar has been family run for over 50 years. Well-fitted rooms in modern tones. Long-standing owner lends a hand in the bar and restaurant.

Foley's Townhouse, 23 High St, (064) 31217, *info@foleystownhouse.com, Fax (064) 34683* – rest, DX e
closed December-January – **Rest** (bar lunch)/dinner 35/45 and a la carte 21/47 – **28 rm** 70/100 – 100/150.
◆ Formerly a posting inn, now a likeable town-centre hotel, still personally owned and run; spacious modern accommodation is individually styled with a good range of mod cons. Appetising range of seafood in restaurant.

Fairview without rest., College St, (064) 34164, *fvk@eircom.net, Fax (064) 71777* – DX a
closed 24-25 December – **18 rm** 50/130 – 158/195.
◆ Stylish, personally run town centre house; smart, leather furnished lounge, linen-clad breakfast room. Bright, up-to-date rooms exude distinctively individualistic flourishes.

Killarney Lodge without rest., Countess Rd, ℘ (064) 36499, *klylodge@iol.i* DX
Fax (064) 31070, – P. VISA.
5 February-1 November – **16 rm** ☐ ☆90/120 – ☆☆110/140.
◆ Run by a likeable couple, a purpose-built hotel offering comfortable, thoughtfully fu nished rooms. Within easy walking distance of the town centre.

Earls Court House without rest., Woodlawn Junction, Muckross Rd, ℘ (064) 3400 DY
info@killarney-earlscourt.ie, Fax (064) 34366, – P. VISA
March-15 November – **24 rm** ☐ ☆70/100 – ☆☆100/180.
◆ Behind an unassuming façade, reproduction furniture combines well with modern faci ties in spotlessly kept rooms. Tasty breakfasts served at antique dining tables.

Old Weir Lodge without rest., Muckross Rd, ℘ (064) 35593, *oldweirlodge@eircom.ne* DY
Fax (064) 35583 – P. VISA.
closed 23-29 December – **30 rm** ☐ ☆55/85 – ☆☆80/130.
◆ Just south of the centre, a sizeable modern hotel owned and run by a welcomir couple. Neat rooms - particularly spacious on the second floor - and hearty breakfasts.

Fuchsia House without rest., Muckross Rd, ℘ (064) 33743, *fuchsiahouse@eircom.ne* DY
Fax (064) 36588, – P. VISA.
closed January-February – **9 rm** ☐ ☆50/85 – ☆☆100/140.
◆ Inviting bedrooms, firelit lounge and a leafy conservatory in carefully chosen fabrics ar patterns; homely without a trace of preciousness or fuss. Personally run.

Kathleens Country House without rest., Tralee Rd, North : 3¼ km on N 22 ℘ (06 32810, *info@kathleens.net, Fax (064) 32340,* – P. VISA.
14 March-October – **17 rm** ☐ ☆60/100 – ☆☆120/140.
◆ Cosy lounge with broad, pine-backed armchairs facing an open fire and neat bedroon in traditional patterns - an extended house run by the eponymous owner for over 20 yea

Abbey Lodge without rest., Muckross Rd, ℘ (064) 34193, *abbeylodgekly@eircom.ne* DY
Fax (064) 35877 – P. VISA.
closed 20-27 December – **15 rm** ☐ ☆50/120 – ☆☆90/120.
◆ Smart accommodation not far from the centre of town. Cosy lounge in cheerful yellow Spotless, well-equipped rooms with Queen size beds and CD players.

Gleann Fia Country House without rest., Old Deerpark, North : 2 km by Er mett's Rd ℘ (064) 35035, *info@gleannfia.com, Fax (064) 35000,* – P. VISA AZ
20 rm ☐ ☆50/85 – ☆☆70/140.
◆ Meaning "Glen of the Deer", a substantial, purpose-built hotel in country house sty ringed by woods. Smartly kept bedrooms are usefully supplied with modern facilities.

Coolclogher House without rest., Mill Rd, ℘ (064) 35996, *info@coolclogh house.com, Fax (064) 30933,* – P. VISA. BZ
February-November – **4 rm** ☐ ☆190 – ☆☆190/280.
◆ Very attractive early Victorian house in acres of parkland. Stylish high ceilings throug out. Conservatory built around 19C specimen camellia! Huge, very comfortable rooms.

Kingfisher Lodge without rest., Lewis Rd, ℘ (064) 37131, *kingfisherguesthouse@ com.net, Fax (064) 39871,* – P. VISA. DX
10 February-11 December – **10 rm** ☐ ☆38/75 – ☆☆60/110.
◆ Friendly owners, a mine of local information, keep this modern guesthouse in immac late order. Affordable accommodation in pastel shades; rear rooms face a quiet garden.

Rivermere without rest., Muckross Rd, South : ¾ km on N 71 ℘ (064) 37933, *info@kil ney-rivermere.com, Fax (064) 37944,* – P. VISA. DY
10 March-4 November – **8 rm** ☐ ☆50/65 – ☆☆100/130.
◆ The enthusiasm of this husband and wife team shows in the running of their mode house. Comfortable, well-appointed bedrooms, bright and airy pine-furnished breakfa room.

Sika Lodge without rest., Ballydowney, Northwest : 1½ km on N 72 ℘ (064) 36304, – P. VISA. AZ
booking essential in winter – **6 rm** ☐ ☆45 – ☆☆65.
◆ Neat, stone built house with a friendly atmosphere, located on the edge of Killarn National Park. Compact but practical en suite bedrooms at reasonable rates.

Hussey's Townhouse without rest., 43 High St, ℘ (064) 37454, *husseys@iol.* DX
Fax (064) 33144 – P. VISA.
Easter-October – **5 rm** ☐ ☆50/70 – ☆☆80/90.
◆ Affable owner runs this hotel, above and adjacent to a little neighbourhood pub. Hom lounge, compact, pleasantly styled and well-priced bedrooms upstairs.

XX **The Old Presbytery,** Cathedral Pl, ☎ (064) 30555, *oldpresbytery@eircom.net, Fax (064) 30557* – ⇔ ▤ P. MC AE D VISA **CX b**
closed Monday-Wednesday November-17 March and Tuesday – **Rest** (dinner only) a la carte 30/49.
◆ Imposing Georgian restaurant opposite St. Mary's Cathedral. Period windows, coal fire - and pianist accompaniment. Varied menu with traditional base and modern elements.

X **The Cooperage,** Old Market Lane, ☎ (064) 37716, *info@cooperagerestaurant.com, Fax (064) 37716* – ⇔ ⇔ 30. MC VISA **DX s**
closed 25 December and Sunday lunch – **Rest** (light lunch)/dinner a la carte 24/40.
◆ Stylish, slate-floored town centre bar-restaurant lit by eye-catching modern "chandeliers". Flavourful modern dinners. Good choice of daily specials.

Beaufort *West : 9¾ km by R 562 – AZ – off N 72 – ✉ Killarney.*

Dunloe Castle ⛭, Southeast : 1 ½ km on Dunloe Golf Course rd ☎ (064) 71350, *sales@kih.liebherr.com, Fax (064) 44583,* ← Gap of Dunloe and Macgillycuddy's Reeks, ⛭, ⛭, ⛭, ⛭, ⛭, ⛭indoor – |⛭| ⇔ P – ⛭ 250. MC AE D VISA. ⛭
May-September – **Rest** (light lunch)/dinner a la carte 34/62 **s.** – **109 rm** ⛭ ✝135/236 – ✝✝256, 1 suite.
◆ Creeper-clad modern hotel offers sizeable, well-equipped rooms and smart conference suites, not forgetting an impressive view of the Gap of Dunloe and Macgilllicuddy's Reeks. Restaurant serves Irish classic dishes.

LLASHANDRA (Cill na Seanrátha) *Cavan* 712 J 5.
Dublin 133.5 – Belturbet 14.5 – Cavan 19.5.

Eonish Lodge ⛭ without rest., Eonish, Northeast : 4 ¾ km by Belturbet rd ☎ (049) 4334487, *eonishlodge@eircom.net,* ←, ⛭, ⛭ – ⇔ P. ⛭
February-November – **4 rm** ⛭ ✝55 – ✝✝80.
◆ Just a stone's throw from Lough Oughter, in Killykeen Forest Park. Perfect for fishermen and walkers. Simple, neatly furnished bedrooms; front two have best views over lough.

LLEAGH (Cill Ia) *Cork* 712 H 12 – *pop. 362.*
Dublin 243 – Cork 37 – Waterford 85.5.

Ballymakeigh House ⛭, North : 1 ½ km ☎ (024) 95184, *ballymakeigh@eircom.net, Fax (024) 95370,* ⛭, ⛭, ⛭ – ⇔ P. MC VISA. ⛭
March-October – **Rest** (by arrangement) 45 – **6 rm** ⛭ ✝65/70 – ✝✝110/120.
◆ Smoothly run modern country house on a working dairy farm. Attractive conservatory lounge and en suite rooms simply but thoughtfully decorated without starchiness or fuss.

LLORGLIN (Cill Orglan) *Kerry* 712 C 11.
⛭18 *Killorglin, Steelroe* ☎ *(066) 9761979.*
Dublin 333 – Killarney 19.5 – Tralee 26.

Bianconi, Annadale Rd, ☎ (066) 9761146, *bianconi@iol.ie, Fax (066) 9761950,* ⛭ – ⇔ rest. MC AE D VISA. ⛭
closed 25-27 December – **Rest** *(closed Sunday)* (bar lunch)/dinner a la carte 27/41 ⛭ – **15 rm** ⛭ ✝65/90 – ✝✝100/115.
◆ Classic street-corner pub; tiled lounge bar with stools and banquettes and likeable mismatch of paintings, old photos and vintage Guinness posters. Trim, soft-toned bedrooms. Open-fired restaurant, lined with books, bottles and local landscapes.

Grove Lodge without rest., Killarney Rd, East : ¾ km on N 72 ☎ (066) 9761157, *info@grovelodge.com, Fax (066) 9762330,* ⛭, ⛭ – ⇔ P. MC AE VISA. ⛭
February-November – **10 rm** ⛭ ✝50/65 – ✝✝90/110.
◆ Comfortable, well-fitted rooms - one with four-poster bed and private patio - in a smoothly run riverside house. Try smoked salmon and eggs or a full Irish breakfast.

LLYBEGS (Na Cealla Beaga) *Donegal* 712 G 4 *Ireland G.*
Exc. : *Glengesh Pass★★, SW : 24 km by N 56 and R 263 – Glencolmcille Folk Village★★, W : by R 263 – Gweebarra Estuary★, NE : 30½ km by R 262 and R 252 – Trabane Strand★.*
Dublin 291 – Donegal 27.5 – Londonderry 103 – Sligo 92.

Bay View, Main St, ☎ (074) 9731950, *info@bayviewhotel.ie, Fax (074) 9731856,* ←, ⛭, ⛭, ⛭ – |⛭|, ⇔ rest, ▤ rest, ⛭ ⛭ – ⛭ 450. MC AE VISA. ⛭
closed 24-27 December – **Rest** (bar lunch)/dinner 32/45 and a la carte 31/39 **s.** – **40 rm** ⛭ ✝70/100 – ✝✝120/150.
◆ Substantial, modern town-centre hotel providing compact but neatly styled rooms, some facing the busy bay. Occasional music in the traditional Wheel House bar. Formal but unelaborate dining room on the first floor.

KILMALLOCK (Cill Mocheallóg) *Limerick* 712 G 10.
Dublin 212.5 – Limerick 34 – Tipperary 32.

Flemingstown House, Southeast : 4 km on R 512 ℘ (063) 98093, *info@flemingstown.com, Fax (063) 98546*, ←, – P. MC VISA.
15 February-15 November – **Rest** (by arrangement) (communal dining) 40 – **5 rm** ★65/75 – ★★120.
◆ Creeper clad, extended 19C house in centre of 200 acre working farm. The attractively decorated bedrooms boast countryside vistas and pieces of antique furniture. Lamb and beef from the farm served at communal dinners.

KILMESSAN *Meath* 712 L/M 7.
Dublin 38.5 – Navan 16 – Trim 11.5.

The Station House, ℘ (046) 9025239, *info@thestationhousehotel.com, Fax (046) 9025588*, – P. 350. MC AE VISA.
Rest 26/45 and a la carte 30/41 – **20 rm** ★85/105 – ★★160/200.
◆ Former 19C railway station. Bedrooms spread around between station house and converted engine shed! The Signal Suite, the original signal box, now offers four poster comforts. Appealing restaurant using local ingredients.

KILRUSH (Cill Rois) *Clare* 712 D 10 – *pop. 2 699.*
Dublin 587.5 – Ennis 43.5 – Limerick 77.

Central without rest., 46 Henry St, ℘ (065) 9051332, *centralguesthouse@eircom.net*, MC VISA.
closed 23-28 December – **6 rm** ★50 – ★★88.
◆ Terraced guesthouse, some of it 100 years old, in main street of small coastal town. Combined breakfast room and lounge. Well kept bedrooms, all with pine furniture.

KINLOUGH (Cionn Locha) *Leitrim* 712 H 4.
Dublin 220.5 – Ballyshannon 11.5 – Sligo 34.

Courthouse with rm, Main St, ℘ (071) 9842391, *thecourthouserest@eircom.net, Fax (071) 9842824* – . MC VISA
closed 1 week spring, Christmas and Tuesday – **Rest** - Italian influences - (dinner only and Sunday lunch) a la carte 35/45 – **4 rm** ★38/42 – ★★70/80.
◆ Simple, unassuming, pink-painted former courthouse has terracotta palette and wall mounted gargoyles. Prominent Italian menus include home-made breads, pasta, desserts.

KINSALE (Cionn tSáile) *Cork* 712 G 12 *Ireland G.* – *pop. 3 554.*
See : *Town*★★ – *St Multose Church*★ **Y** – *Kinsale Regional Museum*★ **ACY M1.**
Env. : *Kinsale Harbour*★ (<★ *from St Catherine's Anglican Church, Charles Fort*★).
Exc. : *Carbery Coast*★, *W : 61 km by R 600.*
Pier Rd ℘ *(021) 4772234 (March-November), user@cktourism.ie.*
Dublin 286.5 – Cork 27.5.

Plan opposite

Actons, Pier Rd, ℘ (021) 4779900, *info@actonshotelkinsale.com, Fax (021) 4772231*, – , rest, P. – 300. MC AE VISA. **Z**
closed 24-26 December and 8-27 January – **Rest** (bar lunch Monday-Saturday)/dinner 25/40 and a la carte 35/46 ♀ – **73 rm** ★100/140 – ★★180/240.
◆ Group owned and business oriented. Smart modern lounge, panelled in warm wood, and well-appointed bedrooms in a classic palette, at their best in two newer wings. Stylish dining room.

Perryville House without rest., Long Quay, ℘ (021) 4772731, *sales@perryville.iol.ie, Fax (021) 4772298* – P. MC AE VISA. **Y**
8 April-30 October – 12 – **26 rm** ★200 – ★★380.
◆ Imposing Georgian house facing the harbour. Antiques and lavish bouquets fill the hall and two period lounges. Rooms are spacious and stylish, the service keen and friendly.

Blue Haven, 3 Pearse St, ℘ (021) 4772209, *info@bluehavenkinsale.com, Fax (021) 4774268*, – rest, rest, . MC AE VISA. **Y**
Rest - Seafood - *(restricted opening in winter)* (bar lunch)/dinner 40 and a la carte 27/44 s. ♀ – **17 rm** ★75/125 – ★★100/180.
◆ Comfortable, traditional hotel in the heart of town. Perennially popular wine bar with large barrel tables and enclosed terrace. Rooms of varying size in neat floral décor. Locally sourced dishes in conservatory restaurant.

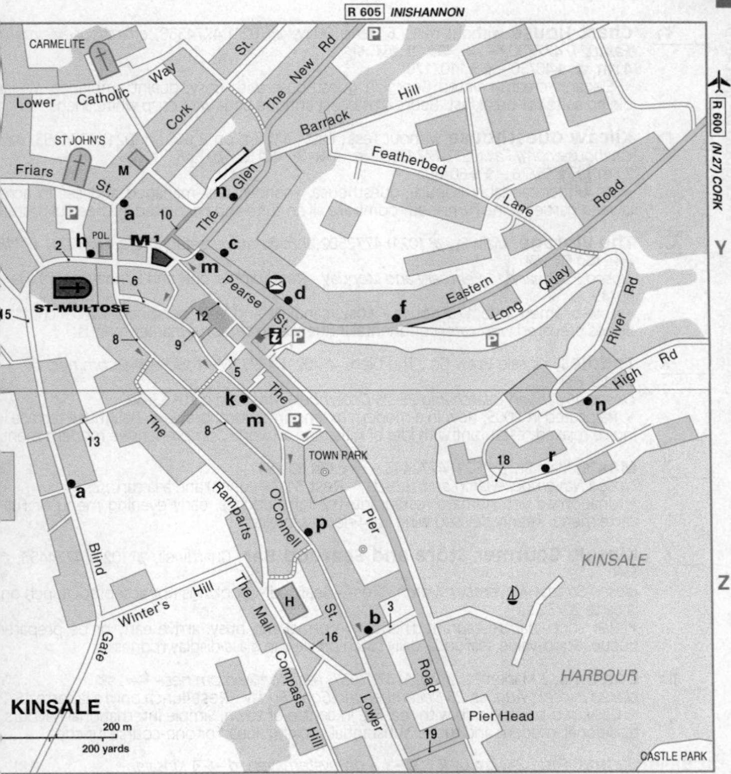

rch St.	Y 2	Main St	Y 9	Rose Abbey	Y 15
is Quay	Z 3	Market Pl.	Y 10	St John's Hill	Z 16
met St	Y 5	Market Quay	Y 12	Seilly Walk	Z 18
rdwell	Y 6	Ramparts Lane	Z 13	World's End	Z 19
ner O'Connel St	YZ 8				

Old Bank House without rest., 11 Pearse St, ☎ (021) 4774075, *oldbank@indigo.ie*, *Fax (021) 4774296* – |‡|. MC AE VISA. ⋇ Y d
closed 1-28 December – **17 rm** ☕ ✝150/170 – ✝✝245/260.
◆ Personally and enthusiastically run town house: cosy lounge and comfortable, neatly kept accommodation - bedrooms above the post office are slightly larger.

The Old Presbytery without rest., 43 Cork St, ☎ (021) 4772027, *info@oldpres.com*, *Fax (021) 4772166* – ⇔ P. MC AE VISA. ⋇ Y a
closed December-14 February – **6 rm** ☕ ✝90 – ✝✝180.
◆ Tucked away down a side street, a Georgian house run by a husband and wife team. Comfortable, thoughtfully furnished bedrooms in old Irish pine.

Blindgate House without rest., Blindgate, ☎ (021) 4777858, *info@blindgatehouse.com*, *Fax (021) 4777868*, ⇔ – ⇔ P. MC AE VISA. ⋇ Z a
17 March-20 December – **11 rm** ☕ ✝115/170 – ✝✝115/170.
◆ Friendly and modern: stylish, clean-lined bedrooms in crisp, light colours, a little front sitting room and smart, wood-floored breakfast room with high backed chairs.

Harbour Lodge without rest., Scilly, ☎ (021) 4772376, *relax@harbourlodge.com*, *Fax (021) 4772675*, ⩽ Kinsale harbour – ⇔ P. MC AE ⦿ VISA. ⋇ Z r
closed Christmas-New Year – **9 rm** ☕ ✝165/198 – ✝✝198/240.
◆ Well kept with a friendly, personally run atmosphere, a modern waterfront house. Spacious conservatory and five of the trim, en suite rooms overlook Kinsale harbour.

Chart House without rest., 6 Denis Quay, (021) 4774568, *charthouse@eircom.ne*
Fax (021) 4777907 – . VISA. Z
4 rm 40/50 – 110/170.
◆ Elegant, cream-painted Georgian guesthouse with cosy, quaint ambience. William
dining suite for breakfast. Bedrooms boast antique beds with crisp white linen.

Kilcaw Guesthouse without rest., East : 1½ km on R 600 (021) 4774155, *info@*
cawhouse.com, Fax (021) 4774755, – P. VISA.
7 rm 35/76 – 60/80.
◆ An understandably popular guesthouse, friendly, well-managed and set in acres
lawned garden. Pine furnished rooms are all en suite and decorated in cheerful pastels.

The Vintage, Main St, (021) 4772502, *info@vintagerestaurant.ie, Fax (021) 477482*
. VISA Z
closed 2 January-11 February and Monday – **Rest** (dinner only and Sunday lunch) a la car
30/49.
◆ Low-beamed little 17C house - cosy, candlelit and very personally run. Rich, classic
dishes prepared with care: continental influence on seasonal market menus.

Toddies, Kinsale Brew Co., The Glen, (021) 4777769, *toddies@eircom.net,* –
VISA Y
closed 15 January-March and 25-26 December – **Rest** a la carte 33/48.
◆ Relocated in 2005; now in a modern extension to local brewery. Delightful terrace lea
ing to relaxed restaurant with lots of glass and artwork. Comprehensive modern menus.

Max's, Main St, (021) 4772443 – . VISA Z
closed November-March and Tuesday – **Rest** 31/46 (lunch) and a la carte.
◆ Unadorned yet intimate restaurant: try light lunches, early evening menu or full à
carte menu. Keenly devised wine list. Friendly service.

Kinsale Gourmet Store and Seafood Bar, Guardwell, (021) 4774453,
Y
closed Sunday November-March – **Rest** - Seafood - (bookings not accepted) (lunch only
la carte 22/32 **s.**
◆ Half shop, half restaurant, friendly, informal and busy: arrive early or be prepared
queue. Good-value seafood - daily catch on view in glass display fridges.

Dalton's, 3 Market St, (021) 4777957, *fedalton@eircom.net* – . Y
closed 2 weeks August, 25 December and Good Friday – **Rest** (lunch only) a la carte 15/25
◆ Cosy, red-painted pub with real fire in centre of town. Simple international flavours n
traditional, modern and rustic: substantial cooking, ideal for one-course lunches.

at Ballinclashet *East : 7¾ km by R 600 – Y – on Oysterhaven rd – Kinsale.*

Oz-Haven, (021) 4770974, – P. VISA
closed Sunday dinner, Monday and Tuesday September-May – **Rest** (dinner only and Su
day lunch)/dinner a la carte 39/45.
◆ Within the traditional white-washed cottage exterior is a modern restaurant with bo
colours and distinctive lighting. The detailed menu lists highly original dishes.

at Barrells Cross *Southwest : 5¾ km on R 600 – Z – Kinsale.*

Rivermount House without rest., Northeast : ¾ km (021) 4778033, *info@riv*
mount.com, Fax (021) 4778225, – P. VISA.
February-November – **6 rm** 50/80 – 70/80.
◆ A friendly and conscientious couple keep this purpose-built guesthouse in good ord
Well-appointed en suite rooms in flowery fabrics overlook the quiet fields.

at Ballinadee *West : 12 km by R 600 – Z – Kinsale.*

Glebe Country House, (021) 4778294, *glebehse@indigo.ie, Fax (021) 47784*
– P. VISA
closed Christmas and New Year – **Rest** *(closed Sunday)* (by arrangement) 35 – **4 rm**
60/65 – 90/100.
◆ Creeper-clad Georgian rectory. Handsomely furnished drawing room; well-chosen fa
rics and fine wooden beds in pretty rooms, one with french windows on to the garde
Guests are welcome to bring their own wine.

KINSALEY *Dublin* 712 N 7 – *see Malahide.*

KINSEALEY *Dublin* 712 N 7 – *see Malahide.*

KINVARRA (Cinn Mhara) *Galway* 712 F 8.
Dublin 228.5 – Galway 27.5 – Limerick 59.5.

Merriman, Main St, (091) 638222, *merrimanhotel@eircom.net, Fax (091) 637686* – rest, P. MO AE VISA.
closed 23-28 December – **Rest** (bar lunch Monday-Saturday)/dinner 26/30 and a la carte 23/35 s. – **32 rm** 70/85 – 100/130.
◆ Named after Irish poet Bryan Merriman; a restored and extended thatched inn on a busy main road. Bright, spacious lobby lounge, neat, modern, well-priced bedrooms. Traditional menus.

Keoghs, Main St, (091) 637145, *keoghsbar@eircom.net, Fax (091) 637028* – . MO AE VISA.
closed 25 December – **Rest** a la carte 18/28.
◆ Centrally located, yellow fronted pub: the eponymous owners have been here for many years. Rear dining room serves appealing, unfussy meals with renowned seafood specials.

KNIGHTS TOWN *Kerry* 712 B 12 – *see Valencia Island.*

KNOCK (An Cnoc) *Mayo* 712 F 6 *Ireland G.*
See : *Basilica of our Lady, Queen of Ireland*★.
Knock (Connaught) Airport : (094) 67222, NE : 14½ km by N 17.
Knock Village (094) 9388193 (May-September) – Knock Airport (094) 9367247 (June-September).
Dublin 212.5 – Galway 74 – Westport 51.5.
Hotels see : **Cong** *SW : 58 km by N 17, R 331, R 334 and R 345.*

LAGHY (An Lathaigh) *Donegal* 712 H 4 – *see Donegal.*

LAHINCH (An Leacht) *Clare* 712 D 9 *Ireland G.*
Env. : *Cliffs of Moher*★★★.
18, 18 Lahinch (065) 7081003 – 9 Spanish Point, Miltown Malbay (065) 7084219.
Dublin 260.5 – Galway 79 – Limerick 66.

Moy House, Southwest : 4 km on N 67 (Milltown Malbay rd) (065) 7082800, *moyhouse@eircom.net, Fax (065) 7082500,* ← Lahinch Bay, – rest, P. MO AE VISA.
closed January and Monday-Friday November-March – **Rest** (residents only) (dinner only) 45 – **9 rm** 127/159 – 200/239.
◆ Early 19C country house in lovely spot away from town and with delightful views of Lahinch Bay. Genuine country house atmosphere with antiques and curios; charming bedrooms. Stylishly understated dining room.

Greenbrier Inn without rest., Ennistymon Rd, (065) 7081242, *gbrier@indigo.ie, Fax (065) 7081247* – P. MO VISA.
March-November – **14 rm** 55/115 – 120/170.
◆ Smartly appointed guesthouse with a modern feel. Conservatory-style breakfast room overlooking Lahinch golf course. Well-kept pine furnished bedrooms.

Dough Mor Lodge without rest., Station Rd, (065) 7082063, *dough@gofree.indigo.ie, Fax (065) 7071384,* – P. MO VISA.
17 March-October – **5 rm** 55/110 – 80/110.
◆ Attractive, well-kept guesthouse with large front garden, a minute's walk from the town centre. Cosy lounge; Gingham-clad breakfast room. Spacious bedrooms in white or cream.

LEENANE (An Líonán) *Galway* 712 C 7 *Ireland G.* – *Clifden.*
See : *Killary Harbour*★.
Env. : *Joyce Country*★★ – *Lough Nafooey*★, *SE : 10 ½ km by R 336* – *Aasleagh Falls*★, *NE : 4 km.*
Exc. : *Connemara*★★★ – *Lough Corrib*★★, *SE : 16 km by R 336 and R 345* – *Doo Lough Pass*★, *NW : 14½ km by N 59 and R 335.*
Dublin 278.5 – Ballina 90 – Galway 66.

Delphi Lodge, Northwest : 13 ¼ km by N 59 on Louisburgh rd (095) 42222, *res@delphilodge.com, Fax (095) 42296,* ←, – rest, P – 25. MO VISA.
closed 20 December-6 January – **Rest** (residents only) (communal dining) (dinner only) (set menu only) 49 – **12 rm** 107/157 – 154/258.
◆ Georgian sporting lodge in a stunning loughside setting with extensive gardens and grounds. Haven for fishermen. Country house feel and simple bedrooms. Communal dining table: fisherman with the day's best catch sits at its head.

LEIXLIP (Léim an Bhradáin) *Kildare* 712 M 7 – *pop. 15 016.*
Dublin 22.5 – Drogheda 63 – Galway 201 – Kilkenny 117.5.

Leixlip House, Captain's Hill, ☎ (01) 624 2268, *info@leixliphouse.com, Fax (01) 624 417* – ⇔ ☏ P – 🏛 100. MC AE ⓓ VISA. ✗
closed 24-26 December – **Rest** – (see ***The Bradaun*** below) – **19 rm** ☕ ✝110/150 ✝✝150/200.
◆ Georgian house on town's main street. Well-geared up to banquets. Luxurious sof furnishings and antiques in bedrooms; front-facing rooms with particularly large window

The Bradaun (at Leixlip House H.), Captain's Hill, ☎ (01) 624 2268, *Fax (01) 624 4177* ⇔ P. MC AE ⓓ VISA
closed 24-26 December and Monday – **Rest** (dinner only and Sunday lunch)/dinner a carte 32/40.
◆ Good size room with high ceilings and large windows commensurate with the age c the property. Simple, fresh décor. Classic dishes with modern and Irish influences.

LEOPARDSTOWN *Dublin* 712 N 7 – *see Dublin.*

LETTERFRACK (Leitir Fraic) *Galway* 712 C 7 *Ireland G.*
Env. : *Connemara★★★ – Sky Road★★ (≤★★) – Connemara National Park★ – Kylemore Ab bey★, E : 4¾ km by N 59.*
Dublin 304 – Ballina 111 – Galway 91.5.

Rosleague Manor ♨, West : 2 ½ km on N 59 ☎ (095) 41101, *info@rosleague.com Fax (095) 41168,* ≤ Ballynakill harbour and mountains, ⛵, ♔, 🎾 – ⇔ rest, P. MC AE VISA
March-November – **Rest** 35 and a la carte 35/45 ♀ – **20 rm** ☕ ✝110/140 – ✝✝170/250.
◆ Imposing, part 19C manor in a secluded, elevated position affording delightful views c Ballynakill harbour and mountains. Antique furnished, old fashioned comfort. Count house-style dining room: distinctive artwork on walls.

LETTERKENNY (Leitir Ceanainn) *Donegal* 712 I 3 *Ireland G. – pop. 15 231.*
Exc. : *Glenveagh National Park★★ (Gardens★★), NW : 19¼ km by R 250, R 251 and R 254 Grianan of Aileach★★ (≤★★) NE : 28 km by N 13 – Church Hill (Glebe House and Gallery★ A NW : 16 km by R 250.*
18 Dunfanaghy ☎ (074) 36335.
Derry Rd ☎ (074) 9121160, donegaltourism@eircom.net.
Dublin 241.5 – Londonderry 34 – Sligo 116.

Clanree, Derry Rd, Southeast : 2 ¾ km on N 14 at junction with N 13 ☎ (074) 912 436 *info@clanreehotel.com, Fax (074) 912 5389,* Lδ, ≘, 🏊 – |♦| ⇔ ▤ ☏ ♿ P – 🏛 1000. MC AE VISA. ✗
closed 23-27 December – **Rest** (carvery lunch)/dinner 15/23 and a la carte 19/37 **s.** **120 rm** ☕ ✝160/270 – ✝✝160/270.
◆ Purpose-built property on edge of town centre. Modern style with an opulent marb floored reception. Well-equipped conference and leisure facilities. Colourful bedroom Full meals from the wood furnished restaurant, including lunchtime carvery.

Castlegrove House ♨, Ramelton Rd, Northeast : 7 ¼ km by N 13 off R 245 ☎ (07 9151118, *marytsweeney@hotmail.com, Fax (074) 9151384,* ≤, ⛳, ⛵, ♔ – ⇔ P. MC ⓓ VISA. ✗
closed 22-30 December – **Rest** *(closed Sunday-Monday November-February)* (dinner on a la carte 38/57 ♀ – **13 rm** ☕ ✝80/120 – ✝✝150/190, 1 suite.
◆ Extended country house, dating from the 17C, in very quiet location. Comfortab sitting room with open fires. All rooms of a good size, the newer ones are most comfort ble. Capacious dining room with views of gardens and grounds.

Letterkenny Court, Main St, ☎ (074) 9122977, *info@letterkennycourthotel. Fax (074) 9122928* – |♦| ⇔, ▤ rest, ♿ P. MC AE ⓓ VISA. ✗
closed 24-25 December – **Rest** (carvery lunch)/dinner a la carte 27/36 **s.** ♀ – ☕ 9 – **59 r** ✝58/89 – ✝✝98/158, 24 suites.
◆ Group owned establishment in brightly painted building in the centre of town. Be rooms decorated in similar modern style with bright, co-ordinated fabrics. Simple, cor fortable restaurant in the basement.

Pennsylvania House ♨ without rest., Curraghleas, Mountain Top, North : 3 ½ km N 56 ☎ (074) 9126808, *info@accommodationdonegal.com, Fax (074) 9128905,* ≤, ⛵ – ⇔ P. MC VISA. ✗
closed 20-27 December – **7 rm** ☕ ✝50/65 – ✝✝90/110.
◆ Comfortable house run by a welcoming couple: rooms in floral fabrics, comfortab lounge decorated with Eastern artefacts, hilltop views towards the Derryveagh Mountain

Ballyraine Guesthouse without rest., Ramelton Rd, East : 2 ¾ km by N 14 on R 245 ✆ (074) 9124460, *ballyraineguesthouse@eircom.net, Fax (074) 9120851* – ⇔ ✆ P. MC VISA.
8 rm ▭ ✝32/40 – ✝✝64/70.
◆ Purpose-built guest house in the suburbs of this busy market town. Wood floored breakfast room in warm pine. En suite bedrooms are spacious and usefully equipped.

MERICK **(Luimneach)** *Limerick* 712 G 9 *Ireland G. – pop. 86 998.*

See : *City*★★ - *St Mary's Cathedral*★★ Y – *Hunt Museum*★★ *AC*Y – *Limerick Museum*★ Z **M2** – *King John's Castle*★ *AC*Y – *John Square*★ Z **20** – *St John's Cathedral*★ Z.

Env. : *Cratloe Wood* (≤★) *NW : 8 km by N 18*Z.

Exc. : *Castleconnell*★, *E : 11¼ km by N 7 – Lough Gur Interpretive Centre*★ *AC, S : 17¾ km by R 512 and R 514* Z – *Clare Glens*★, *E : 21 km by N 7 and R 503* Y – *Monasteranenagh Abbey*★, *S : 21 km by N 20*Z.

✈ *Shannon Airport : ✆ (061) 712000, W : 25 ¾ km by N 18* Z – **Terminal :** *Limerick Railway Station.*

ℹ *Arthur's Quay ✆ (061) 317522*Y, *limericktouristoffice@shannondev.ie.*
Dublin 193 – Cork 93.5.

Plan on next page

Castletroy Park, Dublin Rd, East : 3 ½ km by N 7 ✆ (061) 335566, *sales@castletroy-park.ie, Fax (061) 331117*, ☼, Fø, ⌂s, ▢ – |ǂ| ⇔, ▤ rest, ✆ ♿ P – 🔏 450. MC AE VISA.
closed 25 December – ***McLaughlin's :*** **Rest** (bar lunch Monday-Saturday)/dinner 35/45 and a la carte 32/48 – **105 rm** ▭ ✝215 – ✝✝250, 2 suites.
◆ Large purpose-built property just outside the city. Spacious, stylish public areas and comprehensive conference facilities. Well-appointed modern bedrooms. Dining room themed on traditional arts and crafts.

The Clarion, Steamboat Quay, ✆ (061) 444100, *info@clarionhotellimerick.com, Fax (061) 444101*, ≤ River Shannon and City, Fø, ⌂s, ▢ – |ǂ| ⇔ ▤ ✆ ♿ P – 🔏 110. MC AE ⓓ VISA
Z n
closed 24-25 December – ***Sinergie :*** **Rest** a la carte 29/41 **s.** – ***Kudos :*** **Rest** - Asian - a la carte 16/22 **s.** – **93 rm** ▭ ✝120/200 – ✝✝120/230, 30 suites.
◆ Impressive newly built hotel by the River Shannon with excellent views of the city. Contemporary décor throughout and great views from the pool. Well-appointed, modern rooms. Formal dining room with modern menu. Kudos bar area serves Asian based food.

Radisson SAS, Ennis Rd, Northwest : 6 ½ km on N 18 ✆ (061) 326666, *sales@radissonsas.com/limerick, Fax (061) 327418*, Fø, ⌂s, ▢, ✗ – |ǂ| ⇔, ▤ rest, ✆ ♿ P – 🔏 800. MC AE ⓓ
Porters : **Rest** (carving lunch Monday-Saturday and Sunday dinner) a la carte 25/45 **s.** – **152 rm** ▭ ✝150 – ✝✝150, 2 suites.
◆ Modern hotel with tastefully used chrome and wood interiors. Well-equipped conference rooms and a leisure centre which includes tennis court. Smart, state-of-the-art bedrooms. Informal Porters restaurant with traditional menus.

South Court, Raheen Roundabout, Southwest : 4 ¾ km on N 20 ✆ (061) 4874870, *cro@lynchotels.com, Fax (061) 4874999*, Fø, ⌂s – |ǂ| ⇔, ▤ rest, ✆ P – 🔏 1250. MC AE VISA.
Boru's : **Rest** (carvery lunch)/dinner a la carte approx 25 ♀ – **124 rm** ✝150 – ✝✝180.
◆ Purpose-built hotel near city centre. Spacious public areas include large reception and conference rooms. Oak furnished bedrooms. Informal Boru's serves a bistro-style menu.

Greenhills, Ennis Rd, Northwest : 3 ½ km on R 587 ✆ (061) 453033, *info@greenhillsgroup.com, Fax (061) 453307*, Fø, ⌂s, ▢, ⛱, ✗ – |ǂ| ⇔ ✆ ♿ P – 🔏 500. MC AE ⓓ VISA.
closed 24-25 December – ***Hughs on the Greene :*** **Rest** (carving lunch)/dinner 20/35 – ▭ 8 – **60 rm** ✝90 – ✝✝120.
◆ Low-rise purpose-built property aimed at commercial travellers. Good leisure facilities. Modern reception and open plan bar. Comfortable bedrooms with dark wood furniture. Restaurant specialising in carvery meals.

Jurys Inn Limerick, Lower Mallow St, ✆ (061) 207000, *bookings@jurysinnlimerick.com, Fax (061) 400966* – |ǂ| ⇔ ✆ ♿ 🚗 – 🔏 40. MC AE VISA.
Z a
closed 23-27 December – **Rest** (bar lunch)/dinner a la carte approx 22 – ▭ 11 – **151 rm** ✝59/89 – ✝✝59/89.
◆ Large purpose-built hotel in a well-kept commercial style. Light wood furnished bedrooms, some with views of the River Shannon. Good value and a central location. Basement-based informal restaurant and rustic pub.

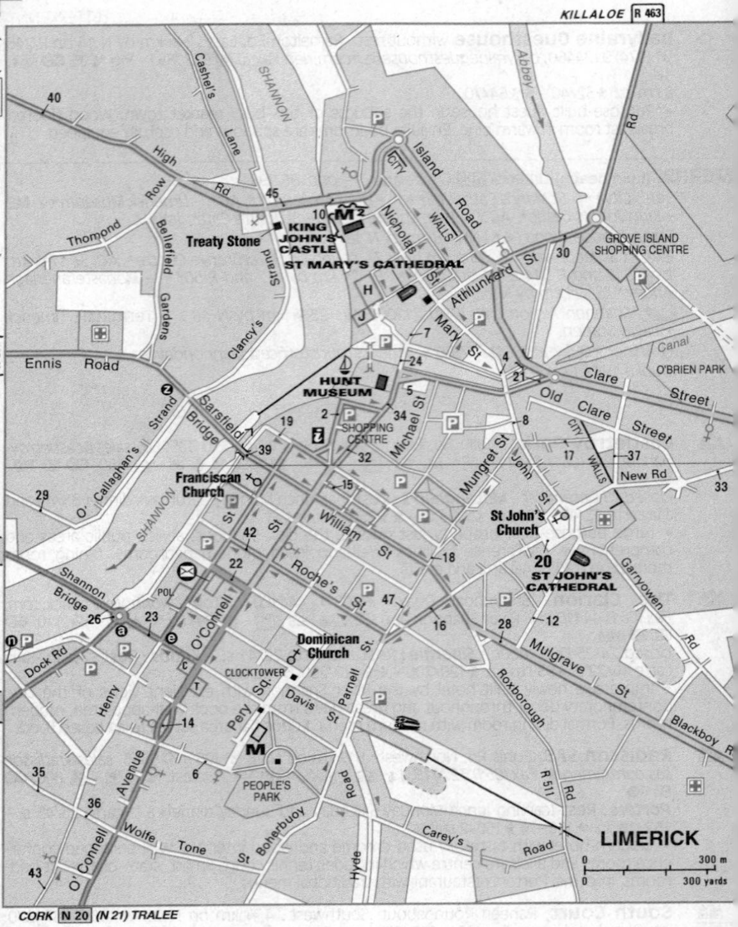

LIMERICK

Arthur Quay Shopping Centre . . . . . Y
Arthur Quay . . . . . Y 2
Baal's Bridge . . . . . Y 4
Bank Pl. . . . . . Y 5
Barrington St . . . . . Z 6
Bridge St . . . . . Y 7
Broad St . . . . . Y 8
Castle St . . . . . Y 10
Cathedral Pl. . . . . . Z 12
Charlotte's Quay . . . . . Y 13
Cruises St. . . . . . Z 15
Gerald Griffen St . . . . . Z 16
Grattan St. . . . . . Y 17
Grove Island Shopping Centre . . . . . Y
High St . . . . . Z 18
Honan's Quay . . . . . Y 19
John Square . . . . . Z 20
Lock Quay . . . . . Y 21
Lower Cecil St . . . . . Z 22
Lower Mallow St. . . . . . Z 23
Mathew Bridge . . . . . Y 24
Mount Kenneth . . . . . Z 26
Newtown Mahon . . . . . Z 28
North Circular Rd . . . . . Z 29
O'Connell St . . . . . Z
O'Dwyer Bridge . . . . . Y 30
Patrick St . . . . . YZ 32
Penniwell Rd . . . . . Z
Roches St . . . . . Z
Rutland St . . . . . Y
St Alphonsus St. . . . . . Z
St Gerard St . . . . . Z
St Lelia St . . . . . YZ
Sarfield St . . . . . Y
Sexton St North. . . . . . Y
Shannon St . . . . . Z
South Circular Rd . . . . . Z
The Crescent . . . . . Z
Thomond Bridge . . . . . Y
Wickham St . . . . . Z
William St. . . . . . Z

For a pleasant stay in a charming hotel, look for the red ... symbols.

Carrig House without rest., No.2, Meadowvale, Raheen, Southwest : 4½ km by N 20 ☎ (061) 309626, *lohanangela@eircom.net*, – P.
closed 23 December-2 January – **4 rm** ☐ ★40/50 – ★★60/70.
◆ Purpose-built house on a residential estate. Colourful décor in the communal rooms is carried through to the fabrics and drapes in the bedrooms.

Brûlées, Corner Mallow/Henry St, ☎ (061) 319931, *brulees@eircom.net* – . MC AE VISA Z e
closed 24 December-2 January, Sunday, Monday and Saturday lunch – **Rest** a la carte 35/45.
◆ Situated on the ground floor of a Georgian building. Three seating levels give spacious feel. Modern Irish cooking with classic base: good emphasis on local produce.

SCANNOR (Lios Ceannúir) *Clare* 712 D 9.

Dublin 272 – Ennistimmon 9.5 – Limerick 72.5.

Vaughan's Anchor Inn, Main St, ☎ (065) 7081548, *info@vaughansanchorinn.com*, *Fax (065) 7086977* – P. MC VISA.
closed 25 December – **Rest** - Seafood - a la carte 25/45.
◆ Close to Cliffs of Moher, this long-standing, family owned pub is awash with nautical bits and bobs. Appealing menus with emphasis on seafood. A bustling venue.

SDOONVARNA (Lios Dúin Bhearna) *Clare* 712 E 8 *Ireland G.*

Env. : *The Burren★★ (Cliffs of Moher★★★, Scenic Routes★★, Aillwee Cave★ AC (Waterfall★★), Corcomroe Abbey★, Kilfenora Crosses★).*
Dublin 268.5 – Galway 63 – Limerick 75.5.

Ballinalacken Castle Country House , Coast Rd, Northwest : 4¾ km by N 67 (Doolin rd) on R 477 ☎ (065) 7074025, *ballinalackencastle@eircom.net*, *Fax (065) 7074025*, <, – P. MC AE VISA.
mid April-mid October – **Rest** *(closed Tuesday)* (dinner only) a la carte 33/55 – **12 rm** ☐ ★120 – ★★180.
◆ 1840's house with purpose-built extension overlooked by imposing ruin of a 15C castle. Characterful communal areas in traditional style. Large, antique furnished bedrooms. Diners greeted by open fireplace and linen-clad tables.

Sheedy's Country House, Sulphir Hill, ☎ (065) 7074026, *info@sheedys.com*, *Fax (065) 7074555*, – P. MC VISA.
15 April-September – **Rest** – (see ***The Restaurant*** below) – **11 rm** ☐ ★85/100 – ★★140/170.
◆ Classic late 19C mustard painted property in an elevated position. Public areas centre around the bright, wicker furnished sun lounge. Neat, well-equipped bedrooms.

Carrigann, ☎ (065) 7074036, *carrigannhotel@eircom.net*, *Fax (065) 7074567*, – P – 40. MC VISA.
10 March-October – **Rest** (bar lunch)/dinner a la carte 31/38 – **20 rm** ☐ ★49/89 – ★★98/138.
◆ Cream coloured building with gardens in centre of the town. Sitting room with open fires and a collection of books. Brightly decorated bedrooms with co-ordinated fabrics. Comfortable dining room.

Kincora House, ☎ (065) 7074300, *kincorahotel@eircom.net*, *Fax (065) 7074490*, – – 40. MC VISA.
April-October – **Rest** *(closed Wednesday lunch)* a la carte 25/37 **s.** ♀ – **14 rm** ☐ ★50/90 – ★★80/130.
◆ Charming hotel; oldest part dating back to 1860. Attractive walled garden to the rear. Comfy sitting room with plenty of local books. Rustic, spacious bar. Light, airy rooms. Smart, relaxing restaurant.

Woodhaven without rest., Doolin Coast Rd, West : 1½ km by N 67 (Doolin rd) off R 477 ☎ (065) 7074017, – P. MC VISA.
closed Christmas – **4 rm** ☐ ★40 – ★★58/65.
◆ Whitewashed house on a country lane with pretty gardens. Traditionally styled interior decoration to the lounge and breakfast room. Simple bedrooms with a homely feel.

The Restaurant (at Sheedy's Country House H.), Sulphir Hill, ☎ (065) 7074026, *Fax (065) 7074555* – P. MC VISA
15 April-September – **Rest** (dinner only) a la carte 31/48 **s.**
◆ Attractive, comfortable restaurant at the front of the building. Linen covered tables and smart place settings. Interesting menus using freshest, local produce.

LISMORE (Lios Mór) *Waterford* 712 I 11.
Dublin 227 – Cork 56.5 – Fermoy 26.

Northgrove without rest., Tourtane, West : 1 ½ km by N 72 on Ballyduff rd ℘ (058) 54325, *johnhoward1@eircom.net*, – P. VISA
3 rm ★30/43 – ★★50/70.
◆ Modern guesthouse providing a keenly priced and accessible resting place for visitors to this historic town. Good sized, pine furnished bedrooms with colourful décor.

Buggys Glencairn Inn with rm, West : 4 ¾ km by N 72 on Ballyduff rd ℘ (058) 56232, *buggysglencairninn@eircom.net, Fax (058) 56232*, ≤, – P. VISA.
closed 24-27 December – **Rest** (booking essential in winter) (dinner only) a la carte 37/40
5 rm ★80 – ★★110/125.
◆ "Pretty as a picture" cottage style inn: picket fence, brass bedsteads in quaint rooms. Cosy bar, restaurant with red gingham tablecloths. Meals broad in scope and flavour.

LISTOWEL (Lios Tuathail) *Kerry* 712 D 10 – *pop. 3 393.*
St John's Church ℘ *(068) 22590 (June-September), tourisminfo@shannon-dev.ie.*
Dublin 270.5 – Killarney 54.5 – Limerick 75.5 – Tralee 27.5.

Allo's with rm, 41-43 Church St, ℘ (068) 22880, *allos@eircom.net, Fax (068) 22803* – VISA
closed 25-26 December – **Rest** *(closed Sunday-Monday)* (booking essential) (dinner only) la carte 22/45 – **3 rm** ★50 – ★★90.
◆ Inviting feel with oak seats and wooden tables. Culinary classics with international touches. Comfortable antique furnished rooms, hand-crafted beds and claw foot baths.

LITTLE ISLAND (An tOileán Beag) *Cork* 712 G/H 12 – *see Cork.*

LONGFORD (An Longfort) *Longford* 712 I 6.
45 Dublin St ℘ *(043) 42577.*
Dublin 124 – Drogheda 120.5 – Galway 112.5 – Limerick 175.5.

Viewmount House without rest., Dublin Rd, Southeast : 1 ½ km on R 393 ℘ (043) 41919, *info@viewmounthouse.com, Fax (043) 42906*, – P. VISA.
6 rm ★50/70 – ★★90/120.
◆ Impressive Georgian house in four acres; breakfast room has attractive vaulted ceiling, lounge reached by fine staircase. Rooms boast antique beds and period furniture.

Longford Country House , East : 8 ¾ km by R 194 off Aghnacliffe rd ℘ (043) 23320, *info@longfordcountryhouse.com, Fax (043) 23516*, – P. VISA.
restricted opening October-March – **Rest** (by arrangement) 40 – **6 rm** ★40/50 ★★78/80.
◆ Pleasant purpose-built house in a rural spot with quiet gardens. Galleried sitting room, parlour with with open fire. Particularly welcoming, individually furnished bedrooms.

LUCAN (Leamhcán) *Dublin* 712 M 7 – *see Dublin.*

MACROOM (Maigh Chromtha) *Cork* 712 F 12 – *pop. 2 985.*
Lackaduve ℘ *(026) 41072.*
Dublin 299.5 – Cork 40 – Killarney 48.5.

Castle, Main St, ℘ (026) 41074, *castlehotel@eircom.net, Fax (026) 41505*, – rest, rest, P – 200. VISA.
closed 23-27 December – **Rest** (carvery lunch)/dinner 35/38 and a la carte 35/39 s. – ***B's*** **Rest** (dinner only) 35/38 and a la carte 35/39 **s.** – **60 rm** ★89/110 – ★★140/170.
◆ A traditional hotel with gabled windows located in the town centre. Boasts a stylish leisure complex and neat, comfortable bedrooms. Informal B's. Local produce proudly used in Castle restaurant.

MALAHIDE (Mullach Íde) *Dublin* 712 N 7 *Ireland G.* – *pop. 13 826.*
See : *Castle*★★.
Env. : *Fingal*★.
18, 9 *Beechwood, The Grange* ℘ *(01) 846 1611.*
Dublin 14.5 – Drogheda 38.5.

XX **Cruzzo,** Marina Village, ☎ (01) 845 0599, *info@cruzzo.ie, Fax (01) 845 0602*, <, – |‡| ⇔ ▤ [P]. MC AE ① VISA
closed 25-26 December, 1 January, Good Friday, Saturday lunch and Monday – **Rest** (light lunch)/dinner a la carte 35/51 ♀.
◆ Modern glass and designer furnishings in a striking marina restaurant above the water. Pleasantly distinctive ground-floor bar for lighter dishes. Tasty, modern cuisine.

XX **Siam Thai,** Gas Yard Lane, off Strand St ☎ (01) 845 4698, *siam@eircom.net, Fax (01) 816 9460* – ⇔ ▤. MC AE ① VISA
closed 25-26 December – **Rest** - Thai - (booking essential) (dinner only) 30/45 and a la carte 31/36 s.
◆ Centrally located restaurant with piano bar providing a light feel. Immaculately set tables and ornate, carved chairs. Richly authentic Thai cuisine, freshly prepared.

XX **Jaipur,** 5 St James Terrace, ☎ (01) 845 5455, *info@jaipur.ie, Fax (01) 845 5456* – ⇔ ▤. MC AE VISA
closed 25-26 December – **Rest** - Indian - (dinner only) 40 and a la carte 23/41.
◆ Friendly basement restaurant in the town centre. Well-run by efficient, welcoming staff. Simple but lively modern decor. Contemporary Indian dishes.

t Kinsaley *Southwest : 4 km by R 106 on R 107 – ✉ Malahide.*

Belcamp Hutchinson without rest., Carrs Lane, Balgriffin, D17, South : 1 ½ km by R 107 ☎ (01) 846 0843, *belcamphutchinson@eircom.net, Fax (01) 848 5703* – [P]. MC VISA
closed 21 December-1 February – **6 rm** ☕ ✝70 – ✝✝140.
◆ Distinguished, creeper clad Georgian country house full of charm and character; eponymously named original owner. Walled garden with maze; airy rooms in strong, dark colours.

MALLARANNY (An Mhala Raithni) *Mayo* 712 C 6.

Dublin 270 – Castlebar 35 – Westport 29.

Park Inn, on N 59 ☎ (098) 36000, *reception.mulranny@rezidorparkinn.com, Fax (098) 36899*, <, ⛹, ≘s, ▢, ⛳, – |‡| ⇔, ▤ rest, ☎ ♿ [P] – 🎪 350. MC ① VISA
closed Christmas – **Rest** *(closed Monday-Saturday lunch)* a la carte 38/44 s. – **41 rm** ☕ ✝75/124 – ✝✝100/198, 20 suites.
◆ Purpose-built business oriented hotel behind 19C façade: lovely Clew Bay views. Impressive leisure and conference facilities. Airy rooms with slightly minimalist interiors. Smart, formal, linen-clad restaurant.

MALLOW (Mala) *Cork* 712 F 11 *Ireland G. – pop. 8 937.*

See : *Town★ – St James' Church★.*

Exc. : *Doneraile Wildlife Park★ AC, NE : 9½ km by N 20 and R 581 – Buttevant Friary★, N : 11¼ km by N 20 – Annes Grove Gardens★, E : 17¾ km by N 72 and minor rd.*

🏌18 *Ballyellis ☎ (022) 21145.*

Dublin 240 – Cork 34 – Killarney 64.5 – Limerick 66.

Longueville House ⛰, West : 5 ½ km by N 72 ☎ (022) 47156, *info@longuevillehouse.ie, Fax (022) 47459*, <, ⛳, – ⇔ [P] – 🎪 30. MC AE VISA. ✂
closed 7 January-16 March – ***Presidents :*** **Rest** (booking essential) (light lunch)/dinner 55 and a la carte approx 47 – **20 rm** ☕ ✝95/260 – ✝✝200/360.
◆ Part Georgian manor; exudes history from oak trees planted in formation of battle lines at Waterloo and views of Dromineen Castle to richly ornate, antique-filled bedrooms. Restaurant offers gourmet cuisine.

Springfort Hall ⛰, North : 7 ½ km by N 20 on R 581 ☎ (022) 21278, *stay@springfort-hall.com, Fax (022) 21557*, ⛳, – ⇔ rest, ♿ [P] – 🎪 300. MC AE VISA. ✂
closed 23 December-2 January – **Rest** 27/42 s. ♀ – **49 rm** ☕ ✝80/92 – ✝✝105/173.
◆ Beyond a porticoed entrance with grand door and fanlight, this part 18C manor offers large, well-proportioned rooms in keeping with the period. Salmon fishing arranged. Pale blond furniture in a richly decorated dining room.

MAYNOOTH (Maigh Nuad) *Kildare* 712 M 7 *Ireland G. – pop. 10 151.*

Env. : *Castletown House★★ AC, SE : 6½ km by R 405.*

Dublin 24.

Moyglare Manor ⛰, Moyglare, North : 3 ¼ km ☎ (01) 628 6351, *info@moyglaremanor.ie, Fax (01) 628 5405*, <, ⛳, – ⇔ [P]. MC AE ① VISA. ✂
closed 23-27 December – **Rest** *(closed Sunday dinner)* 35/60 – **16 rm** (dinner included) ☕ ✝150/200 – ✝✝250.
◆ 18C manor where everything denotes peace and quiet, from location - in sweeping grounds - to individually decorated rooms with canopy beds and four-posters. Antiques abound. Oil paintings hang proudly in fuchsia dining room.

Glenroyal, Straffan Rd, ℘ (01) 629 0909, *info@glenroyal.ie, Fax (01) 629 0919,* – rest, – 450. closed 25 December – ***Bistro :*** **Rest** (carvery lunch)/dinner 27 and a la carte 21/31 **s.** ***Lemongrass :*** **Rest** - Asian - 25 (dinner) and a la carte 27/32 **s.** – **113 rm** 115/130 150/175.
◆ Adjacent to shopping centre, ideal for conferences and weddings. Rooms are furnished in smart fabrics with good quality furniture. Informal bistro. Authentic Asian menus at Lemongrass.

MIDLETON **(Mainistir na Corann)** *Cork* 712 H 12 – *pop. 3 266.*
East Cork, Gortacrue ℘ (021) 4631687.
Jameson Heritage Centre ℘ (021) 4613702.
Dublin 259 – Cork 19.5 – Waterford 98.

Midleton Park, Old Cork Rd, ℘ (021) 4635100, *info@midletonpark.com, Fax (021) 4635101,* – rest, – 300. *closed 24-25 December* – **Rest** *(closed Sunday dinner)* (carvery lunch)/dinner 40 **s.** – **79 rm** 135 – 170, 1 suite.
◆ This large, purpose-built hotel holds a number of spacious, uniformly fitted bedrooms with all mod cons. Up-to-date leisure centre with Canadian hot tub, treatment rooms. Pastel shades invoke relaxed dining.

MILLSTREET *Waterford* 712 I 11 – *see Cappoquin.*

MONAGHAN **(Muineachán)** *Monaghan* 712 L 5 – *pop. 5 936.*
Market House ℘ (047) 81122 (April-October).
Dublin 133.5 – Belfast 69 – Drogheda 87 – Dundalk 35.5 – Londonderry 120.5.

Four Seasons, Coolshannagh, North : 1 ½ km on N 2 ℘ (047) 81888, *info@4seasonshotel.ie, Fax (047) 83131,* – rest, – 200. *closed 25 December* – ***Avenue :*** **Rest** *(closed Monday, Tuesday and Sunday dinner)* (dinner only and Sunday lunch) 38/43 and a la carte 34/42 **s.** – ***The Range :*** **Rest** 25/35 and a la carte 23/38 **s.** – **59 rm** 65/85 – 140/180.
◆ A hotel which offers a blend of the traditional and the modern. Bedrooms are in uniform style and there is an atmospheric pub. Avenue offers modern dining. The Range has a farmhouse feel with beams and dressers.

at Glaslough *Northeast : 9½ km by N 12 on R 185 – Monaghan.*

Castle Leslie, ℘ (047) 88100, *info@castleleslie.com, Fax (047) 88256,* **Rest** (booking essential to non-residents) (dinner only) 54/65 – **20 rm** (dinner included) 220/270 – 370/470.
◆ Family castle in vast parkland with ancient woods and well preserved pike lake. Enjoy walks, boating and fishing. Unique, themed rooms named after personalities in history. Restaurant boasts oil paintings on green hued walls, ornate fireplace.

MONKSTOWN **(Baile na Mhanaigh)** *Cork* 712 G/H 12.
Parkgarriffe ℘ (021) 841376.
Dublin 257.5 – Cork 14.5 – Waterford 120.5.

The Bosun, The Pier, ℘ (021) 4842172, *info@thebosun.ie, Fax (021) 4842008,* rest, rest. *closed 24-26 December and Good Friday* – **Rest** 30/45 and a la carte 25/45 – **15 rm** 65 – 116.
◆ After a walk along the waterway, unwind in the cosy environment of this quayside hotel. There is a private entrance for the bedrooms which are neatly and simply furnished. Seaside location reflected in restaurant menus.

MOUNT PLEASANT *Wexford – see Rosslare Harbour.*

MOYCULLEN **(Maigh Cuilinn)** *Galway* 712 E 7.
Dublin 223.5 – Galway 11.5.

Moycullen House with rm, Mountain Rd, Southwest : 1 ½ km by Spiddle rd ℘ (091) 555621, *info@moycullen.com, Fax (091) 555566,* *closed 5 January-18 March and 23-27 December* – **Rest** *(closed Wednesday)* (dinner only and Sunday lunch)/dinner a la carte 37/54 – **2 rm** 70 – 100.
◆ Built 1890s in "Arts and Crafts" style, set in woodland. Homely rooms, antique furniture. Stone walled dining room with polished oak tables on which tasty meals are served.

MULLINAVAT (Muileann an Bhata) *Kilkenny* 712 K 10.
Dublin 141.5 – Kilkenny 34 – Waterford 13.

Rising Sun, Main St, (051) 898173, *info@therisingsun.ie, Fax (051) 898435* – rest, P. MC AE VISA
closed 25-26 December – **Rest** (carving lunch)/dinner a la carte 25/33 **s.** – **10 rm** 50/70 – 80/120.
◆ A rustic, stone built 17C inn with friendly character. Indoors is a bar with walls hung with brewery themed mirrors. Rooms are of good size and well kept. Sandwiches and steaks served in a traditional dining room.

MULLINGAR (An Muileann gCearr) *Westmeath* 712 J/K 7 *Ireland G. – pop. 15 621.*
Env. : *Belvedere House and Gardens★ AC, S : 5½ km by N 52.*
Exc. : *Multyfarnhan Franciscan Friary★, N : 12 ¾ km by N 4 – Tullynally Castle★ AC, N : 21 km by N 4 and R 394 – Fore Abbey★, NE : 27¼ km by R 394.*
Market House (044) 48761.
Dublin 79 – Drogheda 58.

Mullingar Park, Dublin Rd, East : 2 ½ km on Dublin Rd (N 4) (044) 44446, *info@mullingarparkhotel.com, Fax (044) 35937,* , , , – , rest, P – 1000. MC AE VISA.
closed 24-26 December – **Rest** (buffet lunch)/dinner a la carte 35/40 – **94 rm** 65/95 – 140/360, 1 suite.
◆ Spacious modern hotel with a strong appeal to business and leisure travellers: there's a hydrotherapy pool and host of treatment rooms. Airy, light bedrooms with mod cons. Smart, airy restaurant with international menus.

Turnpike Lodge without rest., Dublin Rd, East : 2 km on Dublin Rd (N 4) (044) 44913, *turnpikelodge@iolfree.ie., Fax (044) 44913,* – P. MC VISA
5 rm 45/50 – 70/80.
◆ Modern guesthouse with mock-Tudor façade. Pleasantly appointed lounge with south facing conservatory breakfast room overlooks countryside. Cosy, welcoming bedrooms.

Marlinstown Court without rest., Dublin Rd, East : 2½ km on Dublin Rd (N 4) (044) 40053, *marlinstownct@eircom.net, Fax (044) 40057,* – P. MC VISA.
5 rm 40/50 – 65/75.
◆ Clean, tidy guesthouse close to junction with N4. Modern rear extension. Light and airy pine-floored lounge and breakfast room overlooking garden. Brightly furnished bedrooms.

Hilltop Country House without rest., Delvin Rd, Rathconnell, Northeast : 4 km by N 52 (044) 48958, *hilltopcountryhouse@eircom.net, Fax (044) 48958,* – P. MC VISA.
April-October – **4 rm** 45 – 70.
◆ Chalet styled house with attractive gardens. Reception and lounge areas cheered by paintings. Good Irish breakfast served. Snug, homely rooms with pleasant views.

at Ballynagall *North : 6 km on R 394 – ✉ Mullingar.*

Belfry, (044) 42488, *belfryrestaurant@eircom.net, Fax (044) 40094* – P. MC VISA
closed 11-24 January, 1 week September, 25 December, Monday-Tuesday and Sunday dinner – **Rest** 20 (lunch) and dinner a la carte 41/49.
◆ Impressive conversion of an early 19C church which retains original elements but applies a contemporary feel. Modern cooking with hints of Mediterranean and Eastern flavours.

NAAS (An Nás) *Kildare* 712 L/M 8 – *pop. 18 288.*
Kerdiffstown, Naas (045) 874644.
Dublin 30.5 – Kilkenny 83.5 – Tullamore 85.5.

Killashee House , South : 1 ½ km on R 448 (Kilcullen Rd) (045) 879277, *reservations@killasheehouse.com, Fax (045) 879266,* , , , , , – , rest, P – 1600. MC AE VISA.
closed 24-25 December – ***Turners*** **: Rest** 35/54 and dinner a la carte 51/76 **s.** – ***Nun's Kitchen*** **: Rest** *(closed lunch Monday-Friday)* a la carte 22/37 **s.** – **130 rm** 155/440 – 198/440, 12 suites.
◆ Imposing part 1860s hunting lodge in acres of parkland. Rooms in the original house are most characterful: French antique furniture, original panelling and fireplaces. Elegant Turners overlooking garden. Informal Nun's Kitchen.

Osprey, Devoy Quarter, ✆ (045) 881111, *info@osprey.ie, Fax (045) 881112,* …, …, … – … 350. MC AE VISA.
closed dinner 24-25 December – **Rest** (carvery lunch Monday-Saturday)/dinner a la car… 41/55 s. – **93 rm** ☐ ★230 – ★★250, 11 suites.
◆ Former barracks, now a smart, stylish hotel. Vast bar area on two levels where carvery … served. Up-to-date leisure and spa. Modish bedrooms in cool colours. Restaurant boas… brown leather chairs and floor-to-ceiling windows overlooking fountain.

Les Olives, 10 South Main St, (above Kavanagh's pub), ✆ (045) 894788, *lesolives@… com.net* – … MC VISA
closed Sunday, Monday and Tuesday after Bank Holidays – **Rest** (booking essential) (dinn… only) a la carte 44/71 ♀.
◆ Above a pub looking down on high street; three sunny rooms complemented by colou… ful artwork, generous sized tables. French inspired cuisine with international flourishes.

NAVAN (An Uaimh) *Meath* 712 L 7 *Ireland G. – pop. 19 417.*

Env. : *Bective Abbey★, S : 6½ km by R 161.*
Exc. : *Trim★ (castle★★), SW : 12¾ km by R 161 – Kells★ (Round Tower and High Crosses★… St Columba's House★), NW : by N 3 – Tara★, S : 9½ km by N 3.*
18 Moor Park, Mooretown ✆ (046) 27661 – 18, 9 Royal Tara, Bellinter ✆ (046) 25244.
Dublin 48.5 – Drogheda 26 – Dundalk 51.5.

Newgrange, Bridge St, ✆ (046) 9074100, *info@newgrangehotel.ie, Fax (046) 9073977* …, rest, P – 450. MC AE VISA.
closed 24-25 December – ***Bridge Brasserie :*** **Rest** (carvery lunch Monday-Saturday)/di… ner a la carte 21/50 ♀ – **62 rm** ☐ ★105 – ★★200.
◆ Warm-toned, well-fitted modern rooms and an inviting, traditionally styled bar, plu… ample meeting space, make this town centre hotel a popular function venue. Smart, brig… brasserie.

Ma Dwyers without rest., Dublin Rd, South : 1 ¼ km on N 3 ✆ (046) 907799… *Fax (046) 9077995* – … P. MC VISA.
11 rm ☐ ★55 – ★★85.
◆ Yellow-painted, mock-Georgian house; comfortable guest lounge, modern breakfa… room. Hospitality trays in equally bright, simple bedrooms.

Killyon without rest., Dublin Rd, South : 1 ½ km on N 3 ✆ (046) 9071224, *info@k… yonguesthouse.ie, Fax (046) 9072766* – … P. MC VISA.
closed 24-25 December – **6 rm** ☐ ★45/50 – ★★70/80.
◆ Very good value, comfortable guesthouse, overlooking the river Boyne, run by husbar… and wife team. Bedrooms are individually decorated. Home baking and good breakfa… choice.

NENAGH (An tAonach) *Tipperary* 712 H 9 *Ireland G. – pop. 6 454.*

See : *Town★ – Heritage Centre★ – Castle★.*
18 Nenagh, Birchwood ✆ (067) 31476.
Connolly St ✆ (067) 31610 (mid May-mid September), tourisminfo@shannon-dev.ie.
Dublin 154.5 – Galway 101.5 – Limerick 42.

Abbey Court, Dublin Rd, East : ½ km ✆ (067) 41111, *info@abbeycourt.i… Fax (067) 41022,* …, …, rest, … P – 450. MC AE VISA.
closed 25-27 December – ***The Cloisters :*** **Rest** (carvery lunch)/dinner a la carte 22/33 **73 rm** ☐ ★69/90 – ★★120/150.
◆ A castellated façade, clock tower and arched windows add a historical theme to a mod… ern hotel. Fitness club offers all amenities including hair salon. Modern bedrooms. Woode… statue of monk distinguishes beamed dining room.

NEWBRIDGE (An Droichead Nua) *Kildare* 712 L 8 *Ireland G. – pop. 12 970.*

Env. : *Irish National Stud★★ AC (Japanese Gardens★★ AC) SW : 9½ km by N 7 – Kildare… (Cathedral★★) SW : 8¾ km by N 7.*
18 Curragh ✆ (045) 441238.
Dublin 45 – Kilkenny 92 – Tullamore 58.

Annagh Lodge without rest., Naas Rd, ½ km on R 445 ✆ (045) 433518, *annag… lodge@eircom.net, Fax (045) 433538,* … – … P. MC VISA.
10 rm ☐ ★60/100 – ★★90/120.
◆ Bungalow guesthouse on main road into town. Small garden with summerhouse; rea… conservatory overlooks it. Bright, modern breakfast room. Spotless, spacious rooms.

EWMARKET-ON-FERGUS (Cora Chaitlín) *Clare* 712 F 7 – *pop. 1 542.*

Dromoland Castle ℘ (061) 368444.

Dublin 219 – Ennis 13 – Limerick 24.

Dromoland Castle, Northwest : 2 ½ km on N 18 ℘ (061) 368144, *sales@dromoland.ie, Fax (061) 363355*, – rest, – 450. VISA.

Earl of Thormond : **Rest** (dinner only and Sunday lunch) 66/120 and a la carte 60/85 – ***Fig Tree*** *(at Dromoland Golf & Country Club) (℘ (061) 368444)* : **Rest** 40 (dinner) and lunch a la carte approx 35 – 26 – **94 rm** 225/417 – 225/417, 6 suites.

◆ Restored 16C castle with 375 acres of woodland and golf course. Sumptuous rooms with plenty of thoughtful extras. Waterford crystal chandeliers and gilded mirrors in the Earl of Thormond restaurant. More informal style in the Fig Tree, popular with golfers.

Clare Inn, Northwest : 3 ¼ km by N 18 ℘ (061) 368161, *cro@lynchotels.com, Fax (061) 368622*, – rest, rest, – 400. VISA.

Rest *(closed weekdays in winter)* (bar lunch)/dinner 30/45 and a la carte 22/42 **s.** – 10 – **182 rm** 99/259 – 159/298, 13 suites.

◆ Elevated hillside location overlooking lush Irish countryside. This modern hotel is a firm favourite with families. Vast leisure centre and spacious bedrooms. Traditional dishes such as Burren lamb or glazed loin of bacon in the family friendly restaurant.

EWPORT (Baile Uí Fhiacháin) *Mayo* 712 D 6 *Ireland G.*

Env. : *Burrishoole Abbey★, NW : 3¼ km by N 59 – Furnace Lough★, NW : 4¾ km by N 59.*

James St, Westport ℘ (098) 25711.

Dublin 264 – Ballina 59.5 – Galway 96.5.

Newport House, ℘ (098) 41222, *info@newporthouse.ie, Fax (098) 41613*, – rest, VISA.

18 March-10 October – **Rest** (dinner only) 59 and a la carte approx 46 **s.** – **18 rm** 177/188 – 302/324.

◆ Mellow ivy-clad Georgian mansion; grand staircase up to gallery and drawing room. Bedrooms in main house or courtyard; some in self-contained units ideal for families. Enjoy the fresh Newport estate produce used in the dishes served in the elegant dining room.

EW QUAY *Clare Ireland G.*

Env. : *Corcomroe Abbey★, S : 4¾ km by N 67.*

Dublin 240 – Ennis 55 – Galway 46.5.

Linnane's Bar, New Quay Pier, ℘ (065) 7078120, – VISA.

closed 25 December and Good Friday – **Rest** - Seafood - a la carte 26/40.

◆ Take lunch here on the terrace beside a sea inlet. Country pub with rustic decor and interesting old photos. Fresh seafood served all day in summer and sold in the pier shop.

EW ROSS (Ros Mhic Thriúin) *Wexford* 712 L 10 *Ireland G. – pop. 6 537 – ✉ Newbawn.*

See : *St Mary's Church★.*

Exc. : *Kennedy Arboretum, Campile★ AC, S : 12 km by R 733 – Dunbrody Abbey★, S : 12 ¾ km by R 733 – Inistioge★, NW : 16 km by N 25 and R 700 – Graiguenamanagh★ (Duiske Abbey★★ AC), N : 17¾ km by N 25 and R705.*

The Quay ℘ (051) 421857 (June-August).

Dublin 141.5 – Kilkenny 43.5 – Waterford 24 – Wexford 37.

Riversdale House without rest., Lower William St, ℘ (051) 422515, *riversdalehouse@eircom.net*, – VISA.

March-December – **4 rm** 50 – 70.

◆ Conservatory lounge and home baking are among the attractions of a good-value guesthouse, run by a friendly owner. Well-tended garden, neat bedrooms with electric blankets.

t Ballynabola *Southeast : 9½ km on N 25 – ✉ New Ross.*

Cedar Lodge, Carrigbyrne, East : 4 ¾ km on N 25 ℘ (051) 428386, *cedarlodge@eircom.net, Fax (051) 428222*, – rest, VISA.

closed 20 December-January – **Rest** (bar lunch)/dinner 50 **s.** – **28 rm** 130/150 – 200.

◆ Family owned hotel beneath slopes of Carrigbyrne Forest, with leafy garden. This is hiking country; owners have compiled walking routes; relax in pastel-toned bedrooms. Dining room menu reflects the area's fruit and honey produce.

NEWTOWNMOUNTKENNEDY (Baile An Chinnéidieh) *Wicklow* 712 N 8.

Dublin 35.5 – Glendalough 22.5 – Wicklow 16.

Marriott Druids Glen H. & Country Club, East : 2 ¾ km off Kilcoole rd ℘ (0 287 0800, *events.druids@marriotthotels.co.uk, Fax (01) 287 0801*, ... – 250. MC AE VISA.

Druids **:** Rest (dinner only) 35 and a la carte 28/39 s. ♀ – ***Flynn's Steakhouse*** **:** Re (dinner only and Sunday lunch) 45 and a la carte 38/51 s. ♀ – **137 rm** ☐ ★195 – ★★22 11 suites.

◆ New hotel in 400 acres, next to golf course. Spacious marble and granite atrium; leisur conference facilities. Very comfortable rooms, with every conceivable facility. Druids offe a popular buffet. Classic grill dishes at Flynn's Steakhouse.

ORANMORE (Órán Mór) *Galway* 712 F 8 *Ireland G.*

Env. : *Galway★★ (St Nicholas Church★, Lynch's Castle★, Roman Catholic Church★, Ey Square, Bank of Ireland Building, sword and mace★), NW : 8 km by N 6.*

Exc. : *Athenry★, NE : 11¼ km by N 6 and R 348 – Dunguaire Castle★, SW : 19¼ km by N and N 67 – Thoor Ballylee★, S : 24 km by N 18 and minor rd – Coole Park★, S : 24 km N 18 and N 66 – Loughrea (St Brendan's Cathedral★), SE : 27 ¼ km by N 6 – Knockm Abbey★, NE : 27¼ km by N 18, N 17 and N 63 – Tuam (St Mary's Cathedral★), N : 29 km N 18 and N 17 – Turoe Stone★, SE : 32¼ km by N 6 and north by R 348.*

Dublin 211 – Galway 11.5.

Quality, North : 1 ¼ km on N 6 ℘ (091) 792244, *sales@qualityhotelgalway.co Fax (091) 792246*, ... rest, ... – 100. MC AE VISA.

closed 24-26 December – ***Lannigans*** **:** Rest (carvery lunch)/dinner 26 and a la carte 19/3 – ☐ 10 – **113 rm** ★69/199 – ★★69/199.

◆ Greystone hotel just a five minute drive from Galway city. Traditional pub with entertai ment. Well-equipped leisure centre. Bright, spacious rooms. Irish whiskey sauces enhan grill styled meals.

Oranmore Lodge, ℘ (091) 794400, *orlodge@eircom.net, Fax (091) 790227*, ... rest, P – 300. MC AE VISA.

closed 24-28 December – ***The Hunt Room*** **:** Rest 25/40 and a la carte 18/38 s. – **62 rm** ★90/300 – ★★180/300.

◆ Former Victorian ancestral home with modern extensions. Characterful public are include traditional bar with ornate ceiling. Airy, spotless rooms with dark wood furnitur Cosy, intimate restaurant with Adam fireplace as focal point.

OUGHTERARD (Uachtar Ard) *Galway* 712 E 7 *Ireland G.*

See : *Town★.*

Env. : *Lough Corrib★★ (Shore road – NW – ≤★★) – Aughnanure Castle★ AC, SE : 3¼ km N 59.*

Gortreevagh ℘ (091) 552131.

Community Office ℘ (091) 552811.

Dublin 240 – Galway 27.5.

Ross Lake House, Rosscahill, Southeast : 7 ¼ km by N 59 ℘ (091) 550109, *r slake@iol.ie, Fax (091) 550184*, ... rest, P. MC AE VISA.

15 March-October – **Rest** (dinner only) 45 ♀ – **12 rm** ☐ ★115 – ★★170, 1 suite.

◆ Georgian country house set in its own estate of woods and attractive gardens. T period theme is carried right through interiors. Bright bedrooms with antiques. Spaciou comfortable dining room with smartly set polished tables.

Currarevagh House, Northwest : 6 ½ km on Glann rd ℘ (091) 552312, *mail@c rarevagh.com, Fax (091) 552731*, ≤, ... rest, P. MC VISA

April-20 October – **Rest** (booking essential) (dinner only) (set menu only) 41 – **15 rm** ★85/140 – ★★175/200.

◆ Victorian manor on Lough Corrib, set in 170 acres. Period décor throughout plus muc fishing memorabilia. Two lovely sitting rooms. Comfortable, well-kept rooms. Countr house style dining room, popular with fishing parties.

Waterfall Lodge without rest., West : ¾ km on N 59 ℘ (091) 552168, *kdolly@e com.net*, ... P.

6 rm ☐ ★50 – ★★80.

◆ Two minutes from the centre, a well-priced guesthouse rebuilt with gleaming wood an original Victorian fittings. A good fishing river flows through the charming gardens.

Railway Lodge without rest., South : ¾ km by Costello rd taking first right ont unmarked road ℘ (091) 552945, *railwaylodge@eircom.net*, ≤, ... P. MC VISA

4 rm ☐ ★60 – ★★90.

◆ Elegantly furnished modern guest house in remote farm location. Communal breakfas with plenty of choice. Open fires, books and magazine but no TV. Beautifully kept bec rooms.

PARKNASILLA (Páirc na Saileach) *Kerry* 712 C 12 *Ireland G.*

Env. : *Sneem★, NW : 4 km by N 70.*

Exc. : *Iveragh Peninsula★★ (Ring of Kerry★★) – Derrynane National Historic Park★★, W : 25¾ km by N 70 – Staigue Fort★, W : 21 km by N 70.*

Dublin 360.5 – Cork 116 – Killarney 55.

Parknasilla Great Southern, (064) 45122, *res@parknasilla-gsh.com, Fax (064) 45323,* ≤ Kenmare Bay and Caha mountains, – rest, – 80. VISA.
Pygmalion : Rest (dinner only) 45 and a la carte 32/59 – **82 rm** (dinner included) ★165/195 – ★★260/320, 1 suite.
◆ Attractive 19C hotel on the wooded coast. Conservatory sun lounge, collection of Irish art. Spacious rooms, in warm, modern shades, have good views, except in the east wing. Restaurant more formal than rest of hotel.

PONTOON *Mayo* 712 E 6 – ✉ *Foxford.*

Dublin 233.5 – Castlebar 14.5 – Sligo 80.5.

Healy's, (094) 9256443, *info@healyspontoon.com, Fax (094) 9256572,* ≤ Lough Cullin, – rest, VISA.
closed 25 December – **Rest** (bar lunch Monday-Saturday)/dinner 39 and a la carte 23/48 –
14 rm ★65 – ★★90.
◆ Extended 19C shooting lodge on shores of Lough Cullin. Well geared up to the fishing fraternity with related paraphernalia and comfortable bars. Bedrooms are simply appointed. Extensive wine list and lough views in the dining room.

PORTLAOISE (Port Laoise) *Laoise* 712 K 8.

Dublin 88.5 – Carlow 40 – Waterford 101.5.

The Heritage, Jessop St, (0502) 78588, *res@theheritagehotel.com, Fax (0502) 78577,* – rest, – 500. VISA.
closed 23-28 December – ***The Fitzmaurice :*** Rest (carvery lunch) a la carte 32/47 **s.** –
Spago : Rest - Italian - *(closed Monday-Wednesday)* (dinner only) a la carte 20/44 **s.** –
109 rm ★170 – ★★240, 1 suite.
◆ Impressive, purpose-built hotel in central location. Extensive leisure facilities include a large pool. Thoroughly spacious throughout. Well equipped bedrooms. Formal Fitzmaurice serving a modern menu. More relaxed Italian-style Spago restaurant.

Ivyleigh House without rest., Bank Pl, Church St, (0502) 22081, *info@ivyleigh.com, Fax (0502) 63343,* – VISA.
6 rm ★65/75 – ★★115/125.
◆ Attractive Georgian listed house with gardens. Breakfast a feature: owner makes it all herself from fresh produce. Charming period drawing room. Airy bedrooms with antiques.

PORTMAGEE (An Caladh) *Kerry* 712 A 12 *Ireland G.*

Exc. : *Iveragh Peninsula★★ (Ring of Kerry★★).*

Dublin 365 – Killarney 72.5 – Tralee 82.

Moorings, (066) 9477108, *moorings@iol.ie, Fax (066) 9477220,* ≤ – , rest, VISA.
Rest *(closed November-March and Monday dinner except Bank Holidays)* (bar lunch)/dinner 33/55 – **18 rm** ★45/55 – ★★80/90.
◆ Pub-style hotel in the high street of this attractive village. Spacious, nautical themed bar and trim upstairs lounge. Bedrooms with views over harbour and its fishing boats. Stone-walled, candlelit dining room with seafaring curios.

PORTMARNOCK (Port Mearnóg) *Dublin* 712 N 7 *Ireland G. – pop. 8 376.*

Env. : *Fingal★.*

Dublin 8 – Drogheda 45.

Portmarnock H. and Golf Links, Strand Rd, (01) 846 0611, *reservations@portmarnock.com, Fax (01) 846 2442,* ≤, – , rest, rest, – 250. VISA.
The Links : Rest 23 (lunch) and a la carte approx 30 **s.** – (see also ***The Osborne*** below) –
98 rm ★235 – ★★315.
◆ Large golf-oriented hotel with challenging 18-hole course. Original fittings embellish characterful, semi-panelled Jamesons Bar. Very comfortable, individually styled rooms. Bright, brasserie styled dining room with shiny wooden tables and blue padded chairs.

XXX **The Osborne** (at Portmarnock H. and Golf Links), ☎ (01) 846 0611 – ⇆ ▤ P. MC AE ⓞ VISA
closed Sunday-Monday – **Rest** (dinner only) a la carte approx 55 s.
• Distinctively formal restaurant named after artist Walter Osborne. Regularly changin menus balance the modern and traditional. Professionally run with good golf course view

PORTSALON *Donegal* 712 J 2.

Croaghross without rest., ☎ (074) 9159548, *jkdeane@croaghross.com* *Fax (074) 59548*, ≤ Knockalla mountain and bay, – ⇆ P. MC VISA
17 March-September – **4 rm** ☕ ★42 – ★★100.
• Rurally set, well-run guesthouse with delightful views of countryside and bay; seve acres of well-tended gardens. Handy for the beach. Pleasant, well-kept rooms.

RANELAGH (Raghnallach) *Dublin* 712 N 7 – *see Dublin.*

RATHGAR (Ráth Garbh) *Dublin* – *see Dublin.*

RATHMELTON (Ráth Mealtain) *Donegal* 712 J 2 *Ireland G.*
See : Town★.
Dublin 248 – Donegal 59.5 – Londonerry 43.5 – Sligo 122.5.

Ardeen without rest., ☎ (074) 9151243, *ardeenbandb@eircom.ne* *Fax (074) 9151243*, , – P. MC VISA.
Easter-September – **5 rm** ☕ ★35/45 – ★★70.
• Simple Victorian house situated on the edge of the village. Homely ambience in th lounge and breakfast room. Immaculately kept bedrooms.

RATHMINES (Ráth Maonais) *Dublin* 712 ⑩ – *see Dublin.*

RATHMULLAN (Ráth Maoláin) *Donegal* 712 J 2 *Ireland G.* – *pop. 491* – ✉ *Letterkenny.*
Exc. : *Knockalla Viewpoint★, N : 12¾ km by R 247 – Rathmelton★, SW : 11¼ km by R 247.*
⛳9 *Otway, Saltpans* ☎ *(074) 58319.*
Dublin 265.5 – Londonderry 58 – Sligo 140.

Rathmullan House, North : ½ m. on R 247 ☎ (074) 9158188, *info@rathmulla house.com, Fax (074) 9158200*, ≤, , , , – ⇆ rest, P. – 80. MC AE VISA.
closed 17-27 December – **Rest** (dinner only) 45 and a la carte July-August 42/57 – **32 rm** ☕ ★85/145 – ★★210/260.
• Part 19C country house with attractive gardens in a secluded site on the shores of Loug Swilly. Rooms range from modern to traditional. Occasional "holistic treatment" weeks Dine at linen-clad tables beneath semi-tented ceiling.

Fort Royal, North : 1 ½ km by R 247 ☎ (074) 9158100, *fortroyal@eircom.net* *Fax (074) 9158103*, ≤, , , – ⇆ rest, P. MC AE ⓞ VISA
April-October – **Rest** (bar lunch)/dinner 37/43 s. – **15 rm** ☕ ★77/122 – ★★154/184.
• Early 19C house in a very quiet location with attractive gardens that run down to the beach. Two comfortable lounges and a spacious bar. Characterful, homely bedrooms Daytime meals are taken in the bar and the main evening meal in the comfortable restaurant.

RATHNEW (Ráth Naoi) *Wicklow* 712 N 8 – *see Wicklow.*

RECESS (Sraith Salach) *Galway* 712 C 7 *Ireland G.*
Exc. : *Connemara★★★ – Cashel★, SW : by N 59 and R 340.*
Dublin 278.5 – Ballina 116 – Galway 58.

Lough Inagh Lodge, Northwest : 7 ¾ km by N 59 on R 344 ☎ (095) 34706 *inagh@iol.ie, Fax (095) 34708*, ≤ Lough Inagh and The Twelve Bens, , – ⇆ rest, P. MC AE ⓞ VISA
mid March-mid December – **Rest** (booking essential to non-residents) (bar lunch)/dinner a la carte 38/46 s. – **13 rm** ☕ ★112/135 – ★★184/264.
• Part 19C former fishing lodge with enchanting views of Lough Inagh and The Twelve Bens. Warm, welcoming feel and ambience; cosy bedrooms. Attentive service in country house-style restaurant.

RINGVILLE *Waterford* 712 J 11 – *see Dungarvan.*

RIVERSTOWN (Baile idir Dhá Abhainn) Sligo 712 G 5.

Dublin 198 – Sligo 21.

Coopershill, (071) 9165108, *ohara@coopershill.com, Fax (071) 9165466*, MC AE VISA.
April-October – **Rest** (booking essential to non-residents) (dinner only) 50/55 s. – **8 rm** 127/143 – 216/258.
◆ Magnificent Georgian country house set within 500 acre estate. Home to six generations of one family. Antique furnished communal areas and rooms exude charm and character. Family portraits, antique silver adorn dining room.

ROSCOMMON (Ros Comáin) Roscommon 712 H 7 *Ireland G.* – *pop. 4 489.*

See : *Castle★.*

Exc. : *Castlestrange Stone★, SW : 11 ¼ km by N 63 and R 362 – Strokestown★ (Famine Museum★ AC, Strokestown Park House★ AC), N : 19¼ km by N 61 and R 368 – Castlerea : Clonalis House★ AC, NW : 30½ km by N 60.*

Moate Park (09066) 26382.

Harrison Hall (090) 6626342 (June-August).

Dublin 151 – Galway 92 – Limerick 151.

Abbey, on N 63 (Galway rd) (090) 6626240, *info@abbeyhotel.ie, Fax (090) 6626021*, – 200. MC AE VISA.
closed 24-26 December – **Rest** 25 (lunch) and dinner a la carte 26/43 s. – **50 rm** 90/100 – 170/180.
◆ Part 19C house with modern extensions, convenient central location and surrounded by attractive gardens. Excellent leisure facilities. Comfortable bedrooms. Spacious restaurant overlooks ruins of Abbey.

Gleeson's Townhouse, Market Sq, (090) 6626954, *info@gleesonstownhouse.com, Fax (090) 6627425*, rest, – 70. MC AE VISA
closed 25-26 December – **Rest** 28/40 (dinner) and a la carte 21/34 s. – **18 rm** 60/75 – 100/150, 1 suite.
◆ 19C former manse with courtyard overlooking the market square. This substantial stone-built edifice was once a minister's residence. Comfortable, well-equipped bedrooms. Meals available in the farmhouse-style restaurant.

Westway without rest., Galway Rd, Southwest : 1 ¼ km on N 63 (090) 6626927, *westwayguests@eircom.net*, MC VISA.
closed 20 December-6 January – **4 rm** 40 – 100/130.
◆ Modern guesthouse with friendly welcome near town centre. Comfy, traditional residents' lounge. Breakfast room with conservatory extension. Brightly decorated rooms.

"Rest" appears in red for establishments with a (star) or (Bib Gourmand).

ROSCREA (Ros Cré) Tipperary 712 I 9.

Dublin 125.5 – Birr 19.5 – Nenagh 34.

Racket Hall, Dublin Rd, East : 2 ¾ km on N 7 (0505) 21748, *racketh@iol.ie, Fax (0505) 23701*, rest, rest, – 400. MC AE VISA.
The Willow Tree : **Rest** (carving lunch Monday-Saturday)/dinner 28/33 and a la carte 24/40 s. – **40 rm** 69/99 – 119/169.
◆ Bright yellow, creeper-clad, extended roadside inn. Huge rustic pubby area with sofas and shelves of books. Bedrooms offer good levels of comfort and modern facilities. Formal dining to the rear.

ROSSES POINT (An Ros) Sligo 712 G 5.

County Sligo (071) 77134.

Dublin 223.5 – Belfast 212.5 – Sligo 9.5.

Yeats Country H., (071) 9177211, *info@yeatscountryhotel.com, Fax (071) 9177203*, MC AE VISA.
closed 20-28 December and 2-25 January – ***Elsinore :*** **Rest** (bar lunch)/dinner 25/32 – **98 rm** 65/85 – 120/170.
◆ Large hotel with attractive views over Sligo Bay. Well-equipped leisure centre and 'kids' organisers' to help keep younger guests busy. Good-sized bedrooms. Attractive bay outlook from some dining room tables.

ROSSLARE (Ros Láir) *Wexford* 712 M 11.

Rosslare Strand ☎ *(053) 32203.*

Kilrane ☎ *(053) 33232 (April-September).*

Dublin 167.5 – Waterford 80.5 – Wexford 19.5.

Kelly's Resort, ☎ (053) 32114, *kellyhot@iol.ie, Fax (053) 32222,* ←, indoor/outdoor – , rest, rest, P. VISA.
closed 11 December-17 February – ***Kelly's :*** Rest 25/45 – ***La Marine :*** Rest a la carte 32/38 – **116 rm** ★77/94 – ★★154/188.
◆ Large, purpose-built hotel on the beachfront of this popular holiday town. Good range of leisure facilities; well-appointed rooms. Kelly's dining room offers a classic popular menu. La Marine is a French inspired, bistro-style restaurant.

ROSSLARE HARBOUR (Calafort Ros Láir) *Wexford* 712 N 11.

to France (Cherbourg and Roscoff) (Irish Ferries) (17 h/15 h) – to Fishguard (Stena Line) 2-4 daily (1 h 40 mn/3 h 30 mn) – to Pembroke (Irish Ferries) 2 daily (3 h 45 mn).

Kilrane ☎ *(053) 33232 (April-October).*

Dublin 169 – Waterford 82 – Wexford 21.

Great Southern, ☎ (053) 33233, *res@rosslare-gsh.com, Fax (053) 33543,* , – rest, rest, P – 250. VISA.
Rest (bar lunch)/dinner 23/35 s. – 13 – **100 rm** ★79/99 – ★★79/99.
◆ Yellow painted modern hotel on a residential road. Comfortable reception lounge and health and beauty facilities. Usefully appointed bedrooms in warm colours. Restaurant boasts excellent views of the Harbour.

Ferryport House, on N 25 ☎ (053) 33933, *info@ferryporthouse, Fax (053) 61707* – P VISA.
closed 25-26 December – **Rest** (carvery lunch Monday-Saturday)/dinner a la carte 25/33 – **16 rm** ★30/50 – ★★60/90.
◆ Contemporary hotel conveniently located for the ferry terminus. Simple communal areas include a pine furnished breakfast room. Comfortable bedrooms with fitted wood furniture. Local produce to fore in dining room.

at Tagoat *West : 4 km on N 25 – Rosslare.*

Churchtown House , North : ¾ km on Rosslare rd ☎ (053) 32555, *info@churchtownhouse.com, Fax (053) 32577,* – P. VISA.
March-October – **Rest** *(closed Sunday-Monday)* (booking essential) (residents only) (dinner only) 39 s. – **12 rm** ★65/85 – ★★110/160.
◆ Part 18C house with extension, set in spacious, well-kept garden. Traditional country house-style lounge and wood furnished dining room. Individually decorated rooms. Fresh country cooking in the Irish tradition.

at Mount Pleasant *West : 14 km by N 25 – Rosslare Harbour.*

Mount Pleasant Country House without rest., ☎ (053) 35631, *mountpleasantbandb@eircom.net, Fax (053) 35631,* , – P. VISA.
April-September – **4 rm** ★50/60 – ★★90/120.
◆ Characterful house dating from 1637, in a very rural setting with extensive grounds. Charming interior furnished with antiques, beds and bedrooms are especially appealing.

ROSSNOWLAGH (Ros Neamhlach) *Donegal* 712 H 4 *Ireland G.*

See : *Rossnowlagh Strand*★★.

Dublin 246 – Donegal 22.5 – Sligo 50.

Sand House , ☎ (071) 985 1777, *info@sandhouse-hotel.ie, Fax (071) 985 2100,* ← bay, beach and mountains, , – P – 80. VISA
February-November – **Rest** (dinner only and Sunday lunch)/dinner 50/55 – **50 rm** ★100/140 – ★★240/280.
◆ Victorian sandstone hotel in coastal location with superb views of bay, beach and mountains. Real fire in the hall and comfortable lounges. Individual, traditional rooms. Attractive dining room with a comfortable atmosphere and classic traditional feel.

Your opinions are important to us:
please write and let us know about your discoveries and experiences – good and bad!

ROUNDSTONE (Cloch na Rón) *Galway* 712 C 7 *Ireland G.*

See : *Town*★.
Exc. : *Connemara*★★★.
Dublin 310.5 – Galway 75.5.

Eldon's without rest., ℘ (095) 35933, *eldonshotel@eircom.net, Fax (095) 35722*, ≤, – MC AE ① VISA. ✗
14 March-2 November – **19 rm** ☐ ★65 – ★★90/120.
◆ Near the harbour of this fishing village with views of the bay and the Twelve Pin Mountains. Wood floored bar with open fires. Annex bedrooms are most comfortable.

SALTHILL (Bóthar na Trá) *Galway* 712 E 8 – *see Galway.*

SCHULL (An Scoil) *Cork* 712 D 13 – *see Skull.*

SHANAGARRY (An Seangharraí) *Cork* 712 H 12 *Ireland G.* – ✉ *Midleton.*

Env. : *Cloyne Cathedral*★, *NW : 6½ km by R 629.*
Dublin 262.5 – Cork 40 – Waterford 103.

Ballymaloe House , Northwest : 2 ¾ km on L 35 ℘ (021) 4652531, *res@ballymaloe.ie, Fax (021) 4652021*, ≤, heated, , , – rest, P. MC AE ① VISA. ✗
closed 22-26 December – **Rest** (booking essential) (buffet dinner Sunday) 35/62 – **33 rm** ☐ ★120/175 – ★★210/300.
◆ Hugely welcoming part 16C, part Georgian country house surrounded by 400 acres of farmland. Characterful sitting room with cavernous ceiling. Warm, comfortable bedrooms. Characterful dining room divided into assorted areas.

SHANNON (Sionainn) *Clare* 712 F 9 – *pop. 8 561.*

Shannon Airport ℘ *(061) 471020.*
Shannon Airport : ℘ (061) 712000.
Shannon Airport, Arrivals Hall ℘ (061) 471664, info@shannondev.ie.
Dublin 219 – Ennis 26 – Limerick 24.

Oak Wood Arms, ℘ (061) 361500, *reservations@oakwoodarms.com, Fax (061) 361414*, , – , rest, P – 650. MC AE ① VISA. ✗
closed 24-25 December – **Rest** (carvery lunch Monday-Saturday)/dinner 25/35 and a la carte 25/40 s. ♀ – **99 rm** ☐ ★90/110 – ★★140/170, 2 suites.
◆ Low rise hotel with good access to Shannon International airport. Large bar with carvery. Lots of small lounges. Good conference facilities. Spacious rooms with fresh décor. Dining room decorated with aeronautical memorabilia.

at Shannon Airport *Southwest : 4 km on N 19 –* ✉ *Shannon.*

Great Southern, ℘ (061) 471122, *res@gsh-shannon.ie, Fax (061) 471982* – , rest, P – 150. MC AE ① VISA. ✗
closed 23-27 December – **Rest** *(closed lunch Saturday and Sunday)* (carvery lunch)/dinner 25 and a la carte 22/38 s. – ☐ 15 – **114 rm** ★160 – ★★160.
◆ Low rise, whitewashed, modern hotel in airport area. Well-kept public areas: marbled lobby, small reading room, rustic bar. Clean, tidy, spacious bedrooms. Restaurant boasts a smart terrace which overlooks gardens and the Shannon estuary.

SHANNON AIRPORT *Clare* 712 F 9 – *see Shannon.*

SKERRIES (Na Sceirí) *Dublin* 712 N 7 *Ireland G.* – *pop. 9 149.*

Env. : *Fingal*★.
Skerries ℘ (01) 849 1204.
Strand St ℘ (01) 849 1439.
Dublin 30.5 – Drogheda 24.

XX **Redbank House** with rm, 7 Church St, ℘ (01) 849 0439, *info@redbank.ie, Fax (01) 849 1598* – MC AE ① VISA
Rest - Seafood - *(closed Sunday dinner)* (dinner only and Sunday lunch)/dinner 29/48 and a la carte 38/55 s. – **18 rm** ☐ ★75/85 – ★★110/140.
◆ One of Ireland's most well-renowned and long-standing restaurants, near the guesthouse. Fresh seafood from Skerries harbour is served simply or in more elaborate fashion.

SKIBBEREEN *Cork* 712 E 13 – *pop. 2 000.*
Town Hall ✆ *(028) 21766.*
Dublin 338 – Cork 85 – Killarney 104.5.

Thai @ Ty ar Mor, First Floor, 46 Bridge St, ✆ (028) 22100, *thai@tyarmor.com* –
MC VISA
closed 4 weeks January-February, 2 weeks October, Sunday and Monday in winter – Rest Thai - (booking essential) a la carte 24/34 **s.**
◆ Compact and popular, above Ty ar Mor. Furnished with Asian ornaments, tapestries an wall blinds. Polite service from staff in national dress. Authentic, well executed dishes.

SKULL/SCHULL **(An Scoil)** *Cork* 712 D 13 *Ireland G.*
See : *Town*★.
Exc. : *Sherkin Island*★ *(by ferry) – Mizen Peninsula (≤★★ from pass).*
Coosheen, Coosheen, Schull ✆ *(077) 28182.*
Dublin 363.5 – Cork 104.5 – Killarney 103.

Corthna Lodge without rest., West : 1¼ km by R 592 ✆ (028) 28517, *info@corthna lodge.net, Fax (028) 28032,* MC VISA.
15 April-September – **6 rm** ★60/70 – ★★85/95.
◆ 100 year old ivy covered guesthouse with many original features remaining. Large ga den. Bright breakfast room. Smart bedrooms boast stencilled walls, modern soft furnish ings.

SLIEVEROE **(Sliabh Rua)** *Waterford – see Waterford.*

SLIGO **(Sligeach)** *Sligo* 712 G 5 *Ireland G. – pop. 17 735.*
See : *Town*★★ *– Abbey*★.
Env. : *SE : Lough Gill*★★ *– Carrowmore Megalithic Cemetery*★ *AC, SW : 4¾ km – Knock narea*★ *(≤★★) SW : 9½ km by R 292.*
Exc. : *Drumcliff*★*, N : by N 15 – Parke's Castle*★ *AC, E : 14½ km by R 286 – Glencar Water fall*★*, NE : 14½ km by N 16 – Creevykeel Court Cairn*★*, N : 25¾ km by N 15.*
Rosses Point ✆ *(071) 77134.*
Sligo Airport, Strandhill : ✆ *(071) 68280.*
Aras Reddan, Temple St ✆ *(071) 9161201.*
Dublin 214 – Belfast 203 – Dundalk 170.5 – Londonderry 138.5.

Clarion, Clarion Rd, Ballinode, Northeast : 3 km by N 16 ✆ (071) 9119000, *info@clario hotelsligo.com, Fax (071) 9119001,* rest, 500. MC AE VISA.
Kudos : Rest - Asian - a la carte 21/33 – ***Sinergie :*** Rest (dinner only and Sunday lunch 37/45 and a la carte 31/50 – 16 – **76 rm** ★190 – ★★190, 91 suites 215/290.
◆ Extensive Victorian building with granite façade: now the height of modernity wit excellent leisure club, and impressive, spacious bedrooms, the majority being plush suite Modern European menus at Sinergie. Informal Asian inspired Kudos.

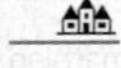

Radisson SAS, Ballincar, Northwest : ¾ km on R 281 ✆ (071) 9140008, *info.sligo@ra ssonsas.com, Fax (071) 9140006,* – 1000. MC VISA
Rest (bar lunch Monday-Saturday)/dinner 35 and a la carte 38/44 – **129 rm** ★90/99 ★★130/180, 3 suites.
◆ Modern, spacious hotel two miles from centre. Impressive conference and leisure facil ties with comprehensive spa treatments. Stylish, airy, modish rooms, some with king beds Smart yet informal restaurant overlooking Sligo Bay.

Sligo Park, Pearse Rd, South : 2 km on N 4 ✆ (071) 9190400, *sligo@leehotels.com Fax (071) 9169556,* – 450. MC AE VISA.
restricted opening at Christmas – ***Hazelwood :*** Rest *(closed Saturday lunch and Ban Holidays)* 22/36 and a la carte 25/37 **s.** – **138 rm** ★74/160 – ★★110/266, 1 suite.
◆ Spacious lobby, with its unique Millennium water feature, leads to bright, moder rooms, thoughtfully equipped for the corporate traveller and overlooking gardens. Con servatory restaurant or hearty bar dining options.

Benwiskin Lodge without rest., Shannon Eighter, North : 2 km by N 15 ✆ (07 9141088, *pquigley@iol.ie, Fax (071) 9141088,* MC VISA.
closed 20 December-4 January – **5 rm** ★40/50 – ★★65/75.
◆ Extensively pine furnished guesthouse in quiet area. 150 year old clock in front hal Open-fired sitting room with shiny wood floor. Cosy breakfast area. Spruce rooms.

Tree Tops without rest., Cleveragh Rd, South : 1 ¼ km by Dublin rd ✆ (071) 9160160, *treetops@iol.ie, Fax (071) 9162301*, – ⇆ P. MC AE VISA.
closed 20 December-10 January – **5 rm** ☕ ✝45/48 – ✝✝66/70.
• Pleasant guesthouse in residential area. Stunning collection of Irish art. Cosy public areas include small lounge and simple breakfast room. Neat, comfortable rooms.

Ard Cuilinn Lodge without rest., Drumiskabole, Southeast : 4 ¾ km by N 4 off R 284 ✆ (071) 9162925, *ardcuiln@esatclear.ie*, – ⇆ P.
20 March-26 October – **3 rm** ☕ ✝60/65 – ✝✝60/65.
• Simple, charming guesthouse located away from the town centre. Homely, spacious lounge. Welcoming breakfast room. Fair sized, immaculately appointed bedrooms.

Carbury House without rest., Donegal Rd, Teesan, North : 3 ¼ km on N 15 ✆ (071) 9143378, *carbury@indigo.ie, Fax (071) 9147433*, – P. MC VISA.
closed 23 December-10 January – **6 rm** ☕ ✝45/50 – ✝✝65/80.
• Large mock-Georgian guesthouse with spacious garden. Oak-floored lounge boasts leather sofas and open fire. Pine-clad breakfast room. Huge bedrooms with modern colours.

Montmartre, Market Yard, ✆ (071) 9169901, *montmartre@eircom.net, Fax (071) 9140065* – ⇆ ▤. MC AE VISA
closed 8-30 January, 24-26 December and Monday – **Rest** (dinner only) a la carte 33/45 **s.** ♀.
• Clear French style at this discreetly located restaurant close to the town's theatre. Polite staff serve broadly influenced French food within simply appointed restaurant.

Do not confuse X with ✿! X defines comfort, while stars are awarded for the best cuisine, across all categories of comfort.

PANISH POINT (Rinn na Spáinneach) *Clare* 712 D 9 – ✉ *Milltown Malbay.*

Dublin 275 – Galway 104.5 – Limerick 83.5.

Admiralty Lodge, ✆ (065) 7085030, *info@admiralty.ie, Fax (065) 7085030*, – ⇆ ▤ ♿ P. MC AE VISA
closed January-February – ***Piano Room*** **: Rest** (dinner only) 39 – **12 rm** ☕ ✝120/165 – ✝✝150/200.
• Purpose-built coastal hotel built around a former 19C seamans lodge. Three warm, comfy lounges bring out period character. Individually stylish rooms a notably strong point. Formal dining in lodge: piano player and French themed menus.

Burkes Armada, ✆ (065) 7084110, *info@burkesarmadahotel.com, Fax (065) 7084632*, <, , – |‡|, ⇆ rest, P – 300. MC VISA.
closed 25 December – **Rest** (bar lunch Monday-Saturday)/dinner a la carte 28/40 – **61 rm** ☕ ✝80/95 – ✝✝120/150.
• Modern, mustard painted hotel in good position overlooking Toormore Bay. Compact bar within otherwise spacious public areas. Sizeable rooms with bright, chintz furnishings. The split-level Cape restaurant has sea-blue décor to complement its fine ocean views.

SPIDDAL/SPIDDLE (An Spidéal) *Galway* 712 E 8.

Dublin 230 – Galway 17.5.

An Cruiscin Lan, ✆ (091) 553148, *info@cruiscinlanhotel.com, Fax (091) 553712*, <, – ⇆ ♿. MC VISA.
closed 25 December – **Rest** 17 (lunch) and a la carte 23/34♀ – **13 rm** ☕ ✝55/70 – ✝✝100/160.
• Personally run, extended inn at the centre of this busy village. Light, comfortable and well-priced rooms, some with bayside views: a useful option for business travel. All-day brasserie facing the water.

Ardmor Country House without rest., West : ¾ km on R 336 ✆ (091) 553145, *ardmorcountryhouse@yahoo.com, Fax (091) 553596*, <, – ⇆ P.
March-December – **7 rm** ☕ ✝45/50 – ✝✝66/70.
• Creamwashed chalet guesthouse with pleasant gardens and spotless, pastel painted back bedrooms with fine views of Galway Bay. Two comfortable lounges and a sun-trap terrace.

SPIDDLE (An Spidéal) *Galway* 712 E 8 – *see Spiddal.*

STILLORGAN *Dublin* 712 N 8 – *see Dublin.*

STRAFFAN (Teach Srafáin) *Kildare* 712 M 8 – *pop. 341.*
Naas, Kerdiffstown ✆ (045) 874644.
Dublin 24 – Mullingar 75.5.

The K Club, ✆ (01) 601 7200, *resortsales@kclub.ie, Fax (01) 601 7297*, , indoor/outdoor, squash – 1000. AE VISA
closed 17-26 September – ***Byerley Turk*** **: Rest** *(closed Sunday-Monday)* (booking essent to non-residents) (dinner only) a la carte 66/122 **s.** – ***Legends*** **: Rest** a la carte 37/69 **s.** ***Monza*** **: Rest** - Italian - a la carte 32/47 **s.** – **70 rm** ★265/495 – ★★315/570, 9 suites.
◆ Part early 19C country house overlooking River Liffey, with gardens, arboretum ar championship golf course. Huge leisure centre. Exquisitely sumptuous rooms. Gran country house style Byerley Turk with river views. Informal Legends. Italian cuisine Monza.

Barberstown Castle, North : ¾ km ✆ (01) 628 8157, *barberstowncastle@i land.com, Fax (01) 627 7027*, – 200. AE VISA
closed 24-26 December – **Rest** (booking essential) a la carte 43/52 – **59 rm** ★150 ★★280.
◆ Whitewashed Elizabethan and Victorian house with 13C castle keep and gardens. Cou try house style lounges exude style. Individually decorated, very comfortable bedroom Dine in characterful, stone-clad keep.

SWINFORD (Béal Atha na Muice) *Galway.*
Dublin 212.5 – Galway 92 – Sligo 59.5.

Gateway, Main St, ✆ (094) 9252156, *info@gatewayswinford.com, Fax (094) 9251328*, rest, – 300. AE VISA
closed 25 December – **Rest** (bar lunch)/dinner 15/18 and a la carte – **15 rm** ★50/70 ★★90/120.
◆ Comfortable, unfussy accommodation at affordable rates in this spacious converte inn. Rear function room is a popular choice for reunions and wedding receptions. Moder formal dining room offers a selection of favourite traditional Irish dishes.

TAGOAT (Teach Gót) *Wexford* 712 M 11 – *see Rosslare Harbour.*

TAHILLA (Tathuile) *Kerry* 712 C 12 *Ireland G.*
Exc. : *Iveragh Peninsula★★ (Ring of Kerry★★) – Sneem★, NW : 6½ km by N 70.*
Dublin 357 – Cork 112.5 – Killarney 51.5.

Tahilla Cove, ✆ (064) 45204, *tahillacove@eircom.net, Fax (064) 45104*, Coong harbour and Caha Mountains, – AE VISA
Easter-15 October – **Rest** *(closed Monday-Tuesday)* (booking essential) (set menu onl (dinner only) 30 **s.** – **9 rm** ★95 – ★★140.
◆ Two houses surrounded by oak forest, with Caha Mountains as a backdrop and garde sweeping down to Coongar harbour. Some bedrooms have balconies from which to s vour views. Locally derived cuisine proudly served by hospitable owner.

TERENURE *Dublin* 712 N 8 – *see Dublin.*

TERMONBARRY *Longford* 712 I 6 *Ireland G.*
Exc. : *Strokestown★ (Famine Museum★ AC, Strokestown Park House★ AC), NW : by N 5.*
Dublin 130.5 – Galway 137 – Roscommon 35.5 – Sligo 100.

Shannonside House without rest., ✆ (043) 26052, *info@keenans.ie, Fax (043) 2619* – AE VISA
closed 25 December and Good Friday – **7 rm** ★40/45 – ★★70/75.
◆ Hospitable owner and well-proportioned bedrooms are among the guesthouse's chie attractions. Good value and comfortable. Located close to the Shannon River.

TERRYGLASS (Tír Dhá Ghlas) *Tipperary* 712 H 8.
Dublin 159.5 – Limerick 66 – Loughrea 43.5.

The Derg Inn, ✆ (067) 22037, *derginn@eircom.net, Fax (067) 22297*, – VISA
closed 25 December and Good Friday – **Rest** a la carte 20/50.
◆ A short walk from lovely Lough Derg. Characterful interior with open fires and pc stoves. Sit on chair, bench or pew as you dine on organic local produce from eclecti menus.

THOMASTOWN (Baile Mhic Andáin) *Kilkenny* 712 K 10 *Ireland G. – pop. 1 600 –* ✉ *Kilkenny.*
Env. : *Jerpoint Abbey★★, SW : 2½ km by N9.*
Dublin 124 – Kilkenny 17.5 – Waterford 48.5 – Wexford 61.

Mount Juliet Conrad ⚲, West : 2 ½ km ✆ (056) 7773000, *mountjulietinfo@conradhotels.com, Fax (056) 7773019,* ← River Nore and park, ⊕, Fδ, ≘s, ⊡, ▶18, ⚲, ⛞, ✕ – ⇔ P. ⓜ AE ⓞ VISA. ⚡
The Lady Helen : Rest (dinner only) 57 and a la carte 40/72 ♀ – (see also ***Hunters Yard*** below) – ☕ 17 – **30 rm** ★290/395 – ★★290/395, 2 suites.
◆ 18C manor in sporting estate, named after wife of original owner. Overlooks the meandering river Nore with stud farm, equestrian centre. Smart, restful rooms. Restaurant features stately stucco work and tall windows.

Hunters Yard & Rose Garden Lodges (at Mount Juliet Conrad H.), West : 2 ½ km ✆ (056) 7773000, *mountjulietinfo@conradhotels.com, Fax (056) 7773019,* Fδ, ≘s, ⊡, ▶18, ⚲, ⛞, ⚲, ✕ – ⇔ rest, ▤ rest, P – 🏛 75. ⓜ AE ⓞ VISA. ⚡
Kendals : Rest (bar lunch Monday-Saturday)/dinner 45 and a la carte 37/42 – ☕ 17 – **26 rm** ★195/220 – ★★195/220.
◆ For those interested in outdoor activities, the well-located club style rooms in the original hunting stables or lodges are ideal. A restful place after a day's exertions. Restaurant with airy yet intimate ambience.

Abbey House without rest., Jerpoint Abbey, Southwest : 2 km on N 9 ✆ (056) 7724166, *abbeyhsejerpoint@eircom.net, Fax (056) 7724192,* ⛞ – ✆ P. ⓜ VISA
closed 20-30 December – **7 rm** ☕ ★40/70 – ★★70/110.
◆ Neat inside and out, this whitewashed house in well-kept gardens offers simple but spacious rooms and pretty wood furnished breakfast room. Read up on area in lounge.

Carrickmourne House ⚲ without rest., New Ross Rd, Southeast : 3 ¼ km by R 700 ✆ (056) 7724124, *carrickmournehouse@eircom.net, Fax (056) 7724124,* ←, ⛞ – ⇔ P. ⓜ VISA. ⚡
closed 15-31 December – **5 rm** ☕ ★40/50 – ★★60/75.
◆ Modern, split-level house looks down on peaceful countryside. Agreeably simple, traditional décor and gleaming wood floors in pristine rooms: homely and well priced.

THURLES (Durlas) *Tipperary* 712 I9 – *pop. 7 425.*
▶18 *Turtulla* ✆ *(0504) 21983.*
Dublin 148 – Cork 114 – Kilkenny 48.5 – Limerick 75.5 – Waterford 93.5.

Inch House ⚲, Northwest : 6 ½ km on R 498 ✆ (0504) 51348, *inchhse@iol.ie, Fax (0504) 51754,* ←, ⛞, ⚲ – ⇔ P. ⓜ ⓞ VISA. ⚡
closed 20-29 December – **Rest** *(closed Sunday-Monday)* (dinner only) 45/50 – **5 rm** ☕ ★65 – ★★110.
◆ 1720s country house on a working farm; lovely rural views. Handsomely restored with a fine eye for decorative period detail. Individually styled en suite bedrooms. Classically proportioned yet intimate dining room.

at Twomileborris *East : 6¾ km on N 75 –* ✉ *Thurles.*

The Castle, ✆ (0504) 44324, *info@thecastletmb.com, Fax (0504) 44352,* ⛞ – ⇔ P. ⓜ AE VISA. ⚡
Rest (by arrangement) 50 – **4 rm** ☕ ★48/60 – ★★80/100.
◆ Charming 17C house adjacent to partly ruined tower of the local castle which runs close to back door. Furnished with numerous period pieces. Pleasantly decorated rooms. Traditionally furnished dining room.

TOORMORE (An Tuar Mór) *Cork* 712 D 13 – ✉ *Goleen.*
Dublin 355.5 – Cork 109.5 – Killarney 104.5.

Fortview House without rest., Gurtyowen, Northeast : 2 ½ km on Durrus rd (R 591) ✆ (028) 35324, *fortviewhousegoleen@eircom.net, Fax (028) 35324,* ⛞ – ⇔ P. ⚡
March-October – **5 rm** ☕ ★45/55 – ★★90.
◆ Stone built farmhouse; antique country pine furniture in coir carpeted rooms and brass, iron bedsteads. Fresh vegetable juice, home-made museli, potato cake for breakfast.

Rock Cottage ⚲, Barnatonicane, Northeast : 3 ¼ km on Durrus rd (R 591) ✆ (028) 35538, *rockcottage@eircom.net, Fax (028) 35538,* ⛞, ⚲ – ⇔ P. ⓜ VISA. ⚡
Rest (by arrangement) 40 – **3 rm** ☕ ★75/90 – ★★110/130.
◆ Georgian former hunting lodge idyllically set in 17 acres of parkland. Very well appointed lounge: modern art on walls. Immaculate, light and airy bedrooms.

TOWER *Cork* 712 G 12 – *see Blarney.*

TRALEE (Trá Lí) *Kerry* 712 C 11 *Ireland G. – pop. 21 987.*

Env. : *Blennerville Windmill★ AC, SW : 3¼ km by N 86 – Ardfert Cathedral★, NW : 8¾ km b R 551.*

Exc. : *Banna Strand★, NW : 12¾ km by R 551 – Crag Cave★ AC, W : 21 km by N 21 – Ratto Round Tower★, N : 19¼ km by R 556.*

Ashe Memorial Hall ☎ (066) 7121288, tourisminfo@shannon-dev.ie.

Dublin 297.5 – Killarney 32 – Limerick 103.

The Meadowlands, Oakpark, Northeast : 1 ¼ km on N 69 ☎ (066) 718 0444 *info@meadowlandshotel.com, Fax (066) 718 0964,* – – 250. VISA.

closed 24-26 December – **Rest** *(closed Sunday dinner)* (bar lunch Monday-Saturday)/dinne 35 and a la carte – **56 rm** ★75/180 – ★★250/300, 2 suites.

◆ Smart, terracotta hotel, a good base for exploring area. Inside are warmly decorated, a conditioned rooms and mellow library lounge with open fire and grandfather clock. Pro prietor owns fishing boats, so seafood takes centre stage in dining room.

The Grand, Denny St, ☎ (066) 7121499, *info@grandhoteltralee.com, Fax (066) 712287* – , rest, – 250. VISA.

Rest 22/35 and a la carte 18/34 **s.** – **44 rm** ★60/75 – ★★120/140.

◆ Established 1928; enjoys a central position in town. Rooms are decorated with ma hogany furniture whilst the popular bar, once a post office, bears hallmarks of bygone era Appetising dinners in restaurant with historic ambience.

Brook Manor Lodge without rest., Fenit Rd, Spa, Northwest : 3 ½ km by R 551 o R 558 ☎ (066) 7120406, *brookmanor@eircom.net, Fax (066) 7127552,* – VISA

8 rm ★60/70 – ★★100/120.

◆ Modern purpose-built manor in meadowland looking across to the Slieve Mish moun tains: good for walks and angling. Breakfast in conservatory. Immaculate bedrooms.

The Forge without rest., Upper Oakpark, Northeast : 2 ½ km on N 69 ☎ (066) 7125245 *theforgeguesthouse@hotmail.com, Fax (066) 7125245,* – VISA.

closed Christmas – **6 rm** ★40/60 – ★★60/70.

◆ Comfortable, family-run house; sporting activities and scenic spots on doorstep. Hallwa with hexagonal light leads upstairs to cosy rooms. Complimentary drinks on arrival.

David Norris, Ivy Terrace, ☎ (066) 7185654, *restaurantdavidnorris@eircom.ne Fax (066) 7126600* – . VISA

closed 2 weeks January-February, 1 week October, Sunday and Monday – **Rest** (dinner only a la carte 31/41.

◆ Pleasant restaurant on first floor of unprepossessing modern building, featuring Renni Macintosh style chairs. Good blend of cuisine: exotic hints and popular favourites.

TRAMORE (Trá Mhór) *Waterford* 712 K 11 – *pop. 8 305.*

☎ *(051) 381572 (June-August).*

Dublin 170.5 – Waterford 9.5.

Glenorney without rest., Newtown, Southwest : 1 ½ km by R 675 ☎ (051) 381056 *glenorney@iol.ie, Fax (051) 381103,* ←, – VISA

6 rm ★50/80 – ★★70/90.

◆ On a hill overlooking Tramore Bay. Inside are personally decorated rooms: family photo graphs and curios; sun lounge with plenty of books. Rear rooms have lovely bay views.

Coast with rm, Upper Branch Rd, ☎ (051) 393646, *coastrestaurant@eircom.ne Fax (051) 393647,* ←, , – . VISA

closed January, Monday, Tuesday and Sunday dinner except July-August and Bank Holiday – **Rest** (dinner only and Sunday lunch)/dinner a la carte 34/47 – **4 rm** ★65/90 ★★120/160.

◆ The exterior gives no hint of the Bohemian style restaurant. Varied menu based on Iris dishes and produce; modern twists. Comfy rooms in eclectic style, best views at front.

TRIM (Baile Átha Troim) *Meath* 712 L 7 *Ireland G. – pop. 5 894.*

See : *Trim Castle★★ – Town★.*

Env. : *Bective Abbey★, NE : 6½ km by R 161.*

County Meath, Newtownmoynagh ☎ (046) 31463.

Old Town Hall, Castle St ☎ (046) 9437227 (May-September).

Dublin 43.5 – Drogheda 42 – Tullamore 69.

Highfield House without rest., Maudlins Rd, ☎ (046) 9436386, *highfieldhousea com@eircom.net, Fax (046) 9438182,* – VISA

closed 23 December-4 January – **7 rm** ★50 – ★★76/78.

◆ 19C former maternity home in lawned gardens overlooking Trim Castle and River Boyne Sizeable bedrooms in cheerful colours offer a welcome respite after sightseeing.

Crannmór without rest., Dunderry Rd, North : 2 km ✆ (046) 9431635, *cranmor@eircom.net, Fax (046) 9438087*, – P. MC VISA.
closed 20 December-8 February – **5 rm** ✶46/48 – ✶✶68/72.
◆ Particularly friendly owners run this creeper-clad Georgian farmhouse in a rural location, offering bright and comfortable bedrooms and a cosy atmosphere.

TULLAMORE (Tulach Mhór) *Offaly* 712 J 8 – *pop. 11 098.*

Tullamore, Brookfield ✆ (0506) 21439.
Bury Quay Tullamore ✆ (0506) 52617.
Dublin 104.5 – Kilkenny 83.5 – Limerick 129.

Tullamore Court, on N 80 (Portlaoise rd) ✆ (0506) 46666, *info@tullamorecourthotel.ie, Fax (0506) 46677*, , , – rest, P – 750. MC AE VISA.
closed 24-26 December – **Rest** 23/50 and dinner a la carte 30/46 **s.** – **72 rm** ✶175 – ✶✶310/350.
◆ Contemporarily styled hotel with curved walls, plenty of marble, glass, rich coloured interiors. Has state-of-the-art leisure centre; children's holiday activities arranged. Stylish, spacious dining room.

Bridge House, off Main St ✆ (0506) 22000, *info@bridgehouse.com, Fax (0506) 25690*, , , – rest, P – 550. MC AE VISA.
closed 24-25 December – **Rest** (bar lunch)/dinner 25/40 and a la carte 30/41 **s.** – **72 rm** ✶95 – ✶✶170/240.
◆ The grand, pillared entrance with steps leading to an ornate reception with crystal chandelier sums up rarified ambience. Polished library bar and impressive bedrooms. Dining options with restaurant or bar carvery.

TULLY CROSS *Galway* 712 C 7.

Dublin 301 – Galway 85.5 – Letterfrack 3.

Maol Reidh, ✆ (095) 43844, *maolreidhhotel@eircom.net, Fax (095) 43784* – P. MC VISA
closed 7 January-1 March and weekends only November-December – **Rest** (bar lunch)/dinner 30 and a la carte 25/37 **s.** – **12 rm** ✶60/75 – ✶✶90/150.
◆ This good value, personally run hotel was built with local stone and a noteworthy attention to detail. Cosy rear bar and sitting room. Good sized bedrooms. Stylish restaurant with modern menus.

TWOMILEBORRIS (Buiríos Léith) *Tipperary* 712 I 9 – *see Thurles.*

VALENCIA ISLAND (Dairbhre) *Kerry* 712 A/B 12.

Dublin 381.5 – Killarney 88.5 – Tralee 92.

Knights Town *Kerry.*

Glanleam House, Glanleam, West : 2 km taking right fork at top of Market St ✆ (066) 9476176, *info@glanleam.com, Fax (066) 9476108*, – P. MC AE VISA.
mid March-October – **Rest** (booking essential to non-residents) (communal dining) (dinner only) 40/50 **s.** – **6 rm** ✶70/105 – ✶✶140/220.
◆ Part 17C and 18C country house in extensive sub-tropical gardens, superbly located off West Kerry coast. Art Deco interiors. Spacious drawing room. Individually styled rooms. Communal dining; produce grown in hotel's 19C walled gardens.

WATERFORD (Port Láirge) *Waterford* 712 K 11 *Ireland G.* – *pop. 46 736.*

See : *Town*★ – *City Walls*★.
Env. : *Waterford Crystal*★, *SW : 2½ km by N 25* **Y**.
Exc. : *Duncannon*★, *E : 19¼ km by R 683, ferry from Passage East and R 374 (south)* **Z** – *Dunmore East*★, *SE : 19¼ km by R 684* **Z** – *Tintern Abbey*★, *E : 21 km by R 683, ferry from Passage East, R 733 and R 734 (south)* **Z**.
Newrath ✆ (051) 874182.
Waterford Airport, Killowen : ✆ (051) 875589.
41 The Quay ✆ (051) 875823 **Y**, *info@southeasttourism.ie – Waterford Crystal Visitor Centre ✆ (051) 358397.*
Dublin 154.5 – Cork 117.5 – Limerick 124.

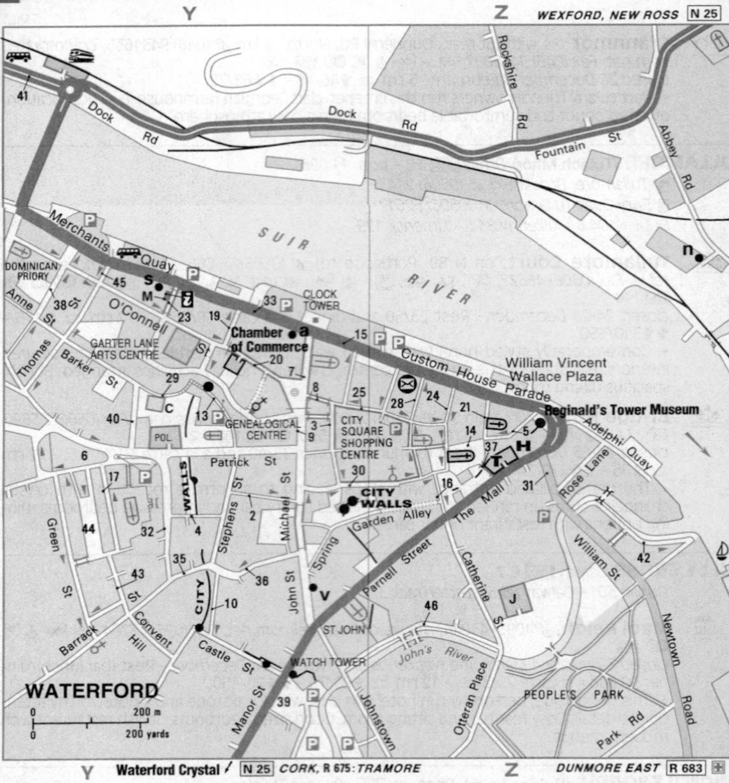

Waterford Castle H. and Golf Club, The Island, Ballinakill, East : 4 km b R 683, Ballinakill Rd and private ferry (051) 878203, *info@waterfordcastle.com Fax (051) 879316*, 18, – P. AE VISA.
closed January – ***The Munster Dining Room :*** Rest (bar lunch Monday-Saturday)/dinne 58 and a la carte approx 52 – 20 – **14 rm** 160/335 – 225/380, 5 suites.
◆ Part 15C and 19C castle in charmingly secluded, historic river island setting. Classic country house ambience amid antiques and period features. Comfortable, elegant rooms Oak panelled dining room with ornate ceilings and evening pianist.

Granville, Meagher Quay, (051) 305555, *stay@granville-hotel.ie, Fax (051) 305566* – , rest, – 200. AE VISA. Y a
closed 24-26 December – ***Bianconi Room :*** Rest (carvery Saturday lunch) 25/28 dinne and a la carte 25/38 – **98 rm** 78/98 – 200/260.
◆ Early 19C hotel that reputedly once hosted Charles Stewart Parnell. Individually styled bedrooms with a consistent traditional standard of décor. Some views of river Suir. Etched glass, drapes and panelling enhance gravitas of classic dining room.

Athenaeum House, Christendom, Ferrybank, Northeast : 1 ½ km by N 25 ☎ (051) 833999, *info@athenaeumhotel.com, Fax (051) 833977,* – rest, – 30. *visa*. Z n
closed 24-26 December – ***Zak's*** **: Rest** a la carte 32/47 **s.** – **26 rm** 100/170 – 120/170.
◆ In a quiet residential area, this extended Georgian house has retained some original features; elsewhere distinctly modern and stylish. Well equipped rooms exude modish charm. Eclectic mix of dishes in restaurant overlooking garden.

Arlington Lodge, Johns Hill, South : 1 ¼ km by N 25, John St and Johnstown Rd ☎ (051) 878584, *info@arlingtonlodge.com, Fax (051) 878127,* – – 25. *visa*.
closed 27 December-2 January – ***Robert Paul*** **: Rest** (residents only Sunday dinner) (dinner only and Sunday lunch) a la carte 27/43 **s.** – **20 rm** 85/150 – 170/250.
◆ Stylish, personally run Georgian former bishop's residence: period style precision. Antiques, gas fires in most of the very comfy and spacious individually styled rooms. Local produce richly employed in tasty menus.

Dooley's, The Quay, ☎ (051) 873531, *hotel@dooleys-hotel.ie, Fax (051) 870262* – – 200. *visa*. Y s
closed 25-28 December – ***The New Ship*** **: Rest** (carvery lunch Monday-Saturday) 25/45 and a la carte 29/46 – 15 – **113 rm** 129 – 198.
◆ Family run hotel, conveniently located for the city centre. Comfy, well-kept bedrooms decorated in uncluttered, up-to-date style. Conference and banqueting facility. Choose formal dining room or the atmospheric John Kirwan bar.

Foxmount Country House without rest., Passage East Rd, Southeast : 7 ¼ km by R 683, off Cheekpoint rd ☎ (051) 874308, *info@foxmountcountryhouse.com, Fax (051) 854906,* –
mid March-October – **5 rm** 65 – 110.
◆ Ivy-clad house, dating from the 17C, on a working farm. Wonderfully secluded and quiet yet within striking distance of Waterford. Neat, cottage-style bedrooms. Breakfast at intimate window alcove table on produce from farm.

Bodéga!, 54 John's St, ☎ (051) 844177, *info@bodegawaterford.com, Fax (051) 384868* – *visa* Y v
closed 25-26 December and Good Friday – **Rest** (dinner only and Sunday lunch) a la carte 30/39.
◆ Tucked away in the heart of the city. Purple exterior; orange interior, augmented by mosaics and wall murals. Classic rustic French menus or warming lunchtime dishes.

at Slieveroe *Northeast : 3½ km by N 25 – Z – ✉ Waterford.*

Diamond Hill without rest., ☎ (051) 832855, *info@diamondhillhouse.com, Fax (051) 832254,* – *visa*.
closed 23-28 December – **17 rm** 40/50 – 70/90.
◆ Relaxed and welcoming accommodation in a large modern house set within pleasant gardens. Warmly decorated public areas. Comfortable, uncluttered bedrooms.

at Butlerstown *Southwest : 8½ km by N 25 – Y – ✉ Waterford.*

Coach House without rest., Butlerstown Castle, Cork Rd, ☎ (051) 384656, *coachhse@iol.ie, Fax (051) 384751,* – *visa*.
closed October-Easter – **7 rm** 70 – 110.
◆ Victorian house in grounds of Butlerstown Castle. Smart traditional communal areas with warmly decorated breakfast room. Tasteful bedrooms offering good comforts.

Undecided between two equivalent establishments?
Within each category, establishments are classified
in our order of preference.

WATERVILLE **(An Coireán)** *Kerry* 712 B 12 *Ireland G.*

EXC. : *Iveragh Peninsula★★ (Ring of Kerry★★) – Skellig Islands★★, W : 12 ¾ km by N 70, R 567 and ferry from Ballinskelligs – Derrynane National Historic Park★★ AC, S : 14½ km by N70 – Leacanabuaile Fort (≤★★), N : 21 km by N 70.*
Ring of Kerry ☎ (066) 9474102.
☎ *(066) 9474646 (June-September).*
Dublin 383 – Killarney 77.

Butler Arms, (066) 9474144, *reservations@butlerarms.com, Fax (066) 9474520,* – P. MC AE VISA.
Easter-October – **Rest** (bar lunch)/dinner 36 and a la carte 30/46 – **37 rm** 110/150 – 180/250.
◆ Built 1862; Charlie Chaplin's holiday retreat. Family owned for three generations. Se views from most bedrooms: spacious junior suites particularly comfortable and luxuriou Unstinting devotion to locally sourced cuisine.

Brookhaven House without rest., New Line Rd, North : 1 ¼ km on N 70 (06 9474431, *brookhaven@esatclear.ie, Fax (066) 9474724,* – P. MC VISA.
closed January-February and 1 week Christmas – **5 rm** 70/85 – 100/120.
◆ Spacious modern guesthouse overlooking Waterville golf course; large and neat, wit restful lounge and cottage style bedrooms. Proud of its home-baked breakfasts.

Do not confuse X with ✿! X defines comfort, while stars are awarded for the best cuisine, across all categories of comfort.

WESTPORT (Cathair na Mart) *Mayo 712 D 6 Ireland G. – pop. 5 634.*

See : *Town★★ (Centre★) – Westport House★★ AC.*
Exc. : *SW : Murrisk Peninsula★★ – Ballintubber Abbey★, SE : 21 km by R 330 – Croag Patrick★, W : 9½ km by R 335 – Bunlahinch Clapper Bridge★, W : 25¾ km by R 335 – Do Lough Pass★, W : 38½ km by R 335 – Aasleagh Falls★, S : 35½ km by N 59.*
James St (098) 25711.
Dublin 262.5 – Galway 80 – Sligo 104.5.

Atlantic Coast, The Quay, West : 1½ km by R 335 (098) 29000, *reservations@atlant coasthotel.com, Fax (098) 29111,* – rest, P – 150. MC AE VISA.
closed 21-26 December – ***Blue Wave :*** **Rest** (bar lunch Monday-Saturday)/dinner 36 **85 rm** 135 – 240, 1 suite.
◆ Striking 18C mill conversion on shores of Clew Bay. Enjoy a seaweed treatment in th hydrotherapy jet bath or a drink in the lively Harbourmaster bar. Well-kept bedroom Top-floor restaurant with harbour and bay views.

Westport, Newport Rd, off Newport Rd (098) 25122, *reservations@hotelwestport.i Fax (098) 26739,* – rest, P – 400. MC AE VISA.
Rest (bar lunch Monday-Saturday)/dinner 38 and a la carte 30/43 – **129 rm** 140 – 240/275.
◆ In attractive grounds running down to Carrowbeg river, a modern hotel appealing t families and conferences alike."Panda Club" and leisure centre will keep the kids bus Sample traditional Irish fare on the daily changing menu in "Islands".

Ardmore Country House, The Quay, West : 2½ km by R 335 (098) 25994, *ardmo ehotel@eircom.net, Fax (098) 27795,* – P. MC AE VISA.
closed January-February and 22-28 December – **Rest** *(closed Sunday and Monday in winte to non-residents)* (dinner only) a la carte 34/50 – **13 rm** 110/170 – 170/240.
◆ Attractive family-run hotel in commanding setting with views across gardens and Clev Bay. Bedrooms are stylishly appointed with a country house feel. Chef owner proudl promotes organic produce.

The Wyatt, The Octagon, (098) 25027, *info@wyatthotel.com, Fax (098) 26316* – – 400. MC AE VISA.
closed 19-27 December – **Rest** (bar lunch Monday-Saturday)/dinner a la carte 29/34 **52 rm** 65/120 – 130/200.
◆ Refurbished hotel with some style located in the very centre of town. Comfortabl furniture and décor from the spacious bar to the deeply carpeted bedrooms. Contempo rary menus served in warmly painted dining room.

Augusta Lodge without rest., Golf Links Rd, North : ¾ km off N 59 (098) 2890 *info@augustalodge.ie, Fax (098) 28995* – P. MC VISA.
closed Christmas – **10 rm** 50/60 – 70/100.
◆ Family run, purpose-built guesthouse, convenient for Westport Golf Club; the owne has a collection of golfing memorabilia. Spacious, brightly decorated rooms.

Ashville House without rest., Castlebar Rd, East : 3 ¼ km on N 5 ✆ (098) 27060, *ashvilleguesthouse@eircom.net, Fax (098) 27060*, ✱, – P. VISA. ✱
17 March-October – **9 rm** ✱80/88 – ✱✱80/88.
◆ Set back from the main road two miles outside town with sun-trap patio to the side of the house. Comfortable appointments throughout and countryside views from the lounge.

Quay West without rest., Quay Rd, West : ¾ km ✆ (098) 27863, *quaywest@eircom.net, Fax (098) 28379* – ✱ P. VISA. ✱
closed 24-26 December – **6 rm** ✱30/45 – ✱✱60/72.
◆ Purpose-built guesthouse located walking distance from the town centre. Simply appointed throughout providing sensibly priced rooms with televisions and phones.

Linenmill, The Demesne, off Newport Rd ✆ (098) 24508, *linenmillrestaurant@eircom.net, Fax (098) 24508* – ✱ P. VISA
closed 3 weeks November, 24-26 December, Tuesday and Wednesday in winter – **Rest** (dinner only) a la carte 29/44 ♀.
◆ Restaurant attached to textile industry museum and its associated shop. Light menu and atmosphere at lunch and candlelit in the evenings. Try daily changing seafood dishes.

Lemon Peel, The Octagon, ✆ (098) 26929, *info@lemonpeel.ie, Fax (098) 26965* – ✱. AE VISA
closed February, 24-26 and 31 December and Monday – **Rest** (booking essential) (dinner only) 17/25 and a la carte 32/44.
◆ Busy atmosphere in a simple, yellow painted dining room popular with locals. Interesting menu offers eclectic selection which may include Cajun shrimp and lamb steaks.

Good food and accommodation at moderate prices? Look for the Bib symbols: red Bib Gourmand ✱ for food, blue Bib Hotel ✱ for hotels

WEXFORD (Loch Garman) *Wexford* 712 M 10 *Ireland G. – pop. 17 235.*

See : *Town*★ – *Main Street*★ YZ – *Franciscan Friary*★ Z – *St Iberius' Church*★ Y D – *Twin Churches*★ Z.
Env. : *Irish Agricultural Museum, Johnstown Castle*★★ *AC, SW : 7 ¼ km* X – *Irish National Heritage Park, Ferrycarrig*★ *AC, NW : 4 km by N 11* V – *Curracloe*★, *NE : 8 km by R 741 and R 743* V.
Exc. : *Kilmoer Quay*★, *SW : 24 km by N 25 and R 739 (Saltee Islands*★ *- access by boat)* X – *Enniscorthy Castle*★ *(County Museum*★ *AC) N : 24 km by N 11* V.
Mulgannon ✆ (053) 42238.
Crescent Quay ✆ (053) 23111.
Dublin 141.5 – Kilkenny 79 – Waterford 61.

Plans on following pages

Ferrycarrig, Ferrycarrig Bridge, Northwest : 4 ½ km on N 11 ✆ (053) 20999, *res.ferrycarrig@ferrycarrighotel.com, Fax (053) 20982*, ≤ River Slaney and estuary, ✱, ✱, ✱, ✱, ✱, ✱ – ✱ ✱, ✱ rest, ✱ P – ✱ 400. AE VISA. ✱ V a
Tides : Rest (dinner only) a la carte 28/47 **s.** ♀ – ***Reeds :*** Rest (dinner only and Sunday lunch)/dinner a la carte 28/47 **s.** ♀ – **98 rm** ✱115/170 – ✱✱160/300, 4 suites.
◆ Imposing hotel idyllically set on River Slaney and estuary. Public areas on enchanting waterfront curve. Good leisure facilities. Modern rooms with super views and balconies. Tides is winningly set at water's edge. Lively, informal Reeds.

Talbot, On the Quay, ✆ (053) 22566, *sales@talbothotel.ie, Fax (053) 23377*, ✱, ✱, ✱ – ✱ ✱, ✱ rest, ✱ ✱ P – ✱ 400. AE VISA. ✱ Z b
Rest (carvery lunch)/dinner 39 and a la carte 19/43 **s.** – **109 rm** ✱95/105 – ✱✱150/170.
◆ Brightly painted property in the city centre. Well-kept communal areas with modern furnishings. Neat, comfortable bedrooms with modern facilities. Carvery restaurant.

Quality, West : 4 km on R 769 ✆ (053) 72000, *info@qualityhotelwexford.com, Fax (053) 72001*, ✱, ✱, ✱ – ✱ ✱, ✱ rest, ✱ P – ✱ 50. AE VISA. ✱
closed 23-26 December – ***Lannigans :*** Rest (dinner only) 26 and a la carte 21/32 – ✱ 10 – **107 rm** ✱199 – ✱✱199.
◆ Just off main road on outskirts of town. Spacious and contemporary lounge and bar. Well equipped leisure club. Spacious uniformly styled rooms with modern facilities. Lannigans offers extensive menus based on steak.

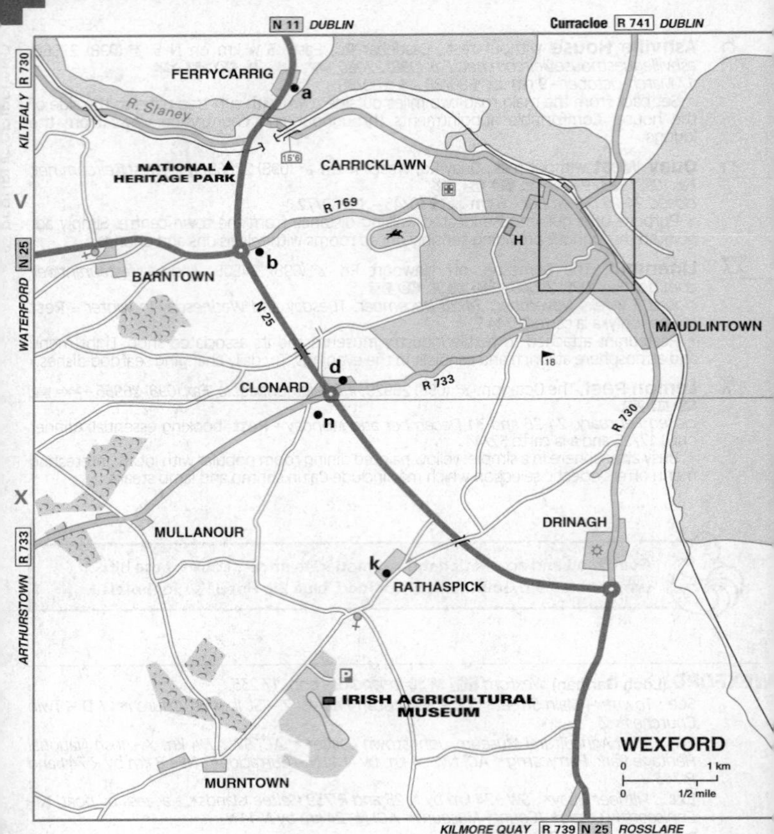

Whitford House, New Line Rd, West : 3 ½ km on R 733 ✆ (053) 43444, *info@whitford.ie, Fax (053) 46399,* ⊠, ☐, – ✂ rest, ▤ rest, ✆ 🅿 – 40. MC AE VISA V d
closed 24-28 December – **Rest** (carvery lunch Monday-Saturday)/dinner 40 and a la carte 25/40 s. ♀ – 36 rm ☐ ★78/178 – ★★110/190.
◆ Late 20C hotel with bright yellow exterior. Lounge bar has traditional food and nightly entertainment. Conference facilities. Spacious, well-kept rooms, some with patios. Dining room has eye-catching lemon interior.

Clonard House without rest., Clonard Great, Southwest : 4 km by R 733 ✆ (053) 43141, *info@clonardhouse.com, Fax (053) 43141,* ≤, – ✂ 🅿. MC VISA X n
May-6 November – 9 rm ☐ ★45/50 – ★★70/80.
◆ Smart Georgian country house with working farm. Behind a massive front door are a high ceilinged lounge in soft peach, cosy breakfast room and appealingly decorated bedrooms.

McMenamin's Townhouse without rest., 3 Auburn Terrace, Redmond Rd, ✆ (053) 46442, *mcmem@indigo.ie, Fax (053) 46442* – ✂ 🅿. MC VISA. Y r
closed 20-31 December – 6 rm ☐ ★60 – ★★100.
◆ Victorian terraced house close to the station. Very traditional interior with an old fashioned-style of comfort. Individually decorated bedrooms with antiques.

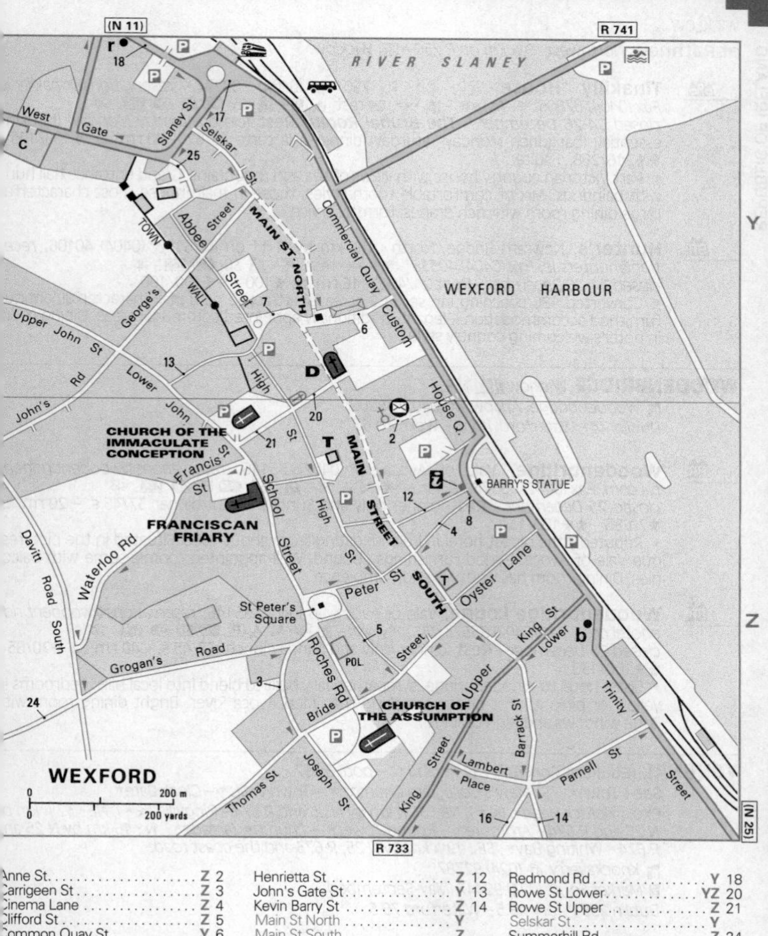

Anne St. . . . . Z 2	Henrietta St . . . . . Z 12	Redmond Rd . . . . . Y 18
Carrigeen St . . . . . Z 3	John's Gate St . . . . . Y 13	Rowe St Lower . . . . . YZ 20
Cinema Lane . . . . . Z 4	Kevin Barry St . . . . . Z 14	Rowe St Upper . . . . . Z 21
Clifford St . . . . . Z 5	Main St North . . . . . Y	Selskar St . . . . . Y
Common Quay St . . . . . Y 6	Main St South . . . . . Z	Summerhill Rd . . . . . Z 24
Cornmarket . . . . . Y 7	Michael St . . . . . Z 16	Temperance Row . . . . . Y 25
Crescent Quay . . . . . Z 8	Redmond Pl. . . . . . Y 17	

Rathaspeck Manor without rest., Rathaspeck, Southwest : 6½ km by Rosslare Rd off Bridgetown rd ☎ (053) 41672, 18, – P. X k

June-October – **4 rm** ☐ ✝50 – ✝✝90.

◆ Georgian country house with 18-hole golf course half a mile from Johnstone Castle. Period furnishings adorn the public rooms. Comfortable, spacious bedrooms.

WICKLOW (Cill Mhantáin) *Wicklow* 712 N 9 *Ireland G. – pop. 9 355.*

Env. : *Mount Usher Gardens, Ashford★ AC, NW : 6½ km by R 750 and N 11 – Devil's Glen★, NW : 12¾ km by R 750 and N 11.*

Exc. : *Glendalough★★★ (Lower Lake★★★, Upper Lake★★, Cathedral★★, Round Tower★, St Kevin's Church★, St Saviour's Priory★) – W : 22½ km by R 750, N 11, R 763, R 755 and R 756 – Wicklow Mountains★★ (Wicklow Gap★★, Sally Gap★★, Avondale★, Meeting of the Waters★, Glenmacnass Waterfall★, Glenmalur★, – Loughs Tay and Dan★).*

ℹ *Fitzwilliam Sq ☎ (0404) 69117, wicklowtouristoffice@eircom.net.*

Dublin 53 – Waterford 135 – Wexford 108.

at Rathnew *Northwest : 3¼ km on R 750 – ✉ Wicklow.*

Tinakilly House, on R 750 ☎ (0404) 69274, *reservations@tinakilly.ie* *Fax (0404) 67806*, ≤, rest, P – 65. MC AE VISA.
closed 24-26 December – ***The Brunel Room*** **: Rest** *(closed Sunday-Monday)* (booking essential) (bar lunch Monday-Saturday)/dinner a la carte 43/52 – **50 rm** ★169/195 ★★216/268, 1 suite.
◆ Part Victorian country house with views of sea and mountains. Grand entrance hall hung with paintings. Mix of comfortable room styles, those in main house most characterful. Large dining room with rich drapes, formal service.

Hunter's, Newrath Bridge, North : 1 ¼ km by N 11 on R 761 ☎ (0404) 40106, *reception@hunters.ie, Fax (0404) 40338*, rest, P – 30. MC VISA.
closed 24-26 December – **Rest** 24/40 – **16 rm** ★100 – ★★180/190.
◆ Converted 18C coaching inn set in 2 acres of attractive gardens. Characterful, antique furnished accommodation. Elegant, traditionally appointed communal areas. Dining room in hotel's welcoming country style.

WOODENBRIDGE *Wicklow* 712 N 9.

18 *Woodenbridge, Arklow ☎ (0402) 35202.*
Dublin 74 – Waterford 109.5 – Wexford 66.

Woodenbridge, Vale of Avoca, ☎ (0402) 35146, *reservations@woodenbridgehotel.com, Fax (0402) 35573*, ≤, P – 250. MC AE VISA.
closed 25 December – **Rest** (dinner only and Sunday lunch)/dinner 37/45 **s.** – **20 rm** ★70/85 – ★★100/130.
◆ Reputedly the oldest hotel in Ireland, dating from about 1608. Situated in the picturesque Vale of Avoca. Period furnishings abound. Well-appointed rooms, some with balconies. Dining room has warm, friendly ambience.

Woodenbridge Lodge, Vale of Avoca, ☎ (0402) 35146, *reservations@woodenbridgehotel.com, Fax (0402) 35573*, P. MC AE VISA.
closed 25 December – **Rest** (dinner only and Sunday lunch) 37/45 **s.** – **40 rm** ★70/85 ★★100/130.
◆ Sister hotel to Woodenbridge, sympathetically built to blend into local hills. Bedrooms in yellow or pink: ask for one overlooking the lyrical Avoca River. Bright dining room with large windows and high ceilings.

YOUGHAL (Eochaill) *Cork* 712 I 12 *Ireland G. – pop. 6 597.*

See : *Town★ – St Mary's Collegiate Church★★ – Town Walls★ – Clock Gate★.*
Exc. : *Helvick Head★ (≤★), NE : 35½ km by N 25 and R 674 – Ringville (≤★), NE : 32¼ km by N 25 and R 674 – Ardmore★ – Round Tower★ – Church★ (arcade★), N : 16 km by N 25 and R 674 – Whiting Bay★, SE : 19¼ km by N 25, R 673 and the coast road.*
18 *Knockaverry ☎ (024) 92787.*
Market Sq ☎ (024) 92447 (May-September).
Dublin 235 – Cork 48.5 – Waterford 75.5.

Glenally House, Copperalley, North : 1 ½ km by old N 25 ☎ (024) 91623, *enquiries@glenally.com, Fax (024) 91623*, P. MC VISA.
March-mid December – **Rest** (by arrangement) (communal dining) 40 – **4 rm** ★80 ★★130.
◆ Affable couple run a stylishly updated 1820s house in paddocks and garden. Notable homebaked breakfasts. Inviting rooms with blend of original and contemporary features. Carefully prepared country cooking in dining room.

Aherne's with rm, 163 North Main St, ☎ (024) 92424, *ahernes@eircom.net* *Fax (024) 93633* – P 20. MC AE VISA
closed 24-29 December – **Rest** - Seafood - (bar lunch)/dinner 40/50 and a la carte 25/42 s – **12 rm** ★110/120 – ★★180/220.
◆ Comfy sofas, books and sitting room fire announce this pleasant restaurant, which has modern art on walls and elegant linen-clad tables. Renowned seafood menus. Smart rooms.

Distances

All distances in this edition are quoted in miles (except for the Republic of Ireland: km). The distance is givenfrom each town to other nearby towns and to the capital of each region as grouped in the guide. To avoid excessive repetition some distances have only been quoted once – you may therefore have to look under both town headings. The distances quoted are not necessarily the shortest but have been based on the roads which afford the best driving conditions and are therefore the most practical.

Distances en miles

Pour chaque région traitée, vous trouverez au texte de chacune des localités sa distance par rapport à la capitale et aux villes environnantes. La distance d'une localité à une autre n'est pas toujours répétée aux deux villes intéressées : voyez au texte de l'une ou de l'autre. Ces distances ne sont pas nécessairement comptées par la route la plus courte mais par la plus pratique, c'est-à-dire celle offrant les meilleures conditions de roulage.

	Belfast	Cork	Dublin	Dundalk	Galway	Killarney	Limerick	Londonderry	Omagh	Sligo	Tullamore
Cork	261										
Dublin	105	155									
Dundalk	53	209	52								
Galway	196	122	135	156							
Killarney	299	56	193	246	136						
Limerick	230	57	123	177	66	71					
Londonderry	72	295	147	103	173	276	207				
Omagh	67	262	114	69	157	243	173	34			
Sligo	123	204	133	105	91	218	148	83	67		
Tullamore	137	125	64	85	83	141	72	152	118	98	
Waterford	207	73	101	154	144	128	79	241	207	182	84

Dublin - Sligo: 133 Miles

Distanze in miglia

Per ciascuna delle regioni trattate, troverete nel testo di ogni località la sua distanza dalla capitale e dalle città circostanti. Le distanza da una località all'altra non è sempre ripetuta nelle due città interessate : vedere nel testo dell'una o dell'altra. Le distanze non sono necessariamente calcolate seguendo il percorso più breve, ma vengono stabilite secondo l'itinerario più pratico, che offre cioè le migliori condizioni di viaggio.

Entfernungsangaben in Meilen

Die Entfernungen der einzelnen Orte zur Landeshauptstadt und zu den nächstgrößeren Städten in der Umgebung sind im allgemeinen Orstext angegeben. Die Entfernung zweier Städte voneinander können Sie aus den Angaben im Ortstext der einen oder der anderen Stadt ersehen. Die Entfernungsangaben gelten nicht immer für der kürzesten, sondern für den günstigsten Weg.

Distances between major towns
Distances entre principales villes
Distanze tra le principali città
Entfernungen zwischen den größeren Stäten

Edinburgh - Southampton 436 Miles

	Aberdeen	Ayr	Birmingham	Blackpool	Brighton	Bristol	Cambridge	Cardiff	Carlisle	Coventry	Dover	Dumfries	Dundee	Edinburgh	Glasgow	Inverness	Ipswich	Kingston-upon-Hull	Leeds	Leicester	Liverpool	London	Manchester	Middlesbrough	Newcastle	Norwich	Nottingham	Oban	Oxford	Plymouth	Portsmouth	Sheffield	Southampton	Stoke-on-Trent	Swansea
Ayr	183																																		
Birmingham	425	294																																	
Blackpool	318	187	128																																
Brighton	594	463	168	297																															
Bristol	508	377	90	211	161																														
Cambridge	469	356	100	221	121	155																													
Cardiff	528	397	110	230	193	42	187																												
Carlisle	223	92	204	96	372	286	265	306																											
Coventry	441	310	22	144	159	98	80	124	219																										
Dover	588	491	203	324	106	199	122	231	400	182																									
Dumfries	203	58	237	129	405	319	298	339	35	252	433																								
Dundee	68	115	358	251	527	441	402	460	156	374	521	136																							
Edinburgh	125	83	302	194	471	385	343	404	100	318	462	79	57																						
Glasgow	146	37	300	192	469	383	362	402	98	316	496	77	79	47																					
Inverness	110	212	460	352	629	543	504	562	258	476	656	237	129	160	176																				
Ipswich	523	411	154	276	127	208	57	240	320	134	128	353	456	398	416	558																			
Kingston-upon-Hull	363	251	145	144	264	237	146	256	160	126	265	193	296	238	256	398	162																		
Leeds	327	214	124	90	266	216	154	236	124	123	273	157	260	201	220	362	208	62																	
Leicester	416	314	44	148	167	122	72	148	224	24	187	257	349	290	320	480	126	102	104																
Liverpool	350	219	103	53	272	185	196	169	128	119	299	161	283	227	225	385	251	132	77	123															
London	540	409	121	243	58	122	58	154	319	100	77	351	473	399	415	575	73	201	205	106	218														
Manchester	347	216	90	54	259	172	169	192	126	106	286	158	280	224	222	382	223	100	45	110	35	205													
Middlesbrough	275	187	181	123	323	273	206	293	96	180	325	129	208	149	192	310	260	91	64	153	146	262	115												
Newcastle	230	147	216	140	358	308	241	328	60	215	360	89	163	104	153	265	295	135	99	188	181	297	149	41											
Norwich	490	378	161	245	168	217	64	249	287	141	169	320	423	365	383	526	43	141	175	119	225	110	191	228	262										
Nottingham	396	283	54	132	196	146	90	165	193	53	216	225	329	270	289	431	145	97	76	28	107	134	75	133	168	121									
Oban	185	127	391	283	559	473	452	493	189	406	587	168	118	124	93	114	507	347	311	411	315	506	313	272	227	474	380								
Oxford	494	363	68	197	109	74	86	106	272	59	146	305	427	371	369	529	137	178	175	76	171	58	158	232	267	148	104	459							
Plymouth	626	495	208	329	219	119	274	155	404	216	294	437	559	503	501	661	312	355	334	240	304	226	290	391	426	334	264	591	198						
Portsmouth	578	447	152	280	52	98	137	139	356	143	142	389	511	455	452	613	163	261	259	160	255	81	242	316	351	197	188	543	87	176					
Sheffield	364	252	88	98	230	179	129	199	161	86	250	194	297	239	257	399	184	70	37	67	77	168	43	101	136	151	40	348	138	297	222				
Southampton	559	428	133	262	64	77	132	118	338	124	152	371	492	436	434	594	170	243	240	141	237	84	224	297	332	192	170	525	68	155	21	204			
Stoke-on-Trent	380	249	48	83	217	131	142	151	159	64	245	192	313	257	255	415	196	134	86	66	58	163	45	155	190	175	50	346	117	249	201	47	182		
Swansea	510	379	136	213	230	79	225	41	289	152	268	321	443	387	385	545	277	283	222	179	172	191	180	319	354	286	192	476	143	193	176	226	155	177	
Wick	[illegible]	[illegible]	[illegible]	[illegible]	[illegible]	[illegible]	[illegible]	[illegible]	[illegible]	[illegible]	[illegible]	[illegible]	[illegible]	[illegible]	[illegible]	[illegible]	[illegible]	[illegible]	[illegible]	[illegible]	[illegible]	[illegible]	[illegible]	[illegible]	[illegible]	[illegible]	[illegible]	[illegible]	[illegible]	[illegible]	[illegible]	[illegible]	[illegible]	[illegible]	[illegible]

Birmingham	Cardiff	Dublin	Glasgow	London	
218	456	380	480	303	**Amsterdam**
908	861	1080	1211	889	**Barcelona**
625	653	787	918	499	**Basel**
778	806	940	1071	652	**Berlin**
684	712	846	978	558	**Bern**
565	514	715	847	610	**Bordeaux**
1061	1089	1223	1355	936	**Bratislava**
1456	1484	1618	1750	1330	**Brindisi**
323	351	485	617	197	**Bruxelles-Brussel**
166	115	315	447	117	**Cherbourg**
531	556	703	835	512	**Clermont-Ferrand**
450	478	612	744	324	**Düsseldorf**
574	602	736	868	449	**Frankfurt am Main**
663	691	825	957	537	**Genève**
674	702	836	488	548	**Hamburg**
409	895	466	356	741	**København**
266	294	428	560	141	**Lille**
1282	1231	1432	1563	1326	**Lisboa**
456	484	618	750	330	**Luxembourg**

Birmingham	Cardiff	Dublin	Glasgow	London	
661	689	823	954	535	**Lyon**
990	939	1140	1271	1034	**Madrid**
1294	1243	1444	1575	1338	**Málaga**
854	882	1016	1148	729	**Marseille**
834	862	996	1128	708	**Milano**
787	815	949	1080	661	**München**
362	311	512	643	313	**Nantes**
1322	1350	1484	1615	1196	**Palermo**
375	403	537	668	249	**Paris**
1176	1125	277	1457	1220	**Porto**
852	880	1014	1145	726	**Praha**
1199	1227	1361	1492	1073	**Roma**
713	662	863	994	757	**San Sebastián**
581	609	743	875	455	**Strasbourg**
691	664	863	994	672	**Toulouse**
1078	1008	1250	1382	1059	**Valencia**
1124	1152	1286	1418	999	**Warszawa**
1013	1041	1175	1307	887	**Wien**
1140	1168	1302	1433	1014	**Zagreb**

For distances refer to the colour key in the table
Les distances sont indiquées dans la couleur du point de passage
Le distanze sono indicate con il colore del punto di passaggio
Die Entfernungen sind angegeben in der Farbe des betroffenen Passagepinktes

● FOLKESTONE (CHANNEL TUNNEL)
● SOUTHAMPTON
● TYNEMOUTH

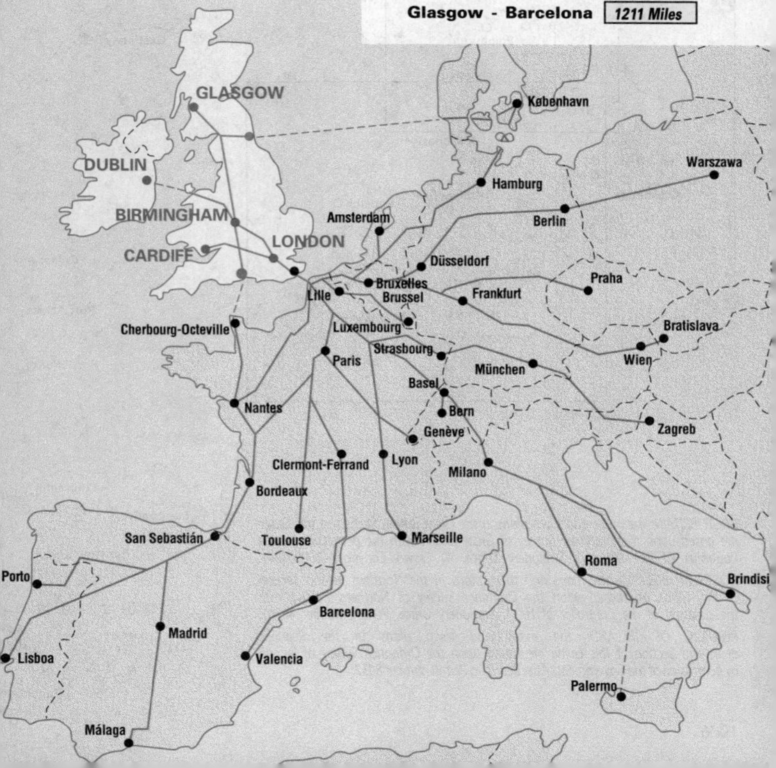

Major roads and principal shipping routes

Motorway

Road number .... A 4. T 35. N 2

Mileage 20

Principales routes et liaisons maritimes

Autoroute

N° de route .... A 4. T 35. N 2

Distance en miles 20

Principali strade e itinerari marittimi

Autostrada

Numero di strada .... A 4. T 35. N 2

Distanza in miglia 20

Hauptverkehrsstraßen und Schiffsverbindungen

Autobahn

Straßennummer .... A 4. T 35. N 2

Entfernung in Meilen 20

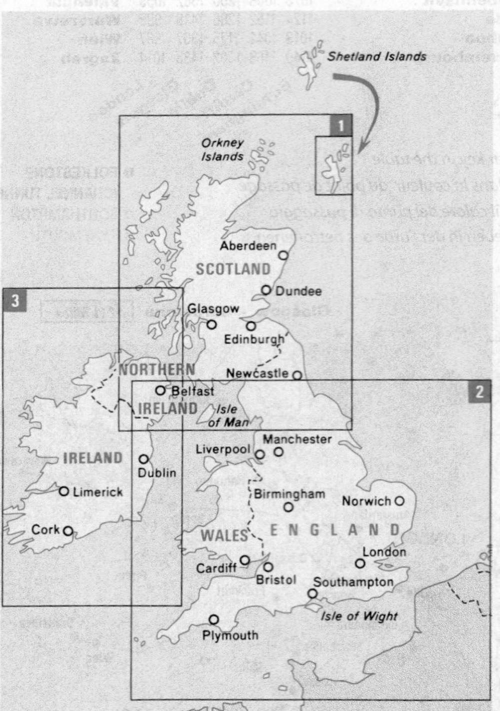

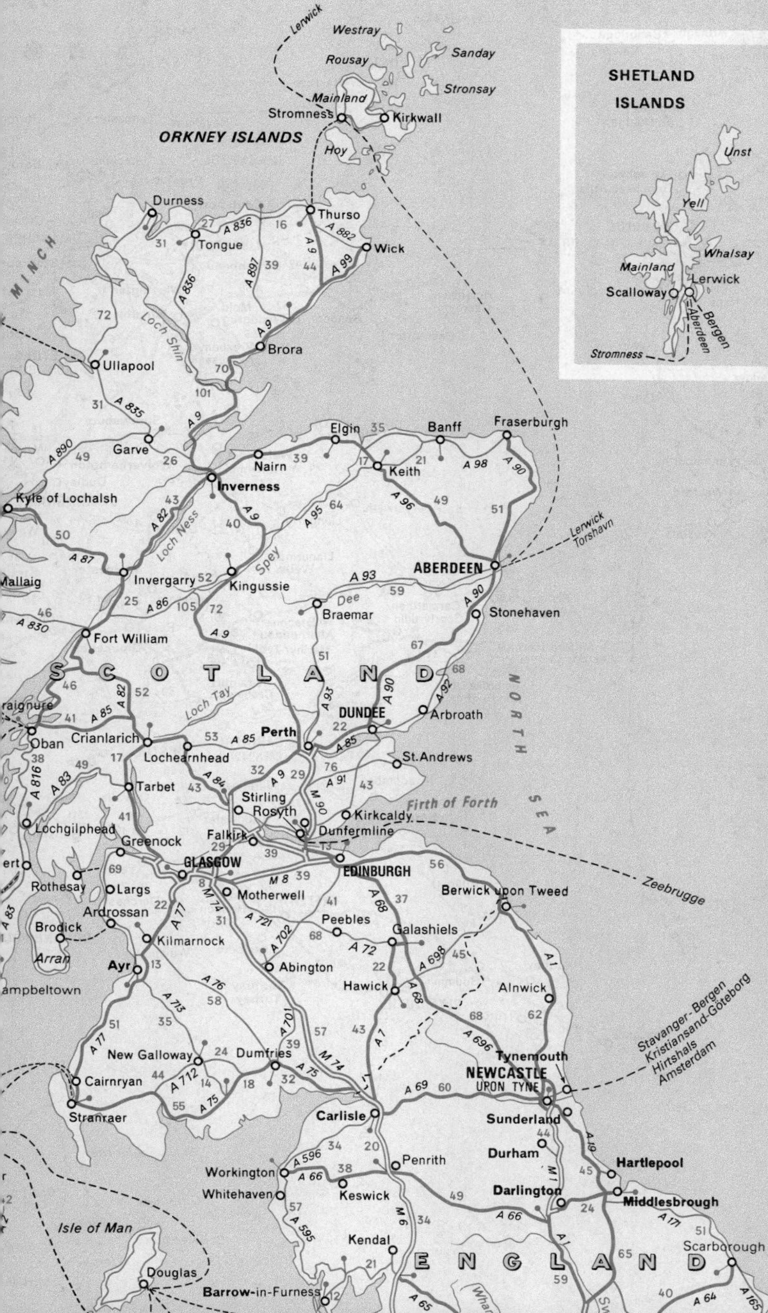
SHETLAND ISLANDS
Unst
Yell
Whalsay
Mainland
Lerwick
Scalloway
Bergen
Aberdeen
Stromness
ORKNEY ISLANDS
Westray
Sanday
Rousay
Stronsay
Mainland
Stromness
Kirkwall
Hoy
Lerwick
MINCH
Durness
Thurso
Tongue
Wick
Loch Shin
Brora
Ullapool
Garve
Elgin
Banff
Fraserburgh
Nairn
Keith
Inverness
Kyle of Lochalsh
Loch Ness
Spey
Lerwick
Torshavn
ABERDEEN
Mallaig
Invergarry
Kingussie
Dee
Braemar
Stonehaven
Fort William
SCOTLAND
NORTH SEA
Loch Tay
DUNDEE
Arbroath
Craignure
Oban
Crianlarich
Perth
Lochearnhead
St. Andrews
Tarbet
Stirling
Rosyth
Firth of Forth
Kirkcaldy
Lochgilphead
Dunfermline
Falkirk
Greenock
GLASGOW
EDINBURGH
Rothesay
Largs
Motherwell
Berwick upon Tweed
Zeebrugge
Ardrossan
Peebles
Brodick
Arran
Kilmarnock
Galashiels
Ayr
Abington
Hawick
Campbeltown
Alnwick
Stavanger-Bergen
Kristiansand-Göteborg
Hirtshals
Amsterdam
New Galloway
Dumfries
Tynemouth
Cairnryan
NEWCASTLE UPON TYNE
Stranraer
Carlisle
Sunderland
Durham
Penrith
Hartlepool
Workington
Whitehaven
Keswick
Darlington
Middlesbrough
Isle of Man
Kendal
Scarborough
ENGLAND
Douglas
Barrow-in-Furness
Wharf

NORTHERN IRELAND
Lough Neagh
BELFAST
Bangor
Strangford Lough
Ballygawley
Armagh
Banbridge
Newcastle
Monaghan
Dundalk / Dun Dealgan
Kells
Drogheda / Droichead Átha
Boyne
DUBLIN / BAILE ÁTHA CLIATH
Naas
Dún Laoghaire
Bray
Wicklow
Carlow
Arklow
Enniscorthy
Wexford
Rosslare
Isle of Man
Douglas
IRISH SEA
ST GEORGE'S CHANNEL
Cherbourg-Octeville
Workington
Whitehaven
Penrith
Keswick
Durham
Kendal
ENG
Barrow-in-Furness
Heysham
Lancaster
Wharfe
BLACKPOOL
Preston
Blackburn
Bradford
Burnley
Halifax
Southport
Wigan
Bolton
Oldham
LIVERPOOL
Birkenhead
MANCHESTER
Stockport
Colwyn Bay / Bae Colwyn
Holyhead / Caergybi
Bangor
Caernarfon
Mold / Yr Wyddgrug
Warrington
Chester
Macclesfield
Wrexham / Wrecsam
STOKE-ON-TRENT
Dolgellau
Shrewsbury
Welshpool / Y Trallwng
Wolverhampton
Walsall
Dudley
BIRMINGHAM
Aberystwyth
Llangurig
Ludlow
Severn
Llandrindod Wells
Worcester
Wye
WALES
Hereford
Fishguard / Abergwaun
Carmarthen / Caerfyrddin
Brecon / Aberhonddu
Ross
Gloucester
Cheltenham
Milford Haven / Aberdaugleddau
Merthyr Tydfil
Pembroke Dock / Doc Penfro
Newport / Casnewydd
Swansea / Abertawe
Swindon
CARDIFF / CAERDYDD
BRISTOL
Bath
Bristol Channel
Ilfracombe
Minehead
Wells
Barnstaple
Bridgwater
Taunton
Salisbury
Yeovil
Bude
EXETER
Honiton
Dorchester
BOURNEMOUTH
Exmouth
Weymouth
Newquay
Bodmin
PLYMOUTH
Torquay Torbay
Truro
Penzance
Falmouth
Isles of Scilly
Roscoff
ENGLISH
Rosslare
Alderney
Guernsey
Sark
St.Peter-Port
Jersey
St.Hélier
St-Malo
Cherbourg-Octeville
M 1
A 3
A 1
A 2
N 2
N 52
N 51
M 4
N 7
N 9
N 11
N 80
A 596
A 66
A 595
M 6
A 65
A 5
A 55
A 483
A 494
A 458
A 41
A 50
A 49
A 456
A 46
A 487
A 470
A 479
M 50
A 40
A 465
M 5
A 39
A 361
A 303
A 37
A 30
A 35
A 38
A 36

2
NORTH SEA
CHANNEL
BELGIË
BELGIQUE
FRANCE
Hartlepool
Middlesbrough
Scarborough
York
KINGSTON UPON HULL
Immingham
Scunthorpe
Grimsby
Rotterdam
Zeebruge
Doncaster
Rotherham
Lincoln
Skegness
Boston
NOTTINGHAM
LEICESTER
Stamford
Wisbech
King's Lynn
Cromer
NORWICH
Great Yarmouth
Lowestoft
Peterborough
Ely
Rugby
Northampton
Bedford
CAMBRIDGE
Bury St.Edmunds
Ipswich
Felixstowe
Harwich
Hoek van Holland
Hamburg
Colchester
Stevenage
Luton
Aylesbury
Harlow
Chelmsford
OXFORD
Southend-on-Sea
Tilbury
THAMES
Reading
Windsor
Newbury
LONDON
Sheerness
Margate
Ramsgate
Canterbury
Deal
Basingstoke
Guildford
Maidstone
Crawley
Royal-Tunbridge Wells
Dover
Folkestone
Channel Tunnel
Winchester
SOUTHAMPTON
BRIGHTON
Hastings
Chichester
Worthing
Eastbourne
Newhaven
PORTSMOUTH
Newport
Isle of Wight
Kingston upon Hull
Rosyth
Zeebrugge
OOSTENDE
BRUGGE
Dunkerque
Calais
Boulogne
St-Omer
LILLE
Arras
Cambrai
Abbeville
AMIENS
Somme
St-Quentin
Dieppe
LE HAVRE
ROUEN
Beauvais
Compiègne
Senlis
CAEN
Lisieux
SEINE

3

ATLANTIC OCEAN

NORTH CHANNEL

Colonsay
Jura
Port Askaig
Islay
Port Ellen

NORTHERN IRELAND

Coleraine
Waterfoot
Londonderry
Letterkenny
Ballymena
Larne
Strabane
Donegal
Omagh
Lough Neagh
BELFAST
Strangford Lough
Ballygawley
Enniskillen
Sligo/
Sligeach
Armagh
Banbridge
Newcastle
Ballina
L. Allen
Monaghan
Boyle
Cavan
Dundalk /
Dun Dealgan
Westport
Castlebar
L. Mask
Longford
Kells
Drogheda/
Droichead Átha
Clifden
Roscommon
L. Corrib
L. Ree
Mullingar
Boyne
Galway/
Gaillimh
Athlone
DUBLIN/
BAILE ÁTHA CLIATH
Ballinasloe
Tullamore
Dún Laoghaire
Naas
Lisdoonvarna

IRELAND

Bray
River Shannon
Roscrea
Ennis/
Inis
Wicklow
Kilkee
Suir
Carlow
Thurles
Arklow
LIMERICK/
LUIMNEACH
Kilkenny /
Cill Chainnigh
Barrow
Cashel/
Caiseal
Enniscorthy
Tralee
Dingle
Caher
Carrick on Suir
Wexford
Killarney/
Cill Airne
Fermoy
R Blackwater
Lismore
Waterford/
Port Lairge
Rosslare
CORK/
CORCAIGH
Youghal
Cobh
Glengarriff
Bantry
Milford
Aberdaugleddau

ST GEORGE'S CHANNEL

CELTIC SEA

Major hotel groups

Central reservation telephone numbers

Principales chaînes hôtelières

Centraux téléphoniques de réservation

Principali catene alberghiere

Centrali telefoniche di prenotazione

Die wichtigsten Hotelketten

Zentrale für telefonische Reservierung

ACCOR HOTELS (IBIS, MERCURE & NOVOTEL)	0208 2834500
CHOICE HOTELS	0800 444444 *(Freephone)*
CORUS HOTELS	08457 334400
DE VERE HOTELS PLC	0870 6063606
HILTON HOTELS	08705 515151
HOLIDAY INN WORLDWIDE	0800 897121 *(Freephone)*
HYATT HOTELS WORLDWIDE	0845 8881234
INTERCONTINENTAL HOTELS LTD	0800 0289387 *(Freephone)*
JURYS/DOYLE HOTELS	0870 9072222
MACDONALD HOTELS PLC	08457 585593
MARRIOTT WORLDWIDE	0800 221222 *(Freephone)*
MILLENNIUM & COPTHORNE HOTELS PLC	0845 3020001
PREMIER TRAVEL INNS	0870 2428000
QUEENS MOAT HOUSES PLC	0500 213214 *(Freephone)*
RADISSON EDWARDIAN HOTELS	0800 374411 *(Freephone)*
SHERATON HOTELS	0800 353535 *(Freephone)*
THISTLE HOTELS	0800 181716 *(Freephone)*

International Dialling Codes

Note: When making an international call, do not dial the first (0) of the city codes (except for calls to Italy).

Indicatifs téléphoniques internationaux

Important : pour les communications internationales, le zéro (0) initial de l'indicatif interurbainn'est pas à composer (excepté pour les appels vers l'Italie).

from \ to	A	B	CH	CZ	D	DK	E	FIN	F	GB	GR
A Austria		0032	0041	00420	0049	0045	0034	00358	0033	0044	0030
B Belgium	0043		0041	00420	0049	0045	0034	00358	0033	0044	0030
CH Switzerland	0043	0032		00420	0049	0045	0034	00358	0033	0044	0030
CZ Czech Republic	0043	0032	0041		0049	0045	0034	00358	0033	0044	0030
D Germany	0043	0032	0041	00420		0045	0034	00358	0033	0044	0030
DK Denmark	0043	0032	0041	00420	0049		0034	00358	0033	0044	0030
E Spain	0043	0032	0041	00420	0049	0045		00358	0033	0044	0030
FIN Finland	0043	0032	0041	00420	0049	0045	0034		0033	0044	0030
F France	0043	0032	0041	00420	0049	0045	0034	00358		0044	0030
GB United Kingdom	0043	0032	0041	00420	0049	0045	0034	00358	0033		0030
GR Greece	0043	0032	0041	00420	0049	0045	0034	00358	0033	0044	
H Hungary	0043	0032	0041	00420	0049	0045	0034	00358	0033	0044	0030
I Italy	0043	0032	0041	00420	0049	0045	0034	00358	0033	0044	0030
IRL Ireland	0043	0032	0041	00420	0049	0045	0034	00358	0033	0044	0030
J Japan	00143	00132	00141	001420	00149	00145	00134	001358	00133	00144	00130
L Luxembourg	0043	0032	0041	00420	0049	0045	0034	00358	0033	0044	0030
N Norway	0043	0032	0041	00420	0049	0045	0034	00358	0033	0044	0030
NL Netherlands	0043	0032	0041	00420	0049	0045	0034	00358	0033	0044	0030
PL Poland	0043	0032	0041	00420	0049	0045	0034	00358	0033	0044	0030
P Portugal	0043	0032	0041	00420	0049	0045	0034	00358	0033	0044	0030
RUS Russia	81043	81032	81041	6420	81049	81045	*	810358	81033	81044	*
S Sweden	0043	0032	0041	00420	0049	0045	0034	00358	0033	0044	0030
USA	01143	01132	01141	001420	01149	01145	01134	01358	01133	01144	01130

** Direct dialling not possible*

** Pas de sélection automatique*

Indicativi Telefonici Internazionali

Importante: per le comunicazioni internazionali, non bisogna comporre lo zero (0) iniziale del prefisso interurbano (escluse le chiamate per l'Italia).

Telefon-Vorwahlnummern International

Wichtig: bei Auslandsgesprächen darf die Null (0) der Ortsnetzkennzahl nicht gewählt werden (außer bei Gesprächen nach Italien).

H	I	IRL	J	L	N	NL	PL	P	RUS	S	USA	
0036	0039	00353	0081	00352	0047	0031	0048	00351	007	0046	001	**A Austria**
0036	0039	00353	0081	00352	0047	0031	0048	00351	007	0046	001	**B Belgium**
0036	0039	00353	0081	00352	0047	0031	0048	00351	007	0046	001	**CH Switzerland**
0036	0039	00353	0081	00352	0047	0031	0048	00351	007	0046	001	**CZ Czech Republic**
0036	0039	00353	0081	00352	0047	0031	0048	00351	007	0046	001	**D Germany**
0036	0039	00353	0081	00352	0047	0031	0048	00351	007	0046	001	**DK Denmark**
0036	0039	00353	0081	00352	0047	0031	0048	00351	007	0046	001	**E Spain**
0036	0039	00353	0081	00352	0047	0031	0048	00351	007	0046	001	**FIN Finland**
0036	0039	00353	0081	00352	0047	0031	0048	00351	007	0046	001	**F France**
0036	0039	00353	0081	00352	0047	0031	0048	00351	007	0046	001	**GB United Kingdom**
0036	0039	00353	0081	00352	0047	0031	0048	00351	007	0046	001	**GR Greece**
	0039	00353	0081	00352	0047	0031	0048	00351	007	0046	001	**H Hungary**
0036		00353	0081	00352	0047	0031	0048	00351	*	0046	001	**I Italy**
0036	0039		0081	00352	0047	0031	0048	00351	007	0046	001	**IRL Ireland**
00136	00139	001353		001352	00147	00131	00148	001351	*	001146	0011	**J Japan**
0036	0039	00353	0081		0047	0031	0048	00351	007	0046	001	**L Luxembourg**
0036	0039	00353	0081	00352		0031	0048	00351	007	0046	001	**N Norway**
0036	0039	00353	0081	00352	0047		0048	00351	007	0046	001	**NL Netherlands**
0036	0039	00353	0081	00352	0047	0031		00351	007	0046	001	**PL Poland**
0036	0039	00353	0081	00352	0047	0031	048		007	0046	001	**P Portugal**
81036	*	*	*	*	*	81031	1048	*		*	*	**RUS Russia**
0036	0039	00353	0081	00352	0047	0031	0048	00351	007		001	**S Sweden**
01136	01139	011353	01181	011352	01147	01131	01148	011351	*	011146		**USA**

** Selezione automatica impossibile*

** Automatische Vorwahl nicht möglich*

Index of towns

Index des localités
Indice delle località
Ortsverzeichnis

D

G

H

M

Y

Manufacture française des pneumatiques Michelin

Société en commandite par actions au capital de 304 000 000 EUR.
Place des Carmes-Déchaux – 63 Clermont-Ferrand (France)
R.C.S. Clermont-Fd B 855 200 507

Dépôt légal Janvier 2006 – ISBN 2-06-711577-4

Printed in Belgium 12-05

Compogravure : A.P.S.-Chromostyle, 37000 TOURS

Impression : CASTERMAN, Tournai (Belgique)

Reliure : S.I.R.C., Martigny-le-Châtel